33rd Conference on Uncertainty in Artificial Intelligence 2017

Sydney, Australia
11-15 August 2017

Volume 1 of 2

Editors:

Gal Elidan **Kristian Kersting**

ISBN: 978-1-5108-4779-8

Printed from e-media with permission by:

Curran Associates, Inc.
57 Morehouse Lane
Red Hook, NY 12571

Some format issues inherent in the e-media version may also appear in this print version.

Printed by Curran Associates, Inc. (2017)

Association For Uncertainty in Artificial Intelligence (AUAI)
Department of Computer Science
University of British Columbia
Vancouver BC Canada V6T 1Z4

Phone: (703) 787-8044
Fax: (703) 478-0829

www.auai.org

Additional copies of this publication are available from:

Curran Associates, Inc.
57 Morehouse Lane
Red Hook, NY 12571 USA
Phone: 845-758-0400
Fax: 845-758-2633
Email: curran@proceedings.com
Web: www.proceedings.com

Uncertainty in Artificial Intelligence

Proceedings of the Thirty-Third Conference (2017)

August 11-15, 2017, Sydney, Australia

Edited by
Gal Elidan, Google Inc. and The Hebrew University, Israel
Kristian Kersting, TU Darmstadt, Germany

General Chair
Alexander Ihler, University of California Irvine, USA

Sponsored by
Google Inc., Microsoft Research, Amazon Web Services, Artificial Intelligence Journal, Disney Research, Uber, NextAI

AUAI Press Corvallis, Oregon

Contents

Preface

The Conference on Uncertainty in Artificial Intelligence (UAI) is the premier international conference on research related to representation, inference, learning and decision making in the presence of uncertainty within the field of Artificial Intelligence. This volume contains the schedule and abstracts of all papers that were accepted for the 33rd UAI Conference, held in Sydney, Australia, from August 11 to 15, 2017.

Papers appearing in this volume were subjected to a rigorous review process. A total of 282 papers were reviewed by at least 3 reviewers each. Of these, 87 papers were accepted, for an acceptance rate of close to 31%. We are very grateful to the program committee and senior program committee members for their diligent efforts. We are confident that the proceedings, like past UAI conference proceedings, will become an important archival reference for the field.

We are pleased to announce that the Best Paper Award is awarded to Shayan Doroudi, Philip S. Thomas, and Emma Brunskill for their paper "Importance Sampling for Fair Policy Selection". The Best Student Paper Award is awarded to David Buchman and David Poole for their paper "Why Rules are Complex: Real-Valued Probabilistic Logic Programs are not Fully Expressive". Finally, a Best Student Paper Honorable Mention is given to Daniel Seita, Xinlei Pan, Haoyu Chen, and John Canny for their paper "An Efficient Minibatch Acceptance Test for Metropolis-Hastings". We are grateful to the members of the best paper committee Tom Heskes (chair), Pascal Poupart, and Sriraam Natarajan.

In addition to the presentation of technical papers, we are very pleased to have five distinguished invited speakers at UAI 2017: Amir Globerson (Tel-Aviv University), Katherine Heller (Duke University), Leslie Pack Kaelbling (MIT), Christopher Ré (Stanford University), and Terry Speed (Walter and Eliza Hall Institute of Medical Research).

The UAI 2017 tutorials program, chaired by Ricardo Silva, consists of four tutorials: "Methods and Models for Large-scale Optimization" by John Duchi (Stanford University), "Representing and Comparing Probabilities with (and without) Kernels" by Arthur Gretton (University College London), "Deep Generative Models" by Shakir Mohamed and Danilo Rezende (DeepMind), and an invited tutorial "Machine Learning and Counterfactual Reasoning for 'Personalized' Decision-Making in Healthcare" by Suchi Saria and Hossein Soleimani (Johns Hopkins University).

UAI 2017 also hosts three workshops, chaired by Guy Van den Broeck: "Statistical Relational AI (StarAI)" organized by Angelika Kimmig, David Poole, Jay Pujara, and Tim Rocktäschel. "Causality: Learning, Inference, and Decision-Making", organized by Elias Bareinboim, Kun Zhang, Caroline Uhler, Jiji Zhang, and Dominik Janzing. "Bayesian Modelling Applications", organized by John Mark Agosta and Tomas Singliar. UAI 2017 will also hold, for the first time, a training event where participants will learn how to code papers with TensorFlow, MXNet, PyTorch, CNTK and more. The event will include six training sessions: Generative Models, Neural Abstract Machines, Reinforcement Learning, LSTMs and Text, Speech and Time series, and Deep Recommender Systems. The session will be led instructors Alex Dimakis, Chris Fregly, and Nikolaos Vasiloglou.

Gal Elidan and Kristian Kersting (Program Co-Chairs),
Alexander Ihler (General Chair)

Organizing Committee

General Chair

Alexander Ihler, University of California Irvine, USA

Program Chairs

Gal Elidan, Google Inc. and The Hebrew University, Israel
Kristian Kersting, TU Darmstadt, Germany

Best Paper Award Committee

Tom Heskes (chair), Radboud University, Netherlands
Pascal Pupart, University of Waterloo, Canada
Sriraam Natarajan, Indiana University, USA

Workshops Chair

Guy Van den Broeck, University of California Los Angeles, USA

Tutorial Chair

Ricardo Silva, University College London, UK

Sponsoring and Social Media Chair

Nikolaos Vasiloglou, Ismion, USA

Local Arrangements Chair

Ann Nicholson, Monash University, Australia

Proceedings Chair

Martin Mladenov, TU Dortmund, Germany

Webmaster and OpenReview Chair

Alejandro Molina, TU Dortmund, Germany

Acknowledgments

The success of UAI depends greatly on the efforts of many individuals who volunteer their time to provide expert and detailed reviews of submitted papers. In particular, the Program Committee and Senior Program Committee for UAI 2017 were responsible for generating reviews and recommendations for the 282 submissions to the conference. Each submitted paper was reviewed by at least 3 members of the Program Committee. The Senior Program Committee then assessed the individual reviews for each paper, moderated discussion among Program Committee members if needed, and generated meta-reviews and recommendations for the program chairs. We are extremely grateful for the efforts of all of the individuals listed below.

Senior Program Committee

Alan Fern	Oregon State University
Amir Globerson	Tel Aviv University
Ann Nicholson	Monash University
Ayesha Ali	University of Guelph
Benjamin Marlin	UMass Amherst
Brian Milch	Google
Cassio de Campos	Queen's University Belfast
Chris Meek	Microsoft Research
Claire Monteleoni	George Washington University
Craig Boutilier	Google
Dhruv Batra	Virginia Tech
Fabio Cuzzolin	Oxford Brookes University
Francisco Diez	UNED
Guy Van den Broek	UCLA
Helene Fargier	Institut de Recherche en Informatique de Toulouse
Jennifer Dy	Northeastern University
Jin Tian	Iowa State University
Jun Zhu	Tsinghua University
Kamalika Chaudhuri	University of California
Marloes Maathuis	ETH Zurich
Michel Besserve	Max Planck Institute
Nevin Zhang	Hong Kong University of Science and Technology
Nuria M. Oliver	Vodafone & Data-Pop Alliance
Ofer Meshi	Google
Pascal Poupart	University of Waterloo
Peter Grnwald	Centrum voor Wiskunde en Informatica
Peter Lucas	Radboud University Nijmegen
Raquel Urtasun	University of Toronto
Rina Dechter	UC-Irvine
Ryan P. Adams	Harvard
Stefano Ermon	Stanford
Thomas Richardson	University of Washington
Tom Heskes	Radboud University Nijmegen
Vibhav Gogate	The University of Texas at Dallas
Wray Buntine	Monash University
Zoltan Szabo	École Polytechnique

Program Committee

Alessandro Antonucci	IDSIA
Alessio Benavoli	IDSIA
Alex Kirillov	TU Dresden
Alex Schwing	University of Illinois at Urbana-Champaign
Alexandre Bouchard-Cote	UBC
Ali Ghodsi	University of Waterloo
Ami Wiesel	Hebrew University
Amit Gruber	Yahoo!
Anders Madsen	Hugin Expert
Andrey Kolobov	Microsoft Research
Antonio Salmeron	Universidad de Almeria
Antti Hyttinen	University of Helsinki
April Liu	The Hong Kong University of Science and Technology
Aram Galstyan	Information Sciences Institute
Aritanan Gruber	University of Sao Paulo
Arjen Hommersom	University of Nijmegen
Arthur Choi	UCLA
Arvind Agarwal	Xerox
Ashish Sabharwal	Allen Institute for Artificial Intelligence
Aurelie Lozano	IBM
Balaji Lakshminarayanan	UCL
Bart Selman	Cornell
Ben London	Amazon
Bob Price	PARC
Bozhena Bidyuk	Google
Brandon Malone	University of Helsinki
Branislav Kveton	Adobe Research
Brian Ruttenberg	Charles River Analytics
Carlo Berzuini	University of Manchester
Changhe Yuan	City University of New York
Changyou Chen	Duke University
Chong Wang	Carnegie Mellon University
Christoph Dann	CMU
Christophe Gonzales	LIP6-UPMC
Clark Glymour	CMU
Cory Butz	University of Regina
Daniel Lowd	University of Oregon
Daniel Malinsky	CMU
David Arbour	University of Massachusetts Amherst
David Balduzzi	Victoria University Wellington
David Jensen	University of Massachusetts Amherst
David Page	UW Madison
David Pennock	Microsoft Research
David Pynadath	USC Institute for Creative Technologies
Debarun Bhattacharjya	IBM Research
Denis Mauá	University of Sao Paulo
Dragomir Anguelov	Google
Dustin Tran	Columbia
Elad Eban	Google
Elias Bareinboim	Purdue University
Erik Cambria	Nanyang Technological University

Ethan Zhao	Monash University
Eunho Yang	KAIST
Eyal Amir	University of Illinois at Urbana-Champaign
Fabio Stella	University of Milan
Farhad Anaraki	University of Colorado
Frederick Eberhardt	Caltech
Georg P Schoenherr	CMU
Gerardo Simari	Universidad Nacional del Sur in Bahia Blanca & CONICET
Greg Ver Steeg	Information Sciences Institute
Hang Su	Tsinghua University
Hong Chang	Institute of Computing Technology
Hung Bui	Adobe
Ilya Shpitser	Johns Hopkins Univeristy
Ioannis Tsamardinos	University of Crete
Jaesik Choi	Ulsan National Institute of Science and Technology
James Cussens	University of York
James Foulds	UC San Diego
Jan Gasthaus	University College London
Janardhan Rao Doppa	Washington State University
Jay Pujara	UC Santa Cruz
Jesse Hoey	University of Waterloo
Jesse Hostetler	Oregon State University
Jian Peng	UIUC
Jiji Zhang	Lingnan University
Jirka Vomlel	Institute of Information Theory and Automation
Joe Suzuki	Osaka University
Johannes Textor	Utrecht University
John Paisley	Columbia University
John Mark Agosta	Toyota Information Technology Center
Jonas Vlasselaer	KU Leuven
Jose Peña	Linköping University
Julian McAuley	UC San Diego
Junxiang Chen	Northeastern University
Justin Domke	University of Massachusetts Amherst
Kacper Chwialkowski	UCL / Gatsby Unit
Kar Wai Lim	ANU
Karthika Mohan	UCLA
Kevin Small	Amazon
Kim-Leng Poh	National University of Singapore
Kun Zhang	CMU
L. Enrique Sucar	INAOE
Lan Du	Monash
Le Song	Georgia Tech
Leonard Poon	Hong Kong Institute of Education
Linbo Wang	University of Washington
Lirong Xia	Rensselaer Polytechnic Institute
Lluis Godo	Artificial Intelligence Research Institute
M. Julia Flores	University of Castilla - La Mancha (UCLM)
Mahesh Mohan	George Washington University
Malik Magdon-Ismail	Rensselear Polytechnic Institute
Manuel Gomez-Olmedo	Universidad de Granada
Manuel Luque	UNED
Marco Valtorta	University of South Carolina

Marcus Hutter	Australian National University
Maria Vanina Martinez	University of Oxford
Mark Crowley	University of Waterloo
Martin Zinkevich	Google
Mathias Niepert	NEC
Mathieu Sinn	IBM Research
Maya Gupta	Google
Michael Lyu	Chinese University of Hong Kong
Mikko Koivisto	University of Helsinki
Mingming Gong	University of Technology Sydney
Minjie Xu	Tsinghua University
Minos Garofalakis	Technical University of Crete
Mohammad Emtiyaz Khan	RIKEN
Nahla Ben Amor	ISG Tunis
Nan Ye	National University of Singapore
Narges Razavian	New York University
Nicolas Drougard	ONERA - The French Aerospace Lab
Nimar Arora	Oracle
Ole Mengshoel	Carnegie Mellon University
Olivier Buffet	LORIA-INRIA
Paola Vicard	Universit degli Studi Roma Tre
Perry Groot	Radboud University Nijmegen
Philipp Geiger	Max Planck Institute for Intelligent Systems
Philipp Hennig	Max Planck Institute
Philippe Leray	University of Nantes
Piyush Rai	IIT Kanpur
Preetam Nandy	ETH
Qi Lou	UCI
Quanquan Gu	University of Virginia
Rafael Rumi	Almeria University
Reza Babanezhad Harikandeh	The University of British Columbia
Robert Castelo	Universitat Pompeu Fabra
Robin Evans	University of Oxford
Roger Baker Grosse	University of Toronto
Roland Ramsahai	University of Cambridge
Roman Garnett	Washington University in St. Louis
Ru He	Amazon
Russell Almond	Florida State University
Scott Sanner	University of Toronto
Sebastien Destercke	CNRS
Shang-Tse Chen	Georgia Tech
Shuai Li	Cambridge University
Silja Renooij	Universiteit Utrecht
Sriraam Natarajan	Indiana University
Steffen Michels	Radboud University Nijmegen
Stephen Bach	Stanford
Su-In Lee	University of Washington
Suriya Gunasekar	TTI
Tameem Adel	University of Manchester
Taneli Mielikainen	Yahoo
Teemu Roos	Helsinki Institute for Information Technology
Tengfei Liu	The Hong Kong University
Thomas Walsh	MIT

Tianjiao Chu	University of Pittsburgh
Tiberio Caetano	Ambiata & University of Sydney
Tom Claassen	Radboud University Nijmegen
Tomas Singliar	Microsoft
Tomi Silander	Xerox Research Centre Europe
Truong-Huy Dinh Nguyen	Texas A&M University
Twan van Laarhoven	Radboud University Nijmegen
Uri Shalit	New York University
Vicenç Gómez	Universitat Pompeu Fabra
Vincent Tan	NUS
Wannes Meert	KU Leuven
Wei Ping	Baidu
William Cheung	Hong Kong Baptist University
Wu-Jun Li	Nanjing University
Xiaotong Yuan	Nanjing University of Information Science & Technology
Yan Liu	USC
Yetian Chen	Amazon
Yexiang Xue	Cornell University
Yi Zhen	Georgia Institute of Technology
Yifeng Zeng	Teesside University
Yingyu Liang	Princeton University
Yoni Halpern	New York University
Yu Zhang	Hong Kong Baptist University
Yuhong Guo	Temple University
Yutian Chen	Google
Zied Eloudi	ISG Tunis

Additional Acknowledgments

A number of other people have made significant contributions towards making UAI 2017 possible. We acknowledge and thank:

- The OpenReview team:

Andrew McCallum	University of Massachusetts Amherst
Melisa Bok	University of Massachusetts Amherst
Michael Spector	University of Massachusetts Amherst

- The following student scholarship volunteers:

Ouali Abdelkader	CNRS & Universit de Caen Normandie
David Arbour	UMass Amherst
Jessa Bekker	KU Leuven
Jagmohan Chauhan	UNSW & Data61 (CSIRO)
Bence Cserna	University of New Hampshire
Shayan Doroudi	Carnegie Mellon University
Jun Han	Dartmouth College
Chait Manapragada	Monash University
Philippe Morere	The University of Sydney
Swetasudha Panda	Vanderbilt University
Niranjani Prasad	Princeton University
Ehsan Shareghi	Monash University

Benjamin van Niekerk	University of the Witwatersrand
Claire Vernade	Télécom ParisTech
Jiasen Yang	Purdue University
Qinyi Zhang	University of Oxford
He Zhao	Monash University
Fujin Zhu	University of Technology Sydney

Sponsors

We gratefully acknowledge the generous support of our sponsors, including support for best paper awards and travel scholarships. Without our sponsors' support it would not be feasible to organize a conference such as UAI 2017 without charging much higher registration fees.

Gold Sponsors

Microsoft

Google™

amazon web services

Artificial Intelligence
www.elsevier.com/locate/artint

Bronze Sponsors

Disney Research

UBER

Startup Sponsor

NEXT Ai

Media Sponsor

AI & MACHINE LEARNING SUMMIT

Best Paper Awards

Best Paper Award

Importance Sampling for Fair Policy Selection

Shayan Doroudi, Philip S. Thomas, and Emma Brunskill

Best Student Paper Award

Why Rules are Complex: Real-Valued Probabilistic Logic Programs are not Fully Expressive

David Buchman and David Poole

Best Student Paper Honorable Mention

An Efficient Minibatch Acceptance Test for Metropolis-Hastings

Daniel Seita, Xinlei Pan, Haoyu Chen, and John Canny

Tutorials

Friday August 11th
Room C3.6

8:45–10:15 Methods and Models for Large-scale Optimization
John C. Duchi, Stanford University

10:15–10:35 **Coffee Break**

10:35–12:05 Representing and Comparing Probabilities with (and without) Kernels
Arthur Gretton, University College London

12:05–14:05 **Lunch Break**

14:05–15:35 Deep Generative Models
Shakir Mohamed and Danilo Rezende, DeepMind

15:35–16:00 **Break**

16:00–17:30 Machine Learning in Healthcare
Suchi Saria and Hossein Soleimani, Johns Hopkins University

Tutorial: Methods and Models for Large-scale Optimization

John C. Duchi

In this tutorial, we cover a biased view of recent movements in optimization and its intersection with machine learning and statistics, with an eye toward applying these algorithms. Broadly, we believe these advances lie in two major areas: the first is in large-scale stochastic optimization problems, where the growing size in dataset - both in sample size and dimension - due to the amount of information we track and collect has led to substantial research in the optimization literature. The second is a more recent trend toward non-convex optimization problems. While, as Rockafellar notes, the justifiable dogma in optimization is that "the great watershed in optimization isnt between linearity and nonlinearity, but convexity and nonconvexity," a number of problems in statistics that are nominally non-convex are in fact still (with high probability) easy to solve using simple gradient-based and other methods. Unifying both of these trends is that the inherent randomness in the problems we solve - sampling randomness from collecting data - lends itself to simple optimization methods with convergence guarantees that are, at least, good enough. Our tutorial addresses these trends in three parts: first, by covering methods for large-scale stochastic optimization, second, by discussing optimization models that arise in large-scale problems, and third, by showing how non-convex problems arising from various nice stochastic problems are in practice (and in theory) relatively easy.

Tutorial: Representing and Comparing Probabilities with (and without) Kernels

Arthur Gretton

The purpose of this tutorial is to provide an introduction to distribution embeddings and their applications, with a focus on recent tools (from 2014-2017) developed to represent and compare probabilty distributions. The first part of the talk will focus entirely on the representation of probability distributions, using both kernel methods and explicit features. The focus will be on designing kernels or features to make two distributions as distinguishable as possible. The second part of the talk will focus on more sophisticated applications of distribution representations: model criticism (using Stein's method to test against a parametric model), learning from probabilities as inputs, testing for independence and testing multi-way interaction. I might also touch on the problem of testing where the inputs are time series.

Tutorial: Deep Generative Models

Shakir Mohamed and Danilo Rezende

This tutorial will be a review of recent advances in deep generative models. Generative models have a long history at UAI and recent methods have combined the generality of probabilistic reasoning with the scalability of deep learning to develop learning algorithms that have been applied to a wide variety of problems giving state-of-the-art results in image generation, text-to-speech synthesis, and image captioning, amongst many others. Advances in deep generative models are at the forefront of deep learning research because of the promise they offer for allowing data-efficient learning, and for model-based reinforcement learning. At the end of this tutorial, audience member will have a full understanding of the latest advances in generative modelling covering three of the active types of models: Markov models, latent variable models and implicit models, and how these models can be scaled to high-dimensional data. The tutorial will expose many questions that remain in this area, and for which there remains a great deal of opportunity from members of the UAI community.

Tutorial: Machine Learning and Counterfactual Reasoning for "Personalized" Decision-Making in Healthcare

Suchi Saria

Electronic health records and high throughput measurement technologies are changing the practice of healthcare to become more algorithmic and data-driven. This offers an exciting opportunity for statistical machine learning techniques to impact healthcare.

The aim of this tutorial is to introduce you to challenges and techniques for developing "personalized decision-making" tools in medicine. Example topics covered will include: scalable joint models for forecasting risk from "messy" clinical streams, estimating individualized treatment response in populations with heterogeneous treatment effects, and examples of counterfactual reasoning or "what-if" analysis for decision-making. We will also cover example data sources and describe ongoing national initiatives that provide a way for you to get involved.

Target audience: The majority of this tutorial will be targeted at an audience with basic machine learning knowledge. No background in medicine or health care is needed. We will make our slides and any relevant documents accessible after the talk.

Conference Program

All the conference talks will be held in **Room C4.8** on the fourth level of the Sydney International Convention Centre. Poster sessions and coffee breaks will be located in **Room C4.9**.

Saturday August 12th

8:30 Welcome

Keynote Talk

8:40 Intelligent Robots in an Uncertain World
Leslie Pack Kaelbling, MIT

Session 1: Deep Models

10:40 - 11:10 Coffee break

Session 2: Machine Learning

12:10 - 14:00 Lunch break

Keynote Talk

14:00 Learning and Inference with Expectations
Amir Globerson, University of Tel Aviv

Session 3: Inference

15:00 160: On Loopy Belief Propagation – Local Stability Analysis for Non-Vanishing Fields 100
Christian Knoll and Franz Pernkopf

15:20 259: Improving Optimization-Based Approximate Inference by Clamping Variables 110
Junyao Zhao, Josip Djolonga, Sebastian Tschiatschek, Andreas Krause

15:40 109: Approximation Complexity of Maximum A Posteriori Inference in Sum-Product Networks 124
Diarmaid Conaty, Cassio P. de Campos, Denis D. Maua

16:00 - 16:20 Coffee break

Session 4: Learning

16:20 291: Learning the Structure of Probabilistic Sentential Decision Diagrams 134
Yitao Liang, Jessa Bekker, Guy Van den Broeck

16:40 278: A Probabilistic Framework for Multi-Label Learning with Unseen Labels 146
Abhilash Gaure and Piyush Rai

17:00 297: Hybrid Deep Discriminative/Generative Models for Semi-Supervised Learning 156
Volodymyr Kuleshov and Stefano Ermon

Poster Spotlights 1

17:20 - 17:50 one minute poster spotlight presentations of papers:

100: Regret Minimization Algorithms for the Followers Behaviour Identification in Leadership Games 166
Lorenzo Bisi, Giuseppe De Nittis, Francesco Trovò, Marcello Restelli, Nicola Gatti

105: On the Complexity of Nash Equilibrium Reoptimization 183
Andrea Celli, Alberto Marchesi, Nicola Gatti

26: Shortest Path under Uncertainty: Exploration versus Exploitation 193
Zhan Wei Lim, David Hsu, Wee Sun Lee

35: Learning with Confident Examples: Rank Pruning for Robust Classification with Noisy Labels 203
Curtis G. Northcutt, Tailin Wu, Isaac L. Chuang

37: Monte-Carlo Tree Search using Batch Value of Perfect Information 228
Shahaf S. Shperberg, Solomon Eyal Shimony, Ariel Felner

45: Submodular Variational Inference for Network Reconstruction 238
Lin Chen, Forrest W. Crawford, Amin Karbasi

70: Bayesian Inference of Log Determinants 253
J. Fitzsimons, K. Cutajar, M. Filippone, M. Osborne, S. Roberts

75: Fast Amortized Inference and Learning in Log-linear Models with Randomly Perturbed Nearest Neighbor Search 264
Stephen Mussmann, Daniel Levy, Stefano Ermon

17:50 - 19:50 Poster Session 1

Will include all papers presented on Saturday.

Sunday August 13th

Keynote Talk

8:30 Snorkel: Beyond Hand-labeled Data
Christopher Ré, Stanford

Session 5: Representations

10:30 - 11:00 Coffee break

Session 6: Reinforcement Learning

12:20 - 14:10 Lunch break

Keynote Talk

14:10 - 15:10 Machine Learning for Healthcare Data
Katherine Heller, Duke University

Poster Spotlights 2

15:10pm - 15:40 one minute poster spotlight presentations of papers:

15:40 - 16:00 Coffee break

16:00 - 18:00 Poster Session 2

Will include all papers presented on Sunday.

18:45 - Banquet Boarding

Banquet Talk: 15 minutes on Artificial Intelligence and Statistical Models
Terry Speed, Walter and Eliza Hall Institute of Medical Research

Monday August 14th

Keynote Talk

8:30 Two current analysis challenges: Single Cell Omics
and Nanopore Long-read Sequence Data
Terry Speed, Walter and Eliza Hall Institute of Medical Research

Session 7: Causality

10:30 - 11:00 Coffee break

Session 8: Sampling

12:20 - 14:10 Lunch break

Session 9: Bandits

Poster Spotlights 3

15:10 - 15:40 one minute poster spotlight presentations of papers:

15:40 - 16:00 Coffee break

16:00 - 16:45 Business Meeting

16:00 - 18:00 Poster Session 3

Will include all papers presented on Monday.

Invited Speakers

Keynote Lecture: Learning and Inference with Expectations

Amir Globerson, School of Computer Science, Tel Aviv University

Probabilistic models can be characterized using expectations of functions of random variables. This can in turn be used to devise methods for learning representations, performing probabilistic inference, and discriminative learning. The talk will survey such methods, highlighting both theoretical results and their practical implications.

Biographical details

Prof. Globerson received his BSc in computer science and physics in 1997 from the Hebrew University, and his PhD in computational neuroscience from the Hebrew University in 2006. After his PhD, he was a postdoctoral fellow at the University of Toronto and a Rothschild postdoctoral fellow at MIT. He joined the Hebrew University school of computer science in 2008, and moved to the Tel Aviv University School of Computer Science in 2015. Prof. Globersons research interests include machine learning, probabilistic inference, convex optimization, neural computation and natural language processing. He is an associate editor for the Journal of Machine Learning Research, and the Associate Editor in Chief for the IEEE Transactions on Pattern Analysis and Machine Intelligence. His work has received several prizes including five paper awards (two at NIPS, two at UAI, and one at ICML), as well as one runner up for best paper at ICML. His research has been supported by several grants and awards from ISF, BSF, GIF, Intel, HP, and Google. In 2015 he was a visiting scientist at Google Mountain View.

Keynote Lecture: Machine Learning for Healthcare Data

Katherine A. Heller, Department of Statistical Science, Duke University

We will discuss multiple ways in which healthcare data is acquired and machine learning methods are currently being introduced into clinical settings. This will include: 1) Modeling disease trends and other predictions, including joint predictions of multiple conditions, from electronic health record (EHR) data using Gaussian processes. 2) Predicting surgical complications and transfer learning methods for combining databases 3) Using mobile apps and integrated sensors for improving the granularity of recorded health data for chronic conditions and 4) The combination of mobile app and social network information in order to predict the spread of contagious disease. Current work in these areas will be presented and the future of machine learning contributions to the field will be discussed.

Biographical details

Katherine is an Assistant Professor at Duke University, in the Department of Statistical Science and at the Center for Cognitive Neuroscience. Prior to joining Duke she was an NSF Postdoctoral Fellow, in the Computational Cognitive Science group at MIT, and an EPSRC Postdoctoral Fellow at the University of Cambridge. Her Ph.D. is from the Gatsby Unit, where her advisor was Zoubin Ghahramani. Katherine's research interests lie in the fields of machine learning and Bayesian statistics. Specifically, she develops new methods and models to discover latent structure in data, including cluster structure, using Bayesian nonparametrics, hierarchical Bayes, techniques for Bayesian model comparison, and other Bayesian statistical methods. She applies these methods to problems in the brain and cognitive sciences, where she strives to model human behavior, including human categorization and human social interactions.

Keynote Lecture: Intelligent Robots in an Uncertain World

Leslie Pack Kaelbling, Department of Electrical Engineering and Computer Science, Massachusetts Institute of Technology

The fields of AI and robotics have made great improvements in many individual subfields, including in motion planning, symbolic planning, reasoning under uncertainty, perception, and learning. Our goal is to develop an integrated approach to solving very large problems that are hopelessly intractable to solve optimally. We make a number of approximations during planning, including serializing subtasks, factoring distributions, and determinizing stochastic dynamics, but regain robustness and effectiveness through a continuous state-estimation and replanning process. I will describe our application of these ideas to an end-to-end mobile manipulation system, as well as ideas for current and future work on improving correctness and efficiency through learning.

Biographical details

Leslie is a Professor at MIT. She has an undergraduate degree in Philosophy and a PhD in Computer Science from Stanford, and was previously on the faculty at Brown University. She was the founding editor-in-chief of the Journal of Machine Learning Research. Her goal is to make intelligent robots, although she is not, herself, a robot.

Keynote Lecture: Snorkel: Beyond Hand-labeled Data

Christopher Ré, Department of Computer Science, Stanford University

This talk describes Snorkel, whose goal is to make routine machine learning tasks dramatically easier. Snorkel focuses on a key bottleneck in the development of machine learning systems: the lack of large training datasets. In Snorkel, a user implicitly defines large training sets by writing simple programs that label data, instead of tediously hand-labeling individual data items. Snorkel then combines these programs using a generative model to produce probabilistic training labels. This talk will cover the underlying theory, including methods to learn both the parameters and structure of generative models without labeled data, and new convergence guarantees for Gibbs sampling and accelerated non-convex optimization. Additionally we'll describe our preliminary evidence that the Snorkel approach may allow a broader set of users to train machine learning models more easily than previous approaches. Snorkel and its predecessor DeepDive are in daily use by scientists in areas including genomics and drug repurposing, by a number of companies involved in various forms of search, and by law enforcement in the fight against human trafficking. DeepDive and Snorkel are open source on github and available from `DeepDive.Stanford.edu` and `Snorkel.Stanford.edu`. Technical blog posts are available at `Snorkel.Stanford.edu`.

Biographical details

Christopher (Chris) Ré is an assistant professor in the Department of Computer Science at Stanford University in the InfoLab who is affiliated with the Statistical Machine Learning

Group, Pervasive Parallelism Lab, and Stanford AI Lab. His work's goal is to enable users and developers to build applications that more deeply understand and exploit data. His contributions span database theory, database systems, and machine learning, and his work has won best paper at a premier venue in each area, respectively, at PODS 2012, SIGMOD 2014, and ICML 2016. In addition, work from his group has been incorporated into major scientific and humanitarian efforts, including the IceCube neutrino detector, PaleoDeepDive and MEMEX in the fight against human trafficking, and into commercial products from major web and enterprise companies. He received a SIGMOD Dissertation Award in 2010, an NSF CAREER Award in 2011, an Alfred P. Sloan Fellowship in 2013, a Moore Data Driven Investigator Award in 2014, the VLDB early Career Award in 2015, the MacArthur Foundation Fellowship in 2015, and an Okawa Research Grant in 2016.

Keynote Lecture: Two Current Analysis Challenges: Single Cell Omics and Nanopore Long-read Sequence Data

Terry Speed, Bioinformatics Division, Walter and Eliza Hall Institute of Medical Research

Abstract. Two of the most exciting recent developments in my field are single cell omics assays, where omics here currently encompasses genomics, transcriptomics and epigenomics, and the long-read DNA sequencing capability introduced by Oxford Nanopore Technologies. Each leads to lots of interesting data permitting biomedical researchers to address questions previously beyond their reach. Each offers numerous opportunities and challenges to those who wish to, or must dive into the data to help the researchers answer these new questions. And each seems likely to drive theoretical developments in areas of interest to participants in UAI 2017. Ive been lucky enough to be associated with research projects in these two areas. Building on my experience with them, Ill discuss some of the opportunities, challenges and areas for theoretical development that I see.

Biographical details

Terry Speed completed a BSc (Hons) in mathematics and statistics at the University of Melbourne and a PhD in mathematics and Dip Ed at Monash University. He has held appointments at the University of Sheffield, U.K., the University of Western Australia in Perth, and the University of California at Berkeley, and with the CSIRO in Canberra. In 1997 he took up an appointment with the Walter & Eliza Hall Institute of Medical Research, where he is now an Honorary Fellow and lab head in the Bioinformatics Division. His research interests lie in the application of statistics and bioinformatics to genetics and genomics, and related fields such as proteomics, metabolomics and epigenomics, with a focus on cancer and epigenetics.

Inverse Reinforcement Learning via Deep Gaussian Process

Ming Jin[*]
UC Berkeley, USA
jinming@berkeley.edu

Andreas Damianou[†]
Amazon.com, Cambridge, UK
damianou@amazon.com

Pieter Abbeel
UC Berkeley, USA
pabbeel@berkeley.edu

Costas Spanos
UC Berkeley, USA
spanos@berkeley.edu

Abstract

We propose a new approach to inverse reinforcement learning (IRL) based on the deep Gaussian process (deep GP) model, which is capable of learning complicated reward structures with few demonstrations. Our model stacks multiple latent GP layers to learn abstract representations of the state feature space, which is linked to the demonstrations through the Maximum Entropy learning framework. Incorporating the IRL engine into the nonlinear latent structure renders existing deep GP inference approaches intractable. To tackle this, we develop a non-standard variational approximation framework which extends previous inference schemes. This allows for approximate Bayesian treatment of the feature space and guards against overfitting. Carrying out representation and inverse reinforcement learning simultaneously within our model outperforms state-of-the-art approaches, as we demonstrate with experiments on standard benchmarks ("object world","highway driving") and a new benchmark ("binary world").

1 INTRODUCTION

The problem of inverse reinforcement learning (IRL) is to infer the latent reward function that the agent subsumes by observing its demonstrations or trajectories in the task. It has been successfully applied in scientific inquiries, e.g., animal and human behavior modeling (Ng et al., 2000; Konstantakopoulos et al., 2017; 2016), as well as practical challenges, e.g., transportation (Ratliff et al., 2006; Abbeel et al., 2008; Ziebart et al., 2008; Gu et al., 2017) and intelligent building controls (Barrett and Linder, 2015). By learning the reward function, which provides the most succinct and transferable definition of a task, IRL has enabled advancing the state of the art in the robotic domains (Abbeel and Ng, 2004; Kolter et al., 2007).

Previous IRL algorithms treat the underlying reward as a linear (Abbeel and Ng, 2004; Ratliff et al., 2006; Ziebart et al., 2008; Syed and Schapire, 2007; Ratliff et al., 2009) or non-parametric function (Levine et al., 2010; 2011) of the state features. Main formulations within the linearity category include maximum margin (Ratliff et al., 2006), which presupposes that the optimal reward function leads to maximal difference of expected reward between the demonstrated and random strategies, and feature expectation matching (Abbeel and Ng, 2004; Syed et al., 2008), based on the observation that it suffices to match the feature expectation of a policy to the expert in order to guarantee similar performances. The reward function can be also regarded as the parameters for the policy class, such that the likelihood of observing the demonstrations is maximized with the true reward function, e.g., the maximum entropy approach (Ziebart et al., 2008).

As the representation power is limited by the linearity assumption, nonlinear formulations (Levine et al., 2010) are proposed to learn a set of composite features based on logical conjunctions. Non-parametric methods, pioneered by (Levine et al., 2011) based on Gaussian Processes (GPs) (Rasmussen and Williams, 2006), greatly enlarge the function space of latent reward to allow for non-linearity, and have been shown to achieve the state of the art performance on benchmark tests, e.g., object world and simulated highway driving (Abbeel and Ng, 2004; Syed and Schapire, 2007; Levine et al., 2010; 2011). Nevertheless,

[*] This research is funded by the Republic of Singapore's National Research Foundation through a grant to the Berkeley Education Alliance for Research in Singapore (BEARS) for the Singapore-Berkeley Building Efficiency and Sustainability in the Tropics (SinBerBEST) Program. BEARS has been established by the University of California, Berkeley as a center for intellectual excellence in research and education in Singapore.

[†] Work done while this author was at the University of Sheffield.

the heavy reliance on predefined or handcrafted features becomes a bottleneck for the existing methods, especially when the complexity or essence of the reward can not be captured by the given features. Finding such features automatically from data would be highly desirable.

In this paper, we propose an approach which performs feature and inverse reinforcement learning simultaneously and coherently within the same model by incorporating deep learning. The success of deep learning in a wide range of domains has drawn the community's attention to its structural advantages that can improve learning in complicated scenarios, e.g., Mnih et al. (2013) recently achieved a deep reinforcement learning (RL) breakthrough. Nevertheless, most deep models require massive data to be properly trained and can become impractical for IRL. On the other hand, deep Gaussian processes (deep GPs) (Damianou and Lawrence, 2013; Damianou, 2015) not only can they learn abstract structures with *smaller* data sets, but they also retain the non-parametric properties which Levine et al. (2011) demonstrated as important for IRL.

A deep GP is a deep belief network comprising a hierarchy of latent variables with Gaussian process mappings between the layers. Analogously to how gradients are propagated through a standard neural network, deep GPs aim at propagating uncertainty through Bayesian learning of latent posteriors. This constitutes a useful property for approaches involving stochastic decision making and also guards against overfitting by allowing for noisy features. However, previous methodologies employed for approximate Bayesian learning of deep GPs (Damianou and Lawrence, 2013; Hensman and Lawrence, 2014; Bui et al., 2015; Mattos et al., 2016) fail when diverging from the simple case of fixed output data modeled through a Gaussian regression model. In particular, in the IRL setting, the reward (output) is only revealed through the demonstrations, which is guided by the policy given by the reinforcement learning (Damianou, 2015).

The main contributions of our paper are below.

- We extend the deep GP framework to the IRL domain (Fig. 1), allowing for learning latent rewards with more complex structures from limited data.
- We derive a variational lower bound on the marginal log likelihood using an innovative definition of the variational distributions. This methodological contribution enables Bayesian learning in our model and can be applied to other scenarios where the observation layer's dynamics cause similar intractabilities.
- We compare the proposed deep GP for IRL with existing approaches in benchmark tests as well as newly defined tests with more challenging rewards.

Table 1: Summary of notations.

t	time step $t \in \{1, 2, \cdots, T\}$
h	index of demonstrations $h \in \{1, \cdots, H\}$
s, a	state $s \in \mathcal{S}$, action $a \in \mathcal{A}$
γ	RL discount factor, $\gamma \in (0, 1)$
$\boldsymbol{r}$	reward vector for all states $s \in \mathcal{S}$
$r(\cdot)$	reward function for states $\mathcal{S} \mapsto \mathbb{R}$
$Q(\cdot)$	Q-value function $\mathcal{S} \times \mathcal{A} \mapsto \mathbb{R}$
$\mathcal{Q}$	variational distribution
$V(\cdot)$	state value function $\mathcal{S} \mapsto \mathbb{R}$
$\pi, \hat{\pi}, \pi^*$	policy $\mathcal{S} \mapsto \mathcal{A}$, and the corresponding estimated and optimal versions
$\mathbf{X}$	m_0-dimensional feature matrix for $\lvert\mathcal{S}\rvert = n$ discrete states, $\mathbf{X} \in \mathbb{R}^{n,m_0}$
$\mathbf{x}_i, \mathbf{x}^m$	features for ith state, $[\mathbf{X}]_{i,:} = \mathbf{x}_i$, the mth feature for all states, $[\mathbf{X}]_{:,m} = \mathbf{x}^m$
$k_{\boldsymbol{\theta}}$	covariance function parametrized by $\boldsymbol{\theta}$
$K_{\mathbf{X},\mathbf{X}}$	covariance matrix, $[K_{\mathbf{X},\mathbf{X}}]_{i,j} = k_{\boldsymbol{\theta}}(\mathbf{x}_i, \mathbf{x}_j)$
$\mathbf{B}$	latent state matrix with m_1-dimensional features, $\mathbf{B} \in \mathbb{R}^{n,m_1}$
$\mathbf{D}$	$\mathbf{B}$ with Gaussian noise, $\mathbf{D} \in \mathbb{R}^{n,m_1}$
$\mathbf{W}, \mathbf{Z}$	inducing inputs, $\mathbf{W} \in \mathbb{R}^{K,m_0}$, $\mathbf{Z} \in \mathbb{R}^{K,m_1}$
$\mathbf{V}, \boldsymbol{f}$	inducing outputs, $\mathbf{V} \in \mathbb{R}^{K,m_1}$, $\boldsymbol{f} \in \mathbb{R}^K$
tilde $\tilde{}$	mean of the corresponding variable distribution, e.g., $\tilde{\boldsymbol{f}}, \tilde{\mathbf{v}}, \tilde{\mathbf{D}}$

In the following, we review the problem of inverse reinforcement learning (IRL). The list of notations used throughout the paper is summarized in Table 1.

1.1 Inverse Reinforcement Learning

The Markov Decision Process (MDP) is characterized by $\{\mathcal{S}, \mathcal{A}, \mathcal{T}, \gamma, \boldsymbol{r}\}$, which represents the state space, action space, transition model, discount factor, and reward function, respectively.

Take robot navigation as an example. The goal is to travel to the goal spot while avoiding stairwells. The state describes the current location and heading. The robot can choose actions from going forward or backward, turning left or right. The transition model specifies $p(s_{t+1}|s_t, a_t)$, i.e., the probability of reaching the next state given the current state and action, which accounts for the kinematic dynamics. The reward is +1 if it achieves the goal, -1 if it ends up in the stairwell, and 0 otherwise. The discount factor, γ, is a positive number less than 1, e.g., 0.9, to discount the future rewards. The optimal policy is then given by maximizing the expected reward, i.e.,

$$\pi^* = \arg\min_{\pi} \mathbb{E}\left[\sum_{t=0}^{\infty} \gamma^t r(s_t) | \pi\right]. \quad (1)$$

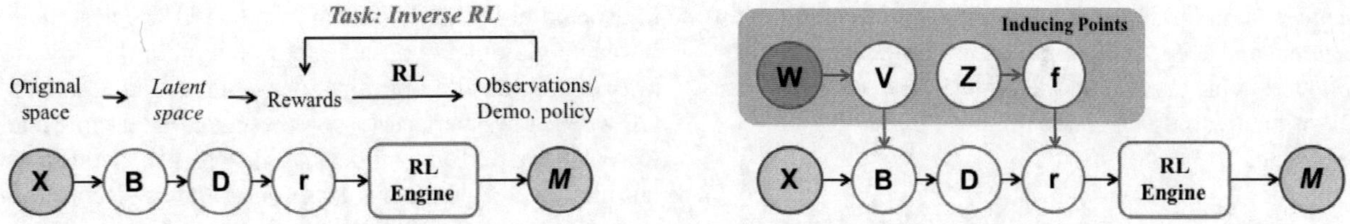

Figure 1: *Left:* The proposed deep GP model for IRL. The two layers of GPs are stacked to generate the latent reward $\boldsymbol{r}$, which is input to the reinforcement learning (RL) engine to produce an optimal control policy and demonstrations. $\mathbf{X}$ denotes the initial feature representation of states. *Right:* Illustration of DGP-IRL augmented with inducing outputs $\boldsymbol{f}, \mathbf{V}$ and corresponding inputs $\mathbf{Z}, \mathbf{W}$.

The IRL task is to find the reward function r^* such that the induced optimal policy matches the demonstrations, given $\{\mathcal{S}, \mathcal{A}, \mathcal{T}, \gamma\}$ and $\mathcal{M} = \{\zeta_1, ..., \zeta_H\}$, where $\zeta_h = \{(s_{h,1}, a_{h,1}), ..., (s_{h,T}, a_{h,T})\}$ is the demonstration trajectory, consisting of state-action pairs. Under the **linearity assumption**, the feature representation of states forms the linear basis of reward, $r(s) = \mathbf{w}^\top \phi(s)$, where $\phi(s) : \mathcal{S} \mapsto \mathbb{R}^{m_0}$ is the m_0-dimensional mapping from the state to the feature vector. From this definition, the *expected reward* for policy π is given by:

$$\mathbb{E}\left[\sum_{t=0}^{\infty} \gamma^t r(s_t) | \pi\right] = \mathbf{w}^\top \mathbb{E}\left[\sum_{t=0}^{\infty} \gamma^t \phi(s_t) | \pi\right]$$

where $\mu(\pi) = \mathbb{E}\left[\sum_{t=0}^{\infty} \gamma^t \phi(s_t)|\pi\right]$ is the feature expectation for policy π. The reward parameter $\mathbf{w}^*$ is learned such that

$$\mathbf{w}^{*\top} \mu(\pi^*) \geq \mathbf{w}^{*\top} \mu(\pi), \forall \pi \tag{2}$$

a prevalent idea that appears in the maximum margin planning (MMP) (Ratliff et al., 2006) and feature expectation matching (Syed and Schapire, 2007).

Motivated by the perspective of expected reward that parametrizes the policy class, the maximum entropy (MaxEnt) model (Ziebart et al., 2008) considers a stochastic decision model, where *the optimal policy randomly chooses the action* according to the associated reward:

$$p(a|s) = \exp\{Q^*(s, a; \boldsymbol{r}) - V^*(s; \boldsymbol{r})\} \tag{3}$$

where $V(s; \boldsymbol{r}) = \log \sum_a \exp(Q(s, a; \boldsymbol{r}))$ follows the Bellman equation, $Q(s, a; \boldsymbol{r})$ and $V(s; \boldsymbol{r})$ are measures of how desirable are the corresponding state s and state-action pair (s, a) under rewards $\boldsymbol{r}$. In principle, for a given state s, the best action corresponds to the highest Q-value, which represents the "desirability" of the action. Assuming independence among state-action pairs from demonstrations, the likelihood of the demonstration corresponds to the joint probability of taking a sequence of actions $a_{i,t}$ under states $s_{h,t}$ according to the Bellman equation:

$$\begin{aligned} p(\mathcal{M}|\boldsymbol{r}) &= \prod_{h=1}^{H} \prod_{t=1}^{T} p(a_{h,t}|s_{h,t}) \\ &= \exp\left(\sum_{h=1}^{H} \sum_{t=1}^{T} (Q(s_{h,t}, a_{h,t}; \boldsymbol{r}) - V(s_{h,t}; \boldsymbol{r}))\right). \end{aligned} \tag{4}$$

Though directly optimizing the above criteria with respect to $\boldsymbol{r}$ is possible, it does not lead to generalized solutions transferrable in a new test case where no demonstrations are available; hence, we need a "model" of $\boldsymbol{r}$. MaxEnt assumes linear structure for rewards, while GPIRL (Levine et al., 2011) uses GPs to relate the states to rewards. In Section 2.1, we will give a brief overview of GPs and GPIRL.

2 THE MODEL

In this section, we start by discussing the reward modeling through Gaussian processes (GPs) following (Levine et al., 2011), proceed to incorporate the representation learning module as additional GP layers, then develop our variational training framework and, finally, develop the transfer between tasks.

2.1 Gaussian Process Reward Modeling

We consider the setup of *discretizing the world* into n states. Assume that observed state-action pairs (demonstrations) $\mathcal{M} = \{\zeta_1, \ldots, \zeta_h\}$ are *generated* by a set of m_0−dimensional state features $\mathbf{X} \in \mathbb{R}^{n, m_0}$ through the reward function r. Throughout this paper we denote points (rows of a matrix) as $[\mathbf{X}]_{i,:} = \mathbf{x}_i$, features (columns) as $[\mathbf{X}]_{:,m} = \mathbf{x}^m$ and single elements as $[\mathbf{X}]_{i,m} = x_i^m$.

In this modeling framework, the reward function r plays the role of an unknown mapping, thus we wish to treat it as *latent* and keep it flexible and non-linear. Therefore, we follow (Levine et al., 2011) and model it with a zero-mean GP prior (Rasmussen and Williams, 2006):

$$r \sim \mathcal{GP}(0, k_{\boldsymbol{\theta}}(\mathbf{x}_i, \mathbf{x}_j)),$$

where $k_{\boldsymbol{\theta}}$ denotes the covariance function, e.g. $k_{\boldsymbol{\theta}}(\mathbf{x}_i, \mathbf{x}_j) = \sigma_k^2 e^{-\frac{\xi}{2}(\mathbf{x}_i - \mathbf{x}_j)^\top(\mathbf{x}_i - \mathbf{x}_j)}$, $\boldsymbol{\theta} = \{\sigma_k, \xi\}$. Given a finite amount of data, this induces the probability $\boldsymbol{r}|\mathbf{X}, \boldsymbol{\theta} \sim \mathcal{N}(\mathbf{0}, K_{\mathbf{XX}})$, where $\boldsymbol{r} \triangleq r(\mathbf{X})$ and the covariance matrix is obtained by $[K_{\mathbf{XX}}]_{i,j} = k_{\boldsymbol{\theta}}(\mathbf{x}_i, \mathbf{x}_j)$. The GPIRL training objective comes from integrating out the latent reward:

$$p(\mathcal{M}|\mathbf{X}) = \int p(\mathcal{M}|\boldsymbol{r}) p(\boldsymbol{r}|\mathbf{X}, \boldsymbol{\theta}) \mathrm{d}\boldsymbol{r} \tag{5}$$

and maximizing over $\boldsymbol{\theta}$, which we drop from our expressions from now on.

The above integral is intractable, because $p(\mathcal{M}|\boldsymbol{r})$ has the complicated expression of (4) (this is in contrast to the tranditional GP regression where $\mathcal{M}|\boldsymbol{r}$ is a Gaussian or other simple distribution). This can be alleviated using the approximation of (Levine et al., 2011). We will describe this approximation in the next section, as it is also used by our approach. Notice that all latent function instantiations are linked through a joint multivariate Gaussian. Thus, prediction of the function value $r^* = r(\mathbf{x}^*)$ at a test input $\mathbf{x}^*$ is found through the conditional

$$r^*|\boldsymbol{r}, \mathbf{X}, \mathbf{x}^* \sim \mathcal{N}\big(K_{\mathbf{x}^*\mathbf{X}} K_{\mathbf{XX}}^{-1} \boldsymbol{r}, k_{\mathbf{x}^*\mathbf{x}^*} - K_{\mathbf{x}^*\mathbf{X}} K_{\mathbf{XX}}^{-1} K_{\mathbf{X}\mathbf{x}^*}\big)$$

As can be seen, the prediction $r(\mathbf{x}^*)$ is reliant on the *effectiveness of feature representation*: states with features close in Euclidean distance are assumed to be associated with similar rewards. This motivates our novel deep GP-IRL method which is obtained by considering additional layers, as we will describe next.

2.2 Incorporating the Representation Learning Layers

The traditional model-based IRL approach is to learn the latent reward $\boldsymbol{r}$ (operating on fixed state features $\mathbf{X}$) that best explains the demonstrations $\mathcal{M}$. In this paper we wish to additionally and simultaneously uncover a highly descriptive state feature representation. To achieve this, we introduce a *latent* state feature representation $\mathbf{B} = \left[\mathbf{b}^1, ..., \mathbf{b}^{m_1}\right] \in \mathbb{R}^{n, m_1}$. $\mathbf{B}$ constitutes the instantiations of an introduced function b which is learned as a non-linear GP transformation from $\mathbf{X}$. To account for noise we further introduce $\mathbf{D}$ as the noisy versions of $\mathbf{B}$, i.e., $d_i^m = b_i^m + \epsilon$, $\epsilon \sim \mathcal{N}(0, \lambda^{-1})$.

Importantly, rather than performing two steps of learning separately (for the GPs on r and on b), we nest them into a single objective function, to maintain the flow of information during optimization. This results in a deep GP whose top layers perform representation learning and lower layers perform model-based IRL. Fig. 1 outlines our model, Deep Gaussian Process for Inverse Reinforcement Learning (**DGP-IRL**). By using $\mathbf{x}^m$ to represent the m-th column of $\mathbf{X}$, and similarly for $\mathbf{D}, \mathbf{B}$ the full generative model is written as follows:

$$\begin{aligned} & p(\mathcal{M}, \boldsymbol{r}, \mathbf{D}, \mathbf{B}|\mathbf{X}) \\ &= \underbrace{p(\mathcal{M}|\boldsymbol{r})}_{\text{IRL}} \underbrace{p(\boldsymbol{r}|\mathbf{D})}_{\mathcal{GP}(\mathbf{0}, k^r(\mathbf{d}_i, \mathbf{d}_j))} \underbrace{p(\mathbf{D}|\mathbf{B})}_{\text{Gaussian noise}} \underbrace{p(\mathbf{B}|\mathbf{X})}_{\mathcal{GP}(\mathbf{0}, k^b(\mathbf{x}_i, \mathbf{x}_j))} \\ &= e^{\sum_{h=1}^H \sum_{t=1}^T \left(Q(s_{h,t}, a_{h,t}; \boldsymbol{r}) - V(s_{h,t}; \boldsymbol{r})\right)} \mathcal{N}(\boldsymbol{r}|\mathbf{0}, K_{\mathbf{DD}}) \\ & \quad \prod_{m=1}^{m_1} \mathcal{N}(\mathbf{d}^m|\mathbf{b}^m, \lambda^{-1}\mathbf{I}) \mathcal{N}(\mathbf{b}^m|\mathbf{0}, K_{\mathbf{XX}}), \end{aligned} \tag{6}$$

where the IRL term $p(\mathcal{M}|\boldsymbol{r})$ takes the form of (4) as suggested by Ziebart et al. (2008). $K_{\mathbf{XX}}$ and $K_{\mathbf{DD}}$ are the covariance matrices in each layer, constructed with covariance functions k^b and k^r respectively. Compared to GPIRL the proposed framework has substantial gain in flexibility by introducing the abstract representation of states in the hidden layers $\mathbf{B}, \mathbf{D}$. Note that the model in Fig. 1 can be extended in depth by introducing additional hidden layers and connecting them with additional GP mappings; it is only for illustration simplicity that we base our derivation on the two layered structure.

We can compress the statistical power of each generative layer into a set of auxiliary variables within a *sparse GP framework* (Snelson and Ghahramani, 2005). Specifically, we introduce *inducing outputs and inputs*, denoted by $\boldsymbol{f} \in \mathbb{R}^K$ and $\mathbf{Z} \in \mathbb{R}^{K, m_1}$ respectively for the lower layer and by $\mathbf{V} \in \mathbb{R}^{K, m_1}$ and $\mathbf{W} \in \mathbb{R}^{K, m_0}$ for the top layer (as in Fig. 1). The inducing outputs and inputs are related with the same GP prior appearing in each layer. For example, $\boldsymbol{f}|\mathbf{Z} \sim \mathcal{N}(\mathbf{0}, K_{\mathbf{ZZ}})$ with $K_{\mathbf{ZZ}} = k^r(\mathbf{Z}, \mathbf{Z})$. By relating the original and inducing variables through the conditional Gaussian distribution, the auxiliary variables are learned to be *sufficient statistics* of the GP. The augmented model, shown in Fig. 1, has the following definition:

$$\begin{aligned} & p(\mathcal{M}, \boldsymbol{r}, \boldsymbol{f}, \mathbf{B}, \mathbf{D}, \mathbf{V}|\mathbf{X}, \mathbf{Z}, \mathbf{W}) \\ &= p(\mathcal{M}|\boldsymbol{r}) p(\boldsymbol{r}|\boldsymbol{f}, \mathbf{D}, \mathbf{Z}) p(\boldsymbol{f}|\mathbf{Z}) p(\mathbf{D}|\mathbf{B}) p(\mathbf{B}|\mathbf{V}, \mathbf{X}, \mathbf{W}) \\ &= e^{\sum_{h=1}^H \sum_{t=1}^T \left(Q(s_{h,t}, a_{h,t}; \boldsymbol{r}) - V(s_{h,t}; \boldsymbol{r})\right)} \cdot \\ & \quad \mathcal{N}(\boldsymbol{r}|K_{\mathbf{DZ}} K_{\mathbf{ZZ}}^{-1} \boldsymbol{f}, \boldsymbol{\Sigma}_r) \mathcal{N}(\boldsymbol{f}|\mathbf{0}, K_{\mathbf{ZZ}}) \cdot \\ & \quad \prod_{m=1}^{m_1} \mathcal{N}(\mathbf{d}^m|\mathbf{b}^m, \lambda^{-1}\mathbf{I}) \mathcal{N}(\mathbf{b}^m|K_{\mathbf{XW}} K_{\mathbf{WW}}^{-1} \mathbf{v}^m, \boldsymbol{\Sigma}_B) \end{aligned} \tag{7}$$

where we adopt the Fully Independent Training Conditional (FITC) to preserve the exact variances in $\mathbf{\Sigma}_B = diag\left(K_{\mathbf{XX}} - K_{\mathbf{XW}}K_{\mathbf{WW}}^{-1}K_{\mathbf{WX}}\right)$, and the Deterministic Training Conditional (DTC) (Quiñonero-Candela and Rasmussen, 2005) in $\mathbf{\Sigma}_r = \mathbf{0}$ as in GPIRL to facilitate the integration of $\boldsymbol{r}$ in the training objective (see next section).

In the following, we will omit the inducing inputs $\mathbf{W}, \mathbf{Z}$ in the conditions, with the convention to treat them as model parameters (Damianou and Lawrence, 2013; Damianou, 2015; Kandemir, 2015). By selecting $K \ll n$ the complexity reduces from $\mathcal{O}(n^3)$ to $\mathcal{O}(nK^2)$. While DGP-IRL resolves the case when the outputs have complex dependencies with the latent layers, the training of the model based on variational inference requires gradients for the parameters, as in backpropagation, whose convergence can be improved by leveraging advancements in deep learning.

Additionally, in DGP-IRL, the role of auxiliary variables goes further than just introducing scalability. Indeed, as we shall see next, the auxiliary variables play a distinct role in our model, by forming the base of a variational framework for Bayesian inference.

2.3 Variational Inference

We wish to optimize the model evidence for training:

$$p(\mathcal{M}|\mathbf{X}) = \int p(\mathcal{M}, \boldsymbol{f}, \boldsymbol{r}, \mathbf{V}, \mathbf{D}, \mathbf{B}|\mathbf{X}) \mathrm{d}(\boldsymbol{f}, \boldsymbol{r}, \mathbf{V}, \mathbf{D}, \mathbf{B})$$

However, this quantity is intractable. Firstly because the latent variables $\mathbf{D}$ appear nonlinearly in the inverse of covariance matrices. Secondly, because the latent rewards $\boldsymbol{f}, \boldsymbol{r}$ relate to the observation $\mathcal{M}$ through the reinforcement learning layer; the choice of $\mathbf{\Sigma}_r = \mathbf{0}$ in (7) does not completely solve this problem because in DGP-IRL there is additional uncertainty propagated by the latent layers. This indicates that Laplace approximation is not practical, neither is the variational method employed for deep GP (Damianou and Lawrence, 2013; Kandemir, 2015), where the output is related to the latent variable in a simple regression framework.

To this end, we show that we can derive an analytic lower bound on the model evidence by constructing a variational framework using the following special form of variational distribution:

$$\mathcal{Q} = q(\boldsymbol{f})q(\mathbf{D})q(\mathbf{B})q(\mathbf{V}), \text{ with :} \tag{8}$$

$$q(\boldsymbol{f}) = \delta(\boldsymbol{f} - \tilde{\boldsymbol{f}})$$

$$q(\mathbf{B}) = p(\mathbf{B}|\mathbf{V}, \mathbf{X}) \tag{9}$$

$$q(\mathbf{D}) = \prod_{m=1}^{m_1} \delta\left(\mathbf{d}^m - K_{\mathbf{XW}}K_{\mathbf{WW}}^{-1}\tilde{\mathbf{v}}^m\right) \tag{10}$$

$$q(\mathbf{V}) = \prod_{m=1}^{m_1} \mathcal{N}\left(\mathbf{v}^m|\tilde{\mathbf{v}}^m, \mathbf{G}^m\right) \tag{11}$$

The delta distribution is equivalent to taking the mean of normal distributions for prediction, which is reasonable in the context of reinforcement learning (Levine et al., 2011). Also note that the delta distribution is *applied only in the bottom layer and not repeatedly*; therefore, representation learning is indeed being manifested in the latent layers.

In addition, $q(\mathbf{B})$ matches the exact conditional $p(\mathbf{B}|\mathbf{V}, \mathbf{X})$ so that these two terms cancel in the fraction of (13) and the number of variational parameters is minimized, as in (Titsias and Lawrence, 2010). As for $q(\mathbf{D})$, it is chosen as delta distributions such that combined with $\mathbf{\Sigma}_r = \mathbf{0}$ the IRL term $p(\mathcal{M}|\boldsymbol{r})p(\boldsymbol{r}|\boldsymbol{f}, \mathbf{D})$ in (12) becomes tractable and information can flow through the latent layers $\mathbf{B}, \mathbf{D}$.

The variational marginal $q(\mathbf{V})$ is factorized across its dimensions with fully parameterized normal densities, as in (Damianou and Lawrence, 2013). Notice that $\tilde{\boldsymbol{f}}$ and $\tilde{\mathbf{v}}$ are the mean of the inducing outputs (Table 1), corresponding to pseudo-inputs $\mathbf{Z}$ and $\mathbf{W}$, where $\mathbf{Z}$ (initialized with random numbers from uniform distributions (Sutskever et al., 2013)) be learned to further maximize the marginaliked likelihood, and $\mathbf{W}$ is chosen as a subset of $\mathbf{X}$.

The variational means of $\mathbf{D}$ can be augmented with input data, $\mathbf{X}$, to improve stability during training (Duvenaud et al., 2014).

The variational lower bound, $\mathcal{L}$, follows from the Jensen's inequality, and can be derived analytically due to the choice of variational distribution $\mathcal{Q}$ (see Section 2 of the Appendix for details):

$$\log p(\mathcal{M}|\mathbf{X}) = \log \int \underbrace{p(\mathcal{M}|\boldsymbol{r})p(\boldsymbol{r}|\boldsymbol{f}, \mathbf{D})}_{p(\mathcal{M}|\boldsymbol{r}=K_{\mathbf{DZ}}K_{\mathbf{ZZ}}^{-1}\boldsymbol{f}) \text{ by DTC: } \mathbf{\Sigma}_r=\mathbf{0}} \quad p(\boldsymbol{f})p(\mathbf{D}|\mathbf{B})p(\mathbf{B}|\mathbf{V}, \mathbf{X})p(\mathbf{V})\mathrm{d}(\boldsymbol{r}, \boldsymbol{f}, \mathbf{V}, \mathbf{D}, \mathbf{B}) \tag{12}$$

$$\geq \int q(\boldsymbol{f})q(\mathbf{D})p(\mathbf{B}|\mathbf{V}, \mathbf{X})q(\mathbf{V}) \log \frac{p(\mathcal{M}|K_{\mathbf{DZ}}K_{\mathbf{ZZ}}^{-1}\boldsymbol{f})p(\boldsymbol{f})p(\mathbf{D}|\mathbf{B})p(\mathbf{V})}{q(\boldsymbol{f})q(\mathbf{D})q(\mathbf{V})} \text{ by Jensen's ineq.} \tag{13}$$

$$= \mathcal{L}_{\mathcal{M}} + \mathcal{L}_{\mathcal{G}} - \mathcal{L}_{\mathrm{KL}} + \mathcal{L}_{\mathcal{B}} - \frac{nm_1}{2}\log(2\pi\lambda^{-1}) \tag{14}$$

where

$$\mathcal{L}_{\mathcal{M}} = \log p(\mathcal{M}|K_{\tilde{\mathbf{D}}\mathbf{Z}}K_{\mathbf{ZZ}}^{-1}\tilde{\boldsymbol{f}})) = \sum_{h=1}^{H}\sum_{t=1}^{T}\Big(Q(s_{h,t},a_{h,t};K_{\tilde{\mathbf{D}}\mathbf{Z}}K_{\mathbf{ZZ}}^{-1}\tilde{\boldsymbol{f}})-V(s_{h,t};K_{\tilde{\mathbf{D}}\mathbf{Z}}K_{\mathbf{ZZ}}^{-1}\tilde{\boldsymbol{f}})\Big) \tag{15}$$

$$\mathcal{L}_{\mathcal{G}} = \log p(\boldsymbol{f} = \tilde{\boldsymbol{f}}|\mathbf{Z}) = \log \mathcal{N}(\boldsymbol{f} = \tilde{\boldsymbol{f}}|\mathbf{0}, K_{\mathbf{ZZ}}) \tag{16}$$

$$\mathcal{L}_{KL} = \text{KL}(q(\mathbf{V})||p(\mathbf{V}|\mathbf{W})) = \sum_{m=1}^{m_1}\text{KL}(\mathcal{N}(\mathbf{v}^m|\tilde{\mathbf{v}}^m, \mathbf{G}^m)||\mathcal{N}(\mathbf{v}^m|\mathbf{0}, K_{\mathbf{WW}}))$$

$$\mathcal{L}_{\mathcal{B}} = -\frac{\lambda}{2}\sum_{m=1}^{m_1}\text{Tr}(\mathbf{\Sigma_B} + K_{\mathbf{XW}}K_{\mathbf{WW}}^{-1}\mathbf{G}^m K_{\mathbf{WW}}^{-1}K_{\mathbf{WX}}) \tag{17}$$

where $|K_{\mathbf{WW}}|$ is the determinant of $K_{\mathbf{WW}}$. $\tilde{\mathbf{D}} = [\tilde{\mathbf{d}}^1, ..., \tilde{\mathbf{d}}^{m_1}]$, where $\tilde{\mathbf{d}}^m = K_{\mathbf{XW}}K_{\mathbf{WW}}^{-1}\tilde{\mathbf{v}}^m$. $\mathcal{L}_{\mathcal{M}}$ is the term associated with RL. $\mathcal{L}_{\mathcal{G}}$ is the Gaussian prior on inducing outputs $\boldsymbol{f}$. $\mathcal{L}_{KL}$ denotes the Kullback – Leibler (KL) divergence between the variational posterior $q(\mathbf{V})$ to the prior $p(\mathbf{V})$, acting as a regularization term. The lower bound $\mathcal{L}$ can be optimized with gradient-based methods, which are computed by backpropagation. In addition, we can find the optimal fixed-point equations for the variational distribution parameters $\tilde{\mathbf{v}}^m, \mathbf{G}^m$ for $q(\mathbf{V})$ using variational calculus, in order to raise the variational lower bound $\mathcal{L}$ further (refer to Section 3 of the supplement for this derivation).

Notice that the approximate marginalization of all hidden spaces, in (14), approximates a Bayesian training procedure, according to which model complexity is automatically balanced through the Bayesian Occam's razor principle. Optimizing the objective $\mathcal{L}$ turns the variational distribution $\mathcal{Q}$ into an approximation to the true model posterior.

2.4 Transfer to New Tasks

The inducing points provide a succinct summary of the data, by the property of FITC (Quiñonero-Candela and Rasmussen, 2005), which means only the inducing points are necessary for prediction. Given a set of new states $\mathbf{X}^*$, DGP-IRL can infer the latent reward through the full Bayesian treatment:

$$p(\boldsymbol{r}^*|\mathbf{X}^*, \mathbf{X}) = \int \Big\{p(\boldsymbol{r}^*|\boldsymbol{f}, \mathbf{D}^*)q(\boldsymbol{f})p(\mathbf{D}^*|\mathbf{B}^*) \\ p(\mathbf{B}^*|\mathbf{V}, \mathbf{X}^*)q(\mathbf{V})\Big\}\text{d}(\boldsymbol{f}, \mathbf{B}^*, \mathbf{D}^*, \mathbf{V}) \tag{18}$$

Given that the above integral is computationally intensive to evaluate, a practical alternative adopted in our implementation is to use point estimates for latent variables; hence, the rewards are given by:

$$\boldsymbol{r}^* = K_{\mathbf{D}^*\mathbf{Z}}K_{\mathbf{ZZ}}^{-1}\tilde{\boldsymbol{f}} \tag{19}$$

where $\mathbf{D}^* = [\mathbf{d}_*^1, ..., \mathbf{d}_*^{m_1}]$, with $\mathbf{d}_*^m = K_{\mathbf{X}^*\mathbf{W}}K_{\mathbf{WW}}^{-1}\tilde{\mathbf{v}}^m$. The above formulae suggest that instead of making inference based on $\mathbf{X}$ layer directly as in Levine et al. (2011), DGP-IRL first estimates the latent representation of the states, $\mathbf{D}^*$, then makes GP regression using the latent variables.

3 EXPERIMENTS

For the experimental evaluation, we employ the *expected value difference* (EVD) as a metric of optimality, given by:

$$\mathbb{E}\left[\sum_{t=0}^{\infty}\gamma^t r(s_t)|\pi^*\right] - \mathbb{E}\left[\sum_{t=0}^{\infty}\gamma^t r(s_t)|\hat{\pi}\right], \tag{20}$$

which is the difference between the expected reward earned under the optimal policy, π^*, given by the true rewards, and the policy derived from the IRL rewards, $\hat{\pi}$. Our software implementation is included in the supplementary and can be also accessed at: `http://www.jinming.tech/software/`.

3.1 Object World Benchmark

The Object World (OW) benchmark, originally implemented by Levine et al. (2011), is a $N \times N$ gridworld where dots of *primary colors*, e.g., red and blue, and *secondary colors*, e.g., purple and green, are placed on the grid at random, as shown in Fig. 2. Each state, i.e., grid block, is described by the shortest distances to dots among each color group. The latent reward is assigned such that if a block is 1 step within a red dot and 3 steps within a blue dot, the reward is +1; if it is 3 steps within a blue dot only, the reward is -1, and the reward is 0 otherwise. The agent maximizes its expected discounted reward by following a policy which provides the probabilities of actions (moving up/down/left/right, or stay still) at each state, subject to a transition probability.

The objective of the experiment is to compare the performances of DGP-IRL with previous methods as the

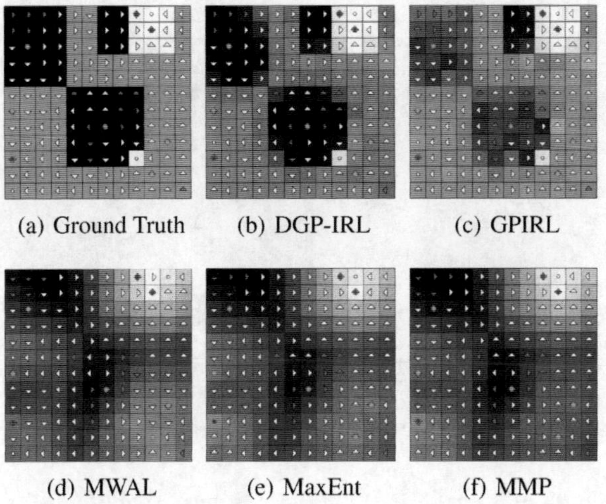

(a) Ground Truth (b) DGP-IRL (c) GPIRL

(d) MWAL (e) MaxEnt (f) MMP

Figure 2: OW benchmark for IRL, evaluated for (a) DGP-IRL, (b) GPIRL, (c) MWAL, (d) MaxEnt, and (e) MMP, with 64 demonstrations and continuous features. Except for DGP-IRL, all the other algorithms are evaluated with the toolbox by Levine et al. (2011).

number of demonstrations varies. Candidates that are evaluated include the Multiplicative Weights for Apprenticeship Learning (MWAL) (Syed and Schapire, 2007), MaxEnt, MMP, which assume a linear reward function, and GPIRL, which is the state-of-the-art method on the benchmark. Linear models, as is shown in Fig. 2, cannot capture the complex structure, while GPIRL learns more accurate yet still noisy rewards, as limited by feature discriminability; DGP-IRL, on the contrary, makes inference closest to the ground truth even with limited data, thanks to the increased representational power and robust training through variational inference.

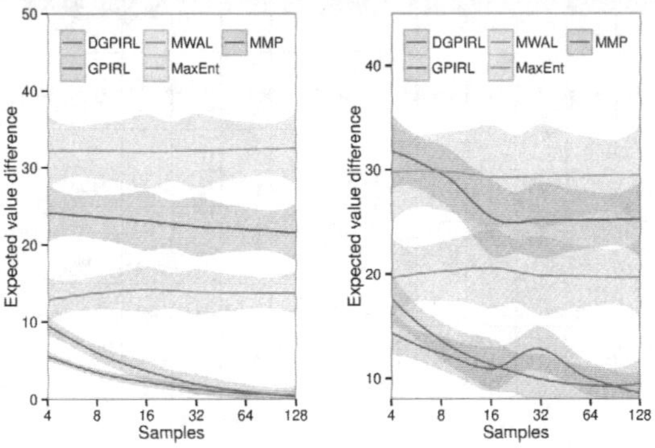

(a) Training (b) Transfer

Figure 3: Plots of EVD in the training (a) and transfer (b) tests for the OW benchmark, where continuous features are employed.

Additionally, the transferability test is carried out by examining EVD in a new world where no demonstrations are available, which requires the ability of knowledge transfer from the previous learning scenario. DGP-IRL outperforms GPIRL and other models in both the training and transfer cases, and the improvement is obvious as more data is accessible (Fig. 3). The shaded area (Fig. 3, 6, 7(a)) are the standard deviation of EVD among independent experiments, which reflect that DGP-IRL and GPIRL are more reliable.

3.2 Binary World Benchmark

Though the rewards in OW are nonlinear functions of the features, they form separated clusters in the subspace spanned by two dimensions, i.e., distances to the nearest red and blue dots. Binary world (BW) is a benchmark introduced by Wulfmeier et al. (2015) whose reward depends on combinatorics of features. More specifically, in a world of $N \times N$ plane where each block is randomly assigned with either a blue or red dot, the state is associated with the +1 reward if there are 4 blues in the 3×3 *neighborhood*, -1 for 5 blues, and 0 otherwise. The feature represents the color of the 9 dots in the neighborhood. BW sets up a challenging scenario, where states that are maximally separated in feature space can have the same rewards, yet those that are close in euclidean distance may have opposite rewards.

The task is to learn the latent rewards of states given limited demonstrations, as is shown in Fig. 4. While linear models are limited by their capacity of representation, the results of GPIRL also deviate from the latent rewards as it cannot generalize from training data with the convoluted features. DGP-IRL, nevertheless, is able to recover the ground truth with the highest fidelity.

By successively warping the original feature space through the latent layers, DGP-IRL can learn an abstract representation that reveals the reward structure. As is illustrated in Fig. 5, though the points are mixed up in the input space, making it impossible to separate those with the same rewards, their positions in the latent space clearly form clusters, which indicates that DGP-IRL has remarkably uncovered the mechanism of reward generation by simply observing the traces of actions.

The advantage of simultaneous representation and inverse reinforcement learning is demonstrated in Fig. 6, which plots the EVD for the training and transfer cases. As the features are interlinked not only with the reward but also with themselves in a very nonlinear way, this scenario is particularly challenging for linear models, such as LEARCH (Ratliff et al., 2009), MaxEnt, and MMP. While both GPIRL and DGP-IRL have satisfactory performance in the training case, DGP-IRL significantly out-

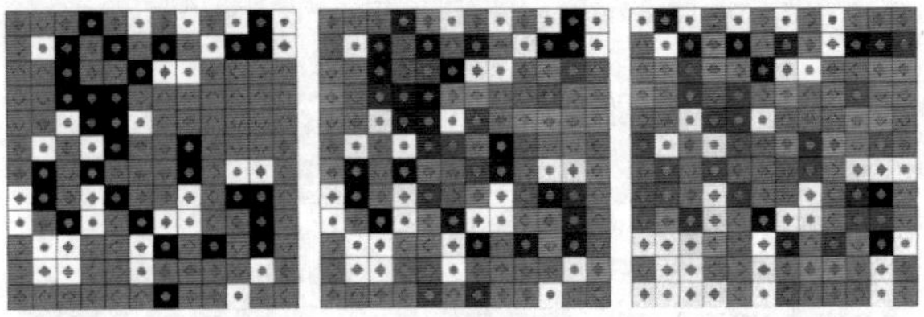

(a) Ground Truth (b) DGP-IRL (c) GPIRL

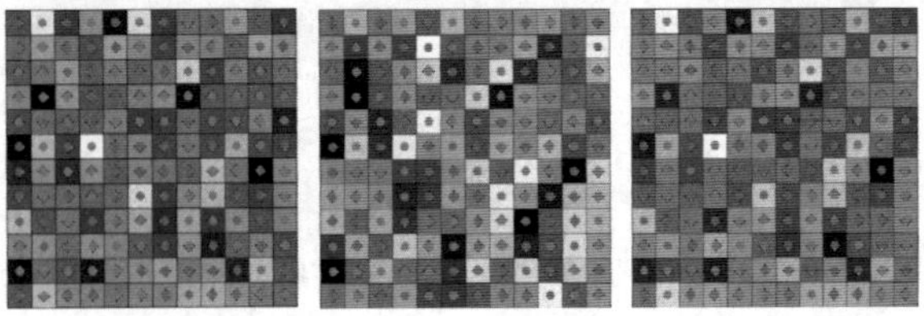

(d) LEARCH (e) MaxEnt (f) MMP

Figure 4: BW benchmark evaluated with 128 demonstrated traces for DGP-IRL, GPIRL, LEARCH Ratliff et al. (2009), MaxEnt, and MMP.

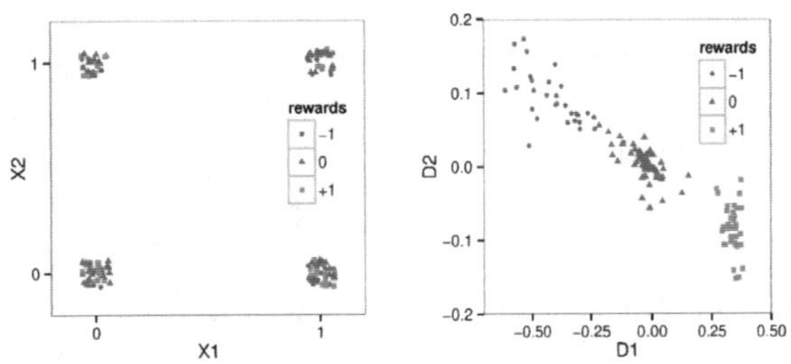

(a) Input space $\mathbf{X}$ (b) Latent space $\mathbf{D}$

Figure 5: Visualization of points along two arbitrary dimensions in the (a) input space $\mathbf{X}$ and (b) latent space $\mathbf{D}$ of DGP-IRL. The points represent features of states and are color-coded with the associated rewards. The rewards are entangled in the input space $\mathbf{X}$ but separated in the latent space $\mathbf{D}$.

performs GPIRL in the transfer task, which indicates that the learned latent space is transferrable across different scenarios.

3.3 Highway Driving Behaviors

Highway driving behavior modeling, as investigated by Levine et al. (2010; 2011), is a concrete example to examine the capacity of IRL algorithms in learning the underlying motives from demonstrations based on a simple simulator. In a three-lane highway, vehicles of specific class (civilian or police) and category (car or motorcycle) are positioned at random, driving at the same constant speed. The robot car can switch lanes and navigate at up to three times the traffic speed. The state is described by a continuous feature which consists of the closest distances to vehicles of each class and category in the same lane, together with the left, right, and any lane, both in the front and back of the robot car, in addition to the current speed and position.

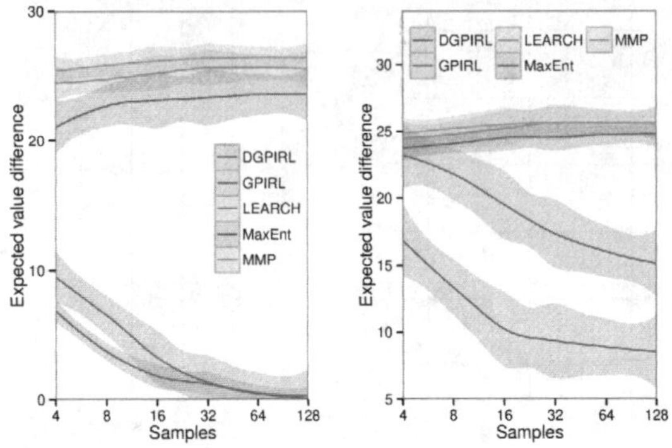

(a) Training (b) Transfer

Figure 6: Plots of EVD in the training (a) and transfer (b) tests for the BW benchmark as the number of training samples varies.

The goal is to navigate the robot car as fast as possible, but avoid speeding by checking that the speed is no greater than twice the current traffic when the police car is 2 car lengths nearby. As the reward is a nonlinear function determined by the current speed and distance to the police, linear models are outrun by GPIRL and DGP-IRL. Performance generally improves with more demonstrations, and DGP-IRL remains to yield the policy closest to the optimal in EVD, and with minimal probability of speeding, as illustrated in Fig. 7(a) and 7(b), respectively.

4 CONCLUSION AND FUTURE WORK

DGP-IRL is proposed as a solution for IRL based on deep GPs. By extending the structure with additional GP layers to learn the abstract representation of the state features, DGP-IRL has more representational capability than linear-based and GP-based methods. Meanwhile, the Bayesian training approach through variational inference guards against overfitting, bringing the advantage of automatic capacity control and principled uncertainty handling.

Our proposed DGP-IRL outperforms state-of-the-art methods in our experiments, and is shown to learn efficiently even from few demonstrations. For future work, the unique properties of DGP-IRL enable easy incorporation of side knowledge (through priors on the latent space) to IRL, but our work also opens up the way for combining

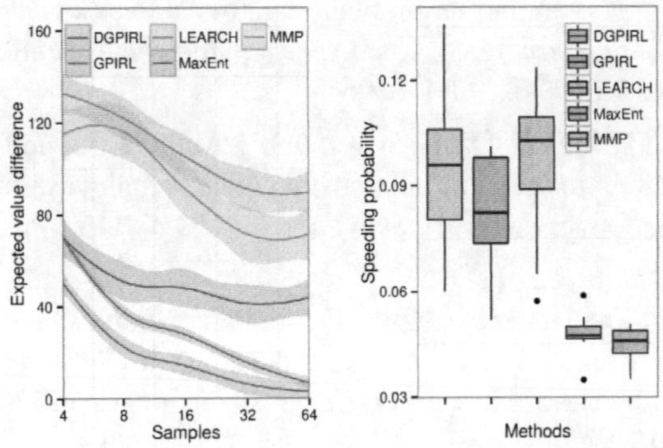

(a) Training EVD (b) Speeding Prob.

Figure 7: Plots of EVD in the training (a) and the probability of speeding (with 64 demonstrations) (b) in the highway driving simulation benchmark, with three lanes and 32 car lengths.

deep GPs with other complicated inference engines, e.g., selective attention models (Gregor et al., 2015). We plan to investigate these ideas in the future. Another promising future direction is to construct transferable models where the latent layer is relied on for knowledge sharing.

Finally, we plan to investigate some of the many applications where DGP-IRL can prove especially beneficial, such as mobile sensing for health (Gu, 2017), building and grid controls (Jin et al., 2017), multiobjective control (Jia et al., 2017), and human-in-the-loop gamification (Ratliff et al., 2014).

References

Pieter Abbeel and Andrew Y Ng. Apprenticeship learning via inverse reinforcement learning. In *Proceedings of the twenty-first international conference on Machine learning*, page 1. ACM, 2004.

Pieter Abbeel, Dmitri Dolgov, Andrew Y Ng, and Sebastian Thrun. Apprenticeship learning for motion planning with application to parking lot navigation. In *Intelligent Robots and Systems, 2008. IROS 2008. IEEE/RSJ International Conference on*, pages 1083–1090. IEEE, 2008.

Enda Barrett and Stephen Linder. Autonomous HVAC control, a reinforcement learning approach. In *Machine Learning and Knowledge Discovery in Databases*, pages 3–19. Springer, 2015.

Thang D Bui, José Miguel Hernández-Lobato, Yingzhen Li, Daniel Hernández-Lobato, and Richard E Turner. Training deep Gaussian processes using stochastic expectation propagation and probabilistic backpropagation. *arXiv preprint arXiv:1511.03405*, 2015.

Andreas Damianou. *Deep Gaussian processes and variational propagation of uncertainty*. PhD thesis, University of Sheffield, 2015.

Andreas Damianou and Neil Lawrence. Deep Gaussian processes. In *Proceedings of the Sixteenth International Conference on Artificial Intelligence and Statistics*, pages 207–215, 2013.

David Duvenaud, Oren Rippel, Ryan P. Adams, and Zoubin Ghahramani. Avoiding pathologies in very deep networks. In *Artificial Intelligence and Statistics*, 2014.

Karol Gregor, Ivo Danihelka, Alex Graves, and Daan Wierstra. Draw: A recurrent neural network for image generation. *arXiv preprint arXiv:1502.04623*, 2015.

Weixi Gu. Non-intrusive blood glucose monitor by multi-task deep learning: Phd forum abstract. In *Proceedings of the 16th ACM/IEEE International Conference on Information Processing in Sensor Networks*, pages 249–250. ACM, 2017.

Weixi Gu, Kai Zhang, Zimu Zhou, Ming Jin, Yuxun Zhou, Xi Liu, Costas J Spanos, Zuo-Jun Max Shen, Wei-Hua Lin, and Lin Zhang. Measuring fine-grained metro interchange time via smartphones. *Transportation Research Part C: Emerging Technologies*, 81:153–171, 2017.

James Hensman and Neil D Lawrence. Nested variational compression in Deep Gaussian Processes. *arXiv preprint arXiv:1412.1370*, 2014.

Ruoxi Jia, Roy Dong, S Shankar Sastry, and Costas J Spanos. Privacy-enhanced architecture for occupancy-based HVAC control. In *Proceedings of the 8th International Conference on Cyber-Physical Systems*, pages 177–186. ACM, 2017.

Ming Jin, Wei Feng, Ping Liu, Chris Marnay, and Costas Spanos. MOD-DR: microgrid optimal dispatch with demand response. *Applied Energy*, 187:758–776, 2017.

Melih Kandemir. Asymmetric transfer learning with Deep Gaussian Processes. In *Proceedings of the 32nd International Conference on Machine Learning (ICML-15)*, pages 730–738, 2015.

J Zico Kolter, Pieter Abbeel, and Andrew Y Ng. Hierarchical apprenticeship learning with application to quadruped locomotion. In *Advances in Neural Information Processing Systems*, pages 769–776, 2007.

I. C. Konstantakopoulos, L. J. Ratliff, M. Jin, S. S. Sastry, and C. J. Spanos. A robust utility learning framework via inverse optimization. *IEEE Transactions on Control Systems Technology*, PP(99):1–17, 2017. doi: 10.1109/TCST.2017.2699163.

Ioannis C Konstantakopoulos, Lillian J Ratliff, Ming Jin, Costas J Spanos, and S Shankar Sastry. Inverse modeling of non-cooperative agents via mixture of utilities. In *Decision and Control (CDC), 2016 IEEE 55th Conference on*, pages 6327–6334. IEEE, 2016.

Sergey Levine, Zoran Popovic, and Vladlen Koltun. Feature construction for inverse reinforcement learning. In *Advances in Neural Information Processing Systems*, pages 1342–1350, 2010.

Sergey Levine, Zoran Popovic, and Vladlen Koltun. Nonlinear inverse reinforcement learning with Gaussian processes. In *Advances in Neural Information Processing Systems*, pages 19–27, 2011.

César Lincoln C Mattos, Zhenwen Dai, Andreas Damianou, Jeremy Forth, Guilherme A Barreto, and Neil D Lawrence. Recurrent Gaussian processes. *International Conference on Learning Representations (ICLR)*, 2016.

Volodymyr Mnih, Koray Kavukcuoglu, David Silver, Alex Graves, Ioannis Antonoglou, Daan Wierstra, and Martin Riedmiller. Playing atari with deep reinforcement learning. *arXiv preprint arXiv:1312.5602*, 2013.

Andrew Y Ng, Stuart J Russell, et al. Algorithms for inverse reinforcement learning. In *Icml*, pages 663–670, 2000.

Joaquin Quiñonero-Candela and Carl Edward Rasmussen. A unifying view of sparse approximate Gaussian process regression. *The Journal of Machine Learning Research*, 6:1939–1959, 2005.

Carl Edward Rasmussen and Christopher KI Williams. *Gaussian processes for machine learning*, volume 1. MIT press Cambridge, 2006.

Lillian J Ratliff, Ming Jin, Ioannis C Konstantakopoulos, Costas Spanos, and S Shankar Sastry. Social game for building energy efficiency: Incentive design. In *52nd Annual Allerton Conference on Communication, Control, and Computing, 2014*, pages 1011–1018, 2014.

Nathan D Ratliff, J Andrew Bagnell, and Martin A Zinkevich. Maximum margin planning. In *Proceedings of the 23rd international conference on Machine learning*, pages 729–736. ACM, 2006.

Nathan D Ratliff, David Silver, and J Andrew Bagnell. Learning to search: Functional gradient techniques for imitation learning. *Autonomous Robots*, 27(1):25–53, 2009.

Edward Snelson and Zoubin Ghahramani. Sparse Gaussian processes using pseudo-inputs. In *Advances in neural information processing systems*, pages 1257–1264, 2005.

Ilya Sutskever, James Martens, George Dahl, and Geoffrey Hinton. On the importance of initialization and momentum in deep learning. In *Proceedings of the 30th International Conference on Machine Learning (ICML-13)*, pages 1139–1147, 2013.

Umar Syed and Robert E Schapire. A game-theoretic approach to apprenticeship learning. In *Advances in neural information processing systems*, volume 20, pages 1–8, 2007.

Umar Syed, Michael Bowling, and Robert E Schapire. Apprenticeship learning using linear programming. In *Proceedings of the 25th international conference on Machine learning*, pages 1032–1039. ACM, 2008.

Michalis K Titsias and Neil D Lawrence. Bayesian Gaussian process latent variable model. In *International Conference on Artificial Intelligence and Statistics*, pages 844–851, 2010.

Markus Wulfmeier, Peter Ondruska, and Ingmar Posner. Deep inverse reinforcement learning. *arXiv preprint arXiv:1507.04888*, 2015.

Brian D Ziebart, Andrew L Maas, J Andrew Bagnell, and Anind K Dey. Maximum entropy inverse reinforcement learning. In *AAAI*, pages 1433–1438, 2008.

Appendix of:
Inverse Reinforcement Learning via Deep Gaussian Process

1 Background: Inverse Reinforcement Learning and DGP-IRL

The Markov Decision Process (MDP) is characterized by $\{\mathcal{S}, \mathcal{A}, \mathcal{T}, \gamma, \boldsymbol{r}\}$, which represents the state space, action space, transition model, discount factor, and reward function, respectively.

The IRL task is to find the reward function r^* such that the induced optimal policy matches the demonstrations, given $\{\mathcal{S}, \mathcal{A}, \mathcal{T}, \gamma\}$ and $\mathcal{M} = \{\zeta_1, ..., \zeta_h\}$, where $\zeta_i = \{(s_{i,1}, a_{i,1}), ..., (s_{i,T}, a_{i,T})\}$ is the demonstration trajectory, consisting of state-action pairs.

Deep Gaussian process for inverse reinforcement learning (DGP-IRL) extends the deep Gaussian process (deep GP) framework to the IRL domain, as shown in Fig. 1. DGP-IRL learns an abstract representation that reveals the reward structure by warping the original feature space through the latent layers, $\mathbf{D}, \mathbf{B}$.

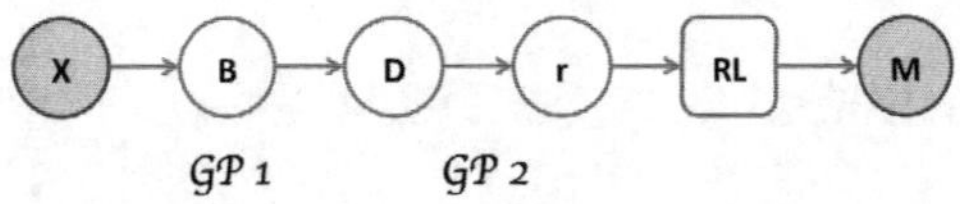

Figure 1: The proposed deep GP model for IRL, where latent Gaussian processes are introduced to learn a representation of the world for the latent reward $\boldsymbol{r}$. The rewards are provided to the reinforcement learning (RL) engine to generate a set of observable trajectories $\mathcal{M}$.

For a set of observed trajectories $\mathcal{M}$, our objective is to optimize the corresponding marginalized log-likelihood given the states in the world as represented by $\mathbf{X}$:

$$\log p(\mathcal{M}|\mathbf{X}) = \log \int p(\mathcal{M}|\boldsymbol{r})p(\boldsymbol{r}|\mathbf{D})p(\mathbf{D}|\mathbf{B})p(\mathbf{B}|\mathbf{X})d(\boldsymbol{r}, \mathbf{D}, \mathbf{B}) \tag{1}$$

where the integration is with respect to the latent layers, including the reward vector $\boldsymbol{r}$. As introduced in the main paper, $\mathbf{d}^m \in \mathbb{R}^n$ is the m-th column of the latent layer $\mathbf{D} = \begin{bmatrix}\mathbf{d}^1 & \cdots & \mathbf{d}^{m_1}\end{bmatrix}$, and similarly for $\mathbf{B} = \begin{bmatrix}\mathbf{b}^1 & \cdots & \mathbf{b}^{m_1}\end{bmatrix}$:

$$p(\mathcal{M}|\boldsymbol{r}) = \sum_{i=1}^{h}\sum_{t=1}^{T}\left(Q(s_{i,t}, a_{i,t}; \boldsymbol{r}) - V(s_{i,t}; \boldsymbol{r})\right) \tag{2}$$

$$p(\boldsymbol{r}|\mathbf{D}) = \mathcal{N}(\boldsymbol{r}|\mathbf{0}, K_{\mathbf{DD}}) \tag{3}$$

$$p(\mathbf{D}|\mathbf{B}) = \prod_{m=1}^{m_1} \mathcal{N}(\mathbf{d}^m|\mathbf{b}^m, \lambda^{-1}\mathbf{I}) \tag{4}$$

$$p(\mathbf{B}|\mathbf{X}) = \prod_{m=1}^{m_1} \mathcal{N}(\mathbf{b}^m|\mathbf{0}, K_{\mathbf{XX}}) \tag{5}$$

where $p(\mathcal{M}|\boldsymbol{r})$ represents the reinforcement learning term, given by:

$$\log p(\mathcal{M}|\boldsymbol{r}) = \sum_{i}\sum_{t}\left(Q(s_{i,t}, a_{i,t}; \boldsymbol{r}) - V(s_{i,t}; \boldsymbol{r})\right) \tag{6}$$

$$= \sum_{t}\sum_{t}\left(\boldsymbol{r}_{s_{i,t},a_{i,t}} - V(s_{i,t}; \boldsymbol{r}) + \sum_{s'} \gamma \mathcal{T}_{s'}^{s_{i,t},a_{i,t}} V(s'; \boldsymbol{r})\right) \tag{7}$$

The Q-value $Q(s_{i,t}, a_{i,t}; \boldsymbol{r})$ used above is a measure of how desirable is the corresponding state-action pair $(s_{i,t}, a_{i,t})$ under rewards $\boldsymbol{r}$ for all the world states, and is defined by:

$$Q(s_{i,t}, a_{i,t}; \boldsymbol{r}) = \boldsymbol{r}_{s_{i,t},a_{i,t}} + \sum_{s'} \gamma \mathcal{T}_{s'}^{s_{i,t},a_{i,t}} V(s'; \boldsymbol{r})$$

where $\boldsymbol{r}_{s_{i,t},a_{i,t}} = r(s_{i,t}, a_{i,t}) \in \mathbb{R}$ is the reward for $(s_{i,t}, a_{i,t})$, γ is the discount factor, $\mathcal{T}_{s'}^{s_{i,t},a_{i,t}} = P(s'|s_{i,t}, a_{i,t})$ is the transition probability by the transition model, and $V(s_{i,t}; \boldsymbol{r})$ is the value associated with state $s_{i,t}$, obtained by the modified Bellman backup operator:

$$V(s_{i,t}; \boldsymbol{r}) = \log \sum_{a \in \mathcal{A}} \exp \left(\boldsymbol{r}_{s_{i,t},a_{i,t}} + \sum_{s'} \gamma \mathcal{T}_{s'}^{s_{i,t},a} V(s'; \boldsymbol{r}) \right)$$

where we apply a **soft-max function** $V(s_{i,t}; \boldsymbol{r}) = \log \sum_{a \in \mathcal{A}} \exp\left(Q(s_{i,t}, a; \boldsymbol{r})\right)$ for the Q-values with all possible actions $a \in \mathcal{A}$. The value function $V(s; \boldsymbol{r})$ for state s can be obtained by repeatedly applying the above Bellman backup operator. For simplicity of notations, we use $V(s_{i,t}; \boldsymbol{r}), Q(s_{i,t}, a_{i,t}; \boldsymbol{r})$ to denote the solution after Bellman backup operators, unlike some literature that uses $V^*(s_{i,t}; \boldsymbol{r}), Q^*(s_{i,t}, a_{i,t}; \boldsymbol{r})$ to denote the difference. Detailed derivation of the above relationships can be found in [4].

2 Variational Lower Bound for DGP-IRL

It is intractable to perform the integration as in (1) for the marginal log-likelihood. In addition to $p(\mathcal{M}|\boldsymbol{r})$, which involves the latent variable $\boldsymbol{r}$ in a way which requires Q-value iterations, the term $p(\boldsymbol{r}|\mathbf{D}) = \mathcal{N}(\boldsymbol{r}|\mathbf{0}, K_{\mathbf{DD}})$ has a nonlinear dependency on $\mathbf{D}$ in the kernel matrix.

To tackle this issue, we introduce inducing outputs $\boldsymbol{f}, \mathbf{V}$ and their corresponding inputs $\mathbf{Z}, \mathbf{W}$, as shown in Fig. 2. The resulting model follows the main paper:

$$p(\mathcal{M}|\boldsymbol{r}) = \sum_{i=1}^{h} \sum_{t=1}^{T} \left(Q(s_{i,t}, a_{i,t}; \boldsymbol{r}) - V(s_{i,t}; \boldsymbol{r})\right) \tag{8}$$

$$p(\boldsymbol{r}|\boldsymbol{f}, \mathbf{D}, \mathbf{Z}) = \mathcal{N}(\boldsymbol{r}|K_{\mathbf{DZ}} K_{\mathbf{ZZ}}^{-1} \boldsymbol{f}, \mathbf{0}) \tag{9}$$

$$p(\boldsymbol{f}|\mathbf{Z}) = \mathcal{N}(\boldsymbol{f}|\mathbf{0}, K_{\mathbf{ZZ}}) \tag{10}$$

$$p(\mathbf{D}|\mathbf{B}) = \prod_{m=1}^{m_1} \mathcal{N}(\mathbf{d}^m|\mathbf{b}^m, \lambda^{-1}\mathbf{I}) \tag{11}$$

$$p(\mathbf{B}|\mathbf{V}, \mathbf{X}, \mathbf{W}) = \prod_{m=1}^{m_1} \mathcal{N}(\mathbf{b}^m|K_{\mathbf{XW}} K_{\mathbf{WW}}^{-1} \mathbf{v}^m, \boldsymbol{\Sigma}_B) \tag{12}$$

We also design the variation distribution as illustrated in the main paper:

$$\begin{aligned}
\mathcal{Q} &= q(\boldsymbol{f}) q(\mathbf{D}) p(\mathbf{B}|\mathbf{V}, \mathbf{X}) q(\mathbf{V}), \text{ with :} \\
q(\boldsymbol{f}) &= \delta(\boldsymbol{f} - \tilde{\boldsymbol{f}}) \\
q(\mathbf{D}) &= \prod_{m=1}^{m_1} \delta\left(\mathbf{d}^m - K_{\mathbf{XW}} K_{\mathbf{WW}}^{-1} \tilde{\mathbf{v}}^m\right) \\
q(\mathbf{V}) &= \prod_{m=1}^{m_1} \mathcal{N}\left(\mathbf{v}^m|\tilde{\mathbf{v}}^m, \mathbf{G}^m\right),
\end{aligned}$$

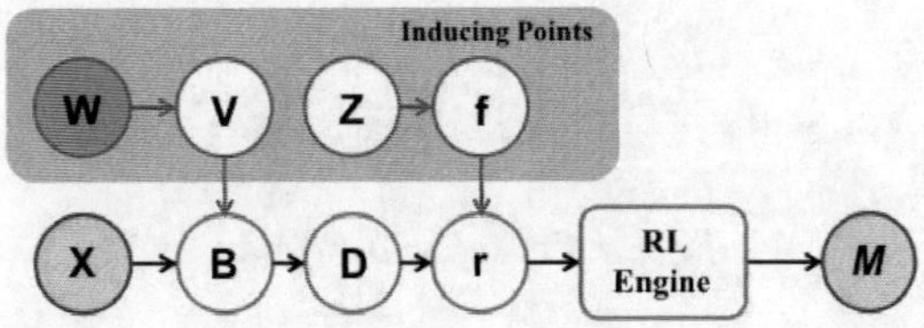

Figure 2: Illustration of DGP-IRL with the inducing outputs $\boldsymbol{f}, \mathbf{V}$ and the corresponding inputs $\mathbf{Z}, \mathbf{W}$.

where the variational distribution $\mathcal{Q}$ is to not be confused with the notation for Q-values, Q. Using the above distribution $\mathcal{Q}$, we can derive the variational lower bound as follows:

$$\log p(\mathcal{M}|\mathbf{X},\mathbf{Z},\mathbf{W}) = \log \int p(\mathcal{M},\boldsymbol{r},\boldsymbol{f},\mathbf{V},\mathbf{D},\mathbf{B}|\mathbf{Z},\mathbf{W},\mathbf{X})d(\boldsymbol{r},\boldsymbol{f},\mathbf{V},\mathbf{D},\mathbf{B}) \tag{13}$$

$$= \log \int \underbrace{p(\mathcal{M}|\boldsymbol{r})p(\boldsymbol{r}|\boldsymbol{f},\mathbf{D},\mathbf{Z})}_{p(\mathcal{M}|K_{\mathbf{DZ}}K_{\mathbf{ZZ}}^{-1}\boldsymbol{f})} p(\boldsymbol{f}|\mathbf{Z})p(\mathbf{D}|\mathbf{B})p(\mathbf{B}|\mathbf{V},\mathbf{W},\mathbf{X})p(\mathbf{V}|\mathbf{W})d(\boldsymbol{r},\boldsymbol{f},\mathbf{V},\mathbf{D},\mathbf{B}) \tag{14}$$

$$\geq \int q(\boldsymbol{f})q(\mathbf{D})p(\mathbf{B}|\mathbf{V},\mathbf{W},\mathbf{X})q(\mathbf{V}) \log \frac{p(\mathcal{M}|K_{\mathbf{DZ}}K_{\mathbf{ZZ}}^{-1}\boldsymbol{f})p(\boldsymbol{f}|\mathbf{Z})p(\mathbf{D}|\mathbf{B})p(\mathbf{V}|\mathbf{W})}{q(\boldsymbol{f})q(\mathbf{D})q(\mathbf{V})} \tag{15}$$

$$= \log p(\mathcal{M}|K_{\tilde{\mathbf{D}}\mathbf{Z}}K_{\mathbf{ZZ}}^{-1}\tilde{\boldsymbol{f}}) + \log p(\boldsymbol{f}=\tilde{\boldsymbol{f}}|\mathbf{Z})$$
$$+ \int q(\mathbf{V})q(\mathbf{D})p(\mathbf{B}|\mathbf{V},\mathbf{W},\mathbf{X}) \log \frac{p(\mathbf{D}|\mathbf{B})p(\mathbf{V}|\mathbf{W})}{q(\mathbf{V})} d(\mathbf{D},\mathbf{B},\mathbf{V}) \tag{16}$$

In the above derivation, the combination of $p(\mathcal{M}|\boldsymbol{r})p(\boldsymbol{r}|\boldsymbol{f},\mathbf{D},\mathbf{Z})$ in (14) uses the deterministic training conditional (DTC) assumption [2], i.e., $p(\boldsymbol{r}|\boldsymbol{f},\mathbf{D},\mathbf{Z}) = \delta(\boldsymbol{r} - K_{\mathbf{DZ}}K_{\mathbf{ZZ}}^{-1}\boldsymbol{f})$, (15) applies Jensen's inequality with the variational distribution $\mathcal{Q}$, (16) is a direct consequence of the choice of $\mathcal{Q}$, and $\tilde{\mathbf{D}} = [\tilde{\mathbf{d}}^1 \ \cdots \ \tilde{\mathbf{d}}^{m_1}]$, with $\tilde{\mathbf{d}}^m = K_{\mathbf{XW}}K_{\mathbf{WW}}^{-1}\tilde{\mathbf{v}}^m$.

Utility 1 (Gaussian identities) *If the marginal and conditional Gaussian distributions for* $\boldsymbol{f}$ *and* $\mathbf{v}$ *are in the form:*

$$p(\boldsymbol{f}|\mathbf{v}) = \mathcal{N}(\boldsymbol{f}|\mathbf{M}\mathbf{v}+\mathbf{m},\boldsymbol{\Sigma}_{\boldsymbol{f}})$$
$$p(\mathbf{v}) = \mathcal{N}(\mathbf{v}|\boldsymbol{\mu}_{\mathbf{v}},\boldsymbol{\Sigma}_{\mathbf{v}})$$

Then the marginal distribution of $\boldsymbol{f}$ *is:*

$$p(\boldsymbol{f}) = \mathcal{N}(\boldsymbol{f}|\mathbf{M}\boldsymbol{\mu}_{\mathbf{v}}+\mathbf{m},\boldsymbol{\Sigma}_{\boldsymbol{f}}+\mathbf{M}\boldsymbol{\Sigma}_{\mathbf{v}}\mathbf{M}^\top) \tag{17}$$

Using the Gaussian identities, the derivation of $\int q(\mathbf{V})p(\mathbf{B}|\mathbf{V},\mathbf{W},\mathbf{X})d\mathbf{V}$ is as follows:

$$\int q(\mathbf{V})p(\mathbf{B}|\mathbf{V},\mathbf{W},\mathbf{X})d\mathbf{V} = \int \prod_{m=1}^{m_1} \mathcal{N}(\mathbf{v}^m|\tilde{\mathbf{v}}^m,\mathbf{G}^m)\mathcal{N}(\mathbf{b}^m|K_{\mathbf{XW}}K_{\mathbf{WW}}^{-1}\mathbf{v}^m,\boldsymbol{\Sigma}_{\mathbf{B}})d\mathbf{V}$$
$$= \prod_{m=1}^{m_1} \mathcal{N}(\mathbf{b}^m|\underbrace{K_{\mathbf{XW}}K_{\mathbf{WW}}^{-1}\tilde{\mathbf{v}}^m}_{\tilde{\mathbf{b}}^m},\underbrace{\boldsymbol{\Sigma}_{\mathbf{B}}+K_{\mathbf{XW}}K_{\mathbf{WW}}^{-1}\mathbf{G}^mK_{\mathbf{WW}}^{-1}K_{\mathbf{WX}}}_{\tilde{\boldsymbol{\Sigma}}_{\mathbf{B}}^m})$$

Therefore, we can obtained a closed form integration for the last term in (16) as follows:

$$\begin{aligned}
&\int q(\mathbf{V})q(\mathbf{D})p(\mathbf{B}|\mathbf{V},\mathbf{W},\mathbf{X})\log p(\mathbf{D}|\mathbf{B})d(\mathbf{D},\mathbf{B},\mathbf{V})\\
&=\int\left(\int q(\mathbf{V})p(\mathbf{B}|\mathbf{V},\mathbf{W},\mathbf{X})d\mathbf{V}\right)q(\mathbf{D})\log p(\mathbf{D}|\mathbf{B})d(\mathbf{D},\mathbf{B})\\
&=\int\prod_{m=1}^{m_1}\mathcal{N}(\mathbf{b}^m|\tilde{\mathbf{b}}^m,\tilde{\boldsymbol{\Sigma}}_{\mathbf{B}}^m)\log\prod_{m=1}^{m_1}\mathcal{N}(\mathbf{d}^m=\tilde{\mathbf{d}}^m|\mathbf{b}^m,\lambda^{-1}\mathbf{I})d\mathbf{B}\\
&=\int\prod_{m=1}^{m_1}\mathcal{N}(\mathbf{b}^m|\tilde{\mathbf{b}}^m,\tilde{\boldsymbol{\Sigma}}_{\mathbf{B}}^m)\log\prod_{m=1}^{m_1}\left((2\pi)^{-n/2}|\lambda^{-1}\mathbf{I}|^{-1/2}e^{-\frac{\lambda}{2}(\tilde{\mathbf{d}}^m-\mathbf{b}^m)^\top(\tilde{\mathbf{d}}^m-\mathbf{b}^m)}\right)d\mathbf{B}\\
&=\int\prod_{m=1}^{m_1}\mathcal{N}(\mathbf{b}^m|\tilde{\mathbf{b}}^m,\tilde{\boldsymbol{\Sigma}}_{\mathbf{B}}^m)\left(-\frac{nm_1}{2}\log(2\pi\lambda^{-1})-\frac{\lambda}{2}\sum_{m=1}^{m_1}(\tilde{\mathbf{d}}^m-\mathbf{b}^m)^\top(\tilde{\mathbf{d}}^m-\mathbf{b}^m)\right)d\mathbf{B}\\
&=-\frac{nm_1}{2}\log(2\pi\lambda^{-1})-\frac{\lambda}{2}\sum_{m=1}^{m_1}\left(Tr(\tilde{\boldsymbol{\Sigma}}_{\mathbf{B}}^m)+(\tilde{\mathbf{d}}^m-\tilde{\mathbf{b}}^m)^\top(\tilde{\mathbf{d}}^m-\tilde{\mathbf{b}}^m)\right)
\end{aligned}$$

where $\tilde{\boldsymbol{\Sigma}}_B^m = \boldsymbol{\Sigma}_B + K_{\mathbf{XW}}K_{\mathbf{WW}}^{-1}\mathbf{G}^m K_{\mathbf{WW}}^{-1}K_{\mathbf{WX}}$, $\tilde{\mathbf{b}}^m = K_{\mathbf{XW}}K_{\mathbf{WW}}^{-1}\tilde{\mathbf{v}}^m$, and $\tilde{\mathbf{d}}^m = K_{\mathbf{XW}}K_{\mathbf{WW}}^{-1}\tilde{\mathbf{v}}^m$, according to the variational distribution Q.

We now express the variational lower bound of the log likelihood as follow:

$$\mathcal{L}=\mathcal{L}_M+\mathcal{L}_G-\mathcal{L}_{KL}+\mathcal{L}_B-\frac{nm_1}{2}\log(2\pi\lambda^{-1}) \tag{18}$$

where

$$\mathcal{L}_M=\log p(\mathcal{M}|K_{\tilde{\mathbf{D}}\mathbf{Z}}K_{\mathbf{ZZ}}^{-1}\tilde{\boldsymbol{f}}) \tag{19}$$

$$\mathcal{L}_G=\log p(\boldsymbol{f}=\tilde{\boldsymbol{f}}|\mathbf{Z})=\log\mathcal{N}(\boldsymbol{f}=\tilde{\boldsymbol{f}}|0,K_{\mathbf{ZZ}}) \tag{20}$$

$$=-\frac{1}{2}\tilde{\boldsymbol{f}}^\top K_{\mathbf{ZZ}}^{-1}\tilde{\boldsymbol{f}}-\frac{n_{inducing}}{2}\log(2\pi)-\frac{1}{2}\log|K_{\mathbf{ZZ}}| \tag{21}$$

$$\mathcal{L}_{KL}=KL(q(\mathbf{V})||p(\mathbf{V}|\mathbf{W}))=\sum_{m=1}^{m_1}KL(\mathcal{N}(\mathbf{v}^m|\tilde{\mathbf{v}}^m,\mathbf{G}^m)||\mathcal{N}(\mathbf{v}^m|0,K_{\mathbf{WW}})) \tag{22}$$

$$=\sum_{m=1}^{m_1}\frac{1}{2}\left(Tr(K_{\mathbf{WW}}^{-1}(\mathbf{G}^m+\tilde{\mathbf{v}}^m\tilde{\mathbf{v}}^{m\top})-n_{inducing}+\log\left(\frac{|K_{\mathbf{WW}}|}{|\mathbf{G}^m|}\right)\right) \tag{23}$$

$$\mathcal{L}_B=-\frac{\lambda}{2}\sum_{m=1}^{m_1}Tr(\boldsymbol{\Sigma}_{\mathbf{B}}+K_{\mathbf{XW}}K_{\mathbf{WW}}^{-1}\mathbf{G}^m K_{\mathbf{WW}}^{-1}K_{\mathbf{WX}}) \tag{24}$$

which is also described in the main paper. The learning of the model involves optimizing over the variational parameters, including $\tilde{\boldsymbol{f}},\tilde{\mathbf{v}}^m,\mathbf{G}^m$, inducing inputs $\mathbf{Z}$, as well as hyperparameters for the kernel functions, which is performed through backpropagation based on the gradients of the variational lower bound (18) with respect to these parameters.

3 Optimizing the Variational Distribution $q(\mathbf{V})$

As can be seen, the variational lower bound (18) depends on the parameters of the variational distribution $q(\mathbf{V})=\prod_{m=1}^{m_1}\mathcal{N}(\mathbf{v}^m|\tilde{\mathbf{v}}^m,\mathbf{G}^m)$, which can be optimized to improve the lower bound further. For the last term in (16), we have

$$\begin{aligned}
&\int q(\mathbf{V})q(\mathbf{D})p(\mathbf{B}|\mathbf{V},\mathbf{W},\mathbf{X})\log\frac{p(\mathbf{D}|\mathbf{B})p(\mathbf{V}|\mathbf{W})}{q(\mathbf{V})}d(\mathbf{D},\mathbf{B},\mathbf{V})\\
&=\int q(\mathbf{V})\left(\int q(\mathbf{D})p(\mathbf{B}|\mathbf{V},\mathbf{W},\mathbf{X})\log\frac{p(\mathbf{D}|\mathbf{B})p(\mathbf{V}|\mathbf{W})}{q(\mathbf{V})}d(\mathbf{D},\mathbf{B})\right)d\mathbf{V}\\
&=\int q(\mathbf{V})\left(\int p(\mathbf{B}|\mathbf{V},\mathbf{W},\mathbf{X})\log\frac{p(\mathbf{D}=\tilde{\mathbf{D}}|\mathbf{B})p(\mathbf{V}|\mathbf{W})}{q(\mathbf{V})}d\mathbf{B}\right)d\mathbf{B}\\
&=\int q(\mathbf{V})\log\frac{e^{\langle\log p(\mathbf{D}=\tilde{\mathbf{D}}|\mathbf{B})\rangle_{p(\mathbf{B}|\mathbf{V},\mathbf{W},\mathbf{X})}}p(\mathbf{V}|\mathbf{W})}{q(\mathbf{V})}d\mathbf{V}
\end{aligned}$$

where we have $\tilde{\mathbf{D}}=\begin{bmatrix}\tilde{\mathbf{d}}^1 & \cdots & \tilde{\mathbf{d}}^{m_1}\end{bmatrix}$, with $\tilde{\mathbf{d}}^m=K_{\mathbf{XW}}K_{\mathbf{WW}}^{-1}\tilde{\mathbf{e}}^m$, and $\tilde{\mathbf{e}}^m$ for $m=1,...,m_1$ are variational parameters to optimize.

To maximize the above quantity, we can reverse the Jensen's inequality to obtin the condition that:

$$\log q(\mathbf{V})=const+\langle\log p(\mathbf{D}=\tilde{\mathbf{D}}|\mathbf{B})\rangle_{p(\mathbf{B}|\mathbf{V},\mathbf{W},\mathbf{X})}+\log p(\mathbf{V}|\mathbf{W})$$

Now for the term $\langle\log p(\mathbf{D}=\tilde{\mathbf{D}}|\mathbf{B})\rangle_{p(\mathbf{B}|\mathbf{V},\mathbf{W},\mathbf{X})}$, we have:

$$\begin{aligned}
&\langle\log p(\mathbf{D}=\tilde{\mathbf{D}}|B)\rangle_{p(\mathbf{B}|\mathbf{V},\mathbf{W},\mathbf{X})}=\sum_{m=1}^{m_1}\langle\log\mathcal{N}(\mathbf{d}^m=\tilde{\mathbf{d}}^m|\mathbf{b}^m,\lambda^{-1}I)\rangle_{p(\mathbf{B}|\mathbf{V},\mathbf{W},\mathbf{X})}\\
&=const+\sum_{m=1}^{m_1}\left\langle-\frac{\lambda}{2}Tr\left(\tilde{\mathbf{d}}^m\tilde{\mathbf{d}}^{m\top}+\mathbf{b}^m\mathbf{b}^{m\top}-2\tilde{\mathbf{d}}^m\mathbf{b}^{m\top}\right)\right\rangle_{\mathcal{N}(\mathbf{b}^m|K_{\mathbf{XW}}K_{\mathbf{WW}}^{-1}\mathbf{v}^m,\boldsymbol{\Sigma}_{\mathbf{B}})}\\
&=const+\sum_{m=1}^{m_1}\left(-\frac{\lambda}{2}Tr\left(\tilde{\mathbf{d}}^m\tilde{\mathbf{d}}^{m\top}+\boldsymbol{\Sigma}_{\mathbf{B}}+\mathbf{v}^{m\top}K_{\mathbf{WW}}^{-1}K_{\mathbf{WX}}K_{\mathbf{XW}}K_{\mathbf{WW}}^{-1}\mathbf{v}^m-2\mathbf{v}^{m\top}K_{\mathbf{WW}}^{-1}K_{\mathbf{WX}}\tilde{\mathbf{d}}^m\right)\right)
\end{aligned}$$

Therefore, we have:

$$\log q(\mathbf{v}^m)=const-\frac{1}{2}\left(\lambda\mathbf{v}^{m\top}K_{\mathbf{WW}}^{-1}K_{\mathbf{WX}}K_{\mathbf{XW}}K_{\mathbf{WW}}^{-1}\mathbf{v}^m-2\lambda\mathbf{v}^{m\top}K_{\mathbf{WW}}^{-1}K_{\mathbf{WX}}\tilde{\mathbf{d}}^m+\mathbf{v}^{m\top}K_{\mathbf{WW}}^{-1}\mathbf{v}^m\right)$$

Therefore by completing the squares we have $q(\mathbf{v}^m)=\mathcal{N}(\mathbf{v}^m|\tilde{\mathbf{v}}_*^m,\boldsymbol{\Sigma}_{\mathbf{v}*}^m)$:

$$\begin{aligned}
\boldsymbol{\Sigma}_{\mathbf{v}*}^m&=(K_{\mathbf{WW}}^{-1}+\lambda K_{\mathbf{WW}}^{-1}K_{\mathbf{WX}}K_{\mathbf{XW}}K_{\mathbf{WW}}^{-1})^{-1}\\
&=\lambda^{-1}K_{\mathbf{WW}}(\lambda^{-1}K_{\mathbf{WW}}+K_{\mathbf{WX}}K_{\mathbf{XW}})^{-1}K_{\mathbf{WW}}\\
\tilde{\mathbf{v}}_*^m&=\lambda\boldsymbol{\Sigma}_{\mathbf{v}*}^mK_{\mathbf{WW}}^{-1}K_{\mathbf{WX}}\tilde{\mathbf{d}}^m\\
&=K_{\mathbf{WW}}\underbrace{(\lambda^{-1}K_{\mathbf{WW}}+K_{\mathbf{WX}}K_{\mathbf{XW}})^{-1}}_{\boldsymbol{\Gamma}}K_{\mathbf{WX}}\tilde{\mathbf{d}}^m
\end{aligned}$$

With the above optimized variational parameters for $q(\mathbf{v}^m)$, we first obtain:

$$\begin{aligned}
&\int q(\mathbf{v}^m)\langle\log p(\mathbf{d}^m=\tilde{\mathbf{d}}^m|\mathbf{b}^m)\rangle_{p(\mathbf{b}^m|\mathbf{v}^m,\mathbf{W},\mathbf{X})}d\mathbf{v}^m=\\
&-\frac{n}{2}\log(2\pi\lambda^{-1})-\frac{\lambda}{2}Tr\Big(\tilde{\mathbf{d}}^m\tilde{\mathbf{d}}^{m\top}+\boldsymbol{\Sigma}_{\mathbf{B}}+K_{\mathbf{WW}}^{-1}K_{\mathbf{WX}}K_{\mathbf{XW}}K_{\mathbf{WW}}^{-1}(\boldsymbol{\Sigma}_{\mathbf{v}*}^m+\tilde{\mathbf{v}}_*^m\tilde{\mathbf{v}}_*^{m\top})-2\tilde{\mathbf{v}}_*^{m\top}K_{\mathbf{WW}}^{-1}K_{\mathbf{WX}}\tilde{\mathbf{d}}^m\Big)
\end{aligned}$$

Next, we calculate $\int q(\mathbf{v}^m)\log p(\mathbf{v}^m|\mathbf{W})d\mathbf{v}^m$:

$$\int q(\mathbf{v}^m)\log p(\mathbf{v}^m|\mathbf{W})=-\frac{n}{2}\log(2\pi)-\frac{1}{2}\log|K_{\mathbf{WW}}|-\frac{1}{2}Tr(K_{\mathbf{WW}}^{-1}(\boldsymbol{\Sigma}_{\mathbf{v}*}^m+\tilde{\mathbf{v}}_*^m\tilde{\mathbf{v}}_*^{m\top}))$$

Finally we have:

$$H(q(\mathbf{v}^m))=q(\mathbf{v}^m)\log\frac{1}{q(\mathbf{v}^m)}=\frac{n}{2}\log(2\pi)+\frac{1}{2}\log|\boldsymbol{\Sigma}_{\mathbf{v}*}^m| \qquad (25)$$

Summarizing, we have:

$$\int q(\mathbf{V})q(\mathbf{D})p(\mathbf{B}|\mathbf{V},\mathbf{W},\mathbf{X})\log\frac{p(\mathbf{D}|\mathbf{B})p(\mathbf{V}|\mathbf{W})}{q(\mathbf{V})}d(\mathbf{D},\mathbf{B},\mathbf{V})$$
$$\leq \sum_{m=1}^{m_1}\Bigg[-\frac{n}{2}\log(2\pi\lambda^{-1})-\frac{1}{2}\log|K_{\mathbf{WW}}|-\frac{1}{2}Tr(K_{\mathbf{WW}}^{-1}(\mathbf{\Sigma}_{\mathbf{V}*}^{m}+\tilde{\mathbf{v}}_*^m\tilde{\mathbf{v}}_*^{m\top}))+\frac{1}{2}\log|\mathbf{\Sigma}_{\mathbf{V}*}^{m}|$$
$$-\frac{\lambda}{2}Tr\Big(\tilde{\mathbf{d}}^m\tilde{\mathbf{d}}^{m\top}+\mathbf{\Sigma_B}+K_{\mathbf{WW}}^{-1}K_{\mathbf{WX}}K_{\mathbf{XW}}K_{\mathbf{WW}}^{-1}(\mathbf{\Sigma}_{\mathbf{V}*}^{m}+\tilde{\mathbf{v}}_*^m\tilde{\mathbf{v}}_*^{m\top})-2\tilde{\mathbf{v}}_*^{m\top}K_{\mathbf{WW}}^{-1}K_{\mathbf{WX}}\tilde{\mathbf{d}}^m\Big)\Bigg]$$

We now express the variational lower bound of the log likelihood as follow:

$$\mathcal{L}=\mathcal{L}_M+\mathcal{L}_G+\mathcal{L}_{DBV} \tag{26}$$

where

$$\mathcal{L}_M=\log p(\mathcal{M}|K_{\tilde{\mathbf{D}}\mathbf{Z}}K_{\mathbf{ZZ}}^{-1}\tilde{\boldsymbol{f}}) \tag{27}$$
$$\mathcal{L}_G=\log p(u=\tilde{u}|Z)=\log\mathcal{N}(u=\tilde{u}|0,K_{ZZ}) \tag{28}$$
$$=-\frac{1}{2}\tilde{u}^\top K_{ZZ}^{-1}\tilde{u}-\frac{K}{2}\log(2\pi)-\frac{1}{2}\log|K_{ZZ}| \tag{29}$$
$$\mathcal{L}_{DBV}=\sum_{m=1}^{m_1}\Bigg[-\frac{n}{2}\log(2\pi\lambda^{-1})-\frac{1}{2}\log|K_{\mathbf{WW}}|-\frac{1}{2}Tr(K_{\mathbf{WW}}^{-1}(\mathbf{\Sigma}_{\mathbf{V}*}^{m}+\tilde{\mathbf{v}}_*^m\tilde{\mathbf{v}}_*^{m\top}))+\frac{1}{2}\log|\mathbf{\Sigma}_{\mathbf{V}*}^{m}|$$
$$-\frac{\lambda}{2}Tr\Big(\tilde{\mathbf{d}}^m\tilde{\mathbf{d}}^{m\top}+\mathbf{\Sigma_B}+K_{\mathbf{WW}}^{-1}K_{\mathbf{WX}}K_{\mathbf{XW}}K_{\mathbf{WW}}^{-1}(\mathbf{\Sigma}_{\mathbf{V}*}^{m}+\tilde{\mathbf{v}}_*^m\tilde{\mathbf{v}}_*^{m\top})-2\tilde{\mathbf{v}}_*^{m\top}K_{\mathbf{WW}}^{-1}K_{\mathbf{WX}}\tilde{\mathbf{d}}^m\Big)\Bigg] \tag{30}$$

where $\tilde{\mathbf{d}}^m=K_{\mathbf{XW}}K_{\mathbf{WW}}^{-1}\tilde{\mathbf{e}}^m$, $\mathbf{\Gamma}=(\lambda^{-1}K_{\mathbf{WW}}+K_{\mathbf{WX}}K_{\mathbf{XW}})^{-1}$,$\Sigma_{\mathbf{V}*}^m=\lambda^{-1}K_{\mathbf{WW}}\mathbf{\Gamma}K_{\mathbf{WW}}$.

The parameters we need to learn in this case include the variational parameters $\tilde{\boldsymbol{f}}$, and $\tilde{\mathbf{e}}^m$ for $m=1,...,m_1$, inducing inputs $\mathbf{Z}$, as well as hyperparameters for kernel functions.

4 Parameters Learning by Derivatives

In this section, we will obtain the derivatives of the marginal log likelihood $\mathcal{L}$ in (26) with respect to the variational parameters $\tilde{\boldsymbol{f}}$, $\tilde{\mathbf{e}}^m$ and inducing inputs $\mathbf{Z}$. The derivative of the reinforcement learning term, $p(\mathcal{M}|\boldsymbol{r})$ in (7), with respect to the reward vectors $\boldsymbol{r}$, is given by:

$$\frac{\partial}{\partial\boldsymbol{r}}\log p(\mathcal{M}|\boldsymbol{r})=\sum_i\sum_t\left(\frac{\partial}{\partial\boldsymbol{r}}\boldsymbol{r}_{s_{i,t},a_{i,t}}-\frac{\partial}{\partial\boldsymbol{r}}V_{s_{i,t}}^{\boldsymbol{r}}+\sum_{s'}\gamma\mathcal{T}_{s'}^{s_{i,t},a_{i,t}}\frac{\partial}{\partial\boldsymbol{r}}V_{s'}^{\boldsymbol{r}}\right) \tag{31}$$

The first term, $\sum_i\sum_t\frac{\partial}{\partial\boldsymbol{r}}\boldsymbol{r}_{s_{i,t},a_{i,t}}$, is simply a vector that counts the number of state-action pairs in the demonstrations $\hat{\mu}$, whose entry corresponding to (s,a) is given by: $\hat{\mu}_{s,a}=\sum_i\sum_t 1_{s_{i,t}=s\wedge a_{i,t}=a}$. The second term involves the derivative of the value function at state s with respect to rewards, as indicated in [4], equal to the expected visitation count of each state-action pair when starting from state s and following the optimal stochastic policy, i.e., $\frac{\partial}{\partial\boldsymbol{r}}V_s^{\boldsymbol{r}}=E[\mu|s]$, where μ is a vector with each entry $\mu_{s,a}$ corresponding to the expected visitation count for (s,a). Therefore, (31) can be written as:

$$\frac{\partial}{\partial\boldsymbol{r}}\log p(\mathcal{M}|\boldsymbol{r})=\hat{\mu}-\sum_i\sum_t E[\mu|s_{i,t}]+\sum_i\sum_t\sum_{s'}\gamma\mathcal{T}_{s'}^{s_{i,t},a_{i,t}}E[\mu|s_{i,t}]$$
$$=\hat{\mu}-\sum_s\hat{\nu}_s E[\mu|s]$$

where $\hat{\nu}_s=\sum_a\hat{\mu}_{s,a}-\sum_i\sum_t\gamma\mathcal{T}_{s'}^{s_{i,t},a_{i,t}}$. The term $\sum_s\hat{\nu}_s E[\mu|s]$ can be computed efficiently by a simple iterative algorithm described in [4], which we do not recount here. Note that the above derivation follows from [1].

For the variational parameters $\tilde{\boldsymbol{f}}$, we need to consider only two terms that involve it, i.e., $\mathcal{L}_{\mathcal{M}}, \mathcal{L}_G$:

$$\frac{\partial \mathcal{L}_M}{\partial \tilde{\boldsymbol{f}}} = \frac{\partial \boldsymbol{r}}{\partial \tilde{\boldsymbol{f}}} \frac{\partial \mathcal{L}_{\mathcal{M}}}{\partial \boldsymbol{r}} = K_{\tilde{\mathbf{D}}\mathbf{Z}} K_{\mathbf{ZZ}}^{-1} \frac{\partial \log p(\mathcal{M}|\boldsymbol{r})}{\partial \boldsymbol{r}}$$

$$\frac{\partial \mathcal{L}_G}{\partial \tilde{\boldsymbol{f}}} = -K_{\mathbf{ZZ}}^{-1} \tilde{\boldsymbol{f}}$$

where $\boldsymbol{r} = K_{\tilde{\mathbf{D}}\mathbf{Z}} K_{\mathbf{ZZ}}^{-1} \tilde{\boldsymbol{f}}$ is the reward vector that we use for reinforcement learning.

For the variational parameters $\tilde{\mathbf{e}}^m$, let $\tilde{\mathbf{D}} = \left[K_{\mathbf{XW}} K_{\mathbf{WW}}^{-1} \tilde{\mathbf{e}}^1, ..., K_{\mathbf{XW}} K_{\mathbf{WW}}^{-1} \tilde{\mathbf{e}}^{m_1}\right] \in \mathbb{R}^{n \times m_1}$, and $\mathbf{E} = [\tilde{\mathbf{e}}^1, ..., \tilde{\mathbf{e}}^{m_1}] \in \mathbb{R}^{K \times m_1}$:

$$\frac{\partial \mathcal{L}_{\mathcal{M}}}{\partial \mathbf{E}} = \frac{\partial \tilde{\mathbf{D}}}{\partial \mathbf{E}} \frac{\partial K_{\tilde{\mathbf{D}}\mathbf{Z}}}{\partial \tilde{\mathbf{D}}} \frac{\partial \boldsymbol{r}}{\partial K_{\tilde{\mathbf{D}}\mathbf{Z}}} \frac{\partial \mathcal{L}_{\mathcal{M}}}{\partial \boldsymbol{r}}$$

In addition, by applying matrix derivatives,

$$\frac{\partial \mathcal{L}_{DBV}}{\partial \mathbf{e}^m} = -\frac{\lambda}{2}\Big(2K_{\mathbf{WW}}^{-1} K_{\mathbf{WX}} K_{\mathbf{XW}} K_{\mathbf{WW}}^{-1} + 2K_{\mathbf{WW}}^{-1} K_{\mathbf{WX}} K_{\mathbf{XW}} \boldsymbol{\Gamma} K_{\mathbf{WX}} K_{\mathbf{XW}} \boldsymbol{\Gamma} K_{\mathbf{WX}} K_{\mathbf{XW}} K_{\mathbf{WW}}^{-1}$$

$$-4K_{\mathbf{WW}}^{-1} K_{\mathbf{WX}} K_{\mathbf{XW}} \boldsymbol{\Gamma} K_{\mathbf{WX}} K_{\mathbf{XW}} K_{\mathbf{WW}}^{-1}\Big) \mathbf{e}^m - K_{\mathbf{WW}}^{-1} K_{\mathbf{WX}} K_{\mathbf{XW}} \boldsymbol{\Gamma} K_{\mathbf{WW}} \boldsymbol{\Gamma} K_{\mathbf{WX}} K_{\mathbf{XW}} K_{\mathbf{WW}}^{-1} \mathbf{e}^m$$

The gradients are provided to minFunc [3], which calls a quasi-Newton strategy, where limited-memory BFGS updates with Shanno-Phua scaling are used in computing the step direction, and a bracketing line-search for a point satisfying the strong Wolfe conditions is used to compute the step direction.

References

[1] S. Levine, Z. Popovic, and V. Koltun. Nonlinear inverse reinforcement learning with Gaussian processes. In *Advances in Neural Information Processing Systems*, pages 19–27, 2011.

[2] J. Quiñonero-Candela and C. E. Rasmussen. A unifying view of sparse approximate Gaussian process regression. *The Journal of Machine Learning Research*, 6:1939–1959, 2005.

[3] M. Schmidt. minFunc: unconstrained differentiable multivariate optimization in matlab. *URL http://www. di. ens. fr/mschmidt/Software/minFunc. html*, 2012.

[4] B. D. Ziebart, J. A. Bagnell, and A. K. Dey. Modeling interaction via the principle of maximum causal entropy. In *International Conference on Machine Learning (ICML)*, pages 1247–1254, 2010.

Holographic Feature Representations of Deep Networks

Martin A. Zinkevich
Google, Inc.

Alex Davies
Google, Inc.

Dale Schuurmans*
University of Alberta

Abstract

It is often asserted that deep networks learn "features", traditionally expressed by the activations of intermediate nodes. We explore an alternative concept by defining features as partial derivatives of model output with respect to model parameters—extending a simple yet powerful idea from generalized linear models. The resulting features are not equivalent to node activations, and we show that they can induce a *holographic* representation of the complete model: the network's output on given data can be exactly replicated by a simple *linear* model over such features extracted from *any* ordered cut. We demonstrate useful advantages for this feature representation over standard representations based on node activations.

1 INTRODUCTION

Deep networks provide an effective foundation for machine learning, having delivered significant advances in computer vision [10, 26, 17, 19, 8], speech recognition [7], spoken dialogue systems [9], and machine translation [9, 22]. Such models are often said to learn useful "features" [4, 23], which are normally considered to be the activations of intermediate nodes. However, we consider a more fundamental concept than node activations, and show that this alternative notion of what constitutes a "feature" can provide more powerful properties.

The standard way to think about the features learned in a deep network—as node activations across a single layer [4, 25, 26, 23]—has led to some insight into what a trained network might be representing. For example, such a perspective has led to impressive visualizations that illustrate how such models might "see" classes [20] or interpret images [15]. The layer-wise embeddings in deep networks trained on text have also been visualized and shown to encode semantically meaningful dimensions [14]. Attempts have also been made to "transfer" useful activation features between tasks [23], and to understand layer-wise representations by using them in linear classifiers [1]. In fact, this latter work bears some similarity to the present investigation, but without considering equally powerful feature representations.

Meanwhile, a key drawback of deep networks remains the stability and repeatability of training. It is well known that non-convex optimization problems can have suboptimal local minima separated from global minima, which also occurs in training deep networks [5]. It is true that local minima do not prevent good outcomes from being obtained in practice [3]; in fact, whenever one is attempting to produce a single model given a fixed training set (i.e. the "offline" scenario) any weak result can simply be discarded and training repeated. *However, the situation is quite different in the typical "online" scenario encountered in industry,* where data arrives continually and models must be constantly retrained or adjusted for user-facing applications. In such cases, training instability can at minimum be a nuisance and at worst be dangerous. The online scenario presents an important challenge for deep networks and raises some of the key questions we attempt to address in this paper. Can features be extracted from a deep network that can be reliably used in other models? Can extracted features be used to more efficiently and stably incorporate new data?

In this paper, we provide a different perspective on what a "feature" might represent about a deep network. We show how the specific features we extract can be used to recover a linear model that *exactly* reproduces the original network on the training data. These features incorporate both the "upstream" information from previous layers, and the "downstream" information from later layers, giving a complete "holographic" representation

* Work supported by Google.

of the network from the perspective of any given layer. An important advantage is that this representation can be rapidly re-trained to global optimality on new data, efficiently obtaining repeatable outcomes. Moreover, the features are "calibrated" in a manner that allows weaknesses in the model versus the chosen training objective to be disambiguated, as we discuss in the next section.

2 FEATURES AND CALIBRATION

To investigate whether the rich notion of "feature" from generalized linear models can be meaningfully applied to deep networks, we leverage the concept of *calibration* (which is a particular form of *moment matching*).

Consider linear least squares regression. If a feature is 1 in each example (e.g., the bias), the average label must equal the average prediction in any optimally trained model. More generally, for any $\{0,1\}$-valued (boolean) feature, the average label must equal the average prediction when the feature is 1 [16, Equation 3]. This calibration property provides a powerful diagnostic: Imagine one is trying to predict the number of minutes someone who searches for "cat videos" will watch `cat_12`. Having a feature that is 1 when the search is "cat videos" and the video shown is `cat_12` guarantees that the average prediction will equal the average label in this subset. Thus, if you wanted to rank videos by how many minutes will be watched, you can disambiguate between mistakes in the label (e.g. `cat_12` is watched more on average than `cat_13` but is a worse video by a different metric: do we need to change our metric?) and mistakes in the modeling (e.g. `cat_12` is watched more on average than `cat_13`, but predicted on average to be watched less).

A similar property holds for logistic regression after distinguishing the *predicted log odds* (a linear combination of the features) from the *predicted probability* (a function of the log odds). In an optimally trained model, the average predicted probability will equal the average label whenever a boolean feature is 1. That is, if we tried to predict the probability someone would click on video `cat_12` given that they search for "cat videos", the average predicted probability would be the average label.

This notion of calibration provides a practical tool for disambiguating problems with the feature representation versus problems with the objective. We use it as a key defining concept in the technical development below.

3 FORMALISM

Our basic strategy is to relate deep networks to generalized linear models—such as linear, logistic and Poisson regression—by considering supervised learning problems defined in terms of exponential families [16, 21].

3.1 EXPONENTIAL FAMILIES

We base our development on full, minimal, 1-dimensional, standard exponential families [2] (see Appendix A for standard definitions), which will be used to formulate the training loss. We will denote the exponential family being used by p, from which one can derive the domain $\Omega_p \subseteq \mathbf{R}$ of possible outcomes, the mean function $\mu_p : \mathbf{R} \to \mathbf{R}$ of the outcome given the parameter, and the loss $\ell_p : \Omega_p \times \mathbf{R} \to \mathbf{R}$ given by the negative log likelihood of the outcome given the parameter.

For example, the Bernoulli family is specified by $\Omega_p = \{0,1\}$, $\ell_p(\omega,\theta) = -\theta\omega + \ln(1+\exp(\theta))$, and $\mu_p(\theta) = \frac{1}{1+\exp(\theta)}$; this family forms the basis of logistic regression. Other examples, such as Gaussian with a fixed variance (least squares regression), and the Poisson family (Poisson regression) are given in Appendix A. The following lemma encapsulates the key facts we require:

Lemma 1 *The Bernoulli family, Gaussian family (fixed variance), and Poisson family are full, minimal, 1-dimensional standard exponential families. For a full, minimal, 1-dimensional standard exponential family p:*

1. *for every $\theta \in \mathbf{R}$, $\omega \in \Omega_p$, $\ell_p(\omega,\theta)$ is differentiable with respect to θ and $\frac{\partial \ell_p(\omega,\theta)}{\partial\theta} = \mu_p(\theta) - \omega$; and*
2. *ℓ_p is **strictly convex in its second argument**: for every $\theta,\theta' \in \mathbf{R}$, if $\theta \neq \theta'$, then for all $\lambda \in (0,1)$ we have $\ell_p(\omega,\lambda\theta + (1-\lambda)\theta') < \lambda\ell_p(\omega,\theta) + (1-\lambda)\ell_p(\omega,\theta')$.*

Proofs for all lemmas and theorems stated in this paper are given in the appendices.

3.2 SUPERVISED LEARNING PROBLEM

Our focus in this paper will be on supervised learning problems. A **model** is defined to be a function $M : X \to \mathbf{R}$. A **model family** is given by a parameterized set of models $\mathcal{M} = \{M_w\}_{w \in \mathbf{R}^S}$ where S is a finite set of parameters. We define a **supervised learning problem** (or just a **problem** for short) to be a tuple $\mathcal{P} = (p, X, \{x_1 \ldots x_m\}, \{y_1 \ldots y_m\})$, where p is a full, minimal, 1-dimensional standard exponential family, X is the domain of instances, $x_1 \ldots x_m \in X$ are the instances, and $y_1 \ldots y_m \in \Omega_p$ are the labels. We define a **loss function** $L_{\mathcal{P}} : \mathbf{R}^X \to \mathbf{R}$ that maps a model M to a scalar loss value via:

$$L_{\mathcal{P}}(M) = \sum_{i=1}^{m} \ell_p(y_i, M(x_i)), \tag{1}$$

the negative log likelihood of the labels given instances.

3.3 CALIBRATION, FEATURES, OPTIMALITY

Definition 2 *Given a supervised learning problem* $\mathcal{P} = (p, X, \{x_1 \ldots x_m\}, \{y_1 \ldots y_m\})$,[1] *a* ***feature*** *is a function* $f : X \to \mathbf{R}$. *We say that a model* M *is* ***calibrated with respect to feature*** f ***on*** $\mathcal{P}$ *if:*

$$\sum_{i=1}^{m} f(x_i)\mu_p(M(x_i)) = \sum_{i=1}^{m} f(x_i)y_i. \quad (2)$$

For example, if the feature $f : X \to \mathbf{R}$ is 1 if the instance comes from the United States, and 0 otherwise, then calibration of a model with respect to this feature would imply that the average prediction given an instance from the United States would equal the average label for an instance from the United States. Note that the concept of calibration with respect to a feature is independent of whether the feature is actually used by the model M. In the literature on regression, there are many results that show how various generalized linear regression problems find models that are calibrated with respect to the features [16, 21]. In this paper, we will consider starting with a model and generating calibrated features from it.

Definition 3 *For a model family* $\{M_w\}_{w \in \mathbf{R}^S}$ *with* $w \in \mathbf{R}^S$ *and* $s \in S$, *we define the* ***feature generated from parameter*** s ***of model*** M_w *to be* $f_s : X \to \mathbf{R}$ *such that:*

$$f_s(x) = \frac{\partial^+ M_w(x)}{\partial w_s} \quad \text{for all } x \in X; \quad (3)$$

in other words, a feature is specified by the right partial derivative of the output of model M_w *acting on* x *with respect to some parameter* s.[2]

Definition 4 *Given a parameter subset* $S' \subseteq S$, *the features generated from* S' *of* M_w *are* ***total for*** $x \in X$ *if:*

$$\lim_{h \to 0} \frac{\left|M_{w+h}(x) - \left(M_w(x) + \sum_{s' \in S} h_{s'} f_{s'}(x)\right)\right|}{\|h\|} = 0 \quad (4)$$

(note $h \in \mathbf{R}^{S'}$*), where* $f_{s'}$ *is the feature generated from* s' *of model* M_w, *and* $w + h \in \mathbf{R}^S$ *obeys* $(w+h)_{s'} = w_{s'} + h_{s'}$ *if* $s' \in S'$, *and* $(w+h)_{s'} = w_{s'}$ *if* $s' \notin S'$. *For brevity, we will also call such a set* S' *itself* ***total***.[3]

First note that the property of a feature set S' being total exhibits downward inheritance: if S' is total for some x, then so is S'' for any $S'' \subseteq S'$. Therefore, if $M_w(x)$ is differentiable at w, implying that the full feature set S is total, then any generated feature set must also be total. Note that it is not sufficient that $M_w(x)$ be be partially differentiable with respect to w to ensure totality; specifically, if the features generated from S' are total, and the features generated from S'' are total, there is no guarantee that the features generated from $S' \cup S''$ are total—Appendix E provides a concrete example.

Definition 5 *Given a problem* $\mathcal{P} = (p, X, \{x_1 \ldots x_m\}, \{y_1 \ldots y_m\})$, *two models* M *and* M' *are* ***equal on the training data*** *if for all* $i \in \{1 \ldots m\}$, $M(x_i) = M'(x_i)$.

Definition 6 *Given a problem* $\mathcal{P}$ *and a model family* $\mathcal{M}$, *we say that* $M \in \mathcal{M}$ *is* ***optimal*** *for* $\mathcal{P}$ *on* $\mathcal{M}$ *if, for all* $M' \in \mathcal{M}$, $L_{\mathcal{P}}(M) \le L_{\mathcal{P}}(M')$.

Notice that optimality is based upon both the problem and the model family: this will become important later when we talk about models outside of a family being equivalent to optimal models inside a family.

In what follows we will distinguish these generated features from the more common node activations. In some cases they are the same, as in the last layer, other times they are related, and sometimes they are completely different, as in the generated features from bias parameters.

4 GENERATED FEATURES

We first show that if the partial derivative of the loss with respect to a parameter is zero, then the feature generated by that parameter must be calibrated.

Theorem 7 *For a problem* $\mathcal{P}$ *and model family* $\mathcal{M} = \{M_w\}_{w \in \mathbf{R}^S}$, *given a* $w \in \mathbf{R}^S$ *and* $s \in S$ *such that* f_s *is the feature generated from parameter* s *of model* M_w: *if* $\{s\}$ *is total on the training data given* M_w *and* $\frac{\partial L_{\mathcal{P}}(M_w)}{\partial w_s} = 0$, *then* M_w *is calibrated with respect to* f_s.

Note that we do not assume that the model family $\mathcal{M}$ is *linearly* parameterized; far from it, below we will be considering model families defined by certain classes of deep neural networks. Nevertheless, the features generated in this way can be exported to an external family of linear models defined over the same feature set. Such an auxiliary family of linear models will possess several strong properties with respect to the original nonlinear model family, as we now show.

Definition 8 *For a finite* S, *given a set of functions* $\{f_s\}_{s \in S}$ *where* $f_s : X \to \mathbf{R}$, *we define the* ***family of linear models induced by*** $\{f_s\}_{s \in S}$, *to be the model family*

[1] When we mention a feature in the context of a model or problem, we assume the feature shares the same domain.

[2] Note that this definition is related but not identical to the Fisher score, given by $\partial \log \ell_p(y, M_w(x))/\partial w_s$. A key difference is that the Fisher score requires the label y, whereas a generated feature is only defined with respect to model output.

[3] Appx. I.1 shows how totality relates to differentiability.

$\{N_w\}_{w \in \mathbf{R}^S}$ *such that for all* $w \in \mathbf{R}^S$ *and* $x \in X$*:*

$$N_w(x) = \sum_{s \in S} w_s f_s(x). \qquad (5)$$

Let this family be denoted by $\mathcal{L}(\{f_s\}_{s \in S})$.

Note that if we were generating features from a model M_w that was already linearly parameterized, we would simply re-generate the original feature set. Next, we need some preliminary results for families of linear models.

Lemma 9 *For finite* S*, given a set of features* $\{f_s\}_{s \in S}$*, the family of linear models* $\mathcal{L}(\{f_s\}_{s \in S})$*, and* $N_w \in \mathcal{L}$*: the set* S *is total for all* $x \in X$ *given* N_w*, and the feature generated from parameter* s *by model* N_w *is* f_s*.*

Lemma 10 *(c.f. [16, Equation 10]) Given a problem* $\mathcal{P}$*, a finite set* S *and a set of features* $\{f_s\}_{s \in S}$*: a model* N *in the family of linear models* $\mathcal{L}(\{f_s\}_{s \in S})$ *is optimal if and only if* N *is calibrated with respect to* f_s *for all* $s \in S$*.*

Lemma 11 *Given a problem* $\mathcal{P}$*, a finite set* S*, a subset* $S' \subseteq S$*, and a set of features* $\{f_s\}_{s \in S}$*: if a model* N *is optimal in the family of linear models* $\mathcal{L}(\{f_s\}_{s \in S'})$ *and* N *is calibrated with respect to* f_s *for all* $s \in S - S'$*, then* N *is also an optimal model in* $\mathcal{L}(\{f_s\}_{s \in S})$*.*

Now consider a general model family $\mathcal{M}$. Even if the models in $\mathcal{M}$ are not linear, our first key result is that a family of linear models defined over the features *generated* from $\mathcal{M}$ (via Definition 3) will satisfy important properties.

Definition 12 *Given a finite* S*, family* $\{M_w\}_{w \in \mathbf{R}^S}$ *of models, subset* $S' \subseteq S$*, and parameters* $w \in \mathbf{R}^{S'}$*: if* f_s *is the feature generated by* s *given* M_w*, then the* ***family of linear models associated with*** S' ***given*** M_w *will be denoted* $\mathcal{L}(\{f_s\}_{s \in S'})$*.*

Lemma 13 *Given a problem* $\mathcal{P}$*, a finite set* S*, a subset* $S' \subseteq S$*, a model family* $\{M_w\}_{w \in \mathbf{R}^S}$*, and a* $w \in \mathbf{R}^S$ *such that* $\frac{\partial L_{\mathcal{P}}(M_w)}{\partial w_s} = 0$ *for all* $s \in S'$*:* ***if*** $\mathcal{L}'$ *is the family of linear models associated with* S' *given* M_w*,* S' *is total on the training data given* M_w*, and* M_w *is equal on the training data to some* $N' \in \mathcal{L}'$*,* ***then*** N' *is optimal in* $\mathcal{L}'$*.*

This next lemma goes one step further, by showing that if a model $M \in \mathcal{M}$ is stationary on a subset of parameters S' and if there is a linear model over features generated on S' that matches M, then there is an optimal linear model over features generated on S that also matches M.

Lemma 14 *Given a problem* $\mathcal{P}$*, a finite set* S*, a subset* $S' \subseteq S$*, a model family* $\{M_w\}_{w \in \mathbf{R}^S}$*, and a* $w \in \mathbf{R}^S$ *such that* $\frac{\partial L_{\mathcal{P}}(M_w)}{\partial w_s} = 0$ *for all* $s \in S$*:* ***if*** $\mathcal{L}'$ *is the family of linear models associated with* S' *given* M_w*,* S' *is total,* M_w *is equal on the training data to some* $N' \in \mathcal{L}'$*, and* $\mathcal{L}''$ *is the family of linear models associated with* S*,* ***then*** *any optimal* $N'' \in \mathcal{L}''$ *equals* M_w *on the training data.*

So a key question will be to understand when a model M_w that is stationary on a subset S' of parameters will also be equal on the training data to a stationary model that uses all the parameters S. To address deep neural networks we will introduce the concept of *homogeneity*, which will allow us to prove that, for certain families of deep models, if a model is stationary with respect to a particular subset of its parameters it will also be equal on the training data to a linear model over the same subset. We will use this construction to show how the generated features can capture *all* of the expressiveness of a given deep model with respect to the training data, while still allowing one to re-train in a linear setting.

5 FEEDFORWARD NETWORKS

We first need to formally define deep neural networks for subsequent analysis. For generality we follow the formalization given in [18] that extends the more conventional layered representation; see also Appendix B.

A **feedforward neural network** D is defined by a directed acyclic graph with objects attached to the vertices and edges: in particular, $D = (V, E, I, \{g_i\}_{i \in I}, o^*, A)$, where V is a set of vertices, $E \subseteq V \times V$ is a set of edges, $I = \{i_1 \dots i_m\} \subset V$ is a set of input vertices, $g_i : X \to \mathbf{R}$ is an input function connected to $i \in I$, $o^* \in V$ is the output vertex, and $A = \{a_v : v \in V\}$ is a set of activation functions, $a_v : \mathbf{R} \to \mathbf{R}$. The parameters are $w \in \mathbf{R}^E$.

We will need to refer to the partial ordering on vertices implied by $G = (V, E)$, where we assume G contains no cycles,[4] the input vertices have no incoming edges (i.e. $(u, i) \notin E$ for all $i \in I$, $u \in V$), the output vertex is not an input (i.e. $o^* \notin I$) and the output vertex has no outgoing edges (i.e. $(o^*, v) \notin E$ for all $v \in V$). A directed acyclic graph defines a partial order $\leq$ on vertices where $u \leq v$ if and only if there is a path from u to v.

Given a training input $x \in X$, the computation of the network D is specified by a circuit function $c_{v,w}$ that assigns values to each vertex based on the partial order:

$$c_{i,w}(x) = a_i(g_i(x)) \text{ for } i \in I; \qquad (6)$$

$$c_{v,w}(x) = a_v\Big(\sum_{u:(u,v) \in E} c_{u,w}(x) w_{(u,v)}\Big) \text{ for } v \in V - I. \quad (7)$$

[4] A **path** $(v_1, ..., v_k)$ is a sequence of vertices such that $(v_j, v_{j+1}) \in E$ for all j. A **cycle** is a path with $v_1 = v_k$.

Note that the activations on input and output nodes are usually the identity, i.e. $a_v(x) = x$ for $v \in I \cup \{o^*\}$. We can also add a bias vertex $b \in I$, with input function $g_b(x) = 1$ for all $x \in X$, so that adding an edge $(b, v) \in E$ ensures that vertex v receives an affine rather than a linear combination of its incoming circuit values.

Definition 15 *Given $D = (V, E, I, \{g_i\}_{i \in I}, o^*, A)$, we will denote the **family of feedforward network models** by $\mathcal{D}(V, E, I, \{g_i\}_{i \in I}, o^*, A) = \{M_w\}_{w \in \mathbf{R}^E}$, where for all $w \in \mathbf{R}^E$ we let $M_w = c_{o^*,w}$.*

6 HOMOGENEOUS MODEL FAMILIES

Our main theoretical development applies to feedforward neural networks with *homogeneous* activation functions.

Definition 16 *A function $f : \mathbf{R}^p \to \mathbf{R}^q$ is **homogeneous** (of degree 1) [11] if for all $v \in \mathbf{R}^p$ and all $\lambda \geq 0$:*

$$f(\lambda v) = \lambda f(v). \tag{8}$$

Homogeneity implies that a function is linear along any ray from the origin, and also that it can be decomposed as an inner product between inputs and partial derivatives.

Lemma 17 (Euler's Homogeneous Function Theorem) (Degree 1 Case) *If a homogeneous function $f : \mathbf{R}^p \to \mathbf{R}^q$ is differentiable at $x \in \mathbf{R}^p$, then for all $k \in \{1 \ldots q\}$,*

$$f_k(x) = \sum_{j=1}^{p} \frac{\partial f_k(x)}{\partial x_j} x_j. \tag{9}$$

An important example of a (degree 1) homogeneous function is the standard neural network activation function $relu : \mathbf{R} \to \mathbf{R}$, given by $relu(x) = \max(x, 0)$.

Fact 18 *The $relu$ and $leaky\ relu$ [13] activation functions are homogeneous. Any linear function is homogeneous, therefore so are projection and identity. The sum or composition of homogeneous functions is homogeneous, therefore constant multiplication of a homogeneous function is also homogeneous.*

We can now state our main results, first in terms of general families of homogeneous functions.

Definition 19 *Given a finite set S, a subset $S' \subseteq S$, and an instance space X: we say that a model family $\{M_w\}_{w \in \mathbf{R}^S}$ is **homogeneous on the parameter set S'** if for all $w \in \mathbf{R}^S$, $x \in X$ and $\lambda \geq 0$,*

$$M_v(x) = \lambda M_w(x), \tag{10}$$

where $v \in \mathbf{R}^S$, $v_s = \lambda w_s$ when $s \in S'$, and $v_s = w_s$ when $s \notin S'$.

Note that under this definition homogeneity is a property of a set of parameters not an individual parameter: if a model family is homogeneous on S' and on S'', that does not imply it is homogeneous on $S' \cup S''$; however, if $S''' \subseteq S'$, it will be homogeneous on S'''.

Our main results show that homogeneity and totality allow a holographic feature set to be extracted, where an auxiliary linear model on the feature set can replicate the output of any model in the family over the training data.

Theorem 20 *If a model family $\mathcal{M}$ is homogeneous on the parameter set S', $M \in \mathcal{M}$, $\mathcal{L}'$ is the family of linear models associated with S' given M, and S' is total on the training data given M, then there exists $N \in \mathcal{L}'$ such that M and N are equivalent on the training data.*

Theorem 21 *Given a problem $\mathcal{P}$, if a model family $\{M_w\}_{w \in \mathbf{R}^S}$ is homogeneous on the parameter set S', then for any $w \in \mathbf{R}^S$:*

1. *if $\mathcal{L}'$ is the family of linear models associated with S' given M_w, S' is total on the training data given M_w, and $\frac{\partial L_{\mathcal{P}}(M_w)}{\partial w_s} = 0$ for all $s \in S'$, then M_w is equal on the training data to any optimal N' in $\mathcal{L}'$.*
2. *if $\mathcal{L}'$ is the family of linear models associated with S given M_w, S' is total on the training data given M_w, and $\frac{\partial L_{\mathcal{P}}(M_w)}{\partial w_s} = 0$ for all $s \in S$, then M_w is equal on the training data to any optimal N' in $\mathcal{L}'$.*

Theorem 21 can be proved simply by combining Theorem 20 with Lemmas 13 and 14. We thus reach the conclusion that homogeneity allows one to generate features and build an auxiliary linear model that can behave equivalently to the original model over the training data.

6.1 APPLICATION TO NEURAL NETWORKS

To apply these results to deep neural networks we need to consider the question of when a model family defined by a network specification can be homogeneous in the sense of Definition 19. Recall the definition from Section 5 where a feedforward neural network is defined in terms of a directed acyclic graph $G = (V, E)$. A **cut** of G is a partition of the vertices in V into two disjoint subsets, where a **cut set** is the set of edges in E between those two sets. We wish to partition G into two sets, $B \subseteq V$ (bottom) and $T \subseteq V$ (top), such that $B \cap T = \emptyset$, $I \subseteq B$ and $o^* \in T$. The cut set consists of edges (u, v) where $u \in B$ and $t \in T$. We will call such a cut an **ordered cut**, since $t \nleq b$ for all $b \in B$, $t \in T$ under the partial order generated by G. Note that, since there are no incoming edges to I and $o^* \notin I$ is assumed, we have the following.

Lemma 22 *For any feedforward neural network, there is an ordered cut, specifically $B = I$ and $T = V \backslash I$.*

Features generated by the parameters on edges in the cut set turn out to be of critical importance. In particular, by considering a partition of the vertices in a feedforward network into an ordered cut—consisting of B, T and the cut set—we reach the deepest result in this paper: that the solutions to the deep network can be mimicked by the solutions to the corresponding linear model defined on the features generated by the ordered cut.

Theorem 23 *Given a problem $\mathcal{P}$ and a family of feedforward network models $\mathcal{D}(V, E, I, \{g_i\}_{i \in I}, o^*, A) = \{M_w\}_{w \in \mathbf{R}^E}$, where all $a \in A$ are homogeneous:* ***if*** *B and T is an ordered cut of the feedforward network, such that E' is the cut set,* ***then****:*

1. *$\{M_w\}_{w \in \mathbf{R}^E}$ is homogeneous on E';*
2. *for some $w \in \mathbf{R}^E$, if E' is total on the training data given M_w, $\mathcal{L}'$ is the family of linear models associated with E' given M_w, and $\frac{\partial L_{\mathcal{P}}(M_w)}{\partial w_e} = 0$ for all $e \in E'$, then M_w is equal on the training data to any optimal model in $\mathcal{L}'$;*
3. *for some $w \in \mathbf{R}^E$, if $\mathcal{L}'$ is the family of linear models associated with E given M_w, if E is total on the training data given M_w, and $\frac{\partial L_{\mathcal{P}}(M_w)}{\partial w_e} = 0$ for all $e \in E$, then M_w is equal on the training data to any optimal model in $\mathcal{L}'$.*

This result is of particular significance to the problem of repeated training, where data is arriving over time and one needs to continually produce new models. In such a scenario, it is important that the models produced behave stably: roughly speaking, there needs to be some form of repeatability in the training process and consistency in the resulting model prediction errors. Such stability is important so that human beings, who must ultimately decide whether a machine learning system can be trusted in a continuous setting, can accept that a subsequent trained model will not make significantly worse mistakes than a trained model makes today. An auxiliary family of linear models improves this notion of stability in two key ways:

1. One can approximate an optimal model with techniques from convex optimization (when it exists).
2. All optimal models are semantically equivalent on the training data.

Thus, we obtain a new form of reproducibility in a continual learning process. Such stability does not imply that the model will remain unchanged in the future, and the data may change, but this provides a solid foundation. Although the features associated with all parameters can be extracted, the fact that one can extract an equivalent linear model over a fraction of the features is a significant result. If one extracted all features, multiple distinct linear models would be optimal on the training data yet differ on new data, which would decrease stability.

It is pointed out in [21], Theorem 3.4, that there is a duality between entropy maximization and maximum likelihood. In fact, if we wish to maximize entropy subject to a set of constraints, then the member of an exponential family that satisfies those constraints maximizes entropy. Thus, when a linear model is calibrated on all of its input features, it is not only maximizing likelihood, it is maximizing entropy.[5] If a deep network is at a local minimum where the derivative is equal to zero, it is equal to one of these linear models: thus, one can consider a locally optimal model in a deep network to be maximizing entropy subject to being calibrated on the extracted features.

7 OTHER ARCHITECTURES

Not all deep models are feedforward networks: recursive neural networks are not defined on a fixed graph, residual networks (ResNets) [8] fix some weights to be constant, and convolutional neural networks (CNNs) [12] have sets of edges with equal weights.

We can handle convolutional and residual neural networks by considering a function $w^* : \mathbf{R}^n \to \mathbf{R}^E$, where we choose $v \in \mathbf{R}^n$ and use $w = w^*(v)$ as the parameters for the network. Thus, for $\mathcal{D}(V, E, I, \{g_i\}_{i \in I}, o^*, A)$ represented as $\{M_w\}_{w \in \mathbf{R}^E}$, we can write $\{Q_v\}_{v \in \mathbf{R}^n}$ such that $Q_v = M_{w^*(v)}$ for all $v \in \mathbf{R}^n$. For ResNets, we need to specify some $E^f \subseteq E$ and $w^f \in \mathbf{R}^{E^f}$, where w^f_e is always the weight of $(w^*(v))_e$. Define $E^d = E - E^f$. For CNNs, we need to specify a partition of the edges: it is easiest to do so with a function $\pi : E^d \to \{1 \ldots n\}$. So, for any $v \in \mathbf{R}^n$ and all $e \in E$:

$$(w^*(v))_e = \begin{cases} w^f_e & \text{if } e \in E^f \\ v_{\pi(e)} & \text{otherwise} \end{cases} \tag{11}$$

Thus, we will consider a **family of RC neural networks**[6] $\mathcal{RC}(V, E, I, \{g_i\}_{i \in I}, o^*, A, w^*) = \{Q_v\}_{v \in \mathbf{R}^n}$. Notice that now, instead of having $|E|$ we have n parameters. Define $E_1 \ldots E_n \subseteq E^d$ such that $E_s = \pi^{-1}(s)$, i.e. the conventional representation of the partition. Given a

[5] There is a nuance: this particular kind of entropy maximization is with respect to a particular measure. For the Bernoulli or any multinomial family, this corresponds with the traditional concept of entropy (entropy with respect to the counting measure). However, conventional differential entropy, which is defined with respect to the Lebesgue measure, is maximized subject to an additional constraint on variance.

[6] RC stands for ResNet and CNN.

family of RC feedforward neural networks, a cut B, T is **well-behaved** if it is an ordered cut and there exists an $S \subseteq \{1 \ldots n\}$ such that the cut set equals $\bigcup_{s \in S} E_s$.

Theorem 24 *For a problem $\mathcal{P}$ and family of RC feedforward network models $\mathcal{RC}(V, E, I, \{g_i\}_{i \in I}, o^*, A, w^*)$ denoted $\{Q_v\}_{v \in \mathbf{R}^n}$, where all $a \in A$ are homogeneous:* ***if*** *$E_1 \ldots E_n$ is the partition of the dynamic parameters, and B and T are a well-behaved cut such that there is an $S \subseteq \{1 \ldots n\}$ where $E' = \bigcup_{s \in S} E_s$ is the cut set;* ***then***

1. *$\{Q_v\}_{v \in \mathbf{R}^n}$ is a homogeneous model family with respect to S;*
2. *if for some $v \in \mathbf{R}^n$, $\frac{\partial L_{\mathcal{P}}(Q_v)}{\partial v_s} = 0$ for all $s \in S$, the set S is total on the training data given Q_v, and $\mathcal{L}'$ is the family of linear models associated with S given Q_v, then Q_v is equal on the training data to any optimal N' in $\mathcal{L}'$;*
3. *if for some $v \in \mathbf{R}^n$, $\frac{\partial L_{\mathcal{P}}(Q_v)}{\partial v_s} = 0$ for all $s \in \{1 \ldots n\}$, the set $\{1 \ldots n\}$ is total on the training data given Q_v, and $\mathcal{L}'$ is the family of linear models associated with $\{1 \ldots n\}$ given Q_v, then Q_v is equal on the training data to any optimal N' in $\mathcal{L}'$.*

Thus, if the cut exists, we can extract all the features.

8 REGULARIZATION

To this point, we have assumed parameters can have any value, and there is no external cost to choosing one set of parameters over another. However, there is evidence that regularization yields better generalization [6, Chapter 7].

In our framework, regularization can be defined in a generic way. Given a model family $\mathcal{M}$, a regularization function $R : \mathcal{M} \rightarrow \mathbf{R}$ assigns a cost to each model, independent of how it fits the data.

Definition 25 *Given a model family $\mathcal{M}$, we say that $M \in \mathcal{M}$* ***is optimal in $\mathcal{M}$ given the problem $\mathcal{P}$ and a regularization function $R : \mathcal{M} \rightarrow \mathbf{R}$****, if for all $M' \in \mathcal{M}$, $L_{\mathcal{P}}(M) + R(M) \leq L_{\mathcal{P}}(M') + R(M')$.*

This kind of optimality can sometimes be interpreted as maximum a posteriori rather than maximum likelihood optimization. For the remainder of this section, we assume we have a finite S and model family $\mathcal{M} = \{M_w\}_{w \in \mathbf{R}^S}$. For a regularization function $R : \mathcal{M} \rightarrow \mathbf{R}$, define $R^* : \mathbf{R}^S \rightarrow \mathbf{R}$ such that $R^*(w) = R(M_w)$. We assume R is (strictly) convex if R^* is (strictly) convex. Given a subset $S' \subseteq S$, we will say that a function $r : \mathbf{R}^S \rightarrow \mathbf{R}$ is **additively separable** with respect to S' if there exists $r^{S'} : \mathbf{R}^{S'} \rightarrow \mathbf{R}^S$, and $r^{S-S'} : \mathbf{R}^{S-S'} \rightarrow \mathbf{R}^S$ such that for all $w \in \mathbf{R}^S$, $r(w) = r^{S'}(\pi^{S \rightarrow S'}(w)) + r^{S-S'}(\pi^{S \rightarrow S-S'}(w))$. R is additively separable with respect to S' if R^* is additively separable with respect to S'. We can consider when, for all $s \in S$, the partial derivative with respect to s is zero:

$$\frac{\partial L_{\mathcal{P}}(M_w) + R(M_w)}{\partial w_s} = 0. \qquad (12)$$

This is a stationary point and might be a saddle point or a local minima. The most common regularizers are L1 (where $R(M_w) = \sum_{s \in S} |w_s|$) and L2 (where $R(M_w) = \sum_{s \in S} w_s^2$), but group lasso [24] and other regularizations are also possible. Note that L1 regularization and group lasso are convex, L2 regularization is strictly convex, L1 and L2 regularization are separable, and group L1 regularization is sometimes separable.

As before, we want to connect homogeneous families (such as some deep networks) with regularization to the associated linear family with regularization.

Theorem 26 *Given a problem $\mathcal{P}$, a set S, a subset $S' \subseteq S$, a model family $\mathcal{M} = \{M_w\}_{w \in \mathbf{R}^S}$ that is homogeneous with respect to S', a strictly convex regularization function $R : \mathcal{M} \rightarrow \mathbf{R}$ that is additively separable with respect to S', and a model M_w where for all $s \in S'$:*

$$\frac{\partial [L_{\mathcal{P}}(M_w) + R(M_w)]}{\partial w_s} = 0, \qquad (13)$$

if *S' is total on the training data given M_w, $\mathcal{L}' = \{N_v\}_{v \in \mathbf{R}^{S'}}$ is the family of linear models associated with S' given M_w, and a new regularizer $R' : \mathcal{L}' \rightarrow \mathbf{R}$ is defined such that $R'(N_v) = (R^*)^{S'}(v)$,* ***then*** *M_w must be equal on the training data to any optimal $N \in \mathcal{L}'$ given the supervised learning problem and regularization R'.*

Thus, in all circumstances where we showed functions were homogeneous (for the generic feedforward networks and some CNNs and ResNets), we now know that for a separable regularizer we can map these to a linear model family. However, we cannot simply add back all the other generated features not present in the ordered cut, because there might be a parameterization across all the generated features that has the same predictions and lower regularization. This requires further study.

9 EXPERIMENTAL EVALUATION

We investigated the main assertions that:

1. In practice, the holographic features generated can faithfully recover the original classifier.
2. The holographic features generated are indeed calibrated with respect to the original classifier.
3. Training with the generated holographic features is more stable than training a neural network.

Data set	# examples	input dim	λ	layer width	hidden layers
Pima	750 of 768	9	1/720	4	2
Census	30000 of 32561	108	1/1490	10	3
MNIST-3v5	9000 of 11552	784	1/1490	100	3

Table 1: Data sets and neural network architectures used.

4. The holographic features support generalization beyond the training set they were generated from.

We used three binary classification data sets, UCI Pima, UCI Census and MNIST (3 vs 5). The details of each data set and the respective neural network architectures used are given in Table 1. Since our experimental design required us to partition each data set into three disjoint subsets, we extracted the number of examples indicated from the initial portion of the original data then split the chosen data into three equal sized subsets. In particular, we consider training the neural network on the first third, training the extracted linear models on the middle third, and using the final third to assess generalization performance. We also normalized the input features in each case by subtracting the means and dividing by the range.

Faithfulness First we evaluate whether a linear classifier trained on holographic features can faithfully reproduce the predictions of the original neural network, whereas using activation features fails to do so. Specifically, we trained the neural network on the first data partition, extracted the holographic and activation feature sets for each layer-wise cut of the neural network, trained a linear model over these feature sets on the same data, then compared the predictions on the same training data against those made by the source neural network. Figures 1 to 3 show the agreement plots for the Pima, Census and MNIST data sets respectively. The plots show the results achieved by trained linear models over the activation and holographic feature sets respectively, as well as using exact weights for the holographic features. There are minor differences due to the neural network not being at a true local minimum, but the assertion appears to be verified.

Calibration Next, we investigate the assertion that the holographic features must be calibrated. To do so, we plot $\sum_{i=1}^{m} f(x_i)\mu_p(M(x_i))$ against $\sum_{i=1}^{m} f(x_i)y_i$ for each extracted set of holographic features over the training data. Figure 4 shows that the holographic features are indeed well calibrated, regardless of which cut was used to generate them, or which data set is considered.

Stability To determine whether a linearized representation improves learning stability compared to re-training a neural network, we conducted the following experiment. We trained a neural network on the first partition, extracted distinct holographic and activation feature sets

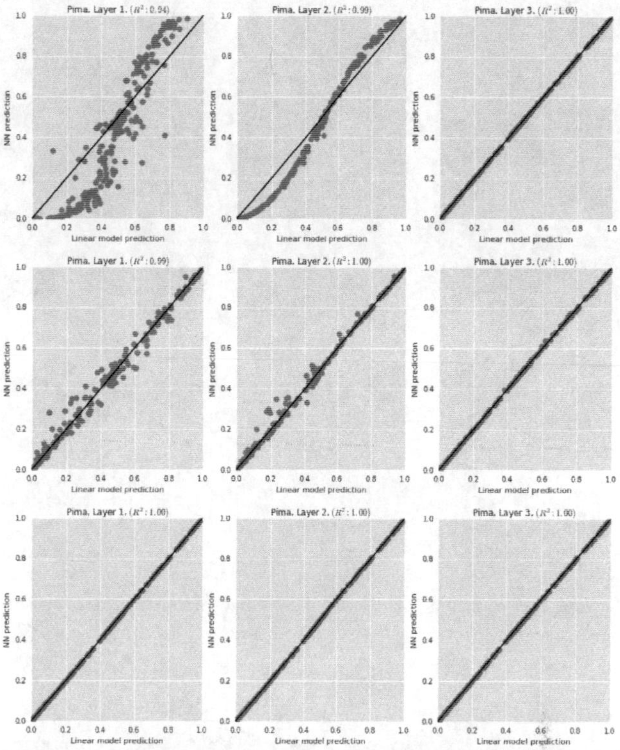

Figure 1: Classifier comparison for *Pima*. Training on activation features (row 1), holographic features (row 2), and closed form solution to holographic weights (row 3).

Model type	Pima	Census	MNIST-3v5
Neural net	5.9×10^{-5}	2.8×10^{-5}	1.1×10^{-4}
Activation	$< 10^{-15}$	$< 10^{-15}$	$< 10^{-15}$
Holographic	$< 10^{-15}$	$< 10^{-15}$	$< 10^{-15}$

Table 2: Average KL divergence between posteriors for different re-trainings of the same model on the same data.

for each layer-wise cut, then repeatedly re-trained the linear models with different random initializations on the second data partition, gathering the predictions made on the third data partition. We then re-trained the neural network on the original training data with different random initializations, and gathered the predictions made on the third data partition. To evaluate learning stability, we measured the average symmetrized KL divergence between the predictions of the different re-trained models for each type. The results are reported in Table 2. As expected, re-training produces nearly identical predictions for the linear models since the problem is convex. However, neural network re-training results in non-negligible variability between the different learned models.

Generalization Finally, we investigate whether holographic features support generalization to data from

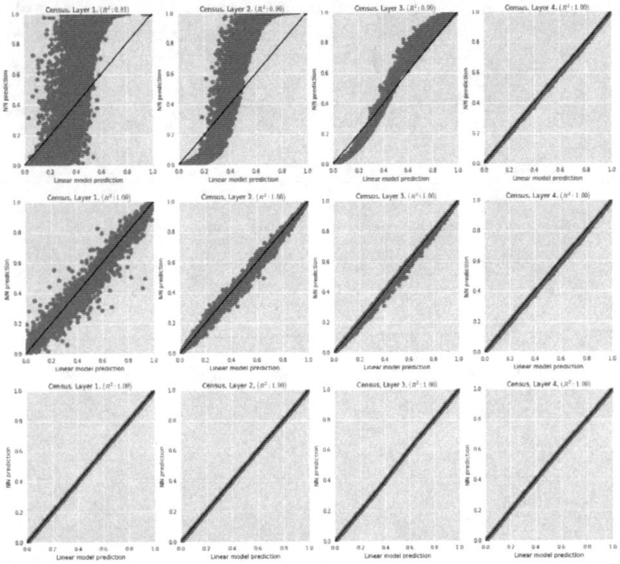

Figure 2: Classifier comparison for *Census*. Training on activation features (row 1), holographic features (row 2), and closed form solution to holographic weights (row 3).

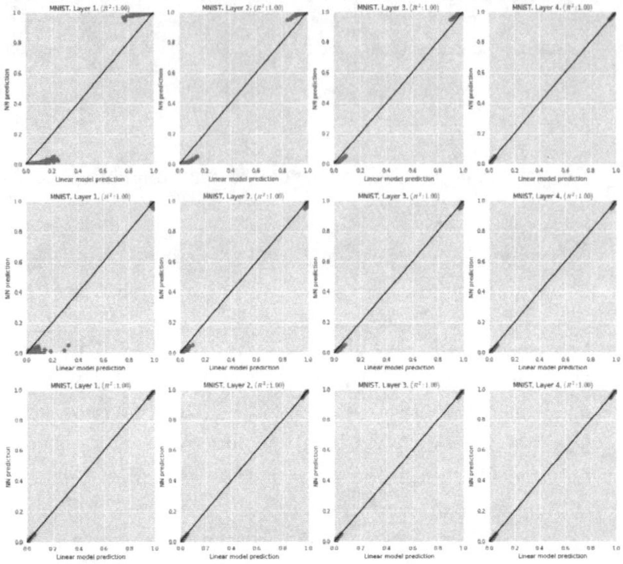

Figure 3: Classifier comparison for *MNIST*. Training on activation features (row 1), holographic features (row 2), and closed form solution to holographic weights (row 3).

	Pima		Census		MNIST-3v5	
Layer	Activ	Holo	Activ	Holo	Activ	Holo
1	.529	.462	.477	.331	.375	.133
2	.536	.455	.494	.339	.249	.085
3	.474	.471	.380	.345	.155	.082

Table 3: Average negative log-likelihood on third partition for linear classifier trained on second partition (after being extracted from first partition).

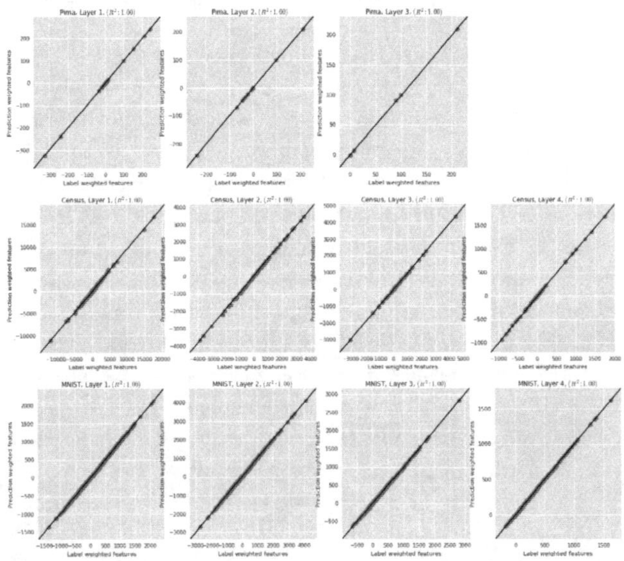

Figure 4: Calibration plots for extracted holographic features from each layer (columns) on each data set (rows).

which they were not inferred. In this case, we generated both holographic and activation features from a neural network that was trained on the first data partition, as above. Then we trained the linear models defined over these extracted feature sets on the second data partition, and assessed their negative log-likelihood on the third data partition. The results are given in Table 3. For comparison, the generalization performance of the neural network is Pima: 0.421, Census: 0.360, and MNIST-3v5: 0.086 (smaller is better). It is clear that the holographic features support better generalization than activation features, while achieving competitive generalization to the original neural network on the larger data sets.

10 CONCLUSION

We have introduced the concept of generated ("holographic") features from a model family, specified by the gradient of the prediction with respect to an appropriate subset of parameters. We have shown that, for any model family, if a model is at a local minimum, then the model is calibrated with respect to features generated from the parameters with respect to the model. Moreover, we have shown that for many standard feedforward networks, an optimal linear model on the generated features will make the same predictions as the original feedforward network. We show that in practice, building linear models with the generated "holographic" features better replicates the original network than building linear models based on intermediate activations.

References

[1] G. Alain and Y. Bengio. Understanding intermediate layers using linear classifier probes. *arXiv e-prints*, abs/1610.01644, October 2016.

[2] L. D. Brown. Fundamentals of statistical exponential families with applications in statistical decision theory. *Lecture Notes-Monograph Series*, 9:i–279, 1986.

[3] Y. Dauphin, R. Pascanu, Ç. Gülçehre, K. Cho, S. Ganguli, and Y. Bengio. Identifying and attacking the saddle point problem in high-dimensional non-convex optimization. *CoRR*, abs/1406.2572, 2014.

[4] D. Erhan, Y. Bengio, A. A. Courville, and P. Vincent. Visualizing higher-layer features of a deep network. Technical report, University of Montreal, 2009.

[5] D. Erhan, P.-A. Manzagol, Y. Bengio, S. Bengio, and P. Vincent. The difficulty of training deep architectures and the effect of unsupervised pre-training. In *AISTATS*, pages 153–160, 2009.

[6] I. Goodfellow, Y. Bengio, and A. Courville. *Deep Learning*. MIT Press, 2016. `http://www.deeplearningbook.org`.

[7] A. Graves, A. Mohamed, and G. E. Hinton. Speech recognition with deep recurrent neural networks. In *ICASSP*, 2013.

[8] K. He, X. Zhang, S. Ren, and J. Sun. Deep residual learning for image recognition. In *CVPR*, 2016.

[9] J. Hirschberg and C. Manning. Advances in natural language processing. *Science*, 349(6245):261–266, Jul 2015.

[10] A. Krizhevsky, I. Sutskever, and G. Hinton. Imagenet classification with deep convolutional neural networks. In *NIPS*, 2012.

[11] L. D. Kudryavtsev. Homogeneous function. In M. Hazewinkel, editor, *Encyclopedia of Mathematics*. Springer, 2001.

[12] Y. LeCun, L. Bottou, Y. Bengio, and P. Haffner. Gradient-based learning applied to document recognition. *Proceedings of the IEEE*, 86(11):2278–2324, 1998.

[13] A. L. Maas, A. Y. Hannun, and A. Y. Ng. Rectifier nonlinearities improve neural network acoustic models. In *ICML*, 2013.

[14] T. Mikolov, I. Sutskever, K. Chen, G. Corrado, and J. Dean. Distributed representations of words and phrases and their compositionality. In *NIPS*, 2013.

[15] A. Mordvintsev, C. Olah, and M. Tyka. Deepdream - a code example for visualizing neural networks. `https://research.googleblog.com/2015/06/inceptionism-going-deeper-into-neural.html`, July 2015.

[16] J. Nelder and R. Wedderburn. Generalized linear models. *Journal of the Royal Statistical Society Series A (General)*, 135(3):370–384, 1972.

[17] O. Russakovsky, J. Deng, H. Su, J. Krause, S. Satheesh, S. Ma, Z. Huang, A. Karpathy, A. Khosla, M. Bernstein, A. C. Berg, and L. Fei-Fei. ImageNet Large Scale Visual Recognition Challenge. *International Journal of Computer Vision (IJCV)*, 115(3):211–252, 2015.

[18] D. Schuurmans and M. Zinkevich. Deep learning games. In *NIPS*, 2016.

[19] P. Sermanet, D. Eigen, X. Zhang, M. Mathieu, R. Fergus, and Y. LeCun. Overfeat: Integrated recognition, localization and detection using convolutional networks. In *ICLR*, 2014.

[20] K. Simonyan, A. Vedaldi, and A. Zisserman. Deep inside convolutional networks: Visualising image classification models and saliency maps. *CoRR*, abs/1312.6034, 2013.

[21] M. J. Wainwright and M. I. Jordan. Foundations and trends®in machine learning. 1(1–2):1–305, 2008.

[22] Y. Wu, M. Schuster, Z. Chen, Q. V. Le, M. Norouzi, W. Macherey, M. Krikun, Y. Cao, Q. Gao, K. Macherey, J. Klingner, A. Shah, M. Johnson, X. Liu, . Kaiser, S. Gouws, Y. Kato, T. Kudo, H. Kazawa, K. Stevens, G. Kurian, N. Patil, W. Wang, C. Young, J. Smith, J. Riesa, A. Rudnick, O. Vinyals, G. Corrado, M. Hughes, and J. Dean. Google's neural machine translation system: Bridging the gap between human and machine translation. *CoRR*, abs/1609.08144, 2016.

[23] J. Yosinski, J. Clune, Y. Bengio, and H. Lipson. How transferable are features in deep neural networks? In *NIPS*, pages 3320–3328, 2014.

[24] M. Yuan and Y. Lin. Model selection and estimation in regression with grouped variables. *Journal of the Royal Statistical Society B*, 68:49–67, 2006.

[25] M. Zeiler, G. Taylor, and R. Fergus. Adaptive deconvolutional networks for mid and high level feature learning. In *ICCV*, 2011.

[26] M. D. Zeiler and R. Fergus. Visualizing and understanding convolutional neural networks. In *ECCV*, 2014.

A EXPONENTIAL FAMILIES

This section reviews the standard results on exponential families in the literature [16, 2, 21]. A 1-dimensional standard exponential family [2, page 2] at its core can be represented by a reference measure $(\mathbf{R}, \mathcal{B}, \rho_p)$, where the set of outcomes (whether possible or not: see the definition of Ω_p below) is given by $\mathbf{R}$, the real numbers; the set of measurable sets is given by $\mathcal{B}$, the Borel algebra of $\mathbf{R}$; and $\rho_p : \mathcal{B} \to [0, \infty]$ is a positive measure (often not a probability measure). Define $A_p : \mathbf{R} \to [-\infty, +\infty]$ to be a normalization function where:

$$A_p(\theta) = \ln \left(\int \exp(\theta\omega) d\rho_p(\omega) \right). \quad (14)$$

If A_p is finite for all $\theta \in \mathbf{R}$, then p is defined to be full [2]. If p is full, then for each $\theta \in \mathbf{R}$, there is a distribution in the family of the form:

$$\forall B \in \mathcal{B}, \Pr[x \in B|\theta] = \int_B \exp(\theta\omega - A_p(\theta))\rho_p(d\omega), \quad (15)$$

Full exponential families are also "regular" [2, page 2]. Define Ω_p to be the support of ρ_p, the minimal closed set $\mathcal{W} \subseteq \mathbf{R}$ such that $\rho_p(\mathbf{R} - \mathcal{W}) = 0$, i.e. the possible outcomes. If p is full and $|\Omega_p| > 1$, it is "minimal" [2, page 2].[7] A full, minimal, 1-dimensional standard exponential family p has a strictly convex A_p [2, Theorem 1.13] that is infinitely differentiable everywhere [2, Theorem 2.2],

The likelihood of ω given θ is $\exp(\theta\omega - A_p(\theta))$. The negative log likelihood of ω given θ is $\ell_p(\omega, \theta) = A_p(\theta) - \theta\omega$. Notice that if A_p is strictly convex, then ℓ_p is strictly convex in its second argument. The mean $\mu_p : \mathbf{R} \to \mathbf{R}$ is:

$$\mu_p(\theta) = \int \exp(\theta\omega - A_p(\theta))\rho_p(d\omega). \quad (16)$$

It is useful to define $\lambda_p : \mathbf{R} \to \mathbf{R}$ to be:

$$\lambda_p(\theta) = \int \exp(\theta\omega)\rho_p(d\omega). \quad (17)$$

Now given these standard defintions, we can prove Lemma 1:

[7] The definition of minimal in [2, page 2] states that p is minimal if the dimension of the convex hull of the support equals the dimension of the set of parameters where A_p is finite, but since we are dealing with full, 1-dimensional, standard exponential families, that complexity is unnecessary, as the dimension of the set of parameters where A_p is finite is always 1, and the dimension of the convex hull of the support is zero if the support has 1 point, and 1 if the support has two or more points.

Lemma 1 *The Bernoulli family, Gaussian family (fixed variance), and Poisson family are full, minimal, 1-dimensional standard exponential families. For a full, minimal, 1-dimensional standard exponential family p:*

1. *for every $\theta \in \mathbf{R}$, $\omega \in \Omega_p$, $\ell_p(\omega, \theta)$ is differentiable with respect to θ and $\frac{\partial \ell_p(\omega,\theta)}{\partial\theta} = \mu_p(\theta) - \omega$; and*
2. *ℓ_p is **strictly convex in its second argument**: for every $\theta, \theta' \in \mathbf{R}$, if $\theta \neq \theta'$, then for all $\lambda \in (0, 1)$ we have $\ell_p(\omega, \lambda\theta + (1 - \lambda)\theta') < \lambda\ell_p(\omega, \theta) + (1 - \lambda)\ell_p(\omega, \theta')$.*

Proof: As we stated before, A_p is strictly convex if p is a full, minimal, 1 dimensional standard exponential family, and this implies that ℓ_p is strictly convex in its second argument. If p is a standard exponential family that is full and minimal, then λ_p is infinitely differentiable everywhere [2, Theorem 2.2], and by [2, page 34]:

$$\lambda_p'(\theta) = \int \omega \exp(\theta\omega)\rho_p(d\omega) \quad (18)$$

We then normalize:

$$\frac{\lambda_p'(\theta)}{\lambda_p(\theta)} = \frac{\int \omega \exp(\theta\omega)\rho_p(d\omega)}{\lambda_p(\theta)} \quad (19)$$

$$= \frac{\int \omega \exp(\theta\omega)\rho_p(d\omega)}{\exp(A_p(\theta))} \quad (20)$$

$$= \int \omega \exp(\theta\omega - A_p(\theta))\rho_p(d\omega) \quad (21)$$

$$= \mu_p(\theta). \quad (22)$$

So, for $\ell_p(\omega, \theta)$:

$$\frac{\partial \ell_p(\omega, \theta)}{\partial\theta} = A_p'(\theta) - \omega \quad (23)$$

$$= \frac{\lambda_p'(\theta)}{\lambda_p(\theta)} - \omega \quad (24)$$

$$= \mu_p(\theta) - \omega. \quad (25)$$

Equation 25 is [16, Equation 3].

We now just have to show that $|\Omega_p| > 1$ and A_p is finite everywhere for the families mentioned. It is natural to think of the definition of ρ_p in terms of the possible outcomes, but Ω_p is defined in terms of ρ_p. So, instead we define $\mathcal{W}$ as a set (that will turn out to be the possible outcomes), define ρ_p in terms of $\mathcal{W}$, and then show $\Omega_p = \mathcal{W}$. Note that if $\mathcal{W}$ is finite, to prove $\Omega_p = \mathcal{W}$, we need only prove that for all $\omega \in \mathcal{W}$, $\rho_p(\omega) > 0$, and $\rho_p(\mathbf{R} - \mathcal{W}) = 0$. If $\mathcal{W} = \mathbf{R}$, then we need to show any finite, nonempty, open interval has positive measure to prove $\Omega_p = \mathcal{W}$ (this is because $\mathbf{R} - \Omega_p$ is open, and if there is some $\omega \in \mathbf{R} - \Omega_p$, then there must be a neighborhood N of ω (a finite, nonempty, open interval) in $\mathbf{R} - \Omega_p$ where $\rho_p(N) = 0$).

1. For the Bernoulli family of distributions, $\mathcal{W} = \{0, 1\}$ and $\rho_p(B) = |B \cap \mathcal{W}|$. Thus, $\rho_p(\{0\}) = \rho_p(\{1\}) = 1$, and $\rho_p(\mathbf{R} - \mathcal{W}) = |(\mathbf{R} - \mathcal{W}) \cap \mathcal{W}| = 0$, so $\Omega_p = \mathcal{W}$. Also, $A_p(\theta) = -\ln(1 + \exp(\theta))$, $\Pr[\omega|\theta] = \frac{\exp(\theta\omega)}{1+\exp(\theta)}$, and $\ell_p(\omega, \theta) = -\theta\omega + \ln(1 + \exp(\theta))$, and $\mu_p(\theta) = \frac{1}{1+\exp(-\theta)}$. Since $A_p(\theta)$ is finite everywhere, the Bernoulli family is full, and since $|\Omega_p| > 1$, the Bernoulli family is minimal.
2. For the Gaussian family of distributions with fixed mean $\sigma^2 = 1$ we have $\mathcal{W} = \mathbf{R}$, but we also need to define a particular ρ_p. Specifically, define some $h(\omega) = \frac{1}{\sqrt{2\pi}} \exp(-\frac{\omega^2}{2})$. For any Borel measurable set, define $\rho_p(B) = \int_B h(\omega) d\omega$, where the right hand side is the standard Lebesgue integral. Note ρ_p itself is a Gaussian with mean zero and variance one. Since $h(\omega) > 0$ and $h(\omega)$ is continuous, on any finite, closed interval $[a, b]$ it has a minimum $m > 0$, and therefore on any finite, nonempty, open interval (a, b), $\rho_p((a, b)) \geq (b - a)m$, so $\Omega_p = \mathcal{W}$. Thus, $A_p(\theta) = \frac{\theta^2}{2}$, $\Pr[\omega \in B|\theta] = \frac{1}{\sqrt{2\pi}} \int_B \exp\big(-\frac{(\omega-\theta)^2}{2}\big) d\omega$, $\mu_p(\theta) = \theta$, the likelihood[8] is $\exp(\theta\omega - \frac{\theta^2}{2})$, and $\ell_p(\theta, \omega) = \frac{\theta^2}{2} - \theta\omega = \frac{1}{2}(\theta - \omega)^2 + \frac{\omega^2}{2}$. Notice that this loss is off by $\frac{\omega^2}{2}$ from squared loss, and this term is independent of θ. Finally, $|\Omega_p| > 1$, A_p is finite everywhere, implying p is a full, minimal, standard, 1-dimensional family.
3. For the Poisson family of distributions $\mathcal{W} = \{0, 1, 2 \ldots\}$. Define $\rho_p(B) = \sum_{\omega \in \mathcal{W} \cap B} \frac{1}{\omega!}$, so $A_p(\theta) = \exp(\theta)$. Moreover, for any non-negative integer ω, $\rho_p(\{\omega\}) = \frac{1}{\omega!}$, and $\rho_p(\mathbf{R} - \mathcal{W})$ is the sum over an empty set, and therefore zero. Finally, $\Pr[\omega|\theta] = \frac{1}{\omega!} \exp(\theta\omega - \exp(\theta))$, and the likelihood[9] is $\exp(\theta\omega - \exp(\theta))$. $\mu_p(\theta) = \exp(\theta)$ and $\ell_p(\omega, \theta) = \exp(\theta) - \theta\omega$. Again, $|\Omega_p| > 1$, and A_p is finite everywhere.

■

B RELATION TO TRADITIONAL LAYERED NEURAL NETWORKS

A more conventional way to represent a network involves writing layers, by interleaving fixed activation functions with learned affine functions. We imagine a sequence of integers $n_0 \ldots n_k$, representing the number of nodes in each layer, with 0 being the input layer (with $X = \mathbf{R}^{n_0}$), and k being the output layer (with $n_k = 1$). We choose an activation function $a_i : \mathbf{R} \to \mathbf{R}$ for each layer $\{0, \ldots k-1\}$, and define $A^i : \mathbf{R}^{n_i} \to \mathbf{R}^{n_i}$ such that $(A^i(v))_j = a_i(v_j)$ for all $v \in \mathbf{R}^{n_i}$, for all $j \in \{1 \ldots n_i\}$. Often a_0 is the identity, and $a_1 \ldots a_{k-1}$ are $relu$, sigmoid, or some other standard function.

Then, in-between these layers, we have a matrix $W^i \in \mathbf{R}^{n_i \times n_{i-1}}$ and a vector $w^i \in \mathbf{R}^{n_i}$. We define $h^0 : \mathbf{R}^{n_0} \to \mathbf{R}^{n_0}$ to be the identity. We can then define $h^i : \mathbf{R}^{n_0} \to \mathbf{R}^{n_i}$ for $i \in \{1 \ldots k\}$ recursively such that $h^i(x) = W^i A^{i-1}(h^{i-1}(x)) + w^i)$. The model in this form is $M_{W,w}(x) = h^k(x)_1$. As we will show, these can be easily modeled in our graph representation. However, we will see that learning affine (as opposed to linear) functions show that the conventional concept of "layer" is not as crisp and neat as one would like.

B.1 REPRESENTATION AS A GRAPH

First of all, this kind of model can be represented in the graph network that we describe in Section 5. Most oddities of the representation come from the bias features.

1. For each $i \in \{1 \ldots k\}$, define $V_i = \{v_{i,1} \ldots v_{i,n_i}\}$, and let v_c be a special vertex (which will be a special input node that will always equal 1).
2. Define $V = \{v_c\} \cup \bigcup_{i=0}^k V_i$.
3. Define $I = V_0 \cup \{v_c\}$.
4. Define $o^* = v_{k,1}$,
5. For $i \in \{0, \ldots k-1\}$, for all $j \in \{1 \ldots n_i\}$, let $a_{v_{i,j}} = a^i$.
6. Define a_{o^*} and a_{v_c} to be the identity.
7. For all $x \in X$, for all $j \in 1 \ldots n_0$, let $g_{v_{0,j}}(x) = x_j$.
8. For all $x \in X$, $g_{v_c}(x) = 1$.
9. The edges associated with W^i are $E_i = V_{i-1} \times V_i$.
10. The edges associated with w^i are $E_i^c = \{v_c\} \times V_i$.
11. Define $E = \bigcup_{i=1}^k E_i \cup E_i^c$.

$D = (V, E, I, \{g_i\}_{i \in I}, o^*, \{a_v\}_{v \in V})$ is a neural network, equivalent to the layered form we described in the previous section.

In the next section, we will show how the edges in E_i^c (associated with the bias parameters) play an unusual role in our work.

B.2 AN ORDERED CUT IN A LAYERED NEURAL NETWORK

We introduced ordered cuts and cut sets in Section 6. The most obvious cut would be $B_i = \{v_c\} \cup \bigcup_{j=0}^{i-1} V_j$ and

[8] Note the distinction here between the conventional density defined with respect to the Lebesgue measure, and this likelihood defined with respect to ρ. However, since we are tuning θ and ω is given, this is simply a constant in ℓ_p.

[9] As before, there is a slight distinction between the conventional probability mass and the likelihood as defined here.

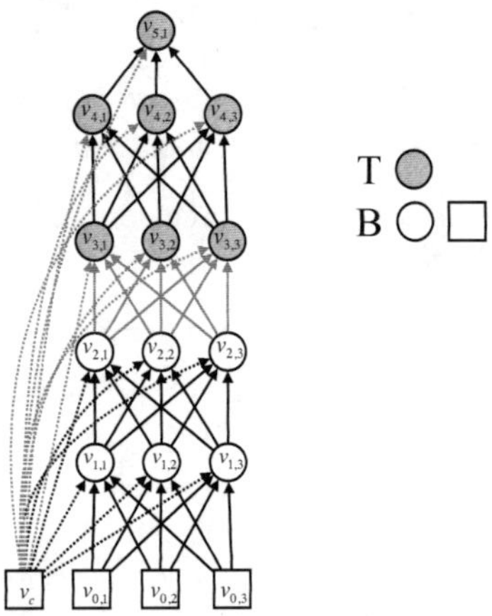

Figure 5: A traditional neural network represented as a graph, with 4 fully connected hidden layers, and a bias parameter for each node. The input nodes are squares, and the internal nodes are circles, with the output node on top. The ordered cut is indicated with the white nodes and the black nodes, and the edges in the cut set are red. Note that while this ordered cut naturally separates the second and third hidden layers, bias parameters from the third, fourth, and fifth layer are in the cut set.

$T_i = \bigcup_{j=i}^{k} V_j$, and these are the ones we use in the experiments.

Suppose $k = 5$, and we consider the cut B_2, T_2, then the cut set E' is the set of edges with one endpoint in B_2 and one endpoint in T_2 (see Figure 5). Obviously, E_2 is a subset of the cut set, as is E_2^c. Less obviously, E_3^c, E_4^c, and E_5^c are also subsets of the cut set.[10] However, upon reflection this makes sense: the proof in Appendix F relies on the network after the cut set to be a homogeneous function, and affine functions with nonzero offsets are certainly not homogeneous functions.

This is the reason that we use the graph representation to introduce our results. Cut sets have very counterintuitive properties in the conventional representation, but once the traditional representations are reduced to a network, they make perfect sense.

[10]Keep in mind, while E_5^c is in the cut set, it only contains one parameter, and the generated (holographic) feature is always 1.

B.3 EXPLORING THE NATURE OF GENERATED FEATURES

So, as we consider these conventional networks, it is natural to ask, what does a generated feature look like? How does it relate to a conventional activation feature? Let us break this down into features generated from weight matrices W (or $E_1 \dots E_k$), and features generated from bias vectors w (or $E_1^c \dots E_k^c$). In this section, for simplicity we assume that partial derivatives exist where necessary: see Appendix I for a deeper discussion of differentiability in deep networks.

We consider the bias features first for some layer $i \in \{1 \dots k-1\}$. For any $j \geq i$, we can recursively define $h^{j,i} : \mathbf{R}^{n_i} \rightarrow \mathbf{R}^{n_j}$ such that $h^{i,i}(v) = v$ and for all $j \in \{i+1 \dots k\}$, $h^{j,i}(v) = W^j A^{j-1}(h^{j-1,i}(v)) + w^j$. This is an accumulation of the transforms after the input of layer i, and for all $x \in X$:

$$M_{W,w}(x) = h^{k,i}(h^i(x)) \quad (26)$$
$$M_{W,w}(x) = h^{k,i}(W^i A^{i-1}(h^{i-1}(x)) + w^i). \quad (27)$$

For some $q \in \{1 \dots n_i\}$, if we define $f_q^i : X \rightarrow \mathbf{R}$ to be the feature generated from $(v_c, v_{i,q})$, then we can write:

$$f_q^i(x) = \frac{\partial M_{W,w}(x)}{\partial w_q^i} \quad (28)$$
$$= \left. \frac{\partial h^{k,i}(v)}{\partial v_q} \right|_{v = W^i A^{i-1}(h^{i-1}(x)) + w^i}. \quad (29)$$

Notice that this is the partial derivative of the prediction with respect to the input of node $v_{i,q}$.

Next, we consider features generated from a weight matrix. Consider some $i \in \{1 \dots k\}$, some $p \in \{1 \dots n_{i-1}\}$ and some $q \in \{1 \dots n_i\}$. Then $(v_{i-1,p}, v_{i,q}) \in E_i$ is the edge related to parameter $W_{q,p}^i$. Define $F_{q,p}^i : X \rightarrow \mathbf{R}$ to be the feature generated from $(v_{i-1,p}, v_{i,q})$. Using $h^{k,i}$ again:

$$F_{q,p}^i(x) = \frac{\partial M_{W,w}(x)}{\partial W_{q,p}^i} \quad (30)$$
$$= \left. \frac{\partial h^{k,i}(v)}{\partial v_q} \right|_{v = W^i A^{i-1}(h^{i-1}(x)) + w^i} A_p^{i-1}(h^{i-1}(x)) \quad (31)$$
$$= f_q^i(x) a^{i-1}(h_p^{i-1}(x)). \quad (32)$$

So, the generated feature from $(v_{i-1,p}, v_{i,q})$ is the activation feature of $v_{i-1,p}$ times the generated feature of $(v_c, v_{i,q})$.

In summary, the generated features of conventional layers have a nice form, and one can take a conventional layered network and translate it into a graph. However, from a mathematical perspective, it is much easier to reason about graphs, because of the clean concept of cuts and cut sets. Moreover, the bias features work in highly counterintuitive ways, and presenting a theory without them tells an incomplete story.

C CONVEXITY

In this section, we will state some known results about convexity.

Fact 27 *Given a supervised learning problem* $\mathcal{P} = (p, X, \{x_1 \dots x_m\}, \{y_1 \dots y_m\})$, *given two models* $M : X \to \mathbf{R}$ *and* $M' : X \to \mathbf{R}$ *that are equal on the training data, if* M *is calibrated on a feature* $f : X \to \mathbf{R}$, *then* M' *is calibrated on* f.

One can think about the model as mapping a matrix of inputs to a vector of predictions, which is then composed with a loss function that maps a vector of predictions to a single loss. Next, we show when this second mapping will be (strictly) convex.

Lemma 28 *Given convex sets* $C_1 \dots C_m \subseteq \mathbf{R}$, *for each* $i \in \{1 \dots m\}$ *a function* $L_i : C_i \to \mathbf{R}$, *then if* $C = \times_{i=1}^{m} C_i$, *and there is a function* $L : C \to \mathbf{R}$ *such that for all* $x \in C$:

$$L(x) = \sum_{i=1}^{m} L_i(x_i), \tag{33}$$

then:

1. *if for all* i, L_i *is convex, then* L *is convex.*
2. *if for all* i, L_i *is strictly convex, then* L *is strictly convex.*

Proof: Consider $x, y \in C$, and $\lambda \in [0, 1]$. Without loss of generality, assume $x \neq y$, and $\lambda \in (0, 1)$. By convexity, for all i, $\lambda L_i(x_i) + (1-\lambda)L_i(y_i) \geq L_i(\lambda x_i + (1-\lambda)y_i)$, so:

$$\begin{aligned} &L(\lambda x + (1-\lambda)y) \\ &= \sum_{i=1}^{m} L_i(\lambda x_i + (1-\lambda)y_i) &(34)\\ &\leq \sum_{i=1}^{m} (\lambda L_i(x_i) + (1-\lambda)L(y_i)) &(35)\\ &\leq \lambda \sum_{i=1}^{m} L_i(x_i) + (1-\lambda)\sum_{i=1}^{m} L(y_i) &(36)\\ &\leq \lambda L(x) + (1-\lambda)L(y). &(37)\end{aligned}$$

To prove the result for strong convexity, we need to be a little more careful. Since $x \neq y$, there exists a $j \in \{1 \dots m\}$ where $x_j \neq y_j$. So $L_j(\lambda x_j + (1-\lambda)y_j) < \lambda L_j(x_j) + (1-\lambda)L_j(y_j)$. Thus:

$$\begin{aligned} &L(\lambda x + (1-\lambda)y) \\ &= L_j(\lambda x_j + (1-\lambda)y_j) \\ &\quad + \sum_{i \neq j} L_i(\lambda x_i + (1-\lambda)y_i) &(38)\\ &< \lambda L_j(x_j) + (1-\lambda)L_j(y_j) \\ &\quad + \sum_{i \neq j} L_i(\lambda x_i + (1-\lambda)y_i) &(39)\\ &< \lambda L_j(x_j) + (1-\lambda)L_j(y_j) \\ &\quad + \sum_{i \neq j} (\lambda L_i(x_i) + (1-\lambda)L_i(y_i)) &(40)\\ &< \sum_{i=1}^{m} (\lambda L_i(x_i) + (1-\lambda)L_i(y_i)) &(41)\\ &< \lambda \sum_{i=1}^{m} L_i(x_i) + (1-\lambda)\sum_{i=1}^{m} L_i(y_i) &(42)\\ &< \lambda L(x) + (1-\lambda)L(y). &(43)\end{aligned}$$

■

D PROOFS OF CALIBRATION ON GENERATED FEATURES

Next we show that if the partial derivative of the loss with respect to a parameter is zero, then the feature generated by that parameter is calibrated.

Theorem 7 *For a problem* $\mathcal{P}$ *and model family* $\mathcal{M} = \{M_w\}_{w \in \mathbf{R}^S}$, *given a* $w \in \mathbf{R}^S$ *and* $s \in S$ *such that* f_s *is the feature generated from parameter* s *of model* M_w: *if* $\{s\}$ *is total on the training data given* M_w *and* $\frac{\partial L_{\mathcal{P}}(M_w)}{\partial w_s} = 0$, *then* M_w *is calibrated with respect to* f_s.

Proof: Define p, m, X, $x_1 \dots x_m$, $y_1 \dots y_m$ such that $\mathcal{P} = (p, X, \{x_1 \dots x_m\}, \{y_1 \dots y_m\})$. We begin with the partial derivative of $L_{\mathcal{P}}$. Note that from Lemma 1, ℓ_p is partially differentiable with respect to its second argument, and since for any $i \in \{1 \dots m\}$ $\{s\}$ is total for x_i given M_w, then $M_w(x_i)$ is partially differentiable with respect to w_s. Therefore:

$$0 = \frac{\partial L_{\mathcal{P}}(M_w)}{\partial w_s} \tag{44}$$
$$= \frac{\partial}{\partial w_s} \sum_{i=1}^{m} \ell_p(y_i, M_w(x_i)) \tag{45}$$
$$= \sum_{i=1}^{m} \frac{\partial \ell_p(y_i, M_w(x_i))}{\partial w_s} \tag{46}$$
$$= \sum_{i=1}^{m} \frac{\partial \ell_p(y_i, \hat{y}_i)}{\partial \hat{y}_i}\bigg|_{\hat{y}_i = M_w(x_i)} \frac{\partial M_w(x_i)}{\partial w_s} \tag{47}$$
$$= \sum_{i=1}^{m} (\mu_p(M_w(x_i)) - y_i) \frac{\partial M_w(x_i)}{\partial w_s}. \tag{48}$$

The last step is because of Lemma 1. For any $i \in \{1 \dots m\}$, since $M_w(x_i)$ is partially differentiable with respect to w_s, we can use $f_s(x_i) = \frac{\partial^+ M_w(x_i)}{\partial w_s} = \frac{\partial M_w(x_i)}{\partial w_s}$ to get:

$$0 = \sum_{i=1}^{m} (\mu_p(M_w(x_i)) - y_i) f_s(x_i) \tag{49}$$
$$\sum_{i=1}^{m} y_i f_s(x_i) = \sum_{i=1}^{m} \mu_p(M_w(x_i)) f_s(x_i). \tag{50}$$

■

Lemma 9 *For finite S, given a set of features $\{f_s\}_{s \in S}$, the family of linear models $\mathcal{L}(\{f_s\}_{s \in S})$, and $N_w \in \mathcal{L}$: the set S is total for all $x \in X$ given N_w, and the feature generated from parameter s by model N_w is f_s.*

Proof: First note that, by definition, a linear model is a linear function of w, and therefore a differentiable function of w regardless of the input or w. Thus, for any $x \in X$, for any w, the set S is total. Notice that, for any $x \in X$:

$$\frac{\partial M_w(x)}{\partial w_s} = \frac{\partial}{\partial w_s} \sum_{t \in S} w_t f_t(x) \tag{51}$$
$$= \sum_{t \in S} \frac{\partial}{\partial w_s} (w_t f_t(x)) \tag{52}$$
$$= f_s(x). \tag{53}$$

■

Another known key result about linear models is that any two linear models that minimize loss will produce the same predictions on the training data.

Theorem 29 *Given a supervised learning problem $\mathcal{P} = (p, X, \{x_1 \dots x_m\}, \{y_1 \dots y_m\})$, a set of features $f_1 \dots f_n : X \to \mathbf{R}$, and a family of linear models $\mathcal{L}(\{f_1 \dots f_n\})$, if two models $M, M' \in \mathcal{L}$ are optimal in $\mathcal{L}$ for $\mathcal{P}$, then they are equal on the training data.*

Proof: Define $L^* : \mathbf{R}^m \to \mathbf{R}$ such that for all $\hat{y} \in \mathbf{R}^m$:

$$L^*(\hat{y}) = \sum_{i=1}^{m} \ell_p(y_i, \hat{y}_i). \tag{54}$$

By Lemma 1, each ℓ_p is strictly convex in its second argument. By Lemma 28,[11] L^* is strictly convex. We define $P : \mathbf{R}^n \to \mathbf{R}^m$, such that for all $v \in \mathbf{R}^n$, for all $i \in \{1 \dots m\}$, $P_i(v) = M_v(x_i)$. Therefore, $L^*(P(v)) = L_{\mathcal{P}}(M_v)$. We need to prove $P(w) = P(w')$.

Consider $w'' = \frac{w+w'}{2}$. Since the models are linear, we know that for all $x \in X$, $M_{w''}(x) = \frac{M_w(x)+M_{w'}(x)}{2}$. Thus, $P(w'') = \frac{P(w)+P(w')}{2}$. Assume for the sake of contradiction, $P(w) \neq P(w')$. Since L^* is strictly convex:

$$L^*(P(w'')) < \frac{L^*(P(w)) + L^*(P(w'))}{2}; \tag{55}$$

since $L^*(P(v)) = L_{\mathcal{P}}(M_v)$:

$$L_{\mathcal{P}}(M_{w''}) < \frac{L_{\mathcal{P}}(M_w) + L_{\mathcal{P}}(M_{w'})}{2}; \tag{56}$$

since $L_{\mathcal{P}}(M_w) = L_{\mathcal{P}}(M_{w'})$:

$$L_{\mathcal{P}}(M_{w''}) < L_{\mathcal{P}}(M_w). \tag{57}$$

This contradicts the original hypothesis that both are minima. Thus, $P(w) = P(w')$, which is the same as saying, for all $i \in \{1 \dots m\}$, $M_w(x_i) = M_{w'}(x_i)$. ■

Lemma 10 *(c.f. [16, Equation 10]) Given a problem $\mathcal{P}$, a finite set S and a set of features $\{f_s\}_{s \in S}$: a model N in the family of linear models $\mathcal{L}(\{f_s\}_{s \in S})$ is optimal if and only if N is calibrated with respect to f_s for all $s \in S$.*

Proof: Define p, m, X, $x_1 \dots x_m$, $y_1 \dots y_m$ such that $\mathcal{P} = (p, X, \{x_1 \dots x_m\}, \{y_1 \dots y_m\})$. Define $\{N_w\}_{w \in \mathbf{R}^S} = \mathcal{L}(\{f_s\}_{s \in S})$ where $N_w(x) = \sum_{s \in S} w_s f_s(x)$. Define $w^* \in \mathbf{R}^S$ such that $N_{w^*} = N$. If N (and therefore N_{w^*}) is calibrated, for all $s \in S$:

$$\sum_{i=1}^{m} \mu_p(N_{w^*}(x_i)) f_s(x_i) = \sum_{i=1}^{m} y_i f_s(x_i) \tag{58}$$
$$0 = \sum_{i=1}^{m} (y_i - \mu_p(N_{w^*}(x_i))) f_s(x_i). \tag{59}$$

[11] Formally, for all $i \in \{1 \dots m\}$, we could define $L_i : \mathbf{R} \to \mathbf{R}$ such that $L_i(\hat{y}_i) = \ell_p(y_i, \hat{y}_i)$.

By Lemma 1:

$$0 = \sum_{i=1}^{m} \frac{\partial \ell_p(y_i, \hat{y}_i)}{\partial \hat{y}_i}\bigg|_{\hat{y}_i = N_{w^*}(x_i)} f_s(x_i) \quad (60)$$

$$0 = \sum_{i=1}^{m} \frac{\partial \ell_p(y_i, N_{w^*}(x_i))}{\partial w_s^*} \quad (61)$$

$$0 = \frac{\partial L_{\mathcal{P}}(N_{w^*})}{\partial w_s^*}. \quad (62)$$

If we define $L^* : \mathbf{R}^n \to \mathbf{R}$ as $L^*(w) = L_{\mathcal{P}}(N_w)$, it is convex, then N_{w^*} (and therefore N) is optimal.

To prove the converse, suppose that there is some $s \in S$ that is not calibrated. Then $\frac{\partial L_{\mathcal{P}}(N_{w^*})}{\partial w_s^*} \neq 0$, implying that there is a model with lower loss. ■

Lemma 11 *Given a problem $\mathcal{P}$, a finite set S, a subset $S' \subseteq S$, and a set of features $\{f_s\}_{s \in S}$: if a model N is optimal in the family of linear models $\mathcal{L}(\{f_s\}_{s\in S'})$ and N is calibrated with respect to f_s for all $s \in S - S'$, then N is also an optimal model in $\mathcal{L}(\{f_s\}_{s\in S})$.*

Proof: Define p, m, X, $x_1 \dots x_m$, $y_1 \dots y_m$ such that $\mathcal{P} = (p, X, \{x_1 \dots x_m\}, \{y_1 \dots y_m\})$. Note that any model in $\mathcal{L}(\{f_s\}_{s\in S'})$ (and specifically N) is in $\mathcal{L}(\{f_s\}_{s\in S})$. Since N is optimal in $\mathcal{L}(\{f_s\}_{s\in S'})$, by Lemma 10, it is calibrated with respect to $\{f_s\}_{s\in S'}$. Moreover, by assumption it is calibrated with respect to $\{f_s\}_{s\in S-S'}$, and therefore it is calibrated with respect to $\{f_s\}_{s\in S}$, and again by Lemma 10, it is optimal with respect to $\mathcal{L}(\{f_s\}_{s\in S})$. ■

Lemma 13 *Given a problem $\mathcal{P}$, a finite set S, a subset $S' \subseteq S$, a model family $\{M_w\}_{w\in\mathbf{R}^S}$, and a $w \in \mathbf{R}^S$ such that $\frac{\partial L_{\mathcal{P}}(M_w)}{\partial w_s} = 0$ for all $s \in S'$:* ***if*** *$\mathcal{L}'$ is the family of linear models associated with S' given M_w, S' is total on the training data given M_w, and M_w is equal on the training data to some $N' \in \mathcal{L}'$,* ***then*** *N' is optimal in $\mathcal{L}'$.*

Proof: Define p, m, X, $x_1 \dots x_m$, $y_1 \dots y_m$ such that $\mathcal{P} = (p, X, \{x_1 \dots x_m\}, \{y_1 \dots y_m\})$. For all $s \in S'$, define $f_s : X \to \mathbf{R}$ to be the feature generated by s given M_w. By Theorem 7, M_w is calibrated with respect to f_s. Moreover, the family of linear models associated with S' given M_w is $\mathcal{L}' = \mathcal{L}(\{f_s\}_{s\in S'})$. Since N' and M_w are equal on the training data, by Fact 27, N' is calibrated with respect to all $\{f_s\}_{s\in S'}$. Thus, by Lemma 10, N' is optimal in $\mathcal{L}'$. ■

Lemma 14 *Given a problem $\mathcal{P}$, a finite set S, a subset $S' \subseteq S$, a model family $\{M_w\}_{w\in\mathbf{R}^S}$, and a $w \in \mathbf{R}^S$ such that $\frac{\partial L_{\mathcal{P}}(M_w)}{\partial w_s} = 0$ for all $s \in S$:* ***if*** *$\mathcal{L}'$ is the family of linear models associated with S' given M_w, S' is total, M_w is equal on the training data to some $N' \in \mathcal{L}'$, and $\mathcal{L}''$ is the family of linear models associated with S,* ***then*** *any optimal $N'' \in \mathcal{L}''$ equals M_w on the training data.*

Proof: For all $s \in S$, define $f_s : X \to \mathbf{R}$ to be the feature generated by s given M_w. By Theorem 7, M_w is calibrated with respect to f_s, and by Fact 27, N' is calibrated with respect to f_s. By Lemma 13, N' is optimal in $\mathcal{L}' = \mathcal{L}(\{f_s\}_{s\in S'})$. By Lemma 11, N' is optimal in $\mathcal{L}'' = \mathcal{L}(\{f_s\}_{s\in S})$. Thus, by Theorem 29, any optimal $N'' \in \mathcal{L}''$ is equal on the training data to N', and transitively to M_w. ■

E EULER'S HOMOGENEOUS FUNCTION THEOREM

This appendix can be skipped, as Lemma 17 is a well known result. However, this section provides a deeper discussion of total differentiability and partial differentiability that can be helpful in understanding the rest of the paper.

Although a variant of Lemma 17 is in [11], we prove the specific variant here.

Lemma 17 (Euler's Homogeneous Function Theorem) (Degree 1 Case) *If a homogeneous function $f : \mathbf{R}^p \to \mathbf{R}^q$ is differentiable at $x \in \mathbf{R}^p$, then for all $k \in \{1 \dots q\}$,*

$$f_k(x) = \sum_{j=1}^{p} \frac{\partial f_k(x)}{\partial x_j} x_j. \quad (9)$$

Proof: If $x = 0$, then for any $k \in \{1 \dots q\}$:

$$\sum_{j=1}^{p} \frac{\partial f_k(x)}{\partial x_j} x_j = \sum_{j=1}^{p} \frac{\partial f_k(x)}{\partial x_j} \times 0 \quad (63)$$

$$= 0 \quad (64)$$

$$= 0 \times f_k(x) \quad (65)$$

$$= f_k(0x) \quad (66)$$

$$= f_k(x). \quad (67)$$

For the remainder, assume $x \neq 0$. Consider a particular x where $f(x)$ is differentiable, and the derivative is a matrix $G \in \mathbf{R}^{q\times p}$ where:

$$\lim_{h\to 0} \frac{\|f(x+h) - f(x) - Gh\|}{\|h\|} = 0. \quad (68)$$

Specifically, we can write:

$$\lim_{\epsilon\to 0} \frac{\|f(x+\epsilon x) - f(x) - G\epsilon x\|}{\|\epsilon x\|} = 0. \quad (69)$$

In the limit, $\epsilon > -1$, so by the homogeneous property:

$$\lim_{\epsilon\to 0}\frac{\|(1+\epsilon)f(x)-f(x)-G\epsilon x\|}{\|\epsilon x\|}=0 \quad (70)$$

$$\lim_{\epsilon\to 0}\frac{\|\epsilon f(x)-G\epsilon x\|}{\epsilon\|x\|}=0 \quad (71)$$

$$\lim_{\epsilon\to 0}\frac{\|f(x)-Gx\|}{\|x\|}=0 \quad (72)$$

$$\frac{\|f(x)-Gx\|}{\|x\|}=0 \quad (73)$$

$$\|f(x)-Gx\|=0 \quad (74)$$

$$f(x)=Gx. \quad (75)$$

Since $G_{k,j}=\frac{\partial f_k(x)}{\partial x_j}$, the result follows. ■

One might wonder, is it possible to prove this for functions that are only partially (and not totally) differentiable? Yes and no: for one or two dimensions partially differentiability is sufficient for Euler's function to hold, but for three or more dimensions, there is no such guarantee, and we can demonstrate this with a counterexample.

Lemma 30 *If a homogeneous function $f:\mathbf{R}^p\to\mathbf{R}^q$ is partially differentiable at a point $x\in\mathbf{R}^p$, and $p\le 2$, then for all $k\in\{1\ldots q\}$:*

$$f_k(x)=\sum_{j=1}^{p}\frac{\partial f_k(x)}{\partial x_j}x_j. \quad (76)$$

Proof: Since partial differentiability implies differentiability when $p=1$, the proof for $p=1$ follows directly from Lemma 17. So, we assume $p=2$. Consider a specific point (x,y) where f is partially differentiable, i.e. $\frac{\partial f(x,y)}{\partial x}$ and $\frac{\partial f(x,y)}{\partial y}$ exist. If $x=0$ or $y=0$, then it is basically analogous to the one dimensional case, as the function along the axis can be considered a 1 dimensional homogeneous function that is differentiable at that point.

Next, assume $x>0$ and $y>0$, i.e. a point in the positive quadrant as in Figure 6: near the end of the proof, we will show how to reduce a problem in a different quadrant to one in the positive quadrant.

We can define $g:(0,x)\to(0,\infty)$ and $h:(0,x)\to(0,\infty)$ such that $g(\epsilon)=\frac{y\epsilon}{x-\epsilon}$ and $h(\epsilon)=\frac{y+g(\epsilon)}{y}$.

Then, for any $\epsilon\in(0,x)$, observe that $h(\epsilon)(x-\epsilon,y)=(x,y+g(\epsilon))$, so $h(\epsilon)f(x-\epsilon,y)=f(x,y+g(\epsilon))$. Since

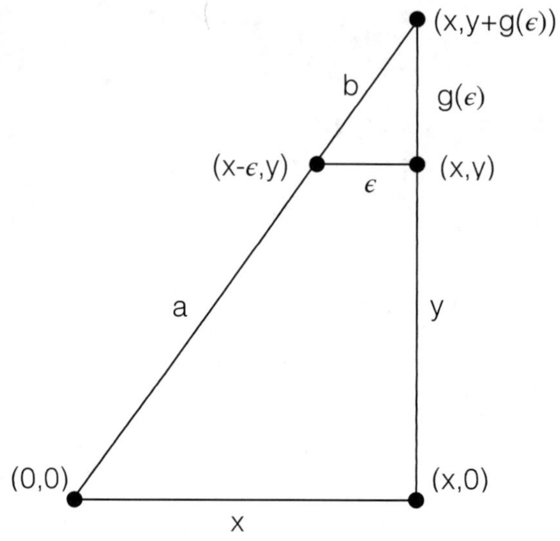

Figure 6: For homogeneous functions with a 2-dimensional domain, the partial derivatives are inextricably linked. Note that the definition of $g(\epsilon)$ can be derived from $\frac{g(\epsilon)+y}{x}=\frac{g(\epsilon)}{\epsilon}$. The function values at $(x-\epsilon,y)$ and $(x,y+g(\epsilon))$ are connected through the homogeneous property.

$\lim_{\epsilon\to 0^+}g(\epsilon)=0$, we know that:

$$\frac{\partial f(x,y)}{\partial y}=\lim_{\epsilon\to 0^+}\frac{f(x,y+g(\epsilon))-f(x,y)}{g(\epsilon)} \quad (77)$$

$$\frac{\partial f(x,y)}{\partial y}=\lim_{\epsilon\to 0^+}\frac{f(x-\epsilon,y)h(\epsilon)-f(x,y)}{g(\epsilon)} \quad (78)$$

$$\frac{\partial f(x,y)}{\partial y}=\lim_{\epsilon\to 0^+}\frac{f(x-\epsilon,y)h(\epsilon)-f(x,y)h(\epsilon)}{g(\epsilon)}+\lim_{\epsilon\to 0^+}\frac{f(x,y)h(\epsilon)-f(x,y)}{g(\epsilon)} \quad (79)$$

$$\frac{\partial f(x,y)}{\partial y}=\lim_{\epsilon\to 0^+}\frac{f(x-\epsilon,y)-f(x,y)}{\epsilon}\lim_{\epsilon\to 0^+}\frac{h(\epsilon)\epsilon}{g(\epsilon)}+f(x,y)\lim_{\epsilon\to 0^+}\frac{h(\epsilon)-1}{g(\epsilon)}. \quad (80)$$

First, observe that $\lim_{\epsilon\to 0^+}\frac{f(x-\epsilon,y)-f(x,y)}{\epsilon}=-\frac{\partial f(x,y)}{\partial x}$. Notice that for $\epsilon\in(0,x)$:

$$\frac{h(\epsilon)-1}{g(\epsilon)}=\frac{\frac{y+g(\epsilon)}{y}-1}{g(\epsilon)}=\frac{1}{y}. \quad (81)$$

Also, since $\lim_{\epsilon \to 0^+} h(\epsilon) = 1$, for $\epsilon \in (0, x)$:

$$\lim_{\epsilon \to 0^+} \frac{h(\epsilon)\epsilon}{g(\epsilon)} = \lim_{\epsilon \to 0^+} \frac{\epsilon}{g(\epsilon)} \quad (82)$$

$$= \lim_{\epsilon \to 0^+} \frac{\epsilon(x-\epsilon)}{y\epsilon} \quad (83)$$

$$= \frac{x}{y}. \quad (84)$$

So, from Equation 80:

$$\frac{\partial f(x,y)}{\partial y} = -\frac{\partial f(x,y)}{\partial x}\frac{x}{y} + f(x,y)\frac{1}{y} \quad (85)$$

$$\frac{\partial f(x,y)}{\partial x}x + \frac{\partial f(x,y)}{\partial y}y = f(x,y), \quad (86)$$

which is Euler's function.

Now if $x < 0$ or $y < 0$, we could flip the function on one axis or on both without affecting homogeneity, partial differentiability, or Euler's function. Specifically, note that if we defined $f^* : \mathbf{R}^2 \to \mathbf{R}$ such that for all $x', y' \in \mathbf{R}$, $f^*(x', y') = f(-x', y')$, then $\frac{\partial f^*(-x,y)}{\partial x} = -\frac{\partial f(x,y)}{\partial x}$, $\frac{\partial f^*(-x,y)}{\partial y} = \frac{\partial f^*(-x,y)}{\partial y}$, and if $f^*(-x,y) = \frac{\partial f^*(-x,y)}{\partial x}(-x) + \frac{\partial f^*(-x,y)}{\partial x}y$ then:

$$f(x,y) = f^*(-x,y) \quad (87)$$

$$= \frac{\partial f^*(-x,y)}{\partial x}(-x) + \frac{\partial f^*(-x,y)}{\partial x}y \quad (88)$$

$$= (-\frac{\partial f(-x,y)}{\partial x})(-x) + \frac{\partial f(-x,y)}{\partial x}y \quad (89)$$

$$= \frac{\partial f(-x,y)}{\partial x}x + \frac{\partial f(-x,y)}{\partial x}y. \quad (90)$$

Similarly for flipping on the x axis. ■

However, if we add a third dimension, things get incredibly complex. Consider the following function:

$$f(x,y,z) = \begin{cases} 7z - x \text{ if } x + y - 2z \geq 0 \text{ and } x - y < 0 \\ 7z - y \text{ if } x - y \geq 0 \text{ and } x + y - 2z > 0 \\ x + 5z \text{ if } x + y - 2z \leq 0 \text{ and } x - z > 0 \\ 7z - x \text{ if } x - z \leq 0 \text{ and } x - y > 0 \\ 7z - y \text{ if } x - y \leq 0 \text{ and } y - z < 0 \\ y + 5z \text{ if } y - z \geq 0 \text{ and } x + y - 2z < 0 \\ y + 5z \text{ if } x = y = z \end{cases} \quad (91)$$

So, we wish to establish five things:

1. f is well-defined.
2. f is continuous.
3. f is homogeneous.
4. f has partial derivatives at $(1,1,1)$.

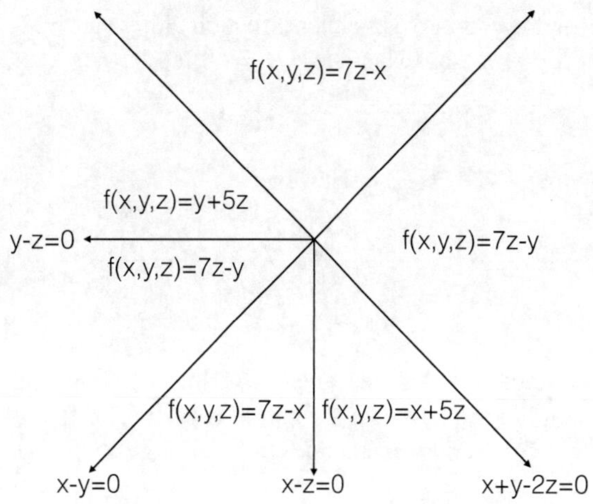

Figure 7: A visual representation of the eight regions of the piecewise linear homogeneous function $f : \mathbf{R}^3 \to \mathbf{R}$. We are looking along the axis $x = y = z$.

5. Euler's formula does not hold at $(1,1,1)$.

To confirm f is well-defined, we must confirm that it is defined everywhere. If one considers Figure 7, one will notice that we have defined each region, starting from the top region and going clockwise, and then defined the center. Each region contains its counterclockwise edge, but not its clockwise edge, and none contain the center. Thus, each point is in exactly one of the cases.

Next, we must establish continuity. First, we establish it at the center. If $x = y = z$, then clearly $7z - x = 7z - y$, and $y + 5z = x + 5z$. If $x = y = z$, then $x + y - 2z = 0$, so $7z - x = 7z - x - (x + y - 2z) = x + 5z$.

Thus, all four linear functions equal each other along the line $x = y = z$. Simple algebra shows us, along the plane $x - y = 0$, $7z - x = 7z - y$, because $7z - x = 7z - x + (x - y) = 7z - y$. Similarly, we can look at each boundary, and prove equality.

Notice that homogeneity is pretty straightforward. Since each constraint is in itself a linear inequality with no constants, given any (x,y,z), $(\lambda x, \lambda y, \lambda z)$ has the exact same constraints hold. Since within each region, the function is linear, then it is also homogeneous.

At the point $(1,1,1)$, notice that:

1. if you move in either direction along the x axis, $f(x,y,z) = 7z - y$, so $\left.\frac{\partial f(x,1,1)}{\partial x}\right|_{x=1} = 0$,
2. if you move in either direction along the y axis, $f(x,y,z) = 7z - x$, so $\left.\frac{\partial f(1,y,1)}{\partial y}\right|_{y=1} = 0$,

3. and if you move in either direction along the z axis, you will stay where $x - y = 0$, so $f(x,y,z) = 7z - x$, so $\left.\frac{\partial f(1,1,z)}{\partial z}\right|_{z=1} = 7$.

Note that $f(1,1,1) = 6$. However:

$$\left.\frac{\partial f(x,1,1)}{\partial x}\right|_{x=1} \times 1 + \left.\frac{\partial f(1,y,1)}{\partial y}\right|_{y=1} \times 1 + \left.\frac{\partial f(1,1,z)}{\partial z}\right|_{z=1} \times 1$$
$$= 0 \times 1 + 0 \times 1 + 7 \times 1 = 7. \quad (92)$$

Thus, since $6 \neq 7$, this function, while homogeneous and continuous, has a point where it is partially differentiable, but Euler's formula does not hold.

With further effort, we can also show that the function can be constructed using *relu* gates. Thus, in a very crucial way, Euler's function requires total differentiability, justifying the large role this concept of total features has in our theoretical analysis. However, as our empirical analysis shows, we can pretty much ignore this concern in practice. In Appendix I, we give a sufficient condition (based on a complex proof) to determine if the model is total on an input.

F PROOFS FOR HOMOGENEOUS FUNCTIONS

Before continuing, it is important to note that when defining the homogeneous property of a model family, we directly appealed to a property of differentiability due to the technical issues described in higher dimensional homogeneous functions in Appendix E.

We now prove Theorem 20:

Theorem 20 *If a model family $\mathcal{M}$ is homogeneous on the parameter set S', $M \in \mathcal{M}$, $\mathcal{L}'$ is the family of linear models associated with S' given M, and S' is total on the training data given M, then there exists $N \in \mathcal{L}'$ such that M and N are equivalent on the training data.*

Proof: Define $\mathcal{M} = \{M'_w\}_{w \in \mathbf{R}^S}$, and $w \in \mathbf{R}^S$ such that $M'_w = M$. Given some x in the training data, since $\mathcal{M}$ is homogeneous with respect to S', and S' is total on x given M'_w, then by Lemma 17:

$$M'_w(x) = \sum_{s \in S'} \frac{\partial M'_w(x)}{\partial w_s} w_s. \quad (93)$$

Since $f_s(x) = \frac{\partial^+ M'_w(x)}{\partial w_s}$ is the feature generated by s given M, if x is in the training data, then$\{s\} \subseteq S'$ is total on x given M'_w, and $f_s(x) = \frac{\partial M'_w(x)}{\partial w_s}$, so:

$$M'_w(x) = \sum_{s \in S'} w_s f_s(x). \quad (94)$$

Note $\mathcal{L}' = \mathcal{L}(\{f_s\}_{s \in S'})$, and if $\{N'_w\}_{w \in \mathbf{R}^{S'}} = \mathcal{L}'$, then for the $w' \in \mathbf{R}^{S'}$ where $w'_s = w_s$ for all $s \in S'$:

$$N'_{w'}(x) = \sum_{s \in S'} w'_s f_s(x) \quad (95)$$
$$= \sum_{s \in S'} w_s f_s(x) \quad (96)$$
$$= M'_w(x) = M(x), \quad (97)$$

so $M(x) = N'_{w'}(x)$ on the training data, and $N'_{w'}$ is in the family of linear models associated with S' given M. ■

We now prove Theorem 23:

Theorem 23 *Given a problem $\mathcal{P}$ and a family of feedforward network models $\mathcal{D}(V, E, I, \{g_i\}_{i \in I}, o^*, A) = \{M_w\}_{w \in \mathbf{R}^E}$, where all $a \in A$ are homogeneous:* ***if*** *B and T is an ordered cut of the feedforward network, such that E' is the cut set,* ***then:***

1. *$\{M_w\}_{w \in \mathbf{R}^E}$ is homogeneous on E';*
2. *for some $w \in \mathbf{R}^E$, if E' is total on the training data given M_w, $\mathcal{L}'$ is the family of linear models associated with E' given M_w, and $\frac{\partial L_{\mathcal{P}}(M_w)}{\partial w_e} = 0$ for all $e \in E'$, then M_w is equal on the training data to any optimal model in $\mathcal{L}'$;*
3. *for some $w \in \mathbf{R}^E$, if $\mathcal{L}'$ is the family of linear models associated with E given M_w, if E is total on the training data given M_w, and $\frac{\partial L_{\mathcal{P}}(M_w)}{\partial w_e} = 0$ for all $e \in E$, then M_w is equal on the training data to any optimal model in $\mathcal{L}'$.*

Proof: We need only prove that the model family is homogeneous: the other two results follow from Theorem 20, Lemma 13, and Lemma 14. We need to construct a function from the inputs passing through the cut set to the second part of the function. First, define $E'' = E - E'$, and given w, define $w'' \in \mathbf{R}^{E''}$ such that for all $e \in E''$, $w''_e = w_e$. Thus, for all $t \in T$, define $d_{t,w''} : \mathbf{R}^{E'} \to \mathbf{R}$ recursively (using the partial ordering of the vertices in the network) such that for all $z \in \mathbf{R}^{E'}$:

$$d_{t,w''}(z) = a_t\Big(\sum_{u:(u,t) \in E'} z_{(u,t)} + \sum_{u:(u,t) \in E''} d_{u,w''}(z) w''_{(u,t)} \Big). \quad (98)$$

We subscript this by w'' to indicate that $d_{t,w''}$ is independent of the weights in E'. An important point to note is that for any $x \in X$, for any $b \in B$, $c_{b,w}(x)$ does not depend upon the weight of any edge in E'. For any

$(b,t) \in E'$, we can write $g_{w''}(x)_{(b,t)} = c_{b,w}(x)$ to formalize this idea. Define $w' \in \mathbf{R}^{E'}$ such that for all $e \in \mathbf{R}^{E'}$, $w'_e = w_e$. Finally, for any $z, z' \in \mathbf{R}^{E'}$ we denote the **Hadamard (entrywise) product** as $(z \circ z')_e = z_e z'_e$. We can prove recursively, for all $t \in T$:

$$c_{t,w}(x) = d_{t,w''}(w' \circ g_{w''}(x)). \tag{99}$$

Importantly, this means:

$$M_w(x) = c_{o^*,w}(x) \tag{100}$$
$$= d_{t,w''}(w' \circ g_{w''}(x)). \tag{101}$$

We can use this formulation to prove $M_w(x)$ is homogeneous in w'. First, we can prove recursively that $d_{t,w''}(z)$ is a homogeneous function of z: since all $a \in A$ are homogeneous, it is a homogeneous function of the sum of a set of projections (and all projections are homogeneous) and a set of homogeneous functions multiplied by a constant. To prove that the overall function is homogeneous, we introduce $\lambda \geq 0$, $v \in \mathbf{R}^E$, $v' \in \mathbf{R}^{E'}$, and $v'' \in \mathbf{R}^{E''}$, such that $v'_s = v_s$ for all $s \in E'$, $v''_s = v_s$ for all $s \in E''$, $v'' = w''$, and $v' = \lambda w'$. Note that:

$$M_v(x) = c_{o^*,v}(x) \tag{102}$$
$$= d_{t,v''}(v' \circ g_{v''}(x)) \tag{103}$$
$$= d_{t,w''}((\lambda w') \circ g_{w''}(x)) \tag{104}$$
$$= d_{t,w''}(\lambda(w' \circ g_{w''}(x))). \tag{105}$$

Since $d_{t,w''}$ is homogeneous:

$$M_v(x) = \lambda d_{t,w''}(w' \circ g_{w''}(x)) \tag{106}$$
$$= \lambda M_w(x). \tag{107}$$

We have established that $M_w(x)$ is homogeneous with respect to w'. Thus, from Theorem 20, Lemma 13, and Lemma 14, the other results hold. ■

G PROOFS FOR RESNETS AND CNNS

Recall the main theorem about ResNets and CNNs:

Theorem 24 *For a problem $\mathcal{P}$ and family of RC feedforward network models $\mathcal{RC}(V, E, I, \{g_i\}_{i\in I}, o^*, A, w^*)$ denoted $\{Q_v\}_{v\in\mathbf{R}^n}$, where all $a \in A$ are homogeneous:* ***if*** *$E_1 \dots E_n$ is the partition of the dynamic parameters, and B and T are a well-behaved cut such that there is an $S \subseteq \{1 \dots n\}$ where $E' = \bigcup_{s\in S} E_s$ is the cut set;* ***then***

1. *$\{Q_v\}_{v\in\mathbf{R}^n}$ is a homogeneous model family with respect to S;*
2. *if for some $v \in \mathbf{R}^n$, $\frac{\partial L_{\mathcal{P}}(Q_v)}{\partial v_s} = 0$ for all $s \in S$, the set S is total on the training data given Q_v, and $\mathcal{L}'$ is the family of linear models associated with S given Q_v, then Q_v is equal on the training data to any optimal N' in $\mathcal{L}'$;*
3. *if for some $v \in \mathbf{R}^n$, $\frac{\partial L_{\mathcal{P}}(Q_v)}{\partial v_s} = 0$ for all $s \in \{1 \dots n\}$, the set $\{1 \dots n\}$ is total on the training data given Q_v, and $\mathcal{L}'$ is the family of linear models associated with $\{1 \dots n\}$ given Q_v, then Q_v is equal on the training data to any optimal N' in $\mathcal{L}'$.*

Proof: We need only prove that the model family is homogeneous: as with Theorem 23, the other two results follow from Theorem 20, Lemma 13, and Lemma 14. We can define $S'' = \{1 \dots n\} - S$, and $v'' \in \mathbf{R}^{S''}$ such that $v''_s = v_s$ for all $s \in S''$. We can define $v' \in \mathbf{R}^S$ such that $v'_s = v_s$ when $s \in S$. We can define $E'' = E - E'$, and $w'' : \mathbf{R}^{S''} \to \mathbf{R}^{E''}$ such that for all $e \in E''$, $w''_e(v'') = w^f_e$ if $e \in E^f$, and $w''_e = v''_{\pi(e)}$ otherwise. As before, we will define $d_{t,v''} : \mathbf{R}^{E'} \to \mathbf{R}$, and we will create a matrix $G^{v''} : X \to \mathbf{R}^{E' \times S}$. As before, for all $t \in T$, for all $z \in \mathbf{R}^{E'}$, we define $d_{t,v''}$ recursively:

$$d_{t,v''}(z) = a_t\Big(\textstyle\sum_{u:(u,t)\in E'} z_{(u,t)} + \displaystyle\sum_{u:(u,t)\in E''} d_{u,v''}(z) w''_{(u,t)}(v'')\Big) \tag{108}$$

Since, for all $b \in B$, $c_{b,w^*(v)}(x)$ does not depend upon parameters in the cut set, we can write $(G^{v''}(x))_{e,s} = 0$ if $\pi(e) \neq s$, and otherwise $(G^{v''}(x))_{(b,t),s} = c_{b,w^*(v)}(x)$. Crucially, neither d nor G is a function of the parameters in S. We can now write the activation energy of a node in the top as a combination of d, G, and v':

$$c_{t,w^*(v)}(x) = d_{t,v''}(G^{v''}(x)v') \tag{109}$$

Notice that $G^{v''}(x)v'$ is the product of a matrix and a vector, and $(G^{v''}(x)v')_{(b,t)} = v'_{\pi(b,t)} c_{b,w^*(v)}(x)$. Moreover, this relies on the fact that the cut set does not include E^f, as this would make the activation energies on the cut set an affine function of v' instead of a linear one. Considering the output of the model is $c_{t,w^*(v)}(x)$ yields:

$$Q_v(x) = d_{o^*,v''}((G^{v''}(x))v'). \tag{110}$$

Consider any $\lambda > 0$. Define $y \in \mathbf{R}^n$, where for all $s \in S''$, $y_s = v_s$, and for all $s \in S$, $y_s = \lambda v_s$. If we define $y' \in \mathbf{R}^S$ such that $y'_s = y_s$ for all $s \in S$, then we can write:

$$Q_y(x) = d_{o^*,v''}((G^{v''}(x))y') \tag{111}$$
$$Q_y(x) = d_{o^*,v''}((G^{v''}(x))(\lambda v')) \tag{112}$$
$$Q_y(x) = d_{o^*,v''}(\lambda(G^{v''}(x))v') \tag{113}$$

As we argued in the proof of Theorem 23, $d_{o^*,v''}(z)$ is a homogeneous function of z. So:

$$Q_y(x) = \lambda d_{o^*,v''}((G^{v''}(x))v') \tag{114}$$
$$Q_y(x) = \lambda Q_v(x) \tag{115}$$

Thus, the RC class is homogeneous with respect to S. ■

H REGULARIZATION AND RESTRICTIONS

Now we prove Theorem 26.

Theorem 26 *Given a problem $\mathcal{P}$, a set S, a subset $S' \subseteq S$, a model family $\mathcal{M} = \{M_w\}_{w \in \mathbf{R}^S}$ that is homogeneous with respect to S', a strictly convex regularization function $R : \mathcal{M} \to \mathbf{R}$ that is additively separable with respect to S', and a model M_w where for all $s \in S'$:*

$$\frac{\partial[L_{\mathcal{P}}(M_w) + R(M_w)]}{\partial w_s} = 0, \tag{13}$$

if *S' is total on the training data given M_w, $\mathcal{L}' = \{N_v\}_{v \in \mathbf{R}^{S'}}$ is the family of linear models associated with S' given M_w, and a new regularizer $R' : \mathcal{L}' \to \mathbf{R}$ is defined such that $R'(N_v) = (R^*)^{S'}(v)$,* ***then*** *M_w must be equal on the training data to any optimal $N \in \mathcal{L}'$ given the supervised learning problem and regularization R'.*

Proof: Define $v' \in \mathbf{R}^{S'}$ such that $v'_s = w_s$ for all $s \in S'$. For all $s \in S'$, define f_s to be the feature generated by s given M_w. We will prove the result by showing that:

1. For all $s \in S'$, for all x in the training data, $f_s(x) = \frac{\partial M_w(x)}{\partial w_s}$.
2. For all x in the training data, $N_{v'}(x) = M_w(x)$.
3. For all $s \in S'$, $\frac{\partial L_{\mathcal{P}}(N_{v'})}{\partial v'_s} = \frac{\partial L_{\mathcal{P}}(M_w)}{\partial w_s}$
4. For all $s \in S'$, $\frac{\partial R'(N_{v'})}{\partial v'_s} = \frac{\partial R(M_w)}{\partial w_s}$
5. Now, we know that $\frac{\partial[L_{\mathcal{P}}(N_{v'}) + R'(N_{v'})]}{\partial v'_s} = \frac{\partial[L_{\mathcal{P}}(M_w) + R(M_w)]}{\partial w_s} = 0$. Then, we use this to prove that $N_{v'}$ is the unique optimal solution in $\mathcal{L}'$.

We begin by proving item 1. By definition, $f_s(x) = \frac{\partial^+ M_w(x)}{\partial w_s}$. Since S' is total on the training data given M_w, M_w is partially differentiable with respect to w_s, so $f_s(x) = \frac{\partial M_w(x)}{\partial w_s}$.

Next we prove item 2 (c.f. Theorem 20). Note that, for any $x \in X$:

$$N_{v'}(x) = \sum_{s \in S'} v'_s f_s(x). \tag{116}$$

By the definition of v':

$$N_{v'}(x) = \sum_{s \in S'} w_s f_s(x). \tag{117}$$

By item 1, if x is in the training data:

$$N_{v'}(x) = \sum_{s \in S'} w_s \frac{\partial M_w(x)}{\partial w_s}. \tag{118}$$

Because the model family $\mathcal{M}$ is homogeneous, and S' is total on the training data given M_w:

$$N_{v'}(x) = M_w(x). \tag{119}$$

Next, we prove item 3. Choose an arbitrary $s \in S'$:

$$\frac{\partial L_{\mathcal{P}}(N_{v'})}{\partial v'_s} = \sum_{i=1}^{m} \left. \frac{\partial L_{\mathcal{P}}(y, \hat{y}'_i)}{\partial \hat{y}'_i} \right|_{\hat{y}'_i = N_{v'}(x_i)} f_s(x_i). \tag{120}$$

By item 1:

$$\frac{\partial L_{\mathcal{P}}(N_{v'})}{\partial v'_s} = \sum_{i=1}^{m} \left. \frac{\partial L_{\mathcal{P}}(y, \hat{y}'_i)}{\partial \hat{y}'_i} \right|_{\hat{y}'_i = N_{v'}(x_i)} \frac{\partial M_w(x_i)}{\partial w_s}. \tag{121}$$

By item 2, $\hat{y}'_i = N_{v'}(x_i) = M_w(x_i)$:

$$\frac{\partial L_{\mathcal{P}}(N_{v'})}{\partial v'_s} = \sum_{i=1}^{m} \left. \frac{\partial L_{\mathcal{P}}(y, \hat{y}'_i)}{\partial \hat{y}'_i} \right|_{\hat{y}'_i = M_w(x_i)} \frac{\partial M_w(x_i)}{\partial w_s} \tag{122}$$

$$= \frac{\partial L_{\mathcal{P}}(M_w)}{\partial w_s}. \tag{123}$$

Now, we prove item 4. Choose an arbitrary $s \in S'$. Note that $\frac{\partial R(M_w)}{\partial w_s} = \frac{\partial R^*(w)}{\partial w_s} = \frac{\partial (R^*)^{S'}(\pi^{S \to S'}(w))}{\partial w_s}$. Since $v' = \pi^{S \to S'}(w)$, $\frac{\partial (R^*)^{S'}(\pi^{S \to S'}(w))}{\partial w_s} = \frac{\partial (R^*)^{S'}(v')}{\partial v'_s}$. Also, by the definition of R', $\frac{\partial (R^*)^{S'}(v')}{\partial v'_s} = \frac{\partial R'(N_{v'})}{\partial v'_s}$. So $\frac{\partial R(M_w)}{\partial w_s} = \frac{\partial R'(N_{v'})}{\partial v'_s}$.

Finally, we must prove item 5. By item 3 and item 4, for any $s \in S'$:

$$\frac{\partial[L_{\mathcal{P}}(N_{v'}) + R'(N_{v'})]}{\partial v'_s} = \frac{\partial[L_{\mathcal{P}}(M_w) + R(M_w)]}{\partial w_s}. \tag{124}$$

Then, by assumption:

$$\frac{\partial[L_{\mathcal{P}}(N_{v'}) + R'(N_{v'})]}{\partial v'_s} = \frac{\partial[L_{\mathcal{P}}(M_w) + R(M_w)]}{\partial w_s} = 0. \tag{125}$$

Now, define a function $g : \mathbf{R}^{S'} \to \mathbf{R}$ such that for all $v \in \mathbf{R}^{S'}$, $g(v) = L_{\mathcal{P}}(N_v) + R'(N_v)$. Notice that the first part is convex, and the second part is strictly convex, implying g is strictly convex. Notice that $\nabla g(v') = 0$. Thus, v' is a minimum of g. Moreover, since g is strictly convex, it can have no more than one minimum. So $N_{v'}$ is the unique optimal model, and it is equivalent to M_w.

■

I SUFFICIENT CONDITIONS FOR TOTAL FEATURE SETS

In this section, we want to focus on when the concept of totality applies in deep networks. Specifically, are there easy rules of thumb to determine whether a feature set is total?

I.1 TOTALITY AND DIFFERENTIABILITY

While we invented the term "totality", it is very similar to the concept of differentiability. Specifically, consider $g : \mathbf{R}^{S'} \to \mathbf{R}$, where for all $h \in \mathbf{R}^{S'}$, $g(h) = M_{w+h}(x)$. Then, $M_w(x)$ is total if $g(h)$ is differentiable at zero.

I.2 TOTALITY AND FEEDFORWARD NETWORKS

Let's focus on feedforward networks with $relu$ gates, as those are relatively simple and have nice homogeneous properties. Specifically, assume that each input and the output have identity transformations, and the internal nodes are $relu$ gates.

Notice that the features will always exist for feedforward networks. If one considers the output of a feedforward network as a function of weights of the edges given a fixed input, the output is a piecewise polynomial function.

The $relu$ function has a single point of non-differentiability at zero. If we "avoid" this point, we will have a total model on an example. More formally, let's take apart deep networks in a different way. Specifically, for all $v \in V - I$, $w \in \mathbf{R}^E$, define $k_{v,w} : X \to \mathbf{R}$ such that:

$$k_{v,w}(x) = \sum_{u:\{u,v\}\in E} c_{u,w}(x) w_{(u,v)}. \tag{126}$$

Notice that, for all $v \in V - I$:

$$c_{v,w}(x) = a_v(k_{v,w}(x)). \tag{127}$$

In this section we assume a_v is the identity for $v \in I \cup \{o^*\}$ and a_v is a $relu$ function elsewhere. Observe[12] that, for some $w \in \mathbf{R}^E$, for some $x \in X$, if $k_{v,w}(x) \neq 0$ for all $v \in V - I$, then E is total for x given M_w. However, notice that if $k_{v,w}(x) = 0$ for some $v \in V - I$, that does not mean that the features are not total. Specifically, if $k_{v,w}(x) = 0$, but for all $u \in V$ where $(v, u) \in E$, $w_{(v,u)} = 0$, then effectively the node v has no effect. Thus, we will define a node to be **soft** given M_w and x if $k_{v,w}(x) \neq 0$ or $\frac{\partial^+ M_w(x)}{\partial c_{v,w}(x)} = 0$. Otherwise, we will say v is **hard**. Notice that any node where all weights on outgoing edges are zero is soft.

Lemma 31 *Given a set $E' \subseteq E$, given a model M_w and an example $x \in X$, if for all $(u, v) \in E'$, for all $v' \geq v$ (in the sense that there exists a path from v to v'), v' is soft, then E' is total on M_w.*

Proof: At a high level, we construct differentiable functions, starting with one that maps the input of o^* to its output, and then incorporating more and more nodes and edges until we have incorporated all of E'. These functions will not be differentiable everywhere, simply where we need them to be.'

Consider V' to be the set of all vertices $v' \in V$ where there is a $(u, v) \in E'$ where $v \leq v'$. Now, without loss of generality, assume $E' = \{(u, v) \in E : v \in V'\}$. Then, we know that all $v' \in V'$ are soft. Without loss of generality, assume $o^* \in V'$.

Now, we can arrange a total ordering on the vertices in V' (in the opposite direction of the partial ordering induced by the graph), beginning with o^*, and we will denote the ordering $v_1 \ldots v_j$, such that there is no path from $v_{i'}$ to v_i for all $i > i'$, and $v_1 = o^*$. We will denote $V_i = \{v_1, \ldots v_i\}$ (such that $V_j = V'$). and $E_i = \{(u, v) \in E : u \in V_i\}$. Define $w^i \in \mathbf{R}^{E_i}$ such that $w^i_{(u,v)} = w_{(u,v)}$ if $(u, v) \in E_i$. Define $\alpha^1_{v_1} = k_{v_1,w}(x)$. We define $d^1 : \mathbf{R}^{V_1} \times \mathbf{R}^{E_1} \to \mathbf{R}$ such that[13] $d^1(\alpha, \emptyset) = a_{v_1}(\alpha) = \alpha$. Thus, $d^1(\alpha^1_{v_1}) = c_{v_1,w}(x)$, and d^1 is differentiable with respect to its arguments.

Now, we recursively define $d^2 \ldots d^j$. Given d^i, we define $m^i : \mathbf{R}^{V_{i+1}} \times \mathbf{R}^{E_{i+1}} \to \mathbf{R}^V_i$ such that $(m^i(\alpha, w'))_v = \alpha_v + a(\alpha_{v_{i+1}}) w'_{v_{i+1},v}$ if $(v_{i+1}, v) \in E$ and $m^i(\alpha, w')_v = \alpha_v$ if $(v_{i+1}, v) \notin E$. Moreover, for any sets S, and $T \subseteq S$, for any $v \in \mathbf{R}^S$, we define $\Pi^T(v)$ such that $\Pi^T(v)_i = v_i$ for all $i \in T$. Then, we can define $d^{i+1} : \mathbf{R}^{V_{i+1}} \times \mathbf{R}^{E_{i+1}} \to \mathbf{R}$ such that $d^{i+1}(\alpha, w') = d^i(m^i(\alpha, w'), \Pi^{E_i}(w'))$.

Recursively, we define $\alpha^{i+1} \in \mathbf{R}^{V_{i+1}}$ such that $\alpha_{v_{i+1}} = k_{v_i,w}(x)$ and for all $v \in V_i$, $\alpha^{i+1}_v = \alpha^i_v - a(k_{v_{i+1},w}(x)) w_{(v_{i+1},v)}$ if $(v_{i+1}, v) \in E$, and $\alpha^{i+1}_v = \alpha^i_v$ otherwise. Thus, observe that $d^{i+1}(\alpha^{i+1}, w^{i+1}) = d^i(\alpha^i, w^i)$, so recursively $d^{i+1}(\alpha^{i+1}, w^{i+1}) = c_{v_1,w}(x)$. Moreover, recursively one can establish that for any $w' \in \mathbf{R}^E$ where $\Pi^{E-E_{i+1}}(w') = \Pi^{E-E_{i+1}}(w)$, $d^{i+1}(\alpha^{i+1}, \Pi^{E_i}(w')) = c_{v_1,w'}(x)$.

Now, we must show differentiability. The inductive hypothesis is d^i is differentiable, or more formally, for

[12] The following may not be obvious: however, it is a corollary of Lemma 31.

[13] Note that E_1 is the emptyset, as there are no outgoing edges from o^*_1.

$h \in \mathbf{R}^{V_i} \times \mathbf{R}^{E_i}$:

$$\lim_{h \to 0} \frac{d^i(\alpha^i + \Pi^{V_i}(h), w^i + \Pi^{E_i}(h))}{\|h\|} = 0 \tag{128}$$

First, we know that v_i is soft. If $k_{v_{i+1},w}(x) \neq 0$, then $\alpha^{i+1}_{v_{i+1}} \neq 0$. If $\alpha^{i+1}_{v_{i+1}} < 0$, then in a region around α^{i+1}, w^{i+1}, $m^i((\alpha^{i+1}, w^{i+1}) + h) = \alpha^i + \Pi^{V_i}(h)$, i.e. is linear. If $\alpha^{i+1}_{v_{i+1}} > 0$, then in a region around α^{i+1}, w^{i+1}, $m^i((\alpha^{i+1}, w^{i+1}) + h)_v = \alpha^i_v + h_v + h_{v_{i+1}}(w^{i+1}_{(v_{i+1},v)} + h_{(v_{i+1},v)})$ if $(v_{i+1}, v) \in E$, and $m^i((\alpha^{i+1}, w^{i+1}) + h)_v = \alpha^i_v + h_v$ otherwise (again, linear).

Thus, if $k_{v_{i+1},w}(x) \neq 0$, then $\alpha^{i+1}_{v_{i+1}} \neq 0$, in a region around α^{i+1} and w^i, m^i is linear. Then d^{i+1} is the composition of a differentiable function, a linear function, and a projection, and therefore differentiable at α^{i+1} and w^i.

On the other hand, if $k_{v_{i+1},w}(x) = 0$, then $\alpha^{i+1}_{v_{i+1}} = 0$. Since v_i is soft, then $\frac{\partial^+ M_w(x)}{\partial c_{v_{i+1},w}(x)} = 0$. This implies $\frac{\partial^+ d^{i+1}(\alpha^{i+1}, w^{i+1})}{\partial \alpha^{i+1}_{v_{i+1}}} = 0$. Using the chain rule for directional derivatives:

$$0 = \frac{\partial^+ d^{i+1}(\alpha^{i+1}, w^{i+1})}{\partial \alpha^{i+1}_{v_{i+1}}} \tag{129}$$

$$0 = \partial_g d^i(\alpha^i, w^i) \tag{130}$$

Where $g = \frac{\partial^+ m^i(\alpha^{i+1}, w^{i+1})}{\partial \alpha^{i+1}_{v_{i+1}}}$, so $g_v = w^{i+1}_{v_{i+1},v}$ if $(v^{i+1}, v) \in E$, and $g_v = 0$ otherwise. If J^i is the derivative of d^i at α^i, w^i, then, because v_{i+1} is soft and $\alpha^{i+1}_{v_{i+1}} = 0$:

$$\sum_{v \in V_i} J^i_v g_v = 0 \tag{131}$$

$$\sum_{(v_{i+1},v) \in E} J^i_v w_{v_{i+1},v} = 0 \tag{132}$$

In order to prove differentiability of d^{i+1}, we introduce a function $\epsilon^i : \mathbf{R}^{V_i} \times \mathbf{R}^{E_i} \to \mathbf{R}$ quantifying the error of the derivative of d^i, such that for any $h^\alpha \in \mathbf{R}^{V_i}$, $h^w \in \mathbf{R}^{E_i}$, $\epsilon(h^\alpha, h^w) = d^i(\alpha^i + h^\alpha, w^i + h^w) - \left(\sum_{v \in V_i} J^i_v h^\alpha_v + \sum_{e \in E_i} J^i_e w^\alpha_e\right)$. Thus, $\lim_{h^\alpha, h^w \to 0} \frac{\epsilon(h^\alpha, h^w)}{\|h^\alpha, h^w\|} = 0$, where $\|h^\alpha, h^w\| = \sqrt{\|h^\alpha\|^2 + \|h^w\|^2}$.

First, although m^i is not differentiable when $\alpha^{i+1}_{v_{i+1}} = 0$, the derivative is "almost" the linear projection operator Π^{V^i}, because the partial derivative of $\alpha^{i+1}_{v_{i+1}} = 0$. We can prove this using a proof similar to the proof of the chain rule. We will denote the following η, and will endeavor to prove it exists and is zero.

$$\eta = \lim_{h^\alpha, h^w \to 0} \frac{d^{i+1}(\alpha^{i+1} + h^\alpha, w^{i+1} + h^w)}{\|h^\alpha, h^w\|} \tag{133}$$

$$- \frac{d^{i+1}(\alpha^{i+1}, w^{i+1}) + \sum_{v \in V_i} J^i_v h^\alpha_v + \sum_{e \in E_i} J^i_e h^w_e}{\|h^\alpha, h^w\|} \tag{134}$$

The last sum is a linear operator: notice that in this case, we are effectively showing $J^{i+1} = J^i$. First, we note that $d^{i+1}(\alpha^{i+1}, w^{i+1}) = d^i(\alpha^i, w^i)$:

$$\eta = \lim_{h^\alpha, h^w \to 0} \frac{d^{i+1}(\alpha^{i+1} + h^\alpha, w^{i+1} + h^w)}{\|h^\alpha, h^w\|} \tag{135}$$

$$- \frac{d^i(\alpha^i, w^i) + \sum_{v \in V_i} J^i_v h^\alpha_v + \sum_{e \in E_i} J^i_e h^w_e}{\|h^\alpha, h^w\|} \tag{136}$$

Furthermore, we study the first term separately:

$$\begin{aligned} &d^{i+1}(\alpha^{i+1} + h^\alpha, w^{i+1} + h^w) \\ &= d^i(m^i(\alpha^{i+1} + h^\alpha, w^{i+1} + h^w), \Pi^{E_i}(w^{i+1} + h^w)) \\ &= d^i(m^i(\alpha^{i+1} + h^\alpha, w^{i+1} + h^w), w^i + \Pi^{E_i}(h^w)) \end{aligned} \tag{137}$$

Write $a = a_{v_{i+1}}$, which is a relu function, because $v_{i+1} \neq o^*$, and $v_{i+1} \notin I$. Using ϵ we get:

$$\begin{aligned} &d^{i+1}(\alpha^{i+1} + h^\alpha, w^{i+1} + h^w) \\ &= d^i(\alpha^i, w^i) + \epsilon^i(m^i(\alpha^{i+1} + h^\alpha, w^{i+1} + h^w), \Pi^{E_i}(w^{i+1} + h^w)) \\ &\quad + \sum_{v \in V_i} J^i_v h^\alpha_v \\ &\quad + \sum_{(v_{i+1},v) \in E} J^i_v a(h^\alpha_{v_{i+1}})(w_{v_{i+1},v} + h^w_{v_{i+1},v}) \\ &\quad + \sum_{e \in E_i} J^i_e h^w_e \end{aligned} \tag{138}$$

Focusing on the most complex term:

$$\begin{aligned} &\sum_{(v_{i+1},v) \in E} J^i_v a(h^\alpha_{v_{i+1}})(w_{v_{i+1},v} + h^w_{v_{i+1},v}) \\ &= a(h^\alpha_{v_{i+1}}) \sum_{(v_{i+1},v) \in E} J^i_v w_{v_{i+1},v} \\ &\quad + a(h^\alpha_{v_{i+1}}) \sum_{(v_{i+1},v) \in E} J^i_v h^w_{v_{i+1},v} \end{aligned} \tag{139}$$

Note that $\sum_{v_{i+1},v} J^i_v w_{v_{i+1},v} = 0$, so:

$$\begin{aligned} &\sum_{(v_{i+1},v) \in E} J^i_v a(h^\alpha_{v_{i+1}})(w_{v_{i+1},v} + h^w_{v_{i+1},v}) \\ &= a(h^\alpha_{v_{i+1}}) \sum_{(v_{i+1},v) \in E} J^i_v h^w_{v_{i+1},v} \end{aligned} \tag{140}$$

So, now we consider the limit:

$$\lim_{h^\alpha,h^w\to 0}\frac{\sum_{(v_{i+1},v)\in E} J_v^i a(h^\alpha_{v_{i+1}})(w_{v_{i+1},v}+h^w_{v_{i+1},v})}{\|h^\alpha,h^w\|} = \lim_{h^\alpha,h^w\to 0}\frac{a(h^\alpha_{v_{i+1}})\sum_{(v_{i+1},v)\in E} J_v^i h^w_{v_{i+1},v}}{\|h^\alpha,h^w\|} \quad (141)$$

Taking the absolute value:

$$\lim_{h^\alpha,h^w\to 0}\frac{\left|\sum_{(v_{i+1},v)\in E} J_v^i a(h^\alpha_{v_{i+1}})(w_{v_{i+1},v}+h^w_{v_{i+1},v})\right|}{\|h^\alpha,h^w\|} = \lim_{h^\alpha,h^w\to 0}\frac{|a(h^\alpha_{v_{i+1}})|\sum_{(v_{i+1},v)\in E} |J_v^i||h^w_{v_{i+1},v}|}{\|h^\alpha,h^w\|} \quad (142)$$

Since $|a(h^\alpha_{v_{i+1}})|\le |h^\alpha_{v_{i+1}}|$:

$$\lim_{h^\alpha,h^w\to 0}\frac{\left|\sum_{(v_{i+1},v)\in E} J_v^i a(h^\alpha_{v_{i+1}})(w_{v_{i+1},v}+h^w_{v_{i+1},v})\right|}{\|h^\alpha,h^w\|} = \lim_{h^\alpha,h^w\to 0}\frac{|h^\alpha_{v_{i+1}}|\sum_{(v_{i+1},v)\in E} |J_v^i||h^w_{v_{i+1},v}|}{\|h^\alpha,h^w\|} \quad (143)$$

The quadratic terms in the numerator mean that the limit is zero, because for any $i,j\in\{1\dots n\}$ $\lim_{z\to 0}\frac{z_i z_j}{\|z\|}=0$.

$$\lim_{h^\alpha,h^w\to 0}\frac{\sum_{(v_{i+1},v)\in E} J_v^i a(h^\alpha_{v_{i+1}})(w_{v_{i+1},v}+h^w_{v_{i+1},v})}{\|h^\alpha,h^w\|}=0 \quad (144)$$

We next consider the term $\epsilon^i(m^i(\alpha^{i+1}+h^\alpha,w^{i+1}+h^w),\Pi^{E_i}(w^{i+1}+h^w))$. In order to bound this, we need to understand how fast m^i is approaching α^i.

$$\begin{aligned}\left\|m^i(\alpha^{i+1}+h^\alpha,w^{i+1}+h^w)-\alpha^i\right\|^2 &= \sum_{v\in V_i:(v_{i+1},v)\in E}(h^\alpha_v+a(h^\alpha_{v_{i+1}})(w^{i+1}_{v_{i+1},v}+h^w_{v_{i+1},v}))^2 \\ &+\sum_{v\in V_i:(v_{i+1},v)\notin E}(h^\alpha_v)^2 \\ &\le \sum_{v\in V_i:(v_{i+1},v)\in E}2(h^\alpha_v)^2 \\ &+\sum_{v\in V_i:(v_{i+1},v)\in E}4(a(h^\alpha_{v_{i+1}}))^2(w^{i+1}_{v_{i+1},v})^2 \\ &+\sum_{v\in V_i:(v_{i+1},v)\in E}4(a(h^\alpha_{v_{i+1}}))^2(h^w_{v_{i+1},v})^2 \\ &+\sum_{v\in V_i:(v_{i+1},v)\notin E}(h^\alpha_v)^2\end{aligned} \quad (145)$$

Define $W^{i+1}=\sum_{v\in V_i:(v_{i+1},v)\in E}(w_{v_{i+1},v})^2$.

$$\left\|m^i(\alpha^{i+1}+h^\alpha,w^{i+1}+h^w)-\alpha^i\right\|^2 \le 2\|h^\alpha\|^2+4(a(h^\alpha_{v_{i+1}}))^2W^{i+1}+4(a(h^\alpha_{v_{i+1}}))^2\|h^w\|^2 \quad (146)$$

In the limit $|h^\alpha_{v_{i+1}}|<1$, so $(a(h^\alpha_{v_{i+1}}))^2<1$, and we can write:

$$\left\|m^i(\alpha^{i+1}+h^\alpha,w^{i+1}+h^w)-\alpha^i\right\|^2 \le 2\|h^\alpha\|^2+4(a(h^\alpha_{v_{i+1}}))^2W^{i+1}+4\|h^w\|^2 \quad (147)$$

Moreover, $a(h^\alpha_{v_{i+1}})^2\le (h^\alpha_{v_{i+1}})^2\le\|h^\alpha,h^w\|^2$:

$$\left\|m^i(\alpha^{i+1}+h^\alpha,w^{i+1}+h^w)-\alpha^i\right\|^2 \le (4+4W^{i+1})\|h^\alpha,h^w\|^2 \quad (148)$$

Since $\Pi^{E_i}(w^{i+1}-h^w)-w^i=\Pi^{E_i}(h^w)$, then $\left\|\Pi^{E_i}(w^{i+1}-h^w)-w^i\right\|^2\le\|h^w\|^2\le\|h^\alpha,h^w\|^2$, so:

$$\left\|m^i(\alpha^{i+1}+h^\alpha,w^{i+1}+h^w)-\alpha^i,\Pi^{E_i}(w^{i+1}-h^w)-w^i\right\| \le \sqrt{5+4W^{i+1}}\|h^\alpha,h^w\| \quad (149)$$

So, considering the limit of the absolute value:

$$\lim_{h^\alpha,h^w\to 0}\frac{|\epsilon^i(m^i(\alpha^{i+1}+h^\alpha,w^{i+1}+h^w),\Pi^{E_i}(w^{i+1}+h^w))|}{\|h^\alpha,h^w\|} = \sqrt{5+4W^{i+1}}\times \lim_{h^\alpha,h^w\to 0}\frac{|\epsilon^i(m^i(\alpha^{i+1}+h^\alpha,w^{i+1}+h^w),\Pi^{E_i}(w^{i+1}+h^w))|}{\sqrt{5+4W^{i+1}}\|h^\alpha,h^w\|} \quad (150)$$

Note that since the denominator is larger than the norm of the vector inside ϵ^i, then the whole thing approaches zero.

$$\lim_{h^\alpha,h^w\to 0}\frac{|\epsilon^i(m^i(\alpha^{i+1}+h^\alpha,w^{i+1}+h^w),\Pi^{E_i}(w^{i+1}+h^w))|}{\|h^\alpha,h^w\|}=0 \quad (151)$$

Now we have established that:

$$\lim_{h^\alpha,h^w\to 0}\frac{d^{i+1}(\alpha^{i+1}+h^\alpha,w^{i+1}+h^w)}{\|h^\alpha,h^w\|} = \lim_{h^\alpha,h^w\to 0}\frac{d^i(\alpha^i,w^i)}{\|h^\alpha,h^w\|} + \frac{\sum_{v\in V_i}J_v^i h^\alpha_v}{\|h^\alpha,h^w\|} + \frac{\sum_{e\in E_i}J_e^i h^w_e}{\|h^\alpha,h^w\|} \quad (152)$$

Plugging this into η yields $\eta = 0$, implying that d^{i+1} is differentiable. Recursively, we have established that d^j is differentiable. However, E_j is a subset of E': by construction, $V' = V_j$ are the nodes that are at the end of the edges in E', not at the beginning, and E_j are the edges that can be reached from V_j. The final step is to construct a function $f : \mathbf{R}^{E'} \to \mathbf{R}$ as a function defined on all the relevant edges. Define $E^* = E' - E_j$. For all $(u, v) \in E^*$, define $\beta_{(u,v)} = c_{u,w}(x)$. Define $w^* \in \mathbf{R}^{E'}$ such that $w^*_e = w_e$ for all $e \in E'$. Then, we define $m^* : \mathbf{R}^{E'} \to \mathbf{R}^{V_j}$ such that for all $v \in V_j$, for all $w' \in \mathbf{R}^{E'}$:

$$m^*(w') = \sum_{(u,v)\in E^*} w'_{(u,v)}\beta_{(u,v)} \qquad (153)$$

Now we can define $f(w') = d^j(m^*(w'), \Pi^{E_j}(w'))$. Note that $f(w^*) = M_w(x)$: moreover, for any $w' \in \mathbf{R}^E$, if $\Pi^{E-E'}(w') = \Pi^{E-E'}(w)$, then $f(\Pi^{E'}(w')) = M_{w'}(x)$. Finally, since d^j is differentiable and m^* is linear, then f is differentiable at w^*. This implies that E' is total on x given $M_w(x)$. ■

Computing Nonvacuous Generalization Bounds for Deep (Stochastic) Neural Networks with Many More Parameters than Training Data

Gintare Karolina Dziugaite
Department of Engineering
University of Cambridge

Daniel M. Roy
Department of Statistical Sciences
University of Toronto

Abstract

One of the defining properties of deep learning is that models are chosen to have many more parameters than available training data. In light of this capacity for overfitting, it is remarkable that simple algorithms like SGD reliably return solutions with low test error. One roadblock to explaining these phenomena in terms of implicit regularization, structural properties of the solution, and/or easiness of the data is that many learning bounds are quantitatively vacuous when applied to networks learned by SGD in this "deep learning" regime. Logically, in order to explain generalization, we need nonvacuous bounds. We return to an idea by Langford and Caruana (2001), who used PAC-Bayes bounds to compute nonvacuous numerical bounds on generalization error for *stochastic* two-layer two-hidden-unit neural networks via a sensitivity analysis. By optimizing the PAC-Bayes bound directly, we are able to extend their approach and obtain nonvacuous generalization bounds for deep stochastic neural network classifiers with millions of parameters trained on only tens of thousands of examples. We connect our findings to recent and old work on flat minima and MDL-based explanations of generalization.

1 INTRODUCTION

By optimizing a PAC-Bayes bound, we show that it is possible to compute nonvacuous numerical bounds on the generalization error of deep *stochastic* neural networks with millions of parameters, despite the training data sets being one or more orders of magnitude smaller than the number of parameters. To our knowledge, these are the first explicit and nonvacuous numerical bounds computed for trained neural networks in the modern deep learning regime where the number of network parameters eclipses the number of training examples.

The bounds we compute are data dependent, incorporating millions of components optimized numerically to identify a large region in weight space with low average empirical error around the solution obtained by stochastic gradient descent (SGD). The data dependence is essential: indeed, the VC dimension of neural networks is typically bounded below by the number of parameters, and so one needs as many training data as parameters before (uniform) PAC bounds are nonvacuous, i.e., before the generalization error falls below 1. To put this in concrete terms, on MNIST, having even 72 hidden units in a fully connected first layer yields vacuous PAC bounds.

Evidently, we are operating far from the worst case: observed generalization cannot be explained in terms the regularizing effect of the size of the neural network alone. This is an old observation, and one that attracted considerable theoretical attention two decades ago: Bartlett [Bar97; Bar98] showed that, in large (sigmoidal) neural networks, when the learned weights are small in magnitude, the fat-shattering dimension is more important than the VC dimension for characterizing generalization. In particular, Bartlett established classification error bounds in terms of the empirical margin and the fat-shattering dimension, and then gave fat-shattering bounds for neural networks in terms of the *magnitudes* of the weights and the depth of the network alone. Improved norm-based bounds were obtained using Rademacher and Gaussian complexity by Bartlett and Mendelson [BM02] and Koltchinskii and Panchenko [KP02].

These norm-based bounds are the foundation of our current understanding of neural network generalization. It is widely accepted that these bounds explain observed generalization, at least "qualitatively" and/or when the weights are explicitly regularized. Indeed, recent work by Neyshabur, Tomioka, and Srebro [NTS14] puts forth the idea that SGD performs implicit norm-based regularization. Somewhat surprisingly, when we investigated state-of-the-art Rademacher bounds for ReLU networks, the bounds were vacuous when applied to solutions obtained by SGD on real networks/datasets. We discuss the details of this analysis in Appendix D. While most theoreticians would assume these bounds were numerically loose to *some* extent, they might be surprised to learn that the bounds do not logically establish generalization on their own. It is worth highlighting that this observation does not necessarily rule out the existence of nonvacuous bounds under the same or similar hypotheses. This is an important avenue to investigate.

1.1 UNDERSTANDING SGD

Our investigation was instigated by recent empirical work by Zhang, Bengio, Hardt, Recht, and Vinyals [Zha+17], who show that stochastic gradient descent (SGD), applied to deep networks with millions of parameters, is:

1. able to achieve ≈ 0 training error on CIFAR10 and IMAGENET and still generalize (i.e., test error remains small, despite the potential for overfitting);
2. still able to achieve ≈ 0 training error even after the labels are *randomized*, and does so with only a small factor of additional computational time.

Taken together, these two observations demonstrate that these networks have a tremendous capacity to overfit and yet SGD does not abuse this capacity as it optimizes the surrogate loss, despite the lack of explicit regularization.

It is a major open problem to explain this phenomenon. A natural approach would be to show that, under realistic hypotheses, SGD performs implicit regularization or tends to find solutions that possess some particular structural property that we already know to be connected to generalization. However, in order to complete the logical connection, we need an associated error bound to be nonvacuous in the regime of model size / data size where we hope to explain the phenomenon.

This work establishes a potential candidate, building off ideas by Langford [Lan02] and Langford and Caruana [LC02]: On a binary class variant of MNIST, we find that SGD solutions are nearby to relatively large regions in weight space with low average empirical error. We find this structure by optimizing a PAC-Bayes bound, starting at the SGD solution, obtaining a nonvacuous generalization bound for a stochastic neural network. Across a variety of network architectures, our PAC-Bayes bounds on the test error are in the range 16–22%. These are far from nonvacuous but loose: Chernoff bounds on the test error based on held-out data are consistently around 3%. Despite the gap, theoreticians aware of the numerical performance of generalization bounds will likely be surprised that it is possible at all to obtain nonvacuous numerical bounds for models with such large capacity trained on so few training examples. While we cannot entirely explain the magnitude of generalization, we can demonstrate nontrivial generalization.

Our approach was inspired by a line of work in physics by Baldassi, Ingrosso, Lucibello, Saglietti, and Zecchina [Bal+15] and the same authors with Borgs and Chayes [Bal+16]. Based on theoretical results for discrete optimization linking computational efficiency to the existence of nonisolated solutions, the authors propose a number of new algorithms for learning discrete neural networks by explicitly driving a local search towards nonisolated solutions. On the basis of Bayesian ideas, they posit that these solutions have good generalization properties. In a recent work with Chaudhari, Choromanska, Soatto, and LeCun [Cha+17], they introduce local-entropy loss and Entropy-SGD, extending these algorithmic ideas to modern deep learning architectures with continuous parametrizations, and obtaining impressive empirical results.

In the continuous setting, nonisolated solutions correspond to "flat minima". The existence and regularizing effects of flat minima in the empirical error surface was recognized early on by researchers, going back at work by Hinton and Camp [HC93] and Hochreiter and Schmidhuber [HS97]. Hochreiter and Schmidhuber discuss sharp versus flat minima using the language of minimum description length (MDL; [Ris83; Grü07]). In short, describing weights in sharp minima requires high precision in order to not incur nontrivial excess error, whereas flat minimum can be described with lower precision. A similar coding argument appears in [HC93].

Hochreiter and Schmidhuber propose an algorithm to find flat minima by minimizing the training error while maximizing the log volume of a connected region of the parameter space that yields similar classifiers with similarly good training error. There are very close connections—at both the level of analysis and algorithms—with the work of Chaudhari et al. [Cha+17] and close connections with the approach we take to compute nonvacuous error bounds by exploiting the local error surface. (We discuss more related work in Section 6.)

Despite the promising underpinnings, the generalization theorems given by [Cha+17] have admittedly unrealistic assumptions, and fall short of connecting local-entropy minimization to observed generalization.

The goal of this work is to identify structure in the solutions obtained by SGD that provably implies small generalization error. Computationally, it is much easier to demonstrate that a randomized classifier will generalize, and so our results actually pertain to the generalization error of a *stochastic* neural network, i.e., one whose weights/biases are drawn at random from some distribution on every forward evaluation of the network. Under bounded loss, Fubini's theorem implies that we also obtain a bound on the expected error of a neural network whose weights have been randomly perturbed. It would be interesting to achieve tighter control on the distribution of error or on the error of the mean neural network.

Returning to the goal of explaining SGD and generalization in deep learning more generally, one could study whether the type of structure we exploit to obtain bounds necessarily arises from performing SGD under natural conditions. (We suspect one condition may be that the Bayes error rate is close to zero.) More ambitiously, perhaps the existence of the same structure can explain the success of SGD in practice.

1.2 APPROACH

Our working hypothesis is that SGD finds good solutions only if they are surrounded by a relatively large volume of solutions that are nearly as good. This hypothesis suggests that PAC-Bayes bounds may be fruitful: if SGD finds a solution contained in a large volume of equally good solutions, then the expected error rate of a classifier drawn at random from this volume should match that of the SGD solution. The PAC-Bayes theorem [McA99] bounds the expected error rate of a classifier chosen from a distribution Q in terms of the Kullback–Liebler divergence from some a priori fixed distribution P, and so if the volume of equally good solutions is large, and not too far from the mass of P, we will obtain a nonvacuous bound.

Our approach will be to use optimization to find a broad distribution Q over neural network parameters that minimizes the PAC-Bayes bound, in effect mapping out the volume of equally good solutions surrounding the SGD solution. This idea is actually a modern take on an old idea by Langford and Caruana [LC02], who apply PAC-Bayes bounds to small two-layer stochastic neural networks (with only 2 hidden units) that were trained on (relatively large, in comparison) data sets of several hundred labeled examples.

The basic idea can be traced back even further to work by Hinton and Camp [HC93], who propose an algorithm for controlling overfitting in neural networks via the minimum description length principle. In particular, they minimize the sum of the empirical squared error and the KL divergence between a prior and posterior distribution on the weights. Their algorithm is applied to networks with 100's of inputs and 4 hidden units, trained on several hundred labeled examples. Hinton and Camp do not compute numerical generalization bounds to verify that MDL principles alone suffice to *explain* the observed generalization.

Our algorithm more directly extends the work by Langford and Caruana, who propose to construct a distribution Q over neural networks by performing a sensitivity analysis on each parameter after training, searching for the largest deviation that does not increase the training error by more than, e.g., 1%. For Q, Langford and Caruana choose a multivariate normal distribution over the network parameters, centered at the parameters of the trained neural network. The covariance matrix is diagonal, with the variance of each parameter chosen to be the estimated sensitivity, scaled by a global constant. (The global scale is chosen so that the training error of Q is within, e.g., 1% of that of the original trained network.) Their prior P is also a multivariate normal, but with zero mean and covariance given by some scalar multiple of the identity matrix. By employing a union bound, they allow themselves to choose the scalar multiple in a data-dependent fashion to optimize the PAC-Bayes bound.

The algorithm sketched by Langford and Caruana does not scale to modern neural networks for several reasons, but one dominates: in massively overparametrized networks, individual parameters often have negligible effect on the training classification error, and so it is not possible to estimate the *relative* sensitivity of large populations of neurons by studying the sensitivity of neurons in isolation.

Instead, we use stochastic gradient descent to directly optimize the PAC-Bayes bound on the error rate of a stochastic neural network. At each step, we update the network weights and their variances by taking a step along an unbiased estimate of the gradient of (an upper bound on) the PAC-Bayes bound. In effect, the objective function is the sum of i) the empirical surrogate loss averaged over a random perturbation of the SGD solution, and ii) a generalization error bound that acts like a regularizer.

Having demonstrated that this simple approach can construct a witness to generalization, it is worthwhile asking whether these ideas can be extended to the setting of local-entropic loss [Cha+17]. If we view the distribution that defines the local-entropic loss as defining a stochastic neural network, can we use PAC-Bayes bounds to establish nonvacuous bounds on its generalization error?

2 PRELIMINARIES

Much of our setup is identical to that of [LC02]: We are working in the batch supervised learning setting. Data points are elements $x \in \mathcal{X} \subseteq \mathbb{R}^k$ with binary class labels

$y \in \{-1, 1\}$. Let S_m denote a training set of size m,

$$S_m = \{(x_i, y_i)\}_{i=1,\ldots,m}, \text{ where } (x_i, y_i) \in (\mathcal{X} \times \mathcal{Y}).$$

Let $\mathcal{M}$ denote the set of all probability measures on the data space $\mathbb{R}^k \times \{-1, 1\}$. We will assume that the training examples are i.i.d. samples from some $\mu \in \mathcal{M}$.

A parametric family of classifiers is a function $H : \mathbb{R}^d \times \mathbb{R}^k \to \{-1, 1\}$, where $h_w := H(w, \cdot) : \mathbb{R}^k \to \{-1, 1\}$ is the classifier indexed by the parameter $w \in \mathbb{R}^d$. The hypotheses space induced by H is $\mathcal{H} = \{h_w : w \in \mathbb{R}^d\}$. A randomized classifier is a distribution Q on $\mathbb{R}^d$. Informally, we will speak of distributions on $\mathcal{H}$ when we mean distributions on the underlying parametrization.

We are interested in the 0–1 loss $\ell : \mathbb{R} \times \{-1, 1\} \to \{0, 1\}$

$$\ell(\hat{y}, y) = \mathbb{I}(\text{sign}(\hat{y}) = y).$$

We will also make use of the logistic loss $\breve{\ell} : \mathbb{R} \times \{-1, 1\} \to \mathbb{R}_+$

$$\breve{\ell}(\hat{y}, y) = \frac{1}{\log(2)} \log\big(1 + \exp(-\hat{y}y)\big),$$

which will serve as a convex surrogate (i.e., upper bound) to the 0–1 loss.

We define the following notions of error:

- $\hat{e}(h, S_m) = \frac{1}{m}\sum_{i=1}^{m} \ell(h(x_i), y_i)$ empirical classification error of hypothesis h for sample S_m;
- $\breve{e}(h, S_m) = \frac{1}{m}\sum_{i=1}^{m} \breve{\ell}(h(x_i), y_i)$ empirical (surrogate) error of a hypothesis h on the training data set S_m. We will use this for training purposes when we need our empirical loss to be differentiable;
- $e_\mu(h) = \mathop{\mathbb{E}}_{S_m \sim \mu^m} [\hat{e}(h, S_m)]$ expected error for hypothesis h under the data distribution μ (we will often drop the subscript μ and just write $e(h)$);
- $\hat{e}(Q, S_m) = \mathop{\mathbb{E}}_{w \sim Q} [\hat{e}(h_w, S_m)]$ expected empirical error under the randomized classifier Q on $\mathcal{H}$;
- $e(Q) = \mathop{\mathbb{E}}_{w \sim Q} [e_\mu(h_w)]$ expected error for Q on $\mathcal{H}$.

2.1 KL DIVERGENCE

Let Q, P be probability measures defined on a common measurable space $\mathcal{H}$, such that Q is absolutely continuous with respect to P, and write $\frac{\mathrm{d}Q}{\mathrm{d}P} : \mathcal{H} \to \mathbb{R}_+ \cup \{\infty\}$ for some Radon–Nikodym derivative of Q with respect to P. Then the Kullback–Liebler divergence (or relative entropy) of P from Q is defined to be

$$\mathrm{KL}(Q||P) := \int \log \frac{\mathrm{d}Q}{\mathrm{d}P}\, \mathrm{d}Q.$$

We will mostly be concerned with KL divergences where Q and P are probability measures on Euclidean space, $\mathbb{R}^d$, absolutely continuous with respect to Lebesgue measure. Let q and p denote the respective densities. In this case, the definition of the KL divergence simplifies to

$$\mathrm{KL}(Q||P) = \int \log \frac{q(x)}{p(x)} q(x) \mathrm{d}x.$$

Of particular interest to us is the KL divergence between multivariate normal distributions in $\mathbb{R}^d$. Let $N_q = \mathcal{N}(\mu_q, \Sigma_q)$ be a multivariate normal with mean μ_q and covariance matrix Σ_q, let $N_p = \mathcal{N}(\mu_p, \Sigma_p)$, and assume Σ_q and Σ_p are positive definite. Then $\mathrm{KL}(N_q||N_p)$ is

$$\frac{1}{2}\Bigg(\mathrm{tr}\left(\Sigma_p^{-1}\Sigma_q\right) - k + (\mu_p - \mu_q)^\top \Sigma_p^{-1}(\mu_p - \mu_q) + \ln\left(\frac{\det \Sigma_p}{\det \Sigma_q}\right)\Bigg). \tag{1}$$

For $p, q \in [0, 1]$, we will abuse notation and define

$$\begin{aligned}\mathrm{KL}(q||p) &:= \mathrm{KL}(\mathcal{B}(q)||\mathcal{B}(p)) \\ &= q \log \frac{q}{p} + (1 - q) \log \frac{1 - q}{1 - p},\end{aligned}$$

where $\mathcal{B}(p)$ denotes the Bernoulli distribution on $\{0, 1\}$ with mean p.

2.2 INVERTING KL BOUNDS

In the following sections, we will encounter bounds on a quantity $p^* \in [0, 1]$ of the form

$$\mathrm{KL}(q||p^*) \leq c$$

for some $q \in [0, 1]$ and $c \geq 0$. Thus, we are interested in

$$\mathrm{KL}^{-1}(q|c) := \sup\{p \in [0, 1] : \mathrm{KL}(q||p) \leq c\}.$$

We are not aware of a simple formula for $\mathrm{KL}^{-1}(q|c)$, although numerical approximations are readily obtained via Newton's method (Appendix A). For the purpose of gradient-based optimization, we can use the well-known inequality, $2(q - p)^2 \leq \mathrm{KL}(q||p)$, to obtain a simple upper bound

$$\mathrm{KL}^{-1}(q|c) \leq q + \sqrt{c/2}. \tag{2}$$

This bound is quantitatively loose near $q \approx 0$, because then $\mathrm{KL}^{-1}(q|c) \approx c$ for $c \ll 1$, versus the upper bound of $\Theta(\sqrt{c})$. On the other hand, when c is large enough that $q + \sqrt{\frac{c}{2}} > 1$, the derivative of $\mathrm{KL}^{-1}(q|c)$ is zero, whereas the upper bound provides a useful derivative.

2.3 BOUNDS

We will employ three probabilistic bounds to control generalization error: the union bound, a sample convergence bound derived from the Chernoff bound, and the PAC-Bayes bound due to McAllester [McA99]. We state the union bound for completeness.

Theorem 2.1 (union). *Let $E_1, E_2, \ldots$ be events. Then* $\mathbb{P}(\bigcup_n E_n) \leq \sum_n \mathbb{P}(E_n)$.

Recall that $\mathcal{B}(p)$ denotes the Bernoulli distribution on $\{0,1\}$ with mean $p \in [0,1]$. The following bound is derived from the KL formulation of the Chernoff bound:

Theorem 2.2 (sample convergence [LC02]). *For every $p, \delta \in (0,1)$ and $n \in \mathbb{N}$, with probability at least $1-\delta$ over $x \sim \mathcal{B}(p)^n$,* $\mathrm{KL}(n^{-1}\sum_{i=1}^{n} x_i || p) \leq \frac{\log \frac{2}{\delta}}{n}$.

Finally, we present a variant of McAllester's PAC-Bayes bound due to Langford and Seeger [LS01]. (See also [Lan02].)

Theorem 2.3 (PAC-Bayes [McA99; LS01]). *For every $\delta > 0$, $m \in \mathbb{N}$, distribution μ on $\mathbb{R}^k \times \{-1, 1\}$, and distribution P on $\mathcal{H}$, with probability at least $1-\delta$ over $S_m \sim \mu^m$, for all distributions Q on $\mathcal{H}$,*

$$\mathrm{KL}(\hat{e}(Q, S_m) || e(Q)) \leq \frac{\mathrm{KL}(Q||P) + \log \frac{m}{\delta}}{m-1}.$$

The PAC-Bayes bound leads to the following learning algorithm [McA99]:

1. Fix a probability $\delta > 0$ and a distribution P on $\mathcal{H}$.
2. Collect an i.i.d. dataset S_m of size m.
3. Compute the optimal distribution Q on $\mathcal{H}$ that minimizes the error bound
$$\mathrm{KL}^{-1}\left(\hat{e}(Q, S_m) \middle| \frac{\mathrm{KL}(Q||P) + \log \frac{m}{\delta}}{m-1}\right). \quad (3)$$
4. Return the randomized classifier given by Q.

In all but the simplest scenarios, making predictions according to the optimal Q is intractable. However, we can attempt to approximate it.

3 PAC-BAYES BOUND OPTIMIZATION

Let H be a parametric family of classifiers and write h_w for $H(w, \cdot)$. We will interpret h_w as a neural network with (weight/bias) parameters $w \in \mathbb{R}^d$, although the development below is more general.

Fix $\delta \in (0,1)$ and a distribution P on $\mathbb{R}^d$, and let $S_m \sim \mu^m$ be m i.i.d. training examples. We aim to minimize the PAC-Bayes bound (Eq. (3)) with respect to Q.

For $w \in \mathbb{R}^d$ and $s \in \mathbb{R}^d_+$, let $\mathcal{N}_{w,s} = \mathcal{N}(w, \mathrm{diag}(s))$ denote the multivariate normal distribution with mean w and diagonal covariance $\mathrm{diag}(s)$. As our first simplifications, we replace the PAC-Bayes with the upper bound described by Eq. (2), replace the empirical loss with its convex surrogate, and restrict Q to the family of multivariate normal distributions with diagonal covariance structure, yielding the optimization problem

$$\min_{w \in \mathbb{R}^d, s \in \mathbb{R}^d_+} \breve{e}(\mathcal{N}_{w,s}, S_m) + \sqrt{\frac{\mathrm{KL}(\mathcal{N}_{w,s}||P) + \log \frac{m}{\delta}}{2(m-1)}}.$$

3.1 THE PRIOR

In order to obtain a KL divergence in closed form, we choose P to be multivariate normal. Symmetry considerations would suggest that we choose $P = \mathcal{N}(0, \lambda I)$ for some $\lambda > 0$, however there is no single good choice of λ. (We will also see that there are good reasons not to choose a zero mean, and so we will let w_0 denote the mean to be chosen a priori.)

In order to deal with the problem of choosing λ, we will follow Langford and Caruana [LC02] and use a union-bound argument to choose λ optimally from a discrete set, at the cost of a slight expansion to our generalization bound. In particular, we will take $\lambda = c\exp\{-j/b\}$ for some $j \in \mathbb{N}$ and fixed $b, c \geq 0$. (Hence, b determines a level of precision and c is an upper bound.) If the PAC-Bayes bound for each $j \in \mathbb{N}$ is designed to hold with probability at least $1 - \frac{6}{\pi^2 j^2}$, then, by the union bound (Theorem 2.1), it will hold uniformly for all $j \in \mathbb{N}$ with probability at least $1-\delta$, as desired.During optimization, we will want to avoid discrete optimization, and so we will treat λ as if it were a continuous variable. (We will then discretize λ when we evaluate the PAC-Bayes bound after the fact.) Solving for j, we have $j = b \log \frac{c}{\lambda}$, and so we will replace j with this term during optimization. Taking into account the choice of P and the continuous approximation to the union bound, we have the following minimization problem:

$$\min_{w \in \mathbb{R}^d, s \in \mathbb{R}^d_+, \lambda \in (0,c)} \breve{e}(\mathcal{N}_{w,s}, S_m) + \sqrt{\frac{1}{2} B_{\mathrm{RE}}(w, s, \lambda; \delta)} \quad (4)$$

where $B_{\mathrm{RE}}(w, s, \lambda; \delta)$ is

$$\frac{\mathrm{KL}(\mathcal{N}_{w,s}||\mathcal{N}(w_0, \lambda I)) + 2\log(b \log \frac{c}{\lambda}) + \log \frac{\pi^2 m}{6\delta}}{m-1}, \quad (5)$$

and, using Eq. (1), the KL term simplifies to

$$\frac{1}{2}\left(\frac{1}{\lambda}\|s\|_1 - d + \frac{1}{\lambda}\|w - w_0\|_2^2 + d \log \lambda - 1_d \cdot \log s\right).$$

We fix $\delta = 0.025$, $b = 100$, and $c = 0.1$.

3.2 STOCHASTIC GRADIENT DESCENT

We cannot optimize Eq. (4) directly because we cannot compute $\breve{e}(\mathcal{N}_{w,s}, S_m)$ or its gradients efficiently. We can, however, compute the gradient of the unbiased estimate $\breve{e}(h_{w+\xi\odot\sqrt{s}}, S_m)$, where $\xi \sim \mathcal{N}_{0,I_d}$. We will use an i.i.d. copy of ξ at each iteration. We did not experiment using mini-batches during bound optimization.

3.3 FINAL PAC-BAYES BOUND

While we treat λ as a continuous parameter during optimization, the union bound requires that λ be of the form $\lambda = c\exp\{-j/b\}$, for some $j \in \mathbb{N}$. We therefore round λ up or down, choosing that which delivers the best bound, as computed below.

According to the PAC-Bayes and union bound, with probability $1-\delta$, uniformly over all $w \in \mathbb{R}^d$, $s \in \mathbb{R}^d_+$, and λ of the form $c\exp\{-j/b\}$, for $j \in \mathbb{N}$, the error rate of the randomized classifier $Q = \mathcal{N}_{w,s}$ is bounded by

$$\mathrm{KL}^{-1}(\hat{e}(Q, S_m)|B_{\mathrm{RE}}(w, s, \lambda; \delta)).$$

We cannot compute this bound exactly because computing $\hat{e}(Q, S_m)$ is intractable. However, we can obtain unbiased estimates and apply the sample convergence bound (Theorem 2.2). In particular, given n i.i.d. samples $w_1, \ldots, w_n$ from Q, we produce the Monte Carlo approximation $\hat{Q}_n = \sum_{i=1}^{n} \delta_{w_i}$, for which $\hat{e}(\hat{Q}_n, S_m)$ is exactly computable, and obtain the bound

$$\begin{aligned}\hat{e}(Q, S_m) &\leq \overline{\hat{e}_{n,\delta'}}(Q, S_m) \\ &:= \mathrm{KL}^{-1}(\hat{e}(\hat{Q}_n, S_m)|n^{-1}\log 2/\delta'),\end{aligned}$$

which holds with probability $1-\delta'$. By another application of the union bound,

$$e(Q) \leq \mathrm{KL}^{-1}(\overline{\hat{e}_{n,\delta'}}(Q, S_m)|B_{\mathrm{RE}}(w, s, \lambda; \delta)), \quad (6)$$

with probability $1-\delta-\delta'$. We use this bound in our reported results.

4 EXPERIMENTS

Starting from neural networks whose weights have been trained by SGD (with momentum) to achieve near-perfect accuracy on a binary class variant of MNIST, we then optimize a PAC-Bayes bound on the error rate of stochastic neural network whose weights are random perturbations of the weights learned by SGD. We consider several different network architectures, varying both the depth and the width of the network.

4.1 DATASET

We use the MNIST handwritten digits data set [LCB10] as provided in Tensorflow [TF], where the dataset is split into the training set (55000 images) and test set (10000 images). (We do not use the validation set.) Each MNIST image is black and white and 28-pixels square, resulting in a network input dimension of $k = 784$. MNIST is usually treated as a multiclass classification problem. In order to use standard PAC-Bayes bounds, we produce a binary classification problem by mapping numbers $\{0, \ldots, 4\}$ to label 1 and $\{5, \ldots, 9\}$ to label -1. In some experiments, we train on random labels, i.e., binary labels drawn independently and uniformly at random.

4.2 INITIAL NETWORK TRAINING BY SGD

All experiments are performed on multilayer perceptrons, i.e., feed-forward neural networks with 2 or more layers, each layer fully connected to the previous and next layer. We choose a standard initialization scheme for the weights and biases: Weights are initialized randomly from a normal distribution (with mean zero and standard deviation $\sigma = 0.04$) that is truncated to $[-2\sigma, 2\sigma]$. Biases are initialized to a constant value of 0.1 for the first layer and 0 for the remaining layers. We let w_0 denote this random initialization of the weights (and biases).

We use REctified Linear Unit (RELU) activations at every hidden node. The last layer is linear. In order to train the weights, we minimize the logistic loss by SGD with momentum (learning rate 0.01; momentum 0.9). SGD is run in mini-batches of size 100. These settings are similar to those in [Zha+17].

On our binary class variant of MNIST, we train several neural network architectures of varying depth and width (see Table 1). In each case, we train for a total of 20 epochs. We also train a small network (with one 600-unit hidden layer) on *random* labels, in order to demonstrate the large capacity of the network. Obtaining ≈0 training error requires 120 epochs. See the first two rows of Table 1 for the train/test error rates.

4.3 PAC-BAYES BOUND OPTIMIZATION

Starting from weights w learned by SGD, we construct a stochastic neural network with a multivariate normal distribution $Q = \mathcal{N}_{w,s}$ over its weights with mean w and covariance $\mathrm{diag}(s)$. We initialize s to $|w|$ and $|w|/10$ for true- and random-label experiments, respectively.

We optimize the PAC-Bayes bound (Eq. (4)) starting from an initial choice of e^{-6} for the prior variance λ and the prior mean fixed at the random initialization w_0. (See Appendix B for a discussion of this subtle but important inno-

Experiment	T-600	T-1200	T-300^2	T-600^2	T-1200^2	T-600^3	R-600
Train error	0.001	0.002	0.000	0.000	0.000	0.000	0.007
Test error	0.018	0.018	0.015	0.016	0.015	0.013	0.508
SNN train error	0.028	0.027	0.027	0.028	0.029	0.027	0.112
SNN test error	0.034	0.035	0.034	0.033	0.035	0.032	0.503
PAC-Bayes bound	0.161	0.179	0.170	0.186	0.223	0.201	1.352
KL divergence	5144	5977	5791	6534	8558	7861	201131
# parameters	471k	943k	326k	832k	2384k	1193k	472k
VC dimension	26m	56m	26m	66m	187m	121m	26m

Table 1: Results for experiments on binary class variant of MNIST. SGD is either trained on (T) true labels or (R) random labels. The network architecture is expressed as N^L, indicating L hidden layers with N nodes each. Errors are classification error. The reported VC dimension is the best known upper bound (in millions) for ReLU networks. The SNN error rates are tight upper bounds (see text for details). The PAC-Bayes bounds upper bound the test error with probability 0.965.

vation.) We transform the constrained optimization over $w \in \mathbb{R}^d$, $s \in \mathbb{R}^d_+$, and $\lambda \in (0, c)$, into an unconstrained optimization over w, $\frac{1}{2}\log(s)$, and $\frac{1}{2}\log(\lambda)$, respectively.

We optimize the objective by gradient descent with the RMSprop optimizer (with decay 0.9, as is typical). We use the unbiased estimate of the gradient of the empirical surrogate error of the randomized classifier $Q = \mathcal{N}_{w,s}$. We set the learning rate to 0.001 for the first 150000 iterations, and then lower it to 0.0001 for the final 50000 iterations. For the random-label experiment, we optimize the bound with a smaller 0.0001 learning rate for 500000 iterations. In both cases, the learning rate is tuned so that the objective decreases smoothly during learning.

Algorithm 1 is pseudo code for optimizing the PAC-Bayes bound. The code implements vanilla SGD, although it can be easily modified to use an optimizer like RMSprop.

4.4 REPORTED VALUES

Reported error rates correspond to classification error. Train and test error rates are empirical averages for networks learned by SGD. In light of 10000 test data points and the observed error rates, upper bounds via Theorem 2.2 are only 0.005 higher.

Reported train and test error rates for the stochastic neural networks (abbreviated SNN) are upper bounds computed by an application of Theorem 2.2 as described in Section 3.3 with $\delta' = 0.01$ and $n = 150000$. These numbers produce estimates within 0.001–0.002.

The PAC-Bayes bound is computed as described in Section 3.3. Each bound holds with probability 0.965 over the choice of the training set and the draws from the learned SNN Q. For the random-label experiment, we report $\sqrt{\frac{1}{2}B_{\mathrm{RE}}(w, s, \lambda; \delta)}$ from Eq. (5), since the PAC-Bayes bound is vacuous when this quantity is greater than 1.

Our VC-dimension bounds for ReLU networks are computed from a formula communicated to us by Bartlett [Bar17]. These bounds are in $O(LW \log W)$, where L is the number of layers and W is the total number of tunable parameters across layers.

5 RESULTS

See Table 1. All SGD trained networks achieve perfect or near-perfect accuracy on the training data. On true labels, the SNN mean training error increases slightly as the weight distribution broadens to minimize the KL divergence. The SGD solution is close to mean of the SNN as measured with respect to the SNN covariance. (See Appendix C for a discussion.) For the random-label experiment, the SNN mean training error rises above 10%. Ideally, it might have risen to nearly 50%, while driving down the KL term to near zero.

The empirical test error of the SGD classifiers does not change much across the different architectures, despite the potential for overfitting. This phenomenon is well known, though still remarkable. For the random-label experiment, the empirical test classification error of 0.508 represents lack of generalization, as expected. The same two patterns hold for the SNN test error too, with slightly higher error rates.

Remarkably, the PAC-Bayes bounds do not grow much despite the networks becoming several times larger, and all true label experiments have classification error bounded by 0.23. (This observation is consistent with [NTS14].) Since larger networks possess many more symmetries, the true PAC-Bayes bounds for our learned stochastic neural network classifier might be substantially smaller. (See Appendix B for a discussion.) While these bounds

Algorithm 1 PAC-Bayes bound optimization by SGD

Input:

$w_0 \in \mathbb{R}^d$ ▷ Network parameters (random init.)

$w \in \mathbb{R}^d$ ▷ Network parameters (SGD solution)

S_m ▷ Training examples

$\delta \in (0,1)$ ▷ Confidence parameter

$b \in \mathbb{N}, c \in (0,1)$ ▷ Precision and bound for λ

$\tau \in (0,1), T$ ▷ Learning rate; # of iterations

Output: Optimal w, s, λ ▷ Weights, variances

procedure PAC-BAYES-SGD

  $\varsigma \leftarrow \text{abs}(w)$ ▷ where $s(\varsigma) = e^{2\varsigma}$

  $\varrho \leftarrow -3$ ▷ where $\lambda(\varrho) = e^{2\varrho}$

  $\text{B}(w, s, \lambda, w') = \check{e}(h_{w'}, S_m) + \sqrt{\tfrac{1}{2} B_{\text{RE}}(w, s, \lambda)}$

  for $t \leftarrow 1, T$ **do** ▷ Run SGD for T iterations.

    Sample $\xi \sim \mathcal{N}(0, I_d)$

    $w'(w, \varsigma) = w + \xi \odot \sqrt{s(\varsigma)}$

    ▷ Gradient step

$$\begin{bmatrix} w \\ \varsigma \\ \varrho \end{bmatrix} \mathrel{-}= \tau \begin{bmatrix} \nabla_w B(w, s(\varsigma), \lambda(\varrho), w'(w,\varsigma)) \\ \nabla_\varsigma B(w, s(\varsigma), \lambda(\varrho), w'(w,\varsigma)) \\ \nabla_\varrho B(w, s(\varsigma), \lambda(\varrho), w'(w,\varsigma)) \end{bmatrix}$$

  return $w, s(\varsigma), \lambda(\varrho)$

are several times larger than the test error estimated on held-out data (approximately, 0.03), they demonstrate nontrivial generalization. The PAC-Bayes bound for the random-label experiment is vacuous.

The VC-dimension upper bounds indicate that data independent bounds will be vacuous by several orders of magnitude. Because the number of parameters exceeds the available training data, lower bounds imply that generalization cannot be explained in a data independent way.

6 RELATED WORK

As we mention in the introduction, our approach scales the ideas in [HC93] and [LC02] to the modern deep learning regime where the networks have millions of parameters, but are trained on one or two orders of magnitude fewer training examples. The objective we optimize is an upper bound on the PAC-Bayes bound, which we know from the discussion in Section 2.2 will be very loose when the empirical classification error is approximately zero. Indeed, in that case, the PAC-Bayes bound is approximately

$$\hat{e}(\mathcal{N}_{w,s}, S_m) + \frac{\text{KL}(\mathcal{N}_{w,s} || P) + \log \frac{m}{\delta}}{(m-1)}. \quad (7)$$

The objective optimized by Hinton and Camp is of the same essential form as this one, except for the choice of squared error and different prior and posterior distributions. We explored using Eq. (7) as our objective with a surrogate loss, but it did not produce different results.

In the introduction we discuss the close connection of our work to several recent papers [Bal+15; Bal+16; Cha+17] that study "flat" or nonisolated minima on the account of their generalization and/or algorithmic properties.

Based on theoretical results for k-SAT that efficient algorithms find nonisolated solutions, Baldassi et al. [Bal+16] model efficient neural network learning algorithms as minimizers of a *replicated* version of the empirical loss surface, which emphasizes nonisolated minima and deemphasizes isolated minima. They then propose several algorithms for learning discrete neural networks using these ideas.

In follow-up work with Chaudhari, Choromanska, Soatto, and LeCun [Cha+17], they translate these ideas into the setting of continuously parametrized neural networks. They introduce an algorithm, called Entropy-SGD, which seeks out large regions of dense local minima: it maximizes the depth and flatness of the energy landscape. Their objective integrates both the energy of nearby parameters and the weighted distance to the parameters. In particular, rather than directly minimizing an error surface $w \mapsto L(h_w, S_m)$, they propose the following minimization problem over the so-called local-entropic loss:

$$\min_{w \in \mathbb{R}^d} \quad \log \mathop{\mathbb{E}}_{W \sim \mathcal{N}_{w,1/\gamma}} [C(\gamma) \exp\{-L(h_W, S_m)\}], \quad (8)$$

where $\gamma > 0$ is a parameter and $C(\gamma)$ a constant. In comparison, our algorithm can be interpreted as an optimization of the form

$$\min_{w \in \mathbb{R}^p, s \in \mathbb{R}^p_+} \quad \mathop{\mathbb{E}}_{W \sim \mathcal{N}_{w,s}} [L(h_W, S_m)] + R(w, s) \quad (9)$$

where R serves as a regularizer that accounts for the generalization error by, roughly speaking, trying to expand the axis-aligned ellipsoid $\{x \in \mathbb{R}^d : (w-x)^T \text{diag}(s)^{-1}(w-x) = 1\}$ and draw it closer to some point w_0 near the origin. Comparing Eqs. (8) and (9) highlights similarities and differences. The local-entropic loss is sensitive to the volume of the regions containing good solutions. While the first term in our objective function looks similar, it does not, on its own, account for the volume of regions. This role is played by the second term, which prefers large regions (but also ones near the initialization w_0). In our formulation, the first term is the empirical error of a stochastic neural network, which is precisely the term whose generalization error we are trying to bound. Entropy-SGD was not designed for the purpose of finding good stochastic neural networks, although it seems possible that having small local-entropic loss would lead to generalization for neural networks whose parameters are drawn from the local Gibbs distribution. Another difference is that, in our formulation, the diagonal covariance of the multivariate normal perturbation is learned adaptively, and driven by the goal of minimizing error. The shape of the normal perturbation is not learned, although the region whose volume is being measured is determined by the error surface, and it seems likely that this volume will be larger than that spanned by a multivariate Gaussian chosen to lie entirely in a region with good loss.

Chaudhari et al. [Cha+17] give an informal characterization of the generalization properties of local-entropic loss in Bayesian terms by comparing the marginal likelihood of two Bayesian priors centered at a solution with small and large local-entropic loss. Informally, a Bayesian prior centered on an isolated solution will lead to small marginal likelihood in contrast to one centered in a wide valley. They give a formal result relying on the uniform stability of SGD [HRS15] to show under some strong (and admittedly unrealistic) conditions that Entropy-SGD generalizes better than SGD. The key property is that the local-entropic loss surface is smoother than the original error surface.

Other authors have found evidence of the importance of "flat" minima: Recent work by Keskar, Mudigere, Nocedal, Smelyanskiy, and Tang [Kes+17] finds that large-batch methods tend to converge to sharp / isolated minima and have worse generalization performance compared to mini-batch algorithms, which tend to converge to flat minima and have good generalization performance. The bulk of their paper is devoted to the problem of restoring good generalization behavior to batch algorithms.

Finally, our algorithm also bears resemblance to *graduated optimization*, an approach toward non-convex optimization attributed to Blake and Zisserman [BZ87] whereby a sequence of increasingly fine-grained versions of an optimization problem are solved in succession. (See [HLS16] and references therein.) In this context, Eq. (8) is the result of a local smoothing operation acting on the objective function $w \mapsto \breve{\ell}(h_w, S_M)$. In graduate optimization, the effect of the local smoothing operation would be decreased over time, eventually disappearing. In our formulation, the act of balancing the empirical loss and generalization error serve to drive the evolution of the local smoothing in an adaptive fashion. Moreover, in the limit, the local smoothing does not vanish in our algorithm, as the volume spanned by the perturbations relates to the generalization error. Our results suggest that SGD solutions live inside relatively large volumes, and so perhaps SGD can be understood in terms of graduated optimization.

7 CONCLUSION AND FUTURE WORK

We obtain nonvacuous generalization bounds for deep neural networks with millions of parameters trained on 55000 MNIST examples. These bounds are obtained by optimizing an objective derived from the PAC-Bayes bound, starting from the solution produced by SGD. Despite the weights changing, the SGD solution remains well within the 1% ellipsoidal quantile, i.e., the volume spanned by the stochastic neural network contains the original SGD solution. (When labels are randomized, however, optimizing the PAC-Bayes bound causes the solution to shift considerably.)

Our experiments look only at fully connected feed forward networks trained on a binary class variant of MNIST. It would be interesting to see if the results extend to multiclass classification, to other data sets, and to other types of architectures, especially convolutional ones.

Our PAC-Bayes bound can be tightened in several ways. Highly dependent weights constrain the size of the axis-aligned ellipsoid representing the stochastic neural network. We can potentially recognize small populations of highly dependent weights, and optimize their covariance parameters, rather than enforcing independence in the posterior.

One might also consider replacing the multivariate normal posterior with a distribution that is more tuned to the loss surface. One promising avenue is to follow the lines of Chaudhari et al. [Cha+17] and consider (local) Gibbs distributions. If the solutions obtained by minimizing the local-entropic loss are flatter than those obtained by SGD, than we may be able to demonstrate quantitatively tighter bounds.

Finally, there is the hard work of understanding the generalization properties of SGD. In light of our work, it may be useful to start by asking whether SGD finds solutions in flat minima. Such solutions could then be lifted to stochastic neural networks with good generalization properties. Going from stochastic networks back to deterministic ones may require additional structure.

Acknowledgments This research was carried out while the authors were visiting the Simons Institute for the Theory of Computing at UC Berkeley. The authors would like to thank Peter Bartlett, Shai Ben-David, Dylan Foster, Matus Telgarsky, and Ruth Urner for helpful discussions. GKD is supported by an EPSRC studentship. DMR is supported by an NSERC Discovery Grant, Connaught Award, and U.S. Air Force Office of Scientific Research grant #FA9550-15-1-0074.

REFERENCES

[Bal+15] C. Baldassi, A. Ingrosso, C. Lucibello, L. Saglietti, and R. Zecchina. "Subdominant Dense Clusters Allow for Simple Learning and High Computational Performance in Neural Networks with Discrete Synapses". *Phys. Rev. Lett.* 115 (12 Sept. 2015), p. 128101.

[Bal+16] C. Baldassi, C. Borgs, J. T. Chayes, A. Ingrosso, C. Lucibello, L. Saglietti, and R. Zecchina. "Unreasonable effectiveness of learning neural networks: From accessible states and robust ensembles to basic algorithmic schemes". *Proceedings of the National Academy of Sciences* 113.48 (2016), E7655–E7662. eprint: http://www.pnas.org/content/113/48/E7655.full.pdf.

[Bar17] P. L. Bartlett. "The impact of the nonlinearity on the VC-dimension of a deep network". Preprint. 2017.

[Bar97] P. L. Bartlett. "For valid generalization the size of the weights is more important than the size of the network". In: *Advances in Neural Information Processing Systems*. 1997, pp. 134–140.

[Bar98] P. L. Bartlett. "The sample complexity of pattern classification with neural networks: the size of the weights is more important than the size of the network". *IEEE transactions on Information Theory* 44.2 (1998), pp. 525–536.

[BM02] P. L. Bartlett and S. Mendelson. "Rademacher and Gaussian complexities: Risk bounds and structural results". *Journal of Machine Learning Research* 3.Nov (2002), pp. 463–482.

[BZ87] A. Blake and A. Zisserman. *Visual Reconstruction*. Cambridge, MA, USA: MIT Press, 1987.

[Cha+17] P. Chaudhari, A. Choromanska, S. Soatto, Y. LeCun, C. Baldassi, C. Borgs, J. Chayes, L. Sagun, and R. Zecchina. "Entropy-SGD: Biasing Gradient Descent Into Wide Valleys". In: *International Conference on Learning Representations (ICLR)*. 2017. arXiv: 1611.01838v4 [cs.LG].

[Grü07] P. D. Grünwald. *The minimum description length principle*. MIT press, 2007.

[HC93] G. E. Hinton and D. van Camp. "Keeping the Neural Networks Simple by Minimizing the Description Length of the Weights". In: *Proceedings of the Sixth Annual Conference on Computational Learning Theory*. COLT '93. Santa Cruz, California, USA: ACM, 1993, pp. 5–13.

[HLS16] E. Hazan, K. Y. Levy, and S. Shalev-Shwartz. "On Graduated Optimization for Stochastic Non-Convex Problems". In: *Proceedings of the 33rd International Conference on Machine Learning (ICML)*. 2016, pp. 1833–1841.

[HRS15] M. Hardt, B. Recht, and Y. Singer. "Train faster, generalize better: Stability of stochastic gradient descent". *CoRR* abs/1509.01240 (2015).

[HS97] S. Hochreiter and J. Schmidhuber. "Flat Minima". *Neural Comput.* 9.1 (Jan. 1997), pp. 1–42.

[Kes+17] N. S. Keskar, D. Mudigere, J. Nocedal, M. Smelyanskiy, and P. T. P. Tang. "On Large-Batch Training for Deep Learning: Generalization Gap and Sharp Minima". In: *International Conference on Learning Representations (ICLR)*. 2017. arXiv: 1609.04836v2 [cs.LG].

[KP02] V. Koltchinskii and D. Panchenko. "Empirical margin distributions and bounding the generalization error of combined classifiers". *Annals of Statistics* (2002), pp. 1–50.

[Lan02] J. Langford. "Quantitatively tight sample complexity bounds". Carnegie Mellon University, 2002.

[LC02] J. Langford and R. Caruana. "(Not) Bounding the True Error". In: *Advances in Neural Information Processing Systems 14*. Ed. by T. G. Dietterich, S. Becker, and Z. Ghahramani. MIT Press, 2002, pp. 809–816.

[LCB10] Y. LeCun, C. Cortes, and C. J. C. Burges. *MNIST handwritten digit database*. http://yann.lecun.com/exdb/mnist/. 2010.

[LS01] J. Langford and M. Seeger. *Bounds for Averaging Classifiers*. Tech. rep. CMU-CS-01-102. Carnegie Mellon University, 2001.

[McA99] D. A. McAllester. "PAC-Bayesian Model Averaging". In: *Proceedings of the Twelfth Annual Conference on Computational Learning Theory*. COLT '99. Santa Cruz, California, USA: ACM, 1999, pp. 164–170.

[NSS15] B. Neyshabur, R. Salakhutdinov, and N. Srebro. "Path-SGD: Path-Normalized Optimization in Deep Neural Networks". In: *Advances in Neural Information Processing Systems*. Vol. 28. NIPS. 2015. arXiv: 1506.02617v1 [cs.LG].

[NTS14] B. Neyshabur, R. Tomioka, and N. Srebro. *In Search of the Real Inductive Bias: On the Role of Implicit Regularization in Deep Learning*. Workshop track poster at ICLR 2015. 2014. arXiv: 1412.6614v4 [cs.LG].

[NTS15] B. Neyshabur, R. Tomioka, and N. Srebro. "Norm-based capacity control in neural networks". In: *Proceedings of the Eigth Annual Conference on Learning Theory*. COLT 2016. 2015, pp. 1376–1401. arXiv: 1503.00036v2 [cs.LG].

[Ris83] J. Rissanen. "A Universal Prior for Integers and Estimation by Minimum Description Length". *Ann. Statist.* 11.2 (June 1983), pp. 416–431.

[TF] M. Abadi, A. Agarwal, P. Barham, E. Brevdo, Z. Chen, C. Citro, G. S. Corrado, A. Davis, J. Dean, M. Devin, S. Ghemawat, I. Goodfellow, A. Harp, G. Irving, M. Isard, Y. Jia, R. Jozefowicz, L. Kaiser, M. Kudlur, J. Levenberg, D. Mané, R. Monga, S. Moore, D. Murray, C. Olah, M. Schuster, J. Shlens, B. Steiner, I. Sutskever, K. Talwar, P. Tucker, V. Vanhoucke, V. Vasudevan, F. Viégas, O. Vinyals, P. Warden, M. Wattenberg, M. Wicke, Y. Yu, and X. Zheng. *TensorFlow: Large-Scale Machine Learning on Heterogeneous Systems*. Software available from tensorflow.org. 2015.

[Zha+17] C. Zhang, S. Bengio, M. Hardt, B. Recht, and O. Vinyals. "Understanding deep learning requires rethinking generalization". In: *International Conference on Representation Learning (ICLR)*. 2017. arXiv: 1611.03530v2 [cs.LG].

A APPROXIMATING $\mathrm{KL}^{-1}(Q|C)$

There is no simple formula for $\mathrm{KL}^{-1}(q|c)$, but we can approximate it via root-finding techniques. For all $q \in (0,1)$ and $c \geq 0$, define $h_{q,c}(p) = \mathrm{KL}(q||p) - c$. Then $h'_{q,c}(p) = \frac{1-q}{1-p} - \frac{q}{p}$. Given a sufficiently good initial estimate p_0 of a root of $h_{q,c}(\cdot)$, we can obtain improved estimates of a root via Newton's method:

$$p_{n+1} = \mathrm{N}(p_n; q, c) \text{ where } \mathrm{N}(p; q, c) = p - \frac{h_{q,c}(c)}{h'_{q,c}(p)}.$$

This suggests the following approximation to $\mathrm{KL}^{-1}(q|c)$:

1. Let $\tilde{b} = q + \sqrt{\frac{c}{2}}$.
2. If $\tilde{b} \geq 1$, then return 1.
3. Otherwise, return $\mathrm{N}^k(\tilde{b})$, for some integer $k > 0$.

Our reported results use five steps of Newton's method.

B NETWORK SYMMETRIES

In an ideal world, we would account for all the network symmetries when computing the KL divergence in the PAC-Bayes bound. However, it does not seem to be computationally feasible to account for the symmetries, as we discuss below. Given this, it makes sense to try to break the symmetries somehow. Indeed, one consequence of randomly initializing a neural network's weights is that some symmetries are broken. If we do not expect SGD to reverse (many of) these symmetries, then the initial weight configuration, w_0, will be a better mean for the PAC-Bayes prior P than the origin. In fact, breaking symmetries in this way lead to much better bounds than setting the means to zero.

B.1 BOUNDS FROM MIXTURES

Fix a neural network architecture $H : \mathbb{R}^d \times \mathbb{R}^k \to \{-1, 1\}$ and write h_w for $H(w, \cdot)$. It has long been appreciated that distinct parametrizations $w, w' \in \mathbb{R}^d$ can lead to the same *functions* $h_w = h_{w'}$, and so the set $\mathcal{H} = \{h_w : w \in \mathbb{R}^d\}$ of classifiers defined by a neural network architecture is a quotient space of $\mathbb{R}^d$.

For the purposes of understanding the generalization error of neural networks, we would ideally work directly with $\mathcal{H}$. Let P, Q be a distributions on $\mathbb{R}^d$, i.e., stochastic neural networks. Then P and Q induce distributions on $\mathcal{H}$, which we will denote by $\bar{P}$ and $\bar{Q}$, respectively. For the purposes of the PAC-Bayes bound, it is the KL divergence $\mathrm{KL}(\bar{Q}||\bar{P})$ that upper bounds the performance of the stochastic neural network Q. In general, $\mathrm{KL}(\bar{Q}||\bar{P}) \leq \mathrm{KL}(Q||P)$, but it is difficult in practice to approximate the former because the quotient space is extremely complex.

One potential way to approach $\mathcal{H}$ is to account for symmetries in the parameterization. A *network symmetry* is a map $\sigma : \mathbb{R}^d \to \mathbb{R}^d$ such that, for all $w \in \mathbb{R}^d$, we have $h_w = h_{\sigma(w)}$. As an example of such a symmetry, in a fully connected network with identical activation functions at every unit, the function computed by the network is invariant to permuting the nodes with a hidden layer. Let $\mathbb{S}$ be any finite set of symmetries possessed by the architecture. For every distribution Q on $\mathbb{R}^d$ and network symmetry σ, we may define $Q_\sigma = Q \circ \sigma^{-1}$ to be the distribution over networks obtained by first sampling network parameters from Q and then applying the map σ to obtain a network that computes the same function.

Define $Q^{\mathbb{S}} = \frac{1}{|\mathbb{S}|} \sum_{\sigma \in \mathbb{S}} Q_\sigma$. Informally, Q and $Q^{\mathbb{S}}$ are identical when viewed as distributions on functions, yet $Q^{\mathbb{S}}$ spreads its mass evenly over equivalent parametrizations. In particular, for any data set S, we have $\hat{e}(Q, S) = \hat{e}(Q^{\mathbb{S}}, S)$. We call $Q^{\mathbb{S}}$ a symmetrized version of Q. The following lemma states that symmetrized versions always have smaller KL divergence with respect to distributions that are invariant to symmetrization: Before stating the lemma, recall that the differential entropy of an absolutely continuous distribution Q on $\mathbb{R}^d$ with density q is $\int q(x) \log q(x) \mathrm{d}x \in \mathbb{R} \cup \{-\infty, \infty\}$.

Lemma B.1. *Let $\mathbb{S}$ be a finite set of network symmetries, let P be an absolutely continuous distribution such that $P = P_\sigma$ for all $\sigma \in \mathbb{S}$, and define $Q^{\mathbb{S}}$ as above for some arbitrary absolutely continuous distribution Q on $\mathbb{R}^d$ with finite differential entropy. Then* $\mathrm{KL}(Q^{\mathbb{S}}||P) = \mathrm{KL}(Q||P) - \mathrm{KL}(Q||Q^{\mathbb{S}}) \leq \mathrm{KL}(Q||P)$.

The above lemma can be generalized to distributions over (potentially infinite) sets of network symmetries.

It follows from this lemma that one can do no worse by accounting for symmetries using mixtures, provided that one is comparing to a distribution P that is invariant to those symmetries. In light of the PAC-Bayes theorem, this means that a generalization bound based upon a KL divergence that does not account for symmetries can likely be improved. However, for a finite set $\mathbb{S}$ of symmetries, it is easy to show that the improvement is bounded by $\log |\mathbb{S}|$, which suggests that, in order to obtain appreciable improvements in a numerical bound, one would need to account for an exponential number of symmetries. Unfortunately, exploiting this many symmetries seems intractable. It is hard to obtain useful lower bounds to $\mathrm{KL}(Q||Q^{\mathbb{S}})$, while upper bounds from Jensen's inequality lead to negative (hence vacuous) lower bounds on $\mathrm{KL}(Q^{\mathbb{S}}||P)$.

In this work, we therefore take a different approach to dealing with symmetries. Neural networks are randomly initialized in order to *break* symmetries. Combined with the idea that the learned parameters will reflect these broken symmetries, we choose our prior P to be located at the random initialization, rather than at zero.

C COMPARING WEIGHTS BEFORE AND AFTER PAC-BAYES OPTIMIZATION

In the course of optimizing the PAC-Bayes bound, we allow the mean w to deviate from the SGD solution w_{SGD} that serves as the starting point. This is necessary to obtain bounds as tight as those that we computed. Do the weights change much during optimization of the bound? How would we measure this change?

To answer these questions, we calculated the p-value of the SGD solution under the distribution of the stochastic neural network.

Let Q_{SNN} denote the distribution obtained by optimizing the PAC-Bayes bound, write w_{SNN} and Σ_{SNN} for its mean and covariance, and let $\|w\|_{\Sigma_{\text{SNN}}} = w^T \Sigma_{\text{SNN}}^{-1} w$ denote the induced norm. Using 10000 samples, we estimated

$$\mathbb{P}_{w \sim Q_{\text{SNN}}} \Big(\|w - w_{\text{SNN}}\|_{\Sigma_{\text{SNN}}} < \|w_{\text{SGD}} - w_{\text{SNN}}\|_{\Sigma_{\text{SNN}}} \Big).$$

The estimate was 0 for all true label experiments, i.e., w_{SGD} is less extreme of a perturbation of w_{SNN} than a typical perturbation. For the random-label experiments, w_{SNN} and w_{SGD} differ significantly, which is consistent with the bound being optimized in the face of random labels.

D EVALUATING RADEMACHER ERROR BOUNDS

Fix a class $\mathcal{F}$ of measurable functions from $\mathbb{R}^D$ to $\mathbb{R}$ and let $\mathcal{R}_m(\mathcal{F})$ denote the Rademacher complexity of $\mathcal{F}$ associated with m i.i.d. samples. For $h \in \mathcal{F}$, we will obtain binary classifications (and measure error and empirical error) by computing the sign of its output, i.e., by thresholding. The following error bound is a straightforward adaptation of [BM02, Thm. 7], which is itself an adaptation of [KP02, Thm. 2].

Theorem D.1. *For every $L > 0$, with probability at least $1 - \delta$ over the choice of $S_m \sim \mu^m$, for all $h \in \mathcal{F}$,*

$$e(h) \leq \hat{e}(h, S_m, L) + 2L\mathcal{R}_m(\mathcal{F}) + \sqrt{\frac{\log(\frac{2}{\delta})}{2m}}, \quad (10)$$

where

$$\hat{e}(h, S_m, L) = \frac{1}{m} \sum_{i=1}^{m} \max(\min(1 - L y_i h(x_i), 1), 0).$$

In order to compute these bounds, we must compute (bounds on) the Rademacher complexity of appropriate function classes. To that end, we will use results by Neyshabur, Tomioka, and Srebro [NTS15] for ReLU networks (i.e., multilayer perceptrons with ReLU activations).

Let w be the weights of a ReLU network and let $w_{i,j}^{(k)}$ denote the weight associated with the edge from neuron i in layer $k-1$ to neuron j in layer k. Neyshabur, Tomioka, and Srebro [NTS15] define the ℓ_1 path norm

$$\phi_1(w) = \sum_j \Big[|w_{j,1}^{(2)}| \sum_i |w_{i,j}^{(1)}| \Big], \quad (11)$$

stated here in the special case of a 2-layer network with 1 output neuron. For any number of layers, the path norm can be computed easily in a forward pass, requiring only a matrix–vector product at each layer.

Neyshabur, Tomioka, and Srebro also provide the follow Rademacher bound in terms of the path norm:

Theorem D.2 ([NTS15, Cor. 7]). *Given m datapoints $x_1, \ldots, x_m \in \mathbb{R}^D$, the Rademacher complexity of the class of depth-d ReLU networks, whose ℓ_1 path norms are bounded by ϕ, is no greater than*

$$2^d \phi \sqrt{\frac{\log(2D)}{m}} \max_i \|x_i\|_\infty. \quad (12)$$

Let $w_j^{(k)}$ for the jth column of $w^{(j)}$, i.e., the vector of weights for edges from layer $k-1$ to neuron j in layer k. The ℓ_1 path norm is closely related to the norm

$$\gamma_{1,\infty}(w) = \prod_{i=1}^{d} \max_j \|w_j^{(k)}\|_1.$$

If the upper bound ϕ appearing in the bound of Theorem D.2 is instead taken to be a bound on $\gamma_{1,\infty}(w)$, then one essentially obtains the Gaussian complexity bounds for neural networks established by Bartlett and Mendelson [BM02] and Koltchinskii and Panchenko [KP02]. However, their bounds apply only to networks with bounded activation functions, ruling out ReLU networks.

Regardless, the path-norm bound is tighter for ReLU networks. In order to establish the connection, let $\mathcal{W}(w)$ denote the set of all weights w' obtained from redistributing the weights w across layers, i.e., by multiplying the weights $w^{(k-1)}$ in a layer by a constant $c > 0$ and multiplying the weights in the subsequent layer $w^{(k)}$ by c^{-1}. Note that the function computed by a ReLU network is invariant to this transformation. This is the key insight of Neyshabur, Tomioka, and Srebro. Obviously, $\phi_1(w) = \phi_1(w')$ for all $w' \in \mathcal{W}(w)$. Neyshabur, Tomioka, and Srebro show that $\phi_1(w) = \inf_{w' \in \mathcal{W}(w)} \gamma_{1,\infty}(w')$, and so the path norm better captures the complexity of a ReLU network.

In our experiments, we will compute the bound obtained by combining Theorems D.1 and D.2.

Note that the constant L in Theorem D.1 must be chosen independently of the data S_m. As in the original result [KP02, Thm. 2], one can use a union bound to allow oneself to choose L based on the data in order to minimize the bound. Even though the effect of this change is usually (relatively) small, its magnitude depends on the particular weight function employed in the union bound. Instead, we will apply the bound with an optimized L, yielding an optimistic bound (formally, a lower bound on any upper bound obtained from a union bound). We optimize L over a grid of values, and handle the vacuous edge cases analytically. Nevertheless, we will see even the resulting (optimistic) bound is vacuous.

D.1 EXPERIMENT DETAILS

We use SGD to train a two-layer 600-hidden-unit ReLU network on the same binary class variant of MNIST used to evaluate our PAC-Bayes bounds. We set the global learning rate to 0.005. As in our PAC-Bayes experiments, we optimize the average logistic loss during training. The random initializations commonly used for ReLU networks lead to initial path norms that produce vacuous error bounds. In order to visualize the behavior of the path-norm bound under SGD, we reduce the standard deviation of the truncated-normal initialization from 0.04 to 0.0001. As before, we use mini-batches of 100 training examples, yielding 550 iterations per epoch.

For comparison, we also train the same network architecture while explicitly regularizing the path norm. (Neyshabur, Salakhutdinov, and Srebro [NSS15] propose training neural networks via steepest descent with respect to the path norm. We leave this comparison to future work.)

D.2 RESULTS

When the network is trained by optimizing the logistic cost function without regularization, the error bound becomes vacuous within a fraction of a single epoch. This occurs before the training error dips appreciable below chance. The bound's behavior is due to the path norm diverging. While the level sets $\hat{e}(h, S, \cdot)^{-1}$ of the empirical margin distribution are growing, they are not growing fast enough to counteract the growth of the path norm. (See the left column of Fig. 1.)

When the network is trained with explicit path-norm regularization, we obtain vacuous error bounds, unless we apply excessive amounts of regularization. We report results when the regularization parameter is 0.01 and 0.05. Both settings are clearly too large, as evidenced by the training error converging to ~20% and ~30%, respectively. A cursory study of overall ℓ_1 and ℓ_2 regularization produced qualitatively similar results. Further study is necessary.

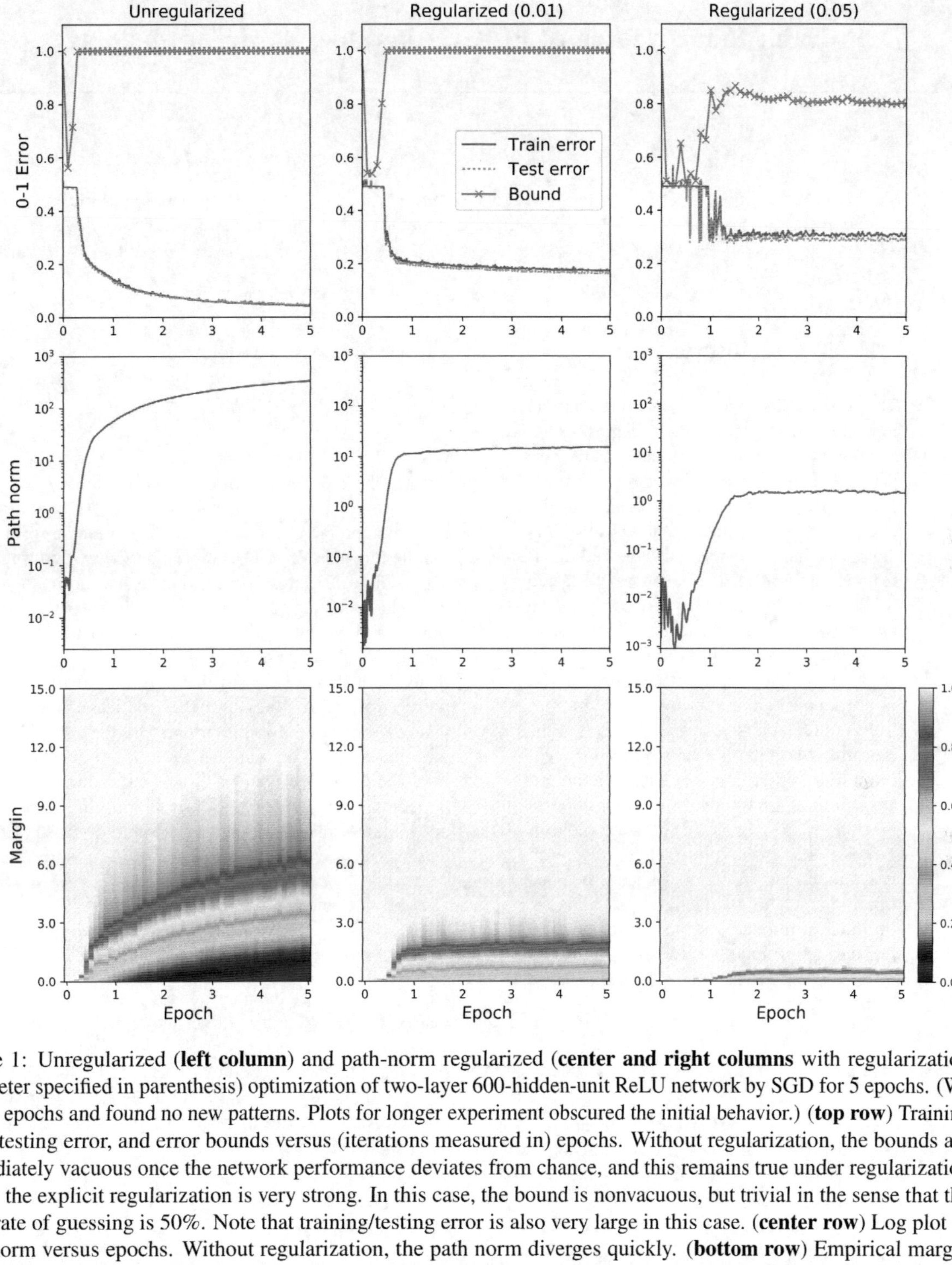

Figure 1: Unregularized (**left column**) and path-norm regularized (**center and right columns** with regularization parameter specified in parenthesis) optimization of two-layer 600-hidden-unit ReLU network by SGD for 5 epochs. (We ran 20 epochs and found no new patterns. Plots for longer experiment obscured the initial behavior.) (**top row**) Training error, testing error, and error bounds versus (iterations measured in) epochs. Without regularization, the bounds are immediately vacuous once the network performance deviates from chance, and this remains true under regularization unless the explicit regularization is very strong. In this case, the bound is nonvacuous, but trivial in the sense that the error rate of guessing is 50%. Note that training/testing error is also very large in this case. (**center row**) Log plot of path norm versus epochs. Without regularization, the path norm diverges quickly. (**bottom row**) Empirical margin distributions versus epochs. The margin that attains a fixed average loss is growing, but not rapidly enough to counteract the rapidly increasing path norm.

Provable Inductive Robust PCA via Iterative Hard Thresholding

U.N. Niranjan*
Microsoft Corporation

Arun Rajkumar†
Conduent Labs India

Theja Tulabandhula‡
University of Illinois Chicago

Abstract

The robust PCA problem, wherein, given an input data matrix that is the superposition of a low-rank matrix and a sparse matrix, we aim to separate out the low-rank and sparse components, is a well-studied problem in machine learning. One natural question that arises is that, as in the inductive setting, if features are provided as input as well, can we hope to do better? Answering this in the affirmative, the main goal of this paper is to study the robust PCA problem while incorporating feature information. In contrast to previous works in which recovery guarantees are based on the convex relaxation of the problem, we propose a simple iterative algorithm based on hard-thresholding of appropriate residuals. Under weaker assumptions than previous works, we prove the global convergence of our iterative procedure; moreover, it admits a much faster convergence rate and lesser computational complexity per iteration. In practice, through systematic synthetic and real data simulations, we confirm our theoretical findings regarding improvements obtained by using feature information.

1 INTRODUCTION

Principal Component Analysis (PCA) (Pearson, 1901) is a very fundamental and ubiquitous technique for unsupervised learning and dimensionality reduction; basically, this involves finding the best low-rank approximation to the given data matrix. To be precise, one common formulation of PCA is the following:

$$\widehat{L} = \arg\min_{L} \|M - L\|_F \quad \text{s.t. } \operatorname{rank}(L) \leq r \tag{1}$$

where $M \in \mathbb{R}^{n_1 \times n_2}$ is the input data matrix, where $\|.\|_F$ denotes the Frobenius norm of a matrix and $1 \leq r \leq \min(n_1, n_2)$. It is well-known that the constrained optimization problem given by Equation (1) can be solved via the Singular Value Decomposition (SVD) and truncating the resultant decomposition to the top-r singular values and singular vectors yields the optimal solution (Eckart & Young, 1936). While this machine learning technique has umpteen number of applications, one of its main shortcomings is that it is not robust to the presence of gross outliers since the optimization involves just an ℓ_2 objective. To address this issue, the *robust PCA* technique – given M such that $M = L^* + S^*$, our aim is to find L^* and S^* which are low-rank and sparse matrix components respectively – was developed. Precisely, one hopes to solve the following problem (or its equivalent formulations):

$$\{\widehat{L}, \widehat{S}\} = \arg\min_{L,S} \|M - L - S\|_F \quad \text{s.t. } \operatorname{rank}(L) \leq r, \quad \|S\|_0 \leq z_0 \tag{2}$$

where $\|.\|_0$ denotes the number of non-zero entries in a matrix, $0 \leq r \leq \min(n_1, n_2)$ and $0 \leq z_0 \leq n_1 n_2$. While Equation (2) may not be always well-posed, under certain identifiability conditions, many recent works over the past decade have advanced our understanding of this problem; we briefly recap some of the existing relevant results in Section 1.2.

1.1 ROBUST INDUCTIVE LEARNING: MOTIVATION

A key point to be noted is that Equation (2) does not incorporate feature information; this is the so-called *transductive* setting. In practical applications, we often have

*Part of work done while at the University of California Irvine and at Xerox Research Centre India.

†Part of work done while at Xerox Research Centre India.

‡Part of work done while at Xerox Research Centre India.

Table 1: Comparison of this work to previous robust PCA works. For simplicity and brevity, we let $n_1 = n_2 = n$ and $d_1 = d_2 = d$; let the number of non-zeros per row/column of S^* be z and the number of non-zero entries in S^* be m; we use $\widetilde{O}$ to suppress log factors. Note that we consider the practically important regime of $d \ll n$.

Work	Features	Approach	Incoherence	Sparsity	Corruption	Comp. complexity
(Candès *et al.* , 2011)	✗	Convex	Strong	Random	$m = O(n^2), r = \widetilde{O}(n)$	$O(\frac{n^3}{\sqrt{\epsilon}})$
(Hsu *et al.* , 2011)	✗	Convex	Weak	Deterministic	$z = O(\frac{n}{r})$	$O(\frac{n^3}{\sqrt{\epsilon}})$
(Netrapalli *et al.* , 2014)	✗	Non-convex	Weak	Deterministic	$z = O(\frac{n}{r})$	$O(r^2 n^2 \log(\frac{1}{\epsilon}))$
(Yi *et al.* , 2016)	✗	Non-convex	Weak	Deterministic	$z = O(\frac{n}{r^{1.5}})$	$O(rn^2 \log(\frac{1}{\epsilon}))$
(Chiang *et al.* , 2016)	✓	Convex	Strong	Random	$m = O(n^2), r = \widetilde{O}(\frac{n^2}{d})$	$O(\frac{dn^2+d^3}{\sqrt{\epsilon}})$
This work	✓	Non-convex	Weak	Deterministic	$z = O(\frac{n}{d})$	$O((dn^2 + d^2 r) \log(\frac{1}{\epsilon}))$

feature information available in the form of feature matrices F_1 and F_2. In the low-rank matrix recovery literature, this is often incorporated as a bilinear form, $L^* = F_1^\top W^* F_2$, which models the feature interactions via the latent space characterized by matrix $W^* \in \mathbb{R}^{d_1 \times d_2}$; this is the so-called *inductive* setting. We now present a motivating real-life situation.

Example 1.1 (Using features for collaborative filtering with grossly corrupted observations). *In recommendation systems, it is often the case that we have user-product ratings matrix along with side information in the form of features corresponding to each user and product. It is common in large-scale machine learning applications that the number of products and users is very large compared to the features available for each user or product. Though a user might not have used a product, we would like to infer how the user might rate that product given the user and product features – unlike the transductive setting this is possible in, and is a key application of, the inductive learning setting. Moreover, the ratings matrix is subject to various kinds of noise including erasures and outliers – in this work, we consider a general noise model using which robust recovery of ratings is possible.*

It is the goal of this paper to focus on the practically useful regime of $\max(d_1, d_2) \ll \min(n_1, n_2)$.

1.2 RELATED WORK

We now present the related work in both transductive and inductive settings.

Transductive setting: This is the relatively more well-explored setting. There are two main solution approaches that have been considered in the literature namely, the convex and the non-convex methods.

Convex methods entail understanding the properties of the convex relaxation of Equation (2) given by:

$$\{\widehat{L}, \widehat{S}\} = \arg\min_{L,S} \|L\|_* + \lambda \|S\|_1 \quad \text{s.t. } M = L + S \tag{3}$$

The works of (Chandrasekaran *et al.* , 2011) and (Hsu *et al.* , 2011) characterize the recovery properties of the convex program assuming a weak deterministic assumption on the support of the sparse matrix that the fraction of corrupted entries; the tightest bounds are that this fraction scales as $O(1/r)$. Under a stronger model of the sparse matrix namely, uniformly sampled support, (Candès *et al.* , 2011) show that it is possible to have $r = O(n/\log(n))$ when $z_0 = O(n^2)$ for exact recovery with high probability. Numerically, the convex program in Equation (3) is most commonly solved by variants of sub-gradient descent (involving iterative soft-thresholding); the convergence rate known for trace-norm programs is $O(1/\sqrt{\epsilon})$ (Ji & Ye, 2009) for an ϵ-close solution.

The underlying theme in non-convex methods involves retaining the formulation in Equation (2), starting with a suitable initialization and performing alternating projections onto non-convex sets (involving iterative hard-thresholding) until convergence. The work of (Netrapalli *et al.* , 2014) provides recovery guarantees under the weaker deterministic support assumptions matching the conditions of (Hsu *et al.* , 2011). However, the computational complexity of their algorithm scales with rank quadratically – to improve this, (Yi *et al.* , 2016) propose a (non-convex) projected gradient approach while paying a cost in the permissible number of sparse corruptions, i.e., $O(1/r^{1.5})$ as opposed to $O(1/r)$. A consequence of the analysis of these non-convex methods is that they admit a faster convergence rate – specifically, $O(\log(1/\epsilon))$ iterations for an ϵ-close solution – as opposed to convex methods.

It is noteworthy that the matrix completion problem (see, for instance, (Recht, 2011) and (Jain & Netrapalli, 2014)), where the goal is to recover an incomplete low-rank matrix, is a special case of the robust PCA problem where S^* is taken to be $-L^*$ for the non-observed entries. Finally, we note that the robust PCA problem has been invoked in several applications including topic modeling (Min *et al.* , 2010), object detection (Li *et al.* , 2004) and so on.

Inductive setting: To the best of our knowledge, currently, there is only one other work due to (Chiang *et al.* , 2016) which considers the robust PCA problem in the inductive setting and presents a guaranteed convex optimization procedure for solving it; incorporating additional feature information into the robust PCA problem, they solve the following convex program, known as *PCPF*:

$$\{\widehat{W}, \widehat{S}\} = \arg\min_{W,S} \|W\|_* + \lambda \|S\|_1 \quad \text{s.t. } M = F_1^\top W F_2 + S \tag{4}$$

For this paragraph, let $m := \|S^*\|_0$, $W^* = U_{W^*}\Sigma_{W^*}V_{W^*}^\top$ be the SVD of W^*, $F_1F_1^\top = I$, $F_2F_2^\top = I$ and e_i denote the ith standard basis vector in $\mathbb{R}^n$; the key recovery guarantee states that $r = O(n^2/d\log(n)\log(d))$ and $m = O(n^2)$; most notably, these guarantees are derived under stronger assumptions namely, (1) strong incoherence property, i.e., $\|U_{W^*}V_{W^*}^\top\|_\infty \leq \mu\sqrt{r/n_1n_2}$, $\max_j \|U_{W^*}^\top F_1 e_j\|_2 \leq \mu_0\sqrt{r/n_1}$, $\max_j \|V_{W^*}^\top F_2 e_j\|_2 \leq \mu_0\sqrt{r/n_2}$, $\max_j \|F_1 e_j\|_2 \leq \mu_{F_1}\sqrt{d/n_1}$, $\max_j \|F_2 e_j\|_2 \leq \mu_{F_2}\sqrt{d/n_2}$ (2) random sparsity, i.e., the support of S^* is drawn uniformly at random from all subsets of $[n_1] \times [n_2]$ of size m. Note that assumptions such as uniform support sampling may not be realistic in practice. In contrast, as we explain in Sections 1.3 and 2.2, our work relaxes the assumptions they require while admitting a simpler algorithm, novel analysis approach and faster convergence result.

In this context, it is also to be mentioned that for the related problem of inductive matrix completion is relatively better understood; recovery guarantees are known for both the convex (see, for instance, (Xu *et al.* , 2013) and (Chiang *et al.* , 2015)) and the non-convex (e.g., (Jain & Dhillon, 2013)) approaches. Other related works based on probabilistic modeling include (Zhou *et al.* , 2012) and (Porteous *et al.* , 2010).

To summarize, we position this paper with respect to other works in Table 1. While we have highlighted the most relevant existing results, note that the list provided here is by no means comprehensive – such a list is beyond the scope of this work.

1.3 OUR CONTRIBUTIONS

To the best of our knowledge, our work is the first to derive a provable and efficient non-convex method for robust PCA in the inductive setting. Our novelty and technical contributions can be summarized along the following axes:

1. *Assumptions (Section 2.2):* We use the weakest assumptions, i.e., (1) weak incoherence conditions on only the feature matrices and (2) (weak) deterministic support of the sparse matrix.
2. *Algorithm (Section 2.4):* Our algorithm (IRPCA-IHT) performs simple steps involving spectral and entry-wise hard-thresholding operations.
3. *Guarantees (Sections 3.2, 3.3 and 3.4:* We show ϵ-close recovery in both the noiseless and noisy cases for problems of general size, feature dimension, rank and sparsity; moreover, our method has the fast (linear) convergence property.
4. *Experiments (Section 4):* We substantiate our theoretical results by demonstrating gains on both synthetic and real-world experiments.

2 PROBLEM SETUP

2.1 NOTATION AND PRELIMINARIES

Let $M = L^* + S^*$, i.e., $\{M, L^*, S^*\} \in \mathbb{R}^{n_1 \times n_2}$ are matrices such that the input data matrix M is the superposition of two component matrix signals namely, the low-rank component L^* and the sparse component S^*. Here, S^* is a sparse perturbation matrix with unknown (deterministic) support and arbitrary magnitude. In our inductive setting, side information or features are present in the bilinear form specified $L^* = F_1^\top W^* F_2$. The feature matrices are denoted as $F_1 \in \mathbb{R}^{d_1 \times n_1}$ and $F_2 \in \mathbb{R}^{d_2 \times n_2}$. Note that the feature dimensions are d_1 and d_2 such that $\max(d_1, d_2) \ll \min(n_1, n_2)$ and $W^* \in \mathbb{R}^{d_1 \times d_2}$ is the rank-r latent matrix to be estimated where $r \leq \min(d_1, d_2)$; intuitively, this latent matrix parameter describes the interaction and correlation among the feature vectors. Now, our optimization problem is given by:

$$\{\widehat{W}, \widehat{S}\} = \arg\min_{W,S} \|M - F_1^\top W F_2 - S\|_F \quad \text{s.t. } \operatorname{rank}(W) \leq r, \|S\|_{0,\infty} \leq z_2, \|S\|_{\infty,0} \leq z_1 \tag{5}$$

Here, for a matrix $A \in \mathbb{R}^{n_1 \times n_2}$, we define the relevant functions, $\|A\|_{0,\infty} := \max_j \sum_{i=1}^{n_2} \mathbf{1}(A_{ij} \neq 0)$, $\|A\|_{\infty,0} := \max_i \sum_{j=1}^{n_1} \mathbf{1}(A_{ij} \neq 0)$, $\|A\|_\infty := \max_{ij} |A_{ij}|$, Frobenius norm $\|A\|_F := \sqrt{\sum_{i=1}^{n_1}\sum_{j=1}^{n_2} A_{ij}^2}$, spectral norm $\|A\|_2 = \max_{\|x\|_2=1, \|y\|_2=1} x^\top A y$ for unit vectors $x \in \mathbb{R}^{n_1}$ and $y \in \mathbb{R}^{n_2}$. Next, for a matrix A, we denote its maximum and minimum singular value by $\sigma_{\max}(A)$ and $\sigma_{\min}(A)$ respectively, and further the condition number of A is denoted by $\kappa(A) := \sigma_{\max}(A)/\sigma_{\min}(A)$. The pseudoinverse of a matrix A is denoted by $B = A^\dagger$ and is computed as $B := (A^\top A)^{-1}A^\top$ where A is assumed to be of full rank. Let I denote the identity matrix whose size will be clear from the context. Finally, we use e_i to denote the ith standard basis vector in the appropriate dimension, which will also be clear from the context.

Remark 2.1 (Noisy case: motivation and setup). *Note that, so far, for simplicity and clarity, we have been focusing on the case when* $M = L^* + S^*$ *where* $L^* = F_1^\top W^* F_2$. *This model posits that* W^* *is exactly a rank-*r *matrix and* S^* *is exactly a sparse matrix which might not be the case in practice. Our approach, for solving Equation 5, in terms of both the algorithm and the analysis, also handles the noisy case* $M = F_1^\top W^* F_2 + S^* + N^*$ *wherein* N^* *is some generic bounded additive noise that renders* L^* *approximately low-rank or* S^* *approximately sparse.*

2.2 ASSUMPTIONS

We now state and explain the intuition behind the (by now standard) identifiability assumptions on the quantities involved in our optimization problem so that it is well-posed. Also, we re-emphasize specifically that Assumptions 2 and 3 are much weaker and generic than previous works such as (Chiang *et al.* , 2016).

1. *Feasibility condition:* We assume that $\text{row}(L^*) \subseteq \text{row}(F_2)$ and $\text{col}(L^*) \subseteq \text{col}(F_1^\top)$.
2. *Weak incoherence of the feature matrices:* Let $F_1 = U_{F_1}\Sigma_{F_1}V_{F_1}^\top$ be the SVD of the feature matrix F_1 such that $U_{F_1} \in \mathbb{R}^{d_1\times d_1}$, $V_{F_1} \in \mathbb{R}^{d_1\times n_1}$ are the matrices of left and right singular vectors respectively, and $\Sigma_{F_1} \in \mathbb{R}^{d_1\times d_1}$ is the diagonal matrix of singular values. Then, we assume $\max_i \left\|e_i^\top V_{F_1}\right\|_2 \leq \mu_{F_1}\sqrt{d_1/n_1}$ where μ_{F_1} is called the incoherence constant of matrix F_1. Similarly, we assume incoherence of F_2 as well.
3. *Bounded deterministic sparsity:* Let the number of non-zeros per row of the sparse matrix S satisfy $z_1 \leq n_1/20\mu^2 d_1\kappa$; similarly, let the number of non-zeros per column of the sparse matrix S satisfy $z_2 \leq n_2/20\mu^2 d_2\kappa$. Here, $\mu = \max(\mu_{F_1}, \mu_{F_2})$ and $\kappa = \max(\kappa(F_1), \kappa(F_2))$.
4. *Bounded latent matrix:* Without loss of generality, we assume that the latent matrix is bounded, ie, $\|W^*\|_2 \leq c_W$ for a global constant c_W.

Having side information always need not help; otherwise, we may always generate random features and obtain improvement over transductive learning. In disallowing this, Assumption 1 is a necessary condition, which ensures that we have informative features F_1 and F_2 in the sense that they are correlated meaningfully in the latent space given by W^*.

In order to make the low-rank component not too sparse

Algorithm 1 IRPCA-IHT: Inductive Robust PCA via Iterative Hard Thresholding

Input: Grossly corrupted data matrix $M \in \mathbb{R}^{n_1\times n_2}$, feature matrices $F_1 \in \mathbb{R}^{d_1\times n_1}, F_2 \in \mathbb{R}^{d_2\times n_2}$, true rank r, noise parameter ν, global constant c_W.
Output: Estimated latent matrix $\widehat{W} \in \mathbb{R}^{d_1\times d_2}$ and sparse perturbation matrix $\widehat{S} \in \mathbb{R}^{n_1\times n_2}$.
Initialize $L_0 \leftarrow 0$ and $\zeta_0 \leftarrow 5\mu_{F_1}\mu_{F_2}\sigma_{\max}(F_1)\sigma_{\max}(F_2)\sqrt{\frac{d_1 d_2}{n_1 n_2}}c_W + \nu$ where μ_{F_1} and μ_{F_2} are the incoherence constants as computed in Assumption 2.
for $t = 1, \ldots, T$ **do**
  $\zeta_t \leftarrow \frac{\mu_{F_1}\mu_{F_2}\sigma_{\max}(F_1)\sigma_{\max}(F_2)\sqrt{d_1 d_2}c_W}{5^{t-1}\sqrt{n_1 n_2}} + \nu$.
  $S_t \leftarrow \mathcal{P}_{\zeta_t}(M - L_{t-1})$.
  $W_t \leftarrow \mathcal{P}_r\left((F_1^\top)^\dagger(M - S_t)(F_2)^\dagger\right)$.
  $L_t \leftarrow F_1^\top W_t F_2$.
end for
Set $\widehat{W} \leftarrow W_T$ and $\widehat{S} \leftarrow S_T$.
return $\widehat{W}, \widehat{S}$.

and distinguishable from the sparse perturbation, we make the weak incoherence assumption on the feature matrices which says that the energy of the right singular vectors of the matrices is well-spread with respect to all the co-ordinate axes. This is precisely quantified by Assumption 2.

In our problem setup we assume that a generic (possibly adversarial) deterministic sparse perturbation is added to the low-rank matrix. This is quantified by Assumption 3. In particular, we *do not* have any specific distributional assumptions on the support of the sparse matrix, and the magnitudes and signs of its non-zero entries.

Remark 2.2 (Noisy case: assumptions). *To obtain recovery guarantees for the noisy case described in Remark 2.1, the only assumption on* N^* *we have is that it is suitably well-behaved – this is quantified by assuming* $\|N^*\|_\infty \leq 1/40\mu^2 d\kappa^2$.

2.3 CORRUPTION RATE

In this work, as give in Table 1, we refer to the rank-sparsity trade-off in Assumption 3 as 'corruption rate' – this is the allowable extent to which the model is robust to gross outliers while retaining identifiability, ie, the number of non-zeros in the sparse corruption matrix. Note that, by using features, we are always able to tolerate $\Omega(n_1/d_1)$ (resp. $\Omega(n_2/d_2)$) gross corruptions per row (resp. column). This is a gain over the transductive setting as in (Netrapalli *et al.* , 2014) where the permissible number of outliers is $O(n_1/r)$ (resp. $O(n_2/r)$) per row (resp. column) and r could be potentially $O(n)$.

2.4 ALGORITHM

Our method, presented in Algorithm 1, uses two non-convex projection operations as building blocks. Our algorithm essentially applies these projections to the low-rank and sparse residuals in an alternating manner until convergence, i.e., at the tth iteration, the residuals $M - L_{t-1}$ and $M - S_t$ are projected onto the set of sparse and low-rank matrices respectively via the following hard-thresholding operations:

1. *Spectral hard thresholding:* This is used for projecting a matrix onto the set of low-rank matrices. It is achieved via the truncated-SVD operation and is denoted by $B = \mathcal{P}_r(A)$. Here, we are finding a matrix rank-r matrix B which best approximates A.
2. *Entry-wise hard thresholding:* This is used for projecting a matrix onto the set of sparse matrices. We compute a matrix $B = \mathcal{P}_a(A)$ where $B_{ij} = A_{ij}$ if $|A_{ij}| > a$ and $B_{ij} = 0$ if $|A_{ij}| \leq a$.

Note that the above hard thresholding operations result in in rank-restricted and sparsity-restricted matrices for appropriate choices of r and a. It is noteworthy that our algorithm, unlike many non-convex optimization procedures, employs the very simple initialization scheme of setting the initial iterates to the all-zeros matrix (L_0) while achieving global convergence.

The algorithm needs (a) the true rank r of W^*, and (b) the noise parameter ν (for which it suffices to have the knowledge of a reasonable bound on $\|N^*\|_\infty (1 + 3\mu^2 d\kappa^2)$). In practice, the knowledge of r and $\|N^*\|_\infty$ can be obtained using cross-validation, grid search or leveraging domain knowledge of the specific application; for instance, in the noiseless setting, $N^* = 0$ and hence, ν is set to zero. Furthermore, efficient ways of estimating the incoherence of a matrix have been studied in the literature; see for instance, (Mohri & Talwalkar, 2011) and (Drineas *et al.* , 2012).

A key difference from related approaches in the transductive setting (Netrapalli *et al.* , 2014) is the more efficient spectral hard thresholding that is possible due to the available feature information, i.e., our approach involves a truncated SVD operation in the feature space rather than the ambient space which is computationally inexpensive. Specifically, since $L^* = F_1^\top W^* F_2$, in Step 7 of Algorithm 1, we find the best matrix $\underline{W}_t$ such that $M - S_t \approx F_1^\top \underline{W}_t F_2$ for every t. This is achieved via a bilinear transformation of the residual $M - S_t$ given by $(F_1^\top)^\dagger (M - S_t)(F_2)^\dagger$ followed by a truncated r-SVD of the resulting $d_1 \times d_2$ matrix $\underline{W}_t$ to obtain W_t. Note that the low-rank iterates may then be computed as $L_t = F_1^\top W_t F_2$; specifically, $\widehat{L} = F_1^\top \widehat{W} F_2$ at termination.

2.5 COMPUTATIONAL COMPLEXITY

We now infer the per-iteration computational complexity from Algorithm 1, specifically Steps 6-8. The entry-wise hard-thresholding in Step 6 has a time complexity of $O(n_1 n_2)$. The spectral hard-thresholding in Step 7 has a time complexity of $O(\max(n_1^2 d_1, n_2^2 d_2) + d_1 d_2 r)$ due to the involved matrix multiplication followed by the truncated SVD operation. Step 8 has a complexity of $O(n_1 n_2 \max(d_1, d_2))$. Unlike previous (Chiang *et al.* , 2016) trace norm based approaches in the inductive setting, we directly perform rank-r SVD in Step 7 leading to a complexity of just $O(d_1 d_2 r)$ as opposed to $O(d_1 d_2 \min(d_1, d_2))$; this is a significant gain when $r \ll \min(d_1, d_2)$. In the transductive setting as well, our method has significant computational gains over the state-of-the art AltProj algorithm of (Netrapalli *et al.* , 2014), especially in the regime $\max(d_1, d_2) < r^2$ while maintaining the corruption rate guarantees as in Section 2.3.

3 ANALYSIS

3.1 PROOF OUTLINE

For simplicity, we first begin with the symmetric noiseless case (Section 3.2). Upon presenting the convergence result for this case, we show how to extend our analysis and result to general cases including the noisy case (Section 3.3) and the asymmetric matrix case (Section 3.4).

The key steps in the proof of convergence of Algorithm 1 involve analyzing the two main hard-thresholding operations and controlling the error decrease, in terms of a suitably chosen potential function, as a result of performing these operations. Since we care about recovering every entry of both the low-rank and the sparse matrix components, we choose the infinity norm of appropriate error matrices as our potential function to track the progress of our algorithm. Bounds in the infinity norm are trickier to obtain than the more usual spectral norm. Consequently, our guarantees are stronger as opposed to showing faithful recovery in the spectral or Frobenius norms. Specifically, for a given t, we show that $\|L^* - L_t\|_\infty \leq 2\|S^* - S_t\|_\infty \leq \frac{1}{5}\|L^* - L_{t-1}\|_\infty$. Upon showing this geometric reduction in error, we use induction to stitch up argument across iterations.

At a high level, the proof techniques involved for a fixed t are as follows:

1. *Entry-wise hard thresholding:* The are two aspects here. First, given that L_{t-1} is close to L^*, we show, by using a case-by-case argument, that S_t is also close to S^*. Second, we show, by contradiction,

that the S_t does not have any spurious entries that are not present in S^* originally.

2. *Spectral hard thresholding:* Given that S_t is close to S^*, we show that L_t gets closer to L^* than L_{t-1}. There are three aspects here. First, we use the weak incoherence property of features to obtain infinity norm bounds. Second, we use Weyl's eigenvalue pertubation lemma to quantify how close the estimate W_t is to the true latent matrix W^*. Third, we bound the spectral norm of a sparse matrix tightly in terms of its infinity norm.

For the noisy case, using Remark 2.1, we simply account for the noise terms as well in the error reduction argument. Extension to the asymmetric case proceeds via the standard symmetric embedding technique, both for the noiseless and the noisy setting, as detailed in Section 3.4; a key point to be noted here is that we maintain the rank-sparsity conditions in the symmetrized matrix.

3.2 SYMMETRIC NOISELESS CASE

Let $N^* = 0$, $W^* = (W^*)^\top$ and $S^* = (S^*)^\top$. For simplicity, let the features be equal i.e., $F_1 = F_2 = F$ and $\mu_{F_1} = \mu_{F_2} = \mu$. Further, let $d_1 = d_2$, $z_1 = z_2 = z$ and $n_1 = n_2 = n$. Also, recall that $\nu = 0$ in the noiseless case. We now state our main result.

Theorem 3.1 (Noiseless case: fast and correct convergence). *Under the assumptions of Section 2.2, after $T > \lceil \log_5(2\mu^2\sigma^2_{\max}(F)\frac{d}{n}\frac{c_W}{\epsilon})\rceil + 1$ iterations of Algorithm 1, we have $\left\|L^* - \widehat{L}\right\|_\infty \leq \epsilon$, $\mathrm{rank}(\widehat{L}) \leq r$, $\left\|S^* - \widehat{S}\right\|_\infty \leq \epsilon$ and $\mathrm{Supp}(\widehat{S}) \subseteq \mathrm{Supp}(S^*)$.*

Remark 3.1. *Several implications are immediate from Theorem 3.1: (1) our algorithm converges to the true parameters at a linear rate; (2) we have faithful latent space recovery as well as outlier detection; (3) assumptions used for deriving the recovery guarantee are weaker than previous works in the inductive setting; (4) we achieve improved corruption rate; (5) guarantees for the transductive robust PCA problem are recovered if the features are identity matrices and $W^* = L^*$; in particular, our corruption rate bounds match up to a factor of d/r.*

We now prove Theorem 3.1.

Proof. We prove this by induction over t. Note that Step 3 of Algorithm 1 initializes $\zeta_0 = 5\mu^2\sigma^2_{\max}(F)\frac{d}{n}c_W$ (as $N^* = 0$) and sets $\zeta_t = \zeta_{t-1}/5$ for all $t \geq 1$. For $t = 1$, since $L_0 = 0$ by our initialization, it is clear that $\|L^* - L_0\|_\infty \leq \|L^*\|_\infty \leq \left\|F^\top W^* F\right\|_\infty \leq \mu^2\sigma^2_{\max}(F)\frac{d}{n}c_W$ and hence the base case holds.

Next, for $t \geq 1$, by using Lemma 3.1, we have $\|S^* - S_t\|_\infty \leq 2\mu^2\sigma^2_{\max}(F)\frac{d}{n}\frac{c_W}{5^{t-1}}$ and $\mathrm{Supp}(S_t) \subseteq \mathrm{Supp}(S^*)$ and further, by Lemma 3.2, we have $\|L^* - L_t\|_\infty \leq \mu^2\sigma^2_{\max}(F)\frac{d}{n}\frac{c_W}{5^t}$. Moreover, setting $T > \lceil \log_5(2\mu^2\sigma^2_{\max}(F)\frac{d}{n}\frac{c_W}{\epsilon})\rceil + 1$, we have $\|L^* - L_T\|_\infty \leq \epsilon$ and $\|S^* - S_T\|_\infty \leq \epsilon$. □

Lemma 3.1 (Noiseless case: faithful support recovery due to entry-wise hard thresholding). *Let L_{t-1} satisfy the error condition that $\|L^* - L_{t-1}\|_\infty \leq \mu^2\sigma^2_{\max}(F)\frac{d}{n}\frac{c_W}{5^{t-1}}$. Then, we have $\|S^* - S_t\|_\infty \leq 2\mu^2\sigma^2_{\max}(F)\frac{d}{n}\frac{c_W}{5^{t-1}}$ and $\mathrm{Supp}(S_t) \subseteq \mathrm{Supp}(S^*)$.*

Proof. Note that $S_t = \mathcal{P}_{\zeta_t}(M - L_{t-1}) = \mathcal{P}_{\zeta_t}(L^* - L_{t-1} + S^*)$. By the definition of our entry-wise hard thresholding operation, we have the following:

1. Term $e_i^\top S_t e_j = e_i^\top (M - L_{t-1})e_j = e_i^\top (L^* + S^* - L_{t-1})e_j$ when $\left|e_i^\top (M - L_{t-1})e_j\right| > \zeta_t$.Thus $\left|e_i^\top (S^* - S_t)e^j\right| = \left|e_i^\top (L^* - L_{t-1})e_j\right| \leq \mu^2\sigma^2_{\max}(F)\frac{d}{n}\frac{c_W}{5^{t-1}}$.
2. Term $e_i^\top S_t e_j = 0$ when $\left|e_i^\top (M - L_{t-1})e_j\right| = \left|e_i^\top (L^* + S^* - L_{t-1})e_j\right| \leq \zeta_t$. Using the triangle inequality, we have $\left|e_i^\top (S^* - S_t)e_j\right| \leq \left|e_i^\top S^* e_j\right| \leq \zeta_t + \left|e_i^\top (L^* - L_{t-1})e_j\right| \leq 2\mu^2\sigma^2_{\max}(F)\frac{d}{n}\frac{c_W}{5^{t-1}}$.

Thus, the above two cases show the validity of the entry-wise hard thresholding operation. To show correct support recovery, we show that for any given (i, j), if $e_i^\top S^* e_j = 0$ then $e_i^\top S_t e_j$ is also zero for all t. Noting that $M = L^* + S^*$ and $e_i^\top S^* e_j = 0$, $e_i^\top S_t e_j = e_i^\top (M - L_{t-1})e_j = e_i^\top (L^* - L_{t-1})e_j \neq 0$ iff $\left|e_i^\top (L^* - L_{t-1})e_j\right| > \zeta_t$. But this is a contradiction since $\left|e_i^\top (L^* - L_{t-1})e_j\right| \leq \mu^2\sigma^2_{\max}(F)\frac{d}{n}\frac{c_W}{5^{t-1}} = \zeta_t$ by the inductive assumption. □

Lemma 3.2 (Noiseless case: error decay due to spectral hard thresholding). *Let S_t satisfy the error condition that $\|S^* - S_t\|_\infty \leq 2\mu^2\sigma^2_{\max}(F)\frac{d}{n}\frac{c_W}{5^{t-1}}$. Then, we have $\|L^* - L_t\|_\infty \leq \mu^2\sigma^2_{\max}(F)\frac{d}{n}\frac{c_W}{5^t}$ and $\mathrm{rank}(L_t) \leq r$.*

Proof. Using the fact that $L^* = F^\top W^* F$ and $L_t = F^\top W_t F$, we have

$$\|L^* - L_t\|_\infty = \left\|F^\top (W^* - W_t)F\right\|_\infty$$

$$= \max_{i,j} \left|e_i^\top F^\top (W^* - W_t)Fe_j\right|$$

$$\stackrel{\xi_1}{=} \max_{i,j} \left|e_i^\top V_F \Sigma_F^\top U_F^\top (W^* - W_t)U_F \Sigma_F V_F^\top e_j\right|$$

$$\stackrel{\xi_2}{\leq} \left(\max_i \left\|e_i^\top V_F \Sigma_F^\top\right\|_2\right)^2 \left\|U_F^\top (W^* - W_t)U_F\right\|_2, \quad (6)$$

where ξ_1 follows by substituting the SVD of F, i.e., $F = U_F \Sigma_F V_F^\top$ and ξ_2 follows from the sub-multiplicative property of the spectral norm. Now, from Assumption 2, we have

$$\max_i \left\| e_i^\top V_F \Sigma_F^\top \right\|_2 \leq \mu \sqrt{\frac{d}{n}} \sigma_{\max}(F). \quad (7)$$

Recall from Step 7 of Algorithm 1 that W_t is computed as $\mathcal{P}_r\left((F_1^\top)^\dagger (M - S_t)(F_2)^\dagger\right)$ where $M = F_1^\top W^* F_2 + S^*$. Let $E_t := S^* - S_t$. Further, let $Q \Lambda Q^\top + Q_\perp \Lambda_\perp Q_\perp^\top$ be the full SVD of $W^* + G^\top E_t G$, where Q and $Q_\perp$ span orthogonal sub-spaces of dimensions r and $d - r$ respectively, and $G := F^\dagger$ is the pseudoinverse of F. Next, using these and the unitary invariance property of the spectral norm, we have

$$\begin{aligned}
&\left\| U_F^\top (W^* - W_t) U_F \right\|_2 \leq \left\| W^* - W_t \right\|_2 \\
&\leq \left\| W^* - \mathcal{P}_r(G^\top (F^\top W^* F + E_t) G) \right\|_2 \\
&\overset{\xi_3}{\leq} \left\| Q \Lambda Q^\top + Q_\perp \Lambda_\perp Q_\perp^\top - G^\top E_t G - Q \Lambda Q^\top \right\|_2 \\
&\overset{\xi_4}{\leq} \left\| G^\top E_t G \right\|_2 + \left\| Q_\perp \Lambda_\perp Q_\perp^\top \right\|_2 \\
&\overset{\xi_5}{\leq} 2 \left\| G^\top E_t G \right\|_2 \leq 2 \left\| G \right\|_2^2 \left\| E_t \right\|_2 \\
&\leq \frac{2 \left\| E_t \right\|_2}{[\sigma_{\min}(F)]^2} \overset{\xi_6}{\leq} \frac{2z \left\| E_t \right\|_\infty}{[\sigma_{\min}(F)]^2}, \quad (8)
\end{aligned}$$

where ξ_3 is obtained by substituting $W^* = Q \Lambda Q^\top + Q_\perp \Lambda_\perp Q_\perp^\top - G^\top E_t G$, ξ_4 by triangle inequality. Inequality ξ_5 is obtained by using Weyl's eigenvalue perturbation lemma (Bhatia, 2013), which is:

$$\left\| Q_\perp \Lambda_\perp Q_\perp^\top \right\|_2 = \left\| \Lambda_\perp \right\|_\infty \leq \left\| G^\top E_t G \right\|_2.$$

Finally, inequality ξ_6 is obtained by using Lemma 4 of (Netrapalli *et al.* , 2014). Combining Equations (6), (7) and (8), we have

$$\left\| L^* - L_t \right\|_\infty \leq 2\mu^2 d z \kappa^2 \left\| E_t \right\|_\infty / n \overset{\xi_7}{\leq} \left\| E_t \right\|_\infty / 10, \quad (9)$$

where $\kappa = \frac{\sigma_{\max}(F)}{\sigma_{\min}(F)}$ and ξ_7 is due to Assumption 3. Substituting the result $\left\| E_t \right\|_\infty = \left\| S^* - S_t \right\|_\infty \leq 2\mu^2 \sigma_{\max}^2(F) \frac{d}{n} \frac{cw}{5^{t-1}}$ from Lemma 3.1 in Equation (9) completes the proof. □

3.3 SYMMETRIC NOISY CASE

Next we consider the general noisy case of $M = L^* + S^* + N^*$, where $L^* = F^\top W^* F$, S^* and N^* are symmetric and N^* is a bounded additive noise matrix satisfying properties as given in Remark 2.2. Note that, in practice, by setting $\nu = c.d$ for a suitably chosen constant c, Algorithm 1 works unchanged. However, in order to establish convergence in theory, the key challenge is to be able to control the perturbation effects of N^* in each iteration. In making this precise, we now state our main result for this section whose proof is given in Appendix A due to space limitations.

Theorem 3.2 (Noisy case: fast and correct convergence). *Under the assumptions of Section 2.2, setting* $T > \lceil \log_5(2\mu^2 \sigma_{\max}^2(F) \frac{d}{n} \frac{cw}{\epsilon}) \rceil + 1$ *in Algorithm 1, we have* $\left\| L^* - \widehat{L} \right\|_\infty \leq \epsilon + 3\mu^2 d \kappa^2 \left\| N^* \right\|_\infty$, $\mathrm{rank}(\widehat{L}) \leq r$, $\left\| S^* - \widehat{S} \right\|_\infty \leq \epsilon + 8\mu^2 d \kappa^2 \left\| N^* \right\|_\infty$ *and* $\mathrm{Supp}(\widehat{S}) \subseteq \mathrm{Supp}(S^*)$.

To prove the above theorem, we need the following key lemmas whose proofs are given in Appendix A as well.

Lemma 3.3 (Noisy case: faithful support recovery due to entry-wise hard thresholding). *Let* L_{t-1} *satisfy the error condition that* $\left\| L^* - L_{t-1} \right\|_\infty \leq \mu^2 \sigma_{\max}^2(F) \frac{d}{n} \frac{cw}{5^{t-1}} + 3\mu^2 d \kappa^2 \left\| N^* \right\|_\infty$. *Then, we have* $\left\| S^* - S_t \right\|_\infty \leq 2\mu^2 \sigma_{\max}^2(F) \frac{d}{n} \frac{cw}{5^{t-1}} + 2(3\mu^2 d \kappa^2 + 1) \left\| N^* \right\|_\infty$ *and* $\mathrm{Supp}(S_t) \subseteq \mathrm{Supp}(S^*)$.

Lemma 3.4 (Noisy case: error decay due to spectral hard thresholding). *Let* S_t *satisfy the error condition that* $\left\| S^* - S_t \right\|_\infty \leq 2\mu^2 \sigma_{\max}^2(F) \frac{d}{n} \frac{cw}{5^{t-1}} + 2(3\mu^2 d \kappa^2 + 1) \left\| N^* \right\|_\infty$. *Then, we have* $\left\| L^* - L_t \right\|_\infty \leq \mu^2 \sigma_{\max}^2(F) \frac{d}{n} \frac{cw}{5^t} + 3\mu^2 d \kappa^2 \left\| N^* \right\|_\infty$ *and* $\mathrm{rank}(L_t) \leq r$.

3.4 ASYMMETRIC CASE

We now show how to extend our analysis for any general asymmetric matrix, both in the noiseless and the noisy inductive settings. Let $M \in \mathbb{R}^{n_1 \times n_2}$ be the input data matrix. The main result can be stated as:

Claim 3.1. *Let* $M = L^* + S^* + N^*$ *where* $L^* = F_1^\top W^* F_2$ *such that* $n_1 \neq n_2$ *and* $d_1 \neq d_2$. *Algorithm 1 executed on this* M *satisfies the guarantees in Theorem 3.1 (resp. Theorem 3.2) for the noiseless case where* $N^* = 0$ *(resp. noisy case where* N^* *satisfies the properties in Remark 2.2).*

Consider the standard symmetric embedding of a matrix given by:

$$\mathrm{Sym}(M) := \begin{pmatrix} 0 & M \\ M^\top & 0 \end{pmatrix}.$$

With $\mathrm{Sym}(M)$ as input, the intermediate iterates of our algorithm also have a similar form. Moreover, note that this embedding preserves the rank, incoherence and sparsity properties – due to space constraints, these details which are needed as the key components of the proof of Claim 3.1 are deferred to Appendix B.

Figure 1: Comparing of RPCA algorithms in terms of running time to reach a solution of a given accuracy. For $n = 1000$, we vary each problem parameter while fixing the others. Specifically, we vary:
(a) sparsity (b) rank (c) feature dimension (d) condition number

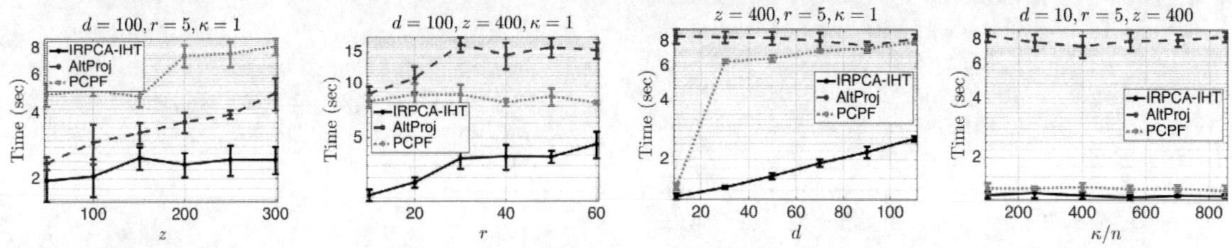

4 EXPERIMENTS

In this section, we conduct a systematic empirical investigation of the performance of our robust subspace recovery method (IRPCA-IHT) and justify our theoretical claims in the previous sections. Specifically, the goal of this study is to show: (1) the correctness of our algorithm, (2) that informative features and feature correlations are indeed useful, and (3) that our algorithm is computationally efficient.

Figure 2: Comparison of robust PCA algorithms on the MovieLens data: running time and recovery error.

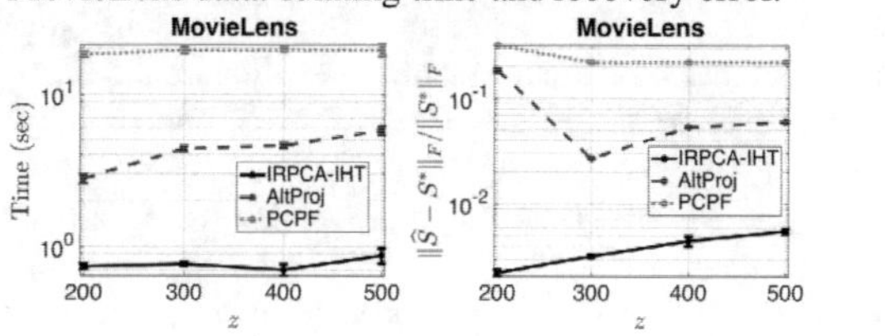

4.1 SYNTHETIC SIMULATIONS

We set the problem size as $n_1 = n_2 = n = 1000$; for simplicity, we take $d_1 = d_2 = d$, $z_1 = z_2 = z$ and $F_1 = F_2 = F$; let κ be the condition number of the feature matrix F. First, we generate approximately well-conditioned weakly incoherent feature matrices by computing $F = U_F \Sigma_F V_F^\top$ where the entries of $U_F \in \mathbb{R}^{d \times d}$ and $V_F \in \mathbb{R}^{d \times n}$ are drawn iid from the standard normal distribution followed by row normalization, and the diagonal entries of Σ_F are set to one. Next, the latent matrix W^* is generated by sampling each entry independently and uniformly at random from the interval $(0, 1)$, performing SVD of this sampled matrix and retaining its top r singular values. The low-rank component L^* is then computed as $F^\top W^* F$. Note that this also ensure the feasibility condition in Assumption 1. Next, we generate the sparse matrix as follows. We first choose the support according to the Bernoulli sampling model, ie, each entry is chosen to be included in the support with probability z/n and then its value is chosen independently and uniformly at random from $(-10r/n, -5r/n) \cup (5r/n, 10r/n)$.

There are four main parameters in the problem namely, (a) the sparsity level z of S^*, (b) the rank r of W^*, (c) the feature dimension d, and (d) condition number κ of the feature matrix F; we vary each of these while fixing the others. We compare the performance of our algorithm to that of two existing algorithms namely, (i) the convex relaxation approach 'PCPF' due to (Chiang *et al.* , 2016) which is a state-of-the-art robust PCA method in the inductive setting, and (ii) 'AltProj' due to (Netrapalli *et al.* , 2014) which is a state-of-the-art robust PCA method in the transductive setting. We execute these algorithms until an accuracy of $\left\|M - \widehat{L} - \widehat{S}\right\|_F / \|M\|_F \leq 10^{-3}$ is achieved and time them individually. All the results presented in the running time plots in Figure 1 are obtained by averaging over five runs.

We note that our algorithm outperforms PCPF and AltProj consistently while increasing the problem hardness in three situations (Figures 1-(a), 1-(b) and 1-(c)) in terms of running time. The gain in terms of scalability of our method over the convex PCPF method is attributed to the fact that the soft thresholding operation for solving the nuclear-norm objective involves computing the partial-SVD of the intermediate iterates which could of potentially much higher rank than r – this leads to $O(d^3)$ worst-case time complexity for the SVD step in PCPF as opposed to our algorithm which has $O(d^2 r)$ worst-case complexity for spectral hard thresholding. The time gain over the transductive AltProj method is attributed to the fact that our spectral hard-thresholding is performed in the d-dimensional (feature) space rather than the n-dimensional (ambient) space; moreover, another factor that adds to the running time of AltProj is that it proceeds in stages unlike Algorithm 1. An interesting point to be noted from the relatively flat plot in Figure 1-(d) is that the condition number dependence in Assumption 3 is merely an artifact of our analysis and is not inherent to the problem; we leave tightening this bound in theory to future work.

4.2 REAL-DATA EXPERIMENTS

As described in Example 1.1, we consider an important application of our method – to robustify estimation in recommendation systems while leveraging feature information; specifically, the task is to predict user-movie ratings accurately despite the presence of gross sparse corruptions. We take the MovieLens [1] dataset which consists of $100,000$ ratings from $n_1 = 943$ users on $n_2 = 1682$ movies. The ground-truth in this dataset is, per se, unavailable. Hence, as the first step, we apply matrix completion techniques (specifically, using the OptSpace algorithm of (Keshavan *et al.* , 2010)) to obtain a baseline complete user-movie ratings matrix, L^*; we take $r = 3$. Next, we form features while ensuring the feasibility condition. For this, we compute the SVD of the baseline matrix, $L^* = U_{L^*}\Sigma_{L^*}V_{L^*}^\top$ followed by setting $F_1 = U_{L^*}Q_U$ (resp. $F_2 = V_{L^*}Q_V$) where $Q_U \in SO(d_1)$ (resp. $Q_V \in SO(d_2)$) are random rotation matrices; we take $d_1 = 20$ and $d_2 = 25$. Note that forming features using the SVD result, as we have done here, is a common technique in inductive matrix estimation problems (see, for instance, (Natarajan & Dhillon, 2014)). We then add a sparse perturbation matrix whose each entry is chosen to be included in the support with probability z/n and the entries are chosen independently and uniformly at random from $(-10r/\sqrt{n_1n_2}, -5r/\sqrt{n_1n_2}) \cup (5r/\sqrt{n_1n_2}, 10r/\sqrt{n_1n_2})$. We compare the performance of PCPF, AltProj and our IRPCA-IHT algorithms; we consider two evaluation metrics, running time and relative recovery error (the latter is measured by $\left\|\widehat{S} - S^*\right\|_F / \|S^*\|_F$). Varying z and averaging over five runs, we note that our algorithm outperforms (Figure 2) both PCPF and AltProj by achieving about an order of magnitude of gain in terms of both the running time as well as the recovery error.

5 CONCLUSION

In this paper, we have presented an novel approach for inductive robust subspace identification by leveraging available informative feature information. We hope our results motivate similar studies of other learning problems in the inductive setting leading to improved statistical and computational performance. Keeping this in mind, some future directions with respect to this work include understanding the following:

1. Minimax rates, both tight lower and upper bounds for learning problems in the inductive setting, are of interest. Relevant techniques include the works by (Negahban & Wainwright, 2012) and (Klopp *et al.* , 2014) in the transductive setting.
2. We note that the corruption rate in Assumption 3 is still sub-optimal by a factor of d/r which is significant when $r \ll d$. In addition to this, removing the condition number dependence in Assumption 3 and also obtaining ϵ-independent results as in matrix completion (see for instance, (Jain & Netrapalli, 2014)) are of interest.

[1] http://grouplens.org/datasets/movielens/

References

Bhatia, Rajendra. 2013. *Matrix analysis*. Vol. 169. Springer Science & Business Media.

Candès, Emmanuel J, Li, Xiaodong, Ma, Yi, & Wright, John. 2011. Robust principal component analysis? *Journal of the ACM (JACM)*, **58**(3), 11.

Chandrasekaran, Venkat, Sanghavi, Sujay, Parrilo, Pablo A, & Willsky, Alan S. 2011. Rank-sparsity incoherence for matrix decomposition. *SIAM Journal on Optimization*, **21**(2), 572–596.

Chiang, Kai-Yang, Hsieh, Cho-Jui, & Dhillon, Inderjit S. 2015. Matrix Completion with Noisy Side Information. *Pages 3447–3455 of: Advances in Neural Information Processing Systems*.

Chiang, Kai-Yang, Hsieh, Cho-Jui, & Dhillon, Inderjit S. 2016. Robust Principal Component Analysis with Side Information. *Pages 2291–2299 of: Proceedings of The 33rd International Conference on Machine Learning*.

Drineas, Petros, Magdon-Ismail, Malik, Mahoney, Michael W, & Woodruff, David P. 2012. Fast approximation of matrix coherence and statistical leverage. *Journal of Machine Learning Research*, **13**(Dec), 3475–3506.

Eckart, Carl, & Young, Gale. 1936. The approximation of one matrix by another of lower rank. *Psychometrika*, **1**(3), 211–218.

Hsu, Daniel, Kakade, Sham M, & Zhang, Tong. 2011. Robust matrix decomposition with sparse corruptions. *IEEE Transactions on Information Theory*, **57**(11), 7221–7234.

Jain, Prateek, & Dhillon, Inderjit S. 2013. Provable inductive matrix completion. *arXiv preprint arXiv:1306.0626*.

Jain, Prateek, & Netrapalli, Praneeth. 2014. Fast exact matrix completion with finite samples. *arXiv preprint*.

Ji, Shuiwang, & Ye, Jieping. 2009. An accelerated gradient method for trace norm minimization. *Pages 457–464 of: Proceedings of the 26th annual international conference on machine learning*. ACM.

Keshavan, Raghunandan H, Montanari, Andrea, & Oh, Sewoong. 2010. Matrix completion from noisy entries. *Journal of Machine Learning Research*, **11**(Jul), 2057–2078.

Klopp, Olga, Lounici, Karim, & Tsybakov, Alexandre B. 2014. Robust matrix completion. *arXiv preprint arXiv:1412.8132*.

Li, Liyuan, Huang, Weimin, Gu, Irene Yu-Hua, & Tian, Qi. 2004. Statistical modeling of complex backgrounds for foreground object detection. *IEEE Transactions on Image Processing*, **13**(11), 1459–1472.

Min, Kerui, Zhang, Zhengdong, Wright, John, & Ma, Yi. 2010. Decomposing background topics from keywords by principal component pursuit. *Pages 269–278 of: Proceedings of the 19th ACM international conference on Information and knowledge management*. ACM.

Mohri, Mehryar, & Talwalkar, Ameet. 2011. Can matrix coherence be efficiently and accurately estimated? *Pages 534–542 of: Proceedings of the Fourteenth International Conference on Artificial Intelligence and Statistics*.

Natarajan, Nagarajan, & Dhillon, Inderjit S. 2014. Inductive matrix completion for predicting gene–disease associations. *Bioinformatics*, **30**(12), i60–i68.

Negahban, Sahand, & Wainwright, Martin J. 2012. Restricted strong convexity and weighted matrix completion: Optimal bounds with noise. *Journal of Machine Learning Research*, **13**(May), 1665–1697.

Netrapalli, Praneeth, Niranjan, UN, Sanghavi, Sujay, Anandkumar, Animashree, & Jain, Prateek. 2014. Non-convex robust PCA. *Pages 1107–1115 of: Advances in Neural Information Processing Systems*.

Pearson, Karl. 1901. LIII. On lines and planes of closest fit to systems of points in space. *The London, Edinburgh, and Dublin Philosophical Magazine and Journal of Science*, **2**(11), 559–572.

Porteous, Ian, Asuncion, Arthur U, & Welling, Max. 2010. Bayesian Matrix Factorization with Side Information and Dirichlet Process Mixtures. *In: AAAI*.

Recht, Benjamin. 2011. A simpler approach to matrix completion. *Journal of Machine Learning Research*, **12**(Dec), 3413–3430.

Xu, Miao, Jin, Rong, & Zhou, Zhi-Hua. 2013. Speedup matrix completion with side information: Application to multi-label learning. *Pages 2301–2309 of: Advances in Neural Information Processing Systems*.

Yi, Xinyang, Park, Dohyung, Chen, Yudong, & Caramanis, Constantine. 2016. Fast Algorithms for Robust PCA via Gradient Descent. *arXiv preprint arXiv:1605.07784*.

Zhou, Tinghui, Shan, Hanhuai, Banerjee, Arindam, & Sapiro, Guillermo. 2012. Kernelized probabilistic matrix factorization: Exploiting graphs and side information. *Pages 403–414 of: Proceedings of the 2012 SIAM international Conference on Data mining*. SIAM.

Appendix of
Provable Inductive Robust PCA via Iterative Hard Thresholding

A PROOFS: NOISY CASE

A.1 Proof of Theorem 3.2

Proof. We prove this by induction over t. Note that Step 3 of Algorithm 1 initializes $\zeta_0 = 5\mu^2\sigma^2_{\max}(F)\frac{d}{n}c_W + \nu$ and sets $\zeta_t = \mu^2\sigma^2_{\max}(F)\frac{d}{n}\frac{c_W}{5^{t-1}} + \nu$ for all $t \geq 1$. Let $\nu = (3\mu^2 d\kappa^2 + 1)\|N^*\|_\infty$. For $t = 1$, since $L_0 = 0$ by our initialization, it is clear that $\|L^* - L_0\|_\infty \leq \mu^2\sigma^2_{\max}(F)\frac{d}{n}c_W$ and hence the base case holds. Next, for $t \geq 1$, by using Lemma 3.3, we have $\|S^* - S_t\|_\infty \leq 2\mu^2\sigma^2_{\max}(F)\frac{d}{n}\frac{c_W}{5^{t-1}} + 2(3\mu^2 d\kappa^2 + 1)\|N^*\|_\infty$ and further, by Lemma 3.4, we have $\|L^* - L_t\|_\infty \leq \mu^2\sigma^2_{\max}(F)\frac{d}{n}\frac{c_W}{5^t} + 3\mu^2 d\kappa^2\|N^*\|_\infty$. Moreover, setting $T > \lceil \log_5(2\mu^2\sigma^2_{\max}(F)\frac{d}{n}\frac{c_W}{\epsilon})\rceil + 1$, we obtain the result. □

A.2 Proof of Lemma 3.3

Proof. Recall that $S_t = \mathcal{P}_{\zeta_t}(M - L_{t-1}) = \mathcal{P}_{\zeta_t}(L^* - L_{t-1} + S^* + N^*)$. By the definition of our entry-wise hard thresholding operation, we have the following:

1. Term $e_i^\top S_t e_j = e_i^\top(M - L_{t-1})e_j = e_i^\top(L^* + S^* + N^* - L_{t-1})e_j$ when $|e_i^\top(M - L_{t-1})e_j| > \zeta_t$. Thus, $|e_i^\top(S^* - S_t)e_j| = |e_i^\top(L^* - L_{t-1})e_j| + |e_i^\top N^* e_j| \leq \mu^2\sigma^2_{\max}(F)\frac{d}{n}\frac{c_W}{5^{t-1}} + 3\mu^2 d\kappa^2\|N^*\|_\infty + \|N^*\|_\infty$.
2. Term $e_i^\top S_t e_j = 0$ when $|e_i^\top(M - L_{t-1})e_j| = |e_i^\top(L^* + S^* + N^* - L_{t-1})e_j| \leq \zeta_t$. Now, using the triangle inequality, we have $|e_i^\top(S^* - S_t)e^j| = |e_i^\top S^* e^j| \leq \zeta_t + |e_i^\top(L^* - L_{t-1})e_j| + |e_i^\top N^* e_j| \leq 2\left(\mu^2\sigma^2_{\max}(F)\frac{d}{n}\frac{c_W}{5^{t-1}} + 3\mu^2 d\kappa^2\|N^*\|_\infty + \|N^*\|_\infty\right)$.

Thus, the above two cases show the validity of the entry-wise hard thresholding operation. Next, we show that for any given (i, j), if $e_i^\top S^* e_j = 0$ then $e_i^\top S_t e_j$ is also zero for all t. Noting that $M = L^* + S^* + N^*$ and $e_i^\top S^* e_j = 0$, $e_i^\top S_t e_j = e_i^\top(M - L_{t-1})e_j = e_i^\top(L^* + N^* - L_{t-1})e_j \neq 0$ iff $|e_i^\top(L^* + N^* - L_{t-1})e_j| > \zeta_t$. But this is a contradiction since $|e_i^\top(L^* + N^* - L_{t-1})e_j| \leq |e_i^\top(L^* - L_{t-1})e_j| + |e_i^\top N^* e_j| \leq \mu^2\sigma^2_{\max}(F)\frac{d}{n}\frac{c_W}{5^{t-1}} + 3\mu^2 d\kappa^2\|N^*\|_\infty + \|N^*\|_\infty = \zeta_t$. □

A.3 Proof of Lemma 3.4

Proof. Using the fact that $F_1 = F_2$, $L^* = F^\top W^* F$ and $L_t = F^\top W_t F$, we have

$$\begin{aligned}
\|L^* - L_t\|_\infty &= \left\|F^\top(W^* - W_t)F\right\|_\infty \\
&= \max_{i,j} \left|e_i^\top F^\top(W^* - W_t)Fe_j\right| \\
&\overset{\xi_{11}}{=} \max_{i,j} \left|e_i^\top V_F\Sigma_F^\top U_F^\top(W^* - W_t)U_F\Sigma_F V_F^\top e_j\right| \\
&\overset{\xi_{12}}{\leq} \left(\max_i \left\|e_i^\top V_F\Sigma_F^\top\right\|_2\right)^2 \left\|U_F^\top(W^* - W_t)U_F\right\|_2
\end{aligned} \tag{10}$$

where ξ_{11} follows by substituting the SVD of $F = U_F\Sigma_F V_F^\top$ and ξ_{12} follows from the sub-multiplicative property of the spectral norm. Similar to the proof of Lemma 3.2, using Assumption 2 we have:

$$\max_i \left\|e_i^\top V_F\Sigma_F^\top\right\|_2 \leq \mu\sqrt{\frac{d}{n}}\sigma_{\max}(F). \tag{11}$$

Let the residual sparse perturbation be defined as $E_t := S - S_t$. Let $Q\Lambda Q^\top + Q_\perp\Lambda_\perp Q_\perp^\top$ be the full SVD of $W^* + G^\top(E_t + N^*)G$ where Q and $Q_\perp$ span orthogonal sub-spaces of dimensions r and $d - r$ respectively, and $G = F^\dagger$ is the pseudoinverse. Also, recall that from Step 7 of Algorithm 1 that W_t is computed as $\mathcal{P}_r\left((F_1^\top)^\dagger(M - S_t)(F_2)^\dagger\right)$

where $M = F_1^\top W^* F_2 + S^* + N^*$. Using these and the unitary invariance property of the spectral norm, we have

$$\begin{aligned}
&\left\|U_F^\top (W^* - W_t) U_F\right\|_2 \le \|W^* - W_t\|_2 \\
&\le \left\|W^* - \mathcal{P}_r(G^\top (F^\top W^* F + E_t + N^*)G)\right\|_2 \\
&\overset{\xi_{13}}{\le} \left\|Q\Lambda Q^\top + Q_\perp \Lambda_\perp Q_\perp^\top - G^\top (E_t + N^*)G - Q\Lambda Q^\top\right\|_2 \\
&\overset{\xi_{14}}{\le} \left\|G^\top (E_t + N^*)G\right\|_2 + \left\|Q_\perp \Lambda_\perp Q_\perp^\top\right\|_2 \\
&\overset{\xi_{15}}{\le} 2\left\|G^\top (E_t + N^*)G\right\|_2 \le 2\left\|G\right\|_2^2 \|E_t + N^*\|_2 \\
&\le \frac{2\|E_t + N^*\|_2}{[\sigma_{\min}(F)]^2} \overset{\xi_{16}}{\le} \frac{2z\|E_t\|_\infty}{[\sigma_{\min}(F)]^2} + \frac{2\|N^*\|_2}{[\sigma_{\min}(F)]^2}
\end{aligned} \tag{12}$$

where ξ_{13} is obtained by substituting $W^* = Q\Lambda Q^\top + Q_\perp \Lambda_\perp Q_\perp^\top - G^\top (E_t + N^*)G$, ξ_{14} by triangle inequality, ξ_{15} by using Weyl's eigenvalue perturbation lemma, ie,

$$\left\|Q_\perp \Lambda_\perp Q_\perp^\top\right\|_2 = \|\Lambda_\perp\|_\infty \le \left\|G^\top (E_t + N^*)G\right\|_2$$

and ξ_{16} by using Lemma 4 of (Netrapalli *et al.* , 2014) along with triangle inequality. Now, combining Equations (10), (11) and (12), we have

$$\begin{aligned}
\|L^* - L_t\|_\infty &\le 2\mu^2 \frac{d}{n} \kappa^2 \left(z\|E_t\|_\infty + \|N^*\|_2\right) \\
&\overset{\xi_{17}}{\le} \frac{\|E_t\|_\infty}{10} + 2\mu^2 d\kappa^2 \|N^*\|_\infty
\end{aligned} \tag{13}$$

where ξ_{17} follows by using Assumption 3 and the inequality that $\|N^*\|_2 \le n\|N^*\|_\infty$. Using the inequality $\|S^* - S_t\|_\infty \le 2\left(\mu^2 \sigma_{\max}^2(F) \frac{d}{n} \frac{cW}{5^{t-1}} + (3\mu^2 d\kappa^2 + 1)\|N^*\|_\infty\right)$ from Lemma 3.3 in Equation (13) completes the proof. □

B PROOFS: ASYMMETRIC CASE

B.1 Proof of Claim 3.1

Proof. Applying the symmetric embedding transformation to our data matrix, we get $\mathrm{Sym}(M) = \mathrm{Sym}(L^*) + \mathrm{Sym}(S^*)$. Now we characterize the properties of this symmetric embedding and show that it satisfies Assumptions 1, 2 and 3. First, we have

$$\begin{aligned}
\mathrm{Sym}(L^*) &= \begin{pmatrix} 0 & L^* \\ L^{*\top} & 0 \end{pmatrix} = \begin{pmatrix} 0 & F_1^\top W^* F_2 \\ F_2^\top W^{*\top} F_1 & 0 \end{pmatrix} \\
&= \begin{pmatrix} F_1^\top & 0 \\ 0 & F_2^\top \end{pmatrix} \begin{pmatrix} 0 & W^* \\ W^{*\top} & 0 \end{pmatrix} \begin{pmatrix} F_1 & 0 \\ 0 & F_2 \end{pmatrix}.
\end{aligned}$$

Thus, $\mathrm{Sym}(L^*)$ is of the form $\widetilde{F}^\top \widetilde{W}^* \widetilde{F}$. If the SVD of W^* is $U_{W^*}\Sigma_{W^*}V_{W^*}^\top$, then the eigenvalue decomposition of $\widetilde{W}^*$ is given by

$$\begin{aligned}
\widetilde{W}^* &= \begin{pmatrix} 0 & W^* \\ W^{*\top} & 0 \end{pmatrix} = \begin{pmatrix} 0 & U_{W^*}\Sigma_{W^*}V_{W^*}^\top \\ V_{W^*}\Sigma_{W^*}^\top U_{W^*}^\top & 0 \end{pmatrix} \\
&= \frac{1}{2} \begin{pmatrix} U_{W^*} & U_{W^*} \\ V_{W^*} & -V_{W^*} \end{pmatrix} \begin{pmatrix} \Sigma_{W^*} & 0 \\ 0 & -\Sigma_{W^*} \end{pmatrix} \begin{pmatrix} U_{W^*} & U_{W^*} \\ V_{W^*} & -V_{W^*} \end{pmatrix}^\top,
\end{aligned}$$

implying that $\mathrm{rank}(\widetilde{W}^*) = 2 \cdot \mathrm{rank}(W^*)$. Next, let the SVDs of F_1 and F_2 be $U_{F_1}\Sigma_{F_1}V_{F_1}^\top$ and $U_{F_2}\Sigma_{F_2}V_{F_2}^\top$ respectively; also, without loss of generality, let $\sigma_{\min}(F_1) > \sigma_{\min}(F_2)$. Then, the SVD of $\widetilde{F} = U_{\widetilde{F}}\Sigma_{\widetilde{F}}V_{\widetilde{F}}^\top$ is given by

$$\widetilde{F} = \begin{pmatrix} F_1 & 0 \\ 0 & F_2 \end{pmatrix} = \begin{pmatrix} U_{F_1}\Sigma_{F_1}V_{F_1}^\top & 0 \\ 0 & U_{F_2}\Sigma_{F_2}V_{F_2}^\top \end{pmatrix}$$
$$= \begin{pmatrix} U_{F_1} & 0 \\ 0 & U_{F_2} \end{pmatrix} \begin{pmatrix} \Sigma_{F_1} & 0 \\ 0 & \Sigma_{F_2} \end{pmatrix} \begin{pmatrix} V_{F_1}^\top & 0 \\ 0 & V_{F_2}^\top \end{pmatrix}$$

Now, we verify that the right singular vectors of this new feature matrix $\widetilde{F}$ satisfies weak incoherence property. Specifically, we expect that the following holds:

$$\max_j \left\| V_{\widetilde{F}} e_j \right\|_2 \leq \mu_{\widetilde{F}} \sqrt{\frac{d_1 + d_2}{n_1 + n_2}} \tag{14}$$

On the other hand, we actually have

$$\max_j \left\| V e_j \right\|_2 \leq \max \left(\mu_{F_1} \sqrt{\frac{d_1}{n_1}}, \mu_{F_2} \sqrt{\frac{d_2}{n_2}} \right). \tag{15}$$

Wlog, let $\mu_{F_1}\sqrt{d_1/n_1} > \mu_{F_2}\sqrt{d_2/n_2}$. Then, combining Equations (14) and (15), we want $\frac{\mu_{\widetilde{F}}}{\mu_{F_1}} \leq \sqrt{\frac{1+n_2/n_1}{1+d_2/d_1}}$. In particular, when $n_2/n_1 = d_2/d_1$, the incoherence constant for $\widetilde{F}$ satisfies $\mu_{\widetilde{F}} = \mu_{F_1}$.

Next, note that $\mathrm{Sym}(S^*)$ is also sparse; specifically, $\|S^*\|_{0,\infty} \leq z$ and $\|S^*\|_{\infty,0} \leq z$ where $z = \max(z_1, z_2)$.

Finally, our algorithm and guarantees hold for general matrices with noise, similar to noiseless case, due to the following observation: $\|\mathrm{Sym}(N^*)\|_\infty = \|N^*\|_\infty$. □

Near-Orthogonality Regularization in Kernel Methods

Pengtao Xie[*†], Barnabas Poczos[*] and Eric P. Xing[†]
[*]Machine Learning Department, Carnegie Mellon University
[†]Petuum Inc.
{pengtaox,bapoczos}@cs.cmu.edu, eric.xing@petuum.com

Abstract

Kernel methods perform nonlinear learning in high-dimensional reproducing kernel Hilbert spaces (RKHSs). Even though their large model-capacity leads to high representational power, it also incurs substantial risk of overfitting. To alleviate this problem, we propose a new regularization approach, *near-orthogonality regularization*, which encourages the RKHS functions to be close to being orthogonal. This effectively imposes a structural constraint over the function space, which reduces model complexity and can improve generalization performance. Besides, encouraging orthogonality reduces the redundancy among functions, which hence can reduce model size without compromising modeling power and better capture infrequent patterns in the data. Here, we define a family of orthogonality-promoting regularizers by encouraging the Gram matrix of the RKHS functions to be close to an identity matrix where the closeness is measured by Bregman matrix divergences. We apply these regularizers to two kernel methods, and develop an efficient ADMM-based algorithm to solve the regularized optimization problems. We analyze how near-orthogonality affects the generalization performance of kernel methods. Our results suggest that the closer the functions are to being orthogonal, the smaller the generalization error is. Experiments demonstrate the efficacy of near-orthogonality regularization in kernel methods.

1 INTRODUCTION

Kernel methods perform learning in reproducing kernel Hilbert spaces (RKHSs) of functions (Schölkopf and Smola, 2002). The RKHS represents a high-dimensional feature space that can capture nonlinear patterns in the lower-dimensional observed data. This Hilbert space is associated with a kernel function k, and the inner product in the RKHS can be implicitly computed by evaluating k in the lower-dimensional input space (known as *kernel trick*). Well-established kernel methods include support vector machine (Schölkopf and Smola, 2002), kernel principal component analysis (Schölkopf et al., 1997), kernel independent component analysis (Bach and Jordan, 2002), to name a few.

One key ingredient in kernel methods is regularization, which reduces overfitting by controlling the complexity of the RKHS functions (Schölkopf and Smola, 2002; Micchelli and Pontil, 2005). Regularizers proposed previously such as RKHS norm, derivatives, green functions, and splines mostly focus on encouraging a small norm (Micchelli and Pontil, 2005) and smoothness of functions (Schölkopf and Smola, 2002). Notably, the most widely-used regularizer is the squared RKHS norm.

In this work, we introduce a new regularization approach that encourages a set of RKHS functions to be close to being orthogonal, so that the correlation and redundancy between these functions can be reduced. Besides alleviating overfitting problems, these regularizers can also (1) reduce model size without sacrificing modeling power (Xie, 2015): near-orthogonal functions bear less redundancy and are highly complementary, and thus a small number of such functions can possess sufficient representational power; (2) capture infrequent latent patterns in the data (Xie et al., 2015a): without near-orthogonality regularization, the majority of RKHS functions are used to capture frequent patterns since these patterns have dominant signals in the dataset; promoting near-orthogonality among the functions can drive them to diversely "spread out", giving both infrequent and frequent patterns a fair treatment. Previously, regularizers that achieved near-orthogonality effects have been investigated in other methods, including latent Dirichlet allocation (Zou and Adams, 2012), neural networks (Cogswell et al., 2015) and restricted Boltzmann machine (Xie et al., 2015a); however, they have not been explored in kernel methods. We aim to bridge this gap in this work.

To promote near-orthogonality among a set of RKHS functions $\{f_i\}_{i=1}^K$, we compute their Gram matrix $\mathbf{G}$ where $G_{ij} = \langle f_i, f_j \rangle$, and encourage $\mathbf{G}$ to be close to an identity matrix $\mathbf{I}$. The off-diagonal elements of $\mathbf{G}$ and $\mathbf{I}$ are $\langle f_i, f_j \rangle$ and zero, respectively. The elements on the diagonal of $\mathbf{G}$ and $\mathbf{I}$ are $\|f_i\|_{\mathcal{H}}^2$ and one, respectively. Making $\mathbf{G}$ close to $\mathbf{I}$ effectively encourages $\langle f_i, f_j \rangle$ to be close to zero and $\|f_i\|_{\mathcal{H}}$ to be close to one, which drives f_i and f_j to be close to being orthogonal. We measure the closeness between $\mathbf{G}$ and $\mathbf{I}$ using Bregman matrix divergences (Dhillon and Tropp, 2007), and define a family of near-orthogonality regularizers thereupon. We apply the proposed regularizers to two kernel methods – kernel distance metric learning (KDML) (Tsang et al., 2003; Jain et al., 2012) and kernel sparse coding (KSC) (Gao et al., 2010), and develop an optimization algorithm based on alternating direction method of multipliers (ADMM) (Boyd et al., 2011) where the RKHS functions are learned using functional gradient descent (FGD) (Dai et al., 2014). We perform analysis to show that the near-orthogonality regularization can reduce generalization error bounds. Experimental results show that the proposed near-orthogonality regularizers (1) greatly improve the generalization performance of KDML and KSC; (2) can reduce model size without sacrificing modeling power; (3) can better capture infrequent patterns in the data; and (4) outperform other orthogonality-promoting regularizers and the squared Hilbert norm.

The major contributions of this paper are:

- We propose a new regularization approach in kernel methods that encourages the RKHS functions to be close to being orthogonal.
- We define a family of near-orthogonality regularizers based on Bregman matrix divergences.
- We apply these regularizers to two kernel methods, and develop an ADMM-based algorithm to solve the regularized optimization problems.
- We analyze how the near-orthogonality regularization affects the generalization performance of kernel methods.
- Experiments demonstrate the efficacy of the proposed regularizers.

The rest of the paper is organized as follows. Section 2 reviews related works. Section 3 introduces the near-orthogonality regularizers and an ADMM-based algorithm. Section 4 and 5 present the generalization error analysis and experimental results respectively. Finally, Section 6 concludes the paper.

2 RELATED WORKS

In non-kernel methods, regularizers that achieve near-orthogonality effects have been investigated. Zou and Adams (2012) employ the determinantal point process (DPP) (Kulesza and Taskar, 2012) to encourage the parallelepiped formed by a set of vectors $\{\mathbf{w}_i\}_{i=1}^K$ to have a large volume which indirectly promotes near-orthogonality among these vectors, because making the vectors close to being orthogonal can effectively enlarge the volume. A major drawback of DPP is its sensitivity to the scaling of vectors, e.g., increasing the magnitude of vectors can also enlarge the volume, but it does not promote near-orthogonality. Xie et al. (2015a) propose an angle-based regularizer, which encourages the angles between a set of vectors to have large mean and small variance, hence encouraging these vectors to become orthogonal. The angle between vector $\mathbf{w}_i$ and $\mathbf{w}_j$ is defined as $\theta_{ij} = \arccos(\frac{|\mathbf{w}_i^\top \mathbf{w}_j|}{\|\mathbf{w}_i\|_2 \|\mathbf{w}_j\|_2})$. An absolute value is used here to ensure the angles are driven to $\frac{\pi}{2}$ (orthogonal), rather than π. The absolute value makes this regularizer non-smooth, which brings in difficulty for optimization. In this paper, we aim to define new near-orthogonality regularizers to overcome the limitations of existing ones.

3 METHOD

We consider kernel methods that are parameterized by a set of RKHS functions. Examples include kernel principal component analysis (PCA) (Schölkopf et al., 1997), kernel independent component analysis (ICA) (Bach and Jordan, 2002), kernel distance metric learning (Tsang et al., 2003; Jain et al., 2012) and kernel sparse coding (Gao et al., 2010), to name a few. We propose to regularize these functions from the perspective of *near-orthogonality*, which encourages these functions to be close to being orthogonal. This can reduce the correlation and redundancy among the functions, which can potentially bring in several benefits: (1) reducing overfitting, (2) shrinking model size (the number of functions) without sacrificing modeling power, and (3) capturing infrequent patterns, as we will verify in experiments.

3.1 NEAR-ORTHOGONALITY REGULARIZERS

In this section, we first define regularizers to achieve near-orthogonality between two RKHS functions f and g. One way to encourage f and g to be close to being orthogonal is to make their inner product $\langle f, g \rangle$ in the

RKHS close to zero and their norms $\|f\|_{\mathcal{H}}$ and $\|g\|_{\mathcal{H}}$ close to one. In light of this, the near-orthogonality among a set of functions $\mathcal{F} = \{f_i\}_{i=1}^{K}$ can be achieved in the following manner: computing the Gram matrix $\mathbf{G}$ where $G_{ij} = \langle f_i, f_j \rangle$, then encouraging $\mathbf{G}$ to be close to an identity matrix. Off the diagonal of $\mathbf{G}$ and $\mathbf{I}$ are $\langle f_i, f_j \rangle$ and zero, respectively. On the diagonal of $\mathbf{G}$ and $\mathbf{I}$ are $\|f_i\|_{\mathcal{H}}^2$ and one, respectively. Making $\mathbf{G}$ close to $\mathbf{I}$ effectively encourages $\langle f_i, f_j \rangle$ to be close to zero and $\|f_i\|_{\mathcal{H}}$ close to one, which as a result encourages f_i and f_j to be close to being orthogonal.

Next, we discuss how to measure the closeness between $\mathbf{G}$ and $\mathbf{I}$. One straightforward way is to use the squared Frobenius norm (SFN): $\|\mathbf{G} - \mathbf{I}\|_F^2$. The SFN measures orthogonality of functions in a pairwise manner since it can be factorized into pairwise inner products: $\sum_{i=1}^{K} \sum_{j \neq i}^{K} (\langle f_i, f_j \rangle)^2 + \sum_{i=1}^{K} (\|f_i\|_{\mathcal{H}}^2 - 1)^2$. We conjecture[1] that measuring orthogonality in a global manner is more desirable. To achieve this goal, we resort to another measure: Bregman matrix divergence (BMD) (Dhillon and Tropp, 2007). Let $\mathbb{S}^n$ denote real, symmetric $n \times n$ matrices. Given a strictly convex, differentiable function $\phi : \mathbb{S}^n \rightarrow \mathbb{R}$, the BMD is defined as: $D_\phi(\mathbf{X}, \mathbf{Y}) = \phi(\mathbf{X}) - \phi(\mathbf{Y}) - \mathrm{tr}((\nabla \phi(\mathbf{Y}))^\top (\mathbf{X} - \mathbf{Y}))$ where $\mathrm{tr}(\cdot)$ denotes the trace of a matrix. Under different choices of ϕ, $D_\phi(\mathbf{X}, \mathbf{Y})$ can be specialized to several instances. Under $\phi(\mathbf{X}) = \mathrm{tr}(\mathbf{X} \log \mathbf{X} - \mathbf{X})$, where $\log \mathbf{X}$ is the matrix logarithm, we have the von Neumann divergence (VND) (Kulis et al., 2009): $D_{vN}(\mathbf{X}, \mathbf{Y}) = \mathrm{tr}(\mathbf{X} \log \mathbf{X} - \mathbf{X} \log \mathbf{Y} - \mathbf{X} + \mathbf{Y})$. $\phi(\mathbf{X}) = -\log \det \mathbf{X}$ results in a log-determinant divergence (LDD) (Kulis et al., 2009): $D_{ld}(\mathbf{X}, \mathbf{Y}) = \mathrm{tr}(\mathbf{X}\mathbf{Y}^{-1}) - \log \det(\mathbf{X}\mathbf{Y}^{-1}) - n$. Interestingly, SFN is a special case of BMD when $\phi(\mathbf{X}) = \|\mathbf{X}\|_F^2$. Given the three instances of BMD, we can use them to measure the closeness between $\mathbf{G}$ and $\mathbf{I}$, and define a family of BMD regularizers (constants are dropped) to promote near-orthogonality. Under VND, the regularizer is

$$\Omega_{vN}(\mathcal{F}) = D_{vN}(\mathbf{G}, \mathbf{I}) \propto \mathrm{tr}(\mathbf{G} \log \mathbf{G} - \mathbf{G}). \tag{1}$$

Under LDD, the regularizer is

$$\Omega_{ld}(\mathcal{F}) = D_{ld}(\mathbf{G}, \mathbf{I}) \propto \mathrm{tr}(\mathbf{G}) - \log \det(\mathbf{G}). \tag{2}$$

Under SFN, the regularizer is

$$\Omega_{sfn}(\mathcal{F}) = D_{sfn}(\mathbf{G}, \mathbf{I}) = \|\mathbf{G} - \mathbf{I}\|_F^2. \tag{3}$$

To apply the VND and LDD regularizers, the Gram matrix $\mathbf{G}$ is required to be positive definite. In our experiments, this condition is always satisfied since VND and LDD encourage the RKHS functions to be close to being orthogonal (therefore linearly independent). Different from the SFN regularizer, VND and LDD do not admit a pairwise factorization, and hence allow one to measure orthogonality globally; this benefit will be demonstrated in experiments as shown below (Section 5). Unlike DPP (Kulesza and Taskar, 2012), LDD utilizes an additional term $\mathrm{tr}(\mathbf{G}) = \sum_{i=1}^{K} \|f_i\|_{\mathcal{H}}^2$ to control the magnitude of RKHS functions, and thus avoiding DPP's sensitivity to scaling. Similarly, VND and SFN are also insensitive to scaling since they encourage $\|f\|_{\mathcal{H}}$ to be close to one. In addition, all three regularizers are smooth and amenable for optimization.

Here, we use these regularizers to encourage near-orthogonality among RKHS functions, and define BMD regularized kernel methods (BMD-KM):

$$\min_{\mathcal{F}} \quad \mathcal{L}(\mathcal{F}) + \lambda \Omega(\mathcal{F}) \tag{4}$$

where $\mathcal{L}(\mathcal{F})$ is the objective function of the kernel method, and λ is the regularization parameter. Compared to kernel PCA and ICA in which the functions are required to be strictly-orthogonal, BMD-KM can be seen as a relaxed counterpart where the functions are encouraged to be close to, but not necessarily strictly, orthogonal. As we will demonstrate in the experiments, strict-orthogonality can compromise performance in certain applications.

3.2 CASE STUDIES

In this section, we apply the BMD regularizers to two instances of kernel methods: kernel distance metric learning and kernel sparse coding.

Kernel Distance Metric Learning with BMD Regularization Distance metric learning (DML) has wide applications in classification, clustering and information retrieval (Xing et al., 2002; Davis et al., 2007; Guillaumin et al., 2009). Given data pairs labeled as similar or dissimilar, DML aims at learning a distance metric such that similar pairs would be placed close to each other and dissimilar pairs are separated apart. Kernel DML (Tsang et al., 2003; Jain et al., 2012) is equipped with K RKHS functions $\mathcal{F} = \{f_i\}_{i=1}^{K}$ that map a data example $\mathbf{x}$ into a vector $\mathbf{h}^{(x)}$ in a K-dimensional latent space, where $\mathbf{h}_i^{(x)} = f_i(\mathbf{x})$. Given two examples $\mathbf{x}$ and $\mathbf{y}$, their distance is defined as $d_{\mathcal{F}}(\mathbf{x}, \mathbf{y}) = \|\mathbf{h}^{(x)} - \mathbf{h}^{(y)}\|_2^2$, which is parameterized by $\mathcal{F}$. Given N training examples, $\{\mathbf{x}_n, \mathbf{y}_n, t_n\}_{n=1}^{N}$, where $\mathbf{x}_n$ and $\mathbf{y}_n$ are similar if the label t_n equals to 1 and dissimilar if $t_n = 0$, following (Guillaumin et al., 2009), we learn the distance metric by minimizing $\sum_{n=1}^{N} \log(1 + \exp((2t_n - 1) d_{\mathcal{F}}(\mathbf{x}_n, \mathbf{y}_n)))$. Using $\Omega(\mathcal{F})$ to promote near-orthogonality, we obtain

[1]The conjecture is validated in experiments.

the BMD-regularized KDML (BMD-KDML) problem:

$$\min_{\mathcal{F}} \sum_{n=1}^{N} \log(1+\exp((2t_n-1)d_{\mathcal{F}}(\mathbf{x}_n,\mathbf{y}_n))+\lambda\Omega(\mathcal{F}). \tag{5}$$

Kernel Sparse Coding with BMD Regularization Sparse coding (SC) (Olshausen and Field, 1997) is widely applied for signal processing, data reconstruction, feature learning, to name a few. To reconstruct an input data $\mathbf{x}$, SC learns a dictionary of basis $\{\mathbf{d}_i\}_{i=1}^K$ and reconstructs $\mathbf{x}$ using a sparse linear combination of the basis: $\mathbf{x} \approx \sum_{i=1}^K \alpha_i \mathbf{d}_i$, where $\{\alpha_i\}_{i=1}^K$ are the sparse coefficients. In the kernel SC (Gao et al., 2010), $\mathbf{x}$ is mapped into $k(\mathbf{x},\cdot)$ in a RKHS induced by kernel function $k(\cdot,\cdot)$ and a dictionary of RKHS functions $\mathcal{F} = \{f_i\}_{i=1}^K$ are learned to reconstruct $k(\mathbf{x},\cdot)$. Given the training data $\{\mathbf{x}_n\}_{n=1}^N$, $\mathcal{F}$ can be learned by minimizing $\frac{1}{2}\sum_{n=1}^N \|k(\mathbf{x}_n,\cdot)-\sum_{i=1}^K a_{ni}f_i\|_{\mathcal{H}}^2+\lambda_1\sum_{n=1}^N\|\mathbf{a}_n\|_1+\frac{\lambda_2}{2}\sum_{i=1}^K\|f_i\|_{\mathcal{H}}^2$, where the reconstruction error is measured by the squared Hilbert norm and $\mathbf{a}_n$ are the linear coefficients. The ℓ_1 regularizer $\|\mathbf{a}_n\|_1$ is applied to encourage the coefficients to be sparse. To avoid the degenerated case where the RKHS functions are of large norm while the coefficients are close to zero, the squared Hilbert norm regularizer $\|f_i\|_{\mathcal{H}}^2$ is applied to the RKHS functions to keep their magnitude small. By adding $\Omega(\mathcal{F})$, we obtain the BMD-regularized KSC (BMD-KSC) problem:

$$\begin{aligned}\min_{\mathcal{F},\mathcal{A}} \quad & \tfrac{1}{2}\sum_{n=1}^{N}\|k(\mathbf{x}_n,\cdot)-\sum_{i=1}^{K} a_{ni}f_i\|_{\mathcal{H}}^2 \\ & +\lambda_1\sum_{n=1}^{N}\|\mathbf{a}_n\|_1+\tfrac{\lambda_2}{2}\sum_{i=1}^{K}\|f_i\|_{\mathcal{H}}^2+\lambda_3\Omega(\mathcal{F})\end{aligned} \tag{6}$$

where $\mathcal{A}$ denotes all the sparse codes.

3.3 ALGORITHM

In this section, we develop an ADMM (Boyd et al., 2011) based algorithm to solve the BMD-KM problem. First, by introducing auxiliary variables $\widehat{\mathcal{F}} = \{\widehat{f}_i\}_{i=1}^K$ which are a set of RKHS functions and $\mathbf{A} \in \mathbb{R}^{K\times K}$, we rewrite the BMD-KM problem into an equivalent form that is amenable for developing ADMM-based algorithms.

$$\begin{aligned}\min_{\mathcal{F},\widehat{\mathcal{F}},\mathbf{A}} \quad & \mathcal{L}(\mathcal{F})+\lambda D_\phi(\mathbf{A},\mathbf{I}) \\ s.t. \quad & \forall i, f_i=\widehat{f}_i \\ & \forall i,j, \langle f_i,\widehat{f}_j\rangle = A_{ij}, \langle f_i,\widehat{f}_j\rangle = A_{ji}\end{aligned} \tag{7}$$

where $\mathbf{A}$ is required to be positive definite when $D_\phi(\mathbf{A},\mathbf{I})$ is an VND or LDD regularizer. The constraints $\langle f_i,\widehat{f}_j\rangle = A_{ij}$ and $\langle f_i,\widehat{f}_j\rangle = A_{ji}$ imply that $\mathbf{A}$ is symmetric. We define augmented Lagrangian with parameter $\rho>0$: $\mathcal{L}(\mathcal{F})+\lambda D_\phi(\mathbf{A},\mathbf{I})+\sum_{i=1}^K\langle g_i, f_i - \widehat{f}_i\rangle+\sum_{i=1}^K\sum_{j=1}^K(P_{ij}(\langle f_i,\widehat{f}_j\rangle-A_{ij})+Q_{ij}(\langle f_i,\widehat{f}_j\rangle-A_{ji})+\frac{\rho}{2}(\langle f_i,\widehat{f}_j\rangle-A_{ij})^2+\frac{\rho}{2}(\langle f_i,\widehat{f}_j\rangle-A_{ji})^2)$, where $\mathcal{G}=\{g_i\}_{i=1}^K$ is another set of RKHS functions, and $\mathbf{P},\mathbf{Q}\in\mathbb{R}^{K\times K}$ are Lagrange multipliers. Then we minimize this Lagrangian function by alternating among $\mathcal{F}$, $\widehat{\mathcal{F}}$, $\mathcal{G}$, $\mathbf{A}$, $\mathbf{P}$, $\mathbf{Q}$.

Solve A Given $\mathbf{H}\in\mathbb{R}^{K\times K}$ where $H_{ij}=\langle f_i,\hat{f}_j\rangle$, we learn $\mathbf{A}$ by minimizing $\lambda D_\phi(\mathbf{A},\mathbf{I})-\langle\mathbf{P},\mathbf{A}\rangle-\langle\mathbf{Q}^\top,\mathbf{A}\rangle+\frac{\rho}{2}\|\mathbf{H}-\mathbf{A}\|_F^2+\frac{\rho}{2}\|\mathbf{H}^\top-\mathbf{A}\|_F^2$, which is a convex problem. $D_\phi(\mathbf{A},\mathbf{I})$ has three cases, which we discuss separately.

When $D_\phi(\mathbf{A},\mathbf{I})$ is VND, we first perform an eigendecomposition of $\mathbf{D}=\mathbf{P}+\mathbf{Q}^\top+\rho(\mathbf{H}+\mathbf{H}^\top)$: $\mathbf{D}=\mathbf{\Phi}\mathbf{\Sigma}\mathbf{\Phi}^{-1}$, then the optimal solution of $\mathbf{A}$ can be obtained as $\mathbf{A}=\mathbf{\Phi}\widehat{\mathbf{\Sigma}}\mathbf{\Phi}^{-1}$ where

$$\widehat{\Sigma}_{ii}=\frac{\lambda\omega\left(\frac{\Sigma_{ii}}{\lambda}-\log\left(\frac{\lambda}{2\rho}\right)\right)}{2\rho} \tag{8}$$

and $\omega(\cdot)$ is the Wright omega function (Gorenflo et al., 2007). It can be shown that $\mathbf{A}$ is positive definite.

When $D_\phi(\mathbf{A},\mathbf{I})$ is LDD, the optimal solution is:

$$\mathbf{A}=-\tfrac{1}{2}\mathbf{B}+\tfrac{1}{2}\sqrt{\mathbf{B}^2-4\mathbf{C}} \tag{9}$$

where $\mathbf{B}=\frac{1}{\rho}(\lambda\mathbf{I}-\mathbf{P}-\mathbf{Q}^\top-\rho(\mathbf{H}+\mathbf{H}^\top))$ and $\mathbf{C}=-\frac{\lambda}{\rho}\mathbf{I}$. It can be verified that $\mathbf{A}$ is positive definite.

When $D_\phi(\mathbf{A},\mathbf{I})$ is SFN, the optimal solution for $\mathbf{A}$ is:

$$\mathbf{A}=(2\lambda\mathbf{I}+\mathbf{P}+\mathbf{Q}^\top+\rho(\mathbf{H}+\mathbf{H}^\top))/(2\lambda+2\rho). \tag{10}$$

Please refer to the supplements for a detailed derivation.

Solve f_i We solve f_i by minimizing $\Upsilon=\mathcal{L}(\mathcal{F})+\langle g_i,f_i\rangle+\sum_{j=1}^K(P_{ij}+Q_{ij})\langle f_i,\widehat{f}_j\rangle+\frac{\rho}{2}\sum_{j=1}^K((\langle f_i,\widehat{f}_j\rangle-A_{ij})^2+(\langle f_i,\widehat{f}_j\rangle-A_{ji})^2)$. The first issue we need to address is how to represent f_i. When $f\in\mathcal{F}$ is regularized by the RKHS norm, according to the representer theorem (Schölkopf and Smola, 2002), the optimal solution f^* can be expressed as a linear combination of kernel functions evaluated at training data: $f^*(\mathbf{x})=\sum_{n=1}^N\alpha_n k(\mathbf{x}_n,\mathbf{x})$, which we refer to as *representer theorem representation* (RTR). This endows f^* an explicit parametrization that greatly eases learning: the search space of f^* is reduced from the infinite-dimensional RKHS $\mathcal{H}$ to an N-dimensional space of coefficients $\{\alpha_n\}_{n=1}^N$. However, in Υ, due to the presence of inner products between f_i with other functions, the representer theorem does not hold and f_i does not admit a RTR form. To address this issue, we learn f_i directly using functional gradient descent (Dai et al., 2014). A *functional* $F:\mathcal{H}\to\mathbb{R}$ maps functions in $\mathcal{H}$ to real numbers. A *functional gradient* $\nabla F[f]$ is defined implicitly as the linear term of the change in a function due to a small perturbation ϵ in its input: $F[f+\epsilon g] = F[f] + \epsilon\langle \nabla F[f], g\rangle + O(\epsilon^2)$. Of particular interest is the *evaluation functional* $F_{\mathbf{x}}[f]$ which is parameterized by an input vector $\mathbf{x}$ and evaluates f at $\mathbf{x}$: $F_{\mathbf{x}}[f] = f(\mathbf{x})$. The functional gradient of $F_{\mathbf{x}}[f]$ is $k(\mathbf{x},\cdot)$ (Dai et al., 2014) where k is the kernel associated with the RKHS. The gradient of an inner product functional $F_g[f] = \langle f, g\rangle$ is g.

$\mathcal{L}(\mathcal{F})$ depends on a specific kernel method. Here, we consider KDML where $\mathcal{L}(\mathcal{F})$ is given in Eq.(5) while leaving the derivation of KSC to the supplements. In KDML, f_i appears in two types of functionals: evaluation functionals in $d_{\mathcal{F}}(\mathbf{x}_n, \mathbf{y}_n)$ (such as $f_i(\mathbf{x}_n)$) and inner product functionals (such as $\langle g_i, f_i\rangle$). The functional gradient of Υ is $\triangle f_i = 2\sum_{n=1}^N \sigma((2t_n - 1)d_{\mathcal{F}}(\mathbf{x}_n, \mathbf{y}_n))(2t_n-1)(f_i(\mathbf{x}_n) - f_i(\mathbf{y}_n))(k(\mathbf{x}_n,\cdot) - k(\mathbf{y}_n,\cdot)) + g_i + \sum_{j=1}^K (P_{ij} + Q_{ij} + \rho(2\langle f_i, \widehat{f}_j\rangle - A_{ij} - A_{ji}))\widehat{f}_j$, where $\sigma(x) = 1/(1+\exp(-x))$ is a sigmoid function. Given this functional gradient, we can perform gradient descent to update f_i until convergence: $f_i \leftarrow f_i - \eta\triangle f_i$, where η is the learning rate. In the algorithm, we initialize f_i, g_i and $\widehat{f}_j$ as zero functions. Then as will be proven in Section 3.3.1, during the algorithm execution, f_i, g_i and $\widehat{f}_j$ are all in the form of RTR. So updating f_i amounts to updating the linear coefficients in the RTR.

Solve $\widehat{f}_j$ The sub-problem defined over $\widehat{f}_j$ is **(T)**: $\min_{\widehat{f}_j} - \langle g_j, \widehat{f}_j\rangle + \sum_{i=1}^K ((P_{ij} + Q_{ij})\langle f_i, \widehat{f}_j\rangle + \frac{\rho}{2}((\langle f_i, \widehat{f}_j\rangle - A_{ij})^2 + (\langle f_i, \widehat{f}_j\rangle - A_{ji})^2))$ which is a convex problem. Setting the derivative of the objective function to zero, we get an equation **(E)**: $(2\rho\sum_{i=1}^K f_i \otimes f_i)\widehat{f}_j = \sum_{i=1}^K (\rho(A_{ij} + A_{ji}) - (P_{ij} + Q_{ij}))f_i + g_j$, where $\otimes$ denotes the outer product in RKHS. As will be proven in Section 3.3.1, $\widehat{f}_j$, g_j and f_i are all in the form of RTR. Let $\Phi = [k(\mathbf{x}_1,\cdot), \cdots, k(\mathbf{x}_N,\cdot)]$, then $f_i = \Phi\mathbf{a}_i$, $\sum_{i=1}^K (\rho(A_{ij} + A_{ji}) - (P_{ij} + Q_{ij}))f_i + g_j = \Phi\mathbf{b}$, $\widehat{f}_j = \Phi\mathbf{c}$, where $\mathbf{a}_i$, $\mathbf{b}$, $\mathbf{c}$ are coefficient vectors. $\mathbf{a}_i$ and $\mathbf{b}$ are known and $\mathbf{c}$ is to be estimated. Then **(E)** can be written as $(2\rho\sum_{i=1}^K \mathbf{a}_i\mathbf{a}_i^\top)\Phi^\top\Phi\mathbf{c} = \mathbf{b}$, where $(\Phi^\top\Phi)_{ij} = k(\mathbf{x}_i, \mathbf{x}_j)$ and $\mathbf{c} = ((2\rho\sum_{i=1}^K \mathbf{a}_i\mathbf{a}_i^\top)\Phi^\top\Phi)^{-1}\mathbf{b}$. In practice, inverting the $N\times N$ matrix $(2\rho\sum_{i=1}^K \mathbf{a}_i\mathbf{a}_i^\top)\Phi^\top\Phi$ is computationally prohibitive when N is large. In that case, we can switch to a stochastic FGD method to solve this problem.

The update rules for $\mathbf{P}$, $\mathbf{Q}$ and g_j are simple:

Update P $\mathbf{P} = \mathbf{P} + \rho(\mathbf{H} - \mathbf{A})$

Update Q $\mathbf{Q} = \mathbf{Q} + \rho(\mathbf{H} - \mathbf{A}^\top)$

Update g_j $g_j = g_j + \rho(f_j - \hat{f}_j)$

3.3.1 RTR Form of RKHS Functions

Next, we present the proof that as long as the RKHS functions f_i, g_i and $\widehat{f}_j$ are initialized to be zero, they are always in the RTR form during the entire execution of the algorithm. We prove this by induction. For the base case (iteration $t=0$), these functions are all zero, hence admitting the RTR form. For the inductive step, assuming the statement is true at iteration $t-1$, we prove it holds for iteration t. We begin with f_i, which is solved by FGD. At iteration t, the input of the algorithm is $f_i^{(t-1)}$ and output is $f_i^{(t)}$. The first term of the functional gradient $\triangle f_i$ is in the RTR form, so are g_i and $\widehat{f}_j$ (according to the inductive hypothesis). Then $\triangle f_i$ is in the RTR form. Starting from $f_i^{(t-1)}$ which is in the RTR form according to the inductive hypothesis, f_i is updated iteratively in the following way: $f_i^{(s)} \leftarrow f_i^{(s-1)} - \eta\triangle f_i^{(s-1)}$ (where s indexes FGD iterations), resulting in $f_i^{(t)}$ which is also in the RTR form.

Next, we prove that if $g_j^{(t-1)}$ and $f_i^{(t-1)}$ are in the RTR form, so will be $\widehat{f}_j$. The proof is similar to that of the representer theorem (Schölkopf and Smola, 2002). We decompose $\widehat{f}_j$ into $\widehat{f}_j^{\parallel}$ and $\widehat{f}_j^{\perp}$, where $\widehat{f}_j^{\parallel}$ is in $S = \{\sum_{n=1}^N \alpha_n k(\mathbf{x}_n, \mathbf{x}), \{\alpha_n\}_{n=1}^N \subset \mathbb{R}\}$ (i.e., in the RTR form) and $\widehat{f}_j^{\perp}$ is perpendicular to S, hence $\langle g_j, \widehat{f}_j^{\perp}\rangle = 0$, $\langle f_i, \widehat{f}_j^{\perp}\rangle = 0$. Problem **(T)** can be equivalently written as: $\min_{\widehat{f}_j^{\parallel}} - \langle g_j, \widehat{f}_j^{\parallel}\rangle + \sum_{i=1}^K ((P_{ij} + Q_{ij})\langle f_i, \widehat{f}_j^{\parallel}\rangle + \frac{\rho}{2}((\langle f_i, \widehat{f}_j^{\parallel}\rangle - A_{ij})^2 + (\langle f_i, \widehat{f}_j^{\parallel}\rangle - A_{ji})^2))$. Hence the optimal solution of $\widehat{f}_j$ is in the RTR form. For g_j, from its update equation $g_j = g_j + \rho(f_j - \hat{f}_j)$, it is easy to see that if $f_j^{(t-1)}$ and $\widehat{f}_j^{(t-1)}$ are in the RTR form, so will be $g_j^{(t)}$. Note that these RKHS functions are in the RTR form because of the algorithmic procedure (namely, initializing these functions as zero and using FGD to solve f) rather than the representer theorem. If we choose another way of initialization, f may not be in the RTR form.

3.3.2 Scalable Representation of RKHS Functions Based on Random Fourier Features

When the RKHS functions are in the RTR form, $O(N^2D)$ computational cost is incurred where N is the number of training examples and D is the input feature dimension. On large-sized datasets, this is not scalable. In this section, we investigate a scalable representation of RKHS functions based on random Fourier features (RFFs) (Rahimi and Recht, 2007). Given a shift-invariant kernel $k(\mathbf{x}, \mathbf{y}) = k(\mathbf{x} - \mathbf{y})$ such as the radial basis function (RBF) kernel, it can be approximated with RFFs: $k(\mathbf{x}, \mathbf{y}) = \langle k(\mathbf{x},\cdot), k(\mathbf{y},\cdot)\rangle \approx z(\mathbf{x})^\top z(\mathbf{y})$, where $z(\mathbf{x}) \in \mathbb{R}^Q$ is the RFF transformation of $\mathbf{x}$, and can be seen as an approximation of $k(\mathbf{x},\cdot)$. $z(\mathbf{x})$ is generated in the following way: (1) compute the Fourier transform $p(\boldsymbol{\omega})$ of the kernel k; (2) draw Q i.i.d samples $\boldsymbol{\omega}_1,\cdots,\boldsymbol{\omega}_Q \in \mathbb{R}^D$ from $p(\boldsymbol{\omega})$ and Q i.i.d samples $b_1,\cdots,b_Q \in \mathbb{R}$ from the uniform distribution on $[0,2\pi]$; (3) let $z(\mathbf{x}) = \sqrt{\frac{2}{Q}}[\cos(\boldsymbol{\omega}_1^\top \mathbf{x}+b_1),\cdots,\cos(\boldsymbol{\omega}_Q^\top \mathbf{x}+b_Q)]^\top$. For $f \in \mathcal{H}$ where $\mathcal{H}$ is a RKHS induced by a shift-invariant kernel, we know that $f(\mathbf{x}) = \langle f, k(\mathbf{x},\cdot)\rangle$. Using $z(\mathbf{x})$ to approximate $k(\mathbf{x},\cdot)$ and $\mathbf{w} \in \mathbb{R}^Q$ to approximate f, we get $f(\mathbf{x}) \approx \mathbf{w}^\top z(\mathbf{x})$. As such, the infinite-dimensional function f can be approximately represented as a finite-dimensional vector $\mathbf{w}$, and the BMD-KM problem defined in Eq.(4) can be written as $\min_{\mathcal{W}} \mathcal{L}(\mathcal{W}) + \lambda\Omega(\mathcal{W})$ where $\mathcal{W} = \{\mathbf{w}_i\}_{i=1}^K$ and $\Omega(\mathcal{W}) = D(\mathbf{G},\mathbf{I})$ with $G_{ij} = \mathbf{w}_i^\top \mathbf{w}_j$. Now, learning can be conducted over $\mathcal{W}$, and the computational cost is reduced from $O(N^2D)$ to $O(NQ)$, where Q is the number of RFFs and is much smaller than ND.

4 ANALYSIS

In this section, we analyze how near-orthogonality regularization affects the generalization performance of kernel methods. Specifically, we choose the LDD regularizer to conduct the study while leaving the other two regularizers (SFN and VND) for future work. Inspired by (Xie et al., 2015a), we perform the analysis in two steps. First, we prove that decreasing LDD amounts to decreasing the absolute value of the cosine similarity (AVCS) of RKHS functions, therefore making the RKHS functions close to being orthogonal. Then we show that the upper bound of generalization error is an increasing function of the AVCS. Combining the two pieces together, we conclude that reducing LDD can decrease the generalization error bound.

We begin with the first step. Given the RKHS function set $\mathcal{F} = \{f_i\}_{i=1}^K$, let $s_{ij} = \frac{|\langle f_i, f_j\rangle|}{\|f_i\|_{\mathcal{H}}\|f_j\|_{\mathcal{H}}}$ be the AVCS between f_i and f_j, and $s(\mathcal{F}) = \max_{1\leq i<j\leq K} s_{ij}$ be the maximal AVCS among all pairs of RKHS functions. Drawing inspiration from (Xie et al., 2015a), we prove that the gradient of LDD $\Omega_{ld}(\mathcal{F})$ is an ascent direction of $s(\mathcal{F})$, which is formally given in the following lemma.

Lemma 1 *Let $\widehat{\mathcal{F}} = \{\widehat{f}_i\}_{i=1}^K$ be a RKHS function set where $\widehat{f}_i = f_i + \eta g_i$ and g_i is the functional gradient of $\Omega_{ld}(\mathcal{F})$ w.r.t f_i. Then $\exists \delta > 0$ such that $\forall \eta \in (0,\delta)$, $s(\widehat{\mathcal{F}}) \geq s(\mathcal{F})$.*

This implies that $\Omega_{ld}(\mathcal{F})$ and $s(\mathcal{F})$ are closely aligned. Decreasing $\Omega_{ld}(\mathcal{F})$ effectively decreases $s(\mathcal{F})$. Next, we show that the generalization error bounds of BMD-KDML and BMD-KSC are increasing functions of $s(\mathcal{F})$, using technique developed in (Xie et al., 2015b).

Kernel Distance Metric Learning In KDML, the hypothesis function is $u(\mathbf{x},\mathbf{y}) = \sum_{i=1}^K (f_i(\mathbf{x}) - f_i(\mathbf{y}))^2$ and the loss function ℓ is the logistic loss $\ell(u(\mathbf{x},\mathbf{y}),t) = \log(1+\exp((2t-1)u(\mathbf{x},\mathbf{y})))$. Let $\mathcal{U} = \{u : (\mathbf{x},\mathbf{y}) \mapsto \sum_{i=1}^K (f_i(\mathbf{x}) - f_i(\mathbf{y}))^2, \{f_i\}_{i=1}^K \subset \mathcal{H}\}$ denote the hypothesis set and $\mathcal{A} = \{\ell : (\mathbf{x},\mathbf{y},t) \mapsto \ell(u(\mathbf{x},\mathbf{y}),t), u \in \mathcal{U}\}$ denote the loss class, which is the composition of the loss function with each of the hypotheses. We assume $\|\mathbf{x}\|_2 \leq C$, $\|f\|_{\mathcal{H}}$ is upper bounded by $B(k)$ which depends on the kernel function k and $|k(\mathbf{x},\mathbf{y})|$ is upper bounded by $B'(k,C)$, which depends on k and C.

Given the joint distribution p^* of input data pair $(\mathbf{x},\mathbf{y})$ and the binary label t indicating whether this data pair is similar or dissimilar, the risk of the hypothesis u is $L(u) = \mathbb{E}_{(\mathbf{x},\mathbf{y},t)\sim p^*}[\ell(u(\mathbf{x},\mathbf{y}),t)]$. Its empirical counterpart (training error) can be defined as $\widehat{L}(u) = \frac{1}{N}\sum_{n=1}^N \ell(u(\mathbf{x}_n,\mathbf{y}_n),t_n)$. The generalization error of a hypothesis u is defined as $L(u) - \widehat{L}(u)$, which represents how well the algorithm can learn and usually depends on the complexity of the hypothesis class and the number of training examples. The generalization error of non-kernelized DML was previously analyzed in (Bellet and Habrard, 2015; Verma and Branson, 2015), focusing on model complexity and sample complexity. Our analysis aims at revealing how near-orthogonality affects the generalization performance.

Next, we analyze how $s(\mathcal{F})$ affects the generalization error bound (GEB) of BMD-KDML. The major result is presented in Theorem 1[2].

Theorem 1 *With probability at least $1-\delta$*

$$\begin{aligned} & L(u) - \widehat{L}(u) \\ & \leq \tfrac{8B(k)^2B'(k,C)^2K}{(1+\exp(-J))\sqrt{N}} + \log(1+\exp(J))\sqrt{\tfrac{2\log(2/\delta)}{N}} \end{aligned} \tag{11}$$

where $J = 4B(k)^2B'(k,C)^2((K-1)s(\mathcal{F})+1)$.

From the GEB (right hand side of Eq.(11)), we can see four implications. First, near-orthogonality can reduce GEB. The smaller $s(\mathcal{F})$ is (which indicates stronger near-orthogonality), the smaller the GEB is. As discussed earlier, decreasing LDD can decrease $s(\mathcal{F})$, hence can reduce the GEB. This is the major insight of this analysis. Second, the GEB admits a $O(N^{-1/2})$ rate of convergence in terms of sample size N, which matches the same rate as the analysis in (Bellet and Habrard, 2015; Verma and Branson, 2015). Third, the GEB grows linearly with K – the number of RKHS functions. In (Verma and Branson, 2015), the GEB is $O(\sqrt{D})$ where D is the feature dimension. As shown in experiments, K is roughly in the same scale as $\sqrt{D}$. Fourth,

[2]Please refer to the supplements for the proof.

Table 1: Statistics of the Datasets

	#Train	#Test	Dim.	#Class
MIMIC-III	40K	18K	7207	2833
Cars	8144	8041	4096	196
Birds	9000	2788	4096	200
Scenes-15	3140	1345	–	15
Caltech-256	20846	8934	–	256
UIUC-Sports	1254	538	–	8

the GEB is affected by the properties of the kernel function via the kernel-dependent bounds including $B(k)$ and $B'(k, C)$.

Kernel Sparse Coding We assume the basis functions of the KSC are in the image of the reproducing kernel feature map $\phi(\cdot)$ associated with the kernel k, i.e., $f = \phi(\mathbf{d})$, where $\mathbf{d}$ is a D-dimensional vector in the input space $\mathcal{R}$. Similar to KDML, we assume $\|\phi(\mathbf{d})\|_{\mathcal{H}} \leq B(k)$. The risk function $L(\Phi)$ of the dictionary $\Phi = \{\phi(\mathbf{d}_i)\}_{i=1}^{K}$ is defined as $\mathbb{E}_{\mathbf{x}\sim p^*}[\min_{\|\mathbf{a}\|_0 \leq m} \|k(\mathbf{x}, \cdot) - \sum_{i=1}^{K} a_i\phi(\mathbf{d}_i)\|_{\mathcal{H}}]$, where m is a parameter that controls the sparsity of linear coefficients $\mathbf{a}$. Let $\widetilde{L}(\Phi)$ denote the empirical risk function on N training examples. We have the following results on the generalization error of KSC:

Theorem 2 *Let $\mathcal{R}$ have ϵ covers of order $(C/\epsilon)^D$ where C is a constant. Let ϕ be uniformly H-Holder of order $\alpha > 0$ over $\mathcal{R}$ and let $\gamma = \max_{\mathbf{d}\in\mathcal{R}}\|\phi(\mathbf{d})\|_{\mathcal{H}}$. Let ν be any distribution on $\mathcal{R}$, then with probability at least $1 - e^{-\delta}$, for all dictionaries Φ, we have:*

$$L(\Phi) - \widehat{L}(\Phi) \leq \gamma\left(\sqrt{\frac{DK\ln\left(\sqrt{N}C^{\alpha}\frac{m\gamma^2 H}{1-mB^2(k)s(\Phi)}\right)}{2\alpha N}} + \sqrt{\frac{\delta}{2N}}\right) + \sqrt{\frac{4}{N}}.$$

This generalization bound is an increasing function of $s(\Phi)$. Hence, if we encourage the RKHS functions to approach orthogonal, i.e., decreasing $s(\Phi)$, then this generalization bound can be reduced.

5 EXPERIMENTS

In this section, we present experimental results on BMD-KDML and BMD-KSC.

Datasets We used six datasets in the experiments: an electronic health record dataset MIMIC-III (Johnson et al., 2016); five image datasets including Stanford-Cars (Cars) (Krause et al., 2013), Caltech-UCSD-Birds (Birds) (Welinder et al., 2010), Scenes-15 (Lazebnik et al., 2006), Caltech-256 (Griffin et al., 2007) and UIUC-Sports (Li and Fei-Fei, 2007). The first three were used for KDML and the last three for KSC. Their statistics are summarized in Table 1. For each dataset, five random train/test splits were performed, and the results were averaged over the five runs. For the MIMIC-III dataset, we extracted features from demographics (including age and gender), clinical notes (including bag-of-words and Word2Vec (Mikolov et al., 2013)) and lab tests (including zero-order, first-order, and second-order temporal features). The total feature dimension is 7207. The features for Cars and Birds datasets were extracted using the VGG16 (Simonyan and Zisserman, 2015) convolutional neural network trained on the ImageNet (Deng et al., 2009) dataset, which were the outputs of the second fully-connected layer with 4096 dimensions. For Scenes-15, Caltech-256 and UIUC-Sport, we extracted pixel-level dense SIFT (Lowe, 2004) features where the step size and patch size were 8 and 16, respectively.

Experimental Setup For BMD-KDML and BMD-KSC, we experimented with six combinations between three regularizers including SFN, LDD and VND, and two representations of RKHS functions including RTR and RFF. In DML experiments, two data examples were labeled as similar if belonging to the same class and dissimilar otherwise. The learned distance metrics were applied for retrieval whose performance was evaluated using precision@k. Precision@k is defined as n/k where n is the number of examples (among the top k retrieved examples) that have the same class label with the query. We compared with three groups of baseline methods: (1) KDML (Eq.(5) without the regularizer $\Omega(\mathcal{F})$) and its variants under different regularizers including squared Hilbert norm (SHN), DPP (Zou and Adams, 2012) and Angle (Xie et al., 2015a); (2) other kernel DML methods including the ones proposed in (Tsang et al., 2003) (Tsang) and (Jain et al., 2012) (Jain), multiple kernels DML (MK-DML) (Wang et al., 2011) and pairwise constrained component analysis (PCCA) (Mignon and Jurie, 2012); (3) non-kernel metric learning (ML) methods, including information theoretic ML (ITML) (Davis et al., 2007), logistic discriminant ML (LDML) (Guillaumin et al., 2009), DML with eigenvalue optimization (DML-Eig) (Ying and Li, 2012), information-theoretic semi-supervised ML via entropy regularization (Seraph) (Niu et al., 2012) and geometric mean ML (GMML) (Zadeh et al., 2016); (4) Euclidean distance (EUC). For methods in group (1), the RKHS functions are represented in the RTR form. In sparse coding experiments, on top of the SIFT features, we used kernel sparse coding to learn a set of RKHS functions and represented each SIFT feature into a sparse code. To obtain image-level features, we applied max-pooling (Yang et al., 2009) and spatial pyramid matching (Lazebnik et al., 2006; Yang et al., 2009) over the pixel-level sparse codes. The following baselines were compared with: sparse coding (SC) (Yang et al., 2009), unregularized kernel SC (KSC) (Gao et al., 2010), KSC regularized by SHN, DPP and Angle. In these methods, the RKHS functions are represented in the RTR form. We used 5-fold

Table 2: Retrieval Precision@10 (%) on Three Datasets

	MIMIC-III	Cars	Birds
EUC	58.3 ± 0.1	37.8 ± 0.0	43.2 ± 0.0
ITML	69.3 ± 0.4	50.1 ± 0.0	52.9 ± 0.3
LDML	70.9 ± 0.9	51.3 ± 0.0	52.1 ± 0.2
DML-Eig	70.6 ± 0.7	50.7 ± 0.0	53.3 ± 0.8
Seraph	71.7 ± 0.2	53.6 ± 0.0	52.9 ± 0.2
GMML	71.2 ± 0.3	54.2 ± 0.0	53.7 ± 0.6
Tsang	73.5 ± 0.2	55.8 ±0.0	53.9 ± 0.4
MKDML	75.1 ± 0.9	53.5 ±0.0	54.4 ± 0.1
Jain	74.9 ± 1.1	53.9 ±0.0	55.9 ± 0.6
PCCA	73.4 ± 0.5	56.4 ±0.0	55.1 ± 0.9
KDML	73.8 ± 0.9	54.9 ±0.0	54.7 ± 0.5
KDML-SHN	74.2 ± 0.6	55.4 ±0.0	54.8 ± 0.9
KDML-DPP	75.5 ± 0.8	56.4 ±0.0	57.3 ± 0.3
KDML-Angle	75.9 ± 0.2	56.8 ±0.0	57.1 ± 0.6
KDML-SFN-RTR	76.3 ± 0.7	56.6 ± 0.0	56.4 ± 0.1
KDML-VND-RTR	**77.1** ± 0.6	**57.7** ± 0.0	58.9 ± 0.7
KDML-LDD-RTR	76.7 ± 0.3	57.4 ± 0.0	**59.2** ± 0.3
KDML-SFN-RFF	75.9 ± 0.1	56.5 ± 0.0	56.0 ± 0.2
KDML-VND-RFF	76.9 ± 0.4	57.2 ± 0.0	58.8 ± 0.6
KDML-LDD-RFF	76.8 ± 0.8	57.1 ± 0.0	58.5 ± 0.4

Table 3: The number of RKHS functions that achieves the precision@10 in Table 2

	MIMIC-III	Cars	Birds	Average
KDML	300	400	300	333
KDML-SHN	300	400	300	333
KDML-DPP	200	300	300	267
KDML-Angle	200	300	200	233
KDML-SFN-RTR	200	200	200	200
KDML-VND-RTR	100	200	200	167
KDML-LDD-RTR	100	200	200	167
KDML-SFN-RFF	100	200	200	167
KDML-VND-RFF	100	200	200	167
KDML-LDD-RFF	100	200	200	167

cross validation to tune the regularization parameters in $\{10^{-5}, 10^{-4}, \cdots, 10^{5}\}$, the number of RKHS functions in $\{50, 100, 200, \cdots, 500\}$ and the dimension of RFF in $\{1, 2, \cdots, 10\} \times D$ where D is the feature dimension of input data. The kernel function was chosen to be the radial basis function (RBF) $\exp(-\gamma\|\mathbf{x}-\mathbf{y}\|_2^2)$ where the scale parameter γ is tuned in $\{10^{-3}, 10^{-2}, \cdots, 10^{3}\}$. The parameter ρ in ADMM-based algorithm was set to 1. The learning rate in functional gradient descent was set to 0.001.

Results Table 2 shows the retrieval precision@10 on three datasets, where we observe the following. First, BMD-KDML methods including KDML-(SFN,VND,LDD)-(RTR,RFF) greatly outperform unregularized and SHN-regularized KDML, which demonstrates that near-orthogonality regularization is an effective way to reduce overfitting. Second, BMD regularizers including SFN, VND and LDD outperform other near-orthogonality regularizers including DPP and Angle, possibly because they are insensitive to vector scaling and amenable for optimization. Third, VND and LDD achieve comparable performance and outperform SFN, possibly because they measure near-orthogonality in a global way while SFN conducts that in a pairwise fashion. Fourth, RFF representation of RKHS functions performs comparably to RTR, in spite of the fact

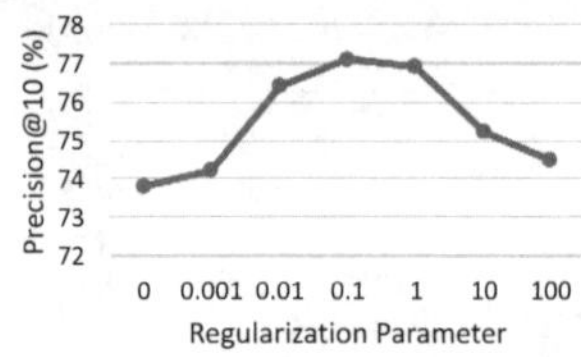

Figure 1: Precision@10 versus the Regularization Parameter λ on MIMIC-III

that it is an approximation method. Finally, the BMD-KDML methods achieve better performance than non-kernel DML methods and other kernel DML methods, suggesting their competitive ability in learning effective distance metrics.

Table 3 shows the number of RKHS functions under which the precision@10 in Table 2 is achieved. It can be seen that the BMD-KDML methods utilize much fewer functions than KDML while achieving better precision@10. For instance, KDML-VND-RTR achieves 77.1% precision@10 with 100 functions on the MIMIC-III dataset while KDML achieves 73.8% precision@10 with 300 functions. These results demonstrate the ability of the BMD regularizers in reducing model size without sacrificing modeling power. By encouraging the functions to be near-orthogonal, the BMD regularizers decrease the redundancy among functions and make the functions highly complementary. As a result, a small number of such functions are able to capture the patterns in the data sufficiently well. In addition, the BMD regularizers achieve better precision@10 with fewer functions than other near-orthogonality regularizers including DPP and Angle, suggesting their better efficacy in promoting near-orthogonality.

In the next experiment, we investigate whether near-orthogonality regularization can better capture infrequent patterns. We select 3 frequent diseases (patterns) and 5 infrequent ones from the MIMIC-III dataset. A disease is regarded as *frequent* if the number of hospital admissions diagnosed with this disease is greater than 300. Table 4 shows the precision@10 on the 8 diseases, from which we observe that: (1) on the 5 infrequent diseases (labeled as D4–D8), the BMD-KDML methods achieve much higher precision@10 than the unregularized KDML, suggesting that by encouraging the functions to be close to being orthogonal, the BMD regularizers can better capture infrequent patterns; (2) on the 3 frequent diseases (labeled as D1–D3), the precision@10 achieved by the BMD-KDML methods is comparable with that achieved by the unregularized KDML, indicating that the BMD regularizers do not compromise the modeling effects on the frequent patterns. On the infrequent diseases, the BMD-KDML methods outperform KDML-DPP and KDML-Angle, suggesting that the BMD regularizers have better abilities in promoting

Table 4: Retrieval precision@10 (%) on three frequent and five infrequent diseases in the MIMIC-III dataset. The number next to a disease ID is its frequency. Note that diseases D1–D3 are frequent diseases, while that D4–D8 are infrequent ones.

	D1 (3566)	D2 (3498)	D3 (2757)	D4 (204)	D5 (176)	D6 (148)	D7 (131)	D8 (121)
Tsang	80.3 ± 0.3	82.8 ± 0.7	81.9 ± 0.4	6.3 ± 0.7	3.9 ± 0.5	4.5 ± 0.5	6.7 ± 0.9	5.1 ± 0.2
MKDML	83.1 ± 0.2	83.4 ± 0.7	82.3 ± 0.6	3.7 ± 1.2	5.5 ± 0.1	9.3 ± 0.8	10.0 ± 0.5	3.7 ± 0.4
Jain	82.7 ± 0.7	84.6 ± 0.5	**82.9** ± 0.4	7.2 ± 0.4	8.2 ± 0.4	3.4 ± 0.9	6.2 ± 0.7	8.7 ± 0.3
PCCA	82.2 ± 0.2	82.1 ± 0.6	82.1 ± 0.3	9.4 ± 0.8	7.7 ± 0.2	5.2 ± 0.4	6.1 ± 0.1	3.2 ± 0.4
KDML	82.6 ± 0.7	83.9 ± 1.2	81.7 ± 0.6	7.4 ± 1.0	5.3 ± 0.9	5.7 ± 0.3	3.8 ± 0.8	3.5 ± 0.4
KDML-SHN	82.1 ± 0.5	83.6 ± 0.4	82.4 ± 0.9	8.3 ± 0.1	5.1 ± 0.8	4.7 ± 0.2	3.4 ± 0.9	3.7 ± 0.8
KDML-DPP	83.4 ± 0.4	**84.7** ± 0.7	82.7 ± 1.0	11.5 ± 0.3	9.7 ± 0.5	10.4 ± 0.4	7.3 ± 0.2	7.9 ± 0.1
KDML-Angle	83.7 ± 0.1	84.3 ± 0.1	81.8 ± 0.3	10.6 ± 0.2	10.2 ± 0.8	9.5 ± 0.6	8.8 ± 0.5	7.2 ± 0.3
KDML-SFN-RTR	82.5 ± 0.8	84.2 ± 1.2	82.2 ± 0.1	15.0 ± 0.3	13.4 ± 0.1	13.8 ± 0.2	12.1 ± 0.6	10.9 ± 0.5
KDML-VND-RTR	**83.9** ± 0.9	84.5 ± 0.8	82.6 ± 0.2	15.5 ± 0.9	16.2 ± 0.7	14.3 ± 0.7	12.4 ± 0.8	14.7 ± 0.8
KDML-LDD-RTR	83.7 ± 0.1	83.8 ± 0.9	82.2 ± 0.6	14.8 ± 0.4	14.2 ± 0.1	13.7 ± 0.3	10.3 ± 0.1	12.8 ± 0.2
KDML-SFN-RFF	82.3 ± 0.9	84.1 ± 0.6	81.1 ± 0.5	15.1 ± 0.2	14.9 ± 0.5	15.2 ± 0.9	13.5 ± 0.1	10.8 ± 0.3
KDML-VND-RFF	83.4 ± 0.2	83.6 ± 0.5	82.7 ± 0.4	15.2 ± 0.5	15.6 ± 0.9	10.6 ± 0.8	12.0 ± 1.1	10.3 ± 0.7
KDML-LDD-RFF	82.9 ± 0.2	84.0 ± 1.0	82.5 ± 0.9	14.4 ± 0.9	13.9 ± 1.2	15.4 ± 0.5	13.9 ± 0.2	14.4 ± 0.1

Table 5: Convergence Time (Hours) on Three Datasets

	MIMIC-III	Cars	Birds
KDML-SFN-RTR	69.4	17.2	18.6
KDML-VND-RTR	69.8	17.4	18.9
KDML-LDD-RTR	69.9	17.5	18.9
KDML-SFN-RFF	12.6	2.7	2.9
KDML-VND-RFF	12.9	2.8	3.1
KDML-LDD-RFF	12.8	2.8	3.1

Table 6: Classification Accuracy (%) on Three Datasets

	Scenes-15	Caltech-256	UIUC-Sports
SC	83.6 ± 0.2	42.3 ± 0.4	87.4 ± 0.5
KSC	85.4 ± 0.5	44.7 ± 0.8	88.2 ± 0.1
KSC-SHN	85.8 ± 0.6	45.4 ± 0.5	88.3 ± 0.3
KSC-DPP	86.3 ± 0.3	47.3 ± 0.8	89.3 ± 0.2
KSC-Angle	86.8 ± 0.1	46.1 ± 0.8	89.5 ± 0.5
KSC-SFN-RTR	87.1 ± 0.5	47.2 ± 0.5	89.9 ± 0.3
KSC-VND-RTR	**87.9** ± 0.7	**48.6** ± 0.3	**91.3** ± 0.5
KSC-LDD-RTR	87.4 ± 0.4	48.1 ± 0.6	90.7 ± 0.2
KSC-SFN-RFF	86.8 ± 0.6	46.5 ± 0.1	89.5 ± 0.7
KSC-VND-RFF	87.5 ± 0.5	48.2 ± 0.4	90.4 ± 0.8
KSC-LDD-RFF	87.2 ± 0.1	47.8 ± 0.2	90.2 ± 0.4

near-orthogonality than DPP and Angle.

Further, Figure 1 shows how the precision@10 on MIMIC-III varies as we increase the regularization parameter λ in KDML-VND-RTR. As can be seen, the best precision@10 is achieved under a modest λ. A very large λ would make the functions strictly orthogonal, as kernel PCA and ICA do, which would result in excessively strong regularization and therefore poor performance.

We also compares the convergence time of BMD-KDML under two representations: RTR and RFF. As shown in Table 5, RFF results in much faster convergence since this representation does not depend on the training data. While computationally efficient, RFF does not sacrifice much modeling power. Table 2 shows that RFF achieves precision@10 that is comparable to RTR.

Next, we present the kernel sparse coding results. Table 6 shows the classification accuracy on three datasets, from which we observe similar results as in the KDML experiments. First, KSC-(SFN,VND,LDD)-(RTR,RFF) achieve better accuracy than the unregularized and the SHN-regularized KSC. Second, the BMD regularizers outperform other near-orthogonality regularizers including DPP and Angle. Third, VND and LDD are superior to SFN. Fourth, the RFF representation of RKHS functions performs comparably to RTR. Finally, the BMD-KSC methods outperform the non-kernel SC methods and other kernel SC methods. These observations demonstrate the efficacy of the BMD regularizers in reducing overfitting and promoting near-orthogonality.

6 CONCLUSIONS AND FUTURE WORKS

In this paper, we propose a new regularization approach for kernel methods – near-orthogonality regularization, which encourages the RKHS functions to be close to being orthogonal, for the sake of reducing overfitting, decreasing model size without compromising modeling power and effectively capturing infrequent patterns. We design a family of near-orthogonality regularizers based on minimizing the Bregman matrix divergences between functions' Gram matrix and an identity matrix, and apply them to promote near-orthogonality in two kernel methods. An efficient ADMM-based optimization algorithm is developed where the RKHS functions are learned using functional gradient descent. The analysis reveals that the near-orthogonality regularization can reduce the generalization error of kernel methods. Experiments demonstrate the effectiveness of the proposed regularizers.

For future work, we plan to apply near-orthogonality regularization to "deep" kernel methods (Cho and Saul, 2009; Wilson et al., 2016) which bridge kernel methods with deep learning.

Acknowledgements

We would like to thank the anonymous reviewers for the helpful suggestions. This research is supported in part by National Institutes of Health P30DA035778, R01GM114311, National Science Foundation IIS1617583, IIS1563887, DARPA FA872105C0003.

References

Francis R Bach and Michael I Jordan. Kernel independent component analysis. *JMLR*, 2002.

A. Bellet and A. Habrard. Robustness and generalization for metric learning. *Neurocomputing*, 2015.

S. Boyd, N. Parikh, E. Chu, B. Peleato, and J. Eckstein. Distributed optimization and statistical learning via alternating direction method of multipliers. *Foundations and Trends® in Machine Learning*, 2011.

Youngmin Cho and Lawrence K Saul. Kernel methods for deep learning. In *Advances in neural information processing systems*, 2009.

M. Cogswell, F. Ahmed, R. Girshick, L. Zitnick, and D. Batra. Reducing overfitting in deep networks by decorrelating representations. *ICLR*, 2015.

Bo Dai, Bo Xie, Niao He, Yingyu Liang, Anant Raj, Maria-Florina F Balcan, and Le Song. Scalable kernel methods via doubly stochastic gradients. In *NIPS*, 2014.

J. Davis, B. Kulis, P. Jain, S. Sra, and I. Dhillon. Information-theoretic metric learning. In *ICML*, 2007.

Jia Deng, Wei Dong, Richard Socher, Li-Jia Li, Kai Li, and Li Fei-Fei. Imagenet: A large-scale hierarchical image database. In *CVPR*, 2009.

Inderjit S Dhillon and Joel A Tropp. Matrix nearness problems with Bregman divergences. *Matrix Analysis and Applications*, 2007.

Shenghua Gao, Ivor Wai-Hung Tsang, and Liang-Tien Chia. Kernel sparse representation for image classification and face recognition. In *ECCV*, 2010.

Rudolf Gorenflo, Yuri Luchko, and Francesco Mainardi. Analytical properties and applications of the Wright function. *arXiv preprint math-ph/0701069*, 2007.

Gregory Griffin, Alex Holub, and Pietro Perona. Caltech-256 object category dataset. 2007.

Matthieu Guillaumin, Jakob Verbeek, and Cordelia Schmid. Is that you? Metric learning approaches for face identification. In *ICCV*, 2009.

P. Jain, B. Kulis, J. Davis, and I. Dhillon. Metric and kernel learning using a linear transformation. *JMLR*, 2012.

A. Johnson, T. Pollard, L. Shen, L. Lehman, M. Feng, M. Ghassemi, B. Moody, P. Szolovits, L. Celi, and R. Mark. MIMIC-III, a freely accessible critical care database. *Scientific data*, 3, 2016.

Jonathan Krause, Michael Stark, Jia Deng, and Li Fei-Fei. 3D object representations for fine-grained categorization. In *ICCV Workshops*, 2013.

Alex Kulesza and Ben Taskar. Determinantal point processes for machine learning. *Foundations and Trends in Machine Learning*, 2012.

Brian Kulis, Mátyás A Sustik, and Inderjit S Dhillon. Low-rank kernel learning with Bregman matrix divergences. *JMLR*, 2009.

Svetlana Lazebnik, Cordelia Schmid, and Jean Ponce. Beyond bags of features: Spatial pyramid matching for recognizing scene categories. In *CVPR*, 2006.

Li-Jia Li and Li Fei-Fei. What, where and who? Classifying events by scene recognition. In *ICCV*, 2007.

David G Lowe. Distinctive image features from scale-invariant keypoints. *IJCV*, 2004.

Charles A Micchelli and Massimiliano Pontil. Learning the kernel function via regularization. *JMLR*, 2005.

A. Mignon and F. Jurie. PCCA: A new approach for distance learning from sparse pairwise constraints. In *CVPR*, 2012.

T. Mikolov, I. Sutskever, K. Chen, G. Corrado, and J. Dean. Distributed representations of words and phrases and their compositionality. In *NIPS*, 2013.

G. Niu, B. Dai, M. Yamada, and M. Sugiyama. Information-theoretic semisupervised metric learning via entropy regularization. *Neural Computation*, 2012.

Bruno A Olshausen and David J Field. Sparse coding with an overcomplete basis set: A strategy employed by v1? *Vision research*, 1997.

Ali Rahimi and Ben Recht. Random features for large-scale kernel machines. In *NIPS*, 2007.

B. Schölkopf, A. Smola, and K. Müller. Kernel principal component analysis. In *ICANN*, 1997.

Bernhard Schölkopf and Alexander J Smola. *Learning with kernels: Support vector machines, regularization, optimization, and beyond.* MIT press, 2002.

K. Simonyan and A. Zisserman. Very deep convolutional networks for large-scale image recognition. *ICLR*, 2015.

Ivor W Tsang, James T Kwok, C Bay, and H Kong. Distance metric learning with kernels. In *ICANN*, 2003.

Nakul Verma and Kristin Branson. Sample complexity of learning Mahalanobis distance metrics. *NIPS*, 2015.

J. Wang, H. Do, A. Woznica, and A. Kalousis. Metric learning with multiple kernels. In *NIPS*, 2011.

P. Welinder, S. Branson, T. Mita, C. Wah, F. Schroff, S. Belongie, and P Perona. Caltech-UCSD birds. 2010.

Andrew Gordon Wilson, Zhiting Hu, Ruslan Salakhutdinov, and Eric P Xing. Deep kernel learning. In *AISTATS*, 2016.

P. Xie, Y. Deng, and E. Xing. Diversifying restricted Boltzmann machine for document modeling. In *SIGKDD*, 2015a.

P. Xie, Y. Deng, and E. Xing. On the generalization error bounds of neural networks under mutual angular regularization. *arXiv:1511.07110*, 2015b.

Pengtao Xie. Learning compact and effective distance metrics with diversity regularization. In *ECML*, 2015.

Eric P Xing, Andrew Y Ng, Michael I Jordan, and Stuart Russell. Distance metric learning with application to clustering with side-information. In *NIPS*, 2002.

Jianchao Yang, Kai Yu, Yihong Gong, and Thomas Huang. Linear spatial pyramid matching using sparse coding for image classification. In *CVPR*, 2009.

Yiming Ying and Peng Li. Distance metric learning with eigenvalue optimization. *JMLR*, 2012.

Pourya Habib Zadeh, Reshad Hosseini, and Suvrit Sra. Geometric mean metric learning. In *ICML*, 2016.

James Y. Zou and Ryan P. Adams. Priors for diversity in generative latent variable models. In *NIPS*, 2012.

Near-Orthogonality Regularization in Kernel Methods – Supplementary Material

1 ADMM-Based Algorithms

1.1 Detailed Derivation of Solving A

Given $\mathbf{H} \in \mathbb{R}^{K\times K}$ where $H_{ij} = \langle f_i, \hat{f}_j \rangle$, the sub-problem defined over $\mathbf{A}$ is

$$\min_{\mathbf{A}} \quad \lambda D_\phi(\mathbf{A}, \mathbf{I}) - \langle \mathbf{P}, \mathbf{A} \rangle - \langle \mathbf{Q}^\top, \mathbf{A} \rangle + \frac{\rho}{2}\|\mathbf{H} - \mathbf{A}\|_F^2 + \frac{\rho}{2}\|\mathbf{H}^\top - \mathbf{A}\|_F^2. \tag{1}$$

$D_\phi(\mathbf{A}, \mathbf{I})$ has three cases, which we discuss separately.
When $D_\phi(\mathbf{A}, \mathbf{I})$ is the squared Frobenius norm, the problem becomes

$$\min_{\mathbf{A}} \quad \lambda\|\mathbf{A} - \mathbf{I}\|_F^2 - \langle \mathbf{P}, \mathbf{A} \rangle - \langle \mathbf{Q}^\top, \mathbf{A} \rangle + \frac{\rho}{2}\|\mathbf{H} - \mathbf{A}\|_F^2 + \frac{\rho}{2}\|\mathbf{H}^\top - \mathbf{A}\|_F^2. \tag{2}$$

Taking the derivative and setting it to zero, we get the optimal solution for $\mathbf{A}$:

$$\mathbf{A} = (2\lambda\mathbf{I} + \mathbf{P} + \mathbf{Q}^\top + \rho(\mathbf{H} + \mathbf{H}^\top))/(2\lambda + 2\rho). \tag{3}$$

When $D_\phi(\mathbf{A}, \mathbf{I})$ is the log-determinant divergence, the problem is specialized to

$$\begin{aligned} \min_{\mathbf{A}} \quad & \lambda(\mathrm{tr}(\mathbf{A}) - \log\det(\mathbf{A})) - \langle \mathbf{P}, \mathbf{A} \rangle - \langle \mathbf{Q}^\top, \mathbf{A} \rangle + \frac{\rho}{2}\|\mathbf{H} - \mathbf{A}\|_F^2 + \frac{\rho}{2}\|\mathbf{H}^\top - \mathbf{A}\|_F^2 \\ s.t. \quad & \mathbf{A} \succ 0 \end{aligned} \tag{4}$$

Taking the derivative of the objective function w.r.t $\mathbf{A}$ and setting it to zero, we get

$$\mathbf{A}^2 + \frac{1}{\rho}(\lambda\mathbf{I} - \mathbf{P} - \mathbf{Q}^\top - \rho(\mathbf{H} + \mathbf{H}^\top))\mathbf{A} - \frac{\lambda}{\rho}\mathbf{I} = 0. \tag{5}$$

Let $\mathbf{B} = \frac{1}{\rho}(\lambda\mathbf{I} - \mathbf{P} - \mathbf{Q}^\top - \rho(\mathbf{H} + \mathbf{H}^\top))$, $\mathbf{C} = -\frac{\lambda}{\rho}\mathbf{I}$, Eq.(5) can be written as

$$\mathbf{A}^2 + \mathbf{B}\mathbf{A} + \mathbf{C} = 0. \tag{6}$$

According to (Higham and Kim, 2001), since $\mathbf{B}$ and $\mathbf{C}$ commute, the solution of this equation is

$$\mathbf{A} = -\frac{1}{2}\mathbf{B} + \frac{1}{2}\sqrt{\mathbf{B}^2 - 4\mathbf{C}}. \tag{7}$$

Taking an eigendecomposition of $\mathbf{B} = \mathbf{\Phi}\mathbf{\Sigma}\mathbf{\Phi}^{-1}$, we can compute $\mathbf{A}$ as $\mathbf{A} = \mathbf{\Phi}\widehat{\mathbf{\Sigma}}\mathbf{\Phi}^{-1}$, where $\widehat{\mathbf{\Sigma}}$ is a diagonal matrix with

$$\widehat{\Sigma}_{kk} = -\frac{1}{2}\Sigma_{kk} + \frac{1}{2}\sqrt{\Sigma_{kk}^2 + \frac{4\lambda}{\rho}}.$$

Since $\sqrt{\Sigma_{kk}^2 + \frac{4\lambda}{\rho}} > \Sigma_{kk}$, we know $\widehat{\Sigma}_{kk} > 0$. Hence $\mathbf{A}$ is positive definite.
When $D_\phi(\mathbf{A}, \mathbf{I})$ is the von Neumann divergence, the problem becomes

$$\begin{aligned} \min_{\mathbf{A}} \quad & \lambda\mathrm{tr}(\mathbf{A}\log\mathbf{A} - \mathbf{A}) - \langle \mathbf{P}, \mathbf{A} \rangle - \langle \mathbf{Q}^\top, \mathbf{A} \rangle + \frac{\rho}{2}\|\mathbf{H} - \mathbf{A}\|_F^2 + \frac{\rho}{2}\|\mathbf{H}^\top - \mathbf{A}\|_F^2 \\ s.t. \quad & \mathbf{A} \succ 0 \end{aligned} \tag{8}$$

Setting the gradient of the objective function w.r.t $\mathbf{A}$ to zero, we get

$$\lambda \log \mathbf{A} + 2\rho\mathbf{A} = \mathbf{P} + \mathbf{Q}^\top + \rho(\mathbf{H} + \mathbf{H}^\top). \tag{9}$$

Let $\mathbf{D} = \mathbf{P} + \mathbf{Q}^\top + \rho(\mathbf{H} + \mathbf{H}^\top)$. We perform an eigendecomposition of $\mathbf{D} = \mathbf{\Phi}\mathbf{\Sigma}\mathbf{\Phi}^{-1}$ and parameterize $\mathbf{A}$ as $\mathbf{A} = \mathbf{\Phi}\widehat{\mathbf{\Sigma}}\mathbf{\Phi}^{-1}$, then we obtain

$$\lambda \log \mathbf{A} + 2\rho\mathbf{A} = \mathbf{\Phi}(\lambda \log \widehat{\mathbf{\Sigma}} + 2\rho\widehat{\mathbf{\Sigma}})\mathbf{\Phi}^{-1}. \tag{10}$$

Plugging this equation into Eq.(9), we get the following equation:

$$\lambda \log \widehat{\mathbf{\Sigma}} + 2\rho\widehat{\mathbf{\Sigma}} = \mathbf{\Sigma} \tag{11}$$

which amounts to solving K independent one-variable equations taking the form

$$\lambda \log \widehat{\Sigma}_{ii} + 2\rho\widehat{\Sigma}_{ii} = \Sigma_{ii} \tag{12}$$

where $i = 1, \cdots, K$. This equation has a closed-form solution:

$$\widehat{\Sigma}_{ii} = \frac{\lambda\omega(\frac{\Sigma_{ii}}{\lambda} - \log(\frac{\lambda}{2\rho}))}{2\rho} \tag{13}$$

where $\omega(\cdot)$ is the Wright omega function Gorenflo et al. (2007). Due to the presence of log, $\widehat{\Sigma}_{ii}$ is required to be positive and the solution always exists since the range of $\lambda \log \widehat{\Sigma}_{ii} + 2\rho\widehat{\Sigma}_{ii}$ and Σ_{ii} are both $(-\infty, \infty)$. Hence $\mathbf{A}$ is guaranteed to be positive definite.

1.2 ADMM-Based Algorithm for BMD-KSC

BMD-KSC has two set of parameters: sparse codes $\{\mathbf{a}_n\}_{n=1}^N$ and a dictionary of RKHS functions $\{f_i\}_{i=1}^K$. We use a coordinate descent algorithm to learn these two parameter sets, which iteratively performs the following two steps: (1) fixing $\{f_i\}_{i=1}^K$, solving $\{\mathbf{a}_n\}_{n=1}^N$; (2) fixing $\{\mathbf{a}_n\}_{n=1}^N$, solving $\{f_i\}_{i=1}^K$, until convergence. We first discuss step (1). The sub-problem defined over $\mathbf{a}_n$ is

$$\min_{\mathbf{a}_n} \quad \tfrac{1}{2}\|k(\mathbf{x}_n, \cdot) - \textstyle\sum_{i=1}^K a_{ni} f_i\|_{\mathcal{H}}^2 + \lambda_1\|\mathbf{a}_n\|_1. \tag{14}$$

$\|k(\mathbf{x}_n, \cdot) - \sum_{i=1}^K a_{ni} f_i\|_{\mathcal{H}}^2 = k(\mathbf{x}_n, \mathbf{x}_n) - 2\mathbf{a}_n^\top \mathbf{h} + \mathbf{a}_n^\top \mathbf{G}\mathbf{a}_n$ where $\mathbf{h} \in \mathbb{R}^K$, $h_i = \langle f_i, k(\mathbf{x}_n, \cdot)\rangle$, $\mathbf{G} \in \mathbb{R}^{K\times K}$ and $G_{ij} = \langle f_i, f_j\rangle$. This is a standard Lasso (Tibshirani, 1996) problem and can be solved using many algorithms.
Next we discuss step (2), which learns $\{f_i\}_{i=1}^K$ using the ADMM-based algorithm outlined in the main paper. The updates of all variables are the same as those in BMD-KDML, except f_i. Let $b_{ni} = k(\mathbf{x}_n, \cdot) - \sum_{j\neq i}^K a_{nj} f_j$, the sub-problem defined over f_i is:

$$\begin{array}{ll} \min_{f_i} & \frac{1}{2}\sum_{n=1}^N \|b_{ni} - a_{ni}f_i\|_{\mathcal{H}}^2 + \frac{\lambda_2}{2}\|f_i\|_{\mathcal{H}}^2 + \langle g_i, f_i\rangle + \sum_{j=1}^K P_{ij}\langle f_i, \hat{f}_j\rangle + \sum_{j=1}^K Q_{ij}\langle f_i, \hat{f}_j\rangle \\ & +\frac{\rho}{2}\sum_{j=1}^K(\langle f_i, \hat{f}_j\rangle - A_{ij})^2 + \frac{\rho}{2}\sum_{j=1}^K(\langle f_i, \hat{f}_j\rangle - A_{ji})^2 \end{array} \tag{15}$$

This problem can be solved with functional gradient descent. The functional gradient of the objective function w.r.t f_i is

$$\sum_{n=1}^N a_{ni}(a_{ni}f_i - b_{ni}) + \lambda_2 f_i + g_i + \sum_{j=1}^K (P_{ij} + Q_{ij} + 2\rho\langle f_i, \hat{f}_j\rangle - \rho(A_{ij} + A_{ji}))\hat{f}_j \tag{16}$$

2 Proof of Lemma 1

For the ease of notation, we use $\langle\cdot,\cdot\rangle$ to denote the inner product in the RKHS and $\|\cdot\|$ to denote the Hilbert norm. To prove Lemma 1, we need the following Lemma, which is an extension of Lemma 4 in (Xie et al., 2015a) from vectors to RKHS functions.

Lemma 2. *Let $\mathcal{F} = \{f_i\}_{i=1}^K$ and $\mathbf{G}$ be the Gram matrix defined on $\mathcal{F}$. Let g_i' be the functional gradient of* $\det(\mathbf{G})$ *w.r.t f_i, then $\langle g_i', f_j\rangle = 0$ for all $j \neq i$, and $\langle g_i', f_i\rangle > 0$.*

Proof. We decompose f_i into $f_i = f_i^{\|} + f_i^{\perp}$. $f_i^{\|}$ is in the span of $\mathcal{F}/\{f_i\}$: $f_i^{\|} = \sum_{j\neq i}^{K} a_j f_j$, where $\{a_j\}_{j\neq i}^{K}$ are the linear coefficients. $f_i^{\perp}$ is orthogonal to $\mathcal{F}/\{f_i\}$: $\langle f_i^{\perp}, f_j\rangle = 0$ for all $j \neq i$.
Let $\mathbf{c}_j$ denote the j-th column of $\mathbf{G}$. Subtracting $\sum_{j\neq i}^{K} a_j \mathbf{c}_j$ from the i-th column, we get

$$\det(\mathbf{G}) = \begin{vmatrix} \langle f_1, f_1\rangle & \cdots & 0 & \cdots & \langle f_1, f_K\rangle \\ \langle f_2, f_1\rangle & \cdots & 0 & \cdots & \langle f_2, f_K\rangle \\ \vdots & \ddots & \vdots & \ddots & \vdots \\ \langle f_i, f_1\rangle & \cdots & \langle f_i^{\perp}, f_i\rangle & \cdots & \langle f_i, f_K\rangle \\ \vdots & \ddots & \vdots & \ddots & \vdots \\ \langle f_K, f_1\rangle & \cdots & 0 & \cdots & \langle f_K, f_K\rangle \end{vmatrix} \tag{17}$$

Expanding the determinant according to the i-th column, we get

$$\det(\mathbf{G}) = \det(\mathbf{G}_{-i})\langle f_i^{\perp}, f_i\rangle \tag{18}$$

where $\mathbf{G}_{-i}$ is the Gram matrix defined on $\mathcal{F}/\{f_i\}$. Then the functional gradient g_i' of $\det(\mathbf{G})$ w.r.t f_i is $\det(\mathbf{G}_{-i})f_i^{\perp}$, which is orthogonal to f_j for all $j \neq i$. Since $\mathbf{G}$ is full rank, we know $\det(\mathbf{G}) > 0$. From Eq.(18) we know $\langle f_i^{\perp}, f_i\rangle$ is non-negative. Hence $\langle g_i', f_i\rangle = \det(\mathbf{G}_{-i})\langle f_i^{\perp}, f_i\rangle > 0$. □

Now we are ready to prove Lemma 1. Some of the proof techniques draw inspiration from (Xie et al., 2015a). We first compute $\hat{s}_{ij}$:

$$\hat{s}_{ij} = \frac{|\langle \widehat{f}_i, \widehat{f}_j\rangle|}{\|\widehat{f}_i\|\|\widehat{f}_j\|} = \frac{|\langle f_i+\eta g_i, f_j+\eta g_j\rangle|}{\sqrt{\|f_i+\eta g_i\|^2}\sqrt{\|f_j+\eta g_j\|^2}} \tag{19}$$

The functional gradient of $\log\det(\mathbf{G})$ w.r.t f_i is computed as $g_i'' = \frac{1}{\det(\mathbf{G})}g_i'$. According to Lemma 1 and the fact that $\det(\mathbf{G}) > 0$, we know $\langle g_i'', f_j\rangle = 0$ for all $j \neq i$, and $\langle g_i'', f_i\rangle > 0$. Then we have

$$\begin{aligned} &|\langle f_i + \eta g_i, f_j + \eta g_j\rangle| \\ &= |\langle f_i + \eta(2f_i - 2g_i''), f_j + \eta(2f_j - 2g_j'')\rangle| \\ &= |\langle (1+2\eta)f_i - 2\eta g_i'', (1+2\eta)f_j - 2\eta g_j''\rangle| \\ &= |(1+2\eta)^2\langle f_i, f_j\rangle + 4\eta^2\langle g_i'', g_j''\rangle| \\ &= |\langle f_i, f_j\rangle||(1+2\eta)^2 + \frac{4\eta^2\langle g_i'', g_j''\rangle}{\langle f_i, f_j\rangle}| \end{aligned} \tag{20}$$

and

$$\begin{aligned} &\frac{1}{\sqrt{\|f_i+\eta g_i\|^2}} \\ &= \frac{1}{\sqrt{\|f_i\|^2 + 2\eta\langle f_i, g_i\rangle + \eta^2\|g_i\|^2}} \\ &= \frac{1}{\sqrt{\|f_i\|^2(1+\frac{2\eta\langle f_i, g_i\rangle}{\|f_i\|^2} + \frac{\eta^2\|g_i\|^2}{\|f_i\|^2})}} \\ &= \frac{1}{\|f_i\|\sqrt{1+\frac{2\eta\langle f_i, g_i\rangle}{\|f_i\|^2} + \frac{\eta^2\|g_i\|^2}{\|f_i\|^2}}} \end{aligned} \tag{21}$$

According to the Taylor expansion, we have

$$\frac{1}{\sqrt{1+x}} = 1 - \frac{1}{2}x + o(x) \tag{22}$$

Then

$$\frac{1}{\sqrt{1+\frac{2\eta\langle f_i, g_i\rangle}{\|f_i\|^2} + \frac{\eta^2\|g_i\|^2}{\|f_i\|^2}}} = 1 - \frac{1}{2}\left(\frac{2\eta\langle f_i, g_i\rangle}{\|f_i\|^2} + \frac{\eta^2\|g_i\|^2}{\|f_i\|^2}\right) + o\left(\frac{2\eta\langle f_i, g_i\rangle}{\|f_i\|^2} + \frac{\eta^2\|g_i\|^2}{\|f_i\|^2}\right) \tag{23}$$

where

$$\frac{2\eta\langle f_i, g_i\rangle}{\|f_i\|^2} = \frac{2\eta\langle f_i, 2f_i - 2g_i''\rangle}{\|f_i\|^2} = 4\eta - 4\eta\frac{\langle f_i, g_i''\rangle}{\|f_i\|^2} \tag{24}$$

Hence

$$\frac{1}{\sqrt{1+\frac{2\eta\langle f_i, g_i\rangle}{\|f_i\|^2} + \frac{\eta^2\|g_i\|^2}{\|f_i\|^2}}} = 1 - 2\eta + 2\eta\frac{\langle f_i, g_i''\rangle}{\|f_i\|^2} + o(\eta) \tag{25}$$

and

$$\frac{1}{\sqrt{1+\frac{2\eta\langle f_i,g_i\rangle}{\|f_i\|^2}+\frac{\eta^2\|g_i\|^2}{\|f_i\|^2}}}\frac{1}{\sqrt{1+\frac{2\eta\langle f_j,g_j\rangle}{\|f_j\|^2}+\frac{\eta^2\|g_j\|^2}{\|f_j\|^2}}}=(1-2\eta)^2+2\eta(\frac{\langle f_i,g_i''\rangle}{\|f_i\|^2}+\frac{\langle f_j,g_j''\rangle}{\|f_j\|^2})+o(\eta) \tag{26}$$

Then

$$\begin{aligned}
\hat{s}_{ij} &= \frac{|\langle f_i,f_j\rangle|}{\|f_i\|\|f_j\|}|(1+2\eta)^2+\frac{4\eta^2\langle g_i'',g_j''\rangle}{\langle f_i,f_j\rangle}|((1-2\eta)^2+2\eta(\frac{\langle f_i,g_i''\rangle}{\|f_i\|^2}+\frac{\langle f_j,g_j''\rangle}{\|f_j\|^2})+o(\eta))\\
&\geq \frac{|\langle f_i,f_j\rangle|}{\|f_i\|\|f_j\|}((1+2\eta)^2+\frac{4\eta^2\langle g_i'',g_j''\rangle}{\langle f_i,f_j\rangle})((1-2\eta)^2+2\eta(\frac{\langle f_i,g_i''\rangle}{\|f_i\|^2}+\frac{\langle f_j,g_j''\rangle}{\|f_j\|^2})+o(\eta))\\
&= s_{ij}(1+2\eta(\frac{\langle f_i,g_i''\rangle}{\|f_i\|^2}+\frac{\langle f_j,g_j''\rangle}{\|f_j\|^2})+o(\eta))\\
&> s_{ij}
\end{aligned} \tag{27}$$

This holds for all i,j, hence $s(\widehat{\mathcal{F}})>s(\mathcal{F})$. The proof completes.

3 Proof of Theorem 1

For the ease of presentation, we use n to denote the number of data examples. Note that this number is denoted by N in the main paper. Some of the proof techniques draw inspiration from (Xie et al., 2015b). A well established result in learning theory is that the generalization error can be upper bounded by the Rademacher complexity. We start from the Rademacher complexity, seek a further upper bound of it and show how $s(\mathcal{F})$ affects this upper bound. The Rademacher complexity $\mathcal{R}_n(\mathcal{A})$ of the loss function set $\mathcal{A}$ is defined as

$$\mathcal{R}_n(\mathcal{A}) \quad = \quad \mathbb{E}[\sup_{\ell\in\mathcal{A}}\tfrac{1}{n}\textstyle\sum_{i=1}^{n}\sigma_i\ell(u(\mathbf{x}_i,\mathbf{y}_i),t_i)] \tag{28}$$

where σ_i is uniform over $\{-1,1\}$ and $\{(\mathbf{x}_i,\mathbf{y}_i,t_i)\}_{i=1}^n$ are i.i.d samples drawn from p^*. Another form of Rademacher complexity Bartlett and Mendelson (2003) can be written as $\mathcal{R}_{||}(\mathcal{A})=\mathbb{E}[\sup_{\ell\in\mathcal{A}}|\frac{2}{n}\sum_{i=1}^{n}\sigma_i\ell(u(\mathbf{x}_i,\mathbf{y}_i),t_i)|]$. The Rademacher complexity can be utilized to upper bound the estimation error, as shown in Lemma 3.

Lemma 3. *(Anthony and Bartlett, 1999; Bartlett and Mendelson, 2003; Liang, 2015) With probability at least* $1-\delta$

$$L(u)-\widehat{L}(u)\leq 4\mathcal{R}_n(\mathcal{A})+\gamma\sqrt{\frac{2\log(2/\delta)}{n}} \tag{29}$$

for $\gamma\geq\sup_{\mathbf{x},\mathbf{y},t,u}|\ell(u(\mathbf{x},\mathbf{y}),t)|$

Our analysis starts from this lemma and we seek further upper bound of $\mathcal{R}_n(\mathcal{A})$. The analysis needs an upper bound of the Rademacher complexity of the hypothesis set $\mathcal{F}$, which is given in Lemma 4.

Lemma 4. *Let* $\mathcal{R}_n(\mathcal{F})$ *denote the Rademacher complexity of the hypothesis set* $\mathcal{F}$*, then*

$$\mathcal{R}_n(\mathcal{F})\leq\frac{8B(k)^2B'(k,C)^2K}{\sqrt{n}} \tag{30}$$

Proof. Let $\mathcal{V}=\{v:(\mathbf{x},\mathbf{y})\mapsto(f(\mathbf{x})-f(\mathbf{y}))^2,f\in\mathcal{H}\}$ denote the set of hypothesis $v(\mathbf{x},\mathbf{y})=(f(\mathbf{x})-f(\mathbf{y}))^2$, we have

$$\begin{aligned}
\mathcal{R}_n(\mathcal{U}) &= \mathbb{E}[\sup_{u\in\mathcal{U}}\tfrac{1}{n}\sum_{i=1}^{n}\sigma_i\sum_{j=1}^{K}(f_j(\mathbf{x}_i)-f_j(\mathbf{y}_i))^2]\\
&= \mathbb{E}[\sup_{u\in\mathcal{U}}\tfrac{1}{n}\sum_{j=1}^{K}\sum_{i=1}^{n}\sigma_i(f_j(\mathbf{x}_i)-f_j(\mathbf{y}_i))^2]\\
&\leq K\mathbb{E}[\sup_{v\in\mathcal{V}}\tfrac{1}{n}\max_j|\sum_{i=1}^{n}\sigma_i(f_j(\mathbf{x}_i)-f_j(\mathbf{y}_i))^2|]\\
&= K\mathbb{E}[\sup_{v\in\mathcal{V}}\tfrac{1}{n}|\sum_{i=1}^{n}\sigma_i(f(\mathbf{x}_i)-f(\mathbf{y}_i))^2|]\\
&= \tfrac{K}{2}\mathcal{R}_{||}(\mathcal{V})
\end{aligned} \tag{31}$$

Let $\mathcal{G} = \{g : (\mathbf{x}, \mathbf{y}) \mapsto f(\mathbf{x}) - f(\mathbf{y}), f \in \mathcal{H}\}$ denote the set of hypothesis $g(\mathbf{x}, \mathbf{y}) = f(\mathbf{x}) - f(\mathbf{y})$ and $h(x) = x^2$, then $\mathcal{R}_{||}(\mathcal{V}) = \mathcal{R}_{||}(h \circ g)$. $h(0) = 0$ and h is Lipschitz continuous with Lipschitz constant L, which can be bounded as follows

$$\begin{array}{rcl} L & = & \sup_{g \in \mathcal{G}} |h'(g)| \\ & = & \sup_{f,\mathbf{x},\mathbf{y}} 2|f(\mathbf{x}) - f(\mathbf{y})| \\ & \leq & 4 \sup_{f,\mathbf{x}} |f(\mathbf{x})| \\ & \leq & 4 \sup_{f,\mathbf{x}} |\langle f, k(\mathbf{x}, \cdot)\rangle| \\ & \leq & 4 \sup_{f,\mathbf{x}} \|f\| \|k(\mathbf{x}, \cdot)\| \\ & \leq & 4B(k)B'(k, C) \end{array} \tag{32}$$

According to the composition property of Rademacher complexity (Theorem 12 in Bartlett and Mendelson (2003)), we have

$$\mathcal{R}_{||}(h \circ g) \leq 4B(k)B'(k, C)\mathcal{R}_{||}(g) \tag{33}$$

Now we bound $\mathcal{R}_{||}(g)$:

$$\begin{array}{rcl} \mathcal{R}_{||}(g) & = & \mathbb{E}[\sup_{g \in \mathcal{G}} |\frac{2}{n} \sum_{i=1}^{n} \sigma_i (f(\mathbf{x}_i) - f(\mathbf{y}_i))|] \\ & = & \mathbb{E}[\sup_{g \in \mathcal{G}} |\frac{2}{n} \sum_{i=1}^{n} \sigma_i (\langle f, k(\mathbf{x}_i, \cdot)\rangle - \langle f, k(\mathbf{y}_i, \cdot)\rangle)|] \\ & \leq & \frac{2}{n}\mathbb{E}[\sup_{g \in \mathcal{G}} \|f\| \| \sum_{i=1}^{n} \sigma_i (k(\mathbf{x}_i, \cdot) - k(\mathbf{y}_i, \cdot))\|] \\ & \leq & \frac{2B(k)}{n}\mathbb{E}[\| \sum_{i=1}^{n} \sigma_i (k(\mathbf{x}_i, \cdot) - k(\mathbf{y}_i, \cdot))\|] \\ & = & \frac{2B(k)}{n}\mathbb{E}_{(\mathbf{x},\mathbf{y})}[\mathbb{E}_{\sigma}[\| \sum_{i=1}^{n} \sigma_i (k(\mathbf{x}_i, \cdot) - k(\mathbf{y}_i, \cdot))\|]] \\ & \leq & \frac{2B(k)}{n}\mathbb{E}_{(\mathbf{x},\mathbf{y})}[\sqrt{\mathbb{E}_{\sigma}[\| \sum_{i=1}^{n} \sigma_i (k(\mathbf{x}_i, \cdot) - k(\mathbf{y}_i, \cdot))\|^2]}] \text{ (concavity of } \sqrt{\cdot}) \\ & = & \frac{2B(k)}{n}\mathbb{E}_{(\mathbf{x},\mathbf{y})}[\sqrt{\mathbb{E}_{\sigma}[\sum_{i=1}^{n} \sigma_i^2 \|k(\mathbf{x}_i, \cdot) - k(\mathbf{y}_i, \cdot)\|^2]}] \; (\forall i \neq j \; \sigma_i \perp\!\!\!\perp \sigma_j) \\ & = & \frac{2B(k)}{n}\mathbb{E}_{(\mathbf{x},\mathbf{y})}[\sqrt{\sum_{i=1}^{n} \|k(\mathbf{x}_i, \cdot) - k(\mathbf{y}_i, \cdot)\|^2}] \\ & = & \frac{2B(k)}{n}\mathbb{E}_{(\mathbf{x},\mathbf{y})}[\sqrt{\sum_{i=1}^{n} (k(\mathbf{x}_i, \mathbf{x}_i) + k(\mathbf{y}_i, \mathbf{y}_i) - 2k(\mathbf{x}_i, \mathbf{y}_i))}] \\ & \leq & \frac{4B(k)B'(k,C)}{\sqrt{n}} \end{array} \tag{34}$$

Putting Eq.(33) and Eq.(34) together, we have

$$\mathcal{R}_{||}(\mathcal{V}) \leq \frac{16B(k)^2 B'(k, C)^2}{\sqrt{n}} \tag{35}$$

Plugging into $\mathcal{R}_n(\mathcal{U}) \leq \frac{K}{2}\mathcal{R}_{||}(\mathcal{V})$ completes the proof. □

In addition, we need the following bound of $u(\mathbf{x}, \mathbf{y})$.

Lemma 5.

$$\sup_{\mathbf{x},\mathbf{y},u} u(\mathbf{x}, \mathbf{y}) \leq \mathcal{J} \tag{36}$$

where $\mathcal{J} = 4B(k)^2 B'(k, C)^2((K - 1)s(\mathcal{F}) + 1)$.

Proof. Let $\mathbf{F} = [f_i, \cdots, f_K]$. We have

$$\begin{array}{rcl} u(\mathbf{x}, \mathbf{y}) & = & \sum_{j=1}^{K} (f_j(\mathbf{x}) - f_j(\mathbf{y}))^2 \\ & = & \sum_{j=1}^{K} (\langle f_j, k(\mathbf{x}, \cdot)\rangle - \langle f_j, k(\mathbf{y}, \cdot)\rangle)^2 \\ & = & \|\mathbf{F}^\top (k(\mathbf{x}, \cdot) - k(\mathbf{y}, \cdot))\|^2 \\ & \leq & \|\mathbf{F}^\top\|_{op}^2 \|k(\mathbf{x}, \cdot) - k(\mathbf{y}, \cdot)\|^2 \\ & = & \|\mathbf{F}\|_{op}^2 \|k(\mathbf{x}, \cdot) - k(\mathbf{y}, \cdot)\|^2 \\ & \leq & (k(\mathbf{x}, \mathbf{x}) + k(\mathbf{y}, \mathbf{y}) - 2k(\mathbf{x}, \mathbf{y}))\|\mathbf{F}\|_{op}^2 \\ & \leq & 4B'(k, C)^2 \|\mathbf{F}\|_{op}^2 \end{array} \tag{37}$$

where $\| \cdot \|_{op}$ denotes the operator norm.

$$\begin{array}{rcl} \|\mathbf{F}\|_{op}^2 & = & \sup_{\|\mathbf{a}\|_2=1} \|\mathbf{F}\mathbf{a}\|_2^2 \\ & = & \sup_{\|\mathbf{a}\|_2=1} \mathbf{a}^\top \mathbf{F}^\top \mathbf{F}\mathbf{a} \\ & = & \sup_{\|\mathbf{a}\|_2=1} \sum_{i=1}^{K} \sum_{j=1}^{K} a_i a_j \langle f_i, f_j\rangle \\ & \leq & \sup_{\|\mathbf{a}\|_2=1} \sum_{i=1}^{K} \sum_{j=1}^{K} |a_i||a_j| \|f_i\| \|f_j\| |\cos\theta_{ij}| \\ & \leq & \sup_{\|\mathbf{a}\|_2=1} \sum_{i=1}^{K} \sum_{j=1}^{K} |a_i||a_j| B(k)^2 |\cos\theta_{ij}| \\ & \leq & B(k)^2 \sup_{\|\mathbf{a}\|_2=1} (\sum_{i=1}^{K} \sum_{j\neq i}^{K} |a_i||a_j| s(\mathcal{F}) + \sum_{i=1}^{K} a_i^2) \end{array} \tag{38}$$

where θ_{ij} is the angle between f_i and f_j. Define $\mathbf{a}' = [|a_1|, \cdots, |a_K|]^T$, $\mathbf{Q} \in \mathbb{R}^{K\times K}$: $Q_{ij} = s(\mathcal{F})$ for $i \neq j$ and $Q_{ii} = 1$, then $\|\mathbf{a}'\|_2 = \|\mathbf{a}\|$ and

$$\begin{aligned} \|\mathbf{F}\|_{op}^2 &\leq B(k)^2 \sup_{\|\mathbf{a}'\|_2=1} \mathbf{a}'^\top \mathbf{Q}\mathbf{a}' \\ &\leq B(k)^2 \sup_{\|\mathbf{a}'\|_2=1} \lambda_1(\mathbf{Q})\|\mathbf{a}'\|_2^2 \\ &\leq B(k)^2 \lambda_1(\mathbf{Q}) \end{aligned} \tag{39}$$

where $\lambda_1(\mathbf{Q})$ is the largest eigenvalue of $\mathbf{Q}$. By simple linear algebra we can get $\lambda_1(\mathbf{Q}) = (K-1)s(\mathcal{F}) + 1$, so

$$\|\mathbf{F}\|_{op}^2 \leq B(k)^2((K-1)s(\mathcal{F}) + 1) \tag{40}$$

Substituting to Eq.(37), we have

$$u(\mathbf{x}, \mathbf{y}) \leq 4B(k)^2 B'(k, C)^2((K-1)s(\mathcal{F}) + 1) \tag{41}$$

Then $\sup_{\mathbf{x},\mathbf{y},u} |u(\mathbf{x}, \mathbf{y})| \leq \mathcal{J}$ with

$$\mathcal{J} = 4B(k)^2 B'(k, C)^2((K-1)s(\mathcal{F}) + 1) \tag{42}$$

The proof completes. □

Given these lemmas, we proceed to prove Theorem 1. Since $|\frac{\partial \ell(u(\mathbf{x},\mathbf{y}),t)}{\partial u(\mathbf{x},\mathbf{y})}| \leq \frac{1}{1+\exp(-u(\mathbf{x},\mathbf{y}))} \leq \frac{1}{1+\exp(-J)}$, $\ell(u(\mathbf{x}, \mathbf{y}), t)$ is Lipschitz continuous with respect to the first argument, and the constant L is $\frac{1}{1+\exp(-J)}$. Applying the composition property of Rademacher complexity, we have

$$\mathcal{R}_n(\mathcal{A}) \leq \frac{1}{1+\exp(-J)} \mathcal{R}_n(\mathcal{U}) \tag{43}$$

Using Lemma 4, we have

$$\mathcal{R}_n(\mathcal{A}) \leq \frac{8B(k)^2 B'(k,C)^2 K}{(1+\exp(-J))\sqrt{n}} \tag{44}$$

In addition, $\sup_{\mathbf{x},\mathbf{y},t,u} |\ell(u(\mathbf{x}, \mathbf{y}), t)| \leq \log(1 + \exp(J))$ Substituting this inequality and Eq.(44) into Lemma 3 completes the proof.

4 Proof of Theorem 2

First, we derive an upper bound of the Babel function Tropp (2004):

$$\begin{aligned} \mu_K(\{f_i\}_{i=1}^K) &= \max_{i\in\{1,\cdots,K\}} \max_{\Lambda\subset\{1,\cdots,K\}\backslash\{i\};|\Lambda|=m} \sum_{j\in\Lambda} |\langle f_j, f_i\rangle| \\ &\leq \max_{i\in\{1,\cdots,K\}} \max_{\Lambda\subset\{1,\cdots,K\}\backslash\{i\};|\Lambda|=m} \sum_{j\in\Lambda} \|f_i\|\|f_j\| s(\mathcal{F}) \\ &\leq mB^2(k)s(\mathcal{F}) \end{aligned} \tag{45}$$

In Theorem 14 of Vainsencher et al. (2011), we set the upper bound of $\mu_{K-1}(\{f_i\}_{i=1}^K)$ to $mB^2(k)s(\mathcal{F})$, then get Theorem 2.

5 Visualization

Given the learned RKHS functions $\{f_i\}_{i=1}^K$, we compute a $K \times K$ matrix $\mathbf{S}$ where S_{ij} is the absolute value of the cosine similarity between f_i and f_j. Then we visualize this matrix using a heatmap obtained by the `imagesc` function in MATLAB. Figure 1 shows the heatmaps of the matrices learned by different methods on the MIMIC-III dataset. The number of RKHS functions was fixed to 200. For all matrices, the diagonal entries equal to 1. From the visualization, we observed the following. For BMD-KDML methods KDML-(SFN,VND,LDD)-(RTR,RFF), the heatmaps have low energy on the off-diagonal entries, which indicates that these matrices are close to an identity matrix and hence the learned RKHS functions are close to being orthogonal. For the unregularized KDML, the heatmap has high energy on the off-diagonal entries. The matrices of KDML-(DPP,Angle) have lower energy compared with KDML and KDML-SHN, but their energy is higher than BMD-KDML methods.

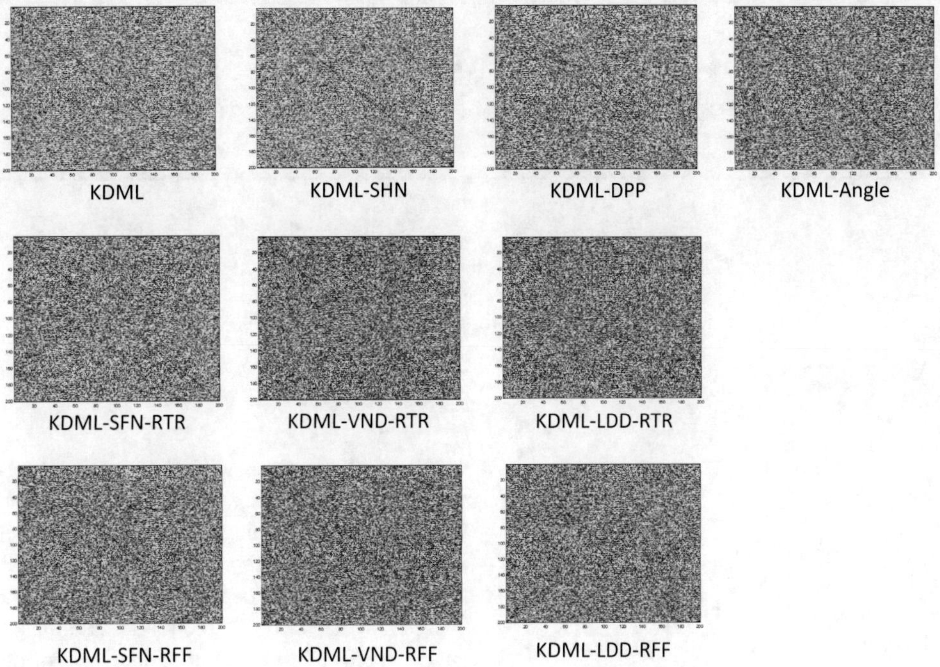

Figure 1: Heatmaps of the Pairwise Cosine Similarities

References

Martin Anthony and Peter L Bartlett. *Neural network learning: Theoretical foundations*. cambridge university press, 1999.

Peter L Bartlett and Shahar Mendelson. Rademacher and gaussian complexities: Risk bounds and structural results. *Journal of Machine Learning Research*, 3:463–482, 2003.

Rudolf Gorenflo, Yuri Luchko, and Francesco Mainardi. Analytical properties and applications of the Wright function. *arXiv preprint math-ph/0701069*, 2007.

Nicholas J Higham and Hyun-Min Kim. Solving a quadratic matrix equation by newton's method with exact line searches. *SIAM Journal on Matrix Analysis and Applications*, 23(2):303–316, 2001.

Percy Liang. Lecture notes of statistical learning theory. 2015.

Robert Tibshirani. Regression shrinkage and selection via the lasso. *Journal of the Royal Statistical Society. Series B (Methodological)*, pages 267–288, 1996.

Joel A Tropp. Greed is good: Algorithmic results for sparse approximation. *IEEE Transactions on Information theory*, 50(10):2231–2242, 2004.

Daniel Vainsencher, Shie Mannor, and Alfred M Bruckstein. The sample complexity of dictionary learning. *Journal of Machine Learning Research*, 12(Nov):3259–3281, 2011.

P. Xie, Y. Deng, and E. Xing. Diversifying restricted Boltzmann machine for document modeling. In *SIGKDD*, 2015a.

P. Xie, Y. Deng, and E. Xing. On the generalization error bounds of neural networks under mutual angular regularization. *arXiv:1511.07110*, 2015b.

How Good Are My Predictions? Efficiently Approximating Precision-Recall Curves for Massive Datasets

Ashish Sabharwal and **Hanie Sedghi**
Allen Institute for Artificial Intelligence (AI2), Seattle, WA, U.S.A.
AshishS,HanieS@allenai.org

Abstract

Large scale machine learning produces massive datasets whose items are often associated with a confidence level and can thus be ranked. However, computing the precision of these resources requires human annotation, which is often prohibitively expensive and is therefore skipped. We consider the problem of cost-effectively approximating precision-recall (PR) or ROC curves for such systems. Our novel approach, called PAULA, provides theoretically guaranteed lower and upper bounds on the underlying precision function while relying on only $O(\log N)$ annotations for a resource with N items. This contrasts favorably with $\Theta(\sqrt{N \log N})$ annotations needed by commonly used sampling based methods. Our key insight is to capitalize on a natural monotonicity property of the underlying confidence-based ranking. PAULA provides tight bounds for PR curves using, e.g., only 17K annotations for resources with 200K items and 48K annotations for resources with 2B items. We use PAULA to evaluate a subset of the much utilized PPDB paraphrase database and a recent Science knowledge base.

1 INTRODUCTION

Precision-recall (PR) curves and receiver operating characteristic (ROC) curves play a fundamental role in understanding the behavior of a variety of systems in the presence of uncertainty. These curves are frequently used in machine learning (ML), electrical engineering, radiology, and many other fields to study the performance of a binary prediction system as a function of a control parameter. As the parameter is varied, one is often able to increase the precision (or decrease the false positive rate) of the system at the expense of lower recall (also known as the true positive rate or sensitivity). PR and ROC curves make this precision-recall tradeoff explicit, enabling users to adaptively choose a parameter value based on the needs of their application, or to compare two systems across the entire spectrum of the control parameter rather than at a single design point. From these curves, one can also "read off" summary performance metrics such as area under the curve (AOC) for classification algorithms, precision of the top k results (Prec@k) or average precision (AP) for ranking algorithms in applications such as Web search, and the F1 score for balancing precision and recall.

A key challenge in this space is cost-effectively approximating PR and ROC curves for massive resources produced by ML systems, when annotating whether an item in the resource is correct or not is expensive. For instance, consider the paraphrase database PPDB (Ganitkevitch et al., 2013; Pavlick et al., 2015) with 169M automatically computed pairs of English paraphrases. Each item in PPDB is associated with a confidence level, with the understanding that higher confidence correlates with being a valid paraphrase. However, the overall precision of PPDB, not to mention its PR tradeoff as a function of the confidence level, is unknown. Instead, PPDB is pre-packaged into six sizes (S, M, L, XL, etc.), ranging from the smallest package containing the highest ranking 6.8M pairs to the largest containing all 169M pairs. Similarly, the NELL system (Mitchell et al., 2012) has collected over 50M beliefs of which 3M are identified as more reliable. Again, its PR tradeoff is not available. Even smaller resources such as a semi-automatically generated Science KB with 217K triples (Dalvi et al., 2017) do not come with an associated PR curve. The bottleneck is the high cost of human annotation.

To address this bottleneck, we propose a novel method, called PAULA for *Precision Approximation Using Logarithmic Annotations*, for cost-effectively (in terms of annotations) computing a constant-factor approximation of the underlying *precision function* $p(r)$, which assigns a precision value (i.e., the fraction of items that are correct) to the top r items in a large, unannotated, ranked list $T = (t_1, \ldots, t_N)$. Note that any resource where each item is associated with a correctness confidence can be viewed as a ranked list. PAULA is able to obtain a pointwise $(1 + \epsilon)$-approximation of p at a large number of points of interest (and roughly a pointwise $(1 + \epsilon)^2$-approximation of entire p) using only roughly $\Delta \log_{1+\epsilon} N$ annotations in total (cf. Theorem 3), where Δ is a monotonicity parameter that is typically in the range 50 to 100. For the Science KB with 217K items, for instance, this translates into 17K annotations when $\epsilon = 0.03$. For a resource with 2B items, PAULA would need only 47K annotations.

The new insight is that one can leverage a natural property of p (and of derived metrics such as PR and ROC curves, to which our results also apply; see Sec. 2), that they are monotonic—when viewed through the lens of a sufficiently wide sliding window and looking beyond the initial few results in T where p is typically more erratic.

To put the benefit of this approach in perspective, we note that naïvely computing $p(r)$ exactly even at a single value of rank r is impractical, as it requires annotating all of the top r items. A common method to approximate PR curves is to randomly draw s samples $T' \subseteq_R T$, annotate T', create the PR curve for T', and use it as a surrogate for the actual PR curve for T. This has the advantage of providing a PR curve that becomes more and more accurate (due to more samples) as we go down the ranked list. We show (cf. Section 4.4.3), however, that it requires $s = \Theta(\sqrt{N \log N})$ annotations to achieve a constant factor approximation of p. E.g., for the 217K Science KB, it requires 47K annotations for a 95% confidence when $\epsilon = 0.03$ as opposed to only 17K annotations needed by PAULA, and this gap widens as N grows.

To analyze the behavior of PAULA, we first derive a general result (cf. Theorem 1) that under a monotonicity assumption, *it is sufficient to estimate* p *at only logarithmically many points* in T. We formalize the assumption and discuss its validity in Sections 4.1 and 4.2.

Building upon this, we consider a refined *stratified sampling* approach that requires only $\Theta(\log N \log \log N)$ annotations (Section 4.4.1, Theorem 2). However, while stratification helps reduce the number of annotations, the probabilistic approach results in cumulative errors, requiring one to be much more precise at estimating p at each individual point. We then develop our main contribution, the PAULA algorithm, in Section 4.4.2, leveraging a stronger form of monotonicity. Our estimates reveal that in typical use cases, *PAULA requires an order of magnitude fewer annotations than the random sampling baseline and half the annotations needed by our refined logarithmic stratified sampling approach.*

We evaluate PAULA on two large resources mentioned earlier: the PPDB dataset from natural language research and the Science KB for common facts about elementary level science. Our experiments show that the lower and upper bounds provided by PAULA are very close in practice—to each other and to the ground truth, when available. The method, being logarithmic and deterministic, easily scales to larger resources.

1.1 RELATED WORK

Much of the existing work in this area has focused on small ranked lists (e.g., the top 10 or 100 Web search results), on aggregating across multiple ranked lists (e.g., multiple search queries), and on summary statistics (e.g., Prec@k for some small k of interest, average precision AP, discounted cumulative gain DCG, etc.). In contrast, our challenge is to compute the entire precision function (and the associated PR, ROC, and precision-yield curves) for a single, large, ranked list. From the entire curve, it is then easy to "read off" various summary statistics.

There has been much interest in random sampling based methods to compute a particular summary statistic of interest (e.g., AP), where the focus is on choosing non-uniform samples in a way that minimizes variance. While very effective for that particular statistic, these methods require different sets of annotations to minimize variance for different metrics (e.g., Prec@k, Prec@k' for $k' \neq k$, Gain@k, DCG, etc.). Our method, on the other hand, relies on a deterministic set of annotations for the entire curve, and hence for any derived summary metrics.

Carterette et al. (2006) focus on the AP metric in the information retrieval (IR) setting, and propose a method to design a test subset that measures AP with high confidence. They choose documents based on the benefit they would provide when fully ranking the system.

Yilmaz et al. (2008) consider large scale retrieval evaluation using incomplete relevance judgments, focusing on a simple yet efficient method. Unlike prior work, they provide confidence intervals for the inferred AP and improve upon two proposals, one that is accurate but complex (Aslam et al., 2006) and another called InfAP that is simple but less efficient (Yilmaz and Aslam, 2006).

Kanoulas (2015) provides a short survey of methods, measures, and designs used in the field of IR to evaluate the quality of search algorithms against collections of observations, considering the use of relevance and observable user behavior to compute search quality.

Schnabel et al. (2016) provide an interesting, comprehensive perspective, recasting nearly all previous approaches with guarantees as Monte Carlo estimation of an expectation, focusing on variance reduction via importance sampling. Their domain of interest is Web search, where importance is placed on the top 10 or so ranked results, aggregation across multiple queries, and specific summary metrics that are used to guide the sampling strategy so as to minimizes variance.

2 PRELIMINARIES

Consider the ranked output $T = (t_1, t_2, \ldots, t_N)$ of an algorithm $\mathcal{A}$, where each t_i comes from some universe U (e.g., all documents on the Web, all paraphrase pairs, all subject-verb-object triples, etc.). Each item $u \in U$ is associated with an unknown true label $v(u) \in \{0, 1\}$ that captures the semantics of some underlying task (e.g., whether a document is relevant to a query, whether a pair of phrases is a linguistic paraphrase, whether a triple denotes a true fact, etc.). The **precision function of $\mathcal{A}$**, $p : [N] \to [0, 1]$, maps each rank $r \in [N]$ to the fraction of the top r items in T that are positive, i.e., labeled as 1:

$$p(r) = \frac{1}{r} \sum_{i=1}^{r} v(t_i) \tag{1}$$

where we omit $\mathcal{A}$ from the notation for brevity. The commonly used metric Prec@k for a specific k (e.g., Prec@10) is simply $p(k)$. The associated *recall of $\mathcal{A}$* at rank r is the fraction of all positive items $U_+ \subseteq U$ that appear among $t_1, \ldots, t_r$; that is, $\frac{r\,p(r)}{|U_+|}$. Since U_+ is unknown in many ranking applications, it is common to instead use its unnormalized variant called *yield*, defined as $\sum_{i=1}^{r} v(t_i)$, which equals $r\,p(r)$.

A plot of $p(r)$ vs. recall (or yield) at r is commonly referred to as the *precision-recall* (or *precision-yield*, resp.) curve for $\mathcal{A}$. One can similarly define a variety of metrics that are derivable from $p(r), r, U_+$, and U, such as Gain@k, accuracy, F1, true positive rate (TPR), false positive rate (FPR), specificity, sensitivity, etc. The ROC curve refers to a plot of FPR vs. TPR, and average precision (AP) is the area under the PR curve. Fawcett (2006) and Majnik and Bosnic (2013) provide good surveys of such metrics, while Davis and Goadrich (2006) explore interesting relationships between PR and ROC curves.

Our goal in this work is to efficiently approximate p, which is a fundamental building block for all of the above metrics—indeed, a pointwise-approximation of p allows one to approximately compute all of these metrics.

Importantly, we operate under a setting where obtaining true labels $v(t_i)$ is costly (e.g., requires a system simulation, human annotation, crowdsourcing, etc.). We aim to *compute a pointwise-approximation of* p *with as few annotations of true labels* $v(t_i)$ as possible.

2.1 POINT ESTIMATES: RANDOM SAMPLING

A simple way to obtain an unbiased point estimate of $p(r)$ for a *fixed* rank r is via random sampling: Sample (with repetition) z indices J independently and uniformly from $\{1, 2, \ldots, r\}$ and compute the empirical average $\tilde{p}(r) = \frac{1}{z} \sum_{j \in J} v(t_j)$. Then $\tilde{p}(r)$ is an unbiased estimator of $p(r)$ and one can apply tail inequalities such as the two-sided Hoeffding bound (Hoeffding, 1963) to compute how tight the estimate is:

$$\Pr[|\tilde{p}(r) - p(r)| \geq \epsilon p(r)] \leq 2 \exp\left(-2z\epsilon^2 p(r)^2\right)$$

For a $1 - \delta$ confidence in the outcome (e.g., a 95% confidence would mean $\delta = 0.05$), it suffices to have $2 \exp\left(-2z\epsilon^2 p(r)^2\right) \leq \delta$, which translates into needing:

$$z \geq \frac{1}{2\epsilon^2 p(r)^2} \ln \frac{2}{\delta} \tag{2}$$

samples in order to achieve a $(1 + \epsilon)$-approximation of $p(r)$. A complementary way of viewing the same result is that the use of z samples results in the following $1 - \delta$ confidence interval (e.g., a 95% confidence interval) which can be used for error bars around the estimate:

$$\tilde{p}(r) \pm \sqrt{\frac{1}{2z} \ln \frac{2}{\delta}} \tag{3}$$

3 PRECISION WITH O($\sqrt{N} \log N$) ANNOTATIONS

A common practice to compute an approximation of the entire precision function p, not only its value at one point, is to draw s uniform random samples T' from the ranked list T, compute the precision function p' for T', and use this as a surrogate for p as $p(r) \approx p'(\frac{rs}{N})$. How close is $p'(\frac{rs}{N})$ an approximation of $p(r)$ is determined by the number $z = \frac{rs}{N}$ of the s random samples that are expected to land in the range $t_1, \ldots, t_r$. We provide a formal analysis of this approach below.

Eqn. (3) indicates that the approximation error starts off large (since we observe very few samples when r is small) and decreases as r increases, scaling proportionally to $1/\sqrt{r}$. To compare this method to our proposal for obtaining a pointwise $(1 + \alpha)$-approximation for entire p, we ask the following question: Given s and N, what is the smallest $n_{\alpha,s} \leq N$ such that for all $r \geq n_{\alpha,s}$, $p'(\frac{rs}{N})$ is a $(1 + \alpha)$-approximation of $p(r)$?

We apply Eqn. (2) to each of the N points, bounding the correctness confidence by $\delta' = \delta/N$ at each point and taking the union bound to guarantee an overall correctness confidence of δ. This yields the requirement that $n_{\alpha,s}s/N$ must be at least $\frac{1}{2\alpha^2 p(r)^2} \ln \frac{2}{\delta'}$. The smallest $n_{\alpha,s}$ satisfying this is:

$$n_{\alpha,s} = \frac{N}{2s\alpha^2 p(r)^2} \ln \frac{2N}{\delta} \tag{4}$$

Thus, we obtain a $(1+\alpha)$-approximation after roughly the first $\frac{N \ln N}{s\alpha^2}$ points.

To obtain a $(1+\alpha)$-approximation of the *entire* precision function, even for low values of r, one possibility is to annotate all of $t_1, \ldots, t_{n_{\alpha,s}}$, in addition to s uniform random samples overall.[1] This would mean annotating $s + n_{\alpha,s}$ items in total. It can be verified that this expression is minimized when s is chosen such that $s = n_{\alpha,s}$, in which case the total number of annotations needed is:

$$\sqrt{\frac{2N}{\alpha^2 p(r)^2} \ln \frac{2N}{\delta}} \tag{5}$$

This expression grows asymptotically as $\Theta(\sqrt{N \log N})$. The methods developed in the next section achieve the same approximation with only $O(\log N)$ annotations.

4 PRECISION WITH $O(\log N)$ ANNOTATIONS

Exactly computing the entire precision function p, in particular computing $p(N)$, requires annotating N labels, which can be prohibitive for massive datasets. To alleviate this, we develop here a novel method called PAULA to efficiently obtain, for any $\epsilon > 0$, a pointwise $\gamma(1+\epsilon)$-approximation of p with roughly only $\Delta \log_{1+\epsilon} N$ deterministically chosen annotation points, where Δ is a constant capturing the level of monotonicity in the underlying data and γ is slightly larger than $1 + \epsilon$.

4.1 LOCAL PRECISION AND MONOTONICITY

We start by defining a Δ-local variant of p and two related notions of monotonicity. Let $T = (t_1, t_2, \ldots, t_N)$ be the ranked output of an algorithm $\mathcal{A}$ with (unknown) true labels $v(t_i) \in \{0, 1\}$ and precision function p.

Definition 1. *Let $\Delta \in \mathbb{N}^+$. The **Δ-precision of $\mathcal{A}$** is a function $p_\Delta : [N] \to [0, 1]$ defined as:*

$$p_\Delta(r) = \begin{cases} \frac{1}{r} \sum_{i=1}^{r} v(t_i) & \text{if } r \leq \Delta \\ \frac{1}{\Delta} \sum_{i=r-\Delta+1}^{r} v(t_i) & \text{otherwise} \end{cases} \tag{6}$$

where we omit $\mathcal{A}$ as before for brevity of notation.

[1] There is a small overlap when counting this way, which we ignore for simplicity of exposition.

Δ-precision may be viewed as a smoothed version of the true label sequence $v(t_1), v(t_2), \ldots, v(t_N)$. Although the actual label sequence, being a sequence of 0s and 1s, is bound to be erratic, we expect the density of 1s in this sequence to decrease as i increases. In other words, a sufficiently smoothed out variant of the true label sequence should be non-increasing, except perhaps for the initial few values. Formally, we use the following two characterizations of monotonicity:

Definition 2 (Weak Monotonicity)**.** *For $m \in \mathbb{N}^+$, p is m-monotone if for all $r_2 \geq r_1 + m$, $p(r_1) \geq p(r_2)$.*

Weak monotonicity guarantees that precision is non-increasing for points ranked at least m apart. We will use this to show that it is sufficient to compute precision at only logarithmically many points.

Definition 3 (Strong Monotonicity)**.** *For $\Delta, m \in \mathbb{N}^+$ s.t. $m \geq \Delta$, p is (Δ, m)-monotone if for all $r_2 \geq r_1 + m$,*

$$p_\Delta(r_1) \geq \frac{\sum_{r=r_1+1}^{r_2} p(r)}{r_2 - r_1} \geq p_\Delta(r_2)$$

Strong monotonicity says that for every large enough rank interval $[r_1, r_2]$, the Δ-precisions at the two ends of the interval bound the average precision across the interval. We will use this property to bound the actual precision function p by functions of local precision p_Δ.

We observe that $p(r)$ is simply $p_r(r)$. Further, when r is a multiple of Δ, $p(r)$ can be decomposed as $\frac{\Delta}{r} \sum_{j=1}^{r/\Delta} p_\Delta(j\Delta)$. Computing all of these uniformly spaced r/Δ local precision terms is, however, still as expensive in terms of the required annotation as computing $p(r)$ directly. We will instead *approximately decompose* $p(r)$ using roughly only $\log_{1+\epsilon} r$ local precision terms that are spaced based on a geometrically increasing spread with geometric ratio $1 + \epsilon$.

4.2 SETUP AND ASSUMPTIONS

Throughout this section, let $T = (t_1, t_2, \ldots, t_N)$ be the ranked output of an algorithm $\mathcal{A}$ with (unknown) true labels $v(t_i) \in \{0, 1\}$. Let p be $\mathcal{A}$'s precision function. Let $\Delta \in \mathbb{N}^+$ and p_Δ be the corresponding local precision function (cf. Definition 1). Let $\epsilon \in (0, 1]$, $\tilde{r} \in \mathbb{N}$ be such that $\tilde{r} \geq \lceil \frac{\Delta+2}{\epsilon} \rceil$, $\ell = \lceil \log_{1+\epsilon} \tilde{r} \rceil$, $m = \lfloor \epsilon(1+\epsilon)^\ell - 1 \rfloor$, $\gamma = 1 + \epsilon + \frac{2+\epsilon}{m}$, and $L = \lfloor \log_{1+\epsilon} N \rfloor$.

Observe that $m > \epsilon(1+\epsilon)^\ell - 2 \geq \epsilon\tilde{r} - 2 \geq \Delta$. The notion of (Δ, m)-monotonicity can thus be applied. Our method will involve annotating the true labels v for all of the first (roughly) $\tilde{r}$ items in the ranked list, followed by fewer than $\Delta \log_{1+\epsilon} N$ annotations for the rest of the list, in order to guarantee a $\gamma(1+\epsilon)$-approximation of p.

Assumptions. The algorithms and results below rely on one or both of the following assumptions:

A.1 p is m-monotone for all $r \geq \tilde{r}$.

A.2 p is (Δ, m)-monotone for all $r \geq \tilde{r}$.

While one intuitively expects monotonicity to hold (for large enough m and Δ) for any dataset produced by a well-designed prediction system, how often this happens in practice is an empirical question. We provide two pieces of support for it in Section 5: (a) visual support via the monotonically non-increasing ground truth points in Figures 2 and 3; and (b) quantitative support via the success of our method on two large and diverse datasets.

We noticed that the assumption fails near the 15K point in Figure 2, where the black ground truth curve starts to rise. Our estimate, as expected, deviates here a little, but then quickly regains accuracy as one moves to the right.

4.3 LOGARITHMIC EVALUATIONS

We start with a general result that evaluating p at $O(\log_{1+\epsilon} N)$ points is sufficient to obtain a $(1+\epsilon)$-approximation of the entire precision function p. The idea is to compute p at the following geometrically spaced points, where the spacing is determined by ϵ:

Definition 4. *For $j \in \mathbb{N}^+$ and $\epsilon > 0$, define $g_{\epsilon,j} = \lceil (1+\epsilon)^j \rceil$.*

For brevity, when ϵ is clear from the context, we write g_j to mean $g_{\epsilon,j}$. Observe that $g_{j+1} - g_j \geq (1+\epsilon)^{j+1} - (1+\epsilon)^j - 1 = \epsilon(1+\epsilon)^j - 1$. When $(1+\epsilon)^j \geq \frac{m+1}{\epsilon}$, we thus have $g_{j+1} - g_j \geq m$. If we assume p is m-monotone for large enough r, we can show that evaluating p at only roughly $\log_{1+\epsilon} N$ points is sufficient to obtain a $(1+\epsilon)$-approximation of the entire precision function p. Formally, we define a step-function approximation:

Definition 5. *Let N, ϵ, ℓ be as in Section 4.2 and $f : [N] \rightarrow [0,1]$. Then $step^f_{\epsilon,\ell} : [N] \rightarrow [0,1]$ is defined as:*

$$step^f_{\epsilon,\ell}(r) = \begin{cases} f(r) & \text{if } r \leq g_\ell \\ f(g_j) \text{ for } j = \lfloor \log_{1+\epsilon} r \rfloor & \text{otherwise} \end{cases}$$

In other words, $step^f_{\epsilon,\ell}(r)$ can be computed using $g_\ell + L - \ell$ evaluations of f, mirrors $f(r)$ for small r, and is a geometrically adjusting step function afterwards. The following theorem, whose proof is deferred to the Appendix, shows that under the weak monotonicity assumption, $step^p_{\epsilon,\ell}$ is a tight approximation of p.

Theorem 1. *Let $p, \epsilon, \tilde{r}, \ell, m, L$ be as in Section 4.2. If Assumption A.1 holds, then $step^p_{\epsilon,\ell}$ is a pointwise $(1+\epsilon)$-approximation of p and can be computed using evaluations of p at points $1, 2, \ldots, g_\ell, g_{\ell+1}, \ldots, g_L$.*

This result as such is not directly helpful when evaluations of p are costly, as computing p *exactly* even at a single point requires a linear number of true label annotations (e.g., computing $p(N)$ exactly requires N annotations). However, what the result shows is that *if we could efficiently compute point-estimates of p, we would need to do so at roughly only $\log_{1+\epsilon} N$ points*:

Corollary 1. *Let $p, \epsilon, \tilde{r}, \ell, m, L$ be as in Sec. 4.2 and $\beta \geq 1$. If Assumption A.1 holds and $q(r)$ is a β-approximation of $p(r)$ for $r \in \{1, 2, \ldots, g_\ell, g_{\ell+1}, \ldots, g_L\}$, then $step^q_{\epsilon,\ell}$ is a pointwise $\beta(1+\epsilon)$-approximation of p.*

4.4 EFFICIENT POINT ESTIMATES

We now consider various ways of efficiently (in terms of required label annotations) computing β-approximations q of p at the $O(\log N)$ points $g_{\ell+1}, \ldots, g_L$, in order to then apply Corollary 1 to obtain a $\beta(1+\epsilon)$-approximation of the entire precision function p.

4.4.1 Stratified Sampling

A simple way is to estimate each of these $L - \ell$ points is to employ random sampling and bound correctness confidence via Hoeffding's inequality, Eqn. (2). Since each point estimate requires many samples, it is substantially more efficient (in terms of evaluations of p) to reuse samples obtained for g_k when evaluating p at g_{k+1}. The resulting lack of independence slightly weakens the probabilistic correctness guarantee (we instead use the union bound), but leads to significantly fewer samples. Specifically, only a $\frac{\epsilon}{1+\epsilon}$ fraction of the required samples need to be obtained afresh; the rest can be reused.

This is formalized in the *stratified sampling* mechanism described in Algorithm 1, where X_k is the set of random samples considered for the point g_k and S_k denotes the precision of X_k. Samples in X_{k+1} are a combination of reusing most samples from X_k and obtaining only a few new samples from the range $g_k + 1, \ldots, g_{k+1}$. For this algorithm, we can derive the following probabilistic correctness guarantees (see Appendix for proofs):

Lemma 1. *Let $T, v, p, \epsilon, \tilde{r}, \ell, L$ be as in Sec. 4.2. Let $\delta > 0$, p_{min} be the minimum value of p, and $\beta > 1$. Then, with probability at least $1 - \delta$, $q(r)$ in Algorithm 1 on input $(T, v, \epsilon, \tilde{r}, \delta, p_{min}, \beta)$ is a β-approximation of $p(r)$ for $r \in \{g_{\ell+1}, \ldots, g_L\}$.*

Putting this together with Corollary 1 and noting that $q(r) = p(r)$ in Algorithm 1 when $r \leq \ell$, we obtain:

Theorem 2 (Logarithmic Stratified Sampling)**.** *Let $T, v, p, \epsilon, \tilde{r}, \ell, m, L$ be as in Sec. 4.2. Let $\delta > 0$, p_{min} be the minimum value of p, and $\beta > 1$. If Assumption A.1 holds, then with probability at least $1 - \delta$, the output of*

Algorithm 1 Logarithmic Stratified Sampling for Approximating Precision Function

input $T = (t_1, t_2, \ldots, t_N), v, \epsilon, \tilde{r}, \delta, p_{\min}, \beta$
  $\ell = \lceil \log_{1+\epsilon} \tilde{r} \rceil$; $L = \lfloor \log_{1+\epsilon} N \rfloor$; $r = (1+\epsilon)^{\ell-1}$
  for $j = \ell$ to L **do**
    $r = r * (1+\epsilon)$; $g_j = \lceil r \rceil$
  end for
  $s = \lceil \frac{1}{2(\beta-1)^2 p_{\min}^2} \ln \frac{L-\ell}{\delta/2} \rceil$
  $X_\ell = s$ random samples from $\{1, \ldots, g_\ell\}$
  $S_\ell = \sum_{i \in X_\ell} v(t_i)$
  for $k = \ell$ to $L - 1$ **do**
    $X_{k+1}^{(1)}$ = include each $i \in X_k$ independently with probability g_k / g_{k+1}
    $X_{k+1}^{(2)} = s - |X_{k+1}^{(1)}|$ random samples from $\{g_k + 1, \ldots, g_{k+1}\}$
    $X_{k+1} = X_{k+1}^{(1)} \cup X_{k+1}^{(2)}$
    $S_{k+1} = \sum_{i \in X_{k+1}} v(t_i)$
  end for
  $q(r) = \frac{1}{r} \sum_{i=1}^{r} v(t_i)$ for $r \in \{1, \ldots, g_\ell\}$
  $q(g_k) = S_k / s$ for $k \in \{\ell + 1, \ldots, L\}$
  Compute $step_{\epsilon,\ell}^q$ using the above values of q
output $step_{\epsilon,\ell}^q$

Algorithm 1 on input $(T, v, \epsilon, \tilde{r}, \delta, p_{min}, \beta)$ is a $\beta(1+\epsilon)$-approximation of $p(r)$. Further, Algorithm 1 evaluates p only at $1, \ldots, g_\ell$ and at $\frac{\epsilon(L-\ell)}{2(\beta-1)^2(1+\epsilon)p_{min}^2} \ln \frac{L-\ell}{\delta/2}$ points chosen randomly via stratified sampling.

Note that since $L = \Theta(\log N)$, the stratified sampling approach requires $\Theta(\log N \log \log N)$ annotations.

4.4.2 New Approach: PAULA

While random sampling provides efficient single point estimates, using it to approximate the entire p with error probability $\leq \delta$ requires bounding the error probability of each point more strictly, namely, by $\frac{\delta}{L-\ell}$, and using the union bound over $L - \ell$ dependent random events.[2]

We develop a novel method called PAULA to obtain γ-approximations of p at points of interest by evaluating p at logarithmically many *deterministically chosen* points. Since there is no probabilistic confidence involved, γ-approximations of the points directly carry over to a tight approximation of entire p, without any loss.

To this end, we employ the notions of local precision and strong monotonicity introduced in Section 4.1. We begin by observing that for any $k \geq \ell$, $g_{k+1} - g_k \geq g_{\ell+1} - g_\ell \geq (1+\epsilon)^{\ell+1} - (1+\epsilon)^\ell - 1 = \epsilon(1+\epsilon)^\ell - 1 \geq m$. The strong monotonicity assumption A.2 thus implies $p_\Delta(g_{k+1}) \leq p_\Delta(g_k)$, i.e., the *local precision is monotonically non-increasing along the geometrically spaced points* of interest. We define our candidates for lower and upper bounds on p via telescopic sums of local precisions at these points, as follows. As we will shortly see (Lemma 3), these terms bound the *yield* of $\mathcal{A}$ at rank g_k, normalizing which by g_k generates bounds on $p(g_j)$.

Definition 6. *Let $\Delta, \epsilon, \ell, L$ be as in Section 4.2 and $k \in \{\ell, \ldots, L\}$. Then:*

$$Y_-(\epsilon, \ell, k, \Delta) = g_\ell\, p(g_\ell) + \sum_{j=\ell}^{k-1} (g_{j+1} - g_j)\, p_\Delta(g_{j+1})$$

$$Y_+(\epsilon, \ell, k, \Delta) = g_\ell\, p(g_\ell) + \sum_{j=\ell}^{k-1} (g_{j+1} - g_j)\, p_\Delta(g_j)$$

Algorithm 2 describes our precision function approximation method, PAULA. We abbreviate $Y_-(\epsilon, \ell, k, \Delta)$ and $Y_+(\epsilon, \ell, k, \Delta)$ as Y_-^k and Y_+^k, resp. The algorithm is, in fact, very simple: compute some derived parameters and then loop over k to compute Y_-^k and Y_+^k via Δ-precision computations as defined above.

A similar idea has been used previously by Ermon et al. (2013), but in a different context, namely discrete integration for probabilistic graphical models. Our more delicate analysis, motivated by a novel use case, extends their finding for $\epsilon = 1$ to any $\epsilon \in (0, 1]$.[3]

Lemma 2 captures the nature of the approximation provided by PAULA:

Lemma 2. *Let $T, v, p, \Delta, \epsilon, \tilde{r}, \ell, m, \gamma, L$ be as in Section 4.2. If Assumption A.2 holds and $p(g_\ell) \geq p_\Delta(g_\ell)$, then $q^-(r)$ and $q^+(r)$ in PAULA on input $(T, v, \Delta, \epsilon, \tilde{r})$ are pointwise γ-approximations of $p(r)$ from below and above, resp., for $r \in \{g_{\ell+1}, \ldots, g_L\}$.*

This follows from Lemmas 3 and 4 below, whose proof is deferred to the Appendix.

Lemma 3. *Let $p, \Delta, \epsilon, \ell, m$ be as in Section 4.2. If Assumption A.2 holds, then for any $k \geq \ell$:*

$$Y_-(\epsilon, \ell, k, \Delta) \;\leq\; g_k\, p(g_k) \;\leq\; Y_+(\epsilon, \ell, k, \Delta)$$

Lemma 4. *Let $p, \Delta, \epsilon, \ell, m, \gamma$ be as in Section 4.2. If Assumption A.2 holds and $p(g_\ell) \geq p_\Delta(g_\ell)$, then for all $k \geq \ell$:*

$$\gamma \cdot Y_-(\epsilon, \ell, k, \Delta) \geq Y_+(\epsilon, \ell, k, \Delta)$$

[2]Even if the samples are not shared and one obtains independent estimates for each point with error probability δ' each, the overall error probability is $1 - (1 - \delta')^{L-\ell}$, which is very close to $\delta'(L - \ell)$ when δ' is small.

[3]Specifically, (a) the notion of (m, Δ)-monotonicity is irrelevant to that work, as the search space there always (implicitly) satisfies monotonicity; (b) Theorems 1 and 2 and Corollary 1 are unrelated to that work; and (c) the 2-approximation that arose there naturally from parity constraints is too loose to be useful as an approximation of the precision function.

Algorithm 2 PAULA for Approximating Precision Function

input $T = (t_1, t_2, \ldots, t_n), v, \Delta, \epsilon, \tilde{r}$
  $\ell = \lceil \log_{1+\epsilon} \tilde{r} \rceil$; $L = \lfloor \log_{1+\epsilon} n \rfloor$; $r = (1+\epsilon)^{\ell-1}$
  for $j = \ell$ to L **do**
    $r = r * (1+\epsilon)$; $g_j = \lceil r \rceil$
  end for
  $Y_-^{\ell} = Y_+^{\ell} = g_\ell \, p(g_\ell)$
  for $k = \ell$ to $L-1$ **do**
    $Y_-^{k+1} = Y_-^k + (g_{k+1} - g_k) \, p_\Delta(g_{k+1})$
    $Y_+^{k+1} = Y_+^k + (g_{k+1} - g_k) \, p_\Delta(g_k)$
  end for
  $q^-(r) = q^+(r) = \frac{1}{r} \sum_{i=1}^{r} v(t_i)$ for $r \in \{1, \ldots, \ell\}$
  $q^-(g_k) = Y_-^k / g_k$ for $k \in \{\ell+1, \ldots, L\}$
  $q^+(g_k) = Y_+^k / g_k$ for $k \in \{\ell+1, \ldots, L\}$
  Compute $step_{\epsilon,\ell}^{q^-}$ and $step_{\epsilon,\ell}^{q^+}$ using the above values of q^- and q^+, resp.
output $(step_{\epsilon,\ell}^{q^-}, step_{\epsilon,\ell}^{q^+})$

The above lemmas, in fact, show that Y_- and Y_+ together provide a γ-approximation *jointly*, in that sense that if Y_- is far from p at some point, then Y_+ must be close to p at that point. For simplicity, Lemma 2 (and Theorem 3 to follow shortly) states a weaker version that each of Y_- and Y_+ is a γ-approximation of p, independently.

Combining Lemma 2 and Corollary 1, we obtain:

Theorem 3 (PAULA). *Let $p, \Delta, \epsilon, \ell, m, \gamma, L$ be as in Section 4.2. If Assumptions A.1 and A.2 hold, and $p(g_\ell) \geq p_\Delta(g_\ell)$, then the output of PAULA on input $(T, v, \Delta, \epsilon, \tilde{r})$ provides pointwise $\gamma(1+\epsilon)$-approximations of p from below and above, resp. Further, PAULA uses evaluations of p only at $g_\ell + \Delta(L-\ell)$ deterministically chosen points.*

In typical use cases, g_ℓ can be taken to be a constant like 500 or 1000, after which the precision function stabilizes. With Δ being a constant (typically 50 to 100) and $L = \Theta(\log N)$, PAULA thus requires $\Theta(\log N)$ annotations.

4.4.3 Comparison With Random Sampling

PAULA starts with zero error in approximating $p(r)$ as long as $r \leq n_0 = \lceil \frac{\Delta+2}{\epsilon} \rceil$. As r increases beyond n_0, the error increases as we only take logarithmically many samples afterwards. Nonetheless, under the monotonicity assumption, the error remains provably bounded by $\gamma(1+\epsilon)$. This contrasts with the common random sampling approach discussed in Section 3, which is inaccurate in the beginning and starts providing a $(1+\alpha)$-approximation, where $\alpha = \gamma(1+\epsilon) - 1$, with confidence $1 - \delta$ once $r \geq n_{\alpha,s}$ as defined in Eqn. (4).

As noted earlier, the random sampling approach requires $\Theta(\sqrt{N \log N})$ samples where as PAULA requires only $\Theta(\log N)$ samples. Further, given the same number s of true label annotations and the same desired approximation factor, *we find that $n_{\alpha,s}$ is often too large*. Asymptotically, since s scales as $\Theta(\log N)$ for PAULA, we see from Eqn. (4) that $n_{\alpha,s}$ scales as $\Theta(N)$ when using the same s. In other words, given the same number of samples, PAULA obtains an approximation that holds everywhere whereas the random sampling method is inaccurate at a linear fraction of the N points.

For concreteness, we provide a numeric example. Consider the Science tensor (to be described later) where $N = 217077$. Using $\epsilon = 0.03$, PAULA requires $s = 17392$ annotations to provide a $\gamma(1+\epsilon)$ approximation of p at every point. In contrast, the random sampling approach from Section 3 needs 47030 annotations to achieve the same approximation (with error probability $\delta = 0.05$ and $p(r) \approx 0.7$). Alternatively, given the same number s of samples, the random sampling baseline has a much larger error initially and provides a pointwise α-approximation of $p(r)$ only for $r \geq n_{\alpha,s} = 41056$.

4.4.4 Comparison With Stratified Sampling

Comparing the number of evaluations of p needed in Theorems 2 vs. 3 to achieve a $\gamma(1+\epsilon)$-approximation, we see that PAULA has an asymptotic advantage over stratified sampling: $\Theta(\log N)$ vs. $\Theta(\log N \log \log N)$.

From a practical perspective, the difference is in the factor multiplying the $L - \ell$ term in each, which is $\frac{\epsilon}{2(\gamma-1)^2(1+\epsilon)p_{\min}^2} \log \frac{L-\ell}{\delta/2}$ for stratified sampling and simply Δ for PAULA. To illustrate how these terms compare in practice, consider a typical application with parameter values $\delta = 0.05$ (i.e., 95% correctness confidence), $\epsilon = 0.03$, and $p_{\min} = 0.5$. If we assume p is stable after the first 1000 points (i.e., $\tilde{r} = 1000$), then $\ell = 234$. In this case, the first expression simplifies to roughly $5.8 \log 40(L - 234)$. For a ranked list T of size $N = 10000$ (or 100000), we have $L = 311$ (389, resp.) and the expression evaluates to 46.6 (50.6, resp.). In contrast, Δ is independent of N and can often be taken safely to be somewhat larger than $1/\epsilon = 20$.

This difference can be small in practice. We note, however, that the stratified sampling approach considered here is substantially more efficient than the conventional one, as it exploits our finding (Theorem 1) that logarithmically many point-estimates are sufficient.

5 EXPERIMENTS

We begin by illustrating how the number of samples needed by various precision function estimation methods scales as the desired approximation factor is varied.[4]

We will then evaluate the accuracy and effectiveness of PAULA on resources from two application domains: natural language processing and knowledge acquisition. In the first case, ground truth is available and we demonstrate that the bounds produced by PAULA are very close to it. In the second case, we compute bounds on the precision function for a larger resource and demonstrate that (a) the bounds are close to each other and (b) match a few independently generated point estimates.

5.1 NUMBER OF ANNOTATIONS NEEDED

For this experiment, we vary the desired approximation factor $(1+\alpha)$ and compute the number of annotations needed by various methods to achieve this level of accuracy in estimating the precision function. Specifically, we consider the random sampling baseline (Section 3), our logarithmic stratified sampling (Section 4.4.1), and our deterministic approach, PAULA (Section 4.4.2). For the last two methods, $1+\alpha$ is a function of ϵ, namely, $\gamma(1+\epsilon)$.

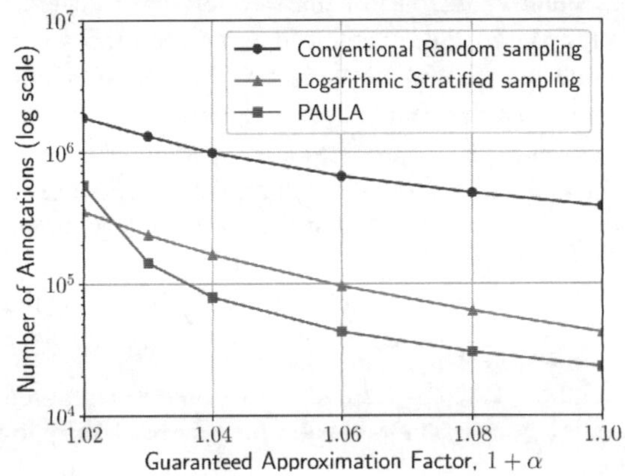

Figure 1: PAULA needs substantially fewer annotations to guarantee various levels of approximation of the precision function. $N = 10^7, p_{\text{min}} = 0.5, \Delta = 100$.

Figure 1 depicts the number of annotations (in log scale) needed when N is 10M, p_{min} for the sampling based methods is taken to be 0.5, and Δ for PAULA is 100. The plot shows that *PAULA requires over an order of magnitude fewer annotations than the random sampling baseline* in order to achieve the same level of guaranteed accuracy. The logarithmic stratified sampling approach, which also exploits our Theorem 1, starts off as more efficient (in terms of annotations) than PAULA when α is small, but requires twice as many annotations when the approximation error is varied from 3% to 10%.

[4]Code and data available at http://allenai.org/software.

5.2 APPLICATION: NLP RESOURCES

We consider the Paraphrase Database PPDB (Ganitkevitch et al., 2013), a massive dataset for major NLP tasks such as paraphrase detection and entailment. Each paraphrase pair in PPDB 2.0 is associated with a validity score generated via supervised learning on 209 features (Pavlick et al., 2015). It also includes entailment relations, word embedding similarities, and style annotations. PPDB 2.0 can be viewed as a list of 169M items, ranked based on the trained paraphrase score.

In the first experiment, our goal is to demonstrate that the bounds provided by PAULA are close to the ground truth. To this end, we consider a subset of PPDB for which Pavlick et al. (2015) provide crowdsourced annotations on a 5-point scale (1-5) using five annotators per phrase pair.[5] If the average human judgment for a phrase pair t_i is at least 3, we consider $v(t_i) = 1$; otherwise, $v(t_i) = 0$.

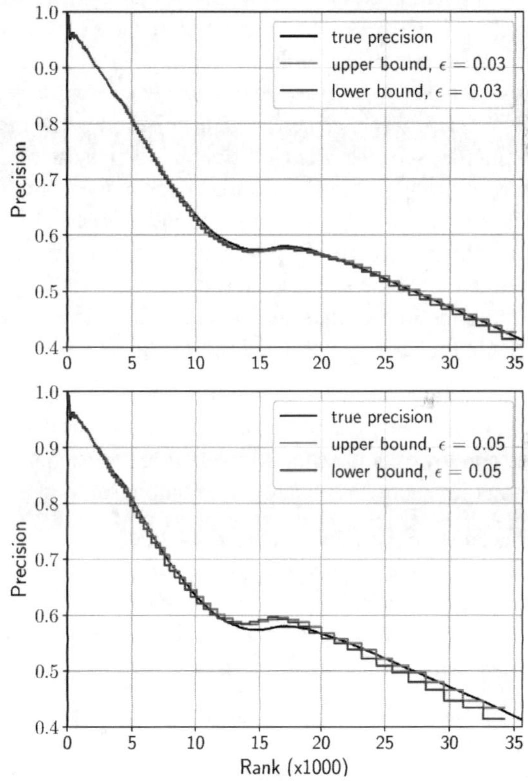

Figure 2: Bounds provided by PAULA with $\Delta = 100$ are very close to the ground truth on a fully annotated subset of PPDB 2.0 of size 36K. Top: $\epsilon = 0.03$, 11K annotations. Bottom: $\epsilon = 0.05$, 8K annotations.

Figure 2 shows the ground truth precision function p (black line) for this dataset of $N = 35615$ items, along

[5]http://www.seas.upenn.edu/~nlp/resources/ppdb-2.0-human-labels.tgz

with step functions corresponding to PAULA's upper (red) and lower (blue) bounds when $\epsilon = 0.03$ (top) and $\epsilon = 0.05$ (bottom), using $\Delta = 100$. The bounds are extremely tight in practice, even though they were obtained using only 11292 and 7822 annotations, resp.

The random baseline can provide a good estimate as well, but is generally less accurate in the earlier part of the curve and resulted in substantial random fluctuations, as also suggested by the error bounds in Figure 1 and the numerical examples discussed in Section 4.4.3.

Finally, we note that using the same setting for ϵ and Δ as in the upper plot would require only 40K annotations to generate a precision function curve for *entire* PPDB 2.0 containing $N = 169$M items.

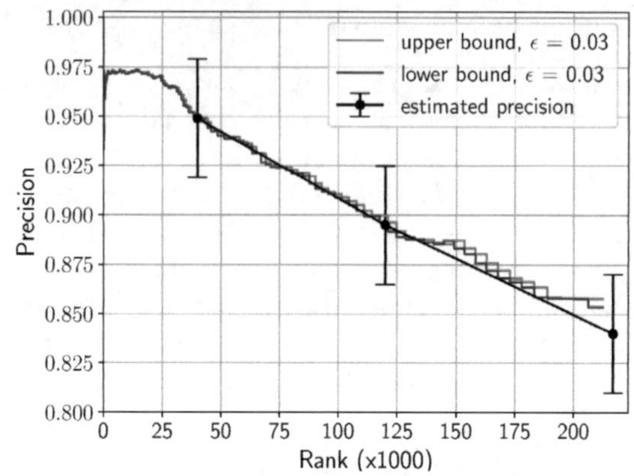

Figure 3: Bounds provided by PAULA with $\epsilon = 0.03, \Delta = 100$ using 17K annotations for Science KB.

5.3 APPLICATION: KNOWLEDGE BASES

As a second application, we consider evaluating the quality of knowledge bases (KBs) which store facts in a structured manner, e.g., in form of *(entity, relation, entity)* triples such as *(EiffelTower, locatedIn, Paris)* or *(butterfly, pollinate, flower)*. Knowledge acquisition is the task of extracting such knowledge from various unstructured resources, such as the Web, while knowledge completion is the task of inferring more facts given a partial KB. In both these tasks, machine learning is commonly employed to model the entities and relations, and score various combinations of them as candidate facts. The triples that score higher are considered more reliable.

In this second experiment, our goal is to demonstrate that PAULA can scale to large resources while still producing upper and lower bounds that are very close to each other and to point estimates obtained via random sampling.

To this end, we consider Science KB (Dalvi et al., 2017), a dataset with facts about elementary science, along with corresponding confidence scores.[6] The KB has $N = 217076$ triples, making it prohibitively expensive to assess its quality by analyzing all triples.

Figure 3 shows the precision function bounds produced by PAULA, using the same setup as earlier ($\epsilon = 0.03, \Delta = 100$), which led to 17392 annotations. Due to the lack of ground truth for this dataset, we compute three point estimates independently by drawing 2000 uniform samples for each and using Eqn. (3) to compute a confidence interval. We observe that the upper (red) and lower (blue) bounds are very close to each other for the entire dataset, and also near the independently obtained point estimates.

[6] Available at http://data.allenai.org/tuple-kb as Aristo Tuple KB v4 (March 2017).

6 CONCLUSION

This is the first work, to our knowledge, that provides a practical way of cost-effectively obtaining guaranteed approximations of the precision function, and associated metrics such as the PR curve, for massive datasets. This is particularly suitable for massive resources generated by today's large scale machine learning algorithms, when assessing individual data items for correctness requires human annotation. While these items are generally associated with a correctness score, and can thus be viewed as a ranked list, naïvely computing the PR curve of this list is prohibitively expensive due to the human annotation step. Consequently, these datasets often do not come with an associated precision-recall analysis, leaving their suitability for downstream applications unclear.

Our method, PAULA, addresses this limitation via tight approximations of the precision function with only logarithmically many annotations. PAULA leverages the fact that the precision function of reliable prediction systems is essentially monotonically non-increasing.[7] Our analysis reveals that sampling techniques require many more annotations (both asymptotically and for typical use cases) to guarantee the same level of approximation. Experiments on two large datasets demonstrate the accuracy of our method and its scalability.

Acknowledgments

The authors would like to thank Peter Clark, Oren Etzioni, Luke Zettlemoyer, and the anonymous reviewers for their valuable feedback, and Ellie Pavlick for sharing crowdsourced annotations for a subset of PPDB 2.0.

[7] For poorly designed prediction systems whose score does not correlate well with correctness, the monotonicity assumption is violated and PAULA's theoretical guarantees do not apply. PAULA can still be used to obtain a cost-effective estimate.

References

J. A. Aslam, V. Pavlu, and E. Yilmaz. A statistical method for system evaluation using incomplete judgments. In *SIGIR*, 2006.

B. Carterette, J. Allan, and R. K. Sitaraman. Minimal test collections for retrieval evaluation. In *SIGIR*, 2006.

B. Dalvi, N. Tandon, and P. Clark. Domain-targeted, high precision knowledge extraction. *TACL*, 2017.

J. Davis and M. Goadrich. The relationship between precision-recall and roc curves. In *ICML*, 2006.

S. Ermon, C. P. Gomes, A. Sabharwal, and B. Selman. Taming the curse of dimensionality: Discrete integration by hashing and optimization. In *Proc. of the 30th International Conference on Machine Learning (ICML)*, 2013.

T. Fawcett. An introduction to roc analysis. *Pattern recognition letters*, 27(8):861–874, 2006.

J. Ganitkevitch, B. V. Durme, and C. Callison-Burch. PPDB: The paraphrase database. In *HLT-NAACL*, 2013.

W. Hoeffding. Probability inequalities for sums of bounded random variables. *Journal of the American statistical association*, 58(301):13–30, 1963.

E. Kanoulas. A short survey on online and offline methods for search quality evaluation. In *RuSSIR*, 2015.

M. Majnik and Z. Bosnic. Roc analysis of classifiers in machine learning: A survey. *Intell. Data Anal.*, 17: 531–558, 2013.

T. M. Mitchell, W. W. Cohen, E. R. Hruschka, P. P. Talukdar, J. Betteridge, A. Carlson, B. D. Mishra, M. Gardner, B. Kisiel, J. Krishnamurthy, N. Lao, K. Mazaitis, T. Mohamed, N. Nakashole, E. A. Platanios, A. Ritter, M. Samadi, B. Settles, R. C. Wang, D. T. Wijaya, A. Gupta, X. Chen, A. Saparov, M. Greaves, and J. Welling. Never-ending learning. In *AAAI*, 2012.

E. Pavlick, P. Rastogi, J. Ganitkevitch, B. Van Durme, and C. Callison-Burch. PPDB 2.0: Better paraphrase ranking, fine-grained entailment relations, word embeddings, and style classification. In *ACL*, 2015.

T. Schnabel, A. Swaminathan, P. I. Frazier, and T. Joachims. Unbiased comparative evaluation of ranking functions. In *ICTIR*, 2016.

E. Yilmaz and J. A. Aslam. Estimating average precision with incomplete and imperfect judgments. In *CIKM*, 2006.

E. Yilmaz, E. Kanoulas, and J. A. Aslam. A simple and efficient sampling method for estimating ap and ndcg. In *SIGIR*, 2008.

A APPENDIX: PROOFS

Proof of Theorem 1. That $p'_{\epsilon,\ell}$ can be computed using the claimed number of evaluations of p follows immediately from Definition 5. Further, the approximation claim holds trivially for $r \leq g_\ell$ since p' and p are identical in this regime. In what follows, we argue that for any $r > g_\ell$, $p'_{\epsilon,\ell}(r)$, which is $p(g_j)$ for $j = \lfloor \log_{1+\epsilon} r \rfloor$, is a $(1+\epsilon)$-approximation of $p(r)$. By definition:

$$p(r) = \frac{p(g_j)\, g_j + \sum_{i=g_j+1}^{r} v(t_i)}{r}$$

Since each $v(t_i) \geq 0$, we have:

$$p(r) \geq \frac{p(g_j)\, g_j}{r} \geq \frac{p(g_j)}{1+\epsilon}$$

where the second inequality can be verified by plugging in the definition of g_j for j as defined above. Thus, $p(g_j)$ is no more than $1+\epsilon$ times $p(r)$.

For the other direction, we rely on the weak monotonicity assumption A.1. In particular, this implies $p(r) \leq p(g_j)$ whenever $r \geq g_j + m$, finishing the proof for such r. When $r < g_j + m$, however, $p(r)$ may be larger than $p(g_j)$. Nevertheless, we use $p(g_j + m) \leq p(g_j)$ and the definition of p to argue that $p(r)$ can be no more than $1+\epsilon$ times $p(g_j)$ when $r < g_j + m$. To this end, consider the sequence of true labels $v(t_i) \in \{0, 1\}$ for $i = g_j + 1, g_j + 2, \ldots, g_j + m$. Since $p(g_j + m) \leq p(g_j)$, it follows from the definition of q that at most a $p(g_j)$ fraction of these m labels is 1. Under these conditions, it can be verified that the largest possible value of $p(r)$ occurs at $r = r^* = g_j + \lfloor p(g_j)\, m \rfloor$ when all true labels $v(t_i)$ for $i = g_j + 1, \ldots, r^*$ are 1. In this case:

$$\begin{aligned}
\frac{p(r^*)}{p(g_j)} &= \frac{1}{p(g_j)} \frac{p(g_j)\, g_j + \lfloor p(g_j)\, m \rfloor}{g_j + \lfloor p(g_j)\, m \rfloor} \\
&\leq \frac{1}{p(g_j)} \frac{p(g_j)\, g_j + p(g_j)\, m}{g_j + p(g_j)\, m} = \frac{g_j + m}{g_j + p(g_j)\, m} \\
&\leq \frac{g_j + m}{g_j} = 1 + \frac{m}{g_j} \\
&\leq 1 + \frac{m}{g_\ell} = 1 + \frac{\lfloor \epsilon(1+\epsilon)^\ell - 1 \rfloor}{\lceil (1+\epsilon)^\ell \rceil} \\
&\leq 1 + \frac{\epsilon(1+\epsilon)^\ell - 1}{(1+\epsilon)^\ell} \\
&\leq 1 + \epsilon
\end{aligned}$$

Thus, we have that for all $r < g_j + m$, $p(r)$ is at most $p(r^*)$ which is no more than $1+\epsilon$ times $p(g_j)$. This finishes the proof. ■

Proof of Lemma 1. At each point g_k, we have s samples in the set X_k. Applying Eqn. (2), it follows that $q(g_k) = S_k/s$, which is the average of the true labels of the s samples in X_k, provides a β-approximation for $p(g_k)$. ■

Proof of Theorem 2. By construction, $q(r) = p(r)$ in Algorithm 1 when $r \in \{1, \ldots, \ell\}$. From Lemma 1, we further have $q(r)$ is a β-approximation of $p(r)$ for $r \in \{g_{\ell+1}, \ldots, g_L$. It now follows from Corollary 1 that $step^q_{\epsilon,\ell}$ is a $\beta(1+\epsilon)$-approximation of p.

For the number of annotated samples used in the whole process, we have ℓ evaluations of v at points $1, \ldots, g_\ell$ for computing $q(1), \ldots, q(g_\ell)$, which subsumes the s samples needed for X_ℓ. For each of $X_{\ell+1}, \ldots, X_L$ in subsequent steps, on average $\frac{\epsilon}{1+\epsilon} s$ new samples are drawn. This yields evaluations of v at a total of g_ℓ initial points and at $(L-\ell)\frac{\epsilon}{1+\epsilon} s = \frac{\epsilon(L-\ell)}{2(\beta-1)^2(1+\epsilon)p_{\min}^2} \ln \frac{L-\ell}{\delta/2}$ points chosen via stratified sampling. ■

Proof of Lemma 3. By the definition of $p(g_k)$, we have:

$$\begin{aligned}
g_k\, p(g_k) &= \sum_{i=1}^{g_k} v(t_i) \\
&= \sum_{i=1}^{g_\ell} v(t_i) + \sum_{j=\ell}^{k-1} \sum_{i=g_j+1}^{g_{j+1}} v(t_i) \\
&= g_\ell\, p(g_\ell) + \sum_{j=\ell}^{k-1} \sum_{i=g_j+1}^{g_{j+1}} v(t_i)
\end{aligned}$$

As observed earlier, $g_{j+1} - g_j \geq (1+\epsilon)^{j+1} - (1+\epsilon)^j - 1 = \epsilon(1+\epsilon)^j - 1$. When $j \geq \ell$, this implies $g_{j+1} - g_j \geq \epsilon(1+\epsilon)^\ell - 1 \geq m$. From the strong monotonicity assumption A.2, the inner summation may be bounded as:

$$p_\Delta(g_{j+1}) \;\leq\; \frac{\sum_{i=g_j+1}^{g_{j+1}} v(t_i)}{g_{j+1} - g_j} \;\leq\; p_\Delta(g_j)$$

Plugging these bounds back into the summation over j, we obtain:

$$\begin{aligned}
g_k\, p(g_k) &\geq g_\ell\, p(g_\ell) + \sum_{j=\ell}^{k-1} (g_{j+1} - g_j)\, p_\Delta(g_{j+1}) \\
&= Y_-(\epsilon, \ell, k, \Delta) \\
g_k\, p(g_k) &\leq g_\ell\, p(g_\ell) + \sum_{j=\ell}^{k-1} (g_{j+1} - g_j)\, p_\Delta(g_j) \\
&= Y_+(\epsilon, \ell, k, \Delta)
\end{aligned}$$

This finishes the proof. ■

Proof of Lemma 4. Using the same argument as in the proof of Lemma 3, for any $j \geq \ell$, we have $g_{j+1} - g_j \geq$

m. Further, by the strong monotonicity assumption A.2, we have $p_\Delta(g_{j+1}) \leq p_\Delta(g_j)$. However, in general, $p_\Delta(g_{j+1})$ may be arbitrarily smaller than $p_\Delta(g_j)$, making it difficult to lower bound the ratio of L and U using the ratio of these local precision terms.

Similar to Ermon et al. (2013), we instead collect all "coefficients" of $p_\Delta(g_j)$ for each $j \in \{\ell, \ell+1, \ldots, k\}$ in the expressions for L and U, resp., and bound each pair of corresponding coefficients. The computations here are more intricate than in prior work because of the non-integrality of ϵ; the previous derivation was for the special case where ϵ is effectively 1.

Using the assumption $p(g_\ell) \geq p_\Delta(g_\ell)$, it can be verified that for the claim it suffices to show two properties:

$$\gamma\, g_\ell \geq g_{\ell+1} \tag{7}$$

$$\gamma\, (g_{j+1} - g_j) \geq g_{j+2} - g_{j+1} \tag{8}$$

for all $j \in \{\ell+1, \ldots, k-1\}$. For the first property:

$$\begin{aligned}
\frac{g_{\ell+1}}{g_\ell} &= \frac{\lceil (1+\epsilon)^{\ell+1} \rceil}{\lceil (1+\epsilon)^{\ell} \rceil} \\
&\leq \frac{(1+\epsilon)^{\ell+1} + 1}{(1+\epsilon)^{\ell} - 1} \\
&= 1 + \epsilon + \frac{2+\epsilon}{(1+\epsilon)^{\ell} - 1} \\
&\leq 1 + \epsilon + \frac{2+\epsilon}{\epsilon(1+\epsilon)^{\ell} - 1} \\
&\leq 1 + \epsilon + \frac{2+\epsilon}{m} = \gamma
\end{aligned}$$

where the second inequality follows from the precondition $\epsilon \in (0, 1]$. For the second property:

$$\begin{aligned}
\frac{g_{j+2} - g_{j+1}}{g_{j+1} - g_j} &= \frac{\lceil (1+\epsilon)^{j+2} \rceil - \lceil (1+\epsilon)^{j+1} \rceil}{\lceil (1+\epsilon)^{j+1} \rceil - \lceil (1+\epsilon)^{j} \rceil} \\
&\leq \frac{(1+\epsilon)^{j+2} - (1+\epsilon)^{j+1} + 1}{(1+\epsilon)^{j+1} - (1+\epsilon)^{j} - 1} \\
&\leq \frac{(1+\epsilon)^{\ell+2} - (1+\epsilon)^{\ell+1} + 1}{(1+\epsilon)^{\ell+1} - (1+\epsilon)^{\ell} - 1} \\
&= 1 + \epsilon + \frac{2+\epsilon}{\epsilon(1+\epsilon)^{\ell} - 1} \\
&\leq 1 + \epsilon + \frac{2+\epsilon}{m} = \gamma
\end{aligned}$$

The second inequality follows from the observation that the ratio under consideration here is a decreasing function of j. This finishes the proof. ■

Proof of Theorem 3. By construction, $q^-(r) = q^+(r) = p(r)$ in Algorithm 2 when $r \in \{1, \ldots, \ell\}$. From Lemma 2, we further have $q^+(r)$ and $q^-(r)$ are γ-approximations of $p(r)$ from below and above, resp., for $r \in \{g_{\ell+1}, \ldots, g_L$. It now follows from Corollary 1 that $step^{q^-}_{\epsilon,\ell}$ and $step^{q^+}_{\epsilon,\ell}$ are $\gamma(1+\epsilon)$-approximations of p from below and above, resp.

That PAULA uses a total of $g_\ell + \Delta(L-\ell)$ evaluations of v follows from the observation that it computes p exactly at points $1, \ldots, g_\ell$, which in total require g_ℓ evaluations, and p_Δ at $L-\ell$ additional points, each of which requires Δ evaluations. ■

On Loopy Belief Propagation – Local Stability Analysis for Non-Vanishing Fields

Christian Knoll
Graz University of Technology
christian.knoll.c@ieee.org

Franz Pernkopf
Graz University of Technology
pernkopf@tugraz.at

Abstract

In this work we obtain all fixed points of belief propagation and perform a local stability analysis. We consider pairwise interactions of binary random variables and investigate the influence of non-vanishing fields and finite-size graphs on the performance of belief propagation; local stability is heavily influenced by these properties. We show why non-vanishing fields help to achieve convergence and increase the accuracy of belief propagation. We further explain the close connections between the underlying graph structure, the existence of multiple solutions, and the capability of belief propagation (with damping) to converge. Finally we provide insights into why finite-size graphs behave better than infinite-size graphs.

1 INTRODUCTION

Belief propagation (BP) is a method that exploits the structure of probabilistic graphical models and performs local operations to approximate the marginal distribution. BP has a long success story with applications including computer vision, speech processing, and medical diagnosis systems (Koller and Friedman, 2009; Pernkopf et al., 2014; Jordan, 2004)

BP may not converge on graphs with loops – only for restricted classes of graphs sufficient conditions are known that guarantee convergence and uniqueness of the solution (Ihler et al., 2005; Heskes, 2004; Weiss, 2000). If BP does not converge or has a bad approximation quality we may be confronted with: (i) multiple solutions where the performance depends on the initialization, or (ii) potentially good approximate solutions that are unstable.

To overcome some of these issues a lot of effort was put into finding provably convergent algorithms. Inspired by the connection between BP and the Bethe free energy (Yedidia et al., 2005) it is natural to minimize the Bethe free energy directly (Welling and Teh, 2001), or find convex surrogates to minimize (Meshi et al., 2009). Alternatively, if multiple fixed points exist, one can try to obtain one stationary point of the Bethe free energy directly (Yuille and Rangarajan, 2003), or get at least some approximation of the stationary points (Shin, 2012). For graphs where fixed points close to the exact solution exist, but BP fails to converge, (Weller and Jebara, 2014) provide a method to obtain an approximation of the best possible fixed point.

All these methods do still raise particular questions, like: under which conditions can we expect BP to perform well?– or, given that multiple fixed points exist, which of these fixed points are stable and how does stability relate to accuracy?

We consider BP as a discrete-time map, and – drawing from the theory of dynamical systems – analyze the local stability of all fixed points. This is inspired by the thorough analysis for Ising models with vanishing local fields (Mooij and Kappen, 2005); for non-vanishing fields, however, local stability analysis was left open. The main difficulty of local stability analysis of Ising models with arbitrary parameters on finite-size graphs is the need for *all* fixed points. To find multiple fixed points one could resort to survey propagation (Braunstein et al., 2005) or its efficient approximation scheme (Srinivasa et al., 2016), but these methods fail to obtain unstable fixed points. Unfortunately, unstable fixed points cannot be obtained in general, which, in general, makes local stability analysis much more intricate.

In this work, we resort to the numerical polynomial-homotopy-continuation (NPHC) method (Knoll et al., 2016), where the update equations of BP are reformulated as a nonlinear system of equations. The NPHC method solves this system of equations and obtains all fixed points of BP – even for Ising graphs with arbitrary parameters. Consequently, we extend the work of (Mooij and Kappen, 2005) and find answers to the following questions: (i) Why does the presence of non-vanishing fields enhance the convergence properties? (ii) Which influence do non-vanishing fields have on the approximation accuracy? (iii) Under which circumstances does damping help to enforce convergence of BP? (iv) How does the number of fixed points and their stability depend on the number of variables for finite-size graphs?

The paper is structured as follows: Section 2 provides a brief background on probabilistic graphical models, belief propagation, and its connection to statistical physics. In Section 3 we present tools from dynamical systems to perform the stability analysis. We discuss empirical observations and extend the stability analysis to graphs with non-vanishing local fields in Section 4 and provide a more formal analysis in Section 5. Finally, we conclude the paper in Section 6.

2 BACKGROUND

Let us consider an undirected graph $G = (\mathbf{X}, \mathbf{E})$ defined by a set of nodes $\mathbf{X} = \{X_1, \ldots, X_N\}$ and a set of undirected edges $\mathbf{E}$. Two nodes X_i and X_j are joined by an edge if $e_{ij} \in \mathbf{E}$. Let the set of neighbors of X_i be defined by $\partial(X_i) = \{X_j \in \mathbf{X} : e_{ij} \in \mathbf{E}\}$ and denote the degree of X_i by $d_i = |\partial(X_i)|$. Consider the adjacency matrix $\boldsymbol{A}$ with rows and columns indexed by the set of nodes; $\boldsymbol{A}$ is a symmetric 0-1-matrix with $a_{ij} = 1$ if and only if $e_{ij} \in \mathbf{E}$. We further define the average degree of G as $\langle d \rangle_G = \frac{|\mathbf{E}|}{N}$. A graph is called bipartite if the set of nodes can be decomposed into two disjoint subsets $\mathbf{Y}$ and $\mathbf{Z}$ so that $\mathbf{X} = \mathbf{Y} \cup \mathbf{Z}$ and where the neighbors $\partial(Y_i) \in \mathbf{Z}$ for all $Y_i \in \mathbf{Y}$ and vice versa. It follows immediately that bipartite graphs are 2-colorable.

Consider a finite set of N binary random variables $\mathbf{X} = \{X_1, \ldots, X_N\}$ with X_i taking values in the finite set $\mathbb{S}_i$. We assume a one-to-one correspondence between the variables and the nodes. The joint probability factorizes as a product of potentials, i.e., $P(\mathbf{X} = \mathbf{x}) = \frac{1}{Z} \prod_{l=1}^{L} \Phi_{C_l}(C_l)$, where the potentials $\Phi_{C_l}(C_l)$ are specified over the maximal cliques C_l of G (Pearl, 1988, p.105). If we restrict all potentials to consist of two variables at most: then, the joint distribution is factorized according to the product

$$P(\mathbf{X} = \mathbf{x}) = \frac{1}{Z} \prod_{(X_i, X_j) : e_{ij} \in \mathbf{E}} \Phi_{X_i, X_j}(x_i, x_j) \prod_{i=1}^{N} \Phi_{X_i}(x_i), \quad (1)$$

where $Z \in \mathbb{R}$ guarantees proper normalization. We refer to $\Phi_{X_i,X_j}(x_i, x_j)$ and $\Phi_{X_i}(x_i)$ as pairwise and local potentials. The marginal probabilities are obtained by summing over all variables except X_i, i.e., $P(X_i = x_i) = \sum_{\sim X_i} P(\mathbf{X})$.

2.1 BELIEF PROPAGATION (BP)

BP[1] approximates the marginals by recursively updating local messages between random variables. The message $\mu_{ij}^{n+1}(x_j)$ from X_i to X_j is given by the recursive update rule

$$\mu_{ij}^{n+1}(x_j) = \alpha_{ij}^{n} \sum_{x_i \in \mathbb{S}_i} \Phi_{X_i, X_j}(x_i, x_j) \Phi_{X_i}(x_i) \prod_{X_k \in \partial(X_{i \setminus j})} \mu_{ki}^{n}(x_i), \quad (2)$$

where n denotes the iteration, and the shorthand notation $\partial(X_{i \setminus j}) = \{\partial(X_i) \setminus X_j\}$ is used. To compute the message, BP collects all messages sent to X_i, except for X_j and multiplies this product with the local potential and the pairwise potential. The sum over all states of X_i is sent to X_j. The messages are often normalized by α_{ij}^{n} so that $\sum_{x_j \in \mathbb{S}_i} \mu_{ij}^{n+1}(x_j) = 1$. If BP is converged the approximate marginals are obtained by

$$\hat{P}(X_i = x_i) = \Phi_{X_i}(x_i) \prod_{X_k \in \partial(X_i)} \mu_{ki}(X_i = x_i). \quad (3)$$

BP is guaranteed to converge and the messages correspond to the correct marginals on tree-structured graphs

2.2 ISING MODELS

We focus on one specific model: the Ising model, in which every variable X_i has an associated spin taking values from $\mathbb{S} = \{+1, -1\}$. Let us define couplings $J_{ij} \in \mathbb{R}$ assigned to each edge $e_{ij} \in \mathbf{E}$ and a local field $\theta_i \in \mathbb{R}$ acting on each variable $X_i \in \mathbf{X}$. Let the Ising potentials be defined as $\Phi_{X_i}(x_i) = \exp(\theta_i x_i)$ and as $\Phi_{X_i,X_j}(x_i, x_j) = \exp(J_{ij} x_i x_j)$. The Boltzmann distribution

$$P(\mathbf{X} = \mathbf{x}) = \frac{1}{Z} \exp\left(\beta \sum J_{ij} x_i x_j + \beta \sum \theta_i x_i\right) \quad (4)$$

gives the probability of a certain configuration $\mathbf{x}$. Instead of changing the inverse temperature $\beta > 0$ we assume that $\beta = 1$ for the remainder of this work and alter the configuration by changing J_{ij} and θ_i. Whenever J_{ij} and θ_i are constant over all edges and variables we drop the subscripts, and – because of its physical interpretation – refer to θ as external field.

Let us distinguish three different interactions on Ising models. First, in the ferromagnetic case all interactions

[1] If BP is applied on graphs with loops it is sometimes named loopy belief propagation; independent of the graph we just stick to the term belief propagation.

J_{ij} are positive; secondly, for antiferromagnetic interactions all J_{ij} are negative. Finally, spin-glass interactions contain both: positive and negative J_{ij}. An Ising model is frustrated whenever local constraints exist that cannot be satisfied simultaneously, i.e., a cycle exists, along which the product of all J_{ij} is negative (Mezard and Montanari, 2009).

BP has a close connection to some concepts from statistical mechanics; in particular the correspondence between fixed points of BP and stationary points of the Bethe free energy motivated a large body of research. An excellent treatment of these connection can be found in (Yedidia et al., 2005; Mezard and Montanari, 2009).

Note that in statistical physics the behavior of graphs is analyzed in the thermodynamical limit (i.e. for $N \to \infty$ many variables) and over ensembles of graphs. In this work, however, we consider finite-size graphs with distinct potentials. Note that we use the term phase transition for the finite-size manifestation of the phase transition in the thermodynamical limit. These two notions are similar but do not coincidence in general (cf. Theorem 3).

2.3 BP FOR BINARY VARIABLES

For binary variables we parametrize the normalized messages as a single message (cf. Mooij and Kappen (2005)) defined by

$$\nu_{ij}^n = \text{atanh}(\mu_{ij}^n(X_j = 1) - \mu_{ij}^n(X_j = -1)). \quad (5)$$

This transformation reduces the number of variables and eases some calculations but does not change the properties of BP. The update rule in (2) can be rewritten for Ising models to:

$$\tanh(\nu_{ij}^{n+1}) = \tanh(J_{ij}) \tanh(h_{ij}), \quad (6)$$

where we define the effective field h_{ij} that acts on X_i while neglecting the incoming message from X_j

$$h_{ij} = \theta_i + \sum_{X_k \in \partial(X_{i \setminus j})} \nu_{ki}. \quad (7)$$

BP corresponds to the cavity method (Mezard et al., 1987) that computes the effect of removing one node and the according edges. This connection becomes obvious by looking at (7) (cf. (Opper and Winther, 2001)).

We can further parametrize the marginals $P(X_i = x_i)$ in (3) by the expected value: $m_i = P(X_i = 1) - P(X_i = -1)$. The mean magnetization of the system $\langle m \rangle = \frac{1}{N} \sum_{i=1}^N m_i$ is often considered to describe the response of the system to an external field (Mezard and Montanari, 2009). Note that the difference between the mean magnetization of an approximate solution $\langle \hat{m} \rangle$ and the exact solution $\langle m \rangle$ is the same as the error averaged over all marginals, i.e., $|\langle m \rangle - \langle \hat{m} \rangle| = \frac{2}{N} |\sum_{i=1}^N P(x_i) - \hat{P}(x_i)|$.

2.4 FIXED POINTS OF BP

At least one fixed point always exists for BP (Yedidia et al., 2000); if the graph has loops, however, multiple fixed points may exist. It further depends on the potentials whether BP converges or not. We obtain all fixed points with the NPHC method and analyze convergence properties.

Let $\underline{\nu}$ be the set of all messages; then BP acts as a map on the messages in discrete time such that $\underline{\nu}^{n+1} = \mathcal{BP}(\underline{\nu}^n)$. If successive messages remain unchanged under this map, then BP did converge to some fixed point

$$\underline{\nu}^* = \mathcal{BP}(\underline{\nu}^*). \quad (8)$$

If, however, the messages oscillate, one can either try to achieve convergence by changing the update rule (Elidan et al., 2006; Sutton and McCallum, 2007; Knoll et al., 2015), or by replacing the messages with a weighted average of the last messages (Murphy et al., 1999). We denote the update map of BP with damping as

$$\mathcal{BP}_D(\underline{\nu}^n) = (1 - \epsilon)\mathcal{BP}(\underline{\nu}^n) + \epsilon\underline{\nu}^n, \quad (9)$$

where $\epsilon \in [0, 1)$. Note that fixed points of $\mathcal{BP}_D(\underline{\nu}^*)$ – if BP with damping did converge – must be fixed points of BP without damping as well, because (8) holds in the equilibrium and $\mathcal{BP}_D(\underline{\nu}^*) = (1 - \epsilon)\mathcal{BP}(\underline{\nu}^*) + \epsilon\underline{\nu}^* = \mathcal{BP}(\underline{\nu}^*)$. Although the fixed points remain unchanged under any form of damping, the local stability of these fixed points may change (cf. Section 4).

3 STABILITY OF FIXED POINTS

We start by considering BP as a discrete-time map and proceed according to the usual procedure in dynamical systems. For an in-depth treatment of dynamical systems we refer the reader to (Teschl, 2003; Scheinerman, 2000).

A fixed point $\underline{\nu}^*$ is locally stable if a neighborhood $U(\underline{\nu}^*)$ exists such that messages inside this neighborhood converge to $\underline{\nu}^*$ under the considered map (Teschl, 2003, pp.170). Local stability of BP cannot be analyzed by looking at the Bethe free energy as: stable fixed points must be local minima, but local minima must not be stable (Heskes et al., 2003).

In general stability can be investigated by the method of Ljapunov (Scheinerman, 2000, pp.93), though it is sufficient for all graphs considered in this work to restrict our analysis to linearization; we therefore obtain *all* fixed points by solving $\mathcal{BP}(\underline{\nu}^*) = \underline{\nu}^*$ and subsequently analyze the Jacobian matrix.

3.1 FINDING FIXED POINTS

As a first step, irrespective of the stability, we have to obtain all fixed points of the map. The trivial solution $\nu_{ij}^* = 0$ for all $e_{ij} \in \mathbf{E}$ is known in the special case of vanishing external field (Mooij and Kappen, 2005). The extension to non-vanishing local fields is not straightforward, because in general the unstable fixed point is not known. There are indeed several methods that aim to capture and combine multiple fixed points of BP (e.g., (Srinivasa et al., 2016)), but none of which does also account for unstable fixed points.

In order to find all fixed point solutions we reformulate the update rule of BP (2) as a system of polynomial equations. To solve this nonlinear system of equations we resort to the NPHC method that overcomes all problems of both iterative (e.g., Newton's method) and symbolic methods (e.g., Gröbner basis). The NPHC method solves a similar, but trivial system of equations and further refines these solutions until all (complex) solutions to the system of interest are obtained. A detailed treatment is beyond the scope of this paper but we refer the interested reader to (Sommese and Wampler, 2005; Chen and Li, 2015) and the references therein. Recently the NPHC method was applied to analyze energy landscapes in general (Mehta et al., 2015; Ballard et al., 2017) and to find *all* solutions of BP (Knoll et al., 2016).

3.2 LINEARIZATION

After obtaining all fixed points the obvious question remains, whether these fixed points are stable or unstable. Therefore, we approximate $\mathcal{BP}(\cdot)$ by a linear function in every fixed point and analyze the behavior of the linearized system. This is done by taking the partial derivatives of all messages, i.e., by analyzing the Jacobian matrix $\boldsymbol{F}'(\underline{\nu}^*)$ with the elements defined as

$$\boldsymbol{F}'(\underline{\nu}^*)_{mn} = \frac{\partial \nu_{ij}^*}{\partial \nu_{kl}^*}, \tag{10}$$

where – given some ordering – ν_{ij}^* and ν_{kl}^* are the mth and the nth message, respectively.

For Ising models parametrized as in Section 2.3 the Jacobian is given as follows: without loss of generality[2] we consider only messages where $e_{ij} \in \mathbf{E}$ and $e_{kl} \in \mathbf{E}$ such that

$$\boldsymbol{F}'(\underline{\nu}^*)_{mn} = \begin{cases} \frac{\tanh(J_{ij})\left(1-\tanh^2(h_{ij})\right)}{1-\tanh^2(J_{ij})\tanh^2(h_{ij})} & \text{if } i=l \text{ and } k\in\partial(X_{i\setminus j}) \\ 0 & \text{else.} \end{cases} \tag{11}$$

Let the spectrum of the Jacobian matrix be the set of all eigenvalues $\Gamma\left(\boldsymbol{F}'(\underline{\nu}^*)\right) = \{\lambda_1, \cdots, \lambda_n\}$ with spectral radius $\rho\left(\boldsymbol{F}'(\underline{\nu}^*)\right) = \max\{|\lambda_1|, \cdots, |\lambda_n|\}$.

A fixed point $\underline{\nu}^*$ is locally stable if all eigenvalues have absolute value strictly smaller than one

$$\rho\left(\boldsymbol{F}'(\underline{\nu}^*)\right) < 1, \tag{12}$$

i.e., all eigenvalues lie inside the unit circle; BP converges to locally stable fixed points if initialized sufficiently close enough. A fixed point is unstable with respect to BP if at least one eigenvalue exists outside the unit circle such that $\rho\left(\boldsymbol{F}'(\underline{\nu}^*)\right) > 1$. For $\rho\left(\boldsymbol{F}'(\underline{\nu}^*)\right) = 1$ stability of the nonlinear system cannot be inferred by just looking at the linear system (Teschl, 2003, Hartman Grobman Theorem).

If we use damping as in (9) the eigenvalue spectrum of $\mathcal{BP}_D(\cdot)$ becomes

$$\Gamma\left(\boldsymbol{F}'_D(\underline{\nu}^*)\right) = \Gamma\left(\boldsymbol{F}'(\underline{\nu}^*)\right) \cdot (1-\epsilon) + \epsilon. \tag{13}$$

It follows, that all eigenvalues are reduced by a factor $(1-\epsilon)$ and experience a shift by ϵ along the real axis, i.e., $\Re\left(\Gamma\left(\boldsymbol{F}'_D(\underline{\nu}^*)\right)\right) = \epsilon + \Re\left((1-\epsilon)\Gamma\left(\boldsymbol{F}'(\underline{\nu}^*)\right)\right)$. A fixed point $\underline{\nu}^*$ is locally stable under $\mathcal{BP}_D(\cdot)$ if

$$\Re\left(\Gamma\left(\boldsymbol{F}'(\underline{\nu}^*)\right)\right) < 1. \tag{14}$$

4 EMPIRICAL STABILITY ANALYSIS OF BP ON ISING MODELS

In this section we present specific instances of the Ising model, compute all fixed points, and analyze the local stability. Then, we compare the results to known results of both: infinite graphs, and finite-size graphs with vanishing local fields. We restrict our analysis to ferromagnetic and antiferromagnetic interactions (cf. Section 2.2), because this allows to change the behavior of BP with just a single parameter.

We briefly present the results of (Mooij and Kappen, 2005) for vanishing fields in Section 4.2. Then we extend the analysis to graphs with non-vanishing fields, discuss some empirical observations, and interpret the implications. We further obtain the exact solution by the junction tree algorithm (Lauritzen and Spiegelhalter, 1988) shown as red line in Figure 2. Fixed points of BP are depicted in blue (stable under $\mathcal{BP}(\cdot)$), black (stable under $\mathcal{BP}_D(\cdot)$), and green (unstable). A more formal analysis is presented in Section 5.

[2] If all possible edges are considered, all rows and columns that correspond to a message ν_{vw}, where $e_{vw} \notin \mathbf{E}$ include only zero-values and do not change the eigenvalues.

4.1 GRAPHS

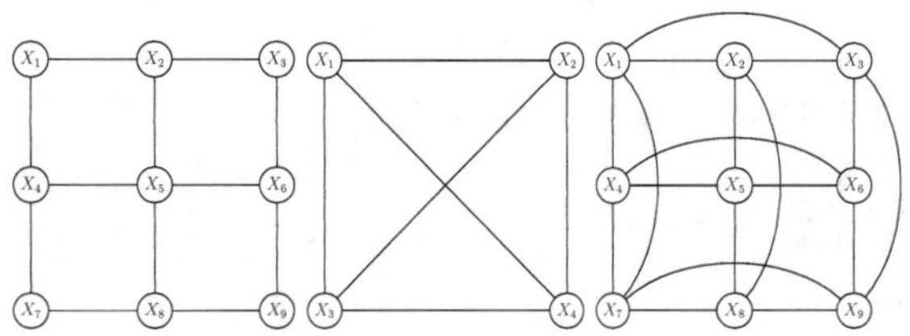

Figure 1: Considered Ising graphs: (a) grid-graph with 9 RVs; (b) complete graph; (c) grid-graph with periodic boundary conditions.

We consider different realizations of the Ising model on complete graphs, grid-graphs, and grid-graphs with periodic boundary conditions (Figure 1).

For the complete graph each pair of nodes is connected by an edge; it follows by definition that it is a regular graph, i.e., all variables have equal degree $d_i = N-1$ for all X_i. Note that we can associate an infinite, connected cycle-free, graph – a Bethe lattice – to the complete graph, which has the same fixed point solutions (Taga and Mase, 2004). The grid-graph has all edges aligned along the two-dimensional square lattice. Finite-size realizations contain variables with varying degree. Further we consider grid-graphs with periodic boundary conditions, where nodes on the boundary are joined by edges so that all variables have equal degree.

4.2 VANISHING LOCAL FIELD

It is assumed that the case of vanishing local fields is the worst case scenario; we will confirm this assumption empirically and analytically. For $\theta = 0$ a trivial solution exists – namely a distribution that is uniform over all states, i.e., for all $X_i \in \mathbf{X}$ the magnetization is $m_i = 0$.

For purely ferromagnetic interactions $J_{ij} > 0$, BP converges to the trivial (paramagnetic) fixed point, which is unique and stable. As coupling-strength increases, the largest eigenvalue λ_{max} increases as well (see Theorem 3) and as λ_{max} crosses the unit circle the paramagnetic fixed point remains unchanged but becomes unstable. At the same time two additional fixed points, however, do appear – these symmetry-broken fixed points are both stable (Figure 2a and 2b).

For purely antiferromagnetic interactions $J_{ij} < 0$ all entries of the Jacobian swap in sign $\boldsymbol{F}'_{-}(\underline{\nu}^*) = -\boldsymbol{F}'_{+}(\underline{\nu}^*)$, where $-$ and $+$ indicate the antiferromagnetic and the ferromagnetic case, respectively. It follows that $\Gamma\left(\boldsymbol{F}'_{-}(\underline{\nu}^*)\right) = -\Gamma\left(\boldsymbol{F}'_{+}(\underline{\nu}^*)\right)$. Consequently the local stability of the fixed point is invariant under a sign-change of J and instability occurs precisely for the same coupling strength as before (Figure 2a and 2b). There is one important difference though – the dominant eigenvalue is negative now, such that damping helps to achieve convergence.

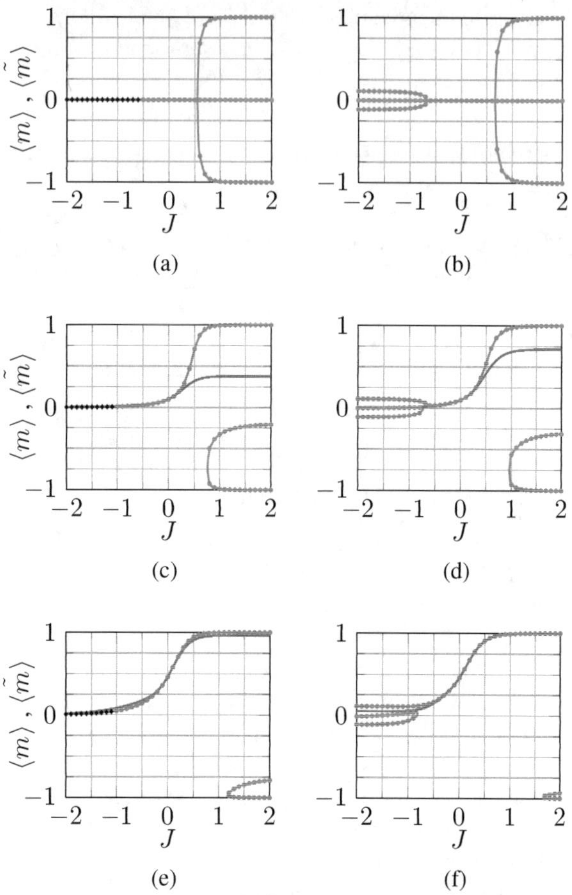

Figure 2: Mean magnetization for couplings $J \in [-2, 2]$ (exact in red, and approximate in blue ($\rho\left(\boldsymbol{F}'(\underline{\nu}^*)\right) < 1$), black ($\rho\left(\boldsymbol{F}'_D(\underline{\nu}^*)\right) < 1$), and green ($\rho\left(\boldsymbol{F}'_D(\underline{\nu}^*)\right) > 1$)); left column shows results for the complete graph with $N = 4$; right column shows results for the grid-graph with $N = 9$. (a) and (b): $\theta = 0$; (c) and (d): $\theta = 0.1$; (e) and (f): $\theta = 0.5$. Increasing θ enhances convergence properties and accuracy of BP.

4.3 NON-VANISHING LOCAL FIELD

For reasons of simplicity we restrict our analysis to graphs where $\theta_i = \theta \neq 0$ for all variables X_i. Because the Ising model is symmetric with respect to the local fields it is sufficient to consider only non-negative local fields. Moreover, the same qualitative results hold if we allow for $\theta_i \geq 0$ in general.

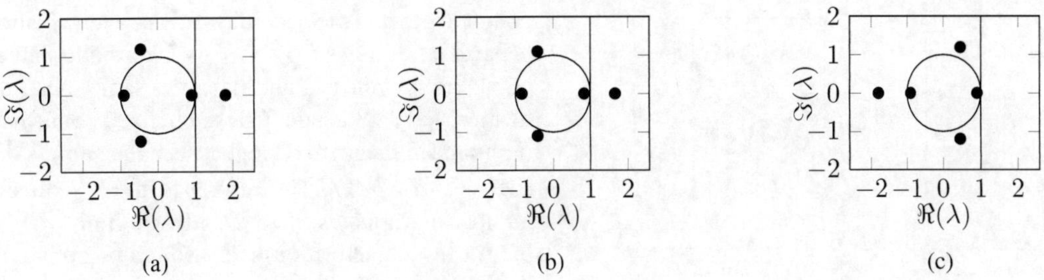

Figure 3: Eigenvalue spectra of the unstable fixed point of the complete graph with $N = 4$. If all eigenvalues are inside the unit-circle BP converges without damping. If no eigenvalues lie on the right-hand side of the vertical line BP converges with damping. (a) $J = 1.5$ and $\theta = 0$: notice that $\Re(\lambda_{max}) > 1$, i.e., damping does not help; (b) $J = 1.5$ and $\theta = 0.5$: notice how the external field reduces the magnitude of the eigenvalues (cf. Theorem 2); (c) $J = -1.5$ and $\theta = 0.5$: the fixed point is unstable but can be stabilized with an damping because $\Re(\lambda_i) < 1$.

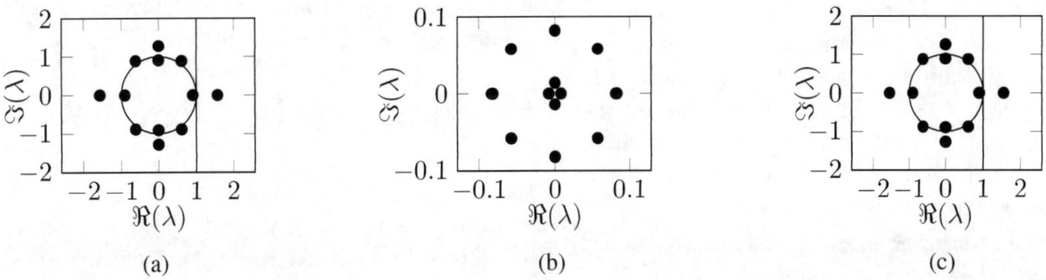

Figure 4: Eigenvalue spectra of the grid-graph with $N = 9$; all eigenvalues are symmetric because the graph is bipartite (cf. Theorem 4). (a) $J = 1.5$, and $\theta = 0$: the shown fixed point is unstable and damping does not help; (b) $J = 1.5$ and $\theta = 0.5$: only a unique stable fixed point exists (cf. Figure 2f); note the qualitative difference in the spectrum; (c) $J = -1.5$ and $\theta = 0.5$: because of the symmetric spectrum, damping does not help in the antiferromagnetic case.

4.3.1 FERROMAGNETIC INTERACTIONS

For small values of $J > 0$ a unique fixed point exists to which BP converges and for which all eigenvalues lie inside the unit circle. If we gradually increase the coupling-strength to the point where instability occurs for vanishing external field, we observe that the spectral radius $\rho\left(\boldsymbol{F}'(\underline{\nu}^*)\right) < 1$ and the fixed point is stable (cf. Theorem 2 for more details). If we further increase θ, the spectral radius decreases and a unique stable fixed point exists for even larger values of J (compare Figure 2c and 2d with Figure 2e and 2f).

Now, if we increase J – although the fixed point remains stable – two additional solutions emerge beyond some critical point J_{C+} (Figure 2c and 2d). As opposed to vanishing local fields, the unique fixed point is continuously deformed and remains stable though. The second stable fixed point corresponds to some self-preserving state of magnetization[3] and is accompanied by another unstable fixed point (Figure 3b).

[3]Self-preserving states are stable fixed points where $\langle \tilde{m} \rangle$ points in the opposite direction as the external field.

The graph structure is supposed to influence the spectral radius as well. This becomes obvious if we enlarge the size of a graph while keeping its local structure unchanged, e.g., by increasing the grid-graph from $N_1 = 9$ to $N_2 = 16$. A comparison of Figure 4 with Figure 5b reveals an increased spectral radius, i.e., $\rho\left(\boldsymbol{F}'_{N_1}(\underline{\nu}^*)\right) < \rho\left(\boldsymbol{F}'_{N_2}(\underline{\nu}^*)\right)$ (cf. Theorem 3). It is interesting that the largest eigenvalue – and its symmetric counterpart for bipartite graphs – are the only eigenvalues that experience a relevant increase in their real part. The real part of all other eigenvalues $\tilde{\lambda}_i \in \Gamma\left(\boldsymbol{F}'(\underline{\nu}^*)\right) \setminus \{\lambda_\rho : |\Re(\lambda_\rho)| = \rho\left(\boldsymbol{F}'(\underline{\nu}^*)\right)\}$ is bounded by $|\Re(\tilde{\lambda}_i)| < 1$.

In terms of accuracy BP performs better for non-vanishing fields; compared to vanishing fields a stable fixed point exists that lies closer to the exact solution. Loosely speaking increased local fields effectively reduce the influence of the couplings. This does not only lead to better convergence properties of BP (cf. Corollary 3.1), but reduces the approximation-error as well.

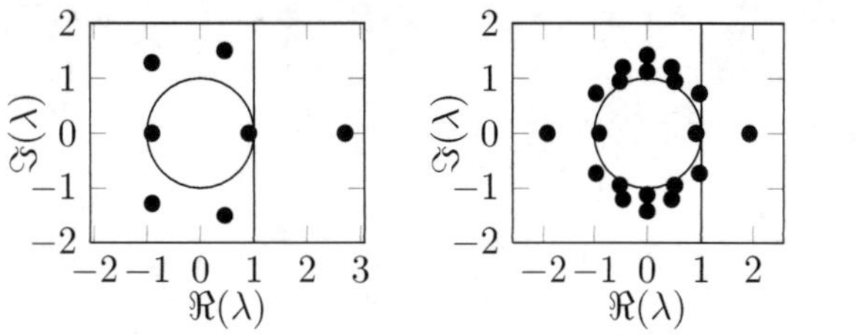

(a) (b)

Figure 5: Eigenvalue spectra for $J = 1.5$ and $\theta = 0.5$ of the (a) grid-graph with $N = 9$ and periodic boundary conditions; (b) grid-graph with $N = 16$.

4.3.2 ANTIFERROMAGNETIC INTERACTIONS

For small values of $J < 0$ a unique fixed point exists for which all eigenvalues lie inside the unit circle. If we further decrease J, a change of behavior can be observed beyond some critical value J_{C-}. Interestingly, $|J_{C-}| \leq |J_{C+}|$ with equality if and only if $\theta = 0$. In Figure 3b and 3c we can also see that $\rho\left(\boldsymbol{F}'_{-}(\underline{\nu}^*)\right) > \rho\left(\boldsymbol{F}'_{+}(\underline{\nu}^*)\right)$, i.e., the invariance of local stability under sign-change of J does not hold in general.

Let $J < J_{C-}$, then it depends on the graph structure whether a unique fixed point exists and if damping is useful. It turns out that these two properties are closely connected: First, consider the complete graph with $N = 4$ or the grid-graph with periodic boundary conditions; these graphs have unique fixed points but frustrations exist because of cycles with odd-length. Consequently $\Gamma\left(\boldsymbol{F}'(\underline{\nu}^*)\right)$ is non-symmetric (cf. Theorem 4). Besides the sign-change, the spectral radius increases as well so that $\rho\left(\boldsymbol{F}'_{-}(\underline{\nu}^*)\right) > \rho\left(\boldsymbol{F}'_{+}(\underline{\nu}^*)\right)$; the dominant eigenvalue, however, has negative sign and $\Re\left(\Gamma\left(\boldsymbol{F}'(\underline{\nu}^*)\right)\right) < 1$ so that an appropriate damping term exists that enforces BP to converge.

Second, consider both grid-graphs with $N_1 = 9$ and $N_2 = 16$; these graphs are bipartite and have a symmetric spectrum $\Gamma\left(\boldsymbol{F}'(\underline{\nu}^*)\right)$ (see Figure 4 and 5b, and Theorem 4). Because of the symmetric spectrum BP behaves similar as in the ferromagnetic case: i.e., no damping term exists that would stabilize the unstable fixed point; however, two additional stable fixed points exist.

Multiple fixed points for graphs with purely antiferromagnetic interactions only exist if the underlying graph is bipartite. Such graphs can be decomposed into two disjoint subsets $\mathbf{X} = \mathbf{Y} \cup \mathbf{Z}$ such that the magnetization follows a "checkerboard-distribution" where for all $X_i \in \mathbf{Y}$ the magnetization is $m_i > 0$ and for all $X_j \in \mathbf{Z}$ the magnetization is $m_j < 0$, or exactly the other way round. This explains the existence of two stable fixed points. Note that the according mean magnetization $\langle \hat{m} \rangle$ behaves as follows: (i) if N is even both stable fixed points are symmetric and have the same mean magnetization; (ii) if N is odd both stable fixed points have different mean magnetization, because the subsets differ in size, i.e., $|\mathbf{Y}| \neq |\mathbf{Z}|$. The difference in $\langle \hat{m} \rangle$ reduces as the number of variables increases. In the limit of $N = \infty$, the mean magnetization of all solutions collapses onto the same value.

To conclude our observations: either a unique fixed point exists, which may be unstable but can be stabilized by damping (black); or a fixed point exists which is unstable under any form of damping (green) but is accompanied by two stable fixed points (blue) (cf. Figure 2). Therefore, non-vanishing fields increase the accuracy of BP (Figure 2) and lead to better convergence properties (Theorem 2) in all experiments.

5 THEORETICAL ANALYSIS

Here we present some more formal arguments and explain the observations made in Section 4. We start with the Perron-Frobenius Theorem and specify some implications for the particular form of $\boldsymbol{F}'(\underline{\nu}^*)$. Then we provide properties of the eigenvalue spectrum $\Gamma\left(\boldsymbol{F}'(\underline{\nu}^*)\right)$ and explain the influence of finite-size graphs in non-vanishing local fields. We consider only connected graphs[4] where all X_i have minimum degree $\min d_i \geq 2$. Note that any X_i with $d_i = 1$ can be absorbed in larger potentials.

Lemma 1. *The Jacobian matrix $\boldsymbol{F}'(\underline{\nu}^*)$ of a connected graph G is irreducible if $\min d_i \geq 2$.*

Proof. The adjacency matrix of a connected undirected graph is irreducible. Let us construct the Jacobian $\boldsymbol{F}'(\underline{\nu}^*)$ as in (10); note that we can partition $\boldsymbol{F}'(\underline{\nu}^*)$ into $N \times N$ block matrices $[\boldsymbol{F}'(\underline{\nu}^*)]_{ik}$ of size $d_i \times d_k$ each. These blocks contain non-zero values if and only if $e_{ij}, e_{kl} \in \mathbf{E}$ for $X_j, X_k \in \mathbf{X}$; i.e., if $a_{ik} = 1$. It follows that $\boldsymbol{F}'(\underline{\nu}^*)$ is irreducible as well. □

Theorem 1 (Perron Frobenius Theorem). *A real non-negative square matrix $\boldsymbol{B}$ has its spectral radius bounded as follows:*

$$\min_i \sum_j b_{ij} \leq \rho(\boldsymbol{B}) \leq \max_i \sum_j b_{ij}. \qquad (15)$$

If $\boldsymbol{B}$ is irreducible the largest eigenvalue is a positive real number $\lambda_{max} = \rho(\boldsymbol{B})$.

[4] A graph G is *connected* if there is a path for all $X_i, X_j \in \mathbf{X}$, i.e., X_j can be reached from X_i along a series of edges.

Corollary 1.1 (Implications for regular graphs). *A regular graph has $d_i = d$ for all $X_i \in \mathbf{X}$. If the couplings and the fields are constant $\sum_n \boldsymbol{F}'(\underline{\nu}^*)_{mn} = c$ is constant for all rows. By the Perron Frobenius Theorem and by Lemma 1 it follows that $\lambda_{max} = c$.*

Consider an infinite-size grid-graph and some constant coupling-strength $J > 0$. Under these assumptions it is fairly straightforward to provide theoretical insights that explain why the existence of non-vanishing fields enhances the convergence properties. We generalize the results subsequently, as the same argument can be applied to finite-size graphs with different J_{ij}.

Theorem 2. *Let G_∞ be an infinite-size graph with $d_i = d$ and purely ferromagnetic interactions $J > 0$. Then, the existence of a non-vanishing external field $\theta \neq 0$ stabilizes BP.*

Proof. First assume a vanishing external field, i.e., $\theta = \theta_0 = 0$, in which case the trivial fixed point is $\nu^*_{ij} = 0$ and (11) reduces to

$$\boldsymbol{F}'_{\theta_0}(\underline{\nu}^*)_{mn} = \begin{cases} \tanh(J) & \text{if } i = l \text{ and } k \in \partial(X_{i\setminus j}) \\ 0 & \text{else.} \end{cases} \quad (16)$$

Because all variables $X_i \in \mathbf{X}(G_\infty)$ have equal degree $\sum_n \boldsymbol{F}'(\underline{\nu}^*)_{mn} = c$ for all m. It follows from (11) and the Perron-Frobenius Theorem that $\rho\left(\boldsymbol{F}'_{\theta_0}(\underline{\nu}^*)\right) = \tanh(J) \cdot (d_i - 1)$. Without loss of generality we exploit symmetry properties and assume an external field $\theta_\delta > 0$. By (2) and (6) it becomes obvious that any fixed point message $\nu^*_{ij} \neq 0$ and $h_{ij} \neq 0$. Note that, qualitatively it does not matter whether h_{ij} is positive or negative as we only consider $\tanh^2(h_{ij})$.

Because $0 \leq \tanh(J) < 1$ it follows that $\tanh(J) > \tanh^2(J)$ and consequently, as

$$\boldsymbol{F}'_{\theta_\delta}(\underline{\nu}^*)_{mn} = \begin{cases} \frac{\tanh(J)\left(1-\tanh^2(h_{ij})\right)}{1-\tanh^2(J)\tanh^2(h_{ij})} & \text{if } i = l \text{ and } k \in \partial(X_{i\setminus j}) \\ 0 & \text{else,} \end{cases} \quad (17)$$

all non-zero entries of $\boldsymbol{F}'_{\theta_0}(\underline{\nu}^*)_{mn}$ are element-wise larger than $\boldsymbol{F}'_{\theta_\delta}(\underline{\nu}^*)_{mn}$. Let us define a field-dependent scaling term $\kappa_\theta \in (0,1)$, then $\boldsymbol{F}'_{\theta_\delta}(\underline{\nu}^*) = \kappa_\theta \boldsymbol{F}'_{\theta_0}(\underline{\nu}^*)$.

Loosely speaking the existence of some non-vanishing field reduces all entries of the Jacobian matrix and consequently reduces the spectral radius. □

Now choose a critical value J_C at the onset of instability[5] so that $\rho\left(\boldsymbol{F}'_{\theta_0}(\underline{\nu}^*)\right) = \lim_{\epsilon \to 0}(1 + \epsilon)$. If the external field dampens the spectral radius, so that $\rho\left(\boldsymbol{F}'(\underline{\nu}^*)\right) < 1$ the unstable fixed point vanishes, and only a unique stable fixed point remains. Interestingly, this observation holds in all experiments, i.e., in the ferromagnetic case an unstable fixed point exists if and only if multiple fixed points are present.

Suppose we either have purely ferromagnetic or purely antiferromagnetic interactions, then all entries of the Jacobian matrix have the same sign as the couplings and are bounded.

Lemma 2. *All entries of the Jacobian are bounded by $\boldsymbol{F}'(\underline{\nu}^*)_{mn} \in [0, 1)$ if $J_{ij} > 0$ and by $\boldsymbol{F}'(\underline{\nu}^*)_{mn} \in (-1, 0]$ if $J_{ij} < 0$.*

Proof. If all couplings have the same sign, the qualitative result of (17) holds as well. For purely antiferromagnetic interactions we just have to swap signs. □

Theorem 3. *The finite-size manifestation of phase transitions occur beyond the theoretical phase transitions. Let us define a parameter-set (J_C, θ_C) for which λ_{max} crosses the unit-circle. Then, for a graph G_N with N nodes, the values of the critical parameters (J_C, θ_C) decrease as N increases.*

Consider two finite-size graphs with identical structure[6] *with different size $N_1 < N_2$, then $\rho\left(\boldsymbol{F}'_{N_1}(\underline{\nu}^*)\right) \leq \rho\left(\boldsymbol{F}'_{N_2}(\underline{\nu}^*)\right) \leq \rho_\infty\left(\boldsymbol{F}'(\underline{\nu}^*)\right)$.*

Proof. Assume $J > 0$ and w.l.g. $\theta = 0$ (for the influence of non-vanishing external field see Theorem 2). Then on G_∞ – or for any other grid-graph with periodic boundary conditions – the degree $d_i = d$ is constant for all $X_i \in \mathbf{X}$. It follows from Corollary 1.1 that the largest eigenvalue is given by $\lambda_{max} = (d_i - 1) \cdot \tanh(J)$[7]. Suppose we increase the couplings to $J^{new} > J$ and denote the change of its parameters as $\kappa = \frac{\tanh(J^{new})}{\tanh(J)}$. It is obvious that $\lambda^{new}_{max} = \kappa \cdot \lambda_{max}$.

Suppose we have some finite-size graph where d_i is not constant but depends on X_i. If the couplings increase as before each row of $\boldsymbol{F}'(\underline{\nu}^*)$ experiences a different amount of scaling. In all generality this is described by

$$\begin{bmatrix} c_1 & & [0] \\ & \ddots & \\ [0] & & c_K \end{bmatrix} \cdot \boldsymbol{F}'(\underline{\nu}^*) \quad (18)$$

[5] If $\lambda_{max} = 1$ we cannot infer from the linearized to the nonlinear map (Teschl, 2003). We introduce an ϵ-small term to avoid this subtlety.

[6] E.g., a grid-graph with $N = 9$ or $N = 16$ variables.

[7] For vanishing fields J_{ij} determines the Jacobian matrix.

where c_k depends on d_i and $K = \sum_{i=1}^{N} d_i$. Let us reformulate (18) in all detail to

$$\boldsymbol{W} = \sum_{m=2}^{\max(d_i)} \boldsymbol{C}_m \boldsymbol{F}'(\underline{\nu}^*), \tag{19}$$

where $\boldsymbol{C}_m$ is a diagonal matrix with values $\boldsymbol{C}_{m;kk} = \kappa_m$ if the kth line of $\boldsymbol{F}'(\underline{\nu}^*)$ corresponds to a variable with $d_k \geq m$ and 0 otherwise. Since the largest eigenvalue is a positive real number it follows that the largest eigenvalue is the sum of the individual eigenvalues, so that

$$\rho(\boldsymbol{W}) = \sum_{m=2}^{\max(d_i)} \rho\left(\boldsymbol{C}_m \boldsymbol{F}'(\underline{\nu}^*)\right). \tag{20}$$

We still have to show that

$$\rho\left(\boldsymbol{F}'_{N_1}(\underline{\nu}^*)\right) \overset{(a)}{\leq} \rho\left(\boldsymbol{F}'_{N_2}(\underline{\nu}^*)\right) \overset{(b)}{\leq} \rho\left(\boldsymbol{F}'_{\infty}(\underline{\nu}^*)\right), \tag{21}$$

where (b) follows from the existence of an associated eigenvector x such that $\rho(\boldsymbol{W})x \leq (d_i - 1) \cdot \tanh(J)$ with equality if and only if all $\boldsymbol{C}_m$ have only non-zero values on the main diagonal, i.e., all variables have equal degree. As G_{N_2} has a larger proportion of nodes with $\max d_i$ than G_{N_1}, the average degree is also higher: $\langle d \rangle_{G_{N_1}} < \langle d \rangle_{G_{N_2}}$. Then (a) follows from (20).

□

By combination of Theorem 2 and Theorem 3 we get:

Corollary 3.1. *The existence of a non-vanishing external field stabilzes BP on finite-size graphs.*

Next we extend the above observations to varying couplings and fields. We assume that, all couplings J_{ij} have the same sign, and all fields θ_i have the same sign, not necessarily the same as the couplings. Then the scaling coefficients c_k in (18) depend not only on d_i, but on J_{ij} and θ_i as well. Still, $\boldsymbol{F}'(\underline{\nu}^*)$ can only contain either positive entries or negative entries; it follows that:

Corollary 3.2. *For infinite-size grid-graphs with either purely ferromagnetic interactions $J_{ij} > 0$ or purely antiferromagnetic interactions $J_{ij} < 0$, the existence of some non-vanishing fields $\theta_i \neq 0$ stabilizes BP.*

Theorem 4. *The eigenvalue-spectrum of the Jacobian $\boldsymbol{F}'(\underline{\nu}^*)$ is symmetric if and only if the underlying graph is bipartite.*

Proof. The adjacency matrix of any bipartite graph can be rearranged and written in block form

$$\boldsymbol{A} = \begin{bmatrix} [0] & \boldsymbol{M} \\ \boldsymbol{M}^T & [0] \end{bmatrix}, \tag{22}$$

so that the eigenvalue-spectrum is symmetric (Brouwer and Haemers, 2011). By the same arguments as in Lemma 1 it follows that $\boldsymbol{F}'(\underline{\nu}^*)$ has the same structure and a symmetric spectrum as well. □

Corollary 4.1. *Assume we only have purely antiferromagnetic interactions. Then a graph is bipartite if and only if no frustrations occur.*

Proof. A cycle is frustrated if and only if the product of all J_{ij} along the corresponding edges is negative (Mezard and Montanari, 2009, p.45). Frustrations can therefore only occur in graphs with cycles of odd length, which implies that the graph cannot be bipartite (Korte and Vygen, 2005, Prop. 2.27). □

6 CONCLUSION

In this paper we applied the NPHC method to belief propagation (BP) and obtained all fixed points – stable and unstable ones. Subsequently we performed a local stability analysis for various Ising models with non-vanishing external field.

On the basis of our empirical observations and our theoretical analysis we answered several questions: (i) graphs with vanishing fields are indeed a worst-case scenario. Non-vanishing fields reduce the magnitude of all eigenvalues and help to achieve convergence. (ii) Additionally, we showed that existence of non-vanishing fields increases the accuracy of the best stable fixed point. (iii) Damping is assumed to work best in the antiferromagnetic case; we argue that damping can only be used to stabilize a fixed point if it is unique. (iv) We showed the influence of the graph structure regarding stability and uniqueness of BP: if the graph increases in size, the eigenvalues tend to increase, and as a result the performance of BP degrades; furthermore, because of the symmetric spectrum, damping does not help on bipartite graphs. Nonetheless, for all bipartite graphs considered a stable fixed point does always exist and BP consequently converges.

Only two types of unstable fixed points could be observed: either the fixed point is unique (which has to be a minimum of the corresponding Bethe free energy) and stable under optimal damping. Or, a fixed point exists that is unstable under any form of damping; then, at least two additional fixed points are present that are both stable.

References

Ballard, A. J., Das, R., Martiniani, S., Mehta, D., Sagun, L., Stevenson, J. D., and Wales, D. J. (2017). Perspective: Energy landscapes for machine learning. *arXiv preprint arXiv:1703.07915*.

Braunstein, A., Mézard, M., and Zecchina, R. (2005). Survey propagation: an algorithm for satisfiability. *Random Structures & Algorithms*, 27(2):201–226.

Brouwer, A. E. and Haemers, W. H. (2011). *Spectra of Graphs*. Springer Science & Business Media.

Chen, T. and Li, T.-Y. (2015). Homotopy continuation method for solving systems of nonlinear and polynomial equations. *Commun. Inf. Syst.*, 15(2):119–307.

Elidan, G., McGraw, I., and Koller, D. (2006). Residual belief propagation: Informed scheduling for asynchronous message passing. In *Proceedings of UAI*, pages 165–173.

Heskes, T. (2004). On the uniqueness of loopy belief propagation fixed points. *Neural Computation*, 16(11):2379–2413.

Heskes, T. et al. (2003). Stable fixed points of loopy belief propagation are minima of the Bethe free energy. In *NIPS*, volume 15, pages 359–366.

Ihler, A., Fisher, J., and Willsky, A. (2005). Loopy belief propagation: convergence and effects of message errors. In *Journal of Machine Learning Research*, pages 905–936.

Jordan, M. (2004). Graphical models. *Statistical Science*, pages 140–155.

Knoll, C., Pernkopf, F., Mehta, D., and Chen, T. (2016). Fixed points of belief propagation–an analysis via polynomial homotopy continuation. *arXiv preprint arXiv:1605.06451*.

Knoll, C., Rath, M., Tschiatschek, S., and Pernkopf, F. (2015). Message scheduling methods for belief propagation. In *Machine Learning and Knowledge Discovery in Databases*, pages 295–310. Springer.

Koller, D. and Friedman, N. (2009). *Probabilistic Graphical Models: Principles and Techniques*. MIT press.

Korte, B. and Vygen, J. (2005). *Combinatorial Optimization*, volume 3. Springer.

Lauritzen, S. and Spiegelhalter, D. (1988). Local computations with probabilities on graphical structures and their application to expert systems. *Journal of the Royal Statistical Society*, pages 157–224.

Mehta, D., Daleo, N. S., Dörfler, F., and Hauenstein, J. D. (2015). Algebraic geometrization of the Kuramoto model: equilibria and stability analysis. *Chaos: An Interdisciplinary Journal of Nonlinear Science*, 25(5):053103.

Meshi, O., Jaimovich, A., Globerson, A., and Friedman, N. (2009). Convexifying the Bethe free energy. In *Proceedings of UAI*, pages 402–410.

Mezard, M. and Montanari, A. (2009). *Information, Physics, and Computation*. Oxford Univ. Press.

Mezard, M., Parisi, G., and Virasoro, M. (1987). *Spin Glass Theory and Beyond: An Introduction to the Replica Method and Its Applications*, volume 9. World Scientific Publishing Co Inc.

Mooij, J. and Kappen, H. (2005). On the properties of the Bethe approximation and loopy belief propagation on binary networks. *Journal of Statistical Mechanics: Theory and Experiment*, 2005(11):P11012.

Murphy, K., Weiss, Y., and Jordan, M. (1999). Loopy belief propagation for approximate inference: an empirical study. In *Proceedings of UAI*, pages 467–475.

Opper, M. and Winther, O. (2001). Tractable approximations for probabilistic models: the adaptive Thouless-Anderson-Palmer mean field approach. *Physical Review Letters*, 86(17):3695.

Pearl, J. (1988). *Probabilistic Reasoning in Intelligent Systems: Networks of Plausible Inference*. Morgan Kaufmann Publishers.

Pernkopf, F., Peharz, R., and Tschiatschek, S. (2014). *Introduction to Probabilistic Graphical Models*. Academic Press Library in Signal Processing.

Scheinerman, E. R. (2000). *Invitation to Dynamical Systems*. Prentice Hall.

Shin, J. (2012). Complexity of Bethe approximation. In *Proceedings of AISTATS*, pages 1037–1045.

Sommese, A. and Wampler, C. (2005). *The Numerical Solution of Systems of Polynomials Arising in Engineering and Science*, volume 99. World Scientific.

Srinivasa, C., Ravanbakhsh, S., and Frey, B. (2016). Survey propagation beyond constraint satisfaction problems. In *Proceedings of AISTATS*, pages 286–295.

Sutton, C. and McCallum, A. (2007). Improved dynamic schedules for belief propagation. In *Proceedings of UAI*, pages 376–383.

Taga, N. and Mase, S. (2004). *On the convergence of belief propagation algorithm for stochastic networks with loops*.

Teschl, G. (2003). *Ordinary Differential Equations and Dynamical Systems*.

Weiss, Y. (2000). Correctness of local probability propagation in graphical models with loops. *Neural Comp.*, 12(1).

Weller, A. and Jebara, T. (2014). Approximating the Bethe partition function. pages 858–867.

Welling, M. and Teh, Y. W. (2001). Belief optimization for binary networks: A stable alternative to loopy belief propagation. In *Proceedings of UAI*, pages 554–561. Morgan Kaufmann Publishers Inc.

Yedidia, J. S., Freeman, W. T., and Weiss, Y. (2005). Constructing free-energy approximations and generalized belief propagation algorithms. *IEEE Transactions on Information Theory*, 51(7):2282–2312.

Yedidia, J. S., Freeman, W. T., Weiss, Y., et al. (2000). Generalized belief propagation. In *NIPS*, volume 13, pages 689–695.

Yuille, A. and Rangarajan, A. (2003). The concave-convex procedure. *Neural Comp.*, 15(4):915–936.

Improving Optimization-Based Approximate Inference by Clamping Variables

Junyao Zhao, Josip Djolonga, Sebastian Tschiatschek, Andreas Krause
Department of Computer Science, ETH Zürich
zhaoju@student.ethz.ch, {josipd,tschiats}@inf.ethz.ch, krausea@ethz.ch

Abstract

While central to the application of probabilistic models to discrete data, the problem of marginal inference is in general intractable and efficient approximation schemes need to exploit the problem structure. Recently, there have been efforts to develop inference techniques that do not necessarily make factorization assumptions about the distribution, but rather exploit the fact that sometimes there exist efficient algorithms for finding the MAP configuration. In this paper, we theoretically prove that for discrete multi-label models the bounds on the partition function obtained by two of these approaches, Perturb-and-MAP and the bound from the infinite Rényi divergence, can be only improved by clamping any subset of the variables. For the case of log-supermodular models we provide a more detailed analysis and develop a set of efficient strategies for choosing the order in which the variables should be clamped. Finally, we present a number of numerical experiments showcasing the improvements obtained by the proposed methods on several models.

1 INTRODUCTION

A key challenge in probabilistic inference is that of computing the normalizing partition function of unnormalized probability distributions, which would enable the evaluation of the probability of evidence and marginal probabilities. While for low tree-width graphs one can use the junction tree algorithm to normalize the distribution, in general the worst case time complexity is exponential in the number of random variables. Consequently, we very often have to resort to techniques for approximating the partition function. In this paper we will focus on a family of such techniques that make assumptions only about the optimization characteristics of the used energy function.

In this paper we will consider discrete probabilistic models $P(X_1, X_2, \ldots, X_N)$ defined over N random variables $X_1, \ldots, X_N$, such that each variable X_i takes on values in $\mathcal{L} = \{0, 1, \ldots, L-1\}$. We will assume that the distribution is given in the form

$$P(\mathbf{x}) = \frac{1}{\mathcal{Z}(f)} \exp(-f(\mathbf{x})), \tag{1}$$

where $f\colon \{0, 1, \ldots, L-1\}^n \to \mathbb{R}$ is an arbitrary *energy function*, and $\mathcal{Z}(f)$ is the *partition function*, which ensures normalization of the distribution. As already suggested, computing $\mathcal{Z}$ is provably hard, and is known to be #P-hard even for binary pairwise models [1, 2].

We make *no factorization assumptions* about f, and thus we cannot directly apply most existing algorithms and techniques relying on a log-linear representation [3]. Instead, we will assume that we can efficiently compute the MAP configuration under any linear perturbation. Specifically, we assume that we can efficiently solve

$$\underset{\mathbf{x}}{\text{minimize}} \quad f(\mathbf{x}) + \sum_{i=1}^{n} g_{i,x_i},$$

for any set of numbers $g_{i,x_i} \in \mathbb{R}$.

The above assumption has two important consequences. First, the energies satisfying this assumption are *closed under clamping*, i.e. if we fix any x_k to have value l, we can solve the problem $\min_{\mathbf{x}\colon x_k=l} f(\mathbf{x}) + \sum_{i=1}^{n} g_{i,x_i}$ by letting $g_{k,l} \to -\infty$. Second, there are at least two techniques for approximate marginal inference which can be directly applied under that sole assumption: *(i)* the Perturb-and-MAP framework of [4], and *(ii)* the minimization of the infinite Rényi divergence [5], known as L-FIELD for log-supermodular models [6, 7]. In this paper, we show both theoretically and experimentally that these two properties can be safely combined to yield better approximate inference results. Specifically, we prove that performing inference after clamping can *only improve* the estimate of the partition function.

An important class of energy functions that satisfies the above assumption, and which we will also analyze as a special case in more detail, is that of *binary* ($L = 2$) log-supermodular distributions. Their energy has to satisfy $f(\mathbf{x} \vee \mathbf{y}) + f(\mathbf{x} \wedge \mathbf{y}) \leq f(\mathbf{x}) + f(\mathbf{y})$ for all $\mathbf{x}, \mathbf{y} \in \{0,1\}^n$, where $\wedge$ and $\vee$ denote element-wise minimum and maximum respectively. These energies can be minimized in polynomial time [8], very efficiently in many cases [9, 10]. The distributions corresponding to these energy functions have non-negative correlations [11], which also explains why they are sometimes referred to as *attractive*. They have been extensively used in computer vision for semantic image segmentation—both pairwise models (also known as graph-cuts) [12], but also models with complicated higher-order potentials [13].

Previous work. In this work we analyze the bound obtained from the infinite Rényi divergence [5], which has been used in [7] for log-supermodular models (in the same paper the authors show that this problem is equivalent to the L-FIELD bound of Djolonga and Krause [6]). We will also study the Perturb-and-MAP method, which was first proposed by Papandreou and Yuille [4] and then analyzed in more detail by Hazan and Jaakkola [14]. Recently, Shpakova and Bach [15] have drawn an interesting connection between these two techniques for log-supermodular models. The idea of improving approximate inference techniques by clamping has been studied by Weller and Jebara [16] and Weller and Domke [17]. In these papers, the authors have answered in the affirmative the question if clamping always helps for mean-field, tree-reweighted belief-propagation and traditional belief propagation (for log-supermodular models) [3]. Unfortunately, these inference techniques can not be easily applied to models with higher order factors without additional factorization assumptions, or a restriction to specific families [18, 19].

Contributions. We prove that clamping can only improve the partition function estimate obtained from Perturb-and-MAP and the bound arising from the infinite Rényi divergence for any discrete model. Furthermore, for log-supermodular models we propose heuristics for choosing which variables to clamp. Finally, we provide an empirical analysis to demonstrate the benefits of clamping and the usefulness of the proposed heuristics.

2 PRELIMINARIES

2.1 MATHEMATICAL SETTING

We will represent each configuration $\mathbf{X} = (X_1 = z_1, X_2 = z_2, \ldots, X_N = z_N)$ by a vector $\mathbf{x} \in \{0,1\}^{NL}$ using the one-hot 1-of-L encoding, i.e. each variable X_i has a corresponding block $\mathbf{x}_i \in \{0,1\}^L$ of $\mathbf{x}$ with a single 1 at the position corresponding to z_i, i.e. $x_{i,j} = [\![z_i = j]\!]$. We also define the set of all admissible vectors $\mathbf{x}$ as

$$\mathcal{X} = \{\mathbf{x} \in \{0,1\}^{NL} \mid \forall i \colon \mathbf{1}^T \mathbf{x}_i = 1\},$$

where $\mathbf{1}$ is the vector of all ones of length L. The partition function is $\mathcal{Z}(f) = \sum_{\mathbf{x} \in \mathcal{X}} \exp(-f(\mathbf{x}))$.

2.2 CLAMPING

The basic idea of clamping is as follows: after selecting any variable X_k, we can re-write the partition function as

$$\mathcal{Z}(f) = \sum_{\mathbf{x}} e^{-f(\mathbf{x})} = \sum_{l=1}^{L} \underbrace{\sum_{\mathbf{x} \in \mathcal{X} \colon \mathbf{x}_{k,l}=1} e^{-f(\mathbf{x})}}_{\mathcal{Z}_{k,l}},$$

i.e. $\mathcal{Z}(f)$ can be computed as the sum of the terms $\mathcal{Z}_{k,l}$, which correspond to the partition functions of distributions induced by the energy function f by fixing X_k to value l. To perform approximate inference, we can now approximate each term $\mathcal{Z}_{k,l}$ independently (this corresponds to performing approximate inference in L separate models) and add up these approximations.

In the remainder of the paper we will work with methods which *guarantee an upper bound* on the partition function. Specifically, if we apply these methods directly to $\mathcal{Z}$ we will obtain some upper bound $\widehat{\mathcal{Z}} \geq \mathcal{Z}$, and similarly applying them to the clamped problem will yield an estimate $\widehat{\mathcal{Z}}_{k,l} \geq \mathcal{Z}_{k,l}$. The important question that arises is if the above strategy will always improve the approximation. Specifically, while we do know that $\mathcal{Z} \leq \sum_{l=1}^{L} \widehat{\mathcal{Z}}_{k,l}$, it is in general not clear if

$$\mathcal{Z} \leq \sum_{l=1}^{L} \widehat{\mathcal{Z}}_{k,l} \leq \widehat{\mathcal{Z}},$$

which is exactly the question studied in §3 and §4.

Also, we would like to point out that while we can use $\sum_{l=1}^{L} \widehat{\mathcal{Z}}_{k,l}$ as an approximation to $\mathcal{Z}$, it is not clear how to obtain approximate marginals after clamping. To motivate the strategy we undertake in the experimental section, let us start by noting that

$$P(X_i = j) = \sum_{l=1}^{L} P(X_i = j \mid X_k = l) P(X_k = l).$$

Then, if in the above formula we approximate $P(X_k = l) = \mathcal{Z}_{k,l}/\mathcal{Z}$ by $\widehat{\mathcal{Z}}_{k,l}/\sum_{l=1}^{L}\widehat{\mathcal{Z}}_{k,l}$, as a natural approximation to $P(X_k = l)$ we will use the following quantity

$$\tau_{i,j} = \frac{\sum_{l=1}^{L}\widehat{\mathcal{Z}}_{k,l}\tau_{i,j}^{l}}{\sum_{l=1}^{L}\widehat{\mathcal{Z}}_{k,l}},$$

where $\tau_{i,j}^{l}$ is the approximation of $P(X_i = j)$ obtained from the sub-problem corresponding to $\widehat{\mathcal{Z}}_{k,l}$. These quantities will be exact if all approximations are also exact, and, as we show in §5, they do improve with the number of clamps when approximate inference is used.

2.3 THE INFINITE RÉNYI DIVERGENCE

The infinite Rényi divergence D_∞ between distributions Q and P is defined as [5]

$$D_\infty(P \,\|\, Q) = \sup_{\mathbf{x}\in\mathcal{X}} \log \frac{P(\mathbf{x})}{Q(\mathbf{x})} \geq 0.$$

Note that this is an *inclusive divergence* [20] in the sense that it will try to cover as much as possible from the distribution. In what follows we will focus our attention to completely factorized distributions Q. Specifically, we will assume that Q has the form

$$\log Q(\mathbf{x}) = -\mathbf{s}^T\mathbf{x} - \sum_{i=1}^{N}\log\sum_{j=1}^{L}\exp(-s_{i,j}),$$

for some parameters $\mathbf{s} \in \mathbb{R}^{NL}$. If we plug this Q and $P(\mathbf{x}) = \exp(-f(\mathbf{x}))/\mathcal{Z}$ in the definition above, we arrive at the following upper bound on the partition function

$$\sum_{i=1}^{N}\log\sum_{j=1}^{L}\exp(-s_{i,j}) + \sup_{\mathbf{x}\in\mathcal{X}}(\mathbf{s}^T\mathbf{x} - f(\mathbf{x})) \geq \log\mathcal{Z}.$$

Note that to minimize this (convex) bound we just need to be able to solve the perturbed MAP problem, where the perturbation is equal to $-\mathbf{s}^T\mathbf{x}$. Djolonga and Krause [7] analyze this bound and discuss algorithms for its optimization for the case when f is submodular.

2.4 PERTURB-AND-MAP

Hazan and Jaakkola [14] proposed using Perturb-and-MAP to estimate the partition function. The idea behind this method is to execute the following procedure several times: (i) perturb the energy by adding a random modular term, and (ii) find the MAP configuration under the perturbation. Then, if we repeatedly perform the above steps, we can obtain both an upper bound $\widehat{\mathcal{Z}}_P$ (in expectation) on $\mathcal{Z}$, and an estimate of the marginals (by treating the configurations found in (ii) as if they had come from the true distributions and computing sample averages). While one can have more complicated perturbation models, in this paper we will focus on the simplest perturbation, i.e. those that only modify the unary potentials, which can be easily applied given the optimization assumption we have made about the energy f. Formally, if $\cup_{i=1}^{N}\cup_{j=1}^{L}\{g_{i,j}(1), g_{i,j}(0)\}$ is a collection of i.i.d. Gumbel variables, we have that

$$\log\mathcal{Z} \leq \mathbb{E}_g[\max_{\mathbf{x}\in\mathcal{X}}\{\sum_{i=1}^{n}\sum_{j=1}^{L} g_{i,j}(x_{i,j}) - f(\mathbf{x})\}].$$

3 CLAMPING WITH D_∞

In this section, we will first prove that clamping can only improve the estimate of the partition function. Then, we will discuss the specific cases of binary and multi-label submodular functions. Finally, we will introduce some strategies for choosing the variables to be clamped.

To prove the main claim, let us first rewrite the D_∞ divergence into a form that is easier to manipulate. Remember from §2.3 that the upper bound has the form

$$\log\mathcal{Z} \leq \sum_{i=1}^{n}\log\sum_{j=1}^{L}\exp(-s_{i,j}) + \sup_{\mathbf{x}\in\mathcal{X}}(\mathbf{x}^T\mathbf{s} - f(\mathbf{x})). \tag{2}$$

As done in [7], we can introduce a new variable $-t$ to capture the supremum and re-write the problem as

$$\begin{aligned} \min_{\mathbf{s},t}.\quad & \sum_{i=1}^{n}\log\sum_{j=1}^{L}\exp(-s_{i,j}) - t \\ \text{s.t.}\quad & \mathbf{x}^T\mathbf{s} + t \leq f(\mathbf{x}),\ \forall\mathbf{x}\in\mathcal{X}. \end{aligned} \tag{$\texttt{OPT}_\infty$}$$

The constraint set of the above problem, which is also known as the upper polyhedron [21], will be denoted as

$$U(f) = \{(\mathbf{s}, t) \mid \mathbf{x}^T\mathbf{s} + t \leq f(\mathbf{x}),\ \forall\mathbf{x}\in\mathcal{X}\}. \tag{3}$$

Now, if we clamp some variable $X_k = l$, the resulting sub-problem will have the form[1]

$$\begin{aligned} \min_{\mathbf{s},t}.\quad & \sum_{i=1,i\neq k}^{n}\log\sum_{j=1}^{L}\exp(-s_{i,j}) - t \\ \text{s.t.}\quad & \forall\mathbf{x}\in\mathcal{X}\colon x_{k,l} = 0 \text{ we have that} \\ & \mathbf{x}^T\mathbf{s} + t \leq f(\mathbf{x} + \mathbf{e}_{k,l}). \end{aligned} \tag{$\texttt{OPT}_\infty^l$}$$

Note that the above optimization problem does not depend the variables in the block $\mathbf{s}_k$, which we have kept to simplify the notation. We will now prove that clamping can only improve the estimate of the partition function.

[1]The vector $\mathbf{e}_{k,l} \in \mathbb{R}^{NL}$ has all coordinates zero, except for the coordinate (k, l), which is equal to one.

Theorem 3.1. *For the D_∞ objective, clamping can only improve the estimate. Specifically, if $\widehat{\mathcal{Z}}$ is the optimal value for* ($\mathtt{OPT}_\infty$) *and $\widehat{\mathcal{Z}}_l$ is the optimal value for* ($\mathtt{OPT}^l_\infty$) *we have $\mathcal{Z} \leq \sum_{l=1}^{L} \widehat{\mathcal{Z}}_l \leq \widehat{\mathcal{Z}}$.*

Proof. The exponential of the objective of problem ($\mathtt{OPT}_\infty$) can be rewritten as

$$\prod_{i=1}^{N}(\sum_{l=1}^{L} e^{-s_{i,l}})e^{-t} = \sum_{l=1}^{L} e^{-s_{k,l}-t} \cdot \prod_{i\neq k}(\sum_{j=1}^{L} e^{-s_{i,j}})$$

Then, it trivially follows that

$$\begin{aligned}\widehat{\mathcal{Z}} &= \min_{(\mathbf{s},t)\in U(f)} \sum_{l=1}^{L}(e^{-s_{k,l}-t} \cdot \prod_{i\neq k}(\sum_{j=1}^{L} e^{-s_{i,j}})) \\ &\geq \sum_{l=1}^{L} \underbrace{\min_{(\mathbf{s},t)\in U(f)} (e^{-s_{k,l}-t} \cdot \prod_{i\neq k}(\sum_{j=1}^{L} e^{-s_{i,j}}))}_{A_l}\end{aligned}$$

Let us now bound $\log A_l$, i.e. the optimal value of

$$\min_{(\mathbf{s},t)\in U(f)} -s_{k,l} - t + \sum_{i\neq k} \log(\sum_{j=1}^{L} e^{-s_{i,j}}).$$

We will show that any feasible pair $(\mathbf{s}, t)$ of this problem can be converted into a feasible pair $(\mathbf{s}', t')$ of problem ($\mathtt{OPT}^l_\infty$) with the same objective value. This would in turn imply that $\log A_l \geq \log \widehat{\mathcal{Z}}_l$, which completes the proof. Define $t' = t + s_{k,l}$, and $\mathbf{s}'$ to be equal to $\mathbf{s}$ with the exception of $s'_{k,l}$, which is set to zero. It is obvious that plugging in $(\mathbf{s}', t')$ into ($\mathtt{OPT}^l_\infty$) will yield the same objective, so we just have to prove that it is feasible. Let $\mathbf{x} \in \mathcal{X}$ have $x_{k,l} = 0$. Define $\mathcal{I} = \{0, 1, \ldots, N-1\} \times \{0, 1, \ldots, L-1\}$. The inequality in $U(f)$ corresponding to $\mathbf{x} + \mathbf{e}_{k,l}$ reads

$$\sum_{(i,j)\in\mathcal{I}-(k,l)} x_{i,j}s_{i,j} + s_{k,l} + t \leq f(\mathbf{x} + \mathbf{e}_{k,l}),$$

which with a little manipulation can be re-written as the inequality corresponding to $\mathbf{x}$ in ($\mathtt{OPT}^l_\infty$), namely

$$\underbrace{\sum_{(i,j)\in\mathcal{I}-(k,l)} x_{i,j}s_{i,j} + \underbrace{0}_{s'_{k,l}}}_{\mathbf{x}^T\mathbf{s}'} + \underbrace{s_{k,l} + t}_{t'} \leq f(\mathbf{x} + \mathbf{e}_{k,l}),$$

which implies that $(\mathbf{s}', t')$ is feasible for ($\mathtt{OPT}^l_\infty$).

In Appendix A.1 we provide a stronger result. i.e. that $A_l = \widehat{\mathcal{Z}}_l$ for submodular functions f. □

3.1 RELAXATIONS

Unfortunately, it can be in general very hard to work with $U(f)$ for arbitrary sets $\mathcal{X}$. For example, even if f is a submodular function, checking if $(\mathbf{s}, t)$ is a member of $U(f)$ requires minimizing $f(\mathbf{x}) - \mathbf{x}^T\mathbf{s}$ subject to $\mathbf{x} \in \mathcal{X}$, which is NP-hard if $L > 2$, as shown by Dahlhaus et al. [22]. However, it is of course tractable if we use $\overline{\mathcal{X}} = \{0, 1\}^{NL}$, which is exactly the approach taken by Zhang et al. [23]. Note that in this case the upper bound is still valid, because replacing $\mathcal{X}$ by $\overline{\mathcal{X}} \supseteq \mathcal{X}$ in Equation (2) can only increase the bound. We would like to point out that in the previous argument would still hold if we replace $\mathcal{X}$ by $\overline{\mathcal{X}}$. In other words, even if a relaxation is used in lieu of the true 1-of-L constraints, the obtained upper bound can only improve after clamping.

3.2 VARIABLE SELECTION FOR PROBABILISTIC SUBMODULAR MODELS

Let us consider the case when f is a submodular set function. This case has been analyzed in more detail by Djolonga and Krause [7]. In that paper, the authors show that for binary models we can simplify the optimization problem as follows. First, because the model is binary for any position i, we have $x_{i,1} = 1 - x_{i,0}$. Then, we can treat only the variables $\mathbf{x}_{i,1}$, and it can be further shown that ($\mathtt{OPT}_\infty$) is equivalent to minimizing the following objective

$$\sum_{i=1}^{N} \log(1 + e^{-x_{i,1}}),$$

over the constraint that requires the concatenation $\mathbf{s}$ of the variables $x_{i,1}$ to be a member of the base-polytope [24]

$$B(f) = \{\mathbf{s} \mid \mathbf{1}^T\mathbf{s} = f(\mathbf{1}), \mathbf{x}^T\mathbf{s} \leq f(\mathbf{x}),\ \forall\mathbf{x} \in \{0, 1\}^n\}. \tag{4}$$

The fact that this object is very well understood (see e.g. [24, 25]) has enabled the development of efficient algorithms for minimizing the D_∞ upper bound. Here, we will also make use of one of the properties of the base polytope to design heuristics for choosing a good clamping order.

We propose two computationally efficient and effective strategies that build on the idea of clamping some random variable X_i whose corresponding optimization variable $s_{i,1}$ can "vary" the most. We quantify this, using the observation that all elements in the base polytope satisfy [25]

$$s_{i,1} \in [f(\mathbf{1}) - f(\mathbf{1} - \mathbf{e}_{i,1}), f(\mathbf{e}_{i,1})]. \tag{5}$$

Actually, the bound is tight in the sense that for both end-points of this interval there exists a vertex whose $(i, 1)$-th coordinate is exactly equal to it. Our experiments show that this range has a strong correlation with the improvement we can make by clamping variable X_i.

The first heuristic that we propose is NAIVEMAXRANGE, that clamps the top k variables with the largest such intervals. In the experiments, we observe that this simple method outperforms random choice. Moreover, we can adaptively apply this strategy — instead of fixing all k variables to clamp in the beginning, we can first clamp the variable with the largest interval and then recursively apply the same strategy to the resulting sub-problems. We call this strategy BRANCHMAXRANGE. This strategy gave the best experimental results.

The BRANCHMAXRANGE algorithm is shown in Algorithm 1. Its input parameters are the energy function f, the number of variables to clamp k and a set of clampings $\mathcal{C}$, i.e. tuples of the form (i, j) denoting that the ith variable is clamped to value j. For the first call, the set of clampings is empty. The output of the algorithm is the approximate partition function $\widehat{\mathcal{Z}}$ and a vector of approximate marginals $\mathbf{p}$. The algorithm recursively identifies the (non-clamped) variable with the largest interval in line 5. It then recurses by clamping the identified variable to both values it can take in lines 6 and 7. Finally, it aggregates the outputs of the recursive calls to compute the approximate partition function and the approximate marginals in lines 8–12. If all k variables are clamped in a call of BRANCHMAXRANGE, it performs approximate inference in line 2, e.g. by using L-FIELD or Perturb-and-MAP.

4 CLAMPING WITH PERTURB-AND-MAP

In this section, we will first prove that clamping can only improve the upper bound estimate from Perturb-and-MAP, and then propose an efficient strategy for selecting the variables to be clamped.

Recall that the bound on the partition function arising from this technique has the form

$$\log \mathcal{Z} \leq \log \widehat{\mathcal{Z}} = \mathbb{E}_g[\max_{\mathbf{x}\in\mathcal{X}}\{\sum_{i=1}^{n}\sum_{j=1}^{L} g_{i,j}(x_{i,j}) - f(\mathbf{x})\}],$$

where $\cup_{i=1}^{N} \cup_{j=1}^{L} \{g_{i,j}(1), g_{i,j}(0)\}$ is a collection of i.i.d. Gumbel random variables. Then we have that

$$\begin{aligned}
&\mathbb{E}_g[\max_{\mathbf{x}\in\mathcal{X}}\{\sum_{i,l} g_{i,l}(x_{i,l}) - f(\mathbf{x})\}] \\
=&\mathbb{E}_g[\max_{\mathbf{x}\in\mathcal{X}}\{\sum_{i,l}(g_{i,l}(1) - g_{i,l}(0))\mathbf{x}_{i,l} + g_{i,l}(0)) - f(\mathbf{x})\}] \\
=&\mathbb{E}_{\mathbf{z}}[\max_{\mathbf{x}\in\mathcal{X}}\{\sum_{i,l} z_{i,l}x_{i,l} - f(\mathbf{x})\}],
\end{aligned}$$

Algorithm 1: BRANCHMAXRANGE clamping for D_∞

Input: f, clampings $\mathcal{C}$, number of variables to clamp k
Output: $\widehat{\mathcal{Z}}(f)$, approximate marginals $\mathbf{p}$

1 **if** $|\mathcal{C}| = k$ **then**
2 | **return** *approx_method*$(f, \mathcal{C})$
3 **end**
4 $\mathcal{V} = [N] \setminus \cup_{(i,l)\in\mathcal{C}}\{i\}$ `// free variables`
5 $i = \arg\max_{i'\in\mathcal{V}} f(\mathbf{e}_{i',1}) - [f(\mathbf{1}) - f(\mathbf{1} - \mathbf{e}_{i',1})]$
6 $(\widehat{\mathcal{Z}}_0, \mathbf{p}^0) =$ BRANCHMAXRANGE$(f, \mathcal{C} \cup \{(i, 0)\}, k)$
7 $(\widehat{\mathcal{Z}}_1, \mathbf{p}^1) =$ BRANCHMAXRANGE$(f, \mathcal{C} \cup \{(i, 1)\}, k)$
8 $\widehat{\mathcal{Z}} = \widehat{\mathcal{Z}}_0 + \widehat{\mathcal{Z}}_1$
9 $p_i = \frac{\widehat{\mathcal{Z}}_1}{\widehat{\mathcal{Z}}}$
10 **for** $j \in \mathcal{V} \setminus \{i\}$ **do**
11 | $p_j = \frac{1}{\widehat{\mathcal{Z}}}[\widehat{\mathcal{Z}}_0 \cdot p_j^0 + \widehat{\mathcal{Z}}_1 \cdot p_j^1]$
12 **end**
13 **return** $(\widehat{\mathcal{Z}}, \mathbf{p})$

where $z_{i,l} = g_{i,l}(1) - g_{i,l}(0)$ is sampled from a logistic distribution. The last equality is by the linearity of expectation, the fact that the Gumbel random variables have a zero mean, and the fact that the difference of two Gumbel variables is a logistic random variable [4]. To simplify notation, we introduce the following set

$$\mathcal{X}_{-i} = \{\Pi_i(\mathbf{x}) \mid \mathbf{x} \in \mathcal{X}\},$$

where the operation Π_i zeroes out the block $\mathbf{x}_i$. We can then rewrite this bound as

$$\mathbb{E}_{\mathbf{z}}[\max_{l=1,2,\ldots,L}\{\max_{\mathbf{x}\in\mathcal{X}_{-i}}\{\mathbf{z}^T\mathbf{x} - f(\mathbf{x} + \mathbf{e}_{i,l}) + z_{i,l}\}\}].$$

If we clamp $x_{i,l}$ to zero and one, we will obtain the following upper bound on $\log \mathcal{Z}$

$$\begin{aligned}
\log\big[&\underbrace{\exp(\mathbb{E}_{\mathbf{z}}[\max_{\mathbf{x}\in\mathcal{X},\mathbf{x}_{i,l}=0}\{\mathbf{z}^T\mathbf{x} - f(\mathbf{x})\}])}_{\widehat{\mathcal{Z}}_-} \\
&+ \underbrace{\exp(\mathbb{E}_{\mathbf{z}}[\max_{\mathbf{x}\in\mathcal{X}_{-i}}\{\mathbf{z}^T\mathbf{x} - f(\mathbf{x} + \mathbf{e}_{i,l})\}])}_{\widehat{\mathcal{Z}}_+}\big].
\end{aligned} \tag{6}$$

Note that both $\widehat{\mathcal{Z}}$ and $\widehat{\mathcal{Z}}_+ + \widehat{\mathcal{Z}}_-$ upper bound the true partition function. The main question is if the second bound dominates the first one, which we show in the following theorem to be indeed the case.

Theorem 4.1. *For multi-label models, if we clamp any arbitrary variable $x_{i,l}$ we have that $\mathcal{Z} \leq \widehat{\mathcal{Z}}_+ + \widehat{\mathcal{Z}}_- \leq \widehat{\mathcal{Z}}$.*

Proof. Before we start with the proof, we would like to explain the strategy that we will use. Instead of showing that clamping X_i helps, we will instead show that clamping $X_{i,l}$ helps, i.e. if we treat $X_{i,l}$ as a variable itself. Then, clamping X_i is equivalent to L consecutive clamps of the variables $X_{i,1}, X_{i,2}, \ldots, X_{i,L}$. As we will show that each of these clamps can only improve the estimate on the partition function, then it must be true that clamping X_i can only improve the estimate.

Let us denote by $\mathbf{z}_{-i,l}$ the vector which has all coordinates of $\mathbf{z}$ except its i, l-th coordinate. Then, for ease of readability let us define

$$G(\mathbf{z}_{-i,l}) = \max_{\mathbf{x}\in\mathcal{X}, \mathbf{x}_{i,l}=0} \{\mathbf{z}^T\mathbf{x} - f(\mathbf{x})\}$$
$$- \max_{\mathbf{x}\in\mathcal{X}_{-i}} \{\mathbf{z}^T\mathbf{x} - f(\mathbf{x} + \mathbf{e}_{i,l})\}.$$

If we define $(x)_+ = \max(x, 0)$, we have that

$$\log \frac{\widehat{\mathcal{Z}}_-}{\widehat{\mathcal{Z}}} = -\mathbb{E}_{\mathbf{z}}[(z_{i,l} - G(\mathbf{z}_{-i,l}))_+]$$
$$= -\mathbb{E}_{\mathbf{z}_{-i,l}}[\int_{G(\mathbf{z}_{-i,l})}^{+\infty} p(z_{i,l}) \cdot (z_{i,l} - G(\mathbf{z}_{-i,l}))dz_{i,l}]$$
$$= \mathbb{E}_{\mathbf{z}_{-i,l}}[-\log(1 + e^{-G(\mathbf{z}_{-i,l})})]$$
$$\leq \log \mathbb{E}_{\mathbf{z}_{-i,l}}[\frac{1}{1 + e^{-G(\mathbf{z}_{-i,l})}}],$$

where the last equality is known for logistic distributions (see e.g. [15]), while the inequality is due to Jensen's inequality. Note the RHS does not depend on $z_{i,l}$, hence this is indeed a function of $\mathbf{z}_{-i,l}$. We can analogously prove that

$$\log \frac{\widehat{\mathcal{Z}}_+}{\widehat{\mathcal{Z}}} \leq \log \mathbb{E}_{\mathbf{z}_{-i,l}}[\frac{1}{1 + e^{G(\mathbf{z}_{-i,l})}}].$$

Combining these two inequalities we obtain

$$\frac{\widehat{\mathcal{Z}}_- + \widehat{\mathcal{Z}}_+}{\widehat{\mathcal{Z}}} \leq \mathbb{E}_{\mathbf{z}_{-i,l}}[\frac{1}{1 + e^{-G(\mathbf{z}_{-i,l})}} + \frac{1}{1 + e^{G(\mathbf{z}_{-i,l})}}]$$
$$= 1,$$

which we had to show. □

Independently of this paper and very recently, Balog et al. [26] derived this result for the Weibull or Fréchet upper bounds, and this actually implies the same result for Perturb-and-MAP because the limit of the Weibull or Fréchet upper bounds, as their distribution parameter approaches 0, is equal to the Perturb-and-MAP upper bound.

4.1 SPEEDING UP GREEDY CLAMPING

Unfortunately, coming up with an easily computable heuristic for clamping variables for Perturb-and-MAP is non-trivial. One possible idea would be to greedily choose a variable that results in the biggest improvement. Unfortunately, if we use M samples for each clamped subproblem we will need to solve in total $O(NLM)$ MAP estimations, which, even though trivially parallelizable, can be still prohibitively expensive.

We will now propose a simple approximation to the greedy strategy, that can sometimes take significantly less time to run and gave promising results in the experiments we performed in §5. Let us start by introducing a related problem, which is that of computing the following quantities

$$\texttt{MIN-MARG}^*_{i,l} = \max_{\mathbf{x}\in\mathcal{X}:\, x_{i,l}=1} \mathbf{s}^T\mathbf{x} - f(\mathbf{x}),$$

for all i, l and some fixed $\mathbf{s} \in \mathbb{R}^{NL}$, which are also known as *min-marginals*. A large family of models where this optimization can be done more efficiently than doing N separate optimization problems are graph-representable submodular functions, as shown by Kohli and Torr [27]. For these models fixing the value of a variable is equivalent to adding a single edge of infinite capacity to the corresponding node, and the authors have developed an algorithm that can more efficiently compute all min-marginals by re-using some intermediate results.

Note that after clamping variable X_k to value l we have to evaluate

$$\mathbb{E}_{\mathbf{s}}[\max_{\mathbf{x}\in\mathcal{X}:\, x_{j,l}=1} \mathbf{s}^T\mathbf{x} - f(\mathbf{x})],$$

by drawing a sample $\mathcal{S}_l = \{\mathbf{s}_{l,1}, \mathbf{s}_{l,2}, \ldots, \mathbf{s}_{l,M}\}$ and solving the M resulting optimization problems. What we suggest then is to estimate these quantities using the min-marginals by tying the samples, i.e. by drawing a single sample $\mathcal{S} = \{\mathbf{s}_1, \mathbf{s}_2, \ldots, \mathbf{s}_M\}$ and setting $\mathcal{S}_l = \mathcal{S}$. Then, we can make use of the faster min-marginal computation from Kohli and Torr [27], but the samples are not independent anymore. However, as substantiated by our experimental results in §5, this approach, which we call Perturb-and-Min-Marginals, works well in practice and performs better than randomly clamping variables.

5 EXPERIMENTS

In this section we want to showcase the following: (1) demonstrate that clamping indeed improves the bounds on the log-partition function, (2) analyze the effect on the estimated marginals, (3) compare the performance of various variable selection strategies. Because in the experiments we focus our attention on submodular models, the minimization of the D_∞ divergence turns into the L-FIELD method of [6], whose code and experimental setup we reuse here. For (1) and (2), we run Perturb-and-MAP (with 200 random samples, labelled `pmap`) and L-FIELD

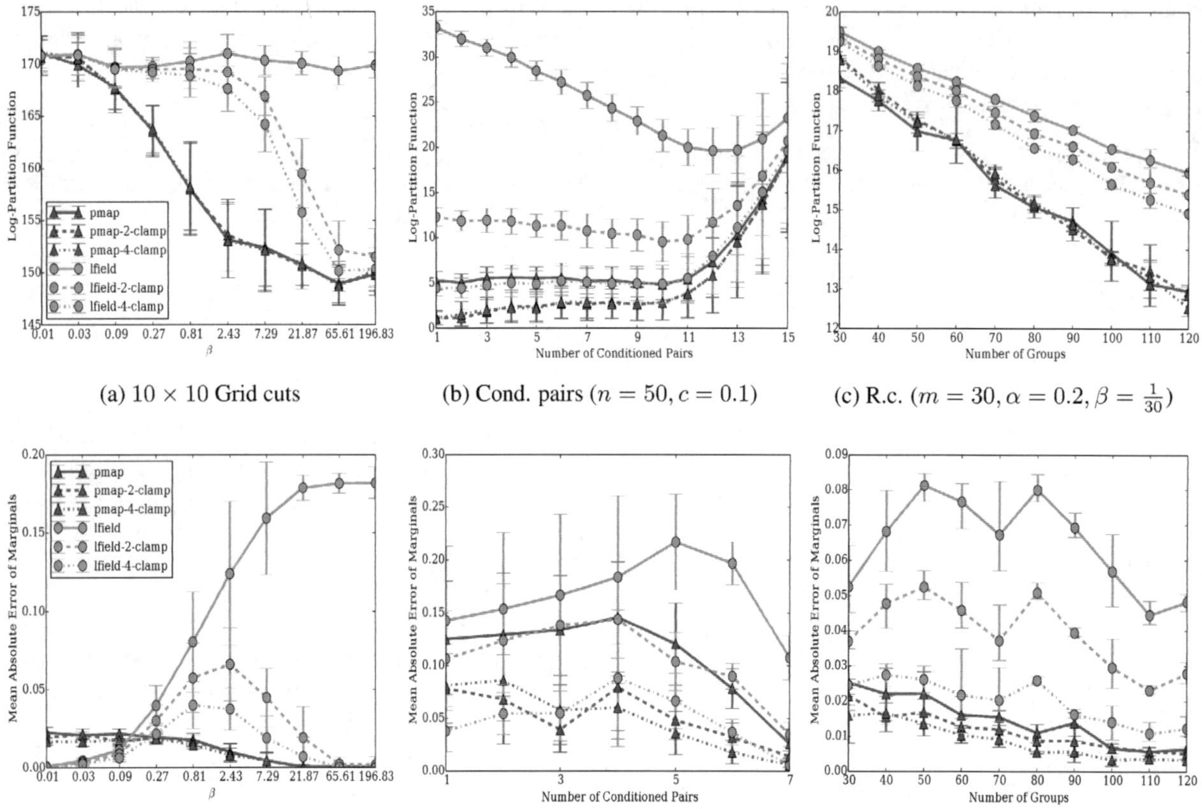

(a) 10×10 Grid cuts (b) Cond. pairs ($n = 50, c = 0.1$) (c) R.c. ($m = 30, \alpha = 0.2, \beta = \frac{1}{30}$)

(d) 4×4 Grid cuts (e) Cond. pairs ($n = 20, c = 0.1$) (f) R.c. ($m = 10, \alpha = 0.2, \beta = \frac{1}{10}$)

Figure 1: In the above plots we show the effects on the estimated partition function (first row) and marginals (second row). We can see that clamping improves the estimates on both $\mathcal{Z}$ and the marginals. Further experiments with different parameter settings can be found in Fig. 4 in appendix.

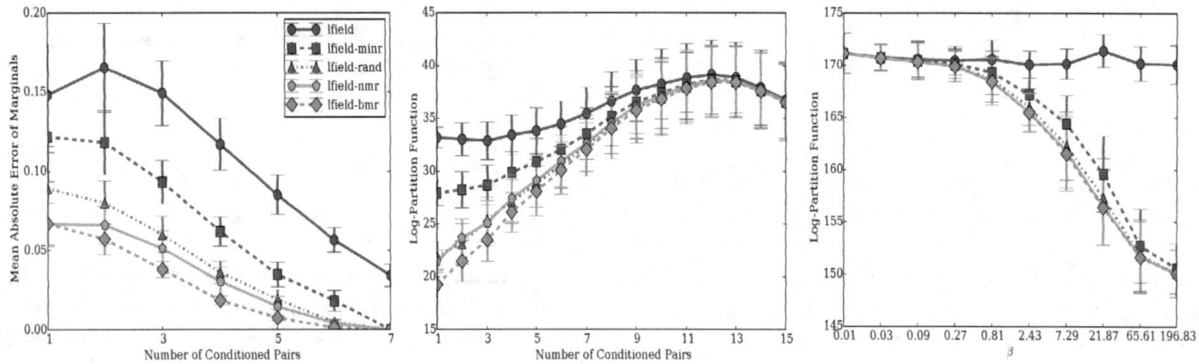

(a) Cond. pairs ($n = 20, c = 1$) (b) Cond. pairs ($n = 50, c = 1$) (c) 10×10 Grid cuts

Figure 2: Comparison of the proposed clamping strategies for L-FIELD. As evident from the plots, `bmr` consistently outperforms the other proposed alternatives.

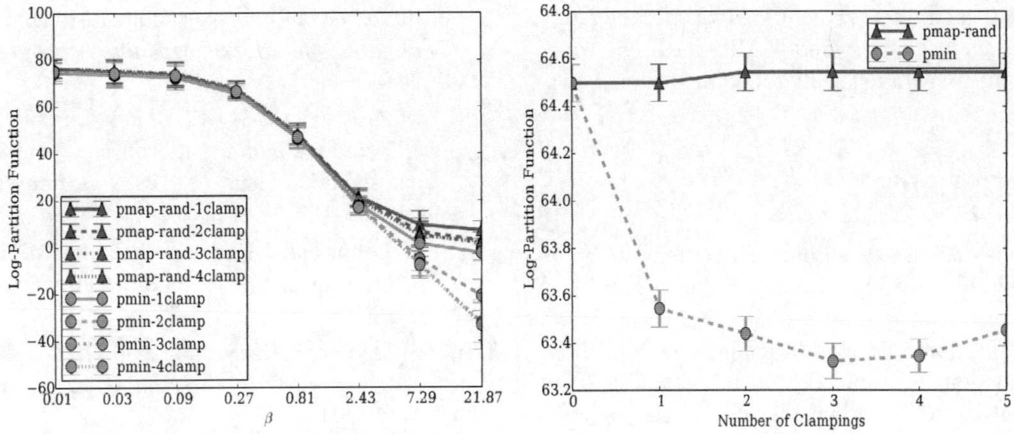

(a) 10×10 Grid cuts

(b) 10×10 G.c. ($\alpha = 0.05, \beta = 0.01$)

Figure 3: Comparison of the proposed clamping strategies for Perturb-and-MAP. The plots show that `pmin` substantially outperforms `pmap-rand`.

after 2 and 4 clamps. For (3), we test different heuristics for variable selection: `bmr` (BRANCHMAXRANGE), `nmr` (NAIVEMAXRANGE) and `rand` (random selection). We also show that Perturb-and-Min-Marginals (`pmin`) does indeed improve over choosing the variables randomly (`pmap-rand`). Finally, to show that using the interval sizes for L-FIELD does make sense, we also include the strategy that chooses variables with the smallest interval size, denoted by `minr`, which we expect to perform poorly. We used the following models, similar to the setup in [6]. As a mincut solver we used the algorithm by Boykov and Kolmogorov [28].

- *Grid cuts.* The first class of models we experiment on are grid-structured pairwise models, i.e. $P(\mathbf{x}) \propto \exp(-\sum_{\{i,j\}\in E} \beta' [\![\mathbf{x}_i \neq \mathbf{x}_j]\!] - \sum_i z_i)$, where E are the grid-structured edges. We sampled $\beta' \sim$ Unif$([0, \beta])$ and $z_i \sim$ Unif$([-1, +1])$, i.e. $P(\mathbf{x})$ is an attractive (log-supermodular) Ising model.

- *Conditioned pairs.* The model has the same functional form as before, but the graph is complete and the edge weights are generated as follows. We first sample two centers from $\mathcal{N}([3, 3], I)$ and $\mathcal{N}([-3, -3], I)$ respectively. Then, around each center we sample n points. These $2n$ points $\{\mathbf{x}_1, \mathbf{x}_2, \ldots, \mathbf{x}_{2n}\}$ are assigned to the elements, and the weight between elements i and j is set to $e^{-c\|\mathbf{x}_i - \mathbf{x}_j\|}$. Then, for $k = 1, 2, \ldots, K$, we perform inference on the posterior distribution after conditioning that k elements from the first cluster are in A and k elements from the second cluster are not contained in A,

- *Random covers.* Motivated by the P^n potentials from vision [13], we generate models with higher-order potentials as follows. We first sample k vectors $\mathbf{x}_1, \mathbf{x}_2 \ldots, \mathbf{x}_k$ of size m from $\{0, 1\}^N$ uniformly at random. Then, we use $f(\mathbf{x}) = \beta \cdot \sum_{i=1}^{k} (\frac{\|\mathbf{x}_i \wedge \mathbf{x}\|_1^\alpha}{\|\mathbf{x}_i\|_1^\alpha}) + \mathbf{z}^T\mathbf{x}$, where $\mathbf{z} \sim$ Unif$([-1, 1]^N)$, which is submodular for $\alpha \in [0, 1]$ and $\beta \geq 0$. We would like to point out that this is a higher-order model because in the i-th factor a total of $\|\mathbf{x}_i\|_1$ variables participate.

The results for different numberd of clampings are shown in Fig. 1, while the performance of the different heuristics for choosing the clamping order can be seen in Fig. 2 and Fig. 3. We can see that clamping *does* improve the estimate on the partition function, and significantly so for L-FIELD. The marginals are likewise generally improved. We can also see that the proposed `bmr` heuristic outperforms the proposed baselines. Moreover, note that if we use the reverse order (`minr`) we obtain results worse than random, thus providing more evidence towards the hypothesis that the possible improvement is related to the "variability" of the corresponding optimization variable. Furthermore, the Perturb-and-Min-Marginals heuristic outperforms random selection consistently. Finally, as one can see, Perturb-and-MAP often gives better estimate of the partition function compared to L-FIELD, but in practice L-FIELD is typically much faster than Perturb-and-MAP, hence it is interesting to compare clamping of these two methods in terms of runtime. However, we can not expect the performance of L-FIELD after clamping to exceed the performance of Perturb-and-MAP, simply because of the large performance gap between these two methods (and because every additional clamping for L-

FIELD roughly doubles the runtime). Nevertheless, we believe that there are cases where MAP queries are rather expensive such that Perturb-and-MAP is infeasible while L-FIELD still enjoys a relatively low computational complexity.

6 CONCLUSION

Perturb-and-MAP and the minimization of the Rényi infinite divergence are approximate inference techniques whose application depends only on the ability to optimize the energy function under a linear perturbation. Since this class of functions is also closed under clamping, it is a natural question to ask if these techniques can be combined without harming the obtained bounds. In this paper we have answered this question in the affirmative, and moreover provided heuristics for choosing the clamping order. Finally, in a set of experiments we have shown the benefits of clamping for these techniques.

Acknowledgements. The research was partially supported by ERC StG 307036 and a Google European PhD Fellowship. This work was done in part while Andreas Krause was visiting the Simons Institute for the Theory of Computing.

References

[1] M. Jerrum and A. Sinclair. "Polynomial-time approximation algorithms for the Ising model". *SIAM Journal on computing* 22.5 (1993), pp. 1087–1116.

[2] L. A. Goldberg and M. Jerrum. "The complexity of ferromagnetic Ising with local fields". *Combinatorics, Probability and Computing* 16.01 (2007), pp. 43–61.

[3] M. J. Wainwright and M. I. Jordan. "Graphical models, exponential families, and variational inference". *Foundations and Trends in Machine Learning* 1.1–2 (2008), pp. 1–305.

[4] G. Papandreou and A. L. Yuille. "Perturb-and-MAP random fields: Using discrete optimization to learn and sample from energy models". *ICCV*. 2011.

[5] T. Van Erven and P. Harremos. "Rényi divergence and Kullback-Leibler divergence". *IEEE Transactions on Information Theory* 60.7 (2014), pp. 3797–3820.

[6] J. Djolonga and A. Krause. "From MAP to Marginals: Variational Inference in Bayesian Submodular Models". *Neural Information Processing Systems (NIPS)*. 2014.

[7] J. Djolonga and A. Krause. "Scalable Variational Inference in Log-supermodular Models". *International Conference on Machine Learning (ICML)*. 2015.

[8] M. Grötschel, L. Lovász, and A. Schrijver. "The ellipsoid method and its consequences in combinatorial optimization". *Combinatorica* 1.2 (1981), pp. 169–197.

[9] P. Stobbe and A. Krause. "Efficient Minimization of Decomposable Submodular Functions". *NIPS*. 2010.

[10] S. Jegelka, F. Bach, and S. Sra. "Reflection methods for user-friendly submodular optimization". *NIPS*. 2013.

[11] S. Karlin and Y. Rinott. "Classes of orderings of measures and related correlation inequalities. I. Multivariate totally positive distributions". *Journal of Multivariate Analysis* 10.4 (1980), pp. 467–498.

[12] Y. Boykov, O. Veksler, and R. Zabih. "Fast approximate energy minimization via graph cuts". *Pattern Analysis and Machine Intelligence, IEEE Transactions on* 23.11 (2001), pp. 1222–1239.

[13] P. Kohli, P. H. Torr, et al. "Robust higher order potentials for enforcing label consistency". *International Journal of Computer Vision* 82.3 (2009), pp. 302–324.

[14] T. Hazan and T. S. Jaakkola. "On the Partition Function and Random Maximum A-Posteriori Perturbations". *ICML*. 2012.

[15] T. Shpakova and F. Bach. "Parameter Learning for Log-supermodular Distributions". *arXiv preprint arXiv:1608.05258* (2016).

[16] A. Weller and T. Jebara. "Clamping variables and approximate inference". *Advances in Neural Information Processing Systems*. 2014, pp. 909–917.

[17] A. Weller and J. Domke. "Clamping Improves TRW and Mean Field Approximations". *AISTATS*. 2016.

[18] D. Tarlow, K. Swersky, R. S. Zemel, and R. P. Adams. "Fast Exact Inference for Recursive Cardinality Models". *Proceedings of the Twenty-Eighth Conference Conference on Uncertainty in Artificial Intelligence*. AUAI Press. 2012.

[19] V. Vineet, J. Warrell, and P. H. Torr. "Filter-based mean-field inference for random fields with higher-order terms and product label-spaces". *International Journal of Computer Vision* 110.3 (2014), pp. 290–307.

[20] T. Minka. *Divergence measures and message passing*. Tech. rep. Microsoft Research, 2005.

[21] R. Iyer and J. Bilmes. "Polyhedral aspects of Submodularity, Convexity and Concavity". *arXiv preprint arXiv:1506.07329* (2015).

[22] E. Dahlhaus, D. S. Johnson, C. H. Papadimitriou, P. D. Seymour, and M. Yannakakis. "The complexity of multiterminal cuts". *SIAM Journal on Computing* 23.4 (1994), pp. 864–894.

[23] J. Zhang, J. Djolonga, and A. Krause. "Higher-Order Inference for Multi-class Log-supermodular Models". *International Conference on Computer Vision (ICCV)*. 2015.

[24] S. Fujishige. *Submodular functions and optimization*. Annals of Discrete Mathematics vol. 58. 2005.

[25] F. Bach. "Learning with submodular functions: a convex optimization perspective". *Foundations and Trends® in Machine Learning* 6.2-3 (2013).

[26] M. Balog, N. Tripuraneni, Z. Ghahramani, and A. Weller. "Lost Relatives of the Gumbel Trick". *arXiv preprint arXiv:1706.04161* (2017).

[27] P. Kohli and P. H. Torr. "Measuring uncertainty in graph cut solutions". *Computer Vision and Image Understanding* 112.1 (2008), pp. 30–38.

[28] Y. Boykov and V. Kolmogorov. "An experimental comparison of min-cut/max-flow algorithms for energy minimization in vision". *IEEE transactions on pattern analysis and machine intelligence* 26.9 (2004), pp. 1124–1137.

A APPENDIX

A.1 D_∞ — A TIGHTER RESULT FOR LOG-SUPERMODULAR MODELS

In the main paper, we prove that clamping always improve D_∞ for general models, and this naturally implies the same result for log-supermodular models. In that proof, we derive the fact that $A_l \geq \widehat{\mathcal{Z}}_l$. Here we provide an auxiliary proof for log-supermodular models, and the purpose of this proof is to stress a stronger result in this special case, *i.e.*, $A_l = \widehat{\mathcal{Z}}_l$. We consider multi-label log-supermodular models for D_∞. In this case, one relaxation of D_∞ reads as following [23],

$$\log \widehat{\mathcal{Z}} = \min_{\mathbf{s} \in B(f)} \sum_{i=1}^{N} \log \sum_{j=1}^{L} \exp(-s_{i,j}),$$

where $B(f) = \{\mathbf{s} \mid \forall x \in \{0,1\}^{NL} : \mathbf{x}^T\mathbf{s} \leq f(x); \mathbf{1}^T\mathbf{s} = f(\mathbf{1})\}$ is the well-known base polytope.

$$\begin{aligned} \mathcal{Z}(f) &= \sum_{\mathbf{x}\in\mathcal{X}} \exp(-f(\mathbf{x})) \\ &= \sum_{l=1}^{L} \sum_{\mathbf{x}\in\mathcal{X}, \mathbf{x}_{k,l}=1} \exp(-f(\mathbf{x})) \\ &= \sum_{l=1}^{L} \underbrace{\sum_{\mathbf{x}\in\mathcal{X}_{-k}} \exp(-f(\mathbf{x}+\mathbf{e}_{k,l}))}_{\mathcal{Z}(f_{+k,l})} \end{aligned} \quad (7)$$

We can obtain the upper bound of $\mathcal{Z}(f_{+k,l})$, denoted by $\widehat{\mathcal{Z}}_l$, using L-FIELD. Because submodular functions are closed under clamping, i.e. f is submodular so are $f_{+k,l}$ (see e.g. [24])[2]. Obviously $\mathcal{Z}(f) = \sum_l \mathcal{Z}(f_{+k,l}) \leq \sum_l \widehat{\mathcal{Z}}_l$, hence $\sum_l \widehat{\mathcal{Z}}_l$ is an upper bound for the partition function.

Theorem A.1. *For multi-label log-supermodular models, i.e., when f is submodular, we have $\sum_l \widehat{\mathcal{Z}}_l \leq \widehat{\mathcal{Z}}$, where k is of arbitrary choice.*

Following the same path, we first decompose the objective used in the optimization problem for solving $\widehat{\mathcal{Z}}$ as follows:

$$\begin{aligned} \exp\Big(\sum_{i=1}^{N} \log \sum_{l=1}^{L} e^{-s_{i,l}}\Big) &= \prod_{i=1}^{N}\Big(\sum_{l=1}^{L} e^{-s_{i,l}}\Big) \\ &= \sum_{l=1}^{L}\Big(e^{-s_{k,l}} \cdot \prod_{i\neq k}\big(\sum_{j=1}^{L} e^{-s_{i,j}}\big)\Big) \end{aligned} \quad (8)$$

[2]Typically $f_{+k,l}$ is defined as $f_{+k,l}(\mathbf{x}) = f(\mathbf{x}+\mathbf{e}_{k,l}) - f(\mathbf{e}_{k,l})$ to make sure that $f_{+k,l}$ is normalized as $f_{+k,l}(\mathbf{0}) = 0$, but this is of course w.l.o.g.

Next we have $A_l = \min_{s\in B(f)} e^{-s_{k,l}} \cdot \prod_{i\neq k}(\sum_{j=1}^{L} e^{-s_{i,j}})$, then it trivially follows that

$$\begin{aligned} \widehat{\mathcal{Z}} &= \min_{s\in B(f)} \sum_{l=1}^{L}\Big(e^{-s_{k,l}} \cdot \prod_{i\neq k}\big(\sum_{j=1}^{L} e^{-s_{i,j}}\big)\Big) \\ &\geq \sum_{l=1}^{L} \min_{s\in B(f)} \Big(e^{-s_{k,l}} \cdot \prod_{i\neq k}\big(\sum_{j=1}^{L} e^{-s_{i,j}}\big)\Big) \\ &= \sum_{l} A_l \end{aligned} \quad (9)$$

The following lemma says that $\forall l, A_l = \widehat{\mathcal{Z}}_l$, hence $\widehat{\mathcal{Z}} \geq \sum_l A_l = \sum_l \widehat{\mathcal{Z}}_l$. Note this is a stronger result compared to the proof for the general case.

Lemma A.2. $A_l = \widehat{\mathcal{Z}}_l$.

Proof. This is equivalent to proving that $\log A_l = \log \widehat{\mathcal{Z}}_l$. Later we will show that $\log A_l$, the minimum of $-s_{k,l} + \sum_{i\neq k} \log \sum_{j=1}^{L}(1+e^{-s_{i,j}})$ for $s \in B(f)$, can still be achieved if we fix $s_{k,l} = f(\mathbf{e}_{k,l})$. If this is true, we can replace $s_{k,l}$ with $f(\mathbf{e}_{k,l})$ in $B(f)$ and get the following explicit form.

$$\begin{cases} \forall \mathbf{x} \in \{0,1\}^{NL}, \mathbf{x}_{k,l} = 0, \mathbf{x}^T s + f(\mathbf{e}_{k,l}) \leq f(\mathbf{x}+\mathbf{e}_{k,l}) \\ \forall \mathbf{x} \in \{0,1\}^{NL}, \mathbf{x}_{k,l} = 0, \mathbf{x}^T s \leq f(\mathbf{x}) \\ (\mathbf{1}-\mathbf{e}_{k,l})^T s + f(\mathbf{e}_{k,l}) = f(\mathbf{1}) \end{cases}$$

Notice that the second constraint is redundant, because the first inequality requires $\forall \mathbf{x} \in \{0,1\}^N, \mathbf{x}_{k,l} = 0, \mathbf{x}^T s \leq f(\mathbf{x}+\mathbf{e}_{k,l}) - f(\mathbf{e}_{k,l})$ and $f(\mathbf{x}+\mathbf{e}_{k,l}) - f(\mathbf{e}_{k,l}) \leq f(\mathbf{x})$ by submodularity, and for the same reason the last equality fulfills the second inequality when $\mathbf{x} = \mathbf{1} - \mathbf{e}_{k,l}$. Thus we can remove the second constraint in above inequality system.

Now we write the explicit form of $B(f_{+k,l})$ as follows.

$$\begin{cases} \forall \mathbf{x} \in \{0,1\}^{NL}, \mathbf{x}_{v_{k,l}} = 0, \mathbf{x}^T s \leq f(\mathbf{x}+\mathbf{e}_{k,l}) - f(\mathbf{e}^{v_{k,l}}) \\ (\mathbf{1}-\mathbf{e}_{k,l})^T s = f(\mathbf{1}) - f(\mathbf{e}_{k,l}) \end{cases}$$

Observe that this is the same as $B(f) \cap \{s \mid s_{k,l} = f(\mathbf{e}_{k,l})\}$. Hence the feasible regions of two minimization problem are exactly the same. Furthermore, since we fix $s_{k,l} = f(\mathbf{e}_{k,l})$, the objective of $\log A_l$ changes into $-f(\mathbf{e}_{k,l}) + \sum_{i\neq k} \log \sum_{j=1}^{L}(1+e^{-s_{i,j}})$, which is also the same as the objective of $\widehat{\mathcal{Z}}_l$. Therefore, $\log A_l = \log \widehat{\mathcal{Z}}_l$, which implies $A_l = \widehat{\mathcal{Z}}_l$. □

Lemma A.3. *By adding $s_{k,l} = f(\mathbf{e}_{k,l})$ to the constraint set, the optimal value of the optimization problem $\min_{s\in B(f)} -s_{k,l} + \sum_{i\neq k} \log \sum_{j=1}^{L}(1+e^{-s_{i,j}})$ does not change.*

Proof. First we define $g(s) = \sum_{i \neq k} \log \sum_{j=1}^{L} (1 + e^{-s_{i,j}}) - s_{k,l}$. Then we have

$$\begin{cases} \frac{\partial g}{\partial s_{k,l}} = -1 \\ \frac{\partial g}{\partial s_{i,j}} = \frac{-\exp(-s_{i,j})}{\sum_{j'=1}^{L}(1+\exp(-s_{i,j'}))} > -1, \forall v_{i,j} \in V \setminus \{v_{k,l}\} \end{cases}$$

Hence it is easy to see exchange $\Delta \geq 0$ between $s_{i,j}$ and $s_{k,l}$, i.e. $s'_{k,l} = s_{k,l} + \Delta, s'_{i,j} = s_{i,j} - \Delta$, can only decrease the objective. Therefore, given optimal solution s^*, we can get a solution at least as good as s^* by setting $s'_{k,l} = s^*_{k,l} + \Delta$ and $s'_{i,j} = s^*_{i,j} - \Delta$ for arbitrary $(i,j) \neq (k,l)$. We can exploit this property to change $s^*_{k,l}$ into $f(\mathbf{e}_{k,l})$, but we need to guarantee that every exchange results in a feasible solution. Hence we need to deal with exchange capacity $\hat{c}(s; (k,l), e') = \min\{f(\mathbf{1}_A) - \mathbf{1}_A^T \mathbf{s}, \forall A \supseteq (k,l), e' \notin A\}$ (e' denotes the element-label pair to exchange with (k,l), $\mathbf{1}_A$ is the indicator vector for set A). Let $S_{e'} \cup \{(k,l)\}$ be the set that achieves $\hat{c}(s; (k,l), e')$, we know $e' \notin S_{e'} \cup \{(k,l)\}$. We propose the following procedure *exchange*, and we will prove later this algorithm will make $s'_{k,l} = f(\mathbf{e}_{k,l})$. Since we already proved that exchange always results in better solution, this will finish the proof.

procedure *exchange*():
Initiate $U = [N] \times [L] \setminus \{(k,l)\}, s = s^*$;
While $U \neq \emptyset$:
    Arbitrarily pick $e' \in U$;
    $s_{k,l} \leftarrow s_{k,l} + \hat{c}(s; (k,l), e')$;
    $s_{e'} \leftarrow s_{e'} - \hat{c}(s; (k,l), e')$;
    $U = U \cap S_{e'}$
end;

We first show that after one exchange with e' the new modular function s' is tight at $S_{e'} \cup \{(k,l)\}$, *i.e.*, $\mathbf{1}^T_{S_{e'} \cup \{(k,l)\}} s' = f(\mathbf{1}_{S_{e'} \cup \{(k,l)\}})$.

$$\begin{aligned} s'_{k,l} &= s_{k,l} + \hat{c}(s; (k,l), e') \\ &= s_{k,l} + f(\mathbf{1}_{S_{e'} \cup \{(k,l)\}}) - \mathbf{1}^T_{S_{e'} \cup \{(k,l)\}} s \\ &= s_{k,l} + f(\mathbf{1}_{S_{e'} \cup \{(k,l)\}}) - \mathbf{1}^T_{S_{e'}} s - s_{k,l} \qquad (10) \\ &= f(\mathbf{1}_{S_{e'} \cup \{(k,l)\}}) - \mathbf{1}^T_{S_{e'}} s \\ \Rightarrow & \mathbf{1}^T_{S_{e'} \cup \{(k,l)\}} s' = f(\mathbf{1}_{S_{e'} \cup \{(k,l)\}}) \end{aligned}$$

Because s' is tight at $S_{e'} \cup \{(k,l)\}$, the element picked next round must be the element in $S_{e'}$ such that the next exchange also results in a feasible solution, otherwise the next exchange will break the tight upper bound for s' at $S_{e'} \cup \{(k,l)\}$ since we only increase $s'_{k,l}$. This is why we let $U = U \cap S_{e'}$ in the algorithm. It is also obvious that once s' is tight at $S_{e'} \cup \{(k,l)\}$, it will always be tight at $S_{e'} \cup \{(k,l)\}$. Moreover, notice that $e' \notin S_{e'}$ but $e' \in U$, hence the intersection operation always strictly decreases the size of U in each round. Therefore, algorithm will terminate and U will definitely turn into $\emptyset$. The final U is $\cap_{e'} S_{e'}$, hence $\cap_{e'}(S_{e'} \cup \{(k,l)\}) = (\cap_{e'} S_{e'}) \cup \{(k,l)\} = \{(k,l)\}$. Since the final s' is tight at each $S_{e'} \cup \{(k,l)\}$ and it is well-known result that the intersection of tight sets is also tight. Therefore the final s' is tight at $\{(k,l)\}$, i.e. $s'_{k,l} = f(\mathbf{e}_{k,l})$, which completes the proof. □

A.2 THE LOWER BOUND FOR BINARY LOG-SUPERMODULAR MODELS: CLAMPING ALWAYS HELPS

Moreover, in [6], the authors also use the properties of submodular functions to obtain lower bounds on $\mathcal{Z}$ for binary log-supermodular models. Likewise, clamping can only improve the lower bounds.

Since we are only concerned with binary models, we change to the set notation for energy function to be in line with [6]. We denote the energy function by $F : 2^V \to \mathbb{R}^n$, where $V = \{1, \cdots, N\}$ is the ground set of all the elements. We notate two operations that preserve submodularity, (a) **contraction**: $F_X(A) = F(X \cup A) - F(X), A \subseteq V \setminus X$, (b) **restriction**: $F^X(A) = F(A), A \subseteq X$.

From the proof of Lemma 4 in [6], we know that by optimizing over bar supergradient, we can derive a lower bound of the log-partition function as follows,

$$\begin{aligned} \log \widehat{\mathcal{Z}}_L(F) = \max_{X \in V} -F(X) + \sum_{j \in X} \log(1 + e^{F(V) - F(V \setminus \{j\})}) \\ + \sum_{j \notin X} \log(1 + e^{-F(\{j\})}). \end{aligned} \tag{11}$$

After clamping i, we also apply this method to get the lower bound for $\mathcal{Z}(F_{\{i\}})$ and $\mathcal{Z}(F^{V \setminus \{i\}})$, denote them by $\widehat{\mathcal{Z}}_L(F_{\{i\}})$ and $\widehat{\mathcal{Z}}_L(F^{V \setminus \{i\}})$ respectively. It is obvious that $\mathcal{Z}(F) = e^{-F(\{i\})} \cdot \mathcal{Z}(F_{\{i\}}) + \mathcal{Z}(F^{V \setminus \{i\}}) \geq e^{-F(\{i\})} \cdot \widehat{\mathcal{Z}}_L(F_{\{i\}}) + \widehat{\mathcal{Z}}_L(F^{V \setminus \{i\}})$, so if $\widehat{\mathcal{Z}}_L(F) \leq e^{-F(\{i\})} \cdot \widehat{\mathcal{Z}}_L(F_{\{i\}}) + \widehat{\mathcal{Z}}_L(F^{V \setminus \{i\}})$, then $e^{-F(\{i\})} \cdot \widehat{\mathcal{Z}}_L(F_{\{i\}}) + \widehat{\mathcal{Z}}_L(F^{V \setminus \{i\}})$ is a better lower bound.

Theorem A.4. $\widehat{\mathcal{Z}}_L(F) \leq e^{-F(\{i\})} \cdot \widehat{\mathcal{Z}}_L(F_{\{i\}}) + \widehat{\mathcal{Z}}_L(F^{V \setminus \{i\}})$.

Proof. We take the exponent of $\log \widehat{\mathcal{Z}}_L(F)$, then $\widehat{\mathcal{Z}}_L(F) = \max_{X \in V} e^{-F(X)} \prod_{j \in X}(1 + e^{F(V) - F(V \setminus \{j\})}) \prod_{j \notin X}(1 + e^{-F(\{j\})})$. We split it into two cases. First, if $i \in X^*$, where X^* is the optimal element set for bar supergradient, we know

$$\begin{aligned}
\widehat{\mathcal{Z}}_L(F) &= \max_{X\in V} e^{-F(X)} \prod_{j\in X\setminus\{i\}} (1+e^{F(V)-F(V\setminus\{j\})}) \cdot \\
&(1+e^{F(V)-F(V\setminus\{i\})}) \prod_{j\notin X}(1+e^{-F(\{j\})}) \\
&= \max_{X\in V} e^{-F(X)} \prod_{j\in X\setminus\{i\}} (1+e^{F(V)-F(V\setminus\{j\})}) \cdot \\
&\prod_{j\notin X}(1+e^{-F(\{j\})}) + e^{F(V)-F(V\setminus\{i\})-F(X)} \cdot \\
&\prod_{j\in X\setminus\{i\}} (1+e^{F(V)-F(V\setminus\{j\})}) \prod_{j\notin X}(1+e^{-F(\{j\})}) \\
&:= \max_{X\in V} A_1 + B_1.
\end{aligned} \tag{12}$$

Otherwise, if $i \notin X^*$

$$\begin{aligned}
\widehat{\mathcal{Z}}_L(F) &= \max_{X\in V\setminus\{i\}} e^{-F(X)} \prod_{j\in X}(1+e^{F(V)-F(V\setminus\{j\})}) \cdot \\
&\prod_{j\notin X\cup\{i\}} (1+e^{-F(\{j\})})(1+e^{-F(\{i\})}) \\
&= \max_{X\in V\setminus\{i\}} e^{-F(X)} \prod_{j\in X}(1+e^{F(V)-F(V\setminus\{j\})}) \cdot \\
&\prod_{j\notin X\cup\{i\}} (1+e^{-F(\{j\})}) + e^{-F(X)-F(\{i\})} \cdot \\
&\prod_{j\in X}(1+e^{F(V)-F(V\setminus\{j\})}) \prod_{j\notin X\cup\{i\}} (1+e^{-F(\{j\})}) \\
&:= A_2 + B_2.
\end{aligned} \tag{13}$$

Since $\widehat{\mathcal{Z}}_L(F_{\{i\}}) = \max_{X\in V\setminus\{i\}} e^{F(\{i\})-F(X\cup\{i\})} \prod_{j\in X}(1+e^{F(V)-F(V\setminus\{j\})}) \prod_{j\notin X}(1+e^{-F(\{i,j\})+F(\{i\})})$ and $\widehat{\mathcal{Z}}_L(F^{V\setminus\{i\}}) = \max_{X\in V\setminus\{i\}} e^{-F(X)} \prod_{j\in X}(1+e^{F(V\setminus\{i\})-F(V\setminus\{i,j\})}) \prod_{j\notin X}(1+e^{-F(\{j\})})$, we explicitly write the lower bound after clamping as follows.

$$\begin{aligned}
&e^{-F(\{i\})}\widehat{\mathcal{Z}}_L(F_{\{i\}}) + \widehat{\mathcal{Z}}_L(F^{V\setminus\{i\}}) \\
&= \max_{X\in V\setminus\{i\}} e^{-F(X\cup\{i\})} \prod_{j\in X}(1+e^{F(V)-F(V\setminus\{j\})}) \cdot \\
&\prod_{j\notin X}(1+e^{F(\{i\})-F(\{i,j\})}) + \max_{X\in V\setminus\{i\}} e^{-F(X)} \cdot \\
&\prod_{j\in X}(1+e^{F(V\setminus\{i\})-F(V\setminus\{i,j\})}) \prod_{j\notin X}(1+e^{-F(\{j\})}) \\
&:= A + B
\end{aligned} \tag{14}$$

We claim that if $i \in X^*$, $A \geq A_1, B \geq B_1$, hence $A+B \geq A_1+B_1$, and if $i \notin X^*$, $B \geq A_2, A \geq B_2$, hence $A+B \geq A_2+B_2$. If this is true, then the expected result follows.

Let $X = X^* \setminus \{i\}$ when $i \in X^*$, then $A_1 = e^{-F(X\cup\{i\})} \prod_{j\in X}(1+e^{F(V)-F(V\setminus\{j\})}) \prod_{j\notin X\cup\{i\}}(1+e^{-F(\{j\})})$. We compare A_1 with $A = e^{-F(X\cup\{i\})} \prod_{j\in X}(1+e^{F(V)-F(V\setminus\{j\})}) \prod_{j\notin X}(1+e^{F(\{i\})-F(\{i,j\})})$. Since $F(\{i\}) - F(\{i,j\}) \geq -F(\{j\})$ by diminishing return, it is easy to see $A \geq A_1$. On the other hand, $B_1 = e^{F(V)-F(V\setminus\{i\})-F(X\cup\{i\})} \prod_{j\in X}(1+e^{F(V)-F(V\setminus\{j\})}) \prod_{j\notin X\cup\{i\}}(1+e^{-F(\{j\})})$. We compare this with $B = e^{-F(X)} \prod_{j\in X}(1+e^{F(V\setminus\{i\})-F(V\setminus\{i,j\})}) \prod_{j\notin X}(1+e^{-F(\{j\})})$. Since $F(V) - F(V\setminus\{i\}) - F(X\cup\{i\}) \leq -F(X)$ and $F(V) - F(V\setminus\{j\}) \leq F(V\setminus\{i\}) - F(V\setminus\{i,j\})$ by diminishing return, it follows that $B \geq B_1$.

Let $X = X^*$ when $i \notin X^*$, then $B_2 = e^{-F(X)-F(\{i\})} \prod_{j\in X}(1+e^{F(V)-F(V\setminus\{j\})}) \prod_{j\notin X\cup\{i\}}(1+e^{-F(\{j\})})$. We compare this with A. Since $-F(X) - F(\{i\}) \leq -F(X\cup\{i\})$ and $-F(\{j\}) \leq F(\{i\}) - F(\{i,j\})$, $A \geq B_2$ follows. Moreover, $A_2 = e^{-F(X)} \prod_{j\in X}(1+e^{F(V)-F(V\setminus\{j\})}) \prod_{j\notin X\cup\{i\}}(1+e^{-F(\{j\})})$, hence $B \geq A_2$ follows because $F(V) - F(V\setminus\{j\}) \leq F(V\setminus\{i\}) - F(V\setminus\{i,j\})$. This completes the proof. ∎

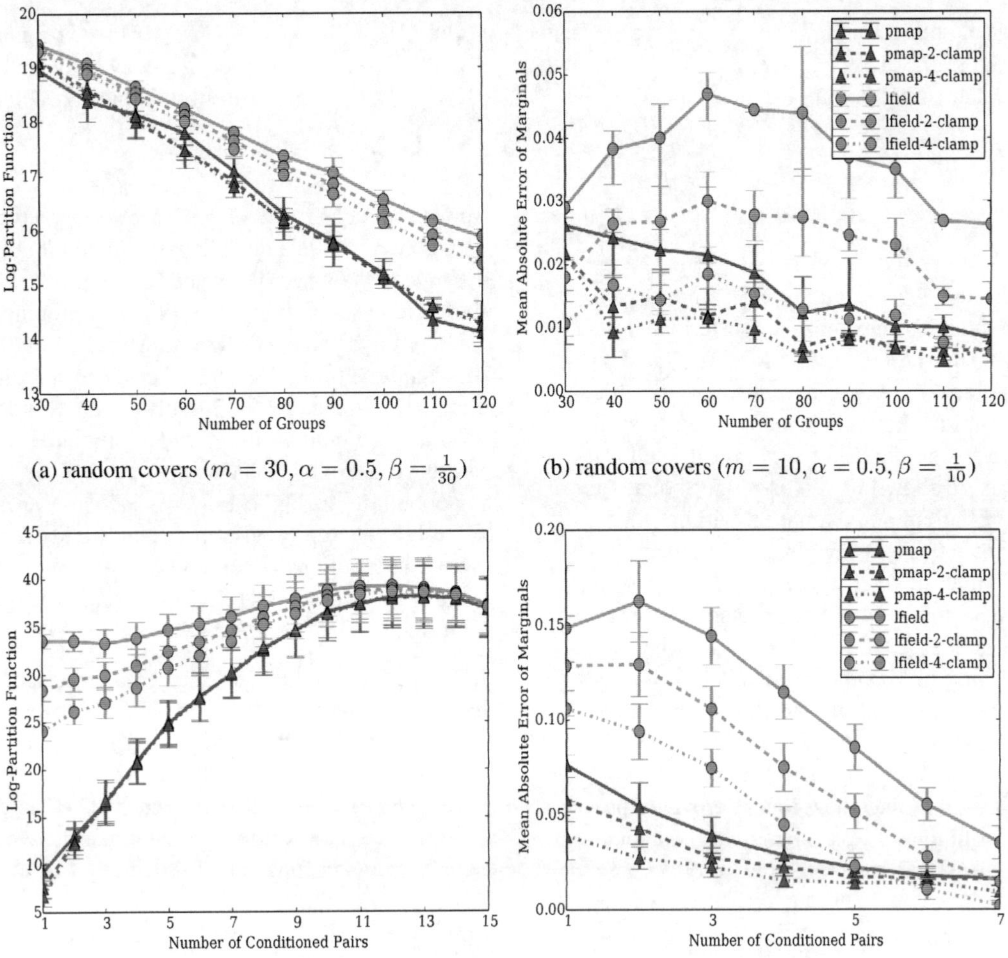

(a) random covers ($m = 30, \alpha = 0.5, \beta = \frac{1}{30}$)

(b) random covers ($m = 10, \alpha = 0.5, \beta = \frac{1}{10}$)

(c) conditioned pairs ($n = 50, c = 1$)

(d) conditioned pairs ($n = 20, c = 1$)

Figure 4: Additional experiments on random covers and conditioned pairs with different parameters. Still we can see that clamping improves the estimates on both $\mathcal{Z}$ and the marginals.

Approximation Complexity of Maximum A Posteriori Inference in Sum-Product Networks

Diarmaid Conaty
Queen's University Belfast
Belfast, United Kingdom

Denis D. Mauá
Universidade de São Paulo
São Paulo, Brazil

Cassio P. de Campos
Queen's University Belfast
Belfast, United Kingdom

Abstract

We discuss the computational complexity of approximating maximum a posteriori inference in sum-product networks. We first show NP-hardness in trees of height two by a reduction from maximum independent set; this implies non-approximability within a sublinear factor. We show that this is a tight bound, as we can find an approximation within a linear factor in networks of height two. We then show that, in trees of height three, it is NP-hard to approximate the problem within a factor $2^{f(n)}$ for any sublinear function f of the size of the input n. Again, this bound is tight, as we prove that the usual max-product algorithm finds (in any network) approximations within factor $2^{c \cdot n}$ for some constant $c < 1$. Last, we present a simple algorithm, and show that it provably produces solutions at least as good as, and potentially much better than, the max-product algorithm. We empirically analyze the proposed algorithm against max-product using synthetic and real-world data.

1 INTRODUCTION

Finding the mode of a probability distribution is a key step of many solutions to problems in artificial intelligence such as image segmentation (Geman and Geman, 1984), 3D image reconstruction (Boykov et al., 1998), natural language processing (Koo et al., 2010), speech recognition (Peharz et al., 2014), sentiment analysis (Zirn et al., 2011), protein design (Szeliski et al., 2008) and multicomponent fault diagnosis (Steinder and Sethi, 2004), to name but a few. This problem is often called (full) maximum a posteriori (MAP) inference, or most likely explanation (MPE).

Sum-Product Networks (SPNs) are a relatively new class of graphical models that allow marginal inference in linear time in their size (Poon and Domingos, 2011). This is therefore in sharp difference with other graphical models such as Bayesian networks and Markov Random Fields that require #P-hard effort to produce marginal inferences (Darwiche, 2009). Intuitively, an SPN encodes an arithmetic circuit whose evaluation produces a marginal inference (Darwiche, 2003). SPNs have received increasing popularity in applications of machine learning due to their ability to represent complex and highly multidimensional distributions (Poon and Domingos, 2011; Amer, 2012; Peharz et al., 2014; Cheng et al., 2014; Nath and Domingos, 2016; Amer and Todorovic, 2016).

In his PhD thesis, Peharz showed a direct proof of NP-hardness of MAP in SPNs by a reduction from maximum satisfiability; his proof however is not correct as it encodes clauses as products (Peharz, 2015, Theorem 5.3).[1] Later, Peharz et al. (2016) noted that NP-hardness can be proved by transforming a Bayesian network with a naive Bayes structure into a distribution-equivalent SPN of height two (this is done by adding a sum node to represent the latent root variable and its marginal distribution, and product nodes as children to represent the conditional distributions). As MAP inference in the former is NP-hard (de Campos, 2011), the result follows.

In this paper, we show a direct proof of NP-hardness of MAP inference by a reduction from maximum independent set, the problem of deciding whether there is a subset of vertices of a certain size in an undirected graph such that no two vertices in the set are connected. This new proof is quite simple, and (as with the reduction from naive Bayesian networks) uses a sum-product network of height two. An advantage of the new proof is that, as a corollary, we obtain the non-approximability of MAP inference within a sublinear factor in networks of height two. This is a tight bound, as we show that there

[1]The proof has been recently rectified in an Erratum note.

HEIGHT	LOWER BOUND	UPPER BOUND
1	1	1
2	$(m-1)^{\varepsilon}$	$m-1$
≥ 3	$2^{s^{\varepsilon}}$	2^{s}

Table 1: Lower and upper bounds on the approximation threshold for a polynomial-time algorithm: s denotes the size of the instance, m is the number of internal nodes, ε is a nonnegative number less than 1.

is a polynomial-time algorithm that produces approximations within a linear factor in networks of height two. For networks of height three or more we prove that it is NP-hard to approximate the problem within any factor $2^{f(n)}$ for any sublinear function f of the input size n, even if the SPN is a tree. This bound is tight, as we show that the usual max-product algorithm by Poon and Domingos (2011), which replaces sums with maximizations, finds an approximation within a factor $2^{c \cdot n}$ for some constant $c < 1$. Table 1 summarizes these results. As far as we are concerned, these are the first results about the complexity of approximating MAP in SPNs.

We also show that a simple modification to the max-product algorithm leads to an algorithm that produces solutions which are never worse and potentially significantly better than the solutions produced by max-product. We compare the performance of the proposed algorithm against max-product in several structured prediction tasks using both synthetic networks and SPNs learned from real-world data. The synthetic networks encode instances of maximum independent set problems. The purpose of these networks is to evaluate the quality of solutions produced by both algorithms on shallow SPNs which (possibly) encode hard to approximate MAP problems. Deeper networks are learned from UCI datasets using the LEARNSPN algorithm by Gens and Domingos (2013). The purpose of these experiments is to assess the relative quality of the algorithms on SPNs from realistic datasets, and their sensitivity to evidence. The empirical results show that the proposed algorithm often finds significantly better solutions than max-product does, but that this improvement is less pronounced in networks learned from real data. We expect these results to foster research in new approximation algorithms for MAP in SPNs.

Before presenting the complexity results in Section 3, we first review the definition of sum-product networks, and comment on a few selected results from the literature in Section 2. The experiments with the proposed modified algorithm and max-product appear in Section 4. We conclude the paper with a review of the main results in Section 5.

2 SUM-PRODUCT NETWORKS

We use capital letters without subscripts to denote random vectors (e.g. X), and capital letters with subscripts to denote random variables (e.g., X_1). If X is a random vector, we call the set $\mathcal{X}$ composed of the random variables X_i in X its *scope*. The scope of a function of a random vector is the scope of the respective random vector. In this work, we constrain our discussion to random variables with finite domains.

Poon and Domingos (2011) originally defined SPNs as multilinear functions of indicator variables that allow for space and time efficient representation and marginal inference. In its original definition SPNs were not constrained to represent valid distributions; this was achieved by imposing properties of consistency and completeness. This definition more closely resembles Darwiche's arithmetic circuits which represent the *network polynomial* of a Bayesian network (Darwiche, 2003), and also allow inference in the size of the circuit.

Later, Gens and Domingos (2013) re-stated SPNs as complex mixture distributions as follows.

- Any univariate distribution is an SPN.
- Any weighted sum of SPNs with the same scope and nonnegative weights is an SPN.
- Any product of SPNs with disjoint scopes is an SPN.

This alternative definition (called generalized SPNs by Peharz (2015)) implies *decomposability*, a stricter requirement than consistency. Peharz et al. (2015) showed that any consistent SPN over discrete random variables can be transformed in an equivalent decomposable SPN with a polynomial increase in size, and that weighted sums can be restricted to the probability simplex without loss of expressivity. Hence, we assume in the following that SPNs are *normalized*: the weights of a weighted sum of SPNs add up to one. This implies that SPNs specify (normalized) distributions. A similar result was obtained by Zhao et al. (2015). We note that the base of the inductive definition can also be extended to accommodate any class of tractable distributions (e.g., Chow-Liu trees) (Rooshenas and Lowd, 2014; Vergari et al., 2015). For the purposes of this work, however, it suffices to consider only univariate distributions.

An SPN is usually represented graphically as a weighted rooted graph where each internal node is associated with an operation $+$ or $\times$, and leaves are associated with variables and distributions. The arcs from a sum node to its children are weighted according to the corresponding convex combinations. The remaining arcs have implicitly weight 1. The height of an SPN is defined as the

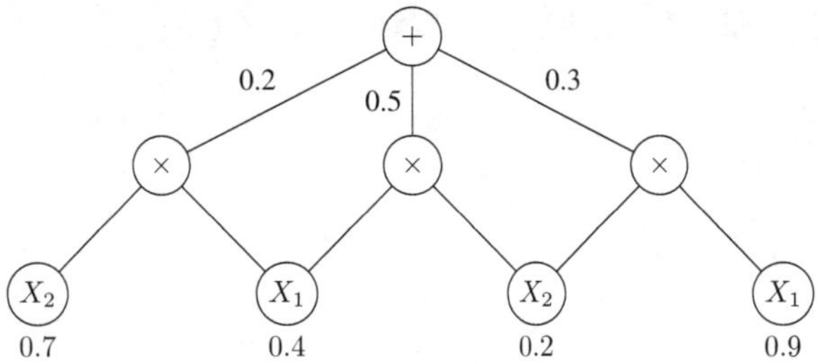

Figure 1: A sum-product network over binary variables X_1 and X_2. Only the probabilities $\mathbb{P}(X_i = 1)$ are shown.

maximum distance, counted as the number of arcs, from the root to a leaf of its graphical representation. Figure 1 shows an example of an SPN with scope $\{X_1, X_2\}$ and height two. Unit weights are omitted in the figure. Note that by definition every node represents an SPN (hence a distribution) on its own; we refer to nodes and their corresponding SPNs interchangeably.

Consider an SPN $S(X)$ over a random vector $X = (X_1, \ldots, X_n)$. The value of S at a point $x = (x_1, \ldots, x_n)$ in its domain is denoted by $S(x)$ and defined recursively as follows. The value of a leaf node is the value of its corresponding distribution at the point obtained by projecting x onto the scope of the node. The value of a product node is the product of the values of its children at x. Finally, the value of a sum node is the weighted average of its children's values at x. For example, the value of the SPN $S(X_1, X_2)$ in Figure 1 at the point $(1, 0)$ is $S(1,0) = 0.2 \cdot 0.3 \cdot 0.4 + 0.5 \cdot 0.4 \cdot 0.8 + 0.3 \cdot 0.8 \cdot 0.9 = 0.4$. Note that since we assumed SPNs to be normalized, we have that $\sum_x S(x) = 1$.

Let $\mathcal{E} \subseteq \{1, \ldots, n\}$ and consider a random vector $X_{\mathcal{E}}$ with scope $\{X_i : i \in \mathcal{E}\}$, and an assignment $e = \{X_i = e_i : i \in \mathcal{E}\}$. We write $x \sim e$ to denote a value of X consistent with e (i.e., the projection of x on $\mathcal{E}$ is e). Given an SPN $S(X)$ representing a distribution $\mathbb{P}(X)$, we denote the marginal probability $\mathbb{P}(e) = \sum_{x \sim e} S(x)$ by $S(e)$. This value can be computed by first marginalizing the variables $\{X_j : j \notin \mathcal{E}\}$ from every (distribution in a) leaf and then propagating values as before. Thus marginal probabilities can be computed in time linear in the network size (assuming that univariate distributions are represented as tables). The marginal probability $\mathbb{P}(X_2 = 0) = 0.7$ induced by the SPN in Figure 1 can be obtained by first marginalizing leaves without $\{X_2\}$ (thus producing the value 1 at the respective leaves), and then propagating values as before.

In this work, we are interested in the following computational problem with SPNs:

Definition 1 (Functional MAP inference problem). *Given an SPN S specified with rational weights and an assignment e, find x^* such that $S(x^*) = \max_{x \sim e} S(x)$.*

A more general version of the problem would be to allow some of the variables to be summed out, while others are maximized. However, the marginalization (i.e., summing out) of variables can performed in polynomial time as a preprocessing step, the result of which is a MAP problem as stated above. We stick with the above definition for simplicity (bearing in mind that complexity is not changed).

To prove NP-completeness, we use the decision variant of the problem:

Definition 2 (Decision MAP inference problem). *Given an SPN S specified with rational weights, an assignment e and a rational γ, decide whether* $\max_{x \sim e} S(x) \geq \gamma$.

We denote both problems by MAP, as the distinction to which particular (functional or decision) version we refer should be clear from context. Clearly, NP-completeness of the decision version establishes NP-hardness of the functional version. Also, approximation complexity always refers to the functional version.

The support of an SPN S is the set of configurations of its domain with positive values: $\text{supp}(S) = \{x : S(x) > 0\}$. An SPN is *selective* if for every sub-SPN T corresponding to a sum node in S it follows that the supports of any two children are disjoint. Peharz et al. (2016) recently showed that MAP is tractable in selective SPNs.

Here, we discuss the complexity of (approximately) solving MAP in general SPNs. We assume that instances of the MAP problem are represented as bitstrings $\langle S, e \rangle$ using a reasonable encoding; for instance, weights and probabilities are rational values represented by two integers in binary notation, and graphs are represented by (a binary encoding of their) adjacency lists.

3 COMPLEXITY RESULTS

As we show in this section, there is a strong connection between the height of an SPN and the complexity of MAP inferences. First, note that an SPN of height 0 is just a univariate distribution (where MAP is trivial). So consider an SPN of height 1. If the root is a sum node, then the network encodes a sum of univariate distributions over the same variable, and MAP can be solved trivially by enumerating all values of that variable. If on the other hand the root is a product node, then the network encodes a distribution of fully independent variables. Also in this case, we can solve MAP easily by optimizing independently for each variable. So MAP in networks of height 1 or less is solvable in polynomial time.

Let us now consider SPNs of height 2. As already discussed in the introduction, Peharz et al. (2016) briefly observed that the MAP problem is NP-hard even for tree-shaped networks of height 2. Here, we give the following alternative, direct proof of NP-hardness of MAP in SPNs, that allows us to obtain results on non-approximability.

Theorem 1. MAP *in sum-product networks is* NP-*complete even if there is no evidence, and the underlying graph is a tree of height 2.*

Proof. Membership is straightforward as we can evaluate the probability of a configuration in polynomial time.

We show hardness by reduction from the NP-hard problem maximum independent set (see e.g. (Zuckerman, 2007)): Given an undirected graph $G = (V, E)$ with vertices $\{1, \ldots, n\}$ and an integer v, decide whether there is an independent set of size v. An independent set is a subset $V' \subseteq V$ such that no two vertices are connected by an edge in E.

Let N_i denote the neighbors of i in V. For each $i \in V$, build a product node S_i whose children are leaf nodes $S_{i1}, \ldots, S_{in}$ with scopes $X_1, \ldots, X_n$, respectively. If $j \in N_i$ then associate S_{ij} with distribution $\mathbb{P}(X_i = 1) = 0$; if $j \notin N_i \cup \{i\}$ associate S_{ij} with $\mathbb{P}(X_j = 1) = 1/2$; finally, associate S_{ii} with distribution $\mathbb{P}(X_i = 1) = 1$. See Figure 2 for an example. Let $n_i = |N_i|$ be the number of neighbors of i. Then $S_i(x) = 1/2^{n-n_i-1}$ if $x_i = 1$ and $x_j = 0$ for all $j \in N_i$; and $S_i(x) = 0$ otherwise. That is, $S_i(x) > 0$ if there is a set V' which contains i and does not contain any of its neighbors. Now connect all product nodes S_i with a root sum node parent S; specify the weight from S to S_i as $w_i = 2^{n-n_i-1}/c$, where $c = \sum_i 2^{n-n_i-1}$. Suppose there is an independent set I of size v. Take x such that $x_i = 1$ if $i \in I$ and $x_i = 0$ otherwise. Then $S(x) = v/c$. For any configuration x of the variables, let $I(x) = \{i : S_i(x) > 0\}$. Then $I(x)$ is an independent set of size $c \cdot S(x)$. So suppose that there is no independent set of size v. Then $\max_x S(x) < v/c$. Thus, there is an independent set if and only if $\max_x S(x) \geq v/c$. □

Consider a real-valued function $f(\langle S, e \rangle)$ of the encoded network S and evidence e. An algorithm for MAP in SPNs is a $f(\langle S, e \rangle)$-approximation if it runs in time polynomial in the size of its input (which specifies the graph, the weights, the distributions, the evidence) and outputs a configuration $\tilde{x}$ such that $S(\tilde{x}) \cdot f(\langle S, e \rangle) \geq \max_{x \sim e} S(x)$. That is, a $f(\langle S, e \rangle)$-approximation algorithm provides, for every instance $\langle S, e \rangle$ of the MAP problem, a solution whose value is at most a factor $f(\langle S, e \rangle)$ from the optimum value. The value $f(\langle S, e \rangle)$ is called the *approximation factor*. We have the following consequence of Theorem 1:

Corollary 1. *Unless* P *equals* NP*, there is no* $(m-1)^{\varepsilon}$*-approximation algorithm for* MAP *in* SPNs *for any* $0 \leq \varepsilon < 1$*, where* m *is the number of internal nodes of the* SPN*, even if there is no evidence and the underlying graph is a tree of height 2.*

Proof. The proof of Theorem 1 encodes a maximum independent set problem and the reduction is a weighted reduction (see Definition 1 in (Bulatov et al., 2012)), which suffices to prove the result. To dispense with weighted reductions, we now give a direct proof. So suppose that there is a $(m-1)^{\varepsilon}$-approximation algorithm for MAP with $0 \leq \varepsilon < 1$. Let $\tilde{x}$ be the configuration returned by this algorithm when applied to the SPN S created in the proof of Theorem 1 for a graph G given as input of the maximum independent set problem. We have that

$$S(\tilde{x}) \cdot c \cdot (m-1)^{\varepsilon} \geq c \cdot \max_x S(x) = \max_{I \in \mathcal{I}(G)} |I| \, ,$$

where $c = \sum_i 2^{n-n_i-1}$, $\mathcal{I}(G)$ is the collection of independent sets of G, n is the number of vertices in G and n_i is the number of neighbors of vertex i in G. Consequently, this algorithm is a n^{ε}-approximation for maximum independent set (note that $n = m - 1$ by construction). We know that there is no n^{ε}-approximation for maximum independent set with $0 \leq \varepsilon < 1$ unless P equals NP (Zuckerman, 2007), so the result follows. □

Corollary 1 shows that there is *probably* no approximation algorithm for MAP with sublinear approximation factor in the size of the input. The following result shows that this lower bound is tight:

Theorem 2. *There exists a* $(m-1)$*-approximation algorithm for* MAP *in sum-product networks whose underlying graph has height at most 2, where* m *is the number of internal nodes.*

Proof. Consider a sum-product network of height 2. If the root is a product node then the problem decomposes into independent MAP problems in SPNs of height 1; each of those problems can be solved exactly. So assume that the root S is a sum node connected either to leaf nodes or to nodes which are connected to leaf nodes. Solve the respective MAP problem for each child S_i independently (which is exact, as the corresponding SPN has height at most 1); denote by x^i the corresponding solution. Note that $S_i(x^i)$ is an upper bound on the value $S_i(x^*)$, where x^* is a (global) MAP configuration. Let $w_1, \ldots, w_{m-1}$ denote the weights from the root to children $S_1, \ldots, S_{m-1}$. Return $\tilde{x} = \arg\max_i w_i \cdot S_i(x^i)$. It follows that $(m-1)S(\tilde{x}) \geq \max_{x \sim e} S(x)$. Note that this is the same value returned by the max-product algorithm by Poon and Domingos (2011). □

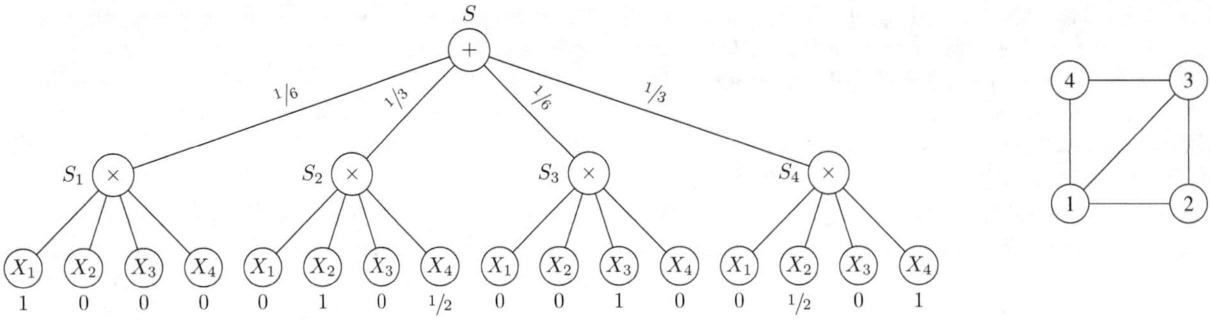

Figure 2: A sum-product network encoding the maximum independent set problem for the graph on the right. Only the values for $\mathbb{P}(X_i = 1)$ are shown.

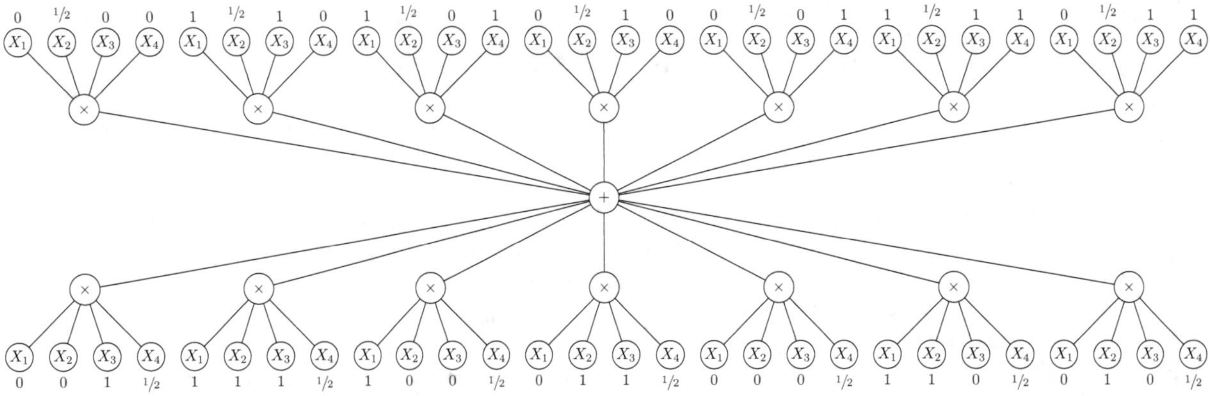

Figure 3: A sum-product network encoding the Boolean formula $(\neg X_1 \vee X_2 \vee \neg X_3) \wedge (\neg X_1 \vee X_3 \vee X_4)$. We represent only the probabilities $\mathbb{P}(X_i = 1)$, and omit the uniform weights $1/14$ associated with the root sum node.

Thus, for networks of height 2, we have a clear divide: there is an approximation algorithm with linear approximation factor in the number of internal nodes, and no approximation algorithm with sublinear approximation factor in the number of internal nodes. Allowing an additional level of nodes reduces drastically the quality of the approximations in the worst case:

Theorem 3. *Unless* P *equals* NP, *there is no* 2^{s^ε}-*approximation algorithm for* MAP *in* SPNs *for any* $0 \leq \varepsilon < 1$, *where s is the size of the input, even if there is no evidence and the underlying graph is a tree of height 3.*

Proof. First, we show how to build an SPN for deciding satisfiability: Given a Boolean formula ϕ in conjunctive normal form, decide if there is a satisfying truth-value assignment. We assume that each clause contains exactly 3 distinct variables (NP-completeness is not altered by this assumption, but if one would like to drop it, then the weights of the sum node we define below could be easily adjusted to account for clauses with less than 3 variables).

Let $X_1, \ldots, X_n$ denote the Boolean variables and $\phi_1, \ldots, \phi_m$ denote the clauses in the formula. For $i = 1, \ldots, m$, consider the conjunctions $\phi_{i1}, \ldots, \phi_{i7}$ over the variables of clause ϕ_i, representing all the satisfying assignments of that clause. For each such assignment, introduce a product node S_{ij} encoding the respective assignment: there is a leaf node with scope X_k whose distribution assigns all mass to value 1 (resp., 0) if and only if X_k appears nonnegated (resp., negated) in ϕ_{ij}; and there is a leaf node with uniform distribution over X_k if and only if X_k does not appear on ϕ_{ij}. See Figure 3 for an example. For a fixed configuration of the random variables, the clause ϕ_i is true if and only if one of the product nodes $S_{i1}, \ldots, S_{i7}$ evaluates to $1/2^{n-3}$. And since these products encode disjoint assignments, at most one such product is nonzero for each configuration. We thus have that $\sum_{ij} S_{ij}(x) = m/2^{n-3}$ if $\phi(x)$ is true, and $\sum_{ij} S_{ij}(x) < m/2^{n-3}$ if $\phi(x)$ is false. So introduce a sum node S with all product nodes as children and with uniform weights $1/7m$. There is a satisfying assignment for ϕ if and only if $\max_x S(x) \geq 2^{3-n}/7$.

We "amplify" the approximation error by multiplying independent copies of the SPN built so far. So take the SPN above and make q copies of it with disjoint scopes: each copy contains different random variables X_k^t, $t = 1, \ldots, q$, at the leaves, but otherwise represents the very same distribution/satisfiability problem. Name each copy S_t, $t = 1, \ldots q$, and let its size be s_t. Denote by $s' = \max_t s_t$ (note that, since they are copies, their size is the same, apart from possible indexing, etc). Connect these copies using a product node S with networks $S_1, \ldots, S_q$ as children, so that $S(x) = \prod_{t=1}^{q} S_t(x)$. Note that $\max_x S_t(x) \geq 2^{3-n}/7$ if there is a satisfying assignment to the Boolean formula, and $\max_x S_t(x) \leq \frac{m-1}{m} \cdot 2^{3-n}/7$ if there is no satisfying assignment. Hence, $\max_x S(x) \geq (2^{3-n}/7)^q$ if there is a satisfying assignment and $\max_x S(x) \leq ((m-1)2^{3-n}/(7m))^q$ if there is no satisfying assignment. Specify

$$q = 1 + \left\lfloor (\ln(2) \cdot m \cdot (s'+2)^{\varepsilon})^{\frac{1}{1-\varepsilon}} \right\rfloor ,$$

which is polynomial in s', so the SPN S can be constructed in polynomial time and space and has size $s < q(s'+2)$. From the definition of q, we have that

$$q > (\ln(2) \cdot m \cdot (s'+2)^{\varepsilon})^{\frac{1}{1-\varepsilon}} .$$

Raising both sides to $1 - \varepsilon$ yields

$$q > q^{\varepsilon} \ln(2) \cdot m \cdot (s+2)^{\varepsilon} = m \ln(2^{(q(s'+2))^{\varepsilon}}) > m \ln 2^{s^{\varepsilon}} .$$

Since $\frac{1}{m} \leq \ln \frac{m}{m-1}$ for any integer $m > 1$, it follows that

$$q \ln \left(\frac{m}{m-1} \right) > \ln 2^{s^{\varepsilon}} .$$

By exponentiating both sides, we arrive at

$$\left(\frac{m}{m-1} \right)^q > 2^{s^{\varepsilon}} \text{ hence } 2^{s^{\varepsilon}} \left(\frac{m-1}{m} \right)^q < 1 ,$$

Finally, by multiplying both sides by $(2^{3-n}/7)^q$, we obtain

$$2^{s^{\varepsilon}} \left(\frac{2^{3-n}(m-1)}{7m} \right)^q < \left(\frac{2^{3-n}}{7} \right)^q .$$

Hence, if we can obtain an $2^{s^{\varepsilon}}$-approximation for $\max_x S(x)$, then we can decide satisfiability: there is a satisfying assignment to the Boolean formula if and only if the approximation returns a value strictly greater than $(2^{3-n}(m-1)/(7m))^q$. □

According to Theorem 3, there is no $2^{f(s)}$-approximation (unless P equals NP) for any sublinear function f of the input size s. The following result is used to show that this lower bound is tight.

Theorem 4. *Let S^+ denote the sum nodes in* SPN *S, and d_i be the number of children of sum node $S_i \in S^+$. Then there exists a $(\prod_{S_i \in S^+} d_i)$-approximation algorithm for* MAP *with input S and evidence e.*

Proof. There are two cases to consider, based on the value of $S(e)$, which can be checked in polynomial time. If $S(e) = 0$, then we can return any assignment consistent with e, as the result will be exact (and equal to zero). If $S(e) > 0$, then take the max-product algorithm by Poon and Domingos (2011), which consists of an upward pass where sums are replaced by maximizations in the evaluation of an SPN, and a downward pass which selects the maximizers of the previous step. Define $\mathrm{pd}(S, e)$ recursively as follows. If S is a leaf then $\mathrm{pd}(S, e) = \max_{x \sim e} S(x)$. If S is a sum node, then $\mathrm{pd}(S, e) = \max_{j=1,\ldots,t} w_j \cdot \mathrm{pd}(S_j, e)$, where $S_1, \ldots, S_t$ are the children of S. Finally, if S is a product node with children $S_1, \ldots, S_t$, then $\mathrm{pd}(S, e) = \prod_{j=1}^{t} \mathrm{pd}(S_j, e)$. Note that $\mathrm{pd}(S, e)$ corresponds to the upward pass of the max-product algorithm; hence it is a lower bound on the value of the configuration obtained by such algorithm. We prove that the max-product algorithm is a $(\prod_{S_i \in S^+} d_i)$-approximation by proving by induction in the height of the SPN that

$$\mathrm{pd}(S, e) \geq \left(\prod_{S_i \in S^+} \frac{1}{d_i} \right) \max_{x \sim e} S(x) .$$

To show the base of the induction, take a network S of height 0 (i.e., containing a single node). Then $\mathrm{pd}(S, e) = \max_{x \sim e} S(x)$ trivially. So take a network S with children $S_1, \ldots, S_t$, and suppose (by inductive hypothesis) that $\mathrm{pd}(S_j, e) \geq (\prod_{S_i \in S_j^+} \frac{1}{d_i}) \max_{x \sim e} S_j(x)$ for every child S_j. If S is a product node, then

$$\begin{aligned}
\mathrm{pd}(S, e) &= \prod_{j=1}^{t} \mathrm{pd}(S_j, e) \\
&\geq \prod_{j=1}^{t} \left(\prod_{S_i \in S_j^+} \frac{1}{d_i} \right) \max_{x \sim e} S_j(x) \\
&= \left(\prod_{S_i \in S^+} \frac{1}{d_i} \right) \prod_{j=1}^{t} \max_{x \sim e} S_j(x) \\
&= \left(\prod_{S_i \in S^+} \frac{1}{d_i} \right) \max_{x \sim e} S(x) ,
\end{aligned}$$

where the last two equalities follow as the scopes of products are disjoints, which implies that the children do not share any node. If S is a sum node, then

$$\begin{aligned}
\mathrm{pd}(S, e) &= \max_{j=1,\ldots,t} w_j \cdot \mathrm{pd}(S_j, e) \\
&\geq \max_{j=1,\ldots,t} \left(\prod_{S_i \in S_j^+} \frac{1}{d_i} \right) w_j \cdot \max_{x \sim e} S_j(x)
\end{aligned}$$

$$
\begin{aligned}
&= \max_{j=1,\dots,t} \left(\frac{t}{t \prod_{S_i \in S_j^+} d_i} \right) w_j \cdot \max_{x \sim e} S_j(x) \\
&\geq \max_{j=1,\dots,t} \frac{t}{\prod_{S_i \in S^+} d_i} \cdot w_j \cdot \max_{x \sim e} S_j(x) \\
&= \frac{t \cdot \max_{j=1,\dots,t} w_j \max_{x \sim e} S_j(x)}{\prod_{S_i \in S^+} d_i} \\
&\geq \left(\prod_{S_i \in S^+} \frac{1}{d_i} \right) \max_{x \sim e} S(x) .
\end{aligned}
$$

The first inequality uses the induction hypothesis. The second inequality follows since $1/(t \cdot \prod_{S_i \in S_j^+} d_i) \geq 1/(t \cdot \prod_{S_i \in S^+, S_i \neq S} d_i) = 1/\prod_{S_i \in S^+} d_i$. The last inequality follows as $\max_j w_j \cdot \max_{x \sim e} S_j(x)$ is an upper bound on the value of any child of S. This concludes the proof. □

We have the following immediate consequence, showing the tightness of Theorem 3.

Corollary 2. *There exists a $2^{\varepsilon \cdot s}$-approximation algorithm for* MAP *for some $0 < \varepsilon < 1$, where s is the size of the* SPN.

Proof. Assume the network has at least one sum node (otherwise we can find an exact solution in polynomial time). Given the result of Theorem 4, we only need to show that there is $\varepsilon < 1$ such that $\prod_{S_i \in S^+} d_i < 2^{\varepsilon \cdot s}$, with S^+ the sum nodes in SPN S and d_i be the number of children of sum node $S_i \in S^+$. Because s is strictly greater than the number of nodes and arcs in the network (as we must somehow encode the graph of S), we know that $s > \sum_{S_i \in S^+} d_i$. One can show that $3^{x/3} > x$ for any positive integer. Hence,

$$
\begin{aligned}
\prod_{S_i \in S^+} d_i \leq \prod_{S_i \in S^+} 3^{d_i/3} = \prod_{S_i \in S^+} 2^{d_i \log_2(3)/3} \\
= 2^{\log_2(3)/3 \cdot \sum_{S_i \in S^+} d_i} < 2^{s \log_2(3)/3} < 2^{\varepsilon \cdot s} ,
\end{aligned}
$$

for some $\varepsilon < 0.5284$. □

The previous result shows that the max-product algorithm by Poon and Domingos (2011) achieves tight upper bounds on the approximation factor. This however does not rule out the existence of approximation algorithms that achieve the same (worst-case) upper bound but perform significantly better on average. For instance, consider the following algorithm that takes an SPN S and evidence e, and returns amap(S, e) as follows, where amap is short for *argmax-product* algorithm. If S is a sum node with children $S_1, \dots, S_t$, then compute

$$
\text{amap}(S, e) = \arg \max_{x \in \{x^1, \dots, x^t\}} \sum_{j=1}^{t} w_j \cdot S_j(x) ,
$$

where $x^k = \text{amap}(S_k, e)$, that is, x^k is the solution of the MAP problem obtained by argmax-product for network S_k (argmax-product is run bottom-up). If S is a product node with children $S_1, \dots, S_t$, then amap(S, e) is the concatenation of amap$(S_1, e), \dots,$ amap(S_t, e). Else, S is a leaf, so return amap$(S, e) = \arg\max_{x \sim e} S(x)$.

The argmax-product has a worst-case time complexity quadratic in the size of the network; that is because the evaluation of all the children of a sum node with the argument which maximizes each of the children takes linear time (with a smart implementation, it might be possible to achieve subquadratic time). For comparison, the max-product (with a smart implementation to keep track of solutions and evaluations) takes linear time. While this is a drawback of the argmax-product algorithm, worst-case quadratic time is still quite efficient. More importantly, argmax-product always produces an approximation at least as good as that of max-product, and possibly exponentially better:

Theorem 5. *For any* SPN *S and evidence e, we have that $S(amap(S, e)) \geq S(PD(S, e))$, where $PD(S, e)$ is the configuration returned by the max-product algorithm. Moreover, there exists S and e such that $S(amap(S, e)) > 2^m S(PD(S, e))$, where m is the number of sum nodes in S.*

Proof. It is not difficult to see that $S(\text{amap}(S, e)) \geq S(\text{PD}(S, e))$, because the configuration that is selected by max-product at each sum node is one of the configurations that are tried by the maximization of argmax-product (and both algorithms perform the same operation on leaves and product nodes). To see that this improvement can be exponentially better, consider the SPN S_i in Figure 4. Let pd(S_i, e) be defined as in the proof of Theorem 4. One can verify that pd$(S_i, e) = 5/16$, while

$$
S_i(\text{amap}(S_i, e)) = 3 \cdot 11/48 = 11/16 > 2 \cdot 5/16 .
$$

Now, create an SPN S with a product root node connected to children $S_1, \dots, S_m$ as described (note that the scope of S is $X_1, \dots, X_m$). Then,

$$
\begin{aligned}
S(\text{amap}(S, e)) &= (11/16)^m \\
&> 2^m (5/16)^m = 2^m \cdot \text{pd}(S, e) .
\end{aligned}
$$

The result follows as (for this network) pd$(S, e) = S(\text{PD}(S, e))$. □

As an immediate result, the solutions produced by argmax-product achieve the upper bound on the complexity of approximating MAP. We hope that this simple result motivates researchers to seek for more sophisticated algorithms that exhibit the time performance of max-product while achieving the accuracy of argmax-product.

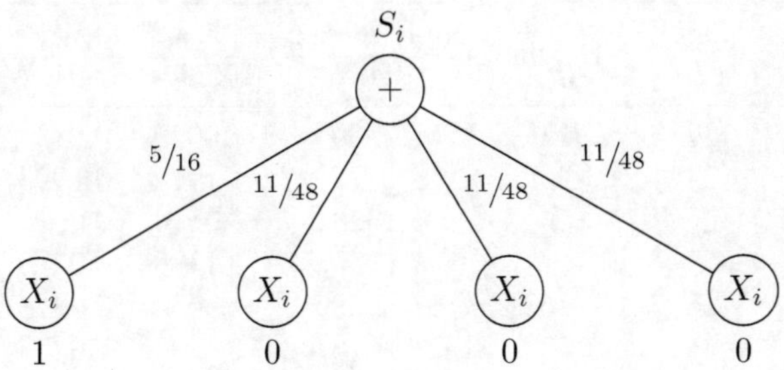

Figure 4: Fragment of the sum-product network used to prove Theorem 5.

4 EXPERIMENTS

We perform two sets of experiments to verify empirically the difference between argmax-product and max-product. We emphasize that our main motivation is to understand the complexity of the problem and how much it can be approximated efficiently in practice. In the light of Theorem 5, one may suggest that a MAP problem instance is easy to approximate when argmax-product and max-product produce similar approximations.

In the first set of evaluations, we build SPNs from random instances for the maximum independent set problem, that is, we generate random undirected graphs with number of vertices given in the first column of Table 2 and number of edges presented as percentage of the maximum number of edges (that is, the number of edges in a complete graph). For each graph, we apply the transformation presented in the proof of Theorem 1 to obtain an SPN. The number of nodes of such SPN is given in the third column of the table. The fourth column shows the ratio of the values of the configurations found by argmax-product and max-product (that is, $S(\text{amap}(S,e))/S(\text{PD}(S,e))$), averaged over 100 random repetitions. Take the first row: On average, the result of argmax-product is 1.58 times better than the result of max-product in SPNs encoding maximum independent set problems with graphs of 5 vertices and 10% of edges (which creates SPNs of 31 nodes: $5 \cdot 5 = 25$ leaves, 5 product nodes and one sum node, same structure as exemplified in Figure 2). The standard deviation for these ratios are also presented (last column in the table). It is clear that argmax-product obtains results that are significantly better than max-product, often surpassing the $2^m = 2$ ratio lower bound in Theorem 5. While in theory argmax-product can be significantly slower than max-product, we did not observe significant differences in running time for these SPNs with up to 6481 nodes (either algorithm terminated almost instantaneously).

In the second set of evaluations, we use realistic SPNs that model datasets from the UCI Repository.[2] The SPNs are learned using the GoSPN library,[3] a freely available implementation of the ideas presented in (Gens and Domingos, 2013). For each dataset, we use a random sample of 90% of the dataset for learning the model and save the remaining 10% to be used as test. Then we perform two types of queries. The first type of query consists in using the learned network to compute the mode of the corresponding distribution, that is, running both algorithms with no evidence. In the second type, we split the set of variables in half; for each instance (row) in the test set, we set the respective evidence for the variables in the first half, and compute the MAP configuration/value for the other half. This allows us to assess the effect of evidence in the approximation complexity. The results are summarized in Table 3. The first three columns display information about the dataset (name, number of variables and number of samples); the middle four columns display information about the learned SPN (total number of nodes, number of sum nodes, number of product nodes and height); the last three columns show the approximation results: the ratio of probabilities of solutions found by argmax-product and max-product

Vertices	% Edges	Nodes	Ratio	StDev
5	10	31	1.58	0.76
5	20	31	1.72	0.78
5	40	31	1.61	0.75
5	60	31	1.57	0.60
10	10	111	1.89	0.95
10	20	111	2.16	1.09
10	40	111	2.12	1.01
10	60	111	2.04	0.89
20	10	421	1.94	0.88
20	20	421	2.89	1.72
20	40	421	3.02	1.24
20	60	421	2.60	1.04
40	10	1641	2.64	1.42
40	20	1641	3.37	1.45
40	40	1641	2.33	0.73
40	60	1641	2.27	0.76
80	10	6481	3.96	1.81
80	20	6481	2.10	0.49
80	40	6481	1.07	0.26
80	60	6481	1.04	0.20

Table 2: Empirical comparison of the quality of approximations produced by argmax-product and max-product in SPNs encoding randomly generated instances of the maximum independent set problem.

[2] Obtained at `http://archive.ics.uci.edu/ml/`.

[3] `http://www.github.com/RenatoGeh/gospn`

Dataset	No. of variables	No. of samples	No. of nodes	No. of nodes +	No. of nodes ×	Height	No Evidence	50% Evidence	
							Ratio	Ratio	StDev
audiology	70	204	13513	28	27	12	1.0000	1.0029	0.0133
breast-cancer	10	258	1357	23	24	24	1.1572	1.1977	0.1923
car	7	1556	16	2	3	3	1.1028	1.0514	0.0514
cylinder-bands	33	487	3129	61	62	62	1.1154	1.1185	0.0220
flags	29	175	787	25	26	26	1.3568	1.3654	0.0363
ionosphere	34	316	603	43	44	42	1.1176	1.1109	0.0273
nursery	9	11665	20	2	3	3	1.6225	1.2060	0.2926
primary-tumor	18	306	804	113	114	114	1.0882	1.0828	0.0210
sonar	61	188	1057	101	102	26	1.2380	1.2314	0.0261
vowel	14	892	23	2	3	3	1.0751	1.0666	0.0229

Table 3: Empirical comparison of the quality of approximations produced by argmax-product and max-product in SPNs learned from UCI datasets with height at least 2.

in the test cases with no evidence, the same ratio in test cases with 50% of variables given as evidence, and the standard deviation for the latter (as it is run over different evidences corresponding to 10% of the data). We only show datasets where the learned SPN has at least one sum node, since in the other cases the MAP can be trivially found and a comparison would be pointless. The results suggest that in these SPNs learned from real data, the difference between argmax-product and max-product is less prominent, yet non negligible. We also see that the complexity of approximation is not considerably affected by the presence of evidence.

5 CONCLUSION

We analyzed the complexity of maximum a posteriori inference in sum-product networks and showed that it relates with the height of the underlying graph. We first provided an alternative (and more direct) proof of NP-hardness of maximum a posteriori inference in sum-product networks. Our proof uses a reduction from maximum independent set in undirected graphs, from which we obtain the non-approximability for any sublinear factor in the size of input, even in networks of height 2 and no evidence. We then showed that this limit is tight, that is, that there is a polynomial-time algorithm that produces solutions which are at most a linear factor for networks of height 2. We also showed that in networks of height 3 or more, complexity of approximation increases considerably: there is no approximation within a factor $2^{f(n)}$, for any sublinear function f of the input size n. This is also a tight bound, as we showed that the usual max-product algorithm by Poon and Domingos (2011) finds an approximation within factor $2^{c \cdot n}$ for some constant $c < 1$. Last, we showed that a simple modification to max-product results in an algorithm that is at least as good, and possibly greatly superior to max-product. We compared both algorithms in two different types of networks: shallow sum-product networks that encode random instances of the maximum independent set problem and deeper sum-product networks learned from real-world datasets. The empirical results show that while the proposed algorithm produces better solutions than max-product does, this improvement is less pronounced in the deeper realistic networks than in the shallower synthetic networks. This suggests that characteristics other than the height of the network might be equally important in determining the hardness of approximating maximum a posteriori inference, and that further (theoretical and empirical) investigations are required. We hope that these results foster research on approximation algorithms for maximum a posteriori inference in sum-product networks.

Acknowledgements

The second author received financial support from the São Paulo Research Foundation (FAPESP) grant #2016/01055-1 and the CNPq grants #303920/2016-5 and #420669/2016-7. We thank Renato Geh for making his source code freely available and promptly answering our questions.

References

Amer, M. R. (2012). Sum-product networks for modeling activities with stochastic structure. In *Proceedings of the IEEE Conference on Computer Vision and Pattern Recognition*, pages 1314–1321.

Amer, M. R. and Todorovic, S. (2016). Sum product networks for activity recognition. *IEEE Transactions on Pattern Analysis and Machine Intelligence*, 38(4):800–813.

Boykov, Y., Veksler, O., and Zabih, R. (1998). Markov random fields with efficient approximations. In *Proceedings of the IEEE Computer Society Conference on Computer Vision and Pattern Recognition*, pages 648–655.

Bulatov, A., Dyer, M., Goldberg, L. A., Jalsenius, M., Jerrum, M., and Richerby, D. (2012). The complexity of weighted and unweighted #CSP. *Journal of Computer and System Sciences*, 78(2):681–688.

Cheng, W.-C., Kok, S., Pham, H. V., Chieu, H. L., and Chai, K. M. A. (2014). Language modeling with sum-product networks. In *Proceedings of the 15th Annual Conference of the International Speech Communication Association.*

Darwiche, A. (2003). A differential approach to inference in Bayesian networks. *Journal of the ACM*, 50(3):280–305.

Darwiche, A. (2009). *Modeling and Reasoning with Bayesian Networks*. Cambridge University Press.

de Campos, C. P. (2011). New complexity results for MAP in Bayesian networks. In *Proceedings of the Twenty-Second International Joint Conference on Artificial Intelligence*, pages 2100–2106.

Geman, S. and Geman, D. (1984). Stochastic relaxation, Gibbs distributions, and the Bayesian restoration of images. *IEEE Transactions on Pattern Analysis and Machine Intelligence*, 6(6):721–741.

Gens, R. and Domingos, P. (2013). Learning the structure of sum-product networks. In *Proceedings of 30th International Conference on Machine Learning*, pages 873–880.

Koo, T., Rush, A. M., Collins, M., Jaakkola, T., and Sontag, D. (2010). Dual decomposition for parsing with non-projective head automata. In *Proceedings of the 2010 Conference on Empirical Methods in Natural Language Processing*, pages 1288–1298.

Nath, A. and Domingos, P. (2016). Learning tractable probabilistic models for fault localization. In *Proceedings of the Thirtieth AAAI Conference on Artificial Intelligence*, pages 1294–1301.

Peharz, R. (2015). *Foundations of sum-product networks for probabilistic modeling*. PhD thesis.

Peharz, R., Gens, R., Pernkopf, F., and Domingos, P. (2016). On the latent variable interpretation in sum-product networks. *IEEE Transactions on Pattern Analysis and Machine Intelligence*, pages 1–14.

Peharz, R., Kapeller, G., Mowlaee, P., and Pernkopf, F. (2014). Modeling speech with sum-product networks: Application to bandwidth extension. In *IEEE International Conference on Acoustics, Speech and Signal Processing*, pages 3699–3703.

Peharz, R., Tschiatschek, S., Pernkopf, F., and Domingos, P. (2015). On theoretical properties of sum-product networks. In *Proceedings of the 18th International Conference on Artificial Intelligence and Statistics*, pages 744–752.

Poon, H. and Domingos, P. (2011). Sum-product networks: A new deep architecture. In *Proceedings of 27th Conference on Uncertainty in Artificial Intelligence*, pages 337–346.

Rooshenas, A. and Lowd, D. (2014). Learning sum-product networks with direct and indirect variable interactions. In *Proceedings of the 31st International Conference on Machine Learning*, pages 710–718.

Steinder, M. and Sethi, A. (2004). Probabilistic fault localization in communication systems using belief networks. *IEEE/ACM Transactions on Networking*, 12(5):809–822.

Szeliski, R., Zabih, R., Scharstein, D., Veksler, O., Kolmogorov, V., Agarwala, A., Tappen, M., and Rother, C. (2008). A comparative study of energy minimization methods for Markov random fields with smoothness-based priors. *IEEE Transactions on Pattern Analysis and Machine Intelligence*, 30(6):1068–1080.

Vergari, A., Mauro, N. D., and Esposito, F. (2015). Simplifying, regularizing and strengthening sum-product network structure learning. In *Proceedings of the European Conference on Machine Learning and Knowledge Discovery in Databases*, pages 343–358.

Zhao, H., Melibari, M., and Poupart, P. (2015). On the relationship between sum-product networks and bayesian networks. In *Proceedings of the 32nd International Conference on Machine Learning*, pages 116–124.

Zirn, C., Niepert, M., and Strube, Heiner Stuckenschmidt, M. (2011). Fine-grained sentiment analysis with structural features. *Proceedings of the 5th International Joint Conference on Natural Language Processing*, pages 336–344.

Zuckerman, D. (2007). Linear degree extractors and the inapproximability of max clique and chromatic number. *Theory of Computing*, 3:103–128.

Learning the Structure of Probabilistic Sentential Decision Diagrams

Yitao Liang
Computer Science Department
University of California, Los Angeles
yliang@cs.ucla.edu

Jessa Bekker
Computer Science Department
KU Leuven
jessa.bekker@cs.kuleuven.be

Guy Van den Broeck
Computer Science Department
University of California, Los Angeles
guyvdb@cs.ucla.edu

Abstract

The probabilistic sentential decision diagram (PSDD) was recently introduced as a tractable representation of probability distributions that are subject to logical constraints. Meanwhile, efforts in tractable learning achieved great success inducing complex joint distributions from data without constraints, while guaranteeing efficient exact probabilistic inference; for instance by learning arithmetic circuits (ACs) or sum-product networks (SPNs). This paper studies the efficacy of PSDDs for the standard tractable learning task without constraints and develops the first PSDD structure learning algorithm, called LEARNPSDD. Experiments on standard benchmarks show competitive performance, despite the fact that PSDDs are more tractable and more restrictive than their alternatives. LEARNPSDD compares favorably to SPNs, particularly in terms of model size, which is a proxy for tractability. We report state-of-the-art likelihood results on six datasets. Moreover, LEARNPSDD retains the ability to learn PSDD structures in probability spaces subject to logical constraints, which is beyond the reach of other representations.

1 INTRODUCTION

Tractable learning aims to induce complex, yet tractable probability distributions from data (Domingos et al., 2014; Mauro and Vergari, 2016). The learned tractable model serves as a certificate to the user that any query that arises can always be answered efficiently. In practice, this means that any conditional marginal can be computed in time linear in the size of the learned model.

Current tractable learning efforts stem from two lines of work. First, probabilistic graphical model learning has long targeted sparse models (Meila and Jordan, 2000; Narasimhan and Bilmes, 2004; Chechetka and Guestrin, 2007). Second, the field of knowledge compilation studies tractable representations, such as *arithmetic circuits* (ACs) for probability distributions (Darwiche, 2003), and NNF circuits for Boolean functions (Darwiche and Marquis, 2002). The superior tractability of these circuits derives from their ability to capture local structure and determinism (Boutilier et al., 1996), which makes compilation to circuits a state-of-the-art technique for probabilistic inference (Darwiche et al., 2008; Choi et al., 2013). Recently, circuits have also become the chosen target representation for tractable learners (Lowd and Domingos, 2008; Lowd and Rooshenas, 2013; Gens and Domingos, 2013; Dennis and Ventura, 2015; Bekker et al., 2015), spurring innovation in arithmetic circuit dialects such as *sum-product networks* (SPNs) (Poon and Domingos, 2011; Peharz et al., 2014) and *cutset networks* (Rahman et al., 2014). While closely related, these representations differ significantly in the types of tractable queries and operations they support.

This paper considers the *probabilistic sentential decision diagram* (PSDD) (Kisa et al., 2014b), which is perhaps the most powerful circuit proposed to date. Owing to their intricate structural properties, PSDDs support closed-form parameter learning, MAP inference, complex queries (Bekker et al., 2015), and even efficient multiplication of distributions (Shen et al., 2016), which are all increasingly rare. These strong properties permit learning of PSDDs in probability spaces that are subject to complex logical constraints disallowing large numbers of possible worlds (Kisa et al., 2014a). In this context, knowledge compilation algorithms can build PSDD structures without looking at the data. These structures are large enough that parameter estimation was shown sufficient to learn distributions over game traces (Choi et al., 2016), configurations, and yield state-of-the-art results learning preference distributions (Choi et al., 2015).

These observations raise two questions: (i) are PSDDs amenable to tractable learning when no logical constraints or compiled circuit are available a priori, and (ii) can we still learn PSDDs that are subject to logical constraints while also fitting the data well; that is, perform true structure learning? To answer both questions, we develop LEARNPSDD, which is the first structure learning algorithm for PSDDs. It uses local operations on the PSDD circuit that maintain the desired circuit properties, while steadily increasing model fit. LEARNPSDD is supported by a vtree learning algorithm that captures the data's independencies in a tree structure, which we empirically show to be an essential step of the learning process. Moreover, using expectation maximization on top of LEARNPSDD, we show competitive results on the standard tractable learning benchmarks. When additionally performing bagging, our PSDD learner reports state-of-the-art results on six datasets. Finally, the proposed algorithm is general and retains the ability to learn in logically constrained probability spaces. Here, we empirically show that LEARNPSDD is able to refine the circuits compiled from constraints, yielding superior likelihood scores.

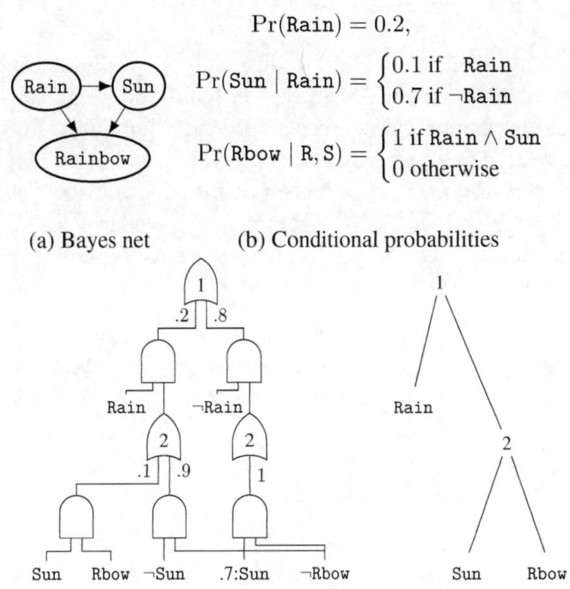

(c) Equivalent PSDD circuit (d) PSDD's vtree

Figure 1: A Bayesian network and its equivalent PSDD.

2 A TRACTABLE REPRESENTATION

This section introduces the notation and circuit representation we employ throughout this paper.

Notation An uppercase letter X denotes a Boolean random variable and a lowercase letter x denotes an assignment to X. Literals X or $\neg X$ respectively assign true or false to variable X. Sets of variables $\mathbf{X}$ and joint assignments $\mathbf{x}$ are denoted in bold. An assignment $\mathbf{x}$ that satisfies logical sentence α is denoted $\mathbf{x} \models \alpha$. Concatenations of sets represent their union. A complete assignment to all variables is a possible world.

PSDDs Probabilistic sentential decision diagrams (PSDDs) are circuit representations of joint probability distributions over binary variables (Kisa et al., 2014b); they are probabilistic extensions of sentential decision diagrams (SDDs) (Darwiche, 2011), which represent Boolean functions as logical circuits. A PSDD is a parametrized directed acyclic graph (DAG), as depicted in Figure 1c. Each inner node is either a logical AND gate with two inputs, or a logical OR gate with an arbitrary number of inputs, and the types of nodes alternate. Each terminal (input) node is a univariate distribution, which could either be X when X is always true, $\neg X$ when it is always false, or $(\theta : X)$ when it is true with probability θ. A decision node is the combination of an OR gate with its AND gate inputs. We refer to the left input of an AND gate as its prime (denoted p) and the right one as its sub (denoted s). The n wires in each decision node are annotated with a normalized probability distribution $\theta_1, \ldots, \theta_n$. Alternatively, we refer to a decision node's labeled AND gates as its elements and represent the decision node itself as a set of elements $\{(p_1, s_1, \theta_1), \ldots, (p_n, s_n, \theta_n)\}$.

Syntactic Restrictions According to the semantics we will detail later, each PSDD node represents a probability distribution over the random variables that appear below it. However, each AND gate must be *decomposable*, meaning that its inputs represent a distribution over disjoint sets of variables. This is enforced uniformly throughout the circuit by a variable tree (vtree): a full, binary tree, whose leaves are labeled with variables; see Figure 1d. The internal vtree nodes split variables into those appearing in the left subtree $\mathbf{X}$ and those in the right subtree $\mathbf{Y}$. This implies that the corresponding PSDD decision nodes must have primes ranging over $\mathbf{X}$ and subs over $\mathbf{Y}$. We say the corresponding PSDD nodes are *normalized* for the vtree node. Figure 1c labels decision nodes with the vtree node they are normalized for.

Each decision node must be *deterministic*, meaning that for any single possible world, it can have at most one prime assign a non-zero probability to that world. In other words, the supports of all distributions represented by primes must be disjoint within the same decision node. We further assume that all elements assign a non-zero probability to at least one world.[1]

Semantics Each PSDD node represents a probability distribution, starting with the terminal nodes' univariate distributions. Each decision node q normalized for a vtree node with $\mathbf{X}$ and $\mathbf{Y}$ in its left and right subtrees respectively, represents a distribution over $\mathbf{XY}$ as $\Pr_q(\mathbf{XY}) = \sum_i \theta_i \Pr_{p_i}(\mathbf{X}) \Pr_{s_i}(\mathbf{Y})$. Under these semantics, the PSDD in Figure 1c represents the same distribution as the Bayesian network in Figure 1a.

Each PSDD node's distribution has an intricate support over which it defines a non-zero probability. We refer to this support as the *base* of node q, written $[q]$. The base of a node can alternatively be defined as a logical sentence using the recursion $[q] = \bigvee_i [p_i] \wedge [s_i]$, where $[X] = X$, $[\neg X] = \neg X$, and $[\theta : X] = $ true.

From a top-down perspective, a decision node presents a choice between its prime bases $[p_i]$: at most one is true in each world. Thus, the PSDD is a decision diagram branching on which sentence $[p_i]$ is true. This generalizes decision trees or binary decision diagrams which only branch on the value of a single variable. To reach node q, all the primes on a path to q must be satisfied; they are the sub-context of q. The disjunction of all q's sub-contexts is its *context* γ_q. This notion lets us precisely characterize PSDD parameter semantics: they are conditional probabilities in root node r's distribution:

$$\theta_i = \Pr_r([p_i] \mid \gamma_q).$$

Inference and Learning PSDDs have several desirable properties. The probability of any (partial) assignment $\mathbf{x}$ can be computed in time linear in the PSDD size (Kisa et al., 2014b). Moreover, PSDDs support efficient complex queries, such as count queries (Bekker et al., 2015), and can be multiplied efficiently (Shen et al., 2016). Most pertinently, the maximum-likelihood estimate for each PSDD parameter is calculated in closed form by observing the fraction of complete examples flowing through the relevant wire. More precisely, out of all the examples that agree with the node context γ_q, the parameter estimate is the fraction of examples that also agrees with the prime base $[p_i]$ (Kisa et al., 2014b):

$$\hat{\theta}_i = \frac{\mathcal{D}\#(\gamma_q, [p_i])}{\mathcal{D}\#(\gamma_q)}. \tag{1}$$

To prevent overfitting, Laplace smoothing is used.

[1] In the original definition this was not required. In fact, primes were required to be exhaustive, which can necessitate a zero-probability element (Kisa et al., 2014b). This is an artifact from defining PSDDs as an extension of SDDs, which require exhaustiveness to support negation or disjunction. These logical operations are not used for our (probabilistic) purpose.

In all current PSDD applications, the learner is given a logical sentence α that encodes domain knowledge (e.g., a constraint encoding rankings or game traces). Using knowledge compilation, sentence α is first transformed into an SDD circuit, and second into a PSDD by parameter learning. Prior work does not perform structure learning: no data is used to come up with PSDD structures.

3 VTREE LEARNING

To learn a vtree from data, it is important to understand the assumptions that are implied by a choice of vtree. PSDDs recursively decompose the distribution by conditioning it on the prime bases $[p_i]$. Specifically, each decision node decomposes the distribution into independent distributions over $\mathbf{X}$ and $\mathbf{Y}$, guided by the vtree.

Proposition 1. *(Kisa et al., 2014b) Prime and sub variables are independent in PSDD q, given a prime base:*

$$\begin{aligned}\Pr_q(\mathbf{XY} \mid [p_i]) &= \Pr_q(\mathbf{X} \mid [p_i]) \Pr_q(\mathbf{Y} \mid [p_i]) \\ &= \Pr_{p_i}(\mathbf{X}) \Pr_{s_i}(\mathbf{Y}).\end{aligned}$$

Independence given a logical sentence is called *context-specific independence* (Boutilier et al., 1996). Which context-specific independencies can be exploited, as specified by the vtree, has a crucial impact on PSDD size.

Prior work always obtained its vtree from compiling logical constraints into SDD circuits (Choi and Darwiche, 2013), disregarding the dependencies that are implied by this choice. We propose a novel method that does induce vtrees based on the independencies found in the data.

A common way to quantify the level of independence between two sets of variables is their mutual information:

$$\mathrm{MI}(\mathbf{X}, \mathbf{Y}) = \sum_{\mathbf{x}} \sum_{\mathbf{y}} \Pr(\mathbf{xy}) \log \frac{\Pr(\mathbf{xy})}{\Pr(\mathbf{x}) \Pr(\mathbf{y})}.$$

Intuitively, low mutual information suggests that $\mathbf{X}$ and $\mathbf{Y}$ are almost independent, and that the data distribution can be approximated by a PSDD that satisfies Proposition 1 using only a small number of primes in each decision node. Therefore, we let mutual information guide the learner: our objective is to induce a vtree that minimizes the mutual information between the $\mathbf{X}$ and $\mathbf{Y}$ variables as they are split in each internal vtree node. Additionally, we will aim to balance the vtrees. We observe that this tends to produce smaller PSDDs in practice.

However, estimating mutual information between large $\mathbf{X}$ and $\mathbf{Y}$ requires estimating an exponential number of terms $\Pr(\mathbf{xy})$, each of which is hard to estimate accurately from data. Therefore, we approximate mutual information by average pairwise mutual information:

$$\mathrm{pMI}(\mathbf{X}, \mathbf{Y}) = \mathrm{avg}_{X \in \mathbf{X}, Y \in \mathbf{Y}} \mathrm{MI}(\{X\}, \{Y\}).$$

Algorithm 1: Split(q, i, Zs, m)

Input: q, i: the ith element of node q to split, Zs: mutually exclusive and exhaustive set of variable assignments, m: depth of PartialCopy
Result: The ith element of node q is split on Zs.

$n2c = \emptyset$ `// maps nodes to copies`
RemoveElement(q, (p_i, s_i))
foreach z $\in Zs$ **do**
  PartialCopy(p_i, **z**, m, $n2c$)
  PartialCopy(s_i, true, m, $n2c$)
  AddElement(q, $(n2c[p_i], n2c[s_i])$)

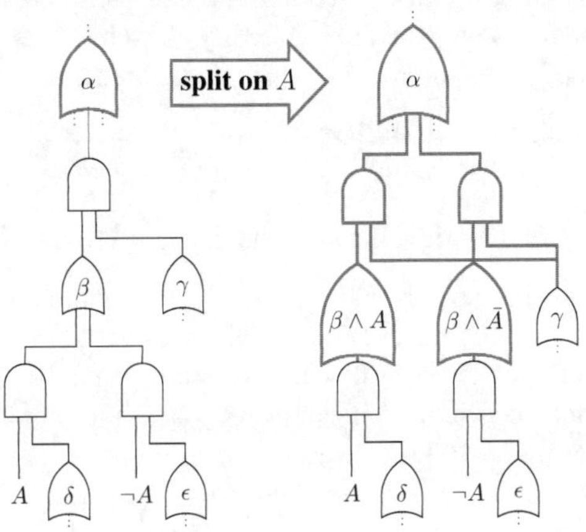

Figure 2: **Minimal Split.** Nodes labels are their base.

We present two algorithms for optimizing a vtree's pMI.

Top-down vtree induction starts with the full variable set and recursively finds splits. Every step divides the variables into two equally-sized subsets with minimal pMI. Finding splits is reduced to a balanced min-cut problem, for which optimized solvers exist (Karypis, 2013).

Bottom-up vtree induction starts with singleton sets of variables at the bottom of the vtree. For each level of the vtree, it pairs two vtrees of the level below, maximizing the pMI of the pairs, in order to minimize the pMI of future pairings at higher levels. Finding pairings of vtrees reduces to the minimum-cost perfect matching problem, for which optimized solvers exist (Kolmogorov, 2009).

Both methods greedily solve the same problem. The difference lies in the direction of the greedy optimization. Top-down induction begins at the root and will therefore get the best splits at the higher levels. Bottom-up starts from the leaves and will therefore get the best pairings at the lower levels. Section 7 will present an empirical comparison showing that bottom-up induction outperforms the top-down approach. Intuitively, most interactions occur between small numbers of variables, which makes the lower levels of the vtree more important.

Algorithm 2: Clone(q, P, m)

Input: q: node to clone, P: parent nodes and elements to redirect to clone, m: depth of PartialCopy
Result: Parents P are redirected to the clone of q.

$n2c = \emptyset$ `// maps nodes to copies`
PartialCopy(q, true, m, $n2c$)
foreach $(\pi, i) \in P$ **do** Update(π, $(i, q, n2c[q])$)

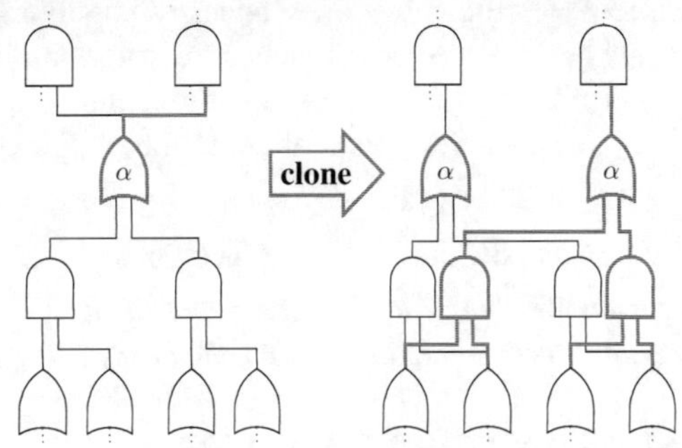

Figure 3: **Minimal Clone.** Base α does not change.

4 PSDD STRUCTURE LEARNING

This section presents the first algorithm to learn PSDD structure from data. The objective is to obtain a compact structure that approximates the data distribution well.

We propose two operations, split and clone, that incrementally change the PSDD structure while keeping the PSDD syntactically sound and the base of the root node unaltered. The soundness criteria guarantees that the learned PSDD follows the syntactic definitions described in Section 2. Not changing the root node's base guarantees that any constraint (i.e., domain knowledge) that is encoded in the PSDD remains intact. Our learner applies these operations greedily to optimize a score function.

4.1 PSDD OPERATIONS

A split or clone operation changes the PSDD structure to represent a different distribution over the same base.

The split operation splits an element (AND node) into multiple elements by constraining the prime. The elements are split based on a mutually exclusive (disjoint) and exhaustive set of partial assignments to the prime variables. This ensures that the decision node remains deterministic. Indeed, for any assignment to the prime variables that had a non-zero probability in the element before the split, there can be at most one element after the split that assigns a non-zero probability to it. To execute a split (Figure 2, Algorithm 1), a new element is created for each partial assignment, where the new prime is a copy of the original prime constrained by the assignment. The new sub is an unconstrained copy. The original element is removed from its decision node.

The clone operation makes a copy of a node and redirects some of the parents to the copy (Figure 3, Algorithm 2).

Both operations need to make partial copies of a decision node and its descendants. Our algorithm can perform these copies up to some specified depth m. A minimal operation ($m = 0$) copies as few nodes as possible, and a complete operation copies all nodes. Any non-minimal operation ($m > 0$) is equivalent to multiple minimal operations. The complete description of the partial-copy algorithm is given in Appendix A.

Finally, Appendix B proves the following result.

Proposition 2. *Splits and clones maintain a PSDD's syntactic properties and do not alter the base of its root.*

4.2 SPLIT AND CLONE ARE LOCAL

Splits and clones are local operations. Only the node that is modified, the parents that are redirected and the copied descendants are affected. Furthermore, key properties of an operation, such as the required change in PSDD structure and improvement in likelihood are typically not affected by operations elsewhere in the PSDD.

Local operations have four desirable properties. First, the complexity of executing an operation is bounded by the number of elements it affects; cheap operations are thus possible in large PSDDs. Second, the difference in PSDD size after an operation can be easily obtained; it is the difference in the affected elements.

Third, the difference in likelihood can be computed by only looking at elements that are affected. Indeed, Kisa et al. (2014b, long version) prove that the log-likelihood decomposes over the PSDD elements as follows.

Proposition 3. *The log-likelihood of PSDD r given data $\mathcal{D}$ is a sum of log-likelihood contributions per node:*[2]

$$\ln \mathcal{L}(r|\mathcal{D}) = \ln \Pr_r(\mathcal{D}) = \sum_{q\in r} \sum_{i\in q} \ln \theta_{q,i}\, \mathcal{D}\#(\gamma_q, [p_{q,i}]),$$

where $\mathcal{D}\#(\gamma_q, [p_{q,i}])$ is the number of examples that satisfy the node context of q and the base of q's prime $p_{q,i}$.

Fourth, we would like to simulate candidate operations before committing to execute them. Because size and likelihood changes are not affected by other operations, we can cache their values when considering a large number of candidate operations during structure search.

Local operations support principled tractable learning, using exact estimates of likelihood and tractability (size).

[2] This equation treats terminal nodes as degenerate decision nodes with primes X and $\neg X$, and subs true and false .

Many other learners, especially traditional ones, are required to approximate the likelihood and have no ability to reliably determine the tractability of a learned model.

4.3 LEARNPSDD ALGORITHM

We build on our split and clone operations to create the first PSDD structure learning algorithm called LEARNPSDD[3]. It incrementally improves the structure of an existing PSDD to better fit the data. In every step, the structure is changed by executing an operation. Learning continues until the log-likelihood on validation data stagnates, or a desired time or size limit is reached. The operation to execute is greedily chosen based on the best likelihood improvement per size increment:

$$\text{score} = \frac{\ln \mathcal{L}(r' \mid \mathcal{D}) - \ln \mathcal{L}(r \mid \mathcal{D})}{\text{size}(r') - \text{size}(r)}$$

where r is the original and r' the updated PSDD.

The algorithm needs to be provided with an initial PSDD and vtree. It can take any PSDD, even one that encodes domain knowledge in its base, as is done in existing applications of PSDDs. It can also be a trivial, maximally uninformative PSDD q whose base $[q] = $ true and whose distribution factorizes completely over the variables. The vtree can either come from compiling those constraints, or can be learn from data as described in Section 3.

In each iteration, LEARNPSDD considers one clone per node and one split per element. The clone is the best clone for that node where at most k parents are moved to the copy. The split is the best split with the partial assignments limited to one prime variable. Only the scores of the operations that use nodes affected by the previous iteration's operation need to be recalculated.

The operation depth parameter m is fixed during learning. The larger this parameter, the more elements are added and the larger the log-likelihood improvement per operation. A large m speeds up the learning but learns larger PSDDs, which are more prone to overfitting. Appendix C provides more implementation details.

5 ENSEMBLES OF PSDDS

This section extends LEARNPSDD to induce mixtures of PSDDs. A mixture of PSDDs $\mathcal{M}$ is a set of pairs (r_i, w_i) where each r_i is a component PSDD and w_i is its mixture weight. A mixture of n PSDDs must have $\sum_{i=1}^{n} w_i = 1$. We further assume that all r_i are normalized for the same vtree. A mixture of PSDDs $\mathcal{M}$ represents the probability distribution $\Pr_{\mathcal{M}}(\mathbf{X}) = \sum_{i=1}^{n} w_i \Pr_{r_i}(\mathbf{X})$.

[3] Open-source code and experiments are available at https://github.com/UCLA-StarAI/LearnPSDD.

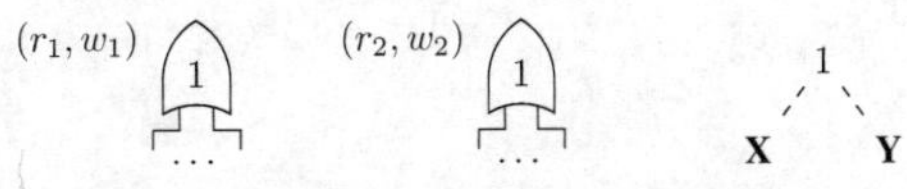

(a) Mixture of two PSDDs with outline of a common vtree.

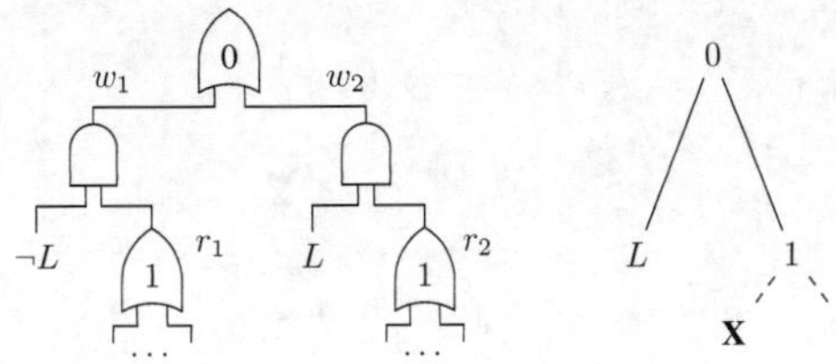

(b) Equivalent single PSDD and vtree with latent variable L.

Figure 4: Representing ensembles as a single PSDD.

An ensemble of PSDDs is equivalent to a single PSDD with latent variables. More precisely, by adding $\lceil \log(n) \rceil$ Boolean variables $\mathbf{L}$ to the top of the vtree (encoding an n-valued latent component identifier), and mixing between the component PSDDs with an additional decision node, one can capture the distribution $\Pr_{\mathcal{M}}(\mathbf{X})$ in a single PSDD circuit. Figure 4 depicts this reduction.

Because the latent variables $\mathbf{L}$ are not observable, the mixture weights w_i cannot be learned from data in closed form. Instead, we appeal to expectation maximization (EM) for optimizing the likelihood $\mathcal{L}(\mathcal{M} \mid \mathcal{D})$ given dataset $\mathcal{D} = \{\mathbf{d}^{(1)}, \mathbf{d}^{(2)}, \ldots, \mathbf{d}^{(M)}\}$.

We propose EM-LEARNPSDD, a variant of the (soft) structural EM algorithm (Friedman, 1998), to learn the structure and parameters of ensembles of PSDDs. In soft EM, each example $\mathbf{x}^{(j)}$ takes part in each component (that is, each PSDD r_i) with weight $\alpha_{i,j}$, resulting in weighted datasets $\bar{\mathcal{D}}_i$ for each component. Weights $\alpha_{i,j}$ represent the probability that example $\mathbf{x}^{(j)}$ belongs to distribution r_i, and therefore $\sum_i \alpha_{i,j} = 1$ for all j.

EM-LEARNPSDD consists of two nested learners: an outer EM for structure learning and an inner EM for parameter learning. The outer E-step is the inner learner. The outer M-step uses LEARNPSDD to improve the structure of all PSDD components given the weighted datasets $\bar{\mathcal{D}}_i$. It also updates the component weights as $w_i = \sum_{j=1}^{M} \alpha_{i,j} / \sum_{k=1}^{n} \sum_{j=1}^{M} \alpha_{k,j}$.

The inner E-step redistributes the data over components r_i. For every example $\mathbf{d}^{(j)}$, it updates the weights in each component's weighted dataset $\bar{\mathcal{D}}_i$ as

$$\alpha_{i,j} = \frac{\Pr_{r_i}(\mathbf{d}^{(j)})}{\sum_{k=1}^{n} \Pr_{r_k}(\mathbf{d}^{(j)})}.$$

The inner M-step learns the parameters in r_i from $\bar{\mathcal{D}}_i$ using closed-form estimates (employing a weighted version of Equation 1). Internal EM steps alternate until convergence, or for a maximum number of iterations. We find empirically that a maximum of 3 inner EM iterations is sufficient to improve the parameters and warrants moving to another iteration of the outer EM structure learner.

The initial weighted datasets $\bar{\mathcal{D}}_i$ are found by k-means clustering on $\mathcal{D}$ and softening these clusters by weighting an example in the cluster with $1 - (n-1)\epsilon$ and one not in the cluster with ϵ (default 0.05). K-means clustering empirically provides a better starting point for EM-LEARNPSDD: worlds belonging to the same component distribution tend to be closer in Euclidean distance.

6 RELATED WORK

The sentential decision diagram (SDD) is a tractable representation that is closely related to the PSDD. Despite being a purely logical circuit, one can reduce statistical models to a weighted model counting task on an SDD encoding (Choi et al., 2013). Bekker et al. (2015) learn Markov networks that have a compact SDD for weighted model counting. The learning algorithm uses bottom-up compilation to incrementally add factors to the SDD. It selects features based on a likelihood vs. size trade-off. Adding features is a global modification and requires all parameters to be re-learned by convex optimization.

PSDDs can be reduced to sum-product networks (SPNs), which are a syntactic variation on arithmetic circuits (ACs). A PSDD can be turned into an equivalent SPN by replacing AND nodes by products and OR nodes by sums. Several learning algorithms for SPNs exist. LearnSPN induces an SPT (an SPN tree structure) by splitting on latent variables (Gens and Domingos, 2013). O-SPN and L-SPN improve this algorithm by merging parts of the SPT back into a DAG (Rahman and Gogate, 2016b). Vergari et al. (2015) describe various improvements to reduce overfitting in LearnSPN. SearchSPN shares with LEARNPSDD that it uses local operators (a combination of a type of minimal split on a latent variable with a type of minimal clone) (Dennis and Ventura, 2015).

Probabilistic decision graphs (PDGs) have a variable forest that defines the dependencies between variables, much like vtrees (Jaeger et al., 2006). To induce a variable forest, one learns small PDGs for different forests and chooses the best one. PDG structure learning applies split, merge and redirect operations to the graph in a fixed order, much like L-SPN and O-SPN.

Beyond these, there is a vast literature on tractable learning algorithms that are less related to LEARNPSDD, include ACBN (Lowd and Domingos, 2008), ACMN (Lowd and Rooshenas, 2013), ID-SPN (Rooshenas and Lowd, 2014) and ECNet (Rahman and Gogate, 2016a).

7 EXPERIMENTS

Next, we evaluate the performance of LearnPSDD and EM-LearnPSDD, and provide deeper insights into PSDD learning. Section 7.2 evaluates how vtrees affect the learner. Section 7.3 to 7.6 demonstrate that PSDDs are amenable to learning in probability spaces without logical constraints. Lastly, Section 7.7 shows that LearnPSDD is able to capture a logically constrained probabilistic space while also fitting the data well.

7.1 SETUP

We evaluate our learners on a standard benchmark suite consisting of 20 real-world datasets (Van Haaren and Davis, 2012); see Table 1. These datasets have been used in various previous works for evaluating the performance of assorted tractable model learners (Gens and Domingos, 2013; Lowd and Rooshenas, 2013; Adel et al., 2015; Rooshenas and Lowd, 2014; Rahman and Gogate, 2016a). These datasets do not assume any prior domain knowledge, and are not associated with any logical constraints. Our experiments run for 24 hours or until convergence on the validation set, whichever happens earlier. The experiments run on servers with 16-core 2.6GHz Intel Xeon CPUs and 256GB RAM.

7.2 IMPACT OF VTREES

Because a PSDD's structure is so strongly constrained by the vtree it is normalized for, we would expect vtrees to play a crucial role in determining the size of a PSDDs, and more importantly, the quality of the probability distributions we can learn with the given data and PSDD size available. To evaluate their impact, and the learners described in Section 3, we generate 3 vtrees per dataset: (i) using top-down induction, (ii) using bottom-up induction, and (iii) a balanced vtree with a random variable ordering. We run LearnPSDD for five hours, with the operation depth parameter m set to 3, using these 3 vtrees. We compare the learned PSDDs in terms of their quality (log-likelihood) as a function of learning time, and their size (number of parameters) as a function of quality.

Figure 5 shows the experimental results for a representative dataset (plants). As expected, bottom-up induction learns superior vtrees, followed by top-down and finally random. The PSDD with a better vtree achieves a higher log-likelihood and is more tractable (smaller). Moreover, a better vtree reduces learning time. In all three cases, LearnPSDD starts from a trivial initial PSDD. Hence, the log-likelihood is the same for all vtrees at the start of learning. Bottom-up vtree induction is used for the remaining experiments.

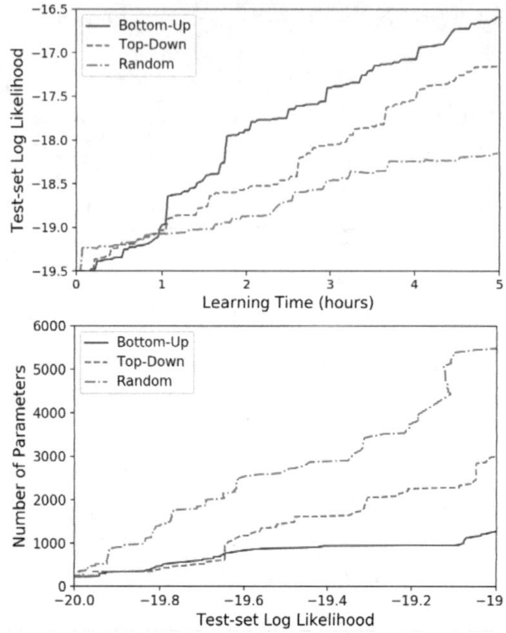

Figure 5: Bottom-up-induced vtrees result in better PSDDs, with higher likelihood and fewer parameters (bottom figure) and are learned in less time (top figure).

7.3 EVALUATION OF LearnPSDD

As discussed in Section 6, the approach LearnPSDD takes is closely related to SearchSPN. We therefore evaluate LearnPSDD's performance in comparison to SearchSPN. The operation copy depth m of LearnPSDD is fixed to 3. As shown in Table 1, LearnPSDD achieves a better test-set log-likelihood than SearchSPN (or ties) in 5 datasets while being competitive in most of the other datasets. In general, LearnPSDD's performance is weaker than SearchSPN. This is expected, because SearchSPN uses many thousands of latent variables, while LearnPSDD uses none, and PSDDs are necessarily more restrictive than SPNs.

7.4 EVALUATION OF EM-LearnPSDD

The structural EM algorithm that augments LearnPSDD essentially decomposes the optimization problems for parameter and structure learning. With a new layer of modeling power, EM-LearnPSDD is expected to learn more effectively. Therefore, we reduce the depth parameter m to learn smaller PSDD components while retaining a high-quality mixture overall. This experiment uses a combination of minimal operations (80%) and operations with a depth of 3 (20%). Minimal operations get chosen most often, resulting in smaller circuits for the same number of operations. We determine the number of components

Table 1: Comparison among LEARNPSDD, EM-LEARNPSDD, SearchSPN, merged L-SPN and merged O-SPN in terms of performance (log-likelihood) and model size (number of parameters). Sizes for SearchSPN are not reported in the original paper. We use the following notation: (1) LL: Average test-set log-likelihood; (2) Size: Number of parameters in the learned model; (3) † denotes a better LL between LEARNPSDD and SearchSPN; (4) * denotes a better LL between LEARNPSDD and EM-LEARNPSDD; (5) Bold likelihoods denote the best LL among EM-LEARNPSDD, merged L-SPN and merged O-SPN.

Datasets	|Var|	|Train|	|Valid|	|Test|	LearnPSDD		EM-LearnPSDD		SearchSPN	Merged L-SPN		Merged O-SPN	
					LL	Size	LL	Size	LL	LL	Size	LL	Size
NLTCS	16	16181	2157	3236	$-6.03^{\dagger *}$	3170	$\mathbf{-6.03}^{*}$	2147	−6.07	−6.04	3988	−6.05	1152
MSNBC	17	291326	38843	58265	$-6.05^{\dagger}$	8977	$\mathbf{-6.04}^{*}$	3891	−6.06	−6.46	2440	−6.08	9478
KDD	64	1800992	19907	34955	$-2.16^{\dagger}$	14974	$\mathbf{-2.12}^{*}$	9182	**−2.16**	−2.14	6670	−2.19	16608
Plants	69	17412	2321	3482	−14.93	13129	-13.79^{*}	13951	$-13.12^{\dagger}$	**−12.69**	47802	−13.49	36960
Audio	100	15000	2000	3000	−42.53	13765	-41.98^{*}	9721	$-40.13^{\dagger}$	**−40.02**	10804	−42.06	6142
Jester	100	9000	1000	4116	−57.67	11322	-53.47^{*}	7014	$-53.08^{\dagger}$	**−52.97**	10002	−55.36	4996
Netflix	100	15000	2000	3000	−58.92	10997	-58.41^{*}	6250	$-56.91^{\dagger}$	**−56.64**	11604	−58.64	6142
Accidents	111	12758	1700	2551	−34.13	10489	-33.64^{*}	6752	$-30.02^{\dagger}$	**−30.01**	13322	−30.83	6846
Retail	135	22041	2938	4408	−11.13	4091	$\mathbf{-10.81}^{*}$	7251	$-10.97^{\dagger}$	−10.87	2162	−10.95	3158
Pumsb-Star	163	12262	1635	2452	−34.11	10489	-33.67^{*}	7965	$-28.69^{\dagger}$	**−24.11**	17604	−24.34	18338
DNA	180	1600	400	1186	-89.11^{*}	6068	−92.67	14864	$-81.76^{\dagger}$	**−85.51**	4320	−87.49	1430
Kosarek	190	33375	4450	6675	$-10.99^{\dagger}$	11034	-10.81^{*}	10179	−11.00	**−10.62**	5318	−10.98	6712
MSWeb	294	29441	32750	5000	$-10.18^{\dagger}$	11389	-9.97^{*}	14512	−10.25	**−9.90**	16484	−10.06	12770
Book	500	8700	1159	1739	−35.90	15197	-34.97^{*}	11292	$-34.91^{\dagger}$	**−34.76**	11998	−37.44	11916
EachMovie	500	4524	1002	591	-56.43^{*}	12483	−58.01	16074	$-53.28^{\dagger}$	**−52.07**	15998	−58.05	19846
WebKB	839	2803	558	838	−163.42	10033	-161.09^{*}	18431	$-157.88^{\dagger}$	**−153.55**	20134	−161.17	10046
Reuters-52	889	6532	1028	1530	−94.94	10585	-89.61^{*}	9546	$-86.38^{\dagger}$	**−83.90**	46232	−87.49	28334
20NewsGrp.	910	11293	3764	3764	−161.41	12222	-161.09^{*}	18431	$-153.63^{\dagger}$	**−154.67**	43684	−161.46	29016
BBC	1058	1670	225	330	−260.83	10585	$\mathbf{-253.19}^{*}$	20327	$-252.13^{\dagger}$	−253.45	21160	−260.59	8454
AD	1556	2461	327	491	-30.49^{*}	9666	−31.78	9521	$-16.97^{\dagger}$	−16.77	49790	**−15.39**	31070

by conducting a grid search over $\{3, 5, 7, 9\}$ on validation data and report the best result for each datasets. EM-LEARNPSDD surpasses or ties the performance of LEARNPSDD in 17 datasets and it learns smaller models in 13 datasets; see Table 1. EM-LEARNPSDD is superior to LEARNPSDD in 12 datasets by being more accurate and more tractable at the same time.

7.5 COMPARISON WITH SPN LEARNERS

SPNs have been demonstrated to be quite effective for tractable learning in probability spaces that are not subject to logical domain constraints. SPN learners have generated state-of-the-art results in the 20 benchmark datasets (Rooshenas and Lowd, 2014; Rahman and Gogate, 2016b). Specifically, merged L-SPN and O-SPN are the first few SPN structure learners that consider a heuristic merging strategy and therefore produce SPNs that have a significant advantage in size with no loss in performance. In fact, merging shows an improvement in test-set log-likelihood for most datasets (Rahman and Gogate, 2016b). We compare our EM-LEARNPSDD with merged L-SPN and merged O-SPN.

Our experiments show that EM-LEARNPSDD is competitive with merged L-SPN and O-SPN. This result is surprising because PSDDs are much more restrictive than SPNs. EM-LEARNPSDD outperforms O-SPN on likelihood in 11 datasets, learns smaller models in 14 datasets, and wins on both measures in 6 datasets; EM-LEARNPSDD outperforms L-SPN on likelihood in 6 datasets, learns smaller models in 14 datasets and wins on both in 2 datasets. See Table 1 for the full results.

7.6 COMPARISON WITH STATE OF THE ART

In this section, we demonstrate that we can achieve near state-of-the art performance using our EM-LEARNPSDD algorithm. It was shown in previous studies that bagged ensembles with expectation maximization can significantly improve results on many of the 20 datasets (Rahman and Gogate, 2016a,b). We therefore build bagging ensembles on top of EM-LEARNPSDD. The result is still equivalent to a single PSDD, by a translation similar to the one shown in Figure 4 for mixture models, except the w_i for bagging represent a uniform distribution. Our goal with this experiment is to match or exceed the state-of-the-art. This is a very strong baseline, consisting of five competitive tractable model learners: (1) ACMN (Lowd and Rooshenas, 2013), (2) ID-SPN (Rooshenas and Lowd, 2014), (3) SPN-SVD (Adel et al., 2015), (4) ECNet (Rahman and Gogate, 2016a) and (6) Merged L-SPN (Rahman and Gogate, 2016b).

When fixing the number of bags to 10, EM-LEARNPSDD is competitive with the state of the art and surpasses it on 6 out of 20 datasets; see Table 2.

Overall, the experiments outlined so far have incrementally demonstrated that the PSDD structure learning algorithms proposed in this paper (LEARNPSDD and EM-

Table 2: Comparison of test-set log-likelihood between LearnPSDD and the state of the art († denotes best).

Datasets	|Var|	LearnPSDD Ensemble	Best-to-Date
NLTCS	16	$-5.99^{\dagger}$	-6.00
MSNBC	17	$-6.04^{\dagger}$	$-6.04^{\dagger}$
KDD	64	$-2.11^{\dagger}$	-2.12
Plants	69	-13.02	$-11.99^{\dagger}$
Audio	100	-39.94	$-39.49^{\dagger}$
Jester	100	-51.29	$-41.11^{\dagger}$
Netflix	100	$-55.71^{\dagger}$	-55.84
Accidents	111	-30.16	$-24.87^{\dagger}$
Retail	135	$-10.72^{\dagger}$	-10.78
Pumsb-Star	163	-26.12	$-22.40^{\dagger}$
DNA	180	-88.01	$-80.03^{\dagger}$
Kosarek	190	$-10.52^{\dagger}$	-10.54
MSWeb	294	-9.89	$-9.22^{\dagger}$
Book	500	-34.97	$-30.18^{\dagger}$
EachMovie	500	-58.01	$-51.14^{\dagger}$
WebKB	839	-161.09	$-150.10^{\dagger}$
Reuters-52	889	-89.61	$-80.66^{\dagger}$
20NewsGrp.	910	-155.97	$-150.88^{\dagger}$
BBC	1058	-253.19	$-233.26^{\dagger}$
AD	1556	-31.78	$-14.36^{\dagger}$

LEARNPSDD) perform competitively in classical probability spaces without domain constraints. This is despite the fact that PSDDs are more tractable and have more syntactic properties than their alternatives.

7.7 EVALUATION IN A CONSTRAINED SPACE

PSDDs pay for their desirable properties, such as their ability to encode domain knowledge into their base, and ability to answer complex queries, by being a more restrictive representation. The experiments so far do not directly exploit these desirable properties, to allow for a comparison with other tractable learners. They therefore only experience the restrictiveness. However, the next experiments show that in practical domains, and spaces with domain constraints in particular, having these desirable properties can be a great advantage.

Many real-world datasets contain discrete multi-valued data, instead of being only binary. The straightforward way to use general ACs for multi-valued domains, is to introduce a binary variable for each value of the multi-valued variable. Unfortunately, in the learned distribution, it will then be possible for a multi-valued variable to have multiple values simultaneously. PSDDs can easily cope with this by encoding into the base that binary variables belonging to the same multi-valued variable must be mutually exclusive, and at least one must be true.

Table 3: Incorporating domain constraints improves the quality of the learned distributions. Compared settings: (i) unconstrained LEARNPSDD, (ii) constrained PSDD (no LEARNPSDD), and (iii) constrained LEARNPSDD.

Datasets	No Constraint	PSDD	LEARNPSDD
Adult	-18.41	-14.14	-12.86
CovType	-14.39	-8.81	-7.32

To assess the advantage of PSDD in this setting, we compare three learning approaches: (i) LEARNPSDD without domain constraints, (ii) parameter learning on an SDD that is compiled from the constraints (as in prior work, for example Kisa et al. (2014b)), and (iii) applying LEARNPSDD on the initial PSDD obtained from (ii). We use the same vtree in all settings and run LEARNPSDD for 5 hours. We conduct the experiments on two real-world datasets from the UCI repository: Adult and CoverType. Continuous features are discretized into four equal-sized bins. Adult has 14 original (125 binary) variables and CoverType has 12 original (84 binary) variables. Adult and CoverType respectively contain 32,562 and 581,012 examples.

As expected, learning structure on top of the constraints yields the best models. Interestingly, only using the constraints to come up with the SDD structure strongly outperforms unconstrained structure learning, which shows that ignoring constraints complicates learning significantly. The improvement is due to the fact that the probabilities of many impossible assignments (given the multi-valued constraint) are set to 0 and hence the probabilities of the remaining assignments correspondingly increase.

8 CONCLUSIONS

The two questions we raised at the beginning of this paper both receive a strong positive answer. LEARNPSDD is an effective algorithm for learning PSDD structures. It achieves some state-of-the-art results learning classical probability distributions that are not subject to constraints. Moreover, it can just as easily induce structure over logically constrained spaces without losing any domain-specific information.

Acknowledgements

The authors thank Arthur Choi and Yujia Shen for helpful discussions. This research was conducted while JB was a visiting student at UCLA. JB is supported by IWT (SB/141744). This work is partially supported by NSF grants #IIS-1657613, #IIS-1633857 and DARPA XAI grant #N66001-17-2-4032.

References

T. Adel, D. Balduzzi, and A. Ghodsi. Learning the structure of sum-product networks via an SVD-based algorithm. *UAI*, pages 32–41, 2015.

J. Bekker, J. Davis, A. Choi, A. Darwiche, and G. Van den Broeck. Tractable learning for complex probability queries. In *NIPS*, pages 2242–2250, 2015.

C. Boutilier, N. Friedman, M. Goldszmidt, and D. Koller. Context-specific independence in Bayesian networks. In *UAI*, pages 115–123, 1996.

A. Chechetka and C. Guestrin. Efficient principled learning of thin junction trees. In *NIPS*, pages 273–280, 2007.

A. Choi and A. Darwiche. Dynamic minimization of sentential decision diagrams. In *AAAI*, 2013.

A. Choi, D. Kisa, and A. Darwiche. Compiling probabilistic graphical models using sentential decision diagrams. In *ECSQARU*, pages 121–132, 2013.

A. Choi, G. Van den Broeck, and A. Darwiche. Tractable learning for structured probability spaces: A case study in learning preference distributions. In *IJCAI*, 2015.

A. Choi, N. Tavabi, and A. Darwiche. Structured features in naive Bayes classification. In *AAAI*, pages 3233–3240, 2016.

A. Darwiche. A differential approach to inference in Bayesian networks. *JACM*, 50(3):280–305, 2003.

A. Darwiche. SDD: A new canonical representation of propositional knowledge bases. In *IJCAI*, pages 819–826, 2011.

A. Darwiche and P. Marquis. A knowledge compilation map. *JAIR*, 17:229–264, 2002.

A. Darwiche, R. Dechter, A. Choi, V. Gogate, and L. Otten. Results from the probablistic inference evaluation of UAI-08. 2008.

A. Dennis and D. Ventura. Greedy structure search for sum-product networks. *IJCAI*, 2015.

P. Domingos, M. Niepert, and D. L. (Eds.). ICML workshop on learning tractable probabilistic models. 2014.

N. Friedman. The Bayesian structural em algorithm. *UAI*, pages 129–138, 1998.

R. Gens and P. Domingos. Learning the structure of sum-product networks. In *ICML*, pages 873–880, 2013.

M. Jaeger, J. D. Nielsen, and T. Silander. Learning probabilistic decision graphs. *IJAR*, 42(1):84–100, 2006.

G. Karypis. METIS a software package for partitioning graphs, partitioning meshes, and computing fill-reducing orderings of sparse matrices, version 5.1.0. Technical report, University of Minnesota, 2013.

D. Kisa, G. Van den Broeck, A. Choi, and A. Darwiche. Probabilistic sentential decision diagrams: Learning with massive logical constraints. In *LTPM*, 2014a.

D. Kisa, G. Van den Broeck, A. Choi, and A. Darwiche. Probabilistic sentential decision diagrams. In *KR*, pages 1–10, 2014b.

V. Kolmogorov. Blossom v: a new implementation of a minimum cost perfect matching algorithm. *Mathematical Programming Computation*, 1(1):43–67, 2009.

D. Lowd and P. Domingos. Learning arithmetic circuits. In *UAI*, pages 383–392, 2008.

D. Lowd and A. Rooshenas. Learning markov networks with arithmetic circuits. In *AISTATS*, pages 406–414, 2013.

N. D. Mauro and A. Vergari. PGM tutorial on learning sum-product networks. 2016.

M. Meila and M. I. Jordan. Learning with mixtures of trees. *JMLR*, 1:1–48, 2000.

C. Meinel and T. Theobald. *Algorithms and Data Structures in VLSI Design: OBDD-foundations and applications*. Springer Science & Business Media, 2012.

M. Narasimhan and J. Bilmes. PAC-learning bounded tree-width graphical models. In *UAI*, 2004.

R. Peharz, R. Gens, and P. Domingos. Learning selective sum-product networks. In *LTPM*, 2014.

H. Poon and P. Domingos. Sum-product networks: A new deep architecture. In *UAI*, 2011.

T. Rahman and V. Gogate. Learning ensembles of cutset networks. In *AAAI*, pages 3301–3307, 2016a.

T. Rahman and V. Gogate. Merging strategies for sum-product networks: From trees to graphs. In *UAI*, 2016b.

T. Rahman, P. Kothalkar, and V. Gogate. Cutset networks: A simple, tractable, and scalable approach for improving the accuracy of Chow-Liu trees. In *ECML PKDD*, pages 630–645, 2014.

A. Rooshenas and D. Lowd. Learning sum-product networks with direct and indirect variable interactions. In *ICML*, pages 710–718, 2014.

Y. Shen, A. Choi, and A. Darwiche. Tractable operations for arithmetic circuits of probabilistic models. In *NIPS*, 2016.

J. Van Haaren and J. Davis. Markov network structure learning: A randomized feature generation approach. In *AAAI*, pages 1148–1154, 2012.

A. Vergari, N. Di Mauro, and F. Esposito. Simplifying, regularizing and strengthening sum-product network structure learning. In *ECML PKDD*, pages 343–358, 2015.

Algorithm 3: PartialCopy($q, \mathbf{z}, m, n2c$)

Input: q: node to copy, $\mathbf{z}$: variable assignment, m: depth of copy, $n2c$: map of nodes to copy

Result: constrained copy of q in $n2c$

1 $E = \emptyset$
2 $\mathbf{X}$ *and* $\mathbf{Y}$ *are the partition variables of* q
3 $\mathbf{z}_p = \exists_{\mathbf{Y}}\mathbf{z}$; $\mathbf{z}_s = \exists_{\mathbf{X}}\mathbf{z}$
4 **for** $i \leftarrow 1$ **to** n **do**
5   **if** $\mathbf{z}_p \models [p_i] \wedge \mathbf{z}_s \models [s_i]$ **then**
6     $p' = p_i$; $s' = s_i$
7   **if** $m > 0$ **or** $[p_i] \not\Rightarrow \mathbf{z}_p$ **then**
8   **if** $p_i \notin n2c$ **then** PartialCopy($p_i, \mathbf{z}_p, m-1, n2c$)
9       $p' = n2c[p_i]$
10   **if** $m > 0$ **or** $[s_i] \not\Rightarrow \mathbf{z}_s$ **then**
11   **if** $s_i \notin n2c$ **then** PartialCopy($s_i, \mathbf{z}_s, m-1, n2c$)
12       $s' = n2c[s_i]$
13     $E = E \cup [(p', s')]$
14 $n2c[q] = \text{NewNode}(E)$

A PARTIAL COPY OF A PSDD

A copy of a node creates a new fold for that node and its descendants up to a specified level (Algorithm 3, lines 8,11). The elements of the copy beyond the specified level redirect to nodes of the original PSDD (line 6). Optionally, the copy can be constrained to a partial assignment for some variables. In this case, only descendants that agree with the assignment are kept in the copy (line 5) and nodes beyond the specified level may have to be copied to enforce the constraint (lines 7,10).

B PROOF OF SYNTACTIC VALIDITY OF OPERATIONS

Definition 1 (Valid PSDD node)**.** *A PSDD node q that is normalized for a vtree node v is valid if: (1) all primes p_i are valid nodes and normalized for the left child of v; (2) all subs s_i are valid nodes and normalized for the right child of v; (3) the primes are mutual exclusive: $\forall i \neq j, [p_i] \wedge [p_j] = \bot$; (4) all elements are satisfiable: $\forall i, [p_i] \wedge [s_i] \neq \bot$.*

A valid operation keeps the PSDD syntactically sound and does not alter the base of the root node.

Lemma 1 (PartialCopy($q, \mathbf{z}, m, n2c$) is valid)**.** *If the following conditions are satisfied: (1) q is valid; (2) $n2c$ is valid (this means that it only contains entries $q \to q'$ where q and q' are normalized for the same vtree, valid and $[q'] = [q] \wedge \mathbf{z}_q$, where $\mathbf{z}_q$ is the projection of the assignment $\mathbf{z}$ to the variables in the vtree of node q); (3) $\mathbf{z}$ only contains variables in the vtree of q and is satisfiable in q: $\mathbf{z} \models [q]$.*

Proof. Proof by induction.

Note the following preconditions hold and we use them in our proof: (1) $n2c$ includes q; (2) $n2c$ is valid.

Base case: $m = 0$ and $[q] \to \mathbf{z}$. In the base case, only one decision node is added according to $n2c$ which is q', the copy of q. Because q and q' have the same elements, q' is valid and $[q] = [q']$. Because $\mathbf{z}$ is implied by $[q]$, $[q'] = [q] \wedge \mathbf{z}_q$.

Induction step: To use the inductive assumption, we first show that the preconditions hold for the calls of PartialCopy. Because q is valid, so are its primes and subs. By induction and precondition, $n2c$ is valid. Finally, $\mathbf{z}_p$ and $\mathbf{z}_s$ only contain the relevant variables because the others are forgotten using existential quantification.

The first postcondition is satisfied because q is added to $n2c$ in line 14. In terms of the second postcondition, we consider 3 cases: (i) The entry is already in $n2c$ when PartialCopy is called, then it is valid because of the precondition. (ii) The entry is added by a recursive call of PartialCopy, then it is valid because of induction. (iii) The entry is $q \to q'$, where q' has an element (p'_i, s'_i) for every element $(p_i, s_i) \in q$, except for those that do not agree with the assignment: $p_i \wedge \mathbf{z}_p = \bot$ or $s_i \wedge \mathbf{z}_s = \bot$. p'_i and s'_i are normalized for the correct vtrees because they either are the original children, or they come from $n2c$ which is valid by the precondition and induction.

We proceed to prove the mutual exclusivity of the copied primes, the satisfiability of the copied elements and the correctness of the base of the copied decision node.

The primes of q' are mutually exclusive:

$$\begin{aligned}[p'_i] \wedge [p'_j] &= [p_i] \wedge \mathbf{z}_p \wedge [p_j] \wedge \mathbf{z}_p \\ &= [p_i] \wedge [p_j] \wedge \mathbf{z}_p \\ &= \bot\end{aligned}$$

All elements of q' are satisfiable because all the elements of q are satisfiable and elements that would become unsatisfied by conditioning on $\mathbf{z}$ are removed.

The base of q' is the base of q constraint by $\mathbf{z}$:

$$[q'] = \bigvee_{i \in q : \mathbf{z}_p \models [p_i] \wedge \mathbf{z}_s \models [s_i]} [p'_i] \wedge [s'_i]$$

$$= \bigvee_{i \in q} [p_i] \wedge \mathbf{z}_p \wedge [s_i] \wedge \mathbf{z}_s$$
$$= \mathbf{z} \wedge \bigvee_{i \in q} [p_i] \wedge [s_i]$$
$$= \mathbf{z} \wedge [q]$$

□

Proposition 4 (Split(q, i, Zs, m) is valid)**.** *If the following conditions are satisfied: (1) q is valid. (2) All $\mathbf{z} \in Zs$ only contain variables of the left children of q's vtree and are satisfiable in the ith element of q: $\mathbf{z} \models [p_i] \wedge [s_i]$. (3) All $\mathbf{z} \in Zs$ are mutually exclusive and exhaustive.*

Proof. Note that the following postconditions hold and we use them in our proof: (1) q is valid; (2) the base of q is not altered: $[q] = [q_{\text{old}}]$.

The primes and subs of q are normalized for the correct vtree because q is valid and $n2c$ is valid (Lemma 1).

The primes of q are mutually exclusive if: (i) the original primes are mutually exclusive, (ii) the new primes are mutually exclusive and (iii) every pair of an original prime and a new prime is mutually exclusive.

All the elements of q are satisfiable, because the precondition states that all the assignments must be satisfiable in the split element.

The original base of q is $[q_{\text{old}}] = \bigvee_j [p_j] \wedge [s_j]$. After the split, the base is:

$$[q] = \bigvee_{j \neq i} [p_j] \wedge [s_j] \vee \bigvee_{\mathbf{z} \in Zs} [p_{i,\mathbf{z}}] \wedge [s_i]$$
$$= \bigvee_{j \neq i} [p_j] \wedge [s_j] \vee \bigvee_{\mathbf{z} \in Zs} [p_i] \wedge \mathbf{z} \wedge [s_i]$$
$$= \bigvee_{j \neq i} [p_j] \wedge [s_j] \vee \Big([p_i] \wedge [s_i] \wedge \bigvee_{\mathbf{z} \in Zs} \mathbf{z} \Big)$$
$$= \bigvee_{j \neq i} [p_j] \wedge [s_j] \vee \Big([p_i] \wedge [s_i] \Big)$$
$$= [q_{\text{old}}]$$

□

Proposition 5 (Clone(q, P, m) is valid)**.** *If the following conditions are satisfied: (1) q is valid; (2) $\forall (\pi, i) \in P$, q is either $p_{\pi,i}$ or $s_{\pi,i}$.*

Proof. Note the following postconditions hold and we use them in our proof: (1) $\forall (\pi, i) \in P$, π is valid; (2) $\forall (\pi, i) \in P$, the base of π is not altered: $[\pi] = [\pi_{\text{old}}]$. Because of lemma 1 and the preconditions, q' is a valid node with the same vtree and base as q. Redirecting the parents to this node therefore keeps the parents valid and also remain the base as unaltered. □

C IMPLEMENTATION DETAILS

We discuss implementation details of LEARNPSDD.

Data In The Nodes The training data is explicitly kept in the PSDD nodes during learning. Every node contains a bitset that indicates which examples agree with the context of that node. This speeds up parameter estimation and log-likelihood calculations, which are needed for every execution and simulation of an operation. For simulation of an operation, a bitmask is used to represent the examples that are moved to a copy.

Unique Node Cache To avoid duplicate calculations when doing inference, the PSDD should not have duplicate nodes. This is accomplished using the unique-node technique, where a cache of the nodes is kept and it is checked every time before creating a new node (Meinel and Theobald, 2012). In general, two nodes are considered equal if they have the same (p, s, θ) elements. During learning, however, we adapt this by considering two nodes different if they might evolve to a different structure, based on the training data that it contains. There are two reasons for a node not to change. First, if the node's base is a complete assignment, i.e. if all descendants of this node have only one element, then there are possible LEARNPSDD operations. A clone would be useless in this case because all the parameters would remain as 1. Second, if the node contains no data. Such a node cannot contribute to the log-likelihood and has therefore no reason to change.

The number of added nodes is no longer a local characteristic of an operation, as it depends on the nodes available in the cache. To cope with this, we consider nodes that can be cached as free nodes: they are not counted in the score. This makes sense because if the node is already in the cache, it does not need to be added, otherwise adding it to the cache can make subsequent operations less expensive to simulate or execute.

SDDs In The Nodes SDDs are kept in the nodes to represent their base. This is not really needed, because the base is implied by the structure of the PSDD. However, during structure learning, PSDDs grow bigger, while SDDs do not. Therefore, if the base needs to be checked, doing this on the SDD is more efficient. Note that before any structure learning is done, the SDD is larger than the PSDD because SDD's primes need to be exhaustive and therefore the SDD may have elements for subs that represent false. However, PSDDs are expected to grow larger than the corresponding SDDs during structure learning.

A Probabilistic Framework for Zero-Shot Multi-Label Learning

Abhilash Gaure, Aishwarya Gupta, Vinay Kumar Verma, Piyush Rai
{agaure,aish,vkverma,piyush}@cse.iitk.ac.in
Department of Computer Science and Engineering
IIT Kanpur, India

Abstract

We present a probabilistic framework for multi-label learning for the setting when the test data may require predicting labels that were not available at training time (i.e., the zero-shot learning setting). We develop a probabilistic model that leverages the co-occurrence statistics of the labels via a joint generative model for the label matrix (which denotes the label presence/absence for each training example) and for the *label co-occurrence matrix* (which denotes how many times a pair of labels co-occurs with each other). In addition to handling the unseen labels at test time, leveraging the co-occurrence information may also help in the standard multi-label learning setting, especially if the number of training examples is very small and/or the label matrix of training examples has a large fraction of missing entries. Our experimental results demonstrate the efficacy of our model in handling unseen labels.

1 Introduction

Multi-label learning (Gibaja and Ventura, 2015, 2014) refers to the problem of annotating an object with a subset of labels from a large label vocabulary (Prabhu and Varma, 2014; Jain et al., 2016; Babbar and Schölkopf, 2017). Unlike standard classification paradigms such as binary or multi-class classification, which associate each object with a *single* label (binary/discrete), in multi-label learning, each object is associated with a binary *label vector* (potentially very large), denoting the presence/absence of each label. Multi-label learning has a wide range of applications in diverse domains such as computer vision (Wang et al., 2016), computational advertising and recommender systems (Prabhu and Varma, 2014; Jain et al., 2016), etc.

To handle the large number of labels and to leverage the label correlations, existing multi-label learning algorithms usually employ certain structural assumptions on the binary label matrix. One such commonly used assumption is the low-rank assumption on the label matrix Yu et al. (2014); Rai et al. (2015). In a probabilistic setting, this is equivalent to modeling the label matrix using a generative latent factor model (Jain et al., 2017) which assumes that each example n and each label ℓ are associated with latent factors $\boldsymbol{u}_n \in \mathbb{R}^K$ and $\boldsymbol{v}_\ell \in \mathbb{R}^K$, respectively, and the *relevance* of the label ℓ for the example n is based on how *similar* $\boldsymbol{u}_n$ and $\boldsymbol{v}_\ell$ are.

One important challenge for multi-label learning that has not been adequately addressed so far is the setting where not all the labels are available at the time of training the model (Zhang et al., 2016; Mensink et al., 2014). In many real-world multi-label learning problems, e.g., in recommender systems, the set of possible labels (e.g., items/products) keeps on increasing and it may not be feasible to re-train the model every time new labels are added to the set of possible labels. This requires collecting fresh training data and annotating it with both existing as well as new labels. This process may be expensive and time-consuming.

To address this issue, we present a generative framework that is based on leveraging the co-occurrence statistics of the *seen* labels (i.e., those present in the training data) with all the labels (both seen and unseen labels). These co-occurrence statistics can usually be obtained from an external source (e.g., a text corpus, such as Wikipedia) and are in form of *counts* of how many times a pair of labels is found to co-occur with each other. We use the train data label matrix and the label co-occurrence matrix to learn the embeddings (in form of low-dimensional latent factors) of both seen and unseen labels using a generative model. Our generative framework employs a negative binomial latent factor model for modeling the (count-valued) co-occurrence of each pair of labels.

We further combine this negative binomial latent factor model with another logistic-Bernoulli latent factor model that is learned exclusively on the binary label matrix of the training data. In order to share information between both generative models, we maintain another set of latent factors (defined only for the seen labels), that are shared between both latent factor models.

We leverage the first set of latent factors (defined for both seen and unseen classes), learned exclusively using the label co-occurrences, and the second set of *shared* latent factors (defined for only seen classes), learned using both label co-occurrences and the binary label matrix, to then learn the label predictors for each of the unseen labels. These label predictors can be used at test time to predict the presence/absence of each of the unseen labels.

In addition to its ability to leverage the label co-occurrences to handle the unseen labels at test time, one of the appealing aspects of our framework is its simplicity. Our generative framework admits a very simple inference procedure, for which both fully Bayesian inference or point estimation based inference can be used. Moreover, using data-augmentation techniques (Polson et al., 2013), our framework enjoys full local-conjugacy, which enables us to develop simple Gibbs sampling, variational inference, or Expectation Maximization (EM) algorithms, for doing inference in our model. In particular, we propose an efficient EM algorithm for our framework, which is extremely simple to implement, with each parameter update only requiring solving a simple weighted ridge-regression style problem.

2 The Model

2.1 Background and Notations

In multi-label learning, the goal is to learn a model to predict, for any example $\boldsymbol{x} \in \mathbb{R}^D$, a binary label vector $\boldsymbol{y} \in \{0,1\}^L$, which denotes the presence/absence of L binary-valued labels for that example. We consider a particularly challenging setting where the training data may only have presence/absence information available for $L_s < L$ labels, with $L = L_s + L_u$, where the subscripts s and u refer to the *seen* and *unseen* labels, respectively. On the other hand, the set of possible labels for test examples can include both seen as well as unseen labels. Our goal is to learn a model that is able to predict the presence/absence for both seen and unseen labels for the test examples.

To learn the model, we assume that we are given N training examples as $\{(\boldsymbol{x}_1, \boldsymbol{y}_1), \ldots, (\boldsymbol{x}_N, \boldsymbol{y}_N)\}$ with $\boldsymbol{x}_n \in \mathbb{R}^D$ and $\boldsymbol{y}_n \in \{0,1\}^{L_s}$, $n = 1, \ldots, N$. We define $\mathbf{X} = \{\boldsymbol{x}_1, \ldots, \boldsymbol{x}_N\}$ to denote the $N \times D$ feature matrix and $\mathbf{Y} = \{\boldsymbol{y}_1, \ldots, \boldsymbol{y}_N\}$ to denote the $N \times L_s$ binary label matrix. Note again that the training data only has the label information for the seen labels.

In addition to the $N \times L_s$ label matrix $\mathbf{Y}$ for the training examples, we also assume that we have access to the label co-occurrence information of each seen label with *all* the labels (both seen and unseen). This information can usually be obtained *unsupervisedly* from an external corpus (e.g., Wikipedia). We assume this information is available in form of an $L_s \times L$ *count-valued* matrix $\mathbf{M}$ where $m_{\ell\ell'}$ denotes the number of times a seen class label $\ell \in \{1, \ldots, L_s\}$ has been found to co-occur with a seen/unseen class label $\ell' \in \{1, \ldots, L\}$ in the external source of data used to compute the label co-occurrences. Our goal will be to leverage the label co-occurrence information to enable our model to also predict the presence/absence of the L_u unseen labels for which have no information in the label matrix $\mathbf{Y}$ of the training data.

Also note that even when $L_s = L$, i.e., when all the labels are available at training time, using the $L \times L$ label co-occurrence matrix $\mathbf{M}$ may still be useful if a large fraction of entries in the label matrix $\mathbf{Y}$ are missing, as is often the case in many multi-label learning problems with partial label information (Yu et al., 2014).

2.2 Modeling the Label Matrix

Given the training data in form of the $N \times D$ feature matrix $\mathbf{X}$ and the $N \times L_s$ label matrix $\mathbf{Y}$ (possibly only partially observed), we assume that each *observed* entry $y_{n\ell} \in \{0,1\}$ of $\mathbf{Y}$ is generated from a latent factor model. Specifically, we assume that each input $\boldsymbol{x}_n$, $n = 1, \ldots, N$ is associated with an *input latent factor* $\boldsymbol{u}_n \in \mathbb{R}^K$ and each label $\ell = 1, \ldots, L_s$ is associated with a *label latent factor* $\boldsymbol{v}_\ell \in \mathbb{R}^K$. These latent factors can be thought of as low-dimensional embeddings. Conditioned on these latent factors, we assume the following model for each observed binary label $y_{n\ell}$ in $\mathbf{Y}$

$$p(y_{n\ell} = 1 | \boldsymbol{u}_n, \boldsymbol{v}_\ell) = \frac{1}{1 + \exp(-\boldsymbol{u}_n^\top \boldsymbol{v}_\ell)} \quad (1)$$

We also assume the following prior distributions on the latent factors $\boldsymbol{u}_n$, $n = 1, \ldots, N$ and $\boldsymbol{v}_\ell$, $\ell = 1, \ldots, L_s$.

$$p(\boldsymbol{u}_n | \boldsymbol{x}_n, \mathbf{W}) = \mathcal{N}(\boldsymbol{u}_n | \mathbf{W}\boldsymbol{x}_n, \lambda_u^{-1}\mathbf{I}) \quad (2)$$

$$p(\boldsymbol{v}_\ell) = \mathcal{N}(\boldsymbol{v}_\ell | \mathbf{0}, \lambda_v^{-1}\mathbf{I}) \quad (3)$$

Note that we condition the latent factors $\boldsymbol{u}_n \in \mathbb{R}^K$ on the corresponding inputs $\boldsymbol{x}_n \in \mathbb{R}^D$ by assuming that mean of the Gaussian prior on $\boldsymbol{u}_n$ depends on $\boldsymbol{x}_n$ via a regression model. Specifically, in Eq. 2, $\mathbf{W}$ is a $K \times D$ matrix of regression weights which maps the feature vector $\boldsymbol{x}_n$ to the latent factors $\boldsymbol{u}_n$. Conditioning the latent factors

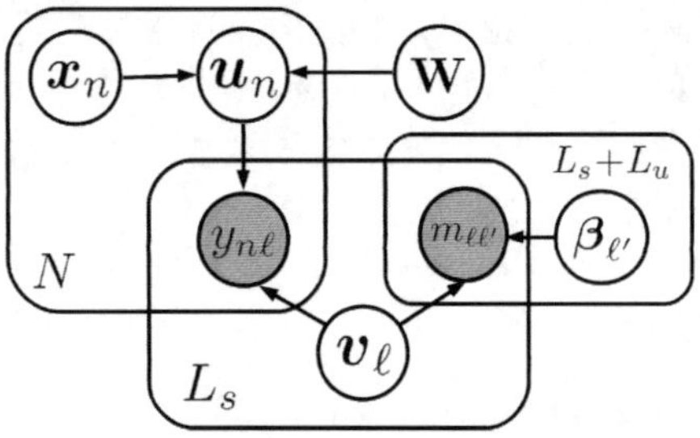

Figure 1: Our generative model in the plate notation. Note: Hyperparameters not shown for brevity.

this way also allows us to predict the latent factors of any test example $\boldsymbol{x}_*$ as $\mathbb{E}[\boldsymbol{u}_*|\boldsymbol{x}_*\mathbf{W}] \approx \mathbf{W}\boldsymbol{x}_*$, which is required to predict the label vector for this test example.

2.3 Modeling Label Co-occurrences

To incorporate the label co-occurrence information in our model, we assume another generative model for the $L_s \times L$ label co-occurrence matrix $\mathbf{M}$ and combine this generative model with the generative model for the label matrix $\mathbf{Y}$, that we described in Sec. 2.2.

To model the label co-occurrence matrix $\mathbf{M}$, we assume another set of label latent factors for each seen/unseen label, $\{\boldsymbol{\beta}_{\ell'}\}_{\ell'=1}^{L}$, with $\boldsymbol{\beta}_{\ell'} \in \mathbb{R}^K$ having a Gaussian prior

$$p(\beta_{\ell'}) = \mathcal{N}(\beta_{\ell'}|\mathbf{0}, \lambda_\beta^{-1}\mathbf{I}) \tag{4}$$

We can then model each count-valued entry $m_{\ell\ell'}$, $\ell = 1, \ldots, L_s, \ell' = 1, \ldots, L$, of $\mathbf{M}$ using a negative binomial distribution, as follows

$$p(m_{\ell\ell'}|r, p_{\ell\ell'}) = \text{NB}(m_{\ell\ell'}|r, p_{\ell\ell'}) \tag{5}$$

where

$$p_{\ell\ell'} = \frac{1}{1 + \exp(-\boldsymbol{v}_\ell^\top \beta_{\ell'})} \tag{6}$$

and r is the overdispersion parameter of the negative binomial distribution,where the negative binomial is

$$\text{NB}(m = k|r, p) \propto (1-p)^r p^k$$

Fig. 1 shows the overall generative model. Note that the label latent factors $\{\boldsymbol{v}_\ell\}_{\ell=1}^{L_s}$, learned exclusively for the seen labels, are shared by both $\mathbf{Y}$ and $\mathbf{M}$, whereas the label latent factors $\{\beta_{\ell'}\}_{\ell'=1}^{L}$ which are defined for both seen and unseen are only used to model $\mathbf{M}$.

One particular benefit of modeling the label co-occurrences via a negative binomial is the fact that it better models the overdispersion in the distribution of count-valued data, as compared to other distributions such as Poisson. Another benefit is that the form of the negative binomial enables us to develop an efficient algorithm based on Pólya-gamma augmentation (Polson et al., 2013) (Sec. 4), which results in very simple ridge-regression like update equations for the latent factors.

3 Handling Unseen Labels at Test Time

The model described in Sec. 2 is able to leverage the label co-occurrences, with the latent factors $\{\boldsymbol{v}_\ell\}_{\ell=1}^{L_s}$, shared by $\mathbf{Y}$ and $\mathbf{M}$, acting as a "conduit". This leads to improved estimates of the model parameters, especially when the label matrix $\mathbf{Y}$ might have a large fraction of its entries as missing. However, this model cannot be used to predict the presence/absence of unseen labels for any test example. To see this, note that although our model learns the label latent factors $\{\beta_{\ell'}\}_{\ell'=1}^{L}$ for seen as well as unseen labels, the $\{\beta_{\ell'}\}_{\ell'=1}^{L}$ only appear in the generative model for the label co-occurrence matrix $\mathbf{M}$ (cf., Fig. 1 and Eq. 5). Therefore these cannot be used to predict the unseen labels $\ell = L_s + 1, \ldots, L$ in the label vector $\boldsymbol{y}_*$ of a test example $\boldsymbol{x}_*$.

In particular, note that, as per Eq. 1, predicting each binary label $y_{*\ell}$ in the label vector $\boldsymbol{y}_* \in \{0,1\}^L$ associated with the test input $\boldsymbol{x}_* \in \mathbb{R}^D$ would require computing

$$p(y_{*\ell} = 1|\boldsymbol{u}_*, \boldsymbol{v}_\ell) = \frac{1}{1 + \exp(-\boldsymbol{u}_*^\top \boldsymbol{v}_\ell)} \tag{7}$$

where the test input's latent factors $\boldsymbol{u}_*$ can be approximated using the test input's feature vector $\boldsymbol{x}_* \in \mathbb{R}^D$ and the $K \times D$ regression weight matrix $\mathbf{W}$ as $\boldsymbol{u}_* \approx \mathbf{W}\boldsymbol{x}_*$.

However, the label latent factors $\boldsymbol{v}_\ell$ required in the evaluation of $p(y_{*\ell} = 1|\boldsymbol{u}_*, \boldsymbol{v}_\ell)$ in Eq. 7 are only available for the *seen* class labels since these are learned using only the $N \times L_s$ label matrix of the training data. In order to compute $p(y_{*\ell} = 1|\boldsymbol{u}_*, \boldsymbol{v}_\ell)$ to predict the presence/absence of labels not seen at training time, we first need an estimate of the latent factors $\boldsymbol{v}_\ell$ for all the unseen labels $\ell = L_s + 1, \ldots, L$. To handle this, we augment our framework with another regression model that will allow us to estimate $\{\boldsymbol{v}_\ell\}_{\ell=L_s+1}^{L}$ for the unseen labels.

To elaborate our regression-based approach for doing this, note that our model, as described in Sec. 2, learns *two* types of latent factors for each label. We will refer to these as *type-1* latent factors $\{\boldsymbol{v}_\ell\}_{\ell=1}^{L_s}$ that are learned for only the seen labels, and *type-2* latent factors $\{\beta_{\ell'}\}_{\ell'=1}^{L}$ are learned for both seen as well as unseen labels.

To predict type-1 latent factors $\{\boldsymbol{v}_\ell\}_{\ell=L_s+1}^{L}$ for unseen labels, we learn a regression model that learns to map the type-2 latent factors to type-1 latent factors using the obtained estimates of type-1 and type-2 latent factors of the *seen* labels. Specifically, given the estimates $\{\hat{\boldsymbol{v}}_\ell\}_{\ell=1}^{L_s}$ and $\{\hat{\boldsymbol{\beta}}_\ell\}_{\ell=1}^{L_s}$ of the type-1 and type-2 latent factors of seen labels learned by our generative model, we learn a regression function f, s.t. $\hat{\boldsymbol{v}}_\ell \approx f(\hat{\boldsymbol{\beta}}_\ell), \ell = 1, \ldots, L_s$, and then use the learned regression function f to predict the type-1 latent factors $\{\boldsymbol{v}_\ell\}_{\ell=L_s+1}^{L}$ for the unseen labels using their corresponding type-2 latent factors.

The function $f : \mathbb{R}^K \to \mathbb{R}^K$ can be modeled as a linear regression model or a nonlinear model (e.g., kernel regression or a deep neural net). In this paper, we consider a linear model defined by a $K \times K$ regression matrix $\mathbf{\Psi}$

$$\arg\min_{\mathbf{\Psi}} \sum_{\ell=1}^{L_s} ||\hat{\boldsymbol{v}}_\ell - \mathbf{\Psi}\hat{\boldsymbol{\beta}}_\ell||^2 + \lambda_{\mathbf{\Psi}}||\mathbf{\Psi}||^2 \tag{8}$$

However, the linear model $\mathbf{\Psi}$ can be replaced by any nonlinear regression model as well.

4 Inference

Inference in our model requires estimating the latent factors $\mathbf{U} = \{\boldsymbol{u}_n\}_{n=1}^N$ of the training examples, the label latent factors $\{\boldsymbol{v}_\ell\}_{\ell=1}^{L_s}$ of the seen labels, the label latent factors $\{\beta_{\ell'}\}_{\ell'=1}^{L}$ of the seen and unseen labels, and the regression matrix $\mathbf{W}$. We learn the regression matrix $\mathbf{\Psi}$ by solving Eq. 8 once we have estimated $\{\boldsymbol{v}_\ell\}_{\ell=1}^{L_s}$ and $\{\beta_{\ell'}\}_{\ell'=1}^{L}$. Note however that learning $\mathbf{\Psi}$ can also be integrated with learning of the rest of the model parameters but we found that learning it separately in the end does almost similarly and therefore we follow this strategy.

Both fully Bayesian inference as well as point estimation is possible under our generative framework. Fully Bayesian posterior inference for our probabilistic framework is, in general, intractable but a number of approximate inference methods such as MCMC (Andrieu et al., 2003) or variational inference (Blei et al., 2017) can be used. Note that our model is not *natively* conjugate due to the presence of the logistic-Bernoulli likelihood (for binary labels - Eq. 1) and negative binomial (for label co-occurrences - Eq. 5) and the Gaussian priors for the model parameters. However, we are able to leverage the recently developed Pólya-gamma augmentation (Polson et al., 2013) technique to handle these non-conjugate likelihoods and are able to transform these likelihoods into Gaussian likelihoods, when conditioned on auxiliary variables. This enables us to develop efficient Gibbs sampling, variational inference, or expectation maximization algorithm for doing inference.

The Pólya-gamma augmentation technique (Polson et al., 2013) is based on the following identity

$$\frac{(\exp(\psi)^a}{(1+\exp(\psi))^b} = 2^{-b}\exp(\kappa\psi)\int_0^\infty \exp\left(-\omega\psi^2/2\right)p(\omega)d\omega$$

where $\kappa = a - b/2$ and $\omega|\psi \sim \text{PG}(b, \psi)$, and PG denotes the Pólya-Gamma distribution (Polson et al., 2013). This identity allows us to write any likelihood of the form $\frac{(\exp(\psi)^a}{(1+\exp(\psi))^b}$ (e.g., logistic-Bernoulli, binomial, negative-binomial) as a Gaussian distribution, when conditioned on another random variable $\omega|\psi \sim \text{PG}(b, \psi)$.

We can thus re-express the logistic-Bernoulli likelihood $p(y_{n\ell} = 1|\boldsymbol{u}_n, \boldsymbol{v}_\ell) = \frac{\exp(\boldsymbol{u}_n^\top \boldsymbol{v}_\ell)}{1+\exp(\boldsymbol{u}_n^\top \boldsymbol{v}_\ell)}$ on the binary labels as a Gaussian, when conditioning on PG auxiliary variables drawn as $\omega_{n\ell} \sim \text{PG}(1, \boldsymbol{u}_n^\top \boldsymbol{v}_\ell)$. In particular, the distribution of $\xi_{n\ell} = \boldsymbol{u}_n^\top \boldsymbol{v}_\ell$, conditioned on $\omega_{n\ell}$, becomes a Gaussian

$$p(\xi_{n\ell}|\omega_{n\ell}) \propto \exp\left(-\kappa_{n\ell}^{(y)}\xi_{n\ell} - \omega_{n\ell}\xi_{n\ell}^2\right) \tag{9}$$

where $\kappa_{n\ell}^{(y)} = y_{n\ell} - 0.5$. This likelihood, combined with the Gaussian priors on the latent factors $\boldsymbol{u}_n$ and $\boldsymbol{v}_\ell$, results in Gaussian posteriors for the $\boldsymbol{u}_n$ and $\boldsymbol{v}_\ell$.

Likewise,the negative binomial likelihood model

$$p(m_{\ell\ell'}|r, p_{\ell\ell'}) = \text{NB}(m_{\ell\ell'}|r, p_{\ell\ell'}) \tag{10}$$

$$\propto (1 - p_{\ell\ell'})^r p_{\ell\ell'}^{m_{\ell\ell'}} \tag{11}$$

with $p_{\ell\ell'} = \frac{1}{1+\exp(-\boldsymbol{v}_\ell^\top \beta_{\ell'})}$, can be written in the form $\frac{(\exp(\psi)^a}{(1+\exp(\psi))^b}$, with $a = m_{\ell\ell'}$ and $b = r + m_{\ell\ell'}$.

The Pólya-gamma technique can be applied to this likelihood as well (Polson et al., 2013), which makes it a Gaussian, when conditioned on another set of PG auxiliary variables $\tau_{\ell\ell'}$. In particular, the distribution of $\gamma_{\ell\ell'} = \boldsymbol{v}_\ell^\top \boldsymbol{\beta}_{\ell'}$, conditioned on $\tau_{\ell\ell'}$, becomes a Gaussian

$$p(\gamma_{\ell\ell'}|\tau_{n\ell}) \propto \exp\left(-\kappa_{\ell\ell'}^{(m)}\gamma_{\ell\ell'} - \tau_{\ell\ell'}\gamma_{\ell\ell'}^2\right) \tag{12}$$

where $\kappa_{\ell\ell'}^{(m)} = \frac{(m_{\ell\ell'}+r)}{2}$. This likelihood, combined with the Gaussian priors on the latent factors $\boldsymbol{v}_n$ and $\boldsymbol{\beta}_{\ell'}$, results in Gaussian posteriors for the $\boldsymbol{v}_\ell$ and $\boldsymbol{\beta}_{\ell'}$.

The Pólya-gamma technique therefore enables us to derive closed-form posteriors on all the latent variables and we can easily perform Gibbs sampling. However, Gibbs sampling can be slow to converge in practice, especially when dealing with large data sets. Another alternative would be to develop a variational Bayes (VB) inference algorithm, which is computationally more efficient. Here we take the approach related to VB inference and develop a fast expectation maximization (EM) algorithm for this model (note that the EM algorithm can also be easily extended to a full VB algorithm).

The EM algorithm we propose also benefits from the Pólya-gamma augmentation because having Gaussian likelihoods and Gaussian priors implies that, *given* the Pólya-gamma variables (estimated in the E step) the maximum-a-posteriori (MAP) objective function to be optimized in the M step will have a structure like a least squares problem, which can be solved efficiently (Scott and Sun, 2013) in closed form.

4.1 The EM Algorithm

The (conditional) EM algorithm for our model alternates between computing the *expectations* of the Pólya-gamma variables $\omega_{n\ell}$ and $\tau_{\ell\ell'}$, where $n = 1, \ldots, N; \ell = 1, \ldots, L_s; \ell' = 1, \ldots, L$, in the E step, and then using these expectations to estimate the other model parameters $\boldsymbol{u}_n$, $\boldsymbol{v}_\ell$, $\boldsymbol{\beta}_{\ell'}$, and $\mathbf{W}$, in the M step.

The E Step: The E step involves computing the expectations of the latent variables $\omega_{n\ell}$ and $\tau_{\ell\ell'}$, given the current values of the other model parameters $\boldsymbol{u}_n$, $\boldsymbol{v}_\ell$, $\boldsymbol{\beta}_{\ell'}$, and $\mathbf{W}$ estimated in the previous M step. The E step update equations are given below:

- Expectations of Pólya-gamma variables $\{\omega_{n\ell}\}$, $\forall n, \ell$ are available in closed form and are given by the following expressions (Scott and Sun, 2013)

$$\hat{\omega}_{n\ell} = \mathbb{E}[\omega_{n\ell}|\xi_{n\ell}] = \frac{1}{2\xi_{n\ell}} \tanh\left(\frac{\xi_{n\ell}}{2}\right) \quad (13)$$

  where $\xi_{n\ell} = \boldsymbol{u}_n^\top \boldsymbol{v}_\ell$ is computed using the estimates of $\boldsymbol{u}_n$ and $\boldsymbol{v}_\ell$ from the previous M step.
- Likewise, expectations of Pólya-gamma variables $\tau_{\ell\ell'}, \forall \ell, \ell'$ are also available in closed form and are given by the following expressions (Scott and Sun, 2013)

$$\hat{\tau}_{\ell\ell'} = \mathbb{E}[\tau_{\ell\ell'}|\gamma_{\ell\ell'}] = \frac{(m_{\ell\ell'} + r)}{2\gamma_{\ell\ell'}} \tanh\left(\frac{\gamma_{\ell\ell'}}{2}\right) \quad (14)$$

  where $\gamma_{\ell\ell'} = \boldsymbol{v}_\ell^\top \boldsymbol{\beta}_{\ell'}$ is computed using the estimates of $\boldsymbol{v}_\ell$ and $\boldsymbol{\beta}_{\ell'}$ and from the previous M step.

The M Step: Given the expectations computed in the E step, the M step minimizes the following negative expected complete data log-likelihood $\mathcal{Q}(\mathbf{U}, \mathbf{V}, \boldsymbol{\mu})$, w.r.t. the rest of the model parameters, namely $\mathbf{U} = \{\boldsymbol{u}_n\}_{n=1}^N$, $\mathbf{V} = \{\boldsymbol{v}_\ell\}_{\ell=1}^{L_s}$, $\mathbf{B} = \{\boldsymbol{\beta}_{\ell'}\}_{\ell'=1}^{L}$, and $\mathbf{W}$.

$$\mathcal{Q}(\mathbf{U}, \mathbf{V}, \mathbf{B}, \mathbf{W}) = \sum_{n,\ell} \frac{(\kappa_{n\ell}^{(y)} - \hat{\omega}_{n\ell}\boldsymbol{u}_n^\top \boldsymbol{v}_\ell)^2}{\hat{\omega}_{n\ell}}$$

$$\sum_{\ell,\ell'} \frac{(\kappa_{\ell\ell'}^{(m)} - \hat{\tau}_{\ell\ell'}\boldsymbol{v}_\ell{}^\top \boldsymbol{\beta}_{\ell'})^2}{\hat{\tau}_{\ell\ell'}} + \lambda_u \sum_{n=1}^N ||\boldsymbol{u}_n - \mathbf{W}\boldsymbol{x}_n||^2$$

$$+ \lambda_v \sum_{\ell=1}^{L_s} ||\boldsymbol{v}_\ell||^2 + \lambda_\beta \sum_{\ell'=1}^{L} ||\boldsymbol{\beta}_{\ell'}||^2 + \lambda_w ||\mathbf{W}||^2 \quad (15)$$

Note that the objective function in Eq. 15 can be broken down into a bunch of independent *weighted* least squares problems (where the weights depend on the expectations of the PG variables estimated in the E step), with ℓ_2 regularizers on the model parameters. Therefore minimizing $\mathcal{Q}(\mathbf{U}, \mathbf{V}, \mathbf{B}, \mathbf{W})$ w.r.t. $\mathbf{U}, \mathbf{V}, \mathbf{B}, \mathbf{W}$ reduces to solving these weighted, regularized least squares problems.

We take an alternating minimization scheme and solve for one variable at a time, treating all other variables as fixed. This yields closed-form updates for each of these variables. Denoting the expectations $\mathbb{E}[\omega_{n\ell}|\xi_{n\ell}] = \hat{\omega}_{n\ell}$ and $\mathbb{E}[\tau_{\ell\ell'}|\gamma_{\ell\ell'}] = \hat{\tau}_{\ell\ell'}$, these update equations for these variables will be as follows:

- Estimating the latent factors $\{\boldsymbol{u}_n\}_{n=1}^N$ is a weighted ridge-regression problem with the updates

$$\boldsymbol{u}_n = \boldsymbol{\Sigma}_{\boldsymbol{u}_n}\left(\sum_{\ell=1}^{L_s} \kappa_{n\ell}^{(y)} \boldsymbol{v}_\ell + \lambda_u \mathbf{W}\boldsymbol{x}_n\right) \quad (16)$$

  where $\boldsymbol{\Sigma}_{\boldsymbol{u}_n} = (\sum_{\ell=1}^{L_s} \hat{\omega}_{n\ell}\boldsymbol{v}_\ell\boldsymbol{v}_\ell^\top + \lambda_u \mathbf{I}_K)^{-1}$. Note that the updates for $\{\boldsymbol{u}_n\}_{n=1}^N$ are all independent of each other and are easily parallelizable.

- Likewise, estimating the latent factors $\{\boldsymbol{v}_\ell\}_{\ell=1}^{L_s}$ is a weighted ridge-regression problem with the updates

$$\boldsymbol{v}_\ell = \boldsymbol{\Sigma}_{\boldsymbol{v}_\ell}\left(\sum_{n=1}^{N} \kappa_{n\ell}^{(y)} \boldsymbol{u}_n + \sum_{\ell'=1}^{L} \kappa_{\ell\ell'}^{(m)} \boldsymbol{\beta}_{\ell'}\right) \quad (17)$$

  where $\boldsymbol{\Sigma}_{\boldsymbol{v}_\ell} = (\mathbf{A} + \lambda_v \mathbf{I}_K)^{-1}$, where $\mathbf{A} = \sum_{n=1}^N \hat{\omega}_{n\ell}\boldsymbol{u}_n\boldsymbol{u}_n^\top + \sum_{\ell'=1}^{L} \hat{\tau}_{\ell\ell'}\boldsymbol{\beta}_{\ell'}\boldsymbol{\beta}_{\ell'}^\top$. Again, note that the updates for $\{\boldsymbol{v}_n\}_{\ell=1}^{L}$ are all independent of each other and are easily parallelizable.

- The updates for estimating the latent factors $\{\boldsymbol{\beta}_{\ell'}\}_{\ell'=1}^{L}$ have the form

$$\boldsymbol{\beta}_{\ell'} = \boldsymbol{\Sigma}_{\boldsymbol{\beta}_{\ell'}}\left(\sum_{\ell=1}^{L_s} \kappa_{\ell\ell'}^{(m)} \boldsymbol{v}_\ell\right) \quad (18)$$

  where $\boldsymbol{\Sigma}_{\boldsymbol{\beta}_{\ell'}} = (\sum_{\ell=1}^{L_s} \hat{\tau}_{\ell\ell'}\boldsymbol{v}_\ell\boldsymbol{v}_\ell^\top + \lambda_\beta \mathbf{I}_K)^{-1}$. The updates for $\{\boldsymbol{\beta}_{\ell'}\}_{\ell'=1}^{L}$ are all independent of each other and are easily parallelizable.

Updates for the regression matrices $\mathbf{W}$ and $\boldsymbol{\Psi}$ are also available in simple closed form. For brevity, we skip it here and provide the update equations in the appendix.

Although the inference algorithm described here works in a batch fashion, it is easy to extend the algorithm to operate in an online fashion using an online EM algorithm (Cappé and Moulines, 2009) where, in each iteration, we only process a small minibatch of training examples. To see this, note that the updates of the latent factors $\boldsymbol{v}_\ell$ depend on sufficient statistics that require summing over latent variables that are computed for all the training example. In the online version, we can compute these latent variables only for the examples in the current minibatch and update the sufficient statistics using a weighted sum of the old sufficient statistics and the contribution to the sufficient statistics from the new minibatch of data.

5 Related Work

A number of methods have been proposed for multi-label learning with the main focus being on exploiting the relatedness of the labels. To this end, a major thrust has been on developing methods that capture the label relatedness by learning a low-dimensional label embedding for each label (Chen and Lin, 2012; Yu et al., 2014; Kapoor et al., 2012; Rai et al., 2015; Bhatia et al., 2015). This amounts to the label matrix being a low-rank matrix. However, none of these methods are designed to handle the challenging setting where the test examples may contain labels that were not used at the time of training the model. Therefore, none of these methods can be applied to the setting of predicting previously unseen labels.

One way to handle the issue of previously unseen labels, motivated by applications in recommender systems, could be to use inductive matrix completion methods (Jain and Dhillon, 2013; Natarajan and Dhillon, 2014; Rai, 2017). Here the label matrix could be modeled using an inductive matrix factorization or inductive matrix completion model. These methods assume that we are given features for both examples as well as labels. However, it may be difficult/impossible to get a predefined set of good features for the labels. Our framework circumvents this need by *unsupervisedly* learning a good set of features (in form of the label latent factors) directly from the label co-occurrence statistics. In this sense, co-occurrence based label embedding aspect of our model is akin to word-embedding methods (Mikolov et al., 2013); however, instead of using models like skip-gram, we are directly using a negative binomial latent factor model for the label co-occurrences, and augment this latent factor model with another latent factor model for the label matrix. This results in a model that is customized for the multi-label learning problem.

Our work is somewhat similar in spirit to (Liang et al., 2016a) which developed a model for matrix factorization based recommender system by leveraging item-item co-occurrences. However, our model differs in several key aspects. In particular, (1) The zero-shot multi-label learning setting requires extrapolating to unseen labels; and (2) while (Liang et al., 2016a) assumed a real-valued user-item matrix and real-valued item-item co-occurrence (as point-wise mutual information), we explicitly model the *binary* labels and *count-valued* label co-occurrences.

We would like to point out that, although, much of the prior work on zero-shot learning models is typically for multi-class learning problems (Socher et al., 2013; Norouzi et al., 2013; Changpinyo et al., 2016), our model is designed for multi-label learning, where we also need to learn and leverage the structural properties of the label matrix (which we accomplish by having another latent factor model on the label matrix itself).

Although some prior works (Zhang et al., 2016; Mensink et al., 2014; Sandouk and Chen, 2016; Fu et al., 2015) have directly applied solutions of zero-shot multi-class learning for the multi-label learning problem, these methods do not take into account the structure of the label matrix, which is known to be of extreme importance, as evidenced by success of multi-label learning algorithms that do take into account such structure (Chen and Lin, 2012; Yu et al., 2014; Kapoor et al., 2012; Rai et al., 2015; Bhatia et al., 2015).

The idea of jointly factorizing multiple matrices with some latent factors shared between matrices has also been used in collective matrix factorization models (Bouchard et al., 2013). However, these are several key difference in motivation as well as the methodology. In particular, the goal in collective matrix factorization is typically only limited to matrix completion and not in solving problems like multi-label learning, where we need the model to predict label vectors for test examples. Moreover, in our framework, we do not factorize every matrix; in particular, the feature matrix $\mathbf{X}$ is used to *condition* the latent factors, which is needed to make the prediction for test examples. Finally, our generative model is customized to specifically handle binary label matrix and count-valued co-occurrence matrix via appropriate likelihood models for the observations.

Another distinguishing aspect of our model is that, unlike most existing model for zero-shot multi-class learning, which require label attributes to be given beforehard, our framework *learns* these attributes (in form the label latent factors) directly using the label co-occurrence statistics. Learning of these embeddings is directly influenced by the information in the label matrix (since the two latent factor models are learned jointly) and therefore these embeddings are customized for the task.

Our generative framework is also amenable for various interesting extensions, which we leave for future work. For example, it can be be extended to a *mixture* of latent factor models, which can handle the situation when the label matrix is not low-rank but a mixture of several low-rank matrices. Such an extension would be a fully generative counter-part of the model in (Bhatia et al., 2015) which learns a locally low-rank model but has to rely on an *ad-hoc* clustering step beforehand, which is known to be unstable in practice (Bhatia et al., 2015). Another nice aspect of our probabilistic framework is that it naturally allows active learning (Kapoor et al., 2012; Vasisht et al., 2014) where we can selectively ask for most informative labels for an unannotated example.

6 Experiments

To evaluate the efficacy of our proposed framework, we simulate a setting where the training data only has the label presence/absence information for a subset of all the labels. To do this, we train the model using only $L_s < L$ labels (randomly chosen) from the training data label matrix. However, for the model to be able to predict the unseen labels, we also provide the model the co-occurrence statistics of these L_s labels with all the L labels (seen and unseen) that the model is required to predict at test time. While, in general, this information can be obtained from an external source (e.g., a text corpus, such as Wikipedia), for our experiments, we generate it *from the training data* itself as follows: Since the *original* training data (from which we simulate the zero-shot setting) consists of all the L label, we simply count how many training examples share a pair of labels (seen/unseen). In particular, we count the number of training examples in which each of the L_s seen labels co-occurs with each of the labels (seen/unseen). This gives us the $L_s \times L$ matrix $\mathbf{M}$ (count-valued). Note that the unseen labels are *not* used in the label matrix $\mathbf{Y}$ used to train our model and therefore the label matrix $\mathbf{Y}$ used by our model is only of size $N \times L_s$. Again, note that, although in our simulated experimental setting, we have generated the co-occurrence statistics this way, in real-world applications, these statistics can also be obtained from an external text corpus (e.g., Wikipedia).

In our experiments, we use half of the total labels as the seen labels and the remaining labels are treated as the unseen labels. At test time, the task is to predict the presence/absence of both seen as well as unseen labels.

Evaluation Protocol: To evaluate our model and the other baselines, we use two evaluation protocols: (1) the combined average prediction accuracy on both seen and unseen labels, and (2) prediction accuracy exclusively on the unseen labels. We use precision@k as the measure of the predict accuracy. The precision@k for each test example is the fraction of the top-k predicted labels (based on the predicted scores) that are indeed 1s in the ground truth label vector of that test example. We report the precision@k scores averaged over the entire set of test examples.

We evaluate our model on three benchmark data sets (the details in Table 1). In the experiments, we will refer to our model as **ML-LCS** (abbreviated for **M**ulti-label **L**earning with **L**abel **C**o-occurrence **S**tatistics)

We compare our model with the following baselines:

- The first baseline we use is a state-of-the-art multi-label learning algorithm based on a latent factor model (Yu et al., 2014) for the label matrix $\mathbf{Y}$ but cannot incorporate any information about the unseen class labels. As expected, this baseline would be able to predict the seen labels well but would not be able to reliably predict the unseen class labels (our experimental results corroborate this). We refer to this baseline as LFM-SL (latent factor model with seen labels only). Note that although such a model can be extended to handle unseen label, it would require pre-defined feature vectors for the seen and unseen labels (Jain and Dhillon, 2013; Natarajan and Dhillon, 2014). This is not a realistic assumption in the problem setting being considered here.

Dataset	N	N_{test}	D	L_s	L_u
Bibtex	4880	2515	1836	80	79
Mediamill	30993	12914	120	50	51
Delicious	12920	3185	500	500	483

Table 1: Dataset used for the experiments. D: number of features Dimensionality, L_s: number of seen labels, L_u: number of unseen labels, N: number of training examples, and N_{test}: number of test examples.

- Although most of the existing multi-label learning algorithms cannot be applied for predicting unseen labels, one baseline that can however be used in this setting is the COSTA algorithm (Mensink et al., 2014). The COSTA algorithm uses the normalized label co-occurrences of seen labels with each of the unseen labels and uses it to "synthesize" predictors for the unseen labels. To do so, COSTA uses a weighted combination of the predictors for seen labels to construct the predict of each unseen label. However, COSTA first requires training *independent* classifiers for each of the seen labels and then combines these independent classifiers to synthesize the predictors for unseen classes. Since the original COSTA algorithm assumes that the seen labels are independent of each other, which is not true in practice, we designed and implemented a variant of COSTA which builds on top of a latent factor model (Yu et al., 2014). The variant uses a latent factor model to factorize the label matrix (using only seen class labels), which gives the latent factors ($\boldsymbol{v}_l, l = 1...L_s$) of all the seen labels. It then computes the latent factors of any unseen label $\ell = L_s + 1, \ldots, L$ using a *weighted combination* of the seen class latent factors ($\boldsymbol{v}_l, l = 1...L_s$). The combination weights are given by the normalized co-occurrence information of that unseen label with all the seen labels.

Experimental Settings: In our experiments, we fix the

	Bibtex			MediaMill			Delicious		
	P@1	P@3	P@5	P@1	P@3	P@5	P@1	P@3	P@5
LFM-SL	0.42	0.23	0.17	0.64	0.34	0.24	0.41	0.28	0.23
COSTA	0.43	0.31	0.25	0.63	0.22	0.13	0.44	0.37	0.30
ML-LCS	**0.51**	**0.37**	**0.30**	**0.73**	**0.60**	**0.48**	**0.52**	**0.45**	**0.41**

Table 2: Precision@k scores comparison (considering both seen and unseen labels) of our model with the other baselines on various data sets.

regularization hyperparameters for the various model parameters equal to 1 (via a 5-fold cross-validation over the range 0.1-10). The negative binomial overdispersion parameter was set to 5. The number of latent factors was set to 80% of the total number of labels. More fine-grained tuning via cross-validation can be tried and can potentially improve the results further. We run the EM algorithm for 500 iterations; however, the algorithm exhibits a fast convergence and converges in about 100 iterations in all the cases (Sec. 6.4 shows a convergence plot).

6.1 Zero-Shot Multi-Label Learning

Table 2 shows the comparison of our model with the two baselines when considering how well the models predict both seen and unseen labels. As shown in Table 2, our model ML-LCS outperforms both LFM-SL (which only uses the seen labels) as well as COSTA which uses information from both seen as well as unseen labels. Between the two baselines, COSTA (which uses label co-occurrences) outperforms LFA-SL (which does not use label co-occurrences) on two out of the three data sets.

Table 3 shows the comparison (on bibtex data) of our model with COSTA when considering how well the models exclusively predict the unseen examples. Since we are reporting precision scores, it shows how well the models can *rank* the unseen labels. Expectedly, the average accuracies are lower for both models; however, our model outperforms COSTA, which shows that our model. For Table 3, we do not report the accuracies of LFM-SL as LFM-SL accuracies were expectedly very poor since it does not use any information about the unseen labels.

	P@1	P@3	P@5
COSTA	0.23	0.16	0.12
ML-LCS	**0.34**	**0.20**	**0.14**

Table 3: Precision@k scores (considering only unseen labels) of our model with COSTA on bibtex data.

6.2 Standard Multi-Label Learning

The label co-occurrence statistics is also expected to help even in the standard multi-label learning setting where all the labels are available at the training time ($L_s = L$). To demonstrate this, we conduct an experiment on bibtex data for this setting and compare our model with the standard latent factor model based multi-label learning baseline (LFM-SL) which does not use label co-occurrences. Note that, for this setting, our model does not requie learning the regression matrix $\mathbf{\Psi}$. As Table 4 show, our model outperforms LFM-SL. Interestingly, note that both models use the same amount of information (the label co-occurrence matrix $\mathbf{M}$ used in our model is constructed using the label matrix $\mathbf{Y}$) and this experiment shows that a simple "re-encoding" of the training data (Liang et al., 2016a), leveraged appropriately, can also help in extracting better latent factors, leading to improved performance.

	P@1	P@3	P@5
LFM-SL	0.628	0.374	0.273
ML-LCS	**0.643**	**0.398**	**0.293**

Table 4: Precision@k scores for the standard multi-label learning setting.

6.3 Varying Fractions of Seen vs Unseen Labels

We also perform an experiment when we vary the fraction of seen labels from 20%-80% in the increments of 10% and evaluate our model and COSTA in terms of the precision@1 and precision@3 scores. As shown in Fig. 2, despite both ML-LCS and COSTA having access to the label co-occurrence information, our model consistently outperform COSTA for the entire range of fraction of split between seen and unseen labels, which shows the effectiveness of our generative model that jointly models the label presence/absence and the label co-occurrences.

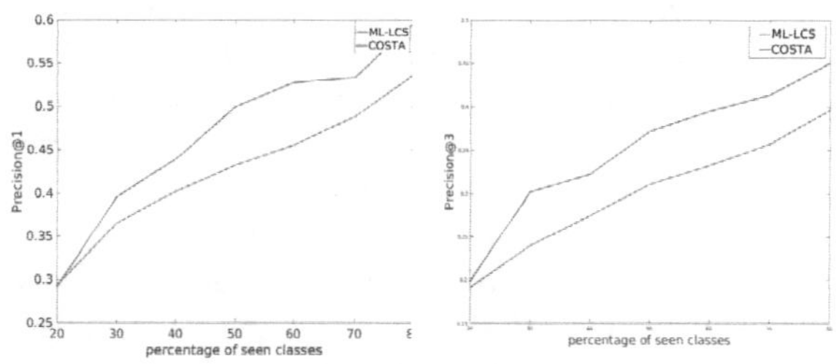

Figure 2: Precision@1 and Prediction@3 comparison of our model (blue curve) with COSTA (red curve) on bibtex data.

6.4 Convergence

The EM algorithm used for our model can only converge to a local optima. However, in practice, we find that our algorithm converges very fast. For example, on the bibtex data, our algorithm converges in about 100 iterations or so, while achieving a significantly better precision@1 score as compared to the COSTA variant we used as a baseline. The convergence plot (also comparing the convergence of COSTA) is shown in Fig. 3. In terms of per-iteration running time, our algorithm is only slightly more expensive than the COSTA baseline as it needs to factorize the label co-occurrence matrix, too.

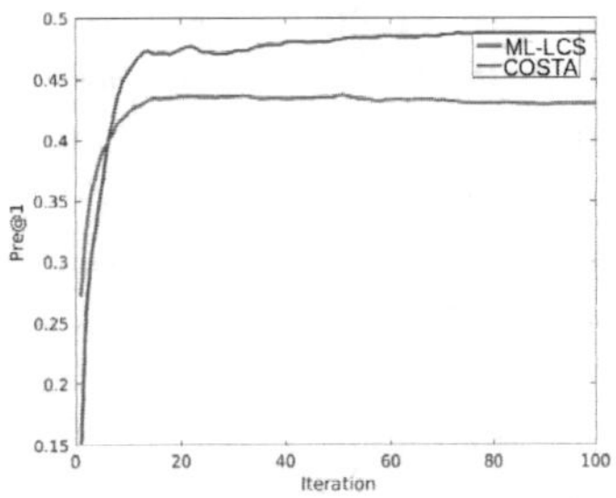

Figure 3: Convergence plot for precision@1 score vs iterations for our model (blue curve) and COSTA (red curve) on bibtex data.

7 Conclusion and Discussion

We have presented a probabilistic framework for multi-label learning that does not require all the labels to be present at the time of training the model. We accomplish this via a generative model that jointly models the label matrix of the training examples and the pairwise label co-occurrence statistics of seen labels (the ones present at training time) with all the labels (seen/unseen). Importantly, the co-occurrence statistics can be computed in an unsupervised fashion using freely available external source of data (e.g., Wikipedia). The joint modeling of the label matrix and the label co-occurrences enables us to learn the predictors for both seen and unseen labels that can be used for predicting the presence/absence of both seen/unseen labels at test time. The generative nature of our framework allows us to also handle missing labels in the label matrix or missing label co-occurrence statistics in the label co-occurrence matrix. Our framework brings to bear the advantage of latent factor models for multi-label learning, while still being capable of handling the labels that were not present at training time. The generative framework also makes it easy to extend our model. For example, it can be extended to a *mixture* of latent factor models, which will allow handling the cases where a single low-rank model does not adequately capture the structure of the label matrix, or replaced by a variational autoencoder style model (Kingma and Welling, 2013; Rezende et al., 2014). Another interesting possible future extension would be to introduce an exposure model (Jain et al., 2017; Liang et al., 2016b) which infers whether a zero in the label matrix is indeed zero or a missing entry (the existing multi-label learning algorithms treat the zeros in the label matrix as true zeros, which may not be the case). Finally, another possible future extension would be to be active learning (Kapoor et al., 2012) in our framework, which can be naturally incorporated since our model produces probabilistic predictions and posterior distributions of various model parameters can be obtained in closed-form.

Appendix

Updating W: Estimating the regression weight matrix $\mathbf{W}$ is equivalent to solving a vector-valued linear regression problem $\boldsymbol{u}_n \approx \mathbf{W}\boldsymbol{x}_n, \forall n$, with the following updates

$$\mathbf{W}^\top = (\mathbf{X}^\top\mathbf{X} + \lambda_w\mathbf{I}_D)^{-1}(\mathbf{X}^\top\mathbf{U}) \tag{19}$$

Note that solving Eq. (19) exactly requires inverting a $D \times D$ matrix which will be expensive for large D. However, the EM algorithm does not require solving for $\mathbf{W}$ *exactly* in each M step. We therefore solve for $\mathbf{W}$ using the conjugate-gradient (CG) method (Bertsekas, 1999), which allows us to also leverage the sparsity in the feature matrix $\mathbf{X}$. Typically, a small number of CG iterations are sufficient in practice.

Updating Ψ: Estimating the regression weight matrix $\boldsymbol{\Psi}$ is equivalent to solving a vector-valued linear regression problem $\hat{\boldsymbol{v}}_\ell \approx \boldsymbol{\Psi}\hat{\boldsymbol{\beta}}_\ell, \forall n$, with the following updates

$$\boldsymbol{\Psi}^\top = (\sum_{\ell=1}^{L_s} \hat{\boldsymbol{\beta}}_\ell\hat{\boldsymbol{\beta}}_\ell^\top + \lambda_\Psi\mathbf{I}_K)^{-1}(\hat{\mathbf{B}}_s^\top\hat{\mathbf{V}}_s) \tag{20}$$

where $\hat{\mathbf{B}}_s$ denotes the $L_s \times K$ matrix consisting of the $\hat{\boldsymbol{\beta}}_\ell$'s along its rows and $\hat{\mathbf{V}}_s$ denotes the $L_s \times K$ matrix consisting of the $\hat{\boldsymbol{v}}_\ell$'s along its rows. If L_s is large, the closed-form update can be replaced by a CG style update for better efficiency.

Acknowledgements: This work is supported by DST (India) SERB Early Career Research Award, a grant from Tower Research CSR, Dr. Deep Singh and Daljeet Kaur Fellowship, and Research-I Foundation, IIT Kanpur. Vinay Verma acknowledges support from Visvesvaraya Ph.D. fellowship.

References

Andrieu, C., De Freitas, N., Doucet, A., and Jordan, M. I. (2003). An introduction to mcmc for machine learning. *Machine learning*, 50(1):5–43.

Babbar, R. and Schölkopf, B. (2017). DiSMEC- distributed sparse machines for extreme multi-label classification. In *WSDM*.

Bertsekas, D. P. (1999). *Nonlinear programming*. Athena scientific Belmont.

Bhatia, K., Jain, H., Kar, P., Varma, M., and Jain, P. (2015). Sparse local embeddings for extreme multi-label classification. In *NIPS*.

Blei, D. M., Kucukelbir, A., and McAuliffe, J. D. (2017). Variational inference: A review for statisticians. *Journal of the American Statistical Association*.

Bouchard, G., Yin, D., and Guo, S. (2013). Convex collective matrix factorization. In *AISTATS*, volume 13, pages 144–152.

Cappé, O. and Moulines, E. (2009). On-line expectation–maximization algorithm for latent data models. *Journal of the Royal Statistical Society: Series B (Statistical Methodology)*, 71(3):593–613.

Changpinyo, S., Chao, W.-L., Gong, B., and Sha, F. (2016). Synthesized classifiers for zero-shot learning. In *Proceedings of the IEEE Conference on Computer Vision and Pattern Recognition*, pages 5327–5336.

Chen, Y.-N. and Lin, H.-T. (2012). Feature-aware label space dimension reduction for multi-label classification. In *NIPS*.

Fu, Y., Yang, Y., Hospedales, T., Xiang, T., and Gong, S. (2015). Transductive multi-label zero-shot learning. *arXiv preprint arXiv:1503.07790*.

Gibaja, E. and Ventura, S. (2014). Multilabel learning: A review of the state of the art and ongoing research. *Wiley Interdisciplinary Reviews: Data Mining and Knowledge Discovery*.

Gibaja, E. and Ventura, S. (2015). A tutorial on multilabel learning. *ACM Comput. Surv.*

Jain, H., Prabhu, Y., and Varma, M. (2016). Extreme multi-label loss functions for recommendation, tagging, ranking & other missing label applications. In *KDD*.

Jain, P. and Dhillon, I. S. (2013). Provable inductive matrix completion. *arXiv preprint arXiv:1306.0626*.

Jain, V., Modhe, N. M., and Rai, P. (2017). Scalable generative models for multi-label learning with missing labels. In *ICML*.

Kapoor, A., Viswanathan, R., and Jain, P. (2012). Multilabel classification using bayesian compressed sensing. In *NIPS*.

Kingma, D. P. and Welling, M. (2013). Auto-encoding variational bayes. *arXiv preprint arXiv:1312.6114*.

Liang, D., Altosaar, J., Charlin, L., and Blei, D. M. (2016a). Factorization meets the item embedding: Regularizing matrix factorization with item co-occurrence. In *RecSys*.

Liang, D., Charlin, L., McInerney, J., and Blei, D. M. (2016b). Modeling user exposure in recommendation. In *WWW*.

Mensink, T., Gavves, E., and Snoek, C. G. (2014). Costa: Co-occurrence statistics for zero-shot classification. In *Proceedings of the IEEE Conference on Computer Vision and Pattern Recognition*, pages 2441–2448.

Mikolov, T., Sutskever, I., Chen, K., Corrado, G. S., and Dean, J. (2013). Distributed representations of words and phrases and their compositionality. In *Advances in neural information processing systems*, pages 3111–3119.

Natarajan, N. and Dhillon, I. S. (2014). Inductive matrix completion for predicting gene–disease associations. *Bioinformatics*.

Norouzi, M., Mikolov, T., Bengio, S., Singer, Y., Shlens, J., Frome, A., Corrado, G. S., and Dean, J. (2013). Zero-shot learning by convex combination of semantic embeddings. *arXiv preprint arXiv:1312.5650*.

Polson, N. G., Scott, J. G., and Windle, J. (2013). Bayesian inference for logistic models using pólya–gamma latent variables. *Journal of the American Statistical Association*, 108(504):1339–1349.

Prabhu, Y. and Varma, M. (2014). FastXML: a fast, accurate and stable tree-classifier for extreme multi-label learning. In *KDD*.

Rai, P. (2017). Non-negative inductive matrix completion for discrete dyadic data. In *AAAI*.

Rai, P., Hu, C., Henao, R., and Carin, L. (2015). Large-scale bayesian multi-label learning via topic-based label embeddings. In *NIPS*.

Rezende, D. J., Mohamed, S., and Wierstra, D. (2014). Stochastic backpropagation and approximate inference in deep generative models. *arXiv preprint arXiv:1401.4082*.

Sandouk, U. and Chen, K. (2016). Multi-label zero-shot learning via concept embedding. *arXiv preprint arXiv:1606.00282*.

Scott, J. G. and Sun, L. (2013). Expectation-maximization for logistic regression. *arXiv preprint arXiv:1306.0040*.

Socher, R., Ganjoo, M., Manning, C. D., and Ng, A. (2013). Zero-shot learning through cross-modal transfer. In *Advances in neural information processing systems*, pages 935–943.

Vasisht, D., Damianou, A., Varma, M., and Kapoor, A. (2014). Active learning for sparse bayesian multilabel classification. In *KDD*.

Wang, J., Yang, Y., Mao, J., Huang, Z., Huang, C., and Xu, W. (2016). CNN-RNN: A unified framework for multi-label image classification. In *CVPR*.

Yu, H.-F., Jain, P., Kar, P., and Dhillon, I. S. (2014). Large-scale multi-label learning with missing labels. In *ICML*.

Zhang, Y., Gong, B., and Shah, M. (2016). Fast zero-shot image tagging. In *CVPR*.

Deep Hybrid Models: Bridging Discriminative and Generative Approaches

Volodymyr Kuleshov
Department of Computer Science
Stanford University
Stanford, CA 94305

Stefano Ermon
Department of Computer Science
Stanford University
Stanford, CA 94305

Abstract

Most methods in machine learning are described as either discriminative or generative. The former often attain higher predictive accuracy, while the latter are more strongly regularized and can deal with missing data. Here, we propose a new framework to combine a broad class of discriminative and generative models, interpolating between the two extremes with a multi-conditional likelihood objective. Unlike previous approaches, we couple the two components through shared latent variables, and train using recent advances in variational inference. Instantiating our framework with modern deep architectures gives rise to deep hybrid models, a highly flexible family that generalizes several existing models and is effective in the semi-supervised setting, where it results in improvements over the state of the art on the SVHN dataset.

1 INTRODUCTION

Modern machine learning techniques rely on the availability of large labeled datasets to achieve state-of-the-art results on tasks such as image classification (Deng et al., 2009), speech recognition (Amodei et al., 2015), and machine translation (Wu et al., 2016) However, obtaining such datasets is often expensive, which has driven significant interest in semi-supervised learning, a class of methods that can leverage unlabeled data to improve the performance of supervised classifiers (Chapelle et al., 2006).

Most semi-supervised algorithms (and, in fact, most machine learning algorithms) can be categorized into one of two general approaches, which differ in how they model input features x and their target labels y (Ng & Jordan, 2002).

Generative methods describe the relationship between x and y using a joint probability distribution $p(x, y)$. As a result, they handle arbitrary queries about the data, such as predicting unknown labels via $p(y|x)$, or imputing missing features x using the distribution $p(x)$. In the semi-supervised setting, they treat y as an unobserved latent variable and optimize the marginal likelihood of the data.

Discriminative methods, on the other hand, focus only on directly predicting y from x via the conditional distribution $p(y|x)$. If prediction is the only goal, this approach will use the model parameters more efficiently, and be more accurate on larger datasets (Ng & Jordan, 2002).

A Framework for Hybrid Models. Choosing between generative and discriminative techniques is a fundamental problem in machine learning. In this work, we propose a framework for designing probabilistic models that can interpolate between a purely generative and a purely discriminative approach. In a semi-supervised context, this enables us to jointly apply both categories of semi-supervised learning algorithms.

A standard approach proposed by several authors (McCallum et al., 2006; Lasserre et al., 2006) is to specify a joint model $p(x, y)$ and assign different weights to the posterior $p(y|x)$ and the marginal $p(x)$ during training. Clearly, this is possible only for simple models in which computing and optimizing $p(y|x)$ and $p(x)$ is tractable. Furthermore, sharing weights between $p(y|x)$ and $p(x)$ limits our modeling flexibility: it is unclear how to tie via shared parameters complex models such as modern neural networks.

Our approach allows choosing very general forms for $p(y|x)$ and $p(x)$ and instead couples them by introducing shared *latent variables* z into the joint model $p(x, y, z)$. The z can be thought of as a latent high-level representation useful for both the discriminative and generative components. We learn the resulting latent-variable model using approximate variational inference, which allows us to handle a wider range of models that otherwise would have been intractable.

Deep Hybrid Models. Instantiating our framework with modern deep architectures gives rise to deep hybrid models (DHMs), a highly flexible family that generalizes several existing deep learning algorithms. For example, a DHM can be defined by modeling the joint probability $p(x, z)$ as a variational auto-encoder (Kingma & Welling, 2013) or a generative adversarial network (Goodfellow et al., 2014), while the discriminative model $p(y|x, z)$ can be a highly flexible convolutional neural network. Our only constraint is that both share the same latent z.

We train the discriminative and the generative component jointly using an objective that places different weights upon the two. This procedure can improve both discriminative accuracy as well the generative log-likelihood by sharing the latent representation z across both models.

Contributions. Our work proposes a new framework for training a broad class of hybrid discriminative-generative models, thus combining the strengths of the two modeling approaches. The practical advantages of our framework over existing approaches are:

- Greater flexibility in the specification of the hybrid model.
- Ability to handle modern machine learning methods based on deep neural networks.
- Compatibility with complex latent-variable models trained using approximate variational inference.
- Ability to apply discriminative and generative semi-supervised learning algorithms on the same model.

Outline. We give a background on generative versus discriminative models and their hybrid extensions in Section 2. In Section 3, we discuss the shortcomings of these methods and introduce our approach and its advantages. We perform an empirical study of our method in Section 4, and conclude with a discussion in Section 5.

2 BACKGROUND

2.1 DISCRIMINATIVE VS. GENERATIVE MODELS

Machine learning models can often be seen as expressing a relationship between features x (e.g., email messages) and labels y (e.g., whether they are spam or not) using a probability distribution p over x, y. Depending of the form of p, these models are characterized as being either generative and discriminative (Ng & Jordan, 2002).

Generative Models. A generative model learns the full relationship between the labels y and the features x, as captured by the full joint distribution $p(x, y)$. This gives the model p maximum flexibility at test-time: we may use $p(y|x)$ to predict labels y from x, impute a missing feature x_i from the other features x_{-i} using $p(x_i|x_{-i})$, as well as

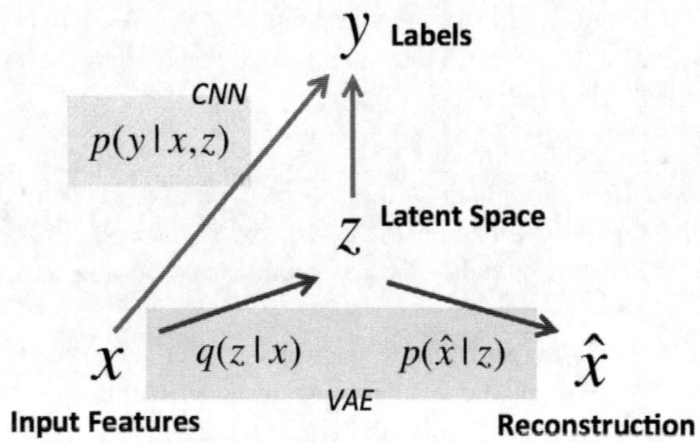

Figure 1: Computational graph describing a deep hybrid model $p(y|x, z)p(x, z)$, whose generative component $p(x, z)$ (blue) is parametrized by a variational auto-encoder with recognition network $q(z|x)$ and whose discriminative component $p(y|x, z)$ (green) is parametrized by a convolutional neural network. We train both models jointly, placing adjustable weights on the two components. The shared representation from $q(z|x)$ is used by both parts, effectively acting as a coupling agent.

sample new data x from $p(x)$. Generative models also offer more flexibility to specify our prior inductive biases; encoding this prior knowledge into p may let us use scarce data more efficiently.

Discriminative Models. If, on the other hand, we are only interested in predicting y from x, it is sufficient to fit a conditional model $p(y|x)$; we refer to this approach as discriminative modeling. Since discriminative models are not concerned with modeling $p(x)$, they may use their parameters more efficiently to capture the relationship $p(y|x)$. This makes them more suitable for purely supasdervised learning. Furthermore, by making fewer modeling assumptions, they may use data more efficiently. However, discriminative models are not suited for tasks like imputation.

2.2 HYBRID DISCRIMINATIVE-GENERATIVE MODELS

The inherent tradeoffs between discriminative and generative modeling have led to the development of hybrid models that attempt to combine the advantages of the two methods. There have been two main approaches to formulating such hybrid models.

Multi-Conditional Learning. Given a probabilistic model $p(x, y; \theta)$ with parameters θ, McCallum et al. (2006) propose optimizing the *multi-conditional likelihood*

$$\alpha \log p(y|x; \theta) + \beta \log p(x; \theta). \quad (1)$$

Here, $\log p(y|x; \theta)$ and $\log p(x; \theta)$ are, respectively, the posterior over y given x and the marginal over x that are both derived from the model $p(x, y; \theta)$. The scalar weights $\alpha, \beta \geq 0$ control the weights assigned to the generative and discriminative components.

Crucially, for any $\alpha, \beta > 0$, we are optimizing a single $p(x, y; \theta)$, albeit with a novel objective. The model p is typically chosen to be a Markov Random Field for which $p(y|x; \theta)$ and $p(x; \theta)$ are tractable to compute and optimize.

Bayesian Parameter Coupling. Lasserre et al. (2006) propose an alternative formulation derived from a Bayesian perspective. Consider a joint model $p(x, y)$ with parameters θ and consider two independent parameter vectors θ_d, θ_g of the same type as θ. Lasserre et al. (2006) propose optimizing the Bayesian model

$$p(x, y, \theta_d, \theta_g) = p_{\theta_d}(y|x) p_{\theta_g}(x) p(\theta_d, \theta_g), \quad (2)$$

where $p(\theta_d, \theta_g)$ is a *parameter coupling prior* that defines a joint distribution over x, y, θ_d, θ_g. Observe that when $p(\theta_d, \theta_g)$ is constant (i.e., the parameter sets are not tied), then we are effectively optimizing two independent models. At test-time, predictions for y will come from a purely discriminative model. Conversely, when $p(\theta_d, \theta_g)$ forces the two sets of weights to be identical, we are optimizing a single generative model.

2.3 SEMI-SUPERVISED LEARNING

In many applications of machine learning, labeled data is scarce, but we have access to large amounts of unlabeled data. Semi-supervised learning (Chapelle et al., 2006) aims to leverage this unlabeled data to improve the performance of purely supervised classifiers.

Discriminative Approaches. One general approach in semi-supervised learning consists in augmenting a discriminative classifier $p(y|x)$ with a regularizer whose goal is generally to place the decision boundary further away from the unlabeled data. Transductive SVMs (Chapelle et al., 2006) define an extension of the hinge loss for unlabeled examples. Entropy regularization (Grandvalet & Bengio, 2004) minimizes the entropy of $p(y|x)$, effectively encouraging the classifier to be maximally certain on unlabeled points. Recently, Laine & Aila (2016) proposed adding a regularizer that encourages the stability of a classifier's predictions over time.

Generative Approaches. Generative semi-supervised models instead formulate semi-supervised learning in the framework of latent variable models, where the variable y is treated as a latent variable for the unlabeled samples $\mathcal{U}$ and as a regular variable for labeled examples $\mathcal{L}$:

$$\sum_{x_i, y_i \in \mathcal{L}} \log p(x_i, y_i) + \sum_{x_i \in \mathcal{U}} \int_y \log p(x_i, y).$$

Recent algorithms implementing this approach include semi-supervised variational auto-encoders (Kingma & Welling, 2013) and auxiliary variable deep generative models (Maaløe et al., 2016).

Approximate Inference. Latent variable models are often optimized using the framework of *variational inference*. The idea is to approximate the intractable marginal likelihood $\log p(x) = \log \int_z p(k, z)$ via a variational lower bound

$$\log p(x) \geq \mathbb{E}_{q(z|x)} [\log p(x, z) - q(z|x)],$$

where $q(z|x)$ is an *approximate posterior* distribution over which we optimize. The difference between the above two terms can be shown to equal $KL(q(z|x)||p(z|x))$. Our work will heavily rely on this variational approach.

3 HYBRID MODELS VIA LATENT VARIABLE COUPLING

In this section, we propose a new way of interpolating between discriminative and generative models. We refer to our approach as *latent-variable coupling*.

Our framework allows the user to choose very general forms for $p(y|x)$ and $p(x)$; we only require them to be contain shared *latent variables* z. The z can be thought of as a latent high-level representation useful for both the discriminative and generative tasks. We learn the resulting joint model $p(x, y, z)$ using approximate variational inference, but assign different weights to each of the two components.

Compared to the previous work of McCallum et al. (2006) and Lasserre et al. (2006), our framework offers much greater modeling flexibility and scales to larger models, particularly ones that make significant use of latent variables. We present the details of this approach below.

3.1 GENERAL FRAMEWORK

Representation. Consider a generative probabilistic model $p(x, y, z)$ over variables $x, y, z \in \mathcal{X} \times \mathcal{Y} \times \mathcal{Z}$. The x are fully-observed, while the y are labels that we only see during training, and the z are unobserved latent variables.

We assume that $p(x, y, z)$ has a parametric form specified by the decomposition

$$p(x, y, z) = p(y|x, z) \cdot p(x, z), \quad (3)$$

where $p(y|x, z)$ and $p(x, z)$ are, respectively, the discriminative and generative components of the model and are directly specified by the user.

Dealing with latent variable models requires us to make use of approximate variational inference and to optimize an approximate posterior $q(z|x)$ to the true learning objective.

Slightly abusing notation, we will use $q(x, y, z)$ to denote the product of the (unknown) data distribution $q(x, y)$ and the user-specified approximate posterior $q(z|x)$; this will let us succinctly represent variational inference algorithms as minimizing a divergence $D(q(x, y, z)||p(x, y, z))$ between q and p.

Learning. At training time, we are given a set of labeled examples $\mathcal{D} = \{x_i, y_i\}_{i=1}^n$ sampled from a data distribution $q(x, y)$; our model also naturally extends to the semi-supervised setting, as we shall see later. We propose training p using a multi-conditional learning objective (McCallum et al., 2006) of the form:

$$\alpha \cdot L_D [q(x, y, z), p(y|x, z)] + \beta \cdot L_G [q(z, x), p(x, z)], \tag{4}$$

where L_D and L_G are two functionals specifying losses for a given choice of p that depend on the true data distribution $q(x, y)$ and the approximate posterior $q(z|x)$.

The L_G term focuses on the generative component of the model and may be any f-divergence between $q(x, z)$ and $p(x, z)$ (Nowozin et al., 2016):

$$L_G [q(z, x), p(x, z)] = D_f (q(z, x)||p(x, z)). \tag{5}$$

We optimize this functional over $q(z|x)$ and $p(x, z)$; the minimum is attained by $q(z|x) = p(z|x)$ and $p(x) = q(x)$.

The L_D term lets us fit the discriminative component of the model. We may choose L_D to be any classification or regression loss, whose expectation is taken over $q(x, y, z)$:

$$L_D = \mathbb{E}_{q(x,y)} \mathbb{E}_{q(z|x)} \ell (y, p(y|x, z)). \tag{6}$$

For example, ℓ may be the log-loss, the ℓ_2-loss, a max-margin objective, or a ranking loss. This objective encourages the discriminative model to achieve high prediction accuracy.

Following the multi-conditional learning framework of McCallum et al. (2006), we assign scalar weights $\alpha, \beta > 0$ to each of the two loss functionals. By shifting weight from α to β, we may smoothly interpolate between a fully discriminative model and a fully generative model that ignores labels y. In between these two extremes is a generative model $p(x, y, z)$ that assigns equal weight to $p(y|x, z)$ and $p(x, z)$.

Next, we look at how to define $p(x, y, z)$ and optimize L_G, L_D. We propose two instantiations of our framework that are compatible with many common models and that are tractable to optimize.

3.1.1 Explicit Density Models

The standard approach for training p is to maximize the *marginal likelihood*

$$\log p(x, y) = \log \int_{z \in \mathcal{Z}} p(x, y, z). \tag{7}$$

In order to trade off the discriminative and generative components of the model, we may follow the approach of McCallum et al. (2006) and optimize the multi-conditional likelihood

$$\log \int_{z \in \mathcal{Z}} p(y|x, z)^\gamma p(x, z). \tag{8}$$

This objective assigns different relative weights to the discriminative and generative components of the model via a scalar $\gamma > 0$.

Unfortunately, this objective is intractable given our assumptions on p. We therefore apply the variational principle to obtain a lower bound:

$$\begin{aligned} &\log \int_{z \in \mathcal{Z}} p(y|x, z)^\gamma p(x, z) \\ &= \log \int_{z \in \mathcal{Z}} \frac{p(y|x, z)^\gamma p(x, z)}{q(z|x)} q(z|x) \\ &\geq \mathbb{E}_{q(z|x)} [\gamma \log p(y|x, z) + \log p(x, z) - \log q(z|x)] \end{aligned} \tag{9}$$

Note that for $\gamma = 1$, Equation 9 reduces to the standard evidence lower bound (ELBO). When $\gamma \neq 1$, this bound may no longer be tight.

The above objective is a special case of our framework if we choose

$$L_D = \mathbb{E}_{q(x,y)} \mathbb{E}_{q(z|x)} [\log p(y|x, z)] \tag{10}$$

$$\approx \frac{1}{n} \sum_{i=1}^{n} \mathbb{E}_{q(z|x_i)} [\log p(y_i|x_i, z)] \tag{11}$$

$$L_G = \text{KL}(q(x, z)||p(x, z)) \tag{12}$$

$$\approx \frac{1}{n} \sum_{i=1}^{n} \mathbb{E}_{q(z|x_i)} [\log p(x_i, z) - \log q(z|x_i)], \tag{13}$$

and $\alpha = \gamma$, $\beta = 1$. The discriminative component is optimized using the log-loss, while the generative component is fit with the reverse KL divergence to $q(x, z)$.

Explicit density hybrid models are very general and encompass many techniques, including most common directed latent variable models, deep generative models, latent-variable Markov random fields with tractable gradients, etc. They can also be trained using recent advances in variational inference, such as stochastic gradient variational Bayes (Kingma & Welling, 2013).

3.1.2 Implicit Density Models

Alternatively, we may specify $p(x, z)$ through an implicit distribution, which only requires us to be able to take samples from a differentiable mechanism $p(x|z)$ operating over input samples from a simple prior $p(z)$. Generative adversarial networks (GANs) (Goodfellow et al., 2014) are perhaps the most well-known class of implicit models. This approach will offer greater modeling flexibility and will potentially allow us to use a greater range of f-divergencies for L_G (Nowozin et al., 2016)

More concretely, we will focus on the following choice of loss functionals:

$$L_D = \mathbb{E}_{q(x,y)}\mathbb{E}_{q(z|x)}\left[\log p(y|x,z)\right] \tag{14}$$

$$\approx \frac{1}{n}\sum_{i=1}^{n}\mathbb{E}_{q(z|x_i)}\left[\log p(y_i|x_i,z)\right] \tag{15}$$

$$L_G = \text{JS}(q(x,z)||p(x,z)) \tag{16}$$

$$\approx \frac{1}{n}\sum_{i=1}^{n}\mathbb{E}_{q(z|x_i)}\log D(x_i,z)+\mathbb{E}_{p(x,z)}\log(1-D(x,z)). \tag{17}$$

The discriminative functional L_D is based on the log loss, as in the previous section; the generative functional L_G is a GAN objective (Goodfellow et al., 2014). The GAN loss introduces an additional *discriminator* function $D(x) : \mathcal{X} \to [0,1]$, whose goal is to discriminate two kinds of tuples: samples $(x,z) \sim p(x|z)p(z)$ from the implicit model $p(x,z)$ as well as real samples x together with their estimated latent $z \sim q(z|x)$. We train D to maximize L_G, whereas p, q are fit to minimize L_G. The resulting objective can be shown to approximate the Jensen-Shannon divergence $\text{JS}(q(x,z)||p(x,z))$ in the limit as the discriminator tends towards optimality (Dumoulin et al., 2016). This objective can be extended to arbitrary f-divergences using standard techniques (Nowozin et al., 2016). Interestingly, it could be used to recover the earlier ELBO objective (Equation 9) within the GAN framework.

The advantage of the above objective over explicit models lies in its modeling flexibility: we may use any sampling mechanism $p(x|z)$. Moreover, in practice, GAN-based techniques tend to produce better-looking samples x and perform well on semi-supervised learning. We expect that implicit hybrid models will be preferred in these settings as well.

3.2 DEEP HYBRID MODELS

Instantiating the components $p(y|x,z)$, $p(x,z)$ using modern deep learning architectures gives rise to deep hybrid models (DHMs), a new family of deep learning algorithms. DHMs are highly flexible and interpolate between several existing models; in several settings they offer accuracy improvements, such as in semi-supervised learning. We examine several classes of DHMs below.

Explicit Density. Explicit density DHMs are naturally formed by combining a deep generative model for $p(x,z)$ with a feed-forward neural network for $p(y|x,z)$. In our experiments, we take $p(x,z)$ to be a auxiliary-variable deep generative model (Maaløe et al., 2016), which is a type of variational autoencoder (VAE; Kingma & Welling (2013)); the discriminative part $p(y|x,z)$ is a convolutional neural network (CNN).

Note that our training objective (10-13) trains each method with its typical objective: the CNN is trained with categorical cross-entropy, while the VAE is trained with the evidence lower-bound. Crucially, the two models are tied via the shared latent z, and hence are trained jointly. By assign each term a suitable weight, we may improve the performance of each individual model. The final joint $p(y|x,z)p(x,z)$ will interpolate betwen the two methods.

For example, while the generative model $p(z|x)$ learns a latent feature representation z for the input x, the discriminative component $p(y|x,z)$ uses these features to accurately predict the labels y. This form of multi-task learning may regularize both models, especially in low-data regimes.

Implicit Density. Implicit density models are inherently tied to neural networks, since they represent a the main way of optimizing implicit density objectives such as (14-17). Furthermore, Equation 17 is equivalent to the adversarially learned inference objective (ALI; Dumoulin et al. (2016)). We augment this construction with an extra discriminative model, in a way that is reminiscent of recent constructions used for semi-supervised learning (Salimans et al., 2016; Dumoulin et al., 2016). We expect implicit density models will inherit the advantages of current GAN-based models, such as visually pleasing samples and good semi-supervised performance.

4 EXPERIMENTS

Next, we study our framework empirically. We focus on deep hybrid models, and start with the fully labeled setting, before moving on to semi-supervised learning.

4.1 EXPERIMENTAL SETUP

4.1.1 Datasets

MNIST. The MNIST dataset consists of 60,000 labeled training images of digits of dimension 28×28 and 10,000 testing images.

SVHN. The Street View House Number (SVHN) dataset consists of 73,257 training examples of 32×32 real-world house number color images; the task is to classify the middle digit. We normalized the inputs in $[-1, 1]$.

CIFAR-10. The CIFAR-10 dataset consists of 50,000 training and 10,000 testing examples of 32×32 color images of different types of animals and vehicles (ten classes in total). Following Laine & Aila (2016), we normalized the input using a whitening transform.

4.1.2 Models

Explicit models. In our experiments with explicit models, we parametrized $p(y|x, z)$ using a neural network with three sets of convolutional layers with 128 filters of size 3×3, each followed by 2×2 max-pooling. We passed the output via a dense hidden layer of size 500, concatenated the result with z and fed the output into a softmax layer.

We parametrized the generative model $p(x, z)$ using an auxiliary-variable deep generative model (ADGM), a more expressive variant of the variational auto-encoder (Maaløe et al., 2016). In brief, an ADGM p has the form $p(a, x, z) = p(a|z)p(x|z)p(z)$, where a are auxiliary latent variables that we introduce into the approximating posterior $q(a, z) = q(z|a)q(a)$ to make it multimodal. We parametrize $q(z|a)$, $p(a|z)$, $p(x|z)$ using dense neural networks with a single hidden layer of size 500; the priors $q(a)$, $p(z)$ were unit normal random variables. We also set $\dim(a) = 10$ and $\dim(z) = 200$.

Implicit Models. In our experiments with implicit models, we used models based on the GAN architectures of Salimans et al. (2016) and Laine & Aila (2016), extending it to the adversarially learned inference (ALI) framework.

For the discriminator, we used two convolutional blocks of three convolutions, each respectively containing 128 and 256 3×3 filters. This was followed by two 1×1 convolutions and global average pooling. We used two dense layers of 256 and 128 filters for the discriminator of z. The two outputs were concatenated and fed to a last dense layer. We used the same architecture in the discriminative model $p(y|x, z)$, and following the approach of Salimans et al. (2016) and Dumoulin et al. (2016), we reuse $p(y|x, z)$ for the discriminator, by introducing an extra class for fake examples.

We use a generator $p(x|z)$ parametrized by a dense layer of size 8,912 followed by three deconvolutional layers with 256, 128, and 3 output filters. The generator $q(z|x)$ consisted of the same three layers in reverse order, followed by a 1×1 convolution and global average pooling.

4.2 INTERPOLATING BETWEEN GENERATIVE AND DISCRIMINATIVE

In this section, we will give examples of how combining both kinds of models improves performance. We start by looking at how a discriminative model benefits from being coupled with a generative component; then, we look at how generative models can use a discriminative signal.

4.2.1 Improvements to the Discriminative Model

To examine the effects of the hyperparameters α and β, we set $\beta = 1$ and varied $\alpha \in \{10^0, 10^1, ..., 10^5\}$ following Druck et al. (2007). We trained an explicit DHM on MNIST for 200 iterations with a learning rate of 0.0003 (decayed to 0 over the last 40 iterations), and evaluated the final test accuracy. We compared our method against a purely discriminative baseline ($\alpha = 1$, $\beta = 0$); note that the baseline uses the exact same number of parameters as our model (namely, both use $p(y|x, z)$ and $q(z|x)$). The results of this experiment are in Figure 2 (a).

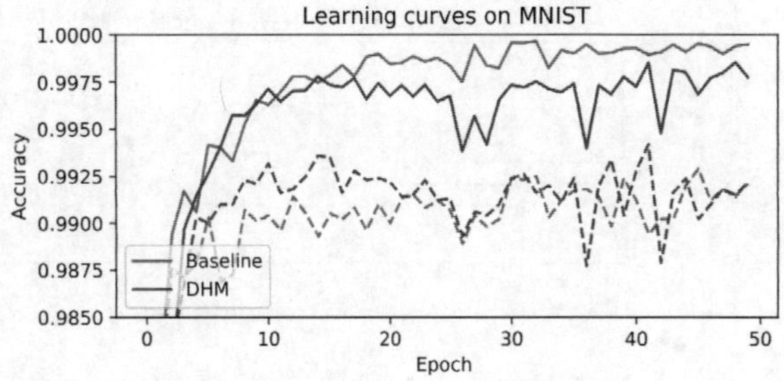

Figure 3: Learning curves of the hybrid (blue) and baseline (green) models on the training (solid line) and test sets (dashed line) for the first 50 epochs. The baseline reaches 0% training error much faster that the hybrid model.

Accuracy. The most obvious improvement over the baseline is an increase in discriminative accuracy. Adding a generative component reduces the test error from about 0.8% for the baseline to about 0.6-0.5%. Varying α does not significantly affect performance; in general, the method appears to be quite robust to this choice of hyperparameter, suggesting there is a lesser need for tuning.

To confirm our findings, we retrained the same network on the SVHN dataset; see Figure 2 (b). Test accuracy again improved from 92.12% to 92.73%, representing about a 0.5% gain in accuracy over same network trained in a purely discriminative fashion. We also noticed slight gains in performance from increasing α.

Regularization. The reason for this gain in accuracy appears to be due to a regularization effect. In Figure 3, we plot the learning curve of the baseline ($\alpha = 1$, $\beta = 0$) and the hybrid method with $\alpha = \beta = 1$. The training error for the baseline very quickly drops to zero; on the other hand, the training error of the hybrid model stays above zero during most of training, and especially at the beginning. Most importantly, the test error of the hybrid method is lower than that of the baseline, and is closer to the training error, indicating that the hybrid model generalizes better.

Intuitively, the network $q(z|x)$ must learn a representation that is useful for both predicting y and reconstructing the data x. This sort of multi-task objective prevents it from significantly overfitting on the prediction task.

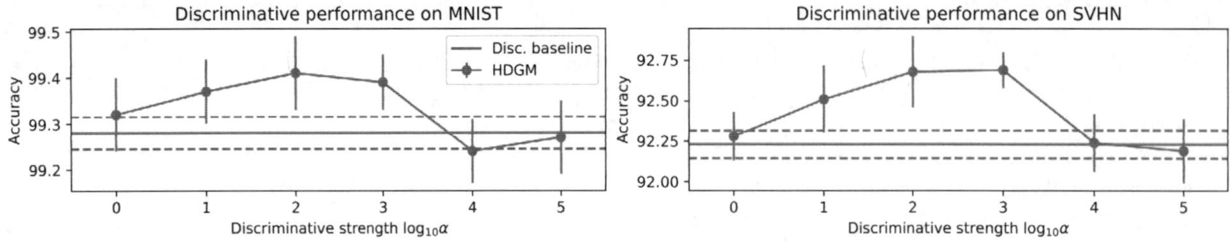

Figure 2: Hybrid model test accuracy for various discriminative weights α on the MNIST (left) and SVHN datasets (right).

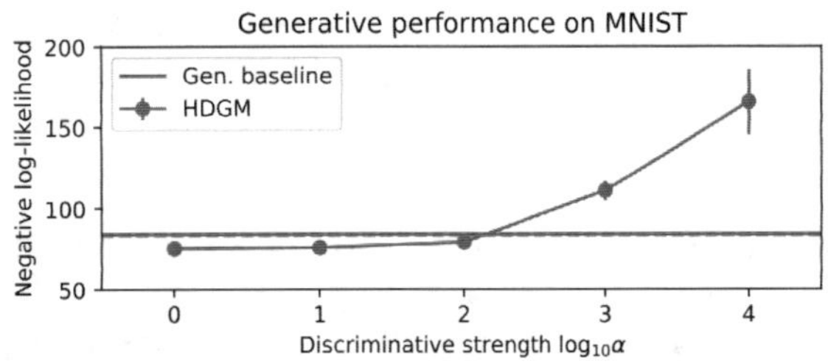

Figure 4: Generative log-likelihood of the hybrid and baseline models as a function of the strength of the discriminative component α on the MNIST dataset.

4.2.2 Improvements to the Generative Model

Conversely, adding a discriminative component to the generative model improves its ability to represent the data and learn useful features.

Generative Log-Likelihood. We evaluated the marginal log-likelihood of the data under the generative component $p(x)$ for each of the runs from the MNIST experiment in the previous section. Figure 4 shows the variational lower bound (ELBO) on the log-likelihood for $\alpha \in \{10^0, 10^1, ..., 10^5\}$, as well as a purely generative baseline with $\alpha = 0, \beta = 1$. The log-likelihood of the hybrid model improves over the baseline and varies with α. Our highest value for the ELBO is -75.5, which is, to the best of our knowledge, higher than any previous purely generative result on MNIST.

This experiment demonstrates that our way of coupling the two components via latent variables allows the discriminative signal to flow from the labels to the generative model, even though it does not share parameters with the discriminative component.

Feature Representation. Next, we trained a linear classifier to predict y from the latent representation learned by our hybrid model with $\alpha = \beta = 1$ and the purely unsupervised baseline ($\alpha = 0, \beta = 1$). In both cases, we used the representation specified by $q(z|x)$. We observed an improvement in accuracy from 97.5% to 98.4% when using the hybrid model. This again indicates that our latent-variable coupling method is effective at propagating signal between the two components of the model.

4.3 SEMI-SUPERVISED LEARNING

In the semi-supervised setting, DHMs can jointly benefit from both discriminative and generative semi-supervised algorithms. We may combine $p(y|x, z)$ with a regularizer (e.g. entropy regularization) while also learning the manifold of unlabeled data using $p(x, z)$. Interpolating between the two models may offer accuracy improvements.

Experimental Setup. We keep the labels of a small random fraction of training examples, and treat the remaining data as unlabeled. Following previous work, we choose 100 labeled points for MNIST, 1000 for SVHN, and 4000 for CIFAR-10. We report results averaged over 10 runs, with error bars corresponding to $\pm 2\sigma$.

Model. We use implicit density DHMs whose architecture we described earlier. We train $p(y|x, z)$ with Π-model discriminative regularization of Laine & Aila (2016), a discriminative semi-supervised technique that adds a penalty $||p(y|x_i) - p'(y|x_i)||_2$ on the difference between two successive applications p, p' of the same model to a given data point x_i (where $p(y|x_i)$ denotes the probability vector of the K classes). The difference between p and p' originates from the internal stochasticity of the model, e.g. dropout regularization, Monte-Carlo sampling, etc.

We use a similar set of hyper-parameters across the three datasets, with $\alpha = \beta = 1$, and the same Π-model hyperparameters as proposed by Laine & Aila (2016).

Results. Our results are summarized in Table 1. We achieve close to state-of-the-art performance on the three datasets. We slightly improve the previous error rate rate on MNIST, while on SVHN we achieve a full 1% in error reduction on the test set. On CIFAR-10, we observe performance comparable to previous state-of-the-art generative models, which is slightly worse than a fully-discriminative approach based on temporal ensembling (Laine & Aila, 2016).

Method	Accuracy
VAE (Kingma et al., 2014)	$3.33 \pm 0.14\%$
SDGM (Maaløe et al., 2016)	$1.91 \pm 0.10\%$
Ladder Network (Rasmus et al.)	$1.06 \pm 0.37\%$
ADGM (Maaløe et al., 2016)	$0.96 \pm 0.02\%$
Improved GAN (Salimans et al., 2016)	$0.93 \pm 0.07\%$
Implicit DHM (ours)	$0.91 \pm 0.06\%$

Table 1: Semi-supervised error on MNIST (100 labels).

Method	Accuracy
VAE (Kingma et al., 2014)	$36.02 \pm 0.10\%$
SDGM (Maaløe et al., 2016)	$16.61 \pm 0.24\%$
Improved GAN (Maaløe et al., 2016)	$8.11 \pm 1.3\%$
ALI (Dumoulin et al., 2016)	$7.42 \pm 0.65\%$
Π-model (Laine & Aila, 2016)	$5.45 \pm 0.25\%$
Implicit DHM (ours)	$4.45 \pm 0.35\%$

Table 2: Semi-supervised error on SVHN (1000 labels).

Method	Accuracy
Ladder Network (Rasmus et al.)	$20.40 \pm 0.47\%$
Improved GAN (Maaløe et al., 2016)	$18.63 \pm 2.32\%$
ALI (Dumoulin et al., 2016)	$17.99 \pm 1.62\%$
Π-model (Laine & Aila, 2016)	$16.55 \pm 0.29\%$
Implicit DHM (ours)	$19.34 \pm 1.05\%$

Table 3: Semi-supervised error on CIFAR-10 (4000 labels).

5 DISCUSSION

Latent-Variable Coupling. Central to our work is a new framework for interpolating between discriminative and generative models. Whereas previous hybrid models were based on parameter sharing (McCallum et al., 2006; Lasserre et al., 2006), our framework combines any two models, as long as they can both incorporate the shared latent variables z. Thus, $p(y|x, z)$ and $p(x, z)$ can be both arbitrarily complex and still be tractable to optimize.

This increased flexibility enables us to define deep hybrid models (DHMs), an instantiation of our framework with modern deep learning architectures.

Multi-Task Regularization. Deep hybrid models jointly train two deep learning models (e.g. a variational autoencoder and a convolutional neural network) and combine some of their advantages. In the end, we obtain a discriminative and a generative model, as well as the joint model defined by the combination of the two. Crucially, these are all trained jointly with a new multi-conditional objective that can improve over standard procedures.

Our approach can be viewed as multi-task regularization, where we train the model to use latent variables z that are useful for both predicting labels y and reconstructing inputs x. This effect is strongest when a large fraction of the data is unlabeled as well as when the architecture of $p(y|x, z)$ relies strongly on z.

Semi-Supervised Learning. Since DHMs involve training both a discriminative and a generative component, we may naturally use both discriminative and generative semi-supervised setting approaches jointly on the same hybrid model. For example, we may use an entropy regularizer on the discriminative predictor while also learning the data manifold with the generative model.

By interpolating between discriminative and generative semi-supervised learning algorithms (by assigning them weights α, β), we may improve classification accuracy. Our framework is also sufficiently general to be combined with most semi-supervised learning algorithms, including improved algorithms that will be proposed in the future.

Alternative Formulations. A different approach to trade-off discriminative and generative modeling power is to assign weights to $p(y|x)$ and $p(x)$ after the latent z variables have been marginalized out, as in the following objective:

$$\alpha \log \int_z p(y, z|x) + \beta \log \int_z p(z, x). \quad (18)$$

Both components can be optimized using variational inference; however the variational lower bound for the first term requires us to efficiently compute $p(y, z|x) = p(y|z, x)p(z|x)$. Since in most modern generative models, the posterior $p(z|x)$ is intractable, it is not immediately obvious how to apply this formulation to such models.

Shu et al. (2016) recently proposed a different formulation of hybrid models. It centers on parameter sharing, and hence is less general than our framework. Our approach also naturally extends to implicit models. Interestingly, their results suggest that choosing $p(y|x, z)$ to be independent of x may be preferable in the context of deep hybrid models.

6 CONCLUSION

In this work, we have proposed a framework for training a broad class of hybrid discriminative-generative models that combines the strengths of the two modeling approaches using latent variable coupling. Our framework offers greater modeling flexibility relative to previous methods and is compatible with modern deep learning architectures and complex latent-variable models. It enables us to apply discriminative and generative semi-supervised learning algorithms on the same model, which results in accuracy improvements over the state-of-the-art on the SVHN dataset. Our modeling ideas are sufficiently general to be combined with most semi-supervised learning algorithms, including improved algorithms that will be proposed in the future.

Acknowledgements. This work is supported by the Intel Corporation, Toyota, NSF (grants 1651565, 1649208, 1522054) and by the Future of Life Institute (grant 2016-158687).

References

Amodei, Dario, Anubhai, Rishita, Battenberg, Eric, Case, Carl, Casper, Jared, Catanzaro, Bryan C., Chen, Jingdong, Chrzanowski, Mike, Coates, Adam, Diamos, Greg, Elsen, Erich, Engel, Jesse, Fan, Linxi, Fougner, Christopher, Han, Tony, Hannun, Awni Y., Jun, Billy, LeGresley, Patrick, Lin, Libby, Narang, Sharan, Ng, Andrew Y., Ozair, Sherjil, Prenger, Ryan, Raiman, Jonathan, Satheesh, Sanjeev, Seetapun, David, Sengupta, Shubho, Wang, Yi, Wang, Zhiqian, Wang, Chong, Xiao, Bo, Yogatama, Dani, Zhan, Jun, and Zhu, Zhenyao. Deep speech 2: End-to-end speech recognition in english and mandarin. *CoRR*, abs/1512.02595, 2015.

Chapelle, Olivier, Schlkopf, Bernhard, and Zien, Alexander. *Semi-Supervised Learning*. 2006.

Deng, J., Dong, W., Socher, R., Li, L.-J., Li, K., and Fei-Fei, L. ImageNet: A Large-Scale Hierarchical Image Database. In *CVPR09*, 2009.

Druck, Gregory, Pal, Chris, Zhu, Xiaojin, and McCallum, Andrew. Semi-supervised classification with hybrid generative/discriminative methods. In *Proceedings of the Thirteenth ACM SIGKDD International Conference on Knowledge Discovery and Data Mining (KDD 2007)*, number 0, pp. 280–289, 2007. Submitted to KDD 2007.

Dumoulin, Vincent, Belghazi, Ishmael, Poole, Ben, Lamb, Alex, Arjovsky, Martin, Mastropietro, Olivier, and Courville, Aaron. Adversarially learned inference. *CoRR*, abs/1606.00704, 2016.

Ghahramani, Zoubin, Welling, Max, Cortes, Corinna, Lawrence, Neil D., and Weinberger, Kilian Q. (eds.). *Advances in Neural Information Processing Systems 27: Annual Conference on Neural Information Processing Systems 2014, December 8-13 2014, Montreal, Quebec, Canada*, 2014.

Goodfellow, Ian J., Pouget-Abadie, Jean, Mirza, Mehdi, Xu, Bing, Warde-Farley, David, Ozair, Sherjil, Courville, Aaron C., and Bengio, Yoshua. Generative adversarial nets. In Ghahramani et al. (2014), pp. 2672–2680.

Grandvalet, Yves and Bengio, Yoshua. Semi-supervised learning by entropy minimization. In *Advances in Neural Information Processing Systems 17 [Neural Information Processing Systems, NIPS 2004, December 13-18, 2004, Vancouver, British Columbia, Canada]*, pp. 529–536, 2004.

Kingma, Diederik P. and Welling, Max. Auto-encoding variational bayes. *CoRR*, abs/1312.6114, 2013.

Kingma, Diederik P., Mohamed, Shakir, Rezende, Danilo Jimenez, and Welling, Max. Semi-supervised learning with deep generative models. In Ghahramani et al. (2014), pp. 3581–3589.

Laine, Samuli and Aila, Timo. Temporal ensembling for semi-supervised learning. *CoRR*, abs/1610.02242, 2016.

Lasserre, Julia A., Bishop, Christopher M., and Minka, Thomas P. Principled hybrids of generative and discriminative models. pp. 87–94, 2006. doi: 10.1109/CVPR.2006.227.

Maaløe, Lars, Sønderby, Casper Kaae, Sønderby, Søren Kaae, and Winther, Ole. Auxiliary deep generative models. In Balcan, Maria-Florina and Weinberger, Kilian Q. (eds.), *Proceedings of the 33nd International Conference on Machine Learning, ICML 2016, New York City, NY, USA, June 19-24, 2016*, volume 48 of *JMLR Workshop and Conference Proceedings*, pp. 1445–1453. JMLR.org, 2016.

McCallum, Andrew, Pal, Chris, Druck, Greg, and Wang, Xuerui. Multi-conditional learning: Generative/discriminative training for clustering and classification. In *Proceedings of AAAI '06: American Association for Artificial Intelligence National Conference on Artificial Intelligence*, pp. 433–439, 2006.

Ng, Andrew Y and Jordan, Michael I. On discriminative vs. generative classifiers: A comparison of logistic regression and naive bayes. *Advances in neural information processing systems*, 2:841–848, 2002.

Nowozin, Sebastian, Cseke, Botond, and Tomioka, Ryota. f-gan: Training generative neural samplers using variational divergence minimization. In Lee, Daniel D., Sugiyama, Masashi, von Luxburg, Ulrike, Guyon, Isabelle, and Garnett, Roman (eds.), *Advances in Neural Information Processing Systems 29: Annual Conference on Neural Information Processing Systems 2016, December 5-10, 2016, Barcelona, Spain*, pp. 271–279, 2016.

Rasmus, Antti, Berglund, Mathias, Honkala, Mikko, Valpola, Harri, and Raiko, Tapani. Semi-supervised learning with ladder networks. In *Advances in Neural Information Processing Systems 28: Annual Conference on Neural Information Processing Systems 2015, December 7-12, 2015, Montreal, Quebec, Canada*, pp. 3546–3554.

Salimans, Tim, Goodfellow, Ian J., Zaremba, Wojciech, Cheung, Vicki, Radford, Alec, and Chen, Xi. Improved techniques for training gans. In *Advances in Neural Information Processing Systems 29: Annual Conference on Neural Information Processing Systems 2016, December 5-10, 2016, Barcelona, Spain*, pp. 2226–2234, 2016.

Shu, Rui, Bui, Hung H, and Ghavamzadeh, Mohammad. Bottleneck conditional density estimation. *arXiv preprint arXiv:1611.08568*, 2016.

Wu, Yonghui, Schuster, Mike, Chen, Zhifeng, Le, Quoc V., Norouzi, Mohammad, Macherey, Wolfgang, Krikun, Maxim, Cao, Yuan, Gao, Qin, Macherey, Klaus, Klingner, Jeff, Shah, Apurva, Johnson, Melvin, Liu, Xiaobing, ukasz Kaiser, Gouws, Stephan, Kato, Yoshikiyo, Kudo, Taku, Kazawa, Hideto, Stevens, Keith, Kurian, George, Patil, Nishant, Wang, Wei, Young, Cliff, Smith, Jason, Riesa, Jason, Rudnick, Alex, Vinyals, Oriol, Corrado, Greg, Hughes, Macduff, and Dean, Jeffrey. Google's neural machine translation system: Bridging the gap between human and machine translation. *CoRR*, abs/1609.08144, 2016.

Regret Minimization Algorithms for the Follower's Behaviour Identification in Leadership Games

Lorenzo Bisi, Giuseppe De Nittis, Francesco Trovò, Marcello Restelli, Nicola Gatti
Dipartimento di Elettronica, Informazione e Bioingegneria
Politecnico di Milano, Milano, 20133, Italy
lorenzo.bisi@mail.polimi.it, {giuseppe.denittis, francesco1.trovo, marcello.restelli, nicola.gatti}@polimi.it

Abstract

We study for the first time, a leadership game in which one agent, acting as *leader*, faces another agent, acting as *follower*, whose behaviour is not known *a priori* by the leader, being one among a set of possible behavioural profiles. The main motivation is that in real-world applications the common game-theoretical assumption of perfect rationality is rarely met, and any specific assumption on bounded rationality models, if wrong, could lead to a significant loss for the leader. The question we pose is *whether* and *how* the leader can learn the behavioural profile of a follower in leadership games. This is a "natural" *online identification* problem: in fact, the leader aims at identifying the follower's behavioural profile to exploit at best the potential non-rationality of the opponent, while minimizing the regret due to the initial lack of information. We propose two algorithms based on different approaches and we provide a regret analysis. Furthermore, we experimentally evaluate the pseudo-regret of the algorithms in concrete leadership games, showing that our algorithms outperform the online learning algorithms available in the state of the art.

1 INTRODUCTION

The study of scenarios in which multiple strategic agents interact is a challenging problem that is central in Artificial Intelligence from many years. The modelling of these scenarios can be elegantly achieved by means of *non-cooperative game theory* tools (Fudenberg and Tirole, 1991), while the task of solving a game is in many cases an open problem, in which the most suitable techniques to adopt strictly depend on information available to the agents. Two extreme situations can be distinguished: when all the information about the game is common to the players (e.g., utility functions and rationality—either perfect or bounded), the problem is basically an *optimization problem*, solvable by means of techniques from *operations research* (Shoham and Leyton-Brown, 2008), conversely, when players have no information about the opponents, the problem is a *multi-learning problem*, and *learning* techniques are commonly employed (Tuyls and Weiss, 2012). Some attempts were also done to pair these two approaches, allowing agents to play at the equilibrium if the opponent is rational and to play off the equilibrium learning to exploit her at best otherwise (Conitzer and Sandholm, 2007).

Recently, there has been an increasing interest in *leadership* games, where an agent—called *leader*—publicly commits to a strategy and subsequently another agent—called *follower*—observes the commitment and then takes her decision. Such a paradigm has been successfully employed in a number of applications in the security domain (Basilico et al., 2017; Pita et al., 2008; Tsai et al., 2009), where a *defender* (acting as leader) must protect some targets in an environment from an *attacker* (acting as follower), who aims at compromising such targets without being detected. The success of leadership games in real-world applications is due to a number of reasons: committing to a strategy is the best the leader can do, the equilibrium finding problem is conceptually simple since the follower can merely play her best response to the commitment of the leader without any strategic reasoning about the leader's behaviour, and the solution is unique except degeneracy. The crucial issue is that in real-world applications the follower may be not perfectly rational, not necessarily playing her best response to the leader's commitment. For instance, a terrorist could decide either to attack a target that is not patrolled, since she is sure to not be caught, or a target not so valuable itself, but that would cause a huge panic reaction in the population (e.g., this is what happened in November 2015 in Paris attacks at the Bataclan theatre). The same challenge may be faced by a company that aims at planning the production of a product and has to decide when and how it is convenient to enter the market when another company is already the leader in such a market—this is the well-known *Stackelberg duopoly* (Von Stackelberg, 1934). Whenever the assumption of perfect rationality is not met, each agent may in principle exploit her opponent's strategy.

In the present paper, we focus on leadership games in which the follower may be not rational. The literature provides a number of models of bounded rationality (An et al., 2013; Nguyen et al., 2013). Probably, the most elegant one is the Quantal Response (QR) (McFadden, 1984), which fixes the probability distribution over the non-optimal actions of an agent on the basis of their optimality gap. The crucial issue is that all the works on bounded rationality make an assumption about the specific behaviour of the opponent and this assumption could be never met in real-world applications. In that case, such an assumption may lead to an arbitrarily loss for the leader. Differently from the existing literature, we study the original single-agent-learning problem in which the behaviour of the follower is one among a set of possible behavioural profiles—e.g., the rational one (i.e., best response), a rationally bounded one based on the QR, a stochastic strategy—and the leader does not initially know it, but she can learn it by exploiting the opponent's behaviour at best. Our goal is to design online learning techniques capable to identify the behaviour of the follower while minimizing the regret due to the initial lack of information. We propose a set of algorithms based on sequential learning techniques (Bubeck et al., 2012) that are able to infer the behaviour of the follower the leader is playing against exploiting the repeated interactions between the two players.

Original contributions The main original contributions we provide in this paper are as follows. We define a novel scenario in which a leader plays against a follower whose behaviour is unknown but it belongs to a set of known profiles. We show that state-of-the-art bandit and expert algorithms—suitable for our problem—suffers from a linear and logarithmic regret, respectively, in the length of the time horizon. Thus, we introduce two novel approaches to deal with our problem, bridging together game-theoretical techniques and online learning tools. In the first approach, the leader has a *belief* about the follower and updates it during the game. We name the algorithm *Follow the Belief* (`FB`) and we provide a finite-time analysis showing that the regret of the algorithm is constant in the length of the time horizon. In the second approach, namely *Follow the Regret* (`FR`), the learning policy is driven directly by the estimated expected regret and is based on a backward induction procedure. Finally, we provide a thorough experimental evaluation in concrete leadership settings inspired to security domains, comparing our algorithms with the main algorithms available in the state of the art of the online learning field and showing that our approaches provide a remarkable improvement in terms of expected pseudo-regret minimization.

2 RELATED WORKS

Here, we mention the main works related to ours. We mainly refer to the literature on security games since most of the works on leadership games with bounded rationality and/or learning deal with these games. Security games model the problem of finding the optimal schedule of scarce resources when facing strategic adversaries. Many of them deal with real-world problems, e.g., in Pita et al. (2008) game theoretic techniques have been applied to ensure the security of the Los Angeles International Airport (LAX), in Tsai et al. (2009) the authors exploit the Stackelberg paradigm to study how to schedule undercover federal air marshals on domestic U.S. flights, while in Pita et al. (2011) such paradigm is employed to allocate the Transportation Security Administration (TSA) scarce resources to provide protection within several U.S. airports. A higher degree of interaction among the agents is captured in Basilico et al. (2017), where an alarm system to detect potential attacks is introduced. The main issue is that such works only deal with a fully rational attacker while in real-life scenarios attackers might be rationally bounded.

Bounded rationality has been introduced in security games models in the so called Green Security Games (GSGs), a generalization of Stackelberg games (Fang et al., 2015). A remarkable example is Qian et al. (2014), in which the problem of protecting natural resources from illegal extraction is studied: since such extractions are frequent, it is possible for the defender to *learn* the distribution of the resources analyzing the attacker's behavior. A recent application in which an *ad hoc* adaption of the QR function, named *Subjective Utility Quantal Response* (SUQR) (Nguyen et al., 2013), has been employed is the prevention from poachers, who hunt endangered species (Ford et al., 2014; Yang et al., 2014). Here, the QR is employed to model the non-rational behavior of the poachers. In a similar setting, Qian et al. (2016) analyze the problem in which the defender is aware only of the attack activities at targets they protect, modeling it with Restless Multi-Armed Bandit and using Whittle index policy to compute patrol strategies.

In security games, Balcan et al. (2015); Blum et al.

(2015); Paruchuri et al. (2008) deal with a single rational attacker whose preferences may be of multiple types in Bayesian fashion. Specifically, the different attackers are discriminated according to the evaluations they give to the targets, thus leading to the problem of solving Bayesian Stackelberg Games.

The main limitation of all the aforementioned works is that the defender plays against an attacker whose behavioral profile is *a priori* known, while in real-world situation it may be unknown. When dealing with sequential decision learning problems, a customary approach consists in exploiting Multi-Armed Bandit (MAB) techniques, as done by Klíma et al. (2014) and Xu et al. (2016). Even though both works focus on minimizing the expected regret, the different actions corresponding to the arms are the possible targets that may be chosen, while in our work we are discriminating among different attacker types.

3 PROBLEM FORMULATION

Although our work can be employed in principle for any leadership scenario, for the sake of clarity, we focus on security domains, thus referring to the leader as *defender* and to the follower as *attacker*.

Let us consider a 2-player normal-form repeated game $\mathcal{G}_N$ defined over a finite number of rounds $N \in \mathbb{N}$, where a defender D and an attacker A play against each other in some environment with some valuable targets $\mathcal{M} = \{1, \dots, M\}$, characterized by values $\mathbf{v} = (v_1, \dots, v_M)^T, v_m \in (0, 1]$. The goal of the defender D is to protect such targets while the attacker A aims at compromising them. The space of actions of D and A is given by the set of targets such that D chooses the target to protect, while A chooses the target to attack. The course of the game is represented in Figure 1. Specifically, at each round $n \in \{1, \dots, N\}$, the defender D announces the strategy she commits to $\boldsymbol{\sigma}_{D,n} \in \Delta_M$ (Line 1), where Δ_M denotes the M-dimensional simplex, while A observes such a commitment (Line 2). Then, they concurrently play their action over the target space (Line 3), i.e., the defender plays actions $i_{D,n} \in \mathcal{M}$ according to $\boldsymbol{\sigma}_{D,n}$ while A, the follower, plays $i_{A,n} \in \mathcal{M}$ according to some attacker model $\boldsymbol{\sigma}_A(\boldsymbol{\sigma}_{D,n}) \in \Delta_M$. The game is zero-sum: if D and A choose the same target at round n, they both get a utility equal to 0, conversely, if A attacks the i-th target while D decides to protect the j-th one, A gets v_i and D gets $-v_i$ since she lost the target. More concisely, the defender incurs in the *loss* (Line 4):

$$l_n := v_{i_{A,n}} \mathcal{I}\{i_{A,n} \neq i_{D,n}\}, \qquad (1)$$

not suffering from any loss if both players select the same target.[1] Hereafter, we assume that the defender is able to compute the best response strategy $\boldsymbol{\sigma}^*_D(A) \in \Delta_M$ if she is given the attacker model she is playing against. Similarly, we denote with $\boldsymbol{\sigma}^*_A(\boldsymbol{\sigma}_D) \in \Delta_M$ the best response A plays against strategy $\boldsymbol{\sigma}_D$ of D. According to such assumption, we can compute the expected loss of D against a generic attacker A as:

> **for each** $n \in \{1, \dots, N\}$
>
> 1. D publicly commits to a strategy $\boldsymbol{\sigma}_{D,n}$
> 2. A observes the strategy D committed to
> 3. D and A play $i_{D,n}$ and $i_{A,n}$, respectively
> 4. D incurs in loss l_n according to Equation (1)

Figure 1: Leader-follower interaction

$$L(A) := \sum_{m \in \mathcal{M}} \sigma_A(\boldsymbol{\sigma}^*_D(A))_m \, v_m \, (1 - \sigma^*_D(A)_m), \qquad (2)$$

where $\sigma_{\cdot}(\cdot)_m$ is the probability associated with target m by the strategy.

The problem we study in this work is defined as follows.

Definition 1. *The Follower's Behaviour Identification in Security Games (FBI-SG) problem is a tuple $(\mathcal{G}_N, \mathcal{A}, A_{k^*})$, where $\mathcal{G}_N$ is a 2-player normal-form repeated game and $\mathcal{A} = \{A_1, \dots, A_K\}$ is a set of possible attacker behavioural profiles, with $A_{k^*} \in \mathcal{A}$ denoting the actual profile of the attacker in $\mathcal{G}_N$, unknown to the defender D.*

In this work, we cast the FBI-SG as a sequential decision learning problem, where, at each round n, the defender aims at selecting her best response to the attacker in order to identify the actual attacker profile $A_{k^*} \in \mathcal{A}$ while minimizing the loss suffered during the learning process.

Definition 2. *A policy $\mathfrak{U}$ is an algorithm able to provide at each round n a strategy profile $\boldsymbol{\sigma}_{D,n}$ for the defender D. Formally:*

$$\mathfrak{U}(h_n) := \boldsymbol{\sigma}_{D,n},$$

where h_n is the history collected so far, i.e., all the strategies declared by the defender $\{\boldsymbol{\sigma}_{D,1}, \dots, \boldsymbol{\sigma}_{D,n-1}\}$, the actions played by the two players $\{i_{D,1}, i_{A,1}, \dots, i_{D,n-1}, i_{A,n-1}\}$ in the past rounds and the corresponding losses $\{l_1, \dots, l_{n-1}\}$.

We evaluate the performance of a given policy $\mathfrak{U}$ over a finite-time horizon of N rounds by means of the expected

[1] Hereafter, we denote with $\mathcal{I}\{E\}$ the indicator function of a generic event E.

cumulative *pseudo-regret*, defined as:

$$R_N(\mathfrak{U}) = \mathbb{E}\left[\sum_{n=1}^{N} l_n\right] - L^* N,$$

where $L^* := L(A_{k^*})$ is the expected loss incurred by the defender if she plays the best response to the actual attacker A_{k^*}, l_n is the loss incurred by using the policy $\mathfrak{U}$ at round n and the expectation $\mathbb{E}[\cdot]$ is taken w.r.t. the stochasticity of the attacker strategy, the defender policy and the policy $\mathfrak{U}$. The goal of a generic policy $\mathfrak{U}$ is to minimize the pseudo-regret $R_N(\mathfrak{U})$ incurred while learning the true attacker's profile.

4 ANALYSED ATTACKER PROFILES

In this section, we describe the different attacker profiles we study in this work and formalize the definition of the attacker strategy $\boldsymbol{\sigma}_{A_{k^*}}(\cdot)$ for two sets of attackers, grouped depending on their ability to change their behavior w.r.t. the strategy D commits to. Specifically, on one side, we take into account stochastic attackers, which disregard the strategy of D, on the other, we focus on strategy-aware attackers, able to modify their strategies depending on the defender announced strategy $\boldsymbol{\sigma}_{D,n}$.

4.1 STOCHASTIC ATTACKER

The first class of attackers is the *Stochastic* (Sto) one, where the attacking player does not take into account the strategy $\boldsymbol{\sigma}_{D,n}$ announced by the defender D and thus has a fixed probability over time to attack the available targets. This class of attackers models opponents focused on specific targets and whose preferences are not influenced by the defender behaviour. At round n, a stochastic attacker Sto plays according to the strategy:

$$\boldsymbol{\sigma}_{Sto}(\boldsymbol{\sigma}) = \mathbf{p}(Sto) \quad \forall \boldsymbol{\sigma} \in \Delta_M,$$

where $\mathbf{p}(Sto) \in \Delta_M$ is a probability distribution over the targets, which is known to D. In this case, the defender best response $\boldsymbol{\sigma}^*_D(\boldsymbol{\sigma}_{Sto})$ is defined as:

$$\sigma^*_D(Sto)_m = \begin{cases} 1 & \text{if } m = \arg\max_{i \in \mathcal{M}} \{v_i\, p(Sto)_i\} \\ 0 & \text{otherwise} \end{cases}.$$

4.2 STRATEGY AWARE ATTACKER

The second class of attackers we examine in this paper consists of strategy aware attackers, corresponding to followers able to modify their strategy depending on the strategy of the defender D. In particular, we study *Stackelberg* (Sta) attackers (Von Stackelberg, 1934), who are able to exploit the information provided by strategy profile declared by the defender D and optimally respond to it, and SUQR attackers (Nguyen et al., 2013), having bounded rationality and being capable to partially exploit the information provided by the defender, disregarding heavily patrolled targets.

Stackelberg Attacker Given a strategy profile declaration $\boldsymbol{\sigma}_{D,n}$, a Stackelberg attacker Sta responds with:

$$\boldsymbol{\sigma}_{Sta}(\boldsymbol{\sigma}) = \arg\max_{\boldsymbol{\sigma}' \in \Delta_M} \sum_{m \in \mathcal{M}} \sigma'_m\, v_m\,(1 - \sigma_m)$$

and the defender best-responds to this attacker is:

$$\boldsymbol{\sigma}^*_D(Sta) = \arg\min_{\boldsymbol{\sigma}' \in \Delta_M} \max_{\boldsymbol{\sigma} \in \Delta_M} \sum_{m \in \mathcal{M}} \sigma'_m\, v_m\,(1 - \sigma_m),$$

as reported in (Conitzer and Sandholm, 2006), where it is proved that, for 2-player zero-sum games, the optimal mixed strategy for the leader to commit to is equivalent to computing the minmax strategy, i.e., to minimize the maximum expected utility that the opponent can obtain.

SUQR Attacker The SUQR attacker responds to the commitment $\boldsymbol{\sigma}_{D,n}$ as:

$$\sigma_{SUQR}(\boldsymbol{\sigma})_m = \frac{\exp\{-\alpha\sigma_m + \beta v_m + \gamma\}}{\sum_{h=1}^{M} \exp\{-\alpha\sigma_h + \beta v_h + \gamma\}},$$

where $\alpha \in \mathbb{R}^+$, $\beta, \gamma \in \mathbb{R}$ are parameters known to the defender, characterizing the attacker and depending on the underlying application. In this case, we do not have a closed form for the best response, but we can compute the minmax solution to the problem following the steps taken in (Yang et al., 2011). We will refer to $\boldsymbol{\sigma}^*_D(SUQR)$ as the best response to an attacker with a SUQR profile.

5 IDENTIFYING THE ATTACKER

Initially, we describe how the state-of-the-art techniques can be adapted to address the FBI-SG problem. Direct approaches are provided by MAB (Bubeck et al., 2012) and expert (Cesa-Bianchi and Lugosi, 2006) algorithms, where arms/experts represent the different attacker behavioural profiles in $\mathcal{A}$. These are general-purpose techniques not exploiting the structure of the problem we are tackling. Summarily, MAB algorithms do not use the expert feedback to learn the attacker behaviour, while expert algorithms do not differentiate among feedbacks received after the defender committed to different strategies. We show below the regret obtained when these algorithms are used in a FBI-SG problem.

When using MAB algorithms, we are able to directly apply the derivation of an upper bound over the pseudo-regret available in the literature to our problem. We can state the following result for the case of UCB1 (Auer et al., 2002).

Theorem 1 (UCB1 Pseudo-regret upper bound). *Let us consider an instance of the FBI-SG problem and apply the UCB1 algorithm, where each possible behavioural profile $A_k \in \mathcal{A}$ is an arm which receives reward $-l_n$ if played. Then, we incur in the following pseudo-regret:*

$$R_N(\mathfrak{U}) \leq 8 \sum_{k \neq k^*} \frac{\ln N}{(\Delta L_k)} + \left(1 + \frac{\pi^2}{3}\right) \sum_{k \neq k^*} \Delta L_k,$$

where $\Delta L_k = \sum_{m=1}^{M} \sigma_{A_{k^*}}(\boldsymbol{\sigma}_D^*(A_k))_m v_m (1 - \sigma_D^*(A_k)_m) - L^*$ *is the expected regret of playing the best response to attacker A_k when the real attacker is A_{k^*}.*

When using an expert algorithm, for instance Follow the Perturbed Leader (FPL) (Cesa-Bianchi and Lugosi, 2006), we could exploit an (expert) feedback over all arms since we can compute the expected loss also for the attacker profiles that have not been played at turn n. Nevertheless, if the attacker is strategy aware and we adopt an expert feedback, D incurs in a linear regret. We formally state this result in the following theorem.

Theorem 2 (Expert pseudo-regret upper bound). *Let us consider an instance of the FBI-SG problem and apply the FPL algorithm, where each possible profile A_k is an expert and receives, at round n, an expert reward equal to minus the loss she would have incurred observing $i_{A_{k^*},n}$ by playing the best response to the attacker A_k. Then, there always exists an attacker set $\mathcal{A}$ s.t. the defender D incurs in an expected pseudo-regret of:*

$$R_N(\mathfrak{U}) \propto \Delta L_k N.$$

The proof of Theorem 2 is reported in Appendix A for reasons of space. The above results show that MAB techniques provide, in the general case, better guarantees than expert algorithms, assuring a worst-case pseudo-regret of $O(\ln N)$ vs. $O(N)$.

In the following, we propose two different techniques that effectively exploit the information both on stochastic and strategy aware attackers, providing better guarantees over the worst-case pseudo-regret. The first algorithm, *Follow the Belief* (`FB`), conducts the learning process taking into account the belief of the learner about the different behavioural profiles. The second method, *Follow the Regret* (`FR`), is based on a value iteration algorithm over the belief space that minimizes the expected regret over the next rounds.

5.1 FOLLOW THE BELIEF

The pseudo-code of `FB` is presented in Algorithm 1. At the beginning, `FB` initializes a set of active attackers

Algorithm 1 `FB`

1: $\mathcal{P} = \mathcal{A}$
2: **for all** $A' \in \mathcal{P}$ **do**
3: $\quad b_1(A') = \frac{1}{K}$
4: **for all** $n \in \{1, \ldots, N\}$ **do**
5: $\quad$ Select $A_{k_n} = \arg\max_{A' \in \mathcal{P}} b_n(A')$
6: $\quad$ Play $\boldsymbol{\sigma}_D^*(A_{k_n})$
7: $\quad$ Observe attacker action $i_{A_{k^*},n}$
8: $\quad$ **for all** $A' \in \mathcal{P}$ **do**
9: $\quad\quad$ **if** $\sigma_{A'}(\boldsymbol{\sigma}_D^*(A_{k_n}))_{i_{A_{k^*},n}} = 0$ **then**
10: $\quad\quad\quad \mathcal{P} \leftarrow \mathcal{P} \setminus A'$
11: $\quad\quad$ **else**
12: $\quad\quad\quad$ Compute $b_{n+1}(A')$ with Equation (3)

$\mathcal{P} = \mathcal{A}$ and a belief $b_1(A_k) = 1/K$ for all the attacker profiles $A_k \in \mathcal{P}$ (Lines 1-3). At each round n, the algorithm selects the attacker A_{k_n} for which the belief is the largest one (where ties are broken arbitrarily), best responds with the strategy $\boldsymbol{\sigma}_D^*(A_{k_n})$ and observes the action actually played by the attacker $i_{A_{k^*},n}$ (Lines 4-7). After that, the belief is updated as follows:

$$b_{n+1}(A') = \frac{w_n(A')}{\sum_{A \in \mathcal{P}} w_n(A)}, \tag{3}$$

where $w_n(A) = b_n(A') \, \sigma_{A_{k^*}}(\boldsymbol{\sigma}_D^*(A_{k_n}))_{i_{A_{k^*},n}}$ (Lines 8-12). In other words, the algorithm updates the likelihood of the sequence of the actions for each profile in $A' \in \mathcal{P}$ according to the observed action $i_{A_{k^*},n}$ at round n (Line 12). If the realization $i_{A_{k^*},n}$ is not consistent for attacker A' (zero likelihood), profile A' is removed from $\mathcal{P}$ (Line 10).

Let $b_{kj,t} := \mathbb{E}_{\sigma_D^*(A_j)}[B_{k,t}]$, be the expected value of the belief we get for attacker A_k when we are best responding to A_j and the true type is $A_{k^*} \neq A_k$ and denote with $\Delta b_k := \min_{j | A_j \in \mathcal{A}} \ln(b_{k^* j,t}) - \ln(b_{kj,t})$ the minimum difference of such values. We can upper bound the regret of `FB` algorithm as stated by the following theorem.

Theorem 3 (`FB` pseudo-regret upper bound). *Given an instance of the FBI-SG problem s.t. $\Delta b_k > 0$ for each $A_k \in \mathcal{A}$ and applying `FB`, the defender incurs in a pseudo-regret of:*

$$R_N(\mathfrak{U}) \leq \sum_{k=1}^{K} \frac{2(\lambda_k^2 + \lambda_{k^*}^2)\Delta L_k}{(\Delta b_k)^2},$$

where $\lambda_k := \max_{m \in \mathcal{M}} \max_{\boldsymbol{\sigma} \in \mathcal{S}} \ln(\sigma_{A_k}(\boldsymbol{\sigma})_m) - \min_{m \in \mathcal{M}} \min_{\boldsymbol{\sigma} \in \mathcal{S}} \ln(\sigma_{A_k}(\boldsymbol{\sigma})_m) \mathcal{I}\{\sigma_{A_k}(\boldsymbol{\sigma})_m \neq 0\}$ *is the range where the logarithm of the beliefs realizations lies (excluding realizations equal to zero, which end the exploration of a profile) and $\mathcal{S} := \cup_k \boldsymbol{\sigma}_D^*(A_k)$ is the set of the available best response to the attackers profile.*

For space reasons, we report the proof of Theorem 3 in Appendix A. Comparing the derived results, we notice that the `FB` algorithm presents an upper bound over the pseudo-regret that is strictly better than that of MAB algorithms, i.e., a constant regret $O(1)$ in N vs. a logarithmic one $O(\ln N)$.

5.2 FOLLOW THE REGRET

`FB` adopts the belief as discriminant factor to select the strategy profile to play in the next round. Conversely, in what follows, we describe the `FR` algorithm which is driven by a value iteration procedure that directly minimizes the expected regret over the remaining rounds $\{n+1, \ldots, N\}$. In principle, one should perform the procedure until the last round N, but, for computational purposes, an approximate solution can be obtained by setting a maximum level of recursion $h_{\max}$ and carry on the optimization only on the rounds $\{n+1, \ldots, \min\{n+h_{\max}, N\}\}$.

Algorithm 2 $\texttt{FR}(h_{\max})$

1: **for all** $A_k \in \mathcal{A}$ **do**
2:     Initialize $b_k^{(1)} = \frac{1}{K}$
3: **for all** $n \in \{1, \ldots, N\}$ **do**
4:     $\hat{\mathbf{R}} = \texttt{RE}(1, \mathbf{b}^{(n)}, h_{\max})$
5:     Select A_{k_n} s.t. $k_n = \arg\min_t \hat{R}_t$
6:     Play $\boldsymbol{\sigma}_D^*(A_{k_n})$
7:     Observe attacker action $i_{A_{k^*},n}$
8:     **for all** $A_k \in \mathcal{A}$ **do**
9:         Compute $b_k^{(n+1)}$ according to Equation (6)

Algorithm 3 $\texttt{RE}(h, \mathbf{b}, h_{\max})$

1: **for all** $A_k \in \mathcal{A}$ **do**
2:     **for all** $(i, j) \in \mathcal{M}^2$ **do**
3:         **for all** $A_t \in \mathcal{A}$ **do**
4:             $\hat{b}_t \leftarrow b_t\, \sigma_{A_t}(\boldsymbol{\sigma}_D^*(A_k))_j$
5:         $\hat{\mathbf{b}} \leftarrow \frac{\hat{\mathbf{b}}}{\sum_m \hat{b}_m}$
6:         Compute $r_{ij,k}$ according to Equation (4)
7:         **if** $h < h_{\max}$ **then**
8:             $\tilde{\mathbf{R}} = \texttt{RE}(h+1, \hat{\mathbf{b}}, h_{\max})$
9:             $r_{ij,k} \leftarrow r_{ij,k} + \min_k \tilde{R}_k$
10:     Compute $\hat{R}_k$ according to Equation (5)
11: Return $\hat{\mathbf{R}}$

The pseudo-code of the `FR` algorithm is presented in Algorithm 2, which recursively exploits the subroutine Algorithm 3. At first, the `FR` algorithm requires to initialize a belief vector $b_k^{(1)} = \frac{1}{K}$ for each attacker $A_k \in \mathcal{A}$ (Line 2, Alg. 2). At each round n, the algorithm computes the estimated expected regret vector $\hat{\mathbf{R}}$ suffered by D if she plays the best response $\boldsymbol{\sigma}_D^*(A_k)$ to A_k for each attacker profile $A_k \in \mathcal{A}$ (Line 4, Alg. 2), by recursively calling the *Regret Estimator* (`RE`) algorithm. Here, for every possible attacker $A_k \in \mathcal{A}$ and for every pair of possible actions of the defender and the attacker $(i, j) \in \mathcal{M}^2$, we create a new belief vector $\hat{\mathbf{b}}$ by updating $\mathbf{b}$ according to the information the attacker played action j (Line 4, Alg. 3). After that, we compute $r_{ij,k}$, i.e., the estimated expected loss in the case the defender D plays action $i_{D,n} = i$ and the attacker A_k plays $i_{A_k,n} = j$ averaged over the beliefs $b_n(A)$, as follows:

$$r_{ij,k} = v_j \mathcal{I}\{i \neq j\} - \sum_{t \in \{1, \ldots, K\}} \hat{b}_t\, L(A_t). \tag{4}$$

If the maximum recursion level $h_{\max}$ has been reached, the above value corresponds to the total estimated expected regret, otherwise we recursively compute the regret by calling `RE` over the following rounds and sum it to the instantaneous one $r_{ij,k}$ (Line 9, Alg. 3). Finally we compute the estimated total regret of choosing a specific attacker A_k for the next turn (Line 10, Alg. 3) as follows:

$$\hat{R}_k := \sum_{i=1}^{M} \sum_{j=1}^{M} r_{ij,k}\, \sigma_D^*(A_k)_i \cdot \sum_{A_{k'} \in \mathcal{A}} b_{k'}\, \sigma_{A_{k'}}(\boldsymbol{\sigma}_D^*(A_k))_j, \tag{5}$$

where the regret $r_{ij,k}$ is weighted with the probabilities that action i is selected by D and action j is selected by A. The defender D plays, for the current round n, the best response to the attacker A_{k_n}, providing the minimum estimated expected regret $\hat{R}_{k_n}$ (Line 6, Alg. 2) and observing action $i_{A_{k^*},n}$ undertaken by the attacker A_{k^*}. Finally, the algorithm updates the beliefs (Line 9, Alg. 2) as follows:

$$b_k^{(n+1)} = \frac{w_{nk}}{\sum_{k' \in \{1, \ldots, K\}} w_{nk'}}, \tag{6}$$

where $w_{nk} = b_k^{(n)}\, \sigma_{A_k}(\boldsymbol{\sigma}_D^*(A_{k_n}))_{i_{A_{k^*},n}}$.

5.3 COMPUTATIONAL COMPLEXITY

In this section, we analyse the proposed algorithms from a computational perspective. `FB` has complexity $O(KN)$, since it performs a belief update for each of the K attacker profiles, repeating this operation over N rounds. Thus, it results being linear both in the number of profiles and the rounds the game is played. Conversely, `FR` requires much more computational time. Indeed, for each attacker profile K, we consider M actions for both players and update the expected regret over the K profiles current beliefs. This leads to

Table 1: Number and type of attacker profiles $\mathcal{A}$ used for the experiments and total number of attacker K.

	Sta	Sto	$SUQR$	U	K
C_1	1	1	-	-	2
C_2	1	-	1	-	2
C_3	1	1	1	-	3
C_4	1	5	-	-	6
C_5	1	-	5	-	6
C_6	1	5	5	-	11
C_7	1	5	5	1	12

a cost of $O(M^2K^2)$ for a single round and an overall computational cost of $O(M^2K^2N)$ over the problem horizon N. If we want to employ the strategy from the current round n to the end of the horizon to compute the estimated expected regret $\hat{R}_n(A_k)$ by means of a forward procedure, the computational cost required by FR is $O(M^{2(N-n)}K^{2(N-n)})$ for a round. Thus, the final computational cost required by FR is $\sum_{n=1}^{N} O(M^{2(N-n)}K^{2(N-n)}) = O\left(\frac{(MK)^{2N}-1}{(MK)^2-1}\right) \approx O(M^{2N}K^{2N})$.

6 EXPERIMENTAL EVALUATION

We compare the proposed algorithms FB and FR (with $h_{\max} = 1$) with the state-of-the-art online learning approaches from the MAB (Bubeck et al., 2012) and expert (Kalai and Vempala, 2005) fields. In particular, We evaluate UCB1 algorithm (Auer et al., 2002), from the MAB literature, and the FPL algorithm (Cesa-Bianchi and Lugosi, 2006), from the expert literature.

In the experiments we also analyse the case in which one of the attacker behavioural profiles, namely U, is stochastic and her strategy is unknown to the defender D (to avoid possible misunderstandings, let us notice that the stochastic behaviour we describe in Section 4 is based on the assumption that the defender knows the strategy). In this case, we are still able to allow the leader to commit to a strategy that somehow minimizes the expected loss. Indeed, we can assign:

$$\boldsymbol{\sigma}^*_{D,n}(U) = FPL(h_n),$$

where $FPL(\cdot) \in \Delta_M$ is the pure strategy prescribed by the FPL algorithm. In this case the algorithm suffers from an additional regret due to the fact that, even if it is able to correctly detect the profile, it does not know the best response $\boldsymbol{\sigma}^*_D(U)$, but it needs to learn it over time.

6.1 EXPERIMENTAL SETTING

The experimental setting is as follows. We use a time horizon of $N = 1000$ rounds, with a different amount of targets $M \in \{5, 10\}$ and different profile configurations C_i, listed in Table 1, in which we report also the number of different stochastic, SUQR, and unknown stochastic behavioural profiles for each configuration. The configurations are ordered from the ones with smallest number of behavioural profiles ($K = 2$) to the largest one ($K = 12$). In principle, these problems should be of increasing difficulty, since the algorithms have to identify the actual behaviour among a larger number of options.

The strategies of the stochastic behavioural profiles Sto are drawn from a Dirichlet distribution with $\boldsymbol{\theta} = \mathbf{1}_M$ (uniform distribution over Δ_M) and the target values $\mathbf{v}$ are uniformly sampled in $[0,1]^M$. The parameters for the SUQR behavioural profiles are drawn from a uniform probability distribution over the intervals $\alpha \in [5, 15]$, $\beta \in [0, 1]$ and $\gamma \in [0, 1]$, whose choice is motivated by the experimental results obtained by Nguyen et al. (2013). For each combination of behavioural profiles and targets size, 10 random configurations (i.e., target values $\mathbf{v}$ and attacker profile sets $\mathcal{A}$) are generated and the actual behavioural profile A_{k^*} is drawn from a uniform probability distribution over the given profiles set $\mathcal{A}$. For each configuration we run 100 independent experiments and we compute the average regret. We evaluate the performance in terms of expected pseudo-regret $R(\mathfrak{U})_n$ with $n \in \{1, \ldots, N\}$ and computational time spent by the algorithms to execute a single run ($N = 1000$ rounds). Each component of the noise vector z in FPL is drawn from a uniform probability distribution over the interval $[0, \hat{v}K\sqrt{N}]$, where $\hat{v} = \max_{m \in M} v_m$, as described in Cesa-Bianchi and Lugosi (2006), Chapter 4.

6.2 EXPERIMENTAL RESULTS

We report in Table 2 the empiric pseudo-regret obtained in the experimental results. It can be observed that the algorithms we propose dramatically outperform the baselines provided by the state of the art. Furthermore, there is no strong statistical evidence that one algorithm between FB or FR outperforms the other. We recall that FR is more computationally demanding than FB, thus one might prefer FB for problems with many attacker behavioural profiles, since it has comparable performance w.r.t. FR and is computationally more efficient. Notably, the FPL algorithm generally improves its performance when tested over larger target space $M = 10$. We think this could be induced by the fact that the specific configurations in which the FPL gets linear regret (i.e., the ones considered in Theorem 2) are less likely to occur when we have a larger amount of targets. Remarkably, our algorithms provide good performance also when a stochastic behavioural profile U whose strategy is unknown to the defender is present among the possible ones.

Table 2: Expected pseudo-regret $R_N(\mathfrak{U})$ over $N = 1000$ rounds and corresponding 95% confidence intervals for different configurations (best results are in boldface).

		C_1	C_2	C_3	C_4	C_5	C_6	C_7
$M = 5$	UCB1	14.12 ± 1.88	8.62 ± 3.73	23.92 ± 5.23	45.75 ± 11.68	1.76 ± 0.41	75.82 ± 19.94	62.31 ± 12.22
	FPL	18.71 ± 35.02	11.16 ± 5.98	38.5 ± 27.18	49.8 ± 62.33	0.77 ± 0.12	68.88 ± 64.13	72.5 ± 53.34
	FB	$\mathbf{0.19 \pm 0.13}$	$\mathbf{0.2 \pm 0.18}$	$\mathbf{0.5 \pm 0.24}$	$\mathbf{0.48 \pm 0.2}$	$\mathbf{0.09 \pm 0.03}$	$\mathbf{0.67 \pm 0.2}$	$\mathbf{7.92 \pm 4.87}$
	FR	$\mathbf{0.1 \pm 0.06}$	$\mathbf{0.27 \pm 0.36}$	$\mathbf{0.42 \pm 0.3}$	$\mathbf{0.62 \pm 0.24}$	$\mathbf{0.07 \pm 0.04}$	$\mathbf{1.07 \pm 1.1}$	$\mathbf{4.84 \pm 3.32}$
$M = 10$	UCB1	16.77 ± 1.2	5.24 ± 2.79	21.2 ± 3.76	60.58 ± 8.89	4.24 ± 5.02	61.52 ± 22.48	58.93 ± 17.42
	FPL	1.08 ± 0.2	5.97 ± 3.5	12.06 ± 4.31	2.63 ± 0.99	3.24 ± 3.96	17.69 ± 16.03	$\mathbf{22.49 \pm 12.26}$
	FB	$\mathbf{0.13 \pm 0.03}$	$\mathbf{0.1 \pm 0.02}$	$\mathbf{0.33 \pm 0.16}$	$\mathbf{0.57 \pm 0.17}$	$\mathbf{0.05 \pm 0.01}$	$\mathbf{0.58 \pm 0.14}$	$\mathbf{16.06 \pm 6.89}$
	FR	$\mathbf{0.06 \pm 0.05}$	$\mathbf{0.12 \pm 0.21}$	$\mathbf{0.21 \pm 0.12}$	$\mathbf{0.43 \pm 0.19}$	$\mathbf{0.02 \pm 0.02}$	$\mathbf{0.6 \pm 0.43}$	$\mathbf{14.65 \pm 8.1}$

In Figures 2 to 7 we show how the pseudo-regret $R_n(\mathfrak{U})$ evolves during the time horizon in the most challenging configurations, namely C_5, C_6 and C_7. The results in other configurations, omitted due to reasons of space, confirm the results obtained in C_5, C_6, C_7 and are reported in Appendix B. The plots are in a semilogarithmic scale for a better comprehension. In all the presented configurations, except in C_7 with $M = 10$, there is statistical significance that the FB and FR algorithms outperform the baselines on average since the confidence intervals do not overlap after the first ≈ 50 rounds. In configuration C_7 with $M = 10$, our algorithms outperform the baselines only on average.

Finally, we analyze the computational effort required by our algorithms to solve instances over $N = 1000$ rounds and $M \in \{5, 10, 20, 40\}$ targets.[2] The average computational times are reported in Table 3 (the full version of Table 3 with confidence intervals is reported in Appendix B). There are three observations we can make. First, we could not report the values for $M \in \{20, 40\}$ for FR since the required computational cost is too high (≥ 3600 seconds). Second, both FB and FR present the same trend w.r.t. the configurations: in fact, when the behavioral profile of the opponent can only be either Sta or Sto, both algorithms are twice more efficient than in cases in which SUQR adversaries are introduced. This is due to the fact that both Sta and SUQR models exploit the strategy the defender commits to, making more difficult to distinguish among them. The most difficult configuration is C_7, where the presence of a stochastic unknown adversary make things even worse since the distribution must also be estimated. Finally, as expected, we notice that FB is *always* faster than FR: in fact, while they are both polynomial in the actions available to the players, i.e., the number of targets, the former is linear while the latter quadratic (since we set $h_{\max} = 1$).

[2]The computational times for the UCB1 and FPL algorithm are omitted since they are in line with the one of FB.

Table 3: Computational time in seconds needed by FB and FR to solve an instance over $N = 1000$ rounds.

		C_1	C_2	C_3	C_4	C_5	C_6	C_7
$M = 5$	FB	6	11	12	4	24	15	15
	FR	77	121	170	146	652	1029	1114
$M = 10$	FB	10	22	23	7	63	47	48
	FR	356	679	887	960	4402	7527	7292
$M = 20$	FB	33	222	138	34	485	227	229
	FR	–	–	–	–	–	–	–
$M = 40$	FB	105	2061	1412	129	2348	1634	1643
	FR	–	–	–	–	–	–	–

7 CONCLUSIONS AND FUTURE RESEARCH

In this work, we study for the first time, a novel leadership game in which the leader plays against a follower whose behaviour is unknown, but it belongs to a set of known profiles. We provide two novel approaches to tackle this problem, namely FB and FR, bridging together game-theoretical techniques and online learning tools. In the FB algorithm the leader is driven by the beliefs on the possible follower profiles, while the FR one is based on a learning policy directly driven by the estimated expected regret, computed according to a value iteration procedure. For the first approach, we provide also a finite-time analysis, showing that the regret of the algorithm is constant in the number of rounds, while bandit and expert algorithms available in the state of the art suffer from a logarithmic and linear regret, respectively. Finally, we experimentally evaluate the performance of our algorithms in leadership settings inspired by concrete security domains, showing that our approaches provide a remarkable improvement in terms of empirical pseudo-regret minimization w.r.t. the main algorithms available in the state of the art of the online learning field.

In the future, we will study an upper bound over the regret of the FR algorithm. Furthermore, we will include new types of attacker profiles and we will extend the framework towards a multi-agent-learning setting, allowing the attacker to exploit a finite/infinite memory.

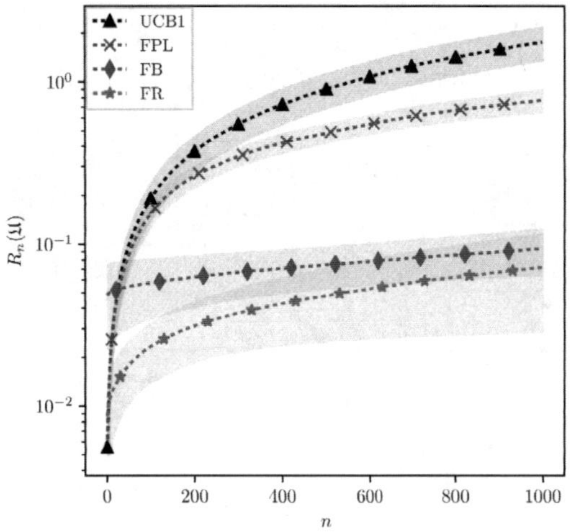

Figure 2: Expected pseudo-regret for the configuration C_5 with $M = 5$ targets.

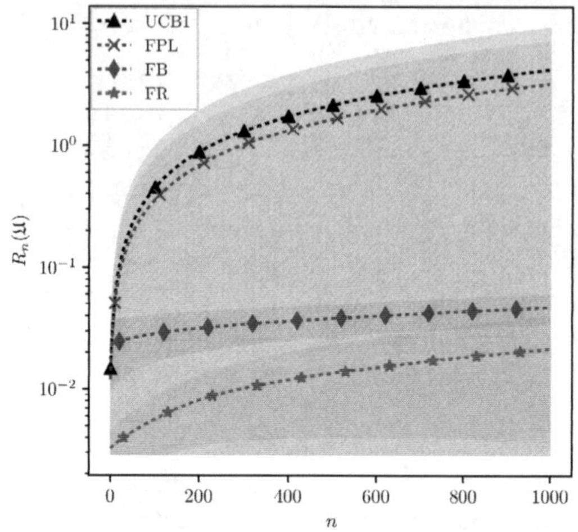

Figure 5: Expected pseudo-regret for the configuration C_5 with $M = 10$ targets.

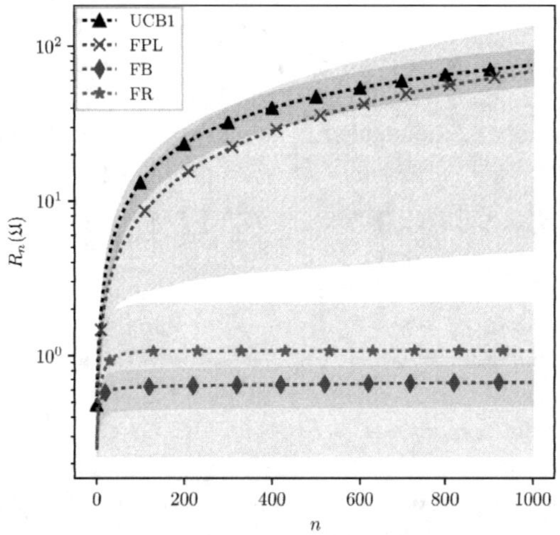

Figure 3: Expected pseudo-regret for the configuration C_6 with $M = 5$ targets.

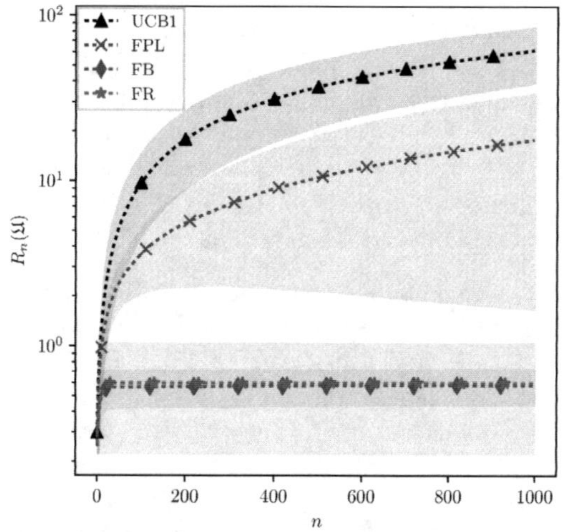

Figure 6: Expected pseudo-regret for the configuration C_6 with $M = 10$ targets.

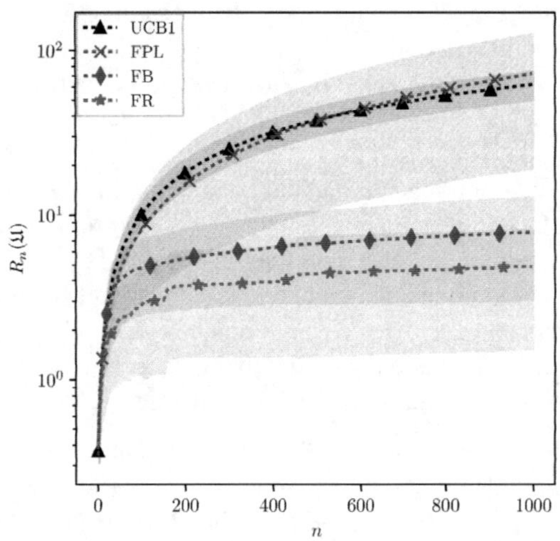

Figure 4: Expected pseudo-regret for the configuration C_7 with $M = 5$ targets.

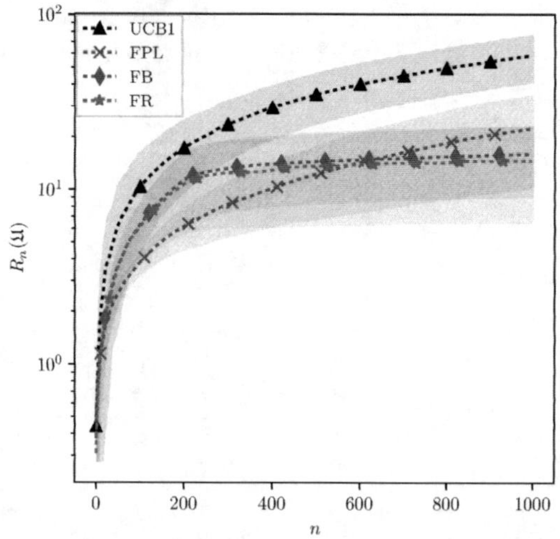

Figure 7: Expected pseudo-regret for the configuration C_7 with $M = 10$ targets.

References

An, B., Brown, M., Vorobeychik, Y., and Tambe, M. (2013). Security games with surveillance cost and optimal timing of attack execution. In *AAMAS*, pages 223–230.

Auer, P., Cesa-Bianchi, N., and Fischer, P. (2002). Finite-time analysis of the multiarmed bandit problem. *MACH LEARN*, 47(2):235–256.

Balcan, M., Blum, A., Haghtalab, N., and Procaccia, A. D. (2015). Commitment without regrets: Online learning in Stackelberg security games. In *EC*, pages 61–78.

Basilico, N., De Nittis, G., and Gatti, N. (2017). Adversarial patrolling with spatially uncertain alarm signals. *ART INT*, 246:220–257.

Blum, A., Haghtalab, N., and Procaccia, A. D. (2015). Learning to play Stackelberg security games. Technical report, Carnegie Mellon University, Computer Science Department.

Bubeck, S., Cesa-Bianchi, N., et al. (2012). Regret analysis of stochastic and nonstochastic multi-armed bandit problems. *Foundations and Trends in Machine Learning*, 5(1):1–122.

Cesa-Bianchi, N. and Lugosi, G. (2006). *Prediction, learning, and games*. Cambridge university press.

Conitzer, V. and Sandholm, T. (2006). Computing the optimal strategy to commit to. In *EC*, pages 82–90.

Conitzer, V. and Sandholm, T. (2007). Awesome: A general multiagent learning algorithm that converges in self-play and learns a best response against stationary opponents. *MACH LEARN*, 67(1-2):23–43.

Fang, F., Stone, P., and Tambe, M. (2015). When security games go green: designing defender strategies to prevent poaching and illegal fishing. In *IJCAI*, pages 2589–2595.

Ford, B., Kar, D., Delle Fave, F. M., Yang, R., and Tambe, M. (2014). PAWS: adaptive game-theoretic patrolling for wildlife protection. In *AAMAS*, pages 1641–1642.

Fudenberg, D. and Tirole, J. (1991). *Game Theory*. MIT Press.

Kalai, A. and Vempala, S. (2005). Efficient algorithms for online decision problems. *J COMPUT SYST SCI*, 71(3):291–307.

Klíma, R., Kiekintveld, C., and Lisỳ, V. (2014). Online learning methods for border patrol resource allocation. In *GameSec*, pages 340–349.

McDiarmid, C. (1989). On the method of bounded differences. *LOND MATH S*, 141(1):148–188.

McFadden, D. L. (1984). Econometric analysis of qualitative response models. *Handbook of econometrics*, 2:1395–1457.

Nguyen, T., Yang, R., Azaria, A., Kraus, S., and Tambe, M. (2013). Analyzing the effectiveness of adversary modeling in security games. In *AAAI*, pages 718–724.

Paruchuri, P., Pearce, J. P., Marecki, J., Tambe, M., Ordóñez, F., and Kraus, S. (2008). Playing games for security: An efficient exact algorithm for solving Bayesian Stackelberg games. In *AAMAS*, pages 895–902.

Pita, J., Jain, M., Western, C., Portway, C., Tambe, M., Ordóñez, F., Kraus, S., and Paruchuri, P. (2008). Deployed ARMOR protection: The application of a game-theoretic model for security at the Los Angeles International Airport. In *AAMAS*, pages 125–132.

Pita, J., Tambe, M., Kiekintveld, C., Cullen, S., and Steigerwald, E. (2011). Guards: game theoretic security allocation on a national scale. In *AAMAS*, pages 37–44.

Qian, Y., Haskell, W. B., Jiang, A. X., and Tambe, M. (2014). Online planning for optimal protector strategies in resource conservation games. In *AAMAS*, pages 733–740.

Qian, Y., Zhang, C., Krishnamachari, B., and Tambe, M. (2016). Restless poachers: Handling exploration-exploitation tradeoffs in security domains. In *AAMAS*, pages 123–131.

Shoham, Y. and Leyton-Brown, K. (2008). *Multiagent systems: Algorithmic, game-theoretic, and logical foundations*. Cambridge University Press.

Tsai, J., Rathi, S., Kiekintveld, C., Ordóñez, F., and Tambe, M. (2009). IRIS-A tool for strategic security allocation in transportation networks. In *AAMAS*, pages 1327–1334.

Tuyls, K. and Weiss, G. (2012). Multiagent learning: Basics, challenges, and prospects. *AI MAG*, 33(3):41.

Von Stackelberg, H. (1934). *Marktform und gleichgewicht*. J. Springer.

Xu, H., Tran-Thanh, L., and Jennings, N. R. (2016). Playing repeated security games with no prior knowledge. In *AAMAS*, pages 104–112.

Yang, R., Ford, B., Tambe, M., and Lemieux, A. (2014). Adaptive resource allocation for wildlife protection against illegal poachers. In *AAMAS*, pages 453–460.

Yang, R., Kiekintveld, C., Ordóñez, F., Tambe, M., and John, R. (2011). Improving resource allocation strategy against human adversaries in security games. In *IJCAI*, pages 458–464.

A SUPPLEMENTAL MATERIAL

Theorem 2 (Expert pseudo-regret upper bound). *Let us consider an instance of the FBI-SG problem and apply the FPL algorithm, where each possible profile A_k is an expert and receives, at round n, an expert reward equal to minus the loss she would have incurred observing $i_{A_{k^*},n}$ by playing the best response to the attacker A_k. Then, there always exists an attacker set $\mathcal{A}$ s.t. the defender D incurs in an expected pseudo-regret of:*

$$R_N(\mathfrak{U}) \propto \Delta L_k N.$$

Proof. Let us analyse the FBI-SG problem in which the attacker profile set is $\mathcal{A} = \{Sta, Sto\}$, the true attacker $A_{k^*} = Sta$ and we use the Follow the Leader algorithm (Cesa-Bianchi and Lugosi, 2006). Assume that the best response $\boldsymbol{\sigma}_D^*(Sto)$ to the stochastic attacker Sto corresponds to the pure strategy played by the Stackelberg attacker at the equilibrium, i.e, $\boldsymbol{\sigma}_{Sta}^*(\boldsymbol{\sigma}_D^*(Sta)) = \boldsymbol{\sigma}_D^*(Sto)$. Assume the chosen target by the two strategies has value $v_{\hat{m}}$ in target $\hat{m}$, maximum value $v_{\bar{m}}$ in target $\bar{m}$ and that the stochastic attacker has strategy $\mathbf{p}$ s.t.:

$$p_m = \begin{cases} \alpha & \text{if } m = \hat{m} \\ 1-\alpha & \text{if } m = \bar{m} \\ 0 & \text{otherwise} \end{cases},$$

where $\alpha = \frac{v_{\bar{m}} - L(Sta)}{v_{\bar{m}}}$ and $\alpha v_{\hat{m}} > (1-\alpha) v_{\bar{m}}$. In this case, the defender might commit to two different strategies:

- if the defender D declares its best response to the Stackerlberg attacker $\boldsymbol{\sigma}_D^*(Sta)$ for the turn, it would provide zero loss as feedback for the stochastic attacker expert and loss equal to $-L(Sta)$ to the Stackelberg one
- if the defender D selects the best response to the stochastic attacker $\boldsymbol{\sigma}_D^*(Sto)$, the defender would gain loss equal to $-(1-\alpha)v_{\bar{m}} = -L(Sta)$ for the stochastic attacker expert and $-L(Sta)$ for the Stackelberg one. Thus, in this case the two types would receive the same feedback.

Summarizing, we have that the Stackelberg attacker expert always incurs in a loss greater or equal to the one of the stochastic one, even if the real attacker is Stackelberg. Thus, with a probability grater than 0.5 we are incurring in a loss of ΔL_k for the entire horizon, with a total regret proportional to $\Delta L_k N$. Even by resorting to randomization, thus even adopting the FPL we would have a probability of at least $0.5 - \varepsilon$ (being ε the probability with which the FPL chooses a suboptimal option) to select the wrong option, thus also the FPL algorithm would incur in a linear regret over the time horizon.

□

Theorem 3 (FB pseudo-regret upper bound). *Given an instance of the FBI-SG problem s.t. $\Delta b_k > 0$ for each $A_k \in \mathcal{A}$ and applying FB, the defender incurs in a pseudo-regret of:*

$$R_N(\mathfrak{U}) \leq \sum_{k=1}^{K} \frac{2(\lambda_k^2 + \lambda_{k^*}^2)\Delta L_k}{(\Delta b_k)^2},$$

where $\lambda_k := \max_{m \in \mathcal{M}} \max_{\boldsymbol{\sigma} \in \mathcal{S}} \ln(\sigma_{A_k}(\boldsymbol{\sigma})_m) - \min_{m \in \mathcal{M}} \min_{\boldsymbol{\sigma} \in \mathcal{S}} \ln(\sigma_{A_k}(\boldsymbol{\sigma})_m) \mathcal{I}\{\sigma_{A_k}(\boldsymbol{\sigma})_m \neq 0\}$ is the range where the logarithm of the beliefs realizations lies (excluding realizations equal to zero, which end the exploration of a profile) and $\mathcal{S} := \cup_k \boldsymbol{\sigma}_D^*(A_k)$ is the set of the available best response to the attackers profile.

Proof. Let us analyze the regret of the FB algorithm. We get some regret if the algorithm selects a strategy profile corresponding to a type different from the real one. Thus, the regret is upper bounded by:

$$R_N(\mathfrak{U}) = \mathbb{E}\left[\sum_{n=1}^{N} l_n\right] - L^* N$$
$$= \mathbb{E}\left[\sum_{n=1}^{N} l_n - L^*\right] = \sum_{k=1}^{K} \Delta L_k \mathbb{E}[T_k(N)],$$

where we recall that:

- $T_i(N) = \sum_{n=1}^{N} \mathcal{I}\{A_{k_n} = A_k\}$ is the number of times we played the best response $\boldsymbol{\sigma}_D^*(A_k)$ to attacker A_k;

- $\Delta L_k = \sum_{m=1}^{M} \sigma_A(\boldsymbol{\sigma}_D^*(A_k))_m v_m (1 - \sigma_D^*(A_k)_m) \; - L^*$ is the expected regret of playing the best response to attacker A_k when the real attacker is A.

Each round in which the algorithm selects a profile s.t. the best response is not equal to the one of A_{k^*} we are getting some regret.

Let us define variables $B_{k,n}$ and $B_{k^*,n}$ denoting the belief we have for the possible attacker A_k and of the real attacker A, respectively, of the action played by the real attacker A at turn n. Moreover, let $b_{kj,t} := \mathbb{E}_{\sigma_D^*(A_j)}[B_{k,t}]$ be the expected value of the belief we get for attacker A_k when we are best responding to A_j and the true type is $A_{k^*} \neq A_k$ at round t. Note that $b_{kj,t} < b_{k^*j,t}, \forall j$, since Δb_k is positive.

For each profile $A_k \neq A_{k^*}$, we have:

$$\mathbb{E}[T_k(N)] \leq \sum_{n=1}^{N} \mathbb{E}\left[\mathcal{I}\left\{\prod_{t=1}^{n} B_{k,t} \geq \prod_{t=1}^{n} B_{k^*,t}\right\}\right] \tag{7}$$

$$\leq \sum_{n=1}^{N} \mathbb{E}\left[\mathcal{I}\left\{\sum_{t=1}^{n} \ln(B_{k,t}) \geq \sum_{t=1}^{n} \ln(B_{k^*,t})\right\}\right] \tag{8}$$

$$= \sum_{n=1}^{N} \mathbb{P}\left(\frac{\sum_{t=1}^{n} \ln(B_{k,t})}{n} \geq \frac{\sum_{t=1}^{n} \ln(B_{k^*,t})}{n}\right) \tag{9}$$

$$= \sum_{n=1}^{N} \mathbb{P}\left(\frac{\sum_{t=1}^{n} \ln(B_{k,t})}{n} - \frac{\sum_{t=1}^{n} \ln(b_{kj_t,t})}{n} - \frac{\sum_{t=1}^{n} \ln(B_{k^*,t})}{n} + \right.$$

$$\left. + \frac{\sum_{t=1}^{n} \ln(b_{k^*j_t,t})}{n} \geq \underbrace{\left(\frac{\sum_{t=1}^{n} \ln(b_{k^*j_t,t})}{n} - \frac{\sum_{t=1}^{n} \ln(b_{kj_t,t})}{n}\right)}_{\geq \Delta b_k}\right) \tag{10}$$

$$\leq \sum_{n=1}^{N} \mathbb{P}\left(\frac{\sum_{t=1}^{n} \ln(B_{k,t})}{n} - \frac{\sum_{t=1}^{n} \ln(b_{kj_t,t})}{n} - \frac{\Delta b_k}{2} - \frac{\sum_{t=1}^{n} \ln(B_{k^*,t})}{n} + \frac{\sum_{t=1}^{n} \ln(b_{k^*j_t,t})}{n} - \frac{\Delta b_k}{2} \geq 0\right) \tag{11}$$

$$\leq \underbrace{\sum_{n=1}^{N} \mathbb{P}\left(\frac{\sum_{t=1}^{n} \ln(B_{k,t})}{n} \geq \frac{\sum_{t=1}^{n} \ln(b_{kj_t,t})}{n} + \frac{\Delta b_k}{2}\right)}_{R_1} +$$

$$+ \underbrace{\sum_{n=1}^{N} \mathbb{P}\left(\frac{\sum_{t=1}^{n} \ln(B_{k^*,t})}{n} \leq \frac{\sum_{t=1}^{n} \ln(b_{k^*j_t,t})}{n} - \frac{\Delta b_k}{2}\right)}_{R_2}, \tag{12}$$

where j_t is the index of the attacker A_{j_t} we selected at round t and we defined $\Delta b_k := \min_{j|A_j \in \mathcal{A}} \ln(b_{k^*j,t}) - \ln(b_{kj,t})$, i.e., the minimum w.r.t. the best response for the available attackers of the difference between the expected value of the loglikelihood of attacker A_{k^*} and A_k if the true profile is A_{k^*}. Equation (9) has been obtained from Equation (8) since $\mathbb{E}\left[\mathcal{I}\left\{\cdot\right\}\right] = \mathbb{P}\left(\cdot\right)$ while Equation (10) has been computed from Equation (9) adding $\left(\frac{\sum_{t=1}^{n} \ln(b_{k^*j_t,t})}{n} - \frac{\sum_{t=1}^{n} \ln(b_{kj_t,t})}{n}\right)$ to both l.h.s. and r.h.s. of the inequality. We would like to point out that Δb_k does not depend on t since the distribution of $B_{k,t}$ and $B_{k^*,t}$ is the same over rounds.

Let us focus on R_1. We use the McDiarmid inequality (McDiarmid, 1989) to bound the probability that the empirical estimate of the loglikelihood expected value is higher than a certain upper bound as follows:

$$
\begin{aligned}
R_1 &= \sum_{n=1}^{N} \mathbb{P}\left(\frac{\sum_{t=1}^{n} \ln(B_{k,t})}{n} \geq \frac{\sum_{t=1}^{n} \ln(b_{kj_t,t})}{n} + \frac{\Delta b_k}{2} \right) \\
&\leq \sum_{n=1}^{\infty} \mathbb{P}\left(\frac{\sum_{t=1}^{n} \ln(B_{k,t})}{n} \geq \frac{\sum_{t=1}^{n} \ln(b_{kj_t,t})}{n} + \frac{\Delta b_k}{2} \right) \\
&\leq \sum_{n=1}^{\infty} \exp\left\{ -\frac{(\Delta b_k)^2 n}{2\lambda_k^2} \right\} \leq \frac{2\lambda_k^2}{(\Delta b_k)^2},
\end{aligned}
$$

where we exploited $\sum_{x=1}^{\infty} e^{-\kappa x} \leq \frac{1}{\kappa}$. We define $\lambda_k := \max_{m\in\mathcal{M}} \max_{\boldsymbol{\sigma}\in\mathcal{S}} \ln(\sigma_{A_k}(\boldsymbol{\sigma})_m) - \min_{m\in\mathcal{M}} \min_{\boldsymbol{\sigma}\in\mathcal{S}} \ln(\sigma_{A_k}(\boldsymbol{\sigma})_m)\mathcal{I}\{\sigma_{A_k}(\boldsymbol{\sigma})_m \neq 0\}$ as the range where the beliefs realizations lie (excluding realizations equal to zero which ends the exploration of a profile), where we used the fact that $\mathbb{E}[B_{k,t}] = b_k \forall k, t$ and $\mathcal{S} := \cup_k \boldsymbol{\sigma}_D^*(A_k)$ is the set of the available best response to the attackers profile.

A similar reasoning can be applied to R_2 getting an upper bound of the following form:

$$
R_2 \leq \frac{2\lambda_{k^*}^2}{(\Delta b_k)^2}.
$$

The regret becomes:

$$
R_N(\mathfrak{U}) = \sum_{i=1}^{K} \Delta L_k \mathbb{E}[T_k(N)] \leq \sum_{i=1}^{K} \Delta L_k \left(\frac{2\lambda_k^2}{(\Delta b_k)^2} + \frac{2\lambda_{k^*}^2}{(\Delta b_k)^2} \right) \leq \sum_{i=1}^{K} \frac{2(\lambda_k^2 + \lambda_{k^*}^2)\Delta L_k}{(\Delta b_k)^2},
$$

which concludes the proof.

□

B ADDITIONAL RESULTS

For the sake of completeness, we report in Figures 8 and 9 all the graphs regarding the regret for all the running configurations $C_1, \dots, C_7$ and for the two dimensions of the target space, namely $M \in \{5, 10\}$. By inspecting these additional set of figures are in line with what has been presented in Section 6 of the main paper, where the proposed techniques, namely FB and FR, are able to outperform the literature methods. Even here, there is not a clear method providing statistical evidence that it is able to outperform the other.

Moreover, we also provide in Figure 10 the results for configuration C_6 with a number of target $M = 40$. In this configuration, we were able to run only the FB algorithm for computational time constraints. The results show that the FB has performance similar to the ones experienced with smaller target space, thus it is able to scale without significant loss in terms of expected pseudo-regret $R_N(\mathfrak{U})$.

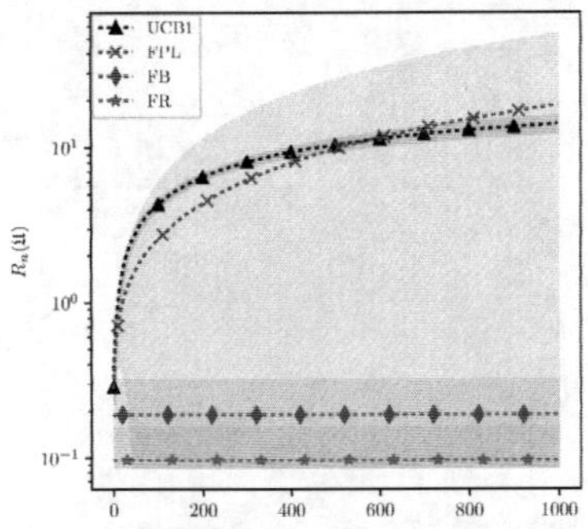

(a) Configuration C_1.

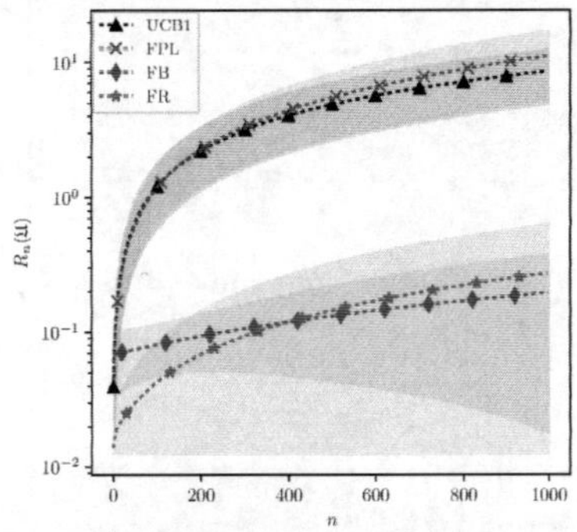

(b) Configuration C_2.

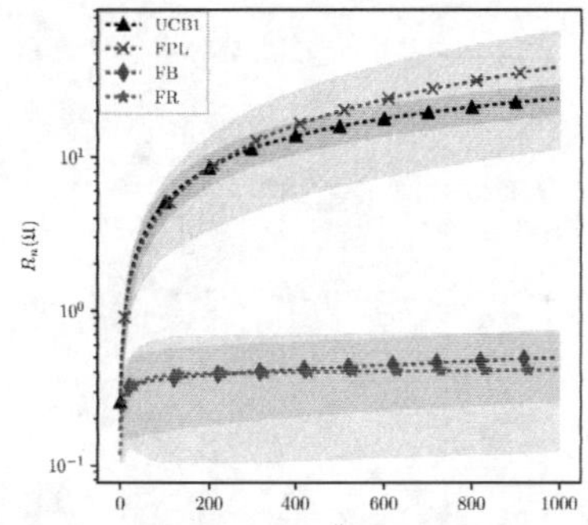

(c) Configuration C_3.

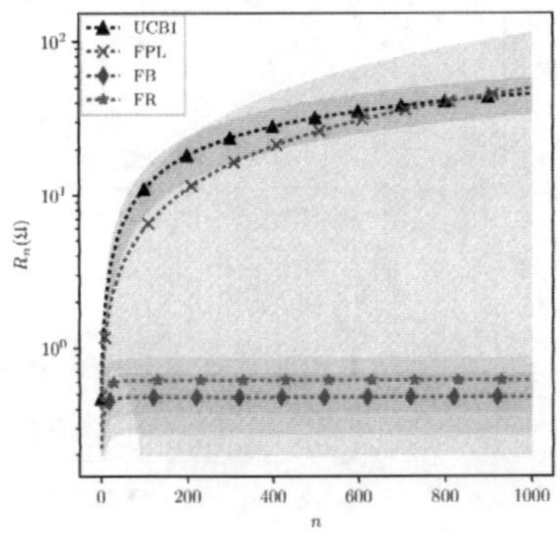

(d) Configuration C_4.

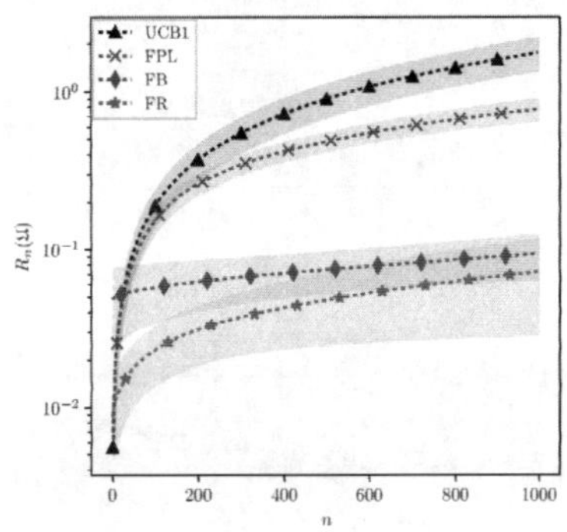

(e) Configuration C_5.

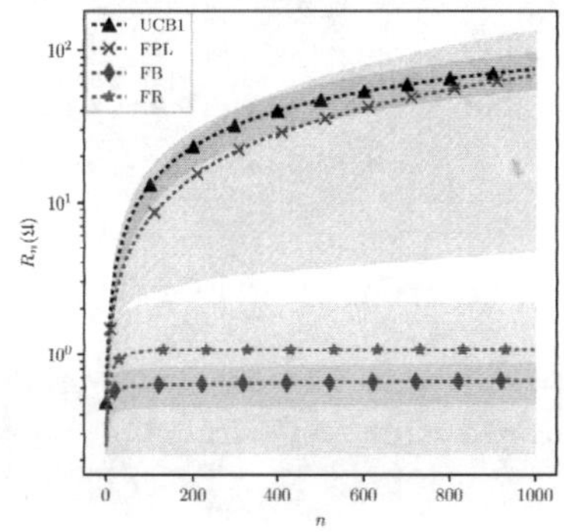

(f) Configuration C_6.

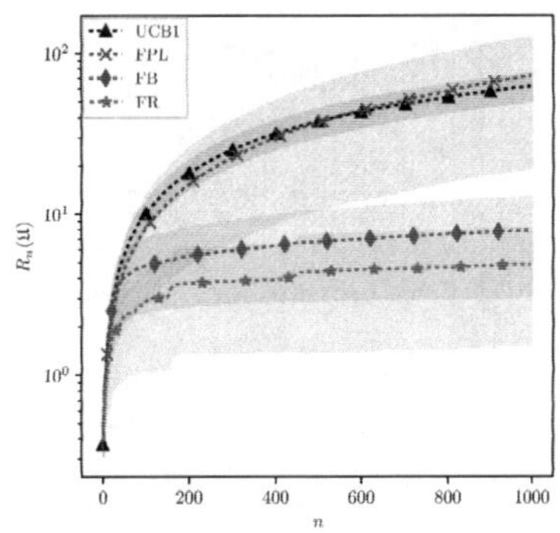

(g) Configuration C_7.

Figure 8: Expected pseudo-regret for the different configurations with $M = 5$ targets.

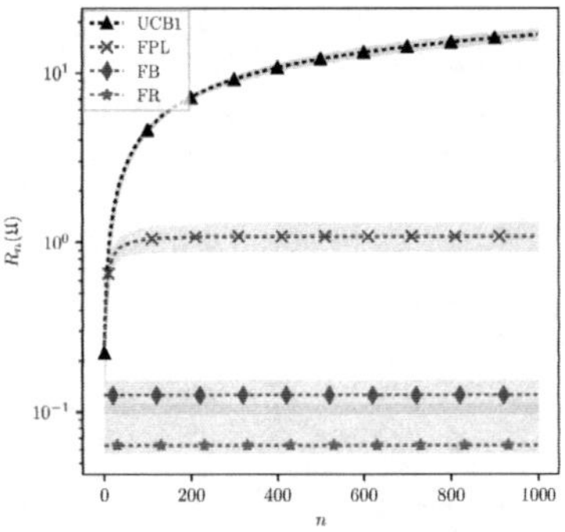

(a) Configuration C_1.

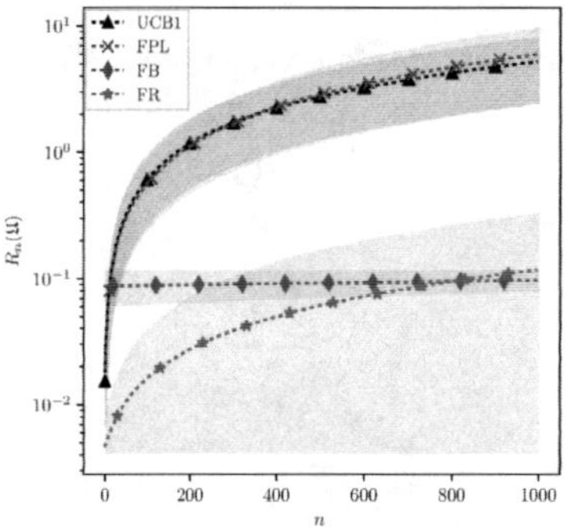

(b) Configuration C_2.

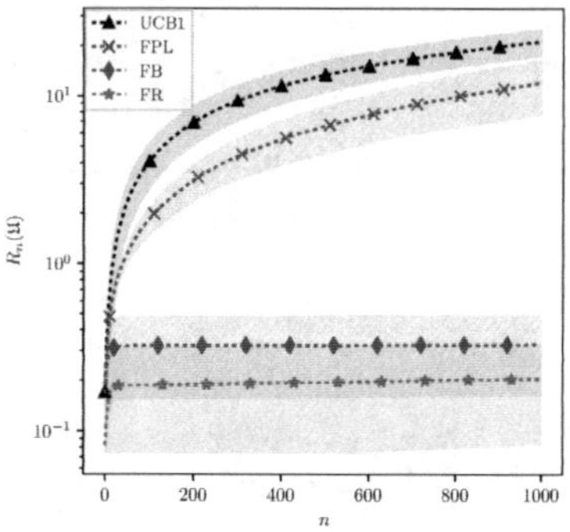

(c) Configuration C_3.

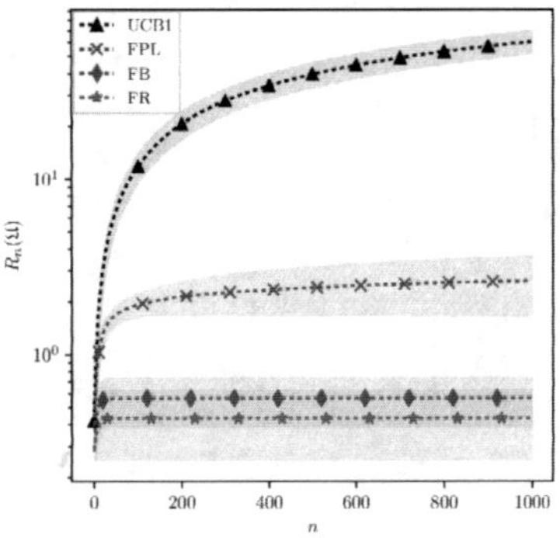

(d) Configuration C_4.

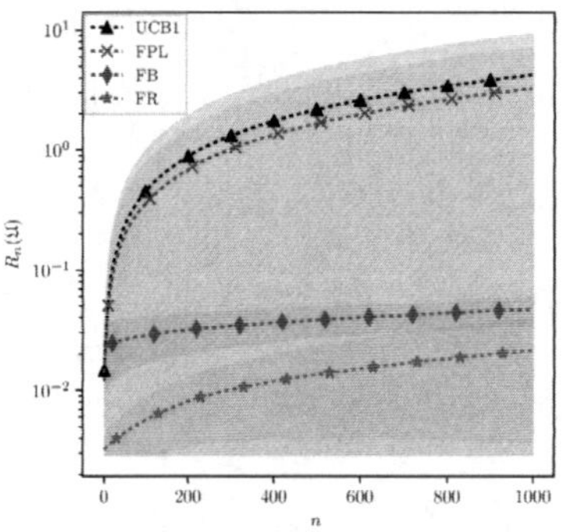

(e) Configuration C_5.

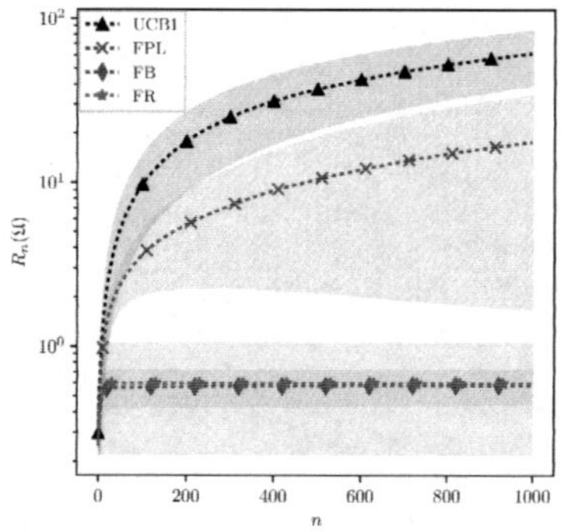

(f) Configuration C_6.

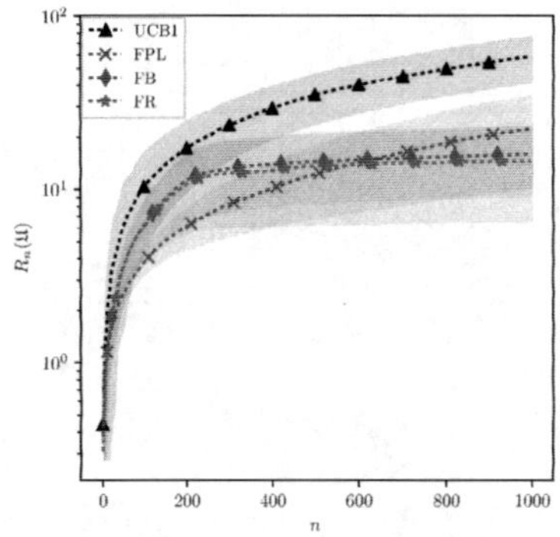

(g) Configuration C_7.

Figure 9: Expected pseudo-regret for the different configurations with $M = 10$ targets.

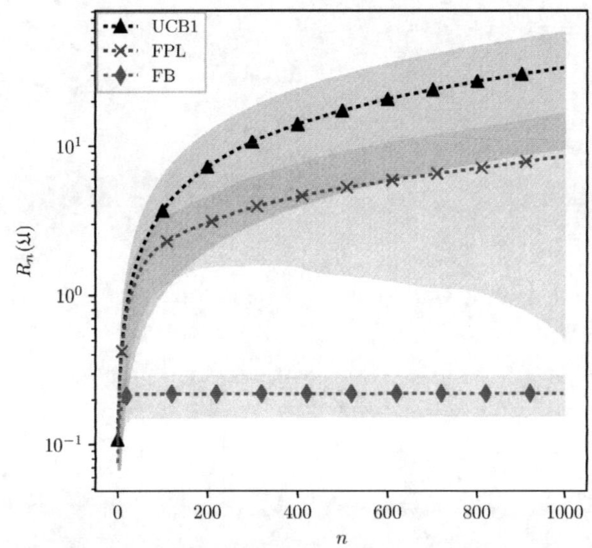

Figure 10: Expected pseudo-regret for the configuration C_6 with $M = 40$ targets.

Table 4: Computational time in seconds needed by FB and FR to solve an instance over $N = 1000$ rounds and the corresponding 95% confidence intervals.

		C_1	C_2	C_3	C_4	C_5	C_6	C_7
$M = 5$	FB	5.9 ± 1.7	11.1 ± 2.2	11.7 ± 2.9	3.5 ± 1.0	23.7 ± 2.4	14.9 ± 4.3	14.7 ± 3.2
	FR	77.0 ± 2.1	121.1 ± 3.2	170.4 ± 4.1	146.2 ± 4.7	651.7 ± 36.6	1029.2 ± 64.7	1113.7 ± 40.2
$M = 10$	FB	10.3 ± 2.6	21.9 ± 13.2	23.0 ± 17.9	7.1 ± 2.3	63.0 ± 7.4	47.22 ± 14.05	48.59 ± 13.48
	FR	356.1 ± 14.3	678.5 ± 15.9	887.0 ± 11.1	960.4 ± 13.0	4402.5 ± 14.2	7526.5 ± 189.9	7291.6 ± 23.7
$M = 20$	FB	33.5 ± 3.0	222.2 ± 126.9	137.8 ± 77.6	33.7 ± 1.2	484.5 ± 107.7	226.8 ± 45.3	229.5 ± 46.44
	FR	–	–	–	–	–	–	–
$M = 40$	FB	104.5 ± 7.1	2061.5 ± 837.2	1412.0 ± 812.1	128.9 ± 16.5	2347.9 ± 1223.2	1634.2 ± 487.6	1643.62 ± 468.8
	FR	–	–	–	–	–	–	–

We also report here Table 4, the full version of Table 3, with the time values up to the first decimal and also specifying the confidence interval.

On the Complexity of Nash Equilibrium Reoptimization

Andrea Celli, Alberto Marchesi, Nicola Gatti
Politecnico di Milano
Piazza Leonardo da Vinci, 32
Milano, Italy
{andrea.celli, alberto.marchesi, nicola.gatti}@polimi.it

Abstract

We provide, to the best of our knowledge, the first study about *reoptimization* complexity of game-theoretical solutions. In a reoptimization problem, we are given an instance, its optimal solution, and a local modification, and we are asked to find the exact or an approximate solution to the modified instance. Reoptimization is crucial whenever an instance needs to be solved repeatedly and, at each repetition, its parameters may slightly change. In this paper, we focus on Nash equilibrium, being the central game-theoretical solution. We study the reoptimization of Nash equilibria satisfying some properties (i.e., maximizing/minimizing the social welfare, the utility of a player or the support size) for some different local modifications of the game (i.e., modification of a payoff or addition/removal of an action), showing that such problems are NP-hard. Furthermore, we assess the approximation complexity of the aforementioned problems, showing that it matches the complexity of the original (non-reoptimization) problems. Finally, we show that, when finding a Nash equilibrium is thought as an optimization problem, reoptimization is useful for finding approximate solutions. Specifically, it allows one to find ϵ-Nash equilibria with smaller ϵ than that of the solutions returned by the best known approximation algorithms.

1 INTRODUCTION

The design of computational tools for tackling strategic scenarios has been a central problem in Artificial Intelligence for several years. The main goal is the development of software/physical agents capable of behaving optimally when facing strategic opponents. This is achieved by modelling a scenario by means of models from non-cooperative game theory [Fudenberg and Tirole, 1991] and by employing algorithmic tools [Nisan et al., 2007] to search for optimal solutions (a.k.a. equilibria), each one specifying the best strategies the agents can play. A crucial issue is the study of the complexity of equilibrium-finding problems and the design of efficient algorithms scaling up in real-world applications, e.g., as in Security Games [Tambe, 2011].

A key solution concept is the Nash Equilibrium (NE), which prescribes strategies so that no player has any incentive in deviating unilaterally. Given the importance of NE concept, there has been a growing interest on settling its computational properties. More precisely, the computational complexity of finding an NE has been recently shown to be PPAD-complete [Daskalakis et al., 2009] even for 2-player games [Chen and Deng, 2006]. Recall that $\mathsf{PPAD} \subseteq \mathsf{FNP}$ but $\mathsf{PPAD} \not\subseteq \mathsf{FNP}$-complete unless $\mathsf{NP} = \text{co-}\mathsf{NP}$ [Megiddo and Papadimitriou, 1991], and it is unlikely that this last equivalence holds. Furthermore, it is generally believed that $\mathsf{PPAD} \neq \mathsf{FP}$ and thus it is unlikely that there is an algorithm finding an NE that requires polynomial time in the size of the game. When, instead, one searches for an optimal NE, e.g., maximizing social welfare or the payoff of a single player, the problem becomes NP-hard [Gilboa and Zemel, 1989, Conitzer and Sandholm, 2008].

Frequently, the same equilibrium-finding problem must be repeated whenever the value of some parameter changes. Practical examples of such a scenario are, e.g., the problems of bargaining among economic agents [Gatti et al., 2008] and games for security [Tambe, 2011]. In these settings, the structure of the game may gradually change during time as, for example, costs in bargaining games could change or, in a security game, the available resources or the values of the targets may vary at different times of the interaction. Another interesting related scenario is when learning tools are paired with optimization algorithms (e.g., in an online fashion, see [Nguyen et al., 2013]) to continuously refine the estimations of some parameters, in the attempt to minimize the regret due to the initial lack of information. In all these scenarios, a central question is whether the knowledge of an optimal solution (e.g., the Nash equilibrium with a certain property) can make the equilibrium-finding problem of the modified game easier. This problem is commonly known as *reoptimization* problem (see [Ausiello et al., 2012, Chapter 4]). Most NP-hard problems maintain the same complexity in reoptimization but, for many of them, reoptimization allows one to find better approximations, changing in some cases the approximation computational complexity class or just improving the approximation ratio in others. This happens, for instance, in scheduling problems [Schäffter, 1997] and in the Travelling Salesman Problem [Archetti et al., 2003]. To the best of our knowledge, the problem of reoptimizing equilibria in games is unexplored in the literature so far. In this paper, we provide the first study on the reoptimization complexity of game-theoretical solutions and, more precisely, of Nash equilibria.

Original contributions. The original contributions provided in this paper are as follows. For the sake of presentation, at first, we focus on the exact reoptimization problem and, subsequently, on the approximation problem, whose treatment is more involved. Specifically, we show that the NE reoptimization problem is NP-hard when searching for NEs maximizing/minimizing the social welfare, a player's utility or the support size, and the local modification is either the modification of the value of some payoffs of the game or the addition/removal of actions. Then, we prove that the aforementioned problems are also hard to approximate, unless P = NP. This happens even when the modification is as small as possible (i.e., a payoff modification arbitrarily close to zero or the addition/removal of one action). We show that, for every modification, maximizing/minimizing social welfare or a player's utility is not in Poly-APX, while maximizing/minimizing the support size is not in Log-APX[1]. In doing that, we also provide a complete picture of the approximation problems for the non-reoptimization case, while, so far, the results provided by the literature are only partial and do not analyze the specific approximation complexity classes. Finally, we study how an NE of the original game maps to those of the locally modified one, proving that, in case of payoff modifications with maximum magnitude δ, an NE of the original game is a δ-NE of the modified game. This shows that reoptimization may be useful when searching for approximate NEs.

[1]See [Ausiello et al., 2012] for the definitions of the classes.

2 PRELIMINARIES

A *normal-form* game [Shoham and Leyton-Brown, 2008] is a tuple (N, A, U) in which $N = \{1, \dots, n\}$ is the set of players, $A = A_1 \times \dots \times A_n$, where A_i is the set of actions available to player $i \in N$, and $U = \{U_1, \dots, U_n\}$, where $U_i : A \to \mathbb{R}$ is the utility function of player $i \in N$. A (*mixed*) *strategy* s_i for player $i \in N$ is a probability distribution over A_i, where we define with $s_i(a)$ the probability that $a \in A_i$ is played by player i. We denote with S_i the set of all mixed strategies of player i, i.e., the $(|A_i| - 1)$-simplex. A strategy s_i is said to be *pure* if there exists an $a \in A_i$ s.t. $s_i(a) = 1$. Letting $S = S_1 \times \dots \times S_n$, a *strategy profile* $s \in S$ is a tuple specifying a strategy for each player. Given strategy s_i, its *support* is the set of actions $\{a | s_i(a) > 0\}$. Moreover, the support of a strategy profile is made by the union of the supports of players' strategies. With a slight abuse of notation, let $U_i(s)$ be the *expected utility* of player i when s is played, i.e., $U_i(s) = \sum_{a\in A} U_i(a) \prod_{j\in N} s_j(a_j)$ (where a_j is the action of player j in a).

A *Nash equilibrium* (NE) [Nash, 1951] is a strategy profile s s.t., for each $i \in N$, for each $s'_i \in S_i$, $U_i(s_i, s_{-i}) \geq U_i(s'_i, s_{-i})$, where s_{-i} denotes the profile of players' strategies except for s_i. It is well known that the problem of finding an NE is PPAD-complete [Daskalakis et al., 2009], even for 2-player games [Chen and Deng, 2006], and therefore it is unlikely to be solvable in polynomial time. Moreover, the problem is FIXP-complete for three or more players [Etessami and Yannakakis, 2010]. Additionally, [Gilboa and Zemel, 1989] and [Conitzer and Sandholm, 2008] study the complexity of finding a NE optimizing certain properties—for instance the social welfare (i.e., the sum of players' utilities), the utility of a given player, and the size of the support at the equilibrium—showing that the problem is also inapproximable. The results that are relevant to our work are summarized in Table 1.

Table 1: Complexity Results.

	Exact solution	Approximate solution
Max/Min social welfare	NP-hard [2]	$\notin$ Poly-APX[3]
Max/Min player utility	NP-hard [2]	$\notin$ Poly-APX[3]
Max support	NP-hard	$\notin$ Log-APX[3]
Min support	NP-hard	$\notin$ Log-APX[4]

[2]Results on Min problems are novel, see Remark 2.

[3]Inapproximability results on Max problems refine those presented in [Conitzer and Sandholm, 2008], where the authors just show that the problems are not in the APX class. The refined results can be derived similarly to Theorems 5-7.

[4]The inapproximability of Min support is a novel result

The literature also explores the idea of approximate NEs. Notice that the computation of an NE can be formulated as an optimization problem as follows. The NE constraints are relaxed so that players can play also non-optimal actions with strictly positive probability, provided they guarantee a regret, w.r.t. a best response, of at most ϵ (in additive sense), and the objective function to be minimized is ϵ. Multiple notions of approximate NE have been proposed. Most of the literature [Lipton et al., 2003, Daskalakis et al., 2007, Tsaknakis and Spirakis, 2007] studies the *ϵ-approximate Nash equilibrium* (ϵ-NE), which is a strategy profile s.t. no player can gain more than ϵ by unilaterally deviating from it. Formally, $s \in S$ is an ϵ-NE if, for each $i \in N$, for each $s'_i \in S_i$, $U_i(s) \geq U_i(s'_i, s_{-i}) - \epsilon$. Some works [Kontogiannis and Spirakis, 2007, Daskalakis et al., 2006] study a stronger notion of approximate equilibrium strategies, called *ϵ-well-supported Nash equilibrium* (ϵ-ws-NE). In an ϵ-ws-NE, a player plays with strictly positive probability only actions guaranteeing her an expected utility within ϵ from the best reachable value, given the strategies of the others. Formally, $s \in S$ is an ϵ-ws-NE if, for each $i \in N$, for each $a \in A_i$, if $s_i(a) > 0$ then, for every $a'_i \in A_i$, it holds $U_i(a, s_{-i}) \geq U_i(a'_i, s_{-i}) - \epsilon$. We remark that, while an ϵ-ws-NE is always an ϵ-NE, the contrary is not generally true. However, given an ϵ-NE, one can construct in polynomial time an ϵ'-ws-NE, where ϵ' polynomially scales with ϵ [Chen et al., 2006].

In the derivation of our original complexity results, we employ two game gadgets introduced in [Conitzer and Sandholm, 2008] and [Gilboa and Zemel, 1989], respectively. They are built starting from instances of SAT and SET-COVER, which are well-known NP-complete problems [Garey and Johnson, 1979]. For clarity, we provide their brief definition.

Definition 1 (SAT) *SAT is defined as follows:*

- ***INSTANCE:*** *A set V of m variables and a collection C of c clauses.*
- ***QUESTION:*** *Is there a satisfying truth assignment for C?*

Definition 2 (SET-COVER) *SET-COVER is defined as follows:*

- ***INSTANCE:*** *A collection R of subsets of a set T, with $|R| = r$ and $|T| = t$, and a positive integer k.*
- ***QUESTION:*** *Does R contain a cover for T of size k i.e., a subset $R' \subseteq R$ with $|R'| = k$ and s.t. $\bigcup_{\rho \in R'} \rho = T$?*

Now, we highlight the structure of the two aforementioned gadgets.

Definition 3 (SAT-gadget) *Given a SAT instance with m variables and c clauses, and a real number $\epsilon > 0$, a* SAT-gadget *is a normal-form game $\Gamma_\epsilon^{SAT} = (\{1,2\}, A^{SAT}, U^{SAT})$, with $|A_1^{SAT}| = |A_2^{SAT}| = 3m+c+1$, s.t.:*

- *there exists an NE where each player's expected utility is $m-1$ iff the SAT instance is satisfiable;*
- *the only other NE provides both players an expected utility of ϵ.*

Remark 1 *In a SAT-gadget, the support size of players' strategies at an equilibrium is, respectively, m for the NE providing $m-1$ utility, 1 for the other one.*

Definition 4 (SET-COVER-gadget) *Given a SET-COVER instance with t items and r subsets of items, a SET-COVER-gadget is a normal-form game $\Gamma^{SC} = (\{1,2\}, A^{SC}, U^{SC})$, with $|A_1^{SC}| = t+1$ and $|A_2^{SC}| = r+1$, s.t. there exists an NE with support for each player no more than k iff the SET-COVER instance has a cover of size k.*

3 REOPTIMIZATION RESULTS

We focus on the following question: does the knowledge of an optimal NE, w.r.t. a certain property, help one in finding a new optimal solution for a slightly modified game? This question is crucial every time the game is repeated in time and, at every repetition, a slight modification to the game may be introduced. Knowing the solution of the original (pre-modified) game could, in principle, avoid one to solve the game from scratch making the optimization problem easier. Roughly speaking, the answer to the above question is no, unless P = NP. To prove such a result, let us formally define the reoptimization framework in the context of NE optimization.

Definition 5 *Given a property π and a local modification μ, the reoptimization problem* RE-NE(π, μ) *is defined as follows:*

- ***INPUT:*** *$(\Gamma, \Gamma', \hat{s})$, where Γ is a normal-form game, Γ' is the modified game obtained by applying μ to Γ, and $\hat{s}$ is the optimal NE w.r.t. π over Γ.*
- ***OUTPUT:*** *the optimal NE $\hat{s}'$ w.r.t. π over Γ'.*

which has never been studied before. We prove this result in Lemma 10.

In this work we focus on the following properties π characterizing a NE:

- maximum (minimum) social-welfare (MAX-SW, MIN-SW);
- maximum (minimum) utility for a given player (MAX-REV, MIN-REV);
- maximum (minimum) support size at the equilibrium (MAX-SUPP, MIN-SUPP).

We denote with Π the set of all properties. Furthermore, we focus on the following local modifications μ to the original game:[5]

- payoff modification of a single outcome (PAYOFF);
- addition and removal of an action (ADD, REM).

For the sake of presentation, let NE(π) be the problem of finding an optimal NE w.r.t. property π in a given normal-form game.

In Sections 4 and 5, we study the intractability of the problems of finding, respectively, an exact and an approximate solution to RE-NE(π, μ), for each pair π, μ. Table 2 summarizes our results.

Table 2: Reoptimization Intractability Results.

	PAYOFF	ADD	REM
MAX/MIN-SW	NP-hard	NP-hard	NP-hard
	$\notin$ Poly-APX	$\notin$ Poly-APX	$\notin$ Poly-APX
MAX/MIN-REV	NP-hard	NP-hard	NP-hard
	$\notin$ Poly-APX	$\notin$ Poly-APX	$\notin$ Poly-APX
MAX/MIN-SUPP	NP-hard	NP-hard	NP-hard
	$\notin$ Log-APX	$\notin$ Log-APX	$\notin$ Log-APX

4 NP-HARDNESS RESULTS

In this section, we give the formal proofs of the hardness of RE-NE(π, μ) for each π and μ. Initially, we focus on the case in which $\mu \in \{\text{PAYOFF}, \text{ADD}\}$.

Theorem 1 *RE-NE(π, μ) is NP-hard for each $\pi \in \Pi$ and for each $\mu \in \{$PAYOFF, ADD$\}$, even for 2-player games.*

Proof 1 *We start by considering the case μ = PAYOFF. We show that the existence of a polynomial-time algorithm $\mathcal{A}$ solving RE-NE(π, μ) would allow one to solve NE(π) in polynomial time, therefore leading to a contradiction. Given a generic normal-form game $\Gamma^k = (\{1,2\}, A^k, U^k)$, where k denotes the number of outcomes of the game, we define $\Gamma^0 = (\{1,2\}, A^0, U^0)$ s.t. $A_i^0 = A_i^k$, for each $i \in \{1,2\}$, and $U_1^0(a) = U_2^0(a) = 0$ for each $a \in A^0$. Clearly, every strategy profile in Γ^0 is an NE. Therefore, we select an appropriate $\hat{s}_0$, according to π, as the initial optimal solution. Specifically, if π = MAX-SUPP, we set $\hat{s}_0$ to any strategy profile with full support for both players, otherwise, if $\pi = \Pi \setminus \{$MAX-SUPP$\}$, we set $\hat{s}_0$ to any pure strategy profile. Then, we can define a sequence of PAYOFF transformations that allows one to obtain Γ^k starting from game Γ^0. Specifically, a transformation that leads from Γ^t to Γ^{t+1}, with $t = 0, \ldots, k-1$, is s.t., for a given $a' \in A^t$ for which $U_1^t(a') \neq U_1^k(a')$ or $U_2^t(a') \neq U_2^k(a')$, it sets $U_i^{t+1}(a') = U_i^k(a')$ for each $i \in \{1,2\}$ and keeps the other payoffs unchanged. Notice that the sequence of games $\Gamma^0, \Gamma^1, \ldots, \Gamma^k$ requires a number of transformations to reach Γ^k that is polynomial in the size of the game[6]. Therefore, starting from $(\Gamma^0, \Gamma^1, \hat{s}_0)$, we can apply $\mathcal{A}$ to any $(\Gamma^t, \Gamma^{t+1}, \hat{s}_i)$ to produce, in polynomial time, $\hat{s}_{t+1}$, up to $\hat{s}_k$. Thus, $\hat{s}_k$ being the optimal NE according to π in Γ^k, we reach the contradiction.*

Let us now consider μ = ADD. A reasoning similar to the one used above applies. In particular, given a generic normal-form game $\Gamma^k = (\{1,2\}, A^k, U^k)$, let Γ^0 be $(\{1,2\}, \{x\} \times \{y\}, U^0)$ s.t. $x \in A_1^k$, $y \in A_2^k$ and $U_i^0(x,y) = U_i^k(x,y)$, for each $i \in \{1,2\}$. The sequence of ADD transformations that allows one to obtain Γ^k from Γ^0 requires a number of steps polynomial in the size of Γ^k, where each step of the sequence adds an action to one of the players. Therefore, by assuming the existence of $\mathcal{A}$, we reach the same contradiction. □

In the following, we focus on the case μ = REM, which is more involved since the reasoning underlying the proof of Theorem 1 cannot be applied.

Theorem 2 *RE-NE(π, μ) is NP-hard for $\pi \in \{$MAX-SW, MIN-SW, MAX-REV, MIN-REV$\}$ and μ = REM, even for 2-player games.*

Proof 2 *In order to prove the result, we show the hardness of the decision version of our problem, which asks for an NE of the modified game having value of π greater than or equal to a given constant. Let us first focus on the case $\pi \in \{$MAX-SW, MAX-REV$\}$, and consider a SAT-gadget Γ_ϵ^{SAT} with $0 < \epsilon < m - 1$, where m is the number of variables of the SAT instance embedded in Γ_ϵ^{SAT}, as in Definition 3 (in the following proofs we omit*

[5] We do not take into consideration the introduction/removal of a player since it cannot be considered a local modification of the game.

[6] k is upper bounded by the number of outcomes of the game, which is its dimension.

the definition of m, giving it the same meaning). Let us define a game $\Gamma = (\{1,2\}, A, U)$ s.t. $A_1 = A_1^{SAT} \cup \{x\}$, $A_2 = A_2^{SAT} \cup \{y\}$ and U is equal to:

- $U_i(a) = U_i^{SAT}(a)$, $\forall i \in \{1,2\}, \forall a \in A^{SAT}$;
- $U_1(x, a_2) = U_2(x, a_2) = -M$, $\forall a_2 \in A_2^{SAT}$;
- $U_1(a_1, y) = U_2(a_1, y) = -M$, $\forall a_1 \in A_1^{SAT}$;
- $U_1(x, y) = U_2(x, y) = m$;

where M is a sufficiently large constant (i.e., any $M \geq 4$), making $-M$ the lowest payoff in the game. Therefore, Γ preserves the NEs of Γ_ϵ^{SAT}, i.e., given an equilibrium s for Γ_ϵ^{SAT}, playing the actions of Γ corresponding to the support of s according to the same probability distribution leads to an equilibrium. Γ has also the new equilibrium (x, y), which is the optimal equilibrium w.r.t π. If we apply REM to Γ removing action x (or, equivalently, y), we obtain a new game Γ' s.t. its NEs are only those of Γ_ϵ^{SAT}. Therefore, Γ' has an equilibrium with value for the property π greater than or equal to $m - 1$ iff the SAT instance embedded in Γ_ϵ^{SAT} is satisfiable.

Similarly, when $\pi = \{$MIN-SW, MIN-REV$\}$, we follow the same reasoning, by setting $\epsilon > m-1$ and $U_1(x, y) = U_2(x, y) = m - 2$. □

The proof of the previous theorem suggests the following result about optimal NEs without reoptimization.

Remark 2 *Using a reduction similar to that due to [Conitzer and Sandholm, 2008], setting $\epsilon > m - 1$, it follows that NE(π), for $\pi \in \{$MIN-SW, MIN-REV$\}$, is NP-hard, even for 2-player games.*

Theorem 3 *RE-NE(MAX-SUPP, REM) is NP-hard, even for 2-player games.*

Proof 3 *Let us focus on the maximization of the overall support size at the equilibrium. The proof for the problem of maximizing the support of a single player follows the same reasoning.*

Consider the decision version of RE-NE(MAX-SUPP, REM), i.e., the problem of deciding whether Γ' has an NE with support size greater than or equal to a given constant. Let Γ_ϵ^{SAT} be a SAT-gadget, with $\epsilon > 0$. Γ is a normal-form game $(\{1,2\}, A, U)$ s.t. $A_1 = A_1^{SAT} \cup \{x_i | 1 \leq i \leq m\}$, $A_2 = A_2^{SAT} \cup \{y_j | 1 \leq j \leq m\}$ and U is defined as:

- $U_i(a) = U_i(a)^{SAT}$, $\forall i \in \{1,2\}$, $\forall a \in A^{SAT}$;
- $U_1(x_i, a_2) = U_2(x_i, a_2) = -M$, $\forall x_i \in A_1 \backslash A_1^{SAT}$, $\forall a_2 \in A_2^{SAT}$;
- $U_1(a_1, y_j) = U_2(a_1, y_j) = -M$, $\forall y_i \in A_2 \backslash A_2^{SAT}$, $\forall a_1 \in A_1^{SAT}$;
- $U_1(x_i, y_j) = U_2(x_i, y_j) = 1$, $\forall x_i \in A_1 \backslash A_1^{SAT}$, $\forall y_j \in A_2 \backslash A_2^{SAT}$;

where $-M$ is s.t. it is the lowest payoff in the game (i.e., any $M \geq 4$). Γ preserves the NEs of Γ_ϵ^{SAT} and also has a new set of equilibria given by all the possible probability distributions over actions in $A_1 \backslash A_1^{SAT}$ and $A_2 \backslash A_2^{SAT}$. Therefore, if the two players randomize uniformly over all x_i and y_j, $\hat{s}$ has support of size $2m$. Suppose to apply a REM transformation to a row in $A_1 \backslash A_1^{SAT}$ (or, equivalently, to a column in $A_2 \backslash A_2^{SAT}$). The resulting Γ' has an NE with support greater than or equal to $2m$ iff the SAT instance contained in Γ_ϵ^{SAT} is satisfiable. □

Theorem 4 *RE-NE(MIN-SUPP, REM) is NP-hard, even for 2-player games.*

Proof 4 *We consider the problem of minimizing the overall support size at the equilibrium. The proof for the problem of minimizing the support size of a single player follows the same reasoning. We show that the reoptimization problem is hard by proving the hardness of its decisional counterpart.*

Given a SET-COVER-gadget Γ^{SC}, we build $\Gamma = (\{1,2\}, A, U)$ s.t. $A_1 = A_1^{SC} \cup \{x\}$, $A_2 = A_2^{SC} \cup \{y\}$ and U is defined as:

- $U_i(a) = U_i^{SC}(a)$, $\forall i \in \{1,2\}$, $\forall a \in A^{SC}$;
- $U_i(x, a_2) = -M$, $\forall i \in \{1,2\}$, $\forall a_2 \in A_2^{SC}$;
- $U_i(a_1, y) = -M$, $\forall i \in \{1,2\}$, $\forall a_1 \in A_1^{SC}$;
- $U_i(x, y) = 1$, $\forall i \in \{1,2\}$;

where $M > 1$ (so that $-M$ is the lowest payoff in the game) and therefore, the set of NEs of Γ is equal to that of Γ^{SC} with the only addition of (x, y), which is the equilibrium minimizing support size. Γ' is obtained by applying REM to row x (or column y). Γ' has an NE with support size less than or equal to k iff the SET-COVER instance in Γ^{SC} has a cover of size k. □

5 INAPPROXIMABILITY RESULTS

We show the inapproximability of RE-NE(π, μ), for every pair of π and μ. We initially focus on searching for an NE maximizing either the social welfare or the utility of a player.

Theorem 5 *RE-NE(π,μ) is not in Poly-APX for each $\pi \in$ {MAX-SW, MAX-REV} and $\mu \in$ {PAYOFF, REM, ADD}, unless P = NP.*

Proof 5 *We provide the proof for π = MAX-SW. The proof for π = MAX-REV follows the same reasoning. Let Γ_ϵ^{SAT} be a SAT-gadget, with $0 < \epsilon < \frac{m-1}{f(m)}$, where $f(m) = 2^m$ (the polynomiality of the reduction is preserved as $f(m)$ can be codified with m bits). Assume, by contradiction, that there exists a polynomial-time algorithm $\mathcal{A}$ providing an approximate solution to RE-NE(MAX-SW,μ), with approximation factor $r = \frac{1}{f(m)}$. Let $\Gamma = (\{1,2\}, A, U)$, where $A_1 = A_1^{SAT} \cup \{x\}$, $A_2 = A_2^{SAT} \cup \{y\}$, and U is so defined:*

- $U_i(a) = U_i^{SAT}(a), \forall i \in \{1,2\}, \forall a \in A^{SAT}$;
- $U_i(x, a_2) = -M, \forall i \in \{1,2\}, \forall a_2 \in A_2^{SAT}$;
- $U_1(a_1, y) = K$, $U_2(a_1, y) = -M, \forall a_1 \in A_1^{SAT}$;
- $U_1(x, y) = K$ *and* $U_2(x, y) = 0$;

where $M \geq 4$ and $K > 2(m-1)$. Let $\hat{s}$ be the NE with maximum social welfare, i.e., the pure strategy profile where $\hat{s}_1(x) = 1$ and $\hat{s}_2(y) = 1$. We define Γ' on the basis of the applied μ as follows:

- *μ = PAYOFF. We build Γ' by applying a PAYOFF transformation to outcome (x, y), setting $U_1(x, y) = K - \delta$, where $\delta > 0$ is an arbitrarily small positive constant.*
- *μ = REM. We build Γ' by applying a REM transformation either to row x or column y.*
- *μ = ADD. We obtain Γ' by adding to Γ a new column y' s.t.:*
  - $U_1(a_1, y') = K, \forall a_1 \in A_1^{SAT}$;
  - $U_2(a_1, y') = -M, \forall a_1 \in A_1^{SAT}$;
  - $U_1(x, y') = 0$ *and* $U_2(x, y') = 1$.

Notice that, in each Γ', the additional equilibrium of Γ w.r.t Γ_ϵ^{SAT} disappears, and no other equilibria are introduced. Therefore, in each of these cases, by employing $\mathcal{A}$, we would be able to obtain an approximate solution of value at least $\frac{2m-2}{f(m)} > 2\epsilon$ iff the SAT instance of Γ_ϵ^{SAT} is satisfiable. Otherwise, if it is unsatisfiable, the value of the approximate solution is less than or equal to 2ϵ. Thus, the existence of $\mathcal{A}$ would allow us to solve SAT in polynomial time. □

The case in which we search for an NE minimizing either the social welfare or the utility of a player is similar to the case studied above.

Theorem 6 *RE-NE(π,μ) is not in Poly-APX for each $\pi \in$ {MIN-SW, MIN-REV} and $\mu \in$ {ADD, REM, PAYOFF}, unless P = NP.*

Proof 6 *The proof follows from that of Theorem 5. The same reasoning applies if we choose $\epsilon > m - 1$ and $K < 2(m-1)$.* □

The next three results focus on the case in which we search for an NE with maximum support.

Theorem 7 *RE-NE(MAX-SUPP, ADD) is not in Log-APX, unless P = NP.*

Proof 7 *Consider a SAT-gadget Γ_ϵ^{SAT} (for any $\epsilon > 0$). Let us define a game $\Gamma = (\{1,2\}, A, U)$ s.t. $A_1 = A_1^{SAT} \cup \{x_i | 1 \leq i \leq m\}$, $A_2 = A_2^{SAT} \cup \{y_j | 1 \leq j \leq m\}$, and U is defined as:*

- $U_i(a) = U_i^{SAT}(a), \forall i \in \{1,2\}, \forall a \in A^{SAT}$;
- $U_1(x_i, a_2) = U_2(x_i, a_2) = -M, \forall x_i \in A_1 \backslash A_1^{SAT}, \forall a_2 \in A_2^{SAT}$;
- $U_1(a_1, y_j) = U_2(a_1, y_j) = -M, \forall y_j \in A_2 \backslash A_2^{SAT}, \forall a_1 \in A_1^{SAT}$;
- $U_1(x_i, y_j) = U_2(x_i, y_j) = 1, \forall x_i \in A_1 \backslash A_1^{SAT}, \forall y_j \in A_2 \backslash A_2^{SAT}$ *with* $i \neq j$;
- $U_1(x_i, y_j) = U_2(x_i, y_j) = -1, \forall x_i \in A_1 \backslash A_1^{SAT}, \forall y_j \in A_2 \backslash A_2^{SAT}$ *with* $i = j$;

where $M \geq 4$. Clearly, all the NEs of Γ_ϵ^{SAT} are preserved in Γ, and every additional NE of Γ does not have actions of A_1^{SAT} and A_2^{SAT} in its support. Moreover, Γ has always an equilibrium $\hat{s} = (\hat{s}_1, \hat{s}_2)$ s.t. $\hat{s}_1(x_i) = \frac{1}{m}$ for every $1 \leq i \leq m$ and $\hat{s}_2(y_j) = \frac{1}{m}$ for every $1 \leq j \leq m$, having support size $2m$. Also note that Γ has no NE with support size greater than $2m$. Suppose to apply an ADD transformation to Γ, leading to a new game, say Γ', by introducing an action x for player 1 s.t. $U_1(x, a_2) = U_2(x, a_2) = -M$ for any $a_2 \in A_2^{SAT}$, $U_1(x, y_j) = 2$ and $U_2(x, y_j) = 1$ for any $1 \leq j \leq m-1$, and $U_1(x, y_m) = U_2(x, y_m) = 2$. Notice that $\hat{s}$ is not an NE of Γ' since player 1 has an incentive to deviate from $\hat{s}_1$, playing x, which provides her a utility of 2, instead of $\frac{m-2}{m}$. In addition, simple arguments allow us to prove that the set of NEs of Γ' is equal to the one of Γ_ϵ^{SAT} with the addition of (x, y_m) (whose support size is 2).

By contradiction, assume there exists a polynomial-time approximation algorithm $\mathcal{A}$ for RE-NE(MAX-SUPP, ADD), which guarantees an approximation factor $r = \frac{1}{g(m)}$, where $g(\cdot)$ is a logarithmic function of the input. Clearly, if the SAT instance embedded in Γ_ϵ^{SAT} is satisfiable, then $\mathcal{A}$, when applied to $(\Gamma, \Gamma', \hat{s})$, produces an *equilibrium $\hat{s}'$ with support size at least $\frac{2m}{g(m)} > 2$. Otherwise, the support size of $\hat{s}'$ is less than or equal to 2. Thus, the existence of such an algorithm would allow us to solve SAT in polynomial time.* □

Theorem 8 *RE-NE(MAX-SUPP, PAYOFF) is not in Log-APX, unless P = NP.*

Proof 8 *Let Γ be defined as in the proof of Theorem 7, where, in this case, U is changed so that:*

- $U_1(x_1, y_j) = 0$ *and* $U_2(x_1, y_j) = (m-1)\delta$, $\forall y_j \in A_2 \backslash A_2^{SAT}, 1 \leq j \leq m-1$;
- $U_1(x_1, y_m) = 1$ *and* $U_2(x_1, y_m) = 0$;
- $U_1(x_2, y_1) = U_2(x_2, y_1) = 0$;
- $U_1(x_i, y_1) = 1$ *and* $U_2(x_i, y_1) = 0$, $\forall x_i \in A_1 \backslash A_1^{SAT}, 3 \leq i \leq m$;
- $U_1(x_i, y_j) = U_2(x_i, y_j) = 0$, $\forall x_i \in A_1 \backslash A_1^{SAT}, 2 \leq i \leq m$, $\forall y_j \in A_2 \backslash A_2^{SAT}, 2 \leq j \leq m-1$;
- $U_1(x_2, y_m) = 1$ *and* $U_2(x_2, y_m) = \delta$;
- $U_1(x_i, y_m) = 0$ *and* $U_2(x_i, y_m) = \delta$, $\forall x_i \in A_1 \backslash A_1^{SAT}, 3 \leq i \leq m$;

where δ is an arbitrarily small positive constant. As before, Γ has all the NEs of Γ_ϵ^{SAT}, with the addition of $\hat{s}$, which has support size $2m$ (the maximum possible). Now, let us apply a PAYOFF transformation to Γ, leading to Γ', by changing the utilities in (x_1, y_m), so that $U_1(x_1, y_m) = 1 - \delta$ and $U_2(x_1, y_m) = 3\delta$. Simple considerations allow us to conclude that the NEs of Γ' are those of Γ_ϵ^{SAT}, with the addition of (x_2, y_m). The result easily follows, by contradiction, as in Theorem 7. □

Theorem 9 *RE-NE(MAX-SUPP, REM) is not in Log-APX, unless P = NP.*

Proof 9 *Let Γ be defined as in the proof of Theorem 7 with the only difference being the definition of U, which is defined in the same way but for the subgame $\{x_1, \ldots, x_m\} \times \{y_1, \ldots, y_m\}$. Specifically:*

- $U_1(x_1, y_1) = U_1(x_1, y_2) = -1$;
- $U_1(x_1, y_j) = 1$, $\forall y_j \in A_2 \setminus A_2^{SAT}, 3 \leq j \leq m$;
- $U_1(x_i, y_m) = -1$, $\forall x_i \in A_1 \setminus A_1^{SAT}, 2 \leq i \leq m-1$;
- $U_1(x_i, y_j) = \mathbb{1}_{i \neq j} - \mathbb{1}_{i=j}$, $\forall x_i \in A_1 \setminus A_1^{SAT}, 2 \leq i \leq m$, $\forall y_j \in A_2 \setminus A_2^{SAT}, 1 \leq j \leq m-1$;
- $U_1(x_m, y_m) = -3$.
- $U_2(x_i, y_j) = -1$, $\forall x_i \in A_1 \backslash A_1^{SAT}, 1 \leq i \leq m-1$, $\forall y_j \in A_2 \setminus A_2^{SAT}, 1 \leq j \leq m-1$;
- $U_2(x_m, y_j) = 1$, $\forall y_j \in A_2 \backslash A_2^{SAT}, 1 \leq j \leq m-1$;
- $U_2(x_i, y_m) = 1$, $\forall x_i \in A_1 \backslash A_1^{SAT}, 1 \leq i \leq m-1$;
- $U_2(x_m, y_m) = -2m + 3$.

Notice that Γ has always an optimal NE, say $\hat{s}$, with support size $2m$, s.t. $\hat{s}_1(x_i) = \frac{1}{m}$ for every $1 \leq i \leq m$ and $\hat{s}_2(y_j) = \frac{1}{m}$ for every $1 \leq j \leq m$. We build Γ' by applying a REM transformation to row x_m. Γ' has only an additional equilibrium w.r.t. Γ_ϵ^{SAT} (this can be shown by deleting strictly dominated rows/columns). The resulting additional equilibrium is (x_1, y_m) and, being in pure strategies, has support of size 2. Therefore, we can prove the theorem by contradiction, with the same reasoning as in the proof of Theorem 7. □

Now, we focus on the problem of searching for an NE with minimum support. Before stating our main results, let us introduce the following lemma, whose proof is useful in the sequel.

Lemma 10 *NE(MIN-SUPP) is not in Log-APX, unless P = NP.*

Proof 10 *NE(MIN-SUPP) was shown to be NP-hard in [Gilboa and Zemel, 1989]. We adapt the reduction to prove also the hardness of finding an approximate solution to the problem. The reduction is based on a SET-COVER gadget Γ^{SC} (for details see [Gilboa and Zemel, 1989]), where, for our purpose, k is set equal to r (see Definition 4). By construction, each of its NEs corresponds to a valid cover for the SET-COVER instance embedded in the gadget. Moreover, the support size of an NE is precisely the size of the cover plus one, since player 1's actions correspond to the subsets composing the cover, whereas player 2 always plays her last action. Denoting with OPT_{NE} the optimal solution value of NE(MIN-SUPP), we have that $OPT_{SC} = OPT_{NE} - 1$, where OPT_{SC} is the size of an optimal cover. By contradiction, assume $\mathcal{A}$ is a polynomial-time approximation algorithm for NE(MIN-SUPP), providing an approximation ratio $r = \frac{1}{g(t)}$, where $g(\cdot)$ is a logarithmic function of the input. Let APX_{NE} be the value (in terms of support size) of the approximate solution which is returned by $\mathcal{A}$ on Γ^{SC}. Clearly, such solution is an NE, and it corresponds to a valid cover for the SET-COVER instance, with size $APX_{SC} = APX_{NE} - 1$ and, thus, we have $\frac{OPT_{SC}}{APX_{SC}} = \frac{OPT_{NE}-1}{APX_{NE}-1}$. Given that $\frac{OPT_{NE}}{APX_{NE}} \geq r$, we have $OPT_{NE} \geq rAPX_{NE}$. Thus, it* *follows* $\frac{OPT_{NE-1}}{APX_{NE-1}} \geq \frac{rAPX_{NE-1}}{APX_{NE-1}} \geq 2r$ *and therefore we have* $\frac{OPT_{SC}}{APX_{SC}} \geq \frac{2}{g(t)}$. *The last inequality leads to a contradiction, since SET-COVER cannot be approximated within a factor* $\frac{c}{g(t)}$, *where c is a constant greater than one [Dinur and Steurer, 2014].* □

Now, we can state the main results.

Theorem 11 *RE-NE(MIN-SUPP,* μ*) is not in Log-APX for each* $\mu \in$ {*PAYOFF, ADD, REM*}, *unless P = NP.*

Proof 11 *Let us first prove the case* μ=*PAYOFF. Given a SET-COVER gadget* Γ^{SC}, *where we set* $k = r$ *(see Definition 4), let us define* $\Gamma = (\{1,2\}, A, U)$ *s.t.* $A_1 = A_1^{SC} \cup \{x\}$, $A_2 = A_2^{SC} \cup \{y\}$, *and U is so defined:*

- $U_i(a) = U_i^{SC}(a)$, $\forall i \in \{1,2\}, \forall a \in A^{SC}$;
- $U_1(x, a_2) = U_2(x, a_2) = -M$, $\forall a_2 \in A_2^{SC}$;
- $U_1(a_1, y) = 1$, $U_2(a_1, y) = -M$, $\forall a_1 \in A_1^{SAT}$;
- $U_1(x, y) = U_2(x, y) = 2$;

where $M > 1$ *and therefore,* $-M$ *is lower than any other payoff in the game. Observe that the NEs of* Γ *are the same as those of* Γ^{SC}, *with the only addition of* (x, y) *(having support size 2). Suppose* Γ' *is built by applying a PAYOFF transformation to* Γ, *by changing U so that* $U_1(x, y) = 1 - \delta$. *Clearly, the set of NEs of* Γ' *coincides with the one of* Γ^{SC}. *Suppose, by contradiction, there exists a polynomial-time approximation algorithm solving RE-NE(MIN-SUPP, PAYOFF), providing an approximation factor* $r = \frac{1}{g(t)}$, *where* $g(\cdot)$ *is a logarithmic function of the input. Following a reasoning similar to that adopted in the proof of Lemma 10, we can show that the existence of such an algorithm would allow us to obtain an* $\frac{1}{g(t)}$*-approximate solution for a generic SET-COVER instance, which is a contradiction.*

The proofs for the other cases follow a similar structure: Γ *is defined as before, while* Γ' *is obtained by applying a specific transformation to* Γ, *which makes the set of NEs of* Γ' *equal to the one of* Γ^{SC}. *In particular, for* μ = ADD, *the result is achieved by applying an ADD transformation which introduces a new action* x' *into* A_1, *s.t.* $U_1(x', a_2) = U_2(x', a_2) = -M$, *for any* $a_2 \in A_2^{SC}$, $U_1(x', y) = 3$, *and* $U_2(x', y) = -M - 1$. *Instead, for* μ = REM, *the considered REM operation simply removes action x from* A_1. □

Given the negative results presented in this section, a natural question is whether the knowledge of an optimal NE in the original game may help in approximating the optimum in the locally modified one when we upper bound the magnitude of the modification. Given that ADD and REM are already elementary operations, since they consider the addition (respectively, the removal) of a single action, we concentrate on PAYOFF modifications where payoffs are either increased or decreased at most of $\delta > 0$, which we call δ-PAYOFF.

The following example shows how the value of an optimal NE of the modified game (in terms of MAX-SW) can be arbitrarily worse than that for the original game, even for δ arbitrarily close to zero.

	a_2^1	a_2^2
a_1^1	$1, 1$	$1, 0$
a_1^2	$0, 0$	$1, M$

Γ

	a_2^1	a_2^2
a_1^1	$1, 1$	$1, 0$
a_1^2	$0, 0$	$1-\delta, M$

Γ'

Figure 1: Arbitrarily small PAYOFF modifications may disrupt social welfare.

Example 1 *Consider the game* Γ *in Figure 1, where M is an arbitrarily large value. In this game, the optimal NE for MAX-SW is the bottom right outcome, which has social welfare* $M + 1$. *Suppose to apply a* δ*-PAYOFF transformation to such outcome, where* $\delta > 0$ *is a constant arbitrarily close to zero, reducing player 1's utility from 1 to* $1 - \delta$ *(see* Γ' *in Figure 1). Clearly,* (a_1^2, a_2^2) *is no more an NE, and the new optimal NE becomes the top left outcome, which has social welfare 2. Therefore, the ratio between the two optimal values is* $\frac{M+1}{2}$, *which goes to infinity as M grows.*

We can construct similar examples showing that the same holds for maximization/minimization of the revenue and of the support size. Indeed, simple modifications of the previous proofs (for μ = PAYOFF) show that the same inapproximability results hold even for μ = δ-PAYOFF with $\delta > 0$ arbitrarily close to zero, as stated in the following remarks.

Remark 3 *For any* $\delta > 0$, *RE-NE(*π*,* δ*-PAYOFF) is not in Poly-APX for each* $\pi \in$ {*MAX-SW, MIN-SW, MAX-REV, MIN-REV*}, *unless P = NP.*

Remark 4 *For any* $\delta > 0$, *RE-NE(*π*,* δ*-PAYOFF) is not in Log-APX for each* $\pi \in$ {*MAX-SUPP, MIN-SUPP*}, *unless P = NP.*

The above remarks directly follow, respectively, from the

construction adopted in the proof of Theorems 5-6 and Theorems 8-11.

6 APPROXIMATE NASH EQUILIBRIA

We observed that even arbitrarily small modifications in the payoffs may generate considerable changes in the equilibria of the game. In particular, it may happen that, given a generic NE s for Γ, a PAYOFF transformation results in s no longer being an equilibrium point (disregarding any concept of optimality). Notice that this may happen even for arbitrarily small payoff modification, as shown in Example 1. Furthermore, the computational complexity of the reoptimization version of the problem of finding an NE (without requiring optimality w.r.t. a certain property) is the same as that of its non-reoptimization counterpart (i.e., finding an ϵ-approximate equilibrium minimizing ϵ). This can be shown with arguments similar to those of Section 4.

A question with useful practical implications, is whether knowing that s is a Nash equilibrium for Γ becomes a completely useless piece of information after a small δ-PAYOFF perturbation is applied to the original game. The answer is that, if we consider approximate Nash equilibria, strategy profile s preserves interesting properties and should be kept into account when considering whether computing a new solution for Γ' is worth it or not. Specifically, if we focus on normalized $[0, 1]$-games[7] (a common assumption in the literature on approximate NEs), we can state the following theorem, which is a refinement of [Chen et al., 2006].[8]

Theorem 12 *Consider a generic normal-form game* $\Gamma = (\{1,2\}, A, U)$ *and a new game* $\Gamma' = (\{1,2\}, A, U')$*, obtained by applying a PAYOFF modification of magnitude* (δ_1, δ_2)*,* $\delta_i \in [-1, 1]$ *for each* $i \in \{1,2\}$*, to an outcome* $(\overline{a}_1, \overline{a}_2) \in A$ *of* Γ *so that* $U_i'(\overline{a}_1, \overline{a}_2) = U_i(\overline{a}_1, \overline{a}_2) + \delta_i$ *and* $U_i'(\overline{a}_1, \overline{a}_2) \in [0, 1]$*, for each* $i \in \{1, 2\}$*. Let* s^* *be an NE of* Γ*. Then,* s^* *is a* δ*-well supported Nash equilibrium for* Γ'*, where* $\delta = \max\{\delta_1, \delta_2\}$*.*

Proof 12 *First, we show that each action played with positive probability by the first player in* s_1^* *leads to a payoff at most* δ_1 *smaller than the payoff at her best response against* s_2^**. We denote with* $S : A \to [-1, 1]$ *a function s.t.* $S(\overline{a}_1, \overline{a}_2) = \delta_1$ *and* $S(a) = 0$ *for every* $a \in A \setminus \{(\overline{a}_1, \overline{a}_2)\}$*. Moreover, let* $\hat{a}_1 \in A_1$ *be an action s.t. strategy* $s_1(\hat{a}_1) = 1$ *is a best response to* s_2^* *in* Γ'*. For each* $a_1 \in A_1$ *s.t.* $s_1^*(a_1) > 0$ *it holds:*

$$\begin{aligned}
&\sum_{a_2 \in A_2} U_1'(\hat{a}_1, a_2) s_2^*(a_2) - \sum_{a_2 \in A_2} U_1'(a_1, a_2) s_2^*(a_2) = \\
&= \sum_{a_2 \in A_2} (U_1(\hat{a}_1, a_2) + S(\hat{a}_1, a_2)) s_2^*(a_2) + \\
&\quad - \sum_{a_2 \in A_2} (U_1(a_1, a_2) + S(a_1, a_2)) s_2^*(a_2) = \\
&= \sum_{a_2 \in A_2} U_1(\hat{a}_1, a_2) s_2^*(a_2) - \sum_{a_2 \in A_2} U_1(a_1, a_2) s_2^*(a_2) + \\
&\quad + \sum_{a_2 \in A_2} S(\hat{a}_1, a_2) s_2^*(a_2) - \sum_{a_2 \in A_2} S(a_1, a_2) s_2^*(a_2) \leq \\
&\leq \sum_{a_2 \in A_2} U_1(\hat{a}_1, a_2) s_2^*(a_2) + \\
&\quad - \sum_{a_1 \in A_1} \sum_{a_2 \in A_2} U_1(a_1, a_2) s_1^*(a_1) s_2^*(a_2) + |\delta_1| \leq |\delta_1|
\end{aligned}$$

The same reasoning holds for the second player, with a final upper bound of $|\delta_2|$*. If we set* $\delta = \max\{\delta_1, \delta_2\}$*, the previous inequalities show that* s^* *is a* δ*-well supported NE for* Γ'*.* □

Notice that, for $\delta < 0.3393$, s^* has better guarantees over Γ' than what we could obtain by applying the best polynomial-time approximation algorithm currently known [Tsaknakis and Spirakis, 2007]. Therefore, on a mildly modified game, strategy profile s^* is still a valuable prescription for both players. This is an example in which reoptimization is useful, allowing one to outperform the best approximation algorithm known so far.

7 CONCLUSIONS

In this paper, we provide, to the best of our knowledge, the first study of the reoptimization complexity of game-theoretical solutions. We focus on Nash equilibria satisfying some specific properties (i.e., maximizing/minimizing the social welfare, the utility of a player, the support size), showing that the reoptimization complexity is NP-hard for some local modifications (i.e., modification of a payoff or addition/removal of an action). Furthermore, we show that reoptimization does not help even when one is searching for approximate solutions and this holds also when the modification is as small as possible. Instead, when one searches for approximate ϵ-Nash equilibria, reoptimization can help, allowing one to find approximations better than those returned by the best known algorithms.

In the future, we are interested in empirically evaluating reoptimization techniques. Although we show in this paper that reoptimization does not help in the worst case when searching for optimal Nash equilibria, preliminary results suggest that in the average case it is very useful. Furthermore, we are interested in investigating reoptimization complexity in Security Games models.

[7]Normalized $[0, 1]$-games are games in which all the payoffs of the players are in $[0, 1]$. We recall that any game is equivalent to a normalized $[0, 1]$-game by means of an affine transformation.

[8]They obtain an ϵ-approximate NE with $\epsilon \leq 4\delta$, when perturbing each payoff with an arbitrary probability distribution over $[-\delta, \delta]$.

References

[Archetti et al., 2003] Archetti, C., Bertazzi, L., and Speranza, M. G. (2003). Reoptimizing the traveling salesman problem. *NETWORKS*, 42(3):154–159.

[Ausiello et al., 2012] Ausiello, G., Crescenzi, P., Gambosi, G., Kann, V., Marchetti-Spaccamela, A., and Protasi, M. (2012). *Complexity and approximation: Combinatorial optimization problems and their approximability properties*. Springer Science & Business Media.

[Chen and Deng, 2006] Chen, X. and Deng, X. (2006). Settling the complexity of two-player Nash equilibrium. In *ANN IEEE SYMP FOUND*, pages 261–272.

[Chen et al., 2006] Chen, X., Deng, X., and Teng, S.-H. (2006). Computing Nash equilibria: Approximation and smoothed complexity. In *FOCS*, pages 603–612.

[Conitzer and Sandholm, 2008] Conitzer, V. and Sandholm, T. (2008). New complexity results about Nash equilibria. *GAME ECON BEHAV*, 63(2):621–641.

[Daskalakis et al., 2009] Daskalakis, C., Goldberg, P. W., and Papadimitriou, C. H. (2009). The complexity of computing a Nash equilibrium. *SIAM J COMPUT*, 39(1):195–259.

[Daskalakis et al., 2006] Daskalakis, C., Mehta, A., and Papadimitriou, C. (2006). A note on approximate Nash equilibria. In *WINE*, pages 297–306. Springer.

[Daskalakis et al., 2007] Daskalakis, C., Mehta, A., and Papadimitriou, C. (2007). Progress in approximate Nash equilibria. In *EC*, pages 355–358.

[Dinur and Steurer, 2014] Dinur, I. and Steurer, D. (2014). Analytical approach to parallel repetition. In *STOC*, pages 624–633.

[Etessami and Yannakakis, 2010] Etessami, K. and Yannakakis, M. (2010). On the complexity of Nash equilibria and other fixed points. *SIAM J COMPUT*, 39(6):2531–2597.

[Fudenberg and Tirole, 1991] Fudenberg, D. and Tirole, J. (1991). *Game theory*. MIT Press.

[Garey and Johnson, 1979] Garey, M. and Johnson, D. (1979). *Computers and Intractability: A Guide to the Theory of NP-Completeness*. Freeman, San Francisco, CA.

[Gatti et al., 2008] Gatti, N., Di Giunta, F., and Marino, S. (2008). Alternating-offers bargaining with one-sided uncertain deadlines: an efficient algorithm. *ARTIF INTELL*, 172(8-9):1119–1157.

[Gilboa and Zemel, 1989] Gilboa, I. and Zemel, E. (1989). Nash and correlated equilibria: Some complexity considerations. *GAME ECON BEHAV*, 1(1):80–93.

[Kontogiannis and Spirakis, 2007] Kontogiannis, S. C. and Spirakis, P. G. (2007). Efficient algorithms for constant well supported approximate equilibria in bimatrix games. In *ICALP*, pages 595–606.

[Lipton et al., 2003] Lipton, R. J., Markakis, E., and Mehta, A. (2003). Playing large games using simple strategies. In *EC*, pages 36–41.

[Megiddo and Papadimitriou, 1991] Megiddo, N. and Papadimitriou, C. H. (1991). On total functions, existence theorems and computational complexity. *THEOR COMPUT SCI*, 81(2):317–324.

[Nash, 1951] Nash, J. (1951). Non-cooperative games. *ANN MATH*, pages 286–295.

[Nguyen et al., 2013] Nguyen, T. H., Yang, R., Azaria, A., Kraus, S., and Tambe, M. (2013). Analyzing the effectiveness of adversary modeling in security games. In *AAAI*.

[Nisan et al., 2007] Nisan, N., Roughgarden, T., Tardos, E., and Vazirani, V. V. (2007). *Algorithmic game theory*, volume 1. Cambridge University Press Cambridge.

[Schäffter, 1997] Schäffter, M. W. (1997). Scheduling with forbidden sets. *DISCRETE APPL MATH*, 72(1-2):155–166.

[Shoham and Leyton-Brown, 2008] Shoham, Y. and Leyton-Brown, K. (2008). *Multiagent systems: Algorithmic, game-theoretic, and logical foundations*. Cambridge University Press.

[Tambe, 2011] Tambe, M. (2011). *Security and game theory: algorithms, deployed systems, lessons learned*. Cambridge University Press.

[Tsaknakis and Spirakis, 2007] Tsaknakis, H. and Spirakis, P. G. (2007). An optimization approach for approximate Nash equilibria. In *WINE*, pages 42–56.

Shortest Path under Uncertainty: Exploration versus Exploitation

Zhan Wei Lim
Movel AI
zhanwei@movel.ai

David Hsu
Department of Computer Science,
National University of Singapore
dyhsu@comp.nus.edu.sg

Wee Sun Lee
Department of Computer Science,
National University of Singapore
leews@comp.nus.edu.sg

Abstract

In the Canadian Traveler Problem (CTP), a traveler seeks a shortest path to a destination through a road network, but unknown to the traveler, some roads may be blocked. This paper studies the Bayesian CTP (BCTP), in which road states are correlated with known prior probabilities and the traveler can infer the states of an unseen road from past observations of other correlated roads. As generalized shortest-path problems, CTP and BCTP have important practical applications. We show that BCTP is NP-complete and give a polynomial-time approximation algorithm, *Hedged Shortest Path under Determinization* (HSPD), which approximates an optimal solution with a polylogarithmic factor. Preliminary experiments show promising results. HSPD outperforms a widely used greedy algorithm and a state-of-the-art UCT-based search algorithm for CTP, especially when significant exploration is required.

1 INTRODUCTION

The Canadian Traveler Problem (CTP) is a generalization of the Shortest Path Problem. A traveler seeks a shortest path through a road network, modeled as a graph, from a source to a destination node. Some roads, however, are impassable. The traveler finds out the state of a road only upon reaching it. CTP has diverse applications in transportation planning, network routing, robot navigation, *etc.* [1, 2, 9, 18], but it is PSPACE-complete [19].

We introduce the Bayesian Canadian Traveler Problem (BCTP), a Bayesian variant of CTP, in which each configuration of the road network has known prior probability. A distinctive feature of BCTP is that road states may be correlated. For example, rain or snow may block all roads in a region; scheduled repair may block roads according to a known pattern. The traveler can infer the state of an unseen road from past observations of other correlated roads. BCTP is thus a more realistic model than CTP for shortest path finding under uncertainty in many applications.

To find a shortest path under uncertain road conditions, the traveler may seek to gain information on road conditions, or proceed directly towards the destination on the presumed best path, despite the uncertainty. The two objectives are sometimes in conflict, and this reflects the exploration-exploitation trade-off, a fundamental issue in reinforcement learning and planning under uncertainty. An optimal solution must balance exploration and exploitation carefully. BCTP is in fact a special case of model-based Bayesian reinforcement learning [5, 7], with deterministic transition dynamics, and provides a simplified setting for studying the exploration-exploitation trade-off.

We show that BCTP is NP-complete and give a polynomial-time approximation algorithm, *Hedged Shortest Path under Determinization* (HSPD), which approximates an optimal solution with a polylogarithmic factor.

HSPD uses two key ideas. The first is to determinize the road network graph according to the *most likely edge* (MLE) assumption: each edge is assumed passable if the marginal probability of it being passable is greater than 0.5. Determinization simplifies the problem by removing uncertainty. The MLE determinization has an important property: if the traveler follows a path in the determinized graph and encounters a road state incompatible with the MLE assumption, then the probability of compatible road configurations is reduced by at least a half. Consequently, the MLE assumption is wrong for at most a logarithmic number of times. After that, the true states of all roads are known, leaving us a simple shortest path problem.

Let us call the shortest path in a determinized graph the *exploitation path*. The exploitation path may be far from being optimal, as all edges with marginal probability less than 0.5 are removed. In fact, the destination node may not even be reachable in the determinized graph. Our second key idea handles this by hedging the exploitation path with the *exploration path*. The exploration path in a determinized graph is the shortest path that gathers information and reduces the probability of incompatible road configurations by at least a half. Somewhat surprisingly, the shorter of the exploitation path and the exploration path has length within a constant factor of the expected length of an adaptive optimal solution.

HSPD is recursive and computes, in each step, the exploitation and exploration paths. It traverses the shorter of the two paths, until it encounters a road state incompatible with the MLE determinization assumption. HSPD then updates the probability distribution over the road configurations, taking advantage of any correlation present, and repeats until it reaches the goal.

We compare HSPD with two alternatives. One is a widely used greedy algorithm that makes an optimistic assumption on road conditions, and the other is a UCT-based heuristic search algorithm, which has achieved some of the best empirical results [8]. The empirical comparison shows promising results for HSPD. It outperforms the greedy algorithm, as expected. It also outperforms the UCT algorithms, even when the UCT algorithm is given substantially more computation time. The performance gap is particularly large, when significant exploration is required.

2 RELATED WORK

The BCTP is tied closely to many planning problems in partially observable domains. One such problem is the *Active Learning* [23] problem where a learner adaptively queries the labels of unlabeled training data to learn a classifier while using as few queries as possible. The unlabeled training data is analogous to the roads in BCTP. However, active learning is only concerned with gathering information efficiently and does not involve proceeding to a goal state whereas BCTP has to balance gathering information and proceeding to the goal. Furthermore, in active learning, taking an action does not affect the future cost of other actions, whereas in BCTP, going to a different location affects the cost of visiting other sites from that location. This latter property is present in adaptive Informative Path Planning (IPP) [15] and the adaptive Travelling Salesperson Problem (TSP) [11]. Both adaptive IPP and adaptive TSP extend active learning to path planning problems where actions move the agent to the next locations in a metric space in order to collect observations and identify the target hypothesis with minimum expected cost. Like active learning, adaptive IPP and adaptive TSP also do not have a goal other than gathering information, hence do not have to balance exploration and exploitation.

Another closely related problem is the Bayesian reinforcement learning problem [5, 7]. In the Bayesian reinforcement learning problem, the environment is modeled as an unknown Markov decision process (MDP) but we have a prior probability distribution over the MDP models. An agent that maximizes its expected long-term reward has to balance exploration and exploitation. As in BCTP, an agent may lose potential higher reward if it explores more than necessary to learn about the true model. On the other hand, it may also lose higher future reward if it stops learning about the model too early and exploits its current knowledge of the model for rewards. The Bayesian reinforcement learning is more complex as its uncertainty is over MDP models, a much richer model than the graphs in BCTP. The BCTP may serve as a simpler problem to further our understanding of Bayesian reinforcement learning problem.

A number of variants of Canadian Traveler problem have been proposed over the year. In [18], an efficient exact algorithm was given for the special case where the graphs contain disjoint paths from source to destination with random two-valued edge costs. Another variant is the remote-sensing Canadian Traveler Problem [3] where an agent can pay a sensing cost to reveal whether a road not incident on its current site is passable. This problem appear to be harder than the Canadian Traveler problem; it is NP-hard even in the special case of disjoint path [10]. BCTP is similar to the remote-sensing Canadian Traveler problem in the sense that the agent can learn about states of roads not incident on its current site. However, BCTP achieves that by correlation between states of road instead of directly sensing it. The most similar variant to BCTP is the one proposed in [21] where the edge costs are correlated. In fact, BCTP can be expressed as a special case of the model in [21] by setting the edge cost to infinity to make an edge impassable. In [21], an approximation algorithm that achieves an approximation factor of $\min(N, R)$, where N is number of graph nodes and R is the number of realizations of edge costs, is described. Our algorithm achieve a polylogarithmic approximation factor (see Theorem 2), which is better in many situations. In a recent variant, [6] modeled the edge costs using Gaussian Process. The Canadian Hacker Problem is a variant of the Canadian Traveler Problem applied to cybersecurity, where the aim is to reach a particular host by compromising network nodes [12].

Our algorithm and analysis follows the intuition of assuming the most likely observation developed in [16] and [15]. However, in those works the graph connectivity is assumed to be known while in BCTP, we assume unknown graph connectivity. Maximum likelihood determinization has also been used in Markov decision process (MDP) planning [24] and partially observable Markov decision process (POMDP) planning [20]. Those cases are planning problems where the probabilistic models are assumed to be known, unlike the Canadian Traveler Problem where the graph needs to be learned while the agent is trying to reach the goal.

Both Bayesian and the original Canadian Traveler Problem can be formulated as partially observable Markov decision process (POMDP) [2] models. While modern POMDP solvers are able to scale up to large state spaces, solving a POMDP remains difficult in practice.

3 BAYESIAN CANADIAN TRAVELER PROBLEM

We represent a road map for a Bayesian Canadian Traveler Problem (BCTP) as a directed graph $\mathcal{G} = (\mathcal{V}, \mathcal{E}, \mathcal{W})$ where $\mathcal{V}$ (the set of nodes) is the set of sites, $\mathcal{E}$ (the set of edges) is the set of roads in the road map, and $\mathcal{W} : \mathcal{E} \to \boldsymbol{R}$ gives the length of the roads on the road map (weight of each edge). While we motivate the problem on road maps, we only require that the weight function forms a metric.

For each edge $e \in \mathcal{E}$, let X_e be the random variable that equals its state. *i.e.*, $X_e = 1$ if the road corresponding to edge e is passable and $X_e = 0$ otherwise. We denote the vector of the states of a set of edges $\mathcal{A}$ as $x_{\mathcal{A}}$. In particular $x_{\mathcal{E}}$ denotes the configuration of edges in the entire graph. We assume that there are n possible configurations $x_{\mathcal{E}}$ for the entire graphs and call the set of possible configurations the hypothesis space $\mathcal{H} = \{x^1_{\mathcal{E}}, \ldots, x^n_{\mathcal{E}}\}$, represented as a n by m binary matrix, where m is the number of edges. In addition, the prior probability $p(h = x_{\mathcal{E}})$ for each hypothesis is given in a vector p. Overall, the Bayesian Canadian Traveler Problem is specified by the tuple $(\mathcal{G}, \mathcal{H}, p, s, t)$ where $\mathcal{G}$ is the graph, $\mathcal{H}$ is the hypothesis space, p is the prior probability, s is the starting node, and t is the destination node. We assume that the destination is reachable for all configurations.

When a traveler arrives at node v, he observes the states of incident edges at node v. For *e.g.*, if edges e_1, e_2 are incident on v, then the traveler observes a vector of states $\langle X_{e_1}, X_{e_2}\rangle$. To simplify notations, we refer to the vector of edge states observed at a site v as an observation $x_v = x_{\mathcal{N}(v)}$, where $\mathcal{N}(v) \subseteq \mathcal{E}$ is the set of edges incident on node v.

The solution to BCTP can be represented as a policy tree π, where the nodes in the policy tree specify a site $v \in \mathcal{V}$ to visit. Each branch is labeled by an observation o_v. To follow a policy specified by a policy tree π, a traveler first travels to the site specified by the current policy node of π, v_i. The traveler then observes the states of edges incident on v_i and takes the branch matching his observation o_{v_i} to go to the next policy node v_j. The procedure is repeated on the subtree rooted at v_j until the traveler reaches a terminal node in policy tree π, which is always labeled with the destination node t. Any two nodes connected in policy tree π must also be connected in G for the policy to be valid. The root node of a policy π must be labeled s; we assume that the traveler is initially located at the graph node s and starts following the policy at the root of the policy tree by observing the states of edges incident to s.

The cost incurred by a traveler is defined as $C(\tau) = \sum_{e\in\tau} \mathcal{W}(e)$, where $\tau = e_1, e_2, \ldots$ is the sequence of graph edges traversed by the traveler.

BCTP seeks an adaptive path to reach destination node t from starting node s with the least expected cost. The expected cost is defined as:

$$\mathrm{E}_H[C(\pi(h))] = \sum_{h\in\mathcal{H}} p(h)C(\pi(h)),$$

where $\pi(h)$ is the path in policy tree taken when $H = h$.

3.1 Computational Complexity

The decision version of BCTP problem is NP-complete. We prove this by a reduction from the Optimal Decision Tree (ODT) problem.

In the ODT problem, $\mathcal{H} = \{h_1, h_2, \ldots, h_n\}$ is a finite set of objects and $\mathcal{E} = \{e_1, \ldots, e_m\}$ is a finite set of tests. A test e_i reveals an outcome $x_i \in \{0, 1\}$ that depends on the unknown object $h \in \mathcal{H}$. We let function $p(e_i, h)$ map a test e_i and true object h to its outcome. In the ODT problem, we aim to find a policy to identify an element in $\mathcal{H}$ with the least expected number of tests, when the hypotheses are uniformly distributed. The policy is a binary decision tree where the root and internal nodes specify a test and the terminal nodes give the true object $h \in \mathcal{H}$. The decision version of the problem, which asks whether there is a policy with expected cost of less than or equal to w is NP-complete [13].

Theorem 1. *We define the decision version of Bayesian Canadian Traveler Problem as the question of whether there is a policy with expected cost less than or equal w. The decision version of BCTP is NP-complete.*

Proof. The solution of a BCTP problem can be represented as a policy tree. To see that an optimal policy tree is of polynomial size, note that every hypothesis can be associated with a path to a leaf in the policy tree, and the size of the tree is no more that the total size of all these paths. Furthermore, the number of observations that can cause branching on a path to a leaf is at most the number of vertices in $\mathcal{G}$ and the path between two such observation locations does not contain a cycle in the graph.

Finally, we can compute the expected cost of an optimal policy in polynomial time by doing a weighted sum of the cost of each $h \in \mathcal{H}$, showing that the problem is in NP.

We prove that BCTP is NP-hard by showing that ODT is polynomial time reducible to BCTP.

Given an instance of ODT$(\mathcal{H}, \mathcal{E})$, we construct an instance of BCTP $(\mathcal{G} = (\mathcal{V}, \mathcal{E}'), \mathcal{H}', P, s, t,)$ as follows.

The graph G consists of two clusters of edges as shown in Figure 1. Given each $h_i \in \mathcal{H}$, we construct the corresponding $h'_i \in \mathcal{H}'$ as follows. The first cluster of edges $e_1, \ldots, e_m, e_{m+1}, \ldots e_{2m}$ mirrors the tests in ODT. Edges $e_1, \ldots, e_m$ are always passable. An agent after traversing an edge $e_j \in \{e_1, \ldots, e_m\}$ will observe whether e_{m+j} is passable. The edge e_{m+j} will be passable if and only if the outcome of test e_j under h_i is 1. The second cluster of edges consists of n disjoint paths from v_i to destination v_t. The first edge in the i-path e_{2m+n+i} is always passable. The second edge e_{2m+i} will be passable if and only if the unknown object is h_i. Hence, only one out of the n paths is passable. All edges has cost of 1 except $e_{2m+n+1}, \ldots, e_{2m+2n}$ where they have cost $2m$. Finally, all $h' \in \mathcal{H}'$ are given equal probability.

We now argue that the expected cost of the ODT instance is less than or equal to w if and only if the expected cost of the BCTP instance is less than or equal to $2m+2+2w$.

First, we note that if the expected cost of the ODT instance is no more than w, then we can traverse the left cluster using the policy tree of the ODT instance and identify the correct h' with cost no more than $2w$, then go directly to t with an additional cost of $2m + 2$. We now argue the converse that if the expected cost of the BCTP instance is no more than $2m + 2 + 2w$, the expected of the ODT instance is no more than w. The case $w \geq m$ is vacuous as the ODT solution can always be found with cost no more than m by running each of the m tests. If $w < m$ then by our assumption, the expected cost of the BCTP instance is less than $2m + 2 + 2m$. This can only be done by identifying the hypothesis first before traversing to the target. To see this, we note that as long as the hypothesis has not been identified, there are at least two equally likely path to reach the target, and the expected cost of any policy that tries to go to the target directly when there are at least two equally likely path is at least $4m + 2$. Hence, the policy must identify h' first at a cost no more than $2w$ before traversing to the target with an additional cost of $2m + 2$.

Thus ODT is reducible to BCTP in polynomial time, and BCTP is NP-complete. □

We note that it is possible to encode $\mathcal{H}$ using representations other than a n by m binary matrix. In particular, factored representations may result in more compact representations of the distribution of hypotheses. With such representations, the BCTP may no longer be in NP. In particular, the original Canadian Traveler problem is PSPACE-complete [10]. Also, in general, there may be no compact representation of the posterior distribution even when there is a compact representation of the prior distribution, unless the distribution has some special structure.

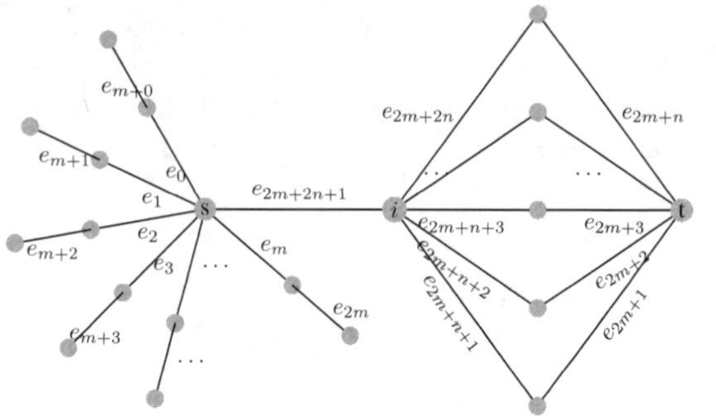

Figure 1: Reduction from Optimal Decision Tree problem

4 HEDGED SHORTEST PATH UNDER DETERMINIZATION

HSPD is a recursive algorithm. In each recursive step, we determinize the state of every edge using the MLE assumption to obtain a determinized graph $\hat{\mathcal{G}} = (\mathcal{V}, \hat{\mathcal{E}}, \mathcal{W})$. This graph is the same as the graph G of BCTP except that its edges whose probability of being passable is less than a half is removed. More formally, $\hat{\mathcal{E}} = \{e \in \mathcal{E} | P(X_e = 1) \geq 0.5\}$.

The idea of determinization is important. First, determinization gives a computational simpler problem whose solution is a path, as opposed to a policy tree that needs to account for all observations at every step. Second, if the observation received disagrees with the determinized graph while following the chosen path, then at least half of the probability mass of the current hypotheses would be eliminated. Furthermore, this happens at most a logarithmic number of times before we identify the true road network.

We call the solution of the shortest path problem in the determinized graph the exploitation path. Unfortunately, the exploitation path alone is not enough to solve the problem. In fact, a path to the goal may not exist in the determinized graph, even if a path exists under the true hypothesis. Furthermore, the exploitation path may be longer than necessary as some passable roads are assumed un-passable.

To hedge against the possibility of a poor exploitation

path, HSPD also plans an exploration path in the determinized graph. To obtain the exploration path, we solve the problem of finding the quickest way to gather information and reduce the probability mass of consistent hypotheses by half. Let the version space size function be $\varphi(x_{\mathcal{A}}) = \sum_{h \in \mathcal{H} \text{ consistent with } x_{\mathcal{A}}} p(H = h)$. Let $\hat{\mathcal{G}}_{\mathcal{A}} = \langle \mathbf{1}(e \in \hat{\mathcal{E}}) \rangle_{e \in \mathcal{A}}$ be the vector of edge states of the set of edges $\mathcal{A}$. For convenience, we normalize the probabilities to get conditional probabilities such that $p'(h) = P(H = h|x_{\mathcal{A}}) = \frac{P(H=h)}{\varphi(x_{\mathcal{A}})}$, and use p' as the input to each recursive step. The information gathering problem seeks to find the shortest path through $\hat{\mathcal{G}}$ such that $\varphi(\hat{\mathcal{G}}_{\mathcal{A}}) \leq 0.5$, where $\mathcal{A}$ is the set of edges observed along the path. The version space size function φ is a submodular function and finding the shortest path to reduce version space size is a submodular orienteering problem.

In a submodular orienteering problem, there is a set of locations X, a metric d that gives the distance between any pair of locations $x, x' \in X$, a starting location r, and a submodular function f of the set of locations. The goal of submodular orienteering problem is to find a tour starting from r that covers the function f. To solve for the exploration path, we give determinized graph $\hat{\mathcal{G}}$, weight of the edges $\mathcal{W}$, version space function φ, and starting node s as input to the submodular orienteering problem. Solving the submodular orienteering problem exactly is computationally hard. We use the polynomial-time approximation procedure described in [17].

Let τ^* be the exploitation path and τ_φ be the exploration path in $\hat{\mathcal{G}}$. HSPD chooses the shorter path τ out of the two paths τ_φ and τ^* or chooses τ_φ if there is no path from s to t on $\hat{\mathcal{G}}$. HSPD then traverses τ until the end unless we receive an observation that violates the MLE assumption, *i.e.*, when we receive an observation o_v at site v such that $o_v \neq \hat{\mathcal{G}}_{\mathcal{N}(v)}$; along the way we add any received observation to the observed set $\mathcal{A}$, denoting the operation as $x_{\mathcal{A}} \| o_v$.

If we had traversed the entire τ^* then we would have reached the destination node t and we are done. Otherwise, we go on to the next recursive step that works on the posterior distribution p' given the states of edges observed $x_{\mathcal{A}}$.

The pseudo-code of the algorithm is shown as Algorithm 1. The algorithm, as presented, always return to the starting site after each recursive call. This simplifies analysis. A practical version may skip this step and resume from the same site after each recursive call.

To fine tune the balance between exploration and exploitation we introduce a parameter $\alpha \geq 1$ that scales the length of the exploration tour τ_φ at Line 7 of Algorithm 1 such that $\tau \leftarrow \arg\min(W(\tau^*), \alpha W(\tau_\varphi))$. The bigger the value of α, the more HSPD will favor exploitation over exploration.

Algorithm 1 HSPD

```
procedure RECURSEHSPD(p)
    construct Ĝ using most likely observation determinization
    τ* ← SHORTESTPATH(Ĝ)
    if max_{h∈H} P(H = h) = 1.0 then
        follow tour τ*
    τ_φ ← ORIENTEER(Ĝ, W, φ, s)
    τ ← arg min(W(τ*), W(τ_φ))
    x_A ← EXECUTEPLAN(τ)
    p' = P(H|x_A)
    RECURSEHSPD(p')

procedure EXECUTEPLAN(τ)
    repeat
        Visit next site v in τ and observe o_v.
        A ← N(v)
        x_A ← x_A || o_v.
    until Ĝ_{N(v)} ≠ o_v or end of tour.
    Move to node s by tracing back its step
    return x_A
```

5 ANALYSIS

This section provides the performance guarantee for HSPD. Each recursive step divides the BCTP problem into smaller subproblems such that each subproblem consists of the subset of the hypotheses that are consistent with observations received, and its prior distribution is the posterior of the original problem given the observations. Note that at run time, only the subproblem corresponding the actual observations received needs to be solve. We show that each recursive step either reduces the size of the problem by a constant factor (as measured by probability mass of consistent hypotheses) or solves the problem completely (by reaching the destination). Furthermore, we show that the distance traveled in each recursive call can be bounded by a constant factor of the cost of the optimal policy. As each recursive call reduces the size of the subsequent subproblems by a constant factor, we can bound the number of the recursive calls needed to solve the BCTP problem and provide a performance bound.

We begin our analysis by bounding the distance traveled in each recursive call. We extract a subpath σ from the optimal solution π^* by following the most likely branch of the optimal policy tree and truncate just before the probability of traversing the path becomes less than 0.5. Lemma 1 gives the properties of this path. Lemma 2 shows that the subpath σ is present on $\hat{\mathcal{G}}$.

Lemma 1. *There is a subpath $\sigma = v_1, \ldots, v_k$ that is* *traversed with probability at least 0.5 under the optimal policy* π^*.

Furthermore, either (1) σ *ends at destination node* t *or (2)* $\varphi(x_{v_1}\|\ldots\|x_{v_{k-1}}\|x_{v_k}) \leq 0.5$, *where* $x_{v_1},\ldots,x_{v_{k-1}}$ *is the sequence of observations that leads to the subpath* σ *under* π^*, *and* x_{v_k} *is any observation.*

Proof. Let $p(\sigma|\pi^*)$ be the probability of traversing a subpath σ under optimal policy π^*. It is equal to the joint probability of the receiving the observation labels of branches in π^* that lead to the subpath σ, $p(\sigma|\pi^*) = p(x_{v_1}, x_{v_2},\ldots,x_{v_{k-1}})$, where $x_{v_1}, x_{v_2},\ldots,x_{v_{k-1}}$ are observation labels on the branches along subpath $\sigma = v_1, v_2,\ldots,v_k$.

We show that such a subpath σ exists by constructing it from the optimal policy π^*. Let σ' be the path from the root node to terminal node in optimal policy tree π^* by assuming we always receive the most likely observation $x_v^* = \arg\max_{x_v} p(x_v|x_{\mathcal{A}})$, where $\mathcal{A}$ is the set of edges observed so far. If $p(\sigma'|\pi^*) \geq 0.5$ then we simply let $\sigma = \sigma'$. Otherwise, we truncate the path σ' up to the node before the probability of traversing it becomes less than 0.5. Specifically, suppose $\sigma' = v_1, v_2,\ldots,v_k, v_{k+1},\ldots$ we truncate σ' up to until a node v_k such that $p(v_1, v_2,\ldots,v_k, v_{k+1}|\pi^*) \leq 0.5$ and $p(v_1, v_2,\ldots,v_k|\pi^*) > 0.5$.

The subpath σ satisfies property (1) if σ ends at terminal node. Otherwise it satisfies property (2) since the probability of the path going one node further down the most likely branch than σ is $p(v_1, v_2,\ldots,v_k, v_{k+1}|\pi^*) \leq 0.5$ and the probability of any observation x_{v_k} is at most the probability of the most likely observation branch, *i.e.*, $p(x_{v_k}|x_{\mathcal{A}}) \leq p(x^*_{v_k}|x_{\mathcal{A}})$. □

Lemma 2. *The sequence of observations* $x_{v_1},\ldots,x_{v_{k-1}}$ *that leads to subpath* σ *under optimal policy* π^* *is consistent with the vector of edge states that* $\hat{\mathcal{G}}$ *generates, i.e.,* $x_{v_1}\|\ldots\|x_{v_{k-1}} = \hat{\mathcal{G}}_{\mathcal{A}}$, *where* $\mathcal{A}$ *is the set of edges observed at every node in* σ *except the last one. As a corollary,* $\hat{\mathcal{G}}$ *contains all edges necessary to connect the subpath* σ.

Proof. We prove the main statement by contradiction. Suppose there is an edge e whose state is observed at a node $v \in \sigma$ and its state is not consistent with $\hat{\mathcal{G}}$, *i.e.*, $x_e \neq \mathbf{1}(e \in \hat{\mathcal{E}})$. By definition of $\hat{\mathcal{G}}$, $p(X_e \neq \mathbf{1}(e \in \hat{\mathcal{E}})) < 0.5$. However, lemma 1 states that $p(\sigma|\pi^*) \geq 0.5$ and $p(\sigma|\pi^*) = p(x_{v_1}, x_{v_2},\ldots,x_{v_{k-1}}) < p(X_e \neq \mathbf{1}(e \in \hat{\mathcal{E}}))$. Thus, we reached a contradiction and the observation sequence $x_{v_1},\ldots,x_{v_{k-1}}$ is consistent with $\hat{\mathcal{G}}$.

The corollary is true because any edge e needed to connect the subpath σ must be observed as $x_e = 1$ in the observation sequence $x_{v_1},\ldots,x_{v_{k-1}}$ and $\hat{\mathcal{G}}$ is consistent with the observation sequence. □

Since the subpath σ is traversed with probability at least 0.5 under the optimal policy and is a feasible solution to the tour required by the recursive call, we can bound the length of the tour generated in each recursive call by a factor of the expected cost of the optimal policy.

Lemma 3. *Assume we compute the optimal solution to* τ^* *and* τ_φ *in each recursive call. The distance traveled for each recursive call is at most* $4C(\pi^*)$.

Proof. From lemma 1 and lemma 2, if σ terminates at the destination t, then it is a feasible solution to the shortest path problem on graph $\hat{\mathcal{G}}$. Otherwise, we show that $\varphi(\hat{\mathcal{G}}_{\mathcal{A}}) \leq 0.5$ and hence σ is a feasible solution to the version space reduction problem, where $\mathcal{A}$ is the set of edges observed in σ.

Lemma 2 states that the observations received on σ under π^* are consistent with $\hat{\mathcal{G}}$ up to the second last node in σ. We get $\hat{\mathcal{G}}_{\mathcal{A}} = x_{v_1}\|\ldots\|x_{v_{k-1}}\|x'_{v_k}$ where $x'_{v_k} = \hat{\mathcal{G}}_{\mathcal{N}(v_k)}$. We need to prove two cases: when the observation generated by $\hat{\mathcal{G}}$ at v_k is consistent with some outgoing branch from v_k and when it is not. In the first case, $x'_{v_k} = x_{v_k}$, where x_{v_k} is some outgoing branch on π^* from v_k. If σ does not terminate at t, then from lemma 1, $\varphi(x_{v_1}\|\ldots\|x_{v_{k-1}}\|x_{v_k}) \leq 0.5$. If, on the other hand, x'_{v_k} is not consistent with any outgoing branch, the version space is immediately set to zero. Hence σ is a feasible solution to the version space reduction problem.

The cost incurred in each recursive call is $W = \min(C(\tau^*, \tau_\varphi)$. If σ terminates at the destination t, then $W \leq C(\tau^*) \leq C(\sigma)$. Otherwise, $W \leq C(\tau_\varphi) \leq C(\sigma)$. Furthermore, subpath σ is traversed with probability at least 0.5 in the optimal policy π^*, then

$$C(\pi^*) \geq 0.5C(\sigma) \geq 0.5W$$
$$W \leq 2C(\pi^*)$$

At the end of EXECUTEPLAN, if it did not reach the destination t, the agent traces its path back to node s for the recursive call. Hence, the distance traveled for each recursive call is at most $4C(\pi^*)$. □

Lemma 4. *Let* $x_{\mathcal{A}}$ *be the states observed after a recursive call of HSPD. Then either: (1) recursive call reached the destination node* t *(2) or we have reduced the probability mass of consistent hypotheses by at least half such that* $\varphi(x_{\mathcal{A}}) \leq 0.5$.

Proof. Suppose the agent completes the tour τ, if the tour chosen in the recursive call is τ^* then it would reach the destination node since τ^* ends at destination node. Otherwise, the tour chosen is τ_φ. As the tour did not terminate early, all states observed must be consistent with the observations of the determinized graph $\hat{\mathcal{G}}$, $x_{\mathcal{A}} = \hat{\mathcal{G}}_{\mathcal{A}}$. By the problem defintion of τ_φ, we have $\varphi(\hat{\mathcal{G}}_{\mathcal{A}}) \leq 0.5$.

Hence, we have reduced the probability mass of consistent hypotheses by at least half.

For the case when the agent did not complete the tour τ, then it must encounter an edge e' whose state $x_{e'}$ is inconsistent with its the determinized graph $\hat{\mathcal{G}}$. From the definition of the set of edges in the determinized graph, $\hat{\mathcal{E}} = \{e \in \mathcal{E} | P(X_e = 1) \geq 0.5\}$, we get the probability of the observed edge state $x_{e'}$ is $P(X_{e'} = x_{e'}) < 0.5$. Since $\varphi(x_{\mathcal{A}}) \leq \sum_{h \in \mathcal{H}} P(H = h | x_{e'}) = P(X_{e'} = x_{e'}) < 0.5$, we have reduce the probability mass of consistent hypotheses by at least half as well. □

After dividing the BCTP problem in smaller subproblems, we show that the sum of cost of optimally solving each subproblem weighted by the probability of its occurence is at most the expected cost of the optimal policy of the original problem. In short, the problem does not become harder when it becomes smaller.

Lemma 5. *Let π^* be an optimal policy for an instance of BCTP $(\mathcal{G}, \mathcal{H}, p, s, t)$. Let $\{\mathcal{H}_1, \ldots, \mathcal{H}_K\}$ be a partition of the hypotheses $\mathcal{H}$. We denote the sum of probabilities of a subset $\mathcal{H}_i$ as $p(\mathcal{H}_i) = \sum_{h' \in \mathcal{H}_i} p(H = h')$. For each $\mathcal{H}_i$ we define the i-th subproblem, BCTP $(\mathcal{G}, \mathcal{H}_i, p_i, s, t)$ where*

$$p_i = p(H) \triangleq \begin{cases} p(H = h)/p(\mathcal{H}_i) & \text{if } h \in \mathcal{H}_i \\ 0 & \text{otherwise} \end{cases} .$$

Let π_i^* be the optimal policy for the ith subproblem. Then we have $\sum_{i=1}^{K} p(\mathcal{H}_i) C(\pi_i^*) \leq C(\pi^*)$.

Proof. We can extract a feasible solution π_i for every subproblem i from the optimal policy of the original problem π^* by combining all paths taken under π^* for each hypothesis $h' \in \mathcal{H}_i$. The combination of these paths is a subtree of π^*. Hence,

$$\begin{aligned} \sum_{i=1}^{K} p(\mathcal{H}_i) C(\pi_i^*) &\leq \sum_{i=1}^{K} p(\mathcal{H}_i) C(\pi_i) \\ &\leq \sum_{i=1}^{K} p(\mathcal{H}_i) \sum_{h \in \mathcal{H}_i} \frac{p(h)}{p(\mathcal{H}_i)} \cdot C(\pi_i, h) \\ &= \sum_{h \in \mathcal{H}} p(h) C(\pi^*, h) = C(\pi^*). \end{aligned}$$

□

Because each recursive call divides the problem into sufficiently small ones by halving the probability mass of consistent hypotheses except when it reaches the destination, we can bound the number of recursive calls required.

Lemma 6. *Suppose we solve the submodular orienteering problem in HSPD optimally. For an instance of $BCTP(G, \mathcal{H}, p, s, t)$, HSPD computes a policy π such that*

$$C(\pi) \leq 4(\log \delta + 1) C(\pi^*),$$

where $\delta = 1/p_{min}$ and $p_{min} = \min_{h \in \mathcal{H}} p(h)$ is the prior probability of the least likely edge configuration.

Proof. From lemma 4, every recursive call either reaches the destination or reduces the probability mass of consistent hypotheses by at least half. In the worst case, the recursive call is repeated until there is only one consistent hypothesis left and then it proceeds to the destination using shortest path on $\hat{\mathcal{G}}$. Hence, the number of recursive call is at most $\log \delta + 1$.

We prove the bound on expected cost of policy π by induction on the number of recursives call. In the base case $i = 1$, lemma 3 gives us $C(\pi) \leq 4C(\pi^*)$. Suppose that $C(\pi) \leq 4(i-1)C(\pi^*)$ when there are at most $i - 1$ recursive calls. We now consider the case where there are i recursive call. The first recursive call partitions $\mathcal{H}$ into K mutually exclusive subsets $\mathcal{H}_1, \ldots, \mathcal{H}_K$ by the location in the tour when it is terminated. Each subset $\mathcal{H}_k$ induce a subproblem k of the original BCTP and it takes at most $i - 1$ recursive calls for each subproblem. By lemma 3, the first call incurs a cost at most $4C(\pi^*)$. By the induction hypothesis, each subproblem k incurs a cost at most $4(i-1)C(\pi_k^*)$. With lemma 5, the total cost is at most $4iC(\pi^*)$. □

Finally, we substitute the optimal orienteering algorithm with a polynomial time approximation and add in the tuning factor α to get the final approximation bound.

Theorem 2. *For an instance of BCTP $(\mathcal{G}, \mathcal{H}, p, s, t)$, assume that prior probability distribution p is represented as non-negative integers with $\sum_{\mathcal{H}} p(h) = P$. HSPD with scaling parameter $\alpha \geq 1$ computes a policy π in polynomial time such that*

$$C(\pi) \in O(\alpha \log |\mathcal{V}|^{2+\epsilon} \log P (\log P + 1)) C(\pi^*)$$

Proof. In each recursive call, HSPD uses a polynomial time β-approximation algorithm in each recursive call to solve the version space reduction orienteering problem to get τ_φ. Let W be the length of the tour chosen in a recursive call when we use an approximation algorithm and let W_φ^* be the length of the optimal version space reduction tour. Then $W = \min(\beta W_\varphi^*, W(\tau^*)) \leq \beta \min(W_\varphi^*, W(\tau^*)) \leq 4\beta C(\pi^*)$. Using lemma 6, we get the approximation bound for HSPD to be $4\beta \log(P + 1) C(\pi^*)$.

The polynomial time approximation for the version space reduction orienteering problem is based on the greedy approximation algorithm in [4] (see [17] for details). The approximation factor for the greedy algorithm is $O(\log |\mathcal{V}|^{2+\epsilon} \log P)$. The scaling factor α can be seen as an additional factor to approximating τ_φ since it makes the tour looks longer. Putting all the factors together gives us the final approximation bound. □

The performance bound of HSPD is dependent on the probability of the least likely edge configuration. It is useful when the number of configurations is moderate but may be vacuous if the outcomes of the edges are independent of each other as in the case of the original CTP. In the experiment section, we show that HSPD can still give good performance with appropriate value of α on a mixture model with a very large number of configurations. The bound show that a bigger value of α gives a worse performance guarantee. However, in practice the parameter α helps to fine tune the balance between exploration and exploitation to give better empirical performance.

6 EXPERIMENTS

6.1 Setup

We implement two baseline algorithms, Optimistic and Upper Confidence Tree (UCT) [14], to compare the performance of HSPD. Optimistic plans a path by assuming a optimistic graph where all roads are passable unless it can be inferred to be otherwise from the observations. The algorithm takes the first step of the path, receives observation and re-plans on an updated optimistic graph where roads observed to be impassable are removed. UCT is a general Monte-Carlo tree search algorithm that uses the upper confidence bound to guide the search. It has been successfully applied to many MDP and POMDP problems [22]. We implement the variant of the UCT algorithm in [8] that is designed for good performance on the Canadian Traveler Problem. This variant of UCT uses Optimistic as rollout policy and incorporates two modifications to place more emphasis on the heuristic value of Optimistic in its search.

It may be tempting to implement a baseline that simply uses shortest path on graph $\hat{\mathcal{G}}$ of the deterministic instance of BCTP we defined in HSPD. That is, HSPD without the version space reduction part. However, this is an incomplete solution as the graph $\hat{\mathcal{G}}$ may not necessary contains a path from the agent's current site to the destination.

In the first experiment, we implement a BCTP that is a reduction from a optimal decision tree problem using Theorem 1. The original optimal decision tree problem has 10 tests and 25 hypotheses. The outcomes of the tests for each hypothesis are randomly generated at the beginning. The second experiment simulates a road network affected by snow. The road network in the experiment is a 10 by 10 grid and every road has length 2. In each simulation, the ground truth road blockages are generated using a mixture model with 100 components. Each component is represented by a generating template, a configuration of blockages that is most likely for that component. To generate the ground truth road network in each simulation, we first sample one of the 100 templates with equal probability. Every road has a 0.9 chance of taking on the state as determined by the sampled template. If the state of a road is not taken from the template, the road state is randomly sampled with a 0.9 chance of being passable and a 0.1 chance of being blocked. To create a template, we simulate snowfall and its effect on the road by randomly choosing an affected area and blocking each road in the affected area with probability 0.5. The affected area is chosen by picking a rectangle whose side lengths are randomly selected to be between 3 and 10, and then randomly placing the rectangle on the 10 by 10 grid. To ensure the BCTP is sufficiently hard, for every template, we repeatedly simulate a snowfall (block each edge with probability 0.5) until more than 30 percent of the roads are blocked. As a finite mixture model, the posterior distribution of this model can be maintained in closed form.

We run HSPD on three different values of α: 1.0, 4.0, and 8.0. For the UCT algorithm, we use 100 and 300 rollouts per step and use an exploration constant of 5.0. For the first experiment, we run every hypothesis in the ODT problem once for Optimistic and HSPD. We run each hypothesis in the ODT 20 times for UCT as it is a randomized algorithm. For the second experiment, we generate 100 scenarios to get the correlated component of the mixture model and then sample 500 blockage configurations from the mixture model for evaluation and we run one simulation for each sample.

The results for the average path cost are shown in Table 1. We also report the 95% confidence and the average time taken per run in seconds. We limit the number of steps per run to 140 for the first experiment and 100 for the second experiment, and count a run as failure if the algorithm does not reach the destination within these number of steps. Failed runs are excluded in the calculation average path cost.

All algorithms are implemented in Clojure language. While care has been taken for efficiency, they are not highly optimized for performance.

6.2 Results

Our algorithm, HSPD, shows promising results compared to the other algorithms across both experiments. In the Optimal Decision Tree reduction experiment (Figure 1), out of the n paths that leads to the goal, only

Table 1: Average Cost

	HSPD $\alpha = 1.0$	HSPD $\alpha = 4.0$	HSPD $\alpha = 8.0$	Optimistic	UCT (100)	UCT (300)
ODT Reduction						
Cost	31.7 ± 0.64	31.7 ± 0.64	31.5 ± 0.456	502 ± 58.9	$566.\pm 32.1$	579 ± 29.1
Time (sec)	6.8	8.8	8.8	0.002	352	1069
Road Network						
Cost	63.3 ± 1.42	44.0 ± 0.774	38.9 ± 0.642	59.1 ± 1.59	44.6 ± 1.55	43.5 ± 1.58
Time (sec)	85.3	71.6	69.1	0.04	85.4	216

the one that corresponds to the true hypothesis is passable. The optimal strategy requires exploration using the "test" edges (e_0 to e_m) on the left to determine the true hypothesis before taking the path corresponding to the identified hypothesis. HSPD has the best result across different values of α. Optimistic performs badly for this problem because it does not gather information about the passable path using the test edges. It repeatedly traverse very expensive edges (e_{2m+n+i}) on the paths before realizing the next edge is not passable. This is because Optimistic assumes those edge are passable until it finds out that they are not. The value of α does not affect the average path cost because the cost of the shortest path on the determinized graph is usually much higher than the cost of the exploration path (often the path to the target is not present at all). UCT fails to improve the result of Optimistic with 100 and 300 rollouts. UCT relies heavily on Optimistic, which performs poorly in this experiment as a rollout policy and as a heuristic in guiding its search. In fact, UCT on this problem provides the only failures in the experiments. With 100 rollouts, it failed to reach the destination within 140 steps for 18 out of 500 runs.

In the second experiment, we only test on cases where the destination is reachable. The optimal strategy is nontrivial and depends on the sampled instances in the mixture model. However, there are instances where Optimistic is obviously sub-optimal. The road network is well-connected in general but there may be situations where there are long dead ends due to blockages. In such instances, Optimistic can incur significant cost traversing these dead ends because it does not reason about the uncertainty about upcoming edges. HSPD on the other hand is able to reason about uncertainty of edges ahead and may choose to gather information about potential dead ends before traversing them.

HSPD outperforms Optimistic for bigger values of α (4.0 and 8.0) but it under-performs Optimistic slightly for $\alpha = 1$. This is because it is often fairly cheap to visit a new location nearby to receive an observation that reduces version space by half, in comparison to reaching the goal by the shortest path. For this problem, the performance guarantee is very weak since the least likely configuration has very small probability. In spite of that, the algorithm is still practically useful as the scaling factor α helps to reduce over-exploration by making the exploration path look longer.

In this experiment, UCT improves the result of Optimistic significantly, by almost 25%. This is likely because Optimistic already has reasonable performance and UCT provides further improvements by searching in belief space and accounting for uncertainty in upcoming edges. However, its performance does not improve much when the number rollouts is increased from 100 to 300, and it still under-performs HSPD with $\alpha = 8.0$.

To apply the algorithm in practice, it would be useful to develop automatic methods for tuning α in each recursive call of HSPD. Computing the probability of reaching the goal with the exploitation path may provide useful information for doing that.

7 CONCLUSION

This paper introduces the Bayesian Canadian Traveler Problem. Compared with CTP, BCTP allows correlations among the unknown states of edges in a graph and provides a more realistic model for short-path finding in many applications. An optimal solution to BCTP requires careful balance between exploration and exploitation, a fundamental issue in reinforcement learning and planning under uncertainty.

We have developed Hedged Shortest Path under Determinization, a polynomial-time algorithm that approximates an optimal solution to BCTP within a polylogarithmic factor. It outperforms a widely used greedy algorithm and a state-of-the-art UCT-based search algorithm in our experiments. The basic ideas behind the algorithm are (i) the most likely edge determinization and (ii) hedging the exploration and exploitation paths. We believe that these ideas are useful in more general settings. A future research direction is to generalize the algorithm to model-based Bayesian reinforcement learning, where the transition dynamics is non-deterministic.

Acknowledgments. This work is supported in part by the Singapore MoE Tier 2 grant MOE2016-T2-2-068 and the US Air Force Research Laboratory under agreement number FA2386-15-1-4010.

References

[1] Amotz Bar-Noy and Baruch Schieber. The Canadian Traveller Problem. In *Proc. ACM-SIAM Symp. on Discrete Algorithms*, volume 91, pages 261–270, 1991.

[2] David Meir Blei and Leslie Pack Kaelbling. Shortest paths in a dynamic uncertain domain. In *Proc. IJCAI Workshop on Adaptive Spatial Representations of Dynamic Environments*, volume 4, page 2, 1999.

[3] Zahy Bnaya, Ariel Felner, and Solomon Eyal Shimony. Canadian traveler problem with remote sensing. In *Proc. Int. Jnt. Conf. on Artificial Intelligence*, pages 437–442, 2009.

[4] Gruia Calinescu and Alexander Zelikovsky. The polymatroid steiner problems. *J. Combinatorial Optimization*, 9(3):281–294, 2005.

[5] Richard Dearden, Nir Friedman, and David Andre. Model based Bayesian exploration. In *Proc. Uncertainty in Artificial Intelligence*, pages 150–159. Morgan Kaufmann Publishers Inc., 1999.

[6] Debadeepta Dey, Andrey Kolobov, Rich Caruana, Ece Kamar, Eric Horvitz, and Ashish Kapoor. Gauss meets Canadian traveler: shortest-path problems with correlated natural dynamics. In *Proceedings of the 2014 international conference on Autonomous agents and multi-agent systems*, pages 1101–1108. International Foundation for Autonomous Agents and Multiagent Systems, 2014.

[7] Michael O'Gordon Duff. *Optimal Learning: Computational procedures for Bayes-adaptive Markov decision processes*. PhD thesis, University of Massachusetts Amherst, 2002.

[8] Patrick Eyerich, Thomas Keller, and Malte Helmert. High-Quality Policies for the Canadian traveler's problem. In *Proc. AAAI Conf. on Artificial Intelligence*, 2010.

[9] Dave Ferguson, Anthony Stentz, and Sebastian Thrun. PAO for planning with hidden state. In *Proc. IEEE Int. Conf. on Robotics & Automation*, volume 3, pages 2840–2847. IEEE, 2004.

[10] Dror Fried, Solomon Eyal Shimony, Amit Benbassat, and Cenny Wenner. Complexity of Canadian traveler problem variants. *Theoretical Computer Science*, 487:1–16, 2013.

[11] Anupam Gupta, Viswanath Nagarajan, and R. Ravi. Approximation Algorithms for Optimal Decision Trees and Adaptive TSP Problems. In *Automata, Languages and Programming*, number 6198, pages 690–701. January 2010.

[12] Jörg Hoffmann. Simulated penetration testing: From "Dijkstra" to "Turing Test++". In *Proc. Int. Conf. on Automated Planning and Scheduling*, pages 364–372, 2015.

[13] Laurent Hyafil and Ronald L Rivest. Constructing optimal binary decision trees is NP-complete. *Information Processing Letters*, 5(1):15–17, 1976.

[14] Levente Kocsis and Csaba Szepesvári. Bandit based monte-carlo planning. In *Machine Learning: ECML 2006*, pages 282–293. Springer, 2006.

[15] Zhan Wei Lim, David Hsu, and Wee Sun Lee. Adaptive informative path planning in metric spaces. In *Workshop on the Algorithmic Foundations of Robotics*, 2014.

[16] Zhan Wei Lim, David Hsu, and Wee Sun Lee. Adaptive stochastic optimization: From sets to paths. In *Advances in Neural Information Processing Systems (NIPS)*, pages 1576–1584, 2015.

[17] Zhan Wei Lim, David Hsu, and Wee Sun Lee. Supplementary material for Adaptive stochastic optimization: From sets to paths. https://papers.nips.cc/paper/6005-adaptive-stochastic-optimization-from-sets-to-paths, 2015. NIPS Supplementary Material. Accessed: 2017-03-28.

[18] Evdokia Nikolova and David R Karger. Route planning under uncertainty: The Canadian Traveller Problem. In *Proc. AAAI Conf. on Artificial Intelligence*, pages 969–974, 2008.

[19] Christos H Papadimitriou and Mihalis Yannakakis. Shortest paths without a map. *Theoretical Computer Science*, 84(1):127–150, 1991.

[20] Robert Platt, Russell Tedrake, Leslie Kaelbling, and Tomás Lozano-Pérez. Belief space planning assuming maximum likelihood observations. In *Proc. Robotics: Science and Systems*, 2010.

[21] George Harry Polychronopoulos, John N Tsitsiklis, et al. Stochastic shortest path problems with recourse. 1993.

[22] David Silver and Joel Veness. Monte-Carlo planning in large POMDPs. In *Advances in Neural Information Processing Systems (NIPS)*, 2010.

[23] Simon Tong and Daphne Koller. Support vector machine active learning with applications to text classification. *The Journal of Machine Learning Research*, 2:45–66, 2002.

[24] Sung Wook Yoon, Alan Fern, and Robert Givan. FF-replan: A baseline for probabilistic planning. In *Proc. Int. Conf. on Automated Planning and Scheduling*, volume 7, pages 352–359, 2007.

Learning with Confident Examples: Rank Pruning for Robust Classification with Noisy Labels

Curtis G. Northcutt, * **Tailin Wu,** * **Isaac L. Chuang**
Massachusetts Institute of Technology
Cambridge, MA 02139

Abstract

$\tilde{P}\tilde{N}$ learning is the problem of binary classification when training examples may be mislabeled (flipped) uniformly with noise rate ρ_1 for positive examples and ρ_0 for negative examples. We propose Rank Pruning (RP) to solve $\tilde{P}\tilde{N}$ learning and the open problem of estimating the noise rates. Unlike prior solutions, RP is efficient and general, requiring $\mathcal{O}(T)$ for any unrestricted choice of probabilistic classifier with T fitting time. We prove RP achieves consistent noise estimation and equivalent expected risk as learning with uncorrupted labels in ideal conditions, and derive closed-form solutions when conditions are non-ideal. RP achieves state-of-the-art noise estimation and F1, error, and AUC-PR for both MNIST and CIFAR datasets, regardless of the amount of noise. To highlight, RP with a CNN classifier can predict if an MNIST digit is a *one* or *not* with only 0.25% error, and 0.46% error across all digits, even when 50% of positive examples are mislabeled and 50% of observed positive labels are mislabeled negative examples.

1 INTRODUCTION

Consider a student with no knowledge of animals tasked with learning to classify whether a picture contains a dog. A teacher shows the student pictures of lone four-legged animals, stating whether the image contains a dog or not. Unfortunately, the teacher may often make mistakes, asymmetrically, with a significantly large false positive rate, $\rho_1 \in [0, 1]$, and significantly large false negative rate, $\rho_0 \in [0, 1]$. The teacher may also include "white noise" images with a uniformly random label. This information is unknown to the student, who only knows of the images and corrupted labels, but suspects that the teacher may make mistakes. Can the student (1) estimate the mistake rates, ρ_1 and ρ_0, (2) learn to classify pictures with dogs accurately, and (3) do so efficiently (e.g. less than an hour for 50 images)? This allegory clarifies the challenges of $\tilde{P}\tilde{N}$ learning for any classifier trained with corrupted labels, perhaps with intermixed noise examples. We elect the notation $\tilde{P}\tilde{N}$ to emphasize that both the positive and negative sets may contain mislabeled examples, reserving P and N for uncorrupted sets.

This example illustrates a fundamental reliance of supervised learning on training labels (Michalski et al., 1986). Traditional learning performance degrades monotonically with label noise (Aha et al., 1991; Nettleton et al., 2010), necessitating semi-supervised approaches (Blanchard et al., 2010). Examples of noisy datasets are medical (Raviv & Intrator, 1996), human-labeled (Paolacci et al., 2010), and sensor (Lane et al., 2010) data. The problem of uncovering the same classifications as if the data was not mislabeled is our fundamental goal.

Towards this goal, we introduce Rank Pruning, an algorithm for $\tilde{P}\tilde{N}$ learning composed of two sequential parts: (1) estimation of the asymmetric noise rates ρ_1 and ρ_0 and (2) removal of mislabeled examples prior to training. The fundamental mantra of Rank Pruning is *learning with confident examples*, i.e. examples with a predicted probability of being positive *near* 1 when the label is positive or 0 when the label is negative. If we imagine non-confident examples as a noise class, separate from the confident positive and negative classes, then their removal should unveil a subset of the uncorrupted data.

An ancillary mantra of Rank Pruning is *removal by rank* which exploits ranking without sorting. Instead of pruning non-confident examples by predicted probability, we estimate the number of mislabeled examples in each class. We then remove the kth-most or k^{th}-least examples, *ranked* by predicted probability, via the BFPRT algorithm (Blum et al., 1973) in $\mathcal{O}(n)$ time, where n is

* Equal Contribution

the number of training examples. *Removal by rank* mitigates sensitivity to probability estimation and exploits the reduced complexity of learning to rank over probability estimation (Menon et al., 2012). Together, *learning with confident examples* and *removal by rank* enable robustness, i.e. invariance to erroneous input deviation.

Beyond prediction, confident examples help estimate ρ_1 and ρ_0. Typical approaches require averaging predicted probabilities on a holdout set (Liu & Tao, 2016; Elkan & Noto, 2008) tying noise estimation to the accuracy of the predicted probabilities, which in practice may be confounded by added noise or poor model selection. Instead, we estimate ρ_1 and ρ_0 as a fraction of the predicted counts of confident examples in each class, encouraging robustness for variation in probability estimation.

1.1 RELATED WORK AND CONTRIBUTIONS

Rank Pruning bridges framework, nomenclature, and application across PU and $\tilde{P}\tilde{N}$ learning. In this section, we consider the contributions of Rank Pruning in both.

1.1.1 PU Learning

Positive-unlabeled (PU) learning is a binary classification task in which a subset of positive training examples are labeled, and the rest are unlabeled. For example, co-training (Blum & Mitchell, 1998; Nigam & Ghani, 2000) with labeled and unlabeled examples can be framed as a PU learning problem by assigning all unlabeled examples the label '0'. PU learning methods often assume corrupted negative labels for the unlabeled examples U such that PU learning is $\tilde{P}\tilde{N}$ learning with no mislabeled examples in P, hence their naming conventions.

Early approaches to PU learning modified the loss functions via weighted logistic regression (Lee & Liu, 2003) and biased SVM (Liu et al., 2003) to penalize more when positive examples are predicted incorrectly. Bagging SVM (Mordelet & Vert, 2014) and RESVM (Claesen et al., 2015) extended biased SVM to instead use an ensemble of classifiers trained by resampling U (and P for RESVM) to improve robustness (Breiman, 1996). RESVM claims state-of-the-art for PU learning, but is impractically inefficient for large datasets because it requires optimization of five parameters and suffers from the pitfalls of SVM model selection (Chapelle & Vapnik, 1999). Elkan & Noto (2008) introduce a formative time-efficient probabilistic approach (denoted *Elk08*) for PU learning that is ~621 times faster than biased SVM and directly estimates ρ_1 by averaging predicted probabilities of a holdout set and dividing predicted probabilities by $1-\rho_1$. However, *Elk08* noise rate estimation is sensitive to inexact probability estimation and both RESVM and

Table 1: Noise rate variable definitions. ρ_1 is also referred to as *contamination* in PU learning literature.

VAR	CONDITIONAL	DESCRIPTION
ρ_0	$P(s=1\|y=0)$	Fraction of N examples mislabeled as positive
ρ_1	$P(s=0\|y=1)$	Fraction of P examples mislabeled as negative
π_0	$P(y=1\|s=0)$	Fraction of mislabeled examples in $\tilde{N}$
π_1	$P(y=0\|s=1)$	Fraction of mislabeled examples in $\tilde{P}$

Elk08 assume $P = \tilde{P}$ and do not generalize to $\tilde{P}\tilde{N}$ learning. Rank Pruning leverages *Elk08* to initialize ρ_1, but then re-estimates ρ_1 using confident examples for both robustness (RESVM) and efficiency (*Elk08*).

1.1.2 $\tilde{P}\tilde{N}$ Learning

Theoretical approaches for $\tilde{P}\tilde{N}$ learning often have two steps: (1) estimate the noise rates, ρ_1, ρ_0, and (2) use ρ_1, ρ_0 for prediction. To our knowledge, Rank Pruning is the only time-efficient solution for the open problem (Liu & Tao, 2016; Yang et al., 2012) of noise estimation.

We first consider relevant work in noise rate estimation. Scott et al. (2013) established a lower bound method for estimating the *inversed* noise rates π_1 and π_0 in Table 1. However, the method can be intractable due to unbounded convergence and assumes that the positive and negative distributions are mutually irreducible. Under additional assumptions, Scott (2015) proposed a time-efficient method for noise rate estimation, but with reportedly poor performance (Liu & Tao, 2016). Liu & Tao (2016) used the minimum predicted probabilities as the noise rates, which often yields futile estimates of min = 0. Natarajan et al. (2013) provide no method for estimation and view the noise rates as parameters optimized with cross-validation, inducing a sacrificial accuracy, efficiency trade-off. In comparison, Rank Pruning noise rate estimation is time-efficient, consistent in ideal conditions, and robust to imperfect probability estimation.

Natarajan et al. (2013) developed two methods for prediction in the $\tilde{P}\tilde{N}$ setting which modify the loss function. The first method constructs an unbiased estimator of the loss function for the true distribution from the noisy distribution, but the estimator may be non-convex even if the original loss function is convex. If the classifier's loss function cannot be modified directly, this method requires splitting each example in two with class-conditional weights and ensuring split examples are in the same batch during optimization. For these reasons, we instead compare Rank Pruning with their second method (*Nat13*), which constructs a label-dependent loss function such that for 0-1 loss, the minimizers of *Nat13*'s risk and the risk for the true distribution are equivalent.

Liu & Tao (2016) generalized *Elk08* to the $\tilde{P}\tilde{N}$ learning setting by modifying the loss function with per-example importance reweighting (*Liu16*), but reweighting terms

Table 2: Summary of state-of-the-art and selected general solutions to $\tilde{P}\tilde{N}$ and PU learning.

RELATED WORK	NOISE ESTIM.	$\tilde{P}\tilde{N}$	PU	ANY PROB. CLASSIFIER	PROB ESTIM. ROBUSTNESS	TIME EFFICIENT	THEORY SUPPORT	ADDED NOISE
ELKAN & NOTO (2008)	✓		✓	✓		✓	✓	
CLAESEN ET AL. (2015)			✓		✓			
SCOTT ET AL. (2013)	✓			✓	✓		✓	
NATARAJAN ET AL. (2013)		✓	✓	✓	✓	✓	✓	
LIU & TAO (2016)		✓	✓	✓		✓	✓	
RANK PRUNING	✓	✓	✓	✓	✓	✓	✓	✓

are derived from predicted probabilities which may be sensitive to inexact estimation. To mitigate sensitivity, Liu & Tao (2016) examine the use of density ratio estimation (Sugiyama et al., 2012). Instead, Rank Pruning mitigates sensitivity by learning from confident examples selected by rank order, not predicted probability. For fairness of comparison across methods, we compare Rank Pruning with their probability-based approach.

Assuming perfect estimation of ρ_1 and ρ_0, we, Natarajan et al. (2013), and Liu & Tao (2016) all prove that the expected risk for the modified loss function is equivalent to the expected risk for the perfectly labeled dataset. However, both *Nat13* and *Liu16* effectively "flip" example labels in the construction of their loss function, providing no benefit for added random noise. In comparison, Rank Pruning will also remove added random noise because noise drawn from a third distribution is unlikely to appear confidently positive or negative. Table 2 summarizes our comparison of $\tilde{P}\tilde{N}$ and PU learning methods.

Procedural efforts have improved robustness to mislabeling in the context of machine vision (Xiao et al., 2015), neural networks (Reed et al., 2015), and face recognition (Angelova et al., 2005). Though promising, these methods are restricted in theoretical justification and generality, motivating the need for Rank Pruning.

2 FRAMING $\tilde{P}\tilde{N}$ LEARNING

In this section, we formalize the foundational definitions, assumptions, and goals of the $\tilde{P}\tilde{N}$ learning problem illustrated by the student-teacher motivational example.

Given n observed training examples $x \in \mathcal{R}^D$ with associated observed corrupted labels $s \in \{0, 1\}$ and unobserved true labels $y \in \{0, 1\}$, we seek a binary classifier f that estimates the mapping $x \to y$. Unfortunately, if we fit the classifier using observed (x, s) pairs, we estimate the mapping $x \to s$ and obtain $g(x) = P(\hat{s} = 1|x)$.

We define the observed noisy positive and negative sets as $\tilde{P} = \{x|s = 1\}, \tilde{N} = \{x|s = 0\}$ and the unobserved true positive and negative sets as $P = \{x|y = 1\}, N = \{x|y = 0\}$. Define the hidden training data as $D = \{(x_1, y_1), (x_2, y_2), ..., (x_n, y_n)\}$, drawn i.i.d. from some true distribution $\mathcal{D}$. We assume that a class-conditional Classification Noise Process (CNP) (Angluin & Laird, 1988) maps y true labels to s observed labels such that each label in P is flipped independently with probability ρ_1 and each label in N is flipped independently with probability ρ_0 ($s \leftarrow CNP(y, \rho_1, \rho_0)$). The resulting observed, corrupted dataset is $D_\rho = \{(x_1, s_1), (x_2, s_2), ..., (x_n, s_n)\}$. Therefore, $(s \perp\!\!\!\perp x)|y$ and $P(s = s|y = y, x) = P(s = s|y = y)$.

The noise rate $\rho_1 = P(s = 0|y = 1)$ is the fraction of P examples mislabeled as negative and the noise rate $\rho_0 = P(s = 1|y = 0)$ is the fraction of N examples mislabeled as positive. Note that $\rho_1 + \rho_0 < 1$ is a necessary condition, otherwise more examples would be mislabeled than labeled correctly. Thus, $\rho_0 < 1 - \rho_1$. We elect a subscript of "0" to refer to the negative set and a subscript of "1" to refer to the positive set. Additionally, let $p_{s1} = P(s = 1)$ be the fraction of corrupted labels that are positive and $p_{y1} = P(y = 1)$ be the fraction of true labels that are positive. It follows that the inversed noise rates are $\pi_1 = P(y = 0|s = 1) = \frac{\rho_0(1-p_{y1})}{p_{s1}}$ and $\pi_0 = P(y = 1|s = 0) = \frac{\rho_1 p_{y1}}{(1-p_{s1})}$. Combining these relations, given any pair in $\{(\rho_0, \rho_1), (\rho_1, \pi_1), (\rho_0, \pi_0), (\pi_0, \pi_1)\}$, the remaining two and p_{y1} are known.

We consider five levels of assumptions for P, N, and g:
Perfect Condition: g is a "perfect" probability estimator iff $g(x) = g^*(x)$ where $g^*(x) = P(s = 1|x)$. Equivalently, let $g(x) = P(s = 1|x) + \Delta g(x)$. Then $g(x)$ is "perfect" when $\Delta g(x) = 0$ and "imperfect" when $\Delta g(x) \neq 0$. g may be imperfect due to the method of estimation or due to added uniformly randomly labeled examples drawn from a third noise distribution.
Non-overlapping Condition: P and N have "non-overlapping support" if $P(y = 1|x) = \mathbb{1}[[y = 1]]$, where the indicator function $\mathbb{1}[[a]]$ is 1 if a is true, else 0.
Ideal Condition[1]: g is "ideal" when both perfect and non-overlapping conditions hold and $(s \perp\!\!\!\perp x)|y$ such that

$$\begin{aligned} g(x) =& g^*(x) = P(s = 1|x) \\ =& P(s = 1|y = 1, x) \cdot P(y = 1|x) + \\ & P(s = 1|y = 0, x) \cdot P(y = 0|x) \\ =& (1 - \rho_1) \cdot \mathbb{1}[[y = 1]] + \rho_0 \cdot \mathbb{1}[[y = 0]] \end{aligned} \tag{1}$$

Range Separability Condition g range separates P and N iff $\forall x_1 \in P$ and $\forall x_2 \in N$, we have $g(x_1) > g(x_2)$.

[1]Eq. (1) is first derived in (Elkan & Noto, 2008) .

Unassuming Condition: g is "unassuming" when perfect and/or non-overlapping conditions may not be true.

Their relationship is: **Unassuming** $\supset$ **Range Separability** $\supset$ **Ideal** $=$ **Perfect** $\cap$ **Non-overlapping**.

We can now state the two goals of Rank Pruning for $\tilde{P}\tilde{N}$ learning. **Goal 1** is to perfectly estimate $\hat{\rho}_1 \triangleq \rho_1$ and $\hat{\rho}_0 \triangleq \rho_0$ when g is ideal. When g is not ideal, to our knowledge perfect estimation of ρ_1 and ρ_0 is impossible and at best **Goal 1** is to provide exact expressions for $\hat{\rho}_1$ and $\hat{\rho}_0$ w.r.t. ρ_1 and ρ_0. **Goal 2** is to use $\hat{\rho}_1$ and $\hat{\rho}_0$ to uncover the classifications of f from g. Both tasks must be accomplished given only observed (x, s) pairs. y, ρ_1, ρ_0, π_1, and π_0 are hidden.

3 RANK PRUNING

We develop the Rank Pruning algorithm to address our two goals. In Section 3.1, we propose a method for noise rate estimation and prove consistency when g is ideal. An estimator is "consistent" if it achieves perfect estimation in the expectation of infinite examples. In Section 3.2, we derive exact expressions for $\hat{\rho}_1$ and $\hat{\rho}_0$ when g is unassuming. In Section 3.3, we develop the entire algorithm, and in Section 3.5, prove that Rank Pruning has equivalent expected risk as learning with uncorrupted labels for both ideal g and non-ideal g with weaker assumptions. Throughout, we assume $n \to \infty$ so that P and N are the hidden distributions, each with infinite examples. This is a necessary condition for Thms. 2, 4 and Lemmas 1, 3.

3.1 NOISE ESTIMATION: IDEAL CASE

We propose the *confident counts* estimators $\hat{\rho}_1^{conf}$ and $\hat{\rho}_0^{conf}$ to estimate ρ_1 and ρ_0 as a fraction of the predicted counts of confident examples in each class, encouraging robustness for variation in probability estimation. To estimate $\rho_1 = P(s = 0|y = 1)$ we count the number of examples that we are confident belong to $s = 0$ and $y = 1$ and divide it by the number of examples that we are confident belong to $y = 1$. More formally,

$$\hat{\rho}_1^{conf} := \frac{|\tilde{N}_{y=1}|}{|\tilde{N}_{y=1}| + |\tilde{P}_{y=1}|}, \hat{\rho}_0^{conf} := \frac{|\tilde{P}_{y=0}|}{|\tilde{P}_{y=0}| + |\tilde{N}_{y=0}|} \quad (2)$$

such that

$$\begin{cases} \tilde{P}_{y=1} = \{x \in \tilde{P} \mid g(x) \geq LB_{y=1}\} \\ \tilde{N}_{y=1} = \{x \in \tilde{N} \mid g(x) \geq LB_{y=1}\} \\ \tilde{P}_{y=0} = \{x \in \tilde{P} \mid g(x) \leq UB_{y=0}\} \\ \tilde{N}_{y=0} = \{x \in \tilde{N} \mid g(x) \leq UB_{y=0}\} \end{cases} \quad (3)$$

where g is fit to the corrupted training set D_ρ to obtain $g(x) = P(\hat{s} = 1|x)$. The threshold $LB_{y=1}$ is the predicted probability in $g(x)$ above which we guess that an example x has hidden label $y = 1$, and similarly for upper bound $UB_{y=0}$. $LB_{y=1}$ and $UB_{y=0}$ partition $\tilde{P}$ and $\tilde{N}$ into four sets representing a *best guess* of a *subset* of examples having labels (1) $s = 1, y = 0$, (2) $s = 1, y = 1$, (3) $s = 0, y = 0$, (4) $s = 0, y = 1$. The threshold values are defined as

$$\begin{cases} LB_{y=1} := P(\hat{s} = 1 \mid s = 1) = E_{x \in \tilde{P}}[g(x)] \\ UB_{y=0} := P(\hat{s} = 1 \mid s = 0) = E_{x \in \tilde{N}}[g(x)] \end{cases}$$

where $\hat{s}$ is the predicted label from a classifier fit to the observed data. $|\tilde{P}_{y=1}|$ counts examples with label $s = 1$ that are *most* likely to be correctly labeled ($y = 1$) because $LB_{y=1} = P(\hat{s} = 1|s = 1)$. The three other terms in Eq. (3) follow similar reasoning. Importantly, the four terms do not sum to n, i.e. $|N|+|P|$, but $\hat{\rho}_1^{conf}$ and $\hat{\rho}_0^{conf}$ are valid estimates because mislabeling noise is assumed to be uniformly random. The choice of threshold values relies on the following two important equations:

$$\begin{aligned} LB_{y=1} =& E_{x \in \tilde{P}}[g(x)] = E_{x \in \tilde{P}}[P(s = 1|x)] \\ =& E_{x \in \tilde{P}}[P(s = 1|x, y = 1)P(y = 1|x) \\ &+ P(s = 1|x, y = 0)P(y = 0|x)] \\ =& E_{x \in \tilde{P}}[P(s = 1|y = 1)P(y = 1|x) \\ &+ P(s = 1|y = 0)P(y = 0|x)] \\ =& (1 - \rho_1)(1 - \pi_1) + \rho_0 \pi_1 \end{aligned} \quad (4)$$

Similarly, we have

$$UB_{y=0} = (1 - \rho_1)\pi_0 + \rho_0(1 - \pi_0) \quad (5)$$

To our knowledge, although simple, this is the first time that the relationship in Eq. (4) (5) has been published, linking the work of Elkan & Noto (2008), Liu & Tao (2016), Scott et al. (2013) and Natarajan et al. (2013). From Eq. (4) (5), we observe that $LB_{y=1}$ and $UB_{y=0}$ are linear interpolations of $1 - \rho_1$ and ρ_0 and since $\rho_0 < 1 - \rho_1$, we have that $\rho_0 < LB_{y=1} \leq 1 - \rho_1$ and $\rho_0 \leq UB_{y=0} < 1 - \rho_1$. When g is ideal we have that $g(x) = (1 - \rho_1)$, if $x \in P$ and $g(x) = \rho_0$, if $x \in N$. Thus when g is ideal, the thresholds $LB_{y=1}$ and $UB_{y=0}$ in Eq. (3) will perfectly separate P and N examples within each of $\tilde{P}$ and $\tilde{N}$. Lemma 1 immediately follows.

Lemma 1 *When g is ideal,*

$$\begin{aligned} &\tilde{P}_{y=1} = \{x \in P \mid s = 1\}, \tilde{N}_{y=1} = \{x \in P \mid s = 0\}, \\ &\tilde{P}_{y=0} = \{x \in N \mid s = 1\}, \tilde{N}_{y=0} = \{x \in N \mid s = 0\} \end{aligned} \quad (6)$$

Thus, when g is ideal, the thresholds in Eq. (3) partition the training set such that $\tilde{P}_{y=1}$ and $\tilde{N}_{y=0}$ contain the correctly labeled examples and $\tilde{P}_{y=0}$ and $\tilde{N}_{y=1}$ contain the mislabeled examples. Theorem 2 follows (for brevity, proofs of all theorems/lemmas are in Appendix 1.1-1.5).

Theorem 2 *When g is ideal,*

$$\hat{\rho}_1^{conf} = \rho_1, \hat{\rho}_0^{conf} = \rho_0 \quad (7)$$

Thus, when g is ideal, $\hat{\rho}_1^{conf}$ and $\hat{\rho}_0^{conf}$ are consistent estimators for ρ_1 and ρ_0 and we set $\hat{\rho}_1 := \hat{\rho}_1^{conf}, \hat{\rho}_0 := \hat{\rho}_0^{conf}$. These steps comprise Rank Pruning noise rate estimation (see Alg. 1). There are two practical observations. First, for any g with T fitting time, computing $\hat{\rho}_1^{conf}$ and $\hat{\rho}_0^{conf}$ is $\mathcal{O}(T)$. Second, $\hat{\rho}_1$ and $\hat{\rho}_0$ should be estimated out-of-sample to avoid over-fitting, resulting in sample variations. In our experiments, we use 3-fold cross-validation, requiring at most $2T = \mathcal{O}(T)$.

3.2 NOISE ESTIMATION: UNASSUMING CASE

Theorem 2 states that $\hat{\rho}_i^{conf} = \rho_i, \forall i \in \{0, 1\}$ when g is ideal. Though theoretically constructive, in practice this is unlikely. Next, we derive expressions for the estimators when g is unassuming, i.e. g may not be perfect and P and N may have overlapping support.

Define $\Delta p_o := \frac{|P \cap N|}{|P \cup N|}$ as the fraction of overlapping examples in $\mathcal{D}$ and remember that $\Delta g(x) := g(x) - g^*(x)$. Denote $LB^*_{y=1} = (1-\rho_1)(1-\pi_1) + \rho_0\pi_1, UB_{y=0} = (1-\rho_1)\pi_0 + \rho_0(1-\pi_0)$. We have

Lemma 3 *When g is unassuming, we have*

$$\begin{cases} LB_{y=1} = LB^*_{y=1} + E_{x\in\tilde{P}}[\Delta g(x)] - \frac{(1-\rho_1-\rho_0)^2}{p_{s1}}\Delta p_o \\ UB_{y=0} = UB^*_{y=0} + E_{x\in\tilde{N}}[\Delta g(x)] + \frac{(1-\rho_1-\rho_0)^2}{1-p_{s1}}\Delta p_o \\ \hat{\rho}_1^{conf} = \rho_1 + \frac{1-\rho_1-\rho_0}{|P|-|\Delta P_1|+|\Delta N_1|}|\Delta N_1| \\ \hat{\rho}_0^{conf} = \rho_0 + \frac{1-\rho_1-\rho_0}{|N|-|\Delta N_0|+|\Delta P_0|}|\Delta P_0| \end{cases} \quad (8)$$

where

$$\begin{cases} \Delta P_1 = \{x \in P \mid g(x) < LB_{y=1}\} \\ \Delta N_1 = \{x \in N \mid g(x) \geq LB_{y=1}\} \\ \Delta P_0 = \{x \in P \mid g(x) \leq UB_{y=0}\} \\ \Delta N_0 = \{x \in N \mid g(x) > UB_{y=0}\} \end{cases}$$

The second term on the R.H.S. of the $\hat{\rho}_i^{conf}$ expressions captures the deviation of $\hat{\rho}_i^{conf}$ from ρ_i, $i = 0, 1$. This term results from both imperfect $g(x)$ and overlapping support. Because the term is non-negative, $\hat{\rho}_i^{conf} \geq \rho_i$, $i = 0, 1$ in the limit of infinite examples. In other words, $\hat{\rho}_i^{conf}$ is an *upper bound* for the noise rates ρ_i, $i = 0, 1$. From Lemma 3, it also follows:

Theorem 4 *Given non-overlapping support condition,*

If $\forall x \in N, \Delta g(x) < LB_{y=1} - \rho_0$, *then* $\hat{\rho}_1^{conf} = \rho_1$.

If $\forall x \in P, \Delta g(x) > -(1-\rho_1-UB_{y=0})$, *then* $\hat{\rho}_0^{conf} = \rho_0$.

Theorem 4 shows that $\hat{\rho}_1^{conf}$ and $\hat{\rho}_0^{conf}$ are robust to imperfect probability estimation. As long as $\Delta g(x)$ does not exceed the distance between the threshold in Eq. (3) and the perfect $g^*(x)$ value, $\hat{\rho}_1^{conf}$ and $\hat{\rho}_0^{conf}$ are consistent estimators for ρ_1 and ρ_0. Our numerical experiments in Section 4 suggest this is reasonable for $\Delta g(x)$. The average $|\Delta g(x)|$ for the MNIST training dataset across different (ρ_1, π_1) varies between 0.01 and 0.08 for a logistic regression classifier, 0.01~0.03 for a CNN classifier, and 0.05~0.10 for the CIFAR dataset with a CNN classifier. Thus, when $LB_{y=1} - \rho_0$ and $1 - \rho_1 - UB_{y=0}$ are above 0.1 for these datasets, from Theorem 4 we see that $\hat{\rho}_i^{conf}$ still accurately estimates ρ_i.

Algorithm 1 Rank Pruning

Input: Examples X, corrupted labels s, classifier clf
Part 1. Estimating Noise Rates:
(1.1) clf.fit(X,s)
$g(x) \leftarrow$clf.predict_crossval_probability($\hat{s} = 1|x$)
$p_{s1} = \frac{\text{count}(s=1)}{\text{count}(s=0 \vee s=1)}$
$LB_{y=1} = E_{x\in\tilde{P}}[g(x)], UB_{y=0} = E_{x\in\tilde{N}}[g(x)]$
(1.2) $\hat{\rho}_1 = \hat{\rho}_1^{conf} = \frac{|\tilde{N}_{y=1}|}{|\tilde{N}_{y=1}|+|\tilde{P}_{y=1}|}$,
$\hat{\rho}_0 = \hat{\rho}_0^{conf} = \frac{|\tilde{P}_{y=0}|}{|\tilde{P}_{y=0}|+|\tilde{N}_{y=0}|}$
$\hat{\pi}_1 = \frac{\hat{\rho}_0}{p_{s1}}\frac{1-p_{s1}-\hat{\rho}_1}{1-\hat{\rho}_1-\hat{\rho}_0}$, $\hat{\pi}_0 = \frac{\hat{\rho}_1}{1-p_{s1}}\frac{p_{s1}-\hat{\rho}_0}{1-\hat{\rho}_1-\hat{\rho}_0}$
Part 2. Prune Inconsistent Examples:
(2.1)Remove $\hat{\pi}_1|\tilde{P}|$ examples in $\tilde{P}$ with least $g(x)$
Remove $\hat{\pi}_0|\tilde{N}|$ examples in $\tilde{N}$ with greatest $g(x)$
Denote the remaining training set (X_{conf}, s_{conf})
(2.2)clf.fit(X_{conf}, s_{conf}), with sample weight
$w(x) = \frac{1}{1-\hat{\rho}_1}\mathbb{1}[[s_{conf} = 1]] + \frac{1}{1-\hat{\rho}_0}\mathbb{1}[[s_{conf} = 0]]$
Output: clf

3.3 THE RANK PRUNING ALGORITHM

Using $\hat{\rho}_1$ and $\hat{\rho}_0$, we must uncover the classifications of f from g. In this section, we describe how Rank Pruning selects confident examples, removes the rest, and trains on the pruned set using a reweighted loss function. First, we obtain the inverse noise rates $\hat{\pi}_1$, $\hat{\pi}_0$ from $\hat{\rho}_1$, $\hat{\rho}_0$:

$$\hat{\pi}_1 = \frac{\hat{\rho}_0}{p_{s1}}\frac{1-p_{s1}-\hat{\rho}_1}{1-\hat{\rho}_1-\hat{\rho}_0}, \hat{\pi}_0 = \frac{\hat{\rho}_1}{1-p_{s1}}\frac{p_{s1}-\hat{\rho}_0}{1-\hat{\rho}_1-\hat{\rho}_0} \quad (9)$$

Next, we prune the $\hat{\pi}_1|\tilde{P}|$ examples in $\tilde{P}$ with smallest $g(x)$ and the $\hat{\pi}_0|\tilde{N}|$ examples in $\tilde{N}$ with highest $g(x)$ and denote the pruned sets $\tilde{P}_{conf}$ and $\tilde{N}_{conf}$. To prune, we define k_1 as the $(\hat{\pi}_1|\tilde{P}|)^{th}$ smallest $g(x)$ for $x \in \tilde{P}$ and k_0 as the $(\hat{\pi}_0|\tilde{N}|)^{th}$ largest $g(x)$ for $x \in \tilde{N}$. BFPRT ($\mathcal{O}(n)$) (Blum et al., 1973) is used to compute k_1 and k_0 and pruning is reduced to the following $\mathcal{O}(n)$ filter:

$$\begin{cases} \tilde{P}_{conf} := \{x \in \tilde{P} \mid g(x) \geq k_1\} \\ \tilde{N}_{conf} := \{x \in \tilde{N} \mid g(x) \leq k_0\} \end{cases} \quad (10)$$

Lastly, we refit the classifier to $X_{conf} = \tilde{P}_{conf} \cup \tilde{N}_{conf}$ by class-conditionally reweighting the loss function for examples in $\tilde{P}_{conf}$ with weight $\frac{1}{1-\hat{\rho}_1}$ and examples in $\tilde{N}_{conf}$ with weight $\frac{1}{1-\hat{\rho}_0}$ to recover the estimated balance of positive and negative examples. The entire Rank Pruning algorithm is presented in Alg. 1 and illustrated step-by-step on a synthetic dataset in Fig. 1.

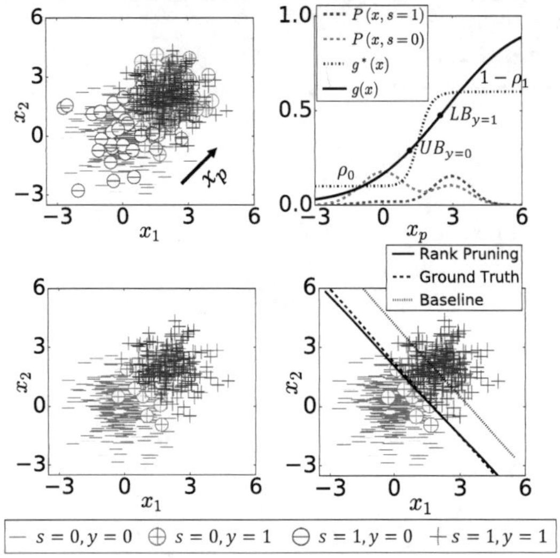

Figure 1: Illustration of RP with a logistic regression classifier ($\mathcal{LR}_\theta$). **Top left**: The corrupted training set D_ρ with noise rates $\rho_1 = 0.4$, $\rho_0 = 0.1$. Corrupted colored labels ($s = 1$,$s = 0$) are observed. y ($+$,$-$) is hidden. **Top right**: D_ρ projected onto the x_p axis (indicated in top left subfigure), and the $\mathcal{LR}_\theta$'s estimated $g(x)$, from which $\hat{\rho}_1^{conf}$=0.42, $\hat{\rho}_0^{conf}$=0.11 are estimated. **Bottom left**: The pruned X_{conf}, s_{conf}. **Bottom right**: The classifier by Rank Pruning ($\hat{f}$=$\mathcal{LR}_\theta$.fit(X_{conf}, s_{conf})), ground truth (f=$\mathcal{LR}_\theta$.fit(X, y)), and baseline (g=$\mathcal{LR}_\theta$.fit(X, s)), with an accuracy of 94%, 94% and 79%, respectively.

We conclude this section with a formal discussion of the loss function and efficiency of Rank Pruning. Define $\hat{y}_i$ as the predicted label of example i for g fit to X_{conf}, s_{conf} and let $l(\hat{y}_i, s_i)$ be the original loss function for $x_i \in D_\rho$. Then the loss function for Rank Pruning is simply the original loss function exerted on the pruned X_{conf}, with class-conditional weighting:

$$\begin{aligned}\tilde{l}(\hat{y}_i, s_i) =& \frac{1}{1-\hat{\rho}_1} l(\hat{y}_i, s_i) \cdot \mathbb{1}[[x_i \in \tilde{P}_{conf}]] \\ &+ \frac{1}{1-\hat{\rho}_0} l(\hat{y}_i, s_i) \cdot \mathbb{1}[[x_i \in \tilde{N}_{conf}]] \qquad (11)\end{aligned}$$

Effectively this loss function uses a zero-weight for pruned examples. Other than potentially fewer examples, the only difference in the loss function for Rank Pruning and the original loss function is the class-conditional weights. These constant factors do not increase the complexity of the minimization of the original loss function. In other words, we can fairly report the running time of Rank Pruning in terms of the running time ($\mathcal{O}(T)$) of the choice of probabilistic estimator. Combining noise estimation ($\mathcal{O}(T)$), pruning ($\mathcal{O}(n)$), and the final fitting ($\mathcal{O}(T)$), Rank Pruning has a running time of $\mathcal{O}(T) + \mathcal{O}(n)$, which is $\mathcal{O}(T)$ for typical classifiers.

3.4 RANK PRUNING: A SIMPLE SUMMARY

Recognizing that formalization can create obfuscation, in this section we describe the entire algorithm in a few sentences. Rank Pruning takes as input training examples X, noisy labels s, and a probabilistic classifier clf and finds a subset of X, s that is likely to be correctly labeled, i.e. a subset of X, y. To do this, we first find two thresholds, $LB_{y=1}$ and $UB_{y=0}$, to *confidently* guess the correctly and incorrectly labeled examples in each of $\tilde{P}$ and $\tilde{N}$, forming four sets, then use the set sizes to estimate the noise rates $\rho_1 = P(s = 0|y = 1)$ and $\rho_0 = P(s = 1|y = 0)$. We then use the noise rates to estimate the number of examples with observed label $s = 1$ and hidden label $y = 0$ and remove that number of examples from $\tilde{P}$ by removing those with lowest predicted probability $g(x)$. We prune $\tilde{N}$ similarly. Finally, the classifier is fit to the pruned set, which is intended to represent a subset of the correctly labeled data.

3.5 EXPECTED RISK EVALUATION

In this section, we prove Rank Pruning exactly uncovers the classifier f fit to hidden y labels when g range separates P and N and ρ_1 and ρ_0 are given.

Denote $f_\theta \in \mathcal{F} : x \to \hat{y}$ as a classifier's prediction function belonging to some function space $\mathcal{F}$, where θ represents the classifier's parameters. f_θ represents f, but without θ necessarily fit to the training data. $\hat{f}$ is the Rank Pruning estimate of f.

Denote the empirical risk of f_θ w.r.t. the loss function $\tilde{l}$ and corrupted data D_ρ as $\hat{R}_{\tilde{l},D_\rho}(f_\theta) = \frac{1}{n}\sum_{i=1}^{n} \tilde{l}(f_\theta(x_i), s_i)$, and the expected risk of f_θ w.r.t. the corrupted distribution $\mathcal{D}_\rho$ as $R_{\tilde{l},\mathcal{D}_\rho}(f_\theta) = E_{(x,s)\sim\mathcal{D}_\rho}[\hat{R}_{\tilde{l},\mathcal{D}_\rho}(f_\theta)]$. Similarly, denote $R_{l,\mathcal{D}}(f_\theta)$ as the expected risk of f_θ w.r.t. the hidden distribution $\mathcal{D}$ and loss function l. We show that using Rank Pruning, a classifier $\hat{f}$ can be learned for the hidden data D, given the corrupted data D_ρ, by minimizing the empirical risk:

$$\hat{f} = \underset{f_\theta \in \mathcal{F}}{\mathrm{argmin}}\, \hat{R}_{\tilde{l},D_\rho}(f_\theta) = \underset{f_\theta \in \mathcal{F}}{\mathrm{argmin}}\, \frac{1}{n}\sum_{i=1}^{n} \tilde{l}(f_\theta(x_i), s_i) \quad (12)$$

Under the *range separability* condition, we have

Theorem 5 *If g range separates P and N and $\hat{\rho}_i = \rho_i$, $i = 0, 1$, then for any classifier f_θ and any bounded loss function $l(\hat{y}_i, y_i)$, we have*

$$R_{\tilde{l},\mathcal{D}_\rho}(f_\theta) = R_{l,\mathcal{D}}(f_\theta) \qquad (13)$$

where $\tilde{l}(\hat{y}_i, s_i)$ is Rank Pruning's loss function (Eq. 11).

The proof of Theorem 5 is in Appendix 1.5. Intuitively, Theorem 5 tells us that if g range separates P and N, then given exact noise rate estimates, Rank Pruning will exactly prune out the positive examples in $\tilde{N}$ and negative examples in $\tilde{P}$, leading to the same expected risk as learning from uncorrupted labels. Thus, Rank Pruning can exactly uncover the classifications of f (with infinite examples) because the expected risk is equivalent for any f_θ. Note Theorem 5 also holds when g is ideal, since *ideal* $\subset$ *range separability*. In practice, *range separability* encompasses a wide range of imperfect $g(x)$ scenarios, e.g. $g(x)$ can have large fluctuation in both P and N or systematic drift w.r.t. to $g^*(x)$ due to underfitting.

4 EXPERIMENTAL RESULTS

In Section 3, we developed a theoretical framework for Rank Pruning, proved exact noise estimation and equivalent expected risk when conditions are ideal, and derived closed-form solutions when conditions are non-ideal. Our theory suggests that, in practice, Rank Pruning should (1) accurately estimate ρ_1 and ρ_0, (2) typically achieve as good or better F1, error and AUC-PR (Davis & Goadrich, 2006) as state-of-the-art methods, and (3) be robust to both mislabeling and added noise.

In this section, we support these claims with an evaluation of the comparative performance of Rank Pruning in non-ideal conditions across thousands of scenarios. These include less complex (MNIST) and more complex (CIFAR) datasets, simple (logistic regression) and complex (CNN) classifiers, the range of noise rates, added random noise, separability of P and N, input dimension, and number of training examples to ensure that Rank Pruning is a general, agnostic solution for $\tilde{P}\tilde{N}$ learning.

In our experiments, we adjust π_1 instead of ρ_0 because binary noisy classification problems (e.g. detection and recognition tasks) often have that $|P| \ll |N|$. This choice allows us to adjust both noise rates with respect to P, i.e. the fraction of true positive examples that are mislabeled as negative (ρ_1) and the fraction of observed positive labels that are actually mislabeled negative examples (π_1). The $\tilde{P}\tilde{N}$ learning algorithms are trained with corrupted labels s, and tested on an unseen test set by comparing predictions $\hat{y}$ with the true test labels y using F1 score, error, and AUC-PR metrics. We include all three to emphasize our apathy toward tuning results to any single metric. We provide F1 scores in this section with error and AUC-PR scores in Appendix 3.

4.1 SYNTHETIC DATASET

The synthetic dataset is comprised of a Guassian positive class and a Guassian negative classes such that negative examples ($y = 0$) obey an m-dimensional Gaussian distribution $N(\mathbf{0}, \mathbf{I})$ with unit variance $\mathbf{I} = diag(1, 1, ...1)$, and positive examples obey $N(d\mathbf{1}, 0.8\mathbf{I})$, where $d\mathbf{1} = (d, d, ...d)$ is an m-dimensional vector, and d measures the separability of the positive and negative set.

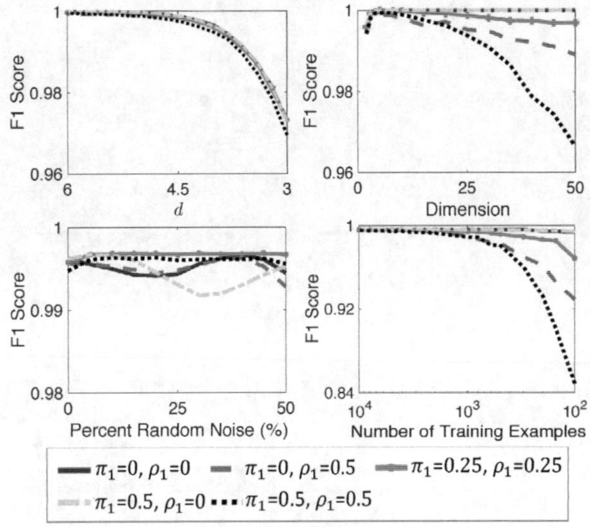

Figure 2: Comparison of Rank Pruning with different noise ratios (π_1, ρ_1) on a synthetic dataset for varying separability d, dimension, added random noise and number of training examples. Default settings for both Fig. 2 and Fig. 3: d = 4, 2-dimension, 0% random noise, and 5000 training examples with p_{y1} = 0.2. The lines are an average of 200 trials.

We test Rank Pruning by varying 4 different settings of the environment: separability d, dimension, number of training examples n, and percent (of n) added random noise drawn from a uniform distribution $U([-10, 10]^m)$. In each scenario, we test 5 different (π_1, ρ_1) pairs: $(\pi_1, \rho_1) \in \{(0, 0), (0, 0.5), (0.25, 0.25), (0.5, 0), (0.5, 0.5)\}$. From Fig. 2, we observe that across these settings, the F1 score for Rank Pruning is fairly agnostic to magnitude of mislabeling (noise rates).

For significant mislabeling (ρ_1=0.5, π_1=0.5), Rank Pruning often outperforms other methods (Fig. 3). In the scenario of different separability d, it achieves nearly the same F1 score as the ground truth classifier. Remarkably, from Fig. 2 and Fig. 3, we observe that when added random noise comprises 50% of total training examples, Rank Pruning still achieves F1 > 0.85, compared with F1 < 0.5 for all other methods. This emphasizes a unique feature of Rank Pruning, it will also remove added random noise because noise drawn from a third distribution is unlikely to appear confidently positive or negative.

4.2 MNIST AND CIFAR DATASETS

We consider the binary classification tasks of one-vs-rest for the MNIST (LeCun & Cortes, 2010) and CIFAR-10

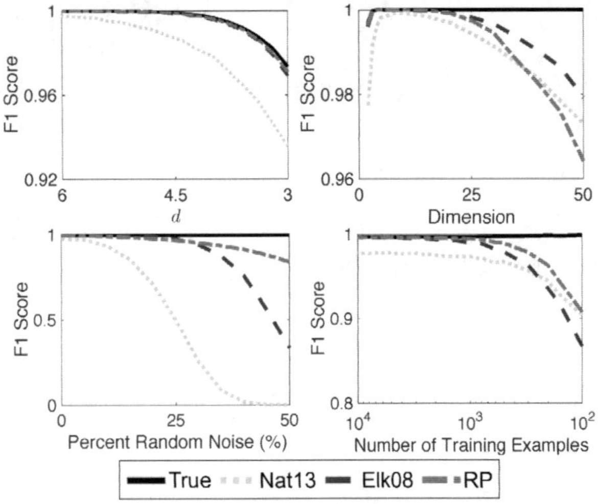

Figure 3: Comparison of $\tilde{P}\tilde{N}$ methods for varying separability d, dimension, added random noise, and number of training examples for π_1=0.5,ρ_1=0.5 (given to all).

(Krizhevsky et al.) datasets, e.g. the "car vs rest" task in CIFAR is to predict if an image is a "car" or "not." ρ_1 and π_1 are given to all $\tilde{P}\tilde{N}$ learning methods for fair comparison, except for RP_ρ which is Rank Pruning including noise rate estimation. RP_ρ metrics measure our performance on the unadulterated $\tilde{P}\tilde{N}$ learning problem.

As evidence that Rank Pruning is dataset and classifier agnostic, we demonstrate its superiority with both (1) a linear logistic regression model with unit L2 regularization and (2) an AlexNet CNN variant with max pooling and dropout, modified to have a two-class output. The CNN structure is adapted from Chollet (2016b) for MNIST and Chollet (2016a) for CIFAR. CNN training ends when a 10% holdout set shows no loss decrease for 10 epochs (max 50 for MNIST and 150 for CIFAR).

We consider noise rates $\pi_1, \rho_1 \in \{(0, 0.5), (0.25, 0.25), (0.5, 0), (0.5, 0.5)\}$ for both MNIST and CIFAR, with additional settings for MNIST in Table 3 to emphasize Rank Pruning performance is noise rate agnostic. The $\rho_1 = 0$, $\pi_1 = 0$ case is omitted because when given ρ_1, π_1, all methods have the same loss function as the ground truth classifier, resulting in nearly identical F1 scores. Note that in general, Rank Pruning does not require perfect probability estimation to achieve perfect F1-score. As an example, this occurs when P and N are range-separable, and the rank order of the sorted $g(x)$ probabilities in P and N is consistent with the rank of the perfect probabilities, regardless of the actual values of $g(x)$.

For MNIST using logistic regression, we evaluate the consistency of our noise rate estimates with actual noise rates and theoretical estimates (Eq. 8) across $\pi_1 \in [0, 0.8] \times \rho_1 \in [0, 0.9]$. The computing time for one set-

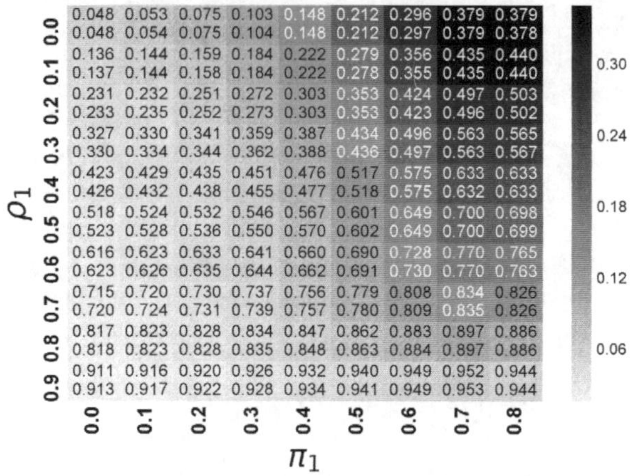

Figure 4: Rank Pruning $\hat{\rho}_1$ estimation consistency, averaged over all digits in MNIST. Color depicts $\hat{\rho}_1$ - ρ_1 with $\hat{\rho}_1$ (upper) and theoretical $\hat{\rho}_1^{thry}$ (lower) in each block.

ting was $\sim$ 10 minutes on a single CPU core. The results for $\hat{\rho}_1$ (Fig. 4) and $\hat{\pi}_1$ (Fig. S2 in Appendix) are satisfyingly consistent, with mean absolute difference $\text{MD}_{\hat{\rho}_1, \rho_1} = 0.105$ and $\text{MD}_{\hat{\pi}_1, \pi_1} = 0.062$, and validate our theoretical solutions ($\text{MD}_{\hat{\rho}_1, \hat{\rho}_1^{thry}}$=0.0028, $\text{MD}_{\hat{\pi}_1, \hat{\pi}_1^{thry}}$=0.0058).

We emphasize two observations from our analysis on CIFAR and MNIST. First, Rank Pruning performs well in nearly every scenario and boasts the most dramatic improvement over prior state-of-the-art in the presence of extreme noise (π_1 = 0.5, ρ_1 = 0.5). This is easily observed in the right-most quadrant of Table 4. The $\pi_1 = 0.5$, $\rho_1 = 0$ quadrant is nearest to $\pi_1 = 0$, $\rho_1 = 0$ and mostly captures CNN prediction variation because $|\tilde{P}| \ll |\tilde{N}|$. Second, RP_ρ often achieves equivalent (MNIST in Table 4) or significantly higher (CIFAR in Tables 3 and 4) F1 score than Rank Pruning when ρ_1 and π_1 are provided, particularly when noise rates are large. This effect is exacerbated for harder problems (lower F1 score for the ground truth classifier) like the "cat" in CIFAR or the "9" digit in MNIST likely because these problems are more complex, resulting in less confident predictions, and therefore more pruning.

Remember that ρ_1^{conf} and ρ_0^{conf} are upper bounds when g is unassuming. Noise rate overestimation accounts for the complexity of harder problems. As a downside, Rank Pruning may remove correctly labeled examples that "confuse" the classifier, instead fitting only the confident examples in each class. We observe this on CIFAR in Table 3 where logistic regression severely underfits so that RP_ρ has significantly higher F1 score than the ground truth classifier. Although Rank Pruning with noisy labels seemingly outperforms the ground truth model, if we lower the classification threshold to 0.3 instead of 0.5, the performance difference goes away by accounting for the lower probability predictions.

Table 3: Comparison of F1 score for one-vs-rest MNIST and CIFAR-10 (averaged over all digits/images) using logistic regression. Except for RP_ρ, ρ_1, ρ_0 are given to all methods. Top model scores are in bold with RP_ρ in red if greater than non-RP models. Due to sensitivity to imperfect $g(x)$, *Liu16* often predicts the same label for all examples.

DATASET	**CIFAR**				**MNIST**														
$\pi_1 =$	**0.0**	**0.25**	**0.5**	**0.5**	π_1 **= 0.0**			π_1 **= 0.25**				π_1 **= 0.5**				π_1 **= 0.75**			
MODEL, $\rho_1 =$	**0.5**	**0.25**	**0.0**	**0.5**	**0.25**	**0.5**	**0.75**	**0.0**	**0.25**	**0.5**	**0.75**	**0.0**	**0.25**	**0.5**	**0.75**	**0.0**	**0.25**	**0.5**	**0.75**
TRUE	0.248	0.248	0.248	0.248	0.894	0.894	0.894	0.894	0.894	0.894	0.894	0.894	0.894	0.894	0.894	0.894	0.894	0.894	0.894
RP$_\rho$	0.301	0.316	0.308	0.261	0.883	0.874	0.843	0.881	0.876	0.863	0.799	0.823	0.831	0.819	0.762	0.583	0.603	0.587	0.532
RP	**0.256**	**0.262**	**0.244**	0.209	**0.885**	**0.873**	**0.839**	**0.890**	**0.879**	**0.863**	**0.812**	**0.879**	**0.862**	**0.838**	**0.770**	**0.855**	**0.814**	**0.766**	0.617
NAT13	0.226	0.219	0.194	0.195	0.860	0.830	0.774	0.865	0.836	0.802	0.748	0.839	0.810	0.777	0.721	0.809	0.776	0.736	**0.640**
ELK08	0.221	0.226	0.228	**0.210**	0.862	0.830	0.771	0.864	0.847	0.819	0.762	0.843	0.835	0.814	0.736	0.674	0.669	0.599	0.473
LIU16	0.182	0.182	0.000	0.182	0.021	0.000	0.000	0.000	0.147	0.147	0.073	0.000	0.164	0.163	0.163	0.047	0.158	0.145	0.164

Table 4: F1 score comparison on MNIST and CIFAR-10 using a CNN. Except for RP_ρ, ρ_1, ρ_0 are given to all methods.

MNIST/CIFAR IMAGE CLASS	**TRUE**	π_1 **= 0.0**, ρ_1 **= 0.5** RP$_\rho$	RP	NAT13	ELK08	LIU16	π_1 **= 0.25**, ρ_1 **= 0.25** RP$_\rho$	RP	NAT13	ELK08	LIU16	π_1 **= 0.5**, ρ_1 **= 0.0** RP$_\rho$	RP	NAT13	ELK08	LIU16	π_1 **= 0.5**, ρ_1 **= 0.5** RP$_\rho$	RP	NAT13	ELK08	LIU16
0	0.993	0.991	**0.988**	0.977	0.976	0.179	0.991	**0.992**	0.982	0.981	0.179	0.991	**0.992**	0.984	0.987	0.985	0.989	**0.989**	0.937	0.964	0.179
1	0.993	0.990	**0.991**	0.989	0.985	0.204	0.992	**0.992**	0.984	0.987	0.204	0.990	0.991	0.992	**0.993**	0.990	0.989	**0.989**	0.984	0.988	0.204
2	0.987	0.973	**0.976**	0.972	0.969	0.187	0.984	**0.983**	0.978	0.975	0.187	0.985	0.986	0.985	0.986	**0.988**	0.971	**0.975**	0.968	0.959	0.187
3	0.990	0.984	**0.984**	0.972	0.981	0.183	0.986	**0.986**	0.978	0.978	0.183	0.990	0.987	**0.989**	**0.989**	0.984	0.981	**0.979**	0.957	0.971	0.183
4	0.994	0.981	0.979	**0.981**	0.977	0.179	0.985	**0.987**	0.971	0.964	0.179	0.987	**0.990**	**0.990**	0.989	0.985	0.977	**0.982**	0.955	0.961	0.179
5	0.989	0.982	**0.980**	0.978	0.979	0.164	0.985	**0.982**	0.964	0.965	0.164	0.988	**0.987**	**0.987**	0.984	**0.987**	0.965	**0.968**	0.962	0.957	0.164
6	0.989	0.986	**0.985**	0.972	0.982	0.175	0.985	**0.987**	0.978	0.981	0.175	0.985	0.985	**0.988**	0.987	0.985	0.983	**0.982**	0.946	0.959	0.175
7	0.987	0.981	**0.980**	0.967	0.948	0.186	0.976	**0.975**	0.971	0.971	0.186	0.976	0.980	**0.985**	0.982	0.983	0.973	**0.968**	0.942	0.958	0.186
8	0.989	0.975	**0.978**	0.943	0.967	0.178	0.982	**0.981**	0.967	0.951	0.178	0.982	**0.984**	0.982	0.979	0.983	0.977	**0.975**	0.864	0.959	0.178
9	0.982	0.966	**0.974**	0.972	0.935	0.183	0.976	**0.974**	0.967	0.967	0.183	0.976	0.975	0.974	**0.978**	0.970	0.959	0.940	0.931	**0.942**	0.183
AVG$_{MN}$	0.989	0.981	**0.981**	0.972	0.970	0.182	0.984	**0.984**	0.974	0.972	0.182	0.985	**0.986**	**0.986**	0.985	0.984	0.976	**0.975**	0.945	0.962	0.182
PLANE	0.755	0.689	**0.634**	0.619	0.585	0.182	0.695	**0.702**	0.671	0.640	0.182	0.757	**0.746**	0.716	0.735	0.000	0.628	**0.635**	0.459	0.598	0.182
AUTO	0.891	0.791	**0.785**	0.761	0.768	0.000	0.832	**0.824**	0.771	0.783	0.182	0.862	0.866	**0.869**	0.865	0.000	0.749	**0.720**	0.582	0.501	0.182
BIRD	0.669	0.504	**0.483**	0.445	0.389	0.182	0.543	**0.515**	0.469	0.426	0.182	0.577	**0.619**	0.543	0.551	0.000	0.447	**0.409**	0.366	0.387	0.182
CAT	0.487	0.350	0.279	0.310	**0.313**	0.000	0.426	0.317	**0.350**	0.345	0.182	0.489	**0.433**	0.426	0.347	0.000	0.394	0.282	0.240	**0.313**	0.182
DEER	0.726	0.593	**0.540**	0.455	0.522	0.182	0.585	0.554	0.480	**0.569**	0.182	0.614	0.630	**0.643**	0.633	0.000	0.458	0.375	0.310	**0.383**	0.182
DOG	0.569	0.544	**0.577**	0.429	0.456	0.000	0.579	0.559	0.569	**0.576**	0.182	0.647	0.637	**0.667**	0.630	0.000	0.516	0.461	0.412	**0.465**	0.182
FROG	0.815	0.746	0.727	**0.733**	0.718	0.000	0.729	**0.750**	0.630	0.584	0.182	0.767	**0.782**	0.777	0.770	0.000	0.635	**0.615**	0.589	0.524	0.182
HORSE	0.805	0.690	0.670	0.624	**0.672**	0.182	0.710	0.669	**0.683**	0.627	0.182	0.761	**0.776**	0.769	0.753	0.000	0.672	**0.569**	0.551	0.461	0.182
SHIP	0.851	0.791	**0.783**	0.719	0.758	0.182	0.810	**0.801**	0.758	0.723	0.182	0.816	0.822	0.830	**0.831**	0.000	0.715	**0.738**	0.569	0.632	0.182
TRUCK	0.861	0.744	**0.722**	0.655	0.665	0.182	0.814	**0.826**	0.798	0.774	0.182	0.812	0.830	**0.826**	0.824	0.000	0.654	0.543	0.575	**0.584**	0.182
AVG$_{CF}$	0.743	0.644	**0.620**	0.575	0.585	0.109	0.672	**0.652**	0.618	0.605	0.182	0.710	**0.714**	0.707	0.694	0.000	0.587	**0.535**	0.465	0.485	0.182

5 DISCUSSION AND CONTRIBUTIONS

To our knowledge, Rank Pruning is the first time-efficient algorithm, w.r.t. classifier fitting time, for $\tilde{P}\tilde{N}$ learning that achieves similar or better F1, error, and AUC-PR than current state-of-the-art methods across practical scenarios for synthetic, MNIST, and CIFAR datasets, with logistic regression and CNN classifiers, across all noise rates, ρ_1, ρ_0, for varying added noise, dimension, separability, and number of training examples. By *learning with confident examples*, we discover provably consistent estimators for noise rates, ρ_1, ρ_0, derive theoretical solutions when g is unassuming, and accurately uncover the classifications of f fit to hidden labels, perfectly when g range separates P and N.

We recognize that disambiguating whether we are in the unassuming or range separability condition may be desirable. Although knowing $g^*(x)$ and thus $\Delta g(x)$ is impossible, if we assume randomly uniform noise, and toggling the $LB_{y=1}$ threshold does not change ρ_1^{conf}, then g range separates P and N. When g is unassuming, Rank Pruning is still robust to imperfect $g(x)$ within a range separable subset of P and N by training with confident examples even when noise rate estimates are inexact.

An important contribution of Rank Pruning is generality, both in classifier and implementation. The use of logistic regression and a CNN in our experiments emphasizes that our findings are not dependent on model complexity. We evaluate thousands of scenarios to avoid findings that are an artifact of problem setup. A key point of Rank Pruning is that we only report the simplest, non-parametric version. For example, we use 3-fold cross-validation to compute $g(x)$ even though we achieved improved performance with larger folds. We tried many variants of pruning and achieved significantly higher F1 for MNIST and CIFAR, but to maintain generality, we present only the basic model.

At its core, Rank Pruning is a simple, robust, and general solution for noisy binary classification by *learning with confident examples*, but it also challenges how we think about training data. For example, SVM showed how a decision boundary can be recovered from support vectors. Yet, when training data contains significant mislabeling, confident examples, many of which are far from the boundary, are informative for uncovering the true relationship $P(y = 1|x)$. Although modern affordances of "big data" emphasize the value of *more* examples for training, through Rank Pruning we instead encourage a rethinking of learning with *confident* examples.

References

Aha, D. W., Kibler, D., and Albert, M. K. Instance-based learning algorithms. *Mach. Learn.*, 6(1):37–66, 1991.

Angelova, A., Abu-Mostafam, Y., and Perona, P. Pruning training sets for learning of object categories. In *CVPR*, volume 1, pp. 494–501. IEEE, 2005.

Angluin, D. and Laird, P. Learning from noisy examples. *Machine Learning*, 2(4):343–370, 1988.

Blanchard, G., Lee, G., and Scott, C. Semi-supervised novelty detection. *J. Mach. Learn. Res.*, 11:2973–3009, December 2010. ISSN 1532-4435.

Blum, A. and Mitchell, T. Combining labeled and unlabeled data with co-training. In *11th Conf. on COLT*, pp. 92–100, New York, NY, USA, 1998. ACM.

Blum, M., Floyd, R. W., Pratt, V., Rivest, R. L., and Tarjan, R. E. Time bounds for selection. *J. Comput. Syst. Sci.*, 7(4):448–461, August 1973. ISSN 0022-0000.

Breiman, L. Bagging predictors. *Machine Learning*, 24 (2):123–140, August 1996. ISSN 0885-6125.

Chapelle, O. and Vapnik, V. Model selection for support vector machines. In *Proc. of 12th NIPS*, pp. 230–236, Cambridge, MA, USA, 1999.

Chollet, F. *Keras CIFAR CNN*, 2016a. bit.ly/2mVKR3d.

Chollet, F. *Keras MNIST CNN*, 2016b. bit.ly/2nKiqJv.

Claesen, M., Smet, F. D., Suykens, J. A., and Moor, B. D. A robust ensemble approach to learn from positive and unlabeled data using svm base models. *Neurocomputing*, 160:73 – 84, 2015. ISSN 0925-2312.

Davis, J. and Goadrich, M. The relationship between precision-recall and roc curves. In *Proc. of 23rd ICML*, pp. 233–240, NYC, NY, USA, 2006. ACM.

Elkan, C. and Noto, K. Learning classifiers from only positive and unlabeled data. In *Proc. of 14th KDD*, pp. 213–220, NYC, NY, USA, 2008. ACM.

Krizhevsky, A., Nair, V., and Hinton, G. Cifar-10 (canadian institute for advanced research).

Lane, N. D., Miluzzo, E., Lu, H., Peebles, D., Choudhury, T., and Campbell, A. T. A survey of mobile phone sensing. *IEEE Communications*, 48(9), 2010.

LeCun, Y. and Cortes, C. MNIST handwritten digit database. 2010.

Lee, W. and Liu, B. Learning with positive and unlabeled examples using weighted logistic regression. In *Proc. of 20th ICML*, volume 1, pp. 448–455, 12 2003.

Liu, B., Dai, Y., Li, X., Lee, W. S., and Yu, P. S. Building text classifiers using positive and unlabeled examples. In *Proc. of 3rd ICDM*, pp. 179–, Washington, DC, USA, 2003. IEEE Computer Society.

Liu, T. and Tao, D. Classification with noisy labels by importance reweighting. *IEEE Trans. Pattern Anal. Mach. Intell.*, 38(3):447–461, March 2016.

Menon, A. K., Jiang, X., Vembu, S., Elkan, C., and Ohno-Machado, L. Predicting accurate probabilities with a ranking loss. *CoRR*, abs/1206.4661, 2012.

Michalski, S. R., Carbonell, G. J., and Mitchell, M. T. *ML an AI Approach*. Morgan Kaufmann Publishers Inc., San Francisco, CA, USA, 1986.

Mordelet, F. and Vert, J. P. A bagging svm to learn from positive and unlabeled examples. *Pattern Recogn. Lett.*, 37:201–209, February 2014. ISSN 0167-8655.

Natarajan, N., Dhillon, I. S., Ravikumar, P. K., and Tewari, A. Learning with noisy labels. In *Adv. in NIPS 26*, pp. 1196–1204. Curran Associates, Inc., 2013.

Nettleton, D. F., Orriols-Puig, A., and Fornells, A. A study of the effect of different types of noise on the precision of supervised learning techniques. *Artificial Intelligence Review*, 33(4):275–306, 2010.

Nigam, K. and Ghani, R. Understanding the behavior of co-training. In *KDD Workshop*, 2000.

Paolacci, G., Chandler, J., and Ipeirotis, P. G. Running experiments on amazon mechanical turk. *Judgment and Decision Making*, 5(5):411–419, 2010.

Raviv, Y. and Intrator, N. Bootstrapping with noise: An effective regularization technique. *Connection Science*, 8(3-4):355–372, 1996.

Reed, S. E., Lee, H., Anguelov, D., Szegedy, C., Erhan, D., and Rabinovich, A. Training deep neural networks on noisy labels with bootstrapping. In *ICLR*, 2015.

Scott, C. A rate of convergence for mixture proportion estimation, with application to learning from noisy labels. *JMLR*, 38:838–846, 2015. ISSN 1532-4435.

Scott, C., Blanchard, G., and Handy, G. Classification with asymmetric label noise: Consistency and maximal denoising. In *COLT*, pp. 489–511, 2013.

Sugiyama, M., Suzuki, T., and Kanamori, T. *Density Ratio Estimation in ML*. Cambridge University Press, New York, NY, USA, 1st edition, 2012.

Xiao, T., Xia, T., Yang, Y., Huang, C., and Wang, X. Learning from massive noisy labeled data for image classification. In *CVPR*, 2015.

Yang, T., Mahdavi, M., Jin, R., Zhang, L., and Zhou, Y. Multiple kernel learning from noisy labels by stochastic programming. In *Proc. of 29th ICML*, pp. 233–240, New York, NY, USA, 2012. ACM.

Appendix

1 PROOFS

In this section, we provide proofs for all the lemmas and theorems in the main paper. We always assume that a class-conditional extension of the Classification Noise Process (CNP) (Angluin & Laird, 1988) maps true labels y to observed labels s such that each label in P is flipped independently with probability ρ_1 and each label in N is flipped independently with probability ρ_0 ($s \leftarrow CNP(y, \rho_1, \rho_0)$), so that $P(s = s|y = y, x) = P(s = s|y = y)$. Remember that $\rho_1 + \rho_0 < 1$ is a necessary condition of minimal information, otherwise we may learn opposite labels.

In Lemma 1, Theorem 2, Lemma 3 and Theorem 4, we assume that P and N have infinite number of examples so that they are the true, hidden distributions.

A fundamental equation we use in the proofs is the following lemma:

Lemma S1 *When g is ideal, i.e. $g(x) = g^*(x)$ and P and N have non-overlapping support, we have*

$$g(x) = (1 - \rho_1) \cdot \mathbb{1}[[y = 1]] + \rho_0 \cdot \mathbb{1}[[y = 0]] \tag{1}$$

Proof: Since $g(x) = g^*(x)$ and P and N have non-overlapping support, we have

$$\begin{aligned} g(x) =& g^*(x) = P(s = 1|x) \\ =& P(s = 1|y = 1, x) \cdot P(y = 1|x) + P(s = 1|y = 0, x) \cdot P(y = 0|x) \\ =& P(s = 1|y = 1) \cdot P(y = 1|x) + P(s = 1|y = 0) \cdot P(y = 0|x) \\ =& (1 - \rho_1) \cdot \mathbb{1}[[y = 1]] + \rho_0 \cdot \mathbb{1}[[y = 0]] \end{aligned}$$

1.1 PROOF OF LEMMA 1

Lemma 1 *When g is ideal, i.e. $g(x) = g^*(x)$ and P and N have non-overlapping support, we have*

$$\begin{cases} \tilde{P}_{y=1} = \{x \in P|s = 1\}, \tilde{N}_{y=1} = \{x \in P|s = 0\} \\ \tilde{P}_{y=0} = \{x \in N|s = 1\}, \tilde{N}_{y=0} = \{x \in N|s = 0\} \end{cases} \tag{2}$$

Proof: Firstly, we compute the threshold $LB_{y=1}$ and $UB_{y=0}$ used by $\tilde{P}_{y=1}$, $\tilde{N}_{y=1}$, $\tilde{P}_{y=0}$ and $\tilde{N}_{y=0}$. Since P and N have non-overlapping support, we have $P(y = 1|x) = \mathbb{1}[[y = 1]]$. Also using $g(x) = g^*(x)$, we have

$$\begin{aligned} LB_{y=1} =& E_{x \in \tilde{P}}[g(x)] = E_{x \in \tilde{P}}[P(s = 1|x)] \\ =& E_{x \in \tilde{P}}[P(s = 1|x, y = 1)P(y = 1|x) + P(s = 1|x, y = 0)P(y = 0|x)] \\ =& E_{x \in \tilde{P}}[P(s = 1|y = 1)P(y = 1|x) + P(s = 1|y = 0)P(y = 0|x)] \\ =& (1 - \rho_1)(1 - \pi_1) + \rho_0 \pi_1 \end{aligned} \tag{3}$$

Similarly, we have

$$UB_{y=0} = (1 - \rho_1)\pi_0 + \rho_0(1 - \pi_0)$$

Since $\pi_1 = P(y = 0|s = 1)$, we have $\pi_1 \in [0, 1]$. Furthermore, we have the requirement that $\rho_1 + \rho_0 < 1$, then $\pi_1 = 1$ will lead to $\rho_1 = P(s = 0|y = 1) = 1 - P(s = 1|y = 1) = 1 - \frac{P(y=1|s=1)P(s=1)}{P(y=1)} = 1 - 0 = 1$

which violates the requirement of $\rho_1 + \rho_0 < 1$. Therefore, $\pi_1 \in [0, 1)$. Similarly, we can prove $\pi_0 \in [0, 1)$. Therefore, we see that both $LB_{y=1}$ and $UB_{y=0}$ are interpolations of $(1 - \rho_1)$ and ρ_0:

$$\rho_0 < LB_{y=1} \leq 1 - \rho_1$$
$$\rho_0 \leq UB_{y=0} < 1 - \rho_1$$

The first equality holds iff $\pi_1 = 0$ and the second equality holds iff $\pi_0 = 0$.

Using Lemma S1, we know that under the condition of $g(x) = g^*(x)$ and non-overlapping support, $g(x) = (1 - \rho_1) \cdot \mathbb{1}[[y = 1]] + \rho_0 \cdot \mathbb{1}[[y = 0]]$. In other words,

$$g(x) \geq LB_{y=1} \Leftrightarrow x \in P$$
$$g(x) \leq UB_{y=0} \Leftrightarrow x \in N$$

Since

$$\begin{cases} \tilde{P}_{y=1} = \{x \in \tilde{P} | g(x) \geq LB_{y=1}\} \\ \tilde{N}_{y=1} = \{x \in \tilde{N} | g(x) \geq LB_{y=1}\} \\ \tilde{P}_{y=0} = \{x \in \tilde{P} | g(x) \leq UB_{y=0}\} \\ \tilde{N}_{y=0} = \{x \in \tilde{N} | g(x) \leq UB_{y=0}\} \end{cases}$$

where $\tilde{P} = \{x | s = 1\}$ and $\tilde{N} = \{x | s = 0\}$, we have

$$\begin{cases} \tilde{P}_{y=1} = \{x \in P | s = 1\}, \tilde{N}_{y=1} = \{x \in P | s = 0\} \\ \tilde{P}_{y=0} = \{x \in N | s = 1\}, \tilde{N}_{y=0} = \{x \in N | s = 0\} \end{cases}$$

1.2 PROOF OF LEMMA 2

We restate Theorem 2 here:

Theorem 2 *When g is ideal, i.e. $g(x) = g^*(x)$ and P and N have non-overlapping support, we have*

$$\hat{\rho}_1^{conf} = \rho_1, \hat{\rho}_0^{conf} = \rho_0$$

Proof: Using the definition of $\hat{\rho}_1^{conf}$ in the main paper:

$$\hat{\rho}_1^{conf} = \frac{|\tilde{N}_{y=1}|}{|\tilde{N}_{y=1}| + |\tilde{P}_{y=1}|}, \ \hat{\rho}_0^{conf} = \frac{|\tilde{P}_{y=0}|}{|\tilde{P}_{y=0}| + |\tilde{N}_{y=0}|}$$

Since $g(x) = g^*(x)$ and P and N have non-overlapping support, using Lemma 1, we know

$$\begin{cases} \tilde{P}_{y=1} = \{x \in P | s = 1\}, \tilde{N}_{y=1} = \{x \in P | s = 0\} \\ \tilde{P}_{y=0} = \{x \in N | s = 1\}, \tilde{N}_{y=0} = \{x \in N | s = 0\} \end{cases}$$

Since $\rho_1 = P(s = 0 | y = 1)$ and $\rho_0 = P(s = 1 | y = 0)$, we immediately have

$$\hat{\rho}_1^{conf} = \frac{|\{x \in P | s = 0\}|}{|P|} = \rho_1, \ \hat{\rho}_0^{conf} = \frac{|\{x \in N | s = 1\}|}{|N|} = \rho_0$$

1.3 PROOF OF LEMMA 3

We rewrite Lemma 3 below:

Lemma 3 *When g is unassuming, i.e., $\Delta g(x) := g(x) - g^*(x)$ can be nonzero, and P and N can have overlapping support, we have*

$$\begin{cases} LB_{y=1} = LB^*_{y=1} + E_{x\in\tilde{P}}[\Delta g(x)] - \frac{(1-\rho_1-\rho_0)^2}{p_{s1}}\Delta p_o \\ UB_{y=0} = UB^*_{y=0} + E_{x\in\tilde{N}}[\Delta g(x)] + \frac{(1-\rho_1-\rho_0)^2}{1-p_{s1}}\Delta p_o \\ \hat{\rho}_1^{conf} = \rho_1 + \frac{1-\rho_1-\rho_0}{|P|-|\Delta P_1|+|\Delta N_1|}|\Delta N_1| \\ \hat{\rho}_0^{conf} = \rho_0 + \frac{1-\rho_1-\rho_0}{|N|-|\Delta N_0|+|\Delta P_0|}|\Delta P_0| \end{cases} \tag{4}$$

where

$$\begin{cases} \Delta p_o := \frac{|P\cap N|}{|P\cup N|} \\ \Delta P_1 = \{x \in P | g(x) < LB_{y=1}\} \\ \Delta N_1 = \{x \in N | g(x) \geq LB_{y=1}\} \\ \Delta P_0 = \{x \in P | g(x) \leq UB_{y=0}\} \\ \Delta N_0 = \{x \in N | g(x) > UB_{y=0}\} \end{cases} \tag{5}$$

Proof: We first calculate $LB_{y=1}$ and $UB_{y=0}$ under unassuming condition, then calculate $\hat{\rho}_i^{conf}$, $i = 0, 1$ under unassuming condition.

Note that Δp_o can also be expressed as

$$\Delta p_o := \frac{|P \cap N|}{|P \cup N|} = P(\hat{y} = 1, y = 0) = P(\hat{y} = 0, y = 1)$$

Here $P(\hat{y} = 1, y = 0) \equiv P(\hat{y} = 1|y = 0)P(y = 0)$, where $P(\hat{y} = 1|y = 0)$ means for a perfect classifier $f^*(x) = P(y = 1|x)$, the expected probability that it will label a $y = 0$ example as positive ($\hat{y} = 1$).

(1) $LB_{y=1}$ and $UB_{y=0}$ under unassuming condition

Firstly, we calculate $LB_{y=1}$ and $UB_{y=0}$ with perfect probability estimation $g^*(x)$, but the support may overlap. Secondly, we allow the probability estimation to be imperfect, superimposed onto the overlapping support condition, and calculate $LB_{y=1}$ and $UB_{y=0}$.

I. Calculating $LB_{y=1}$ and $UB_{y=0}$ when $g(x) = g^*(x)$ and support may overlap

With overlapping support, we no longer have $P(y = 1|x) = \mathbb{1}[[y = 1]]$. Instead, we have

$$\begin{aligned} LB_{y=1} =& E_{x\in\tilde{P}}[g^*(x)] = E_{x\in\tilde{P}}[P(s = 1|x)] \\ =& E_{x\in\tilde{P}}[P(s = 1|x, y = 1)P(y = 1|x) + P(s = 1|x, y = 0)P(y = 0|x)] \\ =& E_{x\in\tilde{P}}[P(s = 1|y = 1)P(y = 1|x) + P(s = 1|y = 0)P(y = 0|x)] \\ =& (1 - \rho_1) \cdot E_{x\in\tilde{P}}[P(y = 1|x)] + \rho_0 \cdot E_{x\in\tilde{P}}[P(y = 0|x)] \\ =& (1 - \rho_1) \cdot P(\hat{y} = 1|s = 1) + \rho_0 \cdot P(\hat{y} = 0|s = 1) \end{aligned}$$

Here $P(\hat{y}=1|s=1)$ can be calculated using Δp_o:

$$\begin{aligned}
P(\hat{y}=1|s=1) &= \frac{P(\hat{y}=1, s=1)}{P(s=1)} \\
&= \frac{P(\hat{y}=1, y=1, s=1) + P(\hat{y}=1, y=0, s=1)}{P(s=1)} \\
&= \frac{P(s=1|y=1)P(\hat{y}=1, y=1) + P(s=1|y=0)P(\hat{y}=1, y=0)}{P(s=1)} \\
&= \frac{(1-\rho_1)(p_{y1}-\Delta p_o) + \rho_0 \Delta p_o}{p_{s1}} \\
&= (1-\pi_1) - \frac{1-\rho_1-\rho_0}{p_{s1}}\Delta p_o
\end{aligned}$$

Hence,

$$P(\hat{y}=0|s=1) = 1 - P(\hat{y}=1|s=1) = \pi_1 + \frac{1-\rho_1-\rho_0}{p_{s1}}\Delta p_o$$

Therefore,

$$\begin{aligned}
LB_{y=1} &= (1-\rho_1)\cdot P(\hat{y}=1|s=1) + \rho_0 \cdot P(\hat{y}=0|s=1) \\
&= (1-\rho_1)\cdot\left((1-\pi_1) - \frac{1-\rho_1-\rho_0}{p_{s1}}\Delta p_o\right) + \rho_0\cdot\left(\pi_1 + \frac{1-\rho_1-\rho_0}{p_{s1}}\Delta p_o\right) \\
&= LB^*_{y=1} - \frac{(1-\rho_1-\rho_0)^2}{p_{s1}}\Delta p_o
\end{aligned} \tag{6}$$

where $LB^*_{y=1}$ is the $LB_{y=1}$ value when $g(x)$ is ideal. We see in Eq. (6) that the overlapping support introduces a non-positive correction to $LB^*_{y=1}$ compared with the ideal condition.

Similarly, we have

$$UB_{y=0} = UB^*_{y=0} + \frac{(1-\rho_1-\rho_0)^2}{1-p_{s1}}\Delta p_o \tag{7}$$

II. Calculating $LB_{y=1}$ and $UB_{y=0}$ when g is unassuming

Define $\Delta g(x) := g(x) - g^*(x)$. When the support may overlap, we have

$$\begin{aligned}
LB_{y=1} &= E_{x\in\tilde{P}}[g(x)] \\
&= E_{x\in\tilde{P}}[g^*(x)] + E_{x\in\tilde{P}}[\Delta g(x)] \\
&= LB^*_{y=1} - \frac{(1-\rho_1-\rho_0)^2}{p_{s1}}\Delta p_o + E_{x\in\tilde{P}}[\Delta g(x)]
\end{aligned} \tag{8}$$

Similarly, we have

$$\begin{aligned}
UB_{y=0} &= E_{x\in\tilde{N}}[g(x)] \\
&= E_{x\in\tilde{N}}[g^*(x)] + E_{x\in\tilde{N}}[\Delta g(x)] \\
&= UB^*_{y=0} + \frac{(1-\rho_1-\rho_0)^2}{1-p_{s1}}\Delta p_o + E_{x\in\tilde{N}}[\Delta g(x)]
\end{aligned} \tag{9}$$

In summary, Eq. (8) (9) give the expressions for $LB_{y=1}$ and $UB_{y=0}$, respectively, when g is unassuming.

(2) $\hat{\rho}_i^{conf}$ under unassuming condition

Now let's calculate $\hat{\rho}_i^{conf}$, $i = 0, 1$. For simplicity, define

$$\begin{cases} PP = \{x \in P | s = 1\} \\ PN = \{x \in P | s = 0\} \\ NP = \{x \in N | s = 1\} \\ NN = \{x \in N | s = 0\} \\ \Delta_{PP_1} = \{x \in PP | g(x) < LB_{y=1}\} \\ \Delta_{NP_1} = \{x \in NP | g(x) \geq LB_{y=1}\} \\ \Delta_{PN_1} = \{x \in PN | g(x) < LB_{y=1}\} \\ \Delta_{NN_1} = \{x \in NN | g(x) \geq LB_{y=1}\} \end{cases} \tag{10}$$

For $\hat{\rho}_1^{conf}$, we have:

$$\hat{\rho}_1^{conf} = \frac{|\tilde{N}_{y=1}|}{|\tilde{P}_{y=1}| + |\tilde{N}_{y=1}|}$$

Here

$$\begin{aligned} \tilde{P}_{y=1} &= \{x \in \tilde{P} | g(x) \geq LB_{y=1}\} \\ &= \{x \in PP | g(x) \geq LB_{y=1}\} \cup \{x \in NP | g(x) \geq LB_{y=1}\} \\ &= (PP \setminus \Delta_{PP_1}) \cup \Delta_{NP_1} \end{aligned}$$

Similarly, we have

$$\tilde{N}_{y=1} = (PN \setminus \Delta_{PN_1}) \cup \Delta_{NN_1}$$

Therefore

$$\begin{aligned} \hat{\rho}_1^{conf} &= \frac{|PN| - |\Delta_{PN_1}| + |\Delta_{NN_1}|}{[(|PP| - |\Delta_{PP_1}|) + (|PN| - |\Delta_{PN_1}|)] + (|\Delta_{NN_1}| + |\Delta_{NP_1}|)} \\ &= \frac{|PN| - |\Delta_{PN_1}| + |\Delta_{NN_1}|}{|P| - |\Delta P_1| + |\Delta N_1|} \end{aligned} \tag{11}$$

where in the second equality we have used the definition of ΔP_1 and ΔN_1 in Eq. (5).

Using the definition of ρ_1, we have

$$\begin{aligned} \frac{|PN| - |\Delta_{PN_1}|}{|P| - |\Delta P_1|} &= \frac{|\{x \in PN | g(x) \geq LB_{y=1}\}|}{|\{x \in P | g(x) \geq LB_{y=1}\}|} \\ &= \frac{P(x \in PN, g(x) \geq LB_{y=1})}{P(x \in P, g(x) \geq LB_{y=1})} \\ &= \frac{P(x \in PN | x \in P, g(x) \geq LB_{y=1}) \cdot P(x \in P, g(x) \geq LB_{y=1})}{P(x \in P, g(x) \geq LB_{y=1})} \\ &= \frac{P(x \in PN | x \in P) \cdot P(x \in P, g(x) \geq LB_{y=1})}{P(x \in P, g(x) \geq LB_{y=1})} \\ &= \rho_1 \end{aligned}$$

Here we have used the property of CNP that $(s \perp\!\!\!\perp x)|y$, leading to $P(x \in PN | x \in P, g(x) \geq LB_{y=1}) = P(x \in PN | x \in P) = \rho_1$.

Similarly, we have

$$\frac{|\Delta_{NN_1}|}{|\Delta N_1|} = 1 - \rho_0$$

Combining with Eq. (11), we have

$$\hat{\rho}_1^{conf} = \rho_1 + \frac{1 - \rho_1 - \rho_0}{|P| - |\Delta P_1| + |\Delta N_1|}|\Delta N_1| \tag{12}$$

Similarly, we have

$$\hat{\rho}_0^{conf} = \rho_0 + \frac{1 - \rho_1 - \rho_0}{|N| - |\Delta N_0| + |\Delta P_0|}|\Delta P_0| \tag{13}$$

From the two equations above, we see that

$$\hat{\rho}_1^{conf} \geq \rho_1, \hat{\rho}_0^{conf} \geq \rho_0 \tag{14}$$

In other words, $\hat{\rho}_i^{conf}$ is an ***upper bound*** of ρ_i, $i = 0, 1$. The equality for $\hat{\rho}_1^{conf}$ holds if $|\Delta N_1| = 0$. The equality for $\hat{\rho}_0^{conf}$ holds if $|\Delta P_0| = 0$.

1.4 PROOF OF LEMMA 4

Let's restate Theorem 4 below:

Theorem 4 *Given non-overlapping support condition,*
If $\forall x \in N, \Delta g(x) < LB_{y=1} - \rho_0$, *then* $\hat{\rho}_1^{conf} = \rho_1$.
If $\forall x \in P, \Delta g(x) > -(1 - \rho_1 - UB_{y=0})$, *then* $\hat{\rho}_0^{conf} = \rho_0$.

Theorem 4 directly follows from Eq. (12) and (13). Assuming non-overlapping support, we have $g^*(x) = P(s = 1|x) = (1 - \rho_1) \cdot \mathbb{1}[[y = 1]] + \rho_0 \cdot \mathbb{1}[[y = 0]]$. In other words, the contribution of overlapping support to $|\Delta N_1|$ and $|\Delta P_0|$ is 0. The only source of deviation comes from imperfect $g(x)$.

For the first half of the theorem, since $\forall x \in N, \Delta g(x) < LB_{y=1} - \rho_0$, we have $\forall x \in N, g(x) = \Delta g(x) + g^*(x) < (LB_{y=1} - \rho_0) + \rho_0 = LB_{y=1}$, then $|\Delta N_1| = |\{x \in N | g(x) \geq LB_{y=1}\}| = 0$, so we have $\hat{\rho}_1^{conf} = \rho_1$.

Similarly, for the second half of the theorem, since $\forall x \in P, \Delta g(x) > -(1 - \rho_1 - UB_{y=0})$, then $|\Delta P_0| = |\{x \in P | g(x) \leq UB_{y=0}\}| = 0$, so we have $\hat{\rho}_0^{conf} = \rho_0$.

1.5 PROOF OF LEMMA 5

Theorem 5 reads as follows:

Theorem 5 *If g range separates P and N and $\hat{\rho}_i = \rho_i$, $i = 0, 1$, then for any classifier f_θ and any bounded loss function $l(\hat{y}_i, y_i)$, we have*

$$R_{\tilde{l},\mathcal{D}_\rho}(f_\theta) = R_{l,\mathcal{D}}(f_\theta) \tag{15}$$

where $\tilde{l}(\hat{y}_i, s_i)$ is Rank Pruning's loss function given by

$$\tilde{l}(\hat{y}_i, s_i) = \frac{1}{1-\hat{\rho}_1} l(\hat{y}_i, s_i) \cdot \mathbb{1}[[x_i \in \tilde{P}_{conf}]] + \frac{1}{1-\hat{\rho}_0} l(\hat{y}_i, s_i) \cdot \mathbb{1}[[x_i \in \tilde{N}_{conf}]] \tag{16}$$

and $\tilde{P}_{conf}$ and $\tilde{N}_{conf}$ are given by

$$\tilde{P}_{conf} := \{x \in \tilde{P} \mid g(x) \geq k_1\}, \tilde{N}_{conf} := \{x \in \tilde{N} \mid g(x) \leq k_0\} \tag{17}$$

where k_1 is the $(\hat{\pi}_1 |\tilde{P}|)^{th}$ smallest $g(x)$ for $x \in \tilde{P}$ and k_0 is the $(\hat{\pi}_0 |\tilde{N}|)^{th}$ largest $g(x)$ for $x \in \tilde{N}$

Proof:

Since $\tilde{P}$ and $\tilde{N}$ are constructed from P and N with noise rates π_1 and π_0 using the class-conditional extension of the Classification Noise Process (Angluin & Laird, 1988), we have

$$\begin{cases} P = PP \cup PN \\ N = NP \cup NN \\ \tilde{P} = PP \cup NP \\ \tilde{N} = PN \cup NN \end{cases} \tag{18}$$

where

$$\begin{cases} PP = \{x \in P | s = 1\} \\ PN = \{x \in P | s = 0\} \\ NP = \{x \in N | s = 1\} \\ NN = \{x \in N | s = 0\} \end{cases} \tag{19}$$

satisfying

$$\begin{cases} PP \sim PN \sim P \\ NP \sim NN \sim N \\ \frac{|NP|}{|\tilde{P}|} = \pi_1, \frac{|PP|}{|\tilde{P}|} = 1 - \pi_1 \\ \frac{|PN|}{|\tilde{N}|} = \pi_0, \frac{|NN|}{|\tilde{N}|} = 1 - \pi_0 \\ \frac{|PN|}{|P|} = \rho_1, \frac{|PP|}{|P|} = 1 - \rho_1 \\ \frac{|NP|}{|N|} = \rho_0, \frac{|NN|}{|N|} = 1 - \rho_0 \end{cases} \tag{20}$$

Here the $\sim$ means obeying the same distribution.

Since g range separates P and N, there exists a real number z such that $\forall x_1 \in P$ and $\forall x_0 \in N$, we have $g(x_1) > z > g(x_0)$. Since $P = PP \cup PN, N = NP \cup NN$, we have

$$\forall x \in PP, g(x) > z;\ \forall x \in PN, g(x) > z;$$
$$\forall x \in NP, g(x) < z;\ \forall x \in NN, g(x) < z \tag{21}$$

Since $\hat{\rho}_1 = \rho_1$ and $\hat{\rho}_0 = \rho_0$, we have

$$\begin{cases} \hat{\pi}_1 = \frac{\hat{\rho}_0}{p_{s1}} \frac{1-p_{s1}-\hat{\rho}_1}{1-\hat{\rho}_1-\hat{\rho}_0} = \frac{\rho_0}{p_{s1}} \frac{1-p_{s1}-\rho_1}{1-\rho_1-\rho_0} = \pi_1 \equiv \frac{\rho_0|N|}{|\tilde{P}|} \\ \hat{\pi}_0 = \frac{\hat{\rho}_1}{1-p_{s1}} \frac{p_{s1}-\hat{\rho}_0}{1-\hat{\rho}_1-\hat{\rho}_0} = \frac{\rho_1}{1-p_{s1}} \frac{p_{s1}-\rho_0}{1-\rho_1-\rho_0} = \pi_0 \equiv \frac{\rho_1|P|}{|\tilde{N}|} \end{cases} \tag{22}$$

Therefore, $\hat{\pi}_1|\tilde{P}| = \pi_1|\tilde{P}| = \rho_0|N|$, $\hat{\pi}_0|\tilde{N}| = \pi_0|\tilde{N}| = \rho_1|P|$. Using $\tilde{P}_{conf}$ and $\tilde{N}_{conf}$'s definition in Eq. (17), and $g(x)$'s property in Eq. (21), we have

$$\tilde{P}_{conf} = PP \sim P, \tilde{N}_{conf} = NN \sim N \tag{23}$$

Hence P_{conf} and N_{conf} can be seen as a uniform downsampling of P and N, with a downsampling ratio of $(1-\rho_1)$ for P and $(1-\rho_0)$ for N. Then according to Eq. (16), the loss function $\tilde{l}(\hat{y}_i, s_i)$ essentially sees a fraction of $(1-\rho_1)$ examples in P and a fraction of $(1-\rho_0)$ examples in N, with a final reweighting to restore the class balance. Then for any classifier f_θ that maps $x \to \hat{y}$ and any bounded loss function $l(\hat{y}_i, y_i)$, we have

$$\begin{aligned}
&R_{\tilde{l},\mathcal{D}_\rho}(f_\theta) \\
&= E_{(x,s)\sim\mathcal{D}_\rho}[\tilde{l}(f_\theta(x), s)] \\
&= \frac{1}{1-\hat{\rho}_1} \cdot E_{(x,s)\sim\mathcal{D}_\rho}\left[l(f_\theta(x), s) \cdot \mathbb{1}[[x \in \tilde{P}_{conf}]]\right] + \frac{1}{1-\hat{\rho}_0} \cdot E_{(x,s)\sim\mathcal{D}_\rho}\left[l(f_\theta(x), s) \cdot \mathbb{1}[[x \in \tilde{N}_{conf}]]\right] \\
&= \frac{1}{1-\rho_1} \cdot E_{(x,s)\sim\mathcal{D}_\rho}\left[l(f_\theta(x), s) \cdot \mathbb{1}[[x \in \tilde{P}_{conf}]]\right] + \frac{1}{1-\rho_0} \cdot E_{(x,s)\sim\mathcal{D}_\rho}\left[l(f_\theta(x), s) \cdot \mathbb{1}[[x \in \tilde{N}_{conf}]]\right] \\
&= \frac{1}{1-\rho_1} \cdot E_{(x,s)\sim\mathcal{D}_\rho}\left[l(f_\theta(x), s) \cdot \mathbb{1}[[x \in PP]]\right] + \frac{1}{1-\rho_0} \cdot E_{(x,s)\sim\mathcal{D}_\rho}\left[l(f_\theta(x), s) \cdot \mathbb{1}[[x \in NN]]\right] \\
&= \frac{1}{1-\rho_1} \cdot (1-\rho_1) \cdot E_{(x,y)\sim\mathcal{D}}\left[l(f_\theta(x), y) \cdot \mathbb{1}[[x \in P]]\right] + \\
&\quad \frac{1}{1-\rho_0} \cdot (1-\rho_0) \cdot E_{(x,y)\sim\mathcal{D}}\left[l(f_\theta(x), y) \cdot \mathbb{1}[[x \in N]]\right] \\
&= E_{(x,y)\sim\mathcal{D}}\left[l(f_\theta(x), y) \cdot \mathbb{1}[[x \in P]] + l(f_\theta(x), y) \cdot \mathbb{1}[[x \in N]]\right] \\
&= E_{(x,y)\sim\mathcal{D}}\left[l(f_\theta(x), y)\right] \\
&= R_{l,\mathcal{D}}(f_\theta)
\end{aligned}$$

Therefore, we see that the expected risk for Rank Pruning with corrupted labels, is exactly the same as the expected risk for the true labels, for any bounded loss function l and classifier f_θ. The reweighting ensures that after pruning, the two sets still remain unbiased w.r.t. to the true dataset.

Since the ideal condition is more strict than the range separability condition, we immediately have that when g is ideal and $\hat{\rho}_i = \rho_i, i = 0, 1$, $R_{\tilde{l},\mathcal{D}_\rho}(f_\theta) = R_{l,\mathcal{D}}(f_\theta)$ for any f_θ and bounded loss function l.

2 ADDITIONAL FIGURES

Figure S1 shows the sum of absolute difference between theoretically estimated $\hat{\rho}_i^{thry}$ (Eq. (8) in main paper) and empirical $\hat{\rho}_i$: $|\hat{\rho}_1 - \hat{\rho}_1^{thry}| + |\hat{\rho}_0 - \hat{\rho}_0^{thry}|$. The deviation of the theoretical and empirical estimates reflects the assumption that we have infinite examples, whereas empirically, the number of examples is finite.

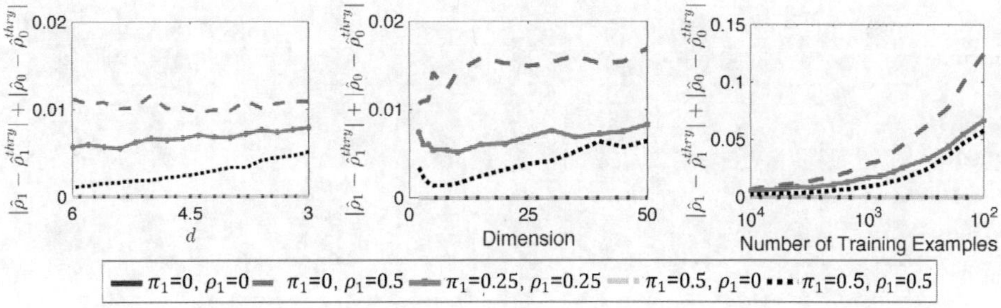

Figure S 1: Sum of absolute difference between theoretically estimated $\hat{\rho}_i^{thry}$ and empirical $\hat{\rho}_i$, $i = 0, 1$, with five different (π_1, ρ_1), for varying separability d, dimension, and number of training examples. Note that no figure exists for percent random noise because the theoretical estimates in Eq. (4) do not address added noise examples. The default parameters are: $d = 4$, 2 dimensional input, 0% random noise, and 5000 training examples with a fraction of $p_{y1} = 0.2$ examples as positive. The lines are an average of 200 trials.

Figure S2 shows the Rank Pruning's noise rate estimation of $\hat{\pi}_1$ for the MNIST dataset using a logistic regression classifier, for varying amount of ($\hat{\pi}_1$,$\hat{\rho}_1$), averaging over 10 digits.

Figure S3 shows the average image for each digit for the binary classification problem "1" or "not 1" in MNIST with logistic regression and high noise ($\rho_1 = 0.5, \pi_1 = 0.5$). The number on the bottom and on the right counts the total number of examples (images). From the figure we see that RP makes few mistakes, and when it does, the mistakes vary greatly in image from the typical digit.

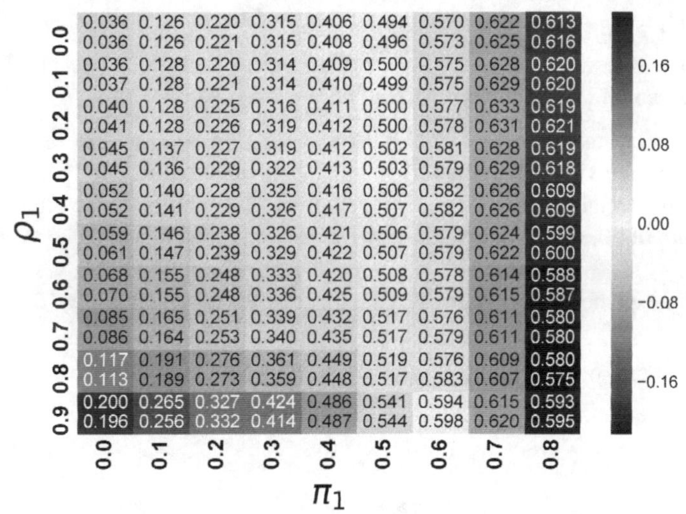

Figure S 2: Rank Pruning $\hat{\pi}_1$ estimation consistency, averaged over all digits in MNIST. Color depicts $\hat{\pi}_1$ - π_1 with $\hat{\rho}_1$ (upper) and theoretical $\hat{\pi}_1^{thry}$ (lower) in each block.

3 ADDITIONAL TABLES

Here we provide additional tables for the comparison of error, Precision-Recall AUC (AUC-PR, Davis & Goadrich (2006)), and F1 score for the algorithms *RP*, *Nat13*, *Elk08*, *Liu16* with ρ_1, ρ_0 given to all methods

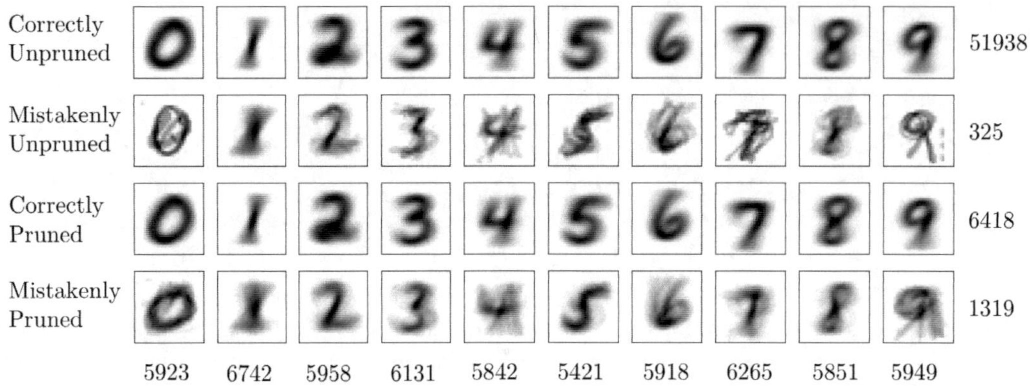

Figure S 3: Average image for each digit for the binary classification problem "1" or "not 1" in MNIST with logistic regression and significant mislabeling ($\rho_1 = 0.5, \pi_1 = 0.5$). The right and bottom numbers count the total number of example images averaged in the corresponding row or column.

for fair comparison. Additionally, we provide the performance of the ground truth classifier (*true*) trained with uncorrupted labels (X, y), as well as the complete Rank Pruning algorithm (RP_ρ) trained using the noise rates estimated by Rank Pruning. The top model scores are in bold with RP_ρ in red if its performance is better than non-RP models. The $\pi_1 = 0$ quadrant in each table represents the "PU learning" case of $\tilde{P}\tilde{N}$ learning.

Whenever $g(x) = P(\hat{s} = 1|x)$ is estimated for any algorithm, we use a 3-fold cross-validation to estimate the probability $g(x)$. For improved performance, a higher fold may be used.

For the logistic regression classifier, we use scikit-learn's LogisticRegression class (scikit learn (2016)) with default settings (L2 regularization with inverse strength $C = 1$).

For the convolutional neural networks (CNN), for MNIST we use the structure in Chollet (2016b) and for CIFAR-10, we use the structure in Chollet (2016a). A 10% holdout set is used to monitor the weighted validation loss (using the sample weight given by each algorithm) and ends training when there is no decrease for 10 epochs, with a maximum of 50 epochs for MNIST and 150 epochs for CIFAR-10.

The following list comprises the MNIST and CIFAR-10 experimental result tables for error, AUC-PR and F1 score metrics:

Table S1: Error for MNIST with logisitic regression as classifier.

Table S2: AUC-PR for MNIST with logisitic regression as classifier.

Table S3: Error for MNIST with CNN as classifier.

Table S4: AUC-PR for MNIST with CNN as classifier.

Table S5: F1 score for CIFAR-10 with logistic regression as classifier.

Table S6: Error for CIFAR-10 with logistic regression as classifier.

Table S7: AUC-PR for CIFAR-10 with logistic regression as classifier.

Table S8: Error for CIFAR-10 with CNN as classifier.

Table S9: AUC-PR for CIFAR-10 with CNN as classifier.

Due to its sensitivity to imperfect probability estimation, here *Liu16* always predicts all labels to be positive or negative, resulting in the same metric score for every digit/image in each scenario. Since $p_{y1} \simeq 0.1$, when predicting all labels as positive, *Liu16* has an F1 score of 0.182, error of 0.90, and AUC-PR of 0.55; when predicting all labels as negative, *Liu16* has an F1 score of 0.0, error of 0.1, and AUC-PR of 0.55.

4 ADDITIONAL RELATED WORK

In this section we include tangentially related work which was unable to make it into the final manuscript.

4.1 ONE-CLASS CLASSIFICATION

One-class classification (Moya et al., 1993) is distinguished from binary classification by a training set containing examples from only one class, making it useful for outlier and novelty detection (Hempstalk et al., 2008). This can be framed as $\tilde{P}\tilde{N}$ learning when outliers take the form of mislabeled examples. The predominant approach, one-class SVM, fits a hyper-boundary around the training class (Platt et al., 1999), but often performs poorly due to boundary over-sensitivity (Manevitz & Yousef, 2002) and fails when the training class contains mislabeled examples.

4.2 $\tilde{P}\tilde{N}$ LEARNING FOR IMAGE RECOGNITION AND DEEP LEARNING

Variations of $\tilde{P}\tilde{N}$ learning have been used in the context of machine vision to improve robustness to mislabeling (Xiao et al., 2015). In a face recognition task with 90% of non-faces mislabeled as faces, a bagging model combined with consistency voting was used to remove images with poor voting consistency (Angelova et al., 2005). However, no theoretical justification was provided. In the context of deep learning, consistency of predictions for inputs with mislabeling enforces can be enforced by combining a typical cross-entropy loss with an auto-encoder loss (Reed et al., 2015). This method enforces label consistency by constraining the network to uncover the input examples given the output prediction, but is restricted in architecture and generality.

Table S 1: Comparison of **error** for one-vs-rest MNIST (averaged over all digits) using a **logistic regression** classifier. Except for RP_ρ, ρ_1, ρ_0 are given to all methods. Top model scores are in bold with RP_ρ in red if better (smaller) than non-RP models.

	π_1 = 0			π_1 = 0.25				π_1 = 0.5				π_1 = 0.75			
MODEL, ρ_1 =	**0.25**	**0.50**	**0.75**	**0.00**	**0.25**	**0.50**	**0.75**	**0.00**	**0.25**	**0.50**	**0.75**	**0.00**	**0.25**	**0.50**	**0.75**
TRUE	0.020	0.020	0.020	0.020	0.020	0.020	0.020	0.020	0.020	0.020	0.020	0.020	0.020	0.020	0.020
RP$_\rho$	**0.023**	**0.025**	**0.031**	**0.024**	**0.025**	**0.027**	**0.038**	0.040	0.037	0.039	0.049	0.140	0.128	0.133	0.151
RP	**0.022**	**0.025**	**0.031**	**0.021**	**0.024**	**0.027**	**0.035**	**0.023**	**0.027**	**0.031**	**0.043**	**0.028**	**0.036**	**0.045**	0.069
NAT13	0.025	0.030	0.038	0.025	0.029	0.034	0.042	0.030	0.033	0.038	0.047	0.035	0.039	0.046	**0.067**
ELK08	0.025	0.030	0.038	0.026	0.028	0.032	0.042	0.030	0.031	0.035	0.051	0.092	0.093	0.123	0.189
LIU16	0.187	0.098	0.100	0.100	0.738	0.738	0.419	0.100	0.820	0.821	0.821	0.098	0.760	0.741	0.820

Table S 2: Comparison of **AUC-PR** for one-vs-rest MNIST (averaged over all digits) using a **logistic regression** classifier. Except for RP_ρ, ρ_1, ρ_0 are given to all methods. Top model scores are in bold with RP_ρ in red if greater than non-RP models.

	$\pi_1 = 0$			$\pi_1 = 0.25$				$\pi_1 = 0.5$				$\pi_1 = 0.75$			
MODEL, $\rho_1 =$	**0.25**	**0.50**	**0.75**	**0.00**	**0.25**	**0.50**	**0.75**	**0.00**	**0.25**	**0.50**	**0.75**	**0.00**	**0.25**	**0.50**	**0.75**
TRUE	0.935	0.935	0.935	0.935	0.935	0.935	0.935	0.935	0.935	0.935	0.935	0.935	0.935	0.935	0.935
RP_ρ	0.921	0.913	0.882	0.928	0.920	0.906	0.853	0.903	0.902	0.879	0.803	0.851	0.835	0.788	0.640
RP	**0.922**	**0.913**	**0.882**	**0.930**	**0.921**	**0.906**	**0.858**	**0.922**	**0.903**	**0.883**	**0.811**	**0.893**	**0.841**	**0.799**	0.621
NAT13	**0.922**	0.908	0.878	0.918	0.909	0.890	0.839	0.899	0.892	0.862	0.794	0.863	0.837	0.784	**0.645**
ELK08	0.921	0.903	0.864	0.917	0.908	0.884	0.821	0.898	0.892	0.861	0.763	0.852	0.837	0.772	0.579
LIU16	0.498	0.549	0.550	0.550	0.500	0.550	0.505	0.550	0.550	0.550	0.549	0.503	0.512	0.550	0.550

Table S 3: Comparison of **error** for one-vs-rest MNIST (averaged over all digits) using a **CNN** classifier. Except for RP_ρ, ρ_1, ρ_0 are given to all methods. Top model scores are in bold with RP_ρ in red if better (smaller) than non-RP models.

		$\pi_1 = 0$, $\rho_1 = 0.5$					$\pi_1 = 0.25$, $\rho_1 = 0.25$					$\pi_1 = 0.5$, $\rho_1 = 0$					$\pi_1 = 0.5$, $\rho_1 = 0.5$				
IMAGE	**TRUE**	**RP_ρ**	**RP**	**NAT13**	**ELK08**	**LIU16**	**RP_ρ**	**RP**	**NAT13**	**ELK08**	**LIU16**	**RP_ρ**	**RP**	**NAT13**	**ELK08**	**LIU16**	**RP_ρ**	**RP**	**NAT13**	**ELK08**	**LIU16**
0	0.0013	0.0018	**0.0023**	0.0045	0.0047	0.9020	0.0017	**0.0016**	0.0034	0.0036	0.9020	0.0017	**0.0016**	0.0031	0.0026	0.0029	0.0021	**0.0022**	0.0116	0.0069	0.9020
1	0.0015	0.0022	**0.0020**	0.0025	0.0034	0.8865	0.0019	**0.0019**	0.0035	0.0030	0.8865	0.0023	0.0020	0.0018	**0.0016**	0.0023	0.0025	**0.0025**	0.0036	0.0027	0.8865
2	0.0027	0.0054	**0.0049**	0.0057	0.0062	0.8968	0.0032	**0.0035**	0.0045	0.0051	0.8968	0.0030	0.0029	0.0031	0.0029	**0.0024**	0.0059	**0.0050**	0.0066	0.0083	0.8968
3	0.0020	0.0032	**0.0032**	0.0055	0.0038	0.8990	0.0029	**0.0029**	0.0043	0.0043	0.8990	0.0021	0.0027	**0.0023**	**0.0023**	0.0032	0.0038	**0.0042**	0.0084	0.0057	0.8990
4	0.0012	0.0037	0.0040	**0.0038**	0.0044	0.9018	0.0029	**0.0025**	0.0055	0.0069	0.9018	0.0026	0.0020	**0.0019**	0.0021	0.0030	0.0044	**0.0035**	0.0086	0.0077	0.9018
5	0.0019	0.0032	**0.0035**	0.0039	0.0038	0.9108	0.0027	**0.0031**	0.0062	0.0060	0.9108	0.0021	0.0024	0.0024	0.0028	**0.0023**	0.0061	**0.0056**	0.0066	0.0074	0.9108
6	0.0021	0.0027	**0.0028**	0.0053	0.0035	0.9042	0.0028	**0.0025**	0.0042	0.0036	0.9042	0.0029	0.0029	**0.0022**	0.0024	0.0028	0.0032	**0.0035**	0.0098	0.0075	0.9042
7	0.0026	0.0039	**0.0041**	0.0066	0.0103	0.8972	0.0050	**0.0052**	0.0058	0.0058	0.8972	0.0049	0.0040	**0.0030**	0.0037	0.0035	0.0054	**0.0064**	0.0113	0.0085	0.8972
8	0.0022	0.0047	**0.0043**	0.0106	0.0063	0.9026	0.0034	**0.0036**	0.0062	0.0091	0.9026	0.0036	**0.0030**	0.0035	0.0041	0.0032	0.0044	**0.0048**	0.0234	0.0077	0.9026
9	0.0036	0.0067	**0.0052**	0.0056	0.0124	0.8991	0.0048	**0.0051**	0.0065	0.0064	0.8991	0.0048	0.0050	0.0051	**0.0043**	0.0059	0.0081	0.0114	0.0131	**0.0112**	0.8991
AVG	0.0021	0.0038	**0.0036**	0.0054	0.0059	0.9000	0.0031	**0.0032**	0.0050	0.0054	0.9000	0.0030	**0.0028**	**0.0028**	0.0029	0.0032	0.0046	**0.0049**	0.0103	0.0074	0.9000

Table S 4: Comparison of **AUC-PR** for one-vs-rest MNIST (averaged over all digits) using a **CNN** classifier. Except for RP_ρ, ρ_1, ρ_0 are given to all methods. Top model scores are in bold with RP_ρ in red if greater than non-RP models.

		$\pi_1 = 0$, $\rho_1 = 0.5$					$\pi_1 = 0.25$, $\rho_1 = 0.25$					$\pi_1 = 0.5$, $\rho_1 = 0$					$\pi_1 = 0.5$, $\rho_1 = 0.5$				
IMAGE	**TRUE**	**RP_ρ**	**RP**	**NAT13**	**ELK08**	**LIU16**	**RP_ρ**	**RP**	**NAT13**	**ELK08**	**LIU16**	**RP_ρ**	**RP**	**NAT13**	**ELK08**	**LIU16**	**RP_ρ**	**RP**	**NAT13**	**ELK08**	**LIU16**
0	0.9998	0.9992	**0.9990**	0.9986	0.9982	0.5490	0.9996	**0.9996**	0.9986	0.9979	0.5490	0.9989	**0.9995**	0.9976	0.9979	0.9956	0.9984	**0.9982**	0.9963	0.9928	0.5490
1	0.9999	0.9995	**0.9995**	0.9976	0.9974	0.5568	0.9996	0.9993	**0.9995**	**0.9995**	0.5568	0.9995	**0.9998**	0.9982	0.9972	0.9965	0.9995	**0.9994**	0.9978	0.9985	0.5568
2	0.9994	0.9971	**0.9969**	0.9917	0.9942	0.5516	0.9980	**0.9977**	0.9971	0.9945	0.5516	0.9988	**0.9992**	0.9958	0.9934	0.9940	0.9938	**0.9947**	0.9847	0.9873	0.5516
3	0.9996	0.9986	**0.9987**	0.9983	0.9984	0.5505	0.9991	**0.9989**	0.9982	0.9980	0.5505	0.9993	**0.9994**	0.9991	0.9971	0.9974	0.9969	**0.9959**	0.9951	**0.9959**	0.5505
4	0.9997	0.9982	**0.9989**	0.9939	0.9988	0.0891	0.9992	**0.9991**	0.9976	0.9965	0.5491	0.9994	**0.9996**	0.9985	0.9978	0.9986	0.9983	**0.9977**	0.9961	0.9919	0.5491
5	0.9993	0.9982	**0.9976**	0.9969	0.9956	0.5446	0.9986	**0.9987**	0.9983	0.9979	0.5446	0.9984	**0.9982**	0.9971	0.9963	0.9929	0.9958	**0.9965**	0.9946	0.9934	0.5446
6	0.9987	0.9976	**0.9970**	0.9928	0.9931	0.5479	0.9974	**0.9980**	0.9956	0.9959	0.5479	0.9968	**0.9983**	0.9933	0.9950	0.9905	0.9964	0.9957	0.9942	**0.9961**	0.5479
7	0.9989	0.9973	**0.9972**	0.9965	0.9944	0.0721	0.9968	0.9973	0.9966	**0.9979**	0.5514	0.9969	**0.9983**	0.9961	0.9958	0.9974	0.9933	**0.9937**	0.9896	0.9886	0.5514
8	0.9996	0.9974	**0.9964**	**0.9964**	0.9946	0.5487	0.9981	**0.9981**	0.9973	0.9971	0.5487	**0.9983**	0.9988	0.9984	0.9976	**0.9989**	0.9976	**0.9975**	0.9873	0.9893	0.5487
9	0.9979	0.9931	**0.9951**	0.9901	0.9922	0.5504	0.9935	**0.9951**	0.9933	0.9920	0.5504	0.9961	**0.9951**	0.9924	0.9922	0.9912	0.9877	**0.9876**	0.9819	0.9828	0.5504
AVG	0.9993	0.9976	**0.9976**	0.9953	0.9957	0.4561	0.9980	**0.9982**	0.9972	0.9967	0.5500	0.9983	**0.9986**	0.9966	0.9960	0.9953	0.9958	**0.9957**	0.9918	0.9917	0.5500

Table S 5: Comparison of **F1 score** for one-vs-rest CIFAR-10 (averaged over all images) using a **logistic regression** classifier. Except for RP_ρ, ρ_1, ρ_0 are given to all methods. Top model scores are in bold with RP_ρ in red if greater than non-RP models.

		$\pi_1 = 0$, $\rho_1 = 0.5$					$\pi_1 = 0.25$, $\rho_1 = 0.25$					$\pi_1 = 0.5$, $\rho_1 = 0$					$\pi_1 = 0.5$, $\rho_1 = 0.5$				
IMAGE	TRUE	RP_ρ	RP	NAT13	ELK08	LIU16	RP_ρ	RP	NAT13	ELK08	LIU16	RP_ρ	RP	NAT13	ELK08	LIU16	RP_ρ	RP	NAT13	ELK08	LIU16
PLANE	0.272	0.311	**0.252**	0.217	0.220	0.182	0.329	**0.275**	0.222	0.224	0.182	0.330	**0.265**	0.231	0.259	0.0	0.266	**0.188**	0.183	0.187	0.182
AUTO	0.374	0.389	**0.355**	0.318	0.320	0.182	0.388	**0.368**	0.321	0.328	0.182	0.372	**0.355**	0.308	0.341	0.0	0.307	0.287	0.287	**0.297**	0.182
BIRD	0.136	0.241	0.167	0.143	0.136	**0.182**	0.248	**0.185**	0.137	0.137	0.182	0.258	**0.147**	0.100	0.126	0.0	0.206	0.153	0.132	0.150	**0.182**
CAT	0.122	0.246	0.170	0.141	0.150	**0.182**	0.232	0.163	0.112	0.127	**0.182**	0.241	**0.125**	0.068	0.103	0.0	0.209	0.148	0.119	0.157	**0.182**
DEER	0.166	0.250	**0.184**	0.153	0.164	0.182	0.259	0.175	0.146	0.163	**0.182**	0.259	**0.177**	0.126	0.164	0.0	0.222	0.162	0.132	0.164	**0.182**
DOG	0.139	0.245	0.174	0.146	0.148	**0.182**	0.262	0.171	0.115	0.126	**0.182**	0.254	**0.152**	0.075	0.120	0.0	0.203	0.151	0.128	0.137	**0.182**
FROG	0.317	0.322	**0.315**	0.289	0.281	0.182	0.350	**0.319**	0.283	0.299	0.182	0.346	**0.305**	0.239	0.279	0.0	0.308	0.252	0.244	**0.269**	0.182
HORSE	0.300	0.300	**0.299**	0.283	0.263	0.182	0.334	**0.313**	0.272	0.281	0.182	0.322	**0.310**	0.260	0.292	0.0	0.275	**0.258**	0.240	0.245	0.182
SHIP	0.322	0.343	**0.322**	0.297	0.272	0.182	0.385	**0.319**	0.287	0.289	0.182	0.350	**0.303**	0.250	0.293	0.0	0.304	**0.248**	0.230	0.237	0.182
TRUCK	0.330	0.359	**0.323**	0.273	0.261	0.182	0.369	**0.327**	0.293	0.290	0.182	0.343	**0.302**	0.278	0.299	0.0	0.313	0.246	0.252	**0.262**	0.182
AVG	0.248	0.301	**0.256**	0.226	0.221	0.182	0.316	**0.262**	0.219	0.226	0.182	0.308	**0.244**	0.194	0.228	0.000	0.261	0.209	0.195	**0.210**	0.182

Table S 6: Comparison of **error** for one-vs-rest CIFAR-10 (averaged over all images) using a **logistic regression** classifier. Except for RP_ρ, ρ_1, ρ_0 are given to all methods. Top model scores are in bold with RP_ρ in red if better (smaller) than non-RP models. Here the logistic regression classifier severely underfits CIFAR, resulting in Rank Pruning pruning out some correctly labeled examples that "confuse" the classifier, hence in this scenario, RP and RP_ρ generally have slightly smaller precision, much higher recall, and hence larger F1 scores than other models and even the ground truth classifier (Table S5). Due to the class inbalance ($p_{y1} = 0.1$) and their larger recall, RP and RP_ρ here have larger error than the other models.

		$\pi_1 = 0$, $\rho_1 = 0.5$					$\pi_1 = 0.25$, $\rho_1 = 0.25$					$\pi_1 = 0.5$, $\rho_1 = 0$					$\pi_1 = 0.5$, $\rho_1 = 0.5$				
IMAGE	TRUE	RP_ρ	RP	NAT13	ELK08	LIU16	RP_ρ	RP	NAT13	ELK08	LIU16	RP_ρ	RP	NAT13	ELK08	LIU16	RP_ρ	RP	NAT13	ELK08	LIU16
PLANE	0.107	0.287	0.133	0.123	**0.122**	0.900	0.177	0.128	**0.119**	0.123	0.900	0.248	0.124	0.110	0.118	**0.100**	0.202	0.147	**0.142**	0.160	0.900
AUTO	0.099	0.184	0.120	**0.110**	**0.110**	0.900	0.132	0.114	**0.105**	0.109	0.900	0.189	0.110	0.105	0.110	**0.100**	0.159	0.129	**0.125**	0.139	0.900
BIRD	0.117	0.354	0.148	0.133	**0.131**	0.900	0.217	0.135	**0.120**	0.125	0.900	0.277	0.135	0.115	0.123	**0.100**	0.226	0.147	**0.139**	0.158	0.900
CAT	0.114	0.351	0.138	**0.129**	**0.129**	0.900	0.208	0.139	**0.122**	0.125	0.900	0.303	0.132	0.114	0.122	**0.100**	0.225	0.151	**0.141**	0.158	0.900
DEER	0.112	0.336	0.143	**0.128**	0.130	0.900	0.194	0.135	**0.120**	0.122	0.900	0.271	0.133	0.118	0.126	**0.100**	0.209	0.150	**0.147**	0.161	0.900
DOG	0.119	0.370	0.150	**0.136**	0.138	0.900	0.205	0.142	**0.129**	0.132	0.900	0.288	0.135	0.120	0.128	**0.100**	0.229	0.154	**0.147**	0.168	0.900
FROG	0.107	0.228	0.128	**0.117**	**0.117**	0.900	0.155	0.124	**0.113**	0.115	0.900	0.228	0.118	0.110	0.116	**0.100**	0.167	0.137	**0.130**	0.142	0.900
HORSE	0.104	0.251	0.127	**0.114**	0.116	0.900	0.153	0.123	**0.110**	0.112	0.900	0.224	0.116	0.108	0.113	**0.100**	0.178	0.134	**0.129**	0.144	0.900
SHIP	0.112	0.239	0.134	**0.121**	0.126	0.900	0.160	0.131	**0.119**	0.123	0.900	0.236	0.122	0.113	0.120	**0.100**	0.193	0.145	**0.139**	0.159	0.900
TRUCK	0.106	0.210	0.130	**0.121**	0.122	0.900	0.145	0.125	**0.113**	0.117	0.900	0.213	0.121	0.108	0.117	**0.100**	0.165	0.142	**0.134**	0.150	0.900
AVG	0.110	0.281	0.135	**0.123**	0.124	0.900	0.175	0.130	**0.117**	0.120	0.900	0.248	0.125	0.112	0.119	**0.100**	0.195	0.144	**0.137**	0.154	0.900

Table S 7: Comparison of **AUC-PR** for one-vs-rest CIFAR-10 (averaged over all images) using a **logistic regression** classifier. Except for RP_ρ, ρ_1, ρ_0 are given to all methods. Top model scores are in bold with RP_ρ in red if greater than non-RP models. Since $p_{y1} = 0.1$, here *Liu16* always predicts all labels as positive or negative, resulting in a constant AUC-PR of 0.550.

		$\pi_1 = 0$, $\rho_1 = 0.5$					$\pi_1 = 0.25$, $\rho_1 = 0.25$					$\pi_1 = 0.5$, $\rho_1 = 0$					$\pi_1 = 0.5$, $\rho_1 = 0.5$				
IMAGE	TRUE	RP_ρ	RP	NAT13	ELK08	LIU16	RP_ρ	RP	NAT13	ELK08	LIU16	RP_ρ	RP	NAT13	ELK08	LIU16	RP_ρ	RP	NAT13	ELK08	LIU16
PLANE	0.288	0.225	0.224	0.225	0.207	**0.550**	0.261	0.235	0.225	0.217	**0.550**	0.285	0.251	0.245	0.248	**0.550**	0.196	0.171	0.171	0.159	**0.550**
AUTO	0.384	0.350	0.317	0.312	0.316	**0.550**	0.342	0.335	0.331	0.331	**0.550**	0.328	0.348	0.334	0.333	**0.550**	0.256	0.257	0.259	0.261	**0.550**
BIRD	0.198	0.160	0.169	0.166	0.161	**0.550**	0.188	0.185	0.179	0.177	**0.550**	0.186	0.173	0.174	0.175	**0.550**	0.150	0.154	0.150	0.147	**0.550**
CAT	0.188	0.164	0.175	0.174	0.175	**0.550**	0.163	0.169	0.168	0.170	**0.550**	0.148	0.156	0.154	0.152	**0.550**	0.145	0.143	0.140	0.145	**0.550**
DEER	0.215	0.161	0.177	0.180	0.183	**0.550**	0.194	0.180	0.180	0.182	**0.550**	0.174	0.175	0.176	0.175	**0.550**	0.151	0.152	0.146	0.151	**0.550**
DOG	0.188	0.162	0.161	0.165	0.155	**0.550**	0.175	0.160	0.161	0.158	**0.550**	0.173	0.169	0.162	0.164	**0.550**	0.145	0.142	0.139	0.133	**0.550**
FROG	0.318	0.246	0.264	0.262	0.258	**0.550**	0.292	0.277	0.272	0.273	**0.550**	0.276	0.274	0.277	0.277	**0.550**	0.239	0.212	0.206	0.212	**0.550**
HORSE	0.319	0.242	0.267	0.269	0.260	**0.550**	0.283	0.264	0.264	0.263	**0.550**	0.288	0.282	0.279	0.278	**0.550**	0.223	0.218	0.208	0.207	**0.550**
SHIP	0.317	0.257	0.267	0.271	0.248	**0.550**	0.296	0.266	0.267	0.259	**0.550**	0.279	0.268	0.259	0.262	**0.550**	0.220	0.212	0.207	0.191	**0.550**
TRUCK	0.329	0.288	0.261	0.271	0.263	**0.550**	0.298	0.275	0.286	0.284	**0.550**	0.289	0.272	0.276	0.277	**0.550**	0.241	0.213	0.208	0.204	**0.550**
AVG	0.274	0.226	0.228	0.229	0.223	**0.550**	0.249	0.235	0.233	0.231	**0.550**	0.243	0.237	0.234	0.234	**0.550**	0.197	0.187	0.183	0.181	**0.550**

Table S 8: Comparison of **error** for one-vs-rest CIFAR-10 (averaged over all images) using a **CNN** classifier. Except for RP_ρ, ρ_1, ρ_0 are given to all methods. Top model scores are in bold with RP_ρ in red if better (smaller) than non-RP models.

		$\pi_1 = 0$, $\rho_1 = 0.5$					$\pi_1 = 0.25$, $\rho_1 = 0.25$					$\pi_1 = 0.5$, $\rho_1 = 0$					$\pi_1 = 0.5$, $\rho_1 = 0.5$				
IMAGE	TRUE	RP_ρ	RP	NAT13	ELK08	LIU16	RP_ρ	RP	NAT13	ELK08	LIU16	RP_ρ	RP	NAT13	ELK08	LIU16	RP_ρ	RP	NAT13	ELK08	LIU16
PLANE	0.044	0.054	**0.057**	0.059	0.063	0.900	0.050	**0.051**	0.054	0.057	0.900	0.048	**0.045**	0.049	0.048	0.100	0.063	**0.061**	0.074	0.065	0.900
AUTO	0.021	0.040	**0.037**	0.041	0.043	0.100	0.032	**0.034**	0.040	0.039	0.900	0.028	**0.026**	**0.026**	**0.026**	0.100	0.047	**0.049**	0.062	0.070	0.900
BIRD	0.055	0.083	**0.078**	0.080	0.082	0.900	0.074	**0.074**	0.077	0.078	0.900	0.072	**0.066**	0.072	0.070	0.100	0.124	**0.084**	0.089	0.093	0.900
CAT	0.077	0.108	**0.091**	0.092	0.095	0.100	0.111	0.090	**0.086**	0.089	0.900	0.113	**0.084**	0.086	0.088	0.100	0.117	0.098	**0.094**	0.100	0.900
DEER	0.049	0.081	**0.078**	**0.078**	0.079	0.900	0.080	**0.069**	0.075	0.070	0.900	0.076	0.062	**0.061**	0.062	0.100	0.106	**0.086**	0.091	0.093	0.900
DOG	0.062	0.075	**0.071**	0.079	0.080	0.100	0.071	0.069	0.070	**0.067**	0.900	0.069	0.061	**0.057**	0.076	0.100	0.103	**0.081**	0.084	0.086	0.900
FROG	0.038	0.050	**0.048**	**0.048**	0.054	0.100	0.047	**0.052**	0.056	0.062	0.900	0.045	**0.040**	0.042	0.043	0.100	0.058	**0.062**	0.066	0.071	0.900
HORSE	0.035	0.050	**0.052**	0.057	0.054	0.900	0.048	**0.051**	0.052	0.057	0.900	0.045	**0.040**	0.042	0.046	0.100	0.065	**0.063**	0.066	0.075	0.900
SHIP	0.028	0.042	**0.042**	0.046	**0.042**	0.900	0.037	**0.036**	0.042	0.047	0.900	0.035	0.033	**0.031**	0.033	0.100	0.051	**0.049**	0.064	0.058	0.900
TRUCK	0.027	0.044	**0.046**	0.054	0.056	0.900	0.034	**0.032**	0.038	0.043	0.900	0.034	**0.031**	0.034	0.034	0.100	0.060	0.066	0.067	**0.065**	0.900
AVG	0.043	0.063	**0.060**	0.064	0.065	0.580	0.059	**0.056**	0.059	0.061	0.900	0.056	**0.049**	0.050	0.053	0.100	0.080	**0.070**	0.076	0.077	0.900

Table S 9: Comparison of **AUC-PR** for one-vs-rest CIFAR-10 (averaged over all images) using a **CNN** classifier. Except for RP_ρ, ρ_1, ρ_0 are given to all methods. Top model scores are in bold with RP_ρ in red if greater than non-RP models.

		$\pi_1 = 0$, $\rho_1 = 0.5$					$\pi_1 = 0.25$, $\rho_1 = 0.25$					$\pi_1 = 0.5$, $\rho_1 = 0$					$\pi_1 = 0.5$, $\rho_1 = 0.5$				
IMAGE	TRUE	RP_ρ	RP	NAT13	ELK08	LIU16	RP_ρ	RP	NAT13	ELK08	LIU16	RP_ρ	RP	NAT13	ELK08	LIU16	RP_ρ	RP	NAT13	ELK08	LIU16
PLANE	0.856	0.779	0.780	**0.784**	0.756	0.550	0.808	**0.797**	0.770	0.742	0.550	0.813	**0.824**	0.792	0.794	0.550	0.710	**0.722**	0.662	0.682	0.550
AUTO	0.954	0.874	**0.889**	0.878	0.833	0.550	0.905	**0.900**	0.871	0.866	0.550	0.931	**0.927**	0.924	0.910	0.550	0.824	**0.814**	0.756	0.702	0.550
BIRD	0.761	0.559	0.566	**0.569**	0.568	0.550	0.619	**0.618**	0.584	0.597	0.550	0.623	**0.679**	0.613	0.619	0.115	0.465	0.492	0.436	0.434	**0.550**
CAT	0.601	0.387	0.447	**0.463**	0.433	0.550	0.423	0.454	0.487	0.480	**0.550**	0.483	**0.512**	0.493	0.473	0.050	0.373	0.375	0.382	0.371	**0.550**
DEER	0.820	0.620	0.600	**0.615**	0.573	0.550	0.646	**0.660**	0.610	0.657	0.550	0.658	**0.707**	0.700	0.703	0.550	0.434	0.487	0.414	0.435	**0.550**
DOG	0.758	0.629	**0.662**	0.617	0.573	0.550	0.673	**0.667**	0.658	0.660	0.550	0.705	0.722	**0.741**	0.705	0.550	0.541	0.545	0.496	0.519	**0.550**
FROG	0.891	0.812	**0.815**	0.812	0.776	0.550	0.821	**0.827**	0.808	0.749	0.550	0.841	**0.851**	0.828	0.831	0.550	0.753	**0.710**	0.691	0.620	0.550
HORSE	0.897	0.810	**0.817**	0.799	0.779	0.550	0.824	**0.809**	0.801	0.772	0.550	0.826	**0.844**	0.818	0.819	0.550	0.736	**0.699**	**0.699**	0.600	0.550
SHIP	0.922	0.870	0.862	**0.864**	0.853	0.550	0.889	**0.885**	0.843	0.848	0.550	0.889	**0.897**	0.891	0.887	0.550	0.800	**0.808**	0.767	0.741	0.550
TRUCK	0.929	0.845	**0.848**	0.824	0.787	0.550	0.887	**0.894**	0.873	0.853	0.550	0.904	**0.902**	0.898	0.883	0.550	0.740	**0.709**	0.695	0.690	0.550
AVG	0.839	0.719	**0.729**	0.722	0.693	0.550	0.750	**0.751**	0.730	0.722	0.550	0.767	**0.787**	0.770	0.762	0.457	0.637	**0.636**	0.600	0.579	0.550

References

Angelova, Anelia, Abu-Mostafam, Yaser, and Perona, Pietro. Pruning training sets for learning of object categories. In *Computer Vision and Pattern Recognition, 2005. CVPR 2005. IEEE Computer Society Conference on*, volume 1, pp. 494–501. IEEE, 2005.

Angluin, Dana and Laird, Philip. Learning from noisy examples. *Machine Learning*, 2(4):343–370, 1988.

Chollet, Francois. *Keras CIFAR CNN*, 2016a. URL http://bit.ly/2mVKR3d.

Chollet, Francois. *Keras MNIST CNN*, 2016b. URL http://bit.ly/2nKiqJv.

Davis, Jesse and Goadrich, Mark. The relationship between precision-recall and roc curves. In *Proceedings of the 23rd International Conference on Machine Learning*, ICML '06, pp. 233–240, New York, NY, USA, 2006. ACM. ISBN 1-59593-383-2. doi: 10.1145/1143844.1143874. URL http://doi.acm.org/10.1145/1143844.1143874.

Hempstalk, Kathryn, Frank, Eibe, and Witten, Ian H. One-class classification by combining density and class probability estimation. In *Proceedings of the 2008 European Conference on Machine Learning and Knowledge Discovery in Databases - Part I*, ECML PKDD '08, pp. 505–519, Berlin, Heidelberg, 2008. Springer-Verlag. ISBN 978-3-540-87478-2. doi: 10.1007/978-3-540-87479-9_51. URL http://dx.doi.org/10.1007/978-3-540-87479-9_51.

Manevitz, Larry M. and Yousef, Malik. One-class svms for document classification. *Journal of Machine Learning Research*, 2:139–154, March 2002. ISSN 1532-4435. URL http://dl.acm.org/citation.cfm?id=944790.944808.

Moya, M. M., Koch, M. W., and Hostetler, L. D. One-class classifier networks for target recognition applications. *NASA STI/Recon Technical Report N*, 93, 1993.

Platt, John, Schlkopf, Bernhard, Shawe-Taylor, John, Smola, Alex J., and Williamson, Robert C. Estimating the support of a high-dimensional distribution. Technical report, Microsoft Research, November 1999. URL https://www.microsoft.com/en-us/research/publication/estimating-the-support-of-a-high-dimensional-distribution/.

Reed, Scott E., Lee, Honglak, Anguelov, Dragomir, Szegedy, Christian, Erhan, Dumitru, and Rabinovich, Andrew. Training deep neural networks on noisy labels with bootstrapping. In *ICLR 2015*, 2015. URL http://arxiv.org/abs/1412.6596.

scikit learn. *LogisticRegression Class at scikit-learn*, 2016. URL http://bit.ly/2o3y6r5.

Xiao, Tong, Xia, Tian, Yang, Yi, Huang, Chang, and Wang, Xiaogang. Learning from massive noisy labeled data for image classification. In *CVPR*, 2015.

Monte-Carlo Tree Search using Batch Value of Perfect Information

Shahaf S. Shperberg
CS Department
Ben Gurion University
shperbsh@post.bgu.ac.il

Solomon Eyal Shimony
CS Department
Ben Gurion University
shimony@cs.bgu.ac.il

Ariel Felner
ISE Department
Ben Gurion University
felner@bgu.ac.il

Abstract

This paper focuses on the selection phase of Monte-Carlo Tree Search (MCTS). We define *batch value of perfect information* (BVPI) in game trees as a generalization of *value of computation* as proposed by Russell and Wefald, and use it for selecting nodes to sample in MCTS. We show that computing the BVPI is NP-hard, but it can be *approximated* in polynomial time. In addition, we propose methods that intelligently find sets of fringe nodes with high BVPI, and quickly select nodes to sample from these sets. We apply our new BVPI methods to partial game trees, both in a stand-alone set of tests, and as a component of a full MCTS algorithm. Empirical results show that our BVPI methods outperform existing node-selection methods for MCTS in different scenarios.

1 INTRODUCTION

Monte-Carlo tree search (MCTS) algorithms, such as the UCT algorithm and its many variants [Browne *et al.*, 2012], are state-of-the-art in numerous domains. A crucial phase in MCTS is the *selection phase* where a fringe node of the partially expanded tree is selected for sampling (initiating rollouts). Although UCT is a prominent approach, its node-selection criterion, based on optimization of *cumulative regret*, is actually inappropriate for move selection: it was shown in [Hay *et al.*, 2012; Feldman and Domshlak, 2013] that *simple regret* and value of information (VOI) criteria are more appropriate, and result in more efficient search. A scheme similar to the "value of computation" of [Russell and Wefald, 1991b; 1991a] can be used to define the VOI (see Section 2.2). Since a single rollout cannot find the true utility of a node, the "blinkered" scheme in [Hay *et al.*, 2012] provided bounds on the VOI for a *number of samples* at a node. Despite its success, the "blinkered" scheme has two shortcomings. First, it applies only at the first level of the tree. Second, it only considers the VOI of individual nodes.

Numerous authors attempted to optimize VOI for multiple sources of information. Such an optimization is intractable in general [Reches *et al.*, 2013; Krause and Guestrin, 2011; 2009]. Approximations thereof using myopic assumptions and greedy search are a common way to alleviate this problem [Krause and Guestrin, 2011]. The myopic-greedy schemes have a basis in theory, due to the fact that if the VOI is submodular, greedy algorithms are provably near-optimal [Krause and Guestrin, 2009; 2011; Papachristoudis and Fisher III, 2012]. However, the VOI is not submodular in general [Krause and Guestrin, 2009], thus myopic-greedy metareasoning can be far from optimal.

We address the above shortcomings by defining **batch value of perfect information** (BVPI) of multiple nodes in game trees, as a generalization of *value of computation* [Russell and Wefald, 1991a]. First, we examine the computational complexity of BVPI, and show a deterministic approximation (Section 3). Second, we introduce algorithmic variants that quickly choose a set of nodes S with high BVPI, and evaluate them on trees generated by MCTS algorithms (Section 4). Third, we present variants that quickly select nodes in S for rollouts. We provide empirical evidence of improved rollouts effectiveness without incurring too much overhead. Finally, we show how all ideas can be plugged into any MCTS algorithm by modifying only its selection phase (Section 5). Experimental results (Section 6) on two disparate domains show that our methods significantly outperform the node selection schemes used by UCT and "blinkered", as well as that of an adaptation of MGSS* [Russell and Wefald, 1991a] to MCTS.

2 BACKGROUND

This paper uses techniques from Monte-Carlo tree search, value of computation (value of information) in game trees, and conspiracy numbers. We briefly examine each below.

2.1 MONTE-CARLO TREE SEARCH

Monte-Carlo tree search (MCTS) is an algorithmic schema commonly used to search huge trees. In general, MCTS grows a search tree, using four phases: node **selection**, node **expansion**, **simulation** (also called rollouts or sampling), and **updating** (also called backup). Algorithm 1 depicts the MCTS, following [Browne *et al.*, 2012]).

Algorithm 1: Monte-Carlo Tree Search

```
1 function MCTS(root):
2     while computation budget not exceeded do
3         v ←TreePolicy(root)
4         U ← DoRollout(v)
5         Backup(v, U)
```

TreePolicy() consists of the **node selection** and **expansion**, DoRollout() performs simulation (sampling) from the selected node v. The computation budget (line 2) can be the number of rollouts, a time limit, etc. There are numerous schemes for deciding which nodes to expand, which nodes to select, how to propagate updates, and how to do rollouts (See [Browne *et al.*, 2012] for a deep survey). A popular approach for node selection is the Upper Confidence Bounds for Trees (UCT) [Kocsis and Szepesvári, 2006], which selects a node recursively, starting from the root, down to the fringe. At each node v, select a child c which maximizes the score:

$$UCTscore(c) = Q(c) + b\sqrt{\frac{2\ln N(v)}{N(c)}} \qquad (1)$$

where $Q(c)$ is the previous average value of c, $N(v)$ is the number of past visits of v, and b is a constant. If v is a fringe node, a rollout is initiated from v.

2.2 INFORMATION GATHERING IN TREES

We are given a game tree T consisting of MAX, MIN, and CHANCE nodes (root r is a MAX node). Each leaf has known utility value distribution P_v, as in Figure 1, but its true utility $u(v)$ is unknown. Leaf utility distributions are assumed independent (the commonly used "subtree independence" assumption [Russell and Wefald, 1991a]). The notation $[p_1 : u_1, ..., p_n : u_n]$ represents P_v, meaning that p_i is the probability that the true utility is u_i.

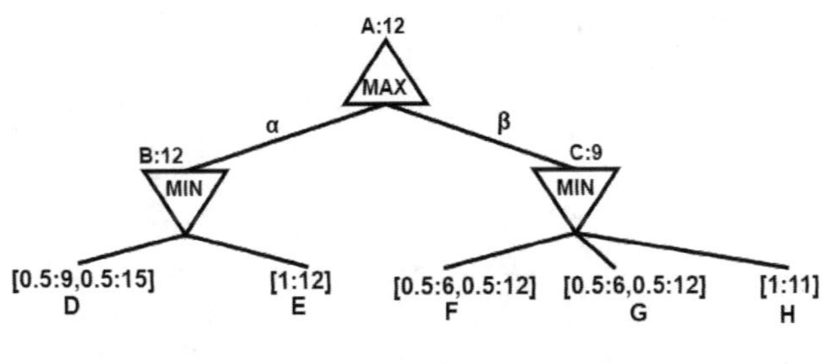

Figure 1: MIN-MAX tree with leaf utility distributions

For each leaf v of T, we can choose to perform a measurement that costs $C(v)$, obtaining further information about v, such as the true utility of v. Optionally, there is also a budget constraint that limits the total number, or cost, of allowed measurements. The problem of *optimal information gathering* is: what is the optimal policy of performing measurements, and then selecting the action at the root, so as to achieve maximum overall expected utility?

There are two standard settings of this problem. In the *batch setting*, all measurements are made in a single batch. Only then, the decision maker gets to observe the results of the measurements. In the *sequential setting*, the decision maker selects a measurement and immediately observes the result. This is repeated until a decision to stop is reached. In both settings, after stopping the measurement process, the decision maker selects the root action that achieves the best expected utility for the tree given all the observations.

In this section, as well as in Section 3, we assume that the distributions P_v are given, and that the measurements are abstract operators that have a known cost and reveal the true utility $u(v)$. But in the context of a search algorithm, T is actually the partially developed game tree, of which v is a fringe node. A measurement is done by a computation, obtaining additional (usually **noisy**) information about v by expanding it, or (in MCTS) by initiating additional rollouts from v. The initial distributions P_v are obtained by heuristics, by rollouts (as in Section 5) etc.

2.2.1 Value of Perfect Information

Suppose that the agent has developed the tree T. If no additional measurements were allowed, a MAX player should compute an EXPECTI-MINI-MAX value $\bar{U}(T)$ of the tree, treating the utility of each leaf v of T as if it were equal to its expected value. Let α be the child of the root which propagated $\bar{U}(T)$ to the root node in EXPECTI-MINI-MAX. We call this move α the "current best" (see Figure 1). In order not to introduce additional notation, as far as utility distributions are concerned, we henceforth refer to a move, and to its respective child node, interchangeably.

In a nutshell (See [Russell and Wefald, 1991a]), the *Value of (Perfect) Information* (VPI), (called *Value of Computation* in [Russell and Wefald, 1991a]) is the expected gain from picking another move β_i as a result of performing the additional measurements either under α or under β_i. Let β_1 be the next-best move after α, and denote by $\bar{U}(\gamma)$ the current expected utility of any move γ. Let S_α be a set of leaves under α, and let $p_{\alpha S_\alpha}(x)$ be the probability density function for the utility of move α, given the utility observations at the leaves S_α. The VPI for S_α is defined as:

$$VPI(S_\alpha) = \int_{-\infty}^{\bar{U}(\beta_1)} p_{\alpha S_\alpha}(x)(\bar{U}(\beta_1) - x)dx \qquad (2)$$

Intuitively, $VPI(S_\alpha)$ is the gain due to preferring β_1 over α because measurements below α revealed that the new value of α (given the observations) is worse than the current expected value of β_1. Likewise, for a move β_i (not the current best), let S_{β_i} be a set of leaves under β_i, and denote by $p_{\beta_i S_{\beta_i}}(x)$ the probability density function for the utility of move β_i, given utility observations at leaves S_{β_i}. Then:

$$VPI(S_{\beta_i}) = \int_{\bar{U}(\alpha)}^{\infty} p_{\beta_i S_{\beta_i}}(x)(x - \bar{U}(\alpha))dx \quad (3)$$

The distributions in Eqs. 2, 3 were defined in [Russell and Wefald, 1991a] for MIN-MAX trees. Equation 4 below is an alternative statement that incorporates CHANCE nodes.

MGSS* (Meta-Greedy Single-Step) [Russell and Wefald, 1991a] uses Eqs. 2, 3, and assumes that the measured node-set S is a single node: their "single-step assumption" of defining the value of computation under the assumption that only one step of computation will be done before the final move decision (see Example 1). The scheme was extended into MGSS2 that estimates the value of computation for more than one node.

Example 1. *In Figure 1, α is the current best move, since $\bar{U}(\alpha) = 12 > 9 = \bar{U}(\beta)$, due to the MIN-MAX computation in the tree, using the expected value of leaf node distributions as a "known value". For example, the value of leaf node D is taken to be 12. Obtaining the true utility $u(v)$ of any one leaf cannot change the move selected by MAX. Thus, the VPI of any individual leaf node here is 0, so MGSS* stops further computational actions. Examining value of computation for multiple nodes under the same move (such as $\{F, G\}$) does not help in this case. But if we measure $\{D, F, G\}$, then with probability 0.5, D will show utility 9, so B will have utility 9 as well. With probability 0.25, both F and G will show utility 12, so C will have a utility of 11. So with overall probability 0.125, C will be better than B, and MAX would change the first move to C. The set $\{D, F, G\}$ has a value of computation greater than 0, and should be measured if its cost is sufficiently low. This paper extends VOI to consider such sets.*

For any set of nodes to be measured, its value of information minus the cost of the measurement is called the **net value of information**. By extension, we likewise use the terms "net VPI" and "net BVPI" (below) to mean the appropriate type of VOI minus measurement costs.

2.3 CONSPIRACY NUMBERS

Conspiracy numbers [McAllester, 1988] denote the minimal number of nodes that need to change their values so as to cause the tree's value to change to a given value u.

Example 2. *In Figure 2, the minimax value of the root is 10. In order to increase its value to any $u \in (10, 15]$, the minimal number of leaf nodes that need to change is 1 (node F), thus, there is a single conspirator required. In order to increase the root's value to $u \in (15, 20]$, the values of both E and F need to change (two conspirators), and three conspirators are required to change it to any $u > 20$.*

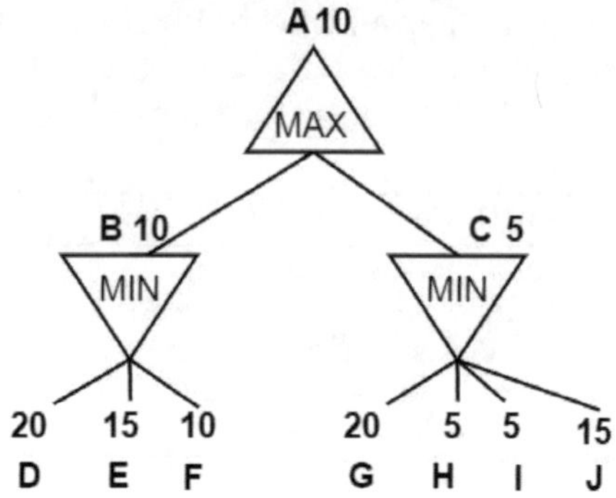

Figure 2: Conspiracy numbers in MIN-MAX trees

Originally the idea was used to focus game tree search on such conspiracy nodes. Although conspiracy numbers are defined for known leaf values, they are loosely related to the value of computation [Russell and Wefald, 1991a]. Generally speaking, a conspiracy number greater than 1 (when true leaf utilities are assumed to be equal to their expected utility as in Example 1 and Figure 1) indicates that MGSS* will see a VPI of 0 for every node, whereas the value of computation for numerous nodes may be non-zero (in which case the VPI is not submodular). In this paper we adapt conspiracy numbers in order to find sets of nodes that have a high *probability* of affecting the value at the root.

3 BATCH VALUE OF INFORMATION

We now define *Batch Value of Perfect Information* (BVPI). The *value of computation* (=VPI) in [Russell and Wefald, 1991a] was defined for nodes all under a single child of the root. BVPI is a straightforward generalization of VPI allowing measurements at arbitrary sets S of leaves. Denote by $U_S(v)$ the utility of node v, given that measurements will be performed at a set of leaf nodes S. Note that before getting the actual observed values, $U_S(v)$ is a random variable. Since measurements are assumed to be perfect, $U_S(v)$ (at leaf nodes) is distributed as P_v. Denote the children of v by $ch(v)$, the probability of a child node c of a chance node by $p(c)$, and use appropriate predicates ($LEAF(v)$ is true if v is a leaf node, etc.) to denote node types. The distribution of $U_S(v)$ is defined recursively in Eq. 4.

$$U_S(v) \sim \begin{cases} P_v & \text{LEAF}(v) \wedge v \in S \\ [1 : E_v[P_v]] & \text{LEAF}(v) \wedge v \notin S \\ \max_{c \in ch(v)}\{U_S(c)\} & \text{MAXnode}(v) \\ \min_{c \in ch(v)}\{U_S(c)\} & \text{MINnode}(v) \\ \sum_{c \in ch(v)} p(c)U_S(c) & \text{CHANCEnode}(v) \end{cases} \quad (4)$$

The *batch value of perfect information* (BVPI) for obtaining perfect information on a set S of nodes is defined as follows. Denote $U_S(\beta) = \max_i\{U_S(\beta_i)\}$, and let $p_{\alpha\beta S}(x, y)$

be the joint probability density function of $(U_S(\alpha), U_S(\beta))$ at (x, y) given the measurements at S. Then:

$$BVPI(S) = \int_{y>x} p_{\alpha\beta S}(x, y)(y - x)dxdy \quad (5)$$

Intuitively, $BVPI(S)$ is the gain due to a change of best move from α to some β_i, because observations at S revealed that the new utility of β_i is better than that of α. Note that if S is a set of leaves limited to a subtree under α then Eq. 5 reduces to Eq. 2. Likewise if S is limited to a subtree under β_i, in which case Eq. 5 reduces to Eq. 3.

In using $BVPI(S)$ (Eq. 5) below, we re-write it as:

$$BVPI(S) = \int_{y>x} p_{\alpha S_\alpha}(x) p_{\beta S_\beta}(y)(y - x)dxdy \quad (6)$$
$$= E[max(U_{S_\beta}(\beta) - U_{S_\alpha}(\alpha), 0)] \quad (7)$$

where $p_{\beta S_\beta}$ is the density function of $U_{S_\beta}(\beta)$, which is the same as $U_S(\beta)$, due to subtree independence. The first equality also follows from the subtree independence, and the second from an algebraic manipulation of the terms.

To optimize (batch setting) information gathering using BVPI, one should find a set of nodes S with the highest net $BVPI(S)$. This is hard because: **(1)** We need to compute the BVPI for each such set. **(2)** There is an exponential number of potential subsets S of leaves of T.

3.1 COMPUTING THE BVPI

Theorem 1. *Computing $BVPI(S)$ for a given set of leaves S in expecti-mini-max trees is NP-hard.*

Proof (outline): by reduction from the Partition problem [Garey and Johnson, 1979] [SP12], defined as follows. Given a multi set S of integers $\{S_1, S_2, ..., S_n\}$ (w.l.o.g. $\sum_{i=1}^n S_i$ is even), is there an equal partition, i.e. a set of indices $I \subseteq [1, ..., n]$ such that $\sum_{i \in I} S_i = \sum_{i \notin I} S_i$?
The reduction uses the three-level expecti-minimax tree of Figure 3, with two-valued distributions at the leaves. The S_i in the figure are the same numbers as in the partition problem. By computing $BVPI(S)$, with S being the set of all children of the chance node, for 2 different values of u_2, we can decide the partition problem, as follows. Denote $\sigma = \sum_{i=1}^n \frac{S_i}{2n}$, the desired partition sum divided by n. Before any measurements are made, the expected utility of each uncertain leaf i is $\frac{S_i}{4}$, and thus the expected utility $\bar{U}(v)$ of the chance node is $\frac{\sigma}{2}$, which is less than u_1 and either value of u_2. So indeed MAX chooses α. If all uncertain leaf nodes are measured, then there is a non-zero probability that $u(v) > u_1$, but if we also have $u(v) > u_2$ then MIN will not pick the chance node, so the gain in such cases is limited by $u_2 - u_1$. Denote $BVPI(S)$ for the case where $u_2 = \sigma + \frac{1}{2n}$ by B_1, and for the case where

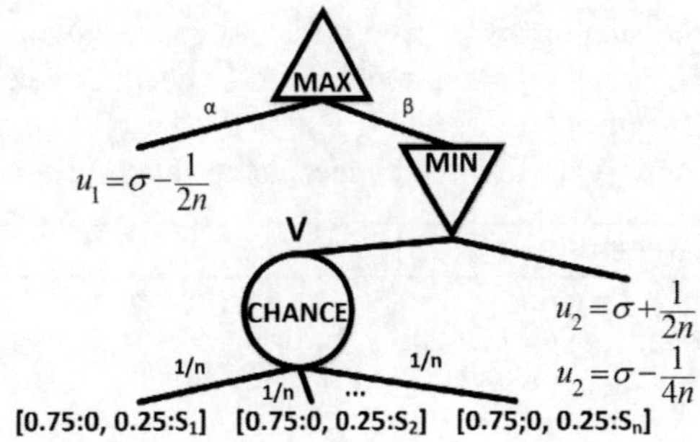

Figure 3: NP-hardness of computing BVPI: reduction

$u_2 = \sigma - \frac{1}{4n}$ by B_2. In the first case we have:

$$B_1 = P(U_S(v) = \sigma)(\sigma - u_1) + \frac{P(U_S(v) > \sigma)}{n}$$

Since the S_i are all integers, then σ and all possible values of $U_S(v)$ are integer multiples of $\frac{1}{n}$, so $P(U_S(v) \in [u_1, u_1 + \frac{1}{4n}]) = 0$. Thus, the BVPI in the second case is:

$$B_2 = \frac{P(U_S(v) > \sigma - \frac{1}{4n})}{4n} = \frac{P(U_S(v) \geq \sigma)}{4n}$$

If we can compute B_1 and B_2 in polynomial time, we can trivially solve for $P(U_S(v) = \sigma)$, which is non-zero just when the partition problem has a solution. □

Note that this reduction also implies NP-hardness of VPI (Eq. 3), as all the uncertain leaves are in the same subtree. However, if the utility of the leaves is bounded, standard *sampling* techniques can be used to approximate $BVPI(S)$. We show a *deterministic* approximation result.

Theorem 2. *Given a game tree T with finite discrete distributions, the value $BVPI(S)$ where S is a subset of the leaves of T can be deterministically approximated within additive error ϵ in time polynomial in the (explicit) description size of T, $\frac{1}{\epsilon}$, and utility span bound $U_{max} - U_{min}$.*

Proof (outline): We approximate $U_S(v)$ bottom up, in a manner similar to [Cohen *et al.*, 2015]. There, an approximate cumulative distribution (CDF) was computed for MAX-SUM trees, in a manner that bounded the Kolmogorov distance ($\max_x |F'(x) - F(x)|$) of the approximate CDF from the exact CDF. As the Kolmogorov distance is unhelpful in our case, we use a different version that provides the appropriate error bound for the expected values in Eq. 7.

Denote by $F_{U_S(v)}(x)$ the CDF of $U_S(v)$ at x. For MAX nodes we have: $F_{U_S(v)}(x) = \Pi_{c \in ch(v)} F_{U_S(c)}(x)$ due to independence. Likewise, for MIN nodes we have: $F_{U_S(v)}(x) = 1 - \Pi_{c \in ch(v)}(1 - F_{U_S(c)}(x))$. Chance nodes are weighted sums of the random variables, so we need to use convolution, which may grow the distributions' support exponentially. To overcome this problem, we bound the support by an appropriately defined $n = f(U_{max} - U_{min}, |T|, \frac{1}{\epsilon})$ and apply a TRIM operator (see Algorithm 2) to the current $U_S(v)$, assumed to be a list of (value, probability) pairs sorted by increasing value.

Algorithm 2: TRIM operator

m ← |support($U_S(v)$)|; $U'_S(v) \leftarrow \emptyset$;
head ← first($U_S(v)$); tail ← rest($U_S(v)$);
while *$m > n$ and tail is non-empty* **do**
  next ← first(tail);
  if *value(next) - value(head)* $< \frac{U_{max}-U_{min}}{n}$ **then**
    prob(head) ← prob(head)+ prob(next);
    tail ← rest(tail); m ← m-1;
  else
    $U'_S(v)$ ← append($U'_S(v)$, head);
    head ← first(tail); tail ← rest(tail);
return append($U'_S(v)$, tail) ;

By construction, $|\text{support}(U'_S(v))| \leq n$ after TRIM. The error introduced by TRIM is bounded by $\delta = \frac{U_{max}-U_{min}}{n}$, i.e.: $F_{U_S(v)}(x+\delta) \geq F_{U'_S(v)}(x) \geq F_{U_S(v)}(x)$ for all x.

We prove lemmas bounding combination errors: in MIN and MAX nodes errors are added, and in CHANCE nodes at worst equal to the maximum error in the children. The (low-order polynomial) function f can be chosen so that $F_{U_S(r)}(x+\epsilon) \geq F_{U'_S(r)}(x) \geq F_{U_S(r)}(x)$ for all x at the root r. These inequalities imply that the Wasserstein distance between $U_S(r)$ and $U'_S(r)$ is at most ϵ, thus $|E[U'_S(r)] - E[U_S(r)]| \leq \epsilon$. Since $|\text{support}(U'_S(v))| \leq n$, for all v, we can then compute the expectations in Eq. 7 in polynomial time. □

Note that we can also handle continuous distributions, by discretizing them into $\frac{U_{max}-U_{min}}{n}$ values, achieving similar approximation guarantees, assuming that we can efficiently compute their CDFs at any given point.

4 PRACTICAL BATCH-SELECTION

We now examine practical methods for choosing batches of nodes with a high net BVPI. Here, we treat this as a stand-alone problem on a partially developed tree T. In Section 5 we incorporate these methods into MCTS.

Optimizing the value of information was shown to be NP-hard even for one-level trees (see, e.g. [Reches *et al.*, 2013; Shperberg and Shimony, 2017]). Thus we are forced to introduce methods suggested by the theory, but which have no guarantees, in order to be able to meet the extremely difficult task of actually improving the runtime or quality of MCTS, which requires that we find node-sets with high BVPI in essentially negligible computation time.

4.1 HIGH-BVPI SETS: USING CONSPIRACIES

This scheme uses an idea based on the above described conspiracy numbers [McAllester, 1988]; it is possible to quickly detect node-sets involved in minimal conspiracies. We desire instead a probabilistic version that can quickly detect node-sets S that have a significant contribution to Eq. 6, and hence should have a high net $BVPI(S)$. Note that we do not need to find even a nearly optimal set, it is sufficient for our search application to find a reasonably good set, and not to return an empty set when sets with a high net BVPI are available.

Algorithm 3: C-VIBES Selection Scheme

function *SelectNodes(root)*:
  foreach $V \in \mathcal{V}$ **do**
    $storeProbabilities(\alpha, V)$
    foreach *Node* $c \in ch(root) - \{\alpha\}$ **do**
      $storeProbabilities(c, V)$
  V, V', c ← values which optimize Equation 8
  $S' \leftarrow \emptyset$; $OpenList.init(\alpha)$; $OpenList.insert(c)$
  while *OpenList not empty* **do**
    $v \leftarrow OpenList.pop()$
    if *v is a fringe node* **then**
      $S' \leftarrow S' \cup \{v\}$
    else
      $Val \leftarrow \begin{cases} V & \text{if } v \in \text{subtree of } \alpha \\ V' & \text{otherwise} \end{cases}$
      foreach $c \in ch(v)$ **do**
        if $\phi[v, Val] \notin \{0,1\}$ *and (CHANCEnode(v) or* $\phi[v, Val] == \phi[c, Val]$*)* **then**
          $OpenList.insert(c)$
  return S'
function *storeProbabilities(v, Val)*:
  foreach $c \in ch(v)$ **do**
    $storeProbabilities(c, Val)$
  $\phi[v, Val] \leftarrow \begin{cases} \hat{P}(U_S(v) \leq Val) & \text{if } v \in \text{subtree of } \alpha \\ \hat{P}(U_S(v) \geq Val) & \text{otherwise} \end{cases}$

We adapt the conspiracy scheme by defining a probabilistic variant of conspiracy numbers, and then by evaluating a modified version of Eq. 6 where we replace integration by maximization, using as S the entire set of leaf nodes, and $U_S(v)$ as in Eq. 4. In MIN-MAX trees, the probability that the value of node v will increase to at least Val if we measure nodes S is: $\uparrow \phi(v, Val) = P(U_S(v) \geq Val)$. Likewise the value v will decrease to be at most Val with probability: $\downarrow \phi(v, Val) = P(U_S(v) \leq Val)$. Now perform the following optimization (note the similarities with Eq. 6), and use its optimum as done within Algorithm 3.

$$\max_{V'>V} ((V'-V)(\downarrow \phi(\alpha, V) \max_{c \in ch(r)-\{\alpha\}} \uparrow \phi(c, V')) \quad (8)$$

The $\hat{P}$ in the algorithm are probabilities approximated as in Theorem 2, except that for CHANCE nodes, our BVPI approximation is still too slow for the desired real-time performance, so we use: $\hat{P}(U_S(v) \leq Val) \approx \sum_{c \in ch(v)} p(c)P(U_S(c) \leq Val)$ instead of convolution in our implementation of the conspiracy scheme. Example 3 below depicts one such node-set recovery instance.

Table 1: BVPI in Trees Generated by UCTO in the CTP (left) and in StarCaft (right)

CTP									
#	Tree Size	Tree Height	Max BF	Full Tree BVPI	Full Tree T (**ms**)	Conspiracy BVPI	Conspiracy T (**ms**)	Greedy BVPI	Greedy T (**ms**)
1	30	9	3	**359**	217	296	**0.28**	92	**0.28**
2	45	13	4	**453**	443	382	0.29	215	**0.28**
3	61	15	3	**126**	1868	103	**0.29**	19	**0.29**
4	106	25	4	**527**	356872	480	**0.34**	319	**0.34**
5	125	20	6	**812**	7129870	681	0.36	681	**0.35**
6	153	42	5	**219**	20676623	**219**	0.4	71	**0.38**
7	1018	33	6	T/O	T/O	**113**	0.78	0	**0.73**
8	3077	29	6	T/O	T/O	**65**	1.89	13	**1.88**
9	6820	37	5	T/O	T/O	**53**	4.2	0	**3.9**
10	15321	69	7	T/O	T/O	**277**	8.5	12	**8**

StarCraft									
#	Tree Size	Tree Height	Max BF	Full Tree BVPI	Full Tree T (**ms**)	Conspiracy BVPI	Conspiracy T (**ms**)	Greedy BVPI	Greedy T (**ms**)
11	30	4	20	**283**	198	234	0.25	205	**0.24**
12	45	4	20	**356**	413	**356**	**0.25**	**356**	**0.25**
13	60	6	20	**326**	1719	312	**0.28**	283	**0.28**
14	100	11	20	**147**	299814	**147**	0.33	105	**0.31**
15	125	11	20	**63**	7088815	**63**	**0.36**	**63**	**0.36**
16	150	12	20	**96**	19938631	71	0.39	0	**0.38**
17	1000	23	20	T/O	T/O	**33**	0.72	**33**	**0.70**
18	3000	28	20	T/O	T/O	**116**	1.85	42	**1.82**
19	7000	42	20	T/O	T/O	**25**	4.33	7	**4.01**
20	15000	79	20	T/O	T/O	**47**	8.41	0	**7.96**

4.1.1 Batch Selection Algorithms

We evaluate three batch selection algorithms:

(1) Full tree (FT): Exhaustively compute net BVPI (using BVPI approximation algorithm from Theorem 2) for every subset S of T's leaves; pick S with the highest net BVPI.

(2) Greedy (G): Start S as an empty set. Estimate the net VPI for every leaf node not in S, and add the best to S. Repeat until no node has a positive net VPI.

(3) Conspiracy (C): The conspiracy-based scheme described above. As the optimization in Eq. 8 is still too slow to perform in real time for MCTS, our implementation optimizes over only a few possible values of V, V' in Eq. 8. In the experiments we used the value set:

$$\mathcal{V} = \{0.8\bar{U}(\alpha), 0.9\bar{U}(\alpha), 0.95\bar{U}(\alpha), \bar{U}(\alpha), 1.05\bar{U}(\alpha)\}$$

Example 3. *In figure 1, α is the current best move, since $\bar{U}(\alpha) = 12 > 9 = \bar{U}(\beta)$. The leaf node set $S = \{D, F, G\}$ is the only one to potentially change the best action from α to β, thus the only set with $BVPI(S) > 0$. FT estimates the BVPI exhaustively, and thus will correctly return S. Greedy suffers from myopic assumptions like MGSS*. Recall that in this example, the VPI of every individual node is 0, hence, Greedy will terminate without finding S and return an empty set. The Conspiracy scheme optimizes Equation 8 in order to find a batch to sample. The optimal solution is achieved with $V' = 11$ and $V = 9$. Using these values, $\downarrow \phi(\alpha, V = 9) = 0.5$, obtained by picking D, and $\uparrow \phi(\beta, V' = 11) = 0.5$ obtained by picking both F and G. Therefore, Conspiracy returns $\{D, F, G\}$ as desired. Note that the values $V' = 11$ and $V = 9$ are outside the range $\mathcal{V}$ used by our actual Conspiracy implementation for optimizing Equation 8. Despite that, using $V = 0.8\bar{U}(\alpha) = 9.6$ and $V' = 0.9\bar{U}(\alpha) = 10.8$, the implementation still finds and returns the correct node-set $S = \{D, F, G\}$.*

4.2 EXPERIMENTS ON GAME TREES

To get a realistic game tree, we used a snapshot of a partially developed game tree T' from a MCTS. T' is cut off so that its fringe nodes become the leaves of our tree T. Values previously returned by rollouts form an empirical distribution at each fringe node (now leaf) v; this distribution is assumed to be the actual distribution P_v of leaf node utilities. E.g. if we had 2 rollouts with value 10, and 6 rollouts with value 20, (from v) then we set $P_v = [0.25 : 10,\ 0.75 : 20]$. Measurement costs assumed are given by Equation 9 (Sec. 5). We obtained trees from the following 2 domains.

Domain 1: (stochastic) Canadian traveler problem [Papadimitriou and Yannakakis, 1991]; we are given a weighted graph $G = (V, E, w)$ where $w : E \rightarrow R^+$. Each edge $e \in E$, has a known probability $p(e)$ of being blocked. The agent starts at vertex $s \in V$, and must reach a vertex $t \in V$. Whether an edge is blocked becomes known upon reaching an incident vertex. The problem is to find a policy that minimizes the expected travel distance (sum of w) before reaching t (the utility here is minus the distance). The decision version of the stochastic CTP is PSPACE complete [Fried *et al.*, 2013]. [Eyerich *et al.*, 2010] present an effective UCT-based algorithm called UCTO which randomly searches the belief states in the given program instance, and generates EXPECTI-MAX trees.

Domain 2: StarCraft, a Real Time Strategy (RTS) game by Blizzard Entertainment, a popular AI competition and research platform. Our StarCraft experiments used code by [Justesen *et al.*, 2014] for playing StarCraft battles against an opposing team. Their code uses a UCT-based MCTS algorithm that generates MAX-MIN trees during the search.

Approximate net-BVPI and CPU time for 10 instances appear in Table 1(left) for CTP and in Table 1(right) for StarCraft. In both domains, FT timed out (T/O denotes timing out after 6 hours) in large instances. Greedy is the fastest, but the BVPI it achieved was only 64% of that of FT on average (over instances where FT did not time out). Conspiracy had the best balance between time and effectiveness. Its BVPI was 89% of that of FT on average, and was only slightly slower (2%) than Greedy. In fact, the conspiracy scheme was also the best in the MCTS below.

5 PLUGGING BVPI INTO MCTS

The next challenge is to use the theory of BVPI for selecting nodes on which rollouts will be performed.

5.1 SELECTING THE ROLLOUTS

We describe a number of BVPI-based selection schemes and evaluate them as well as other related schemes by plugging them into existing UCT based implementations (denoted as "the host MCTS algorithm") by changing only the selection phase. Each scheme has a different trade-off between metareasoning overhead (time for choosing the nodes to sample), and the effectiveness of the resulting rollouts. The first scheme we implemented is the **Blinkered** scheme from [Hay *et al.*, 2012], which replaces the UCT criterion by a VOI bound in the first tree level, resorting to UCT at deeper levels.

We now introduce our BVPI-based schemes, called *Value of Information of a Batch Efficient Selection* (VIBES). The metareasoning overhead in VIBES is relatively high, thus too expensive to use to decide every single rollout. Therefore, after a node v is selected for sampling we perform N rollouts from v. This amortizes the metareasoning overhead over N rollouts. Additionally, some of the schemes below first select a batch S of fringe nodes to sample. This set can be of any size (up to the number of leaf nodes). In order not to over-commit a large number of rollouts in such cases, we choose K nodes from S with the highest individual net VPI, and an additional K randomly selected from S to a total of at most $2K$ nodes for rollouts. The additional K random samples are used to allow measurements on nodes with VPI = 0 inside the selected batch. Below we call this *the batch selection method*, $BSM(N, K)$. Values of $N = 3$, $K = 5$ proved to produce a good balance. That is, K was set to be roughly one quarter of the size of a typical set S observed in a few trial runs. Then N was set such that $2KN$ rollouts per decision delivered a metareasoning overhead of roughly 15% of the runtime.

(1) Full tree VIBES (FT-VIBES): Exhaustively check all possible sets of fringe nodes in the tree, to find a set S with the highest net $BVPI(S)$. Then use $BSM(N, K)$ on S.

(2) First level VIBES (FL-VIBES): Estimate the net BVPI for every subset of the root's children. Choose the subset S which maximizes net $BVPI(S)$. Within S, choose a child c with the maximal individual net VPI. At deeper levels, revert to selection as in the host MCTS algorithm (e.g., the UCT formula if host=UCTO).

(3) Recursive first level VIBES (RFL-VIBES): Use FL-VIBES to select node c at the first level. Then, recursively call FL-VIBES on c until reaching a fringe node.

(4) Blinkered VIBES (B-VIBES): Perform the blinkered algorithm [Hay *et al.*, 2012] until blinkered decides to halt. Then, resort to performing FT-VIBES.

(5) Conspiracy VIBES (C-VIBES):

Select the node-set S using the Conspiracy scheme (Algorithm 3). Then use $BSM(N, K)$ on S.

In all the above methods: (a) generate some random samples to gather statistics before applying VIBES (typically 1% of the sampling budget), (b) stop the entire sampling process if the sampling budget (number of rollouts per move, or a time limit per move) is exhausted or if the scheme did not find a set S with positive net BVPI.

We also tried greedy schemes. The *basic greedy* scheme (G) repeatedly chooses the node v with the greatest individual net VPI and performs rollouts from v. This halts when the net VPI of v is non-positive or the simulation budget has been reached. This method is thus essentially the same as the Meta-Greedy Single Step (MGSS*) method of [Russell and Wefald, 1991a] applied to MCTS.

Basic greedy is fast and performs well when the BVPI is submodular. Otherwise, it suffers from premature stopping, i.e. fails to detect sets of nodes with a high combined BVPI. In order to take advantage of the speed of the greedy scheme but avoid premature stopping, we can combine it with any of the above schemes (X), as follows. Run the greedy scheme. Once the greedy scheme decides to stop due to low VPI, revert to scheme X to decide on any additional samples as long as the budget allows. We denote these combined schemes by G-X (e.g, G-FT-VIBES).

Finally, we need to address the issue of fringe node distributions used in the BVPI, and the resulting distributions after potential additional rollouts. Ideally, use a Bayesian scheme for the distributions: have some prior, and compute distributions given past rollouts, and distributions over the conditional expectation of fringe node utilities given additional potential rollouts. This issue is beyond the scope of this paper, and even if somehow this is done, it would not be obvious how to do so in real time. Instead we performed the following. We assumed that the fringe node distributions P_v are the empirical utility distributions of past rollouts, which is the reason for the initial "statistics gathering" rollouts mentioned above. We then compute the BVPI values as if rollouts from a node result in a perfect measurement of the fringe node utility. As the latter assumption is obviously incorrect, we compensated by modifying the measurement cost of a node. (Note that our BVPI schemes are not sensitive to multiplying all costs and VOI values by a constant, so this compensation makes sense.) Although the latter is somewhat of a hack, it works in practice in a way that is not too sensitive to tunable parameters.

Thus, in the above schemes, as the measurement cost $C(v)$ in the computation of the net BVPI we used:

$$C(v) = \frac{C\sqrt{N(v)}}{B - \bar{U}(\alpha)} \tag{9}$$

with $N(v)$ as in Eq. 1, B the maximal utility bound on the solution. The rationale is: if the $N(v)$ (=number of previous rollouts) is a large number, it will require more future

Table 2: Average results for CTP. The standard deviation was at most 0.36%.

Settings n	Settings p	UCTO	Blink'd	FL-VIBES	RFL-VIBES	FT-VIBES	B-VIBES	C-VIBES	Greedy	G-FL-VIBES	G-RFL-VIBES	G-FT-VIBES	G-C-VIBES
30	0.2	3,006	2,911	2,989	2,830	3,625	2,785	**2,598**	2,902	2,709	2,668	2,973	2,747
	0.4	3,600	3,490	3,564	3,397	4,356	3,336	**3,130**	3,473	3,253	3,224	3,563	3,294
	0.6	4,198	4,070	4,172	3,959	5,095	3,901	**3,630**	4,098	3,804	3,758	4,149	3,829
	0.8	4,801	4,646	4,768	4,510	5,829	4,469	**4,165**	4,599	4,344	4,298	4,742	4,388
	1	5,401	5,241	5,378	5,099	6,521	5,028	**4,675**	5,226	4,893	4,838	5,346	4,933
Avg. of n=30		4,201	4,072	4,174	3,959	5,085	3,904	**3,640**	4,060	3,801	3,757	4,155	3,838
60	0.2	5,049	4,836	4,870	4,804	6,157	4,753	**4,340**	4,842	4,590	4,480	5,091	4,495
	0.4	7,074	6,775	6,805	6,735	8,611	6,665	**6,095**	6,762	6,412	6,252	7,140	6,309
	0.6	8,572	8,237	8,280	8,179	10,465	8,084	**7,396**	8,268	7,745	7,568	8,630	7,651
	0.8	10,082	9,704	9,698	9,603	12,335	9,501	**8,696**	9,667	9,175	8,915	10,224	9,030
	1	11,572	11,091	11,213	11,049	14,179	10,937	**9,968**	11,102	10,534	10,266	11,708	10,366
Avg. of n=60		8,470	8,129	8,173	8,074	10,349	7,988	**7,299**	8,128	7,691	7,496	8,559	7,570
100	0.2	7,506	7,277	7,392	7,210	8,929	6,965	**6,240**	7,299	6,961	6,912	7,273	6,668
	0.4	10,966	10,614	10,763	10,546	13,005	10,160	**9,109**	10,581	10,151	10,139	10,488	9,753
	0.6	13,459	13,032	13,232	12,932	15,961	12,450	**11,162**	13,096	12,424	12,422	12,810	11,957
	0.8	15,916	15,469	15,634	15,264	18,923	14,740	**13,226**	15,490	14,683	14,634	15,157	14,089
	1	18,346	17,886	18,076	17,702	21,851	17,066	**15,273**	17,787	17,005	17,014	17,461	16,284
Avg. of n=100		13,239	12,855	13,019	12,731	15,734	12,276	**11,002**	12,851	12,245	12,224	12,638	11,750

rollouts to change the overall average of all the rollout values by a significant amount (on the order of $B - \bar{U}(\alpha)$). C is empirically determined over a few instances. Results were not very sensitive to C, we used $C = 96$ in our experiments. A more disciplined treatment of the costs is a non-trivial issue beyond the scope of this paper, as the computation time is not on the same scale as the game utilities.

6 EMPIRICAL EVALUATION: MCTS

We now report results where the selection schemes were plugged into existing MCTS algorithms for two domains.

6.1 CANADIAN TRAVELER PROBLEM (CTP)

CTP experiments were on Delaunay graphs following [Bnaya *et al.*, 2009; Eyerich *et al.*, 2010]. Instance parameters were n (number of vertices), and p (probability for each edge to be potentially blocked). For each potentially blocked edge e, $p(e)$ is chosen uniformly from the range $[0, 1)$. Edge travel costs were random, uniform from $\{1, \ldots, 500\}$.

We compared the original UCTO code [Eyerich *et al.*, 2010], with the same code where the node-selection function (a UCT formula variant) was replaced by one of the above described methods. All the algorithms were evaluated as follows. 10 instances were generated for each pair of $n \in \{30, 60, 100\}$ and $p \in \{0.2, 0.4, 0.6, 0.8, 1\}$. We ran every instance 100 times using a time limit of 3 seconds to decide on each move.

Table 2 shows the average cost of the path traveled by the agent for the different algorithms. As can be seen, all the proposed schemes outperformed UCTO, except for FT-VIBES (see below). C-VIBES delivered a good rollout selection at relatively little overhead, thus the best overall performance: a major improvement of more than 15% in the **path-cost** of the resulting solutions over UCTO.

In order to gain additional insight, we chose a typical instance where computing the optimal policy by value iteration (VI) over the belief space was feasible. We examined the runtime and quality of the results vs. the optimal under two budget constraints. **(Const-1:)** a time limit of 3 sec/move (as in Table 2); results appear in Table 3. Here, FT-VIBES timed out after only a few samples. Conspiracy-VIBES was the best here (4.5% from optimal), as it produces good sampling decisions with only a modest overhead. **(Const-2:)** a rollout limit (but no time limit). Runtime vs. path-costs results appear in Figure 4 for a 10K rollout limit for all algorithms. Additional runs with different limits for UCTO and C-VIBES are also shown, labeled as "C-VIBES-3K" (limit 3,000 rollouts per move) etc. C-VIBES-3K already gets better path-cost than UCTO-45K and runs 10 times faster. Furthermore C-VIBES-20K, seems to have found the optimal policy for this instance in many of the runs.

It is also of interest that among all algorithms run with 10,000 samples, FT-VIBES was the best w.r.t. policy quality, as expected. So the BVPI scheme done exhaustively indeed resulted in the most efficient selection of nodes and samples if the meta-reasoning overhead is ignored. However, this scheme is seen here to be completely useless for MCTS due to its huge meta-reasoning overhead. Another interesting point is that for 10,000 samples the greedy scheme was already better than UCT, but only slightly. We conjecture that this is due to cases where the BVPI is not submodular. This is supported by the results for the greedy hybrids, which select further nodes after greedy decides that no nodes should be selected. All the greedy hybrids do better than greedy w.r.t. policy quality, usually with negligible additional overhead.

Table 3: 30 node graphs, p=0.2, time limit 3 sec/move

Selection alg.	Cost	Subopt.	#RollOuts/Move
Optimal (VI)	2,572	0%	N/A
UCTO	3,128	21.6%	**12,371**
Blinkered	3,021	17.5%	11,016
FL-VIBES	3,096	20.4%	4,284
RFL-VIBES	2,931	14.0%	1,576
FT-VIBES	3,778	46.9%	43
B-VIBES	2,890	12.4%	745
C-VIBES	**2,699**	**4.5%**	9,989
Greedy	2,989	16.2%	11,904
G-FL-VIBES	2,823	9.8%	10,978
G-RFL-VIBES	2,784	8.2%	8,732
G-FT-VIBES	3,084	19.9%	611
G-C-VIBES	2,847	10.7%	10,633

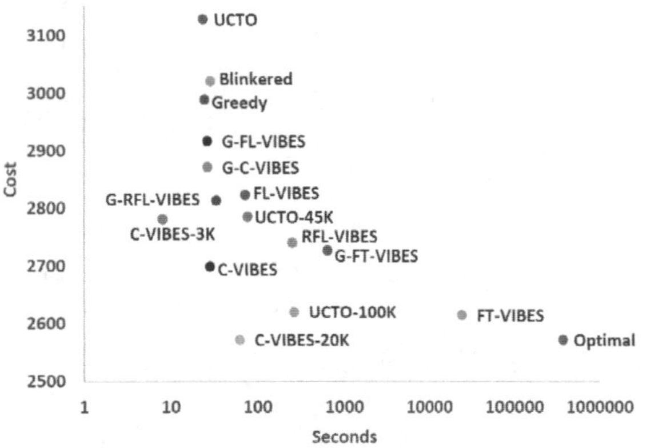

Figure 4: 30 node graphs, p=0.2, w. 10,000 rollouts/move

6.2 STARCRAFT BATTLES

Our experiments used JarCraft, an open-source java StarCraft combat simulator as well as the search algorithms from [Justesen *et al.*, 2014]. These algorithms use UCT on different action spaces as follows:

(1) UCTCD: a UCT variant which handles simultaneous and durative actions. Possible actions are sets of unit commands. [Churchill and Buro, 2013].

(2) Script-based UCTCD: an extension of UCTCD allowing both unit commands and scripts as possible actions [Justesen *et al.*, 2014]. Also presented there were **(3)**, **(4)**: **Cluster-based UCTCD**: two improvements of UCTCD that cluster units in order to decrease the number of possible actions.

We modified these UCT-based algorithms, replacing their node-selection by Blinkered, Greedy, and C-VIBES. The test scenario is based on [Justesen *et al.*, 2014]: each competing algorithm in each run controls $\frac{n}{2}$ Protoss Zealots (close combat unit) and $\frac{n}{2}$ Protoss Dragoons (ranged combat unit) vs. an opposing team of equal size controlled by another algorithm. The units are first lined up by type and then scattered randomly. For each army size n we chose the UCT variant with the best performance according to [Justesen *et al.*, 2014].

Representative results appear in Figure 5 where Blinkered, Greedy, and C-VIBES competed against UCT. C-VIBES was the best, averaging a 77% win rate against UCT (see Figure 5), though both Blinkered and Greedy were also consistently better than UCT. C-VIBES also defeated Greedy and Blinkered in head-to-head matches (not shown).

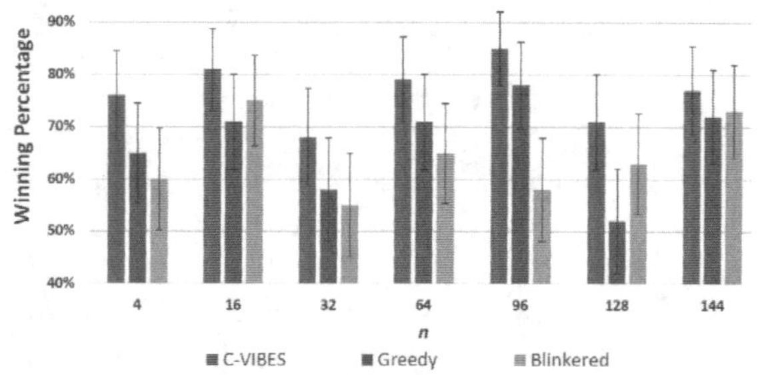

Figure 5: Win rates vs. UCT (100 games). Error bars are 95% confidence intervals.

7 CONCLUSION

Optimizing VOI for individual nodes has been shown to improve allocation of rollouts [Hay *et al.*, 2012; Feldman and Domshlak, 2013], as well as backups [Feldman and Domshlak, 2013] in MCTS. Estimating the VOI for individual nodes is too limiting. We suggested a method based on value of computation that considers large batches, and suggested several effective ways to approximately optimize them. While we confirmed that previously suggested VOI methods (MGSS* and blinkered) outperform UCT, our BVPI-based selection schemes plugged into MCTS implementations outperformed them all.

Although our measurements were assumed to be rollouts in a MCTS, the analysis in Section 3 and the batch selection methods in Section 4 may be applicable to other information-gathering operations; such as computing a static heuristic evaluation function at v, expanding v, or even real-world physical measurements (whenever the latter is meaningful).

Future improvements to our schemes are possible. First, a more disciplined way to estimate the cost of computations (e.g. by learning) would be beneficial. Second, a better defined distribution over fringe node utilities given the future rollouts is desired, such as through Bayesian updating, or estimation methods from [Feldman and Domshlak, 2013], which is essentially orthogonal to our paper, can be attempted.

Acknowledgments

Supported by ISF grant 417/13, and by the Frankel Center. We thank the authors of [Justesen *et al.*, 2014; Eyerich *et al.*, 2010] for providing their code.

References

[Bnaya *et al.*, 2009] Zahy Bnaya, Ariel Felner, and Solomon Eyal Shimony. Canadian traveler problem with remote sensing. In *Proc. of IJCAI*, pages 437–442, San Francisco, CA, USA, 2009. Morgan Kaufmann Publishers Inc.

[Browne *et al.*, 2012] Cameron Browne, Edward Jack Powley, Daniel Whitehouse, Simon M. Lucas, Peter I. Cowling, Philipp Rohlfshagen, Stephen Tavener, Diego Perez Liebana, Spyridon Samothrakis, and Simon Colton. A survey of Monte Carlo tree search methods. *IEEE Trans. Comput. Intellig. and AI in Games*, 4(1):1–43, 2012.

[Churchill and Buro, 2013] David Churchill and Michael Buro. Portfolio greedy search and simulation for large-scale combat in StarCraft. In *2013 IEEE Conference on Computational Inteligence in Games (CIG), Niagara Falls, ON, Canada, August 11-13, 2013*, pages 1–8, 2013.

[Cohen *et al.*, 2015] Liat Cohen, Solomon Eyal Shimony, and Gera Weiss. Estimating the probability of meeting a deadline in hierarchical plans. In Qiang Yang and Michael Wooldridge, editors, *Proceedings of the Twenty-Fourth International Joint Conference on Artificial Intelligence, IJCAI 2015, Buenos Aires, Argentina, July 25-31, 2015*, pages 1551–1557. AAAI Press, 2015.

[Eyerich *et al.*, 2010] Patrick Eyerich, Thomas Keller, and Malte Helmert. High-quality policies for the Canadian traveler's problem. In *In Proc. AAAI 2010*, pages 51–58, 2010.

[Feldman and Domshlak, 2013] Zohar Feldman and Carmel Domshlak. Monte-Carlo planning: Theoretically fast convergence meets practical efficiency. In Ann Nicholson and Padhraic Smyth, editors, *Proceedings of the Twenty-Ninth Conference on Uncertainty in Artificial Intelligence, UAI 2013, Bellevue, WA, USA, August 11-15, 2013*. AUAI Press, 2013.

[Fried *et al.*, 2013] Dror Fried, Solomon Eyal Shimony, Amit Benbassat, and Cenny Wenner. Complexity of Canadian traveler problem variants. *Theor. Comput. Sci.*, 487:1–16, 2013.

[Garey and Johnson, 1979] M. R. Garey and D. S. Johnson. *Computers and Intractability, A Guide to the Theory of NP-completeness*, page 190. W. H. Freeman and Co., 1979.

[Hay *et al.*, 2012] Nicholas Hay, Stuart J. Russell, David Tolpin, and Solomon Eyal Shimony. Selecting computations: Theory and applications. In Nando de Freitas and Kevin P. Murphy, editors, *Proceedings of the Twenty-Eighth Conference on Uncertainty in Artificial Intelligence, Catalina Island, CA, USA, August 14-18, 2012*, pages 346–355. AUAI Press, 2012.

[Justesen *et al.*, 2014] Niels Justesen, Balint Tillman, Julian Togelius, and Sebastian Risi. Script- and cluster-based UCT for StarCraft. In *2014 IEEE Conference on Computational Intelligence and Games, CIG 2014, Dortmund, Germany, August 26-29, 2014*, pages 1–8, 2014.

[Kocsis and Szepesvári, 2006] Levente Kocsis and Csaba Szepesvári. Bandit based Monte-Carlo planning. In *ECML*, pages 282–293, 2006.

[Krause and Guestrin, 2009] Andreas Krause and Carlos Guestrin. Optimal value of information in graphical models. *J. Artif. Intell. Res. (JAIR)*, 35:557–591, 2009.

[Krause and Guestrin, 2011] Andreas Krause and Carlos Guestrin. Submodularity and its applications in optimized information gathering. *ACM TIST*, 2(4):32, 2011.

[McAllester, 1988] David Allen McAllester. Conspiracy numbers for min-max search. *Artificial Intelligence*, 35(3):287 – 310, 1988.

[Papachristoudis and Fisher III, 2012] Georgios Papachristoudis and John W. Fisher III. Theoretical guarantees on penalized information gathering. In *Statistical Signal Processing Workshop (SSP)*, pages 301–304, Aug 2012.

[Papadimitriou and Yannakakis, 1991] Christos H. Papadimitriou and Mihalis Yannakakis. Shortest paths without a map. *Theor. Comput. Sci.*, 84(1):127–150, 1991.

[Reches *et al.*, 2013] Shulamit Reches, Ya'akov (Kobi) Gal, and Sarit Kraus. Efficiently gathering information in costly domains. *Decision Support Systems*, 55(1):326–335, 2013.

[Russell and Wefald, 1991a] Stuart J. Russell and Eric Wefald. *Do the right thing - studies in limited rationality*. MIT Press, 1991.

[Russell and Wefald, 1991b] Stuart J. Russell and Eric Wefald. Principles of metareasoning. *Artif. Intell.*, 49(1-3):361–395, 1991.

[Shperberg and Shimony, 2017] Shahaf S. Shperberg and Solomon Eyal Shimony. Some properties of batch value of information in the selection problem. *J. Artif. Intell. Res. (JAIR)*, 58:777–796, 2017.

Submodular Variational Inference for Network Reconstruction

Lin Chen[1,2], **Forrest W Crawford**[2,3] and **Amin Karbasi**[1,2]
[1]Department of Electrical Engineering, [2]Yale Institute for Network Science, [3]Department of Biostatistics, Yale University
{lin.chen,forrest.crawford,amin.karbasi}@yale.edu

Abstract

In real-world and online social networks, individuals receive and transmit information in real time. Cascading information transmissions (e.g. phone calls, text messages, social media posts) may be understood as a realization of a diffusion process operating on the network. The process only traverses and thereby reveals a limited portion of the edges. The network reconstruction/inference problem is to estimate the unrevealed connections. Most existing approaches derive a likelihood and attempt to find the network topology maximizing the likelihood, yielding a highly intractable problem. In this paper, we focus on the network reconstruction problem for a broad class of real-world diffusion processes, exemplified by a network diffusion scheme called respondent-driven sampling (RDS). We prove that under realistic and general models of network diffusion, the posterior distribution of an observed RDS realization is a Bayesian log-submodular model. We then propose VINE, a novel, accurate, and computationally efficient variational inference algorithm, for the network reconstruction problem under this model. Crucially, we do not assume any particular probabilistic model for the underlying network. VINE recovers any connected graph with high accuracy as shown by our experimental results on real-life networks.

1 INTRODUCTION

The network reconstruction problem, also known as the network inference problem (Daneshmand et al., 2014; Kramer et al., 2009; Farajtabar et al., 2015; Liben-Nowell and Kleinberg, 2007; Linderman and Adams, 2014; Anandkumar et al., 2011; Kim and Leskovec, 2011), arises naturally in a variety of scenarios and has been the focus of great research interest. In the most general setting, we assume there is an underlying unknown graph structure that represents the connections between network subjects, and that we can only observe single or multiple diffusion processes over the graph. Usually propagation of the diffusion process can only occur over network edges; however, there exist many hidden ties untraversed or unrevealed by the diffusion processes, and the goal is to infer such hidden ties. This network reconstruction problem arises in several empirical topic areas:

Blogosphere. Millions of authors in the worldwide blogosphere write articles every day, each triggering a diffusion process of reposts over the underlying blog network structure. The diffusion process initiated by an article can be represented by a directed tree. The observed data consist of multiple directed trees and it is of great interest to understand the underlying structure of information flow (Gomez-Rodriguez et al., 2014). Following inference of the network, researchers may apply community detection algorithms to, e.g., aggregate and further analyze blog sites of different political views.

Online social networks. Weibo is a Twitter-like microblogging service in China (Gao et al., 2012) where users post microblogs and repost those from other users they follow. An explicit repost chain, which indicates the sequence of users that a post passes through, is attached to each repost on Weibo. Similarly, each post initiates a diffusion process. By observing several realizations of diffusion processes, researchers seek to understand the underlying social and information network structure.

Respondent-driven sampling. Respondent-driven sampling (RDS) is a chain-referral peer recruitment procedure that is widely used in epidemiology for studying hidden and hard-to-reach human populations when random sampling is impossible (Heckathorn, 1997). RDS is commonly used in studies of men who have sex with men, homeless people, sex workers, drug users, and other groups at high risk for HIV infection (Woodhouse et al., 1994). An RDS recruitment process is also a diffusion process over an unknown social network structure, and the diffusion tree (who recruited whom) is revealed by the observed process. In addition, when a subject enters the survey, she reports her total number of acquaintances in the population, or graph-theoretically speaking, her degree in the underlying network. Understanding the underlying network structure is a topic of great interest to epidemiologists and sociologists who wish to study the transmission of infectious diseases, and the propagation of health-related behaviors in the networks of high-risk groups (Crawford, 2016). However, in contrast to the aforementioned scenarios where multiple diffusion realizations are available over the same network, in RDS we can only observe a single realization due to limited financial, temporal and human resources to conduct the experiments. As a result, network reconstruction from RDS data is particularly challenging and only heuristic algorithms are known. Crawford (2016) assumes that the recruitment time along any recruitment link is exponentially distributed and thus models RDS as a continuous-time diffusion process. Chen et al. (2016) removes the exponential distribution assumption and extends it to any distribution. Both works use a simulated-annealing-based heuristic to find the most likely configuration.

As a general strategy, for a particular diffusion model, a likelihood function can be derived that measures the probability of a diffusion realization. In this way, the network inference problem can be cast as an optimization problem, in which the researcher seeks the topology that maximizes the likelihood. Unfortunately, the derived likelihood functions are usually intractable for efficient maximization with respect to the graph, and can be computationally prohibitive to evaluate. To address this challenge, approximate solutions have been proposed as an efficient alternative (Gomez-Rodriguez et al., 2010, 2013). For instance, Gomez-Rodriguez et al. (2010), instead of maximizing the likelihood, derived an alternative heuristic formulation by considering only the most likely tree (still an NP-hard problem) rather than all possible propagation trees and showed how a greedy solution can find a near-optimal solution. It enjoys good empirical results when many realizations of the diffusion process can be observed.

In this paper, we consider the challenging instance of network inference where only one realization of the diffusion process is observed. As a motivating empirical example, we study the network reconstruction problem for RDS data and propose VINE (Variational Inference for Network rEconstruction), a computationally efficient variational inference algorithm. Our major contributions are summarized as follows.

Proof of log-submodularity and a variational inference algorithm. We show that under a realistic model of RDS diffusion, the likelihood function is log-submodular. Using variational inference methods, we approximate the submodular function with affine functions and obtain tight upper and lower bounds for the partition function. We then estimate the most probable network configuration, which is the maximizer of the likelihood, as well as the marginal probability of each edge.

Relaxation of constraints. The optimization problem of the RDS likelihood (as shown later) is constrained. First, the observed diffusion results in a directed subgraph and the inferred network must be a supergraph of the diffusion process. Second, for each subject, their degree in the reconstructed subgraph cannot exceed their total network degree. The first constraint is easy to incorporate while the second precludes efficient computation of partition functions of the likelihood (or any linear approximations). We address this challenge by introducing penalty terms in the objective function. This way, the constrained reconstruction problem becomes unconstrained and admits the use of variational methods.

Flexibility for possibly inexact reported degrees. One may not assume that the reported degrees by recruited subjects are exact because subjects may not be able to accurately recall the number of people they know who are members of the target population. We would like to note that the aforementioned relaxation of the second constraint allows for more flexibility of the possible mismatch of the reported degrees from the true ones by introducing an additional term that penalizes the deviation between the reported and true degrees, seeking to preserve the relative accuracy of the reported degrees.

High reconstruction performance and time efficiency using a single realization of RDS diffusion. As shown by our experiments, VINE achieves significantly higher inference performance while running orders of magnitude faster. We should note that the very accurate inference is achieved based on the observation of a single diffusion realization. This is in sharp contrast to previous work that assumes multiple diffusion realizations.

2 NETWORK RECONSTRUCTION FOR RDS DATA

We use the following notational convention throughout this paper. The symbol $\mathbf{1}$ denotes the all-ones column

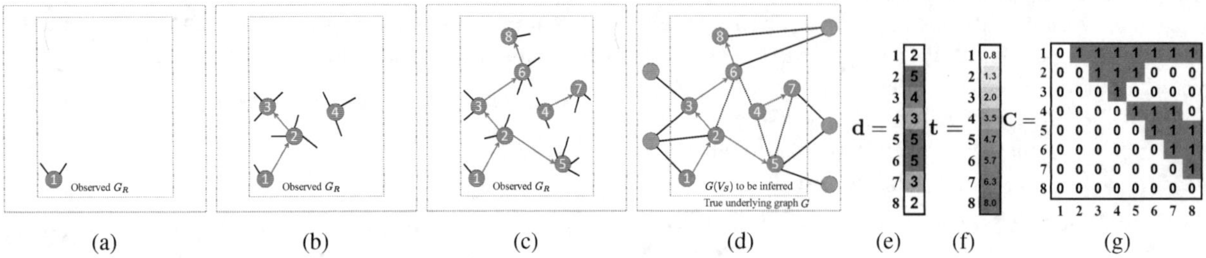

Figure 1: Example RDS recruitment with unobserved and observed data. Nodes 1 and 4 are seed nodes chosen directly by the researchers; however, only node 1 is recruited at the beginning of the study. Every subject except nodes 3 and 4 is given two coupons, while nodes 3 and 4 are given only one. Figs. 1a to 1c show three snapshots of the RDS process at three different times. Fig. 1a shows the snapshot when the seed node 1 just enters the study due to direct recruitment by the researchers. Node 1 reports that her total degree is 2; thus there are two pendant edges attached to her. Fig. 1b presents the snapshot when the other seed node 4 is directly recruited by the researchers. Before node 4 is recruited, node 1 recruits node 2 and then node 2 recruits node 3. Red arrows denote the recruitment relation. Nodes 2, 3, and 4 report that their total degrees are 5, 4, and 3, respectively; thus there are 5, 4, and 3 pendant edges attached to them, respectively. Fig. 1c illustrates the snapshot at the end of the experiment. Fig. 1d reveals the whole picture of the RDS process, containing the observable part (within the inner rectangle) and the unobservable part (outside the inner rectangle), where the inner rectangle denotes the sample and the outer rectangle denotes the entire population. The dashed lines denote the hidden ties to be inferred within the sample. The nodes outside the inner rectangle are marked in gray and they are the unsampled and thereby unobservable nodes. In Fig. 1e, $\mathbf{d} = (\mathbf{d}_1, \mathbf{d}_2, \mathbf{d}_3, \ldots, \mathbf{d}_n)'$ is the degree vector, where $\mathbf{d}_i$ is the total degree of node i in G. In Fig. 1f, $\mathbf{t} = (\mathbf{t}_1, \mathbf{t}_2, \mathbf{t}_3, \ldots, \mathbf{t}_n)'$ is the recruitment time vector, where $\mathbf{t}_i$ is the recruitment time of node i. In Fig. 1g, $\mathbf{C}$ is the coupon matrix; its (i, j)-entry is 1 if node i has at least one coupon just before the jth recruitment event and is 0 otherwise. The observed data consist of $\mathbf{Y} = (\mathbf{C}, \mathbf{d}, \mathbf{t}, G_R)$.

vector. If f is a real-valued function and that $\mathbf{v}$ is a vector, then $f(\mathbf{v})$ is a vector of the same size as vector $\mathbf{v}$, we denote the i-th entry of $f(\mathbf{v})$ by $f(\mathbf{v})_i$, and $f(\mathbf{v})_i = f(\mathbf{v}_i)$. The transposes of matrix $\mathbf{A}$ and vector $\mathbf{v}$ are written as $\mathbf{A}'$ and $\mathbf{v}'$, respectively.

The objective of the RDS sampling method is to obtain a sample from a population for which random sampling is impossible. The network structure of the underlying inaccessible population is modeled as an undirected simple graph $G = (V, E)$, where each vertex represents an individual and edges represent the intra-population connections. The sample obtained via RDS is denoted by $V_S \subseteq V$. Let $n = |V_S|$ be the number of subjects recruited into the study by the end of the RDS process.

In contrast to random sampling, RDS is a chain-referral process that operates by propagating a diffusion process on the edges of the target social network. Subjects enter the study one at a time. The recruitment (diffusion) process is done either by researchers directly or by other subjects already in the study prior to this new recruitment event. If a subject is recruited into the study by researchers directly, she is called a *seed*. Let $M \subseteq V_S$ be the set of all seed nodes. Note that seed nodes may not necessarily be recruited simultaneously; however, we need at least one seed that enters the study at the initial stage of the experiment in order to initiate the chain-referrals over the underlying network. We label the subjects $i = 1, \ldots, n$ in the time-order they enter the study; node $i \in V_S$ is the i-th subject that enters the study. When a subject enters the study (either via researchers directly or other subjects already in the study), she will be given several coupons to recruit other members (each recruitment costs one coupon). Each coupon is marked with a unique ID that can be traced back to the recruiter. Subjects are given a reward for being interviewed and recruiting other eligible subjects. The date/time of every subject's recruitment is recorded and every subject reports their total number of acquaintances (their network *degree*). Let $\mathbf{t}_i$ be the recorded recruitment time of subject i and $\mathbf{d}_i$ be the reported degree of subject i in the population (in the graph G). Let the recruitment time and degree vector be $\mathbf{t} = (\mathbf{t}_1, \mathbf{t}_2, \ldots, \mathbf{t}_n)'$ and $\mathbf{d} = (\mathbf{d}_1, \mathbf{d}_2, \ldots, \mathbf{d}_n)'$, respectively.

Once a subject recruits another subject the (directed) link between them will be revealed. The direction simply indicates who recruited whom. Furthermore, any subject who has entered the study with a coupon may not reenter the study with another coupon, and no participant may enter the study more than once. Thus no subject can recruit others already recruited and thereby already in the study. We can form a directed graph, called the recruitment graph $G_R = (V_R, E_R)$, that has the same vertex set as V_S and reflects the recruitment links; $(i, j) \in E_R$ if and only if subject i directly recruits j. The above requirements will result in a directed recruitment graph G_R being a disjoint union of rooted directed arborescences (a directed graph is a rooted directed arborescence with root r if for every vertex v, there exists a unique directed path from r to v) (Gordon and McMahon, 1989), where the root corresponds to a seed node. Equivalently, an arborescence is a directed, rooted tree in which all edges point away from the root. We illustrate an example of G_R in Fig. 1d, where the red links form the recruitment graph G_R and there are two disjoint arborescences with roots 1 and 4, respectively; the two roots correspond to the two seed nodes.

The first subject enters the study at time $\mathbf{t}_1$. At some time $t \geq \mathbf{t}_1$, any subject in the study who has at least one coupon (recall that each recruitment costs one coupon and that one cannot recruit any subject without a coupon) and has at least one acquaintance not in the study (i.e., has at least one neighbor in G who is not already recruited) is called a *recruiter* at time t; accordingly, any subject who is not in the study and is connected to at least one recruiter is called a *potential recruitee* or a *susceptible subject* at time t; and the edge between a recruiter and a potential recruitee is said to be *susceptible* at time t. Let $R(i)$ and $I(i)$ be the recruiter set and potential recruitee set just before time $\mathbf{t}_i$, respectively. Similarly, If subject u is a recruiter just before time $\mathbf{t}_i$, then $I_u(i)$ denotes the set of potential recruitees connected to subject u just before time $\mathbf{t}_i$, and if u is a potential recruitee just before time $\mathbf{t}_i$, then $R_u(i)$ denotes the set of recruiters connected to subject u just before time $\mathbf{t}_i$.

In what follows, we model RDS as a continuous-time stochastic process on the edges of a hidden graph. Our goal is to estimate the induced subgraph connecting the sampled vertices G_S. To do this, we construct a flexible model for this process and derive its likelihood, conditional on an underlying graph. The inference problem is to find the graph that maximizes this likelihood, subject to the constraint that the graph must be compatible with the observed degrees in the data. We start with making the following assumptions:

Assumption 1. *Upon entering the study, each subject is given coupons and begins to recruit other members (if any) immediately.*

Assumption 2. *Inter-recruitment times between any recruiter and its potential recruitees are i.i.d. continuous random variables with cumulative distribution function (cdf) $D(t;\theta)$ parametrized by $\theta \in \Theta$.*

In fact, Assumption 2 can be relaxed to the case where inter-recruitment times are independent but not necessarily identically distributed. For simplicity we assume that they are i.i.d.

If W_θ is a random variable with cdf $D(t;\theta)$, we have $D(t;\theta) = \Pr[W_\theta \leq t]$ and let $D_s(t;\theta) = \Pr[W_\theta \leq t | W_\theta > s]$. We write $\rho_s(t;\theta) = \frac{\mathrm{d}D_s(t;\theta)}{\mathrm{d}t}$ for the conditional probability density function (pdf). Let $S_s(t;\theta) = 1 - D_s(t;\theta)$ be the conditional survival function and $H_s(t;\theta) = \frac{\rho_s(t;\theta)}{S_s(t;\theta)}$ be the conditional hazard function. Recall that the set of all subjects in the study is denoted by $V_S = \{1, 2, 3, \ldots, n\} \subseteq V$. The recruitment graph $G_R = (V_R, E_R)$ has the same vertex set as V_S and indicates who recruited whom: $(i,j) \in E_R$ if subject i recruits subject j. Note that subject i can recruit subject j only if there is an edge in the underlying network G that connects i and j. The $n \times n$ coupon matrix $\mathbf{C}$ has a 1 in entry $\mathbf{C}_{ij}$ if subject i has at least one coupon just before the j-th recruitment event $\mathbf{t}_j$, and zero otherwise. In addition, we define another $n \times n$ matrix $\mathbf{A}_R$, which is the adjacency matrix of the undirected version of G_R, obtained by replacing all directed edges with undirected edges.

Assumption 3. *The observed data from an RDS process consists of $\mathbf{Y} = (\mathbf{C}, \mathbf{d}, \mathbf{t}, G_R)$.*

Our goal is to infer the induced subgraph $G(V_S)$, denoted by $G_S = (V_S, E_S)$, which encodes all connections among the subjects in the study. We also use $\mathbf{A}$ to denote the adjacency matrix of G_S and throughout this paper $\mathbf{A}$ and G_S are used interchangeably. Obviously the undirectified version of G_R must be a subgraph of G_S. Thus $\mathbf{A}$ must be greater than or equal to $\mathbf{A}_R$ entrywise; formally,

$$\mathbf{A} \geq \mathbf{A}_R \text{ (entrywise).}$$

This will be a constraint in the optimization problem specified later in Problem 1. Fig. 1 shows an example of an RDS process including its unobserved and observed parts.

Recall that M denotes the set of seeds and let $\tau(u;i) = \mathbf{t}_{i-1} - \mathbf{t}_u$. The likelihood of the recruitment time series is given by

$$\begin{aligned} & L(\mathbf{t}|\mathbf{A},\theta) \\ &= \prod_{i=1}^{n} \left(\sum_{u \in R(i)} |I_u(i)| H_{\tau(u;i)}(\mathbf{t}_i - \mathbf{t}_u;\theta) \right)^{1\{i \notin M\}} \\ &\times \prod_{j \in R(i)} S_{\tau(j;i)}^{|I_j|}(\mathbf{t}_i - \mathbf{t}_j;\theta) \end{aligned} \tag{1}$$

(The proof of Eq. (1) is presented in Appendix A). The above model was originally derived in (Chen et al., 2016).

We can represent the log-likelihood in a more compact way using linear algebra. Prior to this, we need some notation. Let $\mathbf{m}$ and $\mathbf{u}$ be column vectors of size n such that $\mathbf{m}_i = 1\{i \notin M\}$ and $\mathbf{u}_i$ is the number of pendant edges of subject i (the reported total degree of subject i minus the number of its neighbors in G_S), i.e.,

$$\mathbf{u}_i = \mathbf{d}_i - |\{j \in V_S : (i,j) \in E_S\}|,$$

and let $\mathbf{H}$ and $\mathbf{S}$ be $n \times n$ matrices, defined as $\mathbf{H}_{ui} = H_{\tau(u;i)}(\mathbf{t}_i - \mathbf{t}_u; \theta)$ and $\mathbf{S}_{ji} = \log S_{\tau(j;i)}(\mathbf{t}_i - \mathbf{t}_j; \theta)$. Furthermore, we form matrices $\mathbf{B} = (\mathbf{C} \circ \mathbf{H})$ and $\mathbf{D} = (\mathbf{C} \circ \mathbf{S})$, where $\circ$ denotes the Hadamard (entrywise) product. We let

$$\begin{aligned}\beta &= \log(\mathbf{B}'\mathbf{u} + \mathrm{LowerTri}(\mathbf{AB})' \cdot \mathbf{1}),\\ \delta &= \mathbf{D}'\mathbf{u} + \mathrm{LowerTri}(\mathbf{AD})' \cdot \mathbf{1},\end{aligned}$$

where the log of a vector is taken entrywise and $\mathrm{LowerTri}(\cdot)$ denotes the lower triangular part (diagonal elements inclusive) of a square matrix. Then the log-likelihood can be written as

$$l(\mathbf{t}|\mathbf{A}, \theta) = \mathbf{m}'\beta + \mathbf{1}'\delta \quad (2)$$

(The proof of Eq. (2) is presented in Appendix B). To adopt a Bayesian approach, we consider maximizing the joint posterior distribution $\Pr(\mathbf{A}, \theta|\mathbf{t}) \propto L(\mathbf{t}|\mathbf{A}, \theta)\pi(\mathbf{A})\phi(\theta)$, where π and ϕ are the prior distribution of $\mathbf{A}$ and θ. The network inference problem of the RDS data is reduced to maximization of $\Pr(\mathbf{A}, \theta|\mathbf{t})$. Our main observation in this paper is that the log-likelihood function is submodular, which opens the possibility of rigorous analysis and variational inference.

If we assume that the reported degrees of subjects are exact, then the vector $\mathbf{u}$ should be set to $\mathbf{d} - \mathbf{A} \cdot \mathbf{1}$ and it must be non-negative entrywise. However, in practice, the reported degree of a subject may be an approximation, but we assume the true degree does not deviate excessively from the reported degree. To be more flexible, we allow $\mathbf{u}$ to be any non-negative integer-valued vector. In this case, the true degree vector will be $\mathbf{d}_{\text{true}} = \mathbf{u} + \mathbf{A} \cdot \mathbf{1}$. We penalize it if $\mathbf{d}_{\text{true}}$ deviates from $\mathbf{d}$ excessively. To be precise, we define the prior distribution $\pi(\mathbf{A})$ as

$$\pi(\mathbf{A}) \propto \exp(-\psi(\max\{\mathbf{u} + \mathbf{A} \cdot \mathbf{1} - \mathbf{d}, \mathbf{0}\})), \quad (3)$$

where max is conducted entrywise and ψ is a multivariate (n-dimensional) convex function and non-decreasing in each argument whenever this argument is non-negative. We can now formulate our inference problem as an optimization problem.

Problem 1. Given the observed data $\mathbf{Y} = (\mathbf{C}, \mathbf{d}, \mathbf{t}, G_R)$, we seek an $n \times n$ adjacency matrix (symmetric, binary and zero-diagonal) and a parameter value $\theta \in \Theta$ that

$$\begin{aligned}&\text{maximizes} \quad L(\mathbf{t}|\mathbf{A}, \theta)\pi(\mathbf{A})\phi(\theta)\\ &\text{subject to} \quad \mathbf{A} \geq \mathbf{A}_R \text{ (entrywise).}\end{aligned}$$

Problem 1 can be solved by maximizing the likelihood with respect to θ and $\mathbf{A}$ alternately. We set an initial guess θ_1 for the parameter θ. In the τ-th iteration ($\tau \geq 1$), setting $\theta = \theta_\tau$ in Problem 1, we optimize the objective function over $\mathbf{A}$ (this step is called the $\mathbf{A}$-step), denoting the maximizer by $\mathbf{A}_\tau$; then setting $\mathbf{A} = \mathbf{A}_\tau$ in Problem 1, we optimize the objective function over θ (this step is called the θ-step), denoting the maximizer by $\theta_{\tau+1}$. The interested reader is referred to Algorithm 1 in (Chen et al., 2016). Note that the parameter space Θ is usually a subset of the Euclidean space. The optimization problem given $\mathbf{A}$ in the θ-step can be solved with off-the-shelf solvers. As a result, we focus on the $\mathbf{A}$-step; equivalently, we study how to solve Problem 1 assuming that θ is known.

3 PROPOSED METHOD

We now present a network reconstruction algorithm, based on submodular variational inference, for respondent-driven sampling data. This method is referred to as VINE in this paper. We first introduce the definition of a submodular function (Jegelka et al., 2011; Iyer and Bilmes, 2015).

Definition 1. A pseudo-Boolean function $f : \{0,1\}^p \to \mathbb{R}$ is *submodular* if $\forall \mathbf{x}, \mathbf{y} \in \{0,1\}^p$, we have $f(\mathbf{x}) + f(\mathbf{y}) \geq f(\mathbf{x} \wedge \mathbf{y}) + f(\mathbf{x} \vee \mathbf{y})$, where $\wedge$ and $\vee$ denote entrywise logical conjunction and disjunction, respectively.

We can trivially identify the domain $\{0,1\}^p$ with $2^{[p]}$, the power set of $[p] = \{1, 2, 3, \ldots, p\}$. Thus a pseudo-Boolean function f can also be viewed as a set function $2^{[p]} \to \mathbb{R}$. We will view f from these two perspectives interchangeably throughout this paper. If we view f as a set function, it is submodular if for every subset $X, Y \subseteq [p]$, we have $f(X) + f(Y) \geq f(X \cap Y) + f(X \cup Y)$. An equivalent definition is that f is submodular if for every $X \subseteq Y \subseteq [p]$ and $x \in [p] \setminus Y$, we have $f(X \cup \{x\}) - f(X) \geq f(Y \cup \{x\}) - f(Y)$; this is also known as the "diminishing returns" property because the marginal gain when an element is added to a subset is no less than the marginal gain when it is added to its superset.

A pseudo-Boolean or set function f is *log-submodular* if $\log(f)$ is submodular; it is *modular* if $f(\mathbf{x}) = \sum_{i=1}^p f_i \mathbf{x}_i$ (if viewed as a pseudo-Boolean function) or equivalently $f(X) = \sum_{i \in X} f_i$ (if viewed as a set function), where $f_i \in \mathbb{R}$ is called the weight of the element i. It is *affine* if $f(\mathbf{x}) = s(\mathbf{x}) + c$, where s is modular and c is some fixed real number; similarly, it is *log-affine* if $\log(f)$ is affine.

3.1 RELAXATION OF CONSTRAINTS

The formulation of Problem 1 makes clear that the network reconstruction problem is a constrained optimization problem. Recall that we have two constraints. One is that the reconstructed subgraph should contain all edges already revealed by the RDS process. This constraint is natural since if a direct recruitment occurs between two subjects, then they must know each other in the underlying social network. The other constraint is that the degree of the subject in the reconstructed subgraph must be bounded by the degree that this subject reports. In this section, we remove these two constraints and cast it into an unconstrained problem. The first constraint is easy to remove by considering only the edges unrevealed by the RDS process. The final objective function results from replacing the second constraint with a penalty function to allow for some room for the deviation of the degree in the inferred subgraph from the reported degree. After relaxing the two constraints, we turn Problem 1 into an unconstrained problem and make submodular variational inference (to be discussed later in Section 3.3) possible.

Specifically, the first constraint requires some entries of $\mathbf{A}$ to be 1; if the (i, j)-entry of $\mathbf{A}_R$ (denoted by $\mathbf{A}_R^{ij}$) is 1, so is $\mathbf{A}$. Only the rest of the entries of $\mathbf{A}$ can either be 0 or 1 and are the free entries. We collect the free entries in a binary vector

$$\boldsymbol{\alpha} = (\mathbf{A}_{ij} : 1 \le i < j \le n, \mathbf{A}_R^{ij} = 0)$$

and view $L(\mathbf{t}|\mathbf{A}, \theta)\pi(\mathbf{A})\phi(\theta)$ as a function of $\boldsymbol{\alpha}$. In fact, there is a one-to-one correspondence between $\mathbf{A}$ and $\boldsymbol{\alpha}$. In this way, we remove the constraint $\mathbf{A} \ge \mathbf{A}_R$. Now we discuss how to relax the second constraint (the degree constraint) to make small deviation from the (usually approximate) reported degree possible.

Representing u as a binary vector and thereby the objective function as a pseudo-Boolean function. We notice that $L(\mathbf{t}|\mathbf{A}, \theta)\pi(\mathbf{A})\phi(\theta)$ is also a function of $\mathbf{u}$; however, $\mathbf{u}$ is an integer-valued vector rather than a binary vector. We consider representing $\mathbf{u}$ as a binary vector and thereby casting $L(\mathbf{t}|\mathbf{A}, \theta)\pi(\mathbf{A})\phi(\theta)$ into a pseudo-Boolean function. We observe that $\mathbf{u}$ is bounded entrywise; to be precise, $\forall 1 \le i \le n$, $0 \le \mathbf{u}_i \le u_{\max}$, where $u_{\max} = \max_{1 \le i \le n}(\mathbf{d} - \mathbf{A} \cdot \mathbf{1})_i$. We can form an $n \times \lceil \log_2 u_{\max} \rceil$ matrix $\boldsymbol{\mu}$ such that the i-th row of $\boldsymbol{\mu}$ is the binary representation of $\mathbf{u}_i$; formally,

$$\mathbf{u} = \boldsymbol{\mu} \cdot \begin{pmatrix} 2^0 & 2^1 & 2^2 & \dots & 2^{\lceil \log_2 u_{\max} \rceil - 1} \end{pmatrix}'.$$

In this way, we represent $L(\mathbf{t}|\mathbf{A}, \theta)\pi(\mathbf{A})\phi(\theta)$ as a pseudo-Boolean function of $\boldsymbol{\alpha}$ and $\boldsymbol{\mu}$. Let $\boldsymbol{\gamma} = (\boldsymbol{\alpha}, \boldsymbol{\mu})$ and define $\tilde{L}(\boldsymbol{\gamma}) = L(\mathbf{t}|\mathbf{A}, \theta)\pi(\mathbf{A})\phi(\theta)$. Therefore $\tilde{L}$ is a pseudo-Boolean function of $\boldsymbol{\gamma}$, whose dimension is $N = \sum_{1 \le i < j \le n} 1_{\{\mathbf{A}_R^{ij} = 0\}} + n \times \lceil \log_2 u_{\max} \rceil$. The likelihood function $\tilde{L}(\boldsymbol{\gamma})$ defines a probability measure over $\{0, 1\}^N$, $\Pr(\boldsymbol{\gamma}) = \tilde{L}(\boldsymbol{\gamma})/\tilde{Z}$, where $\tilde{Z} = \sum_{\boldsymbol{\gamma} \in \{0,1\}^N} \tilde{L}(\boldsymbol{\gamma})$ is the normalizing constant.

3.2 LOG-SUBMODULARITY OF LIKELIHOOD

Theorem 1 below shows that $\tilde{L}(\boldsymbol{\gamma})$ is log-submodular. We know that a submodular function can be approximated by affine functions from above and below. Due to the log-submodularity of $\tilde{L}(\boldsymbol{\gamma})$, it can be approximated by two log-affine functions from above and below. The partition function of a probability distribution proportional to a log-affine function can be computed in a closed form; therefore this distribution can be computed exactly and we have upper and lower bounds of $\Pr(\boldsymbol{\gamma})$; we can conduct variational inference via the two bounds. We will elaborate on this in Section 3.3.

Theorem 1 (Proof in Appendix C). *The function $\tilde{L}(\boldsymbol{\gamma})$ is log-submodular; equivalently, there exists a submodular function $\tilde{F}(\boldsymbol{\gamma})$ such that $\tilde{L}(\boldsymbol{\gamma}) = \exp \tilde{F}(\boldsymbol{\gamma})$ for every $\boldsymbol{\gamma} \in \{0, 1\}^N$.*

Normalizing $\tilde{L}(\boldsymbol{\gamma})$ into $L(\boldsymbol{\gamma})$. Ideally, we want a submodular function F to be *normalized*; i.e., $F(\mathbf{0}) = 0$, or equivalently $F(\varnothing) = 0$ if viewed as a set function. Thus we define $F(\boldsymbol{\gamma}) \triangleq \tilde{F}(\boldsymbol{\gamma}) - \tilde{F}(\mathbf{0})$; this way F is a normalized submodular function (it is a submodular function minus some constant). In addition, we define $L(\boldsymbol{\gamma}) = \exp(F(\boldsymbol{\gamma}))$ and we have $L(\boldsymbol{\gamma}) = \exp(\tilde{F}(\boldsymbol{\gamma}) - \tilde{F}(\mathbf{0})) = \exp(-\tilde{F}(\mathbf{0}))\tilde{L}(\boldsymbol{\gamma})$. Note that the probability measure is proportional to $\tilde{L}(\boldsymbol{\gamma}) = L(\mathbf{t}|\mathbf{A}, \theta)\pi(\mathbf{A})\phi(\theta)$ (up a constant factor) and that $L(\boldsymbol{\gamma})$ only differs from $\tilde{L}(\boldsymbol{\gamma})$ up to a constant factor. Therefore the probability measure remains proportional to $L(\boldsymbol{\gamma})$, thus $L(\boldsymbol{\gamma})$ is also a likelihood function and defines the same probability measure over $\{0, 1\}^N$ as $\tilde{L}(\boldsymbol{\gamma})$ does. As a result, the probability measure can be expressed as $\Pr(\boldsymbol{\gamma}) = \frac{1}{Z}\exp(F(\boldsymbol{\gamma}))$, where $Z = \sum_{\boldsymbol{\gamma} \in \{0,1\}^N} \exp(F(\boldsymbol{\gamma}))$ is the normalizing constant, or the *partition function*.

3.3 VARIATIONAL INFERENCE

Using a variational method lets us consider bounding $F(\boldsymbol{\gamma})$ from above and from below with affine functions. We want to find modular functions s_u and s_l and two real numbers c_u and c_l such that $s_l(\boldsymbol{\gamma}) + c_l \le F(\boldsymbol{\gamma}) \le s_u(\boldsymbol{\gamma}) + c_u$ for all $\boldsymbol{\gamma} \in \{0, 1\}^N$. If this holds for all $\boldsymbol{\gamma} \in \{0, 1\}^N$, then we have the inequality between log-partition functions: $\sum_{\boldsymbol{\gamma} \in \{0,1\}^N} \exp(s_l(\boldsymbol{\gamma}) + c_l) \le \sum_{\boldsymbol{\gamma} \in \{0,1\}^N} \exp F(\boldsymbol{\gamma}) = Z \le \sum_{\boldsymbol{\gamma} \in \{0,1\}^N} \exp(s_u(\boldsymbol{\gamma}) + c_u)$. We define the partition function of the affine function $s(\boldsymbol{\gamma}) + c$ as $Z(s, c) \triangleq \sum_{\boldsymbol{\gamma} \in \{0,1\}^N} \exp(s(\boldsymbol{\gamma}) + c)$. Using this notation, we have $Z(s_l, c_l) \le Z \le Z(s_u, c_u)$. Note that from this we may also obtain the bounds for the marginal probability for each element $i \in [N]$. To be precise, if γ is sampled from the distribution $\Pr(\gamma) = \exp(F(\gamma))/Z$, then the marginal probability $\Pr(i \in \gamma)$ satisfies $\frac{s_l(\{i\})+c_l}{Z(s_u,c_u)} \leq \Pr(i \in \gamma) \leq \frac{s_u(\{i\})+c_u}{Z(s_l,c_l)}$. We may also use $s_u(\gamma) + c_u$ or $s_l(\gamma) + c_l$ as a surrogate for F and make inference via these two affine functions.

Suppose that we already have two affine functions $s_u(\gamma)+c_u$ and $s_l(\gamma)+c_l$ bounding $F(\gamma)$ from above and below. By Lemma 1 in (Djolonga and Krause, 2014), the log-partition function for $s(\gamma) + c$ in the unconstrained case is $\log Z'(s, c) \triangleq \log \sum_{\gamma\in\{0,1\}^N} \exp(s(\gamma) + c) = c + \sum_{i=1}^{N} \log(1 + \exp s_i)$, where $s_i = s(\{i\})$ is the weight of element i. Thus we have $Z'(s_l, c_l) \leq Z = \sum_{\gamma\in\{0,1\}^N} L(\gamma) = \sum_{\gamma\in\{0,1\}^N} \exp F(\gamma) \leq Z'(s_u, c_u)$.

So our goal is to find the upper- and lower-bound affine functions.

Lower-bound affine function. We define $v_j = \arg\max_{k\in[N]\setminus V_j} (F(V_j \cup \{k\}) - F(V_j))$, and $s^g_{v_j} = \max_{k\in[N]\setminus V_j} (F(V_j \cup \{k\}) - F(V_j))$, where $V_1 = \varnothing$, $V_j = \{v_1, v_2, \ldots, v_{j-1}\}$, and $1 \leq j \leq N$ (Djolonga and Krause, 2014; Iyer et al., 2013). Then we have the affine function s^g that assigns to $i \in [N]$ a weight of s^g_i. Let $s_l(\gamma) = s^g(\gamma)$ and $c_l = 0$.

Proposition 1 (Proof in Appendix D). *The affine function s^g is a lower-bound function of the submodular function F; for all $\gamma \in \{0,1\}^N$, $s^g(\gamma) \leq F(\gamma)$.*

Upper-bound affine function. We may find an upper-bound affine function for a submodular function via its supergradients. The set of supergradients of a submodular function F at $\mathbf{x} \in \{0,1\}^N$ (Iyer et al., 2013) is defined as

$$\partial^F(\mathbf{x}) = \{s \text{ is modular}: \forall \mathbf{y} \in \{0,1\}^N, F(\mathbf{y}) \leq F(\mathbf{x}) + s(\mathbf{y}) - s(\mathbf{x})\}.$$

If a modular function s is a supergradient of F at $\mathbf{x}$, then the affine function $s(\gamma) + (F(\mathbf{x}) - s(\mathbf{x}))$ is an upper bound of $F(\gamma)$. The corresponding log-partition function is $Z'_{\mathbf{x}}(s) = Z'(s, F(\mathbf{x}) - s(\mathbf{x}))$.

We consider three families of supergradient, which are grow ($\hat{s}_{\mathbf{x}}$), shrink ($\check{s}_{\mathbf{x}}$) and bar ($\bar{s}_{\mathbf{x}}$) supergradients at $\mathbf{x}$ (Iyer et al., 2013; Iyer and Bilmes, 2012; Djolonga and Krause, 2014). Let us view $F(\gamma)$ as a set function where $\gamma \subseteq [N]$. We define $\Delta_i F(\gamma) = F(\gamma \cup \{i\}) - F(\gamma)$, where $i \in [N]$. These three supergradients are defined as follows. If $j \in \mathbf{x}$, then $\hat{s}_{\mathbf{x}}(\{j\}) = \check{s}_{\mathbf{x}}(\{j\}) = \Delta_j F(\mathbf{x} \setminus \{j\})$ and $\bar{s}_{\mathbf{x}}(\{j\}) = \Delta_j F([N] \setminus \{j\})$ if $j \notin \mathbf{x}$, then $\hat{s}_{\mathbf{x}}(\{j\}) = \Delta_j F(\mathbf{x})$ and $\check{s}_{\mathbf{x}}(\{j\}) = \bar{s}_{\mathbf{x}}(\{j\}) = F(\{j\})$. To make the paper self-contained, we include in the appendix the proof of Proposition 2 showing that they are indeed supergradients.

Algorithm 1 VINE

Input: observed data $\mathbf{Y} = (\mathbf{C}, \mathbf{d}, \mathbf{t}, G_R)$
Output: inferred adjacency matrix $\hat{\mathbf{A}}$

function GETLOWERBOUNDAFFINEFUNCTION
  $V_1 \leftarrow \varnothing$
  for $j \leftarrow 1$ **to** N **do**
    $v_j \leftarrow \arg\max_{k\in[N]\setminus V_j} (F(V_j \cup \{k\}) - F(V_j))$
    $s^g_{v_j} \leftarrow \max_{k\in[N]\setminus V_j} (F(V_j \cup \{k\}) - F(V_j))$
    $V_{j+1} \leftarrow V_j \cup \{v_j\}$
  end for
  return affine function $s_l(\gamma) = \sum_{j=1}^{N} s^g_j \gamma_j$
end function

function GETUPPERBOUNDAFFINEFUNCTION
  $m_i \leftarrow \log\left(1 + e^{-\Delta_i F([N]\setminus\{i\})}\right) - \log\left(1 + e^{F(\{i\})}\right)$
  Define $m(\mathbf{x}) = \sum_{i=1}^{N} m_i \mathbf{x}_i$
  $\mathbf{x} \leftarrow \arg\min_{\mathbf{x}} (F(\mathbf{x}) + m(\mathbf{x}))$
  $S_{\mathbf{x}} = \{\hat{s}_{\mathbf{x}}, \check{s}_{\mathbf{x}}, \bar{s}_{\mathbf{x}}\}$
  $s_u \leftarrow \arg\min_{s\in S_{\mathbf{x}}} Z'_{\mathbf{x}}(s)$
  return affine function $s_u(\gamma) + (F(\mathbf{x}) - s_u(\mathbf{x}))$
end function

function VARIATIONALINFERENCE
  $s \leftarrow$ GETUPPERBOUNDAFFINEFUNCTION() or GETLOWERBOUNDAFFINEFUNCTION()
  Select threshold $\zeta \in [\min_i s^\alpha_i, \max_i s^\alpha_i]$
  $\boldsymbol{\alpha}_i \leftarrow 1_{\{s^\alpha_i \geq \zeta\}}$
  Obtain the inferred adjacency matrix $\hat{\mathbf{A}}$ from $\boldsymbol{\alpha}$
end function

Proposition 2 (Proof in Appendix E). *The modular functions $\hat{s}_{\mathbf{x}}$, $\check{s}_{\mathbf{x}}$ and $\bar{s}_{\mathbf{x}}$ are supergradients of the submodular function F at $\mathbf{x}$.*

Define the modular function

$$m(\{i\}) = \log\left(1 + e^{-\Delta_i F([N]\setminus\{i\})}\right) - \log\left(1 + e^{F(\{i\})}\right).$$

By Lemma 4 in (Djolonga and Krause, 2014), we know that these two optimization problems are equivalent:

$$\min_{\mathbf{x}} \log Z'_{\mathbf{x}}(\bar{s}^{\mathbf{x}}) \equiv \min_{\mathbf{x}} F(\mathbf{x}) + m(\mathbf{x}).$$

The right-hand side is an unconstrained submodular minimization problem, which can be solved efficiently (Jegelka et al., 2011). By solving this problem, we obtain a supergradient $\bar{s}^{\mathbf{x}}$ at $\mathbf{x}$ and thus know its partition function $Z'_{\mathbf{x}}(\bar{s}^{\mathbf{x}})$. Then we compute the partition function of grow and shrink supergradients at $\mathbf{x}$ and let s_u be the one with the smallest partition function. Thus the upper-bound affine function is $s_u(\gamma) + (F(\mathbf{x}) - s_u(\mathbf{x}))$.

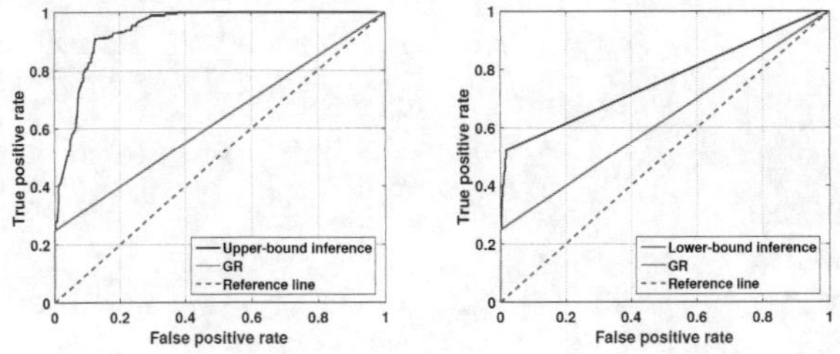

(a) (b)

Figure 2: This figure show an example of the reconstruction results: (a) ROC curves for upper-bound inference and G_R. (b) ROC curves for lower-bound inference and G_R.

When we have an affine approximation for the submodular function, we may make inference via the affine function. Suppose that the affine function is $s(\boldsymbol{\gamma}) + c$, which can be either an upper-bound or lower-bound approximation. Recall that $\boldsymbol{\gamma} = (\boldsymbol{\alpha}, \boldsymbol{\mu})$ and $s(\boldsymbol{\gamma}) = \sum_{i=1}^{N_1} s_i^{\alpha} \boldsymbol{\alpha}_i + \sum_{i=1}^{n} \sum_{j=1}^{N_2} s_{ij}^{\mu} \boldsymbol{\mu}_{ij}$, where $N_1 = \sum_{1 \le i < j \le n} 1_{\{\mathbf{A}_R^{ij}=0\}}$, $N_2 = \lceil \log_2 u_{\max} \rceil$, and $s_i^{\alpha}, s_{ij}^{\mu} \in \mathbb{R}$.

We can select a threshold $\zeta \in [\min_i s_i^{\alpha}, \max_i s_i^{\alpha}]$ and obtain $\boldsymbol{\alpha}(\zeta)$ by thresholding, $\boldsymbol{\alpha}(\zeta)_i = 1_{\{s_i^{\alpha} \ge \zeta\}}$. Thus we obtain an inferred adjacency matrix $\hat{\mathbf{A}}(\zeta)$ from $\boldsymbol{\alpha}(\zeta)$. The proposed method VINE is presented in Algorithm 1.

4 EXPERIMENT

In this section, we evaluate the proposed variational inference algorithm via experimental results. By varying ζ from $\min_i s_i^{\alpha}$ to $\max_i s_i^{\alpha}$, we obtain a series of inferred adjacency matrices $\hat{\mathbf{A}}(\zeta)$. Suppose that the true adjacency matrix of G_S is $\mathbf{A}$. The reconstruction performance of an inferred adjacency matrix $\hat{\mathbf{A}}$ is measured by the true positive rate (TPR) and the false positive rate (FPR), which are defined as $\text{TPR}(\hat{\mathbf{A}}, \mathbf{A}) = \binom{n}{2}^{-1} \sum_{i<j} 1\{\hat{\mathbf{A}}_{ij} = 1 \text{ and } \mathbf{A}_{ij} = 1\}$ and $\text{FPR}(\hat{\mathbf{A}}, \mathbf{A}) = \binom{n}{2}^{-1} \sum_{i<j} 1\{\hat{\mathbf{A}}_{ij} = 1 \text{ and } \mathbf{A}_{ij} = 0\}$, where n is the number of subjects. We plot the TPR and FPR of each $\hat{\mathbf{A}}(\zeta)$ on the ROC plane and obtain the ROC curve. Figs. 2a and 2b show an example of the reconstruction result. In this example, we simulated an RDS process over a real-world network, the Project 90 graph that represents the community structure of heterosexuals at high risk for HIV infection (Woodhouse et al., 1994), with inter-recruitment time distribution $\text{Exp}(1)$ (exponential distribution with rate 1). In the simulation, we choose $n = |V_S| = 50$, and a single seed subject at the initial stage; each subject is given 3 coupons; 1176 missing edges are to be inferred. In practice, the sample size n is usually fixed in advance (according to researchers' study plan). In Fig. 2a, the blue ROC curve corresponds to the upper-bound inference. We choose ψ to be the L^2 norm. The red curve is a baseline reconstruction given by estimating G_S by G_R. Since G_R must be a subgraph of G_S, the FPR of G_R is zero. The red curve is obtained by connecting the point of the TPR of G_R on the vertical axis and the point $(1, 1)$. The performance is quantified by the area of the region under the ROC curve (note that larger is better). In this example, the area of the region under the blue curve is 0.92 and that of the red curve is 0.64. The region under the blue curve is 47% greater than that of the red curve. With the best thresholding, the algorithm can achieve a TPR of 90% while the FPR is only 10%. In Fig. 2b, the blue curve is the ROC curve of the lower-bound inference. We choose ψ to be the L^2 norm. The red curve is a baseline given by G_R. The area under the blue curve is 0.74, which is 18% greater than that of the red curve. Since the lower-bound approximation is obtained from the greedy algorithm while the upper-bound approximation is the solution to an optimization problem, we focus on the upper-bound inference.

4.1 EXPERIMENTS ON FACEBOOK NETWORK

Recall that in Eq. (3), ψ can be any non-decreasing convex function. We may let $\psi(\cdot) = \omega \left\|\cdot\right\|_p$ be ω times the L^p norm ($\omega \ge 0$, $1 \le p \le \infty$). We now study the influence of different choices of ψ.

Influence of p. First we fix $\omega = 1$ and vary p from 1 to 5. We simulated 100 RDS processes over the Facebook network (McAuley and Leskovec, 2012). For each p, we measure the area under the ROC curve of the upper-bound inference for each RDS data and illustrate their distribution with a Tukey boxplot, shown in Fig. 3a. We also record the advantage of the area under the ROC curve of the upper-bound inference over that of G_R; boxplots are given in Fig. 3b. We observe that the variational inference algorithm achieves remarkably high accuracy when $p = 2, 3, 4, 5$.

Influence of ω. We let ψ be $\omega \left\|\cdot\right\|_2$ and vary ω from 0.01 to 100. 100 RDS processes are simulated over the Facebook network. For each ω, we measure the area under the ROC curve of the upper-bound inference for each RDS data and illustrate their distribution with a Tukey boxplot. The result is presented in Fig. 3c. In addition, we also record the advantage of the area under the ROC curve of the upper-bound inference over that of G_R. Accordingly, their boxplots are presented in Fig. 3d. From Figs. 3c and 3d, we can observe that the variational infer-

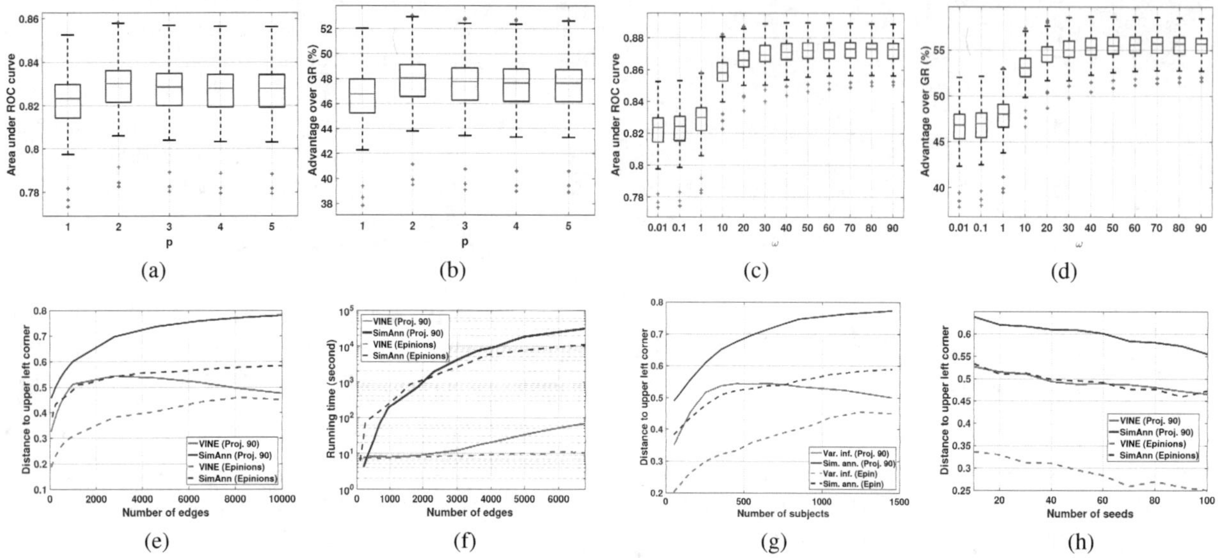

Figure 3: (a) The area under the ROC curve of the upper-bound inference, when ψ is L^p norm and p varies from 1 to 5. (b) Improvement of upper-bound inference over G_R in terms of the area under the ROC curve, as a function of p. (c) Area under the ROC curve for upper-bound inference, when we let ψ be $\omega \|\cdot\|_2$ and ω varies from 0.01 to 100. (d) Improvement of upper-bound inference over G_R in terms of the area under the ROC curve, when we let ψ be $\omega \|\cdot\|_2$ and ω varies from 0.01 to 100. (e) Distance to the upper left corner (the smaller, the better) versus the number of edges in G_S. (f) Running time (in seconds) versus the number of edges in G_S. (g) Distance to the upper left corner versus the number of subjects in the sample (the number of nodes in G_S). (h) Distance to the upper left corner (the smaller, the better) versus the number of seeds.

ence algorithm achieves higher accuracy as ω increases from 0.01 to 10 and that the increase of ω from 10 to 100 leads to lower accuracy of the variational inference.

4.2 EXPERIMENTS ON LARGE PROJECT 90 AND EPINION NETWORKS

We compare VINE with the simulated-annealing-based method proposed in (Chen et al., 2016) (referred to as SIMANN). Since SIMANN only gives a single point on the ROC plane rather than a curve, thus the reconstruction performance in this set of experiments is quantified by the distance from the output point to the upper left corner, $[(1-\text{TPR})^2 + \text{FPR}^2]^{1/2}$. The algorithm with smaller distance is considered to attain better performance. We apply both methods to the large Project 90 network (Woodhouse et al., 1994) and the Epinions social network (Richardson et al., 2003). The Epinions network characterizes the trust relationships between users of a general consumer review site Epinions.com.

Fig. 3e shows the distance to the upper left corner versus the number of edges in G_S, where the ζ value is chosen to minimize the distance of the VINE ROC curve datapoint to the upper-left corner $(0,1)$; we vary from tens of edges to 10000 edges. We generate many RDS processes with different sample sizes and sort them according to the number of edges in G_S and see the reconstruction performance on these datasets. In this way, we plot how the reconstruction performance varies with the number of edges in G_S. Fig. 3g presents the distance to the upper left corner versus the number of subjects in the sample (the number of nodes in G_S). VINE outperforms SIMANN significantly on both datasets. Fig. 3f presents the running time (in seconds) versus of the number of edges in G_S. SIMANN was implemented in C++ while VINE was written in the Julia language and can be implemented as a parallelized version. VINE runs three orders of magnitude faster than SIMANN when there are more edges in G_S and VINE is more scalable for large graphs.

Fig. 3h shows the distance to the upper left corner versus the number of seeds. We vary the number of seeds from 10 to 100, while fixing the sample size. Both algorithms achieve better reconstruction performance with more seeds and that under the same number of seeds, VINE attains a remarkably better performance than SIMANN.

Acknowledgements

LC and AK were supported by DARPA Young Faculty Award (D16AP00046). FWC was funded by NIH grant 1DP2 OD022614-01. LC would like to thank Zheng Wei.

References

Animashree Anandkumar, Avinatan Hassidim, and Jonathan Kelner. Topology discovery of sparse random graphs with few participants. *ACM SIGMETRICS Performance Evaluation Review*, 39(1):253–264, 2011.

Stephen Boyd and Lieven Vandenberghe. *Convex optimization*. Cambridge university press, 2004.

Lin Chen, Forrest W Crawford, and Amin Karbasi. Seeing the unseen network: Inferring hidden social ties from respondent-driven sampling. In *AAAI*, pages 1174–1180, 2016.

Forrest W Crawford. The graphical structure of respondent-driven sampling. *Sociological Methodology*, 46(1):187–211, 2016.

H. Daneshmand, M. Gomez-Rodriguez, L. Song, and B. Schölkopf. Estimating diffusion network structures: Recovery conditions, sample complexity & soft-thresholding algorithm. In *ICML*, 2014.

Josip Djolonga and Andreas Krause. From map to marginals: Variational inference in bayesian submodular models. In *NIPS*, December 2014.

Mehrdad Farajtabar, Manuel Gomez Rodriguez, Mohammad Zamani, Nan Du, Hongyuan Zha, and Le Song. Back to the past: Source identification in diffusion networks from partially observed cascades. In *AISTATS*, pages 232–240, 2015.

Qi Gao, Fabian Abel, Geert-Jan Houben, and Yong Yu. A comparative study of users' microblogging behavior on sina weibo and twitter. In *UMAP*, pages 88–101. Springer, 2012.

M. Gomez-Rodriguez, J. Leskovec, and B. Schölkopf. Structure and dynamics of information pathways in on-line media. In *WSDM*, 2013.

Manuel Gomez-Rodriguez, Jure Leskovec, and Andreas Krause. Inferring networks of diffusion and influence. In *SIGKDD*, pages 1019–1028. ACM, 2010.

Manuel Gomez-Rodriguez, Jure Leskovec, David Balduzzi, and Bernhard Schölkopf. Uncovering the structure and temporal dynamics of information propagation. *Network Science*, 2(01):26–65, 2014.

Gary Gordon and Elizabeth McMahon. A greedoid polynomial which distinguishes rooted arborescences. *Proceedings of the AMS*, 107(2):287–298, 1989.

Steve Hanneke and Eric P Xing. Network completion and survey sampling. In *AISTATS*, pages 209–215, 2009.

Douglas D Heckathorn. Respondent-driven sampling: a new approach to the study of hidden populations. *Social Problems*, 44(2):174–199, 1997.

Rishabh Iyer and Jeff Bilmes. Polyhedral aspects of submodularity, convexity and concavity. *arXiv preprint arXiv:1506.07329*, 2015.

Rishabh Iyer and Jeff A Bilmes. Submodular-Bregman and the Lovász-Bregman divergences with applications. In *NIPS*, pages 2933–2941, 2012.

Rishabh Iyer, Stefanie Jegelka, and Jeff A. Bilmes. Fast semidifferential-based submodular function optimization. In *ICML*, 2013.

Stefanie Jegelka, Hui Lin, and Jeff A Bilmes. On fast approximate submodular minimization. In *NIPS*, pages 460–468, 2011.

Myunghwan Kim and Jure Leskovec. The network completion problem: Inferring missing nodes and edges in networks. In *SDM*, volume 11, pages 47–58, 2011.

Mark A Kramer, Uri T Eden, Sydney S Cash, and Eric D Kolaczyk. Network inference with confidence from multivariate time series. *Physical Review E*, 79(6): 061916, 2009.

David Liben-Nowell and Jon Kleinberg. The link-prediction problem for social networks. *Journal of the American society for information science and technology*, 58(7):1019–1031, 2007.

Scott Linderman and Ryan Adams. Discovering latent network structure in point process data. In *ICML*, pages 1413–1421, 2014.

Julian J McAuley and Jure Leskovec. Learning to discover social circles in ego networks. In *NIPS*, pages 548–56, 2012.

Matthew Richardson, Rakesh Agrawal, and Pedro Domingos. Trust management for the semantic web. In *ISWC*, pages 351–368. Springer, 2003.

Srinivas Gorur Shandilya and Marc Timme. Inferring network topology from complex dynamics. *New Journal of Physics*, 13(1):013004, 2011.

Donald E Woodhouse, Richard B Rothenberg, John J Potterat, William W Darrow, et al. Mapping a social network of heterosexuals at high risk for HIV infection. *AIDS*, 8(9):1331–1336, 1994.

APPENDIX

A LIKELIHOOD OF RECRUITMENT TIME SERIES

We consider the recruitment of subject i. Recall that $R_u(i)$ denotes the set of recruiters of subject u just before time $\mathbf{t}_i$ and that $I_u(i)$ denotes the set of potential recruitees of recruiter u just before time $\mathbf{t}_i$.

We compute the likelihood of the i-th recruitment event (the recruitment of subject i) in the two cases: i enters the study via the recruitment of a subject already in the study (in this case, subject i is not a seed node, which is denoted by $i \notin M$) and via the direct recruitment of the researchers (in this case, subject i is a seed node, which is denoted by $i \in M$).

Suppose that $i \notin M$. The inter-recruitment time between i and its potential recruiter u is denoted $W_{ui} = \mathbf{t}_i - \mathbf{t}_u$ and is greater than $\mathbf{t}_{i-1} - \mathbf{t}_u$ conditional on previous recruitment of i. Let U be the random variable of next recruiter and X be the random variable of next recruitee, namely the subject that will be labeled as subject i. We would like to note here that subject i is in fact random. Let J denote the event $\forall j \in R(i), k \in I(i), W_{jk} > \mathbf{t}_{i-1} - \mathbf{t}_j$.

We first compute the probability that a certain subject $x \in I(i)$ is the next (i-th) recruitee, $u \in R_x(i)$ is its recruiter, and the inter-recruitment time between u and x is greater than or equal to $t - \mathbf{t}_u$, conditional on event J. Intuitively, t is the recruitment time of subject x and in fact we are computing the tail probability of W_{ux}. We condition on the event J because having observed the $(i-1)$-th recruitment event, we know that for all possible recruiter-recruitee pairs in the next (i-th) recruitment event, say $j \in R(i)$ and $x \in I(i)$, their inter-recruitment time W_{jk} should be greater than or equal to $\mathbf{t}_{i-1} - \mathbf{t}_j$ (otherwise, the event that subject j recruits subject x will happen before $\mathbf{t}_i$ and they will not appear in $R(i)$ and $I(i)$, respectively). We have

$$\begin{aligned}&\Pr\left[U = u, X = x, W_{ux} \geq t - \mathbf{t}_u \mid J\right] \\ =&\Pr\left[W_{ux} \geq t - \mathbf{t}_u, \mathbf{t}_j + W_{jk} > \mathbf{t}_u + W_{ux},\right. \\ &\left.\forall j \in R(i), k \in I(i), \{u, x\} \neq \{j, k\} \mid J\right]. \quad (4)\end{aligned}$$

Since the i-th recruitment event is that u recruits x, the inter-recruitment time along this link must be minimum among those along all other links. Therefore, in Eq. (4) we consider W_{jk} for $\forall j \in R(i), k \in I(i), \{u, x\} \neq \{j, k\}$. We require that

$$\mathbf{t}_j + W_{jk} > \mathbf{t}_u + W_{ux},$$

which means exactly that the recruitment time of x ($\mathbf{t}_u + W_{ux}$) is minimum (smaller than the recruitment time of k for all k).

Then we marginalize the above probability in Eq. (4) over all possible combinations of x and u. Recall that any subject in $x \in I(i)$ could possibly be the subject i and any subject in $R_x(i)$ could be her recruiter; therefore we need to sum over all possible recruitee-recruiter combinations, i.e., sum over $x \in I(i)$ and $u \in R_x(i)$:

$$\begin{aligned}&\Pr\left[W_{Ui} \geq t - \mathbf{t}_U \mid J\right] \\ =&\sum_{x\in I(i)}\sum_{u\in R_x(i)} \Pr\left[W_{ux} \geq t - \mathbf{t}_u, \mathbf{t}_j + W_{jk} > \mathbf{t}_u\right. \\ &\left.+W_{ux}, \forall j \in R(i), k \in I(i), \{u, x\} \neq \{j, k\} \mid J\right] \\ =&\sum_{x\in I(i)}\sum_{u\in R_x(i)} \int_{t-\mathbf{t}_u}^{\infty} \rho_{\tau(u;i)}(s)\mathrm{d}s \Pr\left[W_{jk} > s + \mathbf{t}_u\right. \\ &\left.-\mathbf{t}_j, \forall j \in R(i), k \in I(i), \{u, x\} \neq \{j, k\} \mid J\right] \\ =&\sum_{x\in I(i)}\sum_{u\in R_x(i)} \int_{t-\mathbf{t}_u}^{\infty} \rho_{\tau(u;i)}(s) \cdot \\ &\frac{\prod_{j\in R(i)}\prod_{k\in I_j(i)}\left(1 - D_{\tau(j;i)}(s + \mathbf{t}_u - \mathbf{t}_j)\right)}{1 - D_{\tau(u;i)}(s)}\mathrm{d}s \\ =&\sum_{x\in I(i)}\sum_{u\in R_x(i)} \int_{t-\mathbf{t}_u}^{\infty} H_{\tau(u;i)}(s) \cdot \\ &\prod_{j\in R(i)} S_{\tau(j;i)}^{|I_j(i)|}(s + \mathbf{t}_u - \mathbf{t}_j)\mathrm{d}s.\end{aligned}$$

Using the notation that we introduced in Section 2 to rewrite and simplify the above expression, we obtain the likelihood of the i-th recruitment event for $i \notin M$:

$$\begin{aligned}&\sum_{x\in I(i)}\sum_{u\in R_x(i)} H_{\tau(u;i)}(\mathbf{t}_i - \mathbf{t}_u) \prod_{j\in R(i)} S_{\tau(j;i)}^{|I_j(i)|}(\mathbf{t}_i - \mathbf{t}_j) \\ =&\prod_{j\in R(i)} S_{\tau(j;i)}^{|I_j(i)|}(\mathbf{t}_i - \mathbf{t}_j) \sum_{u\in R(i)} |I_u(i)| H_{\tau(u;i)}(\mathbf{t}_i - \mathbf{t}_u)\end{aligned}$$

Now suppose that $i \in M$, which means that subject i is recruited into the study directly by the researchers. Therefore the inter-recruitment time of any possible recruiter-recruitee pairs of the i-th recruitment event, say j and k, should be greater than or equal to $t - \mathbf{t}_j$, where t is the recruitment time of subject i. In the terminology of survival analysis, all these potential recruitment links are censored. So we compute the probability that all these links are censored:

$$\begin{aligned}&\Pr\left[W_{jk} \geq t - \mathbf{t}_j, \forall j \in R(i), k \in I_j(i) \mid J\right] \\ =&\prod_{j\in R(i)}\prod_{k\in I_j(i)} \left(1 - D_{\tau(j;i)}(t - \mathbf{t}_j)\right) \\ =&\prod_{j\in R(i)} S_{\tau(j;i)}^{|I_j(i)|}(t - \mathbf{t}_j).\end{aligned}$$

Plugging in the observed recruitment time of subject i (denoted by $\mathbf{t}_i$), we obtain the likelihood of the i-th recruitment event for $i \in M$:

$$\prod_{j \in R(i)} S_{\tau(j;i)}^{|I_j(i)|}(\mathbf{t}_i - \mathbf{t}_j).$$

So far we have obtained the likelihood of the i-th recruitment event for both cases ($i \notin M$ and $i \in M$); Multiplying the likelihoods with i running from 1 to n, we have the entire likelihood:

$$\prod_{i=1}^{n} \left(\sum_{u \in R(i)} |I_u(i)| H_{\tau(u;i)}(\mathbf{t}_i - \mathbf{t}_u) \right)^{1\{i \notin M\}} \cdot \prod_{j \in R(i)} S_{\tau(j;i)}^{|I_j|}(\mathbf{t}_i - \mathbf{t}_j), \quad (5)$$

where $1\{i \notin M\}$ the indicator random variable for the event that $i \notin M$.

B LOG-LIKELIHOOD OF RECRUITMENT TIME SERIES

According to Eq. (5) in Appendix A , the log-likelihood is

$$\sum_{i=1}^{n} \left[1\{i \notin M\} \log \left(\sum_{u \in R(i)} |I_u(i)| H_{\tau(u;i)}(\mathbf{t}_i - \mathbf{t}_u) \right) + \sum_{j \in R(i)} |I_j(i)| \log S_{\tau(j;i)}(\mathbf{t}_i - \mathbf{t}_j) \right].$$

The number of recruitees of recruiter u just before time $\mathbf{t}_i$ is given by

$$|I_u(i)| = \mathbf{C}_{ui} \left(\sum_{k=i}^{n} \mathbf{A}_{uk} + \mathbf{u}_u \right). \quad (6)$$

The cardinality of $I_u(i)$ is zero if and only if recruiter u has at least one coupon just before $\mathbf{t}_i$, i.e., $\mathbf{C}_{ui} = 1$. Therefore there is a factor $\mathbf{C}_{ui}$ in Eq. (6). When recruiter u has at least one coupon, the number of recruitees of recruiter u just before time $\mathbf{t}_i$ is

$$\sum_{k=i}^{n} \mathbf{A}_{uk} + \mathbf{u}_u,$$

where $\sum_{k=i}^{n} \mathbf{A}_{uk}$ is the number of recruitees in the final sample and $\mathbf{u}_u$ is the number of recruitees outside the final sample. In the expression $\sum_{k=i}^{n} \mathbf{A}_{uk}$, we sum over k from i to n since subjects $i, i+1, \ldots, n$ are those in the final sample and recruited at and after time $\mathbf{t}_i$ and they contribute one to the sum if they are adjacent to subject u (namely $\mathbf{A}_{uk} = 1$).

Recall that $\mathbf{B}$ is the Hadamard product of $\mathbf{C}$ and $\mathbf{H}$, which yields that $\mathbf{B}_{ui} = \mathbf{C}_{ui}\mathbf{H}_{ui}$, and that

$$\mathbf{H}_{ui} = H_{\tau(u;i)}(\mathbf{t}_i - \mathbf{t}_u).$$

Therefore the term

$$\sum_{u \in R(i)} |I_u(i)| H_{\tau(u;i)}(\mathbf{t}_i - \mathbf{t}_u)$$

in the log-likelihood can be written as

$$\begin{aligned} &\sum_{u \in R(i)} |I_u(i)| H_{\tau(u;i)}(\mathbf{t}_i - \mathbf{t}_u) \\ =& \sum_{u} \mathbf{C}_{ui} \left(\sum_{k=i}^{n} \mathbf{A}_{uk} + \mathbf{u}_u \right) \mathbf{H}_{ui} \\ =& (\mathbf{B}'\mathbf{u} + \mathrm{LowerTri}(\mathbf{AB})' \cdot \mathbf{1})_i. \end{aligned}$$

Recall the definition of the matrix $\mathbf{S}$:

$$\mathbf{S}_{ji} = \log S_{\tau(j;i)}(\mathbf{t}_i - \mathbf{t}_j),$$

and that $\mathbf{D}$ is the Hadamard product of $\mathbf{C}$ and $\mathbf{S}$, which yields that $\mathbf{D}_{ji} = \mathbf{C}_{ji}\mathbf{S}_{ji}$. Similarly, the term

$$\sum_{j \in R(i)} |I_j(i)| \log S_{\tau(j;i)}(\mathbf{t}_i - \mathbf{t}_j)$$

in the log-likelihood is given by

$$\begin{aligned} &\sum_{j \in R(i)} |I_j(i)| \log S_{\tau(j;i)}(\mathbf{t}_i - \mathbf{t}_j) \\ =& \sum_{j \in R(i)} \mathbf{C}_{ji} \left(\sum_{k=i}^{n} \mathbf{A}_{jk} + \mathbf{u}_j \right) \mathbf{S}_{ji} \\ =& (\mathbf{D}'\mathbf{u} + \mathrm{LowerTri}(\mathbf{AD})' \cdot \mathbf{1})_i. \end{aligned}$$

Thus the log-likelihood is

$$\sum_{i=1}^{n} [1\{i \notin M\} \log (\mathbf{B}'\mathbf{u} + \mathrm{LowerTri}(\mathbf{AB})' \cdot \mathbf{1})_i + (\mathbf{D}'\mathbf{u} + \mathrm{LowerTri}(\mathbf{AD})' \cdot \mathbf{1})_i] = \mathbf{m}'\beta + \mathbf{1}'\delta.$$

C PROOF OF THEOREM 1

In this section, we will show that $\log \tilde{L}(\boldsymbol{\gamma})$ is submodular in $\boldsymbol{\gamma}$. We have

$$\begin{aligned} & \log \tilde{L}(\boldsymbol{\gamma}) \\ =& \log L(\mathbf{t}|\mathbf{A}, \theta) + \log \pi(\mathbf{A}) + \log \phi(\theta) \\ =& \mathbf{m}'\beta + \mathbf{1}'\delta - \psi(\max\{\mathbf{u} + \mathbf{A} \cdot \mathbf{1} - \mathbf{d}, \mathbf{0}\}) + \log \phi(\theta). \end{aligned}$$

Later we will show that it is submodular part by part.

First, we need to prove that $-\psi(\max\{\mathbf{u}+\mathbf{A}\cdot\mathbf{1}-\mathbf{d},\mathbf{0}\})$ is submodular. We temporarily view them as real-valued vectors and matrices rather than binary vectors and matrices. In light of the fact that

$$\mathbf{u}=\boldsymbol{\mu}\cdot\begin{pmatrix} 2^0 & 2^1 & 2^2 & \ldots & 2^{\lceil \log_2 u_{\max}\rceil -1}\end{pmatrix}',$$

we know that $\mathbf{u}$ is a linear function of $\boldsymbol{\mu}$, which yields that $\mathbf{u}+\mathbf{A}\cdot\mathbf{1}-\mathbf{d}$ is a linear function of $\boldsymbol{\mu}$. We know that if $g(\mathbf{x})$ is a linear function, then $f(\mathbf{x}) = \max\{g(\mathbf{x}),0\}$ is a convex function (see Section 3.2.3 in (Boyd and Vandenberghe, 2004)). Therefore, every entry of $\max\{\mathbf{u}+\mathbf{A}\cdot\mathbf{1}-\mathbf{d},\mathbf{0}\}$ is convex in $\mathbf{u}$. Since ψ is a convex function and non-decreasing in each argument whenever this argument is non-negative, thus $\psi(\max\{\mathbf{u}+\mathbf{A}\cdot\mathbf{1}-\mathbf{d},\mathbf{0}\})$ is convex in $\mathbf{u}$ (see Section 3.2.4 in (Boyd and Vandenberghe, 2004)); equivalently, $-\psi(\max\{\mathbf{u}+\mathbf{A}\cdot\mathbf{1}-\mathbf{d},\mathbf{0}\})$ is concave in $\mathbf{u}$. Thus this term $-\psi(\max\{\mathbf{u}+\mathbf{A}\cdot\mathbf{1}-\mathbf{d},\mathbf{0}\})$ is submodular in $\boldsymbol{\mu}$ if we view $\boldsymbol{\mu}$ as a Boolean vector.

Recall the definitions of β and δ:

$$\begin{aligned}\beta &= \log(\mathbf{B}'\mathbf{u}+\mathrm{LowerTri}(\mathbf{AB})'\cdot\mathbf{1}),\\ \delta &= \mathbf{D}'\mathbf{u}+\mathrm{LowerTri}(\mathbf{AD})'\cdot\mathbf{1}.\end{aligned}$$

The function $\beta(\mathbf{u},\mathbf{A})$ is concave in $\mathbf{u}$ and $\mathbf{A}$ since the inner part

$$\mathbf{B}'\mathbf{u}+\mathrm{LowerTri}(\mathbf{AB})'\cdot\mathbf{1}$$

is linear in $\mathbf{u}$ and $\mathbf{A}$, the logarithm function is concave, and β is the composition of the linear inner part and the concave logarithm function. The function $\delta(\mathbf{u},\mathbf{A})$ is linear in $\mathbf{u}$ and $\mathbf{A}$. Recall that $\mathbf{u}$ and $\mathbf{A}$ are linear in $\boldsymbol{\mu}$ and $\boldsymbol{\alpha}$, respectively. Thus β is concave in $\boldsymbol{\mu}$ and $\boldsymbol{\alpha}$ and δ is linear in $\boldsymbol{\mu}$ and $\boldsymbol{\alpha}$. Therefore β is concave in $\boldsymbol{\gamma}$ and δ is linear in $\boldsymbol{\gamma}$, where

$$\boldsymbol{\gamma}=(\boldsymbol{\alpha},\boldsymbol{\mu}).$$

Thus $\mathbf{m}'\beta+\mathbf{1}'\delta$ is submodular in $\boldsymbol{\gamma}$ if $\boldsymbol{\gamma}$ is viewed as a binary vector.

Hence in light of the fact that the sum of submodular functions is submodular, the whole expression is submodular in $\boldsymbol{\gamma}$. In other words, $\log L(\boldsymbol{\gamma})$ is submodular in $\boldsymbol{\gamma}$.

D PROOF OF PROPOSITION 1

We prove it by induction.

Suppose that $\boldsymbol{\gamma}=\{v_{j_1},v_{j_2},\ldots,v_{j_q}\}$, where $j_1<j_2<\cdots<j_q$ and $q\le N$.

If $q=1$, then

$$\begin{aligned}&F(\boldsymbol{\gamma})-F(\varnothing)=F(\{v_{j_1}\})-F(\varnothing)\\ &\ge F(V_{j_1-1}\cup v_{j_1})-F(V_{j_1-1})=s^g(v_{j_1})=s^g(\boldsymbol{\gamma}),\end{aligned}$$

since $\varnothing$ must be a subset of V_{j_1-1}. Therefore,

$$F(\boldsymbol{\gamma})\ge s^g(\boldsymbol{\gamma})+F(\varnothing)=s^g(\boldsymbol{\gamma}),$$

since F is normalized.

Suppose that the proposition holds for all $q<r$. When $q=r$, we have

$$\begin{aligned}&F(\{v_{j_1},v_{j_2},\ldots,v_{j_r}\})-F(\{v_{j_1},v_{j_2},\ldots,v_{j_{r-1}}\})\\ &\qquad\ge F(V_{j_r-1}\cup\{v_{j_r}\})-F(V_{j_r-1})=s^g(\{v_{j_r}\}),\end{aligned}$$

since $\{v_{j_1},v_{j_2},\ldots,v_{j_{r-1}}\}$ is a subset of V_{j_r-1}. Therefore, we obtain

$$\begin{aligned}F(\boldsymbol{\gamma}) &= F(\{v_{j_1},v_{j_2},\ldots,v_{j_r}\})\\ &\ge s^g(\{v_{j_r}\})+F(\{v_{j_1},v_{j_2},\ldots,v_{j_{r-1}}\})\\ &\ge s^g(\{v_{j_r}\})+s^g(\{v_{j_1},v_{j_2},\ldots,v_{j_{r-1}}\})\\ &= s^g(\{v_{j_1},v_{j_2},\ldots,v_{j_r}\})\end{aligned}$$

by the induction assumption. This completes the proof.

E PROOF OF PROPOSITION 2

In order to show that a modular function s is a supergradient of the submodular function F at $\mathbf{x}$, we have to show that

$$\forall \mathbf{y}\in\{0,1\}^N, F(\mathbf{y})\le F(\mathbf{x})+s(\mathbf{y})-s(\mathbf{x}).$$

Equivalent, if viewed as a set function, we have to show that

$$\forall Y\subseteq[N], F(Y)\le F(X)+s(Y)-s(X),$$

where X is the corresponding subset for $\mathbf{x}$, i.e.,

$$X=\{i\in[N]:\mathbf{x}_i=1\}.$$

Since s is a modular function, it is equivalent to show

$$F(Y)+\sum_{i\in X\setminus Y}s(\{i\})\le F(X)+\sum_{i\in Y\setminus X}s(\{i\}).$$

Grow supergradient We have to show that

$$F(Y)+\sum_{i\in X\setminus Y}\hat{s}(\{i\})\le F(X)+\sum_{i\in Y\setminus X}\hat{s}(\{i\});$$

equivalently,

$$F(Y)+\sum_{i\in X\setminus Y}\Delta_i F(V-\{i\})\leq F(X)+\sum_{i\in Y\setminus X}\Delta_i F(X).$$

We will show that the left-hand side is less than or equal to $F(X\cup Y)$ while the right-hand side is greater than or equal to $F(X\cup Y)$.

Suppose that $Y\setminus X=\{a_1,a_2,a_3,\dots,a_r\}$, $A_i=X\cup\{a_1,a_2,a_3,\dots,a_i\}$ and $A_0=X$. We have

$$\begin{aligned}F(X\cup Y)&=F(X)+\sum_{i=1}^{r}(F(A_i)-F(A_{i-1}))\\&=F(X)+\sum_{i=1}^{r}\Delta_{a_i}F(A_{i-1})\\&\leq F(X)+\sum_{i=1}^{r}\Delta_{a_i}F(X)\\&=F(X)+\sum_{i\in Y\setminus X}\Delta_i F(X).\end{aligned}\tag{7}$$

Suppose that $X\setminus Y=\{b_1,b_2,\dots,b_q\}$, $B_i=Y\cup\{b_1,b_2,\dots,b_i\}$ and $B_0=Y$. We have

$$\begin{aligned}F(X\cup Y)&=F(Y)+\sum_{i=1}^{q}(F(B_i)-F(B_{i-1}))\\&=F(Y)+\sum_{i=1}^{q}\Delta_{b_i}F(B_{i-1})\\&\geq F(Y)+\sum_{i=1}^{q}\Delta_{b_i}F(V-\{b_i\})\\&=F(Y)+\sum_{i\in X\setminus Y}\Delta_i F(V-\{i\}).\end{aligned}\tag{8}$$

Shrink supergradient We have to show that

$$F(Y)+\sum_{i\in X\setminus Y}\check{s}(\{i\})\leq F(X)+\sum_{i\in Y\setminus X}\check{s}(\{i\});$$

equivalently,

$$F(Y)+\sum_{i\in X\setminus Y}\Delta_i F(X-\{i\})\leq F(X)+\sum_{i\in Y\setminus X}F(\{i\}).$$

We will show that the left-hand side is less than or equal to $F(X\cup Y)$ while the right-hand side is greater than or equal to $F(X\cup Y)$.

In light of Eq. (7), we have

$$\begin{aligned}F(X\cup Y)&=F(X)+\sum_{i=1}^{r}\Delta_{a_i}F(A_{i-1})\\&\leq F(X)+\sum_{i=1}^{r}\Delta_{a_i}F(\varnothing)\\&=F(X)+\sum_{i\in Y\setminus X}\Delta_i F(\varnothing)\\&=F(X)+\sum_{i\in Y\setminus X}F(\{i\}).\end{aligned}\tag{9}$$

In light of Eq. (8), we have

$$\begin{aligned}F(X\cup Y)&=F(Y)+\sum_{i=1}^{q}\Delta_{b_i}F(B_{i-1})\\&\geq F(Y)+\sum_{i=1}^{q}\Delta_{b_i}F(X-\{b_i\})\\&=F(Y)+\sum_{i\in X\setminus Y}\Delta_i F(X-\{i\}).\end{aligned}$$

Bar supergradient We have to show that

$$F(Y)+\sum_{i\in X\setminus Y}\bar{s}(\{i\})\leq F(X)+\sum_{i\in Y\setminus X}\bar{s}(\{i\});$$

equivalently,

$$F(Y)+\sum_{i\in X\setminus Y}\Delta_i F(V-\{i\})\leq F(X)+\sum_{i\in Y\setminus X}F(\{i\}).$$

By Eq. (8), we know that the left-hand side is less than or equal to $F(X\cup Y)$. By Eq. (9), we know that the right-hand side is greater than or equal to $F(X\cup Y)$. Therefore, the left-hand side is less than or equal to the right-hand side.

F DISCUSSION

In some ways, RDS resembles a diffusion process and in fact the continuous-time stochastic process that we formulate RDS as in this paper is a diffusion process; but RDS reveals an extra piece of information that makes reconstruction of the induced subgraph possible: the degrees of each vertex visited by the diffusion process.

For other diffusion processes, we can also derive their likelihood functions. If the optimization problem of the likelihood or the posterior is log-submodular and unconstrained, we can use the submodular variational inference method that we used in this paper. If it is a constrained problem, it is natural to relax the constraints with multiplicative log-submodular penalty factor such that the product of the original likelihood/posterior function and the penalty factor remain log-submodular. For example, if the constraint is an equality constraint of the form $q(\mathbf{A}) = \boldsymbol{c}_0$, where q is a linear function (e.g., multiplying $\mathbf{A}$ by some matrix), $\boldsymbol{c}_0$ is a fixed vector, and $\mathbf{A}$ is the adjacency matrix to be optimized over, then we can add a multiplicative factor $e^{-\|q(\mathbf{A})-\mathbf{c}_0\|}$ to the likelihood or posterior function, in light of the fact that every norm is a convex function, which guarantees that $e^{-\|q(\mathbf{A})-\mathbf{c}_0\|}$ is log-submodular with respect to $\mathbf{A}$. If the constraint is given by an inequality, we can mimic the method that we used in Section 3.1 by introducing auxiliary variables $\mathbf{u}$ and adding a multiplicative penalty term similar to Eq. (3).

Bayesian Inference of Log Determinants

Jack Fitzsimons[1] **Kurt Cutajar**[2] **Michael Osborne**[1] **Stephen Roberts**[1] **Maurizio Filippone**[2]

[1] Information Engineering, University of Oxford, UK
[2] Department of Data Science, EURECOM, France

Abstract

The log determinant of a kernel matrix appears in a variety of machine learning problems, ranging from determinantal point processes and generalized Markov random fields, through to the training of Gaussian processes. Exact calculation of this term is often intractable when the size of the kernel matrix exceeds a few thousands. In the spirit of probabilistic numerics, we reinterpret the problem of computing the log determinant as a Bayesian inference problem. In particular, we combine prior knowledge in the form of bounds from matrix theory and evidence derived from stochastic trace estimation to obtain probabilistic estimates for the log determinant and its associated uncertainty within a given computational budget. Beyond its novelty and theoretic appeal, the performance of our proposal is competitive with state-of-the-art approaches to approximating the log determinant, while also quantifying the uncertainty due to budget-constrained evidence.

1 INTRODUCTION

Developing scalable learning models without compromising performance is at the forefront of machine learning research. The scalability of several learning models is predominantly hindered by linear algebraic operations having large computational complexity, among which is the computation of the log determinant of a matrix (Golub & Van Loan, 1996). The latter term features heavily in the machine learning literature, with applications including spatial models (Aune et al., 2014; Rue & Held, 2005), kernel-based models (Davis et al., 2007; Rasmussen & Williams, 2006), and Bayesian learning (Mackay, 2003).

The standard approach for evaluating the log determinant of a positive definite matrix involves the use of Cholesky decomposition (Golub & Van Loan, 1996), which is employed in various applications of statistical models such as kernel machines. However, the use of Cholesky decomposition for general dense matrices requires $\mathcal{O}(n^3)$ operations, whilst also entailing memory requirements of $\mathcal{O}(n^2)$. In view of this computational bottleneck, various models requiring the log determinant for inference bypass the need to compute it altogether (Anitescu et al., 2012; Stein et al., 2013; Cutajar et al., 2016; Filippone & Engler, 2015).

Alternatively, several methods exploit sparsity and structure within the matrix itself to accelerate computations. For example, sparsity in Gaussian Markov random fields (GMRFs) arises from encoding conditional independence assumptions that are readily available when considering low-dimensional problems. For such matrices, the Cholesky decompositions can be computed in fewer than $\mathcal{O}(n^3)$ operations (Rue & Held, 2005; Rue et al., 2009). Similarly, Kronecker-based linear algebra techniques may be employed for kernel matrices computed on regularly spaced inputs (Saatçi, 2011). While these ideas have proven successful for a variety of specific applications, they cannot be extended to the case of general dense matrices without assuming special forms or structures for the available data.

To this end, general approximations to the log determinant frequently build upon stochastic trace estimation techniques using iterative methods (Avron & Toledo, 2011). Two of the most widely-used polynomial approximations for large-scale matrices are the Taylor and Chebyshev expansions (Aune et al., 2014; Han et al., 2015). A more recent approach draws from the possibility of estimating the trace of functions using stochastic Lanczos quadrature (Ubaru et al., 2016), which has been shown to outperform polynomial approximations from both a theoretic and empirical perspective.

Inspired by recent developments in the field of probabilistic numerics (Hennig et al., 2015), in this work we propose an alternative approach for calculating the log determinant of a matrix by expressing this computation as a Bayesian quadrature problem. In doing so, we reformulate the problem of *computing* an intractable quantity as an *estimation* problem, where the goal is to infer the correct result using tractable computations that can be carried out within a given time budget. In particular, we model the eigenvalues of a matrix A from noisy observations of $\mathrm{Tr}(A^k)$ obtained through stochastic trace estimation using the Taylor approximation method (Zhang & Leithead, 2007). Such a model can then be used to make predictions on the infinite series of the Taylor expansion, yielding the estimated value of the log determinant. Aside from permitting a probabilistic approach for predicting the log determinant, this approach inherently yields uncertainty estimates for the predicted value, which in turn serves as an indicator of the quality of our approximation.

Our contributions are as follows.

1. We propose a probabilistic approach for computing the log determinant of a matrix which blends different elements from the literature on estimating log determinants under a Bayesian framework.
2. We demonstrate how bounds on the expected value of the log determinant improve our estimates by constraining the probability distribution to lie between designated lower and upper bounds.
3. Through rigorous numerical experiments on synthetic and real data, we demonstrate how our method can yield superior approximations to competing approaches, while also having the additional benefit of uncertainty quantification.
4. Finally, in order to demonstrate how this technique may be useful within a practical scenario, we employ our method to carry out parameter selection for a large-scale determinantal point process.

To the best of our knowledge, this is the first time that the approximation of log determinants is viewed as a Bayesian inference problem, with the resulting quantification of uncertainty being hitherto unexplored thus far.

1.1 RELATED WORK

The most widely-used approaches for estimating log determinants involve extensions of iterative algorithms, such as the conjugate gradient and Lanczos methods, to obtain estimates of functions of matrices (Chen et al., 2011; Han et al., 2015) or their trace (Ubaru et al., 2016). The idea is to rewrite log determinants as the trace of the logarithm of the matrix, and employ trace estimation techniques (Hutchinson, 1990) to obtain unbiased estimates of these. Chen et al. (2011) propose an iterative algorithm to efficiently compute the product of the logarithm of a matrix with a vector, which is achieved by computing a spline approximation to the logarithm function. A similar idea using Chebyshev polynomials has been developed by Han et al. (2015). Most recently, the Lanczos method has been extended to handle stochastic estimates of the trace and obtain probabilistic error bounds for the approximation (Ubaru et al., 2016). Blocking techniques, such as in Ipsen & Lee (2011) and Ambikasaran et al. (2016), have also been proposed.

In our work, we similarly strive to use a small number of matrix-vector products for approximating log determinants. However, we show that by taking a Bayesian approach we can combine priors with the evidence gathered from the intermediate results of matrix-vector products involved in the aforementioned methods to obtain more accurate results. Most importantly, our proposal has the considerable advantage that it provides a full distribution on the approximated value.

Our proposal allows for the inclusion of explicit bounds on log determinants to constrain the posterior distribution over the estimated log determinant (Bai & Golub, 1997). Nyström approximations can also be used to bound the log determinant, as shown in Bardenet & Titsias (2015). Similarly, Gaussian processes (Rasmussen & Williams, 2006) have been formulated directly using the eigendecomposition of its spectrum, where eigenvectors are approximated using the Nyström method (Peng & Qi, 2015). There has also been work on estimating the distribution of kernel eigenvalues by analyzing the spectrum of linear operators (Braun, 2006; Wathen & Zhu, 2015), as well as bounds on the spectra of matrices with particular emphasis on deriving the largest eigenvalue (Wolkowicz & Styan, 1980; Braun, 2006). In this work, we directly consider bounds on the log determinants of matrices (Bai & Golub, 1997).

2 BACKGROUND

As highlighted in the introduction, several approaches for approximating the log determinant of a matrix rely on stochastic trace estimation for accelerating computations. This comes about as a result of the relationship between the log determinant of a matrix, and the corresponding trace of the log-matrix, whereby

$$\log\big(\mathrm{Det}\,(A)\big) = \mathrm{Tr}\big(\log\,(A)\big). \qquad (1)$$

Provided the matrix $\log(A)$ can be efficiently sampled, this simple identity enables the use of stochastic trace es-

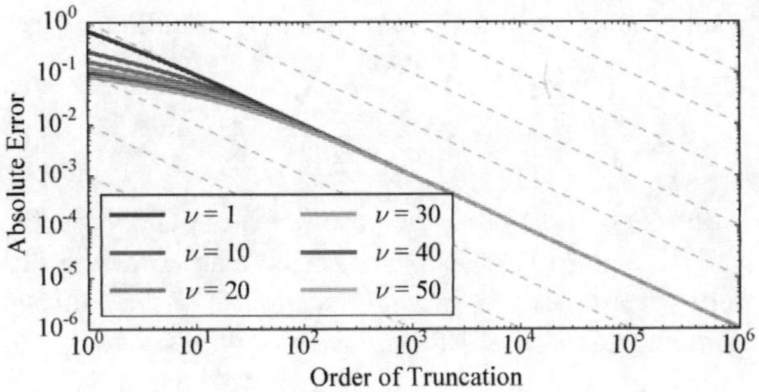

Figure 1: Expected absolute error of truncated Taylor series for stationary ν-continuous kernel matrices. The dashed grey lines indicate $\mathcal{O}(n^{-1})$.

timation techniques (Avron & Toledo, 2011; Fitzsimons et al., 2016). We elaborate further on this concept below.

2.1 STOCHASTIC TRACE ESTIMATION

It is possible to obtain a stochastic estimate of the trace term such that the expectation of the estimate matches the term being approximated (Avron & Toledo, 2011). In this work, we shall consider the Gaussian estimator, whereby we introduce $N_\mathbf{r}$ vectors $\mathbf{r}^{(i)}$ sampled from an independently and identically distributed zero-mean and unit variance Gaussian distribution. This yields the unbiased estimate

$$\operatorname{Tr}(A) = \frac{1}{N_r} \sum_{i=1}^{N_r} \mathbf{r}^{(i)^\top} A\, \mathbf{r}^{(i)}. \tag{2}$$

Note that more sophisticated trace estimators (see Fitzsimons et al., 2016) may also be considered; without loss of generality, we opt for a more straightforward approach in order to preserve clarity.

2.2 TAYLOR APPROXIMATION

Against the backdrop of machine learning applications, in this work we predominantly consider covariance matrices taking the form of a Gram matrix $K = \{\kappa(\mathbf{x}_i, \mathbf{x}_j)\}_{i,j=1,\ldots,n}$, where the kernel function κ implicitly induces a feature space representation of data points $\mathbf{x}$. Assume K has been normalized such that the maximum eigenvalue is less than or equal to one, $\lambda_0 \leq 1$, where the largest eigenvalue can be efficiently found using Gershgorin intervals (Gershgorin, 1931). Given that covariance matrices are positive semidefinite, we also know that the smallest eigenvalue is bounded by zero, $\lambda_n \geq 0$. Motivated by the identity presented in (1), the Taylor series expansion (Barry & Pace, 1999; Zhang & Leithead, 2007) may be employed for evaluating the log determinant of matrices having eigenvalues bounded between zero and one. In particular, this approach relies on the following logarithm identity,

$$\log(I - A) = -\sum_{k=1}^{\infty} \frac{A^k}{k}. \tag{3}$$

While the infinite summation is not explicitly computable in finite time, this may be approximated by computing a truncated series instead. Furthermore, given that the trace of matrices is additive, we find

$$\operatorname{Tr}\big(\log(I - A)\big) \approx -\sum_{k=1}^{m} \frac{\operatorname{Tr}\left(A^k\right)}{k}. \tag{4}$$

The $\operatorname{Tr}(A^k)$ term can be computed efficiently and recursively by propagating $\mathcal{O}(n^2)$ vector-matrix multiplications in a stochastic trace estimation scheme. To compute $\operatorname{Tr}(\log(K))$ we simply set $A = I - K$.

There are two sources of error associated with this approach; the first due to stochastic trace estimation, and the second due to truncation of the Taylor series. In the case of covariance matrices, the smallest eigenvalue tends to be very small, which can be verified by Weyl (1912) and Silverstein (1986)'s observations on the eigenspectra of covariance matrices. This leads to A^k decaying slowly as $k \to \infty$.

In light of the above, standard Taylor approximations to the log determinant of covariance matrices are typically unreliable, even when the exact traces of matrix powers are available. This can be verified analytically based on results from kernel theory, which state that the approximate rate of decay for the eigenvalues of positive definite kernels which are ν-continuous is $\mathcal{O}(n^{-\nu-0.5})$ (Weyl, 1912; Wathen & Zhu, 2015). Combining this result with the absolute error, $E(\lambda)$, of the truncated Taylor approximation we find

$$\begin{aligned} \mathbb{E}\left[E(\lambda)\right] &= \mathcal{O}\left(\int_0^1 \lambda^{\nu+0.5}\left(\log(\lambda) - \sum_{j=1}^{m} \frac{\lambda^j}{j}\right) \mathrm{d}\lambda\right) \\ &= \mathcal{O}\left(\int_0^1 \lambda^{\nu+0.5} \sum_{j=m}^{\infty} \frac{\lambda^j}{j} \mathrm{d}\lambda\right) \\ &= \mathcal{O}\left(\frac{\Psi^{(0)}(m+\nu+1.5) - \Psi^{(0)}(m)}{\nu+1.5}\right), \end{aligned}$$

where $\Psi^{(0)}(\cdot)$ is the Digamma function. In Figure 1, we plot the relationship between the order of the Taylor approximation and the expected absolute error. It can be observed that irrespective of the continuity of the kernel, the error converges at a rate of $\mathcal{O}(n^{-1})$.

3 THE PROBABILISTIC NUMERICS APPROACH

We now propose a probabilistic numerics (Hennig et al., 2015) approach: we reframe a numerical computation (in this case, trace estimation) as probabilistic inference. Probabilistic numerics usually requires distinguishing: an appropriate latent function; data and; the ultimate object of interest. Given the data, a posterior distribution is calculated for the object of interest. For instance, in numerical integration, the latent function is the integrand, f, the data are evaluations of the integrand, $f(x)$, and the object of interest is the value of the integral, $\int f(x)p(x)\mathrm{d}x$ (see § 3.1.1 for more details). In this work, our latent function is the distribution of eigenvalues of A, the data are noisy observations of $\mathrm{Tr}(A^k)$, and the object of interest is $\log(\mathrm{Det}(K))$. For this object of interest, we are able to provide both expected value and variance. That is, although the Taylor approximation to the log determinant may be considered unsatisfactory, the intermediate trace terms obtained when raising the matrix to higher powers may prove to be informative if considered as observations within a probabilistic model.

3.1 RAW MOMENT OBSERVATIONS

We wish to model the eigenvalues of A from noisy observations of $\mathrm{Tr}\left(A^k\right)$ obtained through stochastic trace estimation, with the ultimate goal of making predictions on the infinite series of the Taylor expansion. Let us assume that the eigenvalues are i.i.d. random variables drawn from $P(\lambda_i = x)$, a probability distribution over $x \in [0,1]$. In this setting $\mathrm{Tr}(A) = n\mathbb{E}_x[P(\lambda_i = x)]$, and more generally $\mathrm{Tr}\left(A^k\right) = n\mathbf{R}_x^{(k)}[P(\lambda_i = x)]$, where $\mathbf{R}_x^{(k)}$ is the kth raw moment over the x domain. The raw moments can thus be computed as,

$$\mathbf{R}_x^{(k)}\left[P\left(\lambda_i = x\right)\right] = \int_0^1 x^k P\left(\lambda_i = x\right)\mathrm{d}x. \quad (5)$$

Such a formulation is appealing because if $P\left(\lambda_i = x\right)$ is modeled as a Gaussian process, the required integrals may be solved analytically using Bayesian Quadrature.

3.1.1 Bayesian Quadrature

Gaussian processes (GPs; Rasmussen & Williams, 2006) are a powerful Bayesian inference method defined over functions $X \to \mathbb{R}$, such that the distribution of functions over any finite subset of the input points $X = \{\mathbf{x}_1, \ldots, \mathbf{x}_n\}$ is a multivariate Gaussian distribution. Under this framework, the moments of the conditional Gaussian distribution for a set of predictive points, given a set of labels $\mathbf{y} = (y_1, \ldots, y_n)^\top$, may be computed as

$$\mu = \mu_0 + K_*^\top K^{-1}(\mathbf{y} - \mu_0), \quad (6)$$

$$\Sigma = K_{*,*} - K_*^\top K^{-1} K_*, \quad (7)$$

with μ and Σ denoting the posterior mean and variance, and K being the $n \times n$ covariance matrix for the observed variables $\{\mathbf{x}_i, y_i; i \in (1, 2, \ldots n)\}$. The latter is computed as $\kappa(\mathbf{x}, \mathbf{x}')$ for any pair of points $\mathbf{x}, \mathbf{x}' \in X$. Meanwhile, K_* and $K_{*,*}$ respectively denote the covariance between the observable and the predictive points, and the prior over the predicted points. Note that μ_0, the prior mean, may be set to zero without loss of generality.

Bayesian Quadrature (BQ; O'Hagan, 1991) is primarily concerned with performing integration of potentially intractable functions. In this work, we limit our discussion to the setting where the integrand is modeled as a GP,

$$\int p(x)\, f(x)\, \mathrm{d}x, \quad f \sim \mathrm{GP}(\mu, \Sigma),$$

where $p(x)$ is some measure with respect to which we are integrating. A full discussion of BQ may be found in O'Hagan (1991) and Rasmussen & Ghahramani (2002); for the sake of conciseness, we only state the result that the integrals may be computed by integrating the covariance function with respect to $p(x)$ for both K_*,

$$\kappa\left(\int \cdot\, \mathrm{d}x, x'\right) = \int p\left(x\right)\kappa\left(x, x'\right)\mathrm{d}x,$$

and $K_{*,*}$,

$$\kappa\left(\int \cdot\, \mathrm{d}x, \int \cdot\, \mathrm{d}x'\right) = \iint p\left(x\right)\kappa\left(x, x'\right)p\left(x'\right)\mathrm{d}x\mathrm{d}x'.$$

3.2 KERNELS FOR RAW MOMENTS AND INFERENCE ON THE LOG DETERMINANT

Recalling (5), if $P(\lambda_i = x)$ is modeled using a GP, in order to include observations of $\mathbf{R}_x^{(k)}[P(\lambda_i = x)]$, denoted as $\mathbf{R}_x^{(k)}$, we must be able to integrate the kernel with respect to the polynomial in x,

$$\kappa\left(\mathbf{R}_x^{(k)}, x'\right) = \int_0^1 x^k \kappa\left(x, x'\right)\mathrm{d}x, \quad (8)$$

$$\kappa\left(\mathbf{R}_x^{(k)}, \mathbf{R}_{x'}^{(k')}\right) = \int_0^1 \int_0^1 x^k \kappa\left(x, x'\right) x'^{k'} \mathrm{d}x\mathrm{d}x'. \quad (9)$$

Although the integrals described above are typically analytically intractable, certain kernels have an elegant analytic form which allows for efficient computation. In this section, we derive the raw moment observations for a histogram kernel, and demonstrate how estimates of the log determinant can be obtained. An alternate polynomial kernel is described in Appendix A.

3.2.1 Histogram Kernel

The entries of the histogram kernel, also known as the piecewise constant kernel, are given by $\kappa(x,x') = \sum_{j=0}^{1-m} \mathcal{H}(\frac{j}{m}, \frac{j+1}{m}, x, x')$, where

$$\mathcal{H}\left(\frac{j}{m}, \frac{j+1}{m}, x, x'\right) = \begin{cases} 1 & x, x' \in \left[\frac{j}{m}, \frac{j+1}{m}\right] \\ 0 & \text{otherwise} \end{cases}.$$

Covariances between raw moments may be computed as follows:

$$\begin{aligned} \kappa\left(\mathbf{R}_x^{(k)}, x'\right) &= \int_0^1 x^k \kappa\left(x, x'\right) \mathrm{d}x \\ &= \frac{1}{k+1}\left(\left(\frac{j+1}{m}\right)^{k+1} - \left(\frac{j}{m}\right)^{k+1}\right), \end{aligned} \tag{10}$$

where in the above x lies in the interval $\left[\frac{j}{m}, \frac{j+1}{m}\right]$. Extending this to the covariance function between raw moments we have,

$$\begin{aligned} \kappa\left(\mathbf{R}_x^{(k)}, \mathbf{R}_{x'}^{(k')}\right) &= \int_0^1 \int_0^1 x^k x'^{k'} \kappa\left(x, x'\right) \mathrm{d}x\mathrm{d}x' \\ &= \sum_{j=0}^{m-1} \prod_{\bar{k} \in (k,k')} \frac{1}{(\bar{k}+1)}\left(\left(\frac{j+1}{m}\right)^{\bar{k}+1} - \left(\frac{j}{m}\right)^{\bar{k}+1}\right). \end{aligned} \tag{11}$$

This simple kernel formulation between observations of the raw moments compactly allows us to perform inference over $P(\lambda_i = x)$. However, the ultimate goal is to predict $\log(\mathrm{Det}(K))$, and hence $\sum_{i=1}^{\infty} \frac{\mathrm{Tr}(A^k)}{k}$. This requires a seemingly more complex set of kernel expressions; nevertheless, by propagating the implied infinite summations into the kernel function, we can also obtain the closed form solutions for these terms,

$$\begin{aligned} \kappa\left(\sum_{k=1}^{\infty} \frac{\mathbf{R}_x^{(k)}}{k}, \mathbf{R}_{x'}^{(k')}\right) &= \sum_{j=0}^{m-1} \frac{1}{k'+1}\left(\left(\frac{j+1}{m}\right)^{k'+1} - \right. \\ &\left.\left(\frac{j}{m}\right)^{k'+1}\right)\left(S\left(\frac{j+1}{m}\right) - S\left(\frac{j}{m}\right)\right) \end{aligned} \tag{12}$$

$$\kappa\left(\sum_{k=1}^{\infty} \frac{\mathbf{R}_x^{(k)}}{k}, \sum_{k'=1}^{\infty} \frac{\mathbf{R}_{x'}^{(k')}}{k'}\right) = \sum_{j=0}^{m-1}\left(S\left(\frac{j+1}{m}\right) - S\left(\frac{j}{m}\right)\right)^2 \tag{13}$$

where $S(\alpha) = \sum_{k=1}^{\infty} \frac{\alpha^{k+1}}{k(k+1)}$, which has the convenient identity for $0 < \alpha < 1$,

$$S(\alpha) = \alpha + (1-\alpha)\log(1-\alpha).$$

Following the derivations presented above, we can finally go about computing the prediction for the log determinant, and its corresponding variance, using the GP posterior equations given in (6) and (7). This can be achieved by replacing the terms K_* and $K_{*,*}$ with the constructions presented in (12) and (13), respectively. The entries of K are filled in using (11), whereas $\mathbf{y}$ denotes the noisy observations of $\mathrm{Tr}\left(A^k\right)$.

3.2.2 Prior Mean Function

While GPs, and in this case BQ, can be applied with a zero mean prior without loss of generality, it is often beneficial to have a mean function as an initial starting point. If $P(\lambda_i = x)$ is composed of a constant mean function $g(\lambda_i = x)$, and a GP is used to model the residual, we have that

$$P\left(\lambda_i = x\right) = g\left(\lambda_i = x\right) + f\left(\lambda_i = x\right).$$

The previously derived moment observations may then be decomposed into,

$$\begin{aligned} \int x^k P\left(\lambda_i = x\right) \mathrm{d}x = &\int x^k g\left(\lambda_i = x\right) \mathrm{d}x \\ &+ \int x^k f\left(\lambda_i = x\right) \mathrm{d}x. \end{aligned} \tag{14}$$

Due to the domain of $P\left(\lambda_i = x\right)$ lying between zero and one, we set a beta distribution as the prior mean, which has some convenient properties. First, it is fully specified by the mean and variance of the distribution, which can be computed using the trace and Frobenius norm of the matrix. Secondly, the r-th raw moment of a Beta distribution parameterized by α and β is

$$\mathbf{R}_x^{(k)}\left[g\left(\lambda_i = x\right)\right] = \frac{\alpha + r}{\alpha + \beta + r},$$

which is straightforward to compute.

In consequence, the expectation of the logarithm of random variables and, hence, the 'prior' log determinant yielded by $g\left(\lambda_i = x\right)$ can be computed as

$$\mathbb{E}[\log(X); X \sim g(\lambda_i = x)] = \Psi(\alpha) - \Psi(\alpha + \beta). \tag{15}$$

This can then simply be added to the previously derived GP expectation of the log determinant.

3.2.3 Using Bounds on the log determinant

As with most GP specifications, there are hyperparameters associated with the prior and the kernel. The optimal settings for these parameters may be obtained via optimization of the standard GP log marginal likelihood, defined as

$$\mathrm{LML}_{GP} = -\frac{1}{2}\mathbf{y}^\top K^{-1}\mathbf{y} - \frac{1}{2}\log(\mathrm{Det}(K)) + \mathrm{const.}$$

Borrowing from the literature on bounds for the log determinant of a matrix, as described in Appendix B, we can also exploit such upper and lower bounds to truncate the resulting GP distribution to the relevant domain, which is expected to greatly improve the predicted log determinant. These additional constraints can then be propagated to the hyperparameter optimization procedure by incorporating them into the likelihood function via the product rule, as follows:

$$\mathrm{LML} = \mathrm{LML}_{GP} + \log\left(\Phi\left(\frac{a-\hat{\mu}}{\hat{\sigma}}\right) - \Phi\left(\frac{b-\hat{\mu}}{\hat{\sigma}}\right)\right),$$

with a and b representing the upper and lower log determinant bounds respectively, $\hat{\mu}$ and $\hat{\sigma}$ representing the posterior mean and standard deviation, and $\Phi(\cdot)$ representing the Gaussian cumulative density function. Priors on the hyperparameters may be accounted for in a similar way.

3.2.4 Algorithm Complexity and Recap

Due to its cubic complexity, GP inference is typically considered detrimental to the scalability of a model. However, in our formulation, the GP is only being applied to the noisy observations of $\mathrm{Tr}\left(A^k\right)$, which rarely exceed the order of tens of points. As a result, given that we assume this to be orders of magnitude smaller than the dimensionality n of the matrix K, the computational complexity is dominated by the matrix-vector operations involved in stochastic trace estimation, i.e. $\mathcal{O}(n^2)$ for dense matrices and $\mathcal{O}(ns)$ for s-sparse matrices.

The steps involved in the procedure described within this section are summarized as pseudo-code in Algorithm 1. The input matrix A is first normalized by using Gershgorin intervals to find the largest eigenvalue (line 1), and the expected bounds on the log determinant (line 2) are calculated using matrix theory (Appendix B). The noisy Taylor observations up to an expansion order M (lines 3-4), denoted here as $\mathbf{y}$, are then obtained through stochastic trace estimation, as described in § 2.2. These can be modeled using a GP, where the entries of the kernel matrix K (lines 5-7) are computed using (11). The kernel parameters are then tuned as per § 3.2.3 (line 8). Recall that we seek to make a prediction for the infinite Taylor expansion, and hence the exact log determinant. To this end, we must compute K_* (lines 9-10) and $k_{*,*}$ (line 11) using (12) and (13), respectively. The posterior mean and variance (line 12) may then be evaluated by filling in (6) and (7). As outlined in the previous section, the resulting posterior distribution can be truncated using the derived bounds to obtain the final estimates for the log determinant and its uncertainty (line 13).

Algorithm 1 Computing log determinant and uncertainty using probabilistic numerics

Input: PSD matrix $A \in \mathbb{R}^{n\times n}$, raw moments kernel κ, expansion order M, and random vectors Z
Output: Posterior mean MTRN, and uncertainty VTRN

```
1: A ← NORMALIZE(A)
2: BOUNDS ← GETBOUNDS(A)
3: for i ← 1 to M do
4:     y_i ← STOCHASTICTAYLOROBS(A, i, Z)
5: for i ← 1 to M do
6:     for j ← 1 to M do
7:         K_ij ← κ(i, j)
8: κ, K ← TUNEKERNEL(K, y, BOUNDS)
9: for i ← 1 to M do
10:    K_{*,i} ← κ(*, i)
11: k_{*,*} ← κ(*, *)
12: MEXP, VEXP ← GPPRED(y, K, K_*, k_{*,*})
13: MTRN, VTRN ← TRUNC(MEXP, VEXP, BOUNDS)
```

4 EXPERIMENTS

In this section, we show how the appeal of this formulation extends beyond its intrinsic novelty, whereby we also consistently obtain performance improvements over competing techniques. We set up a variety of experiments for assessing the model performance, including both synthetically constructed and real matrices. Given the model's probabilistic formulation, we also assess the quality of the uncertainty estimates yielded by the model. We conclude by demonstrating how this approach may be fitted within a practical learning scenario.

We compare our approach against several other estimations to the log determinant, namely approximations based on Taylor expansions, Chebyshev expansions and Stochastic Lanczos quadrature. The Taylor approximation has already been introduced in § 2.2, and we briefly describe the others below.

Chebyshev Expansions: This approach utilizes the m-degree Chebyshev polynomial approximation to the function $\log(I-A)$ (Han et al., 2015; Boutsidis et al., 2015; Peng & Wang, 2015),

$$\mathrm{Tr}\left(\log\left(I-A\right)\right) \approx \sum_{k=0}^{m} c_k \mathrm{Tr}\left(T_k\left(A\right)\right), \qquad (16)$$

where $T_k(x) = AT_{k-1}(A) - T_{k-2}(A)$ starting with

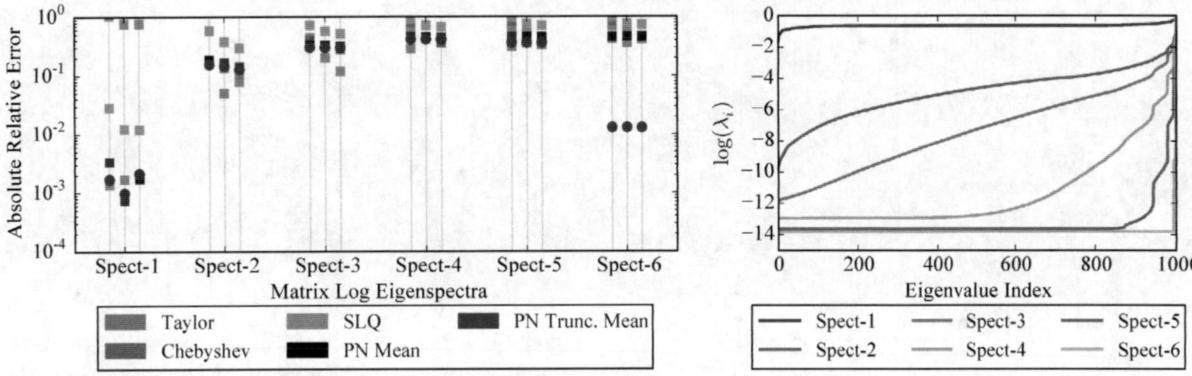

Figure 2: Empirical performance over 6 covariance matrices described in § 4.1. The right figure displays the log eigenspectrum of the matrices and their respective indices. The left figure displays the relative performance of the algorithms for the stochastic trace estimation order set to 5, 25 and 50 (from left to right respectively).

$T_0(A) = 1$ and $T_1(A) = A$, and c_k is defined as

$$\begin{aligned} c_k &= \frac{2}{n+1} \sum_{i=0}^{n} \log\left(I - x_i\right) T_k\left(x_i\right), \\ x_i &= \cos\left(\frac{\left(i + \frac{1}{2}\right)\pi}{n+1}\right). \end{aligned} \tag{17}$$

The Chebyshev approximation is appealing as it gives the best m-degree polynomial approximation of $\log(I - x)$ under the L_∞-norm. The error induced by general Chebyshev polynomial approximations has also been thoroughly investigated (Han et al., 2015).

Stochastic Lanczos Quadrature: This approach (Ubaru et al., 2016) relies on stochastic trace estimation to approximate the trace using the identity presented in (1). If we consider the eigendecomposition of matrix A into $Q\Lambda Q^\top$, the quadratic form in the equation becomes

$$\begin{aligned} \mathbf{r}^{(i)^\top} \log(A) \mathbf{r}^{(i)} &= \mathbf{r}^{(i)^\top} Q \log\left(\Lambda\right) Q^\top \mathbf{r}^{(i)} \\ &= \sum_{k=1}^{n} \log\left(\lambda_k\right) \mu_k^2 \end{aligned},$$

where μ_k denotes the individual components of $Q^\top \mathbf{r}^{(i)}$. By transforming this term into a Riemann-Stieltjes integral $\int_a^b \log(t) \mathrm{d}\mu(t)$, where $\mu(t)$ is a piecewise constant function (Ubaru et al., 2016), we can approximate it as

$$\int_a^b \log(t) \mathrm{d}\mu(t) \approx \sum_{j=0}^{m} \omega_j \log\left(\theta_j\right),$$

where m is the degree of the approximation, while the sets of ω and θ are the parameters to be inferred using Gauss quadrature. It turns out that these parameters may be computed analytically using the eigendecomposition of the low-rank tridiagonal transformation of A obtained using the Lanczos algorithm (Paige, 1972). Denoting the resulting eigenvalues and eigenvectors by θ and y respectively, the quadratic form may finally be evaluated as,

$$\mathbf{r}^{(i)^\top} \log\left(A\right) \mathbf{r}^{(i)} \approx \sum_{j=0}^{m} \tau_j^2 \log\left(\theta_j\right), \tag{18}$$

with $\tau_j = \left[e_1^T y_j\right]$.

4.1 SYNTHETICALLY CONSTRUCTED MATRICES

Previous work on estimating log determinants have implied that the performance of any given method is closely tied to the shape of the eigenspectrum for the matrix under review. As such, we set up an experiment for assessing the performance of each technique when applied to synthetically constructed matrices whose eigenvalues decay at different rates. Given that the computational complexity of each method is dominated by the number of matrix-vector products (MVPs) incurred, we also illustrate the progression of each technique for an increasing allowance of MVPs. All matrices are constructed using a Gaussian kernel evaluated over 1000 input points.

As illustrated in Figure 2, the estimates returned by our approach are consistently on par with (and frequently superior to) those obtained using other methods. For matrices having slowly-decaying eigenvalues, standard Chebyshev and Taylor approximations fare quite poorly, whereas SLQ and our approach both yield comparable results. The results become more homogeneous across methods for faster-decaying eigenspectra, but our method is frequently among the top two performers. For our approach, it is also worth noting that truncating the GP using known bounds on the log determinant indeed

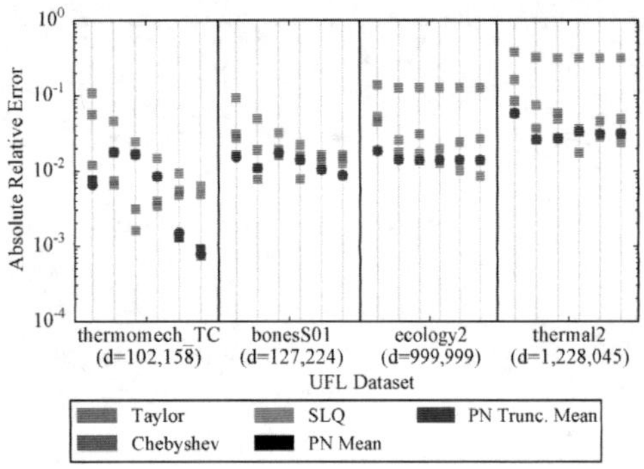

Figure 3: Methods compared on a variety on UFL Sparse Datasets. Each dataset was ran the matrix approximately raised to the power of 5, 10, 15, 20, 25 and 30 (left to right) using stochastic trace estimation.

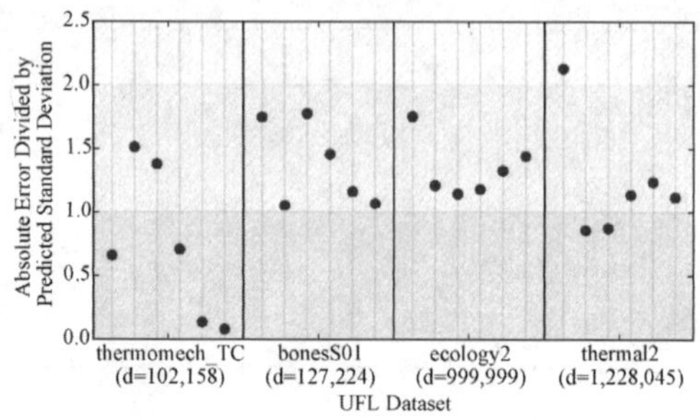

Figure 4: Quality of uncertainty estimates on UFL datasets, measured as the ratio of the absolute error to the predicted variance. As before, results are shown for increasing computational budgets (MVPs). The true value lay outside 2 standard deviations in only one of 24 trials.

results in superior posterior estimates. This is particularly evident when the eigenvalues decay very rapidly. Somewhat surprisingly, the performance does not seem to be greatly affected by the number of budgeted MVPs.

4.2 UFL SPARSE DATASETS

Although we have so far limited our discussion to covariance matrices, our proposed method is amenable to any positive semi-definite matrix. To this end, we extend the previous experimental set-up to a selection of real, sparse matrices obtained from the SuiteSparse Matrix Collection (Davis & Hu, 2011). Following Ubaru et al. (2016), we list the true values of the log determinant reported in Boutsidis et al. (2015), and compare all other approaches to this baseline.

The results for this experiment are shown in Figure 3. Once again, the estimates obtained using our probabilistic approach achieve comparable accuracy to the competing techniques, and several improvements are noted for larger allowances of MVPs. As expected, the SLQ approach generally performs better than Taylor and Chebyshev approximations, especially for smaller computational budgets. Even so, our proposed technique consistently appears to have an edge across all datasets.

4.3 UNCERTAINTY QUANTIFICATION

One of the notable features of our proposal is the ability to quantify the uncertainty of the predicted log determinant, which can be interpreted as an indicator of the quality of the approximation. Given that none of the other techniques offer such insights to compare against, we assess the quality of the model's uncertainty estimates by measuring the ratio of the absolute error to the predicted standard deviation (uncertainty). For the latter to be meaningful, the error should ideally lie within only a few multiples of the standard deviation.

In Figure 4, we report this metric for our approach when using the histogram kernel. We carry out this evaluation over the matrices introduced in the previous experiment, once again showing how the performance varies for different MVP allowances. In all cases, the absolute error of the predicted log determinant is consistently bounded by at most twice the predicted standard deviation, which is very sensible for such a probabilistic model.

4.4 MOTIVATING EXAMPLE

Determinantal point processes (DPPs; Macchi, 1975) are stochastic point processes defined over subsets of data such that an established degree of repulsion is maintained. A DPP, $\mathcal{P}$, over a discrete space $y \in \{1, \ldots, n\}$ is a probability measure over all subsets of y such that

$$\mathcal{P}(A \in y) = \mathrm{Det}(K_A),$$

where K_A is a positive definite matrix having all eigenvalues less than or equal to 1. A popular method for modeling data via K is the *L-ensemble* approach (Borodin, 2009), which transforms kernel matrices, L, into an appropriate K,

$$K = (L + I)^{-1} L.$$

The goal of inference is to correctly parameterize L given observed subsets of y, such that the probability of unseen subsets can be accurately inferred in the future.

Given that the log-likelihood term of a DPP requires the log determinant of L, naïve computations of this term are intractable for large sample sizes. In this experiment, we demonstrate how our proposed approach can be employed to the purpose of parameter optimization for

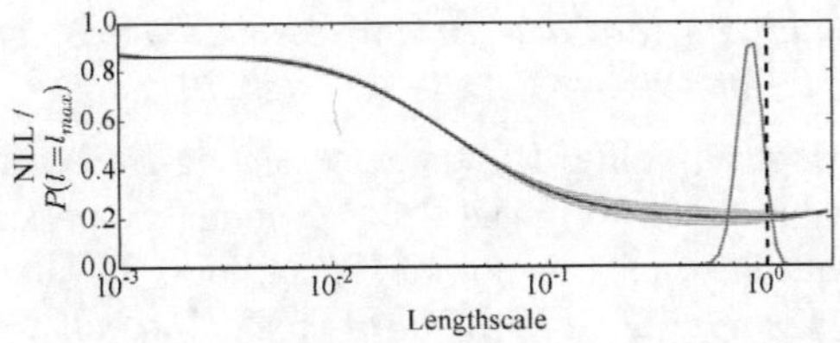

Figure 5: The rescaled negative log-likelihood (NLL) of DPP with varying length scale (blue) and probability of maximum likelihood (red). Cubic interpolation was used between inferred likelihood observations. Ten samples, z, were taken to polynomial order 30.

large-scale DPPs. In particular, we sample points from a DPP defined on a lattice over $[-1, 1]^5$, with one million points at uniform intervals. A Gaussian kernel with lengthscale parameter l is placed over these points, creating the true L. Subsets of the lattice points can be drawn by taking advantage of the tensor structure of L, and we draw five sets of 12,500 samples each. For a given selection of lengthscale options, the goal of this experiment is to confirm that the DPP likelihood of the obtained samples is indeed maximized when L is parameterized by the true lengthscale, l. As shown in Figure 5, the computed uncertainty allows us to derive a distribution over the true lengthscale which, despite using few matrix-vector multiplications, is very close to the optimal.

5 CONCLUSION

In a departure from conventional approaches for estimating the log determinant of a matrix, we propose a novel probabilistic framework which provides a Bayesian perspective on the literature of matrix theory and stochastic trace estimation. In particular, our approach enables the log determinant to be inferred from noisy observations of $\mathrm{Tr}\left(A^k\right)$ obtained from stochastic trace estimation. By modeling these observations using a GP, a posterior estimate for the log determinant may then be computed using Bayesian Quadrature. Our experiments confirm that the results obtained using this model are highly comparable to competing methods, with the additional benefit of measuring uncertainty.

We forecast that the foundations laid out in this work can be extended in various directions, such as exploring more kernels on the raw moments which permit tractable Bayesian Quadrature. The uncertainty quantified in this work is also a step closer towards fully characterizing the uncertainty associated with approximating large-scale kernel-based models.

References

Ambikasaran, S., Foreman-Mackey, D., Greengard, L., Hogg, D. W., and O'Neil, M. Fast Direct Methods for Gaussian Processes. *IEEE Transactions on Pattern Analysis and Machine Intelligence*, 38(2):252–265, 2016.

Anitescu, M., Chen, J., and Wang, L. A Matrix-free Approach for Solving the Parametric Gaussian Process Maximum Likelihood Problem. *SIAM J. Scientific Computing*, 34(1), 2012.

Aune, E., Simpson, D. P., and Eidsvik, J. Parameter Estimation in High Dimensional Gaussian Distributions. *Statistics and Computing*, 24(2):247–263, 2014.

Avron, H. and Toledo, S. Randomized Algorithms for Estimating the Trace of an Implicit Symmetric Positive Semi-definite Matrix. *J. ACM*, 58(2):8:1–8:34, 2011.

Bai, Z. and Golub, G. H. Bounds for the Trace of the Inverse and the Determinant of Symmetric Positive Definite Matrices. *Annals of Numerical Mathematics*, 4:29–38, 1997.

Bardenet, R. and Titsias, M. K. Inference for Determinantal Point Processes Without Spectral Knowledge. In *Proceedings of the 28th International Conference on Neural Information Processing Systems*, pp. 3393–3401, 2015.

Barry, R. P. and Pace, R. K. Monte Carlo Estimates of the Log-Determinant of Large Sparse Matrices. *Linear Algebra and its applications*, 289(1):41–54, 1999.

Borodin, A. Determinantal point processes. *arXiv preprint arXiv:0911.1153*, 2009.

Boutsidis, C., Drineas, P., Kambadur, P., and Zouzias, A. A Randomized Algorithm for Approximating the Log Determinant of a Symmetric Positive Definite Matrix. *CoRR*, abs/1503.00374, 2015.

Braun, M. L. Accurate Error Bounds for the Eigenvalues of the Kernel Matrix. *Journal of Machine Learning Research*, 7:2303–2328, December 2006.

Chen, J., Anitescu, M., and Saad, Y. Computing f(A)b via Least Squares Polynomial Approximations. *SIAM Journal on Scientific Computing*, 33(1):195–222, 2011.

Cutajar, K., Osborne, M., Cunningham, J., and Filippone, M. Preconditioning Kernel Matrices. In *Proceedings of the 33nd International Conference on Machine Learning, ICML 2016, New York City, NY, USA, June 19-24*, 2016.

Davis, J. V., Kulis, B., Jain, P., Sra, S., and Dhillon, I. S. Information-theoretic Metric Learning. In *Proceedings of the Twenty-Fourth International Conference (ICML 2007), Corvallis, Oregon, USA, June 20-24, 2007*, pp. 209–216, 2007.

Davis, T. A. and Hu, Y. The University of Florida Sparse Matrix Collection. *ACM Transactions on Mathematical Software (TOMS)*, 38(1):1, 2011.

Filippone, M. and Engler, R. Enabling Scalable Stochastic Gradient-based inference for Gaussian processes by employing the Unbiased LInear System SolvEr (ULISSE). In *Proceedings of the 32nd International Conference on Machine Learning, ICML 2015, Lille, France, July 6-11*, 2015.

Fitzsimons, J. K., Osborne, M. A., Roberts, S. J., and Fitzsimons, J. F. Improved Stochastic Trace Estimation using Mutually Unbiased Bases. *CoRR*, abs/1608.00117, 2016.

Gershgorin, S. Uber die Abgrenzung der Eigenwerte einer Matrix. *Izvestija Akademii Nauk SSSR, Serija Matematika*, 7(3):749–754, 1931.

Golub, G. H. and Van Loan, C. F. *Matrix computations*. The Johns Hopkins University Press, 3rd edition, October 1996. ISBN 080185413.

Han, I., Malioutov, D., and Shin, J. Large-scale Log-Determinant computation through Stochastic Chebyshev Expansions. In Bach, F. R. and Blei, D. M. (eds.), *Proceedings of the 32nd International Conference on Machine Learning, ICML 2015, Lille, France, 6-11 July 2015*, 2015.

Hennig, P., Osborne, M. A., and Girolami, M. Probabilistic Numerics and Uncertainty in Computations. *Proceedings of the Royal Society of London A: Mathematical, Physical and Engineering Sciences*, 471(2179), 2015.

Hutchinson, M. A Stochastic Estimator of the Trace of the Influence Matrix for Laplacian Smoothing Splines. *Communications in Statistics - Simulation and Computation*, 19(2):433–450, 1990.

Ipsen, I. C. F. and Lee, D. J. Determinant Approximations, May 2011.

Macchi, O. The Coincidence Approach to Stochastic point processes. *Advances in Applied Probability*, 7:83–122, 1975.

Mackay, D. J. C. *Information Theory, Inference and Learning Algorithms*. Cambridge University Press, first edition edition, June 2003. ISBN 0521642981.

O'Hagan, A. Bayes-Hermite Quadrature. *Journal of Statistical Planning and Inference*, 29:245–260, 1991.

Paige, C. C. Computational Variants of the Lanczos method for the Eigenproblem. *IMA Journal of Applied Mathematics*, 10(3):373–381, 1972.

Peng, H. and Qi, Y. EigenGP: Gaussian Process Models with Adaptive Eigenfunctions. In *Proceedings of the 24th International Conference on Artificial Intelligence*, IJCAI'15, pp. 3763–3769. AAAI Press, 2015.

Peng, W. and Wang, H. Large-scale Log-Determinant Computation via Weighted L_2 Polynomial Approximation with Prior Distribution of Eigenvalues. In *International Conference on High Performance Computing and Applications*, pp. 120–125. Springer, 2015.

Rasmussen, C. E. and Williams, C. *Gaussian Processes for Machine Learning*. MIT Press, 2006.

Rasmussen, C. E. and Ghahramani, Z. Bayesian Monte Carlo. In *Advances in Neural Information Processing Systems 15, NIPS 2002, December 9-14, 2002, Vancouver, British Columbia, Canada*, pp. 489–496, 2002.

Rue, H. and Held, L. *Gaussian Markov Random Fields: Theory and Applications*, volume 104 of *Monographs on Statistics and Applied Probability*. Chapman & Hall, London, 2005.

Rue, H., Martino, S., and Chopin, N. Approximate Bayesian inference for latent Gaussian models by using integrated nested Laplace approximations. *Journal of the Royal Statistical Society: Series B (Statistical Methodology)*, 71(2):319–392, 2009.

Saatçi, Y. *Scalable Inference for Structured Gaussian Process Models*. PhD thesis, University of Cambridge, 2011.

Silverstein, J. W. Eigenvalues and Eigenvectors of Large Dimensional Sample Covariance Matrices. *Contemporary Mathematics*, 50:153–159, 1986.

Stein, M. L., Chen, J., and Anitescu, M. Stochastic Approximation of Score functions for Gaussian processes. *The Annals of Applied Statistics*, 7(2):1162–1191, 2013. doi: 10.1214/13-AOAS627.

Ubaru, S., Chen, J., and Saad, Y. Fast Estimation of tr (f (a)) via Stochastic Lanczos Quadrature. 2016.

Wathen, A. J. and Zhu, S. On Spectral Distribution of Kernel Matrices related to Radial Basis functions. *Numerical Algorithms*, 70(4):709–726, 2015.

Weyl, H. Das asymptotische Verteilungsgesetz der Eigenwerte linearer partieller Differentialgleichungen (mit einer Anwendung auf die Theorie der Hohlraumstrahlung). *Mathematische Annalen*, 71(4):441–479, 1912.

Wolkowicz, H. and Styan, G. P. Bounds for Eigenvalues using Traces. *Linear algebra and its applications*, 29: 471–506, 1980.

Zhang, Y. and Leithead, W. E. Approximate Implementation of the logarithm of the Matrix Determinant in Gaussian process Regression. *Journal of Statistical Computation and Simulation*, 77(4):329–348, 2007.

A POLYNOMIAL KERNEL

Similar to the derivation of the histogram kernel, we can also derive the polynomial kernel for moment observations. The entries of the polynomial kernel, given by $k(x, x') = (xx' + c)^d$, can be integrated over as,

$$\begin{aligned} \kappa\left(\mathbf{R}_x^{(k)}, x'\right) &= \int_0^1 \sum_{i=1}^{d} \binom{d}{i} x^{k+i} x'^{i} c^{d-i} dx \\ &= \sum_{i=1}^{d} \binom{d}{i} \frac{x'^{i} c^{d-i}}{k+i+1}, \end{aligned} \tag{19}$$

$$\begin{aligned} \kappa\left(\mathbf{R}_x^{(k)}, \mathbf{R}_{x'}^{(k')}\right) &= \int_0^1 \int_0^1 \sum_{i=1}^{d} \binom{d}{i} x^{k+i} x'^{k'+i} c^{d-i} dx dx' \\ &= \sum_{i=1}^{d} \binom{d}{i} \frac{c^{d-i}}{(k+i+1)(k'+i+1)}. \end{aligned} \tag{20}$$

As with the histogram kernel, the infinite sum of the Taylor expansion can also be combined into the Gaussian process,

$$\begin{aligned} \kappa\left(\sum_{k=1}^{\infty} \frac{\mathbf{R}_x^{(k)}}{k}, \mathbf{R}_{x'}^{(k')}\right) &= \frac{1}{k} \sum_{k=1}^{\infty} \sum_{i=1}^{d} \binom{d}{i} \frac{c^{d-i}}{(k+i+1)(k'+i+1)} \\ &= \sum_{i=1}^{d} \binom{d}{i} \frac{c^{d-i}\left(\Psi^{(0)}(i+2)+\gamma\right)}{(i+1)(k'+i+1)}, \end{aligned} \tag{21}$$

$$\begin{aligned} \kappa\left(\sum_{k=1}^{\infty} \frac{\mathbf{R}_x^{(k)}}{k}, \sum_{k'=1}^{\infty} \frac{\mathbf{R}_{x'}^{(k')}}{k'}\right) &= \frac{1}{kk'} \sum_{k=1}^{\infty} \sum_{k'=1}^{\infty} \sum_{i=1}^{d} \binom{d}{i} \frac{c^{d-i}}{(k+i+1)(k'+i+1)} \\ &= \sum_{i=1}^{d} \binom{d}{i} \frac{c^{d-i}\left(\Psi^{(0)}(i+2)+\gamma\right)^2}{(i+1)^2}. \end{aligned} \tag{22}$$

In the above, $\Psi^{(0)}(\cdot)$ is the digamma function and γ is the Euler-Mascheroni constant. We strongly believe that the polynomial and histogram kernels are not the only kernels which can be analytically derived to include moment observations but act as a reasonable initial choice for practitioners.

B BOUNDS ON LOG DETERMINANTS

For the sake of completeness, we restate the bounds on the log determinants used throughout this paper (Bai & Golub, 1997).

Theorem 1 *Let A be an n-by-n symmetric positive definite matrix, $\mu_1 = Tr(A)$, $\mu_2 = \|A\|_F^2$ and $\lambda_i(A) \in [\alpha; \beta]$ with $\alpha > 0$, then*

$$\begin{bmatrix} \log \alpha \\ \log t \end{bmatrix}^T \begin{bmatrix} \alpha & t \\ \alpha^2 & t^2 \end{bmatrix}^{-1} \begin{bmatrix} \mu_1 \\ \mu_2 \end{bmatrix} \leq Tr(\log(A)) \leq \begin{bmatrix} \log \beta \\ \log \bar{t} \end{bmatrix}^T \begin{bmatrix} \beta & \bar{t} \\ \beta^2 & \bar{t}^2 \end{bmatrix}^{-1} \begin{bmatrix} \mu_1 \\ \mu_2 \end{bmatrix}$$

where,

$$t = \frac{\alpha\mu_1 - \mu_2}{\alpha n - \mu_1}, \quad \bar{t} = \frac{\beta\mu_1 - \mu_2}{\beta n - \mu_1}$$

This bound can be easily computed while loading the matrix as both the trace and Frobenius norm can be readily calculated using summary statistics. However, bounds on the maximum and minimum must also be derived. We chose to use Gershgorin intervals to bound the eigenvalues (Gershgorin, 1931).

Fast Amortized Inference and Learning in Log-linear Models with Randomly Perturbed Nearest Neighbor Search

Stephen Mussmann*, **Daniel Levy***, **Stefano Ermon**
Department of Computer Science
Stanford University
Stanford, CA 94305
{mussmann,danilevy,ermon}@cs.stanford.edu

Abstract

Inference in log-linear models scales linearly in the size of output space in the worst-case. This is often a bottleneck in natural language processing and computer vision tasks when the output space is feasibly enumerable but very large. We propose a method to perform inference in log-linear models with sublinear amortized cost. Our idea hinges on using Gumbel random variable perturbations and a pre-computed Maximum Inner Product Search data structure to access the most-likely elements in sublinear amortized time. Our method yields provable runtime and accuracy guarantees. Further, we present empirical experiments on ImageNet and Word Embeddings showing significant speedups for sampling, inference, and learning in log-linear models.

1 INTRODUCTION

Log-linear models are widely used in machine learning and statistics. These models receive their name from the fact that the log unnormalized probabilities are linear in the parameters and the sufficient statistics. Since the probabilities are defined up to scaling, inference and learning require computing the normalization constant, also known as the partition function (Murphy, 2012).

While defining unnormalized probabilities affords modeling flexibility, it comes at the price of computation time. For factorized models, there are many methods, such as Gibbs sampling and variational inference (Koller & Friedman, 2009), to approximately perform inference. Here we are interested in the setting where the output space is not factorizable, and is large but enumerable (e.g., a few million elements). Such problems with large output spaces occur in many areas including computer vision and natural language processing (NLP) (Joulin et al., 2016; Bengio et al., 2003; Mikolov et al., 2013). While inference is tractable (by brute force, in time linear in the size of the output space), it can be a major bottleneck in learning and even at test time in resource-constrained settings. Clearly, computation time cannot be saved for a *single* inference query as it requires linear time to examine the input. However, as Mussmann & Ermon (2016) establishes, computation time can be saved for a *sequence* of related queries, e.g., sampling from log-linear models with the same sufficient statistics but different (changing) parameters. Such sequences of queries arise naturally in learning and at test time.

In this work, we employ Gumbel random variables to convert sampling into maximizing unnormalized log-probabilities perturbed by Gumbel noise, applied independently to each element in the output space (Hazan et al., 2013; Maddison et al., 2014; Kim et al., 2016). Naively, sampling a Gumbel for each element requires linear runtime which yields no savings. However, we introduce a novel way to lazily instantiate the Gumbel random variables. In order to maximize the Gumbel-perturbed objective, we only examine a (small) subset of the most-likely states and a small number of Gumbel perturbations (the largest ones). This yields asymptotic runtime improvements with provable accuracy guarantees. To find the most likely states, which involves the maximization of the dot product between the parameters and the sufficient statistics, we are able to make use of the large literature on Maximum Inner Product Search (Shrivastava & Li, 2014; Auvolat et al., 2015; Douze et al., 2016; Ram & Gray, 2012; Koenigstein et al., 2012).

The contributions of this work are as follows.

- We present a method to perform sampling using access to the top $O(\sqrt{n})$ most likely states (where n is the number of states), using the Gumbel max trick.

*Both authors contributed equally.

- We present a method to estimate the partition function and expected values using access to the top $O(\sqrt{n})$ values and relying on uniform sampling.
- We present a way to use Maximum Inner Product Search (MIPS) techniques to retrieve the approximate top $O(\sqrt{n})$ elements to provably achieve sublinear amortized query time.
- We demonstrate applications of our method in computer vision and NLP where we achieve 5–10× per-query speedups compared to the naive method.

2 BACKGROUND

2.1 LOG-LINEAR MODELS

Log-linear models are widely used in machine learning and artificial intelligence. Generally, any exponential family distribution can be written as a log-linear model. As examples, very common models like multinomial logistic regression and maximum entropy models (Koller & Friedman, 2009; Murphy, 2012) are log-linear models. Additionally, the last layer of a neural network (softmax) is a log-linear model, e.g. sampling the next element of a sequence for recurrent neural networks.

In this work, we focus on discrete distributions over a set of states $\mathcal{X}$. For a log-linear model, the log unnormalized probabilities are linear in the parameters. More precisely, if the parameters are θ and the features (sufficient statistics) for an element $x \in \mathcal{X}$ are $\phi(x)$, then,

$$\Pr(x;\theta) \propto e^{\theta\cdot\phi(x)} \tag{1}$$

Note that in order to define a distribution, we must normalize these probabilities by

$$Z_\theta = \sum_{x\in\mathcal{X}} e^{\theta\cdot\phi(x)} \tag{2}$$

which is known as the partition function. Unfortunately, computing the partition function Z is expensive as it requires summing over all elements in $\mathcal{X}$. We can also learn a log-linear model by maximizing the likelihood of some training data where evaluating the gradient requires computing the expected value of the sufficient statistics.

Assumption: In our setting, $\mathcal{X}$ is large but feasibly enumerable, so naively computing the partition function is tractable but computationally expensive.

As an example, in the experimental results section, $|\mathcal{X}| \approx 10^6$. As a negative example, Markov Random Fields can be written as a log-linear model but have an exponentially large $\mathcal{X}$ and thus are not amenable to our method.

2.2 GUMBEL VARIABLE

In the context of extremal statistics, Gumbel & Lieblein (1954) defines the Gumbel distribution as

$$\Pr(G < x) = \exp(-\exp(-x)) \tag{3}$$

We can sample a Gumbel random variable using the following scheme,

$$U \sim \text{Uniform}(0,1) \tag{4}$$

$$G = -\ln(-\ln(U)) \tag{5}$$

Our use of the Gumbel distribution is motivated by the so-called "Gumbel Trick" which involves adding Gumbel noise to the log unnormalized probabilities to turn sampling from a log-linear model into finding the maximizing element.

Proposition 2.1 ((Hazan et al., 2013; Maddison et al., 2014)). *For Gumbel variables G_x sampled i.i.d. for each data point x,*

$$\operatorname*{argmax}_x \theta\cdot\phi(x) + G_x \sim \text{Categorical}(\{\frac{e^{\theta\cdot\phi(x)}}{Z_\theta}\}_x) \tag{6}$$

2.3 MAXIMUM INNER PRODUCT SEARCH

A common computational task is retrieving the nearest neighbor to a query from a database of vectors. More specifically, we are given a database of vectors on which we can perform preprocessing and build a data structure, and then, we receive a sequence of queries $\{q_i\}_i$, and for each query, we use the data structure to compute the element in the database that is most similar to q_i. Note that the structure of this problem depends on the similarity measure between vectors.

If n is the number of vectors, we can trivially create an $O(n)$ algorithm (per query): for every query q, iterate through the entire database and find the vector that is most similar to q. Remarkably, for Euclidean distance and cosine similarity, it is possible to achieve *amortized sublinear* query runtime (Indyk & Motwani, 1998; Charikar, 2002).

Because of applications in log-linear models, we will be interested in using the inner product as the similarity measure. This is known as the Maximum Inner Product Search (MIPS) task.

Definition 2.1 (Maximum Inner Product Search). *Given a set of vectors $V = \{v_1, ..., v_n\}$ the MIPS task is to respond to a query vector q with*

$$\operatorname*{argmax}_{v\in V} q\cdot v \tag{7}$$

One common class of techniques for solving MIPS are space-partitioning methods such as k-d trees (Bentley, 1975). Ram & Gray (2012) and Koenigstein et al. (2012) introduce space-partitioning methods based on a branch and bound technique to solve the MIPS problem. Unfortunately, it has been observed that such tree-based methods suffer from the curse of dimensionality (Shrivastava & Li, 2014).

Clustering is another approach for solving the MIPS task (Auvolat et al., 2015; Douze et al., 2016). For this technique, the database vectors are clustered during the preprocessing step. Then, at query time, the algorithm searches the clusters near q for the most similar vector.

Another common class of techniques for MIPS are based on Local Sensitive Hashing (Shrivastava & Li, 2014; Neyshabur & Srebro, 2014), a method introduced by Indyk & Motwani (1998). LSH only requires a family of hash functions with collision probabilities that are monotonic in the similarity. LSH works by combining these basic hashes to form longer hashes, and then building a hash table for each longer hash. Then, at query time, LSH hashes the query, retrieves elements from the colliding hash buckets, and computes the maximum over such elements. More precisely, define $\mathrm{Sim}(x, y)$ as the similarity between x and y and an S-neighbor to a query q as a point x such that $\mathrm{Sim}(q, x) \geq S$.

Theorem 2.1. *Given a set V of size n with a similarity measure and hash family $\mathcal{H}$ such that for scalars $S_1 > S_2$ and $p_1 > p_2$,*

- *For any $x, y \in V$ where $\mathrm{Sim}(x, y) \geq S_1$, $\Pr_{h\in\mathcal{H}}[h(x) = h(y)] \geq p_1$*
- *For any $x, y \in V$ where $\mathrm{Sim}(x, y) \leq S_2$, $\Pr_{h\in\mathcal{H}}[h(x) = h(y)] \leq p_2$*

one can construct a data structure which, given any query q, does the following with high probability: if there exists a S_1-neighbor of q in V, it returns a S_2-neighbor of q in V. Further, this can be done with $O(n^\rho \log n)$ query time and $O(n^{1+\rho})$ space where $\rho = \frac{\log p_1}{\log p_2} < 1$.

Proof. See Indyk & Motwani (1998) □

This theorem states that if there is an S_1-close neighbor, the algorithm will find an S_2-close neighbor. Intuitively, this means that each LSH instance is "tuned" to a different similarity value. We can build a series of LSH instances "tuned" to different values so that we can find the largest element with high probability, no matter the similarity of the nearest neighbor. The theorem states that this can be done in sublinear time.

For the sublinear theoretical guarantees in this paper, we will rely on the reduction from MIPS to Maximum Cosines Similarity Search presented in Neyshabur & Srebro (2014) which adds a single dimension to make all the database vectors have the same norm. For the cosine similarity search problem, we will rely on LSH techniques for cosine similarity search presented in Charikar (2002) based on Signed Random Projections, a binary hash function based on the sign of the dot product with a random vector.

3 METHOD

Suppose we have a log-linear model over a set of n elements $\mathcal{X}$. We wish to perform sampling and inference in sublinear time. This cannot be done for a single value of the parameters θ, but with preprocessing on $\mathcal{X}$, we can achieve sublinear amortized query time.

Our method generally works for any distribution where

$$\Pr(i) = \frac{e^{y_i}}{\sum_j e^{y_j}} \tag{8}$$

which encompasses all distributions with strictly positive probability mass. The requirement for our method is that we have access to the largest $O(\sqrt{n})$ values of y_i in sublinear time. In particular, this method works for log-linear models where $y_i = \theta \cdot \phi(x_i)$ and we use Maximum Inner Product search techniques to access the top values.

3.1 SAMPLING

Recall the Gumbel max technique from the background section. In particular, if we can compute the maximum element and value of $y_i + G_i$ for Gumbel variables G_i, the maximum element will be a sample from the model. We can construct a naive strategy as follows: sample a Gumbel G_i for each y_i and iterate over all elements to find the maximum (perturbed) element. However, this algorithm's runtime is linear and provides no savings.

Ideally, we would like to find a way to preprocess $\{y_i\}_{i=1}^n$ so that we can draw samples and perform inference quickly. Mussmann & Ermon (2016) achieves this by performing preprocessing on fixed Gumbel samples and using MIPS techniques. This "frozen" Gumbel noise makes the samples very correlated; in fact, there are a small fixed number of possible samples for a given parameter value. We wish to find a way that allows us to sample fresh Gumbels for every sample, but only a sublinear number of them.

Intuitively, for an element to maximize $y_i + G_i$, either y_i needs to be large or G_i needs to be large, so we only need to examine indices where either y_i or G_i is large. We

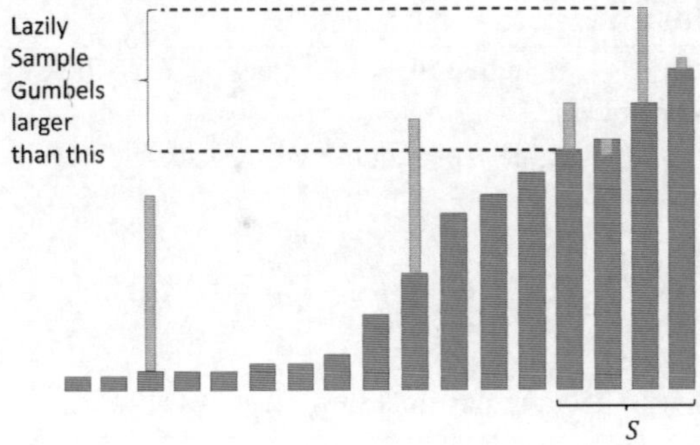

Figure 1: The values of y_i are shown sorted in blue while the Gumbel noise is shown in yellow. We sample a Gumbel for each element of the set S of the largest y_i. Then, we compute the minimum value that a Gumbel must have to yield a candidate solution, represented by the difference between the dotted lines. Finally, we lazily sample Gumbels larger than this value for elements not in S.

can find the largest y_i by performing preprocessing (such as maximum inner product search) and we will find the largest G_i by incorporating a lazy evaluation strategy for the Gumbel variables to only require an expected number of $O(\sqrt{n})$ samples.

First, we describe the method intuitively and with a figure before diving into the details. Let S be the set of the largest $O(\sqrt{n})$ elements of $\{y_i\}_{i=1}^n$. First, we will sample Gumbel values for these S largest elements. Note that the minimal y_i in S is an upper bound on the y_i value of elements not in S. Further, for an element not in S to have the overall maximal $y_i + G_i$, it must exceed the maximal $y_i + G_i$ for elements in S, which is quickly computable. Thus, we have a lower bound on what the value of a Gumbel must be to perturb a point not in S to be the overall maximum. We can lazily sample large Gumbels that exceed this gap, which we will show there will not be too many in expectation. Then, we randomly assign these large Gumbels to the tail of the distribution and check if any of them exceed the maximal $y_i + G_i$ from the largest elements S. See Figure 1.

Note that our method requires the top $k = O(\sqrt{n})$ elements of $\{y_i\}_{i=1}^n$ which we will refer to as S. For lazy sampling the large Gumbels, we will use the fact that a Gumbel can be represented as $G_i = -\ln(-\ln(U_i))$. Then we can sample the number of Gumbels that exceed a threshold B by sampling the number of U_i such that $U_i > \exp(-\exp(-B))$ and then can conditionally sample $U_i > \exp(-\exp(-B))$. Precisely, our method involves several steps shown in Algorithm 1.

Theorem 3.1. *For Algorithm 1, $\hat{x}$ is an exact sample from* $\Pr(i) \propto e^{y_i}$.

Algorithm 1 Fast Sampling with Lazy Gumbels

Input: $\{y_i\}_{i=1}^n$, S as the top k values of y_i
Sample k Gumbel variables G_i for $i \in S$
Compute $M = \max_{i \in S} y_i + G_i$
Compute $S_{\min} = \min_{i \in S} y_i$
Compute the Gumbel cutoff $B = M - S_{\min}$.
Sample $m \sim \text{Binomial}(n - k, 1 - \exp(-\exp(-B))$ as the number of $|\mathcal{X} \setminus S|$ Gumbels with value $> B$
Uniformly sample m points from $\mathcal{X} \setminus S$ and denote T
Sample Gumbels that are conditionally $G_i > B$ for the points $i \in T$ (sample $U_i \sim \text{Uniform}(\exp(-\exp(-B)), 1)$)
$\hat{x} = \text{argmax}_{i \in S \cup T}\, y_i + G_i$
return Sample $\hat{x}$

Proof. This theorem would follow from Proposition 2.1 if we prove that we are finding the maximum of $y_i + G_i$. Note that we do not evaluate the Gumbel for all of the elements in $\mathcal{X} - S - T$. Thus, the only way the lazy sampling strategy will fail is if one of these points is the true maximum. However, these points have Gumbel $G_i < B$ and since they aren't in S, $y_i < S_{\min}$. Together, this implies that $y_i + G_i < S_{\min} + B = M$ which is a value attained by a point in S. Therefore points not in $S \cup T$ cannot be the maximum. □

3.1.1 Runtime

Further, the runtime will be composed of two parts: retrieving the top k elements S and the runtime of Algorithm 1. Let the cost of retrieving the top k elements be $f(n,k)$. For Algorithm 1, including the cost of retrieving S, the runtime will be $O(f(n,k) + m)$ and m has a reasonable expected value.

Theorem 3.2. *For Algorithm 1,* $\mathbb{E}[m] \leq \frac{n}{k}$

The proof is in the appendix. Thus, the expected runtime for our method will be $O(f(n,k) + \frac{n}{k})$ which is sublinear if $k = \sqrt{n}$ and $f(n, \sqrt{n})$ is sublinear.

3.1.2 Fixed B

Note that the technique above has a reasonable expected runtime but no runtime guarantees with high probability. To address this, we can fix B to be a constant so that the value of m is concentrated. Additionally, the technique shown in Algorithm 1 only works if $S_{\min}$ is an upper bound on elements not in S which is brittle to errors in the MIPS technique.

To address these issues, we define a related algorithm with a fixed Gumbel cutoff of $B = -\ln(-\ln(1 - l/n))$ so that there are on average l Gumbel variables that exceed the cutoff. See Algorithm 2.

Algorithm 2 Fast Sampling with Fixed B

Input: $\{y_i\}_{i=1}^n$, S as the top k values of y_i, l
Sample k Gumbel variables G_i for $i \in S$
Set $B = -\ln(-\ln(1 - l/n))$
Sample m as the number of $|\mathcal{X} - S|$ Gumbels with value $> B$
Uniformly sample m points from $\mathcal{X} - S$ and call them T
Sample Gumbels that are conditionally $G_i > B$ for the points $i \in T$
$\hat{x} = \text{argmax}_{i \in S \cup T}\, y_i + G_i$
return Sample $\hat{x}$

Algorithm 3 Partition Function Estimation

Input: $\{y_i\}$, S as the top k values of y_i, l
Uniformly sample l elements with replacement from $[1, n] \setminus S$ and call it T
$\hat{Z} = \sum_{i \in S} e^{y_i} + \frac{n-|S|}{|T|} \sum_{i \in T} e^{y_i}$
return Partition function estimate $\hat{Z}$

Note that for $|S| = k$, the total runtime is $O(f(n, k) + m)$ where $f(n, k)$ is the runtime of gathering the top k elements. Further $m \sim \text{Binomial}(n, l/n)$ so with very high probability, $m < 2l$ and the runtime is $O(f(n, k) + l)$ which will be sublinear if $f(n, k)$ and l are sublinear.

Theorem 3.3. *For Algorithm 2, the sample is an exact sample with probability* $1 - \delta$ *for* $kl \geq n \ln(1/\delta)$.

The proof is in the appendix. Thus, we can set $k = l \geq \sqrt{\ln(1/\delta)}\sqrt{n}$.

3.2 PARTITION FUNCTION ESTIMATION

Similar to sampling, we can estimate the partition function by using the top $k = O(\sqrt{n})$ elements S and a uniform sample T of $l = O(\sqrt{n})$ elements from the remaining elements. We combine these two sets to form an estimate of the partition function with relative error ϵ. See Algorithm 3.

Theorem 3.4. *Algorithm 3 returns an unbiased estimate* $\hat{Z}$ *and for* $kl \geq \frac{2}{3}\frac{1}{\epsilon^2} n \ln(1/\delta)$, *then with* $1-\delta$ *probability,*

$$\frac{|\hat{Z} - Z|}{Z} \leq \epsilon \tag{9}$$

The proof is in the appendix. If we set $k = l$, then the runtime is $O(\frac{1}{\epsilon}\sqrt{n}\sqrt{\ln(1/\delta)})$.

This is closely related to the heuristic presented in Rastogi & Van Durme (2015) as MIMPS. However, this is the first work that provides theoretical guarantees for the method and yields a theoretical understanding for the choice of k and l.

Algorithm 4 Expectation Estimation

Input: $\{y_i\}$, bounded function values f_i, S as the top k values of y_i, l
Uniformly sample l elements with replacement from $[1, n] \setminus S$ and call it T
$\hat{Z} = \sum_{i \in S} e^{y_i} + \frac{n-|S|}{|T|} \sum_{i \in T} e^{y_i}$
$\hat{J} = \sum_{i \in S} e^{y_i} f_i + \frac{n-|S|}{|T|} \sum_{i \in T} e^{y_i} f_i$
$\hat{F} = \hat{J}/\hat{Z}$
return Expectation estimate $\hat{F}$

3.3 EXPECTED VALUE ESTIMATION

In this section we show a way to estimate an expected value with respect to the distribution $\Pr(i) \propto e^{y_i}$. In particular, for bounded function values $\{f_i\}_{i=1}^n$ where $|f_i| \leq C$ we can define the expectation

$$F = \sum_i \frac{e^{y_i}}{Z} f_i \tag{10}$$

where $Z = \sum_i e^{y_i}$. The algorithm we use to create an estimate is very similar to the partition function estimate. More specifically, we compute the largest S values of $\{y_i\}_{i=1}^n$ and then draw uniform samples from the remaining elements and call it T. Then we compute an expected value using S and T (and upweighting the estimate from T). See Algorithm 4.

This algorithm comes with a guarantee on the additive error.

Theorem 3.5. *Algorithm 4 returns an estimate* $\hat{F}$ *such that* $|\hat{F} - F| \leq \epsilon C$ *with probability* δ *if*

$$k^2 l \geq \frac{8n^2}{\epsilon^2} \log(4/\delta) \tag{11}$$

$$kl \geq \frac{8}{3}\frac{1}{\epsilon^2} n \ln(2/\delta) \tag{12}$$

The proof is in the appendix. If we set $k = l$ then

$$k = O(n^{2/3}(1/\epsilon)\sqrt{\log(1/\delta)}) \tag{13}$$

Then, with a sublinear MIPS technique, the total runtime is sublinear. Note that we can use this to compute the expectation of $\phi(x)$ and thus the gradient of data likelihood. This technique will be used in the experiments section for the learning experiment.

3.4 APPROXIMATE TOP ELEMENTS

Many Maximum Inner Product Search (MIPS) methods, including LSH-based techniques, do not solve the exact nearest neighbor problem, but approximate nearest neighbor problem. In this work, we define a similar concept of the approximate top $O(\sqrt{n})$ elements that will suffice for our theoretical arguments. Further, we show that we can use LSH instances to retrieve the approximate top k elements in sublinear time.

We say that an algorithm returns the approximate top k if the gap between the smallest element in S and the largest element *not* in S is bounded by a constant.

Definition 3.1 (Approximate Top k)**.** *A set of elements S is an approximate top k if $|S| = k$ and*

$$\max_{i \notin S} y_i - \min_{i \in S} y_i < c \tag{14}$$

We can create a sequence of LSH instances that are "tuned" to a range of similarity values. Then at query time, we can go through the LSH instances in decreasing order of tuned value, gathering elements until we have k elements. It turns out that these elements will be the approximate top k elements (more details in the appendix). This technique will have a total runtime of

$$O(k + (\log(k) + \log(1/\delta)) \log(n) n^{\rho}) \tag{15}$$

where $\rho < 1$. Thus, we have a sublinear approximate top k element MIPS technique. We state this as a theorem and prove it in the appendix.

Theorem 3.6. *For sublinear k, there exists a MIPS technique that returns the approximate top k elements in sublinear amortized time.*

Note that if we have a MIPS technique that returns an approximate top k set S then we can adapt Algorithm 1 to make $B = M - S_{\min} - c$ for an added increase of e^c in the expected value of m, and thus the runtime.

If we have a MIPS technique that returns an approximate top k set S with constant c, then Algorithm 2 and 3 will have an extra factor of $e^{c/2}$ for k and l and Algorithm 4 will have an extra factor of $e^{2c/3}$ for k and l. These extensions are proved in the appendix and the previously stated theorems are special cases with $c = 0$.

4 EXPERIMENTS

In this section, we present an empirical evaluation of our proposed sampling, inference, and expectation techniques. The use case for our method is when there are fixed feature vectors $\{\phi(x)\}_{x \in \mathcal{X}}$, and a sequence of inference or sampling queries with different parameter vectors $\{\theta_i\}$. Although we cannot achieve gains on a single query, through preprocessing we can decrease the amortized query time. We will evaluate **runtime improvements** and **accuracy**.

4.1 PRELIMINARIES

4.1.1 MIPS technique

We present the MIPS technique used to retrieve the top-k values of the unnormalized log-probabilities. We follow the approximate nearest neighbor search method presented in Douze et al. (2016) as well as the publicly available implementation. However, we will not be making use of the compression component, as we do not optimize for memory usage.

This method relies on the use of a k-means clustering. With the same notations as 2.3, given a query q and a set of vectors V, we aim at finding the k highest values of $\{q \cdot v, v \in V\}$.

We first cluster the vectors in V in n_c clusters. For an incoming query vector q, we look at the inner product with the vectors in the cluster q is assigned to as well as n_p neighboring clusters. While this method doesn't have any theoretical guarantees, it has been shown to perform better than LSH in practice as it more advantageously exploits the distribution of the set of vectors.

In our experiments, we use CPU implementations of all algorithms for fair comparison.

4.1.2 Data

We experiments with two datasets from different domains to demonstrate the effectiveness of our method in real-world use.

Word Embeddings We use a set of word embeddings released by Facebook (Bojanowski et al., 2016). Each embedding is a dense vector representing a word in a given vocabulary. These continuous representations are obtained by training log-bilinear models on large text corpora. The embeddings incorporate structure from character n-grams of the words. We retain words containing only letters and scale each vector to be of unit-norm. The data is composed of $N = 2,000,126$ vectors of dimension $d = 300$.

ImageNet The ImageNet dataset (Russakovsky et al., 2015) from the ILSVRC 2012 competition contains 1.2 million natural images divided into 1000 classes. We extract features using a pre-trained residual network (He et al., 2016) trained on this classification task. More precisely, we represent each image by its activation map from the last layer before the linear classification layer of a ResNet-152. The extracted features are of size $7 \times 7 \times 2048$ for each image. We then take the average along the depth dimension and reduce dimensionality using a PCA. We scale each vector to be of unit-norm.

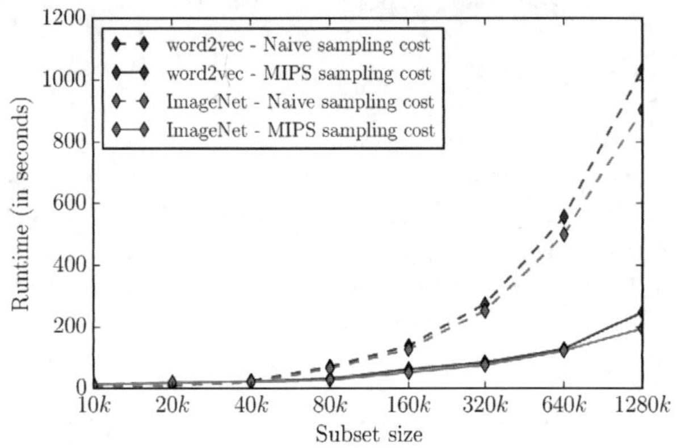

Figure 2: Empirical comparison of the runtime of sampling for $10,000$ randomly chosen θ from a log-linear model on subsets (of varying size) of the datasets. Note the log-scale of the dataset size. This time is the per query runtime and does not include preprocessing.

The data is thus composed of $N = 1,281,167$ vectors of dimension $d = 256$. In the rest of our experiments, we choose the temperature of the log-linear model to be $\tau = 0.05$.

4.2 SAMPLING

In this section, we measure the performance of our method in terms of both sampling quality and speed. We first present empirical results on sampling and then illustrate the efficiency of our method on a specific task: a random walk over ImageNet.

4.2.1 Sampling

Speed We want to evaluate the runtime of our method for sampling on large datasets. Given a dataset $\mathcal{X}$ and a parameter vector θ, we compare the time necessary to sample from $\Pr(x) \propto e^{\theta \cdot \phi(x)}$ using our method or by enumeration (brute force). We compute the sampling time for random vectors $\{\theta_i\}_{i \leq 1000}$ and subsets of varying size for ImageNet ranging from $10,000$ to $1,280,000$. The results are presented in Figure 2.

We can see that the speedup is linear w.r.t the log of the sub-sampled dataset size, achieving up to $5\times$ sampling speedup for the full dataset of size $1,281,167$. If we consider the amortized cost, i.e. including the pre-processing cost of our MIPS data structure, our method starts paying off after approximately $8,600$ samples. The amortized costs are presented in the appendix, in Figure 7.

Accuracy To measure the accuracy of our method, we present a way to establish an upper bound on the total variation distance in closed form for a given θ. Then, we average this upper bound over 100 samples of θ (drawn uniformly from the dataset).

Dataset	Speedup	Total Variation Bound
ImageNet	$4.65\times$	$(2.5 \pm 1.4) \times 10^{-4}$
Word Embeddings	$4.17\times$	$(4.8 \pm 2.2) \times 10^{-4}$

Table 1: Summary of the sampling speedup and bound on the total variation distance for our method on the ImageNet and Word Embeddings datasets.

Note that the lazy sampling strategy is exact unless the true maximum is not in $S \cup T$. Thus, if we can upper bound this probability, it is an upper bound on the total variation distance. For a given threshold x, we can compute the closed form probability that $\max_{i \notin S \cup T} y_i + G_i < x$ and $\max_{i \in S} y_i + G_i > x$. This is the upper bound that we desire and we can optimize x for the tightest upper bound. For both datasets, over 100 samples of θ, the average upper bound was on the order of 10^{-4} proving that our sampling method is accurate even while using an approximate MIPS technique. A summary of our results in terms of accuracy and speedup are provided in Table 1. We provide further empirical evidence in the appendix to show that the distributions closely match on the shown θ.

4.2.2 Random walk over a large set

To showcase the applicability of our method, we perform a random walk over the ImageNet dataset. We define the transition function, i.e. the probability to walk from image j to image i as $\Pr(X_{t+1} = i | X_t = j) \propto e^{\tau \phi(x_i) \cdot \phi(x_j)}$ where τ is the temperature, ϕ is the fixed featurization previously defined, and x_i, x_j are the pixel-values of images i, j. The initial state is sampled uniformly across the dataset. This is similar in spirit to the PageRank algorithm (Page et al., 1999). This setting fits our method because while the MIPS structure can be reused across time steps, no computation can be cached in the naive setting (assuming we do not store the distribution for each element, which would be on the order of Terabytes).

We evaluate the quality of the Markov Chain by comparing the top elements of the empirical sampling distribution. We run two different Markov chains, one with exact sampling and one with our sampling technique. Over one million steps, the two Markov Chains share 73.6% of the top 1000 elements. This percentage looks low because of the finite sampling error. When we compare two different one million element windows within each chain, the top 1000 elements are shared 69.3% and 72.9% for the

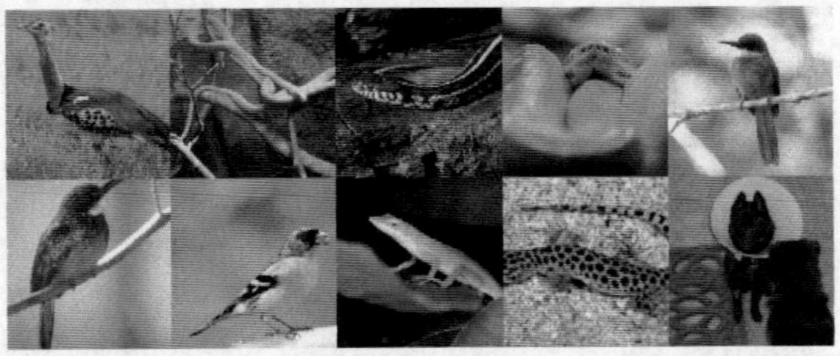

Figure 3: Samples of the Markov chain. The samples are spaced out by 20 time steps.

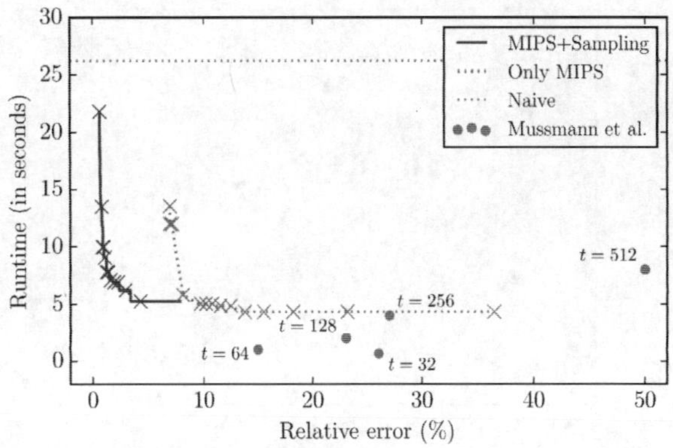

Figure 4: Runtime plotted as a function of relative error of partition function estimate (different points made by varying k and l) on ImageNet (averaged over random values of θ. The red dotted line is the time for the exact partition function computation.

exact sampling and our sampling, respectively. It is seen that the between-chain differences are the same as the within-chain differences, so the Markov chain with our sampling technique yields roughly the same distribution as the chain with exact sampling.

4.3 PARTITION FUNCTION ESTIMATE

We show the performance of our partition function estimate as shown in Algorithm 3. We can trade-off error and runtime by varying k and l. See Figure 4. We average the results over several values of θ, drawn uniformly from the dataset. For comparison, we plot the trade-off for only looking at the top k values and using this as a partition function estimate. Additionally, we compare to the method of Mussmann & Ermon (2016) for different size of noise t. For each value of k, l and t we report the runtime and relative error of the partition function estimate. As shown by the relative error of the top-k estimate, sampling from the tail is necessary to achieve low relative error. We also show that the method from Mussmann & Ermon (2016) cannot come close in terms of relative error, achieving a maximum of 15% relative error for $t = 64$. It is also important to note that their method cannot trade-off speed for accuracy as, when the noise-length t increases, the injected noise destroys the MIPS structure rendering it highly inaccurate.

4.4 LEARNING

We wish to maximize the likelihood of a subset of the data $\mathcal{D} \subseteq \mathcal{X}$ given $\Pr(\cdot; \theta)$. We aim at finding

$$\theta^* = \arg\max_{\theta} \sum_{x \in \mathcal{D}} \log \Pr(x; \theta) \tag{16}$$

using gradient ascent. Evaluating the gradient requires finding the expectation of the features $\phi(x)$ which can be estimated using our method in Algorithm 4. The features are fixed but θ is updated at each step of the gradient ascent algorithm, fitting well into the setting of our method. We choose a small subset $\mathcal{D}$ of ImageNet as images with a commonality. In particular, we handpick 16 images showing the presence of water. We compare computing the gradient with our method to the computation of the exact gradient and to approximating the gradient by considering the truncated distribution on the top k elements (referred to as top-k gradient). The chosen images are shown in the appendix in Figure 9. We perform gradient ascent for 5000 iterations with learning rate $\alpha = 10$, which we halve every 1000 iterations. The results are reported in Table 2. The learning curves are shown in Figure 5. We also show the 10 most probable samples (outside of the dataset $\mathcal{D}$) according to the log-linear model in Figure 6. We can see that these images are semantically similar to the training set, all containing water, showcasing the expressive power of the ResNet features.

Method	Log-likelihood	Speedup
Exact gradient	−3.170	1×
Only top-k	−4.062	22.7×
Our method	−3.175	9.6×

Table 2: Log-likelihood and speedup for the learning of a log-linear model on ImageNet. For our method, we picked $k = 10\sqrt{n}, l = 10k$, for the comparison to only weighing the top-k, we chose $k = 100\sqrt{n}$ as well.

As shown in Figure 5, we can see that the log-likelihood for our method and the exact gradient almost exactly overlap indicating that our estimation of the gradient is very accurate. In contrast, the top-k gradient, while faster, proves to be a poor estimator and thus cannot optimize the log-likelihood. To summarize, **our method converges to the global maximum $9.6\times$ as fast as computing the exact gradient**.

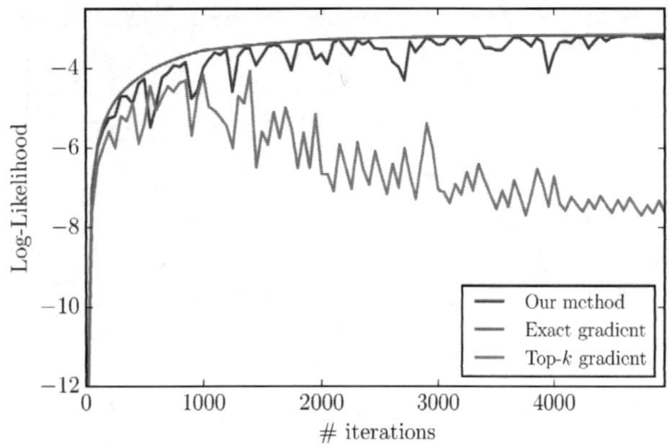

Figure 5: Log-likelihood plotted against the number of iterations for performing gradient ascent on our learning problem for 5000 iterations with a learning rate $\alpha = 10$, halving the learning rate every 1000 iterations.

Figure 6: 10 most probable images (outside of $\mathcal{D}$) from our log-linear model trained to convergence.

5 RELATED WORK

Our method can be viewed in two different comparative perspectives. Our method can be seen as an alternative to only using the top-k most probable elements as is done in Vijayanarasimhan et al. (2014). There, large output spaces for deep learning are handled using Locality Sensitive Hashing. In particular, the top vectors are gathered and the rest of the vectors in the tail are ignored. For spread-out distributions (closer to uniform), this method will fail. Our work provides a scalable method to incorporate the probability mass present in the tail of the distribution by sampling $O(\sqrt{n})$ elements, a small prices compared to retrieving the top elements.

Our method can also be compared to a different way of combining the Gumbel max trick and Maximum Inner Product Search as presented in Mussmann & Ermon (2016). In that work, Gumbel noise is appended to the database vectors and stored in the MIPS data structure. Then, query vectors are chosen to access the frozen Gumbel noise. That work has several major shortcomings that make it unusable in practice. The Gumbel noise is re-used, introducing correlated samples and systematic bias in the partition function estimate. In particular, for any fixed value of the parameters, there are a fixed number of samples "frozen" into the stored Gumbel noise. We avoid this issue by sampling $O(\sqrt{n})$ fresh Gumbel variables for every sample. While real world data often has structure that can be exploited by the MIPS techniques, in Mussmann & Ermon (2016), the structure is destroyed by injecting random Gumbel noise. In our technique, we preserve structure in the database vectors by leaving the vectors unchanged. Finally, the method of Mussmann & Ermon (2016) requires accessing the MIPS data structure many times for independent samples and partition function estimates. In this work, we only require accessing the MIPS data structure once per parameter value.

6 CONCLUSION

In conclusion, we have presented several related methods that are based on the key idea of accessing the large elements in a distribution using Maximum Inner Product Search and accessing the tail of a distribution with uniform sampling. This decreases the runtime from $O(n)$ to $O(\sqrt{n})$ plus the runtime for the MIPS technique.

This work is best suited for cases where the output space is large but enumerable, such as those in NLP and computer vision. This work can be expected to give speedups when the feature vectors of a log-linear model are fixed but it is desired to perform inference and sampling for several different values of the the parameters. Note that our method is as flexible as the MIPS method that is employed; the feature vectors need to only be fixed for the MIPS to work. As an example, if a MIPS system allows for sparse updates, our method will also allow for sparse updates. Since our method treats MIPS as a black-box, advances in the speed and accuracy of MIPS techniques automatically improve our method.

When accessing the top elements is not accurate enough, we present a method to include uniform samples from the tail to provide provably good samples and estimates of the partition function. All this, at the small overhead price of uniform sampling.

7 Acknowledgments

This research was supported by Intel Corporation, Future of Life Institute ($\#2016 - 158687$) and NSF grants 1651565, 1649208, 1522054, and DGE-1656518.

We thank Ludwig Schmidt and Moses Charikar for helpful discussions.

References

Auvolat, Alex, Chandar, Sarath, Vincent, Pascal, Larochelle, Hugo, and Bengio, Yoshua. Clustering is efficient for approximate maximum inner product search. *arXiv preprint arXiv:1507.05910*, 2015.

Bengio, Yoshua, Ducharme, Réjean, Vincent, Pascal, and Jauvin, Christian. A neural probabilistic language model. *Journal of machine learning research*, 3(Feb): 1137–1155, 2003.

Bentley, Jon Louis. Multidimensional binary search trees used for associative searching. *Communications of the ACM*, 18(9):509–517, 1975.

Bojanowski, Piotr, Grave, Edouard, Joulin, Armand, and Mikolov, Tomas. Enriching word vectors with subword information. *arXiv preprint arXiv:1607.04606*, 2016.

Charikar, Moses S. Similarity estimation techniques from rounding algorithms. In *Proceedings of the thiry-fourth annual ACM symposium on Theory of computing*, pp. 380–388. ACM, 2002.

Douze, Matthijs, Jégou, Hervé, and Perronnin, Florent. Polysemous codes. In *European Conference on Computer Vision*, pp. 785–801. Springer International Publishing, 2016.

Gumbel, Emil Julius and Lieblein, Julius. Statistical theory of extreme values and some practical applications: a series of lectures. 1954.

Hazan, Tamir, Maji, Subhransu, and Jaakkola, Tommi. On sampling from the gibbs distribution with random maximum a-posteriori perturbations. In *Advances in Neural Information Processing Systems*, pp. 1268–1276, 2013.

He, Kaiming, Zhang, Xiangyu, Ren, Shaoqing, and Sun, Jian. Deep residual learning for image recognition. In *Computer Vision and Pattern Recognition (CVPR), 2016 IEEE Conference on*, 2016.

Indyk, Piotr and Motwani, Rajeev. Approximate nearest neighbors: towards removing the curse of dimensionality. In *Proceedings of the thirtieth annual ACM symposium on Theory of computing*, pp. 604–613. ACM, 1998.

Joulin, Armand, van der Maaten, Laurens, Jabri, Allan, and Vasilache, Nicolas. Learning visual features from large weakly supervised data. In *European Conference on Computer Vision*, pp. 67–84. Springer, 2016.

Kim, Carolyn, Sabharwal, Ashish, and Ermon, Stefano. Exact sampling with integer linear programs and random perturbations. In *Proc. 30th AAAI Conference on Artificial Intelligence*, 2016.

Koenigstein, Noam, Ram, Parikshit, and Shavitt, Yuval. Efficient retrieval of recommendations in a matrix factorization framework. In *Proceedings of the 21st ACM international conference on Information and knowledge management*, pp. 535–544. ACM, 2012.

Koller, Daphne and Friedman, Nir. *Probabilistic graphical models: principles and techniques.* MIT press, 2009.

Maddison, Chris J, Tarlow, Daniel, and Minka, Tom. A* sampling. In *Advances in Neural Information Processing Systems*, pp. 3086–3094, 2014.

Mikolov, Tomas, Sutskever, Ilya, Chen, Kai, Corrado, Greg S, and Dean, Jeff. Distributed representations of words and phrases and their compositionality. In *Advances in neural information processing systems*, pp. 3111–3119, 2013.

Murphy, Kevin P. *Machine learning: a probabilistic perspective.* MIT press, 2012.

Mussmann, Stephen and Ermon, Stefano. Learning and inference via maximum inner product search. In *Proceedings of The 33rd International Conference on Machine Learning*, pp. 2587–2596, 2016.

Neyshabur, Behnam and Srebro, Nathan. On symmetric and asymmetric lshs for inner product search. *arXiv preprint arXiv:1410.5518*, 2014.

Page, Lawrence, Brin, Sergey, Motwani, Rajeev, and Winograd, Terry. The pagerank citation ranking: Bringing order to the web. Technical report, Stanford InfoLab, 1999.

Ram, Parikshit and Gray, Alexander G. Maximum inner-product search using cone trees. In *Proceedings of the 18th ACM SIGKDD international conference on Knowledge discovery and data mining*, pp. 931–939. ACM, 2012.

Rastogi, Pushpendre and Van Durme, Benjamin. Sublinear partition estimation. *arXiv preprint arXiv:1508.01596*, 2015.

Russakovsky, Olga, Deng, Jia, Su, Hao, Krause, Jonathan, Satheesh, Sanjeev, Ma, Sean, Huang, Zhiheng, Karpathy, Andrej, Khosla, Aditya, Bernstein, Michael, et al. Imagenet large scale visual recognition challenge. *International Journal of Computer Vision*, 115(3):211–252, 2015.

Shrivastava, Anshumali and Li, Ping. Asymmetric lsh (alsh) for sublinear time maximum inner product search (mips). In *Advances in Neural Information Processing Systems*, pp. 2321–2329, 2014.

Vijayanarasimhan, Sudheendra, Shlens, Jonathon, Monga, Rajat, and Yagnik, Jay. Deep networks with large output spaces. *arXiv preprint arXiv:1412.7479*, 2014.

8 APPENDIX

8.1 EMPIRICAL EVALUATION OF SAMPLING

We wish to evaluate the empirical accuracy of our sampling technique on concrete examples. We do this in two ways. First, we can sort the elements by probability and make events of drawing an element in the top 10, or the top 100, top 1000, etc. We show the results for two random θ with different distributions in Figure 8 for $50,000$ samples. Note that our method closely matches the histogram of the true distribution. For a more comprehensive evaluation, we sample 30 values of θ and compute the relative error for exact sampling and our approximate sampling. See Figure 8. We also present in Figure 7 the amortized speedups obtained by our method. The amortized cost is defined as the time needed to train the index, added to the runtime of sampling $10,000$ samples.

8.2 LEARNING TRAINING SET

For the learning experiment, we show the set of images $\mathcal{D}$ that we maximized the probability of. See Figure 9. The common theme of the images is the presence of water.

8.3 VALUE OF c

For all of the proofs, we will include the result with the approximate MIPS with an error of c. To recover the original results in the paper, set $c = 0$.

8.4 SAMPLING

Theorem 3.2. *For Algorithm 1,* $\mathbb{E}[m] \leq \frac{ne^c}{k}$

Proof. Note that m is the number of Gumbels that are larger than $B = M - S_{min} - c$.

Note that Gumbels can be defined by $-\ln(-\ln(U_i))$ where U_i is a uniform random variable on the interval $[0, 1]$. Thus, we can think of each point having a uniform sample U_i and finding places where

$$-\ln(-\ln(U_i)) > M - S_{min} - c \tag{17}$$

$$U_i > \exp(-\exp(S_{min} + c - M)) \tag{18}$$

Thus, if we can find places where $U_i > \exp(-\exp(S_{min}+c-M))$, then we have the value of m. The number of points where this occurs is distributed according to $Bin(n-|S|, 1-\exp(-\exp(S_{min}+c-M))$.

Thus,

$$\mathbb{E}[m|M] = (n - |S|)(1 - \exp(-\exp(S_{min} + c - M))) \tag{19}$$

$$\mathbb{E}[m|M] \leq n\exp(S_{min} + c - M) \tag{20}$$

Note that

$$\Pr[ne^{S_{min}+c-M} > x] = \Pr[M - S_{min} - c < \ln(n/x)] \tag{21}$$

$$= \Pr[(\max_{i \in S} y_i + G_i) - S_{min} - c < \ln(n/x)] \tag{22}$$

$$\leq \Pr[\max_{i \in S} G_i - c < \ln(n/x)] \tag{23}$$

$$\leq \Pr[\ln(|S|) + G - c < \ln(n/x)] \tag{24}$$

$$\leq \Pr[\frac{ne^c e^{-G}}{|S|} > x] \tag{25}$$

$$\leq \Pr[exponential(\frac{ne^c}{|S|}) > x] \tag{26}$$

And thus,

$$\mathbb{E}[ne^{S_{min}+c-M}] \leq \mathbb{E}[exponential(\frac{ne^c}{|S|})] = \frac{ne^c}{|S|} \tag{27}$$

Putting it all together,

$$\mathbb{E}[m] = \mathbb{E}[\mathbb{E}[m|M]] \leq \frac{ne^c}{|S|} \tag{28}$$

□

Theorem 3.3. *For Algorithm 2, the sample is an exact sample with probability* $1 - \delta$ *for* $\delta = \exp(-\frac{kl}{n}e^{-c})$.

Proof. Note that the elements not in $S \cup T$ have values $y_i \leq S_{min} + c$ and $G_i \leq B = -\ln(-\ln(1 - l/n))$. Further, there exists an element in S with $y_i \geq S_{min}$ and with $G_i = \max_{j=1}^{k} G_j$. As long as there is an element in S that exceeds all the elements not in $S \cup T$, the sample will be exact.

$$\Pr[\text{not exact sample}] \leq \tag{29}$$

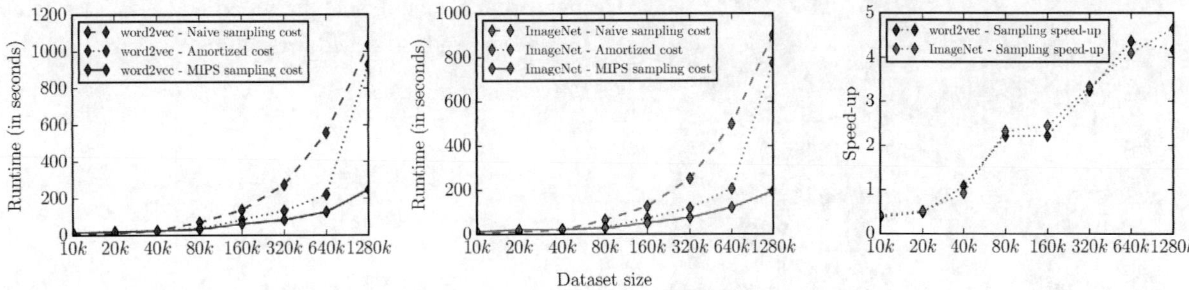

Figure 7: *Left and Center:* empirical comparison of the runtime of sampling for a $10,000$ randomly chosen θ on Word Embeddings and Image Net for varying fraction of the data. The amortized cost is defined as the time necessary for the sampling in addition to the training time of the index. *Right:* Evaluation of the sampling speed-up for both datasets for varying fraction of the data.

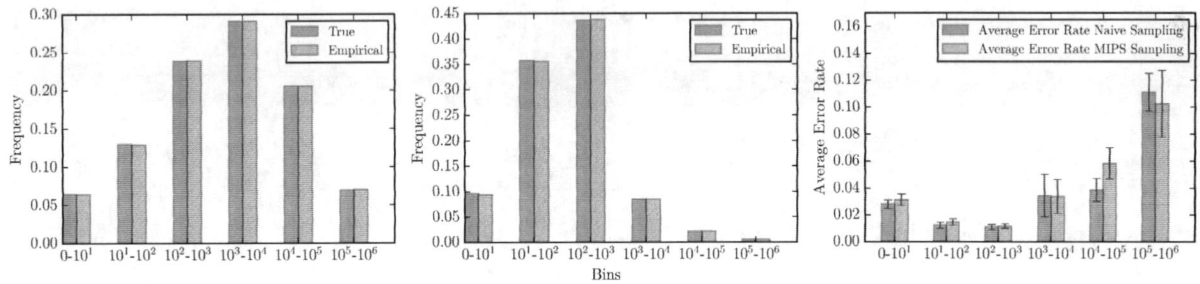

Figure 8: *Left and Center:* Two randomly chosen θ with different bin distributions. We see that the empirical sampling closely matches the true distribution for all the bins. *Right:* Evaluation of the relative error on 30 samples of θ for the exact sampling and our sampling technique. The error bars are for the average error rate between the empirical distribution and the true distribution for both exact sampling and our method. We see that the error rates are not statistically significantly different.

Figure 9: The set of images $\mathcal{D}$ used in the learning experiment. Note that all of the images contain water, though the content of the images is quite different.

$$\leq \Pr[\max_{j=1}^{k} G_j < -\ln(-\ln(1-l/n)) + c] \quad (30)$$

$$\leq \Pr[\ln(k) - \ln(-\ln(U)) < -\ln(-\ln(1-l/n)) + c] \quad (31)$$

$$\leq \Pr[k(-\ln(1-l/n))e^{-c} < -\ln(U)] \quad (32)$$

$$\leq \Pr[\frac{kl}{n} e^{-c} < -\ln(U)] \quad (33)$$

$$\leq \Pr[\exp(-\frac{kl}{n} e^{-c}) > U] \quad (34)$$

$$\leq \exp(-\frac{kl}{n} e^{-c}) \quad (35)$$

Thus, the probability of failure, δ, is bounded by $\exp(-\frac{kl}{n}e^{-c})$ □

8.5 PARTITION FUNCTION ESTIMATE

Theorem 3.4. *Algorithm 3 returns an unbiased estimate $\hat{Z}$ and for $kl \geq \frac{2}{3}\frac{1}{\epsilon^2} n e^c \ln(1/\delta)$, then with $1-\delta$ probability,*

$$\frac{|\hat{Z} - Z|}{Z} \leq \epsilon$$

Proof. Define $Z = \sum_i e^{y_i}$. Let S be the indices of the k largest elements of $\{y_i\}$ and $S' = [1, n] \setminus S$. Denote $||S'||_1 = \sum_{i \in S'} e^{y_i}$ and $||S||_1 = \sum_{i \in S} e^{y_i}$. Thus, the true partition function is $Z = \sum_{i \in S} e^{y_i} + \sum_{i \in S'} e^{y_i} = ||S||_1 + ||S'||_1$.

Let r be the largest value of e^{y_i} for elements in S'. Then for all $i \in S'$, $e^{y_i} \in (0, r]$ and further, for all $i \in S$, $e^{y_i} \geq re^{-c}$. We can scale these values of S' and denote them as $q_i = \frac{e^{y_i}}{r}$ where $q_i \in [0, 1]$.

For the estimate $\hat{Z}$ we will draw l samples with replacement from S' and denote the set as T. Denote the samples as $y^{(j)}$ and the scaled versions as $q^{(j)} = \frac{e^{y^{(j)}}}{r}$.

We use the estimate:

$$\hat{Z} = \sum_{i \in S} e^{y_i} + \frac{|\mathcal{X} - S|}{|T|} \sum_{i \in T} e^{y_i} \quad (36)$$

$$\hat{Z} = ||S||_1 + \frac{(n-k)r}{l} \sum_{j=1}^{l} q^{(j)} \quad (37)$$

Note that

$$\mathbb{E}[\hat{Z}] = (n-k)r\mathbb{E}[q^{(1)}] + ||S||_1 \quad (38)$$

$$\mathbb{E}[\hat{Z}] = (n-k)r \sum_{i \in S'} \frac{1}{|S'|} \frac{e^{y_i}}{r} + ||S||_1 = ||S'||_1 + ||S||_1 = Z \quad (39)$$

This is because $|S'| = n - k$. Thus, $\hat{Z}$ is an unbiased estimator of Z. However, we are concerned if it is well concentrated about its mean.

Let Q be a random variable as the scaled sample from S' and $\bar{Q}$ be the empirical mean over l samples. Thus, $\mathbb{E}[Q] = \frac{||S'||_1}{(n-k)r}$.

Note that

$$|\hat{Z} - Z| = |\frac{(n-k)r}{l} \sum_{j=1}^{l} q^{(j)} - ||S'||_1| \quad (40)$$

$$|\hat{Z} - Z| = |\frac{(n-k)r}{l} \sum_{j=1}^{l} q^{(j)} - (n-k)r\mathbb{E}[Q]| \quad (41)$$

$$|\hat{Z} - Z| = (n-k)r|\frac{1}{l} \sum_{j=1}^{l} q^{(j)} - \mathbb{E}[Q]| \quad (42)$$

$$|\hat{Z} - Z| = (n-k)r|\bar{Q} - \mathbb{E}[Q]| \quad (43)$$

Therefore,

$$\Pr[|\hat{Z} - Z| > \epsilon Z] = \Pr[(n-k)r|\bar{Q} - \mathbb{E}[Q]| > \epsilon(||S'||_1 + ||S||_1)] \quad (44)$$

$$= \Pr[(n-k)r|\bar{Q} - \mathbb{E}[Q]| > \epsilon((n-k)r\mathbb{E}[Q] + ||S||_1)] \quad (45)$$

$$= \Pr[|\bar{Q} - \mathbb{E}[Q]| > \epsilon(\mathbb{E}[Q] + \frac{||S||_1}{(n-k)r})] \quad (46)$$

$$\leq \Pr[|\bar{Q} - \mathbb{E}[Q]| > \epsilon(\mathbb{E}[Q] + \frac{ke^{-c}}{n})] \quad (47)$$

If we use Chernoff (use a convexity argument to bound the MGF in terms of the mean as on page 22 of "Concentration of Measure for the Analysis of Randomised Algorithms" by Dubhashi and Panconesi)

$$\Pr[|\sum_j Q^{(j)} - l\mathbb{E}[Q]| > \delta l\mathbb{E}[Q]] \leq 2\exp(-\frac{1}{3}\delta^2 l\mathbb{E}[Q]) \quad (48)$$

$$\Pr[|\bar{Q} - \mathbb{E}[Q]| > \delta\mathbb{E}[Q]] \leq 2\exp(-\frac{1}{3}\delta^2 l\mathbb{E}[Q]) \quad (49)$$

$$\Pr[|\bar{Q} - \mathbb{E}[Q]| > a] \leq 2\exp(-\frac{1}{3}a^2 l\frac{1}{\mathbb{E}[Q]}) \quad (50)$$

Combining these two by setting $a = \epsilon(\mathbb{E}[Q] + \frac{ke^{-c}}{n})$,

$$\Pr[|\bar{Q} - \mathbb{E}[Q]| > \epsilon(\mathbb{E}[Q] + \frac{ke^{-c}}{n})] \leq \quad (51)$$

$$\leq 2\exp(-\frac{1}{3}\epsilon^2 l(\mathbb{E}[Q] + \frac{ke^{-c}}{n})^2\frac{1}{\mathbb{E}[Q]}) \quad (52)$$

$$\leq 2\exp(-\frac{2}{3}\epsilon^2\frac{kle^{-c}}{n}) \quad (53)$$

Thus, as long as $kl \geq \frac{2}{3}\frac{1}{\epsilon^2}ne^c\ln(1/\delta)$, then with $1-\delta$ probability, $\hat{Z} \in (1 \pm \epsilon)Z$ □

returns an unbiased estimate $\hat{Z}$ and for $kl = \frac{2}{3}\frac{1}{\epsilon^2}n\ln(1/\delta)$, then with $1-\delta$ probability, $\hat{Z} \in (1 \pm \epsilon)Z$

8.6 EXPECTATION ESTIMATE

Theorem 3.5. *Algorithm 4 returns an estimate $\hat{F}$ such that $|\hat{F} - F| \leq \epsilon C$ with probability δ if*

$$lk^2 \geq \frac{8n^2e^{2c}}{\epsilon^2}\ln(4/\delta)$$

and

$$kl \geq \frac{8}{3}\frac{1}{\epsilon^2}ne^c\ln(2/\delta)$$

Proof. Recall

$$J = \sum_i e^{y_i} f_i$$

$$\hat{J} = \sum_{i\in S} e^{y_i} f_i + \frac{n-k}{l}\sum_{i\in T} e^{y_i} f_i$$

Thus, $F = J/Z$ and $\hat{F} = \hat{J}/\hat{Z}$.

To show that

$$|\hat{F} - F| = |\frac{\hat{J}}{\hat{Z}} - \frac{J}{Z}| \leq \epsilon C$$

with probability $1-\delta$, we will show that

$$|\frac{\hat{J}}{\hat{Z}} - \frac{\hat{J}}{Z}| \leq \frac{\epsilon}{2}C$$

$$|\frac{\hat{J}}{Z} - \frac{J}{Z}| \leq \frac{\epsilon}{2}C$$

each with probability $1-\delta/2$. These will be shown as two separate parts.

8.6.1 Part One

Because

$$kl \geq \frac{2}{3}\frac{4}{\epsilon^2}ne^c\ln(2/\delta)$$

from Theorem 3.4, with probability $1-\delta/2$ then $\frac{|\hat{Z}-Z|}{Z} \leq \epsilon$.

$$|\frac{\hat{J}}{\hat{Z}} - \frac{\hat{J}}{Z}| = \frac{|\hat{J}|}{\hat{Z}}\frac{|\hat{Z}-Z|}{Z}$$

$$\leq \frac{|\hat{J}|}{\hat{Z}}\frac{\epsilon}{2}$$

$$\leq \frac{\epsilon}{2}C$$

8.6.2 Part Two

For the second one is written as the following lemma

Lemma 8.1. $|\frac{\hat{J}}{Z} - \frac{J}{Z}| \leq \frac{\epsilon}{2}C$ *with probability* $1-\delta/2$ *for*

$$lk^2 \geq \frac{8n^2}{\epsilon^2}\ln(4/\delta)$$

Proof. Note that the smallest element in S has "probability" $e^{y_i}/Z \leq 1/k$. Thus, for the largest element not in S, $e^{y_i}/Z \leq e^c/k$. Define Q as the random variable of the value of sampling i uniformly from $[1,n] \setminus S$ and returning

$$Q = \frac{ke^{y_i}}{e^cZ}\frac{f_i}{C}$$

Note that $Q \in [-1, 1]$ and that $\mathbb{E}[Q] = \frac{1}{n-k}\frac{k}{ZCe^c}\sum_{i \notin S} e^{y_i} f_i$. The elements of T are samples $\{y^{(j)}\}_i$ and $\{f^{(i)}\}_i$ and thus we can define

$$Q^{(j)} = \frac{ke^{y^{(j)}}}{e^c Z}\frac{f^{(j)}}{C}$$

$$|\frac{J}{Z} - \frac{\hat{J}}{Z}| = \frac{1}{Z}|\sum_{i \notin S} e^{y_i} f_i + \frac{n-k}{l}\sum_{j=1}^{l} e^{y^{(j)}} f^{(j)}|$$

$$= \frac{(n-k)Ce^c}{k}|\mathbb{E}[Q] - \frac{1}{l}\sum_j Q^{(i)}|$$

From Hoeffding's Inequality,

$$\Pr[|\mathbb{E}[Q] - \frac{1}{l}\sum_j Q^{(i)}| > t] \leq 2\exp(-\frac{lt^2}{2})$$

Thus,

$$\Pr[|\frac{J}{Z} - \frac{\hat{J}}{Z}| > \frac{(n-k)Ce^c}{k}t] \leq 2\exp(-\frac{lt^2}{2})$$

Defining $t = \frac{k\epsilon}{2(n-k)e^c}$ we get that $\frac{(n-k)Ce^c}{k}t = \frac{\epsilon}{2}C$, so

$$\Pr[|\frac{J}{Z} - \frac{\hat{J}}{Z}| > \frac{\epsilon}{2}C] \leq 2\exp(-\frac{lk^2\epsilon^2}{8(n-k)^2 e^{2c}})$$

$$\Pr[|\frac{J}{Z} - \frac{\hat{J}}{Z}| > \frac{\epsilon}{2}C] \leq 2\exp(-\frac{lk^2\epsilon^2}{8n^2 e^{2c}})$$

Thus, the conclusion of the Lemma follows for

$$lk^2 \geq \frac{8n^2e^{2c}}{\epsilon^2}\ln(4/\delta)$$

□

With this lemma, the conclusion of the theorem follows. □

Theorem 3.6. *There exists a MIPS technique that returns the approximate top k elements in sublinear time.*

Proof. For the data structure, we create a sequence of LSH instances that are tuned to values that are $c/2$ apart. Thus, if $\|\theta\| \leq M_1$ and $\|\phi(x)\| \leq M_2$, then $|\theta \cdot \phi(x)| \leq M_1 M_2$. And we create $n_{LSH} = \frac{4M_1M_2}{c}$ instances.

Call the LSH instances $\{L_i\}_i$ and for the ith instance, set the lower tuned value to be $S_{i,2} = (c/2)(i-1) - M_1M_2$ and the higher tuned value to be $S_{i,1} = (c/2)i - M_1M_2$. Thus, $S_1 - S_2 = c/2$. Further, set the failure probability of each LSH instance to be $\delta' = \delta k n_{LSH}$ so that with high probability, each of the LSH instances will not fail to find each of the top k values.

At query time, hash the query θ and let B_i be the buckets of neighbors from L_i. From the LSH guarantee, there are a small constant number of elements in B_i that are smaller than $S_{i,2}$ and with high probability, all elements larger than $S_{i,1}$ will be in B_i. Find the neighboring pair of LSH instances L_i and L_{i+1} where $|B_{i+1}| \leq k$ and $|B_i| \geq k$. Collect $k' = k - |B_{i+1}|$ elements $B' \subseteq B_i - B_{i+1}$ where the elements are larger than $S_{i,2}$ (all but a constant number will be larger than $S_{i,2}$). Then return the elements $S = B' \cup B_{i+1}$.

Note that any elements larger than $S_{i+1,1}$ will be in S with high probability because they will be contained in B_{i+1}. So $\max_{x \notin S} \theta \cdot \phi(x) \leq S_{i+1,1}$. Further, by construction, $\min_{x \in S} \theta \cdot \phi(x) \geq S_{i,2}$. Thus, the technique returns the approximate top k elements with high probability with a gap of $S_{i+1,1} - S_{i,2} = 2(c/2) = c$.

This technique will have a total runtime of

$$O(k + (\log(k) + \log(1/\delta))\log(n)n^\rho)$$

where $\rho < 1$. Thus, we have a sublinear approximate top k element MIPS technique. □

Supervised Restricted Boltzmann Machines

Tu Dinh Nguyen, Dinh Phung, Viet Huynh, Trung Le
Center for Pattern Recognition and Data Analytics,
Deakin University, Australia.
{tu.nguyen, dinh.phung, viet.huynh, trung.l}@deakin.edu.au.

Abstract

We propose in this paper the *supervised restricted Boltzmann machine* (sRBM), a unified framework which combines the versatility of RBM to simultaneously learn the data representation and to perform supervised learning (i.e., a nonlinear classifier or a nonlinear regressor). Unlike the current state-of-the-art classification formulation proposed for RBM in (Larochelle *et al.*, 2012), our model is a *hybrid* probabilistic graphical model consisting of a distinguished *generative* component for data representation and a *discriminative* component for prediction. While the work of (Larochelle *et al.*, 2012) typically incurs no extra difficulty in inference compared with a standard RBM, our discriminative component, modeled as a directed graphical model, renders MCMC-based inference (e.g., Gibbs sampler) very slow and unpractical for use. To this end, we further develop scalable variational inference for the proposed sRBM for both classification and regression cases. Extensive experiments on real-world datasets show that our sRBM achieves better predictive performance than baseline methods. At the same time, our proposed framework yields learned representations which are more discriminative, hence interpretable, than those of its counterparts. Besides, our method is probabilistic and capable of generating meaningful data conditioning on specific classes – a topic which is of current great interest in deep learning aiming at data generation.

1 INTRODUCTION

Restricted Boltzmann machine (RBM) is an important generative model that is capable of learning representations from data. It has been successfully applied to diverse data types including: images (Hinton and Salakhutdinov, 2006), mixed low-level features of images (Nguyen *et al.*, 2013c), text (Salakhutdinov and Hinton, 2009a) and medical data (Nguyen *et al.*, 2013a). In these tasks, the RBMs can serve as either fast feature extractors or building blocks to provide a good parameter initialization for deep architectures (Hinton and Salakhutdinov, 2006; Salakhutdinov and Hinton, 2009b). In both cases, one often uses a two-stage pipeline framework that has the RBMs followed by another supervised learning method (a classifier or a regressor). The first stage is to train the RBMs using an unsupervised learning algorithm with efficient MCMC-based learning procedures (Hinton, 2002). Then the supervised learning algorithm is built upon the representations or parameters learned by RBMs to further carry out a discriminative training in the second stage.

These two-stage approaches, however, suffer from two key drawbacks. First, they require to tune hyperparameters for both models (RBM and the supervised model) which is computationally expensive and time consuming. Second, representations learned by RBM may effectively support generating the data, but there is no guarantee that they would be useful for further fitting a supervised model, as they have not seen any label during the unsupervised training. In other words, the models miss the opportunity to use labeled data to 'regularize' the learned representations. Thus separating the feature learning phase from the discriminative training could be suboptimal.

Our solution is to construct a supervised restricted Boltzmann machine (sRBM) – a unified framework that leverages the successful architecture of RBM to simultaneously learn the data representation as a feature extractor and to perform prediction as a nonlinear classifier or a nonlinear regressor. The sRBM uses a hidden layer to associate the outcome with input data in order to model their joint distribution. The resulting *hybrid* probabilistic graphical model consists of two components: an RBM with undirected connections of hidden and visible units, and a predictive model with directed connections from hidden units to outcome variable. The RBM component has generative capability of representing data whilst the discriminative part enables the model to perform prediction by itself. Combining generative and discriminative models allows one to leverage the strength from each other. More precisely, the generative component plays a role as a regularization for discriminative part, at the same time the discriminative part utilizes label statistical information to drive the generative one to learn more expressive representations. Besides, the combined framework facilitates the model selection since no additional hyperparameters from the separate prediction module must be tuned. However, the introduction of the discriminative component into the model makes inferences become much more challenging where standard Gibbs sampler could be very slow for practical use. To this end, we further develop variational inference for the proposed sRBM for both classification and regression.

In addition to predictive capacity, the sRBM offers a principled way to generate data based on the specific labels or classes, and to disentangle the data and labels via the learned latent representations and embedding connection matrix – a capability that is desirable in many cases, especially in natural language processing (Mikolov *et al.*, 2013). As a generative model, once our model has been learned, we can select and fix the labels and then alternatively sample hidden and visible variables using MCMC to obtain the data corresponding to the labels. For disentangling capability, recall that, in the standard RBM, each unit in the hidden layer can act as a feature detector, and together, all the hidden units form a distributed, and discrete representation of data (Nguyen *et al.*, 2013b). In sRBM, they are also linked to the labels via directed connections parameterized by a weight matrix. Due to the *explaining away* effect (Coates and Ng, 2011; Bengio *et al.*, 2013), these hidden units must compete with each other to explain the labels. Thus, the learned representations and weight matrix associating latent factors to the labels are driven to discriminate the labels.

We quantitatively and qualitatively demonstrate the capacity of our proposed model through comprehensive experiments on three tasks – classification, regression and data generation using three real-world datasets: handwritten digits, newsgroup documents, and CT scan images. Our primary target is to verify the predictive and generative capabilities of sRBM, and the effectiveness of learned representations and the embedding discovered by the model. The experimental results show that our method achieves better predictive performance than the baselines. At the same time, its learned representations and embedding matrices are more discriminative than those of the ClassRBM and standard RBM, and the data generated by the proposed model are meaningful and appropriate to respective classes.

In short, our contributions are: (i) a novel unified RBM-based model that can acts as a complete supervised model, thus there is no need to tune additional hyperparameters for the separate predictor; (ii) the derivation of variational inference for the proposed model for both classification and regression cases; and (iii) a comprehensive evaluation of the effectiveness of our method on three learning tasks of three applications: image recognition, text classification and location prediction for CT images.

2 RELATED WORK

We first describe the restricted Boltzmann machine (RBM) for unsupervised learning representation. An RBM is a bipartite undirected graphical model in which the bottom layer contains observed variables called visible units and the top layer consists of latent *representational variables*, known as hidden units (Freund and Haussler, 1994). Two layers are fully connected but there is no connection within layers. The hidden units can capture the latent factors not presented in the observations. As a matter of convention in the literature of RBM, we shall use the term "unit" and "random variable" interchangeably.

More formally, assume a binary RBM with N visible units and K hidden units, let $\mathbf{v}$ denote the set of visible variables: $\mathbf{v} = [\mathrm{v}_1, \mathrm{v}_2, ..., \mathrm{v}_\mathrm{N}]^\top \in \{0,1\}^\mathrm{N}$ and $\mathbf{h}$ indicate the set of hidden ones: $\mathbf{h} = [\mathrm{h}_1, \mathrm{h}_2, ..., \mathrm{h}_\mathrm{K}]^\top \in \{0,1\}^\mathrm{K}$. The RBM assigns an energy function for a joint configuration over the state $(\mathbf{v}, \mathbf{h})$ as:

$$E(\mathbf{v}, \mathbf{h}; \psi) = -\left(\mathbf{a}^\top \mathbf{v} + \mathbf{b}^\top \mathbf{h} + \mathbf{v}^\top \mathbf{W} \mathbf{h}\right) \quad (1)$$

where $\psi = \{\mathbf{a}, \mathbf{b}, \mathbf{W}\}$ is the set of parameters. $\mathbf{a} = [\mathrm{a}_n]_\mathrm{N} \in \mathbb{R}^\mathrm{N}$, $\mathbf{b} = [\mathrm{b}_k]_\mathrm{K} \in \mathbb{R}^\mathrm{K}$ are the biases of hidden and visible units respectively; and $\mathbf{W} = [\mathrm{w}_{nk}]_{\mathrm{N}\times\mathrm{K}} \in \mathbb{R}^{\mathrm{N}\times\mathrm{K}}$ represents the weights connecting the hidden and visible units. The model admits a Boltzmann distribution (also known as Gibbs distribution) as follows:

$$p(\mathbf{v}, \mathbf{h}; \psi) = \exp\{-E(\mathbf{v}, \mathbf{h}; \psi) - A(\psi)\} \quad (2)$$

where $A(\psi)$ is the log-partition function. Since the network has no intra-layer connections, units in one layer become conditionally independent given the other layer. Thus the conditional distributions over visible and hidden units are factorized as:

$$p(\mathbf{h} \mid \mathbf{v}; \psi) = \prod_{k=1}^{\mathrm{K}} p(\mathrm{h}_k \mid \mathbf{v}) \quad (3)$$

$$p(\mathbf{v} \mid \mathbf{h}; \psi) = \prod_{n=1}^{\mathrm{N}} p(\mathrm{v}_n \mid \mathbf{h}) \quad (4)$$

There have been recent approaches that attempt to incorporate label information into the standard RBM (McCallum *et al.*, 2006; Schmah *et al.*, 2009; Li *et al.*, 2015). The main differences from our method are: (i) such methods still require separate classifiers, and (ii) without sharing parameters, they fail to directly capture the latent similarity between classes. Our idea is to focus on the self-contained framework for prediction, which does not need to rely on an additional supervised algorithm. The model introduced in (Yang *et al.*, 2007) and the current state-of-the-art classification formulation proposed for RBM (ClassRBM) in (Larochelle *et al.*, 2012) are closely related to ours, that couple the label to input features of RBMs. These models, however, only support classification whilst our model can perform both classification and regression. Moreover, in these models, the label is considered an additionally observed variable that links to hidden units using undirected connections. On the other hand, our proposed model uses directed connections to construct a discriminative modeling of the label given hidden layer (cf. Fig. 1b). This structure enhances the discriminative latent representations and predictive performance, allowing for better prediction results.

More specifically, our proposed model differs substantially from the ClassRBM from three crucial points: model representation, inference scheme and model expressiveness. For model representation and inference, although one might construct the *moral* graph of our hybrid model, resulting in a similar undirected graphical model (as shown in Fig. 1c), they are technically different since one cannot convert an undirected form of the ClassRBM to our model. As a consequence, the ClassRBM can still be viewed as a standard RBM with some nodes being designated as label variables, hence can still be learned with standard techniques for RBM. Whereas, our directed link has resulted in a technical challenge during the inference process, hence our contribution in the variational inference techniques.

Furthermore, from the conceptual point of view, after being moralized, in both our sRBM and ClassRBM, the data features and label interact indirectly through the hidden layer, thus this layer would play an important role in capturing the relationship between features and label. The difference is that our proposed model now contains the connections among hidden units, which enables hidden units to capture more complex structures than those of the ClassRBM where these connections are not modeled. This view has indeed been considered in semi-restricted Boltzmann machines (Salakhutdinov, 2009), a wider class of RBMs.

In terms of model expressiveness, our sRBM implicitly models the correlations among hidden units, thus it provides flexible capacity to capture a wider class of distributions as discussed in (Salakhutdinov, 2009). In particular, it can model *nonlinear* interactions between label and hidden units (cf. Eq. (7)), whilst all interactions in the ClassRBM are *linear*. Another advantage is that our model, when using the first-order Taylor series, offers more freedom to choose the conditional distribution $p(\mathrm{y} \mid \mathbf{h})$ due to appealing approximation in Eq. (11). This is a promising feature and opens room for further extensions of our approach to cover broader ranges of applications such as multi-task and multi-modal learning (Srivastava and Salakhutdinov, 2012), as well as incorporating different discriminative architectures such as Lasso (Tibshirani, 1996).

In the deep learning literature, the RBMs can be interpreted as stochastic neural networks, pretrained and then stacked layer-by-layer as a building block for deep architectures such as deep belief nets (DBNs) (Hinton and Salakhutdinov, 2006) and deep Boltzmann machines (DBMs) (Salakhutdinov and Hinton, 2009b). These deep models, however, are either trained not completely as generative models (e.g., DBNs are often fine-tuned as a standard feedforward neural nets after pretraining), and known to be extremely difficult to train (e.g., training DBMs requires a very careful weights initialization procedure, i.e., layer-by-layer pretraining followed by weights halving trick). By contrast, our sRBM still enjoys its versatility on efficient learning and inference of standard RBMs where the effective learning algorithm can be used.

Lastly, while we do not claim our main contribution in data generation, we would like to point out its connection to recent important and active research direction in constructing data generators epitomized by two current state-of-the-art density-based approaches, namely the variational autoencoder (VAE) (Kingma and Welling, 2014) and generative adversarial nets (GAN) (Goodfellow *et al.*, 2014). While these methods are still unsupervised, our sRBM provides a conditional probabilistic generator where data can be generated based on specific labels or classes.

3 PROPOSED SUPERVISED RBMs

We now present our main contribution – the supervised RBM (sRBM) that adds to the standard RBM an outcome variable y associated with each data point. This variable is generated from the hidden units via directed connections. The model now consists of two components: an RBM with undirected connections of joint distribution $p(\mathbf{v}, \mathbf{h})$ that has generative capability of representing data, and a predictive model with directed connections of conditional distribution $p(\mathrm{y} \mid \mathbf{h})$ that allows the model to perform prediction on its own right. These components form a *hybrid* probabilistic graphical model of sRBM as illustrated in Fig. 1b.

3.1 MODEL REPRESENTATION

More formally, the target variable represents the target label $\mathrm{y} \in \{1, 2, ...\mathrm{C}\}$ in classification problems or the response value $\mathrm{y} \in \mathbb{R}$ in regression tasks. Without loss of generality, the outcome follows a conditional distribution of exponential family that has the probability density as below:

$$p(\mathrm{y} \mid \mathbf{h}; \boldsymbol{\theta}) = t(\mathrm{y}) \exp\left\{\boldsymbol{\theta}^\top \boldsymbol{\phi}(\mathrm{y}, \mathbf{h}) - B(\boldsymbol{\theta}, \mathbf{h})\right\} \quad (5)$$

wherein $\boldsymbol{\theta}$ denotes the natural or canonical parameters; $\boldsymbol{\phi}(\mathrm{y}, \mathbf{h})$ refers to sufficient statistics; and $B(\boldsymbol{\theta}, \mathbf{h})$ is the log-partition or cumulant function. The function $t(\mathrm{y})$ is independent of the parameter $\boldsymbol{\theta}$. The function $B(\boldsymbol{\theta}, \mathbf{h})$ en-

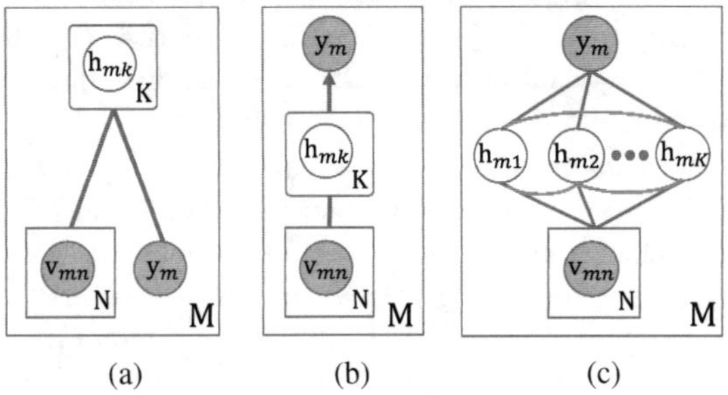

Figure 1: Graphical illustrations of (a) ClassRBM, (b) sRBM, and (c) the moralization form of sRBM. The shaded nodes represents observed variables.

sures $p(\mathrm{y} \mid \mathbf{h}; \boldsymbol{\theta})$ is a proper density, thus:

$$B(\boldsymbol{\theta}, \mathbf{h}) = \log \int_{\mathrm{y}} t(\mathrm{y}) \exp\left[\boldsymbol{\theta}^\top \boldsymbol{\phi}(\mathrm{y}, \mathbf{h})\right] d\mathrm{y} \quad (6)$$

Our aim is to jointly model the data and the outcome in order to learn alternative data representations that simultaneously explain the data and predict the outcome for future unlabeled data. Multiplicatively combining two probability densities in Eq. (5) and Eq. (2), we obtain the joint distribution of sRBM that is also an exponential family distribution: $p(\mathbf{v}, \mathbf{h}, \mathrm{y}; \psi, \boldsymbol{\theta}) = p(\mathrm{y} \mid \mathbf{h}; \boldsymbol{\theta}) p(\mathbf{v}, \mathbf{h}; \psi) =$

$$e^{\log t(\mathrm{y}) + \boldsymbol{\theta}^\top \boldsymbol{\phi}(\mathrm{y}, \mathbf{h}) - B(\boldsymbol{\theta}, \mathbf{h}) - E(\mathbf{v}, \mathbf{h}; \psi) - A(\psi)} \quad (7)$$

3.2 INFERENCE

As in any other graphical models, inference is a key task in sRBM. Suppose that the model parameters have been fully specified, there are various inference tasks to be performed in a sRBM. What we present next are the most typical ones: expectation over hidden posterior and prediction.

3.2.1 Expectation over Hidden Posterior

Our aim is to compute the expectation over the hidden posterior: $\mathbb{E}_{p(\mathbf{h} \mid \mathbf{v}, \mathrm{y})}$, which requires a sum over an exponential space of hidden units. Due to the *explaining away* effect, the hidden units become conditionally dependent given the response y. Therefore the conditional distributions over hidden units are no longer factorized as in Eq. (3) of the standard RBM, resulting in an intractable inference. To overcome this shortcoming, we must resort to approximation methods. In what follows we propose two approximation approaches: Gibbs sampling and variational inference.

Gibbs sampling. Let $\mathbf{h}_{\neg k}$ denote the state of all hidden units except the k-th one. The conditional distribution of a single hidden unit is:

$$p(\mathrm{h}_k \mid \mathbf{h}_{\neg k}, \mathbf{v}, \mathrm{y}) \propto p(\mathrm{h}_k, \mathbf{h}_{\neg k} \mid \mathbf{v}, \mathrm{y}) \propto p(\mathrm{y} \mid \mathbf{h}) p(\mathrm{h}_k \mid \mathbf{v})$$

Thus sampling from the posterior distribution of h_k can be performed using:

$$p(\mathrm{h}_k = 1 \mid \mathbf{h}_{\neg k}, \mathbf{v}, \mathrm{y}) \propto p(\mathrm{y} \mid \mathrm{h}_k = 1, \mathbf{h}_{\neg k}) p(\mathrm{h}_k = 1 \mid \mathbf{v})$$
$$p(\mathrm{h}_k = 0 \mid \mathbf{h}_{\neg k}, \mathbf{v}, \mathrm{y}) \propto p(\mathrm{y} \mid \mathrm{h}_k = 0, \mathbf{h}_{\neg k}) p(\mathrm{h}_k = 0 \mid \mathbf{v})$$

in which the state of a hidden unit being active or inactive given the visible units is:

$$p(\mathrm{h}_k = 1 \mid \mathbf{v}) = \mathrm{sig}\left(\mathrm{b}_k + \mathbf{v}^\top \mathbf{w}_{\bullet k}\right) \quad (8)$$
$$p(\mathrm{h}_k = 0 \mid \mathbf{v}) = \mathrm{sig}\left(-\mathrm{b}_k - \mathbf{v}^\top \mathbf{w}_{\bullet k}\right) \quad (9)$$

where $\mathrm{sig}(x) = 1/1+e^{-x}$ is logistic sigmoid function. We refer to supplementary material for full derivations.

Variational inference. When performing inference in large models or on moderately-sized datasets, the Gibbs sampler can become extremely slow as it must sequentially iterate over every single hidden unit. We hereby choose a faster method – variational inference.

In variational methods (Jordan *et al.*, 1998), the true posterior distribution $p(\mathbf{h} \mid \mathbf{v}, \mathrm{y})$ is approximated by a variational distribution $q(\mathbf{h}; \boldsymbol{\mu})$ with $\boldsymbol{\mu} = [\mu_1, \mu_2, ..., \mu_{\mathrm{K}}]^\top$ is the vector of variational parameters. These parameters are learned in order to maximize the following evidence lower bound (ELBO):

$$\begin{aligned}\mathcal{L}(\psi, \boldsymbol{\theta}, \boldsymbol{\mu}) &= \mathbb{E}_{q(\mathbf{h})}\left[\log p(\mathbf{v}, \mathbf{h}, \mathrm{y})\right] - \mathbb{E}_{q(\mathbf{h})}\left[\log q(\mathbf{h})\right] \\ &= \mathbb{E}_{q(\mathbf{h})}\left[\boldsymbol{\theta}^\top \boldsymbol{\phi}(\mathrm{y}, \mathbf{h}) - B(\boldsymbol{\theta}, \mathbf{h}) - E(\mathbf{v}, \mathbf{h}; \psi)\right] \\ &\quad + \log t(\mathrm{y}) - \mathbb{E}_{q(\mathbf{h})}\left[\log q(\mathbf{h})\right] - A(\psi)\end{aligned}$$

Using a naive mean-field approximation, we choose a variational distribution that is fully factorized into K Bernoulli distributions as: $q(\mathbf{h}; \boldsymbol{\mu}) = \prod_{k=1}^{\mathrm{K}} q(\mathrm{h}_k; \mu_k)$ in which μ_k denotes the probability $q(\mathrm{h}_k = 1)$. The ELBO now reads (c.f. supplementary material for the full derivation): $\mathcal{L}(\psi, \boldsymbol{\theta}, \boldsymbol{\mu}) =$

$$\begin{aligned}&\sum_{k=1}^{\mathrm{K}} \theta_k \left[\mu_k \phi(\mathrm{y}, \mathrm{h}_k = 1) + (1 - \mu_k) \phi(\mathrm{y}, \mathrm{h}_k = 0)\right] \\ &- \mathbb{E}_{q(\mathbf{h})}\left[B(\boldsymbol{\theta}, \mathbf{h})\right] + \sum_{k=1}^{\mathrm{K}} \mu_k \left(\mathrm{b}_k + \sum_{n=1}^{\mathrm{N}} \mathrm{v}_n \mathrm{w}_{nk}\right) \\ &+ \mathrm{K}\left(\sum_{n=1}^{\mathrm{N}} \mathrm{a}_n \mathrm{v}_n\right) + \log t(\mathrm{y}) - A(\psi) \\ &- \sum_{k=1}^{\mathrm{K}} \left[\mu_k \log \mu_k + (1 - \mu_k) \log(1 - \mu_k)\right] \quad (10)\end{aligned}$$

As the model parameters $\psi, \boldsymbol{\theta}$ are fixed, three terms $\mathrm{K}\left(\sum_{n=1}^{\mathrm{N}} \mathrm{a}_n \mathrm{v}_n\right)$, $\log t(\mathrm{y})$ and $A(\psi)$ are constant. Thus we can ignore them in this maximization process. Only the log-partition function $B(\boldsymbol{\theta}, \mathbf{h})$ cannot be decomposed into individual functions of each hidden unit, rendering its expectation intractable. We approximate this expectation using two strategies: the *first-order* and the *second-order*

Taylor series approximations. The first-order approximation evaluated at the first moment $\boldsymbol{\mu} = \mathbb{E}_{q(\mathbf{h})}[\mathbf{h}]$ reads:

$$\mathbb{E}_{q(\mathbf{h})}[B(\boldsymbol{\theta},\mathbf{h})] \approx \mathbb{E}_{q(\mathbf{h})}\left[B(\boldsymbol{\theta},\boldsymbol{\mu}) + (\mathbf{h}-\boldsymbol{\mu})^\top \nabla_{\mathbf{h}} B(\boldsymbol{\theta},\mathbf{h})\right]$$
$$= B(\boldsymbol{\theta},\boldsymbol{\mu}) + \mathbb{E}_{q(\mathbf{h})}[\mathbf{h}-\boldsymbol{\mu}]^\top \nabla_{\mathbf{h}} B(\boldsymbol{\theta},\mathbf{h}) = B(\boldsymbol{\theta},\boldsymbol{\mu}) \quad (11)$$

wherein $\nabla_{\mathbf{h}} B(\boldsymbol{\theta},\mathbf{h})$ denotes the derivative w.r.t $\mathbf{h}$ and then evaluated at $\mathbf{h} = \boldsymbol{\mu}$, thus it is independent with $q(\mathbf{h})$ and can be taken out from the expectation in the second step. Note that we have used $\mathbb{E}_{q(\mathbf{h})}[\mathbf{h}-\boldsymbol{\mu}]^\top = 0$ in the last step. The result offers an interesting property that the expectation can be approximated by the function itself, evaluated at the mean. This allows us more freedom to choose the conditional distribution $p(\mathrm{y} \mid \mathbf{h})$.

Assuming that $B(\boldsymbol{\theta},\mathbf{h})$ is a twice differentiable function of $\mathbf{h}$, the second-order approximation evaluated at $\boldsymbol{\mu}$ is:

$$\mathbb{E}_{q(\mathbf{h})}[B(\boldsymbol{\theta},\mathbf{h})]$$
$$\approx B(\boldsymbol{\theta},\boldsymbol{\mu}) + \mathbb{E}_{q(\mathbf{h})}\left[\frac{1}{2}(\mathbf{h}-\boldsymbol{\mu})^\top \mathbf{H}[B(\boldsymbol{\theta},\boldsymbol{\mu})](\mathbf{h}-\boldsymbol{\mu})\right]$$
$$\overset{(a)}{=} B(\boldsymbol{\theta},\boldsymbol{\mu}) + \frac{1}{2}\sum_{i=1}^{\mathrm{K}}\sum_{j=1}^{\mathrm{K}} \mathrm{H}_{ij}\mathbb{E}_{q(\mathbf{h})}[(\mathrm{h}_i-\mu_i)(\mathrm{h}_j-\mu_j)]$$
$$= B(\boldsymbol{\theta},\boldsymbol{\mu}) + \frac{1}{2}\sum_{i=1}^{\mathrm{K}} \mathrm{H}_{ii}\mu_i(1-\mu_i) \quad (12)$$

where $\mathrm{H}_{ij} \triangleq \partial_{\mathrm{h}_i}\partial_{\mathrm{h}_j} B(\boldsymbol{\theta},\boldsymbol{\mu})$ denotes the second-order derivative of $B(\boldsymbol{\theta},\mathbf{h})$ evaluated at $\mathbf{h} = \boldsymbol{\mu}$, thus H_{ij} is constant w.r.t $\mathbf{h}$ and can be taken out from the expectation as in step (a). We refer to supplementary material for full derivations.

Substituting Eq. (11) into the ELBO in Eq. (10), and then taking the derivative with respect to (w.r.t) variational parameter, we obtain: $\nabla_{\mu_k}\mathcal{L} =$

$$\theta_k[\phi(\mathrm{y},\mathrm{h}_k=1) - \phi(\mathrm{y},\mathrm{h}_k=0)] + \mathrm{b}_k + \sum\nolimits_{n=1}^{\mathrm{N}} \mathrm{v}_n \mathrm{w}_{nk}$$
$$- \nabla_{\mu_k}\mathbb{E}_{q(\mathbf{h})}[B(\boldsymbol{\theta},\mathbf{h})] - [\log \mu_k - \log(1-\mu_k)] \quad (13)$$

Since there is no closed-form solution to compute μ_k by setting the gradient to zero, we update the variational parameters by iterating at the following fixed point:

$$\mu_k \leftarrow \mathrm{sig}(\theta_k[\phi(\mathrm{y},\mathrm{h}_k=1) - \phi(\mathrm{y},\mathrm{h}_k=0)]$$
$$+ \mathrm{b}_k + \sum\nolimits_{n=1}^{\mathrm{N}} \mathrm{v}_n \mathrm{w}_{nk} - \nabla_{\mu_k}\mathbb{E}_{q(\mathbf{h})}[B(\boldsymbol{\theta},\mathbf{h})]) \quad (14)$$

3.2.2 Prediction

The next goal is to predict the outcome given the input data: $p(\mathrm{y} \mid \mathbf{v})$. This conditional probability density can be derived as follows:

$$p(\mathrm{y} \mid \mathbf{v}) = \sum\nolimits_{\mathbf{h}} p(\mathrm{y} \mid \mathbf{h})\, p(\mathbf{h} \mid \mathbf{v}) = \mathbb{E}_{p(\mathbf{h}|\mathbf{v})}[p(\mathrm{y} \mid \mathbf{h})]$$

As can be seen from the graphical model of sRBM, the hidden units are conditionally independent given observed visible units and unobserved outcome variables. Thus the model realizes the hidden factorization (see Eq. (3)) as in the standard RBM. Furthermore, according to Eq. (8) and Eq. (9), the probability of being active of each hidden unit also follows a Bernoulli distribution. Hence, the distribution $p(\mathbf{h} \mid \mathbf{v})$ plays the same role as the one of variational distribution $q(\mathbf{h})$ in Section 3.2.1. This allows us to use the similar approximation approach as the first-order approximation in Eq. (11), that is:

$$p(\mathrm{y} \mid \mathbf{v}) = \mathbb{E}_{p(\mathbf{h}|\mathbf{v})}[p(\mathrm{y} \mid \mathbf{h})] \approx p(\mathrm{y} \mid \boldsymbol{\mu})$$

in which μ_k is the mean of distribution $q(\mathrm{h}_k;\mu_k) \approx p(\mathrm{h}_k \mid \mathbf{v})$.

Interestingly, the predictive inference is reminiscent of the forward pass of an ordinary feedforward neural network. In particular, it could be implemented by a single layer neural network with sigmoid hidden units and softmax (for classification) or identity (for regression) output neurons. This also suggests an approach to pretrain deep models that contain the sRBM as the top layer of a building block of RBMs.

3.3 PARAMETER ESTIMATION

In this section we present how to estimate the parameters of sRBM from training data. Following the learning in the standard RBM, the sRBM also aims to maximize the log-likelihood of data: $\log p(\mathbf{v},\mathrm{y}) = \log \sum_{\mathbf{h}} p(\mathbf{v},\mathbf{h},\mathrm{y})$, but the data now include the features and outcome instead of the features only. The parameters are then updated in a gradient ascent fashion as (cf. supplementary material for more details):

$$\psi \leftarrow \psi + \eta\left(\mathbb{E}_{\tilde{p}}[\nabla_\psi E(\mathbf{v},\mathbf{h})] - \mathbb{E}_p[\nabla_\psi E(\mathbf{v},\mathbf{h})]\right) \quad (15)$$
$$\boldsymbol{\theta} \leftarrow \boldsymbol{\theta} + \eta\left(\mathbb{E}_{\tilde{p}}[\boldsymbol{\phi}(\mathrm{y},\mathbf{h})] - \mathbb{E}_{\tilde{p}}[\nabla_{\boldsymbol{\theta}} B(\boldsymbol{\theta},\mathbf{h})]\right) \quad (16)$$

for a learning rate $\eta > 0$. $\tilde{p}(\mathbf{h} \mid \mathbf{v},\mathrm{y})$ denotes the data distribution, and $p(\mathbf{v},\mathbf{h})$ the model distribution of RBM part in sRBM. It is intractable to compute both two expectations exactly as it requires the sum over exponential space. We choose a stochastic method known as contrastive divergence (CD) (Hinton, 2002) which runs short Markov chains started from the data to approximate the model expectation.

For the data expectation, we use the approximation variational inference of $\mathbb{E}_{p(\mathbf{h}|\mathbf{v},\mathrm{y})}$ as described in Section 3.2. The mean-field update rule in Eq. (14) depends on the forms of sufficient statistics $\boldsymbol{\phi}(\mathrm{y},\mathbf{h})$ and log-partition function $B(\boldsymbol{\theta},\mathbf{h})$. For multiclass classification, the parameter $\boldsymbol{\theta}$ is a $\mathrm{K}\times\mathrm{C}$ matrix, and the probability density $p(\mathrm{y} \mid \mathbf{h};\boldsymbol{\theta},\boldsymbol{\beta})$ in Eq. (5) is given by:

$$\exp\left\{\boldsymbol{\theta}_{\cdot\mathrm{y}}^\top \mathbf{h} + \beta_{\mathrm{y}} - \log\sum\nolimits_c \exp\left(\boldsymbol{\theta}_{\cdot c}^\top \mathbf{h} + \beta_c\right)\right\}$$

in which $\boldsymbol{\theta}_{\bullet c}$ is the c-th column, and we have further introduced the bias β_c for the c-th class, hence:

$$\boldsymbol{\theta}^\top \boldsymbol{\phi}(\mathrm{y}, \mathbf{h}) \triangleq \boldsymbol{\theta}_{\bullet \mathrm{y}}^\top \mathbf{h} + \beta_\mathrm{y}$$

$$B(\boldsymbol{\theta}, \mathbf{h}) = \log \sum_{c=1}^{\mathrm{C}} \exp\left(\boldsymbol{\theta}_{\bullet c}^\top \mathbf{h} + \beta_c\right)$$

The update rule in Eq. (14) when using the first-order approximation in Eq. (11) now reads:

$$\mu_k \leftarrow \mathrm{sig}\left(\theta_{k\mathrm{y}} + \mathrm{b}_k + \sum_{n=1}^{\mathrm{N}} \mathrm{v}_n \mathrm{w}_{nk} - \frac{\sum_c \theta_{kc} e^{\left(\boldsymbol{\theta}_{\bullet c}^\top \boldsymbol{\mu} + \beta_c\right)}}{\sum_l e^{\boldsymbol{\theta}_{\bullet l}^\top \boldsymbol{\mu} + \beta_l}}\right)$$

The derivation for the second-order in Eq. (12) is more complicated, thus we refer to the supplementary material.

For regression problem, the parameter $\boldsymbol{\theta}$ is a K-dimensional vector, and the outcome variable follows the following Gaussian distribution: $p(\mathrm{y} \mid \mathbf{h}; \boldsymbol{\theta}, \beta) =$

$$\frac{1}{\sqrt{2\pi}} \exp\left[-\frac{1}{2\sigma^2}\mathrm{y}^2 + \frac{\boldsymbol{\theta}^\top \mathbf{h} + \beta}{\sigma^2}\mathrm{y} - \frac{\left(\boldsymbol{\theta}^\top \mathbf{h} + \beta\right)^2}{2\sigma^2} - \log \sigma\right]$$

with the standard deviation σ and bias β, thus:

$$\boldsymbol{\theta}^\top \boldsymbol{\phi}(\mathrm{y}, \mathbf{h}) \triangleq -\mathrm{y}^2 / \left(2\sigma^2\right) + \mathrm{y}\left(\boldsymbol{\theta}^\top \mathbf{h} + \beta\right) / \sigma^2$$

$$B(\boldsymbol{\theta}, \mathbf{h}) = \left(\boldsymbol{\theta}^\top \mathbf{h} + \beta\right)^2 / \left(2\sigma^2\right) + \log \sigma$$

Fixing $\sigma = 1$, the update rule in Eq. (14) when using the first-order approximation in Eq. (11) now reads:

$$\mu_k \leftarrow \mathrm{sig}\left[\theta_k \mathrm{y} + \mathrm{b}_k + \sum_{n=1}^{\mathrm{N}} \mathrm{v}_n \mathrm{w}_{nk} - \theta_k \left(\boldsymbol{\theta}^\top \boldsymbol{\mu} + \beta\right)\right]$$

, and using the second-order approximation in Eq. (12) is:

$$\mu_k \leftarrow \mathrm{sig}[\theta_k \mathrm{y} + \mathrm{b}_k + \sum_{n=1}^{\mathrm{N}} \mathrm{v}_n \mathrm{w}_{nk} - \theta_k \left(\boldsymbol{\theta}^\top \boldsymbol{\mu} + \beta\right) - \frac{1}{2}\theta_k^2 (1 - 2\mu_k)]$$

We refer to the supplementary material[1] for the pseudo-code of learning parameters for sRBM using CD-1. Once the model is fully specified, the new representation of an input data can be achieved by computing the posterior vector $\hat{\mathbf{h}} = \left(\hat{\mathrm{h}}_1, \hat{\mathrm{h}}_2, ..., \hat{\mathrm{h}}_\mathrm{K}\right)$, where $\hat{\mathrm{h}}_k$ is shorthand for $\hat{\mathrm{h}}_k = p(\mathrm{h}_k = 1 \mid \mathbf{v})$ in Eq. (8).

4 EXPERIMENTS

In this section, we examine the predictive and generative capabilities of sRBM, and the effectiveness of discriminative representations and semantically related features discovered by the proposed model on three tasks – classification, regression and data generation. For classification, we use identical experimental setups to those of (Larochelle *et al.*, 2012) in order to directly compare our method with the current state-of-the-art – ClassRBM – and other baselines. Here we consider the ClassRBM with generative training objective since it is the most relevant approach to our model that is also learned in a generative fashion. We also would like to note that we do not compare with deep neural nets because our focus is on generative models.

Datasets. We use three datasets: MNIST[2], 20 Newsgroups (Mitchell, 1997) and CT slices obtained from UCI repository[3]. After ordinal preprocessing steps (e.g., normalizing, rescaling), they are not exactly binary data. Following the previous work (Hinton and Salakhutdinov, 2006), we treat their feature values as empirical probabilities on which the RBM-based models are naturally applied. Since the empirical expectations $\mathbb{E}_{\tilde{p}}[\cdot]$ in Eq. (15) and Eq. (16) require the probability $p(\mathbf{v})$, the normalized intensity is a good approximation.

Methods and baselines. We create two versions of our approach: sRBM using the first-order approximation (sRBM-1st) and the second-order (sRBM-2nd). For classification performance comparison, we employ 5 baselines: ClassRBM with generative training strategy (Larochelle *et al.*, 2012), k-nearest neighbors (kNN, where $k = 1$, with cosine similarity measures) and support vector machine (SVM) directly on the hidden posteriors of sRBM (sRBM+kNN, sRBM+SVM), ClassRBM (ClassRBM+kNN, ClassRBM+SVM) and RBM (RBM+kNN, RBM+SVM). We obtain ClassRBM code[4] that reproduces the results of (Larochelle *et al.*, 2012). For regression, we use: ridge regression (RR) – linear regression with ℓ_2-norm regularization, and RR on top of other methods, similar to the setup for classification.

Hyperparameter settings. For RBM-based models, mapping parameters are randomly drawn from $\mathcal{N}(0, 0.01)$, and biases are set to zeros. Learning is terminated after a number of epochs over training set, that was specified using early stopping based on the error of validation set in every interval of 15 epochs. For a fair comparison, we empirically tune the learning rate of each model: $\eta \in \{0.1, 0.05, 0.01, 0.005, 0.001\}$ using cross-validation for the best result on validation part.

4.1 IMAGE AND TEXT CLASSIFICATION

In the first task, we replicate the experimental settings in Sections 7.1 and 7.2 in (Larochelle *et al.*, 2012). In particular, we use MNIST and the "bydate" version of 20 Newsgroups datasets to validate the predictive performance of our proposed model on image and text data. The MNIST consists of $50,000$ training; $10,000$ validation; and $10,000$ testing 28×28 grayscale handwritten digit images whose

[1] https://tund.github.io/papers/tu_etal_uai17_srbm_supp.pdf

[2] http://yann.lecun.com/exdb/mnist/.

[3] https://archive.ics.uci.edu/ml/datasets.html.

[4] https://github.com/skaae/rbm_toolbox

pixel values are then normalized into the range $[0, 1]$. The 20 Newsgroups consists of $9, 578$ training; $1, 691$ validation; and $7, 505$ testing documents. We first extract $5, 000$ most frequent words based on their counts in the training part, then use their appearances as binary bag-of-word features for each document.

The number of hidden units is set to $6, 000$ for MNIST and to $1, 000$ for 20 Newsgroups. Once again, we note that these numbers are identically set to those in (Larochelle *et al.*, 2012). The results for different numbers of hidden units are provided in the supplementary material. Overall, the larger hidden layers yield better classification results, which is plausible since the hidden units need to capture both data and labels. This finding is also consistent with that of the ClassRBM.

Table 1 reports the classification errors on testing set for all methods. For handwritten recognition, our proposed model significantly outperforms all baselines, based on the fact that on MNIST, differences of more than 0.1% are statistically significant. This result, to the best of our knowledge, is the highest among those of standalone RBMs trained in a generative fashion. For document classification, our model, with 5-fold dimensionality reduction from $5, 000$ words to $1, 000$ hidden units, also achieves the best result.

Table 1: Classification errors ($\%$) on testing sets.

	MNIST	20 Newsgroups
RBM+kNN	3.03	56.15
RBM+SVM	1.76	41.79
ClassRBM+kNN	2.98	57.80
ClassRBM+SVM	1.68	40.88
ClassRBM	3.39	24.9
sRBM+kNN	2.94	55.89
sRBM+SVM	1.42	38.43
sRBM-1st	2.27	24.1
sRBM-2nd	**2.21**	**23.2**

Discriminative representations. One could question that whether the discriminative representations learned by sRBM would have more advantages. The first argument is these representations, learned with guidance from labels, could straightforwardly translate into better predictive performance without the need for well-trained classifiers. Looking at the classification errors of sRBM+kNN, ClassRBM+kNN, and RBM+kNN in Table 1, we believe that the learned representations of sRBM would be more naturally discriminative than those of other RBMs. The results on MNIST are much better than those on 20 newsgroups because the MNIST is a clean, well-preprocessed dataset, whilst 20 newsgroups is a more difficult text dataset in higher dimensional space.

For further comparison, we quantitatively compute the pairwise cosine similarities between $6, 000$-dimensional hidden posteriors: $c_{ij} = \text{cosine}(\hat{\mathbf{h}}_i, \hat{\mathbf{h}}_j)$ of data points $(\mathbf{v}_i, y_i)$ and $(\mathbf{v}_j, y_j)$. The similarity between a data sample and the rest is: $c_i^\star = 1/M \left[\sum_{\forall j | y_j = y_i} c_{ij} - \sum_{\forall j | y_j \neq y_i} c_{ij}\right]$ where M is the number of data points. The average similarities over all samples of sRBM, ClassRBM, and RBM are $-\mathbf{0.02}$, -0.36, and -0.61, which demonstrates that our proposed model has significantly higher power of disentangling data from different classes. For quality demonstration, we project $5, 000$ hidden posteriors of sRBM onto 2D using t-SNE[5] (Van der Maaten and Hinton, 2008). Fig. 2 depicts the distribution of where class information is only used for visual labeling. The separation is over satisfactory.

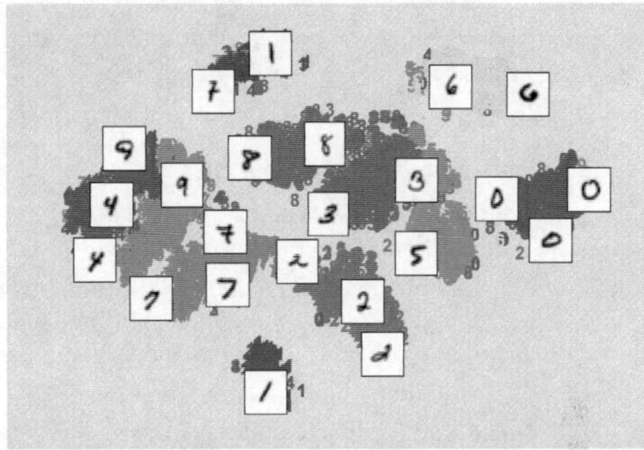

Figure 2: An illustration of 10 digit classes from $5, 000$ MNIST images. t-SNE projection performs on higher representations of images mapped by sRBM.

Topic modeling. The next aspect is whether the sRBM effectively models the topics, so that it can obtain better classification performance. Here we examine the weight connections between the hidden and output layers. This offers a method to embed discrete topics (classes) in a continuous space using $\boldsymbol{\theta}_{\cdot t} \in \mathbb{R}^K$, i.e., the t-th column of weight matrix $\boldsymbol{\theta}$. A topic is now represented by a vector of K dimensions. This embedding is closely related to the word embedding that has found numerous applications in natural language processing (Mikolov *et al.*, 2013).

To assess the correlation between topics, we compute pairwise similarities between embedded vectors: $s_{ij} = \text{sig}(\boldsymbol{\theta}_{\cdot i}^\top \boldsymbol{\theta}_{\cdot j})$ and present them in Fig. 3. It can be seen that the sRBM effectively disentangles different topics, whilst still retains a certain degree of similarity for semantically related topics. More precisely, the bounding squares in the figure indicate groups of topics such as computer (comp.*), science (sci.*) and politics (talk.politics.*), or secondary topics such as sports (rec.sports.*) and other recreational activities (rec.autos and rec.motorcycles). Interestingly, the model can also recognize the resemblance of some separated groups (alt.atheism, soc.religion.christian and talk.*) that are indeed semantically related.

Similar results are obtained by the ClassRBM as shown in

[5]Note that the t-SNE does not perform clustering, it only reduces the dimensionality into 2D for visualization while still strives to preserve the local properties of the data.

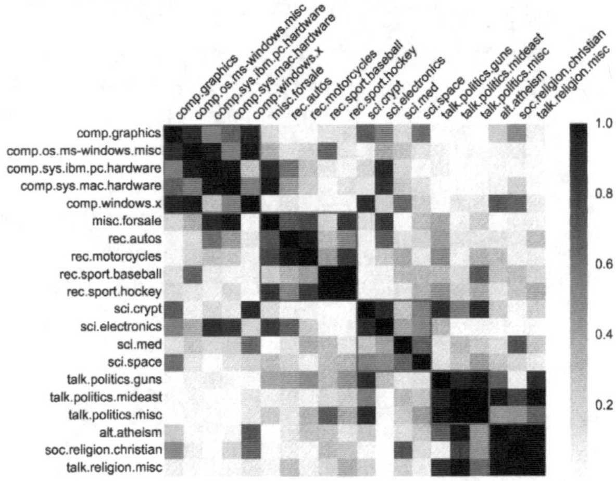

Figure 3: Similarities among weight vectors of the sRBM associated with 20 Newsgroups.

Fig. 3 in (Larochelle *et al.*, 2012)). For quantitative comparison, we compute the correlation of a topic with the rest as: $s_i^\star = {}^1/_{T-1} \sum_{j \neq i} s_{ij}$. The result is favorable toward sRBM with the average correlation over all topics of $\mathbf{0.314}$ that is lower than $\mathbf{0.399}$ of ClassRBM. This, once again, demonstrates that our proposed method disentangles different topics better. The gap is much smaller than that of similarities between hidden posteriors, which can be reflected by the fact that the improvement in classification performances on 20 Newsgroups is much less significant than the one on MNIST dataset (cf. Table 1).

For document modeling task on 20 Newsgroups dataset, we analyze how our proposed model captures words that are coherent in a topic by examining the weight matrices $\boldsymbol{\theta}$ and $\mathbf{W}$. The entry of column $\mathbf{w}_{\bullet k}$ reflects the association strength of a particular word to the latent factor k, and $\boldsymbol{\theta}_{\bullet c}$ the strength of a latent factor to the topic c. We first specify top 100 hidden units with the largest weight for each topic c, then aggregate (by summing) the associated word-to-hidden weight vectors. This reveals the positive contribution of the words to each newsgroup via the hidden layer. Fig. 4 illustrates top 8 words per topic, in descending order of their aggregated association strength, discovered by our model. The chart shows that the words under each feature are semantically related in a coherent way.

4.2 LABEL-DRIVEN DATA GENERATION

As a generative model, it is desirable that our proposed method can generate meaningful data after training. In this experiment, we analyze the capability of sRBM in drawing images and words in documents for specified handwritten digit and news topics. To generate a data sample, we first fix a label y, then randomly initialize $\hat{\mathbf{h}} \in [0,1]^K$. Next we alternatively sample the data $\hat{\mathbf{v}} \sim p(\mathbf{v} \mid \hat{\mathbf{h}})$ and the hidden units $\hat{\mathbf{h}} \sim p(\mathbf{h} \mid \mathbf{v}, y)$ using 100 separate Markov chains, then collect data $\hat{\mathbf{v}}$ at the 1000th sampling step. For handwritten digits, we generate 10 images for each digit. For news groups, we choose to generate documents (bags of words) for three topics: *rec.autos*, *sci.space* and *comp.sys.mac.hardware*. For each group, we generate 100 documents, and then select 50 most frequent words with their frequencies.

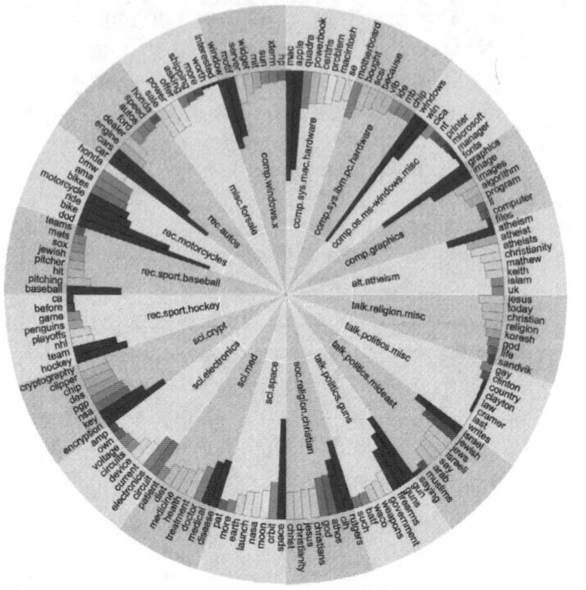

Figure 4: Topics associated with top 8 words discovered by sRBM from 20 Newsgroups dataset. The bar height and color relatively represent the aggregated association strength of a word. (Best viewed in colors and refer to the supplementary material for larger plot).

Fig. 5 (left) and Fig. 6 show images of handwritten digits and top words of three news topics generated by the sRBM. In general, our model can draw correct images on each row from top to bottom for each digit from 0 to 9, and generate words that are semantically related in a coherent way for each topic. In particular, it can capture factors of variation from the data, i.e., digits are sampled with clearly different styles. For reference, we further show the images generated by VAE in Fig. 5 (middle) and GAN in Fig. 5 (right). Here we do not make any qualitative and quantitative comparison since we do not claim our main contribution in data generation.

4.3 LOCATION PROGNOSIS FOR CT IMAGES

In the last application, the aim is to predict the relative location for computed tomography (CT) slice. The dataset consists of $53,500$ CT images captured from 74 different patients (Graf *et al.*, 2011). Two histograms in polar space are extracted from each CT slice, forming a 385-dimensional feature vector. The response variable is the relative location of an image on the axial axis with the value in $[0, 180]$, and then is rescaled into $[0, 1]$.

We divide the dataset into three disjoint parts: 80% for training, 5% for validation and 15% for testing with 42800, 2675 and 8025 data samples respectively. The validation

Figure 5: Handwritten digit images generated by sRBM (left) for 10 classes (each row is generated conditionally on the digit labels from 0 to 9), VAE (middle), and GAN (right). Images generated by VAE and GAN are taken from original work – (Kingma and Welling, 2014) and (Salimans *et al.*, 2016).

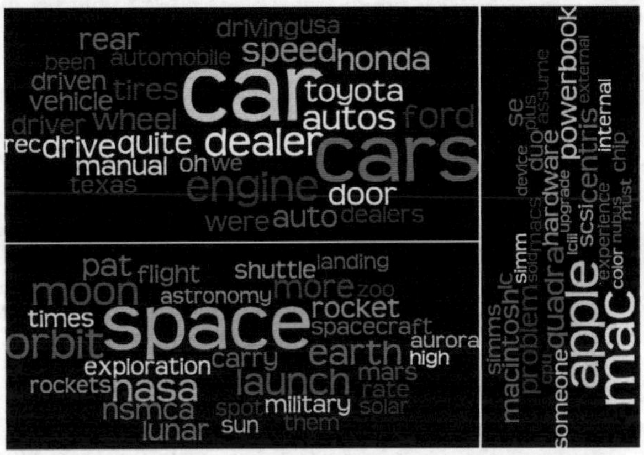

Figure 6: Words generated by sRBM for (*rec.autos*, *sci.space*, *comp.sys.mac.hardware*) news groups.

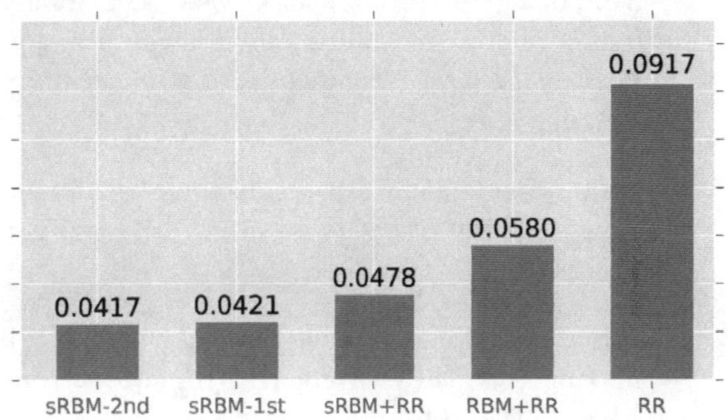

Figure 7: Regression errors (%) on testing data of CT slice dataset (lower is better).

set is used for hyperparameter tuning step wherein the number of hidden units K is varied in $\{100, 200, 500, 1000\}$. In general, we observe that the larger K improves the performance of our method, thus we use $K = 1,000$. Note that we normalize the responses to zero mean and unit variance before training the sRBM. In testing phase, the sRBM maps the prediction values back into the original space.

We use root mean square error (RMSE) to measure the regression results. Fig. 7 shows that our proposed sRBM-1st achieves a regression error that is 54%, 27%, and 12% better than those of ridge regression (RR), RBM+RR, and sRBM+RR respectively, and the second-order version (sRBM-2nd) slightly outperforms the first-order (sRBM-1st). This, again, demonstrates that the unified learning of sRBM results in more discriminative representations and better prediction scores than two-stage framework of unsupervised models followed by predictive models.

5 CONCLUSION

We have introduced a novel self-contained prediction model – supervised restricted Boltzmann machine (sRBM) that leverages the powerful RBM to simultaneously learn data representations and perform supervised learning. Different from the current state-of-the-art classification formulation of RBM – ClassRBM (Larochelle *et al.*, 2012), our model is a *hybrid* probabilistic graphical model with a generative component for data representation and a discriminative component for both classification and regression.

We have further developed variational inference for sRBM to tackle the challenging inference posed by the introduction of the discriminative component. We evaluated the effectiveness of our model using comprehensive experiments on three real-world applications. The results confirm that the integration of the discriminative component into RBM: (i) significantly improves the classification performance of the ClassRBM; (ii) renders more discriminative representations; (iii) generates meaningful data driven by classes; and (iv) achieves better regression results.

ACKNOWLEDGMENT. This work was partially supported by the Australian Research Council (ARC) Discovery Grant Project DP150100031.

References

Yoshua Bengio, Aaron Courville, and Pascal Vincent. Representation learning: A review and new perspectives. *IEEE Transactions on Pattern Analysis and Machine Intelligence (PAMI)*, 35(8):1798–1828, 2013.

Adam Coates and Andrew Y Ng. The importance of encoding versus training with sparse coding and vector quantization. In *The 28th International Conference on Machine Learning (ICML)*, pages 921–928, 2011.

Yoav Freund and David Haussler. Unsupervised learning of distributions on binary vectors using two layer networks. Technical Report UCSC-CRL-94-25, University of California Santa Cruz (UCSC), CA, USA, 1994.

Ian Goodfellow, Jean Pouget-Abadie, Mehdi Mirza, Bing Xu, David Warde-Farley, Sherjil Ozair, Aaron Courville, and Yoshua Bengio. Generative adversarial nets. In *Advances in Neural Information Processing Systems (NIPS)*, pages 2672–2680. 2014.

Franz Graf, Hans-Peter Kriegel, Matthias Schubert, Sebastian Pölsterl, and Alexander Cavallaro. 2d image registration in ct images using radial image descriptors. In *Medical Image Computing and Computer-Assisted Intervention*, pages 607–614. Springer, 2011.

Geoffrey Hinton and Ruslan Salakhutdinov. Reducing the dimensionality of data with neural networks. *Science*, 313(5786):504–507, 2006.

Geoffrey E. Hinton. Training products of experts by minimizing contrastive divergence. *Neural Computation*, 14(8):1771–1800, 2002.

Michael I Jordan, Zoubin Ghahramani, Tommi S Jaakkola, and Lawrence K Saul. *An introduction to variational methods for graphical models*. Springer, 1998.

Diederik P Kingma and Max Welling. Auto-encoding variational bayes. In *The International Conference on Learning Representations (ICLR)*, Banff, 2014.

Hugo Larochelle, Michael Mandel, Razvan Pascanu, and Yoshua Bengio. Learning algorithms for the classiffcation restricted boltzmann machine. *Journal of Machine Learning Research*, pages 643–669, 2012.

Xin Li, Feipeng Zhao, and Yuhong Guo. Conditional restricted boltzmann machines for multi-label learning with incomplete labels. In *Artificial Intelligence and Statistics (AISTATS)*, pages 635–643, 2015.

A. McCallum, C. Pal, G. Druck, and X. Wang. Multi-conditional learning: Generative/discriminative training for clustering and classification. In *The National Conference on AI*, volume 1, pages 433–439, 2006.

Tomas Mikolov, Ilya Sutskever, Kai Chen, Greg S Corrado, and Jeff Dean. Distributed representations of words and phrases and their compositionality. *Neural Information Processing Systems (NIPS)*, pages 3111–3119, 2013.

Thomas M Mitchell. Machine learning. *Artificial Intelligence*, 1997. (citation for 20 newsgroups dataset).

Tu Dinh Nguyen, Truyen Tran, Dinh Phung, and Svetha Venkatesh. Latent patient profile modelling and applications with mixed-variate restricted boltzmann machine. In *The 17th Pacific-Asia Conference on Knowledge Discovery and Data Mining (PAKDD)*, volume 7818, pages 123–135, Gold Coast, Australia, 2013.

Tu Dinh Nguyen, Truyen Tran, Dinh Phung, and Svetha Venkatesh. Learning parts-based representations with nonnegative restricted Boltzmann machine. In *Proceedings of the 5th Asian Conference on Machine Learning (ACML)*, volume 29, pages 133–148, Canberra, Australia, November 13–15 2013.

Tu Dinh Nguyen, Truyen Tran, Dinh Phung, and Svetha Venkatesh. Learning sparse latent representation and distance metric for image retrieval. In *Proceedings of IEEE International Conference on Multimedia and Expo (ICME)*, pages 1–6, USA, 2013.

R. Salakhutdinov and GE Hinton. Replicated softmax: an undirected topic model. In *The 23rd Neural Information Processing Systems (NIPS)*, pages 1607–1614, Vancouver, Canada, December 7–10 2009.

Ruslan Salakhutdinov and Geoffrey Hinton. Deep Boltzmann machines. In *The 12th International Conference on Artificial Intelligence and Statistics (AISTATS)*, volume 5, pages 448–455, USA, 2009.

Ruslan Salakhutdinov. *Learning deep generative models*. PhD thesis, Ph.D. Thesis, University of Toronto, 2009.

Tim Salimans, Ian Goodfellow, Wojciech Zaremba, Vicki Cheung, Alec Radford, and Xi Chen. Improved techniques for training gans. In *Neural Information Processing Systems (NIPS)*, pages 2226–2234, 2016.

T.a Schmah, G.E.a Hinton, R.S.a Zemel, S.L.b Small, and S.c Strother. Generative versus discriminative training of rbms for classification of fmri images. In *Advances in Neural Information Processing Systems 21 (NIPS)*, pages 1409–1416, 2009.

Nitish Srivastava and Ruslan Salakhutdinov. Multimodal learning with deep Boltzmann machines. In *The 26th Neural Information Processing Systems (NIPS)*, volume 3, pages 2222–2230, USA, December 3–6 2012.

Robert Tibshirani. Regression shrinkage and selection via the lasso. *Journal of the Royal Statistical Society. Series B (Methodological)*, pages 267–288, 1996.

L. Van der Maaten and G. Hinton. Visualizing data using t-SNE. *The Journal of Machine Learning Research (JMLR)*, 9:2579–2625, 2008.

J.a Yang, Y.a b Liu, E.P.a Xing, and A.G.a Hauptmann. Harmoniurn models for semantic video representation and classification. In *The 7th SIAM International Conference on Data Mining (SDM)*, pages 378–389, 2007.

Safe Semi-Supervised Learning of Sum-Product Networks

Martin Trapp[1,2], **Tamas Madl**[2], **Robert Peharz**[3], **Franz Pernkopf**[1], and **Robert Trappl**[2]

[1]Signal Processing and Speech Communication Laboratory, Graz University of Technology, Graz, Austria
[2]Austrian Research Institute for Artificial Intelligence, Vienna, Austria
[3]Computational and Biological Learning Lab, University of Cambridge, Cambridge, UK

Abstract

In several domains obtaining class annotations is expensive while at the same time unlabelled data are abundant. While most semi-supervised approaches enforce restrictive assumptions on the data distribution, recent work has managed to learn semi-supervised models in a non-restrictive regime. However, so far such approaches have only been proposed for linear models. In this work, we introduce semi-supervised parameter learning for Sum-Product Networks (SPNs). SPNs are deep probabilistic models admitting inference in linear time in number of network edges. Our approach has several advantages, as it (1) allows generative and discriminative semi-supervised learning, (2) guarantees that adding unlabelled data can increase, but not degrade, the performance (*safe*), and (3) is computationally efficient and does not enforce restrictive assumptions on the data distribution. We show on a variety of data sets that *safe* semi-supervised learning with SPNs is competitive compared to state-of-the-art and can lead to a better generative and discriminative objective value than a purely supervised approach.

1 INTRODUCTION

In several domains, unlabelled observations are abundant and cheap to acquire, while obtaining class labels is expensive and sometimes infeasible for large amounts of data. In such cases, semi-supervised learning can be used to exploit large amounts of unlabelled data in addition to labelled data. Examples include text [30] or image data [17, 27, 22], which are ubiquitous online, but also biological (genomics, proteomics, gene expression) data [31] and speech [28].

One of the challenges facing most semi-supervised learning approaches is scalability, many methods scale quadratically or even cubically with data set size, or require restrictive assumptions such as low dimensionality or sparsity [32, 17]. In fact, if the data violates the assumptions enforced by a learner, the use of additional unlabelled data can even degrade the classification performance.

Several approaches for semi-supervised have been proposed, including self-training, Transductive Support-Vector Machines (TSVM) [5], and graph-based methods. We refer to [32, 14] for comprehensive reviews on the state-of-the-art. As pointed out by [17], self-training is error-prone (it can reinforce poor predictions) and TSVM as well as graph-based methods are difficult to scale. In addition, TSVM, and its recent extensions [19] require that the decision boundary lie in a low density region, yielding sub-optimal accuracy if this is not met. Each of these methods can lead to decreased accuracy when adding unlabelled data. To overcome these limitations, [21] recently proposed a probabilistic formulation for *safe* semi-supervised learning of generative linear models.

In the family of deep probabilistic models, Sum-Product Networks (SPNs) [26] have recently gained popularity, due to their efficiency, i.e. linear-time inference, generality, i.e. they subsume existing approaches such as latent tree models and mixtures, and performance on various tasks including computer vision [26, 10], action recognition [2], speech [24], and language modelling [4].

For probabilistic models, including SPNs, semi-supervised learning with generative models is natural. Data points are assigned to whichever class maximizes $p(\boldsymbol{x}, y) = p(y)p(\boldsymbol{x}|y)$, with $p(\boldsymbol{x}|y)$ being a generative model for the data in class y. Subsequently, the labelled data points can be used to learn the model. Unfortunately, adding unlabelled data can significantly degrade classification accuracy instead of improving it [6].

In this paper, we introduce *safe* semi-supervised parameter learning for SPNs that is *safe*, scalable and non-restrictive. *Safe* means that adding unlabelled data can increase, but not degrade, model performance. The training time scales linearly with added data points and apart from the structure of the underlying SPN, no assumptions are made regarding the data distribution. Unlike other semi-supervised methods, the presented approach does not need low-density or clustering assumptions [3]. In addition to safety, we show competitive results when compared with state-of-the-art approaches in Section 4.

The structure of the paper is as follows: Section 2 introduces the notation used throughout the paper, describes recent approaches for parameter learning in SPNs and introduces the contrastive pessimistic likelihood estimation for *safe* semi-supervised learning of generative models. In Section 3 we propose *safe* semi-supervised learning for SPNs, give derivations for generative and discriminative parameter learning and present the algorithm MCP-SPN for training *safe* semi-supervised SPNs. Experiments are presented in Section 4 showing that *safe* semi-supervised SPNs are able to escape from degenerated supervised solutions, generally outperform purely supervised learning and achieve competitive performance on a variety of data sets. Section 5 concludes the paper and gives future prospects.

2 BACKGROUND

We use capital letters to denote random variables (RVs) and denote a set of RVs as $\boldsymbol{X} = \{X^d\}_{d=1}^D$. Moreover, we denote a realisation of a RV using lower-case letters and indicate a realisation of $\boldsymbol{X}$ using bold lower-case letters, e.g. $\boldsymbol{x} = \{x^d\}_{d=1}^D$. We denote the set of labelled observation as $\mathcal{X} = \{(\boldsymbol{x}_n, \boldsymbol{y}_n)\}_{n=1}^N$ and the set of unlabelled observation as $\mathcal{U} = \{\boldsymbol{u}_m\}_{m=1}^M$ where $\boldsymbol{x}_n$, $\boldsymbol{u}_m$ are the features and $\boldsymbol{y}_n$ the labels in one-hot-encoding. Additionally, we use $\boldsymbol{q} = \{\boldsymbol{q}_m\}_{m=1}^M$ to denote soft labels for the unlabelled observations. We generally write $p(x)$ instead of $p(X = x)$ and write $p(\boldsymbol{x})$ instead of $p(\boldsymbol{X} = \boldsymbol{x})$. For readability, we will refer to the value of an SPN using a calligraphic notation, $\mathcal{S}[\boldsymbol{x}]$, and write $S_i[\boldsymbol{x}]$ for the value of the i_{th} node in an SPN.

2.1 SUM-PRODUCT NETWORKS

SPNs are a deep probabilistic architecture which allows to capture expressive variable interactions, yet guaranteeing exact computations of marginals in linear time. SPNs have its foundation in network polynomials for efficient inference in Bayesian networks introduced by [7]. Poon and Domingos [26] generalized the idea and introduced SPNs over random variables (RVs) with finitely many states.

Definition 1. *(Sum-Product Network [26]) A sum-product network (SPN) over variables $X^1, \dots, X^d$ is a rooted directed acyclic graph whose leaves are the indicators $x^1, \dots, x^d$ and $\bar{x}^1, \dots, \bar{x}^d$ and whose internal nodes are sums and products. Each edge (i, j) emanating from a sum node i has a non-negative weight w_{ij}. The value of a product node is the product of the values of its children. The value of a sum node is $\sum_{j \in Ch(i)} w_{ij} v_j$, where $Ch(i)$ are the children of i and v_j is the value of node j. The value of an SPN $\mathcal{S}[x^1, \bar{x}^1, \dots, x^d, \bar{x}^d]$ is the value of its root.*

SPNs can be generalized by replacing the leaf node indicators with arbitrary input distributions [25]. Thus, we consider SPNs with arbitrary leaf node distributions throughout the paper.

2.1.1 Generative Learning

The parameters of an SPN can be learned efficiently using Expectation Maximisation (EM) [26, 23]. We use the formulation of [23], where the updates for the parameters of the i_{th} sum node are defined as:

$$n_{ij} = w_{ij} \sum_{n=1}^{N} \frac{1}{\mathcal{S}[\boldsymbol{x}_n]} \frac{\partial \mathcal{S}[\boldsymbol{x}_n]}{\partial S_i} S_j[\boldsymbol{x}_n], \text{ and} \tag{1}$$

$$w_{ij} \leftarrow \frac{n_{ij}}{\sum_{l \in Ch(i)} n_{il}}. \tag{2}$$

Furthermore, the parameter update for an exponential family leaf node with scope d and parameter θ is given by the expected sufficient statistic and can be computed as:

$$g_i(\boldsymbol{x}) = \frac{1}{\mathcal{S}[\boldsymbol{x}]} \frac{\partial \mathcal{S}[\boldsymbol{x}]}{\partial S_i} S_i[\boldsymbol{x}], \text{ and} \tag{3}$$

$$\theta_i \leftarrow \frac{\sum_{n=1}^N g_i(\boldsymbol{x}_n) t(x_n^d)}{\sum_{n=1}^N g_i(\boldsymbol{x}_n)}, \tag{4}$$

where $t(x)$ denotes the sufficient statistics. We assume complete evidence for the RVs $\boldsymbol{X}$ and refer to [23] for a derivation of the updates with partial evidence.

2.1.2 Discriminative Learning

The parameters of a discriminative SPN can be learned by optimising the conditional log likelihood using back-propagation [10]. The set of variables of a discriminative SPN are divided into query variables $\boldsymbol{Y}$, hidden variables $\boldsymbol{H}$ and observed RVs $\boldsymbol{X}$. Therefore, the value of a discriminative SPN is denoted as $\mathcal{S}[\boldsymbol{Y} = \boldsymbol{y}, \boldsymbol{H} = \boldsymbol{h} | \boldsymbol{X} = \boldsymbol{x}]$. Furthermore, the conditional probability is estimated by setting all indicator functions of the hidden variables to $\mathbf{1}$ and computing

$$p(\boldsymbol{y}|\boldsymbol{x}) = \frac{\mathcal{S}[\boldsymbol{Y} = \boldsymbol{y}, \boldsymbol{H} = \mathbf{1} | \boldsymbol{X} = \boldsymbol{x}]}{\mathcal{S}[\boldsymbol{Y} = \mathbf{1}, \boldsymbol{H} = \mathbf{1} | \boldsymbol{X} = \boldsymbol{x}]}, \tag{5}$$

where setting the indicators of the hidden variables to one allows the gradients of the conditional log likelihood to be computed in a single upward pass. For the sake of readability, we omit the hidden variables if their indicators are set to one and write $\mathcal{S}[\boldsymbol{y}|\boldsymbol{x}]$ for the value of a discriminative SPN instead.

Given a network structure, one can train a discriminative SPN by gradient ascent using the partial derivatives of the SPN with respect to the parameters of the network. The partial derivatives of the weights take the form

$$\frac{\partial \log p(\boldsymbol{y}|\boldsymbol{x})}{\partial w_{ij}} = \frac{1}{\mathcal{S}[\boldsymbol{y}|\boldsymbol{x}]}\frac{\partial \mathcal{S}[\boldsymbol{y}|\boldsymbol{x}]}{\partial w_{ij}} - \frac{1}{\mathcal{S}[\mathbf{1}|\boldsymbol{x}]}\frac{\partial \mathcal{S}[\mathbf{1}|\boldsymbol{x}]}{\partial w_{ij}}, \tag{6}$$

where $\frac{\partial \mathcal{S}}{\partial w_{ij}} = \frac{\partial \mathcal{S}}{\partial S_i} S_j$ is computed using back-propagation. By setting the gradient of the root node $\frac{\partial \mathcal{S}}{\partial S} = 1$, the gradients of the subsequent nodes are computed in a top-down order. At sum nodes the gradient is propagated to the children using $\frac{\partial \mathcal{S}}{\partial S_j} \leftarrow \frac{\partial \mathcal{S}}{\partial S_j} + w_{ij}\frac{\partial \mathcal{S}}{\partial S_i}$ and at product nodes using $\frac{\partial \mathcal{S}}{S_j} \leftarrow \frac{\partial \mathcal{S}}{S_j} + \frac{\partial \mathcal{S}}{\partial S_i}\prod_{l \in Ch(i)\setminus\{j\}} S_l$. As indicated, the gradient at a node j is accumulated based on the parents gradients. We refer to [10] for further details on the derivation of the gradients and derivations of *hard* gradient updates.

As in network polynomials for Bayesian networks [7], partial derivatives of any parameter in an SPN can be calculated using the chain rule, leading to a straight forward computation of parameter updates for the leaf node distributions, i.e.

$$\frac{\partial \mathcal{S}[\boldsymbol{y}|\boldsymbol{x}]}{\partial \theta} = \frac{\partial \mathcal{S}[\boldsymbol{y}|\boldsymbol{x}]}{\partial S_i}\frac{\partial p(x^d|\theta)}{\partial \theta}, \text{ and} \tag{7}$$

$$\frac{\partial \log p(\boldsymbol{y}|\boldsymbol{x})}{\partial \theta} = \frac{1}{\mathcal{S}[\boldsymbol{y}|\boldsymbol{x}]}\frac{\partial \mathcal{S}[\boldsymbol{y}|\boldsymbol{x}]}{\partial \theta} - \frac{1}{\mathcal{S}[\mathbf{1}|\boldsymbol{x}]}\frac{\partial \mathcal{S}[\mathbf{1}|\boldsymbol{x}]}{\partial \theta}. \tag{8}$$

In the case of univariate Gaussian distributions, the updates are computed by taking the partial derivatives of the mean and the variance of the distribution.

2.2 CONTRASTIVE PESSIMISTIC LIKELIHOOD ESTIMATION

Most semi-supervised learning approaches require strong assumptions, e.g. low density assumption for TSVM, and can lead to decreased performance with increasing number of unlabelled data samples if these assumptions are violated. Loog [21] has proposed Contrastive Pessimistic Likelihood Estimation (CPLE) in order to facilitate performance guarantees while only relying on the assumptions of an underlying generative model.

CPLE maintains soft labels (hypotheses) for each unlabelled data point, and assigns them pessimistically, using a training objective that maximizes the log likelihood on the data $L(\theta|\cdot)$ but minimizes the improvement provided by the unlabelled data. Therefore, CPLE yields in a *safe* semi-supervised objective.

Model parameters under CPLE are estimated according to:

$$\theta^* = \operatorname*{argmax}_{\theta \in \Theta} \arg \min_{\boldsymbol{q} \in \Delta_{K-1}^M} L(\theta|\mathcal{X}, \mathcal{U}, \boldsymbol{q}) - L(\theta^+|\mathcal{X}, \mathcal{U}, \boldsymbol{q}), \tag{9}$$

where $\boldsymbol{q}$ denotes soft labels for every unlabelled data point and θ^+ denotes the parameters of a purely supervised model derived only on $\mathcal{X}$. The introduction of soft labels, respects the fact that classes may be overlapping. In the case of K unique class labels each soft label vector $\boldsymbol{q}_m$ is an element of the $K-1$ simplex Δ_{K-1}.

Since the trained classifier assumes the worst-case improvement, its performance cannot degrade when adding unlabelled data. Loog [21] constrains the CPLE to generative models, and provides a concrete solution for a simple linear classifier based on linear discriminative analysis. In the following, we define a contrastive pessimistic objective for generative and discriminative SPNs, yielding in a *safe* semi-supervised learning procedure with linear computational complexity which only relies on the assumptions intrinsic to the given network structure.

3 SAFE SEMI-SUPERVISED SPNS

Given an SPN $\mathcal{S}[\boldsymbol{x}, \boldsymbol{y}]$ we can find the optimal parameters for generative *safe* semi-supervised learning using the CPLE objective defined in Equation (9). For clarity, we always use the plus operator to indicate parameters of the purely supervised solution, e.g. weights w^+, and indicate parameters of the *safe* semi-supervised solution using an asterisk. Due to the conservative choice of $\boldsymbol{q}$ by minimizing the improvement over the supervised result, and since we can always take $\theta^* = \theta^+$ in the worst case, this objective is guaranteed to lead to a *safe* solution. More formally, as shown in Loog [21], it is guaranteed that

$$L(\theta^*|\mathcal{X}, \mathcal{U}, \boldsymbol{q}) \geqslant L(\theta^+|\mathcal{X}, \mathcal{U}, \boldsymbol{q}). \tag{10}$$

Therefore, if log likelihoods are used in the CPLE objective the *safe* semi-supervised solution has at least the same log likelihood given $\mathcal{X}, \mathcal{U}$ and $\boldsymbol{q}$ as the purely supervised objective.

3.1 GENERATIVE SAFE SEMI-SUPERVISED LEARNING

In the following we derive the Expectation Maximisation (EM) updates for the generative *safe* semi-supervised

SPN. Therefore, let

$$\mathcal{S}[\boldsymbol{x}, \boldsymbol{y}|\theta] = \sum_{k=1}^{K} \mathbb{1}_{y_k} w_k S_k[\boldsymbol{x}|\boldsymbol{y}, \theta] \tag{11}$$

be the likelihood of a semi-supervised SPN for labelled observations $(\boldsymbol{x}, \boldsymbol{y}) \in \mathcal{X}$. We denote $\mathbb{1}_{y_k}$ to be the indicator for class k which is one if y_k is true and zero otherwise. Furthermore, let

$$\mathcal{S}[\boldsymbol{u}, \boldsymbol{q}|\theta] = \sum_{k=1}^{K} q_k w_k S_k[\boldsymbol{u}|\boldsymbol{q}, \theta] \tag{12}$$

be the likelihood of a semi-supervised SPN for unlabelled observations $(\boldsymbol{u}, \boldsymbol{q})$ with $\boldsymbol{q}$ being the soft labels of the data. Note that $\sum_k q_k = 1$ for all unlabelled observations, as each soft label vector is an element of the $K-1$ simplex. We can therefore define the generative log likelihood function of a semi-supervised SPN as the sum of the log likelihood given the labelled data and the unlabelled data. Formally, we define the generative log likelihood of a semi-supervised SPN as

$$\begin{aligned} L(\theta|\mathcal{X}, \mathcal{U}, \boldsymbol{q}) = &\sum_{n=1}^{N} \log \mathcal{S}[\boldsymbol{x}_n, \boldsymbol{y}_n|\theta] \\ &+ \sum_{m=1}^{M} \log \mathcal{S}[\boldsymbol{u}_m, \boldsymbol{q}_m|\theta] \end{aligned} \tag{13}$$

which allows for straightforward derivation of the EM updates. The updates of the weights of sum node S_i in $\mathcal{S}$ can be computed as in Eq. (2) using the following n_{ij}, i.e.

$$\begin{aligned} n_{ij} = w_{ij} &\sum_{n=1}^{N} \frac{1}{\mathcal{S}[\boldsymbol{x}_n, \boldsymbol{y}_n]} \frac{\partial \mathcal{S}[\boldsymbol{x}_n, \boldsymbol{y}_n]}{\partial S_i} S_j[\boldsymbol{x}_n|\boldsymbol{y}_n] \\ + w_{ij} &\sum_{m=1}^{M} \frac{1}{\mathcal{S}[\boldsymbol{u}_m, \boldsymbol{q}_m]} \frac{\partial \mathcal{S}[\boldsymbol{u}_m, \boldsymbol{q}_m]}{\partial S_i} S_j[\boldsymbol{u}_m|\boldsymbol{q}_m], \end{aligned} \tag{14}$$

where we omitted the parametrization of the network for better readability. Furthermore, we can update the parameters of an exponential family leaf node with scope d using the expected sufficient statistics as

$$g_i(\boldsymbol{x}_n, \boldsymbol{y}_n) = \frac{1}{\mathcal{S}[\boldsymbol{x}_n, \boldsymbol{y}_n]} \frac{\partial \mathcal{S}[\boldsymbol{x}_n, \boldsymbol{y}_n]}{\partial S_i} S_i[\boldsymbol{x}_n|\boldsymbol{y}_n], \tag{15}$$

$$g_i(\boldsymbol{u}_m, \boldsymbol{q}_m) = \frac{1}{\mathcal{S}[\boldsymbol{u}_m, \boldsymbol{q}_m]} \frac{\partial \mathcal{S}[\boldsymbol{u}_m, \boldsymbol{q}_m]}{\partial S_i} S_i[\boldsymbol{u}_m|\boldsymbol{q}_m], \tag{16}$$

$$\theta_i \leftarrow \frac{\sum_{n=1}^{N} g_i(\boldsymbol{x}_n, \boldsymbol{y}_n) t(x_n^d) + \sum_{m=1}^{M} g_i(\boldsymbol{u}_m, \boldsymbol{q}_m) t(u_m^d)}{\sum_{n=1}^{N} g_i(\boldsymbol{x}_n, \boldsymbol{y}_n) + \sum_{m=1}^{M} g_i(\boldsymbol{u}_m, \boldsymbol{q}_m)}, \tag{17}$$

where we assume complete evidence for the RVs $\boldsymbol{X}$ and $\boldsymbol{U}$.

Subsequently, the soft label for class k of an unlabelled sample m is updated pessimistically with gradient descent using the partial derivative of q_{mk} which is defined as

$$\frac{\partial L(\theta|\mathcal{X}, \mathcal{U}, \boldsymbol{q})}{\partial q_{mk}} = \frac{w_k S_k[\boldsymbol{u}_m|\boldsymbol{q}_m, \theta]}{\mathcal{S}[\boldsymbol{u}_m, \boldsymbol{q}_m|\theta]}, \text{ and} \tag{18}$$

$$\nabla q_{mk} = \frac{\partial L(\theta^*|\mathcal{X}, \mathcal{U}, \boldsymbol{q})}{\partial q_{mk}} - \frac{\partial L(\theta^+|\mathcal{X}, \mathcal{U}, \boldsymbol{q})}{\partial q_{mk}}. \tag{19}$$

Note that after each gradient update it is necessary to ensure that the soft labels for the unlabelled data points are on the $K-1$ simplex. For this purpose, the soft labels are projected back to the $K-1$ simplex using the approach by Duchi et al. [8].

3.2 DISCRIMINATIVE SAFE SEMI-SUPERVISED LEARNING

Conditional likelihoods instead of generative objectives are a more natural way of learning SPNs for classification tasks in the semi-supervised regime. Formally, the model parameters for discriminative *safe* semi-supervised SPNs are estimated according to

$$\operatorname*{argmax}_{\theta\in\Theta} \operatorname*{arg\,min}_{\boldsymbol{q}\in\Delta_{K-1}^{M}} CL(\theta|\mathcal{X}, \mathcal{U}, \boldsymbol{q}) - CL(\theta^+|\mathcal{X}, \mathcal{U}, \boldsymbol{q}), \tag{20}$$

where we intentionally use $CL(\theta|\cdot)$ to indicate the use of the conditional log likelihood. Extending the formulation for discriminative SPNs allows to define a discriminative learning approach for *safe* semi-supervised SPNs, i.e.,

$$\begin{aligned} CL(\theta|\mathcal{X}, \mathcal{U}, \boldsymbol{q}) = &\sum_{n=1}^{N} \log \mathcal{S}[\boldsymbol{y}_n|\boldsymbol{x}_n, \theta] \\ &+ \sum_{m=1}^{M} \log \mathcal{S}[\boldsymbol{q}_m|\boldsymbol{u}_m, \theta], \end{aligned} \tag{21}$$

where the conditional likelihood for labelled and unlabelled data, respectively, are given as

$$\mathcal{S}[\boldsymbol{y}|\boldsymbol{x}, \theta] = \frac{S_k[\boldsymbol{x}, \boldsymbol{y}|\theta]}{S_k[\boldsymbol{x}, \boldsymbol{1}|\theta]}, \text{ and} \tag{22}$$

$$\mathcal{S}[\boldsymbol{q}|\boldsymbol{u}, \theta] = \frac{S_k[\boldsymbol{u}, \boldsymbol{q}|\theta]}{S_k[\boldsymbol{u}, \boldsymbol{1}|\theta]}. \tag{23}$$

The partial derivatives for the weights of the discriminative semi-supervised SPN therefore become

$$\frac{\partial}{\partial w_{ij}} CL(\theta|\mathcal{X}, \mathcal{U}, \boldsymbol{q}) =$$
$$\sum_{n=1}^{N} \frac{1}{\mathcal{S}[\boldsymbol{y}_n|\boldsymbol{x}_n]} \frac{\partial \mathcal{S}[\boldsymbol{y}_n|\boldsymbol{x}_n]}{\partial w_{ij}} - \frac{1}{\mathcal{S}[\mathbf{1}|\boldsymbol{x}_n]} \frac{\partial \mathcal{S}[\mathbf{1}|\boldsymbol{x}_n]}{\partial w_{ij}}$$
$$+ \sum_{m=1}^{M} \frac{1}{\mathcal{S}[\boldsymbol{q}_m|\boldsymbol{u}_m]} \frac{\partial \mathcal{S}[\boldsymbol{q}_m|\boldsymbol{u}_m]}{\partial w_{ij}} - \frac{1}{\mathcal{S}[\mathbf{1}|\boldsymbol{u}_m]} \frac{\partial \mathcal{S}[\mathbf{1}|\boldsymbol{u}_m]}{\partial w_{ij}}. \tag{24}$$

Similarly, we can derive the partial derivatives of the leaf node parameters by applying the chain rule, leading to the following parameter updates

$$\frac{\partial}{\partial \theta} CL(\theta|\mathcal{X}, \mathcal{U}, \boldsymbol{q}) = \tag{25}$$
$$\sum_{n=1}^{N} \frac{1}{\mathcal{S}[\boldsymbol{y}_n|\boldsymbol{x}_n]} \frac{\partial \mathcal{S}[\boldsymbol{y}_n|\boldsymbol{x}_n]}{\partial \theta} - \frac{1}{\mathcal{S}[\mathbf{1}|\boldsymbol{x}_n]} \frac{\partial \mathcal{S}[\mathbf{1}|\boldsymbol{x}_n]}{\partial \theta} \tag{26}$$
$$+ \sum_{m=1}^{M} \frac{1}{\mathcal{S}[\boldsymbol{q}_m|\boldsymbol{u}_m]} \frac{\partial \mathcal{S}[\boldsymbol{q}_m|\boldsymbol{u}_m]}{\partial \theta} - \frac{1}{\mathcal{S}[\mathbf{1}|\boldsymbol{u}_m]} \frac{\partial \mathcal{S}[\mathbf{1}|\boldsymbol{u}_m]}{\partial \theta}. \tag{27}$$

To pessimistically update the soft labels, one can use gradient descent on the partial derivatives similar as for the generative objective in Eq. (19).

3.3 ALGORITHM

The algorithm Maximum Contrastive Pessimistic SPN (MCP-SPN) for learning *safe* semi-supervised SPNs is illustrated in Algorithm 1 and consists of the following adversarial steps: (1) optimising the *safe* semi-supervised solution on the given soft labels by maximising a generative or discriminative objective (2) minimising the improvement of the semi-supervised solution over the purely supervised solution by adjusting the soft labels pessimistically. As an SPN is a multi-linear function in terms of the model parameters we can apply the generalisation of the minmax theorem for multi-linear functions [16] and interchange the maximisation and the minimisation in our algorithm.

Depending on the choice of the objective, the MCP-SPN procedure first finds a purely supervised solution by only maximising the chosen objective with respect to the labelled data. Secondly, we initialise all soft labels of the unlabelled data either using an optimistic approach or using random draws from a Dirichlet distribution. In the case of a generative objective the purely supervised solution can degenerate to a point mass estimator. It is therefore useful for generative SPNs to initialise the soft labels using random draws instead of starting from an

Algorithm 1: MCP-SPN

Input: A valid SPN structure $\mathcal{S}$, labelled data $\mathcal{X}$, unlabelled data $\mathcal{U}$.
Output: Learned parameters and soft labels.

```
// learn purely supervised SPN
if generative then
  | θ+ ← argmax_{θ∈Θ} log S[x, y|θ]
else
  | θ+ ← argmax_{θ∈Θ} log S[y|x, θ]
end
// initialize soft labels
if optimistic then
  | foreach k ∈ {1, ..., K} do
  |   | q_k ← S_k[u|θ+] / S[1|u, θ+]
  | end
else
  | q ~ Dir(1/K, ..., 1/K)
end
// learn safe semi-supervised SPN
repeat
  | // optimistic parameter learning
  | if generative then
  |   | // Eq. 14 and Eq. 17
  |   | θ* ← argmax_{θ∈Θ} log S[x, y|θ] + log S[u, q|θ]
  | else
  |   | // Eq. 24 and Eq. 27
  |   | θ* ← argmax_{θ∈Θ} log S[y|x, θ] + log S[q|u, θ]
  | end
  | // pessimistic soft label adjustment
  | q ← q − α∇q                                  // Eq. 19
  | q ← projectOnSimplex(q, Δ^M_{K−1})
until convergence or early stopping
return θ* and q
```

optimistic labelling. After initialising all soft labels the MCP-SPN procedure finds a *safe* semi-supervised solution θ^* by alternating between the two adversarial steps. The function call *projectOnSimplex* refers to the approach in [8], which we use to project the soft label assignments back to the $K-1$ simplex (but other approaches for this task could also be used). Note that we found it useful to decrease the learning rate α of the pessimistic soft labels adjustment over time. In our experiments we therefore used a simple decay function $\alpha \leftarrow \alpha/\sqrt{(iteration)}$, if necessary more advanced approaches can be used instead. The source code for *safe* semi-supervised learning of SPNs is available on-line[1].

[1] https://github.com/trappmartin/SSLSPN_UAI2017

4 EXPERIMENTS

We analysed the performance of the *safe* semi-supervised learning approach qualitatively on synthetic data using the generative objective, and quantitatively on various data sets using both objectives.

4.1 Datasets and Model Generation

In addition to the synthetic two moons data set [15], we used various well known data sets from the UCI repository [20] to evaluate the performance of the *safe* semi-supervised parameter learning approaches. We preprocessed the data in the following way: (1) we removed features with zero variance, (2) we applied z-score normalisation. To ensure broad applicability of the approaches, we selected data sets which origin from a variety of domains and cover a wide range of number of samples and dimensions. Details on the selected data sets are shown in Table 1 where the last column lists the number of labelled samples used in all experiments. Note that the number of labelled samples per data set is calculated as in [21].

To consistently learn SPN structures for all experiments we extended the well-known learnSPN [11] algorithm for Gaussian distributed data, similar as in [29]. Additionally, we added a layer that conditions on the class labels resulting in structures that are suitable for supervised and semi-supervised learning [10]. As learnSPN produces large SPN structures, which might lead to over-fitting, we used a two step procedure for regularizing the resulting network. First, we estimate and apply a pruning depth of the network and secondly, we remove degenerated leaf distributions. We further ensured throughout all regularization steps that the resulting SPN is complete and decomposable.

4.2 QUALITATIVE RESULTS ON SYNTHETIC DATA

Due to the non-linearity, flexibility and complexity of SPNs with arbitrary leaf distributions, learning a *safe* semi-supervised objective for such networks, without enforcing prior assumptions on the data distribution, is much more difficult than for linear models such as Linear Discriminant Analysis (LDA) [21]. Therefore, we analysed the behaviour of *safe* semi-supervised SPNs qualitatively on the synthetic two moons data set [15]. Figure 1(a) shows the purely supervised solution for a small subset of labelled observations and the solution found using a generative *safe* semi-supervised SPN over time. For reference the oracle solution, which knows the labels of all observations, is depicted in Figure 1(b).

The purely supervised SPN clearly over-fits the few labelled examples and degenerated almost completely to a kernel density estimator. The *safe* semi-supervised parameter learning approach is initialised using soft labels drawn from a Dirichlet distribution, to allow the model to escape from the local optimum. As shown in Figure 1(c), the generative *safe* semi-supervised approach is able to find a reasonable solution after only three iterations even with a random initialisation of the soft labels. The model converges after only 20 iterations to a stable solution without enforcing restrictive assumptions on the data distribution.

Data Set	N	D	K	$2 \cdot D + K$
BUPA	345	6	2	14
Fertility	100	9	2	20
Haberman	306	3	2	8
ILPD	583	10	2	22
Ionosphere	351	34	2	70
Iris	150	4	3	11
Parkinsons	197	23	2	48
WDBC	569	32	2	66
Wine	178	13	3	29

Table 1: Datasets, details on the number of samples (N), dimensionality (D), number of classes (K) and number of labelled samples used in all evaluations ($2 \cdot D + K$). The number of labelled samples is obtained according to [21].

4.3 GENERATIVE SPN PERFORMANCE FOR SAFE SEMI-SUPERVISED LEARNING

Experimental Setup We constructed truncated network structures using learnSPN [11]. The truncation levels have been estimated using the Akaike information criterion [1]. After the structure construction we initialised all soft labels using random draws from a Dirichlet distribution with equal concentration parameter for all classes.

Furthermore, we lower bounded the variance of the leaf distributions to the ith percentile of the nearest neighbour distances of all data points in $\mathcal{X} \cup \mathcal{U}$. We selected the smallest percentile such that the constructed lower bound is above zero. Imposing a lower bound on the variances of the leaf node distributions in such way prevents the univariate Gaussian distributions from degeneration with minimal influence on the model expressiveness.

We analysed our approach for generative semi-supervised learning of SPNs by: (1) splitting each dataset into training (80%) and testing set (20%), (2) draw $2 \cdot D + K$ labelled samples stratified from each training set as proposed in [21]. We used an additional labelled validation set of $2 \cdot D + K$ samples for early stopping. In addition to

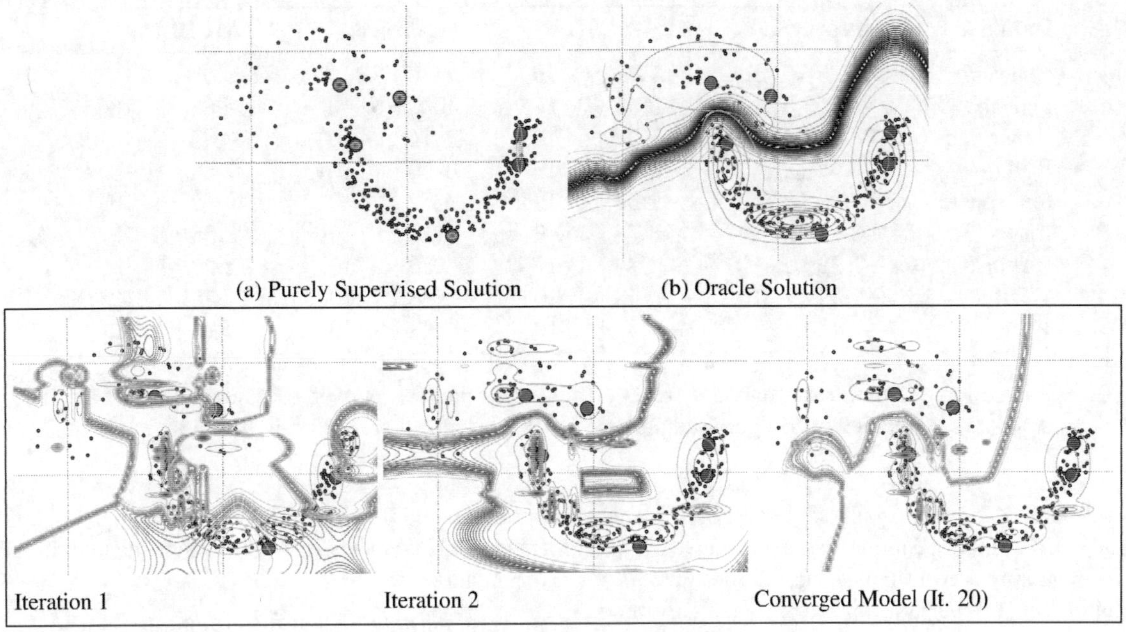

(a) Purely Supervised Solution (b) Oracle Solution

Iteration 1 Iteration 2 Converged Model (It. 20)

(c) Safe Semi-Supervised Solution

Figure 1: Qualitative results on the two moons data set. The colour of the dots indicate their class label and estimated density regions of the classes are shown using coloured density plots. Unlabelled samples are shown as small black dots. The decision boundary of the model is shown using a density plot coloured in grey. (a) Purely supervised solution over-fits the few training examples and degenerates to a point density estimator. (b) Oracle solution, (c) generative *safe* semi-supervised parameter learning is able to find a reasonable solution after only a few iterations without making restrictive assumptions on the data distribution.

the labelled samples, we used all remaining observations in the training set as unlabelled examples.

Results We compare the performance of the *safe* semi-supervised learning (SSL) approach against the purely supervised solution, an oracle solution and the solution found by the recently introduced inductive approach (MC-PLDA) [21]. All models where evaluated on the test set. The resulting average log likelihood values are estimated over 100 independent runs. Table 2 lists the average log likelihood and the standard errors of all approaches. Note that the guarantee of the CPLE is on the training set including unlabelled observations. We expect however, the performance of the SSL approach on the test set in expectation to be better or similar to the purely supervised learner.

In most cases we could indeed find an improvement of the *safe* semi-supervised approach over the purely supervised solution. In the cases of *Parkinsons*, *WDBC* and *Wine* the purely supervised learner already finds solutions which are close to the oracle solution. This might be due to the relative simple geometric properties of those data sets. In this situation, our SSL approach converged to solutions which are close to the purely supervised solution. In some cases, e.g. *BUPA*, *Fertility*, *Haberman* and *ILPD*, we could find an improvement upon the oracle solution or near oracle solution performance. Furthermore, *safe* semi-supervised SPNs generally outperform MCPLDA on almost all data sets in terms of the log likelihood, with one exception being the *Iris* data set. Moreover, our approach generally reaches very stable results and achieves estimated standard errors lower than those of the supervised and the MCPLDA solution.

4.4 DISCRIMINATIVE SPN PERFORMANCE FOR SAFE SEMI-SUPERVISED LEARNING

We assess the classification performance of discriminative *safe* semi-supervised learning below, as optimising a discriminative objective is a more natural way for classification tasks.

Experimental Setup Similar to the quantitative evaluation of the generative approach, we constructed truncated structures for all experiments. To avoid over-fitting we used early truncation of the model, estimated according to the performance on the validation set. We further initialised all soft labels using optimistic predictions from the purely supervised model. To obtain training and test

Data Set	Supervised	SSL	Oracle	MCPLDA
BUPA	$-438.75 \pm 7 \cdot 10^{0}$	$\mathbf{-7.31} \pm 6 \cdot 10^{-2}$	$-8.80 \pm 2 \cdot 10^{-1}$	$-9.07 \pm 3 \cdot 10^{-2}$
Fertility	$-3.31 \pm 3 \cdot 10^{-2}$	$\mathbf{-3.06} \pm 7 \cdot 10^{-3}$	$-3.00 \pm 6 \cdot 10^{-3}$	$-12.68 \pm 5 \cdot 10^{-2}$
Haberman	$-138.63 \pm 4 \cdot 10^{0}$	$\mathbf{-5.05} \pm 6 \cdot 10^{-2}$	$-5.14 \pm 6 \cdot 10^{-2}$	$-7.83 \pm 1 \cdot 10^{-1}$
ILPD	$-5.62 \pm 3 \cdot 10^{0}$	$\mathbf{-1.15} \pm 2 \cdot 10^{-2}$	$-1.00 \pm 1 \cdot 10^{-2}$	$-37.54 \pm 1 \cdot 10^{-1}$
Ionosphere	$-2.83 \pm 5 \cdot 10^{-2}$	$\mathbf{-1.61} \pm 1 \cdot 10^{-2}$	$-1.52 \pm 9 \cdot 10^{-3}$	$-46.12 \pm 5 \cdot 10^{-2}$
Iris	$-20.65 \pm 9 \cdot 10^{-1}$	$-3.78 \pm 3 \cdot 10^{-2}$	$-2.17 \pm 1 \cdot 10^{-2}$	$\mathbf{-2.65} \pm 5 \cdot 10^{-2}$
Parkinsons	$\mathbf{-1.32} \pm 4 \cdot 10^{-3}$	$-1.34 \pm 4 \cdot 10^{-3}$	$-1.30 \pm 2 \cdot 10^{-3}$	$-2.27 \pm 5 \cdot 10^{-2}$
WDBC	$\mathbf{-1.90} \pm 1 \cdot 10^{-3}$	$-1.93 \pm 2 \cdot 10^{-3}$	$-1.88 \pm 3 \cdot 10^{-4}$	$-10.75 \pm 1 \cdot 10^{-2}$
Wine	$\mathbf{-2.47} \pm 4 \cdot 10^{-3}$	$\mathbf{-2.47} \pm 2 \cdot 10^{-3}$	$-2.44 \pm 9 \cdot 10^{-4}$	$-15.28 \pm 2 \cdot 10^{-2}$

Table 2: Averaged log likelihood and standard errors estimated on the test set over 100 independent trials. The best results for each data set obtained by a supervised or semi-supervised model are shown in **bold** face.

sets, we followed the same approach as described for the generative experiments. Similar to the generative evaluation, the randomly drawn labelled subset is obtained from the training set and the performance of each algorithm is estimated over 100 independent trials.

Results We compared the performance of our discriminative approach against the purely supervised solution, the oracle solution and the following state of the art approaches: Transductive SVM (TSVM) [5], Minimum Entropy Regularization (MER) [13] and the recently published Implicitly Constrained Least Squares (ICLS) [18]. To assess the performance of a classification method, we computed the F_1 score for binary classification tasks. In cases of multi-class data sets, we used the macro average F_1 score. To compute multi-class predictions for approaches designed only for binary classification we used the one-vs-rest approach. The average F_1 scores as well as the standard errors of all approaches are shown in Table 3.

The *safe* semi-supervised parameter learning approach achieves competitive results for almost all data sets. In general, our approach produces reasonable results and does not degenerate if certain assumptions are not met. Moreover, in several cases our discriminative approach achieves test F_1 scores which are comparable to those of the oracle solution, e.g. for *Haberman* and *Wine*. We could find the lowest performance of our approach on the *Fertility* data set. Note that the F_1 scores on *Fertility*, *Haberman* and *ILPD* are generally very low as those are imbalanced or skewed data sets.

In general, the proposed *safe* semi-supervised learning for SPNs is a powerful adversarial approach which scales linearly in the number of samples and is non-restrictive. Even though we achieved competitive results even on data sets where low density assumptions are met, e.g. *Wine*, further improvements may be achieved by trading off optimism and pessimism. One way of approaching this issue would be to add a weighting scheme into the CPLE formulation.

Even though optimising the conditional log likelihood inside the CPLE objective provides a reasonable criterion for classification tasks, this approach does not guarantee to improve the classification performance of the learner. It is therefore possible, that better classification performance can be achieved by using a multi-class squared-hinge loss, which was recently used in a related model [12].

5 CONCLUSION AND FUTURE WORK

In this paper, we introduced the first approach for semi-supervised parameter learning with Sum-Product Networks (SPNs). We presented generative and discriminative *safe* semi-supervised learning procedures which guarantee that adding unlabelled data can increase, but not degrade, the performance of the learner on the training set. Furthermore, our approach exploits the tractability of SPNs and scales linear in the number of data points and model parameters. In contrast to other semi-supervised learners, the proposed approach is non-restrictive and does not need prior assumptions on the data distribution. The approach allows broad applicability and is a generic *safe* semi-supervised learning procedure for all models which leverage the sum-product theorem [9] and therefore provides a semi-supervised learning procedure beyond SPNs.

We investigated the performance of our approach quantitatively and qualitatively. In the conducted qualitative analysis we found that the generative *safe* semi-supervised parameter learning approach is able to a find reasonable solution after only a few iterations and is able to escape from the degenerated supervised solutions. We further compared the performance of *safe* semi-supervised parameter learning for SPNs against state-of-the-art approaches.

Data Set	Supervised	SSL	Oracle	TSVM	ICLSC	MER
BUPA	$0.41\pm1\cdot10^{-2}$	$0.40\pm1\cdot10^{-2}$	$0.48\pm5\cdot10^{-3}$	$0.36\pm2\cdot10^{-2}$	**0.47**$\pm7\cdot10^{-3}$	$0.42\pm1\cdot10^{-2}$
Fertility	$0.07\pm2\cdot10^{-2}$	$0.03\pm1\cdot10^{-2}$	$0.06\pm2\cdot10^{-2}$	$0.07\pm2\cdot10^{-2}$	$0.07\pm2\cdot10^{-2}$	**0.12**$\pm2\cdot10^{-2}$
Haber.	$0.23\pm2\cdot10^{-2}$	$0.28\pm2\cdot10^{-2}$	$0.25\pm0.$	$0.20\pm2\cdot10^{-2}$	**0.33**$\pm1\cdot10^{-2}$	$0.27\pm1\cdot10^{-2}$
ILPD	$0.17\pm2\cdot10^{-2}$	$0.20\pm1\cdot10^{-2}$	$0.24\pm4\cdot10^{-3}$	$0.23\pm2\cdot10^{-2}$	$0.29\pm1\cdot10^{-2}$	**0.33**$\pm2\cdot10^{-2}$
Ionos.	$0.79\pm4\cdot10^{-3}$	**0.82**$\pm4\cdot10^{-3}$	$0.87\pm0.$	$0.66\pm9\cdot10^{-3}$	$0.61\pm9\cdot10^{-3}$	$0.70\pm7\cdot10^{-3}$
Iris	$0.73\pm1\cdot10^{-2}$	**0.88**$\pm1\cdot10^{-2}$	$0.93\pm0.$	$0.72\pm1\cdot10^{-2}$	$0.74\pm2\cdot10^{-2}$	$0.80\pm6\cdot10^{-3}$
Parkins.	$0.72\pm1\cdot10^{-2}$	**0.77**$\pm4\cdot10^{-3}$	$0.82\pm4\cdot10^{-3}$	$0.74\pm1\cdot10^{-2}$	$0.66\pm2\cdot10^{-2}$	$0.68\pm1\cdot10^{-2}$
PID	$0.38\pm1\cdot10^{-2}$	$0.45\pm1\cdot10^{-2}$	$0.64\pm8\cdot10^{-4}$	$0.45\pm1\cdot10^{-2}$	$0.54\pm7\cdot10^{-3}$	**0.57**$\pm9\cdot10^{-3}$
WDBC	$0.85\pm3\cdot10^{-3}$	$0.90\pm2\cdot10^{-3}$	$0.92\pm3\cdot10^{-4}$	$0.91\pm4\cdot10^{-3}$	$0.88\pm4\cdot10^{-3}$	**0.92**$\pm3\cdot10^{-3}$
Wine	$0.82\pm7\cdot10^{-3}$	**0.97**$\pm2\cdot10^{-3}$	$0.97\pm4\cdot10^{-3}$	$0.96\pm2\cdot10^{-3}$	$0.95\pm7\cdot10^{-3}$	$0.95\pm9\cdot10^{-3}$

Table 3: Macro-average F1 scores estimated on the test set over 100 independent trials. The best results for each data set obtained by a supervised or semi-supervised model are shown in **bold** face.

The proposed *safe* semi-supervised learning for SPNs achieves competitive performance compared to state-of-the-art approaches, and outperformed supervised SPNs in the majority of cases. Even though our approach is non-restrictive and does not need prior assumptions on the data distribution, *safe* semi-supervised SPNs can utilise low density regions if the structure of the network reflects geometric properties of the data distribution. However, as such assumptions are not enforced in the learning procedure, our *safe* semi-supervised learner is still capable of finding decision boundaries which cross high density regions.

Future research directions include: interleaving network structure learning with semi-supervised parameter learning, extensions to other learning objectives, investigating possibilities for trading off optimism and pessimism in the objective, dealing with covariate shift and analysing instability in *safe* semi-supervised SPNs and its comparison with GANs. Furthermore, we plan to apply our *safe* semi-supervised learning approach to high-dimensional classification problems from medicine, genetics and other domains.

Acknowledgments

This research is partially funded by the Austrian Science Fund (FWF): P 27530 and P 27803-N15.

References

[1] H. Akaike. A new look at the statistical model identification. *Transactions on Automatic Control*, 19(6):716–723, 1974.

[2] M.R. Amer and S. Todorovic. Sum-product networks for modeling activities with stochastic structure. In *Proceedings of Conference on Computer Vision and Pattern Recognition (CVPR)*, pages 1314–1321, 2012.

[3] O. Chapelle, B. Schölkopf, and A. Zien. *Semi-Supervised Learning*. Adaptive computation and machine learning. MIT Press, 2006.

[4] W.C. Cheng, S. Kok, H.V. Pham, H.L. Chieu, and K.M.A. Chai. Language modeling with sum-product networks. In *Proceedings of Annual Conference of the International Speech Communication Association (Interspeech)*, pages 2098–2102, 2014.

[5] R. Collobert, F. Sinz, J. Weston, and L. Bottou. Large scale transductive svms. *Journal of Machine Learning Research*, 7:1687–1712, 2006.

[6] F. G. Cozman, I. Cohen, and M. Cirelo. Unlabeled data can degrade classification performance of generative classifiers. In *Proceedings of International Florida Artificial Intelligence Society Conference*, pages 327–331, 2002.

[7] A. Darwiche. *Modeling and reasoning with Bayesian networks*. Cambridge University Press, 2009.

[8] J. Duchi, S. Shalev-Shwartz, Y. Singer, and T. Chandra. Efficient projections onto the l 1-ball for learning in high dimensions. In *International Conference on Machine Learning (ICML)*, pages 272–279, 2008.

[9] A.L. Friesen and P. Domingos. The sum-product theorem: A foundation for learning tractable models. In *Proceedings of International Conference on Machine Learning (ICML)*, pages 1909–1918, 2016.

[10] R. Gens and P. Domingos. Discriminative learning of sum-product networks. In *Proceedings of Ad-*

vances in Neural Information Processing Systems (NIPS), pages 3248–3256, 2012.

[11] R. Gens and P. Domingos. Learning the structure of sum-product networks. *International Conference on Machine Learning (ICML)*, pages 873–880, 2013.

[12] R. Gens and P. Domingos. Compositional kernel machines. In *Proceedings of International Conference on Learning Representations*, 2017.

[13] Y. Grandvalet and Y. Bengio. Semi-supervised learning by entropy minimization. In *Proceedings of Advances in Neural Information Processing Systems (NIPS)*, pages 529–536, 2004.

[14] M.F.A. Hady and F. Schwenker. Semi-supervised learning. In *Handbook on Neural Information Processing*, pages 215–239. Springer, 2013.

[15] A. K. Jain and M. Law. Data clustering: A users dilemma. In *International Conference on Pattern Recognition and Machine Intelligence (PReMI)*, pages 1–10, 2005.

[16] B. Kalantari. Approximating nash equilibrium via multilinear minimax. *arXiv preprint*, 2016.

[17] D. P. Kingma, S. Mohamed, D. J. Rezende, and M. Welling. Semi-supervised learning with deep generative models. In *Proceedings of Advances in Neural Information Processing Systems (NIPS)*, pages 3581–3589, 2014.

[18] J. H. Krijthe and M. Loog. Implicitly constrained semi-supervised least squares classification. In *Proceedings of International Symposium on Intelligent Data Analysis*, pages 158–169, 2015.

[19] Y.F. Li and Z.H. Zhou. Towards making unlabeled data never hurt. *Transactions on Pattern Analysis and Machine Intelligence (TPAMI)*, 37(1):175–188, 2015.

[20] M. Lichman. UCI machine learning repository, 2013.

[21] M. Loog. Contrastive pessimistic likelihood estimation for semi-supervised classification. *Transactions on Pattern Analysis and Machine Intelligence (TPAMI)*, 38(3):462–475, 2016.

[22] L. Maaloe, C. K. Sonderby, S. K. Sonderby, and O. Winther. Auxiliary deep generative models. In *Proceedings of The International Conference on Machine Learning (ICML)*, pages 1445–1453, 2016.

[23] R. Peharz, R. Gens, F. Pernkopf, and P. Domingos. On the latent variable interpretation in sum-product networks. *IEEE Transactions on Pattern Analysis and Machine Intelligence (TPAMI)*, 2016.

[24] R. Peharz, G. Kapeller, P. Mowlaee, and F. Pernkopf. Modeling speech with sum-product networks: Application to bandwidth extension. In *Proceedings of IEEE International Conference on Acoustics, Speech and Signal Processing (ICASSP)*, pages 3699–3703, 2014.

[25] R. Peharz, S. Tschiatschek, F. Pernkopf, and P. Domingos. On theoretical properties of sum-product networks. In *Proceedings of International Conference on Artificial Intelligence and Statistics (AISTATS)*, pages 744–752, 2015.

[26] H. Poon and P. Domingos. Sum-product networks: A new deep architecture. In *Proceedings of Conference on Uncertainty in Artificial Intelligence (UAI)*, pages 337–346, 2011.

[27] A. Rasmus, M. Berglund, M. Honkala, H. Valpola, and T. Raiko. Semi-supervised learning with ladder networks. In *Proceedings of Advances in Neural Information Processing Systems (NIPS)*, pages 3546–3554, 2015.

[28] S. Thomas, M.L. Seltzer, K. Church, and H. Hermansky. Deep neural network features and semi-supervised training for low resource speech recognition. In *Proceedings of International Conference on Acoustics, Speech and Signal Processing (ICASSP)*, pages 6704–6708, 2013.

[29] A. Vergari, N. Di Mauro, and F. Esposito. Simplifying, regularizing and strengthening sum-product network structure learning. In *Proceedings of European Conference on Machine Learning (ECML-PKDD)*, pages 343–358, 2015.

[30] Z. Yang, W. Cohen, and R. Salakhutdinov. Revisiting semi-supervised learning with graph embeddings. In *Proceedings of International Conference on Machine Learning (ICML)*, pages 40–48, 2016.

[31] X. Zhang, N. Guan, Z. Jia, X. Qiu, and Z. Luo. Semi-supervised projective non-negative matrix factorization for cancer classification. *PloS one*, 10(9):e0138814, 2015.

[32] X. Zhu and A.B. Goldberg. Introduction to semi-supervised learning. *Synthesis lectures on artificial intelligence and machine learning*, 3(1):1–130, 2009.

Green Generative Modeling: Recycling Dirty Data using Recurrent Variational Autoencoders

Yu Wang * **Bin Dai** † **Gang Hua** ♯ **John Aston*** **David Wipf** ♯

* University of Cambridge, Cambridge, UK
† Tsinghua University, Beijing, China
♯ Microsoft Research, Beijing, China

yw323@cam.ac.uk; daib13@mails.tsinghua.edu.cn; ganghua@microsoft.com; jada2@cam.ac.uk; davidwipf@gmail.com

Abstract

This paper explores two useful modifications of the recent variational autoencoder (VAE), a popular deep generative modeling framework that dresses traditional autoencoders with probabilistic attire. The first involves a specially-tailored form of conditioning that allows us to simplify the VAE decoder structure while simultaneously introducing robustness to outliers. In a related vein, a second, complementary alteration is proposed to further build invariance to contaminated or dirty samples via a data augmentation process that amounts to recycling. In brief, to the extent that the VAE is legitimately a representative generative model, then each output from the decoder should closely resemble an authentic sample, which can then be resubmitted as a novel input ad infinitum. Moreover, this can be accomplished via special recurrent connections without the need for additional parameters to be trained. We evaluate these proposals on multiple practical outlier-removal and generative modeling tasks, demonstrating considerable improvements over existing algorithms.

1 INTRODUCTION

Autoencoders can be viewed as nonlinear generalizations of PCA, capable of producing low-dimensional representations of data lying on or near a manifold (Bengio, 2009). The model consists of two parts: an encoder which computes a low-dimensional representation, and a decoder that uses the latent representation to predict the original input. While enjoying a lengthy tenure as one of the most widely-used unsupervised learning approaches, autoencoders are not probabilistic generative models, and hence cannot be directly used to estimate new samples from some target distribution. To address this limitation (among other things), the recently popular variational autoencoder (VAE) replaces the deterministic encoder and decoder with parameterized distributions, and fits them to the data using a principled variational bound that can be optimized using stochastic gradient descent (Kingma and Welling, 2014; Rezende et al., 2014). For both model components, when applied to continuous data it is typical to assume Gaussian distributions with means and covariances computed by individual deep networks.

In addition to its role as a tractable deep generative model, we have argued in a companion work (Dai et al., 2017) that the basic VAE model is sometimes capable of handling large but relatively sparse outliers, at least provided that the decoder covariance is sufficiently complex/deep. This observation represents our launching point herein, where the goal is to explore several modifications of the canonical VAE pipeline that refine its natural ability to digest dirty, or highly corrupted data and produce a viable low-dimensional representation as though the data had been clean to begin with. To this end, we first present detailed background information regarding the basic VAE model in Section 2. We then proceed to our contributions as follows.

In Section 3 we describe a particular form of conditional autoencoder that jettisons the need for explicitly learning a complex decoder covariance model to handle inputs with gross corruptions. In brief, by conditioning on the sample indices themselves in a precise way, we are able to analytically solve for these covariances in terms of other model parameters (without the need for actually training them) leading to a significantly condensed decoder with many nice attributes related to scale invariance and local minima smoothing when removing sparse outliers.

* Y. Wang is sponsored by the EPSRC Centre for Mathematical Imaging in Healthcare, University of Cambridge, EP/N014588/1. B. Dai is finantially supported by Tsinghua University. Y. Wang and B. Dai are partially supported by sponsorship from Microsoft Research Asia.

Nevertheless, any estimation task involving contaminated samples will require a large training set to compensate, the collection and management of which may be untenable. In Section 4 we describe a novel prescription for extracting maximum utility from available data by recycling each sample after its pilgrimage through the VAE pipeline. The premise here is that, to the extent that the VAE is a truly representative generative model, then each output from the decoder should closely resemble an authentic sample, which can then be resubmitted as a novel input ad infinitum as a form of data augmentation. Training is accomplished by adding special recurrent connections to the conditional VAE described above, but no additional parameters are required.

Finally, we empirically examine the above two VAE modifications via a battery of tests in Section 5. Highlights include the ability to remove large outliers from handwritten digits and face data with far greater success than traditional VAE networks. Moreover, generated samples do not display the blurry artifacts commonly associated with the Gaussian decoder model of existing VAE models, a common criticism of this approach. In fact, even when clean training data is applied, our modified decoder model produces crisper samples for reasons we will describe later.

2 VAE BACKGROUND DETAILS

The VAE assumes that there exists a distribution $p_{\boldsymbol{\theta}}(\boldsymbol{x}) = \int p_{\boldsymbol{\theta}}(\boldsymbol{x}|\boldsymbol{z})p(\boldsymbol{z})d\boldsymbol{z}$ over some random variable $\boldsymbol{x} \in \mathbb{R}^d$ of interest, where $\boldsymbol{\theta}$ are unknown parameters that must be estimated from samples $\boldsymbol{X} = \{\boldsymbol{x}^{(i)}\}_{i=1}^n$ collected for this purpose.[1] The latent variables $\boldsymbol{z} \in \mathbb{R}^\kappa$ with agnostic prior $p(\boldsymbol{z}) = \mathcal{N}(\boldsymbol{z}; \boldsymbol{0}, \boldsymbol{I})$ are assumed to reflect a low-dimensional (i.e., $\kappa \ll d$) representation of $\boldsymbol{x}$ that characterize its elemental structure.

For non-trivial models with sufficiently rich parameterizations, the marginalization over $\boldsymbol{z}$ will be intractable and there is no closed-form solution for $\prod_i p_{\boldsymbol{\theta}}(\boldsymbol{x}^{(i)})$, which could otherwise simply be optimized via maximum likelihood. To circumvent this problem, the VAE introduces the upper bound $\mathcal{L}(\boldsymbol{\theta}, \boldsymbol{\phi}; \boldsymbol{X}) \geq -\sum_i \log p_{\boldsymbol{\theta}}(\boldsymbol{x}^{(i)})$ on the negative log-likelihood, where

$$\mathcal{L}(\boldsymbol{\theta}, \boldsymbol{\phi}; \boldsymbol{X}) \triangleq \tag{1}$$
$$-\sum_i \left\{ \log p_{\boldsymbol{\theta}}(\boldsymbol{x}^{(i)}) + \mathbb{KL}\left[q_{\boldsymbol{\phi}}\left(\boldsymbol{z}|\boldsymbol{x}^{(i)}\right) || p_{\boldsymbol{\theta}}\left(\boldsymbol{z}|\boldsymbol{x}^{(i)}\right) \right] \right\},$$

$q_{\boldsymbol{\phi}}\left(\boldsymbol{z}|\boldsymbol{x}^{(i)}\right)$ defines some arbitrary approximating distribution parameterized by $\boldsymbol{\phi}$, and $\mathbb{KL}[\cdot||\cdot]$ denotes the KL divergence between two distributions. The latter is always a non-negative quantity, which ensures that the bound is strict. In this expression, $q_{\boldsymbol{\phi}}(\boldsymbol{z}|\boldsymbol{x})$ can be interpreted as an encoder surrogate that defines a conditional distribution over the latent 'code' $\boldsymbol{z}$, while $p_{\boldsymbol{\theta}}(\boldsymbol{x}|\boldsymbol{z})$ serves as the complementary decoder model since, given a code $\boldsymbol{z}$ it quantifies the distribution over $\boldsymbol{x}$. Additionally, if we first draw random samples from $p(\boldsymbol{z})$, then the decoder can also be used to generate new samples of $\boldsymbol{x}$ for an application-specific purpose.

[1] We will use a superscript $^{(i)}$ to reference all quantities associated with the i-th sample.

By far the most common distributional assumptions for continuous data are

$$q_{\boldsymbol{\phi}}(\boldsymbol{z}|\boldsymbol{x}) = \mathcal{N}(\boldsymbol{z}; \boldsymbol{\mu}_z, \boldsymbol{\Sigma}_z), \quad p_{\boldsymbol{\theta}}(\boldsymbol{x}|\boldsymbol{z}) = \mathcal{N}(\boldsymbol{x}; \boldsymbol{\mu}_x, \boldsymbol{\Sigma}_x), \tag{2}$$

where the moments $\boldsymbol{\mu}_z$ and $\boldsymbol{\Sigma}_z$ are functions of $\boldsymbol{x}$, parameterized by $\boldsymbol{\phi}$, while $\boldsymbol{\mu}_x$ and $\boldsymbol{\Sigma}_x$ are functions of $\boldsymbol{z}$, parameterized by $\boldsymbol{\theta}$. Technically speaking then $\boldsymbol{\mu}_z \equiv \boldsymbol{\mu}_z(\boldsymbol{x}; \boldsymbol{\phi})$, $\boldsymbol{\Sigma}_z \equiv \boldsymbol{\Sigma}_z(\boldsymbol{x}; \boldsymbol{\phi})$, $\boldsymbol{\mu}_x \equiv \boldsymbol{\mu}_x(\boldsymbol{z}; \boldsymbol{\theta})$, and $\boldsymbol{\Sigma}_x \equiv \boldsymbol{\Sigma}_x(\boldsymbol{z}; \boldsymbol{\theta})$; however, for simplicity we will often omit one or both of these arguments when the intended meaning is clear from context. Additionally, the high-dimensional covariance matrix $\boldsymbol{\Sigma}_x$ (as well as sometimes $\boldsymbol{\Sigma}_z$) is typically assumed to be diagonal.

Finally, the *conditional* VAE (Sohn et al., 2015; Walker et al., 2016) represents one relevant alteration of the basic framework from above. Here we assume that our attention is shifted to the conditional distribution $p_{\boldsymbol{\theta}}(\boldsymbol{x}|\boldsymbol{y})$, where $\boldsymbol{y}$ reflects some salient observable quantity, such as a category label or state variable. Using analogous reasoning as before, given $\boldsymbol{Y} = \{\boldsymbol{y}^{(i)}\}_{i=1}^n$ the encoder and decoder distributions from the VAE upper bound are then revised via conditioning to $q_{\boldsymbol{\phi}}\left(\boldsymbol{z}|\boldsymbol{x}^{(i)}, \boldsymbol{y}^{(i)}\right)$ and $p_{\boldsymbol{\theta}}\left(\boldsymbol{x}^{(i)}|\boldsymbol{z}, \boldsymbol{y}^{(i)}\right)$ respectively, and all posterior moments include an additional dependency on $\boldsymbol{y}^{(i)}$.

3 THE iCONDITIONAL VAE AND OUTLIER ARBITRATION

Assuming the decoder covariance $\boldsymbol{\Sigma}_x$ is sufficiently complex, then its diagonal elements can potentially mirror the outlier profile in $\boldsymbol{X}$, with corrupted samples of $\boldsymbol{x}$ producing large values in the corresponding diagonal elements $[\boldsymbol{\Sigma}_x]_{jj}$, and vice versa, clean samples driving $[\boldsymbol{\Sigma}_x]_{jj}$ towards zero, sometimes provably so (Dai et al., 2017). To the extent that we believe our data emerge from such a contaminated source, the VAE represents a viable choice for nonlinear, outlier-robust dimensionality reduction or generative modeling. Of course this comes with a significant cost, namely, in practice we must actually train a complex decoder covariance model capable of detecting dirty samples. In this section we describe a convenient workaround based on the conditional VAE.

More specifically, we assume a conditional VAE where the observed latent variables are simply scalars satisfying $y^{(i)} = i$, the sample index itself, a model we refer to as the *iConditional VAE* or iC-VAE. In a broad sense, this conditioning should interject additional representational flexibility into the model since it allows each of the moment functions $\boldsymbol{\mu}_x$, $\boldsymbol{\Sigma}_x$, $\boldsymbol{\mu}_z$, and $\boldsymbol{\Sigma}_z$ to vary in form across each sample. As it turns out however, without loss of generality we may assume that $\boldsymbol{\mu}_z(\boldsymbol{x}, y; \boldsymbol{\phi}) = \boldsymbol{\mu}_z(\boldsymbol{x}; \boldsymbol{\phi})$, and $\boldsymbol{\Sigma}_z(\boldsymbol{x}, y; \boldsymbol{\phi}) = \boldsymbol{\Sigma}_z(\boldsymbol{x}; \boldsymbol{\phi})$, since given a specific sample $\boldsymbol{x}^{(i)}$, the index parameter $y^{(i)} = i$ actually provides no additional information of value, i.e., all subsequent results will ultimately hold with or without this dependency. So this particular conditioning has no impact on the effective encoder, and the KL regularization term is unaffected. We also constrain that $\boldsymbol{\mu}_x(\boldsymbol{z}, y; \boldsymbol{\theta}) = \boldsymbol{\mu}_x(\boldsymbol{z}; \boldsymbol{\theta})$, leaving the decoder mean unchanged (as discussed later in Section 3.2, this constraint may be invoked *w.l.o.g.* in certain settings anyway).

In contrast, the proposed conditioning opens a convenient entry point for side-stepping the responsibility of training a huge $\boldsymbol{\Sigma}_x$ via the following downstream effects. First, it is convenient to re-express the conditional VAE upper bound as

$$\mathcal{L}(\boldsymbol{\theta}, \boldsymbol{\phi}; \boldsymbol{X}) \equiv \sum_i \Big(\mathbb{KL}\left[q_{\boldsymbol{\phi}}\left(\boldsymbol{z}|\boldsymbol{x}^{(i)}, y^{(i)}\right) || p(\boldsymbol{z})\right] - \mathbb{E}_{q_{\boldsymbol{\phi}}(\boldsymbol{z}|\boldsymbol{x}^{(i)}, y^{(i)})}\left[\log p_{\boldsymbol{\theta}}\left(\boldsymbol{x}^{(i)}|\boldsymbol{z}, y^{(i)}\right)\right]\Big), \quad (3)$$

where given the Gaussian assumptions,

$$2\mathbb{KL}\left[q_{\boldsymbol{\phi}}\left(\boldsymbol{z}|\boldsymbol{x}, y\right) || p(\boldsymbol{z})\right] \equiv \text{tr}\left[\boldsymbol{\Sigma}_z\right] + \|\boldsymbol{\mu}_z\|_2^2 - \log|\boldsymbol{\Sigma}_z|. \quad (4)$$

Then for a single sample, and given the independence of both $\boldsymbol{\mu}_x$ as well as the encoder from $y^{(i)}$, we have

$$\begin{aligned} &-2\mathbb{E}_{q_{\boldsymbol{\phi}}(\boldsymbol{z}|\boldsymbol{x}^{(i)}, y^{(i)})}\left[\log p_{\boldsymbol{\theta}}\left(\boldsymbol{x}^{(i)}|\boldsymbol{z}, y^{(i)}\right)\right] \quad (5) \\ &= \int \left[\left(\boldsymbol{x}^{(i)} - \boldsymbol{\mu}_x\right)^\top \left(\boldsymbol{\Sigma}_x^{(i)}\right)^{-1} \left(\boldsymbol{x}^{(i)} - \boldsymbol{\mu}_x\right) + \log\left|\boldsymbol{\Sigma}_x^{(i)}\right|\right] q_{\boldsymbol{\phi}}\left(\boldsymbol{z}|\boldsymbol{x}^{(i)}\right) d\boldsymbol{z}, \end{aligned}$$

where we adopt the notation $\boldsymbol{\Sigma}_x^{(i)} \triangleq \boldsymbol{\Sigma}_x(\boldsymbol{z}, y^{(i)}; \boldsymbol{\theta}) = \boldsymbol{\Sigma}_x(\boldsymbol{z}, i; \boldsymbol{\theta})$. If for each i we can minimize

$$\left(\boldsymbol{x}^{(i)} - \boldsymbol{\mu}_x\right)^\top \left(\boldsymbol{\Sigma}_x^{(i)}\right)^{-1} \left(\boldsymbol{x}^{(i)} - \boldsymbol{\mu}_x\right) + \log\left|\boldsymbol{\Sigma}_x^{(i)}\right| \quad (6)$$

over $\boldsymbol{\Sigma}_x^{(i)}$ independently for all values of $\boldsymbol{z}$, then we will necessarily also minimize (5). Fortunately this is possible if we grant $\boldsymbol{\Sigma}_x^{(i)}$ unlimited capacity to represent any function and knowledge of i as allowed by conditioning. Hence taking derivatives of (6) with respect to $\boldsymbol{\Sigma}_x^{(i)}$, equating to zero and solving, we find that the optimal covariance, when forced to be diagonal (the default assumption used with VAE models as mentioned previously) is given by

$$\text{diag}\left[\boldsymbol{\Sigma}_x(\boldsymbol{z}, i; \boldsymbol{\theta})\right] = \left(\boldsymbol{x}^{(i)} - \boldsymbol{\mu}_x\right)^2, \quad (7)$$

where the squaring operator is understood to apply element-wise, and diag$[\cdot]$ converts vector-valued inputs to a diagonal matrix, and square matrix-valued inputs to a vector formed from the diagonal (e.g., as defined in the Matlab computing environment). Plugging this value back into (5) and ignoring constants we find that the overall VAE objective reduces to

$$\mathcal{L}(\boldsymbol{\theta}, \boldsymbol{\phi}; \boldsymbol{X}) \equiv \sum_i \left\{ \text{tr}\left[\boldsymbol{\Sigma}_z^{(i)}\right] - \log\left|\boldsymbol{\Sigma}_z^{(i)}\right| + \|\boldsymbol{\mu}_z^{(i)}\|_2^2 + 2\sum_j \mathbb{E}_{q_{\boldsymbol{\phi}}(\boldsymbol{z}|\boldsymbol{x}^{(i)})}\left[\log\left|x_j^{(i)} - \mu_{x_j}\right|\right] \right\}, \quad (8)$$

where $\boldsymbol{\mu}_z^{(i)} \triangleq \boldsymbol{\mu}_z(\boldsymbol{x}^{(i)}; \boldsymbol{\phi})$ and $\boldsymbol{\Sigma}_z^{(i)} \triangleq \boldsymbol{\Sigma}_z(\boldsymbol{x}^{(i)}; \boldsymbol{\phi})$. Therefore, although a potentially high capacity $\boldsymbol{\Sigma}_x$ in the original VAE model is needed to arrive at something even approximating (8), the net effect of this assumption can lead to a dramatic overall simplification.

Furthermore, from this expression we observe that what was once effectively a quadratic penalty on the errors $x_j^{(i)} - \mu_{x_j}$ is now replaced with a $\log(\cdot)^2$ term, which as a concave non-decreasing function (Palmer et al., 2006), heavily favors $x_j^{(i)} - \mu_{x_j} \to 0$, while at the same time applying only soft penalization for large values. Such a regularization effect is the cornerstone of sparse estimation algorithms, and hence we may expect that this construction will ultimately be useful for the removal of large yet sparse outliers. Additionally, this regularizer can be viewed as the negative logarithm of the Jeffreys prior on the squared errors, with a number of notable advantages described next.

3.1 CHARACTERISTICS OF THE JEFFREYS DISTRIBUTION

As a non-informative prior for quantities such as error variances (Berger, 1985), the Jeffreys distribution $p(e) \propto \frac{1}{e}$ (which as an improper prior does not integrate to one) displays a unique form of scale invariance. In particular, the probability that an error $e = (x - \mu_x)^2$ is between 1 and 10, equals the probability that it is within 10 and 10^2, or equivalently, between 10^{-2} and 10^{-1}. More generally, the probability that e is within any scaling window is given by $P\left(e \in \left[\eta^k, \eta^{k+1}\right]\right) \propto \log\eta$ for any scale factor $\eta \geq 1$ and any integer k (positive or negative). Therefore outlier arbitration is carried out equally regardless of how any particular data set or network output is scaled.

In contrast, other selections would require special tuning to align with a scale-appropriate range of the distribution. For example, although robust ℓ_p-norm-based penalties $\sum_j e_j^{p/2}$, $p \leq 1$ (which can be derived from a generalized Gaussian distribution) also discount large errors/outliers (Rao et al., 2003), their behavior will be highly dependent on the scale at which outliers are differentiated from inliers, meaning that data in the $[10, 10^2]$ range will be treated very differently than data in the $[10^{-2}, 10^{-1}]$ range.

But there is a dark side to the aggregate $\log(\cdot)^2$ penalty arising from the Jeffreys distribution if applied in the context of a traditional autoencoder, the latter of which emerges if we fix $\boldsymbol{\Sigma}_z = \mathbf{0}$ in the VAE framework and remove the now undefined KL term. Simply put, this penalty will introduce a combinatorial constellation of locally minimizing solutions owing to the infinite regress as any $\left(x_j^{(i)} - \mu_{x_j}\right)^2$ meanders towards zero. In fact, just a single site with $\left(x_j^{(i)} - \mu_{x_j}\right)^2 \approx 0$ can drive the objective towards minus infinity, regardless of the quality of the overall reconstruction at other locations. Hence the energy landscape will be plagued with a combinatorial number of degenerate, infinitely deep extrema.

Fortunately, within the iC-VAE framework, the Jeffreys-based penalty occurs inside of an expectation operator, which smooths over these degenerate pits.[2] However there exists an important exception: if the covariance $\boldsymbol{\Sigma}_z^{(i)}$ becomes degenerate, e.g., $\boldsymbol{\Sigma}_z^{(i)} \to \varepsilon \boldsymbol{I}$ with ε approaching zero, then $q_{\boldsymbol{\phi}}\left(\boldsymbol{z}|\boldsymbol{x}^{(i)}\right) \approx \delta\left(\boldsymbol{\mu}_z^{(i)}\right)$ and

$$\mathbb{E}_{q_{\boldsymbol{\phi}}(\boldsymbol{z}|\boldsymbol{x}^{(i)})}\left[\log\left|x_j^{(i)} - \mu_{x_j}\right|\right] \approx \log\left|x_j^{(i)} - \mu_{x_j}^{(i)}\right|, \tag{9}$$

where $\mu_{x_j}^{(i)} \triangleq \mu_{x_j}\left(\boldsymbol{\mu}_z^{(i)}; \boldsymbol{\theta}\right)$. But the $-\log\left|\boldsymbol{\Sigma}_z^{(i)}\right|$ term in (8) will normally prevent this from happening since any $\boldsymbol{\Sigma}_z^{(i)} \to \varepsilon \boldsymbol{I}$ would have a large, counteracting positive contribution. Roughly speaking then, within the VAE framework, the only way we can ever encounter degeneracies introduced by the Jeffreys distribution is if

$$\sum_{j=1}^{d} \mathcal{I}\left[\left(x_j^{(i)} - \mu_{x_j}^{(i)}\right)^2 < \varepsilon\right] > \sum_{k=1}^{\kappa} \mathcal{I}\left[s_k\left(\boldsymbol{\Sigma}_z^{(i)}\right) < \varepsilon\right] \tag{10}$$

where $\mathcal{I}[\cdot]$ is and indicator function and $s_k(\cdot)$ returns the k-th singular value of a matrix.[3] In this situation, the higher dimensionality of the data fit term could outweigh the KL regularizer leading to the collapsed situation under review. But the KL regularization from the VAE framework still provides a valuable service by confining these degeneracies to special cases, and these special cases may be desirable solution points to begin with since they often represent a configuration whereby most data are fit snugly, except for a few exceptions that likely correspond with outlier locations. We will discuss this further in the next section with a more concrete example. Additionally, further details about how the VAE (and the iC-VAE by inheritance) smooths away bad degenerate solutions, favoring data fit errors exactly aligned with true outlier locations, can be found in (Dai et al., 2017).

3.2 iCONDITIONAL VAE WITH AFFINE DECODER MEAN

After optimizing $\boldsymbol{\Sigma}_x$ away as described previously, for analysis purposes in this section we consider the case where $\boldsymbol{\mu}_x$ is restricted to be affine, while the encoder moments can have potentially infinite capacity. Although the affine-constrained $\boldsymbol{\mu}_x$ with full conditional plumage would be given by $\boldsymbol{\mu}_x(\boldsymbol{z}, y; \boldsymbol{\theta}) = \boldsymbol{W}\boldsymbol{z} + \boldsymbol{h}y + \boldsymbol{b}$, where $\{\boldsymbol{W}, \boldsymbol{h}, \boldsymbol{b}\} \subset \boldsymbol{\theta}$ represent parameters to learn, it can be shown that in fact the optimal value for $\boldsymbol{h}$ is typically zero. We therefore choose to omit this extra factor consistent with earlier assumptions and ease of presentation.

Even with the affine assumption however, the expectation in (8) remains intractable, compromising further direct analysis. Fortunately though we can construct a more transparent upper bound that both retains important properties of (8) while simultaneously lending itself to more detailed inquiry.

Proposition 1 *Assume that $\boldsymbol{\mu}_x(\boldsymbol{z}, y; \boldsymbol{\theta}) = \boldsymbol{\mu}_x(\boldsymbol{z}; \boldsymbol{\theta}) = \boldsymbol{W}\boldsymbol{z} + \boldsymbol{b}$, while $\boldsymbol{\mu}_z(\boldsymbol{x}, y; \boldsymbol{\phi}) = \boldsymbol{\mu}_z(\boldsymbol{x}; \boldsymbol{\phi})$ and $\boldsymbol{\Sigma}_z(\boldsymbol{x}, y; \boldsymbol{\phi}) = \boldsymbol{\Sigma}_z(\boldsymbol{x}; \boldsymbol{\phi})$ are capable via some internal parameter arrangement of representing any function (infinite capacity). Then given $y^{(i)} = i$, a strict upper-bound on the conditional VAE objective from (8) is given by*

$$\sum_i h^{(i)}(\boldsymbol{W}, \boldsymbol{b}) \geq \mathcal{L}(\boldsymbol{\theta}, \boldsymbol{\phi}; \boldsymbol{X}), \tag{11}$$

where $h^{(i)}(\boldsymbol{W}, \boldsymbol{b}) \triangleq$

$$\inf_{\boldsymbol{\Lambda}^{(i)} \succ \mathbf{0}} \left(\boldsymbol{x}^{(i)} - \boldsymbol{b}\right)^\top \left(\boldsymbol{\Psi}^{(i)}\right)^{-1} \left(\boldsymbol{x}^{(i)} - \boldsymbol{b}\right) + \log\left|\boldsymbol{\Psi}^{(i)}\right|, \tag{12}$$

$\boldsymbol{\Psi}^{(i)} \triangleq \boldsymbol{\Lambda}^{(i)} + \boldsymbol{W}\boldsymbol{W}^\top$, $\boldsymbol{\Lambda}^{(i)} = diag[\boldsymbol{\lambda}^{(i)}]$, and $\boldsymbol{\lambda}^{(i)} \in \mathbb{R}_+^d$ represents a vector of non-negative variational parameters for each i.

There are several important consequences of this result. First, it is not actually required that $\boldsymbol{\mu}_z$ and $\boldsymbol{\Sigma}_z$ have infinite capacity for Proposition 1 to hold. In reality, we only require that much more lenient *stationarity conditions* are satisfied (these emerge from the proof construction; see supplementary). Secondly, assuming centered data or $\boldsymbol{b} = \mathbf{0}$, then the upper bound from (11) corresponds

[2]Note that $\int_{0+}^{\infty} \log u^2 \cdot p(u)du$ is finite and well-behaved when $p(u)$ is a Gaussian distribution, analogous to the last term in (8).

[3]It is also possible to have trivial degeneracies when other subtle technical conditions occur (e.g., a constant decoder mean function fit to a single sample), but such situations are unlikely to substantially influence practical problems and we will defer such considerations to a longer journal version.

with a robust PCA model from (Wipf, 2012) derived using completely different principles tied to convex analysis and Fenchel duality theory (Boyd and Vandenberghe, 2004). This model is designed to decompose a data matrix $\boldsymbol{X}$ via $\boldsymbol{X} = \boldsymbol{L} + \boldsymbol{S}$, where $\boldsymbol{L}$ is a low-rank term, reflecting principal subspaces, and $\boldsymbol{S}$ represents sparse errors or outliers, i.e., a matrix with many zero-valued elements and some possibly large corruptions. So we have tied an established probabilistic robust PCA algorithm directly to a specific conditional VAE model, with the latter inheriting any useful properties of the former, which is decidedly more transparent and devoid of intractable integrals. Thirdly, if both

$$\boldsymbol{x}^{(i)} - \boldsymbol{b} \in \text{span}\left[\boldsymbol{\Psi}^{(i)}\right] \text{ and } \text{rank}\left[\boldsymbol{\Psi}^{(i)}\right] < d, \quad (13)$$

then $h^{(i)}(\boldsymbol{W}, b)$ will be unbounded from below, since the quadratic term can be held fixed at a finite value while the log-det term is driven to minus infinity. Moreover, because $\sum_i h^{(i)}(\boldsymbol{W}, \boldsymbol{b})$ is an upper bound on both the conditional VAE objective, as well as ultimately $-\log p_{\boldsymbol{\theta}}(\boldsymbol{x}|y)$ by design, this result then implies that infinite negative peaks exist in the original conditional distribution at data points $\boldsymbol{x}^{(i)}$ that can be well-represented by *fewer* than d degrees of freedom. Note that *any* $\boldsymbol{x} \in \mathbb{R}^d$ can be trivially represented using d degrees of freedom. However, degeneracies in the iC-VAE only occur when the degrees of freedom κ from the implicit inlier model, combined with the number of sparse errors, i.e., $\|\boldsymbol{\lambda}^{(i)}\|_0 \equiv \text{rank}\left[\boldsymbol{\Psi}^{(i)}\right] - \kappa$, is less than d.[4] This will be a desirable degeneracy to the extent that we seek parsimonious data representations, and is unlikely to occur with samples that do not conform to a robust PCA-like model. Please see (Dai et al., 2017) for more comprehensive analysis of general VAE models and their connection with robust PCA and outlier removal.

4 RECYCLING DIRTY DATA BY ADDING RECURRENCIES

Although the iC-VAE model on its own has merits in dealing with contaminated data, there is no substitute for a rich set of training samples if any clean low-dimensional representation is ultimately to be found. In this section we describe a simple, practical procedure for creating additional, virtual samples by recycling the VAE output via recurrent connections. The initial intuition here is straightforward: *if the VAE has accurately captured the true generative process, then output samples should be indistinguishable from input samples*, or at least a subset of input samples correlated with the initial seed sample. And if this is indeed the case, then outputs repeatedly fed back through the VAE encoder and decoder networks should produce a sequence of valid samples. In contrast, divergence of this sequence would suggest the accumulation of significant deviations from the true generative process.

[4]Here $\|\cdot\|_0$ refers to the ℓ_0 norm, or a count of the number of nonzero elements.

Overall, this recurrent structure serves as a form of automatic data augmentation. The network has technically "seen" a wider range of training data, since each partially corrected sample, or perturbed inlier sample, can be viewed as a new input containing attributes not found in the original training data. This includes samples where only a portion of the outliers have been removed, implying that the network will be forced to deal with a much larger breadth of corrupted support patterns. And crucially, the iC-VAE objective is applied to each recurrent loop, leading to an overall process we refer to as a *recurrent* iC-VAE or RiC-VAE.

4.1 BASIC MODEL DETAILS

To begin, although the integrals embedded in the iC-VAE cost $\mathcal{L}(\boldsymbol{\theta}, \boldsymbol{\phi}; \boldsymbol{X})$ cannot be computed in closed form, the simple stochastic approximation

$$\mathbb{E}_{q_{\boldsymbol{\phi}}(\boldsymbol{z}|\boldsymbol{x}^{(i)})}\left[\log\left|x_j^{(i)} - \mu_{x_j}\right|\right] \approx \log\left|x_j^{(i)} - \mu_{x_j}\left(\boldsymbol{z}^{(i)}\right)\right| \quad (14)$$

has been shown to be a suitable substitute (Kingma and Welling, 2014; Rezende et al., 2014) for the original VAE, where $\boldsymbol{z}^{(i)}$ is a sample drawn from $q_{\boldsymbol{\phi}}\left(\boldsymbol{z}|\boldsymbol{x}^{(i)}\right)$. Using a reparameterization trick, every $\boldsymbol{z}^{(i)}$ can be constructed such that gradients with respect to $\boldsymbol{\mu}_z$ and $\boldsymbol{\Sigma}_z$ can be propagated through the righthand side of (14). This involves drawing a sample $\boldsymbol{\epsilon}^{(i)}$ from $\mathcal{N}(\boldsymbol{\epsilon}; \boldsymbol{0}, \boldsymbol{I})$ and then computing $\boldsymbol{z}^{(i)} = \boldsymbol{\mu}_z^{(i)} + \left(\boldsymbol{\Sigma}_z^{(i)}\right)^{\frac{1}{2}} \boldsymbol{\epsilon}^{(i)}$. See (Kingma and Welling, 2014; Rezende et al., 2014) for more details.

To avoid later confusion, we now redefine our original data as $\boldsymbol{X}_1 = \left\{\boldsymbol{x}_1^{(i)}\right\}_{i=1}^n \equiv \boldsymbol{X}$, where the context of the new subscript '1' will soon become apparent. Likewise we adopt $\boldsymbol{z}_1^{(i)} \equiv \boldsymbol{z}^{(i)}$ for the latent samples described above. Given a specific $\boldsymbol{x}_1^{(i)}$, the basic iC-VAE model will compute the posterior mean $\boldsymbol{\mu}_{x_1}^{(i)} = \boldsymbol{\mu}_x\left(\boldsymbol{z}_1^{(i)}\right)$ via one pass through the network structure. Moreover, by applying (7) we can extract the companion covariance $\text{diag}\left[\boldsymbol{\Sigma}_{x_1}^{(i)}\right] = \left(\boldsymbol{x}_1^{(i)} - \boldsymbol{\mu}_{x_1}^{(i)}\right)^2$ at this same point. From these two moments, we may then draw a new sample $\boldsymbol{x}_2^{(i)}$ from $\mathcal{N}\left(\boldsymbol{x}; \boldsymbol{\mu}_{x_1}^{(i)}, \boldsymbol{\Sigma}_{x_1}^{(i)}\right)$. Continuing this process across all $i = 1, \ldots, n$, we obtain a new dataset $\boldsymbol{X}_2$.

This operation can be repeated N times, effectively producing a set $\widetilde{\boldsymbol{X}} \triangleq \{\boldsymbol{X}_k\}_{k=1}^N$ of separate datasets, with N

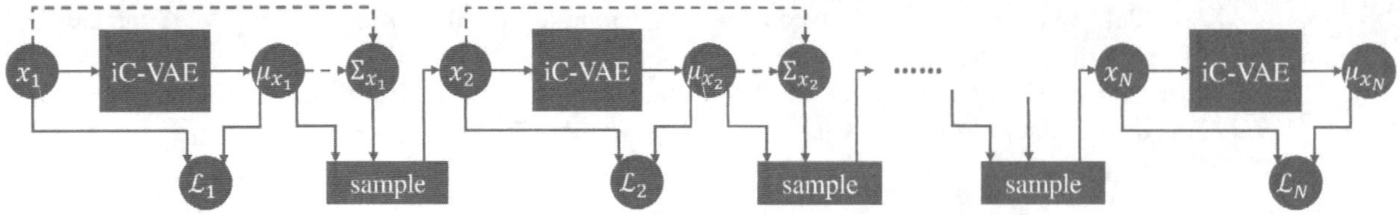

Figure 1: Structure flow of the RiC-VAE network (sample indices $^{(i)}$ are omitted for simplicity). Solid lines indicate paths in which gradients are backpropagated during training, and $\mathcal{L}_k$ indicates the penalty $\mathcal{L}(\boldsymbol{\theta}, \boldsymbol{\phi}; \boldsymbol{X}_k)$. Initial data sample $\boldsymbol{x}_1$ passes through the iC-VAE and produces $\boldsymbol{\mu}_{x_1}$. Using (7) the attendant diagonal covariance $\boldsymbol{\Sigma}_{x_1}$ is also computed. A new $\boldsymbol{x}_2$ is then drawn from $\mathcal{N}\left(\boldsymbol{x}; \boldsymbol{\mu}_{x_1}, \boldsymbol{\Sigma}_{x_1}\right)$ and the process repeats. More details in the supplementary.

times the total number of samples eventually being seen by the network, albeit $N-1$ of these are recycled virtual samples. Nonetheless, these datasets can be used simultaneously during training via the process defined in Figure 1. Importantly, after each pass we include the same iC-VAE objective function applied to the respective recycled data $\boldsymbol{X}_k$, which acts as a form of deep supervision (Lee et al., 2015), giving the overall RiC-VAE cost

$$\mathcal{L}_N(\boldsymbol{\theta}, \boldsymbol{\phi}; \widetilde{\boldsymbol{X}}) \triangleq \sum_{k=1}^{N} \mathcal{L}(\boldsymbol{\theta}, \boldsymbol{\phi}; \boldsymbol{X}_k). \tag{15}$$

By penalizing (15), all the iC-VAE units in Figure 1 are effectively forced to shared the same $\boldsymbol{\theta}$, $\boldsymbol{\phi}$, and hence the overall number of parameters remains unaltered.

4.2 CONNECTIONS WITH ITERATIVE REWEIGHTED COMPRESSIVE SENSING ALGORITHMS

In the spirit of learning-to-learn (Andrychowicz et al., 2016), learning-to-optimize (Li and Malik, 2016), and other recent attempts to replace or augment conventional iterative algorithms with deep networks estimated from training data (Sprechmann et al., 2015; Hershey et al., 2014; Xin et al., 2016), the proposed RiC-VAE framework can be viewed as an unfolded iterative algorithm with many trainable parameters. As an illustrative example, consider the family of iterative reweighted ℓ_1 norm minimization algorithms (IR-ℓ_1) recently developed for sparse estimation and compressive sensing (Candès et al., 2008). Here the objective is to minimize some function $f(\boldsymbol{x})$ that reflects a structured regression task. We now provide a reinterpretation of this approach in the context of the RiC-VAE.

Provided some initial guess $\boldsymbol{x}^0$, the IR-ℓ_1 algorithm proceeds to iteration $t+1$ via two steps:

$$\begin{aligned} \boldsymbol{z}^{t+1} &\leftarrow g\left(\boldsymbol{x}^t; \boldsymbol{A}\right), \\ \boldsymbol{x}^{t+1} &\leftarrow \arg\min_{\boldsymbol{x}} \|\boldsymbol{u} - \boldsymbol{A}\boldsymbol{x}\|_2^2 + \sum_j z_j^{t+1}|x_j|, \end{aligned} \tag{16}$$

where $\boldsymbol{A}$ is a matrix of feature vectors and $\boldsymbol{u}$ is a signal we would like to represent. Here g plays the role of an arbitrary encoder model, sometimes parameterized by $\boldsymbol{A}$ (Wipf and Nagarajan, 2010), that computes a set of weights (or latent variables) $\boldsymbol{z}$. However, given that g is handcrafted in an application-specific manner, often based on gradients of some heuristically chosen sparsity penalty with no clear guidelines on the optimal choice, we might expect that a learned replacement would afford some benefit. Either way, once computed $\boldsymbol{z}^{t+1}$ is used to create a weighted ℓ_1 norm penalty term that is later optimized by a decoder-like step to update $\boldsymbol{x}^{t+1}$. It has been shown that related tasks can be implemented via a DNN-like structure (He et al., 2017), and therefore again, it is reasonable to consider replacing this inner-loop optimization step, which could be computationally expensive, with a trainable decoder module.

Additionally, when we interpret $\{\boldsymbol{A}, \boldsymbol{u}\} \equiv \boldsymbol{y}$ as additional observable latent variables, then a single iteration of (16) accurately maps to a form of handcrafted conditional VAE, strengthening the overall analogy further. And of course in both cases, the incentive to iterate this process is significant. As we will later observe in Section 5, the empirical behavior of our RiC-VAE model subject to multiple recurrent loops mirrors the improvement seen by IR-ℓ_1 algorithms. In both cases, initial iterations focus on localizing the support pattern of the largest components/outliers, and later iterations refine these solutions. So there is no longer any need for a first pass through the VAE to provide a perfect screening.

5 EXPERIMENTAL RESULTS

Training data are not always perfect. Instead of selecting clean images manually, our RiC-VAE is able to recycle dirty data into useful samples. In this section, we demonstrate the advantage brought about by this ability applied to generative tasks and outlier removal problems. Throughout we use N to refer to the number of RiC-VAE passes/recurrencies used during *training*, as distinguished from M, the number of RiC-VAE passes applied at *test* time, or when generating new samples. These need not always be the same given that a learned model can be iterated for any number of passes. We use RiC-VAE(N,M) to describe the generic case, which implies

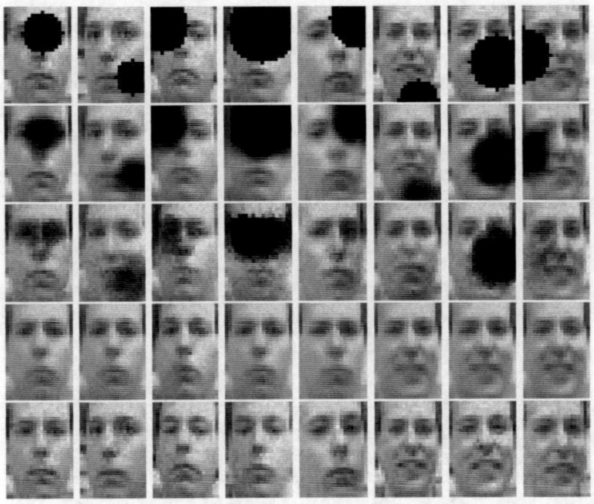

Figure 2: Visualization of recovery results on Frey face data. 1179 of the 1965 images (60%) were corrupted by a randomly positioned dark circle mark with random radius. Each column corresponds to a different database image. *Row 1*: Original contaminated samples. *Row 2*: Reconstructed images using RPCA. *Row 3*: Reconstructed images using an iC-VAE (no recycling). *Row 4*: Reconstructed image from an RiC-VAE(N=2,M=2). *Row 5*: Clean ground truth data without contamination.

that iC-VAE equals RiC-VAE(N=1,M=1).

5.1 EVALUATION OF AFFINE iC-VAE BASELINE

The Google-30 data (Liu et al., 2014) includes images returned from 30 different search queries, with roughly 500 images collected per concept. Human labelers then determine which of these are relevant, and which are considered as outliers or irrelevant. This data has been recently used to assess various unsupervised outlier detection algorithms, where the labels themselves are only used for evaluation purposes (Liu et al., 2014; Xia et al., 2015). We adopt a similar experimental design; however, because the number of samples per query is relatively small, we restrict ourselves to a simple affine iC-VAE model. Regardless, the Google-30 data still provides a useful benchmark for evaluating such a baseline upon which the RiC-VAE ultimately depends.

We learn a affine iC-VAE-based model for each search query, and then predict outliers using the thresholding heuristic from applied to residuals from (Xia et al., 2015). We also assume that $d = \kappa$, meaning that the iC-VAE must automatically learn any latent low-dimensional structure via its natural regularization process (no tuning of the latent dimension is required). F1 scores from this procedure averaged across all 30 search queries are shown in Table 1 along side results from two state-of-the-art approaches: a kernel-based max-margin algorithm called UOCL from (Liu et al., 2014), and

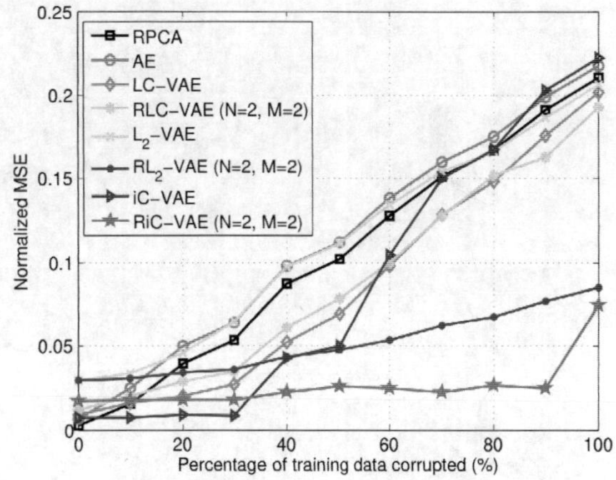

(a) Reconstruction MSE on Frey face training data.

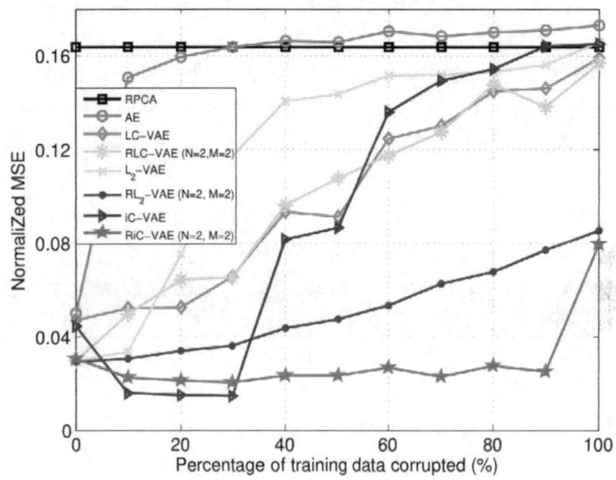

(b) Reconstruction MSE on novel test images.

Figure 3: Evaluation of reconstruction MSE

a autoencoder-based pipeline DRAE from (Xia et al., 2015). Although admittedly these results do not highlight the full flexibility of the RiC-VAE, they nonetheless support the iC-VAE as a viable building block or starting point.

Table 1: Outlier detection accuracy on Google-30 data.

Method	UOCL	DRAE	iC-VAE
Average F1 scores	0.826	0.849	**0.874**

5.2 RiC-VAE OUTLIER REMOVAL PERFORMANCE

Recovery of clean training data: The Frey face dataset (Rezende et al., 2014) includes 1965 images, each of size 28×20. We selectively contaminate these images to varying degree using a randomly positioned dark circle mark with random radius. We vary the percentage of training images corrupted in this way, and compare the ability of 8 different models to recover the original, clean face images given only the contaminated source. These include: (a) a convex robust PCA (RPCA) approach from (Candès et al., 2011) often applied to this problem (Elhamifar and Vidal, 2013), (b) a conventional

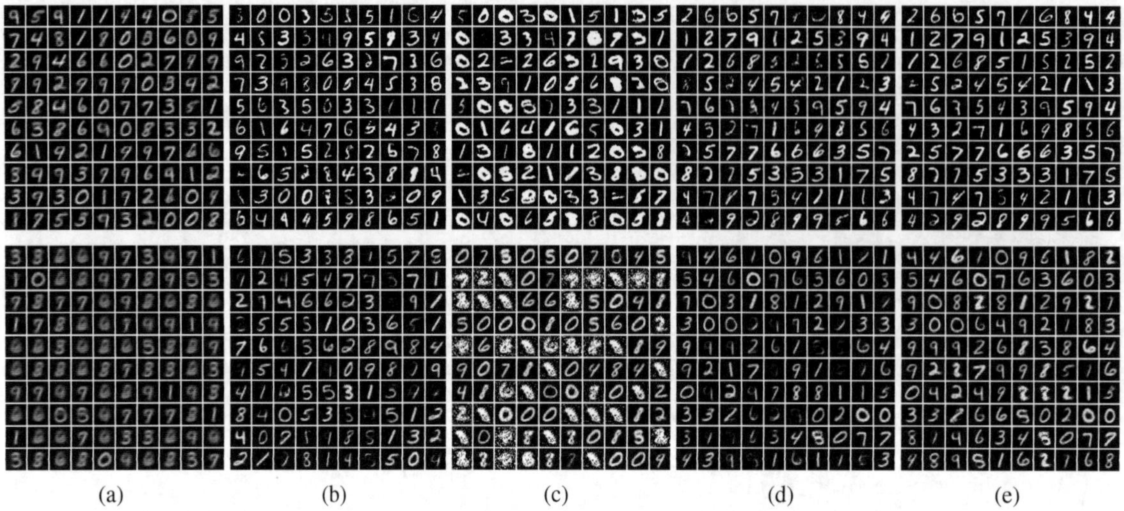

Figure 4: Samples generated from VAE models trained on MNIST data (please zoom for better viewing). *Top Row*: Results using clean training data. *Bottom Row*: Results using noisy training data. *Columns*: Samples generated from (a) ℓ_2-VAE, (b) iC-VAE, (c) RiC-VAE(N=1,M=20), (d) RiC-VAE(N=5,M=1), and (e) RiC-VAE(N=5,M=20).

autoencoder (AE), (c) an ℓ_2-VAE, meaning a standard VAE with fixed decoder covariance $\boldsymbol{\Sigma}_x = \boldsymbol{I}$ as is most commonly assumed (Doersch, 2016), (d) a recurrent ℓ_2-VAE denoted Rℓ_2-VAE(N=2,M=2), i.e., analogous to RiC-VAE(N=2,M=2) but with fixed decoder covariance, (e) a standard VAE with the a learned decoder covariance called LC-VAE, (f) a recurrent LC-VAE version denoted RLC-VAE(N=2,M=2), (g) an iC-VAE, (h) a RiC-VAE(N=2,M=2). For all VAE models, we use $\kappa = 10$ and a common 3-layer encoder/decoder network structure, with details deferred to the supplementary file. Additionally, all VAE and AE networks share common DNN structures with the exception of different loss layers as stated, and only the VAE has encoder/decoder covariance functions and KL terms.

Figure 2 qualitatively illustrates the advantage of the multiple data passes/recycling leveraged by the RiC-VAE at an image corruption level of 60%. In fact, even with huge contaminations (e.g., 4th and 7th columns), the RiC-VAE is still able to reconstruct salient facial details. Moreover, the initial iC-VAE estimate only partially removes the corrupted region, analogous to how initial iterations of IR-ℓ_1 algorithms only partially recovery outlier support patterns as discussed in Section 4.2. Complementary quantitative results are presented in Figure 3(a) for all algorithms. Here we observe that traditional methods (i.e., RPCA, AE, ℓ_2-VAE, LC-VAE) do not produce competitive results, and RLC-VAE exhibits no advantage over LC-VAE since, not surprisingly, learning decoder covariances destabilizes the recycling process. The iC-VAE is adequate at low corruption levels but starts to breaks down above 30%. In contrast, while the Rℓ_2-VAE(N=2,M=2) exploits our proposed recycling strategy, without the iC-VAE base network its performance cannot match the RiC-VAE.

Recovery of a new test set: We also generated a new test dataset by changing the dirty pattern added to the faces. Specifically, instead of using circle-shaped outliers as applied above, we generate new 'rectangle' dirty patterns having random width, length and location. The 1965 clean Frey face images were corrupted by these new rectangle marks, allowing us to examine the resilience of the previously-trained models to outlier distributions distinct from the original data. Figure 3(b) displays the overall reconstruction errors, where the superiority of the RiC-VAE (with $N, M > 1$) is preserved. See the supplementary file for visualization of candidate reconstructions, as well as results on an independent medical imaging application related to anomaly detection.

5.3 RiC-VAE GENERATIVE MODELING PERFORMANCE

Moving beyond outlier removal, arguably the most common application of VAE models is to the task of generating new samples of $\boldsymbol{x}$ (Doersch, 2016). This section explores RiC-VAE capabilities in this revised context using MNIST handwritten digit data (LeCun et al., 1998), which contains 60000 training images of digits, each of size 28×28. We first train different models using this data, both clean and dirty versions, and then compare performance on subsequent generative tasks. Models considered include: (a) a standard ℓ_2-VAE, (b) an iC-VAE, (c) an RiC-VAE(N=1,M=20), (d) an RiC-VAE(N=5,M=1), and (e) an RiC-VAE(N=5,M=20). In all cases $\kappa = 30$, and both encoder and decoder have 3 layers (the supplementary file contains full network

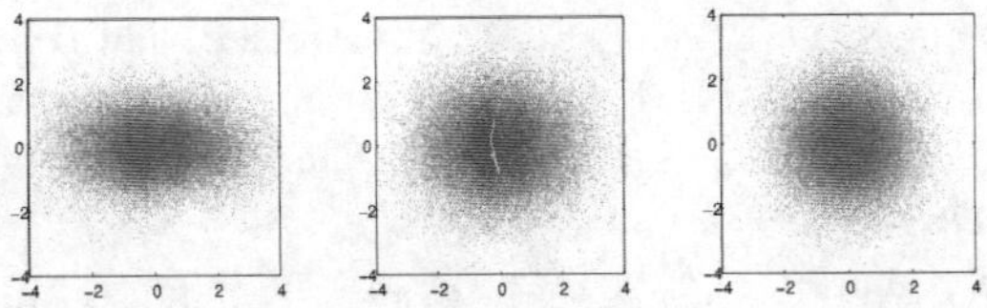

(a) (b) (c)

Figure 5: 2D samples from $\frac{1}{n}\sum_i q_\phi\left(z|x^{(i)}\right)$ when using (a) iC-VAE, and (b) RiC-VAE with N=5. (c) Ideal samples from $\mathcal{N}(z;\mathbf{0},\boldsymbol{I})$.

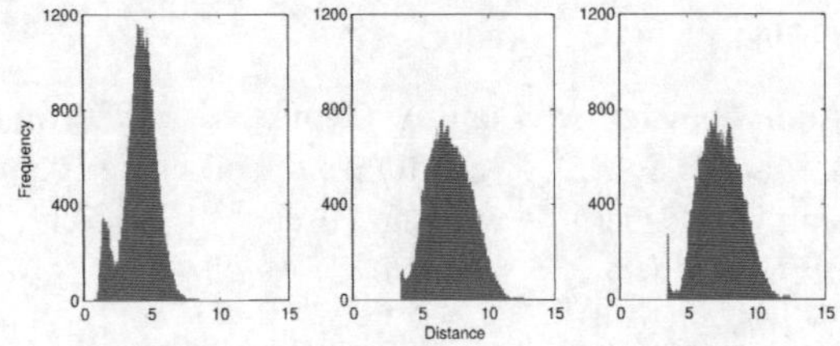

Figure 6: Evaluation of sample diversity. *Left*: Histogram of nearest neighbor distances in original MNIST data. *Middle*: Histogram of distances between 60000 RiC-VAE(N=5,M=1) samples and their nearest neighbors in MNIST data. *Right*: Same for a RiC-VAE(N=5,M=5).

structure and training details). By varying M, we can examine the quality of generated samples after different passes through the networks at test time.

Results using clean training data: Here we first use the original MNIST data for training (no corruptions added) and compare the quality of new generated samples obtained by first drawing a latent z from $\mathcal{N}(z;\mathbf{0},\boldsymbol{I})$ and then passing the resulting value through the decoder to produce a sample of x (Doersch, 2016). Results from 100 random draws are shown for each method in Figure 4(*top row*). In (a) we observe that the ℓ_2-VAE produces overly blurry samples, a common criticism, and although the iC-VAE removes this blur in (b), realistic digit shapes are compromised. Next, (c) reveals that cycling through a learned iC-VAE network (i.e., N=1) when generating samples introduces new artifacts, since recycling was not used during training, and conversely, in (d) we see that the use of recycling during training has limited value without the attendant recycling at test time generating new samples. Finally, we see that the full RiC-VAE structure produces more authentic digit samples, and that this can be achieved even though the number of training and test passes are not equivalent. Please see the supplementary for original MNIST data examples to compare against, as well as further experiments with different numbers of training and testing passes.

Dirty training dataset: We next repeat the above experiment using corrupted training samples. Specifically, 40% of pixels are replaced with random values drawn from a uniform distribution over $[0, 255]$, i.e., salt-and-pepper noise. In this more challenging situation, the value of recycling dirty training samples is readily apparent as shown in Figure 4(*bottom row*).

Statistical validation of generated samples: If an estimated VAE model truly reflects the underlying latent distributions well, then $\int q_\phi(z|x)\,p_\theta(x)dx \approx \frac{1}{n}\sum_i q_\phi\left(z|x^{(i)}\right) \approx p(z) = \mathcal{N}(z;\mathbf{0},\boldsymbol{I})$. To test this hypothesis, we generate samples of z from $\frac{1}{n}\sum_i q_\phi\left(z|x^{(i)}\right)$ and make scatter-plots of two randomly selected dimensions. Figure 5 shows results for both the iC-VAE and a RiC-VAE with N=5 trained on MNIST data; clearly the latter is able to remove some of the heteroscedastic variance of the former. For more detailed analysis of means and variances in higher dimensions, see the supplementary file.

A second important validation issue pertains to sample diversity. In brief, we would like to generate novel samples that are not trivially plagiarized versions of the original training set. To examine this issue, we plot the the mean Euclidean distance between each sample generated by a RiC-VAE and its nearest neighbor in the MNIST data. These distances should be as large or larger than the mean distance between each authentic MNIST sample and its nearest neighbor if no copying has occurred. Figure 6 shows histograms of these distances for the original MNIST data (*left*), a RiC-VAE(N=5,M=1) (*middle*), and a RiC-VAE(N=5,M=5) (*right*). Clearly the RiC-VAE is not copying samples from the original data, and moreover, the additional testing passes used to generate samples for the M=5 case maintain these distances, while nonetheless improving the overall digit visual quality as observed previously.

6 CONCLUSION

Although the VAE has secured itself as a powerful generative modeling paradigm, there remain limitations to its effectiveness in practice. In this work, we have provided targeted enhancements that both reduce the sensitivity to outliers, as well as crystalize new, generated samples devoid of excessive blur. This is possible in large part due to our proposal for leveraging outputs of the generative process as virtual inputs that can be applied during training as a form of data augmentation, and during testing as a source for iterative refinements. The resulting recurrent structure itself resembles the iterative steps of certain influential compressive sensing algorithms that are also capable of incrementally removing sparse outliers. However, while the latter essentially rely on 'hand-crafted' updates derived from potentially heuristic energy function gradients or related, our pipeline is entirely learned from data.

References

M. Andrychowicz, M. Denil, S. Gomez, M. W. Hoffman, D. Pfau, T. Schaul, B. Shillingford, and N. de Freitas. Learning to learn by gradient descent by gradient descent. In *Advances in Neural Information Processing Systems*, 2016.

Y. Bengio. Learning deep architectures for AI. In *Foundations and Trends in Machine Learning*, 2009.

J. O. Berger. *Statistical Decision Theory and Bayesian Analysis*. Springer-Verlag, New York, 2nd edition, 1985.

S. Boyd and L. Vandenberghe. *Convex Optimization*. Cambridge University Press, 2004.

E. Candès, M. Wakin, and S. Boyd. Enhancing sparsity by reweighted ℓ_1 minimization. *Journal of Fourier Analysis and Applications*, 14(5), 2008.

E. Candès, X. Li, Y. Ma, and J. Wright. Robust principal component analysis? *J. ACM*, 58(2), May 2011.

B. Dai, Y. Wang, Aston J., G. Hua, and D. Wipf. Veiled attributes of the variational autoencoder. In *arXiv:1706.05148*, 2017.

C. Doersch. Tutorial on variational autoencoders. *arXiv preprint arXiv:1606.05908*, 2016.

E. Elhamifar and R. Vidal. Sparse subspace clustering: Algorithm, theory, and applications. *IEEE Trans. Pattern Analysis and Machine Intelligence*, 35(11), 2013.

H. He, B. Xin, and D. Wipf. From bayesian sparsity to gated recurrent nets. *arXiv preprint arXiv:1706.02815*, 2017.

J. R. Hershey, J. L. Roux, and F. Weninger. Deep unfolding: Model-based inspiration of novel deep architectures. *arXiv preprint arXiv:1409.2574*, 2014.

D. Kingma and M. Welling. Auto-encoding variational bayes. In *International Conference on Learning Representations*, 2014.

Y. LeCun, L. Bottou, Y. Bengio, and P. Haffner. Gradient-based learning applied to document recognition. *Proceedings of the IEEE*, 86(11), 1998.

C. Y. Lee, S. Xie, and P. W. Gallagher. Deeply supervised nets. In *Artificial Intelligence and Statistics*, 2015.

K. Li and J. Malik. Learning to optimize. *arXiv preprint arXiv:1606.01885*, 2016.

W. Liu, G. Hua, and J. R. Smith. Unsupervised one-class learning for automatic outlier removal. In *Proceedings of the IEEE Conference on Computer Vision and Pattern Recognition*, 2014.

J. A. Palmer, D. P. Wipf, K. Kreutz-Delgado, and B.D. Rao. Variational EM algorithms for non-Gaussian latent variable models. *Advances in Neural Information Processing Systems*, 2006.

B. D. Rao, K. Engan, S. F. Cotter, J. Palmer, and K. Kreutz-Delgado. Subset selection in noise based on diversity measure minimization. *IEEE Trans. Signal Processing*, 51(3), 2003.

D. J. Rezende, S. Mohamed, and D. Wierstra. Stochastic backpropagation and approximate inference in deep generative models. In *International Conference on Machine Learning*, 2014.

K. Sohn, H. Lee, and X. Yan. Learning structured output representation using deep conditional generative models. In *Advances in Neural Information Processing Systems*, pages 3483–3491, 2015.

P. Sprechmann, A. M. Bronstein, and G. Sapiro. Learning efficient sparse and low rank models. *IEEE Trans. Pattern Analysis and Machine Intelligence*, 37 (9), 2015.

J. Walker, C. Doersch, A. Gupta, and M. Hebert. An uncertain future: Forecasting from static images using variational autoencoders. In *European Conference on Computer Vision*, pages 835–851. Springer, 2016.

D. P. Wipf. Non-convex rank minimization via an empirical Bayesian approach. In *Uncertainty in Artificial Intelligence*, 2012.

D. P. Wipf and S. Nagarajan. Iterative reweighted ℓ_1 and ℓ_2 methods for finding sparse solutions. *Journal of Selected Topics in Signal Processing (Special Issue on Compressive Sensing)*, 4(2), 2010.

Y. Xia, X. Cao, F. Wen, G. Hua, and J. Sun. Learning discriminative reconstructions for unsupervised outlier removal. In *Proceedings of the IEEE International Conference on Computer Vision*, 2015.

B. Xin, Y. Wang, W. Gao, D. Wipf, and B. Wang. Maximal sparsity with deep networks? In *Advances in Neural Information Processing Systems*. 2016.

SUPPLEMENTARY FILE
Green Generative Modeling: Recycling Dirty Data using Recurrent Variational Autoencoders

Yu Wang * **Bin Dai** † **Gang Hua** ♯ **John Aston*** **David Wipf** ♯

* **University of Cambridge, Cambridge, UK**
† **Tsinghua University, Beijing, China**
♯**Microsoft Research, Beijing, China**

yw323@cam.ac.uk; daib13@mails.tsinghua.edu.cn; ganghua@microsoft.com; jada2@cam.ac.uk; davidwipf@gmail.com

1. Introduction

This document contains companion technical material regarding our UAI 2017 submission. Note that herein all equation numbers referencing back to the main submission document will be be prefixed with an 'M' to avoid confusion, i.e, (M.#) will refer to equation (#) from the main text. Similar notation differentiates sections, tables, and figures, e.g., Section M.#, etc. Notations without prefix or with the emphasized S.# will refer to the notations in this supplementary file.

2. Contents

This document includes the following supporting materials:

- **Section 3 - Medical Imaging Application:** We present additional results using the BRATS2015 brain tumor dataset (Menze et al., 2015), where the goal is the unsupervised detection of tumors. This provides preliminary evidence for the effectiveness of iC-VAE and RiC-VAE models on a challenging medical application.
- **Section 4 - Proof of Proposition M.1**
- **Section 5 - Alternative iC-VAE Derivation:** Here we re-derive the iC-VAE from the perspective of sparse Bayesian learning, which sheds additional insights into its robustness to outliers.
- **Section 6 - Deep Network Structure and Training Details:** This section specifies the DNN structures used for the RiC-VAE encoder and decoder layers referred to in Section M.5. We also discuss training details, e.g., learning rates, etc.
- **Section 7 - Additional Experimental Results:** Finally we describes additional supplementary experiments referred to in Section M.5 that could not fit in the main paper.

*. Y. Wang is sponsored by the EPSRC Centre for Mathematical Imaging in Healthcare, University of Cambridge, EP/N014588/1. B. Dai is finantially supported by Tsinghua University. Y. Wang and B. Dai are partially supported by sponsorship from Microsoft Research Asia.

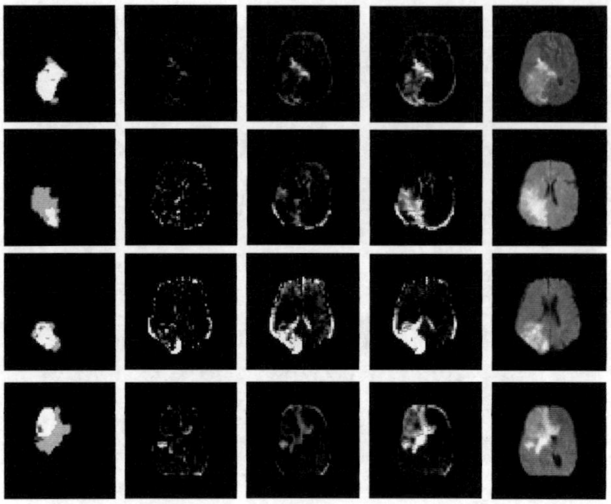

(a) (b) (c) (d) (e)

Figure 1: Unsupervised brain tumor segmentation examples using BRATS2015 data. (a) Ground truth tumor segmentation annotation by human expert. (b) Abnormality segmentation by RPCA. (c) Abnormality segmentation by iC-VAE. (d) Abnormality segmentation by RiC-VAE(N=2,M=2). (e) Original brain image (preprocessed).

3. Medical Imaging Application: Unsupervised Tumor Detection

In this section, we examine various unsupervised learning algorithms with respect to their ability to detect abnormalities in real medical data. The public BRATS2015 data (Menze et al., 2015) consists of 274 multi-contrast MRI scans from brain glioma patients, out of which 54 were acquired from patients with low-grade tumors and 220 from patients with high-grade tumors. Each MRI scan contains a sequence of brain imaging slices consecutively taken from different brain depths. We collect the 80th-100th slices (hence some consistent depth cross different brains) from each flair channel of the high-grade MRI scans, and use these $21 \times 220 = 4620$ images to form training data.

We also resize all the original 240×240-resolution images to 60×60 (because of limited data for learning VAE networks), and normalize to zero mean and unit variance before application to unsupervised learning algorithms for evaluation purposes. The goal here is to compare the accuracy of detected tumor regions with respect to ground truth annotations labeled by human experts.

Table 1: Intersection over Union (BRATS 2015 dataset)

Algo.	Opt. Thr.	RPCA	iC-VAE	RiC-VAE
No D.O.	0.252	0.174	0.270	**0.349**
D.O	0.252	0.174	0.305	**0.352**

We train a iC-VAE for 5000 iterations (learning rate lr=1e-4) and use the resultant network weights to initialize the RiC-VAE(N=2,M=2) (lr=2e-5); the actual network structures used are described in Section 6 below. Both the iC-VAE and RiC-VAE were further trained for another 45000 iterations until convergence (in total 50000 iterations). We use IoU (Intersection over Union) to evaluate the tumor detection accuracy, which is defined as the ratio between the size of 'intersection of support sets' and the 'union of support sets' w.r.t. two sets: the ground truth tumor region and the predicted segmentation region.

In Table 1 we present IoU detection statistics for 4 different methods: (i) Opt. Thr., which denotes a prediction heuristic based on hard-thresholding the raw data set according to an optimal threshold (obtained by empirical search), (ii) Robust PCA (RPCA), a common unsupervised learning method for outlier removal (Candès et al., 2011), (iii) the iC-VAE described above, and (iv) the RiC-VAE(N=2,M=2) also from above. We also consider applying a dropout layer (D.O.) with rate 0.2 for both initialization purposes and final evaluation (this also affect the RiC-VAE via the initialization). Some complementary sample segmentation results are shown in Figure 1.

Both the evaluations in Figure 1 and Table 1 provide preliminary evidence of the effectiveness of iC-VAE and RiC-VAE(N=2,M=2) networks. By introducing the recycling mechanism via the RiC-VAE, multiple passes during training help to alleviate overfitting problems caused by the limited number of training data. Although extra structures and knowledge could be considered for overall performance improvement relative to supervised methods (e.g., to remove the ring artifacts around the brain borders, convolutional layers could be added to encoder and decoder networks), here our goal is merely proof-of-concept using unsupervised learning methods.

4. Proof of Proposition M.1

Using Jensen's inequality, we have that

$$
\begin{aligned}
2\mathbb{E}_{q_\phi(\boldsymbol{z}|\boldsymbol{x}^{(i)})}\left[\log\left|x_j^{(i)}-\mu_{x_j}^{(i)}\right|\right] &\leq \log\mathbb{E}_{q_\phi(\boldsymbol{z}|\boldsymbol{x}^{(i)})}\left[\left(x_j^{(i)}-\mu_{x_j}^{(i)}\right)^2\right] \\
&= \inf_{\lambda_j^{(i)}>0}\frac{\mathbb{E}_{q_\phi(\boldsymbol{z}|\boldsymbol{x}^{(i)})}\left[\left(x_j^{(i)}-\mu_{x_j}^{(i)}\right)^2,\right]}{\lambda_j^{(i)}}+\log\lambda_j^{(i)}
\end{aligned}
\tag{1}
$$

where an irrelevant constant has been omitted and $\boldsymbol{\lambda}^{(i)}\in\mathbb{R}_+^d$ for all i represent arbitrary variational parameters, independent of $\boldsymbol{z}$. Any concave function can be expressed as a minimization of upper-bounding linear functions in this way (Jordan et al., 1999). The expectation now admits a closed-form solution leading to

$$
\begin{aligned}
&\mathbb{E}_{q_\phi(\boldsymbol{z}|\boldsymbol{x}^{(i)})}\left[\left(\boldsymbol{x}^{(i)}-\boldsymbol{W}\boldsymbol{z}-\boldsymbol{b}\right)^\top\left(\boldsymbol{\Lambda}^{(i)}\right)^{-1}\left(\boldsymbol{x}^{(i)}-\boldsymbol{W}\boldsymbol{z}-\boldsymbol{b}\right)\right] \\
&= \left(\boldsymbol{x}^{(i)}-\boldsymbol{W}\boldsymbol{\mu}_z^{(i)}-\boldsymbol{b}\right)^\top\left(\boldsymbol{\Lambda}^{(i)}\right)^{-1}\left(\boldsymbol{x}^{(i)}-\boldsymbol{W}\boldsymbol{\mu}_z^{(i)}-\boldsymbol{b}\right)+\mathrm{tr}\left[\boldsymbol{\Sigma}_z^{(i)}\boldsymbol{W}^\top\left(\boldsymbol{\Lambda}^{(i)}\right)^{-1}\boldsymbol{W}\right].
\end{aligned}
\tag{2}
$$

where $\mathbf{\Lambda}^{(i)} = \text{diag}[\boldsymbol{\lambda}^{(i)}]$. Using these expressions we obtain the new upper bound on the original VAE cost given by

$$\begin{aligned}\mathcal{L}(\boldsymbol{\theta}, \boldsymbol{\phi}; \boldsymbol{X}) \leq & \sum_i \inf_{\mathbf{\Lambda}^{(i)} \succ \mathbf{0}} \left\{ \text{tr}\left[\mathbf{\Sigma}_z^{(i)}\right] - \log\left|\mathbf{\Sigma}_z^{(i)}\right| + \|\boldsymbol{\mu}_z^{(i)}\|_2^2 \right. \\ & + \left(\boldsymbol{x}^{(i)} - \boldsymbol{W}\boldsymbol{\mu}_z^{(i)} - \boldsymbol{b}\right)^\top \left(\mathbf{\Lambda}^{(i)}\right)^{-1} \left(\boldsymbol{x}^{(i)} - \boldsymbol{W}\boldsymbol{\mu}_z^{(i)} - \boldsymbol{b}\right) \\ & + \left. \text{tr}\left[\mathbf{\Sigma}_z^{(i)} \boldsymbol{W}^\top \left(\mathbf{\Lambda}^{(i)}\right)^{-1} \boldsymbol{W}\right] + \log\left|\mathbf{\Lambda}^{(i)}\right| \right\}. \end{aligned} \tag{3}$$

Because $\boldsymbol{\mu}_z^{(i)}$ and $\mathbf{\Sigma}_z^{(i)}$ appear in different terms, we can optimize over each separately in terms of $\mathbf{\Lambda}^{(i)}$ and $\boldsymbol{W}$ by taking gradients, equating to zero, and solving. This leads to the optimal solutions

$$\begin{aligned}\boldsymbol{\mu}_z^{(i)} &= \boldsymbol{W}^\top \left(\mathbf{\Lambda}^{(i)} + \boldsymbol{W}\boldsymbol{W}^\top\right)^{-1} \left(\boldsymbol{x}^{(i)} - \boldsymbol{b}\right), \\ \mathbf{\Sigma}_z^{(i)} &= \left[\boldsymbol{W}^\top \mathbf{\Lambda}^{(i)} \boldsymbol{W} + \boldsymbol{I}\right]^{-1}. \end{aligned} \tag{4}$$

Plugging these values into (3) and ignoring constants, we obtain the stated bound. Moreover, we observe from this development that in fact $\boldsymbol{\mu}_z^{(i)}$ and $\mathbf{\Sigma}_z^{(i)}$ need not involve overly complex deep network structures. By satisfying (4), which can be viewed as simple affine stationary conditions, the result still holds.

5. Alternative iC-VAE Derivation

In this section, we re-derive the iC-VAE objective (M.8) from the perspective of sparse Bayesian learning or automatic relevance determination applied to low-rank modeling (Wipf, 2012).

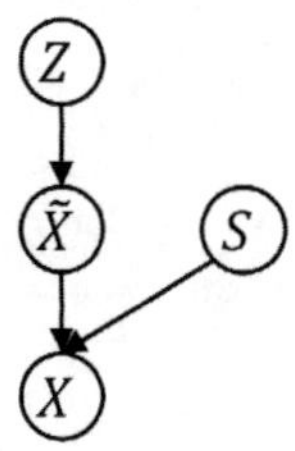

Figure 2: Graphical Model

We begin with the graphical model from Figure 2. We have a latent variable $\boldsymbol{z}$ which determines the 'clean' data $\tilde{\boldsymbol{x}}$, which is then corrupted by some sparse noise $\boldsymbol{s}$, which follows the Jeffreys prior $p(\boldsymbol{s}) \propto \Pi_{j=1}^d \frac{1}{|s_j|}$. Then we obtain the observed data $\boldsymbol{x}$, and $p(\boldsymbol{x})$ can be expressed as

$$p(\boldsymbol{x}) = \int p(\boldsymbol{x}|\boldsymbol{z}, \boldsymbol{s}) p(\boldsymbol{z}, \boldsymbol{s}) d\boldsymbol{z} d\boldsymbol{s} \tag{5}$$

Similarly, we can write a lower bound on the negative log of $p(\boldsymbol{x})$ by replacing the latent $\boldsymbol{z}$ in a conventional VAE with $(\boldsymbol{z}, \boldsymbol{s})$, giving us

$$\mathcal{L} = \mathbb{KL}\left[q(\boldsymbol{z}, \boldsymbol{s}|\boldsymbol{x})||p(\boldsymbol{z}, \boldsymbol{s})\right] + \mathbb{E}_{(\boldsymbol{z},\boldsymbol{s})\sim q(\boldsymbol{z},\boldsymbol{s}|\boldsymbol{x})}\left[-\log p(\boldsymbol{x}|\boldsymbol{z}, \boldsymbol{s})\right]. \tag{6}$$

Note that we omit θ and ϕ in the loss function because they serve different roles in this formulation (in fact they are both absorbed into q). We define the prior of $\boldsymbol{z}$ as a standardized Gaussian distribution and the approximated posterior of $\boldsymbol{z}$ as a Gaussian distribution determined by the encoder. The prior of $\boldsymbol{s}$ is defined as the Jeffreys prior as mentioned before while the approximated posterior of $\boldsymbol{s}$ is a Dirac-delta function. In summary then we have

$$\begin{aligned} q(\boldsymbol{z}, \boldsymbol{s}|\boldsymbol{x}) &= q(\boldsymbol{z}|\boldsymbol{x})q(\boldsymbol{s}|\boldsymbol{z}, \boldsymbol{x}) \\ q(\boldsymbol{z}|\boldsymbol{x}) &\sim \mathcal{N}\left(\boldsymbol{\mu}_z(\boldsymbol{x}), \boldsymbol{\Sigma}_z(\boldsymbol{x})\right) \\ q(\boldsymbol{s}|\boldsymbol{z}, \boldsymbol{x}) &\sim \delta(\boldsymbol{x} - \boldsymbol{\mu}_x(\boldsymbol{z})) \\ p(\boldsymbol{x}|\boldsymbol{z}, \boldsymbol{s}) &\propto \exp\left(-\frac{1}{2\lambda}||\boldsymbol{x} - \boldsymbol{\mu}_x(\boldsymbol{z}) - \boldsymbol{s}||_{\mathcal{F}}^2\right), \end{aligned} \tag{7}$$

where $\delta(\cdot)$ is a Dirac-delta function. Now consider the second term on the r.h.s of (6). It becomes

$$\begin{aligned} &\mathbb{E}_{(\boldsymbol{z},\boldsymbol{s})\sim q(\boldsymbol{z},\boldsymbol{s}|\boldsymbol{x})}\left[\frac{1}{2\lambda}||\boldsymbol{x} - \boldsymbol{\mu}_x - \boldsymbol{s}||_{\mathcal{F}}^2 + C\right] \\ =&\mathbb{E}_{\boldsymbol{z}\sim q(\boldsymbol{z}|\boldsymbol{x})}\left[\int \delta(\boldsymbol{x} - \boldsymbol{\mu}_x)\frac{1}{2\lambda}||\boldsymbol{x} - \boldsymbol{\mu}_x - \boldsymbol{s}||_{\mathcal{F}}^2 ds\right] + C \\ =&\mathbb{E}_{\boldsymbol{z}\sim q(\boldsymbol{z}|\boldsymbol{x})}\left[\frac{1}{2\lambda}||\boldsymbol{x} - \boldsymbol{\mu}_x - (\boldsymbol{x} - \boldsymbol{\mu}_x)||_{\mathcal{F}}^2\right] + C \\ =&C, \end{aligned} \tag{8}$$

where C is a constant, hence we can omit this term. The first term of (6) can be decomposed into two parts as

$$\begin{aligned} &\int q(\boldsymbol{z}|\boldsymbol{x})q(\boldsymbol{s}|\boldsymbol{z}, \boldsymbol{x}) \log \frac{q(\boldsymbol{z}|\boldsymbol{x})q(\boldsymbol{s}|\boldsymbol{z}, \boldsymbol{x})}{p(\boldsymbol{z})p(\boldsymbol{s})} d\boldsymbol{z}d\boldsymbol{s} \\ =&\int q(\boldsymbol{z}|\boldsymbol{x}) \log \frac{q(\boldsymbol{z}|\boldsymbol{x})}{p(\boldsymbol{z})} d\boldsymbol{z} + \int q(\boldsymbol{z}|\boldsymbol{x})q(\boldsymbol{s}|\boldsymbol{z}, \boldsymbol{x}) \log \frac{q(\boldsymbol{s}|\boldsymbol{z}, \boldsymbol{x})}{p(\boldsymbol{s})} d\boldsymbol{z}d\boldsymbol{s} \\ =&\mathbb{KL}\left[q(\boldsymbol{z}|\boldsymbol{x})||p(\boldsymbol{z})\right] + \mathbb{E}_{\boldsymbol{z}\sim q(\boldsymbol{z}|\boldsymbol{x})}\left[\int q(\boldsymbol{s}|\boldsymbol{z}, \boldsymbol{x}) \log \frac{q(\boldsymbol{s}|\boldsymbol{z}, \boldsymbol{x})}{p(\boldsymbol{s})} d\boldsymbol{s}\right]. \end{aligned} \tag{9}$$

The first term is exactly the same as the KL term in the conventional VAE. Plugging $q(\boldsymbol{s}|\boldsymbol{z},\boldsymbol{x}) = \delta(\boldsymbol{s};\boldsymbol{x}-\boldsymbol{\mu}_x(\boldsymbol{z}))$ into the second term gives

$$
\begin{aligned}
&\mathbb{E}_{\boldsymbol{z}\sim q(\boldsymbol{z}|\boldsymbol{x})}\left[\int q(\boldsymbol{s}|\boldsymbol{z},\boldsymbol{x})\log\frac{q(\boldsymbol{s}|\boldsymbol{z},\boldsymbol{x})}{p(\boldsymbol{s})}d\boldsymbol{s}\right] \\
=&\mathbb{E}_{\boldsymbol{z}\sim q(\boldsymbol{z}|\boldsymbol{x})}\left[\int \delta(\boldsymbol{s};\boldsymbol{x}-\boldsymbol{\mu}_x)\log\delta(\boldsymbol{s};\boldsymbol{x}-\boldsymbol{\mu}_x)d\boldsymbol{s} - \int \delta(\boldsymbol{s};\boldsymbol{x}-\boldsymbol{\mu}_x)\log p(\boldsymbol{s})d\boldsymbol{s}\right] \\
=&C - \mathbb{E}_{\boldsymbol{z}\sim q(\boldsymbol{z}|\boldsymbol{x})}\left[\log p(\boldsymbol{s}=\boldsymbol{x}-\boldsymbol{\mu}_x)\right] \\
=&C + \mathbb{E}_{\boldsymbol{z}\sim q(\boldsymbol{z}|\boldsymbol{x})}\left[\sum_j \log|x_j-\mu_{x_j}|\right].
\end{aligned}
\tag{10}
$$

It should be noticed that though $\int \delta(\boldsymbol{s};\boldsymbol{x}-\boldsymbol{\mu}_x)\log\delta(\boldsymbol{s};\boldsymbol{x}-\boldsymbol{\mu}_x)d\boldsymbol{s}$ is infinite, it is not related to the parameters thus it can be treated as a constant. Combining these results, the lower bound of the negative log likelihood can be finally be expressed as

$$
\mathcal{L} = \mathbb{KL}[q(\boldsymbol{z}|\boldsymbol{x})||p(\boldsymbol{z})] + \sum_j \mathbb{E}_{\boldsymbol{z}\sim q(\boldsymbol{z}|\boldsymbol{x})}\left[\log|x_j-\mu_{x_j}|\right] + C, \tag{11}
$$

which is equivalent to (M.8) in the main paper once we account for multiple samples $i = 1,\ldots,n$. This formulation explicitly elucidates the crucial role that outliers play in the iC-VAE development.

6. Deep Network Structure and Training Details

In this section, we illustrate the further particulars of the RiC-VAE framework originally shown in Figure M.1. Here Figure 3 first presents the general structure flow, including additional ingredients pertinent to the iC-VAE.

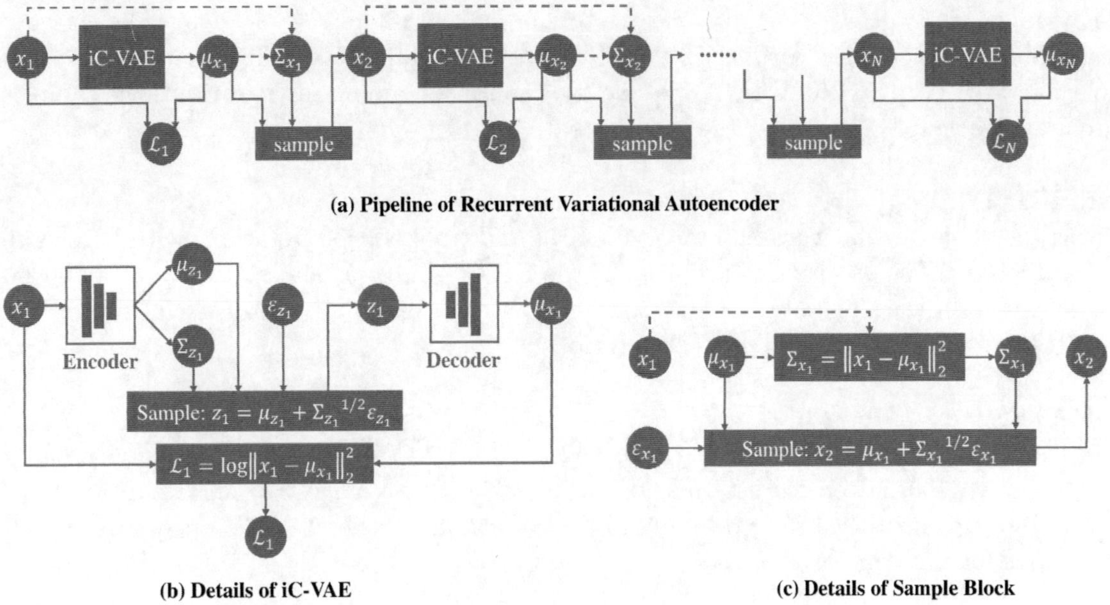

(a) Pipeline of Recurrent Variational Autoencoder

(b) Details of iC-VAE **(c) Details of Sample Block**

Figure 3: Detailed structure flow of the RiC-VAE network.

6.1 RiC-VAE network structure

The dimensions of each input layer, encoder inner-product hidden layers, latent dimension of $\boldsymbol{z}$, decoder inner-product hidden layers, and finally each output layer are listed here for each data set.

Frey face (Section M.5.2)
$560(input) - 1000 - 500 - 250 - 10(\boldsymbol{z}) - 250 - 500 - 1000 - 560(output)$
We use ReLU activations for all inner product layers except the last one which uses sigmoid activations to accommodate the magnitude range of the image pixels.

MNIST (Section M.5.3.)
$784(input) - 1000 - 500 - 250 - 30(\boldsymbol{z}) - 250 - 500 - 1000 - 784(output)$.
The activation scheme is the same as for the Frey face data.

BRATS2015 (Section 3)
$3600(input) - 50 - 10(\boldsymbol{z}) - 50 - 3600(output)$
The activation scheme is also the same as Frey face data except the last layer, after which we use no activation. This is because the format of BRATS2015 is different from ordinary images.

6.2 Training Details

Learning rates and iteration counts are listed below.

Frey face

For iC-VAE, we set the learning rate as 1×10^{-4} and train 150000 iterations with batch size equal to 100. For RiC-VAE(N=2), we use the same training setting. Since the samples are actually doubled, we halve the learning rate to be 5×10^{-5}.

MNIST

For iC-VAE, we set the learning rate as 1×10^{-4} and train 600000 iterations with batch size equal to 100. Then we use this to initialize the RiC-VAE(N=5) and train an extra 100000 iterations with learning rate 2×10^{-5}. To compare iC-VAE and RiC-VAE fairly, we also train the iC-VAE for another 100000 iterations.

BRATS2015

For the iC-VAE, we set the learning rate as 1×10^{-4} and train 5000 iterations with batch size equal to 100. Then we use this to initialize the RiC-VAE(N=2) and train an extra 45000 iterations with learning rate 5×10^{-5}. We also train the iC-VAE for another 45000 iterations for fair comparison.

7. Additional Experimental Results

This section contains a wider range of empirical results that complement those from Section M.5 in the main paper.

7.1 Frey face recovery from new outlier patterns

When testing the models on Frey face dataset (Section M.5.2), we synthesize new test images by changing the corruption patterns seen during training. Instead of using circle outliers as in the training data, new 'rectangle' dirty patterns having random width, length and location were added. In this way, we examine the resilience of models on the outlier distribution distinct from the training data. Figure 4 demonstrates the dirty pattern in test mode and the corresponding reconstruction results when trained at a 60% corruption level.

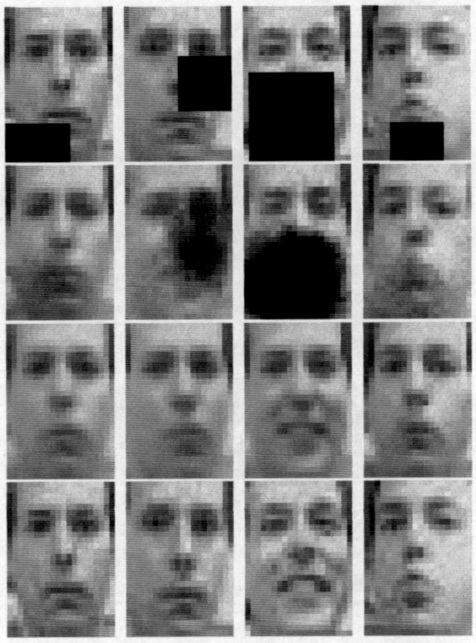

Figure 4: Visualizing reconstructions on Frey face test data. *Row 1*: Dirty test data. *Row 2:* Reconstruction by iC-VAE. *Row 3:* Reconstruction by RiC-VAE (N=2,M=2). *Row 4:* Original clean Frey faces

7.2 Generative performance using MNIST data

This section provides supporting material for Section M.5.3. For illustration purposes, Figure 5 first presents some random samples from both the original clean MNIST data and the corrupted version at a 40% noise level. Later Figures 6-10 visualize samples generated by VAE networks under various clean and dirty scenarios. Among other things, these figures illustrate that once trained, the RiC-VAE can produce reasonable samples after cycling through the network a variable number of times.

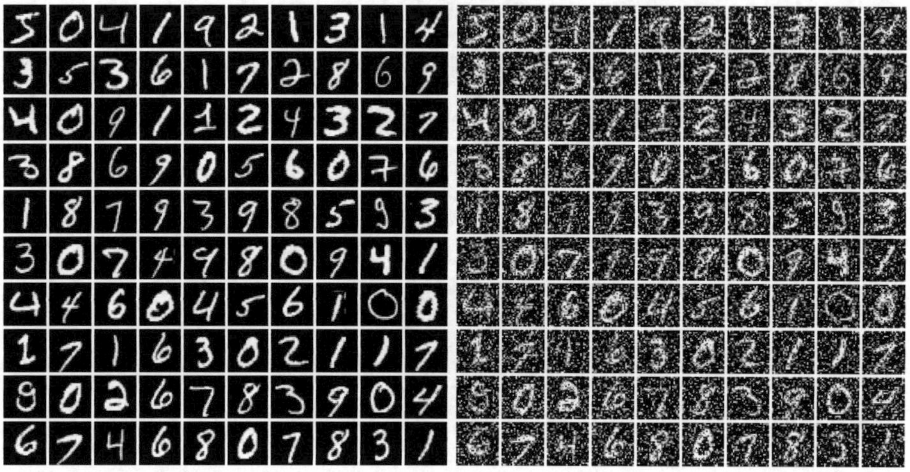

Figure 5: *Left*: Original clean MNIST data. *Right*: MNIST training data corrupted with 40% salt-and-pepper noise.

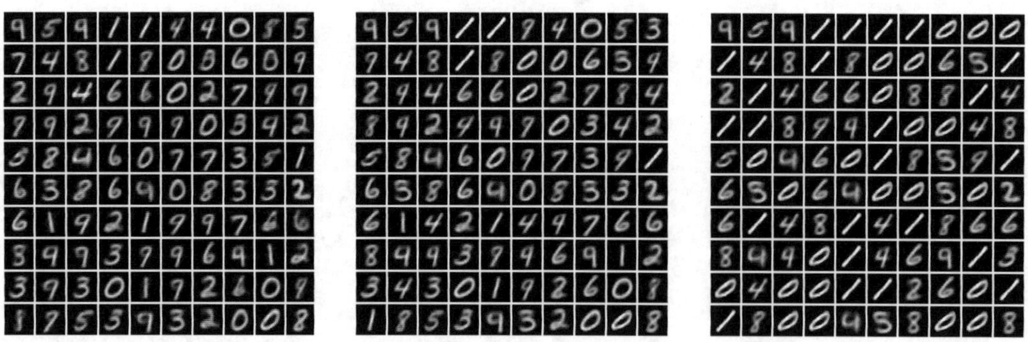

(a) (b) (c)

Figure 6: Samples generated from ℓ_2-VAE and Rℓ_2-VAE models trained on clean MNIST data. (a) ℓ_2-VAE, (b) Rℓ_2-VAE(N=1,M=5), and (c) Rℓ_2-VAE(N=1,M=20).

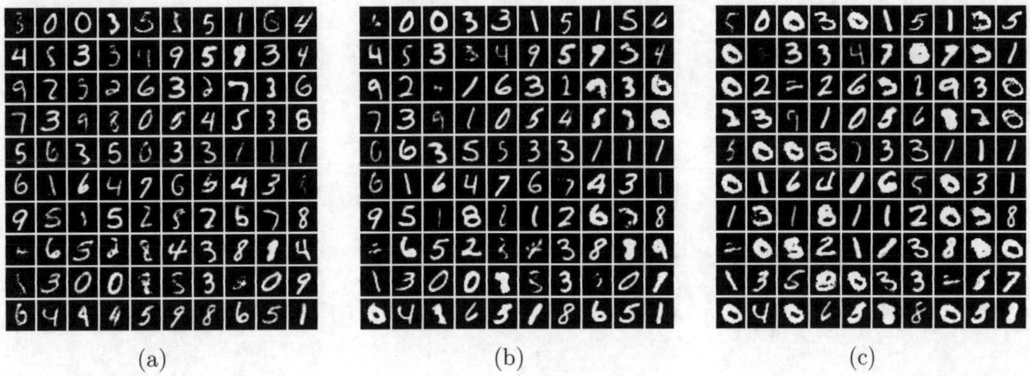

Figure 7: Samples generated from iC-VAE and RiC-VAE models trained on clean MNIST data. (a) iC-VAE, (b) RiC-VAE(N=1,M=5), and (c) RiC-VAE(N=1,M=20).

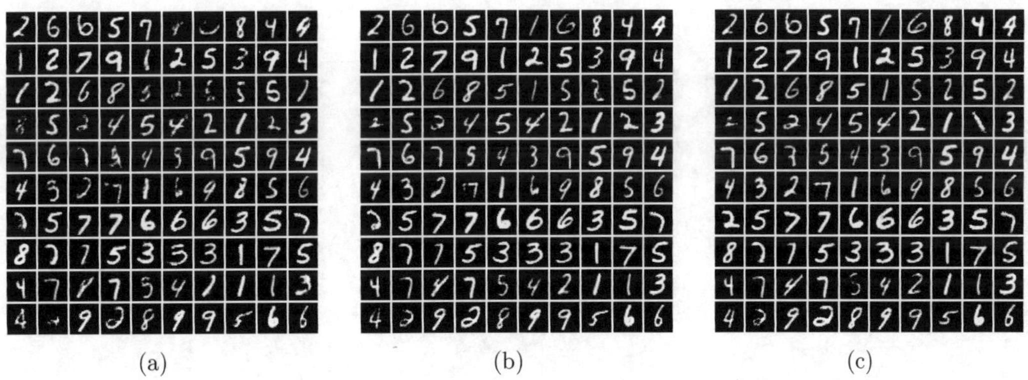

Figure 8: Samples generated from RiC-VAE(N=5,M=#) having different M and trained on clean MNIST data. (a) RiC-VAE(N=5,M=1), (b) RiC-VAE(N=5,M=5), and (c) RiC-VAE(N=5,M=20).

(a) (b) (c)

Figure 9: Samples generated from iC-VAE and RiC-VAE trained on noisy MNIST data. (a) iC-VAE, (b) RiC-VAE(N=1,M=5), and (c) RiC-VAE (N=1,M=20).

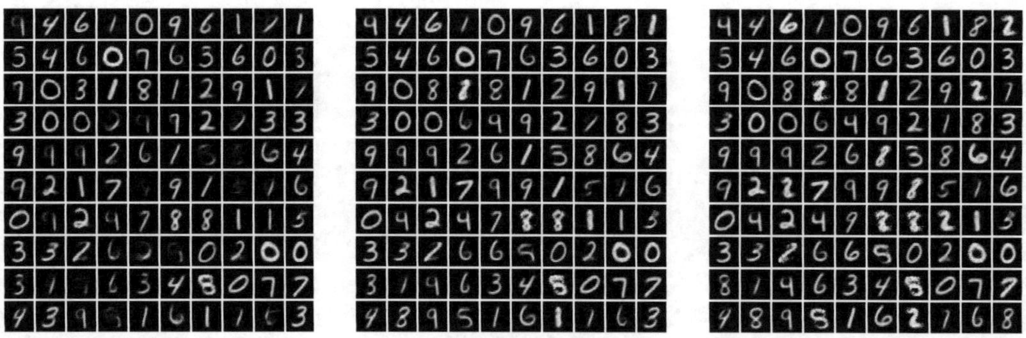

(a) (b) (c)

Figure 10: Samples generated from the dirty training set using RiC-VAE(N=5,M=#) and different M. (a) RiC-VAE(N=5,M=1), (b) RiC-VAE(N=5,M=5), and (c) RiC-VAE(N=5,M=20).

7.3 Further statistical validation of generated samples

The approximate marginal distribution of the latent variable $\boldsymbol{z}$ should satisfy

$$\frac{1}{n}\sum_i q_\phi\left(\boldsymbol{z}|\boldsymbol{x}^{(i)}\right) \approx p(\boldsymbol{z}) = \mathcal{N}(\boldsymbol{z}; \boldsymbol{0}, \boldsymbol{I}) \tag{12}$$

if our estimated distributions are accurate. In the main paper we visualized 2D samples from this distribution to test this approximation. Here we consider a higher dimensional comparisons with a standardized Gaussian.

In particular, we draw 60000 samples from $\frac{1}{n}\sum_i q_\phi\left(\boldsymbol{z}|\boldsymbol{x}^{(i)}\right)$ and then compute the mean and variance of each of the $\kappa = 30$ dimensions in $\boldsymbol{z}$ as used with the MNIST data. Ideally these means should be near zero while the variances should be near one. Figure 11 shows the results for an iC-VAE and a RiC-VAE. From this figure it is immediately apparent that the RiC-VAE statistics are far more consistent with the ideal standardized Gaussian (which emerges if the non-Gaussian underlying latent distributions are approximated well) than the iC-VAE, suggesting that our recycling approach indeed better captures the true underlying distributions. Note also that results are similar as M is varied, implying that the statistics of recycled data or multiple passes at test time are stable.

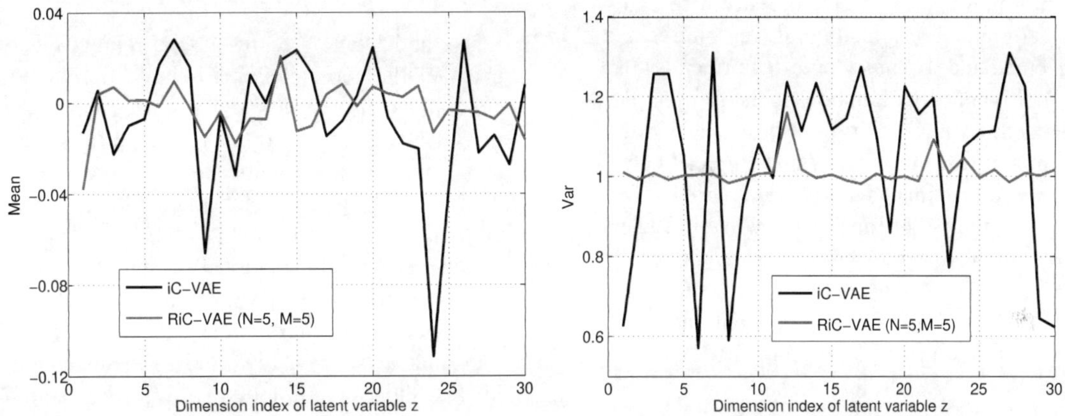

(a) Mean value comparison.

(b) Variance value comparison

Figure 11: Means and variances of samples drawn from $\frac{1}{n}\sum_i q_\phi\left(\boldsymbol{z}|\boldsymbol{x}^{(i)}\right)$.

References

Candès E. J., Li X., Ma Y., et al. Robust principal component analysis?. *Journal of the ACM (JACM)*, 58(3), 2011.

Jordan, M. I., Ghahramani, Z., Jaakkola, T. S., Saul, L. K.. An introduction to variational methods for graphical models *Machine learning*, 37(2): 1999

Menze B H, Jakab A, Bauer S, et al. The multimodal brain tumor image segmentation benchmark (BRATS). *IEEE transactions on medical imaging*,34(10): 2015

Wipf D. Non-convex rank minimization via an empirical Bayesian approach. *Uncertainty in Artificial Intelligence, 2012.*

Approximate Evidential Reasoning Using Local Conditioning and Conditional Belief Functions

Van Nguyen
Defence Science and Technology Group
van.nguyen5@dst.defence.gov.au

Abstract

We propose a new message-passing belief propagation method that approximates belief updating on evidential networks with conditional belief functions. By means of local conditioning, the method is able to propagate beliefs on the original multiply-connected network structure using local computations, facilitating reasoning in a distributed and dynamic context. Further, by use of conditional belief functions in the form of partially defined plausibility and basic plausibility assignment functions, belief updating can be efficiently approximated using only partial information of the belief functions involved. Experiments show that the method produces results with high degree of accuracy whilst achieving a significant decrease in computational and space complexity (compared to exact methods).

1 INTRODUCTION

Network-based approaches for reasoning with uncertainty feature a graphical representation of the knowledge base (commonly a directed acyclic graph) equipped with bi-directional belief propagation, facilitating reasoning in a coherent manner. Such networks dynamically reflect the current state of knowledge through the process of *belief updating* where the impact of an observation presented at a node is propagated to other nodes throughout the network.

This work is concerned with belief updating in evidential networks with conditional belief functions such as ECNs [Xu and Smets1996] and DEVNs [Yaghlane and Mellouli2008] towards their practical application, motivated by a computer network defence (CND) system. Such networks are formulated based on the theory of belief functions (BF theory) [Shafer1976], specifically in the framework of Transferable Belief Models (TBM) [Smets and Kennes1994] which provides a greater expressive power to handle more general forms of knowledge, in particular incomplete knowledge, a vital requirement in our application. In particular, it is crucial to be able to distinguish between conflicting information, missing information and statistical variability (see [Dubois and Prade2009] for further discussion) in order to act appropriately; for instance, deploying additional sensors in the face of incomplete knowledge, or mitigating against adversary manipulation or faulty sensors in the case of conflicting information.

ECNs and DEVNs represent the relations between variables in the form of conditional belief functions which generally consume less space, and provide a more intuitive formalism to encode knowledge (albeit less generic) than joint belief functions on the product space as in well-known valuation networks [Shenoy1993]. Belief updating in networks with belief functions can be efficiently performed using local computations with message-passing mechanisms, provided that the network is singly-connected at *execution* time. This can be achieved by imposing a tree-structure (e.g., [Shenoy and Shafer1986, Shafer, Shenoy, and Mellouli1987]), or simplifying the structure of certain networks using partial dependency (e.g., [Xu and Smets1996]), or generation of a secondary structure for the network, such as a binary join tree (e.g., Figure 1b), using graph-theoretic techniques (e.g., [Shenoy1997, Yaghlane and Mellouli2008]). These methods assume knowledge of the network and/or involve significant pre-processing before belief updating can occur. In the context of our CND system, the reasoning networks of concern are a federation/integration of distributed subnetworks of knowledge dynamically emerging and submerging through activation/deactivation of different sets of sensors, actuators and tasks as demanded by the changing situation. As such not only is the topology and the full knowledge of the reasoning network not available prior to execution, but they may change at run-time.

In this paper, we propose a message-passing belief propagation method that does not assume/require the reasoning network to be singly-connected at and during execution. More specifically, the method operates directly on the *original* multiply-connected network (by means of local conditioning), and within this framework approximate computations using only partial information of the belief functions to be combined and propagated (by means of conditional belief functions represented in the form of partially defined plausibility and basic plausibility assignment functions). The method is thereby adaptive to changes in the network topology while associated with a significant reduction in space and computational complexity. We will present BF theory and networks using conditional belief functions in the next section. In Section 3, we briefly discuss local conditioning in Bayesian networks and how the technique can be extended to our networks of interest. In Section 4, we present our new approximate belief updating method that combines local conditioning with conditional belief functions. Discussions and experimental results are provided in Section 5 before concluding in Section 6.

2 BF THEORY AND NETWORKS OF CONDITIONAL BELIEF FUNCTIONS

Given a frame of discernment Θ, a finite nonempty set of all possible hypotheses, BF theory assigns belief mass to the elements of its powerset 2^Θ, effectively representing incompleteness by means of disjunctive sets. Formally, an (unnormalised) *mass function* over Θ is defined as a mapping $\mathrm{m} : 2^\Theta \to [0, 1]$ such that $\sum_{A \subseteq 2^\Theta} \mathrm{m}(A) = 1$. Those subsets A where $\mathrm{m}(A) > 0$ are called *focal elements*; with $\mathrm{m}(A) = 0$ whenever $|A| > 1$ representing a *Bayesian* belief function, and $\mathrm{m}(\Theta) = 1$ representing total ignorance. A mass function can be equivalently represented in the form of a *belief function* (bel), a *plausibility function* (pl) and a *commonality function* (q) with different semantics[1], given respectively as $\mathrm{bel}(A) = \sum_{B \subseteq A, B \neq \emptyset} \mathrm{m}(B)$, $\mathrm{pl}(A) = \mathrm{bel}(\Theta) - \mathrm{bel}(\bar{A})$ and $\mathrm{q}(A) = \sum_{A \subseteq B \subseteq \Omega} \mathrm{m}(B)$, where $\bar{A} = \Theta - A$. If there are multiple distinct pieces of evidence defined on Θ such as m_1 and m_2, their combined impact is computed through the conjunctive rule of combination (CRC) ⓒ: $\forall A \subseteq \Omega, m_{1 \copyright 2}(A) = \sum_{B,C \subseteq \Omega, B \cap C = A} m_1(B) m_2(C)$, or equivalently $q_{1 \copyright 2}(A) = q_1(A) q_2(A)$ (2.1).

In his work formulating BF theory from a geometric perspective, [Cuzzolin2012] proposed the notion of *basic plausibility assignment* (or b.pl.a) as the Moebius inverse $\mu_{pl} : 2^\Omega \to \Re$ of a plausibility function *pl* such that:

$$\mu_{pl}(A) = \textstyle\sum_{B \subseteq A} (-1)^{|A \setminus B|} pl(B) \qquad (2.2)$$

$$pl(A) = \textstyle\sum_{B \subseteq A} \mu_{pl}(B). \qquad (2.3)$$

We now show that distinct *pl* functions can be combined by means of μ_{pl}, which plays a major role in this work.

Lemma 2.1 *: Let $pl_1, \ldots, pl_n$ be distinct pieces of evidence on Θ, their combined impact on Θ is computed by means of their corresponding $\mu_{pl_1}, \ldots, \mu_{pl_n}$ as: $\forall A \subseteq \Theta$,*

$$\mu_{pl_1 \copyright \ldots \copyright n}(A) = (-1)^{(|A|+1)(n-1)} \textstyle\prod_{k=1}^{n} \mu_{pl_k}(A). \quad (2.4)$$

[1] *m, bel, pl* and *q* can all be referred to as *belief functions*.

Proof By iteratively substituting terms in the RHS of Eq. (2.2) with $pl(A) = \sum_{B \subseteq A} (-1)^{|B|+1} q(B)$ [Shafer1976] for each subset A with increasing size $|A|$, we can derive $q(A) = (-1)^{|A|+1} \mu(A)$ (2.5). Substituting q in Eq. (2.1) with μ according to Eq. (2.5) results in Eq. (2.4). ■

When distinct m^Θ and m^Ω are expressed on different frames, e.g., Θ and Ω, [Smets1994] devised a formalism where the relation between Θ and Ω is represented by means of *conditional belief functions* (cbfs) $pl^\Omega[\theta_i](\omega)$ for each $\omega \subseteq \Omega$ given $\theta_i \in \Theta$. To allow for belief propagation in the presence of incomplete knowledge (e.g., the prior knowledge of Θ can be incomplete or even vacuous), [Smets1994] proposed the *Disjunctive Rule of Combination* (DRC), and conversely the *Generalised Bayes' Theorem* (GBT), to compute $pl^\Omega[\theta](\omega)$ and $pl^\Theta[\omega](\theta)$, respectively, for any $\theta \subseteq \Theta$, $\omega \subseteq \Omega$, from those $pl^\Omega[\theta_i](\omega)$:

$$pl^\Omega[\theta](\omega) = pl^\Theta[\omega](\theta) = 1 - \textstyle\prod_{\theta_i \in \theta}(1 - pl^\Omega[\theta_i](\omega)). (2.6)$$

As Eq. (2.6) is derived from the *principle of minimal commitment* (MCP) [Smets1994], the cbfs between any two nodes constructed in this way are said hereafter to be *MCP-compatible*. By Eq. (2.6), the impacts of m^Θ and m^Ω can be propagated to each other frame through:

$$pl^\Omega(\omega) = \textstyle\sum_{\theta \subseteq \Theta} m^\Theta(\theta) pl^\Omega[\theta](\omega), \forall \omega \subseteq \Omega, \quad (2.7)$$

$$pl^\Theta(\theta) = \textstyle\sum_{\omega \subseteq \Omega} m^\Omega(\omega) pl^\Omega[\omega](\theta), \forall \theta \subseteq \Theta. \quad (2.8)$$

The DRC and GBT allows a knowledge base to be constructed as a *directed acyclic graph* where nodes represent variables, and the directed edge between a node Ω and its parent Θ represents their relationship, initially described by the conditional belief functions $pl^\Omega[\theta_i](\omega), \forall \theta_i \in \Theta, \forall \omega \subseteq \Omega$. When a node receives observation in the form of a belief function, the impact will be propagated throughout the network to reflect the current state of knowledge. When the network or its secondary structure is singly-connected, belief propagation can be performed using a message-passing mechanism similar to that of Bayesian networks (see [Pearl1988]) with (i) beliefs propagated between nodes using DRC and GBT, and (ii) beliefs received at the same node combined using CRC (see [Xu and Smets1996, Yaghlane and Mellouli2008] for further discussion). When all the knowledge involved is complete, belief propagation using the DRC and GBT coincide with that of Bayesian reasoning (see [Smets1994]).

3 BELIEF UPDATING

Message-passing algorithms that compute beliefs directly on the original network have been devised for Bayesian networks (BNs), most notably the *loopy belief propagation* (LBP) and *(local) conditioning* algorithms (LC). LBP [Pearl1988] iteratively propagates beliefs as if the network is a poly-tree until convergence. Though providing a simple and often efficient mechanism for belief propagation, the results from LBP are theoretically known (e.g., in [Pearl1988]), and empirically verified (e.g., in [Weiss1997]) to not represent the posterior marginal of nodes which is of primary concern in belief updating. Thus LBP is not considered in this work. *(Global) conditioning* [Pearl1988] is based on the fact that instantiation of certain nodes (or a *cutset*) in the network will break the loop(s) containing them, rendering the network singly-connected. *Local conditioning* (LC) [Díez1996, Fay and Jaffray2000] improves on the original global method by ensuring that only nodes within a loop are conditioned on the variable that breaks the loop, and allows the impact from multiple observations to be simultaneously propagated. Application of LC in BNs was described in detail in [Díez1996, Fay and Jaffray2000]. In essence, LC is able to integrate belief propagation with the process of breaking loops and forming a tree associated with the network. When a loop is discovered, the method breaks the loop by splitting the conditioning variable into the original and its phantom instances and assigning the variable to every node within the loop (as illustrated in Figure 1c, the loop 3-4-5-6-7-3 is broken by 5, with 4 connected to 'phantom 5', and 3, 4, 6, 7 conditioned on 5). Once the cutset is found, belief propagation with LC in BNs is then similar to the original message-passing algorithm, except that each message now carries the unconditional probabilities on the product space of a node within the loop(s) and its conditioning variables, and no normalisation is performed. It is not hard to prove that LC can be directly extended and applied to networks with conditional belief functions by using the ballooning extension technique [Smets and Kennes1994] to transform the conditional belief functions between a node and its parent into the corresponding belief functions on their product space, and beliefs can be propagated in a classical way. However, this would diminish the original purpose of these types of network, and significantly increase the computational complexity and memory consumption (i.e., the space complexity required to represent a belief function on the product space with n variables of m states would be $\mathcal{O}(2^{m^n})$, rather than $\mathcal{O}(2^{mn})$ as in the case of conditional belief functions).

Our question therefore is *whether it is possible to apply local conditioning directly with conditional belief functions*. Such an approach would encounter two major obstacles. On the one hand, unlike a BN where conditional probabilities are just the normalised version of the unconditional ones, conditional belief functions correspond to only a certain portion of the underlying unconditional (joint) belief functions. On the other hand, while knowledge of the local cutset in a BN is always complete (a necessary condition for loop elimination), such knowledge in networks with cbfs can be incomplete (i.e., the belief function associated with the cutset can be non-Bayesian) and the MCP-compatibility required for DRC/GBT to propagate beliefs in this case is generally not met. The former demands combination of belief functions defined on arbitrary domains which are partially known, while the latter necessitates the devising of an extended version of DRC/GBT without the MCP compatibility assumption.

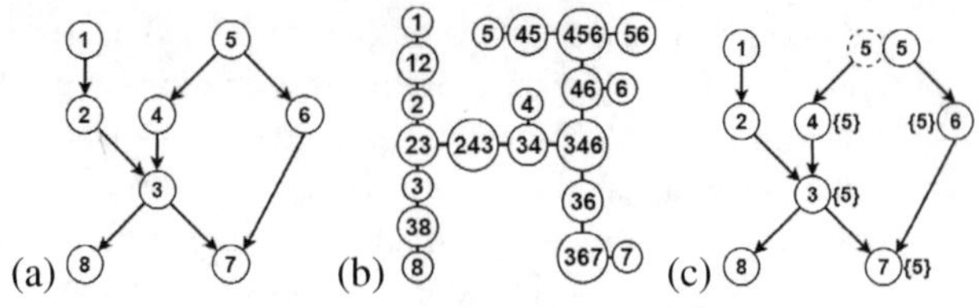

Figure 1: An example network (a), in the form of a binary join tree (adapted from [Yaghlane and Mellouli2008]) (b), or configured for local conditioning (c).

These obstacles will be addressed in Section 4. Specifically, we introduce the notion of (i) partially defined pl function, pl_{r}, that provides a compact and simultaneous encoding of multi-directional cbfs between a group of nodes of interest (e.g., a node and its parents/local cutset); and (ii) its corresponding partially defined $b.pl.a$ function, $\mu_{pl_{\text{r}}}$, that serves as the computational construct facilitating efficient computations. We next devise efficient methods that allow direct combination and propagation of beliefs represented in the form of pl_{r} by means of $\mu_{pl_{\text{r}}}$. The method $\circledcirc_r$ allows exact combination when such pl_{r} are associated with disjoint sets of conditioning variables (see Theorem 4.5). When those pl_r are associated with overlapping sets of conditioning variables, $\circledcirc_r$ enables exact computation of a particular portion, $\mathscr{C}_{pl_{\text{r}}}$, of their combined impact (see Theorem 4.6 Step 1). Based on $\mathscr{C}_{pl_{\text{r}}}$, the entire combined impact can be reconstructed when necessary; either by means of interval approximation as in Theorem 4.6 Step 2, or point estimation using a parameterised version of DRC/GBT. In order to discuss the proposed belief propagation method, we assume that the cutset has been determined and the network has been configured accordingly (e.g., see Figure 1c).

4 BELIEF UPDATING WITH LC & CBFS

It is sufficient to define pl_{r} and $\mu_{pl_{\text{r}}}$ with respect to any three variables X, Y and Z. The following notations are adopted from [Yaghlane, Smets, and Mellouli2002b]:

- XYZ denotes the Cartesian product $X \times Y \times Z$;
- x_i, y_j, z_k denote elements, and x, y, z subsets of X, Y, Z;
- (x, y, z) denotes $\{(x_i, y_j, z_k) : x_i \in x, y_j \in y, z_k \in z\}$ for some x, y and z;
- pl^{Ω} denotes the plausibility function on Ω, $pl^{\Omega\downarrow X}$ the marginal of pl^{Ω} on X, and $pl^{\Omega}[y, z]^{\downarrow X}$ the plausibility function on X that results from conditioning pl^{Ω} on (y, z) and then marginalised on X[2];
- $x^{\uparrow XY}$ is the cylindrical extension of $x \subseteq X$ on XY : $x^{\uparrow XY} = (x, Y)$, and $\omega^{\downarrow X}$ is the projection of $\omega \subseteq \Omega$ on X: $\omega^{\downarrow X} = \{x_i : x_i \in X, x_i^{\uparrow\Omega} \cap \omega \neq \emptyset\}$.

[2]Note that conditioning and marginalisation are not commutative, e.g., $pl^{\Omega}[y, z]^{\downarrow X} \neq pl^{\Omega\downarrow X}[y, z]$.

4.1 PARTIALLY DEFINED pl_{r} AND $\mu_{pl_{\mathrm{r}}}$

Definition 1 *Let* r_Ω *be the set of subsets of* $\Omega = XYZ$ *consisting of* (x, y, z) *for all* $x \subseteq X$, $y \subseteq Y$, *and* $z \subseteq Z$. *A* partially defined pl_{r}^Ω *is a plausibility function on* Ω *whose value is known for only those subsets of* Ω *in* r_Ω.

Such r_Ω can be considered the set of *hyper-rectangle* subsets of Ω. Each pl_{r}^Ω is associated with a set of pl^Ω on Ω (denoted as $\mathscr{P}_{\mathrm{r}}^\Omega$) such that $pl^\Omega(\omega) = pl_{\mathrm{r}}^\Omega(\omega)$, $\forall \omega \in \mathrm{r}_\Omega$; and pl_{r} defined on a single variable corresponds to its marginal (e.g., $pl_{\mathrm{r}}^X \equiv pl^X$). By extending Lemma 1 and 2 in [Yaghlane, Smets, and Mellouli2002a] to a multivariate context, Lemma 4.1 is obtained for all $x \subseteq X$, $y \subseteq Y$, $z \subseteq Z$:

Lemma 4.1 *For any given* pl_{r}^Ω *defined on* Ω, *we have:*

$$pl_{\mathrm{r}}^\Omega(x, y, z) = pl_{\mathrm{r}}^\Omega[z]^{\downarrow XY}(x, y) = pl_{\mathrm{r}}^\Omega[y, z]^{\downarrow X}(x),$$

$$pl_{\mathrm{r}}^{\Omega \downarrow XY}(x, y) = pl_{\mathrm{r}}^\Omega(x, y, Z), pl_{\mathrm{r}}^{\Omega \downarrow X}(x) = pl_{\mathrm{r}}^\Omega(x, Y, Z).$$

As seen above, the collection of conditional belief functions allowing evidence to be propagated between X, Y and Z in a canonical manner corresponds to the partially defined pl_{r}^Ω on Ω. Thus, pl_{r}^Ω can be considered a compact encoding that simultaneously represents the conditional relationship between any nodes of interest, not only between child and parent nodes as presented in Section 2. In singly-connected networks, propagated beliefs are in their marginal form (Eqs. (2.7) and (2.8)). In multiply-connected networks under local conditioning, the beliefs sent and received by a node are potentially conditioned on some variables, represented here in the form of pl_{r}, necessitating methods to combine and propagate those pl_{r}. Combination of (completely defined) pl functions is possible by means of other functions as shown in Section 2. However, since Lemma 4.1 does not hold for any functions other than pl (e.g., $m[x](y) \neq m(x, y) \neq m[y](x)$), attempts to derive a method to combine beliefs in their partial form pl_{r} by means of such functions would result in a significant computational and spatial overhead. In order to facilitate efficient and simultaneous combination of pl_{r} functions, we propose for any given pl_{r} its dual representation $\mu_{pl_{\mathrm{r}}}$.

Definition 2 *For any given* pl_{r}^Ω *on* Ω, *the corresponding* partially defined *b.pl.a* function $\mu_{pl_{\mathrm{r}}^\Omega}$ *is defined by:*

$$\mu_{pl_{\mathrm{r}}^\Omega}(x, y, z) = \textstyle\sum_{\omega'^{\downarrow X}=x, \omega'^{\downarrow Y}=y, \omega'^{\downarrow Z}=z} \mu_{pl^\Omega}(\omega') \quad (4.1)$$

for all $x \subseteq X, y \subseteq Y, z \subseteq Z, \omega' \subseteq \Omega$, *where* μ_{pl^Ω} *is associated with any* pl^Ω *in* $\mathscr{P}_{\mathrm{r}}^\Omega$.

Subsets ω' in Eq. (4.1) are said to be *indistinguishable* with respect to x on X, y on Y and z on Z (i.e., their respective projections on X, Y and Z coincide with each other). Intuitively, $\mu_{pl_{\mathrm{r}}^\Omega}(x, y, z)$ 'clamps' together $\mu_{pl^\Omega}(\omega')$ of all indistinguishable subsets ω' associated with (x, y, z) on Ω, considering only their total μ value rather than any specific μ distribution among ω'.

Lemma 4.2 pl_{r}^Ω *and* $\mu_{pl_{\mathrm{r}}^\Omega}$ *are one-to-one correspondent and related with each other through:* $\forall (x, y, z) \in \mathrm{r}_\Omega$,

$$pl_{\mathrm{r}}^\Omega(x, y, z) = \textstyle\sum_{x' \subseteq x, y' \subseteq y, z' \subseteq z} \mu_{pl_{\mathrm{r}}^\Omega}(x', y', z').$$

Proof Suppose there exists some $\omega' \subseteq \Omega$ such that $\mu_{pl^\Omega}(\omega')$ contributes to (i) more than one element in $\mu_{pl_{\mathrm{r}}^\Omega}$, the elements must be the same (by Def. 2); (ii) none of the elements in $\mu_{pl_{\mathrm{r}}^\Omega}$, ω' must be $\emptyset$ (by Def. 2). From this, $\mu_{pl_{\mathrm{r}}^\Omega}$ can be inferred as a lossless coarsening of μ_{pl^Ω}, and thus by Eq. (2.3), the above relation can be obtained.

Consequently, Lemma 4.1 can be equivalently written in terms of $\mu_{pl_{\mathrm{r}}^\Omega}$ (see Lemma 4.3), and so the initially defined relation between any node and its parent (see Lemma 4.4).

Lemma 4.3 *For any given* pl_{r}^Ω *defined on* Ω, *we have:*

$$\begin{aligned}
\mu_{pl_{\mathrm{r}}^\Omega}^{\downarrow X}(x) &= \textstyle\sum_{y \subseteq Y, z \subseteq Z} \mu_{pl_{\mathrm{r}}^\Omega}(x, y, z), \\
\mu_{pl_{\mathrm{r}}^\Omega}^{\downarrow XY}(x, y) &= \textstyle\sum_{z \subseteq Z} \mu_{pl_{\mathrm{r}}^\Omega}(x, y, z), \\
\mu_{pl_{\mathrm{r}}^\Omega}[z]^{\downarrow XY}(x, y) &= \textstyle\sum_{z' \subseteq z} \mu_{pl_{\mathrm{r}}^\Omega}(x, y, z'), \\
\mu_{pl_{\mathrm{r}}^\Omega}[y, z]^{\downarrow X}(x) &= \textstyle\sum_{y' \subseteq y, z' \subseteq z} \mu_{pl_{\mathrm{r}}^\Omega}(x, y', z'),
\end{aligned}$$

for all $x \subseteq X$, $y \subseteq Y$ *and* $z \subseteq Z$.

Lemma 4.4 *The initial relation between any* Y *and its parent* X *in Eq.* (2.6) *can be equivalently written by means of* $\mu_{pl_{\mathrm{r}}^\Theta}$ *on* $\Theta = XY$ *for all* $x \subseteq X$, $y \subseteq Y$ *and* $\alpha_x \triangleq (-1)^{|x|+1}$ *as*

$$\mu_{pl_{\mathrm{r}}^\Theta}(x, y) = \alpha_x \prod_{x_i \in x} pl_{\mathrm{r}}^\Theta(x_i, y) - \sum_{y' \subset y} \mu_{pl_{\mathrm{r}}^\Theta}(x, y'). \quad (4.2)$$

Proof Eq. (4.2) is obtained by first rewriting Eq. (2.6) as $pl_{\mathrm{r}}^\Theta(x, y) = 1 - \prod_{x_i \in x}(1 - pl_{\mathrm{r}}^\Theta(x_i, y))$ (4.3) using Lemma (4.1), then replacing all pl_{r} terms in Eq. (4.3) with their corresponding $\mu_{pl_{\mathrm{r}}}$ using Lemma 4.2.

With all quantitative aspects of a network represented in the form of pl_{r} (by means of its corresponding $\mu_{pl_{\mathrm{r}}}$), belief propagation is now essentially concerned with combination of such pl_{r}. For instance, pl^{AG} (Figure 2b) is the combined impact of pl_{r}^A, pl_{r}^{AB}, pl_{r}^B and pl_{r}^{BG} (Figure 2a) on AG. We will next show how pl_{r} can be efficiently and directly combined by means of $\mu_{pl_{\mathrm{r}}}$. Since the algorithm is based on the message-passing mechanism, belief combination methods will be presented from the perspective of each node.

4.2 COMBINATION OF pl_{r} FUNCTIONS

At any node X_0 in the network, belief combination using LC can be generalised into two scenarios: the set of pl_{r} to be combined are (1) mutually distinct (they do not share any common conditioning variables) and (2) non-distinct (they are otherwise). Across nodes, Case 1 is concerned with belief combination associated with 'tree' portions of loop(s) (e.g., combination of pl_{r}^{AG} and pl_{r}^{FG} at node G to propagate belief from A to F); while Case 2 with computing the entire impact of one or more loops on X_0 (e.g., combination of pl_{r}^{AG} and $pl_{\mathrm{r}}^{AG'}$ at node G). As such let $\mathbf{X} = \{X_0, \ldots, X_n\}$ be any subset of nodes in the network; $\mathbf{U}_1$ and $\mathbf{U}_2$ respectively be any set of subsets of $\mathbf{X}$ (without loss of generality, assume $\mathbf{X} = \mathbf{U}_1 \cup \mathbf{U}_2$) and $\mathbf{V} = \mathbf{U}_1 \cap \mathbf{U}_2$. Let Θ_1, Θ_2 and Ω be the Cartesian product of the elements in $\mathbf{U_1}$, $\mathbf{U_2}$, and $\mathbf{X}$, respectively, we are interested in the combined impact on Ω for any given $pl_{\mathrm{r}}^{\Theta_1}$ and $pl_{\mathrm{r}}^{\Theta_2}$ where $\mathbf{U}_1$ and $\mathbf{U}_2$ can be arbitrarily overlapping.

4.2.1 Combination of Distinct pl_{r} Functions

Theorem 4.5 is concerned with belief combination at X_0 in Case 1 where $pl_{\mathrm{r}}^{\Theta_1}$ and $pl_{\mathrm{r}}^{\Theta_2}$ to be combined are distinct (i.e., having non-overlapping conditioning variables, or $\mathbf{V} = \{X_0\}$). The theorem proposes a new conjunctive combination rule $\circledcap_r$ such that the combined impact $pl_{\mathrm{r}}^{\Omega}{=}pl_{\mathrm{r}}^{\Theta_1} \circledcap_r pl_{\mathrm{r}}^{\Theta_2}$ on Ω is equivalent to the partially defined pl_{r} associated with $pl^{\Omega} = pl^{\Theta_1} \circledcap pl^{\Theta_2}$ (for any $pl^{\Theta_1} \in \mathscr{P}_{\mathrm{r}}^{\Theta_1}$ and $pl^{\Theta_2} \in \mathscr{P}_{\mathrm{r}}^{\Theta_2}$) without having to perform the latter computations, the knowledge of which is generally not available, and the computations significantly more expensive.

Theorem 4.5 *Given $pl_{\mathrm{r}}^{\Theta_1}$ and $pl_{\mathrm{r}}^{\Theta_2}$ defined on Θ_1 and Θ_2, respectively where $\mathbf{V} = \{X_0\}$, their combined impact $pl_{\mathrm{r}}^{\Omega} = pl_{\mathrm{r}}^{\Theta_1} \circledcap_r pl_{\mathrm{r}}^{\Theta_2}$ on Ω is uniquely determined by means of their corresponding $\mu_{pl_{\mathrm{r}}^{\Omega}}$, $\mu_{pl_{\mathrm{r}}^{\Theta_1}}$ and $\mu_{pl_{\mathrm{r}}^{\Theta_2}}$:*

$$\mu_{pl_{\mathrm{r}}^{\Omega}}(\omega) = (-1)^{|x_0|+1} \mu_{pl_{\mathrm{r}}^{\Theta_1}}(\omega^{\downarrow\Theta_1}) \mu_{pl_{\mathrm{r}}^{\Theta_2}}(\omega^{\downarrow\Theta_2}), \quad (4.4)$$

for all $\omega \in \mathrm{r}_{\Omega}$ and $x_0 = \omega^{\downarrow X_0}$.

Proof See the Appendix.

When there are more than two mutually distinct pl_{r} to be combined at a node, Eq. (4.4) can be carried out in a pairwise fashion. When they are across nodes, application of $\circledcap_r$ in Theorem 4.5 and marginalisation in Lemma 4.1 and 4.3 fulfill the three axioms by Shenoy [Shenoy1993] that make local computations possible. For instance, let $pl_{\mathrm{r}1}, pl_{\mathrm{r}2}$, $pl_{\mathrm{r}3}$ and $pl_{\mathrm{r}12}$ denote pl_{r}^{AB}, pl_{r}^{BG}, pl_{r}^{FG} and pl_{r}^{ABG} in Figure 2, respectively, the following axioms are satisfied for all $a \subseteq A$, $b \subseteq B$, $f \subseteq F$, and $g \subseteq G$:

Commutativity and associativity of combination, e.g.,
$((\mu_{pl_{\mathrm{r}1}} \circledcap_r \mu_{pl_{\mathrm{r}2}}) \circledcap_r \mu_{pl_{\mathrm{r}3}})(a, b, f, g)$
$= (-1)^{|g|+1} \left((-1)^{|b|+1} \mu_{pl_{\mathrm{r}1}}(a, b) \mu_{pl_{\mathrm{r}2}}(b, g)\right) \mu_{pl_{\mathrm{r}3}}(f, g)$
$= (-1)^{|b|+1} \left((-1)^{|g|+1} \mu_{pl_{\mathrm{r}2}}(b, g) \mu_{pl_{\mathrm{r}3}}(f, g)\right) \mu_{pl_{\mathrm{r}1}}(a, b)$
$= (\mu_{pl_{\mathrm{r}1}} \circledcap_r (\mu_{pl_{\mathrm{r}2}} \circledcap_r \mu_{pl_{\mathrm{r}3}}))(a, b, f, g)$
Consonance of marginalisation, e.g,
$pl_{\mathrm{r}}^{ABG\downarrow AB\downarrow A}(a) = \sum_{b \subseteq B} (\sum_{g \subseteq G} \mu_{pl_{\mathrm{r}12}}(a, B, G))$
$= \sum_{b \subseteq B, g \subseteq G} \mu_{pl_{\mathrm{r}12}}(a, B, G) = pl_{\mathrm{r}}^{ABG\downarrow A}(a)$
Distributivity of marginalisation over combination, e.g.,
$(pl_{\mathrm{r}1} \circledcap_r pl_{\mathrm{r}2})^{\downarrow AB} = \sum_g (-1)^{|b|+1} \mu_{pl_{\mathrm{r}1}}(a, b) \mu_{pl_{\mathrm{r}2}}(b, g)$
$= (-1)^{|b|+1} \mu_{pl_{\mathrm{r}1}}(a, b) \sum_g \mu_{pl_{\mathrm{r}2}}(b, g) = pl_{\mathrm{r}1} \circledcap_r (pl_{\mathrm{r}2})^{\downarrow B}$.
When $pl_{\mathrm{r}}^{\Theta_1}$ and $pl_{\mathrm{r}}^{\Theta_2}$ are distinct, pl_{r}^{Ω} can be exactly and uniquely determined due to the cylindrical extension $(\omega^{\downarrow\Theta_1})^{\uparrow\Omega}$ (resp. $(\omega^{\downarrow\Theta_2})^{\uparrow\Omega}$) applied to $\omega^{\downarrow\Theta_1}$ (resp. $\omega^{\downarrow\Theta_2}$) for each $\omega \in \mathrm{r}_{\Omega}$, rendering the product in Eq. (4.4) insensitive to any specific distribution of μ among those *indistinguishable* ω' (see Def. (2)) associated with each $\omega \in \mathrm{r}_{\Omega}$.

4.2.2 Combination of Non-distinct pl_{r} Functions

When $pl_{\mathrm{r}}^{\Theta_1}$ and $pl_{\mathrm{r}}^{\Theta_2}$ are non-distinct (i.e., having common conditioning variables: $|\mathbf{V}|{>}1$ in Case 2), the equality in Eq. (4.4) no longer holds, thus their combination result on Ω is no longer unique. The basic mathematical reasoning for Theorem 4.6 that determines a set of possible pl_{r}^{Ω} resulting from combination of $pl_{\mathrm{r}}^{\Theta_1}$ and $pl_{\mathrm{r}}^{\Theta_2}$ is as follows. Let

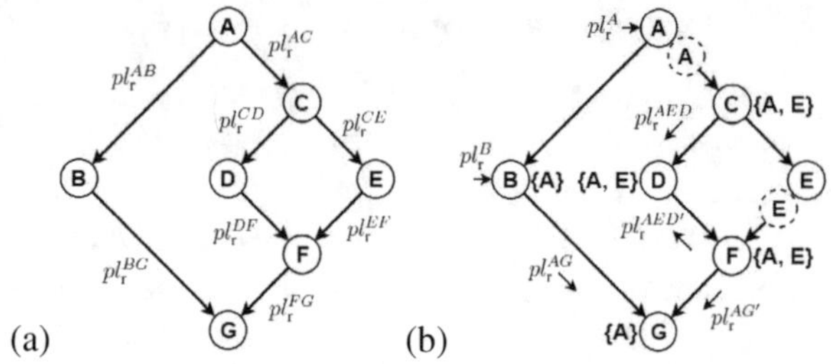

Figure 2: (a) A sample network where the relations between nodes are represented with pl_{r}, and (b) with its loops broken by the cutset $\{A, E\}$, and example messages received by D and G during belief updating.

- $\Phi_i = \Omega \backslash X_i$, $\Phi_{ij} = \Omega \backslash \{X_i, X_j\}$ denote the product of elements in $\mathbf{X} \backslash X_i$ and $\mathbf{X} \backslash \{X_i, X_j\}$, respectively;
- $\omega \in \mathrm{r}_{\Omega}$ be equivalently represented as $\omega = (x_i, \phi_i)$ where $x_i = \omega^{\downarrow X_i}$, $\phi_i = \omega^{\downarrow\Phi_i}$ for any $X_i \in \mathbf{X}$[3], and as $\omega = (x_i, x_j, \phi_{ij})$ for any $X_j (\neq X_i) \in \mathbf{X}$, $x_j = \omega^{\downarrow X_j}$ and $\phi_{ij} = \omega^{\downarrow\Phi_{ij}}$;
- $N(\omega)$ denote the number of $X_i \in \mathbf{V}$ associated with ω s.t. $x_i = \omega^{\downarrow X_i}$ is a non-singleton subset (i.e., $|x_i| > 1$)[4];
- α_{x_i} denote $(-1)^{|x_i|+1}$ for some $x_i \subseteq X_i$; and
- ω be arranged in partial order by increasing size $N(\omega)$.

We are now interested in computing $pl_{\mathrm{r}}^{\Omega}(\omega)$ for all $\omega \in \mathrm{r}_{\Omega}$.

(I) We first consider all those ω with $N(\omega) \leq 1$, i.e., there exists $X_i \in \mathbf{V}$ s.t. $\omega = (x_i, \phi_i)$ and $N(\phi_i) = 0$. Since $pl_{\mathrm{r}}^{\Omega}(x_i, \phi_i) = pl_{\mathrm{r}}^{\Omega}[\phi_i]^{\downarrow X_i}(x_i)$ for all $x_i \subseteq X_i$ (Lemma 4.1) and $N(\phi_i) = N(\phi_i^{\downarrow\Theta_1}) = N(\phi_i^{\downarrow\Theta_2}) = 0$ in this case, only *singleton* subsets of the conditioning variables associated with both $pl_{\mathrm{r}}^{\Theta_1}$ and $pl_{\mathrm{r}}^{\Theta_2}$ hold, thereby eliminating the associated loop(s) and rendering the belief functions induced by $pl_{\mathrm{r}}^{\Theta_1}$ and $pl_{\mathrm{r}}^{\Theta_2}$ on X_i, $pl_{\mathrm{r}}^{\Theta_1}[\phi_i^{\downarrow\Theta_1}]^{\downarrow X_i}$ and $pl_{\mathrm{r}}^{\Theta_2}[\phi_i^{\downarrow\Theta_2}]^{\downarrow X_i}$, distinct. Thus by Theorem 4.5 we have for all $x_i \subseteq X_i$:

$$\mu_{pl_{\mathrm{r}}^{\Omega}}(x_i, \phi_i) = \alpha_{x_i} \mu_{pl_{\mathrm{r}}^{\Theta_1}}(x_i, \phi_i^{\downarrow\Theta_1}) \mu_{pl_{\mathrm{r}}^{\Theta_2}}(x_i, \phi_i^{\downarrow\Theta_2}),$$
$$pl_{\mathrm{r}}^{\Omega}(x_i, \phi_i) = \sum_{x_{i'} \subseteq x_i, \phi_{i'} \subseteq \phi_i, \phi_{i'} \in \mathrm{r}_{\Phi_i}} \mu_{pl_{\mathrm{r}}^{\Omega}}(x_{i'}, \phi_{i'}). \quad (4.5)$$

All $pl_{\mathrm{r}}^{\Omega}(\omega)$ computed by Eq. (4.5) are referred to collectively as the *Core* of pl_{r}^{Ω} ($\mathscr{C}_{pl_{\mathrm{r}}^{\Omega}}$) from which the bounds associated with $pl_{\mathrm{r}}^{\Omega}(\omega)$ where $N(\omega){\geq}2$ are derived below.

(II) We next consider all ω where $N(\omega){=}2$, i.e., there exist X_i and X_j in $\mathbf{V}$ s.t. $\omega = (x_i, x_j, \phi_{ij})$, $|x_i| > 1$, $|x_j| > 1$. With respect to X_i alone, we have by Lemma 4.2:

$$pl_{\mathrm{r}}^{\Omega}(\omega) = pl_{\mathrm{r}}^{\Omega}(x_i, \phi_i) = \sum_{x_{i_k}} pl_{\mathrm{r}}^{\Omega}(x_{i_k}, \phi_i) + \sum_{x_{i*}, \phi_{i'}} \mu_{pl_{\mathrm{r}}^{\Omega}}(x_{i*}, \phi_{i'}), \quad (4.6)$$

for all $x_{i_k} \in x_i$, $x_{i*} (\neq x_{i_k}) \subseteq x_i$, $\phi_{i'} (\in \mathrm{r}_{\Phi_i}) \subseteq \phi_i$.

Regarding the first sum of Eq. (4.6), since $(x_{i_k}, \phi_i) = (x_{i_k}, x_j, \phi_{ij})$ and $N(x_{i_k}, \phi_{ij}) = 0$, $pl_{\mathrm{r}}^{\Omega}(x_{i_k}, \phi_i)$ $\forall x_{i_k} \in x_i$ can be exactly computed using Eq. (4.5). Regarding the second sum, $\mu_{x_{i*}, \phi_{i'}} \triangleq \sum_{x_{i*}, \phi_{i'}} \mu_{pl_{\mathrm{r}}^{\Omega}}(x_{i*}, \phi_{i'})$, $\mu_{x_{i*}, \phi_{i'}}$ can be considered the *total overlapping (belief) mass* and thus constrained by those $pl_{\mathrm{r}}^{\Omega}(x_{i_k}, \phi_i)$ $\forall x_{i_k} \in x_i$. Due to

---

[3]For instance, $\omega = (x_0, ..., x_n)$ can be represented as $\omega = (x_1, \phi_1)$ where $\phi_1 = (x_0, x_2, ..., x_n)$ with respect to X_1.

[4]For instance, given $\omega = (x_0, ..., x_n)$ and $\mathbf{V} = \{X_0, X_1\}$, $N(\omega) = 0$ when $|x_0| = |x_1| = 1$, $N(\omega) = 1$ when $|x_0| > 1$ or $|x_1| > 1$, and $N(\omega) = 2$ when $|x_0| > 1$ and $|x_1| > 1$.

$\alpha_{x_{i*}} \sum_{\phi_{i'}} \mu_{pl_{\mathrm{r}}^{\Omega}}(x_{i*}, \phi_{i'}) \leq \min_{x_{ik*} \in x_{i*}} pl_{\mathrm{r}}^{\Omega}(x_{x_{ik*},\phi_i})$[5] substitution of which into $\mu_{x_{i*},\phi_{i'}}$ of Eq. (4.6) yields:

$$\underline{pl_{\mathrm{r}}^{\Omega}}(\omega) = \underline{pl_{\mathrm{r}}^{\Omega}}(x_i, \phi_i) = \max_{x_{i_k}} pl_{\mathrm{r}}^{\Omega}(x_{i_k}, \phi_i) \quad (4.7)$$

$$\overline{pl_{\mathrm{r}}^{\Omega}}(\omega) = \overline{pl_{\mathrm{r}}^{\Omega}}(x_i, \phi_i) = \min(1, \textstyle\sum_{x_{i_k}} pl_{\mathrm{r}}^{\Omega}(x_{i_k}, \phi_i)) \quad (4.8)$$

corresponding to Fréchet bounds in probability theory. Since x_j is also non-singleton, $\mu_{x_{i*},\phi_{i'}}$ is expected to be further constrained, e.g., through $pl_{\mathrm{r}}^{\Omega}(x_{j_l}, \phi_j), \forall x_{j_l} \in x_j$.

Let pl_{r}^{Θ} denote $pl_{\mathrm{r}}^{\Omega}[\phi_{ij}]^{\downarrow\Theta}$, $\Theta{=}X_iX_j$, we can decompose $pl_{\mathrm{r}}^{\Omega}(\omega)$ with respect to X_j in reference to X_i as

$$\begin{aligned} pl_{\mathrm{r}}^{\Omega}(\omega) &= pl_{\mathrm{r}}^{\Omega}(x_i, x_j, \phi_{ij}) = pl_{\mathrm{r}}^{\Omega}[\phi_{ij}]^{\downarrow\Theta}(x_i, x_j) \\ &= \sum_{x_{j_l}} pl_{\mathrm{r}}^{\Omega}(x_i, x_{j_l}, \phi_{ij}) + \sum_{x_{i'}, x_{j*}, \phi_{ij'}} \mu_{pl_{\mathrm{r}}^{\Omega}}(x_{i'}, x_{j*}, \phi_{ij'}) \\ &= \sum_{x_{j_l}} pl_{\mathrm{r}}^{\Omega}[\phi_{ij}]^{\downarrow\Theta}(x_i, x_{j_l}) + \sum_{x_{i'}, x_{j*}} \mu_{pl_{\mathrm{r}}^{\Omega}}[\phi_{ij}]^{\downarrow\Theta}(x_{i'}, x_{j*}) \\ &= \sum_{x_{j_l}} pl_{\mathrm{r}}^{\Theta}(x_i, x_{j_l}) + \sum_{x_{i'}, x_{j*}} \mu_{pl_{\mathrm{r}}^{\Theta}}(x_{i'}, x_{j*}), \end{aligned} \quad (4.9)$$

for all $x_{i'} \subseteq x_i$, $x_{j_l} \in x_j$, $x_{j*}(\neq x_{j_l}) \subseteq x_j$, $\phi_{ij'}(\in \mathrm{r}_{\Phi_{ij}}) \subseteq \phi_{ij}$; and subsequently $pl_{\mathrm{r}}^{\Theta}(x_i, x_{j_l})$ with respect to X_i as

$$pl_{\mathrm{r}}^{\Theta}(x_i, x_{j_l}) = \textstyle\sum_{x_{i_k}} pl_{\mathrm{r}}^{\Theta}(x_{i_k}, x_{j_l}) + \sum_{x_{i*}} \mu_{pl_{\mathrm{r}}^{\Theta}}(x_{i*}, x_{j_l}) \quad (4.10)$$

for all $x_{i_k} \in x_i$ and $x_{i*}(\neq x_{i_k}) \subseteq x_i$.

From Eqs. (4.6) and (4.10), we have

$$\begin{aligned} \mu_{x_{i*},\phi_{i'}} &\leq \min_{x_{j_l}} \textstyle\sum_{x_{i*}} \mu_{pl_{\mathrm{r}}^{\Theta}}(x_{i*}, x_{j_l})^{6} \\ &\leq \min_{x_{j_l}} (pl_{\mathrm{r}}^{\Theta}(x_i, x_{j_l}) - \textstyle\sum_{x_{i_k}} pl_{\mathrm{r}}^{\Theta}(x_{i_k}, x_{j_l})), \end{aligned}$$

thus the bound in Eq. (4.8) can be further tightened:

$$\begin{aligned} \overline{pl_{\mathrm{r}}^{\Omega}}(\omega) = \min(1, &\textstyle\sum_{x_{i_k}} pl_{\mathrm{r}}^{\Omega}(x_{i_k}, \phi_i) + \\ &\min_{x_{j_l} \in x_j} (pl_{\mathrm{r}}^{\Theta}(x_i, x_{j_l}) - \textstyle\sum_{x_{i_k}} pl_{\mathrm{r}}^{\Theta}(x_{i_k}, x_{j_l}))) \end{aligned} \quad (4.11).$$

(III) Finally, we consider all ω where $N(\omega){>}2$. Each ω in this case is associated with multiple such X_i in Eq. (4.6), each in turn associated with multiple such X_j in Eq. (4.9), this necessitates extending Eqs (4.7) and (4.11) to all $X_i \in \mathbf{X}$, and all $X_j(\neq X_i) \in \mathbf{X}$, respectively. Since $N(x_{i_k}, \phi_i) = N(x_i, \phi_i) - 1$, Eqs (4.7) and (4.11) can be efficiently applied in a dynamic programming manner to all ω with increasing size $N(\omega)$ as shown in Theorem 4.6.

Theorem 4.6 *Given any two non-distinct* $pl_{\mathrm{r}}^{\Theta_1}$ *and* $pl_{\mathrm{r}}^{\Theta_2}$ *defined on* Θ_1 *and* Θ_2*, respectively (i.e.,* $|\mathbf{V}| > 1$*), their combined impact on* Ω*,* pl_{r}^{Ω}*, can be approximated as:*

Step 1: Computation of $\mathscr{C}_{pl_{\mathrm{r}}^{\Omega}}$:

$$\mu_{pl_{\mathrm{r}}^{\Omega}}(x_i, \phi_i) = \alpha_{x_i} \mu_{pl_{\mathrm{r}}^{\Theta_1}}(x_i, \phi_i^{\downarrow\Theta_1}) \mu_{pl_{\mathrm{r}}^{\Theta_2}}(x_i, \phi_i^{\downarrow\Theta_2})$$

$$pl_{\mathrm{r}}^{\Omega}(x_i, \phi_i) = \textstyle\sum_{x_{i'} \subseteq x_i, \phi_{i'}(\in \mathrm{r}_{\Phi_i}) \subseteq \phi_i} \mu_{pl_{\mathrm{r}}^{\Omega}}(x_{i'}, \phi_{i'}) \quad (4.12)$$

for all $\omega = (x_i, \phi_i) \in \mathrm{r}_{\Omega}$ *where* $|x_i| \geq 1$ *and* $N(\phi_i) = 0$.

Step 2: Reconstruction of pl_{r}^{Ω}:

$$\underline{pl_{\mathrm{r}}^{\Omega}}(\omega) = \max_{X_i}(\max_{x_{i_k} \in x_i} \underline{pl_{\mathrm{r}}^{\Omega}}(x_{i_k}, \phi_i)) \quad (4.13)$$

$$\overline{pl_{\mathrm{r}}^{\Omega}}(\omega) = \min_{X_i} (1, \sum_{x_{i_k} \in x_i} \overline{pl_{\mathrm{r}}^{\Omega}}(x_{i_k}, \phi_i) + \min_{X_j} \mu_{x_{i*},\phi_{i'}}) \quad (4.14)$$

$$\mu_{x_{i*},\phi_{i'}} \triangleq \min_{x_{j_l} \in x_j} (\overline{pl_{\mathrm{r}}^{\Omega}}(x_i, x_{j_l}, \phi_{ij}) - \sum_{x_{i_k}} \overline{pl_{\mathrm{r}}^{\Omega}}(x_{i_k}, x_{j_l}, \phi_{ij}))$$

for all ω *s.t.* $N(\omega) > 1$*, all* $X_i, X_j {\in} \mathbf{X}$ *s.t.* $|x_i|{>}1$, $|x_j|{>}1$.

Since $pl_{\mathrm{r}}^{\Omega\downarrow X_i}(x_i) = pl_{\mathrm{r}}^{\Omega}(x_i, \Phi_i)$, Theorem 4.6 allows simultaneous approximation of the posterior marginal of any node X_i in the form of a set of possible belief functions defined by the bounds imposed on $pl_{\mathrm{r}}^{\Omega\downarrow X_i}(x_i)$, $\forall x_i \subseteq X_i$. It is highly desirable however in many cases to approximate a single combination result (which would be more informative, and more efficient with respect to belief propagation). As such, we will now take one step further and devise a method that estimates a specific point value $pl_{\mathrm{r}}^{\Omega}(\omega)$ within the interval approximation $[\underline{pl_{\mathrm{r}}^{\Omega}}(\omega), \overline{pl_{\mathrm{r}}^{\Omega}}(\omega)]$ in Theorem 4.6 in such a way that $pl_{\mathrm{r}}^{\Omega}(\omega)$ *reflects the current state of knowledge* with a high degree of accuracy.

4.2.3 Approximation with parameterised DRC/GBT

Recall from Lemma 4.1 that $pl_{\mathrm{r}}^{\Omega}(x_i, \phi_i) = pl_{\mathrm{r}}^{\Omega}[\phi_i]^{\downarrow X_i}(x_i)$, $\forall x_i \subseteq X_i$. By Eq. (4.12), a 'complete' marginal of pl_{r}^{Ω} on some X_i (i.e., $pl^{\Omega}[\phi_i]^{\downarrow X_i} \equiv pl_{\mathrm{r}}^{\Omega}[\phi_i]^{\downarrow X_i}$) can be exactly computed when ϕ_i holds, rendering $\mathscr{C}_{pl_{\mathrm{r}}^{\Omega}}$ a collective set of such marginals on all $X_i \in X$. As a result, Theorem 4.6 Step 2 can be reformulated as the problem of reconstructing pl_{r}^{Ω} from those marginals. To this end, with respect to X_i and X_j in Eq. (4.9), let us rewrite the equation in the form of conditional belief functions on X_i in reference to X_j:

For all $x_{i_k} \in x_i$, $x_{i*}(\neq x_{i_k}) \subseteq x_i$: $pl_{\mathrm{r}}^{X_i}[x_j] \triangleq pl_{\mathrm{r}}^{\Omega}[x_j, \phi_{ij}]^{\downarrow X_i}$,

$$\begin{aligned} pl_{\mathrm{r}}^{\Omega}(\omega) &= pl_{\mathrm{r}}^{X_i}[x_j](x_i) \\ &= \sum_{x_{i_k}} pl_{\mathrm{r}}^{X_i}[x_j](x_{i_k}) + \sum_{x_{i*}} \mu_{pl_{\mathrm{r}}^{X_i}}[x_j](x_{i*}), \end{aligned} \quad (4.15)$$

where $pl_{\mathrm{r}}^{X_i}[x_j](x_{i_k})$, $\forall x_{i_k} \in x_i$ have been computed in the previous iteration. Applying DRC/GBT as in Eq. (2.6) which directly computes $pl_{\mathrm{r}}^{X_i}[x_j](x_i)$ from $pl_{\mathrm{r}}^{X_i}[x_j](x_{i_k})$ is not eligible since (i) those $pl_{\mathrm{r}}^{X_i}[x_j](x_{i_k})$ are not the only knowledge about $pl_{\mathrm{r}}^{\Omega}(\omega)$, and (ii) they are not initially defined but correspond to pl_{r}^{Ω} on Ω and thus generally not MCP-compatible. This requires us to extend the *Generalised Likelihood Principle* (GLP) [Smets1994] to a multivariate context without the MCP-compatibility assumption.

Extended GLP For any $pl_{\mathrm{r}}^{\Omega}(\omega)$ in Eq. (4.15), we have:

(1) $pl_{\mathrm{r}}^{\Omega}(\omega) = pl_{\mathrm{r}}^{\Omega}[x_j, \phi_{ij}]^{\downarrow X_i}(x_i) = pl_{\mathrm{r}}^{\Omega}[x_i, \phi_{ij}]^{\downarrow X_j}(x_j)$
$= pl_{\mathrm{r}}^{X_i}[x_j](x_i) = pl_{\mathrm{r}}^{X_j}[x_i](x_j)$ for all $X_i, X_j \in \mathbf{X}$

(2) $pl_{\mathrm{r}}^{X_i}[x_j](x_i)$ is related to $pl_{\mathrm{r}}^{X_i}[x_j](x_{i_k})$, $\forall x_{i_k} \in x_i$ for any x_i and x_j through a parameterised function $\mathscr{F}^{s_{[x_j]x_i}}$ where $s_{[x_j]x_i}$ is informed by knowledge of $pl_{\mathrm{r}}^{X_k}[x_i](x_{k_t}) \triangleq pl_{\mathrm{r}}^{\Omega}[x_i, \phi_{ik}]^{\downarrow X_k}(x_{k_t})$, $\forall x_{k_t} \in x_k$, for all $X_k(\neq X_i) \in \mathbf{X}$[7].

The extended GLP allows $pl_{\mathrm{r}}^{\Omega}(\omega)$ to be computed in the form of $pl_{\mathrm{r}}^{X_i}[x_j](x_i)$ for any X_i and X_j through an estimation of the parameter $s_{[x_j]x_i}$. In this regard, estimation of $s_{[x_j]x_i}$ for each $x_j \subseteq X_j$ is motivated by the dual aspect of $pl_{\mathrm{r}}^{\Theta=X_iX_j}$, the conditional form of which is given in Eq. (4.15). With respect to Ω, pl_{r}^{Θ} is a *marginalisation* of

[5] As $(-1)^{|A|+1}\mu(A) \geq (-1)^{|B|+1}\mu(B \supseteq A)$ for any subset A and B, and $\mu_{pl}(A) \equiv pl(A)$ when $|A| = 1$.

[6] $\mu_{x_{i*}\phi_{i'}} = \sum_{x_{i*}x_{j'}} \mu_{pl_{\mathrm{r}}^{\Omega}}[\phi_{ij}]^{\downarrow\Theta}(x_{i*}, x_{j'}) = \sum_{x_{i*}x_{j'},} \mu_{pl_{\mathrm{r}}^{\Theta}}(x_{i*}, x_{j'})$.

[7] Note that all those $pl_{\mathrm{r}}^{X_i}[x_j](x_{i_k})$ and $pl_{\mathrm{r}}^{X_k}[x_i](x_{k_t})$ were already computed in the previous iteration.

pl_{r}^{Ω} on Θ (through conditioning on ϕ_{ij}: $pl_{\mathrm{r}}^{\Theta} = pl_{\mathrm{r}}^{\Omega}[\phi_{ij}]^{\downarrow\Theta}$). With respect to Θ, it can be considered a *specialisation* [Klawonn and Smets1992] of $pl_{\mathrm{r}}^{\Theta o}$ initially defined on Θ which is MCP-compatible[8], thus satisfying DRC/GBT:

$$pl_{\mathrm{r}}^{X_i o}[x_{j'}](x_i) = 1 - \prod_{x_{i_k} \in x_i} (1 - pl_{\mathrm{r}}^{X_i o}[x_{j'}](x_{i_k})) \quad (4.16)$$

for all $x_{j'} \subseteq x_j$. Such $pl_{\mathrm{r}}^{X_i o}[x_{j'}](x_i)$ corresponds to a point within the interval $[\underline{pl_{\mathrm{r}}^{X_i o}}[x_{j'}](x_i), \overline{pl_{\mathrm{r}}^{X_i o}}[x_{j'}](x_i)]$ in Theorem 4.6 Step 2. As $pl_{\mathrm{r}}^{\Theta o}$ is specialised into pl_{r}^{Θ}, the equality in Eq. (4.16) may no longer hold, moving the corresponding $pl_{\mathrm{r}}^{X_i}[x_{j'}](x_i)$ for each $x_{j'} \subseteq x_j$ toward either of its respective bounds. To this end, let $r_{[x_j]x_i} \in [-1, 1]$[9] be associated with $pl_{\mathrm{r}}^{X_i}[x_j](x_i)$ to linearly measure the relative mass overlapping between $pl_{\mathrm{r}}^{X_i}[x_j](x_{i_k}), \forall x_{i_k} \in x_i$ such that $r_{[x_j]x_i} = 0, 1, -1$ when $pl_{\mathrm{r}}^{X_i}[x_j](x_i)$ coincides with its MCP-compatible value (determined by Eq. (4.16)), and its lower bound and upper bound (determined by Eqs. (4.13) and (4.14)), respectively. Then for each $x_j \subseteq X_j$, a parameterised version of DRC/GBT can be defined as the Frank t-conorm [Klement, Mesiar, and Pap2013], $\mathscr{F}^{s_{[x_j]x_i}}$, for any other arbitrary value of $r_{[x_j]x_i}$:

$$pl_{\mathrm{r}}^{X_i}[x_j](x_i) = \mathscr{F}^{s}_{x_{i_k}} (pl_{\mathrm{r}}^{X_i}[x_j](x_{i_k}))$$

$$= 1 - \log_s \left(1 + \frac{\prod_{x_{i_k}} \left(s^{1 - pl_{\mathrm{r}}^{X_i}[x_j](x_{i_k})} - 1 \right)}{(s-1)^{n-1}} \right) \quad (4.17)$$

where $s \triangleq s_{[x_j]x_i}$ is a positive parameter defined in terms of $r_{[x_j]x_i}$ as $s_{[x_j]x_i} = \pi(1 - r_{[x_j]x_i})/4$ [Ferson et al.2004].

This alternative formulation, in place of Eq. (4.15), presents an interesting property when MCP-compatibility holds:

$$r^0_{[x_j]x_i} = r^0_{[x_{j_l}]x_i} = 0 \text{ for all } x_{j_l} \in x_j, \quad (4.18)$$

where $r^0_{[x_{j_l}]x_i}$ are associated with $pl_{\mathrm{r}}^{X_i 0}[x_{j_l}](x_i), \forall x_{j_l} \in x_j$. As $pl_{\mathrm{r}}^{\Theta 0}$ is specialised into pl_{r}^{Θ}, and accordingly $r^0_{[x_{j_l}]x_i}$ to $r_{[x_{j_l}]x_i}, \forall x_{j_l} \in x_j$, we are interested in computing $r_{[x_j]x_i}$ from those $r_{[x_{j_l}]x_i}$ whose knowledge is available from the previous iteration. We conjecture among all the arbitrary $pl_{\mathrm{r}}^{\Theta +}$ that satisfies the constraints imposed by such $r_{[x_{j_l}]x_i}$, the one that exhibits the least divergence from the initial relation in Eq. (4.18) would likely correspond to pl_{r}^{Θ}, e.g.,

$$r_{[x_j]x_i} = \underset{r^+_{[x_j]x_i}}{\arg\min} \sum_{x_{j_l}} pl_{\mathrm{r}}^{X_i}[x_{j_l}](x_i)(r^+_{[x_j]x_i} - r_{[x_{j_l}]x_i})^2,$$

allowing $r_{[x_j]x_i}$ to be approximated as a weighted average:

$$r_{[x_j]x_i} = \sum_{x_{j_l}} w_{[x_{j_l}]x_i} r_{[x_{j_l}]x_i}, \; w_{[x_{j_l}]x_i} = \frac{pl_{\mathrm{r}}^{X_i}[x_{j_l}](x_i)}{\sum_{x_{j_l}} pl_{\mathrm{r}}^{X_i}[x_{j_l}](x_i)}. \quad (4.19)$$

Utilising parameterised t-norms and t-conorms for combining belief functions induced by possibly overlapping bodies of evidence has been studied thoroughly in [Denœux2008] where the relative dependence between the belief functions is (i) defined by a single parameter s (i.e., $s = s_{[x_j]x_i} = s_{[x_{j'}]x_i}, \forall x_{j'} \subset x_j$ in this case) which can be learned from data, and (ii) concerned with positive dependence (i.e., $s \in [0, 1]$). In contrast, our method deals with situations where the parameters $s_{[x_{j_l}]x_i}$ are (i) generally of different values computed during execution time, and (ii) concerned with the entire range of positive and negative dependence (i.e., $s_{[x_{j'}]x_i} \in [0, +\infty), \forall x_{j'} \subseteq x_j$).

By replacing Eqs. (4.13) and (4.14) with (4.17) and (4.19), the interval approximation for each $pl_{\mathrm{r}}^{\Omega}(\omega)$ in Theorem 4.6 Step 2 can be reduced to a point estimation[10] (below), where the pair X_i and X_j in Eq. (4.20) correspond to those in $\mathbf{X}$ such that $pl_{\mathrm{r}}^{\Omega}[\phi_{ij}]^{\downarrow\Theta}$ exhibits the least divergence from its initial MCP-compatible value $pl_{\mathrm{r}}^{\Theta o}$ on $\Theta = X_i X_j$.

Step 2: Reconstruction of $pl_{\mathbf{r}}^{\Omega}$:

$$pl_{\mathrm{r}}^{X_i}[x_j](x_i) \triangleq pl_{\mathrm{r}}^{\Omega}[x_j, \phi_{ij}]^{\downarrow X_i}(x_i)$$

$$pl_{\mathrm{r}}^{\Omega}(\omega) = pl_{\mathrm{r}}^{X_i}[x_j](x_i) = \mathscr{F}^{s_{[x_j]x_i}}_{x_{ik} \in x_i}(pl_{\mathrm{r}}^{X_i}[x_j](x_{i_k})), \quad (4.20)$$

where $s_{[x_j]x_i} = \pi(1 - r_{[x_j]x_i})/4$, $r_{[x_j]x_i} = \min_{X_p} \min_{X_q} |r_{[x_q]x_p}|$ $\forall X_p, X_q \in \mathbf{X}$ s.t. $x_p = \omega^{\downarrow X_p}$, $x_q = \omega^{\downarrow X_q}$ and $|x_p| > 1$, $|x_q| > 1$.

Since both the interval approximation in Theorem 4.6 Step 2, and point estimation in Eq. (4.20), of any $pl_{\mathrm{r}}^{\Omega}(\omega), \omega \in \mathrm{r}_{\Omega}$ is reconstructed based on $\mathscr{C}_{pl_{\mathrm{r}}}$, it is sufficient that beliefs be propagated in the form of $\mathscr{C}_{pl_{\mathrm{r}}}$[11], hence Fact 4.7.

Fact 4.7 *Given a node X_0 associated with $(n-1)$ conditioning variables, all with m states, the messages propagated to X_0 in the form of $\mathscr{C}_{pl_{\mathrm{r}}}$ have space complexity of $\mathcal{O}(2^{mm} - Z)$ where $Z = \sum_{k=2}^{n} \binom{n}{k} m^{n-k}(2^m - m)^k$.*

5 DISCUSSION AND RESULTS

By means of local conditioning (LC), the proposed method enables belief propagation directly on the original multiply-connected network. The advantages of maintaining and propagating beliefs in the original structure of the network are multi-fold, e.g., eliminating the assumption/requirement that the reasoning network is singly-connected at and during runtime, mitigating disruptions during execution associated with generation of a secondary structure due to changes in the network topology, facilitating local computations in a distributed manner and allowing run-time pruning of the network, and enhancing transparency of reasoning and supporting explanation.

By combining local conditioning and conditional belief functions, the proposed method allows combination and propagation of beliefs with a significant reduction in space

[8]By construction, this is the case when X_i and X_j are directly connected; otherwise, they are assumed to have an implicit edge with vacuous cbfs which are naturally MCP-compatible.

[9]Let pl^0, $\underline{pl}$ and $\overline{pl}$ denote the MCP-compatible value, lower and upper bounds associated with the pl to be computed, respectively, the relative mass overlapping r can be defined as follows:

$$r = \begin{cases} (pl - pl^0)/(pl^0 - \overline{pl}), & \overline{pl} \geq pl \geq pl^0 \\ (pl - pl^0/(\underline{pl} - pl^0), & pl^0 > pl \geq \underline{pl} \\ \text{undefined}, & \text{otherwise}. \end{cases}$$

[10]Note that this estimation is not guaranteed to produce a valid belief function, thus a normalisation step may be required.

[11]For instance, in Figure 2b, the beliefs propagated to G would be $\mathscr{C}_{pl_{\mathrm{r}}^{AG}}$ and $\mathscr{C}_{pl_{\mathrm{r}}^{AG'}}$ rather than pl_{r}^{AG} and $pl_{\mathrm{r}}^{AG'}$.

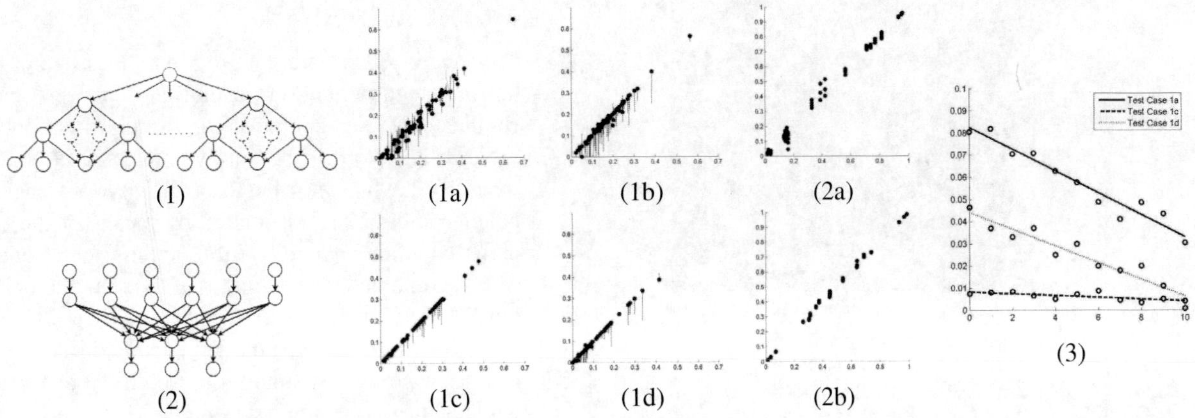

Figure 3: (1) A sample hierarchical network with 10 clusters of loops, and the correlated posterior marginals (normalised beliefs) for Test Case (1a), (1b), (1c) and (1d). (2) A sample densely connected network and the correlated posterior marginals for (2a) a worst case scenario i.e., no observations, and (2b) where three random nodes in the network receive (soft) observations. (3) Average approximation error for Test Case 1a, 1c and 1d as a function of observations received.

and time. As shown in Fact 4.7, the worst case space complexity associated with the messages propagated in the form of $\mathscr{C}_{pl_r}$ is only a fraction of the associated conditional space ($\mathcal{O}(2^{mn})$), and a very small fraction of the product space ($\mathcal{O}(2^{m^n})$) if exact belief updating is to be performed.

One of the rationales for representing beliefs in the form of partially defined pl and $b.pl.a$ functions is to reduce the space complexity of the messages propagated, and thus the computational complexity involved. Reducing the size of belief functions for the purpose of efficient combination has received substantial attention in the literature, resulting in a rich class of belief transformation methods (see [Bauer1997], [Wilson2000], [Cuzzolin2012]). To this end, one could potentially argue that instead of representing the beliefs in the form of pl and $b.pl.a$ functions as proposed, they could be defined on the product space with a smaller number of focal sets by means of belief transformation. However the unsuitability of such alternative approaches can be readily identified at a high level. Specifically, they would suffer from: (i) a significant computational overhead involved with belief transformation during propagation, (ii) information loss due to beliefs being forced to be more 'committed' during propagation, and (iii) inconsistent results due to violation of the axioms that make local computations possible since most belief transforms do not commute with combination. In contrast, our proposed technique does not experience the above problems, specifically (i) no computational overhead since it enables simultaneous combination operating directly on the cbfs initially defined between nodes without requiring any belief transformation, (ii) mitigated information loss: instead of transforming the correct belief function to be propagated into an approximate one with a smaller number of focal elements, it propagates the *Core*, $\mathscr{C}_{pl_r}$, of the 'correct'[12] beliefs on the product space, facilitating reconstruction of the original belief functions on demand, and (iii) consistency of results is also significantly improved as belief combination and propagation between nodes with the same conditioning variables satisfies the axioms facilitating local computations. In another vein, stochastic sampling [Wilson2000, Laâmari, Hariz, and Yaghlane2014] could also be applied to combine beliefs received at a node. However, the methods aim to reduce the computational complexity associated with belief combination, but not to reduce the space complexity involved with each message sent and received.

As mentioned in Section 3, unlike LBP which is known for not producing the correct numerical value for the posterior marginals of nodes, our proposed method is aimed at approximating the correct posterior marginals for the purpose of belief updating. Thus it is important to verify the degree of accuracy of the results produced by the approach. To this end, experiments have been performed to verify the practical accuracy of our approximate algorithm. Due to space limitations, we will primarily present representative cases. In Test Cases 1, we conducted experiments on networks which are instantiations of Figure 3.1. We first started with networks with minimal information and complexity (Test Case 1a), e.g., each branch of the network contains only the simplest form of loop (i.e., dashed-line nodes are excluded), each node is associated with a binary domain, prior beliefs are vacuous, and none of the nodes receive any observations during belief updating. We then introduced more information and complexity to the networks, specifically, a (soft) observation was introduced at every loop in Test Case (1b), the complexity of loops in each branch was increased (i.e., dashed-line nodes included) in Test Case (1c), and the domain size of each node was increased (to tertiary domain) in Test Case (1d). Figures 3.1a, 1b, 1c and 1d present the posterior marginals approximated for every node in Test Case 1a, 1b, 1c and 1d, respectively, correlated with the correct results

[12]Provided that the beliefs propagated to nodes outside the respective loops are correct.

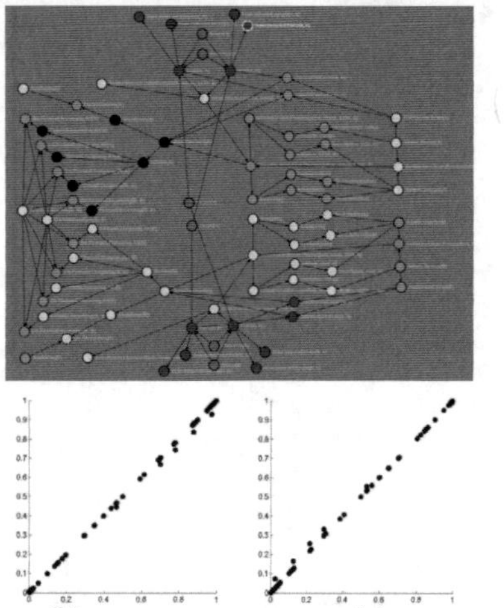
(a) (b) (c)

Figure 4: Correlated posterior marginals in the form of belief (b) and plausibility (c) functions obtained for a real-world (CND) application (a).

generated using the exact method based on LC and joint belief function briefly proposed in Section 3. To illustrate each approximate result with respect to its lower and upper bounds, we also approximated the lower and upper posterior marginals for each node, according to Theorem 4.6, depicted as a vertical bar associated with each marginal. As the figures illustrate, the algorithm produced approximate results with a high degree of accuracy. Even in the worst case scenarios where all the prior beliefs and observations are totally vacuous (Test Case 1a), the approximate marginals are close to exact; and with some increase in the 'informativeness' and complexity of the network, the bounds obtained for Test Case 1b, 1c and 1d were tightened and the approximate marginals are almost exact. Simulating the networks with different sets of randomly generated parameters produces similar results. Figure 3.3 shows the average error (vertical axis) of the approximate marginals — compared to exact, using L_2 norm [Cuzzolin2012] — obtained from 100 randomly generated instances each of Test Case 1a, 1c and 1d, each with 0 to 10 observations (horizontal axis). The results show that on average, the approximation error across all the tests is low even in the absence of any observations, and diminishes with additional observations.

To reveal the behaviour of the algorithm when dealing with more extreme loops and arbitrary networks, we extended our experiments with the densely-connected network in Figure 3.2 and a real-world network drawn from our CND application (Figure 4a). For both cases, the algorithm produced accurate results. Indeed, in cases where the network contains complex loops such as these, $\mathscr{C}_{pl_r}$ tends to become a substantial belief dominant region of pl_r. Not only does this help increase the accuracy of the results, but also the approximation process quickly converges, significantly reducing the space and computational complexity involved.

6 CONCLUSIONS

This paper proposed an approximate message-passing belief propagation method for multiply-connected networks. By means of local conditioning, the algorithm does not require the network to be singly-connected prior to execution. By having knowledge of the network encoded and belief combination formulated by means of the proposed partially defined pl and $b.pl.a$ functions, local conditioning can be combined with (subsets of) conditional belief functions, approximating belief updating in an efficient manner. The empirical results demonstrated that the method is able to produce results with a high degree of accuracy while achieving a significant reduction in space and computational complexity (in comparison to its exact counterpart), promoting the practicality of networks with (conditional) belief functions. Indeed, the algorithm is currently being incorporated into Influx, the inference engine of our CND system, in order to address the aforementioned challenges that motivated this research effort.

Acknowledgement The author thanks Michael Docking for providing advice and discussion throughout this work.

A APPENDIX

Proof (Theorem 4.5) Let $\Phi_1 = \Theta_1 \backslash X_0$, $\Phi_2 = \Theta_1 \backslash X_0$[13], and $\alpha_{x_0} \triangleq (-1)^{|x_0|+1}$. Since the variables associated with Φ_1 and Φ_2 in this case are disjoint, the pieces of evidence induced on X_0 when $\phi_1 \in \mathrm{r}_{\Phi_1}$ and $\phi_2 \in \mathrm{r}_{\Phi_2}$ hold are distinct. Thus the plausibility that ϕ_1 and ϕ_2 jointly induce on X_0 can be obtained by Lemma 2.1, that is:

$$\mu_{pl_r^\Omega}[\phi_1,\phi_2]^{\downarrow X_0}(x_0) = \alpha_{x_0}\mu_{pl_r^{\Theta_1}}[\phi_1]^{\downarrow X_0}(x_0) \mu_{pl_r^{\Theta_2}}[\phi_2]^{\downarrow X_0}(x_0), \forall x_0 \subseteq X, \quad \text{(A.1)}$$

which can be equivalently written by Lemma 4.3 as:

$$\textstyle\sum_{\phi_{1'},\phi_{2'}} \mu_{pl_r^\Omega}(x_0,\phi_{1'},\phi_{2'}) = \alpha_{x_0} \sum_{\phi_{1'}} \mu_{pl_r^{\Theta_1}}(x_0,\phi_{1'}) \sum_{\phi_{2'}} \mu_{pl_r^{\Theta_2}}(x_0,\phi_{2'}), \forall \phi_{i'} \subseteq \phi_i, \phi_{i'} \in \mathrm{r}_{\Phi_i}, i = 1,2. \quad \text{(A.2)}$$

Let us investigate the impact that ϕ_1 and ϕ_2 (with increasing cardinalities) jointly induce on X_0. By Eq. (A.2), we have for all $\omega^* = (x_0,\phi_{1^*},\phi_{2^*})$ s.t. $|\phi_{1^*}| = 1$ and $|\phi_{2^*}| = 1$:

$$\mu_{pl_r^\Omega}(x_0,\phi_{1^*},\phi_{2^*}) = \alpha_{x_0}\mu_{pl_r^{\Theta_1}}(x_0,\phi_{1^*})\mu_{pl_r^{\Theta_2}}(x_0,\phi_{2^*}). \quad \text{(A.3)}$$

For all $\omega' = (x_0,\phi_{1'},\phi_{2^*})$ s.t. $|\phi_{1'}| = 2$ and $|\phi_{2^*}| = 1$:

$$\mu_{pl_r^\Omega}(x_0,\phi_{1'},\phi_{2^*}) = \textstyle\sum_{\phi_{1''}\subseteq\phi_{1'}} \mu_{pl_r^\Omega}(x_0,\phi_{1''},\phi_{2^*})$$
$$= \alpha_{x_0} \textstyle\sum_{\phi_{1''}\subseteq\phi_{1'}} \mu_{pl_r^{\Theta_1}}(x_0,\phi_{1''})\mu_{pl_r^{\Theta_2}}(x_0,\phi_{2^*}). \quad \text{(A.4)}$$

Substitute terms in the LHS of Eq. (A.4) with terms in the RHS of Eq. (A.3) and simplify the result:

$$\mu_{pl_r^\Omega}(x_0,\phi_{1'},\phi_{2^*}) = \alpha_{x_0}\mu_{pl_r^{\Theta_1}}(x_0,\phi_{1'})\mu_{pl_r^{\Theta_2}}(x_0,\phi_{2^*}). \quad \text{(A.5)}$$

For each $x_0 \subseteq X_0$, iteratively applying the above steps to all $\phi_1 \in \mathrm{r}_{\Phi_1}$, $\phi_2 \in \mathrm{r}_{\Phi_2}$ with increasing cardinalities, we have:

$$\mu_{pl_r^\Omega}(x_0,\phi_1,\phi_2) = \alpha_{x_0}\mu_{pl_r^{\Theta_1}}(x_0,\phi_1)\mu_{pl_r^{\Theta_2}}(x_0,\phi_2).$$

Thus for all $\omega \in \mathrm{r}_\Omega$ and $x_0 = \omega^{\downarrow X_0}$:

$$\mu_{pl_r^\Omega}(\omega) = (-1)^{|x_0|+1}\mu_{pl_r^{\Theta_1}}(\omega^{\downarrow\Theta_1})\mu_{pl_r^{\Theta_2}}(\omega^{\downarrow\Theta_2}).$$

[13] Φ_1, Φ_2 denotes the product of the variables associated with Θ_1, Θ_2, respectively, excluding X_0.

References

[Bauer1997] Bauer, M. 1997. Approximation algorithms and decision making in the dempster-shafer theory of evidence – an empirical study. *International Journal of approximate reasoning* 17(2):217–237.

[Cuzzolin2012] Cuzzolin, F. 2012. The geometry of uncertainty. *Information Science and Statistics Series. Springer*.

[Denœux2008] Denœux, T. 2008. Conjunctive and disjunctive combination of belief functions induced by nondistinct bodies of evidence. *Artificial Intelligence* 172(2-3):234–264.

[Díez1996] Díez, F. J. 1996. Local conditioning in bayesian networks. *Artificial Intelligence* 87(1):1–20.

[Dubois and Prade2009] Dubois, D., and Prade, H. 2009. Formal representations of uncertainty. *Decision-Making Process: Concepts and Methods* 85–156.

[Fay and Jaffray2000] Fay, A., and Jaffray, J.-Y. 2000. A justification of local conditioning in bayesian networks. *International Journal of Approximate Reasoning* 24(1):59–81.

[Ferson et al.2004] Ferson, S.; Nelsen, R. B.; Hajagos, J.; Berleant, D. J.; Zhang, J.; Tucker, W. T.; Ginzburg, L. R.; and Oberkampf, W. L. 2004. Dependence in probabilistic modeling, dempster-shafer theory, and probability bounds analysis. *Sandia National Laboratories, Report No. SAND2004-3072*.

[Klawonn and Smets1992] Klawonn, F., and Smets, P. 1992. The dynamic of belief in the transferable belief model and specialization-generalization matrices. In *Proceedings of the Eighth international conference on Uncertainty in artificial intelligence*, 130–137. Morgan Kaufmann Publishers Inc.

[Klement, Mesiar, and Pap2013] Klement, E. P.; Mesiar, R.; and Pap, E. 2013. *Triangular norms*, volume 8. Springer Science & Business Media.

[Laâmari, Hariz, and Yaghlane2014] Laâmari, W.; Hariz, N. B.; and Yaghlane, B. B. 2014. Approximate inference in directed evidential networks with conditional belief functions using the monte carlo algorithm. In *International Conference on Information Processing and Management of Uncertainty in Knowledge-Based Systems*, 486–497. Springer.

[Pearl1988] Pearl, J. 1988. *Probabilistic reasoning in intelligent systems: networks of plausible inference*. Morgan Kaufmann.

[Shafer, Shenoy, and Mellouli1987] Shafer, G.; Shenoy, P. P.; and Mellouli, K. 1987. Propagating belief functions in qualitative markov trees. *International Journal of Approximate Reasoning* 1(4):349–400.

[Shafer1976] Shafer, G. 1976. *A mathematical theory of evidence*, volume 1. Princeton university press Princeton.

[Shenoy and Shafer1986] Shenoy, P. P., and Shafer, G. 1986. Propagating belief functions with local computations. *IEEE Expert* 1(3):43–52.

[Shenoy1993] Shenoy, P. P. 1993. Valuation networks and conditional independence. In *Proceedings of the Ninth international conference on Uncertainty in artificial intelligence*, 191–199. Morgan Kaufmann Publishers Inc.

[Shenoy1997] Shenoy, P. P. 1997. Binary join trees for computing marginals in the shenoy-shafer architecture. *International Journal of approximate reasoning* 17(2):239–263.

[Smets and Kennes1994] Smets, P., and Kennes, R. 1994. The transferable belief model. *Artificial intelligence* 66(2):191–234.

[Smets1994] Smets, P. 1994. Belief functions: the disjunctive rule of combination and the generalized bayesian theorem. *International Journal of approximate reasoning* 9(1):1–35.

[Weiss1997] Weiss, Y. 1997. Belief propagation and revision in networks with loops.

[Wilson2000] Wilson, N. 2000. Algorithms for dempster-shafer theory. In *Handbook of defeasible reasoning and uncertainty management systems*. Springer. 421–475.

[Xu and Smets1996] Xu, H., and Smets, P. 1996. Reasoning in evidential networks with conditional belief functions. *International Journal of Approximate Reasoning* 14(2):155–185.

[Yaghlane and Mellouli2008] Yaghlane, B. B., and Mellouli, K. 2008. Inference in directed evidential networks based on the transferable belief model. *International Journal of Approximate Reasoning* 48(2):399–418.

[Yaghlane, Smets, and Mellouli2002a] Yaghlane, B. B.; Smets, P.; and Mellouli, K. 2002a. Belief function independence: I. the marginal case. *International Journal of Approximate Reasoning* 29(1):47–70.

[Yaghlane, Smets, and Mellouli2002b] Yaghlane, B. B.; Smets, P.; and Mellouli, K. 2002b. Belief function independence: Ii. the conditional case. *International Journal of Approximate Reasoning* 31(1):31–75.

Differentially Private Variational Inference for Non-conjugate Models

Joonas Jälkö **Onur Dikmen** **Antti Honkela***
Helsinki Institute for Information Technology (HIIT), Department of Computer Science,
University of Helsinki, Finland
{joonas.jalko, onur.dikmen, antti.honkela}@helsinki.fi

Abstract

Many machine learning applications are based on data collected from people, such as their tastes and behaviour as well as biological traits and genetic data. Regardless of how important the application might be, one has to make sure individuals' identities or the privacy of the data are not compromised in the analysis. Differential privacy constitutes a powerful framework that prevents breaching of data subject privacy from the output of a computation. Differentially private versions of many important Bayesian inference methods have been proposed, but there is a lack of an efficient unified approach applicable to arbitrary models. In this contribution, we propose a differentially private variational inference method with a very wide applicability. It is built on top of doubly stochastic variational inference, a recent advance which provides a variational solution to a large class of models. We add differential privacy into doubly stochastic variational inference by clipping and perturbing the gradients. The algorithm is made more efficient through privacy amplification from subsampling. We demonstrate the method can reach an accuracy close to non-private level under reasonably strong privacy guarantees, clearly improving over previous sampling-based alternatives especially in the strong privacy regime.

*AH is also with the Department of Mathematics and Statistics and Department of Public Health, University of Helsinki.

1 INTRODUCTION

Using more data usually leads to better generalisation and accuracy in machine learning. With more people getting more tightly involved in the ubiquitous data collection, privacy concerns related to the data are becoming more important. People will be much more willing to contribute their data if they can be sure that the privacy of their data can be protected.

Differential privacy (DP) (Dwork et al., 2006; Dwork and Roth, 2014) is a strong framework with strict privacy guarantees against attacks from adversaries with side information. The main principle is that the output of an algorithm (such as a query or an estimator) should not change much if the data for one individual are modified or deleted. This can be accomplished through adding stochasticity at different levels of the estimation process, such as adding noise to data itself (input perturbation), changing the objective function to be optimised or how it is optimised (objective perturbation), releasing the estimates after adding noise (output perturbation) or by sampling from a distribution based on utility or goodness of the alternatives (exponential mechanism).

A lot of ground-breaking work has been done on privacy-preserving versions of standard machine learning approaches, such as objective-perturbation-based logistic regression (Chaudhuri and Monteleoni, 2008), regression using functional mechanism (Zhang et al., 2012) to name a few. Privacy-preserving Bayesian inference (e.g. (Williams and McSherry, 2010; Zhang et al., 2014)) has only recently started attracting more interest. The result of Dimitrakakis et al. (2014) showing that the posterior distribution is under certain assumptions differentially private is mathematically elegant, but does not lead to practically useful algorithms. Methods based on this approach suffer from the major weakness that the privacy guarantees are only valid for samples drawn from the exact posterior which is usually impossible to guarantee in practice. Methods based on perturbation of data sufficient statistics (Zhang et al., 2016; Foulds et al., 2016; Honkela et al., 2016) are asymptotically efficient, but they are only applicable to exponential family models which limits their usefulness. The sufficient statistic perturbation approach was recently also applied to variational inference (Park et al., 2016), which is again applicable to models where non-private inference can be performed by accessing sufficient statistics.

General differentially private Bayesian inference can be realised most easily using the gradient perturbation mechanism. This was first proposed by Wang et al. (2015), who combine differential privacy by gradient perturbation with stochastic gradient Markov chain Monte Carlo (MCMC) sampling. This approach works in principle for arbitrary models, but because of the gradient perturbation mechanism each MCMC iteration will consume some privacy budget, hence severely limiting the number of iterations that can be run which can cause difficulties with the convergence of the sampler.

Our goal in this work is to apply the gradient perturbation mechanism to devise a generic differentially private variational inference method. Variational inference seems preferable to stochastic gradient MCMC here because a good optimiser should be able to make better use of the limited gradient evaluations and the variational approximation provides a very efficient summary of the posterior. The recently proposed doubly stochastic variational inference Titsias and Lázaro-Gredilla (2014) and the further streamlined automatic differentiation variational inference (ADVI) method (Kucukelbir et al., 2017) provide a generic variational inference method also applicable to non-conjugate models. These approaches apply a series of transformations and approximations so that the variational distributions are Gaussian and can be optimised by stochastic gradient ascent. Here, we propose differentially private variational inference (DPVI) based on gradient clipping and perturbation as well as double stochasticity. We make a thorough case study on the Bayesian logistic regression model with comparisons to the non-private case under different design decisions for DPVI. We also test the performance of DPVI with a Gaussian mixture model.

2 BACKGROUND

2.1 DIFFERENTIAL PRIVACY

Differential privacy (DP) (Dwork et al., 2006; Dwork and Roth, 2014) is a framework that provides mathematical formulation for privacy that enables proving strong privacy guarantees.

Definition 1 (ϵ-Differential privacy). *A randomised algorithm $\mathcal{A}$ is ϵ-differentially private if for all pairs of adjacent data sets, i.e., differing only in one data sample, x, x', and for all sets $S \subset im(\mathcal{A})$*

$$\Pr(\mathcal{A}(x) \in S) \leq e^{\epsilon} \Pr(\mathcal{A}(x') \in S).$$

There are two different variants depending on which data sets are considered adjacent: in *unbounded DP* data sets x, x' are adjacent if x' can be obtained from x by adding or removing an entry, while in *bounded DP* x, x' are adjacent if they are of equal size and equal in all but one of their elements (Dwork and Roth, 2014). The definition is symmetric in x and x' which means that in practice the probabilities of obtaining a specific output from either algorithm need to be similar. The privacy parameter ϵ measures the strength of the guarantee with smaller values corresponding to stronger privacy.

ϵ-DP defined above, also known as *pure DP*, is sometimes too inflexible and a relaxed version called (ϵ, δ)-DP is often used instead. It is defined as follows:

Definition 2 ((ϵ, δ)-Differential privacy). *A randomised algorithm $\mathcal{A}$ is (ϵ, δ)-differentially private if for all pairs of adjacent data sets x, x' and for every $S \subset im(\mathcal{A})$*

$$\Pr(\mathcal{A}(x) \in S) \leq e^{\epsilon} \Pr(\mathcal{A}(x') \in S) + \delta.$$

It can be shown that (ϵ, δ)-DP provides a probabilistic ϵ-DP guarantee with probability $1 - \delta$ (Dwork and Roth, 2014).

2.1.1 Gaussian mechanism

There are many possibilities how to make algorithm differentially private. In this paper we use *objective perturbation*. We use the *Gaussian mechanism* as our method for perturbation. Dwork and Roth (2014, Theorem 3.22) state that given query f with ℓ_2-sensitivity of $\Delta_2(f)$, releasing $f(x)+\eta$, where $\eta \sim N(0, \sigma^2)$, is (ϵ, δ)-DP when

$$\sigma^2 > 2\ln(1.25/\delta)\Delta_2^2(f)/\epsilon^2. \quad (1)$$

The important ℓ_2-sensitivity of a query is defined as:

Definition 3 (ℓ_2-sensitivity). *Given two adjacent data sets x, x', ℓ_2-sensitivity of query f is*

$$\Delta_2(f) = \sup_{\substack{x,x' \\ ||x-x'||=1}} ||f(x) - f(x')||_2.$$

2.1.2 Composition theorems

One of the very useful features of DP compared to many other privacy formulations is that it provides a very natural way to study the privacy loss incurred by repeated use of the same data set. Using an algorithm on a data set multiple times will weaken our privacy guarantee because of the potential of each application to leak more information. The DP variational inference algorithm proposed in this paper is iterative, so we need to use composition theorems to bound the total privacy loss.

The simplest basic composition Dwork and Roth (2014) shows that a k-fold composition of an (ϵ, δ)-DP algorithm provides $(k\epsilon, k\delta)$-DP. More generally releasing joint output of k algorithms $\mathcal{A}_i$ that are individually (ϵ_i, δ_i)-DP will be $(\sum_{i=1}^{k} \epsilon_i, \sum_{i=1}^{k} \delta_i)$-DP. Under pure ϵ-DP when $\delta_1 = \cdots = \delta_k = 0$ this is the best known composition that yields a pure DP algorithm.

Moving from the pure ϵ-DP to general (ϵ, δ)-DP allows a stronger result with a smaller ϵ at the expense of having a larger total δ on the composition. This trade-off is characterised by the Advanced composition theorem of Dwork and Roth (2014, Theorem 3.20), which becomes very useful when we need to use data multiple times

Theorem 1 (Advanced composition theorem). *Given algorithm $\mathcal{A}$ that is (ϵ, δ)-DP and $\delta' > 0$, k-fold composition of algorithm $\mathcal{A}$ is $(\epsilon_{tot}, \delta_{tot})$-DP with*

$$\epsilon_{tot} = \sqrt{2k \ln(1/\delta')}\epsilon + k\epsilon(e^{\epsilon} - 1) \tag{2}$$

$$\delta_{tot} = k\delta + \delta'. \tag{3}$$

The theorem states that with small loss in δ_{tot} and with small enough ϵ, we can provide more strict ϵ_{tot} than just summing the ϵ. This is obvious by looking at the first order expansion for small ϵ of

$$\epsilon_{tot} \approx \sqrt{2k \ln(1/\delta')}\epsilon + k\epsilon^2.$$

2.1.3 Privacy amplification

We use a stochastic gradient algorithm that uses subsampled data while learning, so we can make use of the amplifying effect of the subsampling on privacy. This *Privacy amplification theorem* (Li et al., 2012) states that if we run (ϵ, δ)-DP algorithm $\mathcal{A}$ on randomly sampled subset of data with uniform sampling probability $q > \delta$, privacy amplification theorem states that the subsampled algorithm is $(\epsilon_{amp}, \delta_{amp})$-DP with

$$\epsilon_{amp} = \min(\epsilon, \log(1 + q(e^{\epsilon} - 1))) \tag{4}$$

$$\delta_{amp} = q\delta, \tag{5}$$

assuming $\log(1 + q(e^{\epsilon} - 1)) < \epsilon$.

2.1.4 Moments accountant

The moments accountant proposed by Abadi et al. (2016) is a method to accumulate the privacy cost that provides a tighter bound for ϵ and δ than the previous composition approaches. The moments accountant incorporates both the composition over iterations and privacy amplification due to subsampling into a single bound given by the following Theorem.

Theorem 2. *There exist constants c_1 and c_2 so that given the sampling probability $q = L/N$ and the number of steps T, for any $\epsilon < c_1 q^2 T$, a DP stochastic gradient algorithm that clips the ℓ_2 norm of gradients to C and injects Gaussian noise with standard deviation $2C\sigma$ to the gradients, is (ϵ, δ)-DP for any $\delta > 0$ under bounded DP if we choose*

$$\sigma \geq c_2 \frac{q\sqrt{T \log(2/\delta)}}{\epsilon}. \tag{6}$$

Proof. Abadi et al. (2016) show that injecting gradient noise with standard deviation $C\sigma$ where σ satisfies the inequality (6) yields an $(\epsilon, \frac{1}{2}\delta)$-DP algorithm under unbounded DP. This implies that adding noise with standard deviation $2C\sigma$ yields an $(\frac{1}{2}\epsilon, \frac{1}{2}\delta)$-DP algorithm under unbounded DP.

This proves the theorem as any $(\frac{1}{2}\epsilon, \frac{1}{2}\delta)$ unbounded DP algorithm is an (ϵ, δ) bounded DP algorithm. This follows from the fact that the replacement of an element in the data set can be represented as a composition of one addition and one removal of an element. □

Similar bounds can also be derived using concentrated DP (Dwork and Rothblum, 2016; Bun and Steinke, 2016).

We use the implementation of Abadi et al. (2016) to compute the total ϵ privacy cost with a given δ-budget, standard deviation σ of noise applied in Gaussian mechanism and subsampling ratio q.

In our experiments we report results using both the advanced composition theorem with privacy amplification as well as the moments accountant.

2.2 VARIATIONAL BAYES

Variational Bayes (VB) methods (Jordan et al., 1999) provide a way to approximate the posterior distribution of latent variables in a model when the true posterior is intractable. True posterior $p(\boldsymbol{\theta}|\mathbf{x})$ is approximated with a variational distribution $q_{\boldsymbol{\xi}}(\boldsymbol{\theta})$ that has a simpler form than the posterior, obtained generally by removing some dependencies from the graphical model such as the fully-factorised form $q_{\boldsymbol{\xi}}(\boldsymbol{\theta}) = \prod_d q_{\boldsymbol{\xi}_d}(\theta_d)$. $\boldsymbol{\xi}$ are the variational parameters and their optimal values $\boldsymbol{\xi}^*$ are obtained through minimising the Kullback-Leibler (KL) divergence between $q_{\boldsymbol{\xi}}(\boldsymbol{\theta})$ and $p(\boldsymbol{\theta}|\mathbf{x})$. This is also equivalent to maximising the *evidence lower bound* (ELBO)

$$\mathcal{L}(q_{\boldsymbol{\xi}}) = \int q_{\boldsymbol{\xi}}(\boldsymbol{\theta}) \ln \left(\frac{p(\mathcal{D}, \boldsymbol{\theta})}{q_{\boldsymbol{\xi}}(\boldsymbol{\theta})} \right)$$
$$= -\mathrm{KL}(q_{\boldsymbol{\xi}}(\boldsymbol{\theta}) \,||\, p(\boldsymbol{\theta})) + \sum_{i=1}^{B} \langle \ln p(x_i|\boldsymbol{\theta}) \rangle_{q_{\boldsymbol{\xi}}(\boldsymbol{\theta})},$$

where $\langle\rangle_{q_{\boldsymbol{\xi}}(\boldsymbol{\theta})}$ is an expectation taken w.r.t $q_{\boldsymbol{\xi}}(\boldsymbol{\theta})$ and the observations $\mathcal{D} = \{\mathbf{x}_1, \ldots, \mathbf{x}_N\}$ are assumed to be exchangeable under our model.

When the model is in the conjugate exponential family (Ghahramani and Beal, 2001) and $q_{\boldsymbol{\xi}}(\boldsymbol{\theta})$ is factorised, the expectations that constitute $\mathcal{L}(q_{\boldsymbol{\xi}})$ are analytically available and each $\boldsymbol{\xi}_d$ is updated iteratively by fixed point iterations. Most popular applications of VB fall into this category, because handling of the more general case involves more approximations, such as defining another level of lower bound to the ELBO or estimating the expectations using Monte Carlo integration.

2.2.1 Doubly stochastic variational inference

An increasingly popular alternative approach is the doubly stochastic variational inference framework proposed by Titsias and Lázaro-Gredilla (2014). The framework is based on stochastic gradient optimisation of the ELBO. The expectation over $q_{\boldsymbol{\xi}}(\boldsymbol{\theta})$ is evaluated using Monte Carlo sampling. Exchanging the order of integration (expectation) and differentiation and using the reparametrisation trick to represent for example samples from a Gaussian approximation $q_{\boldsymbol{\xi}_i}(\boldsymbol{\theta}_i) = N(\boldsymbol{\theta}_i; \boldsymbol{\mu}_i, \boldsymbol{\Sigma}_i)$ as $\boldsymbol{\theta}_i = \boldsymbol{\mu}_i + \boldsymbol{\Sigma}_i^{1/2}\mathbf{z}$, $\mathbf{z} \sim N(0, I)$, it is possible to obtain stochastic gradients of the ELBO which can be fed to a standard stochastic gradient ascent (SGA) optimisation algorithm.

For models with exchangeable observations, the ELBO objective can be broken down to a sum of terms for each observation:

$$\mathcal{L}(q_{\boldsymbol{\xi}}) = -\mathrm{KL}(q_{\boldsymbol{\xi}}(\boldsymbol{\theta}) \,||\, p(\boldsymbol{\theta})) + \sum_{i=1}^{N} \langle \ln p(x_i|\boldsymbol{\theta}) \rangle_{q_{\boldsymbol{\xi}}(\boldsymbol{\theta})}$$
$$= \sum_{i=1}^{N} \left(\langle \ln p(x_i|\boldsymbol{\theta}) \rangle_{q_{\boldsymbol{\xi}}(\boldsymbol{\theta})} - \frac{1}{N}\mathrm{KL}(q_{\boldsymbol{\xi}}(\boldsymbol{\theta}) \,||\, p(\boldsymbol{\theta})) \right)$$
$$=: \sum_{i=1}^{N} \mathcal{L}_i(q_{\boldsymbol{\xi}}).$$

This allows considering mini batches of data at each iteration to handle big data sets, which adds another level of stochasticity to the algorithm.

The recently proposed Automatic Derivation Variational Inference (ADVI) framework (Kucukelbir et al., 2017) unifies different classes of models through a transformation of variables and optimises the ELBO using stochastic gradient ascent (SGA). Constrained variables are transformed into unconstrained ones and their posterior is approximated by Gaussian variational distributions, which can be a product of independent Gaussians (mean-field) or larger multivariate Gaussians. Expectations in the gradients are approximated using Monte Carlo integration and the ELBO is optimised iteratively using SGA.

Algorithm 1 DPVI

Input: Data set $\mathcal{D}$, sampling probability q, number of iterations T, SGA step size η, Clipping threshold c_t and initial values $\boldsymbol{\xi}_0$.
for $t \in [T]$ **do**
  Pick random sample U from $\mathcal{D}$ with sampling probability q
  Calculate the gradient $g_t(x_i) = \nabla \mathcal{L}_i(q_{\boldsymbol{\xi}_t})$ for each $i \in U$
  Clip and sum gradients:
  $\tilde{g}_t(x_i) \leftarrow g_t(x_i)/\max(1, \frac{||g_t(x_i)||_2)}{c_t})$
  $\tilde{g}_t \leftarrow \sum_i \tilde{g}_t(x_i)$
  Add noise: $\tilde{g}_t \leftarrow \tilde{g}_t + \mathcal{N}(0, 4c_t^2\sigma^2\mathbf{I})$
  Update AdaGrad parameter. $G_t \leftarrow G_{t-1} + \tilde{g}_t^2$
  Ascent: $\boldsymbol{\xi}_t \leftarrow \boldsymbol{\xi}_{t-1} + \eta\tilde{g}_t/\sqrt{G_t}$
end for

3 DIFFERENTIALLY-PRIVATE VARIATIONAL INFERENCE

Differentially-private variational inference (DPVI) is based on clipping of the contributions of individual data samples to the gradient, $g_t(x_i) = \nabla \mathcal{L}_i(q_{\boldsymbol{\xi}_t})$, at each iteration t of the stochastic optimisation process and perturbing the total gradient. Each $g_t(x_i)$ is clipped in order to calculate gradient sensitivity. Gradient contributions from all data samples in the mini batch are summed and perturbed with Gaussian noise $\mathcal{N}(0, 4c_t^2\sigma^2\mathbf{I})$. The algorithm is presented in Algorithm 1. The algorithm is very similar to the one used for deep learning by Abadi et al. (2016). DPVI can be easily implemented using automatic differentiation software such as Autograd, or incorporated even more easily into automatic inference engines, such as the ADVI implementations in PyMC3 (Salvatier et al., 2016) or Edward (Tran et al., 2017) which also provide subsampling. Python implementation of DPVI based on Autograd can be found at `https://github.com/DPBayes/DPVI-code`.

The sampling frequency q for subsampling within the data set, total number of iterations T and the variance σ^2 of Gaussian noise are important design parameters that determine the privacy cost. c_t is chosen before learning, and does not need to be constant. After clipping $||g_t(x_i)||_2 \leq c_t, \forall i \in U$. Clipping gradients too much will affect accuracy, but on the other hand large clipping threshold will cause large amount of noise to sum of gradients. Parameter q determines how large subsample of the training data we use to for gradient ascent. Small q values enable privacy amplification but may need a need larger T. For a very small q when the mini batches consist of just a few samples, the added noise will dominate over the gradient signal and the optimisation will fail. While in our experiments q was fixed, we could also alter the q during iteration. Next, we show that Algorithm 1 is differentially private and explain how to calculate its privacy budget.

Theorem 3. *Algorithm 1 is (ϵ, δ)-differentially private.*

Proof. The algorithm applies Gaussian mechanism on the total gradient of a subsample of the dataset at every iteration t. If each iteration is ($\epsilon_{\text{subs}}, \delta_{\text{subs}}$)-DP on the subsample, then it is ($\epsilon_{\text{iter}}, \delta_{\text{iter}}$)-DP w.r.t. the whole data set due to privacy amplification theorem with

$$\epsilon_{\text{iter}} = \log(1 + q\,(e^{\epsilon_{\text{subs}}} - 1))\,. \tag{7}$$

Overall algorithm is (ϵ, δ)-DP with

$$\epsilon = \sqrt{2T\ln(1/\delta')}\epsilon_{\text{iter}} + T\epsilon_{\text{iter}}(e^{\epsilon_{\text{iter}}} - 1)\,, \tag{8}$$

due to T-fold composition of ($\epsilon_{\text{iter}}, \delta_{\text{iter}}$)-DP iterations. Determining δ, δ' and σ before running the algorithm, leads to $\delta_{\text{iter}} = (\delta - \delta')/T$ and $\delta_{\text{subs}} = \delta_{\text{iter}}/q$. Then, evaluation of the total privacy budget in (8) is straightforward using (7) with

$$\epsilon_{\text{subs}} = \sqrt{2\ln(1.25/(\delta_{\text{subs}}))}/\sigma\,.$$

This is simpler to show using the moments accountant instead of advanced composition and privacy amplification theorems. Given δ and σ, Algorithm 1 is readily (ϵ, δ)-DP, where ϵ (is the smallest value that) satisfies the conditions in Theorem 2. □

3.1 MODELS WITH LATENT VARIABLES

The simple approach in Algorithm 1 will not work well for models with latent variables. This is because the main gradient contributions to latent variables come from only a single data point, and the amount of noise that would need to be injected to mask the contribution of this point as needed by DP would make the gradient effectively useless.

One way to deal with the problem is to take the EM algorithm view (Dempster et al., 1977) of latent variables as a hidden part of a larger complete data set and apply the DP protection to summaries computed from the complete data set. In this approach, which was also used by Park et al. (2016), no noise would be injected to the updates of the latent variables but the latent variables would never be released.

An alternative potentially easier way to avoid this problem is to marginalise out the latent variables if the model allows this. As the DPVI framework works for arbitrary likelihoods we can easily perform inference even for complicated marginalised likelihoods. This is a clear advantage over the VIPS framework of Park et al. (2016) which requires conjugate exponential family models.

3.2 SELECTING THE ALGORITHM HYPERPARAMETERS

The DPVI algorithm depends on a number of parameters, the most important of which are the gradient clipping threshold c_t, the data subsampling ratio q and the number of iterations T. Together these define the total privacy cost of the algorithm, but it is not obvious how to find the optimal combination of these under a fixed privacy budget. Unfortunately the standard machine learning hyperparameter adaptation approach of optimising the performance on a validation set is not directly applicable, as every test run would consume some of the privacy budget. Developing good heuristics for parameter tuning is thus important for practical application of the method.

Out of these parameters, the subsampling ratio q seems easiest to interpret. The gradient that is perturbed in Algorithm 1 is a sum over qN samples in the mini batch. Similarly the standard deviation of the noise injected with the moments accountant in Eq. (6) scales linearly with q. Thus the signal-to-noise ratio for the gradients will be independent of q and q can be chosen to minimise the number of iterations T.

The number of iterations T is potentially more difficult to determine as it needs to be sufficient but not too large. The moments accountant is somewhat forgiving here as its privacy cost increases only in proportion to $\sqrt{T}$. In practice one may need to simply pick T believed to be sufficiently large and hope for the best. Poor results in the end likely indicate that the number of samples in the data set may be insufficient for good results at the given level of privacy.

The gradient clipping threshold c_t may be the most difficult parameter to tune as that depends strongly on the details of the model. Fortunately our results do not seem overly sensitive to using the precisely optimal value of c_t. Developing good heuristics for choosing c_t is an important objective for future research. Still, the same problem is shared by every DL method based on gradient perturbation including the deep learning work of Abadi et al. (2016) and the DP stochastic gradient MCMC methods of Wang et al. (2015). In the case of stochastic gradient MCMC this comes up through selecting a bound on the parameters to bound the Lipschitz constant appearing in the algorithm. A global Lipschitz constant for the ELBO would naturally translate to a c_t guaranteed not to distort the gradients, but as noted by Abadi et al. (2016), it may actually be good to clip the gradients to make the method more robust against outliers.

4 EXPERIMENTS

4.1 LOGISTIC REGRESSION

We tested DPVI with two different learning tasks. Lets first consider model of logistic regression using the Abalone and Adult data sets from the UCI Machine Learning Repository (Lichman, 2013) for the binary classification task. Our model is:

$$P(y|\mathbf{x}, \mathbf{w}) = \sigma(y\mathbf{w}^T\mathbf{x})$$
$$p(\mathbf{w}) = N(\mathbf{w}; \mathbf{w}_0, \mathbf{S}_0),$$

where $\sigma(x) = 1/(1 + \exp(-x))$.

For Abalone, individuals were divided into two classes based on whether individual had less or more than 10 rings. The data set consisted of 4177 samples with 8 attributes. We learned a posterior approximation for $\mathbf{w}$ using ADVI with SGA using Adagrad optimiser (Duchi et al., 2011) and sampling ratio $q = 0.02$. The posterior approximation $q(\mathbf{w})$ was Gaussian with a diagonal covariance. Classification was done using an additional Laplace approximation. Before training, features of the data set were normalised by subtracting feature mean and dividing by feature standard deviation. Training was done with 80% of data.

The other classification dataset "Adult" that we used with logistic regression consisted of 48842 samples with 14 attributes. Our classification task was to predict whether or not an individual's annual income exceeded $50K. The data were preprocessed similarly as in Abalone: we subtracted the feature mean and divided by the standard deviation of each feature. We again used 80% of the data for training the model.

We first compared the classification accuracy of models learned using two variants of DPVI with the moments accountant and advanced composition accounting as well as DP-SGLD of Wang et al. (2015). The classification results for Abalone and Adult are shown in Fig. 1. We used $q = 0.05$ in Abalone corresponding to mini batches of 167 points and $q = 0.005$ in Adult corresponding to mini batches of 195 points. With Abalone the algorithm was run for 1000 iterations and with Adult for 2000 iterations. Clipping threshold were 5 for Abalone and 75 for Adult. Both results clearly show that even under comparable advanced composition accounting used by DP-SGLD, DPVI consistently yields significantly higher classification accuracy at a comparable level of privacy. Using the moments accountant further helps in obtaining even more accurate results at comparable level of privacy. DPVI with the moments accountant can reach classification accuracy very close to the non-private level already for $\epsilon < 0.5$ for both data sets.

4.1.1 The effect of algorithm hyperparameters

We further tested how changing the different hyperparameters of the algorithm discussed in Sec. 3.2 affects the test set classification accuracy of models learned with DPVI with the moments accountant.

Fig. 2 shows the results when changing the data subsampling rate q. The result confirms the analysis of Sec. 3.2 that larger q tend to perform better than small q although there is a limit how small values of ϵ can be reached with a larger q.

Fig. 3 shows corresponding results when changing the gradient clipping threshold c_t. The results clearly show that too strong clipping can hurt the accuracy significantly. Once the clipping is sufficiently mild the differences between different options are far less dramatic.

4.2 GAUSSIAN MIXTURE MODEL

We also tested the performance of DPVI with a Gaussian mixture model. For K components our model is

$$\pi_k \sim \text{Dir}(\alpha)$$
$$\mu^{(k)} \sim \text{MVNormal}(\mathbf{0}, \mathbf{I})$$
$$\tau^{(k)} \sim \text{Inv-Gamma}(1, 1)$$

with the likelihood

$$p(\mathbf{x}_i|\boldsymbol{\pi}, \boldsymbol{\mu}, \boldsymbol{\tau}) = \sum_{k=1}^{K} \pi_k \mathcal{N}(\mathbf{x_i}; \mu^{(k)}, \tau^{(k)}\mathbf{I}).$$

Unlike standard variational inference that augments the model with indicator variables denoting the component responsible for generating each sample, we performed the inference directly on the mixture likelihood. This lets us avoid having to deal with latent variables that would otherwise make the DP inference more complicated.

The posterior approximation $q(\pi, \mu, \tau) = q(\pi)q(\mu)q(\tau)$ was fully factorised. $q(\pi)$ was parametrised using soft-

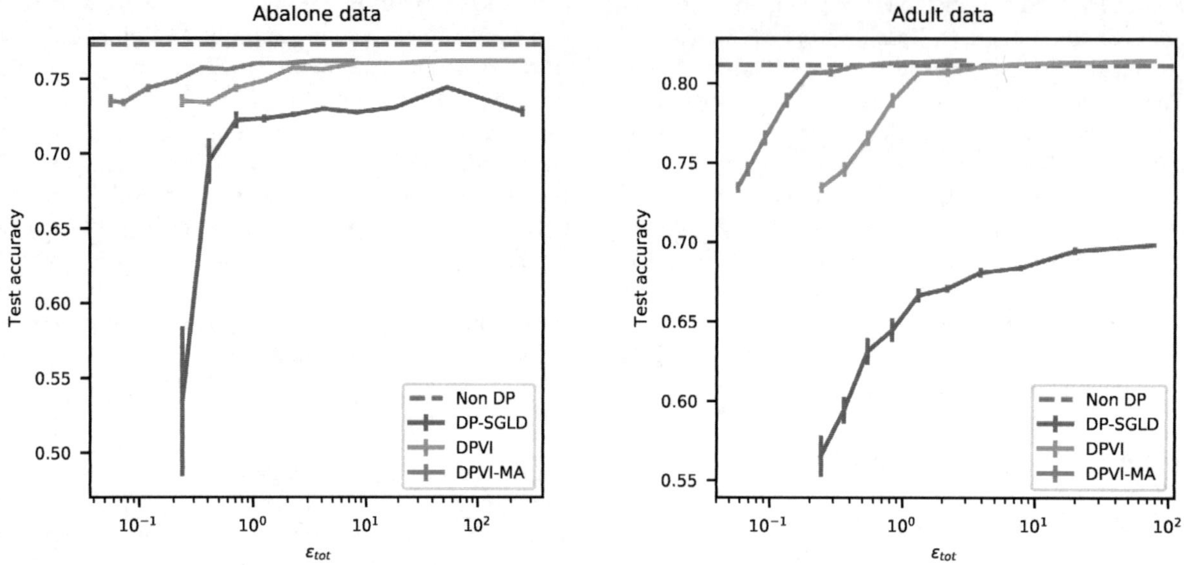

Figure 1: Comparison of binary classification accuracies using the Abalone data set (left) and the Adult data set (right). The figure shows test set classification accuracies of non-private logistic regression, two variants of DPVI with the moments accountant and advanced composition accounting and DP-SGLD of Wang et al. (2015). The curve shows the mean of 10 runs of both algorithms with error bars denoting the standard error of the mean.

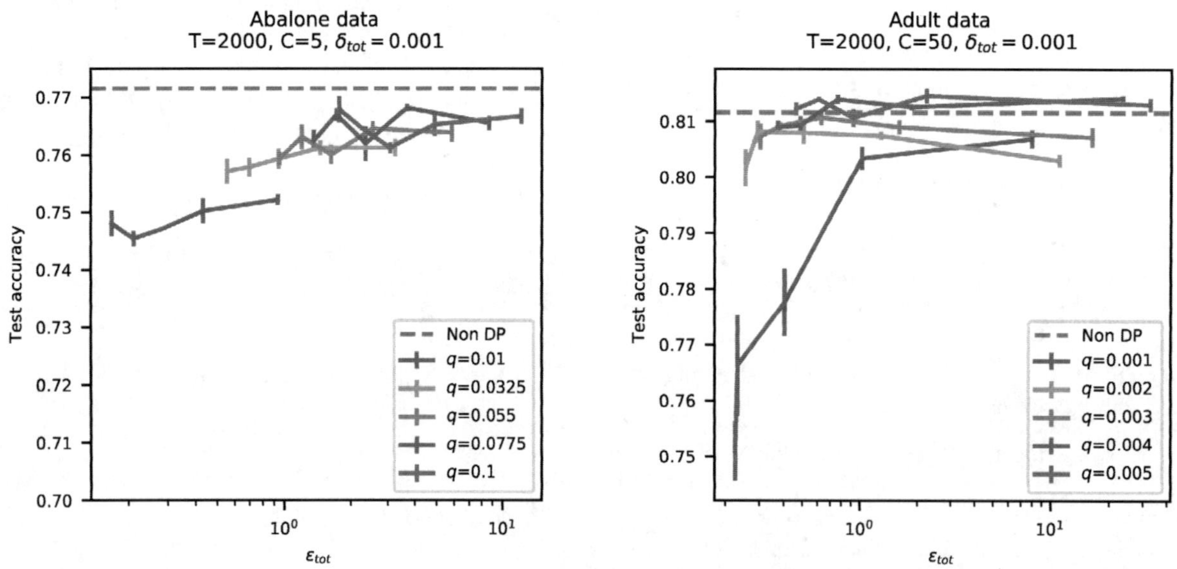

Figure 2: Accuracy vs. total ϵ in Abalone (left) and Adult (right) data sets with several data subsampling ratios q in DPVI with the moments accountant. The curve shows the mean of 10 runs of the DP algorithm with error bars denoting the standard error of the mean. Note that the y-axis scale covers a much smaller range than in Fig. 1.

max transformation from a diagonal covariance Gaussian while $q(\mu)$ was Gaussian with a diagonal covariance and $q(\tau)$ was log-normal with a diagonal covariance.

The synthetic data used in experiments was drawn from mixture of five spherical multivariate Gaussian distribution with means $[0, 0]$, $[\pm 2, \pm 2]$ and covariance matrices $0.5\mathbf{I}$. Similar data has been used previously by Honkela et al. (2010) and Hensman et al. (2012). We used 2000 samples from this mixture for training the model and 100

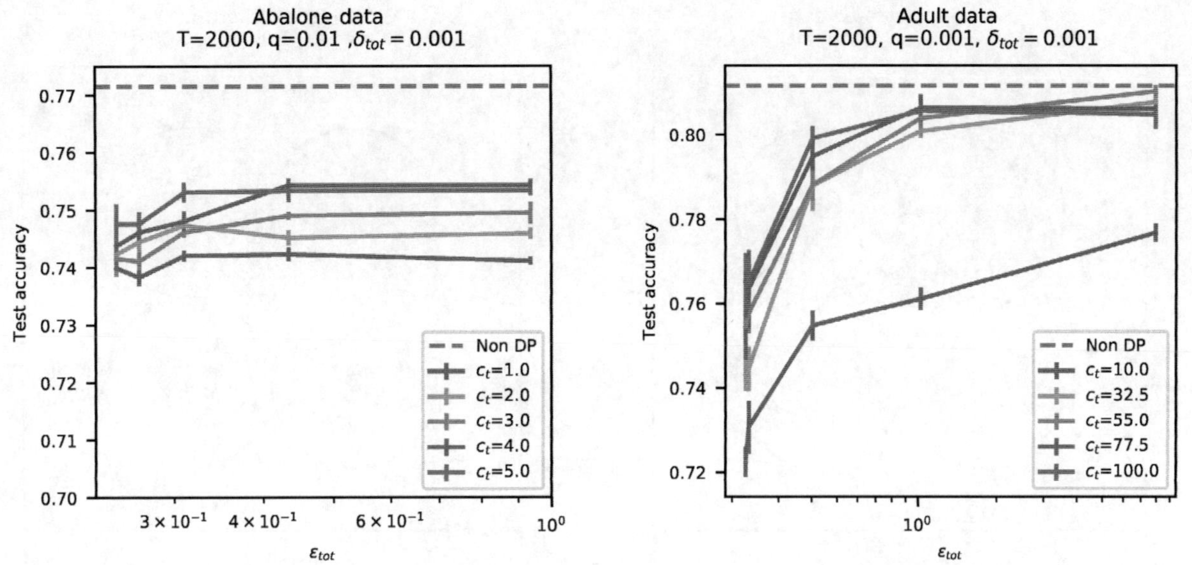

Figure 3: Accuracy vs. total ϵ in Abalone (left) and Adult (right) data sets with several gradient clipping threshold c_t values in DPVI with the moments accountant. The curve shows the mean of 10 runs of the DP algorithm with error bars denoting the standard error of the mean. Note that the y-axis scale covers a much smaller range than in Fig. 1.

samples to test the performance. We used both DPVI and DP-SGLD for this data. Performance comparison was done by computing the predictive likelihoods for both algorithms with several different epsilon values. We also show one example of approximate distribution that DPVI learns from above mixture model.

From Fig. 4 we can see that DPVI algorithm performs well compared to non-private version of DPVI even with relatively small epsilon values. We used $q = 0.003$ for DPVI and $q = 0.03$ for DP-SGLD. For DPVI algorithm number of iterations was 1000 and for DP-SGLD it was 150. Gradient clipping threshold for DPVI was set to $c_t = 1.0$. We used $\delta = 0.001$ in the predictive likelihood comparison. For DPVI predictive likelihood was approximated by Monte-Carlo integration using samples from the learned approximate posterior and for DP-SGLD by using the last 100 samples the algorithm produced. Non-private results were obtained by setting $\sigma = 0$ in DPVI, using $q = 0.003$ and running the DPVI algorithm for 2000 iterations.

Fig. 5 shows a visualisation of the mixture components learned by DPVI and DP-SGLD. Components inferred by DPVI appear much closer to ground truth than those from DP-SGLD.

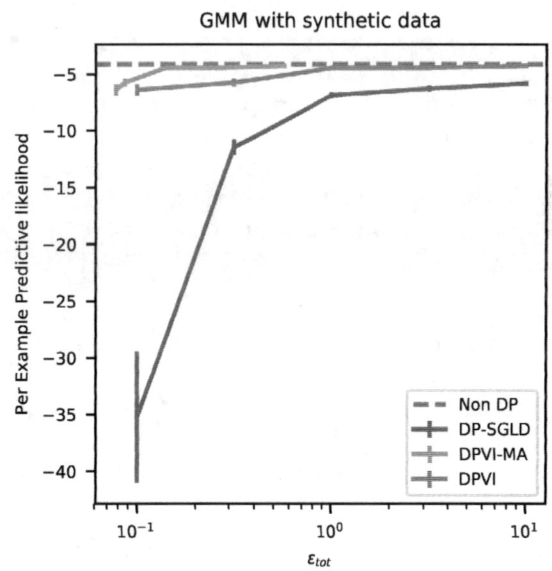

Figure 4: Per example predictive likelihood vs. ϵ. For both DP-SGLD and DPVI, lines show mean between 5 runs of algorithm with error bars denoting the standard error of mean.

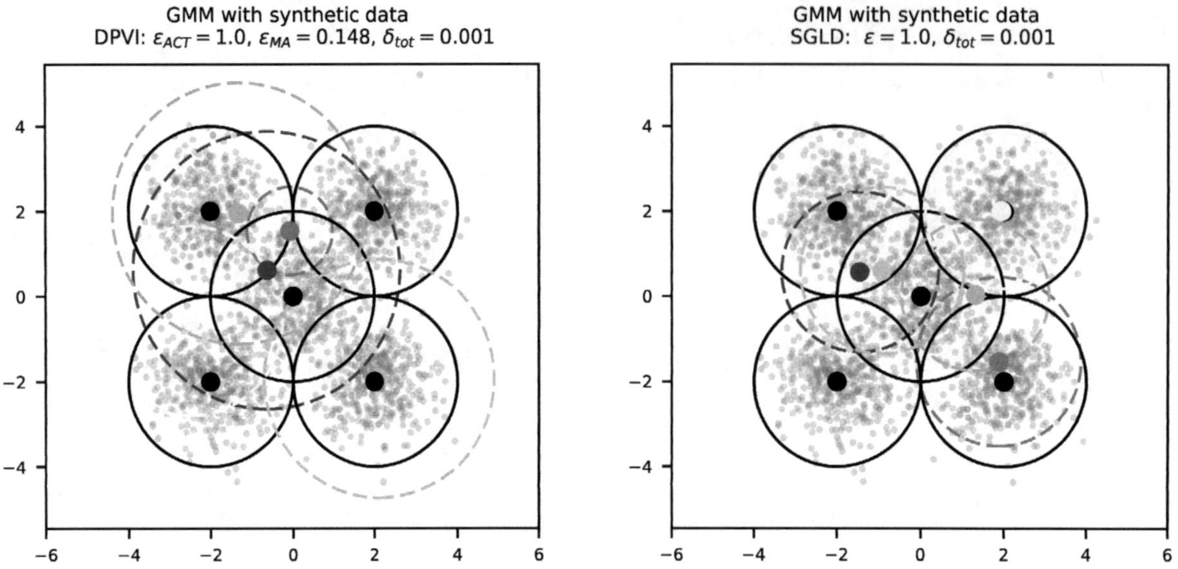

Figure 5: Approximate posterior predictive distribution for the Gaussian mixture model learned with DPVI (left) and DP-SGLD (right). The DP-SGLD distribution is formed as an average over the last 100 samples from the algorithm. Per example predictive log-likelihoods for DPVI and DP-SGLD in these experiments are -5.84 and -7.56 respectively. Predictive log-likelihoods were calculated using 100 test points.

5 DISCUSSION

Our results demonstrate that the proposed DPVI method has the potential to produce very accurate learning results, but this requires finding good values for algorithmic hyperparameters that unfortunately cannot be tuned using standard approaches without compromising the privacy. Finding good heuristics and default values for the hyperparameters is a very important avenue of future research.

It is tempting to think that the effect of gradient clipping would disappear as the algorithm converges and the total gradient becomes smaller. Unfortunately this is not true as the clipping is applied on the level of data point specific gradients which will typically not disappear even at convergence. This also means that aggressive clipping will change the stationary points of the SGA algorithm.

One way to make the problem easier to learn under DP is to simplify it for example through dimensionality reduction. This was noted for exponential family models by Honkela et al. (2016) but the same principle carries over to DPVI too. In DPVI, lower dimensional model typically has fewer parameters leading to a shorter parameter vector whose norm would thus be smaller, implying that smaller c_t is enough. This means that simpler posterior approximations such as Gaussians with a diagonal covariance may be better under DP while without the DP constraint an approximation with a full covariance would usually be better (see also Kucukelbir et al., 2017).

6 CONCLUSIONS

We have introduced the DPVI method that can deliver differentially private inference results with accuracy close to the non-private doubly stochastic variational inference and ADVI. The method can effectively harness the power of ADVI to deal with very general models instead of just conjugate exponential models and the option of using multivariate Gaussian posterior approximations for greater accuracy.

Acknowledgements

This work was funded by the Academy of Finland (Centre of Excellence COIN; and grants 278300, 259440 and 283107).

References

M. Abadi, A. Chu, I. Goodfellow, H. B. McMahan, I. Mironov, K. Talwar, and L. Zhang. Deep learning with differential privacy. In *Proc. CCS 2016*, 2016. arXiv:1607.00133 [stat.ML].

M. Bun and T. Steinke. Concentrated differential privacy: Simplifications, extensions, and lower bounds. May 2016. arXiv:1605.02065 [cs.CR].

K. Chaudhuri and C. Monteleoni. Privacy-preserving logistic regression. In *Adv. Neural Inf. Process. Syst. 21*, pages 289–296, 2008.

A. P. Dempster, N. M. Laird, and D. B. Rubin. Maximum likelihood from incomplete data via the EM algorithm. *Journal of the Royal Statistical Society. Series B (Methodological)*, 39(1):1–38, 1977.

C. Dimitrakakis, B. Nelson, A. Mitrokotsa, and B. I. P. Rubinstein. Robust and private Bayesian inference. In *ALT 2014*, volume 8776 of *Lecture Notes in Computer Science*, pages 291–305. Springer Science + Business Media, 2014.

J. Duchi, E. Hazan, and Y. Singer. Adaptive subgradient methods for online learning and stochastic optimization. *J. Mach. Learn. Res.*, 12:2121–2159, July 2011.

C. Dwork and A. Roth. The algorithmic foundations of differential privacy. *Found. Trends Theor. Comput. Sci.*, 9(3–4):211–407, August 2014.

C. Dwork and G. N. Rothblum. Concentrated differential privacy. 2016. arXiv:1603.01887 [cs.DS].

C. Dwork, F. McSherry, K. Nissim, and A. Smith. Calibrating noise to sensitivity in private data analysis. In S. Halevi and T. Rabin, editors, *Theory of Cryptography: Third Theory of Cryptography Conference, TCC 2006, New York, NY, USA, March 4-7, 2006. Proceedings*, pages 265–284. Springer Berlin Heidelberg, Berlin, Heidelberg, 2006.

J. Foulds, J. Geumlek, M. Welling, and K. Chaudhuri. On the theory and practice of privacy-preserving Bayesian data analysis. In *Proc. 32nd Conf. on Uncertainty in Artificial Intelligence (UAI 2016)*, 2016.

Z. Ghahramani and M. J. Beal. Propagation algorithms for variational Bayesian learning. In T. K. Leen, T. G. Dietterich, and V. Tresp, editors, *Advances in Neural Information Processing Systems 13*, pages 507–513. MIT Press, 2001.

J. Hensman, M. Rattray, and N. D. Lawrence. Fast variational inference in the conjugate exponential family. In *Advances in Neural Information Processing Systems 25*, pages 2897–2905. 2012.

A. Honkela, T. Raiko, M. Kuusela, M. Tornio, and J. Karhunen. Approximate Riemannian conjugate gradient learning for fixed-form variational Bayes. *J Mach Learn Res*, 11:3235–3268, Nov 2010.

A. Honkela, M. Das, A. Nieminen, O. Dikmen, and S. Kaski. Efficient differentially private learning improves drug sensitivity prediction. 2016. arXiv:1606.02109.

M. I. Jordan, Z. Ghahramani, T. S. Jaakkola, and L. K. Saul. An introduction to variational methods for graphical models. *Mach. Learn.*, 37(2):183–233, November 1999.

A. Kucukelbir, D. Tran, R. Ranganath, A. Gelman, and D. M. Blei. Automatic differentiation variational inference. *J Mach Learn Res*, 18(14):1–45, 2017.

N. Li, W. Qardaji, and D. Su. On sampling, anonymization, and differential privacy or, k-anonymization meets differential privacy. In *Proceedings of the 7th ACM Symposium on Information, Computer and Communications Security*, ASIACCS '12, pages 32–33, New York, NY, USA, 2012. ACM.

M. Lichman. UCI machine learning repository, 2013. URL `http://archive.ics.uci.edu/ml`.

M. Park, J. Foulds, K. Chaudhuri, and M. Welling. Variational Bayes in private settings (VIPS). 2016. arXiv:1611.00340 [stat.ML].

J. Salvatier, T. V. Wiecki, and C. Fonnesbeck. Probabilistic programming in Python using PyMC3. *PeerJ Computer Science*, 2:e55, apr 2016.

M. Titsias and M. Lázaro-Gredilla. Doubly stochastic variational Bayes for non-conjugate inference. In *Proc. 31st Int. Conf. Mach. Learn. (ICML 2014)*, pages 1971–1979, 2014.

D. Tran, M. D. Hoffman, R. A. Saurous, E. Brevdo, K. Murphy, and D. M. Blei. Deep probabilistic programming. In *International Conference on Learning Representations*, 2017.

Y. Wang, S. E. Fienberg, and A. J. Smola. Privacy for free: Posterior sampling and stochastic gradient Monte Carlo. In *Proc. 32nd Int. Conf. Mach. Learn. (ICML 2015)*, pages 2493–2502, 2015.

O. Williams and F. McSherry. Probabilistic inference and differential privacy. In *Adv. Neural Inf. Process. Syst. 23*, 2010.

J. Zhang, G. Cormode, C. M. Procopiuc, D. Srivastava, and X. Xiao. PrivBayes: Private data release via Bayesian networks. In *SIGMOD'14*, pages 1423–1434, 2014.

J. Zhang, Z. Zhang, X. Xiao, Y. Yang, and M. Winslett. Functional mechanism: Regression analysis under differential privacy. *PVLDB*, 5(11):1364–1375, 2012.

Z. Zhang, B. Rubinstein, and C. Dimitrakakis. On the differential privacy of Bayesian inference. In *Proc. Conf. AAAI Artif. Intell. 2016*, 2016.

Value Directed Exploration in Multi-Armed Bandits with Structured Priors

Bence Cserna **Marek Petrik** **Reazul Hasan Russel** **Wheeler Ruml**
University of New Hampshire
Durham, NH 03824 USA
bence, mpetrik, rrussel, ruml at cs.unh.edu

Abstract

Multi-armed bandits are a quintessential machine learning problem requiring balancing exploration with exploitation. While there has been progress in developing algorithms with strong theoretical guarantees, there has been less focus on practical near-optimal finite-time performance. In this paper, we propose an algorithm for Bayesian multi-armed bandits that utilizes approximate value functions. Building on previous work on UCB and Gittins index, we introduce *linearly-separable value functions* that capture the benefit of exploration when choosing the next arm to pull. Our algorithm enjoys a sub-linear performance guarantee and our simulation results confirm its strength in problems with structured priors. The simplicity and generality of our approach makes it a strong candidate for use in more complex multi-armed bandit problems.

1 INTRODUCTION

In the multi-armed bandit setup, a decision-maker repeatedly chooses from a finite set of actions. A reward is generated independently from a probability distribution associated with the action. The underlying reward distribution for each action is unknown to the decision-maker, but each action-reward pair can further inform future choices. Strong performance in this setup critically depends on the balance between exploring less well-understood actions and exploiting actions thought to provide high reward. In this sense, the problem captures the quintessence of the interplay between learning and decision-making.

Many approaches to the multi-armed bandit problem have achieved impressive theoretical and empirical results [Bubeck and Cesa-Bianchi, 2012; Kuleshov and Precup, 2014]. There is, however, growing recognition that more wide-spread practical use will require algorithms that can better exploit structured prior information [Russo and Roy, 2014; Lattimore and Szepesvári, 2016]. For example, consider a bandit problem in which the arms represent different levels of customer discounts such as 5% or 10%. The conversion probabilities for the discounts are not known before the promotion starts, but one can safely assume that more customers choose to buy the product when offered a 10% rather than a 5% discount. Such prior information should ideally be used to increase the efficiency of exploration in particular when a large number of discounts is considered. While in some problems such prior information can be captured using parametric models, like GLM-UCB [Filippi *et al.*, 2010], such models make many additional assumptions that are difficult to verify when little or no data is available.

In this paper, we propose a Bayesian bandit algorithm designed to use structured prior information in order to achieve good short-term performance with a small number of arm pulls. We take an approach based on online planning, using lookahead search to consider states to which each possible sequence of actions might lead. Relying on lookahead search makes it possible to easily exploit structured prior information when it is available. Because the state space grows exponentially with the number of arms, it is impossible to enumerate all reachable states to the problem horizon. Thus, this formulation of the problem relies crucially on having a value function that can be applied at a modest depth cut-off in lieu of further state search.

Many methods for computing approximate value functions have been developed in reinforcement learning and some have been used to solve some multi-armed bandit problems [Whittle, 1988; Adelman and Mersereau, 2008]. But they can be computationally intensive and cumbersome to use. As our main contribution, we derive in Section 3 a new method for computing *linearly-separable value functions* that, when used in concert with lookahead search, performs as well as state-of-the-art-algorithms. The method computes value functions by exploiting existing algorithms and the weakly-coupled property of multi-armed bandit problems. It also enjoys sublinear regret as we show in Section 4. Our algorithm is simple to implement and, as we demonstrate in Section 5, performs well in bandit problems with structured prior information.

Given the fundamental simplicity of our approach and its empirical success, we are optimistic that it may provide a basis for addressing more complex problems, such as contextual bandits, in the future. Our approach also opens the door to bandit algorithms that can yield improved performance when additional computation time is available.

2 BACKGROUND

We begin by describing the Bayesian multi-armed bandit problem in more detail. We focus on the case of Bernoulli bandits, deferring discussion of more complex models to Section 5.2. We then briefly review previously proposed algorithms before turning to our new method.

2.1 PROBLEM FORMULATION

The decision-maker in the standard multi-armed bandit problem aims to maximize the cumulative return by repeatedly choosing one of N arms: $\mathcal{A} = \{a_1, \ldots, a_N\}$. Choosing an arm a_i results in receiving a reward $R_i \in \{0, 1\}$ distributed according to a Bernoulli distribution with a mean μ_i. The mean μ_i is not known in advance. To achieve the maximal cumulative return over a horizon of T steps, the decision-maker must balance exploration to learn about the expected returns of arms with exploitation in order to learn which arms are more likely to provide high rewards.

In the Bayesian variant of the problem, the decision-maker has access to a prior distribution over the expected reward $\mu_1, \mu_2, \ldots, \mu_N$ for each arm $a_1, a_2, \ldots, a_N$. We use $\mu = (\mu_1, \ldots, \mu_N)$ to represent the prior parameters of the bandit; each μ_i is distributed according to a Beta distribution. As in most machine learning settings, the Bayesian approach has both advantages and disadvantages —a proper discussion is beyond the scope of this paper and we refer to Kaufmann *et al.* [2012a]; Russo and Van Roy [2014]; Kim and Lim [2015] and the references therein for details.

The Bayesian multi-armed bandit problem can be modeled as a Markov Decision Process (MDP). The state in this MDP represents the sufficient statistic of the history of the observed rewards for each arm. We denote the state space of the MDP that represents the multi-armed bandit problem as $\mathcal{S} = \mathcal{S}_1 \cup \mathcal{S}_2 \cup \ldots \cup \mathcal{S}_T$, where $\mathcal{S}_t$ is the set of states at time t. The actions in this MDP are simply the pulls of arms of the bandit. Fig. 1 shows a fragment of the MDP for a two-arm bandit, illustrating the transition from one state to the four possible successors.

In order for the Markov property to hold, each state of the MDP must represent the posterior distribution of μ_i given the history of rewards for every arm a_i. The posterior estimate $\tilde{\mu}_i$ of μ_i is distributed according to the Beta distribution $\mathrm{Beta}(\alpha, \beta)$ with some parameters α, β since it is the conjugate prior to Bernoulli distribution (e.g., [Gittins *et al.*, 2011]). Any state $s \in \mathcal{S}$ can, therefore, be represented as

$$s = \Big((\alpha_1, \beta_1), (\alpha_2, \beta_2), \ldots, (\alpha_N, \beta_N)\Big),$$

where α_i, β_i represent the Beta distribution parameters for each arm i. We use α_i^0, β_i^0 to denote the parameters of the prior Beta distributions and generally assume that $\alpha_i^0 = \beta_i^0 = 1$ which corresponds to the uniform prior. The parameters α, β of the Beta distribution have a convenient interpretation: after observing n_s successes (value 1) and n_f failures (value 0) for R_i then $\tilde{\mu}_i \sim \mathrm{Beta}(\alpha_i^0 + n_s, \beta_i^0 + n_f)$. Thus the transition, after pulling an arm a_i, consists of merely adding one to the appropriate α_i or β_i based on the observed reward.

When the bandit is in state s_t and the decision maker chooses arm a_i, the subsequent state is represented by a random variable $S_{t+1}(s_t, a_i)$. When $s_t = (\ldots, (\alpha_i, \beta_i), \ldots)$, the random variable $S_{t+1}(s_t, a_i)$ is distributed as

$$\mathbb{P}\left[\, S_{t+1} = (\ldots, (\alpha_i + 1, \beta_i), \ldots) \,\right] = \frac{\alpha_i}{\alpha_i + \beta_i}, \quad (1)$$

$$\mathbb{P}\left[\, S_{t+1} = (\ldots, (\alpha_i, \beta_i + 1), \ldots) \,\right] = \frac{\beta_i}{\alpha_i + \beta_i}, \quad (2)$$

where the transition probabilities follow from the definition of the mean of the Beta distribution. To reduce clutter, we omit s_t and a_i when they are obvious from the context. The rewards received in transitions (1) and (2) are 1 and 0 respectively.

By specifying which arm to pull at any given state, a multi-armed bandit algorithm defines a policy for this bandit MDP. The decision rule at time t is denoted as $\pi_t : \mathcal{S}_t \to \mathcal{A}$ and the policy is the collection of the decision rules $\pi = \{\pi_t \mid t = 1 \ldots T\}$ for each time step t. The celebrated Gittins index defines the optimal policy

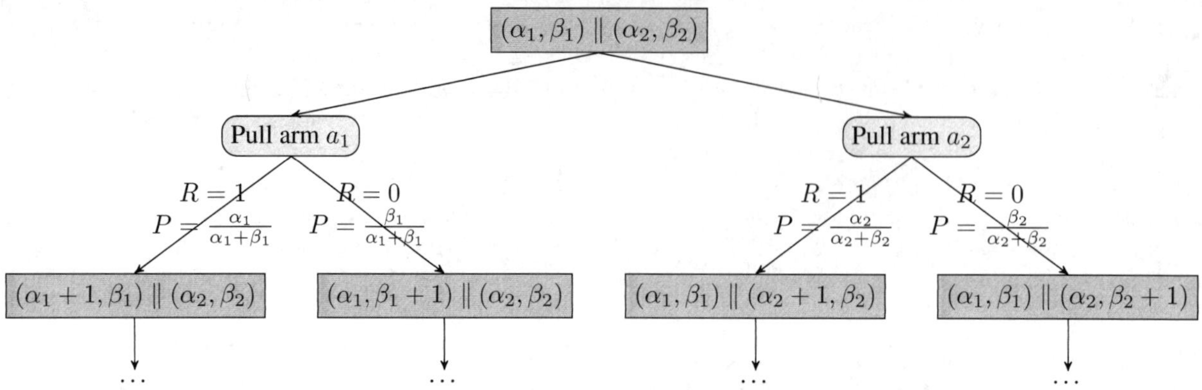

Figure 1: A single transition of the Bernoulli multi-armed bandit problem.

for the discounted infinite-horizon version of the bandit problem, but that method is not based on directly solving the MDP. In most practical problems, it is impossible to compute the optimal policy because the number of states grows exponentially with the number of arms. Unfortunately, while Gittins index may be optimal, it provably does not generalize to most other bandit problems [Gittins *et al.*, 2011].

The established performance measure for classic bandit algorithms is the regret, sometimes referred to as pseudo-regret [Bubeck and Cesa-Bianchi, 2012], which is defined for a particular realization of the bandit parameters μ and policy π as

$$\mathrm{Regret}(\pi, T, \mu) = \sum_{t=1}^{T} \Big(\max_{i=1\ldots N} \mu_i - \mathbb{E}\left[R_{\pi(S_t)} \mid \mu \right] \Big) ,$$

where S_t is a random variable that represents the state of the bandit process. In Bayesian bandits, it is natural to instead evaluate Bayesian regret:

$$\mathrm{BayesRegret}(\pi, T) = \mathbb{E}_\mu \left[\mathrm{Regret}(\pi, T, \mu) \right] .$$

We aim to minimize Bayesian regret with a particular focus on the regret in the first few steps. While the guarantees provided by a small bound on the Bayesian regret are somewhat weaker than that of regular regret, it is a very reasonable measure in most circumstances.

2.2 PREVIOUS WORK

The literature on bandit problems is enormous, so we will focus only on the most relevant algorithms. The UCB family of algorithms [Auer *et al.*, 2002] use the problem structure to derive tight optimistic upper bounds. While these algorithms are simple and have been used in various applications with success, they lack the ability to incorporate structured prior information such as arm dependency or different reward policies without requiring complex and difficult re-analysis of the upper bounds. Kaufmann *et al.* [2012a] propose Bayes-UCB, a Bayesian index policy that improves on UCB in Bayesian bandits by taking advantage of the prior distribution.

Russo and Roy [2014] describe a method that improves on the optimistic approach taken by UCB algorithms. Their method considers the information gain from taking an action to optimize the exploration-exploitation trade-off. They provide a strong Bayesian regret bound that applies for a general class of models. Our new method is based on a similar principle but uses additive value functions to estimate the information gain.

Thompson sampling works by choosing an arm based on its probability of being the best arm. Specifically, the method draws a sample from the decision maker's current belief distribution for each arm and then chooses the arm that yielded the highest sample. The performance of Thompson sampling has been proved to be near optimal, and it is simple and efficient to implement. Thompson sampling can easily be adapted to a wide range of problem structures and prior distributions [Agrawal and Goyal, 2012; Leike *et al.*, 2016; Kaufmann *et al.*, 2012b]. For example, one can reject sets of samples that contradict contextual information. However, the simplicity of the method makes it also difficult to improve its performance.

Gittins indices exploit the weak dependence between actions to compute the optimal action in time that is linear in the number of arms [Gittins, 1979; Chakravorty and Mahajan, 2014]. Gittins indices, however, are guaranteed to be optimal only for the basic multi-armed bandit problem, require a discounted infinite-horizon objective, and provably cannot be extended to most interesting practical problems which involve correlations between arms or an additional context [Gittins *et al.*, 2011].

3 SEPARABLE VALUE FUNCTIONS

We now turn to our new approach, which we call "ELSV" (Exploration via Linearly Separable Value Functions). As described above, our main goal is a method that is flexible and takes advantage of the complex problem structure or prior knowledge in order to reduce the regret. We achieve this by taking a state-space search-based approach and by leveraging the exploration-exploitation trade-off behavior of existing algorithms to build good value functions.

The ELSV algorithm, as described in this section, does not improve the performance of existing methods when applied to Bernoulli bandits. In Section 5, we describe how it can be extended easily to settings with prior information in which it significantly outperforms state-of-the-art methods.

Algorithm 1: One-step lookahead algorithm

Input: Current time step t, current state s_t, and value function $v_t : \mathcal{S}_t \to \mathbb{R}$
Output: Arm to pull at time step t
for $a \in \mathcal{A}$ **do**
  // $q_t(s_t, a)$ is the expected value for action a in state s_t
  $q_t(s_t, a) \leftarrow \mathbb{E}\left[r(s_t, a, S_{t+1}) + v_{t+1}(S_{t+1})\right]$;
return $\arg\max_{a \in \mathcal{A}} q_t(s_t, a)$;

Our general approach is based on an n-step lookahead guided by a specific value function. This is an instance of receding horizon control, a common approach to solving online planning and reinforcement learning problems [Sutton and Barto, 1998]. The state space is enumerated to depth n, at which point a value function is evaluated at the frontier states to avoid further expansion. Note that, because there are multiple ways of reaching a state in the MDP, the state space forms a graph and it is important to detect and merge duplicate states. The values are backed up to the current state at the root and the best-looking action is chosen. After the outcome of pulling the arm is observed, the cycle repeats again with a fresh lookahead. A simplified version of the algorithm, depicted in Algorithm 1, estimates the value of each action by computing the expected value for the next step.

Since Algorithm 1 does not rely on any complex confidence bounds, one would expect that it can easily generalize to many different problems. Choosing a longer lookahead horizon also offers the promise of trading off computational time for more efficient exploration. The quality of this algorithm will clearly depend on whether it is supplied with a good value function v.

There has been little previous work that considered a value function-driven approach to bandit problems, with Adelman and Mersereau [2008] being one notable exception. This is perhaps because UCB is simple and efficient, while computing value functions via approximate dynamic programming requires complex computation and can be unreliable. We show, however, that it is possible to *efficiently* construct good value functions directly from UCB and other popular bandit algorithms. Surprisingly, such value functions are simple and linearly separate over the individual arms.

Before describing how we construct the value function, consider what it is supposed to represent. Consider, for example, a state $s = ((2,3),(10,10))$ in a two-arm bandit problem with 10 steps remaining until the end of the horizon T is reached. The expected returns of the two arms are $2/5 \cdot 10 = 4$ and $1/2 \cdot 10 = 5$ respectively. One could simply assign $v_{10}(s) = \max\{4,5\} = 5$, but this would not be precise. The first arm, while apparently having a lower expected mean, is far less certain than the second arm (because of a smaller number of pulls). In order to achieve good results, and in particular a sub-linear regret guarantee, the value function must consider not only the expected return but also the confidence of the estimates. Another way to put it is that the value function must model both the expected return (exploitation) and the benefit of exploration.

Algorithm 2: Index Policy

Input: Current time step t, current state s_t, and index function $z_t : \mathcal{S}_t \times \mathcal{A} \to \mathbb{R}$
Output: Arm to pull at time step t
return $\arg\max_{a \in \mathcal{A}} z_t(s_t^i, a_i)$;

We seek to take advantage of the implicit value of exploration that is encoded by existing multi-armed bandit index algorithm. Algorithm 2 shows a canonical example of an index-based algorithm. UCB, Gittins index, and many other methods fit this basic mold. Note that the index $z_t(s_t^i, a_i)$ is computed for each arm separately. The notation s_t^i denotes the component of state s_t that corresponds to arm a_i, that is $s_t^i = (\alpha_i, \beta_i)$. For example, if $s_t = ((5,2),(4,6))$ then $s_t^2 = (4,6)$. An important property of the index function $z_t(s_t^i, a_i)$ is that it is completely independent of the states of other arms and can thus be computed efficiently.

The challenge when constructing an index algorithm is how to define the index value z_t. If we use the Bayesian expectation of the immediate return in place of the standard frequentist one, then the value of the index for the

α-UCB algorithm for each arm $a \in \mathcal{A}$ is

$$\begin{aligned} z_t^{\mathrm{UCB}}(s_t^i, a_i) &= r(s_t^i, a_i) + \sqrt{\frac{\alpha \log t}{T_i(s_t^i)}} \\ &= \underbrace{r(s_t^i, a_i)}_{\text{Immediate reward}} + \underbrace{b_t^{\mathrm{UCB}}(s_t^i, a_i)}_{\text{Exploration bonus}} \end{aligned} \tag{3}$$

where $r(s_t^i, a_i) = \mathbb{E}\left[r(s_t^i, a_i, S_{t+1}^i) \right] = {\alpha_i}/{\alpha_i + \beta_i}$ is the expected reward after pulling arm a_i, $T_i(s_t^i) = \alpha_i + \beta_i - 2$ is the number of times the arm has been pulled (recall that the initial states is $\alpha_i^0 = \beta_i^0 = 1$), and b_t^{UCB} is the exploration bonus.

The classic UCB algorithm uses $\alpha = 2$, but sub-linear regret can be in fact shown with $\alpha > 1$ [Bubeck and Cesa-Bianchi, 2012]. Lower values of α typically lead to better empirical performance but also make it more difficult to bound the regret. We use $\alpha = 1$ unless otherwise specified.

Another celebrated example of an index policy is the Gittins index, see for example [Gittins *et al.*, 2011]. While UCB is only *asymptotically* optimal (up to a constant factor), following the Gittins index is truly optimal in some simple bandit settings. For example, Gittins indices are optimal for an infinite-horizon discounted Bernoulli bandit problem. We generally use discount $\gamma = 0.99$ and the horizon of 1000 when approximating the infinite horizon.

Unlike UCB, Gittins index does not have a closed-form expression, but it must be precomputed. Since the index is computed for each arm independently, it can be computed and used efficiently regardless of the number of arms in the bandit problem [Niño-Mora, 2011]. We use $z_t^{\mathrm{Gitt}}(s_t^i, a)$ to denote the value of the Gittins index and $b_t^{\mathrm{Gitt}}(s_t^i, a_i) = z_t^{\mathrm{Gitt}}(s_t^i, a_i) - r(s_t^i, a_i)$ to denote the exploration benefit that it assigns to the arms. Many other multi-armed bandit methods have been proposed, some examples are Bayes-UCB [Kaufmann *et al.*, 2012a] or UCB-V [Audibert *et al.*, 2009] to name a few.

We are now ready to describe ELSV, the new method for constructing linearly-separable value functions. A linearly-separable value function for components $v_t^i : \mathcal{S}_t^i \to \mathbb{R}$ is such that, for each $t \in \mathcal{T}$ and for each state $s_t \in \mathcal{S}_t$,

$$v_t(s_t) = \sum_{a_i \in \mathcal{A}} v_t^i(s_t^i) \,. \tag{4}$$

Linearly separable value functions are attractive due to their simplicity and have been used widely in reinforcement learning and approximate dynamic programming [Powell, 2008; Powell *et al.*, 2004; Rust, 1996] and previously for approximating the value function in bandit problems [Adelman and Mersereau, 2008].

We begin with an arbitrary bandit index function z_t^i and the corresponding exploration bonus function b_t^i. Each component v_t^i must satisfy the following condition for every a_i, t, and $\tau \le t$:

$$\begin{aligned} v_{t+1}^i(s_\tau^i) &= \mathbb{E}\left[v_{t+1}^i(S_{\tau+1}^i) \right] + r(s_\tau^i, a_i) - z_t(s_\tau^i, a_i) \\ &= \mathbb{E}\left[v_{t+1}^i(S_{\tau+1}^i) \right] - b_t(s_\tau^i, a_i) \,, \end{aligned} \tag{5}$$

where $S_{\tau+1}^i$ is short for $S_{\tau+1}^i(s_\tau, a_i)$, the random variable that represents the state following the pull of arm a_i. It is important to note that all v's involved use the same time index $t+1$ while the states are over two time steps τ and $\tau + 1$.

To understand the requirement in (5) more intuitively, we can rewrite it as

$$\mathbb{E}\left[v_{t+1}^i(S_{\tau+1}^i) \right] - v_{t+1}^i(s_\tau^i) = b_t(s_\tau^i, a_i) \,.$$

The term $\mathbb{E}\left[v_{t+1}^i(S_{\tau+1}^i) \right]$ represents the expected value of the state at time $t+1$ after pulling the arm a_i; $S_{\tau+1}$ is a random variable. In contrast, the term $v_{t+1}^i(s_\tau^i)$ represents the expected value of the state s_τ^i at time $t+1$ when arm a_i is not pulled. The difference between these two terms is the change in the value of the current state, or in other words, how much we have learned about the arm after pulling it. And this increase in information about the arm should be equal to the exploration bonus assigned by the index.

Algorithm 3: ELSV: Computing linearly separable value functions that satisfy (5).

Input: Arm a_i, time step $t \in 1, \ldots, T$, and exploration bonus function $b_t : \mathcal{S}_t \times \mathcal{A} \to \mathbb{R}$
Output: Value function v_t^i for arm a_i at time t

```
S_t ← {(α, β) ∈ N²_{>0} | α + β − 2 ≤ t − 1} ;
v_t^i(s) ← 0   ∀s ∈ S_t;
// τ = num. of pulls of a_i so far
for τ = t − 2 to 1 do
    // Iterate possible histories
    foreach (α, β) ∈ {s ∈ S_τ | α + β − 2 = τ} do
        p ← α/(α+β),   q ← β/(α+β) ;
        v_t^i(α, β) ←
            p · v_t^i(α + 1, β) + q · v_t^i(α, β + 1) − b_t(α, β) ;
return v_t^i
```

Theorem 3.1. *Let π_I represent Algorithm 2 with index function $\hat{z}_t$. Suppose a policy π_V represents Algorithm 1 with value function $\hat{v}_t$ as defined in* (4)–(5) *using an index function $\hat{z}_t^i$. Then $\pi_V(s_t) = \pi_I(s_t)$ for each $s_t \in \mathcal{S}_t$.*

We defer the proof of Theorem 3.1 to Appendix A.1. It follows by comparing the value of pulling an arm with the value of a hypothetical state which would have resulted from not pulling any arm. The argument relies on the fact that a policy is not affected by adding or subtracting a constant from the value function for all states in $\mathcal{S}_t$ for any t.

The simplest arm index would simply ignore the exploration bonus by setting it to $b_t(s_t^i, a_i) = 0$. The value function for this setting will be a constant and the 1-step lookahead policy will simply be greedy. Having no exploration bonus, therefore, leads to no exploration and pure exploitation.

The value function in Theorem 3.1 induces the same policy as the index, but it is still an approximation of the true value of each state. Therefore, a value function v constructed from the Gittins index will lead to the optimal policy (for the discounted infinite-horizon bandit) but it is not the optimal value function.

Algorithm 3 describes a dynamic programming method that can be used to compute a value function that satisfies (5). The following proposition, which can be shown readily by algebraic manipulation, states the complexity of the algorithm.

Proposition 3.1. *The linearly separable value function v_t^i can be computed using dynamic programming with computational complexity $O(t^3)$.*

Since the values v are computed independently for each t they do not have to be pre-computed ahead of time but can be computed on as needed basis and only for the states relevant to choosing an action. It is also important to note that the complexity in Proposition 3.1 is independent of the number of arms and the complexity of the 1-step lookahead in Algorithm 1 is linear in the number of arms. ELSV can scale to a large number of arms with no significant difficulties.

Fig. 2 depicts value functions computed by ELSV for Gittins index at $t = 10$ and $t = 200$ for each state. The states in $\mathcal{S}$ are mapped to a 2-dimensional space and the contours indicate the value function at that state. The number of arm pulls on the vertical axis can be smaller than t since the arm may not be pulled in every time step. Fig. 3 shows the value function computed by ELSV for UCB index for comparison. As noted above, the constant offset of the value functions is irrelevant to the quality of the policy. The value functions in the plots are offset to satisfy,

$$v_t^i(s_t) \ge \max\left\{r(s_t^i, a_i) + \mathbb{E}\left[v_{t+1}^i(S_{t+1}^i)\right], v_{t+1}^i(s_t^i)\right\} ,$$

which leads to more reasonable value estimates without influencing the policy.

The value function of UCB is notably simpler than the one for Gittins index. As expected, the UCB value function is *concave* and increasing but independent of the expected success probability. This indicates that exploration in UCB is really driven just by the immediate reward and the certainty in it—the potential long-term benefits of the arm are ignored. On the other hand, the value function for the Gittins index value exhibits a curious structure: it increases toward both low and high probabilities. This is counterintuitive as one would expect the value function to monotonically increase with the success probability. In a multi-armed bandit, however, it is also valuable to learn that an arm is not good which reduces the need for further exploration. Arms with medium success probabilities do not provide high rewards and yet require significant exploration. Notice also that this property is much more exaggerated at $t = 200$.

In the remainder of the paper, we discuss regret bounds ELSV and evaluate its performance experimentally on a bandit problem with additional problem structure.

4 ANALYSIS OF REGRET

In this section, we prove that ELSV with the UCB value function has sublinear regret. The sublinear bound on the regret is not surprising; Theorem 4.1 shows that ELSV with such a value function behaves identically to UCB which enjoys sublinear regret bounds. Instead, the main goal of this section is to establish a new methodology that can be used to analyze regret of multi-armed bandit algorithms driven by value functions.

Our goal is, in particular, to derive regret bounds that depend on some property of the value function used by ELSV. We need additional notation to describe such a property concisely. Let $q_t(s, a)$ stand for the expected value after pulling an action a in state s_t:

$$q_t(s_t, a) = r(s_t, a) + \mathbb{E}\left[v_{t+1}\Big(S_{t+1}(s_t, a)\Big)\right] .$$

As we show below, to bound regret it is sufficient to establish an upper bound on:

$$\varphi_t(\mu, s_t, a_i) = q_t(s_t, a_i) - (\mu_i + v_{t+1}(s_t)) . \qquad (6)$$

This value φ_t compares the estimate of the expected value $q_t(s_t, a_i)$ with a more precise estimate of the same value $(\mu_i + v_{t+1}(s_t))$. The more precise estimate uses the unknown parameter μ. One could also interpret φ_t as a finite-horizon form of the Bellman residual used in bounds on performance loss in reinforcement learning (e.g. [Petrik and Zilberstein, 2011]).

The following lemma plays a key role in establishing the regret bounds. It shows how the regret of ELSV can be decomposed into two components: one is independent of the algorithm and the other one is independent of the optimal action.

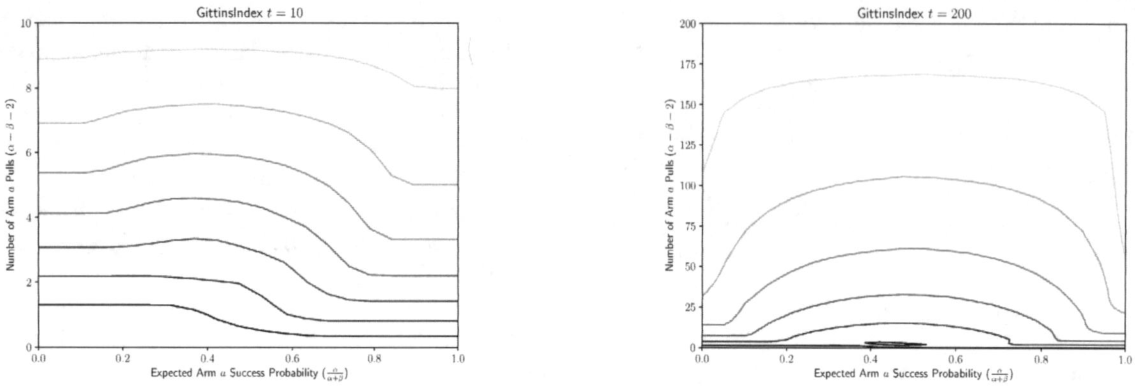

Figure 2: Value functions for Gittins index at $t = 10$ and $t = 200$ (after 10 and 200 pulls of some arm).

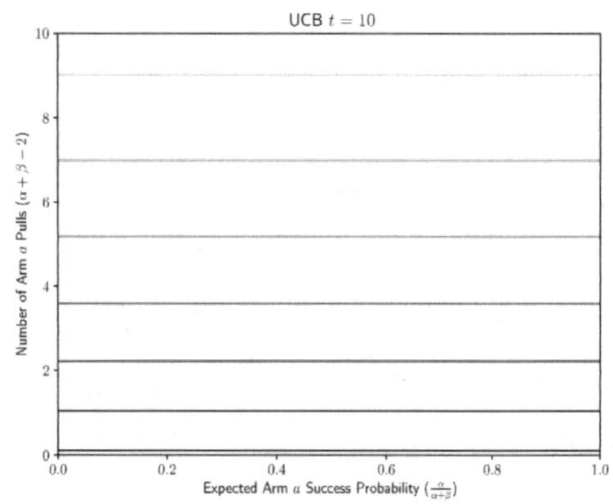

Figure 3: Value function for UCB index at $t = 10$ (after 10 pulls of some arm).

Lemma 4.1. *The regret for any policy π_t computed using 1-step lookahead with respect to value function v_t is upper bounded as follows:*

$$\operatorname{Regret}(\pi, T, \mu) \leq \sum_{t=1}^{T} \mathbb{E}_{S_t}\left[\varphi_t(\mu, S_t, \pi(S_t))\right] - \\ - \sum_{t=1}^{T} \mathbb{E}_{S_t}\left[\varphi_t(\mu, S_t, a_{i^\star_\mu})\right],$$

where S_t is the random variable representing the state at time t under policy π and $i^\star_\mu = \arg\max_{i \in \mathcal{A}} \mu_i$ is the optimal action for the unknown parameter μ.

The proof of the lemma, deferred to Appendix A.2, follows readily from the fact that ELSV chooses actions that maximize q_t.

The actual regret bound depends, of course, on the value function that is used. We now use Lemma 4.1 to bound the regret of the policy that uses UCB derived value function v^{UCB} as described in (5).

Theorem 4.1. *The regret of policy π_U of Algorithm 1 that uses $\hat{v}^{UCB}$ (with $\alpha > 1$) is bounded as:*

$$\operatorname{Regret}(\pi_U, T, \mu) \leq O(\sqrt{T \log(T)}) .$$

The proof of the theorem can be found in Appendix A.3. Note that this bound is not tighter than existing bounds on UCB algorithms, but it does establish sublinear regret of ELSV.

To establish the bound in Theorem 4.1, it is necessary that the difference of the residuals (6) for the arm chosen by ELSV and the optimal arm are not only small but must also decrease at least quickly $1/\sqrt{t}$. In other words, it is not sufficient for the errors in (6) to be small, they also must decrease as more information about the returns of the arms becomes available.

5 EXPERIMENTAL RESULTS

In this section, we compare the performance of ELSV to that of UCB, Bayes-UCB, Thompson sampling, and Gittins indices in simulation. We first analyze in Section 5.1 the impact of the lookahead horizon on the performance in the plain Bernoulli bandit setting. Then, in Section 5.2, we describe the application to a problem in which structured prior information is available.

Unlike UCB and Thompson sampling, Gittins index must be pre-computed in advance. It is also optimal only for infinite-horizon discounted problems. The index that we use in our experiments was computed with a discount factor $\gamma = 0.99$ and horizon of 1000 to approximate the infinite-horizon value. We computed the index using the calibration method with the step size of

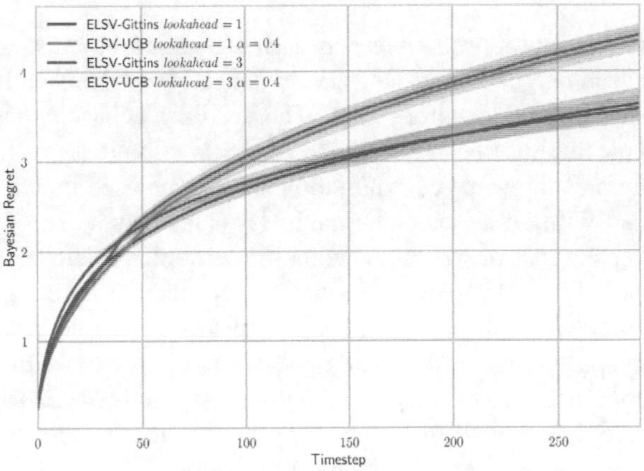

Figure 4: Bernoulli bandit regret with lookahead of 1 and 3 steps.

0.001 as described, for example, in Niño-Mora [2011]. Other approximations for computing the index have been proposed recently [Gutin and Farias, 2016; Lattimore, 2016].

5.1 BERNOULLI BANDITS

Our first set of experiments is in the standard Bernoulli bandit setting as described above in Section 2.1. As shown in Theorem 3.1, ELSV's performance will be identical to the index algorithm it is based upon. And our experiments indeed confirm this fact.

The main purpose of the experimental evaluation in this section is to understand the effect of the size of the lookahead on the performance of the algorithm. A reasonable assumption in online planning algorithms is that their performance generally improves with an increasing horizon size. Fig. 4 compares the Bayesian regret of 1-step and 3-step lookaheads in a 3-armed problem with value functions computed by ELSV. We use two value functions, one computed from the Gittins index and another one from α-UCB with $\alpha = 0.4$ (this α is unrelated to the α value used in each state). The results are averaged over 5200 problem instances with arm success probabilities drawn from the uniform Beta distribution and the shaded areas around the curves show 95% confidence intervals.

Fig. 4 highlights a surprising finding: longer lookahead does not reduce the regret. We observed virtually no improvement in the regret up to a horizon 10 at which point the search becomes computationally intractable. We hypothesize that a more careful, focused, and deeper search would be more likely to yield improvements.

5.2 CONSTRAINED BANDITS

Algorithm 4: Constrained single step lookahead algorithm using rejection sampling

Input: Current time step t, current state s_t, and value function $v_t : \mathcal{S}_t \to \mathbb{R}$

Output: Arm to pull at time step t

$\mathcal{X} \leftarrow \emptyset$

$(\alpha, \beta) \leftarrow s_t$

for $k \in 1 \ldots \mathrm{SampleCount}$ **do**

  Sample $\theta_i \sim \mathrm{Beta}(\alpha_i, \beta_i)$ for each $a_i \in \mathcal{A}$

  if $\theta_1 \geq \theta_2 \geq \ldots \geq \theta_n$ **then**

    $\mathcal{X} \leftarrow \mathcal{X} \cup \{(\theta_1, \theta_2, \ldots, \theta_N)\}$

// compute average

$\tilde{\mu}_i \leftarrow \frac{1}{|\mathcal{X}|} \cdot \sum_{\theta \in \mathcal{X}} \theta_i$;

for $i \in 1 \ldots N$ **do**

  // value of success

  $\mathrm{sc} \leftarrow r(s_t, a_i, (\alpha_i + 1, \beta_i)) + v^i_{t+1}(\alpha_i + 1, \beta_i)$;

  // value of failure

  $\mathrm{fl} \leftarrow v^i_{t+1}(\alpha_i, \beta_i + 1)$;

  // action value

  $q_t(s_t, a_i) \leftarrow \tilde{\mu}_i \cdot \mathrm{sc} + (1 - \tilde{\mu}_i) \cdot \mathrm{sc}$;

return $\arg\max_{a \in \mathcal{A}} q_t(s_t, a)$;

The constrained Bernoulli bandit problem represents a more challenging case that is not handled well by existing algorithms. As described in the introduction, this problem is motivated by an application when trying to optimizing the level of *personalized* discount offers to customers in an e-commerce setting. It has been studied extensively in operations research using customer choice models [Train, 2003]. Although such choice models can be combined with UCB methods, their application with no historical data is often problematic. For the purpose of these experiments, we simply assume that the success probabilities do not increase with a *decreasing* discount percentage: $\mu_1 \geq \mu_2 \geq \ldots \geq \mu_N$. Arm $i + 1$ represents a *smaller* discount than arm i: the experimental results use discount levels of $20\%, 10\%, 0\%$ for arms $1, 2, 3$ respectively. Our approach can be used also with a much more complex set of possible prior assumptions.

Unlike in regular Bernoulli bandits, the rewards r_i depend on arm i. That is, after pulling an arm (choosing a discount level) we received reward r_i if the customer decides to purchase the product and 0 otherwise. Since the arm discount decreases with the index i, the rewards satisfy: $r_1 < r_2 < \ldots < r_N$.

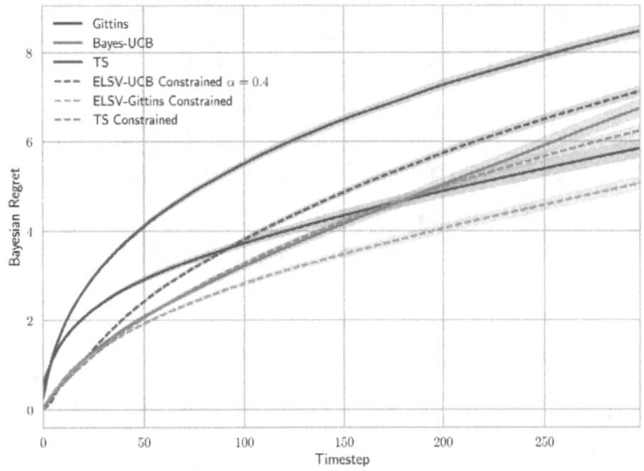

Figure 5: Bayesian Regret of constrained Bernoulli bandit.

Adapting Algorithm 1 to this constrained setting is relatively straightforward. We use the linearly separable value function computed by ELSV and only modify the lookahead to respect the constraints on μ. In particular, we use *rejection sampling* to appropriately adjust the transition probabilities when updating the values in the lookahead. As Algorithm 4 shows, we essentially compute the conditional probability distribution for each μ_i given the observations for that arm as well as the observations for other arms. This probability distribution must be estimated empirically as it does not have a closed form. The algorithm is only a heuristic in this setting and we have no regret bounds yet.

Fig. 5 shows the regret of ELSV (with 1-step lookahead) compared with several state-of-the-art algorithms on the constrained bandit problem with 3 arms and averaged over 5300 problem instances and with 95% confidence intervals. ELSV-UCB and ELSV-Gittins use a value function computed from UCB and Gittins index respectively. We omit the regret of UCB from the plot because its regret was much higher than that of the other algorithms. TS stands for regular Thompson sampling that ignores the constraints on μ, while "TS Constrained" samples from the constrained posterior distribution using rejection sampling similarly to Algorithm 4.

Our results show that ELSV-Gittins outperforms all other algorithms even in a problem with 3 arms. The magnitude of improvement in ELSV-Gittins over Gittins index grows as the number of arms in the problem increases since the constraint becomes more important and more informative. ELSV-UCB performs a bit worse, it but still represents a very significant improvement over plain UCB.

6 CONCLUSION

We have proposed a new approach to bandit problems focused on good short-term performance in problems with structured prior information. The approach is based on a new kind of linearly separable value function that incorporates the value of exploration and can be used in concert with online planning methods. Our method, ELSV, performs close to optimal on basic Bernoulli bandits and can significantly outperform existing methods in problems with prior information. The results on simple bandit problems are promising and we hope to extend the approach also to contextual bandits. We also believe that ELSV is a good first step in developing more sophisticated value-directed methods in the future.

ACKNOWLEDGMENTS

We thank the anonymous reviewers for detailed comments that helped to improve this paper significantly. This work was in part supported by the National Science Foundation under Grant No. IIS-1150068.

REFERENCES

Daniel Adelman and AJ Mersereau. Relaxations of weakly coupled stochastic dynamic programs. *Operations Research*, 56(3):712–727, 2008.

Shipra Agrawal and Navin Goyal. Analysis of Thompson sampling for the multi-armed bandit problem. In *Annual Conference on Learning Theory (COLT)*, pages 39.1–39.26, 2012.

Jean Yves Audibert, Rémi Munos, and Csaba Szepesvári. Exploration-exploitation tradeoff using variance estimates in multi-armed bandits. *Theoretical Computer Science*, 410(19):1876–1902, 2009.

Peter Auer, Nicolo Cesa-Bianchi, and Paul Fischer. Finite time analysis of the multiarmed bandit problem. *Machine Learning*, 47(2-3):235–256, 2002.

Sébastien Bubeck and Nicolò Cesa-Bianchi. Regret Analysis of Stochastic and Nonstochastic Multi-armed Bandit Problems. *Foundations and Trends in Machine Learning*, 5(1):1–122, 2012.

Jhelum Chakravorty and Aditya Mahajan. Multi-Armed Bandits, Gittins Index, and Its Calculation. In *Methods and Applications of Statistics in Clinical Trials*, pages 416–435. 2014.

Sarah Filippi, Olivier Cappe, Aurelien Garivier, and Csaba Szepesvári. Parametric Bandits: The Generalized Linear Case. In *Neural Information Processing Systems (NIPS)*, 2010.

John Gittins, Kevin Glazerbrook, and Richard Weber. *Multi-Armed Bandit Allocation Indices*. John Wiley & Sons, 2nd edition, 2011.

John Gittins. Bandit processes and dynamic allocation indices. *Journal of the Royal Statistical Society. Series B*, 41(2):148–177, 1979.

Eli Gutin and Vivek F. Farias. Optimistic Gittins Indices. In *Conference on Neural Information Processing Systems (NIPS)*, 2016.

Emilie Kaufmann, Olivier Cappé, and Aurélien Garivier. On Bayesian upper confidence bounds for bandit problems. *International Conference on Artificial Intelligence and Statistics*, pages 592–600, 2012.

Emilie Kaufmann, Nathaniel Korda, and Rémi Munos. Thompson Sampling: An Asymptotically Optimal Finite Time Analysis. *Algorithmic Learning Theory*, (1):15, 2012.

Michael Jong Kim and Andrew E.B. Lim. Robust Multiarmed Bandit Problems. *Management Science*, 62(1):264–285, 2015.

Volodymyr Kuleshov and Doina Precup. Algorithms for multi-armed bandit problems. Technical report, 2014.

Tor Lattimore and Csaba Szepesvári. The End of Optimism? An Asymptotic Analysis of Finite-Armed Linear Bandits. Technical report, 2016.

Tor Lattimore. Regret Analysis of the Finite-Horizon Gittins Index Strategy for Multi-Armed Bandits. In *Annual Conference on Learning Theory (COLT)*. arXiv, 2016.

Jan Leike, Tor Lattimore, Laurent Orseau, and Marcus Hutter. Thompson Sampling is Asymptotically Optimal in General Environments. In *Uncertainty in Artificial Intelligence (UAI)*, 2016.

José Niño-Mora. Computing a classic index for finite-horizon bandits. *INFORMS Journal on Computing*, 23(2):254–267, 2011.

Marek Petrik and Shlomo Zilberstein. Robust approximate bilinear programming for value function approximation. *Journal of Machine Learning Research*, 12(1):3027–3063, 2011.

Warren Powell, Andrzej Ruszczynski, and Huseyin Topaloglu. Learning Algorithms for Separable Approximations of Discrete Stochastic Optimization Problems. *Mathematics of Operations Research*, 29(4):814–836, 2004.

Warren B Powell. Value Function Approximation using Multiple Aggregation for Multiattribute Resource Management. *Journal of Machine Learning Research*, 9:2079–2111, 2008.

Daniel Russo and Benjamin Van Roy. Learning to Optimize Via Information-Directed Sampling. pages 1–34, 2014.

Daniel Russo and Benjamin Van Roy. Learning to Optimize via Posterior Sampling. *Mathematics of Operations Research*, 39(4):1221–1243, 2014.

John Rust. Numerical dynamic programming in economics. *Handbook of computational economics*, (November), 1996.

Richard S Sutton and Andrew Barto. *Reinforcement learning*. 1998.

Kenneth E. Train. *Discrete Choice Methods with Simulation*. 2003.

P. Whittle. Restless Bandits: Activity Allocation in a Changing World. *Journal of Applied Probability*, 25(1988):287, 1988.

A PROOFS

A.1 Proof of Theorem 3.1

Proof. To prove the theorem, we need to show that Algorithm 1 will take the same action as the index policy for each state $s \in \mathcal{S}$ that:

$$\arg\max_{a_i \in \mathcal{A}} q_t(s, a_i) = \arg\max_{a_i \in \mathcal{A}} \hat{z}_t(s^i, a_i) .$$

By subtracting a constant from the left-hand side, we get the following equivalent statement:

$$\arg\max_{a_i \in \mathcal{A}} \Big(q_t(s, a_i) - \hat{v}_{t+1}(s) \Big) = \arg\max_{a_i \in \mathcal{A}} \hat{z}_t(s^i, a_i) .$$

Informally, the term $q_t(s, a_i) - \hat{v}_{t+1}(s)$ measures the advantage of pulling an arm a_i in comparison with a virtual action of "pulling no arm" instead. Next we show that $q_t(s, a_i) - \hat{v}_{t+1}(s) = \hat{z}_t(s_i, a_i)$.

Fix an action a_i, let s_τ be some state, and let $S_{\tau+1}$ to be the random variable representing the state that follows s^i_τ after taking action a_i. Than:

$$\begin{aligned} q_t(s_\tau, a_i) - \hat{v}_{t+1}(s_\tau) &= \mathbb{E}\left[\hat{v}_{t+1}(S_{\tau+1}) + r(s_\tau, a_i, S_{\tau+1})\right] - \hat{v}_{t+1}(s_\tau) = \\ &= \mathbb{E}\left[r(s_\tau, a_i, S_{\tau+1})\right] + \mathbb{E}\left[\hat{v}_{t+1}(S_{\tau+1})\right] - \hat{v}_{t+1}(s_\tau) = \\ &= r(s^i_\tau, a_i) + \mathbb{E}\left[\hat{v}_{t+1}(S_{\tau+1})\right] - \hat{v}_{t+1}(s_\tau) \end{aligned}$$

Using the assumed linearly separable form of $\hat{v}_t(s_\tau) = \sum_{a_i \in \mathcal{A}} \hat{v}^i_t(s^i_\tau)$, we get:

$$\begin{aligned} r(s^i_\tau, a_i) + \mathbb{E}\left[\hat{v}_{t+1}(S_{\tau+1})\right] - \hat{v}_{t+1}(s_\tau) &= r(s^i_\tau, a_i) + \mathbb{E}\left[\sum_{a_j \in \mathcal{A}} \hat{v}^j_{t+1}(S^j_{\tau+1})\right] - \sum_{a_j \in \mathcal{A}} \hat{v}^j_{t+1}(s^j_\tau) = \\ &= r(s^i_\tau, a_i) + \sum_{a_j \in \mathcal{A}} \left(\mathbb{E}\left[\hat{v}^{a'}_{t+1}(S^j_{\tau+1})\right] - \hat{v}^j_{t+1}(s^j_\tau) \right) \end{aligned}$$

Notice next that $S^j_{\tau+1} = s^j_\tau$ whenever $a_j \neq a_i$, since the state of an arm does not change unless the arm is pulled. Thus we can further simplify the sum as follows:

$$\begin{aligned} & r(s^i_\tau, a_i) + \sum_{a_j \in \mathcal{A}} \left(\mathbb{E}\left[\hat{v}^j_{t+1}(S^j_{\tau+1})\right] - \hat{v}^j_{t+1}(s^j_\tau) \right) = \\ &= r(s^i_\tau, a_i) + \sum_{a_j \in \mathcal{A} \setminus \{a_i\}} \left(\mathbb{E}\left[\hat{v}^j_{t+1}(S^j_{\tau+1})\right] - \hat{v}^j_{t+1}(s^j_\tau) \right) + \mathbb{E}\left[\hat{v}^i_{t+1}(S^i_{\tau+1})\right] - \hat{v}^i_{t+1}(s^i_\tau) = \\ &= r(s^i_\tau, a_i) + \sum_{a_j \in \mathcal{A} \setminus \{a_i\}} \left(\mathbb{E}\left[\hat{v}^j_{t+1}(s^j_\tau)\right] - \hat{v}^j_{t+1}(s^j_\tau) \right) + \mathbb{E}\left[\hat{v}^i_{t+1}(S^i_{\tau+1})\right] - \hat{v}^i_{t+1}(s^i_\tau) = \\ &= r(s^i_\tau, a_i) + \mathbb{E}\left[\hat{v}^i_{t+1}(S^i_{\tau+1})\right] - \hat{v}^i_{t+1}(s^i_\tau) . \end{aligned}$$

Finally, substituting (5) into the equation above gives us:

$$q_t(s_\tau, a_i) - \hat{v}_{t+1}(s_\tau) = \hat{z}_t(s_\tau, a_i) ,$$

which proves the theorem. □

A.2 Proof of Lemma 4.1

Proof. First, we will use the following decomposition of the regret for a given parameter μ:

$$\begin{aligned}
\text{Regret}(\pi, T, \mu) &= \sum_{t=1}^{T} \mathbb{E}\left[\mu_{i_u^\star} - \mu_{\pi(S_t)}\right] = \\
&\overset{(a)}{=} \sum_{t=1}^{T} \left(\mathbb{E}\left[\mu_{i_u^\star} - (q_t(S_t, \pi(S_t)) - v_{t+1}(S_t))\right] + \mathbb{E}\left[(q_t(S_t, \pi(S_t)) - v_{t+1}(S_t)) - \mu_{\pi(S_t)}\right]\right) = \\
&\overset{(b)}{\leq} \sum_{t=1}^{T} \left(\mathbb{E}\left[\mu_{i_u^\star} - (q_t(S_t, a_{i_u^\star}) - v_{t+1}(S_t))\right] + \mathbb{E}\left[(q_t(S_t, \pi(S_t)) - v_{t+1}(S_t)) - \mu_{\pi(S_t)}\right]\right) = \\
&= \sum_{t=1}^{T} \mathbb{E}\left[\underbrace{(\mu_{i_u^\star} - q_t(S_t, a_{i_u^\star}) + v_{t+1}(S_t))}_{-\varphi_t(\mu, S_t, a_{i_u^\star})}\right] + \sum_{t=1}^{T} \mathbb{E}\left[\underbrace{(q_t(S_t, \pi(S_t)) - v_{t+1}(S_t) - \mu_{\pi(S_t)})}_{\varphi_t(\mu, S_t, \pi(S_t))}\right] = \\
&= \sum_{t=1}^{T} \mathbb{E}_{S_t}\left[\varphi_t(\mu, S_t, \pi(S_t))\right] - \sum_{t=1}^{T} \mathbb{E}_{S_t}\left[\varphi_t(\mu, S_t, a_{i_u^\star})\right]
\end{aligned}$$

The equality (a) follows by simply adding $0 = v_{t+1}(S_t) - v_{t+1}(S_t)$, and the inequality (b) follows from the optimality of $\pi(S_t)$ with respect to v_t:

$$q_t(S_t, \pi(S_t)) \geq q_t(S_t, a),$$

for any action $a \in \mathcal{S}$. □

A.3 Proof of Theorem 4.1

The theorem follows directly from the following two lemmas.

Lemma A.1. *For $\alpha > 1$ and φ_t computed for v^{UCB} the following lower bound holds true:*

$$\sum_{t=1}^{T} \mathbb{E}_{S_t}\left[\varphi_t(\mu, S_t, a_{i_u^\star})\right] \geq -\sum_{t=1}^{T} \frac{1}{t^{2\alpha-1}} \geq O(1)\,.$$

Proof.

$$\begin{aligned}
\mathbb{E}_{S_t}\left[\varphi_t(\mu, S_t, a_{i_u^\star})\right] &= \mathbb{E}_{S_t}\left[q_t(S_t, a_{i_u^\star}) - v_{t+1}(S_t) - \mu_{i_u^\star}\right] = \mathbb{E}\left[z^{\text{UCB}}(S_t, a_{i_u^\star}) - \mu_{i_u^\star}\right] = \\
&= \mathbb{E}\left[r(S_t, a_{i_u^\star}) + \sqrt{\frac{\alpha \log t}{T_{i_u^\star}(S_t^{i_u^\star}, a_{i_u^\star})}} - \mu_{i_u^\star}\right] \geq \\
&\overset{(a)}{\geq} -\mathbb{P}\left[r(S_t, a_{i_u^\star}) - \mu_{i_u^\star} \leq \sqrt{\frac{\alpha \log t}{T_{i_u^\star}(S_t^{i_u^\star}, a_{i_u^\star})}}\right] \geq \\
&\overset{(b)}{\geq} -t \exp\left(-2T_{i_u^\star}(S_t^{i_u^\star}, a_{i_u^\star}) \frac{\alpha \log t}{T_{i_u^\star}(S_t^{i_u^\star}, a_{i_u^\star})}\right) = \\
&= -t \exp(-2\alpha \log t) = -\frac{1}{t^{2\alpha-1}}
\end{aligned}$$

where (a) follows by rewriting expectation and the fact that the rewards are bounded between 0 and 1, and (b) follows from Hoeffding's inequality and the union bound over possible values of $T_{i_u^\star}$. Summing the value above for $t = 1 \ldots T$ proves the lemma. □

Lemma A.2. *Assume $\alpha > 1$ and fix an action $a_i \in \mathcal{A}$. Then for a policy π greedy with respect to v^{UCB} for following inequality holds true:*

$$\sum_{t=1}^{T} \mathbb{E}_{S_t}\left[\varphi_t(\mu, S_t, \pi(S_t))\right] \leq O(\sqrt{T \log T})$$

Proof. Consider the bound for a single action:

$$\begin{aligned}
\mathbb{E}_{S_t}\left[\varphi_t(\mu, S_t, a_i)\right] &= \mathbb{E}_{S_t}\left[q_t(S_t, a_i) - v_{t+1}(S_t) - \mu_i\right] = \mathbb{E}\left[z^{\mathrm{UCB}}(S_t, a_i) - \mu_{i_u^\star}\right] \\
&= \mathbb{E}\left[r(S_t, a_i) + \sqrt{\frac{\alpha \log t}{T_i(S_t^i, a_i)}} - \mu_i\right] = \\
&= \mathbb{E}\left[r(S_t, a_i) - \sqrt{\frac{\alpha \log t}{T_i(S_t^i, a_i)}} + 2\sqrt{\frac{\alpha \log t}{T_i(S_t^i, a_i)}} - \mu_i\right] = \\
&= \mathbb{E}\left[r(S_t, a_i) - \sqrt{\frac{\alpha \log t}{T_i(S_t^i, a_i)}} - \mu_i\right] + \mathbb{E}\left[2\sqrt{\frac{\alpha \log t}{T_i(S_t^i, a_i)}}\right] = \\
&\overset{(a)}{\leq} \mathbb{P}\left[r(S_t, a_i) - \mu_i \leq \sqrt{\frac{\alpha \log t}{T_i(S_t^i, a_i)}}\right] + \mathbb{E}\left[2\sqrt{\frac{\alpha \log t}{T_i(S_t^i, a_i)}}\right] \\
&\overset{(b)}{\leq} \frac{1}{t^{2\alpha-1}} + \mathbb{E}\left[2\sqrt{\frac{\alpha \log t}{T_i(S_t^i, a_i)}}\right]
\end{aligned}$$

The equalities above follow readily using algebra; (a) and (b) follow by an argument that is identical to the proof of Lemma A.1.

Considering just the state in which arm a_i is pulled, it remains to upper bound the following expression:

$$\begin{aligned}
\sum_{t=1}^{T} 2\,\mathbb{E}\left[\mathbf{1}_{a_i=\pi(S_t)}\sqrt{\frac{\alpha \log t}{T_i(S_t^i, a_i)}}\right] &\leq \sum_{t=1}^{T} 2\,\mathbb{E}\left[\mathbf{1}_{a_i=\pi(S_t)}\sqrt{\frac{\alpha \log T}{T_i(S_t^i, a_i)}}\right] \leq \\
&\overset{(d)}{\leq} \sum_{t=1}^{T} 2\,\mathbb{E}\left[\sqrt{\frac{\alpha \log T}{t}}\right] \overset{(e)}{\leq} O(\sqrt{T \log T})\,.
\end{aligned}$$

The inequality (d) follows by upper bounding the error by assuming that the arm was pulled in every step, and (e) follows by upper bounding the sum by an integral. See, for example, the proof of Proposition 2 in Russo and Van Roy [2014]. □

Learning Approximately Objective Priors

Eric Nalisnick
Department of Computer Science
University of California, Irvine
enalisni@uci.edu

Padhraic Smyth
Department of Computer Science
University of California, Irvine
smyth@ics.uci.edu

Abstract

Informative Bayesian priors are often difficult to elicit, and when this is the case, modelers usually turn to noninformative or objective priors. However, objective priors such as the Jeffreys and reference priors are not tractable to derive for many models of interest. We address this issue by proposing techniques for learning reference prior approximations: we select a parametric family and optimize a black-box lower bound on the reference prior objective to find the member of the family that serves as a good approximation. We experimentally demonstrate the method's effectiveness by recovering Jeffreys priors and learning the Variational Autoencoder's reference prior.

1 INTRODUCTION

Bayesian inference is distinguished by its ability to incorporate existing knowledge in a principled way. This knowledge is encoded by the prior distribution, and its specification is widely regarded as "the most important step" in the Bayesian approach given that it can "drastically alter the subsequent inference" [24]. The choice is especially crucial in settings with few observations, as the data cannot overwhelm a harmful prior. Even in situations where there are enough observations to make the prior's influence on the posterior benign, the marginal likelihood is still sensitive to the choice, possibly resulting in the selection of an inferior model.

The best case scenario for specifying a prior is when—unsurprisingly—there is existing information about the phenomenon we wish to model. For example, choosing a good prior for parameters in a model of galaxy formation can usually be done by consulting an astrophysicist or the relevant research literature.

In many practical situations, however, there are no available means for obtaining useful prior information. For example, in high-dimensional problems the parameter space is often inherently unintuitive. The usual way to proceed is to pick a noninformative prior that is *flat* and/or *objective*. By *flat prior* we mean a distribution that does not have any substantial concentration of its mass; maximum entropy priors [9] often exhibit this characteristic. An *objective* prior is one that has some formal invariance property. The two best known examples of objective priors are *Jeffreys* [10] and *reference* [3] priors, which are both invariant to model reparametrization. Some priors are both objective and flat: the Jeffreys prior for the Gaussian mean is the (improper) uniform distribution. However, just because a prior is relatively flat does not mean it is objective. For example, the Bernoulli's Jeffreys prior is the arcsine distribution, which, having vertical asymptotes at 0 and 1, is conspicuously not flat.

Since there are no guarantees that what looks to be a flat prior might not harbor hidden subjectivity, objective priors seem to be the better 'default' choices. However, the mathematical rigor that makes objective priors attractive also makes their use problematic: their derivation is difficult for all but the simplest models. To be specific, solving the calculus of variations problem for a reference prior requires, among other properties, an analytical form for the posterior distribution, which is rarely available.

In this paper we broaden the potential use of objective priors by describing methods for learning high-fidelity reference prior approximations. The proposed method is akin to black-box (posterior) variational inference [20]: we posit a parametric family of distributions and perform derivation-free optimization to find the member of the family closest to the true reference prior. Doing so would be useful, for example, if one wishes to have an objective prior that preserves model conjugacy[1]. The mod-

[1]Reference priors are often improper distributions.

eler could employ the techniques proposed below to find the conjugate prior's parameter setting that makes it closest to objective. Moreover, these methods learn a reference prior for a given model independently of any data source[2], which means that obtaining a reference prior for a particular model needs to be done only once.

In our experimental results we demonstrate that the proposed framework recovers the Jeffreys prior better than existing numerical methods. We also analyze the optimization objective, providing intuition behind a number of hyper-parameter choices. And lastly, we learn a reference prior for a *Variational Autoencoder* [12]. In an interesting case study, we see that the Variational Autoencoder's reference prior differs markedly from the standard Normal distribution that is commonly used as the prior on the latent space.

2 BACKGROUND AND RELATED WORK

We begin by defining reference priors, highlighting their connection to the Jeffreys prior, and summarizing the related work on computing intractable reference priors. We use the following notation throughout the paper. Define the likelihood to be $p(\mathcal{D}|\boldsymbol{\theta}) = \prod_{i=1}^{N} p(\mathbf{x}_i|\boldsymbol{\theta})$ where $\boldsymbol{\theta}$ are the model parameters and $\mathcal{D}$ is the dataset, which is comprised of N i.i.d. observations $\mathbf{x}_i \in \mathcal{X}$. $p(\boldsymbol{\theta})$ denotes the prior, $p(\boldsymbol{\theta}|\mathcal{D})$ the posterior, and $p(\mathcal{D}) = \int_{\boldsymbol{\theta}} p(\mathcal{D}|\boldsymbol{\theta})p(\boldsymbol{\theta})d\boldsymbol{\theta}$ the marginal likelihood (or model evidence). When we refer to the 'likelihood function' we mean the functional form of the data model, $p(\mathbf{x}|\boldsymbol{\theta})$. We write expectations with respect to the dataset likelihood, but because of $\mathcal{D}$'s i.i.d. assumption, these can be written equivalently in terms of each data instance; for example: $\mathbb{H}_{\mathcal{D}|\boldsymbol{\theta}}[\mathcal{D}] = -\int_{\mathcal{D}} p(\mathcal{D}|\boldsymbol{\theta}) \log p(\mathcal{D}|\boldsymbol{\theta}) d\mathcal{D} = -\int_{\mathbf{x}} \prod_i p(\mathbf{x}_i|\boldsymbol{\theta}) \log \prod_i p(\mathbf{x}_i|\boldsymbol{\theta}) d\mathbf{x} = N\mathbb{H}_{\mathbf{x}|\boldsymbol{\theta}}[\mathbf{x}]$.

2.1 REFERENCE PRIORS

Reference priors [1, 4] (RPs) are objective Bayesian prior distributions derived for a given likelihood function by finding the prior that maximizes the data's influence on the posterior distribution. Equivalently, the prior's influence on the posterior is minimized, which is precisely the behavior we desire if we wish to represent a state of ignorance about the model parameters. The RP's data-driven nature yields 'frequentist-esque' posteriors: for large sample sizes, the $1 - \alpha$ credible interval approximates a confidence interval with significance level α [7]. Thus, RPs give results that are the nearest Bayesian equivalent to maximum likelihood estimation, and this behavior is how they derive their name: RPs serve as a *reference* against which to test subjective priors.

Definition. We now state the RP definition formally. A RP $p^*(\boldsymbol{\theta})$ is the distribution that maximizes the mutual information between the parameters $\boldsymbol{\theta}$ and the data $\mathcal{D}$ [1, 3]:

$$\begin{aligned} p^*(\boldsymbol{\theta}) &= \underset{p(\boldsymbol{\theta})}{\operatorname{argmax}} \ I(\boldsymbol{\theta}, \mathcal{D}) \\ &= \underset{p(\boldsymbol{\theta})}{\operatorname{argmax}} \ \underbrace{\mathbb{H}[\boldsymbol{\theta}]}_{\text{maximize prior uncertainty}} - \underbrace{\mathbb{H}[\boldsymbol{\theta}|\mathcal{D}]}_{\text{minimize posterior uncertainty}} . \end{aligned} \tag{1}$$

Here $I(\cdot,\cdot)$ denotes mutual information. In the second line, $I(\cdot,\cdot)$ is (by definition) decomposed into separate marginal and conditional entropy terms, showing that maximizing $I(\boldsymbol{\theta}, \mathcal{D})$ in turn maximizes the prior's uncertainty while minimizing the posterior's uncertainty. The second term reflects the RP's data-driven nature as it encourages the posterior to contract quickly (as N increases). Another way to see how the RP accentuates the data's influence is by writing the mutual information in terms of a Kullback-Leibler divergence (KLD): $I(\boldsymbol{\theta}, \mathcal{D}) = \int_{\mathcal{D}} p(\mathcal{D}) \text{ KLD}[p(\boldsymbol{\theta}|\mathcal{D}) \ || \ p(\boldsymbol{\theta})] \ d\mathcal{D}$. This form shows that increasing $I(\boldsymbol{\theta}, \mathcal{D})$ decreases the similarity between the posterior and prior.

Solution. Solving Equation 1 for p^* is a calculus of variations problem whose solution can be expressed by rewriting the mutual information as

$$\begin{aligned} I(\boldsymbol{\theta}, \mathcal{D}) &= -\int_{\boldsymbol{\theta}} p(\boldsymbol{\theta}) \ \log \frac{p(\boldsymbol{\theta})}{f(\boldsymbol{\theta})} \ d\boldsymbol{\theta} \\ \text{where } f(\boldsymbol{\theta}) &= \exp\{\int_{\mathcal{D}} p(\mathcal{D}|\boldsymbol{\theta}) \ \log p(\boldsymbol{\theta}|\mathcal{D}) \ d\mathcal{D}\}. \end{aligned} \tag{2}$$

Clearly, the mutual information is maximized when $p(\boldsymbol{\theta}) \propto f(\boldsymbol{\theta})$. See Bernardo (1979) for a complete discussion of the derivation. Equation 2 also makes clear the analytical obstacles that need to be overcome to solve the optimization problem for a given model: the functional f requires that the log posterior—which is usually intractable to compute—be integrated over the likelihood function. Note that the solution is commonly not a proper distribution (that integrates to 1).

Relation to Jeffreys Priors. RPs are equal to the Jeffreys[3] in one dimension but not in general. The equivalence is obtained by invoking the *Bernstein Von Mises* theorem: setting $p(\boldsymbol{\theta}|\mathcal{D}) \approx \text{N}(\boldsymbol{\theta}_{\text{MLE}}, \mathcal{F}^{-1}(\boldsymbol{\theta}))$ where $\boldsymbol{\theta}_{\text{MLE}}$ is the maximum likelihood estimate and $\mathcal{F}$ is the Fisher information matrix. RPs, also like the Jeffreys,

[2]Except when the model is for a conditional distribution, i.e. $p(y|x)$. In this case, samples of x are necessary to learn the approximate reference prior.

[3]The Jeffreys prior is defined as $\pi(\boldsymbol{\theta}) \propto \sqrt{\det \mathcal{F}[\boldsymbol{\theta}]}$ where $\mathcal{F}$ denotes the Fisher information matrix.

are invariant to model reparametrization, which follows from the fact that the mutual information is itself invariant to a change in parametrization [1].

2.2 RELATED WORK

Next we review existing techniques for approximating intractable RPs. These methods have a notable lack of scalability, requiring numerical integration over the parameter space. Nonetheless, since they share some fundamental similarities with our proposed method, we reproduce their main components so that we can later discuss how our method handles the same analytical difficulties.

Numerical Algorithm. Berger et al. (2009) proposed a numerical method for computing a RP's value at any given point $\boldsymbol{\theta}_0$. Their method is, simply, to calculate $f(\boldsymbol{\theta})$ numerically via Monte Carlo approximations:

$$p^*(\boldsymbol{\theta}_0) \approx \exp\left\{ \frac{1}{J}\sum_{j=1}^{J} \log \frac{p(\hat{\mathcal{D}}_j|\boldsymbol{\theta}_0)\mathbb{1}_{\boldsymbol{\Theta}}}{\sum_{s=1}^{S} p(\hat{\mathcal{D}}_j|\hat{\boldsymbol{\theta}}_s)} \right\} \quad (3)$$

where $\mathbb{1}_{\boldsymbol{\Theta}}$ is an improper uniform prior over the parameter space. The method proceeds by sampling J datasets from the likelihood function, i.e. $\hat{\mathcal{D}}_j = \{\hat{\mathbf{x}}_{j,i}|\hat{\mathbf{x}} \sim p(\mathbf{x}|\boldsymbol{\theta}_0)\}$, and S parameter values from the prior, i.e. $\hat{\boldsymbol{\theta}}_s \sim \mathbb{1}_{\boldsymbol{\Theta}}$. The posterior is then approximated as $p(\boldsymbol{\theta}|\mathcal{D}) \approx p(\hat{\mathcal{D}}_j|\boldsymbol{\theta}_0)\mathbb{1}_{\boldsymbol{\Theta}} / \sum_{s=1}^{S} p(\hat{\mathcal{D}}_j|\hat{\boldsymbol{\theta}}_s)$. This numerical approximation has two significant downsides. The first is that the user must specify the points at which to compute the prior, and the second is that numerically integrating over the parameter space is computationally expensive in even low dimensions.

MCMC. Lafferty & Wasserman (2001) proposed a Markov Chain Monte Carlo (MCMC) method for sampling from a RP. Their approach involves running the Metropolis-Hastings algorithm on the following ratio [13]:

$$\log \frac{p^{t+1}(\boldsymbol{\theta})}{p^{t+1}(\boldsymbol{\theta}')} = (t+1)(\mathbb{H}_{\mathbf{x}|\boldsymbol{\theta}'}[\mathbf{x}] - \mathbb{H}_{\mathbf{x}|\boldsymbol{\theta}}[\mathbf{x}]) + \sum_{\mathbf{x}\in\mathcal{X}} W^t(\mathbf{x})[p(\mathbf{x}|\boldsymbol{\theta}') - p(\mathbf{x}|\boldsymbol{\theta})] \quad (4)$$

where t is the iteration index, $\mathbb{H}_{\mathbf{x}|\boldsymbol{\theta}}[\mathbf{x}]$ is the entropy of the likelihood function, and $W^t(\mathbf{x}) = W^{t-1}(\mathbf{x}) + \log \frac{1}{S_t}\sum_{s=1}^{S_t} p(\boldsymbol{x}|\hat{\boldsymbol{\theta}}_s^t)$ where $\hat{\boldsymbol{\theta}}_s^t$ are the parameter samples collected during the previous iteration.

While this MCMC approach may look dissimilar to Berger et al.'s method at first glance, the two methods are in fact related. We can see the connection by examining just one of the distributions in the ratio (when $t = 0$):

$$\log p^1(\boldsymbol{\theta}) = -\mathbb{H}_{\mathbf{x}|\boldsymbol{\theta}}[\mathbf{x}] + \sum_{\mathbf{x}\in\mathcal{X}} -W^0(\mathbf{x})p(\mathbf{x}|\boldsymbol{\theta})$$
$$= \sum_{\mathbf{x}\in\mathcal{X}} p(\mathbf{x}|\boldsymbol{\theta}) \left[\log p(\mathbf{x}|\boldsymbol{\theta}) - \log \frac{1}{S_0} \sum_{s=1}^{S_0} p(\boldsymbol{x}|\hat{\boldsymbol{\theta}}_s^0) \right].$$

The line above becomes equivalent to Equation 3 if we use a Monte Carlo approximation of the expectation over $p(\mathbf{x}|\boldsymbol{\theta})$ and then exponentiate both sides. Despite this close connection between the two methods, Lafferty & Wasserman (2001)'s approach is superior to that of Berger et al.'s since it draws samples from the prior instead of merely computing its value at points the user must select. Yet the same costly discrete approximations of the integrals will be required.

Reference Distance Method. The third approach, and the only other that we are aware of for finding approximate RPs, is the *Reference Distance Method* (RDM) proposed by Berger et al. (2015). This method focuses on finding a joint RP by minimizing the divergence between a parametric family and the marginal RPs [2]. Since we are concerned with models for which even the marginal RPs are intractable, the RDM is not a relevant point for comparison.

3 LEARNING REFERENCE PRIOR APPROXIMATIONS

We now turn to the primary contribution of this paper: approximating RPs by *learning* the parameters of the approximation. Our proposed approach contrasts with Berger et al. (2009)'s and Lafferty & Wasserman (2001)'s in that their methods are not model-based. In other words, their procedures produce no parametric artifact for the prior unless a post-hoc step of model fitting is carried out. Our black-box optimization framework subsumes the utility of the numerical and MCMC methods as it can directly learn either a parametric approximation to evaluate the prior's density or a functional sampler that can generate new samples from the prior at any later time.

3.1 METHOD #1: INFORMATION LOWER BOUND

Inspired by recent advances in posterior variational inference (VI), we use similar ideas to optimize an approximate *prior*—call it $p_{\boldsymbol{\lambda}}(\boldsymbol{\theta})$ with parameters $\boldsymbol{\lambda}$—so that it is the distribution in the family closest to the true RP $p^*(\boldsymbol{\theta})$. The mutual information still serves as the natural optimization objective; the difference is that we take the argmax over $\boldsymbol{\lambda}$, instead of the density p itself, such that $p^*(\boldsymbol{\theta}) \approx p_{\boldsymbol{\lambda}^*}(\boldsymbol{\theta})$:

$$\begin{aligned}
\boldsymbol{\lambda}^* &= \underset{\boldsymbol{\lambda}}{\operatorname{argmax}} \;\; I(\boldsymbol{\theta}, \mathcal{D}) \\
&= \underset{\boldsymbol{\lambda}}{\operatorname{argmax}} \int_{\boldsymbol{\theta}} p_{\boldsymbol{\lambda}}(\boldsymbol{\theta}) \int_{\mathcal{D}} p(\mathcal{D}|\boldsymbol{\theta}) \log \frac{p(\mathcal{D}, \boldsymbol{\theta})}{p_{\boldsymbol{\lambda}}(\boldsymbol{\theta}) p(\mathcal{D})} d\mathcal{D} d\boldsymbol{\theta} \\
&= \underset{\boldsymbol{\lambda}}{\operatorname{argmax}} \int_{\boldsymbol{\theta}} p_{\boldsymbol{\lambda}}(\boldsymbol{\theta}) \int_{\mathcal{D}} p(\mathcal{D}|\boldsymbol{\theta}) \log \frac{p(\mathcal{D}|\boldsymbol{\theta})}{p(\mathcal{D})} d\mathcal{D} d\boldsymbol{\theta} \\
&= \underset{\boldsymbol{\lambda}}{\operatorname{argmax}} \; \mathbb{E}_{\boldsymbol{\theta}_{\boldsymbol{\lambda}}} \left[-\mathbb{H}_{\mathcal{D}|\boldsymbol{\theta}}[\mathcal{D}] - \mathbb{E}_{\mathcal{D}|\boldsymbol{\theta}}[\log p(\mathcal{D})] \right].
\end{aligned} \tag{5}$$

In the final line above, we wrote the mutual information as the difference between the negative likelihood entropy and the expected log marginal likelihood because this is $I(\boldsymbol{\theta}, \mathcal{D})$'s most tractable form: it contains only $p(\mathcal{D})$ instead of $p(\mathcal{D})$ *and* $p(\boldsymbol{\theta}|\mathcal{D})$. We use the notional $\boldsymbol{\theta}_{\boldsymbol{\lambda}}$ to emphasize that $\boldsymbol{\theta}$'s distribution is a function of $\boldsymbol{\lambda}$.

Bounding log p($\mathcal{D}$). The marginal likelihood term in Equation 5 is still problematic, and thus, just as in posterior VI, we need some tractable bound to optimize instead. Since we need to bound $I(\boldsymbol{\theta}, \mathcal{D})$ from below, $\log p(\mathcal{D})$ must be bounded from *above*. Hence, unfortunately, we cannot use the *evidence lower bound* (ELBO) common in posterior VI. As an alternative we use the *variational Rényi bound* [14] (VR), which is defined as:

$$\log p(\mathcal{D}) \leq \frac{1}{1-\alpha} \log \mathbb{E}_{\boldsymbol{\theta}} \left[p(\mathcal{D}|\boldsymbol{\theta})^{1-\alpha} \right] \quad \text{for } \alpha \leq 0.$$

Plugging the VR bound into Equation 5 yields a general lower bound on the mutual information:

$$\begin{aligned}
& I(\boldsymbol{\theta}, \mathcal{D}) \\
& \geq \mathbb{E}_{\boldsymbol{\theta}_{\boldsymbol{\lambda}}} \left[-\mathbb{H}_{\mathcal{D}|\boldsymbol{\theta}}[\mathcal{D}] - \frac{1}{1-\alpha} \log \mathbb{E}_{\boldsymbol{\theta}} \left[p(\mathcal{D}|\boldsymbol{\theta})^{1-\alpha} \right] \right].
\end{aligned} \tag{6}$$

In theory, setting $\alpha = 0$ provides the tightest bound, and decreasing α loosens the bound. However, as we discuss next, practical implementation requires a negative value for α.

Optimization Objective. The expectation within the VR bound usually will not be analytically solvable, requiring the use of a Monte Carlo approximation (which we will refer to as MC-VR). Yet, introducing sampling into the VR bound can give rise to numerical challenges. The MC-VR estimator is an exponentiated form of the *harmonic mean estimator* [19], which is notorious for its high variance. Furthermore, approximating the expectation with samples, since they reside inside the logarithm, biases the bound downward. Li & Turner (2016) propose the following *VR-max* estimator, corresponding to $\alpha \to -\infty$, to cope with these issues: $\max_s \log p(\mathcal{D}|\hat{\boldsymbol{\theta}}_s)$ where s indexes samples $\hat{\theta}_s \sim p(\boldsymbol{\theta})$. We find that the VR-max estimator generally preserves the bound and needs to be checked only in high dimensions (100+), which is a regime not well suited for reference priors anyway (due to overfitting).

Introducing the VR-max estimator into Equation 5 yields a tractable lower bound on the mutual information:

$$\begin{aligned}
& I(\boldsymbol{\theta}, \mathcal{D}) \geq \mathcal{J}_{\text{RP}}(\boldsymbol{\lambda}) \\
& = \mathbb{E}_{\boldsymbol{\theta}_{\boldsymbol{\lambda}}} \left[-\mathbb{H}_{\mathcal{D}|\boldsymbol{\theta}}[\mathcal{D}] - \mathbb{E}_{\mathcal{D}|\boldsymbol{\theta}}[\max_s \log p(\mathcal{D}|\hat{\boldsymbol{\theta}}_s)] \right].
\end{aligned} \tag{7}$$

Maximizing $\mathcal{J}_{\text{RP}}(\boldsymbol{\lambda})$ with respect to the prior's parameters $\boldsymbol{\lambda}$ results in $p_{\boldsymbol{\lambda}}(\boldsymbol{\theta}) \approx p^*(\boldsymbol{\theta})$ as long as $p_{\boldsymbol{\lambda}}$ is sufficiently expressive. $\mathcal{J}_{\text{RP}}(\boldsymbol{\lambda})$ can be interpreted as follows. The first term is the entropy of the likelihood function, and thus maximizing its negation encourages certainty in the data model. The second term, the expected value of the VR-max estimator under the likelihood, encourages diversity in $p_{\boldsymbol{\lambda}}$ by forcing a dataset $\mathcal{D}_0 \sim p(\mathcal{D}|\boldsymbol{\theta}_0)$ to have low probability under other parameter settings $\hat{\boldsymbol{\theta}}_s$.

Connection to Previous Work. Further understanding of $\mathcal{J}_{\text{RP}}(\boldsymbol{\lambda})$ can be gained by re-writing it to see its relationship to Berger et al. (2009)'s and Lafferty & Wasserman (2001)'s methods. Pulling out the expectation over the likelihood, we have the equivalent form:

$$\mathcal{J}_{\text{RP}}(\boldsymbol{\lambda}) = \mathbb{E}_{\boldsymbol{\theta}_{\boldsymbol{\lambda}}} \mathbb{E}_{\mathcal{D}|\boldsymbol{\theta}} \left[\log p(\mathcal{D}|\boldsymbol{\theta}) - \max_s \log p(\mathcal{D}|\hat{\boldsymbol{\theta}}_s) \right],$$

which is the difference between the data's log-likelihood under the model (i.e. parameter setting) that generated this data and the data log-likelihood under several samples from the prior. We see that optimization forces the prior to place most of its mass on parameters that generate identifiable datasets—or in other words, datasets that have high probability under only their true generative model. Turning back to Berger et al. (2009)'s Equation 3, and recalling its connection to the MCMC method, we see each method is approximately computing $\log[p(\mathcal{D}|\boldsymbol{\theta})/p(\mathcal{D})]$ with the critical difference being that Berger et al. (2009) and Lafferty & Wasserman (2001) approximate $\log p(\mathcal{D})$ with $\log \frac{1}{S} \sum_s p(\mathcal{D}|\hat{\boldsymbol{\theta}}_s)$ whereas we use $\max_s \log p(\mathcal{D}|\hat{\boldsymbol{\theta}}_s)$ in order to ensure a proper lower bound.

3.1.1 Black-Box, Gradient-Based Optimization

We now address how to compute and optimize $\mathcal{J}_{\text{RP}}(\boldsymbol{\lambda})$ (Equation 7) efficiently using differentiable Monte Carlo approximations.

Computing the Expectations. Consider first the three expectations in Equation 7. Starting with the $\mathbb{H}_{\mathcal{D}|\boldsymbol{\theta}}[\mathcal{D}]$ term, for many predictive models, $p(\mathbf{x}|\boldsymbol{\theta})$ is either Gaussian, as in regression, or Bernoulli, as in binary classification, meaning $\mathbb{H}_{\mathcal{D}|\boldsymbol{\theta}}[\mathcal{D}]$ can be computed analytically[4]. The second term, $\mathbb{E}_{\mathcal{D}|\boldsymbol{\theta}}[\max_s \log p(\mathcal{D}|\hat{\boldsymbol{\theta}}_s)]$, is simply the cross-entropy between $p(\mathcal{D}|\boldsymbol{\theta})$ and $p(\mathcal{D}|\hat{\boldsymbol{\theta}}_{\max})$ where $\hat{\boldsymbol{\theta}}_{\max}$ is the sample that maximizes the likelihood. This term also can usually be calculated analytically for regression and classification models. The only component that will typically be intractable is the expectation over $p_{\boldsymbol{\lambda}}(\boldsymbol{\theta})$, as the parameters are often buried under nonlinear functions and nested hierarchies. To address this we compute the outer expectation with samples $\hat{\boldsymbol{\theta}} \sim p_{\boldsymbol{\lambda}}(\boldsymbol{\theta})$:

$$\begin{aligned}\tilde{\mathcal{J}}_{\text{RP}}(\boldsymbol{\lambda}) &= \frac{1}{S}\sum_{s=1}^{S} \mathbb{H}[p(\mathcal{D}|\hat{\boldsymbol{\theta}}_s)||p(\mathcal{D}|\hat{\boldsymbol{\theta}}_{\max})] - \mathbb{H}_{\mathcal{D}|\hat{\boldsymbol{\theta}}_s}[\mathcal{D}] \\ &= \frac{1}{S}\sum_{s=1}^{S} \text{KLD}[p(\mathcal{D}|\hat{\boldsymbol{\theta}}_s)\ ||\ p(\mathcal{D}|\hat{\boldsymbol{\theta}}_{\max})]\end{aligned} \tag{8}$$

for S samples from the RP approximation and where $\mathbb{H}[p(\mathcal{D}|\hat{\boldsymbol{\theta}}_s)||p(\mathcal{D}|\hat{\boldsymbol{\theta}}_{\max})]$ denotes the cross-entropy term mentioned above. If both entropy terms can be computed analytically, we can write the expression as a KLD, which we do in the second line by using the identity $\text{KLD}[q||p] = \mathbb{H}[q||p] - \mathbb{H}[q]$. If the entropy terms are not analytically tractable, they will need to be estimated by sampling from the likelihood function.

Differentiable Sampling: We can take derivatives through each $\hat{\boldsymbol{\theta}}_s$, thereby allowing for fully gradient-based optimization, by drawing the samples via a differentiable non-centered parametrization (DNCP)—the so-called 'reparametrization trick' [12], i.e.

$$\frac{\partial}{\partial \boldsymbol{\lambda}}\left[\text{KLD}[p(\mathcal{D}|\hat{\boldsymbol{\theta}}_s)\ ||\ p(\mathcal{D}|\hat{\boldsymbol{\theta}}_{\max})]\right] = \frac{\partial}{\partial \hat{\boldsymbol{\theta}}}\left[\text{KLD}[p(\mathcal{D}|\hat{\boldsymbol{\theta}}_s)\ ||\ p(\mathcal{D}|\hat{\boldsymbol{\theta}}_{\max})]\right]\frac{\partial \hat{\boldsymbol{\theta}}}{\partial \boldsymbol{\lambda}}$$

where $\frac{\partial \hat{\boldsymbol{\theta}}}{\partial \boldsymbol{\lambda}}$ is the derivative that needs a DNCP in order to be evaluated. Requiring that p_λ has a DNCP does not significantly limit the approximating family. For instance, most mixture densities have a DNCP. When dealing with discrete data or parameters, we can use the *Concrete distribution* [18, 8], a differentiable relaxation of the discrete distribution, to still have fully gradient-based learning.

3.1.2 Implicit Priors

A crucial detail to note about Equation 8 is that it does not require evaluation of the prior's density. Rather, we need only to draw samples from it. This allows us to use black-box functional samplers as the variational family [21], i.e. $\hat{\boldsymbol{\theta}} = g(\boldsymbol{\lambda}, \hat{\epsilon})$ where $\boldsymbol{\epsilon} \sim p_0$, g is some arbitrary differentiable function (such as a neural network), and p_0 is a fixed noise distribution. We call $p_{\boldsymbol{\lambda}}$ an *implicit prior* in this setting since its density function is unknown.

Thus, the proposed information bound provides a 'built-in' sampling technique in lieu of Lafferty & Wasserman (2001)'s MCMC algorithm. Although we cannot guarantee the same asymptotically unbiased approximation as MCMC, the lack of restrictions on $g(\boldsymbol{\lambda}, \hat{\epsilon})$ should allow for a sufficiently expressive sampler. Furthermore, we can persist the sampler just by saving the values of $\boldsymbol{\lambda}$; there's no need to save the samples themselves. And since learning a RP for a generative model is dataset independent, $\boldsymbol{\lambda}$ could be shared easily via an online repository and users desiring a RP for the same model could download $\boldsymbol{\lambda}$ to generate an unbounded number of their own samples. The same can be done when $p_{\boldsymbol{\lambda}}$ is a proper distribution.

3.1.3 Example: Gaussian Mean

To provide some intuition and to sanity check the proposed approach, consider learning an approximate RP for the mean parameter $\boldsymbol{\mu}$ of a Gaussian density. The RP on $\boldsymbol{\mu}$ is the improper uniform distribution, which can be approximated as a Gaussian with infinite variance: $p^*(\boldsymbol{\mu}) \propto \mathbb{1} \approx \text{N}(\cdot, \infty)$. The analytical solution to the KLD term in Equation 8 in this case is:

$$\text{KLD}[p(\mathcal{D}|\hat{\boldsymbol{\theta}}_s)\ ||\ p(\mathcal{D}|\hat{\boldsymbol{\theta}}_{\max}) = \frac{1}{2}\ ||\ \hat{\boldsymbol{\mu}}_s - \hat{\boldsymbol{\mu}}_{\max}\ ||_2^2,$$

which is the squared distance between two samples from $p_{\boldsymbol{\lambda}}$. Maximizing Equation 8 therefore maximizes the average distance between samples from the RP approximation. If we set $p_{\boldsymbol{\lambda}} = \text{N}(\boldsymbol{\mu}_{\boldsymbol{\lambda}}, \sigma_{\boldsymbol{\lambda}}^2\mathbb{I})$ and transform to the Normal's DNCP $\boldsymbol{\theta} = \boldsymbol{\mu} + \boldsymbol{\sigma} \odot \boldsymbol{\epsilon}$ where $\boldsymbol{\epsilon} \sim \text{N}(\mathbf{0}, \mathbb{I})$, then the optimization objective becomes

$$||\ \hat{\boldsymbol{\mu}}_s - \hat{\boldsymbol{\mu}}_{\max}\ ||_2^2 = ||\ \boldsymbol{\sigma}_{\boldsymbol{\lambda}} \odot (\hat{\boldsymbol{\epsilon}}_s - \hat{\boldsymbol{\epsilon}}_{\max})\ ||_2^2,$$

and optimization would increase $\sigma_{\boldsymbol{\lambda}}^2$ without bound, agreeing with the infinite-variance Normal approximation.

3.2 METHOD #2: PARTICLE DESCENT

Next we present a particle-based approximation method, which we outline below. While the core ideas are not significantly different from those of Method #1, here we use a different rearrangement of the mutual information and a lower bound bound on $\log p(\mathcal{D})$. These changes expose nuances that may be useful if the reader wishes to apply

[4]To keep the notation simple, in our discussion of conditional models the dependence on the features is implicit. Writing the entropy with $\mathbf{X}'$ as the feature matrix and $\mathbf{x}$ as the vector of labels, we have: $\mathbb{H}_{\mathbf{x}|\mathbf{X}',\boldsymbol{\theta}}[\mathbf{x}]$.

other VI techniques to the problem of RP approximation. Other modern VI methods using transformations [22] or importance weighting [5] could also be applied.

A Particle-Based Approximation. *Stein Variational Gradient Descent* [16] (SVGD) is a variational inference technique that exploits a connection between the Stein operator and the derivative of the KLD to derive a deterministic particle update rule. At time step t, each parameter particle $\bar{\boldsymbol{\theta}}_j$ is updated according to:

$$\bar{\boldsymbol{\theta}}_j^{t+1} = \bar{\boldsymbol{\theta}}_j^{t} + \eta\, \phi[\boldsymbol{\theta}] \quad \text{where}$$

$$\phi[\boldsymbol{\theta}] = \frac{1}{K}\sum_{k=1}^{K} \kappa(\bar{\boldsymbol{\theta}}_k^t, \bar{\boldsymbol{\theta}}_j^t)\nabla_{\bar{\boldsymbol{\theta}}_k} \log p(\bar{\boldsymbol{\theta}}_k^t) + \nabla_{\bar{\boldsymbol{\theta}}_k} \kappa(\bar{\boldsymbol{\theta}}_k^t, \bar{\boldsymbol{\theta}}_j^t).$$

η is a learning rate, $\kappa(\cdot,\cdot)$ is a proper kernel function, and p is the cumbersome distribution we wish to approximate. SVGD has the nice property that using one particle reduces to vanilla gradient ascent on p (MAP estimation, in the Bayesian setting).

Similarly to $\tilde{\mathcal{J}}_{\text{RP}}(\boldsymbol{\lambda})$ (Equation 8), SVGD does not require the approximating density be evaluated, and hence we can draw the particles from a black-box function, i.e. $\bar{\boldsymbol{\theta}} = g(\boldsymbol{\lambda}, \hat{\boldsymbol{\epsilon}})$, just as defined in Section 3.1.2. Liu & Feng (2016) call this variant *Amortized SVGD* (A-SVGD), and it estimates the parameters $\boldsymbol{\lambda}$ by finding SVDG's fixed-point solutions [15]:

$$\begin{aligned} \hat{\boldsymbol{\lambda}} &= \operatorname*{argmin}_{\boldsymbol{\lambda}} \; ||\; g(\boldsymbol{\lambda}, \hat{\boldsymbol{\epsilon}}) - (\bar{\boldsymbol{\theta}} + \eta\, \phi[\boldsymbol{\theta}]) \;||_2^2 \\ &= \operatorname*{argmin}_{\boldsymbol{\lambda}} \; ||\; \eta\, \phi[\boldsymbol{\theta}] \;||_2^2 \,. \end{aligned} \tag{9}$$

This formulation is especially beneficial to SVGD because training can be done with a practical number of particles (K), but an unlimited number can be drawn at evaluation time. Lastly, note that the base parameters are updated through the $\bar{\boldsymbol{\theta}}_j^t$ particle, not through the particle in $\nabla_{\bar{\boldsymbol{\theta}}_k^t} \log p(\bar{\boldsymbol{\theta}}_k^t)$.

A-SVGD for RP Approximations. We can use A-SVGD to learn particle approximations of RPs. A-SVGD requires RP learning be formulated as KLD minimization. In this context recall Equation 2 in which we showed that minimizing $\text{KLD}[p(\boldsymbol{\theta}) \;||\; f(\boldsymbol{\theta})]$[5] maximizes $I(\boldsymbol{\theta}, \mathcal{D})$. Hence we can treat the functional f as the intractable density on which to apply the SVGD operator $\phi[\boldsymbol{\theta}]$. The gradient term is then

$$\begin{aligned} \nabla_{\bar{\boldsymbol{\theta}}} \log f(\bar{\boldsymbol{\theta}}) &= \nabla_{\bar{\boldsymbol{\theta}}} \int_{\mathcal{D}} p(\mathcal{D}|\bar{\boldsymbol{\theta}}) \;\log p(\bar{\boldsymbol{\theta}}|\mathcal{D})\; d\mathcal{D} \\ &= \nabla_{\bar{\boldsymbol{\theta}}} \int_{\mathcal{D}} p(\mathcal{D}|\bar{\boldsymbol{\theta}}) \log \frac{p(\mathcal{D}|\bar{\boldsymbol{\theta}})\mathbb{1}_{\Theta}}{p(\mathcal{D})} d\mathcal{D} \\ &= -\nabla_{\bar{\boldsymbol{\theta}}} \mathbb{H}_{\mathcal{D}|\bar{\boldsymbol{\theta}}}[\mathcal{D}] - \nabla_{\bar{\boldsymbol{\theta}}} \mathbb{E}_{\mathcal{D}|\bar{\boldsymbol{\theta}}}[\log p(\mathcal{D})] \end{aligned} \tag{10}$$

[5]While Equation 2, in form, looks like a negated KLD, it will take on positive values due to f being unnormalized.

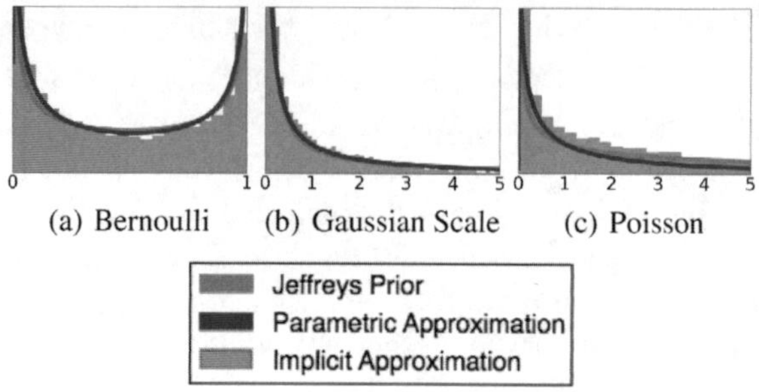

(a) Bernoulli (b) Gaussian Scale (c) Poisson

Figure 1: *Approximation via Lower Bound Optimization.*

where $\bar{\boldsymbol{\theta}}$ is the particle. In line 2, following Berger et al. (2009) in Equation 3, we assume the prior is constant. If a prior is included, it acts as a hyper-prior, regularizing the particles towards a user-specified distribution.

Again we face the problem of evaluating $\log p(\mathcal{D})$. We could use the VR-max estimator, but here we opt for stability and use the ELBO: $\log p(\mathcal{D}) \geq \mathbb{E}_{\boldsymbol{\theta}_{\boldsymbol{\lambda}}}[\log p(\mathcal{D}|\boldsymbol{\theta})]$. Making this substitution reduces the influence of $\partial p(\mathcal{D}|\bar{\boldsymbol{\theta}})/\partial\bar{\boldsymbol{\theta}}$, the term that encourages diversity in $p_{\boldsymbol{\lambda}}$ and the generation of identifiable datasets (as discussed in Section 3.1). Yet the derivative of the kernel, the second term in $\phi[\boldsymbol{\theta}]$, acts as a (locally) repulsive force on the particles, which may compensate for the introduction of the ELBO. Substituting the approximation of the marginal likelihood into Equation 10 yields:

$$\begin{aligned} &\approx -\nabla_{\bar{\boldsymbol{\theta}}}\, \mathbb{H}_{\mathcal{D}|\bar{\boldsymbol{\theta}}}[\mathcal{D}] - \nabla_{\bar{\boldsymbol{\theta}}}\, \mathbb{E}_{\mathcal{D}|\bar{\boldsymbol{\theta}}}\, \mathbb{E}_{\boldsymbol{\theta}_{\boldsymbol{\lambda}}}[\log p(\mathcal{D}|\boldsymbol{\theta})] \\ &= -\nabla_{\bar{\boldsymbol{\theta}}}\, \mathbb{H}_{\mathcal{D}|\bar{\boldsymbol{\theta}}}[\mathcal{D}] + \nabla_{\bar{\boldsymbol{\theta}}}\, \mathbb{E}_{\boldsymbol{\theta}_{\boldsymbol{\lambda}}}\, \mathbb{H}[p(\mathcal{D}|\bar{\boldsymbol{\theta}})||p(\mathcal{D}|\boldsymbol{\theta})] \\ &\approx \nabla_{\bar{\boldsymbol{\theta}}}\, \frac{1}{S}\sum_{s} \mathbb{H}[p(\mathcal{D}|\bar{\boldsymbol{\theta}})||p(\mathcal{D}|\hat{\boldsymbol{\theta}}_s)] - \nabla_{\bar{\boldsymbol{\theta}}}\, \mathbb{H}_{\mathcal{D}|\bar{\boldsymbol{\theta}}}[\mathcal{D}] \\ &= \nabla_{\bar{\boldsymbol{\theta}}}\, \frac{1}{S}\sum_{s} \text{KLD}[p(\mathcal{D}|\bar{\boldsymbol{\theta}}) \;||\; p(\mathcal{D}|\hat{\boldsymbol{\theta}}_s)]. \end{aligned} \tag{11}$$

In the last line we use a Monte Carlo approximation of $\mathbb{E}_{\boldsymbol{\theta}_{\boldsymbol{\lambda}}}$ just as in Method #1, where $\hat{\boldsymbol{\theta}}_s$ denotes a sample from g. Optimization is performed as before as described in Equation 9.

4 EMPIRICAL RESULTS

Below we describe several empirical analyses of the proposed methods. Formulating experiments is somewhat difficult due to the fact that RPs do not necessarily improve a model's ability to generalize to out-of-sample data. In fact, using an RP when a model requires regularization will likely degrade performance. Thus, our main analysis is a case study of the *Variational Autoencoder* [12, 23]. But before analyzing the Variational Autoencoder's RP, we check that our methods do indeed recover known RPs for exponential family models.

For all experiments, we used the *AdaM* optimization algorithm [11] with settings $\beta_1 = 0.9$ and $\beta_2 = 0.999$. Training parameters such as the learning rate, latent dimensionality of the functional sampler $g(\boldsymbol{\lambda}, \hat{\boldsymbol{\epsilon}})$, number of samples were chosen based on which combination gave the highest average value of the information lower bound over the last 50 updates. The number of training iterations was set at 250 and the batch size was set to 100 in all cases.

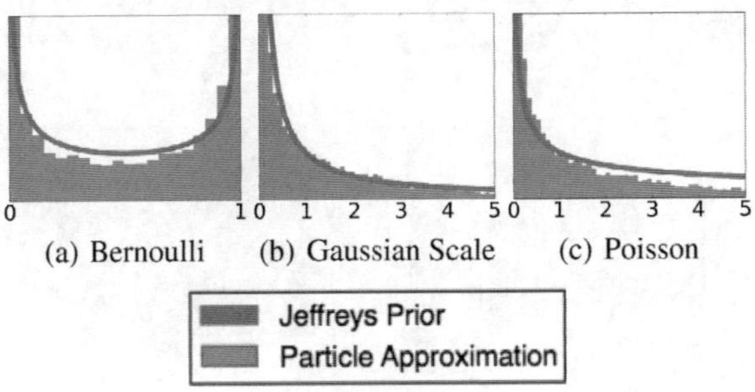

Figure 2: *Approximation via Particle Descent.*

4.1 RECOVERING JEFFREYS PRIORS

We begin experimental evaluation by attempting to recover the true RP for three one-dimensional models: the Bernoulli mean parameter, $p^*(p) \propto \text{Beta}(.5, .5)$, the Gaussian scale parameter, $p^*(\sigma) \propto 1/\sigma$, and the Poisson rate parameter, $p^*(\lambda) \propto 1/\sqrt{\lambda}$. These are also the Jeffreys priors for the respective models (since we are in the univariate case). The chosen learning rate was .001 for the implicit priors and .0001 for the parametric and particle approximations, the number of samples drawn was 50 for all models, and the functional sampler g was a linear model with a latent dimensionality of 5, i.e. $\boldsymbol{\epsilon} \sim \text{N}(\mathbf{0}, \mathbb{I}_{5\times 5})$. We used a logit-normal distribution for the Bernoulli RP's parametric approximation and a log-normal for the Gaussian scale's and Poisson's RP approximation. Both the logit- and log-normal have DNCPs. For A-SVGD, we used the Sobolev kernel (length scale of 2) on the unit interval for the Bernoulli model and an RBF in log space (length scale set via the heuristic in [16]) for the Gaussian scale and Poisson models.

Qualitative Evaluation. Plots of the density functions learned by the lower bound method (Section 3.1) are shown in Figure 1. The red line shows the Jeffreys prior (the gold-standard RP), the blue line shows the parametric approximation, and the gray histogram represents 10,000 samples from the implicit prior. Both approximation types have negligible qualitative difference to the red line.

The density functions learned by A-SGVB (Section 3.2) are shown in Figure 2. Again, the red line denotes the true RP, and the gray histogram represents 10,000 particles sampled from g. Here, we do notice some minor differences. For instance, the Bernoulli prior's right mode seems to be a bit stronger than its left, and the Poisson prior exhibits underestimation in its tail. These defects are likely due to the approximations not being penalized as much as in Method #1 for concentrating their mass in one of the likelihood function's points of low entropy.

Quantitative Evaluation. Next we quantitatively compare our methods via a two-sample test against three baselines: Berger et al. (2009)'s numerical method, Lafferty & Wasserman (2001)'s MCMC algorithm, and a uniform prior, which serves as a naive flat prior. For Berger et al. (2009)'s method, we use the same number of parameter samples (S) as our method, set the J parameter to 100, and sample datasets containing 500 points. To generate samples from Berger et al. (2009)'s method, we calculate the prior at 1000 evenly spaced grid points across the domain and then treat them as a discrete approximation with each point having probability $p(\boldsymbol{\theta}_i)/\sum_j^{1000} p(\boldsymbol{\theta}_j)$. We then sample from this discrete distribution 1000 times. For the MCMC method, we replicate Lafferty & Wasserman (2001)'s simulations by using a uniform proposal distribution and running for 10,000 iterations. We kept the last 1000 samples drawn (no need to account for auto-correlation due to the uniform proposal). For the Gaussian and Poisson cases, we approximated $\mathcal{X}$ using 1000 points. For all settings, we made sure our approximation methods ran no longer than the baselines, but this was never an issue: our methods converged in a fraction of the time the numerical algorithms needed to run.

We quantify the gap in the approximations via a Kolmogorov-Smirnov two-sample test (KST) under the null hypothesis $H_0 : p = q$ where p is the true RP and q is an approximation. We draw samples from the true RP, when it is improper, via the same discrete approximation used for Berger et al. (2009)'s method. The KST computes the distance (KSD) between the distributions as $\text{KSD}(p, q) = \sup_x \mid \hat{F}_p(x) - \hat{F}_q(x) \mid$ where $\hat{F}_p(x)$ is the empirical CDF.

Figure 3 shows the KSD between samples from the Jeffreys prior and the various approximation techniques, as the sample size increases. The black dotted line in conjunction with the gray shaded area denotes the threshold at which the null hypothesis (that the distributions are equal) is rejected. The uniform distribution is denoted by the dark gray line, the numerical algorithm by the black, MCMC by the brown, the parametric approximation by

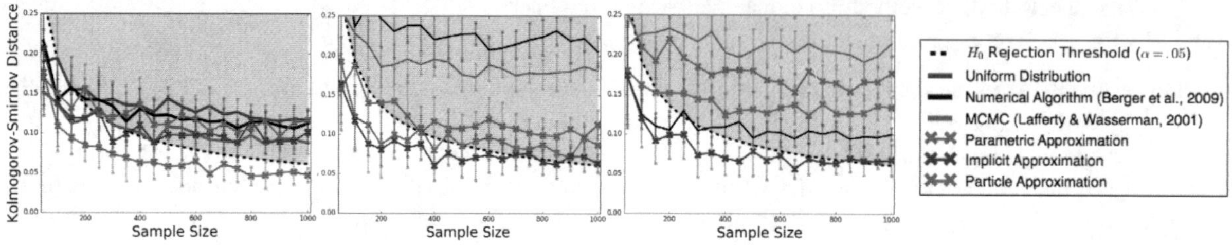

(a) Bernoulli (b) Gaussian Scale (c) Poisson

Figure 3: *Quantifying the Approximation Quality.* The Kolmogorov-Smirnov distance (supremum of distance between empirical CDFs) between the Jeffreys/true reference prior and the various approximation techniques. The gray region denotes where the test's null hypothesis is rejected, meaning there is a statistical difference between the distributions.

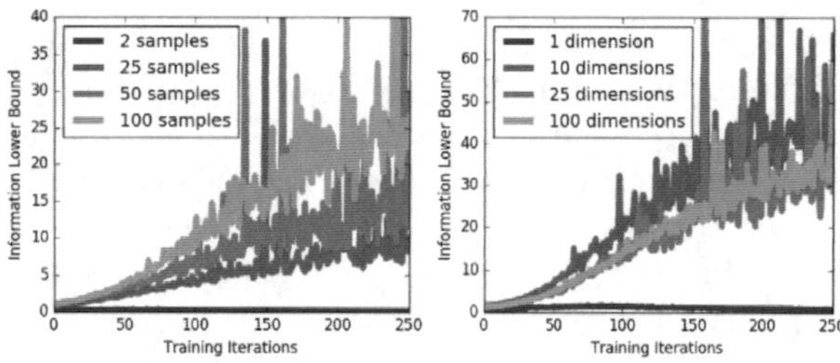

(a) Samples (b) Dimensionality

Figure 4: *Optimization Stability.* We train an implicit prior for a multivariate Gaussian and vary (a) the number of samples used in the VR-max estimator, and (b) the Gaussian's dimensionality.

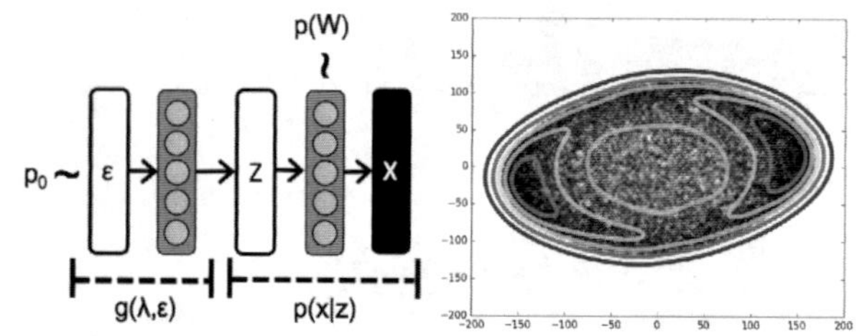

(a) Training Configuration (b) Approximation

Figure 5: *Learning the Variational Autoencoder's Reference Prior.* (a) computational pipeline from the implicit prior through the VAE decoder; (b) RP approximation (contours are generated via kernel density estimation on $10,000$ samples).

the red, the implicit prior by the blue, and the particle approximation by the green. We see that the latter three approximations (ours) have a lower KSD—and thus are closer to the true RP—in almost every experiment. The exceptions are that MCMC is superior to A-SVGD for the Bernoulli (and competitive with the implicit), and the Berger et al. (2009) technique bests A-SVGD and the parametric approximation for the Poisson. The parametric approximation for the Bernoulli and the implicit prior for the Gaussian scale and Poisson are the only methods that achieve conspicuous indistinguishability.

4.2 OPTIMIZATION STABILITY

As discussed in Section 3.1, the VR-max estimator used in Equation 7 has intrinsically high-variance. While we have just shown in the previous section that our approximations better recover the true RP in one dimension, scaling to higher dimensions is a concern (as is also the case for existing techniques). Here we examine optimization progress of an RP approximation for the scale parameters of a multivariate Gaussian with a diagonal covariance matrix. We produce two plots: one showing the information lower bound's progress (for a linear model implicit prior) when using a different number of samples over which to take the maximum (Figure 4a) and another showing progress as the Gaussian's dimensionality increases (Figure 4b). For the former, using a five dimensional Gaussian, we see there is a trade-off between lower bound maximization and the number of samples used: using more samples increases the rate of progress but also the objective's variance. We find that in less than ten dimensions, using around 50 samples (red line) results in a good variance vs progress balance. In Figure 4b, in which we vary the dimensionality of the Gaussian while keeping the number of samples fixed at 100, we see that the objective's variance decreases with dimensionality. While this may seem non-intuitive at first, recall that the VR-max estimator acts as a diversity term, finding points in space that give the data high probability even though it was generated with different parameters. As dimensionality inflates, it becomes harder and harder for a finite number of samples to capture these points and thus the $-\mathbb{H}$ term in Equation 8 becomes prone to mode seeking.

4.3 VAE CASE STUDY

Lastly, we study learning an RP approximation for an intractable, neural-network-based model: a *Variational Autoencoder* [12] (VAE). The standard Normal distribution is often chosen as the prior on the VAE's latent space [12, 23, 5], and this choice is made more for analytical simplicity rather than convictions based on prior information[6]. Thus, we learn an RP for the VAE to investigate the qualities of its objective prior, which was previously intractable.

We trained an implicit prior (IP) for a VAE with 784 output dimensions (MNIST's size), 100 encoder hidden units with hyperbolic tangent activations, and a two-dimensional latent space for purposes of visualization. The IP $g(\boldsymbol{\lambda}, \hat{\boldsymbol{\epsilon}})$ is also a one-hidden layer neural network[7]. The computational pipeline is depicted in Figure 5a, where $p(\mathbf{x}|\mathbf{z})$ denotes the VAE likelihood function (decoder) and $\mathbf{z} = g(\boldsymbol{\lambda}, \hat{\boldsymbol{\epsilon}})$ denotes the functional sampler. Note that the VAE has two sets of parameters: $\mathbf{z}$, the latent variable on which we place the prior, and the weights of the decoder, denoted as $\mathbf{W}$. The weights must have some value during RP training and thus we place a standard normal prior on $\mathbf{W}$ and sample from this prior during optimization of g.

Figure 5b shows samples from the VAE's RP. We see that the learned IP is drastically different than the standard Normal that is typically used: the IP is multimodal and has a much larger variance. Yet, the difference is intuitive: placing most prior mass at opposite sides of the latent space encourages the VAE to space it's latent representations with as much distance as possible, ensuring they are as identifiable w.r.t. the model likelihood, the VAE decoder, as possible. Interestingly, recent work by Hoffman & Johnson (2016) suggests that VAEs can be improved by multimodal priors: "[T]he [VAEs] individual encoding distributions $q(\mathbf{z}_i|\mathbf{x}_i)$ do not have significant overlap. . .then perhaps we should investigate multimodal priors that can meet $q(\mathbf{z})$ halfway" [6]. This suggests using multimodal, dispersed priors encourages flexibility and objectivity in the posterior distribution.

We can also see analytically that the distribution in Figure 5b allows the VAE 'to follow the data' as a good RP should. For simplicity, consider using a bivariate Gaussian as the RP approximation, and assuming it captures the same distribution as in Figure 5 (b), it's parameters would be approximately $\{\boldsymbol{\mu} = \mathbf{0}, \boldsymbol{\Sigma} = 200\, \mathbb{I}_{2\times 2}\}$. Next recall the VAE's optimization objective (the ELBO): $\mathcal{L}_{\text{VAE}} = \mathbb{E}_q[-\log p(\mathbf{x}|\mathbf{z})] + \text{KLD}[q(\boldsymbol{\mu}, \boldsymbol{\Sigma}) \mid\mid p(\mathbf{0}, 200\, \mathbb{I}_{2\times 2})]$. The first term optimizes the model w.r.t. the data and the second acts as regularization, ensuring the variational posterior q is close to the prior. Assuming q's covariance matrix is also diagonal, we can write $\text{KLD}[q(\boldsymbol{\mu}, \boldsymbol{\Sigma}) \mid\mid p(\mathbf{0}, 200\, \mathbb{I}_{2\times 2})] = \text{KLD}[q(\boldsymbol{\mu}, \boldsymbol{\Sigma}) \mid\mid p(\mathbf{0}, \mathbb{I}_{2\times 2})] - \frac{1}{2}\log 200$. This means that using the standard Normal up-weights the regularization (towards the prior) by about a factor of $\sqrt{200}$.

5 CONCLUSIONS

We have introduced two flexible, widely applicable, and derivation-free methods for approximating reference priors. The first optimizes a new lower bound on the reference prior objective and allows for parametric or non-parametric approximations to be employed, depending on whether the user prefers to easily evaluate the prior or to have a maximally expressive approximation. The second method uses a recently proposed particle technique to also allow for free-form approximations. We demonstrated quantitatively and qualitatively that these methods can recover the true reference priors for univariate distributions as well as generalize to more exotic models such as Variational Autoencoders.

Looking forward, we believe using similar techniques for constructing priors that optimize objectives other than mutual information presents a promising next step. For example, Liu et al. (2014) showed that priors that maximize divergence measures other than KLD, such as Hellinger distance, between the prior and posterior have desirable properties. Extending the proposed approximation techniques to these other families of objectives may enable new classes of Bayesian prior distributions.

Acknowledgements

This work was supported by the National Science Foundation under awards IIS-1320527 and DGE-1633631 and by the National Institutes of Health under award NIH-1U01TR001801-01.

References

[1] James O Berger, José M Bernardo, and Dongchu Sun. The formal definition of reference priors. *The Annals of Statistics*, pages 905–938, 2009.

[2] James O Berger, Jose M Bernardo, and Dongchu Sun. Overall objective priors. *Bayesian Analysis*, 10(1):189–221, 2015.

[6] "I chose the simple Gaussian prior N(0,I) because it's simple to demonstrate but also because it results in a relatively friendly objective function." — D. Kingma, comment taken from *r/MachineLearning*, 4/12/16.

[7] Architecture / training paramters: 2000 latent noise dimensions, 1000 hidden dimensions, ReLU activations, .0003 learning rate, 50 samples for VR-max term.

[3] Jose M Bernardo. Reference posterior distributions for Bayesian inference. *Journal of the Royal Statistical Society. Series B (Methodological)*, pages 113–147, 1979.

[4] José M Bernardo. Reference analysis. *Handbook of Statistics*, 25:17–90, 2005.

[5] Yuri Burda, Roger Grosse, and Ruslan Salakhutdinov. Importance weighted autoencoders. *International Conference on Learning Representations (ICLR)*, 2016.

[6] Matthew Hoffman and Matthew Johnson. ELBO surgery: yet another way to carve up the variational evidence lower bound. *NIPS 2016 Workshop on Advances in Approximate Bayesian Inference*, 2016.

[7] Telba Z Irony and Nozer D Singpurwalla. Non-informative priors do not exist: A dialogue with jose m. bernardo. *Journal of Statistical Planning and Inference*, 65(159):189, 1997.

[8] E. Jang, S. Gu, and B. Poole. Categorical reparameterization with Gumbel-softmax. *International Conference on Learning Representations (ICLR)*, 2017.

[9] Edwin T Jaynes. Information theory and statistical mechanics. *Physical Review*, 106(4):620, 1957.

[10] Harold Jeffreys. An invariant form for the prior probability in estimation problems. In *Proceedings of the Royal Society of London A: Mathematical, Physical and Engineering Sciences*, volume 186, pages 453–461. The Royal Society, 1946.

[11] Diederik Kingma and Jimmy Ba. Adam: A method for stochastic optimization. *International Conference on Learning Representations (ICLR)*, 2014.

[12] Diederik P Kingma and Max Welling. Auto-encoding variational Bayes. *International Conference on Learning Representations (ICLR)*, 2014.

[13] John Lafferty and Larry Wasserman. Iterative Markov chain Monte Carlo computation of reference priors and minimax risk. In *Proceedings of the Seventeenth Conference on Uncertainty in Artificial Intelligence*, pages 293–300, 2001.

[14] Yingzhen Li and Richard E Turner. Variational inference with Renyi divergence. *Neural Information Processing Systems (NIPS)*, pages 1073–1081, 2016.

[15] Qiang Liu and Yihao Feng. Two methods for wild variational inference. *ArXiv Preprint*, 2016.

[16] Qiang Liu and Dilin Wang. Stein variational gradient descent: A general purpose Bayesian inference algorithm. *Neural Information Processing Systems (NIPS)*, pages 2378–2386, 2016.

[17] Ruitao Liu, Arijit Chakrabarti, Tapas Samanta, Jayanta K Ghosh, and Malay Ghosh. On divergence measures leading to Jeffreys and other reference priors. *Bayesian Analysis*, 9(2):331–370, 2014.

[18] C. J. Maddison, A. Mnih, and Y. Whye Teh. The concrete distribution: A continuous relaxation of discrete random variables. *International Conference on Learning Representations (ICLR)*, 2017.

[19] Adrian E Raftery, Michael A Newton, Jaya M Satagopan, and Pavel N Krivitsky. Estimating the integrated likelihood via posterior simulation using the harmonic mean identity. *Bayesian Statistics*, pages 1–45, 2007.

[20] Rajesh Ranganath, Sean Gerrish, and David Blei. Black box variational inference. In *Proceedings of the Seventeenth International Conference on Artificial Intelligence and Statistics*, pages 814–822, 2014.

[21] Rajesh Ranganath, Dustin Tran, Jaan Altosaar, and David Blei. Operator variational inference. In *Advances in Neural Information Processing Systems*, pages 496–504, 2016.

[22] Danilo Rezende and Shakir Mohamed. Variational inference with normalizing flows. In *Proceedings of The 32nd International Conference on Machine Learning*, pages 1530–1538, 2015.

[23] Danilo Rezende, Shakir Mohamed, and Daan Wierstra. Stochastic backpropagation and approximate inference in deep generative models. *International Conference on Machine Learning (ICML)*, pages 1278–1286, 2014.

[24] Christian Robert. *The Bayesian Choice*. Springer, 2001.

Learning to Draw Samples with Amortized Stein Variational Gradient Descent

Yihao Feng **Dilin Wang** **Qiang Liu**
Computer Science, Dartmouth College
Hanover, NH, 03755
{yihao.feng.gr, dilin.wang.gr, qiang.liu}@dartmouth.edu

Abstract

We propose a simple algorithm to train stochastic neural networks to draw samples from given target distributions for probabilistic inference. Our method is based on iteratively adjusting the neural network parameters so that the output changes along a Stein variational gradient direction (Liu & Wang, 2016) that maximally decreases the KL divergence with the target distribution. Our method works for any target distribution specified by their unnormalized density function, and can train any black-box architectures that are differentiable in terms of the parameters we want to adapt. We demonstrate our method with a number of applications, including variational autoencoder (VAE) with expressive encoders to model complex latent space structures, and hyper-parameter learning of MCMC samplers that allows Bayesian inference to adaptively improve itself when seeing more data.

1 INTRODUCTION

Modern machine learning increasingly relies on highly complex probabilistic models to reason about uncertainty. A key computational challenge is to develop efficient inference techniques to approximate, or draw samples from complex distributions. Currently, most inference methods, including MCMC and variational inference, are *hand-designed* by researchers or domain experts. This makes it difficult to fully optimize the choice of different methods and their parameters, and exploit the structures in the problems of interest in an automatic way. The hand-designed algorithm can also be inefficient when there is a need to perform fast inference repeatedly on a large number of different distributions with similar structures. This happens, for example, when we need to reason about a number of observed datasets in settings like online learning or personalized prediction, or need fast inference as inner loops for other algorithms such as learning latent variable models (such as variational autoencoder (Kingma & Welling, 2013)) or unnormalized distributions. Therefore, it is highly desirable to develop intelligent probabilistic inference systems that can adaptively improve their own performance to fully optimize the computational efficiency, and generalize to new tasks with similar structures. Developing such systems requires solving the following *learning-to-sample* problem:

Problem 1. *Given a distribution with density $p(z)$ on set $\mathcal{Z}$ and a simulator $z = f(\xi;\, \eta)$, such as a neural network, which takes a parameter η and a random seed ξ drawn from q_0 and outputs a value z in $\mathcal{Z}$, we want to find an optimal parameter η so that the density of the random output $z = f(\xi;\, \eta)$ with $\xi \sim q_0$ closely matches the target p.*

Here, we assume that we do not know the analytical form of the simulator $f(\cdot)$ (which we call inference network), and we can only query it through the output value $f(\xi;\, \eta)$ and derivative $\partial_\eta f(\xi;\, \eta)$ for given η and ξ. We also assume that the random seed distribution q_0 is unknown and we can only access it through the draws of the random input ξ; that is, q_0 can be arbitrarily complex, and can be discrete, continuous or hybrid.

Because of the above assumption, we cannot directly calculate the density $q_\eta(z)$ of the output variable $z = f(\xi;\, \eta)$; this makes it difficult to solve Problem 1 using the typical variational inference (VI) methods. Recall that VI finds an optimal parameter η to approximate the target p with q_η, by minimizing the KL divergence:

$$\mathrm{KL}(q_\eta \,||\, p) = \mathbb{E}_{q_\eta}[\log(q_\eta/p)]. \tag{1}$$

However equation (1) requires calculating the density $q_\eta(z)$ or its derivative, which is intractable by our assumption (and is called implicit models in Mohamed & Lakshminarayanan (2016)). This holds true even when Monte Carlo gradient estimates (Hoffman et al., 2013) and the reparametrization trick (Kingma & Welling, 2013) are applied.

This requirement of calculating $q_\eta(z)$ makes it difficult for

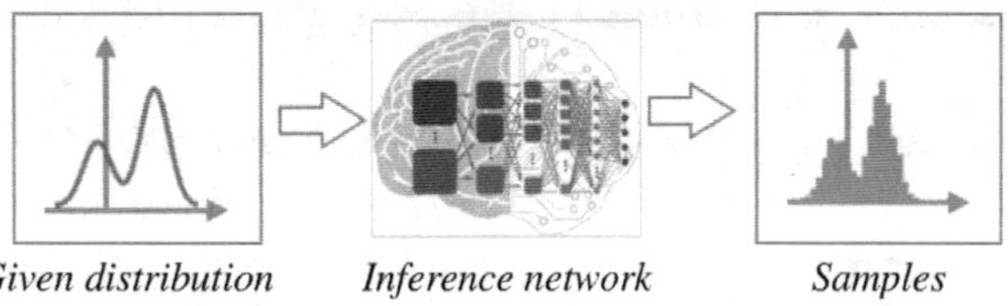

Figure 1: Wild variational inference allows us to train general stochastic neural inference networks to learn to draw (approximate) samples from the target distributions, without restriction on the computational tractability of the density function of the neural inference networks.

practitioners to use variational inference in an automatic way, especially in domains where it is critical to use expressive inference networks to achieve good approximation quality. Methods that do not require to explicitly calculate $q_\eta(z)$, referred to as *wild variational inference*, or *variational programming* (Ranganath et al., 2016), can significantly simplify the design and expand the applications of VI methods, allowing practioners to focus more on choosing proposals that work best with their specific tasks.

A similar problem also appears in importance sampling (IS), where it requires calculating the IS proposal density $q(z)$ in order to calculate the importance weight $w(z) = p(z)/q(z)$. However, there exist methods that use no explicit information of the proposal $q(z)$, and, seemingly counter-intuitively, give better asymptotic variance or converge rate than the typical IS that uses the proposal information (e.g., Liu & Lee, 2016; Briol et al., 2015; Henmi et al., 2007; Delyon & Portier, 2014). Discussions on this phenomenon date back to O'Hagan (1987), who argued that "Monte Carlo (that uses the proposal information) is fundamentally unsound", and developed Bayesian Monte Carlo (O'Hagan, 1991) as an instance that uses no information of proposal $q(z)$, yet gives better convergence rate than the typical Monte Carlo $O(n^{-1/2})$ convergence rate (Briol et al., 2015). Despite the substantial difference between IS and VI, these results intuitively suggest the possibility of developing efficient variational inference without using the information of density function $q(z)$ explicitly.

Main Idea In this work, we study a simple algorithm for Problem 1, motivated by a recent Stein variational gradient descent (SVGD) algorithm. Briefly speaking, SVGD is a nonparametric functional gradient descent algorithm which solves $\min_q \mathrm{KL}(q \,||\, p)$ without parametric assumption on q, and approximates the functional gradient, called the Stein variational gradient, using a set of samples (or particles) $\{z_i\}_{i=1}^n$ which iteratively evolves. See Section 2 for more introduction on SVGD. We can then view Problem 1 as a constrained optimization problem,

$$\min_q \mathrm{KL}(q \,||\, p), \quad s.t. \quad q = q_\eta \text{ for some } \eta, \qquad (2)$$

which motivates us to develop a project gradient like algorithm that iteratively calculates the Stein variational gradient, and projects it to the finite dimensional η-space to update parameter η. At the convergence, the samples drawn from q_η reach the equilibrium state of SVGD, and hence form a good approximation of p. We can view this method as "amortizing" or distilling the SVGD dynamics using parametric family q_η or its inference network $f(\xi;\, \eta)$ and call it amortized SVGD. See Section 3 for the detailed description of amortized SVGD.

Our algorithm provides a simple approach for the wild inference problem in Problem 1, enabling wide application in approximate learning and inference. We explore two examples in this paper. In Section 4.1, we apply amortized SVGD to learn complex encoder functions in variational autoencoder (VAE), allowing it to model complex latent variable space. In Section 4.2 we use amortized SVGD to learn hyper-parameters of MCMC samplers, which allows us to adaptively improve the efficiency of Bayesian computation when performing a large number of similar tasks.

Related Work There has been a number of very recent work that studies advanced variational inference methods that do not require explicitly calculating $q_\eta(z)$ (Problem 1). This includes adversarial variational Bayesian (Mescheder et al., 2017) which approximates the KL divergence with a density ratio estimator, operator variational inference (Ranganath et al., 2016) which replaces the KL divergence with an alternative operator variational objective that is equivalent to Stein discrepancy (see Appendix A for more discussion), and amortized MCMC (Li et al., 2017) which proposes to amortize arbitrary MCMC dynamics to make it applicable to discrete models and gradient-free settings.

The key advantage of our method is its simplicity. both Mescheder et al. (2017) and Ranganath et al. (2016) require training some type of auxiliary networks, while our main algorithm (Algorithm 1 with update (10)) is very simple, and is essentially a generalization of the typical gradient descent rule that replaces the typical gradient with the stein variational gradient.

It is also possible to adopt the auxiliary variational inference methods (e.g., Agakov & Barber, 2004; Salimans et al., 2015) to solve Problem 1 by treating ξ as a hidden variable. however, in order to frame a tractable joint distribution $p(z, \xi)$, one would need to add additional noise on z, e.g., assume $z = f(\xi;\, \eta) + \mathcal{N}(0, \sigma^2)$ with a careful choice of noise variance σ, and also need to introduce an additional auxiliary network to approximate $q(\xi \mid z)$, which makes the algorithm more complex than ours.

The idea of amortized inference (Gershman & Goodman, 2014) has been recently applied in various domains of probabilistic reasoning, including both amortized variational inference (e.g., Kingma & Welling, 2013; Rezende & Mohamed, 2015) and date-driven designs of Monte Carlo based methods (e.g., Paige & Wood, 2016), to name only a few. Snelson & Ghahramani (2005); Balan et al. (2015) also explored the idea of amortizing or distil MCMC samplers to obtain compact fast posterior representation. Most of these methods uses typical variational inference methods and hence need to use simple q_η to ensure tractability.

There is a large literature on traditional adaptive MCMC methods (e.g., Andrieu & Thoms, 2008; Roberts & Rosenthal, 2009) which can be used to adaptively adjust the proposal distribution of MCMC by exploiting the special theoretical properties of MCMC (e.g., by minimizing the autocorrelation). Our method is simpler, more generic, and works efficiently in practice thanks to the use of gradient-based back-propagation. Finally, connections between stochastic gradient descent and variational inference have been discussed and exploited in Mandt et al. (2016); Maclaurin et al. (2015).

2 STEIN VARIATIONAL GRADIENT DESCENT

Stein variational gradient descent (SVGD) (Liu & Wang, 2016) is a nonparametric variational inference algorithm that iteratively transports a set of particles $\{z_i\}_{i=1}^n$ to approximate the target distribution p by performing a type of functional gradient descent on the KL divergence. We give a quick overview of the SVGD in this section.

Let $p(z)$ be a positive density function on $\mathbb{R}^d$ which we want to approximate with a set of particles $\{z_i\}_{i=1}^n$. SVGD starts with a set of initial particles $\{z_i\}_{i=1}^n$, and updates the particles iteratively by

$$z_i \leftarrow z_i + \epsilon \phi(z_i), \quad \forall i = 1, \ldots, n, \tag{3}$$

where ϵ is a step size, and $\phi \colon \mathbb{R}^d \to \mathbb{R}^d$ is a velocity field which should be chosen to push the particle distribution closer to the target distribution. Assume the current particles are drawn from a distribution q, and let $q_{[\epsilon\phi]}$ be the distribution of the updated particles $z' = z + \epsilon\phi(z)$ when $z \sim q$. The optimal choice of ϕ can be framed as the following optimization problem:

$$\phi^* = \arg\max_{\phi \in \mathcal{F}} \left\{ -\frac{d}{d\epsilon} \mathrm{KL}(q_{[\epsilon\phi]} \, || \, p) \Big|_{\epsilon=0} \right\}, \tag{4}$$

that is, ϕ should yield a maximum decreasing rate on the KL divergence between the particle distribution and the target distribution. Here, $\mathcal{F}$ is a function set that includes the possible velocity fields and is chosen to be the unit ball of a vector-valued reproducing kernel Hilbert space (RKHS) $\mathcal{H} = \mathcal{H}_0 \times \cdots \times \mathcal{H}_0$, where $\mathcal{H}_0$ is a RKHS formed by scalar-valued functions associated with a positive definite kernel $k(z, z')$, that is, $\mathcal{F} = \{\phi \in \mathcal{H} \colon ||\phi||_{\mathcal{H}} \leq 1\}$. This choice of $\mathcal{F}$ allows us to consider velocity fields in infinite dimensional function spaces while still obtaining a closed form solution. Liu & Wang (2016) showed that the objective function in (4) equals a simple linear functional of ϕ:

$$-\frac{d}{d\epsilon} \mathrm{KL}(q_{[\epsilon\phi]} \, || \, p) \big|_{\epsilon=0} = \mathbb{E}_{x\sim q}[\mathcal{T}_p \phi(x)], \tag{5}$$

$$\text{with } \mathcal{T}_p \phi(z) = \nabla_x \log p(z)^\top \phi(z) + \nabla_z^\top \phi(z), \tag{6}$$

where $\mathcal{T}_p$ is a linear operator acting on a velocity field ϕ and returns a scalar-valued function; $\mathcal{T}_p$ is called the Stein operator in connection with Stein's identity which shows that the RHS of (5) equals zero if $p = q$:

$$\mathbb{E}_p[\mathcal{T}_p \phi] = \mathbb{E}_p[\nabla_z \log p^\top \phi + \nabla_z \cdot \phi] = 0. \tag{7}$$

This is a result of integration by parts assuming the values of $p(z)\phi(z)$ vanish on the boundary of the integration domain. Therefore, the optimization in (4) reduces to

$$\mathbb{D}(q||p) \overset{def}{=} \max_{\phi \in \mathcal{H}} \{\mathbb{E}_{z\sim q}[\mathcal{T}_p \phi(z)] \quad s.t. \quad ||\phi||_{\mathcal{H}} \leq 1\}, \tag{8}$$

where $\mathbb{D}(q \, || \, p)$ is the kernelized Stein discrepancy defined in (Liu et al., 2016; Chwialkowski et al., 2016), which equals zero if and only if $p = q$ under proper conditions that ensure the function space $\mathcal{H}$ is rich enough.

Observe that (8) is "simple" in that it is a linear functional optimization on a unit ball of a Hilbert space. Therefore, it is not surprise to derive a closed form solution:

$$\phi^*(\cdot) \propto \mathbb{E}_{z\sim q}[\nabla_z \log p(z) k(z, \cdot) + \nabla_x k(z, \cdot)], \tag{9}$$

where $k(z, z')$ is the positive definite kernel associated with RKHS $\mathcal{H}_0$. See Liu et al. (2016) for the derivation. We call ϕ^* the Stein variational gradient direction since it provides the optimal direction for pushing the particles towards the target distribution p.

In the practical SVGD algorithm, we start with a set of initial particles, calculate its corresponding ϕ^* by replacing the expectation under q with the empirical average of particles, and use it to update the particles:

$$z_i \leftarrow z_i + \epsilon \phi^*(z_i), \qquad \forall i = 1, \ldots, n, \tag{10}$$

$$\phi^*(z_i) = \frac{1}{n} \sum_{j=1}^n [\nabla_{z_j} \log p(z_j) k(z_j, z_i) + \nabla_{z_j} k(z_j, z_i)].$$

The two terms in $\phi^*(z_i)$ play two different roles: the term with the gradient $\nabla_z \log p(z)$ drives the particles toward the high probability regions of $p(z)$, while the term with $\nabla_z k(z, z_i)$ serves as a repulsive force to encourage different particles to be different from each other as shown in Liu & Wang (2016). Overall, this procedure provides diverse points for approximating distribution p when it converges.

It is easy to see from (10) that $\phi^*(z_i)$ reduces to the typical gradient $\nabla_z \log p(z_i)$ when there is only a single particle ($n = 1$) and $\nabla_z k(z, z_i) = 0$ when $z = z_i$, in which case SVGD reduces to the standard gradient ascent for maximizing $\log p(z)$ (i.e., maximum *a posteriori* (MAP)).

Algorithm 1 Amortized SVGD for Problem 1

Set batch size m, step-size scheme $\{\epsilon_t\}$ and kernel $k(z, z')$. Initialize η^0.
for iteration t **do**
  Draw random $\{\xi_i\}_{i=1}^m$, calculate $z_i = f(\eta^t;\ \xi_i)$, and the Stein variational gradient $\phi^*(z_i)$ in (10).
  Update parameter η using either (13), (14) or (15).
end for

Computing the Kernelized Stein Discrepancy By substituting the ϕ^* in (9) into (8), one can show that (Liu et al., 2016; Chwialkowski et al., 2016; Oates et al., 2017)

$$\mathbb{D}(q \mid\mid p)^2 = \mathbb{E}_{z,z' \sim\ q}[\kappa_p(z, z')], \tag{11}$$

where $\kappa_p(z, z')$ is a positive definite kernel obtained by applying Stein operator on $k(z, z')$ twice, as a function of z and z', respectively. It has the following computationally tractable form:

$$\begin{aligned}\kappa_p(z, z') =& \boldsymbol{s}_p(z)^\top k(z, z')\boldsymbol{s}_p(z') + \boldsymbol{s}_p(z)^\top \nabla_{z'} k(z, z') \\ &+ \nabla_z k(z, z')^\top \boldsymbol{s}_p(z') + \nabla_z^\top (\nabla_{z'} k(z, z')),\end{aligned}$$

where $\boldsymbol{s}_p(z) = \nabla_z \log p(z)$. The form of KSD in (11) provides a computationally tractable way for estimating the Stein discrepancy between a set of samples $\{z_i\}$ (e.g., drawn from an unknown q) and a distribution p specified by its score function $\nabla_z \log p(z)$ (which is independent of its normalization constant),

$$\hat{\mathbb{D}}_u^2(\{z_i\} \mid\mid p) = \frac{1}{n(n-1)} \sum_{i \neq j} [\kappa_p(z_i, z_j)], \tag{12}$$

where $\hat{\mathbb{D}}_u^2(q \mid\mid p)$ provides an unbiased estimator (hence called a U-statistic) for $\mathbb{D}^2(q \mid\mid p)$. As a side result of this work, we will discuss the possibility of using KSD as an objective function for wild variational inference in Appendix A.

3 AMORTIZED SVGD: TOWARDS AN AUTOMATIC NEURAL SAMPLER

SVGD and other particle-based methods become inefficient when we need to apply them repeatedly on a large number of different, but similar target distributions for multiple tasks, because they can not leverage the similarity between the different distributions and may require a large memory to restore a large number of particles. This problem can be addressed by training a neural network $f(\xi;\ \eta)$ to output particles that would have been produced by SVGD; this amounts to "amortizing" or compressing the nonparametric SVGD into a parametric network, yielding a solution for wild variational inference in Problem 1 of Section 1.

One straightforward way to achieve this is to run SVGD until convergence and train $f(\xi;\ \eta)$ to fit the resulting SVGD particles (e.g., by using generative adversarial networks (GAN) (Goodfellow et al., 2014)). This, however, requires running many epochs of fully converged SVGD and can be slow in practice. We instead propose an *incremental approach* in which η is iteratively adjusted so that the network outputs $z = f(\xi;\ \eta)$ improves by moving along the Stein variational gradient direction in (10), in order to move towards the target distribution.

Specifically, denote by η^t the parameter estimated at the t-th iteration of our method; each iteration of our method draws a batch of random inputs $\{\xi_i\}_{i=1}^m$ and calculate their corresponding output $z_i = f(\xi_i;\ \eta^t)$ based on η^t, where m is a mini-batch size (e.g., $m = 100$). The Stein variational gradient $\phi^*(z_i)$ in (10) would then ensure that $z_i' = z_i + \epsilon\phi^*(z_i)$ forms a better approximation of the target distribution p. Therefore, we should adjust η to make it output $\{z_i'\}$ instead of $\{z_i\}$, that is, we want to update η by

$$\eta^{t+1} \leftarrow \arg\min_{\eta} \sum_{i=1}^{m} ||f(\xi_i;\ \eta) - z_i'||_2^2, \tag{13}$$

where $z_i' = z_i + \epsilon\phi^*(z_i)$. This process is repeated until convergence, in which case the outputs of network f can no longer be improved by SVGD and hence should form a good approximation of the target p. See Algorithm 1.

If we assume ϵ is very small, then (13) can be approximated by a least square optimization. To see this, note that $f(\xi_i;\ \eta) \approx f(\xi_i;\ \eta^t) + \partial_\eta f(\xi_i;\ \eta^t)(\eta - \eta^t)$ by Taylor expansion. Since $z_i = f(\xi_i;\ \eta^t)$, we have

$$||f(\xi_i;\ \eta) - z_i'||_2^2 \approx ||\partial_\eta f(\xi_i;\ \eta^t)(\eta - \eta^t) - \epsilon\phi^*(z_i)||_2^2.$$

As a result, (13) reduces to a least square optimization:

$$\begin{aligned}&\eta^{t+1} \leftarrow \eta^t - \epsilon\Delta\eta^t, \\ &\Delta\eta^t = \arg\min_{\delta} \sum_{i=1}^{m} ||\partial_\eta f(\xi_i;\ \eta^t)\delta - \phi^*(z_i)||_2^2.\end{aligned} \tag{14}$$

It may be still slow to solve a least square problem at each iteration. We can derive a more computationally efficient approximation by performing only one step of gradient descent of (13) starting at η^t (or equivalently (14) starting at $\delta = 0$), which gives

$$\eta^{t+1} \leftarrow \eta^t + \epsilon \sum_{i=1}^{m} \partial_\eta f(\xi_i;\ \eta^t)\phi^*(z_i). \tag{15}$$

Although update (15) is derived as an approximation of (13) or (14), it is computationally faster and it works effectively in practice; this is because when ϵ is small, one step of gradient update can be sufficiently close to the optimum.

Update (15) has a simple and intuitive interpretation: it can be thought as *a "chain rule" that back-propagates the Stein variational gradient to the network parameter* η. This can be justified by considering the special case when we use only a single particle ($n = 1$) in which case $\phi^*(z_i)$ in (10) reduces to the typical gradient $\nabla_z \log p(z_i)$, and update (15) reduces to the typical gradient ascent for maximizing $\mathbb{E}_\xi[\log p(f(\xi;\ \eta))]$, in which case $f(\xi;\ \eta)$ is trained to maximize $\log p(z)$ (that is, *learning to optimize*), instead of *learning to draw samples from* p for which it is crucial to use the Stein variational gradient $\phi^*(z_i)$ to diversify the outputs to capture the uncertainties in p.

Update (15) also has a close connection with the typical variational inference with the reparameterization trick (Kingma & Welling, 2013). Let $q_\eta(z)$ be the density function of $z = f(\xi;\ \eta)$, $\xi \sim q_0$. Using the reparameterization trick, the gradient of $\mathrm{KL}(q_\eta \mid\mid p)$ w.r.t. η equals

$$\nabla_\eta \mathrm{KL}(q_\eta \mid\mid p) = -\mathbb{E}_{\xi\sim q_0}[\partial_\eta f(\eta;\ \xi) \nabla_z \log(p(z)/q_\eta(z))].$$

With $\{\xi_i\}$ i.i.d. drawn from q_0 and $z_i = f(\xi_i;\ \eta)$, $\forall i$, we can obtain a standard stochastic gradient descent for minimizing the KL divergence:

$$\eta^{t+1} \leftarrow \eta^t + \sum_{i=1}^m \partial_\eta f(\xi_i;\ \eta^t) \tilde{\phi}^*(z_i), \quad \text{where} \quad \tilde{\phi}^*(z_i) = \nabla_z \log p(z_i) - \nabla_z \log q_{\eta^t}(z_i). \tag{16}$$

This is similar to (15), but replaces the Stein gradient $\phi^*(z_i)$ defined in (10) with $\tilde{\phi}^*(z_i)$. However, because $\tilde{\phi}^*(z_i)$ depends on the density q_{η^t}, which is assumed to be intractable in Problem 1, (16) is not directly applicable in our setting. Further insights can be obtained by noting that

$$\begin{aligned} \phi^*(z_i) &\approx \mathbb{E}_{z\sim q_{\eta^t}}[\nabla_z \log p(z) k(z, z_i) + \nabla_z k(z, z_i)] \\ &= \mathbb{E}_{z\sim q_{\eta^t}}[(\nabla_z \log p(z) - \nabla_z \log q_{\eta^t}(z)) k(z, z_i)] \\ &= \mathbb{E}_{z\sim q_{\eta^t}}[\tilde{\phi}^*(z) k(z, z_i)], \end{aligned} \tag{17}$$

where (17) is obtained by using Stein's identity (7). Therefore, $\phi^*(z_i)$ can be treated as a smoothed version of $\tilde{\phi}^*(z_i)$ obtained by convolving it with kernel $k(z, z')$.

4 APPLICATIONS OF AMORTIZED SVGD

With amortized SVGD, we can use expressive inference networks to obtain better approximation and explore new applications where traditional VI methods cannot be applied. In this section, we introduce two different applications of amortized SVGD. One is training variational autoencoders (Kingma & Welling, 2013) with complex, non-Gaussian encoders, and the other is training "smart" MCMC samplers that adaptively improve their own hyperparameters from past experience.

4.1 Amortized SVGD For Variational Autoencoders

Variational autoencoders (VAEs) (Kingma & Welling, 2013) are latent variable models of form $p_\theta(x) = \int_z p_\theta(x|z) p_\theta(z) dz$ where x is an observed variable and z is an un-observed latent variable. Assume the empirical distribution of the observed variable is $\hat{p}(x)$, VAE learns the parameter θ using a variational EM algorithm which approximates the posterior distribution $p_\theta(z|x)$ with a simple encoder $q_\eta(z|x)$, and updates θ and η alternatively by

$$\theta \leftarrow \arg\max_\theta \ \mathbb{E}_{\hat{p}(x) q_\eta(z|x)}\big[\log p_\theta(x,\ z)\big], \tag{18}$$

$$\eta \leftarrow \arg\min_\eta \ \mathbb{E}_{\hat{p}(x)}\big[\mathrm{KL}(q_\eta(z \mid x) \mid\mid p_\theta(z \mid x))\big], \tag{19}$$

which alternates between updating θ by maximizing the joint likelihood (M-step (18)) and approximating the posterior distribution $p_\theta(z|x)$ given fixed θ with variational inference (VI) (E-step (19)). In standard VAE, (18) is performed using standard VI with the reparameterization trick (16), which requires q_η to be tractable. Therefore, $q_\eta(z \mid x)$ is often defined as a Gaussian distribution with mean and diagonal covariance parameterized by neural networks with x as input. This Gaussian assumption potentially limits the quality of the resulting generative models, and more expressive encoders can improve the performance as shown in recent works (e.g, Kingma et al., 2016; Mescheder et al., 2017; Kingma et al., 2016, to name a few).

By applying amortized SVGD to solve the posterior inference problem in (19), we obtain simple algorithms that work with more complex inference networks. Specifically, we assume that $z \sim q_\eta(z|x)$ is generated by $z = f(\xi, x;\ \eta)$, and optimize η using update (13)-(15). See Algorithm 2. In our experiment, we take $z = f(\xi, x;\ \eta)$ to be a deep neural network with binary Bernoulli dropout noise at the input layer of the network which is more effective in approximating multi-modal posteriors than the simple Gaussian encoders.

Further, we propose an *entropy regularized VAE* to improve the standard VAE and get more diverse images by adding an entropy regularization term on the encoder networks. Here, we replace the η-update in (19) with

$$\begin{aligned} \eta &\leftarrow \arg\min_\eta \mathbb{E}_{\hat{p}(x)}[\mathrm{KL}(q_\eta(z \mid x) \mid\mid p_\theta(z \mid x))] - \alpha H(q_\eta) \\ &= \arg\min_\eta \mathbb{E}_{\hat{p}(x)}\big[\mathrm{KL}(q_\eta(z \mid x) \mid\mid p_\theta(z \mid x)^{\frac{1}{1+\alpha}})\big], \end{aligned} \tag{20}$$

where $H(q_\eta) = -\mathbb{E}_{\hat{p}(x) q_\eta(z|x)}[\log q_\eta(z|x)]$ is the (conditional) entropy of $q_\eta(z|x)$, and α is a regularization coefficient. (20) can be solved by applying SVGD on the tempered distribution $p_\theta(z \mid x)^{\frac{1}{1+\alpha}}$, which can be done by

Algorithm 2 Amortized SVGD for training VAE

Set batch size m and kernel $k(z, z')$.
Initialize encoder parameter η and decoder parameter θ.
for iteration t **do**
  Pick input $x^{(i)}$ from the training data.
  Draw $\{\xi_k\}_{k=1}^m \sim q_0$, calculate $z_k^{(i)} = f(x^{(i)}, \xi_k;\ \eta)$, and their Stein variational gradients $\phi^*(z_k^{(i)})$ in (10) or (21) related to gradient $\nabla_z \log p_\theta(z_k^{(i)}|x^{(i)})$.
  Update η using either (13), (14) or (15).
  Update θ with
  $\theta \leftarrow \theta + \frac{1}{m}\sum_{k=1}^m \nabla_\theta \log p_\theta(x^{(i)},\ z_k^{(i)})$.
end for

$z_i \leftarrow z_i + \epsilon\phi^*(z_i)$ with

$$\phi^*(z_i) = \frac{1}{n}\sum_{j=1}^{n}[\nabla_{z_j} \log p_\theta(z_j|x)k(z_j, z_i) + \\ + (1+\alpha)\nabla_{z_j} k(z_j, z_i)], \quad (21)$$

where the temperature parameter $(1+\alpha)$ becomes a weight coefficient of the repulsive force; a high temperature (or equivalent a large entropy regularization) yields a strong repulsive force and push the particles to be further away from each other.

4.2 Training Langevin Samplers

By viewing typical MCMC procedures as a simulator $f(\cdot)$, we can apply amortized SVGD to adaptively improve hyperparameters in MCMC inference. This is useful when we need to perform Bayesian inference on a large number of different, but similar datasets or posteriors, where we can adaptively improve the MCMC sampler for future tasks by leveraging the information of the previous tasks. An example of this, which we consider in this work, is adaptively learning optimal step sizes for Langevin dynamics.

To specify the general framework, we assume that we are interested in drawing samples from a set of distributions

$$\mathcal{Q} = \{p_\vartheta(z) \colon \vartheta \in \Theta\},$$

indexed by parameter ϑ. We are interested in learning a network $f(\xi, p_\vartheta;\ \eta)$ which maps the distribution p_ϑ to stochastic posterior samples. Note that this is a generalization of Problem 1 which focuses on approximating an individual distribution. In practice, p_ϑ could be the posterior distributions of unknown parameters of interest conditioning on different observed data, or models of different individuals in hierarchical models.

In order to learn the network $f(\xi, p_\vartheta;\ \eta)$, we modify Algorithm 1, to perform amortized SVGD on a randomly selected p_ϑ from $\mathcal{Q}$ at each iteration. See Algorithm 3. In this way, we expect that the trained network $f(\xi, p_\vartheta;\ \eta)$ can perform well on similar p_ϑ drawn from the same distribution, but never seen by the training algorithm.

Algorithm 3 Amortized SVGD for Learning to Sample a distribution family $\mathcal{Q} = \{p_\vartheta \colon \vartheta \in \Theta\}$

Goal: Learn parameter η to train $z = f(\xi, p_\vartheta;\ \eta)$ drawing samples from p_ϑ.
Set batch size m, and kernel $k(z, z')$. Initialize η^0.
for iteration t **do**
  Randomly select p_ϑ from $\mathcal{Q}$.
  Draw random seed $\{\xi\}_{i=1}^m \sim q_0$.
  Calculate $z_i = f(\xi_i,\ p_\vartheta;\ \eta)$, and the Stein variational gradient $\phi^*(z_i)$ in (10).
  Update parameter η using either (13), (14) or (15).
end for

A useful perspective is that typical MCMC methods can be viewed as neural networks $f(\xi, p_\vartheta;\ \eta)$ handcrafted by researchers, with nice theoretical properties. We can leverage the structure of existing MCMC to design the architecture of $f(\cdot)$, and use amortized SVGD to adaptively improve its parameters across different tasks.

As an example, Langevin dynamics draws samples from p_ϑ by starting with an initial sample z^0 and performing iterative random updates of form $z^{t+1} \leftarrow f_t(z^t)$ with

$$f_t(z^t) = z^t + \eta^t \odot \nabla_z \log p_\vartheta(z^t) + \sqrt{2\eta^t} \odot \xi^t, \quad (22)$$

which performs gradient ascent with a Gaussian perturbation. Here η^t denotes a vector-valued step size at the t-th iteration and "$\odot$" denotes element-wise product, and ξ^t is a standard Gaussian random vector of the same size as z^t.

We can view T iterations of Langevin dynamics as a T-layer neural network:

$$z^T = f(\xi,\ p_\vartheta;\ \eta) = f_{T-1} \circ \cdots \circ f_0(\xi,\ p_\vartheta;\ \eta), \quad (23)$$

in which the initial samples and the Gaussian noise form the random seeds of the network, that is, $\xi = \{\xi^t\}_{t=0}^{T-1} \cup \{z^0\}$, and the step sizes $\eta = \{\eta^t\}_{t=0}^{T-1}$ form the parameters which we can estimate using Algorithm 3. In cases when it is difficult to calculate $\nabla_z \log p_\vartheta$ exactly, such as the case of Bayesian inference with big datasets, we can use stochastic gradient Langevin dynamics (Welling & Teh, 2011) to approximate $\nabla_z \log p_\vartheta$ with subsampling, which introduces another source of randomness. This, however, does not influence the application of Algorithm 3, since our method does not need to know the structure of the random seed distribution.

In practice, a large value of T would result in a deep network and cause a vanishing gradient problem. We address this problem by partitioning the T layers into small blocks of size 5 or 10, and evaluate the gradient of the parameters in each block by back-propagating the Stein variational gradient from the output of its own block.

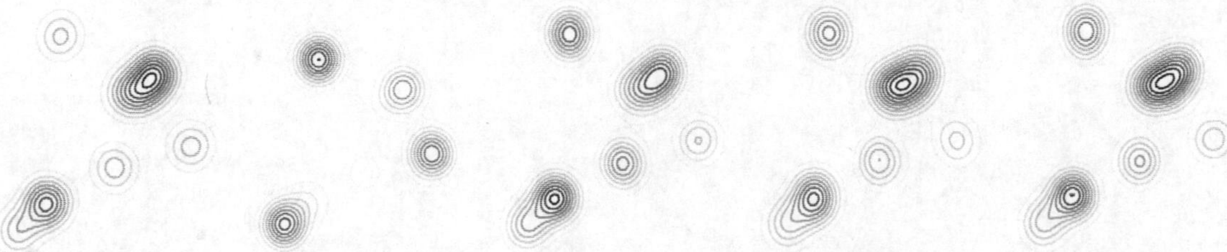

(a) Test Distribution (truth) (b) Power Decay (15 steps) (c) Power Decay (1,000 steps) (d) Amortized SVGD (5 steps) (e) Amortized SVGD (15 steps)

Figure 2: Learning to sample from GMM. We train Langevin samplers using amortized SVGD on a set of randomly generated GMMs, and evaluate the samplers on a new GMM shown in (a) generated randomly in the same way as the training GMMs, but unavailable in the training time. (d)-(e): The Langevin sampler with step size trained by amortized SVGD obtains close approximation with $T = 5$ or 15 steps. (b)-(c): The typical power decay step size requires more Langevin iterations (and hence computation cost) to converge.

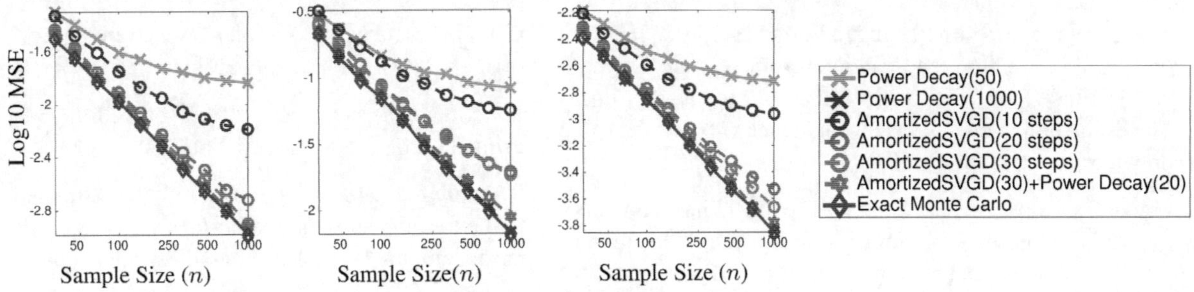

(a) $\mathbb{E}(x)$ (b) $\mathbb{E}(x^2)$ (c) $\mathbb{E}(\cos(wx + b))$

Figure 3: Result on Gaussian-Bernoulli RBM. (a)-(c) show the mean square errors for estimating expectation $\mathbb{E}_p(h(x))$ using Langevin samplers with different numbers T of steps, with either power decay step sizes or adaptive step size trained by amortized SVD. We take $h(x) = x^j, (x^j)^2$ and $\cos(wx^j + b)$ where x^j denotes the j-th coordinate of vector x and $w \sim \mathcal{N}(0, 1)$ and $b \sim \text{Uniform}(0, 2\pi)$ and report the average MSE across all dimensions $j = 1, \ldots, d$, over 20 random trials.

5 EXPERIMENTS

We apply amortized SVGD to the two different applications mentioned in section 4, and demonstrate that our method can train expressive inference networks to draw samples from intractable posterior distributions. For all our experiments, we use the standard RBF kernel $k(z, z') = \exp(-\frac{1}{h}||z - z'||_2^2)$, and take the bandwidth to be $h = \text{med}^2/\log n$, where med is the median of the pairwise distance between the current points $\{z_i\}_{i=1}^n$. We use update (15) in Algorithm 1, which solves Eq (13)-Eq (14) using a single gradient step. We find that using more gradient steps does not change the final results significantly, but may potentially increase the convergence speed (see Appendix B).

5.1 Training Langevin Samplers

In this section, we use amortized SVGD (Algorithm 3) to learn the step size parameters in the Langevin sampler in (23). We test a number of distribution families, including Gaussian Mixture, Gaussian Bernoulli RBM, Bayesian logistic regression and Bayesian neural networks. In all the cases, we train the sampler with a set of "training distributions" and evaluate the sampler on "test distributions" that are not seen by the algorithm during training. We compare our method to the typical Langevin sampler with power decay step size, selected to be the best from $\eta^t = 10^a/(t+b)^\gamma$ where $\gamma = 0.55$, $a \in \{-6, ..., 2\}$, $b \in \{0, ..., 9\}$.

Gaussian Mixture We first train the Langevin samplers to learn to sample from simple Gaussian mixtures. We consider a family of Gaussian Mixtures $q_\vartheta(z) = \frac{1}{10}\sum_{i=1}^{10} \mathcal{N}(z; \vartheta_i, 0.1^2)$, where ϑ is the mean parameter.

We train the sampler by drawing random elements of ϑ from $\text{Uniform}(-1, 1)$ at each iteration of Algorithm 3, and evaluate the quality of the samplers on new values of ϑ drawn from the same distribution, but not seen during training. In Figure 2, we find that the sampler trained by amortized SVGD obtains good approximation with $T = 5$ or 15 steps of Langevin updates (Figure 2(d)-(e)). In comparison, the typical Langevin sampler with the best power decay step size performs much worse (Figure 2(b)).

Restricted Boltzmann Machine (RBM) We test our method on Gaussian-Bernoulli RBM which is high dimensional and multi-modal. Gaussian-Bernoulli RBM is a hidden variable model consisting of a continuous observable variable $z \in \mathbb{R}^d$ and a binary hidden variable $h \in \{\pm 1\}^\ell$ with joint probability $p_\vartheta(z, h) \propto \exp(z^\top Bh + b^\top z + c^\top h - \frac{1}{2}||z||_2^2)$, where the parameters include $\vartheta = \{B, b, c\}$. We obtain the marginal distribution of $p_\vartheta(z)$ by summing over h: $p_\vartheta(z) \propto \exp\left[b^\top z - \frac{1}{2}||z||_2^2 + \sigma(B^\top z + c)\right]$, where $\sigma(h) = \sum_{i=1}^\ell \log(\exp(h_i) + \exp(-h_i))$. In our exper-

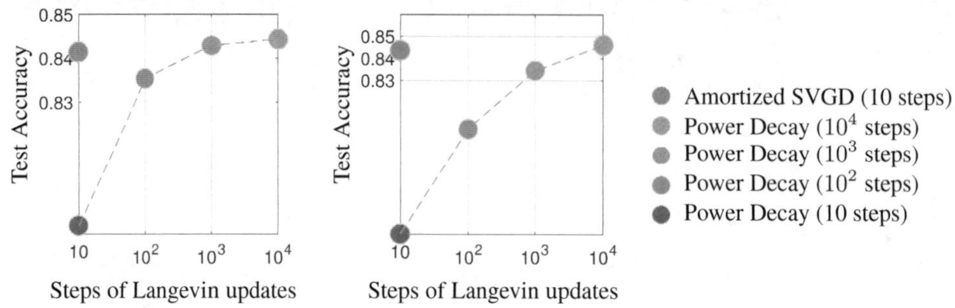

(a) Bayesian logistic regression (b) Bayesian neural networks

Figure 4: By training the step size using amortized SVGD on dataset a9a, we obtain good performance "on" datasets a1a-a8a using Langevin sampler with only $T = 10$ steps of Langevin updates.

iments, we take $\ell = 10$ hidden variables and $d = 100$ observable variables, and randomly draw b and c from $\mathcal{N}(0, I)$ and B uniformly from $\{\pm 0.1\}$ in the training time. The evaluation is on a new set of parameters $\vartheta = \{B, b, c\}$ drawn from the same distribution.

Figure 3 shows the result when we use the trained samplers to estimate integral quantities of form $\mathbb{E}_{p_\vartheta}[h]$ with different testing functions h. The plots show the MSE for estimating $\mathbb{E}_{p_\vartheta}[h]$ using $\sum_i h(z_i)/n$ with z_i generated from the trained sampler $z_i = f(\xi_i, p_\vartheta;\ \eta)$. Here the sample size n is the number of i.i.d. samples generated from the trained sampler in the testing time. In the case of typical, non-adaptive Langevin samplers, it is the number of Langevin Markov chains that we run in parallel. In Figure 3 (a)-(c), we generally find that amortized SVGD allows us to train high quality Langevin samplers with a small number T of Langevin update steps. We observe that we can always further refine the result of our trained samplers using additional typical MCMC steps. For example, in Figure 3, we find that when using 20 steps of typical Langevin dynamics (with a power decay step size) to refine the output of the $T = 30$ layer Langevin sampler trained by amortized SVGD achieves results close to the exact Monte Carlo.

Bayesian Classification We test our method on Bayesian Logistic Regression and Bayesian neural networks for binary classification on real world datasets. In this case, the distribution of interest has a form of $p_\vartheta(z) = p(z|D)$, where z is the network weights in logistic regression and neural networks, and D is the dataset for binary classification, which we view as the parameter ϑ, that is, different dataset D yields different posterior $p(z|D)$, and we are interested in training the Langevin sampler on a set of available datasets, and hope it performs well on future datasets that have similar structures. This setting can be useful, for example, in the streaming setting where we use existing datasets to adaptively improve the Langevin sampler. In our experiment, we take nine similar datasets (a1a-a9) from the libsvm repository[1]; we train our Langevin sampler on a9a, and evaluate the sampler on the remaining 8 datasets (a1a-a8a). Our training and evaluation steps are as follows:

1. Estimate the step sizes $\{\eta^t\}_{t=0}^{T-1}$ of the Langevin sampler using amortized SVGD based on dataset a9a.

2. Apply the Langevin sampler with the estimated step size to the training subsets of aka, $k = 1, \ldots, 8$, to obtain posterior samples $\{z_i^k\}$ of the classification weights.

3. Calculate the test likelihood of $\{z_i^k\}$ on the testing subsets of aka, $k = 1, \ldots, 8$. Report the averaged testing likelihood averaged on the 8 datasets in Figure 4.

Because each dataset is relatively large, we use the stochastic gradient approximation as suggested by Welling & Teh (2011) (with a minibatch size of 100) in Langevin samplers. We find that the $T = 10$ Langevin samplers trained by amortized SVGD on a9a is comparable with the $T = 10^3$ Langevin sampler with the best power decay step size.

5.2 Training VAE With Amortized SVGD

We compare the entropy regularized VAE trained with amortized SVGD (denoted by *ESteinVAE*), which is Algorithm 2 with update (21), with the standard VAE and entropy regularized standard VAE (denoted by *EVAE*) on the dynamically binarized MNIST dataset (Burda et al., 2015). We tested the following settings:

1. A standard VAE (VAE-f) with a fully connected encoder consisting of one hidden layer with 400 hidden units, and a Gaussian output hidden variable with diagonal covariance.

2. A standard convolutional Gaussian VAE (VAE-CNN) with a convolutional encoder consisting of 2 convolution layers with 5×5 filters, stride 2 and $[16, 32]$ features maps, followed by a fully connected layer with 512 hidden units.

3. A convolutional Gaussian entropy regularized (EVAE-CNN) with the same encoder and decoder structures as the standard convolutional VAE (VAE-CNN).

4. Entropy regularized VAEs trained by our amortized SVGD in Algorithm 2, with the same encoder architecture as VAE-f and VAE-CNN, respectively, but removing

[1] https://www.csie.ntu.edu.tw/~cjlin/libsvmtools/datasets/

Table 1: Negative log-likelihood on binarized mnist test dataset.

Model	NLL/nats	ESS
VAE-f	90.32	84.11
ESteinVAE-f	88.85	83.49
VAE-CNN	84.68	85.50
EVAE-CNN	84.43	84.91
ESteinVAE-CNN	84.31	86.57

Table 2: Quantitative imputation experiment based on 2,000 true images and 500 reconstructed images per true image.

Model	Accuracy	Entropy
ESteinVAE-CNN	0.84	0.501
EVAE-CNN	0.82	0.382
VAE-CNN	0.83	0.340

the Gaussian noise on the top layer and adding a multiplicative Bernoulli noise with a dropout rate of 0.3 to the each layer of the encoder. These two cases are denoted by ESteinVAE-f, and ESteinVAE-CNN, respectively.

In all these cases, we use $\dim(z) = 32$ latent variables and the decoders have symmetric architectures as the encoders in all models. Adam is used with a learning rate tuned on the training images. For each training iteration, a batch of 128 images is used, and for each image we draw a batch of $m = 5$ samples to apply amortized SVGD.

Marginal likelihood Table 1 reports the test log-likelihood of all the methods estimated using Hamiltonian annealed importance sampling (HAIS) (Wu et al., 2016) with 100 independent AIS chains and 10,000 intermediate transitions, averaged on 5000 test images. We find that ESteinVAE-f significantly outperforms VAE-f, and ESteinVAE-CNN slightly outperforms VAE-CNN and EVAE-CNN. Table 1 also reports the effective sample size (ESS) of the HAIS estimates. The fact that the effective sample sizes of all the methods are close suggests that accuracy of the different NLL estimates are comparable.

Missing data imputation We demonstrate that ESteinVAE is able to learn multi-modal latent representation with the binary dropout noise. We consider missing data imputation with pixel missing in a square sub-regions of the image (the second column of Figure 5). We use a simple method to reconstruct image by applying one step of encode-decode operation starting from uniform noise $\text{Uniform}(0, 1)$. Specifically, let $x = [x^v, x^m]$ where x^v and x^m denotes the visible and missing parts, respectively. Our imputation procedure consists of the following steps:

1. Draw x^c from $\text{Uniform}(0, 1)$;
2. Draw $z \sim q_\phi(z|x^c,\ x^v)$;
3. Draw $x \sim p(x|z)$.

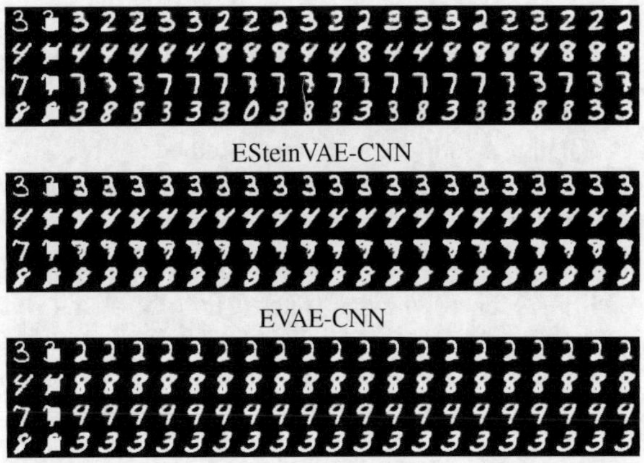

ESteinVAE-CNN

EVAE-CNN

VAE-CNN

Figure 5: Imputation results from benchmark VAE-CNN, EVAE and ESteinVAE-CNN. The first column shows the original image. Col. 2 shows the missing image. The remaining columns show imputations for 20 reconstructed samples.

Each column (starting from the third column) of Figure 5 shows an independent run of this procedure, where we can see that ESteinVAE-CNN is able to generate diverse construction when ambiguity exists, while the EVAE-CNN and VAE-CNN tend to be trapped in a local mode. This suggests that the diagonal variance of the latent variables in the Gaussian encoder of VAE-CNN tends to be small, underestimating the posterior uncertain, while ESteinVAE can capture the multi-modal posterior due to the dropout noise.

Table 2 is the quantitative result of the imputation experiment, in which the "accuracy" column denotes the number of original images whose digit is in its reconstructed images. and the "entropy" column denotes the entropy of the probability of the reconstructed images belonging to different digit classes. We can see that EsteinVAE obtains much more diverse images and slightly more accurate reconstructed images.

6 CONCLUSION

We propose a new method to train neural samplers for given distributions, together with various applications to learning to draw samples using neural samplers. Future directions include exploring more efficient neural architectures and theoretical understanding of our method.

Acknowledgments
This work is supported in part by NSF CRII 1565796. We thank Yingzhen Li from University of Cambridge for her valuable comments and feedbacks.

References

Agakov, Felix V and Barber, David. An auxiliary variational method. In *International Conference on Neural Information Processing*, pp. 561–566. Springer, 2004.

Andrieu, Christophe and Thoms, Johannes. A tutorial on adaptive mcmc. *Statistics and Computing*, 18(4):343–373, 2008.

Balan, Anoop Korattikara, Rathod, Vivek, Murphy, Kevin P, and Welling, Max. Bayesian dark knowledge. In *Advances in Neural Information Processing Systems*, pp. 3438–3446, 2015.

Briol, François-Xavier, Oates, Chris, Girolami, Mark, Osborne, Michael A, Sejdinovic, Dino, et al. Probabilistic integration: A role for statisticians in numerical analysis? *arXiv preprint http://arxiv.org/abs/1512.00933*, 2015.

Burda, Yuri, Grosse, Roger, and Salakhutdinov, Ruslan. Importance weighted autoencoders. *arXiv preprint arXiv:1509.00519*, 2015.

Chwialkowski, Kacper, Strathmann, Heiko, and Gretton, Arthur. A kernel test of goodness of fit. In *Proceedings of the International Conference on Machine Learning (ICML)*, 2016.

Delyon, Bernard and Portier, François. Integral approximation by kernel smoothing. *arXiv preprint arXiv:1409.0733*, 2014.

Gershman, Samuel J and Goodman, Noah D. Amortized inference in probabilistic reasoning. In *Proceedings of the 36th Annual Conference of the Cognitive Science Society*, 2014.

Goodfellow, Ian, Pouget-Abadie, Jean, Mirza, Mehdi, Xu, Bing, Warde-Farley, David, Ozair, Sherjil, Courville, Aaron, and Bengio, Yoshua. Generative adversarial nets. In *Advances in Neural Information Processing Systems*, pp. 2672–2680, 2014.

Henmi, Masayuki, Yoshida, Ryo, and Eguchi, Shinto. Importance sampling via the estimated sampler. *Biometrika*, 94(4):985–991, 2007.

Hoffman, Matthew D, Blei, David M, Wang, Chong, and Paisley, John. Stochastic variational inference. *JMLR*, 2013.

Kingma, Diederik P and Welling, Max. Auto-encoding variational Bayes. In *Proceedings of the International Conference on Learning Representations (ICLR)*, 2013.

Kingma, Diederik P, Salimans, Tim, and Welling, Max. Improving variational inference with inverse autoregressive flow. *arXiv preprint arXiv:1606.04934*, 2016.

Li, Yingzhen, Turner, Richard E, and Liu, Qiang. Approximate inference with amortised mcmc. *arXiv preprint arXiv:1702.08343*, 2017.

Liu, Qiang and Lee, Jason D. Black-box importance sampling. *https://arxiv.org/abs/1610.05247*, 2016.

Liu, Qiang and Wang, Dilin. Stein variational gradient descent: A general purpose bayesian inference algorithm. *arXiv preprint arXiv:1608.04471*, 2016.

Liu, Qiang, Lee, Jason D, and Jordan, Michael I. A kernelized Stein discrepancy for goodness-of-fit tests. In *Proceedings of the International Conference on Machine Learning (ICML)*, 2016.

Maclaurin, Dougal, Duvenaud, David, and Adams, Ryan P. Early stopping is nonparametric variational inference. *arXiv preprint arXiv:1504.01344*, 2015.

Mandt, Stephan, Hoffman, Matthew D, and Blei, David M. A variational analysis of stochastic gradient algorithms. *arXiv preprint arXiv:1602.02666*, 2016.

Mescheder, Lars, Nowozin, Sebastian, and Geiger, Andreas. Adversarial variational bayes: Unifying variational autoencoders and generative adversarial networks. *arXiv preprint arXiv:1701.04722*, 2017.

Mohamed, Shakir and Lakshminarayanan, Balaji. Learning in implicit generative models. *arXiv preprint arXiv:1610.03483*, 2016.

Oates, Chris J, Girolami, Mark, and Chopin, Nicolas. Control functionals for Monte Carlo integration. *Journal of the Royal Statistical Society, Series B*, 2017.

O'Hagan, Anthony. Monte Carlo is fundamentally unsound. *Journal of the Royal Statistical Society. Series D (The Statistician)*, 36(2/3):247–249, 1987.

O'Hagan, Anthony. Bayes–hermite quadrature. *Journal of statistical planning and inference*, 29(3):245–260, 1991.

Paige, Brooks and Wood, Frank. Inference networks for sequential monte carlo in graphical models. *arXiv preprint arXiv:1602.06701*, 2016.

Ranganath, R., Altosaar, J., Tran, D., and Blei, D.M. Operator variational inference. 2016.

Rezende, Danilo Jimenez and Mohamed, Shakir. Variational inference with normalizing flows. In *Proceedings of the International Conference on Machine Learning (ICML)*, 2015.

Roberts, Gareth O and Rosenthal, Jeffrey S. Examples of adaptive mcmc. *Journal of Computational and Graphical Statistics*, 18(2):349–367, 2009.

Salimans, Tim et al. Markov chain monte carlo and variational inference: Bridging the gap. In *International Conference on Machine Learning*, 2015.

Snelson, Edward and Ghahramani, Zoubin. Compact approximations to bayesian predictive distributions. In *Proceedings of the 22nd international conference on Machine learning*, pp. 840–847. ACM, 2005.

Welling, Max and Teh, Yee W. Bayesian learning via stochastic gradient Langevin dynamics. In *Proceedings of the International Conference on Machine Learning (ICML)*, 2011.

Wu, Yuhuai, Burda, Yuri, Salakhutdinov, Ruslan, and Grosse, Roger. On the quantitative analysis of decoder-based generative models. *arXiv preprint arXiv:1611.04273*, 2016.

A KSD Variational Inference

Kernelized Stein discrepancy (KSD) provides a discrepancy measure between distributions and can be in principle used as a variational objective function in replace of KL divergence. In fact, thanks to the special form of KSD ((11)-(12)), one can derive a standard stochastic gradient descent for minimizing KSD without needing to estimate $q_\eta(z)$ explicitly, which provides a conceptually simple wild variational inference algorithm. Although this work mainly focuses on amortized SVGD which we find to be easier to implement and tend to perform superior to KSD variational inference in practice (see Figure 6), we think the KSD approach is of theoretical interest and hence give a brief discussion here.

Specifically, take q_η to be the density of the random output $z = f(\xi;\ \eta)$ when $\xi \sim q_0$, and we want to find η to minimize $\mathbb{D}(q_\eta \mid\mid p)$. Assuming $\{\xi_i\}$ is i.i.d. drawn from q_0, we can approximate $\mathbb{D}^2(q_\eta \mid\mid p)$ unbiasedly using the U-statistics in (12), and derive a standard gradient descent

$$\eta \leftarrow \eta - \epsilon \frac{2}{n(n-1)} \sum_{i \neq j} \partial_\eta f(\xi_i;\ \eta)\, \nabla_{z_i} \kappa_p(z_i, z_j), \quad (24)$$

where $z_i = f(\xi_i;\ \eta)$. This enables a wild variational inference method based on directly minimizing η with standard (stochastic) gradient descent. We call this algorithm *amortized KSD*. Note that (24) is similar to (15) in form, but replaces $\phi^*(z_i)$ with

$$\bar{\phi}^*(z_i) \overset{def}{=} -2 \sum_{j:\ i \neq j} \nabla_{z_i} \kappa_p(z_i, z_j)/(n(n-1)).$$

Here $\bar{\phi}^*$ depends on the second order derivative of $\log p$ because $\kappa_p(z, z')$ depends on $\nabla \log p$, which makes it more difficult to implement amortized KSD than amortized SVGD.

Intuitively, minimizing KSD can be viewed as seeking a stationary point of KL divergence under SVGD updates. To see this, recall that $q_{[\epsilon\phi]}$ denotes the density of $z' = z + \epsilon\phi(z)$ when $z \sim q$. From (4), we have for small ϵ,

$$\mathbb{D}^2(q \mid\mid p) \approx \frac{1}{\epsilon} \max_{\phi \in \mathcal{F}} \big\{ \mathrm{KL}(q \mid\mid p) - \mathrm{KL}(q_{[\epsilon\phi]} \mid\mid p) \big\}.$$

That is, KSD measures the maximum degree of decrease in the KL divergence when we update the particles along the optimal SVGD perturbation direction ϕ^*. If $q = p$, then the decrease of the KL divergence equals zero and $\mathbb{D}^2(q \mid\mid p)$ equals zero. In fact, KSD can be explicitly represented as the magnitude of the functional gradient of the KL divergence w.r.t. ϕ in RKHS (Liu & Wang, 2016),

$$\mathbb{D}(q \mid\mid p) = \Big|\Big| \nabla_\phi F(0) \Big|\Big|_{\mathcal{H}^d}, \qquad F(\phi) \overset{def}{=} \mathrm{KL}(q_{[\epsilon\phi]} \mid\mid p),$$

where $\nabla_\phi F(\phi)$ denotes the functional gradient of the function $F(\phi)$ w.r.t. ϕ defined in RKHS $\mathcal{H}^d$, and $\nabla_\phi F(\phi)$ is also an element in $\mathcal{H}^d$. Therefore, in contrast to amortized SVGD which attends to minimize the KL objective $F(\phi)$, KSD variational inference minimizes the gradient magnitude $||\nabla_\phi F(0)||_{\mathcal{H}^d}$ of KL divergence.

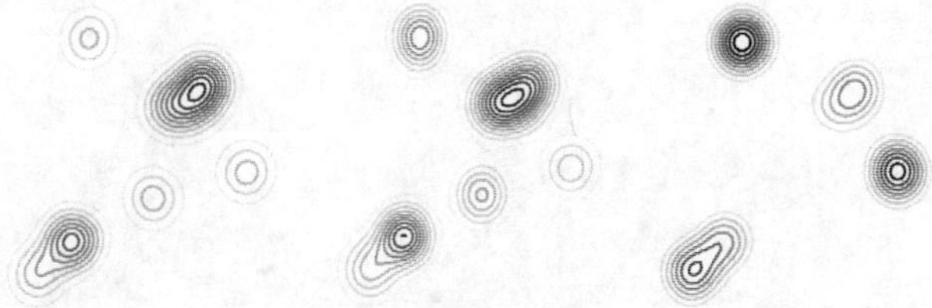

(a) Test Distribution (truth) (b) Amortized SVGD (15 steps) (c) Amortized KSD (15 steps)

Figure 6: Learning to sample from GMM. The Langevin sampler with step size trained by amortized SVGD (b) obtains close approximation with $T = 15$ is close to the true test distribution (a) while amortized KSD (c) which we use equation (24) to perform does not work as well as amortized SVGD.

This idea is closely related to the operator variational inference (Ranganath et al., 2016), which directly minimizes the variational form of Stein discrepancy in (4) and (8) with $\mathcal{F}$ replaced by sets of parametric neural networks. Specifically, Ranganath et al. (2016) assumes $\mathcal{F}$ consists of a neural network $\phi_\tau(z)$ with parameter τ, and find τ jointly with η by solving a min-max game:

$$\min_\eta \max_\tau \mathbb{E}_{z \sim q_\eta}[\mathcal{T}_p \phi_\tau(z)].$$

This yields a more challenging computation problem, although it is possible that the neural networks provide stronger discrimination than RKHS in practice. The main advantage of the KSD based approach is that it leverages the closed form solution in RKHS, yields a simpler optimization formulation based on standard gradient descent.

Figure 6 shows results of Langevin samplers trained by amortized SVGD and amortized KSD, respectively, for learning simple Gaussian mixtures under the same setting as that in Section 5.1. We find that amortized KSD tends to perform worse (Figure 6(c)) than amortized SVGD (Figure 6(b)); given that it is also less straightforward to implement amortized KSD (for requiring calculating $\nabla_z \kappa_p(z, z')$ in (24)), we did not test it in our other experiments.

B Solving the Projection Step Using Different Numbers Gradient Steps

Amortized SVGD requires us to solve the projection step using either (13) or (14) at each iteration. In practice, we approximately solve it using only one step of gradient descent starting from the old values of η for the sake of computational efficiency.

In order to study the trade-off of accuracy and computational cost here, we plot in Figure 7 the results when we

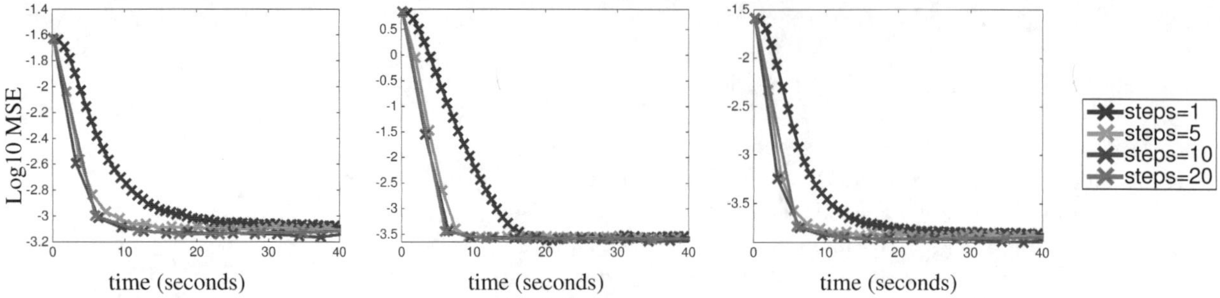

(a) $\mathbb{E}(x)$ (b) $\mathbb{E}(x^2)$ (c) $\mathbb{E}(\cos(wx + b))$

Figure 7: Results when using different numbers of gradient decent steps for solving (14). The setting is the same as that in Figure 2, but we conduct experiments using 1, 5, 10, 20 gradient steps when solving (14), and show their corresponding training time in the x-axis, and their mean square error for estimating $\mathbb{E}_p h$ (for the "testing" distributions) in the y-axis. The Langevin samplers we used have $T = 10$ layers (Langevin update steps). The results are evaluated by drawing 1,000 samples from the trained samplers at different iterations of SVGD. The dimension of the Gaussian Mixtures is $d = 50$.

VAE-CNN EVAE-CNN ESteinVAE-CNN

Figure 8: Images generated by VAE-CNN, EVAE-CNN, and ESteinVAE-CNN

solve Eq (14) using different numbers of gradient descent steps (the result is almost identical when we solve Eq (13) instead). We can see that when using more gradient steps, although the training time per iteration increases, the overall convergence speed may still improve, because it may take less iterations to converge. Figure 7 seems to suggest that using 5, 10, 20 steps gives better convergence than using a single step, but this may vary in different cases. We suggest to search for the best gradient step if the convergence speed is a primary concern. On the other hand, the number of gradient steps seems to have minor influence on the final result at the convergence as shown in Figure 7.

C Images Generated by Different VAEs

Figure 8 shows the images generated by the standard VAE-CNN, the entropy regularized VAE-CNN and ESteinVAE-CNN. We can see that both EVAE-CNN and ESteinVAE-CNN can generate images of good quality.

A Tractable Probabilistic Model for Subset Selection

Yujia Shen and **Arthur Choi** and **Adnan Darwiche**
Computer Science Department
University of California
Los Angeles, CA 90095
{yujias,aychoi,darwiche}@cs.ucla.edu

Abstract

Subset selection tasks, such as top-k ranking, induce datasets where examples have cardinalities that are known a priori. In this paper, we propose a tractable probabilistic model for subset selection and show how it can be learned from data. Our proposed model is interpretable and subsumes a previously introduced model based on logistic regression. We show how the parameters of our model can be estimated in closed form given complete data, and propose an algorithm for learning its structure in an interpretable space. We highlight the intuitive structures that we learn via case studies. We finally show how our proposed model can be viewed as an instance of the recently proposed Probabilistic Sentential Decision Diagram.

1 INTRODUCTION

We consider in this paper the problem of selecting k items from among a set of n alternatives. This *subset selection* problem appears in a number of domains, including resource allocation (what resources shall I allocate?), preference learning (which items do I prefer?), human computation (which labelers should I recruit for my task?), and sports (which players shall play the next game?). In these subset selection tasks, a dataset consists of examples in which a fixed number (k) of variables is set to true from among a total of n variables representing choices. Given such a dataset, the goal is to learn a generative probabilistic model that can accurately represent the underlying processes that govern these selections.

Commonly used representations such as Bayesian and Markov networks are not well-suited for learning from this type of data. In general, the underlying cardinality constraints would lead to fully-connected (and hence intractable) structures—hence more specialized representations are needed to model such subset selection tasks. Recently, a new type of probabilistic model was proposed, called the n-choose-k model (Swersky, Tarlow, Adams, Zemel, & Frey, 2012), that can take into account datasets whose examples have a known cardinality. The proposal includes a view on the popular logistic regression model as a mixture of n-choose-k models (with a component for each k from 0 to n). Both inference and learning are tractable in the n-choose-k model.

In this paper, we propose a more expressive model for subset selection processes, called the *recursive n-choose-k model,* which we derived from a more general tractable representation called the Probabilistic Sentential Decision Diagram (PSDD) (Kisa, Van den Broeck, Choi, & Darwiche, 2014). Our proposed model is *tractable* as it can accommodate a variety of probabilistic queries in polynomial time. It is also *highly interpretable* as its parameters have precise meanings and its underlying structure explicates a generative process for the data. This is in contrast to similar tractable representations such as Arithmetic Circuits (ACs) (Lowd & Domingos, 2008; Lowd & Rooshenas, 2013; Shen, Choi, & Darwiche, 2016; Bekker, Davis, Choi, Darwiche, & Van den Broeck, 2015) and their Sum-Product Networks (SPNs) variant (Poon & Domingos, 2011; Gens & Domingos, 2012; Dennis & Ventura, 2015). We propose a simplified closed-form parameter estimation algorithm for our recursive n-choose-k model, as well as a simple but effective structure learning algorithm. Empirically, we show how our recursive n-choose-k model is more expressive and can provide a better fit for datasets with known cardinalities than previously proposed models for this task.

This paper is organized as follows. In Section 2, we review the subset selection problem and a previously proposed model. In Section 3, we introduce our recursive n-choose-k model. In Section 4, we present the corresponding parameter and structure learning algorithms. In Section 5, we evaluate our model empirically, and present some case studies. In Section 6, we show how the proposed n-choose-k model corresponds to a PSDD for n-choose-k constraints. Section 7 closes with some concluding remarks. Proofs and additional experiments are provided in the supplementary appendix.

2 n-CHOOSE-k MODELS

As a running example, consider the subset selection problem that computer science (CS) students regularly face: selecting k out of n courses to take in a quarter. For simplicity, say that students select three out of the following six courses:

learning (ML)	computability (CP)	linear algebra (LA)
logic (LG)	complexity (CX)	calculus (CL)

By column, we have two AI classes, two CS theory classes, and two math classes.

Let us now consider a dataset over students and the courses that they select. We have six variables $(\mathtt{ML}, \mathtt{LG}, \mathtt{CP}, \mathtt{CX}, \mathtt{LA}, \mathtt{CL})$ representing the classes that a student can select, where $\mathtt{ML}=1$ means the student selected machine learning, whereas $\mathtt{ML}=0$ means they did not. Our dataset consists of examples such as:

$$\mathtt{ML}=0, \mathtt{LG}=1, \mathtt{CP}=1, \mathtt{CX}=1, \mathtt{LA}=0, \mathtt{CL}=0$$
$$\mathtt{ML}=1, \mathtt{LG}=1, \mathtt{CP}=0, \mathtt{CX}=0, \mathtt{LA}=1, \mathtt{CL}=0$$
$$\mathtt{ML}=1, \mathtt{LG}=0, \mathtt{CP}=0, \mathtt{CX}=1, \mathtt{LA}=0, \mathtt{CL}=1.$$

Since students must select three out of six classes, each example in the dataset has exactly three positive entries, and thus three negative entries as well. We refer to such a dataset as an *n-choose-k* dataset: each example has exactly k out of n variables appearing positively, where k is called the example *cardinality*. A CS department with student enrollment data of this type may want to analyze this data and reason about the courses that students choose to take.

In this paper, we assume that the cardinality k is known a priori. For example, in preference learning, we may be provided with data where users have selected their top-10 favorite movies, in which case exactly 10 variables appear positively, and the rest appear negatively.

(Swersky et al., 2012) proposed a probabilistic model, called the *n-choose-k* model, which assumes a prior over k. A simpler form is obtained when k is fixed, leading to the following distribution over a set of n variables $\mathbf{X}$:

$$Pr_k(\mathbf{x}; \boldsymbol{\theta}) = \frac{1}{Z_k(\boldsymbol{\theta})} \prod_{X \in \mathbf{X}} \exp\{\theta_X \cdot \lambda_X\} \qquad (1)$$

for instantiations $\mathbf{x}$ with cardinality k; $Pr(\mathbf{x}) = 0$ otherwise. First, $\boldsymbol{\theta} = (\ldots, \theta_X, \ldots)$ is a vector of n parameters, one parameter θ_X for each variable $X \in \mathbf{X}$. Next, we have a vector $(\ldots, \lambda_X, \ldots)$ of n indicators, one indicator λ_X for each variable $X \in \mathbf{X}$, where λ_X is 1 if $\mathbf{x}$ sets X positively and 0 otherwise. Finally, $Z_k(\boldsymbol{\theta}) = \sum_{\mathbf{x}:\mathsf{Card}(\mathbf{x})=k} \prod_{X \in \mathbf{X}} \exp\{\theta_X \cdot \lambda_X\}$ is the normalizing constant, where $\mathsf{Card}(\mathbf{x})$ is the cardinality of $\mathbf{x}$. When we take a mixture of these models, for k from 0 to n, we obtain the class conditional distribution of the logistic regression model (Swersky et al., 2012):

$$Pr(\mathbf{x}; \boldsymbol{\theta}) = \frac{1}{Z(\boldsymbol{\theta})} \prod_{X \in \mathbf{X}} \exp\{\theta_X \cdot \lambda_X\}$$

for all instantiations $\mathbf{x}$ (of any cardinality), where $Z(\boldsymbol{\theta}) = \prod_{X \in \mathbf{X}} (1 + e^{\theta_X})$. Hence, we refer to the model of Equation 1 as the *logistic n-choose-k* model.

Example 1. In our course selection problem, every course X has a parameter θ_X, where a larger parameter value corresponds to a higher course popularity. For example, the parameters $(\theta_{\mathtt{ML}}, \theta_{\mathtt{LG}}, \theta_{\mathtt{CP}}, \theta_{\mathtt{CX}}, \theta_{\mathtt{LA}}, \theta_{\mathtt{CL}}) = (3, 2, 1, -1, -2, -3)$ suggest that ML is the most popular course. The probability of a student selecting machine learning (ML), logic (LG) and computability (CP) is then

$$Pr(\mathtt{ML}=1, \mathtt{LG}=1, \mathtt{CP}=1, \mathtt{CX}=0, \mathtt{LA}=0, \mathtt{CL}=0)$$
$$= \tfrac{1}{Z} \exp\{\theta_{\mathtt{ML}} + \theta_{\mathtt{LG}} + \theta_{\mathtt{CP}} + 0 + 0 + 0\} = \tfrac{1}{Z} \exp\{6\}$$

where $Z \approx 529.06$ is a normalization constant. □

Next, we propose a more refined model that views course selection as a recursive process.

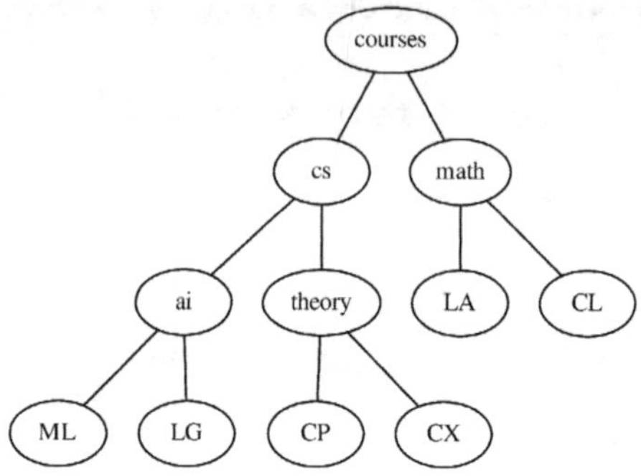

Figure 1: A tree hierarchy of courses.

3 RECURSIVE n-CHOOSE-k MODELS

Consider the following recursive process of course selection that a student may follow, which traces the tree structure of Figure 1. First, at the root courses, a student decides *how many* cs classes to take, compared to the number of math classes to take, out of a total of 3 classes. Say the student decides to take 2 cs classes and 1 math

Algorithm 1 Sample(v, k)

input: Node v in a vtree and a number k, $0 \leq k \leq |\mathbf{X}_v|$
output: A selection of k variables from $\mathbf{X}_v$
main:

```
if v is a leaf node labeled with variable X then
    return {X=0} if k=0 else return {X=1}
else
    v1, v2 ← children of node v
    θ_{v,k} ← distribution over (k1, k2) s.t. k1 + k2 = k
    (k1, k2) ← a cardinality pair drawn from θ_{v,k}
    return Sample(v1, k1) ∪ Sample(v2, k2)
```

class. Following the left branch, the student decides *how many* classes to take, now between ai and theory. Suppose they take one ai class, and hence one theory class. The student then recursively decides between learning (ML) and logic (LG), and independently, between computability (CP) and complexity (CX). We backtrack and decide (independently of the prior choices) between linear algebra (LA) and calculus (CL).

Algorithm 1 describes a probabilistic generative process for subset selection, based on a tree structure similar to the one in Figure 1. This structure is called a variable tree, or *vtree,* and corresponds to a full, binary tree with each leaf node v labeled with a distinct variable $X \in \mathbf{X}$. For a vtree node v, we will use $\mathbf{X}_v$ to denote the set of variables appearing at or below node v. We will also use v_1 and v_2 to represent the left and right children, respectively, of an internal vtree node v.

A call to Sample(v, k) of Algorithm 1 randomly selects k variables from $\mathbf{X}_v$. If v is an internal node, we first sample a cardinality k_1 of variables to select from the left child of v (which implies that we select $k_2 = k - k_1$ variables from the right child of v). If v is a leaf node, then k is either 0 (we do not select a variable), or 1 (we select the variable X at node v).

This generative process describes our new probabilistic model of subset selection, which we call the *recursive n-choose-k model.* We formalize this model next.

3.1 FORMAL DEFINITION

From here on, we assume that $n \geq 1$ and $0 \leq k \leq n$.

To define our recursive n-choose-k model, we first need to define the notion of a *choice distribution*, for deciding how many elements to choose. Such a distribution is defined for three integers n_1, n_2 and k where $n_1, n_2 \geq 1$ and $0 \leq k \leq n_1 + n_2$. The domain of this distribution is the set of pairs (k_1, k_2) such that $k_1 \leq n_1$, $k_2 \leq n_2$ and $k_1 + k_2 = k$. The intuition behind a choice distribution is this. We need to select k items from $n_1 + n_2$ items. Each pair (k_1, k_2) corresponds to a choice of k_1 items from the n_1 items and a choice of k_2 items from the n_2 items. The n_1 and n_2 items will be the variables appearing in the left and right subtrees of a vtree node v; that is, $n_1 = |\mathbf{X}_{v_1}|$ and $n_2 = |\mathbf{X}_{v_2}|$. Hence, we will denote the parameters of a choice distribution by $\theta_{v,k}(k_1, k_2)$, which represents the probability that we will select k_1 items from the left subtree of v and k_2 items from the right subtree of v. This implies that $k \leq |\mathbf{X}_v|$.

Example 2. Consider the following choice distributions from our course selection problem (we are only showing choices with non-zero probability).

v	k	k_1, k_2	$\theta_{v,k}$
courses	3	1, 2	0.1
		2, 1	0.3
		3, 0	0.6
math	2	1, 1	1.0
math	1	1, 0	0.3
		0, 1	0.7
math	0	0, 0	1.0

v	k	k_1, k_2	$\theta_{v,k}$
cs	2	0, 2	0.3
		1, 1	0.6
		2, 0	0.1
cs	1	1, 0	0.4
		0, 1	0.6
ai	1	1, 0	0.4
		0, 1	0.6

For v=courses and $k=3$, the choice distribution $\theta_{v,k}$ is used to select 3 courses from cs and math. For example, we select 1 course from cs and 2 from math with probability $\theta_{v,k}(1, 2) = 0.1$. □

We are now ready to define our subset selection model. A recursive n-choose-k model over n binary variables $\mathbf{X}$ has two components: (1) *structure:* a vtree where each leaf node is labeled with a distinct variable from $\mathbf{X}$, and (2) *parameters:* for each internal vtree node v with m leaves, a choice distribution $\theta_{v,i}$ for each $i = \max(0, k - (n - m)), \ldots, \min(k, m)$. In a recursive n-choose-k model, we will never choose more than k items at any vtree node v, hence we need choice distributions for at most $\min(k, m)$ items at node v. Moreover, since we can choose at most $n - m$ items from outside node v, we must choose at least $k - (n - m)$ items at node v. Hence, we do not need choice distributions for fewer items than $\max(0, k - (n - m))$.

The distribution induced by a recursive n-choose-k model is defined inductively, over instantiations $\mathbf{x}$ whose cardinalities are k. Note that for the inductive cases, we refer to cardinalities by i rather than by k.

For the base case of a leaf vtree node v labeled with variable X, we have $Pr_{v,i}(X = \text{true}) = 1$ if $i=1$ and 0 if $i=0$. For the inductive case of an internal leaf node v:

$$Pr_{v,i}(\mathbf{x}_v) = Pr_{v_1,i_1}(\mathbf{x}_{v_1}) \cdot Pr_{v_2,i_2}(\mathbf{x}_{v_2}) \cdot \theta_{v,i}(i_1, i_2).$$

Here, $\mathbf{x}_{v_1}$ and $\mathbf{x}_{v_2}$ are the subsets of instantiation $\mathbf{x}_v$ pertaining to variables $\mathbf{X}_{v_1}$ and $\mathbf{X}_{v_2}$, respectively. Moreover, i_1 and i_2 are the cardinalities of instantiations $\mathbf{x}_{v_1}$

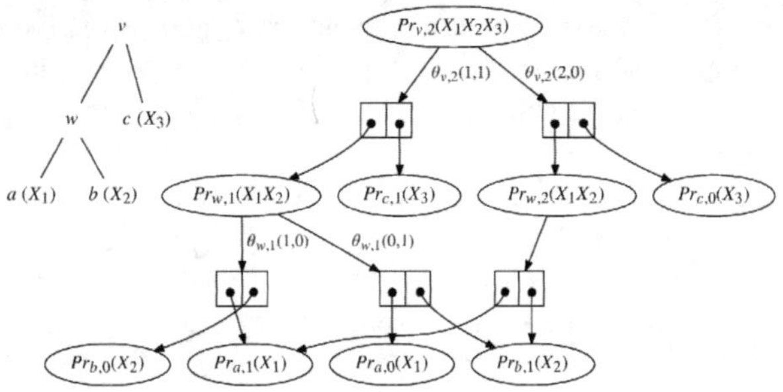

Figure 2: A vtree (upper-left), with a corresponding recursive 3-choose-2 distribution (right). Leaf vtree nodes are labeled with their variables inside parenthesis.

and $\mathbf{x}_{v_2}$, respectively (hence, $i_1 + i_2 = i$). The underlying independence assumption in the above inductive case is this: how we select i_1 elements from v_1 is independent of how we select i_2 elements from v_2, after we have chosen how many elements i_1 and i_2 to select in each.

Figure 2 depicts a vtree and a corresponding 3-choose-2 model. Each circled node represents a recursive n-choose-k model that is associated with an internal vtree node, for particular values of n and k. Each circled node is also associated with a choice distribution, whose parameters annotate the edges outgoing the node.

Example 3. Using the recursive n-choose-k model, and the choice distributions of Example 2, the probability that a student takes machine learning (ML), logic (LG) and linear algebra (LA) is

$$\begin{aligned}
&Pr(\mathtt{ML}=1, \mathtt{LG}=1, \mathtt{CP}=0, \mathtt{CX}=0, \mathtt{LA}=1, \mathtt{CL}=0) \\
&= \theta_{\mathsf{courses},3}(2,1) \cdot \theta_{\mathsf{cs},2}(2,0) \cdot \theta_{\mathsf{math},1}(1,0) \cdot \\
&\quad \theta_{\mathsf{ai},2}(1,1) \cdot \theta_{\mathsf{theory},0}(0,0) \\
&= 0.3 \cdot 0.1 \cdot 0.3 \cdot 1 \cdot 1 = 0.009. \qquad \square
\end{aligned}$$

Finally, we show that our recursive n-choose-k model subsumes the logistic n-choose-k model of Equation 1.

Proposition 1 *For any logistic n-choose-k model, there is a recursive n-choose-k model that induces the same distribution.*

3.2 TRACTABLE INFERENCE

Recursive n-choose-k models are *tractable* probabilistic models: we can perform many probabilistic queries in time linear in the size of the model. For example, we can compute the most probable explanation (MPE), the probability of evidence, and posterior marginals, all in linear time. For example, we can use MPE to extend a partial subset selection to a complete one (e.g., to extend a user's top-3 list of movies to a top-10 list of movies, to provide movie suggestions). We can perform cardinality queries efficiently: given a user's top-3 list, what is the expected number of comedies that would appear on their top-10 list? This tractability is inherited from the Probabilistic Sentential Decision Diagram (Kisa et al., 2014), of which the recursive n-choose-k model is a concrete example. We discuss this connection further in Section 6.

As an example, consider a recursive n-choose-k model and suppose we observed evidence $\mathbf{e}$ on some of its variables $\mathbf{E} \subseteq \mathbf{X}$. We can compute the probability of this evidence recursively, starting from the root vtree node v:

$$Pr_{v,i}(\mathbf{e}) = \sum_{\theta_{v,i}(i_1,i_2)} Pr_{v_1,i_1}(\mathbf{e}_{v_1}) Pr_{v_2,i_2}(\mathbf{e}_{v_2}) \theta_{v,i}(i_1,i_2),$$

which follows from the underlying independence assumptions. In the base case, v is a leaf vtree node with variable X, and $i \in \{0,1\}$. If the evidence $\mathbf{e}$ is empty, then $Pr_{v,i}(\mathbf{e}) = 1$. Otherwise, $Pr_{v_i}(\mathbf{e}) = 1$ iff evidence $\mathbf{e}$ and the 1-choose-i model sets X to the same value.

Example 4. Say we want to compute the probability that a student takes learning (ML) and linear algebra (LA) out of 3 total classes, with the choice distributions of Example 2. With evidence $\mathbf{e} = \{\mathtt{ML}=1, \mathtt{LA}=1\}$, we have:

$$\begin{aligned}
&Pr_{\mathsf{courses},3}(\mathtt{ML}=1, \mathtt{LA}=1) \\
&= Pr_{\mathsf{cs},2}(\mathtt{ML}=1) \cdot Pr_{\mathsf{math},1}(\mathtt{LA}=1) \cdot \theta_{\mathsf{courses},3}(2,1) \\
&+ Pr_{\mathsf{cs},1}(\mathtt{ML}=1) \cdot Pr_{\mathsf{math},2}(\mathtt{LA}=1) \cdot \theta_{\mathsf{courses},3}(1,2) \\
&= Pr_{\mathsf{cs},2}(\mathtt{ML}=1) \cdot 0.3 \cdot 0.3 + Pr_{\mathsf{cs},1}(\mathtt{ML}=1) \cdot 1 \cdot 0.1.
\end{aligned}$$

Recursively, we compute $Pr_{\mathsf{cs},2}(\mathtt{ML}=1) = 0.34$ and $Pr_{\mathsf{cs},1}(\mathtt{ML}=1) = 0.16$, which yields:

$$Pr_{\mathsf{courses},3}(\mathbf{e}) = 0.34 \cdot 0.09 + 0.16 \cdot 0.1 = 0.0466. \quad \square$$

4 LEARNING n-CHOOSE-k MODELS

We show in this section how to estimate the parameters of a recursive n-choose-k model in closed form. We also propose a simple structure learning algorithm for these models, which amounts to learning their underlying vtrees (i.e., the recursive partitioning of variables).

We first consider the number of parameters in a recursive n-choose-k model, which is relevant to our structure learning algorithm. Each leaf vtree node corresponds to a 1-choose-1 or a 1-choose-0 model, which has no parameters. There are $O(n)$ internal nodes in the vtree, and each one has $O(k)$ choice distributions associated with it. Each of these distributions has $O(k)$ parameters, leading to a total of $O(nk^2)$ parameters. Hence, the total number of parameters in a recursive n-choose-k model is bounded by a polynomial in n and k.

To contrast, there are n parameters in a logistic n-choose-k model, which can be learned by iterative methods such as gradient descent (Swersky et al., 2012). Moreover, unlike our recursive model, there is no structure to be learned in a logistic n-choose-k model.

4.1 PARAMETER LEARNING

Suppose we are given a set of n binary variables $\mathbf{X}$. Let $\mathcal{D}$ be a dataset containing N examples, where each example is an instantiation $\mathbf{x}$ of variables $\mathbf{X}$ with exactly k variables set to true (that is, $\mathcal{D}$ is an n-choose-k dataset).

For a set of variables $\mathbf{Y} \subseteq \mathbf{X}$, we will say that an example $\mathbf{x}$ has $\mathbf{Y}$-cardinality equal to m iff exactly m variables in $\mathbf{Y}$ are set to true in the example. We will also use $\mathcal{D}\#(\mathbf{Y}:m)$ to denote the number of examples in dataset $\mathcal{D}$ with $\mathbf{Y}$-cardinality equal to m. This allows us to define the following empirical probability, which is the probability of having $\mathbf{Y}$-cardinality equal to m:

$$Pr_{\mathcal{D}}(\mathbf{Y}:m) = \tfrac{1}{N}\mathcal{D}\#(\mathbf{Y}:m).$$

Example 5. Consider the example

$$\texttt{ML}=0, \texttt{LG}=1, \texttt{CP}=1, \texttt{CX}=0, \texttt{CL}=0, \texttt{LA}=1$$

which has an ai-cardinality of 1 and a cs-cardinality of 2. We can compute the empirical probability that a student takes one ai course and two cs courses by counting examples in the dataset:

$$Pr_{\mathcal{D}}(\mathsf{ai}:1, \mathsf{cs}:2) = \tfrac{1}{N}\mathcal{D}\#(\mathsf{ai}:1, \mathsf{cs}:2).$$

We can also find the conditional probability that a student takes one ai course given that they take two cs courses:

$$Pr_{\mathcal{D}}(\mathsf{ai}:1 \mid \mathsf{cs}:2) = \frac{\mathcal{D}\#(\mathsf{ai}:1, \mathsf{cs}:2)}{\mathcal{D}\#(\mathsf{cs}:2)}. \qquad \square$$

The following theorem provides a closed form for the maximum likelihood estimates of a recursive n-choose-k model given a corresponding dataset $\mathcal{D}$.

Theorem 1 *Consider a recursive n-choose-k model and dataset $\mathcal{D}$, both over variables $\mathbf{X}$. Let v be an internal vtree node of this model. The maximum-likelihood parameter estimates for node v are unique and given by*

$$\begin{aligned}\theta_{v,i}(i_1, i_2) &= Pr_{\mathcal{D}}(\mathbf{X}_{v_1}:i_1 \mid \mathbf{X}_v:i) \\ &= Pr_{\mathcal{D}}(\mathbf{X}_{v_2}:i_2 \mid \mathbf{X}_v:i).\end{aligned}$$

According to this theorem, and given the underlying vtree of a recursive n-choose-k model, we can estimate its maximum likelihood parameters by performing a single pass on the given dataset.

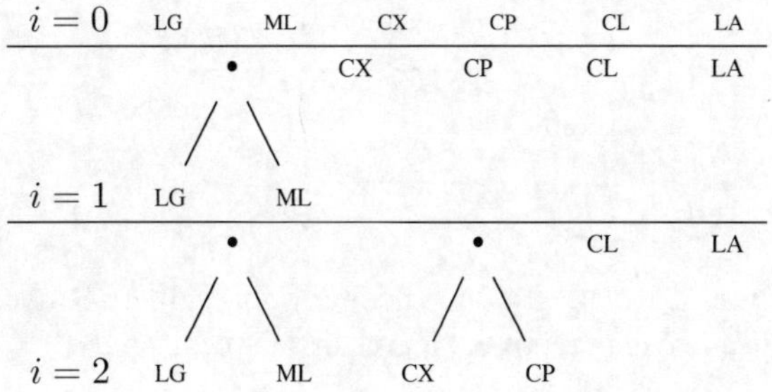

Figure 3: The first few iterations of vtree learning.

4.2 STRUCTURE LEARNING

We now turn to learning the structure of a recursive n-choose-k model, which amounts to learning its underlying vtree. Our approach will be based on maximizing the log-likelihood of the model, without penalizing for structure complexity since the number of parameters of any recursive n-choose-k model is bounded by a polynomial (i.e., regardless of its underlying vtree).

Our approach relies on the following result, which shows that the log-likelihood of a recursive n-choose-k model M, denoted $\mathcal{LL}(M \mid \mathcal{D})$, decomposes over vtree nodes.

Theorem 2 *Consider a recursive n-choose-k model M over variables $\mathbf{X}$ and a corresponding dataset $\mathcal{D}$. Let v be an internal vtree node of this model. We then have*

$$\begin{aligned}\mathcal{LL}(M \mid \mathcal{D}) &= -N \cdot \sum_v H(\mathbf{X}_{v_1} \mid \mathbf{X}_v) \\ &= -N \cdot \sum_v H(\mathbf{X}_{v_2} \mid \mathbf{X}_v)\end{aligned}$$

where $H(\mathbf{X}_{v_1}|\mathbf{X}_v)$ is the (empirical) conditional entropy of the cardinality of $\mathbf{X}_{v_1}$ given the cardinality of $\mathbf{X}_v$:

$$-\sum_{\theta_{v,i}(i_1,i_2)} Pr_{\mathcal{D}}(\mathbf{X}_{v_1}:i_1, \mathbf{X}_v:i) \cdot \log Pr_{\mathcal{D}}(\mathbf{X}_{v_1}:i_1 \mid \mathbf{X}_v:i).$$

Theorem 2 suggests a greedy heuristic for selecting a vtree. We start with n vtrees, each over a single variable $X \in \mathbf{X}$. We greedily pair two vtrees v_a and v_b (i.e., make them children of a new vtree node v) if they have the lowest conditional entropy $H(\mathbf{X}_{v_a} \mid \mathbf{X}_v) = H(\mathbf{X}_{v_b} \mid \mathbf{X}_v)$ over all pairs v_a and v_b. We iterate until we have a single vtree over all variables $\mathbf{X}$.

Example 6. Figure 3 highlights the first few iterations of our vtree learning algorithm, using our course selection example. Initially, at iteration $i = 0$, we have six vtrees, one for each of the six courses. Over all pairs of vtrees, say we obtain the lowest conditional entropy with $H(\{\texttt{LG}\}|\{\texttt{LG}, \texttt{ML}\})$. At iteration $i = 1$, we pair the

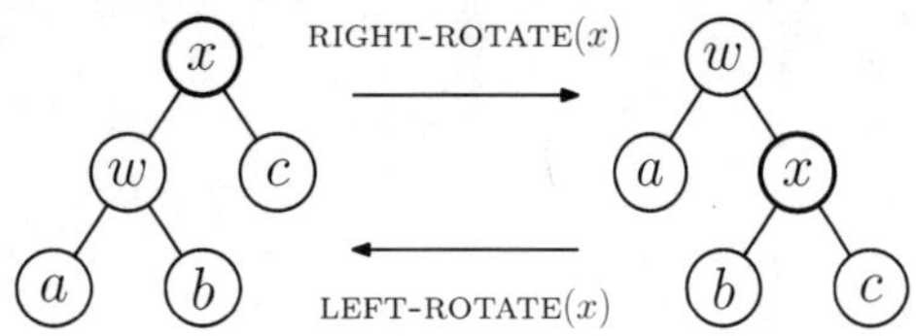

Figure 4: Rotating a vtree node x right and left. Nodes a, b, and c may represent leaves or subtrees.

vtrees of ML and LG to form a new vtree over both. Over all pairs of vtrees, say we now obtain the lowest conditional entropy with $H(\{\text{CX}\}|\{\text{CX}, \text{CP}\})$. At iteration $i = 2$, we again pair the corresponding vtrees to form a new one. We repeat, until we obtain a single vtree. □

Our structure learning algorithm improves the quality of this vtree using local search (simulated annealing in particular). To navigate the full space of vtrees, it suffices to have (left and right) tree rotation operators, and an operator to swap the labels of two vtree leaves.[1] Figure 4 highlights the rotation operator for vtrees. In our experiments, we used simulated annealing with the above operators to navigate the search space of vtrees, using the greedily found vtree we just described as the initial vtree.

Our local search algorithm defines two vtrees as neighbors if one can be obtained from the other by performing a left/right rotation of an internal vtree node, or by swapping the variables of two leaf vtree nodes. We used an exponential cooling schedule for simulated annealing. That is, during each iteration of the algorithm, we first select a neighbor at random. If it has a better log-likelihood score, we move to that neighbor. Otherwise, we move to that neighbor with probability $\exp\{\frac{1}{T_i}\Delta\mathcal{LL}(M \mid \mathcal{D})\}$, where $\Delta\mathcal{LL}(M \mid \mathcal{D})$ is the difference in log-likelihood, and T_i is the temperature at the current iteration. We stop when the temperature drops to a preset threshold.[2] We do not use restarts (empirically, our greedy heuristic appears to obtain a reasonably good initial vtree).

Finally, we remark on the simplicity of our structure learning algorithm, compared to other tractable representations such as the arithmetic circuit (AC) and their sum-product network (SPN) variant (Choi & Darwiche, 2017). In Section 6, we discuss how our recursive n-choose-k model corresponds to a certain type of AC. However, rather than search for ACs (Lowd & Domingos, 2008; Gens & Domingos, 2013; Dennis & Ventura,

[1](Choi & Darwiche, 2013) used rotation operators and an operation that swapped the children of an internal vtree node in order to navigate the space of vtrees. In our recursive n-choose-k model, the log likelihood is invariant to the swapping operator, hence we chose to swap the labels of leaf nodes.

[2]In our experiments, we have an initial temperature of 5.0, a cooling rate of 0.98, and a temperature threshold of 0.001.

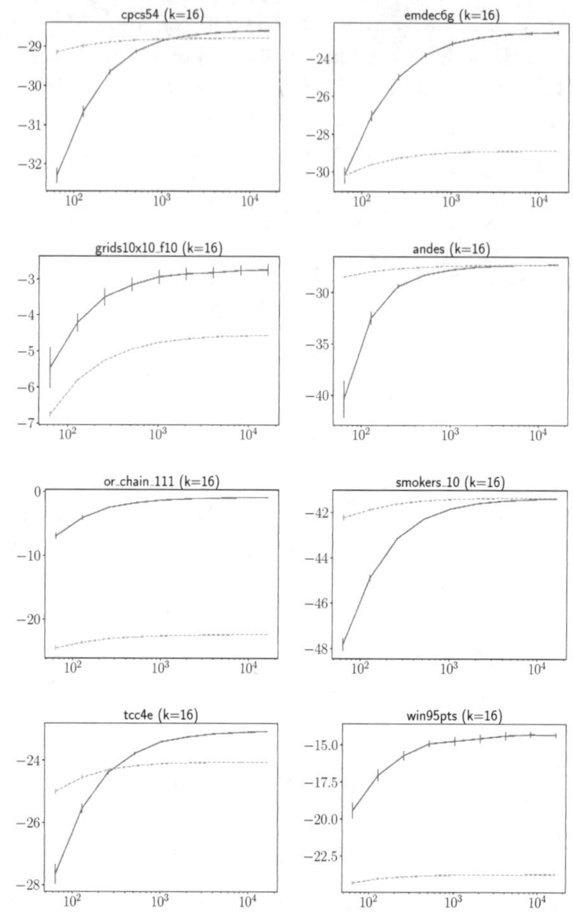

Figure 5: Learning results for cardinality-16: dataset size (x-axis) vs test log likelihood (y-axis). The blue solid lines and orange dashed lines correspond to the recursive and logistic n-choose-k models, respectively.

2015), we only need to search for vtrees (a much simpler space). This is possible due to a property called canonicity, which fixes the structure of the AC once the vtree is fixed (Kisa et al., 2014).

5 EXPERIMENTS AND CASE STUDIES

We next compare our recursive n-choose-k model with the logistic n-choose-k model of (Swersky et al., 2012), using simulated n-choose-k datasets. We later evaluate these models using real-world datasets from the domains of preference learning and sports analytics.

5.1 SIMULATED DATA

Based on Proposition 1, for a given logistic n-choose-k model, there exists a parameterization of a recursive n-choose-k model that induces the same distribution. However, the logistic n-choose-k model has fewer parameters, as discussed before. Thus, for less data we generally expect the logistic version to be more robust to overfitting, and for greater amounts of data we generally expect our recursive version to ultimately provide a better fit.

The first goal in our experiments is to verify this behavior. We simulated n-choose-k datasets, that are independent of both the logistic and recursive n-choose-k models (so that neither model would be able to fit the data perfectly). In particular, we simulated datasets from Bayesian and Markov networks, but subjected the networks to cardinality-k constraints.[3]

We selected a variety of networks from the literature, over binary variables (the corresponding variable count is given in parentheses): `cpcs54` (54), and `win95pts` (76) are classical diagnostic BNs from the literature; `emdec6g`(168) and `tcc4e` (98) are noisy-or diagnostic BNs from HRL Laboratories; `andes` (223) is a Bayesian network for educational assessment; `grid10x10_f10` (100), `or_chain_111` (200), `smokers_10` (120) are networks taken from previously held UAI competitions. We first considered cardinality-16 datasets. For each, we simulated a testing set of size $2,500$ and independently sampled 20 training sets each of size 2^s for s from 6 (64 examples) to 14 (16,384 examples). We trained n-choose-k models from each training set, and evaluated them using the testing set, in Figure 5. Each point in a plot is an average over 20 training sets.

Our recursive n-choose-k model is depicted with a solid blue line, and the logistic n-choose-k model is depicted with a dashed orange line. There are a few general trends. First, the logistic n-choose-k model more often provides a better fit with smaller amounts of data, but in all but two cases (`smokers_10` and `andes`), our recursive alternative will eventually learn a better model given enough data. In Appendix B, we ran analogous experiments except using cardinality-32 datasets, where we observe that our recursive n-choose-k model tends to perform even better, i.e., it tends to overtake the logistic one with fewer examples. Finally, we note that the variance (plotted using error-bars) of the logistic n-choose-k is smaller (since it has fewer parameters).

Figure 6 highlights the impact of varying k, using data simulated from the `win95pts` network. Here, observe the gain obtained from using the recursive model versus the logistic model, in terms of the test log likelihood, i.e., $\mathcal{LL}_{\text{recursive}}(\mathcal{D}) - \mathcal{LL}_{\text{logistic}}(\mathcal{D})$. Hence, if the gain is negative, the logistic model obtained a better likelihood, and if the gain is positive, then our recursive model obtained a better likelihood. Again, as we increase the size of the dataset, our recursive n-choose-k model obtains better likelihoods. As we vary the cardinality of the examples in the data, we see that the performance can vary. Generally, as we increase k from 0 to n, the difference between the models become greater up to a point and then it decreases again. This is expected to an extent since there is an underlying symmetry: a constraint that k values be positive is equivalent to a constraint that $n - k$ values are negative. Hence, for a given n-choose-k model, there is an equivalent n-choose-$(n-k)$ model where the signs have been switched. However, there is not a perfect symmetry in the distribution, since the original distribution generating the data (`win95pts` in this case) does not have this symmetry across cardinalities.

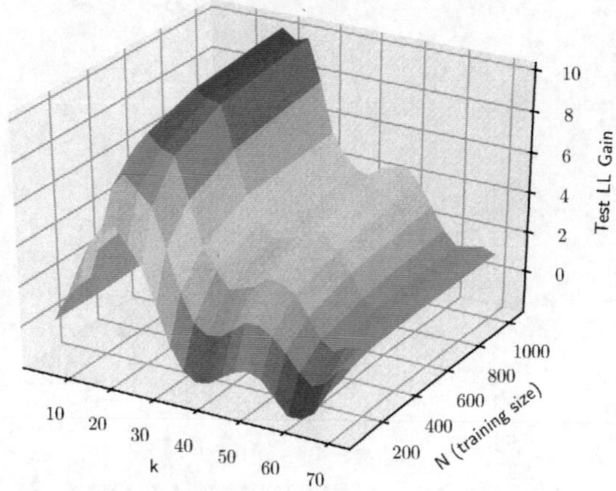

Figure 6: Learning results on the `win95pts` dataset: k vs dataset size vs test log likelihood.

Finally, we remark on the running time of structure learning. On the `win95pts` network, with a 76-choose-32 dataset of size 2^{13}, our structure learning algorithm runs for only 65.02s (on average over 20 runs). On the `andes` network, with a 223-choose-32 dataset of size 2^{13}, it runs for only 367.8s (on average over 20 runs). This is in contrast to other structure learning algorithms for tractable models, such as those based on ACs and their SPNs variant, where learning requires hours for comparably sized learning problems, and even days and weeks for larger scale problems; see, e.g., (Rahman, Kothalkar, & Gogate, 2014) for a discussion. While our recursive n-choose-k model corresponds to a special class of ACs (as we shall discuss in Section 6), it suffices to learn a vtree and not the AC itself.

[3] We remark that it is non-trivial to simulate a Bayesian network, when we condition on logical constraints. To do so, efficiently, we first compiled a Bayesian network to a PSDD, and then multiplied it with a (uniform) PSDD representing a cardinality-k constraint (Shen et al., 2016). The result is a PSDD, which we can now efficiently sample from.

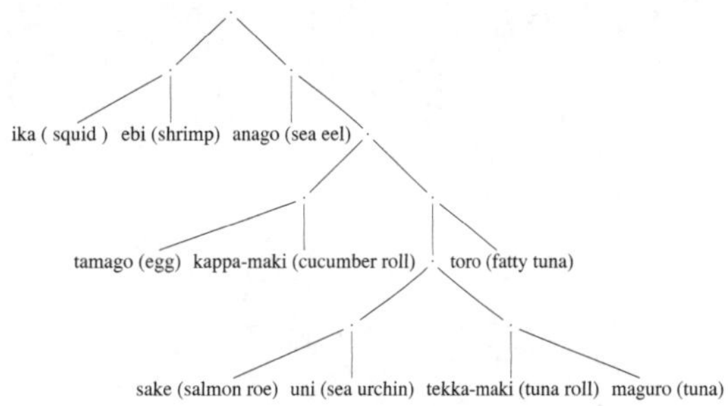

Figure 7: 10-choose-5 model for the `sushi` dataset.

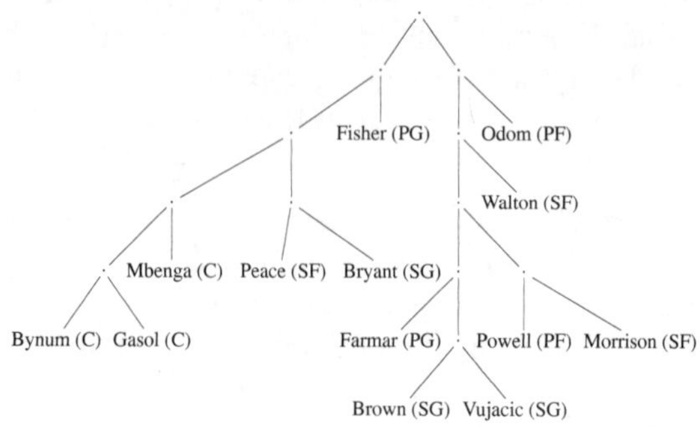

Figure 8: 13-choose-5 model for the 2009-2010 Lakers.

5.2 CASE STUDY: PREFERENCE LEARNING

We consider a case study in preference learning. The `sushi` dataset consists of $5,000$ total rankings of 10 different types of sushi (Kamishima, 2003). From this dataset over total rankings, we can obtain a dataset over top-5 preferred sushi, where we have 10 variables (one for each type of sushi) and a variable is true iff they are in the top-5 of their total ranking; we thus ignore the specific rankings. Note that the resulting dataset is complete, with respect to top-5 rankings. We learned a 10-choose-5 model from this data, using simulated annealing seeded with our conditional entropy heuristic.[4]

Figure 7 highlights the learned vtree structure, which we can view as providing a recursive partitioning to guide a selection of the top-5 preferred sushi, as in Section 3. Going roughly left-to-right, we start with 3 popular non-fish types of sushi: squid, shrimp and sea eel. Next, egg and cucumber roll are relatively not preferred; next, fatty tuna is heavily preferred. Finally, we observe salmon roe and sea urchin (which are both considered acquired tastes) and then tuna roll and tuna. These observations are consistent with previously made observations about the `sushi` dataset; see, e.g., (Lu & Boutilier, 2011; Choi, Van den Broeck, & Darwiche, 2015). In contrast, (Lu & Boutilier, 2011) learned a mixture-of-Mallows model with 6 components, providing 6 different reference rankings (and a dispersion parameter).[5] (Choi et al., 2015) learned a PSDD, but without learning a vtree; a fixed vtree was used based on rankings, which does not reflect any relationships between different types of sushi.

Appendix B compares the recursive and logistic n-choose-k models, where we again observe that the recursive model obtains a better fit when we have more data.

[4]The sushi data was split into a training set of size $3,500$ and a testing set of size $1,500$ as in (Lu & Boutilier, 2011). Our model was learning using just the training set.

[5]The Mallows (1957) model is a probabilistic model for ranking, which assumes a *reference* ranking σ, with other rankings σ' becoming less likely as their distance from σ increases.

5.3 CASE STUDY: SPORTS ANALYTICS

Team sports, such as basketball and soccer, have an inherent n-choose-k problem, where a coach has to select k out of n players to fulfill different roles on a team. For example, in modern basketball, a team consists of five players who play different roles: there are two guards, who are passers and long-distance shooters; there are two forwards, who generally play closer to the basket; and there is the center, who is normally the tallest player and is the one mostly responsible for gathering rebounds and for contesting shots.

`http://stats.nba.com` provides, for a given season and team, a record of all lineups of five players that played together at the same time, and for how many minutes they played. There are 48 minutes played in a basketball game, and 82 games played during the regular season, for a total $3,936$ minutes. For the 2009-2010 Los Angeles Lakers, that season's NBA champions, we obtained a 13-choose-5 dataset with $39,360$ examples, taking lineups in $\frac{1}{10}$-th minute increments, plus some additional examples due to overtime.

Figure 8 highlights the (vtree) structure that we learned from the full dataset. Again, we can view this structure as providing a recursive partitioning to guide our selection of a five-player NBA lineup, as in Section 3. Starting from the left, and rotating around the root: Andrew Bynum, Pao Gasol and Didier Ilunga-Mbenga are the centers; Metta World Peace, Kobe Bryant, Derek Fisher, and Lamar Odom are the starting non-centers; Luke Walton, Josh Powell and Adam Morrison are the reserve forwards; and Jordan Farmar, Shannon Brown, and Sasha Vujacic are the reserve guards.

Appendix B compares the recursive and logistic n-choose-k models, where we again observe that the recursive model obtains a better fit when we have more data.

6 DISCOVERING THE RECURSIVE n-CHOOSE-k MODEL

We now highlight how the recursive n-choose-k model was *discovered* using the Probabilistic Sentential Decision Diagram (PSDD) (Kisa et al., 2014).

A PSDD allows one to define a probability distribution over a *structured probability space,* which is a subset of the Cartesian product of a set of variables—with each element of this subset corresponding to some object of interest. For example, a structured probability space may correspond to the space of permutations, partial rankings or routes on a map (Choi et al., 2015; Choi, Tavabi, & Darwiche, 2016). PSDDs over structured spaces are interpretable in a precise sense. For certain spaces, including those for subset selection, this interpretability may lead to models whose semantics are so clear that they can be described independently, without the need to invoke the notion of a PSDD in the first place. In such cases, we say that the PSDD has enabled *model discovery*.

Underlying the PSDD is the Sentential Decision Diagram (SDD), which is a class of tractable Boolean circuits (Darwiche, 2011). In this framework, the SDD circuit is used to define the structured probability space (a variable instantiation belongs to the structured space iff the SDD circuit outputs one under that instantiation). Once the structured space is defined by an SDD, a PSDD is used to induce a distribution over that space (the PSDD is basically a parameterized SDD).

Consider the recursive 3-choose-2 model of Figure 2. This model corresponds to an SDD circuit when we replace (1) internal circled nodes with or-gates, (2) paired boxes with and-gates, (3) 1-choose-1 leaf nodes with a positive literal X and 1-choose-0 leaf nodes with a negative literal $\neg X$. The result is an SDD circuit whose satisfying instantiations have exactly two positive literals; that is, the structured probability space for 3-choose-2. See Appendix C for an example of this SDD circuit, and its annotation as a PSDD.

More generally, the following theorem describes SDD circuits whose satisfying instantiations are those with exactly k variables set to true (SDDs are also constructed based on vtrees; see (Darwiche, 2011) for details).

Proposition 2 *Let $f_{v,k}$ be an SDD circuit, for a vtree v with n variables $\mathbf{X}$, whose satisfying instantiations $\mathbf{x}$ set exactly k variables to true. This circuit is equivalent to:*

$$\bigvee_{k_1+k_2=k} f_{v_1,k_1} \wedge f_{v_2,k_2}$$

where $0 \leq k_1 \leq |\mathbf{X}_{v_1}|$ and $0 \leq k_2 \leq |\mathbf{X}_{v_2}|$.

Hence, each or-gate of an SDD corresponds to a Boolean formula representing an n-choose-k constraint.

To emphasize the clear semantics of this SDD, consider the number of satisfying instantiations (i.e., model count) that an n-choose-k constraint has: $\binom{n}{k}$. To obtain the model count of an SDD (i.e., the number of satisfying instantiations), we replace each or-gate with a $+$ and each and-gate with a $*$, and all literals with a 1. We then evaluate the circuit bottom-up to evaluate the model count. The model count of the SDD in Figure 2 represents the following computation of $\binom{3}{2}$:

$$\binom{3}{2} = \binom{2}{1}\binom{1}{1} + \binom{2}{2}\binom{1}{0} = 2 \cdot 1 + 1 \cdot 1 = 3.$$

For a more general example, suppose we are given a vtree over a set of n variables $\mathbf{X}$, where the left child of each internal node is a leaf (this is called a right-linear vtree). Computing the model count of an SDD for this vtree, as shown above, yields the well-known recurrence for binomial coefficients:

$$\binom{n}{k} = \binom{1}{0}\binom{n-1}{k} + \binom{1}{1}\binom{n-1}{k-1} = \binom{n-1}{k} + \binom{n-1}{k-1}.$$

To obtain a PSDD from an SDD, one assigns a local distribution on the inputs of each or-gate (Kisa et al., 2014). For the SDDs of Proposition 2, these local distributions correspond to the choice distributions of our recursive n-choose-k model; see Appendix C for an example. This observation allowed us to describe this model in a manner independent of the PSDD framework, and hence enabled *model discovery*.

7 CONCLUSION

We proposed in this paper the recursive n-choose-k model for subset selection problems. We also derived a closed-form parameter estimation algorithm for these models, and a simple structure learning algorithm based on greedy and local search. Empirically, we showed how our recursive n-choose-k models can obtain better fits of the data, compared to a previously proposed model. Moreover, we showed how structure search can lead to an intuitive generative model of the subset selection process (based on vtrees). We finally showed how the proposed model was discovered using the PSDD representation for inducing distributions over structured spaces, with the structured space being the set of variable instantiations having a fixed cardinality.

Acknowledgments

This work has been partially supported by NSF grant #IIS-1514253, ONR grant #N00014-15-1-2339 and DARPA XAI grant #N66001-17-2-4032. We thank Tal Friedman, Yitao Liang and Guy Van den Broeck for comments and discussions on this paper.

References

Bekker, J., Davis, J., Choi, A., Darwiche, A., & Van den Broeck, G. (2015). Tractable learning for complex probability queries. In *Advances in Neural Information Processing Systems 28 (NIPS)*.

Chavira, M., & Darwiche, A. (2008). On probabilistic inference by weighted model counting. *Artificial Intelligence Journal (AIJ)*, *172*(6–7), 772–799.

Choi, A., & Darwiche, A. (2013). Dynamic minimization of sentential decision diagrams. In *Proceedings of the 27th Conference on Artificial Intelligence (AAAI)*.

Choi, A., & Darwiche, A. (2017). On relaxing determinism in arithmetic circuits. In *Proceedings of the Thirty-Fourth International Conference on Machine Learning (ICML)*.

Choi, A., Tavabi, N., & Darwiche, A. (2016). Structured features in naive Bayes classification. In *Proceedings of the 30th AAAI Conference on Artificial Intelligence (AAAI)*.

Choi, A., Van den Broeck, G., & Darwiche, A. (2015). Tractable learning for structured probability spaces: A case study in learning preference distributions. In *Proceedings of the 24th International Joint Conference on Artificial Intelligence (IJCAI)*.

Darwiche, A. (2011). SDD: A new canonical representation of propositional knowledge bases. In *Proceedings of the 22nd International Joint Conference on Artificial Intelligence (IJCAI)*, pp. 819–826.

Dennis, A. W., & Ventura, D. (2015). Greedy structure search for sum-product networks. In *Proceedings of the Twenty-Fourth International Joint Conference on Artificial Intelligence (IJCAI)*, pp. 932–938.

Gens, R., & Domingos, P. M. (2012). Discriminative learning of sum-product networks. In *Advances in Neural Information Processing Systems 25 (NIPS)*, pp. 3248–3256.

Gens, R., & Domingos, P. M. (2013). Learning the structure of sum-product networks. In *Proceedings of the 30th International Conference on Machine Learning (ICML)*, pp. 873–880.

Kamishima, T. (2003). Nantonac collaborative filtering: recommendation based on order responses. In *Proceedings of the Ninth ACM SIGKDD International Conference on Knowledge Discovery and Data Mining*, pp. 583–588.

Kimmig, A., Van den Broeck, G., & De Raedt, L. (2017). Algebraic model counting. *J. Applied Logic*, *22*, 46–62.

Kisa, D., Van den Broeck, G., Choi, A., & Darwiche, A. (2014). Probabilistic sentential decision diagrams. In *Proceedings of the 14th International Conference on Principles of Knowledge Representation and Reasoning (KR)*.

Lowd, D., & Domingos, P. M. (2008). Learning arithmetic circuits. In *Proceedings of the 24th Conference in Uncertainty in Artificial Intelligence (UAI)*, pp. 383–392.

Lowd, D., & Rooshenas, A. (2013). Learning Markov networks with arithmetic circuits. In *Proceedings of the 16th International Conference on Artificial Intelligence and Statistics (AISTATS)*, pp. 406–414.

Lu, T., & Boutilier, C. (2011). Learning Mallows models with pairwise preferences. In *Proceedings of the 28th International Conference on Machine Learning (ICML)*, pp. 145–152.

Mallows, C. L. (1957). Non-null ranking models. *Biometrika*, *44*, 114–130.

Meinel, C., & Theobald, T. (1998). *Algorithms and Data Structures in VLSI Design: OBDD — Foundations and Applications*. Springer.

Poon, H., & Domingos, P. M. (2011). Sum-product networks: A new deep architecture. In *Proceedings of the Twenty-Seventh Conference on Uncertainty in Artificial Intelligence (UAI)*, pp. 337–346.

Rahman, T., Kothalkar, P., & Gogate, V. (2014). Cutset networks: A simple, tractable, and scalable approach for improving the accuracy of Chow-Liu trees. In *European Conference on Machine Learning and Knowledge Discovery in Databases (ECML-PKDD)*, pp. 630–645.

Shen, Y., Choi, A., & Darwiche, A. (2016). Tractable operations for arithmetic circuits of probabilistic models. In *Advances in Neural Information Processing Systems 29 (NIPS)*.

Swersky, K., Tarlow, D., Adams, R. P., Zemel, R. S., & Frey, B. J. (2012). Probabilistic n-choose-k models for classification and ranking. In *Advances in Neural Information Processing Systems 25 (NIPS)*, pp. 3059–3067.

Wegener, I. (2000). *Branching Programs and Binary Decision Diagrams*. SIAM.

A PROOFS

To prove Proposition 1, we reduce the logistic n-choose-k model to a weighted model counting (WMC) problem.

Given a propositional sentence Δ and a set of weights $W(\ell)$ on each literal ℓ, its weighted model count is

$$WMC(\Delta) = \sum_{\mathbf{x} \models \Delta} W(\mathbf{x}) = \sum_{\mathbf{x} \models \Delta} \prod_{\mathbf{x} \models \ell} W(\ell)$$

where the weight of a model $W(\mathbf{x})$ is the product of the weights of its literals $W(\ell)$. For more on weighted model counting see, e.g., (Chavira & Darwiche, 2008; Kimmig, Van den Broeck, & De Raedt, 2017).

A WMC problem induces a distribution over its models:

$$Pr(\mathbf{x}) = \frac{W(\mathbf{x})}{WMC(\Delta)}.$$

If a sentence Δ can be compiled into an SDD, then the SDD can be used to compute its weighted model count. Subsequently, a PSDD can represent the corresponding distribution, as follows.

Lemma 1 *Consider a WMC problem over a propositional sentence Δ with weights $W(\ell)$ on each literal ℓ. Let m be an SDD representing sentence Δ. There is a PSDD with m as its base that induces the same distribution induced by the given WMC problem.*

Proof Given a normalized SDD for Δ, we show how to parameterize it as a PSDD. For an SDD/PSDD node m, let P_m be the distribution induced by the WMC problem on m, and let Q_m be the distribution induced by the PSDD. If m is a terminal node, set $Q_m(\ell) = \eta \cdot W(\ell)$ if ℓ is compatible with the base of m and 0 otherwise, where η is a normalizing constant so that Q_m sums to one. If m is a decision node with elements (p_i, s_i, θ_i), set

$$\theta_i = \frac{WMC(p_i) \cdot WMC(s_i)}{WMC(m)}.$$

We show $P_m(\mathbf{x}) = Q_m(\mathbf{x})$ for all $\mathbf{x}$, by induction. The base case, where m is a terminal node, is immediate. Suppose m is a decision node with elements (p_i, s_i, θ_i) with prime variables $\mathbf{X}$ and sub variables $\mathbf{Y}$, and where $P_{p_i}(\mathbf{x}) = Q_{p_i}(\mathbf{x})$ and $P_{s_i}(\mathbf{y}) = Q_{s_i}(\mathbf{y})$. Given an assignment $\mathbf{xy}$, let the i-th element (p_i, s_i, θ_i) be the one where $\mathbf{x} \models p_i$. We have:

$$\begin{aligned} Q_m(\mathbf{xy}) &= Q_{p_i}(\mathbf{x}) \cdot Q_{s_i}(\mathbf{y}) \cdot \theta_i \\ &= P_{p_i}(\mathbf{x}) \cdot P_{s_i}(\mathbf{y}) \cdot \theta_i \qquad \text{by induction} \\ &= \frac{W(\mathbf{x})}{WMC(p_i)} \cdot \frac{W(\mathbf{y})}{WMC(s_i)} \cdot \frac{WMC(p_i) \cdot WMC(s_i)}{WMC(m)} \\ &= \frac{W(\mathbf{x}) \cdot W(\mathbf{y})}{WMC(m)} = \frac{W(\mathbf{xy})}{WMC(m)} = P_m(\mathbf{xy}). \end{aligned}$$

□

Proof of Proposition 1 We can represent the logistic n-choose-k model of Equation 1 as a weighted model counting problem problem. First, let Δ be a logical n-choose-k constraint as in Proposition 2. If we use the weights $W(X) = \exp\{\theta_X\}$ and $W(\neg X) = 1$, then the weighted model count gives us the partition function of the logistic n-choose-k model of Equation 1.

Using Proposition 2, we can obtain an SDD for Δ of polynomial size. Using the construction of Lemma 1, we obtain a PSDD that corresponds to a recursive n-choose-k model. This distribution is equivalent to the one induced by the WMC problem, and the one induced by the given logistic n-choose-k model. □

Proof of Theorem 1 Under the recursive n-select-k distribution, the probability $Pr_{w,k}(\mathbf{x})$ is a product of $n-1$ choice parameters. Hence, the log likelihood decomposes as follows:

$$\begin{aligned} \mathcal{LL}(M \mid \mathcal{D}) &= \sum_{a=1}^{N} \log Pr_{w,k}(\mathbf{x}) \\ &= \sum_{v,i} \sum_{\theta_{v,i}(i_1,i_2)} \mathcal{D}\#(\mathbf{X}_{v_1}\!:\!i_1, \mathbf{X}_v\!:\!i) \log \theta_{v,i}(i_1, i_2) \\ &= N \cdot \sum_{v,i} \sum_{\theta_{v,i}(i_1,i_2)} Pr_{\mathcal{D}}(\mathbf{X}_{v_1}\!:\!i_1, \mathbf{X}_v\!:\!i) \log \theta_{v,i}(i_1, i_2) \end{aligned}$$

Note that for each v and i, all of the local choice distributions $\theta_{v,i}$ are independent. Hence it suffices to locally maximize each component:

$$\sum_{\theta_{v,i}(i_1,i_2)} Pr_{\mathcal{D}}(\mathbf{X}_{v_1}\!:\!i_1, \mathbf{X}_v\!:\!i) \log \theta_{v,i}(i_1, i_2)$$

which is basically a cross entropy that is maximized at:

$$\begin{aligned} \theta_{v,i}(i_1, i_2) &= Pr_{\mathcal{D}}(\mathbf{X}_{v_1}\!:\!i_1 \mid \mathbf{X}_v\!:\!i) \\ &= Pr_{\mathcal{D}}(\mathbf{X}_{v_2}\!:\!i_2 \mid \mathbf{X}_v\!:\!i). \end{aligned}$$

□

Proof of Theorem 2 If we substitute the maximum likelihood estimates of Theorem 1 into the log likelihood of an n-choose-k model we obtain our result.

First, consider the component contributed by a single vtree node v and their choice distribution $\theta_{v,i}$:

$$\begin{aligned} & N \sum_{\theta_{v,i}(i_1,i_2)} Pr_{\mathcal{D}}(\mathbf{X}_{v_1}\!:\!i_1, \mathbf{X}_v\!:\!i) \log \theta_{v,i}(i_1, i_2) \\ &= N \sum_{\theta_{v,i}(i_1,i_2)} Pr_{\mathcal{D}}(\mathbf{X}_{v_1}\!:\!i_1, \mathbf{X}_v\!:\!i) \log Pr_{\mathcal{D}}(\mathbf{X}_{v_1}\!:\!i_1 | \mathbf{X}_v\!:\!i) \\ &= -N \cdot H(\mathbf{X}_{v_1}\!:\!i_1 | \mathbf{X}_v\!:\!i) \end{aligned}$$

which is the conditional entropy distribution. Hence:

$$\mathcal{LL}(M \mid \mathcal{D}) = -N \sum_{v} H(\mathbf{X}_{v_1}\!:\!i_1 | \mathbf{X}_v\!:\!i)$$

□

Proof of Proposition 2 Consider an n-choose-k constraint $f_{v,k}$ associated with a vtree node v, with children v_1 and v_2 over variables $\mathbf{X}_{v_1}$ and $\mathbf{X}_{v_2}$.

An $\mathbf{X}_{v_1}$-$\mathbf{X}_{v_2}$ decomposition is found by compressing the decomposition:

$$f_{v,k} = \bigvee_{\mathbf{x}_{v_1}} \mathbf{x}_{v_1} \wedge f_{v,k}|\mathbf{x}_{v_1}$$

which is found by disjoining all $\mathbf{x}_{v_1}$ terms that have equivalent terms $f_{v,k}|\mathbf{x}_{v_1}$. For all $\mathbf{x}_{v_1}$ with the same cardinality k_1, the resulting function $f_{v,k}|\mathbf{x}_{v_1}$ is the same. When we disjoin all such $\mathbf{x}_{v_1}$ we obtain the function f_{v_1,k_1}. Further, $f_{v,k}|\mathbf{x}_{v_1} = f_{v_2,k_2}$ for $k_2 = k - k_1$. Hence, the compressed decomposition is:

$$f_{v,k} = \bigvee_{k_1+k_2=k} f_{v_1,k_1} \wedge f_{v_2,k_2}.$$

See also (Meinel & Theobald, 1998; Wegener, 2000) (such as the cardinality-k constraint) for more on symmetric functions on OBDDs. □

B ADDITIONAL EXPERIMENTS

Consider Figure 9, where we ran the same experiments of Figure 5, except where we simulated cardinality-32 datasets instead of cardinality-16 datasets. We observe that our recursive n-choose-k model tends to perform even better here, i.e., they tend to overtake the logistic one with fewer examples.

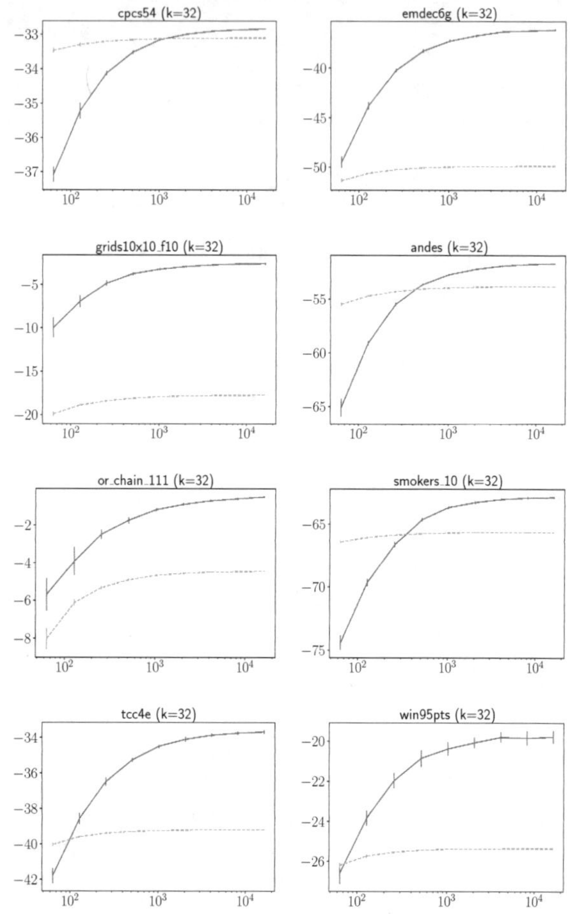

Figure 9: Learning results for cardinality-32: dataset size (x-axis) vs test log likelihood (y-axis). The blue solid lines and orange dashed lines correspond to the recursive and logistic n-choose-k models, respectively.

Consider the preference learning task of Section 5.2, where we considered that `sushi` dataset, which consists of $5,000$ total rankings of 10 different types of sushi (Kamishima, 2003). Consider Figure 10, where we compare our recursive n-choose-k model with the logistic n-choose-k model of (Swersky et al., 2012). First, we split the dataset into a training set (initially, of size 3,500) and a testing set (of size 1,500). Next we simulated training sets of varying sizes, which we used to learn our recursive n-choose-k models, which are then evaluated using the testing set. We used datasets of size 2^s for s from 6 (64 examples) to 11 (2,048 examples), where each was sampled from the original training set, without replacement. Each point of Figure 10 represents an average over 20 simulated training sets. For smaller amounts of data, we see the logistic 10-choose-5 model obtains a better test likelihood. For larger amounts of data, we see our recursive 10-choose-5 model obtains better test likelihoods.

Consider the sports analytics task of Section 5.3, where we considered the 2009-2010 Los Angeles Lakers, that season's NBA champions, and obtained a 13-choose-5 dataset with $39,360$ examples. In Figure 11, we compared our recursive n-choose-k model with the logistic n-choose-k model. First, we split the dataset into a training set and testing set (the testing set had size 2,500, with the rest going to the training set). Next we simulated training sets of varying sizes, which we used to learn our n-choose-k models, which are then evaluated using the testing set. We used datasets of size 2^s for s from 6 (64 examples) to 14 (16,384 examples), where each was sampled from the original training set, without replacement. Each point of Figure 11 represents an average over 20 simulated training sets. Notably, the logistic model (in orange) does not improve much, even from very small amounts of data. The model that we propose (in blue) provides a better fit, even with a small training set, and is further able to provide increasingly better fits given more data.

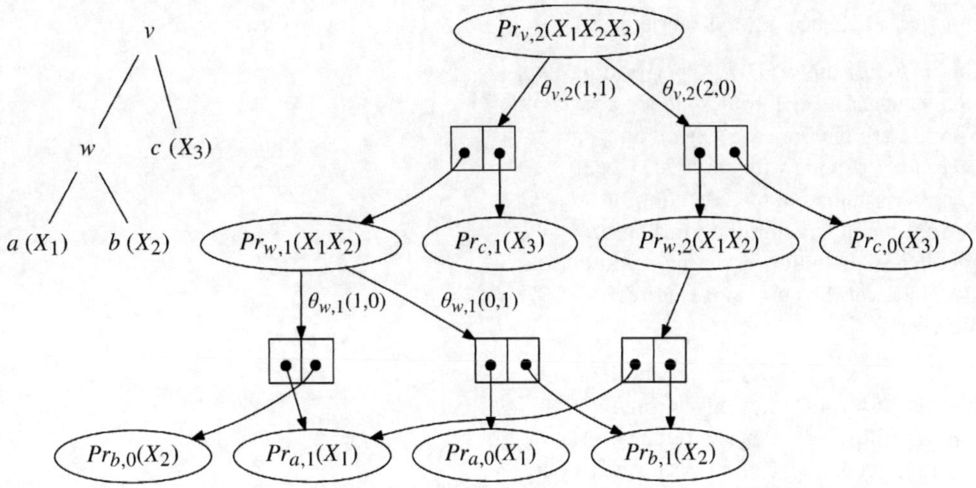

Figure 12: A vtree (upper-left), with a corresponding recursive 3-choose-2 model (right). Leaf vtree nodes are labeled with their variables inside parenthesis. This vtree and model are reproduced from Figure 2.

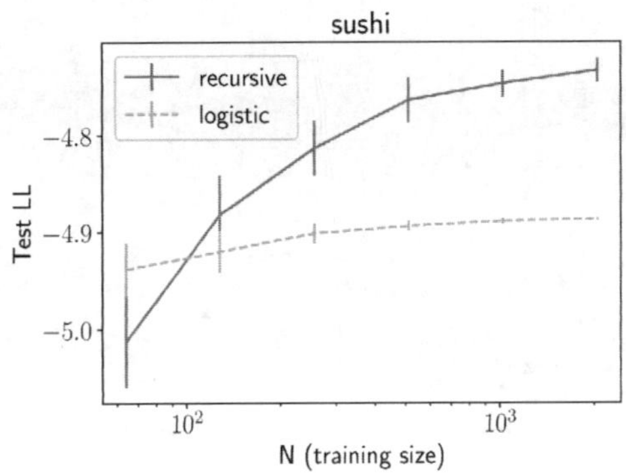

Figure 10: Learning results for the sushi dataset.

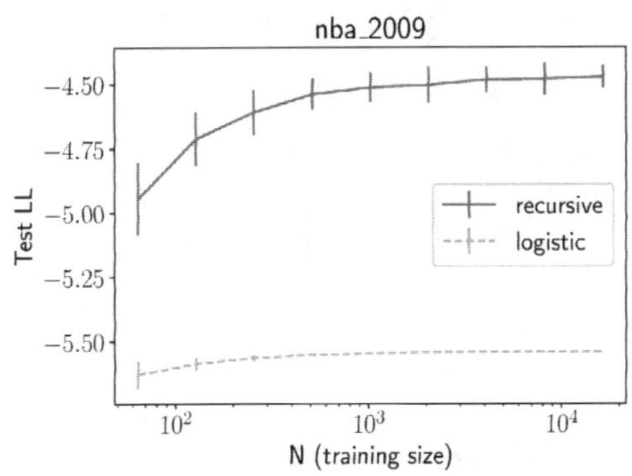

Figure 11: Learning results for the 2009-2010 NBA Champion Los Angeles Lakers.

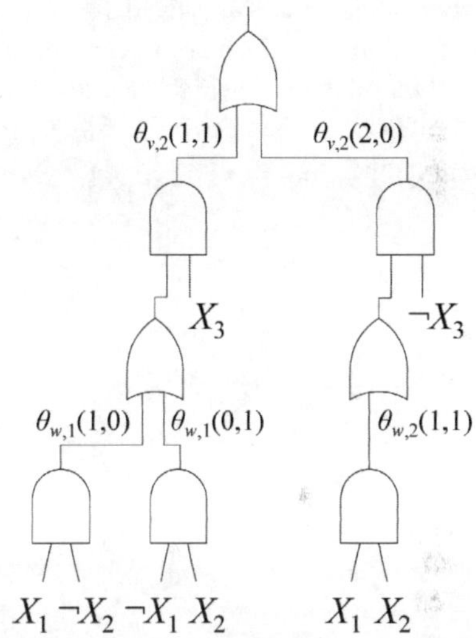

Figure 13: A PSDD corresponding to the vtree and the recursive n-choose-k model of Figure 2 (and Figure 12).

C EXAMPLE PSDD

Figure 13 highlights the SDD/PSDD corresponding to the recursive 3-choose-2 model of Figure 2 using the same vtree. For convenience, we reproduce the vtree and model in Figure 12.

As we highlighted in Section 6, the Boolean circuit of Figure 13 (ignoring the annotated parameters $\theta_{v,k}$) outputs 1 if the circuit input sets exactly 2 out of 3 variables positively, and outputs 0 otherwise. Note that for simplicity, we have omitted inconsistent branches of or-gates that would normally appear in a SDD/PSDD (these branches correspond to instantiations that do not have the required cardinality, and hence, always outputs a 0).

We can obtain an AC of this PSDD by performing two steps: convert each and-gate into a $*$-node, and convert each or-node with children $c_1, \ldots, c_n$ and parameters $\theta_1, \ldots, \theta_n$ into a $+$-node with children $\alpha_1 * c_1, \ldots,$ $\alpha_n * c_n$. Given an instantiation $\mathbf{x}$, the output of the AC is found by setting the inputs to 1/0 according to $\mathbf{x}$ and then evaluating the circuit bottom-up. This output yields the probability $Pr(\mathbf{x})$ of the corresponding recursive 3-choose-2 model.

The properties of SDDs and PSDDs allow certain queries or operations to be performed efficiently, which are otherwise hard on general Boolean and arithmetic circuits. For example, model counting can be performed using SDDs in time that is linear in the size of the SDD (Darwiche, 2011). In PSDDs, queries such as MPE and marginals are similarly tractable (as discussed in Section 3.2). The maximum likelihood parameters of a PSDD can be learned in closed-from from a complete dataset (as in Section 4). Further, one can multiply two PSDDs in polynomial time, which enables incremental learning and inference (Shen et al., 2016).

Structure Learning of Linear Gaussian Structural Equation Models with Weak Edges

Marco F. Eigenmann
Seminar für Statistik
ETH Zurich
Zurich, Switzerland

Preetam Nandy
Department of Biostatistics and Epidemiology
University of Pennsylvania
Philadelphia, PA 19104, USA

Marloes H. Maathuis
Seminar für Statistik
ETH Zurich
Zurich, Switzerland

Abstract

We consider structure learning of linear Gaussian structural equation models with weak edges. Since the presence of weak edges can lead to a loss of edge orientations in the true underlying CPDAG, we define a new graphical object that can contain more edge orientations. We show that this object can be recovered from observational data under a type of strong faithfulness assumption. We present a new algorithm for this purpose, called aggregated greedy equivalence search (AGES), that aggregates the solution path of the greedy equivalence search (GES) algorithm for varying values of the penalty parameter. We prove consistency of AGES and demonstrate its performance in a simulation study and on single cell data from Sachs et al. (2005). The algorithm will be made available in the R-package `pcalg`.

1 INTRODUCTION

We consider structure learning of linear Gaussian structural equation models (SEMs) (Bollen, 1989). A linear SEM is a set of equations of the form $X = B^T X + \varepsilon$, where $X = (X_1, \dots, X_p)^T$, B is a $p \times p$ strictly upper triangular matrix, $\varepsilon = (\varepsilon_1, \dots, \varepsilon_p)^T$, and ε is multivariate Gaussian with mean vector zero and a diagonal covariance matrix D (hence assuming no hidden confounders). Such SEMs can be represented by a directed acyclic graph (DAG) G, where a nonzero entry B_{ij} corresponds to an edge from X_i to X_j. By putting the coefficients B_{ij} along the corresponding edges, one obtains a weighted graph. This weighted graph and the distribution of ε fully determine the distribution of X. Example 1.1 shows a simple instance with $p = 3$, where

$$B = \begin{pmatrix} 0 & 0.1 & 1 \\ 0 & 0 & 1 \\ 0 & 0 & 0 \end{pmatrix}.$$

The weighted DAG is shown in Figure 1a.

Based on n i.i.d. observations from X, we aim to learn the underlying DAG G. However, since G is generally not identifiable from the distribution of X, we learn the so-called Markov equivalence class of G, which can be represented by a completed partially directed acyclic graph (CPDAG) (see Section 2.1). A CPDAG can contain both directed and undirected edges, where undirected edges represent uncertainty about the edge orientation.

Several efficient algorithms have been developed to learn CPDAGs, such as for example the PC algorithm (Spirtes et al., 2000) and the greedy equivalence search algorithm (GES) (Chickering, 2002b). These algorithms have been proved to be sound and consistent (Spirtes et al., 2000; Kalisch and Bühlmann, 2007; Chickering, 2002b; Nandy et al., 2015).

Example 1.1 illustrates a somewhat counter-intuitive behaviour of these algorithms for varying sample size.

Example 1.1. *Consider the following SEM:*

$$X_1 = \varepsilon_1$$
$$X_2 = 0.1 \cdot X_1 + \varepsilon_2$$
$$X_3 = X_1 + X_2 + \varepsilon_3,$$

where $\varepsilon \sim N(0, I)$. *The corresponding CPDAG is the complete undirected graph in Figure 1b. When running PC or GES with a very large sample size, the algorithms will output this CPDAG with high probability. For a smaller sample size, however, the algorithms are likely to miss the weak edge* $X_1 - X_2$, *leading to the CPDAG in Figure 1c. Note that the latter CPDAG contains two edge orientations that are identical to the orientations in the*

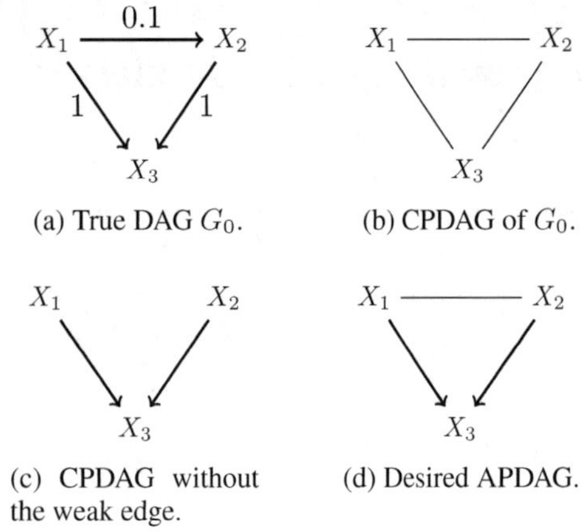

(a) True DAG G_0. (b) CPDAG of G_0. (c) CPDAG without the weak edge. (d) Desired APDAG.

Figure 1: A simple case where the inclusion of a weak edge leads to a loss of edge orientations (see Example 1.1).

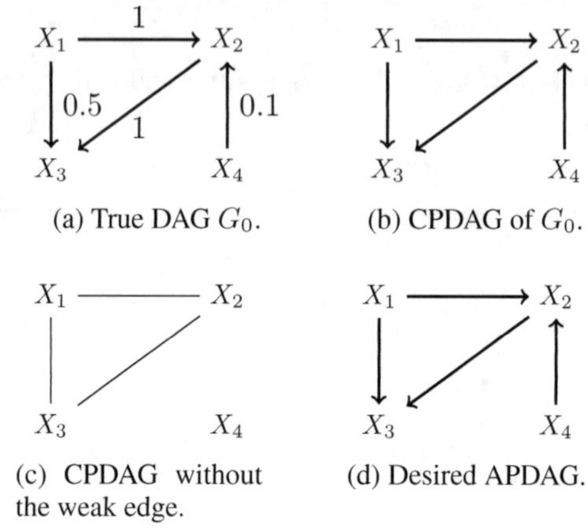

(a) True DAG G_0. (b) CPDAG of G_0. (c) CPDAG without the weak edge. (d) Desired APDAG.

Figure 2: A simple case where the inclusion of a weak edge helps to obtain edge orientations (see Example 1.2).

underlying DAG G_0. Thus, both CPDAGs in Figures 1b and 1c contain some relevant information, one in terms of correct adjacencies and one in terms of correct edge orientations. For this example, GES outputs Figure 1c for a sample size smaller than 100 *and Figure 1b for a sample size larger than 1000, with high probabilities.*

One may think that a simple solution to the above problem is to omit weak edges either by using a strong penalty on model complexity or by truncating edges with small weights. In some cases, however, the inclusion of weak edges can also help to obtain edge orientations. This is illustrated in Example 1.2.

Example 1.2. *Consider the weighted DAG in Figure 2a with $\varepsilon \sim N(0, I)$. Figure 2b represents the corresponding CPDAG, which is fully oriented. For large sample sizes, PC and GES will output this CPDAG with high probability. For smaller sample sizes, however, they are likely to miss the weak edge $X_4 \to X_2$, leading to the CPDAG in Figure 2c, which is fully undirected.*

With a larger sample size we expect to gain more insight into a system, and the fact that we can lose correct edge orientations is undesirable. In the extreme case of a complete DAG with many weak edges, a small sample size yields informative output in terms of certain edge orientations, while a large sample size yields the asymptotically correct CPDAG, which is the uninformative complete undirected graph. This problem is relevant in practice for situations where the underlying system contains many weak effects and the sample size can be very large.

We propose a solution for this problem by defining a new graphical target object that can contain more edge orientations than the CPDAG. This object is a partially directed acyclic graph (PDAG) obtained by aggregating several CPDAGs of sub-DAGs of the underlying DAG G_0, and is called an aggregated PDAG (APDAG). In Example 1.1, we intuitively overlay the CPDAGs of Figures 1b and 1c to obtain the APDAG in Figure 1d, that contains both the correct skeleton and some edge orientations that were present in G_0 but not in the CPDAG of G_0. The APDAG for Example 1.2 is given in Figure 2d, and is in this case identical to the CPDAG of G_0.

Our APDAG is a maximally oriented PDAG, as studied in Meek (1995). We will show that APDAGs can be learned from observational data under a type of strong faithfulness condition, namely strong faithfulness with respect to a sequence of sub-DAGs of the underlying DAG. In this sense, our work is related to other structure learning algorithms that output maximally oriented PDAGs or DAGs under certain restrictions on the model class (e.g., Shimizu et al., 2006; Hoyer et al., 2008; Peters and Bühlmann, 2014; Ernest et al., 2016; Peters et al., 2014). Perković et al. (2017) provide methods for causal reasoning with maximally oriented PDAGs.

We propose an algorithm to learn APDAGs, by aggregating the solution path of the greedy equivalence search (GES) algorithm for varying values of the penalty parameter. The algorithm is therefore called aggregated GES (AGES). We show that the entire solution path can basically be computed at once, similarly to the computation of the solution path of the Lasso (Tibshirani, 1996; Tibshirani and Taylor, 2011). We also prove consistency of the algorithm, and demonstrate its performance in a simulation study and on data from Sachs et al. (2005). All proofs are given in the supplementary material.

2 PRELIMINARIES

2.1 GRAPHICAL MODELS

We now introduce the main terminology for graphical models that we need. Further definitions can be found in Section 1 of the supplementary material.

A *graph* $G = (X, E)$ consists of a set of *vertices* $X = \{X_1, \ldots, X_p\}$ and a set of *edges* E. The edges can be either *directed* $X_i \to X_j$ or *undirected* $X_i - X_j$. A *directed graph* is a graph that contains only directed edges. A *partially directed graph* can contain both directed and undirected edges.

If $X_i \to X_j$, then X_i is a *parent* of X_j. The set of parents of X_i in a graph G is denoted by $\mathrm{Pa}_G(X_i)$. A triple (X_i, X_j, X_k) in a graph G is called a *v-structure* if $X_i \to X_j \leftarrow X_k$ and X_i and X_k are not adjacent in G.

A *directed acyclic graph* (DAG) is a directed graph that does not contain directed cycles. A partially directed graph that does not contain directed cycles is a *partially directed acyclic graph* (PDAG). A PDAG P is *extendible* to a DAG if the undirected edges of P can be oriented to obtain a DAG without additional v-structures. The *skeleton* of a partially directed graph G is the graph obtained by replacing all directed edges by undirected edges, and is denoted by $\mathrm{Skeleton}(G)$. The *directed part* of a partially directed graph G is the graph obtained by removing all undirected edges, and is denoted by $\mathrm{DirPart}(G)$. A DAG G restricted to a graph H is the DAG G' obtained by removing from G all adjacencies not present in H. A DAG $G' = (X, E')$ is a *sub-DAG* of a DAG $G = (X, E)$ if $E' \subseteq E$.

A DAG encodes conditional independence constraints via the concept of d-separation (Pearl, 2009). Several DAGs can encode the same set of d-separations. Such DAGs are called *Markov equivalent*. Markov equivalent DAGs have the same skeleton and the same v-structures (Verma and Pearl, 1990). A Markov equivalence class of DAGs can be represented by a *completed partially directed acyclic graph* (CPDAG) (Andersson et al., 1997; Chickering, 2002a). We denote by $\mathrm{CPDAG}(G)$ the CPDAG of a DAG G. A directed edge $X_i \to X_j$ in a CPDAG means that $X_i \to X_j$ occurs in all DAGs in the Markov equivalence class. An undirected edge $X_i - X_j$ in a CPDAG means that there is a DAG with $X_i \to X_j$ and a DAG with $X_i \leftarrow X_j$ in the Markov equivalence class.

We denote conditional independence of two variables X_i and X_j given a set $S \subseteq X \setminus \{X_i, X_j\}$ by $X_i \perp\!\!\!\perp X_j | S$, and the corresponding d-separation relation in a DAG G is denoted by $X_i \perp_G X_j | S$.

A DAG $G = (X, E)$ is a perfect map of the distribution of X if every conditional independence constraint in the distribution is also encoded by the DAG G via d-separation, and vice versa. The first direction is known as the *faithfulness condition* while the backward direction is known as the *Markov condition*. A multivariate Gaussian distribution is said to be δ-*strong faithful* to a DAG $G = (X, E)$ if for every $X_i, X_j \in X$ and for every $S \subseteq X \setminus \{X_i, X_j\}$ it holds that $X_i \not\perp_G X_j | S \Rightarrow |\rho_{X_i, X_j | S}| > \delta$, where $\rho_{X_i, X_j|S}$ is the partial correlation between X_i and X_j given S (cf., Zhang and Spirtes, 2003). Faithfulness is a special case of δ-strong faithfulness with $\delta = 0$.

Throughout the paper we consider distributions of X that allow a perfect map representation through a DAG $G_0 = (X, E)$. The density f of X then admits the following factorization based on G_0: $f(x) = \prod_{i=1}^{p} f(x_i | \mathrm{Pa}_{G_0}(x_i))$.

We denote n i.i.d. observations of $\tilde{X} \subseteq X$ by $\tilde{X}^{(n)}$. DAGs will be denoted with the letter G, PDAGs with P, CPDAGs with C, and APDAGs with A. We reserve the subscript 0 for graphs associated with the true underlying distribution.

2.2 STRUCTURE LEARNING ALGORITHMS

We will make use of the Greedy Equivalence Search (GES) algorithm of Chickering (2002b). This algorithm is composed of two phases called the forward and the backward phase. Starting generally from the empty graph, the forward phase greedily adds edges, one at a time, minimizing each time a scoring criterion over the set of neighbouring CPDAGs. The forward phase stops when the score can no longer be improved by a single edge addition. At that point, the backward phase starts and removes edges, also one at a time, minimizing each time the same scoring criterion, until the score can no longer be improved.

GES operates on the space of CPDAGs. Conceptually, a move from one CPDAG to the next goes as follows: GES computes all DAGs belonging to the actual CPDAG. It then computes all possible edge additions (deletions) for each of the found DAGs. Among all possible edge additions (deletions) it chooses the one that leads to the maximum score improvement, and then computes the CPDAG of the resulting DAG. Chickering (2002b) presented an efficient way to move from one CPDAG to the next without computing the DAGs as described above.

GES has one tuning parameter which we call penalty parameter and denote by λ. As scoring criterion we take a penalized negative log-likelihood function of the following form:

$$\mathcal{S}_\lambda(G, X^{(n)}) = -\sum_{i=1}^{p} \frac{1}{n} \log(L(X_i^{(n)}, \mathrm{Pa}_G(X_i)^{(n)})) + \lambda |E_G|$$

where L is the likelihood function (cf. Definition 5.1 in Nandy et al., 2015). As oracle version of this scoring criterion, we use the true covariance matrix to compute the expected log-likelihood (see Nandy et al., 2015). We denote the output of the oracle version of GES by $\mathrm{GES}_\lambda(f)$ and the output of the sample version of GES by $\mathrm{GES}_\lambda(X^{(n)})$.

Chickering (2002b) showed consistency for GES for a class of scoring criteria including the Bayesian Information Criterion (BIC), which corresponds to $\lambda = \log(n)/(2n)$. The oracle version of GES is sound for $\lambda = 0$, i.e., $\mathrm{GES}_0(f) = \mathrm{CPDAG}(G_0)$.

Given the density f of X, the *solution path* of the oracle version of GES is defined as the ordered set of CPDAGs $\mathrm{GES}_\lambda(f)$ for increasing values of the penalty parameter λ, $\lambda \geqslant 0$. Given n i.i.d. samples $X^{(n)}$, the solution path of the sample version of GES is defined as the ordered set of estimated CPDAGs $\mathrm{GES}_\lambda(X^{(n)})$ for increasing values of the penalty parameter λ, for $\lambda \geqslant \log(n)/(2n)$.

Nandy et al. (2015) showed that the difference in score between two DAGs $G = (X, E)$ and $G' = (X, E')$ that differ by a single edge, i.e., $E' = E \cup \{X_i \to X_j\}$, is given by

$$S_\lambda(G', X^{(n)}) - S_\lambda(G, X^{(n)}) = \frac{1}{2}\log(1 - \hat{\rho}^2_{X_i, X_j | \mathrm{Pa}_G(X_j)}) + \lambda \quad (1)$$

(see Lemma 1.2 of the supplementary material). An edge is added (or deleted) in the forward (or backward) phase of GES only if this quantity is negative. To obtain the oracle version of Equation (1) we use the true covariance matrix to compute the partial correlation.

3 AGES

The main idea behind our new algorithm, Algorithm 2, is to consider a sequence of sub-DAGs of the underlying DAG G_0, to compute their CPDAGs, and finally to aggregate these CPDAGs. Considering only sub-DAGs of G_0 ensures that if an edge is oriented in one of these CPDAGs it has the same orientation as in G_0. This property makes the aggregation intuitive since all CPDAGs will have compatible edge orientations. To learn these CPDAGs we need to assume a special type of δ-strong faithfulness with respect to the sub-DAGs (see Theorem 3.2). The CPDAGs mentioned above can be computed efficiently using GES (see Section 3.5). Therefore,

Algorithm 1: AggregateCPDAGs

```
input : Ordered set of CPDAGs 𝒞 = {C_0, ..., C_k}
output: APDAG A
A ← C_0
for i ∈ {1, ..., k} do
    Define P ← A
    for All edges in C_i do
        if an edge is oriented in C_i but not in P then
            Orient it in P as in C_i
        end
    end
    if P is extendible to a DAG then
        A ← P
    end
end
return MeekOrient(A) (Sec. 1 of the supp. material)
```

we base our new algorithm on GES and call it aggregated GES (AGES).

3.1 THE APDAG A_0

We construct our new target, the aggregated PDAG (APDAG) A_0, with the following four steps:

S.1 Given a multivariate density f of X, compute the solution path of the oracle version of GES for $\lambda \geqslant 0$ and keep the outputs whose skeletons are contained in the skeleton of $C_0 = \mathrm{GES}_0(f)$. This yields a set of CPDAGs $\mathcal{C} = \{C_0, \cdots, C_k\}$ with associated penalty parameters $\lambda_0 < \ldots < \lambda_k$.[1]

S.2 Construct the set of DAGs $\mathcal{G} = \{G_0, \ldots, G_k\}$ consisting of G_0 restricted to the skeletons of the CPDAGs in $\mathcal{C}$.

S.3 Construct the CPDAGs $\tilde{\mathcal{C}} = \{\tilde{C}_0, \ldots, \tilde{C}_k\}$ where $\tilde{C}_i = \mathrm{CPDAG}(G_i)$, $0 \leqslant i \leqslant k$.

S.4 Let $A_0 = \mathrm{AggregateCPDAGs}(\tilde{\mathcal{C}})$ (Algorithm 1).

We emphasize that A_0 is a theoretical object, since its construction involves the oracle version of GES and the orientations of the true underlying DAG G_0. The construction ensures that $G_1, \ldots, G_k$ are sub-DAGs of G_0. Hence, any oriented edges in the corresponding CPDAGs $\tilde{C}_1, \ldots, \tilde{C}_k$ also correspond to those in G_0. As a result, the APDAG A_0 has the same skeleton as C_0 and

$$\mathrm{DirPart}(C_0) \subseteq \mathrm{DirPart}(A_0) \subseteq \mathrm{DirPart}(G_0).$$

[1] Throughout, we use the convention that any CPDAG computed by GES is associated with the smallest possible value of the penalty parameter λ for which this output can be obtained.

Algorithm 2: AGES (oracle)

input : Distribution of X
output: APDAG A

Compute the solution path of the oracle version of GES for $\lambda \geqslant 0$
Discard all outputs whose skeletons are not contained in the skeleton of the output when $\lambda = 0$. Denote the remaining set of CPDAGs associated with $\lambda_0 < \ldots < \lambda_k$ by $\mathcal{C} = \{C_0, \ldots, C_k\}$
return AggregateCPDAGs($\mathcal{C}$)

This makes A_0 an interesting object to investigate.[2]

3.2 ORACLE VERSION OF AGES AND SOUNDNESS

The oracle version of AGES is given in pseudocode as Algorithm 2. We use Example 3.1 to illustrate it. Soundness of the algorithm is shown in Theorem 3.2.

Example 3.1. *Consider the density f generated by the weighted DAG in Figure 3a with $\varepsilon \sim N(0, D)$, where D is a diagonal matrix with entries $(0.3, 0.4, 0.3, 0.4)$. We compute the solution path of the oracle version of GES, shown in the six CPDAGs in Figures 3b - 3g, corresponding to $\lambda_0 < \cdots < \lambda_5$. We discard C_1 and C_2 since their skeletons are not contained in the skeleton of C_0. We then aggregate the remaining CPDAGs C_0, C_3, C_4, and C_5, using lines 1-12 of Algorithm 1. The result shown in Figure 3h contains additional orientations, coming from the v-structure $X_1 \to X_3 \leftarrow X_2$ in C_3 . The final output in Figure 3i shows two further oriented edges due to MeekOrient.*

Theorem 3.2. *Given a multivariate Gaussian distribution of X with a perfect map $G_0 = (X, E)$, let $\mathcal{G}$ be the set of DAGs constructed in Step S.2, and let $\tilde{\mathcal{C}}$ be the corresponding set of CPDAGs of Step S.3. Assume that for all $1 \leqslant i \leqslant k$ the distribution of X is δ_i-strong faithful with respect to $G_i \in \mathcal{G}$, where δ_i is such that $\lambda_i = -1/2 \log(1 - \delta_i^2)$. Then $\mathrm{GES}_{\lambda_i}(f) = C_i = \tilde{C}_i$ for all $1 \leqslant i \leqslant k$, and the oracle version of AGES returns the APDAG A_0.*

Since the above δ_i-strong faithfulness assumption with respect to G_i for $1 \leqslant i \leqslant k$ is related to the solution path of GES, we refer to it as *path strong faithfulness*.

[2]We note that the if-clause on line 9 of Algorithm 1 is not needed when applying the algorithm to $\tilde{\mathcal{C}}$; it is needed in the context of Algorithms 2 and 3.

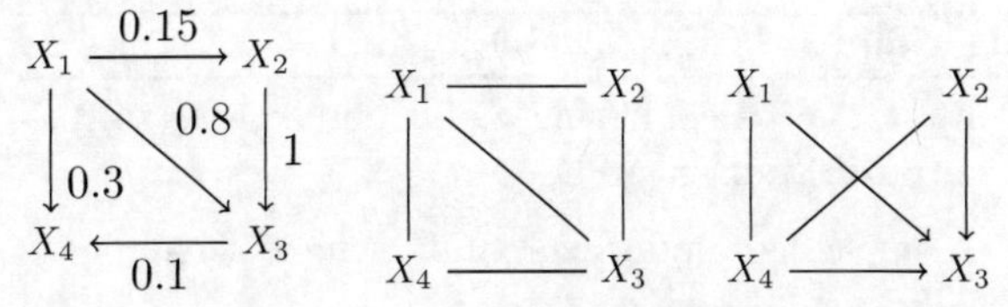

(a) True DAG G_0. (b) True CPDAG $C_0 = \mathrm{GES}_{\lambda_0}(f)$. (c) C_1, not a subskeleton of C_0.

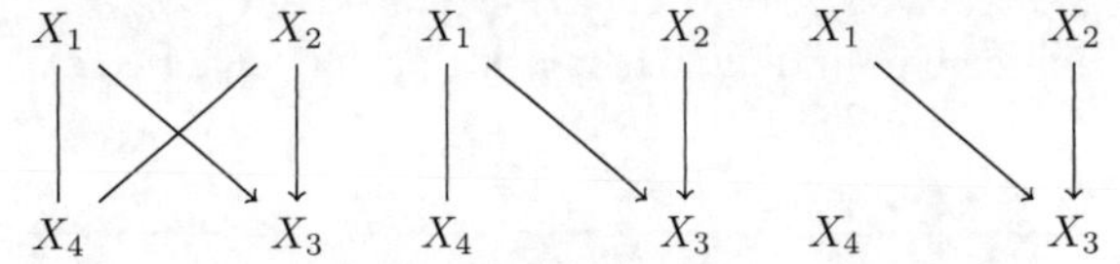

(d) C_2, not a subskeleton of C_0. (e) CPDAG $C_3 = \mathrm{GES}_{\lambda_3}(f)$. (f) CPDAG $C_4 = \mathrm{GES}_{\lambda_4}(f)$.

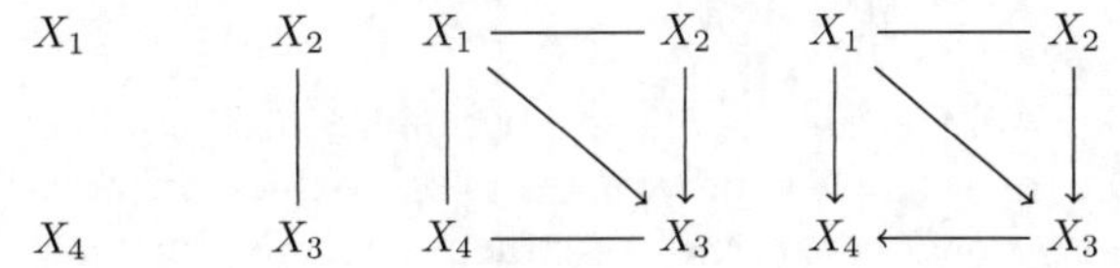

(g) CPDAG $C_5 = \mathrm{GES}_{\lambda_5}(f)$. (h) APDAG without MeekOrient. (i) APDAG with MeekOrient.

Figure 3: Illustration of the oracle AGES algorithm (see Example 3.1).

3.3 SAMPLE VERSION OF AGES AND CONSISTENCY

The sample version of AGES is given in Algorithm 3. We see that the algorithm considers the output of the sample version of GES for all $\lambda \geqslant \log(n)/(2n)$, i.e., by penalizing equally strong or stronger than BIC for model complexity.

In line 2 of Algorithm 3, we may obtain CPDAGs with conflicting orientations. Because of such possible conflicts, we need the if-clause on line 9 of Algorithm 1. The aggregation algorithm is constructed so that orientations in $\hat{C}_\ell$ are only taken into account if they are compatible with the aggregated graph based on $\hat{C}_0, \ldots, \hat{C}_{\ell-1}$. In particular, the algorithm ensures that we stay within the Markov equivalence class defined by $\hat{C}_0 = \mathrm{GES}_{\log(n)/(2n)}(X^{(n)})$, i.e., the output of GES.

Let $\mathrm{AGES}(X^{(n)})$ denote the output of AGES based on a sample $X^{(n)}$. Theorem 3.3 shows consistency of AGES.

Theorem 3.3. *Under the conditions of Theorem 3.2, we have*

$$\lim_{n\to\infty} \mathbb{P}\left(\mathrm{AGES}(X^{(n)}) = A_0\right) \to 1.$$

Algorithm 3: AGES (sample)

input : $X^{(n)}$, containing n i.i.d. observations of X
output: Estimated APDAG $\hat{A}$

1 Compute the solution path of the sample version of GES for $\lambda \geqslant \log(n)/(2n)$
2 Discard all outputs whose skeletons are not contained in the skeleton of the output when $\lambda = \log(n)/(2n)$. Denote the remaining CPDAGs, ordered according to increasing penalty parameter λ, by $\hat{\mathcal{C}} = \{\hat{C}_0, \ldots, \hat{C}_k\}$
3 **return** AggregateCPDAGs($\hat{\mathcal{C}}$)

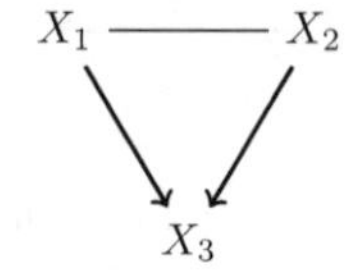

(a) Informative APDAG.

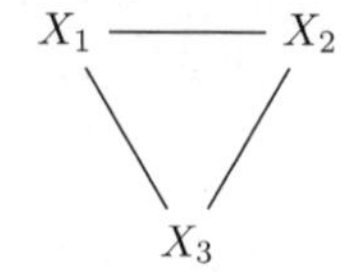

(b) Uninformative APDAG.

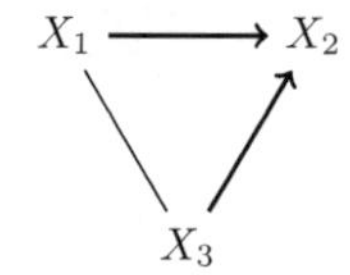

(c) APDAG with one wrong orientation.

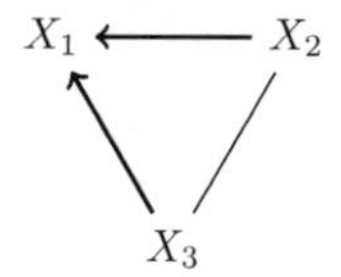

(d) APDAG with two wrong orientations.

Figure 4: The possible outputs of AGES in Example 3.4.

3.4 THE PATH STRONG FAITHFULNESS ASSUMPTION

The δ-strong faithfulness assumption has been used before, for example to prove uniform consistency and high-dimensional consistency of structure learning methods (Kalisch and Bühlmann, 2007; Zhang and Spirtes, 2003). On the other hand, it has been criticised for being too strong (Uhler et al., 2013).

We do not assume the classical δ-strong faithfulness for the underlying distribution with respect to G_0. Instead, we assume δ_i-strong faithfulness of the distribution of X with respect to the sequence of sub-DAGs $G_1, \ldots, G_k$ as defined in Step S.2, with corresponding $\lambda_1 < \cdots < \lambda_k$. Hence, the corresponding δ_is satisfy $\delta_1 < \cdots < \delta_k$. Since smaller values of λ typically yield denser graphs, it follows that for smaller values of δ_i, the assumption has to hold with respect to a denser graph, while for larger values of δ_i, the assumption has to hold with respect to a sparser graph.

Example 3.4. *We first analyse the path strong faithfulness assumption by considering the SEM given in Example 1.1, but with unspecified edge weights B_{13} and B_{23}:*

$$\begin{aligned}X_1 &= \varepsilon_1\\ X_2 &= 0.1 \cdot X_1 + \varepsilon_2\\ X_3 &= B_{13}X_1 + B_{23}X_2 + \varepsilon_3,\end{aligned}$$

and $\varepsilon \sim N(0, I)$.

Depending on the edge weights, A_0 can be either the APDAG in Figure 4a or in Figure 4b. Figure 5 illustrates how A_0 and the path strong faithfulness assumption are related to the edge weights $B_{13} \in [-2, 2]$ and $B_{23} \in [-2, 2]$. We split the $[-2, 2] \times [-2, 2]$ rectangle into the following three regions:

White region: *A_0 equals the APDAG in Figure 4a and the path strong faithfulness assumption is satisfied.*

Grey region: *A_0 equals the APDAG in Figure 4b and the path strong faithfulness assumption is satisfied.*

Black region: *A_0 equals the APDAG in Figure 4b and the path strong faithfulness assumption is violated.*

The output A of the oracle version of AGES can be one of the four APDAGs in Figure 4. Theorem 3.2 guarantees that $A = A_0$ when path strong faithfulness is satisfied, i.e., outside of the black region. Further, for this example, A equals one of the APDAGs in Figures 4c and 4d on the black region. This demonstrates that, in this simple example with $p = 3$, our strong faithfulness assumption is, in fact, a necessary and sufficient condition for having $A = A_0$. We emphasize that for $p > 3$, we may have $A = A_0$ even when the strong faithfulness assumption is violated.

Figure 5 shows that in a large fraction of the plane we gain structural information (white region), on a smaller part we perform as GES (grey region), and on another smaller part we make some errors when orienting edges (black region). Details about the construction of Figure 5 are given in Section 5 of the supplementary material.

The path strong faithfulness assumption is sufficient but not necessary for Theorem 3.2. In Section 6 of the supplementary material we provide a weaker version of the assumption that is necessary and sufficient for equality of $\tilde{\mathcal{C}}$ (as defined in Step S.3) and $\mathcal{C}$ (as defined in line 2 of Algorithm 2). This weaker version is only sufficient for equality of the true APDAG A_0 and the oracle output A of AGES (AggregateCPDAGs($\mathcal{C}$)), since not all orientations of the CPDAGs in $\mathcal{C}$ are used in the aggregation process. The supplementary material also contains empirical results where we evaluated equality of $\tilde{\mathcal{C}}$ and $\mathcal{C}$,

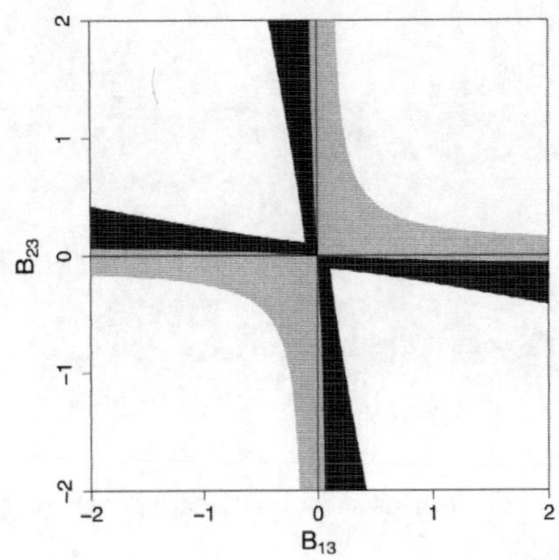

Figure 5: Visual representation of the dependence of A_0 and the path strong faithfulness assumption on the edge weights in Example 3.4.

as well A_0 and A, for the simulation setting described in Section 4.

3.5 COMPUTATION

The forward phase of GES (of both the oracle version and the sample version) can be computed at once for all $\lambda \geqslant 0$. This follows from Equation (1). At each step in the forward phase, GES conceptually searches for the in absolute value largest partial correlation $|\rho_{X_i,X_j|\,\mathrm{Pa}_G(X_j)}|$ among all DAGs G in the current Markov equivalence class, and all pairs X_i and X_j that are not adjacent in G and where X_i is a non-descendant of X_j in G. The algorithm then adds the corresponding edge $X_i \to X_j$ to G if the score is improved, that is, if $1/2\log(1-\rho^2_{X_i,X_j|Pa_G(X_j)}) + \lambda < 0$, and then constructs the CPDAG the resulting DAG.

Thus, starting the forward phase with the empty graph and a very large λ, no edge is added. By decreasing λ so that $\lambda < \max_{i,j} -1/2\log(1-\rho^2_{X_i,X_j})$, the first edge is added. By decreasing λ further, one can compute the entire solution path of the forward phase in one go, analogously to the computation of the solution path of the lasso (Tibshirani, 1996; Tibshirani and Taylor, 2011).

For each distinct output of the forward phase, obtained for a given λ, one has to run the backward phase with this λ. Since the backward phase of GES usually only conducts very few steps, this does not cause a large computational burden.

The fast computation of the entire solution path of GES is one of the reasons for basing our approach on GES, rather than, for example, on the PC-algorithm for a range of different tuning parameters α.

4 EMPIRICAL RESULTS

4.1 SIMULATION SETUP

We simulate data from SEMs of the following form:

$$X = B^T X + \varepsilon,$$

with $\varepsilon \sim \mathcal{N}(0, D)$, where D is a $p \times p$ diagonal matrix whose diagonal entries are drawn independently from a Unif(0.5,1.5) distribution.

In order to vary the concentration of strong and weak edge weights as well as the sparsity of the models, we consider all combinations of pairs $(q_s, q_w) \in \{0.1, 0.3, 0.5, 0.7\}$ such that $q_s + q_w \leqslant 1$. Each entry of the matrix B has a probability of q_s of being strong, of q_w of being weak, and of $(1 - q_s - q_w)$ of being 0. The nonzero edge weights in the B matrix are drawn independently as follows: the absolute values of the weak and the strong edge weights are drawn from Unif(0.1,0.3) and Unif(0.8,1.2), respectively. The sign of each edge weight is chosen to be positive or negative with equal probabilities. Finally, in order to investigate whether our algorithm performs at least as good as GES when we do not encourage the presence of weak edges, we also simulate from SEMs with $q_s \in \{0.1, 0.2, \ldots, 1\}$ and $q_w = 0$.

We simulate from SEMs with $p = 10$ variables. The sample size used in the plots in the main paper is 10000. The number of simulations for each settings is 500.

In Section 3 of the supplementary material we show additional plots corresponding to sample sizes 100 and 1000. Those plots show a similar pattern as the ones in the main paper, but the ability to gain additional edge orientations diminishes for smaller n. Section 4 of the supplementary material also shows simulation results for $p = 100$ and varying sample sizes.

4.2 SIMULATION RESULTS

Since AGES always outputs the same skeleton as GES by construction, we analyse the performance of GES and AGES by comparing their precision and recall in estimating the directed part of the true DAG. The recall is the ratio of the number of correctly oriented edges in the estimated graph and the total number of oriented edges in the true DAG. The precision is the ratio of the number of correctly oriented edges in the estimated graph and the total number of oriented edges in the estimated graph.

Figure 6 summarizes the performance of GES and AGES (with $\lambda = \log(n)/(2n)$) for all combinations of $(q_s, q_w) \in \{0.1, 0.3, 0.5, 0.7\}$ such that $q_s + q_w \leqslant 1$. In each setting, AGES outperforms GES in recall, while achieving a roughly similar performance as GES in pre-

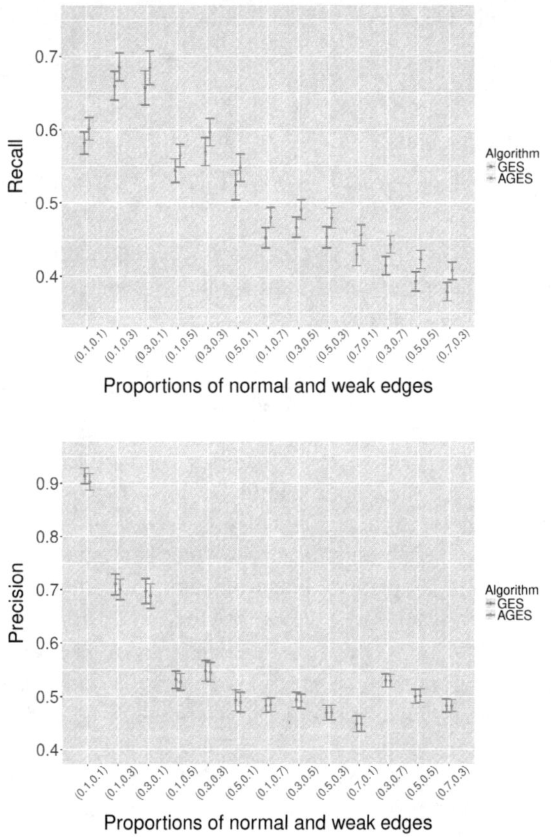

Figure 6: Mean precision and recall of GES and AGES over 500 simulations for all combinations of $(q_s, q_w) \in \{0.1, 0.3, 0.5, 0.7\}$ such that $q_s + q_w \leqslant 1$, using $\lambda = \log(n)/(2n)$ and $n = 10000$ (see Section 4.1). The bars in the plots correspond to $\pm$ twice the standard error of the mean.

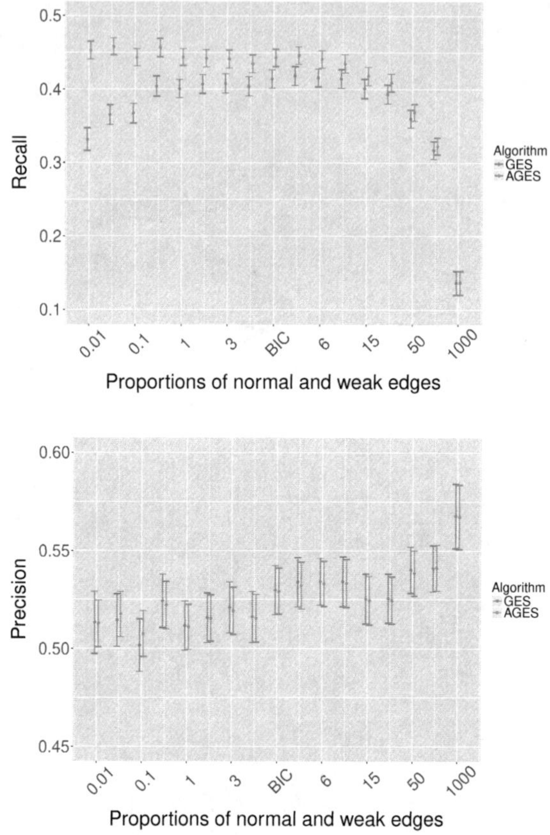

Figure 7: Mean precision and recall of GES and AGES over 500 simulations for $(q_s, q_w) = (0.3, 0.7)$, using $n = 10000$ and varying values of λ (see Section 4.1). The bars in the plots correspond to $\pm$ twice the standard error of the mean.

cision. This demonstrates that AGES is able to orient more edges than GES without increasing the false discovery rate.

Figure 7 compares the performance of GES and AGES for various choices of the penalty parameter λ when $(q_s, q_w) = (0.3, 0.7)$. In each case, we use the chosen penalty of GES as the minimum penalty of AGES, so that the skeletons of both outputs are identical. We see that AGES outperforms GES for all penalty parameters, and that AGES is less sensitive to the choice of the penalty parameter.

Figure 8 compares GES and AGES for $q_s \in \{0.1, 0.2, \ldots, 1\}$ and $q_w = 0$, using again $\lambda = \log(n)(2n)$. We see that AGES outperforms GES in recall for all values of q_s. There tends to be a small loss in precision for the sparser graphs.

4.3 APPLICATION TO SINGLE CELL DATA

We apply AGES to the well-known single cell data of Sachs et al. (2005), consisting of quantitative amounts of 11 proteins in human T-cells that were measured under 14 experimental conditions. In each experimental condition, different interventions were made, concerning the abundance or the activity of the molecules[3] (Sachs et al., 2005; Mooij and Heskes, 2013). We analyze each experimental condition separately, yielding 14 data sets with sample sizes between 700 and 1000.

Sachs et al. (2005) presented a conventionally accepted signalling network for these proteins (Sachs et al., 2005, Figures 2 and 3). We use this to determine a ground truth for each experimental condition (see Section 7 of the supplementary material), so that we can assess the performance of AGES in comparison to GES on these data.

[3]An activity intervention can either activate or inhibit the molecule

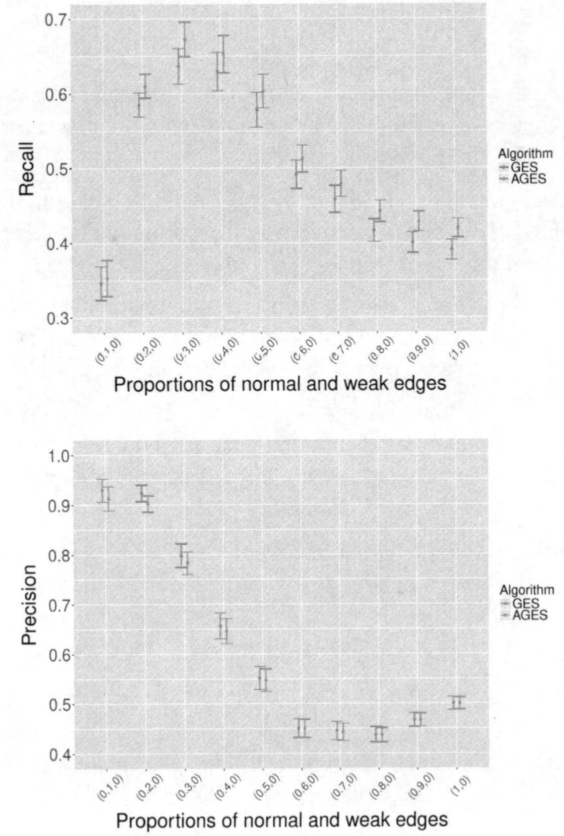

Figure 8: Mean precision and recall over 500 simulations with $q_s \in \{0.1, 0.2, \ldots, 1\}$ and $q_w = 0$, using $\lambda = \log(n)/(2n)$ and $n = 10000$ (see Section 4.1). The bars in the plots correspond to $\pm$ twice the standard error of the mean.

Again, since the skeletons of the outputs of GES and AGES are identical by construction, we only evaluate the directed edges. Moreover, we limit ourselves to adjacencies that are present in the true network. Considering these adjacencies, AGES found additional edge orientations in 6 experimental conditions. Table 1 summarizes the results. In experimental conditions 8 and 9, AGES was able to substantially improve the output, while in the other 4 conditions (4, 5, 13 and 14), AGES and GES had roughly similar performances. Thus, although these data almost certainly violate various assumptions of our methods (acyclicity, Gaussianity, path strong faithfulness, hidden confounders), we obtain encouraging results.

5 DISCUSSION

We considered structure learning of linear Gaussian SEMs with weak edges. We presented a new graphical object, called APDAG, that aggregates the structural information of many CPDAGs, yielding additional orientation information. We proposed a structure learning algorithm that uses the solution path of GES to learn this new object and gave sufficient conditions for its soundness and consistency. The algorithm will be made available in the R-package `pcalg` (Kalisch et al., 2012).

Experimental condition	4	5	8	9	13	14
Correct	0	1	8	5	1	1
Wrong	1	0	0	0	2	0

Table 1: For each of the listed experimental conditions, we report the number of correct and wrong edge orientations among edge orientations that were found by AGES but not by GES. The results are limited to adjacencies that are present in the true network (see Figure 9 of the supplementary material), and correctness of edge orientations was evaluated with respect to this network.

We applied AGES in a simulation study and on data from Sachs et al. (2005). Despite the fact that in both cases the assumptions of Theorem 3.2 are likely violated, we obtained promising results.

Our work can be easily extended to the so called nonparanormal distributions (Liu et al., 2009; Harris and Drton, 2013). In this setting we assume that there is a latent linear Gaussian SEM and that each observed variable is a strictly increasing (or strictly decreasing) transformation of the corresponding latent variable. In this case, the weakness of an edge can be connected to its edge weight in the latent linear Gaussian SEM and we can use AGES with a rank correlation based scoring criterion as defined in Nandy et al. (2015).

Moreover, the Gaussian error assumption can be dropped, i.e., we can consider linear SEMs with arbitrary error distributions. This is due to a one-to-one correspondence between zero partial correlations in a linear SEM with arbitrary error distributions and d-separations in its corresponding DAG (e.g., Hoyer et al., 2008). When all error variables are non-Gaussian, one can use the LiNGAM algorithm (Shimizu et al., 2006) to recover the data generating DAG uniquely. In this case, one would therefore not run GES or AGES. If some error variables are Gaussian and others are non-Gaussian, Hoyer et al. (2008) proposed a combination of PC and LiNGAM. It would be an interesting direction for future work to combine (A)GES with LiNGAM for a mixture of Gaussian and non-Gaussian error variables.

5.1 Acknowledgements

This work was supported in part by the Swiss NSF Grant 200021_172603.

References

Andersson, S. A., Madigan, D., and Perlman, M. D. (1997). A characterization of Markov equivalence classes for acyclic digraphs. *Ann. Stat.*, 25:505–541.

Bollen, K. (1989). *Structural Equations with Latent Variables*. Wiley, New York.

Chickering, D. M. (2002a). Learning equivalence classes of Bayesian-network structures. *J. Mach. Learn. Res.*, 2:445–498.

Chickering, D. M. (2002b). Optimal structure identification with greedy search. *J. Mach. Learn. Res.*, 3:507–554.

Ernest, J., Rothenhäusler, D., and Bühlmann, P. (2016). Causal inference in partially linear structural equation models: identifiability and estimation. arXiv:1607.05980.

Harris, N. and Drton, M. (2013). PC algorithm for nonparanormal graphical models. *J. Mach. Learn. Res.*, 14:3365–3383.

Hoyer, P. O., Hyvarinen, A., Scheines, R., Spirtes, P. L., Ramsey, J., Lacerda, G., and Shimizu, S. (2008). Causal discovery of linear acyclic models with arbitrary distributions. In *Proceedings of UAI 2008*, pages 282–289.

Kalisch, M. and Bühlmann, P. (2007). Estimating high-dimensional directed acyclic graphs with the PC-algorithm. *J. Mach. Learn. Res.*, 8:613–636.

Kalisch, M., Mächler, M., Colombo, D., Maathuis, M. H., and Bühlmann, P. (2012). Causal inference using graphical models with the R package pcalg. *J. Statist. Software*, 47(11):1–26.

Liu, H., Lafferty, J., and Wasserman, L. (2009). The nonparanormal: Semiparametric estimation of high dimensional undirected graphs. *J. Mach. Learn. Research*, 10:2295–2328.

Meek, C. (1995). Causal inference and causal explanation with background knowledge. In *Proceedings of UAI 1995*, pages 403–410.

Mooij, J. M. and Heskes, T. (2013). Cyclic causal discovery from continuous equilibrium data. In *Proceedings of UAI 2013*, pages 431–439.

Nandy, P., Hauser, A., and Maathuis, M. H. (2015). High-dimensional consistency in score-based and hybrid structure learning. arXiv:1507.02608v4.

Pearl, J. (2009). *Causality: Models, Reasoning and Inference*. Cambridge University Press, New York, 2nd edition.

Perković, E., Kalisch, M., and Maathuis, M. H. (2017). Interpreting and using CPDAGs with background knowledge. In *Proceedings of UAI 2017*. To appear; arXiv:1707.02171.

Peters, J. and Bühlmann, P. (2014). Identifiability of Gaussian structural equation models with equal error variances. *Biometrika*, 101:219–228.

Peters, J., Mooij, J. M., Janzing, D., and Schölkopf, B. (2014). Causal discovery with continuous additive noise models. *J. Mach. Learn. Res.*, 15:2009–2053.

Sachs, K., Perez, O., Pe'er, D., Lauffenburger, D. A., and Nolan, G. P. (2005). Causal protein-signaling networks derived from multiparameter single-cell data. *Science*, 308:523–529.

Shimizu, S., Hoyer, P., Hyvärinen, A., and Kerminen, A. (2006). A linear non-Gaussian acyclic model for causal discovery. *J. Mach. Learn. Res.*, 7:2003–2030.

Spirtes, P., Glymour, C., and Scheines, R. (2000). *Causation, Prediction, and Search*. MIT Press, Cambridge, 2nd edition.

Tibshirani, R. (1996). Regression shrinkage and selection via the lasso. *J. Roy. Statist. Soc. Ser. B*, 58:267–288.

Tibshirani, R. J. and Taylor, J. (2011). The solution path of the generalized lasso. *Ann. Statist.*, 39:1335–1371.

Uhler, C., Raskutti, G., Bhlmann, P., and Yu, B. (2013). Geometry of the faithfulness assumption in causal inference. *Ann. Statist.*, 41:436–463.

Verma, T. and Pearl, J. (1990). Equivalence and synthesis of causal models. In *Proceedings of UAI 1990*, pages 255–270.

Zhang, J. and Spirtes, P. (2003). Strong faithfulness and uniform consistency in causal inference. In *Proceedings of UAI 2003*, pages 632–639.

Supplementary material to "Structure Learning of Linear Gaussian Structural Equation Models with Weak Edges"

1 PRELIMINARIES

Two vertices X_i and X_j are *adjacent* if there is an edge between them. A *path* between X_i and X_j is a sequence $(X_i, \ldots, X_j)$ of distinct vertices in which all pairs of successive vertices are adjacent. A *directed path* is a path between X_i and X_j where all edges are directed towards X_j, i.e., $X_i \to \cdots \to X_j$. A directed path from X_i to X_j together with the edge $X_j \to X_i$ forms a *directed cycle*. If $X_i \to X_j \leftarrow X_k$ is part of a path, then X_j is a *collider* on this path.

A vertex X_j is a *child* of the vertex X_i if $X_i \to X_j$. If there is a directed path from X_i to X_j, X_i is a *descendant* of X_j, otherwise it is a non-descendant. We use the convention that X_i is also a descendant of itself.

A DAG encodes conditional independence constraints through the concept of d-separation (Pearl, 2009). For three pairwise disjoint subsets of vertices A, B, and S of X, A is d-separated from B by S, $A \perp B|S$, if every path between a vertex in A and a vertex in B is *blocked* by S. A path between two vertices X_i and X_j is said to be *blocked* by a set S if a non-collider vertex on the path is present in S or if there is a collider vertex on the path for which none of its descendants is in S. If a path is not blocked it is *open*.

The set of d-separation constraints encoded by a DAG G is denoted by $\mathcal{I}(G)$. All DAGs in a Markov equivalence class encode the same set of d-separation constraints. Hence, for a CPDAG C, we let $\mathcal{I}(C) = \mathcal{I}(G)$, where G is any DAG in C. A DAG G_1 is an independence map (I-map) of a DAG G_2 if $\mathcal{I}(G_1) \subseteq \mathcal{I}(G_2)$, with an analogous definition for CPDAGs. A DAG G_1 is a perfect map of a DAG G_2 if $\mathcal{I}(G_1) = \mathcal{I}(G_2)$, again with an analogous definition for CPDAGs.

For the proof of Theorem 3.2 of the main paper we make use of two lemmas of Nandy et al. (2015).

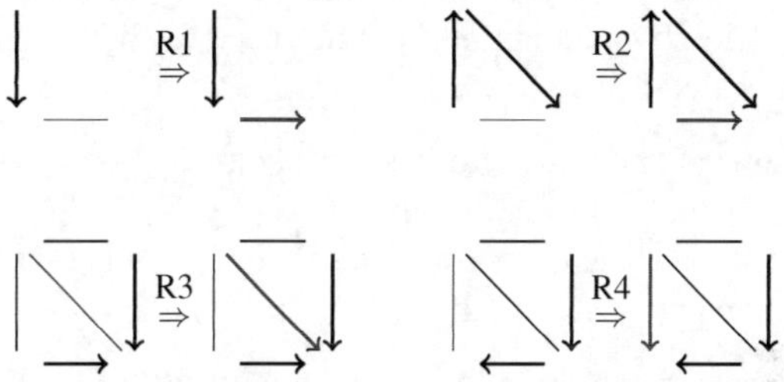

Figure 1: The four orientation rules from Meek (1995). If a PDAG contains one of the graphs on the left-hand-side of the four rules, then orient the blue edge as shown on the right-hand-side.

Lemma 1.1. *(cf. Lemma 9.5 of the supplementary material of Nandy et al. (2015)) Let $G = (X, E)$ be a DAG such that $X_i \to X_j \in E$. Let $G' = (X, E \setminus \{X_i \to X_j\})$. If G is an I-map of a DAG G_1 but G' is not, then $X_i \not\perp_{G_1} X_j \mid \mathrm{Pa}_{G'}(X_i)$.*

Lemma 1.2. *(cf. Lemma 5.1 of Nandy et al. (2015)) Let $G = (X, E)$ be a DAG such that X_i is neither a descendant nor a parent of X_j. Let $G' = (X, E \cup \{X_i \to X_j\})$. If the distribution of X is multivariate Gaussian, then the ℓ_0−penalized log-likelihood score difference between G' and G is*

$$S_\lambda(G', X^{(n)}) - S_\lambda(G, X^{(n)}) \\ = \frac{1}{2}\log(1 - \hat{\rho}^2_{X_i, X_j | \mathrm{Pa}_G(X_j)}) + \lambda.$$

The last step of Algorithm 1 of the main paper consists of MeekOrient. This step applies iteratively and sequentially the four rules depicted in Figure 1. These orientation rules can lead to some additional orientations, and the resulting output is a maximally oriented PDAG (Meek, 1995). For an example of its utility see Example 3.1 and Figure 3 in the main paper.

2 PROOFS

2.1 PROOF OF THEOREM 3.2 OF THE MAIN PAPER

We first establish the following Lemma.

Lemma 2.1. *Consider two CPDAGs C_1 and C_2 where C_1 is an I-map of C_2. If C_1 and C_2 have the same skeleton, then C_1 is a perfect map of C_2.*

Proof. Let G_1 and G_2 be arbitrary DAGs in the Markov equivalence classes described by C_1 and C_2, respectively. Then C_1 is a perfect map of C_2 if and only if G_1 and G_2 have the same skeleton and the same v-structures (Verma and Pearl, 1990). Since G_1 and G_2 have the same skeleton by assumption, we only need to show that they have identical v-structures.

Suppose first that there is a v-structure $X_i \rightarrow X_j \leftarrow X_k$ in G_1 that is not present in G_2. Since G_1 and G_2 have the same skeleton, this implies that X_j is a non-collider on the path (X_i, X_j, X_k) in G_2.

We assume without loss of generality that X_i is a non-descendant of X_k in G_1. Then, $X_i \perp_{G_1} X_k | \mathrm{Pa}_{G_1}(X_k)$, where $X_j \notin \mathrm{Pa}_{G_1}(X_k)$. On the other hand, we have $X_i \not\perp_{G_2} X_k | \mathrm{Pa}_{G_1}(X_k)$, since the path (X_i, X_j, X_k) is open in G_2, since $X_j \notin \mathrm{Pa}_{G_1}(X_k)$. This contradicts that C_1 is an I-map of C_2.

Next, suppose that there is a v-structure $X_i \rightarrow X_j \leftarrow X_k$ in G_2 that is not present in G_1. Since G_1 and G_2 have the same skeleton, this implies that X_j is a non-collider on the path (X_i, X_j, X_k) in G_1.

We again assume without loss of generality that X_i is a non-descendant of X_k in G_1. Then the path (X_i, X_j, X_k) has one of the following forms: $X_i \rightarrow X_j \rightarrow X_k$ or $X_i \leftarrow X_j \rightarrow X_k$. In either case, $X_j \in Pa_{G_1}(X_k)$. Hence, $X_i \perp_{G_1} X_k | \mathrm{Pa}_{G_1}(X_k)$, where $X_j \in \mathrm{Pa}_{G_1}(X_k)$. But X_i and X_k are d-connected in G_2 by any set containing X_j. This again contradicts that C_1 is an I-map of C_2. □

Proof of Theorem 3.2 of the main paper. We need to prove that the CPDAGs in Step S.1 of the main paper and the CPDAGs in Step S.3 of the main paper coincide, i.e., $\mathcal{C} = \tilde{\mathcal{C}}$. We prove this result for one of the CPDAGs. Take for instance $\tilde{C}_\ell$, $1 \leqslant \ell \leqslant k$, the CPDAG of $G_\ell = (V, E_\ell)$. Note that G_ℓ is not a perfect map of the distribution of X, and therefore we cannot directly use the proof of Chickering (2002). We can still use the main idea though, in combination with Lemma 1.2.

Consider running GES with penalty parameter $\lambda = -1/2 \log(1 - \delta_\ell^2)$ and denote by C^f and C^b the output of the forward and backward phase, respectively.

Claim 1: C^f is an I-map of $\tilde{C}_\ell$ i.e., all d-separation constraints true in C^f are also true in $\tilde{C}_\ell$.

Proof of Claim 1:
Assume this is not the case, then there are two vertices $X_i, X_j \in X$ and a DAG $G^f \in C^f$ such that $X_i \perp_{G^f} X_j | \{\mathrm{Pa}_{G^f}(X_j) \setminus X_i\}$ but $X_i \not\perp_{C_\ell} X_j | \{\mathrm{Pa}_{G^f}(X_j) \setminus X_i\}$. Because of the δ_ℓ-strong faithful condition, $|\rho_{X_i, X_j | \mathrm{Pa}_{G^f}(X_j)}| > \delta_\ell$. Thus, adding this edge would improve the score. This is a contradiction to the GES algorithm stopping here.

Claim 2: C^b is an I-map of $\tilde{C}_\ell$ i.e., all d-separation constraints true in C^b are also true in $\tilde{C}_\ell$.

Proof of Claim 2: By Claim 1 the backward phase starts with an I-map of $\tilde{C}_\ell$. Suppose it ends with a CPDAG that is not an I-map of $\tilde{C}_\ell$. Then, at some point there is an edge deletion which turns a DAG G that is an I-map of G_ℓ into a DAG G' that is no longer an I-map of G_ℓ. Suppose the deleted edge is (X_i, X_j). By Lemma 1.1, we have $X_i \not\perp_{G_\ell} X_j | \{\mathrm{Pa}_{G'}(X_j)\}$. Hence, again because of the $\delta_\ell-$strong faithfulness condition, $|\rho_{X_i, X_j | \mathrm{Pa}_{G'}(X_j)}| > \delta$. Thus, deleting this edge would worsen the score. This is a contradiction to the GES algorithm deleting this edge.

Claim 3: $C^b = \tilde{C}_\ell$, i.e., C^b is a perfect map of $\tilde{C}_\ell$.

This claim follows from Lemma 2.1 since we know from the previous claim that C^b is an I-map of $\tilde{C}_\ell$ and by construction the skeletons of C^b and $\tilde{C}_\ell$ are the same.

It follows from $\mathcal{C} = \tilde{\mathcal{C}}$ that $\mathrm{AggregateCPDAGs}(\mathcal{C}) = \mathrm{AggregateCPDAGs}(\tilde{\mathcal{C}})$. □

2.2 PROOF OF THEOREM 3.3 OF THE MAIN PAPER

Recall that AGES combines a collection of CPDAGs obtained in the solution path of GES, where the largest CPDAG corresponds to the BIC penalty with $\lambda = \log(n)/(2n)$. In the consistency proof of GES with the BIC penalty, Chickering (2002) used the fact that the penalized likelihood scoring criterion with the BIC penalty is locally consistent as $\log(n)/(2n) \rightarrow 0$. We note that the other penalty parameters involved in the computation of the solution path of GES do not converge to zero. This prevents us to obtain a proof of Theorem 3.3 of the main paper by applying the consistency result of Chickering (2002). A further complication is that the choices of the penalty parameters in the solution path of GES depend on the data.

In order to prove Theorem 3.3 of the main paper, we rely on the soundness of the oracle version of AGES (Theorem 3.2 of the main paper). In fact, we prove consistency of AGES by showing that the solution path of GES coincides with its oracle solution path as the sample size tends to infinity. Since the number of variables is fixed and the solution path of GES depends only on the partial correlations (see Lemma 1.2 and Section 3.5 of the main paper), the consistency of AGES will follow from the consistency of the sample partial correlations.

Proof of Theorem 3.3 of the main paper. Given a scoring criterion, each step of GES depends on the scores of all DAGs on p variables through their ranking only, where each step in the forward (backward) phase corresponds to improving the current ranking as much as possible by adding (deleting) a single edge. Let $\hat{\boldsymbol{\rho}}$ denote a vector consisting of the absolute values of all sample partial correlations $\hat{\rho}_{X_i,X_j|S}$, $1 \leq i \leq j \leq p$ and $S \subseteq X \setminus \{X_i, X_j\}$, in some order. It follows from Lemma 1.2 that the solution path of GES (for $\lambda \geq \log(n)/(2n)$) solely depends on the ranking of the elements in $\hat{\boldsymbol{\gamma}}$, where $\hat{\boldsymbol{\gamma}}$ contains the elements of $\hat{\boldsymbol{\rho}}$ appended with $(1 - n^{-1/n})^{1/2}$, where the last element results from solving $-\log(1-\rho^2)/2 = \log(n)/(2n)$ for ρ.

Similarly, an oracle solution path of GES solely depends on a ranking of the elements in $\boldsymbol{\gamma}$, where $\boldsymbol{\gamma}$ contains the elements of $\boldsymbol{\rho}$ appended with the value 0, and $\boldsymbol{\rho}$ denotes a vector consisting of the absolute values of all partial correlations in the same order as in $\hat{\boldsymbol{\rho}}$. Note that there can be more than one oracle solution paths of GES depending on a rule for breaking ties. We will write $\mathrm{rank}(\hat{\boldsymbol{\gamma}}) = \mathrm{rank}(\boldsymbol{\gamma})$ if $\mathrm{rank}(\hat{\boldsymbol{\gamma}})$ equals a ranking of $\boldsymbol{\gamma}$ with some rule for breaking ties.

Finally, we define

$$\epsilon = \min\left\{\left||\rho_{X_{i_1},X_{j_1}|S_1}| - |\rho_{X_{i_2},X_{j_2}|S_2}|\right| : |\rho_{X_{i_1},X_{j_1}|S_1}| \neq |\rho_{X_{i_2},X_{j_2}|S_2}|\right\},$$

where the minimum is taken over all $1 \leq i_1 < j_1 \leq p$, $S_1 \subseteq X \setminus \{X_{i_1}, X_{j_1}\}$, $1 \leq i_2 < j_2 \leq p$ and $S_2 \subseteq X \setminus \{X_{i_2}, X_{j_2}\}$. Therefore, it follows from Theorem 3.2 of the main paper and the consistency of the sample partial correlations that

$$\begin{aligned}
&\mathbb{P}\left(\mathrm{AGES}(X^{(n)}) \neq A_0\right) \\
&\leq \mathbb{P}\left(\mathrm{rank}(\hat{\boldsymbol{\gamma}}) \neq \mathrm{rank}(\boldsymbol{\gamma})\right) \\
&\leq \sum_{\substack{1 \leq i < j \leq p, \\ S \subseteq X \setminus \{X_i, X_j\}}} \mathbb{P}\left(\left||\hat{\rho}_{X_i,X_j|S}| - |\rho_{X_i,X_j|S}|\right| \geq \epsilon/2\right)
\end{aligned}$$

converges to zero as the sample size tends to infinity. □

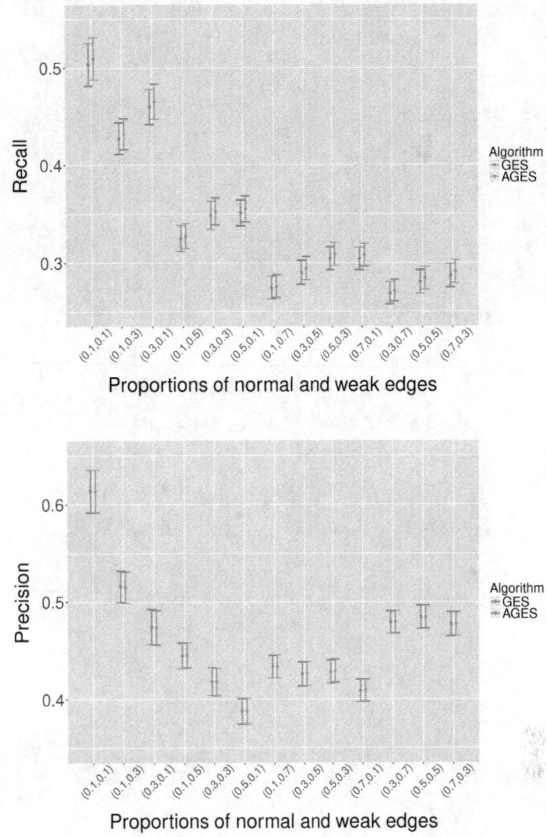

Figure 2: Mean precision and recall of GES and AGES over 500 simulations for all combinations of $(q_s, q_w) \in \{0.1, 0.3, 0.5, 0.7\}$ such that $q_s + q_w \leqslant 1$, for $p = 10$, $\lambda = \log(n)/(2n)$ and $n = 100$ (see Section 3). The bars in the plots correspond to $\pm$ twice the standard error of the mean.

3 ADDITIONAL SIMULATION RESULTS WITH $p = 10$

We also ran AGES on the settings described in the main paper but with smaller sample sizes. Figures 2 and 3 show the results for $n = 100$ and $n = 1000$, respectively, based on 500 simulations per setting.

For the larger sample size, $n = 1000$, we see that we still gain in recall and that the precision remains roughly constant. For the smaller sample size, $n = 100$, the differences become minimal. In all cases AGES performs at least as good as GES.

With a sample size of 100 we expect to detect only partial correlations with an absolute value larger than 0.21. This can be derived solving $1/2\log(1-\rho^2) = -\log(n)/(2n)$ for ρ. This limits the possibility of detecting weak edges, and if an edge is not contained in the output of GES it is also not contained in the output of AGES. This

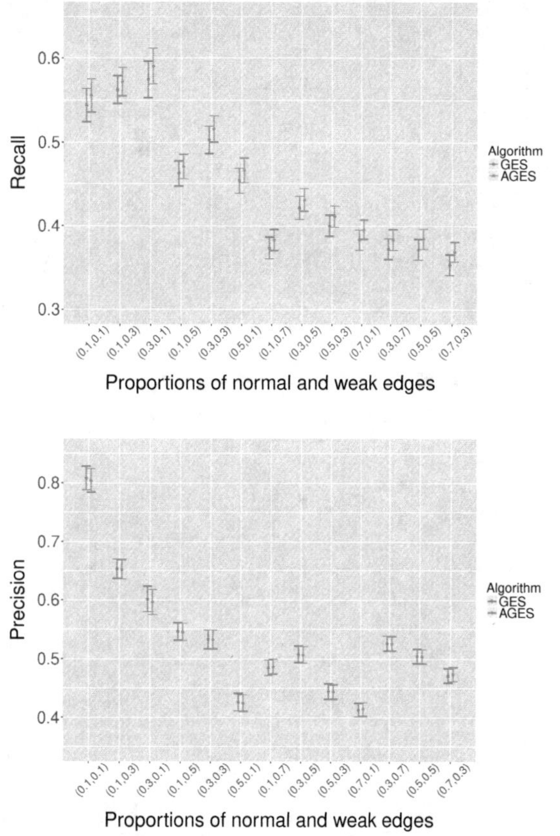

Figure 3: Mean precision and recall of GES and AGES over 500 simulations for all combinations of $(q_s, q_w) \in \{0.1, 0.3, 0.5, 0.7\}$ such that $q_s + q_w \leqslant 1$, for $p = 10$, $\lambda = \log(n)/(2n)$ and $n = 1000$ (see Section 3).The bars in the plots correspond to $\pm$ twice the standard error of the mean.

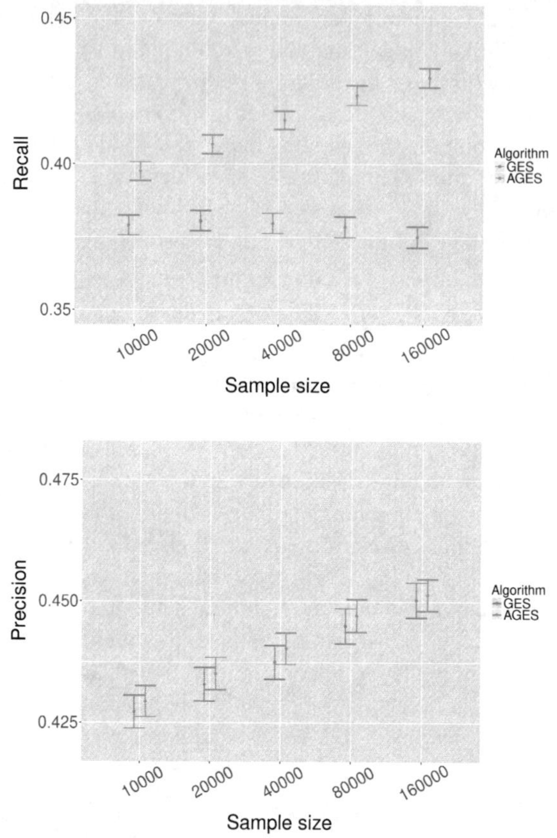

Figure 4: Mean precision and recall of GES and AGES with ARGES-skeleton over 500 simulations for $(q_s, q_w) = (0.3, 0.7)$, $p = 100$, $\lambda = \log(n)/(2n)$, and varying sample sizes (see Section 4). The bars in the plots correspond to $\pm$ twice the standard error of the mean.

explains why we do not see a large improvement with smaller sample sizes. However, AGES then simply returns an APDAG which is very similar, or identical, to the CPDAG returned by GES.

4 FURTHER SIMULATION RESULTS WITH $p = 100$

We randomly generated 500 DAGs consisting of 10 disjoint blocks of complete DAGs, where each block contains strong and weak edges with concentration probabilities $(q_s, q_w) = (0.3, 0.7)$. The absolute values of the strong and weak edge weights are drawn from Unif(0.8,1.2) and Unif(0.1,0.3), respectively. The sign of each edge weight is chosen to be positive or negative with equal probabilities. The variance of the error variables are drawn from Unif(0.5,1.5).

This setting leads more often to a violation of the skeleton condition of Algorithm 3 of the main paper, i.e., the skeleton of the output of GES with $\lambda > \log(n)/(2n)$ is not a subset of the skeleton of the output of GES with $\lambda = \log(n)/(2n)$. This results in almost identical outputs of GES and AGES. In order to alleviate this issue, in each step of AGES with $\lambda > \log(n)/(2n)$, we replace GES with the ARGES-skeleton algorithm of Nandy et al. (2015), based on the skeleton of the output of GES with $\lambda = \log(n)/(2n)$. ARGES-skeleton based on an estimated CPDAG is a hybrid algorithm that operates on a restricted search space determined by the estimated CPDAG and an adaptive modification. The adaptive modification was proposed to retain the soundness and the consistency of GES and it can be easily checked that our soundness and consistency results continue to hold if we replace GES by ARGES-skeleton in each step of AGES with $\lambda > \log(n)/(2n)$. An additional advantage of using ARGES-skeleton is that it leads to a substantial improvement in the runtime of AGES.

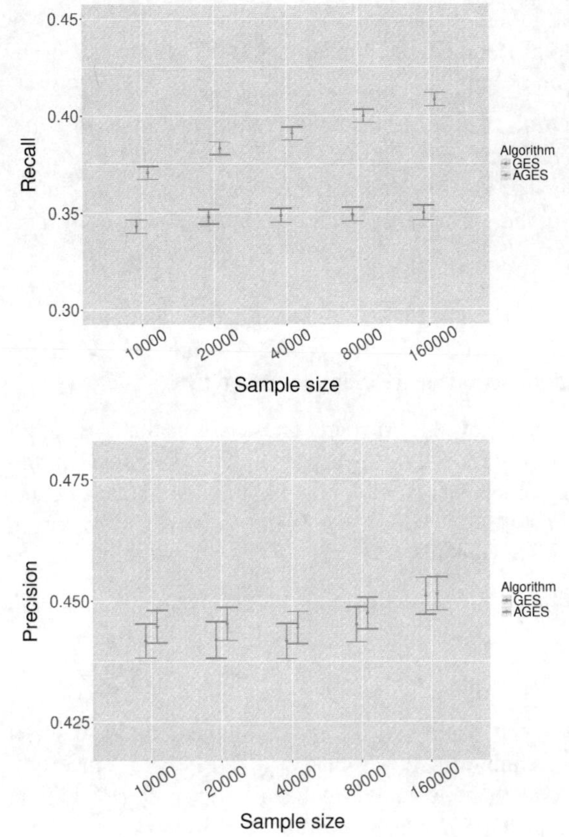

Figure 5: Mean precision and recall of GES and AGES with ARGES-skeleton over 500 simulations for $(q_s, q_w) = (0.3, 0.7)$, $p = 100$, $\lambda = \log(n)/(2n) + \log(p)$, and varying sample sizes (see Section 4). The bars in the plots correspond to $\pm$ twice the standard error of the mean.

Figure 4 shows that AGES (based on ARGES-skeleton) achieves higher recall than GES for estimating the true directions while retaining a similar precision as GES. Unsurprisingly, the difference in the recalls of AGES and GES becomes more prominent for larger sample sizes. We obtain a similar relative performance by using the extended BIC penalty $\lambda = \log(n)/(2n) + \log(p)$ (e.g., Foygel and Drton, 2010) instead of the BIC penalty (Figure 5).

5 PATH STRONG FAITHFULNESS

To produce Figure 5 of the main paper we started by determining the possible APDAGs A_0 for each choice of the edge weights. This is done by considering the four steps in Section 3.1 of the main paper. In Step S.1 we can obtain many CPDAGs (3 with one edge, 6 with two edges, and 1 with three edges). However, once we proceed to Step S.2, we note that only one DAG contains a v-structure. Hence, the orientations in the CPDAGs in Step S.3 are limited to this v-structure. Therefore, the only two possible APDAGs are given in Figures 4a and 4b of the main paper.

Now we consider possible outputs of the oracle version of AGES for every choice of the edge weights. To compute them we have to compute all marginal and partial correlations. Then, we select the in absolute value largest marginal correlation. This corresponds to the first edge addition. Now, we consider the four remaining marginal and partial correlations between non-adjacent vertices. If the in absolute value largest partial correlation is actually a marginal correlation, then we do not obtain a v-structure and the output of AGES is Figure 4b of the main paper. Otherwise, AGES recovers an APDAG with a v-structure.

With these results, we can compute the different areas depicted in Figure 5 of the main paper.

6 AGES δ-STRONG FAITHFULNESS

The path strong faithfulness assumption in Theorem 3.2 of the main paper is sufficient but not necessary for the theorem.

We now present an alternative strong faithfulness assumption which is weaker than path strong faithfulness. This new assumption is necessary and sufficient for Theorem 3.2 of the main paper.

In a CPDAG $C = (V, E)$ we say that $S \subseteq V \setminus \{X_i\}$ is a *possible parent set* of X_i in C if there is a DAG G in the Markov equivalence class represented by C such that $\mathrm{Pa}_G(X_i) = S$.

Definition 6.1. *A multivariate Gaussian distribution is said to be* AGES δ-strong faithful *with respect to a DAG G if it holds that $X_i \not\perp_G X_j | S \Rightarrow |\rho_{X_i, X_j | S}| > \delta$ for every triple (X_i, X_j, S) belonging to at least one of the following two sets:*

1. *Consider the output of the forward phase of oracle GES with penalty parameter $\lambda = -1/2 \log(1 - \delta^2)$. The first set consists of all triples (X_i, X_j, S) such that, in this forward phase output, S is a possible parent set of X_j, X_i is a non-descendant of X_j in the DAG used to define S, and X_i and X_j are not adjacent.*

2. *Consider the backward phase of oracle GES when ran with penalty parameter λ and starting from the output of the forward phase. The second set consists of all triples (X_i, X_j, S) such that the edge between X_i and X_j has been deleted during the backward phase using S as conditioning set.*

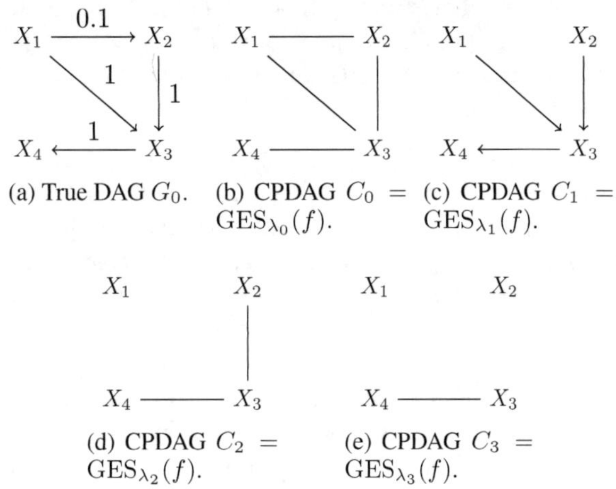

(a) True DAG G_0. (b) CPDAG $C_0 = \mathrm{GES}_{\lambda_0}(f)$. (c) CPDAG $C_1 = \mathrm{GES}_{\lambda_1}(f)$.

(d) CPDAG $C_2 = \mathrm{GES}_{\lambda_2}(f)$. (e) CPDAG $C_3 = \mathrm{GES}_{\lambda_3}(f)$.

Figure 6: Graphs corresponding to Example 6.2. Figure 6a shows the true underlying DAG G_0. Figure 6b - 6e show the sub-CPDAG oracle GES found.

The need for a different condition becomes clear when we think about how GES operates. In Example 6.2, we show why path strong faithfulness is too strong.

Example 6.2. *Consider the distribution f generated from the weighted DAG G_0 in Figure 6a with $\varepsilon \sim N(0, I)$. The solution path of oracle GES is shown in Figures 6b-6e. Note that all sub-CPDAGs found by oracle GES coincide with the CPDAGs constructed as described in Step S.3 of the main paper, i.e., $C_i = \tilde{C}_i$ for $0 \leqslant i \leqslant 3$.*

Intuitively, we would like a condition that is satisfied if and only if the two CPDAGs coincide. However, this is not necessarily the case for the path strong faithfulness condition.

For the CPDAG in Figure 6e, path strong faithfulness imposes δ_3-strong faithfulness with respect to C_3, i.e., $|\rho_{X_3,X_4|S}| > \delta_3$ for all sets S not containing X_3 or X_4. However, the forward phase of GES only checks the marginal correlation between X_3 and X_4. The same is true for the backward phase.

Consider now Figure 6d. Path strong faithfulness imposes δ_2-strong faithfulness with respect to C_2. For instance, it requires that $|\rho_{X_2,X_4|X_1}| > \delta_2$. However, this partial correlation does not correspond to a possible edge addition. Hence, this constraint is not needed, and it is not imposed by AGES δ-strong faithfulness.

In this example, $|\rho_{X_2,X_4|X_1}| < \delta_2 = |\rho_{X_1,X_3|X_2}|$. Hence, f does not satisfy δ_2-strong faithfulness with respect to C_2, but it does satisfy AGES δ_2-strong faithfulness with respect to C_2.

The following lemma states that the AGES δ-strong faithfulness assumption is necessary and sufficient for Claim 1 and Claim 2 in the proof of Theorem 3.2 of the main paper.

Lemma 6.3. *Given a multivariate Gaussian distribution f and a CPDAG C on the same set of vertices, $\mathrm{GES}(f, \lambda)$ with $\lambda = -1/2\log(1-\delta^2)$ is an I-map of C if and only if f is AGES δ-strong faithful with respect to C.*

Proof. For a CPDAG C, we use the notation $X_i \perp_C X_j|S$ to denote that $X_i \perp_G X_j|S$ in any DAG G in the Markov equivalence class described by C.

We first prove the "if" part. Thus, assume that f is AGES δ-strong faithful with respect to C. We consider running oracle GES with $\lambda = -1/2\log(1-\delta^2)$, and denote by C^f and C^b the output of the forward and backward phase, respectively.

Claim 1: C^f is an I-map of C, i.e., all d-separation constraints true in C^f are also true in C.

Proof of Claim 1:

For each triple (X_i, X_j, S) contained in the first set of Definition 6.1, we have $|\rho_{X_i,X_j|S}| < \delta$, since otherwise there would have been another edge addition. From AGES δ-strong faithfulness, it follows that $X_i \perp_C X_j|S$. Since this set of triples characterizes the d-separations that hold in C^f, all d-separations that hold in C^f also hold in C.

Claim 2: C^b is an I-map of C, i.e., all d-separation constraints true in C^b are also true in C.

Proof of Claim 2: By Claim 1 the backward phase starts with an I-map of C. Suppose it ends with a CPDAG that is not an I-map of C. Then, at some point there is an edge deletion which turns a DAG G that is an I-map of C into a DAG G' that is no longer an I-map of C. Suppose the deleted edge is (X_i, X_j). By Lemma 1.1, we have $X_i \not\perp_C X_j|\,\mathrm{Pa}_{G'}(X_j)$. Since the edge has been deleted, the corresponding triple $(X_i, X_j, \mathrm{Pa}_{G'}(X_j))$ is contained in the second set of Definition 6.1. Hence, by AGES δ-strong faithfulness, we obtain $|\rho_{X_i,X_j|\,\mathrm{Pa}_{G'}(X_j)}| > \delta$. Thus, deleting this edge would worsen the score. This is a contradiction to the GES algorithm deleting this edge.

We now prove the "only if" part. Thus, suppose there is a triple (X_i, X_j, S) in one of the sets in Definition 6.1 such that $|\rho_{X_i,X_j|S}| < \delta$ and $X_i \not\perp_C X_j|S$.

Suppose first that this triple concerns the first set. Since all triples in the first set characterize the d-separations that hold in C^f, we know that $X_i \perp_{C^f} X_j|S$. Therefore, C^f is not an I-map of C. Hence, C^b is certainly not an I-map of C.

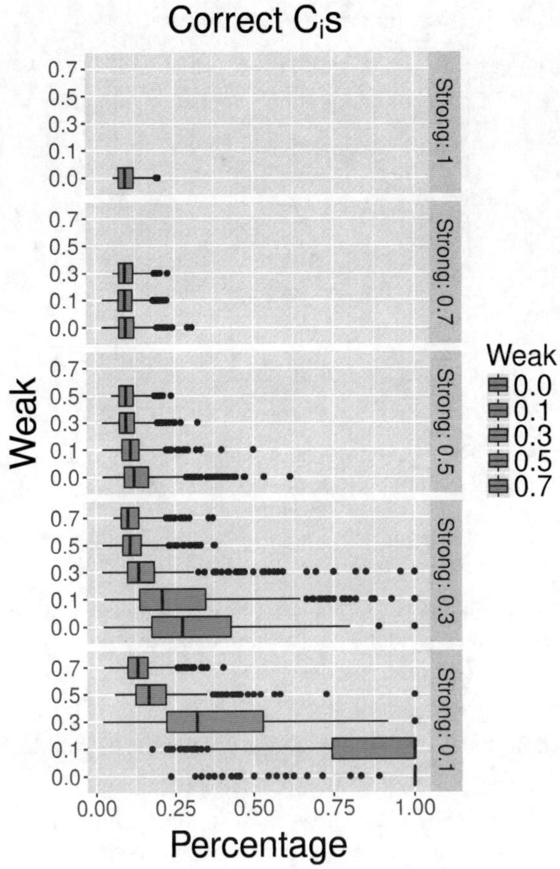

Figure 7: Boxplots of the proportion of correct sub-CPDAGs $\tilde{C}_1, \ldots, \tilde{C}_k$ (as defined in Step S.3 of Section 3.1 of the main paper) found by oracle AGES in each solution path (see Section 6). The different colors represent the different proportions of weak edges. The plots are grouped by the proportion of strong edges.

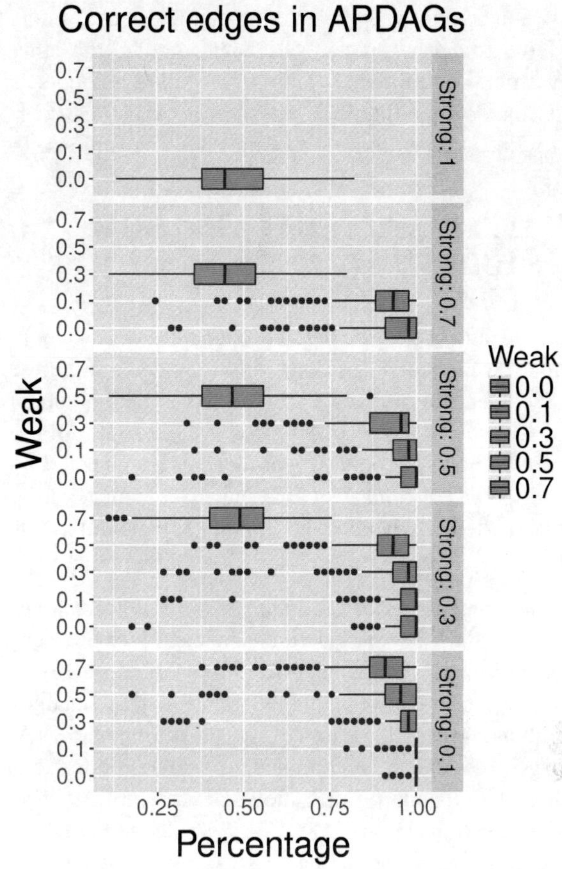

Figure 8: Boxplots of the proportion of edge orientations in the APDAGs found by oracle AGES that are equal to the edge orientations in the true APDAGs (see Section 6). The different colors represent the different proportions of weak edges. The plots are grouped by the proportion of strong edges.

Next, suppose the triple concerns the second set. This means that at some point there is an edge deletion which turns a DAG G into a DAG G' by deleting the edge $X_i \to X_j$, using S as conditioning set. This means that $S = \mathrm{Pa}_G(X_j) \setminus \{X_i\} = \mathrm{Pa}_{G'}(X_j)$. In the resulting DAG G', X_i and X_j are therefore d-separated given S. But we know that $X_i \not\perp_C X_j | S$. Hence, C^b is not an I-map of C. □

We analysed how often the AGES δ-strong faithfulness assumption is met in the simulations presented in the main paper, as well as how often oracle AGES is able to find the correct APDAG. Lemma 6.3 provides a necessary and sufficient condition for the equality of the CPDAGs of Theorem 3.2 of the main paper. For the equality of the APDAGs this condition is only sufficient.

Figure 7 shows the proportion of correct sub-CPDAGs $\tilde{C}_1, \ldots, \tilde{C}_k$ (as defined in Step S.3 of Section 3.1 of the main paper) found by oracle AGES in each solution path and for all simulated settings. We can see that the sparsity of the true underlying DAG plays an important role in the satisfiability of the assumption. We can also see that for the same total sparsity, the settings with more weak edges produce better results.

Even though the AGES δ-strong faithfulness assumption is not very often satisfied for denser graphs, it is much weaker than the classical δ-strong faithfulness assumption. Indeed, we verified that the δ-strong faithfulness assumption is rarely satisfied even for single sub-CPDAGs C_i.

Figure 8 shows the proportion of edge orientations in the APDAGs found by oracle AGES that are equal to the edge orientations in the true APDAGs. With equal edge orientations, we mean that the edges have to be exactly equal. For example, an edge that is oriented in the APDAG found by oracle AGES, but oriented the other way around or unoriented in the true APDAG counts as an error. We see that in many settings AGES can correctly find a large proportion of the edge orientations.

7 APPLICATION TO DATA FROM SACHS ET AL., 2005

We log-transformed the data because they were heavily right skewed. Based on the network provided in Figure 2 of Sachs et al. (2005), we produced the DAG depicted in Figure 9 that we used as partial ground truth. In the presented network, only two variables are connected by a bi-directed edge, meaning that there is a feedback loop between them. To be more conservative, we omitted this edge.

For the comparison of GES and AGES we need to account for the interventions done in the 14 experimental conditions. Following Mooij and Heskes (2013), we distinguish between an intervention that changes the abundance of a molecule and an intervention that changes the activity of a molecule. Interventions that change the abundance of a molecule can be treated as do-interventions (Pearl, 2009), i.e., we delete the edges between the variable and its parents. Activity interventions, however, change the relationship with the children, but the causal connection remains. For this reason, we do not delete edges for such interventions. We also do not distinguish between an activation and an inhibition of a molecule. All this information is provided in Table 1 of Sachs et al. (2005).

The only abundance intervention done in the six experimental conditions we consider in Table 1 of the main paper is experimental condition 5. This intervention concerns $PIP2$. For this reason, when comparing the outputs of GES and AGES we need to consider the DAG in Figure 9 with the edge $PLC_\gamma \to PIP2$ deleted. For the other five experimental conditions we used the DAG depicted in Figure 9 as ground truth.

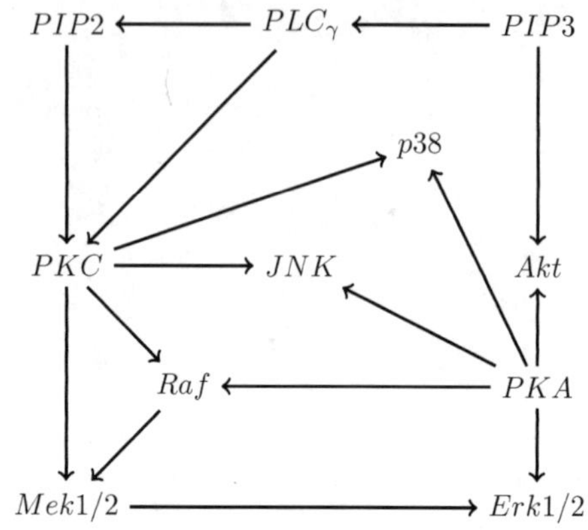

Figure 9: The DAG used as partial ground truth derived from the conventionally accepted network (Sachs et al., 2005).

References

Chickering, D. M. (2002). Optimal structure identification with greedy search. *J. Mach. Learn. Res.*, 3:507–554.

Foygel, R. and Drton, M. (2010). *Extended Bayesian information criteria for Gaussian graphical models.*

Meek, C. (1995). Causal inference and causal explanation with background knowledge. In *Proceedings of UAI 1995*, pages 403–410.

Mooij, J. M. and Heskes, T. (2013). Cyclic causal discovery from continuous equilibrium data. In *Proceedings of UAI 2013*, pages 431–439.

Nandy, P., Hauser, A., and Maathuis, M. H. (2015). High-dimensional consistency in score-based and hybrid structure learning. arXiv:1507.02608v4.

Pearl, J. (2009). *Causality: Models, Reasoning and Inference.* Cambridge University Press, New York, 2nd edition.

Sachs, K., Perez, O., Pe'er, D., Lauffenburger, D. A., and Nolan, G. P. (2005). Causal protein-signaling networks derived from multiparameter single-cell data. *Science*, 308:523–529.

Verma, T. and Pearl, J. (1990). Equivalence and synthesis of causal models. In *Proceedings of UAI 1990*, pages 255–270.

SAT-Based Causal Discovery under Weaker Assumptions

Zhalama
University of South Australia
Adelaide, Australia

Jiji Zhang
Lingnan University
Tuen Mun, NT, Hong Kong

Frederick Eberhardt
Caltech
Pasadena, CA, USA

Wolfgang Mayer
University of South Australia
Adelaide, Australia

Abstract

Using the flexibility of recently developed methods for causal discovery based on Boolean satisfiability (SAT) solvers, we encode a variety of assumptions that weaken the Faithfulness assumption. The encoding results in a number of SAT-based algorithms whose asymptotic correctness relies on weaker conditions than are standardly assumed. This implementation of a whole set of assumptions in the same platform enables us to systematically explore the effect of weakening the Faithfulness assumption on causal discovery. An important effect, suggested by simulation results, is that adopting weaker assumptions greatly alleviates the problem of conflicting constraints and substantially shortens solving time. As a result, SAT-based causal discovery is potentially more scalable under weaker assumptions.

1 INTRODUCTION

In the framework of causal graphical models [Spirtes et al., 2000, Pearl, 2000], the task of causal discovery can be framed as the inference from a statistical dataset of measurements of a set of variables to the underlying causal structure that gave rise to the data. The inference is enabled by a set of assumptions or "bridge principles" that link statistical features of the data to features of the underlying causal structure. Two of the best known assumptions of this kind are the Causal Markov and Faithfulness assumptions. These two assumptions, defined and discussed below, together entail an exact correspondence between conditional independence relations that hold in the distribution (from which the data are drawn) and certain separation features in the underlying causal structure. This correspondence enabled the development of so-called constraint-based causal discovery algorithms — such as PC and FCI [Spirtes et al., 2000] — that exploit the independence structure found in the data, to recover as much as possible about the causal structure.

Although the causal Markov assumption is usually regarded as an ontological principle grounded in the nature of causation, the Faithfulness assumption is often viewed as a methodological assumption in the spirit of Occam's razor [Zhang, 2013]. Moreover, even if Faithfulness holds in the true distribution, there are often "almost violations" of Faithfulness in finite-sample settings that affect causal discovery [Meek, 1996, Robins et al., 2003, Uhler et al., 2013]. These considerations sparked investigations into the possibility of relaxing the Faithfulness assumption in constraint-based causal discovery [Ramsey et al., 2006, Zhang and Spirtes, 2008, Zhang, 2013, Spirtes and Zhang, 2014, Raskutti and Uhler, 2014, Forster et al., 2017], which generated a number of proposals for weakening Faithfulness. However, the impact of these weaker assumptions on causal discovery has not been systematically investigated on a common platform, since constraint-based algorithms have until recently always been custom-built for a specific set of assumptions. In this paper we leverage the recent development of causal discovery algorithms based on general-purpose Boolean satisfiability solvers [Triantafilou et al., 2010, Hyttinen et al., 2013, 2014, Triantafillou and Tsamardinos, 2015, Borboudakis and Tsamardinos, 2016, Magliacane et al., 2016], and show how to implement various weaker assumptions in this flexible approach. We compare the resulting algorithms on synthetic data. Among other things, the results suggest that the weaker assumptions significantly reduce the need for conflict resolution, which translates into substantial gains in solving time.

We will proceed as follows. After introducing the basic terminology in Section 2, we review the Boolean satisfiability and optimization approach to causal discovery in Section 3, focusing on the framework proposed by Hyttinen et al. [2013, 2014]. Then, in Section 4, we go through a number of weakenings of the Faithfulness assumption and show, for all except one, how to encode constraints that correspond to the weaker assumptions. In addition, we "weaken" the causal Markov assumption by implementing constraints associated with the local Markov assumption as opposed to those with the global Markov assumption. Despite their equivalence given a perfect oracle of conditional independence, the former is in general weaker than the latter when the oracle is replaced by finite sample tests. These various constraints in different combinations yield a multitude of algorithms for causal discovery of acyclic, causally sufficient structures, and we report some findings on their empirical performance in Section 5. We conclude in Section 6.

2 PRELIMINARIES

Throughout this paper we consider the setting of a set of observed variables $\mathbf{V}$ that is causally sufficient (there are no unmeasured common causes) and that does not feature causal feedback.[1] The (unknown) causal structure over $\mathbf{V}$ can then be properly represented by a directed acyclic graph (DAG) over $\mathbf{V}$, in which an arrow $X \rightarrow Y$ means that X is a direct cause of Y relative to $\mathbf{V}$.[2]

Some basic graph terminology: Given a DAG G over $\mathbf{V}$, for any $X, Y \in \mathbf{V}$, if there is an edge between X and Y, then X and Y are said to be *adjacent*. If the edge is directed from X to Y, i.e., $X \rightarrow Y$, then X is called a *parent* of Y and Y a *child* of X. A *path* in G is a sequence of distinct vertices $(V_1, ..., V_n)$ such that for $1 \leq i \leq n-1$, V_i and V_{i+1} are adjacent in G. A path between V_1 and V_n is called a *directed path* from V_1 to V_n if V_i is a parent of V_{i+1} for $1 \leq i \leq n-1$. X is called an *ancestor* of Y and Y a *descendant* of X in G if $X = Y$ or there is a directed path from X to Y in G.

An (ordered) triple of distinct vertices (X, Y, Z) in G is called a *collider* if X, Y are adjacent, Y, Z are adjacent, and the edge between X and Y and the edge between Z and Y are both directed at Y, i.e., $X \rightarrow Y \leftarrow Z$. It is called a *non-collider* if X, Y are adjacent, Y, Z are adjacent, and the triple is not a collider. Given a path $(V_1, ..., V_n)$, V_i $(1 < i < n)$ is said to be a collider (non-collider) on the path if the triple (V_{i-1}, V_i, V_{i+1}) is a collider (non-collider).

We are concerned with the constraint-based approach to causal discovery that seeks to recover causal structure from statistically inferred conditional independence (CI) and conditional dependence (CD) statements. A fundamental principle that is almost always assumed (for causally sufficient systems) is the following condition:

(Causal) Markov Assumption: The joint distribution p of $\mathbf{V}$ is Markov to the causal DAG G over $\mathbf{V}$ in the sense that every variable is independent of its non-descendants conditional on its parents in G.

This is a formulation in terms of the *local* Markov property of DAGs. It specifies some CI statements that must be true of p according to G. These CI statements entail others by the laws of probability, all of which are captured by the notion of *d-separation* [Pearl, 1988]. Given $\mathbf{Z} \subseteq \mathbf{V}$, a path in G is blocked by $\mathbf{Z}$ (or not d-connecting given $\mathbf{Z}$) if some non-collider on the path is in $\mathbf{Z}$ or some collider on the path has no descendant in $\mathbf{Z}$. For any distinct $X, Y \notin \mathbf{Z}$, X and Y are d-separated by $\mathbf{Z}$ in G (we write $X \perp_G Y \mid \mathbf{Z}$) if every path between X and Y is blocked by $\mathbf{Z}$. For any $\mathbf{X}, \mathbf{Y}, \mathbf{Z} \subseteq \mathbf{V}$ that are pairwise disjoint, $\mathbf{X}$ and $\mathbf{Y}$ are d-separated by $\mathbf{Z}$ in G if every vertex in $\mathbf{X}$ and every vertex in $\mathbf{Y}$ are d-separated by $\mathbf{Z}$. The Markov assumption can then be reformulated as: for every disjoint $\mathbf{X}, \mathbf{Y}, \mathbf{Z} \subseteq \mathbf{V}$, $\mathbf{X} \perp_G \mathbf{Y} \mid \mathbf{Z} \Rightarrow \mathbf{X} \perp\!\!\!\perp_p \mathbf{Y} \mid \mathbf{Z}$. We will refer to this formulation as the *global* Markov assumption, and we call a CI statement $\mathbf{X} \perp\!\!\!\perp \mathbf{Y} \mid \mathbf{Z}$ *entailed* by G if $\mathbf{X} \perp_G \mathbf{Y} \mid \mathbf{Z}$.

Standard constraint-based methods also assume the converse of the Markov assumption:

(Causal) Faithfulness Assumption: The joint distribution p over $\mathbf{V}$ is faithful to the causal DAG G over $\mathbf{V}$ in the sense that for every disjoint $\mathbf{X}, \mathbf{Y}, \mathbf{Z} \subseteq \mathbf{V}$, $\mathbf{X} \perp\!\!\!\perp_p \mathbf{Y} \mid \mathbf{Z} \Rightarrow \mathbf{X} \perp_G \mathbf{Y} \mid \mathbf{Z}$.

Under these two assumptions, the true causal DAG G is determined by the CI and CD statements that are true of p up to the Markov equivalence class of G. Two DAGs over $\mathbf{V}$ are *Markov equivalent* just in case they entail the exact same CI statements.

3 BOOLEAN SATISFIABILITY AND CONSTRAINED OPTIMIZATION

(Independence-)constraint-based methods that adopt the Markov and Faithfulness assumptions seek to infer the Markov equivalence class of the underlying causal DAG based on CI and CD constraints obtained from data. Standard methods use a graphical representation of the Markov equivalence classes — known as *patterns* (or *essential graphs*) — to perform causal discovery. In contrast, recent approaches to constraint-based causal discovery have attempted to directly encode the d-separation/connection constraints implied by CI/CD

[1] We focus on the relatively simple task of inferring acyclic, causally sufficient structures, because the literature on weakening the Faithfulness assumption has been so focused. However, at least some aspects of this work are readily generalizable to a much more general setting, as we indicate in Section 6.

[2] As usual, we use "variable" and "vertex" interchangeably.

statements in terms of Boolean constraints over the set of possible causal graphs [Hyttinen et al., 2013, 2014, Triantafillou and Tsamardinos, 2015]. Such encodings enable the use of general purpose Boolean constraint solvers and, importantly for our aims here, make the inference from the CI constraints to the graphical constraints flexible: e.g., whether an observed CI only implies that the two independent variables are non-adjacent in the causal graph or whether it implies that there is no d-connecting path of any kind between them, can simply be written into the rules that the solver must respect.

While the specific encodings and the modeling languages vary among extant approaches of this type, the underlying strategy is the same: Define Boolean atoms of the form A = "$X \rightarrow Y \in G$" that specify the presence of a particular edge in the true graph, encode (in a schema) what it means for two variables to be (conditionally) d-connected/separated, and define predicates for the CI/CD-statements that then imply constraints on the d-connections present or absent in the underlying graph. Observed CI/CDs are then encoded as their corresponding predicates and off-the-shelf solvers are used to find truth value assignments to the Boolean atoms that satisfy all the constraints. Any satisfying truth value assignment then describes a causal graph G that is consistent with the input CI/CDs. However, given that the CI/CDs result from a statistical process, the set of observed CI/CDs may contain errors, which may result in a set of constraints that are unsatisfiable. That is, for such a "conflicted" set of constraints, there is no causal graph that satisfies the encoded assumptions. In that case, some method for conflict resolution is required.

Hyttinen et al. [2014], whose encoding forms the basis for our approach here, encoded the standard correspondence between conditional independence and d-separation licensed by the combination of the (global) Markov assumption and the Faithfulness assumption:

$$X \perp\!\!\!\perp_p Y \mid \mathbf{Z} \quad \Leftrightarrow \quad X \perp_G Y \mid \mathbf{Z} \tag{1}$$

In the case of a conflicted set of constraints $\mathbf{K}$, they used the following optimization to determine their output G^*:

$$G^* \in \arg\min_{G \in \mathcal{G}} \sum_{k \in \mathbf{K} \text{ s.t. } G \not\models k} w(k) \tag{2}$$

That is, G^* minimizes the weighted sum of unsatisfied constraints, where the weights $w(.)$ can be set in a variety of ways. Specifically, Hyttinen et al. [2014] consider three weighting schemes: (1) "constant weights" just assigns a weight of 1 to each constraint. (2) "hard dependencies" assigns infinite weight to any observed CD and weight of 1 to any CI. Finally, (3) "log weights" is a pseudo-Bayesian weighting scheme, where the weights depend on the log posterior probability of the CI/CDs being true (see their Sec. 4). Other weighting schemes based on p-values have been developed by Triantafillou and Tsamardinos [2015] and Magliacane et al. [2016].

4 WEAKENING THE ASSUMPTIONS

The Faithfulness assumption has been subject to forceful criticism [Cartwright, 2001, Hoover, 2001]. Examples of violations of Faithfulness are easily constructed by, for example, two causal pathways that cancel each other's effect exactly, resulting in an independence between variables that are (doubly) causally connected. We may find such violations in cases of back-up mechanisms or control systems, where cancellations of causal pathways are part of the design. More problematically, in finite sample inference violations of faithfulness will occur when a (weak) statistical dependence is not detected due to low sample size. Uhler et al. [2013] have shown that such "almost-violations" of Faithfulness are in a measure-theoretic sense fairly common. These considerations together with the recognition that some violations of Faithfulness are in fact testable, have led to a whole set of weaker versions of Faithfulness.

Below we describe a number of weaker assumptions that have been studied in the literature. Let G denote the true causal DAG over $\mathbf{V}$ and p the true joint distribution.

Adjacency-faithfulness: For every distinct $X, Y \in \mathbf{V}$ and $\mathbf{C} \subseteq \mathbf{V} \setminus \{X, Y\}$, if X and Y are adjacent in G, then $X \not\perp\!\!\!\perp_p Y \mid \mathbf{C}$.

Adjacency-faithfulness is a consequence of Faithfulness and is used to justify the step of inferring adjacencies in algorithms like PC [Spirtes et al., 2000]. The Conservative PC algorithm [Ramsey et al., 2006], for example, assumes Adjacency-faithfulness instead of Faithfulness.

Triangle-faithfulness: For every distinct $X, Y, Z \in \mathbf{V}$ such that (X, Z, Y) is a triangle (i.e., they are pairwise adjacent) in G: (i) If (X, Z, Y) is a collider in G, then for every $\mathbf{C} \subseteq \mathbf{V} \setminus \{X, Y\}$ that includes Z, $X \not\perp\!\!\!\perp_p Y \mid \mathbf{C}$; and (ii) If (X, Z, Y) is a non-collider, then for every $\mathbf{C} \subseteq \mathbf{V} \setminus \{X, Y\}$ that excludes Z, $X \not\perp\!\!\!\perp_p Y \mid \mathbf{C}$.

Triangle-faithfulness is much weaker than even Adjacency-faithfulness [Zhang and Spirtes, 2008, Spirtes and Zhang, 2014] and is of particular interest in conjunction with the following, very weak assumption.

SGS-minimality: G is SGS-minimal in the sense that no proper subgraph[3] of G satisfies the Markov assumption with p.

[3] A proper subgraph of G is a DAG over $\mathbf{V}$ whose set of edges is a proper subset of that of G.

SGS-minimality is so weak that given a standard, interventional interpretation of causal DAGs, it is guaranteed to be true if p is positive [Zhang and Spirtes, 2011]. Zhang and Spirtes (2008) showed that under the assumptions of Triangle-faithfulness and SGS-minimality, Faithfulness (and so Adjacency-faithfulness) are in principle testable without knowing the causal structure.

There are also a few minimality assumptions that are stronger than SGS-minimality but nonetheless weaker than Faithfulness. For example, Pearl [2000] discussed the following minimality condition:

P-minimality: G is P-minimal in the sense that no proper independence-submodel of G satisfies the Markov assumption with p.[4]

The GES algorithm [Chickering, 2002] can be viewed as aiming to find a P-minimal pattern [Zhalama et al., 2017]. Finally, there are count-based minimalities that are somewhat stronger. One of them says that the true causal DAG is sparest among all that are Markov to p.

Number-of-Edges(NoE)-minimality: G is NoE-minimal in the sense that no DAG with a smaller number of edges than G satisfies the Markov assumption with p.

Note the contrast to SGS-minimality: Both SGS-minimality and NoE-minimality are concerned with edges, but NoE-minimality is a minimality with respect to the order defined over the number of edges, whereas SGS-minimality is a minimality with respect to the (partial) order defined by the inclusion relation between sets of edges. NoE-minimality is called "Frugality" by Forster et al. [2017], who showed that it is stronger than P-minimality but weaker than Faithfulness. Raskutti and Uhler (2014) proposed a *Sparsest Permutation Algorithm* based on NoE-minimality. Sonntag et al. (2015) applied the same idea in the context of learning chain graphs.

The other minimality condition we will consider states that the true causal DAG entails the greatest number of CI statements among all DAGs that are Markov to p.

Number-of-Independencies(NoI)-minimality: G is NoI-minimal in the sense that no DAG that entails a greater number of conditional independence statements than G does, satisfies the Markov assumption with p.

NoI-minimality is to P-minimality as NoE-minimality is to SGS-minimality: NoI-minimality is a minimality with respect to the order defined over numbers of entailed CI statements, whereas P-minimality is a minimality with respect to the (partial) order defined by the inclusion relation between sets of entailed CI statements. To our knowledge, NoI-minimality has not been explicitly studied in the literature. However, as we will see in Section 4.1, one of the weighting schemes considered by Hyttinen et al. [2014], namely "hard dependencies", can be interpreted as implementing precisely this assumption.

NoI-minimality is obviously stronger than P-minimality, in the same way that NoE-minimality is stronger than SGS-minimality. On the other hand, it is weaker than Faithfulness. It is easy to see that Faithfulness entails NoI-minimality: if p is faithful to G, then any DAG that entails more CIs than G does, must entail some CI that is not satisfied by p and so does not satisfy the Markov assumption with p. Conversely, NoI-minimality does not entail Faithfulness. To show this, it suffices to note that there are distributions over $\mathbf{V}$ that are not both Markov and Faithful to any DAG over $\mathbf{V}$ [Zhang and Spirtes, 2008], but every distribution over $\mathbf{V}$ is Markov to some DAG over $\mathbf{V}$ that is NoI-minimal.

To summarize, we shall consider the following weakenings of the Faithfuless assumption: (i) Adjacency-faithfulness; (ii) the conjunction of SGS-minimality and Triangle-faithfulness; (iii) NoE-minimality; and (iv) NoI-minimality. (We do not consider P-minimality as we have not yet developed a concise encoding of this assumption.) It is worth noting that although these are weaker assumptions than Faithfulness, they become equivalent to Faithfulness for distributions that admit a DAG representation that is both Markov and Faithful. In other words, given the Markov assumption, (i)-(iv) are weaker than Faithfulness *only* because they are consistent with bigger sets of distributions than Faithfulness is [Zhang and Spirtes, 2016]. That is, assuming Faithfulness for distributions from those bigger sets, can result in "conflicted" or unsatisfiable sets of constraints even without statistical errors. Adopting (i) or (ii) significantly reduces but does not completely eliminate conflicts (with or without statistical errors), while adopting (iii) or (iv) completely eliminates conflicts. Indeed, an implementation of (iv) in the SAT approach is precisely a conflict resolution scheme considered by Hyttinen et al. [2014].

4.1 IMPLEMENTATIONS IN ASP

We now show how to implement constraints corresponding to these weaker assumptions in Answer Set Programming (ASP), the framework used in Hyttinen et al. [2014], which we take as basis. ASP is a Prolog-style modeling language expressed in terms of first-order logical rules [Baral, 2010]. None of the details of ASP, the corresponding solvers or even the details of Hyttinen et al.'s encoding are needed to understand what follows.

[4] A *proper independence-submodel* of G is a DAG over $\mathbf{V}$ such that the set of CIs it entails is a proper superset of that entailed by G. We borrow the names "SGS-minimality" (Spirtes, Glymour, and Scheines's minimality) and "P-minimality" (Pearl's minimality) from [Zhang, 2013].

One could similarly express the weakened assumptions in propositional logic and use a standard SAT-solver (or Boolean constraint optimizer) for the inference task.

As mentioned in Section 3, the Markov assumption is encoded as constraints that CD statements impose on the underlying causal structure: $X \not\perp\!\!\!\perp Y \mid \mathbf{C}$ implies that there is a d-connecting path between X and Y given $\mathbf{C}$; the Faithfulness assumption is encoded as constraints that CI statements impose on the underlying causal structure: $X \perp\!\!\!\perp Y \mid \mathbf{C}$ implies that there is no d-connecting path between X and Y given $\mathbf{C}$. Thus, the weakenings of the Faithfulness assumption will be encoded by modifying the constraints imposed by CI statements.

This is most straightforward for Adjacency-faithfulness and Triangle-faithfulness. To encode the former, we simply take a CI statement $X \perp\!\!\!\perp Y \mid \mathbf{C}$ to imply the constraint that there is no edge between X and Y. To encode the latter, we take a CI statement $X \perp\!\!\!\perp Y \mid \mathbf{C}$ to imply the constraint that there is no triangle (X, Z, Y) such that either (X, Z, Y) is a collider and $Z \in \mathbf{C}$, or (X, Z, Y) is a non-collider and $Z \notin \mathbf{C}$.

The minimality assumptions are a little less straightforward. For SGS-minimality, a reformulation will help. Given the Markov assumption, SGS-minimality can be equivalently formulated as: for every $X \in \mathbf{V}$ and every non-empty $\mathbf{P} \subseteq \mathbf{PA}_G(X)$ (where $\mathbf{PA}_G(X)$ denotes the set of parents of X in G), $X \not\perp\!\!\!\perp_p \mathbf{P} \mid \mathbf{PA}_G(X) \setminus \mathbf{P}$. According to this reformulated SGS-minimality, a CI statement $X \perp\!\!\!\perp Y \mid \mathbf{C}$ implies the constraint that $\mathbf{PA}_G(X) \neq \mathbf{C} \cup \{Y\}$ and $\mathbf{PA}_G(Y) \neq \mathbf{C} \cup \{X\}$.

For NoI-minimality and NoE-minimality we employ an optimization of (weak) constraint satisfication, since both essentially assume that the true causal DAG is "optimal" in some sense among all DAGs that satisfy the Markov assumption (that is, satisfy the constraints imposed by CD statements.) The difference is that NoI-minimality aims at maximizing the number of d-separation relations, whereas NoE-minimality aims at maximizing the number of non-adjacencies.

For NoI-minimality, we can keep the original encoding of the constraint associated with a CI statement. We assign each such CI constraint weight 1, while taking every constraint associated with a CD statement as a *hard constraint* that must be satisfied (or assigning them weight ∞). Then, given a perfect oracle of CI statements, the DAGs that minimize the total weight of unsatisfied constraints, as expressed in equation (2), are precisely those that are Markov and NoI-minimal. As we said, this implementation of NoI-minimality is exactly one of the conflict resolution schemes considered by Hyttinen et al. [2014]. Thus, this way of conflict resolution can be motivated from the perspective of weakening Faithfulness.

For NoE-minimality, we can ignore CI statements, and take each possible non-adjacency as a constraint with weight 1 (while taking every constraint associated with a CD statement as a hard constraint). Then, given a perfect oracle of CI statements, the DAGs that minimize the total weight of unsatisfied constraints are precisely those that are Markov and NoE-minimal.

In addition to encoding weaker variations on Faithfulness, we also encode the local Markov assumption in addition to the global Markov assumption. For the local Markov assumption, instead of taking a CD statement $X \not\perp\!\!\!\perp Y \mid \mathbf{C}$ to imply the constraint that X and Y are not d-separated by C (as stated by the global Markov assumption), we take it to imply the constraint that it is not the case that X's parent set is $\mathbf{C}$ and Y is not a descendant of X, or that Y's parent set is $\mathbf{C}$ and X is not a descendant of Y. Although these constraints are equivalent given a perfect oracle of CI statements, the local version is in general weaker given an imperfect one.

Figure 1 summarizes the ASP-encoding of these various assumptions, where, to improve readability, we use the following predicates that are defined in terms of more basic predicates used in Hyttinen et al's encoding.

- $indep(X, Y, \mathbf{C}, w)$: X and Y are independent conditional on C, given as input fact, with weight w.
- $dep(X, Y, \mathbf{C}, w)$: X and Y are independent conditional on C, given as input fact, with weight w.
- $dsep(X, Y, \mathbf{C})$: X and Y are d-separated given $\mathbf{C}$.
- $pa(X, \mathbf{C})$: $\mathbf{C}$ is X's (exact) parent set.
- $ismember(\mathbf{C}, X)$: X is a member of $\mathbf{C}$.
- $desc(X, Y)$: Y is X's descendant.

The constraints are coded in ASP as violation conditions. The ones that begin with :- are *hard* violations that are not allowed in the output, whereas the ones that use the predicate $fail$ are treated as *weak* violations, which are allowed but penalized according to the given weights. In Figure 1, only NoE-minimality and NoI-minimality are encoded with this device (and minimization of the total weight of the violations). In general, any constraint can be treated as a weak constraint with a certain weight for the sake of conflict resolution [Hyttinen et al., 2014].

The encoding in Figure 1 delivers a multitude of SAT-based algorithms that are asymptotically correct under different assumptions. For example, combining the encoding of (global or local) Markov and that of Adjacency-faithfulness in Hyttinen et al.'s general setup

(Variables are arbitrarily ordered so that $indep(X, Y, \mathbf{C}, w)$ and $dep(X, Y, \mathbf{C}, w)$ are considered only if $Y > X$.)

Faithfulness (violations):
$\forall X \forall Y > X, \forall \mathbf{C} \subseteq \mathbf{V} \setminus \{X, Y\},$
:- not $dsep(X, Y, \mathbf{C}), indep(X, Y, \mathbf{C}, w)$

Adjacency-faithfulness (violations):
$\forall X \forall Y > X, \forall \mathbf{C} \subseteq \mathbf{V} \setminus \{X, Y\},$
:- $edge(X, Y), indep(X, Y, \mathbf{C}, w).$
:- $edge(Y, X), indep(X, Y, \mathbf{C}, w).$

Triangle-faithfulness (violations):
$\forall X \forall Y > X, \forall Z \in \mathbf{V} \setminus \{X, Y\}, \forall \mathbf{C} \subseteq \mathbf{V} \setminus \{X, Y\},$
:- $edge(X, Y), edge(X, Z), edge(Y, Z), ismember(\mathbf{C}, Z), indep(X, Y, \mathbf{C}, w).$
:- $edge(Y, X), edge(X, Z), edge(Y, Z), ismember(\mathbf{C}, Z), indep(X, Y, \mathbf{C}, w).$
:- $edge(X, Y), edge(X, Z), edge(Z, Y),$ not $ismember(\mathbf{C}, Z), indep(X, Y, \mathbf{C}, w).$
:- $edge(X, Y), edge(Z, X), edge(Z, Y),$ not $ismember(\mathbf{C}, Z), indep(X, Y, \mathbf{C}, w).$
:- $edge(Y, X), edge(Z, X), edge(Y, Z),$ not $ismember(\mathbf{C}, Z), indep(X, Y, \mathbf{C}, w).$
:- $edge(Y, X), edge(Z, X), edge(Z, Y),$ not $ismember(\mathbf{C}, Z), indep(X, Y, \mathbf{C}, w).$

SGS-minimality (violations):
$\forall X \forall Y > X, \forall \mathbf{C} \subseteq \mathbf{V} \setminus \{X, Y\},$
:- $pa(X, \{Y\} \cup \mathbf{C}), indep(X, Y, \mathbf{C}, w).$
:- $pa(Y, \{X\} \cup \mathbf{C}), indep(X, Y, \mathbf{C}, w).$

NoE-minimality (optimization of weak constraints):
$\forall X \forall Y > X,$
$fail(X, Y, \mathbf{C}, w = 1)$:- $edge(X, Y).$
$fail(X, Y, \mathbf{C}, w = 1)$:- $edge(Y, X).$

:~ $fail(X, Y, \mathbf{C}, w). [w]$

NoI-minimality (optimization of weak constraints):
$\forall X \forall Y > X, \forall \mathbf{C} \subseteq \mathbf{V} \setminus \{X, Y\},$
$fail(X, Y, \mathbf{C}, w = 1)$:- not $dsep(X, Y, \mathbf{C}), indep(X, Y, \mathbf{C}, w).$

:~ $fail(X, Y, \mathbf{C}, w). [w]$

Global Markov (violations):
$\forall X \forall Y > X, \forall \mathbf{C} \subseteq \mathbf{V} \setminus \{X, Y\},$
:- $dsep(X, Y, \mathbf{C}), dep(X, Y, \mathbf{C}, w).$

Local Markov (violations):
$\forall X \forall Y > X, \forall \mathbf{C} \subseteq \mathbf{V} \setminus \{X, Y\},$
:- $pa(X, \mathbf{C})$, not $desc(X, Y), dep(X, Y, \mathbf{C}, w).$
:- $pa(Y, \mathbf{C})$, not $desc(Y, X), dep(X, Y, \mathbf{C}, w).$

Figure 1: ASP Encoding of Various Assumptions

yields a SAT-based algorithm that is correct under the Markov and Adjacency-faithfulness assumptions (together with the assumptions of causal sufficiency and no feedback). Similarly, combining the encoding of Markov and those of SGS-minimality and Triangle-faithfulness yields a SAT-based algorithm that is correct under the Markov, SGS-minimality, and Triangle-faithfulness assumptions. Moreover, it is easy to see that these algorithms are "query-complete" in Hyttinen et al. [2013]'s sense, for the output implicitly contains all DAGs that are compatible with the inputted CI/CD statements given the corresponding assumptions. Consequently, any query about whether certain edge configurations are shared by all those DAGs can be easily computed. By contrast, although the Conservative PC algorithm [Ramsey et al., 2006] is asymptotically correct under the Markov and Adjacency-faithfulness assumptions, it is unknown whether its output entails answers to all such queries. For Triangle-faithfulness (plus Markov and SGS-minimality), Spirtes and Zhang [2014] proposed a Very Conservative SGS algorithm that is asymptotically correct, but it is clear that neither that algorithm nor the variations investigated by Havrilla [2015] are complete in this sense.[5]

So we have the following algorithms:

- **Adj**: Adjacency-faithfulness + Global Markov
- **Tri**: Triangle-faithfulness + SGS-minimality + Global Markov
- **NoE**: NoE-minimality + Global Markov
- **NoI**: NoI-minimality + Global Markov (which is essentially identifical to one of Hyttinen et al.'s conflict resolution algorithms[6], and will also be called **Faith + HW**.)

In each of them, Global Markov can be replaced by Local Markov and we get **AdjLM**, **TriLM**, **NoELM**, and **NoILM**, respectively.

5 SIMULATIONS

In this section, we report some findings from two types of simulations, following the setup of Hyttinen et al. [2013]

[5]For example, in the large sample limit these algorithms will never output any adjacency that violates Adjacency-faithfulness — though if there is any, they will return "don't know" and so do not err — but there are cases in which an edge that violates Adjacency-faithfulness is identifiable under Markov, SGS-minimality, and Triangle-faithfulness, which will be picked up by our algorithm.

[6]Except that NoI outputs all DAGs with the same, optimal weight, whereas Hyttinen et al.'s original, "hard dependencies" algorithm outputs one of them.

and that of Hyttinen et al. [2014], respectively. The former takes a perfect oracle of CI and CD statements as input, whereas the latter uses conditional independence tests on (Gaussian) data of a moderate sample size in place of an oracle.[7] In the experiments reported below, all conditional independence/dependence constraints are taken into account, and the output of an algorithm is the set of *all* DAGs that satisfy all the relevant constraints (with no conflict resolution) or optimize the constraint satisfaction (with conflict resolution).

5.1 SIMULATIONS WITH PERFECT ORACLES

We randomly generate 100 DAGs over 6, 8, and 10 variables, respectively; for each DAG, the average degree of a vertex is set to be 2. We use (the d-separation features of) each DAG as an oracle for CI and CD statements. That is, the input oracle satisfies both Markov and Faithfulness assumptions. We run this simulation (1) to demonstrate the claim that when the input happens to be consistent with Faithfulness (and Markov), all those algorithms based on weaker assumptions will return the exact same result as the algorithm based on Markov and Faithfulness (that is, the extent of underdetermination does not increase even though the Faithfulness assumption is weakened), and (2) to check the effect of adopting weaker assumptions on solving time when there are no conflicts, which provides an interesting contrast to the situation with conflicts.

As expected, in every case all four algorithms — $\mathbf{Adj}, \mathbf{Tri}, \mathbf{NoE}$, and $\mathbf{NoI}$ — return the exact same result (i.e., the Markov equivalence class of the true DAG) as the algorithm $\mathbf{Faith}$, which combines global Markov and Faithfulness. A comparison of the median solving times is given in Table 1.

Table 1: Median Solving Times (in seconds) given Perfect Oracles

|V|	Faith	Adj	Tri	NoI	NoE
6	0.14	0.15	0.22	0.16	0.19
8	1.89	1.91	3.03	4.12	17.22
10	27.97	28.03	51.61	75.04	234.47

Apparently, when there is no conflict, solving times increase as the assumption is weakened. This seems to echo Zhang and Spirtes [2016]'s observation that the Faithfulness assumption may boost computational efficiency over its weaker variants. However, the situation changes dramatically when conflicts are present.

[7]All experiments are done on a virtual machine running RedHat Enterprise Linux 6, with 12 virtual CPUs (Intel(R) Xeon(R) E5-2690 v4 CPU@2.60GHz). We use Clingo 4.5.4 as the ASP solver [Gebser et al., 2011].

5.2 SIMULATIONS WITH FINITE SAMPLES

Following Hyttinen et al. [2014], we randomly generate 200 DAGs over 6 variables (with expected degree of 2 for each vertex) and parameterize each as a linear Gaussian model, in which every edge coefficient is uniformly drawn from $[-0.8, -0.2] \cup [0.2, 0.8]$, and the variance of each error term is $|1 + 0.1Z|$ where Z is drawn from a standard Gaussian distribution. From each model, we draw 20 i.i.d. samples of size 500, and use the CI tests employed in Hyttinen et al. [2014] to obtain, for each sample, an input of (weighted) CI and CD "facts".

For each algorithm that uses classical CI tests, we try 3 threshold values for rejecting the null hypothesis (0.005, 0.01 and 0.05). In these $200 \times 20 \times 3$ runs, $\mathbf{Faith}$ produces results (i.e., returns a non-empty set of DAGs) in about 5% (604/12000) of the cases, whereas $\mathbf{Adj}$ produces results in 44% (5306/12000) of the cases and $\mathbf{Tri}$ produces results in 66% (7917/12000) of the cases. All remaining cases are unsatisfiable under the given assumptions. So weaker assumptions significantly reduce the need of conflict resolution.

To measure the accuracy of inferred adjacencies, we calculate the true positive rate (TPR) and false positive rate (FPR) of *definite* adjacencies in the output, where a definite adjacency is an adjacency that is shared by all DAGs in the output; to measure the accuracy of inferred edge directions, we compare the definite arrows in the output to the definite arrows in the true Markov equivalence class, and calculate arrow precision (AP) and arrow recall (AR) accordingly.

Figure 2 plots the ROC curves for inferred adjacencies (with 3 points on each curve corresponding to the 3 test thresholds), counting only those cases where $\mathbf{Adj}$ produces results. Figure 3 plots the precision-recall curves for inferred arrows.[8] In addition to the four aforementioned algorithms, Hyttinen et al.'s conflict resolution algorithms $\mathbf{Faith} + \mathbf{CW}$ (constant weights) and $\mathbf{Faith} + \mathbf{LW}$ (log weights) are included.[9] For these "no-conflict-for-$\mathbf{Adj}$" cases, $\mathbf{Adj}$'s (or $\mathbf{Tri}$'s) performance is quite comparable even to that of the pseudo-Bayesian algorithm $\mathbf{Faith} + \mathbf{LW}$. For adjacencies, its

[8]It is not hard to prove that when $\mathbf{Adj}$ returns a non-empty set of DAGs, the output of $\mathbf{NoE}$ must be identical to that of $\mathbf{Adj}$. So in Figures 2 and 3, $\mathbf{NoE}$ and $\mathbf{Adj}$ share the same curve. In addition, in Figure 2, $\mathbf{Tri}$ also shares the same curve, for it returns the same definite adjacencies as $\mathbf{Adj}$ does.

[9]$\mathbf{Faith} + \mathbf{LW}$ uses Bayesian tests and we tried 3 values for the prior: 0.05, 0.1, and 0.2.

accuracy seems to be among the best; for orientations, its recall is lower than **Faith + LW** but precision is higher. Since it does not involve constraint optimization, **Adj** also runs significantly faster.

In order to resolve conflicts in the remaining cases, we try **Adj + CW** and **Adj + HW** ("hard dependencies" weights).[10] Figure 4 and Figure 5 show the comparative performance of a number of algorithms. **Adj + HW** and **Faith + HW** (i.e., **NoI**) have very similar performances, with slightly different balances between TPR and FPR, and between AP and AR. **Adj + CW** and **Faith + CW** are also fairly comparable: **Adj + CW** seems to output more accurate adjacencies than **Faith + CW**, but **Faith + CW** is more accurate on arrows when test threshold is 0.05. Overall, **Faith + LW** seems to have the best performance, and **NoELM** acheives the best arrow precision at the cost of arrow recall (in general, using LM instead of global Markov tends to increase precision at a significant cost of decreasing recall.)

Remarkably, however, **Adj + CW/HW** turns out to require much shorter solving times than **Faith + CW/HW/LW**. The differences become dramatic with only 8 variables. We generate 100 linear Gaussian models on 8 variables and from each model draw a sample of size 500. Figure 6 shows the sorted solving times for these 100 cases. The time saving of **Adj + CW/HW** is huge. It is also interesting to note that **Tri + CW** is substantially faster than **Faith + CW**, and **Tri + HW** than **Faith + HW**, even though when there is no conflict, **Tri** is significantly slower than **Faith**.

In addition, we generated 100 datasets on 10 variables, with a 1-hour time-out for each dataset. It turns out that **Faith + CW/HW/LW** fails to finish any case within the time limit, whereas **Adj + HW** finishes $95/100$ and **Adj + CW** finishes $63/100$.

6 CONCLUSION

We have shown how to encode a variety of weakenings of the Faithfulness assumption on top of the framework presented in Hyttinen et al. [2014]. The encoding results in a number of variations on their algorithm that are asymptotically correct and query-complete under assumptions that are weaker than Faithfulness. For some of the weaker assumptions, such as Triangle-faithfulness plus SGS-minimality, no other algorithm that is asymptotically correct and query-complete under them is currently known.

[10]Somehow **Adj + LW** does not work nearly as well as **Faith + LW**, and we are still investigating the reason.

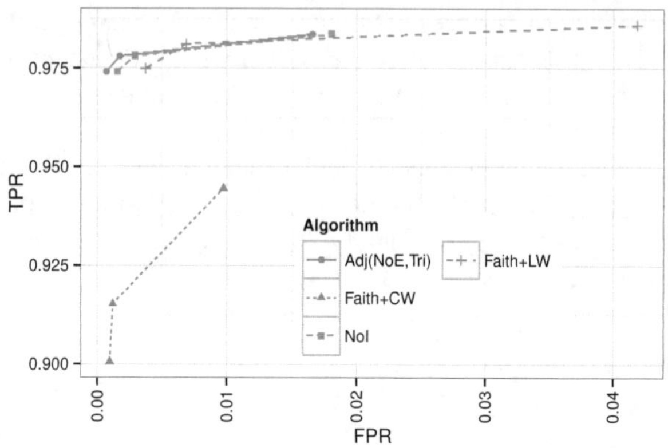

Figure 2: ROC of Adjacencies Among the Cases that **Adj** Produces Results

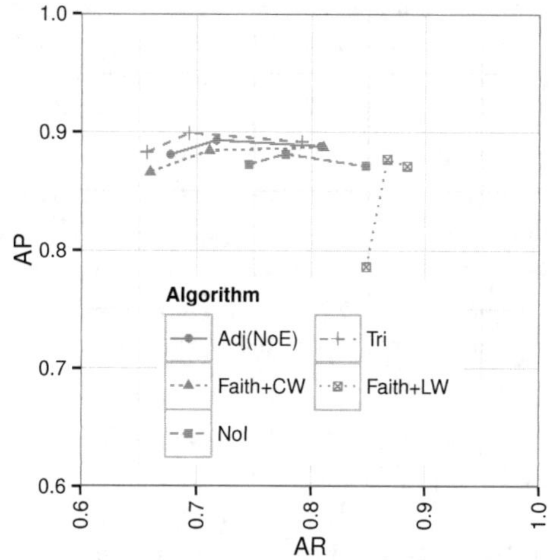

Figure 3: Arrow Precision-Recall Among the Cases that **Adj** Produces Results

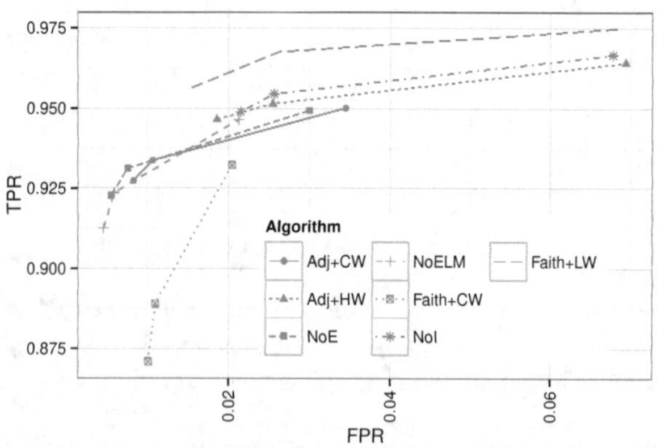

Figure 4: ROC of Adjacencies Among All Cases

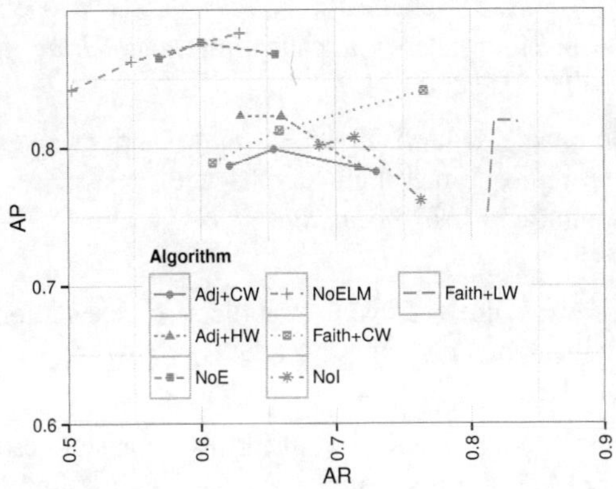

Figure 5: Arrow Precision-Recall Among All Cases

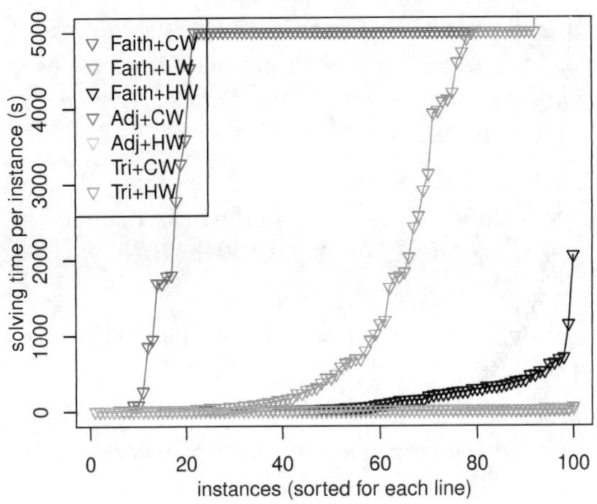

Figure 6: Sorted Solving Times for 8 Variables

These weakenings of Faithfulness are theoretically interesting not only because Faithfulness is a controversial assumption, but more importantly, also because the weaker assumptions are in a sense as inferentially powerful as Faithfulness. For any distribution that is consistent with the Markov and Faithfulness assumptions, adopting any of the weaker assumptions considered in this paper as opposed to Faithfulness does not increase the extent to which the distribution underdetermines the causal structure. This important fact is empirically illustrated by our simulations that take perfect, faithful oracles as inputs.

In this connection, an open problem is how to encode the P-minimality assumption briefly mentioned in Section 4, which is theoretically important for at least two reasons. First, it is even weaker than any of the four weakenings of Faithfulness we encoded. Second, it remains true that when Faithfulness happens to be true, adopting P-minimality does not increase the extent of underdetermination [Zhang, 2013].

The practical value of SAT-based causal discovery algorithms is currently limited by the fact that they do not yet scale well. Our algorithms are no exception. However, the finite-sample simulation results suggest that using a weaker faithfulness such as Adjacency-faithfulness not only reduces the need of conflict resolution, but also leads to substantial savings of solving time when combined with a conflict resolution scheme, compared to using Faithfulness together with the same scheme. It is thus reasonable to expect that our work here will contribute to improving the scalability of SAT-based causal discovery.

On the other hand, we also observed that some conflict resolution strategies, especially the one using "log weights", are less accurate when combined with Adjacency-faithfulness than they are when combined with Faithfulness. It is thus worth exploring whether there are alternative conflict resolution strategies that work better with the weaker constraints.

We have focused in this paper on the task of inferring acyclic, causally sufficient structures, from a single, observational distribution or dataset, because the studies on weakening Faithfulness have been so focused. However, a distinctive power of the SAT-based approach is that it can handle a very general search space, including cyclic structures with latent confounders, as well as multiple, overlapping datasets obtained from observational and/or experimental regimes [Hyttinen et al., 2013]. If the causal structure over $\mathbf{V}$ is possibly cyclic and/or causally insufficient, then in general the causal structure can be represented by a mixed graph over $\mathbf{V}$ that (1) can contain two types of edges, directed and bi-directed ($\leftrightarrow$), where a bi-directed edge between X and Y means that they are confounded by a latent variable, (2) allows multiple edges between any two variables, and (3) allows directed cycles. The notion of d-separation is readily generalized to such a graph, and so are the global Markov[11] and Faithfulness assumptions. We intend to further investigate to what extent the various results on weakening Faithfulness can be generalized to this setting. It is at least clear that Adjacency-faithfulness remains a consequence of Faithfulness, and using the simple, weaker constraint imposed by Adjacency-faithfulness may also speed things up substantially in the general setting.

Acknowledgements

JZ's research was supported by the Research Grants Council of Hong Kong under the General Research Fund LU13600715 and by a Faculty Research Grant from Lingnan University. FE's research was supported by NSF grant #1564330.

[11] The local Markov assumption often fails even in linear cyclic models [Spirtes, 1995].

References

C. Baral. *Knowledge Representation, Reasoning and Declarative Problem Solving*. Cambridge University Press, 2010.

G. Borboudakis and I. Tsamardinos. Towards robust and versatile causal discovery for business applications. In *Proceedings of KDD*, pages 1435–1444, 2016.

N. Cartwright. What is wrong with Bayes nets? *The Monist*, pages 242–264, 2001.

D. M. Chickering. Optimal structure identification with greedy search. *Journal of Machine Learning Research*, 3:507–554, 2002.

M. Forster, G. Raskutti, R. Stern, and N. Weinberger. The frugal inference of causal relations. *British Journal for the Philosophy of Science*, 2017. doi: /10.1093/bjps/axw033.

M. Gebser, B. Kaufmann, R. Kaminski, M. Ostrowski, T. Schaub, and M. T. Schneider. Potassco: The Potsdam Answer Set Solving collection. *AI Communications*, 24(2):107–124, 2011.

N. Havrilla. Exploring very conservative search algorithms. Master's thesis, Department of Philosophy, Carnegie Mellon University, 2015.

K. D. Hoover. *Causality in Macroeconomics*. Cambridge University Press, 2001.

A. Hyttinen, P.O. Hoyer, F. Eberhardt, and M. Järvisalo. Discovering cyclic causal models with latent variables: A general SAT-based procedure. In *Proceedings of UAI*, pages 301–310. AUAI Press, 2013.

A. Hyttinen, F. Eberhardt, and M. Järvisalo. Constraint-based causal discovery: Conflict resolution with Answer Set Programming. In *Proceedings of UAI*, 2014.

S. Magliacane, T. Claassen, and J.M. Mooij. Ancestral causal inference. In *Advances In Neural Information Processing Systems*, pages 4466–4474, 2016.

C. Meek. *Graphical Causal Models: Selecting Causal and Statistical Models*. PhD thesis, Department of Philosophy, Carnegie Mellon University, 1996.

J. Pearl. *Probabilistic Reasoning in Intelligent Systems*. Morgan Kaufmann, 1988.

J. Pearl. *Causality*. Oxford University Press, 2000.

J. Ramsey, J. Zhang, and P. Spirtes. Adjacency-faithfulness and conservative causal inference. In *Proceedings of UAI*, pages 401–408, 2006.

G. Raskutti and C. Uhler. Learning directed acyclic graphs based on sparsest permutations. *arXiv:1307.0366v3*, 2014.

J. M. Robins, R. Scheines, P. Spirtes, and L. Wasserman. Uniform consistency in causal inference. *Biometrika*, 90:491–515, 2003.

D. Sonntag, M. Järvisalo, J. M. Pena, and A. Hyttinen. Learning optimal chain graphs with answer set programming. In *Proceedings of UAI*, pages 822–831, 2015.

P. Spirtes. Directed cyclic graphical representations of feedback models. In *Proceedings of UAI*, pages 491–498, 1995.

P. Spirtes and J. Zhang. A uniformly consistent estimator of causal effects under the k-triangle-faithfulness assumption. *Statistical Science*, 29(4):662–678, 2014.

P. Spirtes, C. Glymour, and R. Scheines. *Causation, Prediction and Search*. MIT Press, 2 edition, 2000.

S. Triantafillou and I. Tsamardinos. Constraint-based causal discovery from multiple interventions over overlapping variable sets. *Journal of Machine Learning Research*, 16:2147–2205, 2015.

S. Triantafilou, I. Tsamardinos, and I. G. Tollis. Learning causal structure from overlapping variable sets. In *Proceedings of AISTATS*, pages 860–867, 2010.

C. Uhler, G. Raskutti, P. Bühlmann, and B. Yu. Geometry of faithfulness assumption in causal inference. *The Annals of Statistics*, 41:436–463, 2013.

Zhalama, J. Zhang, and W. Mayer. Weakening faithfulness: Some heuristic causal discovery algorithms. *International Journal of Data Science and Analytics*, 3: 93–104, 2017.

J. Zhang. A comparison of three Occam's razor for Markovian causal models. *British Jounrnal for the Philosophy of Science*, 64(2):423–448, 2013.

J. Zhang and P. Spirtes. Detection of unfaithfulness and robust causal inference. *Minds and Machines*, 18(2): 239–271, 2008.

J. Zhang and P. Spirtes. Intervention, determinism, and the causal minimality condition. *Synthese*, 182:335–347, 2011.

J. Zhang and P. Spirtes. The three faces of faithfulness. *Synthese*, 193(4):1011–1027, 2016.

Learning to Acquire Information

Yewen Pu
MIT
yewenpu@mit.edu

Leslie P Kaelbling
MIT
lpk@csail.mit.edu

Armando Solar-Lezama
MIT
asolar@csail.mit.edu

Abstract

We consider the problem of diagnosis where a set of simple observations are used to infer a potentially complex hidden hypothesis. Finding the optimal subset of observations is intractable in general, thus we focus on the problem of active diagnosis, where the agent selects the next most-informative observation based on the results of previous observations. We show that under the assumption of uniform observation entropy, one can build an *implication model* which directly predicts the outcome of the potential next observation conditioned on the results of past observations, and selects the observation with the maximum entropy. This approach enjoys reduced computation complexity by bypassing the complicated hypothesis space, and can be trained on observation data alone, learning how to query without knowledge of the hidden hypothesis.

1 INTRODUCTION

In active diagnosis, an agent attempts to discover a hidden hypothesis by asking a series of well chosen questions. For instance, a sushi shop might wish to learn the preference of a customer by asking a series comparison questions; a network monitor might wish to detect a faulty link by making a sequence of connectivity queries.

The difficulty of diagnosis lies in the cost of making observations: it is often too expensive to obtain results for all the observations. A more practical task is to find a subset of observations that yields the most information. Krause and Guestrin (2011) demonstrated that a greedy strategy that iteratively maximizes information gain can obtain a subset of observations that is near-optimal; Golovin and Krause (2011) extended the result to the adaptive case, where the agent chooses the next most-informative observation based on the outcomes of all previous observations. In this paper we consider the setting where the agent is using the greedy strategy in the adaptive case.

However, even in the greedy scheme there can be a significant computational cost. At execution time, the information gain must be computed for each candidate observation, which requires computing entropy terms that sum or integrate over the complex hypothesis space, which can be computationally infeasible. For example, in the case of detecting link failures, the total number of possible failure configurations is 2^M where M is the number of links. Prior work has developed various approximation methods to make information gain computable. Rish (2004), Zhen (2012) and Bellala (2013) simplify the complex hypothesis space by exploiting independence structures in the graphical model and using problem specific assumptions to further restrict the hypothesis space. In cases where observations can rule out a hypothesis completely, one can maintain a version space: a set of hypotheses that are consistent with the observations made so far, and attempt to shrink its size through observations. Tong (2001) and Nowak (2008) directly reduce the size of the version space. Seung (1992) maintains a sample of the version space, called a committee, and selects the observation that maximally reduces the size of the committee. Joshi (2009), Tong (2001), and Lewis (1994) consider the special case where the hypothesis is a classifier and observations are data points. They employ a heuristic that maintains a single current-best classifier, and selects the datapoint that is closest to its decision boundary. Holub (2008) aims to reduce the entropy on the entire dataset, and uses a committee of classifiers to estimate this entropy.

We propose an approach to active diagnosis that is fundamentally different from these previous approaches: We wish to select the next most-informative observation without explicitly modeling or maintaining any notion of the hypothesis space, but by modeling the implications between observations directly. The intuition is that some observations might be redundant given other observations: In the network example if node i is connected to node j via a single path, connectivity between them implies all links on the path are functional. In general, implications may be probabilistic rather than deterministic: Given K current observations $\{O^1 = o^1 \ldots O^K = o^k\}$, one can model the outcome of an unseen observation O' by $P(O'|O^1 = o^1 \ldots O^K = o^k)$. Our key result is that under the assumption of uniform observation entropy (given a particular hypothesis), the next most-informative observation is precisely the observation with the maximum entropy conditioned on the observations already made:

$$O^{best} = \underset{O'}{\operatorname{argmax}} H(O'|O^1 = o^1 \ldots O^K = o^k)$$

This entropy can be easily computed from $P(O'|O^1 = o^1 \ldots O^K = o^k)$, which we model directly with a neural-network called the implication model. It can be trained in a supervised fashion on a dataset of observation data: The dataset with n training examples will contain values for all possible observation dimensions associated with each of n underlying true hypotheses, but does not require that it be labeled with that true hypothesis. Once the implication model is trained, it is used in an observation collection algorithm, OC, which adaptively selects the next most-informative observation conditioned on previous observations. Once a set of informative observations are made, we deliver the best hypothesis from these observations in a problem specific manner.

This work makes the following contributions:

- We prove that under the assumption of uniform observation entropy, the next most-informative observation can be made without explicit modeling of the hypothesis space, but by modeling the implications between observations instead (Section 2). This model has the dual advantages of being computationally efficient to use and being trainable on unlabeled data.
- We describe a method of modeling and training the implication model using a neural network, using techniques from sparsifying auto-encoders (Section 3).
- We evaluate our approach on several distinct benchmark problems, and provide problem-specific algorithms for delivering the best hypothesis after a set of informative observations have been made. We compare our results against reasonable baseline algorithms (Section 4).

2 OVERVIEW

To give an intuition of our approach, consider a simplified, one-player variant of the game BattleShip [1]. Rather than "sinking" all the ships on a given board, the task is to infer the structure of the board itself, which consist of locations and orientations of all the ships.

One algorithm to solve this problem is to keep a set of all possible boards, and with each additional observation, discard all the boards which are incompatible with that observation (for instance, if a query to coordinate $(3,4)$ results in a "miss" then all the boards with a ship occupying the coordinate $(3,4)$ will be discarded). A query is chosen by maximizing the "disagreement" between all the remaining boards in the set (Nowak 2008). Intuitively, if a coordinate (x,y) is occupied by a ship in half of the remaining board and unoccupied in the other half (high disagreement), a query to this coordinate would narrow down the choice of compatible boards by half. This algorithm terminates when there is only 1 board remaining in the set.

The drawback of the aforementioned algorithm is that the computation of disagreement, which requires enumeration over all the remaining boards in the set. In a game such as battleship, there can be an exponentially many number of boards (up to 2^{38} in our experiment), which makes the first query already infeasible to compute.

Instead, we assume the existence of an oracle, which, given a set of past observations (a set of coordinates and whether it resulted in a "hit" or a "miss"), is capable of predicting the probability of "hit" or "miss" of an arbitrary unseen coordinate. Given this oracle, one can ask the following question: Which unseen coordinate is the most "confusing" to the oracle (i.e. closest to a $50\% - 50\%$ split between "hit" and "miss")? It turns out that under the assumption of uniform observation entropy, the most informative query coincides with the query which maximally confuses the oracle. The existence of such an oracle allows one to make the most informative query without having to enumerate over the space of possible boards, saving computation time. We model the oracle as a neural network, which is trained offline on the task of board-completion: Given a complete board B where all the coordinates are labeled as either "hit" or "miss", a random subset of these coordinates are obscured by hiding the labels, forming a partially observable board B'. The neural network is tasked to produce B from B' in via supervised learning.

We will now formalize the specifics of this approach.

[1]For rules of this game see: `https://en.wikipedia.org/wiki/Battleship_(game)`

3 ACTIVE DIAGNOSIS

In this section we formally define the problem of active diagnosis, show that under the uniform observation entropy assumption the next most-informative test is the conditioned observation entropy maximizer, and present our algorithm for active diagnosis.

3.1 PROBLEM DEFINITION

An observation problem is made up of a hidden hypothesis S, which is a random variable that can take on values $s \in dom(S)$, and a finite set of observation random variables $O_1 \ldots O_N$, which can take on values $o_i \in dom(O_i)$. The hypothesis is drawn from a distribution $s \sim P(S)$ and given a hypothesis the observations are drawn from conditional distributions $\forall i, o_i \sim P(O_i|S = s)$. In this work we consider a discrete hypothesis space and observations with discrete domains.

We adopt the greedy strategy proposed by Golovin and Krause (2011) that aims to maximize information gain one observation at a time: Given a (potentially empty) set of current observations $\{O^1 = o^1 \ldots O^K = o^K\}$ the task is to choose an additional observation O' among the set of observations $O_1 \ldots O_N$ that maximizes mutual information between it and the hidden hypothesis. For brevity, we will write the past observations as $O^- := \{O^1 = o^1 \ldots O^K = o^K\}$. The objective is to find

$$O^{best} = \operatorname*{argmax}_{O' \in \{O_1 \ldots O_N\}} I(S, O'|O^-) \ .$$

Rather than computing the mutual information directly, the typical approach solves the equivalent problem of selecting the observation that minimizes posterior conditional entropy:

$$\begin{aligned}\operatorname*{argmax}_{O'} I(S, O'|O^-) &= \operatorname*{argmax}_{O'} H(S|O^-) - H(S|O', O^-) \\ &= \operatorname*{argmin}_{O'} H(S|O', O^-) \ .\end{aligned}$$

This objective of reducing posterior entropy on the hypothesis space is the approach used by Bellala (2013) and Zheng (2012). The posterior conditional entropy $H(S|O', O^-)$ can be computed as:

$$\begin{aligned}&H(S|O', O^-) \\ &= \sum_o P(O' = o|O^-)(\sum_s P(S = s|O' = o, O^-) \\ &\quad \log P(S = s|O' = o, O^-)) \ .\end{aligned}$$

This computation requires a summation over a potentially exponentially large hypothesis space, leading to a time of $O(dom(O)dom(S))$. Zheng (2012) addresses this issue by taking advantage of the independence structures of the graph and develops efficient loopy belief propagation algorithms that approximate this entropy. Bellala (2013) develops a problem-specific ranking function that orders the observations according to their entropy. However, both approaches are problem specific and are difficult to generalize to other kinds of problems.

3.2 APPROACH

Rather than reducing the entropy on the hypothesis space, we consider an alternative decomposition:

$$I(S, O'|O^-) = H(O'|O^-) - H(O'|S, O^-) \ .$$

At first glance this decomposition is no less difficult: both entropy terms depend on O', which would suggest that both need to be computed. We now introduce the assumption of uniform observation entropy, which allows us to simplify $H(O'|S, O^-)$ to a constant.

Definition An observation problem $(S, O_1 \ldots O_N)$ has the *uniform observation entropy* (UOE) property if, for each hypothesis, the conditional entropy for all observation dimensions O_i are equal: $\forall s \in dom(S), \ \forall i, j \in \{1 \ldots N\}$:

$$H(O_i|S = s) = H(O_j|S = s) \ .$$

This is a reasonable assumption for many domains: a common example is when the observations are obtained from a noisy channel that corrupts all observations equally. When observations are deterministic, the uniform observation entropy property holds trivially.

We begin by showing that the entropy of new observations remains uniform when conditioned on past observations:

Lemma.

$$\forall i, j \in \{1 \ldots N\}. \ H(O_i|S, O^-) = H(O_j|S, O^-) \ .$$

Proof. By the definition of conditional entropy, we have

$$\begin{aligned}H(O_i|S, O^-) &= \sum_s P(S = s|O^-)H(O_i|S = s, O^-) \\ &= \sum_s P(S = s|O^-)H(O_i|S = s)\end{aligned}$$

Then applying UOE, we get

$$\begin{aligned}&= \sum_s P(S = s|O^-)H(O_j|S = s) \\ &= H(O_j|S, O^-) \ .\end{aligned}$$

□

We use this lemma to derive a much simpler form of our original problem of maximizing mutual information.

Theorem. *For an observation problem* $(S, O_1 \dots O_N)$ *with the UOE property:*

$$\underset{O'}{\operatorname{argmax}}\, I(S, O'|O^-) = \underset{O'}{\operatorname{argmax}}\, H(O'|O^-) \ .$$

Proof. According to the chain rule for mutual information,

$$\underset{O'}{\operatorname{argmax}}\, I(S, O'|O^-)$$
$$= \underset{O'}{\operatorname{argmax}}\, H(O'|O^-) - H(O'|S, O^-) \ .$$

By the Lemma, the second term is constant for all possible values of O', and hence

$$= \underset{O'}{\operatorname{argmax}}\, H(O'|O^-) \ .$$

□

To compute $H(O'|O^-)$ we require the probability values $P(O'|O^-)$ for each possible O'. Naively, one can compute this probability by summing over the hypothesis space, but this would yield us no benefit. However, we can model this probability directly using a function approximator. The result is an efficient computation for $\operatorname{argmax}_{O'} H(O'|O^-)$ that runs in $O(dom(O)NM)$ time, where N is the total number of observations and M depends on the complexity of our function approximator.

We call the model of $P(O'|O^-)$ an *implication model* because it attempts to deduce the outcome of a future observation based on a set of past observations. We will describe how to train this model in section 3.

3.3 OBSERVATION COLLECTION

We solve the active diagnosis problem in two parts: observation collection (OC) and hypothesis delivery. In OC, an observation is adaptively chosen at each time step by maximizing the entropy $H(O'|O^-)$ until a budget of observations is exhausted. These observations are then used by the hypothesis delivery algorithm to obtain a hypothesis.

The observation collection algorithm is detailed in Algorithm 1. Here, f is a function that models $P(O_j = o|O^-)$; $query$ is a function which returns the value for an observation given a hidden hypothesis s that we are trying to discover. One can only call this function $Budget$ number of times.

Hypothesis delivery is done in a problem specific manner: For some problems it is appropriate to train a classifier that maps the collected observations to the hidden hypothesis; for other problems one can compute the hidden hypothesis directly from the observations. We will discuss the hypothesis delivery in detail in the experiment section.

Require: $f(j, o, [o^1, \dots, o^K]) = P(O_j = o|O^1 = o^1 \dots O^K = o^K)$
Require: $query_s(O)$
$Os = [\,]$
while *size*$(Os) \leq$ *Budget* **do**
  O = $\operatorname{argmax}_{j \in 1 \dots N} H(O_j, Os)$
  o = $query_s(O)$
  $Os \leftarrow Os + [O = o]$
end
where: $H(O_j, Os) = \sum_{dom(O)} f(j, o, Os) \log(f(j, o, Os))$
return: Os

Algorithm 1: Observation Collection

Our scheme is unique in that the observation collection algorithm is completely decoupled from the hypothesis delivery algorithm. This decoupling allows one to explore different hypothesis delivery algorithms with the guarantee that the observations being used to deliver the hypothesis are well chosen. The observation collection algorithm depends only on $P(O'|O^-)$, which can be trained on a dataset that is not annotated with hypothesis-specific information.

4 IMPLICATION MODEL

In this section we describe how to model $P(O' \mid O^-)$. We first describe a neural network model that, given O^-, simultaneously computes $P(O' = o \mid O^-)$ for all possible choices for O' and o; We then describe how to train this neural network in a fashion similar to that of a sparse auto-encoder. Although this strategy can be generalized for non-binary discrete observations, we restrict our attention to the case of binary observations in the following.

4.1 NEURAL NETWORK MODEL

We consider a model that outputs $P(O' \mid O^-)$ for all possible choices of observations simultaneously since the observation collection algorithm must determine the best O' amongst all possible remaining observations. Note that O^- has a variable length depending on how many observations have been made at the time of picking the next one. One may choose to encode this variable-length input with an LSTM, but we found that a simple feed-forward neural network that allows the value of an observation to be UNK, the unknown value, to be more effective.

Our model resembles a simple auto-encoder with a single, fully-connected hidden layer containing M rectified linear units; however, the approach could be straightforwardly extended to use a deeper encoding/decoding network structure in more complex domains. The input to the network is a vector $(x_1^1, x_1^0, x_2^1, x_2^0, \ldots, x_N^1, x_N^0)$, where:

$$(x_i^1, x_i^0) = \begin{cases} (1,0) & \text{if } (O_i = 1) \in O^- \\ (0,1) & \text{if } (O_i = 0) \in O^- \\ (0,0) & \text{if } O_i = \text{UNK} \end{cases}.$$

The output is a vector $(y_1^1, y_1^0, y_2^1, y_2^0, \ldots, y_N^1, y_N^0)$ where the distribution on values of O_i is defined using softmax:

$$\begin{cases} P(O_i = 1) = & \frac{e^{y_i^1}}{e^{y_i^0} + e^{y_i^1}} \\ P(O_i = 0) = & \frac{e^{y_i^0}}{e^{y_i^0} + e^{y_i^1}} \end{cases}.$$

Figure 1 illustrates the architecture.

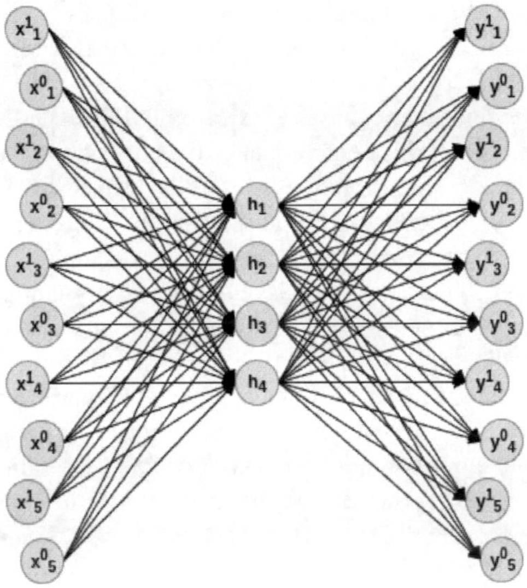

Figure 1: The implication model where there are a total of 5 observations and 4 hidden units

4.2 MODEL TRAINING

Our training data is of the form

$$\{(x_1^{1(j)}, x_1^{0(j)}, x_2^{1(j)}, x_2^{0(j)}, \ldots, x_N^{1(j)}, x_N^{0(j)}\}_{j=1\ldots n}$$

where $(x_i^{1(j)}, x_i^{0(j)})$ corresponds to the value of observation O_i made on hidden hypothesis $s^{(j)} \sim P(S)$. Note that the value of $s^{(j)}$ need not be present in the data.

We perform supervised training of the network using stochastic gradient descent with input-output pairs $(\hat{x}^{(j)}, x^{(j)})$. We draw $x^{(j)}$ randomly from the training data set, and construct $\hat{x}^{(j)}$ from $x^{(j)}$ by randomly changing some elements of $x^{(j)}$ to UNK as follows: We first draw a number $\epsilon \sim uniform(0,1)$, then change each $x_i^{(j)}$ to UNK with probability ϵ. We use cross-entropy as the loss function between the softmax probability of O_i and the expected output $(x_i^{1(j)}, x_i^{0(j)})$. For the experiments in this paper, the hidden layer contains 200 units and is equipped with the ReLU activation function. We implement and train the implication model using TensorFlow.

One can think of this model as a type of sparse autoencoder Le (2013), but rather than sparsifying the hidden layer we are sparsifying the input layer. Intuitively, without any sparsification, the network learns the identity implication, $O_i = o \Rightarrow O_i = o$. Sparsifying the input layer forces the network to learn inter-relationships between the observations, such that a handful of observations is sufficient to recover the full set of observations.

Note that by randomly ablating a subset of the observation features, we learn a model that is capable of working with any subset of observations O^-. This could potentially be more work than necessary, as during observation collection we are following a particular greedy policy that chooses the new observation with the maximum entropy, leading to particular sequences of observations being made, which restricts the set of queries. A good avenue for future work might be to train on observation traces generated by OC so the network can specialize further to a particular distribution of observations.

5 EXPERIMENTS

In this section we evaluate the performance of our active diagnosis algorithm on several simple active diagnosis problems. Here we outline the problems and their characteristics before elaborating them in detail [2].

Battleship This is a variant of the classic battleship game, where the goal is to infer the configurations of all 5 ships on a 10 by 10 board with as few queries to the board as possible. The hypothesis space consists of approximately 2^{38} different configurations, and each query is a (x,y) coordinate that results in "hit" or "miss".

Sushi This is a problem of preference elicitation, where the goal is to learn the full preference order of an unseen user on 10 different types of sushi with as few pair-wise comparison queries as possible. The hypothesis space consists of 10! potential full rankings, and each

[2]For specifics of these experiments see: `https://github.com/evanthebouncy/uai2017_learning_to_acquire_information`

query is a pair-wise comparison between 2 sushi types that results in "true" or "false".

Network We consider a fault localization task on a network of 100 nodes organized as a tree, where each link has 2% chance of failure. The task is to learn an efficient scheme for querying pair-wise connectivities to localize the failure with as few queries as possible. The hypothesis space consists of all 2^{100} combinations of failures. The query is a pair-wise connectivity check, restricted to all 99 direct link checks and 300 additional pairs of fixed nodes with measurement equipment.

5.1 BATTLESHIP

The task is to infer the locations of all the ships with as few queries as possible. The board is a 10 by 10 grid, with 5 ships of size $2 \times 4, 1 \times 5, 1 \times 3, 1 \times 3, 1 \times 3$ placed randomly with arbitrary horizontal or vertical orientations. Adjacent placements are allowed, but the ships may not overlap with each other. See Figure 2 for an example board.

At each stage of the game, our observation collection algorithm OC selects the most-informative observation and updates its belief space. Figure 2 illustrates the belief space at various numbers of observations. Note that without any observations, our model predicts that a ship is more likely to be located near the center of the board rather than toward the edge. In the case of 22 observations, our model queried a "hit" on the lower left without completely observing the 1×5 long ship in the middle of the board.

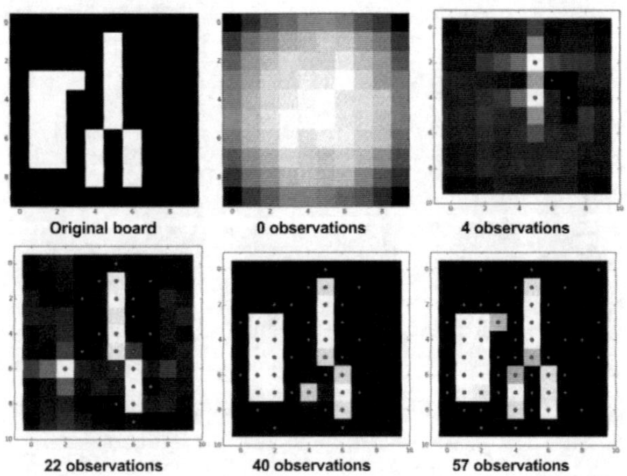

Figure 2: Belief space of observations on a particular board at various numbers of observations. Intensity indicates the probability of a coordinate being a hit, and colored dots indicates past observations: green for "hit" and red for "miss"

We consider two kinds of hypothesis delivery schemes. In the first scheme we deliver the probabilities of all the observations using the implication model $P(O'|O^-)$, implicitly inferring the hidden locations of the ships. In the second scheme we use a constraint solver which takes in the list of observations made by OC and returns a hypothesis s that is consistent with these observations.

For comparison we consider 2 baseline algorithms: The random sampler **rand** samples unseen coordinates at random. The **sink** algorithm samples unseen coordinates at random, and when it has found a hit, it queries all its neighboring coordinates until no "hit" coordinates can be found, then resumes random sampling. Both the random and sink algorithms initially mark all coordinates as "miss" and update them to "hit" when a hit has been recorded.

To evaluate performance under the first hypothesis delivery scheme, we let OC output the maximum likelihood guess for each coordinate. Accuracy is measured as a fraction of correctly guessed coordinates. Figure 3 compares accuracy across all coordinates as a function of number of observations; an accuracy of 1.0 means all coordinates are guessed correctly. In this experiment, we consider 3 different variant of the implication model: **oc_1** is the single hidden-layer fully-connected model originally described, **oc_0** is the 0-layer neural-network model (logistic regression), and **oc_cnn** contains a convolutional neural-network layer before a fully-connected hidden layer. As we can see, the random algorithm improves linearly as expected, the sink heuristic performs better than random, and our approach OC performs the best, with **oc_1** and **oc_cnn** performing better than the logistic regression **oc_0**. Figure 4 considers the same experiment except a 10% observation error is introduced, under this condition all 3 variants of the OC similarly, and more robust to noise than the baseline algorithms.

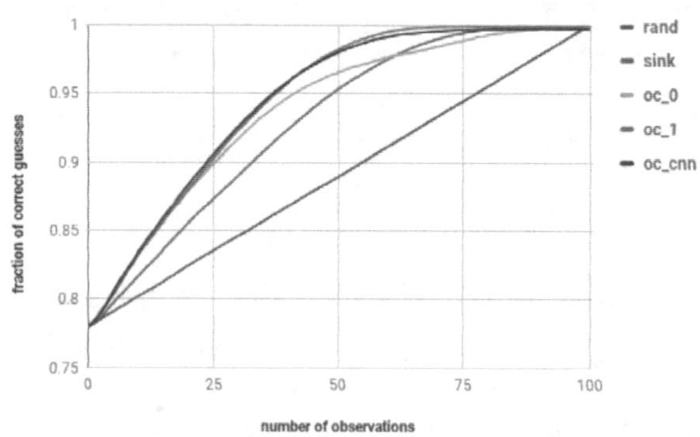

Figure 3: Comparison of our algorithm **oc** against the 2 baselines. Accuracies are averaged over 1000 randomly generated boards

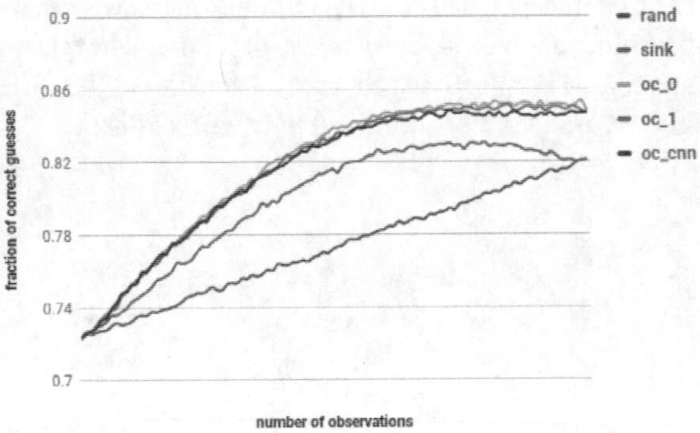

Figure 4: Comparison of our algorithm **oc** against the 2 baselines. Accuracies are averaged over 1000 randomly generated boards with 10% chance of observation error

To evaluate the performance under the second hypothesis delivery scheme, we use a constraint solver to produce a hypothesis in the form of ships' locations and orientations, using observations collected by **rand**, **sink** and **oc** as constraints to the hypothesis. We then measure accuracy by the number of correctly predicted ship's locations and orientations: 5 means all 5 ship's locations and orientations are correctly produced by the constraint solver given the observations collected. Figure 5 compares number of correctly guessed ships as a function of number of observations. As we can see our algorithm OC performs the best, followed by sink with random performing the worst. Note that constraint solvers are known to produce arbitrary hypotheses that satisfy the constraint in an under constrained system, yet despite this, OC was able to consistently out perform the baseline algorithms.

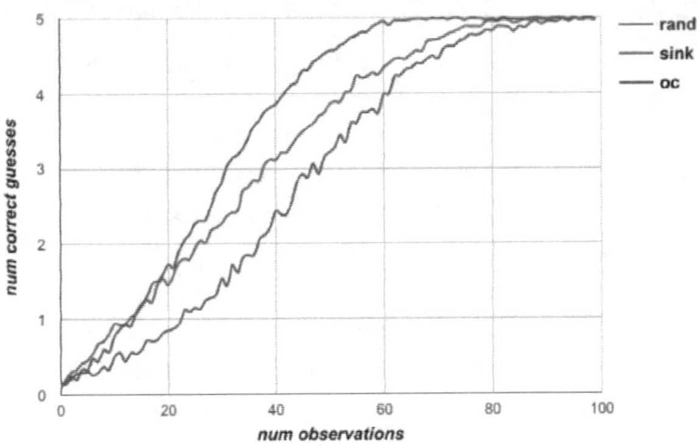

Figure 5: Comparison of our algorithm **oc** against the 2 baselines when using a constraint solver for hypothesis delivery. Accuracies are averaged over 100 randomly generated boards. Only the single-hidden-layer implication model is considered here.

5.2 SUSHI

The sushi data set collected by Kamishima (2003) contains 5000 user preferences for 10 kinds of sushi expressed in *full rankings*. The dataset also contains feature vectors describing each individual type of sushi and describing the users, which in this study we omit. Our task is the following: Given a new user, how to infer the full ranking of this user with as few pair-wise comparison queries as possible? Naively, this is a sorting problem where one can obtain the full ranking of any permutation of items with $O(n \log n)$ comparisons. However, the preference orderings are not uniformly random, for instance, a preference of eel over tuna may indicate a user's liking of cooked sushi over raw sushi. We evaluate accuracy by using the Kendall correlation: a value of 1.0 means all pair-wise orderings of our prediction and the ground truth agree with each other, and a value of -1.0 indicates all pair-wise orderings are in disagreement.

There is no related work on this dataset that attempts to discover the full preference of a new user based on pair-wise queries to the new user. Soufiani (2013) models the sushi preferences as a generative process where the preferences are caused by a combination of user features (such as age and gender) and sushi features (such as price) but does not perform elicitation on a new user in the form of pair-wise queries. Without further elicitation, they are able to infer a new user's preference with a Kendall correlation of 0.75. Guo (2010) performs elicitation on a new user in the form of pair-wise queries but instead of learning the full preference, attempts to recommend the best sushi to the user. They are able to always predict the best sushi after 14 pair-wise comparisons. Thus, for comparison we consider various in-place sorting algorithms as baseline. Each time a pair-wise comparison question is made, we take a snapshot of the current array and extract pair-wise orderings from it.

The 5000 user preferences are split into a 2500 preferences training set and 2500 preferences testing set. In order to train our implication model to handle novel permutations not seen during the training set, we augment the training set by a set of randomly sampled permutations in addition to the 2500 preferences.

For this experiment, we can measure performance directly as Kendall correlation without delivering an explicit ordering as the hypothesis (If one wishes one can easily compute a full ordering from all pair-wise orderings). Figure 6 compares our observation collection algorithm **oc_0** and **oc_1** against various in-place sorting algorithms: BubbleSort **bsort**, QuickSort **qsort**, and MergeSort **msort**. As we can see, even without any observations OC was able to obtain a Kendall correlation of 0.3, indicating the underlying distribution for preferences is not uniform; by comparison, the baseline sorting algorithms make no assumptions on the underlying distribution, thus starts with a correlation around 0. Our scheme was able to infer the full ranking of any user in 26 queries, beating the performance of **qsort**, which takes 40 queries.

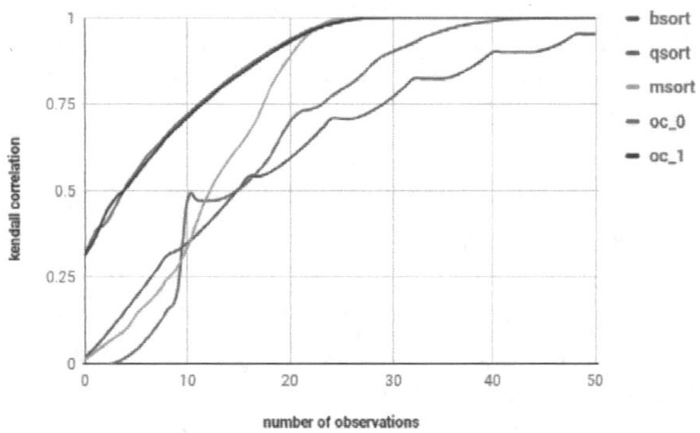

Figure 6: Kendall correlation as a function of number of queries averaged across 2500 testing examples

We also considered the case where the query has a 10% chance of error, the result is shown in Figure 7. Note the OC algorithm is robust in the presence of noise as it improves its pair-wise preferences incrementally with each observation (a property also shared by **bsort**) whereas deterministic baseline such as **qsort** and **msort** sorts the preferences assuming all observations are perfect.

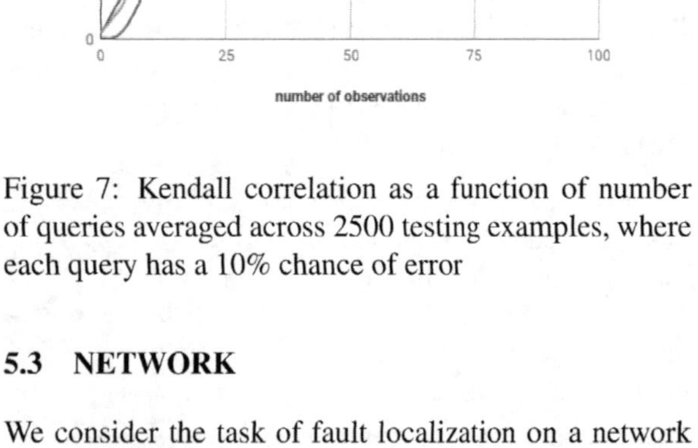

Figure 7: Kendall correlation as a function of number of queries averaged across 2500 testing examples, where each query has a 10% chance of error

5.3 NETWORK

We consider the task of fault localization on a network of nodes organized as a tree. The network without any failure is shown in Figure 8. There are 100 nodes in this network with 99 direct links, forming a spanning tree. The hypothesis space consists of failure cases where each direct link has a probability of 2% of failure. The query is a pair-wise connectivity check, restricted to all 99 direct link checks and 300 additional pairs of fixed nodes.

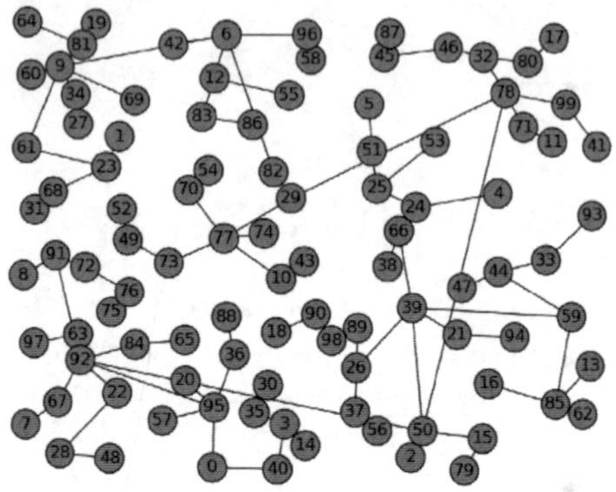

Figure 8: The network without any failure

For hypothesis delivery, we use the implication model $P(O'|O^-)$ to output the probability of failure on the 99 directly connected pairs of nodes. To measure accuracy, we use the maximum likelihood guess for these pairs and measure the fraction of correctly diagnosed link failures.

We compare our approach with the naive localization scheme **rand** that randomly picks an unobserved direct link and checks if it is disconnected. The random scheme will always be able to diagnose all the link failures in 99 observations. However, OC can leverage the network structure to learn an efficient querying scheme by utilizing connectivity queries to the additional pairs of nodes. Figure 9 shows accuracy of OC against the random algorithm. We see OC outperforms the random algorithm most of the time, reaching 99.5% accuracy in 60 observations. OC performs worse than the random scheme for less than 10 observations because OC does not query the direct links for the first few observations: The 300 additional pairs can yield more information without pinpointing an exact failure. OC again performs worse than the random scheme past 80 observations. This is a consequence of the greedy approach: OC maximizes information gain one observation at a time, but the set of observations selected by the random approach (all direct links) is the optimal set of size 99, capable of answering any failure queries. OC fails to find an alternative optimal set partly because there are instances where many links fail simultaneously, which weakens the structures that our implication model depends on.

To quantify the effects of structure on the difficulty to diagnose a link failure, we define the *dependency coeffi-*

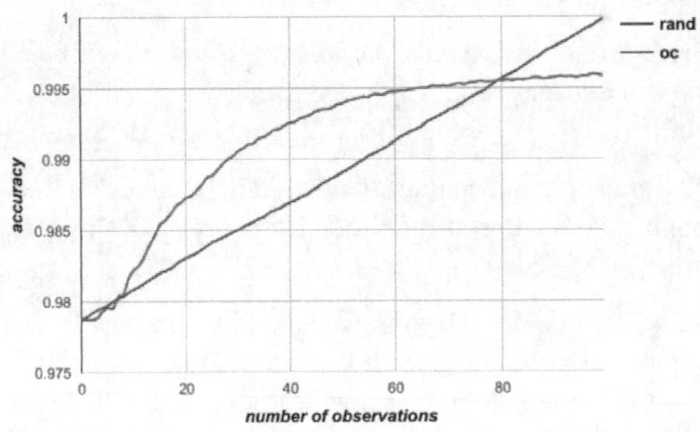

Figure 9: Accuracy of link failure diagnosis averaged across 1400 random instances

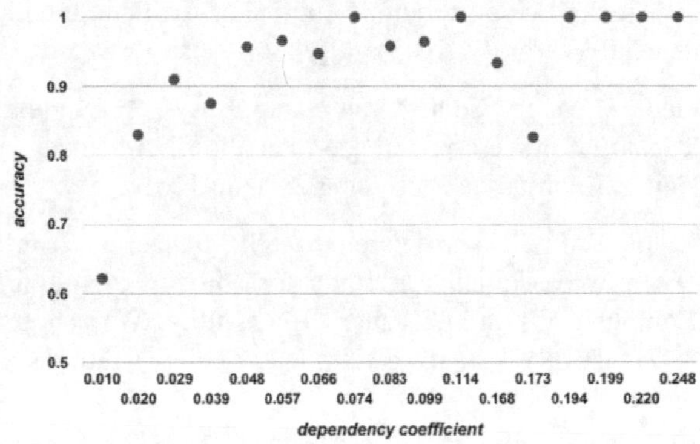

Figure 10: Accuracy of link failure diagnosis as a function of dependency coefficients, averaged over 1400 instances

cient for a direct link e_i as:

$$dep_i = \frac{M_i N_i}{(M_i + N_i)(M_i + N_i - 1)}$$

Where M_i and N_i are the sizes of the disconnected subgraphs when only link e_i fails. The dependency coefficient measures the fraction of pair-wise connectivity which would be affected should e_i fail. When e_i is located next to a leaf node in the network, this coefficient is close to 0.01. When disconnecting e_i breaks the network into 2 equally sized components, the coefficient is close to 0.25.

Figure 10 measures accuracy of diagnosis against dependency coefficient. As one can see, in general higher dependency coefficient means better diagnosis: When many pair-wise connectivities depend on a link, successful pair-wise connection on any of these pairs will imply the link has not failed; conversely, when this link fails all pair-wise connections that depend on this link fail as well. This property is useful because a link which many pair-wise connections depend on would have a better chance of being correctly diagnosed.

6 DISCUSSION

In this paper we present a new approach to active diagnosis in domains with complex hypothesis spaces. We show that given the uniform observation entropy assumption, the problem of choosing the most informative query reduces to maximizing the conditional observation entropy $H(O'|O^-)$, which can be computed from $P(O'|O^-)$ without explicit modeling of the hypothesis space. We describe a neural network modeling of $P(O'|O^-)$ called an implication model, and demonstrate that it can be trained in a supervised fashion. We evaluate our approach on several simple yet distinct benchmarks, demonstrating superior performance against reasonable baseline algorithms.

As our proof and experiments depends on the UOE assumption, the applicability of the UOE assumption is a legitimate concern. While it is true that UOE assumption is not valid under all diagnostic problems, UOE does apply to the class of problems where the same kind of sensor is used to gather signals at different locations of a deterministic environment, including robotic localization, geostatistics, and optimal sensor placements.

A unique feature of our approach is that the implication model can be trained on unlabeled observation data in a supervised fashion. A good direction for future work would be to apply this approach to domains where there are an abundance of observation data without annotations to the hypothesis that generated it. The implication model learns interesting structures of the observation data; it would be instructive to quantify how easy it is to learn different kinds of structures.

Acknowledgements

We would like to thank Rohit Singh for the encoding of the BattleShip SAT formulation, Shachar Itzhaky for insightful discussions, and Twitch Chat for moral supports.

This work was funded by the MUSE program (Darpa grant FA8750-14-2-0242).

References

Bellala, Gowtham, et al. "A rank-based approach to active diagnosis." IEEE transactions on pattern analysis and machine intelligence 35.9 (2013): 2078-2090.

Golovin, Daniel, and Andreas Krause. "Adaptive submodularity: Theory and applications in active learning and stochastic optimization." Journal of Artificial Intelligence Research 42 (2011): 427-486.

Guo, Shengbo, Scott Sanner, and Edwin V. Bonilla. "Gaussian process preference elicitation." Advances in Neural Information Processing Systems. 2010.

Holub, Alex, Pietro Perona, and Michael C. Burl. "Entropy-based active learning for object recognition." Computer Vision and Pattern Recognition Workshops, 2008. CVPRW'08. IEEE Computer Society Conference on. IEEE, 2008.

Joshi, Ajay J., Fatih Porikli, and Nikolaos Papanikolopoulos. "Multi-class active learning for image classification." Computer Vision and Pattern Recognition, 2009. CVPR 2009. IEEE Conference on. IEEE, 2009.

Krause, Andreas, and Carlos Guestrin. "Submodularity and its applications in optimized information gathering." ACM Transactions on Intelligent Systems and Technology (TIST) 2.4 (2011): 32.

Le, Quoc V. "Building high-level features using large scale unsupervised learning." Acoustics, Speech and Signal Processing (ICASSP), 2013 IEEE International Conference on. IEEE, 2013.

Lewis, David D., and William A. Gale. "A sequential algorithm for training text classifiers." Proceedings of the 17th annual international ACM SIGIR conference on Research and development in information retrieval. Springer-Verlag New York, Inc., 1994.

Littman, Michael L., Judy Goldsmith, and Martin Mundhenk. "The computational complexity of probabilistic planning." Journal of Artificial Intelligence Research 9.1 (1998): 1-36.

Mnih, Volodymyr, Nicolas Heess, and Alex Graves. "Recurrent models of visual attention." Advances in neural information processing systems. 2014.

Nowak, Robert. "Generalized binary search." Communication, Control, and Computing, 2008 46th Annual Allerton Conference on. IEEE, 2008.

Rish, Irina, et al. "Real-time problem determination in distributed systems using active probing." Network Operations and Management Symposium, 2004. NOMS 2004. IEEE/IFIP. Vol. 1. IEEE, 2004.

Seung, H. Sebastian, Manfred Opper, and Haim Sompolinsky. "Query by committee." Proceedings of the fifth annual workshop on Computational learning theory. ACM, 1992.

Soufiani, Hossein Azari, David C. Parkes, and Lirong Xia. "Preference elicitation for general random utility models." arXiv preprint arXiv:1309.6864 (2013).

Srivastava, Nitish, et al. "Dropout: a simple way to prevent neural networks from overfitting." Journal of Machine Learning Research 15.1 (2014): 1929-1958.

T. Kamishima, "Nantonac Collaborative Filtering: Recommendation Based on Order Responses", KDD2003, pp.583-588 (2003)

Tong, Simon, and Daphne Koller. "Support vector machine active learning with applications to text classification." Journal of machine learning research 2.Nov (2001): 45-66.

Tong, Simon, and Edward Chang. "Support vector machine active learning for image retrieval." Proceedings of the ninth ACM international conference on Multimedia. ACM, 2001.

Wikipedia contributors. "Battleship (game)." Wikipedia, The Free Encyclopedia. Wikipedia, The Free Encyclopedia, 11 Mar. 2017. Web. 26 Mar. 2017.

Zheng, Alice X., Irina Rish, and Alina Beygelzimer. "Efficient test selection in active diagnosis via entropy approximation." arXiv preprint arXiv:1207.1418 (2012).

Why Rules are Complex: Real-Valued Probabilistic Logic Programs are not Fully Expressive

David Buchman*
davidbuc@cs.ubc.ca
http://www.cs.ubc.ca/~davidbuc

David Poole*
poole@cs.ubc.ca
http://www.cs.ubc.ca/~poole

*Department of Computer Science, University of British Columbia, Vancouver, BC, Canada

Abstract

This paper explores what can and cannot be represented by probabilistic logic programs (PLPs). Propositional PLPs can represent any distribution because they can be acyclic. For relational domains with fixed populations, the probabilistic parameters can be derived as the solutions to polynomial equations. Unfortunately, sometimes they only have complex-valued solutions. Thus PLPs, even with arbitrarily real-valued parameters, cannot represent all distributions. Moreover, they cannot approximate all distributions. Allowing the parameters to be complex numbers, we present a natural truly-cyclic canonical representation that with probability 1 can represent all distributions for (propositional or) relational domains with fixed populations, and, unlike standard representations, has no redundant parameters.

1 INTRODUCTION

Logic programs have the advantage of an intuitive declarative and procedural interpretation (Kowalski, 2014). On the other hand, probabilistic modeling is an established formalism for representing and processing quantified uncertainty. Much attention has been given to formalisms combining logic programming with probabilistic modeling. One such combination is the family of probabilistic logic programs, including ICL (Poole, 1997, 2000), Prism (Sato & Kameya, 1997, 2008), ProbLog (De Raedt et al., 2007), and CP-logic (Vennekens et al., 2009), which separate uncertainty from logic, by encapsulating uncertainty into special variables representing independent probabilistic noise.

Recently, Buchman & Poole (2016, 2017) demonstrated that probabilistic logic programs (PLPs) are incapable of representing some relational distributions, even with a population size of just two. They showed that introducing negations ($\neg$'s) to the language does not help, but allowing negative numeric values as noise probabilities increases expressiveness and solve the problem (in which case $\neg$'s are not needed). They did not, however, examined whether negative probabilities are sufficient for representing arbitrary relational distributions using PLPs.

In this paper, we pick up from where Buchman & Poole (2017) left off. Table 1 describes some of our results. We show that for the relational setting, even for fixed populations, some distributions cannot be represented even using arbitrary real-valued probabilities ($\text{P} \in (-\infty, +\infty)$). We prove that, in general, with probability 1 an arbitrary relational distribution with fixed populations can be represented using complex numbers as rule probabilities; therefore using complex probabilistic values is **essential**.

Furthermore, we expose a natural truly-cyclic canonical form for PLPs, the **Broadcast Canonical Form (BCF)**. BCF is very simple, and it allows to simplify the syntax of the language. We show BCF perfectly strips the redundancy from PLP rules, while maintaining expressiveness in both the propositional and the general (relational) setting (with fixed populations) (using complex probabilities, which are required anyway). We also provide solver algorithms, demonstrating how a BCF PLP representation can be computed, for modeling a given distribution.

In addition, we provide an algorithm for directly computing probabilities of interpretations, which is efficient in domains where few variables are *true* (e.g., applications modeling rare events, system failures, medical conditions, etc.).

Negative probabilities have been used for optimizing inference or computation (Dıez & Galán, 2003; Kisynski & Poole, 2009; Van den Broeck et al., 2013). Meert & Vennekens (2014) suggested a new language feature, using negation in the head of rules in CP-logic, thus facilitat-

Table 1: Properties of languages

		range(P)	BCF (Def. 1)		PLP		PLP with ¬'s
General (Rel.) case:		$\mathrm{P} \in [0,1]$	no		no		no
(fixed popu.)	(Almost-)Fully Expressive?:	$\mathrm{P} \in (-\infty,+\infty)$	no (Thm 2)		no (Thm 2)		
		$\mathrm{P} \in \mathbb{C}$	yes (Thm 5)		yes (Thm 5)		yes (Thm 5)
Prop. case:	**#params:** (Sec. 6)		$2^n - 1$	$<$	$n2^{n-1}$	$\ll$	$n3^{n-1}$
		$\mathrm{P} \in [0,1]$	no		no		yes
	(Almost-)Fully Expressive?:	$\mathrm{P} \in (-\infty,1]$	no		yes		yes
		$\mathrm{P} \in \mathbb{C}$	yes (Thm 4)		yes		yes

ing expressiveness by supporting a cancellation effect of existing rules. Complex probabilities (Cox, 1955; Parisi, 1983; Hamber & Ren, 1985; Salcedo, 1997; Zak, 1998; Hofmann, 2012; Salcedo, 2016) have found use in quantum physics, but much less in the probabilistic modeling of general, non-quantum data.

2 PROGRAMS

We use uppercase letters for (possibly parametrized) Boolean **variables**, and lowercase letters for the corresponding atoms. V represents a set of (unparametrized) Boolean variables. An **interpretation** I is an assignment to all variables in V, and it is represented as the set $I \subseteq V$ of variables that are assigned $true$ (sometimes we use the set of atoms instead).

A (probabilistic) **rule** has the form $p : head \leftarrow body$, where p is a numeric value commonly interpreted as a probability, $head$ is a (non-negated) atom, and $body$ is a conjunction of atoms, some of which may be negated.

Due to Buchman & Poole (2017)'s result that negative probabilities are needed for expressiveness and that ¬'s do not increase expressiveness, we **do not use ¬'s**.

A **(propositional) probabilistic logic program (PLP)** R is a set of rules. A **deterministic program realization (DPR)** for a (propositional or ground) PLP R is a deterministic program, whose rules are a subset of R's. We use the unique stable-model semantics as the semantics for DPRs. A PLP R defines a distribution over its DPRs, where each rule $p : head \leftarrow body$ independently appears with probability p or does not appear with probability $1 - p$. Considering that each DPR represents its stable-model, a PLP represents a distribution over interpretations, i.e., a joint distribution over the variables.

The **relational setting** introduces **populations**, which are sets of **individuals**, and allows variables to be parametrized by **logical variables** (written in uppercase), which refer to individuals. Rules may thus also become parametrized. Once populations are fixed, a PLP can be ground. The ground PLP can be treated as a propositional PLP.

Relational PLPs may use constants, which refer to specific individuals. Once there is a constant for every individual, the PLP can contain rules that refer to any specific ground variable, and the PLP's expressiveness becomes identical to a propositional PLP's. The interesting question is what happens when there are individuals not specifiable using constants. The PLP's expressiveness is reduced; however, the requirement for being "(almost-)fully expressive" (defined later) is also reduced, since the PLP is only required to be able to represent distributions that are symmetric w.r.t. unspecifiable individuals. Therefore, we use no constants in this paper.

Let R be a propositional PLP over variables V, and $V_1, V_2 \subseteq V$. $R_{V_1 \leftarrow V_2} \subseteq R$ is the PLP over $V_1 \cup V_2$ that contains all rules in R whose head is in V_1 and whose bodies only contain variables from V_2; and $R_I \stackrel{\text{def}}{=} R_{I \leftarrow I}$.

In this paper we follow the approach of Buchman & Poole (2015) for simplifying syntax and semantics, and implicitly assume that different logical variables correspond to different individuals, thus a rule $a(X) \leftarrow b(X) \wedge c(Y)$ actually stands for $a(X) \leftarrow b(X) \wedge c(Y) \wedge (X \neq Y)$. There is no loss of generality, as every rule can be converted to multiple rules in which all logical variables correspond to different individuals, such that the overall semantics of the PLP does not change; this can be shown in a manner analogous to Buchman & Poole (2015)'s proof for Markov logic networks.

2.1 USING COMPLEX PROBABILITIES

Buchman & Poole (2017) suggested using negative numerical values as rule probabilities. They defined the semantics, which may either be a proper or improper distribution over interpretations; either way, however, the sum of the interpretations' probabilities is 1. They also argued against the perceived meaninglessness of using negative probabilities, by treating them as meaningless mathematical parameters of a probabilistic model; as long as the mathematical definition of the PLP's semantics is a proper distribution, there is no problem with the negativeness of some rule "probabilities". In this paper, we consider using complex numerical values as rule probabilities. The arguments of Buchman & Poole (2017) about rule "probabilities" not having to be meaningful as probabilities, apply here as well. In addition, their analysis, showing that a PLP's distribution sums to 1 even if some rule probabilities are negative, holds also for complex rule probabilities.

2.2 ALMOST-FULL EXPRESSIVENESS

The space of all (proper) distributions over n binary variables is the standard D-dimensional simplex $S_{\langle D\rangle}$, where $D = 2^n - 1$. Let $S^+_{\mathcal{L}}$ be the set of all (proper) distributions that a language $\mathcal{L}$ can represent, and $S^-_{\mathcal{L}} = S_{\langle D\rangle} \setminus S^+_{\mathcal{L}}$. If $S^-_{\mathcal{L}} = \emptyset$, then $\mathcal{L}$ has **full expressiveness**. Sometimes, $S^-_{\mathcal{L}}$ represents one or more (nonlinear) **"$\neq$" constraints** on the distribution's probabilities that are "$(D-1)$-dimensional", and $S^+_{\mathcal{L}}$ has measure 1. We then say $\mathcal{L}$ has **almost-full expressiveness**. Note that, in this case, if $\mathrm{P} \in S^-_{\mathcal{L}}$, then $\mathcal{L}$ can still represent P, allowing for infinitesimal error. (If this were not the case, then one could draw a D-dimensional sphere around P, such that this sphere, with its positive D-dimensional volume, would be contained in $S^-_{\mathcal{L}}$.)

When $\mathcal{L}$ is not almost-fully expressive, we say $\mathcal{L}$ is **partially-expressive**. This may happen when, e.g., $S^-_{\mathcal{L}}$ is defined by a **"<" constraint** on the distribution's probabilities, leading $S^-_{\mathcal{L}}$ to have "positive D-dimensional volume". This leads to distributions P that cannot even be approximated (to arbitrary accuracy).

3 THE PROPOSITIONAL CASE

Given a propositional PLP R over variables V, the probability of an interpretation $I \subseteq V$ is a complicated function of R's parameters (i.e., rule probabilities). In general, $\mathrm{P}^R(I)$ can be decomposed into a product of two expressions: one sets variables in I to *true*, and one makes sure variables in $V \setminus I$ remain *false*. The following theorem makes this intuitive argument mathematically precise. The "expression that sets variables in I to *true*" is not well-defined, so we replace it with the equivalent "the probability of all variables being *true*, in another ('projected') PLP R_I that only contains the variables I".

Theorem 1. *Let R be a propositional (or grounded) PLP over variables V, and $I \subseteq V$ be an interpretation. Then:*

$$\mathrm{P}^R(I) = \mathrm{P}^{R_I}(I) \prod_{(p:\, head \leftarrow body) \in R_{(V\setminus I)\leftarrow I}} (1-p) \quad (1)$$

$$\mathrm{P}^{R_I}(I) = 1 - \sum_{I' \subsetneq I} \mathrm{P}^{R_I}(I') \quad (2)$$

Proof. Equation (2) holds because for all PLPs, the total probability of all interpretations is always 1 (even with complex probabilities).

The equation for $\mathrm{P}^R(I)$ has two components.

1. First, we make sure the variables in $V \setminus I$ remain *false* even if variables in I are *true*. For this, we must make sure the rules in $R_{(V\setminus I)\leftarrow I}$ do not appear.

2. Second, we must make sure the variables in I are set to *true*. This only depends on the appearance of rules that completely ignore variables in $V \setminus I$. This probability is identical to $\mathrm{P}^{R_I}(I)$, which is the probability of all variables in I being *true*, when the variables in $V \setminus I$ simply do not exist. □

Theorem 1 defines a recursive formulation of interpretation probabilities, by Equation (1) reducing the computation to a computation in a PLP without the variables that are *false*, and Equation (2) reducing the computation further, to interpretations where fewer variables are *true*, for which (1) may again be applied.

Algorithm 1 is a recursive, bottom-up (dynamic programming) algorithm for computing the probability of any interpretation, based on Theorem 1. (Intermediate results can be cached, for efficiency.) Note that the recursion is over both interpretations and PLPs.

Algorithm 1 Compute probability of an interpretation.

Input: V: Set of ground variables,
R: ground PLP over V, $I \subseteq V$: interpretation
Output: `computeP` $(V, R, I) = \mathrm{P}^R(I)$

if $V = \emptyset$ **then**
  return 1
else if $I = V$ **then**
  return $1 - \sum_{I' \subsetneq I}$ `computeP` (V, R, I')
else
  return `computeP` (I, R_I, I)
    $\cdot \prod_{(p:\text{ head}\leftarrow\text{body}) \in R_{(V\setminus I)\leftarrow I}} (1-p)$
end if

While this algorithm takes exponential time in $|I|$, it can be useful for small I's. In addition, its explicit recursive formulation of $\mathrm{P}^R(I)$ makes it useful for theoretical analysis. We use it to derive theoretical results.

4 RELATIONAL PLPS OVER $\{A(X)\}$

We now consider the simplest setting for a relational PLP with fixed populations: a PLP having a single variable $A(X)$. This setting was analyzed by Buchman & Poole (2017) for $n = 2$ individuals; we generalize to $n > 2$.

Every rule in this setting has the following structure (recall that all logical variables may be assumed to be different (Section 2)): $a(X) \leftarrow a(Y) \wedge a(Z) \wedge \ldots$

Thus, for a population of size n, a PLP can be described parametrically, as a set of n rules (some of which may have the probability 0):

$$\begin{aligned} p_0 &: a(X) \\ p_1 &: a(X) \leftarrow a(Y_1) \\ p_2 &: a(X) \leftarrow a(Y_1) \wedge a(Y_2) \\ &\vdots \\ p_{n-1} &: a(X) \leftarrow a(Y_1) \wedge a(Y_2) \wedge \ldots \wedge a(Y_{n-1}) \end{aligned}$$

We use $\mathrm{P}^R_{n_t,n_f}$ for the probability a PLP R assigns to any interpretation where n_t variables are *true* and n_f are *false*, for $n = n_t + n_f$. For example, for $n = 3$, $\mathrm{P}^R(\{a(\text{alice}), a(\text{bob})\}) = \mathrm{P}^R(a(\text{alice}) \wedge \neg a(\text{eve}) \wedge a(\text{bob})) = \mathrm{P}^R_{2,1}$.

The following proposition follows directly from Theorem 1, and it generalizes the derivation used for proving Proposition 1 in Buchman & Poole (2017).

Proposition 1. *Given a PLP R involving only $A(X)$, $\mathrm{P}^R_{n_t,n_f}$ for all interpretations for all population sizes n can be computed using the recursive formulae:*

$$\mathrm{P}^R_{0,0} = 1$$

$$\mathrm{P}^R_{n,0} = 1 - \sum_{m=0}^{n-1} \binom{n}{m} \mathrm{P}^R_{m,n-m} \tag{3}$$

$$\mathrm{P}^R_{n_t,n_f} = \mathrm{P}^R_{n_t,0} \prod_{i=0}^{n_t} (1-p_i)^{\left(n_f \cdot \binom{n_t}{i}\right)} \tag{4}$$

4.1 A BACKTRACKING SOLVER

Let $\mathrm{P}^g > 0$ (for P^{goal}) be an arbitrary positive distribution over $\{A(X)\}$. Algorithm 2 is a recursive backtracking solver for finding a PLP R that represents P^g, if one exists (it is written in rolled-out form). A practical implementation would cache values, to reduce its complexity.

The idea behind the algorithm is as follows. R represents P^g, i.e., $\mathrm{P}^R = \mathrm{P}^g$, if and only if the following n equations hold: $\mathrm{P}^g_{0,n} = \mathrm{P}^R_{0,n}$, $\mathrm{P}^g_{1,n-1} = \mathrm{P}^R_{1,n-1}$, $\ldots$, $\mathrm{P}^g_{n-1,1} = \mathrm{P}^R_{n-1,1}$ (the additional equation $\mathrm{P}^g_{n,0} = \mathrm{P}^R_{n,0}$ is redundant). One can write these equations and use Proposition 1 to express each $\mathrm{P}^R_{n_t,n_f}$ using the parameters, $\{p_0, \ldots, p_{n-1}\}$. Ordering the equations by increasing n_t's, each equation contains exactly one parameter that does not appear in the previous equations. One can then solve each equation in turn. Each equation is polynomial, and may have multiple solutions. If some equation has no solutions, one backtracks. Therefore, the algorithm returns a correct PLP representation if one exists, and "impossible" if one does not exist. There are two reasons why a solution may not exist:

1. An equation's solutions may fall outside the allowed range for rule probabilities. This problem is eliminated by allowing complex rule probabilities.

2. If $\mathrm{P}^R_{n_t,0} = 0$ for some $n_t < n$, then there is no solution. This, however, only creates lower-dimensional manifolds that are (potentially) not representable.

Since $\mathrm{P}^R_{n_t,0}$ depends on values of previous p_i's computed, backtracking and changing their values may make it nonzero. Therefore, it might be the case that complex solutions always exist, and Proposition 2 can be strengthened to prove the language is fully expressive. Whether this is the case is an open problem.

Also note, that since $\mathrm{P}^g > 0$, the p_i's found are not 1, thus $\forall i, (1-p_i) \neq 0$, and the PLPs found have no deterministic rules.

4.2 REAL-VALUED PLPS: NOT FULLY EXPR.

Buchman & Poole (2017) have shown that all positive distributions with $n = 2$ can be represented, if one allows negative probabilities. Whether negative probabilities are enough to represent all positive distributions in general (for fixed n's) was left as an open problem. Unfortunately, the answer is negative:

Example 1. *For $n = 3$, the following positive distribution cannot be represented using PLPs, even allowing negative rule probabilities:*
$\mathrm{P}^g_{0,3} = \frac{1}{3^3} = \frac{1}{27}$, $\mathrm{P}^g_{1,2} = \frac{2^3}{3^3} = \frac{8}{27}$, $\mathrm{P}^g_{2,1} = \frac{1}{54}$, $\mathrm{P}^g_{3,0} = \frac{1}{54}$
Simulating Algorithm 2, (3) and (4) give:

$$\tfrac{1}{27} = \mathrm{P}^g_{0,3} = \mathrm{P}^R_{0,3} = \mathrm{P}^R_{0,0} \prod_{i=0}^{0} (1-p_i)^{\left(3\binom{0}{i}\right)} = (1-p_0)^3 \tag{5}$$

$$\tfrac{8}{27} = \mathrm{P}^g_{1,2} = \mathrm{P}^R_{1,2} = \mathrm{P}^R_{1,0} \cdot \prod_{i=0}^{1} (1-p_i)^{\left(2\cdot\binom{1}{i}\right)} \tag{6}$$
$$= p_0 \cdot (1-p_0)^2 (1-p_1)^2$$

$$\begin{aligned} \mathrm{P}^R_{2,0} &= 1 - \sum_{m=0}^{1} \binom{2}{m} \mathrm{P}^R_{m,2-m} \\ &= 1 - \binom{2}{0} \mathrm{P}^R_{0,2} - \binom{2}{1} \mathrm{P}^R_{1,1} \\ &= 1 - (1-p_0)^2 - 2p_0(1-p_0)(1-p_1) \end{aligned} \tag{7}$$

$$\tfrac{1}{54} = \mathrm{P}^g_{2,1} = \mathrm{P}^R_{2,1} = \mathrm{P}^R_{2,0} \prod_{i=0}^{2} (1-p_i)^{\left(1\cdot\binom{2}{i}\right)} \tag{8}$$

Solving (5) gives $p_0 = \frac{2}{3}$. Substituting into (6) gives $(1-p_1)^2 = 4$, so $p_1 \in \{-1, 3\}$. We required $p_1 < 1$, therefore $p_1 = -1$. Substituting into (7) gives $\mathrm{P}^R_{2,0} = 0$. Substituting $\mathrm{P}^R_{2,0} = 0$ into (8) gives $\mathrm{P}^R_{2,1} = 0 \neq \frac{1}{54}$ irrespective of p_2, thus representing P^g is not possible.

Example 2. *If we also allow rule probabilities above 1, the distribution in Example 1 can be represented.*

Consider Example 1. This time, we can choose $p_1 = 3$. Substituting into (7) gives $\mathrm{P}^R_{2,0} = \frac{16}{9}$. (The PLP thus represents an improper distribution for $n = 2$; however, we are trying to model P^g, which is only defined for $n = 3$. We treat "$\mathrm{P}^R_{2,0}$" as nothing more than a name given to a meaningless expression used in the formula of $\mathrm{P}^R_{2,1}$.) Substituting into (8) gives $p_2 = \frac{127}{128}$. These $\{p_0, p_1, p_2\}$ give $\{\mathrm{P}^g_{0,3} = \mathrm{P}^R_{0,3}, \mathrm{P}^g_{1,2} = \mathrm{P}^R_{1,2}, \mathrm{P}^g_{2,1} = \mathrm{P}^R_{2,1}\}$, thus $\mathrm{P}^g = \mathrm{P}^R$.

Algorithm 2 `find_PLP` $(n, \mathrm{P}^g, range)$: Find a PLP representing a given positive relational dist. P^g over $\{A(X)\}$.

Inputs: n: Population size P^g: Positive relational distribution over $\{A(X)\}$
$range$: Range allowed for rule probabilities
Output: Either a PLP R for P^g, represented using $(p_0, p_1, \ldots, p_{n-1})$ / or "impossible"

Write the n equations (symbolically): $(\ \mathrm{P}^g_{0,n} = \mathrm{P}^R_{0,n}, \quad \ldots, \quad \mathrm{P}^g_{n-1,1} = \mathrm{P}^R_{n-1,1}\ )$
loop over the equations in increasing order of n_t:
Substitute the expression for $\mathrm{P}^R_{n_t,n_f}$ given by (4), into the current equation
// Current equation is now: $\mathrm{P}^g_{n_t,n_f} = \mathrm{P}^R_{n_t,0} \prod_{i=0}^{n_t}(1-p_i)^{\left(n_f \cdot \binom{n_t}{i}\right)}$
Evaluate $\mathrm{P}^R_{n_t,0}$ numerically using $(p_0, \ldots, p_{n_t-1})$ according to Proposition 1
if $\mathrm{P}^R_{n_t,0} = 0$ **then backtrack** *// Current equation cannot be solved:* $\mathrm{P}^g_{n_t,n_f} = 0 \cdot (\prod \ldots)$
Substitute into the equation: $n_t, \quad n_f, \quad \mathrm{P}^g_{n_t,n_f}, \quad \mathrm{P}^R_{n_t,0}, \quad p_0, \ldots, p_{n_t-1}$
// Equation is now: positive real number = nonzero number $\cdot (1-p_{n_t})^{\textit{positive integer}}$
$solutions_{n_t} \leftarrow$ the solutions for p_{n_t} that fall inside $range$ *// Out of* n_f *(possibly complex) solutions*
Try one of $solutions_{n_t}$, and advance to the next equation. If the next equation backtracks, try another solution. If all solutions in $solutions_{n_t}$ backtracked, then **backtrack**.
If all equations were solved then **return** $(p_0, \ldots, p_{n-1})$.
end loop
return "impossible"

In general, p_0 and p_1 can be computed as functions of $\mathrm{P}^g_{0,3}$ and $\mathrm{P}^g_{1,2}$; $\mathrm{P}^R_{2,0}$ is then computed as a function of these, and we then get the constraint $\mathrm{P}^R_{2,0} \neq 0$. (If $\mathrm{P}^R_{2,0} = 0$, then $\mathrm{P}^g > 0$ cannot be represented.) $\mathrm{P}^R_{2,0} \neq 0$ is therefore a complicated non-linear constraint on the values of $\{\mathrm{P}^g_{0,3}, \mathrm{P}^g_{1,2}\}$. This constraint is unexpected and surprising. Given a distribution, it is not immediately obvious if this constraint is violated.

Fortunately, however, since the constraint is $\mathrm{P}^R_{2,0} \neq 0$ (and not, say, $\mathrm{P}^R_{2,0} > 0$), the probability that a "random" distribution P^g violates this constraint is 0, i.e., this constraint has measure 0. It represents a "singularity" of the language, but the language is still useful, since one can use an alternative $\mathrm{P}^{g'}$ that is infinitesimally close to a P^g that violates the constraint.

Unfortunately, there are also constraints with positive "D-dimensional volume". This is a limitation of the language itself, not of any specific program. Adding an arbitrary number of new formulae, or allowing probabilities above 1, does not solve the problem:

Theorem 2. *The language of PLPs with generalized real-valued rule probabilities* ($\mathrm{P} \in (-\infty, +\infty)$) *is only partially-expressive, even with fixed population sizes.*

Proof. We prove by giving a negative example, with a single variable $A(X)$ and $n = 4$. First, we show real-valued PLPs cannot represent any distribution P^g with:

$$\mathrm{P}^g_{0,4} = \tfrac{1}{3^4} = \tfrac{1}{81}, \quad \mathrm{P}^g_{1,3} = \tfrac{2^4+1}{3^4} = \tfrac{17}{81}, \quad \mathrm{P}^g_{2,2} > 0$$

Simulating Algorithm 2, (3) and (4) give:

$$\tfrac{1}{81} = \mathrm{P}^g_{0,4} = \mathrm{P}^R_{0,4} = \mathrm{P}^R_{0,0} \prod_{i=0}^{0}(1-p_i)^{\left(4\binom{0}{i}\right)} = (1-p_0)^4 \quad (9)$$

$$\tfrac{17}{81} = \mathrm{P}^g_{1,3} = \mathrm{P}^R_{1,3} = \mathrm{P}^R_{1,0} \cdot \prod_{i=0}^{1}(1-p_i)^{\left(3\cdot\binom{1}{i}\right)} \quad (10)$$
$$= p_0 \cdot (1-p_0)^3(1-p_1)^3$$

$$\mathrm{P}^R_{2,0} = \ldots \quad \text{(repeating (7))} \quad (11)$$
$$= 1-(1-p_0)^2 - 2p_0(1-p_0)(1-p_1)$$

$$0 < \mathrm{P}^g_{2,2} = \mathrm{P}^R_{2,2} = \mathrm{P}^R_{2,0} \prod_{i=0}^{2}(1-p_i)^{\left(2\cdot\binom{2}{i}\right)} \quad (12)$$
$$= \mathrm{P}^R_{2,0}\left((1-p_0)(1-p_1)^2(1-p_2)\right)^2$$

Solving (9) gives $p_0 \in \{\frac{2}{3}, \frac{4}{3}\}$. We then substitute into (10) to find p_1, then into (11) to compute $\mathrm{P}^R_{2,0}$, and then into (12) to find p_2. Taking $p_0 = \frac{2}{3}$ gives $p_1 = -1.0408$ and $\mathrm{P}^R_{2,0} = -0.0181$. Taking $p_0 = \frac{4}{3}$ gives $p_1 = 2.6198$ and $\mathrm{P}^R_{2,0} = -0.5509$. Either way, we get $\mathrm{P}^R_{2,0} < 0$, and since (12) is "$0 < \mathrm{P}^g_{2,2} = \mathrm{P}^R_{2,0} \cdot (\ldots)^2$", P^g cannot be represented using real numbers.

Since $\mathrm{P}^R_{2,0}$ was computed as a continuous function of p_0 and p_1, which themselves were computed as continuous functions of $\mathrm{P}^g_{0,4}$ and $\mathrm{P}^g_{1,3}$, an infinitesimal perturbation of P^g will not be sufficient to make $\mathrm{P}^R_{2,0} > 0$ and the distribution representable. Thus, there is a D-dimensional region of distributions that are not representable. □

4.3 COMPLEX PLPS: ALMOST-FULLY EXPR.

We suggest extending the PLP language to support **complex** rule probabilities.

Proposition 2. *1. The language of PLPs with* ***complex*** *rule probabilities is almost-fully expressive w.r.t. positive relational distributions over* $\{A(X)\}$ *with a fixed* n.
2. The number of PLP representations for every such distribution is finite.
3. There is at most one such PLP representation where all parameters are real and < 1.

Proof. **1.** We prove by showing that Algorithm 2 finds a PLP representing (almost) any given P^g. Using complex probabilities, the only possibility of Algorithm 2 to fail to find a solution for p_{n_t}, is due to $P^R_{n_t,0} = 0$. The algorithm thus finds a PLP representing P^g if and only if the following n constraints hold: $P^R_{0,0} \neq 0$, $P^R_{1,0} \neq 0$, $\ldots$, $P^R_{n-1,0} \neq 0$. We now show these are lower-dimensional constraints (with measure 0), thus the language is almost-fully expressive.

$P^R_{n_t,0}$ is the sum of the probabilities of the DPRs (for population size n_t) in whose minimal stable model all variables are $true$. The probability of each DPR D is the polynomial $(\prod_{\text{rules} \in D} p_i) \cdot (\prod_{\text{rules} \notin D}(1 - p_i))$. Each $P^R_{n_t,0}$ is therefore a polynomial of $p_0, \ldots, p_{n_t-1}$. Equating a polynomial to 0 gives a lower-dimensional manifold – unless the polynomial happens to be 0 everywhere. This, however, is not the case here, because if we set all rule probabilities to be, say, 0.5, the probability that all variables become $true$ will be positive.

2. Every equation the algorithm solves has a finite number of solutions, thus there is a finite number of PLP representations for P^g.

3. Every parameter is found by solving an equation of the form: positive real number $=$ nonzero number $\cdot(1 - p_{n_t})^{\text{positive integer}}$, i.e., $q_{n_t}^{\text{positive integer}} =$ number, where $q_{n_t} = 1 - p_{n_t}$. q_{n_t} cannot have two positive solutions, thus p_{n_t} cannot have two real solutions below 1. □

5 BROADCAST CANON. FORM (BCF)

PLPs over $\{A(X)\}$ have a special property: every rule has a different body. In general, as we will show, the number of different possible rule **bodies** is identical to the number of degrees of freedom (DoF) the distribution P^g has. PLPs over $\{A(X)\}$ have the exact number of possible rules as the needed DoF, but they cannot represent all distributions, unless they allow their parameters (rule probabilities) to be complex. PLPs over other sets of parametrized variables are overparametrized, i.e., they contain more possible rules (thus more parameters) than P^g's DoF. Overparametrization is inefficient. While practical PLPs do not simultaneously use all possible rules, it is possible that the rules they use contain redundancy, which may be unintuitive and difficult to identify. In the context of learning undirected graphical models with binary variables from data, parametrizations with excessive redundant parameters learn graphical models with excessive parameters (even after pruning un-useful parameters), that are slower to process, without improving learning accuracy (Buchman et al., 2012).

Definition 1. *A program in the* ***Broadcast Canonical Form (BCF) Language*** *(or a* ***BCF PLP****) is a set of negation-free non-deterministic rules with the form:* p : $body$. *Its semantics is that of the corresponding PLP, in which each* p : $body$ *is replaced with the rules* p : $head \leftarrow body$ *for* ***all possible*** *heads. (If* $p = 0$*, then these rules simultaneously do not appear.)*

Bodies that are equivalent, e.g., $a(X) \wedge b(X)$ and $b(Y) \wedge a(Y)$, are considered the same body. "p : $body$" represents a set S_{body} of rules p : $head \leftarrow body$ in the corresponding PLP. In each of its DPRs, some of the rules in S_{body} may appear, and some might not appear.

BCF is a simplified language, and allows to write PLPs in succinct form. A BCF PLP is a PLP with tied weights. We show BCF is a canonical form for PLPs: it is almost-fully expressive, yet without excessive parameters.

We designate BCF parameters by subscripting them with the set of the variables in their bodies; e.g., for $V = \{A, B, C\}$, the BCF $\{p_{\{C\}} : c,\ p_{\{B,C\}} : b \wedge c\}$ corresponds to the PLP $\{p_{\{C\}} : a \leftarrow c,\ p_{\{C\}} : b \leftarrow c,\ p_{\{B,C\}} : a \leftarrow b \wedge c\}$.

Since PLPs over $\{A(X)\}$ can only have a single rule for every possible body, our results for PLPs over $\{A(X)\}$ actually describe results for BCFs over $\{A(X)\}$. Section 4's p_0 is represented by BCF's $p_\emptyset$, p_1 is represented by $p_{\{A(Y_1)\}}$, p_2 is represented by $p_{\{A(Y_1),A(Y_2)\}}$, etc.

BCF is very simple, yet highly unintuitive. For example, all probabilistic facts have the same probability (!). The unintuitiveness is because p : $head \leftarrow body$ is usually interpreted as a probability that is related to the influence that $body = true$ has on $head$. To make sense of BCF, take p : $body$ to mean a "broadcast message" that $body = true$ sends to all other variables, that increases (or decreases, for negative p's) the probabilities of all other variables. If $body = true$ should influence some variables but not others, this is achieved using the combined influence of other rules. The notion of "probabilistic strengths" Buchman & Poole (2017) makes this influence combination additive and intuitive.

6 BCF AND OTHER CANONICAL FORMS FOR PROPOSITIONAL PLPS

As noted in Section 5, PLPs for the simplest relational setting (Section 4) are actually BCF PLPs. We now develop BCF for the simplest (i.e., propositional) multi-variable case. The development and results are similar to those of Section 4.

In the propositional setting, there are n variables, $V = \{V_1, \ldots, V_n\}$, and 2^n possible joint assignments (i.e., interpretations). A ("proper") joint distribution is a non-negative real function summing to 1, over all interpretations, thus it has $2^n - 1$ DoF. An "improper" joint distribution is a function summing to 1, which may contain negative, or even complex, numbers.

PLPs have one DoF for each possible rule (or two DoF, for complex rule probabilities). $\neg$-free (real-valued) PLPs thus have $n2^{n-1}$ DoF (see Table 1), because each rule specifies which variable appears in its head, and the subset of the $n-1$ remaining variables that appears in its body. $\neg$-free PLPs thus have excessive DoF, yet are only partially expressive. Allowing negative probabilities does not add DoF, but it makes $\neg$-free PLPs fully expressive. (It may also allow the representation of improper distributions.) The PLP, however, is still over-parametrized.

(Real-valued) PLPs with $\neg$'s have $n3^{n-1}$ DoF, because each variable (other than the head variable) may either appear in the body, not appear, or appear negated. PLPs with $\neg$'s are fully expressive, but extremely over-parametrized. (They may also be logically inconsistent.)

For PLPs with $\neg$'s, there is a systematic way (a "canonical form") to represent any given distribution: Order the variables arbitrarily $V_1, \ldots, V_n$, and code each $\mathrm{P}(v_i \mid v_1, \ldots, v_{i-1})$ using one rule for each joint assignment to $(v_1, \ldots, v_{i-1})$, with v_i as its head. For $\neg$-free PLPs with negative probabilities there is a similar systematic way, where each $\mathrm{P}(v_i \mid v_1, \ldots, v_{i-1})$ is coded using one rule for each conjunction of subsets of $\{v_1, \ldots, v_{i-1}\}$, with v_i as its head. For both languages, there are a large but finite ($n!$) distinct PLPs that can be considered canonical representations for the given distribution. This finiteness is meaningful: In general, a single redundant real-valued parameter may give ∞ ways for representing any distribution, thus the finiteness means there are no redundant parameters. For both languages, each of the canonical PLP representations only uses a (different) subset of $2^n - 1$ rules out of the $n2^{n-1}$ or $n3^{n-1}$ available rules.

We embrace complex rule probabilities, since they are needed in the general, relational case. We now ask: Allowing complex probabilities, which new systematic ways are there, for representing any given distribution?

We suggest a new systematic way, BCF, to parametrize $\neg$-free propositional PLPs using $2^n - 1$ complex rule probabilities that, for non-extreme distributions, is almost-fully expressive. For some (but not all) distributions, BCF provides a unique canonical BCF PLP that only involves real probabilities in $(-\infty, 1)$. In general, BCF provides any given distribution with a finite number of (complex-valued) canonical BCF PLP representations. (2^n-1 complex rule probabilities have $2\cdot(2^n-1)$ DoF, but they are not overparametrized. This is because PLPs with complex rule probabilities are fully expressive w.r.t. **complex** (improper) distributions, thus adding 2^n-1 DoF to the specification of the distribution.) BCF, however, simplifies the language, and requires no arbitrary ordering. BCF's lack of ordering means that its canonical PLPs are truly cyclic, instead of the Bayes-net semantics of the other two canonical forms. BCF's semantics is intriguing, and not fully understood.

Propositional BCF PLPs have $2^n - 1$ possible parameters: $\{p_s : s \subsetneq V\}$. p_V is excluded (it has no effect). We sometimes subscript by the set of atoms, e.g., $p_{\{a\}}$ instead of $p_{\{A\}}$.

Theorem 3 is the adaptation of Theorem 1 to BCF. It may be expressed as an algorithm, similar to Algorithm 1.

Theorem 3. *Let R be a propositional BCF PLP over variables V, and $I \subseteq V$ be an interpretation. Then:*

$$\mathrm{P}^R(I) = \mathrm{P}^{R_I}(I) \prod_{s \subseteq I} (1 - p_s)^{|V \setminus I|} \tag{13}$$

$$\mathrm{P}^{R_I}(I) = 1 - \sum_{I' \subsetneq I} \mathrm{P}^{R_I}(I')$$

6.1 A BCF BACKTRACKING SOLVER

Algorithm 3 is the adaptation of Algorithm 2 to BCF in the propositional case. Let P^g be a positive distribution over V, and let R be a BCF PLP over V. R represents P^g, i.e., $\mathrm{P}^R = \mathrm{P}^g$, if and only if the following $2^n - 1$ equations hold: $\{\mathrm{P}^g(s) = \mathrm{P}^R(s) : s \subsetneq V\}$. (The additional equation $\mathrm{P}^g(V) = \mathrm{P}^R(V)$ is redundant.)

Example 3. *For two variables, $V = \{A, B\}$, the $2^n - 1$ equations $\mathrm{P}^g(V) = \mathrm{P}^R(V)$ are:*

$$\mathrm{P}^g(\emptyset) = \mathrm{P}^{R_\emptyset}(\emptyset) \prod_{s\subseteq\emptyset} (1-p_s)^2 = (1-p_\emptyset)^2$$
$$\mathrm{P}^g(a) = \mathrm{P}^{R_{\{A\}}}(a) \prod_{s\subseteq\{A\}} (1-p_s)^1 = p_\emptyset(1-p_\emptyset)(1-p_{\{a\}})$$
$$\mathrm{P}^g(b) = \mathrm{P}^{R_{\{B\}}}(b) \prod_{s\subseteq\{B\}} (1-p_s)^1 = p_\emptyset(1-p_\emptyset)(1-p_{\{b\}})$$

The algorithm solves one equation after another, and gives the general solution:

$$p_\emptyset = 1 \pm \sqrt{\mathrm{P}^g(\emptyset)},\ p_{\{a\}} = 1 - \frac{\mathrm{P}^g(\{a\})}{p_\emptyset(1-p_\emptyset)},\ p_{\{b\}} = 1 - \frac{\mathrm{P}^g(\{b\})}{p_\emptyset(1-p_\emptyset)}$$

There is always a solution in real probabilities below 1, and another solution in real probabilities above 1.

Example 4. *Consider running a solver like Algorithm 3, to find a general (non-BCF) PLP for $V = \{A, B\}$. Let*

Algorithm 3 `find_prop_BCF_PLP` (V, P^g): Find a BCF PLP representing a given pos. **propositional** dist. P^g.

Inputs: V: The set of variables P^g: Positive distribution over V
Output: BCF PLP for P^g, represented using $\{p_s : s \subsetneq V\}$ / or "impossible"

Write the $2^n - 1$ equations (symbolically): $\{\mathrm{P}^g(I) = \mathrm{P}^R(I) \ : \ I \subsetneq V\}$.
loop over the equations in (any) increasing partial-order of I:
  Substitute the expression for $\mathrm{P}^R(I)$ given by (13)
  // Current equation is now: $\mathrm{P}^g(I) = \mathrm{P}^{R_I}(I) \prod_{s \subseteq I} (1 - p_s)^{|V \setminus I|}$
  Evaluate $\mathrm{P}^{R_I}(I)$ numerically using $\{p_s : s \subsetneq I\}$ according to Theorem 3
  if $\mathrm{P}^{R_I}(I) = 0$ **then backtrack**
  Substitute into the equation: n_t, n_f, $\mathrm{P}^g(I)$, $\mathrm{P}^{R_I}(I)$, $\{p_s : s \subsetneq I\}$
  // Equation is now: positive real number = nonzero number $\cdot (1 - p_I)^{\text{positive integer}}$
  $solutions_I \leftarrow$ the solutions for p_I *//* $|V \setminus I| \geq 1$ *(possibly complex) solutions*
  Try one of $solutions_I$, and advance to the next equation. If the next equation backtracks,
    try another solution. If all solutions in $solutions_I$ backtracked, then **backtrack**.
    If all equations were solved then **return** $\{p_s : s \subsetneq V\}$.
end loop
return "impossible"

the rule probabilities be $\{p_a, p_b, p_{a \leftarrow b}, p_{b \leftarrow a}\}$. *Its first equation would be:*

$$\mathrm{P}^g(\emptyset) = \ldots = (1 - p_a)(1 - p_b)$$

In general, since PLPs are over-parametrized, equations may simultaneously introduce multiple new parameters. PLPs using only $A(X)$ *are a special case: they are not over-parametrized, so this does not happen. BCF is a technique for resolving the over-parametrization, by effectively forcing simultaneous new parameters to be equal, thus transforming equations to have a single new variable, thus getting rid of the PLP's excessive DoF.*

BCF has tied weights, thus fewer potential parameters; however, it is still almost-fully expressive:

Theorem 4. *1. The language of BCF PLPs with complex rule probabilities is almost-fully expressive for positive propositional distributions.*
2. The number of BCF representations for every such distribution is finite.
3. There is at most one such BCF representation where all parameters are real and < 1.

Proof. The proof is very similar to Proposition 2's, only it relies on Algorithm 3 instead of Algorithm 2, and the constraints are $\{\mathrm{P}^{R_I}(I) \neq 0 \ : \ I \subsetneq V\}$ instead of $\{\mathrm{P}^R_{n_t,0} \neq 0 : n_t \in \{0, \ldots, n-1\}\}$. □

7 GENERAL RELATIONAL BCF PLPS

We now generalize Sections 4 and 6 to general relational PLPs, given fixed populations.

Theorem 5. *1. The language of BCF PLPs with complex rule probabilities is almost-fully expressive for positive relational distributions with fixed population sizes.*
2. The number of BCF representations for every such distribution is finite.
3. There is at most one such BCF representation where all parameters are real and < 1.

Proof. The proof follows from the correctness of Algorithm 4; we only outline the differences with the special cases presented in Sections 4 and 6.

The first step is to ground the PLP, according to the given population sizes. Similarly to Algorithm 3, we write all equations $\mathrm{P}^g(I) = \mathrm{P}^R(I)$ for the ground PLP, and order them in increasing partial-order of I (and omit the last one). Here, however, the ground PLP is exchangeable w.r.t. swapping individuals. Swapping two individuals causes multiple pairs of ground variables to be swapped. Therefore, some interpretations are equivalent. P^g is equal for equivalent interpretations, and the PLP has no rule that can distinguish among them; therefore, they give identical equations, and we only keep the first occurrence of each equation. (This was implicitly done by Algorithm 2, which wrote n equations, although there are 2^n interpretations for $V = \{A(X_1), \ldots, A(X_n)\}$.)

The number of equations that remain after removing duplicate equations is the number of P^g's DoF. Pick an arbitrary I; we need to show that $\mathrm{P}^g(I) = \mathrm{P}^R(I)$ has exactly one new parameter that did not occur in previous equations. This parameter is p_I, which represents the probability of all rules with the form $head \leftarrow \bigwedge_{v \in I} v$. The equations are in increasing partial-order of I, so $\bigwedge_{v \in I} v$ was false for their corresponding interpretations, and p_I did not appear in them. It is also not the case that there was a second new parameter that appears in

Algorithm 4 `find_BCF_PLP` (V, P^g): Find a BCF PLP representing a given **general** pos. (rel.) distribution P^g.

Inputs: V: The set of **ground** variables P^g: Positive distribution over V
Output: BCF PLP for P^g / or "impossible"

Write the $2^{|V|} - 1$ equations (symbolically): $\{\mathrm{P}^g(I) = \mathrm{P}^R(I) \; : \; I \subsetneq V\}$.
Remove recurring equations (keep only the first of each)
loop over the equations in (any) increasing partial-order of I:
  Substitute the expression for $\mathrm{P}^R(I)$ given by (13)
  Evaluate $\mathrm{P}^{R_I}(I)$ numerically using $\{p_s : s \subsetneq I\}$ according to Theorem 3
  if $\mathrm{P}^{R_I}(I) = 0$ **then backtrack**
  Substitute into the equation: n_t, n_f, $\mathrm{P}^g(I)$, $\mathrm{P}^{R_I}(I)$, $\{p_s : s \subsetneq I\}$
  $solutions_I \leftarrow$ the solutions for p_I // $|V \setminus I| \geq 1$ *(possibly complex) solutions*
  Try one of $solutions_I$, and advance to the next equation. If the next equation backtracks,
    try another solution. If all solutions in $solutions_I$ backtracked, then **backtrack**.
    If all equations were solved then **return** $\{p_s : s \subsetneq V\}$.
end loop
return "impossible"

$\mathrm{P}^g(I) = \mathrm{P}^R(I)$ but not before. Every parameter is associated with a body, which is a conjunction. If a parameter contains a ground variable not in I, it will not have an effect on $\mathrm{P}^R(I)$, and thus not appear. If it is a proper subset $I' \subsetneq I$, then the parameter already appeared before, in the equation for I'. □

The proof of Theorem 5 also shows that the number of possible parameters a BCF PLP has, i.e., the number of different rule bodies a PLP may have, is identical to the number of DoF a relational distribution has.

8 CONCLUSIONS

It is perhaps alarming for one to investigate much effort into uncovering why a learning algorithm fails to learn a probabilistic model from data, even given very large amounts of data and a large number of very flexible rules, only to discover that the fault is not the algorithm's; rather, the underlying language is simply incapable of representing the distribution of the data, even approximately.

Before using a language for an application domain, it is therefore advisable to become aware of any limitations the language may have.

A concerning result (Buchman & Poole, 2016, 2017) has recently emerged, demonstrating cases where PLPs are incapable of representing some relational distributions, in which $\neg$'s do not help, but using negative rule probabilities allows the distributions to be represented.

We follow in their footsteps, and investigate general relational settings (with fixed populations). We discovered that, even for a population of size four, PLPs are lacking in their expressiveness, and negative probabilities (or probabilities above 1) do not solve the problem; however, allowing complex probabilities makes PLPs "complete", allowing PLPs to represent any distribution (with probability 1). This is due to a mathematical structure underlying PLPs, in which rule probabilities are determined as solutions of polynomial equations.

We have also provided an algorithm for directly computing the probability of an interpretation. The algorithm is efficient when few variables are $true$. Extending this algorithm, and investigating its usefulness in various applications, is beyond the scope of this paper.

After realizing that complex probabilities are unavoidable, we investigate the question: what is a natural canonical model for PLPs? We expose BCF – a simplified language for representing PLPs, that strips the redundancy among PLP rules by tying their weights (thus avoiding redundant parameters), while maintaining full expressiveness. We also provide solver algorithms, showing how arbitrary relational distributions can be converted into BCF PLPs.

This work raises a few intriguing questions, that suggest that further deep insights may be around the corner. These include questions such as: What is the meaning of complex probabilities? What insights or intuitions are there, for the general interaction of rules with complex probabilities? And: what are further insights and intuitions for BCF? Is there a complimentary (dual) canonical form to BCF, which is more intuitive?

References

Buchman, David and Poole, David. Representing aggregators in relational probabilistic models. In *Proceedings of the 29th AAAI Conference on Artificial Intelligence (AAAI)*, 2015.

Buchman, David and Poole, David. Negation without negation in probabilistic logic programming. In *KR*, pp. 529–532, 2016.

Buchman, David and Poole, David. Negative probabilities in probabilistic logic programs. *International Journal of Approximate Reasoning*, 83:43–59, 2017.

Buchman, David, Schmidt, Mark W., Mohamed, Shakir, Poole, David, and de Freitas, Nando. On sparse, spectral and other parameterizations of binary probabilistic models. *Journal of Machine Learning Research - Proceedings Track*, 22:173–181, 2012.

Cox, David R. A use of complex probabilities in the theory of stochastic processes. In *Mathematical Proceedings of the Cambridge Philosophical Society*, volume 51, pp. 313–319. Cambridge University Press, 1955.

De Raedt, L., Kimmig, A., and Toivonen, H. ProbLog: A probabilistic Prolog and its application in link discovery. In *Proceedings of the 20th International Joint Conference on Artificial Intelligence (IJCAI-2007)*, pp. 2462–2467, 2007.

Dıez, Francisco J and Galán, Severino F. An efficient factorization for the noisy max. *International Journal of Intelligent Systems*, 18(2):165–177, 2003.

Hamber, Herbert W and Ren, Hai-cang. Complex probabilities and the Langevin equation. *Physics Letters B*, 159(4-6):330–334, 1985.

Hofmann, Holger F. Complex joint probabilities as expressions of reversible transformations in quantum mechanics. *New Journal of Physics*, 14(4):043031, 2012.

Kisynski, Jacek and Poole, David. Lifted aggregation in directed first-order probabilistic models. In *Proc. Twenty-first International Joint Conference on Artificial Intelligence (IJCAI-09)*, pp. 1922–1929, Pasadena, California, 2009.

Kowalski, Robert. *Logic for Problem Solving, Revisited.* BoD–Books on Demand, 2014.

Meert, Wannes and Vennekens, Joost. Inhibited effects in cp-logic. In *European Workshop on Probabilistic Graphical Models*, pp. 350–365. Springer, 2014.

Parisi, Giorgio. On complex probabilities. *Physics Letters B*, 131(4-6):393–395, 1983.

Poole, D. The independent choice logic for modelling multiple agents under uncertainty. *Artificial Intelligence*, 94:7–56, 1997. special issue on economic principles of multi-agent systems.

Poole, D. Abducing through negation as failure: stable models in the Independent Choice Logic. *Journal of Logic Programming*, 44(1–3):5–35, 2000.

Salcedo, LL. Representation of complex probabilities. *Journal of Mathematical Physics*, 38(3):1710–1722, 1997.

Salcedo, LL. Gibbs sampling of complex-valued distributions. *Physical Review D*, 94(7):074503, 2016.

Sato, T. and Kameya, Y. PRISM: A symbolic-statistical modeling language. In *Proceedings of the 15th International Joint Conference on Artificial Intelligence (IJCAI-97)*, pp. 1330–1335, 1997.

Sato, T. and Kameya, Y. New advances in logic-based probabilistic modeling by PRISM. In De Raedt, L., Frasconi, P., Kersting, K., and Muggleton, S. (eds.), *Probabilistic Inductive Logic Programming*, volume LNCS 4911, pp. 118–155. Springer, 2008.

Van den Broeck, Guy, Meert, Wannes, and Darwiche, Adnan. Skolemization for weighted first-order model counting. *arXiv preprint arXiv:1312.5378*, 2013.

Vennekens, Joost, Denecker, Marc, and Bruynooghe, Maurice. CP-logic: A language of causal probabilistic events and its relation to logic programming. *TPLP*, 9 (3):245–308, 2009.

Zak, Michail. Incompatible stochastic processes and complex probabilities. *Physics Letters A*, 238(1):1–7, 1998.

Interpreting Lion Behaviour with Nonparametric Probabilistic Programs

Neil Dhir,* **Frank Wood**
Department of Engineering Science
University of Oxford
neild@robots.ox.ac.uk

Matthijs Vákár*, **Andrew Markham**
Department of Computer Science
University of Oxford
matthijs.vakar@cs.ox.ac.uk

Matthew Wijers, Paul Trethowan, Byron Du Preez, Andrew Loveridge, David MacDonald
Department of Zoology
University of Oxford

Abstract

We consider the problem of unsupervised learning of meaningful behavioural segments of high-dimensional time-series observations, collected from a pride of African lions[1]. We demonstrate, by way of a probabilistic programming system (PPS), a methodology which allows for quick iteration over models and Bayesian inferences, which enables us to learn meaningful behavioural segments. We introduce a new Bayesian nonparametric (BNP) state-space model, which extends the hierarchical Dirichlet process (HDP) hidden Markov model (HMM) with an explicit BNP treatment of duration distributions, to deal with different levels of granularity of the latent behavioural space of the lions. The ease with which this is done exemplifies the flexibility that a PPS gives a scientist[2]. Furthermore, we combine this approach with unsupervised feature learning, using variational autoencoders.

1 INTRODUCTION

Animal accelerometer data allows ecologists to identify important correlates and drivers of animal behaviour. Use of accelerometers is widespread within animal biotelemetry as they provide a means of measuring an animal's activity in a meaningful and quantitative way, where direct observation is not possible. In *sequential* acceleration data there is a natural *dependence between observations* of movement or behaviour, a fact that has been largely ignored in most analyses [13]. Recordings are typically sampled at a high temporal resolution, sometimes for years at a time, using tri-axial accelerometer tags [15], which quickly results in terabytes of data that present various challenges regarding transmission, storage, processing and statistical modelling. The latter can be achieved by employing statistical classification methods, and entails observing the animal, *manually assigning labels* corresponding to *known* behaviours to segments of the data, and training a model using the labelled data in order to subsequently classify remaining unlabelled data based on certain *chosen acceleration features* deemed to be salient by domain experts.

Consider the recent work of Pagano et al. [20] wherein the authors use tri-axial accelerometers to identify wild polar bear behaviours. They note that identification of wild animals can be facilitated using captive counterparts, as their accelerometer signatures are generally assumed to be similar to those of their wild kin [20]. They use their captive bears as surrogates for wild ground-truth behaviour, upon which they model polar bear behaviour on sea ice and land, using random forests classification and hand-engineered features. Their results, though of good accuracy, rely on hand-engineered features, large assumptions about captive and wild behaviours and a fundamental need for labelled data to infer behaviour. Along this trail of thought, the work McClune et al. [17] is relevant for our discussion. Therein, the authors fitted tri-axial accelerometers to a tame and captive Eurasian badger, upon which it was allowed to roam free in an enclosure, whilst movements were video recorded and used as ground-truth for its behavioural states. Again, features were hand-engineered using, e.g., acceleration magnitude and principal component analysis. The k-nearest neighbour classifier and decision trees were used to automate classification of behaviours [17]. Their success ranged from 77.4% to 100% classification accuracy, though again deploying a highly laborious process, where a human is necessary for the extraction of the video ground-truth (and classification is conditioned on the ground truth existing at all). The work by Leos-

*Equal contribution

[1] You may be familiar with one of the more famous members of our study, the late Cecil the lion.

[2] Example code: https://goo.gl/14s8Sa

Barajas et al. [13] is faced with precisely this challenge, where they seek to measure an animal's activity in a meaningful and quantitative way where direct observation is not possible [13]. In doing so, they investigate a marine and an aerial system (sharks and eagles). They used the classical HMM to effect supervised and unsupervised learning of animal activity. In the latter case, an HMM is used to segment unlabelled acceleration data into a finite set of pre-specified categories [13]. They go on to show that the metrics that they derive from the learned eagle -states provide meaningful insight into activity levels and thus can lead to biologically interpretable states. Their study is similar to that of Phillips et al. [21], in which the authors applied HMMs in an unsupervised context to model the behaviour of free swimming tuna from vertical movement data collected by data-storage tags [13, §3.3].

As we have thus demonstrated some studies *do* employ models with temporal dependency (e.g., the Markov assumption) but the far more popular method is to deploy classification algorithms that do not, e.g., support vector machines (SVM) or random forests see, e.g., [3]. We, like Leos-Barajas et al. [13], note that disregarding the serial dependence in the acceleration data usually is not a realistic assumption. Moreover, independent and identically distributed statistics (i.i.d.) pose a particular risk if "inferential statistics are applied to the output of say a machine learning algorithm" [13].

In this study, we therefore focus on state-space models like HMMs to model accelerometer data. In doing so we take care to emphasise the two significant disadvantages of a simple HMM: (1) *state duration distributions are necessarily restricted to be of the geometric shape* $\mathbb{P}(d) = a^{d-1}(1-a)$ (and, in particular, monotonically decreasing), where d denotes the duration of a given state and a denotes its self-transition probability, which is not appropriate for many real-world problems like modelling animal behaviour (for instance, a human being usually sleeps for roughly 7-8 hours and, certainly, sleep durations are not monotonically decreasing), and (2) the *number of hidden states must be set a priori* while one of the main objectives of behavioural research is to discover new or more fine-grained behavioural patterns.

Recent work has addressed the latter issue by way of *Bayesian nonparametric HMMs*, which allow us to infer state cardinality from observations, and allows it to grow in a data-driven fashion. The former issue is addressed by variations of the HMM with non-geometric duration distributions like the Hidden semi-Markov model [18]. In the BNP paradigm, inference is usually performed in models with an infinite number of states. Additionally, we consider a BNP treatment of durations.

In this paper, we aim to introduce these *two innovations to the zoology toolbox*, while at the same time showing the value that *unsupervised (behaviour) learning* can have, without reliance on expensive and difficult manual data annotation, as well as *unsupervised feature learning*, reducing the reliance on domain experts to guess the most salient features for possibly unknown kinds of behaviour. We perform full unsupervised nonparametric time-series learning on the observations, resulting in a time-segmented set of waveforms. Such a segmentation can provide useful interpretations which allow us to quantify animal behaviour, energetic expenditure and deepen our insights into individual behaviour as a constituent of populations and ecosystems [13]. Further, we hope to convey the huge value that a *probabilistic programming language* like Anglican can have when exploring the space of possible new models for a novel application domain like ours, in enabling quick implementation and evaluation of many complex models and even design of new ones with minimal mathematical and coding burden to the scientist (e.g., no need to derive custom inference algorithms).

The paper is organised as follows; in section 2, we give an exegesis of BNP HMMs; in section 3, we present the infinite duration HMM and section 4 discusses our choice of using a probabilistic programming framework to implement our models. Experiments and results are presented for the understanding of lion behaviour ecology in section 5. In section 6, we conclude.

2 BAYESIAN NONPARAMETRICS

We motivate our approach by reviewing the principles underpinning BNP staet-space models (SSM), and use this foundation to motivate our contributions in the coming sections, taking our cue from Dhir et al. [5, §II].

We need to be able to infer state cardinality from observations, as well as discover new states as we acquire more data. The former consideration of determining model complexity motivates a Bayesian approach, while the latter suggests a nonparametric model. The defining difference between BNP methods and their parametric cousins is that the size of the representation can grow as we gather more data: for the HDP-HMM, the expectation and variance of the number of states grow logarithmically with the size of the dataset [24]. We can frame our prior through Lo et al. [14]'s suggestion of an infinite dimensional mixture model:

$$\begin{aligned} &G \sim \mathcal{P} \\ &\theta_i \mid G \overset{i.i.d.}{\sim} G && i = 1, 2, \ldots \\ &y_i \mid \theta_i \overset{ind.}{\sim} F(\theta_i) && i = 1, 2, \ldots \end{aligned} \tag{1}$$

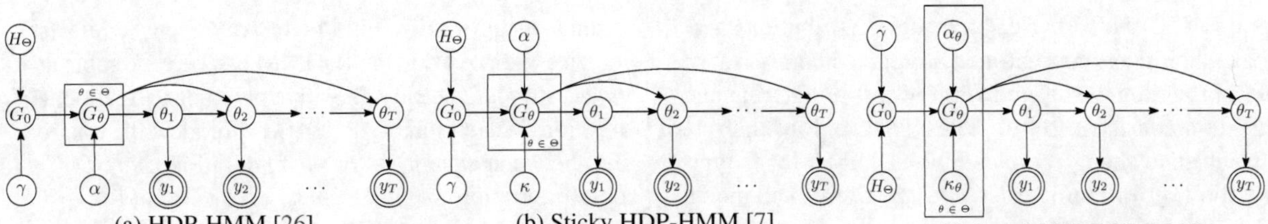

Figure 1: Three types of Bayesian nonparametric hidden Markov models, with various structural prior encoded which, from left to right, induce higher probability of state persistence.

where G is a discrete random probability measure (RPM) with distribution $\mathcal{P}$, $y_{1:n}$ are a collection of continuous and possibly multivariate observations and $\theta_{1:n}$ are the corresponding collection of latent random variables from an i.i.d. sequence directed by G and $F(\theta_i)$ is some continuous distribution parametrised by θ_i [5]. The nonparametric hierarchical model in eq. (1) defines a mixture model (MM) with a potentially countably infinite number of components. Because the RPM in equation eq. (1) is discrete, this means that a pair of consecutive values of θ take on the same value with a strictly positive probability. This value defines a mixture component. By setting the RPM to the Dirichlet process (DP) [6] we obtain the familiar DP mixture model

$$\begin{aligned} G \mid \gamma, H &\sim \mathcal{DP}(\gamma, H), \\ \theta_i \mid G &\sim G, \\ y_i \mid \theta_i &\sim F(\theta_i) \qquad i = 1, 2, \ldots. \end{aligned} \tag{2}$$

The DP, denoted by $\mathcal{DP}(\gamma, H)$, is a distribution over random measures on a parameter space Θ with countably infinite support. It can be parameterised by a base measure H on θ and a concentration parameter γ. The DP is typically used as a prior on the mixture components θ, of a MM of unknown complexity [5]. Note also that, e.g., the Pitman-Yor process or any other distribution over discrete RPMs are valid alternatives to the DP.

In many scenarios we posit that *groups* of data are thought to be produced by related, yet distinct, generative processes [5]. Concurrently, a recurring problem in many areas of information technology is that of segmenting a signal into a set of time intervals that have a useful interpretation in some underlying domain and can be thought of as generated by related but distinct processes [7]. Both of these scenarios describe the problem we face in this work, and both can be analysed through a *hierarchical* BNP approach. Viewed through this lens, observations can be subdivided into a countable collection of groups [5]. Then, we take it that groups of observations are modelled by considering a collection of DPs $\{G_j : j \in \mathcal{J}\}$, defined on a common space Θ, where $\mathcal{J}$ indexes the groups. By placing a global DP prior $\mathcal{DP}(\gamma, H)$ on the base distribution G_0, from whence we draw group specific distributions $G_j \sim \mathcal{DP}(\alpha, G_0)$, we obtain the hierarchical DP (HDP) [26]. Teh et al. [26] explain that the HDP induces sharing of support among the random measures G_j since each inherits its support from the same G_0. This idea is used to develop HMMs with unknown, potentially infinite, state spaces.

2.1 INFINITE HIDDEN MARKOV MODELS

Dhir et al. [5] describe an HMM as a doubly-stochastic Markov chain in which a state sequence $\{\theta_1, \ldots, \theta_T\}$ is drawn according to a Markov chain on a discrete state space Θ with transition kernels $\{G_\theta : \theta \in \Theta\}$ [25]. Corresponding observations $\{y_1, \ldots, y_T\}$, conditional on the state sequence, are drawn from a fixed emission distribution $y_t \mid \theta_t \sim F(\theta_t)\ \forall t \in \{1, \ldots, T\}$. By employing the HDP in an HMM setting, a prior distribution is defined on transition kernels, yielding the HDP-HMM [26] - see fig. 1a; an HMM with a countably infinite state space, with generative model

$$G_0 \mid \gamma, H \sim \mathcal{DP}(\gamma, H), \tag{3}$$

$$G_\theta \mid \alpha, G_0 \sim \mathcal{DP}(\alpha, G_0) \qquad \text{for } \theta \in \Theta, \tag{4}$$

$$\begin{aligned} \theta_t \mid \theta_{t-1}, G_{\theta_{t-1}} &\sim G_{\theta_{t-1}} \qquad \text{for } t = 1, \ldots, T, \\ y_t \mid \theta_t &\sim F(\theta_t). \end{aligned}$$

To frame this discussion, consider two alternatives to eq. (4) (see figs. 1b and 1c). The first extension is by Fox et al. [7]

$$G_\theta \mid \alpha, G_0, \kappa, \theta \sim \mathcal{DP}\left(\alpha + \kappa, \frac{\alpha G_0 + \kappa \delta_\theta}{\alpha + \kappa}\right) \tag{5}$$

and the second by Dhir et al. [5]

$$G_\theta \mid \alpha_\theta, G_0, \kappa_\theta, \theta \sim \mathcal{DP}\left(\alpha_\theta + \kappa_\theta, \frac{\alpha_\theta G_0 + \kappa_\theta \delta_\theta}{\alpha_\theta + \kappa_\theta}\right). \tag{6}$$

We shall consider both in turn, in league with our discussion and motivation of this approach. Hence, consider that each G_θ is a DP draw (this is true for eqs. (4) - (6)), and is interpreted as the transition distribution over $\theta_t \mid \theta_{t-1}$. All transition distributions are linked by the same discrete measure G_0 [5]. Hence, in expectation

$\mathbb{E}[G_\theta] = G_0, \forall\theta \in \Theta$. Thus, transition distributions *tend* to have their mass concentrated around a common set of states, providing the desired bias towards re-entering and re-using a consistent set of states [11, 5]. But, the rate at which state change unfolds in the HDP-HMM is typically too fast for many real-world problems. The model construction furthermore encourages the creation of redundant states and rapid switching amongst these too [11]. To alleviate this the *sticky* HDP-HMM (see fig. 1b) was introduced by Fox et al. [7], with transition kernel in eq. (5), that augment the HDP-HMM with an extra parameter $\kappa > 0$ which encourages self-transitions and thus longer state durations. The model, however, still shares its global self-transition bias with all the other states, and so it does not allow for learning state-specific duration information [11]. An attempt to deal with this restriction was introduced by Dhir et al. [5] with the *stateful* HDP-HMM (fig. 1c), in which the authors propose that by allowing for group-specific self-transition biases κ_θ, greater heterogeneity can be achieved in the dwell-time distribution of the inferred states. Where the transition kernel is given in eq. (6).

Performing inference over these types of models seeks to infer the posterior distributions over the state sequence and, therefore, implicitly, over the persistence of each state. It is with respect to this latter domain, that we propose new methodology for inferring state-specific durations, drawn from an infinite set.

3 INFINITE DURATION HIDDEN MARKOV MODEL

As discussed, in the classic HMM, the duration of a given state has a geometric (in particular, monotonically decreasing) distribution, because of the Markov property. Geometric duration distributions have been found to be deficient not just in behavioural modelling but also in e.g. speech synthesis [1]. Explicit duration HMMs (EDHMM) have been developed [4] to make the duration distribution explicit and allow it to have a more general form. Put simply, in an EDHMM, during a (Markov) state transition, a duration is drawn explicitly from a specified duration distribution depending on the new state. After that, the probability of self-transition is one until the duration has elapsed. We prefer to consider the EDHMM over the hidden semi-Markov model (HSMM), which achieves a similar effect through different, less explicit means [11].

The HDP-HSMM was introduced by Johnson & Willsky [11] and has its graphical model structure shown in fig. 2c (see appendix E for further discussion). Contrast this to the infinite duration HMM (IDHMM), a BNP variant on the EDHMM, which we present herein (see fig. 2a). We posit that the IDHMM can be preferable as it gives a nonparametric rather than parametric treatment of duration distributions. The IDHMM models the relationship between state $\theta_t \in \Theta \subseteq \mathbb{N}$, duration $d_t \in \mathcal{D} \subseteq \mathbb{N}$ and observation $y_t \in \mathcal{Y} \subseteq \mathbb{R}^n, \forall t \in \mathcal{T} \triangleq \{1, \ldots, T\}$, whilst giving a nonparametric treatment of state cardinality and state duration. The base and group distributions, in the generative model, are drawn as

$$G_0 \mid \gamma, H_\Theta \sim \mathcal{DP}(\gamma, H_\Theta)$$
$$D_0 \mid \gamma', H_\mathcal{D} \sim \mathcal{DP}(\gamma', H_\mathcal{D}) \tag{7}$$
$$G_\theta \mid \alpha, G_0 \sim \mathcal{DP}(\alpha, G_0) \qquad \text{for } \theta \in \Theta$$
$$D_\theta \mid \alpha', D_0 \sim \mathcal{DP}(\alpha', D_0) \qquad \text{for } \theta \in \Theta \tag{8}$$

where G_0 and D_0 have support Θ and $\mathcal{D}$ respectively. Noting that G_θ, being a draw from a DP, is a discrete distribution, we can define $G_\theta[\mathbb{P}(\theta) = 0]$ as the measure obtained from G_θ by setting the probability of drawing θ to 0 and renormalising. Next, a sequence of states, durations and emissions are drawn as

$$\theta_t \mid \theta_{t-1}, d_{t-1} \sim \begin{cases} \delta_{\theta_{t-1}}, & \text{if } d_{t-1} > 1 \\ G_{\theta_{t-1}}[\mathbb{P}(\theta_{t-1}) = 0], & \text{otherwise} \end{cases}$$
$$d_t \mid d_{t-1}, \theta_t \sim \begin{cases} \delta_{d_{t-1}-1}, & \text{if } d_{t-1} > 1 \\ D_{\theta_{t-1}}, & \text{otherwise} \end{cases}$$
$$y_t \mid \theta_t \sim F(\theta_t).$$

where δ_a is a δ-distribution with all its mass on a [4]. That is, we keep the state fixed and decrease the duration with one or, if the duration would reach 0, we sample a *different* new state, depending on the old state, and a corresponding new duration, depending on the new state.

Consider that each $G_\theta[\mathbb{P}(\theta) = 0]$ is obtained from a DP draw and is interpreted as the transition distribution over $\theta_t \mid \theta_{t-1}$. All transition distributions are linked by the same discrete measure G_0. Hence, in expectation $\mathbb{E}[G_\theta[\mathbb{P}(\theta) = 0] \mid G_0] = G_0[\mathbb{P}(\theta) = 0], \forall\theta \in \Theta$. Since transition distributions tend to have their mass concentrated around a common set of states, a bias towards re-entering and re-using a common of states is received. Similarly, our choice to extend the representational power of an HDP to durations as well means that the model reuses a common set of state durations.

We can also expose the IDHMM to the stateful representation, fig. 2b, as analogous to that in [5]. As for the stateful HDP-HMM, this adds greater heterogeneity in the state and dwell-time distributions of the inferred states. We will explain in section 4 how general purpose inference allows us to quickly build and experiment with models in this modular fashion, which can give us greater flexibility than using bespoke sampling algorithms such

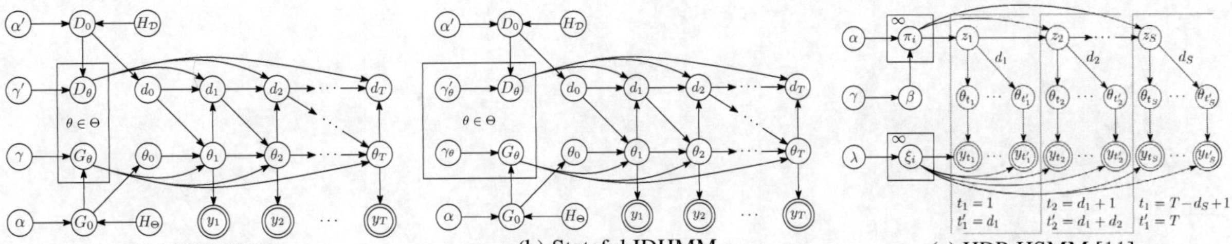

(a) IDHMM. (b) Stateful IDHMM. (c) HDP-HSMM [11].

Figure 2: Bayesian nonparametric state-space models with explicitly modelled state dwell durations.

as those employed by, e.g., Fox et al. [7] and Johnson & Willsky [11], in settings like ours where the computational efficiency of the latter is outweighed by the programmer efficiency of the former.

4 GENERAL PURPOSE INFERENCE

As the optimal model structure, to nonparametrically and in an unsupervised fashion, infer behavioural states from accelerometer data was far from clear, we chose to use a PPS for our analyses, specifically *Anglican* [30]. The idea of a PPS is that it is a programming language with an implementation of many of the basic building blocks for both statistical models and (general purpose) inference algorithms. By composing these building blocks, even a non-expert should be able to quickly build complex statistical models. For instance, Anglican provides a primitive for a Chinese restaurant process which easily allowed us to implement our (H)DPs.

Importantly, Anglican (like many PPS:es) provides a separation between model specification and implementation of inference. In particular, it comes equipped with several general purpose inference algorithms, such as Sequential Monte Carlo (SMC), Markov chain Monte Carlo (MCMC) and Particle MCMC. These can be combined with any model, allowing a user to focus on the modelling task, without having to worry about the implementation of a complicated custom inference algorithm.

A model is a simplified representation of reality, and the simplifications are made to discard unnecessary detail and allow us to focus on the aspect of reality that we want to understand. Depending on the problem, it is important to assess the trade-offs between speed, accuracy, and complexity of different models and algorithms and find a model that works best for that particular problem. Consequently, the pairing of a suitable inference scheme to a model is a notoriously difficult problem; no one method is likely to generalise across the board [29]. A PPS allows us to quickly and accurately iterate over models and inference methods, to find the most optimal pair conditioned on the problem domain.

In our case, this enabled us to quickly experiment with and evaluate many models for lion accelerometer data. The fact that we could quickly design and implement a new model, the IDHMM, speaks to the ease of use and flexibility of the probabilistic programming methodology. In practice, we chose to perform our analyses in Anglican with the SMC inference algorithm. SMC takes as a parameter "the number of particles", where higher numbers increase the expected accuracy of inference.

5 LEARNING LION BEHAVIOUR

We qualify our models and inference methodology, by applying them, and contemporary state-of-the-art, to synthetic followed by lion observations.

5.1 SYNTHETIC OBSERVATIONS

We explore the relative performance between the five models introduced hitherto, by simulating observations $y_t \in \mathbb{R}^{D=2}$, from a very noisy three-state multivariate HSMM with Gaussian emissions – see fig. 3a. Consequently, from the inference perspective, the emission distribution has unknown mean and covariance parameters. The conjugate prior is the normal-inverse-Wishart distribution, denoted by $\mathsf{NIW}(\mu_0, \lambda_0, \Psi, \nu)$. Through conjugacy we seek the posterior distribution of $\{\mu_\theta, \Sigma_\theta\}$ $\forall \theta \in \Theta$, where we index group-specific (i.e., behaviour-specific) parameter samples by θ, given a set of observations $y_t \sim \mathcal{N}(\mu_\theta, \Sigma_\theta)$. For convenience of notation let $\mathbf{Y} = [y_1, \ldots, y_T]^\mathsf{T}$. For brevity, results are only shown for SMC, chosen for its superior performance for this model class. In addition, particle Gibbs (iterated conditional SMC) and lightweight Metropolis-Hastings were all tested as part of our experiments [30]. Model and emissions parameter priors are shown in table 1 in appendix C. We place non-informative hyperpriors on model parameters and then condition the models on the observations and sample state trajectories; i.e. $\theta \to t$, $\forall \theta \in \Theta \wedge \forall t \in \{1, \ldots, T\}$. We use synthetic observations of size $T = 1000$ and use 100 samples for each particle count (see fig. 3).

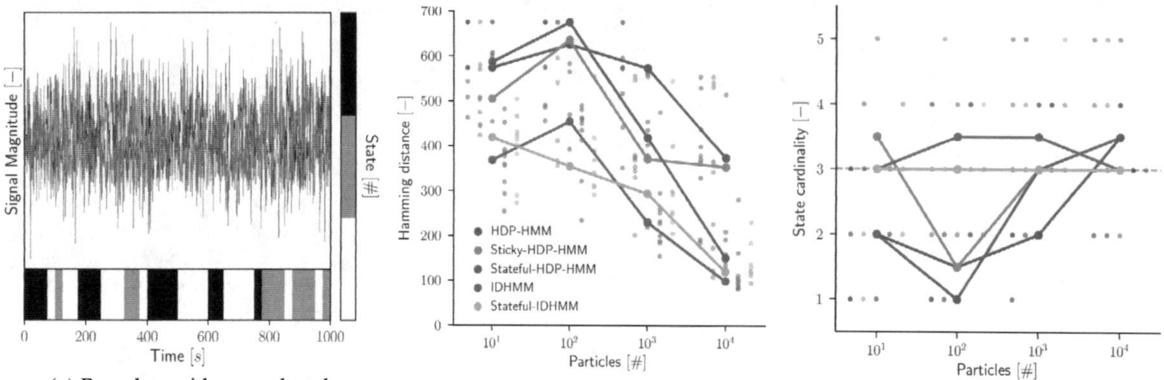

(a) Raw data with ground truth

(b) Hamming distance

(c) State cardinality

Figure 3: Results from experiments on multivariate synthetic Gaussian observations with SMC inference. A three-state HSMM with non-geometric duration distributions was sampled to create the observation set in fig. 3a. All models under discussion are compared and contrasted in fig. 3b and fig. 3c.

Performance is measured with the Hamming distance, a common clustering metric [16]. This distance metric works by mapping the randomly chosen indices of the estimated state sequence, to the set of indices that maximise the overlap with the true sequence [7]. In other words the distance between two sequences, is the number of positions at which the corresponding symbols are different. Hence, the lower, the better.

The results in fig. 3 demonstrate the advantage that our proposed model structure can have for modelling phenomena with non-geometric duration distributions. First, as demonstrated by [5], stateful models yield a clear benefit compared to their contemporaries. This is because we increase the heterogeneity of the dwell-time distribution of the inferred states of the model, by making the model statistics group specific. This is shown in fig. 3b and fig. 3c where the stateful HDP-HMM outperforms the HDP-HMM and sticky HDP-HMM for some particle counts. The benefits of a stateful representation are less clearcut for the IDHMM, but both IDHMMs outperform other state-of-the-art BNP SSMs.

By extending the HDP-HMM and stateful HDP-HMM, by drawing upon explicit-duration semi-Markovianity [11], as was done in the HDP-HSMM, one allows for the *parametric* construction of highly interpretable models which admit prior information on the state durations [11]. We make that model more flexible still by giving a nonparametric treatment treatment to the state cardinality *and* durations. By levering the statistical strength of HDPs for durations, we can model complex duration phenomena, which may be more difficult to treat in a parametric setting. We demonstrate, in appendix D, in fig. 9b and fig. 9c the flexibility that our model structure provides. By employing the duration distributions shown in fig. 9a, we gain approximately the same utility in terms of the Hamming distance, when using a uniform-discrete duration prior. However because we are targeting a duration process of the form shown by the red bars in fig. 9a, it is more appropriate to focus our duration prior density on those regions. Hence, we see that by employing two poorly-specified mixture duration distributions (fig. 9b: $\mathcal{N}(35,15)+\mathcal{N}(85,15)$ and fig. 9c: $\text{Pois}(35)+\text{Pois}(85)$ – with equal mixing proportions), the posterior state cardinality is better specified.

5.2 LION BEHAVIOUR

We demonstrate our methods by applying them to lion behaviour segmentation, to better understand their ecology. Hence, biologger observations are becoming increasingly popular tools for animal behaviour research. The number of studies using accelerometers in particular, has increased rapidly over the last 15 years due to the advantages offered over methods relying solely on direct observation [2]. While direct observation may be the only viable means of studying animal behaviour in certain cases, it can pose several difficulties which may include biases suffered as a result of observer presence [9] or the inability to continuously observe the focal animal if it is an elusive species, or a species that occurs in inaccessible habitats. The African lion is an example of a species for which behavioural research can benefit from accelerometer data-loggers due the challenges associated with keeping study individuals in sight continuously while avoiding influencing their behaviour. However, with the ability to record continuously at sampling frequencies as high as 10,000Hz [2], accelerometers generate extremely large datasets which are impossible to classify manually, which is why unsupervised learning could help.

The majority of studies which make use of machine learning to classify large accelerometry datasets, tend to rely on supervised learning techniques [2] or very coarse quantification of activity [19]. While such techniques have proven effective for many studies focussing on select, broad behavioural states such as 'stationary', 'mobile' and 'feeding' as shown by [8] on the cheetah, they are potentially limiting for those aimed at developing detailed activity budgets, as detailed manual labelling can be labour intensive and difficult. Hence, in this study we seek to dwell deeper by investigating, on a per-second basis, tri-axial accelerometry $(\ddot{x}, \ddot{y}, \ddot{z})$ and magnetometer $(\mathbf{B}_x, \mathbf{B}_y, \mathbf{B}_z)$ observations, collected from a male lion using a 32Hz sampling rate. *Unlike* previous studies, we shall employ a novel form of feature engineering, for our time-series observations, using the recent development of the variational autoencoder [12].

5.3 UNSUPERVISED FEATURE LEARNING

The study by Rahman et al. [22] presented an application of autoencoders (AE) to temporal tri-axial accelerometry observations. They used it to effect unsupervised feature learning, later used for supervised classification of cattle behaviour. This data-driven approach is one which we shall espouse too with the difference that we instead use *variational* AEs (VAE), whose generative nature has the advantage that the learned features are easier to interpret. For further details on the VAE structure and our implementation see appendix B.

5.4 FUZZY GROUND TRUTH

Ground truth (GT), as we have already alluded to, is an elusive property in the zoological domain. In section 1, we noted how, e.g., video was used as a form of GT. In our case, GT, or labelled observations, is received via sound [27]. The collar of each lion, apart from being equipped with sensors that log physical variations (e.g., acceleration), also log the audio of each animal. This enables the zoologist to get a measure of the animal's activity at time t. It also means that in order to ascertain a dataset that can be used for statistical learning, an exceptionally expensive process takes place where a human listens to an audio recording. For it to be of any use though, that recording has to span not hours, but days. Consequently this type of labelling is prohibitive due to its huge cost in man hours, but it also needs to be performed by the same person, as to remove as much bias as possible (e.g., our dataset contains 'trot' and 'walking' - two activities that are perceptively similar). This is another reason why unsupervised learning could prove preferable, being solely observation-driven. Furthermore, whilst it is true that a human does listen to the lion for a significant portion of time, she does *not* listen to the whole recording (which again can span days). Instead, recordings are sub-sampled, where, e.g., every other minute (or five minutes in some cases) are monitored and the inferred label (based on the zoologists' interpretation of the lion's *audible* activity at that point in time) is interpolated until the next sampling point. All of which leads to a form of semi ground truth.

5.5 EXPERIMENTS

Before describing the minutia of our experiments, it is important to re-iterate the purpose of this exercise, and the potential value it could have for zoological studies. Whilst a human will need to be in the semi-GT extraction-loop, we propose that the methods within can function as a conduit for *behaviour discovery*. Differently put, we posit that our methodology can function as a useful tool for zoologist, as the unsupervised segmentation will allow them to hone in on regions of interest, and consequently will allow them to more intelligently choose regions of interest for their work. Upon which their semi-GT can be used in any of the standard supervised classification methods which hitherto have proved their worth in this domain (when good GT is available).

For our experiments, we used 10 hours of labelled[3] observations for one lion, part of a pride currently being studied by our institution. After experimenting with several window sizes, we settled on $3s$ as providing a useful level of granularity. As such, each observation $y \in \mathbb{R}^{96\times6}$ (see appendix B, fig. 8b), was normalised, passed to a VAE, where a low-dimensional latent representation $z \in \mathbb{R}^3$ was extracted. The sequence of latent representations is what we used as input for our models, all of which were written as probabilistic programs (see appendix appendix F, for an example), to which we applied black-box SMC inference. We used the same conjugate prior as in section 5.1. For details see table 2 in appendix C. In summary, the purpose of these methods is not to segment the signal into 'correct' features (given that no true form of the ground truth exists). Rather, the purpose, given limited and noisy information, is to detect regions of interest (as opposed to, e.g., large regions of a resting behaviour). Results are shown in fig. 4.

5.6 DETAILED ANALYSIS: A HUNT

In fig. 5, we demonstrate the utility of the IDHMM and the stateful IDHMM, on a smaller segment of fig. 4. In this experiment, we sought to understand if our methods could accurately segment fast-changing animal behaviour, specifically that related to hunting. Panel four,

[3] In the sense in which this exposition is framed.

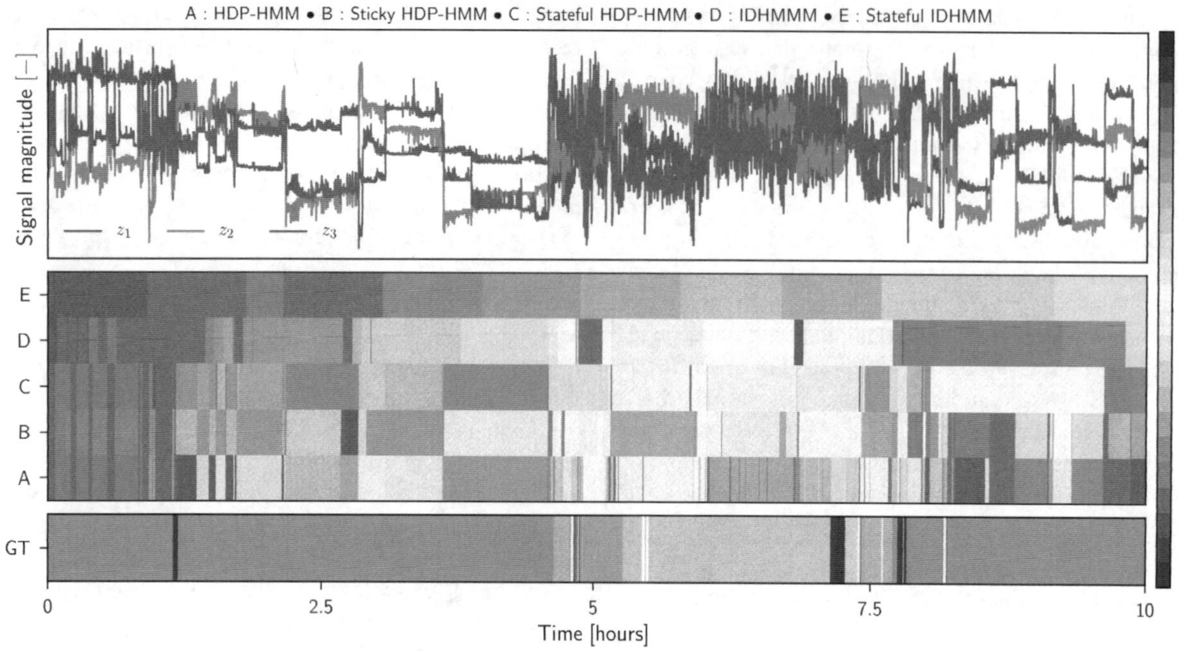

Figure 4: The **top panel** displays the feature-set over which inference was performed. The **middle panel** shows the inferred state trajectories, with the highest log-marginal likelihood $\log \mathbb{P}(y_{1:T})$ for all models. The **bottom panel** displays the manually labelled ground-truth which serves as a comparison to our unsupervised labelling. The colorbar maps the numbers of inferred states to each model heatmap in the middle panel.

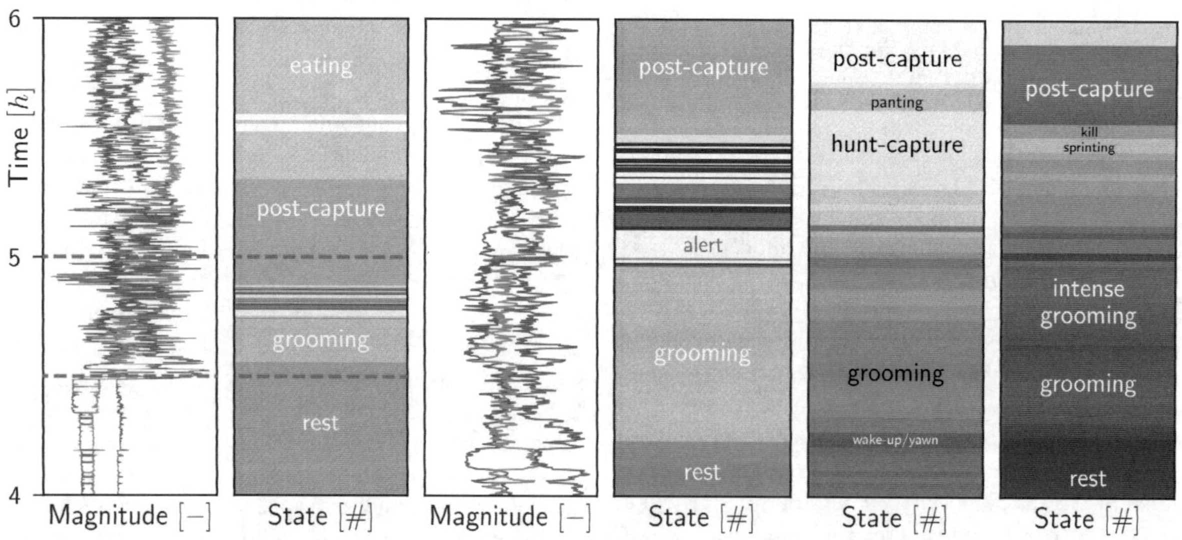

Figure 5: Detailed depiction of a two hour segment which features hunting behaviour, using the IDHMM and the stateful IDHMM. The **first two panels** (from the left) show a two hour segment with 'ground truth', the **second pair of panels** show a zoomed in 30min period in which multiple behaviours exist (some of which have been annotated). The **final two panels** show the inferred behaviour sequences using the IDHMM and the stateful IDHMM (last panel).

from the left, in fig. 5 contains the manual labelling of this segment, followed by the IDHMM and stateful IDHMM inferred state trajectories. For model and conjugate prior details, see table 3 in appendix C.

Post-analysis showed that the models are reasonably successful in segmenting the time-series from a zoological point of view; subtle and short behaviours can be picked out from the audio, which the models 'accurately' recognise from the input sequences. Granted, post-analysis is subject to human error and bias, but is still valuable, if only to validate that *something* has been found and should be studied in more detail. As an example, consider panel four again (from the left), the large top segment labelled 'post-capture' is immediately preceded by a long (minutes) sequence of alert and walking behaviours, all of which eventually lead to a chase and kill. The human labelling of this segment is good, but could be better at picking out subtle behaviours such as the sprint that leads to the kill (behaviours currently folded into the 'post-capture' and 'capture' labels, the latter of which is not shown on the plot). The stateful IDHMM successfully captures this, while the IDHMM does not.

6 DISCUSSION AND CONCLUSION

From the middle panel of fig. 4, a clear trend emerges regarding the nature and behaviour of the models w.r.t. to the observations. The IDHMMs variants (models E and D in fig. 4) allow the practitioner to employ specific domain knowledge regarding the duration distribution of the phenomena being studied. Hence as shown, the model samples from a bespoke duration distribution, where, in this instance, we have employed a simple mixture of discrete-uniform distributions that reflect the duration content as seen in the feature space. In fig. 4, the light grey area preceding the five-hour mark, constitutes an area of less frequent behaviour (as labelled by the zoologists); a hunt (labelled as 'capture'), followed by a kill, followed by post-kill behaviour such as eating and drinking. It is clear that all models segment the onset of this activity sequence, but then differ in the duration properties and number of activities present in this event segment. The HDP-HMM and the sticky HDP-HMM both capture the fast switching dynamics. The other models do not, the IDHMMs do not by design, as they are primed to find *large* regions of interest, with statistical observation similarity. This points towards a scenario where both types of models are used jointly, as the strength of their sum is greater than their individual parts. Viewed this way, we can apply the models of fig. 4 top to bottom. State-space models that better deal with coarse state-space granularity, and observations with non-geometric duration distributions, are labelled top to bottom in the middle panel, according to how much granularity they offer the user for this task. Conversely the IDHMM can be tuned to model bursts of activity as demonstrated in fig. 5.

Having ascertained where large regions of interest are located, we can turn to models A-C of the middle panel in fig. 4. The sticky HDP-HMM, not being as state-persistent as the stateful version, does not smooth out the activity labelling as much, but still quickly introduces new labels for surprising features. The inferred state cardinalities for the HDP-HMM, sticky HDP-HMM and the stateful HDP-HMM were 23, 18 and 20 respectively. The activity set, as labelled by the zoologists consisted of 14. That should not be taken as evidence that these models are converging to the right number. Critical analysis must still be maintained as there are many minor activities, which should be differentiated, such as 'trot' and 'walk' which, from a feature point of view are almost identical.

The unsupervised learning methodology demonstrated in this paper, holds promise when used in conjunction with supervised methods as no prior behavioural states need to be specified, thereby allowing for the recognition of less obvious or unknown behavioural states that may be missed through limited observation. Prior classification of states used in supervised learning may be subject to confirmation bias where an observer may oversimplify a chosen state based upon their expectations and thus exclude a separate, and perhaps more subtle, behavioural class [28]. Moreover, there are many ventures for further exploration from the modelling side, such as training the models in a semi-supervised fashion and then using those models, to segment other regions. We, furthermore, suggest that the methods demonstrated within can be particularly valuable for lion behavioural ecology as the last detailed activity budget for the species was compiled more than four decades ago by [23], where unobservable behaviours may not have been recognised.

Finally, we hope to have conveyed that PPS:es like Anglican hold promise to accelerate modelling innovation in scientific domains like zoology. In areas like these, programmer/scientist time often is a scarcer resource than computation time and the flexibility and ease of use of general purpose inference already weighs up against the downside of extra computation time. With computing power increasing, but our brain power remaining fixed, we expect this to become even more true in the future, particularly when more mature PPS:es are developed.

Acknowledgements

We would like to thank the shareholders of Bubye Valley Conservancy for allowing us to conduct field research on the conservancy. We would also like to thank the management staff of Bubye Valley Conservancy for assistance in the field. Collar design was supported by the John Fell Fund. N. D. is supported by the RCUK Digital Economy Programme grant number EP/G036861/1 (Oxford Centre for Doctoral Training in Healthcare Innovation). M.V. gratefully acknowledges support from the EPSRC and Clarendon Fund. We would like to honour Cecil the lion for his service to science.

References

[1] Bilmes, Jeff A. What HMMs can do. *IEICE TRANSACTIONS on Information and Systems*, 89(3):869–891, 2006.

[2] Brown, Danielle D, Kays, Roland, Wikelski, Martin, Wilson, Rory, and Klimley, A Peter. Observing the unwatchable through acceleration logging of animal behavior. *Animal Biotelemetry*, 1(1):1, 2013.

[3] Carroll, Gemma, Slip, David, Jonsen, Ian, and Harcourt, Rob. Supervised accelerometry analysis can identify prey capture by penguins at sea. *Journal of Experimental Biology*, 217(24):4295–4302, 2014.

[4] Dewar, Michael, Wiggins, Chris, and Wood, Frank. Inference in hidden markov models with explicit state duration distributions. *IEEE Signal Processing Letters*, 19(4): 235–238, 2012.

[5] Dhir, Neil, Perov, Yura, and Wood, Frank. Nonparametric bayesian models for unsupervised activity recognition and tracking. In *Intelligent Robots and Systems (IROS), 2016 IEEE/RSJ International Conference on*, pp. 4040–4045. IEEE, 2016.

[6] Ferguson, Thomas S. A Bayesian analysis of some nonparametric problems. *The annals of statistics*, pp. 209–230, 1973.

[7] Fox, Emily B, Sudderth, Erik B, Jordan, Michael I, and Willsky, Alan S. An HDP-HMM for systems with state persistence. In *Proceedings of the 25th international conference on Machine learning*, pp. 312–319. ACM, 2008.

[8] Grünewälder, Steffen, Broekhuis, Femke, Macdonald, David Whyte, Wilson, Alan Martin, McNutt, John Weldon, Shawe-Taylor, John, and Hailes, Stephen. Movement activity based classification of animal behaviour with an application to data from cheetah (acinonyx jubatus). *PloS one*, 7(11):e49120, 2012.

[9] Gutzwiller, Kevin J, Wiedenmann, Richard T, Clements, Krista L, and Anderson, Stanley H. Effects of human intrusion on song occurrence and singing consistency in subalpine birds. *The Auk*, pp. 28–37, 1994.

[10] Huggins, Jonathan H and Wood, Frank. Infinite structured hidden semi-markov models. *arXiv preprint arXiv:1407.0044*, 2014.

[11] Johnson, Matthew J. and Willsky, Alan S. The hierarchical dirichlet process hidden semi-markov model. In *Proceedings of the Twenty-Sixth Conference on Uncertainty in Artificial Intelligence*, UAI, pp. 252–259, 2010.

[12] Kingma, Diederik P and Welling, Max. Auto-encoding variational bayes. *arXiv preprint arXiv:1312.6114*, 2013.

[13] Leos-Barajas, Vianey, Photopoulou, Theoni, Langrock, Roland, Patterson, Toby A, Watanabe, Yuuki Y, Murgatroyd, Megan, and Papastamatiou, Yannis P. Analysis of animal accelerometer data using hidden markov models. *Methods in Ecology and Evolution*, 8(2):161–173, 2017.

[14] Lo, Albert Y et al. On a class of bayesian nonparametric estimates: I. density estimates. *The annals of statistics*, 12(1):351–357, 1984.

[15] Lush, L, Ellwood, S, Markham, A, Ward, AI, and Wheeler, P. Use of tri-axial accelerometers to assess terrestrial mammal behaviour in the wild. *Journal of Zoology*, 2015.

[16] MacKay, David JC. *Information theory, inference and learning algorithms*. Cambridge university press, 2003.

[17] McClune, David W, Marks, Nikki J, Wilson, Rory P, Houghton, Jonathan DR, Montgomery, Ian W, McGowan, Natasha E, Gormley, Eamonn, and Scantlebury, Michael. Tri-axial accelerometers quantify behaviour in the eurasian badger (meles meles): towards an automated interpretation of field data. *Animal Biotelemetry*, 2(1):5, 2014.

[18] Murphy, Kevin P. Hidden semi-markov models HSMMs. *unpublished notes*, 2, 2002.

[19] Noonan, Michael J, Markham, Andrew, Newman, Chris, Trigoni, Niki, Buesching, Christina D, Ellwood, Stephen A, and Macdonald, David W. Climate and the individual: inter-annual variation in the autumnal activity of the european badger (meles meles). *PLoS One*, 9(1): e83156, 2014.

[20] Pagano, AM, Rode, KD, Cutting, A, Owen, MA, Jensen, S, Ware, JV, Robbins, CT, Durner, GM, Atwood, TC, Obbard, ME, et al. Using tri-axial accelerometers to identify wild polar bear behaviors. *Endangered Species Research*, 32:19–33, 2017.

[21] Phillips, Joe Scutt, Patterson, Toby A, Leroy, Bruno, Pilling, Graham M, and Nicol, Simon J. Objective classification of latent behavioral states in bio-logging data using multivariate-normal hidden markov models. *Ecological Applications*, 25(5):1244–1258, 2015.

[22] Rahman, Ashfaqur, Smith, Daniel, Hills, James, Bishop-Hurley, Greg, Henry, Dave, and Rawnsley, Richard. A comparison of autoencoder and statistical features for cattle behaviour classification. In *Neural Networks (IJCNN), 2016 International Joint Conference on*, pp. 2954–2960. IEEE, 2016.

[23] Schaller, George B. *The Serengeti Lion: A Study of Predator-prey Relations. Drawings by Richard Keane*. University of Chicago Press, 1974.

[24] Teh, Yee Whye. Dirichlet process. In *Encyclopedia of machine learning*, pp. 280–287. Springer, 2011.

[25] Teh, Yee Whye and Jordan, Michael I. Hierarchical bayesian nonparametric models with applications. *Bayesian nonparametrics*, 1, 2010.

[26] Teh, Yee Whye, Jordan, Michael I, Beal, Matthew J, and Blei, David M. Hierarchical dirichlet processes. *Journal of the american statistical association*, 101(476), 2006.

[27] Trethowan, Paul, Fuller, Andrea, Haw, Anna, Hart, Tom, Markham, Andrew, Loveridge, Andrew, Hetem, Robyn, Preez, Byron, and Macdonald, David W. Getting to the core: Internal body temperatures help reveal the ecological function and thermal implications of the lions mane. *Ecology and evolution*, 7(1):253–262, 2017.

[28] van Wilgenburg, Ellen and Elgar, Mark A. Confirmation bias in studies of nestmate recognition: a cautionary note for research into the behaviour of animals. *PloS one*, 8 (1):e53548, 2013.

[29] Wolpert, David H and Macready, William G. No free lunch theorems for optimization. *Evolutionary Computation, IEEE Transactions on*, 1(1):67–82, 1997.

[30] Wood, F., van de Meent, J. W., and Mansinghka, V. A new approach to probabilistic programming inference. In *Proceedings of the 17th International conference on Artificial Intelligence and Statistics*, 2014.

[31] Wood, Frank. Nips probabilistic programming tutorial 2015, December 2015.

APPENDICES

A PROBABILISTIC PROGRAMMING

In fig. 6, we present an HMM as a toy model. Using this, we briefly discuss the idea behind SMC inference.

By way of motivation, consider the generative model $\mathbb{P}(\theta_{1:T}, y_{1:T})$ with hidden variables $\theta_{1:T}$ and observations $y_{1:T}$. In PP, we let the observing random variable y_t be the value of the tth observe, and the hidden variables $\boldsymbol{\theta}_t = \theta_{1:t}$ be the execution trace before this observe (see fig. 7). The goal of, e.g., SMC inference in PP is to approximate $\mathbb{P}(\boldsymbol{\theta}_{1:T} \mid y_{1:T}) = \mathbb{P}(y_{1:t})^{-1}\mathbb{P}(\theta_{1:t}, y_{1:t})\ \forall t \in \{1, \ldots, T\}$. The goal of SMC inference in Anglican is to approximate $\mathbb{P}(\ \theta_{1:T} \mid y_{1:T}) = \mathbb{P}(y_{1:t})^{-1}\mathbb{P}(\theta_{1:t}, y_{1:t})\ \forall t \in \{1, \ldots, T\}$. The weighted approximation to $\mathbb{P}(\theta_{1:T} \mid y_{1:T})$, is achieved by generating a set of particles and importance weights at each time step t: $\{(\theta_{1:n}^{(p)}, w_t^{(p)})\}_{p=1}^{P}$. The approximation to the target distribution is then given by

$$\sum_{p=1}^{P} w_t^{(p)} \delta_{\boldsymbol{\theta}_{1:t}^{(p)}}(\boldsymbol{\theta}_{1:T}). \tag{9}$$

At each time step t particles are generated using a chosen proposal density $q_t(\boldsymbol{\theta}_t \mid \boldsymbol{\theta}_{t-1})$. This is used to propose new particles, given the set of particles $\{\bar{\boldsymbol{\theta}}_{1:t-1}^{(p)}\}$ re-sampled from the previous $t-1$ steps of the SMC estimate of $\mathbb{P}(\boldsymbol{\theta}_{1:t-1} \mid y_{1:t-1})$. The weights of the corresponding particles are given as follows:

$$W_t^{(p)} = \frac{\mathbb{P}\left(\boldsymbol{\theta}_t^{(p)} \mid \bar{\boldsymbol{\theta}}_{1:t-1}^{(p)}\right) \mathbb{P}\left(y_t \mid \boldsymbol{\theta}_t^{(p)}\right)}{q\left(\boldsymbol{\theta}_t^{(p)} \mid \bar{\boldsymbol{\theta}}_{1:t-1}^{(p)}\right)}, \tag{10}$$

and $w_t^{(p)} = W_t^{(p)} \left(\sum_{i=1}^{P} W_t^{(p)}\right)^{-1}$ for $p \in \{1, \ldots, P\}$. Finally, for each t in the proposal, re-sampling and re-weighting steps are iterated. This gives us a particle estimate of our target posterior along with an estimate of the marginal likelihood $\mathbb{P}(y_{1:T})$.

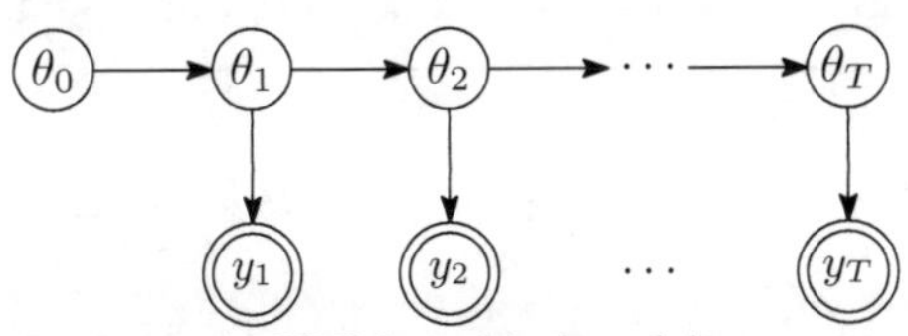

(a) HMM graphical model

```
(defquery hmm
  [observations initial-dist
      transition-dists observation-dists]
  (reduce
    (fn [states observation]
      (let [state (sample (get
           transition-dists (peek states)))]
        (observe (get observation-dists
             state) observation)
        (conj states state)))
    [(sample initial-dist)]
    observations))
```

(b) HMM in Anglican syntax.

Figure 6: The probabilistic programming philosophy illustrated; showing in (a) the graphical model and in (b) the resultant code upon which black-box inference is fully applicable.

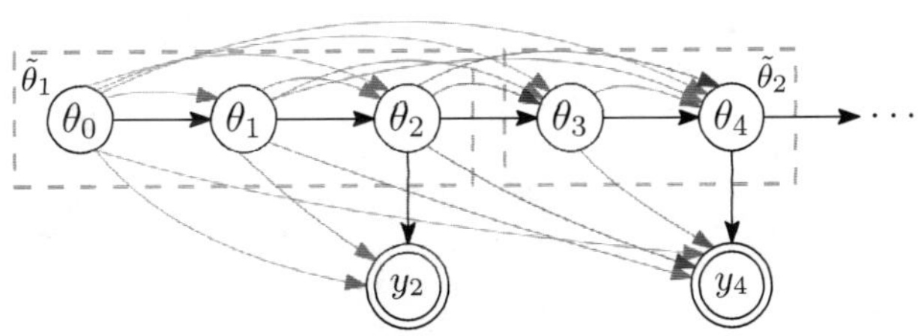

Figure 7: Model traces illustration, adapted from [31]. The execution trace is bounded by the dashed box, wherein $\tilde{\theta}_1 = \theta_1 \times \theta_2 \times \theta_3$ for example.

B NONLINEAR FEATURE LEARNING

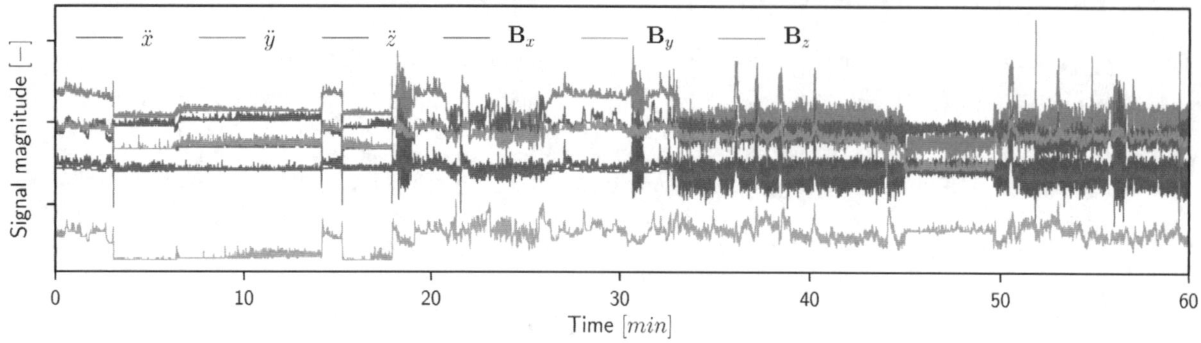

(a) One hour of raw data captured at 32Hz, containing a total of 115,200 multivariate observations.

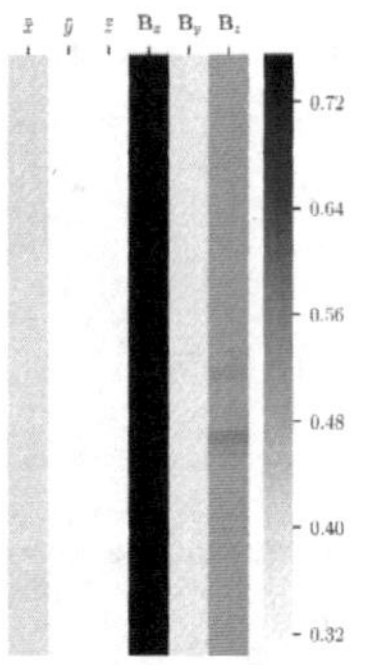

(b) Example of original $3s$ feature (96×6).

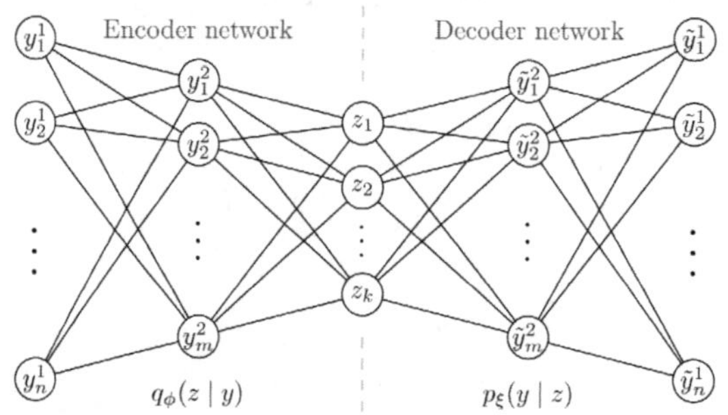

(c) General structure of variational autoencoder.

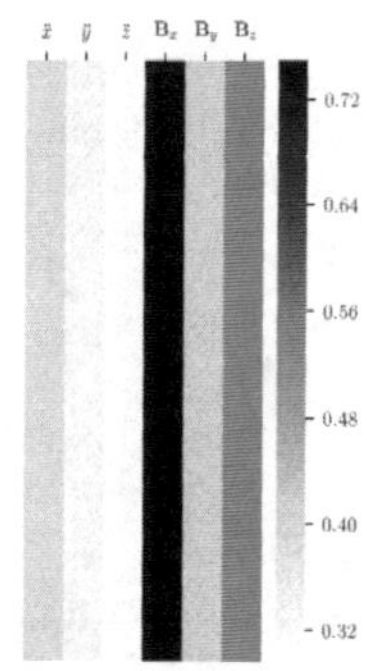

(d) Reconstructed example feature.

Figure 8: The top panel shows the raw data used for this study, consisting of tri-axial accelerometer and magnetometer readings taken from the lion's collar. The bottom figures display the variational autoencoder framework, with original (b) and reconstructed (d) features shown.

In this study, we used a VAE to perform unsupervised feature learning - see fig. 8c. It is on these learned features that we perform our further analyses using state space models implemented in Anglican.

Traditional AEs are models designed to output a reconstruction of their input. VAEs, by extension, ensure that the transformations to or from the hidden representation are useful by sacrificing some fidelity, by imposing some sort of regularization or constraint. VAEs consist of an encoder, a decoder and a loss function. The encoder $q_\phi(z \mid y)$ consists of a neural network. It takes as input an observation y and outputs a latent representation z, and has weights and biases ϕ. The decoder $p_\xi(y \mid z)$ is similarly a neural net. Its input is the latent representation z, it outputs the parameters to the probability distribution of the observations, with weights and biases ξ. The encoder must learn an efficient compression of the data into a lower-dimensional representation z. Because q_ϕ is a Gaussian density, we can sample noisy representations of z. Conversely the decoder p_ξ takes the latent representation z and tries to decode the original input y. Throughout this computational flow, information will be lost, the magnitude of which we measure with the reconstruction log-likelihood $\log p_\xi(y \mid z)$, given by

$$\mathbb{E}_{\mathbf{z}\sim q_\phi(\mathbf{z}|\mathbf{y})}[\log p_\xi(\mathbf{y}|\mathbf{z})] - D_{\mathrm{KL}}(q_\phi(\mathbf{z}|\mathbf{y})||p_\xi(\mathbf{z})) \tag{11}$$

where bold variables contain all data points. This measure tells us how effectively the decoder has learned to reconstruct the input y, given its latent representation z. Consequently we can train the VAE using gradient descent to optimise the loss with respect to the parameters of the encoder and decoder.

Apart from giving us a low-dimensional representation of our sequential observation, the VAE construction lends itself further to our methodological design. We assume that our observation model is Gaussian in our generative modelling framework. The VAE, by construction, yields latent variables which are normally distributed and it is these that we go on to nonparametrically segment. The raw data is *not* normally distributed.

C MODEL PARAMETERS

Table 1: Common model and emission priors used for synthetic data experiments.

Model parameter	Prior
$\alpha, \gamma, \alpha', \gamma'$	$\Gamma(1,1)$
κ	$\Gamma(2,1)$
H_θ	$\mathcal{N}(0,1)$
$H_\mathcal{D}$	$\mathcal{U}(25,100), \mathcal{N}(\mu,\Sigma)^\dagger$, $\text{Pois}(\lambda)^\dagger$
μ_0	$\overline{\mathbf{Y}}$ (empirical average)
λ_0	$D+2$
Ψ	$0.75 \times \text{Cov}(\mathbf{Y})$
ν	0.1

† Used as part of parametric mixture duration distribution

Table 2: Experimental model and emission priors, used for inter-model comparison.

Model parameter	Prior
α, γ	$\Gamma(0.5,1)$
α', γ'	$\Gamma(1,1)$
κ	$\Gamma(5,1)$
H_θ	$\mathcal{N}(0,1)$
$H_\mathcal{D}$	$\mathcal{U}(1000)$
μ_0	$\overline{\mathbf{Y}}$
λ_0	$D+2$
Ψ	$C \times \text{Cov}(\mathbf{Y})$
C	$\mathcal{U}(0.5,2)$
ν	$\mathcal{U}(0.1,2.0)$

Table 3: Experimental model and emission priors, used for detailed analysis of hunt segment.

Model parameter	Prior
α, γ	$\Gamma(1,5)$
α', γ'	$\Gamma(2,1)$
H_θ	$\mathcal{N}(0,1)$
$H_\mathcal{D}$	$\text{Pois}(\lambda)^\dagger$
μ_0	$\overline{\mathbf{Y}}$
λ_0	$D+2$
Ψ	$C \times \text{Cov}(\mathbf{Y})$
C	$\Gamma(5,5)$
ν	$\Gamma(1,0.75)$

† Used as part of parametric mixture duration distribution

D BENEFIT OF NONPARAMETRIC DURATION DISTRIBUTIONS

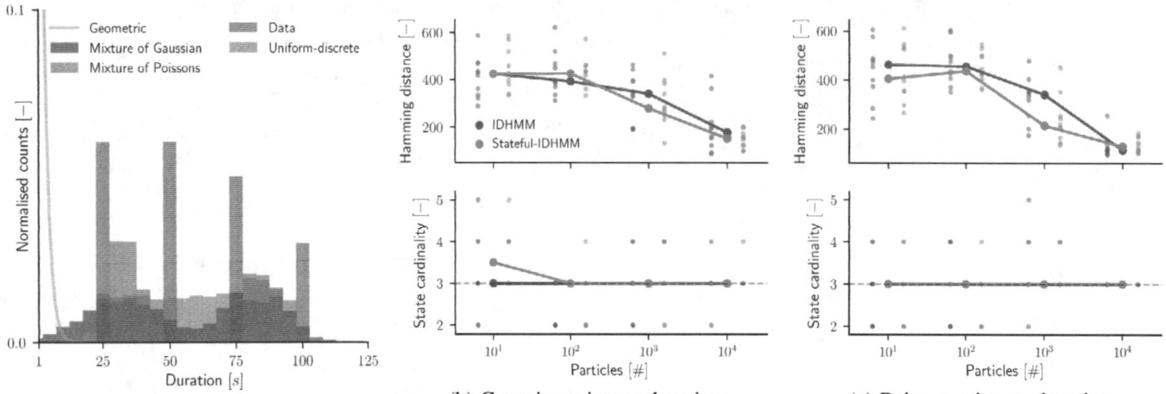

(a) Duration distribution (b) Gaussian mixture duration (c) Poisson mixture duration

Figure 9: Different durations models used as priors, as well as the observations' duration model, are shown in fig. 9a. Our two contributed models are compared, under different durations priors, in fig. 9b and fig. 9c. Shaded small bullets, correspond to the specific experimental results (a total of ten trials were conducted for each particle count, for each model). The solid large bullets correspond to the median error across all trials in each particle count, for that model.

E RELATED MODELS

Hitherto we have alluded to two models which most resemble the construction which we propose: the HDP-HSMM of Johnson & Willsky [11] - see fig. 2c - and the infinite explicit duration HMM (IED-HMM) of Huggins & Wood [10]. We briefly describe these models and compare them to our contribution.

The HDP-HSMM can be seen as similar to the IDHMM with the two key differences that 1) the duration distributions are chosen from a parametric family rather than modelled non-parametrically and 2) the top level DP for state transitions is implemented through a stick-breaking construction. In particular, the model is given by

$$\beta \mid \gamma \sim \text{GEM}(\gamma)$$

$$\pi_i \mid \beta, \alpha \overset{i.i.d.}{\sim} \mathcal{DP}(\alpha, \beta) \qquad (\xi_i, \omega_i) \overset{i.i.d.}{\sim} H \times G \tag{12}$$

$$z_s \mid z_{s-1} \sim \bar{\pi}_{z_{s-1}}$$

$$d_s \mid \omega_{z_s} \sim D(\omega_{z_s}) \tag{13}$$

$$y_{t_s^1:t_s^2} \overset{i.i.d.}{\sim} F(\xi_{z_s}) \qquad t_s^1 = \sum_{\bar{s}<s} d_{\bar{s}} \tag{14}$$

where $t_s^2 = t_s^1 + d_s - 1$. Johnson & Willsky [11] define $\bar{\pi} \triangleq \frac{\pi_{ij}}{1-\pi_{ii}}(1 - \delta_{ij})$ to eliminate self-transitions in what they term their super-state sequence (z_s).

Secondly, the IED-HMM arises from the infinite structured hidden semi-Markov model Bayesian nonparametric framework [10, §5]. This framework, in which the IED-HMM is specified, directly parametrises state duration distributions, allowing for more heterogeneity and specificity, in state dwell durations when compared to the IED-HMM [10].

Summarising, our IDHMM differs from these two precedents primarily (ignoring construction and inference details) by modelling durations non-parametrically. By levering the statistical strength of hierarchical processes also for durations, we can model complex duration phenomena like multi-modal duration distributions which may be more difficult to treat in a parametric setting.

F ANGLICAN CODE

We list here an example of our Anglican code. Specifically, we include our implementation of the IDHMM. Our full code base can be found on https://goo.gl/14s8Sa.

```
(with-primitive-procedures
  [shape
   mmul
   model-params
   DP-ind]
  (defquery idhmm
    "Infinite duration hidden Markov model"
    [observations]
    (let
      [ ;; ==== Initialize Processes for State and Durations Transitions ====

        alpha-trans-0 (sample (model-params :alpha-trans-0-prior))
        _ (store "state-transition-base-process" (DP alpha-trans-0
                                             (model-params :trans-dist)))

        alpha-dur-0 (sample (model-params :alpha-dur-0-prior))
        _ (store "duration-base-process" (DP alpha-dur-0
                                    (model-params :dur-dist)))

        ;; ==== Specify State and Duration Transitions ====

        alpha-dur (sample (model-params :alpha-dur-prior))
        transition-duration
        (fn [S D]
          (if (< 1 D)
            (- D 1)
            (let [ duration-base-process (retrieve "duration-base-process")
                   duration-group-process (or (retrieve ["duration-group-process" S])
                                  (DP-ind alpha-dur (produce duration-base-process)))
                   newpair (sample (produce duration-group-process))
                   newduration (first newpair)
                   newind (second newpair)
                   _ (if newind
                        (store "duration-base-process" (absorb duration-base-process
                            newduration))
                        0)
                   _ (store ["duration-group-process" S] (absorb duration-group-process
                          newduration))]
              newduration)))

        alpha-trans (sample (model-params :alpha-dur-prior))
        transition-state
        (fn [S D]
          (if (< 1 D)
            S
            (let [ transition-base-process (retrieve "state-transition-base-process")
                   transition-group-process (or (retrieve ["state-transition-process" S])
                                    (DP-ind alpha-trans (produce transition-base-process)))
                   ;; Now, we need to exclude self-transtions. We do this by sampling a
                      new state (and indicator) repeatedly
                   ;; and rejecting until we obtain one that is not equal to the state we
                      started from.
                   ;; Note that we only absorb into the DPs after we have sampled a state
                      that we will keep.
                   ;; Again, we always absorb into the group level transition process and
                      depending on the indicator which
                   ;; shows if we sampled from the base distribution of the group level
                      process, we also absorb in the base level
                   ;; transition process.
```

```
        newpair (loop [a [S false]]
        (if (= (first a) S)
          (recur (sample (produce transition-group-process)))
          a))
        newstate (first newpair)
        newind (second newpair)
        _ (if newind
            (store "state-transition-base-process" (absorb
                transition-base-process newstate))
            0)
        _ (store ["state-group-transition-process" S] (absorb
           transition-group-process newstate))]
    newstate)))

  markov-step
  (fn [prev-item]
    (let [s (transition-state (first prev-item) (second prev-item))]
      [s (transition-duration s (second prev-item))]))

  ;; ==== Initialize Observation Process ====

  emperical-observation-mean (mean observations 0)
  rescaled-emperical-observation-cov (mmul
                                       (model-params :cov-mat-scale)
                                       (covariance observations 0))
  dof (+ 2 (second (shape observations)))
  inverse-cov-scale (sample (model-params :inverse-cov-scale))

  obs-base-proc (mvn-niw
                  emperical-observation-mean
                  inverse-cov-scale
                  dof
                  rescaled-emperical-observation-cov)]

;; ==== Condition on observations ====

(reduce
  (fn [states-and-durations obs]
    (let [s_d (markov-step (peek states-and-durations))
          s (first s_d)
          proc (or (retrieve ["observation-process" s])
                   obs-base-proc)]

      (observe (produce proc) obs)
      (store ["observation-process" s] (absorb proc obs))
      (conj states-and-durations s_d)))
  (let [state-transition-base-process (retrieve "state-transition-base-process")
        duration-base-process (retrieve "duration-base-process")
        s (sample (produce state-transition-base-process))
        d (sample (produce duration-base-process))
        _ (store "state-transition-base-process" (absorb
            state-transition-base-process s) )
        _ (store "duration-base-process" (absorb duration-base-process d))]
    [[s d]])
  observations))))
```

Decoupling Homophily and Reciprocity with Latent Space Network Models

Jiasen Yang
Department of Statistics
Purdue University
West Lafayette, IN
jiaseny@purdue.edu

Vinayak Rao
Department of Statistics
Purdue University
West Lafayette, IN
varao@purdue.edu

Jennifer Neville
Depts. of Computer Science and Statistics
Purdue University
West Lafayette, IN
neville@purdue.edu

Abstract

Networks form useful representations of data arising in various physical and social domains. In this work, we consider dynamic networks such as communication networks in which links connecting pairs of nodes appear over continuous time. We adopt a point process-based approach, and study latent space models which embed the nodes into Euclidean space. We propose models to capture two different aspects of dynamic network data: (*i*) communication occurs at a higher rate between individuals with similar features (homophily), and (*ii*) individuals tend to reciprocate communications from other nodes, but in a manner that varies across individuals. Our framework marries ideas from point process models, including Poisson and Hawkes processes, with ideas from latent space models of static networks. We evaluate our models over a range of tasks on real-world datasets and show that a *dual* latent space model, which accounts for heterogeneity in both reciprocity and homophily, significantly improves performance for both static and dynamic link prediction.

1 INTRODUCTION

Latent space models are a valuable tool for modeling social network data. By incorporating an embedding over nodes (*e.g.*, people), such models can account for unobserved preferences, interests, attitudes, etc. Typically, the likelihood of edges (interactions) between two nodes depends on their distance in the embedding space: the closer they are, the more likely they are to be linked. This reflects the notion of *homophily* (McPherson et al., 2001) that has been observed in many social domains: similar entities are more likely to form a tie than two randomly selected entities. As such, including latent spaces in models of static social networks has often improved descriptive and predictive accuracy with respect to modeling the link structure (*e.g.*, Hoff et al. 2002).

In this work, we focus on modeling the structure of dynamic networks, where interactions occur among entities over time. Dynamic networks are more complex than static networks because the temporal interactions can be varied and bursty, reflecting new, repeated, or correlated events. Much of the recent work in modeling temporal networks has typically represented the input networks as a sequence of snapshots taken at discrete time-points and often used Markov assumptions to restrict temporal correlations to the previous time-step.

It is much more natural to model the network dynamics using point processes, particularly when the interactions indicate events that occur in continuous time (*e.g.*, each pair of nodes has a sequence of interactions over time). Previous work have applied various point processes such as Poisson processes (*e.g.*, Iwata et al. 2013), renewal processes (*e.g.*, Min et al. 2011), and Hawkes processes (*e.g.*, Blundell et al. 2012) to modeling network data. Hawkes processes in particular have attracted a great deal of recent interest due to their capability to capture *reciprocity* in interaction data. Reciprocity refers to the act of responding to a particular action with the same type of action (Ekeh, 1974). For example, in social network interactions, if one person sends another a message, the likelihood that the other person will respond and send a message back in the near future increases. However, recent work has focused more on modeling reciprocity with specific individuals (or clusters of people) rather than modeling the dependencies among individuals that may influence reciprocity.

In this work, we bring the strength of latent space models for static networks to point process models for dynamic networks. We make the key observation that the latent dimensions of users which influence link formation may be different from the latent dimensions of users which influence reciprocity. We refer to the former as the user's *homophily* latent space—dimensions which include preferences, interests, attitudes, etc. We refer to the latter as the user's *reciprocal* latent space—dimensions which include prosociality, agreeableness, level of self-monitoring, adherence to social norms, etc. Since the set of temporal interactions in dynamic networks consists of various types of events (some new, some instigated by other events), it is unlikely that all such interactions are governed by the same process. We conjecture that different latent space embeddings will help models to distinguish bursty events due to reciprocation from other types of interactions in a conversation.

To explore these issues, we propose a set of latent space point process models including a Poisson process-based model and multiple Hawkes process-based models with different latent space embeddings. We evaluate the utility of the various models both quantitatively and qualitatively through a set of carefully designed experiments on real-world datasets. Our results show that a *dual* latent space Hawkes process model, which contains latent spaces for both homophily and reciprocity, are more accurate for both dynamic and static link prediction. Moreover, the embeddings themselves can be used for subjective evaluation and provide insights on how various pairs of entities interact in the network.

Contributions. We make the following contributions:

- We propose and study a sequence of latent space point process models, including a Poisson process latent space model, two single-latent space Hawkes process models and a novel dual-latent space model.
- We develop methodology to evaluate the proposed models, including static and dynamic prediction tasks, and exploration of the learned embeddings.
- We evaluate the utility of our models both quantitatively and qualitatively on three real-world datasets. We show that incorporating both the homophily and reciprocal latent spaces improves predictive performance and gives rise to interpretable embeddings.

Outline. Section 2 reviews background on point processes and statistical network models; Section 3 formulates the problem and clarifies modeling assumptions; Section 4 proposes a set of latent space models for dynamic networks; Section 5 empirically evaluates the proposed models; Section 6 covers related work; and finally Section 7 concludes the paper.

2 BACKGROUND

2.1 POINT PROCESS MODELS

Point pattern data, consisting of the counts and locations of objects in some space, occur widely in the physical and social sciences. Our focus is on events occurring in time, so that the underlying space is the non-negative real line $\mathbb{R}_+$. We write realizations of such data as $\{N(t), t \geq 0\}$, where $N(t)$ is non-negative, integer, and non-decreasing, and gives the number of events occurring in the time interval $[0, t)$. The object $\{N(t), t \geq 0\}$ is sometimes called a counting measure, assigning to any interval $[s, t)$ a measure equal to the number of events in that interval. The special structure of the real line, as well as the causal nature of temporal dynamics have led to a variety of models for point process data on the real line. Two are particularly relevant to this paper:

Poisson Processes. The Poisson process is the canonical example of a point process. It is governed by a non-negative intensity (rate) function $\lambda(t)$, and has two properties: (*i*) for any $t > s$, the number of events within the time interval $[s, t)$, *i.e.*, $N(t) - N(s)$, follows a Poisson distribution with mean $\int_s^t \lambda(t)\,\mathrm{d}t$; and (*ii*) the number of events in disjoint time intervals are independent random variables. A Poisson process is homogeneous if its intensity function is constant ($\lambda(t) = \lambda$), otherwise it is referred to as non-homogeneous. If the intensity $\lambda(t)$ itself is random, then the point process is referred to as a Cox process (or a doubly-stochastic Poisson process).

Hawkes Processes. Hawkes processes have attracted much attention recently by capturing deviations from the Poisson process assumptions. Hawkes processes account for causality in the temporal dynamics of point pattern data by modeling self-excitation (when a single point process is involved), and mutual excitation or *reciprocity* (when collections of point processes are under study). The former is relevant to modeling individual activities over time (*e.g.*, hospital visits), while the latter is useful for modeling activities on communication networks (*e.g.*, email communications between members of an organization). In both examples, an initial event is often a trigger for a subsequent burst of activity.

Formally, a Hawkes process is a point process with conditional intensity function

$$\begin{aligned} \lambda(t|\mathcal{H}(t)) &= \gamma + \int_0^t \phi(t-s)\,\mathrm{d}N(s) \\ &= \gamma + \sum_{k:\, t_k < t} \phi(t - t_k) \end{aligned} \tag{1}$$

where $\mathcal{H}(t) = \{t_k : t_k < t\}$ consists of the event history at time t, γ is the base-rate, and $\phi(\cdot)$ is a *triggering* kernel that characterizes the excitatory effect that a past event has on the current event rate. For example, $\phi(\cdot)$ might be the exponential kernel $\phi(t) = \beta e^{-t/\tau}$, $t \geq 0$, implying that an event has an excitatory boost of magnitude β, which decays exponentially with a time scale τ. More generally, when we have m processes

$\{N_1(t), N_2(t), \cdots, N_m(t)\}$ that mutually excite one another, a multivariate Hawkes process has the conditional intensity of the j-th process given by

$$\lambda_j(t|\{\mathcal{H}_i(t)\}_{i=1}^m) = \gamma_j + \sum_{i=1}^{m} \int_0^t \phi_{ij}(t-s)\,\mathrm{d}N_i(s)\,.$$

Here $\mathcal{H}_i(t)$ denotes the event history associated with the i-th process $N_i(t)$ at time t; this consists of all events up to time t that are seen by process i.

We conclude with a technical remark. For any of these point processes, given a set of observed events $\{t_i\}_{i=1}^n$ in an interval $[0, T)$, the likelihood of a conditional intensity $\lambda(t)$ is given by

$$\mathcal{L}(\lambda(t)|\{t_i\}_{i=1}^n) = e^{-\Lambda(0,T)} \prod_{i=1}^{n} \lambda(t_i) \qquad (2)$$

where $\Lambda(0,T) = \int_0^T \lambda(t)\,\mathrm{d}t$ is the cumulative conditional intensity function. Different point process models make different independence assumptions about $\lambda(t)$.

2.2 STATISTICAL NETWORK MODELS

Graphs or networks, are useful representations of *relational* data natural to various physical, social, and informational domains. Mathematically, a graph G is written as $G = (V, E)$ where V is the set of vertices (nodes) and $E \subseteq V \times V$ is the set of edges (links). For example, in a network of individuals on a social media platform like Facebook, V represents users and E encodes undirected friendship relations. In a corporate email network, each node $v \in V$ might represent an employee in the corporation, and each edge (u, v), an email message sent from node u to node v. These two examples represent two different kinds of network data: static and dynamic.

Static Network Models. These models have a rich history, with proposed models including the Erdős-Rényi model (Erdős and Rényi, 1959), the preferential attachment model (Barabasi and Albert, 1999), the small-world model (Watts and Strogatz, 1998), the exponential random graph model (Holland and Leinhardt, 1981), and the stochastic blockmodel (Nowicki and Snijders, 2001), etc.

Of particular interest to us is the seminal work of Hoff et al. (2002), which models the probability p_{uv} of a link between two nodes u and v via a logistic regression model that depends on the observed features of nodes u and v, as well as the Euclidean distance $\|\mathbf{z}_u - \mathbf{z}_v\|_2$ between their *latent* features $\mathbf{z}_u, \mathbf{z}_v \in \mathbb{R}^d$. Young and Scheinerman (2007) proposed a similar model where the Euclidean distance $\|\mathbf{z}_u - \mathbf{z}_v\|_2$ is replaced by the dot-product $\mathbf{z}_u^\mathsf{T}\mathbf{z}_v$. An advantage of latent space models is that by estimating the latent features $\mathbf{z}_v$ for each node v, we obtain a mapping that *embeds* the nodes of the graph into a Euclidean space $\mathbb{R}^d$. Such an embedding is much more amenable to conventional statistical analysis.

Dynamic Network Models. In many real-world applications, the network structure evolves over time, and we have access to fine-grained *temporal* information describing the evolution of the network structure. For instance, new users join a social network like Facebook every day; additionally, existing users may be connected by newly forged friendships. Similarly, in a corporate email network, the server records the precise time-stamps of every message sent between every pair of nodes.

In contrast to the extensive literature on static networks, statistical models for dynamic networks are much less explored. Existing models (Sarkar and Moore, 2005; Miller et al., 2009; Fan and Shelton, 2009; Fu and Xing, 2009; Hanneke and Xing, 2010; Snijders et al., 2010; Durante and Dunson, 2014) typically assume that the available data contain a sequence of graph snapshots captured at discrete time-points, and that the network evolution follows Markov transition. Such approximations discard important information when one has exact time-stamps for each link event, and require modelers to choose a particular temporal resolution to study network dynamics. A much more natural approach is to merge ideas from point process modeling with network models.

3 PROBLEM DEFINITION

In this work, we develop and explore latent space models of dynamic network data. We consider network data with the following properties:

- There exists a fixed set of vertices $V = \{1, \ldots, n\}$ throughout an observation time period $[0, T)$.
- For each ordered pair of vertices (u, v), we observe a set of event-times, corresponding to a sequence of directed links or messages from u to v. We write the overall observed data as $\{(u, v, \mathcal{H}_{uv})\}_{u,v \in V}$, where $\mathcal{H}_{uv} \triangleq \{t_i^{uv}\}_{i=1}^{n_{uv}}$ records the set of all time-points at which u sent v a message. We write $n_{uv} \geq 0$ for the total number of messages from u to v.
- A node never sends a message to itself; and the granularity of measurements is fine enough that the probability of two simultaneous events is zero.

These properties naturally motivate a point process-based approach, and we model the arrival times $\{t_i^{uv}\}$ of each link from node u to v as realizations of a point process $N_{uv}(t)$, $t \in [0, T)$. The dynamic network evolving over time consists of $n^2 - n$ point processes $N_{uv}(t)$, which if treated as independent, involves $\mathcal{O}(n^2)$ parameters. Such an independence assumption however ignores important structure in the dynamics of the point processes. We assume two sources of dependency:

Static dependencies due to homophily, where baseline event rates vary between pairs of nodes because of shared features. Among other things, this accounts for the fact that the two processes $N_{uv}(t)$ and $N_{uw}(t)$ have a node u in common and therefore will share statistical properties. In general, homophily reflects how similarity in node-level properties (such as preferences, interests, and attitudes) affects link formation.

Dynamic interactions due to reciprocity, where activity between pairs of nodes is a function of previous history. At its simplest, this might account for reciprocity in communications between a pair of individuals. More generally, this accounts for how social influence, charisma, and the user-role affects the dynamics in a sequence of interactions. The nature of this reciprocation might depend on shared features between two nodes different from the features relevant to homophily.

Inspired by the work of Hoff et al. (2002), we model these phenomena by assigning to each node $v \in V$ a set of latent features. For the first effect, we write its feature vector as $\mathbf{z}_v \in \mathbb{R}^d$, and assume that the intensity function $\lambda_{uv}(t)$ underlying the process $N_{uv}(t)$ depends on the Euclidean distance between $\|\mathbf{z}_u - \mathbf{z}_v\|_2$. To account for the second effect, we cannot assume that $\lambda_{uv}(t)$ is fixed in time given these latent features, and instead must allow it to depend on previous network activity. This dependency will again be described by latent features associated with each node, but a different set which we write as $\mathbf{x}_v \in \mathbb{R}^d$.

While we do not explicitly assume the availability of any observed features for each node, they can be directly incorporated in our models by augmenting the $\mathbf{x}$- and $\mathbf{z}$-vectors. We also do not assume any additional information (such as message text or topic) for each link apart from its time-stamp, but we note that such information can be utilized by augmenting the hierarchical generative models with another level, as demonstrated in *e.g.*, He et al. (2015); Tan et al. (2016).

4 LATENT SPACE POINT PROCESS MODELS OF DYNAMIC NETWORKS

In this section we present a series of latent space point process models for dynamic network data. We begin with the most straightforward model that only captures homophily, and proceed through a sequence of models of increasing complexity.

4.1 POISSON LATENT SPACE MODEL

Perhaps the simplest latent space network point process model treats messages from a node u to v as a time-homogeneous Poisson process whose intensity is a function of the Euclidean distance between them in a latent feature space. In equations:

Poisson-rate Latent Space (PLS) Model

$$\mathbf{z}_v \sim \mathcal{N}(\mathbf{0}, \sigma^2 \mathbf{I}_{d\times d}) \qquad \forall v \in V$$

$$\lambda_{uv}(t) = \gamma\, e^{-\|\mathbf{z}_u - \mathbf{z}_v\|_2^2} \qquad \forall u \neq v$$

$$N_{uv}(\cdot) \sim \mathsf{PoissonProcess}(\lambda_{uv}(\cdot)) \qquad \forall u \neq v$$

Here, we have placed independent Gaussian priors on the latent features for each node, resulting in a collection of correlated doubly-stochastic Poisson processes. The parameter γ can be assigned a prior if we have node-level or edge-level covariates available, but for identifiability we tie the parameter across all pairs of nodes.

4.2 HAWKES LATENT SPACE MODELS

The remaining models augment the latent-space representation with additional non-Poissonian dynamics that capture reciprocity in communications across a network.

Hawkes Process Model. At its simplest, a node v is much more likely to send node u a message if u had just sent v a message earlier. To incorporate such reciprocity, the intensity function $\lambda_{uv}(t)$ governing the $N_{uv}(t)$ process can be modeled to depend on the events history of the reciprocal process $N_{vu}(t)$. Hawkes processes provide a simple mathematical tool to achieve this.

Specifically, for nodes $u, v \in V$, $u \neq v$, we model the pair of processes $N_{uv}(t)$ and $N_{vu}(t)$, as a bivariate Hawkes process, with intensity depending on the event histories, $\mathcal{H}_{uv} \triangleq \{t_i^{uv}\}_{i=1}^{n_{uv}}$ and $\mathcal{H}_{vu} \triangleq \{t_i^{vu}\}_{i=1}^{n_{vu}}$:

$$\lambda_{uv}(t|\mathcal{H}_{uv}, \mathcal{H}_{vu}) = \gamma_{uv} + \sum_{k:\, t_k^{vu} < t} \phi_{uv}(t - t_k^{vu}). \quad (3)$$

We have removed the self-excitation component since we do not consider self-loops in the network. Similar approaches have appeared in previous work (*e.g.*, Blundell et al. 2012), but we will comment on these in Section 6. While it is standard to parametrize the triggering function $\phi_{uv}(\cdot)$ as an exponential kernel with time scale τ, we found that learning τ suffered from identifiability issues. Instead, we model $\phi_{uv}(\cdot)$ as a weighted combination of basis kernels:

$$\phi_{uv}(t) = \sum_{b=1}^{B} \xi_b^{uv} \phi_b(t) \quad (4)$$

where ξ_b^{uv} is the weight of the kernel ϕ_b. We consider two possible forms for the basis kernel ϕ_b: (*i*) exponential kernels with length-scale τ, $\phi_b(t) = e^{-t/\tau}$; and (*ii*) locally periodic kernels with period p and length-scale τ, $\phi_b(t) = e^{-t/\tau} \sin^2\left(\frac{\pi t}{\tau}\right)$. In our experiments, we utilize kernels with time-scales of an hour, a day, and a week, which are interpretable and realistic for our applications.

We summarize the Hawkes process model below:

Hawkes Process (HP) Model

$$\lambda_{uv}(t) = \gamma + \sum_{k:\, t_k^{vu} < t} \sum_{b=1}^{B} \xi_b \, \phi_b(t - t_k^{vu}) \quad \forall u \neq v$$

$$N_{uv}(\cdot) \sim \mathsf{HawkesProcess}(\lambda_{uv}(\cdot)) \quad \forall u \neq v$$

We have again tied the parameters $\gamma_{uv} \equiv \gamma$ and $\xi_b^{uv} \equiv \xi_b$ across all node-pairs to avoid identifiability issues.

Hawkes Base-Rate Latent Space Model. The most straightforward way of modeling both homophily and reciprocity is to add the Hawkes triggering function term to the intensity functions of the previous PLS model:

Hawkes Base-Rate Latent Space (BLS) Model

$$\mathbf{z}_v \sim \mathcal{N}(\mathbf{0}, \sigma^2 \mathbf{I}_{d\times d}) \quad \forall v \in V$$

$$\lambda_{uv}(t) = \gamma \, e^{-\|\mathbf{z}_u - \mathbf{z}_v\|_2^2} + \sum_{k:\, t_k^{vu} < t} \sum_{b=1}^{B} \xi_b \, \phi_b(t - t_k^{vu}) \quad \forall u \neq v$$

$$N_{uv}(\cdot) \sim \mathsf{HawkesProcess}(\lambda_{uv}(\cdot)) \quad \forall u \neq v$$

Here, and with the Poisson-rate latent space model, we shall refer to the $\mathbf{z}$-space as the *homophily latent space*, with the distance between $\mathbf{z}_u$ and $\mathbf{z}_v$ reflecting how dissimilar u and v are, regardless of their communication history. This distance sets a baseline rate of communication between the two nodes—*i.e.*, the rate at which one node initiates communication with the other. The Hawkes component captures the fact that having initiated a new communication, subsequent messages in that thread will follow different dynamics.

Hawkes Reciprocal Latent Space Model. The previous model assumes heterogeneity only in the rate at which different node-pairs initiate communications, and the Hawkes dynamics are themselves assumed to be homogeneous across all pairs. Our next model modifies Eq. (3) to reverse this assumption, associating latent features with reciprocity rather than the base-rate:

Hawkes Reciprocal Latent Space (RLS) Model

$$\mathbf{x}_v \sim \mathcal{N}(\mathbf{0}, \sigma^2 \mathbf{I}_{d\times d}) \quad \forall v \in V$$

$$\lambda_{uv}(t) = \gamma + \sum_{k:\, t_k^{vu} < t} \sum_{b=1}^{B} \xi_b \, e^{-\|\mathbf{x}_u - \mathbf{x}_v\|_2^2} \, \phi_b(t - t_k^{vu})$$

$$N_{uv}(\cdot) \sim \mathsf{HawkesProcess}(\lambda_{uv}(\cdot)) \quad \forall u \neq v$$

We shall refer to the $\mathbf{x}$-space as the *reciprocal latent space*, since it modulates the magnitude of excitation triggered by each message between the pair of nodes.

Hawkes Dual Latent Space Model. As a final model, we combine the ideas of homophily and reciprocal latent spaces into a single model. Our final Hawkes process latent space model accounts for heterogeneity both in how two users initiate communications, as well as in the dynamics within a particular exchange. Using a mixture of exponential and periodic kernels with various length-scales, we can investigate whether a message sent from node u to v is more likely to trigger an immediate response, a response sometime over a week, or whether communications have a periodic nature.

Hawkes Dual Latent Space (DLS) Model

$$\mathbf{z}_v \sim \mathcal{N}(\mathbf{0}, \sigma^2 \mathbf{I}_{d\times d}) \quad \forall v \in V$$

$$\boldsymbol{\mu}_v \sim \mathcal{N}(\mathbf{0}, \sigma_\mu^2 \mathbf{I}_{d\times d}) \quad \forall v \in V$$

$$\boldsymbol{\varepsilon}_v^{(b)} \sim \mathcal{N}(\mathbf{0}, \sigma_\varepsilon^2 \mathbf{I}_{d\times d}) \quad \forall v \in V,\ b = 1, \ldots, B$$

$$\mathbf{x}_v^{(b)} \sim \boldsymbol{\mu}_v + \boldsymbol{\varepsilon}_v^{(b)} \quad \forall v \in V,\ b = 1, \ldots, B$$

$$\lambda_{uv}(t) = \gamma \, e^{-\|\mathbf{z}_u - \mathbf{z}_v\|_2^2} + \sum_{k:\, t_k^{vu} < t} \sum_{b=1}^{B} \beta \, e^{-\|\mathbf{x}_u^{(b)} - \mathbf{x}_v^{(b)}\|_2^2} \, \phi_b(t - t_k^{vu})$$

$$N_{uv}(\cdot) \sim \mathsf{HawkesProcess}(\lambda_{uv}(\cdot)) \quad \forall u \neq v$$

Notice that we have also placed a hierarchical prior on the B reciprocal latent spaces to enforce consistency between the learned latent features across different kernels.

4.3 INFERENCE

For all the models we have discussed, we perform maximum a posteriori (MAP) inference over the unknown parameters. Recall that we place independent standard Gaussian priors on the latent space vectors $\{\mathbf{z}_v\}_{v\in V}$ and $\{\mathbf{x}_v\}_{v\in V}$. Additionally, we place Gamma priors on the base rate γ and triggering magnitudes $\{\xi_b\}_{b=1}^{B}$ and β. Inference is tractable since it follows from Eq. (2) that the log-likelihood of all communications observed over the entire network $\{(u, v, \{t_i^{uv}\}_{i=1}^{n_{uv}})\}_{u,v\in V}$ can be written as

$$\log \mathcal{L} = \sum_{\substack{u,v=1 \\ u\neq v}}^{n} \left\{ -\Lambda_{uv}(0, T) + \sum_{i=1}^{n_{uv}} \log \lambda_{uv}(t_i^{uv}) \right\} \quad (5)$$

where the intensities $\lambda_{uv}(t)$ are specified for each model, and the cumulative intensities can be found in closed-form by noticing that for the basis kernel ϕ_b, we have

$$\int_0^T \sum_{k:\, t_k^{vu} < t} \phi_b(t - t_k^{vu}) \, \mathrm{d}t = \sum_{k=1}^{n_{vu}} \left[\Phi_b(T - t_k^{vu}) - \Phi_b(0) \right]$$

where $\Phi_b(t) \triangleq \int_0^t \phi_b(s)\, ds$. In fact, the right-hand side, as well as the quantities $\{\sum_{k:\, t_k^{vu} < t_i^{uv}} \phi_b(t_i^{uv} - t_k^{vu})\}_{i=1}^{n_{uv}}$ are data statistics that can be pre-computed and cached for each pair of nodes $u, v \in V$ and kernel ϕ_b. Furthermore, the gradients of the log-posterior function are also available in closed form, and the optimization can be carried out using L-BFGS-B (Byrd et al., 1995). Detailed calculations are provided in the supplementary material.

We conclude this section with a brief summary of the complexity of each proposed model. Assuming that the number of nodes n and the dimensionality of the latent spaces d are both much larger than the number of basis-kernels B, the HP model has $\mathcal{O}(B)$ parameters, while the PLS, BLS, and RLS models have $\mathcal{O}(n \cdot d)$ parameters, and the DLS model has $\mathcal{O}(n \cdot d \cdot B)$ parameters.

5 EXPERIMENTAL EVALUATION

In this section, we evaluate the proposed models of Section 4, both quantitatively and qualitatively, on three real-world datasets. For the quantitative component, we evaluate model performance across multiple tasks, including predictive log-likelihood, dynamic link prediction, and (static) link prediction using the learned embeddings. For the qualitative component, we visualize the learned network embeddings, and demonstrate how the reciprocal latent spaces in the DLS model can be used to characterize different reciprocation patterns.

Dataset Description. We perform experiments on three real-world communication networks:

ENRON This is the "core" network of the Enron email dataset (Klimmt and Yang, 2004) consisting of communications among 155 Enron executives. Each node represents an employee, while each link corresponds to an email message. We consider the period between January 2000 and April 2002, during which the vast majority of communications occurred. The resulting dataset contains 9,646 email messages spanning a period of 453 days.

EMAIL This dataset contains email communications within Purdue University from July 2011 to February 2012. Each node in the network represents an email address, while each link corresponds to an email message. We cleaned up this dataset by filtering out mailing-lists, and extracted the one hundred nodes with largest total degree. The resulting network consists of 34,438 email messages spanning a period of 237 days.

FACEBOOK This dataset contains Facebook wall messages among students of Purdue University from March 2007 to March 2008. Each node in the network represents an anonymized user account, and each link corresponds to a wall message. To focus on the "core" part of the network, we take a subset of the one hundred accounts with largest total degree. The resulting network consists of 18,865 wall messages posted over a period of 385 days.

Experiment Setup. For each network dataset, we sort the messages according to their timestamps, and split the dataset into a training set consisting of the first 70% messages, and a test set consisting of the remaining 30% messages. All models are trained on the training set, and all evaluation tasks are performed on the test set.

For all Hawkes process-based models (*cf.* Section 4.2), we utilize $B = 4$ basis kernels—three exponential kernels with length-scales one hour, one day, and one week, respectively: $\phi_1(t) = e^{-\frac{t}{1/24}}$, $\phi_2(t) = e^{-t}$, $\phi_3(t) = e^{-t/7}$; and a locally periodic kernel with both period and length-scale set to one week: $\phi_4(t) = e^{-t/7}\sin^2\left(\frac{\pi t}{7}\right)$ (all units are in days). For all latent space models, we set the dimensionality of the latent vectors to be $d = 100$.[1] For the BLS, RLS, and DLS models, we set $\sigma^2 = \sigma_\mu^2 = \sigma_\epsilon^2 = 1$. For MAP inference, we perform optimization using the L-BFGS-B solver in the SciPy package with analytical gradients derived for each model.

5.1 PREDICTIVE LOG-LIKELIHOOD

We learn the parameters of all models on the training set, and compute their predictive log-likelihood values on the test-set. From Table 1, we observe that the Hawkes process-based models significantly outperform the Poisson-rate latent space model (PLS), while the test log-likelihood values improve as we move from the base-rate latent space (BLS) and reciprocal latent space (RLS) models to the dual latent space (DLS) model. The DLS model also comfortably outperforms the Hawkes process (HP) model on two of the three datasets. For the Enron dataset, the simple HP model slightly outperforms the other models: we believe this is because the dataset is relatively unstructured, with pairwise reciprocity dominating most exchanges. Also notice that BLS outperforms PLS, which indicates that going beyond homogeneous Poisson processes to model reciprocity in the network indeed yields better predictive performance.

5.2 DYNAMIC LINK PREDICTION

We further gauge the performance of the learned models in a temporal link prediction task. Specifically, we randomly sample 100 time-points t_i during the test period, and ask every model to predict the probability that a link

[1] Since the DLS model contains one homophily latent space and four reciprocal latent spaces, one could argue that the latent spaces in the other models should be $(5\,d)$-dimensional. We experimented with setting $d = 500$ dimensions for all the other models, and obtained similar results to the $d = 100$ setting.

Table 1: Predictive log-likelihood.

Model	ENRON	EMAIL	FACEBOOK
HP	**-16226.155**	-2129.940	-7871.895
PLS	-37803.978	-112684.130	-66742.379
BLS	-21779.686	-9850.932	-12119.869
RLS	-16565.449	-2113.254	-7867.870
DLS	-16422.946	**185.264**	**-6421.609**

will appear between each pair of nodes in the $[t_i, t_i + \delta)$ time window (we set δ to be two weeks). Note that all models are equipped with parameters estimated from the training set, and for Hawkes process models we also condition on all the historical training and test events up to time t_i. For each time-point t_i, we then compute the area under the ROC curve (AUC) measured across all pairs of nodes according to the predicted probabilities given by each model.[2] Finally, we report the mean and standard deviations of the AUC scores across all 100 randomly sampled testing time-points in Table 2.

Table 2: Dynamic link prediction AUC scores.

Model	ENRON	EMAIL	FACEBOOK
HP	0.750 (0.070)	0.881 (0.088)	0.931 (0.095)
PLS	0.681 (0.041)	0.843 (0.087)	0.874 (0.078)
BLS	0.738 (0.065)	0.868 (0.095)	0.927 (0.096)
RLS	0.750 (0.070)	0.881 (0.088)	0.931 (0.095)
DLS	**0.928 (0.018)**	**0.971 (0.006)**	**0.979 (0.008)**

5.3 NETWORK EMBEDDING

As mentioned in Section 2.2, a major motivation for developing latent-space network models is that the learned latent feature vectors for each node effectively provide a mapping that embeds the observed network into Euclidean space. To evaluate the quality of the learned embeddings for each latent space model, we perform link prediction on the test set by collapsing the messages into a single undirected and unweighted graph, where there exists an edge between two nodes if at least one communication exists between them in the test set. Given the learned latent feature vectors $\{\mathbf{z}_v\}_{v \in V}$ (or $\{\mathbf{x}_v^{(b)}\}_{v \in V}$ for reciprocal latent spaces), we compute the predicted probability that an edge exists in the test graph via $p_{uv} \propto e^{-\|\mathbf{z}_u - \mathbf{z}_v\|_2^2}$, $\forall u, v \in V$, and then measure the link prediction AUC scores for all pairs of nodes.

In addition to the latent space models proposed in this work, we also compare with two popular approaches for embedding static networks:

Spectral Laplacian eigenmaps are widely used in spectral clustering (see *e.g.*, von Luxburg, 2007). Given the adjacency matrix $\mathbf{A}$ of the training network, we compute the d eigenvectors corresponding to the smallest eigenvalues of the symmetric normalized Laplacian $\mathbf{L}^{\mathsf{sym}} \triangleq \mathbf{I} - \mathbf{D}^{-1/2}\mathbf{A}\mathbf{D}^{-1/2}$, where $\mathbf{D}$ is a diagonal matrix of node degrees.

node2vec This is a state-of-the-art deep learning approach to learning continuous feature representations for networks (Grover and Leskovec, 2016).[3]

For both Laplacian eigenmaps and node2vec, we form an adjacency matrix of the training network $\mathbf{A}$ by collapsing the messages in the training set into an undirected graph with each edge weighted by the number of communications between the corresponding pair of nodes.[4] We set $d = 100$ for fair comparison.

Table 3 shows the obtained AUC scores, and Figure 1 plots the corresponding ROC curves. Shown alongside the ROC curves are two-dimensional projections (obtained using PCA) of the 100-dimensional latent spaces learned using each method. We observe that DLS performs on par with node2vec, and outperforms all other approaches in terms of AUC score.[5]

Table 3: Static link prediction AUC scores.

Model	ENRON	EMAIL	FACEBOOK
PLS	0.512	0.483	0.505
BLS	0.512	0.483	0.505
RLS	0.601	0.295	0.445
DLS	**0.906**	**0.958**	0.947
Spectral	0.687	0.428	0.452
node2vec	0.829	**0.958**	**0.956**

Homophily and Reciprocal Latent Spaces. For the DLS model, we found that the learned homophily latent spaces $\{\mathbf{z}_v\}_{v \in V}$ always perform much better than the reciprocal latent spaces $\{\{\mathbf{x}_v^{(b)}\}_{v \in V}\}_{b=1}^{B}$ under the static link prediction setup, as shown in the ROC curves for DLS-$\mathbf{z}$ and DLS-$\mathbf{x}^{(1)}$ in Figure 1.[6] Moreover, simply augmenting the homophily latent space with the reciprocal latent spaces actually leads to degraded performance in link prediction AUC. However, notice that the BLS model actually corresponds to a DLS model where

[2]The predicted probability of node u sending v at least one message during the time interval $[t, t + \delta)$ can be computed as $1 - \exp\{-\int_t^{t+\delta} \lambda_{uv}(s)\, \mathrm{d}s\}$.

[3]We utilize the publicly available implementation at `http://snap.stanford.edu/node2vec/`.

[4]For both Laplacian eigenmaps and node2vec, we have also experimented with treating the adjacency matrix $\mathbf{A}$ as binary (unweighted), but both methods exhibit degraded performance.

[4]For the DLS model, the homophily latent space is used.

[5]Notice that the current experiment setup does not yield standard errors for the AUC scores, since there is only a single training/test set split. To investigate the statistical significance of the results, we conducted a further experiment which showed that while DLS significantly outperforms node2vec on ENRON, their performance are comparable on EMAIL and FACEBOOK. See the supplementary material for details.

[6]The other reciprocal latent spaces exhibit similar performance, and we omit them from the plots to reduce clutter.

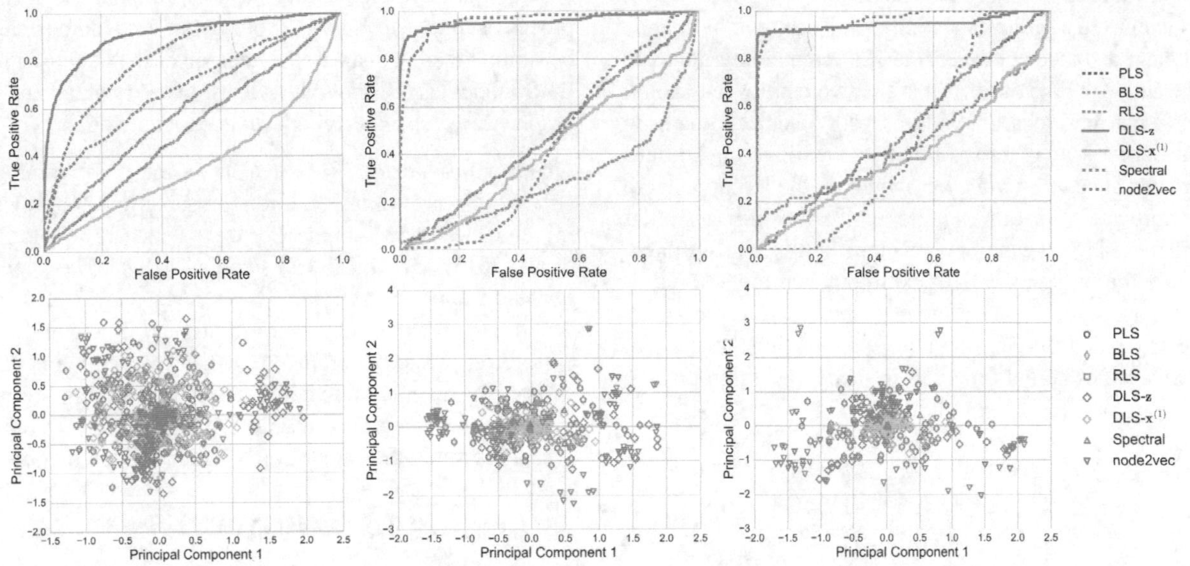

(a) Embedding (ENRON) (b) Embedding (EMAIL) (c) Embedding (FACEBOOK)

Figure 1: Link prediction ROC curves (top row) and visualization of the learned embeddings (bottom row).

we have removed the reciprocal latent spaces, and the BLS results show that in that case the learned homophily latent space performs quite poorly in link prediction as well. This indicates that the reciprocal latent spaces may have a *denoising* effect—*i.e.*, that it "explains away" communications primarily due to reciprocity such that the remaining communications arising from intensities with low reciprocal component has to be due to the fact that the pair of nodes are inherently similar in some way, which is modeled by the homophily latent features.

We further visualize the estimated homophily and reciprocal latent spaces of the DLS model by computing the pair-wise similarities $e^{-\|\mathbf{z}_u-\mathbf{z}_v\|_2^2}$ for every pair of nodes $u, v \in V$, and then plotting a heat-map of the inferred similarity matrices. For the ENRON dataset, Figure 2 shows the heat-maps (colors on log-scale) for both the homophily latent space and the reciprocal latent space corresponding to an hourly exponential kernel (ϕ_1).[7] For each similarity matrix, we performed hierarchical clustering on the rows to obtain a node-ordering and accordingly permuted the rows and columns of the matrix simultaneously. Notice that the similarity matrices exhibit distinct clustering block-structures, indicating that the user-interaction patterns are quite different across the homophily and reciprocal latent spaces.

5.4 EXPLORING RECIPROCATION PATTERNS

While the reciprocal latent spaces in the DLS model may not be directly useful in static link prediction, they do

[7] The complete set of heat-maps for the remaining reciprocal latent spaces as well as those for EMAIL and FACEBOOK are provided in the supplementary material.

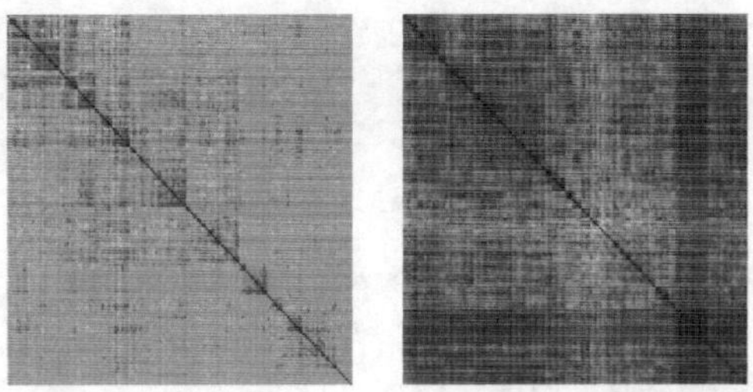

(a) $e^{-\|\mathbf{z}_u-\mathbf{z}_v\|_2^2}$ (b) $e^{-\|\mathbf{x}_u^{(1)}-\mathbf{x}_v^{(1)}\|_2^2}$

Figure 2: Inferred node-similarity matrices in ENRON.

offer a unique tool for examining the varying reciprocation patterns exhibited across different triggering kernels. Specifically, for each pair of nodes u and v, we can compute their *relative* similarities in the b-th kernel via

$$p_{uv}^{(b)} \triangleq \frac{e^{-\|\mathbf{x}_u^{(b)}-\mathbf{x}_v^{(b)}\|_2^2}}{\sum_{h=1}^{B} e^{-\|\mathbf{x}_u^{(h)}-\mathbf{x}_v^{(h)}\|_2^2}}, \quad b = 1, \ldots, B.$$

This allows us to embed each pair of nodes onto a probability simplex where each pair $u, v \in V$ is represented by a point $(p_{uv}^{(1)}, \ldots, p_{uv}^{(B)})^\mathsf{T}$. Note that this simplicial embedding is of a different nature than the latent spaces themselves—if two points are nearby on this simplex, it indicates that the two pairs of nodes exhibit similar relative behavior across the chosen kernels, regardless of the absolute intensities of their communications.

In Figure 3, we selected two nodes in the ENRON network, and for each node v we plot the simplicial embeddings of each pair (v, u), $\forall u \in V$.[8] Figure 3 also plots

[8] For visualization, we have collapsed the kernels ϕ_3 and ϕ_4

node v's total outgoing intensity $\lambda_v(t) \triangleq \sum_{w \in V} \lambda_{vw}(t)$ as well as histograms showing the distribution of the Euclidean distances between v and the remaining nodes in the network. We observe that the two employees exhibit different reciprocation patterns with other employees in the corporation in terms of their active triggering kernels. For instance, the employee shown on the left appears to reciprocate with other employees in much of a similar manner since the points are more tightly concentrated, while the one on the right exhibits much more variability. Also notice that different reciprocating kernels may be active at different time-points, motivating the need for a mixture of kernel functions in modeling reciprocity.

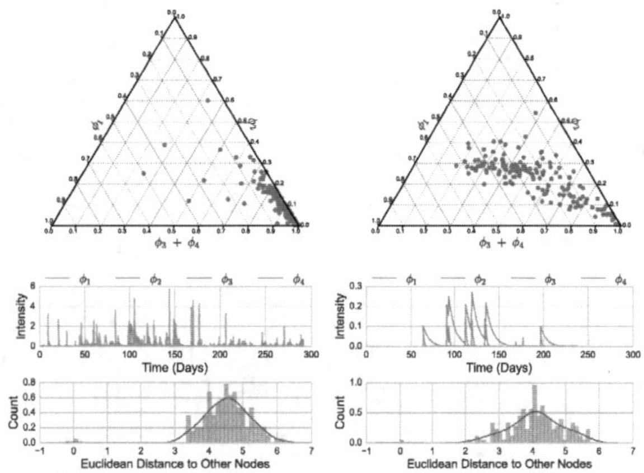

Figure 3: Visualizing reciprocation patterns in ENRON.

6 RELATED WORK

Point Processes. Recent work on point process models of structured temporal data include Simma and Jordan (2010); Perry and Wolfe (2013); DuBois et al. (2013); Guo et al. (2015); He et al. (2015); Farajtabar et al. (2015); Du et al. (2016); Tan et al. (2016). In Blundell et al. (2012), Hawkes processes were combined with the infinite relational model (Kemp et al., 2006) to perform nonparametric clustering of nodes. This forms a simplification to our models, with each node having a latent cluster index rather than a latent embedding. In this model, messages are observed by all nodes in a cluster rather than individual nodes, so that reciprocity operates at the cluster level. Blundell et al. (2012) also do not model heterogeneity in the reciprocating dynamics among users.

In Linderman and Adams (2014), the authors develop a framework that combines random graph priors on the latent network structure with a reciprocating point process observation model. This is roughly equivalent to our RLS model, which we use as a proxy for comparison to Linderman and Adams (2014). However, our focus is not on learning a latent network structure as much as on teasing apart complementary parts of an observed point process. Similar to Figure 2, our latent embeddings can be summarized with an associated graph; in this sense the DLS model can be thought to learn two complementary graph structures underlying events on a network.

Graph Embedding. Recent work in the graph mining community on learning feature representations for nodes in static networks include Perozzi et al. (2014); Tang et al. (2015); Grover and Leskovec (2016). The state-of-the-art approach is node2vec (Grover and Leskovec, 2016), which extends the skip-gram neural network architecture (Mikolov et al., 2013). Our experiments showed that by modeling both homophily and reciprocity in temporal interactions, the DLS model performs comparably or superior to node2vec in static link prediction.

7 CONCLUDING REMARKS

We have proposed latent space models for dynamic network data that embed the network nodes into Euclidean space. Our approach models heterogeneity across two important characteristics of such data—homophily and reciprocity—and connects latent space models of static networks to point process models including Poisson and Hawkes processes. The performance of our proposed dual latent space model shows that it is crucial to account for both characteristics to accurately model dynamic networks. In dynamic link prediction, we find that while the reciprocal latent space is important for accurate predictions, the inclusion of the homophily latent space produces a significant gain across all three real-world datasets. In static link prediction, while the reciprocal latent spaces are not directly useful for prediction, they greatly improve the quality of the estimated homophily latent space, by providing a denoising effect that filters out communications driven primarily by reciprocity.

Our findings shed further light on recent observations in Rudolph et al. (2016), who argue that modeling each observation *conditioned* on a set of other observations improves the quality of the learned embeddings. They refer to the conditioning set as *context* (*e.g.* in natural language the context of a word is its surrounding words). Similarly, one might argue the context of a node in a network is its neighbors. Including reciprocal latent spaces in the model implicitly conditions on the set of reciprocating neighbors, and including homophily latent spaces implicitly conditions on the set of similar neighbors.

Acknowledgements

We thank Shandian Zhe for helpful discussions and the anonymous reviewers for their feedback. This research is supported by NSF under contract numbers IIS-1149789, IIS-1546488, and IIS-1618690.

onto the same axis since they both have length-scale one week.

References

A. Barabasi and R. Albert. Emergence of scaling in random networks. *Science*, 286:509–512, 1999.

C. Blundell, K. Heller, and J. Beck. Modelling reciprocating relationships with Hawkes processes. In *NIPS*, 2012.

R. H. Byrd, P. Lu, J. Nocedal, and C. Zhu. A limited memory algorithm for bound constrained optimization. *SIAM J. Sci. Comput.*, 16(5):1190–1208, 1995.

N. Du, H. Dai, R. Trivedi, U. Upadhyay, M. Gomez-Rodriguez, and L. Song. Recurrent marked temporal point processes: Embedding event history to vector. In *KDD*, 2016.

C. DuBois, C. Butts, and P. Smyth. Stochastic blockmodeling of relational event dynamics. In *AISTATS*, 2013.

D. Durante and D. Dunson. Nonparametric bayes dynamic modelling of relational data. *Biometrika*, 101 (4):883, 2014.

P. Ekeh. *Social exchange theory: The two traditions*. Heinemann London, 1974.

P. Erdős and A. Rényi. On random graphs, I. *Publicationes Mathematicae*, 6:290–297, 1959.

Y. Fan and C. R. Shelton. Learning continuous-time social network dynamics. In *UAI*, 2009.

M. Farajtabar, Y. Wang, M. Gomez-Rodriguez, S. Li, H. Zha, and L. Song. COEVOLVE: A joint point process model for information diffusion and network coevolution. In *NIPS*, 2015.

W. Fu and E. Xing. Dynamic mixed membership blockmodel for evolving networks. In *ICML*, 2009.

A. Grover and J. Leskovec. node2vec: Scalable feature learning for networks. In *KDD*, 2016.

F. Guo, C. Blundell, H. Wallach, and K. Heller. The Bayesian echo chamber: Modeling social influence via linguistic accommodation. In *AISTATS*, 2015.

S. Hanneke and E. Xing. Discrete temporal models of social networks. *Electron. J. Stat.*, 4:585–605, 2010.

X. He, T. Rekatsinas, J. Foulds, L. Getoor, and Y. Liu. Hawkestopic: A joint model for network inference and topic modeling from text-based cascades. In *ICML*, 2015.

P. Hoff, A. Raftery, and M. Handcock. Latent space approaches to social network analysis. *J. Am. Stat. Assoc.*, 97(460):1090–1098, 2002.

P. Holland and S. Leinhardt. An exponential family of probability distributions for directed graphs. *J. Am. Stat. Assoc.*, 76:33–50, 1981.

T. Iwata, A. Shah, and Z. Ghahramani. Discovering latent influence in online social activities via shared cascade Poisson processes. In *KDD*, 2013.

C. Kemp, J. Tenenbaum, and T. Griffiths. Learning systems of concepts with an infinite relational model. In *AAAI*, 2006.

B. Klimmt and Y. Yang. Introducing the enron corpus. In *CEAS*, 2004.

S. Linderman and R. Adams. Discovering latent network structure in point process data. In *ICML*, 2014.

M. McPherson, L. Smith-Lovin, and J. Cook. Birds of a feather: Homophily in social networks. *Annu. Rev. Sociol.*, 27(1):415–444, 2001.

T. Mikolov, I. Sutskever, K. Chen, G. Corrado, and J. Dean. Distributed representations of words and phrases and their compositionality. In *NIPS*, 2013.

K. Miller, T. Griffiths, and M. Jordan. Nonparametric latent feature models for link prediction. In *NIPS*, 2009.

B. Min, K. Goh, and A. Vazquez. Spreading dynamics following bursty human activity patterns. *Phys. Rev. E*, 83(3):036102, 2011.

K. Nowicki and T. Snijders. Estimation and prediction for stochastic blockstructures. *J. Am. Stat. Assoc.*, 96: 1077–1087, 2001.

B. Perozzi, R. Al-Rfou, and S. Skiena. DeepWalk: Online learning of social representations. In *KDD*, 2014.

P. Perry and P. Wolfe. Point process modelling for directed interaction networks. *J. R. Stat. Soc. Ser. B*, 2013.

M. Rudolph, F. Ruiz, S. Mandt, and D. Blei. Exponential family embeddings. In *NIPS*, 2016.

P. Sarkar and A. Moore. Dynamic social network analysis using latent space models. In *NIPS*, 2005.

A. Simma and M. Jordan. Modeling events with cascades of Poisson processes. In *UAI*, 2010.

T. Snijders, G. van de Bunt, and C. Steglich. Introduction to stochastic actor-based models for network dynamics. *Social Networks*, 32(1):44–60, 2010.

X. Tan, S. Naqvi, A. Qi, K. Heller, and V. Rao. Content-based modeling of reciprocal relationships using Hawkes and Gaussian processes. In *UAI*, 2016.

J. Tang, M. Qu, M. Wang, M. Zhang, J. Yan, and Q. Mei. LINE: Large-scale information network embedding. In *WWW*, 2015.

U. von Luxburg. A tutorial on spectral clustering. *Stat. Comput.*, 17(4):395–416, 2007.

D. Watts and S. Strogatz. Collective dynamics of 'small-world' networks. *Nature*, 393:440–42, 1998.

S. Young and E. Scheinerman. Random dot product graph models for social networks. In *WAW*, 2007.

A SUPPLEMENTARY MATERIAL

A.1 MAP ESTIMATION DETAILS

As described in Section 4.3, we perform maximum a posteriori (MAP) inference to estimate the parameters in all the discussed models. In this section, we present the MAP estimation details for the HP and DLS models by deriving the closed form expressions of the log-posterior function and its gradients; the optimization can then be carried out using L-BFGS-B (Byrd et al., 1995). The derivations for the PLS, BLS, RLS models follow analogously, since they can all be viewed as degenerate cases of the DLS model.

Before presenting the MAP estimation details, recall that the observed data $\{(u, v, \mathcal{H}_{uv})\}_{u,v \in V}$ are collected over a time period $[0, T)$, where $\mathcal{H}_{uv} \triangleq \{t_i^{uv}\}_{i=1}^{n_{uv}}$ records the set of all time-points at which u sent v a message.

A.1.1 Hawkes Process (HP) Model

Recall the Hawkes Process (HP) model:

$$\lambda_{uv}(t) = \gamma + \sum_{k:\, t_k^{vu} < t} \sum_{b=1}^{B} \xi_b \, \phi_b(t - t_k^{vu}) \qquad \forall u \neq v$$

$$N_{uv}(\cdot) \sim \mathsf{HawkesProcess}(\lambda_{uv}(\cdot)) \qquad \forall u \neq v$$

Notice that

$$\Lambda_{uv}(0, T) = \int_0^T \lambda_{uv}(t)\, \mathrm{d}t = \gamma T + \sum_{b=1}^{B} \xi_b \sum_{k=1}^{n_{vu}} [\Phi_b(T - t_k^{vu}) - \Phi_b(0)]$$

where $\Phi_b(t) \triangleq \int_0^t \phi_b(s)\, \mathrm{d}s$.

Placing $\mathsf{Gamma}(1, 1)$ priors on γ and each ξ_b, and denoting $\boldsymbol{\xi} \triangleq \{\xi_b\}_{b=1}^{B}$, the joint density can be written as

$$p(\{\mathcal{H}_{uv}\}_{u,v=1}^{n}, \gamma, \boldsymbol{\xi}) \propto \prod_{\substack{u,v=1 \\ u \neq v}}^{n} \left\{ e^{-\Lambda_{uv}(0,T)} \prod_{k=1}^{n_{uv}} \lambda_{uv}(t_i^{uv}) \cdot e^{-\gamma} \cdot \prod_{b=1}^{B} e^{-\xi_b} \right\}$$

and the log-posterior function is given by

$$\begin{aligned} \log p(\gamma, \boldsymbol{\xi} \,|\, \{\mathcal{H}_{uv}\}_{u,v=1}^{n}) &= \sum_{\substack{u,v=1 \\ u \neq v}}^{n} \left\{ -\Lambda_{uv}(0, T) + \sum_{i=1}^{n_{uv}} \log \lambda_{uv}(t_i^{uv}) \right\} - \gamma - \sum_{b=1}^{B} \xi_b \\ &= \sum_{\substack{u,v=1 \\ u \neq v}}^{n} \left\{ -\gamma T - \sum_{b=1}^{B} \xi_b \, \Delta_{b,T}^{vu} + \sum_{i=1}^{n_{uv}} \log \left(\gamma + \sum_{b=1}^{B} \xi_b \, \delta_{b,i}^{uv} \right) \right\} - \gamma - \sum_{b=1}^{B} \xi_b \end{aligned}$$

where $\langle \cdot, \cdot \rangle$ denotes the Euclidean inner-product, and we have adopted the shorthand notations

$$\Delta_{b,T}^{vu} \triangleq \sum_{k=1}^{n_{vu}} [\Phi_b(T - t_k^{vu}) - \Phi_b(0)]$$

$$\delta_{b,i}^{uv} \triangleq \sum_{k:\, t_k^{vu} < t_i^{uv}} \phi_b(t_i^{uv} - t_k^{vu})$$

to denote data statistics that can be pre-computed and cached for each pair of nodes $u, v \in V$ and kernel ϕ_b.

The gradients of the log-posterior are given by

$$\frac{\partial \log p}{\partial \gamma} = -\,(n^2 - n)\,T + \sum_{\substack{u,v=1 \\ u \neq v}}^{n} \sum_{i=1}^{n_{uv}} \left(\gamma + \sum_{b=1}^{B} \xi_b\, \delta_{b,i}^{uv} \right)^{-1} - 1$$

$$\frac{\partial \log p}{\partial \xi_b} = \sum_{\substack{u,v=1 \\ u \neq v}}^{n} \left[-\Delta_{b,T}^{vu} + \sum_{i=1}^{n_{uv}} \delta_{b,i}^{uv} \left(\gamma + \sum_{b=1}^{B} \xi_b\, \delta_{b,i}^{uv} \right)^{-1} \right] - 1\,.$$

A.1.2 Hawkes Dual Latent Space (DLS) Model

Recall the Hawkes Dual Latent Space (DLS) model:

$$\begin{aligned}
\mathbf{z}_v &\sim \mathcal{N}(\mathbf{0}, \sigma^2\, \mathbf{I}_{d\times d}) && \forall v \in V \\
\boldsymbol{\mu}_v &\sim \mathcal{N}(\mathbf{0}, \sigma_\mu^2\, \mathbf{I}_{d\times d}) && \forall v \in V \\
\boldsymbol{\varepsilon}_v^{(b)} &\sim \mathcal{N}(\mathbf{0}, \sigma_\varepsilon^2\, \mathbf{I}_{d\times d}) && \forall v \in V,\ b = 1, \ldots, B \\
\mathbf{x}_v^{(b)} &\sim \boldsymbol{\mu}_v + \boldsymbol{\varepsilon}_v^{(b)} && \forall v \in V,\ b = 1, \ldots, B
\end{aligned}$$

$$\lambda_{uv}(t) = \gamma\, e^{-\|\mathbf{z}_u - \mathbf{z}_v\|_2^2} + \sum_{k:\, t_k^{vu} < t} \sum_{b=1}^{B} \beta\, e^{-\|\mathbf{x}_u^{(b)} - \mathbf{x}_v^{(b)}\|_2^2}\, \phi_b(t - t_k^{vu})$$

$$N_{uv}(\cdot) \sim \mathsf{HawkesProcess}(\lambda_{uv}(\cdot)) \qquad \forall u \neq v$$

Placing $\mathsf{Gamma}(1,1)$ priors on γ and β, setting $\sigma^2 = \sigma_\mu^2 = \sigma_\varepsilon^2 = 1$, and integrating out $\{\boldsymbol{\mu}_v\}_{v=1}^n$, the log-density function can be written as

$$\begin{aligned}
&\log p(\gamma, \beta, \{\mathbf{z}_v\}_{v=1}^n, \{\{\mathbf{x}_v^{(b)}\}_{b=1}^B\}_{v=1}^n \,|\, \{\mathcal{H}_{uv}\}_{u,v=1}^n) \\
&= \sum_{\substack{u,v=1 \\ u \neq v}}^{n} \left\{ -\gamma\, e^{-\|\mathbf{z}_u - \mathbf{z}_v\|_2^2}\, T - \beta \sum_{b=1}^{B} \Delta_{b,T}^{vu}\, e^{-\|\mathbf{x}_u^{(b)} - \mathbf{x}_v^{(b)}\|_2^2} + \sum_{i=1}^{n_{uv}} \log \left(\gamma\, e^{-\|\mathbf{z}_u - \mathbf{z}_v\|_2^2} + \beta \sum_{b=1}^{B} \delta_{b,i}^{uv}\, e^{-\|\mathbf{x}_u^{(b)} - \mathbf{x}_v^{(b)}\|_2^2} \right) \right\} \\
&\quad - \frac{1}{2} \sum_{v=1}^{n} \sum_{b=1}^{B} \|\mathbf{x}_v^{(b)}\|_2^2 + \frac{B^2}{2\,(B+1)} \sum_{v=1}^{n} \|\bar{\mathbf{x}}_v\|_2^2 - \frac{1}{2} \sum_{v=1}^{n} \|\mathbf{z}_v\|_2^2 - \gamma - \beta
\end{aligned}$$

where $\bar{\mathbf{x}}_v \triangleq \frac{1}{B} \sum_{b=1}^{B} \mathbf{x}_v^{(b)}$ denotes the mean latent position of node v across all basis-kernels.

The gradients of the log-posterior are given by

$$\frac{\partial \log p}{\partial \gamma} = \sum_{\substack{u,v=1 \\ u \neq v}}^{n} \left[-T\, e^{-\|\mathbf{z}_u - \mathbf{z}_v\|_2^2} + \sum_{i=1}^{n_{uv}} e^{-\|\mathbf{z}_u - \mathbf{z}_v\|_2^2}\, h^{-1}(u,v,i) \right] - 1$$

$$\frac{\partial \log p}{\partial \beta} = \sum_{\substack{u,v=1 \\ u \neq v}}^{n} \sum_{b=1}^{B} r(u,v,b)\, e^{-\|\mathbf{x}_u^{(b)} - \mathbf{x}_v^{(b)}\|_2^2} - 1$$

$$\nabla_{\mathbf{z}_v} \log p = \sum_{\substack{u=1 \\ u \neq v}}^{n} \left\{ \gamma \left[-2T + \sum_{i=1}^{n_{uv}} \left(h^{-1}(u,v,i) + h^{-1}(v,u,i) \right) \right] e^{-\|\mathbf{z}_u - \mathbf{z}_v\|_2^2} \cdot 2\,(\mathbf{z}_u - \mathbf{z}_v) \right\} - \mathbf{z}_v$$

$$\nabla_{\mathbf{x}_v^{(b)}} \log p = \sum_{\substack{u=1 \\ u \neq v}}^{n} \left\{ \beta\, [r(u,v,b) + r(v,u,b)]\, e^{-\|\mathbf{x}_u^{(b)} - \mathbf{x}_v^{(b)}\|_2^2} \cdot 2\,(\mathbf{x}_v^{(b)} - \mathbf{x}_u^{(b)}) \right\} - \mathbf{x}_v^{(b)} + \frac{B}{B+1} \cdot \bar{\mathbf{x}}_v$$

where

$$h(u,v,i) \triangleq \gamma\, e^{-\|\mathbf{z}_u-\mathbf{z}_v\|_2^2} + \beta \sum_{b=1}^{B} \delta_{b,i}^{uv}\, e^{-\|\mathbf{x}_u^{(b)}-\mathbf{x}_v^{(b)}\|_2^2}$$

$$r(u,v,b) \triangleq -\Delta_{b,T}^{vu} + \sum_{i=1}^{n_{uv}} \delta_{b,i}^{uv}\, h^{-1}(u,v,i)\,.$$

A.2 ADDITIONAL EXPERIMENT RESULTS

A.2.1 Further Experiment on Static Link Prediction

In Section 5.3, we noted that the experiment setup for the static link prediction task did not yield standard errors for the AUC scores reported in Table 3, since there was only one training/test split. To investigate the statistical significance of the results, we conducted a follow-up experiment.

For each dataset, we computed confidence intervals by performing six trials on subsets of the data. Specifically, in the i-th trial, we let the training set to contain all events during the period between the $\lceil \frac{i-1}{10} \rceil$-th and the $\lfloor \frac{i+2}{10} \rfloor$-th event, and the test set to contain all events during the period between the $\lceil \frac{i+2}{10} \rceil$-th and $\lfloor \frac{i+4}{10} \rfloor$-th event. In this way, each trial used 30% training data and 20% test data, with the training and test data being non-overlapping.[9] As in Section 5.3, we fitted the model on the training set, and performed link prediction on the test set. The results are shown in Table 4.[10]

Table 4: Static link prediction AUC scores and standard deviations.

Model	ENRON	EMAIL	FACEBOOK
PLS	0.510 (0.009)	0.496 (0.015)	0.491 (0.013)
BLS	0.510 (0.009)	0.496 (0.015)	0.491 (0.013)
RLS	0.439 (0.073)	0.386 (0.081)	0.456 (0.055)
DLS	**0.864 (0.016)**	**0.934 (0.016)**	**0.892 (0.040)**
Spectral	0.516 (0.020)	0.526 (0.032)	0.492 (0.021)
node2vec	0.749 (0.050)	**0.953 (0.007)**	**0.935 (0.033)**

By conducting two-sided t-tests at the 95% confidence level, we conclude that while DLS significantly outperforms node2vec on ENRON, their performance differences on EMAIL and FACEBOOK are not significant.

A.2.2 Visualization of the Inferred Node-Similarity Matrices

We visualize the estimated homophily and reciprocal latent spaces of the DLS model by computing the pair-wise similarities $e^{-\|\mathbf{z}_u-\mathbf{z}_v\|_2^2}$ for every pair of nodes $u, v \in V$, and then plotting a heat-map of the inferred similarity matrices. Figures 4, 5, and 6 show the heat-maps (colors on log-scale) for both the homophily latent space and the reciprocal latent spaces corresponding to the hourly (ϕ_1), daily (ϕ_2), weekly (ϕ_3) exponential kernels and the weekly locally periodic kernel (ϕ_4) on all three datasets. For each similarity matrix, we performed hierarchical clustering on the rows to obtain a node-ordering and accordingly permuted the rows and columns of the matrix simultaneously. Notice that the similarity matrices exhibit different clustering block-structures, indicating that the user-interaction patterns are quite different across the homophily and reciprocal latent spaces with different kernels and time-scales.

[9] Notice, however, that the training/test data across different trials may share common observations. Thus, strictly speaking, the trials are not independent, and the computed standard error estimates might under-estimate the "true" associated uncertainty.

[10] Note that the overall performance for all methods are slightly degraded since we are only using subsets of the data.

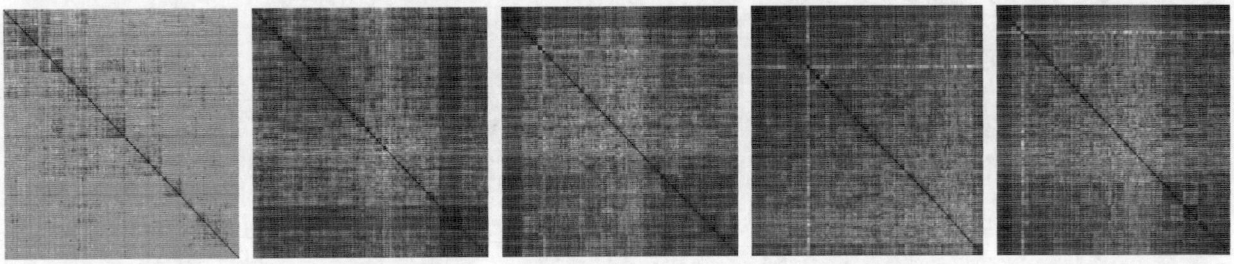

(a) $e^{-\|\mathbf{z}_u-\mathbf{z}_v\|_2^2}$ (b) $e^{-\|\mathbf{x}_u^{(1)}-\mathbf{x}_v^{(1)}\|_2^2}$ (c) $e^{-\|\mathbf{x}_u^{(2)}-\mathbf{x}_v^{(2)}\|_2^2}$ (d) $e^{-\|\mathbf{x}_u^{(3)}-\mathbf{x}_v^{(3)}\|_2^2}$ (e) $e^{-\|\mathbf{x}_u^{(4)}-\mathbf{x}_v^{(4)}\|_2^2}$

Figure 4: Inferred node-similarity matrices in ENRON.

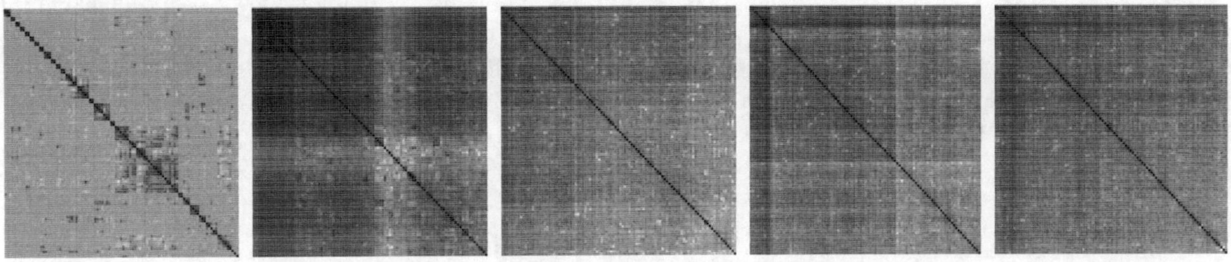

(a) $e^{-\|\mathbf{z}_u-\mathbf{z}_v\|_2^2}$ (b) $e^{-\|\mathbf{x}_u^{(1)}-\mathbf{x}_v^{(1)}\|_2^2}$ (c) $e^{-\|\mathbf{x}_u^{(2)}-\mathbf{x}_v^{(2)}\|_2^2}$ (d) $e^{-\|\mathbf{x}_u^{(3)}-\mathbf{x}_v^{(3)}\|_2^2}$ (e) $e^{-\|\mathbf{x}_u^{(4)}-\mathbf{x}_v^{(4)}\|_2^2}$

Figure 5: Inferred node-similarity matrices in EMAIL.

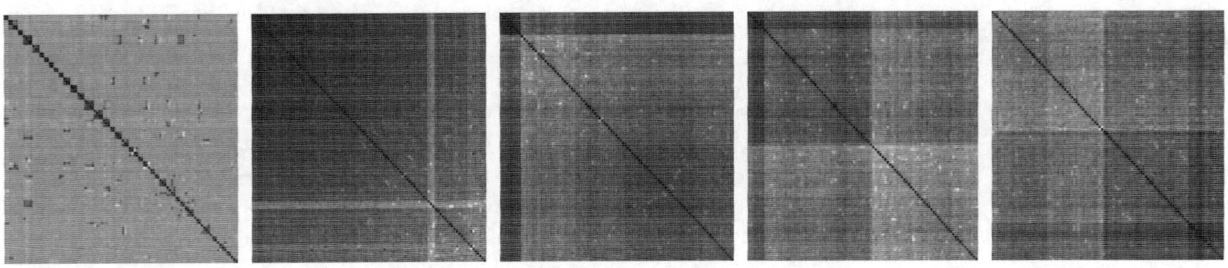

(a) $e^{-\|\mathbf{z}_u-\mathbf{z}_v\|_2^2}$ (b) $e^{-\|\mathbf{x}_u^{(1)}-\mathbf{x}_v^{(1)}\|_2^2}$ (c) $e^{-\|\mathbf{x}_u^{(2)}-\mathbf{x}_v^{(2)}\|_2^2}$ (d) $e^{-\|\mathbf{x}_u^{(3)}-\mathbf{x}_v^{(3)}\|_2^2}$ (e) $e^{-\|\mathbf{x}_u^{(4)}-\mathbf{x}_v^{(4)}\|_2^2}$

Figure 6: Inferred node-similarity matrices in FACEBOOK.

Online Constrained Model-based Reinforcement Learning

Benjamin van Niekerk
School of Computer Science
University of the Witwatersrand
South Africa

Andreas Damianou*
Amazon.com
Cambridge, UK

Benjamin Rosman
Council for Scientific and Industrial Research,
and School of Computer Science
University of the Witwatersrand
South Africa

Abstract

Applying reinforcement learning to robotic systems poses a number of challenging problems. A key requirement is the ability to handle continuous state and action spaces while remaining within a limited time and resource budget. Additionally, for safe operation, the system must make robust decisions under hard constraints. To address these challenges, we propose a model based approach that combines Gaussian Process regression and Receding Horizon Control. Using sparse spectrum Gaussian Processes, we extend previous work by updating the dynamics model incrementally from a stream of sensory data. This results in an agent that can learn and plan in real-time under non-linear constraints. We test our approach on a cart pole swing-up environment and demonstrate the benefits of online learning on an autonomous racing task. The environment's dynamics are learned from limited training data and can be reused in new task instances without retraining.

1 INTRODUCTION

Reinforcement learning has become an important approach to the planning and control of autonomous agents in complex environments. However, recent interest in reinforcement learning is yet to be reflected in robotics applications; possibly due to their specific challenges.

In robotic systems, reinforcement learning methods must deal with continuous, and potentially high-dimensional, state and control spaces. For example, the dynamics of autonomous vehicles are most naturally described in terms of continuous variables like position, velocity, orientation and steering angle. Data efficiency is also critical since collecting experience, or evaluating control policies, with a robot in the loop can be costly and time consuming. Poorly modeled dynamics, due to a slow learning rate, may result in unstable trajectories and dangerous collisions. The system also needs to handle physical constraints — from joint and actuator limitations to the boundaries defined by obstacles. Finally, in fast-paced applications rapid decisions, requiring real-time planning, must be made.

In this paper we propose a method which tackles all of the above challenges simultaneously. Our method achieves this through the marriage of two key components:

1. a learned dynamics model based on sparse spectrum Gaussian processes (GPs), and
2. a planner based on receding horizon control (RHC), and the structure exploiting interior point solver FORCES (Domahidi and Jerez, 2014).

Sparse spectrum GPs allow us to update the learned model online and the RHC framework provides the ability plan in real-time while naturally handling constraints. This means that we can learn and plan online in constrained environments where data collection is expensive. We believe that these are important features for real world applications of reinforcement learning, particularly in safety critical systems. Our proposed method will be referred to as Gaussian Process-Receding Horizon Control (GP-RHC hereafter).

The remainder of the paper is structured as follows. In section 2 we provide an overview of related approaches in model-based reinforcement learning. The receding horizon control framework is presented in section 3. This is followed, in section 4, by a discussion on the application of Gaussian process regression to model learning.

*Work done while this author was at the University of Sheffield.

In section 5 we apply GP-RHC to a cart pole swing-up environment and a challenging autonomous racing task. The results demonstrate that (a) models can be learned quickly from limited data, (b) complex non-linear constraints can be handled in real-time, and (c) online updates improve the rate of learning and result in more consistent performance.

2 RELATED WORK

GP-RHC falls into the class of model-based reinforcement learning methods. These are generally the methods of choice in robotics primarily due to their impressive data efficiency (Kober et al., 2013). Model-based approaches can be broadly classified according to (a) how the dynamics model is learned and, (b) the choice of planner.

PILCO (Deisenroth and Rasmussen, 2011), for example, combines policy search for planning with a Gaussian process model of the dynamics. The policy search relies on analytic gradients of closed form solutions to the long term expected cost. This requires the cost function and policy to take specific functional forms, making it difficult or impossible to incorporate general constraints. In a similar vein, Kim et al. (2004) use policy search with locally weighted linear regression to learn a controller for helicopter flight.

As an alternative, trajectory optimization based on differential dynamic programming is often used for planning. Methods such as PDDP (Pan and Theodorou, 2014) and AGP-iLQR (Boedecker et al., 2014) make use of this idea by combining dynamics models learned by locally weighted projection regression with either an iterative linear quadratic regulator or Gaussian as the planner. These planners can take simple box constraints into account but cannot handle general non-linear constraints.

Our work is most closely related to the RL-RCO method (Andersson et al., 2015) which leverages sparse Gaussian processes for learning the dynamics and trajectory optimization based sequential quadratic programming. We improve upon RL-RCO by proposing an approach which allows the dynamics model to be updated online as the agent interacts with the environment. Furthermore, in contrast to the work of Andersson et al. (2015), we present results that highlight the ability to handle non-linear constraints.

We show how these enhancements improve data efficiency, learning rate and constraint handling, rendering GP-RHC overall more applicable to realistic scenarios.

3 RECEDING HORIZON CONTROL

In this paper, we consider an agent operating in a continuous environment described by a set of differential equations, $\dot{\mathbf{x}} = \mathbf{f}(\mathbf{x}, \mathbf{u})$, where $\mathbf{x} \in \mathbb{R}^n$ represents the agent's state and $\mathbf{u} \in \mathbb{R}^m$ the control signal. The objective of the agent is to select a control $\mathbf{u}$ to minimize a cost function (1a), while conforming to the system dynamics, and additional constraints (1b)-(1d).

We address this overall problem using receding horizon control where the idea is to plan over a finite horizon by iteratively solving an optimization problem. Given a measurement of the current state $\hat{\mathbf{x}}_0$, a trajectory through the state-control space is calculated, and the first step of the control signal is applied to the system. The horizon is then shifted forward and the process repeats. Formally, at each time step the agent must minimize the cost function

$$J(\mathbf{x}_0) = h(\mathbf{x}(t_0+T)) + \int_{t_0}^{t_0+T} \mathcal{L}(\mathbf{x}(t), \mathbf{u}(t))dt, \quad \text{(1a)}$$

where t_0 is the current time, T denotes the length of the planning horizon, $\mathcal{L}$ is an intermediate cost function and h is a terminal cost function. In order to ensure that the trajectory is feasible, the optimization is subject to the constraints:

$$\begin{aligned}
&\mathbf{x}(t_0) = \hat{\mathbf{x}}_0, \\
&\dot{\mathbf{x}}(t) = \mathbf{f}(\mathbf{x}(t), \mathbf{u}(t)), \\
&\underline{\mathbf{u}} \leq \mathbf{u}(t) \leq \overline{\mathbf{u}}, && \text{(1b)} \\
&\underline{\mathbf{x}} \leq \mathbf{x}(t) \leq \overline{\mathbf{x}}, && \text{(1c)} \\
&\mathbf{g}(\mathbf{x}(t), \mathbf{u}(t)) \leq \mathbf{0}, && \text{(1d)} \\
&\text{for all } t \text{ in } [t_0, t_0+T] \,.
\end{aligned}$$

Inequalities (1b) and (1c) specify box constraints on the control and state spaces (described by upper and lower bounds), and can represent operational limits on actuators or joints. On the other hand, (1d) can express non-linear, non-convex constraints through the function $\mathbf{g}$. This can be used, for example, to define road boundaries or obstacles in an autonomous driving task.

The receding horizon formulation differs from other reinforcement learning approaches in a few important ways. First, instead of explicitly maintaining a representation of a policy or value function, the control is recalculated (over the shifting horizon) at each time step. This has the advantage of not requiring a representation for the entire problem *a priori*, but incurs the additional computational burden of repeatedly replanning. Second, hard constraints can be explicitly specified and handled through (1d). This allows agents to safely learn by avoiding dangerous regions of the state and control spaces.

Without some simplifying assumptions we cannot solve problem (1) directly. However, efficient approximate solutions can be found by following the "first discretize, then optimize" approach described in the sections below.

3.1 DIRECT MULTIPLE SHOOTING

Using direct multiple shooting (Bock and Plitt, 1984), problem (1) can be transformed into a structured nonlinear program (NLP). First, the time horizon $[t_0, t_0 + T]$ is partitioned into N equal subintervals $[t_k, t_{k+1}]$ for $k = 0, \ldots, N-1$. Then, taking a piecewise constant approximation of the control signal over each interval, a sequence of initial value problems,

$$\dot{\mathbf{x}}(t) = \mathbf{f}(\mathbf{x}(t), \mathbf{u}_k),\ \mathbf{x}(t_k) = \mathbf{x}_k,\ t \in [t_k, t_{k+1}], \quad (2)$$

can be set up for the state trajectory. Here, the variables $\mathbf{x}_k$ have been added as initial values. Each of these problems can then be integrated to obtain a discretized trajectory. However, in order to enforce continuity over the planning horizon, matching constrains,

$$\mathbf{x}_{k+1} = \mathbf{F}_k(\mathbf{x}_k, \mathbf{u}_k), \qquad k = 0, \ldots, N-1,$$

are placed on $\mathbf{x}_k$ at the boundary of each subinterval. The functions $\mathbf{F}_k$ represent the solutions to the initial value problems (2) at time t_{k+1}.

Finally, the cost function is discretized over each time interval, resulting in the following NLP:

$$\min_{\mathbf{x},\mathbf{u}} \quad h(\mathbf{x}_N) + \sum_{k=0}^{N-1} \mathcal{L}(\mathbf{x}_k, \mathbf{u}_k), \quad (3a)$$

subject to

$$\begin{aligned}
&\mathbf{x}_0 = \hat{\mathbf{x}}_0, && && (3b)\\
&\mathbf{x}_{k+1} = \mathbf{F}_k(\mathbf{x}_k, \mathbf{u}_k), && k = 0, \ldots, N-1 && (3c)\\
&\underline{\mathbf{u}} \leq \mathbf{u}_k \leq \overline{\mathbf{u}}, && k = 0, \ldots, N-1 && (3d)\\
&\underline{\mathbf{x}} \leq \mathbf{x}_k \leq \overline{\mathbf{x}}, && k = 1, \ldots, N && (3e)\\
&\mathbf{g}(\mathbf{x}_k, \mathbf{u}_k) \leq \mathbf{0}. && k = 1, \ldots, N-1 && (3f)
\end{aligned}$$

In principle, any non-linear programming method can be used to solve the above problem (Nocedal and Wright, 2006). However, the computational burden of solving an NLP at each time step is a severe limitation in real-time applications. To address this issue, there has been much interest in efficient optimization for receding horizon control (Domahidi et al., 2012; Vukov et al., 2013) . A particularly successful approach has been the combination of sequential quadratic programming (SQP) with structure exploiting stage-wise solvers (Kouzoupis et al., 2015).

3.2 SEQUENTIAL QUADRATIC PROGRAMMING

In the SQP framework, the NLP (3) is linearized about a given nominal trajectory $\mathbf{w} = [\mathbf{x}_0, \mathbf{u}_0, \ldots, \mathbf{x}_N]$. The trajectory can then be improved according to the update (Nocedal and Wright, 2006),

$$\mathbf{w}^+ = \mathbf{w} + \alpha \Delta \mathbf{w}^*, \quad (4)$$

where α is the step size and $\Delta \mathbf{w}^*$ denotes the solution to the following quadratic program:

$$\begin{aligned}
\min_{\Delta\mathbf{x},\Delta\mathbf{u}} \frac{1}{2} \sum_{k=0}^{N-1} &\begin{bmatrix} \Delta\mathbf{u}_k \\ \Delta\mathbf{x}_k \\ 1 \end{bmatrix}^{\mathsf{T}} \begin{bmatrix} \mathbf{R}_k & \mathbf{S}_k & \mathbf{r}_k \\ \mathbf{S}_k^{\mathsf{T}} & \mathbf{Q}_k & \mathbf{q}_k \\ \mathbf{r}_k^{\mathsf{T}} & \mathbf{q}_k^{\mathsf{T}} & \rho_k \end{bmatrix} \begin{bmatrix} \Delta\mathbf{u}_k \\ \Delta\mathbf{x}_k \\ 1 \end{bmatrix} && (5a)\\
&+ \frac{1}{2} \Delta\mathbf{x}_N^{\mathsf{T}} \mathbf{Q}_N \Delta\mathbf{x}_N + \Delta\mathbf{x}_N \mathbf{q}_N + \rho_N,
\end{aligned}$$

subject to the constraints

$$\begin{aligned}
&\Delta\mathbf{x}_0 = \hat{\mathbf{x}}_0 - \mathbf{x}_0, && (5b)\\
&\Delta\mathbf{x}_{k+1} = \mathbf{A}_k \Delta\mathbf{x}_k + \mathbf{B}_k \Delta\mathbf{u}_k + \mathbf{a}_k, && (5c)\\
&\underline{\mathbf{u}} - \mathbf{u}_k \leq \Delta\mathbf{u}_k \leq \overline{\mathbf{u}} - \mathbf{u}_k, && (5d)\\
&\underline{\mathbf{x}} - \mathbf{x}_k \leq \Delta\mathbf{x}_k \leq \overline{\mathbf{x}} - \mathbf{x}_k, && (5e)\\
&\mathbf{G}_k \Delta\mathbf{x}_k + \mathbf{H}_k \Delta\mathbf{u}_k \leq \mathbf{g}_k. && (5f)
\end{aligned}$$

The objective function (5a) is a quadratic approximation of the discretized cost function (3a) and the constraints correspond to linearizations of (3b) to (3f).

Provided that $\mathbf{Q}_k$ is positive semidefinite and $\mathbf{R}_k$ is strictly positive definite, the trajectory can be shown to converge to a local optimum by iteratively linearizing and optimizing (Nocedal and Wright, 2006). This is guaranteed for least squares cost functions popular in tracking and stabilization tasks. When a more general cost function is desired a positive definite approximation to the Hessian can be obtained using BFGS updates.

In this paper we use FORCES (Domahidi and Jerez, 2014) as the stage-wise solver for the quadratic program (5). FORCES is an interior-point method tailored for problems arising in RHC. In particular, the block diagonal structure of the Hessian (5a) and the fact that the states are only directly coupled to the previous time step are exploited to give linear computational complexity in the planning horizon.

It is often unnecessary to iterate to convergence before a reasonable improvement is found. In real-time settings this is important because we need to maintain a balance between efficiency and accuracy. An example of this trade-off can be seen in figure 1. Given an initial trajectory, the car must maximize its progress along the race track.

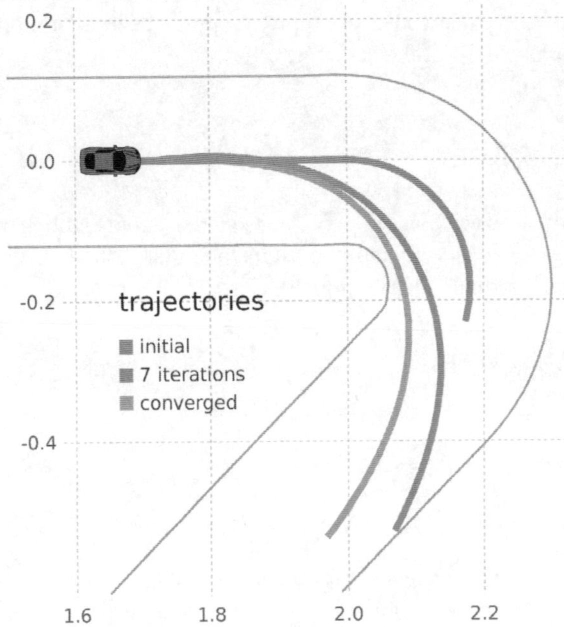

Figure 1: An example of planned trajectories in an autonomous racing task. The agent's objective is to maximize its progress along the racing track over the planning horizon. Note how early termination yields a solution trajectory that is still near-optimal over a short horizon.

The complete algorithm is presented in algorithm 1. In the next section we discuss how sparse online Gaussian process can be used to learn the non-linear dynamics model (3c).

4 DYNAMICS MODEL LEARNING

Typically, trajectory optimization based on receding horizon control relies on an analytic model of the system's dynamics. However, in the setting of reinforcement learning the dynamics are unknown and must be learned by interacting with the environment. In order to effectively plan over the horizon, an accurate model of the system's dynamics needs to be learned quickly.

Gaussian process (GP) regression is a non-parametric, Bayesian approach to model learning that has demonstrated impressive data-efficiency on both simulated and real robotic systems (Deisenroth and Rasmussen, 2011). Unfortunately, GPs do not scale well to large data sets, limiting their applicability in practice. There are, however, a number of approximation schemes that significantly reduce computational costs (Quiñonero-Candela and Rasmussen, 2005). In this paper, we use a sparse spectrum approximation of the kernel function (Lázaro-Gredilla et al., 2010). Sparse spectrum GPs were chosen

```
Data: number of features D, initial training data
foreach episode do
    train GPs on accumulated data (minimize (11));
    linearise dynamics and constraints about x_0;
    solve (5) until convergence;
    while not terminal do
        shift previous trajectory;
        for i = 1 to max iterations do
            linearise about current trajectory;
            solve (5) to get step direction;
            update trajectory (4);
        end
        apply control to the system;
        update dynamics model (12);
    end
end
```

Algorithm 1: The complete GP-RHC algorithm

because (a) online data can be incorporated through incremental updates (Gijsberts and Metta, 2013), and (b) the learned model can be efficiently linearized to form the sequential quadratic programs.

4.1 GAUSSIAN PROCESS REGRESSION

Given an input set of N state-control pairs $\tilde{\mathbf{x}} = (\mathbf{x}, \mathbf{u}) \in \mathbb{R}^{n+m}$ and the resulting (possibly noisy) state transitions $\Delta\mathbf{x} \in \mathbb{R}^n$, GP regression can be used to learn a model of the underlying dynamics. Following Deisenroth and Rasmussen (2011), we train conditionally independent GPs on each component of the state transition vector, so for the remainder of this section we will represent target data as $y \in \mathbb{R}$.

Formally, a Gaussian process is a collection of random variables, any finite number of which have a joint Gaussian distribution (Rasmussen and Williams, 2006). To completely specify a GP we need to choose a mean function $m(\tilde{\mathbf{x}})$ and a covariance function $k(\tilde{\mathbf{x}}, \tilde{\mathbf{x}}')$, parametrized by a set of hyperparameters. A common, but flexible choice for the covariance function is the squared exponential kernel

$$k(\tilde{\mathbf{x}}, \tilde{\mathbf{x}}') = \sigma^2 \exp\left(-\frac{1}{2}\sum_{i=1}^{n+m}\left(\frac{\tilde{x}_i - \tilde{x}_i'}{l_i}\right)^2\right),$$

where the signal variance σ^2 and characteristic length scales l_i constitute the kernel's set of hyperparameters. When modelling noisy targets, an additive noise term with variance σ_n^2 is included in the covariance function.

Since we model the relative rather than absolute state transitions, we choose a zero mean prior. This means that in the absence of data, the state is expected to remain unchanged regardless of the control input.

After defining the input matrix $\mathbf{X} = [\tilde{\mathbf{x}}_1, \ldots, \tilde{\mathbf{x}}_N]$ and the corresponding target vector $\mathbf{y} = [y_1, \ldots, y_N]^\intercal$, the posterior predictive distribution for a set of test points, $\mathbf{X}_*$, is a multivariate Gaussian with mean

$$\mathbb{E}[\mathbf{y}_* | \mathbf{X}_*, \mathbf{X}, \mathbf{y}] = \mathbf{K}(\mathbf{X}_*, \mathbf{X})\mathbf{Q}^{-1}\mathbf{y}, \tag{6}$$

and covariance

$$\mathbf{K}(\mathbf{X}_*, \mathbf{X}_*) - \mathbf{K}(\mathbf{X}_*, \mathbf{X})\mathbf{Q}^{-1}\mathbf{K}(\mathbf{X}, \mathbf{X}_*), \tag{7}$$

where $\mathbf{Q} = \mathbf{K}(\mathbf{X}, \mathbf{X}) + \sigma_n^2\mathbf{I}$, and $\mathbf{K}(\mathbf{X}, \mathbf{X})$ denotes the matrix of covariances evaluated at all pairs of input points. Computing the predictive mean and covariance are $\mathcal{O}(N)$ and $\mathcal{O}(N^2)$ respectively.

A common approach for learning the hyperparameters and the noise variance σ_n^2 is to maximize the marginal likelihood (Rasmussen and Williams, 2006). The negative log marginal likelihood, given by

$$\mathcal{L} = \frac{1}{2}\log|\mathbf{Q}| + \frac{1}{2}\mathbf{y}^\intercal\mathbf{Q}^{-1}\mathbf{y} + \frac{n}{2}\log(2\pi), \tag{8}$$

can be minimized using gradient based optimizers. Since $\mathbf{Q}$ needs to be inverted each time the log marginal likelihood is evaluated, which is an $\mathcal{O}(N^3)$ operation in general, hyperparameter inference represents the main bottleneck for GP regression.

4.2 SPARSE SPECTRUM APPROXIMATION

In this section, we assume that the covariance function is stationary, i.e. that $k(\tilde{\mathbf{x}}, \tilde{\mathbf{x}}')$ is a function of $\mathbf{r} = \tilde{\mathbf{x}} - \tilde{\mathbf{x}}'$. In this case, Bochner's theorem (Rudin, 2011) states that $k(\mathbf{r})$ can be represented as the Fourier transform,

$$k(\mathbf{r}) = \int_{\mathbb{R}^{n+m}} e^{i\boldsymbol{\omega}^\intercal\mathbf{r}} d\mu(\boldsymbol{\omega}), \tag{9}$$

of a positive finite measure μ. If $\mu(\boldsymbol{\omega})$ has a density, then it is called the power spectrum $S(\boldsymbol{\omega})$ of the covariance function and, by the Wiener-Khintchine theorem (Carlson et al., 2009), $S(\boldsymbol{\omega})$ is the Fourier dual of $k(\mathbf{r})$. In particular, this means that S is proportional to some probability measure p over $\mathbb{R}^{n+m}$, and so equation (9) can be rewritten as an expectation

$$k(\mathbf{r}) = \alpha^2\mathbb{E}_p[e^{i\boldsymbol{\omega}^\intercal\mathbf{r}}],$$

where α is the constant of proportionality.

To approximate the expectation, we draw D sample frequencies $\boldsymbol{\omega}_1, \ldots, \boldsymbol{\omega}_D$ from p and take averages. Since the power spectrum is symmetric about zero, we also include $\boldsymbol{\omega}_{-j} = -\boldsymbol{\omega}_j$ for each sample frequency, in order to guarantee that $k(\mathbf{r})$ is real valued for all $\mathbf{r}$. This results in the sparse spectrum approximation (Lázaro-Gredilla et al., 2010) of the covariance function:

$$k(\tilde{\mathbf{x}}, \tilde{\mathbf{x}}') \approx \frac{\alpha^2}{2D}\sum_{j=-D}^{D} e^{i\boldsymbol{\omega}_j^\intercal(\tilde{\mathbf{x}}-\tilde{\mathbf{x}}')}. \tag{10}$$

In the particular case of the squared exponential kernel $\alpha^2 = \sigma^2$, and the frequencies are drawn from the normal distribution $\mathcal{N}(\mathbf{0}, \boldsymbol{\Lambda}^{-1})$, where $\boldsymbol{\Lambda} = \mathrm{diag}([l_1^2, \ldots, l_{n+m}^2])$.

For convenience, we define the feature mapping $\boldsymbol{\phi} : \mathbb{R}^{n+m} \to \mathbb{R}^{2D}$ by,

$$\boldsymbol{\phi}(\tilde{\mathbf{x}}) = \frac{\alpha}{\sqrt{D}}[\, \cos(\boldsymbol{\omega}_1^\intercal\tilde{\mathbf{x}}),\ \sin(\boldsymbol{\omega}_1^\intercal\tilde{\mathbf{x}}),\ \cdots,$$
$$\cos(\boldsymbol{\omega}_D^\intercal\tilde{\mathbf{x}}),\ \sin(\boldsymbol{\omega}_D^\intercal\tilde{\mathbf{x}})\,]^\intercal.$$

In order to make use of the approximation (10), the matrix inversion lemma is applied to equations (6) and (7), giving

$$\mathbb{E}[\mathbf{y}_*] = \boldsymbol{\phi}(\mathbf{X}_*)^\intercal\mathbf{A}^{-1}\boldsymbol{\phi}(\mathbf{X})^\intercal\mathbf{y},$$
$$\mathrm{cov}[\mathbf{y}_*] = \sigma_n^2\boldsymbol{\phi}(\mathbf{X}_*)^\intercal\mathbf{A}^{-1}\boldsymbol{\phi}(\mathbf{X}_*),$$

where $\mathbf{A} = \boldsymbol{\phi}(\mathbf{X})^\intercal\boldsymbol{\phi}(\mathbf{X}) + \sigma_n^2\mathbf{I}$, and $\boldsymbol{\phi}(\mathbf{X})$ is the matrix obtained by applying $\boldsymbol{\phi}$ to each column of $\mathbf{X}$. Instead of inverting the $N \times N$ matrix $\mathbf{Q}$, we now only require the inverse of the $2D \times 2D$ matrix $\mathbf{A}$, which constitutes a significant saving in computational cost if $D \ll N$. Importantly, the size of $\mathbf{A}$ is independent of the number of training points, which makes it amenable to incremental updates (Gijsberts and Metta, 2013).

Applying the same idea to the negative log likelihood (8) gives the expression

$$\mathcal{L} = \frac{1}{2}\log|\mathbf{A}| - \frac{D}{2}\log\sigma_n^2 + \frac{n}{2}\log(2\pi\sigma_n^2) + \frac{1}{2\sigma_n^2}\left(\mathbf{y}^\intercal\mathbf{y} - \mathbf{y}^\intercal\boldsymbol{\phi}(\mathbf{X}_*)\mathbf{A}^{-1}\boldsymbol{\phi}(\mathbf{X}_*)^\intercal\mathbf{y}\right). \tag{11}$$

Again, the smaller size of $\mathbf{A}$ results in reduced computational complexity for hyperparameter inference. In particular, each step of the gradient based optimization is $\mathcal{O}(ND^2)$.

4.3 INCREMENTAL UPDATES

To incrementally handle a stream of data, the matrix $\mathbf{A}$ and the vector $\mathbf{b} = \boldsymbol{\Phi}^\intercal\mathbf{y}$ need to be updated in real time. Given a new sample, $(\tilde{\mathbf{x}}, y)$, the updates are computed according to the rules:

$$\mathbf{A} \leftarrow \mathbf{A} + \boldsymbol{\phi}(\tilde{\mathbf{x}})\boldsymbol{\phi}(\tilde{\mathbf{x}})^\intercal \quad \text{and} \quad \mathbf{b} \leftarrow \mathbf{b} + \boldsymbol{\phi}(\tilde{\mathbf{x}})y. \tag{12}$$

Since **A** remains positive semidefinite after each update, we do not need to store it explicitly. Instead, we can keep track of its upper triangular Cholesky factor. This allows us to make use of fast, numerically stable rank-1 Cholesky updates (Gijsberts and Metta, 2013).

5 EXPERIMENTS

In the following sections we evaluate the performance of GP-RHC on a cart-pole swing up task and an autonomous racing scenario. In all the experiments GP-RHC was able to run in real-time with appropriate choices of the sparsity D and planning horizon N. The choice of D essentially involves a trade-off between model accuracy and the computational costs of both the learning and the prediction routines. Empirically, we found that a value between 20 and 100 allowed us to learn a sufficiently accurate dynamics model while remaining within the real-time constraints. Similarly, the choice of N involves a balance between computational costs and the quality of the controller. Ideally, one would choose a large value of N so that the controller can optimally react to future changes in dynamics or constraints.

5.1 CARTPOLE SWINGUP

Cartpole experiments are a common benchmark in both reinforcement learning and control theory (Kober et al., 2013). The basic set-up consists of a cart with an attached pendulum running along a track. In the swing-up task, the pendulum is initially pointing downwards and the objective is to apply horizontal forces to the cart in order to swing the pendulum up and balance it above the cart in the center of the track. This is a relatively difficult control problem as the dynamics are fairly non-linear. Additionally, a long planning horizon is required because the cart must be pushed back and forth in order to develop enough momentum to swing the pendulum up.

The state of the system, $\mathbf{x} = [x, v, \theta, \omega]$, is described by the position of the cart, the velocity of the cart, the angle of the pendulum and its angular velocity. A horizontal force u in the range of -10N to 10N can be applied to the cart at a sampling rate of 0.025s. The cost function is given by a least squares objective penalizing the distance from the set point $[0, 0, \pi, 0]$.

In the first experiment we compare GP-RHC against PILCO (Deisenroth and Rasmussen, 2011) and the ground-truth analytical model. To initialize each trial, 80 data points were collected from an episode with random control inputs. For the sparse spectrum approximation 50 sample frequencies were drawn and a planning horizon of 50 time steps was used. After each episode the GP models were retrained on all the preceding data using 10 random restarts to avoid poor local minima. PILCO can potentially have problems with least squares costs (Deisenroth, 2010) so we used (the preferred) saturating cost function and post-processed the results. Figure 2 shows that GP-RHC is competitive with PILCO both in terms of sample efficiency and overall performance.

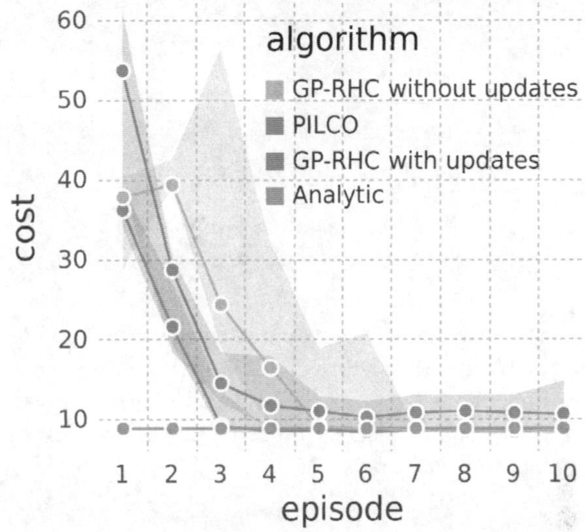

Figure 2: Median cost of the unconstrained cartpole swing-up task (using the saturated cost function). The lower and upper bounds of the confidence envelope represents the first and third quantiles respectively. The results were aggregated over 10 runs.

In the second experiment the length of the track is limited; constraining the cart's position to between -2m and 2m. Since PILCO does not handle constraints we just compare GP-RHC to the analytical model. The GP models were initialized with 20 points of training data collected from an episode with random inputs.

As seen in figures 2 and 3, GP-RHC learns to solve the cartpole swing-up task in just a few episodes. In particular, by updating the dynamics model online we can achieve performance comparable to the optimal analytic model at least a full episode earlier. Another noticeable feature is the reduced variability in cost. GP-RHC, with online updates, performs more consistently and is less susceptible to variations in the initial training data. Finally, table 1 shows that fewer constraint violations can be expected when using online updates. In fact, after the first episode only a single constraint violation was encountered, in contrast to the method without updates which incurred significantly more violations. These results indicate that GP-RHC enables fast learning and planning in safety critical conditions.

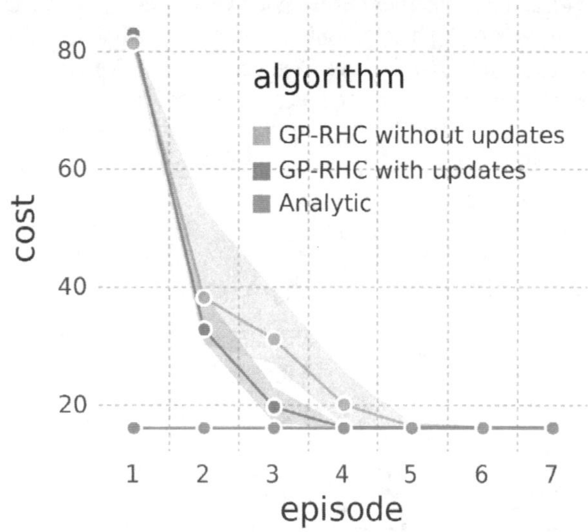

Figure 3: Median cost of the constrained cartpole swing-up task (using the saturated cost function). The lower and upper bounds of the confidence envelope represents the first and third quantiles respectively. The results were aggregated over 22 runs.

Table 1: Percentage of experiments terminated due to constraint violations

EPISODE	UPDATES	NO UPDATES
1	100.0	100.0
2	4.5	18.2
3	0.0	13.6
4	0.0	4.5
5	0.0	0.0
6	0.0	0.0
7	0.0	0.0

5.2 AUTONOMOUS RACING

In this section we apply GP-RHC to the autonomous racing of 1:43 scale remote control cars. Liniger et al. (2015) originally investigated this problem using an analytical model of the cars incorporated into a contouring control framework (see section 5.2.2). The objective is to maximize progress along the race course (depicted in figure 6) while remaining within the track boundaries.

5.2.1 BICYCLE MODEL

Following Liniger et al. (2015), the cars are modeled using a bicycle model. The cars are treated as rigid bodies and symmetry is used to approximate the pairs of front and back tyres as single wheels. Pitch and roll dynamics are neglected so only in-plane motion is considered. In our experiments the additional complexity of tyre dynamics is ignored by assuming a no-slip model.

The state space is described by the vector $[x, y, v, \phi]$, where x and y denote the position of the car, v the longitudinal velocity of the car, and ϕ the car's orientation. The control signal consists of the PWM duty cycle of the electric drive train motor and the steering angle of the front wheels. The duty cycle is constrained to the interval $[0, 1]$ and the steering angle cannot exceed 18 degrees.

5.2.2 CONTOURING CONTROL

Contouring control was originally designed for industrial applications like machine tool control and laser profiling (Lam et al., 2010). The objective of the controller is to track a given reference path while maximizing some measure of progress. Often these are competing interests and we need to find a balance between speed and tracking accuracy. In contrast to standard tracking approaches, the reference path is described only in terms of spatial coordinates. By specifying velocities and orientations the contouring controller is free to determine how the path is followed.

Here we assume that the reference path is given by an arc length parametrized curve

$$\Gamma = \{\mathbf{x} \in \mathbb{R}^q : \mathbf{x} = \gamma(s), s \in [0, l]\},$$

where l is the total length of the path. In our experiments, the center line of the race track is used as the reference path. To find an arc length parametrization, the center line is interpolated by a cubic spline, using the method described by Wang et al. (2002).

Let $p_k = [x_k, y_k]$ denote the position of the car at time t_k. Then, the contouring error,

$$\varepsilon_k^c = \mathbf{n}(s_k^*) \cdot (p_k - \gamma(s_k^*)),$$

is defined as the normal deviation from the path γ, where s_k^* is the value of the path parameter which minimizes the distance between the point p_k and the path, and $\mathbf{n}(s_k^*)$ is the unit normal to γ at s_k^*.

Calculating the contouring error requires us to determine the value of s_k^* at each point along the planned trajectory. This is too computationally intensive to use as a cost function in the iterative SQP framework. To address this issue, approximations to s_k^* at each point are introduced into the state. The dynamics are then augmented by the equation

$$s_{k+1} = s_k + \Delta t v_k, \quad v_k \in [0, v_{\max}],$$

where s_k denotes the approximation to s_k^* at time t_k, and v_k is a virtual control input. Since the path is parameterized by arc length, v_k can be thought of as the velocity of the car along the center line. For the auxiliary state s_k to be a useful approximation we introduce a lag error term ε^l defined as the distance between the points $\gamma(s_k^*)$ and $\gamma(s_k)$ along the reference path.

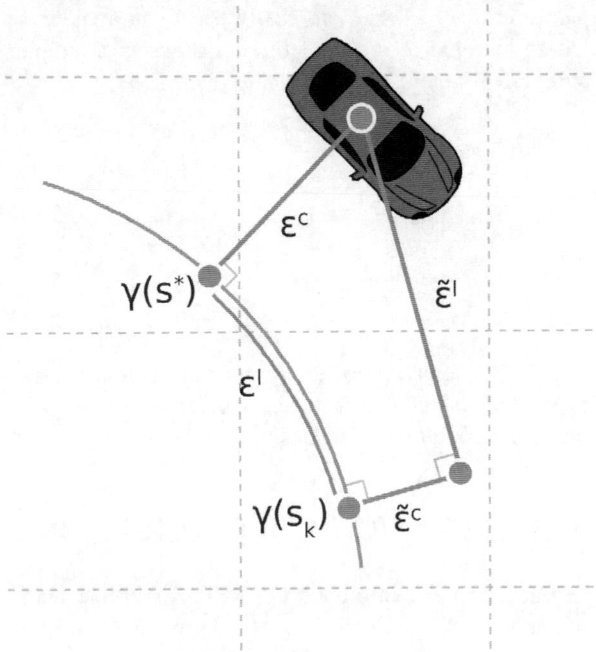

Figure 4: Contouring error ε_c, lag error ε_l and their respective approximations $\tilde{\varepsilon}_c$ and $\tilde{\varepsilon}_l$.

Since neither the contouring nor lag error can be used directly in the cost function, approximations defined only in terms of p_k and s_k are made. The approximate contouring error $\tilde{\varepsilon}_k^c$ and approximate lag error $\tilde{\varepsilon}_k^l$ are defined as the orthogonal and tangential component of the error between the points p_k and $\gamma(s_k)$,

$$\tilde{\varepsilon}_k^c = \mathbf{n}(s_k) \cdot (p_k - \gamma(s_k)),$$
$$\tilde{\varepsilon}_k^l = \mathbf{t}(s_k) \cdot (p_k - \gamma(s_k)),$$

where $\mathbf{t}(s_k)$ is the unit tangent to γ at s_k. It is clear from figure 4 that $\tilde{\varepsilon}_k^c$ approaches ε_k^c, and s_k approaches s_k^* as the lag error is reduced. Therefore, in order to get a good approximation of s_k^* the lag error $\tilde{\varepsilon}^l$ is heavily penalized in the cost function (13).

Using the approximate contouring and lag errors an intermediate cost function can be defined

$$\mathcal{L} = ||\tilde{\varepsilon}^l(x, y, s)||_{q_l}^2 + ||\tilde{\varepsilon}^c(x, y, s)||_{q_c}^2 - \alpha \Delta t v. \quad (13)$$

The term $-\alpha \Delta t v$ can be thought of as a reward for progressing along the track and the weights q_c and α represent the relative importance of fast progress and accurate path tracking.

5.2.3 TRACK CONSTRAINTS

To ensure that the car remains within the track, limits are placed on the x and y components of the car's state. Each point on the planned trajectory is constrained to lie within two half spaces defined by the left and right track boundaries (see figure 5). The relevant tangent lines are found by projecting the point $\gamma(s_k)$ (an approximation to the closest point on the center line) onto the track boundaries.

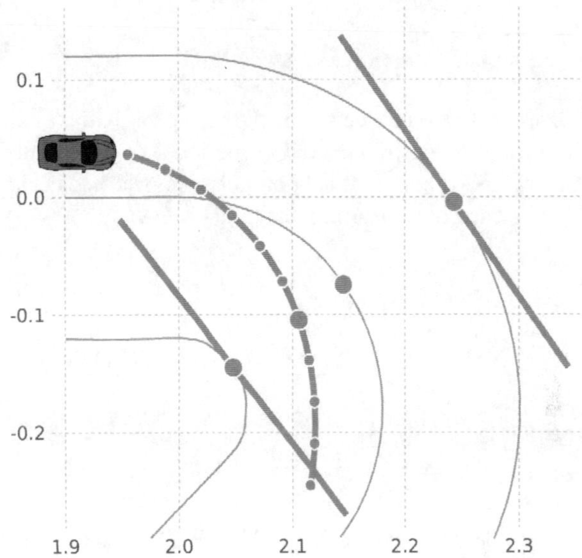

Figure 5: Track constraints (pink lines) corresponding to one point (pink dot) along the planned trajectory. The central dot is the closest point lying on the center line. Tangent lines are found by projecting this point onto the track boundaries.

The planned trajectory is often along the limit of these constraints so in order to avoid infeasibility problems in practice, the constraints are softened by adding slack variables. By penalizing the slack variables heavily in the cost function the original solution of the hard constrained problem is recovered where it would admit a solution.

5.2.4 RESULTS

Initially, 70 points of data were collected from a demonstrated trajectory around a simple oval track. 100 sample frequencies were chosen for the sparse spectrum approximation. A planning horizon of 20 time steps was used at a sampling rate of 0.03s. We found that we could plan in real time by limiting the number of SQP iterations to 30. The race track is shown in figure 6 along with the driven trajectory. The car initially starts at rest the point $[0, 0]$ and the race is completed after one full lap. The track is 7.23m long (measured at the center line).

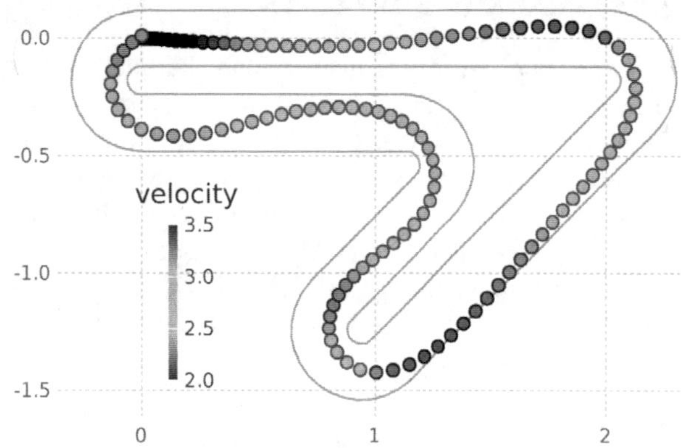

Figure 6: Driven trajectory of the racing car with velocity profile given by GP-RHC. The model was initially trained on 70 points of data on a simple oval track, and was updated online during this task.

Table 2: Lap Times

ANALYTIC	UPDATES	NO UPDATES
2.565	2.639	2.745

Using a learned dynamics model, GP-RHC quickly accelerates from rest and drives trajectories that satisfy the complex track constraints (see figure 6). The sparse spectrum Gaussian processes are very data efficient, learning a sufficiently accurate model of the car's dynamics from just 70 data points. In particular, the training data was collected by driving around a much simpler oval track yet the learned dynamics were able to generalize well enough to effectively navigate the sharp left turn in the new race course. Table 2 shows the lap times of GP-RHC with and without online updates compared to the baseline analytic model. By updating the model online we improve the lap time by more than 0.1s (a relative improvement of about 3.86 percent). This represents a significant saving considering the high speeds and small length scales involved in the problem. In fact, naively scaling up the domain results in a 311m track with a lap time improvement of about 4.56 seconds. This corresponds to a 16.4km/h increase in average speed around the track when using online updates.

In addition to the racing task we also consider an obstacle avoidance problem depicted in figure 7. Static obstacles, represented by the blue cars, are included by adjusting the track constraints. Liniger et al. (2015) determine these adjustments using a high-level planner based on dynamic programming. In our experiments, we manually specify the obstacle constraints but a high level planner could be employed in principle. Since the dynamics are independent of the constraints and cost function, GP-RHC can implicitly take advantage of all the information gained in the racing task by simply reusing the learned model with *no further learning*. This could be useful in safety critical tasks where costly trials can avoided by safely learning a model of the dynamics in a simpler, safer environment.

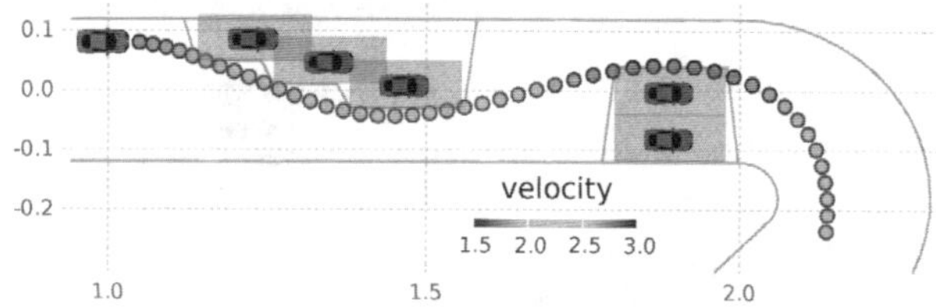

Figure 7: The driven trajectory in an obstacle avoidance task. The car is able to avoid dangerous collisions by planning around the obstacles.

6 CONCLUSION AND FUTURE WORK

In this paper we introduce GP-RHC for online learning and planning in continuous environments with nonlinear constraints. This is achieved by combining receding horizon control for planning with data efficient sparse spectrum Gaussian processes for model learning. We show that incorporating online data results in faster convergence to optimal behaviour while significantly reducing the number of constraint violations during learning — an important feature for safety critical applications. We demonstrate our approach on a complex autonomous racing task, showing that GP-RHC enables learning from only few training points, and the ability to apply the learned model to new tasks with *no additional training*. This method provides a promising approach to deploying online reinforcement learning algorithms on complex systems such as robots.

In future work plan to apply GP-RHC to real robotic systems such as quadrotors or manipulators. To achieve this goal, a possible improvement to the current method would be the ability to handle input noise. GP regression methods typically assume that the training inputs are noise free. However, in real robotic systems, sensors and filtering algorithms can introduce noise into the state estimation. This issue could be addressed, by incorporating ideas from Mchutchon and Rasmussen (2011) for example, to make GP-RHC more robust.

Acknowledgements

We thank the reviewer for their helpful insights and feedback.

References

Olov Andersson, Fredrik Heintz, and Patrick Doherty. Model-based reinforcement learning in continuous environments using real-time constrained optimization. In *Twenty-Ninth AAAI Conference on Artificial Intelligence (AAAI15)*, 2015.

Hans Georg Bock and Karl-Josef Plitt. A multiple shooting algorithm for direct solution of optimal control problems. In *Proceedings of the IFAC world congress*, 1984.

Joschka Boedecker, Jost Tobias Springenberg, Jan Wülfing, and Martin Riedmiller. Approximate real-time optimal control based on sparse gaussian process models. In *2014 IEEE Symposium on Adaptive Dynamic Programming and Reinforcement Learning (ADPRL)*, pages 1–8. IEEE, 2014.

A.B. Carlson, P. Crilly, and P.B. Crilly. *Communication Systems*. McGraw-Hill Education, 2009.

Marc Deisenroth and Carl E Rasmussen. Pilco: A model-based and data-efficient approach to policy search. In *Proceedings of the 28th International Conference on machine learning (ICML-11)*, pages 465–472, 2011.

Marc Peter Deisenroth. *Efficient reinforcement learning using Gaussian processes*. KIT Scientific Publishing, 2010.

Alexander Domahidi and Juan Jerez. FORCES Professional. embotech GmbH (`http://embotech.com/FORCES-Pro`), July 2014.

Alexander Domahidi, Aldo U Zgraggen, Melanie N Zeilinger, Manfred Morari, and Colin N Jones. Efficient interior point methods for multistage problems arising in receding horizon control. In *2012 IEEE 51st IEEE Conference on Decision and Control (CDC)*, pages 668–674. IEEE, 2012.

Arjan Gijsberts and Giorgio Metta. Real-time model learning using incremental sparse spectrum gaussian process regression. *Neural Networks*, 41:59–69, 2013.

H. J. Kim, Michael I. Jordan, Shankar Sastry, and Andrew Y. Ng. Autonomous helicopter flight via reinforcement learning. In *Advances in Neural Information Processing Systems 16*, pages 799–806. MIT Press, 2004.

Jens Kober, J Andrew Bagnell, and Jan Peters. Reinforcement learning in robotics: A survey. *The International Journal of Robotics Research*, 2013.

D Kouzoupis, A Zanelli, Helfried Peyrl, and Hans Joachim Ferreau. Towards proper assessment of qp algorithms for embedded model predictive control. In *Control Conference (ECC), 2015 European*, pages 2609–2616. IEEE, 2015.

Denise Lam, Chris Manzie, and Malcolm Good. Model predictive contouring control. In *Decision and Control (CDC), 2010 49th IEEE Conference on*, pages 6137–6142. IEEE, 2010.

Miguel Lázaro-Gredilla, Joaquin Quiñonero-Candela, Carl Edward Rasmussen, and Aníbal R Figueiras-Vidal. Sparse spectrum gaussian process regression. *The Journal of Machine Learning Research*, 11:1865–1881, 2010.

Alexander Liniger, Alexander Domahidi, and Manfred Morari. Optimization-based autonomous racing of 1:43 scale rc cars. *Optimal Control Applications and Methods*, 36(5):628–647, 2015.

Andrew Mchutchon and Carl E. Rasmussen. Gaussian process training with input noise. In *Advances in Neural Information Processing Systems 24*, pages 1341–1349. Curran Associates, Inc., 2011.

J. Nocedal and S. Wright. *Numerical Optimization*. Springer Series in Operations Research and Financial Engineering. Springer New York, 2006.

Yunpeng Pan and Evangelos Theodorou. Probabilistic differential dynamic programming. In *Advances in Neural Information Processing Systems*, pages 1907–1915, 2014.

Joaquin Quiñonero-Candela and Carl Edward Rasmussen. A unifying view of sparse approximate gaussian process regression. *Journal of Machine Learning Research*, 6(Dec):1939–1959, 2005.

Carl Edward Rasmussen and Christopher K I Williams. Gaussian processes for machine learning. 2006.

Walter Rudin. *Fourier analysis on groups*. John Wiley & Sons, 2011.

Milan Vukov, Alexander Domahidi, Hans Joachim Ferreau, Manfred Morari, and Moritz Diehl. Auto-generated algorithms for nonlinear model predictive control on long and on short horizons. In *52nd IEEE Conference on Decision and Control*, pages 5113–5118. IEEE, 2013.

Hongling Wang, Joseph Kearney, and Kendall Atkinson. Arc-length parameterized spline curves for real-time simulation. In *In in Proc. 5th International Conference on Curves and Surfaces*, pages 387–396, 2002.

A Reinforcement Learning Approach to Weaning of Mechanical Ventilation in Intensive Care Units

Niranjani Prasad
Computer Science
Princeton University

Li-Fang Cheng
Electrical Engineering
Princeton University

Corey Chivers
Penn Medicine

Michael Draugelis
Penn Medicine

Barbara E Engelhardt
Computer Science
Princeton University

Abstract

The management of invasive mechanical ventilation, and the regulation of sedation and analgesia during ventilation, constitutes a major part of the care of patients admitted to intensive care units. Both prolonged dependence on mechanical ventilation and premature extubation are associated with increased risk of complications and higher hospital costs, but clinical opinion on the best protocol for weaning patients off of a ventilator varies. This work aims to develop a decision support tool that uses available patient information to predict time-to-extubation readiness and to recommend a personalized regime of sedation dosage and ventilator support. To this end, we use off-policy reinforcement learning algorithms to determine the best action at a given patient state from sub-optimal historical ICU data. We compare treatment policies from fitted Q-iteration with extremely randomized trees and with feedforward neural networks, and demonstrate that the policies learnt show promise in recommending weaning protocols with improved outcomes, in terms of minimizing rates of reintubation and regulating physiological stability.

1 INTRODUCTION

Mechanical ventilation is one of the most widely used interventions in admissions to the intensive care unit (ICU): around 40% of patients in the ICU are supported on invasive mechanical ventilation at any given hour, accounting for 12% of total hospital costs in the United States (Ambrosino and Gabbrielli [2010], Wunsch et al. [2013]). These are typically patients with acute respiratory failure or compromised lung function caused by some underlying condition such as pneumonia, sepsis, or heart disease, or cases in which breathing support is necessitated by neurological disorders, impaired consciousness, or weakness following major surgery. As advances in healthcare enable more patients to survive critical illness or surgery, the need for mechanical ventilation during recovery has risen.

Closely coupled with ventilation in the care of these patients is sedation and analgesia, which are crucial to maintaining physiological stability and controlling pain levels of patients while intubated. The underlying condition of the patient, as well as factors such as obesity or genetic variations, can have a significant effect on the pharmacology of drugs, and cause high inter-patient variability in response to a given sedative (Patel and Kress [2012]), lending motivation to a personalized approach to sedation strategies.

Weaning refers to the process of liberating patients from mechanical ventilation. The primary diagnostic tests for determining whether a patient is ready to be extubated involve screening for resolution of the underlying disease, haemodynamic stability, assessment of current ventilator settings and level of consciousness, and finally a series of spontaneous breathing trials (SBTs). Prolonged ventilation—and corresponding over-sedation—is associated with post-extubation delirium, drug dependence, ventilator-induced pneumonia, and higher patient mortality rates (Hughes et al. [2012]), in addition to inflating costs and straining hospital resources. Physicians are often conservative in recognizing patient suitability for extubation, however, as failed breathing trials or premature extubations that necessitate reintubation within 48-72 hours can cause severe patient discomfort and result in even longer ICU stays (Krinsley et al. [2012]). Efficient weaning of sedation and ventilation is therefore a priority both for improving patient outcomes and reducing costs, but a lack of comprehensive evidence and the variability in outcomes between individuals and subpopulations means there is little agreement in clinical literature on the best weaning protocol (Conti et al. [2014], Goldstone [2002]).

In this work, we aim to develop a decision support tool that leverages available patient information in the data-rich ICU setting to alert clinicians when a patient is ready for initiation of weaning, and to recommend a personalized treatment protocol. We explore the use of off-policy reinforcement learning algorithms, namely fitted Q-iteration (FQI) with different regressors, to determine the optimal treatment at each patient state from sub-optimal historical patient treatment profiles. The setting fits naturally into the framework of reinforcement learning as it is fundamentally a sequential decision making problem rather than purely a prediction task: we wish to choose the best possible action at each time—in terms of sedation drug and dosage, ventilator settings, initiation of a spontaneous breathing trial, or extubation—while capturing the stochasticity of the underlying process, the delayed effects of actions, and the uncertainty in state transitions and outcomes.

The problem poses a number of key challenges: there are a multitude of factors that can potentially influence patient readiness for extubation, including some not directly observed in ICU chart data, such as a patient's inability to protect their airway due to muscle weakness. The data that is recorded is often sparse and noisy. In addition, there is potentially an extremely large space of possible sedatives and ventilator settings that can be leveraged during weaning. We are also posed with the problem of interval censoring, as in other intervention data: given past treatment and vitals trajectories, observing a successful extubation at time t provides us only with an upper bound on the true time to extubation readiness, $t_e \leq t$; on the other hand, if a breathing trial was unsuccessful, there is uncertainty how premature the intervention was. This presents difficulties both when learning the policy and in evaluating policies.

The rest of the paper is organized as follows: Section 2 explores recent efforts in the use of reinforcement learning in clinical settings. In Section 3, we describe the data and methods used here, and Section 4 presents the results. Finally, conclusions and possible directions for further work are discussed in Section 5.

2 RELATED WORK

The widespread adoption of electronic health records (EHRs) paved the way for a data-driven approach to healthcare, and recent years have seen a number of efforts towards personalized, dynamic treatment regimes. Reinforcement learning in particular has been explored in various settings, from determining the sequence of drugs to be administered in HIV therapy or cancer treatment, to management of anaemia in haemodialysis patients, and insulin regulation in diabetics. These efforts are typically based on estimating the *value*, in terms of clinical outcomes, of different treatment decisions given the state of the patient.

For example, Ernst et al. [2006] applied fitted Q-iteration with a tree-based ensemble method to learn the optimal HIV treatment in the form of structured treatment interruption strategies, in which patients are cycled on and off drug therapy. The observed reward here is defined in terms of the equilibrium point between healthy and unhealthy blood cells in the patient. Zhao et al. [2011] used Q-learning to learn optimal individualized treatment regimens for non-small cell lung cancer. The objective is to choose the optimal first and second lines of therapy and the optimal initiation time for the second line treatment such that the overall survival time is maximized. The Q-function with time-indexed parameters is approximated using a modification of support vector regression (SVR) that explicitly handles right-censored data. In this setting, right-censoring arises in measuring the time of death from start of therapy: given that a patient is still alive at the time of the last follow-up, we have only a lower bound on the exact survival time.

Escandell-Montero et al. [2014] compared the performance of both Q-learning and fitted Q-iteration with current clinical protocol for informing the delivery of erythropoeisis-stimulating agents (ESAs) for treating anaemia. The drug administration strategy is modeled as a Markov decision process (MDP), with the state space expressed by current values and change in haemoglobin levels, the most recent ESA dosage, and the patient subpopulation. The action space is a set of four discretized ESA levels, and the reward function is designed to maintain haemoglobin levels within a healthy range while avoiding abrupt changes.

On the problem of administering anaesthesia in an ICU setting, Moore et al. [2004] applied Q-learning with eligibility traces to the administration of intravenous propofol, modeling patient dynamics according to an established pharmacokinetic model, with the aim of maintaining some level of sedation or consciousness. Padmanabhan et al. [2014] also used Q-learning, for the regulation of both sedation level and arterial pressure as an indicator of physiological stability, using propofol infusion rate. All of the aforementioned work rely on model-based approaches to reinforcement learning, and develop treatment policies on simulated patient data. More recently however, Nemati et al. [2016] consider the problem of heparin dosing to maintain blood coagulation levels within some well-defined therapeutic range, modeling the task as a partially observable MDP, using a dynamic Bayesian network trained on real ICU data, and learning a dosing policy with neural fitted Q-iteration (NFQ).

There exists some literature on machine learning methods for the problem of ventilator weaning: Mueller et al. [2013] and Kuo et al. [2015] look at prediction of weaning outcomes using supervised learning methods, and suggest that classifiers based on neural networks, logistic regression, or naive Bayes, trained on patient ventilator and blood gas data, show promise in predicting successful extubation. Gao et al. [2017] develops association rule networks for naive Bayes classifiers, to analyze the discriminative power of different feature categories toward each decision outcome class, in order to help inform clinical decision making. Our paper is novel in its use of reinforcement learning methods to directly tackle policy recommendation for ventilation weaning. Specifically, we incorporate a larger number of possible predictors of weaning readiness, in a 32-dimensional patient state representation, compared with previous works which typically limit features for classification to at most a couple of key vital signs. Moreover, we make use of current clinical protocols to inform the design and tuning of a reward function.

3 METHODS

3.1 CRITICAL CARE DATA

We use the Multi-parameter Intelligent Monitoring in Intensive Care (MIMIC III) database (Johnson et al. [2016]), a freely available source of de-identified critical care data for 53,423 adult admissions and 7,870 neonates. This data includes patient demographics, time-stamped measurements from bedside monitoring of vitals, administration of fluids and medications, results of laboratory tests, observations and notes charted by care providers, as well as diagnoses, procedures and prescriptions for billing.

We extract from this database a set of 8,860 admissions from 8,182 unique adult patients undergoing invasive ventilation. In order to train and test our weaning policy, we filter further to include only those admissions in which the patient was kept under ventilator support for more than 24 hours. This allows us to exclude the majority of episodes of routine ventilation following surgery, which are at minimal risk of adverse extubation outcomes. We also filter out admissions in which the patient in not successfully discharged from the hospital by the end of the admission, as in cases where the patient expires in the ICU, failure to discharge is largely due to factors beyond the scope of ventilator weaning, and again, a more informed weaning policy is unlikely to have a significant influence on outcomes. *Failure* in our problem setting is instead defined as prolonged ventilation, administration of unsuccessful spontaneous breathing trials, or reintubation within the same admission—all of which are associated with adverse outcomes for the patient. A typical patient timeline is illustrated in Figure 1.

Preliminary guidelines for the weaning protocol, in terms of the desired ranges of physiological parameters (heart rate, respiratory rate, and arterial pH) as well as criteria at time of extubation for the inspired O_2 fraction (FiO_2), oxygenation pulse oxymetry (SpO_2), and positive end-expiratory pressure (PEEP) set, were obtained from clinicians at the Hospital of University of Pennsylvania, HUP (Table 1). These are used in shaping rewards in our MDP to facilitate learning of the optimal policy.

3.1.1 Preprocessing using Gaussian Processes

Measurements of vitals and lab results in the ICU data can be irregular, sparse, and error-prone. Non-invasive measurements such as heart rate or respiratory rate are taken several times an hour, while tests for arterial pH or oxygen pressure, which involve more distress to the patient, may only be administered every few hours as needed. This wide discrepancy in measurement frequency is typically handled by resampling with means in hourly intervals (when we have multiple measurements within an hour), and using sample-and-hold interpolation to impute subsequent missing values. However, patient state—and therefore the need to update management of sedation or ventilation—can change within the space of an hour, and naive methods for interpolation are unlikely to provide the necessary accuracy at higher temporal resolutions. We therefore explore methods for the imputation of patient state that can enable more precise policy estimation.

Physiological Stability	**Oxygenation Criteria**
Respiratory Rate ≤ 30	PEEP (cm H_2O) ≤ 8
Heart Rate ≤ 130	SpO_2 (%) ≥ 88
Arterial pH ≥ 7.3	Inspired O_2 (%) ≤ 50

Table 1: Current extubation guidelines at HUP.

One commonly used approach to resolve missing and irregularly sampled time series data is Gaussian processes (GPs, [Stegle et al., 2008, Dürichen et al., 2015, Ghassemi et al., 2015]). Denoting the observations of the vital signs by $\mathbf{v}$ and the measurement time $\mathbf{t}$, we model

$$\mathbf{v} = f(\mathbf{t}) + \varepsilon,$$

where ε vector represents i.i.d Gaussian noise, and $f(\mathbf{t})$ is the latent noise-free function we would like to estimate. We put a GP prior on the latent function $f(\mathbf{t})$:

$$f(\mathbf{t}) \sim \mathcal{GP}(m(\mathbf{t}), \kappa(\mathbf{t}, \mathbf{t}')),$$

where $m(\mathbf{t})$ is the *mean function* and $\kappa(\mathbf{t}, \mathbf{t}')$ is the *covariance function* or *kernel*, which shapes the temporal properties of $f(\mathbf{t})$. In this work, we use a multi-output GP to account for temporal correlations between physiological signals during interpolation. We adapt the framework in Cheng et al. [2017] to impute the physiological signals jointly by estimating covariance structures between them, excluding the sparse prior settings. We set $m(\mathbf{t}) = \mathbf{0}$ without loss of generality (Rasmussen and Williams [2006]), and $\kappa(\mathbf{t}, \mathbf{t}')$ as the kernel in the linear model of coregionalization using the spectral kernel as the basis kernel, allowing us to model both smooth correlations in time and periodic variations of these vital signs and lab results. The full joint kernel for each patient i is defined as:

$$\kappa_i(\mathbf{t}_i, \mathbf{t}_i') = \sum_{q=1}^{Q} \boldsymbol{B}_q \otimes \kappa_q(\mathbf{t}_{i,*}, \mathbf{t}_{i,*}'),$$

where $\mathbf{t}_{i,*}$ represents the time vector of each vital sign. Note that this is a simplified representation based on the

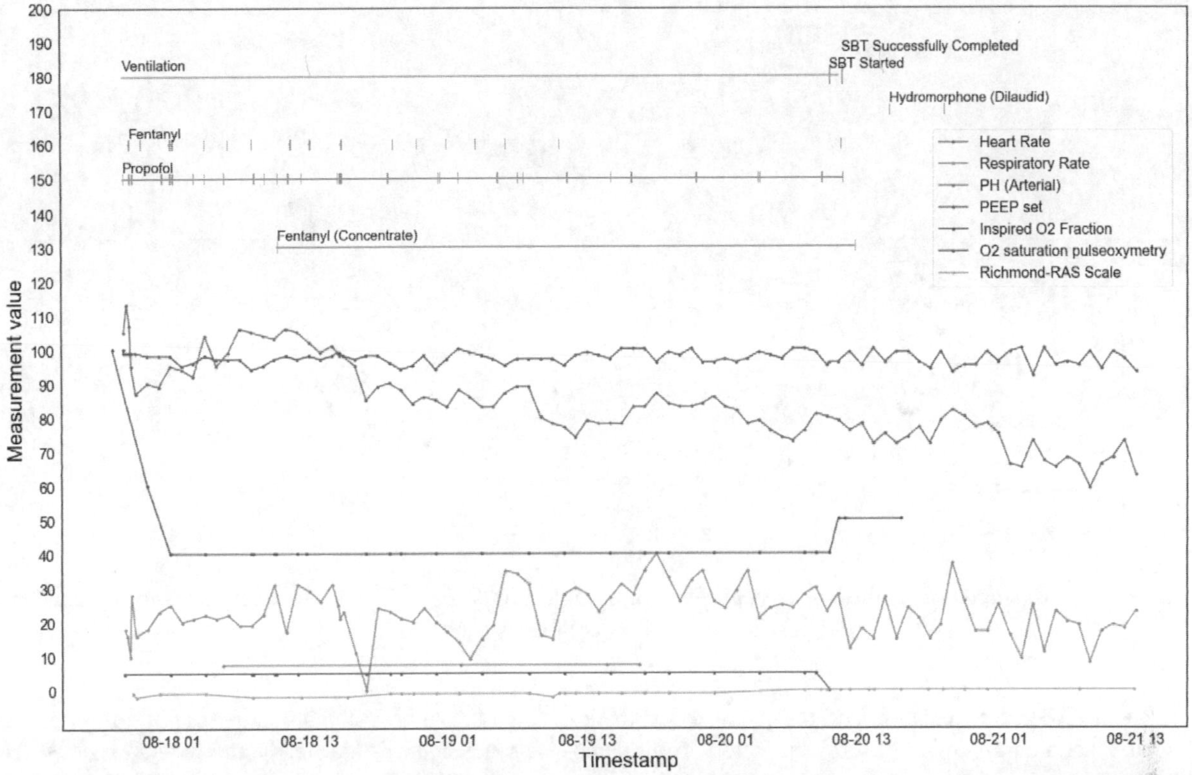

Figure 1: Example ventilated ICU patient. Vitals are measured at a range of sampling intervals. Ventilation times are marked, and multiple administered sedatives (both as continuous IV drips and discrete boli) are shown.

assumption that we have the same input time vector for each signal, which does not hold in our irregularly sampled data. In practice we have to compute each sub-block $\kappa_q(\mathbf{t}_{i,d}, \mathbf{t}'_{i,d'})$ given any pair of input time $\mathbf{t}_{i,d}$ and $\mathbf{t}'_{i,d'}$ from two signals, indexing by d and d'. We use Q to denote the number of mixture kernels, and $\boldsymbol{B}_q$ to encode the scale covariance between any pair of signals, written as

$$\boldsymbol{B}_q = \begin{bmatrix} b_{q,(1,1)} & b_{q,(1,2)} & \cdots & b_{q,(1,D)} \\ b_{q,(1,1)} & \vdots & \ddots & \vdots \\ \vdots & \vdots & \ddots & \vdots \\ b_{q,(D,1)} & b_{q,(D,2)} & \cdots & b_{q,(D,D)} \end{bmatrix} \in \mathbb{R}^{D \times D}.$$

The basis kernel is parameterized as

$$\kappa_q(\mathbf{t}, \mathbf{t}') = \exp\left(-2\pi^2\tau^2 v_q\right)\cos\left(2\pi\tau\mu_q\right),$$
$$\tau = |\mathbf{t} - \mathbf{t}'|.$$

We set $Q = 2$ and $R = 5$ for modeling 12 selected physiological signals ($D = 12$) jointly. For each patient, one structured GP kernel is estimated using the implementation in Cheng et al. [2017]. We then impute the time series with the estimated posterior mean given all the observations across all chosen physiological signals for that patient. In choosing the 12 signals, we exclude vitals that take discrete values, such as ventilator mode or the RASS sedation scale; for these, we simply resample with means and apply sample-and-hold interpolation. After preprocessing, we obtain complete data for each patient, at a temporal resolution of 10 minutes, from admission time to discharge time (Figure 2).

3.2 MDP FORMULATION

A Markov decision process is defined by

(i) A finite **state space** $\mathcal{S}$ such that at each time t, the environment (here, the patient) is in state $s_t \in \mathcal{S}$.

(ii) An **action space** $\mathcal{A}$: at each time t, the agent takes action $a_t \in \mathcal{A}$, which influences the next state, s_{t+1}.

(iii) A **transition function** $P(s_{t+1}|s_t, a_t)$, the probability of the next state given the current state and action, which defines the (unknown) dynamics of the system.

(iv) A **reward function** $r(s_t, a_t, s_{t+1}) \in \mathbb{R}$, the observed feedback following a transition at each time step t.

The goal of the reinforcement learning agent is to learn a **policy**, i.e. a mapping $\pi(s) : \mathcal{S} \to \mathcal{A}$ from states to actions, that maximizes the expected accumulated reward

$$R^{\pi}(s_t) = \lim_{T\to\infty} \mathbb{E}_{s_{t+1}|s_t,\pi(s_t)} \sum_{t=0}^{T} \gamma^t r(s_t, \pi(s_t), s_{t+1})$$

over time horizon T. The discount factor, γ, determines the relative weight of immediate and long-term rewards.

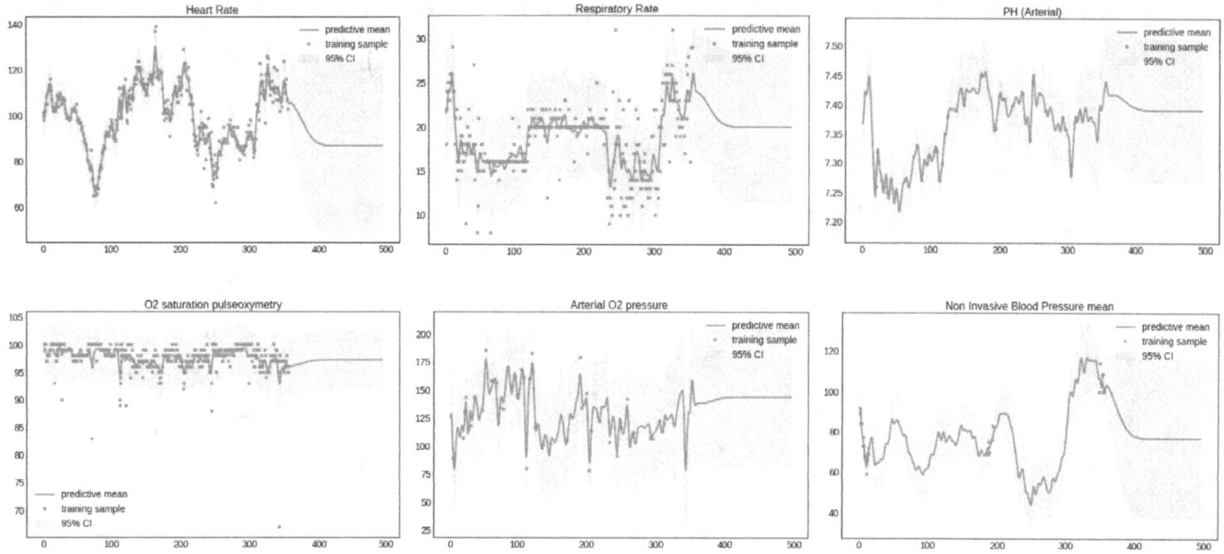

Figure 2: Example trajectories of six vital signs for a single admission, following imputation using Gaussian processes. Twelve vital signs are jointly modeled by the GP.

Patient response to sedation and readiness for extubation can depend on a number of different factors, from demographic characteristics, pre-existing conditions, and comorbidities to specific time-varying vital signs, and there is considerable variability in clinical opinion on the extent of the influence of different factors. Here, in defining each patient state within an MDP, we look to incorporate as many reliable and frequently monitored features as possible, and allow the algorithm to determine the relevant features. The state at each time t is a 32-dimensional feature vector that includes fixed demographic information (patient *age, weight, gender, admit type, ethnicity*), as well as relevant physiological measurements, ventilator settings, level of consciousness (given by the Richmond Agitation Sedation Scale, or RASS), current dosages of different sedatives, time into ventilation, and the number of intubations so far in the admission. For simplicity, categorical variables *admit type* and *ethnicity* are binarized as emergency/non-emergency and white/non-white, respectively.

In designing the action space, we develop an approximate mapping of six commonly used sedatives into a single dosage scale, and choose to discretize this scale to four different levels of sedation. The action $a_t \in \mathcal{A}$ at each time step is chosen from a finite two-dimensional set of eight actions, where $a_t[0] \in \{0,1\}$ indicates having the patient off or on the ventilator, respectively, and $a_t[1] \in \{0,1,2,3\}$ corresponds to the level of sedation to be administered over the next 10-minute interval:

$$\mathcal{A} = \left\{ \begin{bmatrix}0\\0\end{bmatrix}, \begin{bmatrix}0\\1\end{bmatrix}, \begin{bmatrix}0\\2\end{bmatrix}, \begin{bmatrix}0\\3\end{bmatrix}, \begin{bmatrix}1\\0\end{bmatrix}, \begin{bmatrix}1\\1\end{bmatrix}, \begin{bmatrix}1\\2\end{bmatrix}, \begin{bmatrix}1\\3\end{bmatrix} \right\}$$

Finally, we associate a reward signal r_{t+1} with each state transition—defined by the tuple $\langle s_t, a_t, s_{t+1}\rangle$—to encompass (i) time into ventilation, (ii) physiological stability, i.e. whether vitals are steady and within expected ranges, (iii) failed SBTs or reintubation. The reward at each timestep is defined by a combination of sigmoid, piecewise-linear, and threshold functions that reward closely regulated vitals and successful extubation while penalizing adverse events: $r_{t+1} = r_{t+1}^{vitals} + r_{t+1}^{vent\ off} + r_{t+1}^{vent\ on}$, where

$$r_{t+1}^{vitals} = C_1 \sum_v \left[\frac{1}{1+e^{-(v_t - v_{min})}} - \frac{1}{1+e^{-(v_t - v_{max})}} + \frac{1}{2} \right] - C_2 \left[\max\left(0, \frac{|v_{t+1} - v_t|}{v_t} - 0.2\right) \right],$$

$$r_{t+1}^{vent\ off} = \mathbb{1}_{[s_{t+1}(\text{vent on})=0]} \Big[C_3 \cdot \mathbb{1}_{[s_t(\text{vent on})=1]} + C_4 \cdot \mathbb{1}_{[s_t(\text{vent on})=0]} - C_5 \sum_{v^{ext}} \mathbb{1}_{[v_t^{ext} > v_{max}^{ext} \,||\, v_t^{ext} < v_{min}^{ext}]} \Big],$$

$$r_{t+1}^{vent\ on} = \mathbb{1}_{[s_{t+1}(\text{vent on})=1]} \Big[C_6 \cdot \mathbb{1}_{[s_t(\text{vent on})=1]} - C_7 \cdot \mathbb{1}_{[s_t(\text{vent on})=0]} \Big].$$

Here, values v_t are the measurements of those vitals v (included in the state representation s_t) believed to be indicative of physiological stability at time t, with desired ranges $[v_{min}, v_{max}]$. The penalty for exceeding these ranges at each time step is given by a truncated sigmoid function (Figure 3a). The system also receives negative feedback when consecutive measurements see a sharp change (Figure 3b).

Vital signs v_t^{ext} comprise the subset of parameters directly associated with readiness for extubation (FiO_2, SpO_2, and PEEP set) with weaning criteria defined by the ranges $[v_{min}^{ext}, v_{max}^{ext}]$. A fixed penalty is applied when these criteria are not met during extubation. The system also accumulates negative rewards for each additional hour spent on the ventilator, and a large positive reward at the time of successful extubation. Constants C_1 to C_7 determine the relative importance of these reward signals.

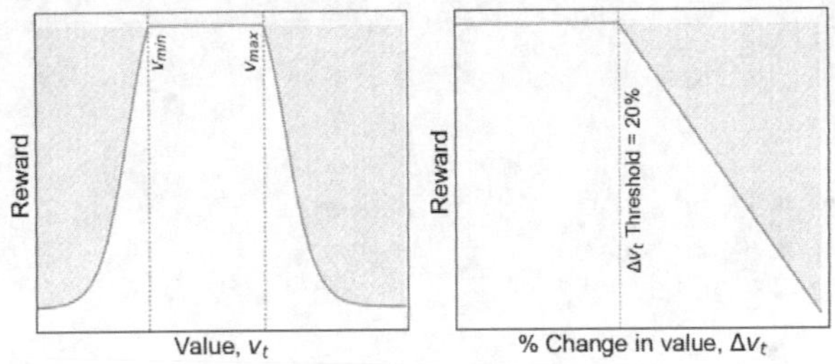

(a) Exceeding threshold values (b) High fluctuation in values

Figure 3: Shape of reward from vitals, $r_t^{vitals}(v_t)$

3.3 LEARNING THE OPTIMAL POLICY

The majority of reinforcement learning algorithms are based on estimation of the Q-function, that is, the expected value of state-action pairs $Q^\pi(s, a) : S \times A \rightarrow \mathbb{R}$, to determine the optimal policy π. Of these, the most widely used is Q-learning, an off-policy reinforcement learning algorithm in which we start with an initial state and arbitrary approximation of the Q-function, and update this estimate using the reward from the next transition using the Bellman recursion for Q-values:

$$\hat{Q}(s_t, a_t) = \hat{Q}(s_t, a_t) + \alpha(r_{t+1} + \gamma \max_{a \in \mathcal{A}} \hat{Q}(s_{t+1}, a) - \hat{Q}(s_t, a_t))$$

where the learning rate α gives the relative weight of the current and previous estimate, and γ is the discount factor.

Fitted Q-iteration (FQI) is a form of off-policy *batch-mode* reinforcement learning that uses a set of one-step transition tuples:

$$\mathcal{F} = \{(\langle s_t^n, a_t^n, s_{t+1}^n \rangle, r_{t+1}^n), n = 1, ..., |\mathcal{F}|\}$$

to learn a sequence of function approximators $\hat{Q}_1, \hat{Q}_2 ... \hat{Q}_K$ of the value of state-action pairs, by iteratively solving supervised learning problems. Both FQI and Q-learning belong to the class of model-free reinforcement learning methods, which assumes no knowledge of the dynamics of the system. In the case of FQI, there are also no assumptions made on the ordering of tuples; these could correspond to a sequence of transitions from a single admission, or randomly ordered transitions from multiple histories. FQI is therefore more data-efficient, with the full set of samples used by the algorithm at every iteration, and hence typically converges much faster than Q-learning.

The training set at the kth supervised learning problem is given by $\mathcal{TS} = \{(\langle s_t^n, a_t^n \rangle, \hat{Q}_k(s_t^n, a_t^n)), n = 1, ..., |\mathcal{F}|\}$. As before, the Q-function is updated at each iteration according to the Bellman equation:

$$\hat{Q}_k(s_t, a_t) \leftarrow r_{t+1} + \gamma \max_{a \in \mathcal{A}} \hat{Q}_{k-1}(s_{t+1}, a)$$

where $\hat{Q}_1(s_t, a_t) = r_{t+1}$. The approximation of the optimal policy after K iterations is then given by:

$$\hat{\pi}^*(s) = \arg\max_{a \in \mathcal{A}} \hat{Q}_K(s, a)$$

FQI guarantees convergence for many commonly used regressors, including kernel-based methods (Ormoneit and Sen [2002]) and decision trees. In particular, extremely randomized trees (Extra-Trees: Geurts et al. [2006], Ernst et al. [2005]), a tree-based ensemble method that extends on random forests by introducing randomness in the thresholds chosen at each split, has been applied in the past to learning large or continuous Q-functions in clinical settings (Ernst et al. [2006], Escandell-Montero et al. [2014]).

Neural Fitted-Q (NFQ, Riedmiller [2005]) on the other hand, looks to leverage the representational power of neural networks as regressors to fitted Q-iteration. Nemati et al. [2016] use NFQ to learn optimal heparin dosages, mapping the patient hidden state to expected return. Neural networks hold an advantage over tree-based methods in iterative settings in that it is possible to simply update network weights at each iteration, rather than rebuilding the trees entirely.

Algorithm 1 Fitted Q-iteration with sampling

Input:
One-step transitions $\mathcal{F} = \{\langle s_t^n, a_t^n, s_{t+1}^n \rangle, r_{t+1}^n\}_{n=1:|\mathcal{F}|}$;
Regression parameters θ;
Action space $\mathcal{A}$; subset size N
Initialize $Q_0(s_t, a_t) = 0 \quad \forall s_t \in \mathcal{F},\ a_t \in \mathcal{A}$
for *iteration* $k = 1 \rightarrow K$ **do**
    $subset_N \sim \mathcal{F}$
    $S \leftarrow []$
    for $i \in subset_N$ **do**
        $Q_k(s_i, a_i) \leftarrow r_{i+1} + \gamma \max_{a' \in \mathcal{A}} (predict(\langle s_{i+1}, a' \rangle, \theta))$
        $S \leftarrow append(S, \langle (s_i, a_i), Q(s_i, a_i) \rangle)$
    end
    $\theta \leftarrow regress(S)$
end
Result: θ
$\pi \leftarrow classify(\langle s_t^n, a_t^n \rangle)$

4 EXPERIMENTAL RESULTS

After extracting relevant ventilation episodes from ICU admissions in the MIMIC III database (Section 3.1), and splitting these into training and test data, we obtain a total of 1,800 distinct admissions in our training set and 664 admissions in our test set. We interpolate time-varying vitals measurements using Gaussian processes or sample-and-hold interpolation, sampling at 10-minute intervals. This yields of the order of 1.5 million one-step transitions in the training set and 0.5 million in the test set respectively, where each transition is a 32-dimensional representation of patient state.

As a baseline, we applied Q-learning to the training data to learn the mapping of continuous states to Q-values, with function approximation using a three-layer feedforward neural network. The network is trained using *Adam*, an efficient stochastic gradient-based optimizer (Kingma and Ba [2014]), and l_2 regularization of weights. Each patient admission k is treated as a distinct episode, with on the order of thousands of state transitions in each; the network weights are incrementally updated following each transition. Studying the change between successive episodes in the predicted Q-values for all state-action pairs in the training set (Figure 4), it is unclear whether the algorithm succeeds in converging within the 1,800 training episodes.

Figure 4: Convergence of $\hat{Q}(s, a)$ using Q-learning, over all transitions for patients in training set.

We then explored the use of FQI to learn our Q-function, first running with an Extra-Trees for function approximation. In our implementation, each iteration of FQI is performed on a random subset of 10% of all transitions in the training set, as described in Algorithm 1, such that on average, each sample is seen in a tenth of all iterations. Though sampling increases the total number of iterations required for convergence, it yields significant speed-ups in building trees at each iteration, and hence in total training time. The ensemble regressor learns 50 trees, with regularization in the form of a minimum leaf node size of 20 samples. We present here results with FQI performed for a fixed number of 100 iterations, though it is possible to use a convergence criterion of the form $\Delta(Q_k, Q_{k-1}) \leq \varepsilon$ for early stopping, to speed up training further.

For comparison, we used he same methods to run FQI with neural networks (NFQ) in place of tree-based regression: we train a feedforward network with architecture and techniques identical to those applied in our function approximation for Q-learning. Convergence of the estimated Q-function for both regressors is measured by the Bellman residual (Ernst et al. [2005]), i.e. the mean squared change in $\hat{Q}$ between consecutive updates (Figure 5), which shows that the algorithm takes roughly 60 iterations to converge in both cases. However, NFQ yields a roughly four-fold gain in runtime speed, as expected, since with neural networks we can simply update network weights at each iteration.

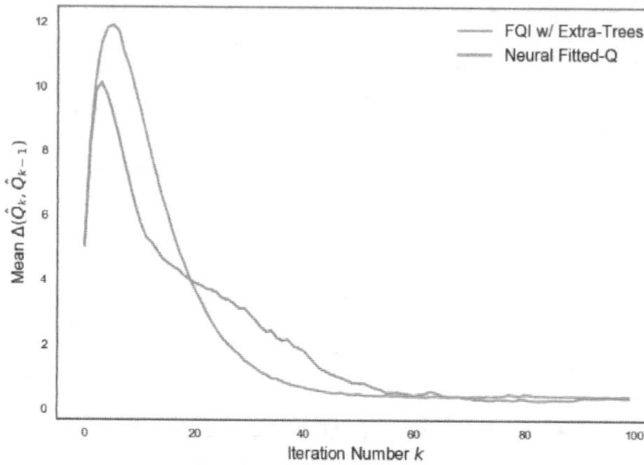

Figure 5: Convergence of estimated Q using FQI, given by the mean change in $\hat{Q}(s, a)$ over successive iterations.

The estimated Q-functions from FQI with Extra-Trees (FQIT) and from NFQ are then used to evaluate the optimal action, i.e. that which maximizes the value of the state-action pair, for each state in the training set. We can then train policy functions $\pi(s)$ mapping a given patient state to the corresponding optimal action $a \in \mathcal{A}$. To allow for clinical interpretation of the final policy, we choose to train an Extra-Trees classifier with an ensemble of 100 trees to represent the policy function.

The relative importance assigned to the top 24 features in the state space for the policy trees learnt, when training on optimal actions from both FQIT and NFQ, show that the five vitals ranking highest in importance across the two policies are arterial O_2 pressure, arterial pH, FiO_2, O_2 flow and PEEP set (Figure 6). These are as expected—Arterial pH, FiO_2, and PEEP all feature in our preliminary HUP guidelines for extubation criteria, and there is considerable literature suggesting blood gases are an important indicator of readiness for weaning (Hoo [2012]). On the other hand, oxygen saturation pulse oxymetry (SpO_2) which is also included in HUP's current extubation criteria, is fairly low in ranking. This may be because these measurements are highly correlated with other factors in the state space, such as arterial O_2 pressure (Collins et al. [2015]), that account for its influence on weaning more directly. The limited importance assigned to heart rate and respiratory rate, which can serve as indicators of blood pressure and blood gases, are also likely to be explained by this dependence between vitals.

In terms of demographics, weight and age play a significant role in the weaning policy learnt: weight is likely to influence our sedation policy specifically, as dosages are typically adjusted for patient weight, while age is strongly correlated with a patient's speed of recovery, and hence the time necessary on ventilator support.

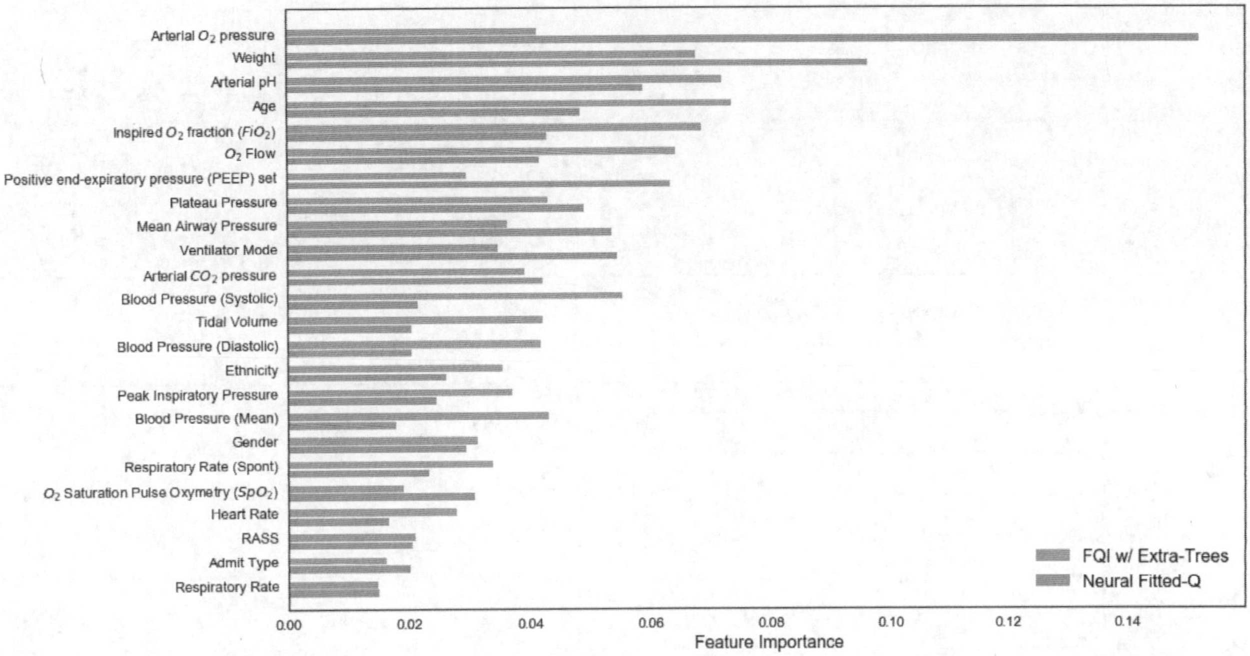

Figure 6: Feature importances (from Gini importance scoring) for policies trained on optimal actions from FQIT & NFQ. The relatively high weighting of indicators *Arterial pH,* FiO_2 and *PEEP set* found is in agreement with typical protocol.

As a preliminary evaluation of the policies learnt, we compare the algorithm's recommendations against the policy implemented by the hospital. Considering ventilation and sedation separately, the policies learnt with FQIT and NFQ achieve similar accuracies in recommending ventilation (both matching the hospital policy in roughly 85% of transitions), while FQIT far outperforms NFQ in the case of sedation policy (achieving 58% accuracy compared with just 28%, barely above random assignment of one of four dosage levels), perhaps due to overfitting of the neural network on this task. More data may be necessary to develop a meaningful sedation policy with NFQ. However, ultimately the goal of the policies learnt is not to simply match the decision-making of clinicians (often biased by timing of shifts or treatment costs, for example) but to maximize a reward function determined solely by clinical outcomes.

We concentrate further analysis of policy recommendations to those produced by FQIT. We divide the 664 test admissions into six groups according to the fraction of FQI policy actions that differ from the hospital's policy: Δ_0 comprises admissions in which the true and recommended policies agree perfectly, while those in Δ_5 show the greatest deviation. Plotting the distribution of number of reintubations and of mean accumulated reward over patient admissions for all patients in each set (Figures 7a and 7b respectively), we see that admissions in Δ_0 undergo no reintubation, and in general the average number of reintubations increases with deviation from the FQIT policy, with up to seven distinct intubations observed in admissions in Δ_5. This trend is reinforced by that in mean rewards across the six admission groups, which serve primarily as an indicator of the regulation of vitals within desired ranges and whether certain criteria were met at extubation: mean reward over a set is highest (and the range lowest) for admissions in which the policies match exactly; mean reward decreases with increasing divergence of the two policies. A less distinct but comparable pattern is seen when grouping admissions instead by similarity of the sedation policy to the true dosage levels administered by the hospital (Figures 7c and 7d).

5 CONCLUSION

In this work, we propose a data-driven approach to the optimization of weaning from mechanical ventilation of patients in the ICU. We model patient admissions as Markov decision processes, developing novel representations of the problem state, action space, and reward function in this framework. Reinforcement learning with fitted Q-iteration using different regressors is then used to learn a simple ventilator weaning policy from examples in historical ICU data. We demonstrate that the algorithm is capable of extracting meaningful indicators for patient readiness and shows promise in recommending extubation time and sedation levels, on average outperforming clinical practice in terms of regulation of vitals and reintubations.

There are a number of challenges that must be overcome before these methods can be meaningfully implemented in a clinical setting, however: first, in order to generate robust treatment recommendations, it is important to ensure policy invariance to reward shaping: the current methods

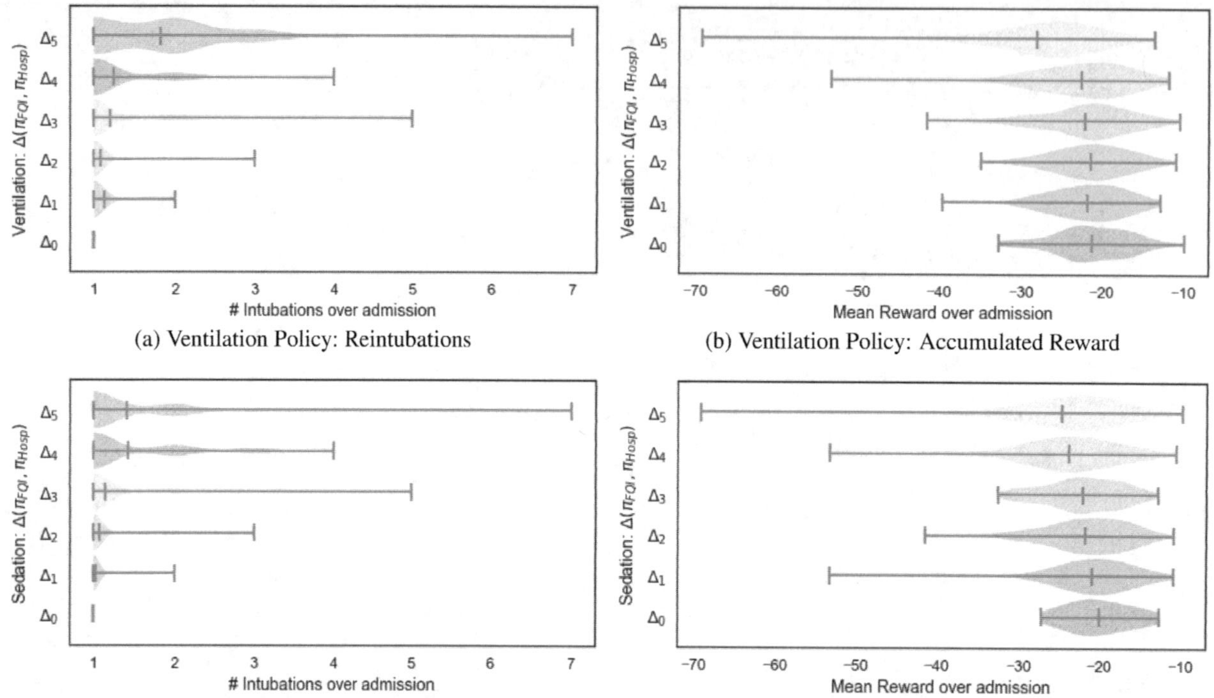

(a) Ventilation Policy: Reintubations

(b) Ventilation Policy: Accumulated Reward

(c) Sedation Policy: Reintubations

(d) Sedation Policy: Accumulated Reward

Figure 7: Evaluating policy in terms of reward and number of reintubations suggests admissions where actions match our policy more closely are generally associated with better patient outcomes, both in terms of number of reintubations and accumulated reward, which reflects in part the regulation of vitals.

display considerable sensitivity to the relative weighting of various components of the feedback received after each transition. A more principled approach to the design of the reward function, for example by applying techniques in inverse reinforcement learning (Ng et al. [2000]), can help tackle this sensitivity. In addition, addressing the question of censoring in sub-optimal historical data and explicitly correcting for the bias that arises from the timing of interventions is crucial to fair evaluation of learnt policies, particularly where they deviate from the actions taken by the clinician. Finally, effective communication of the best action, expected reward, and the associated uncertainty, calls for a probabilistic approach to estimation of the Q-function, which can perhaps be addressed by pairing regressors such as Gaussian processes with Fitted Q-iteration.

Possible directions for future work also include increasing the sophistication of the state space, for example by handling long term effects more explicitly using second-order statistics of vitals, applying techniques in inverse reinforcement learning to feature engineering (as in Levine et al. [2010]), or modeling the system as a partially observable MDP, in which observations map to some underlying state space. Extending the action space to include continuous dosages of specific drug types and settings such as ventilator modes and FiO_2 will also facilitate directly actionable policy recommendations. With further efforts to tackle these challenges, the reinforcement learning methods explored here will play a crucial role in helping to inform patient-specific decisions in critical care.

References

Nicolino Ambrosino and Luciano Gabbrielli. The difficult-to-wean patient. *Expert Review of Respiratory Medicine*, 4(5):685–692, 2010.

Hannah Wunsch, Jason Wagner, Maximilian Herlim, David Chong, Andrew Kramer, and Scott D Halpern. Icu occupancy and mechanical ventilator use in the united states. *Critical care medicine*, 41(12), 2013.

Shruti B Patel and John P Kress. Sedation and analgesia in the mechanically ventilated patient. *American journal of respiratory and critical care medicine*, 185(5):486–497, 2012.

Christopher G Hughes, Stuart McGrane, and Pratik P Pandharipande. Sedation in the intensive care setting. *Clin Pharmacol*, 4:53–63, 2012.

James S Krinsley, Praveen K Reddy, and Abid Iqbal. What is the optimal rate of failed extubation? *Critical Care*, 16(1):111, 2012.

Giorgio Conti, Jean Mantz, Dan Longrois, and Peter Tonner. Sedation and weaning from mechanical ventilation: Time for 'best practice' to catch up with new realities? *Multidisciplinary respiratory medicine*, 9(1):45, 2014.

J Goldstone. The pulmonary physician in critical care: Difficult weaning. *Thorax*, 57(11):986–991, 2002.

Damien Ernst, Guy-Bart Stan, Jorge Goncalves, and Louis Wehenkel. Clinical data based optimal sti strategies for hiv: A reinforcement learning approach. In *2006 45th IEEE Conference on Decision and Control*, pages 667–672. IEEE, 2006.

Yufan Zhao, Donglin Zeng, Mark A. Socinski, and Michael R. Kosorok. Reinforcement learning strategies for clinical trials in nonsmall cell lung cancer. *Biometrics*, 67(4):1422–1433, 2011.

Pablo Escandell-Montero, Milena Chermisi, Jos M. Martnez-Martnez, Juan Gmez-Sanchis, Carlo Barbieri, Emilio Soria-Olivas, Flavio Mari, Joan Vila-Francs, Andrea Stopper, Emanuele Gatti, and Jos D. Martn-Guerrero. Optimization of anemia treatment in hemodialysis patients via reinforcement learning. *Artificial Intelligence in Medicine*, 62(1):47 – 60, 2014.

Brett L Moore, Eric D Sinzinger, Todd M Quasny, and Larry D Pyeatt. Intelligent control of closed-loop sedation in simulated icu patients. In *FLAIRS Conference*, pages 109–114, 2004.

R. Padmanabhan, N. Meskin, and W. M. Haddad. Closed-loop control of anesthesia and mean arterial pressure using reinforcement learning. In *2014 IEEE Symposium on Adaptive Dynamic Programming and Reinforcement Learning (ADPRL)*, pages 1–8, Dec 2014.

S. Nemati, M. M. Ghassemi, and G. D. Clifford. Optimal medication dosing from suboptimal clinical examples: A deep reinforcement learning approach. In *2016 38th Annual International Conference of the IEEE Engineering in Medicine and Biology Society (EMBC)*, pages 2978–2981, Aug 2016.

Martina Mueller, Jonas S Almeida, Romesh Stanislaus, and Carol L Wagner. Can machine learning methods predict extubation outcome in premature infants as well as clinicians? *Journal of neonatal biology*, 2, 2013.

Hung-Ju Kuo, Hung-Wen Chiu, Chun-Nin Lee, Tzu-Tao Chen, Chih-Cheng Chang, and Mauo-Ying Bien. Improvement in the prediction of ventilator weaning outcomes by an artificial neural network in a medical icu. *Respiratory care*, 60(11):1560–1569, 2015.

Yuanyuan Gao, Anqi Xu, Paul Jen-Hwa Hu, and Tsang-Hsiang Cheng. Incorporating association rule networks in feature category-weighted naive bayes model to support weaning decision making. *Decision Support Systems*, 2017.

Alistair EW Johnson, Tom J Pollard, Lu Shen, Li-wei H Lehman, Mengling Feng, Mohammad Ghassemi, Benjamin Moody, Peter Szolovits, Leo Anthony Celi, and Roger G Mark. Mimic-iii, a freely accessible critical care database. *Scientific data*, 3, 2016.

Oliver Stegle, Sebastian V. Fallert, David J. C. MacKay, and Søren Brage. Gaussian process robust regression for noisy heart rate data. *IEEE Transactions on Biomedical Engineering*, 55(9):2143–2151, 2008.

Robert Dürichen, Marco A. F. Pimentel, Lei Clifton, Achim Schweikard, and David A. Clifton. Multitask Gaussian processes for multivariate physiological time-series analysis. *IEEE Transactions on Biomedical Engineering*, 62(1):314–322, 2015.

Marzyeh Ghassemi, Marco A. F. Pimentel, Tristan Naumann, Thomas Brennan, David A. Clifton, Peter Szolovits, and Mengling Feng. A multivariate timeseries modeling approach to severity of illness assessment and forecasting in ICU with sparse, heterogeneous clinical data. In *Proceedings of the Twenty-Ninth AAAI Conference on Artificial Intelligence*, pages 446–453, 2015.

Li-Fang Cheng, Gregory Darnell, Corey Chivers, Michael Draugelis, Kai Li, and Barbara Engelhardt. Sparse Multi-Output Gaussian Processes for Medical Time Series Prediction. *ArXiv e-prints*, March 2017.

Carl Edward Rasmussen and Christopher K. I. Williams. *Gaussian Processes for Machine Learning*. The MIT Press, 2006.

Dirk Ormoneit and Śaunak Sen. Kernel-based reinforcement learning. *Machine learning*, 49(2-3):161–178, 2002.

Pierre Geurts, Damien Ernst, and Louis Wehenkel. Extremely randomized trees. *Machine learning*, 63(1):3–42, 2006.

Damien Ernst, Pierre Geurts, and Louis Wehenkel. Tree-based batch mode reinforcement learning. *Journal of Machine Learning Research*, 6(Apr):503–556, 2005.

Martin Riedmiller. Neural fitted q iteration–first experiences with a data efficient neural reinforcement learning method. In *European Conference on Machine Learning*, pages 317–328. Springer, 2005.

Diederik Kingma and Jimmy Ba. Adam: A method for stochastic optimization. *arXiv preprint arXiv:1412.6980*, 2014.

Guy W Soo Hoo. Blood gases, weaning, and extubation. *Respiratory Care*, 48(11):1019–1021, 2012.

Julie-Ann Collins, Aram Rudenski, John Gibson, Luke Howard, and Ronan ODriscoll. Relating oxygen partial pressure, saturation and content: the haemoglobin–oxygen dissociation curve. *Breathe*, 11(3):194, 2015.

Andrew Y Ng, Stuart J Russell, et al. Algorithms for inverse reinforcement learning. 2000.

Sergey Levine, Zoran Popovic, and Vladlen Koltun. Feature construction for inverse reinforcement learning. In *Advances in Neural Information Processing Systems*, pages 1342–1350, 2010.

Near-Optimal Interdiction of Factored MDPs

Swetasudha Panda and Yevgeniy Vorobeychik
Electrical Engineering and Computer Science
Vanderbilt University
Nashville, TN
swetasudha.panda,yevgeniy.vorobeychik@vanderbilt.edu

Abstract

Stackelberg games have been widely used to model interactions between attackers and defenders in a broad array of security domains. One related approach involves plan interdiction, whereby a defender chooses a subset of actions to block (remove), and the attacker constructs an optimal plan in response. In previous work, this approach has been introduced in the context of Markov decision processes (MDPs). The key challenge, however, is that the state space of MDPs grows exponentially in the number of state variables. We propose a novel scalable MDP interdiction framework which makes use of factored representation of state, using a parity function basis for representing a value function over a Boolean space. We demonstrate that our approach is significantly more scalable than prior art, while resulting in near-optimal interdiction decisions.

1 INTRODUCTION

Stackelberg game approaches to security have received considerable attention in recent years, both in theoretical investigation and practical use [8, 11, 14]. A major challenge in such approaches is high-resolution modeling of adversarial evasion of defensive measures. Letchford and Vorobeychik proposed modeling such evasion in a Stackelberg framework of *plan interdiction* [12], where the Stackelberg leader eliminates a subset of attack actions, and the adversary computes an optimal plan in the restricted action space. This approach was developed both in the context of deterministic (PDDL-based) planning, and planning with Markov decision processes (MDPs). However, while interdiction of deterministic plans was quite scalable, the approach scaled very poorly in the context of MDPs. The central challenge with MDP interdiction is the exponential size of the state space in the number of state variables.

We aim to address the problem of MDP interdiction at scale by leveraging approximation techniques developed for factored MDPs. Scalability in factored MDPs has been achieved by two basic approaches: a) exploting structure in the MDP transition model and reward function [3, 2, 9], and b) value function approximation [1, 9, 10, 4, 16, 5]. Factored MDPs [6] represent the complex state space using state variables and the transition model using a dynamic Bayesian network. This representation allows an exponential reduction in the representation size of structured MDPs. Moreover, efficient approximate solution algorithms have been proposed that exploit structure in factored MDPs.

Starting with the approximation methods for factored MDPs, we develop a mixed-integer linear programming approach for factored MDP interdiction. In doing so, we face two challenges: 1) effective basis representation, and 2) a super-exponential set of constraints corresponding to alternative evasion plans for the attacker. To address the first challenge, we propose using a Fourier (parity function) basis over a Boolean hypercube to represent the value function over a binary factor space. While there always exists an exact Fourier basis for functions over a Boolean space, the representation is exponential in size. We address this challenge by developing iterative basis generation methods. Addressing the second challenge of an intractably large constraint space, we develop a novel constraint generation algorithm using a combination of linear programming factored MDP solvers and novel heuristics for attack plan generation. We demonstrate the effectiveness of the proposed approaches on realistic examples from the international planning competition (IPC). In particular, we show that our approach offers dramatically improved scalability without significantly compromising solution quality.

2 PRELIMINARIES

Our work builds on solution approaches for discounted infinite-horizon MDPs, and particularly for factored MDPs, which we now introduce.

MDPs and Factored MDPs Formally, a discounted infinite-horizon MDP is defined as a tuple $\mathcal{D} = (\mathbf{X}, A, R, P, \gamma)$ where $\mathbf{X}$ is a finite set of $|\mathbf{X}| = N$ states; A is a finite set of actions; R is a *reward function* $R : \mathbf{X} \times A \mapsto \mathbb{R}$, in which $R(\mathbf{x}, a)$ is the reward obtained by the agent in state $\mathbf{x}$ after taking action a; P is a *Markovian transition model* where $P(\mathbf{x}'|\mathbf{x}, a)$ is the probability of moving from state $\mathbf{x}$ to $\mathbf{x}'$, after taking action a; and $\gamma \in [0, 1)$ is the discount factor which exponentially discounts future rewards. It is well-known that such MDPs always admit an optimal *stationary deterministic policy*, which is a mapping $\pi : \mathbf{X} \mapsto A$, where $\pi(\mathbf{x})$ is the action the agent takes at state $\mathbf{x}$ [15]. Each policy can be associated with a *value function* $\mathcal{V}_\pi \in \mathbb{R}^N$, where $\mathcal{V}_\pi(\mathbf{x})$ is the discounted cumulative value obtained by starting at state $\mathbf{x}$ and following policy π. Formally,

$$\mathcal{V}_\pi(\mathbf{x}) = E_\pi\left[\sum_{t=0}^{\infty} \gamma^t R(\mathbf{X}^t, \pi(\mathbf{X}^t)) | \mathbf{x}^{(0)} = \mathbf{x}\right],$$

where $\mathbf{X}^{(t)}$ is a random variable representing the state of the system after t steps.

The discounted reward MDP is a natural model for security, since it captures the fact that attackers prefer to achieve their goals (positive rewards) earlier, and incur costs (negative rewards) later. Additionally, it captures an element of deterrence: the attack which takes too many steps has far more opportunities to fail in practice. Thus, minor (low-reward) goals may be preferred over major (high-reward) goals if they can be achieved much more quickly.

Factored MDPs exploit problem structure to compactly represent MDPs. The set of states is described by a set of *random state variables* $\mathbf{X} = \{X_1, \ldots, X_n\}$. Let $\mathrm{Dom}(X_i)$ be the domain of values for X_i. A state $\mathbf{x}$ defines a value $x_i \in \mathrm{Dom}(X_i)$ for each variable X_i. *Throughout, we assume that all variables are Boolean.* The transition model for each action a is compactly represented as the product of local factors by using a DBN. Let X_i denote the variable X_i at the current time and X_i' the same variable at the next time step. For a given action a, each node X_i' is associated with a conditional probability distribution (CPD) $P_a(X_i'|\mathrm{Parents}_a(X_i'))$. The transition probability is given by $P_a(\mathbf{x}'|\mathbf{x}) = \prod_i P_a(x_i'|\mathbf{x}[\mathrm{Parents}_a(X_i')])$, where $\mathbf{x}[\mathrm{Parents}_a(X_i')]$ is the value in $\mathbf{x}$ to the variables in $\mathrm{Parents}_a(X_i')$. The complexity of this representation is linear in the number of state variables and exponential in the number of variables in the largest factor. The reward function is represented as the sum of a set of localized reward functions. Let $R_1^a, \ldots, R_r^a$ be a set of functions, where the scope of each R_i^a is restricted to the variable cluster $\mathbf{W}_i^a \subset \{X_1, \ldots, X_n\}$. The reward for taking action a at state $\mathbf{x}$ is then $R^a(\mathbf{x}) = \sum_{i=1}^{r} R_i^a(\mathbf{W}_i^a) \in \mathbb{R}$.

Linear Programming Methods for Solving MDPs A common method for computing an optimal policy of an MDP is by using the following linear program (LP):

$$\min \sum_{\mathbf{x}} \alpha(\mathbf{x}) V(\mathbf{x}) \tag{1a}$$

$$\text{s.t.: } \forall \mathbf{x}, a, V(\mathbf{x}) \geq R(\mathbf{x}, a) + \gamma \sum_{\mathbf{x}'} P(\mathbf{x}'|\mathbf{x}, a) V(\mathbf{x}'). \tag{1b}$$

where the variables $V(\mathbf{x})$ represent the value function $\mathcal{V}(\mathbf{x})$, starting at state $\mathbf{x}$. The *state relevance weights* αs are such that $\alpha(\mathbf{x}) > 0$ and $\sum_{\mathbf{x}} \alpha(x) = 1$. The optimal policy π^* can be computed as the greedy policy with respect to $\mathcal{V}^*$, $\pi^* = \arg\max_a [R(\mathbf{x}, a) + \gamma \sum_{\mathbf{x}'} P(\mathbf{x}'|\mathbf{x}, a) V(\mathbf{x}')]$. The dual of this LP (dual LP) maximizes the total expected reward for all actions:

$$\max \sum_{\mathbf{x}} \sum_{a} \phi_a(\mathbf{x}) R(\mathbf{x}, a) \tag{2a}$$

$$\text{s.t.: } \forall \mathbf{x}, a, \quad \phi_a(\mathbf{x}) \geq 0 \tag{2b}$$

$$\forall \mathbf{x}, \sum_a \phi_a(\mathbf{x}) = \alpha(\mathbf{x}) + \gamma \sum_a \sum_{\mathbf{x}'} P(\mathbf{x}|\mathbf{x}', a) \phi_a(\mathbf{x}'). \tag{2c}$$

where $\phi_a(\mathbf{x})$ called the *visitation frequency* for state $\mathbf{x}$ and action a is the (discounted) expected number of times that state $\mathbf{x}$ will be visited and action a will be executed in this state. There is a one-to-one correspondence between policies in the MDP and feasible solutions to the dual LP.

In the case of factored MDPs, there is no guarantee that the structure extends to the value function [9] and linear value function approximation is a common approach. A factored (linear) value function $\mathcal{V}$ is a *linear function* over a set of *basis functions* $H = \{h_1, \ldots, h_k\}$, such that $\mathcal{V}(\mathbf{x}) = \sum_{j=1}^{k} w_j h_j(\mathbf{x})$ for some coefficients $\mathbf{w} = (w_1, \ldots, w_k)'$, where the scope of each h_i is restricted to some subset of variables $\mathbf{C}_i$. The approximate LP corresponding to (1) is given by Guestrin et al. [6]:

$$\min \sum_i \alpha_i w_i \tag{3a}$$

s.t.: $\forall a, \max_{\mathbf{x}} \{R^a(\mathbf{x}) + \sum_i w_i[\gamma g_i^a(\mathbf{x}) - h_i(\mathbf{x})]\} \leq 0.$ (3b)

where for basis h_i, $\alpha_i = \sum_{\mathbf{x}} \alpha(\mathbf{x}) h_i(\mathbf{x})$ is the factored equivalent of α and $g_i^a(\mathbf{x}) = \sum_{\mathbf{x}'} P(\mathbf{x}'|\mathbf{x}, a) h_i(\mathbf{x}')$ is the factored representation of expected future value. The non-linear constraint in LP (3) can be represented by a set of linear constraints using approaches similar to variable elimination in cost networks. The factored dual approximation LP [7] is defined on a set of variable clusters $\mathcal{B} \supseteq \mathcal{B}_{FMDP}$ where $\mathcal{B}_{FMDP} = \{\mathbf{W}_1^a, \ldots, \mathbf{W}_r^a : \forall a\} \cup \{\mathbf{C}_1, \ldots, \mathbf{C}_k\} \cup \{\Gamma_a(\mathbf{C}_1), \ldots, \Gamma_a(\mathbf{C}_k) : \forall a\}$, $\Gamma_a(\mathbf{C}) = \cup_{X_i \in \mathbf{C}} \text{PARENTS}_a(X_i) = \text{Scope}[g]$ is the set of parent state variables of variables in $\mathbf{C}$ (Scope$[h]$) in the DBN for action a. This factored dual LP is given by:

$$\max \sum_a \sum_{j=1}^{r} \sum_{\mathbf{w}_j^a \in \text{Dom}[\mathbf{W}_j^a]} \mu_a(\mathbf{w}_j^a) R_j^a(\mathbf{w}_j^a)$$

s.t.:

$$\forall i = 1, \ldots, k :$$

$$\sum_{\mathbf{c} \in \text{Dom}[\mathbf{C}_i]} \mu(\mathbf{c}) h_i(\mathbf{c}) = \sum_{\mathbf{c} \in \text{Dom}[\mathbf{C}_i]} \alpha(\mathbf{c}) h_i(\mathbf{c})$$

$$+ \gamma \sum_a \sum_{\mathbf{y} \in \text{Dom}[\Gamma_a(\mathbf{C}_i')]} \mu_a(\mathbf{y}) g_i^a(\mathbf{y}) \quad (4a)$$

$$\forall \mathbf{B}_i, \mathbf{B}_j \in \mathcal{B}, \forall \mathbf{y} \in \text{Dom}[\mathbf{B}_i \cap \mathbf{B}_j], \forall a :$$

$$\sum_{\mathbf{b}_i \sim [\mathbf{y}]} \mu_a(\mathbf{b}_i) = \sum_{\mathbf{b}_j \sim [\mathbf{y}]} \mu_a(\mathbf{b}_j) \quad (4b)$$

$$\forall \mathbf{B} \in \mathcal{B}, \forall \mathbf{b} \in \text{Dom}[\mathbf{B}], \forall a, \mu_a(\mathbf{b}) \geq 0 \quad (4c)$$

$$\mu(\mathbf{b}) = \sum_{a'} \mu_{a'}(\mathbf{b}), \quad (4d)$$

$$\sum_{\mathbf{b}' \in \text{Dom}[\mathbf{B}]} \mu(\mathbf{b}') = \frac{1}{1-\gamma} \quad (4e)$$

where $\mu_a(\mathbf{b}) = \sum_{\mathbf{x} \sim [\mathbf{b}]} \phi_a(\mathbf{x}), \forall \mathbf{b} \in \text{Dom}[\mathbf{B}]$ is the *marginal visitation frequency* for a subset of state variables $\mathbf{B} \subset \mathbf{X}$ ($\mathbf{b} \in \text{Dom}[\mathbf{B}]$ represents enumeration of the variables in $\mathbf{B}$ and $\mathbf{x} \sim [\mathbf{b}]$ are the assignments of $\mathbf{x}$ that are consistent with $\mathbf{b}$), and $\mu(\mathbf{b}) = \sum_a \mu_a(\mathbf{b})$. The constraints ensure that these μ_a variables are consistent across variable subsets. The factored dual approximation is guranteed to be equivalent to the dual LP-based approximation [7] if the factored MDP cluster set $\mathcal{B}$ forms a junction tree. Triangulation $\mathbf{Tr}(\mathcal{B}_{FMDP})$ constructs a junction tree by adding cluster sets to $\mathcal{B}$ if needed. Approximate triangulation $\hat{\mathbf{Tr}}(\mathcal{B})$ returns some cluster set $\mathcal{B}'$ such that $\mathcal{B} \subseteq \mathcal{B}'$. The constant basis function h_0—i.e., with scope as the empty set $\{\emptyset\}$—is always included in H for feasibility of the above factored LPs.

Computing Attack Policies Policies in factored MDPs can be compactly represented assuming the default action model [10]. Different actions often have very similar transition dynamics, only differing in their effect on a small subset of variables. In factored MDPs that follow a *default transition model* for each action a, $Effects[a] \subset \mathbf{X}'$ are the variables in the next state whose local probability model is different from the model for the default action d, i.e., $P_a(X_i'|\text{Parents}_a(X_i')) \neq P_d(X_i'|\text{Parents}_d(X_i'))$ [10]. Similarly, in the *default reward model*, there is a set of reward functions for the default action d. The extra reward of any action a has scope restricted to $\mathbf{W}_i^a$. With the above assumptions, the greedy policy relative to a factored value function can be represented as a decision list [6].

However, this default action model is often not applicable in many real world examples. In such cases, we solve the approximate factored dual LP and monitor the values of the μ_a variables as a proxy to determine if a certain action appears in the computed policy. More precisely, if ϕ_a is a feasible solution to the exact dual LP, then in a state $\mathbf{x}$, $\phi_a(\mathbf{x}) > 0$ if $a = \pi(\mathbf{x})$ and $\phi_a(\mathbf{x}) = 0$ for all other actions. In the approximate solution with a subset of basis functions, all ϕ_a variables may not be represented by the set of μ_a variables. However, we can approximately determine the set of actions in a policy by removing those actions a from the set of allowed actions, for which $\mu_a(\mathbf{b}) = 0 \; \forall \mathbf{b} \in \text{Dom}[\mathbf{B}], \forall \mathbf{B} \in \mathcal{B}$.

3 MDP INTERDICTION

3.1 PROBLEM DEFINITION

We model MDP interdiction as a Stackelberg (two-stage, one-shot) game with two players: defender and attacker. The defender, who is the Stackelberg leader, commits to a set of mitigations, and the attacker, who is the follower, computes an MDP policy which optimally responds to (e.g., evades) these mitigations.

Formally, the *MDP interdiction problem (MDPI)* is defined by a tuple $\{\mathcal{M}, C_m, R^D, R^A, \mathbf{X}, A, P, \gamma\}$. $\mathcal{M}$ is the set of mitigation strategies available to the defender, R^D and R^A are the reward functions for the defender and the attacker respectively, C_m is the cost of a mitigation $m \in \mathcal{M}$ to the defender, and $\mathbf{X}, A, P, \gamma$ are the state space, action space, transition function, and discount factor of an infinite-horizon discounted MDPs which the attacker is solving in response to mitigations deployed by the defender. The semantics of a mitigation $m \in \mathcal{M}$ is that it removes (protects against) a subset of attack actions from the original attacker action space

A.[1] For a given set of mitigations $M \subseteq \mathcal{M}$ deployed by the defender, we can define an attacker's resulting MDP, $\tau(M) = [\mathbf{X}, A(M), R^A, P, \gamma]$ over the restricted action space $A(M)$ which includes only the actions which are not removed by any mitigation $m \in M$. In the MDPI Stackelberg game, the defender first chooses $M \subseteq \mathcal{M}$, and the attacker subsequently chooses a policy π in the resulting restricted MDP $\tau(M)$. Since the attacker is effectively facing a decision problem, it will suffice to restrict attention to optimal attacker policies which are deterministic and stationary. Let $\Pi^*(M)$ be the set of optimal deterministic stationary policies of $\tau(M)$. Define $\mathcal{V}^A(\mathbf{x}, \pi)$ to be the attacker's value function for a policy π starting at state $\mathbf{x}$ in MDP $\tau(M)$, and let $\mathcal{V}^D(\mathbf{x}, \pi)$ be the defender's value function (i.e., using the defender's reward function R^D). Let $\mathbf{x}_0$ be the initial state of the MDP. We seek a *strong Stackelberg equilibrium (SSE)* of MDPI, in which the defender solves

$$\max_{M \subseteq \mathcal{M}} \mathcal{V}^D(\mathbf{x}_0, \pi^*(M)) - \sum_{m \in M} C_m,$$

where $\pi^*(M) \in \arg\max_{\pi \in \Pi^*(M)} \mathcal{V}^A(\mathbf{x}_0, \pi)$, and the attacker breaks ties in the defender's favor.

3.2 GENERAL APPROACH

Letchford and Vorobeychik proposed a general approach for MDP interdiction [12] based on a mixed-integer linear programming (MILP). If we define variables D_m which are 1 iff the defender chooses a mitigation m, the defender's objective becomes $\max \sum_{\mathbf{x}} \sum_{a} \phi_a(\mathbf{x}) R^D(\mathbf{x}, a) - \sum_{m \in M} D_m C_m$, where $\phi_a(\mathbf{x})$ are the dual variables of the MDP linear program as before. The attacker's objective is then given by $\max \sum_{\mathbf{x}} \sum_{a} \phi_a(\mathbf{x}) R^A(\mathbf{x}, a)$. To account for the attacker's best response, a set of constraints was introduced for the defender so that a) the optimal attacker policy chosen by the MILP is feasible given the set of defender mitigations, and b) the attacker's utility corresponding to this computed policy is better than that of any other feasible policy. Since the general approach relies on the exact representation of the state space, it fails to scale. Below we introduce our general framework which leverages the factored representation of MDPs, enabling scalability to practical problem instances.

[1] This is quite general; for example, we can model mitigations which modify the initial state by including actions with no preconditions and effects which represent initial state, and allow interdiction of these actions.

3.3 A MILP FORMULATION FOR FACTORED MDP INTERDICTION

We first exhibit the defender and attacker objectives using a factored representation of states. Given a set of basis functions H and the variable cluster set $\mathcal{B}_{FMDP}$ the defender's utility is given by

$$\sum_{a} \sum_{j=1}^{r} \sum_{\mathbf{w}_j^a \in \text{Dom}[\mathbf{W}_j^a]} \mu_a(\mathbf{w}_j^a) R_j^{Da}(\mathbf{w}_j^a) - \sum_{m \in M} D_m C_m,$$

where the expected sum of rewards is represented by the μ_a variables, the factored version of the visitation frequencies with scope restricted to that of the local reward functions. The first term is to minimize the attacker's value of the initial state (we set $R^D = -R^A$ in our experiments) and the second term represents mitigation costs. The attacker's objective, in turn, is

$$\sum_{a} \sum_{j=1}^{r} \sum_{\mathbf{w}_j^a \in \text{Dom}[\mathbf{W}_j^a]} \mu_a(\mathbf{w}_j^a) R_j^{Aa}(\mathbf{w}_j^a).$$

For each mitigation $m \in M$, let $A_{m,a} = 1$ iff m removes action a. To ensure that the computed policy is feasible, we add the constraints 4a-4e in the approximate factored dual LP. Let $\delta_\pi = 1$ if and only if the policy π is interdicted, i.e., there is a deployed mitigation m that removes at least one action from π. We denote the following MILP formulation for *MDPI* by *MDPI_MILP*:

$$\max \sum_{a} \sum_{j=1}^{r} \sum_{\mathbf{w}_j^a \in \text{Dom}[\mathbf{W}_j^a]} \mu_a(\mathbf{w}_j^a) R_j^{Da}(\mathbf{w}_j^a) - \sum_{m} D_m C_m$$

s.t.:

$$\forall a, m, D_m A_{m,a} \leq D_a \leq \sum_{m'} D_{m'} A_{m',a} \quad (5a)$$

$$\forall a, \forall \mathbf{B} \in \mathcal{B}, \forall \mathbf{b} \in \text{Dom}[\mathbf{B}], \quad \mu_a(\mathbf{b}) \leq Z(1 - D_a) \quad (5b)$$

$$\forall \pi, a \in \pi, D_a \leq \delta_\pi \leq \sum_{a' \in \pi} D_{a'} \quad (5c)$$

$$\forall \pi, \sum_{a} \sum_{j=1}^{r} \sum_{\mathbf{w}_j^a \in \text{Dom}[\mathbf{W}_j^a]} \mu_a(\mathbf{w}_j^a) R_j^{Aa}(\mathbf{w}_j^a) \geq \mathcal{V}^A(\mathbf{x}_0, \pi) - Z\delta_\pi \quad (5d)$$

constraints $4a - 4e$

where Z is a large number and $\mathcal{B} = \mathbf{Tr}(\mathcal{B}_{FMDP})$. (We use $\hat{\mathbf{Tr}}(\mathcal{B}) = \mathcal{B}$ so that $\mathcal{B} = \mathcal{B}_{FMDP}$). The constraints 5a compute a variable D_a such that $D_a = 1$ iff there is a mitigation m that interdicts action a. Constraint 5b ensures that if an action is interdicted, the corresponding visitation frequencies are 0. Constraints 5c compute

δ_π. Constraints 5d represents the condition that the policy generated for the attacker is its best response to the defender's choce of mitigations.

If H, the set of basis functions considered is general enough to include the full value function space, the solution to this MILP yields the optimal interdiction decision for the defender. The key challenge, however, is (a) what basis function space we should consider, and (b) given that capturing arbitrary value functions in the basis space is likely intractable, how can we best approximate a value function basis in this space. Finally, the set of constraints captures all possible attack policies, thereby rendering the MILP too large to be tractable even with a compact set of bases. We address these challenges next, starting with the issue of iteratively generating constraints to avoid complete enumeration of the policy space (Section 4), and proceeding to address the basis selection problem thereafter (Section 5).

4 CONSTRAINT GENERATION FOR FACTORED MDP INTERDICTION

The MDP interdiction algorithm requires the addition of policies and the corresponding utilities as constraints (captured by Constraint 5d). To compute the attacker's best response, we solve the approximate primal LP 3 for a given basis set H (we deal with the basis selection problem in Section 5). We can then compute the attacker's policy as discussed in Section 2.

4.1 CONSTRAINT GENERATION WITH BASIS FUNCTION SELECTION

We define the *master* problem *MDPI_MASTER($\hat{\mathcal{P}}$)* as a relaxed version of the MILP with the constraints 5a-5d corresponding to a subset $\hat{\mathcal{P}}$ of all possible policies. For now, suppose that we have a method for selecting a subset of "important" basis functions (Section 5).

The constraint generation procedure (Algorithm 1) works as follows. In any iteration, $\hat{\mathcal{P}}$ contains a small set of attack policies generated thus far. We solve the master problem with $\hat{\mathcal{P}}$ to obtain a set of mitigations $\hat{M} \subseteq \mathcal{M}$, along with a policy $\hat{\pi} \in \hat{\mathcal{P}}$ with a utility of $\hat{V} = \mathcal{V}^A(\mathbf{x}_0, \hat{\pi})$ which is the attacker's best decision from the feasible subset of policies in $\hat{\mathcal{P}}$. Now there are two possibilities: either $\hat{\pi}$ is the actual best response of the attacker, in the presence of the deployed mitigations, or the actual attacker best response is not in $\hat{\mathcal{P}}$. To confirm, we can compute the best response for the attacker by solving a factored MDP (LP 3), removing actions which are blocked by the mitigations $\hat{M}$. At this point, we also improve our basis function set, as described in Section 5 (GENERATEBASIS($A_{\hat{M}}, H$)). The resulting solution will either have a utility of $\hat{V}$ to the attacker, confirming $\hat{M}$ as the optimal set of mitigations, or will be a strict improvement on $\hat{V}$, in which case we add the resulting policy (computed as described in Section 2), and its utility, to the master program, and repeat.

Algorithm 1 Constraint Generation with Basis Selection

```
function CONSTRAINTGENERATION(P̂, H)
    V = ∞
    V̂ = 0
    while V̂ < V do
        (M̂, D_a, V̂) = MDPI_MASTER(P̂, H)
        A_M̂ = ∅
        for a ∈ A do
            if D_a = 0 then
                A_M̂ = A_M̂ ∪ a
        (π, V, Ĥ) = GENERATEBASIS(A_M̂, H)
        if V > V̂ then
            P̂ = P̂ ∪ π
            H = Ĥ
```

This constraint generation procedure suffers from two important bottlenecks: the number of iterations can be large, and each iteration can be computationally costly. Next we improve upon the baseline procedure above by alleviating both of these issues.

4.1.1 Reducing the Number of Iterations of Constraint Generation

A natural way to begin the constraint generation process is with an empty subset of attack policies $\hat{\mathcal{P}}$. However, this results in a large number of iterations of the constraint generation procedure building up enough attack policies to prevent trivial mitigation solutions, which mitigate no actions, or a single action sufficient to make all policies in $\hat{\mathcal{P}}$ infeasible. To address this, we start by selecting a subset of (possibly all) attacker actions $\hat{a} \in A$. For each $\hat{a}$, we solve the attacker's best response with the single action $\hat{a}$, using the approximate primal LP 3. The corresponding attack policies have only a single action. We then define the initial subset $\hat{\mathcal{P}}$ using these sets of attacker policies and the corresponding utilities, allowing us to warm start the constraint iteration procedure and saving a considerable amount of computation time in the process.

4.1.2 Fast Constraint Generation

While warm starting considerably reduces the number of iterations of the constraint generation procedure, each iteration still involves a costly set of computational operations even to evaluate whether new policies need to be added. However, we observe that to make progress in constraint generation, we only need to find *some* policy which yields a better utility for the attacker than the optimal policy computed in the master program.

A major part of the overhead is the size of the basis set. To speed up computation, we propose to attempt generating an improved policy (ATTACKERPOLICY(A, H)) first using only a small subset of the basis function (e.g., H_1 with each basis using a single state variable, as discussed in Section 5). If the attacker's utility computed in the subproblem is greater than the best response computed by the master program, we add this policy to the set of constraints. Otherwise, we fall back on the full combined basis selection and factored MDP solution approach. This approach may need more iterations to converge, but each iteration will be much faster. Algorithm 2 is a formalization of these ideas.

Algorithm 2 Fast Constraint Generation

```
function CONSTRAINTGENERATION(P̂, H_1)
    V = ∞
    V̂ = 0
    while V̂ < V do
        (M̂, D_a, V̂)=MDPI_MASTER(P̂, H_1)
        A_M̂ = ∅
        for a ∈ A do
            if D_a = 0 then
                A_M̂ = A_M̂ ∪ a
        (π, V) = ATTACKERPOLICY(A_M̂, H_1)
        if V > V̂ then
            P̂ = P̂ ∪ π
        else
            (π, V, Ĥ) = GENERATEBASIS(A_M̂, H_1)
```

5 BASIS GENERATION

In this section we address the issue of selecting a basis function space for linear value function approximation and, subsequently, the incremental generation of the "important" set of basis functions H.

5.1 FOURIER BASIS FUNCTIONS ON BOOLEAN FEATURE SPACE

We start by making use of the assumption that all variables are Boolean. In this case, the Fourier (parity) basis for Boolean function is a natural basis choice: every function $f : \{0,1\}^n \to \mathbb{R}$ can be uniquely represented as $f(\mathbf{x}) = \sum_{S\subseteq\{1,\dots,n\}} \hat{f}(S)h_S(\mathbf{x})$ [13], where h_S is a parity function over the subset S of the variables:

$$h_S(\mathbf{x}) = \prod_{i\in S}(-1)^{x_i} = \begin{cases} +1, & \text{if } \sum_{i\in S} x_i \bmod 2 = 0. \\ -1, & \text{if } \sum_{i\in S} x_i \bmod 2 = 1. \end{cases} \quad (6)$$

While the full Fourier representation of the value function is therefore linear, and exact, it has 2^n bases. Consequently, it is crucial to intelligently select a small subset which yields a sufficiently good approximation of the value function for the purposes of computing an approximately optimal set of mitigations. We do this by an iterative basis function selection process described below.

5.2 ITERATIVE BASIS FUNCTION SELECTION

The attacker solves the approximate LP (3) to compute the best response to the imposed mitigations. Observe that the basis functions correspond to variables in this LP. Column generation can be used to generate only those variables which have the potential to improve the objective function. Thus, basis functions can be iteratively generated while computing the attacker's policy. However, since the variables $\mathbf{w}$ corresponding to the basis functions are unconstrained, the concept of reduced cost is not well-defined. In this case, we compute the magnitude of the constraint violation in the dual LP instead.

Recall that the non-linear constraint in the LP (3) $\max_{\mathbf{x}}\{R^a(\mathbf{x}) + \sum_i w_i[\gamma g_i^a(\mathbf{x}) - h_i(\mathbf{x})]\} \leq 0$ is represented as a set of linear constraints using variable elimination [6]. Instead of enumerating the entire state space, one variable is eliminated at a time. There is one set of factored LP constraints for each action a. Let X_j be the variable being eliminated. If X_j appears in any set $\mathbf{C} \cup \Gamma_a(\mathbf{C})$, ($\mathbf{C}$ = Scope[h]), and/or $\mathbf{W}^a$ (the scope of any local reward function) these set of state variables are "relevant" while eliminating X_j. Denote this set of relevant variables by $\mathbf{Z}_j^a$. Only these variables are enumerated while maximizing over X_j. For each enumeration, the linear constraint is of the form $u^{max} \geq u^R + \sum_i w_i u^{\gamma g_i - h_i}$, where u^{max} is the variable introduced after elimination, u^R is the relevant factored reward term and $u^{\gamma g_i - h_i}$ represents $\gamma g_i - h_i$ for a relevant h_i. After all state variables are eliminated, the remaining elimination-introduced variables have empty scope and the final maximization constraint is added. The number of constraints in this LP grows exponentially in the induced width of the *cost network*, the undirected graph defined over the variables $X_1, \dots, X_n$, with an edge between X_l and X_m if they appear together in $\mathbf{Z}_j^a$. Given this construction, we describe our basis function selection approach as follows.

We begin with a subset of basis functions H^0 and solve

the above factored LP. It is necessary to include $h_0 = \emptyset$ in H^0 to ensure feasibility of the LP. Next, we need to determine whether a new basis function will improve the current LP objective. We consider the dual LP

$$\begin{aligned} \max_{\lambda_k \geq 0} \quad & \sum_k u_k^R \lambda_k \\ \text{s.t.:} \quad & \sum_k u_k^{\gamma g_i - h_i} \lambda_k = \alpha_i, \forall i, \end{aligned} \tag{7}$$

where λ_k is the dual variable corresponding to a factored linear constraint k in the primal LP, and u_k^R and $u_k^{\gamma g_i - h_i}$ are the reward function and basis function terms respectively in constraint k. If a new basis h_l is added, it generates a new column in the primal LP, and thus, a new constraint in the dual LP. If the new constraint is not satisfied given the current λ, the objective can be improved by adding this basis. More precisely, if the new constraint is violated given the current λ, the amount of violation $\beta = |\sum_k u_k^{\gamma g_l - h_l} \lambda_k - \alpha_l|$ can be used to decide whether to include the new basis. We compute the magnitude of constraint violation for a possible new basis and choose the basis which maximizes this violation. We add this basis to the primal LP and repeat. Finally, we return the updated set of basis functions. The corresponding LP objective is the attacker's utility, given a set of actions A. We outline this procedure formally in Algorithm 3.

Algorithm 3 Iterative Basis Function Selection

> **function** GENERATEBASIS(A, H)
> $\lambda, V' =$ATTACKERPOLICY(A, H)
>   **for** $s \in \{1, \ldots, s_{max}\}$ **do**
>   **while** $H_s \neq \emptyset$ **do**
> $\beta = 0$
>   **for** $h_l \in H_s$ and $h_l \notin H$ **do**
>   **if** $|\sum_k u_k^{\gamma g_l - h_l} \lambda_k - \alpha_l| > \beta$ **then**
> $\beta = |\sum_k u_k^{\gamma g_l - h_l} \lambda_k - \alpha_l|$
> $\hat{h}_l = h_l$
> $H = H \cup \hat{h}_l$
> $(\lambda, V) =$ATTACKERPOLICY(A, H)
>   **if** $|V - V'| < \theta$ **then return** V', H
> $H_s = H_s \setminus \hat{h}_l$
> $V' = V$

In Algorithm 3, ATTACKERPOLICY(A, H) solves the LP (3) and H_s is the set of parity basis functions over s state variables. To maintain smaller cost networks, we consider all bases of a particular size before moving to the next size until $s = s_{max}$, for some $s_{max} \leq n$. Within a particular size, we consider those variable clusters that are also connected in the underlying DBN of the factored MDP (i.e., one variable is the parent node of the other variable). We observe that many dual variables λ_k will be 0 so that we can restrict all computations to the set of active constraints $\{k, \lambda_k > 0\}$. Finally, using the parity basis functions allows two simplifications. First, we consider the g^a variable corresponding to a basis h: $g^a(\mathbf{y}) = \sum_{\mathbf{c} \in \mathbf{C}} \prod_{i|X_i \in \mathbf{C}} P_a(\mathbf{c}[X_i]|\mathbf{y}) h(c)$, for each assignment $\mathbf{y} \in \Gamma_a(\mathbf{C})$, where $\mathbf{C}$ is the scope of h and the sum is over Dom[$\mathbf{C}$], the enumeration of variables in $\mathbf{C}$. In our case, using the parity basis, this sum of products can be reorganized as a product of sums: $g^a(\mathbf{y}) = \prod_{i|X_i \in \mathbf{C}} P(x_i = 0|\mathbf{y}, a) - P(x_i = 1|\mathbf{y}, a)$. These terms can be precomputed for each state variable allowing efficient computation. Second, we consider $\alpha = \sum_{\mathbf{x}} \alpha(\mathbf{x}) h(\mathbf{x}) = \sum_{\mathbf{c} \in \mathbf{C}} \alpha(\mathbf{c}) h(\mathbf{c})$, where $\alpha(\mathbf{c})$ is the marginal of α over Dom[$\mathbf{C}$]. In the case of parity basis functions, $\alpha_l = 0, \forall l \neq 0$ and $\beta = |\sum_k u_k^{\gamma g_l - h_l} \lambda_k|$.

6 GREEDY INTERDICTION

In this section, we propose a greedy heuristic for factored MDP interdiction which requires the generation of attacker policies in response to specific mitigations. Specifically, we start with a mitigation strategy by randomly choosing an action to block. The attacker then computes a policy with utility V using the restricted set of actions. Next, we evaluate actions in the available set of actions A_{av}, at random, choosing an action to block if it decreases the sum of the attacker utility and total mitigation cost. Here we assume that each mitigation blocks exactly one action. The algorithm proceeds until no action can be found to be blocked so as to improve the defender's utility. This greedy algorithm is outlined as Algorithm 4.

We speed up greedy interdiction similar to fast constraint generation in Section 4.1.2 by computing policies with a small subset of basis functions (e.g., H_1). At the very end, we make further additions to the set of basis functions to compute the attacker's policy in response to the greedily computed mitigation strategy to check whether the attacker can indeed improve on the approximate best response computed over the restricted space.

7 EXPERIMENTS

We evaluate our MDP interdiction algorithms on several instances of three problem domains from the international planning competition (IPC 2014): a) sysadmin b) academic advising and c) wildfire. While these have little direct connection to security, they provide the most meaningful evaluation of our approaches in terms of effectiveness and scalability: prior security-related domains which consider multi-stage attacks use toy examples which would not provide a meaningful evaluation.

Algorithm 4 Greedy Factored MDP Interdiction

$A_{av} = A$
$A_m = \emptyset$
$A_n = A_{av}$
$\hat{V} = \infty$
while $A_n \neq \emptyset$ **do**
  a =CHOOSERANDOM(A_{av})
  V = ATTACKERPOLICY($A_{av} \setminus a, H$)
  if $V^A < \hat{V}$ **then**
    $A_m = A_m \cup a$
    $\hat{V} = V$
    $A_{av} = A_{av} \setminus a$
    $A_n = A_{av}$
    if $A_{av} = \emptyset$ **then**
      break
  else
    $A_n = A_n \setminus a$
return V = GENERATEBASIS($A \setminus A_m, H$)

For all experiments, each defender mitigation $m \in \mathcal{M}$ blocks exactly one action a. We also let $R^A(\mathbf{x}, a) = -R^D(\mathbf{x}, a) - C_a$, where C_a is the cost of action a, which we set to 0 for the default (no-op) action and to 0.5 for all other actions.. We set the cost of imposing a mitigation $C_m = 1$ for all m. We use the discount factor of $\gamma = 0.9$. The experiments are run on a 2.4GHz hyperthreaded 8-core Ubuntu Linux machine with 16 GB RAM, with CPLEX version 12.51 used to solve MILP instances.

7.1 COMPARISON WITH EXACT MDP INTERDICTION

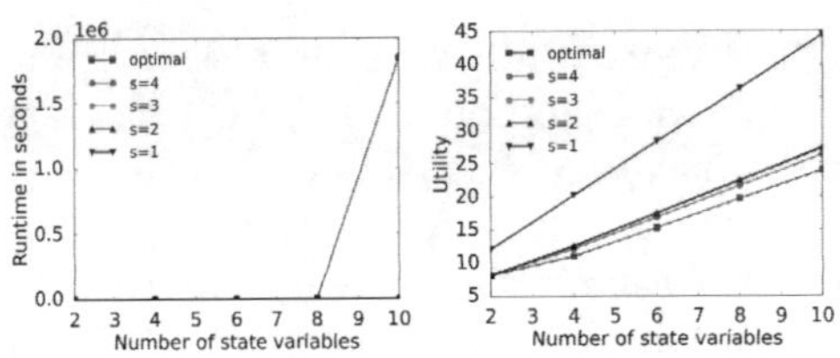

Figure 1: Comparison of exact and approximate MDP interdiction in terms of runtime (left) and attacker utility (right; lower is better for the defender).

First, we compare the performance of the constraint generation with basis selection algorithm to the state-of-the-art optimal solution in MDP interdiction proposed by Letchford and Vorobeychik [12]. We consider the sysadmin domain with $n = 2 - 10$ state variables (2^n states) and 10 actions. We evaluate our approach with $s = 1, 2, 3$ and 4, where s is the maximum number of state variables in the scope of any basis.

As expected, the runtime of the exact MDPI is dominated by our approach for sufficiently many state variables (Figure 1(a)); more significantly, the exact approach runs out of memory for larger problem sizes.

From Figure 1(b) we can see that while the utility of approximate interdiction improves significantly as s increases from 1 to 2, it already becomes close to optimal when $s = 2$, with little added value from increasing it further. The results are similar for other IPC domains. Consequently, our experiments below use $s = 2$.

7.2 SCALABILITY

We evaluate the constraint generation approach on larger problem sizes on the sysadmin domain (up to 60 state variables and 60 actions). Even with constraint generation with only a subset of basis functions, our baseline algorithm (marked as "slow bilevel") scales poorly for $n > 30$. On the other hand, the use of fast constraint generation (Algorithm 2, marked as "fast bilevel"), significantly improves scalability (Figure 2 left). Indeed, the baseline (slow bilevel) becomes intractable for $n \geq 50$, whereas we can successfully solve these with the "fast" approach. Since we compute the utility of the final attacker policy using basis generation, the solution accuracy is not compromised (Figure 2 right).

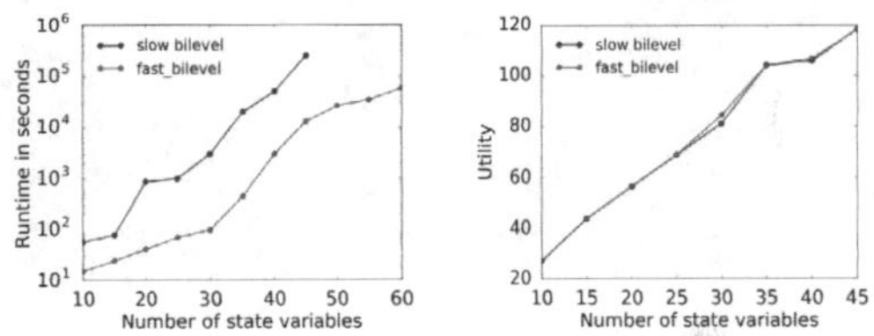

Figure 2: Comparison between baseline (slow) and fast interdiction on the sysadmin domain in terms of runtime (left) and utility (right).

In the second set of scalability experiments, we evaluate our approaches on 10 problem instances of the academic advising domain. The problem size increases with problem number from 10 to 30 courses (20 to 60 state variables and 10 to 30 actions). For each problem size, there are two instances, corresponding to different program requirements and course prerequisites. The first (odd numbered) problem instance is somewhat simpler (fewer prerequisites per course). The second (even numbered) instance is more complicated, with a larger number of prerequisites per course (larger number of connections in the underlying DBN). Problem 10 has the largest problem size with 30 courses, 11 program requirements, 3 prerequisites for most courses and 4 prerequisites for 8 courses. As demonstrated in Figure 3, we observe a similar trend as before: the fast constraint generation approach significantly outperforms baseline without compromising much solution quality. The baseline is intractable for problems 7 to 10 ($n \geq 50$).

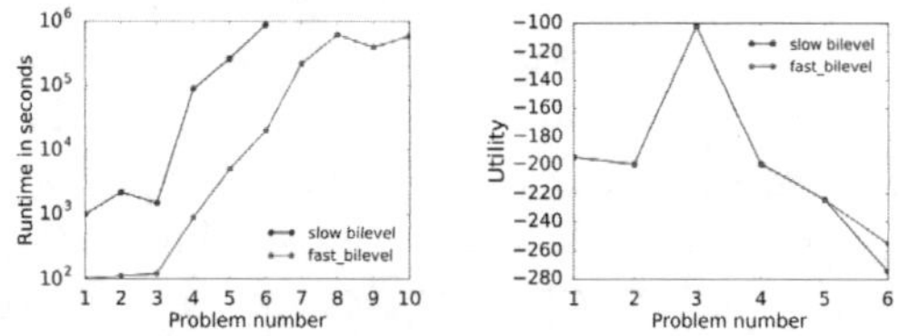

Figure 3: Comparison between baseline (slow) and fast interdiction on the academic advising domain in terms of runtime (left) and utility (right).

In the third set of experiments, we evaluate on 6 problem instances of the wildfire domain. The grid size increases with problem number from $m = 3$ to 5 ($n = 2 \times m^2 =$ 18 to 50 state variables, and 36 to 100 actions). For each grid size, there are two instances, corresponding to different neighbourhood configurations and targets (cells on the grid that need to be protected). The first (odd numbered) problem instance has fewer targets than the second (even numbered) instance. The results are shown in Figure 4. The baseline is again intractable on problems 5 and 6 ($n = 50$) which can be solved by fast bilevel.

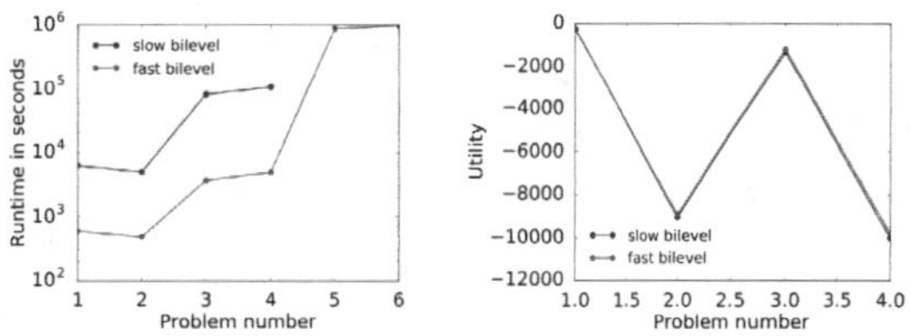

Figure 4: Comparison between baseline (slow) and fast interdiction on the wildfire domain in terms of runtime (left) and utility (right).

7.3 EFFECTIVENESS OF GREEDY INTERDICTION

Finally, we compare the greedy interdiction algorithm to fast constraint generation. As shown in Figures 5-7, the greedy algorithm is faster for larger problem sizes, saving up to an order of magnitude of computation time, without significantly compromising solution quality.

8 CONCLUSION

We presented a MILP approach for factored MDP interdiction, using a parity basis for linear value function approximation over binary state variables. We offered an iterative basis generation approach to select the most effective set of basis functions, and presented several variations of constraint generation, combined with basis selection, to solve the MILP. We evaluated our approaches on several realistic problem instances and demonstrated significantly increased scalability while achieving near-optimal solutions. Finally, we proposed a greedy algorithm for MDP interdiction and showed that it can further improve scalability.

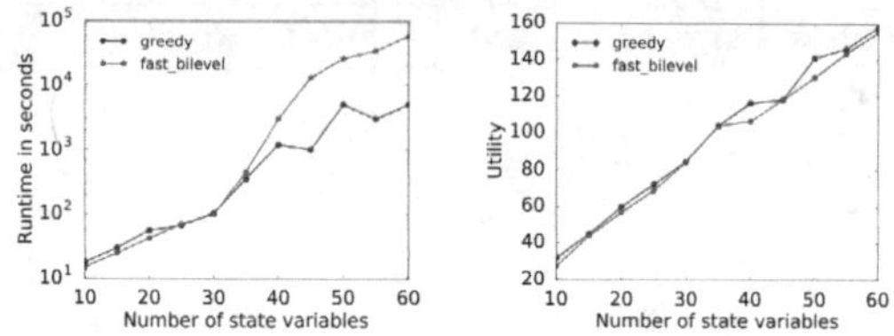

Figure 5: Comparison between fast interdiction and greedy in terms of runtime (left) and utility (right) on the sysadmin domain.

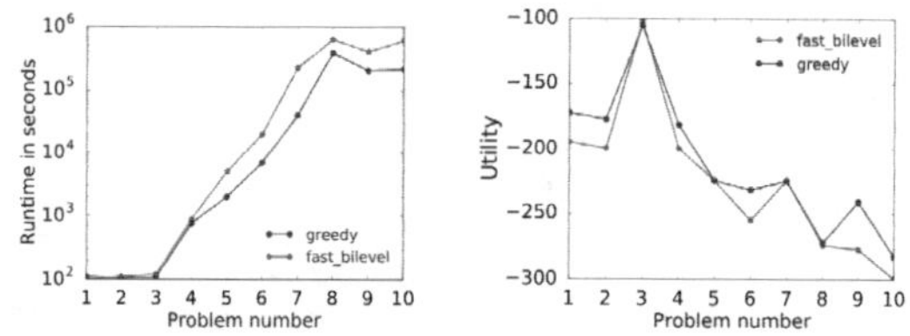

Figure 6: Comparison between fast interdiction and greedy in terms of runtime (left) and utility (right) on the academic advising domain.

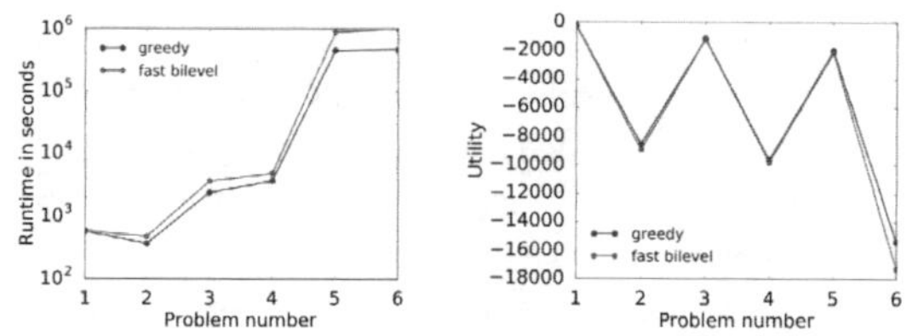

Figure 7: Comparison between fast interdiction and greedy in terms of runtime (left) and utility (right) on the wildfire domain.

In this paper, we only model deterministic mitigation strategies. Related research on Stackelberg games for security often considers randomized defensive resource allocation, which in our case would translate to randomized mitigations that can yield considerably higher utility to the defender. Within our framework, such an extension is quite non-trivial, and remains an important question for future research.

Acknowledgements This research was partially supported by NSF (CNS-1640624, IIS-1526860, IIS-1649972, CNS-1238959), ONR (N00014-15-1-2621), ARO (W911NF-16-1-0069), NIH (UH2 CA203708-01, R01HG006844), and AFRL (FA 8750-14-2-0180).

References

[1] Dimitri P Bertsekas and John N Tsitsiklis. Neuro-dynamic programming: an overview. In *Decision and Control, 1995., Proceedings of the 34th IEEE Conference on*, volume 1, pages 560–564. IEEE, 1995.

[2] Craig Boutilier, Thomas Dean, and Steve Hanks. Decision-theoretic planning: Structural assumptions and computational leverage. *Journal of Artificial Intelligence Research*, 11(1):94, 1999.

[3] Craig Boutilier, Richard Dearden, and Moisés Goldszmidt. Stochastic dynamic programming with factored representations. *Artificial intelligence*, 121(1):49–107, 2000.

[4] Thomas G Dietterich. Hierarchical reinforcement learning with the maxq value function decomposition. *J. Artif. Intell. Res.(JAIR)*, 13:227–303, 2000.

[5] Carlos Guestrin, Daphne Koller, and Ronald Parr. Max-norm projections for factored mdps. In *IJCAI*, volume 1, pages 673–682, 2001.

[6] Carlos Guestrin, Daphne Koller, Ronald Parr, and Shobha Venkataraman. Efficient solution algorithms for factored mdps. *Journal of Artificial Intelligence Research*, 19:399–468, 2003.

[7] Carlos Ernesto Guestrin. *Planning under uncertainty in complex structured environments*. PhD thesis, Stanford University, 2003.

[8] Manish Jain, James Pita, Milind Tambe, Fernando Ordónez, Praveen Paruchuri, and Sarit Kraus. Bayesian stackelberg games and their application for security at los angeles international airport. *ACM SIGecom Exchanges*, 7(2):10, 2008.

[9] Daphne Koller and Ronald Parr. Computing factored value functions for policies in structured mdps. In *IJCAI*, volume 99, pages 1332–1339, 1999.

[10] Daphne Koller and Ronald Parr. Policy iteration for factored mdps. In *Proceedings of the Sixteenth conference on Uncertainty in artificial intelligence*, pages 326–334. Morgan Kaufmann Publishers Inc., 2000.

[11] Dmytro Korzhyk, Zhengyu Yin, Christopher Kiekintveld, Vincent Conitzer, and Milind Tambe. Stackelberg vs. nash in security games: An extended investigation of interchangeability, equivalence, and uniqueness. *J. Artif. Intell. Res.(JAIR)*, 41:297–327, 2011.

[12] Joshua Letchford and Yevgeniy Vorobeychik. Optimal interdiction of attack plans. In *Proceedings of the 2013 international conference on Autonomous agents and multi-agent systems*, pages 199–206. International Foundation for Autonomous Agents and Multiagent Systems, 2013.

[13] Ryan O'Donnell. Some topics in analysis of boolean functions. In *Proceedings of the fortieth annual ACM symposium on Theory of computing*, pages 569–578. ACM, 2008.

[14] Praveen Paruchuri, Jonathan P Pearce, Janusz Marecki, Milind Tambe, Fernando Ordonez, and Sarit Kraus. Playing games for security: An efficient exact algorithm for solving bayesian stackelberg games. In *Proceedings of the 7th international joint conference on Autonomous agents and multiagent systems-Volume 2*, pages 895–902. International Foundation for Autonomous Agents and Multiagent Systems, 2008.

[15] Martin L Puterman. Markov decision processes: Discrete stochastic dynamic programming. 1994.

[16] Robert St-Aubin, Jesse Hoey, and Craig Boutilier. Apricodd: Approximate policy construction using decision diagrams. In *NIPS*, pages 1089–1095, 2000.

Importance Sampling for Fair Policy Selection

Shayan Doroudi
Computer Science Department
Carnegie Mellon University
Pittsburgh, PA 15213
shayand@cs.cmu.edu

Philip S. Thomas
Computer Science Department
Carnegie Mellon University
Pittsburgh, PA 15213
philipt@cs.cmu.edu

Emma Brunskill
Computer Science Department
Stanford University
Stanford, CA 94305
ebrun@cs.stanford.edu

Abstract

We consider the problem of off-policy policy selection in reinforcement learning: using historical data generated from running one policy to compare two or more policies. We show that approaches based on importance sampling can be *unfair*—they can select the worse of two policies more often than not. We give two examples where the unfairness of importance sampling could be practically concerning. We then present sufficient conditions to theoretically guarantee fairness and a related notion of safety. Finally, we provide a practical importance sampling-based estimator to help mitigate one of the systematic sources of unfairness resulting from using importance sampling for policy selection.

1 INTRODUCTION

In this paper, we consider the problem of *off-policy policy selection*: using historical data generated from running one policy to compare two or more policies. Off-policy policy selection methods can be used, for example, to decide which policy should be deployed when two or more batch reinforcement learning (RL) algorithms suggest different policies or when a data-driven policy is compared to a policy designed by a human expert. The primary contribution of this paper is that we show that the *importance sampling* (IS) estimator (Precup et al., 2000), which lies at the foundation of many policy selection and policy search algorithms (Mandel et al., 2014; Levine and Koltun, 2013; Thomas et al., 2015b), is often *unfair* when used for policy selection: when comparing two policies, the worse of the two policies may be returned more than half the time.

After formalizing our notion of fairness, we show that unfairness can occur in both the on-policy and off-policy settings. We further show that in the off-policy setting, using importance sampling for policy selection can be unfair in practically relevant settings. In particular, we show that IS can favor myopic policies—policies that obtain less total reward, but which obtain it early in an episode—as well as favoring policies that produce shorter trajectories. Although IS is an unbiased estimator, this unfairness arises because policy selection involves taking a maximum over estimated quantities. Depending on the distribution of estimates, importance sampling may systematically favor policies that are worse in expectation.

We then present two new approaches for avoiding unfairness when using importance sampling for policy selection. First, we give sufficient conditions under which using importance sampling for policy selection is fair, and provide algorithms that guarantee a related notion of safety. We also describe how our approach to guaranteeing fairness and safety is related to the notions of power analysis and statistical hypothesis testing. Although of theoretical interest, the reliance of this approach on conservative concentration inequalities limits its practicality. Thus, in our second approach, we introduce a new practical IS-based estimator that lacks the theoretical properties of our first approach, but which can help mitigate unfairness due to differing trajectory lengths.

Although there is significant literature surrounding reducing the variance and mean squared error of off-policy policy evaluation methods that use IS-based estimators (Powell and Swann, 1966; Dudík et al., 2011; Jiang and Li, 2016; Thomas and Brunskill, 2017), other challenges associated with off-policy policy selection, such as fairness, have not been explored in the literature. Similar notions of fairness have recently been proposed in the online RL setting, where an algorithm is fair if it never takes a worse action with higher probability than a better action Jabbari et al. (2017). This is similar to our notion of fairness in the offline RL setting, where an algorithm is fair if it does not choose a worse policy with higher probability than the best candidate policy. However, the issues surrounding fairness in the two settings are different due to the different nature of each setting. By introducing a notion of fairness for policy selection and highlighting some limitations of existing IS-based approaches, we hope to motivate further work on developing practical and fair policy selection algorithms.

2 BACKGROUND

We consider sequential decision making settings in stochastic domains. In such domains, an agent interacts with the environment, and in doing so, it generates a *trajectory*, $\tau \triangleq (O_0, A_1, R_1, O_1, A_2, R_2, \ldots, A_T, R_T, O_T)$, which is a sequence of observations, actions, and rewards, with trajectory length T. The observations and rewards are generated by the environment according to a stochastic process—such as a Markov decision process (MDP) or partially observable Markov decision process (POMDP)—that is unknown. The agent chooses actions according to a stochastic policy π, which is a conditional probability distribution over actions A_t given the partial trajectory $\tau_{1:t-1} \triangleq (O_0, A_1, R_1, O_1, A_2, R_2, \ldots, O_{t-1})$ of prior observations, actions, and rewards. The value of a policy π, V^π, is the expected sum of rewards when the policy is used: $V^\pi \triangleq \mathbf{E}\left[\sum_{t=1}^T R_t \middle| \tau \sim \pi\right]$, where $\tau \sim \pi$ means that the actions of τ are sampled according to π. The agent's goal is to find and execute a policy with a large value.

In this paper, we consider offline (batch) reinforcement learning (RL) where we have a batch of data, called historical data, that was generated from some known behavior policy π_b. We are interested in the problem of batch policy selection: identifying a good policy for use in the future. This typically involves policy evaluation or estimating the value of a policy π_e using the historical data that was generated from the behavior policy π_b. If $\pi_e = \pi_b$ this is known as *on-policy policy evaluation*. Otherwise it is known as *off-policy policy evaluation*.

2.1 ON-POLICY POLICY EVALUATION

Although we are primarily interested in the off-policy setting, i.e., the setting where $\pi_b \neq \pi_e$, we will also discuss the problem of on-policy policy evaluation. This problem arises, for example, when running a randomized control trial or A/B test to compare two policies. In this case, the value of each policy is directly estimated by running it to generate n trajectories, $\tau_1, \tau_2, \ldots, \tau_n$, and then estimating the policy's performance using the *Monte Carlo* estimator: $\hat{V}^{\pi_e}_{\text{MC},n} \triangleq \frac{1}{n}\sum_{i=1}^n \sum_{t=1}^{T_i} R_{i,t}$, where $R_{i,t}$ and T_i denote the reward of τ_i at time t and the length of τ_i respectively.

2.2 IMPORTANCE SAMPLING

In this paper, we primarily focus on off-policy policy evaluation and selection. Specifically, we focus on estimators that use importance sampling. Model-based off-policy estimators tend to have lower variance than IS-based estimators, but at the cost of being biased and asymptotically incorrect (not consistent estimators of V^π) (Mandel et al., 2014). In contrast, IS-based estimators can provide unbiased estimates of the value. There has been significant interest in using IS-based techniques in RL for policy evaluation (Precup et al., 2000; Jiang and Li, 2016; Thomas and Brunskill, 2016), as well as growing recent interest in using it for policy selection (Mandel et al., 2014) and the related problems of policy search and policy gradient optimization (Jie and Abbeel, 2010; Levine and Koltun, 2013; Thomas et al., 2015b; Wang et al., 2016).

The IS estimator (Precup et al., 2000) is given by: $\hat{V}^{\pi_e}_{\text{IS}} \triangleq \frac{1}{n}\sum_{i=1}^n w_i \sum_{t=1}^{T_i} R_{i,t}$, where $w_i \triangleq \prod_{t=1}^{T_i} \frac{\pi_e(a_{i,t}|\tau_{i,1:t-1})}{\pi_b(a_{i,t}|\tau_{i,1:t-1})}$. The IS estimator is an unbiased and strongly consistent estimator of V^{π_e} if $\pi_e(a|\tau_{1:t-1}) = 0$ for all actions, a, and partial trajectories, $\tau_{1:t-1}$, where $\pi_b(a_t|\tau_{1:t-1}) = 0$. However, $\hat{V}^{\pi_e}_{\text{IS}}$ often has high variance. The *weighted importance sampling* (WIS) estimator, $\hat{V}^{\pi_e}_{\text{WIS}} \triangleq \frac{1}{\sum_{i=1}^n w_i}\sum_{i=1}^n w_i \sum_{t=1}^{T_i} R_{i,t}$, is a variant of the IS estimator that often has much lower variance, but which is *not* an unbiased estimator of V^{π_e}.

3 FAIR POLICY SELECTION

A policy selection algorithm is given a set of candidate policies and must choose one of the policies for use in the future. Any policy evaluation algorithm (i.e., estimator) can be converted to a policy selection algorithm by simply evaluating each policy using the estimator, and then selecting the policy that has the largest estimated value. Thus we can use the Monte Carlo estimator for on-policy policy selection, and we can use the IS or WIS estimators for off-policy policy selection.

There are two natural properties we would like in a batch policy selection algorithm:

- **Consistency**: In the limit as the amount of historical data goes to infinity, the algorithm should always select the policy that has the largest value.

- **Fairness**: With *any* amount of historical data, the probability that the algorithm selects a policy with the largest value should be greater than the probability that it selects a policy that does not have the largest value. When choosing between two policies, this implies that the algorithm should choose the better policy at least half the time.[1]

Exploring and ensuring the fairness of (IS-based) policy selection algorithms is the focus of this paper. There has been recent interest on combining model-based estimators and IS-based estimators (Jiang and Li, 2016; Thomas and Brunskill, 2016), however as both model-based estimators and (as we will show) IS-based estimators are unfair, it is easy to show that these new estimators must also be unfair. Therefore, we restrict our attention to the standard IS and WIS estimators.

Before proceeding, we formally define a way to rank policies. Let the better-than operator $\succ_B$, be such that $\pi_1 \succ_B \pi_2$ is `True` if π_1 is better than π_2 and `False` otherwise, for some notion of "better". For example, we can define $\succ_V$ to order policies based on their values: $\pi_1 \succ_V \pi_2$ is `True` if $V^{\pi_1} > V^{\pi_2}$ and `False` otherwise. Define the optimal policy π^* in a policy class Π to be the policy where $\pi^* \succ_B \pi'$ for all $\pi' \neq \pi^* \in \Pi$.[2] We will now formally define fairness.

Definition 3.1. A policy selection algorithm that chooses policies from a policy class Π is *fair with respect to a better-than operator* $\succ_B$ if whenever the algorithm outputs a policy, the probability that it outputs π^* is at least as large as the probability that it will output any other policy. The algorithm is strictly fair if the probability of outputting policy π^* is strictly greater than the probability of outputting any other policy.

Notice that the probabilistic guarantee in this definition conditions on when the algorithm outputs a policy. This allows for a policy selection algorithm that does not output any policy in cases when it cannot determine which policy is better. Also, notice that the trivial policy selection algorithm that never outputs a policy is fair. However, ideally we want a policy selection algorithm that outputs a policy as often as possible while maintaining fairness. This is an important distinction: although we *want* an algorithm that often outputs a policy, we *require* the algorithm to at least be fair. We now see that this seemingly straightforward property is not satisfied by even the most natural policy selection algorithms.

We begin by showing that even Monte Carlo estimation is unfair when used for on-policy policy selection. Suppose we want to select the better of two policies, π_1 and π_2, in a multi-armed bandit (MAB) domain with three actions a_1, a_2, and a_3 with rewards and probabilities as described in Table 1. Notice that $V^{\pi_1} = r$ and $V^{\pi_2} = p$. So, if $r < p$, then $V^{\pi_1} < V^{\pi_2}$. However, notice that using one trajectory ($n = 1$), the Monte Carlo estimator is unfair with respect to $\succ_V$ if $r < p < 0.5$ since $\Pr(\hat{V}^{\pi_1}_{\text{MC},1} \leq \hat{V}^{\pi_2}_{\text{MC},1}) = p$. We can similarly show that Monte Carlo policy selection is unfair using n trajectories for $n > 1$, as long as r and p are sufficiently small.

Table 1: The probability of each action under π_1 and π_2 for the example domain where Monte Carlo estimation is unfair. Rewards, R, are deterministic.

	$a_1(R=0)$	$a_2(R=r)$	$a_3(R=1)$
π_1	0	1	0
π_2	$1-p$	0	p

[1]For simplicity, hereafter we assume that there are no two candidate policies that are equally good.

[2]We assume such a best policy exists; however, for some reasonable better-than operators, this may not be true, as we explore in Section 5.1.

4 UNFAIRNESS OF IMPORTANCE SAMPLING POLICY SELECTION

Unsurprisingly, importance sampling is also unfair with respect to $\succ_V$. However, the unfairness of importance sampling can be arbitrarily worse than the unfairness of the Monte Carlo estimator, in that for any n, we can construct a domain such that IS policy selection is unfair even though the Monte Carlo estimator will always pick the correct policy with even a single sample! We provide one such example in Supplementary Material A. In this section, we present two examples that highlight how the unfairness of importance sampling can arise in counter-intuitive ways in practically interesting settings, motivating the importance of caring about satisfying fairness.

4.1 IS FAVORS MYOPIC POLICIES

In the following example we show that even when comparing two policies that are equally close to the behavior policy, importance sampling can still be unfair. In particular, we show that using IS for policy selection could be biased in favor of myopic policies, which could be of significant practical concern. This may come up in practical settings where we are interested in comparing more heuristic methods of planning (e.g., short look-ahead) to full-horizon planning methods. If we have the correct model class, full horizon planning is expected to be optimal, however it is both computationally expensive (so possibly not even tractable) and potentially sub-optimal if our model class is incorrect (e.g., our state representation is inaccurate or the world is a POMDP but we are modeling it as a MDP). Thus, we may be interested in comparing full-horizon planning (or an approximation thereof) to myopic planning, and the following exam-

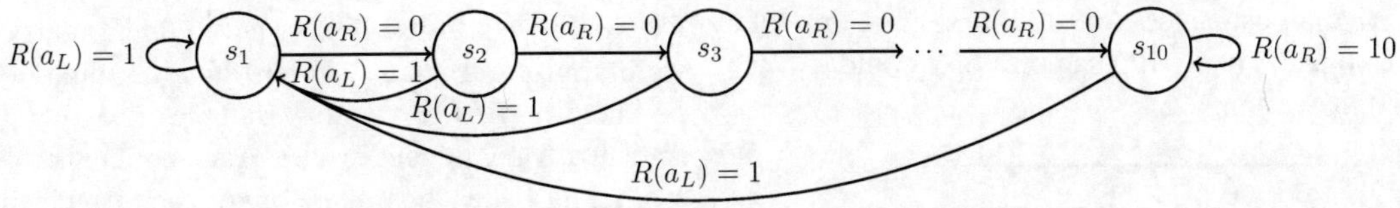

Figure 1: Domain in Section 4.1. The agent is in a chain of length 10. In each state, the agent can either go right (a_R) which progresses the agent along the chain and gives a reward of 0 unless the agent is in s_{10}, in which case it gives a reward of 10 (and keeps the agent in the s_{10}), or go left (a_L), which takes the agent back to state s_1 and gives a reward of 1.

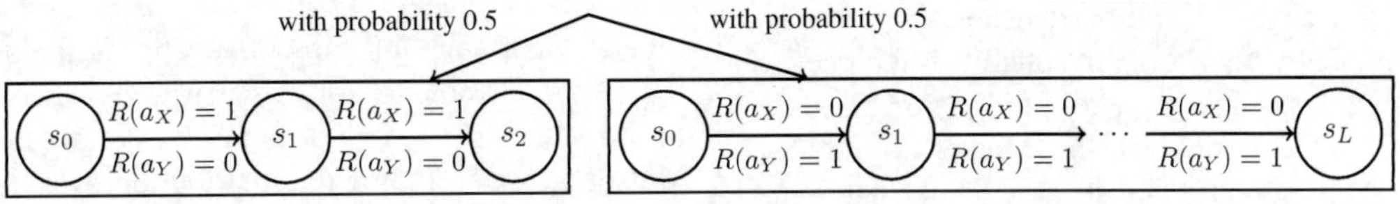

Figure 2: Domain in Section 4.2. The agent is placed uniformly at random in either a chain MDP of length 2 or a chain of length L. At each time step, action a_X deterministically gives a reward of 1 to the agent if the agent is in the chain of length 2 and 0 otherwise, and action a_Y deterministically gives a reward of 1 to the agent if the agent is in the chain of length L and 0 otherwise. Both actions progress the agent along the chain.

ple shows that IS can sometimes favor policies resulting from myopic planning even when full horizon planning is optimal.

Consider the MDP given in Figure 1. Now suppose we have data collected from a behavior policy π_b that takes each action with probability 0.5 and all trajectories have length 200. We want to compare two policies: π_{myopic} which takes a_L with probability 0.99 and a_R with probability 0.01, and π_{opt} which takes a_L with probability 0.01 and a_R with probability 0.99. (Note: the actual optimal policy is to always take a_R, for which π_{opt} is a slightly stochastic version.) Notice that the probability distribution of importance weights is the same for both π_{myopic} and π_{opt}, so both are equally close to the behavior policy in terms of probability distributions over trajectories. However, for datasets that are not large enough, the importance sampling estimate will be larger for π_{myopic} than for π_{opt}, even though it is clearly the worse policy. For example, when we have 1000 samples, (1) around 60% of the time, the importance sampling estimate of π_{myopic} is larger than that of π_{opt}, and (2) around 95% of the time, the weighted importance sampling estimate of π_{myopic} is larger than that of π_{opt}. Thus both the IS and WIS estimators are unfair for policy selection.

The reason IS is unfair in this case is because one policy only gives high rewards in events that are unlikely under the behavior policy, and hence the behavior policy often does not see the high rewards of this policy as compared to a myopic policy. However, note that these events are still likely enough that we can build a model that would suggest choosing the optimal policy. IS is unable to detect simple patterns that a model-based approach (or even a human briefly looking at the data) would easily infer; this is the cost of having an evaluation technique that places virtually no assumptions on policies.

4.2 IS FAVORS SHORTER TRAJECTORIES

Importance sampling can also systematically favor policies that assign higher probability to shorter trajectory lengths in domains where the length of each trajectory may vary. This is a problem that could arise in many practical domains, for example domains where a user is free to leave the system at any time, such as a student solving problems in an educational game or a user chatting with a dialogue system. In such systems, a bad policy may cause a user to leave the system sooner resulting in a short trajectory, which makes it particularly problematic that importance sampling can favor policies that assign higher probability to shorter trajectories. The following example shows that importance sampling can favor policies that generate shorter trajectories even when they are clearly worse.

Consider the domain given in Figure 2. Now suppose we have data collected from a behavior policy π_b that takes each action with probability 0.5. We want to compare two policies: π_X, which takes action a_X with probability 0.99, and π_Y, which takes action a_Y with probability 0.99. Consider the case where $L = 80$. Clearly π_Y is the better policy, because it incurs a lot of reward when we encounter trajectories of length 80, while only los-

Table 2: Median estimates, out of 100 simulations, of different estimators using 100 samples of π_X and π_Y in the domain in Section 4.2.

	$\hat{V}_{\text{MC}}$	$\hat{V}_{\text{IS}}$	$\hat{V}_{\text{WIS}}$
π_X	1.39	0.98	1.98
π_Y	39.52	0.010	0.020

ing out on a small reward when encountering the short trajectories. Table 2 shows the median estimate, out of 100 simulations, of the Monte Carlo estimator, as well as the median IS and WIS estimates using 1000 samples each. We find that while π_Y is, in actuality, much better, IS essentially only weighs the shorter trajectories, so the estimates only reflect how well the policies do on those trajectories. WIS simply (almost) doubles the estimates because half of the samples have extremely low importance weights. So why does this occur? When using IS in settings where trajectories can have varying lengths, the importance weight of shorter trajectories can be much larger than for longer trajectories, because for longer trajectories we are multiplying more ratios of probabilities that are more often smaller than one. This happens even if the policy we are evaluating is more likely to produce longer trajectories than a shorter one (because there are exponentially many longer trajectories and so each individual trajectory has an exponentially smaller weight than an individual short trajectory).

5 A NEW KIND OF FAIRNESS

The examples above illustrate that even the most straightforward way of evaluating policies could misguide someone about which policy is actually better under the objective of maximizing the expected sum of reward. Although we showed that off-policy policy selection using IS can be much less fair than doing on-policy Monte Carlo estimation, the fact that on-policy estimation is also unfair suggests that perhaps we are using the wrong measure of performance to construct our better-than operators. The problem is that, even if π_1 usually produces trajectories with more reward than those produced by π_2, it could still be that $V^{\pi_1} < V^{\pi_2}$ if there is a rare trajectory with very large reward that is more likely under π_2. It is therefore worth considering a different notion of "better-than" that better captures which policy is likely to perform better given a fixed and finite amount of historical data. This can be captured using the following better-than operator, which we refer to as better-than with respect to Monte Carlo estimation: $\pi_1 \succ_{\text{MC},n} \pi_2$ is `True` if $\Pr(\hat{V}^{\pi_1}_{\text{MC},n} > \hat{V}^{\pi_2}_{\text{MC},n}) \geq \Pr(\hat{V}^{\pi_1}_{\text{MC},n} < \hat{V}^{\pi_2}_{\text{MC},n})$, and `False` otherwise.

Notice that this notion of better-than is also exactly what we would want to use if we want to find a policy where we optimize our chance of beating a baseline in an experiment or A/B test with n samples (i.e., obtaining a statistically significant result). Also, notice that we have a different better-than operator for each n, which is not necessarily related to the number of samples that we have from our behavior policy π_b. (For example, we may have collected data from interactions with 1,000 users, but want to deploy a policy and expect one million users to use it; in that case we may want to be fair with respect to $\succ_{\text{MC},10^6}$.) We will use $\succ_{\text{MC}}$ to refer to this notion of better-than in general (even though it is not technically a better-than operator without specifying the number of samples). Of course, for this new better-than operator, the Monte Carlo estimator is fair by definition. It is interesting to note that if the distribution over the sum of rewards under the two policies are symmetric distributions (e.g., normal distributions), then the two better-than operators are equivalent. It may seem as though it is easier to satisfy fairness for importance sampling with respect to $\succ_{\text{MC},n}$ than with respect to $\succ_V$; however, we will show below that, at least in some sense, this is not the case. However, we can present conditions where both are satisfied simultaneously. We will henceforth consider and present results with respect to both notions of fairness (i.e., fairness with respect to $\succ_V$ and fairness with respect to $\succ_{\text{MC},n}$). But we will first consider some counterintuitive properties of this new better-than operator.

5.1 FAIRNESS AND NON-TRANSITIVITY

It is a well-known result in probability theory that there exists random variables X, Y, and Z such that $\Pr(X > Y) > 0.5$ and $\Pr(Y > Z) > 0.5$, but $\Pr(Z > X) > 0.5$ as well, indicating that comparing between random variables in such a way is non-transitive (Trybuła, 1961; Gardner, 1970). We claim that this non-transitivity holds for the ordering induced by the $\succ_{\text{MC},n}$ operator as well. This is shown in Supplementary Material B. In fact, it is possible that for any policy π, there is another policy π' where $\succ_{\text{MC},n} (\pi', \pi) =$ `True`, meaning a best policy might not exist with respect to $\succ_{\text{MC}}$.

The good news is that over fifty years ago, Trybuła (1965) showed that for any m independent random variables $X_1, \ldots, X_m$, $\min\{\Pr(X_1 > X_2), \ldots \Pr(X_{m-1} > X_m), \Pr(X_m > X_1)\} < 0.75$. Thus, in order to avoid such non-transitivity, we motivate a new kind of fairness:

Definition 5.1. An algorithm is *transitively fair* with respect to a better-than operator $\succ_B$ if it is fair with respect to $\succ_B$ and if the algorithm does not output a policy when comparing two policies from a set of policies π_1, $\ldots$, π_k such that $\pi_i \succ_B \pi_{i+1}$ for $i \in \{1, \ldots, k-1\}$ and

$\pi_k \succ_B \pi_1$.

Clearly any algorithm that is fair with respect to $\succ_V$ is also transitively fair, as comparing real numbers is a transitive operation. This is not the case for any algorithm that is fair with respect to $\succ_{\text{MC},n}$, but one way to ensure transitive fairness in this case is to not only be fair with respect to $\succ_{\text{MC},n}$, but to also not output a policy unless $\Pr(\hat{V}^{\pi_1}_{\text{MC},n} > \hat{V}^{\pi_2}_{\text{MC},n}) \geq 0.75$.

6 GUARANTEEING FAIRNESS

Given that importance sampling is not fair in general, we would like to understand under what conditions we can guarantee importance sampling can be used to do fair policy selection. Recall that even Monte Carlo estimation is not fair, so we would also like to give conditions for which we can guarantee on-policy policy selection can be done fairly. Thus, we are interested in guaranteeing the following four notions of fairness: **(1)** fairness with respect to $\succ_V$ when we have samples from each policy, **(2)** fairness with respect to $\succ_{\text{MC},n}$ when we have samples from each policy, **(3)** fairness with respect to $\succ_V$ when we have samples from a behavior policy, and **(4)** fairness with respect to $\succ_{\text{MC},n}$ when we have samples from a behavior policy.

Notice that case (2) is satisfied whenever we use Monte Carlo estimation for policy selection by definition of $\succ_{\text{MC}}$. We now give theorems describing the conditions under which we can satisfy the remaining three cases. Let V^{π}_{Max} be the largest value that could result from policy π and w^{π}_{Max} be the largest importance weight possible for policy π with samples drawn from behavior policy π_b. In what follows, for simplicity, we assume that the minimum possible value of a trajectory for all policies is 0.[3] Our results can be extended in the case that this is not true by considering the minimum possible value for each policy. Theorem 6.1 gives the conditions for which using the on-policy Monte Carlo estimator is fair for policy selection, when comparing between two policies.

Theorem 6.1. *Using the on-policy Monte Carlo estimator for policy selection when we have n samples from each of policies π_1 and π_2 is fair provided that* $V^{\pi_1}_{Max} + V^{\pi_2}_{Max} \leq |V^{\pi_1} - V^{\pi_2}|\sqrt{\frac{2n}{\ln 2}}$ *We can guarantee strict fairness if the inequality above is strict.*

Similarly, Theorem 6.2 gives conditions for which using the importance sampling estimator for policy selection is guaranteed to be fair with respect to $\succ_V$. Algorithm 1 is a fair policy selection algorithm that guarantees fairness whenever the condition in Theorem 6.2 is met, and otherwise returns `No Fair Comparison`, provided that $\epsilon \geq |V^{\pi_1} - V^{\pi_2}|$ and $\delta \geq 0.5$. Setting $\delta = 0.5$ is sufficient to guarantee fairness, but we can guarantee stronger notions of fairness by choosing some $\delta > 0.5$ (i.e., whenever the algorithm outputs a policy, it outputs the better policy with probability at least $\delta > 0.5$). While we only consider comparing between two policies in this section, we can extend our results to the case where we select a policy from a class of $n \geq 2$ policies, as we show in Supplementary Material D.

Theorem 6.2. *Using importance sampling for policy selection when we have n samples from the behavior policy is fair with respect to $\succ_V$, provided that*

$$w^{\pi_1}_{Max} V^{\pi_1}_{Max} + w^{\pi_2}_{Max} V^{\pi_2}_{Max} \leq |V^{\pi_1} - V^{\pi_2}|\sqrt{\frac{2n}{\ln 2}}$$

We can guarantee strict fairness if the inequality above is strict.

Theorems 6.1 and 6.2 can both be shown with a simple application of Hoeffding's inequality; the proofs are given in Supplementary Material C. Alternatively, we can use other concentration inequalities to obtain fairness conditions/algorithms of a similar form. Notice that Theorem 6.2 tells us that as long as neither policy is too far from the behavior policy in terms of the largest possible importance weight, then we can guarantee fairness, which intuitively makes sense; we can only fairly compare policies that are similar to the behavior policy. However, how far we stray will also depend on how different the values of the policies are from each other. This is a quantity we do not know, so we must pick an ϵ where either we think $\epsilon \geq |V^{\pi_1} - V^{\pi_2}|$ or we are comfortable with the possibility of selecting a policy whose value is ϵ worse than that of the better policy. Thus ϵ can be thought of as a hypothetical effect size as would be encountered in hypothesis testing. To make the analogue with hypothesis testing more clear, notice that if we fix the policies that we want to compare, we can instead convert Theorems 6.1 and 6.2 to give lower bounds on n that guarantee fairness; that is, we can ask how many samples do we need before we can fairly compare between two specific policies. This is analogous to doing a power analysis in the hypothesis testing literature. A critical difference is that in hypothesis testing we are typically interested in minimizing the probability of a bad event, whereas here we are ensuring that the better of the two policies is chosen more often. Furthermore, in the off-policy case, we are testing counterfactual hypotheses—hypotheses that we never run in the real-world.

Notice that Theorem 6.2 is satisfied for a much smaller subset of policies than Theorem 6.1 as $w^{\pi_1}_{\text{Max}}$ and $w^{\pi_2}_{\text{Max}}$

[3]In the off-policy case, all our results also hold under the very mild assumption that for each policy we evaluate there is some trajectory that has non-zero probability under π_b but has 0 probability under the evaluation policy.

can be huge (exponential in the trajectory length). This is not surprising and matches our intuition (as seen in the examples above) that IS can be very unfair even in cases where on-policy selection is fair.

Algorithm 1 Off-Policy FPS-$\succ_V$

Require: $\pi_1, \pi_2, V_{\text{Max}}^{\pi_1}, V_{\text{Max}}^{\pi_2}, \epsilon, \delta$
$\tau_1, \tau_2, \ldots, \tau_n \sim \pi_b$
if $w_{\text{Max}}^{\pi_1} V_{\text{Max}}^{\pi_1} + w_{\text{Max}}^{\pi_2} V_{\text{Max}}^{\pi_2} \leq \epsilon\sqrt{\frac{2n}{\ln 1/\delta}}$ **then**
return $\max(\hat{V}_{\text{IS}}^{\pi_1}, \hat{V}_{\text{IS}}^{\pi_2})$
else
return `No Fair Comparison`
end if

In order to satisfy fairness with respect to $\succ_{MC,n}$, the condition on the difference between the two policies will be in terms of the difference between typical Monte Carlo estimates of the value, as shown in Theorem 6.3. We can also satisfy transitive fairness with a stricter assumption on the difference between the two policies.

Theorem 6.3. *For any two policies π_1 and π_2, behavior policy π_b, and for all $k \in \{1, 2, 3, \ldots\}$, using importance sampling for policy selection when we have n samples from the behavior policy is fair with respect to $\succ_{MC,kn}$ provided that there exists $\epsilon > 0$ and $\delta < 0.5$ such that $\Pr\left(|\hat{V}_{MC,kn}^{\pi_1} - \hat{V}_{MC,kn}^{\pi_2}| \geq \epsilon\right) \geq 1 - \delta$ and $(w_{Max}^{\pi_1} + 1)V_{Max}^{\pi_1} + (w_{Max}^{\pi_2} + 1)V_{Max}^{\pi_2} \leq \epsilon\sqrt{\frac{2n}{\ln \frac{1-\delta}{0.5-\delta}}}$. Importance sampling in this setting is transitively fair, provided that $\delta \leq 0.25$.*

The theorem essentially says that as long as the conditions hold, we can guarantee fairness with respect to $\succ_{\text{MC},m}$ for any m that is a multiple of n (which is slightly weaker than being able to satisfy fairness for all $m \geq n$). Notice that if we compare Theorem 6.2 with Theorem 6.3 for the same choice of ϵ and for any choice of $\delta < 0.5$ (in Theorem 6.3), then provided that the conditions on the difference between the two policies for both theorems hold, the latter is satisfied for a strict subset of policies. Thus, we can use Theorem 6.3 to simultaneously guarantee fairness with respect to $\succ_V$ and with respect to $\succ_{\text{MC},m}$ (provided that the policy effect size conditions of both theorems hold). It might seem strange that satisfying $\succ_{\text{MC},n}$ requires a stricter test than for satisfying $\succ_V$, as it might seem as though importance sampling would be more likely to choose the same policy as the Monte Carlo estimator than the policy that has a higher value (when they are not the same). However, this is not necessarily the case, as the policy that importance sampling chooses will depend on the behavior policy.

6.1 SAFETY

As mentioned above, our conditions on fairness require us to have a reasonable estimate of an effect size between the policies we want to compare. It would be worthwhile to have a guarantee that does not require us to speculate about this unknown quantity. In this section, we give another type of guarantee which we refer to as *safety*. Safety has been considered as a property for policy evaluation and policy improvement algorithms (Thomas et al., 2015a,b). Here we extend the property to apply to policy selection algorithms.

Definition 6.1. A policy selection algorithm that chooses policies from a policy class Π is *safe with probability $1 - \delta$ with respect to a better-than operator $\succ_B$* if whenever it outputs any policy π such that there exists another policy $\tilde{\pi} \in \Pi$ where $\tilde{\pi} \not\succ_B \pi$, it does so with probability at most δ for some $\delta \leq 0.5$.

Thus, a safe policy selection algorithm does not output a sub-optimal policy often; however, it is still possible for a safe policy selection algorithm to output a sub-optimal policy more often than the best policy—but in that case, the algorithm won't output any policy often. This definition is weaker than fairness, but as we will see, we can satisfy it without requiring knowledge about an effect size between the policies. Theorem 6.4 gives the conditions for a safe policy selection algorithm with respect to $\succ_V$ and Theorem 6.5 gives analogous conditions for a safe policy selection algorithm with respect to $\succ_{\text{MC}}$, both using Algorithm 2 as the underlying algorithm. The proofs that these algorithms guarantee safety are given in Supplementary Material E.

Algorithm 2 Off-Policy SPS

input $\pi_1, \pi_2, \omega, p,$
$\tau_1, \tau_2, \ldots, \tau_n \sim \pi_b$
$\beta \leftarrow \omega\sqrt{\frac{\ln(2/(1-p))}{2n}}$
if $\hat{V}_{\text{IS}}^{\pi_1} - \hat{V}_{\text{IS}}^{\pi_2} - \beta > 0$ **then**
return π_1
else if $\hat{V}_{\text{IS}}^{\pi_1} - \hat{V}_{\text{IS}}^{\pi_2} + \beta < 0$ **then**
return π_2
else
return `No Fair Comparison`
end if

Theorem 6.4. *For any two policies π_1 and π_2, behavior policy π_b, $\omega = w_{Max}^{\pi_1} V_{Max}^{\pi_1} + w_{Max}^{\pi_2} V_{Max}^{\pi_2}$, and $\delta \leq 0.5$, Algorithm 2 is a safe policy selection algorithm with respect to $\succ_V$ with probability $1 - \delta$.*

Theorem 6.5. *For any two policies π_1 and π_2, where $\Pr\left(|\hat{V}_{MC,kn}^{\pi_1} - \hat{V}_{MC,kn}^{\pi_2}| \geq 0\right) \geq 1 - \delta_{MC}$ any behavior policy π_b, $\omega = (w_{Max}^{\pi_1} + 1)V_{Max}^{\pi_1} + (w_{Max}^{\pi_2} + 1)V_{Max}^{\pi_2}$, $p =$*

$1-\delta_{MC}\delta$ *for some* $\delta \leq 0.5$, *and for all* $k \in \{1,2,3,\dots\}$, *Algorithm 2 is a safe policy selection algorithm with respect to* $\succ_{MC,kn}$ *with probability* $1-\delta$ *when we have* n *samples drawn from* π_b. *It is a transitively fair policy selection algorithm whenever* $\delta_{MC} \leq 0.25$.

Note that these algorithms are analogous to statistical hypothesis testing in that we compare the lower bound of our estimate of the value of one policy with the upper bound of our estimate of the value of another policy. This analogue is similar to how our fair policy selection algorithms shared much in common with doing power analyses for hypothesis testing. Also note that as with fairness, Theorem 6.5 ensures safety with respect to both better-than operators, so if one uses Algorithm 2 with the inputs as described in Theorem 6.5, one does not have to determine which better-than operator one is using. Again, we find that safety with respect to $\succ_{MC}$ is more difficult to satisfy than safety with respect to $\succ_V$. We can formalize this with the following theorem.

Theorem 6.6. *There exists policies* π_1, π_2, *and behavior policy* π_b *for which Algorithm 2 with inputs as described in Theorem 6.4 is not a safe policy selection algorithm with respect to* $\succ_{MC,1}$ *with* $p = 0.5$ *when we have a single sample drawn from* π_b.

7 PRACTICAL FAIRNESS: VARYING TRAJECTORY LENGTHS

While the algorithms above provide a way to guarantee fairness, the concentration inequalities we used are naturally quite loose in most cases, and would likely result in returning `No Fair Comparison` in many cases. Practically, it would be desirable to have algorithms that can provide fair comparisons more often. As a first step in this direction, here we discuss a heuristic approach to policy selection for domains where we have varying trajectory lengths, as seen in Section 4.2. The reason for focusing on this particular aspect of unfairness is because it is systematic (potentially arising in any domain where trajectories vary in length), yet it seems like there should be a way to correct for the systematic preference towards shorter trajectories in practically relevant domains. The idea we propose here is to compute an IS-based estimate for each trajectory length individually and then recombine the estimates to get a new estimate. We propose using the following estimator, which we refer to as the *Per-Horizon Weighted Importance Sampling* (PHWIS) estimator:

$$\hat{V}_{\text{PHWIS}} = \sum_{l \in L} W_l \underbrace{\frac{1}{\sum_{\{\tau_i | T_i = l\}} w_i} \sum_{\{\tau_i | T_i = l\}} w_i \sum_{t=1}^{T_i} R_{i,t}}_{\text{WIS estimate on } l\text{-length trajectories}}$$

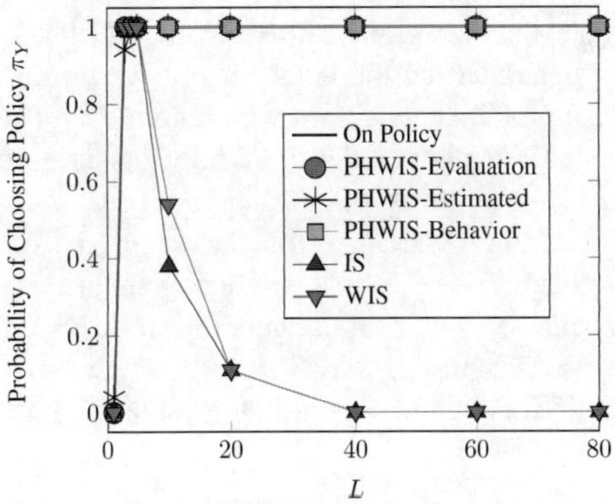

Figure 3: Probability of various estimators choosing π_Y over π_X for different values of L in the domain given in Section 4.2 with 1000 trajectories drawn from the uniform random behavior policy. For each estimator, the probability of outputting π_Y was estimated using 100 independent estimates.

where L is the set of trajectory lengths that appear in the data and W_l is a weight for the relative importance of each trajectory length.

Notice that in the domain in Section 4.2, the length of the trajectories did not depend on the policy that was used to generate them; in such cases, we can use the following weights: W_l (Behavior) $\triangleq \frac{|\{\tau_i | T_i = l\}|}{n}$. The weights simply count the proportion of trajectories in our data (i.e., generated by the behavior policy) that have length l. We will refer to PHWIS with this weighting scheme as PHWIS-Behavior. Now we will see how this estimator performs on the domain in Section 4.2 (Figure 2) where $L \in \{1,3,5,10,20,40,60,80\}$ given 1000 trajectories from the uniform random behavior policy. Figure 3 shows that while IS and WIS are unfair (choose π_X more often than π_Y) when the long trajectories are of length 20, PHWIS-Behavior always chooses the policy that the on-policy Monte Carlo estimator would choose (i.e., π_X when $L = 1$, and π_Y otherwise).

However, note that in cases where different policies may generate trajectories of different lengths (for example, bad policies causing users to dropout sooner), this simple form of weighting might not work too well. Ideally, we would like to use the following weights: W_l (Evaluation) $\triangleq \Pr(\mathbb{1}(|\tau| = l | \tau \sim \pi_e))$, where π_e is the evaluation policy for which we would like to estimate $\hat{V}^{\pi_e}$. We cannot actually compute these weights because we do not know the probability of any trajectory being generated by the evaluation policy, but when we have ground truth, we can use the PHWIS-Evaluation estimator as a point of comparison. To approximate these weights, we can take the weighted importance sampling estimate of the trajectory lengths generated by the behavior policy: W_l (WIS) $\triangleq \frac{1}{\sum_{i=1}^n w_i} \sum_{i=1}^n w_i \mathbb{1}(T_i = l)$

(i.e., rather than reweighing the rewards of all the trajectories generated by the behavior policy, we reweigh the probability that trajectories of length l are generated by the behavior policy). While this is a seemingly reasonable thing to do, this estimate will still suffer from high variance for the same reason the WIS estimator does, which would again lead to assigning small weights for longer trajectories. Instead we propose a heuristic way to make weights for different trajectory lengths have comparable magnitudes: W_l (Estimated) $\triangleq \frac{1}{\sum_{i=1}^{n} w_i} \sum_{i=1}^{n} w_i^{1/T_i} \mathbb{1}\,(T_i = l)$. The idea behind these weights is that they should give us a sense of which weights are preferred by the evaluation policy while maintaining that weights of different trajectory lengths have comparable magnitudes. As we see in Figure 3, PHWIS-Estimated has almost identical performance to PHWIS-Behavior and PHWIS-Evaluation (with just a small probability of choosing the wrong policy when both trajectory lengths are short). However, the true value of using such an estimator comes in domains where the length of a trajectory depends on the policy, and so PHWIS-Behavior may not be sufficient. We now examine one such domain.

7.1 POLICY-DEPENDENT TRAJECTORY LENGTHS

Consider a MDP that has three states—s_0, s_1, and s_2—and two actions—X and Y. The agent starts in s_0 and, on the first time step, if the agent takes action X, they deterministically transition to s_1 and receives a reward of r, and if the agent takes action Y, they transition deterministically to s_2 and receive a reward of 1. Thereafter the agent will always remain in the same state until the trajectory ends and will receive a reward of r whenever it takes action X in state s_1, a reward of 1 whenever it takes action Y in state s_2, and a reward of 0 otherwise. If the first action was X, the trajectory will end with probability 0.05 after each action, and if the first action was Y, the trajectory will end with probability 0.01 after each action. Thus, taking action Y in the beginning will result in a trajectory that is five times as long in expectation.

The behavior policy π_b takes each action with probability 0.5. Again, we want to compare two policies: π_X, which takes action X with probability 0.99, and π_Y, which takes action Y with probability 0.99. Whether π_X or π_Y is better will depend on r. The policies have the same value when $r = 5$, because the difference in rewards offsets the difference in lengths.

Figure 4 shows which policy is chosen when using different estimators for the domain described above with various values for r. We find that the IS, WIS, and even PHWIS-Behavior estimators are unfair regardless of the

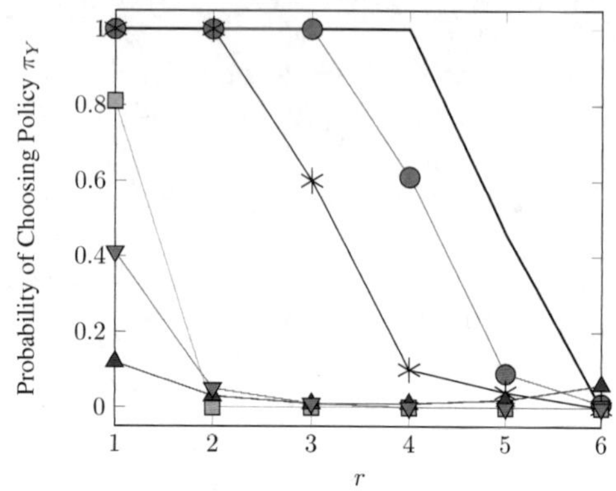

Figure 4: Probability of various estimators choosing π_Y over π_X for different values of r in the domain given in Section 7.1.

value of r (except for PHWIS-Behavior when $r = 1$). PHWIS-Evaluation tracks the on-policy estimator reasonably well, only sometimes choosing the wrong policy in the $r = 4$ case. PHWIS-Estimated similarly tracks the on-policy estimator reasonably well, but it sometimes chooses the wrong policy in the $r = 3$ case and is unfair when $r = 4$. Thus, PHWIS-Estimated seems to be a reasonable policy selection estimator to use in such domains, and can be much better than using PHWIS-Behavior in some cases.

8 CONCLUSION

In this paper, we examined the problem of off-policy policy selection and introduced a new property for policy selection algorithms called fairness. We showed that importance sampling is unfair when used for policy selection even though it is an unbiased estimator for policy evaluation. We presented two approaches to deal with this issue, a theoretical solution and a new practical estimator. This is but a first step in tackling the issue of fairness in off-policy policy selection. Our hope is that our introduction of the notion of fairness for policy selection will result in growing interest on the challenges involved in doing off-policy policy selection, including how unfairness propagates to policy search methods that optimize over an infinite class of policies.

Acknowledgements

The research reported here was supported, in whole or in part, by the Institute of Education Sciences, U.S. Department of Education, through Grants R305A130215 and R305B150008 to Carnegie Mellon University. The opinions expressed are those of the authors and do not represent views of the Institute or the U.S. Dept. of Education. The research was also supported in part by a NSF CAREER grant.

References

M. Dudík, J. Langford, and L. Li. Doubly robust policy evaluation and learning. In *International Conference on Machine Learning*, pages 1097–1104. Omnipress, 2011.

M. Gardner. Paradox of nontransitive dice and elusive principle of indifference. *Scientific American*, 223(6): 110, 1970.

S. Jabbari, M. Joseph, M. Kearns, J. Morgenstern, and A. Roth. Fairness in reinforcement learning. In *International Conference on Machine Learning*, 2017.

N. Jiang and L. Li. Doubly robust off-policy value evaluation for reinforcement learning. In *International Conference on Machine Learning*, pages 652–661, 2016.

T. Jie and P. Abbeel. On a connection between importance sampling and the likelihood ratio policy gradient. In *Advances in Neural Information Processing Systems*, pages 1000–1008, 2010.

S. Levine and V. Koltun. Guided policy search. In *International Conference on Machine Learning*, pages 1–9, 2013.

T. Mandel, Y.-E. Liu, S. Levine, E. Brunskill, and Z. Popovic. Offline policy evaluation across representations with applications to educational games. In *Internatonal Conference on Autonomous Agents and Multi-Agent Systems*, pages 1077–1084. International Foundation for Autonomous Agents and Multiagent Systems, 2014.

M. Powell and J. Swann. Weighted uniform sampling—a Monte Carlo technique for reducing variance. *IMA Journal of Applied Mathematics*, 2(3):228–236, 1966.

D. Precup, R. S. Sutton, and S. Singh. Eligibility traces for off-policy policy evaluation. In *International Conference on Machine Learning*. Citeseer, 2000.

P. S. Thomas and E. Brunskill. Data-efficient off-policy policy evaluation for reinforcement learning. In *International Conference on Machine Learning*, pages 2139–2148, 2016.

P. S. Thomas and E. Brunskill. Importance sampling with unequal support. In *AAAI*, pages 2646–2652, 2017.

P. S. Thomas, G. Theocharous, and M. Ghavamzadeh. High-confidence off-policy evaluation. In *AAAI*, pages 3000–3006, 2015a.

P. S. Thomas, G. Theocharous, and M. Ghavamzadeh. High confidence policy improvement. In *International Conference on Machine Learning*, 2015b.

S. Trybuła. On the paradox of three random variables. *Applicationes Mathematicae*, 4(5):321–332, 1961.

S. Trybuła. On the paradox of n random variables. *Applicationes Mathematicae*, 8(2):143–156, 1965.

Z. Wang, V. Bapst, N. Heess, V. Mnih, R. Munos, K. Kavukcuoglu, and N. de Freitas. Sample efficient actor-critic with experience replay. *arXiv preprint arXiv:1611.01224*, 2016.

SUPPLEMENTARY MATERIAL

A UNFAIRNESS OF IMPORTANCE SAMPLING

Suppose we want to use importance sampling to select the better of two policies, π_e and π_b, where we have prior data collected from π_b, in a MAB with two actions a_1 and a_2, with rewards and probabilities as described in Table 3. Notice that $V^{\pi_b} = p + (1-p)r$ and $V^{\pi_e} = 1$, so a fair policy selection algorithm should choose π_e at least half the time since $p + (1-p)r < 1$. If we draw only a single sample from π_b, we get that with probability $1-p$, IS would select π_b over π_e. Thus as long as $p < 0.5$, IS will be unfair. Furthermore, notice that as we decrease p, the gap between the performance of the policies increases, yet the probability that IS chooses the right policy only decreases!

Now suppose we draw n samples from π_b. Notice that as long as τ_2 is never sampled, IS will choose π_b, since in that case $\hat{V}_{\text{IS}}^{\pi_3} = 0$. π_b will never sample τ_2 with probability $(1-p)^n$. Thus IS is unfair as long as $(1-p)^n \geq 0.5$, or as long as $p \leq 1 - 0.5^{1/n} \approx \ln(2)/n$ for large n.

It may appear that this unfairness is not a big problem when we have a reasonable number of samples, but the practical significance of this problem becomes more pronounced in more realistic domains where we have a large number of possible trajectories, or equivalently, a long horizon. For example consider a domain where there are only two actions and the agent must take 50 sequential actions and receives a reward only at the end of a trajectory. Furthermore, consider that the only valuable trajectory is to take a particular action for the entire trajectory (analogous to a_2 above). In this case, we would need over 10^{14} samples just to get IS to be fair!

Table 3: Domain in Supplementary Material A. Rewards are deterministic. The bottom two rows give the probability distributions for π_e and π_b over the two actions.

	a_1 $(R = r < 1)$	a_2 $(R = 1)$
π_e	0	1
π_b	$1-p$	p

B NON-TRANSITIVITY

Theorem B.1 (Non-Transitivity of $\succ_{\text{MC},n}$). *The relation induced by $\succ_{MC,n}$ is non-transitive. Specifically, there exists policies π_1, π_2, and π_3 where $\Pr(\hat{V}^{\pi_1}_{MC,n} > \hat{V}^{\pi_2}_{MC,n}) = \Pr(\hat{V}^{\pi_2}_{MC,n} > \hat{V}^{\pi_3}_{MC,n}) = \Pr(\hat{V}^{\pi_3}_{MC,n} > \hat{V}^{\pi_1}_{MC,n}) = 1 - \phi \approx 0.618$ where $\phi = \frac{\sqrt{5}+1}{2}$ is the golden ratio. Moreover, it is possible that for any policy π, there is another policy π' where $\succ_{MC,n}$ $(\pi', \pi) =$ `True`.*

Proof of Theorem B.1. Consider a multi-armed bandit where there are three actions: a_1, which gives a reward of $n+1$ with probability p and a reward of 0 with probability $1-p$, a_2 which always gives a reward of 1, and a_3 which gives a reward of $n^2 + n + 1$ with probability $1-q$ and a reward of 0.5 with probability q. Suppose policies π_1, π_2, and π_3 always choose action a_1, a_2, and a_3 respectively. Now suppose we want to estimate the three policies with n on-policy samples from each. We have that π_1 gives a higher reward than π_2 whenever we get the large reward at least once, which happens with probability $1-(1-p)^n$. Thus

$$\Pr(\hat{V}^{\pi_1}_{\text{MC},n} > \hat{V}^{\pi_2}_{\text{MC},n}) = 1 - (1-p)^n$$

Furthermore, clearly π_2 gives a larger reward than π_3 whenever all samples of π_2 give a reward of 0.5, which happens with probability q^n. Now, finally we see that π_3 gives a larger reward than π_1 whenever it gives at least one sample with a large reward or when both of them give only samples of their small rewards, which happens with probability $(1-q^n) + q^n(1-p)^n$, so

$$\Pr(\hat{V}^{\pi_3}_{MC,n} > \hat{V}^{\pi_1}_{\text{MC},n}) = (1-q^n) + q^n(1-p)^n$$

Now let $p = 1 - (2-\phi)^{1/n}$ and $q = (\phi - 1)^{1/n}$, where $\phi = \frac{\sqrt{5}+1}{2} \approx 1.618$ is the golden ratio. Thus we have that:

$$\Pr(\hat{V}^{\pi_1}_{\text{MC},n} > \hat{V}^{\pi_2}_{\text{MC},n}) = \phi - 1$$

$$\Pr(\hat{V}^{\pi_2}_{\text{MC},n} > \hat{V}^{\pi_3}_{\text{MC},n}) = \phi - 1$$

$$\Pr(\hat{V}^{\pi_3}_{\text{MC},n} > \hat{V}^{\pi_1}_{\text{MC},n}) = (2-\phi) + (\phi-1)(2-\phi) = \phi - 1$$

We now show that for this multi-armed bandit, there is no optimal policy with respect to $\succ_{\text{MC},n}$. A policy in this setting is simply a distribution over a_1, a_2, and a_3. Equivalently, we can view any policy as a mix of the policies π_1, π_2, and π_3. Suppose a policy π executes π_1 with probability p, π_2 with probability q, and π_3 with probability r. If p is the largest of the probabilities, then notice that $\Pr(\hat{V}^{\pi_3}_{\text{MC},n} > \hat{V}^{\pi}_{\text{MC},n}) = p(\phi - 1) \geq q(\phi - 1) = \Pr(\hat{V}^{\pi}_{\text{MC},n} > \hat{V}^{\pi_3}_{\text{MC},n})$. We can make a similar argument if q or r are the largest probabilities. Thus, there is no optimal policy. □

C FAIRNESS PROOFS

Theorem 6.1. *Using the on-policy Monte Carlo estimator for policy selection when we have n samples* *from each of policies π_1 and π_2 is fair provided that $V^{\pi_1}_{Max} + V^{\pi_2}_{Max} \leq |V^{\pi_1} - V^{\pi_2}|\sqrt{\frac{2n}{\ln 2}}$ We can guarantee strict fairness if the inequality above is strict.*

Proof of Theorem 6.1. Suppose without loss of generality that $V^{\pi_1} > V^{\pi_2}$. Let $\hat{V}_i^{\pi} = \sum_{t=1}^{T_i} R_{i,t}$ (i.e., the estimate of the value of policy π using only τ_i^{π}). Now let

$$X_i = \hat{V}_i^{\pi_1} - \hat{V}_i^{\pi_2}$$

Note that the range of X_i is $[-V^{\pi_2}_{\text{Max}}, V^{\pi_1}_{\text{Max}}]$. Let ω be the difference between the upper and lower bounds of X_i, that is, $\omega = V^{\pi_1}_{\text{Max}} + V^{\pi_2}_{\text{Max}}$. Because all $\tau_i^{\pi_1}$ and $\tau_i^{\pi_2}$ are independent of $\tau_j^{\pi_1}$ and $\tau_j^{\pi_2}$ for all $i \neq j$, we know that X_i is independent of X_j for all $i \neq j$. Thus we can use Hoeffding's inequality to find that:

$$\Pr\left(\bar{X} \leq 0\right) = \Pr\left(\bar{X} - \mathbf{E}\left[\bar{X}\right] \leq -\mathbf{E}\left[\bar{X}\right]\right)$$
$$\leq \exp\left(\frac{-2n\mathbf{E}\left[\bar{X}\right]^2}{\omega^2}\right)$$

Note that

$$\bar{X} = \frac{1}{n}\sum_{i=1}^{n} X_i = \frac{1}{n}\sum_{i=1}^{n} \hat{V}_i^{\pi_1} - \hat{V}_i^{\pi_2} = \hat{V}^{\pi_1}_{\text{MC},n} - \hat{V}^{\pi_2}_{\text{MC},n}$$

and $\mathbf{E}\left[\bar{X}\right] = V^{\pi_1} - V^{\pi_2}$. Thus, if we want to guarantee

$$\Pr\left(\hat{V}^{\pi_1}_{\text{MC},n} - \hat{V}^{\pi_2}_{\text{MC},n} \leq 0\right) \leq \delta$$

we can simply guarantee

$$\exp\left(\frac{-2n(V^{\pi_1} - V^{\pi_2})^2}{\omega^2}\right) \leq \delta$$

Solving for ω, we must have that:

$$\omega \leq (V^{\pi_1} - V^{\pi_2})\sqrt{\frac{2n}{\ln(1/\delta)}}$$

Substituting $\delta = 0.5$, we can thus guarantee that $\Pr\left(\hat{V}^{\pi_1}_{\text{MC},n} - \hat{V}^{\pi_2}_{\text{MC},n} > 0\right) \geq 0.5$, which guarantees fairness when $V^{\pi_1} > V^{\pi_2}$. Since we do not actually know which policy has a greater value, we can guarantee fairness with the following condition:

$$\omega \leq |V^{\pi_1} - V^{\pi_2}|\sqrt{\frac{2n}{\ln 2}}$$

□

Theorem 6.2. *Using importance sampling for policy selection when we have n samples from the behavior policy is fair with respect to $\succ_V$, provided that*

$$w^{\pi_1}_{Max} V^{\pi_1}_{Max} + w^{\pi_2}_{Max} V^{\pi_2}_{Max} \leq |V^{\pi_1} - V^{\pi_2}|\sqrt{\frac{2n}{\ln 2}}$$

We can guarantee strict fairness if the inequality above is strict.

Proof of Theorem 6.2. Let $\hat{V}_i^{\pi} = \sum_{t=1}^{T_i} w_i^{\pi_e} R_{i,t}$ (i.e., the estimate of the value of policy π using only τ_i). Now let

$$X_i = \hat{V}_i^{\pi_1} - \hat{V}_i^{\pi_2}$$

Note that the range of X_i is $[-w^{\pi_2}_{\text{Max}} V^{\pi_2}_{\text{Max}}, w^{\pi_1}_{\text{Max}} V^{\pi_1}_{\text{Max}}]$. Let ω be the difference between the upper and lower bounds of X_i, that is, $\omega = w^{\pi_1}_{\text{Max}} V^{\pi_1}_{\text{Max}} + w^{\pi_2}_{\text{Max}} V^{\pi_2}_{\text{Max}}$. Because τ_i and τ_j are independent for all $i \neq j$, we know that X_i is independent of X_j for all $i \neq j$. The rest of the proof follows exactly as in the proof of Theorem 6.1. □

Theorem 6.3. *For any two policies π_1 and π_2, behavior policy π_b, and for all $k \in \{1, 2, 3, \dots\}$, using importance sampling for policy selection when we have n samples from the behavior policy is fair with respect to $\succ_{MC,kn}$ provided that there exists $\epsilon > 0$ and $\delta < 0.5$ such that $\Pr\left(|\hat{V}^{\pi_1}_{MC,kn} - \hat{V}^{\pi_2}_{MC,kn}| \geq \epsilon\right) \geq 1 - \delta$ and $(w^{\pi_1}_{Max}+1)V^{\pi_1}_{Max} + (w^{\pi_2}_{Max}+1)V^{\pi_2}_{Max} \leq \epsilon\sqrt{\frac{2n}{\ln\frac{1-\delta}{0.5-\delta}}}$. Importance sampling in this setting is transitively fair, provided that $\delta \leq 0.25$.*

Proof of Theorem 6.3. Suppose without loss of generality that $\Pr\left(\hat{V}^{\pi_1}_{\text{MC},kn} - \hat{V}^{\pi_2}_{\text{MC},kn} \geq \epsilon\right) \geq 1 - \delta$. Recall that IS uses trajectories $\tau_1, \dots, \tau_n \sim \pi_b$. Consider additional random samples $\tau_1^{\pi_1}, \dots, \tau_{kn}^{\pi_1} \sim \pi_1$ and $\tau_1^{\pi_2}, \dots, \tau_{kn}^{\pi_2} \sim \pi_2$. Note that these samples are all independent from each other. For $i \in \{1, 2, \dots, n\}$, let

$$\hat{V}_i^{\pi} = \frac{1}{k}\sum_{j=1}^{k}\sum_{t=1}^{T_{ji}} R_{ji,t}$$

(i.e., the estimate of the value of policy π using only samples $\tau_i^{\pi}, \tau_{2i}^{\pi}, \dots \tau_{ki}^{\pi}$). Furthermore let $\hat{V}^{\pi}_{\text{IS},i} = \sum_{t=1}^{T_i} w_{i,t} R_{i,t}$. Now let

$$X_i = (\hat{V}^{\pi_1}_{\text{IS},i} - \hat{V}^{\pi_2}_{\text{IS},i}) - (\hat{V}_i^{\pi_1} - \hat{V}_i^{\pi_2})$$

Notice that the range of X_i is $[-V^{\pi_2}_{\text{Max}} - w^{\pi_1}_{\text{Max}} V^{\pi_1}_{\text{Max}}, V^{\pi_1}_{\text{Max}} + w^{\pi_2}_{\text{Max}} V^{\pi_2}_{\text{Max}}]$. Let ω be the difference between the upper and lower bounds of X_i, that is, $\omega = (w^{\pi_1}_{\text{Max}} + 1)V^{\pi_1}_{\text{Max}} + (w^{\pi_2}_{\text{Max}} + 1)V^{\pi_2}_{\text{Max}}$.

Notice that

$$\bar{X} = \frac{1}{n}\sum_{i=1}^{n} X_i = \frac{1}{n}\sum_{i=1}^{n}(\hat{V}^{\pi_1}_{\text{IS},i} - \hat{V}^{\pi_2}_{\text{IS},i}) - (\hat{V}_i^{\pi_1} - \hat{V}_i^{\pi_2})$$
$$= (\hat{V}^{\pi_1}_{\text{IS}} - \hat{V}^{\pi_2}_{\text{IS}}) - (\hat{V}^{\pi_1}_{\text{MC},kn} - \hat{V}^{\pi_2}_{\text{MC},kn})$$

and

$$\mathbf{E}\left[\bar{X}\right] = (V^{\pi_1} - V^{\pi_2}) - (V^{\pi_1} - V^{\pi_2}) = 0$$

Thus we have that

$$\Pr\left(\hat{V}^{\pi_1}_{\text{IS}} - \hat{V}^{\pi_2}_{\text{IS}} \leq 0\right) = \Pr\left(\bar{X} \leq -(\hat{V}^{\pi_1}_{\text{MC},kn} - \hat{V}^{\pi_2}_{\text{MC},kn})\right)$$

$$= \Pr\left(\bar{X} - \mathbf{E}\left[\bar{X}\right] \leq -(\hat{V}^{\pi_1}_{\text{MC},kn} - \hat{V}^{\pi_2}_{\text{MC},kn})\right)$$

Thus, we can use Hoeffding's inequality to find that:

$$\Pr\left(\hat{V}^{\pi_1}_{\text{IS}} - \hat{V}^{\pi_2}_{\text{IS}} \leq 0 | \hat{V}^{\pi_1}_{\text{MC},kn} - \hat{V}^{\pi_2}_{\text{MC},kn} \geq \epsilon\right) \leq \exp\left(\frac{-2n\epsilon^2}{\omega^2}\right)$$

So if we want to guarantee

$$\Pr\left(\hat{V}^{\pi_1}_{\text{IS}} - \hat{V}^{\pi_2}_{\text{IS}} \leq 0\right) \leq \gamma$$

we can simply guarantee

$$\exp\left(\frac{-2n(\hat{V}^{\pi_1}_{\text{MC},kn} - \hat{V}^{\pi_2}_{\text{MC},kn})^2}{\omega^2}\right) \leq \gamma$$

Solving for ω, we must have that:

$$\omega \leq (\hat{V}^{\pi_1}_{\text{MC},kn} - \hat{V}^{\pi_2}_{\text{MC},kn})\sqrt{\frac{2n}{\ln(1/\gamma)}}$$

Notice that

$$\Pr\left(\hat{V}^{\pi_1}_{\text{IS}} - \hat{V}^{\pi_2}_{\text{IS}} \geq 0\right)$$

$$\geq \Pr\left(\hat{V}^{\pi_1}_{\text{IS}} - \hat{V}^{\pi_2}_{\text{IS}} \leq 0 | \hat{V}^{\pi_1}_{\text{MC},kn} - \hat{V}^{\pi_2}_{\text{MC},kn} \geq \epsilon\right)$$

$$\times \Pr\left(\hat{V}^{\pi_1}_{\text{MC},kn} - \hat{V}^{\pi_2}_{\text{MC},kn} \geq \epsilon\right)$$

$$\geq (1-\gamma)(1-\delta)$$

If we set $\gamma = \frac{0.5-\delta}{1-\delta}$, we have that

$$\Pr\left(\hat{V}^{\pi_1}_{\text{IS}} - \hat{V}^{\pi_2}_{\text{IS}} \geq 0\right) \geq 0.5$$

which is what we want.

As long as $\delta \leq 0.25$, we have that the IS is transitively fairness since any fair algorithm with respect to $\succ_{\text{MC},kn}$ is transitively fair whenever $\Pr(|\hat{V}^{\pi_1}_{\text{MC},kn} - \hat{V}^{\pi_1}_{\text{MC},kn}| > 0) \geq 0.75$ □

D MULTIPLE COMPARISONS

Here we present an algorithm that uses pairwise comparisons to select amongst $k \geq 2$ policies (Algorithm 3). This algorithm can take as input either of the off-policy fair policy selection algorithms above (or some variant thereof).

Theorem D.1. *For any finite set of k policies* Π, *behavior policy* π_b, $p = 0.5$, *and fair off-policy policy selection algorithm* FPS, *Algorithm 3 is a strictly fair policy selection algorithm with when we have* n *samples drawn from* π_b.

Algorithm 3 Off-Policy FPS for k policies

input Π, V^{Π}_{Max}, ϵ, p
  $\mathcal{T} = \{\tau_1, \tau_2, \ldots, \tau_n \sim \pi_b\}$, FPS
 $\delta \leftarrow (1-p)/(2k+3)$
 $\pi^* \leftarrow \Pi$.next
 Eliminated $\leftarrow \emptyset$
 CurrBeat $\leftarrow \emptyset$
 repeat
  $\pi' \leftarrow (\Pi \backslash \text{CurrBeat})$.next
  winner $\leftarrow$ FPS(π^*, π', $V^{\pi^*}_{\text{Max}}$, $V^{\pi'}_{\text{Max}}$, ϵ, δ, $\mathcal{T}$)
  if winner == $\pi*$ **then**
   Eliminated $\leftarrow$ Eliminated $\cup \{\pi'\}$
   CurrBeat $\leftarrow$ CurrBeat $\cup \{\pi'\}$
  else if winner == π' **then**
   $\pi* \leftarrow \pi'$
   Eliminated $\leftarrow$ Eliminated $\cup \{\pi^*\}$
   CurrBeat $\leftarrow$ CurrBeat $\cup \{\pi^*\}$
  else
   $\pi^* \leftarrow (\Pi \backslash \text{Eliminated})$.next
   Eliminated $\leftarrow$ Eliminated $\cup \{\pi^*, \pi'\}$
   CurrBeat $\leftarrow \emptyset$
  end if
 until len(Eliminated) == $k-1$ or len(CurrBeat) == k
 if len(Eliminated) == $k-1$ **then**
  return π^*
 else
  return No Fair Comparison
 end if

Proof of Theorem D.1. The algorithm essentially applies an algorithm for finding the maximum element of a set, with the exception that whenever it cannot make a fair comparison between two policies, it will eliminate both of those policies from consideration of being better than all other policies with respect to the better-than function. The algorithm must return `No Fair Comparison` if and only if every policy is eliminated. Notice that we only eliminate a policy when it is not returned by `FPS` or when `No Fair Comparison` is returned, which is correct. Notice that until there are $k-1$ policies that are eliminated, at every comparison at least one policy is eliminated and the last of those comparisons must include the only remaining non-eliminated policy. Afterwards it takes at most $k-2$ comparisons with the final policy (comparing it to every other policy other than the one it was already compared to) to determine that no fair comparison is possible, making a total of $2k-3$ comparisons.

On the other hand, the algorithm must return a policy when that policy is outputted by `FPS` from comparisons with every other policy, which is exactly what it does (i.e. when the CurrBeated set includes $k-1$ policies). The maximum number of comparisons it takes to output a policy is the number of comparisons it takes to eliminate $k-1$ other policies plus the number of comparisons it takes to beat $k-2$ policies using the same argument as above, making a total of $2k-3$ comparisons. Thus, if we let $\delta = (1-p)/(2k-3)$ all of the comparisons made by `FPS` will simultaneously hold with probability $1-(2k-3)\delta = p$, and so setting $p = 0.5$ ensures fairness. □

E SAFETY THEOREMS AND PROOFS

In this section, we will prove the theorems for ensuring safety when using importance sampling for policy selection.

Theorem 6.4. *For any two policies π_1 and π_2, behavior policy π_b, $\omega = w^{\pi_1}_{Max}V^{\pi_1}_{Max} + w^{\pi_2}_{Max}V^{\pi_2}_{Max}$, and $\delta \leq 0.5$, Algorithm 2 is a safe policy selection algorithm with respect to $\succ_V$ with probability $1-\delta$.*

Proof of Theorem 6.4. Let $\hat{V}^{\pi}_i = \sum_{t=1}^{T_i} w^{\pi_e}_i R_{i,t}$ (i.e., the estimate of the value of policy π using only τ_i). Now let

$$X_i = \hat{V}^{\pi_1}_i - \hat{V}^{\pi_2}_i$$

Note that the range of X_i is $[-w^{\pi_2}_{\text{Max}}V^{\pi_2}_{\text{Max}}, w^{\pi_1}_{\text{Max}}V^{\pi_1}_{\text{Max}}]$. Because τ_i and τ_j are independent for all $i \neq j$, we know that X_i is independent of X_j for all $i \neq j$. Thus we can use Hoeffding's inequality to find that:

$$\Pr\left(\bar{X} - \mathbf{E}\left[\bar{X}\right] \geq -\omega\sqrt{\frac{\ln(1/\gamma)}{2n}}\right) \geq 1-\gamma$$

and

$$\Pr\left(\bar{X} - \mathbf{E}\left[\bar{X}\right] \leq \omega\sqrt{\frac{\ln(1/\gamma)}{2n}}\right) \geq 1-\gamma$$

where $\omega = w^{\pi_1}_{\text{Max}}V^{\pi_1}_{\text{Max}} + w^{\pi_2}_{\text{Max}}V^{\pi_2}_{\text{Max}}$. Note that

$$\bar{X} = \frac{1}{n}\sum_{i=1}^{n} X_i = \frac{1}{n}\sum_{i=1}^{n} \hat{V}^{\pi_1}_i - \hat{V}^{\pi_2}_i = \hat{V}^{\pi_1}_{\text{IS}} - \hat{V}^{\pi_2}_{\text{IS}}$$

and $\mathbf{E}\left[\bar{X}\right] = V^{\pi_1} - V^{\pi_2}$. Thus, substituting $(1-p)/2$ for γ, we have that the following two statements hold with probability at least $1 - 2\gamma = p$,

$$V^{\pi_1} - V^{\pi_2} \geq \hat{V}^{\pi_1}_{\text{IS}} - \hat{V}^{\pi_2}_{\text{IS}} - \sqrt{\frac{\ln(2/(1-p))}{2n}}$$

and

$$V^{\pi_1} - V^{\pi_2} \leq \hat{V}^{\pi_1}_{\text{IS}} - \hat{V}^{\pi_2}_{\text{IS}} + \sqrt{\frac{\ln(2/(1-p))}{2n}}$$

Thus the probability that $V^{\pi_1} - V^{\pi_2} < 0$ but $\hat{V}^{\pi_1}_{\text{IS}} - \hat{V}^{\pi_2}_{\text{IS}} - \sqrt{\frac{\ln(2/(1-p))}{2n}} > 0$ or $V^{\pi_1} - V^{\pi_2} > 0$ but $\hat{V}^{\pi_1}_{\text{IS}} + \hat{V}^{\pi_2}_{\text{IS}} - \sqrt{\frac{\ln(2/(1-p))}{2n}} < 0$ is less than p, which means for $p = 1-\delta$, we will output the worse policy according to $\succ_V$ with probability at most δ, which is exactly what we need. □

Theorem 6.5. *For any two policies π_1 and π_2, where $\Pr\left(|\hat{V}^{\pi_1}_{MC,kn} - \hat{V}^{\pi_2}_{MC,kn}| \geq 0\right) \geq 1 - \delta_{MC}$ any behavior policy π_b, $\omega = (w^{\pi_1}_{Max}+1)V^{\pi_1}_{Max} + (w^{\pi_2}_{Max}+1)V^{\pi_2}_{Max}$, $p = 1-\delta_{MC}\delta$ for some $\delta \leq 0.5$, and for all $k \in \{1,2,3,\dots\}$, Algorithm 2 is a safe policy selection algorithm with respect to $\succ_{MC,kn}$ with probability $1-\delta$ when we have n samples drawn from π_b. It is a transitively fair policy selection algorithm whenever $\delta_{MC} \leq 0.25$.*

Proof of Theorem 6.5. Recall that Algorithm 2 receives as input $\tau_1, \dots, \tau_n \sim \pi_b$. Consider additional random samples $\tau^{\pi_1}_1, \dots, \tau^{\pi_1}_{kn} \sim \pi_1$ and $\tau^{\pi_2}_1, \dots, \tau^{\pi_2}_{kn} \sim \pi_2$. Note that these samples are all independent from each other. For $i \in \{1, 2, \dots, n\}$, let

$$\hat{V}^{\pi}_i = \frac{1}{k}\sum_{j=1}^{k}\sum_{t=1}^{T_{ji}} R_{ji,t}$$

(i.e., the estimate of the value of policy π using only samples $\tau_i^\pi, \tau_{2i}^\pi, \ldots \tau_{ki}^\pi$). Furthermore let $\hat{V}^\pi_{\text{IS},i} = \sum_{t=1}^{T_i} w_{i,t} R_{i,t}$. Now let

$$X_i = (\hat{V}_i^{\pi_1} - \hat{V}_i^{\pi_2}) - (\hat{V}^{\pi_1}_{\text{IS},i} - \hat{V}^{\pi_2}_{\text{IS},i})$$

Notice that the range of X_i is $[-V^{\pi_2}_{\text{Max}} - w^{\pi_1}_{\text{Max}} V^{\pi_1}_{\text{Max}}, V^{\pi_1}_{\text{Max}} + w^{\pi_2}_{\text{Max}} V^{\pi_2}_{\text{Max}}]$. Thus we can use Hoeffding's inequality to find that:

$$\Pr\left(\bar{X} - \mathbf{E}\left[\bar{X}\right] \geq -\omega\sqrt{\frac{\ln(1/\delta)}{2n}}\right) \geq 1 - \gamma$$

and

$$\Pr\left(\bar{X} - \mathbf{E}\left[\bar{X}\right] \leq \omega\sqrt{\frac{\ln(1/\delta)}{2n}}\right) \geq 1 - \gamma$$

where $\omega = (w^{\pi_1}_{\text{Max}} + 1)V^{\pi_1}_{\text{Max}} + (w^{\pi_2}_{\text{Max}} + 1)V^{\pi_2}_{\text{Max}}$. Notice that

$$\bar{X} = \frac{1}{n}\sum_{i=1}^{n} X_i = \frac{1}{n}\sum_{i=1}^{n}(\hat{V}_i^{\pi_1} - \hat{V}_i^{\pi_2}) - (\hat{V}^{\pi_1}_{\text{IS},i} - \hat{V}^{\pi_2}_{\text{IS},i})$$
$$= (\hat{V}^{\pi_1}_{\text{MC},kn} - \hat{V}^{\pi_2}_{\text{MC},kn}) - (\hat{V}^{\pi_1}_{\text{IS}} - \hat{V}^{\pi_2}_{\text{IS}})$$

and

$$\mathbf{E}\left[\bar{X}\right] = (V^{\pi_1} - V^{\pi_2}) - (V^{\pi_1} - V^{\pi_2}) = 0$$

Thus, substituting $(1-p)/2$ for γ, we have that the following two statements hold with probability at least $1 - 2\gamma = p$,

$$\hat{V}^{\pi_1}_{\text{MC},kn} - \hat{V}^{\pi_2}_{\text{MC},kn} \geq \hat{V}^{\pi_1}_{\text{IS}} - \hat{V}^{\pi_2}_{\text{IS}} - \sqrt{\frac{\ln(2/(1-p))}{2n}}$$

and

$$\hat{V}^{\pi_1}_{\text{MC},kn} - \hat{V}^{\pi_2}_{\text{MC},kn} \leq \hat{V}^{\pi_1}_{\text{IS}} - \hat{V}^{\pi_2}_{\text{IS}} + \sqrt{\frac{\ln(2/(1-p))}{2n}}$$

Thus the probability that $\hat{V}^{\pi_1}_{\text{MC},kn} - \hat{V}^{\pi_2}_{\text{MC},kn} < 0$ but $(\hat{V}^{\pi_1}_{\text{IS}} - \hat{V}^{\pi_2}_{\text{IS}}) - \omega\sqrt{\frac{\ln(2/(1-p))}{2n}} > 0$ or $\hat{V}^{\pi_1}_{\text{MC},kn} - \hat{V}^{\pi_2}_{\text{MC},kn} > 0$ but $\hat{V}^{\pi_1}_{\text{IS}} - \hat{V}^{\pi_2}_{\text{IS}} + \omega\sqrt{\frac{\ln(2/(1-p))}{2n}} < 0$ is less than $1 - p$. Now suppose without loss of generality that $P(\hat{V}^{\pi_1}_{\text{MC},kn} > \hat{V}^{\pi_2}_{\text{MC},kn} = \delta_{\text{MC}} > 0.5$. The probability that we output π_2 is at most p/δ_{MC}. So if $p = 1 - \delta_{\text{MC}}\delta$, we output the worse policy with respect to $\succ_{\text{MC},kn}$ with probability at most δ, which is exactly what we need.

As long as $\delta_{\text{MC}} \leq 0.25$, we have that the algorithm is transitively safe since any fair algorithm with respect to $\succ_{\text{MC},kn}$ is transitively fair whenever $\Pr(|\hat{V}^{\pi_1}_{\text{MC}} - \hat{V}^{\pi_1}_{\text{MC}}| > 0) \geq 0.75$ □

Theorem 6.6. *There exists policies π_1, π_2, and behavior policy π_b for which Algorithm 2 with inputs as described in Theorem 6.4 is not a safe policy selection algorithm with respect to $\succ_{MC,1}$ with $p = 0.5$ when we have a single sample drawn from π_b.*

Proof of Theorem 6.6. Consider a world where there are three trajectories: τ_1 with reward 0.0001, τ_2 with reward 0.0002, and τ_3 with reward 1. We want to select between two policies: π_1, which places probability 1 on τ_2 and π_2 which places probability 0.51 on τ_1 and probability 0.49 on τ_3. When we only have one sample from each policy, $\Pr(\hat{V}^{\pi_1}_{\text{MC},1} > \hat{V}^{\pi_2}_{\text{MC},1}) = 0.51 > 0.5$, but clearly $V^{\pi_1} \ll V^{\pi_2}$. Now consider using IS with behavior policy π_b which places probability 0.48 on τ_1 and probability 0.01 on τ_2 and probability 0.51 on τ_3. If we apply Algorithm 2 with the inputs to guarantee that the algorithm is safe with respect $\succ_V$ (as given in Theorem 6.4), we find that whenever π_b samples from τ_3,

$$V^{\pi_1}_{\text{IS}} - V^{\pi_2}_{\text{IS}} + (w^{\pi_1}_{\text{Max}} V^{\pi_1}_{\text{Max}} + w^{\pi_2}_{\text{Max}} V^{\pi_2}_{\text{Max}})\sqrt{\frac{\ln 4}{2n}}$$
$$= 0(1) - \frac{0.49}{0.51}(1) + \left(\frac{1}{0.01}(0.0002) + \frac{0.51}{0.48}(1)\right)\sqrt{\frac{\ln 4}{2}}$$
$$\approx -0.060 < 0$$

Since this event occurs with probability 0.51, we find that Algorithm 2 returns π_2 more than half the time, indicating that Algorithm 2 is not a safe policy with respect to $\succ_{\text{MC},1}$ □

FROSH: FasteR Online Sketching Hashing

Xixian Chen[1,2], **Irwin King**[1,2], **Michael R. Lyu**[1,2]
[1]Shenzhen Research Institute, The Chinese University of Hong Kong, Shenzhen, China
[2]Department of Computer Science and Engineering,
The Chinese University of Hong Kong, Shatin, N.T., Hong Kong
{xxchen, king, lyu}@cse.cuhk.edu.hk

Abstract

Many hashing methods, especially those that are in the data-dependent category with good learning accuracy, are still inefficient when dealing with three critical problems in modern data analysis. First, data usually come in a streaming fashion, but most of the existing hashing methods are batch-based models. Second, when data become huge, the extensive computational time, large space requirement, and multiple passes to load the data into memory will be prohibitive. Third, data often lack sufficient label information. Although the recently proposed Online Sketching Hashing (OSH) is promising to alleviate all three issues mentioned above, its training procedure still suffers from a high time complexity. In this paper, we propose a FasteR Online Sketching Hashing (FROSH) method to make the training process faster. Compared with OSH, we leverage fast transform to sketch data more compactly. Particularly, we derive independent transformations to guarantee the sketching accuracy, and design a novel implementation to make such transformations applicable to online data sketching without increasing the space cost. We rigorously prove that our method can yield a comparable learning accuracy with a lower time complexity and an equal space cost compared with OSH. Finally, extensive experiments on synthetic and real-world datasets demonstrate the excellent performance of our method.

1 INTRODUCTION

Hashing is an efficient method to conduct an approximate nearest neighbor search, which is critical for machine learning and applications such as clustering, retrieval and matching [43]. It transforms data into a low-dimensional representation, i.e., a short hash code consisting of a sequence of bits in Hamming space. The data distance in original space then is approximated by the Hamming distance that can be calculated extremely fast in modern CPU. Thus, the approximate nearest neighbor search can be accomplished with less time and space costs. Current hashing methods can be categorized broadly as data-independent and data-dependent techniques. Locality Sensitive Hashing (LSH) methods [3, 8, 12, 15, 39] are prime examples of data-independent techniques, which are also unsupervised. They construct hash functions based on random projection, which are typically very fast and theoretically guaranteed, but are developed only for certain distance functions and often require long code length to achieve acceptable search accuracy because of ignoring the data distribution. Compared with data-independent methods, data-dependent hashing techniques achieve better accuracy performance with shorter binary codes, while usually incurring a larger computational cost to train the hashing functions. These data-dependent methods can be categorized as unsupervised and (semi-)supervised techniques. In unsupervised studies [13, 17, 22, 27–29, 33, 37, 44, 49], hash functions are learned from data distribution rather than being randomly generated by preserving a metric induced distance in the Hamming space. Supervised methods [19, 23, 24, 26, 35, 38, 42] additionally leverage the label information, and thus often outperform those unsupervised ones.

Although data-dependent hashing methods have achieved a promising learning accuracy, yet they suffer from some critical problems when confronted with the data such as web images, videos, stocks, genomes and web documents in the big data era. First, data often become available continuously in a streaming fashion, and each data point or data chunk can be processed only once [22, 25]. Hence, batch learning strategies are not allowed. Moreover, with batch-learners, it is unclear how to adapt the hash functions as the dataset continues to grow and new variations appear over time. Second, the data size n and dimension d can be large with $1 \ll d \ll n$ [10], so that the high time complexity and $O(nd)$ space cost [22, 25] are prohibitive. In particular, advanced batch-based unsupervised hashing solutions such as SGH [17] and OCH [27] can avoid the $O(nd)$ space cost merely by performing multiple passes over the data, while the disk IO overhead for loading all data into memory multiple times will be the major performance bottleneck [47]. Third, labels are commonly missing, noisy, and scarce in today's big data situation, and labeling streaming data is also expensive and infeasible [40,46,48].

To tackle the above challenges, we focus on the most recently proposed online hashing, i.e., online sketching hashing (OSH) [22], which is data-dependent, space-efficient, unsupervised, and in a single pass. Note that there have been several other investigations in online hashing. Such hashing methods include online kernel-based hashing (OKH) [14], adaptive online hashing (AOH) [5], and [6] but they all belong to the supervised category, which require extra label information.

However, given $O(d\ell)$ space to store and perform calculation on the streaming data, the OSH method retains a training time of $O(nd\ell + d\ell^2)$ to yield $r \leq O(\ell)$ hashing bits, where n is the data size, d is the data dimension, and ℓ denotes the sketching size satisfying $\ell < d \ll n$. Such training time is still expensive since $1 \ll d \ll n$ [10]. In this paper, we attempt to reduce the running time further. Our contributions are summarized as follows:

- First, we propose a FasteR Online Sketching Hashing (FROSH) method by improving the data sketching procedure in the OSH method. Specifically, we employ a fast transform to reduce the data size, in which independent transformations are applied for different small data chunks to make the sketching compact and accurate.

- Second, we design a more efficient way to implement the fast transform in our FROSH. Compared with the standard way, our strategy reduces the space burden incurred by the fast transform for sketching streaming data while maintaining the same time efficiency.

- Third, we analyze the accuracy of our FROSH, and give an error bound comparable with OSH. Moreover, our FROSH has a smaller time complexity of $\widetilde{O}(n\ell^2 + nd)$ with an equal space usage. Extensive experiments demonstrate the computational efficiency with a competitive learning accuracy.

The remainder of this paper is organized as follows. In Section 2, we review the prior work and techniques. In Section 3, we present our method along with theoretical analysis, and emphasize its advantages from various aspects. In Section 4, we provide extensive empirical results, and Section 5 concludes the whole work.

Notation. Let $[k]$ denote a set of integers $\{1, 2, \ldots, k\}$. Given a matrix $\mathbf{A} \in \mathbb{R}^{n\times d}$, for $i \in [n]$, $j \in [d]$, we let $\mathbf{a}^i \in \mathbb{R}^{1\times d}$ denote the i-th row of $\mathbf{A}$, $\mathbf{a}_j \in \mathbb{R}^n$ denote the j-th column of $\mathbf{A}$, and a_{ij} denote the (i,j)-th element of $\mathbf{A}$ or j-th element of $\mathbf{a}^i$. Let $\{\mathbf{A}_t\}_{t=1}^k$ denote a set of matrices $\{\mathbf{A}_1, \mathbf{A}_2, \ldots, \mathbf{A}_k\}$. Let $a_{t,ij}$ and $\mathbf{a}_{t,i}$ denote the (i,j)-th element and i-th column of matrix $\mathbf{A}_t$, respectively. Let $\mathbf{A}^T$ denote the transpose of $\mathbf{A}$, and $\mathrm{Tr}(\mathbf{A})$ denote its trace. Let $|a|$ denote the absolute value of a. Let $\|\mathbf{A}\|_2$ and $\|\mathbf{A}\|_F$ denote the spectral norm and Frobenius norm of $\mathbf{A}$, respectively. Let $\|\mathbf{a}\|_q = (\sum_{j=1}^d |a_j|^q)^{1/q}$ for $q \geq 1$ be the ℓ_q-norm of $\mathbf{a} \in \mathbb{R}^d$. We denote the SVD of $\mathbf{A}$ by $\mathbf{A} = \mathbf{U}\mathbf{\Sigma}\mathbf{V}^T = \sum_{i=1}^{\rho} \sigma_i \mathbf{u}_i \mathbf{v}_i^T = \mathbf{U}_k\mathbf{\Sigma}_k\mathbf{V}_k^T + \mathbf{U}_k^{\perp}\mathbf{\Sigma}_k^{\perp}\mathbf{V}_k^{\perp T}$, where $\mathrm{rank}(\mathbf{A}) = \rho$, $\mathbf{A}_k = \mathbf{U}_k\mathbf{\Sigma}_k\mathbf{V}_k^T$ represents the best rank k approximation to $\mathbf{A}$, and $\sigma_i(\mathbf{A})$ denotes the i-th largest singular value of $\mathbf{A}$. Finally, $\mathbf{A} \preceq \mathbf{B}$ means that $\mathbf{B} - \mathbf{A}$ is positive semi-definite.

2 RELATED WORK

In this section, we describe the properties of the OSH method. Then, we outline and discuss the fast transforms, especially the Subsampled Randomized Hadamard Transform (SRHT).

2.1 ONLINE SKETCHING HASHING

We rephrase the background and details of the OSH method [22]. Given data $\mathbf{A} \in \mathbb{R}^{n\times d}$ and the unknown projection matrix $\mathbf{W} \in \mathbb{R}^{d\times r}$, the k-th hashing function for a data point $\mathbf{a}^i \in \mathbb{R}^{1\times d}$ is defined as

$$h_k(\mathbf{a}^i) = \mathrm{sgn}((\mathbf{a}^i - \boldsymbol{\mu})\mathbf{w}_k), \tag{1}$$

where $\boldsymbol{\mu} = \bar{\mathbf{A}} = \frac{1}{n}\sum_{i=1}^n \mathbf{a}^i$. By dropping the non-differentiable function $\mathrm{sgn}(\cdot)$ for the binary codes [42], the objective can be reformulated as the same as that of Principal Component Analysis (PCA)

$$\begin{aligned} \max_{\mathbf{W}\in\mathbb{R}^{d\times r}} \quad & \mathrm{Tr}(\mathbf{W}^T(\mathbf{A}-\boldsymbol{\mu})^T(\mathbf{A}-\boldsymbol{\mu})\mathbf{W}) \\ \text{s.t.} \quad & \mathbf{W}^T\mathbf{W} = \mathbf{I}_r, \end{aligned} \tag{2}$$

where $(\mathbf{A}-\boldsymbol{\mu})$ denotes a matrix $[\mathbf{a}^1-\boldsymbol{\mu}; \mathbf{a}^2-\boldsymbol{\mu}; \ldots; \mathbf{a}^n-\boldsymbol{\mu}]$.

The solution to $\mathbf{W} \in \mathbb{R}^{d\times r}$ in Eq. (2) is the top r right eigenvectors of the covariance matrix $(\mathbf{A}-\boldsymbol{\mu})^T(\mathbf{A}-\boldsymbol{\mu})$.

Algorithm 1 Online Sketching Hashing (OSH) [22]

Input: Data $\mathbf{A} = \{\mathbf{A}_j \in \mathbb{R}^{h_j \times d}\}_{j=1}^{s}$, sketching size $\ell < d$, positive integer η, hashing bits r

1: Initialize sketching matrix by $\mathbf{B} = \mathbf{0}^{\ell \times d}$
2: Set $\boldsymbol{\mu}_1$ as the row mean vector of $\mathbf{A}_1$
3: Let $\boldsymbol{\varphi} = \boldsymbol{\mu}_1, \tau = h_1, \xi = 0$
4: Sketch $\mathbf{G}_1 = (\mathbf{A}_1 - \boldsymbol{\mu}_1) \in \mathbb{R}^{h_1 \times d}$ into $\mathbf{B} \in \mathbb{R}^{\ell \times d}$
5: **for** $j = 2 : s$ **do**
6: Set $\boldsymbol{\mu}_j$ as the row mean vector of $\mathbf{A}_j$
7: Set $\boldsymbol{\varsigma} = \sqrt{\frac{\tau h_j}{\tau + h_j}}(\boldsymbol{\mu}_j - \boldsymbol{\varphi}) \in \mathbb{R}^{1 \times d}$
8: Sketch $\mathbf{G}_j = [(\mathbf{A}_j - \boldsymbol{\mu}_j); \boldsymbol{\varsigma}] \in \mathbb{R}^{(h_j+1) \times d}$ into $\mathbf{B} \in \mathbb{R}^{\ell \times d}$
9: Set $\boldsymbol{\varphi} = \frac{\tau \boldsymbol{\varphi}}{\tau + h_j} + \frac{h_j \boldsymbol{\mu}_j}{\tau + h_j}$ # Update the mean vector
10: Set $\tau = \tau + h_j$ # Update the data size
11: Set $\xi = \xi + 1$
12: **if** $\xi == \eta$ **then**
13: Compute the SVD of $\mathbf{B} \in \mathbb{R}^{\ell \times d}$, and assign the top r right singular vectors as $\mathbf{W}^T \in \mathbb{R}^{r \times d}$
14: Set $\xi = 0$
15: **return** $\mathbf{W}$

For $d < n$, it takes $O(nd^2)$ time and $O(nd)$ space, which is infeasible for large n and d [18].

To tackle above computational issues, sketching the data before the training is a promising way. Specifically, a sketch of a data matrix is another matrix that is significantly smaller than the original but still approximates it well and preserves the properties of interest. It implies that the storing and the computing on the sketch will be much easier than with the original large matrix, and the downstream learning algorithms on the sketch can still guarantee the learning accuracy [4, 9, 25, 32, 45].

Leveraging the effectiveness of sketching in the learning, OSH is proposed, and its details are presented in Algorithm 1. It aims at efficiently achieving a small matrix $\mathbf{B} \in \mathbb{R}^{\ell \times d}$ for the centered data $(\mathbf{A} - \boldsymbol{\mu})$, then computing the SVD on $\mathbf{B}$ only takes $O(d\ell^2)$ time and $O(d\ell)$ space for $\ell < d$. The difficulty lies in that sketching cannot be directly applied in each centered data chunk $(\mathbf{A}_j - \boldsymbol{\mu})$, since $\boldsymbol{\mu}$ can only be obtained after observing all data points in $\mathbf{A}$.

Then, the *online centering procedure* in steps 3 to 10 are to ensure that $(\mathbf{A}_{[j]} - \hat{\boldsymbol{\mu}}_j)^T(\mathbf{A}_{[j]} - \hat{\boldsymbol{\mu}}_j) = \mathbf{G}_{[j]}^T \mathbf{G}_{[j]}$ after the j-th iteration, where $\mathbf{A}_{[j]} = [\mathbf{A}_1; \mathbf{A}_2; \cdots; \mathbf{A}_j]$ by stacking all observed $\mathbf{A}_j$ vertically, $\mathbf{G}_{[j]}$ follows a similar definition, and $\hat{\boldsymbol{\mu}}_j$ is the row mean vector of $\mathbf{A}_{[j]}$. Steps 4 and 8 are to get a smaller matrix $\mathbf{B}$ via an efficient sketching such that $\mathbf{B}^T\mathbf{B} \approx \mathbf{G}_{[j]}^T \mathbf{G}_{[j]}$ after the j-th iteration. After all iterations, OSH guarantees that $\mathbf{B}^T\mathbf{B} \approx \mathbf{G}_{[s]}^T \mathbf{G}_{[s]} = (\mathbf{A}_{[s]} - \hat{\boldsymbol{\mu}}_s)^T(\mathbf{A}_{[s]} - \hat{\boldsymbol{\mu}}_s) = (\mathbf{A} - \boldsymbol{\mu})^T(\mathbf{A} - \boldsymbol{\mu})$. If $\sum_{j=1}^{s} h_j = O(n)$, the sketching steps in OSH will take $O(nd\ell)$ time and $O(d\ell)$ space. The SVD in step 13 runs for about ξ/η times. As ξ/η can be manually set to be a small constant, step 13 takes $O(d\ell^2)$ time and $O(d\ell)$ space in total. The computational cost of the online data centering procedure is negligible. In conclusion, OSH consumes $O(nd\ell + d\ell^2)$ time and $O(d\ell)$ space.

Remark 1. To address the problem that most of the information can be contained by only a small number of significant singular vectors in $\mathbf{W} \in \mathbb{R}^{d \times r}$, OSH also empirically applies a random orthogonal rotation $\boldsymbol{\Upsilon} \in \mathbb{R}^{r \times r}$ (the orthonormal bases of an $r \times r$ random Gaussian matrix) to all singular vectors $\mathbf{W} \in \mathbb{R}^{d \times r}$ in Algorithm 1 via $\mathbf{W}\boldsymbol{\Upsilon}$. This step resembles Iterative Quantization [13] but runs much more efficiently with streaming settings maintained and negligible computational cost incurred.

2.2 FREQUENT DIRECTIONS FOR SKETCHING

Algorithm 2 Frequent Directions (FD) [25]

Input: Data $\mathbf{A} \in \mathbb{R}^{n \times d}$, sketching matrix $\mathbf{B} \in \mathbb{R}^{\ell \times d}$

1: **if** $\mathbf{B}$ not exists **then**
2: Set $\mathbf{B} = \mathbf{0}^{\ell \times d}$
3: **for** $i \in [n]$ **do**
4: Insert $\mathbf{a}^i \in \mathbb{R}^{1 \times d}$ into a zero valued row of $\mathbf{B}$
5: **if** $\mathbf{B}$ has no zero valued rows **then**
6: $[\mathbf{U}, \boldsymbol{\Sigma}, \mathbf{V}] = \text{SVD}(\mathbf{B})$
7: $\widehat{\boldsymbol{\Sigma}} = \sqrt{\max(\boldsymbol{\Sigma}^2 - \sigma_{\ell/2}^2 \mathbf{I}_l, 0)}$
8: Set $\mathbf{B} = \widehat{\boldsymbol{\Sigma}}\mathbf{V}^T$

OSH employs the Frequent Directions (FD) as a blackbox to sketch streaming data, which is summarized in Algorithm 2. It operates by keeping collecting row vectors from the data source. Once the sketching matrix $\mathbf{B} \in \mathbb{R}^{\ell \times d}$ has ℓ non-zero rows, the shrinking procedure as shown in steps 5 to 8 will reduce the size of the matrix $\mathbf{B} \in \mathbb{R}^{\ell \times d}$ by a half, *which repeats throughout the entire streaming data*.

In this part, we assume that FD will process n data points. The computational cost of the FD algorithm is dominated by the shrinking procedure that involves computing an exact SVD on $\mathbf{B} \in \mathbb{R}^{\ell \times d}$, which takes $O(d\ell^2)$ time and $O(d\ell)$ space for $\ell < d$. Since the shrinking procedure is operated once nearly every $\ell/2$ iterations of the main loop, the time complexity is $O(d\ell^2 \times n/\ell) = O(nd\ell)$ with $O(d\ell)$ space burden.

Recently, the Sparse FD (SFD) algorithm [11] is proposed to take advantage of the sparsity of $\mathbf{A}$ by applying a powerful randomized SVD [34] instead of an exact SVD in each shrinking procedure. SFD still takes $O(d\ell)$

space but only requires $\widetilde{O}(\text{nnz}(\mathbf{A})\ell + n\ell^2)$ running time, where nnz($\mathbf{A}$) means the number of non-zero entries in $\mathbf{A}$. This time cost is much smaller than $O(nd\ell)$ if $\ell \ll d$ and $\mathbf{A} \in \mathbb{R}^{n\times d}$ is extremely sparse.

Remark 2. FD works well for streaming data. For instance, given two (or more) data chunks like $\mathbf{G}_1 \in \mathbb{R}^{h_1\times d}$ and $\mathbf{G}_2 \in \mathbb{R}^{(h_2+1)\times d}$ in Algorithm 1, we invoke FD and run it on $\mathbf{G}_1$ to yield a sketching matrix $\mathbf{B} = \mathbf{B}_1 \in \mathbb{R}^{\ell\times d}$. Based on the current $\mathbf{B} = \mathbf{B}_1$, we then run FD on $\mathbf{G}_2$ to update $\mathbf{B}$ and get $\mathbf{B} = \mathbf{B}_2 \in \mathbb{R}^{\ell\times d}$. Such procedures are obviously equivalent to that we directly invoke FD for once and run it on $[\mathbf{G}_1; \mathbf{G}_2] \in \mathbb{R}^{(h_1+h_2+1)\times d}$, which also gets an identical $\mathbf{B} = \mathbf{B}_2$.

2.3 FAST TRANSFORM

Given a vector $\mathbf{a} \in \mathbb{R}^m$, its compressed representation $\mathbf{b} \in \mathbb{R}^q$ can be obtained by performing the matrix-vector multiplication like $\mathbf{\Phi a}$, where $q < m$ and $\mathbf{\Phi} \in \mathbb{R}^{q\times m}$ is a random projection matrix (e.g., a Gaussian random matrix). Generally, computing $\mathbf{\Phi a}$ takes $O(qm)$ time. It can be a computational bottleneck of fast implementing numerous learning tasks that involve data compression.

Fast transforms, which are based on the structured projection matrix like Hadamard matrix or Fourier matrix, then are employed to overcome the shortcomings of the classical transformation methods. For Hadamard matrix $\mathbf{H}_m \in \mathbb{R}^{m\times m}$, its entry is defined as

$$\mathbf{H}_{ij} = (-1)^{\langle i-1, j-1\rangle}, \tag{3}$$

where $\langle i-1, j-1\rangle$ is the dot-product of the b-bit vectors of integers $i-1$ and $j-1$ expressed in binary, and $b \le \max(\lceil \log(i+1)\rceil, \lceil \log(j+1)\rceil)$. It can also be defined recursively as

$$\mathbf{H}_m = \begin{bmatrix} \mathbf{H}_{m/2} & \mathbf{H}_{m/2} \\ \mathbf{H}_{m/2} & -\mathbf{H}_{m/2} \end{bmatrix} \quad \text{and} \quad \mathbf{H}_2 = \begin{bmatrix} 1 & 1 \\ 1 & -1 \end{bmatrix}.$$

The normalized Hadamard matrix is defined by $\mathbf{H} = \sqrt{\frac{1}{m}}\mathbf{H}_m$, and by exploring the recursive structure of $\mathbf{H}$, computing $\mathbf{Ha}$ only takes $O(m \log m)$ time with $O(m)$ space [1].

To compress data, we perform the Subsampled Randomized Hadamard Transform (SRHT), i.e., data is transformed via a randomized Hadamard matrix and then uniformly sampled in the resulting entries. For a $q \times m$ SRHT matrix, it is defined as the form $\mathbf{\Phi} = \mathbf{SHD}$, where $\mathbf{D} \in \mathbb{R}^{m\times m}$ is a diagonal matrix with its diagonal elements being i.i.d. Rademacher random variables (i.e., 1 or -1 with equal probability), $\mathbf{S} \in \mathbb{R}^{q\times m}$ is a scaled sampling matrix with each row uniformly sampled *without replacement* from m rows of the identity matrix $\mathbf{I}_m \in \mathbb{R}^{m\times m}$ multiplied by $\sqrt{\frac{m}{q}}$.

Differently, computing $\mathbf{\Phi a}$ only takes $O(m \log q)$ time with $O(m)$ space [1,31].

3 FASTER ONLINE SKETCHING HASHING

In this section, we motivate and present FROSH, whose sketching relies on our Faster FD (FFD). To make FROSH maintain an equal space efficiency with that of OSH, we also derive a new implementation of fast transform in FFD for sketching streaming data. The analysis guarantees the performance of our solution.

3.1 MOTIVATION, METHOD AND RESULTS

The computational cost of OSH is dominated by its sketching method FD. This sketching requires $O(nd\ell)$ time to obtain $\mathbf{B} \in \mathbb{R}^{\ell\times d}$ from the data $\mathbf{A} \in \mathbb{R}^{n\times d}$, which is computationally expensive for $1 \ll d \ll n$ [10]. Even regarding SFD, its $\widetilde{O}(\text{nnz}(\mathbf{A})\ell + nl^2)$ time cost still tends to be $\widetilde{O}(nd\ell + n\ell^2)$ since the centered data $\mathbf{A} - \boldsymbol{\mu}$ are dense.

We first present an FFD sketching method as stated in Algorithm 3 to tackle above issues. In steps 5 to 8, after collecting m data points into $\mathbf{F} \in \mathbb{R}^{m\times d}$, a new SRHT matrix is generated to compress $\mathbf{F}$ with its size reduced to $\ell/2$. Then, the newly compressed data and previously shrunken data form the $\mathbf{B} \in \mathbb{R}^{\ell\times d}$. Steps 9 to 10 employ a shrinking procedure that is similar to that in FD.

Algorithm 3 Faster Frequent Directions (FFD)

Input: Data $\mathbf{A} \in \mathbb{R}^{n\times d}$, sketching matrix $\mathbf{B} \in \mathbb{R}^{\ell\times d}$
1: **if** $\mathbf{B}$ not exists **then**
2:     Set $t = 1$, $\mathbf{B} = \mathbf{0}^{\ell\times d}$
3:     Set $\mathbf{F} = \mathbf{0}^{m\times d}$ with $m = \Theta(d)$ # Only needed for notation
4: **for** $i \in [n]$ **do**
5:     Insert $\mathbf{a}^i$ into a zero valued row of $\mathbf{F}$
6:     **if** $\mathbf{F}$ has no zero valued rows **then**
7:         Generate a fast transform $\mathbf{\Phi}_t = \mathbf{S}_t\mathbf{H}\mathbf{D}_t \in \mathbb{R}^{(\ell/2)\times m}$ in the t-th trial
8:         Insert $\mathbf{\Phi}_t\mathbf{F} \in \mathbb{R}^{(\ell/2)\times d}$ into the last $\frac{\ell}{2}$ rows of $\mathbf{B}$
9:         $[\mathbf{U}, \mathbf{\Sigma}, \mathbf{V}] = \text{SVD}(\mathbf{B})$
10:         $\widehat{\mathbf{\Sigma}} = \sqrt{\max(\mathbf{\Sigma}^2 - \sigma^2_{\ell/2}\mathbf{I}_l, 0)}$
11:         Set $\mathbf{B} = \widehat{\mathbf{\Sigma}}\mathbf{V}^T$
12:         Let $\mathbf{B}_t = \mathbf{B}$, $\mathbf{C}_t = \mathbf{\Phi}_t\mathbf{F}$ # Only needed for proof notations
13:         Set $\mathbf{F} = \mathbf{0}^{m\times d}$, $t = t + 1$

However, there may exist one problem in each iteration of step 8, i.e., computing $\mathbf{\Phi}_t\mathbf{F}$ in the standard way has to take $O(md \log \ell)$ time but with $O(md)$ space to collect all m data points. For a big $m = \Theta(d)$, the space cost of $O(md) = O(d^2)$ is practically prohibitive since space can be severely limited [25], which is also inferior to FD method whose advantages includes that only $O(d\ell)$ space is employed.

Fortunately, we do not have to keep a matrix $\mathbf{F} \in \mathbb{R}^{m \times d}$ explicitly to store m data points. Instead, $\mathbf{F} \in \mathbb{R}^{m \times d}$ here is simply used for easily presenting the algorithm. Furthermore, as data come sequentially, we only take $O(d\ell)$ space to handle $O(\ell)$ data points, save and combine intermediate results. We repeat such procedures until that we have sequentially processed m data points denoted by $\mathbf{F} \in \mathbb{R}^{m \times d}$, which finally still only takes $O(md \log \ell)$ time in total to achieve $\mathbf{\Phi}_t \mathbf{F}$. The detailed implementation is deferred to the subsequent section.

Moreover, we adopt an independent and distinct $\mathbf{\Phi}_t$ in each iteration of step 8, which benefits the sketching accuracy by controlling the variance in all sketchings. Below, we formally characterize the properties of our proposed FFD.

Theorem 1 (FFD). *Given data $\mathbf{A} \in \mathbb{R}^{n \times d}$ and the sketching size $\ell \leq k = \min(m, d)$, let the small sketch $\mathbf{B} \in \mathbb{R}^{\ell \times d}$ be constructed by FFD. Then, with probability at least $1 - p\beta - (2p+1)\delta - \frac{2n}{e^k}$ we have*

$$\|\mathbf{A}^T\mathbf{A} - \mathbf{B}^T\mathbf{B}\|_2 \leq \widetilde{O}\Big(\frac{1}{\ell} + \Gamma(\ell, p, k)\Big)\|\mathbf{A}\|_F^2 \quad (4)$$

where $\Gamma(\ell, p, k) = \sqrt{\frac{k}{\ell p^2}} + \sqrt{\frac{1+\sqrt{k/\ell}}{p}}$ with $p = \frac{n}{m}$, and $\widetilde{O}(\cdot)$ hides logarithmic factors on (β, δ, k, d, m) as given in Eqs. (12)(16)(30).

The running time of the algorithm is $\widetilde{O}(nl^2\frac{d}{m} + nd)$ and its space cost is $O(d\ell)$ before taking $m = \Theta(d)$.

Remark 3. For a fixed n, a smaller m improves the sketching accuracy while taking more time burden. We choose $m = \Theta(d)$ such that the time consumption of FFD is $\widetilde{O}(n\ell^2 + nd)$. If $\ell \ll d$, it is superior to $O(nd\ell)$ time cost in FD and $\widetilde{O}(nd\ell + n\ell^2)$ time usage in SFD for dense centered data.

When data keep coming (i.e., n increases) and/or m decreases, p will get larger, which makes the bound in Eq. (4) tighter. If $p = \Omega(\ell^{3/2}k^{1/2})$, i.e., $n = \Omega(\ell^{3/2}d^{3/2})$ when $m = \Theta(d)$, then the error bound of FFD becomes $\widetilde{O}(\frac{1}{\ell}\|\mathbf{A}\|_F^2)$, which is asymptotically comparable with the bounds $\frac{2}{\ell}\|\mathbf{A}\|_F^2$ of FD and $\widetilde{O}(\frac{1}{\ell}\|\mathbf{A}\|_F^2)$ of SFD.

Thus, FFD is more applicable to the big data situation $1 \ll d \ll n$ with computational cost reduced and accuracy guaranteed. Competitive empirical results suggest there is an opportunity to further tighten our error bound.

Algorithm 4 FasteR Online Sketching Hashing (FROSH)

Input: Data $\mathbf{A} = \{\mathbf{A}_j \in \mathbb{R}^{h_j \times d}\}_{j=1}^s$, sketching size $\ell < d$, positive integer η, hashing bits r

1: Run steps 1 to 3 of Algorithm 1

2: Run steps 4 to 10 of Algorithm 1 with FFD to sketch the centered data into $\mathbf{B} \in \mathbb{R}^{\ell \times d}$

3: Run steps 11 to 15 of Algorithm 1 and return $\mathbf{W} \in \mathbb{R}^{d \times r}$

Based on FFD and OSH, our FROSH is straightforward given in Algorithm 4. Its step 2 contains the online data centering procedure, which is equivalent to that in OSH. Then, combining Theorem 1 and the properties of the online data centering procedure yields the next result.

Theorem 2 (FROSH). *Given data $\mathbf{A} \in \mathbb{R}^{n \times d}$ with its row mean vector $\boldsymbol{\mu} \in \mathbb{R}^{1 \times d}$, let the sketch $\mathbf{B}^{\ell \times d}$ be generated by FROSH in Algorithm 4. Then, with probability defined in Theorem 1 we have*

$$\begin{aligned}&\|(\mathbf{A} - \boldsymbol{\mu})^T(\mathbf{A} - \boldsymbol{\mu}) - \mathbf{B}^T\mathbf{B}\|_2 \\ &\quad \leq \widetilde{O}\Big(\frac{1}{\ell} + \Gamma(\ell, p, k)\Big)\|\mathbf{A} - \boldsymbol{\mu}\|_F^2, \end{aligned} \quad (5)$$

where $(\mathbf{A} - \boldsymbol{\mu}) \in \mathbb{R}^{n \times d}$ means subtracting each row of $\mathbf{A}$ by $\boldsymbol{\mu}$, $\Gamma(\ell, p, k)$ is from Theorem 1, and the top r right singular vectors of $\mathbf{B}^{\ell \times d}$ are used for hashing projections $\mathbf{W}^T \in \mathbb{R}^{r \times d}$ in Remark 1.

The algorithm takes $\widetilde{O}(n\ell^2 + nd + d\ell^2)$ time and $O(d\ell)$ space cost after taking $m = \Theta(d)$ in the FFD of FROSH.

Remark 4. This primary analysis resembles that of OSH [22], which follows the conception that accurate sketching does not harm the learning accuracy [4, 9, 22, 25, 32, 45]. Hence, the $\mathbf{W}$ from $\mathbf{B}$ is expected to well approximate that from $\mathbf{A} - \boldsymbol{\mu}$ (more illustrations on the approximation for $\mathbf{W}$ are deferred into the appendix), and we use this sketching error for the centered data $\mathbf{A} - \boldsymbol{\mu}$ to justify if the sketching-based hashing works properly [22]. Thus, the accuracy comparisons between OSH and FROSH resemble Remark 3. Compared with $\widetilde{O}(nd\ell + d\ell^2)$ time and $O(d\ell)$ space cost in OSH, we improve a lot if $1 < \ell \ll d \ll n$.

3.2 IMPLEMENTATION OF THE FAST TRANSFORM IN FFD

Define $q = \ell/2$, then we show how to simply adopt $O(qd)$ space and perform a single pass through $\mathbf{F} \in \mathbb{R}^{m \times d}$ to achieve $\mathbf{\Phi F}$ with $O(md \log q)$ time, given $\mathbf{\Phi} = \mathbf{SHD} \in \mathbb{R}^{q \times m}$, $q \leq m$, and $\log m \leq O(d \log q)$.

To clarify, we choose an m such that $m = 2^b$ for a positive integer b. We can always find a $q/2 \leq p \leq q$ to define positive integers c and p such that $m = 2^c p$.

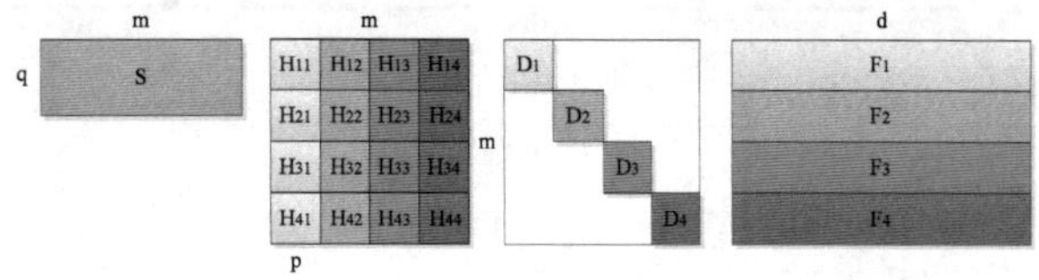

Figure 1: Space-efficient implementation of $\mathbf{\Phi F} = \mathbf{SHDF}$. We set $m/p = 2^c$ with $c = 2$ for clarity.

As shown in Figure 1, we divide data matrix $\mathbf{F} \in \mathbb{R}^{m \times d}$ into 2^c blocks as $\{\mathbf{F}_i \in \mathbb{R}^{p \times d}\}_{i=1}^{2^c}$, and the diagonal matrix $\mathbf{D} \in \mathbb{R}^{m \times m}$ into 2^c square blocks as $\{\mathbf{D}_i \in \mathbb{R}^{p \times d}\}_{i=1}^{2^c}$. Hadamard matrix $\mathbf{H} \in \mathbb{R}^{m \times m}$ can also be divided into $(2^c)^2 = 4^c$ square blocks $\{\mathbf{H}_{ij} \in \mathbb{R}^{p \times p}\}_{i,j=1}^{2^c}$.

We take $O(pd)$ space to receive streaming data from $\mathbf{F}_1 \in \mathbb{R}^{p \times d}$. Then, perform the matrix multiplication through $\mathbf{S}[\mathbf{H}_{11}; \mathbf{H}_{21}; \cdots; \mathbf{H}_{2^c1}]\mathbf{D}_1\mathbf{F}_1 \in \mathbb{R}^{q \times d}$. We first run $\mathbf{H}_{11}\mathbf{D}_1\mathbf{F}_1 \in \mathbb{R}^{p \times d}$, taking $O(pd \log p)$ time and $O(pd)$ space. We then only have to get at most q resulting rows from $\{\mathbf{H}_{i1}\mathbf{F}_1\}_{i \geq 2}^{2^c}$ since $\mathbf{S} \in \mathbb{R}^{q \times m}$ only selects q rows. Fortunately, $\mathbf{H}_{11} = +\mathbf{H}_{i1}$ or $\mathbf{H}_{11} = -\mathbf{H}_{i1}$ holds for any $i \in [2^c]$, and the $\pm$ sign can be determined by calculating the first entry of each $\mathbf{H}_{i1}$ based on Eq. (3) whose running time is at most $O(\log m)$. Hence, the ultimate time complexity is $O(pd \log p) + O(qd) + O(q \log m)$. It is also straightforward to check that $O(pd + qd)$ space suffices for all calculations and saving the compressed data.

Then, we remove $\mathbf{F}_1$, receive data from $\mathbf{F}_2$, do the similar calculations, and update current result based on the previous compressed data from $\mathbf{F}_1$. The time and space costs on $\mathbf{F}_2$ still keep asymptotically unchanged.

Finally, the space usage of computing $\mathbf{\Phi F}$ is $O(pd) = O(qd)$, and its time cost is $2^c[O(pd \log p) + O(qd) + O(q \log m)] = O(md \log q)$ given $q/2 \leq p \leq q$, $m = 2^c p$, and $\log m \leq O(d \log q)$.

3.3 ERROR ANALYSIS

In our analysis, we turn to series of existing theoretical tools. We use the Matrix Bernstein inequality on the sum of zero-mean random matrices given as below.

Theorem 3 ([41]). *Let $\{\mathbf{A}_i\}_{i=1}^L \in \mathbb{R}^{n \times d}$ be independent random matrices with $\mathbb{E}[\mathbf{A}_i] = \mathbf{0}^{n \times d}$ and $\|\mathbf{A}_i\|_2 \leq R$ for all $i \in [L]$. Define a variance parameter as $\sigma^2 = \max\{\| \sum_{i=1}^L \mathbb{E}[\mathbf{A}_i\mathbf{A}_i^T] \|_2, \| \sum_{i=1}^L \mathbb{E}[\mathbf{A}_i^T\mathbf{A}_i] \|_2\}$. Then, for all $\epsilon \geq 0$ we have*

$$\mathbb{P}(\| \sum_{i=1}^{L} \mathbf{A}_i \|_2 \geq \epsilon) \leq (d+n)\exp(\frac{-\epsilon^2/2}{\sigma^2 + R\epsilon/3}). \quad (6)$$

It is also helpful to provide the next result that characterizes the property of compressed data via SRHT matrix.

Theorem 4 ([31]). *Given $\mathbf{A} \in \mathbb{R}^{m \times d}$, let $rank(\mathbf{A}) \leq k \leq \min(m, d)$ and $\mathbf{\Phi} \in \mathbb{R}^{q \times m}$ be the SRHT matrix. Then, with probability at least $1 - (\delta + \frac{m}{e^k})$ we have*

$$(1-\Delta)\mathbf{A}^T\mathbf{A} \preceq \mathbf{A}^T\mathbf{\Phi}^T\mathbf{\Phi}\mathbf{A} \preceq (1+\Delta)\mathbf{A}^T\mathbf{A}, \quad (7)$$

where $\Delta = \Theta(\sqrt{\frac{k \log(2k/\delta)}{q}})$.

With Corollary 3 of [2], it is straightforward to have the next norm bound for compressed data vectors.

Lemma 1. *Give data matrix $\mathbf{A} \in \mathbb{R}^{m \times d}$, and the SRHT matrix $\mathbf{\Phi} \in \mathbb{R}^{q \times m}$. Then, with probability at least $1 - \beta$, we have*

$$\|\mathbf{\Phi a}_i\|_2 \leq \sqrt{2\log(\frac{2md}{\beta})}\|\mathbf{a}_i\|_2, \textit{for all}\, i \in [d]. \quad (8)$$

Before proceeding, we first give the following Lemma together with its proof.

Lemma 2. *Given data matrix $\mathbf{X} \in \mathbb{R}^{m \times d}$, and the scaled sampling matrix $\mathbf{S} \in \mathbb{R}^{q \times m}$ in SRHT. Then, we have*

$$\mathbb{E}[\mathbf{X}^T\mathbf{S}^T\mathbf{S}\mathbf{X}] = \mathbf{X}^T\mathbf{X}. \quad (9)$$

Proof of Lemma 2. It is related to sampling without replacement, and we defer the proof in the appendix. □

We are now ready to prove our main results: Theorem 1 and Theorem 2.

Proof of Theorem 1. To clarify, we let $q = \ell/2$, define p as the times that steps 6 to 11 in Algorithm 3 have been executed, and assume $p = \frac{n}{m}$ without loss of generality for the input $\mathbf{A} = [\mathbf{A}_1; \mathbf{A}_2; \cdots; \mathbf{A}_p] \in \mathbb{R}^{n \times d}$ with $\{\mathbf{A}_t \in \mathbb{R}^{m \times d}\}_{t=1}^p$. By the triangle inequality, we have

$$\|\mathbf{A}^T\mathbf{A} - \mathbf{B}^T\mathbf{B}\|_2 \leq \|\mathbf{A}^T\mathbf{A} - \mathbf{C}^T\mathbf{C}\|_2 + \|\mathbf{C}^T\mathbf{C} - \mathbf{B}^T\mathbf{B}\|_2, \quad (10)$$

where $\mathbf{C} = [\mathbf{C}_1; \mathbf{C}_2; \cdots; \mathbf{C}_p] \in \mathbb{R}^{pq \times d}$ is from compressing each $\mathbf{A}_t$ by $\mathbf{\Phi}_t = \mathbf{S}_t\mathbf{H}\mathbf{D}_t$ in Algorithm 3 such that $\mathbf{C}_t = \mathbf{\Phi}_t\mathbf{A}_t$. Since $\mathbf{B}$ results from running standard FD on $\mathbf{C}$, then with probability at least $1 - p\beta$, we have

$$\|\mathbf{C}^T\mathbf{C} - \mathbf{B}^T\mathbf{B}\|_2 \leq \frac{2}{\ell}\|\mathbf{C}\|_F^2 \quad (11)$$

$$\leq \frac{4}{\ell}\log(\frac{2md}{\beta})\|\mathbf{A}\|_F^2, \quad (12)$$

where Eq. (11) directly follows from the error bound of FD [25], and Eq. (12) holds by combing $\|\mathbf{C}\|_F^2 =$

$\sum_{t=1}^{p}\|\mathbf{C}_t\|_F^2 = \sum_{t=1}^{p}\sum_{i=1}^{d}\|\mathbf{c}_{t,i}\|_2^2$ with Lemma 1 and the union bound.

We next bound $\|\mathbf{A}^T\mathbf{A}-\mathbf{C}^T\mathbf{C}\|_2$. Define $\mathbf{X}_t = \mathbf{H}\mathbf{D}_t\mathbf{A}_t$, then it follows that

$$\|\mathbf{A}^T\mathbf{A} - \mathbf{C}^T\mathbf{C}\|_2 = \|\sum_{t=1}^{p}(\mathbf{A}_t^T\mathbf{A}_t - \mathbf{C}_t^T\mathbf{C}_t)\|_2 \quad (13)$$

$$= \|\sum_{t=1}^{p}(\mathbf{A}_t^T\mathbf{A}_t - \mathbf{X}_t^T\mathbf{S}_t^T\mathbf{S}_t\mathbf{X}_t)\|_2. \quad (14)$$

Let $\mathbf{Z}_t = \mathbf{A}_t^T\mathbf{A}_t - \mathbf{X}_t^T\mathbf{S}_t^T\mathbf{S}_t\mathbf{X}_t$, then obviously $\{\mathbf{Z}_t\}_{t=1}^{p}$ are independent random variables. By Lemma 2, we perform the expectation w.r.t. $\mathbf{S}_t$ and $\mathbf{D}_t$ to obtain that

$$\mathbb{E}[\mathbf{X}_t^T\mathbf{S}_t^T\mathbf{S}_t\mathbf{X}_t] = \mathbb{E}_{\mathbf{D}_t}\mathbb{E}_{\mathbf{S}_t}[\mathbf{X}_t^T\mathbf{S}_t^T\mathbf{S}_t\mathbf{X}_t|\mathbf{D}_t] \quad (15)$$
$$= \mathbb{E}_{\mathbf{D}_t}[\mathbf{X}_t^T\mathbf{X}_t] = \mathbb{E}_{\mathbf{D}_t}[\mathbf{A}_t^T\mathbf{D}_t^T\mathbf{H}^T\mathbf{H}\mathbf{D}_t\mathbf{A}_t] = \mathbf{A}_t^T\mathbf{A}_t,$$

where the second equality follows from Lemma 2 with $\mathbf{D}_t$ fixed, and the last equality holds because $\mathbf{H}$ and $\mathbf{D}_t$ are the unitary matrices. Thus, $\{\mathbf{Z}_t\}_{t=1}^{p}$ satisfy the setting of the Matrix Bernstein inequality in Theorem 3.

Hence, due to that $\|\mathbf{Z}_t\|_2 \le \Delta_t\|\mathbf{A}_t^T\mathbf{A}_t\|_2 = \Delta_t\|\mathbf{A}_t\|_2^2$ resulted from Theorem 4, we first achieve

$$R = \max_{t\in[p]}\Delta_t\|\mathbf{A}_t\|_2^2 \quad (16)$$

with probability at least $1 - (p\delta + \sum_{t=1}^{p}\frac{m}{e^{k_t}})$ after applying union bound, where $\Delta_t = \Theta(\sqrt{\frac{k_t\log(2k_t/\delta)}{q}})$ and $\text{rank}(\mathbf{A}_t) \le k_t \le \min(m,d)$.

Regarding σ^2, due to the symmetry of each matrix $\mathbf{Z}_t$, $\sigma^2 = \|\sum_{t=1}^{p}\mathbb{E}[(\mathbf{Z}_t)^2]\|_2$ holds. Next, we have

$$\mathbf{0}^{d\times d} \preceq \mathbb{E}[(\mathbf{Z}_t)^2] \quad (17)$$
$$= \mathbb{E}[(\mathbf{X}_t^T\mathbf{S}_t^T\mathbf{S}_t\mathbf{X}_t)^2] - (\mathbf{A}_t^T\mathbf{A}_t)^2 \quad (18)$$
$$\preceq \mathbb{E}[\|\mathbf{S}_t\mathbf{X}_t\|_2^2\mathbf{X}_t^T\mathbf{S}_t^T\mathbf{S}_t\mathbf{X}_t] - (\mathbf{A}_t^T\mathbf{A}_t)^2 \quad (19)$$
$$\preceq \mathbb{E}[(1+\Delta_t)\|\mathbf{A}_t\|_2^2\mathbf{X}_t^T\mathbf{S}_t^T\mathbf{S}_t\mathbf{X}_t] - (\mathbf{A}_t^T\mathbf{A}_t)^2 \quad (20)$$
$$= (1+\Delta_t)\|\mathbf{A}_t\|_2^2\mathbf{A}_t^T\mathbf{A}_t - (\mathbf{A}_t^T\mathbf{A}_t)^2 \quad (21)$$

with probability at least $1-(\delta+\frac{m}{e^{k_t}})$, where Eqs. (18)(21) hold because $\mathbb{E}(\mathbf{X}_t^T\mathbf{S}_t^T\mathbf{S}_t\mathbf{X}_t) = \mathbf{A}_t^T\mathbf{A}_t$, Eq. (20) follows from Theorem 4, and Eq. (19) holds because of

$$\mathbf{0}^{d\times d} \preceq (\mathbf{X}_t^T\mathbf{S}_t^T\mathbf{S}_t\mathbf{X}_t)^2 \preceq \|\mathbf{S}_t\mathbf{X}_t\|_2^2\mathbf{X}_t^T\mathbf{S}_t^T\mathbf{S}_t\mathbf{X}_t,$$

which results from that for any $\mathbf{y} \in \mathbb{R}^d$,

$$\mathbf{y}^T(\mathbf{X}_t^T\mathbf{S}_t^T\mathbf{S}_t\mathbf{X}_t)^2\mathbf{y} = \|\mathbf{y}^T\mathbf{X}_t^T\mathbf{S}_t^T\mathbf{S}_t\mathbf{X}_t\|_2^2$$
$$\le \|\mathbf{y}^T\mathbf{X}_t^T\mathbf{S}_t^T\|_2^2\|\mathbf{S}_t\mathbf{X}_t\|_2^2 = \|\mathbf{S}_t\mathbf{X}_t\|_2^2\mathbf{y}^T\mathbf{X}_t^T\mathbf{S}_t^T\mathbf{S}_t\mathbf{X}_t\mathbf{y}.$$

Then, we have

$$\|\sum_{t=1}^{p}\mathbb{E}[(\mathbf{Z}_t)^2]\|_2 \le \sum_{t=1}^{p}\|\mathbb{E}[(\mathbf{Z}_t)^2]\|_2 \quad (22)$$

$$\le \sum_{t=1}^{p}\left\|(1+\Delta_t)\|\mathbf{A}_t\|_2^2\mathbf{A}_t^T\mathbf{A}_t - (\mathbf{A}_t^T\mathbf{A}_t)^2\right\|_2 \quad (23)$$

$$= \sum_{t=1}^{p}\left\|(1+\Delta_t)\|\mathbf{A}_t\|_2^2\mathbf{U}_t\mathbf{\Sigma}_t^2\mathbf{U}_t - \mathbf{U}_t\mathbf{\Sigma}_t^4\mathbf{U}_t\right\|_2 \quad (24)$$

$$= \sum_{t=1}^{p}\left\|(1+\Delta_t)\|\mathbf{A}_t\|_2^2\mathbf{\Sigma}_t^2 - \mathbf{\Sigma}_t^4\right\|_2 \quad (25)$$

$$= \sum_{t=1}^{p}\max_{j\in[d]}|(1+\Delta_t)\sigma_{t1}^2\sigma_{tj}^2 - \sigma_{tj}^4| \quad (26)$$

$$\le \sum_{t=1}^{p}(1+\Delta_t)\sigma_{t1}^4 = \sum_{t=1}^{p}(1+\Delta_t)\|\mathbf{A}_t\|_2^4 \quad (27)$$

$$\le \max_{t\in[p]} p(1+\Delta_t)\|\mathbf{A}_t\|_2^4. \quad (28)$$

where Eq. (23) establishes due to Eq. (21), and $\mathbf{U}_t$ in Eq. (24) is from the SVD of $\mathbf{A}_t$ with $\mathbf{A}_t = \mathbf{U}_t\mathbf{\Sigma}_t\mathbf{V}_t^T$ and the eigenvalues $\sigma_{tj} \triangleq \sigma_{t,jj}$ listed in the descending order in $\mathbf{\Sigma}_t$. By Theorem 3, we have

$$\mathbb{P}(\|\sum_{t=1}^{p}\mathbf{Z}_t\|_2 \ge \epsilon) \le 2d\exp(\frac{-\epsilon^2/2}{\sigma^2 + R\epsilon/3}). \quad (29)$$

Denote the RHS of Eq. (29) by δ, we then obtain that

$$\epsilon = \log(\frac{2d}{\delta})\Big(\frac{R}{3} + \sqrt{(\frac{R}{3})^2 + \frac{2\sigma^2}{\log(2d/\delta)}}\Big) \quad (30)$$

$$\le \log(\frac{2d}{\delta})\frac{2R}{3} + \sqrt{2\sigma^2\log(\frac{2d}{\delta})} \quad (31)$$

$$\le \max_{t\in[p]}\widetilde{O}\Big(\Delta_t\|\mathbf{A}_t\|_2^2\Big) + \max_{t\in[p]}\widetilde{O}\Big(\sqrt{p(1+\Delta_t)}\|\mathbf{A}_t\|_2^2\Big) \quad (32)$$

$$\le \max_{t\in[p]}\widetilde{O}\Big(\big(\sqrt{\frac{k}{\ell p^2}} + \sqrt{\frac{1+\sqrt{k/\ell}}{p}}\big)\frac{\|\mathbf{A}_t\|_2^2}{\|\mathbf{A}_t\|_F^2}\Big)\|\mathbf{A}\|_F^2 \quad (33)$$

$$\le \widetilde{O}\Big(\big(\sqrt{\frac{k}{\ell p^2}} + \sqrt{\frac{1+\sqrt{k/\ell}}{p}}\big)\Big)\|\mathbf{A}\|_F^2. \quad (34)$$

To derive Eq. (33) from Eq. (32), we first substitute $\Delta_t = \Theta(\sqrt{\frac{k_t\log(2k_t/\delta)}{q}})$ into Eq. (32) and set $k = k_t = \min(m,d)$, which allows Eq. (32) to become the maximum of the sum of two functions. Then, we leverage the definition $q = \ell/2$ and apply a common practical assumption of that $p\lambda_1 \le \|\mathbf{A}\|_F^2 = \sum_{t=1}^{p}\|\mathbf{A}_t\|_F^2 \le p\lambda_2$ with each $\|\mathbf{A}_t\|_F^2$ bounded between λ_1 and λ_2 that are very close to each other [2, 36].

Combing Eq. (34) with Eqs. (10)(12) by the union bound achieves the desired result with probability at least $1 - p\beta - (2p+1)\delta - 2p\frac{m}{e^k}$.

The computational analysis is straightforward based on Sections 2.2 and 3.2. □

Proof of Theorem 2. This proof directly follows from that in Section 2.1 and OSH [22] since FROSH differs OSH merely in the sketching techniques. Then, leveraging Theorem 1 immediately yields the desired results.

□

4 EXPERIMENTS

In this section, we conduct three sets of experiments to empirically verify the properties and demonstrate the superiority of our proposed FROSH. The experiments are conducted in MATLAB R2015a and run on a standard workstation with Intel CPU@2.90GHz and 128GB RAM. The MATLAB is set in single thread mode to fairly test time. All results are averaged over 10 independent runs.

4.1 NUMERICAL STUDIES ON SKETCHING

First of all, it is necessary to verify the sketching properties of FD and FFD, which dominate the performance of OSH and FROSH, respectively. We aim to demonstrate that FFD can achieve a comparable sketching accuracy with a faster running speed in comparison with FD.

To make an insightful comparison, we run both algorithms on the synthetic data $\mathbf{A} \in \mathbb{R}^{n \times d}$, which is generated as [25] to verify the sketching methods. Specifically, $\mathbf{A} \in \mathbb{R}^{n \times d}$ is formally defined as $\mathbf{A} = \mathbf{GFU} + \mathbf{W}/\gamma$, where $\mathbf{G} \in \mathbb{R}^{n \times k}$ is the signal coefficient with $g_{ij} \sim \mathcal{N}(0, 1)$, the square diagonal matrix $\mathbf{F} \in \mathbb{R}^{k \times k}$ contains the diagonal entries $f_{ii} = 1 - (i-1)/k$ that gives linearly diminishing signal singular values, $\mathbf{U} \in \mathbb{R}^{k \times d}$ defines the signal row space with $\mathbf{UU}^T = \mathbf{I}_k$ ($k \ll d$), and $\mathbf{W} \in \mathbb{R}^{n \times d}$ consists of noise $w_{ij} \sim \mathcal{N}(0, 1)$.The parameter γ determines if the noise can dominate the signal. Following [25], we set $k = 10$ and $\gamma = 10$.

In the experiments, we vary the sketching size ℓ along $(16, 32, 64, 100, 128, 200, 256)$. We also vary the data size n and dimension d of $\mathbf{A} \in \mathbb{R}^{n \times d}$, and the parameter m in FFD. Such variables can impact the sketching performance in different degrees.

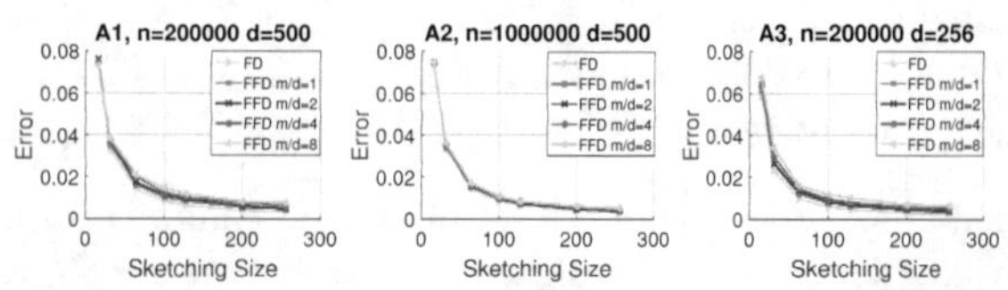

Figure 2: Accuracy comparisons of sketching methods.

We plot the relative error $\|\mathbf{A}^T\mathbf{A} - \mathbf{B}^T\mathbf{B}\|_2 / \|\mathbf{A}\|_F^2$ versus the sketching size ℓ in Figure 2 and compare the running time given in Figure 3. It can be seen that, for data $\mathbf{A}_1$, FFD displays comparable accuracy while enjoying a much lower time cost compared with FD. Besides, when m increases, the sketching accuracy of FFD slightly decreases, but its running speed increases especially for a larger ℓ. Data $\mathbf{A}_2$ differs $\mathbf{A}_1$ only on n, and we observe that a larger n improves the sketching accuracy of FFD. Finally, we decrease the dimension d in $\mathbf{A}_3$, and we find that the improvement of running speed for FFD becomes smaller than that in $\mathbf{A}_1$. All these observations are consistent with the proved results in Theorem 1.

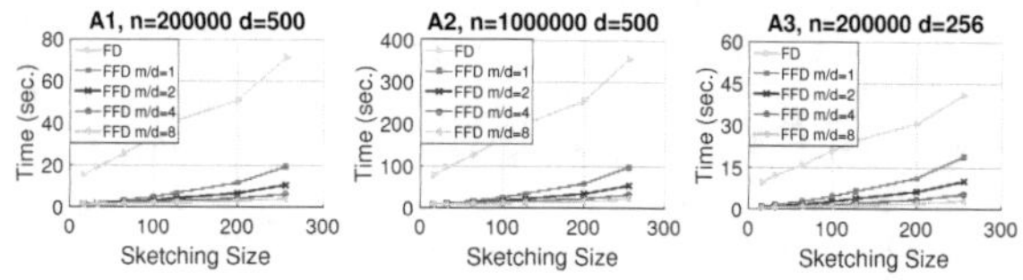

Figure 3: Time comparisons of sketching methods.

All the results indicate that our proposed FFD has the potential to benefit the sketching-based online hashing.

4.2 COMPARISONS WITH LSH AND OSH

In this part, we compare against online unsupervised hashing methods including LSH [8] and OSH. We employ four datasets: CIFAR-10 [21], MNIST [7], GIST-1M [16], and FLICKR-25600 [49]. For CIFAR-10, it consists of 60,000 images in 10 classes with 6000 images per class. We extract 512-dimensional GIST descriptor to represent each image. MNIST contains 70,000 images with 784-dimensional features. GIST-1M consists of one million 960-dimensional GIST descriptors. The FLICKR-25600 dataset contains 100,000 images sampled from a noisy Internet image collection, and each image is represented by a 25,600-dimensional vector normalized to be of unit norm. Following the common setting, we take the top 2% nearest neighbors in Euclidean space as the ground truth for all datasets.

In both OSH and FROSH, we set the sketching size $\ell = 2r$, where r is the code length assigned from $\{32, 64, 128\}$. We train both algorithms in a streaming fashion by evenly dividing each dataset into 10 parts, and evaluate the mean average precision (MAP) score after each round. We also empirically set $m = 4d$ in FROSH during the training. For LSH, it does not require training, and we simply report its MAP at the final round [22].

Figure 4 shows the MAP scores at different rounds on four datasets with 32, 64 and 128 bits codes. On all datasets, it is apparent that our proposed FROSH performs as accurately as OSH and outperforms LSH with a large margin. In addition, both OSH and FROSH stably improve the MAP scores when receiving more data, which demonstrates that a successful adaption to the data variations has been achieved.

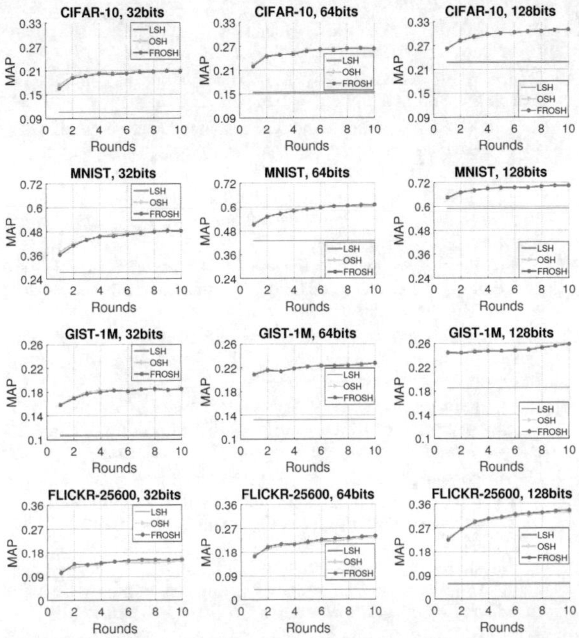

Figure 4: MAP at each round with 32, 64, and 128 bits.

Table 1 provides the accumulated training time of OSH and FROSH with 32, 64, 128 bits codes, respectively. FROSH consistently has the lower training time for each comparison, which achieves about $10 \sim 20$ times speedup than OSH. Thus, our method is highly efficient.

Table 1: Accumulated training time of OSH and FROSH after all rounds (in sec.).

Dataset	**Method**	32bits	64bits	128bits
CIFAR-10	OSH	7.78	11.88	22.09
	FROSH	**0.63**	**0.94**	**2.11**
MNIST	OSH	13.25	18.93	30.75
	FROSH	**1.17**	**1.49**	**2.56**
GIST-1M	OSH	228	331	520
	FROSH	**21**	**27**	**45**
FLICKR-25600	OSH	679	1283	2570
	FROSH	**72**	**92**	**134**

4.3 COMPARISONS WITH BATCH SOLUTIONS

We also compare OSH and our FROSH against two leading batch methods SGH [17] and OCH [27]. Based on the literature [17, 27, 29], we know that SGH maintains a superior tradeoff between the learning accuracy and the scalability, and OCH is the state-of-the-art regarding the accuracy performance compared with the other unsupervised hashing methods such as SpH [44], AGH [30], IsoH [20], DGH [29], and OEH [28].

In Figure 5, we clearly observe that FROSH achieves comparable or even better accuracy in comparison with the two leading batch solutions, which suggests that not only does the online sketching maintain sufficient information necessary for the hash function training but also it owns a good learning ability. In conclusion, considering the properties that FROSH can adapt the hash functions to the new coming data and enjoy superior training efficiency (single pass, lowest costs of space and time), our proposed method is more appropriate for hashing learning on the big streaming unlabeled data. Note that we defer the time comparisons in the appendix.

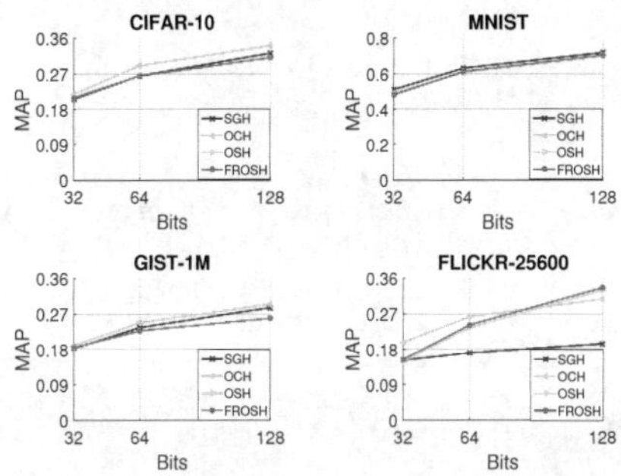

Figure 5: MAP comparisons at different code lengths.

5 CONCLUSION

In this paper, we propose an effective hashing method for streaming unlabeled data. Its basic idea is to reduce the sketching time that is the dominated cost in the OSH method. The analysis shows better time efficiency with accuracy guaranteed. The simulations on both synthetic and real-world datasets support our theoretical findings and demonstrate the practicability of our method.

The sketching designed in this work also provides an insightful view for accelerating general streaming matrix multiplications, which then may be helpful for deriving an online version of OCH. Such extensions can be explored in the future work.

Acknowledgments

We thank the reviewers for their insightful comments to improve the paper quality. We also truly thank Cong Leng for the fruitful discussions and suggestions. This work was fully supported by the National Natural Science Foundation of China (Project No. 61332010), the Research Grants Council of the Hong Kong Special Administrative Region, China ((No. CUHK 14208815 and No. CUHK 14234416 of the General Research Fund), and 2015 Microsoft Research Asia Collaborative Research Program (Project No. FY16-RES-THEME-005).

References

[1] N. Ailon and E. Liberty. Fast dimension reduction using rademacher series on dual bch codes. In *Proceedings of the nineteenth annual ACM-SIAM symposium on Discrete algorithms*, 2008.

[2] F. Anaraki and S. Becker. Preconditioned data sparsification for big data with applications to pca and k-means. *arXiv preprint arXiv:1511.00152*, 2015.

[3] A. Andoni, P. Indyk, T. Laarhoven, I. Razenshteyn, and L. Schmidt. Practical and optimal lsh for angular distance. In *Advances in Neural Information Processing Systems*, 2015.

[4] H. Avron, H. Nguyen, and D. Woodruff. Subspace embeddings for the polynomial kernel. In *Advances in Neural Information Processing Systems*, 2014.

[5] F. Cakir and S. Sclaroff. Adaptive hashing for fast similarity search. In *Proceedings of the IEEE International Conference on Computer Vision*, pages 1044–1052, 2015.

[6] F. Cakir and S. Sclaroff. Online supervised hashing. In *Image Processing (ICIP), 2015 IEEE International Conference on*, pages 2606–2610. IEEE, 2015.

[7] C.-C. Chang and C.-J. Lin. Libsvm: a library for support vector machines. *ACM Transactions on Intelligent Systems and Technology*, 2011.

[8] M. S. Charikar. Similarity estimation techniques from rounding algorithms. In *Proceedings of the thiry-fourth annual ACM symposium on Theory of computing*, pages 380–388. ACM, 2002.

[9] A. Choromanska, K. Choromanski, M. Bojarski, T. Jebara, S. Kumar, and Y. LeCun. Binary embeddings with structured hashed projections. In *ICML*, 2016.

[10] P. Dhillon, Y. Lu, D. P. Foster, and L. Ungar. New subsampling algorithms for fast least squares regression. In *Advances in Neural Information Processing Systems*, pages 360–368, 2013.

[11] M. Ghashami, E. Liberty, and J. M. Phillips. Efficient frequent directions algorithm for sparse matrices. In *Proceedings of the 22nd ACM SIGKDD International Conference on Knowledge Discovery and Data Mining*, pages 845–854. ACM, 2016.

[12] A. Gionis, P. Indyk, R. Motwani, et al. Similarity search in high dimensions via hashing. In *VLDB*, 1999.

[13] Y. Gong, S. Lazebnik, A. Gordo, and F. Perronnin. Iterative quantization: A procrustean approach to learning binary codes for large-scale image retrieval. *IEEE Transactions on Pattern Analysis and Machine Intelligence*, 2013.

[14] L.-K. Huang, Q. Yang, and W.-S. Zheng. Online hashing. In *IJCAI*. Citeseer, 2013.

[15] P. Indyk and R. Motwani. Approximate nearest neighbors: towards removing the curse of dimensionality. In *Proceedings of the thirtieth annual ACM symposium on Theory of computing*, 1998.

[16] H. Jegou, M. Douze, and C. Schmid. Product quantization for nearest neighbor search. *IEEE transactions on pattern analysis and machine intelligence*, 2011.

[17] Q.-Y. Jiang and W.-J. Li. Scalable graph hashing with feature transformation. In *IJCAI*, pages 2248–2254, 2015.

[18] I. Jolliffe. *Principal component analysis*. Wiley Online Library, 2002.

[19] W.-C. Kang, W.-J. Li, and Z.-H. Zhou. Column sampling based discrete supervised hashing. In *Thirtieth AAAI Conference on Artificial Intelligence*, 2016.

[20] W. Kong and W.-J. Li. Isotropic hashing. In *Advances in Neural Information Processing Systems*, 2012.

[21] A. Krizhevsky. Learning multiple layers of features from tiny images. 2009.

[22] C. Leng, J. Wu, J. Cheng, X. Bai, and H. Lu. Online sketching hashing. In *Proceedings of the IEEE conference on computer vision and pattern recognition*, pages 2503–2511, 2015.

[23] W.-J. Li, S. Wang, and W.-C. Kang. Feature learning based deep supervised hashing with pairwise labels. In *IJCAI*, 2016.

[24] Y. Li, R. Wang, H. Liu, H. Jiang, S. Shan, and X. Chen. Two birds, one stone: Jointly learning binary code for large-scale face image retrieval and attributes prediction. In *Proceedings of the IEEE International Conference on Computer Vision*, 2015.

[25] E. Liberty. Simple and deterministic matrix sketching. In *Proceedings of the 19th ACM SIGKDD international conference on Knowledge discovery and data mining*. ACM, 2013.

[26] G. Lin, C. Shen, Q. Shi, A. van den Hengel, and D. Suter. Fast supervised hashing with decision trees for high-dimensional data. In *Proceedings of the IEEE Conference on Computer Vision and Pattern Recognition*, 2014.

[27] H. Liu, R. Ji, Y. Wu, and F. Huang. Ordinal constrained binary code learning for nearest neighbor search. In *AAAI*, 2017.

[28] H. Liu, R. Ji, Y. Wu, and W. Liu. Towards optimal binary code learning via ordinal embedding. In *AAAI*, 2016.

[29] W. Liu, C. Mu, S. Kumar, and S.-F. Chang. Discrete graph hashing. In *Advances in Neural Information Processing Systems*, pages 3419–3427, 2014.

[30] W. Liu, J. Wang, S. Kumar, and S.-F. Chang. Hashing with graphs. In *Proceedings of the 28th international conference on machine learning*, 2011.

[31] Y. Lu, P. Dhillon, D. P. Foster, and L. Ungar. Faster ridge regression via the subsampled randomized hadamard transform. In *Advances in neural information processing systems*, 2013.

[32] H. Luo, A. Agarwal, N. Cesa-Bianchi, and J. Langford. Efficient second order online learning by sketching. In *Advances in Neural Information Processing Systems*, 2016.

[33] L. Mukherjee, S. N. Ravi, V. K. Ithapu, T. Holmes, and V. Singh. An nmf perspective on binary hashing. In *Proceedings of the IEEE International Conference on Computer Vision*, 2015.

[34] C. Musco and C. Musco. Randomized block krylov methods for stronger and faster approximate singular value decomposition. In *Advances in Neural Information Processing Systems*, pages 1396–1404, 2015.

[35] B. Neyshabur, N. Srebro, R. R. Salakhutdinov, Y. Makarychev, and P. Yadollahpour. The power of asymmetry in binary hashing. In *Advances in Neural Information Processing Systems*, 2013.

[36] J. Pennington, F. Yu, and S. Kumar. Spherical random features for polynomial kernels. In *Advances in Neural Information Processing Systems*, pages 1846–1854, 2015.

[37] F. Shen, W. Liu, S. Zhang, Y. Yang, and H. T. Shen. Learning binary codes for maximum inner product search. In *International Conference on Computer Vision*. IEEE, 2015.

[38] F. Shen, C. Shen, W. Liu, and H. Tao Shen. Supervised discrete hashing. In *Proceedings of the IEEE Conference on Computer Vision and Pattern Recognition*, 2015.

[39] A. Shrivastava and P. Li. Asymmetric lsh (alsh) for sublinear time maximum inner product search (mips). In *Advances in Neural Information Processing Systems*, pages 2321–2329, 2014.

[40] J. Song, L. Gao, Y. Yan, D. Zhang, and N. Sebe. Supervised hashing with pseudo labels for scalable multimedia retrieval. In *Proceedings of the 23rd ACM international conference on Multimedia*, pages 827–830. ACM, 2015.

[41] J. A. Tropp. An introduction to matrix concentration inequalities. *Foundations and Trends in Machine Learning*, 2015.

[42] J. Wang, S. Kumar, and S.-F. Chang. Semi-supervised hashing for scalable image retrieval. In *Computer Vision and Pattern Recognition, 2010 IEEE Conference on*, pages 3424–3431. IEEE, 2010.

[43] J. Wang, T. Zhang, J. Song, N. Sebe, and H. T. Shen. A survey on learning to hash. *arXiv preprint arXiv:1606.00185*, 2016.

[44] Y. Weiss, A. Torralba, and R. Fergus. Spectral hashing. In *Advances in neural information processing systems*, 2009.

[45] D. P. Woodruff et al. Sketching as a tool for numerical linear algebra. *Foundations and Trends® in Theoretical Computer Science*, 2014.

[46] C. Woolam, M. M. Masud, and L. Khan. Lacking labels in the stream: classifying evolving stream data with few labels. In *International Symposium on Methodologies for Intelligent Systems*, pages 552–562. Springer, 2009.

[47] S. Wu, S. Bhojanapalli, S. Sanghavi, and A. G. Dimakis. Single pass pca of matrix products. In *Advances in Neural Information Processing Systems*, 2016.

[48] L. Xie, L. Zhu, and G. Chen. Unsupervised multi-graph cross-modal hashing for large-scale multimedia retrieval. *Multimedia Tools and Applications*, pages 1–20, 2016.

[49] F. X. Yu, S. Kumar, Y. Gong, and S.-F. Chang. Circulant binary embedding. In *ICML*, 2014.

Appendix

1 Proof of Lemma 2

Proof. According to the definition, each column vector in the scaled sampling matrix $\mathbf{S} \in \mathbb{R}^{q\times m}$ is sampled without replacement from $\{\mathbf{s}^i = \sqrt{\frac{m}{q}}\mathbf{e}_i^T\}_{i=1}^m \in \mathbb{R}^{1\times m}$ uniformly. Note that

$$\mathbb{E}[\mathbf{X}^T\mathbf{S}^T\mathbf{S}\mathbf{X}] = \mathbb{E}[\mathbf{X}^T\sum_{i=1}^q {\mathbf{s}^i}^T\mathbf{s}^i\mathbf{X}] \tag{1}$$

$$= \mathbf{X}^T\sum_{i=1}^q \mathbb{E}[{\mathbf{s}^i}^T\mathbf{s}^i]\mathbf{X}. \tag{2}$$

Without loss of generality, we assume that we sample and determine the value of $\{\mathbf{s}^i\}_{i=1}^q$ in the order of the smallest to the largest index. Then, due to that

$$\mathbb{P}(\mathbf{s}^i = \sqrt{\frac{m}{q}}\mathbf{e}_k^T) \tag{3}$$

$$= \mathbb{P}(\mathbf{s}^i = \sqrt{\frac{m}{q}}\mathbf{e}_k^T|\mathbf{s}^j \neq \sqrt{\frac{m}{q}}\mathbf{e}_k^T, \forall j \in [i-1])$$

$$* \, \mathbb{P}(\mathbf{s}^j \neq \sqrt{\frac{m}{q}}\mathbf{e}_k^T, \forall j \in [i-1]) \tag{4}$$

$$= \frac{1}{m-(i-1)}\frac{m-(i-1)}{m-(i-2)}\cdots\frac{m-1}{m} = \frac{1}{m}, \tag{5}$$

we have

$$\mathbb{E}[{\mathbf{s}^i}^T\mathbf{s}^i] = \sum_{k=1}^m \mathbb{P}(\mathbf{s}^i = \sqrt{\frac{m}{q}}\mathbf{e}_k^T)\frac{m}{q}\mathbf{e}_k\mathbf{e}_k^T \tag{6}$$

$$= \sum_{k=1}^m \frac{1}{m}\frac{m}{q}\mathbf{e}_k\mathbf{e}_k^T = \frac{1}{q}\mathbf{I}_m. \tag{7}$$

Thus, substituting Eq. (7) into Eq. (2) concludes the proof. □

2 More Comparisons with Batch Solutions

We also compare OSH and our FROSH against two leading batch methods SGH [3] and OCH [7]. Based on the literature [3, 7, 9], we know that SGH maintains a superior tradeoff between the learning accuracy and the scalability, and OCH is the state-of-the-art regarding the accuracy performance compared with the other unsupervised hashing methods such as SpH [11], AGH [10], IsoH [4], DGH [9], and OEH [8].

Distinguished with the bath methods, OSH and FROSH are able to adapt the hash functions to the new coming data. Besides, FROSH enjoys superior training efficiency, i.e., *single pass, lowest costs of space ($O(\ell d)$) and time*, while the unsupervised batch methods such as SGH and OCH require either $O(nd)$ space or multiple passes over the data to load all data into memory or both. Regarding the space cost, OSH and FROSH can throw away the used data and update only on the newly coming data via $O(\ell d)$ space while SGH and OCH should maintain a large extern storage to keep all observed data and the newly coming data. Moreover, given the 19GB data FLICKR-25600 that is merely a small subset of the entire FLICKR image collection, if avoiding multiple passes is required, both the SGH and OCH methods have to maintain the entire FLICKR-25600 data in the memory and keep the intermediate computational results (can be several times larger than FLICKR-25600 itself) in the memory as well, which is infeasible for common computers.

In Table 2, we also provide the empirical time comparisons because it is not clear enough to directly compare the associated time complexities when all methods have different parameters. Note that the released OCH codes have been highly optimized by the authors in contrast to the version used in its original paper [7]. We report the accumulated time after all rounds for OSH and FROSH and provide the time consumptions of training SGH and OCH only on all observed data. Overall, our FROSH offers about $10 \sim 70$ times speed-up than the other com-

Table 2: Comparisons of the training time (in sec.). We report the accumulated time after all rounds for OSH and FROSH and provide the time consumptions of training SGH and OCH only on all observed data.

Dataset	Method	32bits	64bits	128bits
CIFAR-10	SGH	7.83	11.35	19.49
	OCH	26.89	26.95	27.49
	OSH	7.78	11.88	22.09
	FROSH	**0.63**	**0.94**	**2.11**
MNIST	SGH	10.47	14.59	23.47
	OCH	40.45	40.49	41.10
	OSH	13.25	18.93	30.75
	FROSH	**1.17**	**1.49**	**2.56**
GIST-1M	SGH	231	275	290
	OCH	1042	1089	1192
	OSH	228	331	520
	FROSH	**21**	**27**	**45**
FLICKR-25600	SGH	3032	3541	4903
	OCH	4981	5300	5441
	OSH	679	1283	2570
	FROSH	**72**	**92**	**134**

pared solutions. If considering the case where batch-learners should repeatedly do batch learning on both the newly coming data and the currently observed data, SGH and OCH would require significantly more training time than that in Table 2.

3 Approximation for the Projection Matrix W

In this part, we offer more details to show how the project matrix $\mathbf{W}^T \in \mathbb{R}^{r\times d}$ can be approximated. We let $m = \Theta(d)$, and assume $n = \Omega(\ell^{3/2}d^{3/2})$ for simplicity, then the error bound of Eq. (5) in Theorem 2 of the main text becomes $\widetilde{O}(\frac{1}{\ell}\|(\mathbf{A}-\boldsymbol{\mu})\|_F^2)$. Based on it, we give Theorem 3.

Theorem 3. *Given data $\mathbf{A} \in \mathbb{R}^{n\times d}$ with its row mean vector $\boldsymbol{\mu} \in \mathbb{R}^{1\times d}$, let the sketching matrix $\mathbf{B}^{\ell\times d}$ be generated by FROSH in Algorithm 4. Let $m = \Theta(d)$, and assume $n = \Omega(\ell^{3/2}d^{3/2})$ for simplicity. Given $(\mathbf{A}-\boldsymbol{\mu}) \in \mathbb{R}^{n\times d}$ that means subtracting each row of $\mathbf{A}$ by $\boldsymbol{\mu}$, let $h = \|(\mathbf{A}-\boldsymbol{\mu})\|_F^2/\|(\mathbf{A}-\boldsymbol{\mu})\|_2^2$ and σ_i be the i-th largest singular value of $(\mathbf{A}-\boldsymbol{\mu})$. If the sketching size $\ell = \Omega(\frac{h\sigma_1^2}{\epsilon\sigma_{r+1}^2})$, then with probability defined in Theorem 1 we have*

$$\begin{aligned}&\|(\mathbf{A}-\boldsymbol{\mu}) - (\mathbf{A}-\boldsymbol{\mu})\mathbf{W_B}\mathbf{W_B}^T\|_2^2 \\ &\le (1+\epsilon)\|(\mathbf{A}-\boldsymbol{\mu}) - (\mathbf{A}-\boldsymbol{\mu})\mathbf{W}\mathbf{W}^T\|_2^2, \end{aligned} \quad (8)$$

where $0 < \epsilon < 1$, $\mathbf{W_B}^T \in \mathbb{R}^{r\times d}$ contains the top r right singular vectors of $\mathbf{B}^{\ell\times d}$, and $\mathbf{W}^T \in \mathbb{R}^{r\times d}$ contains the top r right singular vectors of $(\mathbf{A}-\boldsymbol{\mu}) \in \mathbb{R}^{n\times d}$.

Remark. The bound on $\|(\mathbf{A}-\boldsymbol{\mu}) - (\mathbf{A}-\boldsymbol{\mu})\mathbf{W_B}\mathbf{W_B}^T\|_2^2$ shows the similarity between $\mathbf{W_B}\mathbf{W_B}^T$ and $\mathbf{W}\mathbf{W}^T$. If $\epsilon = 0$, we will have $\mathbf{W_B}\mathbf{W_B}^T = \mathbf{W}\mathbf{W}^T$. However, it cannot characterize the similarity between $\mathbf{W_B} \in \mathbb{R}^{d\times r}$ and $\mathbf{W} \in \mathbb{R}^{d\times r}$, because Eq. (8) of Theorem 3 may also indicate that $\mathbf{W_B}$ approximates $\mathbf{W}\boldsymbol{\Upsilon}$, where $\boldsymbol{\Upsilon} \in \mathbb{R}^{r\times r}$ is an arbitrary unitary matrix with $\boldsymbol{\Upsilon}\boldsymbol{\Upsilon}^T = \mathbf{I}_r$ and $\mathbf{I}_r$ being an identity matrix so that $\mathbf{W}\boldsymbol{\Upsilon}\boldsymbol{\Upsilon}^T\mathbf{W}^T = \mathbf{W}\mathbf{W}^T$. Fortunately, due to that $\boldsymbol{\Upsilon}\boldsymbol{\Upsilon}^T = \mathbf{I}_r$ (i.e., $\boldsymbol{\Upsilon} \in \mathbb{R}^{r\times r}$ is an orthogonal rotation), $\mathbf{W}\boldsymbol{\Upsilon}$ will still retain all information of $\mathbf{W}$ and even empirically get better hashing accuracy, which has been mentioned in Remark 1 of the main text. Therefore, Theorem 3 shows how $\mathbf{W_B}$ approximates $\mathbf{W}$ or $\mathbf{W}\boldsymbol{\Upsilon}$, which can be used to show the effectiveness of the related hashing algorithm.

Here, we restate Remark 1 of the main text: To address the problem that most of the information can be contained by only a small number of significant singular vectors in $\mathbf{W} \in \mathbb{R}^{d\times r}$, OSH [5] also empirically applies a random orthogonal rotation $\boldsymbol{\Upsilon} \in \mathbb{R}^{r\times r}$ (the orthonormal bases of an $r \times r$ random Gaussian matrix) to all singular vectors $\mathbf{W} \in \mathbb{R}^{d\times r}$ returned by Algorithm 1 via $\mathbf{W}\boldsymbol{\Upsilon}$. This step resembles Iterative Quantization [2] but runs much more efficiently with streaming settings maintained and negligible computational cost incurred. Thus, following OSH, our method FROSH also applies $\boldsymbol{\Upsilon} \in \mathbb{R}^{r\times r}$ to the obtained top r right singular vectors of $\mathbf{B}^{\ell\times d}$.

3.1 Proof of Theorem 3

The proof follows by combining our proposed Theorem 2 and Section 1.4 of [6].

Proof. Since $\mathbf{W_B}^T \in \mathbb{R}^{r\times d}$ contains the top r right singular vectors of $\mathbf{B}^{\ell\times d}$, we have $\mathbf{W_B}\mathbf{W_B}^T \in \mathbb{R}^{d\times d}$ as the projection matrix of $\mathbf{B}^{\ell\times d}$. Via Lemma 4 in [1], we have

$$\begin{aligned}&\|(\mathbf{A}-\boldsymbol{\mu}) - (\mathbf{A}-\boldsymbol{\mu})\mathbf{W_B}\mathbf{W_B}^T\|_2^2 \\ &\le \sigma_{r+1}^2 + 2\|(\mathbf{A}-\boldsymbol{\mu})^T(\mathbf{A}-\boldsymbol{\mu}) - \mathbf{B}^T\mathbf{B}\|_2, \end{aligned} \quad (9)$$

where σ_i is the i-th largest singular value of $(\mathbf{A}-\boldsymbol{\mu})$.

For simplicity, when $m = \Theta(d)$ and $n = \Omega(\ell^{3/2}d^{3/2})$, the error bound of Eq. (5) in Theorem 2 of the main text will become $\widetilde{O}(\frac{1}{\ell}\|(\mathbf{A}-\boldsymbol{\mu})\|_F^2)$, which is then incorporated into Eq. (9) to get that

$$\begin{aligned}&\|(\mathbf{A}-\boldsymbol{\mu}) - (\mathbf{A}-\boldsymbol{\mu})\mathbf{W_B}\mathbf{W_B}^T\|_2^2 \\ &\le \sigma_{r+1}^2 + \widetilde{O}(\frac{1}{\ell}\|(\mathbf{A}-\boldsymbol{\mu})\|_F^2). \end{aligned} \quad (10)$$

Let $h = \|(\mathbf{A}-\boldsymbol{\mu})\|_F^2 / \|(\mathbf{A}-\boldsymbol{\mu})\|_2^2$ be the numeric rank of $(\mathbf{A}-\boldsymbol{\mu}) \in \mathbb{R}^{n\times d}$, which could be much smaller than d for a low-rank matrix $(\mathbf{A}-\boldsymbol{\mu}) \in \mathbb{R}^{n\times d}$ with $d < n$. If $\ell = \Omega(\frac{h\sigma_1^2}{\epsilon\sigma_{r+1}^2})$, then from Eq. (10) we have

$$\|(\mathbf{A}-\boldsymbol{\mu}) - (\mathbf{A}-\boldsymbol{\mu})\mathbf{W_B}\mathbf{W_B}^T\|_2^2 \leq (1+\epsilon)\sigma_{r+1}^2$$
$$= (1+\epsilon)\|(\mathbf{A}-\boldsymbol{\mu}) - (\mathbf{A}-\boldsymbol{\mu})\mathbf{W}\mathbf{W}^T\|_2^2, \quad (11)$$

where $\sigma_1^2 = \|(\mathbf{A}-\boldsymbol{\mu})\|_2^2$ and $\sigma_{r+1}^2 = \|(\mathbf{A}-\boldsymbol{\mu}) - (\mathbf{A}-\boldsymbol{\mu})\mathbf{W}\mathbf{W}^T\|_2^2$ according to the definition. □

References

[1] P. Drineas and R. Kannan. Pass efficient algorithms for approximating large matrices. In *SODA*, volume 3, pages 223–232, 2003.

[2] Y. Gong, S. Lazebnik, A. Gordo, and F. Perronnin. Iterative quantization: A procrustean approach to learning binary codes for large-scale image retrieval. *IEEE Transactions on Pattern Analysis and Machine Intelligence*, 35(12):2916–2929, 2013.

[3] Q.-Y. Jiang and W.-J. Li. Scalable graph hashing with feature transformation. In *IJCAI*, pages 2248–2254, 2015.

[4] W. Kong and W.-J. Li. Isotropic hashing. In *Advances in Neural Information Processing Systems*, pages 1646–1654, 2012.

[5] C. Leng, J. Wu, J. Cheng, X. Bai, and H. Lu. Online sketching hashing. In *Proceedings of the IEEE conference on computer vision and pattern recognition*, pages 2503–2511, 2015.

[6] E. Liberty. Simple and deterministic matrix sketching. In *Proceedings of the 19th ACM SIGKDD international conference on Knowledge discovery and data mining*, pages 581–588. ACM, 2013.

[7] H. Liu, R. Ji, Y. Wu, and F. Huang. Ordinal constrained binary code learning for nearest neighbor search. In *AAAI*, 2017.

[8] H. Liu, R. Ji, Y. Wu, and W. Liu. Towards optimal binary code learning via ordinal embedding. In *AAAI*, pages 1258–1265, 2016.

[9] W. Liu, C. Mu, S. Kumar, and S.-F. Chang. Discrete graph hashing. In *Advances in Neural Information Processing Systems*, pages 3419–3427, 2014.

[10] W. Liu, J. Wang, S. Kumar, and S.-F. Chang. Hashing with graphs. In *Proceedings of the 28th international conference on machine learning (ICML-11)*, pages 1–8, 2011.

[11] Y. Weiss, A. Torralba, and R. Fergus. Spectral hashing. In *Advances in neural information processing systems*, pages 1753–1760, 2009.

Self-Discrepancy Conditional Independence Test

Sanghack Lee and **Vasant Honavar**
Artificial Intelligence Research Laboratory
College of Information Sciences and Technology
The Pennsylvania State University, University Park, PA 16802
{sxl439, vhonavar}@ist.psu.edu

Abstract

Tests of conditional independence (CI) of random variables play an important role in machine learning and causal inference. Of particular interest are kernel-based CI tests which allow us to test for independence among random variables with complex distribution functions. The efficacy of a CI test is measured in terms of its power and its calibratedness. We show that the Kernel CI Permutation Test (KCIPT) suffers from a loss of calibratedness as its power is increased by increasing the number of bootstraps. To address this limitation, we propose a novel CI test, called Self-Discrepancy Conditional Independence Test (SDCIT). SDCIT uses a test statistic that is a modified unbiased estimate of maximum mean discrepancy (MMD), the largest difference in the means of features of the given sample and its permuted counterpart in the kernel-induced Hilbert space. We present results of experiments that demonstrate SDCIT is, relative to the other methods: (i) competitive in terms of its power and calibratedness, outperforming other methods when the number of conditioning variables is large; (ii) more robust with respect to the choice of the kernel function; and (iii) competitive in run time.

1 INTRODUCTION

Random variables X and Y are said to be conditionally independent given Z, denoted by $X \perp\!\!\!\perp Y \mid Z$, if a joint probability distribution $\mathrm{P}_{xyz} = \mathrm{P}_{xz}\mathrm{P}_{y|xz}$ can be expressed as $\mathrm{P}_{xz}\mathrm{P}_{y|z}$. Tests of conditional independence (CI) play a central role in statistics (Dawid, 1979), machine learning including dimensionality reduction (Fukumizu et al., 2004, 2009), independent component analysis (Bach and Jordan, 2002), probabilistic graphical models (Koller and Friedman, 2009) and causal inference (Pearl, 2000; Spirtes et al., 2000).

In principle, testing for conditional independence is quite straightforward: Obtain a sample S of i.i.d. observations drawn from a distribution P_{xyz}, and evenly split into two subsamples S_1 and S_2 of equal size. Leaving S_1 is intact, permute S_2 so as to simulate a sample from $\mathrm{P}_{xz}\mathrm{P}_{y|z}$ (i.e., $X \perp\!\!\!\perp Y \mid Z$); Apply a two-sample test to determine if S_1 and S_2 are different. Based on the results of the test if the null hypothesis $\mathrm{P}_{xyz} = \mathrm{P}_{xz}\mathrm{P}_{y|z}$ cannot be rejected, we conclude that X is independent of Y given Z. This procedure can be repeated multiple times (i.e., bootstrap Efron, 1979) to improve the power of the test.

In order for the preceding approach to CI testing is feasible, we need an effective two-sample test to determine if S_1 and S_2 are different. Gretton et al. (2012) introduced a framework for designing such tests using a well-behaved (e.g., smooth) function, which is large on the points drawn from one distribution and small on the points from the other distribution. The framework uses as test statistic, MMD, the largest difference between the mean function values on the two samples; when MMD is large, the samples are likely from different distributions. In order for MMD to be effective in practice, the class of functions used to define it should be (i) rich enough to ensure that the MMD vanishes if and only if the two distributions being compared are identical; and (ii) sufficiently restricted so as to ensure that the empirical estimate of MMD converges quickly to its expected value as the sample size is increased. As shown by Gretton et al. (2012), these requirements are met by unit balls in reproducing kernel Hilbert spaces (RKHS).

Doran et al. (2014) introduced the Kernel Conditional Independence Permutation Test (KCIPT), using MMD in a kernel-induced feature space as the test statistic for determining whether $X \perp\!\!\!\perp Y \mid Z$. Doran et al. (2014)

evaluated several kernel-based independence tests based on how well a test correctly rejects the null hypothesis $P_{xyz} = P_{xz}P_{y|z}$ by estimating the *power* of the test (as measured by the Area Under the Power Curve) and the *calibratedness* of the test, i.e., the extent to which it accurately estimates the probability distribution of the test statistic under the null hypothesis (as measured by a Kolmogorov-Smirnov divergence of the observed distribution of p-values from the uniform distribution). Using the preceding procedure, with the number of bootstraps B set equal to 25, Doran et al. (2014) asserted that KCIPT "has power competitive with existing kernel-based approaches" and that it is well-calibrated compared to other kernel independence tests such as KCIT (Zhang et al., 2011) and CHSIC (Fukumizu et al., 2008).

Because increasing the number of bootstraps *always* improves its power, it is natural to ask: How does the power and calibratedness of KCIPT change as a function of B? We present results that show that as B increases, the calibratedness of KCIPT degrades. This suggests that increase in the power of KCIPT comes at the expense of its calibratedness. Based on our analysis of the limitations of KCIPT, we propose a new CI test, which we call the Self-Discrepancy CI Test (SDCIT). SDCIT is based on a modified unbiased estimate of MMD and its distribution under the null hypothesis based on half-sampling without replacement. We present results of experiments that demonstrate several advantages of SDCIT over the existing kernel-based CI tests.

2 PRELIMINARIES

We mostly follow notational conventions of (Doran et al., 2014): We use upper case letters, e.g., X, to denote random variables, and the corresponding lowercase letters $x \in \mathcal{X}$ to denote an instantiation of X in its domain $\mathcal{X}$. We use a bold lowercase letters to denote sets (or vectors) of instantiations, e.g., $\mathbf{x} = (x_i)_{i=1}^n$. We denote by $x \sim \mathbf{x}$ the fact that x is an observation of a random variable sampled from the empirical distribution constructed from the finite sample $\mathbf{x}$. We denote by $\binom{\mathbf{x}}{\ell}$ a set of all ℓ-sized subsets of $\mathbf{x}$. Let $\boldsymbol{\pi}(n)$ be a group of all possible permutations of $(1, 2, \ldots, n)$ with an additional constraint that every permutation $\pi \in \boldsymbol{\pi}(n)$ satisfies that $\forall_{i=1}^n \pi(i) \neq i$. We denote the application of a permutation π to a sequence $\mathbf{y}$ by $\pi\mathbf{y} := (y_{\pi(i)})_{i=1}^n$. We use μ, the average function, to denote the average of a given parameter, e.g., a vector, set, or matrix.

2.1 KERNEL TWO-SAMPLE TEST

Let k_x be a kernel function $k_x : \mathcal{X} \times \mathcal{X} \to \mathbb{R}$. Let $\mathcal{H}_k$ be a reproducing kernel Hilbert space induced by a kernel k. For instance, $k_x(x', x'') = \langle \phi_x(x'), \phi_x(x'') \rangle_{\mathcal{H}_{k_x}}$ where ϕ_x is a feature mapping from $\mathcal{X}$ to $\mathcal{H}_{k_x}$. We use K to denote a Gram matrix (i.e., kernel matrix) corresponding to a kernel function k. Thus, $\mathrm{K}_x(\mathbf{x}, \mathbf{x}')_{ij} := k_x(x_i, x'_j)$. We use k_{xy} to denote the product of kernels k_x and k_y and define it as $k_{xy}((x_i, y_i), (x_j, y_j)) := k_x(x_i, x_j) k_y(y_i, y_j)$. Kernel mean embedding (KME) allows us to represent a probability distribution as a point in the kernel-induced Hilbert space (Berlinet and Thomas-Agnan, 2004; Smola et al., 2007; Sriperumbudur et al., 2010), $\mu_\mathrm{P} := \int k(\cdot, x) \mathrm{P}(dx) \in \mathcal{H}_k$. Maximum mean discrepancy (MMD) is an integral probability metric that provides a measure of distance between the two probability distributions P and Q: $\mathrm{MMD}^2[\mathcal{F}, \mathrm{P}, \mathrm{Q}] := \left[\sup_{f \in \mathcal{F}} (\mathbf{E}_{x\sim \mathrm{P}} f(x) - \mathbf{E}_{x \sim \mathrm{Q}} f(x))\right]^2 = \|\mu_\mathrm{P} - \mu_\mathrm{Q}\|^2_{\mathcal{H}_{k_x}}$ where $\mathcal{F}$ is a unit ball in $\mathcal{H}_{k_x}$. Given a characteristic kernel, $\mathrm{MMD}(\mathrm{P}, \mathrm{Q})$ is 0 if and only if distributions $\mathrm{P} = \mathrm{Q}$ (Sriperumbudur et al., 2010). Given two independent samples of the same size, $\mathbf{x}^{(1)} = \{x_i^{(1)}\}_{i=1}^m$ and $\mathbf{x}^{(2)} = \{x_i^{(2)}\}_{i=1}^m$, let $u_i := (x_i^{(1)}, x_i^{(2)})$. Then, an empirical unbiased estimate of squared MMD

$$\mathrm{MMD}_u^2(\mathbf{x}^{(1)}, \mathbf{x}^{(2)}) := \frac{1}{m(m-1)} \sum_{i \neq j=1}^m h(u_i, u_j) \quad (1)$$

is a one-sample unbiased statistic (U-statistic) where

$$h(u_i, u_j) := k(x_i^{(1)}, x_j^{(1)}) + k(x_i^{(2)}, x_j^{(2)}) - k(x_i^{(1)}, x_j^{(2)}) - k(x_j^{(1)}, x_i^{(2)}).$$

A kernel two-sample test (Gretton et al., 2007, 2009, 2012) uses MMD as the test statistic and its distribution under the null hypothesis to test for homogeneity. The distribution of MMD can be estimated in a number of ways including moment-based approximation (Gretton et al., 2012), Gram matrix spectrum (Gretton et al., 2009), and resampling procedure. For instance, KCIPT uses a bootstrap procedure to repeatedly measure the MMD between two equal-sized random subsamples of the union of the two given samples.

3 KCIPT

We now proceed to describe KCIPT and discuss its limitations that motivate our proposal for SDCIT. Suppose we are given a sample $\Omega = \{(x_i, y_i, z_i)\}_{i=1}^n = (\mathbf{x}, \mathbf{y}, \mathbf{z})$ of n observations drawn i.i.d. from P_{xyz}. We split Ω randomly into two subsamples of equal size: $\Omega^{(1)} = (\mathbf{x}^{(1)}, \mathbf{y}^{(1)}, \mathbf{z}^{(1)})$ and $\Omega^{(2)} = (\mathbf{x}^{(2)}, \mathbf{y}^{(2)}, \mathbf{z}^{(2)})$. The second split sample $\Omega^{(2)}$ is permuted so as to simulate sample from $\mathrm{P}_{xz}\mathrm{P}_{y|z}$.[1] Such permutation $\pi \in \boldsymbol{\pi}(n/2)$ must

[1] One can either permute X or Y. For consistency, we will stick with permuting Y as in (Doran et al., 2014).

Algorithm 1 KCIPT (Doran et al., 2014) with an *unbiased* estimator of MMD.

Input: B: the number of bootstraps, b: the size of sample for a null distribution per bootstrap, M: the size of sample for a bootstrap null distribution, Ω: a sample $(\mathbf{x}, \mathbf{y}, \mathbf{z})$ of size n

1: **for** $i \in 1 \cdots B$ **do**
2: $\quad \Omega_i^{(1)}, \Omega_i^{(2)} \leftarrow$randomly split Ω evenly
3: $\quad \pi \leftarrow$ learn a permutation given δ and $\mathbf{z}^{(2)}$
4: $\quad \Omega_{i,\pi}^{(2)} \leftarrow$ apply π to Y values of $\Omega_i^{(2)}$
5: $\quad T_i \leftarrow \mathrm{MMD}_u^2(\Omega_i^{(1)}, \Omega_{i,\pi}^{(2)})$
6: $\quad$ **for** $j \in 1 \cdots b$ **do**
7: $\quad\quad \Omega', \Omega'' \leftarrow$randomly split $\Omega_i^{(1)} \cup \Omega_{i,\pi}^{(2)}$ evenly
8: $\quad\quad (\mathbf{N})_{ij} \leftarrow \mathrm{MMD}_u^2(\Omega', \Omega'')$
9: $T \leftarrow$average of $\{T_i\}_{i=1}^B$
10: $\mathbf{N} \leftarrow \{\text{average of } \{s_{ij}\}_{i=1}^B \mid \forall_{i=1}^B s_{ij} \sim \mathbf{N}_i\}_{j=1}^M$
11: **return** a p-value of T from $\mathbf{N}$

satisfy that $z_i^{(2)} = z_{\pi(i)}^{(2)}$ to preserve the relationship between Y and Z while breaking ties between X and Y. In many interesting cases, including $\mathcal{Z} = \mathbb{R}$, $\mathbf{z}$ often consists of unique values and such a permutation may not exist. Hence, under the assumption $\mathrm{P}(Y \mid z) \approx \mathrm{P}(Y \mid z')$ if $z \approx z'$, we relax the requirement to learn a permutation $\pi \in \boldsymbol{\pi}(n/2)$ by minimizing $\delta(\mathbf{z}^{(2)}, \pi\mathbf{z}^{(2)})$ where δ is a user-defined distortion measure. A common choice for δ is the sum of distances between permuted $\mathbf{z}$ values, $\sum_{i=1}^{n/2} d_z(z_i^{(2)}, z_{\pi(i)}^{(2)})$ where d_z is induced by k_z, i.e., $d_z^2(z', z'') := k_z(z', z') + k_z(z'', z'') - 2k_z(z', z'')$ or a regression-based distance $d_z(z', z'') := \|f(z') - f(z'')\|_2$ where f is a function relating Z and Y that can be learned, for instance, using a Gaussian process regression (GPR) (Zhang et al., 2011; Doran et al., 2014).

We apply the learned permutation π to $\mathbf{y}^{(2)}$ in $\Omega^{(2)}$ to obtain $\Omega_\pi^{(2)} := (\mathbf{x}^{(2)}, \pi\mathbf{y}^{(2)}, \mathbf{z}^{(2)})$. We then perform a two-sample test between $\Omega^{(1)}$ and $\Omega_\pi^{(2)}$ where we compute a p-value using $\mathrm{MMD}_u^2(\Omega^{(1)}, \Omega_\pi^{(2)})$ as the test statistic. We obtain the empirical distribution of the p-value under the null hypothesis by repeatedly measuring MMD_u^2 between the split samples $\Omega^{(1)}$ and $\Omega_\pi^{(2)}$ (see line 6–8).

We can repeat the test to increase the power of KCIPT. Suppose we bootstrap the aforementioned two-sample test B times. Let T_i and $\mathbf{N}_i$ be the ith MMD_u^2 estimate and a corresponding null distribution (called the 'inner' null distribution). The bootstrapped test statistic is simply the average of test statistics over each of the splits, i.e., $\mu(\{T_i\}_{i=1}^B)$. The null distribution of the bootstrapped test statistic is obtained using a Monte Carlo simulation by averaging together the draws from each individual statistic's null distribution, $\{\mu(\{s_{ij}\}_{i=1}^B) \mid \forall_{i=1}^B s_{ij} \sim \mathbf{N}_i\}_{j=1}^M$, where M is the number of points drawn from each of the B null distributions.

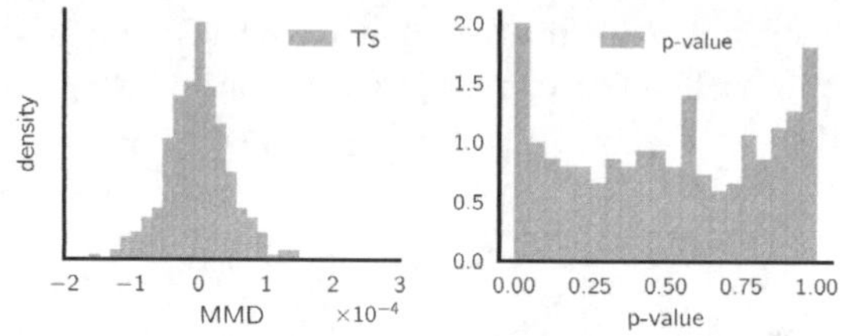

Figure 1: The distribution of test statistics of KCIPT with $B = 5000$ on 300 samples generated under the null hypothesis and a corresponding p-value distribution where B around 2000 is a good choice to balance between power and calibratedness (see Section 5.4)

Doran et al. (2014) evaluated three kernel-based CI tests, KCIT, CHSIC, and KCIPT, based on how well a test correctly rejects the null hypothesis (power) and how similar are the distribution of p-values under the null hypothesis and the uniform distribution between 0 and 1 (calibratedness). Doran et al. (2014) concluded that KCIPT "has power competitive with existing kernel-based approaches" and that it is well-calibrated.

3.1 LIMITATIONS OF KCIPT

Clearly, the larger the number *B* of bootstraps, the larger the power of KCIPT. However, we observe that the increase in the power of KCIPT comes at the expense of its calibratedness. Consider for example, the case where the expected test statistic is a small positive number. As *B* increases, the test statistic converges to its expected value (which is close to 0) and the null distribution of the test statistic will be degenerate at 0. Consequently, KCIPT with a sufficiently large *B* will reject the null hypothesis more often than it should. See Figure 1, where KCIPT with $B = 5000$ results around 10% of type I error given $\alpha = 0.05$. We will examine this phenomenon more closely later in Section 5.

Further, different runs of KCIPT with different random seeds will yield different *random* splits of a given sample (line 2, Algorithm 1) and, hence, potentially different p-values. If the given sample exhibits strong conditional dependence, the differences in random splits have little impact on the resulting p-values. However, if the sample is generated under the null hypothesis, the p-values follow a distribution close to the uniform distribution between 0 and 1 (unless B is so large that KCIPT simply loses its calibratedness). This problem makes it difficult to interpret or reproduce the p-values returned by KCIPT. This calls into question the conclusion of Doran et al. (2014) that KCIPT is well-calibrated.

In summary, KCIPT, in the absence of clear guidance on how to determine the optimal number of bootstraps, fails

Algorithm 2 MMSD

Input K_{xz}, K_y: Gram matrices for $\{(x_i, z_i)\}_{i=1}^n$ and $\{y_i\}_{i=1}^n$; D: a pairwise distance matrix for $\mathbf{z}$

$\pi \leftarrow$ find $\pi \in \boldsymbol{\pi}(n)$ minimizing δ given D

$\mathcal{I} \leftarrow \{(i,j) \mid 1 \leq i \neq j \leq n,\ i \neq \pi(j),\ j \neq \pi(i)\}$

$\mathrm{K}_1, \mathrm{K}_2, \mathrm{K}_3 \leftarrow \mathrm{K}_{xz} \odot \mathrm{K}_y, \mathrm{K}_{xz} \odot \mathrm{K}_y[\pi,\pi], \mathrm{K}_{xz} \odot \mathrm{K}_y[:,\pi]$

$T \leftarrow |\mathcal{I}|^{-1} \cdot \sum_{i,j\in\mathcal{I}} (\mathrm{K}_1 + \mathrm{K}_2 - \mathrm{K}_3 - \mathrm{K}_3^\top)_{i,j}$

return $T, \pi, \mathcal{I}$

to provide informative p-values when it is either underpowered (small B) or not well calibrated (large B).

4 SELF-DISCREPANCY CI TEST

We proceed to introduce Self-Discrepancy Conditional Independence Test (SDCIT), a new permutation and kernel-based CI test, using a new test statistic MMSD, which is based on an unbiased squared MMD estimate. We specify the empirical distribution of the MMSD and that under the null hypothesis. We further establish the *asymptotic consistency* of MMSD as a test statistic for CI (its convergence in probability to zero if and only if the null hypothesis holds).

4.1 MAXIMUM MEAN SELF-DISCREPANCY

One way to get around the limitations of KCIPT noted above is to ensure that the test statistic is determined by the given sample Ω, and *not* the any particular random splits of Ω, and thereby eliminate the dependence of the result of KCIPT on the choice of the random seed (line 2, Algorithm 1). We proceed to show how this can be achieved by replacing MMD_u^2 estimated from the samples obtained by randomly splitting Ω into two parts where one part is left intact and the other is permuted to break the ties that violate conditional independence by a variant of MMD_u^2 between the given sample Ω and its permuted counterpart. We learn a permutation π of Ω by minimizing distortion measure δ on $\mathbf{z}$. Let Ω_π be a sample where the permutation π is applied to $\mathbf{y}$ of Ω. However, because Ω_π is *not* obtained independently from Ω (see Equation 1), we cannot naively measure MMD_u^2 between Ω and Ω_π. Hence, we introduce a new test statistic, which we call Maximum Mean Self-Discrepancy (MMSD), which estimates the discrepancy between a sample Ω and its conditionally independent counterpart Ω_π by removing spurious correlations between elements of Ω and Ω_π arising from the dependence of Ω_π on Ω. Let

$$h(i,j) := k_{xyz}((\Omega)_i, (\Omega)_j) + k_{xyz}((\Omega_\pi)_i, (\Omega_\pi)_j) - k_{xyz}((\Omega)_i, (\Omega_\pi)_j) - k_{xyz}((\Omega)_j, (\Omega_\pi)_i)$$

where $(\cdot)_i$ represents the ith observation of the argument. We count $h(i,j)$ only if two triples from the two observations in each of four terms are independently obtained. For example, we exclude the case $i = j$ since $(x_i, y_i, z_i) \not\perp\!\!\!\perp (x_j, y_j, z_j)$ if $i = j$ based on the first term. Similarly, we exclude the case $i = \pi(j)$ since $(x_i, y_i, z_i) \not\perp\!\!\!\perp (x_j, y_{\pi(j)}, z_j)$ based on the third term. Now, given a permutation π, we denote by

$$\mathcal{I} := \{(i,j) \mid i \neq \pi(j),\ j \neq \pi(i)\}_{i \neq j=1}^n$$

a set of pairs of indices of independent observations conditioning on π. Based on the extent to which the permutation is reciprocal (i.e., $i = (\pi \circ \pi)(i)$), the size of $\mathcal{I}$ ranges from $n^2 - 3n$ to $n^2 - 2n$. We proceed to estimate MMSD as follows:

$$T := \tfrac{1}{|\mathcal{I}|} \textstyle\sum_{i,j\in\mathcal{I}} h(i,j). \qquad (2)$$

MMSD is closely related to the expectation of the test statistic of KCIPT. However, MMSD depends only on a single learned permutation π and eliminates the need for bootstrapping. We now proceed to prove the asymptotic consistency of MMSD by extending a theorem in (Doran et al., 2014).

Theorem 1. *Let the kernel k_{xyz} be universal and the sample space be compact. Given $\max_{\Omega_i \in (\mathcal{X},\mathcal{Y},\mathcal{Z})} \|\phi_{xyz}(\Omega_i)\| \leq C$ for some constant C, the test statistic MMSD is asymptotically consistent if the distortion measure based on RKHS distance, $\frac{1}{n}\sum_{i=1}^n \|\phi(z_i) - \phi(z_{\pi(i)})\|$, converges in probability to zero as $n \to \infty$.*

Proof. Based on Theorem 1 (Doran et al., 2014), the embedding of permuted sample Ω_π converges to the embedding of $\mathrm{P}_{xz}\mathrm{P}_{y|z}$. Thus, $\mathrm{MMD}_u^2(\Omega, \Omega_\pi) \xrightarrow{\mathrm{P}} 0$ under the null hypothesis. Since $h(i,j) \leq 4C^2$ and there are at most $2n$ excluded values in $\mathcal{I}$ except the diagonal elements, $\left|\mathrm{MMD}_u^2(\Omega, \Omega_\pi) - \mathrm{MMSD}(\Omega)\right| \leq \frac{2n \cdot 4C^2}{n(n-1)} = \frac{8C^2}{n-1}$. Hence, $\mathrm{MMSD}(\Omega) \xrightarrow{\mathrm{P}} 0$. □

Note that C is equal to 1 if a Gaussian kernel is used. We describe the pseudocode for MMSD estimate in Algorithm 2 where $\mathbf{M}[\mathbf{a}, \mathbf{b}]$ denotes a submatrix of $\mathbf{M}$ where its rows and columns are selected and ordered by $\mathbf{a}$ and $\mathbf{b}$, respectively, that is, $(\mathbf{M}[\mathbf{a}, \mathbf{b}])_{i,j} = \mathbf{M}_{a_i, b_j}$. A colon ':' represents entire rows or columns. An operator $\odot$ denotes a Hadamard product (i.e., element-wise multiplication).

4.2 EMPIRICAL DISTRIBUTION OF MMSD

We now turn our attention to obtaining the empirical distribution of MMSD, the test statistic used by SDCIT. Although the distribution of MMD_u^2 has been thoroughly

Algorithm 3 EMPMMSD

Input K_{xz}, K_y: Gram matrices for $\{(x_i, z_i)\}_{i=1}^n$ and $\{y_i\}_{i=1}^n$; D: a pairwise distance matrix for $\mathbf{z}$; b: a number of samples to be generated.

```
T′ ←initialize a vector of size b.
for b times do
    i ←randomly choose n/2 unique integers from (1, ..., n)
    T′_i, ·, · ← MMSD(K_xz [i, i] , K_y [i, i] , D[i, i])
return 1/2 · (T′ − μ(T′)) + μ(T′)
```

Algorithm 4 SDCIT

Input K_{xz}, K_y: Gram matrices for $\{(x_i, z_i)\}_{i=1}^n$ and $\{y_i\}_{i=1}^n$; D: a pairwise distance matrix for $\mathbf{z}$; b: the size of empirical null distribution.

```
T, π, J ← MMSD(K_xz, K_y, D)
D_J ←D with D_{i,j} = ∞ for every (i, j) ∈ J
·, π_2, J_2 ← MMSD(K_xz, K_y, D_J)
D_{J_2} ←D with D_{i,j} = ∞ for every (i, j) ∈ J_2
N ← EMPMMSD (K_xz, K_y [π_2, π_2] , D_{J_2}, b)
return a p-value with T and N − μ (N).
```

analyzed (Gretton et al., 2012), it is not at all immediately obvious how the analysis of MMD_u^2, which is based on two independent distributions, is applicable to the case of MMSD, which is defined with respect to two *dependent* distributions. Unlike other point estimates such as mean, MMSD on a bootstrap sample can be problematic: it is possible that pairs of the repeated observations in a bootstrap sample are permuted to each other thereby violating the conditional independence desired in the permuted sample. The resulting test statistic from such bootstrap sample will be closer to 0 than it should be.

Hence, we consider an alternative approach to estimating MMSD using sampling without replacement. We exploit the observation that half-sampling without replacement yields a very similar result to bootstrapping (Buja and Stuetzle, 2006; Friedman and Hall, 2007). Let $\mathbf{\Omega'}$ be b half-samples via sampling without replacement procedure, $\mathbf{\Omega'} := \{\Omega'_i \mid \Omega'_i \sim \binom{\Omega}{n/2}\}_{i=1}^b$. We compute the test statistic on each of randomly chosen half-samples. Since the estimate is based on the average of less than $n^2/4$ values, the expected distribution will be about twice as wide as the empirical distribution of test statistic, which is the average of fewer than n^2 values. Hence, the empirical distribution of MMSD is obtained by shrinking the width of the distribution by half: $\mathbf{T} := \frac{1}{2}(\mathbf{T}' - \mu(\mathbf{T}')) + \mu(\mathbf{T}')$ where $\mathbf{T}' := \{\mathrm{MMSD}(\Omega', \mathrm{D}) \mid \Omega' \in \mathbf{\Omega'}\}$. A pseudocode is given in Algorithm 3. Now, we provide an approximate null distribution based on the analysis in this section.

4.3 APPROXIMATE NULL DISTRIBUTION OF MMSD

An approximate null distribution of test statistic can often be obtained by applying the statistic on many samples generated under the null hypothesis ($\mathrm{P}_{xz}\mathrm{P}_{y|z}$ in this case). Since we do have access to neither $\mathrm{P}_{xz}\mathrm{P}_{y|z}$ nor the model for the distribution, we will apply half-sampling without replacement on the permuted sample Ω_π to approximate the null distribution of MMSD. As described in the previous section, we generate $\mathbf{\Omega'_\pi}$, b half-samples of Ω_π via sampling without replacement. However, we need to be careful in obtaining the test statistic from the resulting half samples. Let a half-sample $\Omega'_\pi = \{(x'_c, y'_c, z'_c)\}_{c=1}^{n/2} \in \mathbf{\Omega'_\pi}$, where $\Omega'_\pi \subset \Omega_\pi$, contain the following two observations at its ath and bth indices, $(x'_a, y'_a, z'_a) = (x_i, y_{\pi(i)}, z_i) = (x_i, y_j, z_i)$ and $(x'_b, y'_b, z'_b) = (x_k, y_{\pi(k)}, z_k) = (x_k, y_i, z_k)$ where indices i, j, and k are originally from Ω. We can infer that $z_j \approx z_i \approx z_k$. Hence, a permutation π' to be learned for Ω'_π will likely permute y's in the two observations. If that is the case (i.e., $\pi'(a) = b$), then the permuted half-sample $(\mathbf{x}', \pi'\mathbf{y}', \mathbf{z}')$ will contain the observation $(x'_a, y'_{\pi'(a)}, z'_a) = (x_i, y'_b, z_i) = (x_i, y_i, z_i)$. That is, applying the permutation π' recovers an original observation in Ω failing to simulate conditional independence in $\Omega'_{\pi\pi'}$. Hence, the following constraints should be imposed in computing a permutation for Ω'_π, $\forall_{1 \le c \le \frac{n}{2}} (f^{-1} \circ \pi \circ f \circ \pi')(c) \neq c$ where f is a mapping between the index of an observation in a subsample to that in Ω_π. In the preceding example, $\pi'(a) = b$, $f(b) = k$, $\pi(k) = i$, and $f^{-1}(i) = a$. In other words, simply disallow permutations that associate y_i back to $(x_i, \cdot, z_i)$. In addition to constraints on the allowed permutations, identifying independent observation pairs is more complicated by the need for additional bookkeeping for tracking the composition of every observation in the half-samples of Ω_π.

Hence, we consider an alternative approach to using the permuted sample Ω_π in MMSD by modifying the distance on $\mathbf{z}$. If we have a pre-computed pairwise distance matrix from the previous step, setting the entries of the matrix at index pairs that appear in $\mathcal{J}$ to infinity will do the trick. We denote by $\mathrm{D}_\mathcal{J}$ a distance matrix D with values at each $(i, j) \in \mathcal{J}$ replaced with infinity. Then, $\mathrm{EMPMMSD}(\mathrm{K}_{xz}, \mathrm{K}_y[\pi, \pi], \mathrm{D}_\mathcal{J}, b)$ is a b sample approximation to the distribution of test statistics under the null hypothesis. We additionally correct the biases by ensuring the average of the distribution is 0. Consequently, the approximate null distribution is given by $\mathbf{N} := \frac{1}{2}(\mathbf{N}' - \mu(\mathbf{N}'))$ where $\mathbf{N}' := \{\mathrm{MMSD}(\Omega'_\pi, \mathrm{D}_\mathcal{J}) \mid \Omega'_\pi \in \mathbf{\Omega'_\pi}\}$.

4.4 ALGORITHM

We combine the new test statistic MMSD and its empirical null distribution to compute a p-value for testing

$X \perp\!\!\!\perp Y \mid Z$ given a sample Ω in the form of Gram matrices $K_{xz} = K_x \odot K_z$ and K_y (see Algorithm 4). We introduce a simple heuristic to improve the quality of approximate null distribution. We say a permutation π for Ω is of good quality if Ω_π closely approximates to the factorized distribution $P_{xz}P_{y|z}$. Consider a permutation π' to be learned from $\Omega'_\pi = (\mathbf{x}', \mathbf{y}', \mathbf{z}')$, a half-sample of Ω_π, with the penalized distance matrix $D_\mathfrak{J}$ (as shown in the previous section). Since the size of sample is half the size of the original sample, $\mathbf{z}'$ is less dense than $\mathbf{z}$, and the quality of π' becomes worse than that of π. Furthermore, since penalized distance is used, two *originally* close z values, say z'_i and z'_j in Ω'_π, will not be considered in computing π' if the pair is permuted in Ω_π. For these reasons, permutations to be learned for half-samples will not be of as high quality as that of π, which is learned from a full sample without any restrictions. We can rectify this situation using a simple trick. In line 3, permutation π_2 is learned from Ω with a penalized matrix $D_\mathfrak{J}$. Although Ω_{π_2} will not be as good as Ω_π in approximating $P_{xz}P_{y|z}$, permutations to be learned for half-samples of Ω_{π_2} will be better than those of Ω_π. We empirically observed that the resulting null distributions are more consistent when we used this trick. In Appendix, a further adjustment to the test statistic and null distribution is provided. The key differences between SDCIT and KCIPT are also summarized in Table 2 in Appendix.

5 EXPERIMENTS

We compare the performance of SDCIT with that of other kernel-based CI tests, including KCIT, CHSIC, and KCIPT, with respect to the following two criteria: (i) Area Under Power Curve (AUPC) which estimates how powerful the test is by measuring the area under the cumulative density function (CDF) of $\mathbf{p}$, a set of p-values produced by running a test on a set of samples; and (ii) Kolmogorov-Smirnov (KS) statistic (a measure of the largest discrepancy between cumulative density functions of the two distributions), applied to $\mathbf{p}$ and a uniform distribution to assess the degree to which the p-values produced by the test given samples under the null hypothesis are distributed uniformly in the interval [0,1]. We also compare the different tests with respect to their type I error rates (given a significance level $\alpha = 0.05$) and their run time. We examine the robustness of the different tests with respect to the choice of the kernel function. We contrast SDCIT with KCIPT when the latter uses a large number of bootstraps.

We implemented SDCIT and KCIPT.[2] Unlike the original implementation of KCIPT which employs a simplex algorithm to learn permutations, all permutations are *approximately* learned using minimum cost perfect matching algorithm (BLOSSOM-V, Kolmogorov, 2009) with heuristics for local improvement where three 2-cycles are transformed to two 3-cycles and a 2-cycle and a 3-cycle are transformed to a 5-cycle. Gaussian RBF kernel $k(v, w) := \exp(-\|v - w\|_2^2/(2\sigma^2))$ is used across all experiments where σ is determined by the median heuristic (Gretton et al., 2005). SDCIT uses empirical null distributions of size 10^3. We used the recommended settings for KCIPT (i.e., $B = 25$ and $b, M = 10^4$) and for CHSIC. For KCIT, we used *both* the original implementation, in which variables are normalized to unit variance and kernel parameters are set empirically (Zhang et al., 2011), and a modified implementation, where the variables are not normalized and the kernel parameters are set by median heuristic. For both implementations, GPR is used to optimize the regularization parameter.

[2]The code is available online at `https://github.com/sanghack81/SDCIT`

5.1 EXPERIMENTAL SETTING

Following previous work (Fukumizu et al., 2008; Zhang et al., 2011; Doran et al., 2014), we conducted experiments on two synthetic datasets, post-nonlinear noise and chaotic time series identical to those used in Doran et al. (2014), where each data has two modes, i.e., $X \perp\!\!\!\perp Y \mid Z$ and $X \not\!\perp\!\!\!\perp Y \mid Z$.

Post-nonlinear noise data is generated using the model described by Zhang and Hyvärinen (2009); Zhang et al. (2011). X and Y are constructed from functions of the form $G_X(F_X(Z_1) + E)$ and $G_Y(F_Y(Z_1) + E)$, respectively, where $G.$ and $F.$ are smooth nonlinear functions, E is a Gaussian error, and Z_1 is a random variable in an m dimension conditioning variable $Z := \{Z_i\}_{i=1}^m$. The conditioning variable Z satisfies that $\forall_{i=2}^m Z_i \perp\!\!\!\perp \{X, Y, Z_1\}$ for some m making only Z_1 relevant to X and Y. Since $X \perp\!\!\!\perp Y \mid Z_1$ by construction, we also generate samples under the alternative, $X \not\!\perp\!\!\!\perp Y \mid Z$, by adding identical Gaussian noise to both X and Y.

Chaotic time series is based on the coupled Hénon map. Each X_t and Y_t is four-dimensional, $X_t = (X_{i,t})_{i=1}^4$ and $Y_t = (Y_{i,t})_{i=1}^4$ where

$$X_{1,t} := 1.4 - X_{1,t-1}^2 + 0.3X_{2,t-1}$$
$$Y_{1,t} := 1.4 - \gamma X_{1,t-1}Y_{1,t-1} + (1-\gamma)Y_{1,t-1}^2 + 0.3Y_{2,t-1}$$

and $X_{2,t}$ and $Y_{2,t}$ inherits $X_{1,t-1}$ and $Y_{1,t-1}$, respectively. The third and fourth dimensions of X_t and Y_t correspond to Gaussian noise $\mathcal{N}(0, 0.5^2)$ to make the data more challenging. The parameter γ controls dependence. Regardless of γ, $X_{t+1} \perp\!\!\!\perp Y_t \mid X_t$ holds and given $\gamma > 0$, $Y_{t+1} \not\!\perp\!\!\!\perp X_t \mid Y_t$.

Following Doran et al. (2014), a set of 300 samples are

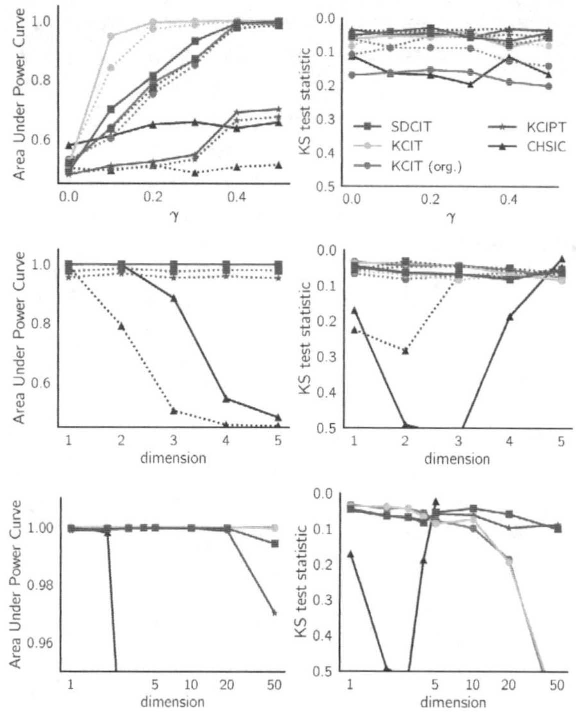

Figure 2: AUPC and KS statistics for (**Top**) Chaotic time series (**Middle**) Post-nonlinear noise data (**Bottom**) High-dimensional conditioning variables on post-nonlinear noise dataset. Dotted and solid lines are for the samples of size 200 and 400, respectively. For high-dimensional setting, CHSIC is excluded.

generated for post-nonlinear noise data per each condition based on the combination of: two variants ($X \perp\!\!\!\perp Y \mid Z$ and $X \not\perp\!\!\!\perp Y \mid Z$), different dimensions $m \in \{1, 2, 3, 4, 5, 10, 20, 50\}$, and different sizes (200 and 400). Similarly, we generated sets of 300 samples of chaotic time series data for two variants, two sample sizes, and γ ranging from 0 to 0.5 by 0.1. Datasets under the null hypothesis are used to report KS statistic and datasets under the alternative hypothesis are used to report AUPCs. SDCIT and KCIPT used RKHS distance for chaotic time series data and, for post-nonlinear noise data, regression-based distance is used where functions are learned based on GPR with automatic relevance determination.

5.2 COMPARISONS AMONG KERNEL-BASED CI TESTS

Figure 2 illustrates the performance of the four tests on the two datasets under various conditions. Note that the original implementation of KCIT with recommended setting is labeled as KCIT (org.) in the figure. Plots in the left column represent AUPCs and those in the right column show KS statistic which measures the degree to which

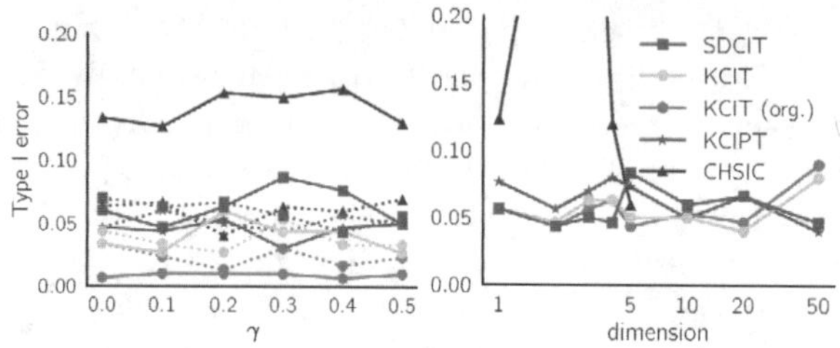

Figure 3: Type I error rates with $\alpha = 0.05$ (**Left**) chaotic time series data (**Right**) post-nonlinear noise data

the distribution of p-values under the null hypothesis deviates from the uniform distribution. Note that the plots for the different tests may differ in the range of values plotted on the y-axis and the values on the y-axis for plots of KS statistic are in descending order.

With respect to power, SDCIT is ranked right below KCIT for both data although SDCIT is more powerful than the implementation of KCIT used in the experiments reported by Doran et al. (2014) for chaotic time series. On post-nonlinear noise data, all tests except CHSIC showed comparable power although the permutation-based methods (SDCIT and KCIPT) show a slight loss in power when $n = 200$. When the number of conditioning variables increases ($m = 50$), SDCIT slightly loses its power (AUPC=0.9944). In the case of KCIPT, we observed a far smaller loss in power (AUPC=0.9703) compared to that reported (around 0.79, Doran et al., 2014). We conclude that SDCIT achieves better power that is comparable to or better than that of all other CI tests except KCIT. We conjecture that the observed difference in power of KCIT relative to SDCIT may be due to the differences in the respective hypotheses, $\mathrm{P}_{xyz} = \mathrm{P}_{x|z}\mathrm{P}_{y|z}\mathrm{P}_z$ versus $\mathrm{P}_{xy|z} = \mathrm{P}_{x|z}\mathrm{P}_{y|z}$.

Next, we compare the tests based on their calibratedness. For both datasets, SDCIT and KCIPT have very consistent null distributions with the KS statistics generally below 0.1. Also the results vary little with sample size. KCIT demonstrates difficulty obtaining accurate null distributions for CI tests with high-dimensional conditional variables. We also report the type I error rates on the two datasets in Figure 3. All tests except CHSIC and the KCIT (org.) reject around 5% of samples under the null hypothesis given a significance level α set to 0.05.

We report the run time of SDCIT and KCIT in Table 1. Based on a set of 300 samples of chaotic time series data, we measured the running time on an iMac with Core i7 3.5Ghz CPU allowing only a single thread. In the case of SDCIT, we expect the learning of permutations will dominate the run time since BLOSSOM-V has $O(nm \log n)$ time complexity where $m = \frac{n(n-1)}{2}$ is the number of edges. However, we see that the run time of

n	SDCIT $b = 500$	SDCIT $b = 1000$	KCIT
200	0.50±0.02	0.96±0.02	1.17±0.19
400	2.41±0.07	4.60±0.07	4.68±0.75

Table 1: Running time in seconds averaged over 300 samples of chaotic time series data (including time for kernel and distance matrices computation)

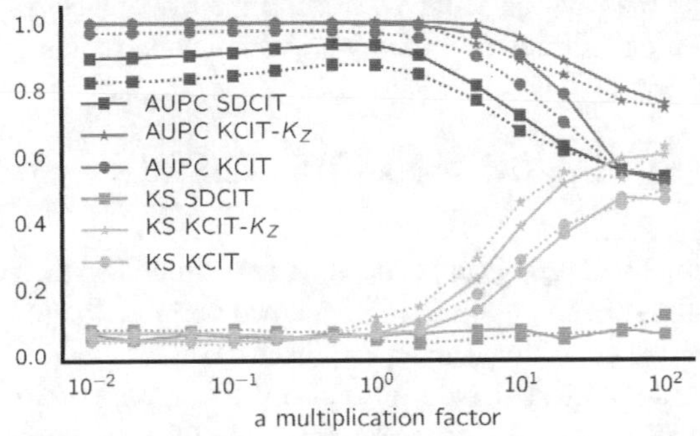

Figure 4: Changes of performance of KCIT and SDCIT with different choice of kernel parameters (relative to the default median heuristic). Solid and dotted lines represent $n = 400$ and 200, respectively.

SDCIT increased by a factor less than 5 when the size of data is doubled. The run time is proportional to b, the size of empirical null distribution. Since SDCIT is trivially parallelizable, the run time can be significantly reduced making the use of modern processors. Note that KCIPT is about 10 times slower even when $B = 25$ due to $B\,(b + 1)$ MMD computations.

5.3 ROBUSTNESS WITH RESPECT TO KERNEL CHOICE

The median heuristic to determine the kernel parameter for an RBF kernel works well for both SDCIT and KCIT in previous experiments. However, the kernel choice is entirely at the user's discretion. A well-designed kernel-based test should be robust with respect to the choice of kernel parameters and should have a consistent null distribution. Consider a parametrized RBF kernel, $k^{(C)}(x, x') = \exp\left(-C\|x - x'\|^2/2\sigma^2\right)$, where σ^2 is chosen based on the median heuristic. We explore how KCIT and SDCIT behave as C varies from 10^{-2} to 10^2. We report AUPC and KS statistics based on a set of 300 chaotic time series datasets with 'dependent' and 'independent' modes, respectively, both with $\gamma = 0.3$.

The original implementation of KCIT uses GPR to learn a regularization parameter only with a real vector Z. Hence, we also provide a result where empirical kernel map for Z is approximately inferred from K_Z (labeled as KCIT-K_Z in Figure 4). Our results demonstrate that SDCIT is robust with respect to the choice of kernel without sacrificing well-calibratedness whereas KCIT degrades in calibratedness as C increases.

5.4 COMPARISON OF SDCIT AND KCIPT WITH INCREASING NUMBER OF BOOTSTRAPS

Unlike other tests, the power of KCIPT can be adjusted by controlling B. Hence, we compare the performance of KCIPT with that of SDCIT as we increase the number of bootstraps used by KCIPT. For computational reasons, we replace the bootstrap procedure for the null distribution of KCIPT by an analytic one to cope with a large number of bootstraps (e.g., $B \geq 1000$). Since the inner null distributions are very similar to each other, we aggregated inner null distributions $\{\mathbf{N}_i\}_{i=1}^{B}$ where each distribution consists of a relatively small number of observations (100). We approximate the null distribution by $\mathcal{N}(0, \mathrm{Var}(\bigcup_{i=1}^{B}\mathbf{N}_i)/B)$, which is nearly identical to the bootstrap-based null distribution (line 10 in Alg. 1).

We used 300 samples of chaotic time series data of $n = 400$ and $\gamma = 0$. We inferred the appropriate value of B to be 2145 for KCIPT to obtain power comparable to that of SDCIT by matching the variance of null distribution of KCIPT to that of SDCIT based on the first of the 300 samples. The rationale behind the matching is that 1) given a sample, the test statistic of SDCIT and expected test statistic of KCIPT (i.e., $B = \infty$) are close to each other since both are based on the RKHS distance to measure the effect of applying permutation(s), and 2) similar null distributions mean similar critical values for rejecting the null hypothesis. Note, however, that the appropriate B may vary by a given sample.

With the first sample, we compared empirical null distributions of SDCIT and KCIPT together with a test statistic for SDCIT and a distribution of test statistics for KCIPT through repeated trials with varying random seeds on the sample (recall p-value inconsistency of KCIPT) (see top of Figure 5). The null distribution of SDCIT are positively-skewed (0.80), which is similar to the null distribution of MMD_u^2 in a two-sample test setting (Gretton et al., 2012) whereas KCIPT demonstrates normality because of large B. Since KCIPT test statistic is stochastic, the p-value is also stochastic. In this example, p-value is nearly uniformly distributed between 0 and 1. For other samples, we observed distributions of either negative or positive skew, shaped like staircases.

In bottom of Figure 5, we plot test statistics of KCIPT and SDCIT on 300 samples. We observe that the p-values of SDCIT are fairly uniformly distributed, ensuring that it

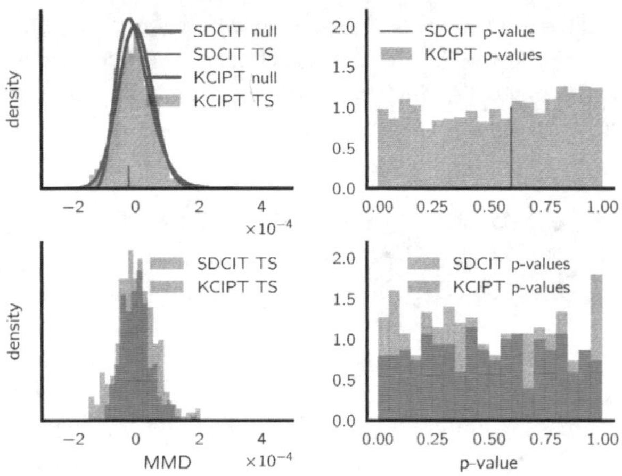

Figure 5: Empirical distributions and p-value distributions of SDCIT and KCIPT with $B = 2145$ based on the first sample (**Top**) and all 300 samples (**Bottom**) with $\gamma = 0.0$ and $n = 400$.

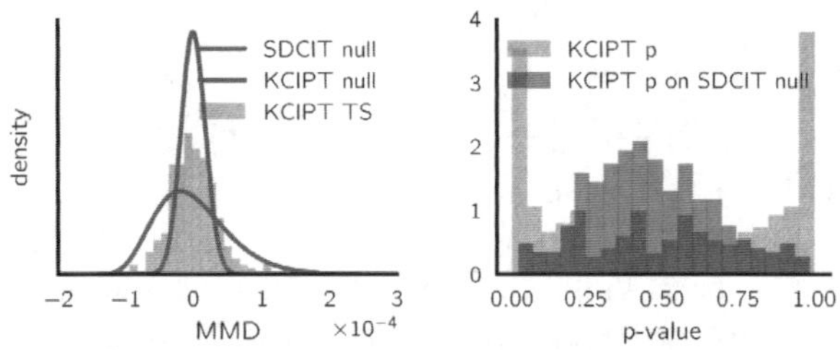

Figure 6: Null distributions of SDCIT and KCIPT, and an empirical distribution of test statistics of KCIPT with $B = 20000$ under the null hypothesis.

is well-calibrated. However, KCIPT starts to lose its calibratedness as the number of bootstraps is increased, resulting in more p-values concentrated around the two extremes, 0 and 1. The analysis presented in Section 3.1 offers an explanation of the loss of calibratedness of KCIPT that is different from that conjectured by Doran et al. (2014), namely, an approximation error in representing $\mathrm{P}_{xz}\mathrm{P}_{y|z}$ due to imperfect permutations.

In Figure 6, with the 300 samples, we illustrate the null distribution of KCIPT and an empirical distribution of its statistics with $B = 20000$. Given a very large B, each test statistic quite accurately reflects conditional (in)dependence of the given sample. That is, the empirical distribution will not shrink as B increases unlike a null distribution will. On the right side, we plot two p-value distributions of KCIPT against null distributions from KCIPT and SDCIT. The dome-shaped p-value distribution is similar to what we have observed, in another simulation, with SDCIT using a bagged statistic of MMSD (i.e., the average of empirical distribution of MMSD) as a test statistic without modifying the null distribution.

Our results suggest that SDCIT is not simply equivalent to KCIPT with some unknown but sufficiently large number of bootstraps B with respect to its power and calibratedness. Further, the run time of SDCIT is generally smaller than that of KCIPT because KCIPT requires a large, data-dependent number (say greater than 1000) to achieve power that is comparable to that of SDCIT even if we factor in the savings achieved in run time by replacing the empirical null distribution by an analytic approximation.

6 SUMMARY AND DISCUSSION

Doran et al. (2014) introduced KCIPT, which has the advantage of relying on a single learned permutation to reduce the conditional independence (CI) test to an easier two-sample test. Based on their experimental comparison of KCIPT with other kernel-based CI tests (CHSIC and KCIT), they concluded that KCIPT has power competitive with that of KCIT and is well-calibrated compared to other alternatives. We observed the previously unobserved behavior of KCIPT when the number of bootstraps is increased: KCIPT suffers from a loss of calibratedness as its power increases with increase in the number of bootstraps. Careful analysis of the behavior of KCIPT leads us to propose SDCIT, a novel kernel-based CI test with a new test statistic based on modified MMD estimate, called Maximum Mean Self-Discrepancy. The resulting test statistic is parameter-free for a given choice of kernel and distortion measure whereas KCIPT requires the user to specify the number of bootstraps. The results of our experiments with two benchmark datasets demonstrate several advantages of SDCIT over other existing kernel-based CI tests. The main drawback of SDCIT is the absence of analytic method to approximate the null distribution. In addition, when there are many permutations minimizing given distortion measure, our test statistic can become non-deterministic. In particular, SDCIT when used to test unconditional independence might yield inconsistent p-values under the null hypothesis despite maintaining its calibratedness.

Acknowledgements

The authors are grateful to UAI 2017 anonymous reviewers for their thorough reviews. This research was supported by the Edward Frymoyer Endowed Professorship, the Center for Big Data Analytics and Discovery Informatics at the Pennsylvania State University, and the Sudha Murty Distinguished Visiting Chair in Neurocomputing and Data Science at the Indian Institute of Science.

References

Bach, F. R. and Jordan, M. I. (2002). Kernel Independent Component Analysis. *Journal of Machine Learning Research*, 3:1–48.

Berlinet, A. and Thomas-Agnan, C. (2004). *Reproducing Kernel Hilbert Spaces in Probability and Statistics*. Springer US, Boston, MA.

Buja, A. and Stuetzle, W. (2006). Observations on bagging. *Statistica Sinica*, 16(2):323–351.

Dawid, A. P. (1979). Conditional Independence in Statistical Theory. *Journal of the Royal Statistical Society. Series B (Methodological)*, 41(1):1–31.

Doran, G., Muandet, K., Zhang, K., and Schölkopf, B. (2014). A Permutation-Based Kernel Conditional Independence Test. In *Proceedings of the Thirtieth Conference on Uncertainty in Artificial Intelligence*, pages 132–141, Corvallis, Oregon. AUAI Press.

Efron, B. (1979). Bootstrap Methods: Another Look at the Jackknife. *The Annals of Statistics*, 7(1):1–26.

Friedman, J. H. and Hall, P. (2007). On bagging and nonlinear estimation. *Journal of Statistical Planning and Inference*, 137(3):669–683.

Fukumizu, K., Bach, F. R., and Jordan, M. I. (2004). Dimensionality Reduction for Supervised Learning with Reproducing Kernel Hilbert Spaces. *Journal of Machine Learning Research*, 5:73–99.

Fukumizu, K., Bach, F. R., and Jordan, M. I. (2009). Kernel dimension reduction in regression. *Annals of Statistics*, 37(4):1871–1905.

Fukumizu, K., Gretton, A., Sun, X., and Schölkopf, B. (2008). Kernel Measures of Conditional Dependence. In *NIPS 2007*, pages 489–496.

Gretton, A., Borgwardt, K. M., Rasch, M. J., Scholkopf, B., and Smola, A. (2012). A Kernel Two-Sample Test. *Journal of Machine Learning Research*, 13:723–773.

Gretton, A., Borgwardt, K. M., Schölkopf, B., and Smola, A. J. (2007). A kernel method for the two sample problem. In *NIPS 2006*, pages 513–520. MIT Press.

Gretton, A., Bousquet, O., Smola, A., and Schölkopf, B. (2005). Measuring Statistical Dependence with Hilbert-Schmidt Norms. In *Algorithmic Learning Theory. ALT 2005*, pages 63–77. Springer.

Gretton, A., Fukumizu, K., Harchaoui, Z., and Sriperumbudur, B. K. (2009). A Fast, Consistent Kernel Two-Sample Test. In *NIPS 2009*, pages 673–681.

Koller, D. and Friedman, N. (2009). *Probabilistic Graphical Models: Principles and Techniques*, volume 2009. MIT Press.

Kolmogorov, V. (2009). Blossom V: a new implementation of a minimum cost perfect matching algorithm. *Mathematical Programming Computation*, 1(1):43–67.

Pearl, J. (2000). *Causality: Models, Reasoning, and Inference*. Cambridge University Press, 2nd edition.

Smola, A., Gretton, A., Song, L., and Schölkopf, B. (2007). A Hilbert space embedding for distributions. In *Proceedings of the 18th International Conference on Algorithmic Learning Theory*, pages 13–31.

Spirtes, P., Glymour, C. N., and Scheines, R. (2000). *Causation, Prediction, and Search*. MIT Press, second edition.

Sriperumbudur, B. K., Gretton, A., Fukumizu, K., Schölkopf, B., and Lanckriet, G. R. G. (2010). Hilbert space embeddings and metrics on probability measures. *Journal of Machine Learning Research*, 11:1517–1561.

Zhang, K. and Hyvärinen, A. (2009). On the identifiability of the post-nonlinear causal model. *Proceedings of the Twenty-Fifth Conference on Uncertainty in Artificial Intelligence*, pages 647–655.

Zhang, K., Peters, J., Janzing, D., and Schölkopf, B. (2011). Kernel-based Conditional Independence Test and Application in Causal Discovery. In *Proceedings of the 27th Conference on Uncertainty in Artificial Intelligence*, pages 804–813, Corvallis, Oregon. AUAI Press.

A ALGORITHMIC COMPARISON

	SDCIT	KCIPT
H_0	$\Omega = \Omega_\pi$	$\{\Omega_i^{(1)} = \Omega_{\pi,i}^{(2)}\}_{i=1}^B$
T	modified MMD	averaged MMDs
null distribution	half-sampling without replacement	aggregated bootstrap null distributions
# of permutations	1 for T $b+1$ for null.	B for T
# of MM(S)Ds	1 for T $b+1$ for null.	B for T Bb for null.

Table 2: Comparison of SDCIT and KCIPT

B TAKING PERMUTATION ERROR INTO ACCOUNT

Our test statistic measures the distance between the original sample (representing P_{xyz}) and a pseudo-null sample (representing $P_{xz}P'_{y|z}$), where $P'_{y|z}$ approximates $P_{y|z}$. Ideally, the test statistic and its null distribution will be reliably estimated if permutation error is small and, hence, $P'_{y|z}$ approximates $P_{y|z}$ well.

We first relate an MMSD estimate and its corresponding permutation error during the estimate, and provide a means to adjust MMSD estimates. Let T be an MMSD estimate given K_{xz}, K_y, and D (see Algorithm 2). Let τ be an MMSD estimate assuming $K_x = \mathbf{1}_{n\times n}$, that is $\tau = \text{MMSD}(K_z, K_y, D)$. In other words, τ is the MMSD estimate between $P'_{y|z}P_z$ and $P_{y|z}P_z$. While T is, roughly, about the conditional dependence between X and Y given Z, τ measures permutation error, i.e., discrepancy between $(\mathbf{y}, \mathbf{z})$ and $(\pi\mathbf{y}, \mathbf{z})$. We illustrate a null distribution $\{T_i\}_{i=1}^b$ and its associated $\{\tau_i\}_{i=1}^b$ in Figure 7. We can clearly observe that the distribution of τ is centered at 0 but still there are lots of null samples associating non-negligible errors.

We then formulate T (under a permutation error) is the function of unknown T^* (under zero permutation error) and τ. We assume a linear model $T = T^* + \beta\tau + \epsilon$ where ϵ is *assumed* a zero-mean Gaussian noise. Given a null distribution $\{(T_i, \tau_i)\}_{i=1}^b$, we can learn β by fitting a linear model. Then, the null distribution $\{T_i\}_{i=1}^b$ is adjusted to $\{T_i - \beta\tau_i\}_{i=1}^b$ and our test statistic is also adjusted similarly. Such adjustment yields a null distribution with smaller variance as shown in Figure 8. The adjustment slightly improves both power and calibratedness.

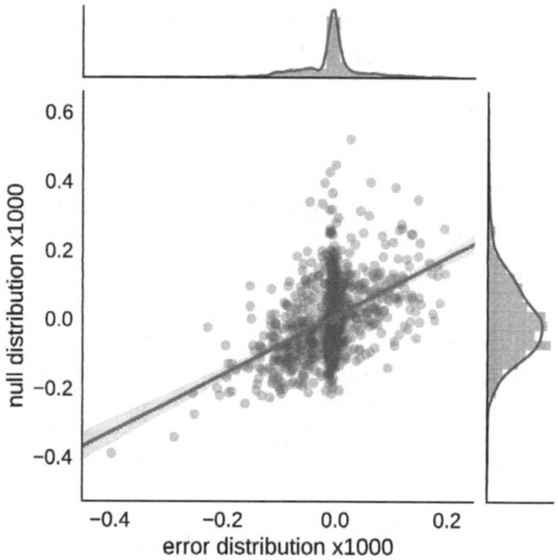

Figure 7: A null distribution and its corresponding errors measured with MMSD. A red cross near origin indicates the test statistic and its corresponding error. A red line indicates a fitted linear model.

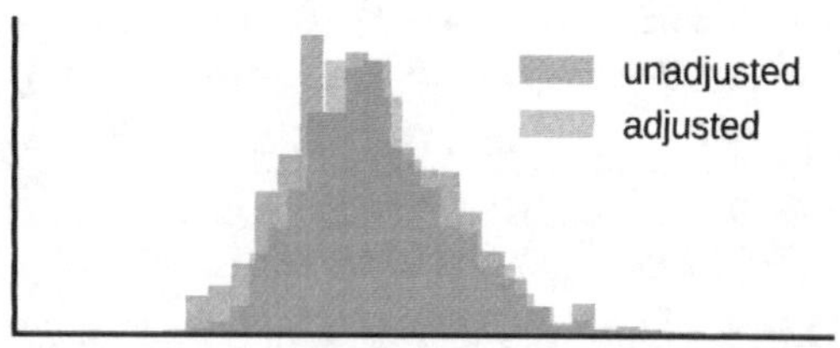

Figure 8: Unadjusted and adjusted null distributions.

A Kernel Conditional Independence Test for Relational Data

Sanghack Lee and **Vasant Honavar**
Artificial Intelligence Research Laboratory
College of Information Sciences and Technology
The Pennsylvania State University, University Park, PA 16802
{sxl439, vhonavar}@ist.psu.edu

Abstract

Conditional independence (CI) tests play a central role in statistical inference, machine learning, and causal discovery. Most existing CI tests assume that the samples are independently and identically distributed (i.i.d.). However, this assumption often does not hold in the case of *relational data*. We define *Relational Conditional Independence* (RCI), a generalization of CI to the relational setting. We show how, under a set of structural assumptions, we can test for RCI by reducing the task of testing for RCI on non-i.i.d. data to the problem of testing for CI on several data sets each of which consists of i.i.d. samples. We develop *Kernel Relational CI test* (KRCIT), a nonparametric test as a practical approach to testing for RCI by relaxing the structural assumptions used in our analysis of RCI. We describe results of experiments with synthetic relational data that show the benefits of KRCIT relative to traditional CI tests that don't account for the non-i.i.d. nature of relational data.

1 INTRODUCTION

Observational and experimental data represent systematic interactions among a set of random variables of interest. Conditional independence (CI) tests constitute essential tools for understanding such interactions. Random variables X and Y are said to be conditionally independent given Z, denoted by $X \perp\!\!\!\perp Y \mid Z$, if and only if the joint distribution P_{xyz} can be factorized as $\mathsf{P}_{x|z}\mathsf{P}_{y|z}\mathsf{P}_{z}$. The notion of CI plays a central role in statistical inference (Dawid, 1979), probabilistic graphical models (Koller and Friedman, 2009), and causal discovery (Pearl, 2000; Spirtes et al., 2000). A variety of methods including, in particular, non-parametric methods (Fukumizu et al., 2008; Zhang et al., 2011; Doran et al., 2014; Lee and Honavar, 2017) have been developed to test for CI in settings where the parametric form of the underlying distribution is unknown but a measure of closeness between data samples can be defined, e.g., using a kernel function. However, these methods implicitly or explicitly assume that the data samples are independently and identically distributed (i.i.d.).

Many sources of real-world data, e.g., the WWW, citation networks, social networks, biomolecular networks, exhibit a *relational* structure, wherein the data are naturally represented as collections of interlinked entities. In the resulting relational data, e.g., a citation network, the entities, e.g., authors, articles, and institutions, clearly do not constitute i.i.d. observations. Methods for learning causal models from relational data rely on oracles that can answer CI queries from such data (Maier et al., 2013; Lee and Honavar, 2016). Practical realizations of such algorithms will need to replace such oracles by CI tests against relational data. However, in the relational setting, with the exception of autocorrelated data, e.g., time series (Chwialkowski et al., 2014), where 'closeness' in time, space, or network is well-defined (Flaxman et al., 2016), effective ways to define and test for CI have been lacking. Any attempt to generalize the notion of CI to the relational setting needs to overcome several challenges: What are relational counterparts of random variables? How can we define their marginal distributions?

Against this background, inspired by the notion of relational d-separation (Maier et al., 2013), which generalizes a graphical criterion for CI to a specific model of relational data, we (i) Formalize Relational Conditional Independence (RCI), the relational counterpart of CI. (ii) Examine the dependence and heterogeneity of relational variables in terms of the underlying relational structure. (iii) Based on the preceding analyses, devise a Kernel Relational CI Test (KRCIT) that, to the best of our knowledge, offers the first practical method for testing for RCI.

(iv) Describe results of experiments with synthetic relational data that show the benefits of KRCIT relative to traditional CI tests that don't account for the non-i.i.d. nature of relational data. RCI and KRCIT offer new ways to understand dependencies in relational data across a broad range of practical applications.

2 PRELIMINARIES

We follow the notational conventions from statistics, graph theory, and relational models. We use a capital letter X to denote a random variable; $\mathcal{X}$ to denote the range of X; and a lowercase letter x to denote the value of X. Calligraphic letters are also used to represent mathematical objects, e.g., graphs.

We define a labeled (directed or undirected) *graph* $\mathcal{G} = \langle \mathcal{V}, \mathcal{E}, \mathcal{L} \rangle$ where $\mathcal{V}$ denotes a set of vertices (or nodes) and $\mathcal{E}$ a set of edges. Each vertex is assigned a discrete label by a labeling function $\mathcal{L} : \mathcal{V} \mapsto \Sigma$ where Σ is a set of labels. We disallow self-loops. Given an undirected graph $\mathcal{G}$, a *connected component* $\mathcal{G}'$ is a vertex-induced subgraph of $\mathcal{G}$ where there exists a path between every pair of vertices in $\mathcal{G}'$. We denote all connected components in $\mathcal{G}$ by $\text{CC}^{\mathcal{G}}$ and a connected component containing $v \in \mathcal{V}$ by $\text{CC}_v^{\mathcal{G}}$. Two labeled graphs $\mathcal{G}$ and $\mathcal{G}'$ are said to be *isomorphic,* denoted by $\mathcal{G} \cong \mathcal{G}'$, if there exists a bijective function $f : \mathcal{V} \mapsto \mathcal{V}'$ such that $\forall_{v \in \mathcal{V}} \mathcal{L}(v) = \mathcal{L}'(f(v))$ and $\forall_{u,v \in \mathcal{V}} (u, v) \in \mathcal{E} \Leftrightarrow (f(u), f(v)) \in \mathcal{E}'$.

We use a simplified version of Entity-Relationship (ER) model (Chen, 1976) to describe relational data (Friedman et al., 1999; Heckerman et al., 2007; Maier et al., 2013). A relational schema $\mathcal{S} = \langle \mathbf{E}, \mathbf{R}, \mathbf{A} \rangle$ describes the relational domain of interest with a set of entity classes $\mathbf{E}$ (e.g., *person*, *student*), relationship classes $\mathbf{R}$ (e.g., *friend-of*, *son-of*), and attribute classes $\mathbf{A}$ (e.g., *gender*, *income*). We refer to the union $\mathbf{E} \cup \mathbf{R}$ as the set of item classes $\mathbf{I}$. In general, a relationship class $R \in \mathbf{R}$ can be n-ary where $n \geq 2$ (e.g., *contract* is a set of ternary relationships involving products, buyers, and sellers). We use $\mathbf{A}(I)$ to denote an item class I's attribute classes, and $\mathbf{A}^{-1}(X)$ by to denote the item class of X.

A relational skeleton $\sigma \in \Sigma_{\mathcal{S}}$ is an instantiation of a given relational schema, which can be viewed as an undirected bipartite graph. We denote by $\sigma(I)$ a set of items of an item class $I \in \mathbf{I}$. Given an item $i \in \sigma(I)$, we use $i.X$ to denote the item i's attribute class X. Note that $i.X$ is a random variable which takes a value $i.x \in \mathcal{X}$. An edge $(i, r) \in \sigma$ represents the participation of an entity i in a relationship r. For simplicity, we represent a skeleton, whose relationship classes are binary, as an undirected graph of entities. We use "relational structure" to mean the the graphical structure of a relational skeleton, and "relational data" to mean a set of data that conform to a given relational schema. We use letters such as i and j to stand for integers or items (e.g., the letters i and j to refer two items in $\sigma(I)$).

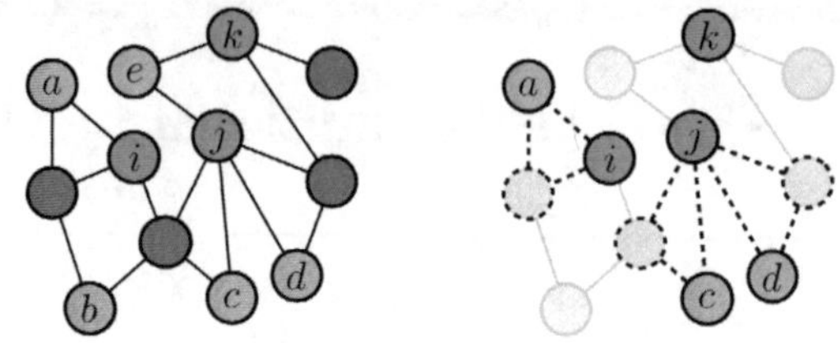

Figure 1: (**Left**) a small relational skeleton σ as an undirected graph of entities of three classes, Blue, Magenta, and Gray; and (**Right**) an example of a relational variable V where $V(\ell)$ refers to the multiset of attribute X of a set of Gray items forming a triangle with the given Blue item ℓ and a Magenta item. Hence, $V(i) = \{a.X\}$; $V(j) = \{c.X, d.X\}$; and $V(k) = \emptyset$;

3 CI TEST WITH RELATIONAL DATA

We define the notion of relational variables followed by the notion of Relational Conditional Independence (RCI). We provide both a theoretical characterization of RCI as well as a practical approach to testing for RCI.

Consider attribute classes (attributes for short) X, Y, and Z of a relational schema. In the absence of any relational structure, the "data" corresponding to instantiations of these random variables in a dataset can be naturally indexed so that (x_i, y_i, z_i) denotes the ith instance drawn from P_{xyz}. However, in the relational setting, there is no such natural index. Hence, we can use a set of items of each item class to serve the role of an index. This indexing scheme generalizes the notion of the 'ith instance' in an i.i.d. setting to the notion of 'instantiated by item i' where $i \in \sigma(I)$ for some $I \in \mathbf{I}$. Note that different item classes provide different ways to index relational data.

Definition (Relational Variable)**.** Let $\mathcal{S} = \langle \mathbf{E}, \mathbf{R}, \mathbf{A} \rangle$ be a relational schema and $\sigma \in \Sigma_{\mathcal{S}}$ be an arbitrary relational skeleton. A *relational variable* V is a function from $\sigma(I)$ for some item class $I \in \mathbf{I}$ to a subset of $\{j.X \mid j \in \sigma(J)\}$ for some attribute class X and item class J such that $X \in \mathbf{A}(J)$:

$$V : \sigma(I) \mapsto 2^{\{j.X \mid j \in \sigma(J)\}}$$

where every $i \in \sigma(I)$ is connected to $j \in \sigma(J)$ such that $j.X \in V(i)$.

As a simple but concrete example, a relational variable V, 'smoking status of one's neighbors', is defined with

I, J both being the 'Person' item class, X corresponding to the attribute class 'smoking', where $j \in \sigma(J)$ where $j.X \in V(i)$ is i's neighbor for every person $i \in \sigma(I)$. Given a person Arthur who has two neighbors Sally and Sean, V (arthur) $= \{$sally.$Smoke$ sean.$Smoke\}$ results a 2-dimensional random variable. In Fig. 1, we illustrate another example of relational variables involving three entity classes.

Understanding an item attribute, e.g., $j.X$, as a random variable, $V(i)$ (or V_i for short) is a set of random variables. The 'value' of V_i is denoted by $v_i = (j.x)_{j.X \in V_i} \in \mathcal{X}^{|V_i|}$, indexed with item attributes in V_i. In the preceding example, $v_{\text{arthur}} = \{\text{sally} : False, \text{sean} : True\}$. Noting that a relational variable itself is *not* a random variable, we proceed to carefully define *relational conditional independence*. Without loss of generality, we consider the case where the conditioning is on a single relational variable although, in general, the conditioning can be on a set of relational variables.

Definition (Relational Conditional Independence). Let $\{U, V, W\}$ be relational variables with a common domain, $\sigma(I)$, defined on a relational schema $\mathcal{S}$ where $\sigma \in \Sigma_{\mathcal{S}}$. Let item attributes $\bigcup_{i \in \sigma(I)} U_i \cup V_i \cup W_i$ be random variables. Then, U and V are said to be independent to each other given W, denoted by $(U \perp\!\!\!\perp V \mid W)_\sigma$, if and only if

$$\forall_{i \in \sigma(I)} \mathsf{P}_{u_i v_i w_i} = \mathsf{P}_{u_i|w_i} \mathsf{P}_{v_i|w_i} \mathsf{P}_{w_i}.$$

It is easy to see that this definition of relational CI (RCI) generalizes traditional CI where i.i.d. samples are drawn from P_{xyz}. Let U be "smoking status of oneself" and W be "smoking status of one's parents", e.g., U (arthur) $= \{$arthur.$Smoke\}$. We might ask $(U \perp\!\!\!\perp V \mid W)_\sigma$: "Is one's smoking status independent of one's neighbors' smoking status given one's parents' smoking status?" While, in the real world, answering such question can be quite difficult because of the complexity and partial observability of interactions among people, the notion of relational CI, once operationalized, can help extract useful insights from relational data.

3.1 RELATIONAL VARIABLES AND PARAMETER TYING

In the relational setting, assuming that each item attribute of the same attribute class is identically distributed (e.g., sally.$Smoke \overset{d}{=}$ arthur.$Smoke$), would be tantamount to ignoring the relational structure of the data. On the other hand, if we were to let each item attribute share no commonality whatsoever with any other item attribute, checking for RCI becomes nearly impossible. Hence, we restrict our attention to the practically relevant setting where the item attributes of each attribute class share some commonality, e.g., the joint probability distribution of *all* item attributes can be modeled as a directed acyclic graph $\mathcal{G}$ of item attributes (Friedman et al., 1999) (n.b. $pa^{\mathcal{G}}$ and $an^{\mathcal{G}}$ denote values of parental and ancestral nodes in $\mathcal{G}$, respectively),

$$\mathsf{P}(\mathbf{v}) = \prod_{X \in \mathbf{A}} \prod_{i \in \sigma(\mathbf{A}^{-1}(X))} \mathsf{P}\left(i.x \mid pa^{\mathcal{G}}(i.X)\right)$$

where $\mathbf{v}$ represents values of all item attributes in σ. For every item of the same item class, e.g., $i, j \in \sigma(I)$, $\mathsf{P}(i.X \mid pa^{\mathcal{G}}(i.X)) = \mathsf{P}(j.X \mid pa^{\mathcal{G}}(j.X))$ is often assumed if $pa^{\mathcal{G}}(i.X)$ and $pa^{\mathcal{G}}(j.X)$ are matched under model-specific assumption, e.g., their averages are the same (Friedman et al., 1999) (i.e., the ratio of one's smoking neighbors to one's neighbors). This is called *parameter-tying* or *templating* (Koller, 1999) and is widely used in relational or temporal domains to capture time-invariant aspects of the domain. We relate parameter tying and item attributes to the homogeneity (in the sense of being identically distributed) and independence of random variables. Let $\mathcal{G} \cong_{i,j} \mathcal{G}'$ denote graph isomorphism between $\mathcal{G}$ and $\mathcal{G}'$ subject to the constraint that vertex $i \in \mathcal{G}$ must be matched to $j \in \mathcal{G}'$.

Proposition 1 (Identically Distributed Random Variables). *Let $\mathcal{G}$ be a directed acyclic graph representing a conditional independence structure of item attributes where each item attribute, e.g., $k.X$, is labeled with its attribute class, e.g., X. Given that the parameters are tied, random variables $i.X$ and $j.X$ in $\mathcal{G}$ are identically distributed if $\mathcal{G}\left[an^{\mathcal{G}}(i.X)\right] \cong_{i.X, j.X} \mathcal{G}\left[an^{\mathcal{G}}(j.X)\right]$.*

Proposition 2 (Independent Random Variables). *Two random variables $i.X$ and $j.X$ are independent if $\mathcal{G}\left[an^{\mathcal{G}}(i.X)\right] \cap \mathcal{G}\left[an^{\mathcal{G}}(j.X)\right] = \emptyset$.*

Proofs for both propositions directly follow from Markov condition that a random variable is independent of its non-descendants given its parents in a DAG $\mathcal{G}$. For an undirected graph $\mathcal{G}$ of item attributes (e.g, Markov random field) labeled as above, $\mathrm{CC}^{\mathcal{G}}_{i.X} \cong_{i.X, j.X} \mathrm{CC}^{\mathcal{G}}_{j.X}$ and $\mathrm{CC}^{\mathcal{G}}_{i.X} \neq \mathrm{CC}^{\mathcal{G}}_{j.X}$ would be a sufficient condition for $i.X, j.X \overset{\text{i.i.d.}}{\sim} \mathsf{P}$ for some distribution P under the parameter-tying assumption where graph isomorphic maximal cliques share the same parameters.

However, we have no access to the underlying CI structure $\mathcal{G}$ of *item attributes*. Hence, we deduce an i.i.d. condition through *items* on an observed skeleton σ:

Assumption 3. *Let $\mathcal{S} = \langle \mathbf{E}, \mathbf{R}, \mathbf{A} \rangle$ be a relational schema and σ be a relational skeleton of $\mathcal{S}$. Let i and j be items in σ and $X \in \mathbf{A}(I)$ of $I \in \mathbf{I}$. Then, random variables $i.X$ and $j.X$ are independent and identically distributed if*

$$(\mathrm{CC}^{\sigma}_{i} \cong_{i,j} \mathrm{CC}^{\sigma}_{j}) \wedge (\mathrm{CC}^{\sigma}_{i} \neq \mathrm{CC}^{\sigma}_{j})$$

Note that the condition is sufficient but not necessary for the random variables corresponding to the item attributes to be i.i.d. This is based on our understanding of how parameter-tying assumption is realized in a given relational structure and determines the qualitative aspects (i.e., homogeneity and independence) of the random variables corresponding to the item attributes.

3.2 HANDLING NON-I.I.D. VARIABLES

It is possible that a relational structure induces dependent and non-identically distributed (i.e., heterogeneous) item attributes even when parameter tying is assumed. Hence, we cannot simply apply a traditional CI test to test $(U \perp\!\!\!\perp V \mid W)_\sigma$ on the flattened version of relational data $\{(u_i, v_i, w_i)\}_{i \in \sigma(I)}$ where $\sigma(I)$ is the common domain of U, V, and W.

Our solution to this problem is to perform CI tests by decomposing, with respect to a given RCI query, the set of items $\sigma(I)$ into subsets of items such that each subset yields a set of i.i.d. observations under the above assumption. Consider a function $id : \sigma(I) \mapsto \mathbb{Z}$ such that for $id(i) = id(j)$ only if $(u_i, v_i, w_i) \overset{d}{=} (u_j, v_j, w_j)$ and $(u_i, v_i, w_i) \perp\!\!\!\perp (u_j, v_j, w_j)$ (i.e., $\mathrm{CC}_i^\sigma \cong_{i,j} \mathrm{CC}_j^\sigma$ and $\mathrm{CC}_i^\sigma \neq \mathrm{CC}_j^\sigma$ given that U, V, and W are *isomorphism-invariant*, see Appendix for definition). Then, a traditional CI test, treating U, V, and W as random variables,

$$U \perp\!\!\!\perp V \mid W, id$$

will remove bias introduced by the relational structure provided we have large enough samples per condition (i.e., a large number of CCs per isomorphic class). Such a naive solution, however, has severe limitations in practice: i) It is possible, in the worst case, that all items in relational data are connected and ii) Each connected component might be non-isomorphic to others.

4 A KERNEL RELATIONAL CI TEST

To address the limitations noted above, we will relax the requirements that the connected components be isomorphic and that items be partitioned into non-overlapping connected components. Recent progress in kernel-based nonparametric tests (e.g., two-sample tests or CI) allows us to utilize the notion of *closeness* between samples to test for homogeneity or conditional independence. We proceed to show how kernel-based conditional independence tests, originally introduced for testing independence of i.i.d. random variables from data, can be adapted to the relational setting, by defining a novel kernel function for relational variables.

4.1 KERNEL FOR RELATIONAL VARIABLES

We provide kernels for relational variables that reflect our understanding of relational structure as in Section 3.1. Consider a relational variable U, associated with the attribute class X. A kernel function for U, k_U, measures *similarity* between two instantiations of U where each instantiation, e.g., $u_i \in \mathcal{X}^{|U_i|}$, consists of a set of item attributes. We illustrate our approach using the R-convolution kernel (Haussler, 1999), which computes the kernel over two sets as the sum of kernel values for every pair of elements from two sets. Thus, we define k_U as

$$k_U\left(u_i, u_j; k_{\mathrm{IA}}^X\right) = \sum_{a.X \in U_i} \sum_{b.X \in U_j} k_{\mathrm{IA}}^X\left(a.X, b.X\right) \tag{1}$$

where the base kernel $k_{\mathrm{IA}}^X(a.X, b.X)$ measures the similarity between two item attributes. Based on the analysis in Section 3.1, U_i and U_j do not necessarily yield identically-distributed item attributes. Hence, we design $k_{\mathrm{IA}}^X(a.X, b.X)$ by taking both homogeneity and attribute values into consideration: k_{IA}^X is defined as a product kernel of the kernel for homogeneity k_σ and a kernel for attribute values k_x:

$$k_{\mathrm{IA}}^X(a.X, b.X) = k_\sigma(a, b)\, k_x(a.x, b.x)$$

where the kernel for attribute values is typically defined using a standard kernel for the data type, for example, a Gaussian RBF kernel if $\mathcal{X} \subseteq \mathbb{R}^d$. We elaborate the kernel for homogeneity k_σ below.

Kernel for Homogeneity (Among Item Attributes) We postulate that two random variables $a.X$ and $b.X$ will be *similarly distributed* if the corresponding items appear in *similar contexts* in σ, i.e., similarly interconnected neighbors in σ. Therefore, the degree to which two item attributes $a.X$ and $b.X$ are identically distributed can be approximated by the similarity of the context of *a* and the context of *b* in σ.

We use h-hop neighbors of an item in σ to induce a context of the item for practicality since a connected component, e.g., CC_a^σ, can be as large as the given relational skeleton σ. Thus, we design the kernel for homogeneity $k_\sigma(a, b)$ as a graph kernel between two labeled graphs $\sigma[ne_h^\sigma(a)]$ and $\sigma[ne_h^\sigma(b)]$ where $ne_h^\sigma(a)$ is a set of items in σ that are reachable in no more than h hops from item a in σ. Each item in a context, e.g., $\sigma[ne_h^\sigma(a)]$, is labeled with its item class except the item a, which is assigned to a special label allowing a graph kernel between $\sigma[ne_h^\sigma(a)]$ and $\sigma[ne_h^\sigma(b)]$ to match a and b. This reflects '$\approxeq_{i,j}$', graph isomorphism with an additional constraint (Assumption 3).

We choose to exploit an existing graph kernel for labeled graphs. For example a shortest-path kernel (Borgwardt and Kriegel, 2005) is given by

$k_{SP}(\mathcal{G}, \mathcal{G}') = \sum_{c,d \in \mathcal{V}} \sum_{c',d' \in \mathcal{V}'} k_n(c, c') \cdot k_n(d, d') \cdot k_l(d_{\mathcal{G}}(c,d), d_{\mathcal{G}'}(c', d'))$ with the choice of kernels on node (i.e., item) k_n and on shortest path length k_l where $d_{\mathcal{G}}(c,d)$ is a shortest path length between c and d in $\mathcal{G}$. We use the Dirac kernel for both k_n and k_l, that is, k_n is 1 if two items have the same label and 0, otherwise, and k_l is 1 if two lengths are the same and 0, otherwise.

Kernel for Homogeneity (Among Observations) The use of contexts does not supplant the role of the indicator id. Hence, we introduce a new variable G to play the role of id without dealing with dependent observations. With G, the question of RCI, $(U \perp\!\!\!\perp V \mid W)_\sigma$, becomes that of traditional CI, $U \perp\!\!\!\perp V \mid W, G$ and, similarly, an unconditional query $(U \perp\!\!\!\perp V)_\sigma$ becomes $U \perp\!\!\!\perp V \mid G$.

We have already seen the kernel for relational variable which considered both contexts and values. Taking the value part out from the definition of the kernel, we can get a kernel for homogeneity among observations. Since an observation consists of three (two if unconditional) relational variables, we use a product kernel. We define

$$k_G(i,j) = k_U(u_i, u_j; k_\sigma)\, k_V(v_i, v_j; k_\sigma)\, k_W(w_i, w_j; k_\sigma) \qquad (2)$$

Note that while we have used the R-convolution kernel for relational variables and the shortest-path kernel as our graph kernel to illustrate our idea, the approach can accommodate other kernels, e.g., the optimal assignment kernel (Kriege et al., 2016) for relational variables and a Weisfeiler-Lehman kernel (Shervashidze et al., 2011) for graphs. In practice, the choice of kernel can be guided by the knowledge of the domain.

4.2 TREATING DEPENDENT OBSERVATIONS

Now we briefly discuss how we can handle dependent observations. In relational data, the dependencies among observations can arise for different reasons. In previous section, we showed that two item attributes become dependent if they share the same ancestors (Proposition 2). However, in some settings, we can ignore some types of dependence among observations. For instance, consider a hidden Markov model with hidden variables X and observed variables Y where $X_{t-1} \perp\!\!\!\perp Y_t \mid X_t$ and $\mathsf{P}(Y_t \mid X_t)$ and $\mathsf{P}(X_t \mid X_{t-1})$ are time-invariant. Simply running a traditional CI test on a sample $\{(x_{t-1}, y_t, x_t)\}_{t=2}^n$ would likely result in the null hypothesis not being rejected in spite of correlations among observations, e.g., (X_{t-1}, Y_t, X_t) and $(X_{t-2}, Y_{t-1}, X_{t-1})$. Variables like X_t and X_{t-1} are naturally represented as (temporally) related variables, the dependencies among which can be broken by conditioning on an appropriate set of variables. In this regard, we treat 'dependent observations' to be resolved explicitly through conditionals instead of being implicitly removed, e.g., non-i.i.d. CI test for *autocorrelated* data (Flaxman et al., 2016).

Algorithm 1 KRCIT

Input: σ: relational data; U, V, W: relational variables of base item class I; k_U, k_V, k_W: kernels for U, V, W; k_σ: a kernel for subgraphs of items; CI: the base kernel-based CI test

$\Omega \leftarrow \{(u_i, v_i, w_i)\}_{i \in \sigma(I)}$, which is $(\mathbf{u}, \mathbf{v}, \mathbf{w})$
$k_G(\cdot,\cdot) \leftarrow k_U(\cdot,\cdot; k_\sigma) k_V(\cdot,\cdot; k_\sigma) k_W(\cdot,\cdot; k_\sigma)$
$\mathbf{K}_u, \mathbf{K}_v, \mathbf{K}_w \leftarrow$kernel matrices for $\mathbf{u}$, $\mathbf{v}$, and $\mathbf{w}$.
$\mathbf{K}_g \leftarrow$kernel matrix for $(\mathbf{u}, \mathbf{v}, \mathbf{w})$ with k_G
$\mathbf{K}_{wg} \leftarrow \mathbf{K}_w \odot \mathbf{K}_g$
return CI $(\mathbf{K}_u, \mathbf{K}_v, \mathbf{K}_{wg})$

4.3 VALIDITY OF FLATTENING APPROACH

We provide a sufficient condition under which a flattened sample of relational data conditioned on G correctly transforms the question of an RCI query $(U \perp\!\!\!\perp V \mid W)_\sigma$ to a traditional CI query $U \perp\!\!\!\perp V \mid W, G$. We consider the alternative hypothesis $(U \not\perp\!\!\!\perp V \mid W)_\sigma$ to satisfy $\forall_{i \in \sigma(I)} U_i \not\perp\!\!\!\perp V_i \mid W_i$ instead of just $\exists_{i \in \sigma(I)} U_i \not\perp\!\!\!\perp V_i \mid W_i$.

Condition 4. $U_i, V_i \perp\!\!\!\perp U_j, V_j \mid W_i$ and $(w_i, g_i = w_j, g_j) \rightarrow (U_i, V_i) \overset{d}{=} (U_j, V_j)$ for every $i \neq j \in \sigma(I)$.

This condition simply makes a set of (U, V) samples into a set of i.i.d. samples where either $U \perp\!\!\!\perp V$ or $U \not\perp\!\!\!\perp V$ holds for each condition. In addition to the first condition, we provide a relaxed sufficient condition only for the null hypothesis.

Condition 5. $V_i \perp\!\!\!\perp V_j \mid W_i$ and $(w_i, g_i = w_j, g_j) \rightarrow V_i \overset{d}{=} V_j$ for every $i \neq j \in \sigma(I)$.

This condition only makes V i.i.d. for each condition. However, it is sufficient to observe $U \perp\!\!\!\perp V$ if $\forall_{i \in \sigma(I)} U_i \perp\!\!\!\perp V_i \mid W_i$. Otherwise, $U \not\perp\!\!\!\perp V \mid W, G$ will hold in *most cases* unless the aggregation of (U_i, V_i) per condition makes such dependence vanish.

4.4 ALGORITHM

By supplying customized kernels for U, V, W, and G (Equation 1 and 2), a kernel CI test in an i.i.d. setting will decide whether to accept or reject the null hypothesis given a flattened sample Ω. We illustrate the pseudocode of the kernel relational conditional independence test, KRCIT, in Algorithm 1. If the given query is unconditional such that W is undefined, then $\mathbf{K}_w = 1$.

We considered the following two kernel-based conditional independence tests as a base CI test for KRCIT:

Kernel CI Test (KCIT, Zhang et al., 2011) which uses the norm of conditional cross-covariance operator in RKHS (reproducing kernel Hilbert space); and Self-Discrepancy CI Test (SDCIT, Lee and Honavar, 2017) which uses RKHS distance between the given sample representing P_{xyz} and the sample modified to mimic $\mathsf{P}_{x|z}\mathsf{P}_{y|z}\mathsf{P}_z$. The time complexity of KRCIT will depend not only on the size of flattened sample but also the cardinality of relational variables, and the size of subgraphs (i.e., hops), etc. If the cardinality of relational variables and the number of hops used to specify contexts are fixed to small constants, computing kernel matrices requires $O\left(n^2\right)$ time where n is the size of flattened sample. Then, the time complexity of KRCIT with KCIT as a base CI test is $O\left(n^3\right)$ since that of KCIT is $O\left(n^3\right)$.

5 EMPIRICAL EVALUATION

We report results of experiments that examine the performance of KRCIT in testing RCI on relational data using synthetic relational data where we know the ground truth RCI. We used RCM (Maier et al., 2013; Lee and Honavar, 2016), which is a generative model for relational data where a set of assumed causal relationships among relational variables specifies how values of item attributes are generated given a relational skeleton.

5.1 METHODS

We compare the performance of KRCIT, traditional CI tests that do not account for the relational structure of the data, and an alternative RCI test that makes use of context using residualization (Flaxman et al., 2016) where regression is used to remove dependence of a variable on a set of conditionals. For example, assume that one wants to test $X \perp\!\!\!\perp Y$ where X and Y are two time series. By regressing each X and Y on time T, one can obtain $\epsilon_{x|t} = X - \hat{E}\left[X|T\right]$ and $\epsilon_{y|t} = Y - \hat{E}\left[Y|T\right]$. Then, the test becomes $\epsilon_{x|t} \perp\!\!\!\perp \epsilon_{y|t}$ under a set of assumptions. In the case of RCI, one can residualize values in the given relational skeleton to remove dependence on the 'context' of each attribute value. Formally, let $X, Z \in \mathbb{R}^m$ be two random variables where we seek for $\epsilon_{x|z}$ such that $X = f\left(Z\right) + \epsilon_{x|z}$. We can train a Gaussian process regression, i.e., $f \sim \mathcal{GP}\left(0, k\right)$, by maximizing total marginal likelihood. Then, $\epsilon_{x|z} = X - \hat{X} = \left(I + \sigma^{-2}\mathbf{K}_z^*\right)^{-1} X$. Both $\mathbf{K}_z^*$ and σ^2 are learned through Gaussian process regression employing, e.g., a Gaussian RBF kernel and a white noise kernel.

Assume that we only have access to kernel matrices $\mathbf{K}_x$ and $\mathbf{K}_z$. Following Zhang et al. (2011), we can use the empirical kernel map for $\mathbf{x}$, $\psi_x = \mathrm{V}\Lambda^{\frac{1}{2}}$, where V and Λ are obtained through the eigendecomposition of the kernel matrix $\mathbf{K}_x = \mathrm{V}^\top\Lambda\mathrm{V}$. Similarly, we can obtain ψ_z. Then, a Gaussian process regression with a linear kernel and a white noise kernel can be used to learn $\mathbf{K}_z^*$. In this case, we focus on the kernel matrix for residuals given by $\mathbf{K}_{x|z} = \mathbf{R}\mathbf{K}_x\mathbf{R}$ where $\mathbf{R} = \left(I + \sigma^{-2}\mathbf{K}_z^*\right)^{-1}$. Following Flaxman et al. (2016), we use the expectation of $\mathbf{K}_{x|z}$, which is given by $\mathbf{K}_z^*\mathbf{R} + \mathbf{R}\mathbf{K}_x\mathbf{R}$.

We list methods to be compared in our experiments. **(Naive)**: We use Hilbert-Schmidt Independence Criterion (HSIC, Gretton et al., 2005) for unconditional cases which uses the eigenspectrum of covariance operators in RKHS. Otherwise, either KCIT or SDCIT is used. **(Residualized)**: We residualize values of a given relational skeleton based on contexts (i.e., replace values to its residuals). Then, aforementioned naive tests are used. We append a prefix 'R-' to denote 'residualized'. **(Residual Kernel)**: Residuals are computed in RKHSs and the kernel for residuals is obtained as described above. Then, naive tests are used where computing kernel for two values (e.g., an RBF kernel) is replaced by looking up the residual kernel matrix. We append a prefix 'RK-'. **(KRCIT)**: We use a postfix '-K' or '-SD' to denote KRCIT with KCIT or with SDCIT, respectively.

We implemented KRCIT and other kernel CI tests in Python.[1] Throughout experiments, we considered real-valued attributes and an RBF kernel, e.g., $k_x\left(x', x''\right) = \exp\left(-\gamma_x\|x' - x''\|^2\right)$, is used for each attribute where $\gamma_\cdot$ is chosen as $\left(2\sigma^2\right)^{-1}$ where $\sigma^2 = 0.1^2$ is the variance of Gaussian noise we used in data generating processes. Additionally, we normalized both R-convolution kernel and shortest-path kernel, i.e., $k'\left(a,b\right) = k\left(a,b\right)/\sqrt{k\left(a,a\right)k\left(b,b\right)}$. We report how correctly null hypothesis is rejected by a given test (power) measured by Area Under Power Curve (AUPC), which is area under cumulative density function of p-values, and how incorrectly null hypothesis is rejected measured by type-I error rates given $\alpha = 0.05$.

5.2 A SIMPLE EXAMPLE FOR VISUALIZATION

We start with a simple example that explains how and why KRCIT is better for relational CI testing than standard CI tests that assume i.i.d. data. For the sake of readability, we omit unnecessary details (detailed descriptions are provided in Appendix). We considered a relational schema where attribute class X and Y associates with entity class 'circle' and 'square', respectively. There are other item classes and attribute classes in the schema. A relational skeleton σ consists of CCs of four differ-

[1]Codes are available online at https://github.com/sanghack81/KRCIT and https://github.com/sanghack81/SDCIT.

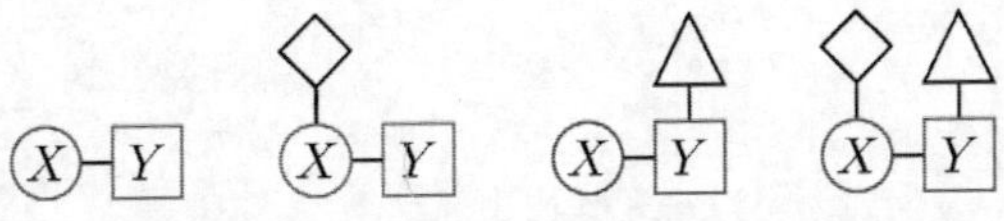

Figure 2: Four connected components composing a relational skeleton.

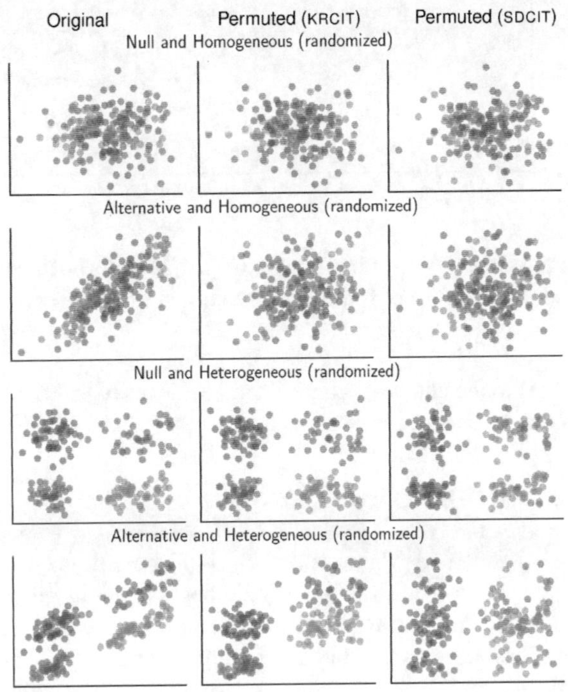

Figure 3: Comparisons of the given data (**left**) and two samples under the null hypothesis using KRCIT with SDCIT (**center**) and by SDCIT (**right**), respectively, with randomized relationships

ent structures as shown in Fig. 2. We designed a generative model such that X is a function of the value in an adjacent 'rhombus' item and Y is a function of X in an adjacent circle and the value in an adjacent 'triangle' item. That is, we make sure that $i.X$ and $j.X$ are not identically-distributed if i is adjacent to a rhombus item while j is not. The same idea also applies to Ys.

We controlled *randomness* of relationships between circles and squares: non-random relationship represents that a resulting relational skeleton consists only circles adjacent to a rhombus are connected to squares adjacent to a triangle (1st and 4th components in Fig. 2) while randomized relationship exhibits a relational skeleton where all four components are balanced. We also controlled *heterogeneity*: the extent to which distributions of (X, Y) of different components diverges from each other.

In the **left** column of Fig. 3, we visualize four relational data based on the combinations of underlying hypothe-

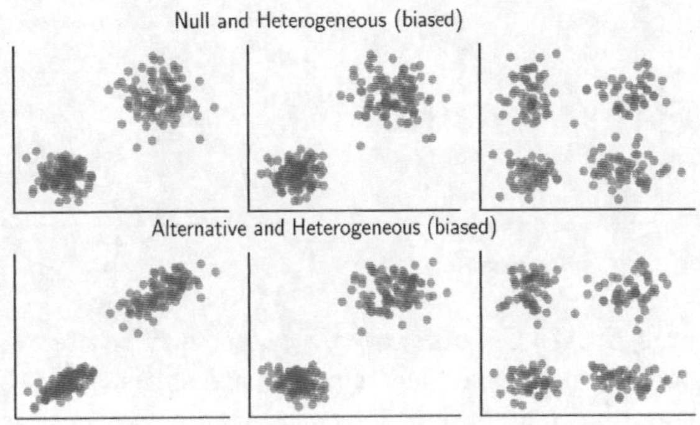

Figure 4: Comparisons with fully biased relationship

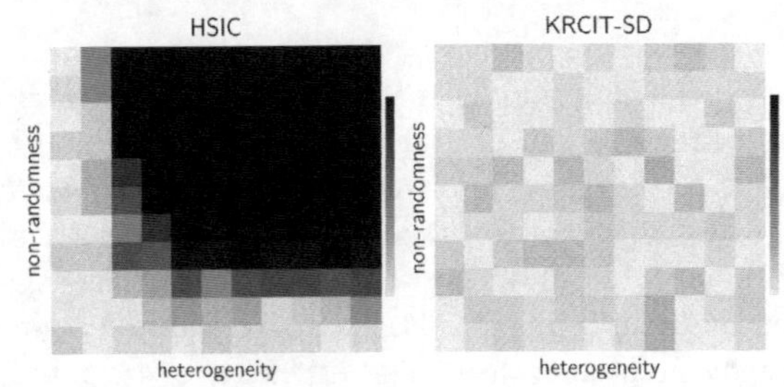

Figure 5: Type-I errors (with 20 trials) varying both non-randomness and heterogeneity

sis and heterogeneity where color codes correspond to the types of structure which associates with the value (x, y) in Fig. 2. Utilizing *permuted* samples, we visualize how KRCIT (with SDCIT) and SDCIT, which is a permutation-based test, produce data consistent with the null hypothesis. KRCIT permutes Ys conditioning on G, which corresponds to 'color', while SDCIT simply shuffles Ys. The **center** and **right** columns correspond to the permuted sample under KRCIT and a naive test, respectively. When contexts more strongly correlate with values, we can more clearly observe the difference between the permuted samples by KRCIT and by SDCIT.

For each row, if the **center** plot is significantly different from its corresponding **left** plot, KRCIT would reject the null hypothesis. For example, KRCIT correctly rejects the null hypothesis for the samples from the alternative hypothesis (row **2nd** and **4th**). Interestingly, SDCIT also correctly rejects samples from the alternative hypothesis. In Fig. 4, we plot null samples when relational skeletons exhibit biased relationships. We can similarly observe difference between two tests. Fig. 5 illustrates type-I errors (given $\alpha = 0.05$) of a naive test (HSIC) and KRCIT-SD based on relational skeletons generated with various degrees of heterogeneity and non-randomness of relationship. KRCIT-SD is robust to heterogeneity and non-random relationships while HSIC is not. Note that residualization approaches utilizing contexts perform similar

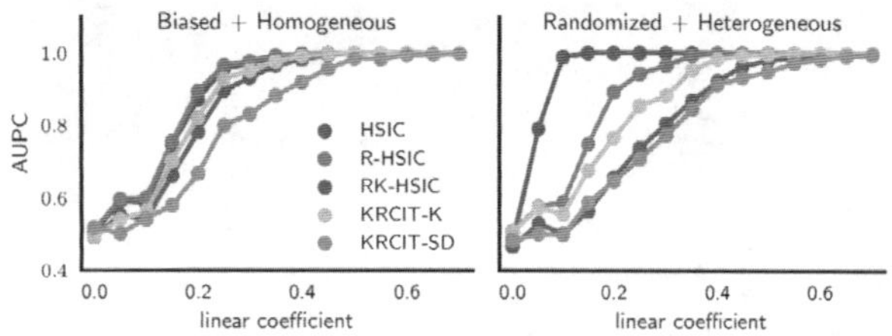

Figure 6: AUPCs with varying dependency where relational skeletons are generated with homogeneous and randomized relationships (**left**) and with heterogeneous and biased relationships (**right**).

to KRCIT (see Appendix).

Finally, we illustrate the changes of power of different tests as the strength of dependency between X and Y is increased (Fig. 6). Tests that use contexts *consistently* estimates dependency without regard to the underlying conditions while HSIC over-rejects samples from weak dependence in certain conditions where rejection comes partially from other than linear dependence (**4th** row in Fig. 3). In summary, whenever contexts provide sufficient information to infer (non-)identically distributed observations, KRCIT is able to eliminate suspicious dependencies due to such heterogeneity.

5.3 MORE COMPLICATED STRUCTURES

We conduct a similar experiment but with more complicated and larger structures where the cardinality of relational variables is not one and observations are dependent. Such dependence among observations, e.g., two circles, is due to their sharing a *common cause,* e.g., a rhombus. In this experiment, we additionally investigate how different sizes of subgraphs as contexts affect the performance of RCI tests. Contexts based on 1-hop subgraphs contain sufficient information while 2-hop subgraphs will include information about other variable, e.g., a 2-hop subgraph of a circle includes triangle and other circles connected to common rhombuses.

For tests for the null hypothesis, we obtained similar results as in the previous section. However, the kernel-based residualization approach (RK-HSIC) shows higher type-I errors than expected when larger contexts are employed (see Appendix). KRCIT performed as desired even with larger contexts. For tests for alternative hypothesis, we report AUPC in Fig. 7. With properly-sized contexts (hop=1), both residualization-based methods perform well. However, they are sensitive to the choice of contexts – the power of both R-HSIC and RK-HSIC drops. Both these KRCIT methods are relatively weaker than any other tests when dependence between relational variables is not strong enough. However, KRCIT with SDCIT seems

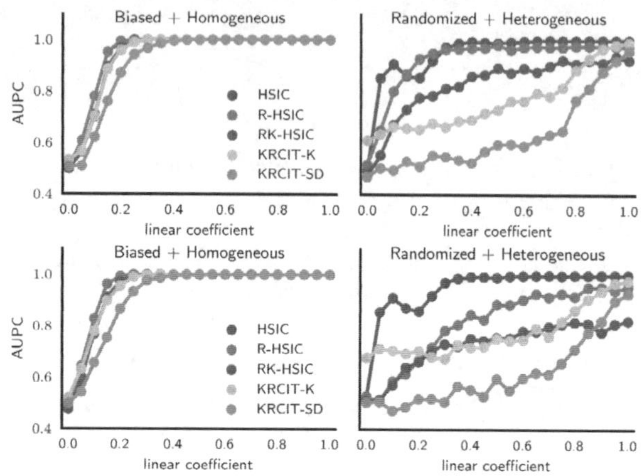

Figure 7: AUPCs with hop=1 (**top**) and hop=2 (**bottom**) under two different settings for relational skeletons

robust to the choice of contexts and achieves high AUPC as the dependence increases.

5.4 CONDITIONAL TESTS

We investigated whether KRCIT would be able to discover the causal structure of synthetic relational data generated from an RCM. Thus, we focus on testing 1) relational version of Markov condition, which is essential to learn the undirected causal structure, and 2) conditional dependence, which is critical to infer the orientation of undirected causal relationships. We constructed a set of relational skeletons of 3 entity classes and 3 relationship classes between every pair of entity classes. We controlled for the maximum number of neighbors of the same item class of an item (e.g., a circle item can have at most three square neighbors) and the number of entities per entity class. We generate relational skeletons to exhibit correlation among different relationships (see Appendix for details). Then, values are generated based on two hypotheses. For the null hypothesis, we generate values, roughly, in a causal order $X \rightarrow Z \rightarrow Y$ or $X \leftarrow Z \rightarrow Y$. For the alternative hypothesis, a relational data is generated based on a causal order $X \rightarrow Z \leftarrow Y$. We test $(U \perp\!\!\!\perp V \mid W)_\sigma$ where U, V, and W associates with X, Y, and Z, respectively.

In Fig. 8, we plot AUPCs and type-I error rates under different sizes of flattened sample, maximum cardinalities of relationships, and the sizes of contexts in terms of hops. The **left** plots demonstrate that the power of all tests increases as larger sample is used (with max 3 relationships and hop 1). However, KRCIT with KCIT as a base CI test suffers high type-I error rates. The **center** plots depict the negative effect of more complex structure on both power and type-I errors. This implies the general

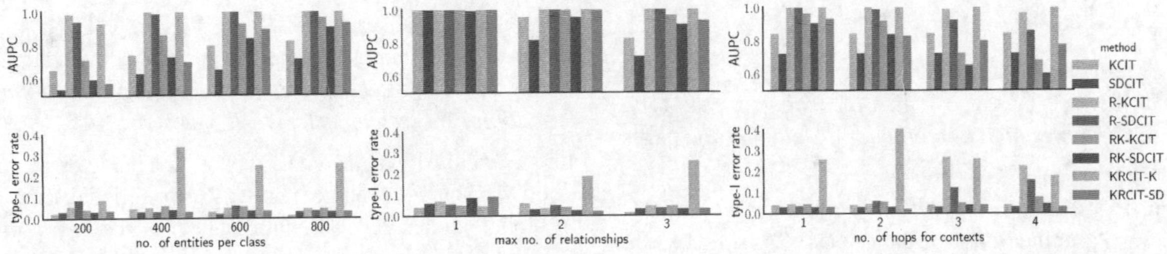

Figure 8: AUPCs and type-I error rates of various tests with relational skeletons generated with different settings and tests employed different size of subgraphs as contexts.

approach to handling multiple values (i.e., using an R-convolution kernel) should properly modified when large relationships are involved (e.g., friends). Unlike previous experiments with unconditional RCI tests, it is surprising to observe that the power of naive tests decreases as underlying structure is more complex. Finally, contexts larger than *necessary* makes some tests weaker and less-calibrated (**right** plots). However, we observed that contexts with hop set to 4 are similar to each other. That is, the kernel matrix obtained by applying shortest-path kernel on contexts contains similar values and can not clearly inform heterogeneity among random variables.

Overall, the naive tests that do not account for relational structure performed well for the null hypothesis yielding type-I error rate around 0.05 since, in our generative model, Z 'values' provide all the necessary information to infer Y. However, they showed weak power compared to others in general. Both residualization approaches perform very well when proper contexts are employed. KRCIT performs very differently depending on the choice of base CI test. KCIT, which also uses residualization as an internal mechanism to handle conditionals, seems to have problems dealing with G, a conditioning variable playing a role of id. KRCIT with SDCIT is, in general, a good choice since it provides a reasonable power with a precise control of type-I error rates.

6 DISCUSSION

Maier et al. (2013) considered relational d-separation, a problem closely related to RCI. However, they relied on a traditional CI test by simply flattening and aggregating relational data (i.e., average) without incorporating structural information. As we have shown, such an approach biases the results of independence tests (Section 5.2). An independence test on two non-i.i.d. data sets is addressed by Zhang et al. (2009), who considered generalizing HSIC to the setting of structured and interdependent observations. However, their work focused on explicitly known CI structures which can be represented as undirected graphical models utilizing factorization provided by the exponential family.

In this paper, we have defined CI in the relational setting and provided an effective approach to testing for RCI. Our definition makes use of a definition of a relational variable that subsumes the notions of *slot chains* in probabilistic relational models (Friedman et al., 1999), *relational path* in relational causal models with *bridge burning semantics* (Maier et al., 2013) and *path semantics* (Lee and Honavar, 2016), and *first order expression* in DAPER (Heckerman et al., 2007).

7 SUMMARY AND FUTURE WORK

In this work, we defined relational conditional independence (RCI), the generalization of CI to a relational setting with the language of Entity-Relationship model. We proposed kernel RCI test (KRCIT), a first practical and general design of RCI test which reduces bias caused by an underlying relational structure. We empirically demonstrated benefits of KRCIT compared to naive CI tests on simulated relational data.

Some directions for future work include: improving KRCIT by employing appropriately designed graph kernels and optimizing the kernel parameters; a more comprehensive experimental study of KRCIT using real-world relational data; investigating a way to incorporate network analysis before performing RCI test to guide the design of kernels; and applying RCI to discover causal relationships in relational domains (Maier et al., 2013; Lee and Honavar, 2016).

Acknowledgements

The authors are grateful to UAI 2017 anonymous reviewers for their thorough reviews. This research was supported by the Edward Frymoyer Endowed Professorship, the Center for Big Data Analytics and Discovery Informatics at the Pennsylvania State University, and the Sudha Murty Distinguished Visiting Chair in Neurocomputing and Data Science at the Indian Institute of Science.

References

Borgwardt, K. M. and Kriegel, H.-P. (2005). Shortest-path kernels on graphs. In *Proceedings of the Fifth IEEE International Conference on Data Mining*, pages 74–81.

Chen, P. P.-S. (1976). The entity-relationship model – toward a unified view of data. *ACM Transactions on Database Systems*, 1(1):9–36.

Chwialkowski, K., Sejdinovic, D., and Gretton, A. (2014). A Wild Bootstrap for Degenerate Kernel Tests. In *Advances in Neural Information Processing Systems 27*, pages 3608–3616.

Dawid, A. P. (1979). Conditional Independence in Statistical Theory. *Journal of the Royal Statistical Society. Series B (Methodological)*, 41(1):1–31.

Doran, G., Muandet, K., Zhang, K., and Schölkopf, B. (2014). A Permutation-Based Kernel Conditional Independence Test. In *Proceedings of the Thirtieth Conference on Uncertainty in Artificial Intelligence*, pages 132–141.

Flaxman, S. R., Neill, D. B., and Smola, A. J. (2016). Gaussian Processes for Independence Tests with Non-iid Data in Causal Inference. *ACM Transactions on Intelligent Systems and Technology*, 7(2):1–23.

Friedman, N., Getoor, L., Koller, D., and Pfeffer, A. (1999). Learning Probabilistic Relational Models. In *Proceedings of the Sixteenth International Joint Conference on Artificial Intelligence*, pages 1300–1309.

Fukumizu, K., Gretton, A., Sun, X., and Schölkopf, B. (2008). Kernel Measures of Conditional Dependence. In *Advances in Neural Information Processing Systems 20*, pages 489–496.

Gretton, A., Bousquet, O., Smola, A., and Schölkopf, B. (2005). Measuring Statistical Dependence with Hilbert-Schmidt Norms. In *Algorithmic Learning Theory. ALT 2005*, pages 63–77.

Haussler, D. (1999). Convolution Kernels on Discrete Structures. Technical report, University of California, Santa Cruz.

Heckerman, D., Meek, C., and Koller, D. (2007). Probabilistic Entity-Relationship Models, PRMs, and Plate Models. In Getoor, L. and Taskar, B., editors, *Introduction to Statistical Relational Learning*, pages 201–238.

Koller, D. (1999). Probabilistic Relational Models. In *Proceedings of the 9th International Workshop on Inductive Logic Programming*, pages 3–13.

Koller, D. and Friedman, N. (2009). *Probabilistic Graphical Models: Principles and Techniques*. MIT Press.

Kriege, N. M., Giscard, P.-L., and Wilson, R. C. (2016). On valid optimal assignment kernels and applications to graph classification. In *Advances in Neural Information Processing Systems 29*, pages 1623–1631.

Lee, S. and Honavar, V. (2016). A Characterization of Markov Equivalence Classes of Relational Causal Models under Path Semantics. In *Proceedings of the 32nd Conference on Uncertainty in Artificial Intelligence*, pages 387–396.

Lee, S. and Honavar, V. (2017). Self-Discrepancy Conditional Independence Test. In *Proceedings of the 33rd Conference on Uncertainty in Artificial Intelligence*. (to appear).

Maier, M., Marazopoulou, K., Arbour, D., and Jensen, D. (2013). A Sound and Complete Algorithm for Learning Causal Models from Relational Data. In *Proceedings of the Twenty-Ninth Conference on Uncertainty in Artificial Intelligence*, pages 371–380.

Pearl, J. (2000). *Causality: Models, Reasoning, and Inference*. Cambridge University Press, 2nd edition.

Shervashidze, N., Schweitzer, P., van Leeuwen, E. J., Mehlhorn, K., and Borgwardt, K. M. (2011). Weisfeiler-Lehman graph kernels. *Journal of Machine Learning Research*, 12:2539–2561.

Spirtes, P., Glymour, C. N., and Scheines, R. (2000). *Causation, Prediction, and Search*. MIT Press, 2nd edition.

Zhang, K., Peters, J., Janzing, D., and Schölkopf, B. (2011). Kernel-based Conditional Independence Test and Application in Causal Discovery. In *Proceedings of the Twenty-Seventh Conference on Uncertainty in Artificial Intelligence*, pages 804–813.

Zhang, X., Song, L., Gretton, A., and Smola, A. (2009). Kernel Measures of Independence for non-iid Data. In *Advances in Neural Information Processing Systems 21*, pages 1937–1944.

A ISOMORPHISM-INVARIANT RELATIONAL VARIABLE

We describe a desired property of a relational variable. This property ensures that the interpretation of relational variable is consistent across graph isomorphic connected components of any relational skeleton $\sigma \in \Sigma_{\mathcal{S}}$. Let $\mathcal{S} = \langle \mathbf{E}, \mathbf{R}, \mathbf{A} \rangle$ be a relational schema and $\sigma \in \Sigma_{\mathcal{S}}$ be an arbitrary instantiation of the schema. Let $\mathrm{CC}_a^\sigma = \langle \mathcal{V}_a, \mathcal{E}_a, \mathcal{L}_a \rangle$ and $\mathrm{CC}_b^\sigma = \langle \mathcal{V}_b, \mathcal{E}_b, \mathcal{L}_b \rangle$ where each item is labeled with its item class. Let $\mathbf{f}_{a,b}^\sigma$ be a set of mapping functions demonstrating $\mathrm{CC}_a^\sigma \cong_{a,b} \mathrm{CC}_b^\sigma$, that is, $\mathbf{f}_{a,b}^\sigma = \{f \mid \forall_{v \in \mathcal{V}_a} \mathcal{L}_a(v) = \mathcal{L}_b(f(v)) \wedge \forall_{u,v \in \mathcal{V}_a} (u,v) \in \mathcal{E}_a \Leftrightarrow (f(u), f(v)) \in \mathcal{E}_b \wedge f(a) = b\}$. Let U be a relational variable with domain $\sigma(I)$ where $I \in \mathbf{E} \cup \mathbf{R}$. If

$$\forall_{f \in \mathbf{f}_{a,b}^\sigma} \{f(i) \mid i.X \in U_a\} = \{j \mid j.X \in U_{f(a)}\}$$

for any $a, b \in \sigma(I)$ for any $\sigma \in \Sigma_{\mathcal{S}}$, then, U is said to be *isomorphism-invariant.*

B EXPERIMENTAL SETUP

We describe experimental settings with the language of relational causal model (Maier et al., 2013). For simplicity, we represent a relational skeleton as an undirected graph of entities. Hence, $(a, b) \in \sigma$ represents that two entities a and b are, in fact, connected to a common relationship item in the relational skeleton σ.

B.1 SIMPLE EXPERIMENTS

Relational Schema There are four entity classes A, B, C, and D where each associates with attribute class X, Y, S, and T, respectively. There are three relationship classes between A and B, A and C, and B and D. We used circle, square, rhombus, and triangle to refer A, B, C, and D.

Relational Skeleton We generate relational skeletons varying degrees of randomness from 0 to 1 where randomness of 0 is referred to as 'biased'. Given randomness $0 \leq p \leq 1$, we initially generate a fully biased relational skeleton σ, then randomize some of edges between $\sigma(A)$ and $\sigma(B)$ to acquire a relational skeleton of desired randomness p.

Let n be the number of entities for each of A and B (we set $n = 200$). There are $n/2$ entities for C and D, respectively. Hence, let $\sigma(A) = \{a_i\}_{i=1}^n$, $\sigma(B) = \{b_i\}_{i=1}^n$, $\sigma(C) = \{c_i\}_{i=1}^{n/2}$, and $\sigma(D) = \{d_i\}_{i=1}^{n/2}$. We connect C items to A items and D items to B items, $\{(a_i, c_i)\}_{i=1}^{n/2} \subset \sigma$ and $\{(b_i, d_i)\}_{i=1}^{n/2} \subset \sigma$. Then, we "initially" connect a_i and b_i, $\{(a_i, b_i)\}_{i=1}^n \subset \sigma$. That is, by design, an A item having (or not having) a C neighbor is connected to a B item having (or not having) a D neighbor. Given the randomness p, we randomly pick np B items and shuffle their A neighbors.

Relational Causal Model We use a linear Gaussian noise model with sum aggregators as follows:

$$\begin{aligned}
&\forall_{c \in \sigma(C)} \quad c.S = \mu + \epsilon_c \\
&\forall_{d \in \sigma(D)} \quad d.T = \mu + \epsilon_d \\
&\forall_{a \in \sigma(A)} \quad a.X = \sum_{c \in ne^\sigma(a) \cap \sigma(C)} c.S + \mu + \epsilon_a \\
&\forall_{b \in \sigma(B)} \quad b.Y = \sum_{a \in ne^\sigma(b) \cap \sigma(A)} \beta \cdot a.X + \\
&\qquad \sum_{d \in ne(b;\sigma) \cap \sigma(D)} d.T + \mu + \epsilon_b
\end{aligned}$$

where every ϵ is an independent Gaussian noise with zero mean and variance 0.1^2. We control the correlation between connected X and Y by adjusting β where $\beta = 0$ implies that X and Y are independently generated, or more precisely, $[A].X$ and $[A, R_{AB}, B].Y$ are independent. The pair of X and Y values generated from this model can be understood as a mixture of four bivariate normal distributions and μ controls the distance between distributions. When $\mu = 0$, all four distributions are centered at $(0, 0)$. Although, we described four distributions having the same mean as 'homogeneous', they have different variances.

We test unconditional independence between $[A].X$ and $[A, R_{AB}, B].Y$.

B.2 MORE COMPLICATED EXPERIMENTS

We only change how skeletons are generated. We use the same relational schema and relational causal model as shown above.

Relational Skeleton Similarly, we generate $n = 400$ items for A and B and $n/2$ items for C and D. Then, each $a_i \in \sigma(A)$ randomly chooses C neighbor(s) so that a_i has one C neighbor if $1 \leq i \leq \frac{n}{3}$, two neighbors if $\frac{n}{3} < i \leq \frac{2n}{3}$, and three neighbors if $\frac{2n}{3} < i \leq n$. Similarly, each $b_i \in \sigma(B)$ randomly chooses D neighbor(s). As shown in the previous setup, we initialize relational skeleton with biased relationships between A and B, that is, $\{(a_i, b_i)\}_{i=1}^n \subset \sigma$. Then, we randomize the connection based on randomness parameter. We further add n random connections between $\sigma(A)$ and $\sigma(B)$.

This setup yields more complicated structure than the previous setup since each of $\{a.X\}_{a \in \sigma(A)}$ and

$\{b.Y\}_{b\in\sigma(B)}$ is made of dependent observations and A and B are in many-to-many relationships.

B.3 CONDITIONAL TESTS

Relational Schema We have three entity classes A, B, and C, which associates with X, Y, and Z, respectively. There are binary relationship classes for each pair of entity classes, i.e., R_{AB}, R_{AC}, and R_{BC}. All cardinalities are '*many*', hence an entity can have *many* neighbors of the other entity class.

Relational Skeleton We control the maximum number of neighbors of the same kind. For example, an item of A can have at most k neighbors of B. In other words, $\forall_{a_i\in\sigma(A)} |ne^\sigma(a_i)\cap\sigma(B)| \leq k$. We similarly put restrictions between B and C and between A and C, as well.

We construct relational skeletons where relationships of all three classes (R_{AB}, R_{BC}, and R_{AC}) are correlated. To do so, we adopt the idea of latent space modeling. Given n, the number of entities per entity class, we generate n points in $[0,1]^2 \subset \mathbb{R}^2$ for each entity class. Let $\phi(\cdot)$ be the coordinate of an item. Let $\mathbf{D}^{AB}$ be a squared Euclidean distance where $\left(\mathbf{D}^{AB}\right)_{i,j} = \|\phi(a_i) - \phi(b_i)\|_2^2$. Then, a kernel matrix $\mathbf{K}^{AB}$ is $\left(\mathbf{K}^{AB}\right)_{i,j} = \exp\left(-\gamma\cdot\left(\mathbf{D}^{AB}\right)_{i,j}\right)$ where we chose $\gamma = 50$. By normalization, we get a probability matrix $\mathbf{P}^{AB} = \frac{\mathbf{K}^{AB}}{(\mathbf{1}^\top\cdot\mathbf{K}^{AB}\cdot\mathbf{1})}$ to (approximately) model $\Pr((a_i,b_j)\in\sigma) \propto 2\left(\mathbf{P}^{AB}\right)_{i,j}$. With this probability, we sample $nk/2$ edges to form a relational skeleton while satisfying maximum number of neighbors k. For example, if we limit an item of A can have three neighbors of B, then, there are, on average, 1.5 B neighbors for an item of A. Edges between A and C and between B and C are similarly obtained.

Relational Causal Model We consider three different models: two for conditional independence and one for conditional dependence. For testing null hypothesis, we randomly choose one of following two models:

$$\begin{aligned}
&\forall_{a\in\sigma(A)} \quad a.X = \mu + \epsilon_a \\
&\forall_{c\in\sigma(C)} \quad c.Z = \sum_{a\in ne^\sigma(c)\cap\sigma(A)} a.X + \mu + \epsilon_c \\
&\forall_{b\in\sigma(B)} \quad b.Y = \sum_{c\in ne^\sigma(b)\cap\sigma(C)} c.Z + \mu + \epsilon_b
\end{aligned}$$

and

$$\begin{aligned}
&\forall_{c\in\sigma(C)} \quad c.Z = \mu + \epsilon_c \\
&\forall_{a\in\sigma(A)} \quad a.X = \sum_{c\in ne^\sigma(a)\cap\sigma(C)} c.Z + \mu + \epsilon_a \\
&\forall_{b\in\sigma(B)} \quad b.Y = \sum_{c\in ne^\sigma(b)\cap\sigma(C)} c.Z + \mu + \epsilon_b.
\end{aligned}$$

For testing alternative hypothesis, we use the following model where (roughly speaking) Z is a common effect of X and Y,

$$\begin{aligned}
&\forall_{a\in\sigma(A)} \quad a.X = \mu + \epsilon_a \\
&\forall_{b\in\sigma(B)} \quad b.Y = \mu + \epsilon_b \\
&\forall_{c\in\sigma(C)} \quad c.Z = \sum_{a\in ne^\sigma(c)\cap\sigma(A)} a.X + \\
&\qquad\qquad \sum_{b\in ne^\sigma(c)\cap\sigma(B)} b.Y + \mu + \epsilon_c.
\end{aligned}$$

In all experiments, we set $\mu = 0.3$. We test

$$[B].Y \perp\!\!\!\perp [B, R_{AB}, A].X \mid [B, R_{BC}, C].Z$$

for the null hypothesis and test

$$[C, R_{AC}, A].X \perp\!\!\!\perp [C, R_{BC}, B].Y \mid [C].Z$$

for the alternative hypothesis.

C TYPE I ERRORS FOR DIFFERENT METHODS

We illustrate type-I error plots for Section 5.2 and 5.3.

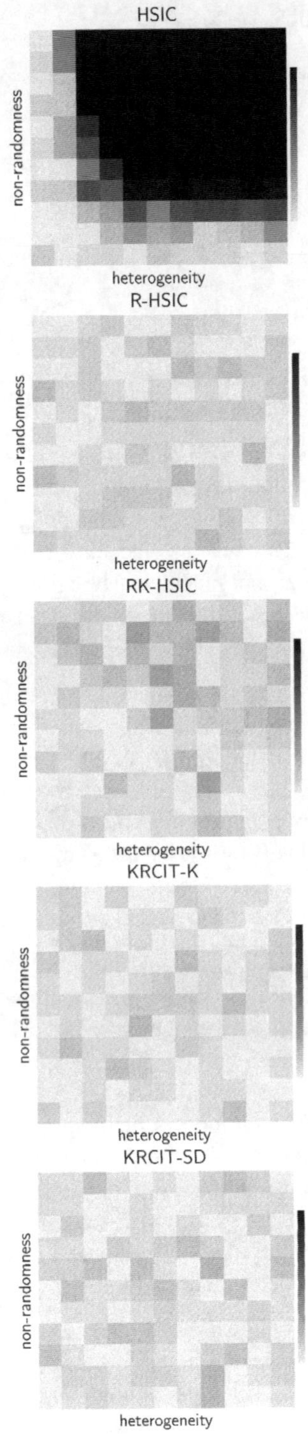

Figure 9: Type-I errors of different methods for Section 5.2.

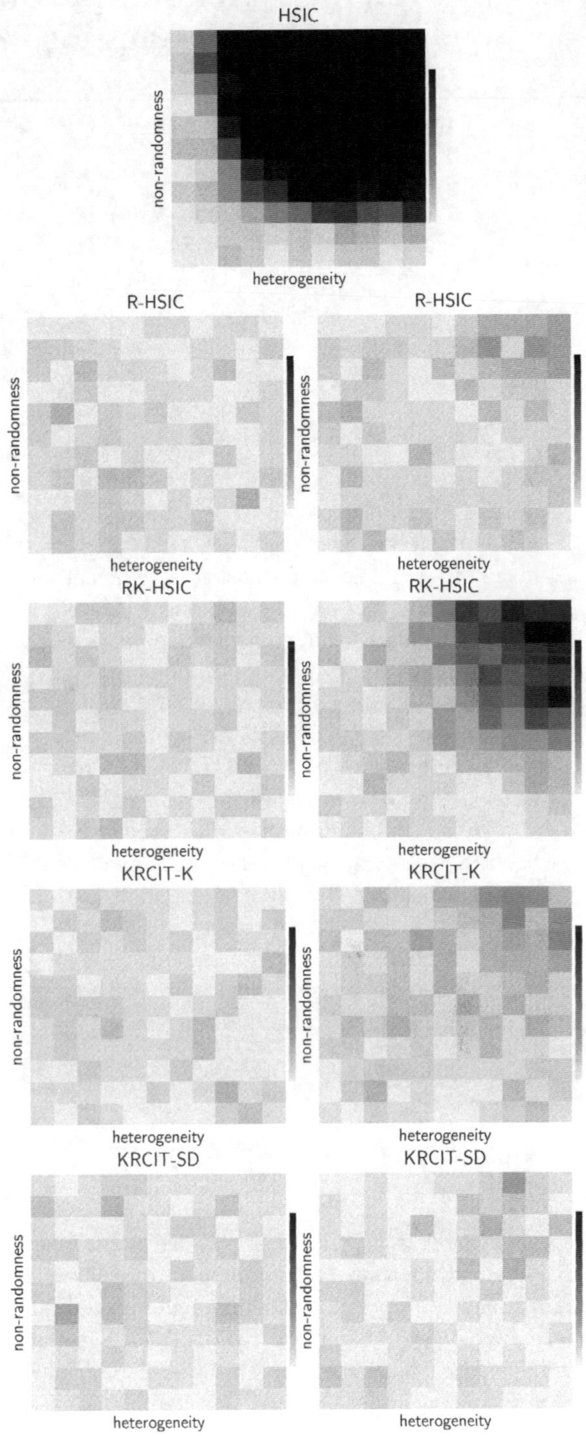

Figure 10: Type-I errors of different methods with two different contexts based on hop=1 (left) and hop=2 (right) for Section 5.3. HSIC does not use contexts.

AutoGP: Exploring the Capabilities and Limitations of Gaussian Process Models

Karl Krauth **Edwin V. Bonilla**
The University of New South Wales
karl.krauth@gmail.com e.bonilla@unsw.edu.au

Kurt Cutajar **Maurizio Filippone**
EURECOM
{kurt.cutajar, maurizio.filippone}@eurecom.fr

Abstract

We investigate the capabilities and limitations of Gaussian process (GP) models by jointly exploring three complementary directions: (i) scalable and statistically efficient inference; (ii) flexible kernels; and (iii) objective functions for hyperparameter learning alternative to the marginal likelihood. Our approach outperforms all previous GP methods on the MNIST dataset; performs comparatively to kernel-based methods using the RECTANGLES-IMAGE dataset; and breaks the 1% error-rate barrier in GP models on the MNIST8M dataset, while showing unprecedented scalability (8 million observations) in GP classification. Overall, our approach represents a significant breakthrough in kernel methods and GP models, bridging the gap between deep learning and kernel machines.

1 INTRODUCTION

Recent advances in deep learning (DL) have revolutionized the application of machine learning in areas such as computer vision speech recognition and natural language processing (LeCun et al., 2015). Although certain kernel-based methods have also been successful in such domains (Cho and Saul, 2009; Mairal et al., 2014), it is still unclear whether these methods can indeed catch up with the recent DL breakthroughs.

Aside from the benefits obtained from using compositional representations, we believe that the main components contributing to the success of DL techniques are: (i) their scalability to large datasets and efficient computation via GPUs; (ii) their large representational power; and (iii) the use of well-targeted objective functions for the problem at hand.

In the kernel world, Gaussian process (GP; Rasmussen and Williams, 2006) models are attractive because they are elegant Bayesian nonparametric approaches to learning from data. Nevertheless, besides the limitations intrinsic to local kernel machines (Bengio et al., 2005), it is clear that GP-based methods have not fully explored the desiderata mentioned above.

Firstly, with regards to (i) scalability, despite recent advances in inducing-variable approaches and variational inference in GP models (Titsias, 2009; Hensman et al., 2013, 2015a; Dezfouli and Bonilla, 2015), the study of truly large datasets in problems other than regression and the investigation of GPU-based acceleration in GP models are still under-explored areas. We note that these issues are shared by non-probabilistic kernel methods such as support vector machines (SVMs).

Furthermore, concerning (ii) representational power, kernel methods have been plagued by the overuse of very limited kernels such as the squared exponential kernel, also known as the radial-basis-function (RBF) kernel. Even worse, it is common in methods such as SVMs to constrain the kernel to having a single length-scale (or bandwidth in SVM parlance) shared across all inputs instead of using a different length-scale for each dimension. The latter approach is commonly known as automatic relevance determination (ARD).

Finally, and perhaps most importantly, GP methods have largely ignored defining (iii) well-targeted objective functions, and instead have focused heavily on optimizing the marginal likelihood (Rasmussen and Williams, 2006, Ch. 5). This includes variational approaches that optimize a lower bound of the marginal likelihood (Titsias, 2009). Although different approaches for hyperparameter learning in GP models are discussed by Rasmussen and Williams (2006, §5.4.2), and indeed carried out by Sundararajan and Keerthi (2001); Sundararajan et al. (2007); Sundararajan and Keerthi (2008) and more recently by Vehtari et al. (2016), their performance results are somewhat limited by their disregard for other directions of improvement (scalability and greater representational power) mentioned above.

In this work we push the capabilities of GP-models, while also investigating their limitations, by addressing the above issues jointly. In particular,

1. we develop scalable and statistically efficient inference methods for GP models using GPU computation and stochastic variational inference along with the reparameterization trick (Kingma and Welling, 2014);
2. we investigate the flexibility of models using ARD kernels for high-dimensional problems, as well as "deep" ARC-COSINE kernels (Cho and Saul, 2009); and
3. we study the impact of employing a leave-one-out-based objective function on hyperparameter learning.

As we rely on automatic differentiation (Baydin et al., 2015) for the implementation of our model in TensorFlow (Abadi et al., 2015), we refer to our approach as AutoGP. Our most significant results show that AutoGP: (i) has superior performance to previous GP-based methods on the MNIST dataset; (ii) achieves comparable performance to previous kernel-based methods using the RECTANGLES-IMAGE dataset; and (iii) breaks the 1% error-rate barrier in GP models using the MNIST8M dataset, while showing unprecedented scalability (8 million observations) in multiclass GP classification.

Overall, AutoGP represents a significant breakthrough in kernel methods in general and in GP models in particular, bridging the gap between deep learning approaches and kernel machines.

2 RELATED WORK

The majority of works related to scalable kernel machines primarily target issues pertaining to the storage and computational requirements of algebraic operations involving kernel matrices. Low-rank approximations are ubiquitous among these approaches, with the Nyström approximation being one of the most popular methods in this category (Williams and Seeger, 2001). Nevertheless, most of these approximations can be understood within the unifying probabilistic framework of Quiñonero-Candela and Rasmussen (2005).

The optimization of inducing inputs using Nyström approximations for GPs made significant progress with the work on sparse-GP variational inference in Titsias (2009). This exposed the possibility to develop stochastic gradient optimization for GP models (Hensman et al., 2013) and handle non-Gaussian likelihoods (Nguyen and Bonilla, 2014; Dezfouli and Bonilla, 2015; Hensman et al., 2015a; Sheth et al., 2015), which has sparked interest in the implementation of scalable inference frameworks such as those in Hensman et al. (2016) and Deisenroth and Ng (2015). These developments greatly improved the generality and applicability of GP models to a variety of applications, and our work follows from this line of ideas.

Other independent works have focused on kernel design (Wilson and Adams, 2013; Cho and Saul, 2009; Mairal et al., 2014; Wilson et al., 2016). This has sparked some debate as to whether kernel machines can actually compete with deep nets. Evidence suggests that this is possible; notable examples include the work by Huang et al. (2014); Lu et al. (2014). These works also provide insights into the aspects that make kernel methods less competitive to deep neural networks, namely lack of application specific kernels, and scalability at the price of poor approximations. These observations are corroborated by our experiments, which report how the combination of these factors impacts performance of GPs.

Because GPs are probabilistic kernel machines, it is natural to target the optimization of the marginal likelihood. However, alternative objective functions have also been considered, in particular the leave-one-out cross-validation (LOO-CV) error. Originally this was done by Sundararajan and Keerthi (2001) for regression; later extended by Sundararajan et al. (2007) to deal with sparse GP formulations; and broadened by Sundararajan and Keerthi (2008); Vehtari et al. (2016) to handle non-Gaussian likelihoods. While the results in these papers seem inconclusive as to whether this can generally improve performance, LOO-CV learning may allow to better accommodate for incorrect model specifications (Wahba, 1990, §4.8). Motivated by this observation, we explore this direction by extending the variational formulation to optimize a LOO-CV error. We also note that none of these previous approaches can actually handle large datasets.

3 GP MODELS

We are interested in supervised learning problems where we are given a training dataset of input-output pairs $\mathcal{D} = \{\mathbf{x}_n, \mathbf{y}_n\}_{n=1}^{n}$, with $\mathbf{x}_n$ being a D-dimensional input vector and $\mathbf{y}_n$ being a P-dimensional output. Our main goal is to learn a probabilistic mapping from inputs to outputs so that for a new input $\mathbf{x}_\star$, we can estimate the probability of its associated label $p(\mathbf{y}_\star|\mathbf{x}_\star)$.

To this end, we follow a Gaussian process modeling approach (GP; Rasmussen and Williams, 2006), where latent functions are assumed to be distributed according to a GP, and observations are modeled via a suitable conditional likelihood given the latent functions. A function f_j is said to be distributed according to a Gaussian process with mean function $\mu_j(\mathbf{x})$ and covariance function $\kappa_j(\mathbf{x}, \mathbf{x}'; \boldsymbol{\theta}_j)$, which we denote with $f_j \sim \mathcal{GP}(\mu_j(\mathbf{x}), \kappa_j(\mathbf{x}, \mathbf{x}'; \boldsymbol{\theta}_j))$, if any subset of function values follow a Gaussian distribution.

Since we are dealing with multiple outputs $\{\mathbf{y}_n\}$, we follow the standard practice of considering Q underlying latent functions $\{f_j\}_{j=1}^{Q}$ which are drawn independently from zero-mean GP priors along with i.i.d. conditional likelihood models. Such a modeling approach encompasses a large class of machine learning problems, including GP-regression, GP-classification and modeling of count data (Rasmussen and Williams, 2006).

Consequently, when realized at the observed data, our probabilistic model is given by:

$$p(\mathbf{f}|\mathbf{X}, \boldsymbol{\theta}) = \prod_{j=1}^{Q} p(\mathbf{f}_{\cdot j}|\mathbf{X}, \boldsymbol{\theta}_j) = \prod_{j=1}^{Q} \mathcal{N}(\mathbf{f}_{\cdot j}; \mathbf{0}, \mathbf{K}_j), \quad (1)$$

$$p(\mathbf{y}|\mathbf{f}) = \prod_{n=1}^{N} p(\mathbf{y}_n|\mathbf{f}_{n\cdot}), \quad (2)$$

where $\mathbf{f}$ is the $(N \times Q)$-dimensional vector of latent function values; $\mathbf{f}_{\cdot j} = \{f_j(\mathbf{x}_n)\}_{n=1}^{N}$ denotes the latent values corresponding to the jth GP; $\mathbf{K}_j$ is the covariance matrix obtained by evaluating the covariance function $\kappa_j(\cdot, \cdot; \boldsymbol{\theta})$ at all pairs of training inputs; $\mathbf{y}$ is the vector of all $(N \times P)$ output observations, with $\mathbf{y}_n$ being nth output observation, and $\mathbf{f}_{n\cdot} = \{f_j(\mathbf{x}_n)\}_{j=1}^{Q}$ being the corresponding vector of latent function values. We refer to the covariance parameters $\boldsymbol{\theta}$ as the hyperparameters.

One commonly used covariance function is the so-called squared exponential (or RBF kernel):

$$\kappa(\mathbf{x}, \mathbf{x}'; \boldsymbol{\theta}) = \sigma^2 \exp\left(-\sum_{i=1}^{D} \frac{(x_i - x_i')^2}{\ell_i^2}\right), \quad (3)$$

where $\boldsymbol{\theta} = \{\sigma^2, \ell_1^2, \ldots, \ell_D^2\}$ and D is the input dimensionality. When all the length-scales, ℓ_i, are constrained to be the same we refer to the above kernel as *isotropic*; otherwise, we refer to it as the squared exponential covariance with automatic relevance determination (ARD).

3.1 INFERENCE PROBLEMS

The main inference problems in GP models are (i) estimation of the posterior over the latent functions $p(\mathbf{f}|\mathbf{X}, \mathbf{y}, \boldsymbol{\theta})$ and subsequent estimation of the predictive distribution $p(\mathbf{y}_\star|\mathbf{x}_\star, \mathbf{X}, \mathbf{y}, \boldsymbol{\theta})$; and (ii) inference over the hyperparameters $\boldsymbol{\theta}$.

For general likelihood models, both inference problems are analytically intractable, as they require the computation of non-trivial high-dimensional integrals. Furthermore, even for the simplest case when the conditional likelihood is Gaussian, evaluating the posterior and hyperparameter estimation is computationally prohibitive, as they entail time and memory requirements of $\mathcal{O}(N^3)$ and $\mathcal{O}(N^2)$ respectively.

In addition to dealing with general likelihoods and scalability issues, the performance of GP models (and kernel machines), is highly dependent on the covariance function (or kernel) used. Most previous work on GP methods and SVMs in the machine learning literature, use the squared exponential kernel in Equation (3). Furthermore, especially in high dimensions, this kernel is constrained to its isotropic version. As pointed out by Bengio et al. (2005), such an approach is severely limited by the curse of dimensionality when learning complex functions.

Finally, the estimation of hyperparameters based solely on marginal likelihood optimization can be very sensitive to model misspecification, with predictive approaches such as those in Sundararajan and Keerthi (2001) being seemingly more appealing for this task, especially in problems such as classification, where we are ultimately interested in having lower error rates and better calibrated predictive probabilities.

In the following sections, we show how to deal with the above issues, namely non-Gaussian likelihood models and scalability; more flexible kernels; and better objective functions for hyperparameter learning, with the endmost goal of improving performance significantly over current GP approaches.

4 VARIATIONAL INFERENCE

In this section we detail our method for scalable and statistically efficient inference in Gaussian process models with general likelihoods as specified by Equations (1) and (2). We adopt the variational framework of Dezfouli and Bonilla (2015), which we prefer over the MCMC method of Hensman et al. (2015b) as we avoid the sampling overhead which is especially significant in very large datasets.

4.1 AUGMENTED MODEL

In order to have a scalable inference framework, we augment our prior with M inducing variables $\{\mathbf{u}_{\cdot j}\}$ per latent process and corresponding inducing inputs $\{\mathbf{Z}_j\}$ such that,

$$p(\mathbf{u}) = \prod_{j=1}^{Q} \mathcal{N}(\mathbf{u}_{\cdot j}; \mathbf{0}, \mathbf{K}_{\mathbf{zz}}^{j}), \tag{4}$$

$$p(\mathbf{f}|\mathbf{u}) = \prod_{j=1}^{Q} \mathcal{N}(\mathbf{f}_{\cdot j}; \tilde{\boldsymbol{\mu}}_j, \widetilde{\mathbf{K}}_j), \text{ where} \tag{5}$$

$$\tilde{\boldsymbol{\mu}}_j = \mathbf{K}_{\mathbf{xz}}^{j} (\mathbf{K}_{\mathbf{zz}}^{j})^{-1} \mathbf{u}_{\cdot j}, \text{ and} \tag{6}$$

$$\widetilde{\mathbf{K}}_j = \mathbf{K}_{\mathbf{xx}}^{j} - \mathbf{A}_j \mathbf{K}_{\mathbf{zx}}^{j} \text{ with } \mathbf{A}_j = \mathbf{K}_{\mathbf{xz}}^{j} (\mathbf{K}_{\mathbf{zz}}^{j})^{-1}, \tag{7}$$

where $\mathbf{K}_{\mathbf{uv}}^{j}$ is the covariance matrix obtained by evaluating the covariance function $\kappa_j(\cdot, \cdot; \boldsymbol{\theta})$ at all pairwise columns of matrices $\mathbf{U}$ and $\mathbf{V}$. We note that this prior is equivalent to that defined in Equation (1), which is obtained by integrating out $\mathbf{u}$ from the joint $p(\mathbf{f}, \mathbf{u})$. However, as originally proposed by Titsias (2009), having an explicit representation of $\mathbf{u}$ will allow us to derive a scalable variational framework without additional assumptions on the train or test conditional distributions (Quiñonero-Candela and Rasmussen, 2005).

We now define our approximate joint posterior as:

$$q(\mathbf{f}, \mathbf{u}|\boldsymbol{\lambda}) \stackrel{\text{def}}{=} p(\mathbf{f}|\mathbf{u}) q(\mathbf{u}|\boldsymbol{\lambda}), \text{ with} \tag{8}$$

$$q(\mathbf{u}|\boldsymbol{\lambda}) = \sum_{k=1}^{K} \pi_k \prod_{j=1}^{Q} \mathcal{N}(\mathbf{u}_{\cdot j}; \mathbf{m}_{kj}, \mathbf{S}_{kj}), \tag{9}$$

where $p(\mathbf{f}|\mathbf{u})$ is the conditional prior given in Equation (5) and $q(\mathbf{u}|\boldsymbol{\lambda})$ is our variational posterior with $\boldsymbol{\lambda} = \{\pi_k, \mathbf{m}_{kj}, \mathbf{S}_{kj}\}$, which we will refer to as variational parameters. Note that we assume a variational posterior in the form of a mixture-of-Gaussians for added flexibility compared to using a single distribution.

4.2 EVIDENCE LOWER BOUND

Such a definition of the variational posterior allows for simplification of the log-evidence lower bound ($\mathcal{L}_{\text{elbo}}$) such that no $\mathcal{O}(N^3)$ operations are required,

$$\mathcal{L}_{\text{elbo}}(\boldsymbol{\lambda}, \boldsymbol{\theta}) = -\text{KL}(q(\mathbf{u}|\boldsymbol{\lambda}) \| p(\mathbf{u})) + \sum_{n=1}^{N} \sum_{k=1}^{K} \pi_k \mathbb{E}_{q_{k(n)}(\mathbf{f}_{n\cdot}|\boldsymbol{\lambda}_k)} [\log p(\mathbf{y}_n | \mathbf{f}_{n\cdot})], \tag{10}$$

where $\text{KL}(q\|p)$ denotes the KL divergence between distributions q and p; $\mathbb{E}_{p(X)}[g(X)]$ denotes the expectation of $g(X)$ over distribution $p(X)$; and $q_{k(n)}(\mathbf{f}_{n\cdot}|\boldsymbol{\lambda}_k)$ is a Q-dimensional diagonal Gaussian with means and variances given by

$$b_{knj} = \mathbf{a}_{jn}^T \mathbf{m}_{kj}, \tag{11}$$

$$\sigma_{knj}^2 = [\widetilde{\mathbf{K}}_j]_{n,n} + \mathbf{a}_{jn}^T \mathbf{S}_{kj} \mathbf{a}_{jn}, \tag{12}$$

where $\mathbf{a}_{jn} \stackrel{\text{def}}{=} [\mathbf{A}_j]_{:,n}$ denotes the M-dimensional vector corresponding to the nth column of matrix $\mathbf{A}_j$; $\widetilde{\mathbf{K}}_j$ and $\mathbf{A}_j$ are given in Equation (7); and, $[\widetilde{\mathbf{K}}_j]_{n,n}$ denotes the (n, n)th entry of matrix $\widetilde{\mathbf{K}}_j$.

In order to compute the log-evidence lower bound in Equation (10) and its gradients, we use Jensen's inequality to bound the KL term (as in Dezfouli and Bonilla, 2015) and estimate the expected likelihood term using Monte Carlo (MC).

4.3 THE REPARAMETERIZATION TRICK

One of the key properties of the log-evidence lower bound in Equation (10) is its decomposition as a sum of expected likelihood terms on the individual observations. This allows for the applicability of stochastic optimization methods and, therefore, scalability to very large datasets.

Due to the expectation term in the expression of $\mathcal{L}_{\text{elbo}}$, gradients of $\mathcal{L}_{\text{elbo}}$ need to be estimated. Dezfouli and Bonilla (2015) follow a similar approach to that in general black-box variational methods (Ranganath et al., 2014), and use the property $\nabla_{\boldsymbol{\lambda}} \mathbb{E}_{q(\mathbf{f}|\boldsymbol{\lambda})}[\log p(\mathbf{y}|\mathbf{f})] = \mathbb{E}_{q(\boldsymbol{\lambda})}[\nabla_{\boldsymbol{\lambda}} \log q(\mathbf{f}|\boldsymbol{\lambda}) \log p(\mathbf{y}|\mathbf{f})]$ and Monte Carlo (MC) sampling to produce unbiased estimates of these gradients.

While such an approach is truly black-box in that it does not require detailed knowledge of the conditional likelihood and its gradients, the estimated gradients may have significantly large variance, which could hinder the optimization process. In fact, Dezfouli and Bonilla (2015) and Bonilla et al. (2016) use variance-reduction techniques (Ross, 2006, §8.2) to ameliorate this effect. Nevertheless, the experiments in Bonilla et al. (2016) on complex likelihood functions such as those in Gaussian process regression networks (GPRNs; Wilson et al., 2012) indicate that such techniques may be insufficient to control the stability of the optimization process, and a large number of MC samples may be required.

In contrast, if one is willing to relax the constraints of a truly black-box approach by having access to the implementation of the conditional likelihood and its gradients, then a simple trick proposed by Kingma and Welling (2014) can significantly reduce the variance in the gradients and make the stochastic optimization of $\mathcal{L}_{\text{elbo}}$ much more practical. This has come to be known as the *reparameterization trick*.

We now present explicit expressions of our estimated $\mathcal{L}_{\text{elbo}}$, focusing on an individual expected likelihood term in Equation (10). Thus, the individual expectations can be estimated as:

$$\epsilon_{knj} \sim \mathcal{N}(0,1), \tag{13}$$

$$f_{nj}^{(k,i)} = b_{knj} + \sigma_{knj}\epsilon_{knj}, \quad j = 1, \dots, Q, \tag{14}$$

$$\widehat{\mathcal{L}}_{\text{ell}}^{(n)} = \frac{1}{S}\sum_{k=1}^{K}\pi_k \sum_{i=1}^{S} \log p(\mathbf{y}_n|\mathbf{f}_{n\cdot}^{(k,i)}), \tag{15}$$

where S is the number of MC samples and $f_{nj}^{(k,i)}$ is an element in the vector of latent functions $\mathbf{f}_{n\cdot}^{(k,i)}$.

4.4 MINI-BATCH OPTIMIZATION

We can now obtain unbiased estimates of the gradients of $\mathcal{L}_{\text{elbo}}$ to use in mini-batch stochastic optimization. In particular, for a mini-batch Ω of size B we have that the estimated gradient is given by:

$$\nabla_{\boldsymbol{\eta}}\widehat{\mathcal{L}}_{\text{elbo}} = -\nabla_{\boldsymbol{\eta}}\text{KL}(q(\mathbf{u}|\boldsymbol{\lambda})\|p(\mathbf{u})) + \frac{N}{B}\sum_{n\in\Omega}\nabla_{\boldsymbol{\eta}}\widehat{\mathcal{L}}_{\text{ell}}^{(n)},$$

where $\boldsymbol{\eta} \in \{\boldsymbol{\lambda}, \boldsymbol{\theta}\}$, and $\boldsymbol{\theta}$ now includes, in addition to the hyperparameters, the inducing inputs across all latent processes $\mathbf{Z}_j$. The corresponding gradients are obtained through automatic differentiation using TensorFlow.

4.5 FULL APPROXIMATE POSTERIOR

An important characteristic of our approach is that, unlike most previous work that uses stochastic optimization in variational inference along with the reparameterization trick (see e.g. Kingma and Welling, 2014; Dai et al., 2016), we do not require a fully factorized approximate posterior to estimate our gradients using only simple scalar transformations of uncorrelated Gaussian samples, as given in Equation (14). Indeed, the posterior over the latent functions is fully correlated and is given by

$$q(\mathbf{f}|\boldsymbol{\lambda}) = \sum_{k=1}^{K}\pi_k \prod_{j=1}^{Q}\mathcal{N}(\mathbf{f}_{\cdot j}; \mathbf{b}_{kj}, \boldsymbol{\Sigma}_{kj}), \text{ where} \tag{16}$$

$$\mathbf{b}_{kj} = \mathbf{A}_j\mathbf{m}_{kj}, \text{ and} \tag{17}$$

$$\boldsymbol{\Sigma}_{kj} = \widetilde{\mathbf{K}}_j + \mathbf{A}_j\mathbf{S}_{kj}\mathbf{A}_j^T. \tag{18}$$

This result is a property inherited from the original framework of Nguyen and Bonilla (2014) and Dezfouli and Bonilla (2015), who showed that, even when having a full approximate posterior, only expectations over univariate Gaussians are required in order to estimate the expected log likelihood term in $\mathcal{L}_{\text{elbo}}$. A less general result, for the case of one latent function and a single Gaussian posterior, has been shown by Nickisch and Rasmussen (2008); Opper and Archambeau (2009).

5 FLEXIBLE KERNELS

We now turn our attention to increase the flexibility of GP models through the investigation of kernels beyond the isotropic RBF kernel. This is a complementary direction for exploring the capabilities of GP models, but it benefits from the results of the previous section in terms of large-scale inference and computation of gradients via (automatic) back-propagation.

For the RBF kernel, we limit our experiments to the automatic relevance determination (ARD) setting in Equation (3), including problems of large input dimensionality such as MNIST and CIFAR10.

Furthermore, given the interesting results reported by Cho and Saul (2009), we investigate their ARC-COSINE kernel, which was proposed as a kernel that mimics the computation of neural networks. In particular, they define an ARC-COSINE kernel of degree d and depth l using the following recursion:

$$\kappa_d^{(l+1)}(\mathbf{x},\mathbf{x}') = \frac{1}{\pi}\left(\kappa_d^{(l)}(\mathbf{x},\mathbf{x})\kappa_d^{(l)}(\mathbf{x}',\mathbf{x}')\right)^{d/2} J_d(\phi_d^{(l)}),$$

where the kernel at depth $l = 1$ is $\kappa_d^{(1)}(\mathbf{x},\mathbf{x}') = \frac{1}{\pi}\|\mathbf{x}\|^d\|\mathbf{x}'\|^d J_d(\phi)$ and the angle corresponding to degree d and depth l is given by

$$\phi_d^{(l)} = \cos^{-1}\left(\kappa_d^{(l)}(\mathbf{x},\mathbf{x}')\left(\kappa_d^{(l)}(\mathbf{x},\mathbf{x})\kappa_d^{(l)}(\mathbf{x}',\mathbf{x}')\right)^{-1/2}\right).$$

All the angular dependences are then modeled with the function

$$J_d(\phi) = (-1)^d(\sin\phi)^{2d+1}\left(\frac{1}{\sin\phi}\frac{\partial}{\partial\phi}\right)^d\left(\frac{\pi-\phi}{\sin\phi}\right),$$

with the base angle defined as $\phi = \cos^{-1}\left(\frac{\mathbf{x}\cdot\mathbf{x}'}{\|\mathbf{x}\|\|\mathbf{x}'\|}\right)$.

6 LEAVE-ONE-OUT LEARNING

Here we focus on the average leave-one-out log predictive probability for hyperparameter learning, as an alternative to optimization of the marginal likelihood. This

Algorithm 1 $\mathcal{L}_{\text{oo}}$-based hyperparameter learning.

repeat
  repeat
    $(\boldsymbol{\theta}, \boldsymbol{\lambda}) \leftarrow (\boldsymbol{\theta}, \boldsymbol{\lambda}) + \alpha \nabla_{\boldsymbol{\theta}, \boldsymbol{\lambda}} \widehat{\mathcal{L}}_{\text{elbo}}(\boldsymbol{\theta}, \boldsymbol{\lambda})$
  until satisfied
  repeat
    $\boldsymbol{\theta} \leftarrow \boldsymbol{\theta} + \alpha \nabla_{\boldsymbol{\theta}} \widehat{\mathcal{L}}_{\text{oo}}(\boldsymbol{\theta})$
  until satisfied
until satisfied

can be particularly useful in problems such as classification where one is mainly interested in having lower error rates and better calibrated predictive probabilities.

This objective function is obtained by leaving one datapoint out of the training set and computing its log predictive probability when training on the other points; the resulting values are then averaged across all the datapoints. Interestingly, in our GP model this can be computed without the need for training N different models, as the resulting expression is given by:

$$\mathcal{L}_{\text{oo}}(\boldsymbol{\theta}) \approx -\frac{1}{N} \sum_{n=1}^{N} \log \int \frac{q(\mathbf{f}_{n\cdot}|\mathcal{D}, \boldsymbol{\lambda}, \boldsymbol{\theta})}{p(\mathbf{y}_n|\mathbf{f}_{n\cdot})} \, d\mathbf{f}_{n\cdot}, \quad (19)$$

where the approximation stems from using the variational marginal posterior $q(\mathbf{f}_{n\cdot}|\mathcal{D}, \boldsymbol{\theta})$ instead of the true marginal posterior $p(\mathbf{f}_{n\cdot}|\mathcal{D}, \boldsymbol{\theta})$ for datapoint n. We also note that we have made explicit the dependency of the posterior on all the data. The derivation of this expression is given in the supplement. Since $\mathcal{L}_{\text{oo}}(\boldsymbol{\theta})$ contains an expectation with respect to the marginal posterior we can also estimate it via MC sampling.

Equation (19) immediately suggests an alternating optimization scheme where we estimate the approximate posterior $q(\mathbf{f}_{n\cdot}|\mathcal{D}, \boldsymbol{\theta})$ through optimization of $\mathcal{L}_{\text{elbo}}$, as described in §4, and then learn the hyperparameters via optimization of $\mathcal{L}_{\text{oo}}$. Algorithm 1 illustrates such an alternating scheme for hyperparameter learning in our model using the leave-one-out objective and vanilla stochastic gradient descent (SGD), where $\widehat{\mathcal{L}}_{\text{elbo}}$ and $\widehat{\mathcal{L}}_{\text{oo}}$ denote estimates of the corresponding objectives when using mini-batches.

7 EXPERIMENTS

We evaluate AutoGP across various datasets with number of observations ranging from $12,000$ to 8.1M and input dimensionality between 31 and 3072. The aim of this section is (i) to demonstrate the effectiveness of the reparameterization trick in reducing the number of samples needed to estimate the expected log likelihood; (ii) to evaluate non-isotropic kernels across a large number of dimensions; (iii) to assess the performance obtained by LOO-CV hyperparameter learning; and (iv) to analyze the performance of AutoGP as a function of time. Details of the experimental set-up can be found in the supplementary material.

7.1 STATISTICAL EFFICIENCY

Bonilla et al. (2016) has shown that sparse variational approaches to GP models can be as accurate as MCMC (which are only applicable to small-scale problems) but orders of magnitude faster and as good as approaches that have been hard-coded for specific likelihood models (e.g. EP and quadratic lower bounds). Here we show that we can improve on the method of Bonilla et al. (2016) by enhancing its statistical efficiency.

Therefore, For our first experiment we look at the behavior of our model as we vary the number of samples used to estimate the expected log likelihood. We trained our model on the SARCOS dataset (Vijayakumar and Schaal, 2000), an inverse dynamics problem for a seven degrees-of-freedom anthropomorphic robot arm.

We used the Gaussian process regression network (GPRN) model of Wilson et al. (2012) as our likelihood function. Bonilla et al. (2016) found that GPRNs require a large number of samples ($10,000$) to yield stable optimization of the $\mathcal{L}_{\text{elbo}}$ in their method. This is most likely due to the increased variance induced by multiplying latent samples together. The high variance of this likelihood model makes it an ideal candidate for us to evaluate how the performance of AutoGP varies with the number of samples.

As shown in Figure 1, increasing the number of samples decreased the number of epochs it took for our model to converge; however, our model always converged to the same optimal value. This is in stark contrast to SAVIGP (Bonilla et al., 2016) which was able to converge to the optimal value of 0.0195 with $10,000$ samples, but converged to sub-optimal values (> 0.05) as the number of samples was lowered. This shows that our MC estimator is significantly more stable than SAVIGP's black-box estimator, without requiring any variance reduction methods. In practice, reducing the number of samples leads to an improved runtime. A gradient update using $10,000$ samples takes around 0.17 seconds, whereas an update using 10 samples only takes around 0.03 seconds, which makes up for the extra epochs needed to converge.

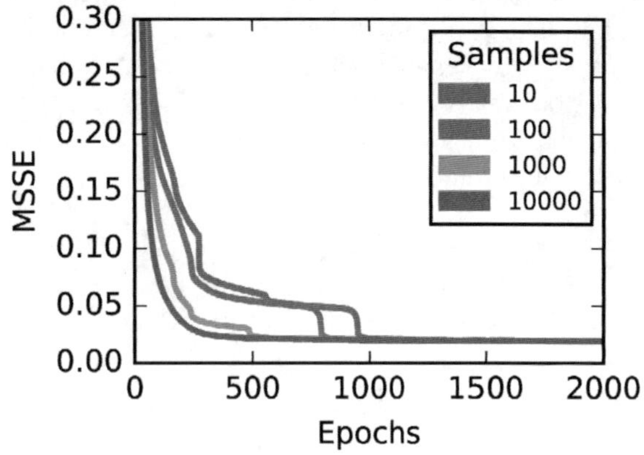

Figure 1: The mean standardized square error (MSSE) of AutoGP for different number of MC samples on the SARCOS dataset. The MSSE was averaged across all 7 joints and 50 inducing inputs were used to train the model. An epoch represents a single pass over the entire training set.

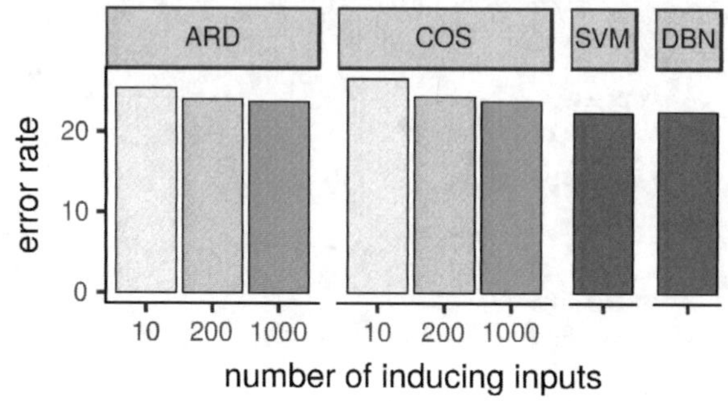

Figure 2: Error rates for binary classification using a logistic likelihood on RECTANGLES-IMAGE. ARD and COS refer to AutoGP with a RBF-ARD kernel, and a 3-layer ARC-COSINE kernel of degree 1 respectively. DBN refers to a 3-layer deep belief network and SVM denotes a support vector machine with a ARC-COSINE kernel of depth 6 and degree 0.

7.2 KERNEL PERFORMANCE

In this section we compare the performance of AutoGP across two different kernels on a high-dimensional dataset.

We trained our model on the RECTANGLES-IMAGE dataset (Larochelle et al., 2007) which is a binary classification task that was created to compare shallow models (e.g. SVMs), and deep learning architectures. The task involves recognizing whether a rectangle has a larger width or height. Randomized images were overlaid behind and over the rectangles, which makes this task particularly challenging.

We compare the multilayer arc-cosine kernel (ARC-COSINE) described by Cho and Saul (2009) with an RBF kernel with automatic relevance determination (RBF-ARD). ARC-COSINE was devised to mimic the architecture of deep neural networks through successive kernel compositions, and has shown good results when combined with non-Bayesian kernel machines (Cho and Saul, 2009). Unlike ARC-COSINE, RBF-ARD is commonly used with Gaussian processes (Hensman et al., 2013). However, RBF-ARD has not been applied to large-scale datasets with a large input dimensionality due to limitations in scalability. Given that our implementation uses automatic differentiation, and is thus able to efficiently compute gradients, we can use RBF-ARD with no noticeable performance overhead.

We trained our model using 10, 200, and 1000 inducing points across both kernels. We experimented with various different depths and degrees for ARC-COSINE and found that 3 layers and a degree of 1 worked best with AutoGP. As such, we ran all ARC-COSINE experiments with these settings.

For reference, Cho and Saul (2009) report an error rate of 22.36% using SVMs with ARC-COSINE. Larochelle et al. (2007) report error rates of 24.04% on SVMs with a simple RBF kernel and 22.50% with a deep belief network with 3 hidden layers (DBN).

Figure 2 shows that AutoGP is competitive with previous approaches, except when using 10 inducing points. Our results also show that RBF-ARD performs comparatively (and sometimes better) than ARC-COSINE. This is likely because ARC-COSINE is better suited to deep architectures, such as the multilayer kernel machine of Cho and Saul (2009).

7.3 LOO-CV HYPERPARAMETER LEARNING

In this section we analyze our approach when learning hyperparameters via optimization of the leave-one-out objective ($\widehat{\mathcal{L}}_{\text{oo}}$), as described in §6, and compare it with the standard variational method that learns hyperparameters via sole optimization of the variational objective ($\widehat{\mathcal{L}}_{\text{elbo}}$). To this end, we use the MNIST dataset using 10, 200, and 1000 inducing points and the RBF-ARD kernel across all settings.

Our results indicate that optimizing the leave-one-out objective leads to a significant performance gain. While Figure 3 shows the corresponding error rates, we refer the reader to the supplementary material for similar re-

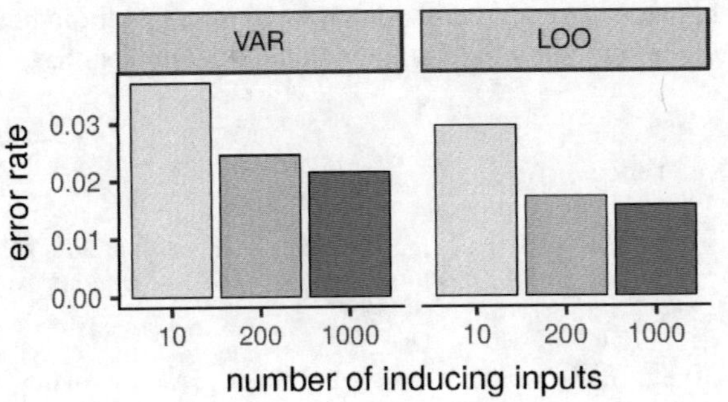

Figure 3: Error rates of AutoGP for multiclass classification using a softmax likelihood on MNIST. VAR refers to learning using only the variational objective $\widehat{\mathcal{L}}_{\text{elbo}}$, while LOO refers to learning hyperparameters using the leave-one-out objective $\widehat{\mathcal{L}}_{\text{oo}}$.

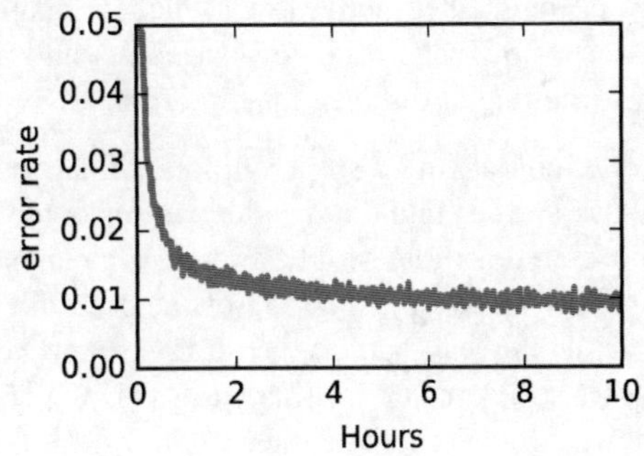

Figure 4: Error rate of AutoGP over time for multiclass classification using a softmax likelihood on MNIST8M. Training was done with 200 inducing points and $\mathcal{L}_{\text{oo}}$ for hyperparameter learning.

sults on negative log probabilities (NLPs). In summary, at 1000 inducing points our LOO-CV approach attains an error rate of 1.55% and a mean NLP of 0.061; At 200 inducing points it obtains an error rate of 1.71% and a mean NLP of 0.063. This represents a 40%–45% decrease in mean NLP and error rate from the equivalent model that only optimized the variational objective. Furthermore, our results outperform the work of Hensman et al. (2015b), Gal et al. (2014), and Bonilla et al. (2016) who reported error rates of 1.96%, 5.95% and 2.74% respectively, that are the best results reported on this data set in the GP literature.

We have shown that our approach reduces the error rate on the test set down to 1.55% without artificially extending the MNIST dataset through transformations, or doing any kind of pre-processing of the data. These results, while not on par with state-of-the-art vision results, show that Gaussian process models can perform competitively with non-Bayesian methods, while solving the harder problem of full posterior estimation. For example, standard convolutional neural networks achieve an error rate of 1.19% without any pre-processing (Benenson, 2013). We will show in the following section how we can further improve our results by artificially extending the training data on MNIST through distortions and affine transformations.

7.4 AUTOGP ALL TOGETHER

We finish by evaluating the performance of AutoGP using all its main components simultaneously, namely statistical efficiency, flexible kernels and LOO-CV hyperparameter learning, using three datasets: RECTANGLES-IMAGE, CIFAR10, and MNIST8M. Our goal is to gain further insights as to how our model compares against other works in the machine learning community. As before, we optimized our model with 200 inducing points and used the RBF-ARD kernel across all experiments.

We begin by looking at the RECTANGLES-IMAGE dataset which we have already investigated in Section 7.2. Optimizing $\widehat{\mathcal{L}}_{\text{oo}}$ slightly improves performance in this case, with a reduction in error rate from 24.06% to 24.04% and a reduction in mean NLP from 0.495 to 0.485, when using 200 inducing points. The error rate can be further reduced to 23.6% when using 1,000 inducing points (with corresponding NLP of 0.478). As a reference, performance of recent deep architectures is: deep trans-layer autoencoder networks (ER = 13.01%, Zhu et al., 2015), PCANet (ER = 13.94%, Chan et al., 2014), and two-layer stacked contractive auto-encoders (ER = 21.54%, Rifai et al., 2011). Bruna and Mallat (2013) have reported results using invariant scattering convolutional networks with an error rate of 8.01%.

We now turn our attention to the MNIST8M (Loosli et al., 2007) dataset, which artificially extends the MNIST dataset to 8.1 million training points by pseudo-randomly transforming existing MNIST images. To the best of our knowledge, no other GP models have been shown to scale to such a large dataset. We were able to achieve an error rate of 0.89% and a mean NLP of 0.033, breaking the 1% error-rate barrier in GP models. This shows that our model is able to perform on par with deep architectures with some pre-processing of the MNIST dataset. We also note that we were able to rapidly converge given the dataset size. As shown in Figure 4 AutoGP achieves near optimal results within the first hour, and converges to the optimal value within 10 hours. As a reference, Henao and Winther (2012) achieved similar performance (0.86% error rate) on MNIST when considering an augmented active set (which is analogous to the concept of inducing inputs/variables) and a 9th-degree polynomial covariance function.

Finally, we look at CIFAR10, a multiclass image classification task and we find that results are less conclusive. We achieve an error rate of 44.95% and a mean NLP of 1.33, which is well below the state-of-the-art, with some models achieving less than 10% error rate. However, we note that we still compare favorably to SVMs which have been shown to achieve error rates of 57.7% (Le et al., 2013). We also perform on par with older deep architectures (Rifai et al., 2011). We believe these results provide a strong motivation for investigating application-specific kernels (such as those studied by Mairal et al., 2014) in GP models.

Table 1: Test error rate and mean NLP of AutoGP trained with 200 inducing points on various datasets. The $\widehat{\mathcal{L}}_{oo}$ objective was used for hyperparameter learning.

Dataset	Error rate	mean NLP
RECTANGLES-IMAGE	24.06%	0.485
MNIST8M	0.89%	0.033
CIFAR10	44.95%	1.333

8 CONCLUSION & DISCUSSION

We have developed AutoGP, an inference framework for GP models that pushes the performance of current GP methods by exploring three complementary directions: (i) scalable and statistically efficient variational inference; (ii) flexible kernels; and (iii) objective functions for hyperparameter learning alternative to the marginal likelihood.

We have shown that our framework outperforms all previous GP approaches on MNIST; achieves comparable performance to previous kernel approaches on the RECTANGLES-IMAGE dataset; and can break the 1% error barrier using MNIST8M. Overall, this represents a significant breakthrough in Gaussian process methods and kernel machines. While our results on CIFAR10 are well below the state-of-the-art achieved with deep learning, we believe we can further reduce the gap between kernel machines and deep architectures by using application-specific kernels such as those recently proposed by Mairal et al. (2014).

One of the latest works that investigates LOO-CV and its connections with other information criteria for model selection can be found in Vehtari et al. (2017). We believe these connections are under-explored in the GP literature, where the marginal likelihood is the preferred choice.

References

Martín Abadi, Ashish Agarwal, Paul Barham, et al. TensorFlow: Large-scale machine learning on heterogeneous systems, 2015.

Atilim Gunes Baydin, Barak A Pearlmutter, Alexey Andreyevich Radul, and Jeffrey Mark Siskind. Automatic differentiation in machine learning: a survey. *arXiv preprint arXiv:1502.05767*, 2015.

Rodrigo Benenson. What is the class of this image? discover the current state of the art in objects classification. http://rodrigob.github.io/are_we_there_yet/build/classification_datasets_results.html, 2013. [Online; accessed 13-October-2016].

Yoshua Bengio, Olivier Delalleau, and Nicolas L Roux. The curse of highly variable functions for local kernel machines. In *NIPS*, 2005.

Edwin V Bonilla, Karl Krauth, and Amir Dezfouli. Generic inference in latent Gaussian process models. *arXiv preprint arXiv:1609.00577*, 2016.

Joan Bruna and Stephane Mallat. Invariant scattering convolution networks. *TPAMI*, pages 1872–1886, 2013.

Tsung-Han Chan, Kui Jia, Shenghua Gao, Jiwen Lu, Zinan Zeng, and Yi Ma. PCANet: A simple deep learning baseline for image classification? *arXiv preprint arXiv:1404.3606*, 2014.

Youngmin Cho and Lawrence K. Saul. Kernel methods for deep learning. In *NIPS*. 2009.

Zhenwen Dai, Andreas Damianou, Javier González, and Neil Lawrence. Variational Auto-encoded Deep Gaussian Processes. In *ICLR*, 2016.

Marc Peter Deisenroth and Jun Wei Ng. Distributed Gaussian processes. In *ICML*, 2015.

Amir Dezfouli and Edwin V. Bonilla. Scalable inference for Gaussian process models with black-box likelihoods. In *NIPS*. 2015.

Yarin Gal, Mark van der Wilk, and Carl Rasmussen. Distributed variational inference in sparse Gaussian process regression and latent variable models. In *NIPS*. 2014.

Ricardo Henao and Ole Winther. Predictive active set selection methods for Gaussian processes. *Neurocomputing*, 80: 10–18, 2012.

James Hensman, Nicolo Fusi, and Neil D Lawrence. Gaussian processes for big data. In *UAI*, 2013.

James Hensman, Alexander Matthews, and Zoubin Ghahramani. Scalable variational Gaussian process classification. In *AISTATS*, 2015a.

James Hensman, Alexander G Matthews, Maurizio Filippone, and Zoubin Ghahramani. MCMC for variationally sparse Gaussian processes. In *NIPS*. 2015b.

James Hensman, Alexander G. de G. Matthews, Alexis Boukouvalas, Keisuke Fujii, Pablo Leon, Valentine Svensson, and Mark van der Wilk. GPflow. https://github.com/GPflow/GPflow, 2016.

Po-Sen Huang, Haim Avron, Tara N. Sainath, Vikas Sindhwani, and Bhuvana Ramabhadran. Kernel methods match deep neural networks on TIMIT. In *ICASSP*, 2014.

Diederik P Kingma and Max Welling. Auto-encoding variational Bayes. In *ICLR*, 2014.

Hugo Larochelle, Dumitru Erhan, Aaron Courville, James Bergstra, and Yoshua Bengio. An empirical evaluation of deep architectures on problems with many factors of variation. In *ICML*, 2007.

Quoc V. Le, Tamás Sarlós, and Alexander J. Smola. Fastfood - computing Hilbert space expansions in loglinear time. In *ICML*, 2013.

Yann LeCun, Yoshua Bengio, and Geoffrey Hinton. Deep learning. *Nature*, 521(7553):436–444, 2015.

Gaëlle Loosli, Stéphane Canu, and Léon Bottou. Training invariant support vector machines using selective sampling. In *Large Scale Kernel Machines*, pages 301–320. MIT Press, Cambridge, MA., 2007.

Zhiyun Lu, Avner May, Kuan Liu, Alireza Bagheri Garakani, Dong Guo, Aurélien Bellet, Linxi Fan, Michael Collins, Brian Kingsbury, Michael Picheny, and Fei Sha. How to scale up kernel methods to be as good as deep neural nets. *CoRR*, abs/1411.4000, 2014.

Julien Mairal, Piotr Koniusz, Zaid Harchaoui, and Cordelia Schmid. Convolutional kernel networks. In *NIPS*, pages 2627–2635, 2014.

Trung V. Nguyen and Edwin V. Bonilla. Automated variational inference for Gaussian process models. In *NIPS*. 2014.

Hannes Nickisch and Carl Edward Rasmussen. Approximations for binary Gaussian process classification. *JMLR*, 9(10), 2008.

Manfred Opper and Cédric Archambeau. The variational Gaussian approximation revisited. *Neural Computation*, 21 (3):786–792, 2009.

Joaquin Quiñonero-Candela and Carl Edward Rasmussen. A unifying view of sparse approximate Gaussian process regression. *JMLR*, 6:1939–1959, 2005.

Rajesh Ranganath, Sean Gerrish, and David M. Blei. Black box variational inference. In *AISTATS*, 2014.

Carl Edward Rasmussen and Christopher K. I. Williams. *Gaussian processes for machine learning*. The MIT Press, 2006.

Salah Rifai, Pascal Vincent, Xavier Muller, Xavier Glorot, and Yoshua Bengio. Contractive auto-encoders: Explicit invariance during feature extraction. In *ICML*, 2011.

Sheldon M Ross. *Simulation*. Burlington, MA: Elsevier, 2006.

Rishit Sheth, Yuyang Wang, and Roni Khardon. Sparse variational inference for generalized GP models. In *ICML*, 2015.

S Sundararajan and S Sathiya Keerthi. Predictive approaches for choosing hyperparameters in Gaussian processes. *Neural Computation*, 13(5):1103–1118, 2001.

S. Sundararajan and S. Sathiya Keerthi. Predictive approaches for Gaussian process classifier model selection. Technical report, 2008.

S. Sundararajan, S. Sathiya Keerthi, and Shirish Shevade. Predictive approaches for sparse Gaussian process regression. Technical report, 2007.

Michalis Titsias. Variational learning of inducing variables in sparse Gaussian processes. In *AISTATS*, 2009.

Aki Vehtari, Tommi Mononen, Ville Tolvanen, Tuomas Sivula, and Ole Winther. Bayesian leave-one-out cross-validation approximations for Gaussian latent variable models. *Journal of Machine Learning Research*, 17(103):1–38, 2016.

Aki Vehtari, Andrew Gelman, and Jonah Gabry. Practical Bayesian model evaluation using leave-one-out cross-validation and WAIC. *Statistics and Computing*, 27(5):1413–1432, Sep 2017.

Sethu Vijayakumar and Stefan Schaal. Locally weighted projection regression: An O(n) algorithm for incremental real time learning in high dimensional space. In *ICML*, 2000.

Grace Wahba. *Spline models for observational data*. CBMS-NSF Regional Conference series in applied mathematics. Society for Industrial and Applied Mathematics, 1990.

Christopher Williams and Matthias Seeger. Using the Nyström method to speed up kernel machines. In *NIPS*, 2001.

Andrew G. Wilson, David A. Knowles, and Zoubin Ghahramani. Gaussian process regression networks. In *ICML*, 2012.

Andrew Gordon Wilson and Ryan Prescott Adams. Gaussian process kernels for pattern discovery and extrapolation. In *ICML*, pages 1067–1075, 2013.

Andrew Gordon Wilson, Zhiting Hu, Ruslan Salakhutdinov, and Eric P. Xing. Deep kernel learning. In *AISTATS*, 2016.

Wentao Zhu, Jun Miao, Laiyun Qing, and Xilin Chen. Deep trans-layer unsupervised networks for representation learning. *arXiv preprint arXiv:1509.08038*, 2015.

AutoGP: Exploring the Capabilities and Limitations of Gaussian Process Models — Supplementary Material

Karl Krauth **Edwin V. Bonilla**
The University of New South Wales
karl.krauth@gmail.com e.bonilla@unsw.edu.au

Kurt Cutajar **Maurizio Filippone**
EURECOM
{kurt.cutajar, maurizio.filippone}@eurecom.fr

1 DERIVATION OF LEAVE-ONE-OUT OBJECTIVE

In this section we derive an expression for the leave-one-out objective and show that this does not require training of N models. A similar derivation can be found in Vehtari et al. (2016). Let $\mathcal{D}_{\neg n} = \{\mathbf{X}_{\neg n}, \mathbf{y}_{\neg n}\}$ be the dataset resulting from removing observation n. Then our leave-one-out objective is given by:

$$\mathcal{L}_{\text{oo}}(\boldsymbol{\theta}) = \frac{1}{N}\sum_{n=1}^{N} \log p(\mathbf{y}_n|\mathbf{x}_n, \mathcal{D}_{\neg n}, \boldsymbol{\theta}). \tag{1}$$

We now that the marginal posterior can be computed as:

$$p(\mathbf{f}_{n\cdot}|\mathcal{D}) = p(\mathbf{f}_{n\cdot}|\mathbf{X}_{\neg n}, \mathbf{y}_{\neg n}, \mathbf{x}_n, \mathbf{y}_n) = \frac{p(\mathbf{y}_n|\mathbf{f}_{n\cdot})p(\mathbf{f}_{n\cdot}|\mathbf{x}_n, \mathcal{D}_{\neg n})}{p(\mathbf{y}_n|\mathbf{x}_n, \mathcal{D}_{\neg n}, \boldsymbol{\theta})} \tag{2}$$

and re-arranging terms

$$\int p(\mathbf{f}_{n\cdot}|\mathbf{x}_n, \mathcal{D}_{\neg n}, \boldsymbol{\theta}) d\mathbf{f}_{n\cdot} = \int \frac{p(\mathbf{f}_{n\cdot}|\mathcal{D}, \boldsymbol{\theta})p(\mathbf{y}_n|\mathbf{x}_n, \mathcal{D}_{\neg n}, \boldsymbol{\theta})}{p(\mathbf{y}_n|\mathbf{f}_{n\cdot})} d\mathbf{f}_{n\cdot} \tag{3}$$

$$p(\mathbf{y}_n|\mathbf{x}_n, \mathcal{D}_{\neg n}, \boldsymbol{\theta}) = 1/\int \frac{p(\mathbf{f}_{n\cdot}|\mathcal{D}, \boldsymbol{\theta})}{p(\mathbf{y}_n|\mathbf{f}_{n\cdot})} d\mathbf{f}_{n\cdot} \tag{4}$$

$$\log p(\mathbf{y}_n|\mathbf{x}_n, \mathcal{D}_{\neg n}; \boldsymbol{\theta}) = -\log \int \frac{p(\mathbf{f}_{n\cdot}|\mathcal{D}, \boldsymbol{\theta})}{p(\mathbf{y}_n|\mathbf{f}_{n\cdot})} d\mathbf{f}_{n\cdot}, \tag{5}$$

and substituting this expression in Equation (1) we have

$$\mathcal{L}_{\text{oo}}(\boldsymbol{\theta}) = -\frac{1}{N}\sum_{n=1}^{N} \log \int p(\mathbf{f}_{n\cdot}|\mathcal{D}, \boldsymbol{\theta}) \frac{1}{p(\mathbf{y}_n|\mathbf{f}_{n\cdot})}\, d\mathbf{f}_{n\cdot}. \tag{6}$$

We see that the objective only requires estimation of the marginal posterior $p(\mathbf{f}_{n\cdot}|\mathcal{D}, \boldsymbol{\theta})$, which we can approximate using variational inference, hence:

$$\mathcal{L}_{\text{oo}}(\boldsymbol{\theta}) \approx -\frac{1}{N}\sum_{n=1}^{N} \log \int q(\mathbf{f}_{n\cdot}|\mathcal{D}, \boldsymbol{\theta}) \frac{1}{p(\mathbf{y}_n|\mathbf{f}_{n\cdot})}\, d\mathbf{f}_{n\cdot}, \tag{7}$$

where $q(\mathbf{f}_{n\cdot}|\mathcal{D}, \boldsymbol{\theta})$ is our approximate variational posterior.

Table 1: The datasets used in the experiments and the corresponding models used. N_{train}, N_{test}, D are the number of training points, test points and input dimensions respectively.

Dataset	N_{train}	N_{test}	D	Model
SARCOS	$44,484$	$4,449$	21	GPRN
RECTANGLES-IMAGE	$12,000$	$50,000$	784	Binary classification
MNIST	$60,000$	$10,000$	784	Multi-class classification
CIFAR10	$50,000$	$10,000$	3072	Multi-class classification
MNIST8M	8.1M	$10,000$	784	Multi-class classification

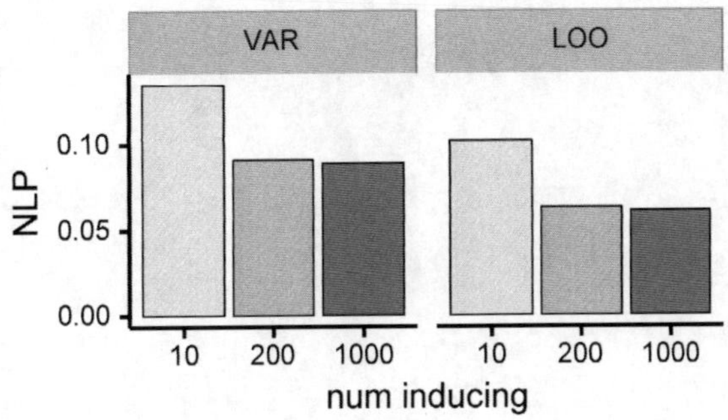

Figure 1: NLP for multiclass classification using a softmax likelihood model on the MNIST dataset. VAR shows the performance of AutoGP where all parameters are learned using only the variational objective $\widehat{\mathcal{L}}_{\text{elbo}}$, while LOO represents the performance of AutoGP when hyperparameters are learned using the leave-one-out objective $\widehat{\mathcal{L}}_{\text{oo}}$.

2 ADDITIONAL DETAILS OF EXPERIMENTS

2.1 EXPERIMENTAL SET-UP

The datasets used are described in Table 1. We trained our model stochastically using the RMSProp optimizer provided by TensorFlow (Abadi et al., 2015) with a learning rate of 0.003 and mini-batches of size 1000. We initialized inducing point locations by using the k-means clustering algorithm, and initialized the posterior mean to a zero vector, and the posterior covariances to identity matrices. When jointly optimizing $\widehat{\mathcal{L}}_{\text{oo}}$ and $\widehat{\mathcal{L}}_{\text{elbo}}$, we alternated between optimizing each objective for 100 epochs. Unless otherwise specified we used 100 Monte-Carlo samples to estimate the expected log likelihood term.

All timed experiments were performed on a machine with an Intel(R) Core(TM) i5-4460 CPU, 24GB of DDR3 RAM, and a GeForce GTX1070 GPU with TensorFlow 0.10rc.

2.2 ADDITIONAL RESULTS

Figure 1 shows the NLP for our evaluation of the LOO-CV-based hyperparameter learning. As with the error rates described in the main text, the NLP obtained with LOO-CV are significantly better than those obtained with a purely variational approach.

References

Martín Abadi, Ashish Agarwal, Paul Barham, et al. TensorFlow: Large-scale machine learning on heterogeneous systems, 2015.

Aki Vehtari, Tommi Mononen, Ville Tolvanen, Tuomas Sivula, and Ole Winther. Bayesian leave-one-out cross-validation approximations for Gaussian latent variable models. *Journal of Machine Learning Research*, 17(103): 1–38, 2016.

A Fast Stochastic Riemannian Eigensolver

Zhiqiang Xu
King Abdullah University of
Science and Technology (KAUST)
CEMSE Division
Thuwal, 23955, Saudi Arabia

Yiping Ke
Nanyang Technological University
Singapore

Xin Gao
King Abdullah University of
Science and Technology (KAUST)
CEMSE Division
Thuwal, 23955, Saudi Arabia

Abstract

We propose a fast stochastic Riemannian gradient eigensolver for a real and symmetric matrix, and prove its local, eigengap-dependent and linear convergence. The fast convergence is brought by deploying the variance reduction technique which was originally developed for the Euclidean strongly convex problems. In this paper, this technique is generalized to Riemannian manifolds for solving the geodesically non-convex problem of finding a group of top eigenvectors of such a matrix. We first propose the general variance reduction form of the stochastic Riemannian gradient, giving rise to the stochastic variance reduced Riemannian gradient method (SVRRG). It turns out that the operation of vector transport is necessary in addition to using Riemannian gradients and retraction operations. We then specialize it to the problem in question resulting in our SVRRG-EIGS algorithm. We are among the first to propose and analyze the generalization of the stochastic variance reduced gradient (SVRG) to Riemannian manifolds. As an extension of the linearly convergent VR-PCA, it is significant and nontrivial for the proposed algorithm to theoretically achieve a further speedup and empirically make a difference, due to our respect to the inherent geometry of the problem.

1 INTRODUCTION

The problem of finding a group of top eigenvectors of a symmetric matrix $\mathbf{A} \in \mathbb{R}^{n\times n}$ is among the core and long-standing topics in numerical computing (Wilkinson, 1988), and plays fundamental roles in various scientific and engineering computing problems, such as numerical computation (Golub and Van Loan, 1996; Press et al., 2007), structural analysis (Torbjorn Ringertz, 1997), kernel approximation (Drineas and Mahoney, 2005) and spectral clustering (Ng et al., 2002; Xu and Ke, 2016b) in machine learning. Varieties of solvers for this problem have been proposed such as the deterministic power iteration (Golub and Van Loan, 1996) and (block) Lanczos algorithm (Parlett, 1998), randomized SVD (Halko et al., 2011), Oja's stochastic PCA (Oja and Karhunen, 1985), online learning of eigenvectors (Garber et al., 2015), stochastic PCA with variance reduction (Shamir, 2015, 2016), and so on. Studies from the optimization perspective are popular as well, including the trace penalty minimization (Wen et al., 2013) and notably the unconstrained maximization in the Riemannian setting (Edelman et al., 1999; Absil et al., 2008; Wen and Yin, 2013). The Riemannian formulation yields a geodesically non-convex problem:

$$\max_{\mathbf{X}\in \mathrm{St}(n,k)} f(\mathbf{X}) \triangleq (1/2)\mathrm{tr}(\mathbf{X}^\top \mathbf{A}\mathbf{X}), \tag{1}$$

where $\mathrm{St}(n,k) = \{\mathbf{X} \in \mathbb{R}^{n\times k} : \mathbf{X}^\top\mathbf{X} = \mathbf{I}\}$ constitutes a Riemannian manifold that is called the Stiefel manifold. Inspired by the success of the recently proposed stochastic variance reduced gradient (SVRG) method, in this paper, we generalize this technique from the Euclidean space to Riemannian manifolds. First, the general form of the stochastic variance reduced Riemannian gradient (SVRRG) method is proposed in the stochastic Riemannian gradient optimization framework. It then is specialized to Problem (1) and gives rise to our SVRRG-EIGS algorithm. In addition to the use of Riemannian gradients and retraction operations, we need to introduce one new ingredient, i.e., parallel/vector transport, in order to legitimize SVRG in the Riemannian setting. Built upon the analysis of VR-PCA (Shamir, 2015, 2016), we prove the local, eigengap-dependent and linear convergence of the proposed SVRRG-EIGS. In addition, it is shown that SVRRG-EIGS achieves a further speedup both theoretically and empirically on top of the fast VR-

PCA, due to our respect to the Riemannian geometry of the problem. This speedup is significant and nontrivial, because VR-PCA already converges at a rate of a best possible order with first-order methods, i.e., $O(\log \frac{1}{\epsilon})$. The main contributions of the paper are summarized as follows:

- We generalize SVRG to Riemannian manifolds to obtain the general SVRRG method and the SVRRG-EIGS algorithm special for Problem (1).
- We establish the local, eigengap-dependent and linear convergence of the proposed SVRRG-EIGS algorithm for the underlying geodesically non-convex problem. We are among the first to propose and analyze the generalization of SVRG to Riemannian manifolds.
- We show that SVRRG-EIGS improves over VR-PCA in both theory and practice.

2 RELATED WORK

We briefly review those recently proposed and closely related work on the stochastic (Riemannian) eigensolvers and refer readers to cited papers and references theirin for more relevant work.

There has been a large body of work emerging recently on stochastic eigensolvers. Balsubramani et al. (2013) proved the local, eigengap-dependent and sub-linear convergence of Oja's stochastic PCA (Oja and Karhunen, 1985) for the case $k = 1$. Shamir proposed VR-PCA based on Oja's algorithm, and proved its local, eigengap-dependent and linear convergence for $k = 1$ (i.e., vector version) in (Shamir, 2015) and its nontrivial extension to $k \geq 1$ (i.e., block version) in (Shamir, 2016). The analysis of our proposed algorithm SVRRG-EIGS is built upon and meanwhile significantly extends/improves over that of VR-PCA for the block version, as is shown largely in the supplementary material. Garber et al. (2016) proved the global and eigengap-dependent linear convergence of PCA and the global, eigengap-free and sub-linear convergence of PCA, both for the case $k = 1$, by giving a robust analysis of the shift-and-invert preconditioning method to reduce the target problem to a sequence of linear systems and then leveraging the SVRG for the system solver. Jain et al. (2016) provides an eigengap-dependent, linear-time and single-pass streaming algorithm for the case $k = 1$. Ge et al. (2016) proved the global, eigengap-dependent and linear convergence of generalized eigenvalue problem for the case $k = 1$. Allen-Zhu and Li (2016) proposed a fast SVD decomposition with the global, eigengap-free and sub-linear convergence for the case $k > 1$ via recursive calls to the vector version of SVD, i.e., $k = 1$. As we can see, most of these studies focus on the vector case $k = 1$, while we work on the block case $k \geq 1$ in this paper. Note that some work on PCA rely on the special data representation $\mathbf{A} = \mathbf{B}\mathbf{B}^\top$ where $\mathbf{B} \in \mathbb{R}^{n \times m}$ consists of m n-dimensional vector samples, and manipulate $\mathbf{B}$ instead of $\mathbf{A}$ in analysis. Their results might be inapplicable to the case where we are given only $\mathbf{A}$ without $\mathbf{B}$.

Our work falls into the category of the stochastic Riemannian optimization. From this point of view, Bonnabel (2013) proposed the general form of the Riemannian stochastic gradient descent (SGD) method and proved its global and almost sure convergence to Riemannian stationary points. The results naturally apply to the Riemannian SGD solver for Problem (1). However, as we know, any k eigenvectors of $\mathbf{A}$ constitutes a Riemannian stationary point of the problem. Thus, theoretically, they are not necessarily the top k eigenvectors. Xu et al. (2016) proved the local, eigengap-dependent and sub-linear convergence to a globally optimal solution. Recently the variance reduction technique has been generalized to Riemannian manifolds by three groups of researchers in parallel. Zhang et al. (2016) proposed the general Riemannian SVRG for compact manifolds and proved the global, eigengap-free and sub-linear convergence to Riemannian stationary points for geodesically nonconvex problems including Problem (1). However, their results only apply to the case $k = 1$ for our problem, because the gradient dominance property was only proven to hold for this case. For $k > 1$, it is unclear thus far. Moreover, their method is computationally costly, because it is built upon the geodesic based operations and thus needs the computation of matrix exponential on Stiefel manifolds. And the parallel transport they used has no closed forms for Stiefel manifolds when $k > 1$. In contrast, we use a closed-form vector transport. Kasai et al. (2016) proposed the Riemannian SVRG for Grassmann manifolds and proved its local, eigengap-free and linear convergence. However, they require the Riemannian Hessian at the locally optimal solution to be positive definite, which does not hold for Problem (1). And their method incurs the computational issue similarly. For example, in each inner iteration, their method needs to do SVD twice in order to complete three operations, i.e., logarithmic map, parallel transport and exponential map. In contrast, we use their cheap counterparts (i.e., first-order approximation) without SVD and do not need the logarithmic map operation. A preliminary version of this paper is also among the first to propose the Riemannian SVRG (Xu and Ke, 2016a).

3 PRELIMINARIES

Suppose that λ_i represents the i-th largest eigenvalue of $\mathbf{A}$, $\mathbf{\Sigma} = \mathrm{diag}(\lambda_1, \ldots, \lambda_k)$ and $\mathbf{U}$ is the collection of corresponding top k eigenvectors in columns. Then $\mathbf{A} = \mathbf{U\Sigma U}^\top + \mathbf{U}_\perp \mathbf{\Sigma}_\perp \mathbf{U}_\perp^\top$, where $\mathbf{\Sigma}_\perp$ is a diagonal matrix with diagonal entries consisting of the other eigenvalues λ_i, $k < i \leq n$ and $\mathbf{U}_\perp$ is the orthogonal complement of $\mathbf{U}$ corresponding to the other eigenvectors. It is easy to see that an arbitrary globally optimal solution of Problem (1) is given by $\mathbf{X}^\star = \mathbf{UQ}$ where $\mathbf{Q} \in \mathrm{St}(k, k)$ is an orthogonal matrix, under the assumption that the eigengap $\tau = \lambda_k - \lambda_{k+1} > 0$.

3.1 RIEMANNIAN OPTIMIZATION

Given a Riemmanian manifold $\mathcal{M}$, its tangent space at a point $\mathbf{X} \in \mathcal{M}$, denoted as $T_\mathbf{X}\mathcal{M}$, is a Euclidean space that is tangential to and locally linearizes $\mathcal{M}$ around this point (Lee, 2012). One update step of the first-order Riemannian optimization on $\mathcal{M}$ can be written as (Absil et al., 2008):

$$\mathbf{X}_{t+1} = R_{\mathbf{X}_t}(\alpha_{t+1}\xi_{\mathbf{X}_t}), \tag{2}$$

where $\xi_{\mathbf{X}_t} \in T_{\mathbf{X}_t}\mathcal{M}$ is called a tangent vector of $\mathcal{M}$ at $\mathbf{X}_t$ and used as the t-th search direction, $\alpha_{t+1} > 0$ is the learning rate (a.k.a. step size), and $R_{\mathbf{X}_t}(\cdot)$ represents the retraction at $\mathbf{X}_t$ that maps a tangent vector $\xi \in T_{\mathbf{X}_t}\mathcal{M}$ to a point on $\mathcal{M}$. Tangent vectors serving as search directions are generally gradient-related. The gradient of a function $f(\mathbf{X})$ on $\mathcal{M}$, denoted as $\mathrm{Grad}f(\mathbf{X})$, depends on the Riemannian metric, which is a family of smoothly varying inner products on tangent spaces, i.e., $\langle \xi, \eta \rangle_\mathbf{X}$, where $\xi, \eta \in T_\mathbf{X}\mathcal{M}$ for any $\mathbf{X} \in \mathcal{M}$. The Riemannian gradient $\mathrm{Grad}f(\mathbf{X}) \in T_\mathbf{X}\mathcal{M}$ is the unique tangent vector that satisfies

$$\langle \mathrm{Grad}f(\mathbf{X}), \xi \rangle_\mathbf{X} = Df(\mathbf{X})[\xi] \tag{3}$$

for any $\xi \in T_\mathbf{X}\mathcal{M}$, where $Df(\mathbf{X})[\xi]$ represents the directional derivative of $f(\mathbf{X})$ in the tangent direction ξ. Setting $\xi_{\mathbf{X}_t} = \mathrm{Grad}f(\mathbf{X}_t)$ in (2) leads to the Riemannian gradient (RG) ascent method:

$$\mathbf{X}_{t+1} = R_{\mathbf{X}_t}(\alpha_{t+1}\mathrm{Grad}f(\mathbf{X}_t)), \tag{4}$$

while setting $\xi_{\mathbf{X}_t} = G(y_{t+1}, \mathbf{X}_t)$ in (2) gives us the stochastic Riemannian gradient (Bonnabel, 2013) (SRG) ascent method:

$$\mathbf{X}_{t+1} = R_{\mathbf{X}_t}(\alpha_{t+1}G(y_{t+1}, \mathbf{X}_t)), \tag{5}$$

where y_{t+1} is a random variable such that $\mathbb{E}[f(y_{t+1}, \mathbf{X}_t)|\mathbf{X}_t] = f(\mathbf{X}_t)$, and $G(y_{t+1}, \mathbf{X}_t) \in T_{\mathbf{X}_t}\mathcal{M}$ is the stochastic Riemannian gradient such that $\mathbb{E}[G(y_{t+1}, \mathbf{X}_t)|\mathbf{X}_t] = \mathrm{Grad}f(\mathbf{X}_t)$. According to (Bonnabel, 2013), the SRG method can converge globally and almost surely to a stationary point under mild conditions including $\sum_t \alpha_t = \infty$ and $\sum_t \alpha_t^2 < \infty$ (the latter condition implies that $\alpha_t \to 0$ as $t \to \infty$).

3.2 RIEMANNIAN EIGENSOLVER

For Problem (1), note that $\mathrm{St}(n, k)$ is an embedded Riemannian sub-manifold of the Euclidean space $\mathbb{R}^{n\times k}$. With the metric inherited from the embedding space $\mathbb{R}^{n\times k}$, i.e., $\langle \xi, \eta \rangle_\mathbf{X} = \mathrm{tr}(\xi^\top \eta)$, and by (3), we can get the Riemannian gradient[1] of $f(\mathbf{X})$ in Problem (1), i.e.,

$$\mathrm{Grad}f(\mathbf{X}) = (\mathbf{I} - \mathbf{XX}^\top)\mathbf{AX} \in T_\mathbf{X}\mathrm{St}(n, k).$$

The orthogonal projection onto $T_\mathbf{X}\mathrm{St}(n, k)$ under this metric is given by

$$P_\mathbf{X}(\zeta) = (\mathbf{I} - \mathbf{XX}^\top)\zeta + \mathbf{X}\mathrm{skew}(\mathbf{X}^\top\zeta) \tag{6}$$

for any $\zeta \in \mathbb{R}^{n\times k}$, where $\mathrm{skew}(H) = (H - H^\top)/2$. We use the polar decomposition based retraction (Absil et al., 2008)

$$R_\mathbf{X}(\xi) = (\mathbf{X} + \xi)(\mathbf{I} + \xi^\top\xi)^{-1/2} \tag{7}$$

for any $\xi \in T_\mathbf{X}\mathrm{St}(n, k)$. The deployment of (4) and (5) to Problem (1) generates one Riemannian eigensolver denoted as RG-EIGS and one stochastic Riemannian eigensolver denoted as SRG-EIGS, respectively.

4 SVRRG

Recall that SVRG (Johnson and Zhang, 2013) is built on the vanilla stochastic gradient and achieves the variance reduction through constructing control variates in epoches (Wang et al., 2013). Control variates are of stochastic zero-mean and serve to augment and correct stochastic gradients towards the true gradients. Following (Johnson and Zhang, 2013), SVRG reads

$$g_t(\xi_t, w^{(t-1)}, \tilde{w}) = \nabla\psi_{i_t}(w^{(t-1)}) - (\nabla\psi_{i_t}(\tilde{w}) - \nabla P(\tilde{w})),$$

where $\tilde{w}$ is a version of the variable w estimated at the snapshot point after every m SGD steps, and $\nabla P(\tilde{w}) = \frac{1}{n}\sum_{i=1}^n \nabla\psi_i(\tilde{w})$ is the full gradient at $\tilde{w}$.

Our goal here is to develop the Riemannian counterpart of SVRG, termed as SVRRG and denoted as

[1] Due to the symmetry of $\mathbf{A}$, Riemannian gradients under the Euclidean metric and the canonical metric are the same (Wen and Yin, 2013). However, since the orthogonal projector used in the sequel requires the metrics for the embedded Riemannian sub-manifold and the embedding space to be the same, we choose the Euclidean metric here.

$G(y_{t+1}, \mathbf{X}_t, \tilde{\mathbf{X}})$. One naive extension of SVRG to Riemannian manifolds by substituting Riemannian gradients only can be written as

$$\begin{aligned} & G(y_{t+1}, \mathbf{X}_t, \tilde{\mathbf{X}}) \\ = \; & G(y_{t+1}, \mathbf{X}_t) - (G(y_{t+1}, \tilde{\mathbf{X}}) - \mathrm{Grad} f(\tilde{\mathbf{X}})), \end{aligned}$$

where $G(y_{t+1}, \tilde{\mathbf{X}})$, $\mathrm{Grad} f(\tilde{\mathbf{X}}) \in T_{\tilde{\mathbf{X}}}\mathcal{M}$ and $G(y_{t+1}, \mathbf{X}_t) \in T_{\mathbf{X}_t}\mathcal{M}$. However, this is unsound theoretically, as the stochastic Riemannian gradient $G(y_{t+1}, \mathbf{X}_t)$ and the control variate $G(y_{t+1}, \tilde{\mathbf{X}}) - \mathrm{Grad} f(\tilde{\mathbf{X}})$ reside in two different tangent spaces and it hence renders their difference $G(y_{t+1}, \mathbf{X}_t, \tilde{\mathbf{X}})$ not well-defined in a Riemannian space. To rectify this issue, we need the operation that can move tangent vectors from one point to another along the geodesics in parallel, namely parallel transport. Our control variate thus need be parallel transported from $\tilde{\mathbf{X}}$ to $\mathbf{X}_t$. For computational efficiency, vector transport as its first-order approximation is often used in practice (Absil et al., 2008).

Vector transport of a tangent vector from point $\tilde{\mathbf{X}}$ to point $\mathbf{X}_t$, denoted as $\mathcal{T}_{\tilde{\mathbf{X}} \to \mathbf{X}_t}$, is a mapping from the tangent space $T_{\tilde{\mathbf{X}}}\mathcal{M}$ to the tangent space $T_{\mathbf{X}_t}\mathcal{M}$. When $\mathcal{M}$ is an embedded Riemannian sub-manifold of a Euclidean space, it can be simply defined as $\mathcal{T}_{\tilde{\mathbf{X}} \to \mathbf{X}_t}(\xi_{\tilde{\mathbf{X}}}) = P_{\mathbf{X}_t}(\xi_{\tilde{\mathbf{X}}})$. With vector transport, we now have a well-defined SVRRG in $T_{\mathbf{X}_t}\mathcal{M}$, i.e.,

$$\begin{aligned} & G(y_{t+1}, \mathbf{X}_t, \tilde{\mathbf{X}}) \\ = \; & G(y_{t+1}, \mathbf{X}_t) - \mathcal{T}_{\tilde{\mathbf{X}} \to \mathbf{X}_t}(G(y_{t+1}, \tilde{\mathbf{X}}) - \mathrm{Grad} f(\tilde{\mathbf{X}})). \end{aligned}$$

The use of Riemannian gradients and vector transport makes SVRRG significantly different from SVRG. We then arrive at the SVRRG method:

$$\mathbf{X}_{t+1} = R_{\mathbf{X}_t}(\alpha_{t+1} G(y_{t+1}, \mathbf{X}_t, \tilde{\mathbf{X}})). \tag{8}$$

Note that the SVRRG method is naturally subsumed into the SRG method (5), and thus enjoys all its properties including the almost sure convergence.

Algorithm 1 SVRRG

Require: $\mathbf{A}$, $\tilde{\mathbf{X}}_0$, α, epoch length m

for $s = 1, 2, \cdots$ **do**
  Compute $\mathrm{Grad} f(\tilde{\mathbf{X}}_{s-1})$
  $\mathbf{X}_0 = \tilde{\mathbf{X}}_{s-1}$
  for $t = 1, 2, \cdots, m$ **do**
    Pick $y_t \in \mathcal{Y}$ uniformly at random
    Compute $\mathbf{X}_t = R_{\mathbf{X}_{t-1}}(\alpha G(y_t, \mathbf{X}_{t-1}, \tilde{\mathbf{X}}_{s-1}))$
  end for
  $\tilde{\mathbf{X}}_s = \mathbf{X}_m$
end for

5 SVRRG-EIGS

In this section, we deploy the SVRRG method to Problem (1), then giving rise to a new eigensolver termed as SVRRG-EIGS. Assume that $\mathbf{A} = \frac{1}{L}\sum_{i=1}^{L} \tilde{\mathbf{A}}_i$, y is a random variable taking values in $\mathcal{Y} = \{1, 2, \cdots, L\}$ and $\mathbf{A}_{t+1} = \tilde{\mathbf{A}}_{y_{t+1}}$. In practice, $\tilde{\mathbf{A}}_i$ can be obtained from a partitioning of $\mathbf{A}$. We then can write the stochastic gradient and control variate as

$$\begin{aligned} G(y_{t+1}, \mathbf{X}_t) &= (\mathbf{I} - \mathbf{X}_t \mathbf{X}_t^\top)\mathbf{A}_{t+1}\mathbf{X}_t, \\ G(y_{t+1}, \tilde{\mathbf{X}}) - \mathrm{Grad} f(\tilde{\mathbf{X}}) &= (\mathbf{I} - \tilde{\mathbf{X}}\tilde{\mathbf{X}}^\top)(\mathbf{A}_{t+1} - \mathbf{A})\tilde{\mathbf{X}}, \end{aligned}$$

respectively. Using the orthogonal projector (6), the transported control variate can be written as

$$\begin{aligned} & \mathcal{T}_{\tilde{\mathbf{X}} \to \mathbf{X}_t}(G(y_{t+1}, \tilde{\mathbf{X}}) - \mathrm{Grad} f(\tilde{\mathbf{X}})) \\ = \; & (\mathbf{I} - \mathbf{X}_t \mathbf{X}_t^\top)(\mathbf{I} - \tilde{\mathbf{X}}\tilde{\mathbf{X}}^\top)(\mathbf{A}_{t+1} - \mathbf{A})\tilde{\mathbf{X}} \\ & + \mathbf{X}_t \mathrm{skew}(\mathbf{X}_t^\top(\mathbf{I} - \tilde{\mathbf{X}}\tilde{\mathbf{X}}^\top)(\mathbf{A}_{t+1} - \mathbf{A})\tilde{\mathbf{X}}) \\ = \; & (\mathbf{I} - \mathbf{X}_t \mathbf{X}_t^\top)(\mathbf{A}_{t+1} - \mathbf{A})\tilde{\mathbf{X}} \\ & - (\mathbf{I} - \mathbf{X}_t \mathbf{X}_t^\top)\tilde{\mathbf{X}}\tilde{\mathbf{X}}^\top(\mathbf{A}_{t+1} - \mathbf{A})\tilde{\mathbf{X}} \\ & + \mathbf{X}_t \mathrm{skew}(\mathbf{X}_t^\top(\mathbf{I} - \tilde{\mathbf{X}}\tilde{\mathbf{X}}^\top)(\mathbf{A}_{t+1} - \mathbf{A})\tilde{\mathbf{X}}). \end{aligned}$$

SVRRG then reads

$$\begin{aligned} & G(y_{t+1}, \mathbf{X}_t, \tilde{\mathbf{X}}) \\ = \; & (\mathbf{I} - \mathbf{X}_t \mathbf{X}_t^\top)\mathbf{A}_{t+1}\mathbf{X}_t \\ & - \mathcal{T}_{\tilde{\mathbf{X}} \to \mathbf{X}_t}(G(y_{t+1}, \tilde{\mathbf{X}}) - \mathrm{Grad} f(\tilde{\mathbf{X}})) \\ = \; & (\mathbf{I} - \mathbf{X}_t \mathbf{X}_t^\top)\mathbf{A}\mathbf{X}_t \\ & + (\mathbf{I} - \mathbf{X}_t \mathbf{X}_t^\top)(\mathbf{A}_{t+1} - \mathbf{A})(\mathbf{X}_t - \tilde{\mathbf{X}}) \\ & + (\mathbf{I} - \mathbf{X}_t \mathbf{X}_t^\top)\tilde{\mathbf{X}}\tilde{\mathbf{X}}^\top(\mathbf{A}_{t+1} - \mathbf{A})\tilde{\mathbf{X}} \\ & - \mathbf{X}_t \mathrm{skew}(\mathbf{X}_t^\top(\mathbf{I} - \tilde{\mathbf{X}}\tilde{\mathbf{X}}^\top)(\mathbf{A}_{t+1} - \mathbf{A})\tilde{\mathbf{X}}) \\ \triangleq \; & \mathrm{Grad} f(\mathbf{X}_t) + \mathbf{W}_t, \end{aligned}$$

where $\mathbf{W}_t \in T_{\mathbf{X}_t}\mathrm{St}(n, k)$ is a stochastic zero-mean term conditioned on $\mathbf{X}_t$. As we see above, SVRRG has significantly extended SVRG used in VR-PCA. Although the factor $(\mathbf{X}_t - \tilde{\mathbf{X}})$ present in $\mathbf{W}_t$ works well empirically, in order for ease of theoretical analysis we follow (Shamir, 2016) to replace $\tilde{\mathbf{X}}$ with $\tilde{\mathbf{X}}\mathbf{Q}_t$, where $\mathbf{Q}_t = \mathbf{P}_2\mathbf{P}_1^\top$ and $\mathbf{X}_t^\top\tilde{\mathbf{X}} = \mathbf{P}_1\mathbf{\Lambda}\mathbf{P}_2^\top$ is the SVD of $\mathbf{X}_t^\top\tilde{\mathbf{X}}$. With a bit abuse of the notation for $\mathbf{W}$, we have the final SVRRG for Problem (1) written as,

$$\begin{aligned} & G(y_{t+1}, \mathbf{X}_t, \tilde{\mathbf{X}}, \mathbf{Q}_t) \\ = \; & (\mathbf{I} - \mathbf{X}_t \mathbf{X}_t^\top)\mathbf{A}\mathbf{X}_t \\ & + (\mathbf{I} - \mathbf{X}_t \mathbf{X}_t^\top)(\mathbf{A}_{t+1} - \mathbf{A})(\mathbf{X}_t - \tilde{\mathbf{X}}\mathbf{Q}_t) \\ & + (\mathbf{I} - \mathbf{X}_t \mathbf{X}_t^\top)\tilde{\mathbf{X}}\tilde{\mathbf{X}}^\top(\mathbf{A}_{t+1} - \mathbf{A})\tilde{\mathbf{X}}\mathbf{Q}_t \\ & - \mathbf{X}_t \mathrm{skew}(\mathbf{X}_t^\top(\mathbf{I} - \tilde{\mathbf{X}}\tilde{\mathbf{X}}^\top)(\mathbf{A}_{t+1} - \mathbf{A})\tilde{\mathbf{X}}\mathbf{Q}_t) \\ \triangleq \; & \mathrm{Grad} f(\mathbf{X}_t) + \mathbf{W}_t. \end{aligned}$$

Thus the intermediate update in the tangent space is

$$\text{SVRRG-EIGS}: \mathbf{X}_t + \alpha_{t+1}\text{Grad}f(\mathbf{X}_t) + \alpha_{t+1}\mathbf{W}_t.$$

For comparison, the counterparts for RG-EIGS and SRG-EIGS are given similarly as follows

$$\begin{aligned} \text{RG-EIGS}: \quad & \mathbf{X}_t + \alpha_{t+1}\text{Grad}f(\mathbf{X}_t), \\ \text{SRG-EIGS}: \quad & \mathbf{X}_t + \alpha_{t+1}\text{Grad}f(\mathbf{X}_t) \\ & + \alpha_{t+1}(\mathbf{I} - \mathbf{X}_t\mathbf{X}_t^\top)(\mathbf{A}_{t+1} - \mathbf{A})\mathbf{X}_t. \end{aligned}$$

We can see that intermediate steps in both SRG-EIGS and SVRRG-EIGS amount to moving forward along the Riemannian gradient direction that is perturbed by a stochastic zero-mean noise term in the tangent space. However, the stochastic zero-mean term with SRG-EIGS, i.e., $(\mathbf{I} - \mathbf{X}_t\mathbf{X}_t^\top)(\mathbf{A}_{t+1} - \mathbf{A})\mathbf{X}_t$, always carries a constant variance. It thus needs a diminishing learning rate α_t in order to reduce the variance and to ensure the convergence. As a result, the convergence rate is compromised. On the contrary, SVRRG-EIGS keeps boosting the variance reduction of the stochastic zero-mean term $\mathbf{W}_t$ during iterations. The variance of $\mathbf{W}_t$ is dominated by quantities $\|\mathbf{X}_t - \tilde{\mathbf{X}}\mathbf{Q}_t\|$, $\|(\mathbf{I} - \mathbf{X}_t\mathbf{X}_t^\top)\tilde{\mathbf{X}}\mathbf{Q}_t\|$ and $\|\mathbf{X}_t^\top(\mathbf{I} - \tilde{\mathbf{X}}\tilde{\mathbf{X}}^\top)\|$. Instead of learning rate, these quantities repeatedly decay till vanishing, as $\mathbf{X}_t$ and $\tilde{\mathbf{X}}\mathbf{Q}_t$ become increasingly close to each other. Since it ensures a decaying variance without learning rate involved, SVRRG-EIGS is able to use a fixed learning rate $\alpha_t = \alpha$ and thus to achieve a much faster convergence rate.

The algorithmic steps of SVRRG-EIGS are given in Algorithm 2.

Algorithm 2 SVRRG-EIGS

Require: $\mathbf{A}, \tilde{\mathbf{X}}_0, \alpha, m$
- **for** $s = 1, 2, \cdots$ **do**
  - $\tilde{\mathbf{G}}^{s-1} = (\mathbf{I} - \tilde{\mathbf{X}}_{s-1}\tilde{\mathbf{X}}_{s-1}^\top)\mathbf{A}\tilde{\mathbf{X}}_{s-1}$
  - $\mathbf{X}_0 = \tilde{\mathbf{X}}_{s-1}$
  - **for** $t = 1, 2, \cdots, m$ **do**
    - Pick $y_t \in \{1, 2, \cdots, L\}$ uniformly at random
    - $\tilde{\mathbf{G}}_{t-1}^{s-1} = (\mathbf{I} - \tilde{\mathbf{X}}_{s-1}\tilde{\mathbf{X}}_{s-1}^\top)\mathbf{A}_t\tilde{\mathbf{X}}_{s-1}$
    - $\mathbf{X}_{t-1}^\top\tilde{\mathbf{X}}_{s-1} \overset{\text{svd}}{=} \mathbf{P}_1\mathbf{\Lambda}\mathbf{P}_2^\top$
    - $\Delta_{t-1}^{s-1} = (\tilde{\mathbf{G}}_{t-1}^{s-1} - \tilde{\mathbf{G}}^{s-1})\mathbf{P}_2\mathbf{P}_1^\top$
    - $\mathcal{T}(\Delta_{t-1}^{s-1}) = \Delta_{t-1}^{s-1} - \mathbf{X}_{t-1}\text{sym}(\Delta_{t-1}^{s-1})$
    - $\mathbf{G}_{t-1} = (\mathbf{I} - \mathbf{X}_{t-1}\mathbf{X}_{t-1}^\top)\mathbf{A}_t\mathbf{X}_{t-1}$
    - $\hat{\mathbf{G}}_{t-1}^{s-1} = \mathbf{G}_{t-1} - \mathcal{T}(\Delta_{t-1}^{s-1})$
    - $\mathbf{Y}_t = \mathbf{X}_{t-1} + \alpha\hat{\mathbf{G}}_{t-1}^{s-1}$
    - $\mathbf{X}_t = \mathbf{Y}_t(\mathbf{Y}_t^\top\mathbf{Y}_t)^{-1/2}$
  - **end for**
  - $\tilde{\mathbf{X}}_s = \mathbf{X}_m$
- **end for**

5.1 THEORETICAL ANALYSIS

We now study theoretical properties of SVRRG-EIGS, which is built upon the analysis of VR-PCA in (Shamir, 2016). The potential function is defined as $\Theta_t \triangleq \Theta(\mathbf{X}_t, \mathbf{U}) = k - \|\mathbf{U}^\top\mathbf{X}_t\|_F^2$. It is easy to see that $\Theta_t \in [0, k]$ and $\Theta_t = 0$ if and only if $\mathbf{X}_t = \mathbf{U}\mathbf{Q}$, where $\mathbf{Q} \in \text{St}(k, k)$. Note that the only assumptions we make in the analysis are that the eigengap $\tau > 0$ and $\Theta_0 < \delta$, where $\delta \in (0, 1)$. In what follows, we use a fixed learning rate α. In addition, let $\beta = \|\mathbf{A}\|_2$, $\tilde{\Theta}_s = \Theta(\tilde{\mathbf{X}}_s, \mathbf{U})$ and $\mathbf{Y}_t = \mathbf{X}_t + \alpha\text{Grad}f(\mathbf{X}_t)$. All the proofs of lemmas herein for the analysis are provided in the supplementary material.

First, we can write

$$\begin{aligned} & \|\mathbf{X}_{t+1}^\top\mathbf{U}\|_F^2 \\ = \; & \|R_{\mathbf{X}_t}(\alpha G(y_{t+1}, \mathbf{X}_t, \tilde{\mathbf{X}}, \mathbf{Q}_t))^\top\mathbf{U}\|_F^2 \\ = \; & \text{tr}((a_1(\mathbf{X}_t) + b_1(\mathbf{W}_t))(a_2(\mathbf{X}_t) + b_2(\mathbf{W}_t))^{-1}), \end{aligned}$$

where[2]

$$\begin{aligned} a_1(\mathbf{X}_t) &= \mathbf{Y}_t^\top\mathbf{U}\mathbf{U}^\top\mathbf{Y}_t + \alpha^2\mathbf{W}_t^\top\mathbf{U}\mathbf{U}^\top\mathbf{W}_t, \\ b_1(\mathbf{W}_t) &= 2\alpha\,\text{sym}(\mathbf{Y}_t^\top\mathbf{U}\mathbf{U}^\top\mathbf{W}_t), \\ a_2(\mathbf{X}_t) &= \mathbf{Y}_t^\top\mathbf{Y}_t + \alpha^2\mathbf{W}_t^\top\mathbf{W}_t, \\ b_2(\mathbf{W}_t) &= 2\alpha\,\text{sym}(\mathbf{Y}_t^\top\mathbf{W}_t). \end{aligned}$$

Note that $\mathbb{E}[b_1(\mathbf{W}_t)|\mathbf{X}_t] = \mathbb{E}[b_2(\mathbf{W}_t)|\mathbf{X}_t] = \mathbf{0}$, $a_1(\mathbf{X}_t) \succcurlyeq \mathbf{Y}_t^\top\mathbf{U}\mathbf{U}^\top\mathbf{Y}_t$ and $a_2(\mathbf{X}_t) \preccurlyeq \mathbf{Y}_t^\top\mathbf{Y}_t + \alpha^2\nu_t^2\mathbf{I}$ due to the following lemma.

Lemma 5.1. *Let* $\tilde{\beta} = \max_i \|\tilde{\mathbf{A}}_i - \mathbf{A}\|_2$. *Then*

$$\begin{aligned} \|\mathbf{W}_t\|_2 &\leq \mu \triangleq 4\tilde{\beta}, \\ \|\mathbf{W}_t\|_F^2 &\leq \nu_t^2 \triangleq 24\tilde{\beta}^2(\Theta_t + \tilde{\Theta}_{s-1}). \end{aligned}$$

Note that ν_t is a constant conditioned on $\mathbf{X}_t$. Despite a more complicated stochastic zero-mean term $\mathbf{W}_t$, we manage to bound it by a quantity about $\Theta_t + \tilde{\Theta}_{s-1}$ which will help the subsequent analysis.

Lemma 5.2. *If* $\mathbf{C}_1 \succcurlyeq \mathbf{0}$, $\mathbf{C}_2 \succcurlyeq \mathbf{0}$ *and* $\mathbf{D}_2 \succcurlyeq \mathbf{D}_1 \succ \mathbf{0}$, *then* $\text{tr}(\mathbf{C}_1\mathbf{D}_1^{-1}) \geq \text{tr}((\mathbf{C}_1 - \mathbf{C}_2)\mathbf{D}_2^{-1})$.

By Lemma 5.2 and abusing notations for $a_i(\mathbf{X}_t)$, $i = 1, 2$, we get

$$\begin{aligned} & \|\mathbf{X}_{t+1}^\top\mathbf{U}\|_F^2 \\ \geq & \text{tr}((a_1(\mathbf{X}_t) + b_1(\mathbf{W}_t))(a_2(\mathbf{X}_t) + b_2(\mathbf{W}_t))^{-1}), \end{aligned}$$

where $a_1(\mathbf{X}_t) = \mathbf{Y}_t^\top\mathbf{U}\mathbf{U}^\top\mathbf{Y}_t$ and $a_2(\mathbf{X}_t) = \mathbf{Y}_t^\top\mathbf{Y}_t + \alpha^2\nu_t^2\mathbf{I}$ now. And note that $a_i(\mathbf{X}_t)$, $i = 1, 2$, become deterministic conditioned on $\mathbf{X}_t$.

[2] $\text{sym}(H) = \frac{1}{2}(H + H^\top)$.

Lemma 5.3. *For $i = 1, 2$ and any $\varsigma \in [0, 1]$,*

$$\|b_i(\mathbf{W}_t)\|_F \leq 2(1+\alpha\beta)\alpha\nu,$$
$$\|a_1(\mathbf{X}_t)\|_2 + \|b_1(\mathbf{W}_t)\|_2 \leq (1+\alpha\beta)\left(1+\alpha\left(\beta+2\mu\right)\right),$$
$$a_2(\mathbf{X}_t) + \varsigma b_2(\mathbf{W}_t) \succcurlyeq (1 - 2(1+\alpha\beta)\alpha\mu)\,\mathbf{I}.$$

By Lemma 5 in (Shamir, 2016) and Lemma 5.3 above, we can get

$$\mathbb{E}[\|\mathbf{X}_{t+1}^\top \mathbf{U}\|_F^2 | \mathbf{X}_t] \geq \operatorname{tr}(a_1(\mathbf{X}_t)a_2^{-1}(\mathbf{X}_t)) - \eta\alpha^2\nu_t^2,$$

where $(1+\alpha\beta)\alpha\mu < \frac{1}{2}$ and $\eta = \frac{4(1+\alpha\beta)^2(2+(1+\alpha\beta)^2)}{(1-2(1+\alpha\beta)\alpha\mu)^3}$.

Lemma 5.4. $\operatorname{tr}(\mathbf{X}_t^\top \mathbf{U}\mathbf{U}^\top(\mathbf{I} - \mathbf{X}_t\mathbf{X}_t^\top)\mathbf{A}\mathbf{X}) \geq \tau(\|\mathbf{X}_t^\top\mathbf{U}\|_F^2 - \|\mathbf{X}_t^\top\mathbf{U}\mathbf{U}^\top\mathbf{X}_t\|_F^2)$.

This lemma is the key to the improvement brought by our algorithm over the VR-PCA as we will see shortly, and is used in proving the following lemma.

Lemma 5.5. *If $\alpha^2(\beta^2 + 48k\tilde{\beta}^2) < 1$, then*

$$\begin{aligned}
&\operatorname{tr}(a_1(\mathbf{X}_t)a_2^{-1}(\mathbf{X}_t)) \\
&\geq 2\alpha\tau(\|\mathbf{X}_t^\top\mathbf{U}\|_F^2 - \|\mathbf{U}^\top\mathbf{X}_t\mathbf{X}_t^\top\mathbf{U}\|_F^2) \\
&\quad + \|\mathbf{X}_t^\top\mathbf{U}\|_F^2 - \alpha^2(1+2\alpha\beta)(2\beta^2\Theta_t + k\nu_t^2).
\end{aligned}$$

Note that the proof of Lemma 5.5 is different from (Shamir, 2016). See the supplementary material for details.

If $\min\{2(1+\alpha\beta)\alpha\mu, \alpha^2(\beta^2+48k\tilde{\beta}^2)\} < 1$, then by Lemma 5.5 above and Lemma 7 in (Shamir, 2016) we can arrive at

$$\begin{aligned}
\mathbb{E}[\Theta_{t+1}|\mathbf{X}_t] \leq &(1 - \alpha(\frac{2}{k}\tau\sigma_t^2\|\mathbf{X}_t^\top\mathbf{U}\|_F^2 - \gamma\alpha))\Theta_t \\
&+ \rho\tilde{\Theta}_{s-1},
\end{aligned}$$

where $\sigma_t \triangleq \sigma_{\min}(\mathbf{X}_t^\top\mathbf{U})$ represents the smallest singular value of $\mathbf{X}_t^\top\mathbf{U}$, $\gamma = (1+2\alpha\beta)(2\beta^2+24k\tilde{\beta}^2) + 24\eta\tilde{\beta}^2$ and $\rho = 24(k(1+2\alpha\beta)+\eta)\alpha^2\tilde{\beta}^2$. It is worth noting that the coefficient for the dominating first-order term about α above is $\frac{2}{k}\tau\sigma_t^2\|\mathbf{X}_t^\top\mathbf{U}\|_F^2$, while the counterpart[3] in (Shamir, 2016) is $\frac{4/5}{k}\tau\sigma_t^2\|\mathbf{X}_t^\top\mathbf{U}\|_F^2$. We thus achieve an improvement by about $\frac{6/5}{k}\tau\sigma_t^2\|\mathbf{X}_t^\top\mathbf{U}\|_F^2$ for each single iteration, and it increases with iterations because both σ_t and $\|\mathbf{X}_t^\top\mathbf{U}\|_F$ keep increasing. For a small α that is often the case in our context, this improvement is indeed negligible. However, that is only for one single iteration. With a large number of iterations which is also often the case in our context, the accumulation of such small improvements can no longer be negligible and will make a visible difference as observed in our experiments.

[3]This is the most appropriate time for the comparison because Shamir (2016) uses implicit constants afterwards.

If $\|\mathbf{X}_t^\top\mathbf{U}\|_F^2 > k - \delta$, i.e., $\Theta_t < \delta$, then $\sigma_t^2 > 1 - \delta$ otherwise we get the contradiction that $\|\mathbf{X}_t^\top\mathbf{U}\|_F^2 \leq k - 1 + \sigma_t^2 \leq k - 1 + 1 - \delta = k - \delta$. In this case, we get

$$\begin{aligned}
\mathbb{E}[\Theta_{t+1}] =&\mathbb{E}[\mathbb{E}[\Theta_{t+1}|\mathbf{X}_t]] \\
\leq&(1 - \alpha(2\xi\tau - \gamma\alpha))\mathbb{E}[\Theta_t] + \rho\mathbb{E}[\tilde{\Theta}_{s-1}], \quad (9)
\end{aligned}$$

where $\xi = 1 - \frac{(k+1-\delta)\delta}{k}$.

In order for the recurrence of the above inequality, we need that $\Theta_t < \delta$ holds for a number of consecutive iterations with high probability, given that $\tilde{\Theta}_{s-1} < \delta$. We can make it by following the concentration of martingale argument. In fact, based on the above inequality, we can construct a super-martingale with bounded differences. By the Azuma-Hoeffding inequality we then can get the following lemma,

Lemma 5.6. *For any $\tilde{\iota} \in (0, 1)$, if α and m satisfy that $\alpha < 2\xi\tau/\gamma$, $\min\{2(1+\alpha\beta)\alpha\mu, \alpha^2(\beta^2+48k\tilde{\beta}^2)\} < 1$ and $\tilde{\Theta}_{s-1} + km\rho + \theta\sqrt{2m\log(1/\iota)} < \delta$, then $\Theta_t < \delta$ holds for all $t = 1, 2, \cdots, m$ with probability at least $1 - \tilde{\iota}$, where $\theta = \frac{4k(\beta+4\tilde{\beta})\alpha}{1-(\beta+4\tilde{\beta})\alpha} + k\rho$.*

Note that given a fixed m, α that satisfies $\tilde{\Theta}_{s-1} + km\rho + \theta\sqrt{2m\log(1/\iota)} < \delta$ depends on the epoch. Thus it is denoted as $\alpha_s(m)$. Let $\kappa = 1 - \alpha(2\xi\tau - \gamma\alpha)$. Under the conditions of Lemma 5.6, we now can call (9) recursively and get

$$\begin{aligned}
&\mathbb{E}[\tilde{\Theta}_{s+1}] \\
=&\mathbb{E}[\Theta_m] \leq \kappa\mathbb{E}[\Theta_{m-1}] + \rho\mathbb{E}[\tilde{\Theta}_s] \\
\leq&\kappa^m\mathbb{E}[\Theta_0] + \rho\sum_{i=0}^{m-1}\kappa^i\mathbb{E}[\tilde{\Theta}_s] \\
=&(\kappa^m + \rho\sum_{i=0}^{m-1}\kappa^i)\mathbb{E}[\tilde{\Theta}_s] \leq (\kappa^m + \frac{\rho}{1-\kappa})\mathbb{E}[\tilde{\Theta}_s] \\
\leq&\left(\exp\{-m\alpha(2\xi\tau - \gamma\alpha)\} + \frac{\rho}{1-\kappa}\right)\mathbb{E}[\tilde{\Theta}_s].
\end{aligned}$$

For any $\omega \in (0, \frac{1}{2})$, when[4]

$$\alpha < \min\{(\beta^2 + 48k\tilde{\beta}^2)^{-1/2}, \frac{1}{4\mu}, \frac{2\xi\tau}{\gamma}, \alpha_s(m)\}$$

and additionally

$$\exp\{-m\alpha(2\xi\tau - \gamma\alpha)\} < \omega, \quad \frac{\rho}{1-\kappa} < 1 - 2\omega,$$

namely $\alpha < \frac{2(1-2\omega)\xi\tau}{24(3k+\eta)\tilde{\beta}+(1-2\omega)\gamma} < \frac{2\xi\tau}{\gamma}$ and $m > \frac{-\log\omega}{\alpha(2\xi\tau-\gamma\alpha)}$, we have $\mathbb{E}[\tilde{\Theta}_{s+1}] \leq (1-\omega)\mathbb{E}[\tilde{\Theta}_s]$. Then,

[4]If $\alpha^2(\beta^2 + 48k\tilde{\beta}^2) < 1$, then $\alpha\beta < 1$ and thus $2(1+\alpha\beta)\alpha\mu < 4\alpha\mu$. If $4\alpha\mu < 1$ then $2(1+\alpha\beta)\alpha\mu < 1$.

$\mathbb{E}[\tilde{\Theta}_S] \leq (1-\omega)^S \tilde{\Theta}_0$ with probability at least $1 - S\tilde{\iota}$ if we further have $\alpha < \min_{1 \leq s \leq S} \alpha_s(m)$, where the number of epoches S for an ϵ-accurate solution is set such that $(1-\omega)^S \leq \epsilon$, i.e., $S = O(\frac{1}{1-\omega} \log \frac{1}{\epsilon})$, corresponding to the number of iterations $T = mS = O(\frac{1}{\xi^2 \tau^2} \log \frac{1}{\epsilon})$. If we set $\tilde{\iota} \in (0, \frac{\iota}{S})$ where $\iota \in (0,1)$, then we get an ϵ-accurate solution with probability at least $1 - \iota$.

Therefore, we arrive at the following theorem.

Theorem 5.7. *Given $\mathbf{A} \in \mathbb{R}^{n \times n}$ with $\mathbf{A}^\top = \mathbf{A}$, for any $\iota \in (0,1)$, $\delta \in (0,1)$ and $\omega \in (0, \frac{1}{2})$, if $\tau > 0$ and $\tilde{\Theta}_0 < \delta$, then with probability at least $1 - \iota$ the SVRRG-EIGS algorithm is able to reach a globally ϵ-optimal solution by running $T = O(\frac{1}{\xi^2 \tau^2} \log \frac{1}{\epsilon})$ iterations in expectation, provided that $0 < \alpha < \min\{(\beta^2 + 48k\tilde{\beta}^2)^{-\frac{1}{2}}, \frac{1}{4\mu}, \frac{2(1-2\omega)\xi\tau}{24(3k+\eta)\tilde{\beta}+(1-2\omega)\gamma}, \min_{1 \leq s \leq S} \alpha_s(m)\}$ and $m > \frac{-\log \omega}{\alpha(2\xi\tau - \gamma\alpha)}$, where $S = O(\frac{1}{1-\omega} \log \frac{1}{\epsilon})$.*

Note that if the constant factor with ξ is considered, SVRRG-EIGS and VR-PCA actually have the iteration complexity $O(\frac{1}{4\xi^2\tau^2} \log \frac{1}{\epsilon})$ and $O(\frac{1}{\frac{9}{25}\xi^2\tau^2} \log \frac{1}{\epsilon})$, respectively. Thus, SVRRG-EIGS achieves the linear convergence[5] at an improved rate over VR-PCA.

Last, suppose that the single column sampling of $\mathbf{A}$ is used. Then each epoch will have the complexity equal to $O(k\text{nnz}(\mathbf{A}) + nk^2)$ from computing a full gradient plus $O(m(k\frac{\text{nnz}(\mathbf{A})}{n} + nk^2))$ for the inner loop in the amortised sense. Thus, the total complexity of Algorithm 2 is $O(k(\text{nnz}(\mathbf{A}) + nk + (\frac{\text{nnz}(\mathbf{A})}{n} + nk)\frac{1}{\xi^2\tau^2}) \log \frac{1}{\epsilon})$ for an ϵ-optimal solution.

6 EXPERIMENTS

In this section, we empirically verify the linear convergence rate of the SVRRG-EIGS algorithm and compare its performance with that of RG-EIGS, SRG-EIGS and VR-PCA. Among various implementations of the RG-EIGS with different choices of a Riemannian metric and a retraction in (2), we choose the one with the canonical metric and the Cayley transformation based retraction (Wen and Yin, 2013), because it is frequently cited and its code is publicly available[6]. This version of the RG-EIGS uses a non-monotone line search with the well-known Barzilai-Borwein step size, which significantly reduces the iteration number and performs well in practice. We adapt the code of VR-PCA provided by the author to our case, because it was originally designed to handle vectorial data[7]. All the three solvers, RG-EIGS, SRG-EIGS and VR-PCA, are fed with the same random initial value of $\mathbf{X}$, where each entry is sampled from the standard normal distribution $\mathcal{N}(0,1)$ and then all entries as a whole are orthogonalized. SRG-EIGS uses the decaying learning rate $\alpha_t = \frac{c}{t}$, where c will be tuned. In order to generate an initial point $\tilde{\mathbf{X}}_0$ with $\tilde{\Theta}_0 < \delta$ for both SVRRG-EIGS and VR-PCA, we use the SRG-EIGS to produce a low-precision solution as $\tilde{\Theta}_0$. But note that other types of solvers are also applicable such as deterministic solvers (Wen and Yin, 2013) and doubly stochastic solvers (Xu et al., 2016).

Different solvers are tested on a real and symmetric matrix, **Schenk**[8], of size $10,728 \times 10,728$ having $85,000$ nonzero entries. It is partitioned into column blocks of block size $10,724 \times 100$ such that $\mathbf{A} = \frac{1}{L}\sum_{i=1}^{L} \tilde{\mathbf{A}}_i$ where $L = \lceil \frac{10728}{100} \rceil$ and the i-th column block in each $\tilde{\mathbf{A}}_i$ is equal to that of $L\mathbf{A}$ and all others are zero blocks. We set $k = 3$. Both VR-PCA and SVRRG-EIGS are able to use a fixed learning rate $\alpha = \frac{d}{\|\mathbf{A}\|_1 \sqrt{n}}$, where d will be tuned and $\|\mathbf{A}\|_1$ represents the matrix 1-norm. The best-tuned values of d for VR-PCA and SVRRG-EIGS are $d = 21.50$ and $d = 4.06$ in the following experiments, respectively. The epoch length is set to $m = \frac{1}{2}L$, i.e., each epoch takes 1.5 passes over $\mathbf{A}$ (including one pass for computing the full gradient). Accordingly, the epoch length of SRG-EIGS is set to $m = \frac{3}{2}L$. In addition, we set $\mathbf{Q}_t = \mathbf{I}$.

The performance of algorithms is evaluated using four quality measures: feasibility $\|\mathbf{X}^\top\mathbf{X} - \mathbf{I}\|_F$, relative error function $E(\mathbf{X}) \triangleq 1 - \frac{\text{tr}(\mathbf{X}^\top\mathbf{A}\mathbf{X})}{\max_{\mathbf{X}\in\text{St}(n,k)} \text{tr}(\mathbf{X}^\top\mathbf{A}\mathbf{X})}$, normalized potential function $\mathbf{\Theta}(\mathbf{X})/k = 1 - \frac{\|\mathbf{X}^\top\mathbf{U}\|_F^2}{k}$ and the potential function used in (Xu et al., 2016) that is defined as $1 - \cos^2 \angle_{\max}(\mathbf{U}, \mathbf{X})$, where $\angle_{\max}(\mathbf{U}, \mathbf{X})$ represents the maximal principal angle between $\mathbf{U}$ and $\mathbf{X}$. The ground truths in these measures, including both $\mathbf{U}$ and $\max_{\mathbf{X}\in\text{St}(n,k)} \text{tr}(\mathbf{X}^\top\mathbf{A}\mathbf{X})$ that is set to $\sum_{i=1}^{k} \lambda_i$, are obtained using Matlab's EIGS function for benchmarking. For each measure, lower values indicate higher quality.

Given a solution $\tilde{\mathbf{X}}_0$ of low precision at $E(\tilde{\mathbf{X}}_0) \leq 10^{-6}$, one solver targets a solution of double precision, that is, $E(\tilde{\mathbf{X}}) \leq 10^{-12}$ or $\mathbf{\Theta}(\tilde{\mathbf{X}})/k \leq 10^{-12}$ or $1 - \cos^2 \angle_{\max}(\mathbf{U}, \mathbf{X}) \leq 10^{-12}$. Each algorithm terminates when the precision requirement is met or the maximum number of epoches (set as 20) is reached.

We report the convergence curves in terms of each mea-

[5]Strictly speaking, the linear rate is achievable only if $\epsilon = o(\tau^2)$.

[6]optman.blogs.rice.edu/

[7]It handles data $\mathbf{B} \in \mathbb{R}^{n \times m}$ consisting of m n-dimensional samples in $\mathbb{R}^n$, instead of data $\mathbf{A} \in \mathbb{R}^{n \times n}$ directly, where $\mathbf{A} = \mathbf{B}\mathbf{B}^\top$.

[8]www.cise.ufl.edu/research/sparse/matrices/

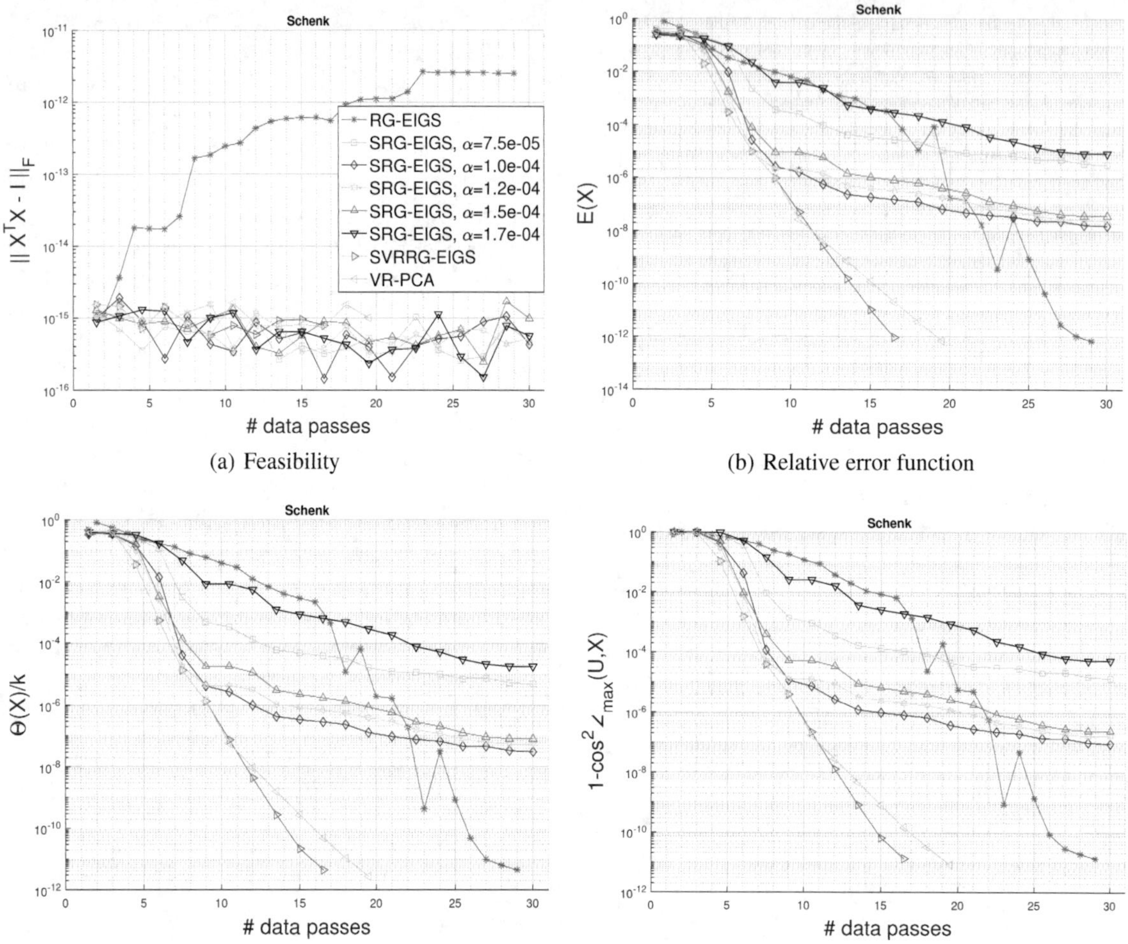

(a) Feasibility

(b) Relative error function

(c) Normalized potential function

(d) Maximal principal angle

Figure 1: Performance on Schenk. Note that the y-axis in each figure is in log scale.

sure, on which empirical convergence rates of the algorithms can be observed. Figure 1 reports the performance of different algorithms. In terms of the feasibility, all solvers but RG-EIGS perform well, while RG-EIGS produces much poorer results. This is because the Cayley transformation based retraction used therein relies heavily on the Sherman-Morrison-Woodbury formula, which suffers from the numerical instability. From Figure 1(b) to Figure 1(d), we observe similar convergence trends for each algorithm under the three different measures. All the four algorithms improve their solutions with more iterations. There are several exceptions in RG-EIGS. This is due to the non-monotone step size used in its implementation. We also observe that SRG-EIGS presents an exponential convergence rate at an early stage thanks to a relatively large learning rate. However, it subsequently steps into a long period of sub-exponential convergence, which leads to small progress towards the optimal solution. In contrast, VR-PCA and SVRRG-EIGS inherit the initial momentum from SRG-EIGS and keep the exponential convergence rate throughout the entire process. This enables it to approach the optimal solution at a fast speed. In particular, compared to VR-PCA, SVRRG-EIGS takes less passes over data to reach the required precision and is about one order of magnitude more accurate after the same number of data passes at a later stage. RG-EIGS has a different trend. It converges sub-exponentially at the beginning and performs worst. Though it converges fast subsquently, it still needs more passes over data than SVRRG-EIGS and VR-PCA in order to achieve the target precision.

More experimental results can be found in (Jiang et al., 2017), where experiments conducted on synthetic datsets also show the superior performance of our algorithm to that of VR-PCA when a large k is chosen.

7 Conclusion

In this paper, we proposed a fast stochastic Riemannian eigensolver by leveraging the recently proposed variance reduction technique in the stochastic Riemannian gradient optimization scheme. In addition to Riemannian gradients and retractions, the operation of vector transport as a new ingredient needs to be introduced in order to generalize SVRG properly to Riemannian manifolds. It has been deployed for the eigenvalue problem to yield a new eigensolver, i.e., the SVRRG-EIGS algorithm. And built upon the analysis of VR-PCA, we proved its local, eigengap-dependent and linear convergence at an improved rate in theory and with empirical support. However, as the learning rate is hand-tuned currently, we find it a difficult task in practice. In the future, we may conduct more empirical investigations towards automatically adjusting learning rates. And it is also important to address SVRRG-EIGS' limitations for $k \geq 1$, such as nontrivial initialization and eigen-gap dependence.

Acknowledgements

We thank anonymous reviewers for suggestions that help improve the quality of the paper. This research is supported in part by the funding from King Abdullah University of Science and Technology (KAUST), the AcRF Tier-1 Grant (RG135/14) from Ministry of Education of Singapore and the SUG Grant M4081416.020 from Nanyang Technological University.

References

P-A Absil, Robert Mahony, and Rodolphe Sepulchre. *Optimization algorithms on matrix manifolds*. Princeton University Press, 2008.

Zeyuan Allen-Zhu and Yuanzhi Li. Even faster svd decomposition yet without agonizing pain. In *Advances in Neural Information Processing Systems*, pages 974–982, 2016.

Akshay Balsubramani, Sanjoy Dasgupta, and Yoav Freund. The fast convergence of incremental pca. In *Advances in Neural Information Processing Systems*, pages 3174–3182, 2013.

Silvere Bonnabel. Stochastic gradient descent on riemannian manifolds. *IEEE Trans. Automat. Contr.*, 58(9): 2217–2229, 2013. doi: 10.1109/TAC.2013.2254619.

Petros Drineas and Michael W. Mahoney. On the nyström method for approximating a gram matrix for improved kernel-based learning. *J. Mach. Learn. Res.*, 6:2153–2175, December 2005. ISSN 1532-4435.

Alan Edelman, Tomás A. Arias, and Steven T. Smith. The geometry of algorithms with orthogonality constraints. *SIAM J. Matrix Anal. Appl.*, 20(2):303–353, April 1999. ISSN 0895-4798. doi: 10.1137/S0895479895290954.

Dan Garber, Elad Hazan, and Tengyu Ma. Online learning of eigenvectors. In *Proceedings of the 32nd International Conference on Machine Learning, ICML 2015, Lille, France, 6-11 July 2015*, pages 560–568, 2015.

Dan Garber, Elad Hazan, Chi Jin, Sham M. Kakade, Cameron Musco, Praneeth Netrapalli, and Aaron Sidford. Faster eigenvector computation via shift-and-invert preconditioning. In *International Conference on Machine Learning*, pages 2626–2634, 2016.

Rong Ge, Chi Jin, Sham M. Kakade, Praneeth Netrapalli, and Aaron Sidford. Efficient algorithms for large-scale generalized eigenvector computation and canonical correlation analysis. In *International Conference on Machine Learning*, pages 2741–2750, 2016.

Gene H. Golub and Charles F. Van Loan. *Matrix Computations (3rd Ed.)*. Johns Hopkins University Press, Baltimore, MD, USA, 1996. ISBN 0-8018-5414-8.

N. Halko, P. G. Martinsson, and J. A. Tropp. Finding structure with randomness: Probabilistic algorithms for constructing approximate matrix decompositions. *SIAM Rev.*, 53(2):217–288, May 2011. ISSN 0036-1445. doi: 10.1137/090771806.

Prateek Jain, Chi Jin, Sham M. Kakade, Praneeth Netrapalli, and Aaron Sidford. Streaming PCA: matching matrix bernstein and near-optimal finite sample guarantees for oja's algorithm. In *Proceedings of the 29th Conference on Learning Theory, COLT 2016, New York, USA, June 23-26, 2016*, pages 1147–1164, 2016. URL `http://jmlr.org/proceedings/papers/v49/jain16.html`.

Bo Jiang, Shiqian Ma, Anthony Man-Cho So, and Shuzhong Zhang. Vector transport-free svrg with general retraction for riemannian optimization: Complexity analysis and practical implementation. *arXiv preprint arXiv:1705.09059*, 2017.

Rie Johnson and Tong Zhang. Accelerating stochastic gradient descent using predictive variance reduction. In C. J. C. Burges, L. Bottou, M. Welling, Z. Ghahramani, and K. Q. Weinberger, editors, *Advances in Neural Information Processing Systems 26*, pages 315–323. Curran Associates, Inc., 2013.

Hiroyuki Kasai, Hiroyuki Sato, and Bamdev Mishra. Riemannian stochastic variance reduced gradient on grassmann manifold. *CoRR*, abs/1605.07367, 2016.

John M. Lee. *Introduction to smooth manifolds.* Springer, 2012.

A. S. Lewis. Convex analysis on the hermitian matrices. *SIAM Journal on Optimization*, 6:164–177, 1996.

Michael Mitzenmacher and Eli Upfal. *Probability and Computing: Randomized Algorithms and Probabilistic Analysis.* Cambridge University Press, New York, NY, USA, 2005. ISBN 0521835402.

Andrew Y. Ng, Michael I. Jordan, and Yair Weiss. On spectral clustering: Analysis and an algorithm. In T.G. Dietterich, S. Becker, and Z. Ghahramani, editors, *Advances in Neural Information Processing Systems 14*, pages 849–856. MIT Press, 2002.

Erkki Oja and Juha Karhunen. On stochastic approximation of the eigenvectors and eigenvalues of the expectation of a random matrix. *Journal of mathematical analysis and applications*, 106(1):69–84, 1985.

Beresford N. Parlett. *The Symmetric Eigenvalue Problem.* Prentice-Hall, Inc., Upper Saddle River, NJ, USA, 1998. ISBN 0-89871-402-8.

William H. Press, Saul A. Teukolsky, William T. Vetterling, and Brian P. Flannery. *Numerical Recipes 3rd Edition: The Art of Scientific Computing.* Cambridge University Press, New York, NY, USA, 3 edition, 2007. ISBN 0521880688, 9780521880688.

Ohad Shamir. A stochastic PCA and SVD algorithm with an exponential convergence rate. In *Proceedings of the 32nd International Conference on Machine Learning, ICML 2015, Lille, France, 6-11 July 2015*, pages 144–152, 2015.

Ohad Shamir. Fast stochastic algorithms for SVD and PCA: convergence properties and convexity. In *International Conference on Machine Learning*, pages 248–256, 2016.

U. Torbjorn Ringertz. Eigenvalues in optimum structural design. *Institute for Mathematics and Its Applications*, 92:135, 1997.

Chong Wang, Xi Chen, Alex J Smola, and Eric P Xing. Variance reduction for stochastic gradient optimization. In C. J. C. Burges, L. Bottou, M. Welling, Z. Ghahramani, and K. Q. Weinberger, editors, *Advances in Neural Information Processing Systems 26*, pages 181–189. Curran Associates, Inc., 2013.

Zaiwen Wen and Wotao Yin. A feasible method for optimization with orthogonality constraints. *Math. Program.*, 142(1-2):397–434, 2013. doi: 10.1007/s10107-012-0584-1.

Zaiwen Wen, Chao Yang, Xin Liu, and Yin Zhang. Trace-penalty minimization for large-scale eigenspace computation. Technical report, RICE UNIV HOUSTON TX DEPT OF COMPUTATIONAL AND APPLIED MATHEMATICS, 2013.

J.H. Wilkinson. *The Algebraic Eigenvalue Problem.* Monographs on numerical analysis. Clarendon Press, 1988. ISBN 9780198534181. URL `https://books.google.com.sg/books?id=5wsK1OP7UFgC`.

Zhiqiang Xu and Yiping Ke. Stochastic variance reduced riemannian eigensolver. *CoRR*, abs/1605.08233, 2016a.

Zhiqiang Xu and Yiping Ke. Effective and efficient spectral clustering on text and link data. In *Proceedings of the 25th ACM International on Conference on Information and Knowledge Management*, CIKM '16, pages 357–366, New York, NY, USA, 2016b. ACM. ISBN 978-1-4503-4073-1. doi: 10.1145/2983323.2983708. URL `http://doi.acm.org/10.1145/2983323.2983708`.

Zhiqiang Xu, Peilin Zhao, and Jianneng Cao. Matrix eigen-decomposition via doubly stochastic riemannian optimization. In *International Conference on Machine Learning*, pages 1660–1669, 2016.

Hongyi Zhang, Sashank J. Reddi, and Suvrit Sra. Riemannian SVRG: fast stochastic optimization on riemannian manifolds. In *Advances in Neural Information Processing Systems, Barcelona, Spain*, pages 4592–4600, 2016.

Supplementary Material

Martingale

A filtration, defined on a measurable probability space, is an increasing sequence of sub-sigma algebras $\{\mathcal{F}_t\}$ for $t \geq 0$, meaning that $\mathcal{F}_s \subset \mathcal{F}_t$ for all $s \leq t$. In our context, $\mathcal{F}_t$ encodes the set of all the random variables seen thus far (i.e., from 0 to t). For brevity, $\mathbb{E}[\,\cdot\,|\mathbf{X}_t] \triangleq \mathbb{E}[\,\cdot\,|\mathcal{F}_t]$. Let $H = \{H_t\}$ and $\mathcal{F} = \{\mathcal{F}_t\}$ be a stochastic process and a filtration on the same probability space, respectively. H then is called a martingale (super-martingale) with respect to $\mathcal{F}$ if for each t, H_t is $\mathcal{F}_t$-measurable, $\mathbb{E}[|H_t|] < \infty$, and $\mathbb{E}[H_{t+1}|\mathcal{F}_t] = H_t$ ($\mathbb{E}[H_{t+1}|\mathcal{F}_t] \leq H_t$). Given a random variable $X \geq 0$ and a constant $a > 0$, we have the Markov inequality $P(X \geq a) \leq \mathbb{E}[X]/a$. Let $X_0, X_1, \cdots, X_T$ be a martingale or supermartingale such that $|X_t - X_{t-1}| \leq d_t$ (i.e., bounded difference) where d_t is a deterministic function of t. We then have the Azuma-Hoeffding (Mitzenmacher and Upfal, 2005) inequality $P(X_t - X_0 \geq a) \leq \exp\{-a^2/(2\sum_{s=1}^t d_t^2)\}$ for all $t \geq 0$ and any $a > 0$.

von Neumann's Trace Inequality

For any two real and symmetric $n \times n$ matrices $\mathbf{B}$ and $\mathbf{C}$ with eigenvalues indexed in descending order, it holds that

$$\max\left\{\sum_{i=1}^{n} \lambda_{n-i+1}(\mathbf{B})\lambda_1(\mathbf{C}), \sum_{i=1}^{n} \lambda_i(\mathbf{B})\lambda_{n-i+1}(\mathbf{C})\right\} \leq \mathrm{tr}(\mathbf{BC}) \leq \sum_{i=1}^{n} \lambda_i(\mathbf{B})\lambda_i(\mathbf{C}).$$

Proof. See (Lewis, 1996) for the right inequality. The proof of the left one is completed by replacing $\mathbf{B}$ with $-\mathbf{B}$ or replacing $\mathbf{C}$ with $-\mathbf{C}$ in the right one. □

Lemma 5.1. Let $\tilde{\beta} = \max_i \left\|\tilde{\mathbf{A}}_i - \mathbf{A}\right\|_2$. Then

$$\begin{aligned} \|\mathbf{W}_t\|_2 \leq \mu &\triangleq 4\tilde{\beta}, \\ \|\mathbf{W}_t\|_F^2 \leq \nu_t^2 &\triangleq 24\tilde{\beta}^2\left(\Theta(\mathbf{X}_t, \mathbf{U}) + \Theta(\tilde{\mathbf{X}}_{s-1}, \mathbf{U})\right). \end{aligned}$$

Proof. For brevity, let's omit subscripts with $\mathbf{X}$, $\tilde{\mathbf{X}}$, $\mathbf{W}$ and $\mathbf{Q}$ herein. $\mathbf{W}$ then can be written as

$$\begin{aligned} \mathbf{W} = {} & \mathbf{X}_\perp\mathbf{X}_\perp^\top(\mathbf{A}_{t+1} - \mathbf{A})\left(\mathbf{X} - \tilde{\mathbf{X}}\mathbf{Q}\right) + \mathbf{X}_\perp\mathbf{X}_\perp^\top\tilde{\mathbf{X}}\tilde{\mathbf{X}}^\top(\mathbf{A}_{t+1} - \mathbf{A})\tilde{\mathbf{X}}\mathbf{Q} \\ & -\mathbf{X}\mathrm{skew}\left(\mathbf{X}^\top\tilde{\mathbf{X}}_\perp\tilde{\mathbf{X}}_\perp^\top(\mathbf{A}_{t+1} - \mathbf{A})\tilde{\mathbf{X}}\mathbf{Q}\right). \end{aligned}$$

We then have

$$\begin{aligned} \|\mathbf{W}\|_2 \leq {} & \left\|\mathbf{X}_\perp\mathbf{X}_\perp^\top(\mathbf{A}_{t+1} - \mathbf{A})(\mathbf{X} - \tilde{\mathbf{X}}\mathbf{Q})\right\|_2 + \left\|\mathbf{X}_\perp\mathbf{X}_\perp^\top\tilde{\mathbf{X}}\tilde{\mathbf{X}}^\top(\mathbf{A}_{t+1} - \mathbf{A})\tilde{\mathbf{X}}\mathbf{Q}\right\|_2 \\ & + \left\|\mathbf{X}\mathrm{skew}\left(\mathbf{X}^\top\tilde{\mathbf{X}}_\perp\tilde{\mathbf{X}}_\perp^\top(\mathbf{A}_{t+1} - \mathbf{A})\tilde{\mathbf{X}}\mathbf{Q}\right)\right\|_2 \\ \leq {} & \tilde{\beta}\left(\|\mathbf{X}\|_2 + \left\|\tilde{\mathbf{X}}\mathbf{Q}\right\|_2\right) + 2\tilde{\beta} = 4\tilde{\beta}, \end{aligned}$$

and

$$\begin{aligned}
\|\mathbf{W}\|_F^2 &\le \left(\left\|\mathbf{X}_\perp\mathbf{X}_\perp^\top(\mathbf{A}_{t+1}-\mathbf{A})(\mathbf{X}-\tilde{\mathbf{X}}\mathbf{Q})\right\|_F + \left\|\mathbf{X}_\perp\mathbf{X}_\perp^\top\tilde{\mathbf{X}}\tilde{\mathbf{X}}^\top(\mathbf{A}_{t+1}-\mathbf{A})\tilde{\mathbf{X}}\mathbf{Q}\right\|_F\right. \\
&\quad \left. + \left\|\mathbf{X}\mathrm{skew}\left(\mathbf{X}^\top\tilde{\mathbf{X}}_\perp\tilde{\mathbf{X}}_\perp^\top(\mathbf{A}_{t+1}-\mathbf{A})\tilde{\mathbf{X}}\mathbf{Q}\right)\right\|_F\right)^2 \\
&\le \left(\left\|\mathbf{X}_\perp\mathbf{X}_\perp^\top(\mathbf{A}_{t+1}-\mathbf{A})\right\|_2\left\|\mathbf{X}-\tilde{\mathbf{X}}\mathbf{Q}\right\|_F + \|\mathbf{X}_\perp\|_2\left\|\mathbf{X}_\perp^\top\tilde{\mathbf{X}}\right\|_F\left\|\tilde{\mathbf{X}}^\top(\mathbf{A}_{t+1}-\mathbf{A})\tilde{\mathbf{X}}\mathbf{Q}\right\|_2\right. \\
&\quad \left. + \|\mathbf{X}\|_2\left\|\mathbf{X}^\top\tilde{\mathbf{X}}_\perp\right\|_F\left\|\tilde{\mathbf{X}}_\perp^\top(\mathbf{A}_{t+1}-\mathbf{A})\tilde{\mathbf{X}}\mathbf{Q}\right\|_2\right)^2 \\
&\le \tilde{\beta}^2\left(\left\|\mathbf{X}-\tilde{\mathbf{X}}\mathbf{Q}\right\|_F + \left\|\mathbf{X}_\perp^\top\tilde{\mathbf{X}}\right\|_F + \left\|\mathbf{X}^\top\tilde{\mathbf{X}}_\perp\right\|_F\right)^2 \\
&\le 3\tilde{\beta}^2\left(\left\|\mathbf{X}-\tilde{\mathbf{X}}\mathbf{Q}\right\|_F^2 + \left\|\mathbf{X}_\perp^\top\tilde{\mathbf{X}}\right\|_F^2 + \left\|\mathbf{X}^\top\tilde{\mathbf{X}}_\perp\right\|_F^2\right).
\end{aligned}$$

From the proof of Lemma 11 in (Shamir, 2016), we have $\left\|\mathbf{X}-\tilde{\mathbf{X}}\mathbf{Q}\right\|_F^2 \le 4\left(\Theta(\mathbf{X},\mathbf{U})+\Theta(\tilde{\mathbf{X}},\mathbf{U})\right)$. Further noting that $\mathbf{I}=\mathbf{U}\mathbf{U}^\top+\mathbf{U}_\perp\mathbf{U}_\perp^\top=\mathbf{X}\mathbf{X}^\top+\mathbf{X}_\perp\mathbf{X}_\perp^\top$, we have

$$\begin{aligned}
\left\|\mathbf{X}_\perp^\top\tilde{\mathbf{X}}\right\|_F^2 &= \left\|\mathbf{X}_\perp^\top(\mathbf{U}\mathbf{U}^\top+\mathbf{U}_\perp\mathbf{U}_\perp^\top)\tilde{\mathbf{X}}\right\|_F^2 \le \left(\left\|\mathbf{X}_\perp^\top\mathbf{U}\mathbf{U}^\top\tilde{\mathbf{X}}\right\|_F + \left\|\mathbf{X}_\perp^\top\mathbf{U}_\perp\mathbf{U}_\perp^\top\tilde{\mathbf{X}}\right\|_F\right)^2 \\
&\le \left(\|\mathbf{X}_\perp^\top\mathbf{U}\|_F\left\|\mathbf{U}^\top\tilde{\mathbf{X}}\right\|_2 + \left\|\mathbf{X}_\perp^\top\mathbf{U}_\perp\|_2\|\mathbf{U}_\perp^\top\tilde{\mathbf{X}}\right\|_F\right)^2 \le \left(\|\mathbf{X}_\perp^\top\mathbf{U}\|_F + \left\|\mathbf{U}_\perp^\top\tilde{\mathbf{X}}\right\|_F\right)^2 \\
&\le 2\left(\|\mathbf{X}_\perp^\top\mathbf{U}\|_F^2 + \left\|\mathbf{U}_\perp^\top\tilde{\mathbf{X}}\right\|_F^2\right) \\
&= 2\left(k-\|\mathbf{U}^\top\mathbf{X}\|_F^2 + k - \left\|\mathbf{U}^\top\tilde{\mathbf{X}}\right\|_F^2\right) = 2\left(\Theta(\mathbf{X},\mathbf{U})+\Theta(\tilde{\mathbf{X}},\mathbf{U})\right),
\end{aligned}$$

and similarly $\left\|\mathbf{X}^\top\tilde{\mathbf{X}}_\perp\right\|_F^2 \le 2\left(\Theta(\mathbf{X},\mathbf{U})+\Theta(\tilde{\mathbf{X}},\mathbf{U})\right)$. Therefore, we arrive at

$$\|\mathbf{W}\|_F^2 \le 24\tilde{\beta}^2\left(\Theta(\mathbf{X},\mathbf{U})+\Theta(\tilde{\mathbf{X}},\mathbf{U})\right).$$

□

Lemma 5.2. If $\mathbf{C}_1 \succcurlyeq \mathbf{0}$, $\mathbf{C}_2 \succcurlyeq \mathbf{0}$ and $\mathbf{D}_2 \succcurlyeq \mathbf{D}_1 \succ \mathbf{0}$, then $\mathrm{tr}(\mathbf{C}_1\mathbf{D}_1^{-1}) \ge \mathrm{tr}((\mathbf{C}_1-\mathbf{C}_2)\mathbf{D}_2^{-1})$.

Proof.

$$\begin{aligned}
\mathbf{C}_1\mathbf{D}_1^{-1} &= \mathbf{C}_1\left(\mathbf{D}_2-(\mathbf{D}_2-\mathbf{D}_1)\right)^{-1} \\
&= \mathbf{C}_1\mathbf{D}_2^{-1/2}\left(\mathbf{I}-\mathbf{D}_2^{-1/2}(\mathbf{D}_2-\mathbf{D}_1)\mathbf{D}_2^{-1/2}\right)^{-1}\mathbf{D}_2^{-1/2}.
\end{aligned}$$

By Lemmas 2 and 3 in (Shamir, 2016), we have

$$\begin{aligned}
\mathrm{tr}\left(\mathbf{C}_1\mathbf{D}_1^{-1}\right) &= \mathrm{tr}\left(\mathbf{C}_1\mathbf{D}_2^{-1/2}(\mathbf{I}-\mathbf{D}_2^{-1/2}(\mathbf{D}_2-\mathbf{D}_1)\mathbf{D}_2^{-1/2})^{-1}\mathbf{D}_2^{-1/2}\right) \\
&= \mathrm{tr}\left(\mathbf{D}_2^{-1/2}\mathbf{C}_1\mathbf{D}_2^{-1/2}\left(\mathbf{I}-\mathbf{D}_2^{-1/2}(\mathbf{D}_2-\mathbf{D}_1)\mathbf{D}_2^{-1/2}\right)^{-1}\right) \\
&\ge \mathrm{tr}\left(\mathbf{D}_2^{-1/2}\mathbf{C}_1\mathbf{D}_2^{-1/2}\left(\mathbf{I}+\mathbf{D}_2^{-1/2}(\mathbf{D}_2-\mathbf{D}_1)\mathbf{D}_2^{-1/2}\right)\right) \\
&\ge \mathrm{tr}\left(\mathbf{D}_2^{-1/2}\mathbf{C}_1\mathbf{D}_2^{-1/2}\right) = \mathrm{tr}\left(\mathbf{C}_1\mathbf{D}_2^{-1}\right) \ge \mathrm{tr}\left((\mathbf{C}_1-\mathbf{C}_2)\mathbf{D}_2^{-1}\right).
\end{aligned}$$

□

Lemma 5.3. For $i = 1, 2$ and any $\varsigma \in [0, 1]$,

$$\begin{aligned}
\|b_i(\mathbf{W}_t)\|_F &\leq 2(1+\alpha\beta)\alpha\nu_t, \\
\|a_1(\mathbf{X}_t)\|_2 + \|b_1(\mathbf{W}_t)\|_2 &\leq (1+\alpha\beta)\left(1+\alpha\left(\beta+2\mu\right)\right), \\
a_2(\mathbf{X}_t) + \varsigma b_2(\mathbf{W}_t) &\succcurlyeq (1 - 2(1+\alpha\beta)\alpha\mu)\,\mathbf{I}.
\end{aligned}$$

Proof. We omit subscripts for brevity herein. Since $\|\mathbf{Y}\|_2 = \left\|\left(\mathbf{I} + \alpha\mathbf{X}_\perp\mathbf{X}_\perp^\top\mathbf{A}\right)\mathbf{X}\right\|_2 \leq 1 + \alpha\beta$, we have

$$\begin{aligned}
\|b_1(\mathbf{W})\|_F &= 2\alpha\left\|\mathrm{sym}(\mathbf{Y}^\top\mathbf{U}\mathbf{U}^\top\mathbf{W})\right\|_F \leq 2\alpha\left\|\mathbf{Y}^\top\mathbf{U}\mathbf{U}^\top\mathbf{W}\right\|_F \leq 2\alpha(1+\alpha\beta)\nu_t, \\
\|b_2(\mathbf{W})\|_F &= 2\alpha\left\|\mathrm{sym}(\mathbf{Y}^\top\mathbf{W})\right\|_F \leq 2\alpha\left\|\mathbf{Y}^\top\mathbf{W}\right\|_F \leq 2\alpha(1+\alpha\beta)\nu_t.
\end{aligned}$$

In addition, we can write

$$\|a_1(\mathbf{X})\|_2 + \|b_1(\mathbf{W})\|_2 \leq \left\|\mathbf{Y}^\top\mathbf{U}\right\|_2\left(\left\|\mathbf{Y}^\top\mathbf{U}\right\|_2 + 2\alpha\left\|\mathbf{U}^\top\mathbf{W}\right\|_2\right) \leq (1+\alpha\beta)\left(1+\alpha\left(\beta+2\mu\right)\right).$$

Further we note that $\mathbf{Y}^\top\mathbf{Y} = \mathbf{I} + \alpha\mathbf{X}^\top\mathbf{A}\mathbf{X}_\perp^\top\mathbf{X}_\perp\mathbf{A}\mathbf{X}$.

$$a_2(\mathbf{X}) + \varsigma b_1(\mathbf{W}) \succcurlyeq (1 - \|b_1(\mathbf{W})\|_2)\,\mathbf{I} \succcurlyeq (1 - 2\alpha(1+\alpha\beta)\mu)\,\mathbf{I}.$$

□

Lemma 5.4. $\mathrm{tr}\left(\mathbf{X}_t^\top\mathbf{U}\mathbf{U}^\top\left(\mathbf{I} - \mathbf{X}_t\mathbf{X}_t^\top\right)\mathbf{A}\mathbf{X}\right) \geq \tau\left(\left\|\mathbf{X}_t^\top\mathbf{U}\right\|_F^2 - \left\|\mathbf{X}_t^\top\mathbf{U}\mathbf{U}^\top\mathbf{X}_t\right\|_F^2\right).$

Proof. Since $\mathbf{A} = \mathbf{U}\mathbf{\Sigma}\mathbf{U}^\top + \mathbf{U}_\perp\mathbf{\Sigma}_\perp\mathbf{U}_\perp^\top$, then

$$\begin{aligned}
&\mathrm{tr}\left(\mathbf{X}^\top\mathbf{U}\mathbf{U}^\top\mathbf{X}_\perp\mathbf{X}_\perp^\top\mathbf{A}\mathbf{X}\right) \\
=\ &\mathrm{tr}\left(\mathbf{X}^\top\mathbf{U}\mathbf{U}^\top\mathbf{X}_\perp\mathbf{X}_\perp^\top\mathbf{U}\mathbf{\Sigma}\mathbf{U}^\top\mathbf{X}\right) + \mathrm{tr}\left(\mathbf{X}^\top\mathbf{U}\mathbf{U}^\top\mathbf{X}_\perp\mathbf{X}_\perp^\top\mathbf{U}_\perp\mathbf{\Sigma}_\perp\mathbf{U}_\perp^\top\mathbf{X}\right) \\
=\ &\mathrm{tr}\left(\mathbf{U}^\top\mathbf{X}\mathbf{X}^\top\mathbf{U}\mathbf{U}^\top\mathbf{X}_\perp\mathbf{X}_\perp^\top\mathbf{U}\mathbf{\Sigma}\right) + \mathrm{tr}\left(\mathbf{U}_\perp^\top\mathbf{X}\mathbf{X}^\top\mathbf{U}\mathbf{U}^\top\mathbf{X}_\perp\mathbf{X}_\perp^\top\mathbf{U}_\perp\mathbf{\Sigma}_\perp\right).
\end{aligned}$$

By von Neumann's trace inequality, we have

$$\begin{aligned}
\mathrm{tr}\left(\mathbf{U}^\top\mathbf{X}\mathbf{X}^\top\mathbf{U}\mathbf{U}^\top\mathbf{X}_\perp\mathbf{X}_\perp^\top\mathbf{U}\mathbf{\Sigma}\right) &\geq \sum_{i=1}^{k}\lambda_i\left(\mathbf{U}^\top\mathbf{X}\mathbf{X}^\top\mathbf{U}\mathbf{U}^\top\mathbf{X}_\perp\mathbf{X}_\perp^\top\mathbf{U}\right)\lambda_{k-i+1}\left(\mathbf{\Sigma}\right), \\
\mathrm{tr}\left(\mathbf{U}_\perp^\top\mathbf{X}\mathbf{X}^\top\mathbf{U}\mathbf{U}^\top\mathbf{X}_\perp\mathbf{X}_\perp^\top\mathbf{U}_\perp\mathbf{\Sigma}_\perp\right) &\geq \sum_{i=1}^{n-k}\lambda_i\left(\mathbf{U}_\perp^\top\mathbf{X}\mathbf{X}^\top\mathbf{U}\mathbf{U}^\top\mathbf{X}_\perp\mathbf{X}_\perp^\top\mathbf{U}_\perp\right)\lambda_{n-k-i+1}\left(\mathbf{\Sigma}_\perp\right).
\end{aligned}$$

Note that both matrices above, i.e., $\mathbf{U}^\top\mathbf{X}\mathbf{X}^\top\mathbf{U}\mathbf{U}^\top\mathbf{X}_\perp\mathbf{X}_\perp^\top\mathbf{U}$ and $\mathbf{U}_\perp^\top\mathbf{X}\mathbf{X}^\top\mathbf{U}\mathbf{U}^\top\mathbf{X}_\perp\mathbf{X}_\perp^\top\mathbf{U}_\perp$, are symmetric and thus von Neumann's trace inequality can be applied. In fact,

$$\begin{aligned}
\mathbf{U}^\top\mathbf{X}\mathbf{X}^\top\mathbf{U}\mathbf{U}^\top\mathbf{X}_\perp\mathbf{X}_\perp^\top\mathbf{U} &= \mathbf{U}^\top\mathbf{X}\mathbf{X}^\top\mathbf{U}\mathbf{U}^\top\left(\mathbf{I} - \mathbf{X}\mathbf{X}^\top\right)\mathbf{U} \\
&= \mathbf{U}^\top\mathbf{X}\mathbf{X}^\top\mathbf{U} - \mathbf{U}^\top\mathbf{X}\mathbf{X}^\top\mathbf{U}\mathbf{U}^\top\mathbf{X}\mathbf{X}^\top\mathbf{U} \\
&= \mathbf{U}^\top\mathbf{X}\mathbf{X}^\top\mathbf{U} - \left(\mathbf{U}^\top\mathbf{X}\mathbf{X}^\top\mathbf{U}\right)^2,
\end{aligned}$$

which is symmetric. Furthermore, it is positive semi-definite, because

$$\left\|\mathbf{U}^\top\mathbf{X}\mathbf{X}^\top\mathbf{U}\right\|_2 \leq \left(\|\mathbf{X}^\top\|_2\|\mathbf{U}\|_2\right)^2 = 1$$

and thus

$$\lambda_i\left(\mathbf{U}^\top\mathbf{X}\mathbf{X}^\top\mathbf{U}\mathbf{U}^\top\mathbf{X}_\perp\mathbf{X}_\perp^\top\mathbf{U}\right) = \lambda_i\left(\mathbf{U}^\top\mathbf{X}\mathbf{X}^\top\mathbf{U}\right) - \lambda_i^2\left(\mathbf{U}^\top\mathbf{X}\mathbf{X}^\top\mathbf{U}\right) \geq 0.$$

Likewise,

$$\begin{aligned}
\mathbf{U}_\perp^\top\mathbf{X}\mathbf{X}^\top\mathbf{U}\mathbf{U}^\top\mathbf{X}_\perp\mathbf{X}_\perp^\top\mathbf{U}_\perp &= \mathbf{U}_\perp^\top\left(\mathbf{I} - \mathbf{X}_\perp\mathbf{X}_\perp^\top\right)\mathbf{U}\mathbf{U}^\top\mathbf{X}_\perp\mathbf{X}_\perp^\top\mathbf{U}_\perp \\
&= -\mathbf{U}_\perp^\top\mathbf{X}_\perp\mathbf{X}_\perp^\top\left(\mathbf{I} - \mathbf{U}_\perp\mathbf{U}_\perp^\top\right)\mathbf{X}_\perp\mathbf{X}_\perp^\top\mathbf{U}_\perp \\
&= -\left(\mathbf{U}_\perp^\top\mathbf{X}_\perp\mathbf{X}_\perp^\top\mathbf{U}_\perp - \left(\mathbf{U}_\perp^\top\mathbf{X}_\perp\mathbf{X}_\perp^\top\mathbf{U}_\perp\right)^2\right),
\end{aligned}$$

which is symmetric but negative semi-definite now, because

$$\left\|\mathbf{U}_\perp^\top \mathbf{X}_\perp \mathbf{X}_\perp^\top \mathbf{U}_\perp\right\|_2 \leq \left(\|\mathbf{X}_\perp^\top\|_2 \|\mathbf{U}_\perp\|_2\right)^2 = 1$$

and thus

$$\lambda_i\left(\mathbf{U}_\perp^\top \mathbf{X}\mathbf{X}^\top \mathbf{U}\mathbf{U}^\top \mathbf{X}_\perp \mathbf{X}_\perp^\top \mathbf{U}_\perp\right) = -\left(\lambda_i(\mathbf{U}_\perp^\top \mathbf{X}_\perp \mathbf{X}_\perp^\top \mathbf{U}_\perp) - \lambda_i^2\left(\mathbf{U}_\perp^\top \mathbf{X}_\perp \mathbf{X}_\perp^\top \mathbf{U}_\perp\right)\right) \leq 0.$$

We now can write

$$\begin{aligned}
& \operatorname{tr}\left(\mathbf{U}^\top \mathbf{X}\mathbf{X}^\top \mathbf{U}\mathbf{U}^\top \mathbf{X}_\perp \mathbf{X}_\perp^\top \mathbf{U}\boldsymbol{\Sigma}\right) + \operatorname{tr}(\mathbf{U}_\perp^\top \mathbf{X}\mathbf{X}^\top \mathbf{U}\mathbf{U}^\top \mathbf{X}_\perp \mathbf{X}_\perp^\top \mathbf{U}_\perp \boldsymbol{\Sigma}_\perp) \\
\geq & \sum_{i=1}^{k} \lambda_i\left(\mathbf{U}^\top \mathbf{X}\mathbf{X}^\top \mathbf{U}\mathbf{U}^\top \mathbf{X}_\perp \mathbf{X}_\perp^\top \mathbf{U}\right) \lambda_{k-i+1}\left(\boldsymbol{\Sigma}\right) + \sum_{i=1}^{n-k} \lambda_i\left(\mathbf{U}_\perp^\top \mathbf{X}\mathbf{X}^\top \mathbf{U}\mathbf{U}^\top \mathbf{X}_\perp \mathbf{X}_\perp^\top \mathbf{U}_\perp\right) \lambda_{n-k-i+1}\left(\boldsymbol{\Sigma}_\perp\right) \\
\geq & \sum_{i=1}^{k} \lambda_i\left(\mathbf{U}^\top \mathbf{X}\mathbf{X}^\top \mathbf{U}\mathbf{U}^\top \mathbf{X}_\perp \mathbf{X}_\perp^\top \mathbf{U}\right) \lambda_k\left(\mathbf{A}\right) + \sum_{i=1}^{n-k} \lambda_i\left(\mathbf{U}_\perp^\top \mathbf{X}\mathbf{X}^\top \mathbf{U}\mathbf{U}^\top \mathbf{X}_\perp \mathbf{X}_\perp^\top \mathbf{U}_\perp\right) \lambda_{k+1}\left(\mathbf{A}\right),
\end{aligned}$$

where we find that

$$\begin{aligned}
\sum_{i=1}^{k} \lambda_i\left(\mathbf{U}^\top \mathbf{X}\mathbf{X}^\top \mathbf{U}\mathbf{U}^\top \mathbf{X}_\perp \mathbf{X}_\perp^\top \mathbf{U}\right) &= \sum_{i=1}^{k} \lambda_i\left(\mathbf{U}^\top \mathbf{X}\mathbf{X}^\top \mathbf{U}\right) - \sum_{i=1}^{k} \lambda_i^2\left(\mathbf{U}^\top \mathbf{X}\mathbf{X}^\top \mathbf{U}\right) \\
&= \operatorname{tr}\left(\mathbf{U}^\top \mathbf{X}\mathbf{X}^\top \mathbf{U}\right) - \operatorname{tr}\left(\left(\mathbf{U}^\top \mathbf{X}\mathbf{X}^\top \mathbf{U}\right)^2\right) \\
&= \left\|\mathbf{X}^\top \mathbf{U}\right\|_F^2 - \left\|\mathbf{U}^\top \mathbf{X}\mathbf{X}^\top \mathbf{U}\right\|_F^2
\end{aligned}$$

and similarly

$$\sum_{i=1}^{k} \lambda_i\left(\mathbf{U}_\perp^\top \mathbf{X}\mathbf{X}^\top \mathbf{U}\mathbf{U}^\top \mathbf{X}_\perp \mathbf{X}_\perp^\top \mathbf{U}_\perp\right) = -\left(\left\|\mathbf{X}_\perp^\top \mathbf{U}_\perp\right\|_F^2 - \left\|\mathbf{U}_\perp^\top \mathbf{X}_\perp \mathbf{X}_\perp^\top \mathbf{U}_\perp\right\|_F^2\right).$$

Note that

$$\begin{aligned}
\left\|\mathbf{X}_\perp^\top \mathbf{U}_\perp\right\|_F^2 &= \operatorname{tr}\left(\mathbf{U}_\perp^\top \mathbf{X}_\perp \mathbf{X}_\perp^\top \mathbf{U}_\perp\right) = \operatorname{tr}\left(\mathbf{U}_\perp \mathbf{U}_\perp^\top \mathbf{X}_\perp \mathbf{X}_\perp^\top\right) = \operatorname{tr}\left(\left(\mathbf{I} - \mathbf{U}\mathbf{U}^\top\right)\left(\mathbf{I} - \mathbf{X}\mathbf{X}^\top\right)\right) \\
&= \operatorname{tr}\left(\mathbf{I} - \mathbf{U}\mathbf{U}^\top - \mathbf{X}\mathbf{X}^\top + \mathbf{U}\mathbf{U}^\top \mathbf{X}\mathbf{X}^\top\right) \\
&= n - 2k + \left\|\mathbf{X}^\top \mathbf{U}\right\|_F^2
\end{aligned}$$

and

$$\begin{aligned}
& \left\|\mathbf{U}_\perp^\top \mathbf{X}_\perp \mathbf{X}_\perp^\top \mathbf{U}_\perp\right\|_F^2 \\
= & \operatorname{tr}\left(\left(\mathbf{I} - \mathbf{U}\mathbf{U}^\top\right)\left(\mathbf{I} - \mathbf{X}\mathbf{X}^\top\right)\left(\mathbf{I} - \mathbf{U}\mathbf{U}^\top\right)\left(\mathbf{I} - \mathbf{X}\mathbf{X}^\top\right)\right) \\
= & \operatorname{tr}\left(\left(\mathbf{I} - \mathbf{U}\mathbf{U}^\top\right)\left(\mathbf{I} - \mathbf{X}\mathbf{X}^\top\right)\left(\mathbf{I} - \mathbf{U}\mathbf{U}^\top - \mathbf{X}\mathbf{X}^\top + \mathbf{U}\mathbf{U}^\top \mathbf{X}\mathbf{X}^\top\right)\right) \\
= & \operatorname{tr}\left(\left(\mathbf{I} - \mathbf{U}\mathbf{U}^\top\right)\left(\mathbf{I} - \mathbf{X}\mathbf{X}^\top\right)\left(\mathbf{I} + \mathbf{U}\mathbf{U}^\top \mathbf{X}\mathbf{X}^\top\right)\right) \\
= & \operatorname{tr}\left(\mathbf{I} - \mathbf{U}\mathbf{U}^\top - \mathbf{X}\mathbf{X}^\top + \mathbf{U}\mathbf{U}^\top \mathbf{X}\mathbf{X}^\top + \left(\mathbf{I} - \mathbf{U}\mathbf{U}^\top - \mathbf{X}\mathbf{X}^\top + \mathbf{U}\mathbf{U}^\top \mathbf{X}\mathbf{X}^\top\right)\mathbf{U}\mathbf{U}^\top \mathbf{X}\mathbf{X}^\top\right) \\
= & \operatorname{tr}\left(\mathbf{I} - \mathbf{U}\mathbf{U}^\top - \mathbf{X}\mathbf{X}^\top + \mathbf{U}\mathbf{U}^\top \mathbf{X}\mathbf{X}^\top \mathbf{U}\mathbf{U}^\top \mathbf{X}\mathbf{X}^\top\right) \\
= & n - 2k + \left\|\mathbf{U}^\top \mathbf{X}\mathbf{X}^\top \mathbf{U}\right\|_F^2.
\end{aligned}$$

Therefore, we arrive at

$$\begin{aligned}
& \operatorname{tr}\left(\mathbf{U}^\top \mathbf{X}\mathbf{X}^\top \mathbf{U}\mathbf{U}^\top \mathbf{X}_\perp \mathbf{X}_\perp^\top \mathbf{U}\boldsymbol{\Sigma}\right) + \operatorname{tr}(\mathbf{U}_\perp^\top \mathbf{X}\mathbf{X}^\top \mathbf{U}\mathbf{U}^\top \mathbf{X}_\perp \mathbf{X}_\perp^\top \mathbf{U}_\perp \boldsymbol{\Sigma}_\perp) \\
\geq & \lambda_k \sum_{i=1}^{k} \lambda_i\left(\mathbf{U}^\top \mathbf{X}\mathbf{X}^\top \mathbf{U}\mathbf{U}^\top \mathbf{X}_\perp \mathbf{X}_\perp^\top \mathbf{U}\right) + \lambda_{k+1} \sum_{i=1}^{n-k} \lambda_i\left(\mathbf{U}_\perp^\top \mathbf{X}\mathbf{X}^\top \mathbf{U}\mathbf{U}^\top \mathbf{X}_\perp \mathbf{X}_\perp^\top \mathbf{U}_\perp\right) \\
= & \left(\lambda_k - \lambda_{k+1}\right)\left(\left\|\mathbf{X}^\top \mathbf{U}\right\|_F^2 - \left\|\mathbf{U}^\top \mathbf{X}\mathbf{X}^\top \mathbf{U}\right\|_F^2\right) \\
= & \tau\left(\left\|\mathbf{X}^\top \mathbf{U}\right\|_F^2 - \left\|\mathbf{X}^\top \mathbf{U}\mathbf{U}^\top \mathbf{X}\right\|_F^2\right).
\end{aligned}$$

□

Lemma 5.5. If $\alpha^2\left(\beta^2+48k\tilde{\beta}^2\right)<1$, then

$$\begin{aligned}\operatorname{tr}\left(a_1\left(\mathbf{X}_t\right)a_2^{-1}\left(\mathbf{X}_t\right)\right) \;\geq\;& \left\|\mathbf{X}_t^\top\mathbf{U}\right\|_F^2+2\alpha\tau\left(\left\|\mathbf{X}_t^\top\mathbf{U}\right\|_F^2-\left\|\mathbf{U}^\top\mathbf{X}_t\mathbf{X}_t^\top\mathbf{U}\right\|_F^2\right)\\ &-2\left(1+2\alpha\beta\right)\alpha^2\beta^2\Theta(\mathbf{X}_t,\mathbf{U})-k(1+2\alpha\beta)\alpha^2\nu_t^2.\end{aligned}$$

Proof. First, we have $a_1\left(\mathbf{X}\right)\succcurlyeq\mathbf{0}$ and $a_2\left(\mathbf{X}\right)\succ\mathbf{0}$. By Lemma 3 in (Shamir, 2016), we then get

$$\operatorname{tr}\left(a_1\left(\mathbf{X}\right)a_2^{-1}\left(\mathbf{X}\right)\right)\geq\operatorname{tr}\left(a_1\left(\mathbf{X}\right)\left(2\mathbf{I}-a_2\left(\mathbf{X}\right)\right)\right),$$

where if $\alpha^2\left(\beta^2+48k\tilde{\beta}^2\right)<1$ then

$$\begin{aligned}2\mathbf{I}-a_2\left(\mathbf{X}\right) &= \mathbf{I}-\alpha^2\mathbf{X}^\top\mathbf{A}\mathbf{X}_\perp\mathbf{X}_\perp^\top\mathbf{A}\mathbf{X}-\alpha^2\nu_t^2\mathbf{I}\\ &\succcurlyeq \left(1-\alpha^2\left\|\mathbf{X}^\top\mathbf{A}\mathbf{X}_\perp\mathbf{X}_\perp^\top\mathbf{A}\mathbf{X}\right\|_2-\alpha^2\nu_t^2\right)\mathbf{I}\succcurlyeq\left(1-\alpha^2\left(\beta^2+48k\tilde{\beta}^2\right)\right)\mathbf{I}\succ\mathbf{0}.\end{aligned}$$

Then by Lemma 2 in (Shamir, 2016) we have

$$\begin{aligned}\operatorname{tr}\left(a_1\left(\mathbf{X}\right)a_2^{-1}(\mathbf{X})\right) &\geq \operatorname{tr}\left(\left(a_1\left(\mathbf{X}\right)-\alpha^2\mathbf{X}^\top\mathbf{A}\mathbf{X}_\perp\mathbf{X}_\perp^\top\mathbf{U}\mathbf{U}^\top\mathbf{X}_\perp\mathbf{X}_\perp^\top\mathbf{A}\mathbf{X}\right)\left(2\mathbf{I}-a_2\left(\mathbf{X}\right)\right)\right)\\ &= \operatorname{tr}\left(\tilde{a}_1\left(\mathbf{X}\right)\right)-\alpha^2\operatorname{tr}\left(\tilde{a}_1\left(\mathbf{X}\right)\mathbf{X}^\top\mathbf{A}\mathbf{X}_\perp\mathbf{X}_\perp^\top\mathbf{A}\mathbf{X}\right)-\alpha^2\nu_t^2\operatorname{tr}\left(\tilde{a}_1\left(\mathbf{X}\right)\right),\end{aligned}$$

where $\tilde{a}_1\left(\mathbf{X}\right)=\mathbf{X}^\top\mathbf{U}\mathbf{U}^\top\mathbf{X}+2\alpha\,\mathrm{sym}\left(\mathbf{X}^\top\mathbf{U}\mathbf{U}^\top\mathbf{X}_\perp\mathbf{X}_\perp^\top\mathbf{A}\mathbf{X}\right)$. We now further lower bound the right hand side of the above inequality. By Lemma 5.4., we get

$$\begin{aligned}\operatorname{tr}\left(\tilde{a}_1\left(\mathbf{X}\right)\right) &= \operatorname{tr}\left(\mathbf{X}^\top\mathbf{U}\mathbf{U}^\top\mathbf{X}\right)+2\alpha\operatorname{tr}\left(\mathbf{X}^\top\mathbf{U}\mathbf{U}^\top\mathbf{X}_\perp\mathbf{X}_\perp^\top\mathbf{A}\mathbf{X}\right)\\ &\geq \left\|\mathbf{X}^\top\mathbf{U}\right\|_F^2+2\alpha\tau\left(\left\|\mathbf{X}^\top\mathbf{U}\right\|_F^2-\left\|\mathbf{X}^\top\mathbf{U}\mathbf{U}^\top\mathbf{X}\right\|_F^2\right).\end{aligned}$$

On the other hand, by the Cauchy-Schwarz inequality, we can obtain

$$\begin{aligned}\operatorname{tr}\left(\tilde{a}_1\left(\mathbf{X}\right)\right) &= \operatorname{tr}\left(\mathbf{X}^\top\mathbf{U}\mathbf{U}^\top\mathbf{X}\right)+2\alpha\operatorname{tr}\left(\mathbf{X}^\top\mathbf{U}\mathbf{U}^\top\mathbf{X}_\perp\mathbf{X}_\perp^\top\mathbf{A}\mathbf{X}\right)\\ &\leq \left\|\mathbf{X}^\top\mathbf{U}\mathbf{U}^\top\right\|_F\left\|\mathbf{X}\right\|_F+2\alpha\left\|\mathbf{X}^\top\mathbf{U}\mathbf{U}^\top\mathbf{X}_\perp\mathbf{X}_\perp^\top\mathbf{A}\right\|_F\left\|\mathbf{X}\right\|_F\\ &\leq \left\|\mathbf{X}^\top\right\|_F\left\|\mathbf{U}\mathbf{U}^\top\right\|_2\left\|\mathbf{X}\right\|_F+2\alpha\left\|\mathbf{X}^\top\right\|_F\left\|\mathbf{U}\mathbf{U}^\top\mathbf{X}_\perp\mathbf{X}_\perp^\top\mathbf{A}\right\|_2\left\|\mathbf{X}\right\|_F\\ &\leq \left(1+2\alpha\beta\right)\left\|\mathbf{X}\right\|_F^2=\left(1+2\alpha\beta\right)k.\end{aligned}$$

In addition,

$$\begin{aligned}&\operatorname{tr}\left(\tilde{a}_1\left(\mathbf{X}\right)\mathbf{X}^\top\mathbf{A}\mathbf{X}_\perp\mathbf{X}_\perp^\top\mathbf{A}\mathbf{X}\right)\\ \leq\;& \left\|\tilde{a}_1(\mathbf{X})\mathbf{X}^\top\mathbf{A}\mathbf{X}_\perp\right\|_F\left\|\mathbf{X}_\perp^\top\mathbf{A}\mathbf{X}\right\|_F\leq\left\|\tilde{a}_1(\mathbf{X})\right\|_2\left\|\mathbf{X}^\top\mathbf{A}\mathbf{X}_\perp\right\|_F^2\\ \leq\;& \left(\left\|\mathbf{X}^\top\mathbf{U}\mathbf{U}^\top\mathbf{X}\right\|_2+2\alpha\left\|\mathbf{X}^\top\mathbf{U}\mathbf{U}^\top\mathbf{X}_\perp\mathbf{X}_\perp^\top\mathbf{A}\mathbf{X}\right\|_2\right)\left\|\mathbf{X}^\top\mathbf{A}\mathbf{X}_\perp\right\|_F^2\\ \leq\;& \left(1+2\alpha\beta\right)\left\|\mathbf{X}^\top\mathbf{A}\mathbf{X}_\perp\right\|_F^2=\left(1+2\alpha\right)\left\|\mathbf{X}^\top(\mathbf{U}\boldsymbol{\Sigma}\mathbf{U}^\top+\mathbf{U}_\perp\boldsymbol{\Sigma}_\perp\mathbf{U}_\perp^\top)\mathbf{X}_\perp\right\|_F^2\\ \leq\;& \left(1+2\alpha\beta\right)\left(\left\|\mathbf{X}^\top\mathbf{U}\boldsymbol{\Sigma}\mathbf{U}^\top\mathbf{X}_\perp\right\|_F+\left\|\mathbf{X}^\top\mathbf{U}_\perp\boldsymbol{\Sigma}_\perp\mathbf{U}_\perp^\top\mathbf{X}_\perp\right\|_F\right)^2\\ \leq\;& \left(1+2\alpha\beta\right)\left(\left\|\mathbf{X}^\top\mathbf{U}\boldsymbol{\Sigma}\right\|_2\left\|\mathbf{U}^\top\mathbf{X}_\perp\right\|_F+\left\|\mathbf{X}^\top\mathbf{U}_\perp\right\|_F\left\|\boldsymbol{\Sigma}_\perp\mathbf{U}_\perp^\top\mathbf{X}_\perp\right\|_2\right)^2\\ \leq\;& \left(1+2\alpha\beta\right)\left(\left\|\mathbf{A}\right\|_2\left\|\mathbf{U}^\top\mathbf{X}_\perp\right\|_F+\left\|\mathbf{X}^\top\mathbf{U}_\perp\right\|_F\left\|\mathbf{A}\right\|_2\right)^2\\ \leq\;& \beta^2\left(1+2\alpha\beta\right)\left(\left\|\mathbf{U}^\top\mathbf{X}_\perp\right\|_F+\left\|\mathbf{X}^\top\mathbf{U}_\perp\right\|_F\right)^2=2\beta^2\left(1+2\alpha\beta\right)\Theta(\mathbf{X},\mathbf{U}).\end{aligned}$$

Therefore, we arrive at

$$\begin{aligned}\operatorname{tr}\left(a_1\left(\mathbf{X}\right)a_2^{-1}\left(\mathbf{X}\right)\right) \;\geq\;& \left\|\mathbf{X}^\top\mathbf{U}\right\|_F^2+2\alpha\tau\left(\left\|\mathbf{X}^\top\mathbf{U}\right\|_F^2-\left\|\mathbf{U}^\top\mathbf{X}\mathbf{X}^\top\mathbf{U}\right\|_F^2\right)\\ &-2\left(1+2\alpha\beta\right)\alpha^2\beta^2\Theta(\mathbf{X},\mathbf{U})-k\left(1+2\alpha\beta\right)\alpha^2\nu_t^2.\end{aligned}$$

□

Lemma 5.6. For any $\iota \in (0,1)$, if α and m satisfy that $\alpha < 2\xi\tau/\gamma$, $\min\{2(1+\alpha\beta)\alpha\mu, \alpha^2(\beta^2+48k\tilde{\beta}^2)\} < 1$ and $\Theta_0 + km\rho + \theta\sqrt{2m\log(1/\iota)} < \delta$, then $\Theta_t < \delta$ holds for all $t = 1, 2, \cdots, m$ with probability at least $1-\iota$, where $\theta = \frac{4k(\beta+4\tilde{\beta})\alpha}{1-(\beta+4\tilde{\beta})\alpha} + k\rho$.

Proof. Consider the stochastic process $\{\Theta_0, \Theta_1, \ldots, \Theta_m\}$ and the filtration $\mathcal{F} = \{\mathcal{F}_t\}$ about random draws y_t. Since $\mathbb{E}[\Theta_{t+1}|\mathbf{X}_t] \le (1-\alpha(2\xi\tau-\gamma\alpha))\Theta_t + \rho\tilde{\Theta}_{s-1}$, we have $\mathbb{E}[\Theta_{t+1}|X^{(t)}] \le \Theta_t + k\rho$ if $\alpha < 2\xi\tau/\gamma$. Define $\Psi_t = \Theta_t - k\rho t$ for $t = 0, 1, 2, \cdots, m$. Note that $\{\Psi_t : t = 0, 1, 2, \cdots, m\}$ is a finite sequence of random variables and thus the natural continuation can be applied to get an infinite sequence such that $|\Psi_t| \le \Theta_t + k\rho m \le k(1+\rho m)$ for all t including $t > m$. In addition,

$$\mathbb{E}[\Psi_t|\mathbf{X}_{t-1}] = \mathbb{E}[\Theta_t|\mathbf{X}_{t-1}] - k\rho t \le \Theta_{t-1} + k\rho - k\rho t = \Theta_{t-1} - k\rho(t-1) = \Psi_{t-1}.$$

$\{\Psi_t\}$ thus is a super-martingale. Next, we prove that it has bounded differences. Note that the intermediate update in the tangent space is $\mathbf{X}_t + \alpha_{t+1}\mathrm{Grad}f(\mathbf{X}_t) + \alpha_{t+1}\mathbf{W}_t$, for which we have

$$\|\mathrm{Grad}f(\mathbf{X}_t) + \mathbf{W}_t\|_2 \le \|\mathrm{Grad}f(\mathbf{X}_t)\|_2 + \|\mathbf{W}_t\|_2 \le \beta + 4\tilde{\beta}$$

using Lemma 5.1. Based on the proof of Lemma 9 in (Shamir, 2016), we have that

$$\left| \|\mathbf{X}_{t+1}^\top \mathbf{U}\|_F^2 - \|\mathbf{X}_t^\top \mathbf{U}\|_F^2 \right| \le \frac{4k(\beta+4\tilde{\beta})\alpha}{1-(\beta+4\tilde{\beta})\alpha}.$$

Thus, we get the bounded difference

$$|\Psi_{t+1} - \Psi_t| \le \left| \|\mathbf{X}_{t+1}^\top \mathbf{U}\|_F^2 - \|\mathbf{X}_t^\top \mathbf{U}\|_F^2 \right| + k\rho \le \frac{4k(\beta+4\tilde{\beta})\alpha}{1-(\beta+4\tilde{\beta})\alpha} + k\rho \triangleq \theta.$$

We now are able to apply the Azuma-Hoeffding inequality, i.e., for any $0 \le t \le m$ and $a > 0$

$$P(\Psi_t - \Psi_0 \ge a) \le \exp\{-\frac{a^2}{2\sum_{s=1}^t \theta^2}\} = \exp\{-\frac{a^2}{2t\theta^2}\} \le \exp\{-\frac{a^2}{2m\theta^2}\} \triangleq \iota \in (0,1).$$

Solving $\iota = \exp\{-\frac{a^2}{2m\theta^2}\}$ with respect to a yields $a = \theta\sqrt{2m\log(1/\iota)}$. Therefore, we get that $\Psi_t - \Psi_0 < a$, i.e.,

$$\Theta_t \le \Theta_0 + k\rho t + a \le \Theta_0 + km\rho + \theta\sqrt{2m\log(1/\iota)} < \delta$$

for all $t = 1, 2, \cdots, m$, with probability at least $1-\iota$. □

AUTHOR INDEX

AUTHOR INDEX

AUTHOR INDEX

33rd Conference on Uncertainty in Artificial Intelligence 2017

Sydney, Australia
11-15 August 2017

Volume 2 of 2

Editors:

Gal Elidan **Kristian Kersting**

ISBN: 978-1-5108-4779-8

Printed from e-media with permission by:

Curran Associates, Inc.
57 Morehouse Lane
Red Hook, NY 12571

Some format issues inherent in the e-media version may also appear in this print version.

Printed by Curran Associates, Inc. (2017)

Association For Uncertainty in Artificial Intelligence (AUAI)
Department of Computer Science
University of British Columbia
Vancouver BC Canada V6T 1Z4

Phone: (703) 787-8044
Fax: (703) 478-0829

www.auai.org

Additional copies of this publication are available from:

Curran Associates, Inc.
57 Morehouse Lane
Red Hook, NY 12571 USA
Phone: 845-758-0400
Fax: 845-758-2633
Email: curran@proceedings.com
Web: www.proceedings.com

Conference Program

All the conference talks will be held in **Room C4.8** on the fourth level of the Sydney International Convention Centre. Poster sessions and coffee breaks will be located in **Room C4.9**.

Saturday August 12th

8:30 Welcome

Keynote Talk

8:40 Intelligent Robots in an Uncertain World
Leslie Pack Kaelbling, MIT

Session 1: Deep Models

10:40 - 11:10 Coffee break

Session 2: Machine Learning

12:10 - 14:00 Lunch break

Keynote Talk

14:00 Learning and Inference with Expectations
Amir Globerson, University of Tel Aviv

Session 3: Inference

15:00 160: On Loopy Belief Propagation – Local Stability Analysis for Non-Vanishing Fields 100
Christian Knoll and Franz Pernkopf

15:20 259: Improving Optimization-Based Approximate Inference by Clamping Variables 110
Junyao Zhao, Josip Djolonga, Sebastian Tschiatschek, Andreas Krause

15:40 109: Approximation Complexity of Maximum A Posteriori Inference in Sum-Product Networks 124
Diarmaid Conaty, Cassio P. de Campos, Denis D. Maua

16:00 - 16:20 Coffee break

Session 4: Learning

16:20 291: Learning the Structure of Probabilistic Sentential Decision Diagrams 134
Yitao Liang, Jessa Bekker, Guy Van den Broeck

16:40 278: A Probabilistic Framework for Multi-Label Learning with Unseen Labels 146
Abhilash Gaure and Piyush Rai

17:00 297: Hybrid Deep Discriminative/Generative Models for Semi-Supervised Learning 156
Volodymyr Kuleshov and Stefano Ermon

Poster Spotlights 1

17:20 - 17:50 one minute poster spotlight presentations of papers:

100: Regret Minimization Algorithms for the Followers Behaviour Identification in Leadership Games 166
Lorenzo Bisi, Giuseppe De Nittis, Francesco Trovò, Marcello Restelli, Nicola Gatti

105: On the Complexity of Nash Equilibrium Reoptimization 183
Andrea Celli, Alberto Marchesi, Nicola Gatti

26: Shortest Path under Uncertainty: Exploration versus Exploitation 193
Zhan Wei Lim, David Hsu, Wee Sun Lee

35: Learning with Confident Examples: Rank Pruning for Robust Classification with Noisy Labels 203
Curtis G. Northcutt, Tailin Wu, Isaac L. Chuang

37: Monte-Carlo Tree Search using Batch Value of Perfect Information 228
Shahaf S. Shperberg, Solomon Eyal Shimony, Ariel Felner

45: Submodular Variational Inference for Network Reconstruction 238
Lin Chen, Forrest W. Crawford, Amin Karbasi

70: Bayesian Inference of Log Determinants 253
J. Fitzsimons, K. Cutajar, M. Filippone, M. Osborne, S. Roberts

75: Fast Amortized Inference and Learning in Log-linear Models with Randomly Perturbed Nearest Neighbor Search 264
Stephen Mussmann, Daniel Levy, Stefano Ermon

106: Supervised Restricted Boltzmann Machines 279
Tu Dinh Nguyen, Dinh Phung, Viet Huynh, Trung Le

108: Safe Semi-Supervised Learning of Sum-Product Networks 289
Martin Trapp, Tamas Madl, Robert Peharz, Franz Pernkopf, Robert Trappl

142: Green Generative Modeling: Recycling Dirty Data using Recurrent Variational Autoencoders 299
Yu Wang, Bin Dai, Gang Hua, John Aston, David Wipf

146: Approximate Evidential Reasoning Using Local Conditioning and Conditional Belief Functions 322
Van Nguyen

152: Differentially Private Variational Inference for Non-conjugate Models 332
Joonas Jälkö, Antti Honkela, Onur Dikmen

162: Value Directed Exploration in Multi-Armed Bandits with Structured Priors 342
Bence Cserna, Marek Petrik, Reazul Hasan Russel, Wheeler Ruml

188: Learning Approximately Objective Priors 355
Eric Nalisnick and Padhraic Smyth

206: Learning to Draw Samples with Amortized Stein Variational Gradient Descent 365
Yihao Feng, Dilin Wang, Qiang Liu

220: A Tractable Probabilistic Model for Subset Selection 377
Yujia Shen, Arthur Choi, Adnan Darwiche

229: Structure Learning of Linear Gaussian Structural Equation Models with Weak Edges 391
Marco Eigenmann, Preetam Nandy, Marloes Maathuis

234: SAT-Based Causal Discovery under Weaker Assumptions 409
Zhalama, Jiji Zhang, Frederick Eberhardt, Wolfgang Mayer

237: Learning to Acquire Information 419
Yewen Pu, Leslie Pack Kaelbling, Armando Solar-Lezama

17:50 - 19:50 Poster Session 1

Will include all papers presented on Saturday.

Sunday August 13th

Keynote Talk

8:30 Snorkel: Beyond Hand-labeled Data
Christopher Ré, Stanford

Session 5: Representations

9:30 263: Why Rules are Complex: Real-Valued Probabilistic Logic Programs are not Fully Expressive 429
David Buchman and David Poole

9:50 292: Interpreting Lion Behaviour as Probabilistic Programs 439
Neil Dhir, Matthjis Vakar, Matthew Wijers, Andrew Markham, Frank Wood

10:10 147: Decoupling Homophily and Reciprocity with Latent Space Network Models 456
Jiasen Yang, Vinayak Rao, Jennifer Neville

10:30 - 11:00 Coffee break

Session 6: Reinforcement Learning

11:00 276: Online Constrained Model-based Reinforcement Learning 470
Benjamin van Niekerk, Andreas Damianou, Benjamin Rosman

11:20 209: A Reinforcement Learning Approach to Weaning of Mechanical Ventilation in Intensive Care Units 480
Niranjani Prasad, Li-Fang Cheng, Corey Chivers, Michael Draugelis, Barbara E. Engelhardt

11:40 62: Near-Optimal Interdiction of Factored MDPs 490
Swetasudha Panda and Yevgeniy Vorobeychik

12:00 225: Importance Sampling for Fair Policy Selection 500
Shayan Doroudi, Philip Thomas, Emma Brusnkill

12:20 - 14:10 Lunch break

Keynote Talk

14:10 - 15:10 Machine Learning for Healthcare Data
Katherine Heller, Duke University

Poster Spotlights 2

15:10pm - 15:40 one minute poster spotlight presentations of papers:

12: FROSH: FasteR Online Sketching Hashing 515
Xixian Chen, Irwin King, Michael R. Lyu

16: Self-Discrepancy Conditional Independence Test 528
Sanghack Lee and Vasant Honavar

15:40 - 16:00 Coffee break

16:00 - 18:00 Poster Session 2

Will include all papers presented on Sunday.

18:45 - Banquet Boarding

Banquet Talk: 15 minutes on Artificial Intelligence and Statistical Models
Terry Speed, Walter and Eliza Hall Institute of Medical Research

Monday August 14th

Keynote Talk

8:30 Two current analysis challenges: Single Cell Omics and Nanopore Long-read Sequence Data
Terry Speed, Walter and Eliza Hall Institute of Medical Research

Session 7: Causality

10:30 - 11:00 Coffee break

Session 8: Sampling

12:20 - 14:10 Lunch break

Session 9: Bandits

Poster Spotlights 3

15:10 - 15:40 one minute poster spotlight presentations of papers:

15:40 - 16:00 Coffee break

16:00 - 16:45 Business Meeting

16:00 - 18:00 Poster Session 3

Will include all papers presented on Monday.

Branch and Bound for Regular Bayesian Network Structure Learning

Joe Suzuki* **and Jun Kawahara**†
∗ Osaka University, Japan. j-suzuki@sigmath.es.osaka-u.ac.jp
† Nara Institute of Science and Technology, Japan. jkawahara@is.naist.ac.jp

Abstract

We consider efficient Bayesian network structure learning (BNSL) based on scores using branch and bound. Thus far, as a BNSL score, the Bayesian Dirichlet equivalent uniform (BDeu) has been used most often, but it is recently proved that the BDeu does not choose the simplest model even when the likelihood is maximized whereas Jeffreys' prior and MDL satisfy such regularity. Although the BDeu has been preferred because it gives Markov equivalent models the same score, in this paper, we introduce another class of scores (quotient scores) that satisfies the property, and propose a pruning rule for the quotient score based on Jeffreys' prior. We find that the quotient score based on Jeffreys' prior is regular, and that the proposed pruning rule utilizes the regularity, and is applied much more often than that of the BDeu, so that much less computation is required in BNSL. Finally, our experiments support the hypothesis that the regular scores outperform the non-regular ones in the sense of computational efficiency as well as correctness of BNSL.

1 INTRODUCTION

We consider learning stochastic relations among variables from data. If we mean by the relations conditional independence (CI) among variables, and if we express them via a directed acyclic graph (DAG), then such a graphical model will be a Bayesian network (BN) (Pearl, 1988). The factorization of the distribution determines its Bayesian network. Figure 1 shows four BNs consisting of three nodes and two edges. For example, if the distribution is factorized as $P(X)P(Y|X)P(Z|Y)$ and $P(Y)P(X|Y)P(Z|Y)$, then the BN will be (a) and (b), respectively. However, if we express them as $P(X,Y)P(Y,Z)/P(Y)$, we find that they share the same factorization and that both imply the same CI statement: "X and Z are conditionally independent given Y". In this paper, we say the two BNs are Markov equivalent, and do not distinguish them. In a broad sense, the BN is defined in terms of the structure and parameters, i.e., its topology of nodes and edges and the conditional probabilities of variables given other variables.

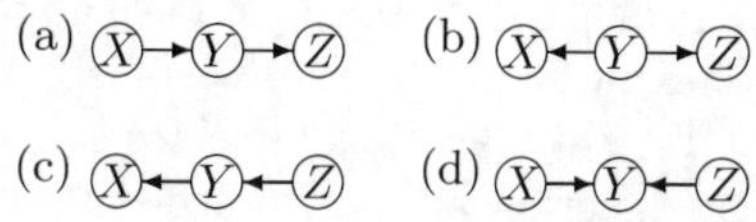

Figure 1: Four BNs with three nodes and two edges.

There are several approaches for Bayesian network structure learning (BNSL). We may test each CI statement between two variable sets given another variable set with the three sets exclusive each other based on an existing statistical method (PC algorithm (Spirtes et al., 1993)). In this paper, however, we focus on the score based approach such as maximizing the posterior probability of a selected structure based on the prior probability and data, or minimizing the description length (MDL (Rissanen, 1978)) of data w.r.t. a selected structure: given data, we compute its score for each structure and select a structure with the optimal value.

We consider four criteria of giving a score to each structure. For many years, the Bayesian Dirichlet equivalent uniform (BDeu) (Buntine, 1991; Heckerman et al., 1995) has been used most often as a criterion that maximizes the posterior probability. The main reason is that the BDeu assures Markov equivalent BNs to have the same score value. Suppose that given n examples w.r.t. X, Y, we assign scores $Q^n(X)$, $Q^n(Y)$, $Q^n(X|Y)$, and $Q^n(Y|X)$ to factors $P(X)$, $P(Y)$, $P(X|Y)$, and $P(Y|X)$, respectively. Then, under the BDeu, $Q^n(X|Y)Q^n(Y) = Q^n(Y|X)Q^n(X)$ holds. The same property holds for any number of variables and any factors. This paper says such BNSL to be normal.

The discussion in this paper is motivated by the paper (Suzuki, 2017) that claims that the BDeu leads to fatal situations in BNSL (see Section 3.1).

In any model selection, given data, simplicity of a model and fitness of the data to the model should be balanced. Any scientific discovery in the history has been found in this way. For example, there would have been many theories that explain mechanics as well as Newton's laws of motion does, but Newton's was selected because it contains only three laws. It is reasonable to think that any belief made by an intelligent activity satisfies such regularity. However, the BDeu violates it. Suppose that given data, we choose a parent set of X from $\{Y\}$ and $\{Y, Z\}$ by comparing $Q^n(X|Y)$ and $Q^n(X|Y, Z)$. Then, the BDeu always chooses $\{Y, Z\}$ when the (empirical) conditional entropy of X given Y is zero (see (Suzuki, 2017) for the proof). In fact, some claim (Silander, 2016) that for small n, the BDeu chooses an over fitted structure.

In this paper, we claim another merit of using the regular scores over the non-regular ones, i.e, BNSL based on the regular scores can be computed more efficiently than BNSL based on the non-regular ones, as explained below.

BNSL consists of finding the optimal parent sets and ordering the variables (Silander and Myllymaki, 2006; Singh and Moore, 2005). We note that as the number of variables grows, the computation exponentially increases (Chickering et al., 2003). For many years, many authors of BNSL have been considering pruning the computation when searching the optimal parent sets in a depth first manner. (Suzuki, 1996) proposed a pruning rule for the MDL principle to reduce the computation; (Tian, 2000) proposed variants of the procedure (Suzuki, 1996); (Campos and Ji, 2011) pointed out that finding the optimal parent sets w.r.t. the MDL principle takes at most polynomial time of p when the sample size n is a constant; (Campos and Ji, 2011) also proposed a pruning rule for the BDeu; and recently, (Suzuki, 2016) proposed a pruning rule for maximizing the posterior probability based on Jeffreys' prior (see Section 3.2 for the details).

Table 1: Normality and regularity (see Sections 2.3 and 3.1 for the definitions, respectively) in the conditional and quotient scores.

Score	BDeu	Jeffreys'
Conditional	normal NOT regular	NOT normal regular
Quotient	N/A	normal regular

In this paper, we point out that BNSL based on the MDL (Suzuki, 1996) and Jeffreys' prior (Suzuki, 2016) are regular, and claims that the pruning rules for those criteria are efficient by utilizing regularity whereas BNSL that maximizes the posterior probability based on Jeffreys' prior (Suzuki, 2016) is not normal.

In order to avoid such inconvenience (not being normal), we consider another framework of constructing scores. For two variables, we only assign four scores $Q^n(\cdot) = 1$, $Q^n(X)$, $Q^n(Y)$, $Q^n(X, Y)$ and compute $Q^n(X|Y) = Q^n(X, Y)/Q^n(Y)$ and $Q^n(Y|X) = Q^n(X, Y)/Q^n(X)$ (quotient scores) rather than assign $Q^n(\cdot) = 1$, $Q^n(X)$, $Q^n(Y)$, $Q^n(X|Y)$, and $Q^n(Y|X)$ (conditional scores). The same idea can be extended into p variables. For the quotient scores, the resulting BNSL will be normal.

In this paper, we propose a pruning rule for the quotient score based on Jeffreys' prior. We prove (Theorem 1) that the resulting BNSL is regular. Although (Suzuki, 2016) has already proposed a pruning rule for the score, we find from Theorem 3 and experiments that the proposed pruning rule significantly improves the existing one (Suzuki, 2016).

Besides, we prove that the minus logarithms of the scores and bounds of the proposed procedure are close to those of the MDL procedure (Theorem 4). While it is known (Campos and Ji, 2011) that the pruning rule for the MDL applies much more often than that for the BDeu, we find that the proposed procedure is much faster than the BDeu as well.

Our contribution is to establish that the regular scores including the quotient ones based on Jeffreys' prior outperform the non-regular ones in the sense of computational efficiency as well as correctness of BNSL.

This paper is organized as follows: Section 2

overviews related matters to the results in Section 3, in particular, Sections 2.1,2.2,2.3 and 2.4 explain BNSL, BDeu, branch and bound, and conditional and quotient scores, respectively; Section 3.1 explains why and how the BDeu faces fatal situation and proves Theorem 1; Section 3.2 claims that the existing pruning rules except the BDeu utilize the fact that the score is regular; Section 3.3 proposes the new bound (Theorem 2), and proves Theorem 3 (it is tighter than the existing one) and Theorem 4; Section 4 shows the results of experiments using the Alarm database (Beinlich et al., 1989); and Section 5 concludes the discussion and raises future works.

2 BACKGROUND

In this section, we overview the notions of Bayesian network structure learning, BDeu, branch and bound for finding the parent sets, and conditional and quotient scores to understand the results in Section 3.

2.1 BAYESIAN NETWORK STRUCTURE LEARNING

Suppose that given n tuples of examples

$$X^{(1)} = x_{i,1}, X^{(2)} = x_{i,2}, \cdots, X^{(p)} = x_{i,p} \ , \qquad (1)$$

$i = 1, 2, \cdots, n$, w.r.t. p variables $X^{(1)}, X^{(2)}, \cdots, X^{(p)}$, we wish to estimate its BN structure that have generated those np examples. We find a BN structure with the maximum posterior probability given the np examples and prior probabilities over structures and parameters (Cooper and Herskovits, 1992).

If X is a binary variable with unknown probability $\theta := P(X = 1)$, the probability of a sequence $X = x_1, X = x_2, \cdots, X = x_n$ with c ones and $n - c$ zeros can be expressed by

$$Q^n(X) := \int_0^1 \theta^c (1-\theta)^{n-c} w(\theta) d\theta \qquad (2)$$

using a prior probability $w(\theta)$ over parameter $0 \leq \theta \leq 1$. It is known (Krichevsky and Trofimov, 1981) that if we assume $w(\theta)$ is proportional to $\theta^{a-1}(1-\theta)^{b-1}$ for real constants $a, b > 0$, (2) can be expressed by

$$Q^n(X) = \prod_{i=1}^{n} \frac{c_{i-1}(x_i) + a(x_i)}{i - 1 + \sum_x a(x)} \ , \qquad (3)$$

where $c_{i-1}(x)$ is the number of occurrences of x in $(x_1, \cdots, x_{i-1}) \in \{0,1\}^{i-1}$, and $a(x) := a$ and $a(x) := b$ for $x = 1$ and for $x = 0$, respectively. For example, if $a = 0.1$, $b = 0.2$, $(x_1, \cdots, x_5) = (0,1,0,1,1)$, then we have

$$Q^5(X) = \frac{0+0.2}{0+0.3} \cdot \frac{0+0.1}{1+0.3} \cdot \frac{1+0.2}{2+0.3} \cdot \frac{1+0.1}{3+0.3} \cdot \frac{2+0.1}{4+0.3} \ .$$

In a similar way, if X, Y are binary variables whose probability is unknown, then the conditional probability of $X = x_1, X = x_2, \cdots, X = x_n$ given $Y = y_1, Y = y_2, \cdots, Y = y_n$ can be expressed by

$$Q^n(X|Y) = \prod_{i=1}^{n} \frac{c_{i-1}(x_i, y_i) + a(x_i, y_i)}{c_{i-1}(y_i) + \sum_x a(x, y_i)} \ , \qquad (4)$$

where $c_{i-1}(x, y)$ is the number of occurrences of $(X, Y) = (x, y)$ in $(X, Y) = (x_1, y_1), \cdots, (x_{i-1}, y_{i-1})$, and $a(x, y) > 0$ is a constant associated with $(X, Y) = (x, y)$. Note that the quantities $Q^n(X)$ and $Q^n(X|Y)$ can be defined even if X and Y are not binary.

If an additional variable Z is available, we can construct $Q^n(X|Y, Z)$ as well as $Q^n(X|Z)$ by regarding (Y, Z) as a single variable that takes a finite number of values. In the same way, we further construct $Q^n(Y|\cdot)$ and $Q^n(Z|\cdot)$, which enables us to express the probabilities of the examples (1) with $p = 3$ and $(X^{(1)}, X^{(2)}, X^{(3)}) = (X, Y, Z)$ given the structures among X, Y, Z. In Figure 1 (a), (b), (c), and (d), those probabilities (scores) are $Q^n(X)Q^n(Y|X)Q^n(Z|Y)$, $Q^n(Y)Q^n(X|Y)Q^n(Z|Y)$, $Q^n(Z)Q^n(Y|Z)Q^n(X|Y)$, and $Q^n(X)Q^n(Z)Q^n(Y|X, Z)$, respectively.

Furthermore, if we have the prior probabilities over the structures, we obtain a BN structure with the maximum posterior probability, where the theory can be extended to p variables each of which takes a finite number of values.

2.2 BDeu

From Section 2.2, we find that $Q^n(X)Q^n(Y|X)Q^n(Z|Y)$, $Q^n(Y)Q^n(X|Y)Q^n(Z|Y)$, and $Q^n(Z)Q^n(Y|Z)Q^n(X|Y)$ should have the same value, which implies

$$Q^n(X)Q^n(Y|X) = Q^n(Y)Q^n(X|Y) \qquad (5)$$

and $Q^n(Y)Q^n(Z|Y) = Q^n(Z)Q^n(Y|Z)$ are required in order for Figure 1 (a)(b)(c) to have the same score. In this paper, we say scores and their BNSL to be *normal* if any Markov equivalent structures share the same score. In particular, in this subsection, we specify $Q^n(\cdot)$ and $Q^n(\cdot|\cdot)$ such that the BNSL is normal.

Let α and β be the numbers of values that X and Y take, respectively. Then, one can check (Buntine, 1991; Heckerman et al., 1995) from (3) and (4) that (5) requires $a(x) = \delta/\alpha$, $a(y) = \delta/\beta$, and $a(x,y) = \delta/\alpha\beta$ for some positive constant δ, if $a(x)$ and $a(x,y)$ take the same values for each of x and for each of (x,y), respectively. Then, we see that (5) has the value

$$\prod_{i=1}^{n} \frac{c_{i-1}(x_i, y_i) + \delta/\alpha\beta}{i - 1 + \delta} .$$

Thus, the BDeu gives normal BNSL.

In this paper, we refer to setting $a(\cdot)$ and $a(\cdot,\cdot)$ in this way as the Bayesian Dirichlet equivalent uniform (BDeu) (Buntine, 1991; Ueno, 2008). On the other hand, some use $a(\cdot) = a(\cdot,\cdot) = 0.5$ while the setting does not give normal BNSL as $Q^n(Y)Q^n(X|Y) \neq Q^n(X)Q^n(Y|X)$ for the case. We say that the latter approach is based on Jeffreys' prior (Jeffreys, 1939; Krichevsky and Trofimov, 1981).

2.3 BRANCH AND BOUND FOR FINDING THE PARENT SETS

In order to obtain a BN structure that maximizes the posterior probability, we need to find a subset U of S that maximizes $Q^n(X|U)$ for each $X \in V$ and $S \subseteq V \backslash \{X\}$, where $V := \{X^{(1)}, X^{(2)}, \cdots, X^{(p)}\}$. For computing $R^n_X(S) := \max_{U \subseteq S} Q^n(X|U)$ and $\pi^n(S) := \mathrm{argmax}_{U \subseteq S} Q^n(X|U)$ (the parent set of X w.r.t. S) for $S \subseteq V \backslash \{X\}$, we put $R^n_X(\{\}) = Q^n(X)$, and recursively compute

$$R^n_X(S) = \max_{Y \in S} \{Q^n(X|S), R^n_X(S \backslash \{Y\})\} \quad (6)$$

for $S \neq \{\}$. Then, we note that the original computation based on dynamic programming takes much time for computing $Q^n(X|S)$, $S \subseteq V \backslash \{X\}$. However, for example, in Figure 2, if we know for $S = \{Y, Z\}$,

$$R^n_X(S) \geq \sup_{T \supseteq S} Q^n(X|T)$$

in some way, we can avoid computing $Q^n(X|Y, Z)$ and $Q^n(X|Y, Z, W)$.

For the BDeu scores, (Campos and Ji, 2011) and (Cussens and Bartlett, 2015) derived

$$\sup_{T \supseteq S} Q^n(X|T) \leq R^n_{X,*}(S) := \alpha^{-d(S)} , \quad (7)$$

where α is the number of values that X takes and $d(S)$ is the number of different states S that actually have occurred in the n tuples of examples. The

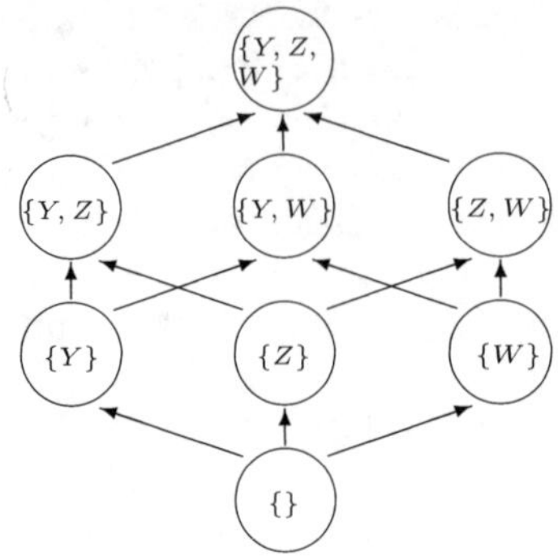

Figure 2: The ordered graph from {} to $\{Y, Z, W\}$: compute $\pi^n(S)$ and its maximum value $R^n_X(S)$ in a bottom-up manner.

bound (7) can be applied to branch and bound technique: if $\max_{Y \in S} R^n_X(S \backslash \{Y\}) \geq \alpha^{-d(S)}$ in (6), neither $Q^n(X|S)$ in (6) nor $Q^n(X|T)$ for $T \supsetneq S$ have to be computed.

2.4 CONDITIONAL AND QUOTIENT SCORES

There are some alternative ways to evaluate the probabilities (scores) for the structures. One of the most promising methods (Silander, 2016; Suzuki, 2017) is to compute the local scores $Q^n(S)$ for the $2^p - 1$ subsets S of V to compute global scores by dividing those values (Silander, 2016; Suzuki, 2017). For example, if $S = \{X, Y\}$, then similar to (3), we can compute the score

$$Q^n(X, Y) = \prod_{i=1}^{n} \frac{c_{i-1}(x_i, y_i) + a(x_i, y_i)}{i - 1 + \sum_x a(x, y_i)} . \quad (8)$$

Then, if we have three variables X, Y, Z ($p = 3$), we can compute seven local scores $Q^n(X)$, $Q^n(Y)$, $Q^n(Z)$, $Q^n(Y,Z)$, $Q^n(Z,X)$, $Q^n(X,Y)$, $Q^n(X,Y,Z)$ and eleven global scores such as

$$\frac{Q^n(X,Y)Q^n(Y,Z)}{Q^n(Y)} , \frac{Q^n(X)Q^n(Z)Q^n(X,Y,Z)}{Q^n(X,Z)}$$

for (a)(b)(c) and (d) in Figure 1, respectively.

We refer the scores in Section 2.1 and the current subsection as the conditional and quotient scores, respectively. For the latter score, we define $Q^n(X|Y)$ by $Q^n(X|Y) := Q^n(X,Y)/Q^n(Y)$, so that the conditions such as (5) are automatically satisfied for any constants $a(\cdot,\cdot)$ (normal BNSL). In particular, we assume $a(\cdot) = a(\cdot,\cdot) = 0.5$ (Jeffreys' prior (Jeffreys, 1939; Krichevsky and Trofimov, 1981)) for the latter score. See Table 1.

Table 2: Dataframe consisting of X, Y, Z with $n = 8$, $\alpha = \gamma = 2$, and $\beta = 4$.

X	0	1	0	1	1	0	1	0
Y	0	1	2	3	3	2	1	0
Z	0	0	1	1	1	1	0	0

It is known (Suzuki, 2016) that the quantities (3), (4), and (8) satisfy

$$\frac{Q^n(X,Y)}{Q^n(Y)} \leq Q^n(X|Y) \quad (9)$$

when $a(\cdot) = a(\cdot,\cdot)$. The quotient score requires to assume its equality in (9).

3 BRANCH AND BOUND FOR REGULAR BNSL

In this section, we propose an improved BNSL pruning rule for the quotient score based on Jeffreys' prior.

3.1 REGULAR BNSL

In this subsection, we illustrate and define the notion of regular BNSL that will be discussed throughout this section.

Suppose that we estimate the parent sets $\pi(X,S)$ of $X \in V$ w.r.t. $S \subseteq V\backslash\{X\}$ from examples. Then, the values of variables in $\pi(X,S)$ determine states, and each example is classified into one of the states. For example, if $\pi(X,S) = \{Y,Z\}$, each example is classified into one of the $\beta\gamma$ states based on the values of (Y,Z) when Y and Z take β and γ values, respectively. Then, the conditional probability of each $X = x$ given each state $(Y,Z) = (y,z)$ is to be estimated. In this sense, as the parent set $\pi(X,S)$ contains more variables, the states are divided into smaller ones that contain fewer examples. In this sense, if X takes only one value in each of the states, it is reasonable to stop dividing the states.

We can see that the BDeu violates such regularity. For example, suppose that for $S = \{Y,Z\}$, we determine either $\pi(X,S) = \{Y\}$ or $\pi(X,S) = \{Y,Z\}$ from the examples in Table 2. We observe that $X = 0$ and $X = 1$ for $Y = 0,2$ and $Y = 1,3$, respectively, so that the states have been fully explained by Y, which means that we should not add any more variable to $\pi(X,S) = \{Y\}$. However, the BDeu further adds Z to $\pi(X,S) = \{Y\}$.

In fact, we have for the BDeu with $\delta = 1$,

$$Q^n(X|Y) = (\frac{1/8}{1/4} \cdot \frac{1+1/8}{1+1/4})^4 = (\frac{9}{10})^4 \cdot 2^{-4}\ , \text{ and}$$

$$Q^n(X|Y,Z) = (\frac{1/16}{1/8} \cdot \frac{1+1/16}{1+1/8})^4 = (\frac{17}{18})^4 \cdot 2^{-4}\ ,$$

so that the latter is larger. However, if we use the quotient score based on Jeffreys' prior, we have $Q^n(Y) = \frac{(3/4)^4}{2\cdot 3\cdots 9}$, $Q^n(X,Y) = Q^n(Y,Z) = \frac{(3/4)^4}{4\cdot 5\cdots 11}$, and $Q^n(X,Y,Z) = \frac{(3/4)^4}{8\cdot 9\cdots 15}$, which means

$$\frac{3}{55} = Q^n(X|Y) = \frac{Q^n(X,Y)}{Q^n(Y)}$$
$$> \frac{Q^n(X,Y,Z)}{Q^n(Y,Z)} = Q^n(X|Y,Z) = \frac{1}{39}\ .$$

Let $(x_1,\cdots,x_n)$ and $(s_1,\cdots,s_n)$ be n realizations of $X \in V$ and $S \subseteq V\backslash\{X\}$, respectively. For example, a realization of $S = \{Y,Z\}$ is that of (Y,Z).

Definition 1 If $Q^n(X|S) \geq Q^n(X|T)$ for any $S \subseteq T$ whenever each $X = x_i$ is uniquely determined by the $S = s_i$, we say scores and their BNSL to be *regular*.

We have seen that the BDeu does not give regular BNSL. On the other hand, for the quotient score based on Jeffreys' prior, we have a positive result:

Theorem 1 The BNSL based on the quotient score based on Jeffreys' prior is regular.

Proof: See Appendix A.

Now we consider the procedure based on the minimum description length (MDL) (Rissanen, 1978) principle (the Bayesian information criterion (Schwarz, 1978)): if we define the empirical conditional entropy of X given Y by

$$H(X|Y) = \sum_x \sum_y \frac{c_n(x,y)}{n} \log \frac{c_n(x,y)}{c_n(y)}$$

with $c_n(y) = \sum_{x'} c_n(x',y)$, then the MDL procedure chooses $\pi(X,S)$ by comparing

$$L^n(\{Y\}) = H(X|Y) + \frac{(\alpha-1)\beta}{2n}\log n \text{ and}$$

$$L^n(\{Y,Z\}) = H(X|Y,Z) + \frac{(\alpha-1)\beta\gamma}{2n}\log n$$

when X,Y,Z take α,β,γ values, respectively: choose either $\pi(X,S) = \{Y\}$ or $\pi(X,S) = \{Y,Z\}$ depending on which description length is smaller. The BNSL satisfies regularity. In fact, among the structures with the empirical conditional entropy zero, it chooses a structure with the smallest number of states.

Table 3: The scores and their pruning bounds in BNSL, where $\delta > 0$ is a constant, $\sigma(S)$ is the number of different values that S takes, and $d(S)$ ($\le \sigma(S)$)is the number of values that S actually occurs at least once in the n examples.

Prior	Score $Q^n(X\|S)$	Bound $R^n_*(S)$
BDeu (Campos and Ji, 2011)	$\prod_{i=1}^n \frac{c_{i-1}(x_i,s_i)+\delta/\alpha\sigma(S)}{c_{i-1}(s_i)+\delta/\sigma(S)}$	$\alpha^{-d(S)}$
Conditional Jeffreys' (Suzuki, 2016)	$\prod_{i=1}^n \frac{c_{i-1}(x_i,s_i)+0.5}{c_{i-1}(s_i)+0.5\alpha}$	$\prod_{i=1}^n \frac{c_{i-1}(x_i,s_i)+0.5}{c_{i-1}(x_i,s_i)+0.5\alpha}$
Quotient Jeffreys' (PROPOSED)	$\prod_{i=1}^n \frac{c_{i-1}(x_i,s_i)+0.5}{c_{i-1}(s_i)+0.5} \cdot \prod_{i=1}^n \frac{i-1+0.5\sigma(S)}{i-1+0.5\alpha\sigma(S)}$	$\prod_{i=1}^n \frac{i-1+0.5\sigma(S)}{i-1+0.5\alpha\sigma(S)}$

3.2 BRANCH AND BOUND FOR REGULAR BNSL

In this subsection, we illustrate the branch and bound procedures in Section 2.4 for regular BNSL.

It has been pointed out that the branch and bound procedure based on (7) is not so efficient (Silander, 2016). In particular, for irregular BNSL, even when the empirical conditional entropy of X given S is zero, the procedure continues to seek candidate states with more variables, as we have seen in Section 3.1.

On the other hand, for the MDL procedure in Section 3.1 that gives a regular BNSL, the pruning works as follows (Suzuki, 1996): suppose

$$H(X|\{Y\}) + \frac{(\alpha-1)\beta}{2n}\log n \le \frac{(\alpha-1)\beta\gamma}{2n}\log n\ . \tag{10}$$

Then, we do not have to compute the values of $L^n(T)$ for $T \supseteq \{Y,Z\}$ because $H(X|\{Y,Z\}) \ge 0$, and the number of values that T takes is no less than $\beta\gamma$, so that $L^n(T)$ exceeds the both sides when (10) holds. This means that we can utilize the fact for branch and bound:

$$H(X|S\backslash\{Y\})+\frac{(\alpha-1)\sigma(S)/\beta}{2n}\log n \le \frac{(\alpha-1)\sigma(S)}{2n}\log n$$

for some $Y \in S$ implies

$$\inf_{T\supseteq S}\{H(X|T)+\frac{(\alpha-1)\sigma(T)}{2}\log n\} \ge \frac{(\alpha-1)\sigma(S)}{2}\log n\ ,$$

where $\sigma(T)$ is the number of values that T takes. Note that the bound is obtained by assuming that $X = x_i$ is determined by $S = s_i$, so that $c_{i-1}(s_i) = c_{i-1}(x_i,s_i)$, $i = 1,\cdots,n$ (see Table 3).

Furthermore, for the conditional score based on Jeffreys' prior $a(x,y) = 0.5$, we have $Q^n(X|Y) = \prod_{i=1}^n \frac{c_{i-1}(x_i,y_i)+0.5}{c_{i-1}(y_i)+0.5\alpha}$, which is upperbounded by

$$\sup_{T\supseteq S} Q^n(X|T) \le R^n_{X,*}(S) := \prod_{i=1}^n \frac{c_{i-1}(x_i,s_i)+0.5}{c_{i-1}(x_i,s_i)+0.5\alpha} \tag{11}$$

for $S \subseteq V\backslash\{X\}$.

Note that the bound is obtained by assuming that $X = x_i$ is determined by $S = s_i$, so that $c_{i-1}(s_i) = c_{i-1}(x_i,s_i)$, $i = 1,\cdots,n$ (see Table 3).

3.3 BRANCH AND BOUND FOR THE QUOTIENT SCORES BASED ON JEFFREYS' PRIOR

In this subsection, we seek a similar scenario for the quotient score based on Jeffreys' prior as in Section 3.2.

First of all, the reference (Suzuki, 2016) pointed out that $R^n_{X,*}(S)$ in (11) can be used for pruning unnecessary computation for the quotient score based on Jeffreys' prior as well. In fact, from (9), $R^n_{X,*}(S)$ in (11) is an upperbound for all quotient scores $Q^n(X|T)$ with $T \supseteq S$, so that if $\max_{Y\in S} Q^n(X|S\backslash\{Y\})$ exceeds $R^n_{X,*}(S)$ in (11), no values of $Q^n(X|T)$ with $T \supseteq S$ have to be computed.

In this paper, however, we propose a different bound that will be found to be tighter. From (3) and (8) with $a(\cdot) = a(\cdot,\cdot) = 0.5$, the quantity $Q^n(X|Y) = Q^n(X,Y)/Q^n(Y)$ will be

$$\prod_{i=1}^n \frac{i-1+0.5\beta}{i-1+0.5\alpha\beta}\prod_{i=1}^n \frac{c_{i-1}(x_i,y_i)+0.5}{c_{i-1}(y_i)+0.5}\ ,$$

from which $Q^n(X|S)$ can be expressed by

$$\prod_{i=1}^n \frac{i-1+0.5\sigma(S)}{i-1+0.5\alpha\sigma(S)}\prod_{i=1}^n \frac{c_{i-1}(x_i,s_i)+0.5}{c_{i-1}(s_i)+0.5}\ . \tag{12}$$

We obtain a pruning rule for the quotient score based on Jeffreys' prior:

Theorem 2 For $S \subseteq V \backslash \{X\}$, we have

$$\sup_{T \supseteq S} Q^n(X|T) \leq R^n_*(S) := \prod_{i=1}^{n} \frac{i-1+0.5\sigma(S)}{i-1+0.5\alpha\sigma(S)} . \quad (13)$$

Note that the bound is obtained by assuming that $X = x_i$ is determined by $S = s_i$, so that $c_{i-1}(s_i) = c_{i-1}(x_i, s_i)$, $i = 1, \cdots, n$ (see Table 3).

Proof of Theorem 2: Checking the inequality $Q^n(X|S) \leq R^n_*(S)$ is straightforward. From Proposition 1, when $c_{i-1}(s_i) = c_{i-1}(x_i, s_i)$, $i = 1, \cdots, n$, if we divide the states, no larger value of $Q^n(X|\cdot)$ than $Q^n(X|S)$ is obtained, which completes the proof.

We compare the values of $R^n_{*,X}(S)$ in (11) and (13):

Theorem 3 The value of $R^n_{X,*}(S)$ in (13) is no more than that of (11):

$$\prod_{i=1}^{n} \frac{i-1+0.5\sigma(S)}{i-1+0.5\alpha\sigma(S)} \leq \prod_{i=1}^{n} \frac{c_{i-1}(x_i, s_i)+0.5}{c_{i-1}(x_i, s_i)+0.5\alpha}$$

Proof: When $c_{i-1}(x_i, s_i) = c_{i-1}(s_i)$, $i = 1, \cdots, n$, the left hand side is $Q^n(X|Y)$ for the quotient score that is upperbounded by $Q^n(X|Y)$ for the conditional score. On the other hand, the right hand side is an upperbound of $Q^n(X|Y)$ for the conditional score, which completes the proof.

Theorem 3 implies that the obtained bound improves the existing one, and we expect that the computation is reduced for obtaining the optimal parent sets w.r.t. the quotient score based on Jeffreys' prior, unless the overhead for computing the bound $R^n_*(S)$ is too large. In the next section, we evaluate the total computation time as well as the number of subsets S for which $Q^n(X|S)$ are actually computed, and examine that both of them are much improved.

Theorem 4 For (12), we have two equations:

$$-\log\{\prod_{i=1}^{n} \frac{i-1+0.5\sigma(S)}{i-1+0.5\alpha\sigma(S)}\} = \frac{(\alpha-1)\sigma(S)}{2}\log n + \log \frac{\Gamma(\frac{\sigma(S)}{2})}{\Gamma(\frac{\alpha\sigma(S)}{2})} + O(\frac{1}{n}) \quad (14)$$

and

$$-\log\{\prod_{i=1}^{n} \frac{c_{i-1}(x_i, s_i)+0.5}{c_{i-1}(s_i)+0.5}\} = nH(X|S) + O(1) \quad (15)$$

where $\Gamma(\cdot)$ is the Gamma function, and $f = g + O(1)$ implies $f - g$ is bounded by constants from above and below.

Proof: See Appendix B.

Theorem 4 implies that maximizing $Q^n(X|S)$ in (12) is equivalent to minimizing its description length $L^n(S)$ plus $O(1)$ terms, which means that the computation of the quotient score based on Jeffreys' prior is close to that of the MDL procedure. Although many authors of BNSL know that the MDL is an approximation of maximizing the posterior probability w.r.t. some prior probability over the parameters, no efficient pruning rule has been found for maximizing the posterior probability. For example, a pruning rule was proposed by (Campos and Ji, 2011) for the BDeu, the search is not efficient, which will be seen in Section 4 as well. Although (Suzuki, 2016) proposed a pruning rule for the conditional score based on Jeffreys' prior, the BNSL is not normal while the BDeu gives normal BNSL.

4 EXPERIMENTS

In this section, we compare the proposed procedure with the existing ones using the Alarm database (Beinlich et al., 1989) that is a standard benchmark for BNSL.

The algorithm is executed via Rcpp (Eddelbuettel, 2013): each compiled Rcpp procedure runs as an R function almost as fast as when the same procedure runs as a C++ function. The CPU we used in the experiments was Core M-5Y10(Broadwell)/800MHz/2.

The correctness of the BNSL procedures is guaranteed because branch and bound only removes unnecessary computations. Thus, we evaluate for each procedure with pruning computations: the number m of subsets that were actually computed among the 2^{p-1} subsets of $V \backslash \{X\}$; and the execution time for the prepared machine. For the first index, we compare the ratio $r := m/2^{p-1}$; the second one depends on the used machine but it takes into account how large the overhead is: if the computation of the bound was heavy and r is close to one, the execution would take longer than without pruning. However, it does not seem that the relative difference between the procedures depends on the used machine so much.

Because we execute many times we restrict the dataframe to that consisting of the first $n = 200$ and $n = 1000$ rows and first $p = 20$ columns.

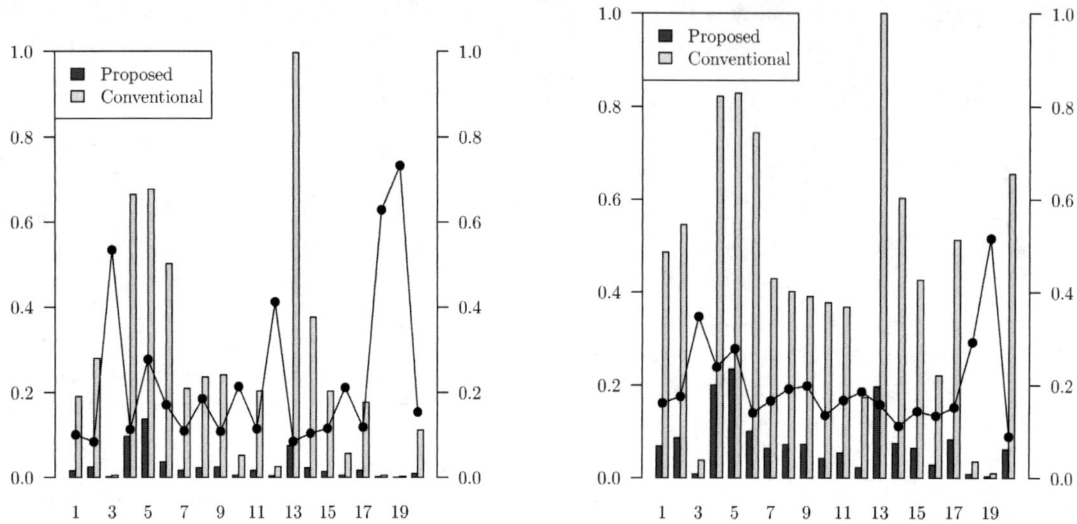

Figure 3: The first experiment for $n = 200$ (Left) and $n = 1000$ (Right): the axis $1 \leq i \leq 20$ indicates the variable $X = X^{(i)}$, and the two bars in each $1 \leq i \leq 20$ indicate the rates r for the proposed and existing procedures while the line graph indicates the ratio of the execution times.

4.1 IMPROVEMENTS IN THE QUOTIENT SCORE BASED ON JEFFREYS' PRIOR

The first experiment examines difference between the existing and proposed bounds for the quotient score based on Jeffreys' prior. As we have seen in Theorem 2, the proposed bound is no larger than the existing one, so that the former prunes unnecessary computation more often than the latter does. But, the actual difference depends on the data, and if we consider the overhead, the execution time for the latter might be small.

Figure 3 shows the two indexes for $n = 200$ (Left) and $n = 1000$ (Right). The axis that ranges over $1 \leq i \leq 20$ indicates the variable $X = X^{(i)}$, and each procedure finds the parent set $\pi(X, S)$ for all $S \subseteq V \backslash \{X\}$. The two bars in each $1 \leq i \leq 20$ indicate the rates r for the proposed and existing procedures, respectively, while the line graph indicates the ratio of the execution times (the proposed divided by the existing) for the 20 variables.

From Figure 3, we see that the numbers of subsets S for which actually $Q^n(X|S)$ were computed for the proposed procedure is less than one tenth and one fifth in many variables for $n = 200$ and $n = 1000$, respectively, and that the execution time ratio is one third and one fifth for $n = 200$ and $n = 1000$, respectively.

In general, how efficiently a pruning rule of branch and bound works depends on the database. In this sense, we cannot say any general statement of the efficiency. However, the significance is rather large, and it seems that the tendency holds for many databases.

4.2 BDeu VS THE QUOTIENT SCORE BASED on JEFFREYS' PRIOR

In this section, we compare the performances among the four criteria: the conditional and quotient scores based on Jeffreys', BDeu, and MDL.

Figure 4 shows the ratio r (Above) and the execution time (Below) for $n = 1000$. The axes that ranges over $1 \leq i \leq 20$ indicates the variable $X = X^{(i)}$, and each procedure finds the parent set $\pi(X, S)$ for all $S \subseteq V \backslash \{X\}$. The four bars in each $1 \leq i \leq 20$ show the performance for the four criteria.

From Figure 4, we have a couple of insights. First of all, the pruning rule for the BDeu is much less efficient compared with those for the other three criteria. It seems that this is due to the fact that the BDeu does not give regular BNSL while the other three criteria do: the BDeu does not stop computing $Q^n(X|T)$ for $T \supsetneq S$ even if the subset S fully divides the examples. Some claim (Silander, 2016) that the BDeu tends to select a complicated structure in particular for small n, which is consistent

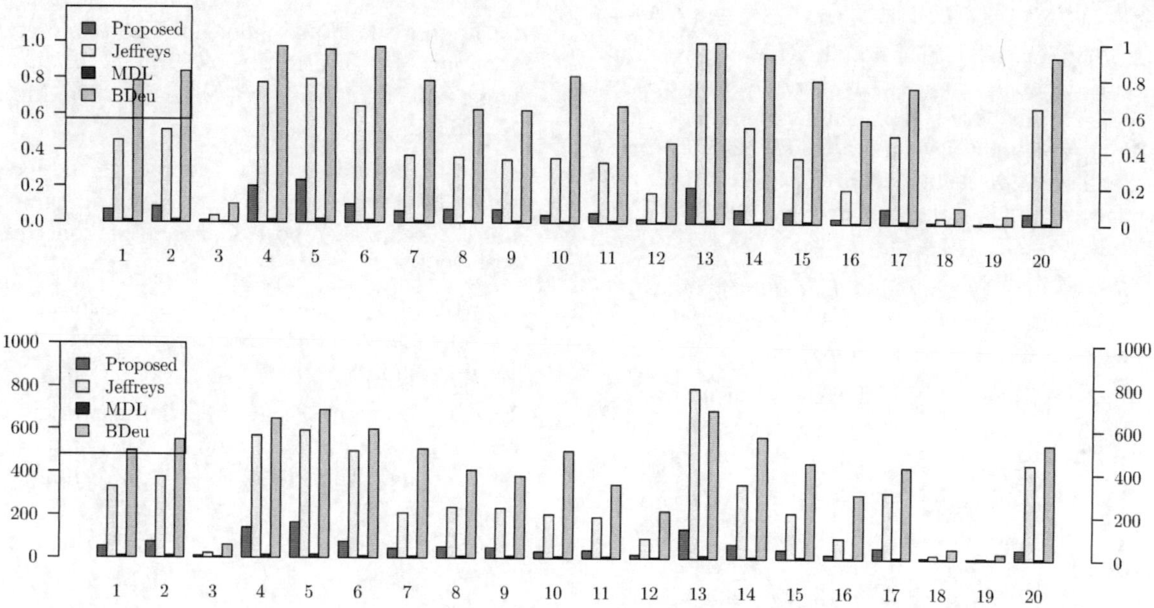

Figure 4: The ratio r (Above) and the execution time (Below) for $n = 1000$: the four bars in each $1 \leq i \leq 20$ shows the performance for the four criteria.

with irregularity of the BDeu.

Secondly, BNSL based on the quotient score based on Jeffreys' prior is much more efficient than the other two Bayesian criteria. It has been known that the pruning bound of the MDL is much more efficient than that of the BDeu (Campos and Ji, 2011). As expected from Theorem 4, the performance of the quotient score based on Jeffreys' prior is close to that of the MDL.

However, the performance is less efficient than the MDL, which seems to be due to the constant term $\log \frac{\Gamma(\sigma(S)/2)}{\Gamma(\alpha\sigma(S)/2)}$ in (14): if $\sigma(S)$ is too large for fixed n, then the bound (14) is too small, so that the pruning rule will be applied less often.

5 CONCLUDING REMARKS

In this paper, we proposed the pruning rule for the quotient score based on Jeffreys' prior. We found that the proposed bound is tighter than the existing one, and examined by the experiments that it runs much faster.

Also, we obtained a novel insight that regular BNSL has a tight pruning bound. We do not have any proof, but have illustrated how the phenomenon occurs, and have experimentally seen that for the three criteria (quotient and conditional Jeffreys' and MDL) that satisfy regularity, the pruning rules are applied more often than for the criterion (BDeu) that is not regularity.

Another significant contribution of this paper is that we obtained an efficient pruning rule for maximizing the posterior probability. Thus far, no efficient pruning rule has been obtained except for the MDL procedure. The result is related to the fact that the score and bound of the quotient score based on Jeffreys' prior behave similarly to those of the MDL procedure.

A problem to consider in the future would be to make the difference clear in correctness between the quotient and conditional scores. In general, each of us has his/her own prior probability over parameters, and a Bayesian solution depends on the belief, so that no one can reject any prior that other holds. However, even if we chose Jeffreys' prior, we see difference in correctness between the quotient and conditional scores. It is worth while considering whether we need to choose one of them.

Appendices A and B are in the Supplementary Material file. They will appear in arXiv math.

References

I. A. Beinlich, H. J. Suermondt, R. M. Chavez, and G. F. Cooper. The ALARM monitoring system: A case study with two probabilistic inference techniques for belief networks. In *The 2nd European Conference on Artificial Intelligence in Medicine*, pages 247–256, London, England, 1989. Springer-Verlag.

W. Buntine. Theory refinement on Bayesian networks. In *Uncertainty in Artificial Intelligence*, pages 52–60, Los Angels, CA, 1991.

C. P. Campos and Q. Ji. Efficient structure learning of Bayesian networks using constraints. *Journal of Machine Learning Research*, 12:663–689, 3 2011.

D. M. Chickering, C. Meek, and D. Heckerman. Large-sample learning of Bayesian networks is NP-hard. In *Uncertainty in Artificial Intelligence*, pages 124–133, Acapulco, Mexico, 2003. Morgan Kaufmann.

G.F. Cooper and E. Herskovits. A Bayesian method for the induction of probabilistic networks from data. *Machine Learning*, 9(4):309–347, 1992.

J. Cussens and M. Bartlett. *GOBNILP 1.6.2 User/Developer Manual1.* University of York, 2015.

D. Eddelbuettel. *Seamless R and C++ Integration with Rcpp.* Springer-Verlag, 2013.

D. Heckerman, D. Geiger, and D. M. Chickering. Learning Bayesian networks: the combination of knowledge and statistical data. *Machine Learning*, 20(3):197–243, 1995.

H. Jeffreys. *Theory of Probability.* Oxford University Press, 1939.

R. E. Krichevsky and V. K. Trofimov. The performance of universal encoding. *IEEE Trans. Information Theory*, IT-27(2):199–207, 1981.

J. Pearl. *Probabilistic Reasoning in Intelligent Systems: Networks of Plausible Inference (Representation and Reasoning).* Morgan Kaufmann, 2nd edition, 1988.

J. Rissanen. Modeling by shortest data description. *Automatica*, 14:465–471, 1978.

G. E. Schwarz. Estimating the dimension of a model. *Annals of Statistics*, 6(2):461–464, 1978.

T. Silander. Bayesian network structure learning with a quotient normalized maximum likelihood criterion. In *Proceedings of the Ninth Workshop on Information Theoretic Methods in Science and Engineering*, 2016.

T. Silander and P. Myllymaki. A simple approach for finding the globally optimal Bayesian network structure. In *Uncertainty in Artificial Intelligence*, pages 445–452, Arlington, Virginia, 2006. Morgan Kaufmann.

A. P. Singh and A. W. Moore. Finding optimal Bayesian networks by dynamic programming. Technical report, Carnegie Mellon University, 2005.

P. Spirtes, C. Glymour, and R. Scheines. *Causation,Prediction and Search.* Springer Verlag, Berlin, 1993.

J. Suzuki. Learning Bayesian belief networks based on the minimum description length principle: An efficient algorithm using the b & b technique. In *International Conference on Machine Learning*, pages 462–470, Bari, Italy, 1996. Morgan Kaufmann.

J. Suzuki. An efficient Bayesian network structure learning strategy. *Next Generation Computation Journal*, 1, 2016.

J. Suzuki. A theoretical analysis of the BDeu scores in Bayesian network structure learning. *Behaviormetrika*, 1:1–20, 2017.

J. Tian. A branch-and-bound algorithm for MDL learning Bayesian networks. In *Uncertainty in Artificial Intelligence*, pages 580–588, Stanford, CA, 2000. Morgan Kaufmann.

M. Ueno. Learning likelihood-equivalence Bayesian networks using an empirical Bayesian approach. *Behaviormetrika*, 35(2):115–135, 2008.

Branch and Bound for Regular Bayesian Network Structure Learning: Supplementary Material

Joe Suzuki* and **Jun Kawahara**†
* Osaka University, Japan. j-suzuki@sigmath.es.osaka-u.ac.jp
† Nara Institute of Science and Technology, Japan. jkawahara@is.naist.ac.jp

Appendix A

Under $c_n(x,y) = c_n(y)$ for each (x,y), we have

$$Q^n(X|Y) \ge Q^n(X|YZ)$$

$$\iff \frac{\Gamma(\frac{\alpha\beta}{2})}{\Gamma(n+\frac{\alpha\beta}{2})}\prod_{x,y}\frac{\Gamma(c_n(x,y)+\frac{1}{2})}{\Gamma(\frac{1}{2})}\cdot\frac{\Gamma(\frac{\beta\gamma}{2})}{\Gamma(n+\frac{\beta\gamma}{2})} \cdot\prod_{y,z}\frac{\Gamma(c_n(y,z)+\frac{1}{2})}{\Gamma(\frac{1}{2})}$$

$$\ge \frac{\Gamma(\frac{\alpha\beta\gamma}{2})}{\Gamma(n+\frac{\alpha\beta\gamma}{2})}\prod_{x,y,z}\frac{\Gamma(c_n(x,y,z)+\frac{1}{2})}{\Gamma(\frac{1}{2})} \cdot\frac{\Gamma(\frac{\beta}{2})}{\Gamma(n+\frac{\beta}{2})}\prod_{y}\frac{\Gamma(c_n(y)+\frac{1}{2})}{\Gamma(\frac{1}{2})}$$

$$\iff \frac{\Gamma(\frac{\alpha\beta}{2})}{\Gamma(n+\frac{\alpha\beta}{2})}\cdot\frac{\Gamma(\frac{\beta\gamma}{2})}{\Gamma(n+\frac{\beta\gamma}{2})} \ge \frac{\Gamma(\frac{\alpha\beta\gamma}{2})}{\Gamma(n+\frac{\alpha\beta\gamma}{2})}\cdot\frac{\Gamma(\frac{\beta}{2})}{\Gamma(n+\frac{\beta}{2})}\ .$$

The last inequality can be proved using induction w.r.t. n, which completes the proof.

Appendix B

From Stirling's formula $\log\Gamma(z) = z\log z - z + \frac{1}{2}\log\frac{2\pi}{z} + \epsilon(z)$ with $\frac{1}{12z} < \epsilon(z) < \frac{1}{12z+1}$, we have for $\beta = \sigma(S)$

$$\log\Gamma(n+\frac{\alpha\beta}{2}) - \log\Gamma(n+\frac{\beta}{2})$$

$$= -(n+\frac{\beta}{2})\log(n+\frac{\beta}{2}) + (n+\frac{\beta}{2}) - \frac{1}{2}\log\frac{2\pi}{n+\frac{\beta}{2}} +(n+\frac{\alpha\beta}{2})\log(n+\frac{\alpha\beta}{2}) - (n+\frac{\alpha\beta}{2}) +\frac{1}{2}\log\frac{2\pi}{n+\frac{\alpha\beta}{2}} + O(\frac{1}{n})$$

$$= -n\log\frac{n+\frac{\beta}{2}}{n+\frac{\alpha\beta}{2}} - \frac{\beta}{2}\log(n+\frac{\beta}{2}) +\frac{\alpha\beta}{2}\log(n+\frac{\alpha\beta}{2}) - \frac{1}{2}\log(n+\frac{\alpha\beta}{2}) +\frac{1}{2}\log(n+\frac{\beta}{2}) - \frac{\alpha\beta-\beta}{2} + O(\frac{1}{n})$$

$$= \frac{(\alpha-1)\beta}{2}\log n + O(\frac{1}{n})\ ,$$

which means

$$-\log\{\prod_{i=1}^{n}\frac{i-1+0.5\beta}{i-1+0.5\alpha\beta}\} = \log\frac{\Gamma(n+\frac{\alpha\beta}{2})\Gamma(\frac{\beta}{2})}{\Gamma(n+\frac{\beta}{2})\Gamma(\frac{\alpha\beta}{2})} = \frac{(\alpha-1)\beta}{2}\log n + \log\frac{\Gamma(\frac{\beta}{2})}{\Gamma(\frac{\alpha\beta}{2})} + O(\frac{1}{n})\ .$$

For the second statement, from

$$\log\Gamma(c_n(x,s)+\frac{1}{2}) = c_n(x,s)\log\{c_n(x,s)+\frac{1}{2}\} - \{c_n(x,s)+\frac{1}{2}\} +\frac{1}{2}\log(2\pi) = c_n(x,s)\log c_n(x,s) - c_n(x,s) + O(\frac{1}{c_n(x,s)})$$

and

$$\log\Gamma(c_n(s)+\frac{1}{2}) = c_n(s)\log c_n(s) - c_n(s) + O(\frac{1}{c_n(s)})\ ,$$

we have

$$-\log\{\prod_{i=1}^{n}\frac{c_{i-1}(x_i,s_i)+0.5}{c_{i-1}(s_i)+0.5}\} = -\log\prod_{s}\{\frac{\prod_x\Gamma(c_n(x,s)+\frac{1}{2})}{\Gamma(c_n(s)+\frac{1}{2})}\}$$

$$= -\sum_s \sum_x c_n(x,s) \log \frac{c_n(x,s)}{c_n(s)} + O(1)$$

$$= -n \sum_s \frac{c_n(s)}{n} \sum_x \frac{c_n(x,s)}{c_n(s)} \log \frac{c_n(x,s)}{c_n(s)} + O(1) .$$

Since $H(X|S) = -\sum_s \frac{c_n(s)}{n} \sum_x \frac{c_n(x,s)}{c_n(s)} \log \frac{c_n(x,s)}{c_n(s)}$, this completes the proof.

Effective sketching methods for value function approximation

Yangchen Pan, Erfan Sadeqi Azer and Martha White
Department of Computer Science
Indiana University Bloomington
yangpan@iu.edu, esadeqia@iu.edu, martha@indiana.edu

Abstract

High-dimensional representations, such as radial basis function networks or tile coding, are common choices for policy evaluation in reinforcement learning. Learning with such high-dimensional representations, however, can be expensive, particularly for matrix methods, such as least-squares temporal difference learning or quasi-Newton methods that approximate matrix step-sizes. In this work, we explore the utility of sketching for these two classes of algorithms. We highlight issues with sketching the high-dimensional features directly, which can incur significant bias. As a remedy, we demonstrate how to use sketching more sparingly, with only a left-sided sketch, that can still enable significant computational gains and the use of these matrix-based learning algorithms that are less sensitive to parameters. We empirically investigate these algorithms, in four domains with a variety of representations. Our aim is to provide insights into effective use of sketching in practice.

1 INTRODUCTION

A common strategy for function approximation in reinforcement learning is to overparametrize: generate a large number of features to provide a sufficiently complex function space. For example, one typical representation is a radial basis function network, where the centers for each radial basis function are chosen to exhaustively cover the observation space. Because the environment is unknown—particularly for the incremental learning setting—such an overparameterized representation is more robust to this uncertainty because a reasonable representation is guaranteed for any part of the space that might be visited. Once interacting with the environment, however, it is likely not all features will become active, and that a lower-dimensional subspace will be visited.

A complementary approach for this high-dimensional representation expansion in reinforcement learning, therefore, is to use projections. In this way, we can overparameterize for robustness, but then use a projection to a lower-dimensional space to make learning feasible. For an effectively chosen projection, we can avoid discarding important information, and benefit from the fact that the agent only visits a lower-dimensional subspace of the environment in the feature space.

Towards this aim, we investigate the utility of sketching: projecting with a random matrix. Sketching has been extensively used for efficient communication and solving large linear systems, with a solid theoretical foundation and a variety of different sketches (Woodruff, 2014). Sketching has been previously used in reinforcement learning, specifically to reduce the dimension of the features. Bellemare et al. (2012) replaced the standard biased hashing function used for tile coding Sutton (1996), instead using count-sketch.[1] Ghavamzadeh et al. (2010) investigated sketching features to reduce the dimensionality and make it feasible to run least-squares temporal difference learning (LSTD) for policy evaluation. In LSTD, the value function is estimated by incrementally computing a $d \times d$ matrix $\mathbf{A}$, where d is the number of features, and an d-dimensional vector $\mathbf{b}$, where the parameters are estimated as the solution to this linear system. Because d can be large, they randomly project the features to reduce the matrix size to $k \times k$, with $k \ll d$.

For both of these previous uses of sketching, however, the resulting value function estimates are biased. This bias, as we show in this work, can be quite significant, resulting in significant estimation error in the value function for a given policy. As a result, any gains from us-

[1] They called the sketch the tug-of-war sketch, but it is more standard to call it count-sketch.

ing LSTD methods—over stochastic temporal difference (TD) methods—are largely overcome by this bias. A natural question is if we can benefit from sketching, with minimal bias or without incurring any bias at all.

In this work, we propose to instead sketch the linear system in LSTD. The key idea is to only sketch the constraints of the system (the left-side of $\mathbf{A}$) rather than the variables (the right-side of $\mathbf{A}$). Sketching features, on the other hand, by design, sketches both constraints and variables. We show that even with a straightforward linear system solution, the left-sided sketch can significantly reduce bias. We further show how to use this left-sided sketch within a quasi-Newton algorithm, providing an unbiased policy evaluation algorithm that can still benefit from the computational improvements of sketching.

The key novelty in this work is designing such system-sketching algorithms when also incrementally computing the linear system solution. There is a wealth of literature on sketching linear systems, to reduce computation. In general, however, many sketching approaches cannot be applied to the incremental policy evaluation problem, because the approaches are designed for a static linear system. For example, Gower & Richtárik (2015) provide a host of possible solutions for solving large linear systems. However, they assume access to $\mathbf{A}$ upfront, so the algorithm design, in memory and computation, is not suitable for the incremental setting. Some popular sketching approaches, such as Frequent Directions (Ghashami et al., 2014), has been successfully used for the online setting, for quasi-Newton algorithms (Luo et al., 2016); however, they sketch symmetric matrices, that are growing with number of samples.

This paper is organized as follows. We first introduce the policy evaluation problem—learning a value function for a fixed policy—and provide background on sketching methods. We then illustrate issues with only sketching features, in terms of quality of the value function approximation. We then introduce the idea of using asymmetric sketching for policy evaluation with LSTD, and provide an efficient incremental algorithm that is $O(dk)$ on each step. We finally highlight settings where we expect sketching to perform particularly well in practice, and investigate the properties of our algorithm on four domains, and with a variety of representation properties.

2 PROBLEM FORMULATION

We address the policy evaluation problem within reinforcement learning, where the goal is to estimate the value function for a given policy[2]. As is standard, the agent-environment interaction is formulated as a Markov decision process $(\mathcal{S}, \mathcal{A}, \Pr, r)$, where $\mathcal{S}$ is the set of states, $\mathcal{A}$ is the set of actions, and $\Pr : \mathcal{S} \times \mathcal{A} \times \mathcal{S} \rightarrow [0, \infty)$ is the one-step state transition dynamics. On each time step $t = 1, 2, 3, ...$, the agent selects an action according to its policy π, $A_t \sim \pi(S_t, \cdot)$, with $\pi : \mathcal{S} \times \mathcal{A} \rightarrow [0, \infty)$ and transitions into a new state $S_{t+1} \sim \Pr(S_t, A_t, \cdot)$ and obtains scalar reward $R_{t+1} \overset{\text{def}}{=} r(S_t, A_t, S_{t+1})$.

For policy evaluation, the goal is to estimate the value function, $v_\pi : \mathcal{S} \rightarrow \mathbb{R}$, which corresponds to the expected return when following policy π

$$v_\pi(s) \overset{\text{def}}{=} \mathbb{E}_\pi[G_t | S_t = s],$$

where $\mathbb{E}_\pi$ is the expectation over future states when selecting actions according to π. The return, $G_t \in \mathbb{R}$ is the discounted sum of future rewards given actions are selected according to π:

$$\begin{aligned} G_t &\overset{\text{def}}{=} R_{t+1} + \gamma_{t+1} R_{t+2} + \gamma_{t+1}\gamma_{t+2} R_{t+3} + ... \quad (1) \\ &= R_{t+1} + \gamma_{t+1} G_{t+1} \end{aligned}$$

where $\gamma_{t+1} \in [0, 1]$ is a scalar that depends on S_t, A_t, S_{t+1} and discounts the contribution of future rewards exponentially with time. A common setting, for example, is a constant discount. This recent generalization to state-dependent discount (Sutton et al., 2011; White, 2016) enables either episodic or continuing problems, and so we adopt this more general formalism here.

We consider linear function approximation to estimate the value function. In this setting, the observations are expanded to a higher-dimensional space, such as through tile-coding, radial basis functions or Fourier basis. Given this nonlinear encoding $x : \mathcal{S} \rightarrow \mathbb{R}^d$, the value is approximated as $v_\pi(S_t) \approx \mathbf{w}^\top \mathbf{x}_t$ for $\mathbf{w} \in \mathbb{R}^d$ and $\mathbf{x}_t \overset{\text{def}}{=} x(S_t)$.

One algorithm for estimating $\mathbf{w}$ is least-squares temporal difference learning (LSTD). The goal in LSTD(λ) (Boyan, 1999) is to minimize the mean-squared projected Bellman error, which can be represented as solving the following linear system

$$\begin{aligned} \mathbf{A} &\overset{\text{def}}{=} \mathbb{E}_\pi[\mathbf{e}_t(\mathbf{x}_t - \gamma_{t+1}\mathbf{x}_{t+1})^\top] \\ \mathbf{b} &\overset{\text{def}}{=} \mathbb{E}_\pi[R_{t+1}\mathbf{e}_t]. \end{aligned}$$

where $\mathbf{e}_t \overset{\text{def}}{=} \gamma_{t+1}\lambda\mathbf{e}_{t-1} + \mathbf{x}_t$ is called the eligibility trace for trace parameter $\lambda \in [0, 1]$. To obtain $\mathbf{w}$, the system $\mathbf{A}$ and $\mathbf{b}$ are incrementally estimated, to solve $\mathbf{A}\mathbf{w} = \mathbf{b}$. For a trajectory $\{(S_t, A_t, S_{t+1}, R_{t+1})\}_{t=0}^{T-1}$,

[2]To focus the investigation on sketching, we consider the simpler on-policy setting in this work. Many of the results, however, generalize to the off-policy setting, where data is generated according to a behavior policy different than the given target policy we wish to evaluate.

let $\mathbf{d}_t \stackrel{\text{def}}{=} \mathbf{x}_t - \gamma_{t+1}\mathbf{x}_{t+1}$, then the above two expected terms are usually computed via sample average that can be recursively computed, in a numerically stable way, as

$$\mathbf{A}_{t+1} = \mathbf{A}_t + \frac{1}{t+1}\left(\mathbf{e}_t\mathbf{d}_t^\top - \mathbf{A}_t\right)$$

$$\mathbf{b}_{t+1} = \mathbf{b}_t + \frac{1}{t+1}\left(\mathbf{e}_t R_{t+1} - \mathbf{b}_t\right)$$

with $\mathbf{A}_0 = \mathbf{0}$ and $\mathbf{b}_0 = \mathbf{0}$. The incremental estimates $\mathbf{A}_t$ and $\mathbf{b}_t$ converge to $\mathbf{A}$ and $\mathbf{b}$. A naive algorithm, where $\mathbf{w} = \mathbf{A}_t^{-1}\mathbf{b}_t$ is recomputed on each step, would result in $\mathcal{O}(d^3)$ computation to compute the inverse $\mathbf{A}_t^{-1}$. Instead, $\mathbf{A}_t^{-1}$ is incrementally updated using the Sherman-Morrison formula, with $\mathbf{A}_0^{-1} = \xi$ for a small $\xi > 0$

$$\mathbf{A}_t^{-1} = \left(\frac{t-1}{t}\mathbf{A}_{t-1} + \frac{1}{t}\mathbf{e}_t\mathbf{d}_t^\top\right)^{-1}$$
$$= \frac{t}{t-1}\left(\mathbf{A}_{t-1}^{-1} + \frac{\mathbf{A}_{t-1}^{-1}\mathbf{e}_t\mathbf{d}_t^\top\mathbf{A}_{t-1}^{-1}}{t-1+\mathbf{d}_t^\top\mathbf{A}_{t-1}^{-1}\mathbf{e}_t}\right)$$

requiring $\mathcal{O}(d^2)$ storage and computation per step. Unfortunately, this quadratic cost is prohibitive for many incremental learning settings. In our experiments, even $d = 10,000$ was prohibitive, since $d^2 = 100$ million.

A natural approach to improve computation to solve for $\mathbf{w}$ is to use stochastic methods, such as TD(λ) (Sutton, 1988). This algorithm incrementally updates with $\mathbf{w}_{t+1} = \mathbf{w}_t + \alpha\delta_t\mathbf{e}_t$ for stepsize $\alpha > 0$ and TD-error $\delta_t = R_{t+1} + (\gamma_{t+1}\mathbf{x}_{t+1} - \mathbf{x}_t)^\top\mathbf{w}_t$. The expectation of this update is $\mathbb{E}_\pi[\delta_t\mathbf{e}_t] = \mathbf{b} - \mathbf{A}\mathbf{w}_t$; the fixed-point solutions are the same for both LSTD and TD, but LSTD corresponds to a batch solution whereas TD corresponds to a stochastic update. Though more expensive than TD—which is only $O(d)$—LSTD does have several advantages. Because LSTD is a batch method, it summarizes all samples (within $\mathbf{A}$), and so can be more sample efficient. Additionally, LSTD has no step-size parameter, using a closed-form solution for $\mathbf{w}$.

Recently, there has been some progress in better balancing between TD and LSTD. Pan et al. (2017) derived a quasi-Newton algorithm, called accelerated gradient TD (ATD), giving an unbiased algorithm that has some of the benefits of LSTD, but with significantly reduced computation because they only maintain a low-rank approximation to $\mathbf{A}$. The key idea is that $\mathbf{A}$ provides curvature information, and so can significantly improve step-size selection for TD and so improve the convergence rate. The approximate $\mathbf{A}$ can still provide useful curvature information, but can be significantly cheaper to compute. We use the ATD update to similarly obtain an unbiased algorithm, but use sketching approximations instead of low-rank approximations. First, however, we investigate some of the properties of sketching.

3 ISSUES WITH SKETCHING THE FEATURES

One approach to make LSTD more feasible is to project—sketch—the features. Sketching involves sampling a random matrix $\mathbf{S} : \mathbb{R}^{k\times d}$ from a family of matrices $\mathcal{S}$, to project a given d-dimensional vector $\mathbf{x}$ to a (much smaller) k-dimensional vector $\mathbf{S}\mathbf{x}$. The goal in defining this class of sketching matrices is to maintain certain properties of the original vector. The following is a standard definition for such a family.

Definition 1 (Sketching). *Let d and k be positive integers, $\delta \in (0,1)$, and $\epsilon \in \mathbb{R}^+$. Then, $\mathcal{S} \subset \mathbb{R}^{k\times d}$ is called a family of sketching matrices with parameters (ϵ, δ), if for a random matrix, $\mathbf{S}$, chosen uniformly at random from this family, we have that $\forall \mathbf{x} \in \mathbb{R}^d$*

$$\mathbb{P}\Big[(1-\epsilon)\|\mathbf{x}\|_2^2 \le \|\mathbf{S}\mathbf{x}\|_2^2 \le (1+\epsilon)\|\mathbf{x}\|_2^2\Big] \ge 1-\delta.$$

where the probability is w.r.t. the distribution over $\mathbf{S}$.

We will explore the utility of sketching the features with several common sketches. These sketches all require $k = \Omega(\epsilon^{-2}\ln(1/\delta)\ln d)$.

Gaussian random projections, also known as the JL-Transform (Johnson & Lindenstrauss, 1984), has each entry in $\mathbf{S}$ i.i.d. sampled from a Gaussian, $\mathcal{N}(0, \frac{1}{k})$.

Count sketch selects exactly one uniformly picked non-zero entry in each column, and sets that entry to either 1 or -1 with equal probability (Charikar et al., 2002; Gilbert & Indyk, 2010). The Tug-of-War sketch (Alon et al., 1996) performs very similarly to Count sketch in our experiments, and so we omit it.

Combined sketch is the product of a count sketch matrix and a Gaussian projection matrix (Wang, 2015; Boutsidis & Woodruff, 2015).

Hadamard sketch—the Subsampled Randomized Hadamard Transform—is computed as $\mathbf{S} = \frac{1}{\sqrt{kd}}\mathbf{D}\mathbf{H}_d\mathbf{P}$, where $\mathbf{D} \in \mathbb{R}^{d\times d}$ is a diagonal matrix with each diagonal element uniformly sampled from $\{1, -1\}$, $\mathbf{H}_d \in \mathbb{R}^{d\times d}$ is a Hadamard matrix and $\mathbf{P} \in \mathbb{R}^{d\times k}$ is a column sampling matrix (Ailon & Chazelle, 2006).

Sketching provides a low-error between the recovery $\mathbf{S}^\top\mathbf{S}\mathbf{x}$ and the original $\mathbf{x}$, with high probability. For the above families, the entries in $\mathbf{S}$ are zero-mean i.i.d. with variance 1, giving $\mathbb{E}[\mathbf{S}^\top\mathbf{S}] = \mathbf{I}$ over all possible $\mathbf{S}$. Consequently, in expectation, the recovery $\mathbf{S}^\top\mathbf{S}\mathbf{x}$ is equal to $\mathbf{x}$. For a stronger result, a Chernoff bound can be used to bound the deviation of $\mathbf{S}^\top\mathbf{S}$ from this expected value: for the parameters (ϵ, δ) of the matrix family, we get that $\mathbb{P}\Big[(1-\epsilon)I \prec \mathbf{S}^\top\mathbf{S} \prec (1+\epsilon)I\Big] \ge 1-\delta$.

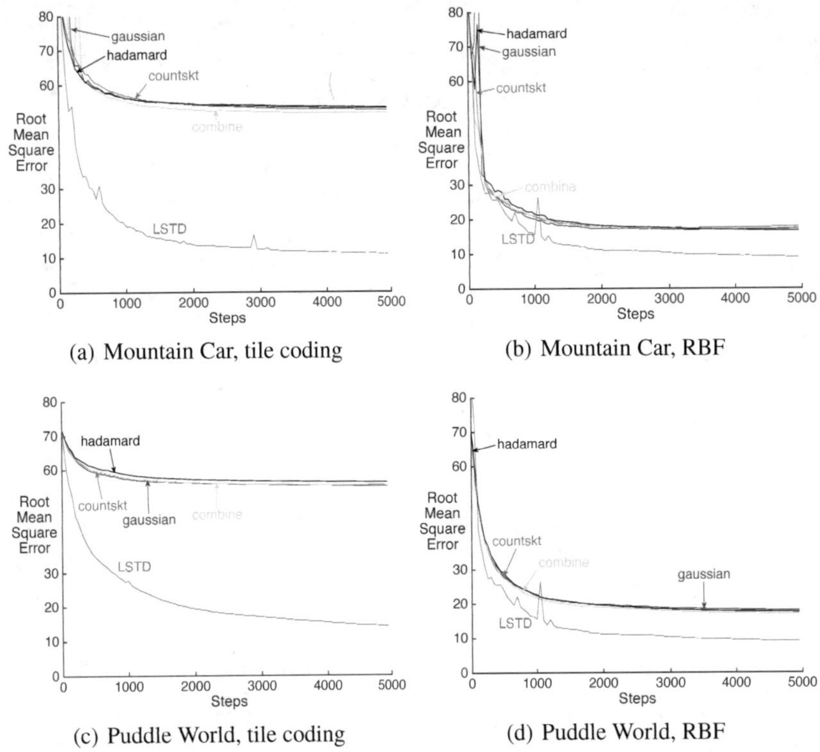

(a) Mountain Car, tile coding

(b) Mountain Car, RBF

(c) Puddle World, tile coding

(d) Puddle World, RBF

Figure 1: Efficacy of different sketches for sketching the features for LSTD, with $k = 50$. The RMSE is w.r.t. the optimal value function, computed using rollouts. LSTD(λ) is included as the baseline, with $\mathbf{w} = \mathbf{A}^{-1}\mathbf{b}$, with the other curves corresponding to different sketches of the features, to give $\mathbf{w} = (\mathbf{SAS}^\top)^{-1}\mathbf{Sb}$ as used for the random projections LSTD algorithm. The RBF width in Mountain Car is $\sigma = 0.12$ times the range of the state space and in Puddle World is $\sigma = \sqrt{0.0072}$. The 1024 centers for RBFs are chosen to uniformly cover the 2-d space in a grid. For tile coding, we discretize each dimension by 10, giving 10×10 grids, use 10 tilings, and set the memory size as 1024. The bias is high for tile coding features, and much better for RBF features, though still quite large. The different sketches perform similarly.

These properties suggest that using sketching for the feature vectors should provide effective approximations. Bellemare et al. (2012) showed that they could use these projections for tile coding, rather than the biased hashing function that is typically used, to improve learning performance for the control setting. The efficacy, however, of sketching given features, versus using the unsketched features, is less well-understood.

We investigate the properties of sketching the features, shown in Figure 1 with a variety of sketches in two benchmark domains for RBF and tile-coding representations (see (Sutton & Barto, 1998, Chapter 8) for an overview of these representations). For both domains, the observations space is 2-dimensional, with expansion to $d = 1024$ and $k = 50$. The results are averaged over 50 runs, with ξ, λ swept over 13 values, with ranges listed in Appendix C. We see that sketching the features can incur significant bias, particularly for tile coding, even with a reasonably large $k = 50$ to give $O(dk)$ runtimes. This bias reduces with k, but remains quite high and so is likely too unreliable for practical use.

4 SKETCHING THE LINEAR SYSTEM

All of the work on sketching within reinforcement learning has investigated sketching the features; however, we can instead consider sketching the linear system, $\mathbf{Aw} = \mathbf{b}$. For such a setting, we can sketch the left and right subspaces of $\mathbf{A}$ with different sketching matrices, $\mathbf{S}_L \in \mathbb{R}^{k_L \times d}$ and $\mathbf{S}_R \in \mathbb{R}^{k_R \times d}$. Depending on the choices of k_L and k_R, we can then solve the smaller system $\mathbf{S}_L\mathbf{A}\mathbf{S}_R^\top\mathbf{S}_R\mathbf{w} = \mathbf{S}_L\mathbf{b}$ efficiently. The goal is to better take advantage of the properties for the different sides of an asymmetric matrix $\mathbf{A}$.

One such natural improvement should be in one-sided sketching. By only sketching from the left, for example, and setting $\mathbf{S}_R = \mathbf{I}$, we do not project $\mathbf{w}$. Rather, we only project the constraints to the linear system $\mathbf{Aw} = \mathbf{b}$. Importantly, this does not introduce bias: the original solution $\mathbf{w}$ to $\mathbf{Aw} = \mathbf{b}$ is also a solution to $\mathbf{SAw} = \mathbf{Sb}$ for any sketching matrix $\mathbf{S}$. The projection, however, removes uniqueness in terms of the solutions $\mathbf{w}$, since the system is under-constrained. Conversely, by only sketching from the right, and setting $\mathbf{S}_L = \mathbf{I}$, we constrain the space of solutions to a unique set, and do not remove any constraints. For this setting, however, it is unlikely that $\mathbf{w}$ with $\mathbf{Aw} = \mathbf{b}$ satisfies $\mathbf{AS}^\top\mathbf{w} = \mathbf{b}$.

The conclusion from many initial experiments is that the key benefit from asymmetric sketching is when only sketching from the left. We experimented with all pairwise combinations of Gaussian random projections, Count sketch, Tug-of-War sketch and Hadamard sketch for $\mathbf{S}_L$ and $\mathbf{S}_R$. We additionally experimented with only sketching from the right, setting $\mathbf{S}_L = \mathbf{I}$. In all of these experiments, we found asymmetric sketching provided little to no benefit over using $\mathbf{S}_L = \mathbf{S}_R$ and that sketching only from the right also performed similarly to using $\mathbf{S}_L = \mathbf{S}_R$. We further investigated column and row selection sketches (see Wang (2015) for a thorough overview), but also found these to be ineffective. We therefore proceed with an investigation into effectively using left-side sketching. In the next section, we provide an efficient $\mathcal{O}(dk)$ algorithm to compute $(\mathbf{S}_L\mathbf{A})^\dagger$, to enable computation of $\mathbf{w} = (\mathbf{S}_L\mathbf{A})^\dagger\mathbf{S}_L\mathbf{b}$ and for use within an unbiased quasi-Newton algorithm.

We conclude this section with an interesting connection to a data-dependent projection method that has been used for policy evaluation, that further motivates the utility of sketching only from the left. This algorithm, called truncated LSTD (tLSTD) (Gehring et al., 2016), incrementally maintains a rank k approximation of $\mathbf{A}$ matrix, using an incremental singular value decomposition. We show below that this approach corresponds to projecting $\mathbf{A}$ from the left with the top k left singular vectors. This is called a data-dependent projection, because the projection depends on the observed data, as opposed to the data-independent projection—the sketching matrices—which is randomly sampled independently of the data.

Proposition 1. *Let $\mathbf{A} = \mathbf{U}\boldsymbol{\Sigma}\mathbf{V}^\top$ be singular value decomposition of the true $\mathbf{A}$. Assume the singular values are in decreasing order and let $\boldsymbol{\Sigma}_k$ be the top k singular values, with corresponding k left singular vectors $\mathbf{U}_k$ and k right singular vectors $\mathbf{V}_k$. Then the solution $\mathbf{w} = \mathbf{V}_k\boldsymbol{\Sigma}_k^\dagger\mathbf{U}_k^\top\mathbf{b}$ (used for tLSTD) corresponds to LSTD using asymmetric sketching with $\mathbf{S}_L = \mathbf{U}_k^\top$ and $\mathbf{S}_R = \mathbf{I}$.*

Proof. We know $\mathbf{U} = [\mathbf{u}_1, \ldots, \mathbf{u}_d]$ for singular vectors $\mathbf{u}_i \in \mathbb{R}^d$ with $\mathbf{u}_i^\top\mathbf{u}_i = 1$ and $\mathbf{u}_i^\top\mathbf{u}_j = 0$ for $i \neq j$. Since $\mathbf{U}_k = [\mathbf{u}_1, \ldots, \mathbf{u}_k]$, we get that $\mathbf{U}_k^\top\mathbf{U} = [\mathbf{I}_k \;\; \mathbf{0}_{d-k}] \in \mathbb{R}^{k\times d}$ for k-dimensional identity matrix $\mathbf{I}_k$ and zero matrix $\mathbf{0}_{d-k} \in \mathbb{R}^{k\times(d-k)}$. Then we get that $\mathbf{S}_L\mathbf{b} = \mathbf{U}_k^\top\mathbf{b}$ and $\mathbf{S}_L\mathbf{A} = [\mathbf{I}_k \;\; \mathbf{0}_{d-k}]\boldsymbol{\Sigma}\mathbf{V}^\top = \boldsymbol{\Sigma}_k\mathbf{V}^\top = \boldsymbol{\Sigma}_k\mathbf{V}_k^\top$. Therefore, $\mathbf{w} = (\mathbf{S}_L\mathbf{A})^\dagger\mathbf{S}_L\mathbf{b} = \mathbf{V}_k\boldsymbol{\Sigma}_k^\dagger\mathbf{U}_k^\top\mathbf{b}$. □

5 LEFT-SIDED SKETCHING ALGORITHM

In this section, we develop an efficient approach to use the smaller, sketched matrix $\mathbf{SA}$ for incremental policy evaluation. The most straightforward way to use $\mathbf{SA}$ is to incrementally compute $\mathbf{SA}$, and periodically solve $\mathbf{w} = (\mathbf{SA})^\dagger\mathbf{Sb}$. This costs $O(dk)$ per step, and $O(d^2k)$ every time the solution is recomputed. To maintain $O(dk)$ computation per-step, this full solution could only be computed every d steps, which is too infrequent to provide a practical incremental policy evaluation approach. Further, because it is an underconstrained system, there are likely to be infinitely many solutions to $\mathbf{SAw} = \mathbf{Sb}$; amongst those solutions, we would like to sub-select amongst the unbiased solutions to $\mathbf{Aw} = \mathbf{b}$.

We first discuss how to efficiently maintain $(\mathbf{SA})^\dagger$, and then describe how to use that matrix to obtain an unbiased algorithm. Let $\tilde{\mathbf{A}} \stackrel{\text{def}}{=} \mathbf{SA} \in \mathbb{R}^{k\times d}$. For this underconstrained system with $\tilde{\mathbf{b}} \stackrel{\text{def}}{=} \mathbf{Sb}$, the minimum norm solution to $\tilde{\mathbf{A}}\mathbf{w} = \tilde{\mathbf{b}}$ is[3] $\mathbf{w} = \tilde{\mathbf{A}}^\top(\tilde{\mathbf{A}}\tilde{\mathbf{A}}^\top)^{-1}\tilde{\mathbf{b}}$ and $\tilde{\mathbf{A}}^\dagger = \tilde{\mathbf{A}}^\top(\tilde{\mathbf{A}}\tilde{\mathbf{A}}^\top)^{-1} \in \mathbb{R}^{d\times k}$. To maintain $\tilde{\mathbf{A}}_t^\dagger$ incrementally, therefore, we simply need to maintain $\tilde{\mathbf{A}}_t$ incrementally and the $k\times k$-matrix $(\tilde{\mathbf{A}}_t\tilde{\mathbf{A}}_t^\top)^{-1}$ incrementally. Let $\tilde{\mathbf{e}}_t \stackrel{\text{def}}{=} \mathbf{Se}_t$, $\mathbf{d}_t \stackrel{\text{def}}{=} \mathbf{d}_t$ and $\mathbf{h}_t \stackrel{\text{def}}{=} \tilde{\mathbf{A}}_t\mathbf{d}_t$. We can update the sketched system in $O(dk)$ time and space

$$\tilde{\mathbf{A}}_{t+1} = \tilde{\mathbf{A}}_t + \tfrac{1}{t+1}\left(\tilde{\mathbf{e}}_t\mathbf{d}_t^\top - \tilde{\mathbf{A}}_t\right)$$
$$\tilde{\mathbf{b}}_{t+1} = \tilde{\mathbf{b}}_t + \tfrac{1}{t+1}\left(\tilde{\mathbf{e}}_t R_{t+1} - \tilde{\mathbf{b}}_t\right)$$

To maintain $(\tilde{\mathbf{A}}_t\tilde{\mathbf{A}}_t^\top)^{-1}$ incrementally, notice that the unnormalized update is

$$\begin{aligned}\tilde{\mathbf{A}}_{t+1}\tilde{\mathbf{A}}_{t+1}^\top &= (\tilde{\mathbf{A}}_t + \tilde{\mathbf{e}}_t\mathbf{d}_t^\top)(\tilde{\mathbf{A}}_t + \tilde{\mathbf{e}}_t\mathbf{d}_t^\top)\\ &= \tilde{\mathbf{A}}_t\tilde{\mathbf{A}}_t^\top + \tilde{\mathbf{e}}_t\mathbf{h}_t^\top + \mathbf{h}_t\tilde{\mathbf{e}}_t^\top + ||\mathbf{d}_t||_2^2\|\tilde{\mathbf{e}}_t\tilde{\mathbf{e}}_t^\top.\end{aligned}$$

Hence, $(\tilde{\mathbf{A}}_{t+1}\tilde{\mathbf{A}}_{t+1}^\top)^{-1}$ can be updated from $(\tilde{\mathbf{A}}_t\tilde{\mathbf{A}}_t^\top)^{-1}$ by applying the Sherman-Morrison update three times. For a normalized update, based on samples, the update is

$$\begin{aligned}\tilde{\mathbf{A}}_{t+1}\tilde{\mathbf{A}}_{t+1}^\top = &\left(\tfrac{t}{t+1}\right)^2\tilde{\mathbf{A}}_t\tilde{\mathbf{A}}_t^\top + \tfrac{t}{(t+1)^2}\left(\tilde{\mathbf{e}}_t\mathbf{h}_t^\top + \mathbf{h}_t\tilde{\mathbf{e}}_t^\top\right)\\ &+ \tfrac{1}{(t+1)^2}||\mathbf{d}_t||_2^2\|\tilde{\mathbf{e}}_t\tilde{\mathbf{e}}_t^\top\end{aligned}$$

We can then compute $\mathbf{w}_t = \tilde{\mathbf{A}}_t(\tilde{\mathbf{A}}_t\tilde{\mathbf{A}}_t^\top)^\dagger\tilde{\mathbf{b}}_t$ on each step.

This solution, however, will provide the minimum norm solution, rather than the unbiased solution, even though the unbiased solution is feasible for the underconstrained system. To instead push the preference towards this unbiased solution, we use the stochastic approximation algorithm, called ATD (Pan et al., 2017). This method is a quasi-second order method, that relies on a low-rank approximation $\hat{\mathbf{A}}_t$ to $\mathbf{A}_t$; using this approximation, the update is $\mathbf{w}_{t+1} = \mathbf{w}_t + (\alpha_t\hat{\mathbf{A}}_t^\dagger + \eta\mathbf{I})\delta_t\mathbf{e}_t$. Instead of being used to explicitly solve for $\mathbf{w}$, the approximation matrix is used to provide curvature information. The inclusion of η constitutes a small regularization component, that pushes the solution towards the unbiased solution.

We show in the next proposition that for our alternative approximation, we still obtain unbiased solutions. We use results for iterative methods for singular linear systems (Shi et al., 2011; Wang & Bertsekas, 2013), since

[3]We show in Proposition 2, Appendix A, that $\tilde{\mathbf{A}}$ is full row rank with high probability. This property is required to ensure that the inverse of $\tilde{\mathbf{A}}\tilde{\mathbf{A}}^\top$ exists. In practice, this is less of a concern, because we initialize the matrix $\tilde{\mathbf{A}}_0\tilde{\mathbf{A}}_0^\top$ with a small positive value, ensuring invertibility for $\tilde{\mathbf{A}}_t\tilde{\mathbf{A}}_t^\top$ for finite t.

$\mathbf{A}$ may be singular. $\mathbf{A}$ has been shown to be positive semi-definite under standard assumptions on the MDP (Yu, 2015); for simplicity, we assume $\mathbf{A}$ is positive semi-definite, instead of providing these MDP assumptions.

Assumption 1. *For $\mathbf{S} \in \mathbb{R}^{k \times d}$ and $\mathbf{B} = \alpha(\mathbf{SA})^{\dagger}\mathbf{S} + \eta\mathbf{I}$ with $\mathbf{B} \in \mathbb{R}^{d \times d}$, the matrix $\mathbf{BA}$ is diagonalizable.*

Assumption 2. *$\mathbf{A}$ is positive semi-definite.*

Assumption 3. *$\alpha \in (0, \frac{1}{2})$ and $0 < \eta \leq \frac{1}{2\lambda_{max}(\mathbf{A})}$ where $\lambda_{max}(\mathbf{A})$ is the maximum eigenvalue of $\mathbf{A}$.*

Theorem 1. *Under Assumptions 1-3, the expected updating rule $\mathbf{w}_{t+1} = \mathbf{w}_t + \mathbb{E}_\pi[\mathbf{B}\delta_t \mathbf{e}_t]$ converges to a fixed-point $\mathbf{w}^\star = \mathbf{A}^\dagger \mathbf{b}$.*

Proof. The expected updating rule is $\mathbb{E}_\pi[\mathbf{B}\delta_t\mathbf{e}_t] = \mathbf{B}(\mathbf{b} - \mathbf{A}\mathbf{w}_t)$. As in the proof of convergence for ATD (Pan et al., 2017, Theorem 1), we similarly verify the conditions from (Shi et al., 2011, Theorem 1.1).

Notice first that $\mathbf{BA} = \alpha(\mathbf{SA})^\dagger\mathbf{SA} + \eta\mathbf{A}$.

For singular value decomposition, $\mathbf{SA} = \mathbf{U}\boldsymbol{\Sigma}\mathbf{V}^\top$, we have that $(\mathbf{SA})^\dagger\mathbf{SA} = \mathbf{V}\boldsymbol{\Sigma}^\dagger\mathbf{U}^\top\mathbf{U}\boldsymbol{\Sigma}\mathbf{V}^\top = \mathbf{V}[\mathbf{I}_{\tilde{k}}\ \mathbf{0}_{d-k}]\mathbf{V}^\top$, where $\tilde{k} \leq k$ is the rank of $\mathbf{SA}$. The maximum eigenvalue of $(\mathbf{SA})^\dagger\mathbf{SA}$ is therefore 1.

Because $(\mathbf{SA})^\dagger\mathbf{SA}$ and $\mathbf{A}$ are both positive semidefinite, $\mathbf{BA}$ is positive semi-definite. By Weyl's inequalities,

$$\lambda_{\max}(\mathbf{BA}) \leq \alpha\lambda_{\max}((\mathbf{SA})^\dagger\mathbf{SA}) + \eta\lambda_{\max}(\mathbf{A}).$$

Therefore, the eigenvalues of $\mathbf{I} - \mathbf{BA}$ have absolute value strictly less than 1, because $\eta \leq (2\lambda_{\max}(\mathbf{A}))^{-1}$ and $\alpha < 1/2 = (2\lambda_{\max}((\mathbf{SA})^\dagger\mathbf{SA}))^{-1}$ by assumption.

For the second condition, since $\mathbf{BA}$ is PSD and diagonalizable, we can write $\mathbf{BA} = \mathbf{Q}\boldsymbol{\Lambda}\mathbf{Q}^{-1}$ for some matrices $\mathbf{Q}$ and diagonal matrix $\boldsymbol{\Lambda}$ with eigenvalues greater than or equal to zero. Then $(\mathbf{BA})^2 = \mathbf{Q}\boldsymbol{\Lambda}\mathbf{Q}^{-1}\mathbf{Q}\boldsymbol{\Lambda}\mathbf{Q}^{-1} = \mathbf{Q}\boldsymbol{\Lambda}^2\mathbf{Q}^{-1}$ has the same rank.

For the third condition, because $\mathbf{BA}$ is the sum of two positive semi-definite matrices, the nullspace of $\mathbf{BA}$ is a subset of the nullspace of each of those matrices individually: nullspace$(\mathbf{BA})$ = nullspace$(\alpha(\mathbf{SA})^\dagger\mathbf{SA} + \eta\mathbf{A}) \subseteq \eta$nullspace$(\eta\mathbf{A})$ = nullspace$(\mathbf{A})$. In the other direction, for all $\mathbf{w}$ such that $\mathbf{Aw} = \mathbf{0}$, its clear that $\mathbf{BAw} = \mathbf{0}$, and so nullspace$(\mathbf{A}) \subseteq$ nullspace$(\mathbf{BA})$. Therefore, nullspace$(\mathbf{A})$ = nullspace$(\mathbf{BA})$. □

6 WHEN SHOULD SKETCHING HELP?

To investigate the properties of these sketching approaches, we need to understand when we expect sketching to have the most benefit. Despite the wealth of literature on sketching and strong theoretical results, there seems to be fewer empirical investigations into when sketching has most benefit. In this section, we elucidate some hypotheses about when sketching should be most effective, which we then explore in our experiments.

In the experiments for sketching the features in Section 3, it was clear that sketching the RBF features was much more effective than sketching the tile coding features. A natural investigation, therefore, is into the properties of representations that are more amenable to sketching. The key differences between these two representations is in terms of smoothness, density and overlap. The tile coding representation has non-smooth 0,1 features, which do not overlap in each grid. Rather, the overlap for tile coding results from overlapping tilings. This differs from RBF overlap, where centers are arranged in a grid and only edges of the RBF features overlap. The density of RBF features is significantly higher, since more RBFs are active for each input. Theoretical work in sketching for regression (Maillard & Munos, 2012), however, does not require features to be smooth. We empirically investigate these three properties—smoothness, density and overlap.

There are also some theoretical results that suggest sketching could be more amenable for more distinct features—less overlap or potentially less tilings. Balcan et al. (2006) showed a worst-case setting where data-independent sketching results in poor performance. They propose a two-stage projection, to maintain separability in classification. The first stage uses a data-dependent projection, to ensure features are not highly correlated, and the second uses a data-independent projection (a sketch) to further reduce the dimensionality after the orthogonal projection. The implied conclusion from this result is that, if the features are not highly correlated, then the first step can be avoided and the data independent sketch should similarly maintain classification accuracy. This result suggests that sketching for feature expansions with less redundancy should perform better.

We might also expect sketching to be more robust to the condition number of the matrix. For sketching in regression, Fard et al. (2012) found a bias-variance trade-off when increasing k, where for large k, estimation error from a larger number of parameters became a factor. Similarly, in our experiments above, LSTD using an incremental Sherman-Morrison update has periodic spikes in the learning curve, indicating some instability. The smallest eigenvalue of the sketched matrix should be larger than that of the original matrix; this improvement in condition number compensates for the loss in information. Similarly, we might expect that maintaining an incremental singular value decomposition, for ATD, could be less robust than ATD with left-side sketching.

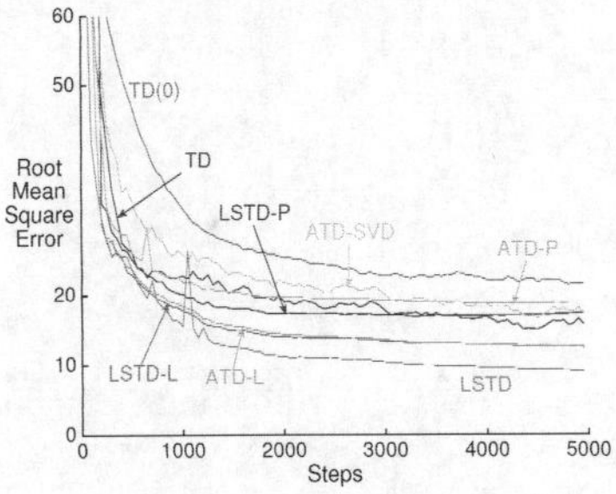

(a) Mountain Car, RBF

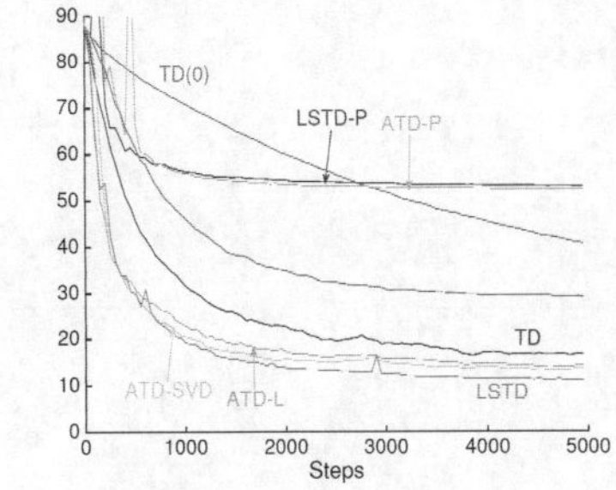

(b) Mountain Car, Tile coding

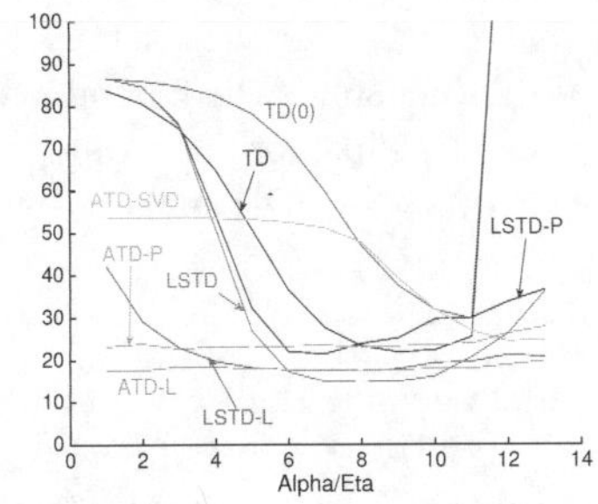

(c) Mountain Car, RBF, Sensitivity

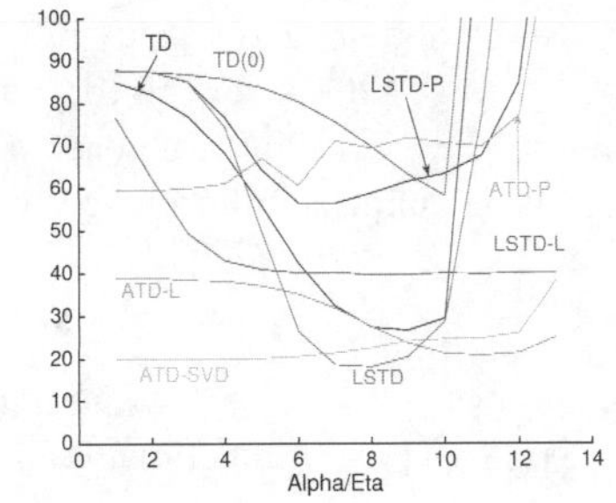

(d) Mountain Car, Tile coding, Sensitivity

Figure 2: **(a)** and **(b)** are learning curves on Mountain Car with $k = 50$, and **(c)** and **(d)** are their corresponding parameter-sensitivity plots. The sensitivity plots report average RMSE over the entire learning curve, for the best λ for each parameter. The stepsize α is reported for TD, the initialization parameter ξ for the LSTD methods and the regularization parameter η for the ATD methods. The initialization for the matrices in the ATD methods is fixed to the identity. The range for the regularization term η is 0.1 times the range for α. As before, the sketching approaches with RBFs perform better than with tile coding. The sensitivity of the left-side projection methods is significantly lower than the TD methods. ATD-L also seems to be less sensitive than ATD-SVD, and incurs less bias than LSTD-L.

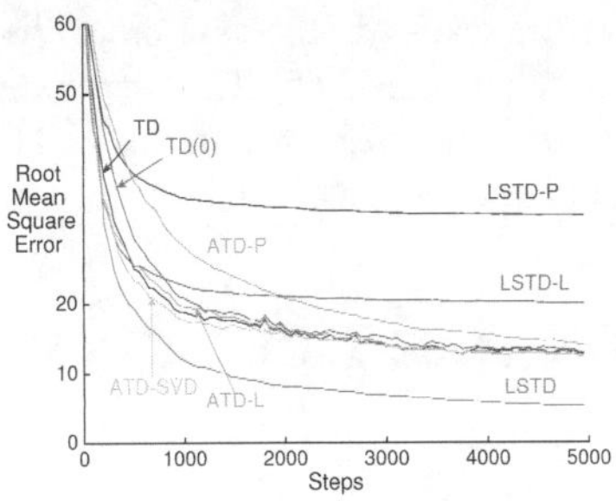

(a) Puddle World, RBF, $k = 25$

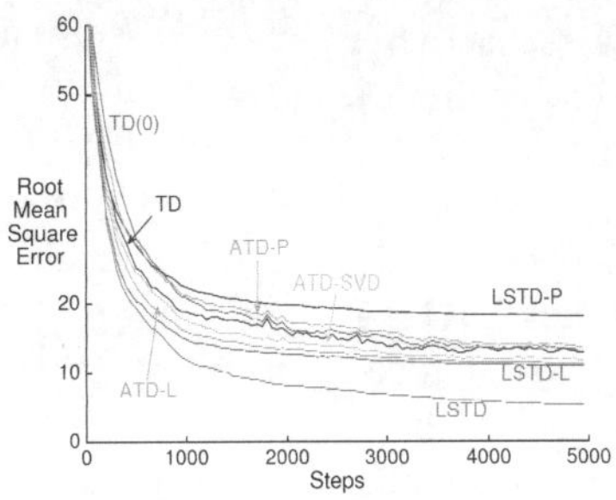

(b) Puddle World, RBF, $k = 50$

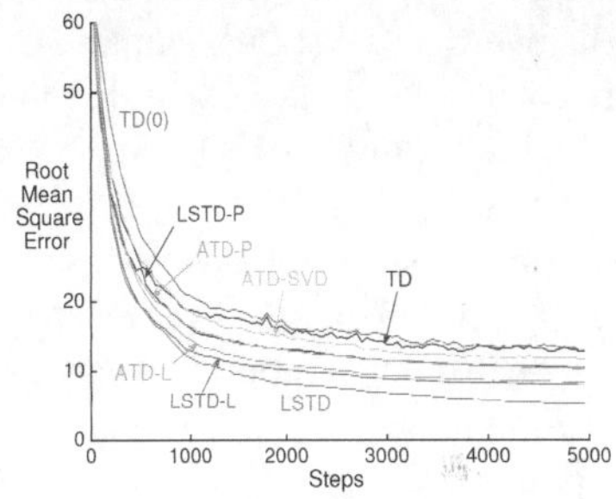

(c) Puddle World, RBF, $k = 75$

Figure 3: Change in performance when increasing k, from 25 to 75. Two-sided projection (i.e., projecting the features) significantly improves with larger k, but is strictly dominated by left-side projection. At $k = 50$, the left-side projection methods are outperforming TD and are less variant. ATD-SVD seems to gain less with increasing k, though in general we found ATD-SVD to perform more poorly than ATD-P particularly for RBF representations.

7 EXPERIMENTS

In this section, we test the efficacy of sketching for LSTD and ATD in four domains: Mountain Car, Puddle World, Acrobot and Energy Allocation. We set $k = 50$, unless otherwise specified, average all results over 50 runs and sweep parameters for each algorithm. Detailed experimental settings, such as parameter ranges, are in Appendix C. To distinguish projections, we add -P for two-sided and -L for left-sided to the algorithm name.

We conclude that 1) two-sided projection—projecting the features—generally does much worse than only projecting the left-side of $\mathbf{A}$, 2) higher feature density is more amenable to sketching, particularly for two-sided sketching, 3) smoothness of features only seems to impact two-sided sketching, 4) ATD with sketching decreases bias relative to its LSTD variant and 5) ATD with left-sided sketching typically performs as well as ATD-SVD, but is significantly faster.

Performance and parameter sensitivity for RBFs and Tile coding. We first more exhaustively compare the algorithms in Mountain Car and Puddle World, in Figures 2 and 3 with additional such results in the appendix. As has been previously observed, TD with a well-chosen stepsize can perform almost as well as LSTD in terms of sample efficiency, but is quite sensitive to the stepsize.

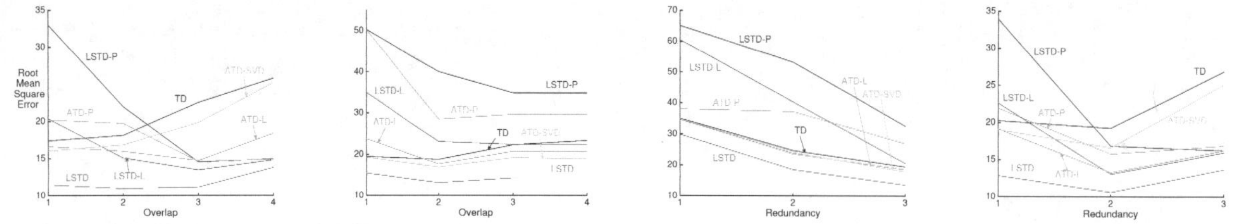

(a) RBF, $k = 50$ (b) Spline, $k = 50$ (c) Tile coding, $k = 50$ (d) RBFs with tilings, $k = 50$

Figure 4: The effect of varying the representation properties, in Puddle World with $d = 1024$. In **(a)** and **(b)**, we examine the impact of varying the overlap, for both smooth features (RBFs) and 0-1 features (Spline). For spline, the feature is 1 if $||\mathbf{x} - \mathbf{c}_i|| < \sigma$ and otherwise 0. The spline feature represents a bin, like for tile coding, but here we adjust the widths of the bins so that they can overlap and do not use tilings. The x-axis has four width values, to give a corresponding feature vector norm of about $20, 40, 80, 120$. In **(c)** and **(d)**, we vary the redundancy, where number of tilings is increased and the total number of features kept constant. We generate tilings for RBFs like for tile coding, but for each grid cell use an RBF similarity rather than a spline similarity. We used $4 \times 16 \times 16$, $16 \times 8 \times 8$ and $64 \times 4 \times 4$.

Here, therefore, we explore if our matrix-based learning algorithms can reduce this parameter sensitivity. In Figure 2, we can indeed see that this is the case. The LSTD algorithms look a bit more sensitive, because we sweep over small initialization values for completeness. For tile coding, the range is a bit more narrow, but for RBFs, in the slightly larger range, the LSTD algorithms are quite insensitive for RBFs. Interestingly, LSTD-L seems to be more robust. We hypothesize that the reason for this is that LSTD-L only has to initialize a smaller $k \times k$ symmetric matrix, $(\mathbf{SA}(\mathbf{SA})^\top)^{-1} = \eta\mathbf{I}$, and so is much more robust to this initialization. In fact, across settings, we found initializing to $\mathbf{I}$ was effective. Similarly, ATD-L benefits from this robustness, since it needs to initialize the same matrix, and then further overcomes bias using the approximation to $\mathbf{A}$ only for curvature information.

Impact of the feature properties. We explored the feature properties—smoothness, density, overlap and redundancy—where we hypothesized sketching should help, shown in Figure 4. The general conclusions are 1) the two-side sketching methods improve—relative to LSTD—with increasing density (i.e., increasing overlap and increasing redundancy), 2) the smoothness of the features (RBF versus spline) seems to affect the two-side projection methods much more, 3) the shape of the left-side projection methods follows that of LSTD and 4) ATD-SVD appears to follow the shape of TD more. Increased density generally seemed to degrade TD, and so ATD-SVD similarly suffered more in these settings. In general, the ATD methods had less gain over their corresponding LSTD variants, with increasing density.

Experiments on high dimensional domains. We finally apply our sketching techniques on two high dimensional domains to illustrate practical usability: Acrobot and Energy allocation. The Acrobot domain (Sutton & Barto, 1998) is a four dimensional episodic task, where the goal is to raise an arm to a certain height. The Energy allocation domain Salas & Powell (2013) is a five-dimensional continuing task, where the goal is to store and allocate energy to maximize profit. For Acrobot, we used $14,400$ uniformly-spaced centers and for Energy allocation, we used the same tile coding of 8192 features as Pan et al. (2017). We summarize the results in the caption of Figure 5, with the overall conclusion that ATD-L provides an attractive way to reduce parameter sensitivity of TD, and benefit from sketching to reduce computation.

8 CONCLUSION AND DISCUSSION

In this work, we investigated how to benefit from sketching approaches for incremental policy evaluation. We first showed that sketching features can have significant bias issues, and proposed to instead sketch the linear system, enabling better control over how much information is lost. We highlighted that sketching for radial basis features seems to be much more effective, than for tile coding, and further that a variety of natural asymmetric sketching approaches for sketching the linear system are not effective. We then showed that more carefully using sketching—particularly with left-side sketching within a quasi-Newton update—enables us to obtain an unbiased approach that can improve sample efficiency without incurring significant computation. Our goal in this work was to provide practical methods that can benefit from sketching, and start a focus on empirically investigating settings in which sketching is effective.

Sketching has been used for quasi-Newton updates in online learning; a natural question is if those methods are applicable for policy evaluation. Luo et al. (2016) consider sketching approaches for an online Newton-update, for general functions rather than just the linear func-

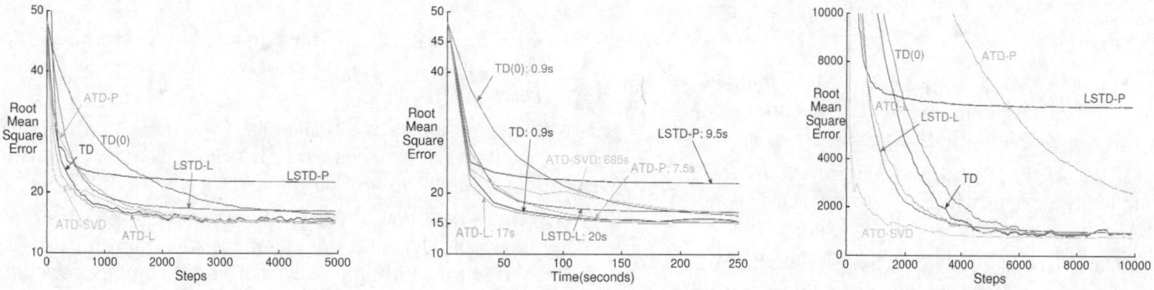

(a) Acrobot, RBF (b) Acrobot, RMSE vs Time (c) Energy allocation, Tile coding

Figure 5: Results in domains with high-dimensional features, using $k = 50$ and with results averaged over 30 runs. For Acrobot, the (left-side) sketching methods perform well and are much less sensitive to parameters than TD. For runtime, we show RMSE versus time allowing the algorithms to process up to 25 samples per second, to simulate a real-time setting learning; slow algorithms cannot process all 25 within a second. With computation taken into account, ATD-L has a bigger win over ATD-SVD, and does not lose relative to TD. Total runtime in seconds for one run for each algorithm is labeled in the plot. ATD-SVD is much slower, because of the incremental SVD. For the Energy Allocation domain, the two-side projection methods (LSTD-P, ATD-P) are significantly worse than other algorithms. Interestingly, here ATD-SVD has a bigger advantage, likely because sketching the tile coding features is less effective.

tion approximation case we consider here. They similarly have to consider updates amenable to incrementally approximating a matrix (a Hessian in their case). In general, however, porting these quasi-Newton updates to policy evaluation for reinforcement learning is problematic for two reasons. First, the objective function for temporal difference learning is the mean-squared projected Bellman error, which is the product of three expectations. It is not straightforward to obtain an unbiased sample of this gradient, which is why Pan et al. (2017) propose a slightly different quasi-Newton update that uses $\mathbf{A}$ as a preconditioner. Consequently, it is not straightforward to apply quasi-Newton online algorithms that assume access to unbiased gradients. Second, the Hessian can be nicely approximated in terms of gradients, and is symmetric; both are exploited when deriving the sketched online Newton-update (Luo et al., 2016). We, on the other hand, have an asymmetric matrix $\mathbf{A}$.

In the other direction, we could consider if our approach could be beneficial for the online regression setting. For linear regression, with $\gamma = 0$, the matrix $\mathbf{A}$ actually corresponds to the Hessian. In contrast to previous approaches that sketched the features (Maillard & Munos, 2012; Fard et al., 2012; Luo et al., 2016), therefore, one could instead sketch the system and maintain $(\mathbf{SA})^{\dagger}$. Since the second-order update is $\mathbf{A}^{-1}\mathbf{g}_t$ for gradient $\mathbf{g}_t$ on iteration t, an approximate second-order update could be computed as $((\mathbf{SA})^{\dagger}\mathbf{S} + \eta\mathbf{I})\mathbf{g}_t$.

In our experiments, we found sketching both sides of $\mathbf{A}$ to be less effective and found little benefit from modifying the chosen sketch; however, these empirical conclusions warrant further investigation. With more understanding into the properties of $\mathbf{A}$, it could be possible to benefit from this variety. For example, sketching the left-side of $\mathbf{A}$ could be seen as sketching the eligibility trace, and the right-side as sketching the difference between successive features. For some settings, there could be properties of either of these vectors that are particularly suited to a certain sketch. As another example, the key benefit of many of the sketches over Gaussian random projections is in enabling the dimension k to be larger, by using (sparse) sketching matrices where dot product are efficient. We could not easily benefit from these properties, because $\mathbf{SA}$ could be dense and computing matrix-vector products and incremental inverses would be expensive for larger k. For sparse $\mathbf{A}$, or when $\mathbf{SA}$ has specialized properties, it could be more possible to benefit from different sketches.

Finally, the idea of sketching fits well into a larger theme of random representations within reinforcement learning. A seminal paper on random representations (Sutton & Whitehead, 1993) demonstrates the utility of random threshold units, as opposed to more carefully learned units. Though end-to-end training has become more popular in recent years, there is evidence that random representations can be quite powerful (Aubry & Jaffard, 2002; Rahimi & Recht, 2007, 2008; Maillard & Munos, 2012), or even combined with descent strategies (Mahmood & Sutton, 2013). For reinforcement learning, this learning paradigm is particularly suitable, because data cannot be observed upfront. Data-independent representations, such as random representations and sketching approaches, are therefore particularly appealing and warrant further investigation for the incremental learning setting within reinforcement learning.

References

Ailon, Nir and Chazelle, Bernard. Approximate nearest neighbors and the fast Johnson-Lindenstrauss transform. *ACM Symposium on Theory of Computing*, 2006.

Alon, Noga, Matias, Yossi, and Szegedy, Mario. The space complexity of approximating the frequency moments. In *ACM Symposium on Theory of Computing*, 1996.

Aubry, Jean-Marie and Jaffard, Stéphane. Random Wavelet Series. *Communications in Mathematical Physics*, 2002.

Balcan, Maria-Florina, Blum, Avrim, and Vempala, Santosh. Kernels as features: On kernels, margins, and low-dimensional mappings. *Machine Learning*, 2006.

Bellemare, Marc, Veness, Joel, and Bowling, Michael. Sketch-Based Linear Value Function Approximation. In *Advances in Neural Information Processing Systems*, 2012.

Boutsidis, Christos and Woodruff, David P. Communication-optimal distributed principal component analysis in the column-partition model. *arXiv:1504.06729*, 2015.

Boyan, J and Moore, A W. Generalization in Reinforcement Learning: Safely Approximating the Value Function. *Advances in Neural Information Processing Systems*, 1995.

Boyan, J A. Least-squares temporal difference learning. *International Conference on Machine Learning*, 1999.

Charikar, M, Chen, K, and Farach-Colton, M. Finding frequent items in data streams. *Theoretical Computer Science*, 2002.

Fard, Mahdi Milani, Grinberg, Yuri, Pineau, Joelle, and Precup, Doina. Compressed Least-Squares Regression on Sparse Spaces. *AAAI*, 2012.

Gehring, Clement, Pan, Yangchen, and White, Martha. Incremental Truncated LSTD. *International Joint Conference on Artificial Intelligence*, 2016.

Ghashami, M, Desai, A, and Phillips, J M. Improved practical matrix sketching with guarantees. *European Symposium on Algorithms*, 2014.

Ghavamzadeh, M, Lazaric, A, Maillard, O A, and Munos, R. LSTD with random projections. In *Advances in Neural Information Processing Systems*, 2010.

Gilbert, A and Indyk, P. Sparse recovery using sparse matrices. *Proceedings of the IEEE*, 2010.

Gower, Robert M and Richtárik, Peter. Randomized Iterative Methods for Linear Systems. *arXiv:1506.03296*, 2015.

Johnson, William B and Lindenstrauss, Joram. Extensions of Lipschitz mappings into a Hilbert space. *Contemporary mathematics*, 1984.

Luo, Haipeng, Agarwal, Alekh, Cesa-Bianchi, Nicolò, and Langford, John. Efficient Second Order Online Learning by Sketching. *Advances in Neural Information Processing Systems*, 2016.

Mahmood, A R and Sutton, R.S. Representation search through generate and test. In *Proceedings of the AAAI Workshop on Learning Rich Representations from Low-Level Sensors*, 2013.

Maillard, Odalric-Ambrym and Munos, Rémi. Linear Regression With Random Projections. *Journal of Machine Learning Research*, 2012.

Pan, Yangchen, White, Adam, and White, Martha. Accelerated Gradient Temporal Difference Learning. In *AAAI Conference on Artifical Intelligence*, 2017.

Rahimi, A and Recht, B. Random features for large-scale kernel machines. In *Advances in Neural Information Processing Systems*, 2007.

Rahimi, Ali and Recht, Benjamin. Uniform approximation of functions with random bases. In *Annual Allerton Conference on Communication, Control, and Computing*, 2008.

Salas, D F and Powell, W B. Benchmarking a Scalable Approximate Dynamic Programming Algorithm for Stochastic Control of Multidimensional Energy Storage Problems. *Dept Oper Res Financial Eng*, 2013.

Shi, X, Wei, Y, and Zhang, W. Convergence of general nonstationary iterative methods for solving singular linear equations. *SIAM Journal on Matrix Analysis and Applications*, 2011.

Sutton, Richard S, Modayil, J, Delp, M, Degris, T, Pilarski, P.M., White, A, and Precup, D. Horde: A scalable real-time architecture for learning knowledge from unsupervised sensorimotor interaction. In *International Conference on Autonomous Agents and Multiagent Systems*, 2011.

Sutton, R.S. Learning to predict by the methods of temporal differences. *Machine Learning*, 1988.

Sutton, R.S. Generalization in reinforcement learning: Successful examples using sparse coarse coding. In *Advances in Neural Information Processing Systems*, 1996.

Sutton, R.S. and Barto, A G. *Reinforcement Learning: An Introduction*. MIT press, 1998.

Sutton, RS and Whitehead, SD. Online learning with random representations. In *International Conference on Machine Learning*, 1993.

Wang, Mengdi and Bertsekas, Dimitri P. On the convergence of simulation-based iterative methods for solving singular linear systems. *Stochastic Systems*, 2013.

Wang, Shusen. A Practical Guide to Randomized Matrix Computations with MATLAB Implementations. *arXiv:1505.07570*, 2015.

White, Martha. Unifying task specification in reinforcement learning. *arXiv:1609.01995*, 2016.

Woodruff, David P. Sketching as a tool for numerical linear algebra. *arXiv:1411.4357*, 2014.

Yu, Huizhen. On convergence of emphatic temporal-difference learning. In *Annual Conference on Learning Theory*, 2015.

A Row-rank properties of SA

To ensure the right pseudo-inverse is well-defined in Section 5, we show that the projected matrix $\mathbf{SA}$ is full row-rank with high probability, if $\mathbf{A}$ has sufficiently high rank. We know that the probability measure of row-rank deficient matrices for $\mathbf{S}$ has zero mass. However in the following, we prove a stronger and practically more useful claim that $\mathbf{SA}$ is far from being row-rank deficient. Formally, we define a matrix to be *δ-full row-rank* if there is no row that can be replaced by another row with distance at most δ to make that matrix row-rank deficient.

Proposition 2. *Let $\mathbf{S} \in \mathbb{R}^{k\times d}$ be any Gaussian matrix with 0 mean and unit variance. For $r_A = rank(\mathbf{A})$ and for any $\delta > 0$, $\mathbf{SA}$ is δ-full row-rank with probability at least $1 - \exp(-2\frac{(r_A(1-0.8\delta)-k)^2}{r_A})$.*

Proof. Let $\mathbf{A} = \mathbf{U\Sigma V}^\top$ be the SVD for $\mathbf{A}$. Since $\mathbf{U}$ is an orthonormal matrix, $\mathbf{S}' = \mathbf{SU}$ has the same distribution as $\mathbf{S}$ and the rank of $\mathbf{SA}$ is the same as $\mathbf{S}'\mathbf{\Sigma}$. Moreover notice that the last $d - r_A$ columns of $\mathbf{S}'$ get multiplied by all-zero rows of $\mathbf{\Sigma}$. Therefore, in what follows, we assume we draw a random matrix $\mathbf{S}' \in \mathbb{R}^{k\times r_A}$ (similar to how $\mathbf{S}$ is drawn), and that $\mathbf{\Sigma} \in \mathbb{R}^{r_A\times r_A}$ is a full rank diagonal matrix. We study the rank of $\mathbf{S}'\mathbf{\Sigma}$.

Consider iterating over the rows of $\mathbf{S}'$, the probability that any new row is δ-far from being a linear combination of the previous ones is at least $1 - 0.8\delta$. To see why, assume that you currently have i rows and sample another vector $\mathbf{v}$ with entries sampled i.i.d. from a standard Gaussian as the candidate for the next row in $\mathbf{S}'$. The length corresponding to the projection of any row $\mathbf{S}'_{j:}$ onto $\mathbf{v}$, i.e., $\mathbf{S}'_{j:}\mathbf{v} \in \mathbb{R}$, is a Gaussian random variable. Thus, the probability of the $\mathbf{S}'_{j:}\mathbf{v}$ being within δ is at most 0.8δ. This follows from the fact that the area under probability density function of a standard Gaussian random variable over $[0, x]$ is at most $0.4x$, for any $x > 0$.

This stochastic process is a Bernoulli trial with success probability of at least $1-0.8\delta$. The trial stops when there are k successes or when the number of iterations reaches r_A. The Hoeffding inequality bounds the probability of failure by $\exp(-2\frac{(r_A(1-0.8\delta)-k)^2}{r_A})$. □

B Alternative iterative updates

In addition to the proposed iterative algorithm using a left-sided sketch of $\mathbf{A}$, we experimented with a variety of alternative updates that proved ineffective. We list them here for completeness.

We experimented with a variety of iterative updates. For a linear system, $\mathbf{Aw} = \mathbf{b}$, one can iteratively update using $\mathbf{w}_{t+1} = \mathbf{w}_t + \alpha(\mathbf{b} - \mathbf{Aw}_t)$ and $\mathbf{w}_t$ will converge to a solution of the system (under some conditions). We tested the following ways to use sketched linear systems.

First, for the two-sided sketched $\mathbf{A}$, we want to solve for $\mathbf{S}_L\mathbf{AS}_R^\top\mathbf{w} = \mathbf{S}_L\mathbf{b}$. If $\tilde{\mathbf{A}}_t = \mathbf{S}_L\mathbf{A}_t\mathbf{S}_R^\top$ is square, we can use the iterative update

$$\begin{aligned}
\tilde{\mathbf{A}}_{t+1} &= \tilde{\mathbf{A}}_t + \frac{1}{t+1}\left(\mathbf{S}_L\mathbf{e}_t(\mathbf{S}_R\mathbf{d}_t)^\top - \tilde{\mathbf{A}}_t\right)\\
\tilde{\mathbf{b}}_{t+1} &= \tilde{\mathbf{b}}_t + \frac{1}{t+1}\left(r_{t+1}\mathbf{S}_L\mathbf{e}_t - \tilde{\mathbf{b}}_t\right)\\
\mathbf{w}_{t+1} &= \mathbf{w}_t + \alpha_t(\tilde{\mathbf{b}}_{t+1} - \tilde{\mathbf{A}}_{t+1}\mathbf{w}_t)\\
&= \mathbf{w}_t + \alpha_t(\mathbf{S}_L\mathbf{b}_{t+1} - \mathbf{S}_L\mathbf{A}_{t+1}\mathbf{S}_R^\top\mathbf{w}_t)
\end{aligned}$$

and use $\mathbf{w}$ for prediction on the sketched features. Another option is to maintain the inverse incrementally, using Sherman-Morrison

$$\begin{aligned}
\mathbf{a}_d &= \mathbf{d}_t^\top\mathbf{S}_R^\top\tilde{\mathbf{A}}_t^{-1}\\
\mathbf{a}_u &= \tilde{\mathbf{A}}_t^{-1}\mathbf{S}_L\mathbf{e}_t\\
\tilde{\mathbf{A}}_t^{-1} &= \tilde{\mathbf{A}}_t^{-1} - \frac{\mathbf{a}_u\mathbf{a}_d}{1+\mathbf{d}_t^\top\mathbf{a}_u}\\
\tilde{\mathbf{b}}_t &= \tilde{\mathbf{b}}_t + \frac{r_{t+1}\mathbf{S}_L\mathbf{e}_t - \tilde{\mathbf{b}}_t}{t}\\
\mathbf{w} &= \tilde{\mathbf{A}}_t^{-1}\tilde{\mathbf{b}}_t
\end{aligned}$$

If $\mathbf{S}_L\mathbf{AS}_R^\top$ is not square (e.g., $\mathbf{S}_R = \mathbf{I}$), we instead solve for $\mathbf{S}_L^\top\mathbf{S}_L\mathbf{AS}_R^\top\mathbf{S}_R\mathbf{w} = \mathbf{S}_L^\top\mathbf{S}_L\mathbf{b}$, where applying $\mathbf{S}_L^\top$ provides the recovery from the left and $\mathbf{S}_R$ the recovery from the right.

Second, with the same sketching, we also experimented with $\mathbf{S}_L^\dagger$, instead of $\mathbf{S}_L^\top$ for the recovery, and similarly for $\mathbf{S}_R$, but this provided no improvement.

For this square system, the iterative update is

$$\begin{aligned}
\mathbf{w}_{t+1} &= \mathbf{w}_t + \alpha_t\mathbf{S}_L^\dagger(\tilde{\mathbf{b}}_{t+1} - \tilde{\mathbf{A}}_{t+1}\mathbf{S}_R\mathbf{w}_t)\\
&= \mathbf{w}_{t+1} + \alpha_t\mathbf{S}_L^\dagger(\mathbf{S}_L\mathbf{b}_{t+1} - \mathbf{S}_L\mathbf{A}_{t+1}\mathbf{S}_R^\top\mathbf{S}_R\mathbf{w}_t)
\end{aligned}$$

for the same $\tilde{\mathbf{b}}_t$ and $\tilde{\mathbf{A}}_t$ which can be efficiently kept incrementally, while the pseudoinverse of $\mathbf{S}_L$ only needs to be computed once at the beginning.

Third, we tried to solve the system $\mathbf{S}_L^\top\mathbf{S}_L\mathbf{Aw} = \mathbf{b}$, using the updating rule $\mathbf{w}_{t+1} = \mathbf{w}_t + \alpha_t(\mathbf{b}_{t+1} - \mathbf{S}_L^\top\mathbf{S}_L\mathbf{A}_{t+1}\mathbf{w}_t)$, where the matrix $\mathbf{S}_L\mathbf{A}_{t+1}$ can be incrementally maintained at each step by using a simple rank-one update.

Fourth, we tried to explicitly regularize these iterative updates by adding a small step in the direction of $\delta_t\mathbf{e}_t$.

In general, none of these iterative methods performed well. We hypothesize this may be due to difficulties in choosing stepsize parameters. Ultimately, we found the sketched updated within ATD to be the most effective.

C Experimental details

Mountain Car is a classical episodic task with the goal of driving the car to the top of mountain. The state is 2-dimensional, consisting of the (position, velocity) of the car. We used the specification from (Sutton & Barto, 1998). We compute the true values of 2000 states, where each testing state is sampled from a trajectory generated by the given policy. From each test state, we estimate the value—the expected return—by computing the average over 1000 returns, generated by rollouts. The policy for Mountain Car is the energy pumping policy with 20% randomness starting from slightly random initial states. The discount rate is 1.0, and is 0 at the end of the episode, and the reward is always -1.

Puddle World Boyan & Moore (1995) is an episodic task, where the goal is for a robot in a continuous gridworld to reach a goal state within as fewest steps as possible. The state is 2-dimensional, consisting of (x, y) positions. We use the same setting as described in (Sutton & Barto, 1998), with a discount of 1.0 and -1 per step, except when going through a puddle that gives higher magnitude negative reward. We compute the true values from 2000 states in the same way as Mountain Car. A simple heuristic policy choosing the action leading to shortest Euclidean distance with 10% randomness is used.

Acrobot is a four-dimensional episodic task, where the goal is to raise an arm to certain level. The reward is -1 for non-terminal states and 0 for goal state, again with discount set to 1.0. We use the same tile coding as described in (Sutton & Barto, 1998), except that we use memory size $2^{15} = 32,768$. To get a reasonable policy, we used true-online Sarsa(λ) to go through 15000 episodes with stepsize $\alpha = 0.1/48$ and bootstrap parameter $\lambda = 0.9$. Each episode starts with a slight randomness. The policy is $\epsilon-$greedy with respect to state value and $\epsilon = 0.05$. The way we compute true values and generate training trajectories are the same as we described for the above two domains.

Energy allocation (Salas & Powell, 2013) is a continuing task with a five-dimensional state, where we use the same settings as in Pan et al. (2017). The matrix $\mathbf{A}$ was shown to have a low-rank structure (Pan et al., 2017) and hence matrix approximation methods are expected to perform well.

For radial basis functions, we used format $k(\mathbf{x}, \mathbf{c}) = \exp(-\frac{||\mathbf{x}-\mathbf{c}||_2^2}{2\sigma^2})$ where σ is called RBF width and $\mathbf{c}$ is a feature. On Mountain Car, because the position and velocity have different ranges, we set the bandwidth separately for each feature using $k(\mathbf{x}, \mathbf{c}) = \exp(-((\frac{\mathbf{x}_1-\mathbf{c}_1}{0.12r_1})^2 + (\frac{\mathbf{x}_2-\mathbf{c}_2}{0.12r_2})^2))$, where r_1 is the range of the first state variable and r_2 is the range of second state variable.

In Figure 4, we used a relatively rarely used representation which we call spline feature. For sample $\mathbf{x}$, the ith spline feature is set to 1 if $||\mathbf{x} - \mathbf{c}_i|| < \delta$ and otherwise set as 0. The centers are selected in exactly the same way as for the RBFs.

Parameter optimization. We swept the following ranges for stepsize (α), bootstrap parameter (λ), regularization parameter (η_t), and initialization parameter ξ for all domains:

1. $\alpha \in \{0.1 \times 2.0^j | j = -7, -6, ..., 4, 5\}$ divided by l_1 norm of feature representation, 13 values in total.
2. $\lambda \in \{0.0, 0.1, ..., 0.9, 0.93, 0.95, 0.97, 0.99, 1.0\}$, 15 values in total.
3. $\eta \in \{0.01 \times 2.0^j | j = -7, -6, ..., 4, 5\}$ divided by l_1 norm of feature representation, 13 values in total.
4. $\xi \in \{10^j | j = -5, -4.25, -3.5, ..., 2.5, 3.25, 4.0\}$, 13 values in total.

To choose the best parameter setting for each algorithm, we used the sum of RMSE across all steps for all the domains Energy allocation. For this domain, optimizing based on the whole range causes TD to pick an aggressive step-size to improve early learning at the expense of later learning. Therefore, for Energy allocation, we instead select the best parameters based on the sum of the RMSE for the second half of the steps.

For the ATD algorithms, as done in the original paper, we set $\alpha_t = \frac{1}{t}$ and only swept the regularization parameter η, which can also be thought of a (smaller) final stepsize. For this reason, the range of η is set to 0.1 times the range of α, to adjust this final stepsize range to an order of magnitude lower.

Additional experimental results. In the main paper, we demonstrated a subset of the results to highlight conclusions. For example, we showed the learning curves and parameter sensitivity in Mountain Car, for RBFs and tile coding. Due to space, we did not show the corresponding results for Puddle World in the main paper; we include these experiments here. Similarly, we only showed Acrobot with RBFs in the main text, and include results with tile coding here.

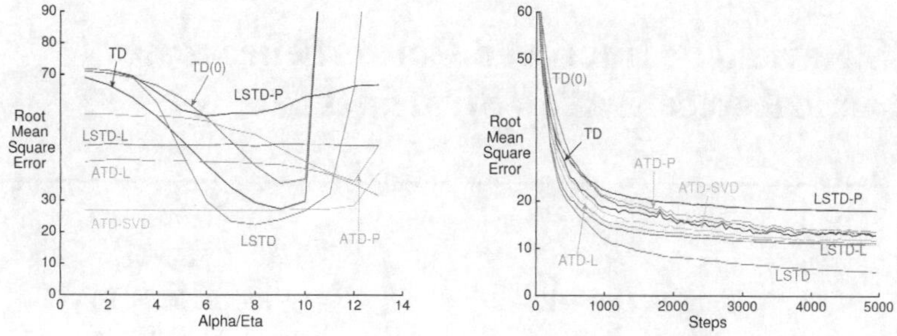

(a) Puddle World, tile coding, $k = 50$ (b) Puddle World, RBF, $k = 50$

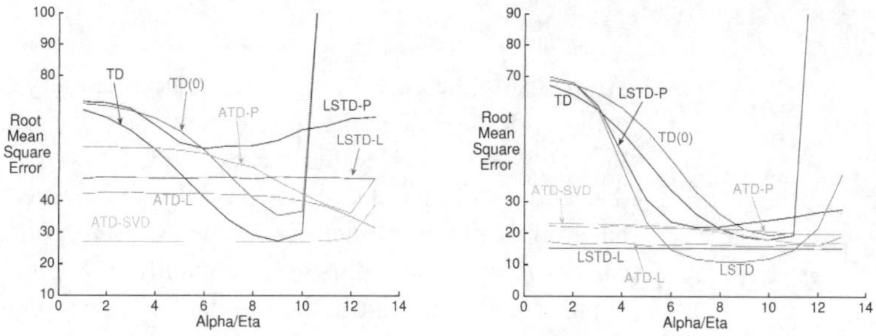

(c) Puddle World, tile coding, $k = 50$ (d) Puddle World, RBF, $k = 50$

Figure 6: The two sensitivity figures are corresponding to the above two learning curves on Puddle World domain. Note that we sweep initialization for LSTD-P, but keep initialization parameter fixed across all other settings. The one-side projection is almost insensitive to initialization and the corresponding ATD version is insensitive to regularization. Though ATD-SVD also shows insensitivity, performance of ATD-SVD is much worse than sketching methods for the RBF representation. And, one should note that ATD-SVD is also much slower as shown in the below figures.

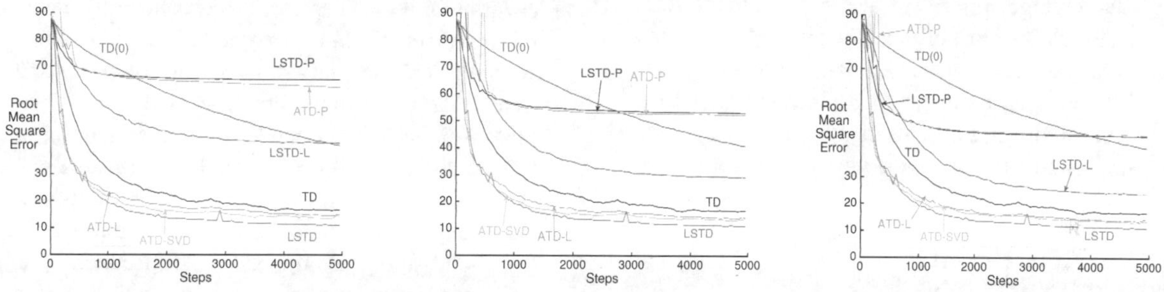

(a) Mountain Car, Tile coding, $k = 25$ (b) Mountain Car, Tile coding, $k = 50$ (c) Mountain Car, Tile coding, $k = 75$

Figure 7: Change in performance when increasing k, from 25 to 75. We can draw similar conclusions to the same experiments in Puddle World in the main text. Here, the unbiased of ATD-L is even more evident; even with as low a dimension as 25, it performs similarly to LSTD.

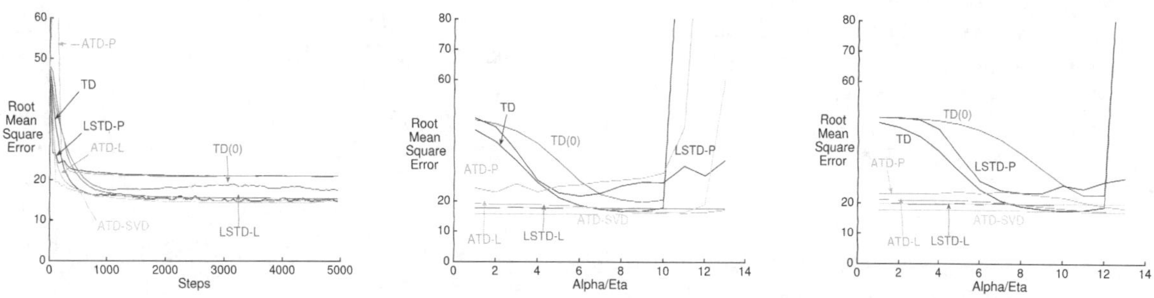

(a) Acrobot, tile coding, $k = 50$ (b) Acrobot, tile coding, $k = 50$ (c) Acrobot, RBF, $k = 75$

Figure 8: Additional experiments in Acrobot, for tile coding with $k = 50$ and for RBFs with $k = 75$.

Stochastic L-BFGS Revisited: Improved Convergence Rates and Practical Acceleration Strategies

Renbo Zhao
Dept. ECE, ISEM & Math
National University of Singapore
elezren@nus.edu.sg

William B. Haskell
Dept. ISEM
National University of Singapore
isehwb@nus.edu.sg

Vincent Y. F. Tan
Dept. ECE & Math
National University of Singapore
vtan@nus.edu.sg

Abstract

We revisit the stochastic limited-memory BFGS (L-BFGS) algorithm. By proposing a new framework for analyzing convergence, we theoretically improve the (linear) convergence rates and computational complexities of the stochastic L-BFGS algorithms in previous works. In addition, we propose several practical acceleration strategies to speed up the empirical performance of such algorithms. We also provide theoretical analyses for most of the strategies. Experiments on large-scale logistic and ridge regression problems demonstrate that our proposed strategies yield significant improvements via-à-vis competing state-of-the-art algorithms.

1 INTRODUCTION

In this work, we are interested in the following (unconstrained) convex finite-sum minimization problem

$$\min_{\mathbf{x}\in\mathbb{R}^d} \left[f(\mathbf{x}) \triangleq \frac{1}{n}\sum_{i=1}^{n} f_i(\mathbf{x}) \right], \tag{1}$$

where d and n denote the dimension of decision vector and the number of component functions respectively. Problems in the form of (1) play important roles in machine learning and signal processing. One important class of such problems is the *empirical risk minimization* (ERM) problem, where each f_i assumes the form

$$f_i(\mathbf{x}) \triangleq \ell(\mathbf{a}_i^T\mathbf{x}, b_i) + \lambda R(\mathbf{x}). \tag{2}$$

In (2), $\ell : \mathbb{R}\times\mathbb{R} \to \mathbb{R}_+$ denotes a smooth loss function, $R : \mathbb{R}^d \to \mathbb{R}_+$ a smooth convex regularizer (e.g., Tikhonov), $\lambda \geq 0$ the regularization weight and $\{(\mathbf{a}_i, b_i)\}_{i=1}^n \subseteq \mathbb{R}^{d+1}$ the set of feature-response pairs. Depending on the form of ℓ and R, many important machine learning problems are special cases of ERM, such as logistic regression, ridge regression and soft-margin support vector machine.

We focus on the case where both n and d are large, and f is ill-conditioned (i.e., the condition number of f is large).[1] In the context of ERM, this means the dataset $\{(\mathbf{a}_i, b_i)\}_{i=1}^n$ that defines (1) has large size and the feature vectors $\mathbf{a}_i$ have high ambient dimension. However, the points typically belong to a low-dimensional manifold. Such a setting is particularly relevant in the big-data era, due to unprecedented data acquisition abilities.

When n is large, the computational cost incurred by the batch optimization methods (both first- and second-order) are prohibitive. Therefore, stochastic (randomized) optimization methods have become very popular in this setting. At each iteration, only a subset of component functions, rather than all of them, are processed. In this way, much more progress can be made towards global optima in the time that only allows batch methods to take a single step. When d is large, Newton- or quasi-Newton-based methods (both batch and stochastic) incur both high computational and storage complexities. Consequently only first-order and limited-memory quasi-newton methods (e.g., L-BFGS (Liu and Nocedal, 1989)) are feasible in this setting.

When both n and d are large, as in our setting, most of research efforts have been devoted to *stochastic first-order methods*, which include stochastic gradient descent (SGD) (Bottou, 1998; Bottou and LeCun, 2004) and its variance-reduced modifications (Defazio et al., 2014; Harikandeh et al., 2015; Johnson and Zhang, 2013; Schmidt et al., 2017). However, these methods do not make use of the curvature information. This limits their abilities to find highly accurate solutions for ill-conditioned problems. In order to incorporate the curvature information in the limited-memory setting, recently much progress have been made toward developing *stochastic L-BFGS* algorithm. A partial list of such works includes Bordes et al. (2009); Byrd et al. (2016); Gower et al. (2016); Mokhtari and Ribeiro (2015); Moritz et al. (2016); Schraudolph et al. (2007); Sohl-Dickstein et al. (2014). Among them, the SQN method (Byrd et al., 2016) innovatively makes use of

[1]In this work, the condition number of a (strongly) convex function refers to that of its Hessian.

the subsampled Hessian-vector products to form the correction pairs (as opposed to using difference of stochastic gradients) and achieves better results than previous methods. However, the convergence rate is sublinear (in the strongly-convex case), similar to that of SGD. Later, Moritz et al. (2016) combines this method with *stochastic variance-reduced gradient* (SVRG) and proves linear convergence of the resulting algorithm. Gower et al. (2016) maintains the structure of this algorithm but incorporates the *block BFGS update* to collect more curvature information in the optimization process. Although the convergence rate of this new method remains similar to that in Moritz et al. (2016), experimental results have demonstrated practical speedup introduced by the block BFGS update.

1.1 MOTIVATIONS AND CONTRIBUTIONS

Our work can be motivated from both theory and practice. In terms of theory, although linear convergence has been shown for both algorithms in Moritz et al. (2016) and Gower et al. (2016), the convergence rates (and hence computational complexities) therein can be potentially further improved.[2] In terms of practice, in addition to block BFGS update, there may exist several other practical strategies that can potentially further accelerate[3] the algorithm in Moritz et al. (2016). Based on these two aspects, our work makes the following contributions.

1) We propose a *coordinate transformation framework* to analyze the stochastic L-BFGS-type algorithms in Moritz et al. (2016) and Gower et al. (2016). Our framework yields a much improved convergence rate and computational complexity. Indeed, our approach can be applied to many other *stochastic second-order algorithms* as well (e.g., SQN algorithm in Byrd et al. (2016)); thus it has great generalizability and wide potential impacts. The essential idea of our method is to unify the analysis of stochastic first-order and second-order method, as a result, it *opens new avenues of designing and analyzing* other variants of stochastic second-order algorithms based on their first-order counterparts. Among these variants, two important examples include proximal (quasi-)Newton methods and momentum-based accelerated (quasi-)Newton methods.

2) We derive *two novel technical lemmas* on variance bound of stochastic gradient with *nonuniform mini-batch sampling* and spectral bound of the sequence of metric matrices $\{\mathbf{H}_r\}_{r\geq 0}$ in stochastic L-BFGS algorithms. These two lemmas are of independent interest. For example, the lemma on the spectral bound is equally applicable to batch L-BFGS algorithms.

3) We conduct a *systematic computational complexity analysis* for the stochastic L-BFGS algorithms. To the best of our knowledge, such an analysis is among the first for stochastic L-BFGS methods. Similar to our convergence analysis framework, our complexity analysis method can be easily generalized to other stochastic (quasi-)Newton methods as well.

4) We propose *several practical acceleration strategies* to speed up the convergence of the stochastic L-BFGS algorithm in Moritz et al. (2016). We demonstrate the efficacy of our strategies through numerical experiments on logistic and ridge regression problems. Theoretically, we also prove linear convergence for most strategies.

2 PRELIMINARIES

Notations. We use lowercase, bold lowercase and bold uppercase letters to denote scalars, vectors and matrices respectively. For a matrix $\mathbf{U} \in \mathbb{R}^{m_1 \times m_0}$, we denotes its (p, q)-th entry as u_{pq}. For a function $f : \mathbb{R}^{m_1} \to \mathbb{R}^{m_2}$, define a function $f \circ \mathbf{U}$ such that $(f \circ \mathbf{U})(\mathbf{z}) \triangleq f(\mathbf{U}\mathbf{z})$, for any $\mathbf{z} \in \mathbb{R}^{m_0}$. We use $\mathbb{N}$ to denote the set of natural numbers excluding zero. For any $n \in \mathbb{N}$, we define $[n] \triangleq \{1, \ldots, n\}$ and $(n) \triangleq \{0, 1, \ldots, n\}$. Accordingly, define $\mathcal{A}_{(n)} \triangleq \{\mathcal{A}_0, \ldots, \mathcal{A}_n\}$. We use $\|\cdot\|$ to denote both the ℓ_2 norm of a vector and the spectral norm of a matrix. We use $\mathbf{B}$ and $\mathbf{H}$ (with subscripts and superscripts) to denote the approximate Hessian and approximate inverse Hessian in L-BFGS algorithms respectively, following the convention in Nocedal and Wright (2006). $\mathbf{H}$ is also known as the *metric matrix* (Goldfarb, 1970). Sections and lemmas with indices beginning with 'S' will appear in the supplemental material.

Assumptions. We make two blanket assumptions on the component functions $\{f_i\}_{i\in[n]}$.

Assumption 1. *For each $i \in [n]$, f_i is convex and twice differentiable on $\mathbb{R}^d$. For ERM problems* (2), *we assume these two properties are satisfied by the loss function ℓ in its first argument on $\mathbb{R}$ and by the regularizer R on $\mathbb{R}^d$.*

Assumption 2. *For each $i \in [n]$, f_i is μ_i-strongly convex and L_i-smooth on $\mathbb{R}^d$, where $0 < \mu_i \leq L_i$.*

Remark 1. Assumptions 1 and 2 are standard in the analysis of second-order optimization methods, for both deterministic and stochastic cases. The strong convexity of f_i in Assumption 2 ensures *positive* curvature at any point in $\mathbb{R}^d$, which in turn guarantees the well-definedness of the BFGS update. As a common practice in the literature (Byrd et al., 2016; Moritz et al., 2016), this condition can typically be enforced by adding a strongly convex regularizer (e.g., Tikhonov) to f_i. Due to the strong convexity, (1) has a unique solution, denoted as $\mathbf{x}^*$.

[2] The analysis method in Gower et al. (2016) mainly follows that in Moritz et al. (2016), so we treat the analyses in both works in a unified manner.

[3] In this work, we refer "acceleration" to general strategies that speed up the algorithm, not necessarily the ones based on momentum methods.

3 ALGORITHM

We present the pseudo-code of the algorithm in Moritz et al. (2016) in Algorithm 1. (Our acceleration strategies for this algorithm will be shown and discussed in Section 6.) In this algorithm, s denotes the outer iteration index, t the inner iteration index and r the index of metric matrices $\{\mathbf{H}_r\}_{r\geq 0}$. We use $\mathbf{x}_{s,t}$ and $\mathbf{x}^s$ to denote an inner iterate and outer iterate respectively. Each outer iteration consists of m inner iterations. The only modification that we make on the original algorithm in Moritz et al. (2016) is sampling the index set $\mathcal{B}_{s,t} \subseteq [n]$ of size b with replacement *nonuniformly*. Specifically, the elements in $\mathcal{B}_{s,t}$ are sampled i.i.d. from a discrete distribution $P \triangleq (p_1, \ldots, p_n)$, such that for any $i \in [n]$, $p_i = L_i / \sum_{i=1}^n L_i$. As will be seen in Lemma 3, compared to uniform sampling, nonuniform sampling leads to a better variance bound on the stochastic gradient $\mathbf{v}_{s,t}$. Using $\mathcal{B}_{s,t}$ and $\nabla f(\mathbf{x}^s)$, we then compute $\mathbf{v}_{s,t}$ according to (5) in Algorithm 1, where for any $\mathbf{x} \in \mathbb{R}^d$,

$$\nabla f_{\mathcal{B}_{s,t}}(\mathbf{x}) \triangleq \frac{1}{b} \sum_{i\in\mathcal{B}_{s,t}} \frac{1}{np_i} \nabla f_i(\mathbf{x}). \tag{3}$$

Next we compute the search direction formed by the product of the metric matrix $\mathbf{H}_r$ and $\mathbf{v}_{s,t}$. In the limited-memory setting, we do not store $\mathbf{H}_r$, but only a set $\mathcal{H}_r$, which consists of $M' \triangleq \min\{r, M\}$ recent *correction pairs* $\{(\mathbf{s}_j, \mathbf{y}_j)\}_{j=r-M'+1}^r$. The correction pairs are constructed from the averaged past iterates $\{\overline{\mathbf{x}}_r\}_{r\geq 0}$ (defined in line 13), and thus contains the "smoothed" curvature information in recent iterates. Following Byrd et al. (2016), in computing $\mathbf{y}_r$, we first sample an index set $\mathcal{T}_r \subseteq [n]$ of size b_{H} uniformly without replacement, and then let $\mathbf{y}_r = \nabla^2 f_{\mathcal{T}_r}(\overline{\mathbf{x}}_r)\mathbf{s}_r$, where

$$\nabla^2 f_{\mathcal{T}_r}(\overline{\mathbf{x}}_r) \triangleq \frac{1}{b_{\mathrm{H}}} \sum_{i\in\mathcal{T}_r} \nabla^2 f_i(\overline{\mathbf{x}}_r), \tag{4}$$

denotes the sub-sampled Hessian at $\overline{\mathbf{x}}_r$.

In computing $\mathbf{H}_r\mathbf{v}_{s,t}$, a direct approach would be to compute $\mathbf{H}_r$ first and form the product. Computing $\mathbf{H}_r$ involves applying M' BFGS updates to the matrix $\mathbf{H}_r^{(r-M')} \triangleq (\mathbf{s}_r^T\mathbf{y}_r)/\|\mathbf{y}_r\|^2\,\mathbf{I}$ using $\{(\mathbf{s}_j, \mathbf{y}_j)\}_{j=r-M'+1}^r$. For each $k \in \{r - M' + 1, \ldots, r\}$, the update is

$$\mathbf{H}_r^{(k)} = \left(\mathbf{I} - \frac{\mathbf{y}_k {\mathbf{s}_k}^T}{{\mathbf{y}_k}^T \mathbf{s}_k}\right) \mathbf{H}_r^{(k-1)} \left(\mathbf{I} - \frac{\mathbf{s}_k {\mathbf{y}_k}^T}{{\mathbf{y}_k}^T \mathbf{s}_k}\right) + \frac{\mathbf{s}_k {\mathbf{s}_k}^T}{{\mathbf{y}_k}^T \mathbf{s}_k}.$$

Finally we set $\mathbf{H}_r = \mathbf{H}_r^{(r)}$. Instead of using this direct approach, we adopt the two-loop recursion algorithm (Nocedal and Wright, 2006, Algorithm 7.4) to compute $\mathbf{H}_r\mathbf{v}_{s,t}$ as a whole. This approach has the same effect as the direct one, but with much reduced computation.

At the end of each outer iteration, the starting point of next outer iteration, $\mathbf{x}^{s+1}$ is either uniformly sampled (option I) or averaged (option II) from all the past inner iterates $\{\mathbf{x}_{s,t}\}_{t\in[m]}$. As shown in Theorem 1, these two options can be analyzed in a unified manner.

Algorithm 1 Stochastic L-BFGS Algorithm with Nonuniform Mini-batch Sampling

1: **Input**: Initial decision vector $\mathbf{x}^0$, mini-batch sizes b and b_{H}, parameters m, M and Υ, step-size η, termination threshold ϵ
2: **Initialize** $s := 0$, $r := 0$, $\overline{\mathbf{x}}_0 = \mathbf{0}$, $\mathbf{H}_0 := \mathbf{I}$, $\mathcal{H}_0 := \emptyset$
3: **Repeat**
4: Compute a full gradient $\mathbf{g}_s \triangleq \nabla f(\mathbf{x}^s)$
5: $\mathbf{x}_{s,0} := \mathbf{x}^s$
6: **for** $t = 0, 1, \ldots, m-1$
7: Sample a set $\mathcal{B}_{s,t}$ with size b
8: Compute a variance-reduced gradient

$$\mathbf{v}_{s,t} := \nabla f_{\mathcal{B}_{s,t}}(\mathbf{x}_{s,t}) - \nabla f_{\mathcal{B}_{s,t}}(\mathbf{x}^s) + \mathbf{g}_s \tag{5}$$

9: Compute $\mathbf{H}_r\mathbf{v}_{s,t}$ from $\mathcal{H}_r$ and $\mathbf{v}_{s,t}$
10: $\mathbf{x}_{s,t+1} := \mathbf{x}_{s,t} - \eta\mathbf{H}_r\mathbf{v}_{s,t}$
11: **if** $sm + t > 0$ **and** $(sm + t) \equiv 0 \mod \Upsilon$
12: $r := r + 1$
13: $\overline{\mathbf{x}}_r := \frac{1}{\Upsilon}\sum_{l=t-\Upsilon+1}^t \mathbf{x}_{s,l}$
14: Sample a set $\mathcal{T}_r$ with size b_{H}
15: $\mathbf{s}_r := \overline{\mathbf{x}}_r - \overline{\mathbf{x}}_{r-1}$, $\mathbf{y}_r := \nabla^2 f_{\mathcal{T}_r}(\overline{\mathbf{x}}_r)\mathbf{s}_r$
16: Update $\mathcal{H}_r := \{(\mathbf{s}_j, \mathbf{y}_j)\}_{j=r-M'+1}$
17: **end if**
18: **end for**
19: **Option I**: Sample τ_s uniformly randomly from $[m]$ and set $\mathbf{x}^{s+1} := \mathbf{x}_{s,\tau_s}$
20: **Option II**: $\mathbf{x}^{s+1} := \frac{1}{m}\sum_{t=1}^m \mathbf{x}_{s,t}$
21: $s := s + 1$
22: **Until** $\left|f(\mathbf{x}^s) - f(\mathbf{x}^{s-1})\right| < \epsilon$
23: **Output**: $\mathbf{x}^s$

4 CONVERGENCE ANALYSIS

4.1 DEFINITIONS

Let $\{\underline{i}_j\}_{j\in[n]}$ and $\{\overline{i}_j\}_{j\in[n]}$ be permutations of $[n]$ such that $\mu_{\min} \triangleq \mu_{\underline{i}_1} \leq \cdots \leq \mu_{\underline{i}_n}$ and $L_{\overline{i}_1} \leq \cdots \leq L_{\overline{i}_n} \triangleq L_{\max}$. Given any $\widetilde{n} \in [n]$, define

$$\overline{\mu}_{\widetilde{n}} \triangleq \frac{1}{\widetilde{n}} \sum_{j=1}^{\widetilde{n}} \mu_{\underline{i}_j} \quad \text{and} \quad \overline{L}_{\widetilde{n}} \triangleq \frac{1}{\widetilde{n}} \sum_{j=n-\widetilde{n}+1}^{n} L_{\overline{i}_j}. \tag{6}$$

Accordingly, define $\kappa_{\max} \triangleq L_{\max}/\mu_{\min}$ and $\kappa_{\widetilde{n}} \triangleq \overline{L}_{\widetilde{n}}/\overline{\mu}_{\widetilde{n}}$. In particular, define $\overline{\mu} \triangleq \overline{\mu}_n$, $\overline{L} \triangleq \overline{L}_n$ and $\kappa \triangleq \overline{L}/\overline{\mu}$. We also define a filtration $\{\mathcal{F}_{s,t}\}_{s\geq 0, t\in(m-1)}$ such that $\mathcal{F}_{s,t}$ contains all the information up to the time (s, t). Formally, $\mathcal{F}_{s,t} \triangleq \sigma(\{\tau_j\}_{j=0}^{s-1} \cup \{\mathcal{B}_{i,j}\}_{i\in(s-1), j\in(m-1)} \cup \{\mathcal{B}_{s,j}\}_{j=0}^{t-1} \cup \{\mathcal{T}_j\}_{j=0}^{\lfloor (sm+t)/L \rfloor})$, where $\sigma\left(\{x_j\}_{j=1}^n\right)$ denotes the σ-algebra generated by random variables $\{x_j\}_{j=1}^n$. We also define $\mathcal{F}_s \triangleq \mathcal{F}_{s,0}$.

To introduce our coordinate transformation framework, we define some transforms of variables appearing in Algorithm 1. Specifically, for any $s, t, r \geq 0$, define $\widetilde{\mathbf{x}}_{s,t,r} \triangleq \mathbf{H}_r^{-1/2}\mathbf{x}_{s,t}$, $\widetilde{\mathbf{x}}^{s,r} \triangleq \mathbf{H}_r^{-1/2}\mathbf{x}^s$, $\widetilde{\mathbf{x}}_r^* \triangleq \mathbf{H}_r^{-1/2}\mathbf{x}^*$ and $\widetilde{\mathbf{v}}_{s,t,r} \triangleq \mathbf{H}_r^{1/2}\mathbf{v}_{s,t}$.[4] We also define transformed functions $\widetilde{f}_{i,r} \triangleq f_i \circ \mathbf{H}_r^{1/2}$ and $\widetilde{f}_r \triangleq \frac{1}{n}\sum_{i=1}^n \widetilde{f}_{i,r}$, for any $i \in [n]$ and $r \geq 0$.

4.2 PRELIMINARY LEMMAS

From the definitions of transformed variables and functions in Section 4.1, we immediately have the following lemmas.

Lemma 1. *For any $s, t, r \geq 0$ and $i \in [n]$, we have*

$$\widetilde{f}_{i,r}(\widetilde{\mathbf{x}}_{s,t,r}) = f_i(\mathbf{x}_{s,t}), \tag{7}$$

$$\nabla \widetilde{f}_{i,r}(\widetilde{\mathbf{x}}_{s,t,r}) = \mathbf{H}_r^{1/2}\nabla f_i(\mathbf{x}_{s,t}), \tag{8}$$

$$\nabla^2 \widetilde{f}_{i,r}(\widetilde{\mathbf{x}}_{s,t,r}) = \mathbf{H}_r^{1/2}\nabla f_i(\mathbf{x}_{s,t})\mathbf{H}_r^{1/2}. \tag{9}$$

Lemma 2. *If there exist $0 < \gamma' \leq \Gamma'$ such that $\gamma'\mathbf{I} \preceq \mathbf{H}_r \preceq \Gamma'\mathbf{I}$ for all $r \geq 0$, then for any $i \in [n]$ and $r \geq 0$, $\widetilde{f}_{i,r}$ is twice differentiable, $(\mu_i\gamma')$-strongly convex and $(L_i\Gamma')$-smooth on $\mathbb{R}^d$. Consequently, $\widetilde{f}_r$ is twice differentiable, $(\gamma'\overline{\mu})$-strongly convex and $(\Gamma'\overline{L})$-smooth on $\mathbb{R}^d$.*

Next we derive two other lemmas that will not only be used in the analysis later, but have potential to be applied to more general problem settings. Specifically, Lemma 3 can be applied to any stochastic optimization algorithms based on SVRG and Lemma 4 can be applied to any finite-sum minimization algorithms based on L-BFGS methods (not necessarily stochastic in nature). The proofs for Lemmas 3 and 4 are deferred to Sections S-3 and S-4 respectively.

Lemma 3 (Variance bound of $\mathbf{v}_{s,t}$). *In Algorithm 1, we have $\mathbb{E}_{\mathcal{B}_{s,t}}[\mathbf{v}_{s,t}|\mathcal{F}_{s,t}] = \nabla f(\mathbf{x}_{s,t})$ and*

$$\mathbb{E}_{\mathcal{B}_{s,t}}\left[\|\mathbf{v}_{s,t} - \nabla f(\mathbf{x}_{s,t})\|^2 |\mathcal{F}_{s,t}\right] \leq \frac{4\overline{L}}{b}\left(f(\mathbf{x}_{s,t}) - f(\mathbf{x}^*) + f(\mathbf{x}^s) - f(\mathbf{x}^*)\right). \tag{10}$$

Remark 2. In previous works (Gower et al., 2016; Moritz et al., 2016), a uniform mini-batch sampling of $\mathcal{B}_{s,t}$ was employed, and different variance bounds of $\mathbf{v}_{s,t}$ were derived. In Moritz et al. (2016, Lemma 6), the bound was

$$4L_{\max}\left(f(\mathbf{x}_{s,t}) - f(\mathbf{x}^*) + f(\mathbf{x}^s) - f(\mathbf{x}^*)\right). \tag{11}$$

In Gower et al. (2016, Lemma 2), this bound was slightly improved to be

$$4L_{\max}((f(\mathbf{x}_{s,t}) - f(\mathbf{x}^*)) + (1 - 1/\kappa_{\max})(f(\mathbf{x}^s) - f(\mathbf{x}^*))). \tag{12}$$

However, both of these bounds fail to capture the dependence on the mini-batch size b. In contrast, in this work we consider a nonuniform mini-batch sampling (with replacement). Due to division by b and $\overline{L} \leq L_{\max}$ (indeed in many cases, $\overline{L} \ll L_{\max}$), our bound in (10) is much superior to (11) and (12). As will be seen in Theorem 1, our better bound (10) leads to a faster (linear) convergence rate of Algorithm 1.

Lemma 4 (Uniform Spectral Bound of $\{\mathbf{H}_r\}_{r\geq 0}$). *The spectra of $\{\mathbf{H}_r\}_{r\geq 0}$ are uniformly bounded, i.e., for each $r \geq 0$, $\gamma\mathbf{I} \preceq \mathbf{H}_r \preceq \Gamma\mathbf{I}$, where*[5]

$$\gamma \triangleq \frac{1}{(M+1)\overline{L}_{b_{\mathrm{H}}}} \quad \text{and} \quad \Gamma \triangleq \frac{\kappa_{b_{\mathrm{H}}}^{M+1}}{\overline{\mu}_{b_{\mathrm{H}}}(\kappa_{b_{\mathrm{H}}} - 1)}. \tag{13}$$

Remark 3. In Byrd et al. (2016) and Moritz et al. (2016), the authors make use of a classical technique in Liu and Nocedal (1989) to derive a different uniform spectral bound of $\{\mathbf{H}_r\}_{r\geq 0}$. Their technique involves applying $\mathrm{tr}(\cdot)$ and $\det(\cdot)$ recursively to the BFGS update rule

$$\mathbf{B}_r^{(k)} = \mathbf{B}_r^{(k-1)} - \frac{\mathbf{B}_r^{(k-1)}\mathbf{s}_k\mathbf{s}_k{}^T\mathbf{B}_r^{(k-1)}}{\mathbf{s}_k{}^T\mathbf{B}_r^{(k-1)}\mathbf{s}_k} + \frac{\mathbf{y}_k\mathbf{y}_k^T}{\mathbf{s}_k^T\mathbf{y}_k}, \tag{14}$$

where $\mathbf{B}_r^{(k)} \triangleq (\mathbf{H}_r^{(k)})^{-1}$ denotes the approximate Hessian matrix at step k in the reconstruction of $\mathbf{B}_r \triangleq (\mathbf{H}_r)^{-1}$. The lower and upper bounds derived by this technique are

$$\widetilde{\gamma} = \frac{1}{(d+M)L_{\max}} \quad \text{and} \quad \widetilde{\Gamma} = (d+M)^{d+M-1}\frac{\kappa_{\max}^{d+M-1}}{\mu_{\min}}$$

respectively. As will be seen in Proposition 1, the overall computational complexity of Algorithm 1 heavily depends on the estimated (uniform) condition number of $\{\mathbf{H}_r\}_{r\geq 0}$. Therefore, it is instructive to compute this quantity for both (γ, Γ) and $(\widetilde{\gamma}, \widetilde{\Gamma})$ as

$$\kappa_{\mathrm{H}} \triangleq \frac{\Gamma}{\gamma} = (M+1)\frac{\kappa_{b_{\mathrm{H}}}^{M+2}}{\kappa_{b_{\mathrm{H}}} - 1} \approx (M+1)\kappa_{b_{\mathrm{H}}}^{M+1}, \tag{15}$$

$$\widetilde{\kappa}_{\mathrm{H}} \triangleq \frac{\widetilde{\Gamma}}{\widetilde{\gamma}} = (M+d)^{M+d}\kappa_{\max}^{M+d}, \tag{16}$$

where the approximation in (15) follows from $\kappa_{b_{\mathrm{H}}} \gg 1$ (see Footnote 5). By comparing (15) and (16), we notice our estimate for the condition number of $\{\mathbf{H}_r\}_{r\geq 0}$, namely κ_{H}, is smaller than those in Byrd et al. (2016) and Moritz et al. (2016), namely $\widetilde{\kappa}_{\mathrm{H}}$, in several aspects. First, κ_{H} does not grow (exponentially) with the data dimension d. Second, κ_{H} depends on $\kappa_{b_{\mathrm{H}}}$, which is usually much smaller than $\kappa_{\max}$. Third, even if we set $d = 1$ in (16), the factor $M+1$ in (15) is much smaller than the factor $(M+1)^{M+1}$ in (16). As a result, our improved estimate of the condition number of $\{\mathbf{H}_r\}_{r\geq 0}$ will lead to a much better computational complexity estimate (see Proposition 1).

[4] As will be shown in Lemma 4, for any $r \geq 0$, $\mathbf{H}_r \succeq \gamma\mathbf{I}$ for some $\gamma > 0$. Therefore, $\mathbf{H}_r^{1/2}$ (and $\mathbf{H}_r^{-1/2}$) are well-defined.

[5] We assume $\kappa_{b_{\mathrm{H}}} > 1$ for any $b_{\mathrm{H}} \in [n]$ since we focus on the setting where f is ill-conditioned, i.e., $\kappa_{b_{\mathrm{H}}} \geq \kappa \gg 1$. If $\kappa_{b_{\mathrm{H}}} = 1$ for some $b_{\mathrm{H}} \in [n]$, then $\Gamma = (\kappa_{b_{\mathrm{H}}}^M + M)/\overline{\mu}_{b_{\mathrm{H}}}$ and γ remains the same. The proof for this case can be straightforwardly adapted from that in Section S-4.

4.3 MAIN RESULT

Theorem 1 presents our main convergence result. For the complete proof, we refer readers to Section S-2.

Theorem 1. *In Algorithm 1, if we choose* $\eta < \min\{b/12, 1\}/(\Gamma\overline{L})$ *and* m *sufficiently large, then with either option I or II, we have*

$$\mathbb{E}\left[f(\mathbf{x}^s) - f(\mathbf{x}^*)\right] \leq \rho^s \left(f(\mathbf{x}^0) - f(\mathbf{x}^*)\right), \text{ where} \quad (17)$$

$$\rho = \frac{b}{\gamma\overline{\mu}m\eta(b - 4\eta\Gamma\overline{L})} + \frac{4\eta\Gamma\overline{L}}{b - 4\eta\Gamma\overline{L}}\left(1 + \frac{1}{m}\right) < 1. \quad (18)$$

Remark 4. We compare our linear convergence rate ρ in (18) with those in Moritz et al. (2016) and Gower et al. (2016). Since the convergence rates in these two works are almost the same, we use the rate in Moritz et al. (2016) for comparison. The linear rate $\widetilde{\rho}$ in Moritz et al. (2016) equals

$$\frac{1}{2\widetilde{\gamma}\mu_{\min}m\eta(1 - \eta\widetilde{\Gamma}L_{\max}\kappa_{\max}\widetilde{\kappa}_{\mathrm{H}})} + \frac{\eta\widetilde{\Gamma}L_{\max}\kappa_{\max}\widetilde{\kappa}_{\mathrm{H}}}{1 - \eta\widetilde{\Gamma}L_{\max}\kappa_{\max}\widetilde{\kappa}_{\mathrm{H}}}.$$

For simplicity, if we let $b = 1$, $\mu_{\min} = \overline{\mu}$, $L_{\max} = \overline{L}$, $\widetilde{\gamma} = \gamma$, $\widetilde{\Gamma} = \Gamma$ and ignore other constant factors,[6] we notice that there is an additional multiplicative factor $\kappa\kappa_{\mathrm{H}}$ associated with $\eta\Gamma\overline{L}$ in $\widetilde{\rho}$. As a result $\widetilde{\rho} > \rho$. A more direct way to observe the detrimental effects of this additional $\kappa\kappa_{\mathrm{H}}$ is to compare the computational complexities resulting from ρ and $\widetilde{\rho}$. See Remark 6 for details. The reason that we manage to avoid this factor in our rate ρ is precisely because we adopt the *coordinate transformation framework* in our analysis (see proof sketch below). Specifically, by absorbing the sequence of metric matrices $\{\mathbf{H}_r\}_{r\geq 0}$ into decision vectors and functions, we are able to proceed through bounding the (expected squared Euclidean) distance between $\widetilde{\mathbf{x}}_{s,t+1,r}$ and $\widetilde{\mathbf{x}}_r^*$, instead of directly bounding $f(\mathbf{x}_{s,t+1})$ via the smoothness property of f (cf. proof of Theorem 7 in Moritz et al. (2016)). Thus in our analysis, we avoid the additional appearance of $\overline{L}$ and Γ (which leads to the additional factor $\kappa\kappa_{\mathrm{H}}$).

Proof Sketch. Fix an outer iteration s and consider an inner iteration t. Define $r \triangleq \lfloor (sm + t)/L \rfloor$,[7] then the iteration in (10) becomes

$$\widetilde{\mathbf{x}}_{s,t+1,r} = \widetilde{\mathbf{x}}_{s,t,r} - \eta\widetilde{\mathbf{v}}_{s,t,r}. \quad (19)$$

From Lemmas 1, 3 and 4, we have $\mathbb{E}_{\mathcal{B}_{s,t}}\left[\widetilde{\mathbf{v}}_{s,t,r} \middle| \mathcal{F}_{s,t}\right] = \nabla\widetilde{f}_r(\widetilde{\mathbf{x}}_{s,t,r})$ and

$$\mathbb{E}_{\mathcal{B}_{s,t}}\left[\|\widetilde{\mathbf{v}}_{s,t,r} - \nabla\widetilde{f}_r(\widetilde{\mathbf{x}}_{s,t,r})\|^2 \middle| \mathcal{F}_{s,t}\right] \leq \frac{4\Gamma\overline{L}}{b}(\widetilde{f}_r(\widetilde{\mathbf{x}}_{s,t,r}) - \widetilde{f}_r(\widetilde{\mathbf{x}}_r^*) + \widetilde{f}_{r'}(\widetilde{\mathbf{x}}^{s,r'}) - \widetilde{f}_{r'}(\widetilde{\mathbf{x}}_{r'}^*)), \quad (20)$$

where $r' \triangleq \lfloor sm/L \rfloor$. Define $\widetilde{\boldsymbol{\delta}}_{s,t,r} \triangleq \widetilde{\mathbf{v}}_{s,t,r} - \nabla\widetilde{f}_r(\widetilde{\mathbf{x}}_{s,t,r})$. Using $\eta \leq 1/(\Gamma\overline{L})$ and Lemma 2, we are able to show that

$$\|\widetilde{\mathbf{x}}_{s,t+1,r} - \widetilde{\mathbf{x}}_r^*\|^2 \leq \|\widetilde{\mathbf{x}}_{s,t,r} - \widetilde{\mathbf{x}}_r^*\|^2 - 2\eta(\widetilde{f}_r(\widetilde{\mathbf{x}}_{s,t+1,r}) - \widetilde{f}_r(\widetilde{\mathbf{x}}_r^*)) + 2\eta^2\|\widetilde{\boldsymbol{\delta}}_{s,t,r}\|^2 - 2\eta\left\langle\widetilde{\boldsymbol{\delta}}_{s,t,r}, \widetilde{\mathbf{x}}_{s,t,r} - \widetilde{\mathbf{x}}_r^*\right\rangle.$$

Taking expectation w.r.t. $\mathcal{B}_{s,t}$ and using (S-8), we have

$$\mathbb{E}_{\mathcal{B}_{s,t}}\left[\|\widetilde{\mathbf{x}}_{s,t+1,r} - \widetilde{\mathbf{x}}_r^*\|^2 + 2\eta(\widetilde{f}_r(\widetilde{\mathbf{x}}_{s,t+1,r}) - \widetilde{f}_r(\widetilde{\mathbf{x}}_r^*))\middle|\mathcal{F}_{s,t}\right] \leq \|\widetilde{\mathbf{x}}_{s,t,r} - \widetilde{\mathbf{x}}_r^*\|^2 + \frac{8}{b}\Gamma\overline{L}\eta^2(\widetilde{f}_r(\widetilde{\mathbf{x}}_{s,t,r}) - \widetilde{f}_r(\widetilde{\mathbf{x}}_r^*) + \widetilde{f}_{r'}(\widetilde{\mathbf{x}}^{s,r'}) - \widetilde{f}_{r'}(\widetilde{\mathbf{x}}_{r'}^*)). \quad (21)$$

Telescoping (S-20) over $t \in (0, m-1]$ and noting that both options I and II in Algorithm 1 yield

$$\frac{1}{m}\sum_{t=1}^{m}\mathbb{E}_{\mathcal{B}_{s,(t-1)}}\left[\widetilde{f}_r(\widetilde{\mathbf{x}}_{s,t,r}) - \widetilde{f}_r(\widetilde{\mathbf{x}}_r^*)\middle|\mathcal{F}_{s,t-1}\right] \geq \mathbb{E}_{\mathcal{B}_{s,(m-1)}}\left[\widetilde{f}_{r''}(\widetilde{\mathbf{x}}^{s+1,r''}) - \widetilde{f}_{r''}(\widetilde{\mathbf{x}}_{r''}^*)\middle|\mathcal{F}_s\right], \quad (22)$$

where $r'' \triangleq \lfloor (s+1)m/L \rfloor$, we have

$$2m\eta(1 - \frac{4}{b}\Gamma\overline{L}\eta)\mathbb{E}_{\mathcal{B}_{s,(m-1)}}\left[\widetilde{f}_{r''}(\widetilde{\mathbf{x}}^{s+1,r''}) - \widetilde{f}_{r''}(\widetilde{\mathbf{x}}_{r''}^*)\middle|\mathcal{F}_s\right] \leq \|\widetilde{\mathbf{x}}^{s,r'} - \widetilde{\mathbf{x}}_{r'}^*\|^2 + \frac{8}{b}\Gamma\overline{L}\eta^2(1+m)(\widetilde{f}_{r'}(\widetilde{\mathbf{x}}^{s,r'}) - \widetilde{f}_{r'}(\widetilde{\mathbf{x}}_{r'}^*)).$$

Using $(\gamma\overline{\mu})$-strong convexity of $\widetilde{f}_{r'}$, we can derive the bound $\|\widetilde{\mathbf{x}}^{s,r'} - \widetilde{\mathbf{x}}_{r'}^*\|^2 \leq \frac{2}{\gamma\overline{\mu}}(\widetilde{f}_{r'}(\widetilde{\mathbf{x}}^{s,r'}) - \widetilde{f}_{r'}(\widetilde{\mathbf{x}}_{r'}^*))$. Finally, using Lemma 1 and rearranging, we have

$$\mathbb{E}\left[f(\mathbf{x}^{s+1}) - f(\mathbf{x}^*)\middle|\mathcal{F}_s\right] \leq \rho(f(\mathbf{x}^s) - f(\mathbf{x}^*)). \quad (23)$$

Taking expectation on both sides, we reach (17). ☐

5 COMPLEXITY ANALYSIS

In this section we provide a systematic framework for analyzing the computational complexity of the stochastic L-BFGS algorithm in Algorithm 1. Note that our framework can be easily generalized to other stochastic second-order algorithms, e.g., SQN algorithm in Byrd et al. (2016). To begin with, we make two additional assumptions.

Assumption 3. *For any* $\mathbf{x} \in \mathbb{R}^d$ *and* $i \in [n]$, *the gradient* $\nabla f_i(\mathbf{x})$ *can be computed in* $O(d)$ *operations.*[8]

Assumption 4. *For any* $\mathbf{x}, \mathbf{y} \in \mathbb{R}^d$ *and* $i \in [n]$, *the Hessian-vector product* $\nabla^2 f_i(\mathbf{x})\mathbf{y}$ *can be computed in* $O(d)$ *operations.*

Remark 5. These two assumptions are naturally satisfied for ERM problems (2) with Tikhonov regularization. For these problems, $R(\mathbf{x}) = \frac{1}{2}\|\mathbf{x}\|^2$ and

$$\nabla\ell(\mathbf{a}_i^T\mathbf{x}, b_i) = \ell'(\mathbf{a}_i^T\mathbf{x}, b_i)\mathbf{a}_i + \lambda\mathbf{x}, \quad (24)$$

$$\nabla^2\ell(\mathbf{a}_i^T\mathbf{x}, b_i)\mathbf{y} = \ell''(\mathbf{a}_i^T\mathbf{x}, b_i)(\mathbf{a}_i^T\mathbf{y})\mathbf{a}_i + \lambda\mathbf{y}, \quad (25)$$

[6] However, bear in mind that by doing all these substitutions, $\widetilde{\rho}$ has already been much improved.

[7] To avoid cluttered notations, we omit showing the dependence of r on s and t.

[8] An operation refers to evaluation of an elementary function, such as addition, multiplication and logarithm.

where $\ell'(\cdot,\cdot)$ and $\ell''(\cdot,\cdot)$ are first and second derivatives of $\ell(\cdot,\cdot)$ w.r.t. the first argument. We easily see that the right-hand sides of both (24) and (25) can be computed in $O(d)$ operations.

From Algorithm 1, we observe that its total computational cost C can be split into three parts. The first part C_1 involves computing the variance-reduced gradient $\mathbf{v}_{s,t}$ in (5), the second part C_2 involves computing $\mathbf{H}_r\mathbf{v}_{s,t}$ (via two-loop recursion) in line 9, and the third part C_3 involves computing the correction pair $(\mathbf{s}_r, \mathbf{y}_r)$ in line 15.

Proposition 1. *Assume Assumptions 1 to 4. In Algorithm 1,*

$$C_1 = O\left((n + \kappa\kappa_{\mathrm{H}})d\log(1/\epsilon)\right), \tag{26}$$

$$C_2 = O\left(\kappa\kappa_{\mathrm{H}} d\log(1/\epsilon)\right), \tag{27}$$

$$C_3 = O\left(d\log(1/\epsilon)\right). \tag{28}$$

Thus the total computational cost $C \triangleq \sum_{i=1}^{3} C_i$ *equals*

$$O\left((n + \kappa\kappa_{\mathrm{H}})\, d\log(1/\epsilon)\right). \tag{29}$$

Proof. We leverage techniques that have become standard in the SVRG literature (e.g., Xiao and Zhang (2014)). In (18), if we choose $\eta = \theta b/(\Gamma\overline{L})$ for some $0 < \theta < 1/12$, $m = \theta'\kappa\kappa_{\mathrm{H}}/b$ for some sufficiently large positive constant θ', and use $1 + 1/m \le 2$, then $\rho = \frac{1}{\theta'\theta(1-4\theta)} + \frac{8\theta}{1-4\theta} < 1$. As a result, the required number of outer iterations to achieve ϵ-suboptimality is $O(\log(1/\epsilon))$. Thus (26) follows from Assumption 3 and that $2mb$ gradients (of component functions) are computed in each inner iteration. If we further choose $M = \Theta(b)$, then (27) follows from the fact that two-loop recursion can be done in $O(Md)$ time (Nocedal and Wright, 2006, Chapter 7). Lastly, if we choose $b_{\mathrm{H}} = \Theta(\Upsilon)$, then we obtain (28) using Assumption 4. □

Remark 6. Following a similar argument, we can deduce the total complexity estimate $\widetilde{C}$ based on the linear rate $\widetilde{\rho}$ (see Remark 4) derived in Moritz et al. (2016) as

$$\widetilde{C} = O\left(\left(n + b(\kappa_{\max}\widetilde{\kappa}_{\mathrm{H}})^2\right) d\log(1/\epsilon)\right). \tag{30}$$

Compared with $\widetilde{C}$, we observe that our complexity estimate C in (29) is much better, in several aspects. First, the dependence of C on the condition number $\kappa\kappa_{\mathrm{H}}$ is linear, rather than quadratic. The quadratic dependence of $\kappa_{\max}\widetilde{\kappa}_{\mathrm{H}}$ in $\widetilde{C}$ is precisely caused by the additional $\kappa_{\max}\widetilde{\kappa}_{\mathrm{H}}$ in $\widetilde{\rho}$ (see Remark 4). Second, C is independent of the minbatch size b. The appearance of b in $\widetilde{C}$ is a result of the loose bound on variance of $\mathbf{v}_{s,t}$ (cf. (11) and (12)). Third, the condition number $\kappa\kappa_{\mathrm{H}}$ in C is much more smaller than $\kappa_{\max}\widetilde{\kappa}_{\mathrm{H}}$ in $\widetilde{C}$ for ill-conditioned problems. This is a result of non-uniform sampling of $\mathcal{B}_{s,t}$ and our improved bound on the spectra of $\{\mathbf{H}_r\}_{r\ge 0}$ (see Lemma 4).

Remark 7. As our coordinate transformation framework unifies the design and analysis of stochastic first- and second-order algorithms, we believe that momentum-based acceleration techniques for stochastic first-order methods (Allen-Zhu, 2016; Lin et al., 2015) can be applied to Algorithm 1 as well. (Details are left to future work.) In this case, the dependence on $\kappa\kappa_{\mathrm{H}}$ in C may be further improved to $\sqrt{\kappa\kappa_{\mathrm{H}}}$ (Allen-Zhu, 2016).

6 ACCELERATION STRATEGIES

In this section, we propose three practical acceleration strategies. We follow the notations in Section 3 and Algorithm 1. As will be shown in Section 7.1, all of these strategies result in faster convergence in practice. For first and second strategies, we also provide their theoretical analyses in Propositions 2 and 3 respectively. See Sections S-5 and S-6 for the proofs of these two propositions.

6.1 GEOMETRIC SAMPLING AND AVERAGING

Instead of choosing $\mathbf{x}^{s+1}$ according to option I or II in Algorithm 1, inspired by Konečný and Richtárik (2013), we can introduce a "forgetting" effect by considering two other sampling or averaging schemes:

option III: Sample τ_s randomly from $[m]$ according to the distribution $Q \triangleq (\beta^{m-1}/c, \beta^{m-2}/c, \ldots, 1/c)$ and set $\mathbf{x}^{s+1} := \mathbf{x}_{s,\tau_s}$,

option IV: $\mathbf{x}^{s+1} := \frac{1}{c}\sum_{t=1}^{m}\beta^{m-t}\mathbf{x}_{s,t}$,

where $0 < \beta \le 1 - \eta\gamma\overline{\mu} < 1$ and the normalization constant $c \triangleq \sum_{t=1}^{m}\beta^{m-t}$. Since $\beta \in (0,1)$, we observe that in both options III and IV, more recent iterates (i.e., iterates $\mathbf{x}_{s,t}$ with larger indices t) will have larger contributions to $\mathbf{x}^{s+1}$. Theoretically, these two schemes can be analyzed in a unified manner, as shown in the following proposition.

Proposition 2. *In Algorithm 1, if we choose* $\eta < \min\{b/12, 1\}/(\Gamma\overline{L})$ *and* m *sufficiently large, then with either option III or IV, we have*

$$\mathbb{E}\left[f(\mathbf{x}^s) - f(\mathbf{x}^*)\right] \le \overline{\rho}^s\left(f(\mathbf{x}^0) - f(\mathbf{x}^*)\right), \text{ where} \tag{31}$$

$$\overline{\rho} \triangleq \frac{b}{\gamma\overline{\mu}c'\eta\left(b - 4\eta\Gamma\overline{L}/(1-\eta\gamma\overline{\mu})\right)} + \frac{4\eta\Gamma\overline{L}}{b - 4\eta\Gamma\overline{L}/(1-\eta\gamma\overline{\mu})}\left(1 + \frac{1}{c'}\right) < 1 \tag{32}$$

and $c' \triangleq c/(1-\eta\gamma\overline{\mu})^m$.

Remark 8. In the literature (Gower et al., 2016; Moritz et al., 2016), usually option I or II (in Algorithm 1) is analyzed theoretically to prove that the stochastic L-BFGS algorithms therein converge linearly. However, for faster convergence in practice, $\mathbf{x}^{s+1}$ is chosen to be the last inner iterate $\mathbf{x}_{s,m}$. However, the latter is not amenable to linear convergence analysis. This *gap between theory and practice* is filled in by our geometric sampling or averaging scheme, i.e., option III or IV. Specifically, as shown in

Figure 2, our scheme not only yields linear convergence in theory, but also performs as well as the "last inner iterate" scheme in practice.

6.2 SUBSAMPLED GRADIENT STABILIZATION

In Algorithm 1, at the beginning of each outer iteration s, we compute a full gradient $\mathbf{g}_s$ to stabilize the subsequent (inner) iterations. Inspired by Harikandeh et al. (2015), we propose a strategy that only computes a subsampled gradient $\widetilde{\mathbf{g}}_s$ at the start of each outer iteration s. Specifically, we uniformly sample a subset $\widetilde{\mathcal{B}}_s$ of $[n]$ with size $\widetilde{b}_s$ *without replacement* and then form $\widetilde{\mathbf{g}}_s \triangleq (1/\widetilde{b}_s)\sum_{i\in\widetilde{\mathcal{B}}_s}\nabla f_i(\mathbf{x}^s)$. The size of $\widetilde{\mathcal{B}}_s$, namely $\widetilde{b}_s$, increases with the index s until it reaches n. By judiciously choosing $\widetilde{b}_s$, we can show that the resulting algorithm still enjoys linear convergence with rate $\overline{\rho}$, when integrated with the geometric sampling/averaging scheme in Section 6.1. Before we formally state this result in Proposition 3, we first make an assumption in additional to Assumptions 1 and 2.

Assumption 5. *The inner iterates $\{\mathbf{x}_{s,t}\}_{s\geq 0,t\in[m]}$ generated by the modified algorithm in Section 6.2 are bounded almost surely, i.e., there exists $B<\infty$ such that for any $s\geq 0$ and $t\in[m]$, $\|\mathbf{x}_{s,t}-\mathbf{x}^*\|\leq B$.*

Proposition 3. *Let Assumptions 1, 2 and 5 hold. For any $\xi>0$ and $S\in\mathbb{N}$, and for any $s\in(S]$, if we choose $\widetilde{b}_s\geq\underline{b}_s\triangleq nS^2\alpha_s/(S^2\alpha_s+(n-1)\xi^2\overline{\rho}^{2s})$, where $\alpha_s\triangleq 1/n\sum_{i=1}^n\|\nabla f_i(\mathbf{x}^s)\|^2$, we have*

$$\mathbb{E}\left[f(\mathbf{x}^s)-f(\mathbf{x}^*)\right]\leq\overline{\rho}^s\Bigg\{\left(f(\mathbf{x}^0)-f(\mathbf{x}^*)\right)$$
$$+\left(1+\frac{1}{c'}\right)\frac{\xi b}{b-4\Gamma\overline{L}\eta/(1-\eta\gamma\overline{\mu})}\left(\kappa_{\mathrm{H}}^{1/2}B+\eta\Gamma\xi\right)\Bigg\}.$$

Remark 9. Several remarks are in order. First, we remark that assumptions involving almost sure boundedness of iterates (e.g., Assumption 5) have appeared many times in the literature of stochastic optimization (Borkar, 2008; Harikandeh et al., 2015; Hu et al., 2009) and are always observed to hold in our experiments. Second, under this assumption, we can show that $\{\alpha_s\}_{s\geq 0}$ are bounded almost surely using Lipschitz continuity of ∇f_i, for any $i\in[n]$ in Assumption 2. Consequently, there exists $B'<\infty$ such that $\alpha_s\leq B'$ for any $s\geq 0$ and hence

$$\underline{b}_s\leq\frac{nS^2B'}{S^2B'+(n-1)\xi^2\overline{\rho}^{2s}} \tag{33}$$
$$\leq\frac{nS^2B'}{(n-1)\xi^2}\left(\overline{\rho}^{-2}\right)^s. \tag{34}$$

As a sanity check, we observe that (33) increases to n as $s\to\infty$. By further upper bounding (33) by (34), we obtain a practical rule to select $\widetilde{b}_s$. Namely, it suffices to choose $\widetilde{b}_s=\min\{\zeta v^s,n\}$, for some constants $\zeta>0$ and $v>1$. As shown in Section 7, this rule works well in practice. Third, for any $\epsilon>0$, we can choose $S\in\mathbb{N}$ such that our algorithm achieves ϵ-suboptimality, i.e., $\mathbb{E}\left[f(\mathbf{x}^S)-f(\mathbf{x}^*)\right]<\epsilon$.

6.3 SMALL APPROXIMATE HESSIANS

In additional to high dimensionality and large size, *sparsity* is also a typical attribute for modern data, i.e., many feature vectors only have a few nonzero entries. For ERM problems (2) (with Tikhonov regularization), this implies that the Hessian of f in (1),

$$\nabla^2 f(\mathbf{x})=\frac{1}{n}\sum_{i=1}^n\ell''(\mathbf{a}_i^T\mathbf{x},b_i)(\mathbf{a}_i\mathbf{a}_i^T)+\lambda\mathbf{I}, \tag{35}$$

tends to be sparse. Based on this observation, we propose a strategy that aims to approximate $\nabla^2 f(\mathbf{x})$ by several smaller Hessian matrices and update them efficiently. For sparse data, collecting curvature information via smaller dense Hessians can be more effective than directly manipulating the high-dimensional sparse Hessian. As a result, the algorithm converges faster in practice (see Figure 4).

Before describing our strategy, we first introduce some notations. We partition $[n]$ into K groups, and denote the set of partitions as $\mathcal{P}\triangleq\{\mathcal{P}_1,\ldots,\mathcal{P}_K\}$. For any $i\in[K]$, we define $\mathcal{S}_i\triangleq\cup_{j\in\mathcal{P}_i}\operatorname{supp}(\mathbf{a}_j)$, where $\operatorname{supp}(\mathbf{a}_j)$ denotes the support of the vector $\mathbf{a}_j$. We define $d_i\triangleq|\mathcal{S}_i|$ and denote the elements in $\mathcal{S}_i$ as $\{s_{i,1},\ldots,s_{i,d_i}\}$. We also define $F_i=\sum_{j\in\mathcal{P}_i}f_j$ so that $f=\frac{1}{n}\sum_{i=1}^K F_i$. We define a *projection matrix* $\mathbf{U}_i\in\mathbb{R}^{d_i\times d}$ such that for any $p\in[d_i]$ and $q\in[d]$, $u_{pq}=1$ if $q=s_{i,p}$ and 0 otherwise. Accordingly, for any $l\in\mathcal{P}_i$, define a function $\phi_{i,l}:\mathbb{R}^{d_i}\to\mathbb{R}$ such that $f_l\triangleq\phi_{i,l}\circ\mathbf{U}_i$. Note that $\phi_{i,l}$ is uniquely defined by the definition $\mathbf{U}_i$. Also define $\phi_i\triangleq\sum_{l\in\mathcal{P}_i}\phi_{i,l}$. Therefore,

$$\nabla^2 f(\mathbf{x})=\frac{1}{n}\sum_{i=1}^K\mathbf{U}_i^T\nabla^2\phi_i(\mathbf{U}_i\mathbf{x})\mathbf{U}_i,\ \forall\mathbf{x}\in\mathbb{R}^d. \tag{36}$$

We now describe our strategy. In Algorithm 1, for any $i\in[K]$ and any $j\in\{r-M'+1,\ldots,r\}$, define correction pairs $\mathbf{s}_{j,i}\triangleq\mathbf{U}_i(\overline{\mathbf{x}}_j-\overline{\mathbf{x}}_{j-1})$ and $\mathbf{y}_{j,i}\triangleq\sum_{l\in\mathcal{T}_{r,i}}\nabla^2\phi_{i,l}(\mathbf{U}_i\overline{\mathbf{x}}_j)\mathbf{s}_{j,i}$, where $\mathcal{T}_{r,i}$ with size b_{H}/K is uniformly sampled from $\mathcal{P}_i$. Accordingly, define $\mathbf{S}_{r,i}\triangleq[\mathbf{s}_{r-M'+1,i},\ldots,\mathbf{s}_{r,i}]$, $\mathbf{Y}_{r,i}\triangleq[\mathbf{y}_{r-M'+1,i},\ldots,\mathbf{y}_{r,i}]$. Instead of storing $\mathcal{H}_r$, we only store matrices $\{(\mathbf{S}_{r,i},\mathbf{Y}_{r,i})\}_{i=1}^K$. To reconstruct approximation $\mathbf{B}_{r,i}$ for each $\nabla^2\phi_i$ at $\mathbf{U}_i\overline{\mathbf{x}}_r$, as usual, we apply M' BFGS updates (S-51) (using the correction pairs stored in $\mathbf{S}_{r,i}$ and $\mathbf{Y}_{r,i}$) to $\mathbf{B}_{r,i}^{(0)}\triangleq\delta_{r,i}\mathbf{I}$, where $\delta_{r,i}\triangleq\|\mathbf{y}_{r,i}\|^2/\mathbf{s}_{r,i}^T\mathbf{y}_{r,i}$. This procedure can be implemented *efficiently* via a *compact representation* (Nocedal and Wright, 2006), i.e.,

$$\mathbf{B}_{r,i}=\delta_{r,i}\mathbf{I}-\mathbf{W}_{r,i}\mathbf{M}_{r,i}^{-1}\mathbf{W}_{r,i}^T, \tag{37}$$

$$\mathbf{M}_{r,i}\triangleq\begin{bmatrix}\delta_{r,i}\mathbf{S}_{r,i}{}^T\mathbf{S}_{r,i} & \mathbf{L}_{r,i}\\ \mathbf{L}_{r,i}{}^T & -\mathbf{D}_{r,i}\end{bmatrix}, \tag{38}$$

where $\mathbf{W}_{r,i} \triangleq [\delta_r^{(i)}\mathbf{S}_r^{(i)}, \mathbf{Y}_r^{(i)}]$ and $\mathbf{L}_{r,i}$ and $\mathbf{D}_{r,i}$ are the lower triangular matrix (excluding diagonal) and diagonal matrix of $\mathbf{S}_{r,i}^T\mathbf{Y}_{r,i}$ respectively. Analogous to (36), we define the approximation of $\nabla^2 f$ at $\mathbf{U}_i\bar{\mathbf{x}}_r$, denoted as $\mathbf{B}_r$, as

$$\mathbf{B}_r \triangleq \frac{1}{n}\sum_{i=1}^{K} \mathbf{U}_i^T\mathbf{B}_{r,i}\mathbf{U}_i. \tag{39}$$

We remark that the strong convexity of each function f_i (see Assumption 2), together with the full-row-rank property of $\mathbf{U}_i$, ensures $\nabla^2\phi_i \succ 0$ on $\mathbb{R}^{d_i}$. This implies *positive curvature* $\mathbf{s}_{r,i}^T\mathbf{y}_{r,i} > 0$ and hence the positive definiteness of $\mathbf{B}_{r,i}$, for any $r \geq 0$ and $i \in [K]$. As a result, $\mathbf{B}_r \succ 0$ on $\mathbb{R}^d$. This suggests the usage of the *conjugate gradient* (CG) method to compute the search direction at time (s,t), namely $\mathbf{p}_{s,t} \triangleq -\mathbf{B}_r^{-1}\mathbf{v}_{s,t}$, via solving the positive definite system $\mathbf{B}_r\mathbf{p}_{s,t} = -\mathbf{v}_{s,t}$. In particular, for any $\mathbf{z} \in \mathbb{R}^d$, $\mathbf{B}_r\mathbf{z}$ and $\mathbf{z}^T\mathbf{B}_r\mathbf{z}$ in CG can be computed very efficiently using (37) and (39). For example, $\mathbf{z}^T\mathbf{B}_r\mathbf{z}$ equals

$$\frac{1}{n}\sum_{i=1}^{K} \delta_{r,i}\left\|\mathbf{z}_i\right\|^2 - (\mathbf{W}_{r,i}^T\mathbf{z}_i)^T\mathbf{M}_{r,i}^{-1}(\mathbf{W}_{r,i}^T\mathbf{z}_i), \tag{40}$$

where $\mathbf{z}_i \triangleq \mathbf{U}_i\mathbf{z}$. We observe that the total computational cost in (40) is $O(M'(M'^2+d'))$, where $d' \triangleq \sum_{i=1}^K d_i$. For sparse data, usually $d' = O(d)$, so this cost is still linear in d. In addition, we can compute (40) *in parallel* across $i \in [K]$. (Intuitively, this amounts to *collecting curvature* from each function ϕ_i in parallel.) In this case, the computational time will be greatly reduced to $O(M'(M'^2 + \max_i d_i))$. Since typically $\max_i d_i \ll d$, the computational savings from *parallel curvature collection* can be significant.[9]

7 NUMERICAL EXPERIMENTS

We consider two ERM problems, including logistic regression (with Tikhonov regularization) and ridge regression. For logistic regression, $b_i \in \{-1, 1\}$ and

$$f_i(\mathbf{x}) \triangleq \log\left(1 + e^{-b_i(\mathbf{a}_i^T\mathbf{x})}\right) + \frac{\lambda}{2}\left\|\mathbf{x}\right\|^2, \ \forall i \in [n]. \tag{41}$$

For ridge regression, $b_i \in \mathbb{R}$ and

$$f_i(\mathbf{x}) \triangleq \left(\mathbf{a}_i^T\mathbf{x} - b_i\right)^2 + \frac{\lambda}{2}\left\|\mathbf{x}\right\|^2, \ \forall i \in [n]. \tag{42}$$

Simple calculations show the smoothness parameters L_i for (41) and (42) are $\left\|\mathbf{a}_i\right\|^2/4+\lambda$ and $2\left\|\mathbf{a}_i\right\|^2+\lambda$ respectively. In both (41) and (42), we choose $\lambda = 1/n$, following the convention in the literature (e.g., Konečný et al. (2016)).

We test logistic and ridge regression on `rcv1.binary` and `E2006-tfidf` datasets respectively (Chang and Lin, 2011). (In the sequel we abbreviate them as `rcv1` and `E2006`.) The size-dimension statistics (n, d) for these two datasets are $(20242, 47236)$ and $(16087, 15036)$ respectively. From (35), we define a sparsity estimate of $\nabla^2 f$ at any $\mathbf{x} \in \mathbb{R}^d$ as $\sigma \triangleq \left|\mathrm{supp}(\mathbf{A}\mathbf{A}^T + \mathbf{I})\right|/d^2$, where $\mathbf{A} \triangleq [\mathbf{a}_1, \ldots, \mathbf{a}_n]$ is the data matrix. For `rcv1` and `E2006`, σ equals 0.0154 and 0.0404 respectively. For both datasets, the norms of all feature vectors $\{\mathbf{a}_i\}_{i=1}^n$ have been normalized to unit. Since the the smoothness parameters L_i for both ERM problems only depend on $\|\mathbf{a}_i\|$ and λ, we have $L_i = L_j$ for any $i, j \in [n]$. Thus the nonuniform distribution P in Section 3 becomes uniform, and the advantage of nonuniform sampling of $\mathcal{B}_{s,t}$ cannot be observed.

To estimate the global optimum $\mathbf{x}^*$ as ground truth, we use batch L-BFGS-B algorithm (Zhu et al., 1997). We randomly initialize $\mathbf{x}^0$ according to a scaled standard normal distribution.[10] We use the number of data passes (i.e., number of data points accessed divided by n), rather than time, to measure the efficiency of algorithms. This has been a well-established convention in the literature since execution time highly depends on implementation of algorithms.

Finally we describe the parameter setting. We set the mini-batch size $b = \sqrt{n}$, Hessian update period $\Upsilon = 10$ and the memory parameter $M = 10$. We set $b_{\mathrm{H}} = b\Upsilon$ so that the computation for $\mathbf{y}_r$ can be amortized to each inner iteration. We set the number of inner iterations $m = n/b$, so that each outer iteration will access $2n$ data points. Lastly, we set $\eta = 1 \times 10^{-2}$. From Figure 1, we observe that when η is too large, e.g., $\eta = 0.1$, Algorithm 1 only converges sublinearly; whereas when η is too small, e.g., $\eta = 1 \times 10^{-3}$, Algorithm 1 converges linearly but slowly. This corresponds well to our theoretical analysis in Theorem 1, which indicates that when η falls below a threshold, ρ increases as η decreases. For both ERM problems, we find $\eta = 1 \times 10^{-2}$ yields fast linear convergence.

7.1 PERFORMANCE OF ACCELERATION STRATEGIES

We first examine the performance of Algorithm 1 with different schemes of choosing $\mathbf{x}^{s+1}$. We consider five schemes in total, including (a) uniform sampling (option I), (b) uniform averaging (option II), (c) geometric sampling (option III), (d) geometric averaging (option IV) and (e) last inner iterate (in Remark 8). For options III and IV, we set $\beta = 1/2$. From Figure 2, we observe that options III and IV perform as well as the "last inner iterate" scheme, on both ERM problems, and outperform the schemes based on uniform sampling/averaging significantly. For all the subsequent experiments, we use option IV to select $\mathbf{x}^{s+1}$.

We next compare the performance of Algorithm 1 with and without using the subsampled gradient stabilization strategy in Section 6.2. As suggested by Remark 9, we choose

[9] The memory parameter M (note that $M' \leq M$) is usually set to a small constant, e.g., 5 or 10. Thus it has much less effects on the computational complexity compared to d or $\max_i d_i$.

[10] The performance of our algorithms were observed to be insensitive to the initialization of $\mathbf{x}^0$.

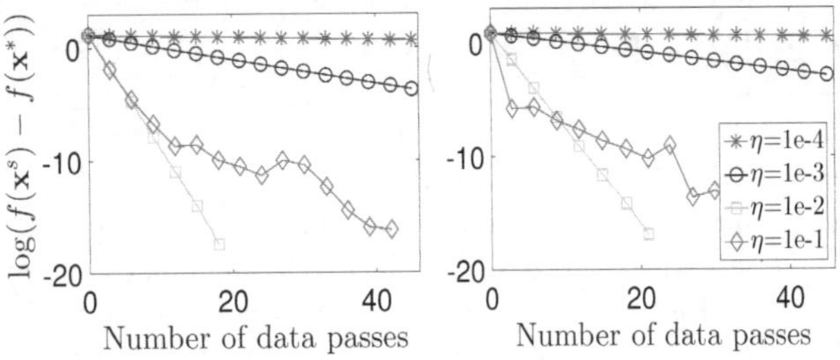

(a) logistic regression (`rcv1`) (b) ridge regression (`E2006`)

Figure 1: Log suboptimality versus number of passes through data of Algorithm 1 with different step sizes η.

$\widetilde{b}_s = \min\{\zeta v^s, n\}$, where $\zeta = n/v^q$, $v = 3$ and $q = 8$. That is, the number of component gradients in $\widetilde{\mathbf{g}}_s$ exponentially increases in the first $p = 8$ outer iterations and then remains at n. From Figure 3, we observe that this simple parameter selection method works well on both ERM problems, especially in the initial phase (when s is small). In addition, we also observe when s is large, both algorithms have almost the same (linear) convergence rates. This corroborates our analysis in Proposition 3.

We finally compare the performance of Algorithm 1 with and without using the low-dimensional approximate Hessian strategy in Section 6.3. We set the number of partitions $K = 5$ and partition $[n]$ evenly and randomly. From Figure 4, we observe that our strategy leads to improvements of convergence on both logistic and ridge regression problems, and the improvement on the latter is *very significant*. Moreover, our strategy *preserves the linear convergence* of Algorithm 1 on both problems. As discussed in Section 6.3, our strategy can be even more efficient in scenarios where parallel computational resources are available.

7.2 COMPARISON TO OTHER ALGORITHMS

We combine all of our acceleration strategies in Section 6 and compare the resulting algorithm with three benchmarking algorithms, including SVRG in Johnson and Zhang (2013) and two state-of-the-art stochastic L-BFGS algorithms in Moritz et al. (2016) and Gower et al. (2016). For the algorithm in Gower et al. (2016), we focus on its variant (b), since it consistently outperformed other variants in experiments. We tested all the three benchmarking algorithms on both ERM problems with different step sizes $\eta \in \{10^{-4}, 10^{-3}, \ldots, 1\}$ and selected the best η for each algorithm. The outer iterate $\mathbf{x}^{s+1}$ in all these algorithms are selected via "the last iterate" scheme. From Figure 5, we observe that on both ERM problems, our algorithm has faster convergence compared to all the benchmarking algorithms. The improvement of convergence is particularly significant on the ridge regression problem. This observation is consistent with our observations in Section 7.1.
Future work and open problems: see Section S-7.

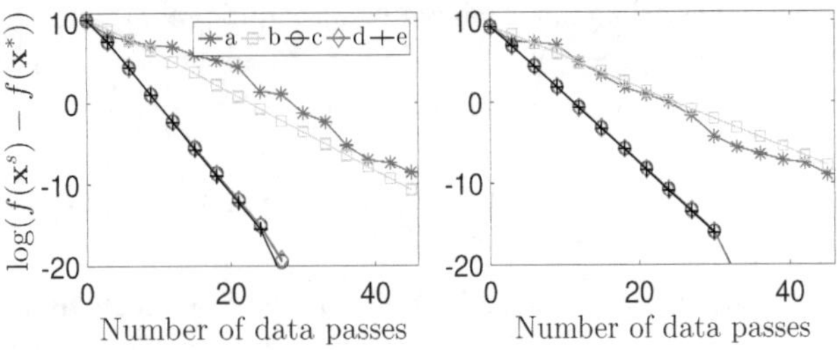

(a) logistic regression (`rcv1`) (b) ridge regression (`E2006`)

Figure 2: Comparison of Algorithm 1 with different selection schemes for $\mathbf{x}^{s+1}$.

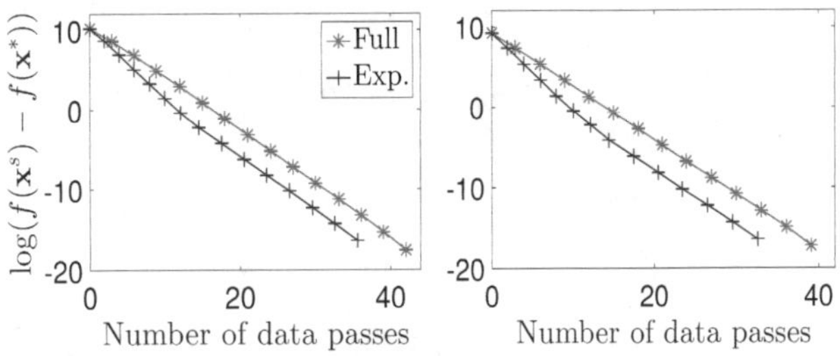

(a) logistic regression (`rcv1`) (b) ridge regression (`E2006`)

Figure 3: Comparison of Algorithm 1 without (Full) and with (Exp.) using the strategy in Section 6.2.

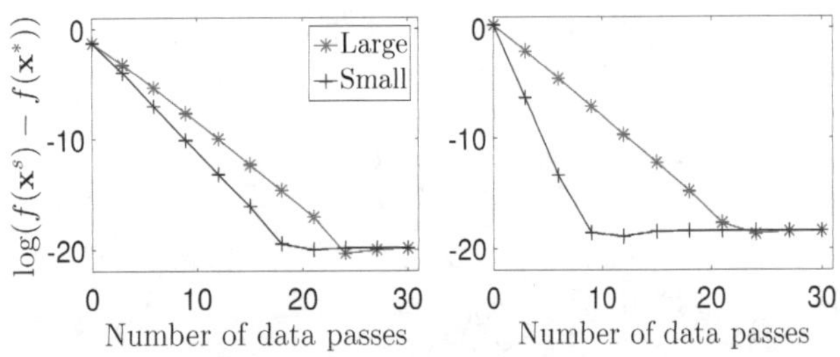

(a) logistic regression (`rcv1`) (b) ridge regression (`E2006`)

Figure 4: Comparison of Algorithm 1 without (Large) and with (Small) using the strategy in Section 6.3.

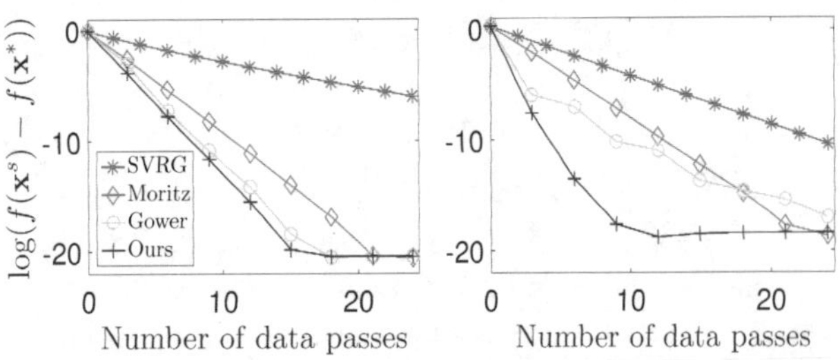

(a) logistic regression (`rcv1`) (b) ridge regression (`E2006`)

Figure 5: Comparison of our algorithm (Ours) with benchmarking algorithms (SVRG, Moritz and Gower).

References

Z. Allen-Zhu. Katyusha: The first direct acceleration of stochastic gradient methods. arXiv:1603.05953, 2016.

A. Bordes, L. Bottou, and P. Gallinari. SGD-QN: Careful quasi-newton stochastic gradient descent. *J. Mach. Learn. Res.*, 10:1737–1754, Dec. 2009.

V. S. Borkar. *Stochastic approximation: a dynamical systems viewpoint*. Cambridge, 2008.

L. Bottou. Online algorithms and stochastic approximations. In *Online Learning and Neural Networks*. Cambridge University Press, 1998.

L. Bottou and Y. LeCun. Large scale online learning. In *Proc. NIPS*, pages 1361–1368. Vancouver, BC, Canada, Dec. 2004.

S. Boyd and L. Vandenberghe. *Convex Optimization*. Cambridge University Press, 2004.

R. H. Byrd, S. L. Hansen, J. Nocedal, and Y. Singer. A stochastic quasi-newton method for large-scale optimization. *SIAM J. Optim.*, 26(2):1008–1031, 2016.

C.-C. Chang and C.-J. Lin. LIBSVM: A library for support vector machines. *ACM Trans. Intell. Syst. Technol.*, 2: 27:1–27:27, 2011.

A. Defazio, F. Bach, and S. Lacoste-Julien. Saga: A fast incremental gradient method with support for non-strongly convex composite objectives. In *Proc. NIPS*, pages 1646–1654, Montréal, Québec, Canada, 2014.

D. Goldfarb. A family of variable metric updates derived by variational means. *Math. Comput.*, 24(109):23–26, 1970.

R. M. Gower, D. Goldfarb, and P. Richtárik. Stochastic block BFGS: squeezing more curvature out of data. In *Proc. ICML*, pages 1869–1878, New York City, NY, USA, June 2016.

R. Harikandeh, M. O. Ahmed, A. Virani, M. Schmidt, J. Konečný, and S. Sallinen. Stopwasting my gradients: Practical svrg. In *Proc. NIPS*, pages 2251–2259. Montréal, Quebec, Canada, 2015.

C. Hu, W. Pan, and J. T. Kwok. Accelerated gradient methods for stochastic optimization and online learning. In *Porc. NIPS*, pages 781–789. Vancouver, B.C., Canada, 2009.

R. Johnson and T. Zhang. Accelerating stochastic gradient descent using predictive variance reduction. In *Proc. NIPS*, pages 315–323, Lake Tahoe, Nevada, USA, 2013.

J. Konečný and P. Richtárik. Semi-stochastic gradient descent methods. arXiv:1312.1666, 2013.

J. Konečný, J. Liu, P. Richtárik, and M. Takáč. Mini-batch semi-stochastic gradient descent in the proximal setting. *IEEE J. Sel. Top. Signal Process.*, 10(2):242–255, 2016.

H. Lin, J. Mairal, and Z. Harchaoui. A universal catalyst for first-order optimization. In *Proc. NIPS*, pages 3384–3392, 2015.

D. C. Liu and J. Nocedal. On the limited memory bfgs method for large scale optimization. *Math. Program.*, 45 (3), Dec. 1989.

A. Mokhtari and A. Ribeiro. Global convergence of online limited memory BFGS. *J. Mach. Learn. Res.*, 16(1): 3151–3181, Jan 2015.

P. Moritz, R. Nishihara, and M. I. Jordan. A linearly-convergent stochastic L-BFGS algorithm. In *Proc. AISTATS*, pages 249–258, Cadiz, Spain, May 2016.

J. Nocedal and S. J. Wright. *Numerical Optimization*. Springer, New York, 2nd edition, 2006.

M. Schmidt, N. Le Roux, and F. Bach. Minimizing finite sums with the stochastic average gradient. *Math. Program.*, 162(1):83–112, 2017.

N. N. Schraudolph, J. Yu, and S. Günter. A stochastic quasi-Newton method for online convex optimization. In *Proc. ATSTATS*, San Juan, Puerto Rico, March 2007.

J. Sohl-Dickstein, B. Poole, and S. Ganguli. Fast large-scale optimization by unifying stochastic gradient and quasi-newton methods. In *Proc. ICML*, pages 604–612, Beijing, China, June 2014.

D. Williams. *Probability with Martingales*. Cambridge University Press, 1991.

L. Xiao and T. Zhang. A proximal stochastic gradient method with progressive variance reduction. *SIAM J. Optim.*, 24(4):2057–2075, 2014.

C. Zhu, R. H. Byrd, P. Lu, and J. Nocedal. Algorithm 778: L-bfgs-b: Fortran subroutines for large-scale bound-constrained optimization. *ACM Trans. Math. Softw.*, 23 (4), Dec 1997.

Supplemental Material for "Stochastic L-BFGS Revisited: Improved Convergence Rates and Practical Acceleration Strategies"

S-1 Technical Lemmas

We first provide some technical lemmas that will be used in our subsequent proofs. Lemma S-1 states two classical inequalities of a strongly convex and smooth function, and its proof can be found in Boyd and Vandenberghe (2004, Chapter 9). Lemma S-2 states some results about importance sampling, and can be derived using definition of expectation and Lemma S-1. For a complete proof, see Xiao and Zhang (2014, Section 3). Lemma S-3 states a classical result on the distance between (uniformly) subsampled mean and (global) mean of a finite number of vectors. Its proof can be found in Konečný et al. (2016, Appendix B.A).

Lemma S-1. *If a function $f : \mathbb{R}^d \to \mathbb{R}$ is μ-strongly convex and L-smooth, then for any $\mathbf{x} \in \mathbb{R}^d$,*

$$\frac{\mu}{2} \|\mathbf{x} - \mathbf{x}^*\|^2 \le f(\mathbf{x}) - f(\mathbf{x}^*) \le \frac{1}{2\mu} \|\nabla f(\mathbf{x})\|^2, \tag{S-1}$$

$$\frac{1}{2L} \|\nabla f(\mathbf{x})\|^2 \le f(\mathbf{x}) - f(\mathbf{x}^*) \le \frac{L}{2} \|\mathbf{x} - \mathbf{x}^*\|^2, \tag{S-2}$$

where $\mathbf{x}^*$ denotes the unique minimizer of f on $\mathbb{R}^d$.

Lemma S-2. *Let f be defined as in (1) and satisfies Assumption 2. Define a distribution p with support $[n]$ such that $p_i = L_i/(n\overline{L})$, for any $i \in [n]$. Then for any $\mathbf{x} \in \mathbb{R}^d$,*

$$\mathbb{E}_{i\sim p}\left[\frac{1}{np_i}\nabla f_i(\mathbf{x})\right] = \nabla f(\mathbf{x}), \tag{S-3}$$

$$\mathbb{E}_{i\sim p}\left[\left\|\frac{1}{np_i}\left(\nabla f_i(\mathbf{x}) - \nabla f_i(\mathbf{x}^*)\right)\right\|^2\right] \le 2\overline{L}(f(\mathbf{x}) - f(\mathbf{x}^*)), \tag{S-4}$$

where $\mathbf{x}^*$ denotes the unique minimizer of f on $\mathbb{R}^d$.

Lemma S-3. *Let $\{\mathbf{z}_i\}_{i=1}^n \subseteq \mathbb{R}^d$ and define $\overline{\mathbf{z}} \triangleq 1/n\sum_{i=1}^n \mathbf{z}_i$. Uniformly sample a random subset $\mathcal{S}$ of $[n]$ with size b without replacement. Then*

$$\mathbb{E}_{\mathcal{S}}\left[\left\|\frac{1}{n}\sum_{i\in\mathcal{S}}^{n}\mathbf{z}_i - \overline{\mathbf{z}}\right\|^2\right] \le \frac{n-b}{b(n-1)}\left(\frac{1}{n}\sum_{i=1}^{n}\|\mathbf{z}_i\|^2\right). \tag{S-5}$$

S-2 Proof of Theorem 1

Proof. Fix an outer iteration s and consider an inner iteration t. Define $r \triangleq \lfloor(\sum_{i=0}^{s-1} T_i + t)/L\rfloor$,[11] then the iteration in (10) becomes

$$\widetilde{\mathbf{x}}_{s,t+1,r} = \widetilde{\mathbf{x}}_{s,t,r} - \eta\widetilde{\mathbf{v}}_{s,t,r}. \tag{S-6}$$

In addition, from Lemmas 1 and 3, we have

$$\mathbb{E}_{\mathcal{B}_{s,t}}\left[\widetilde{\mathbf{v}}_{s,t,r}\middle|\mathcal{F}_{s,t}\right] = \mathbf{H}_r^{1/2}\nabla f(\mathbf{x}_{s,t}) = \nabla\widetilde{f}_r(\widetilde{\mathbf{x}}_{s,t,r}), \tag{S-7}$$

$$\begin{aligned}\mathbb{E}_{\mathcal{B}_{s,t}}\left[\left\|\widetilde{\mathbf{v}}_{s,t,r} - \nabla\widetilde{f}_r(\widetilde{\mathbf{x}}_{s,t,r})\right\|^2\middle|\mathcal{F}_{s,t}\right] &\le \left\|\mathbf{H}^{1/2}\right\|^2\frac{4\overline{L}}{b}\left(f(\mathbf{x}_{s,t}) - f(\mathbf{x}^*) + f(\mathbf{x}^s) - f(\mathbf{x}^*)\right)\\ &\le \frac{4\Gamma\overline{L}}{b}\left(\widetilde{f}_r(\widetilde{\mathbf{x}}_{s,t,r}) - \widetilde{f}_r(\widetilde{\mathbf{x}}_r^*) + \widetilde{f}_{r'}(\widetilde{\mathbf{x}}^{s,r'}) - \widetilde{f}_{r'}(\widetilde{\mathbf{x}}_{r'}^*)\right),\end{aligned} \tag{S-8}$$

where $r' \triangleq \lfloor sm/L\rfloor$. Next we express the distance between $\widetilde{\mathbf{x}}_{s,t+1,r}$ and $\widetilde{\mathbf{x}}_r^*$ as

$$\|\widetilde{\mathbf{x}}_{s,t+1,r} - \widetilde{\mathbf{x}}_r^*\|^2 = \|\widetilde{\mathbf{x}}_{s,t,r} - \eta\widetilde{\mathbf{v}}_{s,t,r} - \widetilde{\mathbf{x}}_r^*\|^2 \tag{S-9}$$

$$= \|\widetilde{\mathbf{x}}_{s,t,r} - \widetilde{\mathbf{x}}_r^*\|^2 + 2\eta\left(\frac{\eta}{2}\|\widetilde{\mathbf{v}}_{s,t,r}\|^2 - \langle\widetilde{\mathbf{v}}_{s,t,r}, \widetilde{\mathbf{x}}_{s,t,r} - \widetilde{\mathbf{x}}_r^*\rangle\right). \tag{S-10}$$

[11] To avoid cluttered notations, we omit showing the dependence of r on s and t.

Defining $\widetilde{\boldsymbol{\delta}}_{s,t,r} \triangleq \widetilde{\mathbf{v}}_{s,t,r} - \nabla \widetilde{f}_r(\widetilde{\mathbf{x}}_{s,t,r})$, we now bound

$$\frac{\eta}{2}\left\|\widetilde{\mathbf{v}}_{s,t,r}\right\|^2 - \langle \widetilde{\mathbf{v}}_{s,t,r}, \widetilde{\mathbf{x}}_{s,t,r} - \widetilde{\mathbf{x}}_r^*\rangle \le -\left(\widetilde{f}_r(\widetilde{\mathbf{x}}_{s,t+1,r}) - \widetilde{f}_r(\widetilde{\mathbf{x}}_r^*)\right) - \left\langle \widetilde{\boldsymbol{\delta}}_{s,t,r}, \widetilde{\mathbf{x}}_{s,t+1,r} - \widetilde{\mathbf{x}}_r^*\right\rangle - \frac{\gamma\overline{\mu}}{2}\left\|\widetilde{\mathbf{x}}_{s,t,r} - \widetilde{\mathbf{x}}_r^*\right\|^2. \quad \text{(S-11)}$$

This is because

$$\widetilde{f}_r(\widetilde{\mathbf{x}}_{s,t+1,r}) + \frac{\eta}{2}\left\|\widetilde{\mathbf{v}}_{s,t,r}\right\|^2 - \langle \widetilde{\mathbf{v}}_{s,t,r}, \widetilde{\mathbf{x}}_{s,t,r} - \widetilde{\mathbf{x}}_r^*\rangle + \left\langle \widetilde{\boldsymbol{\delta}}_{s,t,r}, \widetilde{\mathbf{x}}_{s,t+1,r} - \widetilde{\mathbf{x}}_r^*\right\rangle + \frac{\gamma\overline{\mu}}{2}\left\|\widetilde{\mathbf{x}}_{s,t,r} - \widetilde{\mathbf{x}}_r^*\right\|^2 \quad \text{(S-12)}$$

$$= \widetilde{f}_r(\widetilde{\mathbf{x}}_{s,t+1,r}) - \left\langle \widetilde{\mathbf{v}}_{s,t,r}, \widetilde{\mathbf{x}}_{s,t+1,r} + \frac{\eta}{2}\widetilde{\mathbf{v}}_{s,t,r} - \widetilde{\mathbf{x}}_r^*\right\rangle + \left\langle \widetilde{\boldsymbol{\delta}}_{s,t,r}, \widetilde{\mathbf{x}}_{s,t+1,r} - \widetilde{\mathbf{x}}_r^*\right\rangle + \frac{\gamma\overline{\mu}}{2}\left\|\widetilde{\mathbf{x}}_{s,t,r} - \widetilde{\mathbf{x}}_r^*\right\|^2 \quad \text{(S-13)}$$

$$\overset{\text{(a)}}{\le} \widetilde{f}_r(\widetilde{\mathbf{x}}_{s,t+1,r}) - \frac{\Gamma\overline{L}}{2}\eta^2\left\|\widetilde{\mathbf{v}}_{s,t,r}\right\|^2 - \left\langle \widetilde{\mathbf{v}}_{s,t,r} - \widetilde{\boldsymbol{\delta}}_{s,t,r}, \widetilde{\mathbf{x}}_{s,t+1,r} - \widetilde{\mathbf{x}}_r^*\right\rangle + \frac{\gamma\overline{\mu}}{2}\left\|\widetilde{\mathbf{x}}_{s,t,r} - \widetilde{\mathbf{x}}_r^*\right\|^2 \quad \text{(S-14)}$$

$$= \widetilde{f}_r(\widetilde{\mathbf{x}}_{s,t+1,r}) - \left\langle \nabla\widetilde{f}_r(\widetilde{\mathbf{x}}_{s,t,r}), \widetilde{\mathbf{x}}_{s,t+1,r} - \widetilde{\mathbf{x}}_{s,t,r}\right\rangle - \frac{\Gamma\overline{L}}{2}\left\|\eta\widetilde{\mathbf{v}}_{s,t,r}\right\|^2 - \left\langle \nabla\widetilde{f}_r(\widetilde{\mathbf{x}}_{s,t,r}), \widetilde{\mathbf{x}}_{s,t,r} - \widetilde{\mathbf{x}}_r^*\right\rangle + \frac{\gamma\overline{\mu}}{2}\left\|\widetilde{\mathbf{x}}_{s,t,r} - \widetilde{\mathbf{x}}_r^*\right\|^2 \quad \text{(S-15)}$$

$$\overset{\text{(b)}}{\le} \widetilde{f}_r(\widetilde{\mathbf{x}}_{s,t,r}) + \left\langle \nabla\widetilde{f}_r(\widetilde{\mathbf{x}}_{s,t,r}), \widetilde{\mathbf{x}}_r^* - \widetilde{\mathbf{x}}_{s,t,r}\right\rangle + \frac{\gamma\overline{\mu}}{2}\left\|\widetilde{\mathbf{x}}_r^* - \widetilde{\mathbf{x}}_{s,t,r}\right\|^2 \quad \text{(S-16)}$$

$$\overset{\text{(c)}}{\le} \widetilde{f}_r(\widetilde{\mathbf{x}}_r^*), \quad \text{(S-17)}$$

where (a) follows from $\eta \le 1/(\Gamma\overline{L})$, (b) follows from the $(\Gamma\overline{L})$-smoothness of $\widetilde{f}_r$ and (c) follows from the $(\gamma\overline{\mu})$-strong convexity of $\widetilde{f}_r$ (see Lemma 2). Substituting (S-11) into (S-10), we have

$$\left\|\widetilde{\mathbf{x}}_{s,t+1,r} - \widetilde{\mathbf{x}}_r^*\right\|^2 \le (1-\eta\gamma\overline{\mu})\left\|\widetilde{\mathbf{x}}_{s,t,r} - \widetilde{\mathbf{x}}_r^*\right\|^2 - 2\eta\left(\widetilde{f}_r(\widetilde{\mathbf{x}}_{s,t+1,r}) - \widetilde{f}_r(\widetilde{\mathbf{x}}_r^*)\right) - 2\eta\left\langle \widetilde{\boldsymbol{\delta}}_{s,t,r}, \widetilde{\mathbf{x}}_{s,t+1,r} - \widetilde{\mathbf{x}}_r^*\right\rangle \quad \text{(S-18)}$$

$$= (1-\eta\gamma\overline{\mu})\left\|\widetilde{\mathbf{x}}_{s,t,r} - \widetilde{\mathbf{x}}_r^*\right\|^2 - 2\eta\left(\widetilde{f}_r(\widetilde{\mathbf{x}}_{s,t+1,r}) - \widetilde{f}_r(\widetilde{\mathbf{x}}_r^*)\right) + 2\eta^2\left\|\widetilde{\boldsymbol{\delta}}_{s,t,r}\right\|^2 - 2\eta\left\langle \widetilde{\boldsymbol{\delta}}_{s,t,r}, \widetilde{\mathbf{x}}_{s,t,r} - \widetilde{\mathbf{x}}_r^*\right\rangle. \quad \text{(S-19)}$$

Taking expectation with respect to (w.r.t.) $\mathcal{B}_{s,t}$ and using (S-7) and (S-8), we have

$$\mathbb{E}_{\mathcal{B}_{s,t}}\left[\left\|\widetilde{\mathbf{x}}_{s,t+1,r} - \widetilde{\mathbf{x}}_r^*\right\|^2 \middle| \mathcal{F}_{s,t}\right] + 2\eta\mathbb{E}_{\mathcal{B}_{s,t}}\left[\widetilde{f}_r(\widetilde{\mathbf{x}}_{s,t+1,r}) - \widetilde{f}_r(\widetilde{\mathbf{x}}_r^*)\middle| \mathcal{F}_{s,t}\right]$$
$$\le (1-\eta\gamma\overline{\mu})\left\|\widetilde{\mathbf{x}}_{s,t,r} - \widetilde{\mathbf{x}}_r^*\right\|^2 + \frac{8}{b}\Gamma\overline{L}\eta^2\left(\widetilde{f}_r(\widetilde{\mathbf{x}}_{s,t,r}) - \widetilde{f}_r(\widetilde{\mathbf{x}}_r^*) + \widetilde{f}_{r'}(\widetilde{\mathbf{x}}^{s,r'}) - \widetilde{f}_{r'}(\widetilde{\mathbf{x}}_{r'}^*)\right). \quad \text{(S-20)}$$

By relaxing the factor $1-\eta\gamma\overline{\mu}$ to 1, we are able to telescope (S-20) over $t = 0, \ldots, m-1$ using the tower property of conditional expectations (Williams, 1991, Chapter 9.7) and obtain

$$\mathbb{E}_{\mathcal{B}_{s,(m-1]}}\left[\left\|\widetilde{\mathbf{x}}_{s,m,r} - \widetilde{\mathbf{x}}_r^*\right\|^2 \middle| \mathcal{F}_s\right] + 2m\eta\left(1 - \frac{4}{b}\Gamma\overline{L}\eta\right)\frac{1}{m}\sum_{t=1}^{m}\mathbb{E}_{\mathcal{B}_{s,(t-1]}}\left[\widetilde{f}_r(\widetilde{\mathbf{x}}_{s,t,r}) - \widetilde{f}_r(\widetilde{\mathbf{x}}_r^*)\middle| \mathcal{F}_{s,t-1}\right]$$
$$\le \left\|\widetilde{\mathbf{x}}^{s,r'} - \widetilde{\mathbf{x}}_{r'}^*\right\|^2 + \frac{8}{b}\Gamma\overline{L}\eta^2(1+m)\left(\widetilde{f}_{r'}(\widetilde{\mathbf{x}}^{s,r'}) - \widetilde{f}_{r'}(\widetilde{\mathbf{x}}_{r'}^*)\right), \quad \text{(S-21)}$$

where $\mathcal{B}_{s,(m-1]} \triangleq \{\mathcal{B}_{s,i}\}_{i=0}^{m-1}$. If we use option II to choose $\mathbf{x}^{s+1}$ (in line 20), we have $\widetilde{\mathbf{x}}^{s+1,r''} = 1/m\sum_{i=1}^{m}\widetilde{\mathbf{x}}_{s,t,r''}$, where $r'' \triangleq \lfloor (s+1)m/L \rfloor$. Using (7) and Jensen's inequality, we have

$$\frac{1}{m}\sum_{t=1}^{m}\left(\widetilde{f}_r(\widetilde{\mathbf{x}}_{s,t,r}) - \widetilde{f}_r(\widetilde{\mathbf{x}}_r^*)\right) = \frac{1}{m}\sum_{t=1}^{m}\left(\widetilde{f}_{r''}(\widetilde{\mathbf{x}}_{s,t,r''}) - \widetilde{f}_{r''}(\widetilde{\mathbf{x}}_{r''}^*)\right) \ge \widetilde{f}_{r''}(\widetilde{\mathbf{x}}^{s+1,r''}) - \widetilde{f}_{r''}(\widetilde{\mathbf{x}}_{r''}^*). \quad \text{(S-22)}$$

Therefore, we have

$$\frac{1}{m}\sum_{t=1}^{m}\mathbb{E}_{\mathcal{B}_{s,(t-1]}}\left[\widetilde{f}_r(\widetilde{\mathbf{x}}_{s,t,r}) - \widetilde{f}_r(\widetilde{\mathbf{x}}_r^*)\middle| \mathcal{F}_{s,t-1}\right] \ge \mathbb{E}_{\mathcal{B}_{s,(m-1]}}\left[\widetilde{f}_{r''}(\widetilde{\mathbf{x}}^{s+1,r''}) - \widetilde{f}_{r''}(\widetilde{\mathbf{x}}_{r''}^*)\middle| \mathcal{F}_s\right]. \quad \text{(S-23)}$$

Alternatively, if we use option I to determine $\mathbf{x}^{s+1}$ (in line 19), we still have (S-23) (with inequality replaced by equality). If we further use (S-1) in Lemma S-1 to bound $\|\widetilde{\mathbf{x}}^{s,r'} - \widetilde{\mathbf{x}}^*_{r'}\|^2$ in (S-21), we have

$$2m\eta\left(1-\frac{4}{b}\Gamma\overline{L}\eta\right)\mathbb{E}_{\mathcal{B}_{s,(m-1]}}\left[\widetilde{f}_{r''}(\widetilde{\mathbf{x}}^{s+1,r''})-\widetilde{f}_{r''}(\widetilde{\mathbf{x}}^*_{r''})\middle|\mathcal{F}_s\right]$$
$$\leq\left(\frac{8}{b}\Gamma\overline{L}\eta^2(1+m)+\frac{2}{\gamma\overline{\mu}}\right)\left(\widetilde{f}_{r'}(\widetilde{x}^{s,r'})-\widetilde{f}_{r'}(\widetilde{\mathbf{x}}^*_{r'})\right). \tag{S-24}$$

Using (7) again and rearranging, we have

$$\mathbb{E}\left[f(\mathbf{x}^{s+1})-f(\mathbf{x}^*)\middle|\mathcal{F}_s\right]\leq\rho(f(\mathbf{x}^s)-f(\mathbf{x}^*)). \tag{S-25}$$

Taking expectation on both sides and we complete the proof. □

S-3 Proof of Lemma 3

First from (S-4) we immediately have $\mathbb{E}_{\mathcal{B}_{s,t}}\left[\mathbf{v}_{s,t}|\mathcal{F}_{s,t}\right]=\nabla f(\mathbf{x}_{s,t})$. Then

$$\mathbb{E}_{\mathcal{B}_{s,t}}\left[\left\|\mathbf{v}_{s,t}-\nabla f(\mathbf{x}_{s,t})\right\|^2|\mathcal{F}_{s,t}\right] \tag{S-26}$$

$$=\mathbb{E}_{\mathcal{B}_{s,t}}\left[\left\|\frac{1}{b}\sum_{j=1}^{b}\left(1/(np_{i_j})\left(\nabla f_{i_j}(\mathbf{x}_{s,t})-\nabla f_{i_j}(\mathbf{x}^s)\right)+\nabla f(\mathbf{x}^s)-\nabla f(\mathbf{x}_{s,t})\right)\right\|^2\middle|\mathcal{F}_{s,t}\right] \tag{S-27}$$

$$\overset{(a)}{=}\frac{1}{b^2}\sum_{j=1}^{b}\mathbb{E}_{i_j}\left[\left\|1/(np_{i_j})\left(\nabla f_{i_j}(\mathbf{x}_{s,t})-\nabla f_{i_j}(\mathbf{x}^s)\right)+\nabla f(\mathbf{x}^s)-\nabla f(\mathbf{x}_{s,t})\right\|^2\middle|\mathcal{F}_{s,t}\right] \tag{S-28}$$

$$\overset{(b)}{\leq}\frac{1}{b^2}\sum_{j=1}^{b}\mathbb{E}_{i_j}\left[\left\|1/(np_{i_j})\left(\nabla f_{i_j}(\mathbf{x}_{s,t})-\nabla f_{i_j}(\mathbf{x}^s)\right)\right\|^2\middle|\mathcal{F}_{s,t}\right] \tag{S-29}$$

$$=\frac{1}{b^2}\sum_{j=1}^{b}\mathbb{E}_{i_j}\left[\left\|1/(np_{i_j})\left(\nabla f_{i_j}(\mathbf{x}_{s,t})-\nabla f_{i_j}(\mathbf{x}^*)\right)+1/(np_{i_j})\left(\nabla f_{i_j}(\mathbf{x}^*)-\nabla f_{i_j}(\mathbf{x}^s)\right)\right\|^2\middle|\mathcal{F}_{s,t}\right] \tag{S-30}$$

$$\overset{(c)}{\leq}\frac{2}{b^2}\sum_{j=1}^{b}\mathbb{E}_{i_j}\left[\left\|1/(np_{i_j})\left(\nabla f_{i_j}(\mathbf{x}_{s,t})-\nabla f_{i_j}(\mathbf{x}^*)\right)\right\|^2\middle|\mathcal{F}_{s,t}\right]+\mathbb{E}_{i_j}\left[\left\|1/(np_{i_j})\left(\nabla f_{i_j}(\mathbf{x}^s)-\nabla f_{i_j}(\mathbf{x}^*)\right)\right\|^2\middle|\mathcal{F}_{s,t}\right] \tag{S-31}$$

$$\overset{(d)}{\leq}\frac{2}{b^2}\sum_{j=1}^{b}2\overline{L}(f(\mathbf{x}_{s,t})-f(\mathbf{x}^*))+2\overline{L}(f(\mathbf{x}^s)-f(\mathbf{x}^*)) \tag{S-32}$$

$$=\frac{4\overline{L}}{b}\left(f(\mathbf{x}_{s,t})-f(\mathbf{x}^*)+f(\mathbf{x}^s)-f(\mathbf{x}^*)\right), \tag{S-33}$$

where (a) follows from the independence of i_j and $i_{j'}$ when $j\neq j'$ and

$$\mathbb{E}_{i_j}\left[1/(np_{i_j})\left(\nabla f_{i_j}(\mathbf{x}_{s,t})-\nabla f_{i_j}(\mathbf{x}^s)\right)+\nabla f(\mathbf{x}^s)-\nabla f(\mathbf{x}_{s,t})\middle|\mathcal{F}_{s,t}\right]=0, \tag{S-34}$$

(b) follows from (S-3) and $\mathbb{E}\left[\left\|\mathbf{a}-\mathbb{E}[\mathbf{a}]\right\|^2\middle|\mathcal{G}\right]\leq\mathbb{E}\left[\left\|\mathbf{a}\right\|^2\middle|\mathcal{G}\right]$ almost surely, for any σ-algebra $\mathcal{G}$, (c) follows from $\left\|\mathbf{a}+\mathbf{b}\right\|^2\leq2\left\|\mathbf{a}\right\|^2+2\left\|\mathbf{b}\right\|^2$, and (d) follows from (S-4).

S-4 Proof of Lemma 4

For any $\mathbf{x}\in\mathbb{R}^d$ and $\mathcal{T}\subseteq[n]$ with cardinality b_{H},

$$\overline{\mu}_{b_{\mathrm{H}}}\mathbf{I}\preceq\nabla^2 f_{\mathcal{T}}(\mathbf{x})\preceq\overline{L}_{b_{\mathrm{H}}}\mathbf{I}, \tag{S-35}$$

Define

$$\mathbf{V}_k \triangleq \mathbf{I} - \frac{\mathbf{y}_k {\mathbf{s}_k}^T}{{\mathbf{y}_k}^T \mathbf{s}_k} \quad \text{and} \quad \mathbf{Q}_k \triangleq \frac{\mathbf{s}_k {\mathbf{s}_k}^T}{{\mathbf{y}_k}^T \mathbf{s}_k}. \tag{S-36}$$

Fix any $r \in \mathbb{N}$. Since

$$\mathbf{y}_k = \nabla^2 f_{\mathcal{T}_r}(\overline{\mathbf{x}}_r)\mathbf{s}_k, \tag{S-37}$$

we have

$$\mathbf{V}_k = \mathbf{I} - \frac{\nabla^2 f_{\mathcal{T}_r}(\overline{\mathbf{x}}_r)\mathbf{s}_k {\mathbf{s}_k}^T}{{\mathbf{s}_k}^T \nabla^2 f_{\mathcal{T}_r}(\overline{\mathbf{x}}_r)\mathbf{s}_k} \tag{S-38}$$

$$= \nabla^2 f_{\mathcal{T}_r}(\overline{\mathbf{x}}_r)^{1/2} \left(\mathbf{I} - \frac{\widetilde{\mathbf{s}}_k \widetilde{\mathbf{s}}_k^T}{\widetilde{\mathbf{s}}_k^T \widetilde{\mathbf{s}}_k} \right) \nabla^2 f_{\mathcal{T}_r}(\overline{\mathbf{x}}_r)^{-1/2}, \tag{S-39}$$

where $\widetilde{\mathbf{s}}_k \triangleq \nabla^2 f_{\mathcal{T}_r}(\overline{\mathbf{x}}_r)^{1/2}\mathbf{s}_k$. Hence

$$\|\mathbf{V}_k\| \le \left\| \nabla^2 f_{\mathcal{T}_r}(\overline{\mathbf{x}}_r)^{1/2} \right\| \left\| \mathbf{I} - \frac{\widetilde{\mathbf{s}}_k \widetilde{\mathbf{s}}_k^T}{\|\widetilde{\mathbf{s}}_k\|^2} \right\| \left\| \nabla^2 f_{\mathcal{T}_r}(\overline{\mathbf{x}}_r)^{-1/2} \right\| \tag{S-40}$$

$$\le \overline{L}_{b_{\mathrm{H}}}^{1/2} \overline{\mu}_{b_{\mathrm{H}}}^{-1/2} = \kappa_{b_{\mathrm{H}}}^{1/2}. \tag{S-41}$$

Similarly,

$$\|\mathbf{Q}_k\| = \frac{\|\mathbf{s}_k\|^2}{{\mathbf{s}_k}^T \nabla^2 f_{\mathcal{T}_r}(\overline{\mathbf{x}}_r)\mathbf{s}_k} \le \frac{1}{\overline{\mu}_{b_{\mathrm{H}}}}. \tag{S-42}$$

By (5), we have

$$\left\| \mathbf{H}_r^{(k)} \right\| \le \|\mathbf{V}_k\|^2 \left\| \mathbf{H}_r^{(k-1)} \right\| + \|\mathbf{Q}_k\| \le \kappa_{b_{\mathrm{H}}} \left\| \mathbf{H}_r^{(k-1)} \right\| + \frac{1}{\overline{\mu}_{b_{\mathrm{H}}}}. \tag{S-43}$$

Now, apply (S-43) repeatedly over $k = r - M' + 1, \ldots, r$ and we have

$$\|\mathbf{H}_r\| = \left\| \mathbf{H}_r^{(r)} \right\| \le \kappa_{b_{\mathrm{H}}}^{M'} \left\| \mathbf{H}_r^{(r-M')} \right\| + \frac{1}{\overline{\mu}_{b_{\mathrm{H}}}} \sum_{i=0}^{M'-1} \kappa_{b_{\mathrm{H}}}^i \tag{S-44}$$

$$\overset{(a)}{\le} \frac{1}{\overline{\mu}_{b_{\mathrm{H}}}} \left(\kappa_{b_{\mathrm{H}}}^{M'} + \frac{\kappa_{b_{\mathrm{H}}}^{M'} - 1}{\kappa_{b_{\mathrm{H}}} - 1} \right) \tag{S-45}$$

$$\le \frac{1}{\overline{\mu}_{b_{\mathrm{H}}}} \kappa_{b_{\mathrm{H}}}^{M'} \left(1 + \frac{1}{\kappa_{b_{\mathrm{H}}} - 1} \right) \tag{S-46}$$

$$\overset{(b)}{\le} \frac{\kappa_{b_{\mathrm{H}}}^{M+1}}{\overline{\mu}_{b_{\mathrm{H}}}(\kappa_{b_{\mathrm{H}}} - 1)}, \tag{S-47}$$

where (a) follows from

$$\mathbf{H}_r^{(r-M')} = \frac{{\mathbf{s}_r}^T \mathbf{y}_r}{{\mathbf{y}_r}^T \mathbf{y}_r} \mathbf{I} \tag{S-48}$$

and

$$\frac{{\mathbf{s}_r}^T \mathbf{y}_r}{{\mathbf{y}_r}^T \mathbf{y}_r} = \frac{\widetilde{\mathbf{s}}_r^T \widetilde{\mathbf{s}}_r}{\widetilde{\mathbf{s}}_r^T \nabla^2 f_{\mathcal{T}_r}(\overline{\mathbf{x}}_r)\widetilde{\mathbf{s}}_r} \le \frac{1}{\overline{\mu}_{b_{\mathrm{H}}}}, \tag{S-49}$$

and (b) follows from $\kappa_{b_{\mathrm{H}}} \ge 1$ and $M' \le M$. To show $\gamma = 1/(M+1)\overline{L}_{b_{\mathrm{H}}}$, it suffices to show

$$\|\mathbf{B}_r\| \le (M+1)\overline{L}_{b_{\mathrm{H}}}, \tag{S-50}$$

where $\mathbf{B}_r \triangleq \mathbf{H}_r^{-1}$. To begin with, we rewrite (5) as Nocedal and Wright (2006, Chapter 6)

$$\mathbf{B}_r^{(k)} = \mathbf{B}_r^{(k-1)} - \frac{\mathbf{B}_r^{(k-1)} \mathbf{s}_k {\mathbf{s}_k}^T \mathbf{B}_r^{(k-1)}}{{\mathbf{s}_k}^T \mathbf{B}_r^{(k-1)} \mathbf{s}_k} + \frac{\mathbf{y}_k \mathbf{y}_k^T}{\mathbf{s}_k^T \mathbf{y}_k}, \tag{S-51}$$

where $\mathbf{B}_r^{(k)} \triangleq \left(\mathbf{H}_r^{(k)}\right)^{-1}$, for each $k \in [r - M' + 1 : r]$. Since the update rule (5) preserves positive definiteness of $\mathbf{H}_r^{(k)}$ (Nocedal and Wright, 2006), we have that $\mathbf{B}_r^{(k)} \succ 0$ for all $k \in [r - M' + 1 : r]$. Define $\widehat{\mathbf{s}}_k \triangleq \left(\mathbf{B}_r^{(k)}\right)^{1/2} \mathbf{s}_k$, then

$$\left\| \mathbf{B}_r^{(k-1)} - \frac{\mathbf{B}_r^{(k-1)} \mathbf{s}_k \mathbf{s}_k{}^T \mathbf{B}_r^{(k-1)}}{\mathbf{s}_k{}^T \mathbf{B}_r^{(k-1)} \mathbf{s}_k} \right\| \leq \left\| \left(\mathbf{B}_r^{(k-1)}\right)^{1/2} \right\|^2 \left\| \mathbf{I} - \frac{\widehat{\mathbf{s}}_k \widehat{\mathbf{s}}_k^T}{\|\widehat{\mathbf{s}}_k\|^2} \right\| = \left\| \mathbf{B}_r^{(k-1)} \right\|. \tag{S-52}$$

By (S-51), we have that

$$\left\| \mathbf{B}_r^{(k)} \right\| \leq \left\| \mathbf{B}_r^{(k-1)} \right\| + \left\| \frac{\mathbf{y}_k \mathbf{y}_k^T}{\mathbf{s}_k^T \mathbf{y}_k} \right\| \leq \left\| \mathbf{B}_r^{(k-1)} \right\| + \overline{L}_{b_{\mathrm{H}}}, \tag{S-53}$$

since

$$\left\| \frac{\mathbf{y}_k \mathbf{y}_k^T}{\mathbf{s}_k^T \mathbf{y}_k} \right\| = \frac{\|\mathbf{y}_k\|^2}{\mathbf{s}_k^T \mathbf{y}_k} = \frac{\widetilde{\mathbf{s}}_k^T \nabla^2 f_{\mathcal{T}_r}(\overline{\mathbf{x}}_r) \widetilde{\mathbf{s}}_k}{\widetilde{\mathbf{s}}_k^T \widetilde{\mathbf{s}}_k} \leq \overline{L}_{b_{\mathrm{H}}}. \tag{S-54}$$

Then we have

$$\|\mathbf{B}_r\| = \left\| \mathbf{B}_r^{(r)} \right\| \leq \left\| \mathbf{B}_r^{(r-M')} \right\| + M' \overline{L}_{b_{\mathrm{H}}} \overset{(a)}{\leq} (M+1) \overline{L}_{b_{\mathrm{H}}}, \tag{S-55}$$

where (a) follows from (S-48) and (S-54).

S-5 Proof of Proposition 2

Our proof leverages a refined telescoping of (S-20). For each $t \in [m]$, we multiply both sides of (S-20) by $(1 - \eta\gamma\overline{\mu})^{m-t}$ and obtain

$$\begin{aligned} &(1 - \eta\gamma\overline{\mu})^{m-t} \left(\mathbb{E}_{\mathcal{B}_{s,t}} \left[\|\widetilde{\mathbf{x}}_{s,t,r} - \widetilde{\mathbf{x}}_r^*\|^2 \middle| \mathcal{F}_{s,t} \right] + 2\eta \mathbb{E}_{\mathcal{B}_{s,t}} \left[\widetilde{f}_r(\widetilde{\mathbf{x}}_{s,t,r}) - \widetilde{f}_r(\widetilde{\mathbf{x}}_r^*) \middle| \mathcal{F}_{s,t} \right] \right) \\ &\quad \leq (1 - \eta\gamma\overline{\mu})^{m-t} \left((1 - \eta\gamma\overline{\mu}) \|\widetilde{\mathbf{x}}_{s,t-1,r} - \widetilde{\mathbf{x}}_r^*\|^2 + \frac{8}{b} \Gamma \overline{L} \eta^2 \left(\widetilde{f}_r(\widetilde{\mathbf{x}}_{s,t-1,r}) - \widetilde{f}_r(\widetilde{\mathbf{x}}_r^*) + \widetilde{f}_{r'}(\widetilde{\mathbf{x}}^{s,r'}) - \widetilde{f}_{r'}(\widetilde{\mathbf{x}}_{r'}^*) \right) \right). \end{aligned} \tag{S-56}$$

Telescope (S-56) over $t = 1, \ldots, m$ and we have

$$\begin{aligned} &2c\eta \left(1 - \frac{4}{b} \frac{\Gamma \overline{L} \eta}{1 - \eta\gamma\overline{\mu}}\right) \frac{1}{c} \sum_{t=1}^{m} (1 - \eta\gamma\overline{\mu})^{m-t} \mathbb{E}_{\mathcal{B}_{s,(t]}} \left[\widetilde{f}_r(\widetilde{\mathbf{x}}_{s,t,r}) - \widetilde{f}_r(\widetilde{\mathbf{x}}_r^*) \middle| \mathcal{F}_s \right] \\ &\quad \leq (1 - \eta\gamma\overline{\mu})^m \left\| \widetilde{\mathbf{x}}^{s,r'} - \mathbf{x}_{r'}^* \right\|^2 + \frac{8}{b} \Gamma \overline{L} \eta^2 \left((1 - \eta\gamma\overline{\mu})^m + c \right) \left(\widetilde{f}_{r'}(\widetilde{\mathbf{x}}^{s,r'}) - \widetilde{f}_{r'}(\widetilde{\mathbf{x}}_{r'}^*) \right). \end{aligned} \tag{S-57}$$

Now we consider using option IV to choose $\mathbf{x}^{s+1}$. Since $0 < \beta \leq 1 - \eta\gamma\overline{\mu}$, using (7) and Jensen's inequality in a similar manner as in (S-22) and taking expectations, we have

$$\frac{1}{c} \sum_{t=1}^{m} (1 - \eta\gamma\overline{\mu})^{m-t} \mathbb{E}_{\mathcal{B}_{s,(t]}} \left[\widetilde{f}_r(\widetilde{\mathbf{x}}_{s,t,r}) - \widetilde{f}_r(\widetilde{\mathbf{x}}_r^*) \middle| \mathcal{F}_s \right] \geq \mathbb{E}_{\mathcal{B}_{s,(m]}} \left[\widetilde{f}_{r''}(\widetilde{\mathbf{x}}^{s+1,r''}) - \widetilde{f}(\widetilde{\mathbf{x}}_{r''}^*) \middle| \mathcal{F}_s \right]. \tag{S-58}$$

Alternatively, if $\mathbf{x}^{s+1}$ is determined using option III, the definition of distribution q still yields (S-58). Finally, using (S-1) in Lemma S-1 to bound $\|\widetilde{\mathbf{x}}^{s,r'} - \widetilde{\mathbf{x}}_{r'}^*\|^2$ in (S-57), we have

$$\begin{aligned} &2c'\eta \left(1 - \frac{4}{b} \frac{\Gamma \overline{L} \eta}{1 - \eta\gamma\overline{\mu}}\right) \mathbb{E}_{\mathcal{B}_{s,(m]}} \left[\widetilde{f}_{r''}(\widetilde{\mathbf{x}}^{s+1,r''}) - \widetilde{f}(\widetilde{\mathbf{x}}_{r''}^*) \middle| \mathcal{F}_s \right] \\ &\quad \leq \left(\frac{8}{b} \Gamma \overline{L} \eta^2 (1 + c') + \frac{2}{\gamma\overline{\mu}} \right) \left(\widetilde{f}_{r'}(\widetilde{\mathbf{x}}^{s,r'}) - \widetilde{f}_{r'}(\widetilde{\mathbf{x}}_{r'}^*) \right). \end{aligned} \tag{S-59}$$

Taking expectation on both sides, rearranging and using (7), we reach (31).

S-6 Proof of Proposition 3

The subsampled gradient strategy essentially introduces errors in $\{\mathbf{g}_s\}_{s\geq 0}$. Therefore, we explicit model this error by $\mathbf{e}_s \triangleq \widetilde{\mathbf{g}}_s - \mathbf{g}_s$. We first bound the second moment of $\mathbf{e}_s$. Since $\mathbf{g}_s = \nabla f(\mathbf{x}^s)$, by Lemma S-3 and $\widetilde{b}_s \geq nS^2\alpha_s/(S^2\alpha_s + (n-1)\xi^2\overline{\rho}^{2s})$, we have for any $s \in (S]$,

$$\mathbb{E}_{\widetilde{\mathcal{B}}_s}\left[\|\mathbf{e}_s\|^2\right] \leq \frac{n - \widetilde{b}_s}{\widetilde{b}_s(n-1)}\alpha_s \leq \frac{\xi^2}{S^2}\overline{\rho}^{2s}. \tag{S-60}$$

As a result,

$$\mathbb{E}_{\widetilde{\mathcal{B}}_s}\left[\|\mathbf{e}_s\|\right] \leq \frac{\xi}{S}\overline{\rho}^{s}. \tag{S-61}$$

The introduction of random sets $\{\widetilde{\mathcal{B}}_s\}_{s\geq 0}$ requires us to redefine the filtration $\{\mathcal{F}_{s,t}\}_{s\geq 0, t\in(m-1]}$ as

$$\mathcal{F}_{s,t} \triangleq \sigma\left(\{\tau_j\}_{j=0}^{s-1} \cup \{\widetilde{\mathcal{B}}_j\}_{j\in(s]} \cup \{\mathcal{B}_{i,j}\}_{i\in(s-1],j\in(m-1]} \cup \{\mathcal{B}_{s,j}\}_{j=0}^{t-1} \cup \{\mathcal{T}_j\}_{j=0}^{\lfloor(sm+t)/L\rfloor}\right). \tag{S-62}$$

As usual, we define $\mathcal{F}_s \triangleq \mathcal{F}_{s,0}$. In the sequel, we follow the naming convention in coordinate transformation framework as in Section 4.1. In particular, we define $\widetilde{\mathbf{e}}_{s,r'} \triangleq \mathbf{H}_{r'}^{1/2}\mathbf{e}_s$. Now, define $\widetilde{\mathbf{v}}'_{s,t,r} \triangleq \widetilde{\mathbf{v}}_{s,t,r} + \widetilde{\mathbf{e}}_{s,r'}$, then from (S-7) and (S-8), we have

$$\mathbb{E}_{\mathcal{B}_{s,t}}\left[\widetilde{\mathbf{v}}'_{s,t,r}\middle|\mathcal{F}_{s,t}\right] = \nabla\widetilde{f}_r(\widetilde{\mathbf{x}}_{s,t,r}) + \widetilde{\mathbf{e}}_{s,r'}, \tag{S-63}$$

$$\mathbb{E}_{\mathcal{B}_{s,t}}\left[\left\|\widetilde{\mathbf{v}}'_{s,t,r} - \nabla\widetilde{f}_r(\widetilde{\mathbf{x}}_{s,t,r})\right\|^2\middle|\mathcal{F}_{s,t}\right] \leq \frac{4\Gamma\overline{L}}{b}\left(\widetilde{f}_r(\widetilde{\mathbf{x}}_{s,t,r}) - \widetilde{f}_r(\widetilde{\mathbf{x}}_r^*) + \widetilde{f}_{r'}(\widetilde{\mathbf{x}}^{s,r'}) - \widetilde{f}_{r'}(\widetilde{\mathbf{x}}_{r'}^*)\right) + \|\widetilde{\mathbf{e}}_{s,r'}\|^2, \tag{S-64}$$

Following a similar argument as in the proof of Theorem 1, we have

$$\|\widetilde{\mathbf{x}}_{s,t+1,r} - \widetilde{\mathbf{x}}_r^*\|^2 \leq (1-\eta\gamma\overline{\mu})\|\widetilde{\mathbf{x}}_{s,t,r} - \widetilde{\mathbf{x}}_r^*\|^2 - 2\eta\left(\widetilde{f}_r(\widetilde{\mathbf{x}}_{s,t+1,r}) - \widetilde{f}_r(\widetilde{\mathbf{x}}_r^*)\right) + 2\eta^2\left\|\widetilde{\boldsymbol{\delta}}'_{s,t,r}\right\|^2 - 2\eta\left\langle\widetilde{\boldsymbol{\delta}}'_{s,t,r}, \widetilde{\mathbf{x}}_{s,t,r} - \widetilde{\mathbf{x}}_r^*\right\rangle, \tag{S-65}$$

where $\widetilde{\boldsymbol{\delta}}'_{s,t,r} \triangleq \widetilde{\mathbf{v}}'_{s,t,r} - \nabla\widetilde{f}_r(\widetilde{\mathbf{x}}_{s,t,r})$. Taking expectation w.r.t. $\mathcal{B}_{s,t}$ and using (S-63) and (S-64), we have

$$\begin{aligned}\mathbb{E}_{\mathcal{B}_{s,t}}\left[\|\widetilde{\mathbf{x}}_{s,t+1,r} - \widetilde{\mathbf{x}}_r^*\|^2\middle|\mathcal{F}_{s,t}\right] + 2\eta\mathbb{E}_{\mathcal{B}_{s,t}}\left[\widetilde{f}_r(\widetilde{\mathbf{x}}_{s,t+1,r}) - \widetilde{f}_r(\widetilde{\mathbf{x}}_r^*)\middle|\mathcal{F}_{s,t}\right] &\leq (1-\eta\gamma\overline{\mu})\|\widetilde{\mathbf{x}}_{s,t,r} - \widetilde{\mathbf{x}}_r^*\|^2 \\ + \frac{8}{b}\Gamma\overline{L}\eta^2\left(\widetilde{f}_r(\widetilde{\mathbf{x}}_{s,t,r}) - \widetilde{f}_r(\widetilde{\mathbf{x}}_r^*) + \widetilde{f}_{r'}(\widetilde{\mathbf{x}}^{s,r'}) - \widetilde{f}_{r'}(\widetilde{\mathbf{x}}_{r'}^*)\right) &+ 2\eta^2\|\widetilde{\mathbf{e}}_{s,r'}\|^2 - 2\eta\langle\widetilde{\mathbf{e}}_{s,r'}, \widetilde{\mathbf{x}}_{s,t,r} - \widetilde{\mathbf{x}}_r^*\rangle.\end{aligned} \tag{S-66}$$

Using Cauchy-Schwartz inequality, we have

$$-2\eta\langle\widetilde{\mathbf{e}}_{s,r'}, \widetilde{\mathbf{x}}_{s,t,r} - \widetilde{\mathbf{x}}_r^*\rangle \leq 2\eta\|\widetilde{\mathbf{e}}_{s,r'}\|\|\widetilde{\mathbf{x}}_{s,t,r} - \widetilde{\mathbf{x}}_r^*\| \leq 2\eta\|\widetilde{\mathbf{e}}_{s,r'}\|\left\|\mathbf{H}_r^{-1/2}\right\|\|\mathbf{x}_{s,t} - \mathbf{x}^*\| \leq 2\eta B\gamma^{-1/2}\|\widetilde{\mathbf{e}}_{s,r'}\|. \tag{S-67}$$

Substituting (S-67) into (S-66), and using the telescoping techniques in Section S-5, we have

$$\begin{aligned}2c\eta\left(1 - \frac{4}{b}\frac{\Gamma\overline{L}\eta}{1-\eta\gamma\overline{\mu}}\right)\frac{1}{c}\sum_{t=1}^{m}(1-\eta\gamma\overline{\mu})^{m-t}\mathbb{E}_{\mathcal{B}_{s,(t]}}\left[\widetilde{f}_r(\widetilde{\mathbf{x}}_{s,t,r}) - \widetilde{f}_r(\widetilde{\mathbf{x}}_r^*)\middle|\mathcal{F}_s\right] \leq (1-\eta\gamma\overline{\mu})^m\left\|\widetilde{\mathbf{x}}^{s,r'} - \mathbf{x}_{r'}^*\right\|^2 \\ + \frac{8}{b}\Gamma\overline{L}\eta^2\left((1-\eta\gamma\overline{\mu})^m + c\right)\left(\widetilde{f}_{r'}(\widetilde{\mathbf{x}}^{s,r'}) - \widetilde{f}_{r'}(\widetilde{\mathbf{x}}_{r'}^*)\right) + 2\eta\left((1-\eta\gamma\overline{\mu})^m + c\right)\left(B\gamma^{-1/2}\|\widetilde{\mathbf{e}}_{s,r'}\| + \eta\|\widetilde{\mathbf{e}}_{s,r'}\|^2\right).\end{aligned} \tag{S-68}$$

With either option III or IV and (S-1), we have

$$\begin{aligned}&2c'\eta\left(1 - \frac{4}{b}\frac{\Gamma\overline{L}\eta}{1-\eta\gamma\overline{\mu}}\right)\mathbb{E}_{\mathcal{B}_{s,(m]}}\left[\widetilde{f}_{r''}(\widetilde{\mathbf{x}}^{s+1,r''}) - \widetilde{f}(\widetilde{\mathbf{x}}_{r''}^*)\middle|\mathcal{F}_s\right] \\ &\leq \left(\frac{8}{b}\Gamma\overline{L}\eta^2(1+c') + \frac{2}{\gamma\overline{\mu}}\right)\left(\widetilde{f}_{r'}(\widetilde{\mathbf{x}}^{s,r'}) - \widetilde{f}_{r'}(\widetilde{\mathbf{x}}_{r'}^*)\right) + 2\eta(1+c')\left(B\gamma^{-1/2}\|\widetilde{\mathbf{e}}_{s,r'}\| + \eta\|\widetilde{\mathbf{e}}_{s,r'}\|^2\right).\end{aligned} \tag{S-69}$$

Taking expectation on both sides and using (7), we have

$$\mathbb{E}\left[f(\mathbf{x}^{s+1}) - f(\mathbf{x}^*)\right] \le \overline{\rho}\mathbb{E}\left[f(\mathbf{x}^s) - f(\mathbf{x}^*)\right] + \left(1 + \frac{1}{c'}\right)\frac{b}{b - 4\Gamma\overline{L}\eta/(1-\eta\gamma\overline{\mu})}\left(B\gamma^{-1/2}\mathbb{E}\left[\|\widetilde{\mathbf{e}}_{s,r'}\|\right] + \eta\mathbb{E}\left[\|\widetilde{\mathbf{e}}_{s,r'}\|^2\right]\right). \tag{S-70}$$

From (S-60) and (S-61), we have

$$\mathbb{E}\left[\|\widetilde{\mathbf{e}}_{s,r'}\|\right] \le \frac{\Gamma^{1/2}\xi}{S}\overline{\rho}^s, \tag{S-71}$$

$$\mathbb{E}\left[\|\widetilde{\mathbf{e}}_{s,r'}\|^2\right] \le \frac{\Gamma\xi^2}{S^2}\overline{\rho}^{2s}. \tag{S-72}$$

Substituting (S-71) and (S-72) into (S-70), we have

$$\begin{aligned}\mathbb{E}\left[f(\mathbf{x}^{s+1}) - f(\mathbf{x}^*)\right] &\le \overline{\rho}\mathbb{E}\left[f(\mathbf{x}^s) - f(\mathbf{x}^*)\right] + \left(1 + \frac{1}{c'}\right)\frac{b}{b - 4\Gamma\overline{L}\eta/(1-\eta\gamma\overline{\mu})}\left(\frac{\kappa_{\mathrm{H}}^{1/2}B\xi}{S}\overline{\rho}^s + \frac{\eta\Gamma\xi^2}{S^2}\overline{\rho}^{2s}\right)\\ &\le \overline{\rho}\mathbb{E}\left[f(\mathbf{x}^s) - f(\mathbf{x}^*)\right] + \left(1 + \frac{1}{c'}\right)\frac{b}{b - 4\Gamma\overline{L}\eta/(1-\eta\gamma\overline{\mu})}\left(\kappa_{\mathrm{H}}^{1/2}B + \eta\Gamma\xi\right)\frac{\xi}{S}\overline{\rho}^s\end{aligned} \tag{S-73}$$

Applying (S-73) recursively and we complete the proof.

S-7 Future Work and Open Problems

For future work, we propose to pursue from the following two directions:

- Based on our novel coordinate transformation framework, *proximal* and momentum-based stochastic L-BFGS algorithms can be developed and analyzed. The proximal variant can greatly enable our algorithm to handle composite (convex) objective function, thereby greatly extending the applications of our method. The accelerated variant can potentially improve the linear convergence rate of our algorithm, and thus reduce the total computational complexity.
- The linear convergence of the strategy in Section 6.3 can be analyzed theoretically. In Figure 4, we observed the linear convergence empirically. This indicates that linear convergence of Algorithm 1 may still hold under such a strategy.

Besides future work, there also exists an open problem. Although we have improved the linear convergence rate and computational complexity of Algorithm 1 as compared to those in Moritz et al. (2016) and Gower et al. (2016), it seems our improved complexity in (29) is still inferior to the computational complexity of SVRG. In SVRG, the complexity is $O((n+\kappa)d\log(1/\epsilon))$ (Xiao and Zhang, 2014), so our complexity (29) has an additional multiplicative factor κ_{H}. This contradicts the experimental results in Moritz et al. (2016), Gower et al. (2016) and Section 7.2, where stochastic L-BFGS-type algorithms have been repeatedly shown to outperform their first-order counterparts. A careful analysis will reveal that the additional κ_{H} arises from the uniform spectral bound of the metric matrices $\{\mathbf{H}_r\}_{r\ge 0}$. This uniform bound is effectively a worst-case bound, and does not reflect the *local curvature information* contained in recent iterates at any time (s,t). Since the judicious use of curvature information serves as a very important reason for the fast convergence of stochastic quasi-Newton algorithms, such information should also be reflected in theoretical analysis as well (possibly in an adaptive spectral bound for $\{\mathbf{H}_r\}_{r\ge 0}$). We also believe an effective adaptive bound can potentially improve the complexity result (29). *In short, how to obtain a (computational) complexity bound of stochastic L-BFGS algorithm that is better (or at least as good as) that of SVRG will be an interesting problem to consider.*

The Binomial Block Bootstrap Estimator for Evaluating Loss on Dependent Clusters

Matt Barnes
The Robotics Institute
Carnegie Mellon University
Pittsburgh, PA 15213
mbarnes1@cs.cmu.edu

Artur Dubrawski
The Robotics Institute
Carnegie Mellon University
Pittsburgh, PA 15213
awd@cs.cmu.edu

Abstract

In this paper, we study the non-IID learning setting where samples exhibit *dependency within latent clusters*. Our goal is to estimate a learner's loss on new clusters, an extension of the out-of-bag error. Previously developed cross-validation estimators are well suited to the case where the clustering of observed data is known a priori. However, as is often the case in real world problems, we are only given a noisy approximation of this clustering, likely the result of some clustering algorithm. This subtle yet potentially significant issue afflicts domains ranging from image classification to medical diagnostics, where naive cross-validation is an optimistically biased estimator. We present a novel bootstrap technique and corresponding cross-validation method that, somewhat counterintuitively, injects additional dependency to asymptotically recover the loss in the independent setting.

1 Introduction

The assumption of independent and identically distributed (IID) samples is fundamental to many machine learning algorithms [1, 2]. Some exploration outside this setting has occurred — notably in time-series data, clusters of independent data and less explicitly in active learning [3, 4]. In this paper, we study the setting where samples exhibit dependency both within latent clusters.

To illustrate, consider samples generated according to the simple k-mixture model

$$\begin{aligned} \phi_j &\overset{iid}{\sim} H(\gamma) && \text{for } j = 1, \dots, k \\ c_i &\overset{iid}{\sim} \text{Categorical}(\pi) && \\ x_i, y_i &\overset{iid}{\sim} G(\phi_{c_i}) && \text{for } i = 1, \dots, n_x \end{aligned} \tag{1}$$

where ϕ are latent cluster parameters; c are (potentially latent) cluster assignments; $X = x_1, \dots, x_{n_x}$ are n_x samples; y are the corresponding labels; H is some distribution over cluster parameters; γ, π, k, n_x are model parameters and π is in the k-dimensional probability simplex. This includes, for example, many mixture models and topic models. Note that without conditioning on the latents ϕ, samples within the same cluster are dependent while samples in different clusters are independent. Our goal in this setting is to find a learner $f : \mathcal{X} \to \mathcal{Y}$ which performs well on new clusters, i.e. has small out-of-cluster loss $\mathbb{E}_{x',y'}\ell(y', f(x' \mid X_{1:n_x}, y_{1:n_x}))$, where ℓ is a continuous loss function, $x', y' \sim G(\phi')$ and $\phi' \sim H(\gamma)$.

To address this problem, previous work has considered the case where the partition c is observed and the leave-one-cluster-out (LOCO[1]) estimator is used for cross-validation [1, 2, 5, 6],

$$\widehat{\text{Err}}_{\text{LOCO}} = \frac{1}{n}\sum_{i=1}^{k}\sum_{j \in c_i^{-1}} \ell(y_j, f(x_j \mid x_{\bar{c}_i^{-1}}, y_{\bar{c}_i^{-1}})), \tag{2}$$

where c_i^{-1} and $\bar{c}_i^{-1}$ denote all sample indices belonging and not belonging to cluster i, respectively. For f, we allow any (possibly stochastic) function, which will realistically be some classifier or regressor. This strategy, which creates independent training and testing folds, is referred to as *conditioning on the partition*. By training and testing on disjoint clusters, LOCO is a very nearly unbiased estimate of the out-of-cluster loss, with a small

[1] also referred to as leave-one-label-out cross-validation, terminology we avoid due to potential confusion between sample and cluster labels

amount of bias due to training on $k - 1$ clusters instead of k clusters.

The primary focus of this paper is that the partition c is often unknown a priori or uncertain. Instead of c, we are given an approximation $\hat{c}$, which is usually the result of some unsupervised clustering of X. For example, our original motivation for studying this issue arose from a common problem found in medical applications. Here, medical records correspond to samples X and patients correspond to clusters $i = 1, \ldots, k$. In other words, each patient may have multiple medical records. For tasks such as cancer screening and medical imaging, LOCO prevents the learner from overfitting to patient-specific features such as social security number, name, and date-of-birth, which are not useful for prediction on new patients [5, 6, 7]. Better predictors generalize across patients, e.g. unexplained weight loss, fatigue, and tumor image features. This overfitting need not be blatant. An image classifier could learn the shapes of each patient's bone structure to predict whether they have lung cancer, which is not useful for new patients and difficult to inspect for without using LOCO.

The problem in the medical domain is we only observe X and y, and must infer an approximation $\hat{c}$ through clustering or entity resolution of records across hospitals and providers. Using $\hat{c}$ as a surrogate for c in LOCO presents a subtle yet potentially significant issue: cross-validation folds which were previously independent are now dependent due to incorrectly clustered samples. It is equivalent to mistakingly placing testing fold samples in the training folds, and vice versa. These mistakes enable the learner to, once again, overfit to patient-specific features — the exact problem we intended to avoid by using LOCO. We term this phenomenon *dependency leakage* and show that even at small approximation errors in $\hat{c}$, it can cause significant bias in cross-validation results.

Outside of the medical domain, we are familiar with similar problems in the census and counter-human-trafficking communities. At the US Census Bureau, matching persons across censuses is a challenging, imperfect process and the impact of using $\hat{c}$ for demographic, socioeconomic, and other statistical analysis is unclear [8, 9]. Similarly, imperfect record linkage results are used to estimate death counts in Syria and to both estimate and predict human trafficking in the United States [10, 11]. A major concern in these domains is that dependency leakage can bias a learner against certain sub-populations (i.e. clusters). For example, in Section 4 we empirically demonstrate how dependency leakage causes bias against certain demographics in US Census data. This is increasingly relevant as data science plays a greater role in credit and policy decisions [12, 13].

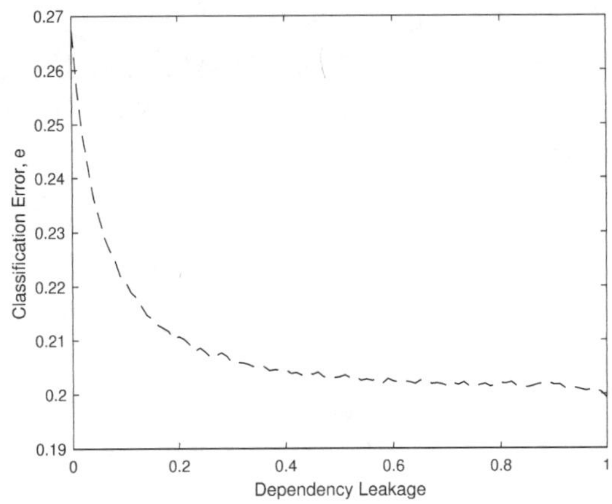

Figure 1: Simulation study on the heart disease dataset showing dependency leakage optimistically biases cross-validation results on clusters of dependent samples by allowing some learning on the test distribution.

In computer vision, consider the task of activity detection from videos. Given many videos of pole vaulters, it is common to have multiple videos of the same event (e.g. the 2016 Olympics). A concern here is the learner may overfit to scene features rather than learning a useful understanding of the activity. Splitting videos by event tags is comparable to using LOCO, which encourages learning activity features which generalize across events. However, event tags and the corresponding clustering are imperfect, and thus this problem may suffer from dependency leakage. One can imagine similar challenges for larger image datasets constructed through un- or semi-supervised means (e.g. knowledge bases).

In this paper, we contribute a novel bootstrap technique for learning on blocks of dependent data, which both estimates and corrects for dependency leakage. This enables learning on clusters of dependent data, where we only observe a noisy approximation of the true clustering, likely the result of some clustering or record linkage algorithm. The key insight is to increase dependency by further corrupting $\hat{c}$, in order to extrapolate an unbiased and consistent estimator for the true c. Simulation studies in the non-asymptotic case show our method significantly outperforms standard cross-validation techniques.

2 Learning in dependent data

The problem of constructing estimators for dependent data has been studied since Singh [14], who provided the first theoretical confirmation of the naive bootstrap's performance with IID data, and also showed its inadequacy for dependent data. Since then, the bootstrap has been extended to both time-series and cluster data. In time-series data, blocks of data are dependent according to some stochastic process [15, 16]. By varying the size and separation of the blocks, these block bootstrap methods can limit the dependency and thus control the bias and variance of the estimator, while sometimes achieving consistency. We refer the reader to [17] for a more thorough overview of the subject.

In cluster data, within-cluster samples are dependent while inter-cluster samples are typically assumed to be independent. This is the same formulation as Eq. 1. Many bootstrap methods have been proposed for variance estimation in the clustering setting, as classical bootstrap estimators will typically be downward biased [18]. Model-based methods assume a parametric model for the within-cluster error correlation. Model-free methods perform post-estimation bias-correction, such as the cluster-robust variance estimator (CRVE) for ordinary least squares [19] and non-linear settings [20]. CRVE suffers from having unbalanced or a small number of clusters, which is addressed in [21]. Field and Welsh [22] provide theoretical asymptotic analysis for several cluster bootstrap techniques, including the randomized cluster bootstrap, two-stage bootstrap [23] and residual bootstrap [24]. Multi-way bootstrap clustering is slightly more general, but still assumes samples belonging to none of the same clusters are independent [25]. Neither these bootstrap techniques nor LOCO cross-validation account for inter-cluster dependency, and will be inadequate for $\hat{c}$ and non-trivial f, ℓ, X and y.

In practice, when the clustering c is latent, researchers choose a coarse clustering $\hat{c}$ to ensure intra-cluster samples are as independent as possible [18]. A coarser clustering decreases bias and increases variance. This approach both lacks guarantees and requires choosing an appropriate clustering coarseness, which is an open problem. The key differentiation of our work is we directly address the issue of inter-cluster dependency due to $\hat{c}$.

Dependency leakage may have a significant impact on cross-validation results and model selection, both in theory and in practice. To illustrate, consider the simulation results depicted in Figure 1. We use heart disease data from hospitals in Cleveland, Hungary, Switzerland and California (see additional details in Section 4) [26]. Each location is a cluster and each sample is a single patient, thus the LOCO estimator generalizes performance at new hospitals. To simulate the effect of using $\hat{c}$ as a surrogate for c, we move samples from the test set into the train set with uniform probability (horizontal axis). Dependency leakage optimistically biases the cross-validation accuracy estimate by more than 25%. We will return to this example in Section 4.

3 The Binomial Block Bootstrap estimator

We now introduce the binomial block bootstrap (B3) class of estimators for cross-validating with dependent blocks of data. First, we begin by formalizing notation to simplify analysis of the core problem. We then proceed with the simplest leakage scenario and gradually build complexity until arriving at our final result. In section 3.2 we begin with the case where samples are moved with known probability in a single direction, from the test blocks to the train blocks or vice versa. Then we show how to solve for the unidirectional dependency leakage in section 3.3 and generalize to the bidirectional case in section 3.4.

3.1 Problem Setup

Broadly, we address the problem of LOCO cross-validation when a noisy approximation of the true latent partition c. For the remainder of the paper, we consider some arbitrary fixed i in Eq. 2 (i.e. a single fold). In the LOCO estimator with known partitioning c, each fold is created such that $\mathcal{T}$ and $\mathcal{V}$ are sets of training and testing samples, respectively, split by the partition, i.e. $c(i) \neq c(j)\ \forall x_i \in \mathcal{T}, x_j \in \mathcal{V}$. Without conditioning on the latent cluster parameters in Eq. 1, samples within the same cluster are dependent while samples in different clusters are independent. Thus, $\mathcal{T}$ and $\mathcal{V}$ are independent.

Using this notation, we think about the core problem as a learner f trained on samples $\mathcal{T}$ drawn IID from distribution $P_\mathcal{T}$ and tested on samples $\mathcal{V}$ drawn IID from a related but different distribution $P_\mathcal{V}$, a form of transfer learning.

Now, suppose we instead observe noisy datasets $\hat{\mathcal{T}}$ and $\hat{\mathcal{V}}$, where samples have randomly moved between $\mathcal{T}$ and $\mathcal{V}$. This question arises naturally when we only have $\hat{c}$, an approximation of c, likely obtained through clustering. Most importantly, $\hat{\mathcal{T}}$ and $\hat{\mathcal{V}}$ are dependent — which provides additional information to the learner and biases our cross-validation estimator. Our goal then is to answer questions regarding the continuous loss function ℓ evaluated on new clusters, for example $\mathbb{E}_{\mathcal{T}\sim P_\mathcal{T}}\mathbb{E}_{(x,y)\sim P_\mathcal{V}}\ell(f(x \mid \mathcal{T}), y)$, given only noisy datasets $\hat{\mathcal{T}}$ and $\hat{\mathcal{V}}$.

3.2 Unidirectional leakage with known probability

First, consider the case where samples move with known uniform probability from either $\mathcal{V}$ to $\mathcal{T}$ or vice versa to

[2] $M_{S_1,S_2}(w_1, w_2)$ is a mixture distribution of sets S_1 and S_2, where the probability of sampling from the sets are $w_1 + w_2 = 1$, respectively. Within set samples are drawn uniformly.

Algorithm 1 B3: Unidirectional leakage with known probability

procedure KNOWNUNIDIRECTIONAL($f, \hat{\mathcal{T}}, \hat{\mathcal{V}}, p_0, dir, n', t$)
  $\bar{b} \leftarrow \vec{0}$
  for p_i in $\{p_0, p_0 + \delta, p_0 + 2\delta, \dots, 1\}$ **do** ▷ Choose $\delta > 0$ s.t. $|\{p_i\}| > n'$
    $p' \leftarrow \frac{p_i - p_0}{1 - p_0}$
    for $j \leftarrow 1$ to t **do**
      if dir is $\mathcal{V}$ to $\mathcal{T}$ **then**
        $\mathcal{T}'_j \overset{n'}{\sim} M_{\hat{\mathcal{T}},\hat{\mathcal{V}}}(1 - p', p')$ ▷ M is a mixture distribution[2]
        $\mathcal{V}'_j \leftarrow \hat{\mathcal{V}} \setminus \mathcal{T}'_j$
      else
        $\mathcal{V}'_j \overset{n'}{\sim} M_{\hat{\mathcal{T}},\hat{\mathcal{V}}}(p', 1 - p')$
        $\mathcal{T}'_j \leftarrow \hat{\mathcal{T}} \setminus \mathcal{V}'_j$
      end if
      $\hat{b}_i \leftarrow \frac{1}{|\mathcal{V}'_j|} \sum_{(x,y) \in \mathcal{V}'_j} \ell(y, f(x \mid \mathcal{T}'_j))$ ▷ ℓ is any continuous loss function
      $\bar{b}_i \leftarrow \bar{b}_i + \frac{\hat{b}_i}{t}$
    end for
  end for
  $A_{ij} \leftarrow \mathbb{P}(\text{Binomial}(n', p_i) = j) \quad \forall p_i \in p, j \in \{0, 1, \dots, n'\}$
  $\hat{e}, residual \leftarrow A(A^\intercal A)^{-1} A^\intercal \bar{b}$
  return $\hat{e}_0, residual$
end procedure

create $\hat{\mathcal{V}}$ and $\hat{\mathcal{T}}$. Without loss of generality, we consider the case where samples move from $\mathcal{V}$ to $\mathcal{T}$. In other words, $\hat{\mathcal{V}}$ contains only samples from $P_{\mathcal{V}}$ while $\hat{\mathcal{T}}$ contains samples from both $P_{\mathcal{T}}$ and $P_{\mathcal{V}}$. Let p_0 be the fraction of samples in $\hat{\mathcal{T}}$ from $\mathcal{V}$, i.e. $p_0 = \frac{|\hat{\mathcal{T}} \cap \mathcal{V}|}{|\hat{\mathcal{T}}|}$. The analysis for the other direction is identical.

The unidirectional B3 estimator (presented in Algorithm 1) is based on the observation that the number of corrupted samples in a bootstrap sample $\mathcal{T}'$ from $\hat{\mathcal{T}}$ is binomially distributed according to p_0 and $n' = |\mathcal{T}'|$. The bootstrap sample $\mathcal{T}'$ is formed by resampling with replacement n' times from $\hat{\mathcal{T}}$, which we notate as $\mathcal{T}' \overset{n'}{\sim} \hat{\mathcal{T}}$. Let b_0 be the expected bootstrap loss estimate, $b_0 = \mathop{\mathbb{E}}_{(x,y)\sim\hat{\mathcal{V}}} \mathop{\mathbb{E}}_{\mathcal{T}' \overset{n'}{\sim} \hat{\mathcal{T}}} \ell(f(x|\mathcal{T}'), y)$. We can express b_0 as a binomial weighting of the expected error at all numbers of corrupted samples in $\mathcal{T}'$. Formally,

$$b_0 = \langle a_0, e \rangle \tag{3}$$

where a_0 is the probability mass function (pmf) of $\text{Binomial}(n', p_0)$, e_i is the expected loss with i corrupted samples in $\mathcal{T}'$ and $\langle \cdot, \cdot \rangle$ denotes the inner product operation. Our goal is to recover e_0, the loss with zero corruption.

At first, this may seem difficult as $b_0 = \langle a_0, e \rangle$ is a very underdetermined system (even assuming we know p_0). To overcome this deficiency, the key insight of our bootstrap technique is to artificially inject additional leakage by further mixing $\mathcal{V}$ into $\hat{\mathcal{T}}$ to create a fully or over defined system. This increases p, alters the binomial pmf a_0, and generates a new linear equality $b_1 = \langle a_1, e \rangle$ where a_1 is the pmf of $\text{Binomial}(n', p_1)$. Repeating this process many times results in the linear system

$$\begin{array}{c} \\ p_0 \\ p_1 \\ \cdot \\ \cdot \\ 1 \end{array} \begin{array}{c} 0 \quad 1 \quad \cdot \quad \cdot \quad n' \\ \begin{pmatrix} \leftarrow \text{Binomial pmf} \rightarrow \\ \cdot \\ \cdot \\ \cdot \\ \leftarrow \text{Binomial pmf} \rightarrow \end{pmatrix} \end{array} \begin{pmatrix} \\ \\ e \\ \\ \\ \end{pmatrix} = \begin{pmatrix} \\ \\ b \\ \\ \\ \end{pmatrix} \tag{4}$$

$$A(p_0) \qquad\qquad e \;=\; b$$

For any unique choice of $p = (p_0, p_1, \dots, p_m) \in [0, 1]^m$, this system will be well-defined (by Lemma 3.1) and can be readily solved for e_0. A somewhat similar clustering randomization idea is used in [27] for estimating treatment effects, though their formulation is quite different than Eq. 4.

Lemma 3.1. *Let matrix A be defined such that*

$$A_{ij} = \mathbb{P}(\text{Binomial}(n', p_i) = j). \tag{5}$$

Then A has full rank for any choice of unique parameters $p = (p_0, p_1, \dots, p_m) \in [0, 1]^m$.

Proof. See Appendix A.1. □

Algorithm 2 B3: Unidirectional leakage with unknown probability

procedure UNKNOWNUNIDIR($f, \hat{\mathcal{T}}, \hat{\mathcal{V}}, dir, n', t$)
    $residual^* \leftarrow \infty$
    $n \leftarrow |\hat{\mathcal{T}}|$
    for $\hat{p}_0$ in $\{\frac{0}{n}, \frac{1}{n}, \ldots, \frac{n-1}{n}\}$ **do**
        $\hat{e}_0, residual \leftarrow$ KNOWNUNIDIR($f, \hat{\mathcal{T}}, \hat{\mathcal{V}}, \hat{p}_0, dir, n', t$)
        if $residual < residual^*$ **then**
            $\hat{e}_0^* \leftarrow \hat{e}_0$
            $\hat{p}_0^* \leftarrow \hat{p}_0$
            $residual^* \leftarrow residual$
        end if
    end for
    return $\hat{e}_0^*, \hat{p}_0^*$
end procedure

Roughly speaking, Algorithm 1 is estimating the loss at increasing levels of dependency leakage, and then extrapolating the loss at zero dependency. It is possible to achieve reasonable results in practice because we know the true formulation to be a binomial weighted regression problem and thus know matrix A exactly. Further, the extrapolation does not extend far beyond the known range for practical clusterings $\hat{c}$ with small p_0.

The estimator $\hat{e}_0$ in Algorithm 1 is consistent, unbiased and has variance decreasing linearly with respect to the number of bootstrap samples t.

Theorem 3.2. *The estimator $\hat{e}_0$ in Algorithm 1 satisfies*

1. *Consistent:* $\hat{e}_0 \xrightarrow{p} \mathbb{E}_{\mathcal{T}' \overset{n'}{\sim} P_{\mathcal{T}}} \mathbb{E}_{(x,y)\sim P_{\mathcal{V}}} \ell(y, f(x \mid \mathcal{T}'))$ *as* $t, |\hat{\mathcal{T}}|, |\hat{\mathcal{V}}| \to \infty$
2. *Unbiased:* $\mathbb{E}[\hat{e}_0] = e_0$ *for finite* t *and infinite* $|\hat{\mathcal{T}}|, |\hat{\mathcal{V}}|$.
3. $\text{Var}(\hat{e}_0) =$

$$\sum_{i=0}^{n'} \left[\frac{\sum\limits_{\substack{0 \le m_0 < \cdots < m_{n'-1} \le n' \\ m_0, \ldots, m_{n'-1} \ne i}} p_{m_0} \cdots p_{m_{n'-1}}}{\prod\limits_{0 \le m \le n', m \ne i} (p_m - p_i)} \right]^2 \frac{\sigma_{b_i}^2}{t}$$

where $\sigma_{b_i}^2$ is the variance of $\hat{b}_i$ in Algorithm 1, which is a function of f, ℓ and the data.

Proof. See Appendix A.2. □

Remark For classification error ℓ, note $\sigma_{b_j}^2 \le \frac{1}{4}$ by Popoviciu's inequality. Generally speaking, there exists a variance tradeoff when choosing $p_0, \ldots, p_{n'}$ — we can expect lower variance as the values are spaced further apart (larger denominator) and when they are closer to p_0 (smaller numerator), which are competing choices.

Remark The quality of the clustering $\hat{c}$ plays an important role in the performance of our estimator. As p_0 increases, the estimator remains unbiased but the variance increases according to Statement 3.

3.3 Unidirectional leakage with unknown probability

We now extend the unidirectional leakage scenario from Section 3.2 to the situation where p_0 is unknown a priori. The general strategy is to minimize the residual $||A(\hat{p}_0)e - \bar{b}||$ over $\hat{p}_0$ and show that a unique minimum exists and it is always the true leakage probability p_0. The most basic optimization procedure detailed in Algorithm 2 searches over the discrete set of possible solutions, though one can imagine other optimization procedures. The search space will be, at most, the one dimensional line defined by $[0, \frac{n-1}{n}]$ where $n = |\hat{\mathcal{T}}|$.

Our optimization routine in Algorithm 2 converges to the true leakage probability p_0 if the following assumption holds

Assumption 1. *b is independent of the columns of $A(\hat{p}_0)$ (except, obviously, at $\hat{p}_0 = p_0$).*

Remark This is a weak assumption when choosing $m >> n'$: it is unlikely the loss vector b happens to fall in the column space of A.

Theorem 3.3. *If Assumption 1 holds, then the estimators $\hat{p}_0^*$ and $\hat{e}_0^*$ in Algorithm 2 are consistent, i.e. $\hat{p}_0^* \xrightarrow{p} p_0$ and $\hat{e}_0^* \xrightarrow{p} e_0$ as $t, |\mathcal{T}|, |\mathcal{V}| \to \infty$ and for $p_0 < 1$.*

Proof. Without loss of generality, we prove the case where samples move in the direction from $\mathcal{V}$ to $\mathcal{T}$. We begin by proving the convergence of $\hat{p}_0^*$. Let $n = |\hat{\mathcal{T}}|$. In Algorithm 2, $\hat{p}_0^{*(t)} = \arg\min_{p_0 \in \{\frac{0}{n}, \frac{1}{n}, \ldots, \frac{n-1}{n}\}} g^{(t)}(p_0)$, where the function

$g^{(i)}(p_0) = ||A(p_0)(A^\intercal(p_0)A(p_0))^{-1}A^\intercal(p_0)\bar{b}^{(i)} - \bar{b}^{(i)}||_2^2$ if $p_0 \in \left[0, \frac{n-1}{n}\right]$ and else infinity. We use $\bar{b}^{(i)}$ to denote the mean estimator $\bar{b}$ in Algorithm 1 after $t = i$ samples. Let $g(p_0) = ||A(p_0)(A^\intercal(p_0)A(p_0))^{-1}A^\intercal(p_0)b - b||_2^2$ if $p_0 \in \left[0, \frac{n-1}{n}\right]$ and else infinity.

Both g and the sequence of functions $\{g^{(0)}, g^{(1)}, \dots\}$ are level-bounded, lower semi-continuous and proper. By Lemma 3.4, $g^{(i)} \xrightarrow{e} g$ where $\xrightarrow{e}$ denotes convergence in epigraph. Thus, $residual = \min_{p_0 \in [0, \frac{n-1}{n}]} g^{(t)}(p_0) \xrightarrow{p} \min_{p_0} g(p_0)$ [28]. We know at least one perfect solution $g(p_0) = 0$ exists, that this solution is unique (by Assumption 1) and that this solution is in $\left\{0, \frac{1}{n}, \dots, \frac{n-1}{n}\right\}$. Thus, $p_0^* \xrightarrow{p} p_0$ and $residual \xrightarrow{p} 0$. □

Lemma 3.4. *Let*

$$g^{(i)}(p_0) = \begin{cases} ||A(p_0)(A^\intercal(p_0)A(p_0))^{-1}A^\intercal(p_0)\bar{b}^{(i)} - \bar{b}^{(i)}||_2^2 & \\ & \textit{if} \;\; p_0 \in \left[0, \frac{n-1}{n}\right] \\ \infty & \textit{else} \end{cases}$$

$$g(p_0) = \begin{cases} ||A(p_0)(A^\intercal(p_0)A(p_0))^{-1}A^\intercal(p_0)b - b||_2^2 & \\ & \textit{if} \;\; p_0 \in \left[0, \frac{n-1}{n}\right] \\ \infty & \textit{else} \end{cases}$$

Then $g^{(i)} \xrightarrow{e} g$, where we use $\xrightarrow{e}$ to denote convergence in epigraph.

Proof. Recall, $g^{(i)} \xrightarrow{e} g$ if and only if at each point e

$$\liminf_i g^{(i)}(e^{(i)}) \geq g(e), \text{ for every } e^{(i)} \to e \quad (6a)$$

$$\limsup_i g^{(i)}(e^{(i)}) \leq g(e), \text{ for some } e^{(i)} \to e \quad (6b)$$

Let $\mathcal{N}_\infty^\# = \{N \in \mathbb{N} | N \text{ is infinite}\}$ be all infinite sets of natural numbers, which we require for cases of periodicity. To establish Eq. 6a, it is sufficient to show that whenever $e^{(i)} \underset{N}{\to} e$ and $f^{(i)}(e^{(i)}) \underset{N}{\to} \alpha$, then $f(e) \leq \alpha$. We consider three cases, when $e \in \left(0, \frac{n-1}{n}\right)$, when $e \notin \left[0, \frac{n-1}{n}\right]$ and when $e \in \left\{0, \frac{n-1}{n}\right\}$. The first case is readily established from the proof of Theorem 3.2, where we showed that $\bar{b}^{(i)} \underset{N}{\to} b \; \forall N \in \mathcal{N}_\infty^\#$, $A(e^{(i)})(A^\intercal(e^{(i)})A(e^{(i)}))^{-1}A^\intercal(e^{(i)}) \underset{N}{\to} A(e)(A^\intercal(e)A(e))^{-1}A^\intercal(e)$, and thus $f^{(i)}(e^{(i)}) \underset{N}{\to} f(e) \; \forall N \in \mathcal{N}_\infty^\#$. In the case where $e \notin \left[0, \frac{n-1}{n}\right]$, $g^{(i)}(e) = \infty$ readily establishes the inequality. In the boundary cases $e \in \left\{0, \frac{n-1}{n}\right\}$, note either $g^{(i)}(e^{(i)}) \underset{N}{\to} \infty$ or $g^{(i)}(e^{(i)}) \underset{N}{\to} g(e)$, respectively. To establish Eq. 6b, choose the sequence $\{e^{(i)}\} = e \; \forall i \in \mathbb{N}$. □

3.4 Bidirectional leakage with unknown probabilities

Lastly, we extend the unidirectional leakage results in Sections 3.2 and 3.3 to the full bidirectional setting, where samples move with unknown uniform probability between $\mathcal{T}$ and $\mathcal{V}$. More specifically, let $p_{\mathcal{T},0} = \frac{|\hat{\mathcal{T}} \cap \mathcal{V}|}{|\hat{\mathcal{T}}|}$ and $p_{\mathcal{V},0} = \frac{|\hat{\mathcal{V}} \cap \mathcal{T}|}{|\hat{\mathcal{V}}|}$ be the probabilities a sample in $\hat{\mathcal{T}}$ and $\hat{\mathcal{V}}$ do not belong in that set, respectively. Similar to the unidirectional case, we independently resample with replacement $n'_\mathcal{T}$ and $n'_\mathcal{V}$ samples from $\mathcal{T}$ and $\mathcal{V}$ to form the bootstrap sample sets $\mathcal{T}'$ and $\mathcal{V}'$, respectively. Thus, the number of corrupted samples in $\mathcal{T}'$ and $\mathcal{V}'$ is drawn according to a joint distribution of two independent binomials. We then formulate a regression problem analogous to Eq. 4,

$$\begin{array}{c} \\ p_{\mathcal{T},0}, p_{\mathcal{V},0} \\ \cdot \\ \cdot \\ \cdot \\ p_{\mathcal{T},n_\mathcal{T}}, p_{\mathcal{V},n_\mathcal{V}} \end{array} \begin{array}{c} 0 \quad 1 \quad \cdot \quad \cdot \quad n' \\ \left(\begin{array}{c} \leftarrow \text{Joint Bin pmf} \rightarrow \\ \cdot \\ \cdot \\ \cdot \\ \leftarrow \text{Joint Bin pmf} \rightarrow \end{array}\right) \\ A(p_{\mathcal{T},0}, p_{\mathcal{V},0}) \end{array} \begin{array}{c} \\ \left(\begin{array}{c} \\ e \\ \\ \end{array}\right) = \left(\begin{array}{c} \\ b \\ \\ \end{array}\right) \\ e \;=\; b \end{array}$$

where $n' = (n'_\mathcal{T} + 1)(n'_\mathcal{V} + 1) - 1$. Note since the joint pmf is defined for $(n'_\mathcal{T} + 1)(n'_\mathcal{V} + 1)$ values, we must bootstrap at $(n'_\mathcal{T} + 1)(n'_\mathcal{V} + 1)$ levels of leakage.

In the case where the leakage probabilities $p_{\mathcal{T},0}$ and $p_{\mathcal{V},0}$ are unknown, we again minimize the residual. The resulting methods for the bidirectional leakage scenario with known and unknown probabilities are presented in Algorithms 3 and 4 (see Appendix B), respectively.

Here, we show the full rank and consistency results for Algorithms 1 and 2 extend to Algorithms 3 and 4. The main difference is we consider the *joint* binomial matrix A, which is also full rank and thus the regression problem is well defined.

Lemma 3.5. *Joint binomial matrix A has full rank for any choice of unique parameters $p_\mathcal{T} = (p_{\mathcal{T},0}, p_{\mathcal{T},1}, \dots, p_{\mathcal{T},m}) \in [0,1]^m$ and $p_\mathcal{V} = (p_{\mathcal{V},0}, p_{\mathcal{V},1}, \dots, p_{\mathcal{V},m'}) \in [0,1]^{m'}$.*

Likewise, the consistency results in Theorems 3.2 and 3.3 extend to the bidirectional leakage scenario.

Theorem 3.6. *For $p_{\mathcal{T},0}, p_{\mathcal{V},0} < 1$ in Algorithm 3, e_0 converges to the expected error on uncorrupted distributions $\mathcal{T}$ and $\mathcal{V}$, $\hat{e}_0 \to \mathbb{E}_{\mathcal{T}' \overset{n'_\mathcal{T}}{\sim} P_\mathcal{T}} \mathbb{E}_{(x,y)\sim P_\mathcal{V}} \ell(y, f(x \mid \mathcal{T}'))$ as $t, |\mathcal{T}|, |\mathcal{V}| \to \infty$.*

Theorem 3.7. *For $p_{\mathcal{T},0}, p_{\mathcal{V},0} < 1$ in Algorithm 4,*

$p^*_{\mathcal{T},0} \xrightarrow{p} p_{\mathcal{T},0}$, $p^*_{\mathcal{V},0} \xrightarrow{p} p_{\mathcal{V},0}$ *and* $\hat{e}^* \xrightarrow{p} e^*$ *as* $t, |\mathcal{T}|, |\mathcal{V}| \to \infty$.

Proofs are in Appendices A.3-A.5.

4 Simulation study

Thus far, we have appealed to asymptotic theory and bias-variance analysis. This is not uncommon for bootstrap and cross-validation analysis, and like others, we now turn to empirical arguments. In this section, we present simulation study results which demonstrate our core method in Algorithm 1 significantly outperforms conventional methods. For all experiments, we consider the more difficult direction where samples move from $\mathcal{V}$ to $\mathcal{T}$.

Our estimators are unbiased and consistent, but they may have large variance (see Theorem 3.2). When practically implementing these estimators, it is beneficial to add a small amount of regularization to achieve a better bias–variance tradeoff. Although we know from Lemma 3.1 and 3.5 that matrix A is full rank, it may be ill-conditioned. Adding regularization helps to improve the condition number of matrix A. Evidence suggests this is a tradeoff worth making. Specifically, in the linear system objective function within Algorithms 1 and 4 we instead solve some variation of

$$\begin{aligned} &\underset{\hat{e}}{\text{minimize}} \quad ||A\hat{e} - \bar{b}||_2^2 + \lambda R(\hat{e}) \\ &\text{subject to} \quad \hat{e}_{j-1} \geq \hat{e}_j \geq 0 \quad \text{for all } j = 1, \ldots, n'. \end{aligned}$$

where λ is a regularization constant and R is some regularization function. We choose the trend filter regularizer $R(\hat{e}) = ||D\hat{e}||_2^2$ to ensure $\hat{e}$ is smooth [29]. For a second-order filter, which regularizes the second derivative of $\hat{e}$, D is the difference matrix

$$D = \begin{bmatrix} 1 & -2 & 1 & & & & \\ & 1 & -2 & 1 & & & \\ & & \ddots & \ddots & \ddots & & \\ & & & 1 & -2 & 1 & \\ & & & & 1 & -2 & 1 \end{bmatrix}$$

where unshown entries are zero. Matrices D for higher order trend filters follow similarly. Intuitively, we expect the estimator error to degrade both monotonically (the constraint) and somewhat smoothly (the regularizer). Later results validate these assumptions.

Experiment I For the synthetic simulation study, we use a partition model with $k = 2$ parts and n sufficiently large such that duplicate resamples are improbable, a subsample of which is depicted in Figure 2. We choose the number of corruption levels $m = 2n$ following the

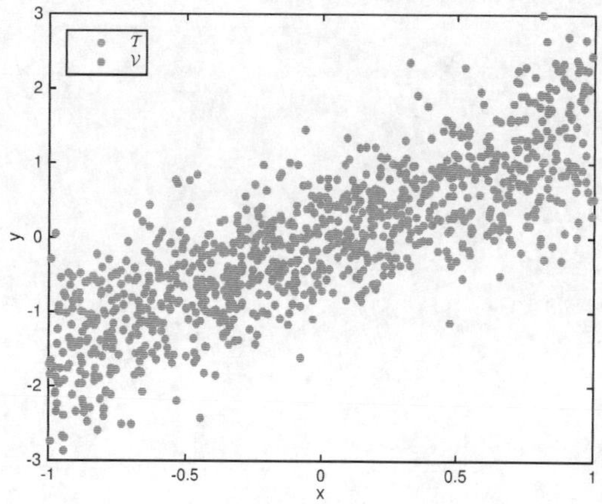

Figure 2: Subsample of data used in the synthetic Experiment I.

arguments in Assumption 1 and perform $t = 1000$ bootstrap samples at each p_i. For f, we use a linear regression model and set the loss ℓ as the mean squared error. To simulate the effects of noisy clusters $\hat{c}$, we move samples between the two parts $\mathcal{T}$ and $\mathcal{V}$ with initial uniform probability $p_0 = 0.1$. All experiments use either a second (T2), third (T3) or fourth (T4) order trend filter with $\lambda = 0.1$ and/or a monotonic constraint. For baselines, we compare against naive IID k-fold and the current state-of-the-art LOCO cross-validation.

Our main synthetic results are presented in the Figure 3a boxplot. LOCO outperforms traditional IID cross-validation, which suggests blocking on the corrupted clusters $\hat{c}$ partially limits the effects of dependency leakage. However, even at $p_0 = 0.1$, LOCO is still unacceptably biased. Our methods, with various forms of regularization, all significantly outperform both existing estimators. Figure 3a also suggests a bias-variance trade-off among all the tested methods. IID cross-validation has high bias and low variance, whereas our methods have low bias and higher variance. Ultimately, this tradeoff allows our methods to achieve lower MSE by choosing an appropriate form and strength of regularization.

An interesting consequence of our method is that in addition to recovering the independent partition performance e_0, we also recover the performance $e_1, e_2, \ldots$ at all levels of dependency leakage, as depicted in Figure 3a. The true loss e (dashed black line) decays monotonically and smoothly, which justifies our regularization choices.

Experiment II In the second experiment, we use data from the 1994 US Census to validate our claim that conventional cross-validation introduce bias against subpopulations due to dependency leakage [26]. Empirical

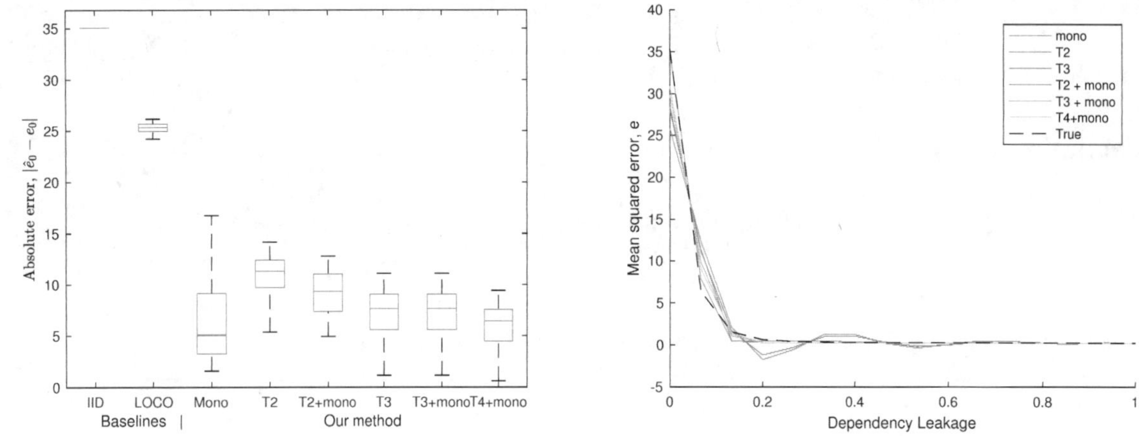

(a) Synthetic simulation study results

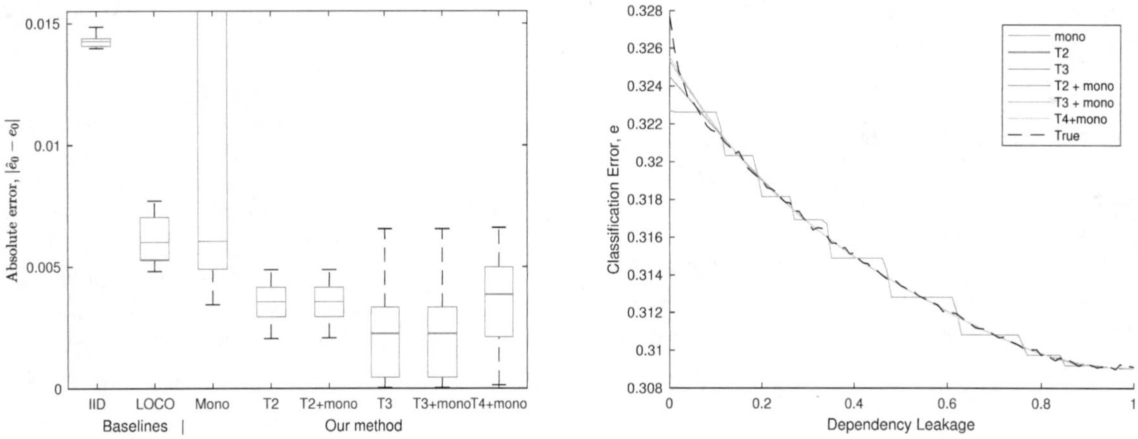

(b) Experimental study results on the 1994 Census dataset.

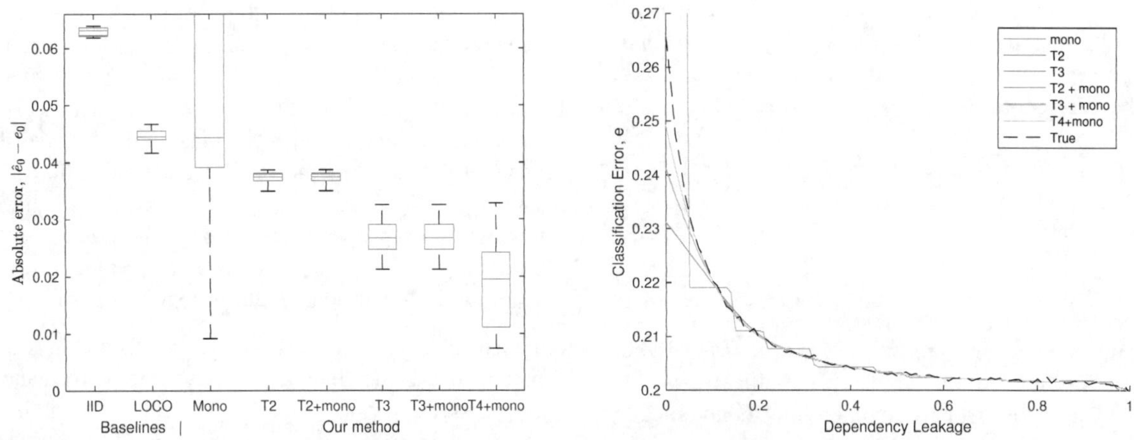

(c) Experimental study results on the heart disease dataset.

Figure 3: **Left** Estimating the generalization loss e_0. Our class of B3 estimators, with various forms of regularization (monotonic; second, third or fourth-order trend filter) outperform existing estimators. Baseline cross-validation methods are biased against the sub-populations we studied, and our class of B3 estimators help correct this bias. **Right** The B3 estimator recovers the full loss vector e. Empirically, the true loss decays monotonically and smoothly in practice, justifying our regularization choices.

results show our class of B3 estimators outperform the baseline methods in practical, non-asymptotic situations.

Here, we consider the task of predicting a person's income given their demographic, educational and occupational information. Our training set consists of samples from certain origin countries and we wish to train a learner which performs well for people of all countries. In other words, we minimize the LOCO generalization loss, where clusters correspond to origin countries. For this experiment, we use 30368 persons from the United States, El Salvador, Germany, Mexico, Philippines and Puerto Rico for training set $\mathcal{T}$ and validate with $\mathcal{V}$ on 221 immigrants from India and Canada. We set $p_0 = 0.1$, $\lambda = 10$, $n' = 100$, $m = 2n'$ and $t = 2500$. For features, we consider their age, years of education, work hours per week, race, and occupation. We trained an SVM classifier to predict whether their yearly income is greater than US$50k per year.

The boxplot in Figure 3b shows small error in origin country causes the learner to be biased against Indian and Canadian immigrants, due to dependency leakage. In other words, the classifier is rewarded for learning attributes specific to the training countries, even though they do not generalize across all countries. Similarly to the synthetic study, the B3 estimators outperform the baseline methods and accurately recover the full loss vector e, which decays monotonically and smoothly.

Experiment III In the third experiment, we use heart disease data collected from Cleveland, USA; VA Long Beach, USA; Switzerland and Hungary [26]. The task is to predict whether a patient has heart disease, given their demographic information and vital signs. We need to train a classifier which performs well at new hospitals – given data from only these 4 locations. Thus, clusters correspond to hospital location and we use LOCO to estimate the generalization error. Training clusters correspond to 479 patients in Cleveland, Long Beach and Switzerland, testing clusters correspond to 262 patients in Hungary. All other experimental details are the same as Experiment II. The results are shown in Figure 3c.

5 Extensions

This work poses several additional questions, some of which we briefly address now. For example, we have extended these methods from estimating the expected loss e to estimating an expected loss histogram E in Eq. 4. To do so, one can simply store the empirical bootstrap histogram $\bar{B}$ in lieu of the empirical bootstrap mean $\bar{b}$. The downside is estimating the additional information in E increases the variance by a linear factor according to the number of histogram bins.

To improve the numerical solution in Algorithm 1 in the direction where samples move from $\mathcal{T}$ to $\mathcal{V}$, note that e will be a linear vector, i.e. $e_{i+1} - e_i = \beta\ \forall i \in \{0, \ldots, n' - 1\}$. This is because the training set $\mathcal{T}'$ has zero corruption, the expected number of corrupted samples in $\hat{\mathcal{V}}$ varies linearly with p_i for fixed δ, and the empirical loss is a mean loss of the samples in $\hat{\mathcal{V}}$. Enforcing this constraint on $\hat{e}$ would improve the solution quality for the direction where samples move from $\mathcal{T}$ to $\mathcal{V}$. We always considered the more difficult $\mathcal{V}$ to $\mathcal{T}$ leakage direction, where we have no prior knowledge of e.

The question of unbalanced clusters for CRVE was addressed in [21]. In our cross-validation method, small Var($|\hat{\mathcal{T}}|$) and Var($|\hat{\mathcal{V}}|$) across the cross-validation folds improves convergence. With unbalanced clusters, instead of leaving one cluster out, we could leave multiple clusters out such that $|\hat{\mathcal{T}}|$ and $|\hat{\mathcal{V}}|$ have lower variance even with high variance cluster sizes. CRVE also suffers from having a small number of clusters k [18]. Our estimator will be nearly unbiased but have high variance with a small number of clusters, due to the same properties as LOCO (see Section 1).

Though we have shown asymptotic convergence of our methods, there are several open questions. Notably, we use a naive discrete optimization routine in Algorithms 2 and 4 to solve for $p_{\mathcal{T},0}$ and $p_{\mathcal{V},0}$. The functions $g(i)(p_0)$ are non-convex, but they are smooth with finite support and faster convergence may be possible.

6 Conclusions

In this paper, we addressed the issue of evaluating a learner on blocks of dependent data. Unlike existing bootstrap methods, which assume a perfect clustering, we allow for imperfect clusterings $\hat{c}$ such that inter-cluster samples may be dependent. Real world applications ranging from medical diagnostics to computer vision fall into this class of problems. Empirical evidence on synthetic data, the 1994 US Census and heart disease data shows dependency leakage biases cross-validation results and thus affects model selection. We presented the B3 class of estimators, which significantly outperform existing cross-validation methods in this setting. The key insight of our bootstrapping methods is that by injecting additional dependency, we can extrapolate an unbiased and asymptotically consistent estimator of the performance on independent clusters.

Acknowledgements

This work has been partially supported by DARPA under awards FA8750-14-2-0244 and FA8750-12-2-0324.

References

[1] Trevor Hastie, Robert Tibshirani, and Jerome Friedman. *The Elements of Statistical Learning*, volume 2. Springer, 2009.

[2] Gareth James, Daniela Witten, Trevor Hastie, and Robert Tibshirani. *An Introduction to Statistical Learning*, volume 6. Springer, 2013.

[3] Daniel Joseph McDonald. *Generalization Error Bounds for Time Series*. PhD thesis, Carnegie Mellon University, 2012.

[4] Burr Settles. *Active Learning*. Morgan & Claypool, 2012.

[5] Chao Liu, Hernando Gomez, Bridget Deasy, Brian Zuckerbraun, Srinivasa G Narasimhan, Artur Dubrawski, and Michael R Pinsky. Micro-vascular Video Analysis for Critical Care. *IEEE Transactions on Medical Imaging*, 2017.

[6] Sohrab Saeb, Luca Lonini, Arun Jayaraman, David C Mohr, and Konrad P Kording. Voodoo Machine Learning for Clinical Predictions. *bioRxiv*, 2016.

[7] Pavel Krepelka and Petr Drexler. A Fiber Optic Biosensor Improved with NIR Spectroscopy for Bacterial Identification. In *International Conference on Near Infrared Spectroscopy*, 2015.

[8] William E. Winkler and Yves Thibaudeau. An application of the Fellegi-Sunter model of record linkage to the 1990 US decennial census. Technical report, U.S. Census Bureau, 1990.

[9] William E. Winkler. Overview of record linkage and current research directions. Technical report, U.S. Census Bureau, 2006.

[10] Peter Sadosky, Anshumali Shrivastava, Megan Price, and Rebecca C Steorts. Blocking Methods Applied to Casualty Records from the Syrian Conflict. *arXiv*, 2015.

[11] Artur Dubrawski, Kyle Miller, Matt Barnes, Benedikt Boecking, and Emily Kennedy. Leveraging Publicly Available Data to Discern Patterns of Human-Trafficking Activity. *Journal of Human Trafficking*, 1:65–85, 2015.

[12] Cynthia Dwork, Moritz Hardt, Toniann Pitassi, Omer Reingold, and Richard Zemel. Fairness Through Awareness. In *Proceedings of the 3rd Innovations in Theoretical Computer Science Conference*, pages 214–226, 2011.

[13] Moritz Hardt, Eric Price, and Nati Srebro. Equality of opportunity in supervised learning. In *Advances in Neural Information Processing Systems*, pages 3315–3323, 2016.

[14] Kesar Singh. On the Asymptotic Accuracy of Efron's Bootstrap. *The Annals of Statistics*, 9(6):11877–1195, 1981.

[15] Peter Hall. Resampling a coverage pattern. *Stochastic Processes and their Applications*, 20(2):231–246, 1985.

[16] Regina Y. Liu and Kesar Singh. Moving blocks jackknife and bootstrap capture weak dependence. In *Exploring the Limits of Bootstrap*, pages 225–248. Wiley-Interscience, 1992.

[17] Soumendra Nath Lahiri. *Resampling methods for dependent data*. Springer Science & Business Media, 2003.

[18] R. C. Cameron and Douglas L. Miller. A Practitioner's Guide to Cluster-Robust Inference. *Journal of Human Resources*, 50(2):317–372, 2015.

[19] Halbert White. *Asymptotic theory for econometricians*. Academic Press, 1984.

[20] Kung-Yee Liang and Scott L. Zeger. Longitudinal data analysis using generalized linear models. *Biometrika*, 73(1):13–22, 1986.

[21] James G. MacKinnon and Matthew D. Webb. Wild Bootstrap Inference for Wildly Different Cluster Sizes. *Journal of Applied Econometrics*, 32:233–254, 2017.

[22] C. A. Field and A. H. Welsh. Bootstrapping clustered data. *Journal of the Royal Statistical Society. Series B: Statistical Methodology*, 69(3):369–390, 2007.

[23] Anthony Christopher Davison and David Victor Hinkley. *Bootstrap methods and their application*, volume 1. Cambridge University Press, 1997.

[24] Michael K Andersson and Sune Karlsson. Bootstrapping error component models. *Computational Statistics*, 16(2):221–231, 2001.

[25] Douglas Miller, A. Cameron, and Jonah Gelbach. Robust Inference with Multi-way Clustering. *Journal of Business & Economic Statistics*, 29(2), 2011.

[26] Moshe Lichman. UCI Machine Learning Repository, 2013.

[27] Johan Ugander, Brian Karrer, Lars Backstrom, and Jon Kleinberg. Graph Cluster Randomization: Network Exposure to Multiple Universes. *Proceedings of the 19th ACM SIGKDD International Conference on Knowledge Discovery and Data Mining*, pages 329–337, 2013.

[28] R. Tyrrell Rockafellar and Roger J-B Wets. *Variational Analysis*. Springer, 2009.

[29] Seung-Jean Kim, Kwangmoo Koh, Stephen Boyd, and Dimitry Gorinevsky. L1 Trend Filtering. *Society for Industrial and Applied Mathematics (SIAM) Review*, 51(2):339–360, 2009.

[30] Nathaniel Macon and Abraham Spitzbart. Inverses of Vandermonde matrices. *The American Mathematical Monthly*, 65(2):95–100, 1958.

Appendix for "The Binomial Block Bootstrap Estimator for Evaluating Loss on Dependent Clusters"

A Proofs

A.1 Lemma 3.1

Proof. Let A_j denote column j of matrix A. The entries of A_j correspond to polynomial $g_j(q) = \binom{n'}{j} q^j (1 - q)^{(n'-j)}$ evaluated at points $q = p_0, p_1, \ldots, p_m$. First, we show polynomials $g(q) = \{g_0(q), \ldots, g_{n'}(q)\}$ are linearly independent.

We look for a non-trivial solution $\kappa \in \mathbb{R}^{(n'+1)}$ to $\langle \kappa, g(q) \rangle = 0, \forall q \in [0, 1]$. The binomial coefficient is a constant in each polynomial and can be dropped. Expanding and collecting terms,

$$\begin{aligned} 0 &= \kappa_0 (1-q)^{n'} + \kappa_1 q^1 (1-q)^{n'-1} + \ldots + \kappa_{n'} q^{n'} \\ &= \sum_{i=0}^{n'} q^i \sum_{j=0}^{i} \kappa_j \binom{n'-j}{i-j} (-1)^j \end{aligned}$$

for all $q \in \left[0, \frac{n-1}{n}\right]$ which implies

$$0 = \sum_{j=0}^{i} \kappa_j \binom{n'-j}{i-j} (-1)^j$$

for all $i \in \{0, 1, \ldots, n'\}$ and all $q \in \left[0, \frac{n-1}{n}\right]$. Clearly, $\kappa_0 = 0$, and the remainder of the terms follow by induction to $\kappa = \vec{0}$. Thus the polynomials $\{g_0, \ldots, g_{n'}\}$ are linearly independent.

Next, the polynomials $\{g_0, \ldots, g_{n'}\}$ are unisolvent by the unisolvence theorem, which implies the vectors

$$\begin{bmatrix} g_0(p_0) \\ g_0(p_1) \\ \vdots \\ g_0(p_m) \end{bmatrix}, \begin{bmatrix} g_1(p_0) \\ g_1(p_1) \\ \vdots \\ g_1(p_m) \end{bmatrix}, \ldots, \begin{bmatrix} g_{n'}(p_0) \\ g_{n'}(p_1) \\ \vdots \\ g_{n'}(p_m) \end{bmatrix}, \tag{7}$$

are also linearly independent for any unique $p_0, \ldots, p_m$, $m \geq n'$. Thus, matrix A is full rank. □

A.2 Theorem 3.2

A.2.1 Statement 1

Proof. Without loss of generality, we prove the corruption direction from $\mathcal{V}$ to $\mathcal{T}$. The empirical loss of KNOWNUNIDIRECTIONAL at corruption level p_i is $\bar{b}_i$.

$$\begin{aligned}
\bar{b}_i &= \frac{1}{t|\hat{\mathcal{V}}|} \sum_{\mathcal{T}' \in \{\mathcal{T}'_0, \ldots, \mathcal{T}'_t\}} \sum_{(x,y)\in\hat{\mathcal{V}}} \ell(y, f(x \mid \mathcal{T}')) \\
&= \frac{1}{t|\hat{\mathcal{V}}|} \sum_{(x,y)\in\hat{\mathcal{V}}} \sum_{j=0}^{n'} \sum_{\mathcal{T}' : |\mathcal{T}' \cap \mathcal{V}| = j, \mathcal{T}' \in \{\mathcal{T}'_0, \ldots, \mathcal{T}'_t\}} \ell(y, f(x \mid \mathcal{T}')) \\
&\xrightarrow[t\to\infty]{p} \frac{1}{|\hat{\mathcal{V}}|} \sum_{(x,y)\in\hat{\mathcal{V}}} \sum_{j=0}^{n'} A_{ij} \mathbb{E}_{\mathcal{T}''(j)} \ell(y, f(x \mid \mathcal{T}'')) \\
&\xrightarrow[|\mathcal{V}|, |\mathcal{T}| \to\infty]{p} \mathop{\mathbb{E}}_{(x,y)\sim P_{\mathcal{V}}} \sum_{j=0}^{n'} A_{ij} \mathbb{E}_{\mathcal{T}'''(j)} \ell(y, f(x \mid \mathcal{T}''')) \\
&= \sum_{j=0}^{n'} A_{ij} e_j = b_i
\end{aligned}$$

where A_{ij} is the probability of sampling j samples from $\mathcal{V}$ at corruption p_i as defined in Eq. 5 and

$$\begin{aligned}
\mathcal{T}''(j) &= \left\{ \{\mathcal{T}'''' \overset{n'-j}{\sim} \mathcal{T}\} \cup \{\mathcal{V}'' \overset{j}{\sim} \mathcal{V}\} \right\} \\
\mathcal{T}'''(j) &= \left\{ \{\mathcal{T}'''' \overset{n'-j}{\sim} P_{\mathcal{T}}\} \cup \{\mathcal{V}'' \overset{j}{\sim} P_{\mathcal{V}}\} \right\} \\
e_j &= \mathbb{E}_{\mathcal{T}'''(j), (x,y)\sim P_{\mathcal{V}}} \ell(y, f(x \mid \mathcal{T}'))
\end{aligned}$$

The proof can be understood as splitting the t bootstraps into bins $j = 0, \ldots, n'$ each with probability A_{ij}. Then $\hat{e} = A(A^\intercal A)^{-1} A^\intercal \bar{b} \xrightarrow{p} A(A^\intercal A)^{-1} A^\intercal b = e$ by the continuous mapping theorem and Lemma 3.1. We require $|\mathcal{V}|, |\mathcal{T}| \to \infty$ sufficiently faster than $t \to \infty$, such that the probability of resampling the same data sample in Algorithm 1 also goes to 0. □

A.2.2 Statement 2

Proof. Recall $\hat{e} = A(A^\intercal A)^{-1} A^\intercal b$ and $\hat{e} = A(A^\intercal A)^{-1} A^\intercal \bar{b}$. Then

$$\begin{aligned}
\mathbb{E}[\hat{e}] &= \mathbb{E}[A(A^\intercal A)^{-1} A^\intercal \bar{b}] \\
&= A(A^\intercal A)^{-1} A^\intercal \mathbb{E}[\bar{b}] \\
&= A(A^\intercal A)^{-1} A^\intercal b \\
&= e
\end{aligned}$$

for finite t but infinitely large $|\hat{\mathcal{V}}|$ and $|\hat{\mathcal{T}}|$. For finite sample sets, bias may be introduced due to resampling the same data sample more than once. □

A.2.3 Statement 3

Proof. We consider the case where A is square for analysis simplicity. Let $\sigma_{b_i}^2$ be the variance of $\hat{b}_i$ in line 13 of Algorithm 1. Then

$$\begin{aligned}\mathrm{Var}(\hat{e}_0) &= \sum_{i=0}^{n'} (A^{-1})_{0i}^2 \mathrm{Var}(\hat{b}_i) \\ &= \sum_{i=0}^{n'} (A^{-1})_{0i}^2 \frac{\sigma_{b_i}^2}{t} \\ &= \frac{1}{t} u^\intercal (A^{-1})^\intercal \Sigma A^{-1} u\end{aligned}$$

where Σ is the diagonal matrix with entires $\Sigma_{ii} = \sigma_{b_i}^2$ and u denotes a standard unit vector, such that $u_0 = 1$. Let $z = A^{-1}u$. Now solving for z

$$Az = u$$

$$\binom{n'}{j} \sum_{i=0}^{n'} p_i^j (1-p_i)^{n'-j} e_i = \begin{cases} 1 & j = 0 \\ 0 & j = 1, \ldots, n' \end{cases}$$

For $j = n'$, note $\sum_{i=0}^{n'} p_i^{n'} z_i = 0$. Then expanding terms for $j = n' - 1$

$$\begin{aligned}\sum_{i=0}^{n'} p_i^{n'-1}(1-p_i) z_i &= 0 \\ \sum_{i=0}^{n'} p_i^{n'-1} z_i - p_i^{n'} z_i &= 0 \\ \sum_{i=0}^{n'} p_i^{n'-1} z_i &= 0\end{aligned}$$

Continuing these expansion and substitution steps for $j = n' - 1, n' - 2, \ldots, 1, 0$ results in

$$\sum_{i=0}^{n'} p_i^k z_i = u_k \quad \text{for } k = 0, \ldots, n'$$

which is a transposed Vandermonde system

$$\begin{bmatrix} 1 & 1 & 1 & \cdots & 1 \\ p_0 & p_1 & p_2 & \cdots & p_{n'} \\ p_0^2 & p_1^2 & p_2^2 & \cdots & p_{n'}^2 \\ \vdots & \vdots & \vdots & \ddots & \vdots \\ p_0^{n'} & p_1^{n'} & p_2^{n'} & \cdots & p_{n'}^{n'} \end{bmatrix} \begin{bmatrix} z_0 \\ z_1 \\ z_2 \\ \vdots \\ z_{n'} \end{bmatrix} = \begin{bmatrix} 1 \\ 0 \\ 0 \\ \vdots \\ 0 \end{bmatrix}$$

$$\begin{aligned} W^\intercal z &= u \\ z &= (W^{-1})^\intercal u \end{aligned}$$

Thus, $\mathrm{Var}(\hat{e}_0) = \frac{1}{t} u^\intercal W^{-1} \Sigma (W^{-1})^\intercal u$ and the inverse of the Vandermonde matrix is known [30]

$$(W^{-1})_{ij} = \begin{cases} (-1)^i \left(\frac{\sum_{0 \le m_0 < \cdots < m_{n'-1} \le n', m_0, \ldots, m_{n'-i} \neq j} p_{m_0} \cdots p_{m_{n'-i}}}{\prod_{0 \le m \le n', m \neq j} (p_m - p_j)} \right) & \text{for } 0 \le i \le n' \\ \frac{1}{\prod_{0 \le m \le n', m \neq j} (p_m - p_j)} & \text{for } k = n' \end{cases}$$

which gives the result. □

A.3 Lemma 3.5

Proof. Let $A_{k+n'_{\mathcal{T}}l}$ denote column $k + n'_{\mathcal{T}}l$ of matrix A. The entries of $A_{k+n'_{\mathcal{T}}l}$ correspond to polynomial $g_{k+n'_{\mathcal{T}}l}(q_1, q_2) = \binom{n'_{\mathcal{T}}}{k} q_1^k (1-q_1)^{(n'_{\mathcal{T}}-k)} \binom{n'_{\mathcal{V}}}{l} q_2^l (1-q_2)^{(n'_{\mathcal{V}}-l)}$ evaluated at points $q_1 = p_{\mathcal{T},0}, p_{\mathcal{T},1}, \ldots, p_{\mathcal{T},m}$ and $q_2 = p_{\mathcal{V},0}, p_{\mathcal{V},1}, \ldots, p_{\mathcal{V},n}$. First, we show polynomials $g = \{g_0, \ldots, g_{(n'_{\mathcal{T}}+1)(n'_{\mathcal{V}}+1)-1}\}$ are linearly independent.

We look for a non-trivial solution $K \in \mathbb{R}^{(n'_{\mathcal{T}}+1, n'_{\mathcal{V}}+1)}$ to $\langle c, g(q_1, q_2)\rangle = 0, \forall q_1, q_2 \in [0,1]$ where κ is a flattened version of K. The binomial coefficient is a constant in each polynomial and can be dropped. Expanding and collecting terms,

$$
\begin{aligned}
0 &= \sum_{i=0}^{n'_{\mathcal{T}}} \sum_{j=0}^{n'_{\mathcal{V}}} K_{ij} q_1^i (1-q_1)^{n'_{\mathcal{T}}-i} q_2^j (1-q_2)^{n'_{\mathcal{V}}-j} \\
&= \sum_{j=0}^{n'_{\mathcal{V}}} q_2^j (1-q_2)^{n'_{\mathcal{V}}-j} \sum_{i=0}^{n'_{\mathcal{T}}} q_1^i \sum_{k=0}^{i} K_{kj} \binom{n'_{\mathcal{T}}-k}{i-k} (-1)^k \\
&= \sum_{i=0}^{n'_{\mathcal{T}}} q_1^i \sum_{k=0}^{i} \binom{n'_{\mathcal{T}}-k}{i-k} (-1)^k \sum_{j=0}^{n'_{\mathcal{V}}} K_{kj} q_2^j (1-q_2)^{n'_{\mathcal{V}}-j} \\
&= \sum_{i=0}^{n'_{\mathcal{T}}} q_1^i \sum_{k=0}^{i} \binom{n'_{\mathcal{T}}-k}{i-k} \sum_{j=0}^{n'_{\mathcal{V}}} q_2^j \sum_{l=0}^{j} K_{kl} \binom{n'_{\mathcal{V}}-l}{j-l} (-1)^{k+l}
\end{aligned}
$$

which implies,

$$
0 = \sum_{k=0}^{i} \sum_{l=0}^{j} K_{kl} \binom{n'_{\mathcal{T}}-k}{i-k} \binom{n'_{\mathcal{V}}-l}{j-l} (-1)^{k+l}
$$

for all $i \in \{0, 1, \ldots, n'_{\mathcal{T}}\}$ and $j \in \{0, 1, \ldots, n'_{\mathcal{V}}\}$. When $i = 0, j = 0 \Rightarrow K_{00} = 0$ and the remainder of the terms follow by induction to $K = \mathbb{0}^{(n'_{\mathcal{T}}+1)\times(n'_{\mathcal{T}}+1)}$. Thus the polynomials $\{g_0, \ldots, g_{(n'_{\mathcal{T}}+1)(n'_{\mathcal{V}}+1)-1}\}$ are linearly independent and A is full rank by the unisolvence theorem. □

A.4 Theorem 3.6

Proof. The empirical loss at corruption levels $(p_{\mathcal{T},i}, p_{\mathcal{V},j})$ is $\bar{b}_{ij}$ in Algorithm 3.

$$
\begin{aligned}
\bar{b}_{ij} &= \frac{1}{t n'_{\mathcal{V}}} \sum_{\mathcal{T}' \in \{\mathcal{T}'_0, \ldots, \mathcal{T}'_t\}} \sum_{\mathcal{V}' \in \{\mathcal{V}'_0, \ldots, \mathcal{V}'_t\}} \sum_{(x,y)\in\mathcal{V}'} \ell(y, f(x \mid \mathcal{T}')) \\
&= \frac{1}{t n'_{\mathcal{V}}} \sum_{l=0}^{n'_{\mathcal{V}}} \sum_{\mathcal{V}' : |\mathcal{V}'\cap\mathcal{T}|=l, \mathcal{V}' \in \{\mathcal{V}'_0, \ldots, \mathcal{V}'_t\}} \sum_{(x,y)\in\mathcal{V}'} \\
&\qquad \sum_{k=0}^{n'_{\mathcal{T}}} \sum_{\mathcal{T}' : |\mathcal{T}'\cap\mathcal{V}|=k, \mathcal{T}' \in \{\mathcal{T}'_0, \ldots, \mathcal{T}'_t\}} \ell(y, f(x \mid \mathcal{T}')) \\
&\xrightarrow[t\to\infty]{p} \sum_{l=0}^{n'_{\mathcal{V}}} \sum_{k=0}^{n'_{\mathcal{T}}} A_{ijkl} \mathbb{E}_{\mathcal{T}''(k),(x,y)\in\mathcal{V}''(l)} \ell(y, f(x \mid \mathcal{T}'')) \\
&\xrightarrow[|\mathcal{V}|,|\mathcal{T}|\to\infty]{p} \sum_{l=0}^{n'_{\mathcal{V}}} \sum_{k=0}^{n'_{\mathcal{T}}} A_{ijkl} \mathbb{E}_{\mathcal{T}'''(k),(x,y)\in\mathcal{V}'''(l)} \ell(y, f(x \mid \mathcal{T}''')) \\
&= \sum_{l=0}^{n'_{\mathcal{V}}} \sum_{k=0}^{n'_{\mathcal{T}}} A_{ijkl} x_{kl} \qquad (8)
\end{aligned}
$$

where A_{ijkl} is the probability of k corrupted samples in $\mathcal{T}'$ and l corrupted samples in $\mathcal{V}'$ at corruption levels $p_{\mathcal{T},i}$ and $p_{\mathcal{V},j}$, i.e.

$$A_{ijkl} = \mathbb{P}(\text{Binomial}(n'_{\mathcal{T}}, p_{\mathcal{T},i}) = k)\mathbb{P}(\text{Binomial}(n'_{\mathcal{V}}, p_{\mathcal{V},j}) = l)$$

and

$$\begin{aligned}
\mathcal{T}''(k) &= \left\{\{\mathcal{T}'''' \overset{n'_{\mathcal{T}}-k}{\sim} \mathcal{T}\} \cup \{\mathcal{V}'''' \overset{k}{\sim} \mathcal{V}\}\right\} \\
\mathcal{V}''(l) &= \left\{\{\mathcal{T}'''' \overset{l}{\sim} \mathcal{T}\} \cup \{\mathcal{V}'''' \overset{n'_{\mathcal{V}}-l}{\sim} \mathcal{V}\}\right\} \\
\mathcal{T}'''(k) &= \left\{\{\mathcal{T}'''' \overset{n'_{\mathcal{T}}-k}{\sim} P_{\mathcal{T}}\} \cup \{\mathcal{V}'''' \overset{k}{\sim} P_{\mathcal{V}}\}\right\} \\
\mathcal{V}'''(l) &= \left\{\{\mathcal{T}'''' \overset{l}{\sim} P_{\mathcal{T}}\} \cup \{\mathcal{V}'''' \overset{n'_{\mathcal{V}}-l}{\sim} P_{\mathcal{V}}\}\right\} \\
x_{kl} &= \mathbb{E}_{\mathcal{T}'''(k),(x,y)\in\mathcal{V}'''(l)}\ell(y, f(x \mid \mathcal{T}'''))
\end{aligned}$$

We flatten x, b and appropriately reshape the tensor A into a matrix such that Eq. 8 is always satisfied in the linear system $Ax = b$. Then, $\hat{e} = A(A^\intercal A)^{-1}A^\intercal \bar{b} \overset{p}{\to} A(A^\intercal A)^{-1}A^\intercal b = x$ by the continuous mapping theorem and Lemma 3.1. □

A.5 Theorem 3.7

Proof. We begin by proving the convergence of $p^*_{\mathcal{T},0}$ and $p^*_{\mathcal{V},0}$. Let $n_{\mathcal{T}} = |\hat{\mathcal{T}}|$ and $n_{\mathcal{V}} = |\hat{\mathcal{V}}|$. In Algorithm 4, $(p^*_{\mathcal{T},0}, p^*_{\mathcal{V},0}) = \arg\min_{p_{\mathcal{T},0}\in\left\{\frac{0}{n_{\mathcal{T}}},\frac{1}{n_{\mathcal{T}}},\ldots,\frac{n_{\mathcal{T}}-1}{n_{\mathcal{T}}}\right\}, p_{\mathcal{V},0}\in\left\{\frac{0}{n_{\mathcal{V}}},\frac{1}{n_{\mathcal{V}}},\ldots,\frac{n_{\mathcal{V}}-1}{n_{\mathcal{V}}}\right\}} g^{(t)}(p_{\mathcal{T},0}, p_{\mathcal{V},0})$, where the function $g^{(i)}$ is defined as

$$g^{(i)}(p_{\mathcal{T},0}, p_{\mathcal{V},0}) = \begin{cases} ||A(p_{\mathcal{T},0}, p_{\mathcal{V},0})(A^\intercal(p_{\mathcal{T},0}, p_{\mathcal{V},0})A(p_{\mathcal{T},0}, p_{\mathcal{V},0}))^{-1}A^\intercal(p_{\mathcal{T},0}, p_{\mathcal{V},0})\bar{b}^{(i)} - \bar{b}^{(i)}||_2^2 \\ \qquad \text{if } p_{\mathcal{T},0} \in \left[0, \frac{n_{\mathcal{T}}-1}{n_{\mathcal{T}}}\right], p_{\mathcal{V},0} \in \left[0, \frac{n_{\mathcal{V}}-1}{n_{\mathcal{V}}}\right] \\ \infty \qquad \text{else} \end{cases}$$

$$g(p_{\mathcal{T},0}, p_{\mathcal{V},0}) = \begin{cases} ||A(p_{\mathcal{T},0}, p_{\mathcal{V},0})(A^\intercal(p_{\mathcal{T},0}, p_{\mathcal{V},0})A(p_{\mathcal{T},0}, p_{\mathcal{V},0}))^{-1}A^\intercal(p_{\mathcal{T},0}, p_{\mathcal{V},0})b - b||_2^2 \\ \qquad \text{if } p_{\mathcal{T},0} \in \left[0, \frac{n_{\mathcal{T}}-1}{n_{\mathcal{T}}}\right], p_{\mathcal{V},0} \in \left[0, \frac{n_{\mathcal{V}}-1}{n_{\mathcal{V}}}\right] \\ \infty \qquad \text{else} \end{cases}$$

Both g and the sequence of functions $\{g^{(0)}, g^{(1)}, \ldots\}$ are level-bounded, lower semi-continuous and proper. By Lemma A.1, $g^{(i)} \overset{e}{\to} g$ where $\overset{e}{\to}$ denotes convergence in epigraph. Thus, $residual = \min_{p_{\mathcal{T},0}\in\left[0,\frac{n_{\mathcal{T}}-1}{n_{\mathcal{T}}}\right], p_{\mathcal{V},0}\in\left[0,\frac{n_{\mathcal{V}}-1}{n_{\mathcal{V}}}\right]} g^{(t)}(p_{\mathcal{T},0}, p_{\mathcal{V},0}) \overset{p}{\to} \min_{p_{\mathcal{T},0},p_{\mathcal{V},0}} g(p_{\mathcal{T},0}, p_{\mathcal{V},0})$ [28]. We know at least one perfect solution $g(p_{\mathcal{T},0}, p_{\mathcal{V},0}) = 0$ exists, that this solution is unique (by Assumption 2) and that this solution is in $\left\{0, \frac{1}{n_{\mathcal{T}}}, \ldots, \frac{n_{\mathcal{T}}-1}{n_{\mathcal{T}}}\right\} \mathcal{X} \left\{0, \frac{1}{n_{\mathcal{V}}}, \ldots, \frac{n_{\mathcal{V}}-1}{n_{\mathcal{V}}}\right\}$. Thus, $p^*_{\mathcal{T},0} \overset{p}{\to} p_{\mathcal{T},0}, p^*_{\mathcal{V},0} \overset{p}{\to} p_{\mathcal{V},0}$ and $residual \overset{p}{\to} 0$. □

Assumption 2. *b is independent of the columns of $A(p_{\hat{\mathcal{T}},0}, p_{\hat{\mathcal{V}},0})$ (except, obviously, at $p_{\hat{\mathcal{T}},0}, p_{\hat{\mathcal{V}},0} = p_{\mathcal{T},0}, p_{\mathcal{V},0}$). This is a very weak assumption when choosing $m >> n_{\mathcal{T}}n_{\mathcal{V}}$. It is unlikely the loss vector b happens to fall in the column space of A.*

Lemma A.1. *$g^{(i)} \overset{e}{\to} g$, where we use $\overset{e}{\to}$ to denote convergence in epigraph.*

Proof. Let $x = (p_{\mathcal{T},0}, p_{\mathcal{V},0})$. Then the proof follows exactly from the proof of Lemma 3.4. □

B Algorithms

Algorithm 3: B3 — Bidirectional leakage with known probabilities

procedure KNOWNBIDIRECTIONAL($f, \hat{\mathcal{T}}, \hat{\mathcal{V}}, p_{\mathcal{T},0}, p_{\mathcal{V},0}, n'_{\mathcal{T}}, n'_{\mathcal{V}}, t$)
  $\bar{b} \leftarrow \mathbb{0}^{(n_{\mathcal{T}'}+1)\times(n_{\mathcal{V}'}+1)}$
  for p_i in $\{p_{\mathcal{T},0}, p_{\mathcal{T},0}+\delta_{\mathcal{T}}, p_{\mathcal{T},0}+2\delta_{\mathcal{T}}, \ldots, 1\}$ **do** ▷ Choose $\delta_{\mathcal{T}} > 0$ s.t. $|\{p_i\}| > n_{\mathcal{T}}$
    $p'_{\mathcal{T}} \leftarrow \frac{p_i + p_{\mathcal{V},0} - 1}{p_{\mathcal{T},0} + p_{\mathcal{V},0} - 1}$
    for p_j in $\{p_{\mathcal{V},0}, p_{\mathcal{V},0}+\delta_{\mathcal{V}}, p_{\mathcal{V},0}+2\delta_{\mathcal{V}}, \ldots, 1\}$ **do** ▷ Choose $\delta_{\mathcal{V}} > 0$ s.t. $|\{p_j\}| > n_{\mathcal{V}}$
      $p'_{\mathcal{V}} \leftarrow \frac{p_j + p_{\mathcal{T},0} - 1}{p_{\mathcal{V},0} + p_{\mathcal{T},0} - 1}$
      for $k \leftarrow 1$ to t **do**
        $\mathcal{T}'_k \overset{n'_{\mathcal{T}}}{\sim} M_{\hat{\mathcal{T}},\hat{\mathcal{V}}}(p'_{\mathcal{T}}, 1 - p'_{\mathcal{T}})$ ▷ M is a mixture distribution[2]
        $\mathcal{V}'_k \overset{n'_{\mathcal{V}}}{\sim} M_{\hat{\mathcal{V}},\hat{\mathcal{T}}}(p'_{\mathcal{V}}, 1 - p'_{\mathcal{V}})$
        $\hat{b}_{ij} \leftarrow \frac{1}{|\mathcal{V}'_k|} \sum_{(x,y)\in\mathcal{V}'_k} \ell(y, f(x \mid \mathcal{T}'_k))$ ▷ ℓ is any continuous loss function
        $\bar{b}_{ij} \leftarrow \bar{b}_{ij} + \frac{\hat{b}_{ij}}{t}$
      end for
    end for
  end for
  $\bar{b} \leftarrow \text{flatten}(\bar{b})$
  $A_{ijkl} \leftarrow \mathbb{P}(\text{Bin}(n'_{\mathcal{T}}, p_i) = k)\mathbb{P}(\text{Bin}(n'_{\mathcal{V}}, p_j) = l) \quad \forall p_i, p_j, k \in \{0, 1, \ldots, n'_{\mathcal{T}}\}, l \in \{0, 1, \ldots, n'_{\mathcal{V}}\}$
  $A \leftarrow reshape(A \in \mathbb{R}^{|\{p_i\}||\{p_j\}|\times(n'_{\mathcal{T}}+1)(n'_{\mathcal{V}}+1)})$ ▷ Each row of A is a joint binomial pmf
  $\hat{e}, residual \leftarrow A(A^{\intercal}A)^{-1}A^{\intercal}\bar{b}$
  return $\hat{e}_0, residual$
end procedure

Algorithm 4: B3 — Bidirectional leakage with unknown probabilities

procedure UNKNOWNBIDIRECTIONAL($f, \hat{\mathcal{T}}, \hat{\mathcal{V}}, n'_{\mathcal{T}}, n'_{\mathcal{V}}, t$)
  $residual^* \leftarrow \infty$
  $n_{\mathcal{T}} \leftarrow |\hat{\mathcal{T}}|, n_{\mathcal{V}} \leftarrow |\hat{\mathcal{V}}|$
  for $p_{\mathcal{T},0}$ in $\left\{\frac{0}{n_{\mathcal{T}}}, \frac{1}{n_{\mathcal{T}}}, \ldots, \frac{n_{\mathcal{T}}-1}{n_{\mathcal{T}}}\right\}$ **do**
    for $p_{\mathcal{V},0}$ in $\left\{\frac{0}{n_{\mathcal{V}}}, \frac{1}{n_{\mathcal{V}}}, \ldots, \frac{n_{\mathcal{V}}-1}{n_{\mathcal{V}}}\right\}$ **do**
      $e, residual \leftarrow$ KNOWNBIDIRECTIONAL($f, \hat{\mathcal{T}}, \hat{\mathcal{V}}, p_{\mathcal{T},0}, p_{\mathcal{V},0}, n'_{\mathcal{T}}, n'_{\mathcal{V}}, t$)
      if $residual < residual^*$ **then**
        $e^* \leftarrow x$
        $p^*_{\mathcal{T},0} \leftarrow p_{\mathcal{T},0}$
        $p^*_{\mathcal{V},0} \leftarrow p_{\mathcal{V},0}$
        $residual^* \leftarrow residual$
      end if
    end for
  end for
  return $e^*, p^*_{\mathcal{T},0}, p^*_{\mathcal{V},0}$
end procedure

Data-Dependent Sparsity for Subspace Clustering

Bo Xin
Microsoft Research, Beijing

Yizhou Wang
Peking University

Wen Gao
Peking University

David Wipf
Microsoft Research, Beijing

Abstract

Subspace clustering is the process of assigning subspace memberships to a set of unlabeled data points assumed to have been drawn from the union of an unknown number of low-dimensional subspaces, possibly interlaced with outliers or other data corruptions. By exploiting the fact that each inlier point has a sparse representation with respect to a dictionary formed by all the other points, an ℓ_1 regularized sparse subspace clustering (SSC) method has recently shown state-of-the-art robustness and practical extensibility in a variety of applications. But there remain important lingering weaknesses. In particular, the ℓ_1 norm solution is highly sensitive, often in a detrimental direction, to the very types of data structures that motivate interest in subspace clustering to begin with, sometimes leading to poor segmentation accuracy. However, as an alternative source of sparsity, we argue that a certain data-dependent, non-convex penalty function can compensate for dictionary structure in a way that is especially germane to subspace clustering problems. For example, we demonstrate that this proposal displays a form of invariance to feature-space transformations and affine translations that commonly disrupt existing methods, and moreover, in important settings we reveal that its performance quality is lower bounded by the ℓ_1 solution. Finally, we provide empirical comparisons on popular benchmarks that corroborate our theoretical findings and demonstrate superior performance when compared to recent state-of-the-art models.

1 INTRODUCTION

Subspace clustering is the process of segmenting a set of unlabeled data points that were drawn from the union of an unknown number of low-dimensional subspaces, possibly corrupted with outliers. As a generalization of traditional PCA, and a fundamental tool for data analysis in high dimensional settings, subspace clustering is relevant to numerous practical applications, including image representation and compression, motion segmentation, and face clustering (Elhamifar and Vidal, 2009; Soltanolkotabi and Candes, 2012; Elhamifar and Vidal, 2013; Liu et al., 2010; Rao et al., 2010; Lu et al., 2012; Liu et al., 2013; Feng et al., 2014; Lu et al., 2013; Soltanolkotabi et al., 2014). We define this problem more formally as follows.

Definition 1 *Let $\{\mathcal{S}_k\}_{k=1}^m$ denote a set of m linear (or possibly affine) subspaces in $\mathbb{R}^d$, where $\dim[\mathcal{S}_k] = d_k < d \quad \forall k = 1, \ldots, m$. Moreover, suppose we have drawn n_k points from each subspace forming data matrices $\boldsymbol{X}_k \in \mathbb{R}^{d \times n_k}$. We then concatenate the points from each subspace and combine them with a matrix $\boldsymbol{X}_0 \in \mathbb{R}^{d \times n_0}$ whose columns represent outlying points with no subspace membership. Finally, the full arrangement of $n = n_0 + \sum_{k=1}^m n_k$ points is scrambled with an unknown permutation matrix $\boldsymbol{P} \in \mathbb{R}^{n \times n}$. The entire ensemble can then be expressed as*

$$\boldsymbol{X} \triangleq [\boldsymbol{x}_1, \ldots, \boldsymbol{x}_n] = [\boldsymbol{X}_0, \boldsymbol{X}_1, \ldots, \boldsymbol{X}_K]\boldsymbol{P} \in \mathbb{R}^{d \times n}. \tag{1}$$

Subspace clustering *is defined as the process of estimating the subspace membership of each point $\boldsymbol{x}_i$ while discarding the outliers, without any a prior knowledge of the dimensionality or cardinality of the underlying union of subspaces.*

Given some means of first isolating and removing outliers, spectral clustering represents one of the most robust approaches to obtaining accurate data segmentations. This process involves forming an affinity matrix $\boldsymbol{A}$, where the ij-th element a_{ij} quantifies the strength of the relationship between points $\boldsymbol{x}_i$ and $\boldsymbol{x}_j$. In traditional clustering, this affinity is typically computed using a Gaussian kernel $\exp[-\alpha\|\boldsymbol{x}_i - \boldsymbol{x}_j\|_2^2]$ with $\alpha > 0$, but this ignores the subspace structure we want to reflect.

To this end, we instead form $\boldsymbol{A}$ to honor the desired subspace arrangement by exploiting a *self-expressiveness property* of $\boldsymbol{X}$ (Elhamifar and Vidal, 2013), namely that any $\boldsymbol{x}_i$ can be represented as a linear combination of other data points in $\boldsymbol{X}$ within the same subspace. This of course assumes a suitable sampling of points in $\boldsymbol{X}$, i.e., each n_k is sufficiently large with points in general position. Overall, with $n > d$ there will exist an infinite number of such self-expressive representations; however, in constructing a viable affinity matrix it is paramount that we find representations that heavily favor *only* using points from the same subspace.

For the moment, assume that no outliers are present (i.e., $n_0 = 0$). At a motivational level, sparse subspace clustering (SSC) (Elhamifar and Vidal, 2013) attempts to learn subspace-aware representations by solving

$$\min_{\boldsymbol{Z}} \|\boldsymbol{Z}\|_0 \text{ s.t. } \boldsymbol{X} = \boldsymbol{X}\boldsymbol{Z},\ \text{diag}[\boldsymbol{Z}] = 0, \quad (2)$$

where $\|\boldsymbol{Z}\|_0$ is the matrix ℓ_0 norm, or a count of the number of nonzero elements in $\boldsymbol{Z}$, a penalty function that heavily favors zero-valued elements or a sparse $\boldsymbol{Z}$. The diagonal constraint is included to prevent each point from using itself in the representation (e.g., the degenerate solution $\boldsymbol{Z}^* = \boldsymbol{I}$), ideally deferring to others in the same subspace. Provided that each individual subspace satisfies $d_k < d$ for all k, and sampled points are sufficiently dense in general position, then up to a permutation matrix $\boldsymbol{P}$, the solution to (2) will be block diagonal and aligned with the true clusters revealing subspace memberships. Note that if noise or other modeling errors are present the equality constraint $\boldsymbol{X} = \boldsymbol{X}\boldsymbol{Z}$ can be relaxed with the inclusion of an additional trade-off parameter, e.g., $\|\boldsymbol{X} - \boldsymbol{X}\boldsymbol{Z}\|_{\mathcal{F}} \leq \epsilon$.

From a practical standpoint, theoretical analysis from (Elhamifar and Vidal, 2013; Soltanolkotabi and Candes, 2012) suggests that in certain cases as long as the angles between subspaces are not too small and points within are suitably arranged, then we can replace the intractable, NP-hard matrix ℓ_0-norm minimization in (2) with $\|\boldsymbol{Z}\|_1$ and still compute the same desirable block-diagonal structure. We will henceforth refer to this algorithm as ℓ_1-SSC. If the data $\boldsymbol{X}$ ideally follow the union of subspace model and the ℓ_1-SSC solution matches the solution of (2), then it is possible to extract subspace memberships directly from $\boldsymbol{Z}^*$. However, in practical situations with noise and model mismatch, it is highly beneficial to first form a symmetric affinity matrix as $\boldsymbol{A} = |\boldsymbol{Z}^*| + |\boldsymbol{Z}^*|^\top$ and then apply traditional spectral clustering (Luxburg, 2007) to the normalized Laplacian of $\boldsymbol{A}$ to obtain a more robust segmentation (Elhamifar and Vidal, 2013).

Regardless, the more the self-expressive representation obtained by ℓ_1-SSC reflects the subspace alignments and sizes, the more effective the final spectral clustering step will be. But is the ℓ_1 norm the optimal objective? Certainly a variety of surrogates for producing a block diagonal $\boldsymbol{Z}$ have been proposed in the literature such as the nuclear norm or other rank penalties (Babacan et al., 2012; Liu et al., 2013), the Frobenius norm (Lu et al., 2012), and the Trace Lasso (Lu et al., 2013). Likewise, a multi-task learning approach from (Wang et al., 2015) introduces an additional penalty and tuning paramter to encourage subspace-aware group-sparse representations. But from a theoretical standpoint, of the existing methods ℓ_1-SSC enjoys some of the strongest recovery guarantees (Soltanolkotabi and Candes, 2012), requires minimal tuning or a priori knowledge across broad operating conditions, and moreover, it is perhaps one of the most straightforward to adapt for handling practical situations where outliers or other data corruptions are present (Elhamifar and Vidal, 2013).

And yet there remains critical lingering issues with ℓ_1-SSC (issues that also affect many other algorithms in the literature). The equivalence between the ℓ_0 and ℓ_1 solutions will be quite sensitive to correlation structure in $\boldsymbol{X}$ as well as the particular feature representation used for each $\boldsymbol{x}_i$ and its interrelationship with the corresponding column norms. In brief, while the ℓ_1 norm regularizer is an order-wise optimal substitution for the ℓ_0 norm with iid Gaussian or similar designs (see (Candes et al., 2006) and the vast literature on compressive sensing), this relationship completely breaks down with the types of highly-structured data required by subspace clustering problems. And of course the reality is, *if such confounding structures were not present, there would be little value in attempting subspace clustering to begin with.*[1]

Fortunately though, unlike the ℓ_1 norm or other typical penalty functions, there exist data-dependent regularization techniques that can directly compensate for correlated data in finding maximally sparse or minimal ℓ_0-norm representations (Wipf, 2011), suggesting a seemingly natural surrogate for sparse subspace segmentation. In Section 2 we will introduce one specific, so-called *data-dependent* penalty for *sparse subspace clustering* (DD-SSC) procedure, as well as principled modifications to handle outliers and affine subspaces.

Note that nearly all recent subspace clustering work be-

[1]Technically speaking, it is sometimes possible to achieve a correct clustering even when ℓ_0-ℓ_1 norm equivalency does not hold (You and Vidal, 2015). However, it is still well-known that the ℓ_0 norm will provably produce a correct subspace clustering under *much* broader conditions than the ℓ_1 norm (e.g., see (Yang et al., 2016)).

gins with some existing algorithm or penalty function over $\boldsymbol{Z}$ that is then optimized to produce a viable affinity matrix. The novelty then lies in the attendant technical arguments for why a particular approach is likely to produce the desired, subspace-aligned block-diagonal structure, and ultimately the correct segmentation. In most cases (e.g.,(Liu et al., 2013; Lu et al., 2012, 2013)), theoretical recovery guarantees are restricted to the simplified setting where the subspaces are independent, in which case virtually any regularizer for $\boldsymbol{Z}$ is provably adequate. In contrast, much stronger guarantees have been shown for convex ℓ_1-SSC using rigorous geometric considerations (Elhamifar and Vidal, 2013; Soltanolkotabi and Candes, 2012; You and Vidal, 2015). Building upon these results, Section 3 presents our two primary analytical contributions, which can be summarized as follows:

- We demonstrate broad, challenging conditions under which DD-SSC will provably perform as well or better than ℓ_1-SSC in a sense that no existing algorithm can match.
- Several important factors can conspire to significantly disrupt the performance of current state-of-the-art subspace clustering algorithms, often in subtle underappreciated ways. These include the aggregate effects of feature space transformations (meaning invertible, potentially ill-conditioned transformations of the columns of $\boldsymbol{X}$), affine subspace translations, and the effects of disparate column norms $\|\boldsymbol{x}_i\|_2$. We precisely characterize the nature of these confounds and demonstrate that DD-SSC is largely invariant to all three factors, unlike existing approaches.

Finally, Section 4 provides complementary empirical results using both simulated and real-world data that confirm our main theoretical insights. Additionally, after preparing an initial version of our paper, we noticed an interesting recent work that also emphasizes the importance of minimizing the ℓ_0 norm as opposed to defaulting to the convex ℓ_1 relaxation (Yang et al., 2016). However, the proposed algorithmic strategy for actually accomplishing this, which amounts to regular ℓ_1 norm minimization followed by non-convex iterative hard-thresholding (IHT) iterations (Blumensath and Davies, 2008) to approximate the ℓ_0 norm, is radically different from ours. Importantly, it does not actually address any of the issues we raise above. In fact, this approach will be highly sensitive to feature space transformations and affine subspace translations since both algorithmic components, meaning the ℓ_1 and IHT steps, are heavily influenced by correlations and scaling factors in the data $\boldsymbol{X}$, and provably do not possess the desirable invariances of DD-SSC. Moreover, empirically we find that DD-SSC consistently outperforms the method from (Yang et al., 2016) on a battery of tests drawn from the latter.

2 DATA-DEPENDENT SPARSE SUBSPACE CLUSTERING (DD-SSC)

Model Development: The original sparse subspace clustering problem from (2) decouples into n individual NP-hard sparse estimation tasks of the form

$$\min_{\boldsymbol{z}_i} \|\boldsymbol{z}_i\|_0 \quad \text{s.t. } \boldsymbol{x}_i = \boldsymbol{X}_{\bar{i}}\boldsymbol{z}_i, \tag{3}$$

where $\boldsymbol{X}_{\bar{i}}$ denotes the full data matrix $\boldsymbol{X}$ with the i-th column removed.[2] Instead of the tractable convex substitution $\|\boldsymbol{z}_i\|_1$ adopted by ℓ_1-SSC, we advocate an alternative, data-dependent penalty that ultimately emerges from manipulations of a seemingly-unrelated Bayesian model from (Tipping, 2001) applied to each $\boldsymbol{x}_i$. For completeness, we briefly introduce the high-level derivations as follows.

For the i-th data point we first define the Gaussian likelihood

$$p(\boldsymbol{x}_i|\boldsymbol{z}_i; \boldsymbol{X}_{\bar{i}}, \alpha) \propto \exp\left[-\tfrac{1}{2\alpha}\|\boldsymbol{X}_{\bar{i}}\boldsymbol{z}_i - \boldsymbol{x}_i\|_2^2\right]. \tag{4}$$

We also note that in the limit as $\alpha \to 0$, this likelihood will enforce the same constraint set as in (3) with probability one. For other values of α we may of course account for measurement noise or model mismatch errors as appropriate. Next we assume parameterized zero-mean Gaussian distributions as priors over each $\boldsymbol{z}_i$. Specifically, we have

$$p(\boldsymbol{z}_i; \boldsymbol{\gamma}_i) \propto \exp\left[-\tfrac{1}{2}\boldsymbol{z}_i^\top \boldsymbol{\Gamma}_i^{-1}\boldsymbol{z}_i\right], \quad \boldsymbol{\Gamma}_i \triangleq \text{diag}[\boldsymbol{\gamma}_i], \tag{5}$$

where $\boldsymbol{\gamma}_i$ denotes a vector of unknown variance hyperparamters. Given that both likelihood and prior are Gaussian, the posterior $p(\boldsymbol{z}_i|\boldsymbol{x}_i; \boldsymbol{X}_{\bar{i}}, \boldsymbol{\gamma}_i, \alpha)$ is also Gaussian, with mean $\hat{\boldsymbol{z}}_i$ given by

$$\hat{\boldsymbol{z}}_i = \boldsymbol{\Gamma}_i \boldsymbol{X}_{\bar{i}}^\top \boldsymbol{\Sigma}_{\boldsymbol{x}_i}^{-1}\boldsymbol{x}_i, \quad \text{with} \tag{6}$$

$$\boldsymbol{\Sigma}_{\boldsymbol{x}_i} \triangleq \boldsymbol{X}_{\bar{i}}\boldsymbol{\Gamma}_i\boldsymbol{X}_{\bar{i}}^\top + \alpha \boldsymbol{I}. \tag{7}$$

From the above expressions it is clear that if $\boldsymbol{\gamma}_i$ is a sparse vector with mostly zero-valued entries, then by virtue of its diagonal positioning and lefthand-side multiplication in (6), the estimator $\hat{\boldsymbol{z}}_i$ will have a matching sparsity profile or support. Of course for this framework to be a successful entry point for producing sparsity, we require some way of determining a viable estimate for $\boldsymbol{\gamma}_i$.

[2] Note that per this definition, the dimension of $\boldsymbol{z}_i$ will technically be reduced by one relative to the original columns of $\boldsymbol{Z}$ since we have removed the zero-valued elements enforced by the constraint; however, we retain this admittedly inconsistent notation for convenience.

If we temporarily treat the unknown z_i as a nuisance variable and γ_i as the parameter of interest, a typical empirical Bayesian estimation strategy is to marginalize over z_i and then maximize the resulting type-II likelihood function with respect to γ_i (MacKay, 1992). Fortunately, the resulting convolution of Gaussians integral is available in closed-form (Tipping, 2001) such that we can equivalently minimize the negative log-likelihood

$$\mathcal{L}(\gamma_i) = -\log \int p(\boldsymbol{x}_i|\boldsymbol{z}_i;\boldsymbol{X}_{\bar{i}},\alpha)p(\boldsymbol{z}_i;\gamma_i)d\boldsymbol{z}_i \equiv \boldsymbol{x}_i^\top \boldsymbol{\Sigma}_{\boldsymbol{x}_i}^{-1}\boldsymbol{x}_i + \log|\boldsymbol{\Sigma}_{\boldsymbol{x}_i}|. \quad (8)$$

Once we have an estimate of γ_i for all data points, we can compute a final estimator $\hat{\boldsymbol{Z}}$ by concatenating the respective posterior means computed via (6).

Thus far we have essentially just deferred a direct search for a sparse estimator of $\boldsymbol{z}_i$ to the search for a (hopefully) sparse γ_i. However, if we apply (Wipf et al., 2011, Theorem 2), we can convert the estimation problem of minimizing $\mathcal{L}(\gamma_i)$ in γ_i-space to an equivalent problem in z_i-space, facilitating direct analysis and comparison with more traditional sparse estimators. In particular, it can be shown that minimizing (8) and then computing $\hat{\boldsymbol{z}}_i$ using (6) is equivalent to minimizing

$$\mathcal{L}(\boldsymbol{z}_i) \triangleq \tfrac{1}{\alpha}\|\boldsymbol{x}_i - \boldsymbol{X}_{\bar{i}}\boldsymbol{z}_i\|_2^2 + f(\boldsymbol{z}_i;\boldsymbol{X}_{\bar{i}},\alpha), \quad \text{where} \quad (9)$$

$$f(\boldsymbol{z}_i;\boldsymbol{X}_{\bar{i}},\alpha) \triangleq \inf_{\gamma_i \succcurlyeq \mathbf{0}} \sum_j \frac{z_{ij}^2}{\gamma_{ij}} + \log|\boldsymbol{X}_{\bar{i}}\boldsymbol{\Gamma}_i\boldsymbol{X}_{\bar{i}}^\top + \alpha\boldsymbol{I}| \quad (10)$$

is a data-dependent penalty function, parameterized by $\boldsymbol{X}_{\bar{i}}$ and α, that is only expressible in variational form.[3] Of course once we view this Bayesian model in terms of (9), we need no longer enforce that the α embedded in f equal the α scale factor found in the ℓ_2-norm error term. This emergent flexibility facilitates later analysis of f restricted to the feasible region but with arbitrary α, and contributes to a broader class of viable algorithms. Finally, although there is generally no closed-form solution for f, it nonetheless can be shown to be a strictly concave, non-decreasing function of each coefficient magnitude $|z_{ij}|$ for all $\alpha \geq 0$, and hence it naturally favors exactly sparse solutions (Wipf et al., 2011), meaning many $z_{ij} = 0$. Therefore we propose to attack (2) by replacing the ℓ_0 norm with f for each point, rather than the standard convex ℓ_1 norm alternative.

Once we have some $\hat{\boldsymbol{Z}}$ obtained by optimizing this revised penalty across all i, we may then form an affinity matrix $\boldsymbol{A}$ just as with previous methods to facilitate the subsequent spectral clustering step. We will henceforth refer to this procedure as DD-SSC, for *data-dependent sparse subspace clustering*. Like the original ℓ_1-SSC, DD-SSC naturally handles extensions to account for both outlier removal and affine subspaces.

[3]If some $z_{ij} = 0$, then we allow by definition the corresponding variational parameter γ_{ij} to exactly equal zero as well; given that the log-det term is a concave, non-decreasing function of each γ_{ij}, zero will in fact be the minimizing value in such a case.

Outlier Removal: In many applications it is quite common to have outlying data points, meaning that some columns of $\boldsymbol{X}$ do not adhere to the union of subspaces model. If such outliers are not properly accounted for, virtually all clustering algorithms, sparsity-based or not, will fail. Fortunately, the SSC framework provides a natural mechanism for removing such divisive points (Soltanolkotabi and Candes, 2012), and DD-SSC can seamlessly piggyback this agency. DD-SSC can also handle element-wise corruptions in a principled fashion, but we postpone this analysis to the supplementary file.

The basic idea proceeds as follows. First we run DD-SSC on each point $\boldsymbol{x}_i$ and compute the corresponding $\hat{\boldsymbol{z}}_i$, which we expect to be sparse. However, because the outliers do not lie in one of the low-dimensional subspaces, we envisage that the support set will be considerably larger (less sparse) than for inlier points. Hence we declare $\boldsymbol{x}_i$ to be an outlier if and only if the number of nonzero entries of $\hat{\boldsymbol{z}}_i$ surpasses a certain threshold, i.e., $\|\hat{\boldsymbol{z}}_i\|_0 \geq \tau$. Moreover, it is our hope that, presuming the DD-SSC penalty f is able to produce even greater sparsity for inlier points, the gap between normal and outlying points will be more pronounced. In Section 4, we will empirically show that this is indeed the case. Finally, once outliers have been identified, the affinity matrix is constructed using the remaining inliers for subsequent spectral clustering.

Affine Subspaces: Real-World data often lie in a union of affine subspaces, a more general model which includes linear subspaces as a special case.[4] For example, motion segmentation problems require the clustering of data that lie in the union of 3-dimensional affine subspaces (Tomasi and Kanade, 1992). To enforce an affine subspace model, it is sufficient in principle to include the additional constraint $\sum_j z_{ij} = 1$, which leads to translation invariance of SSC algorithms (Rao et al., 2010; Elhamifar and Vidal, 2013), at least assuming columns of $\boldsymbol{X}$ are not normalized (more on this in Section 3). This constraint can be incorporated into DD-SSC by updating the likelihood model (4) and then performing the associated marginalization. The net result is that we only need to replace $\boldsymbol{X}_{\bar{i}}$ and $\boldsymbol{I}$ in the objective with $\boldsymbol{X}^+$ and $\boldsymbol{I}^+$ respectively, where $\boldsymbol{X}^+ \triangleq [\boldsymbol{X};\mathbf{1}_{(n)}^\top]$ (i.e., a length

[4]An affine subspace is merely defined as a standard linear subspace that has been translated away from the origin via an arbitrary offset.

n row of ones is appended to the bottom of $\boldsymbol{X}$), and $\boldsymbol{I}^{+} \triangleq \left[[\boldsymbol{I}, \mathbf{0}_{(n-1)}]; \mathbf{0}_{(n)}^{\top}\right]$.

3 ANALYSIS OF DD-SSC

Motivating data-dependent terms for SSC: When we apply sparse regularization such as the ℓ_1 norm penalty (or essentially any other sparsity penalty in the literature), results are highly sensitive to correlation structure in the data matrix $\boldsymbol{X}$, meaning strong off-diagonal elements in $\boldsymbol{X}^{\top}\boldsymbol{X}$ (see (Candes et al., 2006)). In tackling this problem, we observed that it makes sense to include a data-dependent penalty that effectively compensates for this correlation structure. To see this, a simple analogy is in order. Suppose we would like to solve a regularized regression problem of the form

$$\min_{\boldsymbol{z}} \|\boldsymbol{y} - \boldsymbol{X}\boldsymbol{z}\|^2 + \textstyle\sum_i g(z_i), \tag{11}$$

where g is some regularizer that favors small magnitudes. Generally speaking, the solution will be highly dependent on the column norms of $\boldsymbol{X}$, meaning that if the norm of some column $\boldsymbol{x}_i$ is very small, then the corresponding coefficient z_i needs to be made large to compensate, and this will be more heavily penalized by g. Of course in this case there is a trivial solution: If we replace $g(z_i)$ with $g(\|\boldsymbol{x}_i\| z_i)$, then elements of $\boldsymbol{z}$ associated with small column norms will be penalized proportionally less, and the aggregate behavior will be exactly as though the design matrix $\boldsymbol{X}$ had normalized columns.

In this example, we have effectively used a *column-norm-dependent penalty* $\sum_i g(\|\boldsymbol{x}_i\| z_i)$ to counterbalance potentially disparate scale factors. Drawing from this experience though, if our concern is also strong off-diagonal factors in $\boldsymbol{X}^{\top}\boldsymbol{X}$, and not just disparate scales along the diagonal as represented by $\|\boldsymbol{x}_i\|$, it makes sense to consider some new penalty $f(\boldsymbol{z}; \boldsymbol{X}^{\top}\boldsymbol{X})$ that explicitly depends on this correlation structure. The subspace clustering penalty we proposed does exactly this. In particular, given the general determinant identity

$$\log\left|\boldsymbol{X}\boldsymbol{D}\boldsymbol{X}^{\top} + \alpha\boldsymbol{I}\right| = \log\left|\tfrac{1}{\alpha}\boldsymbol{X}^{\top}\boldsymbol{X} + \boldsymbol{D}^{-1}\right| + C \tag{12}$$

where $C{=}\log|\boldsymbol{D}|{+}\log|\alpha\boldsymbol{I}|$ and $\boldsymbol{D}$ is a non-negative diagonal matrix, when we optimize (10), the resulting penalty will explicitly depend on $\boldsymbol{X}^{\top}\boldsymbol{X}$ through the action of this volumetric log-det measure that is highly sensitive to correlations. Moreover, although there is no closed-form solution for the actual penalty, we can nonetheless analyze its behavior in the specific context of SSC, revealing both theoretically and empirically in the coming sections, that it directly solves many previously-unaddressed limitations (and the computational complexity is proportional to the original ℓ_1-SSC).

Improvement over ℓ_1-SSC: For purposes of the simplest practical deployment in a few lines of code, DD-SSC can be implemented using a form of the EM algorithm treating each latent $\boldsymbol{z}_i$ as hidden data (Dempster et al., 1981). However, an alternative implementation can be designed using iterative reweighted ℓ_1-norm updates (Wipf et al., 2011) more amenable to analysis and the elucidation of an explicit advantage of the DD-SSC penalty function over the convex ℓ_1-SSC standard, especially when correlated subspaces confound the latter.

In the present context, iterative reweighted ℓ_1 minimization, which is a specific variant of a majorization-minimization algorithm (Hunter and Lange, 2004), proceeds by forming a convex, first-order Taylor-series approximation to the non-convex penalty function f in (10). More concretely, for the i-th data point, we begin from an initial weight vector $\boldsymbol{w}^{(0)} = \mathbf{1}$ and then proceed to the $(t+1)$-th iteration by computing

$$\boldsymbol{z}_i^{(t+1)} \leftarrow \arg\min_{\boldsymbol{z}_i} \sum_j w_j^{(t)} |z_{ij}| \;\; \text{s.t. } \boldsymbol{x}_i = \boldsymbol{X}_{\bar{i}}\boldsymbol{z}_i,$$

$$\boldsymbol{w}^{(t+1)} \leftarrow \left.\frac{\partial f(\boldsymbol{z}_i; \boldsymbol{X}_{\bar{i}}, \alpha)}{\partial |\boldsymbol{z}|}\right|_{\boldsymbol{z}=\boldsymbol{z}_i^{(t+1)}}, \tag{13}$$

where the $|\cdot|$ operator is understood to apply element-wise. Furthermore, in certain cases the required gradient is available in closed-form even though the original penalty f is not. For example, let

$$\eta_j(\boldsymbol{z}_i; \alpha, q) \triangleq \left[\boldsymbol{x}_j^{\top}\left(\alpha I + \boldsymbol{X}_{\bar{i}}\left|Z_i^{(t+1)}\right|^2 \boldsymbol{X}_{\bar{i}}^{\top}\right)^{-1}\boldsymbol{x}_j\right]^q, \tag{14}$$

where $\left|Z_i^{(t+1)}\right|$ denotes a diagonal matrix with j-th diagonal entry given by $|z_{ij}^{(t+1)}|$. Then when $\alpha \to 0$, $\boldsymbol{w}^{(t+1)}$ can be updated using $w_j^{(t+1)} = \eta_j(\boldsymbol{z}_i; 0, 1/2)$, $\forall j$. Using straightforward application of results from (Sriperumbudur and Lanckriet, 2012), the resulting iterations are guaranteed to converge to the set of local minima (or possibly saddle points) of f in the feasible region $\boldsymbol{x}_i = \boldsymbol{X}_{\bar{i}}\boldsymbol{z}_i$. Additionally, for other values of α and q we obtain a valid, generalized weighting function, although it need not directly correspond with the original Bayesian model from which DD-SSC was derived.

Proceeding further, it is thus far unclear what intrinsic advantage this overall class of estimators has over the canonical ℓ_1-SSC, nor if the required $\eta_j(\boldsymbol{z}_i; 0, 1/2)$ terms are even a suitable choice of weighting factor. However, we will now demonstrate that the above generalized, iterative reweighted ℓ_1 form of DD-SSC is guaranteed to do as well or better than ℓ_1-SSC in certain circumstances.

For this purpose, we first say that a candidate solution $\hat{\boldsymbol{z}}_i$

is *subspace optimal* if its nonzero elements occur only at locations associated with data points from the subspace to which $\boldsymbol{x}_i$ belongs. Note that if an aggregate solution $\hat{\boldsymbol{Z}}$ is subspace optimal for all i, it is a trivial matter to design a clustering wrapper (spectral or otherwise), such that the correct final clustering is obtained. So clearly if we can guarantee subspace optimal sparse representations, the brunt of our work is complete.

Theorem 1 *The DD-SSC updates produced by (13) satisfy the following:*

1. *If at any iteration we compute a subspace optimal solution $\boldsymbol{z}_i^{(t)}$, then all subsequent iterations are guaranteed to be subspace optimal for any $\alpha \in (0, \alpha']$, provided α' is sufficiently small.*
2. *For any identifiable configuration of subspaces, some $q \geq 1/2$, $\alpha \in (0, \alpha']$, and α' sufficiently small, there will always exist configurations of points within each subspace such that the iterations are guaranteed to produce a subspace optimal solution for all i.*

Given that we initialize DD-SSC using $\boldsymbol{w}^{(0)} = \mathbf{1}$, the first iteration is nothing more than ℓ_1-SSC. Combined with the first property from Theorem 1, this ensures that we automatically inherit whatever desirable theoretical properties of the ℓ_1 solution that exist (Soltanolkotabi and Candes, 2012), and we need not worry about subsequent iterations diverging from a subspace correct solution found by ℓ_1-SSC. Extra iterations can only improve our chances, they can never make things worse.[5]

Moreover, the second property from above guarantees that no matter how entwined the various subspaces are, for at least some constellations of the points additional iterations will indeed improve the situation. While the proof construction contains further details (see supplementary), in brief, sufficiently clustered point clouds (lying within a region of non-zero Lebesgue measure inside each subspace), will ensure optimal recovery. In contrast, no other algorithm we are aware of satisfies a similar result. We also emphasize that the ℓ_1 norm solution itself can be quite difficult to improve upon, largely because in failure cases it is frequently positioned (often provably so) in a poor basin of attraction with respect to more complex, non-convex regularizers, *especially* when correlated data $\boldsymbol{X}$ is involved. Therefore further iterations cannot escape, unlike the DD-SSC updates.

[5]Note that prior conditions have been established based on the distribution of nonzero elements in a sparse representation such that guaranteed improvement is possible using iterative reweighted ℓ_1 minimization (Wipf and Nagarajan, 2010). However, these results are inapplicable in the present subspace clustering context and Theorem 1 above relies on an entirely different proof construction (see supplementary file).

When combined together then, we believe that these components of Theorem 1 suggest that there is minimal risk in deploying DD-SSC, but potentially much to gain, especially in challenging recovery conditions with dense, correlated subspaces that can cause existing algorithms to fail. While perhaps not immediately obvious, all of this is possible because the DD-SSC penalty function f depends on the design matrix $\boldsymbol{X}_{\bar{i}}$ in such a way that compensation for subspace structure is possible. In contrast, virtually all existing subspace clustering algorithms rely on *data-independent* penalties, e.g., the ℓ_1, ℓ_2, or nuclear norm, or the hybrid method from (Yang et al., 2016). However, one noteworthy exception is the correlation adaptive subspace segmentation algorithm (CASS) (Lu et al., 2013), which adopts the Trace Lasso penalty function $g(\boldsymbol{z}_i; \boldsymbol{X}_{\bar{i}}) = \|\boldsymbol{X}_{\bar{i}} |Z_i|\|_*$ (Grave et al., 2011). Although this selection does compensate to some extent for correlation structure to increase the number of nonzeros in the correct subspace, it is *not* a concave function of the coefficients $|z_{ij}|$ (unlike both ℓ_1-SSC and DD-SSC), and therefore subspace optimal solutions are essentially impossible to guarantee, except in the trivial case where the subspaces are independent and virtually any algorithm is subspace optimal. Additionally, CASS and other state-of-the-art algorithms do not benefit from the invariance properties discussed next.

Desirable Invariances: The original ℓ_1-SSC algorithm was motivated, at least initially, by its theoretical ability to recover maximally sparse solutions in the context of compressive sensing (CS) (Candes et al., 2006). But there remain several crucial differences between CS and SSC applications. Most importantly, CS typically relies on randomized dictionaries with suitable concentration properties in high dimensions such that different columns are roughly orthogonal with equivalent column ℓ_2 norms. But in SSC we are not free to choose the dictionaries $\boldsymbol{X}_{\bar{i}}$, rather, they are determined by the subspace structure of the data and may display both high degrees of correlation and columns with vastly different norms, both of which can severely bias ℓ_1 regularization dramatically. With regard to the latter, we could of course consider first normalizing each point $\boldsymbol{x}_i$ of the full data $\boldsymbol{X}$ by dividing with $\|\boldsymbol{x}_i\|_2$, but unlike in the CS domain, this may actually hurt performance more than it helps depending on how the data are structured.

For example, consider data generated as $\boldsymbol{X} = \boldsymbol{\Phi}\boldsymbol{S} + \beta\boldsymbol{L}$, where $\boldsymbol{\Phi}$ reflects some arbitrary subspace structure involving embedded points with unit ℓ_2 norm, $\boldsymbol{S}$ is a diagonal scaling matrix, $\boldsymbol{L}$ is a low-rank additive component, and β is a positive scalar. Now suppose we try to recover $\boldsymbol{x}_i$ using $\boldsymbol{X}_{\bar{i}}$ as the dictionary using ℓ_1-SSC. Without column normalization, the scaling via $\boldsymbol{S}$ can completely disrupt the effectiveness of the ℓ_1 norm solution by favoring points in the wrong subspace that happen to have large magnitudes. However, if we do apply normalization and β is large, then the resulting ℓ_2 column norms will be overshadowed by the low-rank term contributing to arbitrarily bad solutions as well. Moreover, this is not some contrived situation. In the case of affine subspaces, such an additive low-rank term will always be present to enforce each subspaces' translation away from zero, namely, $\boldsymbol{L} = [\boldsymbol{b}_1 \mathbf{1}_{n_1}^\top, \boldsymbol{b}_2 \mathbf{1}_{n_2}^\top, \ldots]$, where each $\boldsymbol{b}_k$ is a bias vector and rank$[\boldsymbol{L}] = m$, the number of subspaces.

Further compounding the problem is that there is ambiguity in the constraint set from (2) in that $\boldsymbol{W}\boldsymbol{X} = \boldsymbol{W}\boldsymbol{X}\boldsymbol{Z}$ represents an equivalent feasible region whenever $\boldsymbol{W}$ is an invertible feature transformation. While such a $\boldsymbol{W}$ has no effect on the constraint per se, it will have a major impact on the column sizes should we choose to normalize. Hence even beyond the intrinsic subspace structure and correlation discussed above, issues of feature representations, affine translations, and column scaling can act as a major disruptive force to ℓ_1-SSC, as well as virtually all other existing subspace clustering algorithms we are aware of. For example, the CASS algorithm will be particularly sensitive to these effects since the data-dependent Trace Lasso penalty function is highly dependent on both transformations via $\boldsymbol{W}$ or translations via $\boldsymbol{L}$. Likewise for algorithms built upon IHT (Yang et al., 2016).

It is here that DD-SSC maintains another considerable advantage over existing methods as follows:

Theorem 2 *Let $\widetilde{\boldsymbol{X}} \triangleq \boldsymbol{W}\boldsymbol{X}\boldsymbol{S}$ denote a transformed and rescaled version of $\boldsymbol{X}$, where $\boldsymbol{W}$ is an arbitrary matrix and $\boldsymbol{S}$ is a diagonal matrix. Then the support set (and therefore subspace optimality) of any local or global minimizer of*

$$\min_{\boldsymbol{z}_i} f(\boldsymbol{z}_i; \widetilde{\boldsymbol{X}}_{\bar{i}}, 0) \quad s.t.\ \widetilde{\boldsymbol{x}}_i = \widetilde{\boldsymbol{X}}_{\bar{i}} \boldsymbol{z}_i \qquad (15)$$

is invariant to $\boldsymbol{W}$ and $\boldsymbol{S}$ provided that both are invertible.

This result follows by extending (Wipf, 2011, Lemma 1); details are omitted here. The consequences of the invariance afforded by Theorem 2 in the context of SSC are profound. First, we need not worry about feature transformations/representations and their effect on column norm scalings given that DD-SSC is *jointly* invariant to either. And secondly, assuming $\boldsymbol{L}$ is sufficiently low rank, then the projection operator onto null$[\boldsymbol{L}^\top]$, which is the orthogonal complement of range$[\boldsymbol{L}]$, will be nearly invertible. Therefore if we assign $\boldsymbol{W}$ to be an invertible approximation to this operator, we can transform $\boldsymbol{X} = \boldsymbol{\Phi}\boldsymbol{S} + \beta\boldsymbol{L}$ via

$$\boldsymbol{W}\boldsymbol{X} = \boldsymbol{W}\boldsymbol{\Phi}\boldsymbol{S} + \beta\boldsymbol{W}\boldsymbol{L} \approx \boldsymbol{W}\boldsymbol{\Phi}\boldsymbol{S}, \qquad (16)$$

and so DD-SSC should be nearly invariant to affine transformations as well. Experimental results will confirm this conclusion revealing the sensitivity of ℓ_1-SSC.

4 EXPERIMENTS

Challenging Subspace Detection: In (Soltanolkotabi and Candes, 2012) a series of synthetic experiments were designed to challenge the performance of ℓ_1-SSC. We embed DD-SSC into publicly available code[6] and conduct the same experiments. We begin by testing the ability to cluster subspaces with intersection. Specifically, two subspaces of dimension $d_1 = d_2 = 10$ are embedded in $\mathbb{R}^{20}$ with an intersection of dimension $t \leq d_1$, all generated uniformly at random. Then, $n_1 = n_2 = 20d_1$ points are selected from each subspace also uniformly at random. All data are normalized to have unit ℓ_2 norm.

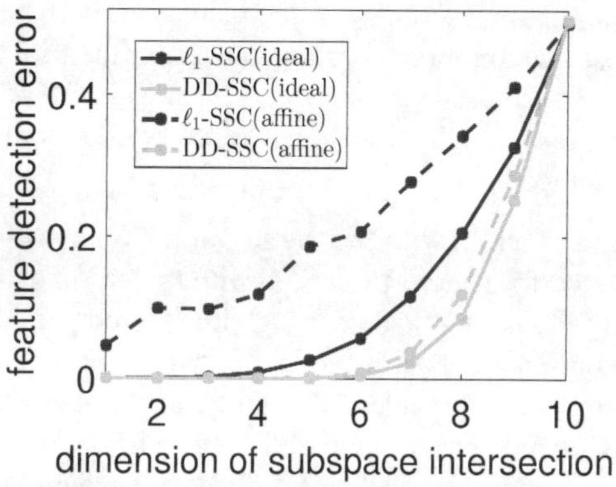

Figure 1: Feature detection error as a function of the subspace intersection dimension. Any algorithm will not have error below 0.5 on average once $t = 10$ where the two subspaces merged to one.

Although this experiment introduces some confounding structure by virtue of the subspace intersections, the remaining conditions of this experiment are rather ideal for ℓ_1-SSC since all points are effectively sampled uniformly on the unit ℓ_2 norm ball. To investigate further disruption of such idyllic conditions, we first remove the original column normalization from above and then shift each subspace away from the origin to form affine subspaces. Ultimately this means that the data matrix $\boldsymbol{X} = [\boldsymbol{X}_1, \boldsymbol{X}_2]$ is modified to $\boldsymbol{X}\boldsymbol{S} + [\boldsymbol{b}_1 \mathbf{1}_{n_1}^\top\ \boldsymbol{b}_2 \mathbf{1}_{n_2}^\top]$, where $\boldsymbol{S}$ is a diagonal matrix of column scalings (which range roughly between 3 and 6 with high probability) and $\boldsymbol{b}_i \triangleq b_i \mathbf{1}_d$ with b_i sampled from a normal distribution with standard deviation 10.

In Figure 1, we show results under both the original (ideal) setting and this more challenging affine setting. Following (Soltanolkotabi and Candes, 2012), we define the *feature detection error* as $\frac{1}{n}\sum_{i=1}^{n} 1 - \frac{\|\boldsymbol{z}_{ik_i}\|_1}{\|\boldsymbol{z}_i\|_1}$,

[6] http://www-bcf.usc.edu/~soltanol/code.html

where z_{ik_i} is the portion of z_i corresponding to points from the i-th subspace and use it for evaluation. This metric goes to zero when each data point is reconstructed using only points from its own subspace, while it tends to one when each point is reconstructed using points from the other subspaces. Figure 1 displays the feature detection error averaged across 20 randomized trials.

As in (Soltanolkotabi and Candes, 2012), under the original ideal setting, we observed failure (error $\neq 0$) of ℓ_1-SSC at $t = 4$. Meanwhile DD-SSC only starts to fail at $t = 6$ and consistently maintains a lower error up to the non-identifiable limit when $t = 10$ and the two subspaces merge to one. (Note that, any possible algorithm will not have error below 0.5 on average once $t = 10$.) Moreover, the affine transformation significantly biases the estimation results of ℓ_1-SSC. ℓ_1-SSC begins to fail even with an intersection dimension of only $t = 1$, and the error continues to grow much more sharply than before (and column-normalization cannot fix the problem because of the affine component). Meanwhile DD-SSC results are essentially unchanged as predicted by our invariance theory.[7]

Outlier Detection with Synthetic Data: We now compare the performance of DD-SSC with ℓ_1-SSC in detecting outliers, noting that other algorithms producing diffuse representations such as CASS or LSR do not naturally facilitate this added flexibility, and existing theory is limited to sparsity-based approaches. We first consider the most demanding problem in (Soltanolkotabi and Candes, 2012), where $m = 20$ subspaces of dimension $d_k = 5, \forall k$ are generated in $\mathbb{R}^{50}$ uniformly at random. From each subspace, 25 points are drawn uniformly at random so that the total number of data points is 500. Data points are *not* normalized such that modest differences remain in the corresponding column norms. We then shift points away from the origin as above.

Next $n_0 = 500$ outliers, equal to the number of inlier points, are chosen uniformly at random and appended to the inliers $\boldsymbol{X}$. We then run ℓ_1-SSC and DD-SSC and compare the degree of sparsity in each recovered $\hat{z}_i$, with the hope that inlier samples with have a lower value than the outliers as described in Section 2. For DD-SSC we simply measure sparsity via $\|\hat{z}_i\|_0$, but we observed empirically that ℓ_1-SSC works poorly with this metric. So instead, consistent with (Soltanolkotabi and Candes, 2012) we report $\|\hat{z}_i\|_1$ values for ℓ_1-SSC.

Figure 2 displays the results. All plots were rescaled for visualization purposes. Clearly DD-SSC's invariance to scalings and translations is also a significant advantage when it comes to locating outliers, with a clear distinction between inliers (points on the left half of each subplot) and outliers (points on the right half), and a simple threshold around 0.3 would nearly resolve every instance. In contrast, ℓ_1-SSC almost completely fails for any threshold.

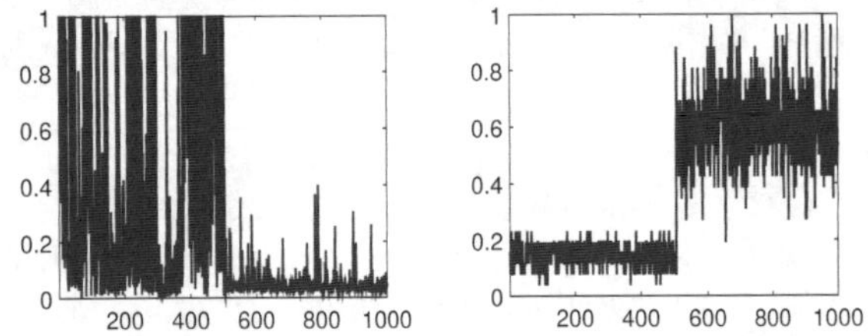

(a) ℓ_1-SSC (b) DD-SSC

Figure 2: Outlier detection in affine subspaces via sparsity measurements.

Clustering Accuracy with Real Data: Following the literature, we test DD-SSC on two challenging benchmarks, the Extended Yale B (Wright et al., 2009) and the MNIST,[8] using the same testing protocol from (Lu et al., 2013). The Yale B consists of 2,432 frontal face images of 38 subjects under various lighting, poses and illumination conditions. Here we use the first 10 subjects' face images for subspace clustering (which have been previously shown to be most difficult), after first projecting onto a 60-dimensional subspace using PCA. The MNIST benchmark includes the handwritten digits 0-9 from 10 subjects. Following (Lu et al., 2013), we select a subset consisting of the first 50 samples from each subject.

Table 1: Final clustering accuracies (%) on the Extended Yale B and the MNIST data sets.

	kNN	LRR	LSR	CASS	ℓ_1-SSC	DD-SSC
YaleB	50.94	65.00	73.59	81.88	78.44	**84.84**
MNIST	61.00	66.80	68.00	73.80	71.60	**75.40**

In Table 1, we report clustering accuracies of DD-SSC, after a final spectral clustering step for both benchmarks. Reported performances from (Lu et al., 2013) for other algorithms under equivalent conditions are included for comparison purposes. These include low rank representation (LRR) (Liu et al., 2013), least-squares representation (LSR) (Lu et al., 2012), and CASS (Lu et al., 2013), and a k-Nearest Neighbor (kNN) baseline. Because outliers are absent, non-adversarial feature representations are used, and the final clustering accuracies are largely influenced by external factors and post-processing, these data sets do not fully showcase the ability of DD-SSC. Regardless, our method displays the best performance.

[7] As a side note, IHT iterations applied to an ℓ_1-SSC initialization, such as proposed in (Yang et al., 2016), cannot appreciably improve results over ℓ_1-SSC alone in these experiments (not shown).

[8] http://yann.lecun.com/exdb/mnist/

Outlier Detection in Motion Segmentation Data: A principled mechanism for generating outlying trajectories for the Hopkins 155 data[9] has been introduced in (Rao et al., 2010). Specifically, outliers were produced by choosing a random initial point in the first frame and then selecting a random increment between successive frames. Each increment is generated by taking the difference between the coordinates of a randomly chosen point in two randomly chosen consecutive frames. In this way the outlying trajectories may qualitatively have the same statistical properties as the other trajectories, but will not be consistent with any particular motion model. Here we examine the most difficult sequence "1R2RC" for evaluation with outliers.

In Table 2, we show the performance of ℓ_1-SSC and DD-SSC using the outlier detection strategy described in Section 2. Given a varying number n_0 of outliers have been added, we sort the learned representations for all points via the sparsity measures, i.e. ℓ_1 norm for ℓ_1-SSC and ℓ_0 norm for DD-SSC; the highest n_0 are then declared outliers and compared to ground truth. To evaluate the performance, we define a detection accuracy as $\frac{\#\ correctly\ found\ inliers}{\#\ total\ inliers}$. When we increase the number of outliers (measured by its percentage with regard to the number of inliers), ℓ_1-SSC gradually failed to find all correct inliers. Meanwhile, DD-SSC can achieve almost 100% success even when there are twice as many outliers as the number of inliers. Typical ROC curves can be found in the supplementary file.

Table 2: Outlier detection on Hopkins 155 motion data.

[%]	0	15	30	50	100	150	200
ℓ_1-SSC	1.00	0.91	0.83	0.77	0.61	0.49	0.43
DD-SSC	**1.00**	**1.00**	**1.00**	**1.00**	**1.00**	**1.00**	**0.99**

Comparisons with (Yang et al., 2016) Using Real Data: As described in Section 1, the very recent approach from (Yang et al., 2016) attempts to approximately solve (2) by first computing an ℓ_1 solution and then later refining it via IHT iterations. Note that IHT is just a projected gradient method for locally minimizing the ℓ_0 norm, and the particular extrema to which it converges will be highly sensitive to the types of correlation structure we described in Section 3 (Blumensath and Davies, 2009). Moreover, in many circumstances it can be proven that the ℓ_1 norm initialization will be at or near a local minima of the IHT objective, in which case improvement is not even feasible. Still (Yang et al., 2016) nonetheless presents some nice theory for when this proposed *approximate* ℓ_0-SSC pipeline, termed Aℓ_0-SSC, is likely to produce good solutions; however, the required, idealized conditions on the data $\boldsymbol{X}$ are similar to those in the compressive sensing literature and disallow the types of correlations commonly found in clustering problems.

Table 3: Final clustering accuracies (%) compared with Aℓ_0-SSC on UCI and COIL data sets.

	SMCE	OMP-SSC	ℓ_1-SSC	Aℓ_0-SSC	DD-SSC
Ionosphere	68.09	63.53	51.28	76.92	**84.90**
Heart	59.63	55.19	63.70	64.44	**77.41**
COIL-20	75.49	33.89	78.54	84.72	**90.00**
COIL-100	56.39	16.67	52.75	76.83	**80.83**

We compare the capability of both Aℓ_0-SSC and DD-SSC to improve upon ℓ_1-SSC using representative experiments from (Yang et al., 2016) involving real-world UCI and COIL data sets. Specifically, the UCI Ionosphere data contains 351 data points from 2 classes of dimensionality 34, while UCI Heart data contains 270 points from 2 classes of dimensionality 13. The COIL-20 and COIL-100 databases have respectively 20 and 100 objects with 72 images of size 32×32 for each object, and therefore 1440 and 7200 total images overall. The images were taken 5 degrees apart as an object was rotated on a turntable.

Our comparisons with Aℓ_0-SSC are shown is Table 3, together with the results of two additional competing algorithms included in (Yang et al., 2016), namely, sparse manifold clustering and embedding (SMCE) Elhamifar and Vidal (2011), and orthogonal matching pursuit or OMP-SSC Dyer et al. (2013), which applies a greedy sparse estimation strategy. Note that, for COIL-20 and COIL-100, we provide results using all 20 and 100 clusters respectively, the hardest cases, and along with the Ionosphere and Heart data, these arguably represent the most demanding experimental conditions from (Yang et al., 2016). As shown in Table 3, our model outperforms Aℓ_0-SSC. Moreover, we observe that in the most difficult case, the Heart data, Aℓ_0-SSC is not able to significantly improve upon the ℓ_1-SSC solution, unlike DD-SSC which consistently supplies an advantage.

5 CONCLUSION

Sparsity promoting algorithms such as what we have advocated are certainly not new. However, deployment of our particular proposal in the context of subspace clustering is firmly supported by the novel theoretical arguments and strong, state-of-the-art empirical evidence presented herein. Simply put, the DD-SSC pipeline displays a remarkable degree of invariance to the very types of confounding factors, e.g., dictionary structures, distracting feature transformations, translations, and outlying data points etc., that otherwise derail existing segmentation algorithms.

[9]http://www.vision.jhu.edu/data/hopkins155/

References

S. Babacan, S. Nakajima, and M. Do. Probabilistic low-rank subspace clustering. In *Advances in Neural Information Processing Systems*, pages 2744–2752, 2012.

T. Blumensath and M.E. Davies. Iterative thresholding for sparse approximations. *J. Fourier Analysis and Applications*, 14(5), 2008.

T. Blumensath and M.E. Davies. Iterative hard thresholding for compressed sensing. *Applied and Computational Harmonic Analysis*, 27(3), 2009.

E. Candes, J. Romberg, and T. Tao. Robust uncertainty principles: Exact signal reconstruction from highly incomplete frequency information. *Information Theory, IEEE Transactions on*, 52(2):489–509, 2006.

A. Dempster, D. Rubin, and R. Tsutakawa. Estimation in covariance components models. *Journal of the American Statistical Association*, 76(374):341–353, June 1981.

Eva L Dyer, Aswin C Sankaranarayanan, and Richard G Baraniuk. Greedy feature selection for subspace clustering. *Journal of Machine Learning Research*, 14(1):2487–2517, 2013.

E. Elhamifar and R. Vidal. Sparse subspace clustering. In *Computer Vision and Pattern Recognition, CVPR 2009.*, pages 2790–2797. IEEE, 2009.

E. Elhamifar and R. Vidal. Sparse subspace clustering: Algorithm, theory, and applications. *Pattern Analysis and Machine Intelligence, IEEE Transactions on*, 35(11):2765–2781, 2013.

Ehsan Elhamifar and René Vidal. Sparse manifold clustering and embedding. In *Advances in neural information processing systems*, pages 55–63, 2011.

J. Feng, Z. Lin, H. Xu, and S. Yan. Robust subspace segmentation with block-diagonal prior. In *Computer Vision and Pattern Recognition (CVPR), 2014 IEEE Conference on*, pages 3818–3825. IEEE, 2014.

E. Grave, G. Obozinski, and F. Bach. Trace lasso: a trace norm regularization for correlated designs. In *Advances in Neural Information Processing Systems*, 2011.

D. Hunter and K. Lange. A tutorial on mm algorithms. *The American Statistician*, 58(1):30–37, 2004.

G. Liu, Z. Lin, and Y. Yu. Robust subspace segmentation by low-rank representation. In *Proceedings of the 27th International Conference on Machine Learning (ICML-10)*, pages 663–670, 2010.

G. Liu, Z. Lin, S. Yan, J. Sun, Y. Yu, and Y. Ma. Robust recovery of subspace structures by low-rank representation. *Pattern Analysis and Machine Intelligence, IEEE Transactions on*, 35(1):171–184, 2013.

C. Lu, H. Min, Z. Zhao, L. Zhu, D. Huang, and S. Yan. Robust and efficient subspace segmentation via least squares regression. In *Computer Vision–ECCV 2012*, pages 347–360. Springer, 2012.

C. Lu, J. Feng, Z. Lin, and S. Yan. Correlation adaptive subspace segmentation by trace lasso. In *Computer Vision (ICCV), 2013 IEEE International Conference on*, pages 1345–1352. IEEE, 2013.

U. Luxburg. A tutorial on spectral clustering. *Statistics and computing*, 17(4):395–416, 2007.

D. MacKay. Bayesian interpolation. *Neural computation*, 4(3): 415–447, 1992.

S. Rao, R. Tron, R. Vidal, and Y. Ma. Motion segmentation in the presence of outlying, incomplete, or corrupted trajectories. *Pattern Analysis and Machine Intelligence, IEEE Transactions on*, 32(10):1832–1845, 2010.

M. Soltanolkotabi and E. Candes. A geometric analysis of subspace clustering with outliers. *The Annals of Statistics*, 40 (4):2195–2238, 2012.

M. Soltanolkotabi, E. Elhamifar, and E. Candes. Robust subspace clustering. *The Annals of Statistics*, 42(2):669–699, 2014.

B. Sriperumbudur and G. Lanckriet. A proof of convergence of the concave-convex procedure using zangwill's theory. *Neural computation*, 24(6):1391–1407, 2012.

Michael E Tipping. Sparse bayesian learning and the relevance vector machine. *The journal of machine learning research*, 1:211–244, 2001.

C. Tomasi and T. Kanade. Shape and motion from image streams under orthography: a factorization method. *International Journal of Computer Vision*, 9(2), 1992.

Y. Wang, D. Wipf, Q. Ling, W. Chen, and I. Wassell. Multi-task learning for subspace segmentation. In *Proceedings of the 32nd International Conference on Machine Learning (ICML-15)*, pages 1209–1217, 2015.

D. Wipf and S. Nagarajan. Iterative reweighted ℓ_1 and ℓ_2 methods for finding sparse solutions. *Selected Topics in Signal Processing, IEEE Journal of*, 4(2):317–329, 2010.

D. Wipf, B. Rao, and S. Nagarajan. Latent variable bayesian models for promoting sparsity. *Information Theory, IEEE Transactions on*, 57(9):6236–6255, 2011.

D.P. Wipf. Sparse estimation with structured dictionaries. *Advances in Neural Information Processing 24*, 2011.

J. Wright, A. Yang, A. Ganesh, S. Sastry, and Y. Ma. Robust face recognition via sparse representation. *Pattern Analysis and Machine Intelligence, IEEE Transactions on*, 31(2): 210–227, 2009.

Y. Yang, J. Feng, N. Jojic, J. Yang, and T. Huang. ℓ_0-sparse subspace clustering. In *Computer Vision–ECCV 2016*. Springer, 2016.

C. You and R. Vidal. Geometric conditions for subspace-sparse recovery. In *Proceedings of the 32nd International Conference on Machine Learning (ICML-15)*, pages 1585–1593, 2015.

Supplementary File: Data-Dependent Sparsity for Subspace Clustering

Bo Xin
Microsoft Research, Beijing

Yizhou Wang
Peking University

Wen Gao
Peking University

David Wipf
Microsoft Research, Beijing

1 INTRODUCTION

This document contains companion information regarding our UAI 2017 submission, including supporting experiments and technical proofs. Note that herein all equation numbers referencing back to the main submission document will be be prefixed with an 'M' to avoid confusion, i.e, (M.#) will refer to equation (#) from the main text. Similar notation differentiates sections, tables, and figures, e.g., Section M.#.

2 COMPARISONS WITH Aℓ_0-SSC USING SYNTHETIC DATA

The Aℓ_0-SSC algorithm (Yang et al., 2016) attempts to approximately solve (M.3) by first computing an ℓ_1 norm initialization and then later refining it via iterative hard thresholding (IHT) iterations (Blumensath and Davies, 2008). However, as we have discussed in Section M.4 and elsewhere in our submission, both the ℓ_1 norm and IHT iterations are quite sensitive to data correlations, and the latter may not be able to appreciable improve upon the former in recovering maximally sparse, subspace-aligned representations. To the extent that this claim is true, we would then expect ℓ_1-SSC and Aℓ_0-SSC to display similar performance in difficult practical situations where such correlation structure is unavoidable.

Indeed an existing experimental paradigm originally from (Soltanolkotabi and Candes, 2012), and investigated in Section M.4, serves to illustrate this point. In particular, Figure 1 represents a reproduction of Figure M.1 under the ideal linear setting (meaning no affine translations), but with the inclusion of results for Aℓ_0-SSC. Note that the released code from (Yang et al., 2016) does not directly address affine subspaces, and there is no standard way of adapting IHT iterations to include the required equality constraints used with existing methods (Elhamifar and Vidal, 2013) to handle the affine model. Hence we restrict our comparisons with Aℓ_0-SSC to ideal, linear subspaces using released code.[1] Additionally, we experiment with different threshold values for the IHT step; however, if this value is set too low, there is no improvement at all as IHT becomes provably stuck at the ℓ_1-norm based initialization, and if it is set too high, the performance can actually become *worse* than just ℓ_1-SSC itself. In contrast, for DD-SSC we do not tune any parameters, and just set $\alpha = 10^{-10}$ to closely enforce the constraint (see Section M.2), a rather arbitrary default setting near zero.[2]

From Figure 1 we observe that with Aℓ_0-SSC, the results are not much improved beyond that of ℓ_1-SSC, while DD-SSC produces considerably lower errors than both methods. For example, when the subspace intersection dimension (a measure of problem difficulty as described in Section M.4) is 8, the error rate of DD-SSC is less than half that of both ℓ_1-SSC and Aℓ_0-SSC. This reinforces our original claim that Aℓ_0-SSC may provide negligible gain over ℓ_1-SSC in challenging practical conditions, unlike DD-SSC which consistently supplies an advantage. And it should be emphasized that this experiment, which originated from (Soltanolkotabi and Candes, 2012), involves a somewhat ideal, uniform distribution of data points within subspaces. If we were to introduce further correlations within or between subspaces, both the ℓ_1 solution and IHT iterations can become even less reliable.

3 ADDITIONAL MOTION DATA EXPERIMENTS

Here we provide additional experiments that reflect real-world situations involving corrupted and outlying motion data.

[1] https://github.com/yingzhenyang/L0-SSC

[2] In fact any small value for α produces the same results, but $\alpha = 0$ can lead to some numerical instability upon nearing convergence because of a potentially ill-conditioned matrix inverse. With additional effort however, even this special case can be technically handled using judicious use of pseudoinverses.

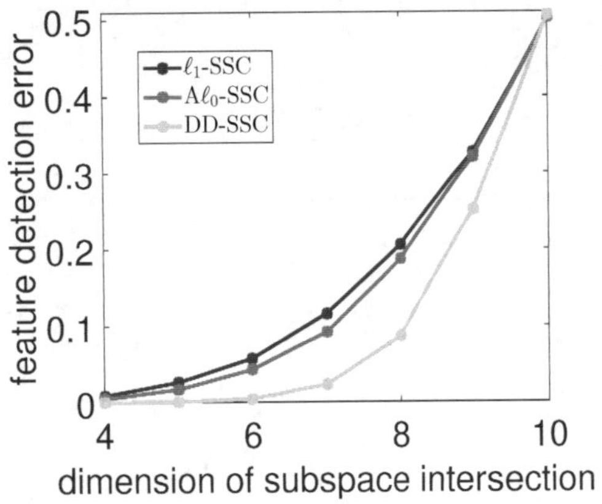

Figure 1: Feature detection error as a function of the subspace intersection dimension t. Any possible algorithm cannot have error below 0.5 on average once $t = 10$, at which point the two subspaces merge into one, the problem is no longer identifiable, and random guessing will achieve a 50% error rate. This plot corresponds to the ideal setting of Figure M.1 (the affine case is omitted here because the released code for Aℓ_0-SSC does not presently handle the additional embedded equality constraint).

3.1 Recovery of Partially Corrupted Trajectories

The Hopkins 155 motion data set contains 156 video sequences, each of which has 39-550 data points drawn from two or three motions (a motion corresponds to a subspace). Conventionally, subspace clustering works were evaluated on this data and the performance of most algorithms achieved nearly perfect segmentation accuracy (over 95%). Therefore using this dataset is difficult to differentiate the ability of different algorithms. However, as shown in (Rao et al., 2010), many additional confounding factors can be introduced to this data set to make it more challenging. These factors include missing or corrupted trajectories and outlying trajectories. We have discussed outlier detection on this dataset in the main text and will focus on dealing with corrupted trajectories here.

Following the protocol from (Rao et al., 2010), we partially corrupt 12 motion sequences from the Hopkins data with missing entries, including 9 with 2 motions, and 3 with 3 motions. The corruption rate is between 4% and 35% of the entries in the data matrix of trajectories. These entries were manually located and labeled. In the ground truth image of Figure 2, we illustrate the corrupted positions in a representative data matrix derived from this set.

For DD-SSC to incorporate such sparse element-wise corruptions, we simply need to concatenate an identity matrix of size $d+1$ to the original dictionary forming $\boldsymbol{X}^{++} \triangleq [\boldsymbol{X}^{+}, \boldsymbol{I}^{+}]$ (where $\boldsymbol{X}^{+} \triangleq [\boldsymbol{X}; \boldsymbol{1}_{(n)}^{\top}]$ and $\boldsymbol{I}^{+} \triangleq \left[[\boldsymbol{I}, \boldsymbol{0}_{(n-1)}]; \boldsymbol{0}_{n}^{\top}\right]$ were introduced in Section M.2) and update the dimensionality of the sparse prior (M.5) and hyperparameters accordingly. Nonzero entries in the expanded γ_i vector that correspond with this extra $\boldsymbol{I}^{+}$ factor will then reflect corrupted entries.

We compared this corruption estimation strategy using DD-SSC with a competing ℓ_1-SSC enhancement for dealing with missing/corrupted entries (Elhamifar and Vidal, 2013). On average, we achieve a feature detection error (defined in Section M.4) of 0.029 for DD-SSC on all these corrupted sequences. As a comparison, the average detection error of ℓ_1-SSC is 0.064. Moreover, in order to check the estimated positions of the corrupted entries with respect to the ground truth label, we define the estimation error as $\frac{\#\text{mismatch entries}}{\#\text{total entries}}$. The average error of DD-SSC is 11.4% whereas that of ℓ_1-SSC is 14.2%. In Figure 2, we illustrate one representative estimation example. We see that while DD-SSC can successfully detect most of the corruptions without many false positive, ℓ_1-SSC exhibits many false positives even after we truncate minor values (those less than 0.0001).

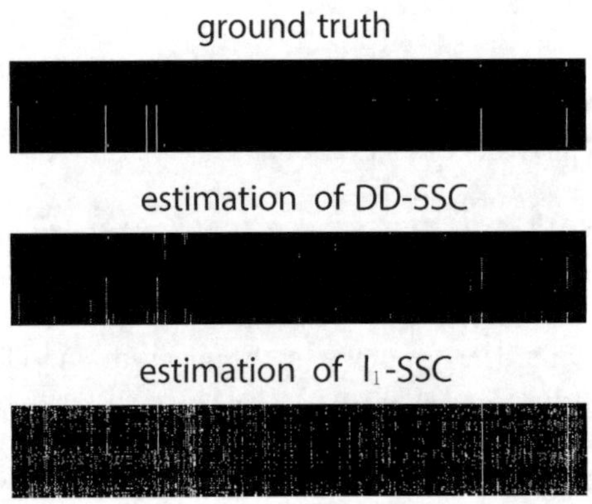

Figure 2: Estimates of the corrupted positions in a representative data matrix of Hopkins 155 data set. The data matrix $\boldsymbol{X}$ is presented as a black rectangle with white pixels indicating corrupted positions.

3.2 Outlier Detection ROC Curve

In Table M.2, we displayed the the performance of ℓ_1-SSC and DD-SSC using an outlier detection accuracy defined as $\frac{\#\text{ correctly found inliers}}{\#\text{ total inliers}}$. Following the literature, in Figure 3, we provide an additional, complementary ROC curve associated with the case where the number of inliers and outliers are equal (other ROC curves show a similar pattern).

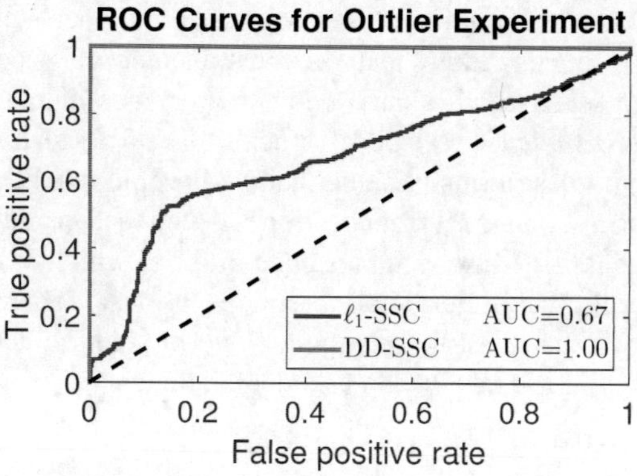

Figure 3: ROC curves for outlier detection.

4 TECHNICAL DETAILS REGARDING THEOREM 1

For the i-th data point, we begin from an initial weight vector $\boldsymbol{w}^{(0)} = \mathbf{1}$ and then proceed to the $(t+1)$-th iteration by computing

$$\begin{aligned} \boldsymbol{z}_i^{(t+1)} &\leftarrow \arg\min_{\boldsymbol{z}_i} \sum_j w_j^{(t)} |z_{ij}| \quad \text{s.t. } \boldsymbol{x}_i = \boldsymbol{X}_{\bar{i}} \boldsymbol{z}_i \\ \boldsymbol{w}^{(t+1)} &\leftarrow \eta_j(\boldsymbol{z}_i^{(t+1)}; \alpha, q), \end{aligned} \tag{1}$$

where the $|\cdot|$ operator is understood to apply element-wise and

$$\eta_j(\boldsymbol{z}_i; \alpha, q) \triangleq \left[\boldsymbol{x}_j^\top \left(\alpha I + \boldsymbol{X}_{\bar{i}} |Z_i|^2 \boldsymbol{X}_{\bar{i}}^\top \right)^{-1} \boldsymbol{x}_j \right]^q . \tag{2}$$

These updates comprise the generalized iterative reweighted ℓ_1 variant of DD-SSC.

Theorem 1 *The DD-SSC updates produced by (1) satisfy the following:*

1. *If at any iteration we compute a subspace optimal solution $\boldsymbol{z}_i^{(t)}$, then all subsequent iterations are guaranteed to be subspace optimal for any $\alpha \in (0, \alpha']$, provided α' is sufficiently small.*
2. *For any identifiable configuration of subspaces, some $q \geq 1/2$, $\alpha \in (0, \alpha']$, and α' sufficiently small, there will always exist configurations of points within each subspace such that the iterations are guaranteed to produce a subspace optimal solution for all i.*

Proof: For convenience we will adopt the notation $f(x) = \mathrm{O}(h(\epsilon))$ to indicate that $|f(x)| < C|h(\epsilon)|$ for some constant C independent of x or ϵ, and $f(x) = \Omega(h(\epsilon))$ to indicate that $|f(x)| > C|h(\epsilon)|$ for some constant C independent of x or ϵ. Likewise, we say $f(x) = \Theta(h(\epsilon))$ iff $f(x) = \mathrm{O}(h(\epsilon))$ and $f(x) = \Omega(h(\epsilon))$.

We begin with the first part of the theorem and the following qualification to ensure that $\eta_j(\boldsymbol{z}_i; \alpha, q)$ is well-defined even in the limit $\alpha \to 0$. Given that

$$\lim_{\epsilon \to 0} \boldsymbol{U}^\top \left(\epsilon \boldsymbol{I} + \boldsymbol{U}\boldsymbol{U}^\top \right)^{-1} \boldsymbol{U} = \boldsymbol{U}^\dagger \boldsymbol{U} = \boldsymbol{U}^\top \left(\boldsymbol{U}\boldsymbol{U}^\top \right)^\dagger \boldsymbol{U} \tag{3}$$

for any matrix $\boldsymbol{U}$, we have that

$$\lim_{\alpha \to 0} \eta_j(\boldsymbol{z}_i; \alpha, q) = \left[\boldsymbol{x}_j^\top \left(\boldsymbol{X}_{\bar{i}} |Z_i|^2 \boldsymbol{X}_{\bar{i}}^\top \right)^\dagger \boldsymbol{x}_j \right]^q \tag{4}$$

if $\boldsymbol{x}_j$ is in the span of the right singular vectors of $\boldsymbol{X}_{\bar{i}} |Z_i|$, and

$$\lim_{\alpha \to 0} \eta_j(\boldsymbol{z}_i; \alpha, q) \triangleq \infty \tag{5}$$

otherwise.

Now suppose that for some arbitrary point $\boldsymbol{x}_i \in \mathcal{S}_k$ we have computed a subspace optimal solution at any iteration t with $\alpha \in (0, \alpha']$. Then based on the above, the corresponding weight $w_j^{(t)} = \eta_j \left(\boldsymbol{z}_i^{(t)}; \alpha, q \right)$ will be $\Theta(1)$ if j indexes a point in the correct subspace, while $w_j^{(t)} = \Theta(\alpha^{-q})$ if j is not in the correct subspace (i.e., $j \notin \mathcal{S}_k$), where $\lim_{\alpha \to 0} w_j^{(t)} = \infty$. Therefore at the next iteration we must solve

$$\boldsymbol{z}_i^{(t+1)} \leftarrow \arg\min_{\boldsymbol{z}_i} \sum_j w_j^{(t)} |z_{ij}| \quad \text{s.t. } \boldsymbol{x}_i = \boldsymbol{X}_{\bar{i}} \boldsymbol{z}_i. \tag{6}$$

Based on (Rao and Kreutz-Delgado, 1999), any minimum of (6) can be achieved at a so-called basic feasible solution satisfying $\|\boldsymbol{z}_i\|_0 \leq d$ (Luenberger and Ye, 1984) (of which there exist a finite number with points in general position, although this is not a strict requirement). Let η^- denote the smallest value of $\sum_{j \notin C_k} |z_{ij}|$ for any non-subspace-optimal basic feasible solution, and define

$$\eta^+ = \min_{\boldsymbol{z}_i} \sum_{j \notin C_k} |z_{ij}| \quad \text{s.t. } \boldsymbol{x}_i = \boldsymbol{X}_{\bar{i}} \boldsymbol{z}_i, \; z_{ij} = 0, \forall j \notin C_k. \tag{7}$$

It then follows that any non-subspace optimal solution to (6) will have

$$\begin{aligned} \sum_j w_j^{(t)} |z_{ij}| &\geq \sum_{j \notin C_k} w_j^{(t)} |z_{ij}| \\ &\equiv \Theta(\alpha^{-q}) \sum_{j \notin C_k} |z_{ij}| > \Theta(\alpha^{-q}) \eta^- \equiv \Theta(\alpha^{-q}). \end{aligned} \tag{8}$$

Furthermore, any subspace optimal solution will satisfy

$$\sum_j w_j^{(t)} |z_{ij}| \equiv \Theta(1) \eta^+ \equiv \Theta(1) < \Theta(\alpha^{-q}) \tag{9}$$

if α' (and therefore any allowable α) are sufficiently small. This implies that a subspace optimal solution, with $z_{ij}^{(t+1)} = 0$ for all $j \notin \mathcal{S}_k$, is preserved if α' (and therefore α) are sufficiently small, otherwise the weighted ℓ_1 norm will be driven to an arbitrarily large value, possibly infinity. Hence subsequent iterations can only change the support set *within* the optimal subspace; they cannot tarnish an existing subspace optimal solution.

We now turn to the second part of the theorem. Our strategy will be to demonstrate that for certain selections of α and q, we can guarantee that reweighted ℓ_1 using $\eta_j(\boldsymbol{z}_i;\alpha,q)$ is guaranteed to produce a subspace optimal solution if the columns of $\boldsymbol{X}$ associated with each subspace $\mathcal{S}_k$ are sufficiently close together. More precisely, suppose every column of $\boldsymbol{X}$ originally drawn from $\mathcal{S}_k$ can be expressed as

$$\boldsymbol{x}_i = \boldsymbol{\mu}_k + \mathrm{O}(\delta), \qquad (10)$$

where $\boldsymbol{\mu}_i \in \mathcal{S}_k$. In other words, every column within the k-th subspace can be expressed as a small offset $\mathrm{O}(\delta)$ from some mean vector $\boldsymbol{\mu}_k$ that can be made arbitrarily small as $\delta \to 0$, which is similar in spirit to a correlated dictionary model from (Wu and Wipf, 2012). We also assume that $\|\boldsymbol{x}_i\|_2 = 1$ for all i. This decision is not limiting given that we are allowed to choose points within each subspace per the theorem statement; however, it is nonetheless not a requirement. This selection merely simplifies the exposition.

The subspace support $\Psi_{\boldsymbol{z}_i} \subset \{1,2,\ldots,m\}$ is defined as the set of subspace indices whereby some arbitrary $\boldsymbol{z}_i$ has at least one associated nonzero element. We also let $C_k \subset \{1,2,\ldots,n\}$ denote the set of dictionary column indices associated with $\mathcal{S}_k$.

Now consider the i-th data point $\boldsymbol{x}_i$ assumed to be drawn from $\mathcal{S}_k$ without loss of generality. If δ is sufficiently small, then after the first iteration (with unit weights) $k \in \Psi_{\boldsymbol{z}_i^{(1)}}$, i.e., the optimal subspace support will be a subset of the current subspace support. Moreover, it will be the case that

$$\sum_{j\in C_k} z_{ij}^{(1)} = 1 + \mathrm{O}(\delta). \qquad (11)$$

These points are a consequence of the well-known stability of the ℓ_1 norm solution to small errors (Candes et al., 2006) (we may consider the variability $\mathrm{O}(\delta)$ within subspaces as a form of error) and the fact that $\Psi_{\boldsymbol{z}_i^{(1)}} = k$ when hypothetically $d_k = 1$ (the k-th subspace has dimension one) and the subspaces are unique/identifiable. In other words, the ℓ_1 norm will always locate the maximally sparse solution if the cardinality of such a solution is one, and will accurately approximate such solutions that are sufficiently close.

However with multiple non-degenerate points per subspace, it remains likely that a few extraneous subspaces are also selected with small compensatory coefficients. These coefficients will be of order $\mathrm{O}(\delta)$. To see this in the simplest terms, assume that we have adopted the data corruption model from Section 3.1 such that an additional identity $\boldsymbol{I}$ has been appended to $\boldsymbol{X}$, in which case there will always exist such feasible solutions.[3] Therefore any other feasible minimum ℓ_1 norm solution certainly could not involve larger order coefficients.

For the second iteration we must solve

$$\boldsymbol{z}_i^{(2)} \leftarrow \arg\min_{\boldsymbol{z}_i} \sum_j w_j^{(1)}|z_{ij}| \;\text{ s.t. } \boldsymbol{x}_i = \boldsymbol{X}_{\bar{i}}\boldsymbol{z}_i \qquad (12)$$

where

$$w_j^{(1)} \triangleq \left[\boldsymbol{x}_j^\top\left(\alpha I + \boldsymbol{X}_{\bar{i}}\left|Z_i^{(1)}\right|^2\boldsymbol{X}_{\bar{i}}^\top\right)^{-1}\boldsymbol{x}_j\right]^q. \qquad (13)$$

When we choose $\alpha = \Theta(\delta)$, then for all j within C_k, it follows that

$$w_j^{(1)} = \Theta(1). \qquad (14)$$

To see this, note that under the stated conditions $\boldsymbol{X}_{\bar{i}}\left|Z_i^{(1)}\right|^2\boldsymbol{X}_{\bar{i}}^\top = \boldsymbol{\mu}_k\boldsymbol{\mu}_k^\top + \mathrm{O}(\delta)$. In contrast, for all $j \notin C_k$, we have

$$w_j^{(1)} = \Theta(\delta^{-q}). \qquad (15)$$

This occurs since $\boldsymbol{x}_j = \boldsymbol{\mu}_{\bar{k}} + \mathrm{O}(\delta)$ with $\bar{k} \neq k$ for all $j \notin C_k$ and

$$\begin{aligned}&\boldsymbol{\mu}_{\bar{k}}^\top\left(\alpha I + \boldsymbol{X}_{\bar{i}}\left|Z_i^{(1)}\right|^2\boldsymbol{X}_{\bar{i}}^\top\right)^{-1}\boldsymbol{\mu}_{\bar{k}}\\ &= \boldsymbol{\mu}_{\bar{k}}^\top\left(\alpha I + \boldsymbol{\mu}_k\boldsymbol{\mu}_k^\top + \mathrm{O}(\delta)\right)^{-1}\boldsymbol{\mu}_{\bar{k}} = \Theta(\delta^{-1}),\end{aligned} \qquad (16)$$

noting that for the subspaces to be identifiable, there will always be distinct selections such that $\boldsymbol{\mu}_k \neq \boldsymbol{\mu}_{\bar{k}}$.

We will now compute the weighted ℓ_1 norm of a subspace optimal solution and compare it to any other non-subspace-optimal feasible solution, demonstrating that it is necessarily smaller. We can always choose points within $\mathcal{S}_k$, consistent with the above stipulations and arguments, such that a representation with $|z_{ij}| = \mathrm{O}\left(\delta^{-1}\right)$ for all j exists and is computable using the appropriate pseudo-inverse. Therefore a subspace optimal solution will always exist such that

$$\sum_j w_j^{(1)}|z_{ij}| = \sum_{j\in C_k} w_j^{(1)}|z_{ij}| = \mathrm{O}\left(\delta^{-1}\right). \qquad (17)$$

[3]This assumption can be relaxed, but we avoid additional details here for the sake of simplicity.

Any other feasible solution, which again will be a basic feasible solution, must necessarily have nonzero coefficients in subspaces outside of $\mathcal{S}_k$. Let $\eta^-(\delta)$ denote the δ-dependent smallest value of $\sum_{j \notin C_k} |z_{ij}|$ for any non-subspace-optimal basic feasible solution. Similar to before, it follows that any such solution will satisfy

$$\sum_j w_j^{(1)} |z_{ij}| > \sum_{j \notin C_k} w_j^{(1)} |z_{ij}| \\ \equiv \Theta(\delta^{-q}) \sum_{j \notin C_k} |z_{ij}| > \Theta(\delta^{-q}) \eta^-(\delta). \quad (18)$$

Because we may always pick some q sufficiently large such that the lower bound from (18) is larger than the upper bound from (17), a subspace optimal solution will be produced via (12). Similar analysis applies at subsequent updates to ensure that the solution will not change, completing the proof.

To summarize, the intuition behind the proof is relatively simple at a high level. If we assume that the data points are sufficiently clustered within each subspace, then at the first iteration the regular ℓ_1 norm solution selects the correct subspace support with its largest magnitude coefficients, while the second, weighted iteration prunes away small spurious coefficients associated with other subspaces. Note that the proposed algorithm accomplishes this without any particular tuning to such a clustered data model and thus similar results likely hold in many other cases as well. ■

References

T. Blumensath and M.E. Davies. Iterative thresholding for sparse approximations. *J. Fourier Analysis and Applications*, 14(5), 2008.

Emmanuel J Candes, Justin K Romberg, and Terence Tao. Stable signal recovery from incomplete and inaccurate measurements. *Communications on pure and applied mathematics*, 59(8):1207–1223, 2006.

E. Elhamifar and R. Vidal. Sparse subspace clustering: Algorithm, theory, and applications. *Pattern Analysis and Machine Intelligence, IEEE Transactions on*, 35(11):2765–2781, 2013.

David G Luenberger and Yinyu Ye. *Linear and nonlinear programming*, volume 2. Springer, 1984.

Bhaskar D Rao and Kenneth Kreutz-Delgado. An affine scaling methodology for best basis selection. *Signal Processing, IEEE Transactions on*, 47(1):187–200, 1999.

S. Rao, R. Tron, R. Vidal, and Y. Ma. Motion segmentation in the presence of outlying, incomplete, or corrupted trajectories. *Pattern Analysis and Machine Intelligence, IEEE Transactions on*, 32(10):1832–1845, 2010.

M. Soltanolkotabi and E. Candes. A geometric analysis of subspace clustering with outliers. *The Annals of Statistics*, 40 (4):2195–2238, 2012.

Yi Wu and David P Wipf. Dual-space analysis of the sparse linear model. In *Advances in Neural Information Processing Systems*, pages 1745–1753, 2012.

Y. Yang, J. Feng, N. Jojic, J. Yang, and T. Huang. ℓ_0-sparse subspace clustering. In *Computer Vision–ECCV 2016*. Springer, 2016.

Weighted Model Counting With Function Symbols*

Vaishak Belle
University of Edinburgh
United Kingdom
vaishak@ed.ac.uk

Abstract

Probabilistic relational languages lift the syntax of relational logic for the specification of large-scale probabilistic graphical models, often admitting concise descriptions for interacting random variables over classes, hierarchies and constraints. The emergence of weighted model counting as an effective and general approach to probabilistic inference has further allowed practitioners to reason about heterogeneous representations, such as Markov logic networks and ProbLog programs, by encoding them as a logical theory. However, much of this work has been limited to an essentially propositional setting: the logical model is understood in terms of ground formulas over a fixed and finite domain; no infinite domains, and certainly no function symbols (other than constants). On the one hand, this is not surprising, because such features are very problematic from a decidability viewpoint, but on the other, they turn out to be very attractive from the point of view of machine learning applications when there is uncertainty about the existence and identity of objects. In this paper, we reconsider the problem of probabilistic reasoning in a logical language with function symbols, and establish some key results that permit effective algorithms.

1 INTRODUCTION

Unifying logic and probability is the one of the long-standing goals of AI [Russell, 2015]. Early efforts attempted the design of general-purpose representation languages [Bacchus, 1990], but were found to be too expressive as they fell off the computational cliff. As a consequence, more modest proposals, such as *probabilistic relational languages*, were developed that lift the syntax of finite-domain relational logic for the specification of large-scale probabilistic graphical models. These often admit concise descriptions for interacting random variables over classes, hierarchies and constraints [Getoor and Taskar, 2007, Wu et al., 2012]. The emergence of *weighted model counting* (WMC) as an effective and general approach to probabilistic inference has further allowed practitioners to reason about heterogeneous representations, such as Markov logic networks and ProbLog programs [Richardson and Domingos, 2006, Fierens et al., 2011], by encoding them as a logical theory. Indeed, the decision versions of both model counting and Bayesian inference are #P-complete, and there are polynomial-time reductions from each problem to the other [Bacchus et al., 2009]. The last decade has seen significant progress in exact and approximate WMC technology [Chavira and Darwiche, 2008, Gogate and Domingos, 2011, Ermon et al., 2013], which enable deterministic reasoning and exploit context-specific independencies.

In so much as the representation language determines the *expressiveness* of the probabilistic framework, however, much of this work has been limited to an essentially propositional setting. (Notable exceptions will be discussed in the final section.) That is, the logical model is understood in terms of ground formulas over a fixed and finite domain for a relational vocabulary; no infinite domains, and certainly no function symbols (other than constants). But these latter features turn out to be very attractive from the point of view of statistical experiments and machine learning pipelines, especially when there is uncertainty about the existence and identity of objects. Consider, for example, a *target tracking* application where we observe a 171 cm tall female individual believed to be James Bond's fiancee [Srivastava et al., 2014]. This can be expressed as:

$$\exists x\, (scanned(x) \land height(x) = 171 \land isFemale(x) \land fiancee(james) = x) \tag{1}$$

which uses an existential for the unknown individual, and functions and relations to express her properties. Perhaps more significantly, functions can be used to express classes and hierarchies exactly as relations would

* The author is grateful to Gerhard Lakemeyer for discussions on the compactness property.

allow, but can additionally enable equational reasoning over complex terms. For example, suppose we are interested in *knowledge base completion* over incomplete data [Nickel et al., 2016]. Consider the sentence:

$$\begin{aligned}&\mathit{advisor}(\mathit{advisor}(\mathit{mary})) \neq \mathit{john} \wedge \\ &\mathit{fiancee}(\mathit{advisor}(\mathit{mary})) = \mathit{beth} \wedge \\ &\mathit{advisor}(\mathit{mary}) = \mathit{adam} \vee \mathit{advisor}(\mathit{mary}) = \mathit{dave}\end{aligned} \qquad (2)$$

Although we do not know who *mary*'s advisor is, learning about *beth*'s betrothed, or otherwise evaluating who among $\{\mathit{adam}, \mathit{dave}\}$ are not *john*'s academic descendants may allow us to infer just that.

Unfortunately, functions are very problematic from a decidability viewpoint [Boerger et al., 1997], with many elementary cases involving function symbols leading to undecidable properties. The hope then is to identify reasonable fragments that suffice for practical purposes. Most of the well-studied fragments [Boerger et al., 1997] seem to have little relevance to the encodings considered for graphical models. To that end, there have been some attempts that allow function symbols in probabilistic programming languages. Distribution semantics [Sato, 1995] underlies languages like ProbLog [Fierens et al., 2011], which in principle support proofs (chains of inference) of infinite length. For example, the following instantiates the set of natural numbers:

$$\mathit{nat}(0) \wedge \forall x(\mathit{nat}(x) \supset \mathit{nat}(\mathit{next}(x)))$$

where $\mathit{next}(x)$ returns the successor of x understood as $x + 1$. How such programs can be well-defined in a probabilistic context has received considerable attention [Poole, 1997], leading to definitive results such as [Riguzzi, 2015]. However, the concern here is that for queries which require infinite support and which admit infinite explanations, probabilities are computed over worlds that instantiate infinitely many terms. Moreover, logic programs were never designed for equational reasoning over complex terms like in (2), where to find a model, possibly infinitely many values need to be attempted for $\mathit{advisor}(\mathit{advisor}(\mathit{mary}))$.

The language BLOG [Milch et al., 2005a] also recognizes the importance of function symbols, but avoids instantiating infinitely many terms by sampling values for function symbols. When it comes to termination, however, a number of structural conditions need to hold, including one that the quantifiers over formulas can only range over finite sets. It is also unclear how the methodology should cope in the presence of negated atoms involving functions, like in (2), where infinitely many substitutions and deterministic reasoning are needed to arrive at the right answer.

In this paper, we reconsider the problem of probabilistic reasoning in a logical language with function symbols. Akin to WMC for propositional logic, our goal is to investigate a general framework that supports an expressive fragment of a logical language, while avoiding issues like instantiations of infinitely many terms. In that regard, we obtain *very encouraging results*: we show that for first-order CNF formulas – as is standard in probabilistic relational languages [Van den Broeck et al., 2014] – mentioning functions in an *arbitrary* way, logical reasoning (validity, satisfiability) is not only computable, but obtainable by means of grounding the formulas wrt a small set of constants. The essential idea is to *exploit symmetries over unmentioned constants*. In fact, we allow *existential quantifiers*, *nested function terms*, and *quantifiers over infinite sets*. With regards to probabilistic reasoning, we show that the above construction yields a simple WMC-style definition for conditional probabilities; this definition is shown to enjoy a number of attractive properties tied to logical equivalence and additivity. Throughout the paper, we demonstrate how the methodology can be *encoded* as a propositional theory, making it straightforward to use existing exact or approximate WMC technology.

2 LANGUAGE WITH RELATIONS

To prepare for the logical language with function symbols, we begin with the well-understood relational counterpart, and discuss the definition of weighted model counting.

2.1 Syntax and Semantics

We let $\mathcal{L}_D^{\text{Rel}}$ be a be a first-order language with equality, relational symbols $\{P(x), \ldots, Q(x, y), \ldots, R(x, y, z), \ldots\}$, variables $\{x, y, z, \ldots\}$, connectives $\vee, \wedge, \neg, \forall$ and a finite set of constants D, serving as the domain of discourse for quantification. Usual abbreviations hold for connectives: we write $\alpha \supset \beta$ (material implication) to mean $\neg\alpha \vee \beta$, $\alpha \equiv \beta$ (equivalence) to mean $(\alpha \supset \beta) \wedge (\beta \supset \alpha)$ and $\exists x\alpha$ (existential quantification) to mean $\neg\forall x\neg\alpha$.

The set of (ground) atoms is obtained as:[1]

$$\text{ATOMS} = \{P(a_1, \ldots, a_k) \mid P \text{ is a predicate, } a_i \in D\}.$$

A $\mathcal{L}_D^{\text{Rel}}$-model M is a $\{0, 1\}$ assignment to the elements of ATOMS. Using $\models$ to denote satisfaction, the semantics for $\phi \in \mathcal{L}_D^{\text{Rel}}$ is defined as usual inductively, but with equality as identity: $M \models (a = b)$ iff a and b are the same constants, and quantification is understood substitutionally over all elements of D: $M \models \forall x\phi(x)$ iff $M \models \phi(a)$ for

[1] Because equality is treated separately, atoms do not include equalities.

all $a \in D$. We say ϕ is *satisfiable* iff there is a $\mathcal{L}_D^{\text{Rel}}$-model M such that $M \models \phi$. We say that ϕ is *valid*, written $\models \phi$, iff for every $\mathcal{L}_D^{\text{Rel}}$-model M, $M \models \phi$.

It is not hard to see that $\mathcal{L}_D^{\text{Rel}}$ is essentially propositional. That is, let $\mathcal{L}^{\text{Prop}}$ be a propositional language over propositions $\{p, q, \ldots\}$ and connectives $\{\neg, \vee, \wedge\}$. Understanding a $\mathcal{L}^{\text{Prop}}$-model to mean $\{0, 1\}$ assignments to $\mathcal{L}^{\text{Prop}}$-formulas, we have:

Proposition 1 *Suppose $*$ is a bijection from* ATOMS *to the propositions in $\mathcal{L}^{Prop}$. For any $\alpha \in \mathcal{L}_D^{Rel}$, let α^* be α with every atom p replaced by the proposition p^*. A quantifier and equality-free formula $\phi \in \mathcal{L}_D^{Rel}$ is satisfiable iff $\phi^* \in \mathcal{L}^{Prop}$ is satisfiable.*

2.2 Weighted Model Counting

In a nutshell, WMC extends #SAT in summing the weights of the models of a propositional formula ϕ:

$$\text{WMC}(\phi, w) = \sum_{M \models \phi} w(M)$$

where M is an $\mathcal{L}_D^{\text{Rel}}$-model, and w is a *weight function.* The weight function is usually *factorized*. For example [Van den Broeck et al., 2014], suppose $v, \overline{v}$ map predicate symbols from ϕ to $\mathbb{R}^+$, $p \in M$ are those atoms that are true at M, and $p \notin M$ are those that are false. Then:[2]

$$w(M) \doteq \prod_{p \in M} v(\text{PRED}(p)) \times \prod_{p \notin M} \overline{v}(\text{PRED}(p))$$

where PRED maps an atom to its predicate.

WMC has emerged as a basic computational framework for encoding many formalisms, such as Markov logic networks [Van den Broeck et al., 2014] and ProbLog programs [Fierens et al., 2011].

Finally, given a query Q and evidence E, both of which are propositional formulas, we define the probability of Q given E wrt (ϕ, w) as:

$$\Pr_{(\phi,w)} (Q \mid E) = \text{WMC}(\phi \wedge Q \wedge E, w)/\text{WMC}(\phi \wedge E, w).$$

3 LANGUAGE WITH FUNCTIONS

We now define the logical language in a general way.

3.1 Syntax and Semantics

Let $\mathcal{L}_{\mathbb{N}}^{\text{FUN}}$ be a first-order language with function symbols $\{f(x), \ldots, g(x, y), \ldots, h(x, y, z), \ldots\}$, variables, equality, logical connectives $\{\vee, \neg, \wedge, \forall\}$ and a countably infinite set of constants (say) $\mathbb{N}$. For presentation purposes, we often use identifiers such as Latin alphabets $(a, b, \ldots)$ and proper names (*john*, *jane*, ...) to implicitly mean elements of $\mathbb{N}$. We understand $\{\supset, \equiv, \exists\}$ as usual.

The *terms* of the language form the least set containing the variables, constants, and function symbols applied to terms (e.g., $f(g(x), x, a, b)$.) A *primitive term* is a function symbol applied to constants only. A *primitive atom* is of the form $t = a$, where t is a primitive term and $a \in \mathbb{N}$. In other words, the set of primitive atoms is obtained as:

$$\text{ATOMS} = \{f(a_1, \ldots, a_k) = a_0 \mid f \text{ is a function}, a_i \in \mathbb{N}\}.$$

In general, atoms may be positive or negative, that is, they are of the form $t = t'$ or $\neg(t = t')$, and *formulas* are built from atoms and connectives as usual. We write $t \neq t'$ to mean $\neg(t = t')$. A *clause* is a disjunction of atoms. Ground formulas and terms are those not mentioning any variables.

A $\mathcal{L}_{\mathbb{N}}^{\text{FUN}}$-model M maps primitive terms to $\mathbb{N}$. We extend the notion of *co-referring* constants to arbitrary ground terms as follows. For any ground term t and M, we define $|t|_M$ as:

- if $t \in \mathbb{N}$, $|t|_M = t$;
- $|f(t_1, \ldots, t_k)|_M = M[f(a_1, \ldots, a_k)]$ where $a_i = |t_i|_M$.

The semantics for $\phi \in \mathcal{L}_{\mathbb{N}}^{\text{FUN}}$ is defined as usual inductively, but with equality as identity over co-reference: $M \models (t = t')$ iff $|t|_M$ and $|t'|_M$ are the same constants, and quantification is understood substitutionally over all constants: $M \models \forall x \phi(x)$ iff $M \models \phi(a)$ for all $a \in \mathbb{N}$. Satisfaction and validity is defined as usual.

3.2 A Propositional Fragment

Our intuitions from $\mathcal{L}_D^{\text{Rel}}$ and $\mathcal{L}^{\text{Prop}}$ do not carry over to $\mathcal{L}_{\mathbb{N}}^{\text{FUN}}$ in an obvious way as it is defined over infinitely many terms and an infinite domain. In fact, even disallowing nesting of function symbols does not make it any easier. To see this, call a formula *flat* iff the argument to a function is either a constant or a variable. A ground flat clause is then of the form $f(a_1, \ldots, a_k) = a_0 \vee \ldots \vee g(b_1, \ldots, b_k) \neq b_0$. So, consider the formula $f(1) \neq 1$. Clearly, this has infinitely many models: $\{f(1) = c \mid c \in \mathbb{N} - \{1\}\}$, and moreover, WMC would also be ill-defined in general.

However, if we define the fragment $\mathcal{L}_D^{\text{FUN}} \subset \mathcal{L}_{\mathbb{N}}^{\text{FUN}}$ as the set of ground flat formulas over a finite set of constants $D \subsetneq \mathbb{N}$, then we note that ATOMS is finite, and every formula of $\mathcal{L}_D^{\text{FUN}}$ has finitely many models.

[2] Alternatively, a weight function could map atoms themselves to positive reals [Chavira and Darwiche, 2008]. The nature of the weight function is irrelevant for most of the technical development in this paper.

We can also intuit a definition for WMC. Given a ground flat formula ϕ, a domain D, and a weight functions $v, \overline{v}$ that map function symbols to positive reals, we have:

$$\text{WMC}(\phi, D, w) = \sum_{M \models \phi} \prod_{p \in M} v(\text{FUN}(p)) \times \prod_{p \notin M} \overline{v}(\text{FUN}(p))$$

where FUN maps a primitive atom to its function symbol, and as usual $p \in M$ are those primitive atoms that are true at M, and $p \notin M$ are those that are false.[3]

Example 2 Consider $f(a) \neq a$ over domain $\{a, b\}$. We have primitive atoms $\{f(a) = b, f(b) = b, f(a) = a, f(b) = a\}$, and models $M_1 = \{f(a) = b, f(b) = a\}$ and $M_2 = \{f(a) = b, f(b) = b\}$. Then the atoms in $\{f(a) = b, f(b) = a, f(a) \neq a, f(b) \neq b\}$ are satisfied at M_1 and those in $\{f(a) = b, f(b) = b, f(a) \neq a, f(b) \neq a\}$ at M_2. Suppose v maps f to 2 and $\overline{v}$ maps it to 1. Then, $w(M_1) = w(M_2) = 2 \times 2 \times 1 \times 1 = 4$. So WMC is 8.

3.3 More Expressiveness

We are caught between two extremes. The language $\mathcal{L}_{\mathbb{N}}^{\text{FUN}}$ is undecidable, but on the other hand, $\mathcal{L}_{D}^{\text{FUN}}$ is clearly too limited as we have gained nothing over $\mathcal{L}^{\text{Prop}}$. We will now attempt to motivate a fragment with first-order features in between these extremes. Consider that the fragment will determine the expressiveness of our knowledge bases.

Perhaps the simplest way to go beyond $\mathcal{L}_{D}^{\text{FUN}}$ is to limit our attention to ground flat formulas from $\mathcal{L}_{\mathbb{N}}^{\text{FUN}}$. As mentioned earlier, this fragment has infinitely many atoms, and formulas such as $f(1) \neq 1$ has infinitely many models. Thus, it already represents a non-trivial and challenging extension to $\mathcal{L}^{\text{Prop}}$.

What the fragment does not yet allow is existential quantifiers. One of our primary motivations was to allow for identity uncertainty in an unrestricted manner: that is, admitting sentences such as $\exists x f(x) \neq 1$ in our KBs. Of course, we can use Skolemization: introduce a new nullary function g and concern ourselves instead with the sentence $f(g) \neq 1$. Moreover, this formula can be brought to a flat form: $\forall z (g = z \supset f(z) \neq 1)$. The very same recipe can also be applied to nesting of function symbols: consider $\forall x(next(x) \neq x \supset next(next(x)) \neq x)$, which says that if the successor of x is not x, then neither is the successor of the successor of x. This is equivalent to $\forall x, z(next(x) \neq x \supset (next(x) = z \supset next(z) \neq x))$.

These reformulations notwithstanding, it should be clear that since quantifiers range over $\mathbb{N}$, a formula such as $\forall z(g = z \supset f(z) \neq 1)$ is logically equivalent to infinitely many clauses: $(g = 1 \supset f(1) \neq 1), (g = 2 \supset f(2) \neq 1)$, and so on. We will identify a way to effectively reason over such knowledge bases. Concretely, let a *basic* clause be a disjunction of atoms of the form $f(x_1, \ldots, x_k) \circ x_0$, where $\circ \in \{=, \neq\}$ and x_i are either constants or variables. (So, a ground basic clause is a disjunction of positive or negative primitive atoms.) Then:

An *acceptable knowledge base* is a satisfiable, *compact* and finite set of *universally quantified basic clauses.*

This is a very expressive fragment that handles existential quantifiers, nested functions, and infinite domains. (We need to assume that knowledge bases are *compact,* a property we formally define in a short while.) To handle acceptable KBs, however, we will first need to solve the problem of reasoning about ground flat formulas from $\mathcal{L}_{\mathbb{N}}^{\text{FUN}}$.

4 SATISFIABILITY AND VALIDITY

Before we discuss model counting, we will need to consider the problem of logical reasoning for which we first turn to ground flat formulas from $\mathcal{L}_{\mathbb{N}}^{\text{FUN}}$ before considering quantified formulas.

4.1 Ground Flat Formulas

Since formulas such as $f(1) \neq 1$ has infinitely many models over infinitely many literals, we cannot readily apply existing propositional techniques. Our key result here is to show that logical reasoning is possible by considering finitely many values for terms.

To achieve the result, a crucial observation is this: when considering assignments to primitive terms in a ground flat clause, constants that are outside the KB behave identically, at least as far as satisfiability is concerned. For example, consider $f \neq 1$. Then, $(f = 2) \wedge (f \neq 1)$ is satisfiable, but so is $(f = 3) \wedge (f \neq 1)$.

More precisely, given a ground flat formula ϕ in CNF (that is, conjunctions of clauses), define:

- TERMS(ϕ) as the set of primitive terms in ϕ;
- CONS(ϕ) is the set of constants in ϕ;
- $\text{XOR}(t, C) = \bigvee_{a \in C}(t = a)$, for any $C \subset \mathbb{N}$;
- $\text{XOR}(\phi) = \phi \wedge \bigwedge_{t \in \text{TERMS}(\phi)} \text{XOR}(t, D)$, where $D =$

[3]Our definition of WMC is reasonable when considering the simulation of a predicate $P(x_1, \ldots, x_k)$ by a function $f(x_1, \ldots, x_k)$ as follows: $P(x_1, \ldots, x_k) \doteq f(x_1, \ldots, x_k) = 1$ with the additional constraint: $f(x_1, \ldots, x_k) = 1 \vee f(x_1, \ldots, x_k) = 0$. It is then not hard to see that our definition of WMC for functions coincides with the relational version. While variant formulations are conceivable, much of the technical contributions in this paper do not hinge on the definition.

$\text{CONS}(\phi) \cup \{b\}$ and b is any constant not mentioned in $\text{CONS}(\phi)$.

So, $\text{XOR}(t, D)$ is a disjunction over possible assignments to t, which includes every constant in ϕ plus an arbitrary new one, and $\text{XOR}(\phi)$ conjoins this constraint for all terms to ϕ.

Example 3 Let $\phi = (f \neq 1 \vee g(1) = 2) \wedge g(1) \neq 1$. Then for $t \in \{f, g(1)\}$, $\text{XOR}(t, D) = (t = 1 \vee t = 2 \vee t = 3)$, where $D = \{1, 2, 3\}$ and 3 is some arbitrary new constant. So $\text{XOR}(\phi) = \phi \wedge \text{XOR}(f, D) \wedge \text{XOR}(g(1), D)$.

It is worth remarking that repeated applications of XOR do not change the meaning of the formula:

Proposition 4 $\text{XOR}(\phi) \equiv \text{XOR}(\text{XOR}(\phi))$.

Proof: Suppose $\text{CONS}(\phi) = \{a_1, \ldots, a_k\}$, and let $D = \text{CONS}(\phi) \cup \{b\}$. Then, for every $t \in \text{TERMS}(\phi)$, $\text{XOR}(\phi)$ includes $\text{XOR}(t, D)$. Observe that $\text{TERMS}(\text{XOR}(\phi)) = \text{TERMS}(\phi)$. So, for for every $t \in \text{TERMS}(\phi)$, $\text{XOR}(\text{XOR}(\phi))$ includes $\text{XOR}(t, D)$ (from $\text{XOR}(\phi)$) and $\text{XOR}(t, D')$, where $D' = D \cup \{c\}$ and c is some new constant. But then $\text{XOR}(t, D) \equiv \text{XOR}(t, D) \wedge \text{XOR}(t, D')$, since $\text{XOR}(t, D')$ is a weaker constraint. ∎

Putting it together, here is the main theorem:

Theorem 5 *Suppose ϕ, α are ground flat formulas. Then $\phi \models \alpha$ iff $\text{XOR}(\phi \wedge \neg\alpha)$ is unsatisfiable.*

Essentially, the forcing constraints for primitive terms added to a formula limit the number of possible assignments, making it essentially equivalent to a propositional theory, a point we return to later. But first, to establish the theorem, we proceed as follows:

Lemma 6 *Suppose ϕ is a ground flat formula, and $t \in \text{TERMS}(\phi)$. For any $a, b \notin \text{CONS}(\phi)$, $\phi \wedge (t = a)$ is satisfiable iff $\phi \wedge (t = b)$ is satisfiable.*

Proof: Suppose $M \models \phi \wedge (t = a)$ iff by definition, $M \models \phi$ and $M[t] = a$ iff $M \models \phi^t_a$, where ϕ^t_a is ϕ with every occurrence of t replaced by a. Now, ϕ^t_a does not mention t, and moreover, every occurrence of $t = c$ for some $c \in \text{CONS}(\phi)$ is replaced by $a = c$, and every occurrence of $t \neq c$ is replaced by $a \neq c$. But because $a \notin \text{CONS}(\phi)$ and equality is understood as identity, $a = c$ is false everywhere, and $a \neq c$ is true everywhere. By extension, because $b \notin \text{CONS}(\phi)$, ϕ^t_a is logically equivalent to ϕ^t_b. Since ϕ^t_b does not actually mention t, construct a M' such that $M'[t] = b$ and for all terms $t' \neq t$, $M'[t'] = M[t']$. Clearly, $M' \models \phi \wedge (t = b)$. ∎

Lemma 7 *Suppose ϕ, D and t are as above. Then ϕ is satisfiable iff $\phi \wedge \text{XOR}(t, D)$ is satisfiable.*

Proof: The if direction is obvious, since the satisfiability of $\phi \wedge \text{XOR}(t, D)$ immediately implies that of ϕ.

So suppose $M \models \phi$. By construction, there is some $a \in \mathbb{N}$ such that $M[t] = a$. So $\phi \wedge (t = a)$ is satisfiable.

Suppose $(t = a)$ is mentioned in $\text{XOR}(t, D)$, then $M \models \text{XOR}(t, D)$ and so we are done. Suppose not, that is, $a \notin D$. Then, $a \notin \text{CONS}(\phi)$ as well. Suppose $b \in (D - \text{CONS}(\phi))$. So we have that $\phi \wedge (t = a)$ is satisfiable iff by Lemma 6, $\phi \wedge (t = b)$ is satisfiable, which means that $\phi \wedge (t = a_1 \vee \ldots \vee t = a_k \vee t = b)$ must be as well. ∎

Corollary 8 *Suppose ϕ is above. Then ϕ is satisfiable iff $\text{XOR}(\phi)$ is satisfiable.*

We are now prepared for the proof of Theorem 5.

Proof: Here, $\phi \models \alpha$ iff $\phi \wedge \neg\alpha$ is unsatisfiable iff by Corollary 8, $\text{XOR}(\phi \wedge \neg\alpha)$ is unsatisfiable. ∎

The added constraints essentially limit the number of assignments to primitive terms, and in fact, we can think of each atom in $\text{XOR}(t, D)$ as a proposition, and thereby return to the familiar setting of $\mathcal{L}^{\text{Prop}}$. First, let us introduce the *logical exclusive-or* symbol $\oplus$ with the understanding that for any model M, $M \models p_1 \oplus \ldots \oplus p_k$ iff $M \models p_i$ for some i and $M \not\models p_j$ for all $j \neq i$. Observe that, in $\mathcal{L}^{\text{FUN}}_{\mathbb{N}}$, replacing the disjunctions in $\text{XOR}(t, D)$ with $\oplus$ does not affect logical equivalence, since the semantics enforces it anyway.

Proposition 9 *Suppose $\text{XOR}(\phi)$ is as above, and $\text{XOR}'(\phi)$ denote the same formula but with every $\text{XOR}(t, D) = (t = a_1 \vee \ldots \vee t = a_k)$ replaced by $(t = a_1 \oplus \ldots \oplus t = a_k)$. Then $\text{XOR}(\phi) \equiv \text{XOR}'(\phi)$.*

However, the point is that by making the exclusive-or explicit preserves satisfaction in the simpler $\mathcal{L}^{\text{Prop}}$.

Proposition 10 *Suppose $*$ is a bijection from the atoms in $\text{XOR}(\phi)$ to the propositions in $\mathcal{L}^{Prop}$. Then ϕ is satisfiable iff $(\text{XOR}'(\phi))^* \in \mathcal{L}^{Prop}$ is satisfiable.*

Example 11 Suppose $\phi = (f \neq 1)$, then $\text{XOR}(\phi) = \phi \wedge (f = 1 \vee f = 2)$. Then the $\mathcal{L}^{\text{FUN}}_{\mathbb{N}}$-model $M \models (f = 2) \wedge (f \neq 1)$ is the only one satisfying $\text{XOR}(\phi)$. Alternatively, suppose p and q are propositions from $\mathcal{L}^{\text{Prop}}$, and suppose $*$: $[f = 1, f = 2] \rightarrow [p, q]$ is a bijection, then $(\text{XOR}'(\phi))^* = \neg p \wedge (p \oplus q)$, and the $\mathcal{L}^{\text{Prop}}$-model $M = \{q, \neg p\}$ is the only one satisfying $(\text{XOR}'(\phi))^*$.

Corollary 12 *Suppose ϕ, α are ground flat formulas.*

Then there is a formula $\beta = (\mathrm{XOR}'(\phi \wedge \neg\alpha))^* \in \mathcal{L}^{Prop}$ *such that* $\phi \models \alpha$ *iff* β *is unsatisfiable.*

4.2 Acceptable Knowledge Bases

Here, we will be interested in a version of Corollary 12 but under the generalization that ϕ is an acceptable KB. Unfortunately, in general, acceptable KBs are logically equivalent to a possibly infinite set of ground clauses, so we cannot simply apply Corollary 12. Our key result will be to show that grounding the KB wrt a finite set of constants is sufficient for checking satisfiability.

First, some notation. Given a universally quantified basic clause such as $\forall x, y(f(x) = y \vee g(y) = x)$, let its *rank* be the maximum number of variables mentioned (here 2). A ground clause, then, has 0 rank. The *rank* of an acceptable KB is the maximum of the ranks of its clauses.

Given an acceptable KB ϕ, a ground theory is obtained by substituting variables with constants. Suppose θ denotes a substitution. For any set of names $D \subseteq \mathbb{N}$, we write $\theta \in D$ to mean substitutions are only allowed wrt the constants in D. Then, define:

- $\mathrm{GND}(\phi) = \{c\theta \mid (\forall x, \ldots, y\ c) \in \phi, \theta \in \mathbb{N}\}$;
- $\mathrm{GND}(\phi, k) = \{c\theta \mid (\forall x, \ldots, y\ c) \in \phi, \theta \in D\}$, where $k \geq 0$ and D is the set of constants mentioned in ϕ plus k (arbitrary) new ones;
- $\mathrm{RGND}(\phi) = \mathrm{GND}(\phi, k)$ where k is the rank of ϕ;
- $\mathrm{XOR}(\phi) = \psi \wedge \bigwedge_{t \in \mathrm{TERMS}(\psi)} \mathrm{XOR}(t, D)$ where $\psi = \mathrm{RGND}(\phi)$, and $D = \mathrm{CONS}(\psi) \cup \{b\}$ and b is any constant not mentioned in $\mathrm{CONS}(\psi)$.

Note that $\mathrm{XOR}(\phi)$ for acceptable KBs and ground flat formulas is compatible: if ϕ is a ground flat formula, then its rank is 0, and so, in fact, $\mathrm{RGND}(\phi) = \phi$.

Example 13 Let ϕ denote $\{\forall x(\mathit{father}(x) \neq \mathit{adam} \supset \mathit{mother}(x) \neq \mathit{beth})\}$. Abbreviating symbols to their first letters, we have:

- $\mathrm{GND}(\phi, 0) = \{f(a) \neq a \supset m(a) \neq b, f(b) \neq a \supset m(b) \neq b\}$;
- $\mathrm{RGND}(\phi) = \mathrm{GND}(\phi, 0) \cup \{f(c) \neq a \supset m(c) \neq b\}$, because ϕ's rank is 1 and where c is arbitrarily chosen from $\mathbb{N} - \{a, b\}$;
- $\mathrm{XOR}(\phi) = \mathrm{RGND}(\phi) \cup \{\mathrm{XOR}(t, D) : t \in T\}$, where $T = \{f(a), m(a), f(b), m(b), f(c), m(c)\}$ and $D = \{a, b, c, d\}$.
- $\mathrm{GND}(\phi) = \mathrm{RGND}(\phi) \cup \{f(d) \neq a \supset m(d) \neq b, f(e) \neq a \supset m(e) \neq b, \ldots\}$.

We are now in a position to formally discuss the *compact* property we expect of our knowledge bases.

Definition 14 Suppose ϕ is a conjunction of universally quantified clauses, of rank k. Suppose $\mathrm{GND}(\phi)$ is satisfiable iff $\mathrm{GND}(\phi, j)$ is satisfiable for all $j \geq k$. Then we say ϕ is *compact.*

Recall that the compactness theorem [Enderton, 1972] says that a possibly infinite set of sentences S is satisfiable iff every finite subset of S is satisfiable. This property does not hold $\mathcal{L}_{\mathbb{N}}^{\mathrm{FUN}}$, not even when restricted to universally quantified basic clauses. Therefore, we explicitly require that our knowledge bases are compact.[4]

The main theorem for the section is:

Theorem 15 *Suppose* ϕ *is an acceptable KB, and* α *is any ground flat formula. Then* $\phi \models \alpha$ *iff* $\mathrm{XOR}(\phi \wedge \neg\alpha)$ *is unsatisfiable.*

Proof: Let us suppose ϕ's rank is k. We first begin with some observations. Note that $\phi \models \alpha$ iff $\phi \wedge \neg\alpha$ is unsatisfiable iff $\mathrm{GND}(\phi) \wedge \neg\alpha$ is unsatisfiable. Also note that $\psi = \phi \wedge \neg\alpha$ is also an acceptable KB, since $\neg\alpha$ can be converted to a ground flat clause. Finally, by Corollary 8, $\mathrm{RGND}(\psi)$ is satisfiable iff $\mathrm{XOR}(\psi)$ is, and so in the arguments below, we only make use of $\mathrm{RGND}(\psi)$.

The if direction is immediate, because if $\mathrm{RGND}(\phi \wedge \neg\alpha)$ is unsatisfiable, then so is $\mathrm{GND}(\phi \wedge \neg\alpha) = \mathrm{GND}(\phi) \wedge \neg\alpha$ since $\mathrm{RGND}(\phi \wedge \neg\alpha) \subseteq \mathrm{GND}(\phi \wedge \neg\alpha)$.

For the only-if direction, suppose $\phi \models \alpha$ but $\mathrm{RGND}(\phi \wedge \neg\alpha)$ is satisfiable. It suffices to show that for the acceptable KB $\psi = \phi \wedge \neg\alpha$ of rank k if $\Delta = \mathrm{RGND}(\psi) = \mathrm{GND}(\psi, k)$, is satisfiable then so is $\Delta' = \mathrm{GND}(\psi, j)$ for any $j \geq k$. Then, by the compact property assumption, this means $\mathrm{GND}(\psi) = \mathrm{GND}(\phi) \wedge \neg\alpha$ is also satisfiable, which contradicts $\phi \models \alpha$.

Without loss of generality, assume $\mathrm{CONS}(\Delta') = \mathrm{CONS}(\Delta)$ plus n new ones, where $n = j - k$. By assumption, there is a M such that $M \models \Delta$. Construct a M':

1. for all $t \in \mathrm{TERMS}(\Delta)$, $M'[t] = M[t]$;

[4] Our view is that KBs not enjoying the compact property do not come up often in practice. To see an example of such a KB, imagine a language with 2 function symbols that simulate relations $R(x, y)$ and $P(x)$ respectively. Then, let ϕ be $\{\forall x, y, z\ (R(x, y) \wedge R(y, z) \supset R(x, z)), \forall x\ (\neg R(x, x)), \forall x\ (P(x) \supset \exists y\ (R(x, y) \wedge P(y))), \forall x\ (\neg P(x) \supset \exists y\ (R(x, y) \wedge \neg P(y))), P(1), \neg P(2)\}$. That is, R is irreflexive but transitive. After Skolemization and flattening, it can be seen that $\mathrm{XOR}(\phi)$ (and hence, $\mathrm{RGND}(\phi)$) is unsatisfiable, but strangely, $\mathrm{GND}(\phi)$ is indeed satisfiable in a $\mathcal{L}_{\mathbb{N}}^{\mathrm{FUN}}$-model where infinitely many instances of P are true and infinitely many instances of P are false.

2. for all $t \notin$ TERMS(Δ'), $M'[t] = M[t]$;

3. for all $t \in$ TERMS($\Delta' - \Delta$), do as follows. Consider that t is mentioned in some $c\theta \in (\Delta' - \Delta)$ such that $\forall x, \ldots, y\ c \in \psi$, and θ is a substitution possibly using constants from ψ and Δ, but at least some, say $a_1, \ldots, a_l$, $l \leq k$, from $(\Delta' - \Delta)$. (Otherwise, $c\theta \notin (\Delta' - \Delta)$.) But by that account, θ does not mention l constants from CONS(Δ) − CONS(ψ), say $b_1, \ldots, b_l$. Let $*$ be a bijection from $\mathbb{N}$ to $\mathbb{N}$ such that maps a_i with b_i but otherwise maps constants to themselves.

   By construction, $(c\theta)^*$, that is, $c\theta^* \in \Delta$. In other words, for every $f(e_1, \ldots, e_z) = e_0$ appearing in $c\theta$, $(f(e_1, \ldots, e_z) = e_0)^*$, that is, $(f(e_1^*, \ldots, e_z^*) = e_0^*) \in c\theta^*$. Let $M'[f(e_1, \ldots, e_z)] = M[f(e_1^*, \ldots, e_z^*)]$.

We have completed the construction of M'. It is easy to show (by induction) that M' satisfies Δ because of construction step (1). Similarly, it is easy to show that M' satisfies $\Delta' - \Delta$ because of construction step (3). Thus, M' satisfies Δ' and we are done. ∎

Example 16 Suppose ϕ is the conjunction of *female(beth)* $= 1$, $\forall x$(*female*(x) $= 1 \lor$ *female*(x) $= 0$), and $\forall x$(*female*(x) $= 1 \supset \forall y$(*father*(y) $\neq x$)), that is, if x is a female than she is not a father to any y.

Suppose α is *father(beth)* $\neq$ *beth*. Suppose RGND($\phi \land \neg\alpha$) is wrt constants {*beth*, *adam*, *dave*}, since ($\phi \land \neg\alpha$)'s rank is 2. Observe that XOR($\phi \land \neg\alpha$) includes *father(beth)* $\neq$ *beth* from ϕ and *father(beth)* $=$ *beth* from $\neg\alpha$, which is inconsistent. So $\phi \models \alpha$.

Suppose $\beta =$ (*father(adam)* $=$ *beth*). It is not hard to see that XOR($\phi \land \neg\beta$) is satisfiable, and so $\phi \not\models \beta$.

At this point, it should be clear that the familiar setting of $\mathcal{L}^{\text{Prop}}$ is sufficient here as well:

Proposition 17 *Suppose $*$ is a bijection from the atoms in* XOR($\phi \land \neg\alpha$) *to the propositions in $\mathcal{L}^{Prop}$, and* XOR$'(\phi)$ *is as before. Then $\phi \models \alpha$ iff* (XOR$'(\phi \land \neg\alpha))^* \in$ *$\mathcal{L}^{Prop}$ is unsatisfiable.*

5 WEIGHTED MODEL COUNTING

We now propose an account of WMC for acceptable KBs, which will then lead to a notion of conditional probabilities. The proposal is motivated from a logical point of view, that is, the definition of probabilities obeys a number of non-trivial properties that respect logical entailment over possibly infinitely many atoms.[5] In essence, the definition satisfies the following properties in a *first-order setting*:

1. *If the query is believed*, it has probability 1.
2. *If the query contradicts what is believed*, it has probability 0.
3. *If the query mentions unknown individuals*, these individuals are interchangeable with other unknowns.
4. *If two queries are logically equivalent*, then they have the same probability.
5. Probabilities satisfy the *addition laws* over Boolean connectives [Fagin and Halpern, 1994].

The proposal, as one would surmise, leverages Theorem 15 as this has the advantage of grounding the KB wrt finitely many constants. Moreover, from a representational viewpoint, no structural assumptions are needed about the encoding. Recall that we provided a definition for WMC(ϕ, D, w) earlier, that is, where the domain was fixed to a finite set of constants D. If the D is implicit, as enabled by a set of possible assignments like XOR(t, D), we simply write WMC(ϕ, w). Turning now to a countably infinite domain, such as $\mathbb{N}$, we define:

$$\text{WMC}(\phi, \mathbb{N}, w) = \text{WMC}(\text{XOR}(\phi), w)$$

That is, we compute the WMC of XOR(ϕ) (where the domain is implicit).

Suppose Q, E are ground flat formulas.[6] Then, the probability of Q given E wrt (ϕ, w) is defined as:

$$\Pr_{(\phi,\mathbb{N},w)}(Q \mid E) = \text{WMC}(\phi \land Q \land E, \mathbb{N}, w) / \text{WMC}(\phi \land E, \mathbb{N}, w).$$

We drop the subscript $(\phi, \mathbb{N}, w)$ when the context is clear, and often write Pr(Q) to mean $E =$ *true*. Of course, by means of Proposition 17, probabilities can be computed using propositional WMC. For the sake of completeness, Algorithm 1 provides the pseudocode.

Overall, the definition is reasonable in terms on the following properties:

Theorem 18 *Suppose ϕ is any acceptable KB, α, β ground flat formulas, and w any weight function mapping function symbols to positive reals. Then*

[5] Other accounts of probabilities in the presence of infinitely many atoms are also conceivable [Singla and Domingos, 2007, Riguzzi, 2015].

[6] Observe that the WMC formulation is sensitive to the set of ground atoms over which the set of interpretations are considered. So, for purely technical reasons, we need to assume that all the primitive atoms in $\{Q, E\}$ are also mentioned in ϕ. This is without loss of generality: let $\gamma = \{(p \lor \neg p) \mid$ atom p is mentioned in $Q \land E\}$. Since $\phi \land \gamma \equiv \phi$, replace ϕ with $\phi \land \gamma$ when computing the model count.

Algorithm 1 $\Pr_{(\phi,\mathbb{N},w)}(Q \mid E)$ using propositional WMC

1: $\alpha_1 = \phi \wedge Q \wedge E, \alpha_2 = \phi \wedge E$
2: $\beta_i = \text{XOR}'(\alpha_i)$
3: ▷ Construct bijection $*$ to map atoms in $\text{XOR}(\alpha_i)$ to propositions $p_1, \ldots, p_n$
4: $\gamma_i = (\beta_i)^*$
5: ▷ Construct u to map a $\mathcal{L}^{\text{Prop}}$ model to the weight of the corresponding $\mathcal{L}^{\text{FUN}}_{\mathbb{N}}$ model, which is obtained by mapping propositions back to $\mathcal{L}^{\text{FUN}}_{\mathbb{N}}$-atoms using $*$
6: return $\text{WMC}(\gamma_1, u)/\text{WMC}(\gamma_2, u)$

1. $\Pr(\alpha) = 1$ *if* $\models \phi \supset \alpha$*;*

2. $\Pr(\alpha) = 0$ *if* $\models \phi \supset \neg\alpha$*;*

3. $\Pr(\alpha) = \Pr(\alpha^*)$ *for any bijection* $*$ *from* $\mathbb{N}$ *to* $\mathbb{N}$ *such that it maps names from* ϕ *to themselves and otherwise arbitrary;*

4. $\Pr(\alpha) = \Pr(\beta)$ *if* $\alpha \equiv \beta$*;*

5. $\Pr(\alpha \vee \beta) = \Pr(\alpha) + \Pr(\beta) - \Pr(\alpha \wedge \beta)$*;*

6. $\Pr(\alpha) = \Pr(\alpha \wedge \beta) + \Pr(\alpha \wedge \neg\beta)$.

Proof: For (1), since $\models \phi \supset \alpha$, $\phi \equiv \phi \wedge \alpha$. For (2), if $\phi \models \neg\alpha$, $\phi \wedge \alpha$ has no model. For (3), by construction, $(\phi \wedge \alpha)^* = \phi \wedge \alpha^*$. By induction on α, we can show that for any model M of $\phi \wedge \alpha$, we can construct a model M' of $\phi \wedge \alpha^*$, and vice versa. For (4), assume α and β mention the same set of atoms. (If not, augment the formulas appropriately in a equivalence-preserving manner.) Then, $M \models \phi \wedge \alpha$ iff by definition, $M \models \phi$ and $M \models \alpha$ iff by assumption, $M \models \phi$ and $M \models \beta$ iff $M \models \phi \wedge \beta$. So every model of $\text{XOR}(\phi \wedge \alpha)$ is a model of $\text{XOR}(\phi \wedge \beta)$ and vice versa. For (5), $M \models \phi \wedge (\alpha \vee \beta)$ iff $M \models \phi \wedge \alpha$ or $M \models \phi \wedge \beta$. It is not hard to see that the models of $\text{XOR}(\phi \wedge (\alpha \vee \beta))$ is the union of $\text{XOR}(\phi \wedge \alpha)$ and $\text{XOR}(\phi \wedge \beta)$. By applying the cardinality property for set union, we avoid double counting by subtracting the intersection, which is precisely the set of models for $\text{XOR}(\phi \wedge (\alpha \wedge \beta))$. The proof for (6) is analogous, but we recognize that the models for $\phi \wedge \alpha \wedge \beta$ and those for $\phi \wedge \alpha \wedge \neg\beta$ are disjoint. ∎

Example 19 Suppose ϕ is the conjunction of *father(adam)* = *dave*, and $\forall x(\textit{father}(x) \neq x)$. Suppose the weight function is factorized in terms of $v, \overline{v}$ (that is, positive and negative instances) which map *father* to 1 and 1 respectively, for simplicity. Here are a few examples corresponding to items 1, 3 and 5 from Theorem 18:

- Suppose α is *father(dave)* $\neq$ *dave*. Since ϕ's rank is 1, and letting *beth* be the new constant, it is easy to see that $\text{XOR}(\phi)$ includes formulas such as *father(adam)* $\neq$ *adam* and *father(dave)* $\neq$ *dave*, and so $\text{XOR}(\phi)$ is identical to $\text{XOR}(\phi \wedge \alpha)$, and thus, $\Pr(\alpha) = 1$.

- Suppose α is *father(john)* = *dave*. Since *john* is not mentioned in ϕ, let $*$ be a bijection that maps *john* to *jane* but otherwise maps constants to themselves. So $\alpha^* = (\textit{father(jane)} = \textit{dave})$.

  Recall that, prior to computing the model counts, we need to ensure that the atoms in the query are also mentioned in ϕ. So, let $\phi' = \phi \wedge (\alpha \vee \neg\alpha)$. Then $\text{RGND}(\phi')$ involves grounding ϕ' wrt the constants in ϕ' plus one new one, say, *mary*. Next, $\text{XOR}(\phi')$ over a new constant *beth* essentially boils down to the ground terms *father*(x), $x \in \{\textit{dave}, \textit{john}, \textit{mary}\}$ taking on possible values $y \in \{\textit{dave}, \textit{adam}, \textit{john}, \textit{beth}, \textit{mary}\}$ under the constraint $x \neq y$. Note that ϕ' already assigns *dave* to *father(adam)*, and so this ground term is not significant. In sum, each of the 3 ground terms can take on 4 possible values, and so the model count of $\text{XOR}(\phi) = 4^3$. In contrast, $\text{XOR}(\phi' \wedge \alpha)$ additionally assigns a value to the term *father(john)* and therefore its model count is 4^2, yielding $\Pr(\alpha) = 1/4$.

  Now, consider α^* and to account for the unmentioned atoms, let $\phi'' = \phi \wedge (\alpha^* \vee \neg\alpha^*)$. It is not hard to see that the model count of $\text{XOR}(\phi'') = 4^3$ and that of $\text{XOR}(\phi'' \wedge \alpha^*) = 4^2$ and so $\Pr(\alpha^*) = 1/4$.

- Suppose α is *father(john)* = *dave* and β is *father(john)* = *adam*. To account for the unmentioned atoms, let $\phi' = \phi \wedge (\alpha \vee \neg\alpha) \wedge (\beta \vee \neg\beta)$. Analogous to how we proceeded before, $\text{XOR}(\phi')$ has a model count of 4^3, and $\text{XOR}(\phi' \wedge \alpha), \text{XOR}(\phi' \wedge \beta)$ a model count of 4^2. Since $\alpha \wedge \beta$ is unsatisfiable, $\text{XOR}(\phi' \wedge (\alpha \wedge \beta))$ has a model count of 0. So, $\Pr(\alpha) = 1/4$, $\Pr(\beta) = 1/4$, $\Pr(\alpha \wedge \beta) = 0$ and therefore, $\Pr(\alpha \vee \beta) = 1/2$.

To reiterate the intuition, these probabilities account for the unknowns: $\text{RGND}(\phi)$ accounts for unknown terms, $\text{XOR}(\phi)$ accounts for unknown values to these terms, which is then used to define Pr.

6 LINEAGE AND DISCUSSION

In the literature on extending graphical models to handle first-order features, several influential papers have appeared. We sketch the main directions that are most closely related to our own work, and refer interested readers to [Milch et al., 2005a, Russell, 2015] for a more comprehensive list.

While existential quantifiers are already discussed in finite-domain Markov logic networks [Richardson and Domingos, 2006], these are, in fact, interpreted as a disjunction over ground instances, which is possible because the domain is finite. To avoid such expansions, [Van den Broeck et al., 2014] suggest an elegant alternative. There is also extensive work in database theory on labeled unknowns [Farré et al., 2007], and in the verification community on functions in ground formulas against background axioms (e.g., theory of arithmetic) [Barrett et al., 2009]. In that vein, logical languages with arithmetic constraints have been shown to be useful for probabilistic reasoning in mixed discrete-continuous spaces [Sanner and Abbasnejad, 2012, Belle et al., 2015, Alberti et al., 2016, de Salvo Braz et al., 2016]. Using the relational structure to speed-up inference has also received attention [Gogate and Domingos, 2011, de Salvo Braz et al., 2005, Van den Broeck et al., 2014]. A synthesis of both threads is further investigated in [de Salvo Braz and O'Reilly, 2017].

The starting point for our work was a recent attempt to lift the finite domain assumption in probabilistic relational languages [Belle, 2017]. The thrust of our results follows the style of that work; however, function symbols necessitated a completely new set of technical devices. Recall that a key construction throughout this paper was a way to reason about possible assignments to ground terms in a finite manner; this is based on a reformulation and generalization of the development in [Belle and Lakemeyer, 2011]. Moreover, when limited to universally quantified clauses over a relational vocabulary, the compactness theorem from propositional logic is applicable [Belle, 2017, Theorem 8]. As we saw, compactness does not hold for us. Finally, from an expressiveness point of view, functions are more powerful. Recall that functions can simulate predicates easily. For a function $f(x)$ to be simulated by a predicate, we need an extra argument for the value: $f(x) = z$ can be represented by $P(x, z)$. The trouble is that functions are implicitly assumed to be assigned a value, but then we would need a constraint $\exists z\ (P(x, z))$ in the knowledge base, but this cannot be represented in [Belle, 2017], because no existential quantifiers are allowed. (It cannot be replaced by a disjunction because the range of z is $\mathbb{N}$.) Of course, with functions, we are able to also handle nesting of terms.

In general, the crux of our work is in handling infinite domains. In that regard, [Singla and Domingos, 2007] handle infinite domains in Markov logic networks using locality constraints over Gibbs measures, [Jaeger, 1998] proves decidability in infinite-domain relational BNs given independence constraints in query atoms, [Laskey and da Costa, 2005] provides a semantics for infinite-state BNs assuming stratification conditions, and [Milch et al., 2005b] provide a semantics for infinite-state BNs while assuming that only a finite number of ancestors affect a variable, which drives the formal foundations of BLOG. Readers may want to consult [Milch et al., 2005a, Singla and Domingos, 2007] for a better understanding on how other known methods in the literature, e.g. [Gilks et al., 1994], compare to those listed here. Finally, as mentioned earlier, most languages based on distribution semantics admit infinite instantiations [Sato, 1995].

In our view, all of these approaches are interesting, and it is difficult, from a formal angle, to suggest that one approach subsumes another. What we have attempted in this paper is a new algorithmic contribution that: (a) makes *no assumptions about the syntax* (outside of assuming it is in CNF, which is usual), (b) can embody full logical reasoning over *complex, nested terms* and *unbounded quantification*, and (c) can simply use any standard exact or approximate model counter.

While we investigated general results, it is conceivable that more restricted fragments are sufficient for the application at hand. Perhaps ground flat formulas in $\mathcal{L}_{\mathbb{N}}^{\text{FUN}}$ (discussed in Section 4.1) represents the most useful but non-trivial extension to the propositional fragment from Section 3.2, the latter being virtually identical to existing probabilistic relational languages. Roughly, if we think of the propositional fragment as an instantiation of a first-order language where both the *arguments* and *values* come from finite sets, Section 4.1 can be thought of as an instantiation where only the *arguments* come from finite sets. Thus, while standard probabilistic relational languages are restricted to finite-outcome discrete distributions, the fragment from Section 4.1 could be used for a richer class of distributions.

For the future, it would be worthwhile to better relate the semantics of other infinite domain approaches and our proposal. Moreover, in this paper, we exploited symmetries over unmentioned constants, and it would be worth exploring how symmetries over instances can be additionally exploited [Van den Broeck et al., 2014, Belle, 2017].

In the last decade, weighted model counting has enabled efficient probabilistic reasoning in a number of challenging domains and over heterogeneous representations. Like classical model counting, our approach supports a general grammar where logical connectives $\{\vee, \wedge, \neg\}$ can be used freely. In this spirit, the methodology in this paper could serve as a *general framework* onto which one would encode *expressive first-order* probabilistic logical and probabilistic programming languages involving functions and quantifiers.

References

[Alberti et al., 2016] Alberti, F., Ghilardi, S., and Pagani, E. (2016). Counting constraints in flat array fragments. In *IJCAR*.

[Bacchus, 1990] Bacchus, F. (1990). *Representing and Reasoning with Probabilistic Knowledge*. MIT Press.

[Bacchus et al., 2009] Bacchus, F., Dalmao, S., and Pitassi, T. (2009). Solving #SAT and Bayesian inference with backtracking search. *JAIR*, 34:391–442.

[Barrett et al., 2009] Barrett, C., Sebastiani, R., Seshia, S. A., and Tinelli, C. (2009). Satisfiability modulo theories. In *Handbook of Satisfiability*, pages 825–885. IOS Press.

[Belle, 2017] Belle, V. (2017). Open-universe weighted model counting. In *AAAI*.

[Belle and Lakemeyer, 2011] Belle, V. and Lakemeyer, G. (2011). On progression and query evaluation in first-order knowledge bases with function symbols. In *Proc. IJCAI*.

[Belle et al., 2015] Belle, V., Passerini, A., and Van den Broeck, G. (2015). Probabilistic inference in hybrid domains by weighted model integration. In *IJCAI*.

[Boerger et al., 1997] Boerger, E., Grädel, E., and Gurevich, Y. (1997). *The classical decision problem*. Springer Verlag.

[Chavira and Darwiche, 2008] Chavira, M. and Darwiche, A. (2008). On probabilistic inference by weighted model counting. *Artif. Intell.*, 172(6-7):772–799.

[de Salvo Braz et al., 2005] de Salvo Braz, R., Amir, E., and Roth, D. (2005). Lifted first-order probabilistic inference. In *Proc. IJCAI*, pages 1319–1325.

[de Salvo Braz and O'Reilly, 2017] de Salvo Braz, R. and O'Reilly, C. (2017). Exact inference for relational graphical models with interpreted functions: Lifted probabilistic inference modulo theories. In *Proc. UAI*.

[de Salvo Braz et al., 2016] de Salvo Braz, R., O'Reilly, C., Gogate, V., and Dechter, R. (2016). Probabilistic inference modulo theories. In *Proc. IJCAI*, pages 3591–3599.

[Enderton, 1972] Enderton, H. (1972). *A mathematical introduction to logic*. Academic press New York.

[Ermon et al., 2013] Ermon, S., Gomes, C. P., Sabharwal, A., and Selman, B. (2013). Embed and project: Discrete sampling with universal hashing. In *NIPS*.

[Fagin and Halpern, 1994] Fagin, R. and Halpern, J. Y. (1994). Reasoning about knowledge and probability. *J. ACM*, 41(2):340–367.

[Farré et al., 2007] Farré, C., Nutt, W., Teniente, E., and Urpí, T. (2007). Containment of conjunctive queries over databases with null values. In *ICDT*.

[Fierens et al., 2011] Fierens, D., den Broeck, G. V., Thon, I., Gutmann, B., and Raedt, L. D. (2011). Inference in probabilistic logic programs using weighted CNF's. In *UAI*.

[Getoor and Taskar, 2007] Getoor, L. and Taskar, B., editors (2007). *An Introduction to Statistical Relational Learning*. MIT Press.

[Gilks et al., 1994] Gilks, W. R., Thomas, A., and Spiegelhalter, D. J. (1994). A language and program for complex Bayesian modelling. *The Statistician*, pages 169–177.

[Gogate and Domingos, 2011] Gogate, V. and Domingos, P. (2011). Probabilistic theorem proving. In *UAI*.

[Jaeger, 1998] Jaeger, M. (1998). Reasoning about infinite random structures with relational Bayesian networks. In *KR*.

[Laskey and da Costa, 2005] Laskey, K. B. and da Costa, P. C. G. (2005). Of starships and klingons: Bayesian logic for the 23rd century. In *UAI*.

[Milch et al., 2005a] Milch, B., Marthi, B., Russell, S. J., Sontag, D., Ong, D. L., and Kolobov, A. (2005a). BLOG: Probabilistic models with unkonwn objects. In *Proc. IJCAI*.

[Milch et al., 2005b] Milch, B., Marthi, B., Sontag, D., Russell, S. J., Ong, D. L., and Kolobov, A. (2005b). Approximate inference for infinite contingent Bayesian networks. In *AISTATS*.

[Nickel et al., 2016] Nickel, M., Murphy, K., Tresp, V., and Gabrilovich, E. (2016). A review of relational machine learning for knowledge graphs. *Proceedings of the IEEE*, 104(1):11–33.

[Poole, 1997] Poole, D. (1997). The independent choice logic for modelling multiple agents under uncertainty. *Artificial intelligence*, 94(1):7–56.

[Richardson and Domingos, 2006] Richardson, M. and Domingos, P. (2006). Markov logic networks. *Machine learning*, 62(1):107–136.

[Riguzzi, 2015] Riguzzi, F. (2015). The distribution semantics is well-defined for all normal programs. In *PLP@ ICLP*.

[Russell, 2015] Russell, S. J. (2015). Unifying logic and probability. *Commun. ACM*, 58(7):88–97.

[Sanner and Abbasnejad, 2012] Sanner, S. and Abbasnejad, E. (2012). Symbolic variable elimination for discrete and continuous graphical models. In *AAAI*.

[Sato, 1995] Sato, T. (1995). A statistical learning method for logic programs with distribution semantics. In *ICLP*, pages 715–729.

[Singla and Domingos, 2007] Singla, P. and Domingos, P. M. (2007). Markov logic in infinite domains. In *UAI*.

[Srivastava et al., 2014] Srivastava, S., Russell, S. J., Ruan, P., and Cheng, X. (2014). First-order open-universe POMDPs. In *UAI*.

[Van den Broeck et al., 2014] Van den Broeck, G., Meert, W., and Darwiche, A. (2014). Skolemization for weighted first-order model counting. In *KR*.

[Wu et al., 2012] Wu, W., Li, H., Wang, H., and Zhu, K. Q. (2012). Probase: A probabilistic taxonomy for text understanding. In *Proc. Int. Conf. on Management of Data*, pages 481–492.

Triply Stochastic Gradients on Multiple Kernel Learning

Xiang Li[*] Bin Gu[‡] Shuang Ao[*] Huaimin Wang[†] Charles X. Ling[*]
[*]Computer Science Department, University of Western Ontario, Canada
[†]School of Computer, National University of Defense Technology, China
[‡]Nanjing University of Information Science and Technology, China
{lxiang2, sao, charles.ling}@uwo.ca, jsgubin@nuist.edu.cn, hmwang@nudt.edu.cn

Abstract

Multiple Kernel Learning (MKL) is highly useful for learning complex data with multiple cues or representations. However, MKL is known to have poor scalability because of the expensive kernel computation. Dai et al (2014) proposed to use a doubly Stochastic Gradient Descent algorithm (doubly SGD) to greatly improve the scalability of kernel methods. However, the algorithm is not suitable for MKL because it cannot learn the kernel weights. In this paper, we provide a novel extension to doubly SGD for MKL so that both the decision functions and the kernel weights can be learned simultaneously. To achieve this, we develop the triply Stochastic Gradient Descent (triply SGD) algorithm which involves three sources of randomness – the data points, the random features, and the kernels, which was not considered in previous work. We prove that our algorithm enjoys similar convergence rate as that of doubly SGD. Comparing to several traditional MKL solutions, we show that our method has faster convergence speed and achieved better accuracy. Most importantly, our method makes it possible to learn MKL problems with millions of data points on a normal desktop PC.

1 INTRODUCTION

Kernel methods provide a principled way of learning with non-linear representations. However, finding the best kernel for a specific task is not always easy. Meanwhile, many applications may have several candidate data representations, such as learning with multi-modal or multi-source data. In either situation, we may need the learning system to find an optimal combination of several base kernels or data representations. To serve this purpose, Multiple Kernel Learning algorithms (Lanckriet et al, 2004) have been proposed to automatically learn the decision functions as well as the weights for combining the base kernels.

In theory, there are infinite ways of combining kernels, most MKL methods focus on linear kernel combination for efficiency. To prevent overfitting, l_1 and $l_p(p > 1)$ are commonly used norms to regularize the kernel weights. In this paper, we focus on linear kernel combination and l_p-normalization because of its many successful applications and its strong convexity which greatly benefits optimization. To learn a good kernel combination under l_p regularization, many optimization strategies have been proposed. For example, (1). directly solving the problem using Sequential Minimal Optimization (Sun et al, 2010); (2). alternating optimization methods (Kloft et al, 2011) and (3). online learning approaches which process one training instance at a time (Orabona and Jie, 2011). See Bucak et al (2014); Gönen and Alpaydın (2011) for a survey.

In the big data era, machine learning systems often have to deal with very large datasets. However, existing MKL algorithms require computing all the kernel matrices beforehand, which severely hinders scalability: the computation and storage cost is $O(m \cdot l^2)$, where l is the number of data instances and m is the number of kernels. To improve efficiency, random feature methods (Rahimi et al, 2007) have been proposed to approximate a kernel matrix using explicit feature mappings in a lower-dimensional space. However, to achieve accurate solution, the number of random features has to be $O(l)$ even for a single kernel (Rahimi and Recht, 2009). The indication is that the random feature matrix is still at the order of $O(l^2)$, which is hardly scalable.

Recently, doubly stochastic gradients (doubly SGD) (Dai et al, 2014; Xie et al, 2015) have been proposed which sample training points and random features stochastically and update the model parameters according to the functional gradient in the RKHS (Reproducing Kernels Hilbert Space) induced by the kernel function. These methods show strong empirical performance on large-scale classification tasks which are dominated by Deep Neural Networks. To deal with multiple kernels, doubly SGD methods already support the concatenation of random features from several kernels, which is equivalent to learning with the summation of base kernels with fixed weights. However, fixing the kernel weights may not lead to the best classification performance. One of the key advantages of Multiple Kernel Learning is to learn the optimal combination of base kernels.

In this paper, we extend the doubly SGD algorithm for the l_p-MKL setting. The problem is more complicated than the original one considered by doubly SGD: l_p-MKL problem requires learning not only the decision functions but also the optimal weights of kernel combination.

To achieve this, we develop the triply Stochastic Gradient Descent (triply SGD) algorithm whose basic idea is to insert a third level of randomness to the stochastic optimization process. Specifically, we randomly select a kernel, a data point and a set of random features (of the corresponding kernel) in each SGD iteration. This triple-stochastic process was not considered in previous work.

We theoretically demonstrate how such an algorithmic design together with a proper learning rate can lead to an optimization program with $O(1/t)$ convergence rate, where t is the number of iterations. In other words, our algorithm achieves the same order of convergence rate as doubly SGD. As demonstrated in our experiments, triply SGD has faster convergence rate and achieved better accuracy on various classification tasks compared to traditional MKL solutions.

This paper makes two major contributions:

1. We extend the theoretic framework of doubly SGD to learn not only the decision functions but also the weights of kernel combination.

2. We provide an online algorithm that can learn MKL problems with millions of data points on a normal desktop PC.

The rest of the paper is organized as follows. We first review the technical background of l_p Multiple Kernel Learning and doubly stochastic gradient methods. We provide our algorithm in Section 4 and the theoretic analysis in Section 5. In Section 6, we conduct extensive experiments to demonstrate the advantage of our algorithm over traditional MKL methods. The last section concludes the paper.

2 PRELIMINARIES

2.1 MULTIPLE KERNEL LEARNING

In this paper, we focus on the MKL problem. Suppose we have m kernels, in general, MKL optimizes the following goal

$$\min_{\{\beta,\alpha\}} \mathbf{E}(Y, \alpha \sum_{r=1}^{m} \beta_r K_r) + \mathbf{R}(\alpha, K') \tag{1}$$

where α are the dual coefficients, β are the kernel weights. If we use a Lipschitz loss function $l(\cdot)$ in the error term $\mathbf{E}(\cdot)$ and l_2 norm in the regularizer $\mathbf{R}(\cdot)$, Eq. (1) is equivalent to

$$\min_{\{f,\beta\}} R_{\text{MKL}}(f,\beta) :=$$

$$\mathbb{E}_{(x,y)}\left[l(\sum_{r=1}^{m} f_r(x), y)\right] + \frac{\nu}{2}\sum_{r=1}^{m} \beta_r ||f_r||^2_{\mathcal{H}_r}; \tag{2}$$

where $\mathcal{H}_r$ is the RKHS induced by kernel K_r and f_r is a functional in space $\mathcal{H}_r$.

In particular, the l_p-MKL ($p > 1$) problem (Kloft et al, 2011) constrains the kernel weights to be within the p-norm simplex $\Delta_p = \{||\beta||_p < 1, \beta_r > 0\}$. Under this constraint, Xu et al (2010) have shown that (2) is equivalent to

$$\min_{\{f,\beta\}} R_{l_p\text{MKL}}(f,\beta)$$

$$:= \mathbb{E}_{(x,y)}\left[l(\sum_{r=1}^{m} f_r(x), y)\right] + \frac{\nu}{2}\sum_{r=1}^{m} \frac{||f_r||^2_{\mathcal{H}_r}}{\beta_r};$$

$$s.t., \beta \in \Delta_p, p > 1 \tag{3}$$

This problem can be solved by alternative optimization approaches (Xu et al, 2010; Kloft et al, 2011) which can exploit off-the-shelf SVM solvers in each iteration. l_p MKL can also be optimized using online learning approaches (Orabona and Jie, 2011; Orabona et al, 2012) that use stochastic optimization to process the data one point at a time. However, all these traditional l_p MKL solutions require computing and storing all the m kernels, which sets up obstacles for scaling-up.

2.2 RANDOM FEATURE APPROXIMATION

There have been many attempts to make kernel methods scalable, such as the Nyström method (Williams and Seeger, 2001), divide-and-conquer SVM solver (Hsieh et al, 2014) and budget online kernel learning (Lu et al,

2015). In this paper, we focus on the random feature method (Rahimi et al, 2007), which explicitly maps the decision function $f(\cdot)$ to a lower dimensional space through random processes.

By Bochner's Theorem, for any PSD (Positive Semi-Definitive) kernel $k(\cdot,\cdot)$, there exists a set Ω, a probability measure $\mathbb{P}$ and a random feature $\phi_\omega(x)$, such that

$$k(x,x') = \int_\Omega \phi_\omega(x)\phi_\omega(x')d\mathbb{P}(\omega) \quad (4)$$

Random feature approximation methods explicitly compute $\phi_\omega(x)$ for many kernel functions such as RBF kernels (Rahimi et al, 2007), dot-product kernels (Kar and Karnick, 2012), Laplacian kernels (Yang et al, 2014), to name a few. They approximate a kernel using

$$k(x,x') \approx \frac{1}{D}\sum_{j=1}^{D} \phi_{\omega_j}(x)\phi_{\omega_j}(x') \quad (5)$$

where D is the number of random features for each instance. It requires $O(lDd)$ computation and $O(lD)$ storage to generate random features for a dataset of l instances. Subsequent algorithm can do efficient linear classification on the generated random features:

$$Z(x) = [\phi_{\omega_1}(x)\ \phi_{\omega_2}(x)\ \dots\ \phi_{\omega_D}(x)] \quad (6)$$

Unfortunately, previous studies (Rahimi and Recht, 2009) have shown that we need $D = O(l)$ to get accurate predictive performance, which implies that the random feature matrix still needs to be $O(l^2)$.

2.3 DOUBLY STOCHASTIC FUNCTIONAL GRADIENTS

To further improve the scalability of random feature methods, Dai et al (2014) have proposed the Doubly Stochastic Functional Gradient (Doubly SGD) algorithm which applies classical SGD procedure to stochastic random feature learning. Specifically, whenever the SGD procedure receives a new data point (or a batch of points), doubly SGD will also generate its corresponding random features on-the-fly, and compute the stochastically-approximated functional gradient to update the model parameters. For the prediction purpose, the system only needs to store the seeds used for generating the random features, which leads to great improvement in scalability. Algorithm 1 and 2 describe the doubly SGD procedure. On the theoretic side, Dai et al (2014) have proved that the doubly SGD algorithm can achieve $O(1/t)$ convergence rate under certain reasonable assumptions.

Notice that the doubly SGD algorithm can be used for multidimensional random features, i.e., $\phi_\omega(x) = [\phi_{\omega_1}(x)\phi_{\omega_2}(x),\dots,\phi_{\omega_m}(x)] \in \mathbb{R}^m$, and each dimension r corresponds to a different kernel $k_r(\cdot,\cdot)$. This formulation is actually equivalent to Multiple Kernel Learning with fixed kernel weights, i.e., Eq. (2) with $\beta = \mathbf{1}$. However, fixed kernel weights unavoidably compromises model expressiveness, and the generalization performance may suffer especially when we are dealing with large datasets. Meanwhile, directly applying doubly SGD to MKL means that we have to generate random features for all the m kernels in each iteration, this could hinder the scalability especially when the number of kernels m is large.

Algorithm 1 $\{\alpha_i\}_{i=1}^t$ =**DoublySGD**($\mathbb{P}(x,y),\theta$)

```
for i = 1, ..., t do
    sample (x_i, y_i);
    sample ω_i ~ P(ω) seed i;
    f(x_i) = DoublySgdPredict(x_i, {α_j}_{j=1}^{i-1});
    γ_i = θ/i;
    α_i = −γ_i l'(f(x_i), y_i) φ_{ω_i}(x_i);
    α_j = (1 − γ_i ν) α_j for j = 1, ..., i − 1;
end for
```

Algorithm 2 $f(x)$ =**Predict**($x,\{\alpha_i\}_{i=1}^t$)

```
set f(x) = 0
for i = 1, ..., t do
    sample ω_i ~ P(ω) seed i;
    f(x) = f(x) + α_i φ_{ω_i}(x);
end for
```

In order to address these challenges, we propose the Triply Stochastic Functional Gradient method (triply SGD), which can learn the kernel weights as well as the decision functions. Most importantly, it only requires generating random features for one stochastically selected kernel in each SGD update, which also opens the door for developing parallel implementations.

3 STOCHASTIC FUNCTIONAL GRADIENTS FOR l_p MKL

It is known that the convex combination of PSD kernels is also a PSD kernel. The RKHS $\mathcal{H}$ in MKL learning can be constructed by the sum space of functions (Sindhwani and Rosenberg, 2008). i.e.,

$$\mathcal{H} := \{\mathcal{H}_1 \oplus \mathcal{H}_2 \oplus \dots \oplus \mathcal{H}_m\}$$

$$:= \{F|F(x) = \sum_{r=1}^{m} f_r(x), \forall f_r \in \mathcal{H}_r\} \quad (7)$$

For the RKHS $\mathcal{H}$ defined by (7), we always have

$$\sum f_r(x) \in \mathcal{H} \tag{8}$$

$$||\sum f_r||^2_{\mathcal{H}} = \sum ||f_r||^2_{\mathcal{H}_r} \tag{9}$$

$$\nabla(\sum f_r) = \sum(\nabla f_r) \tag{10}$$

From Xu et al (2010), we know that l_p MKL problem (3) is equivalent to

$$\min_{\{f_r \in \mathcal{H}_r\}_{r=1}^m} \mathbb{E}_{(x,y)}\Big[l(F(x), y)\Big] + \frac{\nu}{2} \cdot \Psi \tag{11}$$

where

$$F(x) := \sum_{r=1}^m f_r(x)$$

$$\Psi := (\sum_{r=1}^m ||f_r||^q_{\mathcal{H}_r})^{2/q}$$

and $q = \frac{2p}{p+1}$. From $p > 1$, we know that $1 < q < 2$. This leads to a $\frac{\nu(p-1)}{2p}$-strongly convex problem (Orabona et al, 2012). [1]

Using this formulation, the functional gradient w.r.t. one of the decision functions would be

$$\nabla R(f_r) = \mathbb{E}_{(x,y)}[\xi_r(\cdot)] + \frac{\nu}{2}\nabla\Psi(f_r) \tag{12}$$

where $\nabla\Psi(f_r)$ is the functional gradient due to the regularization term and $\xi_r(\cdot) = l'(F(x), y)k_r(x, \cdot)$ is that of the error term. Since we use stochastically generated random features, we cannot compute the decision functional $k_r(x, \cdot)$ explicitly. Instead, we compute the *stochastic* functional gradient with respect to each decision function f_r:

$$\zeta_r(\cdot) = l'(F(x), y)\phi_{\omega_r}(x)\phi_{\omega_r}(\cdot)$$

which satisfies $\xi_r(\cdot) = \mathbb{E}_{\omega_r}[\zeta_r(\cdot)]$.

Using some basic algebraic transformation, $\nabla\Psi(f_r)$ can be represented as:

$$\nabla\Psi(f_r) = 2f_r\psi_r \tag{13}$$

where we define

$$\psi_r := \Big[\frac{\sum_{s=1}^m ||f_s||^q_{\mathcal{H}_s}}{||f_r||^q_{\mathcal{H}_r}}\Big]^{\frac{2-q}{q}} \tag{14}$$

In this paper, we will use the convention that $\frac{t}{0} = 0$ when $t = 0$ and $+\infty$ otherwise (Kloft et al, 2011).

So far we have derived the stochastic functional gradients w.r.t. each individual decision function of the l_p MKL problem. We next develop the triply SGD algorithm based on these stochastic gradients.

[1]Equivalently, $\frac{\nu(q-1)}{q}$-strongly convex.

4 TRIPLY STOCHASTIC GRADIENT DESCENT

The main idea of the triply SGD algorithm is to optimize the l_p MKL objective (11) with three levels of stochastic samplings: data points, kernels and random features; and update the model using stochastic functional gradients with respect to each decision function. The pseudo code is given in Algorithms 3 and 4, where $\phi_{\omega_{r,j}}$ and $\alpha_{r,j}$ denote the random feature and dual coefficient for kernel r sampled in iteration j, respectively. Agian, compared to the multi-kernel extension of the original doubly SGD, triply SGD only needs to sample one kernel in each iteration, which makes it more efficient in memory usage.

Algorithm 3 $\{\alpha_{1:r,i}\}_{i=1}^t$ =**TriplySGD**($\mathbb{P}(x, y), \theta$)

1: **for** $i = 1, \ldots, t$ **do**
2: sample (x_i, y_i);
3: sample kernel $r_i \sim 1 \ldots m$ seed i;
4: sample $\omega_{r_i,i} \sim \mathbb{P}_{r_i}(\omega)$ seed i;
5: $\{f_r(x_i)\}_{r=1}^m$ = **Predict**($x_i, \{\alpha_{1:r,j}\}_{j=1}^{i-1}$);
6: $\psi_i = \Big[\frac{\sum_{s=1}^m ||f_s||^q_{\mathcal{H}_s}}{||f_r||^q_{\mathcal{H}_r}}\Big]^{\frac{2-q}{q}}$;
7: $\gamma_i = \frac{\theta}{i}$;
8: $\eta_i = \frac{\gamma_i}{\psi_i}$;
9: $\alpha_{r_i,i} = -\eta_i l'(\sum_{r=1}^m f_r(x_i), y_i)\phi_{\omega_{r_i,i}}(x_i)$;
10: $\forall r, \alpha_{r,j} = (1 - \gamma_i\nu)\alpha_{r,j}$ for $j = 1, \ldots, i-1$;
11: **end for**

Algorithm 4 $\{f_r(x)\}_{r=1}^m$ =**Predict**($x, \{\alpha_{1:r,i}\}_{i=1}^t$)

1: set $f_1(x) = f_2(x) = \ldots = f_m(x) = 0$
2: **for** $i = 1, \ldots, t$ **do**
3: sample kernel $r_i \sim 1 \ldots m$ seed i;
4: sample $\omega_{r_i,i} \sim \mathbb{P}_{r_i}(\omega)$ seed i;
5: $f_{r_i}(x) = f_{r_i}(x) + \alpha_{r_i,i}\phi_{\omega_{r_i,i}}(x)$;
6: **end for**

Next we illustrate how lines 8-10 of the algorithm update the functional of each kernel K_r and the global functional F.

At iteration t, denote r_t as the chosen kernel, $\mathcal{D}^t = (x_t, y_t)$ as the selected data point and $f_{r,t}$ as the decision function of kernel r. For brevity, we use ψ_t to denote ψ_{r_t}. We have $f_{r,1}(\cdot) = 0$ and

$$f_{r,t+1}(\cdot) = \begin{cases} f_{r,t}(\cdot) - \nu\gamma_t f_{r,t}(\cdot) - \eta_t\zeta_{r,t}(\cdot) & \text{if } r_t = r \\ f_{r,t}(\cdot) - \nu\gamma_t f_{r,t}(\cdot) & \text{else} \end{cases} \tag{15}$$

$$F_{t+1}(\cdot) = F_t(\cdot) - \nu\gamma_t F_t(\cdot) - \eta_t\zeta_{r_t,t}(\cdot) \tag{16}$$

In other words, since we only sampled one kernel at a time, the gradient $\zeta_{r_t,t}(\cdot)$ will only be used to update the functional of that kernel r_t. All other functionals ($f_r, r \neq r_t$) will only shrink by a constant factor $(1-\nu\gamma_t)$.

Meanwhile, since $f_r(\cdot)$ and $F(\cdot)$ may not be in the corresponding RKHS $\mathcal{H}_r$ and $\mathcal{H}$ during the stochastic learning process, we will also construct intermediate functionals $h_r(\cdot)$ and $H(\cdot)$ as did in Dai et al (2014). Accordingly, $h_{r,1}(\cdot) = 0$ and

$$h_{r,t+1}(\cdot) = \begin{cases} h_{r,t}(\cdot) - \nu\gamma_t h_{r,t}(\cdot) - \hat{\eta}_t \xi_{r,t}(\cdot) & \text{if } r_t = r \\ h_{r,t}(\cdot) - \nu\gamma_t h_{r,t}(\cdot) & \text{else} \end{cases} \tag{17}$$

$$H_{t+1}(\cdot) = H_t(\cdot) - \nu\gamma_t H_t(\cdot) - \hat{\eta}_t \xi_{r_t,t}(\cdot) \tag{18}$$

where we have set $\hat{\eta}_t = \frac{\gamma_t}{\hat{\psi}_t}$, in which

$$\hat{\psi}_t := \left[\frac{\sum_{s=1}^m ||h_{s,t}||_{\mathcal{H}_s}^q}{||h_{r,t}||_{\mathcal{H}_{r_t}}^q}\right]^{\frac{2-q}{q}} \tag{19}$$

corresponds to Eq. (14).

Since the kernels are stochastically selected, for ease of illustration, we further denote the following auxiliary variables:

(1). $I^i(r) := \{j | r_j = r\}$, all iterations (up to i) where kernel r gets selected;

(2). $T^i(r) := \max\{I^i(r)\}$, the most recent iteration (up to i) that kernel r gets selected;.

(3). $C^i(r) := |I^i(r)|$, the number of iterations (up to i) that kernel r gets selected.

By these definitions, $T^i(r_i) = i$ and $C^{T^i(r)}(r) = C^i(r)$ always true. We can rewrite (15)(17) as

$$f_{r,t+1}(\cdot) = \sum_{i \in I^t(r)} u_t^i(r) \zeta_{r,i}(\cdot) \tag{20}$$

$$h_{r,t+1}(\cdot) = \sum_{i \in I^t(r)} \hat{u}_t^i(r) \xi_{r,i}(\cdot) \tag{21}$$

where

$$u_t^i(r) = -\eta_{T^i(r)} \prod_{j=T^i(r)+1}^{t} (1-\nu\gamma_j) \tag{22}$$

$$\hat{u}_t^i(r) = -\hat{\eta}_{T^i(r)} \prod_{j=T^i(r)+1}^{t} (1-\nu\gamma_j) \tag{23}$$

Notice that $u_t^i(r), \hat{u}_t^i(r)$ are indeterministic sequences, which depend on the orders of kernel sampling. However, if we look at the global functionals $F(\cdot), H(\cdot)$, we can rewrite (16)(18) as

$$F_{t+1}(\cdot) = \sum_{i=1}^{t} v_t^i \zeta_{r_i,i}(\cdot) \tag{24}$$

$$H_{t+1}(\cdot) = \sum_{i=1}^{t} \hat{v}_t^i \xi_{r_i,i}(\cdot) \tag{25}$$

where

$$v_t^i = -\eta_i \prod_{j=i+1}^{t} (1-\nu\gamma_j) = u_t^i(r_i) \tag{26}$$

$$\hat{v}_t^i = -\hat{\eta}_i \prod_{j=i+1}^{t} (1-\nu\gamma_j) = \hat{u}_t^i(r_i) \tag{27}$$

are deterministic sequences.

Notice that

$$v_t^i = -\frac{a_t^i}{\psi_i}; \quad \hat{v}_t^i = -\frac{a_t^i}{\hat{\psi}_i}$$

where $a_t^i = -\gamma_i \prod_{j=i+1}^t (1-\nu\gamma_j)$ is the same as defined in Dai et al (2014), with step size $\gamma_t = \frac{\theta}{t}$. These settings help us connect to the theoretic framework of Dai et al (2014).

5 ANALYSIS

In this section, we analyze Algorithm 3 and 4 under the following practical assumptions:

A1. Both the loss function $l(u, y)$ and its first-derivative $l'(u, y)$ are L-Lipschitz continuous.

A2. For any data $\{(x_i, y_i)\}_{i=1}^t$ and any sequence of functionals $\{F_i\}_{i=1}^t$, the first-derivative of loss is bounded: $l'(F_i(x_i), y_i) \leq M$.

A3. There exists $\kappa > 0$ and $\phi > 0$, such that for any kernel $r \in \{1, \ldots, m\}$, $\forall x, \omega$: $|k_r(x, x')| \leq \kappa$, $|\phi_\omega(x)\phi_\omega(x')| \leq \phi$.

A4. There exists $C_q > 1$, such that, $\forall \{f_r\}_{r=1}^m$

$$1 \leq \left[\frac{\sum_{s=1}^m ||f_s||_{\mathcal{H}_s}^q}{||f_r||_{\mathcal{H}_r}^q}\right]^{\frac{2-q}{q}} \leq C_q$$

For A4, the first inequality always holds because $q \in (1, 2)$. It implies that $\hat{\psi}_t \in [1, C_q]$ and $\psi_t \in [1, C_q]$.

Under the above conditions, we are able to prove the following theorem, which implies that the algorithm has $O(1/t)$ convergence rate.

Theorem 5.1 (Convergence in Expectation) *Set $\gamma_i = \frac{\theta}{i}(1 \leq i \leq t)$, $\theta > 0$ and $\theta\nu \in (1, 2) \cup \mathbb{Z}_+$ for Algorithm 3 and 4, we always have*

$$\mathbb{E}_{\mathcal{D}^t, r^t, \omega^t}\left[|F_{t+1}(x) - F_*(x)|^2\right] \leq \frac{2C^2 + 2\kappa Q_1^2}{t} \tag{28}$$

Table 1: Dataset information and experiment settings. In the experiments of Figure 1, we only use a subset of training data as indicated in the 5th column of this table.

data	classes	PCA dim	total size	subset size	kernels	kernel size	λ
covtype	2	40	581,012	20,000	5 rbf	22 GB	10^{-5}
epsilon	2	100	400,000	20,000	5 rbf	22 GB	10^{-5}
mnist8m (binary)	2	100	1,625,000	20,000	5 rbf	22 GB	10^{-5}
cifar10 (binary)	2	100	50,000	20,000	5 rbf	22 GB	10^{-5}
mnist8m	10	100	8,100,000	20,000	5 rbf	22 GB	10^{-5}
cifar10	10	100	50,000	25,000	3 rbf	15 GB	10^{-5}

where we define $Q_1 = \max\{||F_*||_{\mathcal{H}}, \frac{Q_0+\sqrt{Q_0^2+(2\nu'\theta-1)\kappa M^2(1+\nu\theta)^2(\theta)^2}}{(2\nu'\theta-1)}\}$, *and* $Q_0 = 2\sqrt{2}\kappa^{1/2}LM(\kappa+\phi)\theta^2$, $C = 4(\kappa+\phi)^2M^2\theta^2$ *and* $\nu' = \frac{\nu(p-1)}{2pC_q}$.

Remarks. Notice that $F_*(\cdot)$ is the optimal functional in the RKHS for solving the l_p MKL problem (11). The above theorem implies that after $t+1$ iterations the functional found by triply SGD will converge to $F_*(\cdot)$, and the difference is no more than $\frac{2C^2+2\kappa Q_1^2}{t}$.

Proof: (sketch) The basic flow of the proof follows that of doubly SGD. In other words, we also decompose the errors into the error due to random features and the error due to random data, i.e.,

$$|F_{t+1}(x) - F_*(x)|^2 \leq 2|F_{t+1}(x) - H_{t+1}(x)|^2 + 2\kappa||H_{t+1} - F_*||_{\mathcal{H}} \quad (29)$$

we use Lemma 5.2 and 5.3 to bound each error term respectively. Detailed proofs are deferred to the appendix. □

Lemma 5.2 *For any* $x \in \mathcal{X}$,

$$\mathbb{E}_{\mathcal{D}^t,r^t,\omega^t}\left[\left|F_{t+1}(x) - H_{t+1}(x)\right|^2\right] \leq B_{1,t+1}^2 \quad (30)$$

where $B_{1,t+1}^2 := M^2(\kappa+\phi)^2\sum_{i=1}^t |a_t^i|^2$.

Lemma 5.3 *Set* $\gamma_i = \frac{\theta}{i}(1 \leq i \leq t)$, $\theta > 0$ *and* $\theta\nu \in (1,2) \cup \mathbb{Z}_+$, *we have*

$$\mathbb{E}_{\mathcal{D}^t,r^t,\omega^t}\left[||H_{t+1} - F_*||_{\mathcal{H}}^2\right] \leq \frac{Q_1^2}{t} \quad (31)$$

where Q_1 *is as defined in Theorem 5.1.*

In the next section, we use experiments to demonstrate the effectiveness and efficiency of triply SGD on l_p MKL tasks.

6 EXPERIMENTS

In this section, we compare the proposed triply SGD algorithm to several traditional MKL methods with various experiments.

6.1 BASELINES

Among the many traditional MKL methods, we select OBSCURE (Orabona et al, 2012), UFO (Orabona and Jie, 2011) and p-norm MKL (Kloft et al, 2011) as the baselines in this paper. OBSCURE and UFO are online algorithms that can directly optimize the l_p-MKL goal using stochastic sub-gradient descent (Shalev-Shwartz et al, 2011) while the p-norm MKL algorithm optimizes kernel weights β and the SVM problem with fixed β alternatively. They are highly competitive MKL solvers in terms of convergence speed and accuracy according to extensive experiments on medium size datasets. (Orabona et al, 2012; Orabona and Jie, 2011; Kloft et al, 2011). Besides, in order to show the benefit of MKL and why doubly SGD is not enough, we include the straightforward extension of doubly SGD as a baseline. To make doubly SGD compatible with the MKL scenario, we generate and concatenate the random features from all the kernels in each iteration of Algorithm 1 and 2. We denote this naive extension as *DoublySGD-MK*.

6.2 DATASETS

The purpose of our experiments is to demonstrate the scalability of the proposed method. For this purpose, we choose large scale datasets on which traditional MKL algorithms are hardly scalable. For binary classification tasks, we have used the *epsilon*, *covtype*, *mnist8m-binary* from the LibSVM DATA collection[2] and the *cifar10-binary* (Krizhevsky et al, 2012) dataset. The *cifar10-binary* task requires to classify whether an image is animal or not, *mnist8m-binary* classifies the digits '6' and '8'. For multi-class problems, we consider all the 10 classes in *cifar10* and *mnist8m*. The dataset information

[2]https://www.csie.ntu.edu.tw/ cjlin/libsvmtools/datasets/

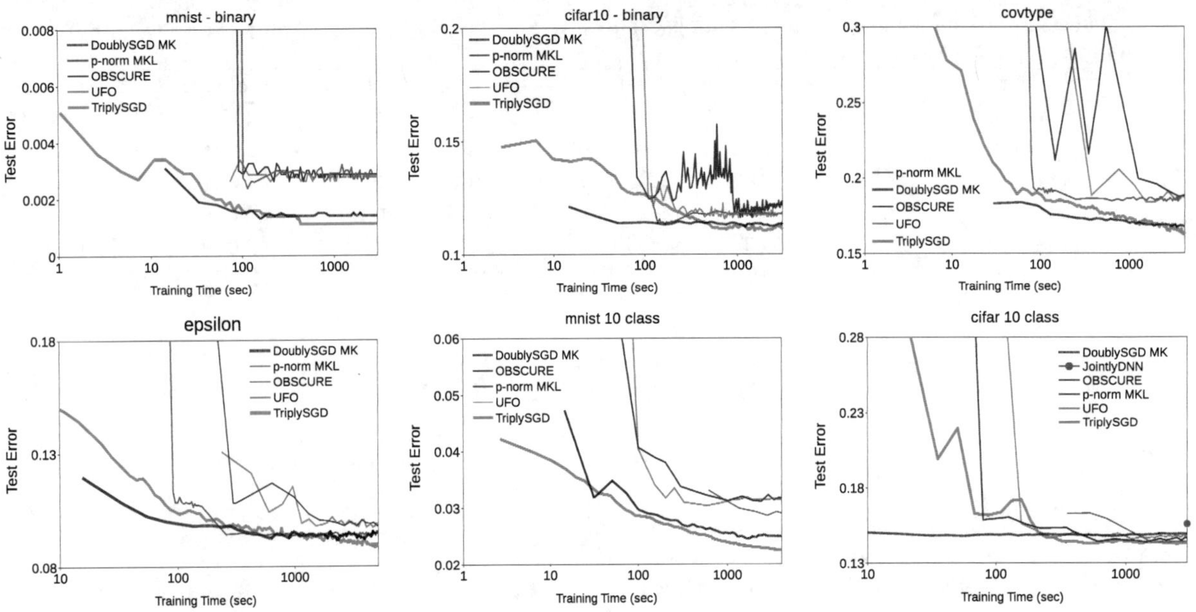

Figure 1: Learning curves on datasets with fixed training sizes. Experiment settings are given in Table 1 and Section 6.3. Best performance of the CNN we used for feature extraction is also indicated as a blue circle. Notice that the curves of traditional MKL solvers start at around 100 seconds, because they need to compute the kernel matrices before training. *Compared to Triply SGD, Doubly SGD converges faster at the beginning since it does not need to learn the kernel weights. However, as a result, its generalization error is higher than triply SGD in the long run.*

Table 2: Comparison of the final test error rates between doubly and triply SGD in Figure 1.

	mnist-bin	cifar-bin	covtype-bin	epsilon-bin	cifar-10	mnist-10
DoublySGD-MK	0.0014	0.1190	0.1680	0.095	0.1497	0.0250
TriplySGD	**0.0011**	**0.1120**	**0.1630**	**0.088**	**0.1407**	**0.0220**

and parameter settings are shown in Table 1.

6.3 MULTIPLE KERNELS

In order to build a multi-kernel scenario for the *cifar10-multiclass* dataset, we use 3 sets of CNN-pretrained features to construct three different RBF kernels. The first set of features are extracted from the last dense layer (512 dimensions) of a well-trained 18-layer-ResNet (He et al, 2016) with 15.6% test error rate after 190 training epochs. The other two sets of features are extracted from a lightly-trained (5 epochs of training) CNN (Lin et al, 2013) with 29% test error rate. We use the last dense layer (512 dimensions) and the last max-pooling layer (2304 dimensions), respectively. In this way, we intentionally made one of the kernels more informative than the other two, so that adjusting the kernel weights is important. We apply PCA to reduce the dimensionality of each feature representation to 100 before computing the RBF functions.

For all other datasets, we apply PCA on the original features or raw pixels for dimensionality reduction. We construct 5 kernels on the PCA dimensions. The first kernel is simply computed using all PCA dimensions. The other 4 kernels are constructed from each $\frac{1}{4}$ of the PCA dimensions. In this way, we still intentionally make the first kernel more informative. The bandwidths of all RBF kernels are determined by the median trick.

6.4 IMPLEMENTATION DETAILS

We run all experiments on a desktop computer with an 8 core Intel i7 CPU and 24 gigabyte memories. All algorithms are implemented in MATLAB. For the baseline methods, the computer memory can only accommodate the kernels of a subset of data, which is $20,000/8,000$ (train/test) instances for the five kernel experiments and $25,000/10,000$ instances for the three kernel experiments. For the triply SGD algorithm, we set the number of random features as 2^{13} and the batch size is set as 2^{15}. With this setting, the triply SGD program never exceeds 16 GB memory-usage, irrespective of the training size.

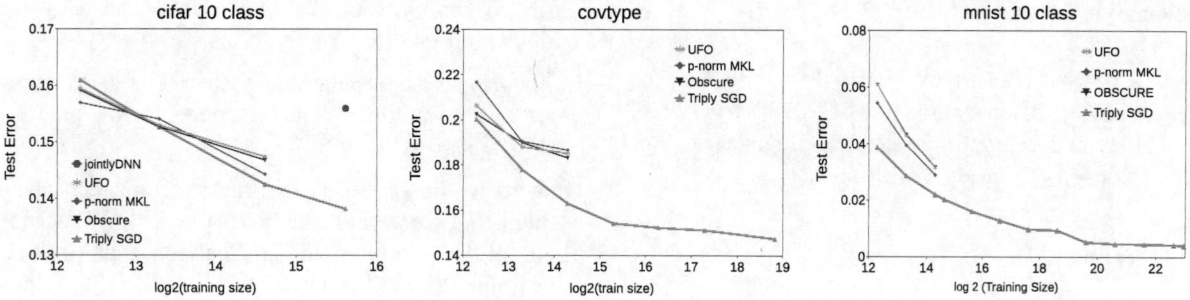

Figure 2: Experiments with different training sizes. The baselines can only handle a small subset of each dataset. For each sample size of a given dataset, we set a time budget of $10,000$ seconds. The other settings including the construction of kernels are the same as Figure 1.

For the parameter p and q in the l_p MKL objective (3), we use $q = \frac{2\log m}{2\log m - 1}$ as suggested in Orabona and Jie (2011).

All the candidate algorithms use hinge loss for the binary classification tasks. To handle multi-class scenarios, the OBSCURE and UFO algorithms have used the 'max-of-hinge' loss (Crammer and Singer, 2001). While the original p-norm MKL approach focuses on binary classification, we use the One-Versus-Rest strategy to extend it to the multi-class setting. For the triply SGD algorithm, we use the multi-class logistic (i.e., softmax) loss as did in Dai et al (2014); Li and Póczos (2016).

6.5 EXPERIMENTS AND RESULTS

We first evaluate the convergence speed and accuracy of all candidate methods with the same training size. In other words, we restrict the triply SGD algorithm to use the same subsets of data as the baselines. See Table 1 for our settings. We use a time budget of $3,000$ seconds for each experiment which includes kernel computation and random feature generation as well as training. Figure 1 depicts the learning curves of test error for different tasks.

Observation 1. *Compared to traditional MKL solvers, Triply SGD has a faster learning convergence speed and achieves higher predictive performance.*

Table 2 shows the final test error of triplySGD and doublySGD-MK (after $3,000$ seconds). In all six experiments, TriplySGD has better performance. This is because doublySGD-MK simply concatenates the random features from multiple kernels and cannot adjust the kernel weights. As a result, this naive extension of doublySGD can hardly take full advantage of the flexibility of Multiple Kernel Learning.

Observation 2. *Compared to Doubly SGD, Triply SGD can achieve better accuracy in the MKL scenario.*

In order to show how triply SGD can handle larger datasets and gain better performance, we conduct experiments with various training sizes using the *covtype*, *mnist8m* and *cifar10* datasets. We keep the same parameter settings and kernel composition as our previous experiments. For baseline methods, they can only process a subset of each data. For the triply SGD algorithm, we are always able to increase the training size until the entire datasets are used. For each sample size of a given dataset, we set a running time budget of $10,000$ second and report the final test accuracy. The results are shown in Figure 2.

Observation 3. *Triply SGD is scalable to large datasets and achieves improved accuracy as the data size increases.*

The experiment on *mnist8m* data also indicates that triply SGD can learn l_p-MKL problem with millions of data points.

7 CONCLUSION

In this paper, we provide a novel extension to doubly SGD for MKL problems so that both the decision functions and the kernel weights can be learned. To achieve this, we develop the triply Stochastic Gradient Descent (triply SGD) algorithm which involves three sources of randomness – the data points, the random features, and the kernels, which was not considered in previous work. We prove that our algorithm has $O(1/t)$ convergence rate. Comparing to several traditional MKL solutions, our experiments show that triply SGD has faster convergence speed and achieved better accuracy. Most importantly, it is possible to learn MKL problems with millions of data points on a normal desktop PC.

Acknowledgments

This work is supported by National Natural Science Foundation of China (grants 61432020, 61472430, 61573191) and Natural Sciences and Engineering Research Council of Canada (NSERC).

References

Bucak S. S., Jin R., Jain A. K. (2014) Multiple kernel learning for visual object recognition: A review. IEEE Transactions on Pattern Analysis and Machine Intelligence 36(7):1354–1369

Crammer K., Singer Y. (2001) On the algorithmic implementation of multiclass kernel-based vector machines. Journal of machine learning research 2(Dec):265–292

Dai B., Xie B., He N., Liang Y., Raj A., Balcan M.-F. F., Song L. (2014) Scalable kernel methods via doubly stochastic gradients. In: Advances in Neural Information Processing Systems, pp. 3041–3049

Gönen M., Alpaydın E. (2011) Multiple kernel learning algorithms. Journal of Machine Learning Research 12(Jul):2211–2268

He K., Zhang X., Ren S., Sun J. (2016) Deep residual learning for image recognition. In: Proceedings of the IEEE Conference on Computer Vision and Pattern Recognition, pp. 770–778

Hsieh C.-J., Si S., Dhillon I. (2014) A divide-and-conquer solver for kernel support vector machines. In: International Conference on Machine Learning, pp. 566–574

Kar P., Karnick H. (2012) Random feature maps for dot product kernels. In: Proceedings of The 15th International Conference on Artificial Intelligence and Statistics(AISTATS)

Kloft M., Brefeld U., Sonnenburg S., Zien A. (2011) Lp-norm multiple kernel learning. Journal of Machine Learning Research 12(Mar):953–997

Krizhevsky A., Sutskever I., Hinton G. E. (2012) Imagenet classification with deep convolutional neural networks. In: Advances in neural information processing systems, pp. 1097–1105

Lanckriet G. R., De Bie T., Cristianini N., Jordan M. I., Noble W. S. (2004) A statistical framework for genomic data fusion. Bioinformatics 20(16):2626–2635

Li C.-L., Póczos B. (2016) Utilize old coordinates: faster doubly stochastic gradients for kernel methods. In: Proceedings of the Thirty-Second Conference on Uncertainty in Artificial Intelligence, AUAI Press, pp. 467–476

Lin M., Chen Q., Yan S. (2013) Network in network. arXiv preprint arXiv:13124400

Lu J., Hoi S. C., Sahoo D., Zhao P. (2015) Budget online multiple kernel learning. arXiv preprint arXiv:151104813

Orabona F., Jie L. (2011) Ultra-fast optimization algorithm for sparse multi kernel learning. In: Proceedings of the 28th International Conference on Machine Learning (ICML-11), pp. 249–256

Orabona F., Jie L., Caputo B. (2012) Multi kernel learning with online-batch optimization. Journal of Machine Learning Research 13(Feb):227–253

Rahimi A., Recht B. (2009) Weighted sums of random kitchen sinks: Replacing minimization with randomization in learning. In: Advances in neural information processing systems, pp. 1313–1320

Rahimi A., Recht B., et al (2007) Random features for large-scale kernel machines. In: Advances in Neural Information Processing Systems

Shalev-Shwartz S., Singer Y., Srebro N., Cotter A. (2011) Pegasos: Primal estimated sub-gradient solver for svm. Mathematical programming 127(1):3–30

Sindhwani V., Rosenberg D. S. (2008) An rkhs for multiview learning and manifold co-regularization. In: Proceedings of the 25th international conference on Machine learning, ACM, pp. 976–983

Sun Z., Ampornpunt N., Varma M., Vishwanathan S. (2010) Multiple kernel learning and the smo algorithm. In: Advances in neural information processing systems, pp. 2361–2369

Williams C. K., Seeger M. (2001) Using the nyström method to speed up kernel machines. In: Advances in neural information processing systems, pp. 682–688

Xie B., Liang Y., Song L. (2015) Scale up nonlinear component analysis with doubly stochastic gradients. In: Advances in Neural Information Processing Systems, pp. 2341–2349

Xu Z., Jin R., Yang H., King I., Lyu M. R. (2010) Simple and efficient multiple kernel learning by group lasso. In: Proceedings of the 27th international conference on machine learning (ICML-10), pp. 1175–1182

Yang J., Sindhwani V., Fan Q., Avron H., Mahoney M. W. (2014) Random laplace feature maps for semigroup kernels on histograms. In: Proceedings of the IEEE Conference on Computer Vision and Pattern Recognition, pp. 971–978

A Supplementary Materials

All our proofs follow the framework of Dai et al (2014).

Lemma 5.2

Proof: Denote $V_i(x) = V_i(x; \mathcal{D}^i, r^i, \omega^i) := [v_t^i \zeta_{r_i,i}(x) - v_t^i \xi_{r_i,i}(x)]$. We have

$$|V_i(x)| \leq |v_t^i|\phi M + |\hat{v}_t^i|\kappa M =$$

$$|a_t^i|[\frac{\phi M}{\psi_i} + \frac{\kappa M}{\hat{\psi}_i}] \leq |a_t^i|(\kappa + \phi)M$$

The last inequality is because $\psi_i \geq 1, \hat{\psi}_i \geq 1$. The rest of the proofs can follow Dai et al (2014) Lemma 7. □

Lemma 5.3

Proof: Now define:

$$g_t := l'(F_t(x_t), y_t)k_{r_t}(x_t, \cdot) + \nu\hat{\psi}_t h_{r_t,t} \tag{32}$$

$$\hat{g}_t := \nabla R_t(h_{r_t}) = \hat{\xi}_{r_t,t} + \nu\hat{\psi}_t h_{r_t,t}$$

$$= l'(H_t(x_t), y_t)k_{r_t}(x_t, \cdot) + \nu\hat{\psi}_t h_{r_t,t} \tag{33}$$

$$\bar{g}_t := \mathbb{E}_{D_t}[\nabla R_t(h_{r_t})] = \mathbb{E}_{D_t}[\hat{g}_t]$$

$$= \mathbb{E}_{D_t}[l'(H_t(x_t), y_t)k_{r_t}(x_t, \cdot)] + \nu\hat{\psi}_t h_{r_t,t} \tag{34}$$

Denote $A_t = ||H_t - F_*||^2_{\mathcal{H}}$. We have $A_{t+1} =$

$$||H_t - F_* - \eta_t g_t||^2_{\mathcal{H}} = A_t + \eta_t^2 ||g_t||^2_{\mathcal{H}} - 2\eta_t \langle H_t - F_*, g_t \rangle_{\mathcal{H}}$$

$$= A_t + \eta_t^2 ||g_t||^2_{\mathcal{H}} - 2\eta_t \langle H_t - F_*, \bar{g}_t \rangle_{\mathcal{H}}$$

$$+2\eta_t \langle H_t - F_*, \bar{g}_t - \hat{g}_t \rangle_{\mathcal{H}} + 2\eta_t \langle H_t - F_*, \hat{g}_t - g_t \rangle_{\mathcal{H}} \tag{35}$$

Since (11) is $\frac{\nu(p-1)}{2p}$-strongly convex, the optimality condition gives:

$$\langle H_t - F_*, \bar{g}_t \rangle_{\mathcal{H}} \geq \frac{\nu(p-1)}{2p} ||H_t - F_*||^2_{\mathcal{H}} \tag{36}$$

thus, $A_{t+1} \leq$

$$(1 - \frac{\eta_t \nu(p-1)}{p})A_t + \eta_t^2 ||g_t||^2_{\mathcal{H}} - 2\eta_t \langle H_t - F_*, \bar{g}_t \rangle_{\mathcal{H}}$$

$$+2\eta_t \langle H_t - F_*, \bar{g}_t - \hat{g}_t \rangle_{\mathcal{H}} + 2\eta_t \langle H_t - F_*, \hat{g}_t - g_t \rangle_{\mathcal{H}} \tag{37}$$

denote

$$\mathcal{M}_t = ||g_t||^2_{\mathcal{H}} \tag{38}$$

$$\mathcal{N}_t = \langle H_t - F_*, \bar{g}_t - \hat{g}_t \rangle_{\mathcal{H}} \tag{39}$$

$$\mathcal{R}_t = \langle H_t - F_*, \hat{g}_t - g_t \rangle_{\mathcal{H}} \tag{40}$$

which will be separately bounded in the Lemma A.1. Denote $e_t = \mathbb{E}_{\mathcal{D}^{t-1}, r^{t-1}, \omega^{t-1}}[A_t]$, using the bounds derived in Lemma A.1, we have

$$e_{t+1} \leq (1 - \frac{\eta_t \nu(p-1)}{p})e_t + \kappa M^2 \gamma_t^2 (1 + \nu c_t)^2$$

$$+2\gamma_t \kappa^{1/2} L B_{1,t} \sqrt{e_t} \tag{41}$$

Applying $|a_t^i| \leq \frac{\theta}{t}$ (Lemma 8(1) in Dai et al (2014)). We have $c_t =$

$$\sqrt{\sum_{i,j \in I^{t-1}(r_t)} |\hat{v}_{t-1}^i||\hat{v}_{t-1}^j|} = \sqrt{\sum_{i,j \in I^{t-1}(r_t)} \frac{|a_{t-1}^i||a_{t-1}^j|}{\hat{\psi}_i \hat{\psi}_j}}$$

$$\leq \sqrt{(\frac{\theta}{t-1})^2 \sum_{i,j \in I^{t-1}(r_t)} \frac{1}{\hat{\psi}_i \hat{\psi}_j}}$$

$$\leq \sqrt{(\frac{\theta}{t-1})^2 \cdot [C^{t-1}(r_t)]^2} = \theta \frac{C^{t-1}(r_t)}{t-1} \leq \theta \tag{42}$$

where we have used the fact that $\hat{\psi}_i \geq 1$, and $\sum_{i \in I^{t-1}(r_t)} 1 = C^{t-1}(r_t)$, i.e., the number of iterations up to $t-1$ that kernel r_t gets selected.

From Lemma 5.2 and $\sum_{i=1}^t |a_t^i|^2 \leq \frac{\theta^2}{t}$ (Lemma 8(1) in Dai et al (2014)), we have

$$B_{1,t}^2 \leq 4M^2(\kappa + \phi)^2 \frac{\theta^2}{t-1} \tag{43}$$

Plug it into (37) together with

$$\frac{\gamma_t}{C_q} \leq \eta_t \leq \gamma_t = \frac{\theta}{t} \tag{44}$$

leads to

$$e_{t+1} \leq (1 - \frac{2\nu'\theta}{t})e_t + \kappa M^2 (\frac{\theta}{t})^2 (1 + \nu\theta)^2$$

$$+2\kappa^{1/2} L \frac{\theta}{t} \sqrt{4M^2(\kappa + \phi)^2 \frac{\theta^2}{t-1}} \sqrt{e_t} \tag{45}$$

where $\nu' = \frac{\nu(p-1)}{2pC_q}$ further rewritten as

$$e_{t+1} \leq (1 - 2\frac{\nu'\theta}{t})e_t + \frac{\beta_2}{t^2} + \frac{\beta_1}{t}\sqrt{\frac{e_t}{t}} \tag{46}$$

with $\beta_1 = 4\sqrt{2}\kappa^{1/2} LM(\kappa + \phi)\theta^2$, $\beta_2 = \kappa M^2(1 + \nu\theta)^2\theta^2$.

Using Lemma 14 of Dai et al (2014), we have

$$e_t \leq \frac{R}{t} \tag{47}$$

where $R = \max\{||F_*||_{\mathcal{H}}, R_0^2\}$,

$$R_0 = \frac{Q_0 + \sqrt{Q_0^2 + (2\nu'\theta - 1)\kappa M^2(1+\nu\theta)^2(\theta)^2}}{(2\nu'\theta - 1)}$$

where $Q_0 = 2\sqrt{2}\kappa^{1/2}LM(\kappa+\phi)\theta^2$. □

The following is an auxiliary lemma used in the above proof, which follows the logic flow of Lemma 10 in Dai et al (2014).

Lemma A.1 *(1)* $\eta_t^2\mathcal{M}_t \leq \kappa M^2(1+\nu c_t)^2$ *where* $c_t = \sqrt{\sum_{i,j\in I^{t-1}(r_t)} |\hat{v}_{t-1}^i||\hat{v}_{t-1}^j|}$ *for* $t \geq 2$ *and* $\forall r, c_1(r) = 0$*;*
(2) $\mathbb{E}_{\mathcal{D}^t,r^t,\omega^t}[\eta_t\mathcal{N}_t] \leq 0$*;*
(3) $\mathbb{E}_{\mathcal{D}^t,r^t,\omega^t}[\eta_t\mathcal{R}_t] \leq \kappa^{1/2}LB_{1,t}\sqrt{\mathbb{E}_{\mathcal{D}^{t-1},\omega^{t-1}}[A_t]}$, *where* $B_{1,t}^2 := 4M^2(\kappa+\phi)^2\sum_{i=1}^{t-1}|\hat{a}_t^i|^2$ *for* $t \geq 2$ *and* $B_{1,1} = 0$*;*

Proof: (1) $\mathcal{M}_t = ||g_t||_{\mathcal{H}}^2 = ||\xi_{r_t,t} + \nu\hat{\psi}_t h_{r_t,t}||_{\mathcal{H}}^2$

$$\leq (||\xi_{r_t,t}||_{\mathcal{H}} + \nu\hat{\psi}_t||h_{r_t,t}||_{\mathcal{H}})^2$$

where

$$||\xi_{r_t,t}||_{\mathcal{H}} = ||l'(F_t(x_t),y_t)k_{r_t}(x_t,\cdot)||_{\mathcal{H}} \leq \kappa^{1/2}M$$

and $||h_{r_t,t}||_{\mathcal{H}}^2$ equals

$$\langle \sum_{i\in I^{t-1}(r_t)} \hat{u}_{t-1}^i(r_t)\xi_{r_t,i}(\cdot), \sum_{j\in I^{t-1}(r_t)} \hat{u}_{t-1}^j(r_t)\xi_{r_t,i}(\cdot)\rangle_{\mathcal{H}}$$

$$= \sum_{i\in I^{t-1}(r_t)}\sum_{j\in I^{t-1}(r_t)} \Big[\hat{u}_{t-1}^i(r_t)\hat{u}_{t-1}^j(r_t)\cdot$$

$$l'(\sum_{s=1}^m f_s(x_i), y_i)l'(\sum_{s=1}^m f_s(x_j), y_j)k_{r_t}(x_i,x_j)\Big]$$

$$\leq \kappa M^2 \sum_{i\in I^{t-1}(r_t)}\sum_{j\in I^{t-1}(r_t)} |\hat{u}_{t-1}^i(r_t)|\cdot|\hat{u}_{t-1}^j(r_t)|$$

$$= \kappa M^2 \sum_{i\in I^{t-1}(r_t)}\sum_{j\in I^{t-1}(r_t)} |\hat{v}_{t-1}^i||\hat{v}_{t-1}^j|$$

thus

$$\eta_t^2\mathcal{M}_t \leq \kappa M^2\eta_t^2(1+\nu\hat{\psi}_t c_t)^2$$
$$= \kappa M^2(\eta_t + \nu\gamma_t c_t)^2 \leq \gamma_t^2\kappa M^2(1+\nu c_t)$$

(2) because $\mathcal{N}_t = \langle H_t - F_*, \bar{g}_t - \hat{g}_t\rangle_{\mathcal{H}}$, thus

$$\mathbb{E}_{\mathcal{D}^t,r^t,\omega^t}[\eta_t\mathcal{N}_t] \leq \mathbb{E}_{\mathcal{D}^t,r^t,\omega^t}[\gamma_t\mathcal{N}_t]$$

$$\leq \gamma_t\cdot\mathbb{E}_{\mathcal{D}^{t-1},r^t,\omega^t}\left[\mathbb{E}_{\mathcal{D}^t}[\langle H_t - F_*, \bar{g}_t - \hat{g}_t\rangle_{\mathcal{H}}|\mathcal{D}^{t-1}, r^t, \omega^t]\right]$$

$$= \gamma_t\cdot\mathbb{E}_{\mathcal{D}^{t-1},r^t,\omega^t}\left[\langle H_t - F_*, \mathbb{E}_{\mathcal{D}^t}[\bar{g}_t - \hat{g}_t]\rangle_{\mathcal{H}}|\mathcal{D}^{t-1}, r^t, \omega^t\right]$$

$$= 0$$

(3) because $\mathcal{R}_t = \langle H_t - F_*, \hat{g}_t - g_t\rangle_{\mathcal{H}}$, then

$$\mathbb{E}_{\mathcal{D}^t,r^t,\omega^t}[\mathcal{R}_t] = \mathbb{E}_{\mathcal{D}^t,r^t,\omega^t}\left[\langle H_t - F_*, \hat{g}_t - g_t\rangle_{\mathcal{H}}\right]$$

$$= \mathbb{E}_{\mathcal{D}^t,r^t,\omega^t}\big[\langle H_t - F_*, [l'(F_t(x_t),y_t)$$
$$-l'(H_t(x_t),y_t)]k_{r_t}(x_t,\cdot)\rangle_{\mathcal{H}}\big]$$

$$\leq \mathbb{E}_{\mathcal{D}^t,r^t,\omega^t}\big[|l'(F_t(x_t),y_t) - l'(H_t(x_t),y_t)|$$
$$\cdot||k_{r_t}(x_t,\cdot)||_{\mathcal{H}}\cdot||H_t - F_*||_{\mathcal{H}}\big]$$

$$\leq \kappa^{1/2}L\cdot\mathbb{E}_{\mathcal{D}^t,r^t,\omega^t}\left[|F_t(x_t) - H_t(x_t)|\cdot||H_t - F_*||_{\mathcal{H}}\right]$$

$$\leq \kappa^{1/2}L\sqrt{\mathbb{E}_{\mathcal{D}^t,r^t,\omega^t}|F_t(x_t) - H_t(x_t)|^2}$$
$$\cdot\sqrt{\mathbb{E}_{\mathcal{D}^t,r^t,\omega^t}||H_t - F_*||_{\mathcal{H}}^2}$$

$$= \kappa^{1/2}LB_{1,t}\sqrt{\mathbb{E}_{\mathcal{D}^{t-1},r^{t-1},\omega^{t-1}}||A_t||_{\mathcal{H}}^2}$$

1st and 3rd inequalities: Cauchy-Schwarz;
2nd inequality: L-Lipschitz of $l'(\cdot,\cdot)$ and $||k_{r_t}(x_t,\cdot)||_{\mathcal{H}} = ||k_{r_t}(x_t,\cdot)||_{\mathcal{H}_r} \leq \kappa$
last step: due to Lemma 5.2 and definition of A_t. Thus

$$\mathbb{E}_{\mathcal{D}^t,r^t,\omega^t}[\eta_t\mathcal{R}_t] \leq \gamma_t\mathbb{E}_{\mathcal{D}^t,r^t,\omega^t}[\mathcal{R}_t]$$

$$\leq \gamma_t\kappa^{1/2}LB_{1,t}\sqrt{\mathbb{E}_{\mathcal{D}^{t-1},r^{t-1},\omega^{t-1}}||A_t||_{\mathcal{H}}^2} \quad (48)$$

□

Coupling Adaptive Batch Sizes with Learning Rates

Lukas Balles
MPI for Intelligent Systems
Tübingen, Germany

Javier Romero*
Body Labs Inc.
New York, NY, USA

Philipp Hennig
MPI for Intelligent Systems
Tübingen, Germany

Abstract

Mini-batch stochastic gradient descent and variants thereof have become standard for large-scale empirical risk minimization like the training of neural networks. These methods are usually used with a constant batch size chosen by simple empirical inspection. The batch size significantly influences the behavior of the stochastic optimization algorithm, though, since it determines the variance of the gradient estimates. This variance also changes over the optimization process; when using a constant batch size, stability and convergence is thus often enforced by means of a (manually tuned) decreasing learning rate schedule.

We propose a practical method for dynamic batch size adaptation. It estimates the variance of the stochastic gradients and adapts the batch size to decrease the variance proportionally to the value of the objective function, removing the need for the aforementioned learning rate decrease. In contrast to recent related work, our algorithm couples the batch size to the learning rate, directly reflecting the known relationship between the two. On popular image classification benchmarks, our batch size adaptation yields faster optimization convergence, while simultaneously simplifying learning rate tuning. A TensorFlow implementation is available.

1 INTRODUCTION

In parametric machine learning models, like logistic regression or neural networks, the performance of a parameter vector $w \in \mathbb{R}^d$ on datum x is quantified by a loss function $\ell(w; x)$. Assuming the data comes from a distribution $x \sim p$, the goal is to minimize the expected loss, or *risk*,

$$\mathcal{R}(w) = \mathbf{E}_{x\sim p}[\ell(w; x)]. \tag{1}$$

We consider *empirical risk minimization* tasks of the form

$$\min_{w\in\mathbb{R}^d} F(w) = \frac{1}{M}\sum_{i=1}^{M} \ell(w; x_i), \tag{2}$$

where the risk is approximated using a training set $\{x_1, \dots, x_M\}$ of data sampled (approximately) from p. Typical optimization algorithms used to minimize (2) repeatedly evaluate the gradient

$$\nabla F(w) = \frac{1}{M}\sum_{i=1}^{M} \nabla\ell(w; x_i). \tag{3}$$

For large-scale problems where M and/or d are large, it is inefficient or impossible to evaluate the exact gradient (3), and one typically resorts to stochastic gradients by randomly drawing a mini-batch $\mathcal{B} \subset \{1, \dots, M\}$, $|\mathcal{B}| = m \ll M$, at each step of the optimization algorithm and using the gradient approximation

$$g(w) = \frac{1}{m}\sum_{i\in\mathcal{B}} \nabla\ell(w; x_i). \tag{4}$$

The simplest, but still widely used, stochastic optimization algorithm is stochastic gradient descent (SGD, Robbins & Monro, 1951), which updates

$$w_{k+1} = w_k - \alpha_k g(w_k), \tag{5}$$

where $\alpha_k \in \mathbb{R}_+$ is the step size parameter, often called *learning rate* in the machine learning context. Variants of SGD include ADAGRAD (Duchi et al., 2011), ADADELTA (Zeiler, 2012), and ADAM (Kingma & Ba, 2015). We restrict our considerations to SGD in this paper.

* Work done while at MPI for Intelligent Systems.

1.1 THE EFFECT OF THE BATCH SIZE

If i is drawn uniformly at random from $\{1, \ldots, M\}$, $\nabla \ell_i(w) = \nabla \ell(w; x_i)$ is a random variable with mean

$$\mathbf{E}[\nabla \ell_i(w)] = \frac{1}{M} \sum_{i=1}^{M} \nabla \ell_i(w) = \nabla F(w), \tag{6}$$

and covariance matrix

$$\Sigma(w) := \mathbf{cov}\left[\nabla \ell_i(w)\right] = \frac{1}{M} \sum_{i=1}^{M} (\nabla \ell_i(w) - \nabla F(w))(\nabla \ell_i(w) - \nabla F(w))^T. \tag{7}$$

Likewise, a stochastic gradient $g(w)$ computed on a randomly-drawn mini-batch $\mathcal{B}$ is a random variable with mean $\nabla F(w)$. Assuming that it is composed of m samples drawn independently with replacement, its covariance matrix is

$$\mathbf{cov}[g(w)] = \frac{\Sigma(w)}{m} \tag{8}$$

and, by the Central Limit Theorem, $g(w)$ is approximately normally distributed:

$$g(w) \sim \mathcal{N}\left(\nabla F(w), \frac{\Sigma(w)}{m}\right). \tag{9}$$

When sampling without replacement, as is usually done in practice, the same holds *approximately* as long as $m \ll M$.

In practice, the batch size m is often set to a fixed value, which is chosen ad hoc or by simple empirical tests. But it is actually a crucial variable, which poses an intricate trade-off that affects the optimizer's performance. On the one hand, the variance of the stochastic gradients *decreases linearly* with m, so small batches give vague gradient information, thus slow convergence in the number of optimization steps. On the other hand, the cost per step *increases linearly* with m. (This assumes that batch sizes are large enough to fully utilize the available parallel computing resources, which can easily be guaranteed by enforcing an appropriate minimal batch size.) While we can thus linearly trade off variance and cost, the gradient variance does *not* linearly affect the performance of the optimizer; its effect depends on the local structure of the objective and interacts with other parameter choices of the optimizer, notably the learning rate. In general, there should thus be an *optimal* batch size that balances these two aspects. Choosing such good batch sizes is an important aspect in the design of a numerical optimizer.

Below, we propose an algorithm that adapts the batch size based on the gradient variance observed by the optimizer at runtime. The exact variance over the entire data set (7) is prohibitively costly to compute, but it can be estimated by the sample variance computed on a mini-batch. As will be described below, we only require the diagonal elements of $\Sigma(w)$, corresponding to the variances of the individual components. These can be estimated by

$$S(w) = \frac{1}{m} \sum_{i \in \mathcal{B}} \nabla \ell_i(w)^{\cdot 2} - g(w)^{\cdot 2} \in \mathbb{R}^d, \tag{10}$$

where $^{\cdot 2}$ signifies an element-wise square.

1.2 NOTATION

The following discussion addresses the choice of batch size for a single SGD step, assuming that we are currently at some arbitrary but fixed point w in parameter space. For notational convenience, we will thus drop w from the notation and write $F = F(w)$, $\nabla F = \nabla F(w)$, et cetera.

2 RELATED WORK

The dynamic adaption of batch sizes has already attracted attention in other recent works. Friedlander & Schmidt (2012) derive decreasing series of bounds on the gradient variance that provably yield fast convergence rates with a *constant* learning rate, showing that an increasing batch size can replace a decreasing learning rate. To realize these bounds in practice, they propose to increase the batch size by a pre-specified constant factor in each iteration, without adaptation to (an estimate of) the gradient variance.

The prior works closest to ours in spirit are by Byrd et al. (2012) and De et al. (2017), who propose to adapt the batch size based on variance estimates. Their criterion is based on the observation that $-g$ is a descent direction if

$$\|g - \nabla F\| \leq \theta \|g\|, \quad \text{with} \quad 0 \leq \theta < 1 \tag{11}$$

(proof in Appendix A). While the left-hand side of (11) is of course unknown, one *can* compute its expected square

$$\begin{aligned} \mathbf{E}\left[\|g - \nabla F\|^2\right] &= \sum_{j=1}^{d} \mathbf{E}\left[(g_j - \nabla F_j)^2\right] \\ &= \sum_{j=1}^{d} \frac{\sigma_{jj}^2}{m} = \frac{\text{tr}(\Sigma)}{m}. \end{aligned} \tag{12}$$

Consequently, (11) holds *in expectation* if $\text{tr}(\Sigma)/m \leq \theta^2 \|g\|^2$ or (with equality)

$$m = \frac{1}{\theta^2} \frac{\text{tr}(\Sigma)}{\|g\|^2}. \tag{13}$$

While this is a practical and intuitive method, the "descent direction" criterion is agnostic of the actual step being taken, which depends on the learning rate α in addition to the direction $-g$. Moreover, the method introduces an additional free parameter θ. In this work we strive to alleviate these issues, while the resulting batch size adaptation rule will stay close to (13) in form and spirit.

A somewhat related line of research aims to reduce the variance of stochastic gradients by incorporating gradient information from previous iterations into the current gradient estimate. Notable methods are SVRG (Johnson & Zhang, 2013) and SAGA (Defazio et al., 2014). Both are not mini-batch methods, since they update after gradient evaluations on individual training examples (which are then modified using stored gradient information). However, two recent papers (Harikandeh et al., 2015; Daneshmand et al., 2016) combine these variance-reduced methods with increasing sample sizes, i.e., the effective size of the training set is increased over time. In both, a sample size schedule has to be pre-specified and is not adapted at runtime.

We note that another recent line of work on non-uniform sampling of training samples with the goal of variance reduction (including, but not limited to, Needell et al., 2014; Zhao & Zhang, 2015; Schmidt et al., 2015; Csiba & Richtárik, 2016) is orthogonal to our work, since it is concerned with the composition of batches rather than their size.

More generally, our work fits into a recent effort to automate or simplify the tuning of parameters in stochastic optimization algorithms, most notably the learning rate (Schaul et al., 2013; Mahsereci & Hennig, 2015).

3 COUPLED ADAPTIVE BATCH SIZE

We will cast the problem of finding a "good" batch size as maximizing a lower bound on the expected *gain* per computational cost for an individual optimization step. While the resulting rule is similar in form to (13), it provides a new interpretation and introduces an explicit interaction with the learning rate. This criterion will subsequently be simplified, removing all unknown quantities and free parameters from the equation.

3.1 MAXIMIZING A BOUND ON THE EXPECTED GAIN

We define the *gain* of the SGD step from w to $w_+ = w - \alpha g$ as the drop in function value, $F - F_+$, where $F_+ = F(w_+)$. In order to quantify this gain, we will assume that F has Lipschitz-continuous gradients, i.e., there is a constant $L > 0$ such that

$$\|\nabla F(u) - \nabla F(v)\| \leq L\|u - v\| \quad \forall u, v \in \mathbb{R}^d. \quad (14)$$

This is a standard assumption in the analysis of stochastic optimization algorithms, setting a not overly restrictive bound on how fast the gradient can change when moving in parameter space. As a consequence, the change in F from $v \in \mathbb{R}^d$ to $u \in \mathbb{R}^d$ is bounded (see, e.g., Bottou et al. (2016), Eq. 4.3) by

$$F(u) \leq F(v) + \nabla F(v)^T(u - v) + \frac{L}{2}\|u - v\|^2. \quad (15)$$

Inserting $v = w$ and $u = w_+ = w - \alpha g$ and rearranging yields a lower bound $\mathcal{G}$ on the gain:

$$F - F_+ \geq \mathcal{G} := \alpha \nabla F^T g - \frac{L\alpha^2}{2}\|g\|^2. \quad (16)$$

To derive the expectation of $\mathcal{G}$, recall from Equation (9) that $\mathbf{E}[g] = \nabla F$ and

$$\begin{aligned} \mathbf{E}\left[\|g\|^2\right] &= \sum_{j=1}^{d} \mathbf{E}\left[g_j^2\right] = \sum_{j=1}^{d} \left(\nabla F_j^2 + \frac{\sigma_{jj}^2}{m}\right) \\ &= \|\nabla F\|^2 + \frac{\operatorname{tr}(\Sigma)}{m}, \end{aligned} \quad (17)$$

where we used that, for $X \sim \mathcal{N}(\mu, \sigma^2)$, the second moment is $\mathbf{E}[X^2] = \mu^2 + \sigma^2$. Thus,

$$\mathbf{E}[\mathcal{G}] = \left(\alpha - \frac{L\alpha^2}{2}\right)\|\nabla F\|^2 - \frac{L\alpha^2}{2m}\operatorname{tr}(\Sigma). \quad (18)$$

The first term in (18) is the gain in absence of noise, determined by α and ∇F. It is reduced by a term that depends on the gradient variance and drops with m. We see from (18) that, for an expected descent, $\mathbf{E}[\mathcal{G}] > 0$, we require

$$\alpha < \frac{2\|\nabla F\|^2}{L\left(\|\nabla F\|^2 + \operatorname{tr}(\Sigma)/m\right)}, \quad (19)$$

which exhibits a clear relationship between learning rate and batch size. Small batch sizes require a small learning rate, while larger batch sizes enable larger steps. We will exploit this relationship later on by explicitly coupling the two parameters. As a side note, for zero variance, we recover the well-known condition $\alpha < 2/L$ that guarantees convergence of gradient descent in the deterministic case.

Obviously, the larger m, the larger $\mathbf{E}[\mathcal{G}]$, so that the deterministic case is optimal if we ignore computational cost. Since that cost scales linearly with m, the optimal batch size is the one that maximizes expected gain per cost,

$$\max_m \frac{\mathbf{E}[\mathcal{G}]}{m}. \quad (20)$$

A recent workshop paper (Pirotta & Restelli, 2016) used a similar idea, although on a different quantity (a statistical lower bound on the linearized improvement). In our setting, maximal gain per cost is achieved by (derivation in Appendix A)

$$m = \frac{2L\alpha}{2 - L\alpha} \frac{\operatorname{tr}(\Sigma)}{\|\nabla F\|^2}. \tag{21}$$

3.2 THE CABS CRITERION

The result in (21) poses two practical problems. First, the Lipschitz constant L is an unknown property of the objective function. Even more importantly, it is difficult to reliably and robustly estimate the squared norm of the true gradient $\|\nabla F\|^2$ from a single batch. One might be tempted to replace it with $\|g\|^2$, recovering a criterion similar to (13), but this is not an unbiased estimator for the true gradient norm, as Equation (17) shows. Depending on the noise level and, intriguingly, the batch size m, the second term in (17) can introduce a significant bias.

In an effort to address these practical problems, we propose to replace Eq. (21) with the following simpler rule, which we term the *Coupled Adaptive Batch Size* (CABS):

$$m = \alpha \frac{\operatorname{tr}(\Sigma)}{F}. \tag{22}$$

A formal justification for this simplification will be given in §3.3, but first we want to highlight some intuitive benefits of this batch size adaptation scheme.

A major advantage of the CABS rule, emphasized in its name, is the direct *coupling* of learning rate and batch size. We have established that a large learning rate demands large batches while a smaller, more cautious learning rate can be used with smaller batches (Equation 19). The CABS rule explicitly reflects this known relationship. Using CABS can thus be seen as "tailoring" the noise level to the learning rate the user has chosen. We show experimentally, see §5, that this makes finding a well-performing learning rate easier.

Apart from that, theoretical considerations (Friedlander & Schmidt, 2012) and experimental evidence show that it is beneficial to have small batches in the beginning and larger ones later in the optimization process. Hence, one may want to think of the denominators of (22), (21) and (13) as a measure of "optimization progress". The function value F used in our CABS rule is, by definition, *the* measure for training progress. The norm of the true gradient $\|\nabla F\|^2$ conveys similar information (even though it might be misleading near non-optimal stationary points like saddle points or plateaus), but can not simply be estimated by $\|g\|^2$ as previously noted. We have also investigated unbiased estimators for $\|\nabla F\|^2$ by correcting the bias in $\|g\|^2$ using the variance estimate S, but these turned out to be too unreliable in experiments. Additionally, Equation (17) also shows that using $\|g\|^2$ in the denominator leads to a disadvantageous feedback: larger batches cause $\|g\|^2$ to become smaller in expectation which, in turn, leads to larger batches according to (13) (and the other way round).

Readers who are rightly worried about the change of "unit" or "type" when replacing the gradient norm in (21) with the function value in (22) may find it helpful to consider the units of measure for the quantities in (22). Let $[w]$ and $[F]$ denote the units of the parameters and the objective function, respectively. The gradient has unit $[F]/[w]$ and its variance $[F]^2/[w]^2$. It is a key insight that a well-chosen learning rate has to be driven by quantities with unit $[w]^2/[F]$ (see MacKay (2003) §34.4 for more discussion). If this was not the case, the gradient descent update $-\alpha_k \nabla F(w_k)$ would not be *covariant*, i.e., independent of the units of measure of w and F. It is also evident in Newton's method: in the one-dimensional case, a Newton update step is $-F''(w_k)^{-1}F'(w_k)$, corresponding to a "learning rate" that is given by the inverse second derivative, having unit $[F]/[w]^2$. Putting it all together, the right-hand side of (22) has unit

$$\frac{[w]^2}{[F]} \frac{[F]^2/[w]^2}{[F]} = [1]. \tag{23}$$

Hence, the chosen batch size is invariant under rescaling of the objective.

Lastly, CABS realizes a bound on the gradient variance that is decreasing with the distance to optimality, similar to that in Theorem 2.5 of Friedlander & Schmidt (2012), which they have shown to guarantee convergence of SGD with a constant, non-decreasing learning rate.

3.3 MATHEMATICAL MOTIVATION FOR CABS

For a more systematic motivation for the CABS rule, we will show that it is approximately equal to (21), and hence optimal in the sense of (20), if we assume that F locally has an approximately scalar Hessian, i.e.,

$$\nabla^2 F(w) \approx hI, \quad h > 0. \tag{24}$$

First, note that under this assumption, the Lipschitz constant L is exactly h and the optimal batch size according to (21) becomes

$$m = \frac{2h\alpha}{2 - h\alpha} \frac{\operatorname{tr}(\Sigma)}{\|\nabla F\|^2}. \tag{25}$$

Furthermore, the second-order Taylor expansion of F around w now reads

$$F(u) \approx F(w) + \nabla F(w)^T (u - w) + \frac{h}{2}\|u - w\|^2. \tag{26}$$

We minimize both sides with respect to u. The left-hand side takes on the optimal value F_*. For the right-hand side, we set the gradient with respect to u, $\nabla F(w) + h(u - w)$, to zero, which yields the minimizer $u = -\nabla F(w)/h + w$. Inserting this back into (26) and rearranging yields

$$\|\nabla F(w)\|^2 \approx 2h(F(w) - F_*). \tag{27}$$

That is, we can replace the squared gradient norm with a scaled distance to optimality. Doing so in (25) reads

$$m = \frac{\alpha}{2 - h\alpha} \frac{\text{tr}(\Sigma)}{F - F_*}. \tag{28}$$

We eliminate h from this equation by realizing that, under the scalar Hessian assumption, a good learning rate is $\alpha = 1/h$. It corresponds both to the Newton step, as well as to the optimal constant learning rate $1/L$ for gradient descent, given that (24) holds. Hence, if we assume a well-chosen learning rate with $h\alpha \approx 1$, then Eq. (28) further simplifies to

$$m = \alpha \frac{\text{tr}(\Sigma)}{F - F_*}. \tag{29}$$

Assuming a scalar Hessian is, of course, a substantial simplification. The result can partly be generalized to the less restrictive assumption of μ-strong convexity, under which we still have (see Appendix A)

$$\|\nabla F\|^2 \geq 2\mu(F - F_*), \tag{30}$$

If the problem is well-conditioned in that μ and L are not too far from each other, the above argument carries through as an upper bound on the batch size.

To finally arrive at the CABS rule, we drop F_*. This is based on the assumption of a non-negative loss, which holds for all standard loss functions like least-squares or cross-entropy. In this case, $F \geq F - F_*$, i.e., the function value F is a non-trivial upper bound on the distance to optimality. If the optimum is close to zero, F will be a good proxy for $F - F_*$. If not, which is not uncommon, the denominator of the CABS rule has a small positive offset compared to (29), but this will not fundamentally alter its implications, as long as we do not come too close to the optimum, which is usually the case for even modestly complex problems. The more general form (29) can be used in lieu of (22) if one has access to a tighter lower bound on F_*, e.g., due to prior experience from similar problems. In fact, when the objective function includes an additive regularization term, we suggest to use the unregularized loss as a proxy for $F - F_*$.

4 PRACTICAL IMPLEMENTATION

We outline a practical implementation of the CABS criterion. Obviously, neither F nor tr(Σ) are known exactly at each individual SGD step, but estimates of both quantities can be obtained from a mini-batch. This is straightforward for the objective F. For the variance, we use the estimate S explained in Equation (10). Since S only estimates the diagonal elements of the covariance matrix, it is tr$(\Sigma) \approx \|S\|_1$. Considerations on how to practically compute S can be found in §4.2.

4.1 MECHANICAL DETAILS

We realize the CABS criterion in a predictive manner, meaning that we do *not* find the exact batch size that satisfies (22) in each single optimization step. To achieve such an exact enforcement of their criterion, Byrd et al. (2012) and De et al. (2017) increase the batch size by a small increment whenever the criterion is not satisfied, and only then perform the update. This incremental computation introduces an overhead and, when the increment is small, can lead to under-utilization of computing resources. Instead, we leverage the observation that gradient variance and function value change only slowly from one optimization step to the next, which allows us to use our current estimates of F and tr(Σ) to set the batch size used for the *next* optimization step. It also allows for a smoothing of both quantities over multiple optimization steps. The estimates can be fairly noisy, especially that of tr(Σ) at small batch sizes. We use exponential moving averages (see Algorithm 1) to obtain more robust estimates.

The resulting batch size is rounded to the nearest integer and clipped at minimal and maximal batch sizes. A minimal batch size avoids under-utilization of the computational resources with very small batches and provides additional stability of the algorithm in the small-batch regime. A maximal batch size is necessary due to hardware limitations: In contemporary deep learning, GPU memory limits the number of samples that can be processed at once. Our implementation has such a limit but it was never reached in our experiments. We note in passing that *algorithmic* batch size (the number of training samples used to compute a gradient estimate before updating the parameters) and *computational* batch size (the number of training samples that are processed simultaneously) are in principle independent—a future implementation could split an algorithmic batch into feasible computational batches when necessary, freeing the algorithm from hardware-specific constraints. Algorithm 1 provides pseudo-code.

Algorithm 1 SGD with Coupled Adaptive Batch Size

Require: Learning rate α, initial parameters w_0, number of steps K, batch size bounds $(m_{\text{min}}, m_{\text{max}})$, running average constant $\mu = 0.95$

$w \leftarrow w_0, m \leftarrow m_{\text{min}}, F_{\text{avg}} \leftarrow 0, \xi \leftarrow 0$
for $k = 1, \ldots, K$ **do**
  Draw a mini-batch $\mathcal{B}$ of size m
  $F, g, S \leftarrow$ EVALUATE$(w, \mathcal{B})$
    $w \leftarrow w - \alpha g$
    $\xi \leftarrow \mu\xi + (1-\mu)\|S\|_1$
  $F_{\text{avg}} \leftarrow \mu F_{\text{avg}} + (1-\mu)F$
    $m \leftarrow$ROUND_&_CLIP$(\alpha\xi/F_{\text{avg}}, m_{\text{min}}, m_{\text{max}})$
end for

Note: EVALUATE$(w, \mathcal{B})$ denotes an evaluation of function value $F(w)$, stochastic gradient $g(w)$ and variance estimate $S(w)$ (Eq. 10) using mini-batch $\mathcal{B}$. ROUND_&_CLIP$(m, m_{\text{min}}, m_{\text{max}})$ rounds m to the nearest integer and clips it at the provided minimal and maximal values.

4.2 VARIANCE ESTIMATE

If the individual gradients $\nabla\ell_i$ in the mini-batch are accessible, then S can be computed directly by Eq. (10), adding only the computational cost of squaring and summing the gradients. Unfortunately, these individual gradients are not available in practical implementations of the backpropagation algorithm (Rumelhart et al., 1986) used to compute gradients in the training of neural networks. A complete discussion of this technical issue is beyond the scope of this paper, but we briefly sketch a solution.

Consider a fully-connected layer in a neural network with weight matrix $W_{l+1} \in \mathbb{R}^{n_l \times n_{l+1}}$. During the forward pass, the matrix of activations $A_l \in \mathbb{R}^{m \times n_l}$ (containing the activations for each of the m input training samples) is propagated forward by a matrix multiplication,

$$Z_{l+1} = A_l W_{l+1} \in \mathbb{R}^{m \times n_{l+1}}. \tag{31}$$

Once the backward pass arrives at this layer, the gradient with respect to W_{l+1} is computed as

$$dW_{l+1} = A_l^T dZ_{l+1}. \tag{32}$$

The aggregation of individual gradients is *implicit* in this matrix multiplication. Practical implementations rely on the efficiency of these matrix operations and, even more importantly, it is infeasible to store m individual gradients in memory if the number of parameters d is high.

However, one can similarly compute the *second moment* of the gradients, $\frac{1}{m}\sum_i (\nabla\ell_i)^{\cdot 2}$, that is needed in (10) without giving up efficient batch processing. It is straight-forward to verify that this second moment of gradients with respect to $W^{(l+1)}$ can be computed as

$$\left(A_l^T\right)^{\cdot 2} (dZ_{l+1})^{\cdot 2}. \tag{33}$$

In this form, the computation of the gradient variance adds non-negligible but manageable computational cost. Since it duplicates half of the operations in the backward pass, the additional cost can be pinned down to roughly 25%. This is primarily an implementation issue; the cost could be reduced by implementing special matrix operations to compute (32) and (33) jointly.

5 EXPERIMENTS

We evaluate the proposed batch size adaptation method by training convolutional neural networks (CNNs) on four popular image classification benchmark data sets: MNIST (LeCun et al., 1998), Street View House Numbers (SVHN) (Netzer et al., 2011), as well as CIFAR-10 and CIFAR-100 (Krizhevsky, 2009). While these are small to medium-scale problems by contemporary standards, they exhibit many of the typical difficulties of neural network training. We opted for these benchmarks to keep the computational cost for a *thorough* evaluation of the method manageable (this required approximately 60 training runs per benchmark, see the following section).

5.1 EXPERIMENT DESIGN

We compare against constant batch sizes 16, 32, 64, 128, 256 and 512. To keep the plots readable, we only report results for batch sizes 32, 128 and 512 in the main text; results for the other batch sizes can be found in the supplements. We also compare against a batch size adaptation based on the criterion (13) used in Byrd et al. (2012) and De et al. (2017). Since implementation details differ between these two works, and both combine batch size adaptation with other measures (Newton-CG method in Byrd et al. (2012) and a backtracking line search in De et al. (2017)), we resort to a custom implementation of said criterion. For a fair comparison, we realize it in a similar manner as CABS. That is, we use criterion (13), while keeping the predictive update mechanism for the batch size, the smoothing via exponential moving averages, rounding and clipping exactly as in our CABS implementation described in §4.1 and Algorithm 1. This method will simply be referred to as *Competitor* in the remainder of this section.

During the optimization process, we periodically evaluate the training loss as well as the classification accuracy on a held-out test set. Since each method uses a different batch size, both quantities are tracked as a function of the number of accessed training examples, instead of the

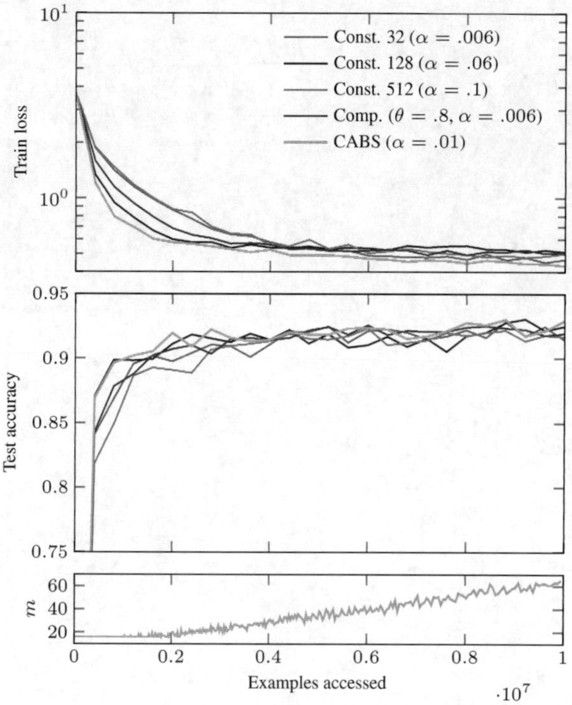

Figure 1: Results for SVHN. Shared horizontal axis indicates the number of examples used for training. Top and middle panel depict evolution of training loss and test accuracy, respectively, color-coded for different batch size methods, each with its optimal learning rate. Bottom panel shows batch size chosen by CABS.

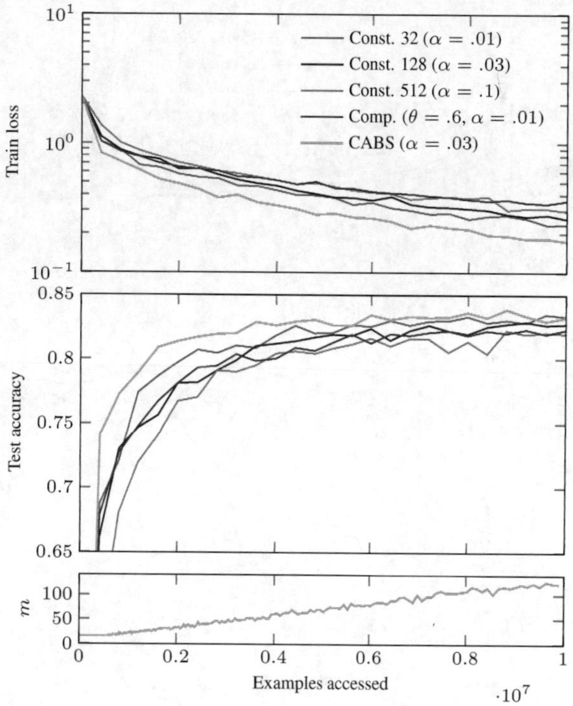

Figure 2: Results for CIFAR-10. Set-up as in Fig. 1.

number of optimization steps. This measure is proportional to wall-clock time up to per-batch overheads that depend on the specific problem and implementation.

The (constant) learning rate for each batch size method was tuned for maximum test accuracy given the fixed budget of accessed training examples. We tried six candidates $\alpha \in \{0.3, 0.1, 0.06, 0.03, 0.01, 0.006\}$; this relevant range has been determined with a few exploratory experiments. In addition to the learning rate, the competitor method has a free parameter θ. De et al. (2017) suggest setting it to 1.0, the highest possible noise tolerance, by default. In our experiments, we found the performance of the method to be fairly sensitive to the choice of θ. We thus tried $\theta \in \{0.6, 0.8, 1.0\}$ and report results for the best-performing choice. For CABS, there is no analogous parameter to tune.

MNIST We start with experiments on the well-known MNIST image classification task of identifying handwritten digits in 28×28 pixel gray scale images. Our network has two convolutional layers with 5×5 filters (32 and 64 filters, respectively) and subsequent max-pooling over 2×2 windows. This is followed by a fully-connected layer with 1024 units. The activation function is ReLU for all layers. The output layer has 10 units with softmax activation and we use cross-entropy loss.

SVHN Next, we train a CNN on the digit classification task of the Street View House Numbers (SVHN) data set. While the task is similar to MNIST, the images are in RGB and larger (32×32). They exhibit real-world views of digits in house numbers, partially with clutter, misalignment and distracting digits at the sides. We train a CNN with two convolutional layers, each with 64 filters of size 5×5 and subsequent max-pooling over 3×3 windows with stride 2. They are followed by two fully-connected layers with 256 and 128 units, respectively. The activation function is ReLU for all layers. The output layer has 10 units with softmax activation and we use cross-entropy loss. We apply L_2-regularization and perform data augmentation operations (random cropping of 24×24 pixel subimages, left-right mirroring, color distortion) on the training inputs.

CIFAR-10 and CIFAR-100 Finally, we train CNNs on the CIFAR-10 and CIFAR-100 data sets, where the task is to classify 32×32 pixel RGB images into one of 10 and 100 object categories, respectively. For CIFAR-10, we crop the images to 24×24 pixels and train a CNN with two convolutional layers, each with 64 filters of size

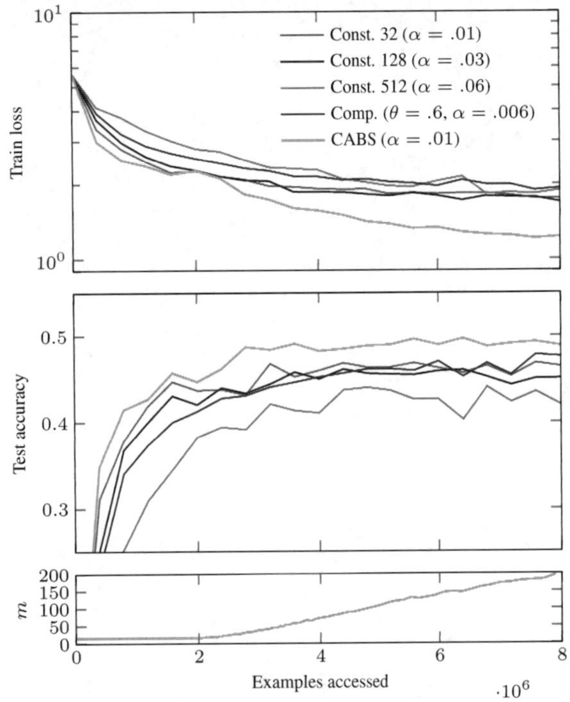

Figure 3: Results for CIFAR-100. Set-up as in Fig. 1.

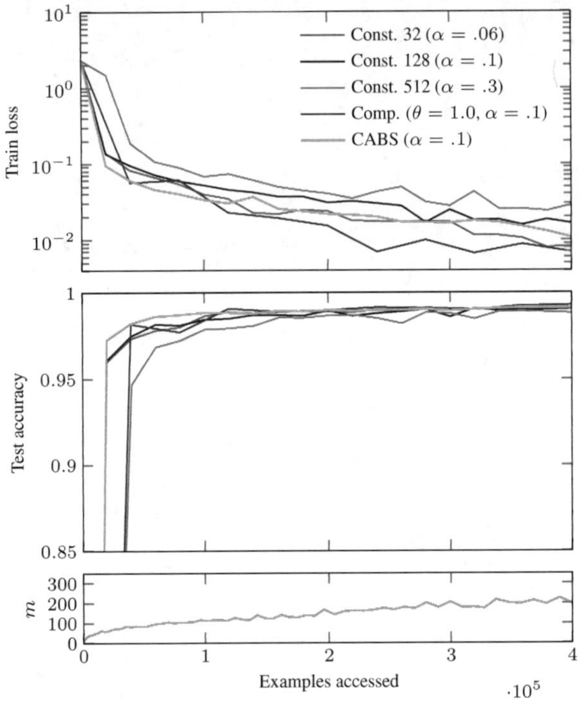

Figure 4: Results for MNIST. Set-up as in Fig. 1.

5x5 and subsequent max-pooling over 3x3 windows with stride 2. They are followed by two fully-connected layers with 384 and 192 units, respectively. The activation function is ReLU for all layers. The output layer has 10 units with softmax activation and we use cross-entropy loss. We perform data augmentation operations (random cropping, left-right mirroring, color distortion) on the training set.

For CIFAR-100, we use the full 32×32 image and add a third convolutional layer (64 filters of size 5×5 followed by max pooling). The fully-connected layers have 512 and 256 units, respectively, and the output layer has 100 units. We add L_2-regularization.

5.2 RESULTS AND DISCUSSION

On SVHN, CIFAR-10 and CIFAR-100 (Figures 1, 2 and 3), CABS yields significantly faster decrease in training loss with the curve contiuously lying below all others. It also achieves the best test set accuracy of all methods on all three problems. While the margin over the second-best method is very small on SVHN, it amounts to a noticeable 0.4 percentage points on CIFAR-10 and even 1.4 points on CIFAR-100.

Surprisingly, on MNIST—the *least* complex of the benchmark problems we investigated—our method is outperformed by the small constant batch size of 32 and the competitor method, which also chooses very small batch sizes throughout. Our method does, however, surpass non-adaptive larger batch sizes (128, 512) in terms of speed and all contenders reach virtually the same test set accuracy on this problem. CABS makes rapid progress initially, but seems to choose unnecessarily large batch sizes later on. The resulting high per-iteration cost evidently can not be compensated by the higher learning rate it enables (.1 for CABS compared to .01 with constant batch size of 32). We conjecture that CABS overestimates the gradient variance due to the homogeneous structure of the MNIST data set; if the distribution of gradients is very closely-centered, outliers in a few coordinate directions lead to comparably high variance estimates.

Overall, CABS outperforms alternative batch size schemes on three out of the four benchmark problems we investigated and the benefits seem to increase with the complexity of the problem (MNIST $\rightarrow$ SVHN $\rightarrow$ CIFAR-10 $\rightarrow$ CIFAR-100). When considering the CABS batch size schedules, depicted in the bottom panels of Figures 1 to 4, a common behavior (with the exception of MNIST) seems to be that CABS uses the minimal batch size (16 in our experiments) for a considerable portion of the training process and increases approximately linearly afterwards.

Finally, we present our findings regarding the sensitivity to the choice of learning rate when using CABS. As

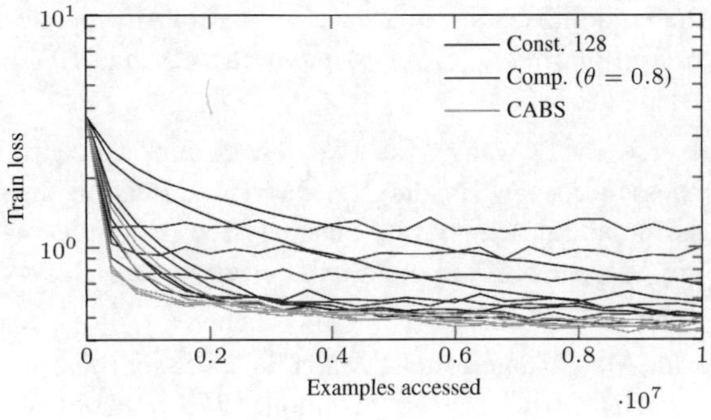

Figure 5: Learning rate sensitivity on SVHN. Families of training loss curves for CABS, Competitor and a constant batch size (color-coded). Each individual curve corresponds to a learning rate $\alpha \in \{.1, .06, .03, .01, .006\}$.

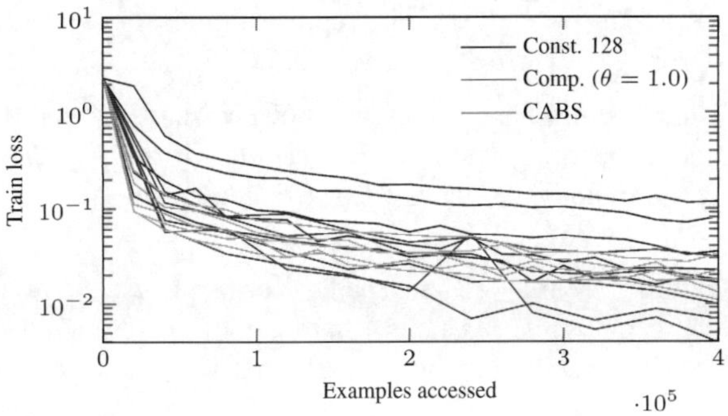

Figure 6: Learning rate sensitivity on MNIST. Set-up as in Fig. 5.

detailed above, the coupling of learning rate and batch size in CABS can be seen as tayloring the noise level to the chosen learning rate. This suggests that the performance of the optimizer should be less sensitive to the choice of learning rate when adapting the batch size with our method. Indeed, this became evident in our experiments by considering the families of training loss curves for various learning rates. Figures 5 and 6 compare a constant batch size, the competitor method and CABS on the SVHN and MNIST benchmark problems, respectively. CABS significantly reduces the dependency of the performance on the learning rate compared to both the constant batch size and the competing adaptive method. In practical applications, this finding could drastically simplify the often tedious process of learning rate tuning.

6 CONCLUSION

We proposed CABS, a practical rule for dynamic batch size adaptation based on estimates of the gradient variance and coupled to the chosen learning rate as well as optimization progress represented by the function value. In our experiments, CABS was able to speed up SGD training in neural networks and simplify the tuning of the learning rate. In contrast to existing methods, it does not introduce any additional free parameters. A TensorFlow[1] implementation of SGD with CABS can be found on `http://github.com/ProbabilisticNumerics/cabs`.

A MATHEMATICAL DETAILS

Proof of Equation (11) By the Cauchy-Schwarz inequality, $\langle g, \nabla F\rangle = \langle g, g\rangle - \langle g, g - \nabla F\rangle \geq \|g\|^2 - \|g\|\|g - \nabla F\| = \|g\|(\|g\| - \|g - \nabla F\|)$. This becomes positive if $\|g - \nabla F\| < \|g\|$.

Solving the Maximization Problem (20) We want to maximize

$$U(m) = \frac{\mathbf{E}[\mathcal{G}]}{m} = \frac{2\alpha - L\alpha^2}{2m}\|\nabla F\|^2 - \frac{L\alpha^2}{2m^2}\text{tr}(\Sigma). \tag{34}$$

Setting the derivative

$$U'(m) = -\frac{2\alpha - L\alpha^2}{2m^2}\|\nabla F\|^2 + \frac{L\alpha^2}{m^3}\text{tr}(\Sigma) \tag{35}$$

to zero and rearranging yields (21).

Proof of Equation (30) The definition of strong convexity is that, for all $w, u \in \mathbb{R}^d$

$$F(u) \geq F(w) + \nabla F(w)^T(u - w) + \frac{\mu}{2}\|u - w\|^2 \tag{36}$$

for $\mu > 0$. From there, the proof is identical to that of Equation (27) in the main text. We minimize both sides of the inequality. The left-hand side has minimal value F_*. The gradient with respect to u of the right-hand side is $\nabla F(w) + \mu(u - w)$. By setting this to zero we find the minimizer $u = -\nabla F(w)/\mu + w$. Inserting this back into (36) and rearranging yields (30). □

References

Bottou, Léon, Curtis, Frank E, and Nocedal, Jorge. Optimization methods for large-scale machine learning. *arXiv preprint arXiv:1606.04838*, 2016.

Byrd, Richard H, Chin, Gillian M, Nocedal, Jorge, and Wu, Yuchen. Sample size selection in optimization methods for machine learning. *Mathematical Programming*, 134(1):127–155, 2012.

Csiba, Dominik and Richtárik, Peter. Importance sampling for minibatches. *arXiv preprint arXiv:1602.02283*, 2016.

[1] `http://tensorflow.org`

Daneshmand, Hadi, Lucchi, Aurelien, and Hofmann, Thomas. Starting small—learning with adaptive sample sizes. In *Proceedings of the 33nd International Conference on Machine Learning (ICML)*, pp. 1463–1471, 2016.

De, Soham, Yadav, Abhay, Jacobs, David, and Goldstein, Tom. Automated inference with adaptive batches. In *Proceedings of the 20th International Conference on Artificial Intelligence and Statistics (AISTATS)*, 2017.

Defazio, Aaron, Bach, Francis, and Lacoste-Julien, Simon. SAGA: A fast incremental gradient method with support for non-strongly convex composite objectives. In *Advances in Neural Information Processing Systems 27*, pp. 1646–1654. 2014.

Duchi, John, Hazan, Elad, and Singer, Yoram. Adaptive subgradient methods for online learning and stochastic optimization. *Journal of Machine Learning Research*, 12(Jul):2121–2159, 2011.

Friedlander, Michael P and Schmidt, Mark. Hybrid deterministic-stochastic methods for data fitting. *SIAM Journal on Scientific Computing*, 34(3):A1380–A1405, 2012.

Harikandeh, Reza, Ahmed, Mohamed Osama, Virani, Alim, Schmidt, Mark, Konečný, Jakub, and Sallinen, Scott. StopWasting my gradients: Practical SVRG. In *Advances in Neural Information Processing Systems 28*, pp. 2251–2259. 2015.

Johnson, Rie and Zhang, Tong. Accelerating stochastic gradient descent using predictive variance reduction. In *Advances in Neural Information Processing Systems 26*, pp. 315–323. 2013.

Kingma, Diederik and Ba, Jimmy. Adam: A method for stochastic optimization. *The International Conference on Learning Representations (ICLR)*, 2015.

Krizhevsky, Alex. Learning multiple layers of features from tiny images. Technical report, University of Toronto, 2009.

LeCun, Yann, Bottou, Léon, Bengio, Yoshua, and Haffner, Patrick. Gradient-based learning applied to document recognition. *Proceedings of the IEEE*, 86 (11):2278–2324, 1998.

MacKay, David JC. *Information Theory, Inference and Learning Algorithms*. Cambridge University Press, 2003.

Mahsereci, Maren and Hennig, Philipp. Probabilistic line searches for stochastic optimization. In *Advances in Neural Information Processing Systems 28*, pp. 181–189. 2015.

Needell, Deanna, Ward, Rachel, and Srebro, Nati. Stochastic gradient descent, weighted sampling, and the randomized Kaczmarz algorithm. In *Advances in Neural Information Processing Systems 27*, pp. 1017–1025. 2014.

Netzer, Yuval, Wang, Tao, Coates, Adam, Bissacco, Alessandro, Wu, Bo, and Ng, Andrew Y. Reading digits in natural images with unsupervised feature learning. *NIPS Workshop on Deep Learning and Unsupervised Feature Learning*, 2011.

Pirotta, Matteo and Restelli, Marcello. Cost-sensitive approach for batch size optimization. *NIPS Workshop on Optimizing the Optimizer*, 2016.

Robbins, Herbert and Monro, Sutton. A stochastic approximation method. *The Annals of Mathematical Statistics*, pp. 400–407, 1951.

Rumelhart, David E., Hinton, Geoffrey E., and Williams, Ronald J. Learning representations by back-propagating errors. *Nature*, 323:533–536, 1986.

Schaul, Tom, Zhang, Sixin, and LeCun, Yann. No more pesky learning rates. In *Proceedings of the 30th International Conference on Machine Learning (ICML)*, pp. 343–351, 2013.

Schmidt, Mark, Babanezhad, Reza, Ahmed, Mohamed Osama, Defazio, Aaron, Clifton, Ann, and Sarkar, Anoop. Non-uniform stochastic average gradient method for training conditional random fields. In *Proceedings of the 18th International Conference on Artificial Intelligence and Statistics (AISTATS)*, 2015.

Zeiler, Matthew D. ADADELTA: An adaptive learning rate method. *arXiv preprint arXiv:1212.5701*, 2012.

Zhao, Peilin and Zhang, Tong. Stochastic optimization with importance sampling for regularized loss minimization. In *Proceedings of The 32nd International Conference on Machine Learning (ICML)*, 2015.

Supplementary Material

Figures 7 to 10 show results for constant batch sizes 16, 64 and 256, which have been omitted from the main text for lack of space.

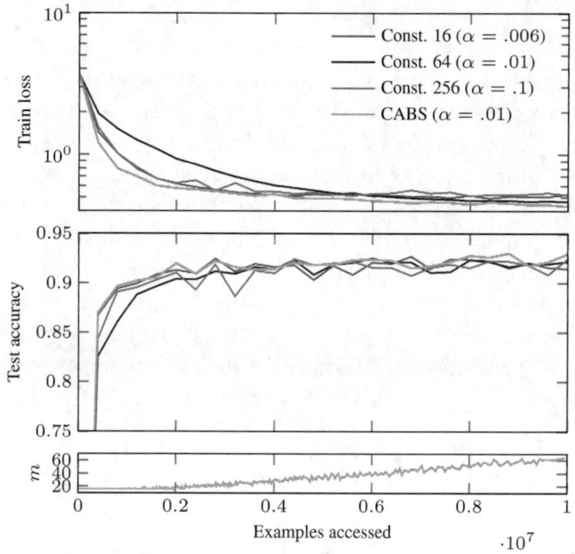

Figure 7: Additional results for SVHN.

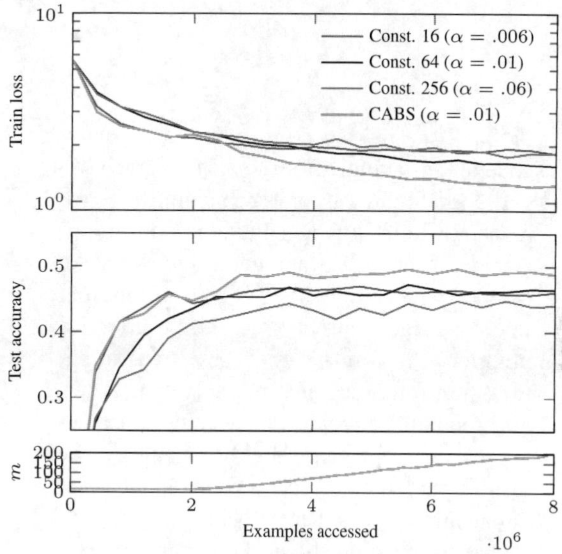

Figure 9: Additional results for CIFAR-100.

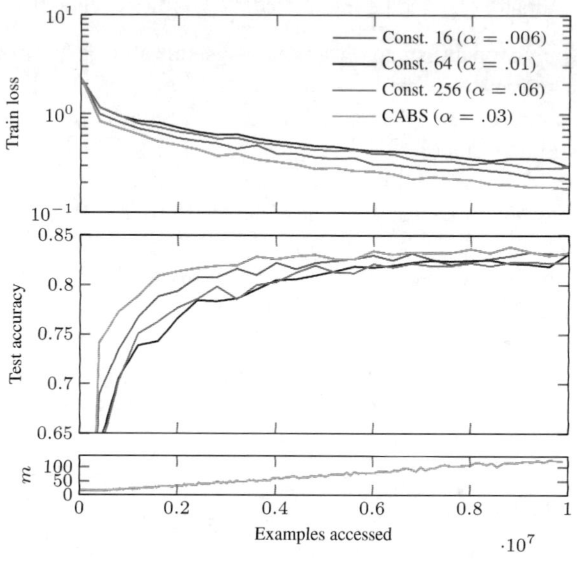

Figure 8: Additional results for CIFAR-10.

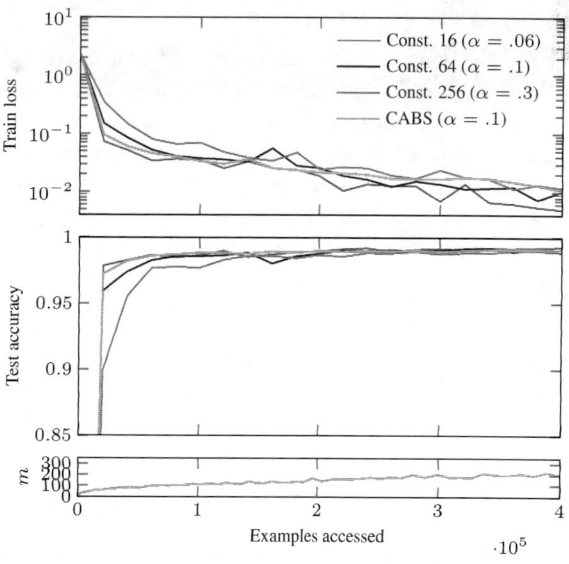

Figure 10: Additional results for MNIST.

Composing inference algorithms as program transformations

Robert Zinkov
Indiana University
Bloomington, IN 47408 USA
zinkov@iu.edu

Chung-chieh Shan
Indiana University
Bloomington, IN 47408 USA
ccshan@indiana.edu

Abstract

Probabilistic inference procedures are usually coded painstakingly from scratch, for each target model and each inference algorithm. We reduce this effort by generating inference procedures from models automatically. We make this code generation modular by decomposing inference algorithms into reusable program-to-program transformations. These transformations perform exact inference as well as generate probabilistic programs that compute expectations, densities, and MCMC samples. The resulting inference procedures are about as accurate and fast as other probabilistic programming systems on real-world problems.

1 INTRODUCTION

Writing inference algorithms for probabilistic models is tedious and error-prone. Conceptually, these algorithms are combinations of simpler operations, such as computing the density of a distribution at a given point. So it is unfortunate that these algorithms are traditionally implemented from scratch. In this paper, we show how to describe these building blocks in code, so that they need not be rewritten for every new inference algorithm or model.

We contribute the first method for composing multiple inference algorithms over the same model, even exact and approximate ones over the same factor. Our approach is to express inference in terms of operations that transform one probabilistic program into another. We use probabilistic programs to represent distributions, though our approach is compatible with other representations such as factor graphs. The goal of our transformations is to turn a program that denotes a model into another program that, when interpreted to draw a weighted sample, is equivalent to the desired inference algorithm.

Because the output of an inference transformation is still a probabilistic program, we can apply further inference transformations to the program. In this way, we can subject a single model to multiple inference methods without coding them from scratch. We thus reduce the informal problem of combining inference methods to the formal and more automatable problem of composing program transformations. In particular, approximate inference methods can be composed with taking advantage of exact mathematical equivalences such as conjugacy.

2 MOTIVATION AND RELATED WORK

Developing inference algorithms that work on a variety of models has long been a goal of probabilistic inference, including graphical models and probabilistic programming. The composability of inference algorithms has unfortunately lagged behind the composability of models.

Many probabilistic programming systems allow a choice of inference methods, both exact and approximate. For example, the probabilistic language Church (Goodman et al. 2008) has many interpreters, each of which implements a different inference method. Systems such as Figaro, Factorie, Anglican and Wolfe (Pfeffer 2009; McCallum et al. 2008; Wood et al. 2014; Riedel et al. 2014) also allow adding inference methods, as new code in the host language where the systems are embedded. However, the end result of applying these inference methods is behavior or code in a different language, no longer a probabilistic program. Thus, it is difficult in these systems to apply one method to the result of another method.

More similar to our approach is Ścibior et al.'s (2015; 2016). Like us, they express and compose inference methods as transformations that produce probabilistic programs in the same language. Thus for example they reuse Sequential Monte Carlo to implement Particle Independent MH. But because their probabilistic language reuses many primitives from the host language Haskell, their transformations cannot inspect most of the input code, notably deterministic computations and code under a binding. In contrast, we can perform exact inference (Section 5), we can compute densities and conditional distributions (Section 4.3) in the face of deterministic dependencies, and we can generate MH samplers (Section 4.5) using a variety of proposal distributions.

So in general, transformations need to take programs as input as well as produce them as output in order to support the variety of inference composition found in the literature. To illustrate the need and the variety, below we recall some patterns of inference composition where we want to *reuse* existing implementations in ways unsupported by existing systems such as those named above.

Sometimes, we apply approximate inference to a model, then post-process the results using exact inference. For example, a popular way to perform inference for latent Dirichlet allocation (LDA) is to use Gibbs sampling (Griffiths and Steyvers 2004) to infer topic markers for each word, then infer from these topic markers the exact distribution on words given each topic.

Other times, we apply exact inference to parts of our model, and use an approximate method for the rest. As an example, Hughes et al. (2015) develop an inference algorithm for hierarchical Dirichlet processes that samples the truncation dictating the number of topics then performs variational inference for the other model parameters. This inference combination requires that sampling a truncation still leave in place a representation on which we can perform variational inference.

Another composition pattern emerges from recent work on parallelizing an inference algorithm to run on multiple machines (Neiswanger et al. 2014; Xu et al. 2014; Gelman et al. 2014). The pattern is to transform a posterior distribution for a parameter given the data into a model that lets us infer noisy versions of the parameter given subsets of the data. We then combine these noisy parameter estimates to infer the underlying parameter.

Finally, given a linear sequential model, we often want to predict future states of the system and the dynamics that govern them. Given the dynamics, for systems like Kalman filters, we may use exact inference to derive the state transition functions in closed form. Learning the dynamics, on the other hand, is usually treated as an approximate inference problem where we sample different possible dynamics given some observed states. This joint learning and exact inference again composes two inference algorithms. Section 6.1 shows our inference composition at work in a tiny instance of this case. We illustrate our approach using this example in Section 3.

3 EXAMPLE OF INFERENCE COMPOSITION

We illustrate our program-transformation approach to inference composition using a simple linear dynamical system. Our model below defines a joint distribution:

$$\begin{aligned}
\text{noise}_T &\sim \text{Uniform}(3,8)\\
\text{noise}_E &\sim \text{Uniform}(1,4)\\
x_1 \mid \text{noise}_T &\sim \text{Normal}(0,\text{noise}_T)\\
m_1 \mid x_1,\text{noise}_E &\sim \text{Normal}(x_1,\text{noise}_E)\\
x_2 \mid x_1,\text{noise}_T &\sim \text{Normal}(x_1,\text{noise}_T)\\
m_2 \mid x_2,\text{noise}_E &\sim \text{Normal}(x_2,\text{noise}_E)
\end{aligned}$$

We would like to draw samples from the posterior distribution over noise_T and noise_E given observations m_1 and m_2, using a Metropolis-Hastings (MH) sampler.

We start by representing the model in our language:

```
kalman =
 noiseT <~ Uniform(3, 8);
 noiseE <~ Uniform(1, 4);
 x1     <~ Normal( 0, noiseT);
 m1     <~ Normal(x1, noiseE);
 x2     <~ Normal(x1, noiseT);
 m2     <~ Normal(x2, noiseE);
 Dirac(((m1, m2), (noiseT, noiseE)))
```

The use of `Dirac` at the bottom shows that this distribution ranges over pairs of pairs of reals.

We first apply the *disintegration* transformation to get another program. As detailed in Section 4.3, disintegration takes as input a joint distribution and produces a program representing a family of posterior distributions. The new program is a function from the observations to the posterior distribution. For example, disintegrating `kalman` produces the program `kalman2` below. It takes as input `(m1, m2)` and returns the distribution over `(noiseT, noiseE)` given those values for `m1` and `m2`.

```
kalman2 = Lam((m1,m2),
 noiseT <~ Uniform(3, 8);
 noiseE <~ Uniform(1, 4);
 x1     <~ Normal( 0, noiseT);
 x2     <~ Normal(x1, noiseT);
 Weight( exp(-(m2-x2)^2/(2*noiseE^2))
         /noiseE/sqrt(2*pi)
       * exp(-(m1-x1)^2/(2*noiseE^2))
         /noiseE/sqrt(2*pi)
       , (noiseT, noiseE) ))
```

The use of `Lam` at the top and `Weight` at the bottom shows that this is a function from pairs of reals `(m1, m2)` to measures over pairs of reals `(noiseT, noiseE)`.

The next step is to apply the *simplification* transformation to `kalman2` to get `kalman3`.

```
kalman3 = Lam((m1,m2),
 noiseT <~ Uniform(3, 8);
 noiseE <~ Uniform(1, 4);
 Weight(P, (noiseT, noiseE)))
```

This program is equivalent to `kalman2`, except the simplification transformation has symbolically integrated out the `Normal`-distributed random variables `x1` and `x2` and replaced them by an observation likelihood in closed form, which we elide above as P.

We next apply to `kalman3` another program transformation we call *mh*, which implements MH sampling. The mh transformation takes as input two programs. The first program represents a proposal distribution, or more precisely a function from the current sample to a distribution over proposed samples. Here we use a proposal distribution that with equal probability resamples one of `noiseT` and `noiseE` while keeping the other fixed:

```
proposal = Lam((noiseT, noiseE),
 Superpose((1/2, n <~ Uniform(3, 8);
                 Dirac((n, noiseE))),
           (1/2, n <~ Uniform(1, 4);
                 Dirac((noiseT, n)))))
```

The second input to the mh transformation represents the target distribution. In this example, it is the part of `kalman3` above after the top line `Lam((m1,m2),`. From these inputs, the mh transformation computes a symbolic formula for the MH acceptance ratio and embeds it in a program representing a transition kernel. The new program, `kalman4` below, is a function from the current sample to a distribution over pairs of proposed samples and acceptance ratios:

```
kalman4 = Lam((noiseT, noiseE),
 proposed <~ Superpose(
   (1/2, n <~ Uniform(3, 8);
         Dirac((n, noiseE))),
   (1/2, n <~ Uniform(1, 4);
         Dirac((noiseT, n)))),
 Dirac((proposed, A)))
```

The elided part A is a symbolic formula that computes the acceptance ratio using the current sample `(noiseT, noiseE)` and the sample `proposed` by the `Superpose`. This acceptance ratio can then be used to decide whether to accept or reject the `proposed`.

We then perform further optimizations on `kalman4`, including algebraic simplifications and rewriting the program to use fewer <~s. We describe in more detail the kinds of optimizations we perform in Section 5. The resulting program, `kalman5`, has the following structure:

```
kalman5 = Lam((noiseT, noiseE),
 Superpose(
  (1/2, n <~ Uniform(3, 8);
        Dirac(((n, noiseE), A_T))),
  (1/2, n <~ Uniform(1, 4);
        Dirac(((noiseT, n), A_E)))))
```

The elided parts A_T and A_E are algebraically simplified formulas for the acceptance ratio in each of the two cases.

Finally we feed this last program `kalman5` to a sampler (Algorithm 1). Given an observation and a current sample, this sampler produces a proposed sample and the MH acceptance ratio of that sample.

```
sample(App(App(kalman5, (0,1)),(5,2)),
       [])
>>> (((5,1.6811397),0.7924639),1.0)
```

In the command above, `(0,1)` is the observation, and `(5,2)` is the current sample. In the output above, `(5,1.6811397)` is the proposed sample, and `0.7924639` is its acceptance ratio.

4 INFERENCE METHODS AS PROGRAM TRANSFORMATIONS

To compose inference methods, we pose them as transformations of one probabilistic program into another. We then achieve the desired inference method for the former program by applying a simpler inference method, such as exact inference or weighted sampling, to the latter program. For example, in Section 3 we feed a program to disintegration (Section 4.3), then mh (Section 4.5), then simplification (Section 5), and finally sampling. Only in the final sampling step is any random choice made!

We first define our probabilistic language, then describe various program transformations that work in concert.

4.1 LANGUAGE DESCRIPTION

Below is our core grammar of probabilistic programs:

$$
\begin{aligned}
e \;::=\;& x \mid 1 \mid e-e \mid e<e \mid \texttt{exp}(e) \mid \texttt{If}(e,e,e) \mid \ldots \\
\mid\;& \texttt{Sum}(e,e,x,e) \mid \texttt{Int}(e,e,x,e) \\
\mid\;& \texttt{Lam}(x,e) \mid \texttt{App}(e,e) \mid (e,e) \mid e\texttt{[0]} \mid e\texttt{[1]} \\
\mid\;& \texttt{Uniform}(e,e) \mid \texttt{Normal}(e,e) \\
\mid\;& \texttt{Gamma}(e,e) \mid \texttt{Weight}(e,e) \\
\mid\;& \texttt{Categorical}((e,e),\ \ldots) \\
\mid\;& \texttt{Superpose}((e,e),\ \ldots) \mid x \mathrel{<\!\sim} e\,;\,e
\end{aligned}
$$

The first line of this grammar says that our language includes ordinary programming support for variables, math, and `If`. The second line adds primitives to represent `Sum`mation and `Int`egration, used in Section 4.2. The third line adds functions and tuples.

The remainder of the grammar is what makes our language probabilistic: we add primitives that represent and compose measures. To start with, `Uniform(1,2)` represents the uniform distribution over real numbers between 1 and 2, and `Normal(3,4)` represents the normal distribution with mean 3 and standard deviation 4.

`Weight(1,8)` represents the probability distribution that assigns its entire probability mass 1 to the single outcome 8. We write `Dirac(8)` as syntactic sugar for it. In contrast, `Weight(0.7,8)` represents the measure, or unnormalized distribution, that assigns the probability 0.7 to the single outcome 8. This primitive lets our language represent (unnormalized) measures in general, not just (normalized) probability distributions. This expressivity lets us separately reuse a transformation that produces an unnormalized measure (Section 4.3) and a transformation that subsequently normalizes a measure (Section 4.4). Also, `Weight` lets us represent a distribution by combining a base measure and a density function.

`Categorical` represents the categorical distribution with a sequence of zero or more pairs. The first element of each pair is the probability of selecting the outcome that is the second element of the pair. If the first elements of the pairs do not sum to 1, they are normalized.

`Superpose` is like `Categorical`, except it does not normalize, so it can represent measures in general. We can define `Superpose` in terms of `Categorical` and `Weight`, but it is actually more convenient to define `Weight` and `Categorical` in terms of `Superpose`.

The final primitive `<~` (pronounced "bind") composes two distributions `e1` and `e2`. The second distribution `e2` may depend on the outcome `x` of `e1`. The outcome of the composed distribution `x<~e1;e2` is the outcome of `e2`. This primitive lets our language represent sequential and hierarchical models. A simple example is this model:

$$x \sim \text{Uniform}(0,2) \qquad y|x \sim \text{Uniform}(x,3)$$

We write the marginal distribution over y as

```
x <~ Uniform(0, 2); Uniform(x, 3)
```

and the joint distribution over (x, y) as

```
x <~ Uniform(0, 2);
y <~ Uniform(x, 3); Dirac((x,y))
```

To make the semantics of our language more concrete, Algorithm 1 shows a sampler that takes a probabilistic program as input and returns a draw from the distribution it represents. It is our only operation that calls a random number generator. We apply it last in a sequence of transformations to perform approximate inference.

Like a typical interpreter, Algorithm 1 takes as input not only a program but also an environment, which is a table

---

Algorithm 1: Weighted sampler: sample(m, *env* = [])

Input: program representing a measure: m
Input: environment: *env*
Output: pair of values (outcome, weight)
Examine m
if *m has the form* `Weight(`w_1`,`e_1`)` **then**
  Evaluate e_1 in the environment *env*, obtaining v_1
  Return (v_1, w_1)
else if *m has the form* `Normal(`e_1`,`e_2`)` **then**
  Evaluate e_1 in the environment *env*, obtaining v_1
  Evaluate e_2 in the environment *env*, obtaining v_2
  Sample from the normal distribution with mean v_1 and standard deviation v_2, obtaining v_3
  Return $(v_3, 1)$
else if *m has the form* x`<~`m_1`;`m_2 **then**
  Call Algorithm 1 on m_1 with the environment *env*, obtaining (v_1, w_1)
  Let *env*′ be the environment *env* extended with x having the value v_1
  Call Algorithm 1 on m_2 with the environment *env*′, obtaining (v_2, w_2)
  Return $(v_2, w_1 \cdot w_2)$
else
  The other cases are similar to above
end

---

mapping variable names to values. Also, because our language includes unnormalized measures, this sampler returns not only a draw but also an importance weight.

4.2 EXPECTATION TRANSFORMATION

The rest of this section describes various inference transformations that we apply to our probabilistic programs. Because we implement some transformations in terms of others, we describe the transformations not in the order we apply them but in the order we implement them.

Our expectation transformation turns any program that represents a distribution into another program that represents its expected value. This transformation is exact and simple even though the expected values of many distributions have no closed form, because our language represents integrals symbolically with `Int`. For example, the expectation transformation turns the program `x<~Uniform(0, 2); Uniform(x, 3)` into

```
Int(0,2,x, Int(x,3,y, y)/(3-x))/(2-0)
```

The latter program represents the integral $\frac{1}{2-0}\int_0^2 \frac{1}{3-x}\int_x^3 y\,dy\,dx$. To compute this integral in closed form is to perform exact inference on the given distribution. The expectation transformation itself does not do so; nor does it approximate the integral by sampling.

Algorithm 2: Expectation transformation: expect(m, f)

Input: program representing a measure: m
Input: program representing a function: f
Output: program representing a number
Examine m
if *m has the form* `Weight` *(*w_1*,*e_1*)* **then**
  Return $w_1 \cdot$ `App` (f, e_1)
else if *m has the form* `Normal` *(*e_1*,*e_2*)* **then**
  Return `Int` ($-\infty$, ∞, `x`, $e_3 \cdot$ `App` (f, `x`))
  where the program e_3 computes the density of the `Normal`(e_1, e_2) distribution at `x`
else if *m has the form* x<~m_1;m_2 **then**
  Call Algorithm 2 with m_2 and f obtaining e_3
  Call Algorithm 2 with m_1 and `Lam` (x, e_3)
else
  The other cases are similar to above
end

Specified more generally, the expectation transformation turns any program that represents a measure, along with a function from the sample space to numbers, into another program that represents the integral of the given function with respect to the given measure. We show this transformation as Algorithm 2. It handles primitive distributions such as `Normal` by looking up their density from a table.

4.3 DENSITY AND DISINTEGRATION

Turning a distribution into its density function is naturally expressed as a program transformation (Bhat et al. 2012, 2013). More precisely, the density transformation takes as input a probabilistic program representing a distribution, and returns another program representing a function that maps each point in the sample space to the density at that point. Note that this transformation does not compute any density numerically. It only returns a program that computes densities when interpreted by our weighted sampler (Algorithm 1). For example, the density transformation turns the probabilistic program

```
x <~ Uniform(0, 2);
y <~ Uniform(x, 3); Dirac((x, y))
```

into the density function `Lam((x,y), If(0<x<2, If(x<y<3, 1/(3-x), 0)/(2-0), 0))`.

We implement density in terms of another program transformation, *disintegration* (Shan and Ramsey 2017; Narayanan and Shan 2017). Disintegration is similar to conditioning in that it takes a probabilistic program representing a joint distribution $\Pr(X, Y)$ as input, but instead of returning a conditional distribution $\Pr(Y \mid X = x)$, disintegration returns an unnormalized slice $\Pr(Y, X = x)$ of the original distribution. More precisely, disintegration returns a program representing a function from values of x to measures $\Pr(Y, X = x)$. Such a (measurable) function is also known as a *kernel*.

Algorithm 3: Density transformation: density(m, t)

Input: program representing a measure: m
Input: program representing value drawn from m: t
Output: program representing a nonnegative number
1. Disintegrate `x<~`m`; Dirac((x,Unit))`, obtaining e_1
2. Call Algorithm 2 on `App` (e_1, t) and `Lam(y,1)`

Algorithm 4: Observation transformation: observe(m, t)

Input: program representing a measure: m
Input: program representing value drawn from m: t
Output: program representing a measure
Examine m
if *m has the form* `Uniform` *(*e_1*,*e_2*) or* `Normal` *(*e_1*,*e_2*) or* `Gamma` *(*e_1*,*e_2*)* **then**
  Let d be a program that computes the density of the distribution m
  Return `Weight` (`App` (d, t), t)
else if *m has the form* x<~m_1;m_2 **then**
  Call Algorithm 4 recursively with m_2 and t obtaining m_3
  Return x<~m_1;m_3
else
  Raise an error about not being able to handle m
end

Taking advantage of the fact that disintegration does not normalize the measures it returns, we implement the density transformation in terms of disintegration and expectation. This implementation is shown in Algorithm 3. It invokes disintegration (letting Y be the space that consists of a single point `Unit`) then expectation (letting the integrand f be the function that maps `Unit` to 1).

Disintegration is useful independently of the density transformation. For example, Section 3 uses it to turn the prior `kalman` into the posterior `kalman2`.

We sketch how disintegration works in terms of a simpler program transformation, which we call *observation* (Algorithm 4). This transformation takes as input a measure m and a value t that could have been drawn from m, and returns a measure which only returns t, weighted by how likely that value was to be drawn from m. For example, the observation transformation turns the program

```
x <~ Uniform(0, 2); Uniform(x, 3)
```

and the variable `y` into the program

```
x <~ Uniform(0, 2);
Weight(If(x<y<3, 1/(3-x), 0), y)
```

Algorithm 5: Normalization transformation: normalize(m)

Input: program representing a measure: m

Output: program representing a probability distribution

1. Call Algorithm 2 on m and `Lam(x,1)` obtaining the program e_1
2. Return `x<~`m`; Weight(1/`e_1`, x)`

As indicated at the bottom in Algorithm 4, the observation transformation only handles a subset of our language. In particular, it does not handle `Dirac`, so it does not handle the typical program `kalman` in Section 3. In general, if the input program performs arithmetic or any other deterministic computation to produce the observation t, then we need to invert this deterministic computation and insert any Jacobian factors required. This inversion is what the disintegration provides over observation.

To relate observation and disintegration more precisely, suppose the program m represents a measure over X, the program e represents a value in Y, and observation turns m and x into m_1. Then disintegrating the program `...; x<~`m`; Dirac((x,`e`))` yields a program equivalent to `Lam(x, ...; dummy<~`m_1`; Dirac(`e`))`.

4.4 NORMALIZATION AND CONDITIONING

The presence of `Weight` in our language enables the observation and disintegration transformations to return measures that are typically unnormalized. To recover a probability distribution, we must reweight the measure. We define this *normalization* operation as a program transformation as well, shown as Algorithm 5.

Conditioning can now be defined by composition: it is just disintegration, followed by normalizing the measure.

4.5 MCMC SAMPLING TRANSFORMATIONS

A major contribution of this paper is to implement Markov chain Monte Carlo (MCMC) methods, such as MH sampling and Gibbs sampling, in a way that applies to a variety of target distributions and composes with other inference techniques. We express an MCMC method as a transformation from a program representing the target distribution to a program representing the transition kernel. Whereas the transformation itself makes no random choices, the latter program can be interpreted by our weighted sampler (Algorithm 1) to generate a random chain, or subject to simplification (Section 5).

Following this approach, our MCMC implementations closely resemble their textbook presentation. As shown in Algorithm 6, where the textbook presentation of the acceptance ratio refers to the target and proposal densities, our implementation invokes the density transformation (Algorithm 3) on two probabilistic programs, representing the target and proposal distributions. Using the fact that the density transformation symbolically handles free variables such as `old` and `new`, we perform the transformation just once (not once per sampler iteration) to generate a program that takes the current state as input.

Algorithm 6: Metropolis-Hastings sampling transformation: mh(*proposal, target*)

Input: program representing the proposal kernel: *proposal*

Input: program representing the target distribution: *target*

Output: program representing MCMC transition kernel with acceptance ratio

1. Let `old` and `new` be fresh variable names
2. Call Algorithm 3 on *target* and `old`, obtaining p_{old}
3. Call Algorithm 3 on *target* and `new`, obtaining p_{new}
4. Call Algorithm 3 on `App(`*proposal*`, new)` and `old`, obtaining $q_{\text{old;new}}$
5. Call Algorithm 3 on `App(`*proposal*`, old)` and `new`, obtaining $q_{\text{new;old}}$
6. Let e_1 be $(p_{\text{new}} \cdot q_{\text{old;new}})/(p_{\text{old}} \cdot q_{\text{new;old}})$
7. Return `Lam(old, new<~App(`*proposal*`,old); Dirac((new, `e_1`)))`

Algorithm 7: Gibbs sampling transformation: gibbs(*target*)

Input: program representing the n-dimensional target distribution: *target*

Output: program representing MCMC transition kernel

Let $\mathbf{x}$ be the set of the n variables in the *target*

Initialize *choices* to the empty sequence `[]`

For each $x_i \in \mathbf{x}$:

1. Let x_{-i} be the rest of the variables
2. Let e_1 be $\mathbf{x}$`<~`*target*`; Dirac((`x_{-i}`,`x_i`))`
3. Disintegrate e_1, obtaining e_2
4. Let e_3 be `App(`e_2`, `x_{-i}`)`
5. Call Algorithm 5 on e_3, obtaining e_4
6. Let $\mathbf{y}$ be $\mathbf{x}$ except replacing x_i by `new`
7. Let e_5 be `new<~`e_4`; Dirac(`$\mathbf{y}$`)`
8. Add the pair `(1/`n`, `e_5`)` to *choices*

Return `Lam(`$\mathbf{x}$`, Superpose(`*choices*`))`

Gibbs sampling is a special case of MH, where the proposal kernel combines the results of conditioning the target distribution along each dimension. The acceptance ratio is then always 1, so it need not be computed. To produce such a proposal kernel automatically, we implement Gibbs sampling as a separate transformation, Algorithm 7. The input is a program representing an n-dimensional distribution $\Pr(x_1, \ldots, x_n)$. For each random variable x_i, we condition (Section 4.4) on the other variables x_{-i} to get a program that resamples x_i. We then combine these n programs to form the proposal kernel.

5 SIMPLIFICATION

Because we express each inference technique as a transformation that produces a probabilistic program, rather than as an interpreter that makes immediate random choices, we can optimize and simplify the produced programs. To this end, we apply the optimizations discussed by Carette and Shan (2016). This *simplification* transformation does not change the measure represented by a program but tries to place the program in a form that, when interpreted by our weighted sampler (Algorithm 1), draws samples faster and with more uniform weights.

Based on computer algebra, the simplification transformation recognizes conjugacy relationships, integrates out latent variables, and performs algebraic simplifications. Like other transformations, simplification operates on a program before any variables receive their values, so in particular its efficacy is independent of data sizes. The rest of this section briefly describes these optimizations.

Conjugacy relationships Simplification recognizes when a density represented by `Weight` matches the density of a primitive distribution. A simple example arises from the joint distribution $\Pr(Y, X)$ represented below:

```
x <~ Normal(a, s);
y <~ Normal(x, t); Dirac((y, x))
```

Disintegrating this program (Section 4.3) produces

```
x <~ Normal(a, s);
Weight( exp(-(y-x)^2/(2*t^2))
        /t/sqrt(2*pi)          , x )
```

This latter program scales the measure `Normal(a,s)` with the density `exp(...)/t/sqrt(2*pi)` to represent the conditional distribution $\Pr(X \mid Y)$ up to a constant factor. Normalizing and simplifying it yields

```
Normal( (y*s^2+a*t^2)/(s^2+t^2),
        s*t/sqrt(s^2+t^2) )
```

using the conjugacy relationship between `Normals` (assuming `s` and `t` are positive). This simplified program runs faster; it draws samples without weighting them.

This optimization is symbolic, in the sense that it works even when the initial program contains free variables such as `a`, `s`, and `t`, whose values are unknown.

This optimization is robust because it recognizes not words like `Normal` but the densities they denote. Thus it works even if we express `Normal(0,1)` by spelling out its density, whether we expand the polynomial `-(y-x)^2`. All conjugacies among `Normal`, `Gamma`, and `Beta` thus fall out from recognizing their densities.

Integrating out a variable When a distribution is described using a latent random variable, it usually helps to eliminate the variable. Such latent variables include `x1` and `x2` in Section 3, as well as `x` in

```
x <~ Normal(0, 1); Normal(x, 1)
```

The simplification transformation eliminates these variables. In particular, it integrates out continuous latent variables symbolically. The density-recognition machinery just described then produces simpler, faster, and equivalent programs, such as `Normal(0,sqrt(2))`.

This integration is symbolic, again in the sense that it works even when the initial program contains free variables whose values are unknown. For example, the program `x <~ Normal(a, s); Normal(x, t)` simplifies to `Normal(a, sqrt(s^2+t^2))`.

Algebraic simplifications When we produce a program that calculates acceptance ratios, the numerator and denominator share many factors, which are usually canceled out by hand. The simplification transformation automates this optimization using computer algebra, so an expression like $(a*b)$ / $(a*c)$ becomes b/c.

6 EXPERIMENTAL RESULTS

To demonstrate that our approach is modular and practical, we apply multiple inference methods (MH, Gibbs) to a variety of models. We conduct three experiments using the Hakaru system (Narayanan et al. 2016).

Modular means we can re-use the components in Section 4 and Section 5 to produce all three samplers. In each experiment, a pipeline composed of reusable inference transformations turns a concise generative model into an executable MCMC sampler in seconds.

Practical means our approach can solve real-world problems by expressing popular models and inference methods discussed in the literature. The largest of our three experiments is the third, a document classification task using the 20 Newsgroups corpus.

We measure the accuracy and speed of our automatically generated samplers, showing they are in line with solutions from commonly used probabilistic programming languages. Our samplers are more accurate across the board because simplification eliminates all latent continuous variables, regardless of the dimensionality of the problem (that is, input and output array sizes).

Table 1: MH sampler run times for linear dynamics

Inference method	Run time (msecs) Mean	SD
WebPPL	1078	16
Hakaru without simplifications	1321	93
Hakaru with simplifications	269	10
Handwritten	207	4

Table 2: MH sampler ESS rates for linear dynamics

Inference method	ESS per sample noise_T	noise_E
WebPPL	0.03	0.01
Hakaru	0.09	0.34

All measurements were produced on a quad-core Intel i5-2540M processor running 64-bit Ubuntu 16.04. Our samplers use Glasgow Haskell Compiler 8.0.1 `-O2`.

6.1 MH SAMPLING FOR DYNAMICS

In our first experiment, we use MH to sample the random parameters of the linear dynamical system in Section 3. We compare our generated samplers with one produced by WebPPL, a state-of-the-art probabilistic programming system, and with one written by hand. The WebPPL sampler was compiled to JavaScript using Node 0.10.28.

Table 1 shows that our system generates a fast sampler, measured by using each sampler to draw 20,000 samples 10 times. Thanks to the simplifications that turn `kalman4` into `kalman5`, the Hakaru sampler is 4 times as fast as the WebPPL sampler for the conditional distribution `kalman2`. (These times exclude the few seconds each system takes to compile the model into a sampler.)

Table 2 shows that our samplers generate good samples, quantified by the Effective Sample Size (ESS). Our ESS is higher per sample compared to WebPPL, because latent variables have been integrated out in `kalman3`.

6.2 GIBBS SAMPLING FOR CLASSIFICATION

In our second and third experiments, we generate Gibbs samplers and compare them to JAGS (v4.20), a probabilistic programming system widely considered practical for Gibbs sampling. We measure accuracy by how well the samplers recover true classifications, and speed by the time it takes to produce samples. This time consists of *initialization* time and time spent actually sampling. Initialization time is the time a system takes from receiving the model to generating the first sample: for JAGS to load the model into memory, and for Hakaru to simplify the model and compile the result into machine code.

Our second experiment is to classify synthetic data using a Gaussian mixture model that has 3 components.

Figure 1 shows that Hakaru requires fewer sweeps than JAGS to achieve the same accuracy. Each curve plots the accuracy of one chain over the course of 15 sweeps on 250 data points. After just one sweep, all 20 Hakaru chains are $> 50\%$ accurate, unlike the 20 JAGS chains, which take a few sweeps to catch up. The cause is that Hakaru's simplification transformation recovers a collapsed Gibbs sampler that computes the sample mean and variance of each mixture component in closed form.

Figure 2 shows Hakaru is about one order of magnitude slower than JAGS, measured by how long 6 sweeps take, varying data size from 500 to 2500 points. The top two curves represent two samplers generated by Hakaru with different lower-level optimizations: the second-from-top curve adds a *histogram* optimization to compute summary statistics such as the per-mixture-component sum $\sum_{i=1}^{N} \left\{ \begin{smallmatrix} t_i & \text{if } z_i = z^* \\ 0 & \text{otherwise} \end{smallmatrix} \right.$ in a single pass over the data for all components z^*. The bottom two curves show the run time of JAGS, with and without initialization. JAGS's speed advantage can be explained by Hakaru's current inability to reuse computation between updates during a sweep. Still, Hakaru is practical for this real-world task.

In our third experiment, Hakaru generates a classifier for the 20 Newsgroups corpus that is more accurate than JAGS and comparable in speed. We use the same Multinomial Naive Bayes model and 20 Newsgroups corpus as McCallum and Nigam (1998). We hold out 10% of the labels and use Gibbs sampling to infer them. We evaluate the samplers on data sizes ranging from 200 to all 19997 documents, evenly distributed among newsgroups.

Because the sampler generated by Hakaru is collapsed, it is more accurate than JAGS in two ways. First, Figure 3 shows Hakaru achieves better accuracy than JAGS after one sweep, and continues to for at least 1000 sweeps. Each curve there plots the accuracy (moving average with window size 20) of one chain on 400 documents. Second, Figure 4 shows Hakaru more accurate than JAGS across data sizes. We use 2 sweeps there since JAGS does not perform above chance with only 1 sweep.

Figure 5 shows Hakaru is as fast as JAGS, measured by how long 2 sweeps take, varying data size. JAGS's initialization time grows with the data size, while Hakaru's is constant. Whereas JAGS unrolls loops into a pointer-based stochastic graph whose size grows with the data, Hakaru generates tight loops over unboxed arrays irrespective of the data size. Even disregarding initialization time, JAGS is at best 4 times faster than Hakaru.

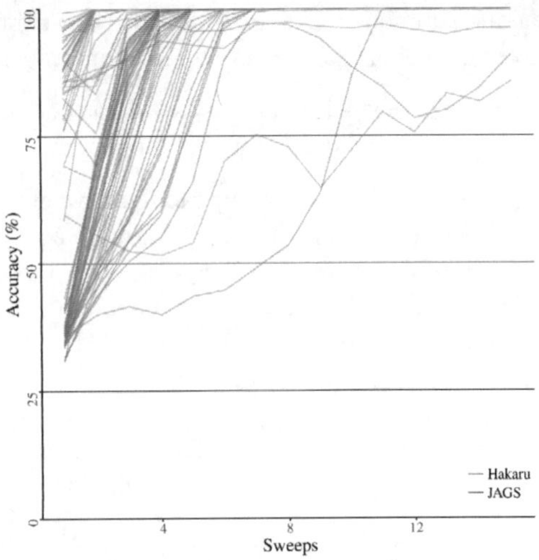

Figure 1: Gibbs sampler accuracy for Gaussian mixture

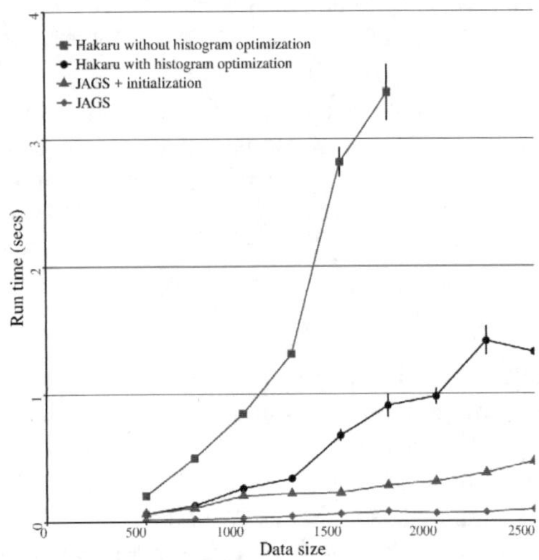

Figure 2: Gibbs sampler run times for Gaussian mixture

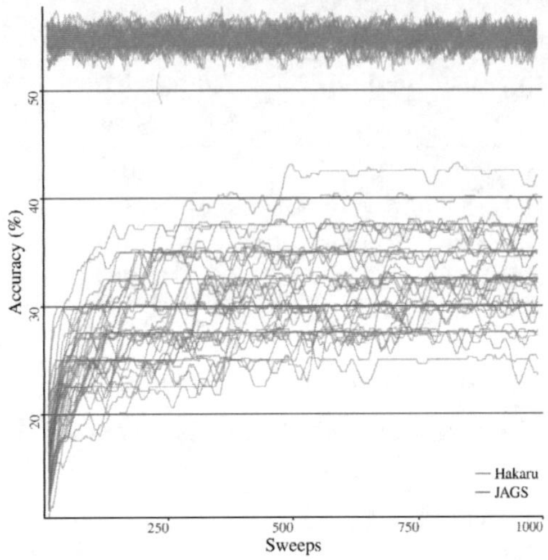

Figure 3: Document classification accuracy by sweeps

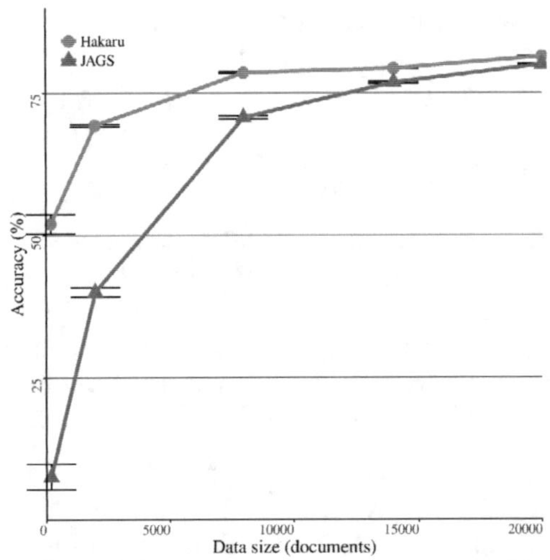

Figure 4: Document classification accuracy by data size

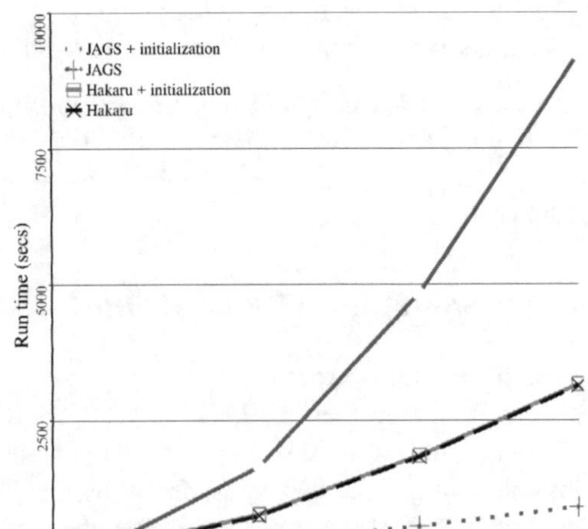

Figure 5: Document classification run times. Error bars were too small to display.

7 CONCLUSIONS

We express inference methods by composing program transformations such as disintegration and expectation. The resulting modular inference procedures perform comparably to other probabilistic programming systems and are usable for practical problems. This technique makes it easier and faster to create and test inference procedures and to explore novel inference methods.

Acknowledgements

We thank David Belanger, Jacques Carette, and Chad Scherrer for helpful discussions, feedback, and suggestions. This research was supported by DARPA contract FA8750-14-2-0007, NSF grant CNS-0723054, Lilly Endowment, Inc., and the Indiana METACyt Initiative.

References

Sooraj Bhat, Ashish Agarwal, Richard Vuduc, and Alexander Gray. A type theory for probability density functions. In *POPL '12: Conference Record of the Annual ACM Symposium on Principles of Programming Languages*, pages 545–556. ACM Press, January 2012.

Sooraj Bhat, Johannes Borgström, Andrew D. Gordon, and Claudio Russo. Deriving probability density functions from probabilistic functional programs. In *19th International Conference on Tools and Algorithms for the Construction and Analysis of Systems (TACAS)*, 2013.

Jacques Carette and Chung-chieh Shan. Simplifying probabilistic programs using computer algebra. In *Practical Aspects of Declarative Languages - 18th International Symposium, PADL 2016, St. Petersburg, FL, USA, January 18-19, 2016. Proceedings*, pages 135–152, 2016.

A. Gelman, A. Vehtari, P. Jylänki, C. Robert, N. Chopin, and J. P. Cunningham. Expectation Propagation as a Way of Life. *ArXiv e-prints*, December 2014.

Noah D. Goodman, Vikash K. Mansinghka, Daniel M. Roy, Keith Bonawitz, and Joshua B. Tenenbaum. Church: a language for generative models. In *Proc. of Uncertainty in Artificial Intelligence*, 2008.

Thomas L Griffiths and Mark Steyvers. Finding scientific topics. *Proceedings of the National Academy of Sciences*, 101(suppl 1):5228–5235, 2004.

Michael Hughes, Dae Il Kim, and Erik Sudderth. Reliable and scalable variational inference for the hierarchical Dirichlet process. In *Proceedings of the Eighteenth International Conference on Artificial Intelligence and Statistics*, pages 370–378, 2015.

Andrew McCallum and Kamal Nigam. A comparison of event models for naive Bayes text classification. In *AAAI-98 workshop on learning for text categorization*, volume 752, pages 41–48. Citeseer, 1998.

Andrew McCallum, Khashayar Rohanemanesh, Michael Wick, Karl Schultz, and Sameer Singh. Factorie: Efficient probabilistic programming for relational factor graphs via imperative declarations of structure, inference and learning. In *NIPS Workshop on Probabilistic Programming*, 2008.

Praveen Narayanan and Chung-chieh Shan. Symbolic conditioning of arrays in probabilistic programs. In *ICFP '16: Proceedings of the ACM International Conference on Functional Programming*. ACM Press, 2017.

Praveen Narayanan, Jacques Carette, Wren Romano, Chung-chieh Shan, and Robert Zinkov. Probabilistic inference by program transformation in Hakaru (system description). In Oleg Kiselyov and Andy King, editors, *Proceedings of FLOPS 2016: 13th International Symposium on Functional and Logic Programming*, number 9613 in Lecture Notes in Computer Science, pages 62–79. Springer, 2016.

Willie Neiswanger, Chong Wang, and Eric Xing. Asymptotically exact, embarrassingly parallel MCMC. In *The Conference on Uncertainty in Artificial Intelligence (UAI)*, 2014.

Avi Pfeffer. Figaro: An object-oriented probabilistic programming language. *Charles River Analytics Technical Report*, 137, 2009.

Sebastian Riedel, Sameer Singh, Vivek Srikumar, Tim Rocktäschel, Larysa Visengeriyeva, and Jan Noessner. WOLFE: Strength Reduction and Approximate Programming for Probabilistic Programming. In *International Workshop on Statistical Relational AI (StarAI)*, 2014.

Adam Ścibior and Zoubin Ghahramani. Modular construction of Bayesian inference algorithms. In *NIPS Workshop on Advances in Approximate Bayesian Inference*, 2016.

Adam Ścibior, Zoubin Ghahramani, and Andrew D. Gordon. Practical probabilistic programming with monads. In *Proceedings of the 8th ACM SIGPLAN Symposium on Haskell, Haskell 2015, Vancouver, BC, Canada, September 3-4, 2015*, pages 165–176, 2015.

Chung-chieh Shan and Norman Ramsey. Exact Bayesian inference by symbolic disintegration. In *POPL '17: Conference Record of the Annual ACM Symposium on Principles of Programming Languages*, pages 130–144. ACM Press, 2017.

Frank Wood, Jan Willem van de Meent, and Vikash Mansinghka. A new approach to probabilistic programming inference. In *Proceedings of the 17th International conference on Artificial Intelligence and Statistics*, pages 1024–1032, 2014.

Minjie Xu, Balaji Lakshminarayanan, Yee Whye Teh, Jun Zhu, and Bo Zhang. Distributed Bayesian posterior sampling via moment sharing. In Z. Ghahramani, M. Welling, C. Cortes, N.D. Lawrence, and K.Q. Weinberger, editors, *Advances in Neural Information Processing Systems 27*, pages 3356–3364, 2014.

Iterative Decomposition Guided Variable Neighborhood Search for Graphical Model Energy Minimization

Abdelkader Ouali[a,b], **David Allouche**[c], **Simon de Givry**[c], **Samir Loudni**[b], **Yahia Lebbah**[a], **Francisco Eckhardt**[c] and **Lakhdar Loukil**[a]

(a) University of Oran 1 Ahmed Ben Bella, Lab. LITIO, 31000 Oran, Algeria.

(b) University of Caen Normandy, CNRS, UMR 6072 GREYC, 14032 Caen, France.

(c) INRA, MIA Toulouse, UR-875, 31320 Castanet-Tolosan, France.

Abstract

Graphical models factorize a global probability distribution/energy function as the product/sum of local functions. A major inference task, known as MAP in Markov Random Fields and MPE in Bayesian Networks, is to find a global assignment of all the variables with maximum a posteriori probability/minimum energy. A usual distinction on MAP solving methods is complete/incomplete, i.e. the ability to prove optimality or not. Most complete methods rely on tree search, while incomplete methods rely on local search. Among them, we study Variable Neighborhood Search (VNS) for graphical models. In this paper, we propose an iterative approach above VNS which uses (partial) tree search inside its local neighborhood exploration. The resulting hybrid method offers a good compromise between completeness and anytime behavior than existing tree search methods while still being competitive for proving optimality. We further propose a parallel version of our method improving its anytime behavior on difficult instances coming from a large graphical model benchmark. Last we experiment on the challenging minimum energy problem found in Computational Protein Design, showing the practical benefit of our parallel version. Solver at `www.inra.fr/mia/T/toulbar2` v1.0.

1 INTRODUCTION

Probabilistic graphical models (Koller and Friedman, 2009) are formed by variables linked to each other by stochastic relationships. They enable to model complex systems with heterogeneous data and to capture uncertainty. Graphical models have been applied in a wide range of areas such as image analysis, speech recognition, bioinformatics, and ecology.

We focus on models with discrete variables like Markov Random Field and Bayesian Network. Our goal is to find a global assignment of all the variables with maximum a posteriori probability. This optimization task defines an NP-complete problem (Shimony, 1994). Solving methods can be categorized in two groups: exact and local search methods. Exact methods rely on tree search, variable elimination, linear programming, or a combination of them (Marinescu and Dechter, 2009; Otten and Dechter, 2012; Allouche *et al.*, 2015). Graph-cut and message-passing algorithms like loopy belief propagation and variational approaches (Kolmogorov, 2006; Wainwright and Jordan, 2008; Sontag *et al.*, 2008; 2012; Wang and Koller, 2013) are exact only in some particular cases (*e.g.,* Potts model or tree structure). Local search methods are stochastic algorithms like Gibbs sampling, Guided Local Search (Park, 2002; Hutter *et al.*, 2005), and Stochastic Greedy Search (Mengshoel *et al.*, 2011). Some of them have theoretical asymptotic proof of convergence, *i.e.,* the optimal solution is guaranteed to be found if infinite time is available. In practice, they may exhibit a better anytime behavior than exact methods on large and difficult problems (Marinescu *et al.*, 2003; Hutter *et al.*, 2005; Mengshoel *et al.*, 2011), *i.e.,* they produce better solutions in less time.

A few attempts have been done to combine exact and local search methods. A simple way is to run sequentially a local search algorithm then tree search, where solutions found by local search will be used as initial upper bounds for branch and bound exact methods. Another approach is to design a local search framework where the neighborhood exploration is performed by tree search in a systematic or non-systematic way. VNS/LDS+CP (Loudni and Boizumault, 2003) combines a metaheuristic, Variable Neighborhood Search (VNS) (Mladenović and Hansen, 1997) with Limited Discrepancy Search (LDS) (Harvey and Ginsberg, 1995), a partial tree search method (Section 2). We propose in Section 3 an iterative variant of VNS/LDS+CP called `UDGVNS`, adapted to graphical models and able to prove optimality when the neighborhood size is maximal and with unbounded tree search. In Section 4, we describe a coarse-grained parallel version called `UPDGVNS` with asynchronous cooperative execution of `UDGVNS` processes with centralized information exchange as in (Davidovic and Crainic, 2012; Ouali *et al.*, 2015). We report experimental results in Sections 5-6.

2 PRELIMINARIES

2.1 GRAPHICAL MODEL

Definition 1 *A* probabilistic graphical model *(or Gibbs distribution) (Koller and Friedman, 2009) is a triplet* $(\mathcal{X}, \mathcal{D}, \mathcal{F})$ *with* $\mathcal{X} = \{X_1, \ldots, X_n\}$*, a set of* n *random variables,* $\mathcal{D} = \{D_1, \ldots, D_n\}$*, a set of finite domains of values of maximum size* $d = \max_{i=1}^{n} |D_i|$*, and* $\mathcal{F}$*, a set of potential functions. Each variable* X_i *takes values in* D_i*. An assignment of* $\mathcal{X}$ *is a set* $x = (x_1, \ldots, x_n)$*, with* $x_i \in D_i$*. The set of all possible assignments of* $\mathcal{X}$ *is denoted* $\Delta = \prod_{i=1}^{n} D_i$*. Let* $A = \{D'_1, \ldots, D'_n\}$ *with* $D'_i \subseteq D_i$ *represent a restricted set of* Δ *called a* partial assignment*. If* S *is a subset of* $V = \{1, \ldots, n\}$*,* X_S*,* x_S *and* Δ_S *are respectively the subset of random variables* $\{X_i, i \in S\}$*, the assignment* $(x_i, i \in S)$ *obtained from* x*, and the set of all possible assignments of* X_S*. Given a set* $\mathcal{S}$ *of part of* V*, the set* $\mathcal{F} = \{f_S\}_{S \in \mathcal{S}}$ *of maps from* Δ_S *to* $\mathbb{R}^+$*, called* potential functions*, is said to factorize a joint probability distribution* $\mathbb{P}$ *iff:*

$$\mathbb{P}(x) = \frac{1}{Z} \prod_{f_S \in \mathcal{F}} f_S(x_S) \tag{1}$$

where $Z = \sum_{x \in \Delta} \prod_{f_S \in \mathcal{F}} f_S(x_S)$ *is the normalizing constant, also called partition function.*

Among the various tasks, the *Most Probable Explanation* (MPE) problem is to find the most likely assignment $x \in \Delta$ to all the variables in $\mathcal{X}$ maximizing $\mathbb{P}(x)$. By taking the opposite of the logarithm of $\mathbb{P}(x)$, *i.e.*, $-\log \mathbb{P}(x) = \sum_{f_S \in \mathcal{F}} -\log f_S(x_S) - \log Z$, we obtain an additive model with $\varphi(x_S) = -\log f_S(x_S)$ called *energy functions*. Finding a solution of minimum energy is equivalent to MPE. In the rest of the paper, we consider energy minimization. When $\varphi(x_S)$ maps to $\mathbb{N}^+ \cup \{\infty\}$, the corresponding deterministic graphical model is called a *Cost Function Network* (CFN) (Meseguer *et al.*, 2006). Finding a solution of minimum cost is the same as doing energy minimization on the equivalent probabilistic model (Hurley *et al.*, 2016).

2.2 TREE DECOMPOSITION

Definition 2 *A tree decomposition of a connected graphical model is a pair* (C_T, T) *where* $T = (I, A)$ *is a tree with nodes set* I *and edges set* A *and* $C_T = \{C_i \mid i \in I\}$ *is a family of subsets of* $\mathcal{X}$*, called clusters, such that: (i)* $\cup_{i \in I} C_i = \mathcal{X}$*, (ii)* $\forall f_S \in \mathcal{F}, \exists\, C_i \in C_T$ *s.t.* $S \subseteq C_i$*, (iii)* $\forall i, j, k \in I$*, if* j *is on the path from* i *to* k *in* T*, then* $C_i \cap C_k \subseteq C_j$*.*

Definition 3 *The intersection of two clusters* C_i *and* C_j *is called a separator, and noted* $sep(C_i, C_j)$*.*

Definition 4 *A graph of clusters for a tree decomposition* (C_T, T) *is an undirected graph* $G = (C_T, E)$ *that has a vertex for each cluster* $C_i \in C_T$*, and there is an edge* $(C_i, C_j) \in E$ *when* $sep(C_i, C_j) \neq \emptyset$*.*

As finding an optimal tree decomposition is NP–hard, we use fast approximate algorithms like *min-fill* heuristic.

2.3 DFBB & LIMITED DISCREPANCY SEARCH

Depth-First Branch and Bound (DFBB) methods explore a search tree in a systematic way by recursively choosing the next unassigned variable to assign and by choosing a value in its domain for the assignment (the *branch* part) until a better solution is found or it can be proved that the subtree rooted at the current search node has no better solutions and it can be pruned (the *bound* part). DFBB depends on its variable and value ordering heuristics for branching in order to find good solutions rapidly and to reduce the size of the search tree to be explored.

Limited Discrepancy Search (LDS) (Harvey and Ginsberg, 1995) is a heuristic method that explores the search tree in a non-systematic way by making a limited number of *wrong* decisions w.r.t. its value ordering heuristic. We assume a binary search tree where at each search node either the selected variable is assigned to its chosen preferred value (left branch) or the value is removed from the domain (right branch). Each value removal corresponds to a wrong decision made by the search, it is called a *discrepancy*. The number of discrepancies is limited by a parameter denoted ℓ. See Algorithm 1 where `lb`(A) gives a lower bound on the minimum energy $\min_{x \in \prod_{D_i \in A} D_i} -\log \mathbb{P}(x)$ of the partial assignment A.

In order to produce good quality solutions as time passes, a simple strategy is to iterate `LDS` with an increasing number of discrepancies ℓ going from ℓ_{min} to ℓ_{max}. Each iteration does at most ℓ discrepancies along the path from the root search node to a terminal node. Let h be the maximum height of the explored search tree, the number of terminals with ℓ discrepancies is bounded by $\binom{h}{\ell}$. Thus, `LDS` has a time complexity in $O(h^{\ell+1})$ (for $\ell < h/2$ (Larrosa *et al.*, 2016)) and a linear space complexity (thanks to the depth-first search principle as in DFBB). Notice that $h \leq n + \ell$ (ℓ right branches followed by n left branches). Without any discrepancy limit, we have at most $n(d-1)$ value removals (right branches)

Algorithm 1: Pseudo-code of mono LDS

Procedure

LDS ($\ell, A, ub : In/Out, x : In/Out, opt : In/Out$)
- **if** ($\exists D_i \in A, |D_i| > 1$) **then**
  - Choose an unassigned variable $X_i \in \mathcal{X}, |D_i| > 1$;
  - Choose a value $x_i \in D_i$;
  - $A' \leftarrow (A \setminus \{D_i\}) \cup \{\{x_i\}\}$; // left branch
  - **if** ($\texttt{lb}(A') < ub$) **then** LDS (ℓ, A', ub, x, opt) ;
  - 1 **if** ($\ell > 0$) **then**
    - $A'' \leftarrow (A \setminus \{D_i\}) \cup \{D_i \setminus \{x_i\}\}$; // right b
    - **if** ($\texttt{lb}(A'') < ub$) **then**
      - LDS ($\ell - 1, A'', ub, x, opt$)
  - **else**
    - 2 $opt \leftarrow$ **false** ;
- **else**
  - 3 $ub \leftarrow \texttt{lb}(A), x \leftarrow A$; // new sol. found

to reach a terminal node, where d is the maximum domain size of all variables. In order to be able to prove optimality, we set $\ell_{max} = n(d-1)$, *i.e.*, the last iteration is complete. In practice, optimality may be proved with a much smaller ℓ[1], and we just have to check if the discrepancy limit was reached during the search (falsified condition at line 1 of Alg. 1) to detect an incomplete search (flag *opt* set to false at line 2).

2.4 VARIABLE NEIGHBORHOOD SEARCH

Variable Neighborhood Search (VNS) (Mladenović and Hansen, 1997) is a metaheuristic that uses a finite set of pre-selected neighborhood structures $N_k, k = 1, 2, ..., k_{max}$ to escape from local minima by systematically changing the neighborhood structure if the current one does not improve the current incumbent solution. VNS repeatedly performs three major steps. In the first one, called *shaking*, a solution x' is randomly generated in the neighborhoods of x denoted $N_k(x)$. In the second one, a local search method is applied from x' to obtain a local optimum x''. In the third one, called *neighborhood change*, if x'' is better than x, x is replaced with x'' and k is set to 1; otherwise, k is increased by one.

2.5 VNS METHODS IN GRAPHICAL MODELS

The use of VNS scheme for solving deterministic graphical models started with VNS/LDS+CP (Loudni and Boizumault, 2003). This approach is related to LNS (Shaw, 1998), but it adjusts dynamically the neighborhood size when search seems to stagnate as in VNS.

VNS/LDS+CP algorithm. Let N_k be the neighborhood structure of size k; N_k denotes the set of all subsets of k variables among $\mathcal{X}$. Let x be the current solution. First, x is partially destroyed by un-assigning a subset of k variables and an exploration of its (large) neighborhood is performed until the solution is repaired with a new one. The core of VNS/LDS+CP is its reconstruction phase. It runs LDS with a fixed discrepancy to explore the neighborhood of the solution. One advantage of this choice is its exploration speed that improves the quality profile and allows a more balanced exploration of the search tree.

Decomposition Guided VNS. More recently, Fontaine *et al.* (Fontaine *et al.*, 2013) investigated the incorporation of tree decomposition within VNS/LDS+CP in order to efficiently guide the exploration of large neighborhoods. They proposed DGVNS, a first local search approach that exploits the graph of clusters provided by a tree decomposition to build relevant neighborhood structures. For both DGVNS and VNS/LDS+CP, the reconstruction phase is performed using LDS with a fixed discrepancy ℓ, but neighborhood structures are managed in a different way. Instead of the neighborhood structures N_k used by VNS/LDS+CP, DGVNS uses neighborhood structures $N_{k,c}$, where k is the neighborhood size and C_c is the cluster where the variables will be selected from. If ($k > |C_c|$), we complete the set of candidate variables to be unassigned by adding clusters adjacent to C_c. The neighborhood change in DGVNS is performed in the same way as in VNS. However, DGVNS considers successively all the clusters. This ensures a better diversification by covering a large number of different regions.

3 AN ITERATIVE DGVNS METHOD

We present UDGVNS (see Algorithm 2), unifying two complete and incomplete search methods. As done by iterative LDS, it restores the completeness of DGVNS by applying successive calls with an increasing discrepancy limit, controlling if tree search was partial using *opt* flag and the fact that the current neighborhood kept some variables assigned in A (test at line 9). In UDGVNS, optimality can be proven in two cases: (i) when the current neighborhood corresponds to the whole problem and the discrepancy value is greater than or equal to the maximum number of right branches or (ii) by examining the bounds at the root node ($ub = \texttt{lb}(\mathcal{D})$ at lines 5 and 8). In this case, the search space is implicitly explored by the algorithm, therefore optimality is proven.

The initial solution of UDGVNS is obtained at line 4 by a modified version of LDS, denoted LDS^r, that stops immediately after a first solution is found[2]. Thus LDS^r ($\infty, \mathcal{D}, ub, x, opt$) will return a solution with non-zero probability (*i.e.,* satisfying the constraints).

UDGVNS has two main parameters for tuning its compromise between optimality proof and anytime behavior: the discrepancy limit (ℓ) and the local search neighbor-

[1] It was less than or equal to 128 for all instances completely solved by LDS and VNS methods in Section 5.

[2] It stops the recursive LDS procedure at line 3 of Alg. 1 and set the optimality flag *opt* to false.

Algorithm 2: Unified DGVNS algorithm.

Function UDGVNS ($\ell_{min}, \ell_{max}, +_\ell, k_{min}, k_{max}, +_k, ub : In/Out, x : In/Out$) : *boolean*

let (C_T, T) be a tree decomposition of $(\mathcal{X}, \mathcal{D}, \mathcal{F})$;
opt ← **true** ;
4 LDS^r ($\infty, \mathcal{D}, ub, x, opt$) ; // initial solution
5 **if** ($ub = $ lb$(\mathcal{D})$) **then** *opt* ← **true**;
$c \leftarrow 1$; // current cluster index
$r \leftarrow 0$; // number of iterations
$\ell \leftarrow \ell_{min}$; // initial discrepancy limit
while ($\neg opt \wedge \ell \leq \ell_{max}$) **do**
  $i \leftarrow 0$; // nb. of failed neighbor.
6   $k \leftarrow k_{min}$; // init. neighbo. size
  while ($\neg opt \wedge k \leq k_{max}$) **do**
    $A \leftarrow$ getNeighborhood(x, C_c, k) ;
    $ub' \leftarrow ub$, *opt* ← **true** ;
7   LDS^r (ℓ, A, ub', x', opt) ; // nei. search
8   **if** ($ub' = $ lb$(\mathcal{D})$) **then** *opt* ← **true**;
9   **else if** ($A \neq \mathcal{D}$) **then** *opt* ← **false**;
10   **if** ($ub' < ub$) **then**
      $x \leftarrow x'$, $ub \leftarrow ub'$; // new best sol
11       $i \leftarrow 0$, $k \leftarrow k_{min}$;
12       $r \leftarrow 0$, $\ell \leftarrow \ell_{min}$;
    else
      $i \leftarrow i + 1$;
      if ($k < k_{max}$) **then**
        $k \leftarrow \min(k_{max}, k_{min} +_k i)$;
      else $k \leftarrow \infty$;
13     $c \leftarrow 1 + c \bmod |C_T|$; // get next clus.
  $r \leftarrow r + 1$;
  if ($\ell < \ell_{max}$) **then**
    $\ell \leftarrow \min(\ell_{max}, \ell_{min} +_\ell r)$;
  else $\ell \leftarrow \infty$;
14 **return** *opt* ;

hood size (k). Recall that inside DGVNS, the maximum tree height for LDS^r is $h \leq k + \ell \leq k(d-1)$, so LDS^r has time complexity in $O((k\min(\ell, d))^{\ell+1})$. The complexity increases exponentially with ℓ and polynomially with k. As soon as a better solution is found by the current neighborhood search (line 7), we stop the search in order to reinitialize the two parameters to their minimum value, as it is faster to explore small neighborhoods (lines 11-12). For each parameter, ℓ and k, we have tested three updating rules: increase by one at each iteration ($+_{\ell/k} = +$), multiply by two at each iteration ($a +_{\ell/k} b = \texttt{mult2}(a, b) = a \times 2^b$), and apply a Luby strategy (Luby *et al.*, 1993) ($a +_{\ell/k} b = \texttt{Luby}(a, b) = a \times luby(1 + b)$)[3].

Operator $+_k$ controls the compromise between intensification and diversification. The goal of the Luby strategy is to exponentially increase the number of small neighborhoods explored compared to the number of larger ones. Whereas classical VNS algorithms will stuck on large problems, trying to diversify the search by exploring larger neighborhoods, VNS using Luby will spend more time on small neighborhoods in order to locally improve the current solution, favoring intensification. The mult2 strategy reduces the number of neighborhood explorations at a given discrepancy limit, in order to try larger discrepancy limits more rapidly. If the problem is solvable by a complete search within the time limit, it will also speed-up the optimality proof.

Operator $+_\ell$ controls the compromise between incomplete and complete search. Using a fast growing strategy emphasis completeness whereas a slow growth should favor anytime behavior. We noticed that it is worthwhile to cover all the variables by the union of the explored neighborhoods in order to not miss some important variables. We tested a forth strategy for k which consists in a slow increment (by $+1$) at the beginning until $k = \max_{i \in I}(|C_i|) + |C_T| - 1$ then it *jumps* directly to $k = k_{max}$. This ensures that k grows slowly until the largest cluster has been totally explored by at least one neighborhood search. Then, when $k = k_{max} = |\mathcal{X}|$, UDGVNS does a restart, looking for an improved starting solution, using LDS^r applied on the whole problem. If it fails to find a better solution, a larger discrepancy can be selected and UDGVNS continues its intensification process starting with a small neighborhood size (line 6).

4 A PARALLEL VERSION OF UDGVNS

This section describes how UDGVNS can been parallelized. We denote the resulting algorithm UPDGVNS for Unified Parallel DGVNS. It relies on asynchronous cooperative execution of several UDGVNS (i.e. workers) processes with centralized information exchange. In the proposed parallelization one global best solution is shared among the worker processes. Initially, the master initiates the search by launching npr worker processes in parallel with the same initial solution (line 4 done in the master). Each worker process obtains from the master a copy of the current best solution x, the index c of the cluster to be processed and performs destroy and repair operations on its local copy. As soon as a new solution is found by a worker, it is sent to the master and a new cluster is requested (line 13 done in the master) to restart a new exploration starting from the best available overall solution. Like UDGVNS, each worker process controls locally how the discrepancy limit ℓ and the neighborhood size k evolve during successive explorations (except that ub comes from the master at line 10). The whole process stops as soon as a worker terminates (line 14) with an optimality proof or it reaches ℓ_{max} and k_{max}.

[3]Recall $luby(i) = \{1, 1, 2, 1, 1, 2, 4, 1, 1, 2, 1, 1, 2, 4, 8, \ldots\}$.

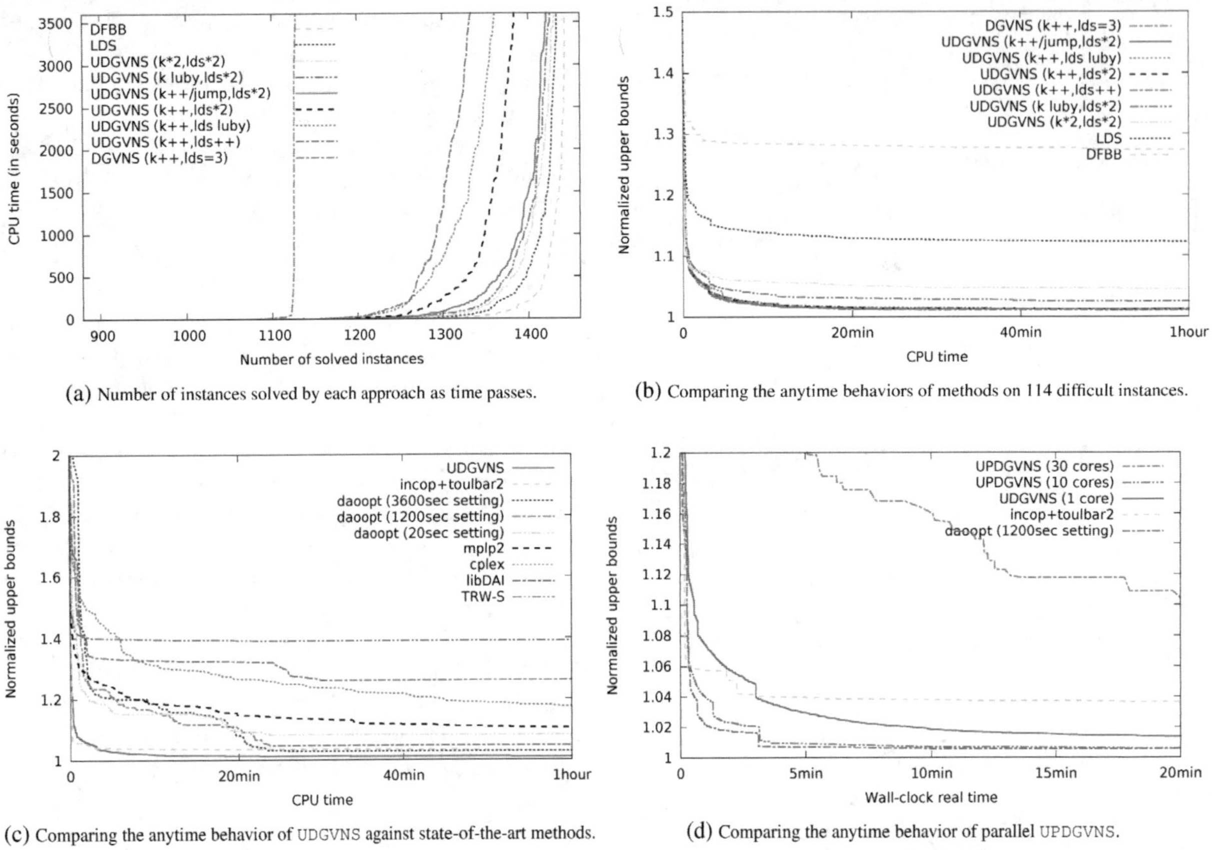

(a) Number of instances solved by each approach as time passes.

(b) Comparing the anytime behaviors of methods on 114 difficult instances.

(c) Comparing the anytime behavior of UDGVNS against state-of-the-art methods.

(d) Comparing the anytime behavior of parallel UPDGVNS.

Figure 1: Comparative evaluation on probabilistic and deterministic graphical models

5 UAI EVALUATION RESULTS

Benchmarks description. We performed experiments on probabilistic and deterministic graphical models coming from a large multi-paradigm benchmark repository (Hurley *et al.*, 2016)[4]. Among the 3016 available instances, we selected all the instances that were used in previous UAI competitions, in image analysis, or in Cost Function Network optimization. It includes 319 instances from *UAI 2008 Evaluation* and *Probabilistic Inference Challenge* (PIC 2011)[5], 1461 instances from the Computer Vision and Pattern Recognition (CVPR) OpenGM2 benchmark[6] (Kappes *et al.*, 2015), and 281 instances from the Cost Function Library[7]. In order to have a fair comparison between solvers, we preprocessed all the instances by polynomial-time problem reformulations and simplifications that remove variables (using bounded and functional variable elimination (Favier *et al.*, 2011)), values (using *dead-end elimination* (de Givry *et al.*, 2013)), and fixed-value potentials, after an initial lower bound computation by *Equivalence Preserving Transformations* (Cooper *et al.*, 2010) (enforcing *Virtual Arc Consistency* (VAC) as a message-passing algorithm). The resulting instances are smaller while preserving the same optimum. We used TOULBAR2 with options *-A -z=2* for this preprocessing step. We kept 1669 non-trivial instances (with more than one variable) for the experiments. The number of variables n ranges from 4 (CVPR-GeomSurf-3-gm13) to 48,566 (CVPR-ColorSeg-8-crops-small) with mean value $n \approx 403.4$ (instead of $1,316.5$ before preprocessing). For DGVNS methods, we built tree decompositions using *min-fill* heuristic. Because the number of clusters $m = |C_T|$ can be very large ($m \approx 256.7$), we merged any pair of connected clusters (C_i, C_j) when the separator size is too large compared to the individual cluster sizes ($|sep(C_i, C_j)| > 0.7 \min(|C_i|, |C_j|)$), resulting in $m \approx 19.9$ and mean tree width $\max_{i \in I}(|C_i|) \approx 76.9$ (instead of 49.6 without merging). In order to experiment sequential and parallel methods on the most difficult instances, we selected a subset of instances unsolved in 1 hour by all our DFBB, LDS, and VNS algorithms. We took at most twenty instances per problem category (avoiding over-representation issues by some categories), resulting

[4] genoweb.toulouse.inra.fr/~degivry/evalgm

[5] graphmod.ics.uci.edu/uai08/Evaluation/Report/Benchmarks, www.cs.huji.ac.il/project/PASCAL

[6] hci.iwr.uni-heidelberg.de/opengm2

[7] costfunction.org/benchmark

in a selection of 114 difficult instances[8].

Experimental protocol. $\texttt{LDS}^r$ employs a randomized (for breaking ties) dynamic variable ordering heuristic[9]. Its value ordering heuristic chooses the EAC value as the preferred value and lower bounds are deduced by enforcing EDAC, as explained in (Larrosa *et al.*, 2005). In the following, we set $k_{min} = 4$, $k_{max} = n = |\mathcal{X}|$, $l_{min} = 1$, and $l_{max} = n(d-1)$. Here, DFBB corresponds to UDGVNS $(\infty, \infty, +, \infty, \infty, +)$, LDS to UDGVNS $(1, \infty, \texttt{mult2}, |\mathcal{X}|, |\mathcal{X}|, +)$, and DGVNS to UDGVNS $(3, 3, +, k_{min}, k_{max}, +)$.

We compared with state-of-the-art exact solvers. DAOOPT[10] won PIC 2011. It has a time-bounded initial phase of lower bound computation based on *Message Passing Linear Programming* algorithm (Sontag *et al.*, 2008; 2012; Ihler *et al.*, 2012) and mini-bucket elimination (Dechter and Rish, 2003) with iterative *min-fill* heuristic. It also finds good initial upper bounds using stochastic local search *GLS*$^+$ (Hutter *et al.*, 2005). We tested three parameter settings as suggested in (Otten *et al.*, 2012), controlling the time spent to compute initial lower and upper bounds. In the 3600sec setting, SLS is run 20 times with 10 seconds per run. The best solution found is used as an initial upper bound for an AND/OR exhaustive tree search. INCOP+TOULBAR2[11] (Hurley *et al.*, 2016) won the *UAI 2010 Evaluation* at 20 min. time limit. TOULBAR2 takes a starting solution from the best result of three runs of the *IDWalk* (Neveu *et al.*, 2004) local search algorithm (100,000 local moves per run). It is followed by an exhaustive hybrid best-first search (Allouche *et al.*, 2015). IBM ILOG CPLEX 12.7.0.0 (using parameters EPAGAP, EPGAP, and EPINT set to zero to avoid premature stop) was reported as being very competitive on some image analysis (Kappes *et al.*, 2015) and Markov Random Field problems (Hurley *et al.*, 2016). CPLEX explores its search tree using best-first search. It applies several heuristics methods to find good solutions before and during the search. We also compared with message-passing algorithms: LIBDAI[12] (Mooij, 2010), winner of the *UAI 2010 Evaluation* at 20sec. and 1hour time limits, MPLP2[13] (Sontag *et al.*, 2008; 2012), and TRW-S[14] (Kolmogorov, 2006). Note that LIBDAI and TRW-S are applied on the original instances rather than the preprocessed ones as we found they produced better results without applying VAC first. All solvers read problems in *uai* tabular format, except CPLEX which uses the local polytope formulation (called support encoding in (Hurley *et al.*, 2016)). All computations were performed on a cluster of 48-core AMD Opteron 6176 at 2.3 GHz and 384 GB of RAM with a 1-hour CPU time limit[15].

Optimality results. The efficiency of DFBB, LDS, and VNS methods to prove optimality is shown in the cactus plot of Figure 1a. DFBB was slightly more efficient than LDS and solved 1442 (resp. 1433) instances among 1669 in 1-hour time limit. They are followed by three UDGVNS strategies with $(k\ \texttt{mult2}, \ell\ \texttt{mult2})$ (1430 solved), $(k\ \texttt{Luby}, \ell\ \texttt{mult2})$ (1425 solved) and $(k\ \texttt{add1/jump}, \ell\ \texttt{mult2})$ (1421 solved), remaining very close in terms of performance. Next, a set of three less-and-less efficient UDGVNS strategies rise: $(k\ \texttt{add1}, \ell\ \texttt{mult2})$ (1384 solved), $(k\ \texttt{add1}, \ell\ \texttt{Luby})$ (1361 solved) and $(k\ \texttt{add1}, \ell\ \texttt{add1})$ (1333 solved), showing the importance of faster discrepancy increase to speed up optimality proofs. The worst strategy here was using a fixed discrepancy level ($\ell = 3$ as originally proposed in (Fontaine *et al.*, 2013)) which solved 1128 instances. For comparison, DAOOPT (3600sec setting) solved 1409 instances, CPLEX solved 1423, and INCOP+TOULBAR2 1440 instances (results in Supp. material).

Anytime upper bound profiles. In order to summarize the evolution of upper bounds as time passes, we took a subset of 114 difficult instances, unsolved in 1 hour by our DFBB, LDS, and VNS methods (whereas CPLEX could solve 17 instances). Specifically, for each instance I we normalize all energies as follows: the best, potentially suboptimal solution found by any algorithm is 1, the worst solution is 2. This normalization is invariant to translation and scaling. Figure 1b shows the upper bound behavior for different VNS strategies compared to DFBB and LDS (see Supp. material for a zoom). The ranking of best methods is the opposite of the cactus plot order, except for $(k\ \texttt{add1/jump}, \ell\ \texttt{mult2})$ which comes in second position. The $\ell = 3$ strategy got the best upper bounds in average, but still very close to the other VNS strategies, except may-be $(k\ \texttt{Luby}, \ell\ \texttt{mult2})$ and $(k\ \texttt{mult2}, \ell\ \texttt{mult2})$. We conclude that our new iterative UDGVNS method (especially $(k\ \texttt{add1/jump}, \ell\ \texttt{mult2})$) offers a good compromise between anytime behavior and optimality proof. These results also show that variable neighborhood search is by far superior to classical systematic (DFBB) or non-systematic (LDS) tree search methods, improving by more than 20% (resp. 10%) the quality of the solu-

[8] UAI DBN, Grid, Linkage, ObjectDetection, CVPR ChineseChars, ColorSeg-8, InPainting-4, InPainting-8, ProteinInteraction, and CFN CELAR, ProteinDesign, SPOT5, Warehouse categories.

[9] *Weighted degree heuristic* (Boussemart *et al.*, 2004).

[10] graphmod.ics.uci.edu/group/DAOOPT-UAI12

[11] www.inra.fr/mia/T/toulbar2 version 0.9.8 with parameters *-i -dee -hbfs*.

[12] bitbucket.org/jorism/libdai.git version 0.3.2 using UAI 2010 settings.

[13] cs.nyu.edu/~dsontag/code/README_v2.html using 2.10^{-7} int gap thres.

[14] github.com/opengm/opengm v2.3.5 with TRW-S v1.3 stopping after $100,000$ iterations or 10^{-5} gap thres.

[15] Using parameter *-pe parallel_smp* $\min(2x, 30)$ on a SUN Grid Engine for a method exploiting x core(s) to ensure half-load of the nodes on the cluster.

tions. In the following figures, we assume UDGVNS with (k add1/jump, ℓ mult2) strategy.

Figure 1c compare UDGVNS with state-of-the-art methods. Message-passing algorithms like TRW-S and LIBDAI gave the worst results. They could not find any solution for 20 (resp. 19) instances (mostly in UAI/Linkage and CFN/SPOT5 categories, both containing hard constraints). The same problem occurred for MPLP2 on 5 instances (SPOT5), but it obtained much better results on the remaining instances. CPLEX ran out of memory on two instances without producing any solution due to the heavy local polytope encoding (CFN/Warehouse/capb,capmq5). All other methods got better results in average and produced at least one solution per instance. According to its initial phase setting, DAOOPT provides different anytime behaviors, very close to the best solutions in 1 hour. UDGVNS performed the best, slightly better than INCOP+TOULBAR2, improving by 1.7% (resp. 2.3%) on average after 1 hour (20 min).

Parallelization. Finally, in order to evaluate the impact of core numbers, we consider the anytime upper bound behavior of the parallel release: UPDGVNS using (k add1/jump, ℓ mult2) with $\ell_{min} = 3$, taken from the best strategies enlightened by UDGVNS. We made a comparison with CPLEX using 10 and 30 cores (results in Supp. material), improving its anytime behavior, but still being far from the other competitors (30 cores gave solutions 10% higher than UPDGVNS after 1 hour). We could not compare with the parallel version of DAOOPT as it is based on a different cluster engine (*condor*) and it does not parallelize its initial phase.

Figure 1d shows that UPDGVNS (with 10 or 30 cores) provides slightly better upper bounds than UDGVNS (using 1 core) in less than 20 min. The results seems to be, in average, poorly sensitive to the cores number, due to the fact than the 10-core curve is extremely close from the 30-core one. The 10 and 30-core UPDGVNS curves converge quickly in less than 2min. INCOP+TOULBAR2 quickly drops out around 1 min and never reaches the same quality level. UDGVNS converges slower but still going down after 20 min. DAOOPT (1200sec setting) gave results 10% in average worse than UPDGVNS with either 10 and 30 processors.

6 COMPUTATIONAL PROTEIN DESIGN

Benchmarks description. One main challenge in Computational Protein Design (CPD) lies in the exploration of the amino-acid sequence space, while considering, to some extent, side chain flexibility. The exorbitant size of the search space urges for the development of efficient exact deterministic search methods enabling identification of low-energy sequence-conformation models, corresponding to the Global Minimum Energy Conformation (GMEC). The GMEC corresponds to a maximum probability mass due to the Boltzmann relation between molecular energy and probability, which is, for that matter, equivalent in the Markov Random Field modeling with Maximum A Posteriori probability (MAP-MRF) estimation.

CPD has been recently modeled as CFN, and various intensive benchmarking had demonstrated that in most cases CFN techniques are more efficient than other discrete optimization methods (Allouche *et al.*, 2014), especially for full design of instances lesser than 100 Amino acid (Simoncini *et al.*, 2015) . In this paper we would like to evaluate VNS methods capability to solve difficult instances. Accordingly, we tried to generate new larger ones supposed to be more difficult to solve than those generated in (Simoncini *et al.*, 2015). For this aims, in a first stage, we selected proteins structure in the PDB databases with size between 100 and 300 amino-acid. On the basis of a database query described in the supplementary material, we obtained a first set including 438 PDB references, which has been sorted according to the average volume per variable calculated using the radius of gyration of each instance (see Supp. material). At last, we extracted for benchmarking only the 20th first elements and used as benchmarking set. Each protein structure was fully redesigned according to (Simoncini *et al.*, 2015) protocol. On the basis of energy matrix generated with a modified release of PYROSETTA.4 script (Simoncini *et al.*, 2015) in order to use the last released Rosetta force-field (aka Beta November 2016) (Alford and others, 2017). The instances (see Supp. material) contain from 130 up to $n = 282$ variables with maximum domain size from 383 to 438, and between 1706 and 6208 cost/energy functions, and besides the tree width ranges from 21 to 68 and from 0.16 to 0.34 for a normalized tree width.

In this section, we evaluate the effectiveness of UDGVNS and UPDGVNS on CPD instances in terms of optimality proof (cf. **part (a)**) and solution quality vs. CPU time (cf. **part (b)**). All computations were performed on a cluster of 96-core AMD Opteron 6174 at 2.2 GHz and 256 GB of RAM. The parallelization has been done in MPI.

Experimental Protocol. We compared UDGVNS and UPDGVNS with VNS/LDS+CP and FIXBB (CPD dedicated algorithm provided by Rosetta package). We also compared with TOULBAR2. We tested TOULBAR2 using Virtual Arc Consistency (Cooper *et al.*, 2010) as preprocessing combined with hybrid best-first search with tree decomposition (BTD-HBFS) using *min-fill* heuristic. Dead end elimination is turned off, according to (Simoncini *et al.*, 2015) (the resulting command line is: `toulbar2-B=1-A-dee:-O=-3`). The TOULBAR2 experiments use a 24-hour CPU time limit.

Concerning the VNS methods, in order to evaluate variability due to the random selection of neighborhoods, a set of 10 runs per instance with different seeds has been performed with a time limit of 1-hour per run. For the parallel strategy, the number of processes npr is set to 96 (i.e. maximum number of available processes). For UDGVNS and UPDGVNS, following the results observed in Section 5, we considered the following two settings for operators $+_k$ and $+_\ell$: (k add1, $\ell = 3$) which yields the best anytime performances and (k add1/jump, ℓ *mult*2) which offers the best compromise between both anytime performances and optimality proof. k_{min}, k_{max} and ℓ_{min} have been respectively set to 4, n (the total number of variables) and 3 (they correspond to the same parameter settings as those described in (Fontaine *et al.*, 2013)).

(a) Optimality results. Our first set of experiments aims at evaluating the efficiency of UDGVNS and UPDGVNS in terms of optimality proof comparing with TOULBAR2. As indicated before, we used the setting (k add1/jump, ℓ *mult*2). For all methods (see Supp. material), the CPU-time is the time to find and prove an optimal solution. TOULBAR2 clearly outperforms the two VNS methods: UDGVNS and UPDGVNS were able to prove optimality only on 3 instances among the 10 ones closed by TOULBAR2. However, the VNS methods are faster (except on 5dbl), despite the fact that BTD-HBFS benefits from the lower bounds reported by HBFS in individual clusters to improve the anytime behavior and from the global pruning lower bounds of BTD. This greatly improves the overall performance of TOULBAR2 compared to VNS methods.

(b) CPU time and solution quality results. Our second set of experiments aims at evaluating VNS capability with respect to finding the optimal solution or a solution of better quality on instances for which optimal solutions are unavailable. For this aims, we selected (k add1, $\ell = 3$) as setting for operators $+_k$ and $+_\ell$.

Table 1 shows a comparative evaluation of VNS methods with FIXBB and TOULBAR2. For each instance and each VNS method, we report the number of successful runs to reach the optimum (or the best found solution for unsolved instances) within a 3600-second time limit, the average CPU times (in seconds) over the 10 runs (for unsuccessful runs, the CPU time is set to the time limit) $\pm$ the standard deviation. The Energy gap ΔE between the best VNS solution and the two external references FIXBB and TOULBAR2 are also given. For TOULBAR2, reported CPU times correspond to times to find an optimal solution (for solved instances) or a best one (for unsolved ones) within the 24-hour time limit.

VNS methods vs. FIXBB. Rosetta Modeling suite is one of the most popular software package used in CPD field. It provides a Monte Carlo based Simulated Annealing algorithm called FIXBB. In this work, the best solutions exhibited by 1000 FIXBB cycles performed on each CPD instance have been used as base-line to compare solution quality of the solution provided by VNS methods when TOULBAR2 BTD-HBFS fails to solve the instance.

The FIXBB CPU times are two orders of magnitude higher than the 1h time limit imposed for VNS evaluation. They are not reported as they exceed 100-hours in sequential mode, even if FIXBB cycles are independent and thus be easy to parallelize. As we can see in Table 1 (see column ΔE of (4)), the solution quality of FIXBB is in all cases inferior to the best solution found by the VNS methods. The Energetic gap ΔE between FIXBB solution and the best VNS overall solution ranges between +0.16 and +5.20 Rosetta Energy Unit (R.E.U). As shown in (Simoncini *et al.*, 2015) such a level of energy difference can strongly impact the designed protein solution (i.e. the corresponding sequences of the two methods can be far in terms of hamming distance).

VNS methods vs. TOULBAR2. The comparison between best solutions found by VNS methods and TOULBAR2 shows that, excepted VNS/LDS+CP, both UDGVNS and UPDGVNS provide in all case the same or even better solution than TOULBAR2 (see column ΔE of (5) in Table 1). The Energetic gap ΔE in the worst case reaches 17.86 R.U.E. Concerning the number of successful runs reported over the 10 runs, VNS/LDS+CP seems less robust respectively than UDGVNS and the parallel release UPDGVNS. This last one provides in all cases the best solution over all. Table 1 also compares the VNS methods in terms of speedups. We observe that speedup values are fluctuating from one instance to another, very likely due to the tree decomposition resulting from the 3D shape of each instance. For VNS/LDS+CP and UDGVNS, it range between 0.62 and 2.86 over the 14 instances solved by both methods. As expected, when tree decomposition and parallelization are used, not only the speed of resolution increases but the reliability too (speedup values between 4.1 and 18.5). Moreover, the comparison between UDGVNS and UPDGVNS shows significant accelerations (between 2.06 and 9.22), thus confirming the practical interest of parallelization in addition to the exploitation of problem decomposition. We can observe (in Supp. material) that both UDGVNS and UPDGVNS find optimal solutions more quickly than TOULBAR2 within the one hour time limit (with the exception of UDGVNS

Instance	ncl	(1)		(2)		(3)		(4)	(5)		Speed-up		
		Succ.	Time (s)	Succ.	Time (s)	Succ.	Time (s)	ΔE	Time (s)	ΔE	(1/2)	(1/3)	(2/3)
5dbl	87	10/10	2,761± 67	10/10	963± 53	10/10	149± 18	0.27	783	0	2.86	18.53	6.46
5jdd	168	0/10	TO	10/10	3,248 ± 162	10/10	646± 72	4.08	20,662	0.04	-	-	5.02
3r8q	157	0/10	TO	10/10	3,478± 82	10/10	397± 47	4.19	12,762	0	-	-	8.76
4bxp	108	10/10	1,213± 32	10/10	1,352± 40	10/10	216± 24	0.26	2,966	0	0.89	5.61	6.26
1f00	177	0/10	TO	10/10	2,575± 29	10/10	542± 30	4.38	9,749	0	-		4.75
2x8x	131	10/10	3,312± 111	4/10	2,801± 1,071	10/10	521± 58	4.16	69,213	3.61	1.18	6.35	5.37
1xaw	66	0/10	TO	10/10	581± 38	10/10	260± 57	2.73	2,804	0	-	-	2.23
5e10	74	10/10	1,667± 86	10/10	1,412± 21	10/10	132± 24	0.26	1,171	0	1.18	12.62	10.7
1dvo	82	10/10	940± 22	10/10	940± 22	10/10	197± 25	2.90	34,142	0.18	1	4.77	4.77
1ytq	67	10/10	2,235± 211	10/10	1,304± 40	10/10	280± 26	1.67	17,063	0.31	1.71	7.98	4.65
2af5	140	0/10	TO	10/10	2,659± 75	10/10	894± 247	4.37	86,029	0.60	-	-	2.97
1ng2	86	10/10	1,065± 69	10/10	547± 18	10/10	260± 26	1.14	38,730	5.93	1.94	4.09	2.10
3sz7	79	0/10	TO	10/10	2,952± 276	10/10	320± 50	3.11	82,625	0.54	-	-	9.22
2gee	110	10/10	1,647± 8	10/10	1,276± 19	10/10	286± 38	1.68	5,021	0	1.29	5.75	4.46
5e0z	73	10/10	621± 15	10/10	995± 18	10/10	105± 8	0.16	999	0	0.62	5.91	9.47
1yz7	87	10/10	2,148± 9	10/10	945± 24	10/10	457± 85	2.91	83,816	3.20	2.27	4.70	2.06
3lf9	72	10/10	1,636± 31	10/10	894± 41.17	10/10	216± 21	2.41	2,667	0	1.82	7.57	4.13
3e3v	91	0/10	TO	10/10	2,327± 621	10/10	263± 38	2.57	81,574	0.15	-	-	8.84
1is1	107	10/10	3,178± 51	10/10	2,274± 421	10/10	329± 48	3.45	63,832	0.42	1.39	9.65	6.91
5eqz	89	10/10	1,849± 49	10/10	697± 6	10/10	225± 16	2.20	12,768	0	2.65	8.21	3.097
4uos	118	10/10	2,304± 988	10/10	2,109± 62	10/10	469± 79	5.20	58,589	17.86	1.09	4.91	4.5

TO: TimeOut **(1):** VNS/LDS+CP(k add1, $\ell = 3$) **(2):** UDGVNS (k add1, $\ell = 3$) **(3):** UPDGVNS (npr, k add1, $\ell = 3$) **(4):** FIXBB **(5):** TOULBAR2

Table 1: Comparative evaluation on CPD instances. In bold instances solved by TOULBAR2. ncl is the number of clusters. ΔE is in Rosetta Energy unit. It has been obtained by the difference of solutions costs divided by the cost shift used during modeling, in this case 10^8.

on 5dbl and 5e10). For UDGVNS, speedup values range from 0.81 to 18.3 with a mean of 4.23 over all the solved instances. For UPDGVNS, the ratio in terms of speedup is greatly amplified (between 5.25 and 56.74 with a mean of 18.48 over all the solved instances). For unsolved instances, we measured the CPU times spent by the three VNS methods (within the 3600-second time limit) to reach the best solution produced by TOULBAR2. Results (in Supplementary material) show a clear ordering in terms of CPU times across different solvers, from TOULBAR2, VNS/LDS+CP, UDGVNS, and UPDGVNS. The speedup values are significantly improved, in particular with UPDGVNS (between 32.3 and 354.6 with a mean of 168.7 over all the unsolved instances). These results confirm the superiority of VNS methods in terms of anytime performance as compared to TOULBAR2.

CONCLUSION

In this paper we proposed a unified view of VNS methods including various LDS and neighborhood evolution strategies. Experiments performed on difficult instances, coming from a large graphical model benchmark, showed that our hybrid method has a much better anytime behavior than existing tree search methods and still being competitive for proving optimality. We further proposed a parallel version of our method improving its anytime behavior. It remains as future work to automatically choose the best parameter settings per instance.

Acknowledgements This work has been partially funded by the french "Agence nationale de la Recherche", reference ANR-16-C40-0028. We are grateful to the genotoul bioinformatics platform Toulouse Midi-Pyrenees (Bioinfo Genotoul) and the HPC HAYTHAM of university of Oran 1 for providing computing and storage resources. We thank Mathieu Fontaine for his contribution to the code of DGVNS.

References

[Alford and others, 2017] R Alford et al. The Rosetta all-atom energy function for macromolecular modeling and design. *bioRxiv*, 2017.

[Allouche *et al.*, 2014] D Allouche, J Davies, S de Givry, G Katsirelos, T Schiex, S Traoré, I André, S Barbe, S Prestwich, and B O'Sullivan. Computational Protein Design as an Optimization Problem. *Artif. Intell.*, 212:59–79, 2014.

[Allouche *et al.*, 2015] D Allouche, S de Givry, G Katsirelos, T Schiex, and M Zytnicki. Anytime Hybrid Best-First Search with Tree Decomposition for Weighted CSP. In *Proc. of CP*, pages 12–28, 2015.

[Boussemart *et al.*, 2004] F Boussemart, F Hemery, C Lecoutre, and L Sais. Boosting systematic search by weighting constraints. In *Proc. of ECAI*, 2004.

[Cooper *et al.*, 2010] M Cooper, S de Givry, M Sanchez, T Schiex, M Zytnicki, and T Werner. Soft arc consistency revisited. *Artificial Intelligence*, 174:449–478, 2010.

[Davidovic and Crainic, 2012] T Davidovic and T Crainic. MPI parallelization of variable neighborhood search. *Electronic Notes in Discrete Mathematics*, 39:241–248, 2012.

[de Givry *et al.*, 2013] S de Givry, S Prestwich, and B O'Sullivan. Dead-end elimination for weighted CSP. In *Proc. of CP*, pages 263–272, 2013.

[Dechter and Rish, 2003] R Dechter and I Rish. Mini-buckets: A general scheme for bounded inference. *Journal of the ACM (JACM)*, 50(2):107–153, 2003.

[Favier *et al.*, 2011] A Favier, S Givry, A Legarra, and T Schiex. Pairwise decomposition for combinatorial optim. in graphical models. In *Proc. of IJCAI*, pages 2126–2132, 2011.

[Fontaine *et al.*, 2013] M Fontaine, S Loudni, and P Boizumault. Exploiting tree decomposition for guiding neighborhoods exploration for VNS. *RAIRO OR*, 47(2):91–123, 2013.

[Harvey and Ginsberg, 1995] W Harvey and M Ginsberg. Limited discrepancy search. In *Proc. of IJCAI*, pages 607–615, 1995.

[Hurley *et al.*, 2016] B Hurley, B O'Sullivan, D Allouche, G Katsirelos, T Schiex, M Zytnicki, and S de Givry. Multi-Language Evaluation of Exact Solvers in Graphical Model Discrete Optimization. *Constraints*, 21(3):413–434, 2016.

[Hutter *et al.*, 2005] F Hutter, H Hoos, and T Stützle. Efficient stochastic local search for MPE solving. In *Proc. of IJCAI*, pages 169–174, 2005.

[Ihler *et al.*, 2012] A Ihler, N Flerova, R Dechter, and L Otten. Join-graph based cost-shifting schemes. In *Proc. of UAI*, pages 397–406, 2012.

[Kappes *et al.*, 2015] J Kappes, B Andres, F Hamprecht, C Schnörr, S Nowozin, D Batra, S Kim, B Kausler, T Kröger, J Lellmann, N Komodakis, B Savchynskyy, and C Rother. A comparative study of modern inference techniques for structured discrete energy minimization problems. *Int. J. of Computer Vision*, 115(2):155–184, 2015.

[Koller and Friedman, 2009] D Koller and N Friedman. *Probabilistic graphical models: principles and techniques*. The MIT Press, 2009.

[Kolmogorov, 2006] V Kolmogorov. Convergent Tree-Reweighted Message Passing for Energy Minimization. *IEEE T. Patt. Anal. Mach. Intell.*, 28(10):1568–1583, 2006.

[Larrosa *et al.*, 2005] J Larrosa, S de Givry, F Heras, and M Zytnicki. Existential arc consistency: getting closer to full arc consistency in weighted CSPs. In *Proc. of IJCAI*, pages 84–89, 2005.

[Larrosa *et al.*, 2016] J Larrosa, E Rollon, and R Dechter. Limited discrepancy AND/OR search and its application to optimization tasks in graphical models. In *Proc. of IJCAI*, pages 617–623, 2016.

[Loudni and Boizumault, 2003] S Loudni and P Boizumault. Solving constraint optimization problems in anytime contexts. In *Proc. of IJCAI*, pages 251–256, 2003.

[Luby *et al.*, 1993] M Luby, A Sinclair, and D Zuckerman. Optimal speedup of Las Vegas algorithms. In *Proc. of TCS*, pages 128–133, 1993.

[Marinescu and Dechter, 2009] R. Marinescu and R. Dechter. Memory intensive and/or search for combinatorial optimization in graphical models. *AI*, 173(16-17):1492–1524, 2009.

[Marinescu *et al.*, 2003] R Marinescu, K Kask, and R Dechter. Systematic vs. non-systematic algorithms for solving the MPE task. In *Proc. of UAI*, pages 394–402, 2003.

[Mengshoel *et al.*, 2011] O Mengshoel, D Wilkins, and D Roth. Initialization and Restart in Stochastic Local Search: Computing a Most Probable Explanation in Bayesian Networks. *IEEE Trans. Knowl. Data Eng.*, 23(2):235–247, 2011.

[Meseguer *et al.*, 2006] P. Meseguer, F. Rossi, and T. Schiex. Soft constraints processing. In *Handbook of Constraint Programming*, chapter 9. Elsevier, 2006.

[Mladenović and Hansen, 1997] N Mladenović and P Hansen. Variable Neighborhood Search. *Comput. Oper. Res.*, 24(11):1097–1100, November 1997.

[Mooij, 2010] Joris M. Mooij. libDAI: A free and open source C++ library for discrete approximate inference in graphical models. *Journal of Machine Learning Research*, 11:2169–2173, 2010.

[Neveu *et al.*, 2004] B Neveu, G Trombettoni, and F Glover. ID Walk: A Candidate List Strategy with a Simple Diversification Device. In *Proc. of CP*, pages 423–437, 2004.

[Otten and Dechter, 2012] L Otten and R Dechter. Anytime AND/OR depth-first search for combinatorial optimization. *AI Communications*, 25(3):211–227, 2012.

[Otten and Dechter, 2017] L Otten and R Dechter. And/or branch-and-bound on a computational grid. page 84p., 2017. Unpublished.

[Otten *et al.*, 2012] L Otten, A Ihler, K Kask, and R Dechter. Winning the PASCAL 2011 MAP challenge with enhanced AND/OR branch-and-bound. In *NIPS W. DISCML*, 2012.

[Ouali *et al.*, 2015] A Ouali, S Loudni, L Loukil, P Boizumault, and Y Lebbah. Replicated parallel strategies for decomposition guided VNS. *ENDM*, 47:93–100, 2015.

[Park, 2002] J Park. Using weighted MAX-SAT engines to solve MPE. In *Proc. of AAAI*, pages 682–687, 2002.

[Shaw, 1998] P Shaw. Using constraint programming and local search methods to solve vehicle routing problems. In *Proc. of CP*, pages 417–431, 1998.

[Shimony, 1994] S Shimony. Finding MAPs for belief networks is NP-hard. *Artificial Intelligence*, 68:399–410, 1994.

[Simoncini *et al.*, 2015] D Simoncini, D Allouche, S de Givry, C Delmas, S Barbe, and T Schiex. Guaranteed discrete energy optimization on large protein design problems. *J. of Chemical Theo. and Comput.*, 11(12):5980–5989, 2015.

[Sontag *et al.*, 2008] D Sontag, T Meltzer, A Globerson, Y Weiss, and T Jaakkola. Tightening LP relaxations for MAP using message-passing. In *Proc. of UAI*, pages 503–510, 2008.

[Sontag *et al.*, 2012] D Sontag, D Choe, and Y Li. Efficiently searching for frustrated cycles in MAP inference. In *Proc. of UAI*, pages 795–804, 2012.

[Wainwright and Jordan, 2008] M Wainwright and M Jordan. Graphical models, exponential families, and variational inference. *F&T. in Machine Learning*, 1(1–2):1–305, 2008.

[Wang and Koller, 2013] H Wang and D Koller. Subproblem-tree calibration: A unified approach to max-product message passing. In *Proc. of ICML*, pages 190–198, 2013.

Supplementary Material

July 11, 2017

1 Cactus plot of UDGVNS versus CPLEX, DAOOPT, and INCOP+TOULBAR2

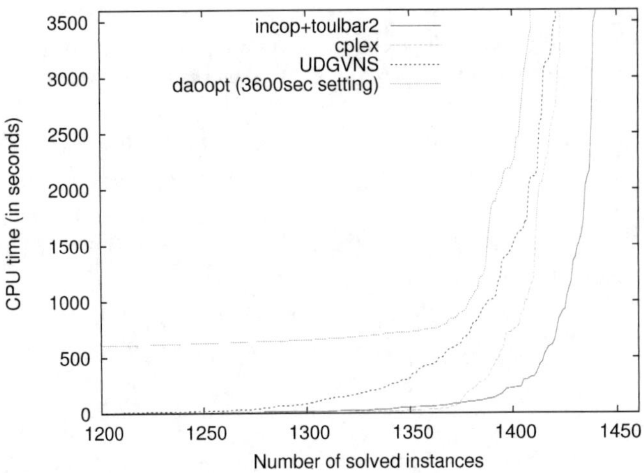

Figure 1: Number of instances solved by each method as time passes (UDGVNS = UDGVNS(k add1/jump, ℓ mult2)).

2 Anytime upper bound zoom for UDGVNS versus LDS

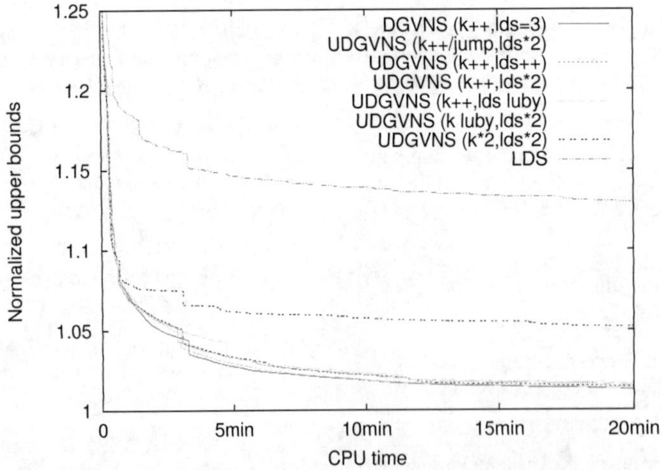

Figure 2: Anytime upper bound zoom for UDGVNS versus LDS.

3 Anytime upper bound of UDGVNS and UPDGVNS versus CPLEX

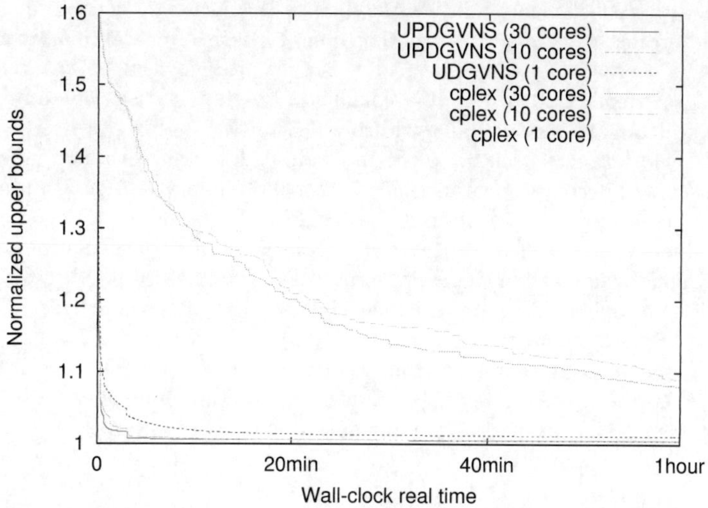

Figure 3: Anytime upper bound with 1 , 10 and 30 processors respectively for `cplex` and `UPDGVNS` (`UPDGVNS` = `UPDGVNS`(k `add1/jump`, ℓ `mult2`)).

4 Solving time and anytime behavior of U(P)DGVNS versus CPLEX and DAOOPT on UAI-Linkage category

Linkage *(optimum / worst solution)*	pedigree19 *(4625/21439)*	pedigree31 *(5258/166553)*	pedigree44 *(6651/104904)*	pedigree51 *(6406/629929)*
CPLEX (1 core)	790	59.3	6.35	36.23
CPLEX (10 cores)	191	9.00	2.48	9.43
CPLEX (30 cores)	**75**	**7.17**	**2.69**	**5.34**
DAOOPT (1 core)	375,110	16,238	95,830	101,788
DAOOPT (20 cores)	27,281	1,055	6,739	6,406
DAOOPT (100 cores)	7,492	201	1,799	1,578
UDGVNS (1 core)	- *(4949)*	- *(5258)*	- *(6722)*	- *(6406)*
UPDGVNS (10 cores)	- *(4762)*	3,341	- *(6651)*	- *(6406)*
UPDGVNS (30 cores)	- *(4626)*	1,775	- *(6651)*	- *(6406)*

Table 1: Best CPU time (in seconds) for sequential versions and best wall-clock time for multiple-core ones to find and prove optimality on Pedigree instances. A "-" means no proof of optimality in 1 hour (except DAOOPT with no time limit) (in parenthesis, unnormalized upper bound founds after 1 hour).

We report DAOOPT time from (OD17), obtained on a cluster of dual 2.67 GHz Intel Xeon X5650 6-core CPUs and 24 GB of RAM.

5 CPD instances filtering

In this paper we would like to evaluate VNS methods capability to solve difficult instances. Accordingly, we tried to generate new larger ones supposed to be more difficult to solve than those generated in (SAdG$^+$15). For this aims, in a first stage, we selected protein structures in the PDB databases (http://www.rcsb.org/pdb/home/home.do) with sizes range between 100 and 300 amino-acid. The resulting query has been filtered with the following criteria: resolution has to be lower than 2.5 A, membrane proteins, proteins complex, as well as proteins with disulfur bright have been removed, in addition, with proteins including non natural amino acid. We also discarded proteins with missing residues, out of the N and C terminal part of the sequence in order to select a protein subset without any hole. Proteins with identity sequences higher than 90% are unselected. The corresponding remaining set includes 438 PDB references. Therefore, we sorted the 438 putative instances according to the average volume per variable and we extracted for benchmarking only the 20th first elements and used as benchmarking set. Each protein structure was fully redesigned according to (SAdG$^+$15) protocol. On the basis of energy matrix generated with a modified release of PYROSETTA.4 script (SAdG$^+$15) in order to use the last released Rosetta force-field (aka Beta November 2016) (A$^+$17). The instances characteristic contain from 130 up to $n = 282$ variables width maximum domain size from 383 to 438, and between 1706 and 6208 cost functions. The tree width ranges from 21 to 68, and from 0.16 to 0.34 for a normalized tree width.

In order to select well decomposable instances, after preliminary reorientation of each protein according to his inertial moment, we filtered the resulting PDB set by 3D geometrical criteria. By construction, due to the cutoff distance used for pairwise energy calculation and his related constraints in the model, Globular protein (.i.e spherical one) will correspond to CFN very nearby as click. In practice, the spherical shape which can be detected by a symmetric repartition of the Radius of gyration (Rg) component Rg(x), Rg(y), Rg(z). Indeed, Rg and his subcomponent are defined as the root mean square distance from each atom of the protein to their centroid or in the orthogonal plan to the related axis (x,y,z). Thus, for selecting non spherical protein , we first calculated the Rg_i respectively around x , y and z axis as and we filtered the proteins characterized by a ratio:

$$min(Rg(x)/Rg + Rg(y)/Rg + Rg(z)/Rg) \tag{1}$$

The $min(Rg(i)/Rg)$ is one figure to detect putative well structured instances.

Another structural criterion that can be used for structured instances filtering is a decreasing sort according to the approximated means space volume occupied associated to each variable. This volume is also related to the Gyration radius by the following equation:

$$\bar{V} = \frac{\frac{4}{3} * \pi * Rg^3}{|X|} \tag{2}$$

This criterion does not give at first sight a direct information about fold shape, but interestingly, both structural criteria produce the same 15th first instances set, with only few re-ranking, very likely because protein compactness got maximum bound and indeed a minimum average volume per amino-acid when the protein fold is close to sphere or vice versa for linear protein fold. After the 15th instances, the two critters remains less correlated. As a matter of fact, in the 5 next instances, the covering between the two sorted list is 2 over 5. On Account of computer power for benchmarking, we can not bench the full protein set.

pdbid	$\|\mathcal{X}\|$	d	e	tw	$tw/\|\mathcal{X}\|$	min(Rg_x/Rg)	$\bar{V}(^3/var)$
5dbl	130	384	1,706	21	0.16	0.150	1,212.49
5jdd	263	406	5,220	41	0.16	0.239	655.58
3r8q	271	418	5,518	43	0.16	0.341	472.88
4bxp	170	439	2,636	33	0.19	0.316	457.81
1f00	282	430	6,208	51	0.18	0.269	439.28
2x8x	235	407	4,745	44	0.19	0.354	404.42
1xaw	107	412	1,623	28	0.26	0.308	378.04
5e10	133	400	2,286	34	0.26	0.294	344.68
1dvo	152	389	2,587	51	0.34	0.420	343.38
1ytq	181	415	3,449	54	0.30	0.392	332.69
2af5	292	410	5,693	68	0.23	0.427	330.23
1ng2	176	397	3,135	60	0.34	0.473	309.16
3sz7	151	450	2805	49	0.32	0.403	304.87
2gee	188	397	3,715	38	0.20	0.367	293.25
5e0z	136	420	2,367	36	0.26	0.362	279.00
1yz7	176	418	3,538	49	0.28	0.414	276.35
3e3v	154	436	2,976	37	0.26	0.367	251.97
3lf9	120	416	2,133	31	0.24	0.323	251.51
1is1	185	431	3,740	48	0.26	0.459	245.58
5eqz	138	434	2,567	33	0.24	0.338	241.93
4uos	188	383	4,161	44	0.23	0.347	234.11

Table 2: Characteristics of PDB instances: pdbid is the code reference in PDB database, $|\mathcal{X}|$ is the number of variable, d is the maximum domain size, e is number of cost functions, tw is the Min-fill tree width and $tw/|\mathcal{X}|$ a normalized tree width by $|\mathcal{X}|$. The two last columns correspond to structural criteria respectively defined in (1) and (2). Grey color corresponds to the re-ranking when one min(Rg_x/Rg) or $\bar{V}$ is used for PDB list sorting.

6 Comparing best solutions of TOULBAR2 vs VNS methods

Instance	Time (s)			Speed-up		
	(1)	(2)	(3)	(5/1)	(5/2)	(5/3)
5jdd	-	3,248±162	639±76	-	6.3	32.3
2x8x	2,087±62	1,012±64	475±54	33.1	68.3	145.7
1dvo	885±20	830±24	191±25	38.5	41.1	178.7
1ytq	2,215±231	1,280±40	277±26	7.7	13.3	61.6
2af5	-	2,217±57	856.±246	-	38.8	100.5
1ng2	542±2	400±12	241±26	71.4	96.8	160.7
3sz7	3,178±421	1,948±484	277±48	26	42.4	298.2
1yz7	970±4	675±16	428±83	86.4	124.1	195.8
3o3v	2,332±46	1,137±37	230±29	34.9	71.7	354.6
1is1	2,986±47	2,159±376	317±53	21.3	29.5	201.36
4uos	465±3	467±9	427±83,81	126	125.4	137.2

(a) Unsolved CPD instances.

Instance	Speed-up		
	(5/1)	(5/2)	(5/3)
5dbl	0.28	0.81	5.25
3r8q	-	3.66	32.14
4bxp	2.44	2.19	13.73
1f00	-	3.78	17.98
1xaw	-	4.82	10.78
5e10	0.70	0.83	8.87
2gee	3.04	3.93	17.55
5e0z	1.6	1.00	9.51
3lf9	1.63	2.98	12.34
5eqz	6.90	18.31	56.74

(b) Solved CPD instances.

Instance	Time(s)		
	(2*)	(3*)	(5)
5dbl	1,828.27	791.16	783.18
3r8q	-		41,700.1
4bxp	-		4,261.67
1f00	-		-
1xaw	-		2,917.04
5e10	839.52	196.43	1,171.98
2gee	-		9,795.59
5e0z	416.12	172.96	999.66
3lf9	-		2,960.64
5eqz	-		41,813

(c) Optimality proof.

Table 3: Tables (3a) and (3b) report, for each instance, the CPU times spent by VNS methods (within the 3600-seconds time limit) to obtain the best solution computed by TOULBAR2 (5). A '–' indicates that the corresponding solver was not able to compute a solution of equal/better quality than `toulbar2`. (1) : `VNS`(k `add1`, $\ell = 3$) (2): `UDGVNS`(k `add1`, $\ell = 3$) (3): `UPDGVNS`(npr, k `add1`, $\ell = 3$). Table (3c) reports the CPU-times required by `UDGVNS`, `UPDGVNS` and TOULBAR2 to prove the optimum within the 24-hours time limit. A '–' indicates that the corresponding solver failed to prove optimality. (2*): `UDGVNS`(k `add1/jump`, ℓ `mult2`) (3*): `UPDGVNS`(npr, k `add1/jump`, ℓ `mult2`).

References

[A+17] R Alford et al. The Rosetta all-atom energy function for macromolecular modeling and design. *bioRxiv*, 2017.

[OD17] L Otten and R Dechter. And/or branch-and-bound on a computational grid. page 84p., 2017. Unpublished.

[SAdG+15] D Simoncini, D Allouche, S de Givry, C Delmas, S Barbe, and T Schiex. Guaranteed discrete energy optimization on large protein design problems. *J. of Chemical Theo. and Comput.*, 11(12):5980–5989, 2015.

Fair Optimal Stopping Policy for Matching with Mediator

Yang Liu
yangl@seas.harvard.edu, SEAS, Harvard University

Abstract

In this paper we study an optimal stopping policy for a multi-agent delegated sequential matching system with *fairness constraints*. We consider a setting where a mediator/decision maker matches a sequence of arriving assignments to multiple groups of agents, with agents being grouped according to certain sensitive attributes that needs to be protected. The decision maker aims to maximize total rewards that can be collected from above matching process (from all groups), while making the matching fair among groups. We discuss two types of fairness constraints: (i) each group has a certain expected deadline before which the match needs to happen; (ii) each group would like to have a guaranteed share of average reward from the matching. We present the exact characterization of fair optimal strategies. Example is provided to demonstrate the computation efficiency of our solution.

1 INTRODUCTION

We consider a delegated multi-agent sequential matching problem [Derman et al., 1972, Moscarini, 2005, Le Ny et al., 2006], where the decision maker (mediator) helps decide on matching a set of sequentially arriving assignments to a set of arriving groups of agents. This setting can model various application scenarios in a sequential and dynamical system:

- *Ride sharing*: UBER matches arriving ride requests to drivers from different groups (according to race, gender, neighborhood, income etc.)
- *Job matching*: On employment market, the mediator matches arriving job opportunities to job candidates from different groups (again race, gender, or social status, background etc).

Serving as the proxy mediator, the decision maker receives reward from each successful matching, which realization depends on the quality of matching. For example, the proxy extracts subsidies proportionally from the payments issued for each matched and completed task.

This decision making problem for sequential matching has been studied and has been shown to be solvable elegantly under an optimal stopping rule solution framework [Ferguson, 2006]. This line of works typically focus on finding the optimal stopping strategy by matching agents with assignments judiciously such that the total average reward (over time) being collected is maximized. The optimal matching policy is shown to have a stopping structure, with the core idea of skipping certain matching if the observed reward realization is low. Often the optimal stopping policy has a simple threshold structure w.r.t. the reward realization.

Recently fairness issues have raised a lot of discussions and concerns on designing and implementing different decision making policies, e.g., see discussion of fairness in social decision making [Radke et al., 2012], algorithmic bias in data mining [Hajian et al., 2016], fairness in a bandit decision making framework [Joseph et al., 2016], and fair action within a Markovian decision making framework [Jabbari et al., 2016]. Our problem setting shares similar concerns. For example, when different groups (differ in sensitive features, such as gender, race etc) of agents have different chances of seeing a high reward matching, the decision maker may bias towards *not* matching such agents. Or consider another example where different agents may have different matching constraints that are supposed to be protected under certain policy. Yet from technical perspectives, much less results has been developed towards understanding the issue of fairness constraints for this multi-agent optimal sequential matching problems.

In this paper we set out to explore this topic. We will devote more to the algorithmic aspects of such a problem, rather than the policy level in that we will characterize the optimal stopping policy under a set of *given* fairness constraints within the optimal stopping rule's framework. Specifically we consider the following *fair* multi-agent matching problem. Suppose there are multiple groups of agents trying to be matched with a sequence of arriving assignments in discrete time slots. Agents's availabilities follow an IID process. The available agent will be allowed to be matched to an assignment. Over the successful matches both the decision maker and agents will accumulate rewards. Rewards follow certain distribution and are generated according to an IID process over matching periods. Therefore due to the fact that the reward statistics vary dynamically, the decision maker needs to decide whether to match or not when facing the opportunity depending on the currently observed reward of the potential matching, in order to improve the total rewards collected. For this classical stopping rule setting, we are going to show that the optimal matching strategy gives up matching opportunity when the observed reward statistics is low, and individual groups of agents may suffer from losing matching opportunities. We consider two fairness constrained versions of above problem. For the first one, each group of agents has a deadline, which the group's expected matching time cannot go beyond of. In the second case, each group of agents would like a certain amount of average reward (over the waiting time) to be guaranteed from the matching.

1.1 OUR RESULTS AND CONTRIBUTIONS

Our contributions summarize as follows. (1) We formulate the fairness constrained multi-agent sequential matching problems into a set of constrained optimal stopping ones, and show their equivalences with a set of constrained optimization problems. (2) We characterize the fair optimal stopping policy under delay and reward constraints respectively. Our characterization also reveals the fundamental limits in fair optimal stopping problems, e.g. our results help characterize the feasible region w.r.t. individual fairness constraints. Properties of the derived optimal strategies are also studied. (3) We demonstrate the efficiency of computing the optimal stopping strategy within our solution framework. To our best knowledge, none of the existing works has tackled this type of matching/stopping problem with groups of agents facing individual fairness constraints.

1.2 RELATED WORKS

Fairness issues in decision making and machine learning systems, or more generally in Artificial Intelligence, have attracted an increasing amount of attentions recently [Hardt, 2011, Dwork et al., 2012, Radke et al., 2012, Joseph et al., 2016, Kleinberg et al., 2017]. More specifically, [Radke et al., 2012] studied the effect of fairness concerns in social decision making processes, while [Joseph et al., 2016] analyzed fairness in candidate option selection within the classical Multi-Armed Bandit decision making framework. While a growing number of works [Hardt, 2011, Dwork et al., 2012, Chouldechova, 2017, Hardt et al., 2016] have studied the fairness issues for one-shot decision making problems, much less has been understood for a fair decision making process. Our results try to fill in this direction.

On a higher level, our matching problem can also be viewed as a multi-agent scheduling problem. [Ferguson, 2006, Xu et al., 2013, Zheng et al., 2009] have established the equivalence between a large category of such a multi-agent scheduling problem with the classical optimal stopping rule problem, where the optimal policy has proven to have a simple characterizable threshold structure. [Ferguson, 2006] gives a good summary of the stopping rule problems for different types (e.g., selfish v.s. collaborative) of agents/users. In [Kennedy, 1982] an optimal stopping problem for multi-agents under delay constraint is considered. Nonetheless the above work considered only the *average delay* (average over all agents) constraint, while the issues with individual *fairness* constraints have not been addressed in this type of scheduling problems.

The rest of our paper is organized as follows. In Section 2, we detail our model and revisit the optimal stopping rule based multi-agent sequential matching problem. Formulations of the sequential matching problems with delay and reward fairness constraints are presented in Section 3. We then state the solutions for above problems in Section 4. In Section 5, we present an specific example to demonstrate the efficiency of computing the optimal strategy. Section 6 concludes the paper.

2 PRELIMINARIES

Consider the following sequential delegated assignment problem. We have $M > 1$ groups of agents facing a sequence of arriving assignments and denote them by the set $\mathcal{U} = \{1, 2, ..., M\}$. We can view the agents as companies looking for job candidates (assignments), or freelancers (UBER drivers) looking for job offers (ride requests). They form groups according to certain attributes, for instance race, gender, or residency. The decision maker (DM) is delegating the matching procedure. Note that the group to be matched is the same as there is an arriving agent from that group to be matched.

The decision making process proceeds as follows. At each time n (discrete time slot), there is an arrival of possible assignment (deterministically) to be matched. We model the availabilities of groups (of agents) as a stochastic process with a constant expected inter-arrival time t_c that $\tau := \mathbb{E}[t_c]$ stays as a constant. Denote by p_i^s the probability that there is an agent from group i is ready to be matched to an assignment upon an arrival time, and $\sum_{i \in \mathcal{U}} p_i^s = 1$ [1].

Both agents and DM are collecting rewards from the matching process. Per each match, reward is generated according to a random variable $R_i \in \mathbb{R}^+$ (non-negative real numbers) for group i, with its cumulative distribution function (CDF) $F_{R_i}(x)$ defined on $x \in \mathbb{R}^+$. Jointly the DM observes reward R:

$$R \sim \sum_i p_i^s F_{R_i}(x) := F_R(x), x \in \mathbb{R}^+.$$

Before each matching, the DM observes the current reward realization $R(\omega)$ (ω denotes a realization of R). Then he makes a decision between two options : *stop* and *continue*. By *stop* the DM will proceed to match the agent with the assignment, which takes one unit time slot to finish. As a consequence, a total reward $\delta \cdot R(\omega), 1 > \delta > 0$ will be collected. δ can be thought of the fraction DM charges for his service. By *continue*, the DM will forgo the current matching opportunity, and the above process repeats by itself. Clearly by *continue* a potentially higher reward may be collected in the future if the current matching happens to be a bad realization. The trade-off is also clear as due to availabilities, coordinating for a new matching takes away non-negligible amount of resources (time in our case). For simplicity of analysis, we assume the matching process repeats over time, and the system clock resets to 0 after each successful match.

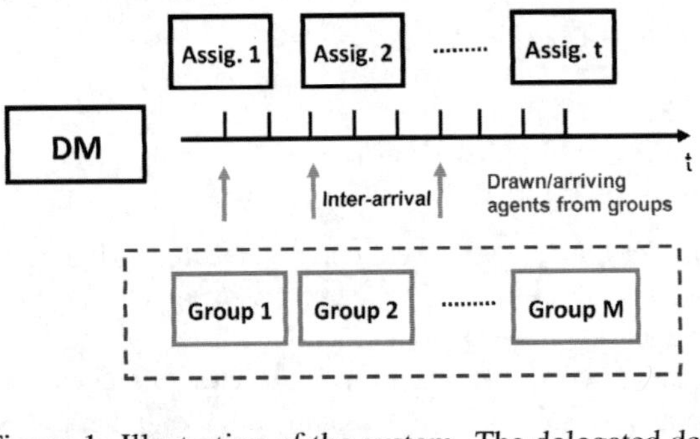

Figure 1: Illustration of the system. The delegated decision maker makes decision on matching arriving assignments to groups of agents.

[1]This modeling choice is mainly for simplicity of presentation; our results can extend to the case when there is not always an available group of agents.

Example: Consider the ride-sharing example. When ride-sharing company (e.g. UBER) schedules drivers, t_c models the coordination cost, such as time for scheduling drivers (sending notification, making calls etc). The reward R captures the per ride earning. Each individual driver has either an expected delay in receiving a job (delay constraints), or an expected hourly payment (reward constraints).

2.1 UN-CONSTRAINED SEQUENTIAL MATCHING: REVISIT

We now rigorously describe our sequential matching problem with the DM's objective being maximizing the average return of reward over successful matches. For each such successful match, denote by π a matching policy $\pi := \{\eta_1, \eta_2, \cdots \eta_{\gamma(\pi)}\}$, where η_k denotes the k-th action taken by the k-th to-be-matched agent for this particular matching cycle. Notice we have

$$\eta_k = continue, \forall k = 1, \cdots, \gamma(\pi) - 1,$$

and $\eta_{\gamma(\pi)} = stop$. Note decision is only made upon the availability of groups of agents, and $\gamma(\pi)$ denotes the stopping time at which the process terminates with decision being *stop and match*. Denote by $R(k)$ as the realized reward of the matching at k-th decision epoch, and we assume within each matching period, the sequence of rewards $\{R(k)\}_k$ forms an IID process.

Let $R^\pi(k)$ denotes the matching reward obtained during the k-th decision epoch under policy π. Clearly for $k < \gamma(\pi)$ we will have $R^\pi(k) = 0$, that is no reward will be collected when no matching happened, and $R^\pi(\gamma(\pi)) = R(\gamma(\pi))$. Let T_k^π denotes the total amount of time that has been spent up to decision epoch k under policy π, which includes the inter-arrival times (denoting as t_n):

$$T_k^\pi = \begin{cases} \sum_{n=1}^k t_n, \ \forall k < \gamma(\pi). \\ \sum_{n=1}^k t_n + 1, \ k = \gamma(\pi) . \end{cases}$$

The goal is to maximize the average return of reward (average reward per time unit) over the duration of this decision process. This is rigorously stated as follows:

$$\begin{aligned} J^* &= \max_{\pi \in \Pi} \mathbb{E}[\frac{\sum_{k=1}^{\gamma(\pi)} \delta \cdot R^\pi(k)}{T_{\gamma(\pi)}^\pi}] \\ &= \max_{\pi \in \Pi} \frac{\mathbb{E}[R^\pi(\gamma(\pi))]}{\mathbb{E}[T_{\gamma(\pi)}^\pi]}, \end{aligned} \quad (1)$$

with Π denoting the admissible set of policies. The second equality is due to renewal theory [Ferguson, 2006]. Maximizing this rate-of-return leads to the problem of choosing a stopping policy π to maximize the ratio defined in Eqn.(1).

Classical results [Ferguson, 2006] have established that the optimal strategy for above problem is simply a threshold based stopping policy. Further the threshold can be easily obtained by solving a fixed point equation:

Theorem 2.1 (Chapter 6 of [Ferguson, 2006], [Zheng et al., 2009]). *The optimal action for each matching of deciding between* stop *and* continue *is given by a stopping rule: the state space of the reward can be divided into a stopping set Δ^s and continuation set Δ^c, such that whenever the reward is observed to be in either set above, the corresponding action (*stop *v.s.* continue*) is taken. Furthermore these two sets are given by the following threshold property ($\forall$ steps n):*

$$\Delta^s = \{R(n) : R(n) \geq x^*\}, \tag{2}$$

and this threshold x^* at time n is given by the unique solution to the following fixed point equation:

$$\mathbb{E}[R(n) - x]^+ = x \cdot \tau\,. \tag{3}$$

The optimal stopping time N^* is then given as

$$N^* = \min\{n \geq 1 : R(n) \geq x^*\}\,. \tag{4}$$

For detailed proof please refer to [Chapter 6, [Ferguson, 2006]],[Zheng et al., 2009] and we will not restate. Also the following iterative algorithm has been developed to compute the exact threshold:

$$x(k+1) := \frac{\int_{x(k)}^{\infty} y dF_R(y)}{\tau + [1 - F_R(x(k))]}\,, \tag{5}$$

with an arbitrarily chosen initial belief $x(0)$. Convergence is defined as observing negligible successive change and is guaranteed [Zheng et al., 2009].

3 FAIR SEQUENTIAL MATCHING

The above results imply that implementing the optimal decision rule via setting an universal threshold may bias towards groups that tend to have higher realized reward statistically. We define our fairness constrained sequential matching problems in this section.

3.1 DELAY FAIR MATCHING

Now we consider a fair matching setting. We start with a matching problem with delay constraints. For each group i, we assume the expected delay before matching one of its agents should be no larger than a certain constant $\nu_i > 0$, and denote $\nu = [\nu_1, \nu_2, ..., \nu_M]$ as the vector form of the constraints. Such fairness constraints may come from regulations, or may come as functions of different groups' protected attributes. Note setting the constraints blindly equal is not regarded as fair. For instance, even for people with the same educational background , which might be a strong indicator of success, fairness constraints may not be necessarily the same for all individuals, as it is likely less so for individuals from a protected subgroup that has fewer financial resources. In fact, such fairness constraints should also take into consideration of the differences in individuals' ability, as well as their commitments for using it. This is similar to the notion of Rawlsian fairness [Braybrooke et al., 1963]. We are not getting into details on how such fairness constraints are generated – instead we assume they are certain outputs of a fairness policy or regulation, and we would like to implement them in our decision making setting. So we will take them as given.

We shorthand the stopping time $\gamma(\pi)$ as N. Denote T_N as the total time spent for one successful match with stopping time N. We first have the following lemma formulating the fairness constrained matching problem.

Lemma 3.1. *The optimal matching strategy under individual group delay constraints is given by a stopping rule with threshold strategy $\mathbf{x}^* = [x_1^*, ..., x_M^*]$ such that for each to-be-matched agent from group i, the decision will be matching if observed reward is no less than x_i^*. $\mathbf{x}^*$ can be characterized by solving the following constrained optimization problem:*

$$\begin{aligned}
\text{(PD)} \quad \max_{\mathbf{x}} \quad & \mathbb{E}[R(N)] - \textstyle\sum_i p_i^s x_i \mathbb{E}[T_N] \\
\text{s.t.} \quad & \frac{1-\sum_{j \in \mathcal{U}} p_j^s F_R(x_j)}{p_i^s[1-F_R(x_i)]}\mathbb{E}[T_N] \leq \nu_i, \forall i \in \mathcal{U}. \\
& x_i \geq 0, \forall i \in \mathcal{U}\,.
\end{aligned}$$

The proof first borrows results from optimal stopping theory, via which we can transfer the rate-of-return objective to the one in (PD). The constraints are given by formulating a system of equations characterizing agents' delay in matching.

Proof. Following results from [Ferguson, 2006, Tan et al., 2010] we know the rate-of-return problem is equivalent with the optimal stopping problem, which can be equivalently formulated as solving the following optimization problem to obtain a set of thresholds $\mathbf{x} = \{x_1, ..., x_M\}$:

$$\sup_{\mathbf{x}} \mathbb{E}[R(N) - \sum_{i \in \Omega} p_i^s x_i T_N]\,.$$

Showing this is equivalent with showing $\sup \mathbb{E}[R(N) - \sum_{i\in\Omega} p_i^s x_i T_N]$ returns the optimal rate of reward, which can be done similarly as in [Ferguson, 2006]. We then have the constrained matching problem stated as follows:

$$\max_{\mathbf{x}} \mathbb{E}[R(N)] - \sum_{i \in \mathcal{U}} p_i^s x_i \mathbb{E}[T_N]$$

subject to

$$x_i \geq 0, \;\; D(N, x_i, \mathbf{x}_{-i}) \leq \nu_i, \forall i \in \mathcal{U},$$

where $D(N, x_i, \mathbf{x}_{-i})$ denotes the expected delay for group i before a (successful)-match, with the threshold policy $\mathbf{x}$ and stopping time N. Now we quantify $D(\cdot)$. Notice the following equation holds:

$$\begin{aligned} &D(N, x_i, \mathbf{x}_{-i}) \\ &= \tau + p_i^s[(1 - F_R(x_i)) + F_R(x_i) D(N, x_i, \mathbf{x}_{-i})] \\ &+ (1 - p_i^s) \sum_{j \neq i} p^s(j|\bar{i})[F_R(x_j) D(N, x_i, \mathbf{x}_{-i}) \\ &+ (1 - F_R(x_j))(1 + D(N, x_i, \mathbf{x}_{-i}))] \,, \end{aligned}$$

where $p^s(j|\bar{i})$ is the probability agent from group $j \neq i$ to be matched (upon the arrival of agents), conditional on the fact group i is not the one to be matched.

We explain the implication of RHS of above equation. The first term corresponds to the expected inter-arrival time. The second term corresponds to the case group i is to be matched: with probability $1 - F_R(x_i)$ agent from group i will be matched immediately while the DM will forgo the match with probability $F_R(x_i)$. The terms associated with the third part correspond to the events when agent from group j other than i is to be matched. From above, re-arrange we have

$$D(N, x_i, \mathbf{x}_{-i}) = \frac{\sum_{j \in \mathcal{U}} p_j^s (1 - F_R(x_j)) + \tau}{p_i^s(1 - F_R(x_i))} \,.$$

Similarly we have (details of explanation omitted)

$$\begin{aligned} \mathbb{E}[T_N] = \tau + &\sum_{j \in \mathcal{U}} p_j^s (1 - F_R(x_j)) \\ &+ \sum_{j \in \mathcal{U}} p_j^s F_R(x_j) \mathbb{E}[T_N] \,, \end{aligned}$$

which further this gives us

$$\mathbb{E}[T_N] = \frac{\sum_{j \in \mathcal{U}} p_j^s (1 - F_R(x_j)) + \tau}{1 - \sum_{j \in \mathcal{U}} p_j^s F_R(x_j)} \,.$$

We thus establish the following

$$D(N, x_i, \mathbf{x}_{-i}) = \frac{1 - \sum_{j \in \mathcal{U}} p_j^s F_R(x_j)}{p_i^s(1 - F_R(x_i))} \mathbb{E}[T_N] \,. \quad (6)$$

Moreover since the thresholds policy can only be non-negative, we have established that the constrained optimal stopping problem is equivalent with (PD).

□

In the constraints, when $1 - F_R(x_i) = 0$ we will follow the convention that $1/0 = +\infty$. The only case that gives us a $0/0$ in the constraints is when $F_R(x_j) = 1, \forall j$. This is an extreme case stating that the DM will only match a pair when the realization of R reaches its maximum (zero measure event for continuous random variable). We rule out this case.

3.2 REWARD FAIR MATCHING

Now we consider another fair setting with each group requiring to be guaranteed for an average rate of returned reward (e.g., minimum hourly wage). Denote individual group's average (per time unit) expected reward demand as $\mu = [\mu_1, ..., \mu_M]$. Re-denote $\mu_i := \frac{\mu_i}{1-\delta}$: since each agent only collects $1 - \delta$ fraction of the realized reward of each matching, this is a normalization step to simplify the notation. We similarly prove the following:

Lemma 3.2. *The optimal matching strategy under individual fairness reward constraints is given by a stopping rule policy with thresholds* $\mathbf{x}^* = [x_1^*, ..., x_M^*]$, *which can be characterized by solving the following optimization problem:*

$$\begin{aligned} \text{(PR)} \quad \max_{\mathbf{x}} \quad & \mathbb{E}[R(N)] - \textstyle\sum_{i \in \mathcal{U}} p_i^s x_i \mathbb{E}[T_N] \\ \textit{s.t.} \quad & \mu_i \frac{1 - \sum_{j \in \mathcal{U}} p_j^s F_R(x_j)}{p_i^s[1 - F_R(x_i)]} \mathbb{E}[T_N] \leq \mathbb{E}[R(N)], \forall i. \\ & x_i \geq 0, \forall i \in \mathcal{U}. \end{aligned}$$

Proof. By renewal theory, with stopping time N, agent from group i's average expected reward is given by

$$(1 - \delta) \frac{\mathbb{E}[R(N)]}{D(N, x_i, \mathbf{x}_{-i})} \,.$$

Then similar with last section, we have the following problem formulation for obtaining $\mathbf{x}^*$:

$$\begin{aligned} \max_{\mathbf{x}} \quad & \mathbb{E}[R(N)] - \textstyle\sum_{i \in \mathcal{U}} p_i^s x_i \mathbb{E}[T_N] \\ \text{s.t.} \quad & \frac{\mathbb{E}[R(N)T]}{D(N, x_i, \mathbf{x}_{-i})} \geq \mu_i, \forall i. \\ & x_i \geq 0, \forall i \in \mathcal{U}. \end{aligned}$$

Remember μ_i is normalized by $1 - \delta$ in above. Since we have (Eqn.(6))

$$D(N, x_i, \mathbf{x}_{-i}) = \frac{1 - \sum_{j \in \mathcal{U}} p_j^s F_R(x_j)}{p_i^s[1 - F_R(x_i)]} \mathbb{E}[T_N]$$

re-arrange the terms we have the constraints being equivalent with

$$\mu_i \frac{1 - \sum_{j \in \mathcal{U}} p_j^s F_R(x_j)}{p_i^s[1 - F_R(x_i)]} \mathbb{E}[T_N] - \mathbb{E}[R(N)] \leq 0 \,,$$

which finishes the proof. □

4 FAIR OPTIMAL MATCHING

We studied the structure of optimal solutions for delay fair matching, and have shown that solving the fair matching problems is equivalent with solving a set of constrained optimization problems. In this section we present the details towards characterizing the optimal solutions to (PD). We obtain very similar results as for the reward fair matching. The proof is also similar to the case with delay constraints – we leave out the details for a concise presentation.

4.1 WHEN IS FAIRNESS UN-ACHIEVABLE?

We start by presenting a characterization result. Denote

$$\nu_{\mathcal{U}} := (\sum_{i \in \Delta} \frac{1}{\nu_i})^{-1}.$$

$\nu_{\mathcal{U}}$ is the geometric mean of all groups' constraints on average matching delay. We first argue $\nu_{\mathcal{U}}$ controls the feasibility region of the fairness problem.

Lemma 4.1. *(PD) is feasible only if* $\nu_{\mathcal{U}} \geq 1 + \tau$.

Proof. To see this, denote by $D_i(N, \mathbf{x})$ the expected delay for group i before each of its matching with matching policy (stopping time) N and thresholds $\mathbf{x}$, we will have (Eqn.(6) of Proof for Lemma 3.1)

$$D_i(N, \mathbf{x}) = \frac{1 - \sum_{j \in \mathcal{U}} p^s_j F_R(x_j)}{p^s_i (1 - F_R(x_i))} \mathbb{E}[T_N] .$$

From above we easily obtain

$$\sum_{i \in \mathcal{U}} \frac{1}{D_i(N, \mathbf{x})} = \frac{1}{\mathbb{E}[T_N]} .$$

For a feasible solution we have $D_i(N, \mathbf{x}) \leq \nu_i$, and thus

$$\sum_{i \in \mathcal{U}} \frac{1}{D_i(N, \mathbf{x})} \geq \sum_{i \in \mathcal{U}} \frac{1}{\nu_i} .$$

Then we arrive at a necessary condition:

$$\frac{1}{\sum_i \frac{1}{\nu_i}} \geq \mathbb{E}[T_N] \geq 1 + \tau .$$

The second inequality is due to the fact each matching attempt takes up at least 1 (the matching time)+ τ (inter-arrival time) time units. □

This result can also be seen as an impossibility results stating the region where the fairness profiles are unable to satisfy. Therefore for this part of study we focus on the case when $\nu_{\mathcal{U}} \geq 1 + \tau$.

4.2 RESULTS

We first introduce a parameter in helping characterize the optimal stopping policy:

Lemma 4.2. *There exists a unique solution for* $\nu \geq 1+\tau$ *for the following equation:*

$$F_R^{-1}(1 - \frac{\tau}{\nu - 1}) = \frac{1}{\tau} \mathbb{E}[R - F_R^{-1}(1 - \frac{\tau}{\nu - 1})]^+ .$$

Denote the unique solution as ν^*. Simple algebras show that the above fact holds. Intuitively speaking (as well as we will show later) ν^* is a threshold determining the strictness of the set of constraints.[2] When $\nu_{\mathcal{U}} < \nu^*$, we will see the constraints are more strict; while when $\nu_{\mathcal{U}} \geq \nu^*$, the set of delay constraints will be easier to satisfy.

When constraints are tight ($\nu_{\mathcal{U}} < \nu^*$)**:** When constraints are tight we have the following theorem:

Theorem 4.3. *When* $\nu_{\mathcal{U}} < \nu^*$, *there exists a computable constant* $x^*_{\mathcal{U}}$ *(computable in* $O(1)$ *time) such that the optimal solution* $\mathbf{x}^* = [x^*_1, ..., x^*_M]$ *for* (PD) *is given by the solution to the following system of equations:*

$$\begin{cases} \frac{1 - F_R(x_i)}{1 - F_R(x_j)} = \frac{p^s_j \nu_j}{p^s_i \nu_i}, \forall i \neq j, i, j \in \mathcal{U}. \\ \sum_{i \in \mathcal{U}} p^s_i x_i = x^*_{\mathcal{U}} . \end{cases}$$

when the following condition holds

$$\sum_{j \in \mathcal{U}} p^s_j F_R^{-1}\left(1 - \frac{\min_{i \in \mathcal{U}} p^s_i \nu_i}{p^s_j \nu_j}\right) \leq x^*_{\mathcal{U}} .$$

This strikingly clean structure of optimal solution has a very intuitive structural property: roughly speaking the probability of matching (with the assigned threshold) should be inversely proportional to different groups' availability probability, as well as their delay constraints $p^s_i \nu_i$. This result also looks similar to proportional fairness [Kelly et al., 1998], may it be in a resource allocation or a cooperative game setting.

When constraints are loose ($\nu_{\mathcal{U}} \geq \nu^*$)**:** Consider now $\nu_{\mathcal{U}} \geq \nu^*$, in which case the constraints are regarded as being loose (the larger the $\nu_{\mathcal{U}}$ is, the larger the ν_is can be.) The idea for solving this case is simple: we can then afford to make a set of strictly tighter constraints out from the one we have, and reuse the results from the case when $\nu < \nu^*$.

[2] For details please refer to the proof.

First denote $\tilde{\nu} = [\tilde{\nu}_1, ..., \tilde{\nu}_M]$ as the solution for the following optimization problem.

$$\begin{array}{lll} \text{(TIGHT)} & \min_{\tilde{\nu}} & \sum_{j\in\mathcal{U}} p_j^s F_R^{-1}(1 - \frac{\min_{i\in\mathcal{U}} p_i^s \tilde{\nu}_i}{p_j^s \tilde{\nu}_j}) \\ & \text{s.t.} & 0 \le \tilde{\nu}_i \le \nu_i, \forall i \in \mathcal{U} \\ & & \sum_{j\in\mathcal{U}} \frac{1}{\tilde{\nu}_j} = \frac{1}{\nu^* - \epsilon}, \end{array}$$

where $\epsilon > 0$ is an arbitrarily small quantity. This is a "tightening" step that we will refer to. The optimization step is to relax the conditions for the solutions to be non-negative as much as we can. Notice technically we should have $\tilde{\nu}_i > 0$. However $\tilde{\nu}_i = 0$ clearly violates the second equality constraint with an appropriately selected ϵ, which leads to the current equivalent formulation.

Theorem 4.4. *When $\nu_{\mathcal{U}} \ge \nu^*$, there exists a computable constant x_ν^* (computable in $O(1)$ time) such that one optimal solution $\mathbf{x}^* = [x_1^*, ..., x_M^*]$ for (PD) is given by the solution to the following system of equations:*

$$\begin{cases} \frac{1-F_R(x_i)}{1-F_R(x_j)} = \frac{p_j^s \tilde{\nu}_j}{p_i^s \tilde{\nu}_i}, \forall i \ne j, i, j \in \mathcal{U}. \\ \sum_{i\in\mathcal{U}} p_i^s x_i = x_\nu^* . \end{cases}$$

when the following condition holds

$$\sum_{j\in\mathcal{U}} p_j^s F_R^{-1} \left(1 - \frac{\min_{i\in\mathcal{U}} p_i^s \tilde{\nu}_i}{p_j^s \tilde{\nu}_j}\right) \le x_\nu^* .$$

The following remarks end this subsection: (1) Our results extend the ones reported in [Kennedy, 1982]. In particular if there is only one global delay constraint ν, the individual group delay becomes ν/p_i^s (the delay before matching of each particular group). Then $\nu_{\mathcal{U}}$ will degenerate to ν and the results degenerate to the ones reported in [Kennedy, 1982]. Further Theorem 4.3 and 4.4 become the two cases that have been discussed in above work. (2) The second observation is when the constraints are loose ($\nu_{\mathcal{U}} \ge \nu^*$), we could simply make the constraint set to be more strict and solve it according to the case when constraints are tight. However this "tightening" step requires solving another optimization problem. We will show later with specific reward distributions the optimization problem can be solved efficiently. (3) The closed-form of the system of equations characterizing the optimal solution in Theorem 4.3 and 4.4 is not clear so far in terms of computation complexity, e.g., linearity, convexity etc. We will discuss this matter in Section 5.

4.3 MAIN IDEAS OF THE PROOF

We provide the main ideas of the proof for Theorem 4.3 and 4.4[3]. The proof builds on the Lagrange relaxation and primal dual analysis of (PD), as well as the optimization formulation of an optimal stopping problem.

[3]Full proof can be found in the supplementary materials.

(Theorem 4.3) We will first introduce the Lagrange relaxation for (PD):

$$V^* := \mathbb{E}[R(N)] - \sum_i (p_i^s x_i + \lambda_i \frac{1 - \sum_j p_j^s F_R(x_j)}{p_i^s[1 - F_R(x_i)]}) \mathbb{E}[T_N] . \quad (7)$$

Following standard stopping rule results [Ferguson, 2006] the optimal stopping time for maximizing V^* is:

$$N^* = \min\{n \ge 1 : R(n) \ge \sum_i (p_i^s x_i + \lambda_i \frac{1 - \sum_j p_j^s F_R(x_j)}{p_i^s[1 - F_R(x_i)]}) + V^* .$$

The intuition is that the stopping time is characterized by when the excessive expected return of reward is no less than V^*, which characterizes the expected excessive return from the stopping policy. Further the optimal set of thresholds satisfy the following fixed-point equation:

$$\mathbb{E}\left[R(N) - \sum_i (p_i^s x_i + \lambda_i \frac{1 - \sum_j p_j^s F_R(x_j)}{p_i^s[1 - F_R(x_i)]}) - V^*\right]^+ = \sum_i (p_i^s x_i + \lambda_i \frac{1 - \sum_j p_j^s F_R(x_j)}{p_i^s[1 - F_R(x_i)]}) \tau . \quad (8)$$

The LHS of above equation characterizes the expected additional reward for not stopping. While the RHS is the additional reward collected when stop.

Meanwhile with above characterization, the expected stopping time can be written as (geometric distribution):

$$\mathbb{E}[T_N] = 1 + \frac{\tau}{1 - F_R(\sum_i (p_i^s x_i + \lambda_i \frac{1-\sum_j p_j^s F_R(x_j)}{p_i^s[1-F_R(x_i)]}) + V^*)} . \quad (9)$$

From KKT condition on the set of threshold policies.

$$\lambda_i^* \frac{1 - \sum_{j\in\mathcal{U}} p_j^s F_R(x_j)}{p_i^s[1 - F_R(x_i)]} \mathbb{E}[T_N] - \lambda_i^* \nu_i = 0, \forall i \in \mathcal{U}. \quad (10)$$

Plug Eqn.(9) into Eqn.(10), we will be able to show

$$p_i^s[1 - F_R(x_i)]\nu_i = C(\mathbf{x}, \lambda) ,$$

where $C(\mathbf{x}, \lambda)$ is a constant that is independent of group index i. From above we know that for $\lambda_i^*, \lambda_j^* > 0, i \ne j$ we have

$$\frac{1 - F_R(x_i)}{1 - F_R(x_j)} = \frac{p_j^s \nu_j}{p_i^s \nu_i} .$$

This give us the first set of equations in Theorem 4.3. For our primal and dual problems we have

$$L(\mathbf{x}^*, \lambda^*) := V^* + \lambda^{*\mathbf{T}}\nu = 0\,. \tag{11}$$

$\lambda^{*\mathbf{T}}\nu$ can further be calculated as follows:

$$\lambda_i^*\nu_i = \lambda_i^* \frac{1-\sum_j p_j^s F_R(x_j)}{p_i^s[1-F_R(x_i)]} \cdot \frac{p_i^s[1-F_R(x_i)]}{1-\sum_j p_j^s F_R(x_j)} \nu_i\,.$$

Plug in V^* (Eqn.(7)) and above into Eqn. (11) we have

$$\exists\, x^*_{\mathcal{U}},\ \text{s.t.} \sum_{i\in\mathcal{U}} p_i^s x_i = x^*_{\mathcal{U}}\,.$$

(Theorem 4.4) Consider $\nu_{\mathcal{U}} \geq \nu^*$, i.e., not all constraints are active. Notice since $\frac{1}{\sum_{i\in\mathcal{U}}\frac{1}{\nu_i}} \geq \nu^*$, we could find a set of $\tilde{\nu}$ such that

$$0 \leq \tilde{\nu}_i \leq \nu_i, \forall i \in \mathcal{U}, \text{ and } \frac{1}{\sum_{i\in\mathcal{U}}\frac{1}{\tilde{\nu}_i}} < \nu^*\,.$$

In particular choose a small $\epsilon > 0$ and set $\frac{1}{\sum_{i\in\mathcal{U}}\frac{1}{\tilde{\nu}_i}} = \nu^* - \epsilon$. Under this case the average optimal reward rate x^*_ν ($O(1)$ computable) associated with $\nu^* - \epsilon$ is achieved. Since we have a set of more strict constraints we know the original constraints $[\nu_1, ..., \nu_M]$ will all be met if the new one gets satisfied. The rest of the proof is similar to the one for Theorem 4.3 and will be omitted.

Meanwhile we would like to choose the set of $\tilde{\nu}$ that will make the constraint

$$\sum_{i\in\mathcal{U}} F_R^{-1}\left(1 - \frac{\min_{j\in\mathcal{U}} p_j^s\tilde{\nu}_j}{p_i^s\tilde{\nu}_i}\right) \leq x^*_\nu$$

less strict, i.e., we choose the set of $\tilde{\nu}$ minimizing $\sum_{i\in\mathcal{U}} F_R^{-1}\left(1 - \frac{\min_{j\in\mathcal{U}} p_j^s\tilde{\nu}_j}{p_i^s\tilde{\nu}_i}\right)$ and we have the following optimization problem for charactering $[\tilde{\nu}_1, ..., \tilde{\nu}_M]$:

$$\begin{array}{ll} \min_{\tilde{\nu}} & \sum_{j\in\mathcal{U}} p_j^s F_R^{-1}\left(1 - \frac{\min_{i\in\mathcal{U}} p_i^s\tilde{\nu}_i}{p_j^s\tilde{\nu}_j}\right) \\ \text{s.t.} & 0 \leq \tilde{\nu}_i \leq \nu_i, \forall i \in \mathcal{U} \\ & \sum_{j\in\mathcal{U}} \frac{1}{\tilde{\nu}_j} = \frac{1}{\nu^*-\epsilon}. \end{array}$$

4.4 REWARD FAIR MATCHING

We show the results we proved for the delay fairness case can be largely extended to the reward fairness case. First denote the maximum reward rate that can be achieved by the group of agents for un-constrained rate-of-return problem as x^* (solution to Eqn.(3)). Obviously when $\sum_{i\in\mathcal{U}} \mu_i > x^*$, there is no solution to the constrained system. This is because we know the objective value of a constrained setting can never exceed the one for its unconstrained counterpart. We then focus on the case with $\sum_{i\in\mathcal{U}} \mu_i \leq x^*$. We have the following theorems leading to the characterization of the fair optimal solution.

When constraints are tight ($\sum_{i\in\mathcal{U}} \mu_i = x^*$):

Theorem 4.5. *When $\sum_{i\in\mathcal{U}} \mu_i = x^*$, the optimal solution $\mathbf{x}^* = [x_1^*, ..., x_M^*]$ for (PR) is given by the solution to the following system of equations:*

$$\begin{cases} \frac{1-F_R(x_i)}{1-F_R(x_j)} = \frac{p_j^s\mu_i}{p_i^s\mu_j}, \forall i \neq j, i, j \in \mathcal{U}. \\ \sum_{i\in\mathcal{U}} p_i^s x_i = x^*\,. \end{cases}$$

when the following condition holds

$$\sum_{j\in\mathcal{U}} p_j^s F_R^{-1}\left(1 - \frac{\mu_j/p_j^s}{\max_{i\in\mathcal{U}} \mu_i/p_i^s}\right) \leq x^*\,.$$

When constraints are loose ($\sum_{i\in\mathcal{U}} \mu_i < x^*$): When $\sum_i \mu_i < x^*$, we similarly have a less restricted scenario. The constraints will be firstly tightened. Denote $\tilde{\mu} = [\tilde{\mu}_1, ..., \tilde{\mu}_M]$ as the solution for the following optimization problem:

$$\begin{array}{ll} \min_{\tilde{\mu}} & \sum_{j\in\mathcal{U}} p_j^s F_R^{-1}\left(1 - \frac{\tilde{\mu}_j/p_j^s}{\max_{i\in\mathcal{U}} \tilde{\mu}_i/p_i^s}\right) \\ \text{s.t.} & \tilde{\mu}_i \geq \mu_i, \forall i \in \mathcal{U}. \\ & \sum_{j\in\mathcal{U}} \tilde{\mu}_j = x^*. \end{array}$$

And then we have the following set of results:

Theorem 4.6. *When $\sum_i \mu_i < x^*$, one optimal solution $\mathbf{x}^* = [x_1^*, ..., x_M^*]$ for (PR) is given by the solution to the following system of equations:*

$$\begin{cases} \frac{1-F_R(x_i)}{1-F_R(x_j)} = \frac{p_j^s\tilde{\mu}_i}{p_i^s\tilde{\mu}_j}, \forall i \neq j, i, j \in \mathcal{U}\,. \\ \sum_{i\in\mathcal{U}} p_i^s x_i = x^*\,. \end{cases}$$

when the following condition holds

$$\sum_{j\in\mathcal{U}} p_j^s F_R^{-1}\left(1 - \frac{\tilde{\mu}_j/p_j^s}{\max_{i\in\mathcal{U}} \tilde{\mu}_i/p_i^s}\right) \leq x^*\,.$$

It is worth to note though (PD) and (PR) appear to be different, their solution structures are similar. The two problems can then share the same solver with setting different parameters (replacing $(\{\nu_i\}, x^*_{\mathcal{U}})$ with $(\{\mu_i\}, x^*)$ to reach (PR) from (PD).

5 COMPUTATION AND EXAMPLES

Our main results have reduced the original constrained stopping rule problem to solving a set of closed-form equations. Despite the clean structure, solving the problem will further rely on the reward distributions, where the computation issue merits a further clarification. We could show these equations reduce to system of *linear* *equations* for simple distributions such as exponential distribution and uniform distribution etc. Take exponential distribution for example (for some ρ): $F_R(x) = 1 - \exp(-\rho x), \forall x \geq 0$, with $F_R^{-1}(y) = -\log(1-y)/\rho$, $0 \leq y \leq 1$. We take the delay constrained case for demonstration, and we start with the case $\nu_{\mathcal{U}} < \nu^*$. From $\frac{1-F_R(x_i)}{1-F_R(x_j)} = \frac{p_j^s \nu_j}{p_i^s \nu_i}$ we know

$$x_i - x_j = -1/\rho \cdot \log p_j^s \nu_j / p_i^s \nu_i \,. \quad (12)$$

Meanwhile we know $\sum_{i \in \mathcal{U}} p_i^s x_i = x_{\mathcal{U}}^*$. Combining this and Eqn.(12) returns us a linear system of equations for all x_i; we can then solve for $\mathbf{x}^*$. This can be done in polynomial time.

For the case $\nu_{\mathcal{U}} \geq \nu^*$, we need to solve the optimization problem (TIGHT). Make the following substitute: $y_i = \frac{\min_{j \in \mathcal{U}} p_j^s \tilde{\nu}_j}{p_i^s \tilde{\nu}_i}$, $y_{\min} = \min_{j \in \mathcal{U}} p_j^s \tilde{\nu}_j$, and the constraint $\sum_{j \in \mathcal{U}} \frac{1}{\tilde{\nu}_j} = \frac{1}{\nu^* - \epsilon}$ then becomes $\sum_{j \in \mathcal{U}} p_j^s \cdot y_j = \frac{y_{\min}}{\nu^* - \epsilon}$. And the constraints $\tilde{\nu}_i \leq \nu_i, \forall i \in \mathcal{U}$ become $\frac{y_{\min}}{p_i^s y_i} \leq \nu_i, \forall i \in \mathcal{U}$, which is further equivalent with $y_{\min} \leq p_i^s y_i \nu_i$. Hence (TIGHT) becomes equivalent with the one below:

$$\begin{aligned} \min \quad & -\textstyle\sum_{i \in \mathcal{U}} p_j^s \cdot \log y_i / \rho \\ \text{s.t.} \quad & 0 \leq y_{\min} \leq p_i^s y_i \nu_i, \forall i \in \mathcal{U} \\ & \textstyle\sum_{j \in \mathcal{U}} p_j^s \cdot y_j = \frac{y_{\min}}{\nu^* - \epsilon}. \end{aligned}$$

Since $-\log x$ is a convex function, the above programming problem is convex and can be solved efficiently.

A sub-optimal but easy-to-compute solution It is worth to mention for the case with $\nu_{\mathcal{U}} \geq \nu^*$ we can also easily obtain a feasible solution that is sub-optimal by setting: $\tilde{\nu} = \frac{\nu^* - \epsilon}{\nu_{\mathcal{U}}} \nu$, and it is easy to verify under this case solving the system of equations reduces to the case with $\nu_{\mathcal{U}} < \nu^*$, which is much easier to solve.

In summary, solving for the optimal solution only requires solving (1) a linear system of equation and (2) a convex optimization problem. Existing solver or methods (e.g., interior point etc) can then be applied to obtain a solution in polynomial time.

5.1 SIMULATION

We numerically simulate a simple two groups scenario. For parameter settings please refer to caption of Figure 2. The figure pictures the heat map for expected reward under different delay constraints: dark blue indicates infeasible area, and dark red implies reaching the maximum. Along with relaxing constraints, our solution gradually converges to the un-constrained optimal ones. It is clear our solution help characterize the trade-off between fairness and social optimality.

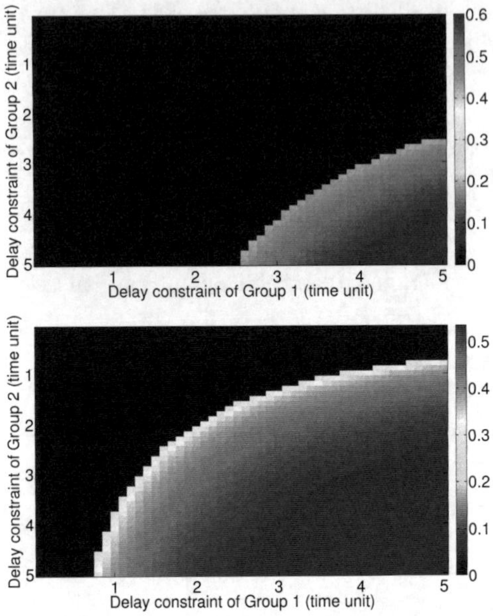

Figure 2: Fairness satisfiability & reward (heat map) for different combination of delay constraints ν_1, ν_2. $p_1^s = p_2^s = 1/2, \rho = 0.05$ (parameter for exp. distribution). Top: $\tau = 1$, max reward = 0.6006 (un-constrained). Bottom: $\tau = 0.5$, max reward = 0.5299 (un-constrained).

6 CONCLUSION

In this paper, we discussed optimal multi-agent matching strategies with individual fairness constraints. We first show the equivalence between this problem and the locally constrained optimal stopping problem, and then a set of constrained programings. We considered two different types of constraints: one with matching deadlines (delay) and the other with reward requirements. We characterized the fair optimal solutions for above two problems respectively. Via practical example, we demonstrated that our solutions can be computed efficiently. The reported results can also be leveraged to obtain scheduling policies with other fairness concerns, by setting the local constraints appropriately.

Our work aims to kick off fairness studies in the sequential decision making framework. One interesting and immediate followup would be to study a fair policy when the decisions made in the past will in fact affect different groups' status (e.g., reward statistics, availability etc) in the future.

Acknowledgements

The author would like to acknowledge the support of the National Science Foundation under grant CCF-1301976.

References

Cyrus Derman, Gerald J Lieberman, and Sheldon M Ross. A sequential stochastic assignment problem. *Management Science*, 18(7):349–355, 1972.

Giuseppe Moscarini. Job matching and the wage distribution. *Econometrica*, 73(2):481–516, 2005.

Jerome Le Ny, Munther Dahleh, and Eric Feron. Multi-agent task assignment in the bandit framework. In *Decision and Control, 2006 45th IEEE Conference on*, pages 5281–5286. IEEE, 2006.

Thomas S. Ferguson. Optimal stopping and applications. *Mathematics Department, UCLA*, 2006.

Sina Radke, Berna Güroğlu, and Ellen RA de Bruijn. There's something about a fair split: intentionality moderates context-based fairness considerations in social decision-making. *PloS One*, 7(2):e31491, 2012.

Sara Hajian, Francesco Bonchi, and Carlos Castillo. Algorithmic bias: From discrimination discovery to fairness-aware data mining. In *Proceedings of the 22nd ACM SIGKDD International Conference on Knowledge Discovery and Data Mining*, pages 2125–2126. ACM, 2016.

Matthew Joseph, Michael Kearns, Jamie Morgenstern, and Aaron Roth. Fairness in learning: Classic and contextual bandits. *arXiv preprint arXiv:1605.07139*, 2016.

Shahin Jabbari, Matthew Joseph, Michael Kearns, Jamie Morgenstern, and Aaron Roth. Fair learning in markovian environments. *arXiv preprint arXiv:1611.03071*, 2016.

Moritz AW Hardt. *A study of privacy and fairness in sensitive data analysis*. PhD thesis, Princeton University, 2011.

Cynthia Dwork, Moritz Hardt, Toniann Pitassi, Omer Reingold, and Richard Zemel. Fairness through awareness. In *ITCS*, pages 214–226. ACM, 2012.

Jon Kleinberg, Sendhil Mullainathan, and Manish Raghavan. Inherent trade-offs in the fair determination of risk scores. *ITCS*, 2017.

Alexandra Chouldechova. Fair prediction with disparate impact: A study of bias in recidivism prediction instruments. *arXiv preprint arXiv:1703.00056*, 2017.

Moritz Hardt, Eric Price, Nati Srebro, et al. Equality of opportunity in supervised learning. In *Advances in Neural Information Processing Systems*, pages 3315–3323, 2016.

Yuhua Xu, Alagan Anpalagan, Qihui Wu, Liang Shen, Zhan Gao, and Jinglong Wang. Decision-theoretic distributed channel selection for opportunistic spectrum access: Strategies, challenges and solutions. *Communications Surveys & Tutorials, IEEE*, 15(4):1689–1713, 2013.

Dong Zheng, Weiyan Ge, and Junshan Zhang. Distributed opportunistic scheduling for ad hoc networks with random access: an optimal stopping approach. *IEEE Trans. Inf. Theor.*, 55(1):205–222, January 2009. ISSN 0018-9448.

DP Kennedy. On a constrained optimal stopping problem. *Journal of Applied Probability*, pages 631–641, 1982.

David Braybrooke, Charles Edward Lindblom, et al. strategy of decision; policy evaluation as a social process. 1963.

Sheu-Sheu Tan, Dong Zheng, Junshan Zhang, and James Zeidler. Distributed opportunistic scheduling for ad-hoc communications under delay constraints. In *INFOCOM'10*, pages 2874–2882, Piscataway, NJ, USA, 2010. IEEE Press. ISBN 978-1-4244-5836-3.

Frank P Kelly, Aman K Maulloo, and David KH Tan. Rate control for communication networks: shadow prices, proportional fairness and stability. *Journal of the Operational Research society*, 49(3):237–252, 1998.

$$L(x,\lambda) = \mathbb{E}[R(N)] - \sum_{i\in\mathcal{U}} p_i^s x_i \mathbb{E}[T_N] - \sum_{i\in\mathcal{U}} \lambda_i (\frac{1-\sum_j p_j^s F_R(x_j)}{p_i^s[1-F_R(x_i)]}\mathbb{E}[T_N] - \nu_i)$$

$$= \mathbb{E}[R(N)] - \sum_{i\in\mathcal{U}} (p_i^s x_i + \lambda_i \frac{1-\sum_j p_j^s F_R(x_j)}{p_i^s[1-F_R(x_i)]})\mathbb{E}[T_N] + \sum_{i\in\mathcal{U}} \lambda_i \nu_i \,. \tag{13}$$

$$0 = -\lambda_i^* \nu_i + \lambda_i^* \frac{1-\sum_j p_j^s F_R(x_j)}{p_i^s[1-F_R(x_i)]} \cdot \Big[\frac{\tau}{1-F_R(\sum_i (p_i^s x_i + \lambda_i^* \frac{1-\sum_j p_j^s F_R(x_j)}{p_i^s[1-F_R(x_i)]}) + V^*)} + 1\Big] \,. \tag{14}$$

$$\Rightarrow p_i^s[1-F_R(x_i)]\nu_i = (1-\sum_j p_j^s F_R(x_j)) \cdot \Big[\frac{\tau}{1-F_R(\sum_i (p_i^s x_i + \lambda_i^* \frac{1-\sum_j p_j^s F_R(x_j)}{p_i^s[1-F_R(x_i)]}) + V^*)} + 1\Big] \,. \tag{15}$$

Supplementary materials: Proof of Theorem 4.3

To solve the constrained optimization problem, we introduce its corresponding Lagrange relaxation in Eqn.(13). Denote

$$V^* := \mathbb{E}[R(N)] - \sum_i (p_i^s x_i + \lambda_i \frac{1-\sum_j p_j^s F_R(x_j)}{p_i^s[1-F_R(x_i)]})\mathbb{E}[T_N] \,.$$

Following previous work [Ferguson, 2006] we know the optimal stopping time for maximizing V^* is given by

$$N^* = \min\{n \geq 1 : R(n) \geq \sum_i (p_i^s x_i + \lambda_i \frac{1-\sum_j p_j^s F_R(x_j)}{p_i^s[1-F_R(x_i)]}) + V^*\} \,,$$

and the optimal set of thresholds satisfy the following fixed-point equation:

$$\mathbb{E}\Big[R(N) - \sum_i (p_i^s x_i + \lambda_i \frac{1-\sum_j p_j^s F_R(x_j)}{p_i^s[1-F_R(x_i)]}) - V^*\Big]^+ = \sum_i (p_i^s x_i + \lambda_i \frac{1-\sum_j p_j^s F_R(x_j)}{p_i^s[1-F_R(x_i)]})\tau \,. \tag{16}$$

Again following the results of [Ferguson, 2006], we are able to characterize the expected stopping time as follows,

$$\mathbb{E}[T_N] = \frac{\tau}{1-F_R(\sum_i (p_i^s x_i + \lambda_i \frac{1-\sum_j p_j^s F_R(x_j)}{p_i^s[1-F_R(x_i)]}) + V^*)} + 1 \,. \tag{17}$$

Consider the dual problem $L(\mathbf{x},\lambda) = V^* + \lambda^{\mathbf{T}}\nu$. By complementary slackness we have:

$$\lambda_i^* \frac{1-\sum_{j\in\mathcal{U}} p_j^s F_R(x_j)}{p_i^s[1-F_R(x_i)]}\mathbb{E}[T_N] - \lambda_i^* \nu_i = 0, \forall i \in \mathcal{U}. \tag{18}$$

Substitute (17) into (18) we have $\forall i \in \mathcal{U}$, we have Eqn.(14).

We first consider active constraints, i.e., constraints with $\lambda_i^* > 0$. (recall in the dual problem we have the variables $\lambda_i^* \geq 0, \forall i \in \mathcal{U}$.) For these active constraints we will get Eqn.(15). Notice the RHS of above equation does not depend on any specific index i. Therefore we have

$$p_i^s[1-F_R(x_i)]\nu_i = C(\mathbf{x},\lambda^*) \,,$$

where $C(\mathbf{x},\lambda^*)$ is a constant that is independent of indices. Moreover for $\lambda_i^*, \lambda_j^* > 0, i \neq j$ we have

$$\frac{1-F_R(x_i)}{1-F_R(x_j)} = \frac{p_j^s \nu_j}{p_i^s \nu_i} \,.$$

Denote $\nu(\mathbf{x}) := \frac{p_i^s[1-F_R(x_i)]\nu_i}{1-\sum_j p_j^s F_R(x_j)}$, we will get

$$\sum_i \Big(p_i^s x_i + \lambda_i^* \frac{1-\sum_j p_j^s F_R(x_j)}{p_i^s[1-F_R(x_i)]} \Big) + V^* = F_X^{-1}(1 - \frac{\tau}{\nu(\mathbf{x})-1}) .$$

Plug above to Eqn.(16), the following establishes

$$\mathbb{E}\Big[R(N) - F_R^{-1}(1-\frac{\tau}{\nu(\mathbf{x})-1})\Big]^+ = \sum_i (p_i^s x_i + \lambda_i^* \frac{1-\sum_j p_j^s F_R(x_j)}{p_i^s[1-F_R(x_i)]})\tau ,$$

and

$$V^* = F_R^{-1}(1-\frac{\tau}{\nu(\mathbf{x})-1}) - \frac{1}{\tau}\cdot \mathbb{E}\Big[R(N) - F_R^{-1}(1-\frac{\tau}{\nu(\mathbf{x})-1})\Big]^+ .$$

Also for our primal and dual problems we have

$$0 = L(\mathbf{x}^*, \lambda^*) = V^* + \lambda^{*\mathbf{T}}\nu .$$

Consider the $\lambda^{*\mathbf{T}}\nu$ term. Notice

$$\begin{aligned}\lambda_i^*\nu_i &= \lambda_i^* \frac{1-\sum_j p_j^s F_R(x_j)}{p_i^s[1-F_R(x_i)]} \cdot \frac{p_i^s[1-F_R(x_i)]}{1-\sum_j p_j^s F_R(x_j)}\nu_i \\ &= \nu(\mathbf{x})\cdot \lambda_i^* \frac{1-\sum_j p_j^s F_R(x_j)}{p_i^s[1-F_R(x_i)]} .\end{aligned}$$

Therefore we have

$$\begin{aligned}\lambda^{*\mathbf{T}}\nu &= \nu(\mathbf{x})\cdot \sum_i \lambda_i^* \frac{1-\sum_j p_j^s F_R(x_j)}{p_i^s[1-F_R(x_i)]} \\ &= \nu(\mathbf{x})\cdot \Big[\frac{\mathbb{E}[R(N)-F_R^{-1}(1-\frac{\tau}{\nu(\mathbf{x})-1})]^+}{\tau} - \sum_i p_i^s x_i\Big] .\end{aligned}$$

Moreover we have Eqn.(19):

$$\begin{aligned} & F_R^{-1}(1-\frac{\tau}{\nu(\mathbf{x})-1}) - \frac{1}{\tau}\cdot \mathbb{E}\Big[R(N) - F_R^{-1}(1-\frac{\tau}{\nu(\mathbf{x})-1})\Big]^+ \\ & + \nu(\mathbf{x})\cdot \left\{ \frac{\mathbb{E}\Big[R(N) - F_R^{-1}(1-\frac{\tau}{\nu(\mathbf{x})-1})\Big]^+}{\tau} - \sum_i p_i^s x_i \right\} = 0 . \end{aligned} \quad (19)$$

Notice the following holds:

$$\nu(\mathbf{x}) = \frac{p_i^s[1-F_R(x_i)]\nu_i}{1-\sum_j p_j^s F_R(x_j)} = \frac{p_i^s[1-F_R(x_i)]\nu_i}{\sum_j p_j^s(1-F_R(x_j))} ,$$

where the second equality is due to $\sum_j p_j^s = 1$. Substitute in

$$1 - F_R(x_j) = \frac{p_i^s\nu_i}{p_j^s\nu_j}(1-F_R(x_i))$$

we have

$$\nu(\mathbf{x}) = \frac{p_i^s[1 - F_R(x_i)]\nu_i}{\sum_j p_j^s \frac{p_i^s \nu_i}{p_j^s \nu_j}(1 - F_R(x_i))} = \frac{1}{\sum_{j\in\mathcal{U}} \frac{1}{\nu_j}} = \nu_{\mathcal{U}} ,$$

which is a constant. From which we have

$$F_R^{-1}(1 - \frac{\tau}{\nu(\mathbf{x}) - 1}) = C_1 ,$$

$$\frac{1}{\tau} \cdot \mathbb{E}[R(N) - F_R^{-1}(1 - \frac{\tau}{\nu(\mathbf{x}) - 1})]^+ = C_2 ,$$

with C_1, C_2 being some constant. Notice $C_1 - C_2$ is our previously defined function g evaluated at $\nu(\mathbf{x})$. Therefore we have

$$C_1 - C_2 + \nu_{\mathcal{U}}(C_2 - \sum_i p_i^s x_i) = 0 .$$

Theoretically with the other equations $\frac{1-F_R(x_i)}{1-F_R(x_j)} = \frac{p_j^s \nu_j}{p_i^s \nu_i}$ we can solve $\mathbf{x}^*$. The above equation can be reduced to

$$\sum_{i\in\mathcal{U}} p_i^s x_i = x_{\mathcal{U}}^* .$$

The rest is to check whether the corresponding λ^*s are positive. This is equivalent with deciding whether the current constraints are active or not. In fact from previous derivations we know

$$\lambda^T \nu = \frac{\mathbb{E}[R(N) - F_R^{-1}(1 - \frac{\tau}{\nu_{\mathcal{U}}-1})]^+}{\tau} - \sum_i p_i^s x_i^*$$

therefore we could derive a positive set of λ if the following holds,

$$\frac{\mathbb{E}[R(N) - F_R^{-1}(1 - \frac{\tau}{\nu_{\mathcal{U}}-1})]^+}{\tau} - \sum_i p_i^s x_i^* > 0$$

which further gives us

$$\frac{1}{\tau}\mathbb{E}[R(N) - F_R^{-1}(1 - \frac{\tau}{\nu_{\mathcal{U}} - 1})]^+ - F_R^{-1}(1 - \frac{\tau}{\nu_{\mathcal{U}} - 1}) > 0 ,$$

since ν^* is the solution for above equation when equality holds, and by simple algebra we could show for $\nu_{\mathcal{U}} < \nu^*$ the above condition holds.

Now we show under what condition the solutions $\mathbf{x}^*$ is non-negative. Note from

$$\frac{1 - F_R(x_i)}{1 - F_R(x_j)} = \frac{p_j^s \nu_j}{p_i^s \nu_i} ,$$

we know

$$x_i = F_R^{-1}\left(1 - [1 - F_R(x_j)]\frac{p_j^s \nu_j}{p_i^s \nu_i}\right) .$$

Not hard to see the smallest x_j associated with the minimum $p_j^s \nu_j$. Therefore

$$\sum_{i\in\mathcal{U}\setminus j} F_R^{-1}\left(1 - [1 - F_R(x_j)]\frac{\min_{j\in\mathcal{U}} p_j^s \nu_j}{p_i^s \nu_i}\right) + x_j = x_{\mathcal{U}}^* .$$

In order to make sure $\mathbf{x}^*$ is non-negative, we need $x_j \geq 0$, i.e.,

$$\sum_{i\in\mathcal{U}} F_R^{-1}\left(1 - \frac{\min_{j\in\mathcal{U}} p_j^s \nu_j}{p_i^s \nu_i}\right) \leq x_{\mathcal{U}}^* .$$

Exact Inference for Relational Graphical Models with Interpreted Functions: Lifted Probabilistic Inference Modulo Theories

Rodrigo de Salvo Braz **Ciaran O'Reilly**
Artificial Intelligence Center
SRI International
Menlo Park, CA USA

Abstract

Probabilistic Inference Modulo Theories (PIMT) is a recent framework that expands exact inference on graphical models to use richer languages that include arithmetic, equalities, and inequalities on both integers and real numbers. In this paper, we expand PIMT to a *lifted* version that also processes random functions and relations. This enhancement is achieved by adapting *Inversion*, a method from Lifted First-Order Probabilistic Inference literature, to also be modulo theories. This results in the first algorithm for exact probabilistic inference that efficiently and simultaneously exploits random relations and functions, arithmetic, equalities and inequalities.

1 INTRODUCTION

Graphical models such as Bayesian networks and Markov networks (Pearl, 1988) are a well-principled way of representing probabilistic models. They represent the dependences between random variables in a factorized form that can be exploited by probabilistic inference algorithms (such as Variable Elimination (Zhang and Poole, 1994) and Belief Propagation (Pearl, 1988)) for greater efficiency.

However, traditional graphical models representations are unable to represent other types of useful structures:

- **Relational structure** occurs when families of random variables share the same dependences. Suppose a model involves random variables $sunny$, $happy(Ann)$, $happy(Bob), \ldots$ and the analogous dependences $P(happy(Ann)|sunny)$, $P(happy(Bob)|sunny)$ and so on. Intuitively, this structure can be exploited for greater efficiency since the same inference can often be performed only once for an entire family of random variables. Traditional graphical model representations cannot explicitly indicate this structure and thus algorithms cannot directly exploit it.
- **Algebraic structure** occurs when dependences between random variables (such as conditional probabilities) can be compactly described by an algebraic expression. For example, it may be that $P(x \in \{1, \ldots, 1000\}|y \in \{1, \ldots, 1000\})$ is equal to $\texttt{if}\, x = y \,\texttt{then}\, 0.8 \,\texttt{else}\, 0.2/999$. Intuitively, this can be exploited for greater efficiency because large groups of values can be treated in the same way (in this case, all pairs of values (x, y) for which $x \neq y$ are equally probable). Traditional graphical model representations, however, represent such functions as a lookup table (a large 1000×1000 one for this example)[1], thus not explicitly representing the algebraic structure, which prevents algorithms from directly exploiting it.

These types of structure are commonly found in real-world applications and fields such as probabilistic programming, so research has been conducted on exploiting both:

- **Lifted probabilistic inference** (Poole, 2003; de Salvo Braz, 2007; Milch *et al.*, 2008; Van den Broeck *et al.*, 2011; Kersting, 2012) exploits **relational structure** that is explicitly represented with richer languages generally known as **Probabilistic Relational Models**. These representations resemble universal quantification in first-order logic such as $\forall x \in People\, P(happy(x)|sunny)$ for $People$ a discrete set $\{Ann, Bob, \ldots\}$. In logic terminology, this employs **uninterpreted functions**, since the random relations are Boolean functions without a fixed interpretation (for example, the value of $happy(Ann)$ is not fixed in advance).
- **Probabilistic Inference Modulo Theories (PIMT)** (de Salvo Braz *et al.*, 2016) exploits **algebraic structure** by explicitly representing and manipulating function definitions of random variable dependences in the form of algebraic expressions. In logic terminology, this employs **interpreted functions**, because functions like equality

[1] But note exceptions in Boutilier *et al.* (1996); Sanner and Abbasnejad (2012).

(=) and arithmetic functions (+, × etc), among others, have *fixed* interpretations: $3 = 3$ is always TRUE, and $1 + 3$ is always 4.

In this paper, we present the **first lifted probabilistic algorithm on languages with interpreted functions**. This is done by **unifying these two lines of research** by incorporating uninterpreted functions and an important lifted probabilistic inference operation, **Inversion**, into PIMT. (Another major lifted operation, Counting (de Salvo Braz, 2007; Milch *et al.*, 2008), is left for future work.) We call this fusion of lifted inference and PIMT **Lifted Probabilistic Inference Modulo Theories (LPIMT)**.

Moreover, we achieve this unification *modularly*, by using PIMT's ability to be extended by solvers for specific theories, and by encapsulating lifted inference into it as an *uninterpreted functions theory solver*. This means the algorithm can apply lifted inference even to unanticipated theories, because solvers for different theories are orthogonally applied by the general, theory-agnostic level of PIMT.

Casting lifted inference in the PIMT framework also makes it simpler and more powerful than previous lifted inference methods. Besides the above mentioned advantages, it also uses standard mathematical notation (e.g., not making a hard distinction between "logical" and "random" variables); does not separate constraints from potential function definitions; and accepts random function applications even as arguments to other functions (nested applications).

2 BACKGROUND

2.1 Graphical Models and Variable Elimination

Graphical models are a standard framework for reasoning with uncertainty. The most common types are Bayesian networks and Markov networks. In both cases, a **joint probability distribution** for each assignment tuple $\mathbf{x}$ to N random variables is defined as a normalized product of non-negative real functions $\{\phi_i\}_{i \in 1..M}$, where $1..M$ is short for $\{1, \ldots, M\}$, each of them applied to a subtuple $\mathbf{x}_i$ of $\mathbf{x}$:[2]

$$P(\mathbf{x}) = \frac{1}{Z} \prod_i \phi_i(\mathbf{x}_i),$$

where Z is a normalization constant equal to $\sum_{\mathbf{x}} \prod_i \phi_i(\mathbf{x}_i)$. Functions ϕ_i are called **factors** and map each assignment on their arguments to a **potential**, a non-negative real number that represents how likely the assignment $\mathbf{x}_i$ is. This representation is called **factorized** due to its breaking the joint probability into this product. In Bayesian networks, $M = N$ and factors are conditional probabilities $P(x_i|Pa_i)$, for each random variable x_i in $\mathbf{x}$, where Pa_i are its parents in a directed acyclic graph.

[2]For simplicity, we use the same symbols for both random variables and their values, but the meaning should be clear.

The **marginal probability (MAR)** problem consists of computing $P(\mathbf{q}) = \sum_{\mathbf{r}} P(\mathbf{x})$, where $\mathbf{q}$ is a subtuple of $\mathbf{x}$ containing queried variables, and $\mathbf{r}$ are all the remaining variables in $\mathbf{x}$. It can be shown that $P(\mathbf{q}) = \frac{1}{Z_{\mathbf{q}}} \sum_{\mathbf{r}} \prod_i \phi_i(\mathbf{x}_i)$ for $Z_{\mathbf{q}}$ a normalization constant over $\mathbf{q}$. Therefore, the problem can be easily reduced to computing a **summation over products of factors**, which the rest of the paper focuses on.

The **belief update (BEL)** problem consists of computing $P(\mathbf{q}|\mathbf{e})$, the posterior probability on variables $\mathbf{q}$ given assignment $\mathbf{e}$ to evidence variables (an observation). BEL can be easily reduced to two instances of MAR, since Bayes' theorem establishes that $P(\mathbf{q}|\mathbf{e}) = P(\mathbf{q}, \mathbf{e})/P(\mathbf{e})$, where $P(\mathbf{q}, \mathbf{e})$ is the joint value of $\mathbf{q}$ and $\mathbf{e}$.

Computing $\sum_{\mathbf{r}} \prod_i \phi_i(\mathbf{x}_i)$ is crucial for inference with graphical models, but solving it naively has exponential cost in the size of $\mathbf{r}$. **Variable Elimination (VE)** is an algorithm that takes advantage of the factorized representation to more efficiently compute this sum. For example, consider the following summation given a factorization on the variables (h)appy, (w)eekday, (t)emperature, (m)onth with range sizes of 2 (true or false), 7 (weekdays), 3 (hot, $mild$, $cold$), and 12 (months) respectively:

$$\sum_{h,w,t,m} P(h|w,t)P(w)P(t|m)P(m).$$

A naive computation iterates over 504 assignments to (h, w, t, m). However, the joint probability factorization enables us to manipulate the expression and compute it with iterations over fewer assignments:

$$\sum_{h,w,t,m} P(h|w,t)P(w)P(t|m)P(m)$$
$$= \sum_{h,w,t} P(h|w,t)P(w) \sum_m P(t|m)P(m).$$

Now, we **sum** m **out** (or **eliminate** it), obtaining a new factor ϕ, defined on t alone, that replaces the last summation. This requires going over each value t and computing $\phi(t) = \sum_m P(t|m)P(m)$ (thus iterating over the values of m). Therefore, computing ϕ takes iterating over 36 assignments to t, m and we are left with the following new summation of a product of functions:

$$\sum_{h,w,t} P(h|w,t)P(w)\phi(t)$$
$$= \sum_w P(w) \sum_{h,t} P(h|w,t)\phi(t)$$
$$= \sum_w P(w)\phi'(w) \text{ (after 42 assignments to } w, h, t)$$
$$= \phi'' \text{ (after 7 assignments to } w).$$

Variable Elimination therefore decreases the number of required iterations to 85, a six-fold reduction, by exploiting the fact that not all variables share factors with all variables (for example, m only shares a factor with t).

VE applies not only to summations of products, but to any commutative associative semiring (Bistarelli *et al.*, 1997): maximization of products, disjunctions of conjunctions, conjunctions of disjunctions, and so on. We use $\oplus$ and $\otimes$ for the **additive and multiplicative operators** of the semiring. We call **quantifiers** the intensional versions of operators: $\forall$ for $\wedge$, $\exists$ for $\vee$, $\sum$ and $\int$ for $+$ (for discrete and continuous indices respectively), $\prod$ for $\times$, Max for max, and so on. Quantifiers corresponding to $\oplus$ and $\otimes$ are denoted $\bigoplus$ and $\bigotimes$, respectively. We use $\bigodot$ for denoting any type of quantifier. VE works by selecting the next variable v in $\mathbf{r}$ to be eliminated and computing a new factor

$$\phi(\mathbf{u}) = \bigoplus_{v} \bigotimes_{i \in \mathbf{f}(v)} \phi_i(\ldots, v, \ldots),$$

where $\mathbf{f}(v)$ is the set of indices of factors of v and $\mathbf{u}$ are the variables sharing factors with v. It then includes ϕ in the product of factors and proceeds until all variables in $\mathbf{r}$ are eliminated.

2.2 Probabilistic Inference Modulo Theories

Typically, graphical model inference algorithms assume that factors can only be accessed as opaque lookup tables, that is, by providing an assignment to its random variables. This requires Variable Elimination to iterate over all assignments to all random variables in a summation, as seen in the example for computing $\phi(t)$ with Variable Elimination.

However, often the *definitions* of factors are available in the form of **symbolic algebraic expressions** that use operators from specific theories. For example, the conditional probability of temperature given month, and the prior probability of month in our original example could be represented by[3]

$$\begin{aligned} P(t|m) = {}& \texttt{if } m \leq 3 \\ & \qquad \texttt{then if } t = \textit{cold} \texttt{ then } 0.8 \texttt{ else } 0.1 \\ & \qquad \texttt{else if } t = \textit{cold} \texttt{ then } 0.4 \texttt{ else } 0.3 \\ P(m) = {}& 1/12. \end{aligned}$$

While this form does not preclude regular VE to access it as a lookup table (by computing its result given an assignment to t and m), the symbolic expression is itself available as a data structure. This makes the structure of the factor evident; for example, specific values of m do not matter, but only whether $m \leq 3$.

Probabilistic Inference Modulo Theories (PIMT), exploits this available symbolic information for much faster inference. It does so by using **Symbolic Evaluation Modulo Theories (SEMT)**, which is a method for simplifying (and, when possible, completely evaluating) symbolic algebraic expressions, including eliminating quantifiers such as $\sum$, $\prod$, $\exists$, and $\forall$. SEMT applies to general expressions, and not only probabilistic reasoning-related ones. PIMT is simply the use of SEMT applied to expressions that happen to be (unnormalized) marginal probabilities, so we mostly refer to SEMT from now on, keeping in mind that it includes PIMT as a special case.

SEMT and PIMT are similar to **Satisfiability Modulo Theories (SMT)** solvers (Barrett *et al.*, 2009; de Moura *et al.*, 2007), which also take modular theory-specific solvers to solve multi-theory problems. However, they generalize SMT in two important ways: they are **quantifier-parametric**, that is, they eliminate multiple types of quantifiers and deal with expressions of any type, including Boolean, numeric and categorical, as opposed to SMT only solving existential quantification on Boolean-valued formulas; and they are **symbolic**, that is, can process free variables and return results expressed in terms of them, as opposed to assuming all variables to be existentially quantified as in SMT.

SEMT is a variant of SGDPLL(T) (de Salvo Braz *et al.*, 2016) slightly generalized to deal with any expression, and not just sequences of nested quantifiers, and to make use of *contexts*, defined below. We give an overview of SEMT here but refer to the SGDPLL(T) reference for details.

SEMT receives a pair (E, C) as input. E is the expression being evaluated, and C the **context**. Let $\mathbf{x}$ be the free variables in E. Context C is a formula on $\mathbf{x}$ that indicates that *only* the assignments on $\mathbf{x}$ satisfying C need be considered. For example, the expression $\texttt{if } x \neq 1 \texttt{ then } 2 \texttt{ else } 4$, under context $x = 2 \vee x = 3$, can be safely evaluated to 4 because $x \neq 1$ is never true under that context.

SEMT traverses the expression top-down and evaluates each sub-expression according to a set of **rewriting rules** (presented below) until no rule applies to any sub-expressions. It also keeps track of the context holding for sub-expression, depending on the expressions above it. For example, in $\texttt{if } x = 1 \texttt{ then } \sum_{i \in 1..10 : i \neq 3} \gamma \texttt{ else } \varphi$, γ is evaluated under context $x = 1 \wedge i \neq 3$.

Let $E[\alpha/\beta]$ be the **substitution** of all occurrences of expression α in expression E by β. The SEMT rewriting rules are the following (an example is provided afterwards):

- **simplification**: simplifiers for each theory are applied when possible: examples are $1+2 \rightarrow 3$, $x = x \rightarrow \textit{true}$, $\texttt{if } \textit{true} \texttt{ then } 1 \texttt{ else } 2 \rightarrow 1$, $0 \times x \rightarrow 0$ and so on. These always decrease the size of the expression.
- **literal determination**: if the expression is a literal L under a context C and $\forall V : C \Rightarrow L$, where V are the free variables in C and L, rewrite the expression to TRUE; if $\forall V : C \Rightarrow \neg L$, rewrite it to FALSE; the tautology may be decided by SEMT itself or an SMT solver;

[3]Note that $P(t|m)$ sums up to 1 for each m because *hot* and *mild* both have the else case probability mass.

- **factoring out**: if ϕ_1 does not involve index i, $\bigodot_{i\in D:C}(\phi_1 \odot \phi_2) \to \phi_1 \odot \bigodot_{i\in D:C}\phi_2$.

- **if-splitting**: if the expression is ϕ and contains a literal L undefined by the context C, rewrite it to $\texttt{if}\, L\, \texttt{then}\, \phi[L/\text{TRUE}]\, \texttt{else}\, \phi[L/\text{FALSE}]$.

- **quantifier-splitting**: rewrite expressions of the form $\bigodot_{i\in D:C}\phi$, where i is a variable of type D, F is a conjunction of literals in the theory for type D, and ϕ is expression containing a literal L containing i, to a new expression containing two quantified expressions, each with one less literal in its body: $\left(\bigodot_{i:F\wedge L}\phi[L/\text{TRUE}]\right) \odot \left(\bigodot_{i:F\wedge\neg L}\phi[L/\text{FALSE}]\right)$.

- **theory-specific quantifier elimination**: if ϕ does not contain any literals, solve $\bigodot_{i\in D:F}\phi$ with a provided, modular *theory-specific* solver for the type of i.

SEMT always returns a quantifier-free expression since the theory-specific quantifier elimination is eventually invoked for each quantifier. For an expression representing a marginal over a product of factors, it reproduces Variable Elimination by summing out one variable at a time, with the advantage of exploiting factors represented symbolically.[4]

Consider the computation of $\phi(t) = \sum_m P(t|m)P(m)$ below. Regular VE requires iterating over 36 assignments to t, m, but SEMT only needs to consider the 4 truth assignments for literals $t = cold$ and $m \le 3$:

$$\sum_m (\texttt{if } m \le 3 \texttt{ then if } t = \mathit{cold} \texttt{ then } 0.8 \texttt{ else } 0.1$$
$$\texttt{else if } t = \mathit{cold} \texttt{ then } 0.4 \texttt{ else } 0.3)/12$$
$$\to \text{(by if-splitting on } t = \mathit{cold} \text{ and simplification)}$$
$$\texttt{if } t = \mathit{cold}$$
$$\texttt{then } \sum_m (\texttt{if } m \le 3 \texttt{ then } 0.8 \texttt{ else } 0.4)/12$$
$$\texttt{else } \sum_m (\texttt{if } m \le 3 \texttt{ then } 0.1 \texttt{ else } 0.3)/12$$
$$\to \text{(by quantifier-splitting on } m \le 3 \text{ in first summation)}$$
$$\texttt{if } t = \mathit{cold}$$
$$\texttt{then } \sum_{m:m\le 3} (\texttt{if TRUE then } 0.8 \texttt{ else } 0.4)/12$$
$$+ \sum_{m:\neg(m\le 3)} (\texttt{if FALSE then } 0.8 \texttt{ else } 0.4)/12$$
$$\texttt{else } \sum_m (\texttt{if } m \le 3 \texttt{ then } 0.1 \texttt{ else } 0.3)/12$$
$$\to \text{(by simplification and quantifier-splitting on } m \le 3)$$
$$\texttt{if } t = \mathit{cold} \texttt{ then } 0.8/12 \times 3 + 0.4/12 \times 9$$
$$\texttt{else } 0.1/12 \times 3 + 0.3/12 \times 9$$
$$\to \texttt{if } t = \mathit{cold} \texttt{ then } 0.5 \texttt{ else } 0.25,$$

which represents the resulting new factor $\phi(t)$ (which happens to be $P(t)$) to be used in the next steps of VE. Note that the expressions above are *not* just a mathematical argument, but the actual data structures manipulated by SEMT.

SEMT (and consequently PIMT) is **modulo theories** because symbolic evaluation is **theory-agnostic**, working for any theory T given an encapsulated **theory solver** that provides quantifier elimination solvers and simplification rules for T. Theory solvers must be provided only for the simpler expressions of the type $\bigodot_{i\in D:F}\phi$ where ϕ is literal-free and F is a conjunction of literals in the theory. de Salvo Braz *et al.* (2016) details a solver for summation over polynomials, with literals in difference arithmetic on bounded integers. A similar solver for integrals over polynomials and linear real arithmetic literals has also been defined since. An example of SEMT on multiple theories with only 4 cases is:

$$\sum_{i\in 1..7}\int_{x\in[0;10]} \texttt{if } i \ge 3 \texttt{ then if } x < 5 \texttt{ then } x^2 \texttt{ else } 0 \texttt{ else } i$$
$$\to \sum_{i\in 1..7} \texttt{if } i \ge 3 \texttt{ then } \int_{x\in[0;10]} \texttt{if } x < 5 \texttt{ then } x^2 \texttt{ else } 0$$
$$\texttt{else } \int_{x\in[0;10]} i$$
$$\to \sum_{i\in 1..7} \texttt{if } i \ge 3 \texttt{ then } \int_{x\in[0;10]:x<5} x^2 + \int_{x\in[0;10]:x\ge 5} 0$$
$$\texttt{else } 10i$$
$$\to \sum_{i\in 1..7} \texttt{if } i \ge 3 \texttt{ then } 125/3 \texttt{ else } 10i$$
$$\to \Big(\sum_{i\in 1..7:i\ge 3} 125/3\Big) + \Big(\sum_{i\in 1..7:i<3} 10i\Big)$$
$$\to 625/3 + 30 \to 715/3.$$

2.3 Relational Graphical Models

Relational graphical models (RGM) specify probability distributions over families of random variables that can be seen as relations. There are many RGM languages in the literature; they vary significantly in syntax and superficial features, but are typically equivalent and convertible to one another. Markov Logic Networks (MLN) (Richardson and Domingos, 2004) is a well-known one. It consists of a set of weight formulas, an example of which is

$$2.5 : \mathit{Smoker}(\mathit{Bob})$$
$$1.4 : \mathit{Smoker}(X) \wedge \mathit{Friends}(X,Y) \Rightarrow \mathit{Smoker}(Y)$$

for **logical** variables X and Y ranging over a finite set $D = \{\mathit{Ann}, \mathit{Bob}, \mathit{Charlie}, \dots\}$.

[4]The variable order used by VE is encoded in the order of quantifiers, and efficient ordering can be introduced by a rule that re-orders sequences of quantifiers.

The random variables in this MLN are the **groundings**, or **instantiations**, of the relations in it for every assignment to the logical variables: $Sm(Ann)$, $Sm(Bob)$, $\ldots$, $Fr(Ann, Ann)$, $Fr(Ann, Bob)$, $\ldots$ (we abbreviate $Smoker$ and $Friends$ from now on). A formula with weight w defines a factor for each of its instantiations (one for each assignments to its logical variables). The potential assigned by such factors is e^w if the formula is true, and 1 otherwise. Therefore, some of the factors of this MLN are: $\phi_1(Sm(Bob))$, $\phi_2(Sm(Ann), Fr(Ann, Bob), Sm(Bob))$, $\phi_2(Sm(Ann), Fr(Ann, Charlie), Sm(Charlie))$, and $\phi_2(Sm(Bob), Fr(Bob, Ann), Sm(Ann))$, where ϕ_1 and ϕ_2 are potential functions applied to all factors instantiated from the first and second formulas respectively:

$$\phi_1(s) = \texttt{if } s \texttt{ then } e^{2.5} \texttt{ else } 1$$

$$\phi_2(s_1, f, s_2) = \texttt{if } s_1 \wedge f \Rightarrow s_2 \texttt{ then } e^{1.4} \texttt{ else } 1.$$

Because the number of instantiations can be huge, performing inference on RGMs by simply instantiating them as regular graphical models is often infeasible. The next section describes **Inversion**, one of the operations used in **lifted probabilistic inference**, which exponentially improves efficiency in RGMs in many cases.

3 INVERSION AND INVERSION MODULO THEORIES

This section presents this paper's main contributions. We present a new formulation for RGMs and Inversion that is more algebraically standard, and then use this formulation to generalize Inversion to Inversion Modulo Theories.

3.1 RGMS with Function-Valued Random Variables

While the RGM literature considers $Sm(Ann)$, $Sm(Bob), \ldots$ as individual (Boolean) random variables, it is conceptually simpler, and more mathematically standard, to talk about Sm as a single random variable that happens to be *function-valued*. From this point of view, this MLN has only two random variables: Sm and Fr, and defines the following joint probability distribution:

$$P(Sm, Fr) = \frac{1}{Z} \times \phi_1(Sm(Bob)) \times \prod_{X \in D} \prod_{Y \in D} \phi_2(Sm(X), Fr(X, Y), Sm(Y))$$

where Z is defined as usual, as well as marginalization:

$$P(Sm) = \sum_{Fr \in D \times D \rightarrow Boolean} P(Sm, Fr).$$

Note that, given the form of $P(Sm, Fr)$, marginal probabilities in RGMs are **sums of products of factors**, including *intensional* products using $\prod$. This fact is heavily exploited by Inversion.

To compute the marginal of a specific function application, say, $Sm(Ann)$, we need to marginalize over all *remaining* random variables, that is, Fr and all $Sm(x)$ for $x \in D \setminus \{Ann\}$. This requires splitting the variable Sm into two distinct function-valued random variables: $Sm' : \{Ann\} \rightarrow Boolean$ and $Sm'' : D \setminus \{Ann\} \rightarrow Boolean$, and replace each application $Sm(\theta)$ of the original Sm on argument expression θ by
$\texttt{if } \theta = Ann \texttt{ then } Sm'(Ann) \texttt{ else } Sm''(\theta)$. Then we can compute

$$P(Sm') = \sum_{Sm'' : D \setminus \{Ann\} \rightarrow Boolean} \sum_{Fr} P(Sm', Sm'', Fr).$$

The above shows that solving RGMs is simply equivalent to allowing function-valued random variables in the model. However, summations over functions are expensive due to their high number of possible values ($2^{|D|^2}$ for Fr, for instance). The next section describes a method that exponentially decreases this cost in some cases.

3.2 Inversion on Function-Valued Variables

Lifted probabilistic inference algorithms seek to exploit the structure of random functions for greater efficiency. It includes a few operations, but in this paper we consider only one: **Inversion** (also called Lifted Decomposition).

Inversion uses the fact that summations indexed by functions of products of factors may under certain conditions be transformed into exponentially cheaper summations over "slices" of the original function. Its name comes from the fact that a summation of products becomes a cheaper product of a summation ($\sum \prod \rightarrow \prod \sum$), thus "inverting" the quantifiers. Consider an example in which the body ϕ of the sum-product depends on a single application of a function f ranging over the set of functions $1..10 \rightarrow 1..5$:

$$\sum_{f \in (1..10 \rightarrow 1..5)} \prod_{x \in 1..10} \phi(f(x)) = \prod_{x \in 1..10} \sum_{f \in (\{x\} \rightarrow 1..5)} \phi(f(x)).$$

Note that, while f ranges over $(1..10 \rightarrow 1..5)$ on the left-hand side, and thus over 5^{10} possible values, the domain of f on the right-hand side is a singleton set, because x is bound by the now outer $\prod_x$. This reduces the number of possible values of f to only 5, making iterating over it exponentially cheaper.

The equality holds because x "slices" f into independent portions:

$$\sum_{f \in (1..10 \rightarrow 1..5)} \prod_{x \in 1..10} \phi(f(x))$$
$$= \sum_{f_1 \in \{1\} \rightarrow 1..5} \cdots \sum_{f_{10} \in \{10\} \rightarrow 1..5} \phi(f_1(1)) \times \ldots \times \phi(f_{10}(10))$$
$$= \sum_{f_1 \in \{1\} \rightarrow 1..5} \phi(f_1(1)) \cdots \sum_{f_{10} \in \{10\} \rightarrow 1..5} \phi(f_{10}(10)) \quad (*)$$

$$= \Big(\sum_{f_1 \in \{1\} \to 1..5} \phi(f_1(1)) \Big) \cdots \Big(\sum_{f_{10} \in \{10\} \to 1..5} \phi(f_{10}(10)) \Big)$$

$$= \Big(\sum_{f \in \{1\} \to 1..5} \phi(f(1)) \Big) \cdots \Big(\sum_{f \in \{10\} \to 1..5} \phi(f(10)) \Big)$$

$$= \prod_{x \in 1..10} \sum_{f \in (\{x\} \to 1..5)} \phi(f(x)).$$

Once transformed in this way, we proceed as follows:

$$\prod_{x \in 1..10} \phi(1) + \phi(2) + \phi(3) + \phi(4) + \phi(5)$$

$$= \prod_{x \in 1..10} \phi' \quad = \quad (\phi')^{10} \quad = \quad \phi''$$

by using the fact that constant ϕ' does not depend on x.

The above transformation is valid because $\prod_x \phi(f(x))$ contains 10 factors, each of them only involving the application of f to a *single* value of x. This means they can be factored out of the summations indexed by other applications of the function, resulting in smaller and equivalent summations that are computed only once and then exponentiated. Similar transformations may be applied even if there are products over more than one variable:

$$\sum_{f \in A_1 \times A_2 \to B} \prod_x \prod_y \phi(f(x,y)) = \prod_x \prod_y \sum_{f \in \{(x,y)\} \to B} \phi(f(x,y))$$

by an analogous argument.

However, the transformation is not always valid:

$$\sum_{f \in A_1 \times A_2 \to B} \prod_x \prod_y \phi(f(x,y), f(y,x))$$
$$\neq \prod_x \prod_y \sum_{f \in \{(x,y)\} \to B} \phi(f(x,y), f(y,x)).$$

To see this, consider a pair $(a, b) \in A_1 \times A_2$. The summation $\sum_{f \in \{(a,b)\} \to B} \phi(f(a,b), f(b,a))$ depends on $f(a,b)$ and $f(b,a)$, which both occur in $\sum_{f \in \{(b,a)\} \to B} \phi(f(b,a), f(a,b))$, and this shared dependence prevents factoring as in step (*) above.

This does not mean that having more than one application of f in ϕ admits no Inversion, but it may restrict the inversion to just *some* of the products:

$$\sum_{f \in ((A_1 \times A_2 \times A_3) \to B)} \prod_x \prod_y \phi(f(x,y,x), f(x,3,x)) \quad (1)$$

$$= \prod_x \sum_{f \in ((\{x\} \times A_2 \times \{x\}) \to B)} \prod_y \phi(f(x,y,x), f(x,3,x)),$$

which does not decrease the function's domain size to 1 but still exponentially decreases the evaluation cost.

All these cases are covered by the following theorem:

Theorem 3.1 (Inversion). *Let E be an expression in which* all *applications of a function f have their first k arguments (without loss of generality because they can be permutated) equal to $x_{i_1}, \ldots, x_{i_k}$ for i a k-tuple of indices in $\{1, \ldots, m\}$. If operator $\oplus$ distributes over operator $\otimes$,*

$$\bigoplus_{f \in (A_1 \times \cdots \times A_n) \to B} \bigotimes_{x_1} \cdots \bigotimes_{x_m} E$$
$$= \bigotimes_{x_1} \cdots \bigotimes_{x_m} \bigoplus_{f \in (\{(x_{i_1}, \ldots, x_{i_k})\} \times A_{k+1} \times \cdots \times A_n) \to B} E,$$

which is exponentially cheaper to evaluate.

Note that E may contain quantifiers itself; this was the case in Equation (1). The theorem's proof mirrors the operations shown in the examples above.

Crucially, Theorem 3.1 uses a *syntactic* check that relies on the language allowing only simple terms (variables and constants) as arguments to functions. It therefore does not apply to the important extensions in which more complex terms, using theory-specific operators such as arithmetic or inequalities, or even operators from unanticipated theories, are used as function arguments. We will see how this can be done with a *semantic* check in the next section.

3.3 Inversion Modulo Theories

We now present this paper's main contribution: **Inversion Modulo Theories**, which is a version of the lifted probabilistic inference operation Inversion in the presence of factors defined through symbolic algebraic expressions involving multiple theories. Like regular Inversion, Inversion Modulo Theories does not cover every possible problem, in which case one must fall back to currently used methods like grounding or sampling. Future work includes generalizing other lifted inference methods like Counting (de Salvo Braz, 2007; Milch *et al.*, 2008) to also be modulo theories, thus decreasing the need for the fallback methods.

Previous work on Inversion assumed RGMs expressed in a simple language in which the only allowed arguments in function applications are variable or constant symbols. This enables the Inversion condition to consist of a *syntactic* check. However, once we allow function arguments to be arbitrary terms from any of the available theories, these syntactic tests no longer apply, since the arguments semantics depends on the particular theory and the syntactic check does not take semantics into account. The new Inversion test must apply to arguments from any theory and, in fact, to arguments in even *new, as of yet unanticipated* theories. This requires this new test to be theory-agnostic, and defined in such a way that theory solvers may be transparently employed.

We start by defining $oc_f[E]$, an expression representing the portion of the domain of a given function f involved in a given expression E.

Definition 3.1. *The* ***set of argument tuples for*** $f : A \to B$ ***occurring in an expression*** E *is denoted* $oc_f[E]$ *and inductively defined as follows:*

- *if* E *does not contain* f*,* $oc_f[E]$ *is* $\emptyset$*;*
- *if* E *is* $f(t)$ *for* t *a tuple,* $oc_f[E]$ *is* $\{t\}$*;*
- *if* E *is* f*,* $oc_f[E]$ *is* A*;*
- *if* E *is* $\texttt{if}\, C\, \texttt{then}\, E_1\, \texttt{else}\, E_2$ *and* C *does not contain* f*, then* $oc_f[E]$ *is* $\texttt{if}\, C\, \texttt{then}\, oc_f[E_1]\, \texttt{else}\, oc_f[E_2]$*; otherwise,* $oc_f[E]$ *is* $oc_f[C] \cup oc_f[E_1] \cup oc_f[E_2]$*;*
- *if* E *is* $g(t_1, \ldots, t_k)$ *for* g *a function symbol distinct from* f*, or* E *is* $\{t_1, \ldots, t_k\}$*,* $oc_f[E]$ *is* $oc_f[t_1] \cup \cdots \cup oc_f[t_k]$*;*
- *if* E *is* $Q_{x \in T:C} E'$ *for* Q *an arbitrary quantifier,*
  - *if* C *does not contain* f*, then* $oc_f[E]$ *is* $oc_f[T] \cup \bigcup_{x \in T:C} oc_f[E']$*;*
  - *otherwise,* $oc_f[E]$ *is* $oc_f[T] \cup \bigcup_{x \in T}(oc_f[C] \cup oc_f[E'])$*.*

For example,

$$oc_f\Big[f(x,y) + \sum_{z \in 1..10:z!=3} f(x,z) \prod_{w \in 1..10} f(w,z)\Big]$$
$$= \{(x,y)\} \cup \bigcup_{z \in 1..10:z!=3} (\{(x,z)\} \cup \bigcup_{w \in 1..10} \{(w,z)\}),$$

in which x and y are free variables.

As a further preliminary step, we add simplification rules for tuples, and for testing whether sets are empty, to be used by SEMT. This will be useful later in manipulating $oc_f[E]$ expressions.

Theorem 3.2 (Tuple and Empty Set Simplifiers)**.** *The following* ***tuple and empty set simplifiers***

1. $(r_1, \ldots, r_n) = (s_1, \ldots, s_n) \to r_1 = s_1 \wedge \cdots \wedge r_m = s_m$ *(or its negation for* $\neq$*).*
2. $t \in \{t_1, \ldots, t_n\} \to (t = t_1) \vee t \in \{t_2, \ldots, t_n\}$*.*
3. $t \in \bigcup_{i \in D:C} \phi \to \exists i \in D : (C \wedge t \in \phi)$*.*
4. $(\bigcup_{i \in D:C} \phi) = \emptyset \to \forall i \in D : (\neg C \vee \phi = \emptyset)$*.*
5. $S \cap \emptyset = \emptyset \to$ TRUE*.*
6. $S \cup \emptyset = \emptyset \to S = \emptyset$*.*
7. $S \cap \{t_1, \ldots, t_n\} = \emptyset \to (t_1 \notin S) \wedge (S \cap \{t_2, \ldots, t_n\} = \emptyset)$*.*
8. $(\bigcup_{i \in D:C} \phi) \cap (\bigcup_{i' \in D':C'} \phi') = \emptyset \to \forall i \in D : C \Rightarrow \forall i' \in D' : C' \Rightarrow (\phi \cap \phi' = \emptyset)$*.*
9. $(S_1 \cup S_2) \cap S_3 = \emptyset \to (S_1 \cap S_3) \cup (S_2 \cap S_3) = \emptyset$*.*
10. $S_1 \cup S_2 = \emptyset \to S_1 = \emptyset \wedge S_2 = \emptyset$*.*
11. $\{t_1, \ldots, t_n\} = \emptyset \to$ FALSE *if* $n > 0$*,* TRUE *otherwise,*

when included in SEMT, rewrite $oc_f[E] = \emptyset$ *expressions to equivalent formulas free of tuple and set expressions.*

The proof is presented in Supplementary Materials. It is based on gradual distribution of $\cap$ over $\cup$, and conversion of intersections to comparisons between set elements:

$$\bigcup_{x \in 1..5} \Big(\{(x,y)\} \cup \bigcup_{z \in 3..5} \{(z,3)\}\Big) \cap \bigcup_{w \in 1..10} \{(1,w)\} = \emptyset$$

$\to$ (rule 8)

$\forall x \in 1..5 : \forall w \in 1..10 :$

$$\Big(\{(x,y)\} \cup \bigcup_{z \in 3..5} \{(z,3)\}\Big) \cap \{(1,w)\} = \emptyset$$

$\to$ (rule 9 distributes $\cap$ over $\cup$)

$\forall x \in 1..5 : \forall w \in 1..10 :$

$$\{(x,y)\} \cap \{(1,w)\} \cup \Big(\bigcup_{z \in 3..5} \{(z,3)\}\Big) \cap \{(1,w)\} = \emptyset$$

$\to$ (rule 10)

$\forall x \in 1..5 : \forall w \in 1..10 :$

$$\{(x,y)\} \cap \{(1,w)\} = \emptyset \wedge \Big(\bigcup_{z \in 3..5} \{(z,3)\}\Big) \cap \{(1,w)\} = \emptyset$$

$\to$ (rules 7, 2, and 8)

$\forall x \in 1..5 : \forall w \in 1..10 :$

$$(x,y) \neq (1,w) \wedge \forall z \in 3..5 : \{(z,3)\} \cap \{(1,w)\} = \emptyset$$

$\to$ (rule 1 on first conjunct, rules 7 and 2 on second one)

$\forall x \in 1..5 : \forall w \in 1..10 :$

$$(x \neq 1 \vee y \neq w) \wedge \forall z \in 3..5 : (z,3) \neq (1,w)$$

$\to$ (rule 1 for breaking tuples)

$\forall x \in 1..5 : \forall w \in 1..10 :$

$$(x \neq 1 \vee y \neq w) \wedge \forall z \in 3..5 : z \neq 1 \vee 3 \neq w$$

$\to$ (integer-specific solver for $\bigodot = \forall$ for z, w and x)

$\forall x \in 1..5 : \forall w \in 1..10 : (x \neq 1 \vee y \neq w) \wedge 3 \neq w$

$\to \forall x \in 1..5 :$ FALSE $\to$ FALSE.

Deciding whether a set expression is equivalent to the empty set is crucial for Inversion Modulo Theories, which can now be formally stated:

Theorem 3.3 (Inversion Modulo Theories)**.** *Let* E *be an expression and* T_i*,* C_i *be type and constraint, respectively, in a theory for which we have a satisfiability solver. Then,*

$$\bigoplus_{f \in A \to B} \bigotimes_{x_1 \in T_1:C_1} \cdots \bigotimes_{x_k \in T_k:C_k} E,$$

where $A = oc_f[\bigotimes_{x_1 \in T_1:C_1} \cdots \bigotimes_{x_k \in T_k:C_k} E]$ *(this is relaxed in Section 3.4), is equivalent to , and therefore can be rewritten as,*

$$\bigotimes_{x_1 \in T_1 : C_1} \cdots \bigotimes_{x_k \in T_k : C_k} \bigoplus_{f \in oc_f[E] \to B} E,$$

if $\bigotimes$ *distributes over* $\bigoplus$ *and*

$$\forall x'_1 \in T_1 \ldots \forall x'_k \in T_k \quad \forall x''_1 \in T_1 \ldots \forall x''_k \in T_k$$
$$\begin{pmatrix} C_1[x_1/x'_1] \wedge \cdots \wedge C_k[x_k/x'_k] \\ \wedge\, C_1[x_1/x''_1] \wedge \cdots \wedge C_k[x_k/x''_k] \\ \wedge\, (x'_1, \ldots, x'_k) \neq (x''_1, \ldots, x''_k) \end{pmatrix}$$
$$\Rightarrow \begin{pmatrix} oc_f[E][x_1/x'_1, \ldots, x_k/x'_k] \\ \cap \\ oc_f[E][x_1/x''_1, \ldots, x_k/x''_k] \end{pmatrix} = \emptyset \qquad (2)$$

(that is, the set of argument tuples in applications of f in E for different value assignments to $x_1, \ldots, x_k$ are always disjoint — we refer to this as ***Condition (2)*** *from now on). Moreover, the rewritten expression is exponentially ($O(2^{\prod_i |\{x_i \in T_i : C_i\}|})$) cheaper to evaluate than the original.*

The theorem (proven in Supplementary Materials) covers significantly more general cases than the original examples may suggest: f may have any arity; its arguments need not be only variables or constants, but even other (interpreted or uninterpreted) function applications; E may contain quantifiers itself; and quantifiers may involve constraints (C_i). The following example involves all these characteristics:

Example 3.4. *Let w and g be free variables.*

$$\sum_{f \in 1..10 \times (1..10 \setminus \{8\}) \times \{w+3\} \to 1..5} \;\prod_{x \in (1+g(w))..(10+g(w))} \;\prod_{y \in 1..10 : y \neq 8} \;\sum_{z \in 1..10} f(x - g(w), y, w+3) z$$

$\rightarrow$ *(Inversion on x, y; see Eqn. (3) for Condition (2))*

$$\prod_{x \in (1+g(w))..(10+g(w))} \;\prod_{y \in 1..10 : y \neq 8} \;\sum_{f \in \{(x - g(w), y, w+3)\} \to 1..5} \;\sum_{z \in 1..10} f(x - g(w), y, w+3) z$$

$\rightarrow$ *(f has a singleton domain since x, y, g and w are fixed in the first summation, so it behaves like a variable v)*

$$\prod_{x \in (1+g(w))..(10+g(w))} \;\prod_{y \in 1..10 : y \neq 8} \;\sum_{v \in 1..5} \;\sum_{z \in 1..10} vz.$$

This transformation decreases the time complexity of the first summation from the time to iterate over $5^{10 \times 9}$ values of f to 5 values of v only. But, in fact, from now on SEMT completes the calculation with no iteration at all by using symbolic integer-specific solvers for $\sum$ and $\prod$:

$$\prod_{x \in (1+g(w))..(10+g(w))} \;\prod_{y \in 1..10 : y \neq 8} \;\sum_{v \in 1..5} \;\sum_{z \in 1..10} vz$$
$$\rightarrow \prod_{x \in (1+g(w))..(10+g(w))} \;\prod_{y \in 1..10 : y \neq 8} \;\sum_{v \in 1..5} 55v$$
$$\rightarrow \prod_{x \in (1+g(w))..(10+g(w))} \;\prod_{y \in 1..10 : y \neq 8} 55 \times 15 \rightarrow 825^{10 \times 9} \rightarrow 825^{90}.$$

In this example, Condition (2) is

$$\forall x' \in (1 + g(w))..(10 + g(w)) \quad \forall y' \in 1..10$$
$$\forall x'' \in (1 + g(w))..(10 + g(w)) \quad \forall y'' \in 1..10$$
$$(x', y') \neq (x'', y'') \wedge y' \neq 8 \wedge y'' \neq 8 \Rightarrow$$
$$\bigcup_{z \in 1..10} (x' - g(w), y', w + 3)$$
$$\cap \bigcup_{z \in 1..10} (x'' - g(w), y'', w + 3) = \emptyset \qquad (3)$$

which can be solved by SEMT with $\bigoplus$ instantiated as $\forall$ over difference arithmetic, after including tuple and empty set simplifiers from Definition 3.2).

Example 3.5. *Consider monitoring crop growth from satellite images to alert against famine. The growth (g) of crops can be determined from their color (c) in the images, and depends on whether the region was in drought (d) 3 months previously. This can be modeled as:*

$$\forall m \in Months, f \in Fields:$$
$$P(c(f, m) | g(f, m)) = \textit{if } g(f, m) > 2.3 \textit{ then if } c(f, m) \ldots$$
$$P(g(f, m + 3) | d(m)) = \textit{if } d(m) \textit{ then if } g(f, m + 3) \ldots$$

The query $P(d|c)$ requires solving the following marginalization over growth:

$$\sum_g \prod_m \prod_f P(c(f, m{+}3) | g(f, m{+}3)) P(g(f, m{+}3) | d(m))$$

Inversion Modulo Theories applies (because each (f, m) involves a single instance of $g(f, m + 3)$) and we obtain

$$\prod_m \prod_f \sum_{g(f, m+3)} P(c(f, m{+}3) | g(f, m{+}3)) P(g(f, m{+}3) | d(m))$$

which makes the summation on growth exponentially cheaper to compute and produces

$$\prod_m \prod_f \phi(c(f, m + 3), d(m)),$$

for ϕ the summation result. This can then be evaluated directly, given the evidence on color for each m and f, producing a factorized representation of the marginal on $drought(m)$, for each month. If the number of fields is 2000, and growths domain size is 5, this cuts the cost of exactly eliminating growth from 5^{2000} iterations to only 5.

3.4 Dealing with Arbitrary Domains for f

Let OC_f be $oc_f[\bigotimes_{x_1 \in T_1:C_1} \cdots \bigotimes_{x_k \in T_k:C_k} E]$. Theorem 3.3 requires that $A = OC_f$, that is, that the domain of f coincide with its portion being used inside $\bigoplus_{f \in A \to B}$. When $A \neq OC_f$, we use function splitting (Section 3.1):

$$\bigoplus_{f \in A \to B} \Psi = \bigoplus_{f' \in (A \setminus OC_f) \to B} \bigoplus_{f'' \in (OC_f \setminus A) \to B} \bigoplus_{f \in (A \cap OC_f) \to B} \Psi'$$

for Ψ' obtained from Ψ after replacing each $f(\alpha)$ by

$$\texttt{if } \alpha \in A \\ \texttt{then if } \alpha \in OC_f \texttt{ then } f(\alpha) \texttt{ else } f'(\alpha) \texttt{ else } f''(\alpha).$$

This technique splits the original f into three different functions f, f', f'', and replaces each of its applications by the one corresponding to its arguments. After this, the domain of f coincides with OC_f, satisfying the corresponding requirement in Theorem 3.3.

3.5 Dealing with Multiple Separate $\bigotimes$ Quantifiers

Theorem 3.3 requires a single nested sequence of $\bigotimes$ quantifiers inside $\bigoplus$. However, summations on products of *separate* $\bigotimes$ quantifiers can be rewritten to the required form:

$$\bigoplus_{f \in A \to B} \left(\left(\bigotimes_{x \in T_x:C_x} E_x \right) \left(\bigotimes_{y \in T_y:C_y} E_y \right) \right)$$

$$\to \bigoplus_{f \in A \to B} \bigotimes_{x \in T_x:C_x} \bigotimes_{y \in T_y:C_y} E_x^{\frac{1}{|\{y \in T_y:C_y\}|}} E_y^{\frac{1}{|\{x \in T_x:C_x\}|}},$$

where the exponents compensate for the extra multiplications of E_x and E_y by moving them inside $\bigotimes_y$ and $\bigotimes_x$ respectively (this is sometimes called **scaling**). Set cardinalities can be computed as a special case of summation.

In the special case in which x and y range over the same values (that is, $\{x \in T_x : C_x\} = \{y \in T_y : C_y\}$, which can be evaluated by SEMT), the two $\bigotimes$ quantifiers can be merged into a single one (or **aligned**), and the original expression is rewritten instead to the cheaper $\bigoplus_{f \in A \to B} \bigotimes_{x \in T_x:C_x} E_x E_y[y/x]$. These transformations can be easily generalized to cases with more than two $\bigotimes$ quantifications, and nested $\bigotimes$ expressions.

3.6 A Proof-of-concept Experiment

Since SEMT and Inversion Modulo Theories are elaborate symbolic algorithms, two immediate questions are whether they can be effectively implemented and how they compare with simpler alternatives such as sampling. As a proof-of-concept test, we used our implementation of SEMT for computing Example 3.4 using two alternatives: one, in which the sum-product is simplified by Inversion Modulo Theories, and another in which the sum and product are computed by sampling. As expected, Inversion Modulo Theories vastly outperforms sampling in this example, computing the exact answer (825^{90}) in less than 300 ms, whereas sampling requires 10 minutes, and 10,000 samples per quantifier, to be within an order of magnitude of the exact answer, and 17 minutes to be within 10% error.

4 RELATED WORK AND CONCLUSION

As mentioned in the introduction, LPIMT generalizes work in the lifted inference, probabilistic inference modulo theories, and satisfiability modulo theories literatures. It is also related to Probabilistic Programs (PP) (Goodman *et al.*, 2012; Milch *et al.*, 2005), a class of high-level representations for probabilistic models that uses interpreted and uninterpreted functions. The current prevalent inference method in PPs is sampling, which is approximate and whose convergence rate depends on the size of the grounded model, that is, on the size of the domain. LPIMT can be applied to some fragments of PPs and is an exact inference alternative that avoids iterating over the domain. The closest approach to LPIMT in the PP area is Hakaru (Carette and Shan, 2016; Narayanan *et al.*, 2016), which employs symbolic methods for simplification and integration of PPs, but does not include lifted inference on random functions. Model Counting Modulo Theories (Phan, 2015) leverages SMT solvers to compute model counts, but does not cover weighted model counting (and thus probabilistic reasoning), and does not exploit factorization. Weighted Model Counting and Integration (Michels *et al.*, 2015; Belle *et al.*, 2015; Michels *et al.*, 2016) and Symbolic Variable Elimination (Sanner and Abbasnejad, 2012) are similar in spirit to PIMT, but not to LPIMT; they apply to Boolean and linear real arithmetic random variables, but not yet to random functions. (Belle, 2017) focuses on weighted model counting (WMC) with function symbols on infinite domains, reducing it to standard WMC, but does not currently use lifting techniques. Group Inversion (Taghipour *et al.*, 2012) expands Inversion to cover some extra cases, but not interpreted functions. Extending it to do so, along with Counting, is the most immediate possibility for future work.

To conclude, we have defined Inversion Modulo Theories, an expansion of the lifted inference operation Inversion for the case with interpreted functions, and added it to Probabilistic Inference Modulo Theories framework, thus defining the first algorithm to perform exact lifted inference in the presence of interpreted functions.

ACKNOWLEDGMENTS We gratefully acknowledge the support of the Defense Advanced Research Projects Agency (DARPA) Probabilistic Programming for Advanced Machine Learning Program under Air Force Research Laboratory (AFRL) prime contract no. FA8750-14-C-0005.

References

Barrett, C. W., Sebastiani, R., Seshia, S. A., and Tinelli, C. Satisfiability Modulo Theories. In Biere, A., Heule, M., van Maaren, H., and Walsh, T., editors, *Handbook of Satisfiability*, volume 185 of *Frontiers in Artificial Intelligence and Applications*, pages 825–885. IOS Press, 2009.

Belle, V., Passerini, A., and Van den Broeck, G. Probabilistic inference in hybrid domains by weighted model integration. In *Proceedings of 24th International Joint Conference on Artificial Intelligence (IJCAI)*, 2015.

Belle, V. Weighted model countingwith function symbols. In *Proceedings of the Conference on Uncertainty in Artificial Intelligence (UAI)*, 2017.

Bistarelli, S., Montanari, U., and Rossi, F. Semiring-based constraint satisfaction and optimization. *J. ACM*, 44(2):201–236, March 1997.

Boutilier, C., Friedman, N., Goldszmidt, M., and Koller, D. Context-Specific Independence in Bayesian Networks. In *Proceedings of UAI*, pages 115–123, 1996.

Carette, J. and Shan, C. Simplifying probabilistic programs using computer algebra. In *Practical Aspects of Declarative Languages - 18th International Symposium, PADL 2016, St. Petersburg, FL, USA, January 18-19, 2016. Proceedings*, pages 135–152, 2016.

de Moura, L., Dutertre, B., and Shankar, N. A tutorial on satisfiability modulo theories. In *Computer Aided Verification, 19th International Conference, CAV 2007, Berlin, Germany, July 3-7, 2007, Proceedings*, volume 4590 of *Lecture Notes in Computer Science*, pages 20–36. Springer, 2007.

de Salvo Braz, R., O'Reilly, C., Gogate, V., and Dechter, R. Probabilistic Inference Modulo Theories. In *Proceedings of the Twenty-Fifth International Joint Conference on Artificial Intelligence*, New York, USA, 2016.

de Salvo Braz, R. *Lifted First-Order Probabilistic Inference*. PhD thesis, University of Illinois at Urbana-Champaign, 2007.

Goodman, N. D., Mansinghka, V. K., Roy, D. M., Bonawitz, K., and Tarlow, D. Church: a language for generative models. *CoRR*, abs/1206.3255, 2012.

Kersting, K. Lifted probabilistic inference. In *European Conference on Artificial Intelligence*, 2012.

Michels, S., Hommersom, A., Lucas, P. J. F., and Velikova, M. A new probabilistic constraint logic programming language based on a generalised distribution semantics. *Artificial Intelligence*, 228(C):1–44, November 2015.

Michels, S., Hommersom, A., and Lucas, P. J. F. Approximate probabilistic inference with bounded error. In *Proceedings of the Twenty-Fifth International Joint Conference on Artificial Intelligence*, New York, USA, 2016.

Milch, B., Marthi, B., Russell, S., Sontag, D., Ong, D. L., and Kolobov, A. BLOG: probabilistic models with unknown objects. In *IJCAI'05: Proceedings of the 19th international joint conference on Artificial intelligence*, pages 1352–1359, San Francisco, CA, USA, 2005. Morgan Kaufmann Publishers Inc.

Milch, B., Zettlemoyer, L., Kersting, K., Haimes, M., and Kaelbling, L. P. Lifted probabilistic inference with counting formulas. In *Proceedings of the Twenty-Third AAAI Conference on Artificial Intelligence (AAAI-2008)*, Chicago, Illinois, USA, July 2008 2008.

Narayanan, P., Carette, J., Romano, W., Shan, C.-c., and Zinkov, R. Probabilistic inference by program transformation in hakaru (system description). In Kiselyov, O. and King, A., editors, *Functional and Logic Programming: 13th International Symposium, FLOPS 2016, Kochi, Japan, March 4-6, 2016, Proceedings*, pages 62–79. Springer International Publishing, Cham, 2016.

Pearl, J. *Probabilistic reasoning in intelligent systems: networks of plausible inference*. Morgan Kaufmann, San Mateo (Calif.), 1988.

Phan, Q.-S. *Model Counting Modulo Theories*. PhD thesis, Queen Mary University of London, 2015.

Poole, D. First-order probabilistic inference. In *Proceedings of the 18th International Joint Conference on Artificial Intelligence*, pages 985–991, 2003.

Richardson, M. and Domingos, P. Markov Logic Networks. Technical report, Department of Computer Science, University of Washington, 2004.

Sanner, S. and Abbasnejad, E. Symbolic variable elimination for discrete and continuous graphical models. In *Proceedings of the Twenty-Sixth AAAI Conference on Artificial Intelligence*, 2012.

Taghipour, N., Fierens, D., den Broeck, G. V., Davis, J., and Blockeel, H. Lifted variable elimination: A novel operator and completeness results. *CoRR*, abs/1208.3809, 2012.

Van den Broeck, G., Taghipour, N., Meert, W., Davis, J., and Raedt, L. D. Lifted probabilistic inference by first-order knowledge compilation. In *In Proceedings of the 22nd International Joint Conference on Artificial Intelligence*, pages 2178–2185, 2011.

Zhang, N. L. and Poole, D. A simple approach to Bayesian network computations. In *Proceedings of the Tenth Biennial Canadian Artificial Intelligence Conference*, 1994.

A SUPPLEMENTARY MATERIALS

A.1 Theorems 3.2 and 3.3 and their proofs

Theorem 3.2 (Tuple and Empty Set Simplifiers)**.** *The following* ***tuple and empty set simplifiers***

1. $(r_1, \ldots, r_n) = (s_1, \ldots, s_n) \rightarrow$ $r_1 = s_1 \wedge \cdots \wedge r_m = s_m$ *(or its negation for* $\neq$*).*

2. $t \in \{t_1, \ldots, t_n\} \rightarrow (t = t_1) \vee t \in \{t_2, \ldots, t_n\}$.

3. $t \in \bigcup_{i \in D:C} \phi \rightarrow \exists i \in D : (C \wedge t \in \phi)$.

4. $(\bigcup_{i \in D:C} \phi) = \emptyset \rightarrow \forall i \in D : (\neg C \vee \phi = \emptyset)$.

5. $S \cap \emptyset = \emptyset \rightarrow$ TRUE.

6. $S \cup \emptyset = \emptyset \rightarrow S = \emptyset$.

7. $S \cap \{t_1, \ldots, t_n\} = \emptyset \rightarrow$ $(t_1 \notin S) \wedge (S \cap \{t_2, \ldots, t_n\} = \emptyset)$.

8. $(\bigcup_{i \in D:C} \phi) \cap (\bigcup_{i' \in D':C'} \phi') = \emptyset \rightarrow$ $\forall i \in D : C \Rightarrow \forall i' \in D' : C' \Rightarrow (\phi \cap \phi' = \emptyset)$.

9. $(S_1 \cup S_2) \cap S_3 = \emptyset \rightarrow (S_1 \cap S_3) \cup (S_2 \cap S_3) = \emptyset$.

10. $S_1 \cup S_2 = \emptyset \rightarrow S_1 = \emptyset \wedge S_2 = \emptyset$.

11. $\{t_1, \ldots, t_n\} = \emptyset \rightarrow$ FALSE *if* $n > 0$, TRUE *otherwise,*

when included in SEMT, rewrite $oc_f[E] = \emptyset$ *expressions to equivalent formulas free of tuple and set expressions.*

Proof. Intuitively, this theorem is analogous to an algorithm that converts propositional formulas into an equivalent disjunctive normal form (DNF), that is, a disjunction of conjunctive clauses (that is, conjunctions of literals). Once a DNF is reached, contradictory conjunctive clauses are eliminated, and therefore the formula is satisfiable if and only if there is at least one conjunctive clause with at least one literal. In this analogy, conjunctions and disjunctions correspond to intersection and union, and sets correspond to conjunctive clauses. Empty sets are eliminated, and if at the end we have a union of sets, and the empty ones have been eliminated, this means that the resulting set is not empty.

Formally, the theorem is proven by induction on the *distance vector*, a tuple that measures how far an expression is from being solved. Before we define the distance vector, we need to inductive define, for any expression E, the **intersection-union nesting** $N_{\cap\cup}(E)$:

$$N_{\cap\cup}(E) = \begin{cases} \sum_i N_{\cap\cup}(E_i), \text{ if } E = E_1 \cap \cdots \cap E_n \\ 1 + \max_i N_{\cap\cup}(E_i), \text{ if } E = E_1 \cup \cdots \cup E_n \\ 0, \text{ if } E \text{ is any other expression.} \end{cases}$$

Intuitively, $N_{\cap\cup}$ measures how far we are from a "flat" union of intersections.

The **distance vector** of an expression E is a vector of non-negative integers that is lexicographically ordered, with the most significant component listed first:

1. $N_{\cap\cup}(E)$;

2. number of intensional unions ($\bigcup$);

3. number of existential and universal quantifications;

4. number of $\cap$ applications;

5. sum of lengths of extensionally defined sets ($\{\ldots\}$);

6. number of $\in$ applications;

7. number of comparisons to $\emptyset$;

8. number of tuples.

In the base case, the distance vector is a tuple of zeros, and therefore the expression is a formula without any tuple or set operators, satisfying the theorem.

Otherwise, the distance vector contains at least one non-zero component. If we can show that there is always at least one applicable simplifier, and that every simplifier application results in an expression with a smaller distance vector with respect to the lexicographical order, then the theorem will have been proven by induction.

There is always an applicable simplifier to expressions with non-zero distance vector, because in that case there is at least one tuple operator or a comparison between a set expression and $\emptyset$:

- if there is a set expression, it must be one of $\cap$, $\cup$ applications or $\bigcup$, and there is at least one simplifier for each of these;

- If there is a tuple anywhere, it is either inside a tuple comparison, or inside a set; if it is in a comparison, simplifier 1 applies; if it is in a set, one of the set simplifiers applies.

Once it is established that there is always an applicable simplifier, the next step is whether the distance vector is always decreased according to its lexicographical order. Simplifiers 1, 2, 4, 5, 6, 10, and 11 strictly decrease one or more of the distance vector components without increasing any other, so for expressions for which any of them apply, the theorem is proven by induction on the distance vector.

The remaining simplifiers decrease a distance vector component while increasing others, but the ones increased are always less significant in the lexicographical order than the one decreased:

- Simplifier 3 decreases the number of intensional unions at the cost of the less significant number of existential quantifications;
- Simplifier 7 decreases the sum of lengths of extensionally defined sets at the cost of the less significant number of $\in$ applications;
- Simplifier 8 decreases the number of intensional unions at the cost of the less significant number of universal quantifications;
- Simplifier 9 duplicates S_3 and therefore *doubles* all distance vector components in S_3, with the exception the most significant one, $N_{\cap\cup}$, which is decreased:

$$\begin{aligned}
&N_{\cap\cup}((S_1 \cup S_2) \cap S_3 = \emptyset)\\
&= \max(N_{\cap\cup}((S_1 \cup S_2) \cap S_3), 0)\\
&= N_{\cap\cup}((S_1 \cup S_2) \cap S_3)\\
&= N_{\cap\cup}(S_1 \cup S_2) + N_{\cap\cup}(S_3)\\
&= 1 + \max(N_{\cap\cup}(S_1), N_{\cap\cup}(S_2)) + N_{\cap\cup}(S_3)\\
&= 1 + \max(N_{\cap\cup}(S_1) + N_{\cap\cup}(S_3),\\
&\qquad N_{\cap\cup}(S_2) + N_{\cap\cup}(S_3))\\
&= 1 + \max(N_{\cap\cup}(S_1 \cap S_3),\\
&\qquad N_{\cap\cup}(S_2 \cap S_3))\\
&= 1 + N_{\cap\cup}((S_1 \cap S_3) \cup (S_2 \cap S_3))\\
&> \quad N_{\cap\cup}((S_1 \cap S_3) \cup (S_2 \cap S_3))\\
&= \quad N_{\cap\cup}((S_1 \cap S_3) \cup (S_2 \cap S_3) = \emptyset).
\end{aligned}$$

To summarize, we have shown that, for every expression in the language of interest, there is always an applicable simplifier, and that all simplifiers decrease the distance vector until it reaches the base case all-zero distance vector, which is free of tuple and set operators. □

Theorem 3.3 (Inversion Modulo Theories)**.** *Let E be an expression and T_i, C_i be type and constraint, respectively, in a theory for which we have a satisfiability solver. Then,*

$$\bigoplus_{f \in A \to B} \bigotimes_{x_1 \in T_1 : C_1} \cdots \bigotimes_{x_k \in T_k : C_k} E,$$

where $A = oc_f[\bigotimes_{x_1 \in T_1:C_1} \cdots \bigotimes_{x_k \in T_k:C_k} E]$ (this is relaxed in Section 3.4), is equivalent to , and therefore can be rewritten as,

$$\bigotimes_{x_1 \in T_1 : C_1} \cdots \bigotimes_{x_k \in T_k : C_k} \bigoplus_{f \in oc_f[E] \to B} E,$$

if $\bigotimes$ distributes over $\bigoplus$ and

$$\forall x'_1 \in T_1 \ldots \forall x'_k \in T_k \quad \forall x''_1 \in T_1 \ldots \forall x''_k \in T_k$$
$$\begin{pmatrix} C_1[x_1/x'_1] \wedge \cdots \wedge C_k[x_k/x'_k] \\ \wedge\, C_1[x_1/x''_1] \wedge \cdots \wedge C_k[x_k/x''_k] \\ \wedge\, (x'_1, \ldots, x'_k) \neq (x''_1, \ldots, x''_k) \end{pmatrix}$$
$$\Rightarrow \begin{pmatrix} oc_f[E][x_1/x'_1, \ldots, x_k/x'_k] \\ \cap \\ oc_f[E][x_1/x''_1, \ldots, x_k/x''_k] \end{pmatrix} = \emptyset \qquad (2)$$

(that is, the set of argument tuples in applications of f in E for different value assignments to $x_1, \ldots, x_k$ are always disjoint — we refer to this as **Condition (2)** *from now on). Moreover, the rewritten expression is exponentially ($O(2^{\prod_i |\{x_i \in T_i : C_i\}|})$) cheaper to evaluate than the original.*

Proof. Let m be the number of possible assignments to $x_1, \ldots, x_m$. We prove the theorem by induction on m. If m is 0,

$$\begin{aligned}
&\bigoplus_{f \in A \to B} \bigotimes_{x_1 \in T_1 : C_1} \cdots \bigotimes_{x_k \in T_k : C_k} E\\
&= \bigoplus_{f \in \emptyset \to B} 1\\
&= \bigotimes_{x_1 \in T_1 : C_1} \cdots \bigotimes_{x_k \in T_k : C_k} \bigoplus_{f \in \emptyset \to B} 1\\
&= \bigotimes_{x_1 \in T_1 : C_1} \cdots \bigotimes_{x_k \in T_k : C_k} \bigoplus_{f \in \emptyset \to B} E\\
&= \bigotimes_{x_1 \in T_1 : C_1} \cdots \bigotimes_{x_k \in T_k : C_k} \bigoplus_{f \in oc_f[E] \to B} E,
\end{aligned}$$

because the empty products allow the substitution of 1 by E and $\emptyset$ by $oc_f[E]$ without change.

If $m > 0$, let $\bar{x}$ be the first possible assignment to $x_1, \ldots, x_k$ satisfying $C_1 \wedge \cdots \wedge C_k$. Then

$$\begin{aligned}
&\bigoplus_{f \in A \to B} \bigotimes_{x_1 \in T_1 : C_1} \cdots \bigotimes_{x_k \in T_k : C_k} E\\
&= \text{(separating } \bar{x} \text{ from other assignments)}\\
&\bigoplus_{f_1 \in oc_f[E][x_1, \ldots, x_k/\bar{x}] \to B}\\
&\bigoplus_{f \in (A \setminus oc_f[E][x_1, \ldots, x_k/\bar{x}]) \to B}\\
&E_1 \quad \otimes\\
&\bigotimes_{(x_1, \ldots, x_k) \in T_1 \times \cdots \times T_k : C_1 \wedge \cdots \wedge C_k \wedge (x_1, \ldots, x_k) \neq \bar{x}} E,
\end{aligned}$$

where $E_1 = E[f/f_1]$

$= (E_1$ has no occurrences of $f)$

$$\Big(\bigoplus_{f_1 \in oc_f[E][x_1,\dots,x_k/\bar{x}] \to B} E_1\Big) \otimes \bigoplus_{f \in (A \setminus oc_f[E][x_1,\dots,x_k/\bar{x}]) \to B} \ \bigotimes_{(x_1,\dots,x_k) \in T_1 \times \cdots \times T_k : C_1 \wedge \cdots \wedge C_k \wedge (x_1,\dots,x_k) \neq \bar{x}} E$$

$=$ (by induction on m)

$$\Big(\bigoplus_{f_1 \in oc_f[E][x_1,\dots,x_k/\bar{x}] \to B} E_1\Big) \otimes \bigotimes_{(x_1,\dots,x_k) \in T_1 \times \cdots \times T_k : C_1 \wedge \cdots \wedge C_k \wedge (x_1,\dots,x_k) \neq \bar{x}} \ \bigoplus_{f \in oc_f[E] \to B} E$$

$=$ (renaming f_1 to f and using the fact that $E_1 = E[f/f_1]$)

$$\Big(\bigoplus_{f \in oc_f[E][x_1,\dots,x_k/\bar{x}] \to B} E\Big) \otimes \bigotimes_{(x_1,\dots,x_k) \in T_1 \times \cdots \times T_k : C_1 \wedge \cdots \wedge C_k \wedge (x_1,\dots,x_k) \neq \bar{x}} \ \bigoplus_{f \in oc_f[E] \to B} E$$

$=$ (introducing intensional products on $x_1, \dots, x_k$ bound to $\bar{x}$)

$$\bigotimes_{(x_1,\dots,x_k) \in T_1 \times \cdots \times T_k : C_1 \wedge \cdots \wedge C_k \wedge (x_1,\dots,x_k) = \bar{x}} \Big(\bigoplus_{f \in oc_f[E][x_1,\dots,x_k/\bar{x}] \to B} E\Big) \otimes \bigotimes_{(x_1,\dots,x_k) \in T_1 \times \cdots \times T_k : C_1 \wedge \cdots \wedge C_k \wedge (x_1,\dots,x_k) \neq \bar{x}} \ \bigoplus_{f \in oc_f[E] \to B} E$$

$=$ (merging $\bigotimes$ by disjuncting their constraints)

$$\bigotimes_{(x_1,\dots,x_k) \in T_1 \times \cdots \times T_k : C_1 \wedge \cdots \wedge C_k \wedge \big((x_1,\dots,x_k) = \bar{x} \vee (x_1,\dots,x_k) \neq \bar{x}\big)} \ \bigoplus_{f \in oc_f[E] \to B} E$$

$=$ (eliminating tautology on $\bar{x}$ and separating $\bigotimes$ per index)

$$\bigotimes_{x_1 \in T_1 : C_1} \cdots \bigotimes_{x_k \in T_k : C_k} \ \bigoplus_{f \in oc_f[E] \to B} E$$

The final expression is $O(2^{\prod_i |\{x_i \in T_i : C_i\}|})$ cheaper to evaluate because the final f has all x_i bound to a single value, mapping each of their $\prod_i |\{x_i \in T_i : C_i\}|$ assignments to a single one and thus dividing the total size of the domain over which one must iterate. □

Neighborhood Regularized ℓ^1-Graph

Yingzhen Yang[1], Jiashi Feng[2], Jiahui Yu[3], Jianchao Yang[1], Pushmeet Kohli[4], Thomas S. Huang[3]
[1] Snap Research
[2] Department of ECE, National University of Singapore, Singapore
[3] Beckman Institute, University of Illinois at Urbana-Champaign
[4] Google DeepMind

Abstract

ℓ^1-Graph, which learns a sparse graph over the data by sparse representation, has been demonstrated to be effective in clustering especially for high dimensional data. Although it achieves compelling performance, the sparse graph generated by ℓ^1-Graph ignores the geometric information of the data by sparse representation for each datum separately. To obtain a sparse graph that is aligned to the underlying manifold structure of the data, we propose the novel Neighborhood Regularized ℓ^1-Graph (NRℓ^1-Graph). NRℓ^1-Graph learns sparse graph with locally consistent neighborhood by encouraging nearby data to have similar neighbors in the constructed sparse graph. We present the optimization algorithm of NRℓ^1-Graph with theoretical guarantee on the convergence and the gap between the sub-optimal solution and the globally optimal solution in each step of the coordinate descent, which is essential for the overall optimization of NRℓ^1-Graph. Its provable accelerated version, NRℓ^1-Graph by Random Projection (NRℓ^1-Graph-RP) that employs randomized data matrix decomposition, is also presented to improve the efficiency of the optimization of NRℓ^1-Graph. Experimental results on various real data sets demonstrate the effectiveness of both NRℓ^1-Graph and NRℓ^1-Graph-RP.

This work is supported in part by US Army Research Office grant W911NF-15-1-0317. The work of Jiashi Feng was supported by NUS startup R-263-000-C08-133, MOE R-263-000-C21-112 and IDS R-263-000-C67-646. Pushmeet Kohli was at Microsoft Research during this project.

1 INTRODUCTION

Similarity-based clustering methods, e.g. K-means (Duda et al., 2000), Affinity Propagation (AP) (Frey and Dueck, 2007) and Spectral Clustering (Ng et al., 2001), segment the data based on the similarity measure between data points. In this manner, similarity-based methods alleviate the difficulty of parameter estimation that model-based methods face, such as modeling data distribution by a mixture of parameterized distributions (Fraley and Raftery, 2002). Among various similarity-based clustering methods, sparse graph based methods, which build sparse graph with only a few edges for each vertex and the data similarity serves as edge weight, are demonstrated to be effective, especially for clustering high dimensional data. Examples of sparse graph based clustering methods include ℓ^1-Graph (Yan and Wang, 2009; Cheng et al., 2010) and Sparse Subspace Clustering (SSC) (Elhamifar and Vidal, 2013), which build the sparse graph by reconstructing each datum with all the other data by sparse representation. In the sparse graph produced by ℓ^1-Graph or SSC, the vertices represent the data, and an edge is between two vertices whenever one participates the spare representation of the other. The weight of the edge is the average of the associated elements in the sparse codes corresponding to the two vertices. Throughout this paper, data point or data may also refer to the corresponding vertex or vertices in the sparse graph if no confusion arises. A sparse similarity matrix is then obtained as the weighted adjacency matrix of the constructed sparse graph by ℓ^1-Graph or SSC, and spectral clustering is performed on the sparse similarity matrix to obtain the data clusters. ℓ^1-Graph and SSC have been shown to be robust to noise and capable of producing superior results for high-dimensional data, compared to spectral clustering on similarity computed by the widely used Gaussian kernel. Such sparse graph has also been successfully applied to a novel deep neural network architecture for the first time (Peng et al., 2016).

While ℓ^1-Graph demonstrates compelling performance for clustering, it performs sparse representation for each datum independently without considering the geometric information of the data, and consequently the generated sparse graph ignores the geometric information of the data. In order to obtain the sparse graph that accounts for the geometric information and manifold structure of the data, regularized ℓ^1-Graph (Yang et al., 2014) employs a manifold assumption which imposes local smoothness on the sparse codes of nearby data, namely nearby data are encouraged to have similar sparse codes in the sense of ℓ^2-distance. This method is also termed ℓ^2-Rℓ^1-Graph in this paper. Moreover, various regularized sparse coding methods, such as (Liu et al., 2010; He et al., 2011; Zheng et al., 2011; Gao et al., 2013), also utilize manifold assumption (Belkin et al., 2006) to obtain locally smooth sparse codes by ℓ^2-distance based graph regularization term.

ℓ^2-Rℓ^1-Graph imposes locally smoothness or consistency on the sparse codes of the data (i.e. the vertices of the graph), not directly on the local structure of the sparse graph. Consistency of the sparse codes indicates that the codes are similar to each other. In this paper, we propose a novel Neighborhood Regularized ℓ^1-Graph, abbreviated as NRℓ^1-Graph, which learns locally consistent neighborhood in the sparse graph, i.e. nearby points have similar neighborhoods. In this manner, manifold assumption is employed directly on the structure of the graph so as to obtain the sparse graph that accounts for the local manifold structure of the data. NRℓ^1-Graph embodies the local consistency on the neighborhood by the novel neighborhood regularization term in the objective function. It should be emphasized that the widely used ℓ^2 graph regularization term cannot represent the neighborhood consistency. Another benefit of local consistency on the neighborhood in the sparse graph is that, instead of choosing neighbors by itself, each data point is encouraged to coordinate with its nearby points on the data manifold (usually specified by its K nearest neighbors by Euclidean distance) to choose its neighbors in the sparse graph (See Figure 1). This makes the sparse graph more robust to outliers while preserving the freedom in the spare representation of data without constraints on the magnitude of the sparse codes. We present the efficient proximal gradient descent (PGD) style iterative method for the optimization problem of NRℓ^1-Graph with theoretical guarantee on the convergence and bounded gap between the sub-optimal solution and the globally optimal solution for each step of coordinate descent for the optimization. Furthermore, NRℓ^1-Graph by Random Projection (NRℓ^1-Graph-RP) is proposed to accelerate the optimization of NRℓ^1-Graph by randomized rank-k approximation of the data matrix. Such low rank approximation reduces the time complexity of the gradient descent step in the PGD-style iterative method from $\mathcal{O}(nd)$ to $\mathcal{O}(nk+dk)$, where d and n are dimension and size of the data, leading to the significantly improved efficiency when $k \ll \min\{d,n\}$ compared to the original NRℓ^1-Graph.

We use bold letters for matrices and vectors, and regular lower letter for scalars throughout this paper. The bold letter with superscript indicates the corresponding column of a matrix, e.g. $\mathbf{Z}^i$ indicates the i-th column of the matrix $\mathbf{Z}$, and the bold letter with subscript indicates the corresponding element of a matrix or vector. $\|\cdot\|_F$ and $\|\cdot\|_p$ denote the Frobenius norm and the ℓ^p-norm, and $\mathrm{diag}(\cdot)$ indicates the diagonal elements of a matrix. $\sigma_{\max}(\cdot)$ and $\sigma_{\max}(\cdot)$ indicate the maximum and minimum singular value of a matrix.

2 PRELIMINARIES: ℓ^1-GRAPH, ℓ^2-Rℓ^1-GRAPH

ℓ^1-Graph (Yan and Wang, 2009; Cheng et al., 2010) and SSC (Elhamifar and Vidal, 2009, 2013) apply the idea of sparse coding where the data similarity is represented by sparse codes. Given data $\boldsymbol{X} = [\mathbf{x}_1, \ldots, \mathbf{x}_n] \in \mathbb{R}^{d \times n}$, ℓ^1-Graph and SSC solve the following optimization problem to obtain a sparse representation for each data point

$$\min_{\mathbf{Z}^i \in \mathbb{R}^n, \mathbf{Z}^i_i = 0} \|\mathbf{Z}^i\|_1 \quad s.t.\ \mathbf{x}_i = \boldsymbol{X}\mathbf{Z}^i \tag{1}$$

SSC (Elhamifar and Vidal, 2009, 2013) also proves that the above sparse representation recovers the underlying independent or disjoint subspaces from which the data are generated when certain conditions on the geometric properties of the subspaces, such as the principle angle between different subspaces, hold. Allowing some tolerance for inexact representation and robustness to noise (Wang and Xu, 2013; Soltanolkotabi et al., 2014), the following Lasso-type problem is solved instead of (1):

$$\min_{\mathbf{Z}^i \in \mathbb{R}^n, \mathbf{Z}^i_i = 0} \|\mathbf{x}_i - \boldsymbol{X}\mathbf{Z}^i\|_2^2 + \lambda^{(\ell^1)}\|\mathbf{Z}^i\|_1 \quad i = 1, \ldots, n \tag{2}$$

for some weighting parameter $\lambda > 0$, and $\mathbf{Z}^i \in \mathbb{R}^n$, $\mathbf{Z} = [\mathbf{Z}^1, \ldots, \mathbf{Z}^n] \in \mathbb{R}^{n \times n}$ is the sparse code matrix with the element $\mathbf{Z}_{ij} = \mathbf{Z}^j_i$. The diagonal elements of $\mathbf{Z}$ are enforced to be zero, i.e. $\mathbf{Z}_{ii} = 0$ for $1 \le i \le n$, so as to avoid trivial solution $\mathbf{Z} = \mathbf{I}_n$ where $\mathbf{I}_n$ is a $n \times n$ identity matrix.

ℓ^1-Graph constructs the sparse graph $G = (\boldsymbol{X}, \mathbf{W}^{(\ell^1)})$ where $\boldsymbol{X}$ is the set of vertices, $\mathbf{W}$ is the weighted adjacency matrix of G and $\mathbf{W}_{ij}$ indicates the edge weight, or the similarity, between $\mathbf{x}_i$ and $\mathbf{x}_j$. $\mathbf{W}$ is set by the sparse codes:

$$\mathbf{W}_{ij}^{(\ell^1)} = (|\mathbf{Z}_{ij}| + |\mathbf{Z}_{ji}|)/2 \quad 1 \le i,j \le n \qquad (3)$$

And there is an edge between $\mathbf{x}_i$ and $\mathbf{x}_j$ if and only if $\mathbf{W}_{ij}^{(\ell^1)} \neq 0$, i.e. either $\mathbf{x}_i$ chooses $\mathbf{x}_j$ as its neighbor by nonzero $\mathbf{Z}_{ji}$, or $\mathbf{x}_j$ chooses $\mathbf{x}_i$ as its neighbor by nonzero $\mathbf{Z}_{ij}$. ℓ^1-Graph then performs spectral clustering on $\mathbf{W}^{(\ell^1)}$ to obtain the data clusters, with better performance than spectral clustering on the similarity matrix produced by the widely used Gaussian kernel. ℓ_1-Graph features robustness to data noise and adaptive neighborhood, specified by the non-zero entries in the sparse codes. It should be emphasized that the above sparse graph construction method is used for almost all the sparse graph based clustering methods (Yan and Wang, 2009; Cheng et al., 2010; Elhamifar and Vidal, 2009, 2013, 2011) while the sparse codes are learnt in different ways.

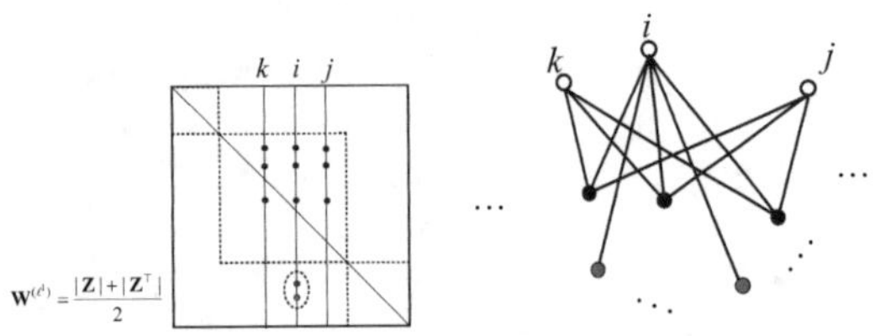

(a) (b)

Figure 1: (a) Illustration of the weighted adjacency matrix of the sparse graph shown in (b), where the three black dots indicate three common neighbors of points $\mathbf{x}_k$, $\mathbf{x}_i$ and $\mathbf{x}_j$. The inner dashed box specifies the scope of correct neighbors, i.e. the ones in the same ground truth cluster. The locally consistent neighborhood encourages $\mathbf{x}_i$ to abandon the wrong neighbors marked with red dots encompassed by the dashed ellipse. (b) The sparse graph corresponding to the weighted adjacency matrix in (a).

The widely adopted manifold assumption assumes that high-dimensional data always lie on or close to a submanifold of low intrinsic dimension, and clustering the data according to its underlying manifold structure is important and challenging in machine learning. While ℓ^1-Graph demonstrates better performance than many traditional similarity-based clustering methods, it performs sparse representation for each datum independently without considering the geometric information and manifold structure of the entire data. On the other hand, in order to obtain the embedding of the data that accounts for the geometric information and manifold structure of the data, manifold assumption (Belkin et al., 2006) is usually employed (Liu et al., 2010; He et al., 2011; Zheng et al., 2011; Gao et al., 2013). Interpreting the sparse code of a data point as its embedding, most existing methods that employ manifold assumption in the sparse representation literature require that if two points $\mathbf{x}_i$ and $\mathbf{x}_j$ are close in the intrinsic geometry of the manifold, their corresponding sparse codes $\mathbf{Z}^i$ and $\mathbf{Z}^j$ are also expected to be similar to each other in the sense of ℓ^2-distance (Zheng et al., 2011; Gao et al., 2013). In other words, $\mathbf{Z}$ varies smoothly along the geodesics in the intrinsic geometry.

Based on the spectral graph theory (Chung, 1997), extensive literature uses graph Laplacian to impose local smoothness of the embedding and preserve the local manifold structure (Belkin et al., 2006; Zheng et al., 2011; Gao et al., 2013). Given a proper symmetric similarity matrix $\mathbf{S}$ that encodes the intrinsic manifold structure of the data, the sparse code $\mathbf{Z}$ in accordance with the manifold assumption by graph Laplacian minimizes the following ℓ^2 regularization term below:

$$\frac{1}{2}\sum_{i=1}^{n}\sum_{j=1}^{n} \mathbf{S}_{ij}\|\mathbf{Z}^i - \mathbf{Z}^j\|_2^2 = \mathrm{Tr}(\mathbf{Z}\mathbf{L}_\mathbf{S}\mathbf{Z}^\top) \qquad (4)$$

where the ℓ^2-norm is used to measure the distance between sparse codes. $\mathbf{L}_\mathbf{S} = \mathbf{D}_\mathbf{S} - \mathbf{S}$ is the graph Laplacian using the adjacency matrix $\mathbf{S}$, the degree matrix $\mathbf{D}_\mathbf{S}$ is a diagonal matrix with each diagonal element being the sum of the elements in the corresponding row of $\mathbf{S}$, namely $(\mathbf{D}_\mathbf{S})_{ii} = \sum_{j=1}^{n} \mathbf{S}_{ij}$. To the best of our knowledge, such ℓ^2 regularization is employed by most methods that use graph regularization for sparse representation. *Incorporating the ℓ^2 graph regularization term into the objective of ℓ^1-Graph, the optimization problem of ℓ^2-Rℓ^1-Graph*, is presented below:

$$\min_{\mathbf{Z}\in\mathbb{R}^{n\times n}, \mathrm{diag}(\mathbf{Z})=\mathbf{0}} \sum_{i=1}^{n} \|\mathbf{x}_i - \boldsymbol{X}\mathbf{Z}^i\|_2^2 + \lambda^{(\ell^2)}\|\mathbf{Z}^i\|_1 \qquad (5)$$
$$+ \gamma^{(\ell^2)}\mathrm{Tr}(\mathbf{Z}\mathbf{L}_\mathbf{S}\mathbf{Z}^\top)$$

where $\gamma^{(\ell^2)} > 0$ is the weighting parameter for the ℓ^2 graph regularization term. Regularized ℓ^1-Graph (Yang et al., 2014) employs the formulation with the same form as (5. Following the representative ℓ^2 graph regularized sparse coding methods (Zheng et al., 2011; Gao et al., 2013), $\mathbf{S}$ is typically chosen as the adjacency matrix of K-Nearest-Neighbor (KNN) graph to represent the local manifold structure of the data, i.e. $\mathbf{S}_{ij} = 1$ if and only if $\mathbf{x}_i$ is among the K nearest neighbors of $\mathbf{x}_j$. Note that KNN is extensively used in the manifold learning literature, such as Locally Linear Embedding (Roweis and Saul, 2000), Laplacian Eigenmaps (Belkin and Niyogi, 2003) and Sparse Manifold Clustering and Embedding (Elhamifar and Vidal, 2011), to reveal the local structure in the manifold. Although $\mathbf{S}$ is not symmetric, letting $\mathbf{S}' = \frac{\mathbf{S}+\mathbf{S}^\top}{2}$, then a symmetric adjacency matrix can be used in the graph regularization term without changing its value: $\mathrm{Tr}(\mathbf{Z}\mathbf{L}_{\mathbf{S}'}\mathbf{Z}^\top) = \mathrm{Tr}(\mathbf{Z}\mathbf{L}_\mathbf{S}\mathbf{Z}^\top)$.

In the next section, we propose NRℓ^1-Graph which learns locally consistent neighborhood in the sparse graph by a novel neighborhood regularization term rather than the ℓ^2 graph regularization term with superior clustering performance.

Algorithm 1 Learning NRℓ^1-Graph

Input:
The data set $\boldsymbol{X} = \{\mathbf{x}_i\}_{i=1}^n$, the number of clusters c, the parameter $\lambda^{(\ell^2)}$, $\gamma^{(\ell^2)}$, K for NRℓ^1-Graph, maximum iteration number M_c for coordinate descent, and maximum iteration number M_p for the iterative proximal method, stopping threshold ε.

```
r = 1, initialize the sparse code matrix as Z^(0) = Z^(ℓ1).
while r ≤ M_c do
    Obtain Z^(r) from Z^(r−1) by coordinate descent. In i-th (1 ≤ i ≤ n) step of the r-th iteration of coordinate descent, solve (8) using the PGD-style iterative method (11), (12) and (13) to update Z^i in each iteration of the iterative proximal method.
    if |L(Z^(r)) − L(Z^(r−1))| < ε then
        break
    else
        r = r + 1.
    end if
end while
Obtain the sub-optimal sparse code matrix Z* when the above iterations converge or maximum iteration number is achieved.
Build the pairwise similarity matrix by symmetrizing Z*: W* = (|Z*| + |Z*|^T) / 2
```

Output: The sparse graph whose weighted adjacency matrix is $\mathbf{W}^*$.

---

3 NEIGHBORHOOD REGULARIZED ℓ^1-GRAPH

In this section, we propose Neighborhood Regularized ℓ^1-Graph (NRℓ^1-Graph) which learns locally consistent neighborhood in the sparse graph. Instead of imposing local smoothness on the sparse codes in the existing regularized ℓ^1-Graph (Yang et al., 2014), NRℓ^1-Graph learns locally consistent neighborhood so as to capture the local manifold structure of the data in the construction of the sparse graph. In addition, NRℓ^1-Graph benefits from robustness to noise or outliers by encouraging each point to choose its neighbors in the sparse graph via coordinating with its nearby points on the manifold. Note that ℓ^2-distance based graph regularization cannot enjoy this benefit since small ℓ^2-distance between the sparse codes of nearby data points does not guarantee their consistent neighborhood in the sparse graph. The optimization problem of NRℓ^1-Graph is presented below:

$$\min_{\mathbf{Z}\in\mathbb{R}^{n\times n}, \mathrm{diag}(\mathbf{Z})=\mathbf{0}} L(\mathbf{Z}) = \sum_{i=1}^{n} \|\mathbf{x}_i - \boldsymbol{X}\mathbf{Z}^i\|_2^2 + \lambda\|\mathbf{Z}^i\|_1 + \gamma \mathbf{R}_{\mathbf{S}}(\mathbf{Z}) \quad (6)$$

where $\mathbf{R}_{\mathbf{S}}(\mathbf{Z}) = \sum_{i,j=1}^{n} \mathbf{S}_{ij} d(\mathbf{Z}^i, \mathbf{Z}^j)$ is the novel neighborhood regularization term, $\mathbf{S}$ is the adjacency matrix of the KNN graph, $\gamma > 0$ is the weighting parameter. $d(\mathbf{Z}^i, \mathbf{Z}^j)$ indicates the neighborhood distance between two points $\mathbf{x}_i$ and $\mathbf{x}_j$ in terms of the sparse code matrix $\mathbf{Z}$ through the weighted adjacency matrix $\mathbf{W}$ (3), which measures the number of different neighbors these two points have in the sparse graph:

$$d(\mathbf{Z}^i, \mathbf{Z}^j) = \sum_{1\le k\le n, k\ne i,j} \left(\mathbb{I}_{\mathbf{W}_{ki}=0, \mathbf{W}_{kj}\ne 0} + \mathbb{I}_{\mathbf{W}_{ki}\ne 0, \mathbf{W}_{kj}=0}\right) \quad (7)$$

where $\mathbf{W} = \frac{|\mathbf{Z}|+|\mathbf{Z}^\top|}{2}$ and $\mathbb{I}$ is the indicator function. Indices i and j are excluded when computing the neighborhood distance between points $\mathbf{x}_i$ and $\mathbf{x}_j$ since any point is not a neighbor of itself in the sparse graph, so it is not necessary to impose penalty on $\mathbf{x}_i$ in the calculation of $d(\mathbf{Z}^i, \mathbf{Z}^j)$ if it does choose $\mathbf{x}_j$ as its neighbor, and vice versa.

3.1 OPTIMIZATION ALGORITHM

We use coordinate descent to optimize (6). In each iteration of coordinate descent, the optimization is performed with respect to $\mathbf{Z}^i$ sequentially for $1 \le i \le n$, while fixing all the other sparse codes $\{\mathbf{Z}^j\}_{j\ne i}$. In the i-th step of each iteration of coordinate descent, the optimization problem for $\mathbf{Z}^i$ is below:

$$\min_{\mathbf{Z}^i\in\mathbb{R}^n, \mathbf{Z}_i^i=0} F(\mathbf{Z}^i) = \|\mathbf{x}_i - \boldsymbol{X}\mathbf{Z}^i\|_2^2 + \lambda\|\mathbf{Z}^i\|_1 + \gamma \mathbf{R}_{\tilde{\mathbf{S}}}(\mathbf{Z}^i) \quad (8)$$

where $\mathbf{R}_{\tilde{\mathbf{S}}}(\mathbf{Z}^i) = \sum_{j=1}^{n} \tilde{\mathbf{S}}_{ij} d(\mathbf{Z}^i, \mathbf{Z}^j)$, $\tilde{\mathbf{S}} = \mathbf{S} + \mathbf{S}^\top$.

We employ proximal gradient descent method (PGD) to optimize the nonconvex problem (8) inspired by the proximal linearized method (Bolte et al., 2014). Although the proximal mapping is typically associated with a lower semicontinuous function (Bolte et al., 2014) and it can be verified that $\mathbf{R}_{\tilde{\mathbf{S}}}$ is not always lower semicontinuous, we can still derive a PGD-style iterative method to optimize (8).

Define $\mathbf{F}^{\tilde{\mathbf{S}}} \in \mathbb{R}^{n\times n}$ as $\mathbf{F}^{\tilde{\mathbf{S}}}_{ki} = \sum_{j\ne k} \tilde{\mathbf{S}}_{ij} \mathbb{I}_{\mathbf{W}_{kj}=0} - \sum_{j\ne k} \tilde{\mathbf{S}}_{ij} \mathbb{I}_{\mathbf{W}_{kj}\ne 0}$ where $\mathbb{I}$ is the indicator function, then $\mathbf{F}^{\tilde{\mathbf{S}}}_{ki}$ indicates the degree to which $\mathbf{Z}_{ki}$ is discouraged to be nonzero and it can be verified that up to a constant irrelevant to $\mathbf{Z}^i$,

$$\mathbf{R}_{\tilde{\mathbf{S}}}(\mathbf{Z}^i) = \sum_{1 \le k \le n, k \ne i} \mathbb{I}_{\mathbf{Z}_{ik}=0} \mathbf{F}_{ki}^{\tilde{\mathbf{S}}} \mathbb{I}_{\mathbf{Z}_{ki} \ne 0} = \sum_{k \in \Lambda_i} \mathbf{F}_{ki}^{\tilde{\mathbf{S}}} \mathbb{I}_{\mathbf{Z}_{ki} \ne 0} \tag{9}$$

where Λ_i is defined as the set comprising all the possible indices k other than i such that $\mathbf{Z}_{ik} = 0$:

$$\Lambda_i \triangleq \{k \colon 1 \le k \le n, k \ne i, \mathbf{Z}_{ik} = 0\} \tag{10}$$

Since each indicator function $\mathbb{I}_{\mathbf{Z}_{ki} \ne 0}$ is lower semicontinuous, it can be verified that $\mathbf{R}_{\tilde{\mathbf{S}}}$ is lower semicontinuous if $\mathbf{F}_{ki}^{\tilde{\mathbf{S}}} \ge 0$ for each $k \in \Lambda_i$. In the following text, we let $Q(\mathbf{Z}^i) = \frac{1}{2}\|\mathbf{x}_i - \boldsymbol{X}\mathbf{Z}^i\|_2^2$. The superscript with bracket indicates the iteration number of PGD or the iteration number of the coordinate descent without confusion. The PGD-style iterative method for optimizing (8) is as follows:

$$\tilde{\mathbf{Z}^i}^{(t)} = \mathbf{Z}^{i^{(t-1)}} - \frac{2}{\tau s}(\boldsymbol{X}^\top \boldsymbol{X} \mathbf{Z}^{i^{(t-1)}} - \boldsymbol{X}^\top \mathbf{x}_i) \tag{11}$$

where $\tau > 1$ is any constant greater than 1 and s is the Lipschitz constant for the gradient of function $Q(\cdot)$, namely

$$\|\nabla Q(\mathbf{y}) - \nabla Q(\mathbf{z})\|_2 \le s\|\mathbf{y} - \mathbf{z}\|_2, \ \forall \mathbf{y}, \mathbf{z} \in \mathbb{R}^n$$

$\mathbf{Z}_{ii} = 0$. For all the other k such that $k \notin \Lambda_i$,

$$\mathbf{Z}_{ki}^{(t)} = \begin{cases} \mathbf{u}_k & : \ k \ne i \\ 0 & : \ k = i \end{cases} \tag{12}$$

and for all $k \in \Lambda_i$

$$\mathbf{Z}_{ki}^{(t)} = \begin{cases} \underset{v \in \{\mathbf{u}_k, 0\}}{\arg\min} H_k(v) & : \ \mathbf{u}_k \ne 0 \text{ or } \mathbf{u}_k = 0 \text{ and } \mathbf{F}_{ki}^{\tilde{\mathbf{S}}} \ge 0 \\ \varepsilon & : \ \mathbf{u}_k = 0 \text{ and } \mathbf{F}_{ki}^{\tilde{\mathbf{S}}} < 0 \end{cases} \tag{13}$$

where ε is any real number such that $\varepsilon \ne 0$ and $H_k(\varepsilon) \le H_k(\mathbf{Z}_{ki}^{(t-1)})$. For each $k \in 1 \ldots n$ and $k \ne i$, H_k is defined below

$$H_k(v) = \frac{\tau s}{2}(v - \tilde{\mathbf{Z}}_{ki}^{(t)})^2 + \lambda|v| + \gamma \mathbb{I}_{\mathbf{Z}_{ik}=0} \mathbf{F}_{ki}^{\tilde{\mathbf{S}}} \mathbb{I}_{v \ne 0} \tag{14}$$

for $v \in \mathbb{R}$. $\mathbf{u}$ is defined as

$$\mathbf{u} = \max\{|\tilde{\mathbf{Z}^i}^{(t)}| - \frac{\lambda}{\tau s}, 0\} \circ \operatorname{sign}(\tilde{\mathbf{Z}^i}^{(t)}) \tag{15}$$

where $\circ$ means element-wise multiplication.

Proposition 1 shows that the PGD-style iterative method decreases the value of the objective function in each iteration.

Proposition 1. *Let the sequence $\{\mathbf{Z}^{i^{(t)}}\}_t$ be generated by the PGD-style iterative method with (11), (12) and (13), then the sequence of the objective $\{F(\mathbf{Z}^{i^{(t)}})\}_t$ decreases, and the following inequality holds for $t \ge 1$:*

$$F(\mathbf{Z}^{i^{(t)}}) \le F(\mathbf{Z}^{i^{(t-1)}}) - \frac{(\tau - 1)s}{2}\|\mathbf{Z}^{i^{(t)}} - \mathbf{Z}^{i^{(t-1)}}\|_2^2 \tag{16}$$

And it follows that the sequence $\{F(\mathbf{Z}^{i^{(t)}})\}_t$ converges.

Remark 1. (11), (12) and (13) in each iteration of the proposed PGD-style iterative method are similar to the update rules of the ordinary PGD. (11) performs gradient descent on the differential part, (12) and (13) can be viewed as an approximate solution to the proximal mapping $\min_{\mathbf{v} \in \mathbb{R}^n} H(\mathbf{v}) = \frac{\tau s}{2}\|\mathbf{v} - \tilde{\mathbf{Z}^i}^{(t)}\|_2^2 + \lambda\|\mathbf{v}\|_1 + \gamma \mathbf{R}_{\tilde{\mathbf{S}}}(\mathbf{v})$. Since $\mathbf{R}_{\tilde{\mathbf{S}}}(\mathbf{Z}^i)$ is not always lower semicontinuous, $\arg\min_{\mathbf{v} \in \mathbb{R}^n} H(\mathbf{v})$ is not guaranteed to exist. One can see a simple example wherein $\mathbf{u}_k = 0$ and $\mathbf{F}_{ki}^{\tilde{\mathbf{S}}} < 0$ for some $k \in \Lambda_i$. In this case, $\inf_{v \in \mathbb{R}} H_k(v) = \frac{\tau s}{2}(\tilde{\mathbf{Z}}_{ki}^{(t)})^2 + \gamma \mathbf{F}_{ki}^{\tilde{\mathbf{S}}}$ but this infinitum can not be achieved.

The PGD-style iterative proximal method starts from $t = 1$ and continues until the sequence $\{F(\mathbf{Z}^{i^{(t)}})\}$ converges or maximum iteration number is achieved. When the proximal method converges or terminates for each $\mathbf{Z}^i$, the step for $\mathbf{Z}^i$ in one iteration of coordinate descent is finished and the optimization algorithm proceed to optimize other sparse codes. We initialize $\mathbf{Z}$ as $\mathbf{Z}^{(0)} = \mathbf{Z}^{(\ell^1)}$ and $\mathbf{Z}^{(\ell^1)}$ is the sparse codes generated by solving (2) with some proper weighting parameter $\lambda^{(\ell^1)}$. In all the experimental results shown in the next section, we empirically set $\lambda = 0.1$. The algorithm of learning NRℓ^1-Graph is described in Algorithm 1.

3.2 TIME COMPLEXITY

Let the maximum iteration number of coordinate descent be M_c, and maximum iteration number be M_p for the PGD-style iterative method solving (8), then the time complexity of running the coordinate descent for NRℓ^1-Graph is $\mathcal{O}(M_c M_p n^2 d)$.

3.3 THEORETICAL ANALYSIS FOR OPTIMIZATION

It can be observed that optimization by coordinate descent in Section 3.1 is essential for the overall optimization of NRℓ^1-Graph, and each step of the coordinate descent (8) is a difficult nonconvex problem and crucial for obtaining the support regularized sparse code, where the nonconvexity comes from the neighborhood regularization term $\mathbf{R}_{\tilde{\mathbf{S}}}(\mathbf{Z}^i)$ (9). Therefore, the optimization of (8) plays an important role in the overall optimization of NRℓ^1-Graph. In the previous section, a PGD-style iterative method is proposed to decrease the value of the objective in each iteration. In this section, we provide further theoretical analysis on the optimization of problem (8) when $\mathbf{F}_{ki}^{\tilde{\mathbf{S}}} \ge 0$ for all $k \in \Lambda_i$. This condition is equivalent to the condition that the neighborhood regularization function $\mathbf{R}_{\tilde{\mathbf{S}}}(\cdot)$ is lower semicontinuous. Under this condition, we prove that the sequence $\{\mathbf{Z}^{i^{(t)}}\}_t$ produced by the PGD-style iterative method converges to the sub-optimal solution which is a critical point of the objective (8). By connecting the support regularized function to the capped-ℓ^1 norm and the nonconvexity analysis of the support regularization term, we present the bound for ℓ^2-distance between the sub-optimal solution and the globally optimal solution to (8) in Theorem 1. Note that our analysis is valid for all $1 \le i \le n$.

Therefore, if $\mathbf{F}_{ki}^{\tilde{\mathbf{S}}} \ge 0$ for all $k \in \Lambda_i$, the neighborhood regularization term $\mathbf{R}_{\tilde{\mathbf{S}}}(\mathbf{Z}^i)$ is lower semicontinuous with respect to $\mathbf{Z}^i$ in (9). In this case, the PGD-style iterative method proposed in Section 3.1 for each iteration $t \ge 1$ becomes

$$\tilde{\mathbf{Z}^i}^{(t)} = {\mathbf{Z}^i}^{(t-1)} - \frac{2}{\tau s}(\boldsymbol{X}^\top \boldsymbol{X} {\mathbf{Z}^i}^{(t-1)} - \boldsymbol{X}^\top \mathbf{x}_i) \tag{17}$$

$$\mathbf{Z}_{ki}{}^{(t)} = \begin{cases} \underset{v \in \{\mathbf{u}_k, 0\}}{\arg\min} H_k(v) & : \ k \in \Lambda_i \\ \mathbf{u}_k & : \ k \notin \Lambda_i \end{cases} \tag{18}$$

which is equivalent to the updates rules in the ordinary proximal gradient descent method. The supplemetary explains the meaning of the condition that $\mathbf{F}_{ki}^{\tilde{\mathbf{S}}} \ge 0$ for all $k \in \Lambda_i$.

In the following lemma, we show that the sequence $\{{\mathbf{Z}^i}^{(t)}\}_t$ generated by (11), (12) and (13) converges to a critical point of $F(\mathbf{Z}^i)$, denoted by $\hat{\mathbf{Z}}^i$. Denote by ${\mathbf{Z}^i}^*$ the globally optimal solution to the original optimization problem (8). The following lemma also shows that both $\hat{\mathbf{Z}}^i$ and ${\mathbf{Z}^i}^*$ are local solutions to the capped-ℓ^1 regularized problem (19). Before stating the lemma, the following definitions are introduced which are essential for our analysis.

Definition 1. *(Critical points) Given the non-convex function $f \colon \mathbb{R}^n \to R \cup \{+\infty\}$ which is a proper and lower semi-continuous function.*

- *for a given $\mathbf{x} \in \mathrm{dom} f$, its Frechet subdifferential of f at $\mathbf{x}$, denoted by $\tilde{\partial} f(x)$, is the set of all vectors $\mathbf{u} \in \mathbb{R}^n$ which satisfy*

$$\limsup_{\mathbf{y} \neq \mathbf{x}, \mathbf{y} \to \mathbf{x}} \frac{f(\mathbf{y}) - f(\mathbf{x}) - \langle \mathbf{u}, \mathbf{y} - \mathbf{x} \rangle}{\|\mathbf{y} - \mathbf{x}\|} \ge 0$$

- *The limiting-subdifferential of f at $\mathbf{x} \in \mathbb{R}^n$, denoted by written $\partial f(x)$, is defined by*

$$\partial f(x) = \{\mathbf{u} \in \mathbb{R}^n \colon \exists \mathbf{x}^k \to \mathbf{x}, f(\mathbf{x}^k) \to f(\mathbf{x}), \\ \tilde{\mathbf{u}}^k \in \tilde{\partial} f(\mathbf{x}^k) \to \mathbf{u}\}$$

The point $\mathbf{x}$ is a critical point of f if $0 \in \partial f(x)$.

Also, we are considering the following capped-ℓ^1 regularized problem, which replaces the indicator function in the support regularization term $\mathbf{R}_{\tilde{\mathbf{S}}}(\mathbf{Z}^i)$ with the continuous capped-ℓ^1 regularization term $\mathbf{T}$:

$$\min_{\boldsymbol{\beta} \in \mathbb{R}^n, \boldsymbol{\beta}_i = 0} L_{\text{capped}-\ell^1}(\boldsymbol{\beta}) = \|\mathbf{x}_i - \boldsymbol{X}\boldsymbol{\beta}\|_2^2 + \lambda \|\boldsymbol{\beta}\|_1 + \mathbf{T}(\boldsymbol{\beta}; b) \tag{19}$$

where $\mathbf{T}(\boldsymbol{\beta}; b) = \sum_{1 \le k \le n, k \neq i} T_k(\boldsymbol{\beta}_k; b)$, $T_k(t; b) = \gamma \mathbb{I}_{\mathbf{Z}_{ik}=0} \mathbf{F}_{ki}^{\tilde{\mathbf{S}}} \frac{\min\{|t|, b\}}{b}$ for some $b > 0$. It can be seen that the objective function of the capped-ℓ^1 problem approaches that of (8) when $\frac{\min\{|t|, b\}}{b}$ approaches the indicator function $\mathbb{I}_{t \neq 0}$ as $b \to 0+$. Define $\mathbf{P}(\cdot; b) = \lambda \|\cdot\|_1 + \mathbf{T}(\cdot; b)$, the location solution to the capped-ℓ^1 problem is defined as follows. In the following, $\boldsymbol{X}^{(-i)}$ is the matrix comprising all but the i-th columns of $\boldsymbol{X}$, and $\mathbf{v}_{-i} \in \mathbb{R}^{n-1}$ indicates the vector comprising of all but the i-th elements of any vector $\mathbf{v} \in \mathbb{R}^n$.

Definition 2. *(Local solution) A vector $\tilde{\boldsymbol{\beta}}$ is a local solution to the problem (19) if*

$$\|2{\boldsymbol{X}^{(-i)}}^\top (\boldsymbol{X}^{(-i)} \tilde{\boldsymbol{\beta}}_{-i} - \mathbf{x}_i) + \dot{\mathbf{P}}(\tilde{\boldsymbol{\beta}}; b)\|_2 = 0 \tag{20}$$

where

$$\dot{\mathbf{P}}(\tilde{\boldsymbol{\beta}}; b) = [\dot{P}_1(\tilde{\boldsymbol{\beta}}_1; b) \ldots, \dot{P}_{i-1}(\tilde{\boldsymbol{\beta}}_{i-1}; b) \\ \dot{P}_{i+1}(\tilde{\boldsymbol{\beta}}_{i+1}; b) \ldots \dot{P}_n(\tilde{\boldsymbol{\beta}}_n; b)]^\top,$$

$P_k(t; b) = \lambda |t| + T_k(t; b)$ for $k = 1, \ldots, n$, $k \neq i$.

Note that in the above definition and the following text, $\dot{P}_k(t; b)$ can be chosen as any value between the right differential $\frac{\partial P_k}{\partial t}(t+; b)$ (or $\dot{P}_k(t+; b)$) and left differential $\frac{\partial P_k}{\partial t}(t-; b)$ (or $\dot{P}_k(t-; b)$) for $k = 1, \ldots, n$, $k \neq i$.

Definition 3. *(Degree of Nonconvexity of a Regularizer) For $\kappa \ge 0$ and $t \in \mathbb{R}$, define*

$$\theta(t, \kappa) := \sup_s \{-\mathrm{sgn}(s-t)(\dot{P}(s; b) - \dot{P}(t; b)) - \kappa |s - t|\}$$

as the degree of nonconvexity for function P. If $\mathbf{u} = (u_1, \ldots, u_n)^\top \in \mathbb{R}^n$, $\theta(\mathbf{u}, \kappa) = [\theta(u_1, \kappa), \ldots, \theta(u_n, \kappa)]$. sgn is the sign function.

Note that $\theta(t, \kappa) = 0$ for convex function P, and it is also used in the analysis of sparse estimation with concave regularization (Zhang and Zhang, 2012).

Let $\hat{\mathbf{S}}_i = \mathrm{supp}(\hat{\mathbf{Z}}^i)$ where $\mathrm{supp}(\cdot)$ indicates the support of a vector, i.e. the indices of its nonzero elements. Denote by ${\mathbf{Z}^i}^*$ the globally optimal solution to (8), and $\mathbf{S}_i^* = \mathrm{supp}({\mathbf{Z}^i}^*)$, then we have

Lemma 1. *For any $1 \le i \le n$, if $\mathbf{F}_{ki}^{\tilde{\mathbf{S}}} \ge 0$ for all $k \in \Lambda_i$, then the sequence $\{{\mathbf{Z}^i}^{(t)}\}_t$ generated by (17) and (18) converges to a critical point of $F(\mathbf{Z}^i)$, which is denoted by $\hat{\mathbf{Z}}^i$. Moreover, if*

$$0 < b < \min\{\min_{k \in \hat{\mathbf{S}}_i} |\hat{\mathbf{Z}}_k^i|, \max_{k \notin \hat{\mathbf{S}}_i, \mathbf{F}_{ki}^{\tilde{\mathbf{S}}} \neq 0, k \in \Lambda_i} \frac{\gamma \mathbf{F}_{ki}^{\tilde{\mathbf{S}}}}{(\frac{\partial Q}{\partial \mathbf{Z}_k^i}|_{\mathbf{Z}^i = \hat{\mathbf{Z}}^i} - \lambda)_+}, \tag{21}$$

$$\min_{k \in \mathbf{S}_i^*} |{\mathbf{Z}_k^i}^*|, \max_{k \notin \mathbf{S}_i^*, \mathbf{F}_{ki}^{\tilde{\mathbf{S}}} \neq 0, k \in \Lambda_i} \frac{\gamma \mathbf{F}_{ki}^{\tilde{\mathbf{S}}}}{(\frac{\partial Q}{\partial \mathbf{Z}_k^i}|_{\mathbf{Z}^i = \mathbf{Z}^{i*}} - \lambda)_+}\}$$

(if the denominator is 0, $\frac{\cdot}{0}$ is defined to be $+\infty$ in the above inequality), then both $\hat{\mathbf{Z}}^i$ and ${\mathbf{Z}^i}^*$ are local solutions to the capped-ℓ^1 regularized problem (19).

Using the degree of nonconvexity of the regularizer $\mathbf{P}$, we have the following theorem showing that the sub-optimal solution $\hat{\mathbf{Z}^i}$ obtained by our PGD-style iterative method can be close to the globally optimal solution to the original problem (8), i.e. ${\mathbf{Z}^i}^*$. In the following text, $\mathbf{B}_{\mathbf{I}}$ indicates a submatrix of $\mathbf{B}$ whose columns correspond to the nonzero elements of $\mathbf{I}$, and $\sigma_{\min}(\cdot)$ indicates the smallest singular value of a matrix.

Theorem 1. (Sub-optimal solution is close to the globally optimal solution) For any $1 \le i \le n$, let $\mathbf{E}_i = \hat{\mathbf{S}}_i \cup \mathbf{S}_i^*$. Suppose $\mathbf{F}_{ki}^{\tilde{\mathbf{S}}} \ge 0$ for all $k \in \Lambda_i$, $\boldsymbol{X}_{\mathbf{E}_i}$ is not singular with $\kappa_0 \triangleq \sigma_{\min}(\boldsymbol{X}_{\mathbf{E}_i}) > 0$, $2\kappa_0^2 > \kappa > 0$, and b is chosen according to (28) as in Lemma 1. Let $\mathbf{U}_i = (\hat{\mathbf{S}}_i \setminus \mathbf{S}_i^*) \cup (\mathbf{S}_i^* \setminus \hat{\mathbf{S}}_i)$ be the symmetric difference between $\hat{\mathbf{S}}_i$ and $\mathbf{S}_i^*$, then

$$\begin{aligned} &\|{\mathbf{Z}^i}^* - \hat{\mathbf{Z}}^i\|_2 \\ &\le \frac{1}{2\kappa_0^2 - \kappa}\Bigg(\Big(\sum_{k \in \mathbf{U}_i \cap \hat{\mathbf{S}}_i} (\max\{0, \frac{\gamma \mathbb{1}_{\mathbf{Z}_{ik}=0} \mathbf{F}_{ki}^{\tilde{\mathbf{S}}}}{b} - \kappa|\hat{\mathbf{Z}}_{ki} - b|\})^2 \\ &+ \sum_{k \in \mathbf{U}_i \setminus \hat{\mathbf{S}}_i} (\max\{0, \frac{\gamma \mathbb{1}_{\mathbf{Z}_{ik}=0} \mathbf{F}_{ki}^{\tilde{\mathbf{S}}}}{b} - \kappa b\})^2\Big)^{\frac{1}{2}} + \|\mathbf{t}\|_2\Bigg) \end{aligned} \tag{22}$$

where $\mathbf{t} \in \mathbb{R}^n$, $\mathbf{t}_m = 2\lambda \mathbb{1}_{{\mathbf{Z}_m^i}^* \hat{\mathbf{Z}}_m^i < 0} + 0 \mathbb{1}_{{\mathbf{Z}_m^i}^* \hat{\mathbf{Z}}_m^i > 0}$ for $m \in \hat{\mathbf{S}}_i \cap \mathbf{S}_i^*$, and $\mathbf{t}_m = 0$ for all other m.

Remark 2. Note that the bound for distance between the sub-optimal solution and the globally optimal solution presented in Theorem 1 does not require typical Restricted Isometry Property (RIP) conditions as those in (Candès, 2008). Also, when $\frac{\gamma \mathbb{1}_{\mathbf{Z}_{ik}=0} \mathbf{F}_{ki}^{\tilde{\mathbf{S}}}}{b} - \kappa|\hat{\mathbf{Z}}_{ki} - b|$ and $\frac{\gamma \mathbb{1}_{\mathbf{Z}_{ik}=0} \mathbf{F}_{ki}^{\tilde{\mathbf{S}}}}{b} - \kappa b$ are no greater than 0 and ${\mathbf{Z}^i}^*$ and $\hat{\mathbf{Z}}^i$ has the same sign in the intersection of their support, the sub-optimal solution $\hat{\mathbf{Z}}^i$ is equal to the globally optimal solution. When $\frac{\gamma \mathbb{1}_{\mathbf{Z}_{ik}=0} \mathbf{F}_{ki}^{\tilde{\mathbf{S}}}}{b} - \kappa|\hat{\mathbf{Z}}_{ki} - b|$ and $\frac{\gamma \mathbb{1}_{\mathbf{Z}_{ik}=0} \mathbf{F}_{ki}^{\tilde{\mathbf{S}}}}{b} - \kappa b$ are small positive numbers and ${\mathbf{Z}^i}^*$ and $\hat{\mathbf{Z}}^i$ has similar sign in the intersection of their support, $\hat{\mathbf{Z}}^i$ is close to the globally optimal solution.

4 ACCELERATION BY RANDOM PROJECTION

The gradient descent step (11) in the proposed PGD-style iterative method has time complexity of $\mathcal{O}(nd)$, leading to the time complexity of $\mathcal{O}(M_c M_p n^2 d)$ for the overall optimization of NRℓ^1-Graph. The literature has extensively employed randomized algorithms for accelerating the numeral computation of different kinds of matrix optimization problems including low rank approximation and matrix decomposition (Frieze et al., 2004; Drineas et al., 2004; Mahoney and Drineas, 2009; Drineas et al., 2011; Halko et al., 2011). In order to accelerate the numerical computation involved in the proposed PGD-style iterative method, we adopt the randomized low rank approximation by random projection (Halko et al., 2011) to obtain a low rank approximation of the data matrix $\boldsymbol{X}$ so as to accelerate the computation of gradient for PGD. Low rank approximation by random projection has also employed in the most recent sparse linear regression method (Zhang et al., 2016). (Zhang et al., 2016) focuses on the convex ℓ^1-regularized sparse linear model, and it remains interesting to explore the provable efficient PGD-style optimization by low rank approximation via random projection on the nonconvex and nonsmooth optimization problem of NRℓ^1-Graph.

Formally, a random matrix $\Omega \in \mathbb{R}^{n \times k}$ is computed such that each element Ω_{ij} is sampled independently from the Gaussian distribution $\mathcal{N}(0, 1)$. With the QR decomposition of $\boldsymbol{X}\Omega$, i.e. $\boldsymbol{X}\Omega = \mathbf{QR}$ where $\mathbf{Q} \in \mathbb{R}^{d \times k}$ is an orthogonal matrix of rank k and $\mathbf{R} \in \mathbb{R}^{k \times k}$ is an upper triangle matrix. The columns of $\mathbf{Q}$ form the orthogonal basis for the sample matrix $\boldsymbol{X}\Omega$. Then $\boldsymbol{X}$ is approximated by projecting $\boldsymbol{X}$ onto the range of $\boldsymbol{X}\Omega$: $\mathbf{Q}\mathbf{Q}^\top \boldsymbol{X} = \mathbf{QW} = \tilde{\boldsymbol{X}}$ where $\mathbf{W} = \mathbf{Q}^\top \boldsymbol{X} \in \mathbb{R}^{k \times n}$. Replacing $\boldsymbol{X}$ with its low rank approximation $\tilde{\boldsymbol{X}}$, we resort to solve the following reduced NRℓ^1-Graph problem termed NRℓ^1-Graph by Random Projection (NRℓ^1-Graph-RP):

$$\begin{aligned} \min_{\mathbf{Z} \in \mathbb{R}^{n \times n}, \mathrm{diag}(\mathbf{Z}) = \mathbf{0}} \tilde{L}(\mathbf{Z}) = \sum_{i=1}^{n} \|\mathbf{x}_i - \tilde{\boldsymbol{X}}\mathbf{Z}^i\|_2^2 + \lambda\|\mathbf{Z}^i\|_1 \\ + \gamma \mathbf{R}_{\mathbf{S}}(\mathbf{Z}) \end{aligned} \tag{23}$$

Similar to NRℓ^1-Graph, the PGD-style iterative method is used in each step of coordinate descent for the optimization of NRℓ^1-Graph-RP which solves the following reduced problem for $\mathbf{Z}^i$:

$$\min_{\mathbf{Z}^i \in \mathbb{R}^n, \mathbf{Z}_i^i = 0} \tilde{F}(\mathbf{Z}^i) = \|\mathbf{x}_i - \tilde{\boldsymbol{X}}\mathbf{Z}^i\|_2^2 + \lambda\|\mathbf{Z}^i\|_1 + \gamma \mathbf{R}_{\tilde{\mathbf{S}}}(\mathbf{Z}^i) \tag{24}$$

And the gradient descent step of the PGD-style iterative method (11) is reduced to

$$\begin{aligned} \tilde{\mathbf{Z}^i}^{(t)} &= {\mathbf{Z}^i}^{(t-1)} - \frac{2}{\tau s}(\tilde{\boldsymbol{X}}^\top \tilde{\boldsymbol{X}} {\mathbf{Z}^i}^{(t-1)} - \tilde{\boldsymbol{X}}^\top \mathbf{x}_i) \\ &= {\mathbf{Z}^i}^{(t-1)} - \frac{2}{\tau s}(\mathbf{W}^\top \mathbf{Q}^\top \mathbf{Q} \mathbf{W} {\mathbf{Z}^i}^{(t-1)} - \mathbf{W}^\top \mathbf{Q}^\top \mathbf{x}_i) \end{aligned} \tag{25}$$

The complexity of this step is reduced from $\mathcal{O}(nd)$ to $\mathcal{O}(nk + dk)$ wherein $k \ll \min\{d, n\}$ and significant efficiency improvement is achieved. Note that the computational cost of QR decomposition for $\boldsymbol{X}\Omega$ is less than $2dk^2$, which is acceptable with a small k.

The subsequent steps of the PGD-style iterative method (12), (13) remain unchanged for NRℓ^1-Graph-RP, therefore, the overall complexity of the optimization of NRℓ^1-Graph-RP by the PGD-style iterative method is reduced from $\mathcal{O}(M_c M_p n^2 d)$ to $\mathcal{O}(M_c M_p n(nk+dk))$ using such randomized low rank decomposition of the data matrix $\boldsymbol{X}$.

(Halko et al., 2011) proved that the low rank approximation $\tilde{\boldsymbol{X}}$ is close to $\boldsymbol{X}$ in terms of the spectral norm:

Lemma 2. *(Corollary 10.9 by (Halko et al., 2011)) Let $k_0 \ge 2$ and $p = k - k_0 \ge 4$, then with probability at least $1 - 6e^{-p}$, then the spectral norm of $\boldsymbol{X} - \hat{\boldsymbol{X}}$ is bounded by*

$$\|\boldsymbol{X} - \hat{\boldsymbol{X}}\|_2 \le C_{k,k_0} \tag{26}$$

where

$$C_{k,k_0} = \left(1 + 17\sqrt{1 + \frac{k_0}{p}}\right)\sigma_{k_0+1} + \frac{8\sqrt{k}}{p+1}\Big(\sum_{j>k_0} \sigma_j^2\Big)^{\frac{1}{2}}$$

and $\sigma_1 \ge \sigma_2 \ge \ldots$ are the singular values of $\boldsymbol{X}$.

Let $\tilde{\mathbf{Z}}^i$ be the globally optimal solution to (24), and $\tilde{\mathbf{S}}_i = \mathrm{supp}(\tilde{\mathbf{Z}}^i)$. We have the following theorem establishing the upper bound for the gap between $\tilde{\mathbf{Z}}^i$ and ${\mathbf{Z}^i}^*$.

Theorem 2. (Optimal solution to the reduced problem (24) is close to the that to the original problem) For any $1 \le i \le n$, let $\mathbf{G}_i = \tilde{\mathbf{S}}_i \cup \mathbf{S}_i^*$. Suppose $\mathbf{F}_{ki}^{\tilde{\mathbf{S}}} \ge 0$ for all $k \in \Lambda_i$, $\boldsymbol{X}_{\mathbf{G}_i}$ is not singular with $\tau_0 \triangleq \sigma_{\min}(\boldsymbol{X}_{\mathbf{G}_i}) > 0$, $2\tau_0^2 > \tau > 0$. Then under the conditions of Lemma 2, with probability at least $1 - 6e^{-p}$,

$$\|{\mathbf{Z}^i}^* - \tilde{\mathbf{Z}}^i\|_2 \le \frac{(A_1 + A_2)^{\frac{1}{2}} + \|\mathbf{t}\|_2 + C_{k,k_0} A(2\sigma_{\max}(\boldsymbol{X}) + C_{k,k_0})}{2\tau_0^2 - \tau} \tag{27}$$

where $A_1 = \sum_{k \in \mathbf{G}_i \cap \hat{\mathbf{S}}_i} (\max\{0, \frac{\gamma \mathbb{1}_{\mathbf{Z}_{ik}=0} \mathbf{F}_{ki}^{\tilde{\mathbf{S}}}}{b} - \kappa|\tilde{\mathbf{Z}}_{ki} - b|\})^2$, $A_2 = \sum_{k \in \mathbf{G}_i \setminus \hat{\mathbf{S}}_i} (\max\{0, \frac{\gamma \mathbb{1}_{\mathbf{Z}_{ik}=0} \mathbf{F}_{ki}^{\tilde{\mathbf{S}}}}{b} - \kappa b\})^2$, $\mathbf{t} \in \mathbb{R}^n$, $\mathbf{t}_m = 2\lambda \mathbb{1}_{\mathbf{Z}_m^i * \tilde{\mathbf{Z}}_m^i < 0} + 0\mathbb{1}_{\mathbf{Z}_m^i * \tilde{\mathbf{Z}}_m^i > 0}$ for $m \in \tilde{\mathbf{S}}_i \cap \mathbf{S}_i^*$, and $\mathbf{t}_m = 0$ for all other m. Moreover, $A = \frac{(\|\mathbf{x}_i\|_2 + \sqrt{\mathbf{R}_{\tilde{\mathbf{S}}}(\mathbf{0}) + \|\mathbf{x}_i\|_2^2})}{\sigma_{\min}(\boldsymbol{X}_{\tilde{\mathbf{S}}_i}) - C_{k,k_0}}$, and b satisfies

$$0 < b < \min\{\min_{k \in \tilde{\mathbf{S}}_i} |\tilde{\mathbf{Z}}_k^i|, \max_{k \notin \tilde{\mathbf{S}}_i, \mathbf{F}_{ki}^{\tilde{\mathbf{S}}} \neq 0, k \in \Lambda_i} \frac{\gamma \mathbf{F}_{ki}^{\tilde{\mathbf{S}}}}{(\frac{\partial Q}{\partial \mathbf{Z}_k^i}|_{\mathbf{Z}^i = \tilde{\mathbf{Z}}^i} - \lambda)_+}, \tag{28}$$

$$\min_{k \in \mathbf{S}_i^*} |{\mathbf{Z}_k^i}^*|, \max_{k \notin \mathbf{S}_i^*, \mathbf{F}_{ki}^{\tilde{\mathbf{S}}} \neq 0, k \in \Lambda_i} \frac{\gamma \mathbf{F}_{ki}^{\tilde{\mathbf{S}}}}{(\frac{\partial Q}{\partial \mathbf{Z}_k^i}|_{\mathbf{Z}^i = {\mathbf{Z}^i}^*} - \lambda)_+}\}$$

Combining Theorem 1 and Theorem 2, we have the bounded gap between the sub-optimal solution obtained by the PGD-style iterative method for the reduced problem (24) and the globally optimal solution to the original problem (8) for each step of coordinate descent. To the best of our knowledge, our result is among the very few results on the provable efficient optimization by randomized matrix decomposition on nonconvex and nonsmooth optimization problems.

5 EXPERIMENTAL RESULTS

We apply NRℓ^1-Graph to data clustering by performing spectral clustering on the weighted adjacency matrix $\mathbf{W}^*$ of the sparse graph by Algorithm 1. The superior clustering performance of NRℓ^1-Graph is demonstrated by extensive experimental results on various data sets. NRℓ^1-Graph is compared to K-means (KM), Spectral Clustering (SC), ℓ^1-Graph, Sparse Manifold Clustering and Embedding (SMCE) (Elhamifar and Vidal, 2011), and ℓ^2-Rℓ^1-Graph introduced in Section 2. Two measures are used to evaluate the performance of different clustering methods, i.e. the Accuracy (AC) and the Normalized Mutual Information (NMI) (Zheng et al., 2004).

5.1 CLUSTERING ON COIL-20, COIL-100, FACE DATA SETS AND MNIST DATA

COIL-20 Database has 1440 images of resolution 32×32 for 20 objects with background removed in all images. The dimensionality of this data is 1024. The extended version of COIL-20, COIL-100 Database, contains 100 objects with 72 images of resolution 32×32 for each object. The images of each object were taken 5 degrees apart when each object was rotated on a turntable. we also demonstrate the clustering result on popular face data sets including Yale-B, CMU PIE, CMU Multi-PIE, UMIST Face Data. The Extended Yale Face Database B contains 64 frontal face images for each of the 38 subjects, and the face images are taken under different illuminations for each subject. CMU PIE face data contains 11554 cropped face images of size 32×32 for 68 persons, and there are around 170 facial images for each person under different illumination and expressions. CMU Multi-PIE (MPIE) data (Gross et al., 2010) contains the facial images captured in four sessions. The UMIST Face Database consists of 575 images of size 112×92 for 20 people. Each person is shown in a range of poses from profile to frontal views. MNIST is comprised of 60000 training images and 10000 test images of ten dig-

Table 1: Clustering Results on Various Data Sets, the top two results for each measure and data set are in bold.

Data Set	Measure	KM	SC	ℓ^1-Graph	SMCE	ℓ^2-Rℓ^1-Graph	NRℓ^1-Graph	NRℓ^1-Graph-RP
COIL-20	AC	0.6504	0.4271	0.7854	0.7549	0.7854	**0.9174**	**0.9257**
	NMI	0.7616	0.6202	0.9148	0.8754	0.9148	**0.9671**	**0.9716**
COIL-100	AC	0.4928	0.2833	0.5310	0.5625	0.5625	**0.7846**	**0.7972**
	NMI	0.7522	0.5913	0.8015	0.8057	0.8059	**0.9238**	**0.9284**
Yale-B	AC	0.0948	0.1060	0.7850	0.3409	**0.7850**	**0.8111**	0.7092
	NMI	0.1254	0.1524	0.7760	0.3909	0.7760	**0.8095**	**0.7216**
CMU PIE	AC	0.0829	0.0718	0.2318	0.1603	**0.3012**	**0.3190**	0.2965
	NMI	0.1865	0.1760	0.3378	0.3406	**0.5121**	0.4993	**0.5103**
MPIE S1	AC	0.1167	0.1309	0.5892	0.1721	**0.5892**	**0.6582**	0.5729
	NMI	0.5021	0.5289	0.7653	0.5514	0.7653	**0.8540**	**0.8052**
MPIE S2	AC	0.1330	0.1437	0.6994	0.1898	**0.6994**	**0.7226**	0.6584
	NMI	0.4847	0.5145	0.8149	0.5293	0.8149	**0.8826**	**0.8505**
MPIE S3	AC	0.1322	0.1441	0.6316	0.1856	**0.6316**	**0.6753**	0.6194
	NMI	0.4837	0.5150	0.7858	0.5155	0.7858	**0.8657**	**0.8134**
MPIE S4	AC	0.1313	0.1469	0.6803	0.1823	**0.6803**	**0.7260**	0.6563
	NMI	0.4876	0.5251	0.8063	0.5294	0.8066	**0.8926**	**0.8413**
UMIST	AC	0.4216	0.4174	0.4417	0.4452	0.4991	**0.6765**	**0.7078**
	NMI	0.6377	0.6095	0.6489	0.6641	0.6893	**0.7982**	**0.8084**
MNIST	AC	0.5338	0.3557	0.6105	**0.6546**	0.6110	0.6353	**0.6395**
	NMI	0.4830	0.3713	0.6310	**0.6684**	0.6315	**0.6526**	0.6514

its from 0 to 9, and each image is of size 28×28 and represented as a 784-dimensional vector.

All the clustering results on various data sets are shown in Table 1. For MNIST data, we randomly sample 1000 images from each class to constitute a total number of 10000 images on which clustering is performed. We conduct such random sampling by 10 times and record the average performance. It can be observed from Table 1 that ℓ^2-Rℓ^1-Graph produces better clustering accuracy than ℓ^1-Graph on COIL-100, since graph regularization produces locally smooth sparse codes aligned to the local manifold structure of the data. Using the neighborhood regularization term to render locally consistent neighborhood in the sparse graph so that the local structure of the sparse graph is aligned to the manifold structure of the data, NRℓ^1-Graph and NRℓ^1-Graph-RP always perform better than all the other clustering methods. Randomized rank-k decomposition of the data matrix is employed in NRℓ^1-Graph-RP to accelerate NRℓ^1-Graph with $k = \frac{\min\{d,n\}}{10}$. Compared to NR$\ell^1$-Graph, we observe that NRℓ^1-Graph-RP usually exhibits competitive or even better results, revealing its compelling performance with reduced computational complexity. For example, NRℓ^1-Graph-RP is around 8.7 times faster than NRℓ^1-Graph for each iteration of the PGD-style iterative method on the COIL-100 data, which is consistent to our complexity analysis in Section 4.

5.2 PARAMETER SETTING

There are two essential parameters for NRℓ^1-Graph, i.e. γ for the neighborhood induced graph regularization term and K for building the KNN graph. We use the sparse codes generated by ℓ^1-Graph with weighting parameter $\lambda^{(\ell^1)} = 0.1$ in (2) to initialize both NRℓ^1-Graph and ℓ^2-Rℓ^1-Graph, and set $\lambda = \gamma = 0.1$, $K = 5$ for NRℓ^1-Graph (6) empirically throughout all the experiments. The maximum iteration number M is 100 and the stopping threshold ε is 10^{-5}. The weighting parameter for the ℓ^1-norm in ℓ^1-Graph, $\lambda^{(\ell^1)}$, and that in ℓ^2-Rℓ^1-Graph, $\lambda^{(\ell^2)}$, and the regularization weight for ℓ^2-Rℓ^1-Graph, $\gamma^{(\ell^2)}$, are chosen from $[0.1, 1]$ for the best performance. Moreover, results on the parameter sensitivity are included in the supplementary of this paper.

6 CONCLUSION

We propose a novel NRℓ^1-Graph which align the sparse graph to the local manifold structure of the data by learning locally consistent neighborhood in the sparse graph. In contrast to most existing methods that use ℓ^2-norm to measure the distance between sparse codes in graph regularization, NRℓ^1-Graph employs the novel neighborhood distance to measure the distance between data points so as to impose the local smoothness on the neighborhood. The optimization algorithm using the proposed PGD-style iterative method and its theoretical properties are analyzed. The optimization of NRℓ^1-Graph is further accelerated by randomized low rank decomposition of the data matrix with theoretical guarantee, leading to the more efficient NRℓ^1-Graph by Random Projection. The effectiveness of NRℓ^1-Graph and its accelerated version for data clustering is demonstrated by experiments on various data sets.

References

Mikhail Belkin and Partha Niyogi. Laplacian eigenmaps for dimensionality reduction and data representation. *Neural Computation*, 15(6):1373–1396, 2003.

Mikhail Belkin, Partha Niyogi, and Vikas Sindhwani. Manifold regularization: A geometric framework for learning from labeled and unlabeled examples. *Journal of Machine Learning Research*, 7:2399–2434, 2006.

Jérôme Bolte, Shoham Sabach, and Marc Teboulle. Proximal alternating linearized minimization for nonconvex and nonsmooth problems. *Math. Program.*, 146(1-2):459–494, August 2014. ISSN 0025-5610.

Emmanuel J. Candès. The restricted isometry property and its implications for compressed sensing. *Comptes Rendus Mathematique*, 346(910):589 – 592, 2008. ISSN 1631-073X.

Bin Cheng, Jianchao Yang, Shuicheng Yan, Yun Fu, and Thomas S. Huang. Learning with l1-graph for image analysis. *IEEE Transactions on Image Processing*, 19(4):858–866, 2010.

F. R. K. Chung. *Spectral Graph Theory*. American Mathematical Society, 1997.

P. Drineas, A. Frieze, R. Kannan, S. Vempala, and V. Vinay. Clustering large graphs via the singular value decomposition. *Machine Learning*, 56(1):9–33, 2004. ISSN 1573-0565.

Petros Drineas, Michael W. Mahoney, S. Muthukrishnan, and Tamás Sarlós. Faster least squares approximation. *Numerische Mathematik*, 117(2):219–249, 2011. ISSN 0945-3245.

Richard O. Duda, Peter E. Hart, and David G. Stork. *Pattern Classification (2nd Edition)*. Wiley-Interscience, 2000.

Ehsan Elhamifar and René Vidal. Sparse subspace clustering. In *CVPR*, pages 2790–2797, 2009.

Ehsan Elhamifar and René Vidal. Sparse manifold clustering and embedding. In *NIPS*, pages 55–63, 2011.

Ehsan Elhamifar and René Vidal. Sparse subspace clustering: Algorithm, theory, and applications. *IEEE Trans. Pattern Anal. Mach. Intell.*, 35(11):2765–2781, 2013.

Chris Fraley and Adrian E. Raftery. Model-Based Clustering, Discriminant Analysis, and Density Estimation. *Journal of the American Statistical Association*, 97(458):611–631, June 2002. ISSN 0162-1459.

Brendan J. Frey and Delbert Dueck. Clustering by passing messages between data points. *Science*, 315:2007, 2007.

Alan Frieze, Ravi Kannan, and Santosh Vempala. Fast monte-carlo algorithms for finding low-rank approximations. *J. ACM*, 51(6):1025–1041, November 2004. ISSN 0004-5411.

Shenghua Gao, Ivor Wai-Hung Tsang, and Liang-Tien Chia. Laplacian sparse coding, hypergraph laplacian sparse coding, and applications. *IEEE Trans. Pattern Anal. Mach. Intell.*, 35(1):92–104, 2013.

Ralph Gross, Iain Matthews, Jeffrey Cohn, Takeo Kanade, and Simon Baker. Multi-pie. *Image Vision Comput.*, 28(5):807–813, May 2010. ISSN 0262-8856.

N. Halko, P. G. Martinsson, and J. A. Tropp. Finding structure with randomness: Probabilistic algorithms for constructing approximate matrix decompositions. *SIAM Rev.*, 53(2):217–288, May 2011. ISSN 0036-1445.

Xiaofei He, Deng Cai, Yuanlong Shao, Hujun Bao, and Jiawei Han. Laplacian regularized gaussian mixture model for data clustering. *Knowledge and Data Engineering, IEEE Transactions on*, 23(9):1406–1418, Sept 2011. ISSN 1041-4347.

Jialu Liu, Deng Cai, and Xiaofei He. Gaussian mixture model with local consistency. In *AAAI*, 2010.

Michael W. Mahoney and Petros Drineas. Cur matrix decompositions for improved data analysis. *Proceedings of the National Academy of Sciences*, 106(3):697–702, 2009.

Andrew Y. Ng, Michael I. Jordan, and Yair Weiss. On spectral clustering: Analysis and an algorithm. In *NIPS*, pages 849–856, 2001.

Xi Peng, Shijie Xiao, Jiashi Feng, Wei-Yun Yau, and Zhang Yi. Deep subspace clustering with sparsity prior. In *Proceedings of the 25 International Joint Conference on Artificial Intelligence*, pages 1925–1931, New York, NY, USA, 9-15 July 2016.

Sam T. Roweis and Lawrence K. Saul. Nonlinear dimensionality reduction by locally linear embedding. *SCIENCE*, 290: 2323–2326, 2000.

Mahdi Soltanolkotabi, Ehsan Elhamifar, and Emmanuel J. Candès. Robust subspace clustering. *Ann. Statist.*, 42(2): 669–699, 04 2014.

Yu-Xiang Wang and Huan Xu. Noisy sparse subspace clustering. In *Proceedings of the 30th International Conference on Machine Learning, ICML 2013, Atlanta, GA, USA, 16-21 June 2013*, pages 89–97, 2013.

Shuicheng Yan and Huan Wang. Semi-supervised learning by sparse representation. In *SDM*, pages 792–801, 2009.

Yingzhen Yang, Zhangyang Wang, Jianchao Yang, Jiangping Wang, Shiyu Chang, and Thomas S. Huang. Data clustering by laplacian regularized l1-graph. In *Proceedings of the Twenty-Eighth AAAI Conference on Artificial Intelligence, July 27 -31, 2014, Québec City, Québec, Canada.*, pages 3148–3149, 2014.

Lihi Zelnik-manor and Pietro Perona. Self-tuning spectral clustering. In L. K. Saul, Y. Weiss, and L. Bottou, editors, *Advances in Neural Information Processing Systems 17*, pages 1601–1608. MIT Press, 2005.

Cun-Hui Zhang and Tong Zhang. A general theory of concave regularization for high-dimensional sparse estimation problems. *Statist. Sci.*, 27(4):576–593, 11 2012.

Weizhong Zhang, Lijun Zhang, Rong Jin, Deng Cai, and Xiaofei He. Accelerated sparse linear regression via random projection. In *Proceedings of the 30th AAAI Conference on Artificial Intelligence (AAAI)*, pages 2337–2343, 2016.

Miao Zheng, Jiajun Bu, Chun Chen, Can Wang, Lijun Zhang, Guang Qiu, and Deng Cai. Graph regularized sparse coding for image representation. *IEEE Transactions on Image Processing*, 20(5):1327–1336, 2011.

Xin Zheng, Deng Cai, Xiaofei He, Wei-Ying Ma, and Xueyin Lin. Locality preserving clustering for image database. In *Proceedings of the 12th Annual ACM International Conference on Multimedia*, MULTIMEDIA '04, pages 885–891, New York, NY, USA, 2004. ACM.

7 SUPPLEMENTARY

7.1 PROOFS

Proof of Proposition 1. Note that $\mathbf{u}$ is the optimal solution to the lasso problem: $\mathbf{u} = \arg\min_{\mathbf{v}\in R^n} \frac{\tau s}{2}\|\mathbf{v} - \tilde{\mathbf{Z}}_{ki}^{(t)}\|_2^2 + \lambda\|\mathbf{v}\|_1$.

Suppose $k \in \Lambda_i$. Define $T_k(v) = \frac{\tau s}{2}(v - \tilde{\mathbf{Z}}_{ki}^{(t)})^2 + \lambda|v|$ for $v \in \mathbb{R}$, then $\mathbf{u}_k = \arg\min_{v\in\mathbb{R}} T_k(v)$. Since the two functions $H_k(v)$ and $T_k(v)$ only differ at $v = 0$, $\arg\min_{v\in\{\mathbf{u}_k,0\}} H_k(v)$ is the optimal solution to $\min_{v\in R} H_k(v)$ when $\mathbf{u}_k \neq 0$ or $\mathbf{u}_k = 0$ and $\mathbf{F}_{ki}^{\tilde{\mathbf{S}}} \geq 0$.

When $\mathbf{u}_k = 0$ and $\mathbf{F}_{ki}^{\tilde{\mathbf{S}}} < 0$, when $\varepsilon \to 0$ and $\varepsilon \neq 0$, $H_k(\varepsilon) \to \frac{\tau s}{2}(\tilde{\mathbf{Z}}_{ki}^{(t)})^2 + \gamma\mathbf{F}_{ki}^{\tilde{\mathbf{S}}}$ and $\inf_{v\in\mathbb{R}} H_k(v) = \frac{\tau s}{2}(\tilde{\mathbf{Z}}_{ki}^{(t)})^2 + \gamma\mathbf{F}_{ki}^{\tilde{\mathbf{S}}}$. Note that the infimum can never be achieved. Since $\inf_{v\in\mathbb{R}} H_k(v) < H_k(\mathbf{Z}_{ki}^{(t-1)})$, we can always find $\varepsilon \neq 0$ such that $H_k(\varepsilon) \leq H_k(\mathbf{Z}_{ki}^{(t-1)})$.

Suppose $k \notin \Lambda_i$, then $\mathbf{u}_k$ is the optimal solution to $\min_{v\in R} H_k(v)$ for $k \neq i$.

Define $H(\mathbf{v}) = \frac{\tau s}{2}\|\mathbf{v} - \tilde{\mathbf{Z}^i}^{(t)}\|_2^2 + \lambda\|\mathbf{v}\|_1 + \gamma\mathbf{R}_{\tilde{\mathbf{S}}}(\mathbf{v})$. Based on the above argument, $H(\mathbf{Z}^{i^{(t)}}) \leq H(\mathbf{Z}^{i^{(t-1)}})$ which indicates that

$$\frac{\tau s}{2}\|\mathbf{Z}^{i^{(t)}} - \mathbf{Z}^{i^{(t-1)}}\|_2^2 + \langle\mathbf{Z}^{i^{(t)}} - \mathbf{Z}^{i^{(t-1)}}, \nabla Q(\mathbf{Z}^{i^{(t-1)}})\rangle \tag{29}$$

$$+ \lambda\|\mathbf{Z}^{i^{(t)}}\|_1 + \gamma\mathbf{R}_{\tilde{\mathbf{S}}}(\mathbf{Z}^{i^{(t)}}) \leq \lambda\|\mathbf{Z}^{i^{(t-1)}}\|_1 + \gamma\mathbf{R}_{\tilde{\mathbf{S}}}(\mathbf{Z}^{i^{(t-1)}}) \tag{30}$$

Also, since s is the Lipschitz constant for the gradient of function $Q(\cdot)$, we have

$$Q(\mathbf{Z}^{i^{(t)}}) \leq Q(\mathbf{Z}^{i^{(t-1)}}) + \langle\mathbf{Z}^{i^{(t)}} - \mathbf{Z}^{i^{(t-1)}}, \nabla Q(\mathbf{Z}^{i^{(t-1)}})\rangle \tag{31}$$

$$+ \frac{s}{2}\|\mathbf{Z}^{i^{(t)}} - \mathbf{Z}^{i^{(t-1)}}\|_2^2$$

Combining (29) and (31),

$$F(\mathbf{Z}^{i^{(t)}}) \leq F(\mathbf{Z}^{i^{(t-1)}}) - \frac{(\tau-1)s}{2}\|\mathbf{Z}^{i^{(t)}} - \mathbf{Z}^{i^{(t-1)}}\|_2^2$$

□

Proof of Lemma 1. We first prove that the sequences $\{\mathbf{Z}^{i^{(t)}}\}_t$ is bounded for any $1 \leq i \leq n$. By Proposition 1, the sequence $\{F(\mathbf{Z}^{i^{(t)}})\}_t$ decreases, so we have

$$F(\mathbf{Z}^{i^{(t)}}) = \|\mathbf{x}_i - \boldsymbol{X}\mathbf{Z}^{i^{(t)}}\|_2^2 + \lambda\|\mathbf{Z}^{i^{(t)}}\|_1 + \gamma\mathbf{R}_{\tilde{\mathbf{S}}}(\mathbf{Z}^{i^{(t)}})$$
$$\leq F(\mathbf{Z}^{i^{(0)}})$$

for $t \geq 1$. Therefore,

$$\|\mathbf{Z}^{i^{(t)}}\|_1 \leq \frac{1}{\lambda}F(\mathbf{Z}^{i^{(0)}})$$

It follows that $\|\mathbf{Z}^{i^{(t)}}\|_1$ is bounded, and $\|\mathbf{Z}^{i^{(t)}}\|_2$ is also bounded. Since $\mathbf{F}_{ki}^{\tilde{\mathbf{S}}} \geq 0$ for all $k \in \Lambda_i$ and the indicator function $\mathbb{I}_{\cdot\neq 0}$ is semi-algebraic function, $\mathbf{R}_{\tilde{\mathbf{S}}}(\cdot)$ is also a semi-algebraic function and lower semicontinuous. Therefore, according to Theorem 1 by Bolte et al. (2014), $\{\mathbf{Z}^{i^{(t)}}\}_t$ converges to a critical point of $F(\mathbf{Z}^i)$, denoted by $\hat{\mathbf{Z}}^i$.

Let $\hat{\mathbf{v}} = 2\boldsymbol{X}^{(-i)^\top}(\boldsymbol{X}^{(-i)}\hat{\mathbf{Z}^i}_{-i} - \mathbf{x}_i) + \dot{\mathbf{P}}(\hat{\mathbf{Z}^i}_{-i}; b)$. For k such that $\mathbf{F}_{ki}^{\tilde{\mathbf{S}}} = 0$ or $k \notin \Lambda_i$, since $\hat{\mathbf{Z}}^i$ is a critical point of $F(\mathbf{Z}^i)$, $\hat{\mathbf{v}}_{k_{-i}} = 0$.

Now we consider the case that $\mathbf{F}_{ki}^{\tilde{\mathbf{S}}} \neq 0$ and $k \in \Lambda_i$. In the following text we denote by k_{-i} the index of the element of the vector $\mathbf{v}_{-i}$ corresponding to the element $\mathbf{v}_k$ of $\mathbf{v}$, i.e. $(\mathbf{v}_{-i})_{k_{-i}} = \mathbf{v}_k$ for any $\mathbf{v} \in \mathbb{R}^n$.

For $k \in \hat{\mathbf{S}}_i$, since $\hat{\mathbf{Z}}^i$ is a critical point of $F(\mathbf{Z}^i) = \|\mathbf{x}_i - \boldsymbol{X}\mathbf{Z}^i\|_2^2 + \lambda\|\mathbf{Z}^i\|_1 + \gamma\mathbf{R}_{\tilde{\mathbf{S}}}(\mathbf{Z}^i)$. then $\frac{\partial(Q+\lambda\|\mathbf{Z}^i\|_1)}{\partial\mathbf{Z}_k^i}|_{\mathbf{Z}^i=\hat{\mathbf{Z}}^i} = 0$ because $\frac{\partial\mathbf{R}_{\tilde{\mathbf{S}}}(\mathbf{Z}^i)}{\partial\mathbf{Z}_k^i}|_{\mathbf{Z}^i=\hat{\mathbf{Z}}^i} = 0$. Note that $\min_{k\in\hat{\mathbf{S}}_i}|\hat{\mathbf{Z}}_k^i| > b$, so $\frac{\partial\mathbf{T}}{\partial\mathbf{Z}_k^i}|_{\mathbf{Z}^i=\hat{\mathbf{Z}}^i} = 0$. It follows that $\hat{\mathbf{v}}_{k_{-i}} = 0$.

For $k \notin \hat{\mathbf{S}}_i$, since $\frac{dP_k}{d\mathbf{Z}_k^i}(\hat{\mathbf{Z}}_k^i+; b) = \frac{\gamma\mathbf{F}_{ki}^{\tilde{\mathbf{S}}}}{b} + \lambda$ and $\frac{dP_k}{d\mathbf{Z}_k^i}(\hat{\mathbf{Z}}_k^i-; b) = -\frac{\gamma\mathbf{F}_{ki}^{\tilde{\mathbf{S}}}}{b} - \lambda$, $\frac{\gamma\mathbf{F}_{ki}^{\tilde{\mathbf{S}}}}{b} + \lambda \geq |\frac{\partial Q}{\partial\mathbf{Z}_k^i}|_{\mathbf{Z}^i=\hat{\mathbf{Z}}^i}|$, we can choose the k_{-i}-th element of $\dot{\mathbf{P}}(\hat{\mathbf{Z}}^i; b)$ such that $\hat{\mathbf{v}}_{k_{-i}} = 0$. Therefore, $\|\hat{\mathbf{v}}\|_2 = 0$, and $\hat{\mathbf{Z}}^i$ is a local solution to the problem (19).

Now we prove that $\mathbf{Z}^{i^*}$ is also a local solution to (19). Let $\mathbf{v}^* = 2\boldsymbol{X}^{(-i)^\top}(\boldsymbol{X}^{(-i)}\mathbf{Z}^{i^*}_{-i} - \mathbf{x}_i) + \dot{\mathbf{P}}(\mathbf{Z}^{i^*}_{-i}; b)$, and Q is defined as before. For k such that $\mathbf{F}_{ki}^{\tilde{\mathbf{S}}} = 0$ or or $k \notin \Lambda_i$, since $\mathbf{Z}^{i^*}$ is the globally optimal solution of $F(\mathbf{Z}^i)$, $\mathbf{v}_{k_{-i}}^* = 0$.

Again we consider the case that $\mathbf{F}_{ki}^{\tilde{\mathbf{S}}} \neq 0$ and $k \in \Lambda_i$.

For $k \in \mathbf{S}_i^*$, since $\mathbf{Z}^{i^*}$ is the globally optimal solution to problem (8), we also have $\frac{\partial(Q+\lambda\|\mathbf{Z}^i\|_1)}{\partial\mathbf{Z}_k^i}|_{\mathbf{Z}^i=\mathbf{Z}^{i^*}} = 0$. If it is not the case and $\frac{\partial(Q+\lambda\|\mathbf{Z}^i\|_1)}{\partial\mathbf{Z}_k^i}|_{\mathbf{Z}^i=\mathbf{Z}^{i^*}} \neq 0$, then we can change $\mathbf{Z}_k^i$ by a small amount in the direction of the gradient $\frac{\partial(Q+\lambda\|\mathbf{Z}^i\|_1)}{\partial\mathbf{Z}_k^i}$ at the point $\mathbf{Z}^i = \mathbf{Z}^{i^*}$ while $\mathbf{Z}_k^i$ is still nonzero, leading to a smaller value of the objective $F(\mathbf{Z}^i)$.

Note that $\min_{k\in\mathbf{S}_i^*}|\mathbf{Z}_k^{i^*}| > b$, so $\frac{\partial\mathbf{T}}{\partial\mathbf{Z}_k^i}|_{\mathbf{Z}^i=\hat{\mathbf{Z}}^i} = 0$, and it follows that $\mathbf{v}_{k_{-i}}^* = 0$.

For $k \notin \mathbf{S}_i^*$, since $\frac{\gamma\mathbf{F}_{ki}^{\tilde{\mathbf{S}}}}{b} + \lambda \geq \max_{k\notin\hat{\mathbf{S}}_i}|\frac{\partial Q}{\partial\mathbf{Z}_k^i}|_{\mathbf{Z}^i=\mathbf{Z}^{i^*}}|$, we can choose the k_{-i}-th element of $\dot{\mathbf{P}}(\mathbf{Z}^{i^*}; b)$ such that $\mathbf{v}_{k_{-i}}^* = 0$. It follows that $\|\mathbf{v}^*\|_2 = 0$, and $\mathbf{Z}^{i^*}$ is also a local solution to the problem (19). □

Proof of Theorem 1. According to Lemma 1, both $\hat{\mathbf{Z}}^i$ and $\mathbf{Z}^{i^*}$ are local solutions to problem (19). In the following text, let $\boldsymbol{\beta}_{\mathbf{I}}$ indicates a vector whose elements are those of $\boldsymbol{\beta}$ with indices in $\mathbf{I}$. Let $\Delta = {\mathbf{Z}^{i^*}}_{-i} - \hat{\mathbf{Z}}^i_{-i}$, $\tilde{\Delta} = \dot{\mathbf{P}}(\mathbf{Z}^{i^*}) - \dot{\mathbf{P}}(\hat{\mathbf{Z}}^i)$. By Lemma 1, we have

$$\|2{\boldsymbol{X}^{(-i)}}^\top \boldsymbol{X}^{(-i)}\Delta + \tilde{\Delta}\|_2 = 0$$

It follows that

$$2\Delta^\top {\boldsymbol{X}^{(-i)}}^\top \boldsymbol{X}^{(-i)}\Delta + \Delta^\top\tilde{\Delta} \le \|\Delta\|_2\|2{\boldsymbol{X}^{(-i)}}^\top \boldsymbol{X}^{(-i)}\Delta + \tilde{\Delta}\|_2 = 0$$

Also, by the proof of Lemma 1, for $k \in \hat{\mathbf{S}}_i \cap \mathbf{S}^*_i$, $(2{\boldsymbol{X}^{(-i)}}^\top \boldsymbol{X}^{(-i)}\Delta)_{k_{-i}} = 2\lambda \mathbb{I}_{\mathbf{Z}^{i}_k{}^* \hat{\mathbf{Z}}^i_k < 0} + 0\mathbb{I}_{\mathbf{Z}^{i}_k{}^* \hat{\mathbf{Z}}^i_k > 0}$. We now present another property on any nonconvex function P using the degree of nonconvexity in Definition 3: $\theta(t,\kappa) := \sup_s\{-\mathrm{sgn}(s-t)(\dot{P}(s;b) - \dot{P}(t;b)) - \kappa|s-t|\}$ on the regularizer $\mathbf{P}$. For any $s, t \in \mathbb{R}$, we have

$$-\,\mathrm{sgn}(s-t)\big(\dot{P}(s;b) - \dot{P}(t;b)\big) - \kappa|s-t| \le \theta(t,\kappa)$$

by the definition of θ. It follows that

$$\begin{aligned}&\theta(t,\kappa)|s-t| \ge -(s-t)\big(\dot{P}(s;b) - \dot{P}(t;b)\big) - \kappa(s-t)^2\\ &-(s-t)\big(\dot{P}(s;b) - \dot{P}(t;b)\big) \le \theta(t,\kappa)|s-t| + \kappa(s-t)^2\end{aligned} \tag{32}$$

Let $\hat{\mathbf{S}}_i^{-i} = \mathrm{supp}(\hat{\mathbf{Z}}^i_{-i})$, $\mathbf{S}_i^{-i^*} = \mathrm{supp}({\mathbf{Z}^{i^*}}_{-i})$, $\mathbf{U}_i^{-i} = (\hat{\mathbf{S}}_i^{-i}\setminus\mathbf{S}_i^{-i^*})\cup(\mathbf{S}_i^{-i^*}\setminus\hat{\mathbf{S}}_i^{-i})$. Applying (32) with $P = P_k$ for $k = 1,\ldots,n$, $k \ne i$, we have

$$\begin{aligned}&2\Delta^\top {\boldsymbol{X}^{(-i)}}^\top \boldsymbol{X}^{(-i)}\Delta \le -\Delta^\top\tilde{\Delta}\\ &= -\Delta^\top_{\mathbf{U}_i^{-i}}\tilde{\Delta}_{\mathbf{U}_i^{-i}} - \Delta^\top_{\hat{\mathbf{S}}_i^{-i}\cap\mathbf{S}_i^{-i^*}}\tilde{\Delta}_{\hat{\mathbf{S}}_i^{-i}\cap\mathbf{S}_i^{-i^*}}\\ &\le |({\mathbf{Z}^{i^*}}_{-i})_{\mathbf{U}_i^{-i}} - (\hat{\mathbf{Z}}^i_{-i})_{\mathbf{U}_i^{-i}}|^\top\theta((\hat{\mathbf{Z}}^i_{-i})_{\mathbf{U}_i^{-i}},\kappa)\\ &+ \kappa\|({\mathbf{Z}^{i^*}}_{-i})_{\mathbf{U}_i^{-i}} - (\hat{\mathbf{Z}}^i_{-i})_{\mathbf{U}_i^{-i}}\|_2^2 + \|\Delta_{\hat{\mathbf{S}}_i^{-i}\cap\mathbf{S}_i^{-i^*}}\|_2\|\tilde{\Delta}_{\hat{\mathbf{S}}_i^{-i}\cap\mathbf{S}_i^{-i^*}}\|_2\\ &\le \|\theta((\hat{\mathbf{Z}}^i_{-i})_{\mathbf{U}_i^{-i}},\kappa)\|_2\|({\mathbf{Z}^{i^*}}_{-i})_{\mathbf{U}_i^{-i}} - (\hat{\mathbf{Z}}^i_{-i})_{\mathbf{U}_i^{-i}}\|_2\\ &+ \kappa\|\Delta\|_2^2 + \|\Delta\|_2\|\tilde{\Delta}_{\hat{\mathbf{S}}_i^{-i}\cap\mathbf{S}_i^{-i^*}}\|_2\\ &\le \|\theta((\hat{\mathbf{Z}}^i_{-i})_{\mathbf{U}_i^{-i}},\kappa)\|_2\|\Delta\|_2 + \kappa\|\Delta\|_2^2 + \|\Delta\|_2\|\tilde{\Delta}_{\hat{\mathbf{S}}_i^{-i}\cap\mathbf{S}_i^{-i^*}}\|_2\end{aligned} \tag{33}$$

On the other hand, $\Delta^\top {\boldsymbol{X}^{(-i)}}^\top \boldsymbol{X}^{(-i)}\Delta \ge \kappa_0^2\|\Delta\|_2^2$. It follows from (33) that

$$\begin{aligned}&2\kappa_0^2\|\Delta\|_2^2 \le \|\theta((\hat{\mathbf{Z}}^i_{-i})_{\mathbf{U}_i^{-i}},\kappa)\|_2\|\Delta\|_2 + \kappa\|\Delta\|_2^2\\ &+ \|\Delta\|_2\|\tilde{\Delta}_{\hat{\mathbf{S}}_i^{-i}\cap\mathbf{S}_i^{-i^*}}\|_2\end{aligned}$$

When $\|\Delta\|_2 \ne 0$, we have

$$2\kappa_0^2\|\Delta\|_2 \le \|\theta((\hat{\mathbf{Z}}^i_{-i})_{\mathbf{U}_i^{-i}},\kappa)\|_2 + \kappa\|\Delta\|_2 + \|\tilde{\Delta}_{\hat{\mathbf{S}}_i^{-i}\cap\mathbf{S}_i^{-i^*}}\|_2$$

$$\Rightarrow \|\Delta\|_2 \le \frac{\|\theta((\hat{\mathbf{Z}}^i_{-i})_{\mathbf{U}_i^{-i}},\kappa)\|_2 + \|\tilde{\Delta}_{\hat{\mathbf{S}}_i^{-i}\cap\mathbf{S}_i^{-i^*}}\|_2}{2\kappa_0^2 - \kappa} \tag{34}$$

According to the definition of θ, it can be verified that $\theta((\hat{\mathbf{Z}}^i_{-i})_{k_{-i}},\kappa) = \max\{0, \frac{\gamma\mathbb{I}_{\mathbf{Z}_{ik}=0}\mathbf{F}^{\tilde{\mathbf{S}}}_{ki}}{b} - \kappa|\hat{\mathbf{Z}}_{ki} - b|\}$ for $k_{-i} \in \mathbf{U}_i^{-i}\cap\hat{\mathbf{S}}_i^{-i}$, and $\theta((\hat{\mathbf{Z}}^i_{-i})_{k_{-i}},\kappa) = \max\{0, \frac{\gamma\mathbb{I}_{\mathbf{Z}_{ik}=0}\mathbf{F}^{\tilde{\mathbf{S}}}_{ki}}{b} - \kappa b\}$ for $k_{-i} \in \mathbf{U}_i^{-i}\setminus\hat{\mathbf{S}}_i^{-i}$. Therefore,

$$\begin{aligned}&\|\theta((\hat{\mathbf{Z}}^i_{-i})_{\mathbf{U}_i^{-i}},\kappa)\|_2\\ &= \Big(\sum_{k\in\mathbf{U}_i\cap\hat{\mathbf{S}}_i}(\max\{0, \frac{\gamma\mathbb{I}_{\mathbf{Z}_{ik}=0}\mathbf{F}^{\tilde{\mathbf{S}}}_{ki}}{b} - \kappa|\hat{\mathbf{Z}}_{ki} - b|\})^2 +\\ &\sum_{k\in\mathbf{U}_i\setminus\hat{\mathbf{S}}_i}(\max\{0, \frac{\gamma\mathbb{I}_{\mathbf{Z}_{ik}=0}\mathbf{F}^{\tilde{\mathbf{S}}}_{ki}}{b} - \kappa b\})^2\Big)^{\frac{1}{2}}\end{aligned} \tag{35}$$

and it follows that

$$\begin{aligned}&\|\mathbf{Z}^{i^*} - \hat{\mathbf{Z}}^i\|_2 = \|\Delta\|_2\\ &\le \frac{1}{2\kappa_0^2 - \kappa}\Bigg(\Big(\sum_{k\in\mathbf{U}_i\cap\hat{\mathbf{S}}_i}(\max\{0, \frac{\gamma\mathbb{I}_{\mathbf{Z}_{ik}=0}\mathbf{F}^{\tilde{\mathbf{S}}}_{ki}}{b} - \kappa|\hat{\mathbf{Z}}_{ki} - b|\})^2 +\\ &\sum_{k\in\mathbf{U}_i\setminus\hat{\mathbf{S}}_i}(\max\{0, \frac{\gamma\mathbb{I}_{\mathbf{Z}_{ik}=0}\mathbf{F}^{\tilde{\mathbf{S}}}_{ki}}{b} - \kappa b\})^2\Big)^{\frac{1}{2}} + \|\tilde{\Delta}_{\hat{\mathbf{S}}_i^{-i}\cap\mathbf{S}_i^{-i^*}}\|_2\Bigg)\end{aligned} \tag{36}$$

where $\tilde{\Delta}_{m_{-i}} = -(2{\boldsymbol{X}^{(-i)}}^\top \boldsymbol{X}^{(-i)}\Delta)_{m_{-i}} = -2\lambda\mathbb{I}_{\mathbf{Z}^i_m{}^*\hat{\mathbf{Z}}^i_m<0} - 0\mathbb{I}_{\mathbf{Z}^i_m{}^*\hat{\mathbf{Z}}^i_m>0}$ for $m \in \hat{\mathbf{S}}_i \cap \mathbf{S}^*_i$. This proves the result of this theorem. □

Proof of Theorem 2. Let $\boldsymbol{Y} = \tilde{\boldsymbol{X}}$. By the proof of Lemma 1, we have

$$\|2{\boldsymbol{Y}^{(-i)}}^\top \boldsymbol{Y}^{(-i)}\tilde{\mathbf{Z}}^i_{-i} + \dot{\mathbf{P}}(\tilde{\mathbf{Z}}^i)\|_2 = 0$$

It follows that

$$\begin{aligned}&\|2{\boldsymbol{X}^{(-i)}}^\top \boldsymbol{X}^{(-i)}\tilde{\mathbf{Z}}^i_{-i} + \dot{\mathbf{P}}(\tilde{\mathbf{Z}}^i)\|_2\\ &= \|2{\boldsymbol{X}^{(-i)}}^\top \boldsymbol{X}^{(-i)}\tilde{\mathbf{Z}}^i_{-i} - 2{\boldsymbol{Y}^{(-i)}}^\top \boldsymbol{Y}^{(-i)}\tilde{\mathbf{Z}}^i_{-i}\\ &+ 2{\boldsymbol{Y}^{(-i)}}^\top \boldsymbol{Y}^{(-i)}\tilde{\mathbf{Z}}^i_{-i} + \dot{\mathbf{P}}(\tilde{\mathbf{Z}}^i)\|_2\\ &\le \|2{\boldsymbol{X}^{(-i)}}^\top \boldsymbol{X}^{(-i)}\tilde{\mathbf{Z}}^i_{-i} - 2{\boldsymbol{Y}^{(-i)}}^\top \boldsymbol{Y}^{(-i)}\tilde{\mathbf{Z}}^i_{-i}\|_2\\ &+ \|2{\boldsymbol{Y}^{(-i)}}^\top \boldsymbol{Y}^{(-i)}\tilde{\mathbf{Z}}^i_{-i} + \dot{\mathbf{P}}(\tilde{\mathbf{Z}}^i)\|_2\\ &= \|2{\boldsymbol{X}^{(-i)}}^\top \boldsymbol{X}^{(-i)}\tilde{\mathbf{Z}}^i_{-i} - 2{\boldsymbol{Y}^{(-i)}}^\top \boldsymbol{Y}^{(-i)}\tilde{\mathbf{Z}}^i_{-i}\|_2\\ &\le \|2{\boldsymbol{X}^{(-i)}}^\top(\boldsymbol{X}^{(-i)} - \boldsymbol{Y}^{(-i)})\tilde{\mathbf{Z}}^i_{-i}\|_2\\ &+ \|2(\boldsymbol{X}^{(-i)} - \boldsymbol{Y}^{(-i)})^\top \boldsymbol{Y}^{(-i)}\tilde{\mathbf{Z}}^i_{-i}\|_2\end{aligned} \tag{37}$$

By $\tilde{F}(\mathbf{Z}^i) \le \tilde{F}(\mathbf{0})$, we have $\|\tilde{\mathbf{Z}}^i_{-i}\|_2 \le A$. Let $k_0 \ge 2$ and $p = k - k_0 \ge 4$. By Lemma 2, with probability at least $1 - 6e^{-p}$, $\|\boldsymbol{X} - \boldsymbol{Y}\|_2 \le C_{k,k_0}$. It follows from (37) that

$$\|2{\boldsymbol{X}^{(-i)}}^\top \boldsymbol{X}^{(-i)}\tilde{\mathbf{Z}}^i_{-i} + \dot{\mathbf{P}}(\tilde{\mathbf{Z}}^i)\|_2$$

$$\leq \sigma_{\max}(\boldsymbol{X})C_{k,k_0}A + C_{k,k_0}(\sigma_{\max}(\boldsymbol{X}) + C_{k,k_0})A$$
$$= C_{k,k_0}A(2\sigma_{\max}(\boldsymbol{X}) + C_{k,k_0})$$

Also, by Lemma 1,

$$\|2\boldsymbol{X}^{(-i)\top}\boldsymbol{X}^{(-i)}\mathbf{Z}^{i*}_{-i} + \dot{\mathbf{P}}(\mathbf{Z}^{i*}_{-i})\|_2 = 0$$

Let $\Delta = \mathbf{Z}^{i*}_{-i} - \tilde{\mathbf{Z}}^{i}_{-i}$, $\tilde{\Delta} = \dot{\mathbf{P}}(\mathbf{Z}^{i*}) - \dot{\mathbf{P}}(\tilde{\mathbf{Z}}^{i})$.

$$\|2\boldsymbol{X}^{(-i)\top}\boldsymbol{X}^{(-i)}\Delta + \tilde{\Delta}\|_2 \leq C_{k,k_0}A(2\sigma_{\max}(\boldsymbol{X}) + C_{k,k_0})$$

Now following the proof of Theorem 1, we have

$$\|\mathbf{Z}^{i*} - \tilde{\mathbf{Z}}^{i}\|_2 = \|\Delta\|_2$$
$$\leq \frac{1}{2\tau_0^2 - \tau}\Bigg(\Big(\sum_{k\in\mathbf{G}_i\cap\hat{\mathbf{S}}_i}(\max\{0, \frac{\gamma \mathbb{I}_{\mathbf{Z}_{ik}=0}\mathbf{F}^{\tilde{\mathbf{S}}}_{ki}}{b} - \kappa|\tilde{\mathbf{Z}}_{ki} - b|\})^2$$
$$+ \sum_{k\in\mathbf{G}_i\setminus\hat{\mathbf{S}}_i}(\max\{0, \frac{\gamma \mathbb{I}_{\mathbf{Z}_{ik}=0}\mathbf{F}^{\tilde{\mathbf{S}}}_{ki}}{b} - \kappa b\})^2\Big)^{\frac{1}{2}} + \|\mathbf{t}\|_2$$
$$+ C_{k,k_0}A(2\sigma_{\max}(\boldsymbol{X}) + C_{k,k_0})\Bigg) \tag{38}$$

□

7.2 MORE DETAILS IN THE PAPER AND MORE EXPERIMENTAL RESULTS

The SC baseline in this paper uses the self-tuning spectral clustering method (Zelnik-manor and Perona, 2005), and we choose this method due to its advantage of adaptively setting the kernel bandwidth for the Gaussian kernel similarity. More concretely, we construct a similarity matrix using Gaussian kernel, and the bandwidth of the Gaussian kernel similarity between two points is determined by the local statistics of the neighborhoods of these two points. We set the distance to the 7-th nearest neighbor as the local statistics, which is also the default choice suggested by the paper, then perform spectral clustering on such similarity matrix to obtain the clustering results for SC in Table 1. In addition, various sparse graph methods, including ℓ^1-Graph, ℓ^2-Rℓ^1-Graph and NRℓ^1-Graph, constructs a sparse graph upon which spectral clustering is applied to find the clusters.

It is worthwhile to mention the meaning of the condition that $\mathbf{F}^{\tilde{\mathbf{S}}}_{ki} \geq 0$ for all $k \in \Lambda_i$ in (9). Let $k \in \Lambda_i$, if the number of point $\mathbf{x}_i$'s neighbors with zero k-th element of the sparse codes is larger than that with nonzero k-th element of the sparse codes, which indicates that the neighbors of $\mathbf{x}_i$ suggest that a zero k-th element of the sparse code of $\mathbf{x}_i$ is preferable, then $\mathbf{F}^{\tilde{\mathbf{S}}}_{ki} \geq 0$ and $\mathbf{F}^{\tilde{\mathbf{S}}}_{ki}$ quantitatively measures the penalty if the sparse code element $\mathbf{Z}^i_k$ is nonzero while the neighbors of $\mathbf{x}_i$ suggest that $\mathbf{Z}^i_k = 0$ is preferable. The optimization helps point $\mathbf{x}_i$ make a sensible choice by considering the suggestion of its neighbors. We observe that $\mathbf{F}^{\tilde{\mathbf{S}}}_{ki} \geq 0$ for all $k \in \Lambda_i$ happens in all the data sets used in the experiments.

The standard deviation values of the NMI by different clustering methods on the MNIST data is as follows. NRℓ^1-Graph-RP: 0.0118; NRℓ^1-Graph: 0.0137; ℓ^2-Rℓ^1-Graph: 0.0114; SMCE: 0.0166; ℓ^1-Graph: 0.0039; SC: 0.0071; KM: 0.0094. We have conducted paired t-test and conclude that both NRℓ^1-Graph and NRℓ^1-Graph-RP are statistically better than other baseline methods with p-value less than 0.05 in many cases. For example, the p-value of the paired t-test between the accuracy of NRℓ^1-Graph and SMCE is less than 0.05 on the COIL-20, COIL-100 and Yale-B data.

We also present clustering results on the first c clusters for COIL-100, CMU PIE and UMIST Face Data in Table 2, 3 and 4 respectively.

In order to investigate the parameter sensitivity of our model, namely how the performance of NRℓ^1-Graph varies with parameter γ and K, we vary γ and K and illustrate the result on the UMIST Face Database in Figure 2 and Figure 3 respectively in this supplementary. The performance of NRℓ^1-Graph is noticeably better than other competing algorithms over a relatively large range of both λ and K, which demonstrates the robustness of our algorithm with respect to the parameter settings. We also observe that a too small K (near to 1) results in under regularization, and a too big K (near to 15) or too big γ (close to 0.45) risks over regularization.

Table 2: Clustering Results on COIL-100 Database. c in the left column is the cluster number, i.e. the first c clusters of the entire data are used for clustering. c has the same meaning in the following tables.

COIL-100 / # Clusters	Measure	KM	SC	ℓ^1-Graph	SMCE	ℓ^2-Rℓ^1-Graph	NRℓ^1-Graph
c = 20	AC	0.5875	0.4493	0.5340	0.6208	0.6681	**0.9236**
	NMI	0.7448	0.6680	0.7681	0.7993	0.7933	**0.9610**
c = 40	AC	0.5774	0.4160	0.5819	0.6028	0.5944	**0.8771**
	NMI	0.7662	0.6682	0.7911	0.7919	0.7991	**0.9504**
c = 60	AC	0.5330	0.3225	0.5824	0.5877	0.6009	**0.7808**
	NMI	0.7603	0.6254	0.8310	0.7971	0.8310	**0.8924**
c = 80	AC	0.5062	0.3135	0.5380	0.5740	0.5632	**0.8177**
	NMI	0.7458	0.6071	0.8034	0.7931	0.8036	**0.9208**
c = 100	AC	0.4928	0.2833	0.5310	0.5625	0.5625	**0.7846**
	NMI	0.7522	0.5913	0.8015	0.8057	0.8059	**0.9238**

Table 3: Clustering Results on CMU PIE Data

CMU PIE / # Clusters	Measure	KM	SC	ℓ^1-Graph	SMCE	ℓ^2-Rℓ^1-Graph	NRℓ^1-Graph
c = 20	AC	0.1327	0.1288	0.2435	0.2321	0.3212	**0.3606**
	NMI	0.1220	0.1342	0.2895	0.2942	0.4007	**0.4876**
c = 40	AC	0.1054	0.0867	0.2443	0.1752	0.3412	**0.3555**
	NMI	0.1534	0.1422	0.3344	0.2976	0.4789	**0.4834**
c = 68	AC	0.0829	0.0718	0.2318	0.1603	0.3012	**0.3190**
	NMI	0.1865	0.1760	0.3378	0.3406	**0.5121**	0.4993

Table 4: Clustering Results on UMIST Face Data

UMIST Face / # Clusters	Measure	KM	SC	ℓ^1-Graph	SMCE	ℓ^2-Rℓ^1-Graph	NRℓ^1-Graph
c = 8	AC	0.4330	0.4789	0.4930	0.4695	0.5399	**0.6056**
	NMI	0.5373	0.5236	0.5516	0.5744	0.5721	**0.5749**
c = 12	AC	0.4478	0.4655	0.5195	0.4955	0.5706	**0.6246**
	NMI	0.6121	0.6049	0.6086	0.6445	0.6994	**0.7244**
c = 16	AC	0.4297	0.4539	0.4539	0.4747	0.4700	**0.6982**
	NMI	0.6343	0.6453	0.6582	0.6909	0.6714	**0.7816**
c = 20	AC	0.4216	0.4174	0.4417	0.4452	0.4991	**0.6765**
	NMI	0.6377	0.6095	0.6489	0.6641	0.6893	**0.7982**

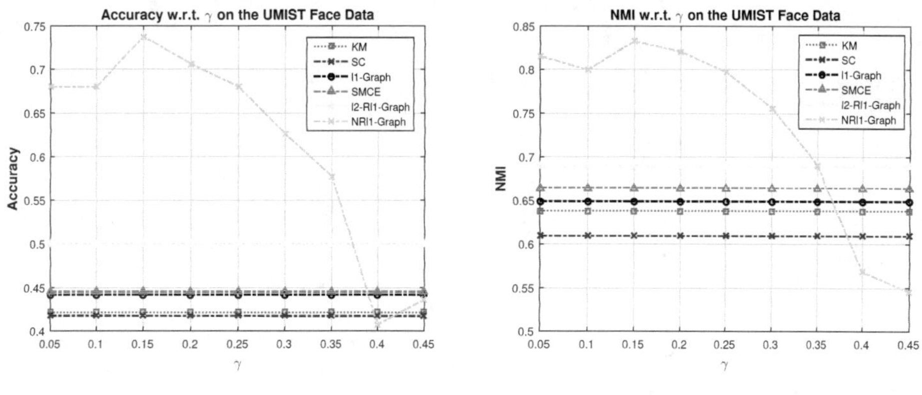

Figure 2: Clustering performance with different values of γ, i.e. the weight for the regularization term in NRℓ^1-Graph, on the UMIST Face Data. Left: Accuracy; Right: NMI

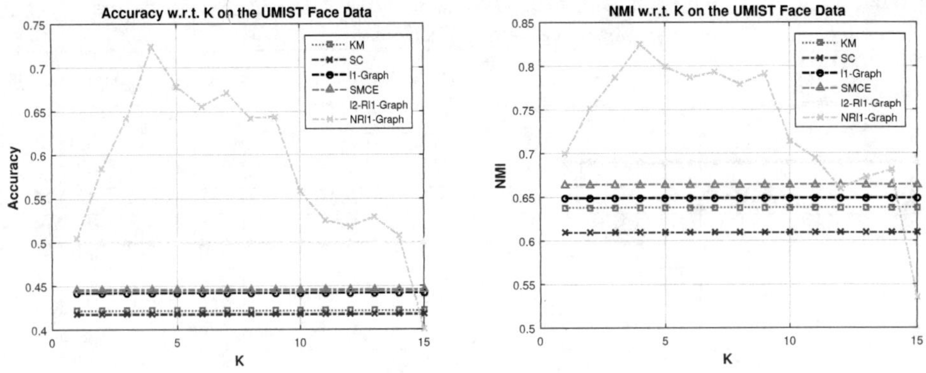

Figure 3: Clustering performance with different values of K, i.e. the number of nearest neighbors for the regularization term in NRℓ^1-Graph, on the UMIST Face Data. Left: Accuracy; Right: NMI

Feature-to-Feature Regression for a Two-Step Conditional Independence Test

Qinyi Zhang
Department of Statistics
University of Oxford
qinyi.zhang@stats.ox.ac.uk

Sarah Filippi
School of Public Health
Department of Mathematics
Imperial College London
s.filippi@imperial.ac.uk

Seth Flaxman
Department of Statistics
University of Oxford
flaxman@stats.ox.ac.uk

Dino Sejdinovic
Department of Statistics
University of Oxford
dino.sejdinovic@stats.ox.ac.uk

Abstract

The algorithms for causal discovery and more broadly for learning the structure of graphical models require well calibrated and consistent conditional independence (CI) tests. We revisit the CI tests which are based on two-step procedures and involve regression with subsequent (unconditional) independence test (RESIT) on regression residuals and investigate the assumptions under which these tests operate. In particular, we demonstrate that when going beyond simple functional relationships with additive noise, such tests can lead to an inflated number of false discoveries. We study the relationship of these tests with those based on dependence measures using reproducing kernel Hilbert spaces (RKHS) and propose an extension of RESIT which uses RKHS-valued regression. The resulting test inherits the simple two-step testing procedure of RESIT, while giving correct Type I control and competitive power. When used as a component of the PC algorithm, the proposed test is more robust to the case where hidden variables induce a switching behaviour in the associations present in the data.

1 INTRODUCTION

Conditional independence tests are an important component of causal discovery (cf. [Shalizi, 2016, Chapter 28]). For example, the popular PC algorithm [Spirtes et al., 2000] for recovering dependence structure among a set of variables starts from a complete undirected graph and recursively removes the edges between variables based on conditional independence testing. With normally distributed variables and linear relationships, conditional independence testing can be performed using estimates of partial correlation. Namely, when testing the hypothesis that $X \perp\!\!\!\perp Y | Z$, partial correlation is the correlation of the residuals of X and Y after linearly regressing each of them on Z separately. However, in the presence of nonlinearities and when one needs to condition on a random vector Z of larger dimensions, conditional independence testing is a challenging problem [Bergsma, 2004]. A popular approach for conditional independence testing within PC algorithm is RESIT (REgression with Subsequent Independence Test) [Hoyer et al., 2009, Peters et al., 2014], which can incorporate nonlinearities by extending the partial correlation approach in the following two ways: (1) it uses a flexible nonparametric regression of X and Y on Z, and (2) the subsequent test is based on a nonlinear dependence measure between the resulting residuals. While RESIT greatly broadens the class of models in which causal discovery with conditional independence tests is possible, as we will see, it is sensitive to departures from its modelling assumption, which itself is not straightforward to verify. In particular, it is likely to give an inflated number of false positives in the presence of associations which do not directly conform to functional relationships (as illustrated in Figure 1).

In the last decade, kernel embeddings of probability measures [Smola et al., 2007, Sriperumbudur et al., 2010] have been widely used to construct nonparametric hypothesis tests, including tests for the two-sample problem [Gretton et al., 2007, 2012], independence [Gretton et al., 2008, Chwialkowski et al., 2015], conditional independence [Fukumizu et al., 2008, Zhang et al., 2011, Doran et al., 2014], three-variable interaction [Sejdinovic et al., 2013], joint independence [Pfister et al., 2016], and goodness of fit [Chwialkowski et al., 2016]. The various kernel-based tests for conditional independence [Fukumizu et al., 2008, Zhang et al., 2011, Doran et al., 2014] allow to measure more general forms of conditional dependence than RESIT. However, these approaches typically involve complex statistics and computationally expensive procedures to estimate their distributions under the null hypothesis. In this paper we propose a kernel-based conditional independence approach which aims to strike a balance between the simplicity of the RESIT approach and the robustness to the functional association and additive noise assumptions made by the RESIT. The procedure we introduce is a test for *weak conditional independence* as defined by [Daudin, 1980] since, like RESIT, it focuses on individual effects[1] of the conditioning variable Z on X and Y. As such, it does not fully characterise conditional independence, but does benefit from a simpler testing procedure and an improved power in comparison to the "strong" tests which do characterise conditional independence. When these individual effects are not present and as such weak CI tests are insufficient to detect a complex joint effect on (X, Y), they can be combined with tests for multivariate interaction [Sejdinovic et al., 2013].

An independent recent work, Strobl et al. [2017], considers a very similar approach to ours – indeed, the method we propose is essentially equivalent to the RCoT approach of Strobl et al. [2017], which in addition operates on explicit primal representations of feature maps leading to a decreased computational cost. However, Strobl et al. [2017] do not comment on the connections with the two-step procedures for CI testing and RESIT. Hence, our contribution is to provide the unifying framework which places the proposed method as a generalisation of RESIT, pointing the deficiencies of RESIT and the interplay between its structural assumptions and nonlinear dependencies. In addition, while RCoT uses approximations to the null distributions with parametric families, we simply employ a permutation-based approach using the two-step interpretation of the proposed test, and do not observe any deviations from the desired significance level in the experiments. The test maintains correct Type I control even under the challenging switching associations induced by hidden variables, where RESIT is inappropriate.

In Section 2, we overview the key notion of weak conditional independence and the existing approach for testing it as well as three related tests for general conditional independence using kernel methods. In Section 3 we develop our novel procedure for weak conditional independence testing. Section 4 evaluates the performance of our approach and compares it to RESIT and other conditional independence tests on both synthetic and real-world data.

2 BACKGROUND

We start by introducing notation and reviewing the existing kernel-based conditional independence tests. Let $\mathcal{X}$, $\mathcal{Y}$ and $\mathcal{Z}$ be non-empty measurable spaces, with Borel σ-algebras $\mathcal{B}_\mathcal{X}$, $\mathcal{B}_\mathcal{Y}$ and $\mathcal{B}_\mathcal{Z}$ respectively. Let k, l and m be measurable positive definite kernels on these respective domains with the corresponding reproducing kernel Hilbert spaces (RKHSs) $\mathcal{H}_\mathcal{X}$, $\mathcal{H}_\mathcal{Y}$, $\mathcal{H}_\mathcal{Z}$. Let (X, Y, Z) be a triple of random variables with the joint probability law P_{XYZ} on $(\mathcal{X} \times \mathcal{Y} \times \mathcal{Z}, \mathcal{B}_\mathcal{X} \times \mathcal{B}_\mathcal{Y} \times \mathcal{B}_\mathcal{Z})$. We will assume $\mathbb{E}_{X\sim P_X}[k(X,X)] < \infty$ and similarly for l and m, which will ensure that $\mathcal{H}_\mathcal{X} \subset L^2_\mathcal{X}(P_X) = \{f : \mathbb{E}[f^2(X)] < \infty\}$, and similarly $\mathcal{H}_\mathcal{Y} \subset L^2_\mathcal{Y}(P_Y)$ and $\mathcal{H}_\mathcal{Z} \subset L^2_\mathcal{Z}(P_Z)$ [Steinwart and Christmann, 2008, Section 4.3]. We will also assume that the kernels k, l and m are characteristic, such that their RKHSs are dense in the corresponding L^2-spaces [Sriperumbudur et al., 2010].

[1] Since regressions of X and Y on Z are done separately and hence cannot capture the joint dependence of (X, Y).

2.1 WEAK CONDITIONAL INDEPENDENCE

Conditional independence $X \perp\!\!\!\perp Y | Z$ is equivalent to

$$\mathbb{P}(X \in \mathsf{A} \,|\, Z)\,\mathbb{P}(Y \in \mathsf{B} \,|\, Z) = \mathbb{P}(X \in \mathsf{A}, Y \in \mathsf{B} \,|\, Z) \quad (1)$$

as random variables, for all measurable sets $\mathsf{A} \in \mathcal{B}_\mathcal{X}$ and $\mathsf{B} \in \mathcal{B}_\mathcal{Y}$, which in turn can be written as

$$\begin{aligned}&\mathbb{E}_Z\left[\mathbf{1}\{Z \in \mathsf{C}\}\mathbb{P}(X \in \mathsf{A} \,|\, Z)\,\mathbb{P}(Y \in \mathsf{B} \,|\, Z)\right]\\ &= \mathbb{E}_Z\left[\mathbf{1}\{Z \in \mathsf{C}\}\mathbb{P}(X \in \mathsf{A}, Y \in \mathsf{B} \,|\, Z)\right]\\ &= \mathbb{P}(X \in \mathsf{A}, Y \in \mathsf{B}, Z \in \mathsf{C})\end{aligned}$$

for all measurable sets $\mathsf{A} \in \mathcal{B}_\mathcal{X}$, $\mathsf{B} \in \mathcal{B}_\mathcal{Y}$ and $\mathsf{C} \in \mathcal{B}_\mathcal{Z}$. Relaxation of this property which only requires it to hold for $\mathsf{C} = \mathcal{Z}$ gives rise to the notion of *weak conditional independence*, i.e. that $\forall \mathsf{A} \in \mathcal{B}_\mathcal{X}, \mathsf{B} \in \mathcal{B}_\mathcal{Y}$

$$\mathbb{E}_Z\left[\mathbb{P}(X \in \mathsf{A} \,|\, Z)\,\mathbb{P}(Y \in \mathsf{B} \,|\, Z)\right] = \mathbb{P}(X \in \mathsf{A}, Y \in \mathsf{B}), \quad (2)$$

which we can write as $\mathbb{E}_Z[P_{X|Z} \otimes P_{Y|Z}] = P_{XY}$, understood as the equality of probability measures defined on $(\mathcal{X} \times \mathcal{Y}, \mathcal{B}_\mathcal{X} \times \mathcal{B}_\mathcal{Y})$. Weak conditional independence is studied by Daudin [1980], who interprets it in terms of zero expected conditional covariances of square integrable functions, i.e.

$$\mathbb{E}_Z\left[\mathrm{Cov}\left[f(X), g(Y)|Z\right]\right] = 0 \quad (3)$$

for all $f \in L^2_\mathcal{X}(P_X)$ and $g \in L^2_\mathcal{Y}(P_Y)$. In other words, the residuals in all square integrable functions of X and Y, given Z, are uncorrelated. Fukumizu et al. [2004] give another characterisation of weak conditional independence using conditional cross-covariance operators between RKHSs. Namely, they define the operator $\Sigma_{YX|Z} \colon \mathcal{H}_\mathcal{X} \to \mathcal{H}_\mathcal{Y}$, such that $\forall f \in \mathcal{H}_\mathcal{X}, g \in \mathcal{H}_\mathcal{Y}$

$$\langle g, \Sigma_{YX|Z} f\rangle_{\mathcal{H}_\mathcal{Y}} = \mathbb{E}_Z\left[\mathrm{Cov}\left[f(X), g(Y)|Z\right]\right], \quad (4)$$

under the additional smoothness assumptions on conditioning variables, i.e. that $\forall f \in \mathcal{H}_\mathcal{X}, g \in \mathcal{H}_\mathcal{Y}$, $\mathbb{E}[f(X)|Z = \cdot]$ and $\mathbb{E}[g(Y)|Z = \cdot]$ both belong to $\mathcal{H}_\mathcal{Z}$ [Fukumizu et al., 2004, Proposition 4], [Alpay, 2001]. Theorem 8 of Fukumizu et al. [2004] then shows that, for characteristic kernels, this operator vanishes if and only if weak conditional independence holds. i.e.

$$\Sigma_{YX|Z} = 0 \iff \mathbb{E}[P_{X|Z} \otimes P_{Y|Z}] = P_{XY}. \quad (5)$$

The conditional independence clearly implies weak conditional independence but the converse is not true. A simple counterexample is where X, Y and Z are all pairwise independent, but are jointly dependent due to a three-variable interaction. For a concrete case, similar to the one described in Sejdinovic et al. [2013], let $X, Y, W \overset{i.i.d.}{\sim} \mathcal{N}(0, 1)$ and define $Z = \operatorname{sign}(XY)|W|$. In this case, $\mathbb{E}(f(X)|Z) = \mathbb{E}(f(X))$ and $\mathbb{E}(g(Y)|Z) = \mathbb{E}(g(Y))$ implying that LHS in (3) vanishes. However, given Z, the pair (X, Y) can only take values in two out of four quadrants, so that X and Y are clearly conditionally dependent given Z. Essentially, whenever the variables are pairwise independent but jointly dependent, any two variables are weakly conditionally independent given the third and need not be "strongly" conditionally independent. We note however that nonparametric tests exist which are directly aimed at such multivariate interaction: Sejdinovic et al. [2013] reports stronger power than the conditional independence tests in these cases. Thus, we challenge the paradigm by which all departures from conditional independence should be tested with the same procedure and instead choose to focus on weak conditional independence testing. When multivariate interaction is present and the individual effects of Z on X and on Y are weak or non-existing and only the joint dependence of (X, Y) on Z is possible to detect, then arguably (X, Y) should be considered a single random vector.

2.2 RESIT: THE TWO-STEP APPROACH

RESIT approach [Hoyer et al., 2009, Peters et al., 2014, Flaxman et al., 2015] converts a conditional independence testing problem into an unconditional one by removing the effect of a confounder Z through a flexible nonparametric regression. More specifically, it assumes an additive noise model where X and Y are expressed as some deterministic functions of Z plus an additive zero-mean noise term, i.e.

$$X = f(Z) + n_x \quad (6)$$

$$Y = g(Z) + n_y \quad (7)$$

where n_x and n_y are zero-mean random variables independent of Z. Under the assumptions (6) and (7), the conditional independence can be characterised as:

$$X \perp\!\!\!\perp Y | Z \iff n_x \perp\!\!\!\perp n_y. \quad (8)$$

Thus, the test proceeds by first regressing X on Z and Y on Z, and then testing for the (unconditional) independence between the fitted residuals of these regressions $\hat{\epsilon}_x = X - \hat{\mathbb{E}}[X|Z]$ and $\hat{\epsilon}_y = Y - \hat{\mathbb{E}}[Y|Z]$. This approach obviously crucially depends on the regression procedure in order to remove the effect of Z by using an appropriate model of regression functions f and g. Gaussian Process regression and kernel ridge regression are often used for the first step, whereas Hilbert-Schmidt Independence Criterion [Gretton et al., 2008] can be used in the second step in order to capture potentially *nonlinear dependence* between residuals. Because of its focus on individual effects of the conditioning variable Z on X and on Y, it is clear that RESIT only tests for weak conditional independence.

As we will demonstrate below, RESIT can result in a substantial inflation of false discoveries when assumptions (6) and (7) are violated. Indeed, RESIT is unable to handle non-functional dependence between the variables X and Y and the conditioning variable Z – the regression will not remove the dependence on Z and the fitted residuals will be dependent even in the cases where X and Y are independent given Z. We see this as an undesirable property for many real data applications, especially when conditioning on a multivariate Z, as these assumptions are difficult to verify and may be violated. In particular, there could be hidden categorical confounders which introduce a switching behaviour in the way X and Y depend on Z, i.e. X and Y are functionally dependent on Z and those confounders, but not on Z itself. An example of such a relationship is illustrated in Figure 2 which plots the total expenditure on health per capita vs the gross national income per capita for 178 countries: there is a superposition of two functional relationships corresponding to two subsets of countries depending on whether their economy relies on oil [WHO, 2009].

For a simple example of how brittle the RESIT approach is, consider the dataset presented in Figure 1. Here, the dependence of both X and Y on Z is a mixture of two functional relationships (linear for X, quadratic for Y), arguably very simple – but also indicating the presence of some latent switching mechanism for both X and Y. However, the conditional expectations in both cases are constant and thus independent of Z. Hence, the fitted regression functions do not capture any dependence on Z and as a result, the residuals (rightmost plot) are clearly dependent, regardless of whether in fact $X \perp\!\!\!\perp Y | Z$ (indeed, in this case, as described in Section 4.2, the conditional independence does hold because switching variables are independent). RESIT with a nonlinear independence test on these residuals will therefore falsely reject the null hypothesis. This is a highly undesirable property as it leads to an inflated number of false positives, and when the same method is used inside PC algorithm, it can potentially result in reporting spurious causal links as illustrated in Section 4.3. This problem is exacerbated for Z being a random vector, even of a small dimension, since such cases which go beyond simple functional relationships become difficult to notice. One way to avoid the inflation of false positives in these cases is to only test for *linear dependence* between the residuals. However, this clearly results in a reduction of power as it misses many alternative models where (6) and (7) are satisfied and n_x and n_y are nonlinearly dependent.

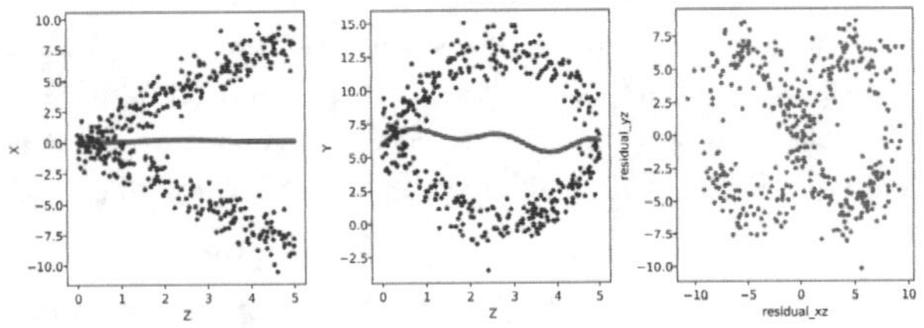

Figure 1: Data generated from the null model of Section 4.2 and kernel ridge regressions are used to remove dependency on Z. Left: X against Z. Middle: Y against Z. Simulated data (blue) and fitted values (red). Right: residuals of the regression for Y against residuals of the regression for X which clearly exhibits non-linear dependency.

2.3 KERNEL TESTS FOR "STRONG" CONDITIONAL INDEPENDENCE

In contrast to the RESIT test, there have been several approaches in the literature that aim to measure all forms of conditional dependence, typically at the expense of more complex statistics which have the distribution under the null hypothesis that is more difficult to estimate.

Cross-Covariance Operators Fukumizu et al. [2008] proposed a general nonparametric characterisation of conditional independence based on the conditional cross-covariance operators between RKHSs. The cross-covariance operator $\Sigma_{YX} : \mathcal{H}_{\mathcal{X}} \to \mathcal{H}_{\mathcal{Y}}$ is defined through

$$\langle g, \Sigma_{YX} f\rangle = \text{Cov}(f(X), g(Y)), \;\; f \in \mathcal{H}_{\mathcal{X}},\, g \in \mathcal{H}_{\mathcal{Y}},$$

i.e., it is a nonlinear extension of the cross-covariance matrix (cf. Baker [1973], Fukumizu et al. [2004]). The conditional cross covariance operator $\Sigma_{YX|Z}$ is then defined as

$$\Sigma_{YX|Z} = \Sigma_{YX} - \Sigma_{YZ}\Sigma_{ZZ}^{-1}\Sigma_{ZX} \tag{9}$$

in analogy to the conditional cross-covariance matrix $C_{YX|Z} = C_{YX} - C_{YZ}C_{ZZ}^{-1}C_{ZX}$ formula for jointly Gaussian random vectors.

The conditional dependence measure can then be based on estimating $\|\Sigma_{\ddot{Y}\ddot{X}|Z}\|_{HS}^2$, where $\ddot{Y} = (Y, Z)$ and $\ddot{X} = (X, Z)$, as it can be shown [Fukumizu et al., 2008] that $\Sigma_{\ddot{Y}\ddot{X}|Z} = 0$ if and only if $X \perp\!\!\!\perp Y|Z$ when the product of the three positive definite kernels, klm, results in a characteristic kernel on $\mathcal{X} \times \mathcal{Y} \times \mathcal{Z}$. In addition, Fukumizu et al. [2008] considers the conditional cross-correlation operators, which can be expressed as $V_{YX|Z} = \Sigma_{YY}^{-1}\Sigma_{YX|Z}\Sigma_{XX}^{-1}$.

The test statistics with these approaches however do not have clear asymptotic null distributions. Consequently, one needs to adopt a *local permutation-based approach* which needs to take into account an artificial discretisation of condition Z (e.g. through clustering) so that the marginal structures are preserved. As remarked by Zhang et al. [2011], this usually requires large sample size and the results become unreliable when the dimension of Z increases.

Kernel Conditional Independence Test (KCI-Test[2]) Following similar reasoning, Zhang et al. [2011] characterise conditional independence based on partial association [Daudin, 1980] where it was shown that

$$X \perp\!\!\!\perp Y|Z \iff \mathbb{E}(\tilde{f}\tilde{g}) = 0 \tag{10}$$

for all $\tilde{f} \in \mathcal{E}_{XZ} := \{\tilde{f} \in L^2_{\mathcal{X}\times\mathcal{Z}}(P_{XZ})|\mathbb{E}(\tilde{f}|Z) = 0\}$ and $\tilde{f}(\ddot{X}) = f(\ddot{X}) - \mathbb{E}(f|Z)$ for $f \in L^2_{\mathcal{X}\times\mathcal{Z}}(P_{XZ})$. The notations for $\tilde{g}$, g and $\mathcal{E}_{YZ}$ are defined similarly. As noted, if the functions f and g are restricted to the spaces $\mathcal{H}_{\mathcal{X}\times\mathcal{Z}}$ and $\mathcal{H}_{\mathcal{Y}\times\mathcal{Z}}$, then such characterisation is exactly the same as Fukumizu et al. [2008]. Zhang et al. [2011] derive an explicit formulae for the asymptotic null distribution and propose an approach for approximating it based on eigendecompositions of kernel matrices or fitting a parametric family. However, this null distribution becomes harder to accurately approximate in practice as the dimension of the conditioning variable increases.

Permutation-based Maximum Mean Discrepancy (MMD) Following the difficulties faced by the approaches of Fukumizu et al. [2008] and Zhang et al. [2011] in estimating the null distributions, Doran et al. [2014] introduce a reduction of the conditional independence testing problem into a two-sample testing one, by considering a carefully selected permutation which mimics a sample from $P_Z P_{X|Z} P_{Y|Z}$ for which the null hypothesis of conditional independence holds. While casting the problem as a simple two-sample test is attractive, promising a better calibration and improved performance in the cases where dimensionality of the conditioning variable is high, this approach does require a costly optimization procedure over the space of doubly stochastic matrices in order to select the required permutation.

3 PROPOSED METHOD

We have seen that RESIT, although a simple and effective conditional independence test for additive noise models, can lead to undesirable properties when the additive noise modelling assumption is violated. On the other hand, strong kernel-based independence tests require no restrictive assumptions on the type of the underlying relationships

[2]Termed by Zhang et al. [2011]

between the variables, but need complex and difficult to tune testing procedures, often requiring to solve difficult side-problems in order to have an estimate of the distribution under the null hypothesis (clustering the conditioning variable or optimisation over the space of permutations). Therefore, our goal is to identify an approach which aims to strike a balance between these two approaches, and construct a test which is more robust to the departures from the modelling assumption in (6) and (7). At the same time, we seek an approach which can be cast as an unconditional independence test on some form of regression residuals – allowing us to employ the well established existing methodology for unconditional tests, including straightforward permutation-based approaches for estimation of the null distribution. Using heuristic arguments, we derive in this section an intuitive test based on well known empirical mean RKHS quantities. The rigorous statistical analysis of this approach is left to further work.

We first note that the assumptions (6) and (7) specify that the conditional distributions $P_{X|Z=z}$ and $P_{Y|Z=z}$ depend on z only through the expectations $\mathbb{E}[X|Z=z]$ and $\mathbb{E}[Y|Z=z]$. Therefore, any additional dependence on z, e.g. in the conditional variance: $\text{Var}[X|Z=z] \neq \text{Var}[X]$ will not be captured by the regression approaches, implying that the residuals remain dependent by construction, leading to spurious rejections when nonlinear dependence tests on residuals are employed. Therefore, we are interested in also modelling how higher-order moments of these distributions depend on z, leading us to consider *conditional expectations of feature maps* $\mathbb{E}[\phi(X)|Z=z]$ and $\mathbb{E}[\psi(Y)|Z=z]$ for some $\phi\colon \mathcal{X} \to \mathcal{H}_{\mathcal{X}}$, $\psi\colon \mathcal{Y} \to \mathcal{H}_{\mathcal{Y}}$ and Hilbert spaces $\mathcal{H}_{\mathcal{X}}$, $\mathcal{H}_{\mathcal{Y}}$, i.e. the mean embeddings of the corresponding conditional distributions. For characteristic kernels [Sriperumbudur et al., 2010], these embeddings fully characterise the corresponding distributions (and thus, their dependence on z).

We thus propose the following two-step approach: first construct feature representations of X and Y and then perform the *vector-valued regression* of these feature representations of each of them on Z separately. Just like in RESIT, the second step is a test of independence between the resulting residuals, but note that the residuals are themselves elements of the corresponding (potentially infinite-dimensional) feature spaces. Fortunately, as we show in the remainder of this section, using the kernel trick allows to perform each of these steps without ever explicitly computing the feature maps. The final result is a simple test statistic, very similar to HSIC of Gretton et al. [2008], which lends itself to direct computation. Moreover, its null distribution can be straightforwardly estimated using a permutation-based approach. Thus, the key step of the procedure is the feature transformation of the responses in regression – we will see that this greatly relaxes the modelling assumptions and in particular allows to model complex dependencies between the responses and the conditioning variable which cannot be expressed in functional forms with additive noise.

Consider now k, l and m to be measurable positive definite kernels with the corresponding RKHSs $\mathcal{H}_{\mathcal{X}}$, $\mathcal{H}_{\mathcal{Y}}$, $\mathcal{H}_{\mathcal{Z}}$. We denote by $\phi(x) \in \mathcal{H}_{\mathcal{X}}$ and $\psi(y) \in \mathcal{H}_{\mathcal{Y}}$ the feature map representations of k and l. Note that Daudin's condition (3) for weak conditional independence can be written as

$$\begin{aligned} 0 &= \mathbb{E}_Z\left[\text{Cov}\left[f(X), g(Y)|Z\right]\right] \\ &= \mathbb{E}_{XYZ}\left[\left(f(X) - \mathbb{E}f(X|Z)\right)\left(g(Y) - \mathbb{E}g(Y|Z)\right)\right] \\ &= \mathbb{E}_{XYZ}\left[n_f(X,Z)n_g(Y,Z)\right] \end{aligned} \tag{11}$$

where we denoted $n_f(X,Z) = f(X) - \mathbb{E}f(X|Z)$, $n_g(Y,Z) = g(Y) - \mathbb{E}g(Y|Z)$ to be the regression residuals for X and Y transformed through square integrable functions $f \in L^2_{\mathcal{X}}(P_X)$ and $g \in L^2_{\mathcal{Y}}(P_Y)$. Note that these residuals would in general depend on Z and that they have mean zero by construction. Thus, weak conditional independence is equivalent to *uncorrelatedness* of residuals $n_f(X,Z)$ and $n_g(Y,Z)$ for all $f \in L^2_{\mathcal{X}}(P_X)$ and $g \in L^2_{\mathcal{Y}}(P_Y)$. Moreover, when $\mathcal{H}_{\mathcal{X}}$ and $\mathcal{H}_{\mathcal{Y}}$ are dense in $L^2_{\mathcal{X}}(P_X)$ and $L^2_{\mathcal{Y}}(P_Y)$, it suffices to consider $f \in \mathcal{H}_{\mathcal{X}}$ and $g \in \mathcal{H}_{\mathcal{Y}}$. But then

$$\begin{aligned} &\mathbb{E}_{XYZ}\left[\left(f(X) - \mathbb{E}f(X|Z)\right)\left(g(Y) - \mathbb{E}g(Y|Z)\right)\right] \\ &= \mathbb{E}_{XYZ}\langle f, \phi(X) - \mathbb{E}\phi(X|Z)\rangle_{\mathcal{H}_{\mathcal{X}}}\langle g, \psi(Y) - \mathbb{E}\psi(Y|Z)\rangle_{\mathcal{H}_{\mathcal{Y}}} \\ &= \langle f, \mathbb{E}_{XYZ}\left(\phi(X) - \mathbb{E}\phi(X|Z)\right) \otimes \left(\psi(Y) - \mathbb{E}\psi(Y|Z)\right) g\rangle_{\mathcal{H}_{\mathcal{X}}} \\ &= \langle f, \mathbb{E}_{XYZ}\left[n_\phi(X,Z) \otimes n_\psi(Y,Z)\right] g\rangle_{\mathcal{H}_{\mathcal{X}}}. \end{aligned}$$

This suggests the method which regresses $\phi(X)$ and $\psi(Y)$ on Z using vector-valued kernel ridge regression and tests for unconditional linear independence of the residuals $n_\phi(X,Z)$ and $n_\psi(Y,Z)$ which are elements of RKHSs.

The resulting regression functions are now simply the empirical mean embeddings of the conditional distributions $P_{X|Z=z}$ and $P_{Y|Z=z}$ [Fukumizu et al., 2011, Theorem 1] and can be expressed as follows [Song et al., 2009, Theorem 5]:

$$\hat{\mathbb{E}}(\phi(X)|Z=z) = \sum_{i=1}^{n} \beta_i^{\mathbf{x}}(z)\phi(x_i) = \Phi_{\mathbf{x}}^\top \beta^{\mathbf{x}}(z) \tag{12}$$

$$\hat{\mathbb{E}}(\psi(Y)|Z=z) = \sum_{i=1}^{n} \beta_i^{\mathbf{y}}(z)\psi(y_i) = \Psi_{\mathbf{y}}^\top \beta^{\mathbf{y}}(z) \tag{13}$$

with $\beta^{\mathbf{x}}(z) = (M + \lambda^{\mathbf{x}} I_n)^{-1}(m(z,z_1), ..., m(z,z_n))^\top$, M is the $n \times n$ matrix such that $M_{ij} = m(z_i, z_j)$, $\Phi_{\mathbf{x}} = (\phi(x_1), ..., \phi(x_n))^\top$ and $\Psi_{\mathbf{y}} = (\psi(y_1), ..., \psi(y_n))^\top$. The notation $\beta^{\mathbf{x}}$ emphasises the fact that the coefficient vector may differ for $\mathbf{x}$ and $\mathbf{y}$; this difference would only be due to different choice of the regularisation parameters $\lambda^{\mathbf{x}}$ and $\lambda^{\mathbf{y}}$. Note that the procedure can straightforwardly be amended to use different kernels $m^{\mathbf{x}}$ and $m^{\mathbf{y}}$ for the two responses, but we do not pursue this further for simplicity of exposition. We have enclosed two parameter optimisation schemes in the Appendix.

The residual of the kernel ridge regression of X on Z for the i-th data point is given by

$$\begin{aligned}\hat{\epsilon}_{x,i} &= \phi(x_i) - \hat{\mathbb{E}}(\phi(X)|Z = z_i) \\ &= \Phi_{\mathbf{x}}^\top \mathbf{e}_i - \Phi_{\mathbf{x}}^\top \beta^{\mathbf{x}}(z_i) \in \mathcal{H}_k \end{aligned} \quad (14)$$

so that the whole set of residuals $\hat{\epsilon}_x = (\epsilon_{x,1}, ..., \epsilon_{x,n})^\top$ can be written as:

$$\hat{\epsilon}_x = (I_n - B_{\mathbf{x}})\Phi_{\mathbf{x}} = (\frac{1}{\lambda^{\mathbf{x}}} M + I_n)^{-1}\Phi_{\mathbf{x}} \quad (15)$$

with $B_{\mathbf{x}} = M(M + \lambda^{\mathbf{x}} I_n)^{-1}$ and $\lambda^{\mathbf{x}} > 0$, so that $I_n - B_{\mathbf{x}} = (\frac{1}{\lambda^{\mathbf{x}}} M + I_n)^{-1}$. Similarly the residual of the kernel ridge regression of Y on Z is given by

$$\hat{\epsilon}_y = (\frac{1}{\lambda^{\mathbf{y}}} M + I_n)^{-1}\Psi_{\mathbf{y}}. \quad (16)$$

The problem of testing weak conditional independence between X and Y given Z then translates into testing if $\hat{\epsilon}_x$ and $\hat{\epsilon}_y$ are correlated.

Since they are elements of RKHSs, we can use the Hilbert-Schmidt independence criterion (HSIC) of Gretton et al. [2008] with linear (inner product) kernels on these residuals, i.e. $\kappa_x(\epsilon_{x,i}, \epsilon_{x,j}) = \langle \epsilon_{x,i}, \epsilon_{x,j} \rangle_{\mathcal{H}_X}$ and $\kappa_y(\epsilon_{y,i}, \epsilon_{y,j}) = \langle \epsilon_{y,i}, \epsilon_{y,j} \rangle_{\mathcal{H}_Y}$. Let the empirically centred residuals be $\hat{\epsilon}^c_{x_i} := \hat{\epsilon}_{x_i} - \frac{1}{n}\sum_{j=1}^n \hat{\epsilon}_{x_j}$ and $\hat{\epsilon}^c_{y_i} := \hat{\epsilon}_{y_i} - \frac{1}{n}\sum_{j=1}^n \hat{\epsilon}_{y_j}$. Essentially, we build an empirical cross covariance operator between the residuals $\hat{\epsilon}_x$ and $\hat{\epsilon}_y$, and HSIC is then the squared Hilbert-Schmidt norm of such operator:

$$\begin{aligned}\Xi(\hat{\epsilon}_x, \hat{\epsilon}_y) &= \left\| \frac{1}{n}\sum_{i=1}^n \hat{\epsilon}^c_{x_i} \otimes \hat{\epsilon}^c_{y_i} \right\|^2_{HS} &(17)\\ &= \frac{1}{n^2}\sum_{i=1}^n \sum_{j=1}^n \langle \hat{\epsilon}^c_{x_i}, \hat{\epsilon}^c_{x_j} \rangle \langle \hat{\epsilon}^c_{y_i}, \hat{\epsilon}^c_{y_j} \rangle &(18)\\ &= \frac{1}{n^2} Trace(H\hat{\epsilon}_x\hat{\epsilon}_x^\top H H \hat{\epsilon}_y \hat{\epsilon}_y^\top H) &(19)\end{aligned}$$

where $H := I_n - \frac{1}{n}\mathbf{1}\mathbf{1}^\top$ is the centering matrix. By definition of $\hat{\epsilon}_x$, we have

$$\hat{\epsilon}_x\hat{\epsilon}_x^\top = (\frac{1}{\lambda^{\mathbf{x}}} M + I_n)^{-1}\Phi_{\mathbf{x}}\Phi_{\mathbf{x}}^\top(\frac{1}{\lambda^{\mathbf{x}}} M + I_n)^{-1} \quad (20)$$

and similarly

$$\hat{\epsilon}_y\hat{\epsilon}_y^\top = (\frac{1}{\lambda^{\mathbf{y}}} M + I_n)^{-1}\Psi_{\mathbf{y}}\Psi_{\mathbf{y}}^\top(\frac{1}{\lambda^{\mathbf{y}}} M + I_n)^{-1} \quad (21)$$

where $\Phi_{\mathbf{x}}\Phi_{\mathbf{x}}^\top = K$ and $\Psi_{\mathbf{y}}\Psi_{\mathbf{y}}^\top = L$ are the $n \times n$ matrices such as $K_{ij} = k(x_i, x_j)$ and $L_{ij} = l(y_i, y_j)$. Combining equations (19), (20) and (21), we obtain

$$\Xi(\hat{\epsilon}_x, \hat{\epsilon}_y) = \frac{1}{n^2} Trace(\tilde{H}_{\mathbf{z,x}} K \tilde{H}_{\mathbf{z,x}}^\top \tilde{H}_{\mathbf{z,y}} L \tilde{H}_{\mathbf{z,y}}^\top)$$

where $\tilde{H}_{\mathbf{z,x}} = H(\frac{1}{\lambda^{\mathbf{x}}} M + I_n)^{-1}$ and $\tilde{H}_{\mathbf{z,y}} = H(\frac{1}{\lambda^{\mathbf{y}}} M + I_n)^{-1}$. Note that the HSIC statistic between the two residuals can be seen as the inner product between transformations of the kernel matrices K and L through the centering terms $\tilde{H}_{\mathbf{z,x}}$ and $\tilde{H}_{\mathbf{z,y}}$ which encompass information regarding the impact of Z on respectively X and Y. To obtain the test threshold, standard permutation approach can be used to estimate the null distribution. It is tempting to also consider the nonlinear tests on RKHS residuals, i.e. one may specify some kernel which only depends on RKHS distances (e.g. Gaussian RBF kernels), however, this results in inflated false positive rates for the same reasons as RESIT.

Related Work Our proposed conditional independence test which we term KRESIT[3] (Kernel RESIT) is a generalisation of the RESIT approach in which the regressions on Z are done after feature transforming both responses X and Y. KRESIT is closely related to the method of Zhang et al. [2011]. More precisely, Zhang et al. [2011] can be understood as performing ridge regressions of the feature transformations of pairs (X, Z) and (Y, Z) on Z in order to achieve full characterisation of conditional independence. This makes the method more difficult to interpret in terms of two-step procedures. Recent extension by Strobl et al. [2017] of Zhang et al. [2011] presents the test called RCoT which essentially computes the same statistic as KRESIT, but uses a different estimation procedure of the asymptotic null distribution. RCoT can be viewed as a large scale approximation of KRESIT through the use of random Fourier features (RFF), similarly RCIT of Strobl et al. [2017] provides an approximation of the KCI-test via RFF. Strobl et al. [2017] has shown that RCIT and RCoT give similar performance as KCI-test but they are orders of magnitude faster in large-scale settings. While the large-scale approximations are not the focus of the present work, methods such as RFF or Nyström approximation can readily be employed in KRESIT (for comparisons of these approximation methods in unconditional independence testing, cf. Zhang et al. [2017]).

4 EXPERIMENTS

We apply the proposed method, KRESIT, to both synthetic and real data to evaluate its performance in terms of Type I error and statistical power. We start with a motivating real data example comparing KRESIT and RESIT on two socio-economic and health indicators from the World Health Organisation (WHO) data [WHO, 2009, Rosling, 2008]. Following this, we compare the performance of the proposed approach against RESIT and the three "strong" conditional independence tests described in Section 2.3 on a synthetic experiment with increasing dimensional-

[3] Code available at https://github.com/oxmlcs/kerpy.

ity of the conditioning variable Z and sample sizes. We then apply the two "weak" conditional independence tests (RESIT and KRESIT) to unravel causal relationships in a synthetic dataset, the Boston Housing dataset [Pace and Gilley, 1997, Harrison and Rubinfeld, 1978] and the Ozone dataset [Breiman and Friedman, 1985] (presented in the Appendix).

Unless otherwise stated, the significance level is kept at $\alpha = 0.05$. For KRESIT, Gaussian kernels with median heuristic are used for all three random variables in regression, but the parameters λ^{x} and λ^{y} are optimised using grid search to find the minimum total 5-fold cross validation error over a grid of 30 evenly spaced values in the interval $(10^{-6}, 10^{1})$. For RESIT, Gaussian kernels with median heuristic are used for kernel ridge regression and on the residuals. The regularisation parameters are tuned in the same way as in KRESIT.

4.1 SIMPLE MOTIVATING EXAMPLE BASED ON WHO DATA

As a motivating example, we apply the proposed approach to two variables in the WHO data set used in Reshef et al. [2011]. We denote by Z the log transformed gross national income per capita and by Y the total expenditure on health per capita. Figure 2 (left) can be thought of as the superposition of two relationships where the small minority curve consists of countries whose economies rely largely on oil [WHO, 2009]. We have taken the log transform of the gross national income per capita so that the values are more evenly distributed. After removing all missing values, we have 178 data points. We then construct a synthetic X with non-functional dependence on Z as follows

$$x_i = \begin{cases} (z_i - 10)^2 + n_i^x & \text{if } c_i^x = 1 \\ -(z_i - 10)^2 + 35 + n_i^x & \text{if } c_i^x = 0 \end{cases} \quad (22)$$

where $c_i^x \overset{i.i.d.}{\sim} Bernoulli(0.5)$ and $n_i^x \overset{i.i.d.}{\sim} \mathcal{N}(0, 1)$. X and Y are conditionally independent given Z by construction.

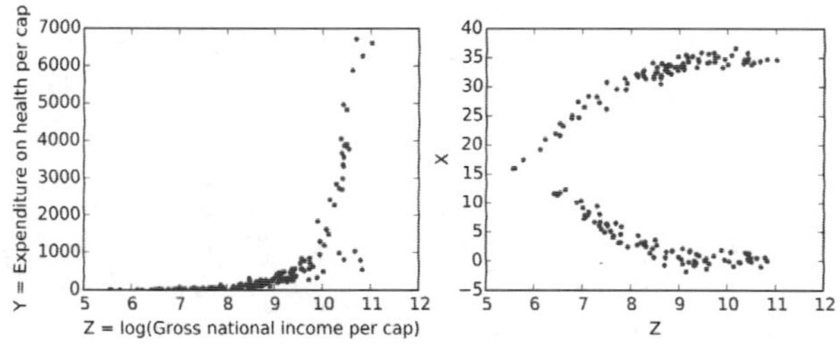

Figure 2: Left: Expenditure on health per cap against the logarithm of gross national income per cap (Z). Right: Synthetic data X against Z.

RESIT incorrectly rejected the null hypothesis at 5% significance level with a p-value of 0.0025 owing to the fact that kernel ridge regression is unable to remove the dependency of Z from X and Y and HSIC using Gaussian kernels is able to detect such nonlinear dependency between the residuals. KRESIT, on the other hand, gives a p-value of 0.91 and hence does not reject the null hypothesis that X and Y are weakly conditionally independent. By relaxing the modelling assumption of additive noise and allowing more complex dependencies between responses and the conditioning variable, KRESIT is able to provide a better calibrated test.

4.2 EFFECT OF DIMENSIONALITY OF Z AND SAMPLE SIZE

We examine the probability of Type I and Type II errors of the "strong" conditional independence tests vs. the "weak" conditional independence tests when the dimensionality of the conditioning set Z is increasing ($d = 1, 2, 3, 4, 5, 6, 7$) and the sample sizes take values in $\{40, 80, 120, 160, 200\}$.

Let us consider the following non-functional dependence as the null model:

$$Z_i^j \overset{i.i.d.}{\sim} Uniform(0, 5), \ j = 1, \dots, d$$
$$C_i^x, C_i^y \overset{i.i.d.}{\sim} Bernoulli(0.5)$$
$$n_i^x, n_i^y \overset{i.i.d.}{\sim} \mathcal{N}(0, 1)$$
$$X_i \in \mathbb{R} = \begin{cases} 1.7Z_i^1 + n_i^x & \text{if } c_i^x = 1 \\ -1.7Z_i^1 + n_i^x & \text{if } c_i^x = 0 \end{cases}$$
$$Y_i \in \mathbb{R} = \begin{cases} (Z_i^1 - 2.7)^2 + n_i^y & \text{if } c_i^y = 1 \\ -(Z_i^1 - 2.7)^2 + 13 + n_i^y & \text{if } c_i^y = 0 \end{cases}$$

Note, X and Y only depend on the first dimension of the conditioning vector Z. To obtain the alternative model, we couple the latent variables C^x and C^y:

$$u_i \overset{i.i.d.}{\sim} Uniform(0, 1)$$
$$C_i^x \overset{i.i.d.}{\sim} Bernoulli(0.5)$$
$$C_i^y = \begin{cases} C_i^x & \text{if } u_i < 0.3 \\ \overset{i.i.d.}{\sim} Bernoulli(0.5) & \text{if } u_i \geq 0.3 \end{cases}$$

We compare the "weak" conditional independence tests: the proposed KRESIT, RESIT and LRESIT (RESIT with linear kernels on residuals) with the "strong" conditional independence tests: CIperm by Fukumizu et al. [2008], KCIPT by Doran et al. [2014] and KCI-test by Zhang et al. [2011]. The rejection rates are calculated out of 100 trials. Each rejection rate is associated with a 95% Wald confidence interval.

For a given dimension, we observe in Figure 3 that the Type I error of RESIT is increasing with the number of samples. As a simple kernel ridge regression cannot remove the dependency of Z from X and Y, the nonlinear dependency pattern in the residuals are more visible as sample size increases. As expected, the proposed approach, KRESIT, has correct Type I control together with LRESIT and the other "strong" conditional independence tests.

To establish sensible comparison in the alternative model (Figure 4), we only compare those methods with correct Type I control. When Z is of dimension 1, KRESIT performs similarly to KCI test where the probability of Type II error (1-power) for both decreases to zero as the number of samples increases to 200, while the other tests give weaker power. In dimension 7, KRESIT again gives strong performance, outperforming other tests. Although LRESIT also tests for weak conditional independence, as expected, it has a reduced power comparing to KRESIT in both cases. While KCI test and KCIPT give similar power performance, CIperm struggles to detect the conditional dependence across all sample sizes.

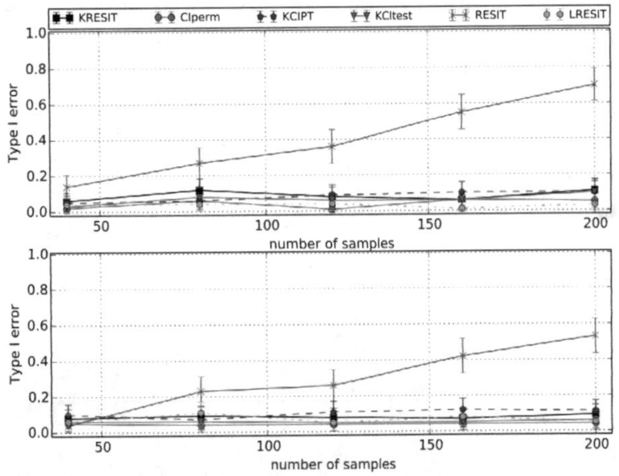

Figure 3: Null model experiments for $d = 1$ (Top) and $d = 7$ (Bottom).

4.3 APPLICATION IN CAUSAL DISCOVERY

Conditional independence tests are frequently used in causal discovery to recover the dependence relationships among a set of variables represented as a directed acyclic graph (DAG). Assuming causal Markov condition (i.e., any variable/node is conditionally independent of its non-descendents given its parents [Hausman and Woodward, 1999]) and faithfulness (i.e., the conditional independences of the distribution can be inferred from the d-separation in the graph and vice-versa [Kalisch and Buhlmann, 2007]),

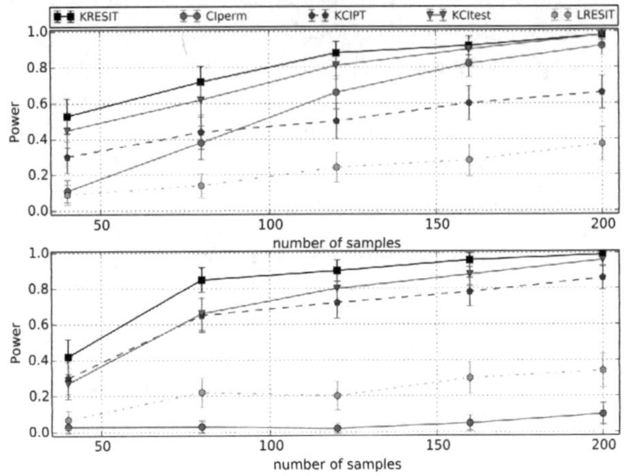

Figure 4: Alternative model experiments for $d = 1$ (Top) and $d = 7$ (Bottom).

the popular constraint-based PC-algorithm [Spirtes et al., 2000] is often used to estimate a Markov equivalence class of DAGs (i.e. a set of graphs that impose the same independences and conditional independences). The estimation starts from a complete undirected graph and recursively deletes edges based on conditional independence decisions. The result is an undirected graph (skeleton) which is then partially directed and further extended to represent the underlying equivalence class of DAG [Kalisch and Buhlmann, 2007]. The quality of the conditional independence tests are hence crucial for the performance of the PC algorithm.

The PC algorithm used in this section is a modified version of the pcalg implementation in python[4] with conditional independence test using KRESIT/RESIT and independence test using HSIC with Gaussian kernel using median heuristic. Completed partially acyclic graph (CPDAG) are used to visualise the equivalence classes of DAGs. Whenever an undirected edge $i - j$ is shown, there exists a DAG with $i \to j$ and a DAG with $i \leftarrow j$ in the equivalence class.

4.3.1 Synthetic Data

Consider variables of the null model from Section 4.2 and additionally let $A_i = (Y_i - 5)^2/3 + 5 + n_i^A$ and $B_i = 5.5\tanh(Y_i) + n_i^B$ where $n_i^A, n_i^B \overset{i.i.d.}{\sim} \mathcal{N}(0,1)$.

We compare the results obtained from the PC algorithm with the variables $\{X, Y, Z, C^x, C^y, A, B\}$ using KRESIT and RESIT. Using a sample of size 800, we obtain Figure 5 (Left). Both KRESIT and RESIT recover the correct structure of the model.

We now turn to investigating the robustness of the method

[4] https://github.com/keiichishima/pcalg

upon removing the variables C^x and C^y. PC algorithm with KRESIT is still able to discover the correct skeleton as shown in Figure 5 (Right). An incorrect graph is obtained with RESIT, reporting a spurious causal link $X - Y$. We note that when the switching variables C^x, C^y are present, all associations are functional, but this is no longer the case when C^x, C^y are unobserved.

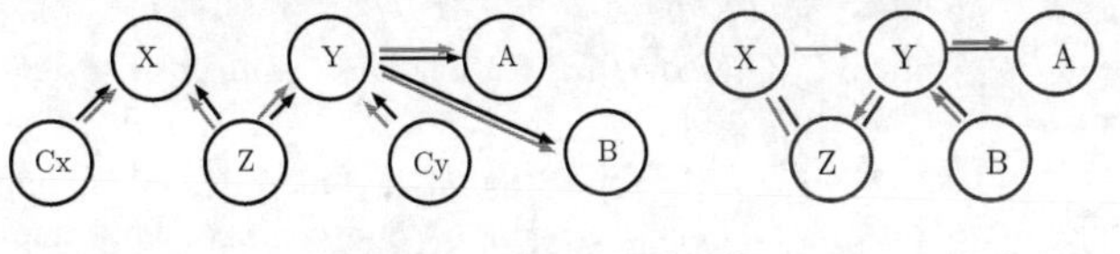

Figure 5: Left: The DAG obtained by using KRESIT (black) fully recovers the causal structure, but the one using RESIT (green) does not. Right: The DAG obtained by PC algorithm using KRESIT and RESIT with C^x and C^y being latent variables.

4.3.2 Boston Housing Data

We consider the corrected Boston Housing dataset of Pace and Gilley [1997] and pre-whiten each variable using the spatial coordinates with a GP regression as in Flaxman et al. [2015] since there is significant spatial clustering in every single variable in the dataset. There are 14 variables in total and each with 506 observations. For a detailed explanation of each variable, we refer to the original paper [Harrison and Rubinfeld, 1978]. To correct for multiple testing, we set the significance level to $\alpha = 0.001$.

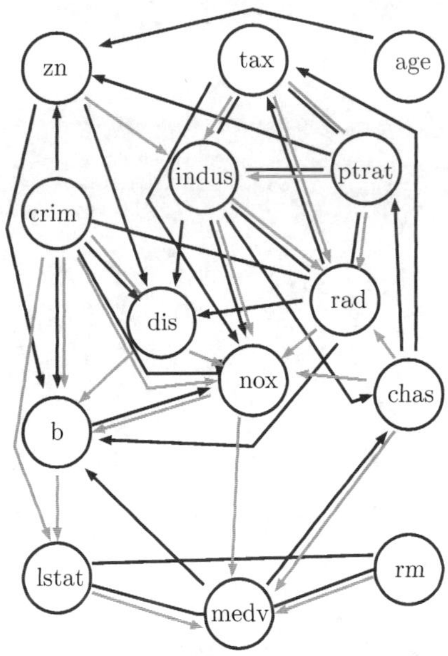

Figure 6: Results of PC algorithm with KRESIT (black) and RESIT [Flaxman et al., 2015] (orange) using pre-whitened Boston Housing dataset.

Overall, the CPDAG obtained by our proposed method is substantially different from previous results in the literature [Zhang et al., 2011, Flaxman et al., 2015]. We argue that many potentially unobserved variables could be driving such differences. The details and some possible interpretations are given in the Appendix: Boston Housing Data. Therefore, the links discovered using RESIT and KRESIT within PC algorithm may need further investigation and one should analyse the results with potential hidden variables in mind and be cautious about any conclusion drawn due to potential violation of structural assumptions.

5 CONCLUSION

We proposed a weak conditional independence test that extends the popular two-step approach RESIT, which combines regression with an unconditional independence test. We consider RKHS-valued ridge regressions and subsequently use a test for linear independence on RKHS-valued residuals. While maintaining simple and effective testing procedures of RESIT, the resulting test has a correct Type I control under more challenging scenarios where the modelling assumptions required by RESIT are violated. It also yields competitive or improved power performance to that of the other conditional independence tests. When used in the PC algorithm, the proposed method is more robust than RESIT to hidden variables inducing associations more complex than functional ones with additive noise.

Acknowledgements

QZ was supported by EPSRC (EP/M50659X/1), SF and DS were supported in part by ERC (FPT/617071).

References

World health organization statistical information systems (whosis). World Health Organization Statistical Information Systems (WHOSIS), 2009. www.who.int/whosis/en/.

D. Alpay. *The Schur Algorithm, Reproducing Kernel Spaces and System Theory*. American Mathematics Society, 2001.

C.R. Baker. Joint Measures and Cross-Covariance Operators. *Transactions of the American Mathematical Society*, 186:273–289, 1973.

W. Bergsma. Testing Conditional Independence for Continuous Random Variable. *EURANDOM-report 2004-049*, 2004.

L. Breiman and J.H. Friedman. Estimating Optimal Transformations for Multiple Regression and Correlation. *Journal of the American Statistical Association*, 80(391):580 – 598, 1985.

K. Chwialkowski, A. Ramdas, D. Sejdinovic, and A. Gretton. Fast Two-Sample Testing with Analytic Representations of Probability Measures. In *Advances in Neural Information Processing Systems (NIPS)*, 2015.

K. Chwialkowski, H. Strathmann, and A. Gretton. A Kernel Test of Goodness of Fit. In *Proceedings of the International Conference on Machine Learning (ICML)*, 2016.

J. Dattorro. *Convex Optimisation & Euclidean Distance Geometry*. Meboo Publishing USA, second edition, 2016.

J.J. Daudin. Partial association measures and an application to qualitative regression. *Biometrika*, 67(3):581–590, 1980.

G. Doran, K. Muandet, K. Zhang, and B. Schölkopf. A Permutation-Based Kernel Conditional Independence Test. In *Uncertainty in Artificial Intelligence (UAI)*, 2014.

S.R. Flaxman, D.B. Neill, and A.J. Smola. Gaussian Processes for Independence Tests with Non-iid Data in Causal Inference. *ACM Transactions on Intelligent Systems and Technology*, 7 (2):22:1–22:23, 2015.

K. Fukumizu, F.R. Bach, and M.I. Jordan. Dimensionality Reduction for Supervised Learning with Reproducing Kernel Hilbert Spaces. *Journal of Machine Learning Research (JMLR)*, 5: 73–99, 2004.

K. Fukumizu, A. Gretton, X. Sun, and B. Schölkopf. Kernel Measures of Conditional Dependence. In *Advances in Neural Information Processing Systems (NIPS)*, 2008.

K. Fukumizu, Le Song, and A. Gretton. Kernel Bayes' Rule. In *Advances in Neural Information Processing Systems (NIPS)*, 2011.

A. Gretton, K. Borgwardt, M. Rasch, B. Schölkopf, and A. Smola. A Kernel Method for the Two-Sample problem. *Advances in Neural Information Processing Systems (NIPS)*, 2007.

A. Gretton, K. Fukumizu, B. Schölkopf, C.H. Teo, L. Song, and A.J. Smola. A Kernel Statistical Test of Independence. *Advances in Neural Information Processing Systems (NIPS)*, 2008.

A. Gretton, K.M. Borgwardt, M.J. Rasch, B. Schölkopf, and A. Smola. A Kernel Two-Sample Test. *Journal of Machine Learning Research (JMLR)*, 13:723–773, 2012.

DJ.R. Harrison and D.L. Rubinfeld. Hedonic Housing Prices and the Demand for Clean Air. *Journal of Environmental Economics and Management*, 5:81–102, 1978.

D.M. Hausman and J. Woodward. Independence, Invariance, and the Causal Markov Condition. *British Journal of Philosophy and Science*, 50(4):521–583, 1999.

P.O. Hoyer, D. Janzing, J.M. Mooij, J. Peters, and B. Schölkopf. Nonlinear Causal Discovery with Additive Noise Models. In *Advances in Neural Information Processing Systems (NIPS)*. 2009.

M. Kalisch and P. Buhlmann. Estimating High-Dimensional Directed Acyclic Graphs with the PC-Algorithm. *Journal of Machine Learning Research (JMLR)*, 8:613–636, 2007.

R. Kelley Pace and Otis W. Gilley. Using the Spatial Configuration of the Data to Improve Estimation. *The Journal of Real Estate Finance and Economics*, 14(3):333–340, 1997.

J. Peters, J.M. Mooij, D. Janzing, and B. Schölkopf. Causal Discovery with Continuous Additive Noise Models. *Journal of Machine Learning Research (JMLR)*, 15(1), 2014.

N. Pfister, P. Bühlmann, B. Schölkopf, and J. Peters. Kernel-based Tests for Joint Independence. *Journal of the Royal Statistical Society*, page to appear, 2016.

D.N. Reshef, Y.A. Reshef, H.K. Finucane, S.R. Grossman, G. McVean, P.J. Turnbaugh, E.S. Lander, M. Mitzenmacher, and P.C. Sabeti. Detecting Novel Associations in Large Data Sets. *Science*, 334(6062):1518–1524, 2011.

H. Rosling. Indicators in Gapminder World. Gapminder, 2008.

D. Sejdinovic, A. Gretton, and W. Bergsma. A Kernel Test for Three-Variable Interactions. In *Advances in Neural Information Processing Systems (NIPS)*. 2013.

C. Shalizi. *Advanced Data Analysis from an Elementary Point of View*. 2016.

A. Smola, A. Gretton, L. Song, and B. Schölkop. A Hilbert Space Embedding for Distributions. In *Algorithmic Learning Theory: 18th International Conference*, 2007.

L. Song, J. Huang, A. Smola, and K. Fukumizu. Hilbert Space Embeddings of Conditional Distributions with Applications to Dynamical Systems. In *Proceedings of the International Conference on Machine Learning (ICML)*, 2009.

P. Spirtes, C. Glymour, and R. Scheines. *Causation, Prediction, and Search*. MIT Press, 2000.

B. K. Sriperumbudur, A. Gretton, K. Fukumizu, B. Schölkopf, and G. R. G. Lanckriet. Hilbert Space Embeddings and Metrics on Probability Measures. *Journal of Machine Learning Research (JMLR)*, 11:1297–1322, 2010.

I. Steinwart and A. Christmann. *Support Vector Machines*. Springer, 2008.

E.V. Strobl, S. Visweswaran, and K. Zhang. Approximate Kernel-based Conditional Independence Tests for Fast Non-Parametric Causal Discovery. *ArXiv e-prints*, 2017.

K. Zhang, J. Peters, D. Janzing, and B. Schölkopf. Kernel-based Conditional Independence Test and Application in Causal Discovery. In *Uncertainty in Artificial Intelligence (UAI)*, 2011.

Q. Zhang, S. Filippi, A. Gretton, and D. Sejdinovic. Large-scale kernel methods for independence testing. *Statistics and Computing*, Jan 2017.

APPENDIX

Parameters Optimisation

For the proposed method where Gaussian radial basis function (RBF) kernels are used on all three random variables of interest, there are two groups of hyper-parameters. The first one includes the kernel bandwidths for the kernel matrices K, L and M. The bandwidth for K and L are fixed by using median heuristic. Although we also fixed the bandwidth for M by median heuristic in the main text, here we include a discussion on the optimisation of such parameter when one has a different kernel bandwidth for the regression on the feature space of X and on that of Y. Let's call them σ^2_{xz} and σ^2_{yz} respectively. The second group contains the regularisation parameters λ^{x} and λ^{y} for the kernel ridge regressions. These parameters can be optimised through grid search or gradient descent on the total cross-validation error as follows.

For a K-fold cross-validation, we aim to minimise the sum of the square of the residuals of each unseen fold given the model trained on the other $K-1$ folds over some (λ, σ^2) values. Here, we present detailed derivation for X and that of Y follows similarly. For a pair of fixed $(\lambda^x, \sigma^2_{xz})$, the cross-validation error of the kth fold is:

$$CVerror^k_\lambda = \frac{1}{u}\sum_{i\in tst} \|\phi(x^{tst}_i) - \Phi^T_{tr}\beta^x(z^{tst}_i)\|^2 \tag{23}$$

where $\{x^{tr}_i, z^{tr}_i\}_i$ and $\{x^{tst}_i, z^{tst}_i\}_i$ denote respectively the training and testing sets for the kth fold, $\Phi_{tr} = (\phi(x^{tr}_1), \phi(x^{tr}_2), ...)^\top$ and u is the size of the testing set. Then, the overall cross-validation error is

$$CVerror_\lambda = \frac{1}{K}\sum_{k=1}^{K} CVerror^k_\lambda . \tag{24}$$

To simplify (23), we note that

$$\sum_{i\in tst} \|\phi(x^{tst}_i) - \Phi^T_{tr}\beta^x(z^{tst}_i)\|^2 \tag{25}$$

$$= \sum_{i\in tst} \|\phi(x^{tst}_i) - \Phi^T_{tr}(M_{tr,tr} + \lambda^x I)^{-1}$$

$$(m(z^{tst}_i, z^{tr}_1), m(z^{tst}_i, z^{tr}_2), ..., m(z^{tst}_i, z^{tr}_m))^T\|^2 \tag{26}$$

$$= Tr([\Phi_{tst} - \mathcal{M}_z][\Phi_{tst} - \mathcal{M}_z]^T) \tag{27}$$

$$= Tr(\Phi_{tst}\Phi^T_{tst} - \Phi_{tst}\mathcal{M}^T_z - \mathcal{M}_z\Phi^T_{tst} + \mathcal{M}_z\mathcal{M}^T_z) \tag{28}$$

where $\mathcal{M}_z = M_{tst,tr}(M_{tr,tr} + \lambda^x I)^{-1}\Phi_{tr}$. Such prediction error for the kth fold (i.e. (28)) can be explicitly formulated in terms of $(\lambda^x, \sigma^2_{xz})$ by writing the gram matrices in terms of square distance matrices:

$$M_{*,\cdot} = \exp(-0.5\ D_{*,\cdot}/\sigma^2_{xz}) \tag{29}$$

where $D_{*,\cdot}$ is the square distance matrix computed on the respective sets, i.e. $(D_{*,\cdot})_{ij} = \|z_i - z_j\|^2_2$. Note, no explicit feature map representation is required.

Since both parameters are constrained to be positive, we can rewrite $\lambda^x = \exp(\eta)$ and $\sigma^2_{xz} = \exp(\gamma)$ and take first order derivate with respect to η and γ to obtain a gradient descent algorithm. Given the expression in (24), taking the first order derivative with respect to η (Appendix D of Dattorro [2016]):

$$\frac{d}{d\eta}Error_{(\lambda^x, \sigma^2_{xz})}$$
$$= 2\,Tr\{K_{tst,tr}\mathcal{M}_\eta M_{tr,tst} - M_{tst,tr}\mathcal{M}_\eta K_{tr,tr}\mathcal{M}_{inv}M_{tr,tst}\}$$

where $\mathcal{M}_\eta := (M_{tr,tr} + \lambda^x I)^{-1}[\exp(\eta)I](M_{tr,tr} + \lambda^x I)^{-1}$ and $\mathcal{M}_{inv} := (M_{tr,tr} + \lambda^x I)^{-1}$. Similarly, take the first order derivative with respect to γ:

$$\frac{d}{d\gamma}Error_{(\lambda^x, \sigma^2_{xz})}$$
$$= Tr\{2\ K_{tst,tr}\mathcal{M}_{inv}\mathcal{D}_{tr,tr}\mathcal{M}_{inv}M_{tr,tst} - 2\ K_{tst,tr}\mathcal{M}_{inv}\mathcal{D}_{tr,tst} + \mathcal{D}_{tst,tr}\mathcal{M}_{inv}K_{tr,tr}\mathcal{M}_{inv}M_{tr,tst} - M_{tst,tr}\mathcal{M}_{inv}\mathcal{D}_{tr,tr}\mathcal{M}_{inv}K_{tr,tr}\mathcal{M}_{inv}M_{tr,tst} - M_{tst,tr}\mathcal{M}_{inv}K_{tr,tr}\mathcal{M}_{inv}\mathcal{D}_{tr,tr}\mathcal{M}_{inv}M_{tr,tst} + M_{tst,tr}\mathcal{M}_{inv}K_{tr,tr}\mathcal{M}_{inv}\mathcal{D}_{tr,tst}\} \tag{30}$$

where

$$\mathcal{D}_{tr,\cdot} := [0.5D_{tr,\cdot} \times \exp(-0.5D_{tr,\cdot}\exp(-\gamma))\exp(-\gamma)I].$$

At iteration i, we update η and γ according to

$$\eta_i = \eta_{i-1} - \alpha\frac{d}{d\eta}Error_{(\lambda^x, \sigma^2_{xz})}\Big|_{\eta_{i-1},\gamma_{i-1}} \tag{31}$$

$$\gamma_i = \gamma_{i-1} - \alpha\frac{d}{d\gamma}Error_{(\lambda^x, \sigma^2_{xz})}\Big|_{\eta_{i-1},\gamma_{i-1}} \tag{32}$$

with learning rate α until convergence. Various adaptive learning rate schemes can be used for faster convergence.

Boston Housing Data

The main variable of interest is the median value of occupied homes (medv). Based on the result using KRESIT (Figure 6), the proportion of lower status people (lstat) and (medv) are conditionally dependent given the rest of the variables, so is average number of rooms per unit (rm) and (medv). However, the estimated CPDAG cannot be more specific on the direction of the causation. Additionally, (medv) has been identified to cause the percentage of black population (b). We observe that such link is indeed plausible. In the US around the time of the 1970 census, residential segregation was common place, and neighbourhoods with a higher percentage of blacks were regarded as less desirable to live in. Banks and the federal government itself refused to give loans to blacks in general, and specifically refused to give them loans when they wanted to buy homes in neighbourhoods that had historically been white.

The variable (medv) has also been identified to cause whether the house is next to the Charles River (chas). However, this edge seems to be misdirected. The result of Flaxman et al. [2015] (using RESIT) has shown the opposite (chas) $\rightarrow$ (medv) which agrees with authors' belief in the original paper [Harrison and Rubinfeld, 1978]. Besides this, they also showed that (nox), (lstat) and (rm) are the causes for (medv). While the strong independence test of Zhang et al. [2011] also identified (lstat) and (rm) as the causes, it additionally concludes crime rates (crim) and proportion of unit built before 1940 (age) as causes. The strong CI test of Fukumizu et al. [2008] agrees with Zhang et al. [2011] on (lstat) and (age).

Ozone Data

We consider the ozone dataset used in Breiman and Friedman [1985] and pre-whitened each variable using time with a GP regression [Flaxman et al., 2015] as the dataset consists of 330 daily observations with clear temporal autocorrelation. We refer to [Breiman and Friedman, 1985] for the details of each variable and the main variable of interest is the ozone concentration (Ozone). We set the significance level to be $\alpha = 0.05$ as the number of variables is only 9.

Figure 7 illustrates that though some edges are present in both our result and the one obtained by Flaxman et al. [2015], the two graphs are quite different. The CPDAG obtained using KRESIT shows that there is no cause of (Ozone) among the variables under consideration, but (Ozone) causes temperature (Temp), humidity (Hum) and inversion base height (InvHt). Flaxman et al. [2015] also concludes that there is no cause of (Ozone) among the variables under consideration, but (Ozone) is one of the causes for visibility (Vis).

The correlations between the concentration of ozone, temperature, inversion base height and humidity in the atmosphere have been shown to exist in many research on meteorology, public health and environmental science. However, the causal directions are less clear as the interaction between them are complex and there are additional factors that plays a part which have not been considered in this dataset. For example, the ratio of volatile organic compounds (VOC) and nitrogen oxides (Nox), the concentration of other green house gases, if heavy cloud is present, etc. We regard our method as promising as it discovers the links between these variables.

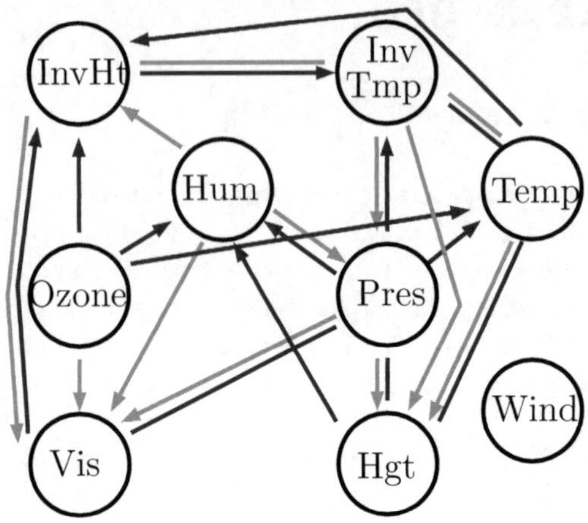

Figure 7: Results of PC algorithm with KRESIT (black) and RESIT [Flaxman et al., 2015] (orange) using pre-whitened Ozone dataset.

Algebraic Equivalence of Linear Structural Equation Models

Thijs van Ommen
Informatics Institute
University of Amsterdam
The Netherlands

Joris M. Mooij
Informatics Institute
University of Amsterdam
The Netherlands

Abstract

Despite their popularity, many questions about the algebraic constraints imposed by linear structural equation models remain open problems. For causal discovery, two of these problems are especially important: the enumeration of the constraints imposed by a model, and deciding whether two graphs define the same statistical model. We show how the half-trek criterion can be used to make progress in both of these problems. We apply our theoretical results to a small-scale model selection problem, and find that taking the additional algebraic constraints into account may lead to significant improvements in model selection accuracy.

1 INTRODUCTION

In a linear structural equation model (SEM), each variable of interest is a linear function of the other variables and a noise term, with possibly correlated noise terms. Linear SEMs are popular in many fields of science, in no small part due to their causal interpretability (Spirtes et al., 2000; Pearl, 2000). However, many questions about these models remain unanswered. For example, it is known that many of these models impose equality constraints on the observational distribution which do not correspond to (conditional) independences (Richardson and Spirtes, 2002). One example of these is the Verma constraint (Robins, 1986; Verma and Pearl, 1991). But no general method exists which enumerates all constraints that hold in a model given its graphical representation. Figure 1 shows another example of a graph that imposes an equality constraint in the linear case; for this type of constraint, no systematic approach exists yet.

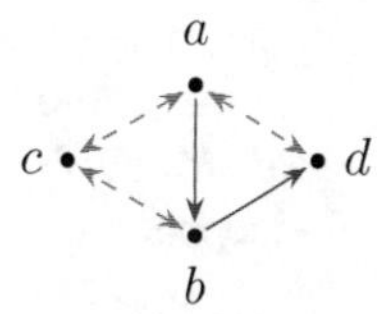

Figure 1: A mixed graph imposing the non-independence constraint (3) on the observational distribution.

Relatedly, given graphical representations of two models, it is often unclear whether the models can be distinguished based on observational data alone. Both of these problems are great impediments to the development of methods that learn the structure of a linear SEM from observational data: constraint-based methods (e.g. PC and FCI (Spirtes et al., 2000)) cannot test for constraints that are not yet well understood and may thus miss signals in the data, while score-based methods (e.g. (Chickering, 2002; Silva and Ghahramani, 2006)) would currently require the scoring of many models that then turn out to be indistinguishable.

The theoretical results of this paper achieve progress in addressing both problems mentioned above. For example, we provide an efficient method to find the constraint imposed by the graph in Figure 1, as well as similar constraints for many other graphs. Our results apply to models with latent confounders (represented by bidirected edges), including confounders between nodes that are also related by a direct causal effect (a structure known as a *bow*), and even to models with directed cycles. We show how these results enable practical improvements on model selection problems.

Suppose we see that our observational data obeys a non-independence equality constraint, such as the one imposed by the graph in Figure 1, and no other constraints. Then we can often draw very specific conclusions about the graph structure. Without knowledge of these constraints, automated methods for causal discovery would

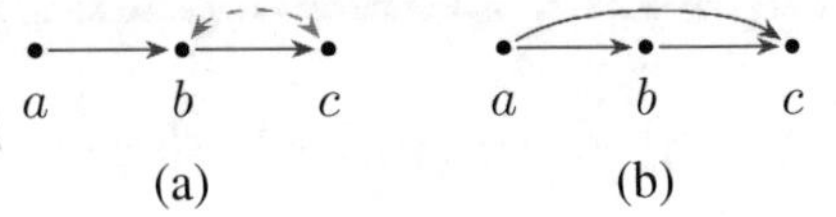

Figure 2: Two graphs whose statistical models are almost, but not entirely identical: (a) the instrumental variable model; (b) a saturated model.

likely select a *saturated* model (one imposing no constraints). This tells us very little about the graph structure, so e.g. it does not allow us to predict the results of interventions. Constraint-based methods generally use only (conditional) independence constraints, so they would not be able to draw any conclusions in the situation described here. For purposes of model selection, we are thus interested in a notion of model equivalence that is more fine-grained than Markov equivalence (which only takes conditional independence constraints into account), yet not so fine-grained as to be impractical

The equivalence concept we propose in this paper is *algebraic equivalence*: Two linear structural equation models are algebraically equivalent if they impose the same algebraic (i.e. equality) constraints on the observational distribution.[1] These constraints take the form of polynomial equations over covariances σ_{vw} of the observed variables. Because the graph in Figure 1 imposes such a constraint, it is not algebraically equivalent to the saturated model on four nodes, so a model selection method based on algebraic equivalence is able to distinguish the two, while a method based on Markov equivalence is not.

For an example of models not distinguished by algebraic equivalence, consider the mixed graph in Figure 2(a), often called the instrumental variable model. This model contains all multivariate Gaussian distributions on the three variables with $\sigma_{ab} \neq 0$, but excludes some with $\sigma_{ab} = 0$. Because it imposes no equality constraints, it is algebraically equivalent to the saturated model on three nodes, represented for example by the graph in Figure 2(b). The difference between the two models is a measure zero subset of their union, so that in a model selection problem, it would rarely be possible to distinguish between these models based on observational data alone. Thus it is appropriate that our proposed equivalence concept treats these models as equivalent.

By considering only equality constraints, we are also treating models as equivalent if they differ only by inequality constraints (of the form $f(\Sigma) \geq 0$). It is known that linear Gaussian models with latent variables may impose inequality constraints. For example, consider the graph with three observed variables and a latent confounder between every pair of observed variables. The corresponding mixed graph has three nodes and a bidirected edge between each pair of nodes. This corresponds to the saturated model. However, if we consider the entire graph on 6 nodes and then marginalize out the latent variables, the resulting set of distributions obeys a nontrivial inequality constraint (Richardson and Spirtes, 2002). By using mixed graphs instead of including latent variables in our models explicitly, we are already simplifying away such inequality constraints. However, as we will show in Section 3.3, using mixed graphs does not get rid of all inequality constraints. We found that for models imposing an inequality constraint, maximum likelihood estimation can be challenging, so score-based methods for causal discovery would benefit significantly from being able to ignore these models. Algebraic equivalence provides a way to do this, as many models that impose an inequality constraint are algebraically equivalent to a model that imposes no such constraints.[2]

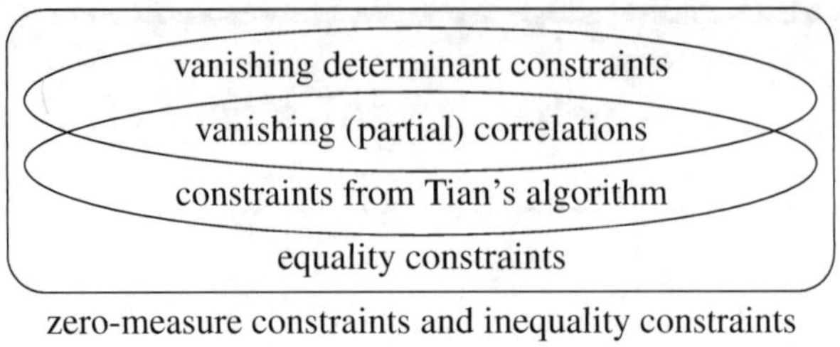

Figure 3: The types of constraints imposed by linear structural equation models.

1.1 RELATIONS TO OTHER TYPES OF CONSTRAINTS

When defining linear structural equation models statistically, often the noise terms are chosen to be Gaussian. For Gaussian variables, independence is equivalent to having zero covariance (and in turn to having zero correlation), and conditional independence is equivalent to zero *partial correlation*. Because we do not want to assume that the data are generated by a Gaussian distribution, we need to distinguish between conditional independence and vanishing partial correlation. The equality constraints we consider express vanishing partial correlations, not conditional independences, so we will use that terminology from now on.

A partial correlation $\rho_{vw.S}$ is zero precisely when a certain submatrix of the observed covariance matrix has

[1]Using terminology from algebraic geometry, the statistical models have the same Zariski closure (Cox et al., 2015).

[2]In a model selection task, we can of course still check for inequality constraints, but we propose to do this *after* selecting the algebraic equivalence class.

zero determinant. Sullivant et al. (2010) give a graphical characterization for the more general type of constraint where an arbitrary square submatrix has zero determinant; this also includes the vanishing tetrad constraints (Spirtes et al., 2000). Together these are called *vanishing determinant constraints* (see Figure 3).

The questions of constraint enumeration and model equivalence that we study here for the linear case, are studied for the general nonparametric case by Tian and Pearl (2002) and Shpitser et al. (2014). Tian's algorithm gives a sound enumeration of constraints in the general case, and Evans (2015) shows it to be complete in the discrete case. If other parametric assumptions are made, there may be additional constraints. Indeed this happens in the linear Gaussian case: Tian's algorithm returns no constraints for the graph in Figure 1, even though one exists.

Lists of algebraic constraints can also be obtained using algorithms from computer algebra, but these are in general impractically slow, sometimes taking many days even for very small graphs (García-Puente et al., 2010). The methods we propose are based on the graphical criteria proposed by Foygel et al. (2012), which can be checked in polynomial time.

The rest of this paper is structured as follows. Section 2 discusses preliminaries about linear SEMs, the half-trek criterion, algebraic geometry, and our notation for sets of graphs. Our main theoretical contributions are in Section 3, addressing the enumeration of algebraic constraints in Section 3.1, and a sufficient graphical criterion for algebraic equivalence in Section 3.2; further, Section 3.3 gives an example of how inequality constraints may arise in linear SEMs. Experimental results demonstrating the practical usefulness of our results are presented in Section 4. Section 5 concludes the paper. All proofs are in the supplementary material in Appendix A, and a complete description of all algebraic equivalence classes on four nodes (acyclic) can be found in Appendix B.

2 PRELIMINARIES

We follow Foygel et al. (2012) for most of the notation defined in this section.

A *mixed graph* $G = (V, D, B)$ consists of a set of nodes V, a set of directed edges D which are ordered pairs of distinct nodes, and a set of bidirected edges B which are unordered pairs of nodes. In this article, the word 'graph' without qualification refers to mixed graphs. A node $x \in V$ with $(x, v) \in D$ is called a *parent* of v, and the set of parents is denoted by $\mathrm{pa}(v)$; similarly, a node x with $\{x, v\} \in B$ is called a *sibling* of v and the set is denoted $\mathrm{sib}(v)$. G is called *acyclic* if it contains no directed cycle (such a G is also called *acyclic directed mixed graph (ADMG)*). If G is acyclic and contains no bidirected edges, it is called a *directed acyclic graph (DAG)*.

Together with parameter vector λ_0 and parameter matrices Λ and Ω, the graph G describes a distribution on observed variables X via

$$X_v = \lambda_{0v} + \sum_{w \in \mathrm{pa}(v)} \lambda_{wv} X_w + \epsilon_v \qquad \text{for } v \in V,$$

where the noise terms have covariances $\mathrm{Cov}(\epsilon_v, \epsilon_w) = \omega_{vw}$. The parameter space is defined as follows. Let $n = |V|$. $\mathbb{R}^D$ is the set of all $n \times n$ matrices Λ with $\Lambda_{vw} \neq 0$ only if $(v, w) \in D$, and $\mathbb{R}^D_{\text{reg}}$ is the subset of $\mathbb{R}^D$ for which $I - \Lambda$ is invertible (for acyclic G, $\mathbb{R}^D = \mathbb{R}^D_{\text{reg}}$). PD_n is the set of all positive definite $n \times n$ matrices, and $\mathrm{PD}(B)$ is the subset consisting of all Ω with $\Omega_{vw} \neq 0$ only if $v = w$ or $\{v, w\} \in B$. The parameterization map ϕ_G maps parameters $(\Lambda, \Omega) \in \mathbb{R}^D_{\text{reg}} \times \mathrm{PD}(B)$ to covariance matrices $\Sigma \in \mathrm{PD}_n$ on the observed variables X as follows:

$$\phi_G(\Lambda, \Omega) = (I - \Lambda)^{-T} \Omega (I - \Lambda)^{-1}.$$

The *model* defined by a graph G then consists of all covariance matrices Σ that can be obtained for some setting of the parameters:

$$\mathcal{M}(G) := \{\phi_G(\Lambda, \Omega) \mid (\Lambda, \Omega) \in \mathbb{R}^D_{\text{reg}} \times \mathrm{PD}(B)\}. \quad (1)$$

Note that the mean of X can be set arbitrarily by choosing appropriate values for the parameter vector $\lambda_0 \in \mathbb{R}^n$, regardless of the structure of G. Thus these aspects of the model carry no information for model selection, and we will ignore them here.

2.1 THE HALF-TREK CRITERION

A central question about a mixed graph G is that of *(parameter) identifiability*: can the parameters (Λ, Ω) be uniquely recovered from Σ? A graph is called *generically identifiable* (or almost-everywhere identifiable) if this is true of $\phi_G(\Lambda, \Omega)$ for all but a measure zero subset of $\mathbb{R}^D_{\text{reg}} \times \mathrm{PD}(B)$. Similarly, G is called *generically finite-to-one* if for almost all (Λ, Ω), the number of parameter values mapped by ϕ_G to the same Σ is finite, and *generically infinite-to-one* if this number is infinite for almost all parameter values. We will sometimes omit the qualifier 'generically' when talking about (in)finite-to-one models.

Foygel et al. (2012) present two graphical criteria to decide in which of the above categories a graph G belongs. A graph is called *HTC-identifiable* if it meets the condition for being generically identifiable; *HTC-nonidentifiable* if it meets the condition for being generically infinite-to-one; and *HTC-inconclusive* otherwise. Because neither criterion is necessary, the class of HTC-inconclusive graphs contains generically identifiable, finite-to-one, and infinite-to-one graphs. While the criteria are not complete, they are quite powerful. For example, all bow-free acyclic graphs are HTC-identifiable (thus implying the earlier identification result of Brito and Pearl (2002)), and so are many graphs containing bows or directed cycles.

The proof of HTC-identifiability in (Foygel et al., 2012) is constructive: it gives an algorithm that, given $\Sigma \in \mathcal{M}(G)$, computes parameters such that $\Sigma = \phi_G(\Lambda, \Omega)$ (except for a measure zero subset). To apply our Theorem 1 below, some details of HTC-identifiability and this algorithm are needed; for the rest, we refer to (Foygel et al., 2012, proof of Theorem 1). A *half-trek* from v to w is either a directed path, or a path consisting of one bidirected edge followed by directed edges towards w. We write $\mathrm{htr}(v)$ (*half-trek reachable*) for the set of nodes that are reachable from v by half-treks.[3] HTC-identifiability of a graph G requires that for each node $v \in V$, a set $Y_v \subseteq V \setminus (\{v\} \cup \mathrm{sib}(v))$ exists, consisting of nodes y with $v \in \mathrm{htr}(y)$, and the set as a whole satisfying $|Y_v| = |\mathrm{pa}(v)|$. There are some additional restrictions which we omit here, except to point out that for all $v, w \in V$, at most one of $v \in Y_w$ and $w \in Y_v$ can hold. As an example, the instrumental variable model (Figure 2(a)) is HTC-identifiable with $Y_a = \varnothing$ and $Y_b = Y_c = \{a\}$.

Using these sets Y_v, the algorithm for finding Λ solves a sequence of linear systems, one for each $v \in V$: Let $Y_v = \{y_1, \dots, y_n\}$ and $\mathrm{pa}(v) = \{p_1, \dots, p_n\}$, and define $\mathbf{A} \in \mathbb{R}^{n \times n}$ and $\mathbf{b} \in \mathbb{R}^n$ as

$$\mathbf{A}_{ij} = \begin{cases} [(I - \Lambda)^T \Sigma]_{y_i p_j} & \text{if } y_i \in \mathrm{htr}(v), \\ \Sigma_{y_i p_j} & \text{if } y_i \notin \mathrm{htr}(v); \end{cases}$$

$$\mathbf{b}_i = \begin{cases} [(I - \Lambda)^T \Sigma]_{y_i v} & \text{if } y_i \in \mathrm{htr}(v), \\ \Sigma_{y_i v} & \text{if } y_i \notin \mathrm{htr}(v). \end{cases}$$

Then the vector $\Lambda_{\mathrm{pa}(v),v}$ is found by solving $\mathbf{A} \cdot \Lambda_{\mathrm{pa}(v),v} = \mathbf{b}$. After the entire matrix Λ has been found this way, Ω is given by $(I - \Lambda)^T \Sigma (I - \Lambda)$.

2.2 SOME TERMINOLOGY FROM ALGEBRAIC GEOMETRY

This section very briefly highlights the main terms from algebraic geometry; we refer to Cox et al. (2015) for further reading.

[3]Here we follow the (more natural) definition of Chen et al. (2014) rather than that of Foygel et al. (2012).

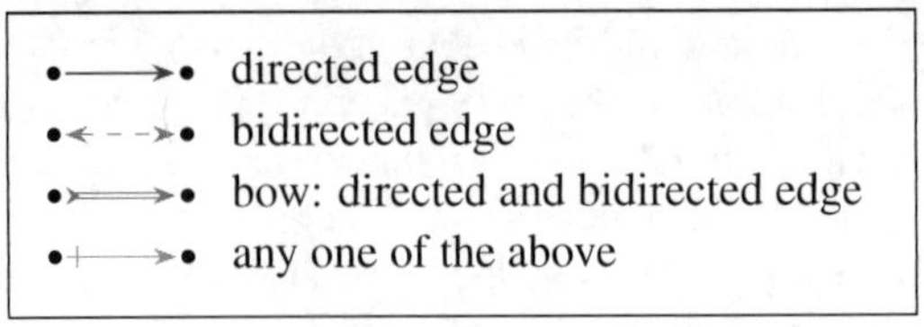

Figure 4: Legend for the edges we use to denote (sets of) graphs.

Algebraic geometry studies sets of points defined by systems of polynomial equations. For points in $\mathbb{R}^n$, such a set is called an *affine variety*. The set of polynomials that are identically zero on some set of points form an *ideal*. The *Zariski closure* of a set of points is obtained by first finding the ideal of the set, then taking all points for which the polynomials in the ideal all vanish.

2.3 NOTATION FOR SETS OF GRAPHS

The notation described here will be used in the remaining figures in this paper, and extensively in Appendix B in the supplementary material. When drawing a mixed graph, we draw directed edges in solid blue and bidirected edges in dashed red (see Figure 4; note that the colours are redundant but may aid visual distinction). Because we often want to show a set of graphs with a common node set V (e.g., an algebraic equivalence class of graphs), we use some new notation to avoid listing all graphs one by one. This notation is based on the *skeletons* of the graphs. Formally, the skeleton $S(G)$ of $G = (V, D, B)$ is the undirected graph on V that has an edge between a pair of nodes if there is at least one edge of any type between them in G. Similarly, our *graph patterns* also have at most one edge between each pair of nodes, with different markings to show what (combinations of) edges may occur between those nodes. For example, in this notation, a bow (a directed and a bidirected edge between two nodes) is represented visually as a double magenta line with 'fletching' at the back.

In a pattern representing a set of graphs, other edges occur in places where the graphs differ. The only such edge that appears in the patterns in the main paper is a green arrow with a plus sign as its tail. In all of these patterns, it can be understood to mean either a directed edge, a bidirected edge, or both. Its meaning changes if another edge is incident at the endpoint with the plus sign; for this case, additional markings are used and defined in Appendix B.

3 THEORETICAL RESULTS

We now present our main theoretical results.

3.1 ALGEBRAIC CONSTRAINTS

The statistical model $\mathcal{M}(G)$ for a graph G is defined by (1) in terms of the parameterization ϕ_G. This makes it hard to decide whether a given Σ belongs to a model, or whether two models differ. For these purposes, a more usable description of $\mathcal{M}(G)$ would be as a set of constraints that must hold for any $\Sigma \in \mathcal{M}(G)$: a set of functions $f_1, \ldots, f_k : \Sigma \to \mathbb{R}$ such that

$$\mathcal{M}(G) \subseteq \{\Sigma \in \mathrm{PD}_{|V|} \mid f_1(\Sigma) = \ldots = f_k(\Sigma) = 0\},$$

with the set difference a measure zero subset of the right-hand set.[4] For a DAG G, this can be done by choosing each f_i to be a partial correlation: $f_i(\Sigma) = \rho_{v_i w_i . S_i}(\Sigma)$ (Richardson and Spirtes, 2002). Put differently, vanishing partial correlation constraints fully describe such models.

In the more general case where G is allowed to contain bidirected edges and directed cycles, vanishing partial correlation constraints are not always expressive enough to describe $\mathcal{M}(G)$ (as we saw in the example of Figure 1). Below we present a method that allows us to write down a list of equality constraints that together describe $\mathcal{M}(G)$, for any *HTC-identifiable graph G* (Foygel et al., 2012).

Any model $\mathcal{M}(G)$ is a *semi-algebraic* subset of $\mathrm{PD}_{|V|}$: it can be described by a set of polynomial (in)equalities (Sullivant et al., 2010). Thus we may use the terms 'equality constraint' and 'algebraic (i.e. polynomial) constraint' interchangeably, and similarly for 'inequality' and 'semi-algebraic'.

The question of finding constraints that describe $\mathcal{M}(G)$ is related to the question of parameter identifiability. Identifiability of a graph G means that for given Σ, *at most* one pair of parameter values (Λ, Ω) exists for which $\phi_G(\Lambda, \Omega) = \Sigma$ (in other words, the *fibre* $\phi_G^{-1}(\Sigma)$ has cardinality at most one). We ask for what Σ (up to measure zero subsets as above) *exactly one* such pair exists. The main tool used here is the algorithm for retrieving the parameters of an HTC-identifiable graph that appears in the proof of Theorem 1 of Foygel et al. (2012), and that we sketched in Section 2.1. For given G and $\mathcal{Y} = (Y_v)_v$ (which we will call *HTC-identifying sets*) satisfying the conditions of the HTC-identifiability theorem, this algorithm defines a rational function that maps Σ to Λ by solving a sequence of linear equation systems. We write this function as $\Lambda_{\mathcal{Y}}(\Sigma)$.[5] Points Σ for which the algorithm encounters a singular matrix are excluded from the domain of $\Lambda_{\mathcal{Y}}$.

[4]Put more precisely, the difference is contained in an affine variety of lower dimension.

[5]Note that this function does not depend on the ordering $\prec$ that also appears in the HTC-identifiability theorem.

Theorem 1 below shows that a graph G imposes the following constraints:

$$[(I - \Lambda_{\mathcal{Y}}(\Sigma))^T \Sigma (I - \Lambda_{\mathcal{Y}}(\Sigma))]_{vw} = 0 \quad \text{for all } \{v, w\} \notin B \text{ with } v \notin Y_w \text{ and } w \notin Y_v. \quad (2)$$

Each left-hand side in these equations is a rational function of Σ: a function of the form $p(\Sigma)/q(\Sigma)$, with p and q polynomials. Instead of these rational constraints, it will often be useful to consider the polynomial constraints $p(\Sigma) = 0$ obtained by multiplying out the denominator. For Σ with $q(\Sigma) \neq 0$, $p(\Sigma) = 0$ iff $p(\Sigma)/q(\Sigma) = 0$, so the two forms of the constraints agree whenever both are defined (see the proof of Theorem 1 for details). The polynomial constraints have the advantage that they are defined everywhere.

As an example, consider again the graph in Figure 1. For $\mathcal{Y}$ with $Y_b = \{a\}$, $Y_d = \{c\}$ and $Y_a = Y_c = \varnothing$, (2) gives us one rational constraint (for $v = b$, $w = d$):

$$\begin{bmatrix} 1 & -\Lambda_{\mathcal{Y}}(\Sigma)_{ab} \end{bmatrix} \begin{bmatrix} \sigma_{bd} & \sigma_{bb} \\ \sigma_{ad} & \sigma_{ab} \end{bmatrix} \begin{bmatrix} 1 \\ -\Lambda_{\mathcal{Y}}(\Sigma)_{bd} \end{bmatrix} = 0,$$

where $\Lambda_{\mathcal{Y}}(\Sigma)_{ab} = \sigma_{ab}/\sigma_{aa}$ and $\Lambda_{\mathcal{Y}}(\Sigma)_{bd} = \sigma_{cd}/\sigma_{bc}$. Multiplying out the denominators, we obtain the polynomial constraint

$$\sigma_{aa}\sigma_{bd}\sigma_{bc} - \sigma_{aa}\sigma_{bb}\sigma_{cd} - \sigma_{ab}\sigma_{ad}\sigma_{bc} + \sigma_{ab}^2\sigma_{cd} = 0. \quad (3)$$

Theorem 1. *For an HTC-identifiable graph G with HTC-identifying sets $\mathcal{Y} = (Y_v)_v$ and generic Σ, $\Sigma \in \mathcal{M}(G)$ iff $\Lambda_{\mathcal{Y}}(\Sigma) \in \mathbb{R}^D_{reg}$ and Σ satisfies the rational constraints (2). A stronger statement holds in one direction:* All *(not merely generic) $\Sigma \in \mathcal{M}(G)$ satisfy the polynomial constraints described above.*

This means that the constraints (2) define the model $\mathcal{M}(G)$ up to a measure zero set that may satisfy all constraints, but still be missing from $\mathcal{M}(G)$. In particular, it shows that the model of an HTC-identifiable graph imposes no semi-algebraic (i.e. inequality) constraints. This is not true for general graphs, as we will see in Section 3.3.

The HT-overidentifying constraints from Chen et al. (2014) are also based on (a version of) the half-trek criterion, but unlike (2), they do not give a full description of the algebraic constraints imposed by a graph G: no constraint is found for pairs $\{v, w\}$ with $v \notin \mathrm{htr}(w)$ and $w \notin \mathrm{htr}(v)$. An example is given in Appendix A.

There may often be several ways of expressing Λ in terms of Σ, using different HTC-identifying sets $\mathcal{Y}$. As a result, the rational constraints may look very different, though they may become the same when converted to polynomial form. For example, a different choice of $\mathcal{Y}$ for the graph in Figure 1 would have led to a different rational expression than we found above. Similarly, sets of constraints may be found which are different when compared one by one, even in polynomial form, but which together still define the same model (in the terminology of algebraic geometry, they generate the same ideal). For example, if $\sigma_{ab} = 0$, then $\sigma_{ac} = 0$ iff $\rho_{ac.b} = 0$, so that a model satisfying all these constraints can be described in two ways using two constraints, or redundantly using all three constraints. So while the set of constraints (2) is not unique, Theorem 1 shows that they are a complete description of $\mathcal{M}(G)$: the model imposes no algebraic constraints beyond these.

Theorem 1 only applies to HTC-identifiable graphs. This immediately excludes graphs which are not generically identifiable; we will revisit those in Sections 3.2 and 3.3. However, it also excludes graphs that are generically identifiable but not HTC-identifiable. For the case of acyclic graphs on four variables, HTC-identifiability is complete (in the sense that all generically identifiable graphs are also HTC-identifiable), but this is no longer true when either more nodes or cycles are allowed. Finding more general sufficient graphical criteria for generic identifiability is the topic of ongoing research (Chen et al., 2014; Chen, 2016; Drton and Weihs, 2016; Chen et al., 2017). Because these criteria are extensions of HTC-identifiability, our Theorem 1 might be extended to work with these criteria as well.

3.2 ALGEBRAIC EQUIVALENCE AND INFINITE-TO-ONE GRAPHS

We now turn to the second central problem we address in this paper, namely checking whether two graphs G_1 and G_2 are algebraically equivalent. Theorem 1 from the previous section in principle allows us to do this: we need to check that each equality constraint imposed by G_1 is implied by G_2's equality constraints, and vice versa. However, the general solution for such tasks from algebraic geometry (computing Gröbner bases (Cox et al., 2015)) is computationally extremely expensive. The theorem below gives a sufficient condition for algebraic equivalence that relies only on graphical criteria that can be checked efficiently.

Another limitation of Theorem 1 is that it only applies to HTC-identifiable graphs, so it does not help us in finding equivalences involving graphs that are not HTC-identifiable. This issue is also addressed by the following theorem.

Theorem 2. *If G is generically infinite-to-one, G' generically finite-to-one and obtained by deleting k edges from G, and this k is the smallest number for which such a G' exists, then G and G' are algebraically equivalent. If further G' imposes no inequality constraint, $\mathcal{M}(G)$ and $\mathcal{M}(G')$ are equal up to a measure zero subset.*

A relation between forms of model equivalence and lack of parameter identifiability has been shown previously by Bekker et al. (1994). The following two corollaries serve to illustrate the power of this theorem.

Corollary 3. *All infinite-to-one graphs are algebraically equivalent to some finite-to-one graph.*

This implies that it is not a limitation that Theorem 1 does not apply to infinite-to-one graphs: for any such graph, these always exists a finite-to-one graph that we can consider instead. In particular, if this finite-to-one graph is HTC-identifiable, then this gives us a complete description of the infinite-to-one graph as a set of equality constraints.

Corollary 4. *If two generically finite-to-one graphs G'_1, G'_2 are each obtained by deleting an edge from a single generically infinite-to-one graph G, then G'_1 and G'_2 are algebraically equivalent to each other (and their models are equal up to a measure zero subset if they impose no inequality constraints).*

Combined with graphical criteria for generic (in)finite-to-oneness, this gives a sufficient *graphical* condition for model equivalence. As an example, take G'_1 and G'_2 to be the two graphs in Figure 2, and G to be their union (thus having three nodes and four edges). G'_1 and G'_2 are generically finite-to-one, while G is generically infinite-to-one (it is HTC-nonidentifiable). Then Corollary 4 states that G'_1 and G'_2 are algebraically equivalent. In fact, both graphs are HTC-identifiable, so they impose no inequality constraints, and their models are thus equal up to measure zero subsets.

By repeatedly applying Corollary 4, equivalence of many more pairs of models may be established. This is illustrated by the following proposition (which is similar to (Nowzohour et al., 2017, Theorem 2), though there the stronger relation of distributional equivalence is shown).

Proposition 5. *If two bow-free acyclic graphs have the same skeleton, and any 2-edge path through three distinct nodes that is a collider in one graph is a collider in both, the graphs are algebraically equivalent.*

3.2.1 Algebraic Equivalence Classes on Four Nodes

Using Theorems 1 and 2 and information on the identifiability of the acyclic graphs on four nodes, we can determine the algebraic equivalence classes of these graphs. An explicit description of these classes is given in Appendix B. Here we describe some details of how these results were derived.

Using HTC-identifiability and HTC-nonidentifiability, almost all acyclic graphs on four nodes can be classified as either generically identifiable or generically infinite-to-one. With the additional information from (Foygel et al., 2012) that the remaining graphs are generically finite-to-one (see Section 3.3), we can apply Theorem 2 to all these graphs. Together with transitivity, this partitions the set of graphs into 419 subsets, which we will call *clusters* here. Because the theorem only gives a sufficient condition for algebraic equivalence, this partition may be finer than the partition into algebraic equivalence classes. We still need to check if algebraic equivalences exist between different clusters.

Among clusters imposing two or more equality constraints, all but three (up to graph isomorphism) can be described by vanishing (partial) correlation constraints. Because graphs in different Markov equivalence classes must also be in different algebraic equivalence classes, we only need to focus on these remaining three clusters. One of these imposes the Verma constraint (Verma and Pearl, 1991); the other two both impose the constraints $\sigma_{cd} = 0$ and $\sigma_{ac}\sigma_{bd} - \sigma_{ad}\sigma_{bc} = 0$ (a vanishing tetrad constraint). These two latter clusters are shown in Figure 5(a) and (b). So those two clusters are algebraically equivalent, while no other algebraic equivalences among these graphs were missed by Theorem 2.

For graphs imposing only one equality constraint, it is much easier to check if two graphs impose the same equality constraint, as we do not need to worry about the possibility of two equality constraints implying a third (see Section 3.1). In algebraic terminology, these models are described by principal ideals; for these, equality can be checked by normalizing the generating polynomials so that their leading coefficients equal one (Cox et al., 2015). This way, we find that among graphs imposing one equality constraint, the three clusters (up to isomorphism) shown in Figure 5(c), (d) and (e) are actually algebraically equivalent to each other, while all others are different. This leaves a total of 389 algebraic equivalence classes.

Interestingly, the graphs imposing a vanishing tetrad constraint and no other equality constraints were all determined to be algebraically equivalent by Theorem 2.

3.2.2 Consequences for Model Selection

The theoretical results we presented above offer enormous benefits to model selection, in particular to score-based methods. Without any knowledge of model equivalence, a score-based method for model selection may in principle need to score all different graphs. Even for the limited case of acyclic graphs on four nodes, there are 34752 distinct graphs, making such an approach clearly not practical. For this reason, most score-based methods for model selection rely on a coarser concept of equivalence such as Markov equivalence, or even limit themselves to DAGs, ignoring the possibility of latent confounders entirely (Drton and Maathuis, 2017). As demonstrated in Section 3.2.1, our theoretical results can be used to determine the 389 algebraic equivalence classes. Scoring just one representative of each class leads to huge computational savings, making algebraic equivalence class selection feasible. As will be elaborated on in Section 4, the gains become even larger when these representatives are chosen cleverly: for example, the maximum likelihood parameters of a DAG are generally much easier to compute than those of a graph which also includes bidirected edges, so by picking a DAG from each class that contains one, we can avoid many relatively expensive score computations on more complex graphs.

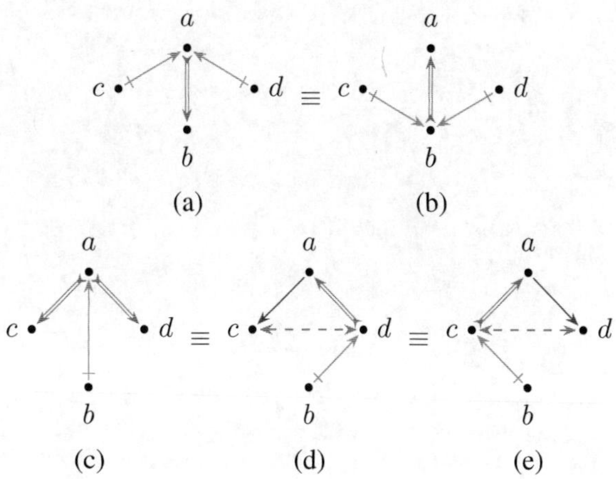

Figure 5: The algebraic equivalences not detected by Theorem 2: clusters (a) and (b) are algebraically equivalent to each other, and the same is true for clusters (c), (d) and (e).

When we are looking for maximum likelihood parameters for an HTC-identifiable graph G but our maximum likelihood fitting procedure has difficulty converging, it may be beneficial to apply the procedure to an 'easier' algebraically equivalent graph G' instead. After maximum likelihood parameters (Λ', Ω') have been found, we can compute $\Sigma = \phi_{G'}(\Lambda', \Omega')$, the point in $\mathcal{M}(G')$ where the likelihood is maximized; this will be the same point for all algebraically equivalent models (up to the nongeneric case where $\Sigma \notin \mathcal{M}(G)$—though then points arbitrarily close to Σ will be included in $\mathcal{M}(G)$). For this Σ, we can compute parameters (Λ, Ω) for which $\phi_G(\Lambda, \Omega) = \Sigma$ using the algorithm in the proof of Theorem 1 of Foygel et al. (2012).

Because Theorem 2 only provides a sufficient condition

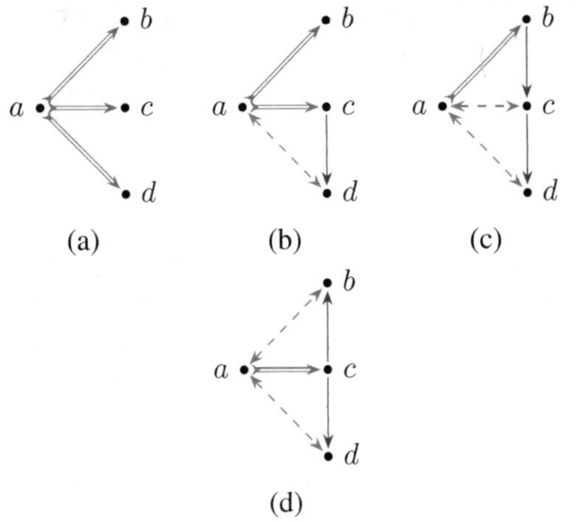

Figure 6: Four acyclic finite-to-one graphs.

for algebraic equivalence, an automatic procedure for model selection based on this theorem may sometimes fail to recognize that two classes of graphs are equivalent, and consider both separately (unless the results of Theorem 1 are also considered by the algorithm, similar to how we used them above). While this means that some redundant computational work is done, it does not hurt the quality of model selection, and the gains in computation time are still enormous compared to testing all models individually: 34752 acyclic mixed graphs on four nodes are grouped into 419 clusters by Theorem 2, which is very close to the 389 algebraic equivalence classes we would find by also looking at the constraints.

3.3 FINITE-TO-ONE GRAPHS AND INEQUALITY CONSTRAINTS

Among the acyclic graphs on four nodes, four (up to graph isomorphism) are HTC-inconclusive. These graphs are shown in Figure 6. By (Foygel et al., 2012, Table 1), these graphs are generically finite-to-one but not identifiable. We used this in Section 3.2.1 to assign them to algebraic equivalence classes, and found that all are algebraically equivalent to the saturated model.

Because these graphs are not generically identifiable, Theorem 1 does not apply to them, so we cannot rule out the possibility that they impose inequality constraints. Indeed, the proposition below shows that one of the graphs imposes such a constraint, so that its model differs from the saturated model by a subset of nonzero measure. We believe the other graphs listed here impose similar constraints, and expect that the same is true for many other graphs that are generically finite-to-one but not generically identifiable.

Proposition 6. *The model of the graph in Figure 6(a) imposes the inequality constraint* $\rho_{bc.a} \cdot \rho_{cd.a} \cdot \rho_{bd.a} \leq 0$.

4 EXPERIMENTAL RESULTS

In Section 4.2, we will describe the results of a model selection experiment using algebraic equivalence classes, choosing the class with the best BIC score from among those found in Section 3.2.1. We define the BIC score of an equivalence class as the best score among its models; this can be determined by computing the maximum likelihood of just one member model. RICF (Drton et al., 2009) was used to find maximum likelihood parameters. We will first describe some empirical results about its convergence behaviour.

4.1 CONVERGENCE BEHAVIOUR OF RICF

As already mentioned in Section 3.2.2, knowing the algebraic equivalence classes is very useful in a model selection problem. Here we elaborate on this, based on Monte Carlo results.

RICF finds maximum likelihood parameters in its first iteration if the graph is a DAG (Drton et al., 2009). For all algebraic equivalence classes not containing a DAG (so all graphs in the class contain a bidirected edge), we saw evidence of local optima: when RICF was run with the same random data on different graphs in the same class, or with different initialization values, there would be different runs that all reported convergence but achieved different likelihoods. This could be addressed by random restarts. However, Drton and Richardson (2004) observe that for one of these graphs, local optima only present themselves when the model is misspecified. If the same is true for all graphs with bidirected edges, then it would follow that local minima will not change the results of model selection, as they only affect the scores of models that would not have scored well anyway. Either way, it is clearly advantageous to run RICF on a DAG, for every algebraic equivalence class that contains one.

For equivalence classes where all graphs contain a bow, RICF failed to converge relatively often (in fact, Drton et al. (2009) only discuss bow-free graphs). These equivalence classes contain graphs having different skeletons; as an example, the nine graphs represented by the pattern in Figure 5(a) have a different skeleton than those in Figure 5(b), but all are algebraically equivalent to each other. We found that for many data sets, RICF failed to converge on all graphs in such a class having one skeleton, even with random restarts, but did converge easily on graphs with a different skeleton. Knowing the algebraic equivalence classes is a great benefit here, as it would be very difficult to determine scores for all graphs in this situation otherwise. When scoring a model, if we find that RICF fails to converge on a graph of this type (e.g., one from Figure 5(a)), then we run RICF again on an alge-

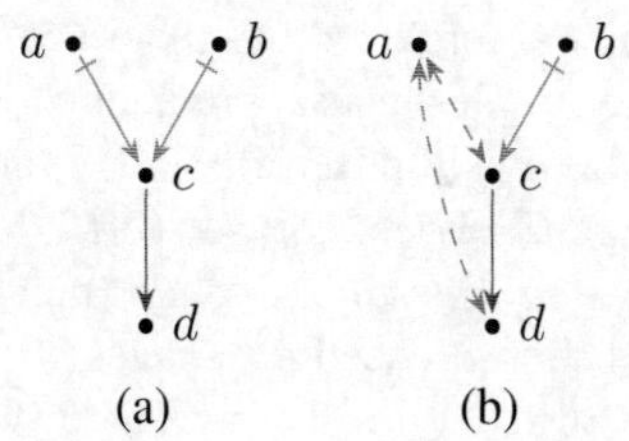

Figure 7: (a) A Y-structure; (b) an extended Y-structure.

braically equivalent graph with a different skeleton (one from Figure 5b).

4.2 USING ALGEBRAIC EQUIVALENCE CLASS SELECTION TO DETECT Y-STRUCTURES

To demonstrate the practical usefulness of algebraic equivalence class selection, we consider the setup of Mooij and Cremers (2015).[6] In a simulated dataset with $p \in \{10, 30, 50\}$ variables (with acyclic ground truth), they look at each ordered 4-tuple of distinct nodes, and use several independence tests to detect whether or not these nodes form a *Y-structure* or an *extended Y-structure* (see Figure 7). These are two of the simplest Markov equivalence classes (coinciding with algebraic equivalence classes) that must contain a directed edge in a fixed place that is not part of a bow, so detecting these structures in observational data allows us to draw conclusions about the results of interventions.

Mooij and Cremers observed that detecting 4-tuples which were in either of these two classes yielded poor precision, especially for larger p. Precision improved when additional tests were added so that only Y-structures were detected.

We applied algebraic equivalence class selection to this problem by taking the 4-tuples that tested positively according to one of these sets of tests, and then filtering out those for which the algebraic equivalence class with the best BIC score was different from the class / pair of classes being tested for. The resulting precisions are shown in Figure 8. The gains of this filtering procedure are significant when testing for both classes together: the precision is close to 0.1 larger for all p. We also show the results of filtering using only Maximal Ancestral Graphs (MAGs) (Richardson and Spirtes, 2002), thus only computing BIC scores of classes which can be described using vanishing partial correlations. This already yields a large improvement, but the gains from considering all algebraic equivalence classes instead are still significant, especially for the larger p. On the other hand, for 4-tuples

[6]The code for reproducing these results is available online at `https://github.com/caus-am/aelsem`.

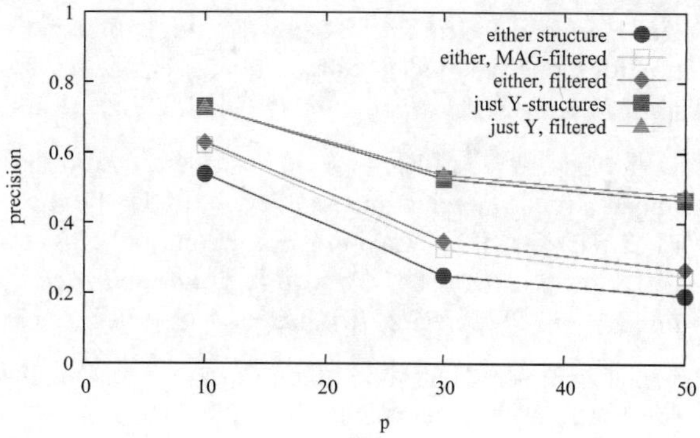

Figure 8: Precision of (extended) Y-structure detection.

that passed the more stringent Y-structure tests, the benefit of filtering is much smaller. Importantly, these gains in precision came at a very small cost in recall: of the true positives detected by a set of independence tests, at least 98% passed through the filter for each p.

5 CONCLUSION

We proposed the notion of algebraic equivalence for use in model selection among linear structural equation models, and showed how graphical criteria can be used to efficiently establish the equivalence of many models. Our experimental results show that the finer granularity of the resulting equivalence classes sometimes allows for improvements in model selection accuracy, compared to methods that only consider vanishing partial correlations.

While the experimental model selection results we show are limited to four nodes, we believe that the theoretical results described here can form the foundation of efficient causal inference algorithms on (much) larger numbers of nodes. For this, more work will need to be put into finding an efficient algorithm, for example by using ideas from Chickering (2002).

Acknowledgements

This project has received funding from the European Research Council (ERC) under the European Union's Horizon 2020 research and innovation programme (grant agreement n° 639466). The authors would like to thank Patrick Forré, Tom Claassen and the anonymous reviewers for their valuable comments.

References

Paul A. Bekker, Arjen Merckens, and Tom J. Wansbeek. *Identification, Equivalent Models, and Computer Algebra*. Academic Press, Boston, 1994.

Carlos Brito and Judea Pearl. A new identification condition for recursive models with correlated errors. *Structural Equation Modeling*, 9(4):459–474, 2002.

Bryant Chen. Identification and overidentification of linear structural equations models. In D. D. Lee, M. Sugiyama, U. V. Luxburg, I. Guyon, and R. Garnett, editors, *Advances in Neural Information Processing Systems 29 (NIPS 2016)*, pages 1579–1587, 2016.

Bryant Chen, Jin Tian, and Judea Pearl. Testable implications of linear structural equations models. In C. E. Brodley and P. Stone, editors, *Proceedings of the Twenty-Eighth AAAI Conference on Artificial Intelligence (AAAI)*, 2014.

Bryant Chen, Daniel Kumor, and Elias Bareinboim. Identification and model testing in linear structural equation models using auxiliary variables. Technical Report R-27-L, Purdue AI Lab, 2017.

David Maxwell Chickering. Optimal structure identification with greedy search. *Journal of Machine Learning Research*, 3:507–554, 2002.

David A. Cox, John Little, and Donal O'Shea. *Ideals, Varieties, and Algorithms*. Springer, New York, fourth edition, 2015.

Mathias Drton and Marloes H. Maathuis. Structure learning in graphical modeling. *Annual Review of Statistics and Its Applications*, 4:365–393, 2017.

Mathias Drton and Thomas S. Richardson. Multimodality of the likelihood in the bivariate seemingly unrelated regression model. *Biometrika*, 91(2):383–392, 2004.

Mathias Drton and Luca Weihs. Generic identifiability of linear structural equation models by ancestor decomposition. *Scandinavian Journal of Statistics*, 43: 1035–1045, 2016.

Mathias Drton, Michael Eichler, and Thomas S. Richardson. Computing maximum likelihood estimates in recursive linear models with correlated errors. *Journal of Machine Learning Research*, 10:2329–2348, 2009.

Robin J. Evans. Margins of discrete Bayesian networks. *arXiv preprint arXiv:1501.02103*, 2015.

Rina Foygel, Jan Draisma, and Mathias Drton. Half-trek criterion for generic identifiability of linear structural equation models. *The Annals of Statistics*, 40(3): 1682–1713, 2012.

Luis D. García-Puente, Sarah Spielvogel, and Seth Sullivant. Identifying causal effects with computer algebra. In P. Grünwald and P. Spirtes, editors, *Proceedings of the Twenty-Sixth Conference on Uncertainty in Artificial Intelligence (UAI 2010)*, 2010.

Joris M. Mooij and Jerome Cremers. An empirical study of one of the simplest causal prediction algorithms. In Ricardo Silva, Ilya Shpitser, Robin J. Evans, Jonas Peters, and Tom Claassen, editors, *UAI 2015 Workshop on Advances in Causal Inference*, number 1504 in CEUR Workshop Proceedings, pages 30–39, Aachen, 2015. URL `http://ceur-ws.org/Vol-1504/uai2015aci_paper2.pdf`.

Christopher Nowzohour, Marloes H. Maathuis, Robin J. Evans, and Peter Bühlmann. Structure learning for bow-free acyclic path diagrams. *arXiv preprint arXiv:1508.01717v3*, 2017.

Judea Pearl. *Causality: Models, Reasoning, and Inference*. Cambridge University Press, New York, NY, USA, 2000.

Thomas S. Richardson and Peter Spirtes. Ancestral graph Markov models. *The Annals of Statistics*, 30 (4):962–1030, 2002.

James Robins. A new approach to causal inference in mortality studies with a sustained exposure period—application to control of the healthy worker survivor effect. *The Annals of Statistics*, 7:1393–1512, 1986.

Ilya Shpitser, Robin J. Evans, Thomas S. Richardson, and James M. Robins. Introduction to nested Markov models. *Behaviormetrika*, 41(1):3–39, 2014.

Ricardo Silva and Zoubin Ghahramani. Bayesian inference for Gaussian mixed graph models. In *Proceedings of the Twenty-Second Conference on Uncertainty in Artificial Intelligence (UAI 2006)*, pages 453–460, 2006.

Peter Spirtes, Clark Glymour, and Richard Scheines. *Causation, Prediction, and Search.* MIT Press, Cambridge, MA, second edition, 2000.

Seth Sullivant, Kelli Talaska, and Jan Draisma. Trek separation for Gaussian graphical models. *The Annals of Statistics*, 38(3):1665–1685, 2010.

Jin Tian and Judea Pearl. On the testable implications of causal models with hidden variables. In *Proceedings of the 18th Conference on Uncertainty in Artificial Intelligence (UAI 2002)*, 2002.

T. S. Verma and Judea Pearl. Equivalence and synthesis of causal models. In *Proceedings of the Sixth Conference on Uncertainty in Artificial Intelligence (UAI 1991)*, 1991.

SUPPLEMENTARY MATERIAL

A PROOFS

Proof of Theorem 1. First assume $\Sigma \in \mathcal{M}(G)$, and consider the equations

$$[(I-\Lambda)^T\Sigma(I-\Lambda)]_{vw} = 0 \quad \text{for all } \{v,w\} \notin B \quad (4)$$

(this is equation (9.2) in Foygel et al. (2012)). Treating the entries of Λ and Σ as variables λ and σ, define the rational function $\delta := \det(I-\Lambda)^{-1}$. Then the left-hand sides of (4) are polynomials in $\mathbb{R}[\lambda,\sigma,\delta]$ generating an ideal $\mathcal{I}$. This ideal consists of all polynomials that are zero everywhere on the set of all (λ,σ) with δ well-defined and $\Sigma = \phi_G(\Lambda,\Omega)$ for some $\Omega \in \mathrm{PD}(B)$ (Foygel et al., 2012, Section 8 of the supplement). In addition to the left-hand sides of (4), (using that G is rationally identifiable) the ideal $\mathcal{I}$ contains for each directed edge $(u,v) \in D$ an element $a(\sigma)\lambda_{uv} - b(\sigma)$ for some nonzero polynomials $a, b \in \mathbb{R}[\sigma]$. By multiplying a left-hand side of (4) by some polynomial and adding polynomial multiples of the ideal elements mentioned above, we can eliminate λ and find an element in $\mathcal{I} \cap \mathbb{R}[\sigma]$. This represents a polynomial constraint that *all* $\Sigma \in \mathcal{M}(G)$ must satisfy, and we see that the polynomial constraints described in the main text can be obtained in this way. This implies that also the rational constraints (2) are satisfied for any Σ that is additionally in the domain of $\Lambda_{\mathcal{Y}}$.

If $\Sigma \in \mathcal{M}(G)$, then there exist $\Lambda \in \mathbb{R}^D_{\text{reg}}$ and $\Omega \in \mathrm{PD}(B)$ for which $\Sigma = \phi_G(\Lambda,\Omega)$. In the generic case, $\Lambda_{\mathcal{Y}}$ will recover the parameter matrix Λ; in particular, $\Lambda_{\mathcal{Y}}(\Sigma) \in \mathbb{R}^D_{\text{reg}}$.

Conversely, suppose Σ is in the domain of $\Lambda_{\mathcal{Y}}$, $\Lambda_{\mathcal{Y}}(\Sigma) \in \mathbb{R}^D_{\text{reg}}$, and Σ satisfies (2). Let $\Lambda = \Lambda_{\mathcal{Y}}(\Sigma)$ and $\Omega = (I-\Lambda)^T\Sigma(I-\Lambda)$. Σ and Λ again satisfy (4):

For $\{v,w\}$ with $v \notin Y_w$ and $w \notin Y_v$: by (2);

For $\{v,w\}$ with $w = y_i \in Y_v \cap \mathrm{htr}(v)$:

$$\left[(I-\Lambda)^T\Sigma\Lambda\right]_{wv} = (\mathbf{A}\cdot\Lambda_{\mathrm{pa}(v),v})_i = \mathbf{b}_i = \left[(I-\Lambda)^T\Sigma\right]_{wv}$$

(with $\mathbf{A}$ and $\mathbf{b}$ as in Foygel et al. (2012) / in Section 2.1), which implies (4) for $\{v,w\}$;

For $\{v,w\}$ with $w \in Y_v \setminus \mathrm{htr}(v)$: Fix any node v, and let $W = Y_v \setminus \mathrm{htr}(v)$ and $I = \{i \mid y_i \in W\}$. Then

$$[\Sigma\Lambda]_{Wv} = (\mathbf{A}\cdot\Lambda_{\mathrm{pa}(v),v})_I = \mathbf{b}_I = \Sigma_{Wv},$$

from which follows

$$\begin{aligned}\mathbf{0} &= [\Sigma(I-\Lambda)]_{Wv} \\ &= \left[(I-\Lambda)^{-T}(I-\Lambda)^T\Sigma(I-\Lambda)\right]_{Wv} \\ &= \left[(I-\Lambda)^{-T}\Omega\right]_{Wv} = \sum_{x\in V}[(I-\Lambda)^{-T}]_{Wx}\Omega_{xv}.\end{aligned}$$

In the case distinction that follows, we use that for all $x \neq v$ with $x \notin \mathrm{sib}(v)$, we have $x \in Y_v$, $v \in Y_x$, or neither. For x in one of the sets $Y_v \cap \mathrm{htr}(v)$, $\{x \mid v \in Y_x \cap \mathrm{htr}(x)\}$, or $\{x \mid x \neq v, x \notin \mathrm{sib}(v), x \notin Y_v, v \notin Y_x\}$, we know from the previous two cases that $\Omega_{xv} = \Omega_{vx} = 0$. For $x = v$ or $x \in \mathrm{sib}(v)$, $[(I-\Lambda)^{-T}]_{wx} = 0$ for any $w \in W$, because such a directed path from such x to w would form a half-trek from v to w. Similarly, for x such that $v \in Y_x \setminus \mathrm{htr}(x)$, also $[(I-\Lambda)^{-T}]_{wx} = 0$, or there would again be a half-trek from v to w. The above covers all cases except $x \in W$. So all terms in the previous sum with $x \notin W$ are zero, and we get

$$\mathbf{0} = [(I-\Lambda)^{-T}]_{WW}\Omega_{Wv}.$$

The entries of $[(I-\Lambda)^{-T}]_{WW}$ are polynomials in the variables Λ_{ij} and $\delta := \det(I-\Lambda)^{-1}$. The matrix $(I-\Lambda)^{-1}$ equals δ times the adjugate matrix of $(I-\Lambda)$; this adjugate matrix includes the constant term 1 in each diagonal entry, and no constant terms in any other entries. We see that the determinant of $[(I-\Lambda)^{-T}]_{WW}$ contains the term $\delta^{|W|}$ so it is not the zero polynomial. It follows that $[(I-\Lambda)^{-T}]_{WW}$ is generically invertible, so the only solution to the above equation is $\Omega_{wv} = 0$ for all $w \in W$. This again implies (4).

Then $\Omega = (I-\Lambda)^T\Sigma(I-\Lambda)$ is positive definite (using that Σ is positive definite and $I-\Lambda$ is invertible) and obeys $\Omega_{vw} = 0$ for $\{v,w\} \notin B$. For these parameters, $\Sigma = \phi_G(\Lambda,\Omega)$, showing that $\Sigma \in \mathcal{M}(G)$.

For generic $\Sigma \in \mathcal{M}(G)$, the matrices $\mathbf{A}$ that occur in the HTC-identifiability algorithm are invertible by (Foygel et al., 2012, Lemma 2), so the assumption above that Σ is in the domain of $\Lambda_{\mathcal{Y}}$ holds in the generic case. □

Example of a constraint that is not HT-overidentifying. Figure 9 gives an example graph which imposes one equality constraint, namely a vanishing tetrad constraint, which is not reported by Algorithm 2 of Chen et al. (2014). The graph is HTC-identifiable, so Theorem 1 will report the constraint. □

Figure 9: Graph imposing an equality constraint that is not HT-overidentifying.

Proof of Theorem 2. Define the *rank deficiency* of a graph as the difference between the number of columns and the generic rank of the Jacobian in (Foygel et al., 2012, proof of Theorem 2). The rank deficiency of a graph is zero iff that graph is finite-to-one, so the rank deficiency of G' is zero. Removing a directed edge from a graph removes a column from the Jacobian, which will not increase the rank, so this reduces the rank deficiency by at most one; removing a bidirected edge adds a row, which will increase the largest order of a non-vanishing minor (this order equals the rank) by at most one. It follows that the rank deficiency of G is at most k. In fact, it must be equal to k: suppose the rank deficiency of G is $k' < k$. Then by deleting k' columns from the Jacobian, a matrix of full column rank can be obtained. By deleting the corresponding k' directed edges from G, a graph with rank deficiency 0 is obtained; however, this is a contradiction with the conditions of the theorem, which imply that all such graphs are infinite-to-one.

By the statements in the beginning and end of the proof of Lemma 2 in the supplement of (Foygel et al., 2012), the dimensions of the images of ϕ_G and $\phi_{G'}$ (i.e. of $\mathcal{M}(G)$ and $\mathcal{M}(G')$) equal the ranks of the respective Jacobians as considered above plus the respective numbers of (co)variance parameters in Ω. It follows that the models' dimensions are equal. Because the models are defined by rational parameterizations, their Zariski closures are irreducible affine varieties (Cox et al., 2015, Proposition 4.5.6). For two such varieties, $W \subsetneq V$ would imply that the dimension of W is smaller than that of V. Because $\mathcal{M}(G') \subseteq \mathcal{M}(G)$, the models' Zariski closures must be equal; in other words, the models are algebraically equivalent.

If additionally G' imposes no inequality constraints, then $\mathcal{M}(G')$ is equal to its Zariski closure up to a measure zero subset. Using again that $\mathcal{M}(G') \subseteq \mathcal{M}(G)$ and that $\mathcal{M}(G)$ is contained in the models' common Zariski closure, we find that $\mathcal{M}(G')$ and $\mathcal{M}(G)$ are equal up to a measure zero subset. □

Proof of Proposition 5. First consider the special case of two acyclic bow-free graphs G'_1, G'_2 that differ in only one arrowhead which does not form a collider. Then the graph G containing the union of their edges (so having a bow where G'_1 and G'_2 had a different type of edge) is HTC-nonidentifiable, as the directed edge of the bow cannot be identified. An application of Corollary 4 shows that G'_1 and G'_2 are algebraically equivalent.

The algebraic equivalence of two arbitrary graphs G'_1, G'_2 with the same skeleton and colliders can now be shown using a finite sequence of such steps. Let G_1^Δ be the subgraph consisting of the edges of G'_1 that are not in G'_2, and let $W \subseteq V$ be the set of nodes where G'_1 and G'_2 have different incoming arrowheads. In G_1^Δ, at each node $w \in W$, there is at most one arrowhead (otherwise there is a collider in either G'_1 or G'_2 that is not in the other) and at most one arrowtail (two tails would become two colliding heads in G'_2), so each node $w \in W$ has degree at most 2 in G_1^Δ.

Now find the finest partition of the edges in G_1^Δ that groups two edges together if they are incident at a node $w \in W$. The edge sets in this partition form paths that may only meet each other at the endpoints, at nodes not in W. None of these paths can have two directed edges pointing away from each other (with possibly other edges in between), as that would imply G'_2 contains a collider not in G'_1. So each of these paths is a half-trek. At each step, modify the first edge of such a half-trek by adding an arrowhead that appears in G'_2 or removing one that does not. □

Proof of Proposition 6. Assume w.l.o.g. that Σ is normalized to a correlation matrix (with ones on the diagonal). Let $W = \{b, c, d\}$. Then for each pair of distinct nodes $x, y \in W$,

$$\begin{aligned}\sigma_{xy} &= \lambda_{ax}\lambda_{ay} + \lambda_{ax}\omega_{ay} + \omega_{ax}\lambda_{ay} \\ &= (\lambda_{ax} + \omega_{ax})(\lambda_{ay} + \omega_{ay}) - \omega_{ax}\omega_{ay} \\ &= \sigma_{ax}\sigma_{ay} - \omega_{ax}\omega_{ay}.\end{aligned}$$

It follows that

$$\omega_{ax}\omega_{ay} = \sigma_{ax}\sigma_{ay} - \sigma_{xy}. \tag{5}$$

We have three of these equations for the three possible pairs in W. If all three ω_{aw}'s have the same sign, all these expressions will be positive; otherwise, two will be negative and one positive. Other combinations of positive and negative cannot be attained by any choice of Ω. Using that (5) has the same sign as $-\rho_{xy.a}$, we can write this as the inequality constraint $\rho_{bc.a} \cdot \rho_{cd.a} \cdot \rho_{bd.a} \leq 0$.

The observed covariance matrix

$$\Sigma = \begin{bmatrix} 1 & 0 & 0 & 0 \\ 0 & 1 & 1/2 & 1/2 \\ 0 & 1/2 & 1 & 1/2 \\ 0 & 1/2 & 1/2 & 1 \end{bmatrix}$$

is an example of a positive definite matrix (so an element of the saturated model) that does not satisfy this inequality constraint. In fact, it is easy to see that an open ball around Σ has this property, showing that the inequality constraint rules out a part of the saturated model having nonzero measure. □

B ACYCLIC ALGEBRAIC EQUIVALENCE CLASSES ON FOUR NODES

Before presenting in Section B.2 a full description of the algebraic equivalence classes of four-node acyclic graphs, we first introduce the additional graph notation we will use.

B.1 NOTATION FOR SETS OF GRAPHS, CONTINUED

In Section 2.3, we described how our graph patterns represent directed edges, bidirected edges, and bows. The full list of markings we use in Section B.2 is displayed in Figure 10. To describe these markings, we need to extend the well-known concept of colliders (see e.g. Spirtes et al. (2000)) to graph skeletons. A 2-edge path in the skeleton $S(G)$ of G along three distinct nodes (v_1, v_2, v_3) is called a *collider* if for both edges of the path, a corresponding edge exists in the original graph G with an arrowhead at v_2. Such an edge could be either bidirected, or directed towards v_2. We distinguish two cases: if *all* corresponding edges in the original graph G have arrowheads at v_2 (in other words, there are no directed edges in G from v_2 to either v_1 or v_3), we call the path a *full collider*; otherwise we call it a *partial collider*. An example of a partial collider is the path (a, b, c) in the instrumental variable model (Figure 2(a)). When looking at the endpoint at v_2 of an edge in $S(G)$ between v_1 and v_2, we say that it *forms a (full/partial) collider* if a node v_3 exists for which the path along (v_1, v_2, v_3) is a (full/partial) collider. Note that an endpoint can simultaneously form a full collider and a partial collider, for different choices of v_3.

In a graph pattern denoting a set of graphs, if all graphs in the set have the same edge(s) between two given nodes, this edge is displayed as for a single graph, as in Section 2.3. If the graphs in the set have different edges between two nodes, these are represented in the graph pattern by a green edge, which may have different endpoint markings. First of all, if all edges to be represented have an arrowhead at an endpoint, then the graph pattern will also show an arrowhead. Otherwise, the following special markings are used (illustrated in Figure 10): a plus sign if the endpoint never forms a collider in any of the graphs; a bracket if it always forms a partial collider; and a star in all other cases. Finally, if two nodes are adjacent in some graphs in the set but not in others, then an edge is shown in dotted grey; other aspects of the edge's appearance are determined using only the graphs in which the nodes are adjacent.

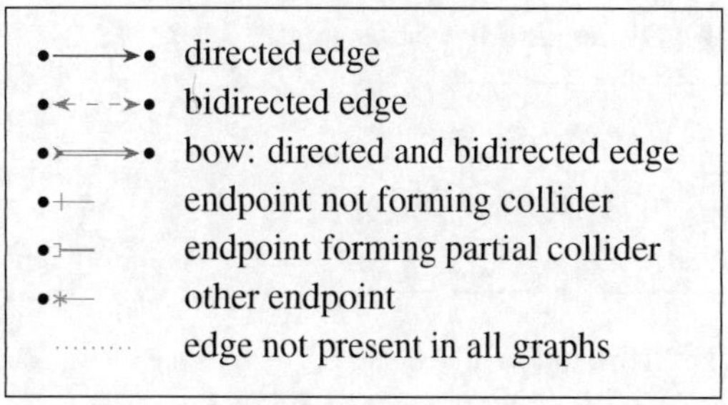

Figure 10: Legend for the edges and endpoints we use to denote (sets of) graphs.

B.2 TABLE OF EQUIVALENCE CLASSES

Each entry in the table below represents one algebraic equivalence class and its isomorphisms (obtained by relabelling the nodes). The leftmost column shows the set of graphs in this equivalence class, using the notation for graph patterns explained in Sections 2.3 and B.1. For each equivalence class, its algebraic constraints (found by Theorem 1 and converted to polynomial form) are also listed.

For many equivalence classes, the set of graphs that fit the pattern in the leftmost column is a superset of the equivalence class: some acyclic graphs that match the pattern do not actually belong in the class, but our notation is not expressive enough to show the precise inclusions in one figure. For each equivalence class where this is the case, a second column of smaller graph patterns appears. The union of the sets of graphs described by these patterns equals the equivalence class exactly. Because many of the graph patterns in the union are graph isomorphisms of each other, we show only one member of each isomorphism class, and indicate how many isomorphisms there are by writing '$n\times$'. (Each of these isomorphisms is an automorphism of the leftmost graph pattern, and there are always exactly n such isomorphic patterns, so no information is lost by not listing them explicitly.) For example, the first equivalence class listed in Section B.2.3 consists of all acyclic graphs with at least one edge of any type between each pair of nodes in $\{a, b, c\}$, as well as all graphs in which one of those pairs has no edge between it, but the other two pairs make up a partial collider.

The equivalence classes are split out below according to their dimension. This refers to the dimension of the set of *correlation* rather than covariance matrices, thus normalizing out the variance Σ_{vv} associated with each node. This number has the convenient property that it equals the minimum number of edges among all graphs in an equivalence class.

B.2.0 Dimension 0

$\sigma_{ab} = 0, \sigma_{ac} = 0, \sigma_{ad} = 0,$
$\sigma_{bc} = 0, \sigma_{bd} = 0, \sigma_{cd} = 0$

B.2.1 Dimension 1

$\sigma_{ac} = 0, \sigma_{ad} = 0, \sigma_{bc} = 0, \sigma_{bd} = 0, \sigma_{cd} = 0$

B.2.2 Dimension 2

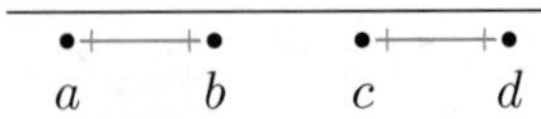

$\sigma_{ac} = 0, \sigma_{ad} = 0, \sigma_{bc} = 0, \sigma_{bd} = 0$

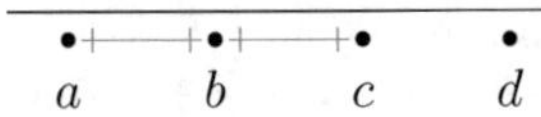

$\rho_{ac.b} = 0, \sigma_{ad} = 0, \sigma_{bd} = 0, \rho_{cd.b} = 0$

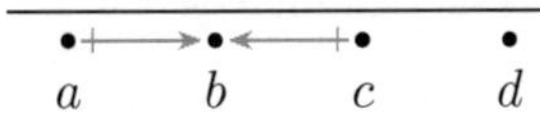

$\sigma_{ac} = 0, \sigma_{ad} = 0, \sigma_{bd} = 0, \sigma_{cd} = 0$

B.2.3 Dimension 3

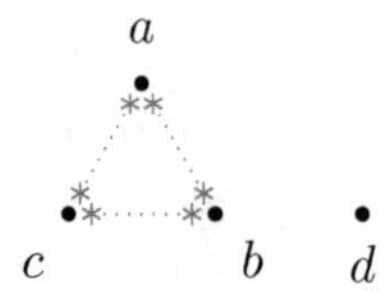

$\sigma_{ad} = 0, \sigma_{bd} = 0,$
$\sigma_{cd} = 0$

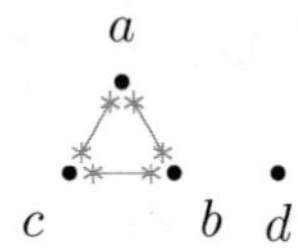

1×

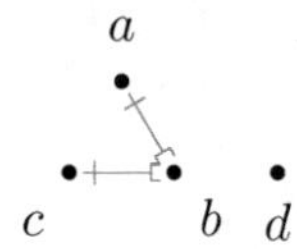

3×

$\rho_{ac.b} = 0, \rho_{ad.b} = 0, \rho_{bd.c} = 0$

$\sigma_{ac} = 0, \sigma_{ad} = 0, \rho_{bd.c} = 0$

$\sigma_{ac} = 0, \sigma_{ad} = 0, \sigma_{bd} = 0$

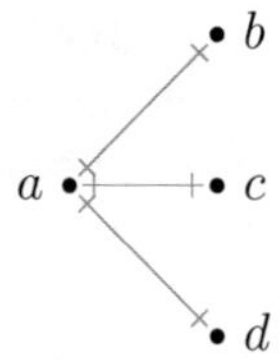

$\rho_{bc.a} = 0, \rho_{bd.a} = 0, \rho_{cd.a} = 0$

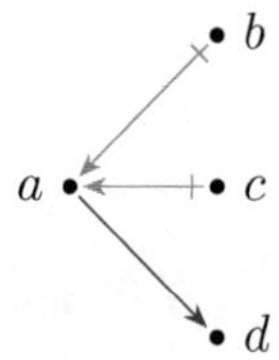

$\sigma_{bc} = 0, \rho_{bd.a} = 0, \rho_{cd.a} = 0$

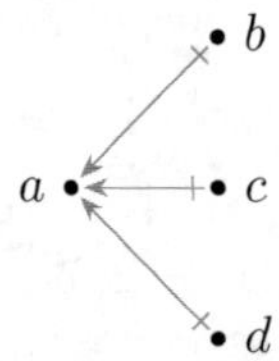

$\sigma_{bc} = 0, \sigma_{bd} = 0, \sigma_{cd} = 0$

B.2.4 Dimension 4

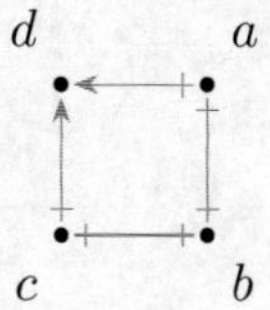

$\rho_{ac.b} = 0$, $\rho_{bd.ac} = 0$

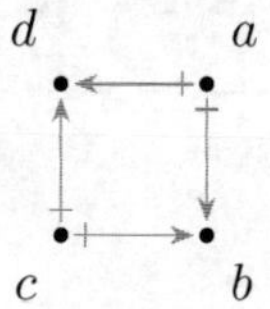

$\sigma_{ac} = 0$, $\rho_{bd.ac} = 0$

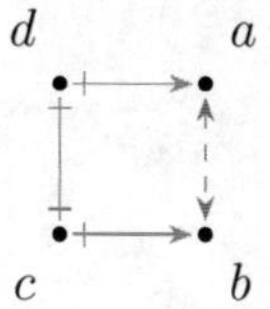

$\rho_{ac.d} = 0$, $\rho_{bd.c} = 0$

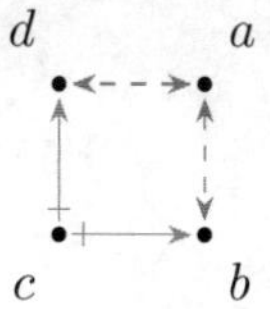

$\sigma_{ac} = 0$, $\rho_{bd.c} = 0$

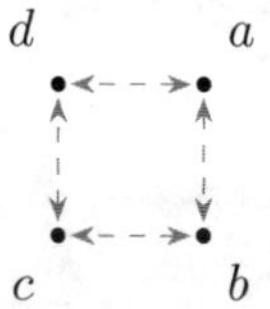

$\sigma_{ac} = 0$, $\sigma_{bd} = 0$

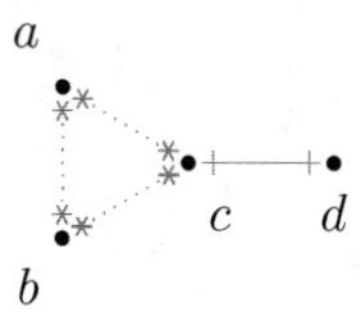

$\rho_{ad.c} = 0$, $\rho_{bd.c} = 0$

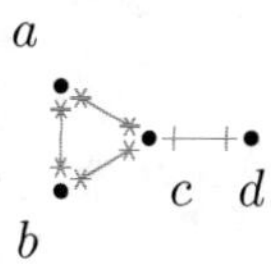

1×

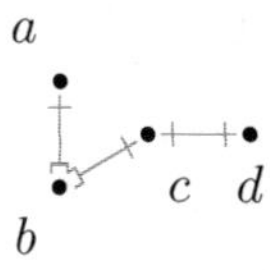

2×

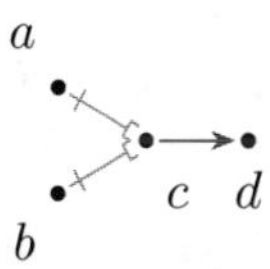

1×

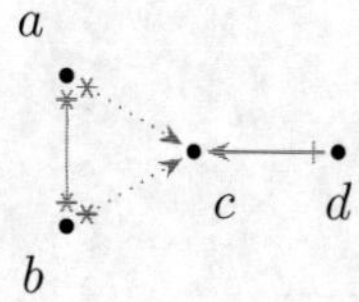

$\sigma_{ad} = 0$, $\sigma_{bd} = 0$

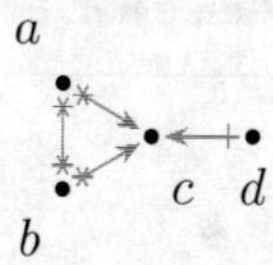

1×

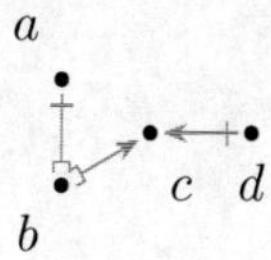

2×

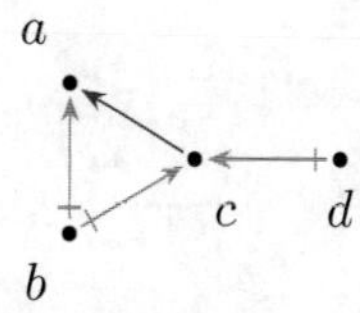

$\rho_{ad.bc} = 0$, $\sigma_{bd} = 0$

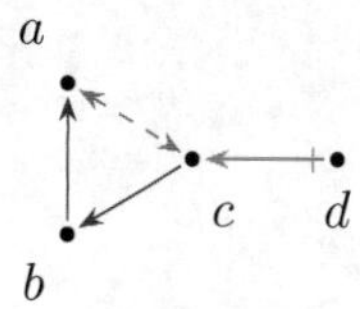

$\rho_{bd.c} = 0$,
$\sigma_{cc}\sigma_{ab}\sigma_{bd} - \sigma_{cc}\sigma_{bb}\sigma_{ad} - \sigma_{bc}\sigma_{ac}\sigma_{bd} + \sigma_{bc}^2\sigma_{ad} = 0$

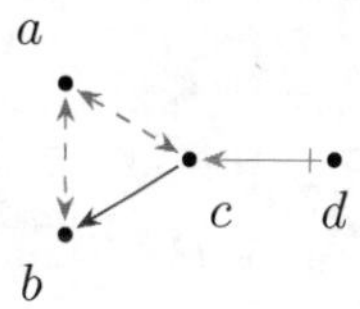

$\sigma_{ad} = 0$, $\rho_{bd.c} = 0$

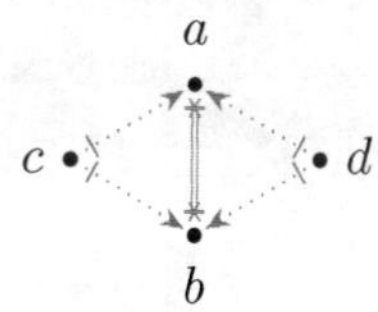

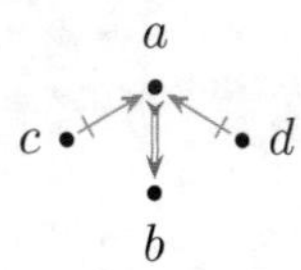

2×

$\sigma_{cd} = 0$, $\sigma_{ac}\sigma_{bd} - \sigma_{ad}\sigma_{bc} = 0$

B.2.5 Dimension 5

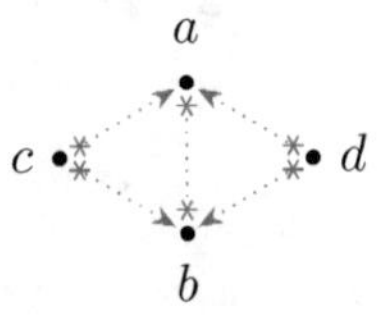

$\sigma_{cd} = 0$

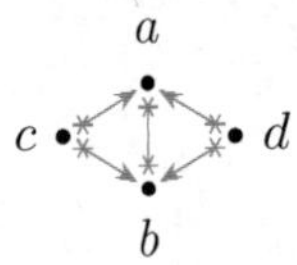

1×

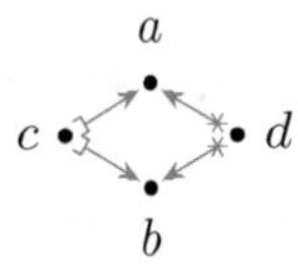

2×

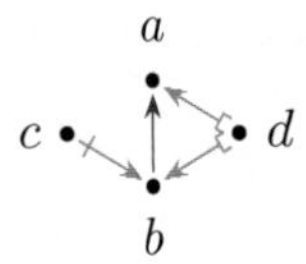

4×

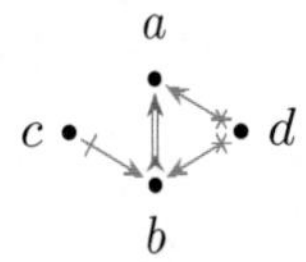

4×

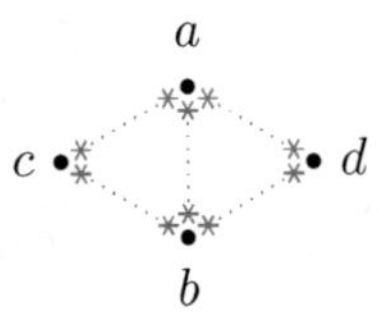

$\rho_{cd.ab} = 0$

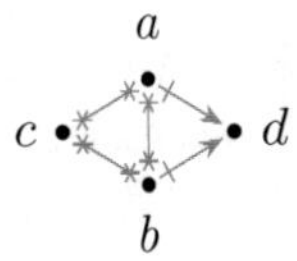

2×

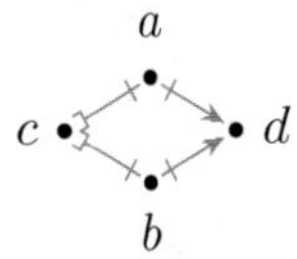

2×

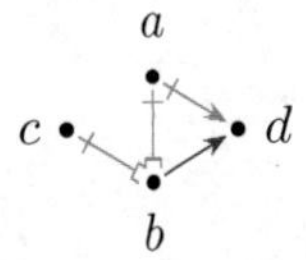

4×

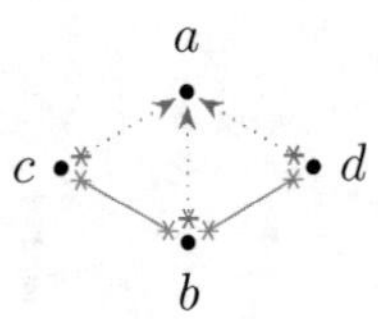

$\rho_{cd.b} = 0$

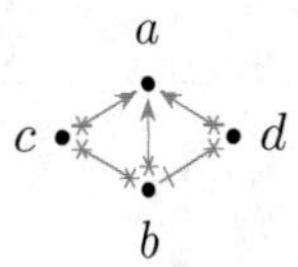

2×

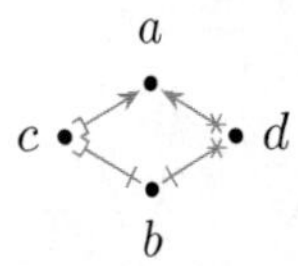

2×

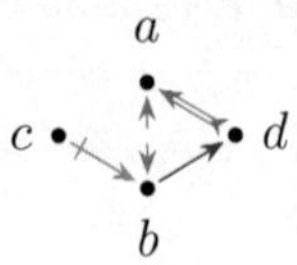

2×

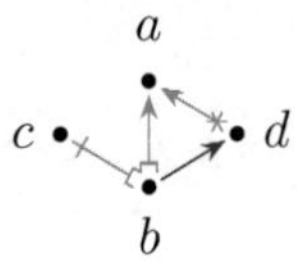

2×

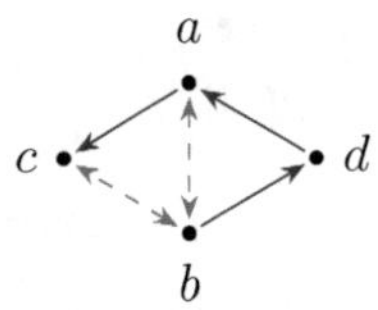

$(p_1\sigma_{aa} - p_2\sigma_{ad})(\sigma_{cd}\sigma_{bb} - \sigma_{bc}\sigma_{bd})$
$- (p_2\sigma_{cd} - p_1\sigma_{ac})(\sigma_{ab}\sigma_{bd} - \sigma_{ad}\sigma_{bb}) = 0$
where $p_1 = \sigma_{bb}\sigma_{dd} - \sigma_{bd}^2$ and $p_2 = \sigma_{ad}\sigma_{bb} - \sigma_{bd}\sigma_{ab}$

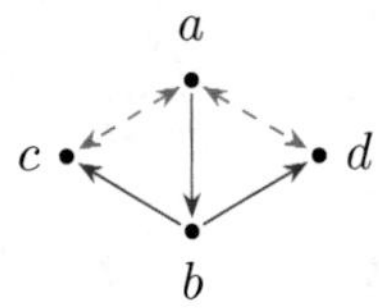

$p_0^2\sigma_{cd} + p_0\sigma_{cb}p_2 + p_1\sigma_{bd}p_0 + p_1\sigma_{bb}p_2 = 0$
where $p_0 = \sigma_{aa}\sigma_{bb} - \sigma_{ab}^2$,
$p_1 = \sigma_{ab}\sigma_{ac} - \sigma_{aa}\sigma_{bc}$, and $p_2 = \sigma_{ab}\sigma_{ad} - \sigma_{aa}\sigma_{bd}$

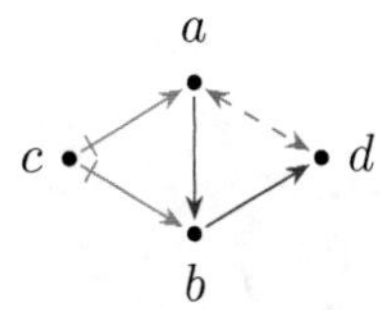

$(\sigma_{aa}\sigma_{cc} - \sigma_{ac}^2)(\sigma_{bd}\sigma_{bc} - \sigma_{bb}\sigma_{cd})$
$+ (\sigma_{ac}\sigma_{bc} - \sigma_{cc}\sigma_{ab})(\sigma_{ad}\sigma_{bc} - \sigma_{ab}\sigma_{cd}) = 0$

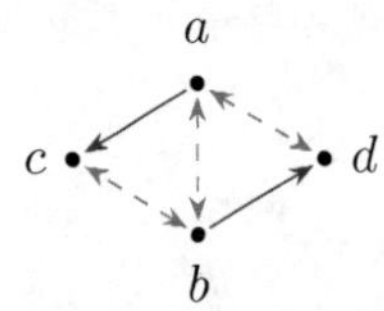

$\sigma_{aa}\sigma_{cd}\sigma_{bb} - \sigma_{aa}\sigma_{cb}\sigma_{bd}$
$- \sigma_{ac}\sigma_{ad}\sigma_{bb} + \sigma_{ac}\sigma_{ab}\sigma_{bd} = 0$

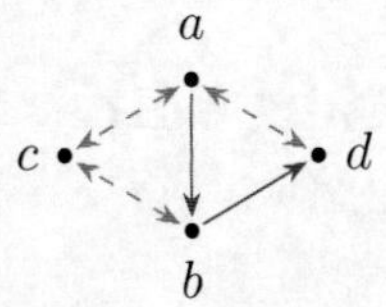

$\sigma_{aa}\sigma_{bd}\sigma_{bc} - \sigma_{aa}\sigma_{bb}\sigma_{cd} - \sigma_{ab}\sigma_{ad}\sigma_{bc} + \sigma_{ab}^2\sigma_{cd} = 0$

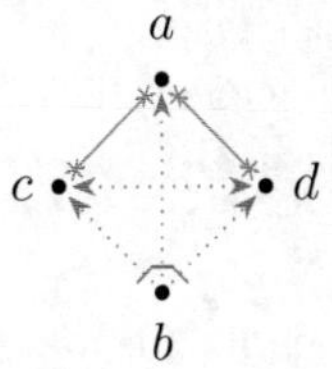

$\sigma_{bd}\sigma_{ac}\sigma_{ab} - \sigma_{bd}\sigma_{aa}\sigma_{bc}$
$- \sigma_{ab}^2\sigma_{cd} + \sigma_{ab}\sigma_{ad}\sigma_{bc} = 0$

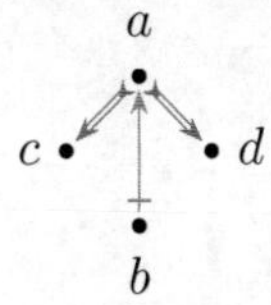

1×

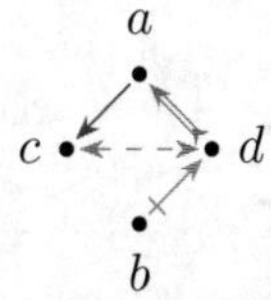

2×

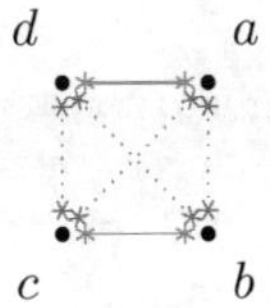

$\sigma_{ab}\sigma_{cd} - \sigma_{ac}\sigma_{bd} = 0$

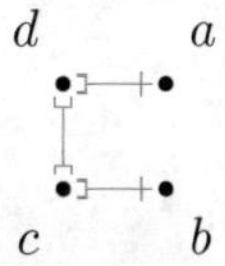

4×

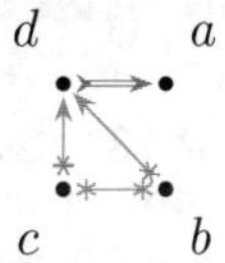

4×

B.2.6 Dimension 6

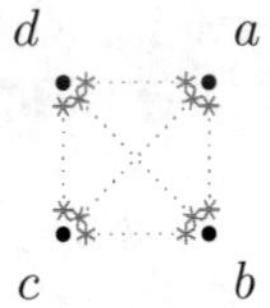

(No algebraic constraints)

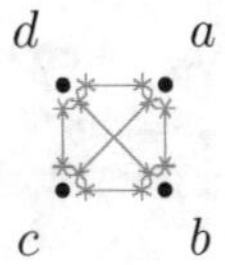

1×

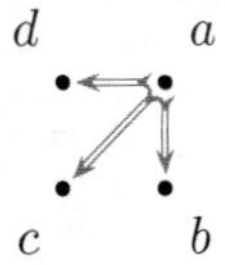

4×

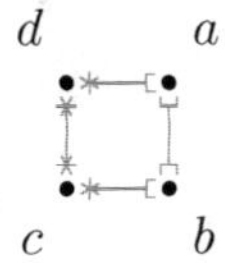

12×

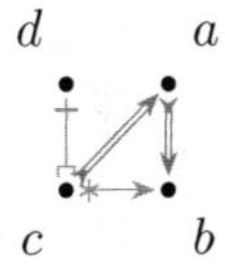

24×

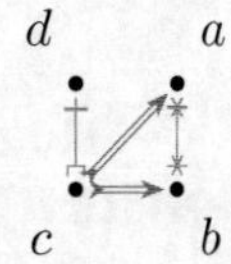

12×

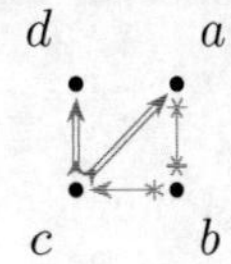

24×

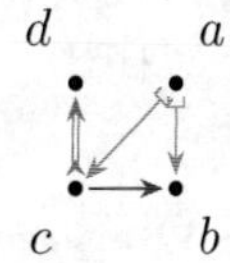

24×

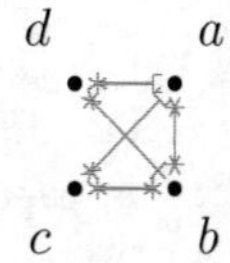

24×

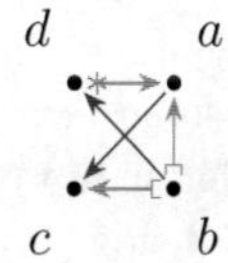

24×

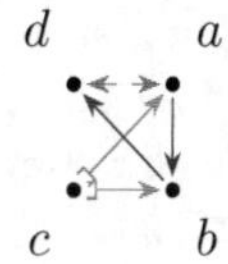

24×

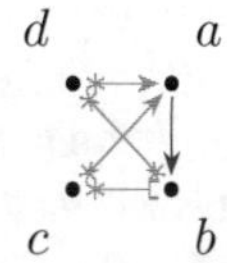

24×

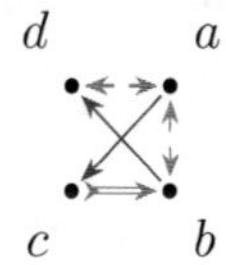

24×

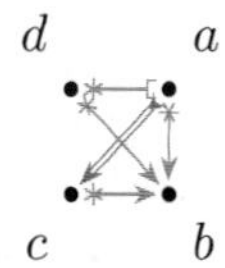

24×

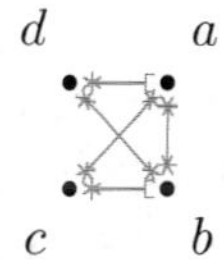

12×

Treatment-Response Models for Counterfactual Reasoning with Continuous-time, Continuous-valued Interventions

Hossein Soleimani*
Computer Science Dept.
Johns Hopkins University
Baltimore, MD 21218

Adarsh Subbaswamy*
Computer Science Dept.
Johns Hopkins University
Baltimore, MD 21218

Suchi Saria
Computer Science Dept.
Johns Hopkins University
Baltimore, MD 21218

Abstract

Treatment effects can be estimated from observational data as the difference in potential outcomes. In this paper, we address the challenge of estimating the potential outcome when treatment-dose levels can vary continuously over time. Further, the outcome variable may not be measured at a regular frequency. Our proposed solution represents the treatment response curves using linear time-invariant dynamical systems—this provides a flexible means for modeling response over time to highly variable dose curves. Moreover, for multivariate data, the proposed method: uncovers shared structure in treatment response and the baseline across multiple markers; and, flexibly models challenging correlation structure both across and within signals over time. For this, we build upon the framework of multiple-output Gaussian Processes. On simulated and a challenging clinical dataset, we show significant gains in accuracy over state-of-the-art models.

1 INTRODUCTION

As computer storage is becoming cheaper, observational data from tracking user behavior are becoming increasingly available in many problem areas. In medicine, electronic health records contain data tracking a patient's disease progression over time. On the web, it is common for websites to track usage patterns over time. These data can be cheap and valuable sources for learning about the efficacy of interventions. For example, using health record data to study the effects of different drugs can accelerate our ability to generate hypotheses about drug responsiveness and design downstream experiments to discover unknown biology linked to efficacy (Wilke et al., 2011). Similarly, on the web, we can leverage observational data about visit and click patterns to measure user responses to interventions (e.g., a new ad campaign or a specific change to the website), allowing us to rapidly improve their web experiences; e.g., Bottou et al. (2013); Li et al. (2015); Schnabel et al. (2016).

In recent years, numerous studies have sought to use such non-experimental datasets for evaluating effects of interventions. For example, Westreich et al. (2012) use the parametric g-formula (Robins, 1987) to estimate the effect of an antiretroviral therapy on time until AIDS or death from an observational cohort study. Hong and Yu (2008) use propensity score methods (Rosenbaum and Rubin, 1984) to examine the effect of kindergarten retention on self-perceived social health.

In this paper, we focus on the task of estimating effects in the setting where *multiple* attributes (or outcome variables) are being measured over time. For example, in tracking kidney function, physicians measure several markers—creatinine, potassium levels, urine output—over time. The timing for when these measurements are made is driven by whether a patient's past measurements suggest that they may be deteriorating. This means the markers are not sampled at regular intervals; rather, they may be missing at random (Rubin, 1976). Further, there may be similarities in how individual markers change in response to treatment: for example, blood urea nitrogen (BUN) and creatinine, waste products in the blood, are filtered at similar rates during dialysis. Therefore, the treatment response to interventions for these markers are likely to be correlated.

As an example, consider three signals from a patient, receiving the treatment of dialysis, shown in Fig. 1. We show fits from the proposed model (blue) and its learned treatment response curves (red). We see that the trajectories of BUN and creatinine are closely tied with simi-

*These authors contributed equally to this work.

lar responses (shown in red) to dialysis, while heart rate is less correlated with only a slight response to treatment. We wish to infer such *shared latent structure* in the treatment response curves from multivariate longitudinal data. Doing so allows a better understanding of markers that may be coupled via a common latent process.

In causal inference, the problem of estimating the effect of the intervention (i.e. the treatment effect) has been studied extensively (Robins, 1987; Robins et al., 2000; Gill and Robins, 2001; Bang and Robins, 2005). Typically, the effect can be quantified as a difference in potential outcomes: the outcome under treatment and what the outcome would have been if no treatment were given (Rubin, 1974; Pearl et al., 2009). Under specific assumptions about the data-generating process, the effect of the intervention is said to be identified and can be expressed as a function of the observational data. Once the effect has been determined to be identifiable, *a key challenge is to posit an accurate and flexible estimation model for the outcome conditioned on history and treatment information*. In recent causal inference challenges, Bayesian additive regression trees (BART) (Chipman et al., 2010), a Bayesian non-parametric method, have become an increasingly popular choice of model to wide success (Hill, 2011; Green and Kern, 2012). However, popular outcome models from cross-sectional scenarios, such as BART, do not naturally extend to functional data.

Recently, Xu et al. (2016) proposed a flexible Bayesian non-parametric approach for estimating *univariate* treatment response curves and predicting disease trajectories. Their approach, which attempts to model the impact of a treatment over time, is limited to discrete-time treatments. This is consistent with most existing methods which model treatments as discrete events with potentially continuous doses (Greenland, 1995; Silva, 2016). While some treatments are administered discretely (e.g., diuretics when given orally), in practice, many others, such as dialysis or intravenous diuretics, are administered continuously over a period of time. Naturally, these treatments should be modeled as continuous processes.

In this paper, we propose a semi-parametric Bayesian framework to model treatment effects in *multivariate longitudinal data*. The proposed framework makes the following contributions. Contrary to past work, it unifies response modeling for both discrete and *continuously-administered* treatments. We build upon linear time-invariant (LTI) systems (Golnaraghi and Kuo, 2010) to flexibly represent the *dynamic* response of physiologic signals to arbitrary treatments (treatment response curves). LTI systems and more generally differential equations are a natural and intuitive representation for describing the way in which an intervention causes

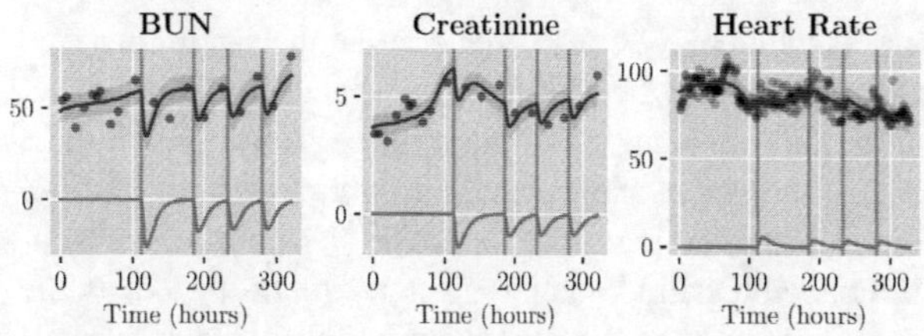

Figure 1: The proposed model fits multivariate longitudinal data (blue) and extracts an estimated treatment response (red). Vertical purple lines denote the start of 3 hour dialysis sessions.

change in the outcome over time. They are also used in pharmacokinetics for modeling concentration of drugs within the body over time (Cutler, 1978; Shargel et al., 2005; Rich et al., 2016).

Second, because data are sparse and irregularly sampled, rather than using imputation methods, we use multiple-output Gaussian Processes (GPs) to jointly model correlated multivariate signals through a shared low-dimensional latent function space. This has multiple advantages including flexibility to fit the complex variation seen within signals and across individuals in clinical data. However, GPs scale poorly with the number of observations. To circumvent this, we employ a fast, approximate inference algorithm using sparse variational inference techniques (Titsias, 2009; Hensman et al., 2013; Hensman and Matthews, 2015).

The rest of the paper is organized as follows. We discuss related work in section 2. In section 3, we describe the proposed model. In section 4, we present experimental results on a simulated and clinical dataset. Finally, concluding remarks are in section 5.

2 RELATED WORK

Continuous-Dose Treatment Modeling: Standard causal inference methods for estimating treatment effects primarily focus on discrete-valued, discrete-time interventions. Here, the effect of the intervention is typically estimated at a single point in time after the treatment is administered. For example, Card (1999) measures the effect of an individual's number of years of education (discrete-valued treatment) on their income. Other studies have considered the effect of continuous-valued treatments. For instance, several studies have focused on estimating the effect of treatment on the outcome variable as a function of the treatment's continuous-valued dose; see, e.g., (Greenland, 1995; Silva, 2016). Others (Moodie and Stephens, 2012) estimate the effect of continuous-valued dose on multivariate longitudinal data using generalized propensity scores.

Most existing studies focus on the settings where the treatment is given at discrete time points. A few works which have considered continuously-administered treatments have been limited to special cases of dose-response learning. For example, Johnson and Tsiatis (2005) consider a problem in which treatment assignment is randomized, but the dose (the duration of continuous Integrilin therapy) is not. In this case, while the treatment is administered continuously, its duration is modeled as the dose and the effect is defined with respect to the outcome at a fixed moment in time. Tao (2016) also considers continuously-administered treatments in a similar way by modeling the time at which the treatment is discontinued as a time-to-event random variable for developing dynamic treatment regimes. Both these approaches apply to the setting where the treatment dose is fixed upfront and does not vary within the duration of the treatment administration period.

Modeling Irregularly-Sampled Multivariate Longitudinal Data: Generalized mixed-effects models (Verbeke and Molenberghs, 2009) have been widely used to model multivariate longitudinal data. However, these models rely on strong parametric assumptions and thus cannot be easily applied to challenging data such as physiologic signals.

Several flexible probabilistic approaches have been proposed for modeling sparse and irregularly sampled longitudinal data. Bayesian non-parametric models based on Gaussian processes (GPs) have been particularly effective in modeling physiologic time series. For example, Ghassemi et al. (2015) use multi-task GPs, Schulam and Saria (2016) use coupled GPs, and Liu and Hauskrecht (2016) combine state-space models with GPs.

Other flexible methods such as recurrent neural networks have also been used for modeling multivariate longitudinal data (Lipton et al., 2016). These methods require alignment of the measurements across signals. When observations are not aligned, imputation and other smoothing methods are used to fill in missing observations.

In this paper, we leverage multi-output GPs to jointly model multivariate physiologic signals. In contrast to above-mentioned methods, we aim to model shared structure across signals and estimate dynamic response to both discrete-time and continuous-time treatments.

3 METHODS

Here, we first review linear dynamic systems and describe their applicability to learning treatment response curves. We then develop a semi-parametric approach for modeling multivariate longitudinal signals with shared structure and treatment response curves.

3.1 BACKGROUND: LTI SYSTEMS

As we see in Fig. 1, the observed values of BUN and creatinine (black dots) decrease in response to dialysis.

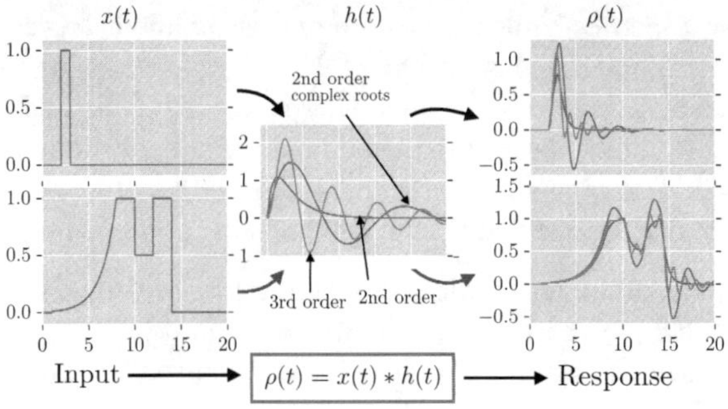

Figure 2: Sample responses ($\rho(t)$) of three LTI systems, characterized by $h(t)$, to input signals ($x(t)$).

However, this response is not instantaneous; rather, BUN and creatinine decrease slowly after the treatment is initiated. Similarly, after the treatment is discontinued, the effect does not disappear immediately; e.g., in Fig. 1, the observed values of BUN and creatinine start to increase and eventually return to the elevated level prior to treatment. To capture this *dynamic* behavior, we use linear time-invariant (LTI) systems.

Consider the examples of LTI dynamic systems shown in Fig. 2. Given an input (e.g., drug dose) $x(t)$, the treatment response function $\rho(t)$ is generated by convolving $x(t)$ with an impulse response function $h(t)$ (Golnaraghi and Kuo, 2010):

$$\rho(t) = x(t) * h(t) = \int_{-\infty}^{\infty} x(\tau)h(t-\tau)\,\mathrm{d}\tau\,. \quad (1)$$

LTI systems make the following two assumptions:

A1) Linearity: Suppose $(x_1(t), \rho_1(t))$ and $(x_2(t), \rho_2(t))$ are two pairs of input-output signals for the system. The response to the input $ax_1(t) + bx_2(t)$ is $a\rho_1(t) + b\rho_2(t), \forall a, b \in \mathbb{R}$. Thus, treatment responses are additive when multiple treatments are given in the same interval.

A2) Time-Invariance: If $\rho(t)$ is the output of the system to input $x(t)$, the response to a shifted input signal $x(t - t_0)$ is $\rho(t - t_0)$ for every choice of $t_0 \in \mathbb{R}$.

In the top and bottom left subplots of Fig. 2, we show two different dose functions. The middle panel, shows impulse response functions, $h(t)$, for three LTI systems. Convolving the input (dose functions) with different impulse functions leads to varying treatment response curves as shown in the top and bottom right subplots.

The input-output relationship of LTI dynamical systems can also be characterized using differential equations. Consider, for instance, the differential equations for a second order LTI system $\frac{d^2\rho(t)}{dt^2} + (\alpha+\beta)\frac{d\rho(t)}{dt} + \alpha\beta = \alpha\beta x(t)$, where $\alpha \neq \beta$ are positive constants. The impulse response for this system is:

$$h(t) = \frac{\alpha\beta}{\beta-\alpha}(\mathrm{e}^{-\alpha t} - \mathrm{e}^{-\beta t})\mathbb{1}(t \geq 0)\,. \quad (2)$$

Here, the indicator function, $\mathbb{1}(c)$, equals 1 or 0 when c is true or false, respectively. The family of impulse response functions can be made more flexible by adding higher order derivatives to the differential equation.

3.2 PROPOSED MODEL

In this section, we describe our proposed approach for modeling multiple outcomes and estimating dynamic treatment responses from multivariate longitudinal data. We model the disease trajectory of every signal d for patient i as follows:

$$y_{id}(t) = \underbrace{\sum_{j=1}^{J} a_{ijd}(t; x_{ij}^{0:t})}_{\text{treatment response}} + \underbrace{\phi_{id}(t)}_{\substack{\text{fixed-effects}\\ \text{component}}} + \underbrace{f_{id}(t)}_{\substack{\text{random-effects}\\ \text{component}}} + \epsilon_{id}(t). \tag{3}$$

Our model described in (3) consists of three major components: treatment response, fixed-effects, and random-effects components. The treatment response component is the sum of responses to each treatment type $j = 1, 2, ..., J$. We denote the response of signal d to the treatment of type j given the treatment input (dose) signal from time 0 to t, $x_{ij}^{0:t}$, by $a_{ijd}(t; x_{ij}^{0:t})$. Example treatment inputs are shown in the left column of Fig. 2.

The fixed-effects and random-effects components, which together we denote as the mixed-effects component, model the natural evolution of the signal independently of the treatments. For example, aging adults have higher baseline creatinine levels. Further, creatinine may drift upward when left untreated (e.g., patients with acute kidney injury). The fixed-effects term is specific to each signal, whereas the random-effects term captures the correlations across and within each signal. Finally, we assume an additive Gaussian noise term $\epsilon_{id}(t) = \mathcal{N}(0, \sigma_{id}^2), \forall d = 1, 2, ..., D, \forall t$.

We expand on each of these components in the next sections. Specifically, we describe the *sharing* mechanism built into these components that allows us to jointly model all D longitudinal signals for each individual.

3.2.1 Treatment Response Component

We develop the treatment response component of our model based on the structure of second order LTI dynamic systems described in section 3.1.

Some treatments affect multiple signals in similar forms. For instance, creatinine and blood urea nitrogen (BUN), measures of kidney function, are similarly affected by dialysis. However, their responses differ from those of vital signs such as heart rate. To capture these differences, we posit that the total treatment response of signal d is a mixture of two terms: a response shared across signals, $\rho^{(0)}$, and a response specific to d, $\rho^{(d)}$.

Specifically, we model the response of treatment type j on signal d as follows:

$$\begin{aligned} a_{ijd}(t; x_{ij}^{0:t}) = &\chi_{ijd}\big(\psi_{ijd}\, \underbrace{\rho_{ij}^{(0)}(t; x_{ij}^{0:t})}_{\text{shared}} \\ &+ (1 - \psi_{ijd})\, \underbrace{\rho_{ij}^{(d)}(t; x_{ij}^{0:t})}_{\text{signal-specific}}\big), \end{aligned} \tag{4}$$

Here, $\psi_{ijd} \in [0, 1]$ controls the degree of mixing between the shared and signal-specific terms, while $\chi_{ijd} \in \mathbb{R}$ defines the direction and influences the magnitude of the response. To improve interpretability of the estimated treatment response terms, we place sparsity inducing priors on ψ so that $a_{ijd}(t; x_{ij}^{0:t})$ is primarily determined by either the shared *or* the signal-specific component.

We use second order LTI systems, introduced in section 3.1, as the form of the shared and signal-specific treatment response components. We compute each of these as the convolution of a treatment input signal which encodes dose and duration information, $x_{ij}^{0:t}$, and an impulse response function, $h_{ij}(t) = \frac{\alpha_{ij}\beta_{ij}}{\beta_{ij}-\alpha_{ij}}(\mathrm{e}^{-\alpha_{ij}t} - \mathrm{e}^{-\beta_{ij}t})\mathbb{1}(t \geq 0)$. The signal-specific impulse response function, $h_{ijd}(t)$, has distinct parameters $\alpha_{ijd}, \beta_{ijd}$ for each signal d, while the shared-impulse response function, $h_{ijd}(t)$ only has one pair of parameters $\alpha_{ij0}, \beta_{ij0}$.

Priors: Since the treatment response parameters are individual-specific, we posit a population-level prior on them. This enables sharing statistical strength across individuals and prevents over-fitting.

Specifically, we posit a Gaussian prior on the weighting coefficients: $\chi_{ijd} \sim \mathcal{N}(\bar{\chi}; 1), \forall i, j, d$. We also place log-normal priors on parameters of the treatment functions (since they have to be positive) $\alpha_{ijd} \sim \log\mathcal{N}(\bar{\alpha}, 1), \beta_{ijd} \sim \log\mathcal{N}(\bar{\beta}, 1), \forall d = 0, 1, ..., D, \forall i, j$. Further, we impose a Beta prior on the mixing coefficient ψ: $\psi_{ijd} \sim \text{Beta}(\lambda_{\psi}^{-1}, \lambda_{\psi}^{-1})$.

3.2.2 Fixed-Effects Component

To capture covariate-dependent general trends in the progressions of particular markers (e.g., rate of deterioration can depend on age), we define the fixed-effects term, $\phi_{id}(t) = \boldsymbol{\gamma}_{id}^T \boldsymbol{c}_{it}$ as a deterministic linear regression term. Here, $\boldsymbol{c}_{it}$ is a vector of individual-specific covariates including observation time, and $\boldsymbol{\gamma}_{id}$ is the vector of regression parameters. We place Gaussian priors on the parameters of the baseline regression: $\boldsymbol{\gamma}_{id} \sim \mathcal{N}(\bar{\boldsymbol{\gamma}}, I), \forall i, d$.

3.2.3 Random-Effects Component

The random-effects component captures correlations within and across signals. Since physiologic signals typically have very challenging structure, which is difficult to capture using simple parametric functions, we use Gaussian processes as the building block of the random-effects component.

In particular, the random-effects component is comprised of a latent function shared across signals, $g_i(t) \sim \mathcal{GP}$, and a signal-specific latent function for every d, $v_{id}(t) \sim \mathcal{GP}$. Some physiologic signals are expected to be strongly correlated; e.g., BUN and creatinine, or heart rate and blood pressure. The shared latent component captures the common structure and correlations across signals. Further, each marker may have its own unique structure which cannot be modeled by $g_i(t)$; this signal-specific structure is modeled by $v_{id}(t)$.

The structure used in the random-effects component is similar to the linear models of coregionalization (Seeger et al., 2005; Álvarez and Lawrence, 2009), which is used to jointly model multiple correlated signals.

Specifically, we define the random-effects component for each signal d of every individual using a shared and a signal-specific term:

$$f_{id}(t) = \underbrace{\rho_{id} g_i(t)}_{\text{shared component}} + \underbrace{\kappa_{id} v_{id}(t)}_{\text{signal-specific component}}. \tag{5}$$

Here, $\rho_{id}, \kappa_{id}, \forall i, d$, are the mixing coefficients, and $g_i(t)$, is a shared latent function drawn from a GP prior with zero mean and kernel function K_i; i.e., $\mathbf{g}_i = g_i(\mathbf{t}_{id}) \sim \mathcal{GP}(\mathbf{0}, \mathbf{K}^{(i)}_{N_{id}N_{id}})$ where $\mathbf{K}^{(i)}_{N_{id}N_{id}} = K_i(\mathbf{t}_{id}, \mathbf{t'}_{id})$, and N_{id} is the number of observations from signal d. The signal-specific component is another latent function with a GP prior: $\mathbf{v}_{id} = v_{id}(\mathbf{t}_{id}) \sim \mathcal{GP}(\mathbf{0}, \mathbf{K}^{(id)}_{N_{id}N_{id}})$ where $\mathbf{K}^{(id)}_{N_{id}N_{id}} = K_{id}(\mathbf{t}_{id}, \mathbf{t'}_{id})$. In contrast to the shared latent function, the latent functions $\mathbf{v}_{id}$ are drawn independently from a GP with a signal-specific kernel function.

We use Matérn-3/2 kernel for each latent function (see, e.g., Rasmussen and Williams (2006)) with variance set to 1 and length-scale as the only free parameter ($l_i^{(g)}$ for shared and $l_{id}^{(v)}$ for signal-specific latent functions). The variance is set to 1 since we can scale each latent function using the mixing coefficients ρ and κ.

Priors: We place Gaussian priors on the mixing coefficients: $\rho_{id} \sim \mathcal{N}(\bar{\rho}_d, \lambda_{\omega\kappa}^{-1})$ and $\kappa_{id} \sim \mathcal{N}(\bar{\kappa}_d, \lambda_{\omega\kappa}^{-1})$, and log-normal priors on the length-scales of the kernels: $l_i^{(g)} \sim \log\mathcal{N}(\bar{l}^g, 1), \forall i$ and $l_{id}^{(v)} \sim \log\mathcal{N}(\bar{l}_d^v, 1), \forall i$.

3.2.4 Learning and Inference

In this section, we describe the learning and inference for our proposed model. Our model has *local* and *global* parameters. Local parameters are individual-specific which we denote by $\Theta_i = \{\chi_{ijd}, \psi_{ijd}, \alpha_{ijd}, \beta_{ijd}, \alpha_{ij0}, \beta_{ij0}, \rho_{id}, \kappa_{id}, l_i^{(g)}, l_{id}^{(v)}, \sigma_{id}^2\}$. The global parameters, denoted by Θ_0, are the parameters of the prior distributions which are shared across individuals; $\Theta_0 = \{\bar{\chi}, \bar{\alpha}, \bar{\beta}, \bar{\gamma}, \bar{\rho}_d, \bar{\kappa}_d, \bar{l}^g, \bar{l}_d^v, \forall d\}$.

We take a maximum a posteriori (MAP) approach and compute point-estimates of all model parameters. We treat $\lambda_{\omega\kappa}$ and λ_ψ as regularization terms. For each individual i, we observe the longitudinal samples and the treatment inputs. Computing the log-likelihood for each individual requires integrating out all latent stochastic function g_i and v_{id} in the random effects component (5).

The main bottleneck for learning and inference in our model is the use of GPs in $f_{id}(t)$. Due to requiring covariance matrix inversion, GP inference scales cubically in the number of observations. To reduce this computational complexity, we develop the learning and inference algorithms for our model using the sparse variational techniques (Titsias, 2009; Hensman et al., 2013; Hensman and Matthews, 2015).

Using these techniques, we compute the evidence lower bound for each individual: ELBO_i. Detailed derivation of ELBO is provided in Appendix A.

Learning: The overall objective function for our model (ELBO) is additive over the lower bound for each of the I individuals: $\text{ELBO} = \sum_{i=1}^{I} \text{ELBO}_i$. We use stochastic gradient techniques for learning. At each iteration of the algorithm, we randomly select a mini-batch of individuals and update their local parameters, keeping the global parameters fixed. We then compute the gradients of ELBO on the mini-batch with respect to Θ_0 and perform one step of stochastic gradient ascent to update the global parameters. We use AdaGrad (Byrd et al., 1995) for stochastic gradient optimization. We repeat this process until either the relative change in global parameters is less than a threshold or the maximum number of iterations is reached.

We use TensorFlow (Abadi et al., 2014) and GPflow (Hensman et al., 2016) to implement our model. TensorFlow automatically computes gradients of the objective function with respect to model parameters.

4 EXPERIMENTS

In this section, we evaluate the proposed model using two datasets. First, we perform a simulation study to show that in the presence of known shared structure (in signals and treatment effects) the proposed model can recover the true decomposition. In order to do this, we construct a synthetic dataset that mimics the conditions we expect to see in clinical data. Then, to demonstrate that

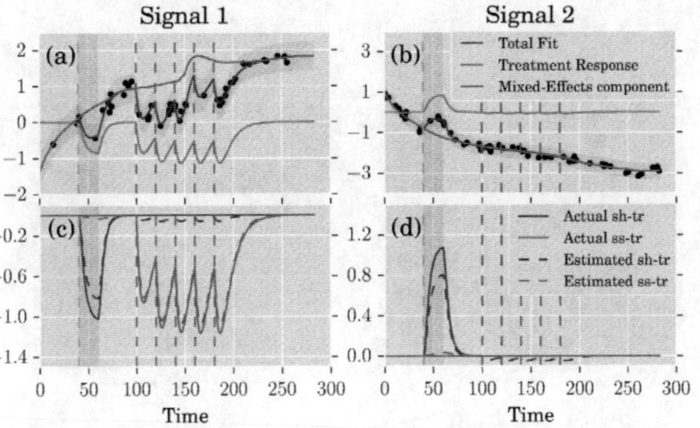

Figure 3: Decomposition of the fit for the disease trajectory of one synthetic patient. (a)-(b) show the observations (dots) and the total fit's (blue curve) separation into mixed-effects (green curve) and treatment response (red curve) components for each signal. (c)-(d) show the estimated shared (sh-tr) and signal-specific (ss-tr) treatment response components against the true treatment response curves used to generate the data.

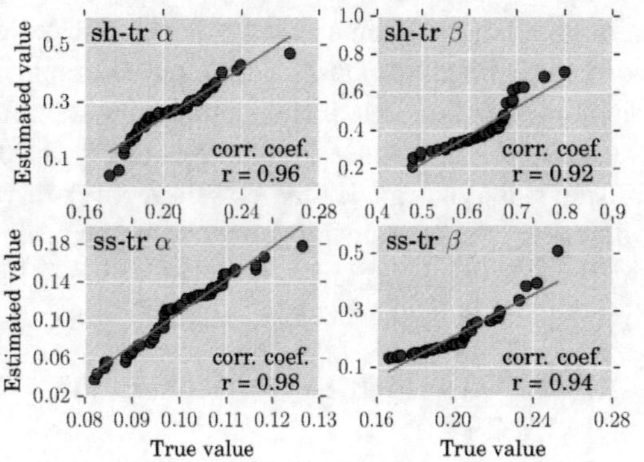

Figure 4: Q-Q plot for the estimated and the true α, β of shared and signal-specific treatment response functions.

the model can accurately represent complex multivariate longitudinal data, we compare the model against state-of-the-art baselines on the task of predicting disease trajectories under treatment in a challenging, publicly available clinical dataset. We also assess the use of the model as an exploratory tool for discovering shared structure in data of this sort by validating the learned treatment responses against clinical knowledge.

4.1 SIMULATION STUDY

Data: We generate the synthetic dataset consistent with the settings typically encountered in clinical observational studies. We generated sparse and irregularly sampled observations for each marker; observation times are drawn from a Poisson process. Specifically, we generated a synthetic dataset consisting of 50 patients, each with two *irregularly-sampled longitudinal signals*. To simulate the unalignment of the signals, for every marker of each patient, we first randomly chose the number of observations from a Poisson distribution with mean 50, and then generated the observation times from a Poisson process with rate 0.2.

We assume each signal consists of a mixed-effects and a treatment response component. We generated the signals with *shared mixed-effects* components. In particular, the signals have opposite fixed-effect trends with similar rates and shared random-effect component drawn from a GP. For each patient i, we computed the mixed-effects component using $\gamma_{id1} \log(t + 10) + \gamma_{id2} + f_i(t)$, where $\gamma_{id1}, \gamma_{id2}$ are signal-specific coefficients and $f_i \sim \mathcal{GP}(0, K)$ with a shared patient-specific RBF kernel with length-scale 20 and variance 0.05. We assume patients in the population have similar fixed-effect components; we draw $\gamma_{i1} \sim \mathcal{N}(1, 0.1), \gamma_{i2} \sim \mathcal{N}(-4, 0.1)$ for signal 1 and $\gamma_{i1} \sim \mathcal{N}(-1, 0.1), \gamma_{i2} \sim \mathcal{N}(4, 0.1), \forall i$ for signal 2.

In clinical data, some treatments affect multiple physiologic markers whereas others may only change one marker. To simulate this setting, we consider two treatments, a continuous one which has shared effect on both signals and a discrete treatment with signal-specific effect only on the first marker. We generate treatment 1 with $\alpha_{i1} \sim \log\mathcal{N}(0.2, 0.1), \beta_{i1} \sim \log\mathcal{N}(0.6, 0.1)$, and treatment type 2 with $\alpha_{i2} \sim \log\mathcal{N}(0.1, 0.1), \beta_{i2} \sim \log\mathcal{N}(0.2, 0.1)$. Treatment type 1 has shared effects on both signals, with $\chi_{i11} \sim \mathcal{N}(-1, 0.1)$ and $\chi_{i12} \sim \mathcal{N}(1, 0.1)$. This treatment was administered continuously in the time interval $[40, 60]$ with dose 1. Treatment 2, on the other hand, only has signal-specific effect on marker 1 with $\chi_{i21} \sim \mathcal{N}(1, 0.05)$ and $\chi_{i22} = 0$, and was given discretely at times 100, 120, 140, 160, and 180, each with dose 20.

We train our model on the trajectories from all 50 patients, setting the maximum number of iterations for optimization to 1000 with mini-batch size 2.

Results: To evaluate the ability of the proposed model to fit disease trajectories, in Fig. 3 we show the decomposition of the model's fit for one patient. Fig. 3a-b shows, for each of the signals, the observations (dots) and the total fit's (blue curve) separation into mixed-effects (green curve) and treatment response (red curve) components. The purple vertical lines correspond to treatment type 2, and the shaded cyan regions indicate the duration of treatment type 1. These plots qualitatively show that the estimated signal values closely fit the disease trajectory under the given treatments. Note that the proposed model is able to uncover that treatment type 2 only affects signal 1, and, as a result, learns that there are no shared effects. Rather, the effect on signal 1 is correctly captured using the signal-specific component.

To analyze the correctness of the decomposition, in Fig. 3c-d we plot the estimated (dashed lines) shared and signal-specific treatment response components against the true (solid lines) treatment response curves used to generate the data. We can see that the model does learn the correct treatment responses. Further, we compare the true and estimated α, β parameters of the treatment functions for all patients using the Q-Q plots in Fig. 4. This figure shows that our model can closely recover the true α and β since the relationship between the quantiles of the distributions of the estimated and true values is linear (with correlation coefficients greater than 0.92).

4.2 REAL DATA: MODELING RESPONSE TO DIALYSIS

Dataset: We apply and evaluate our model on the MIMIC II Clinical Database (Saeed et al., 2002), which consists of electronic health records for ICU patients from the Beth Israel Deaconess Medical Center. In particular, we examine the effect of two types of dialysis: Continuous Renal Replacement Therapy (CRRT) and Intermittent Hemodialysis (IHD).

Dialysis is used to filter blood in place of the kidneys when patients are suffering from acute kidney injury (AKI). While CRRT and IHD are both types of hemodialysis, they differ in their administration: IHD is typically administered 3 times a week with each session lasting 3 hours, whereas CRRT must be administered in the ICU and is typically given 24 hours a day (Pannu and Gibney, 2005). In the ICU, CRRT is used as an alternative for IHD with no significant differences in effect (Pannu and Gibney, 2005).

Elevated levels of waste products like blood urea nitrogen (BUN) and creatinine, which indicate poor kidney function, are reduced over the course of dialysis. Similarly, dialysis is used to regulate the concentration of electrolytes like potassium and calcium in the blood. Dialysis sometimes also indirectly affects other signals which are not primarily controlled by the kidneys; e.g., it can reduce blood pressure causing hypotension (Chou et al., 2006). Therefore, we chose to model BUN and creatinine as primary measures of kidney function, potassium and calcium since they are dialysis-regulated solutes in blood, and blood pressure and heart rate as signals which may be affected by dialysis but are typically not primary factors of interest when prescribing dialysis.

We included acute kidney injury patients who had at least 10 measured values in each signal and received no treatments other than dialysis for AKI, resulting in 67 relevant patients. For every patient, we use the first 70% of the observed marker trajectories for training and the rest for prediction. On average, each patient has 106 training observations and 46 test observations per signal. The training and test regions have average lengths of 11 and 6 days, respectively.

The learning algorithm for the proposed model alternates

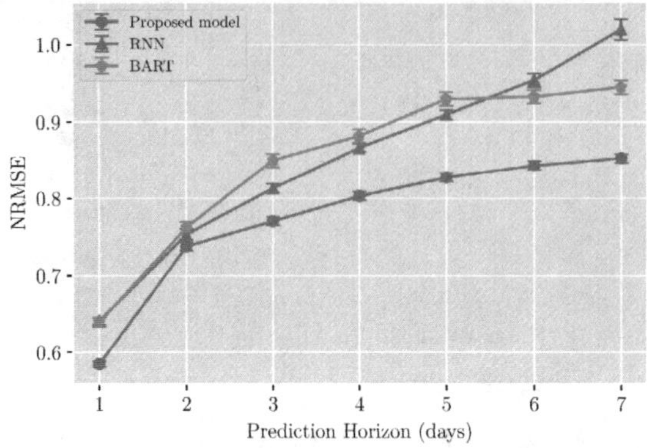

Figure 5: Normalized root mean square error (NRMSE) for the proposed model and the baselines.

between optimization of local and global variables. We set the learning rate and the maximum number of iterations for the global optimization step to 0.05 and 200, respectively. The local optimization for each individual is terminated when the relative change in the objective function (ELBO_i) is less than 10^{-4} or the maximum number of iterations (500) is reached. We also set the regularization terms $\lambda_\psi = 100$ and $\lambda_{\omega\kappa} = 0.1$. These were determined on held-out training data from a subset of the patients. We found that the model performance was not highly sensitive to the choice of the regularization terms within a reasonable range.

Baselines: We compare the proposed model's ability to predict marker trajectories against two state-of-the-art regression and time series prediction methods: Bayesian additive regression trees (BART) (Chipman et al., 2010), and long short-term memory (LSTM) (Hochreiter and Schmidhuber, 1997).

For both baselines, we train separate models for each signal by binning the data into 6 hour intervals. For non-empty intervals, we take the average value. When there are no observations in an interval, we take the value of the previous bin; i.e., we use last-observation-carried-forward imputation. We use the bin midpoint, time since last treatment, dose of last treatment, and the marker value as features. We train BART and LSTM with the features from the previous L bins as covariates and the current value of the marker as the outcome. We determine L for each method via cross-validation. These methods are trained for one-step ahead prediction. For predictions longer than one step, we use the model's predicted value as a feature for predicting the next step.

Performance Criterion: We compute the root mean square error normalized by the standard deviation for each signal (NRMSE) and then average across markers. We also performed non-parametric bootstrap with sample size 50 on the test set to measure the statistical significance of the results.

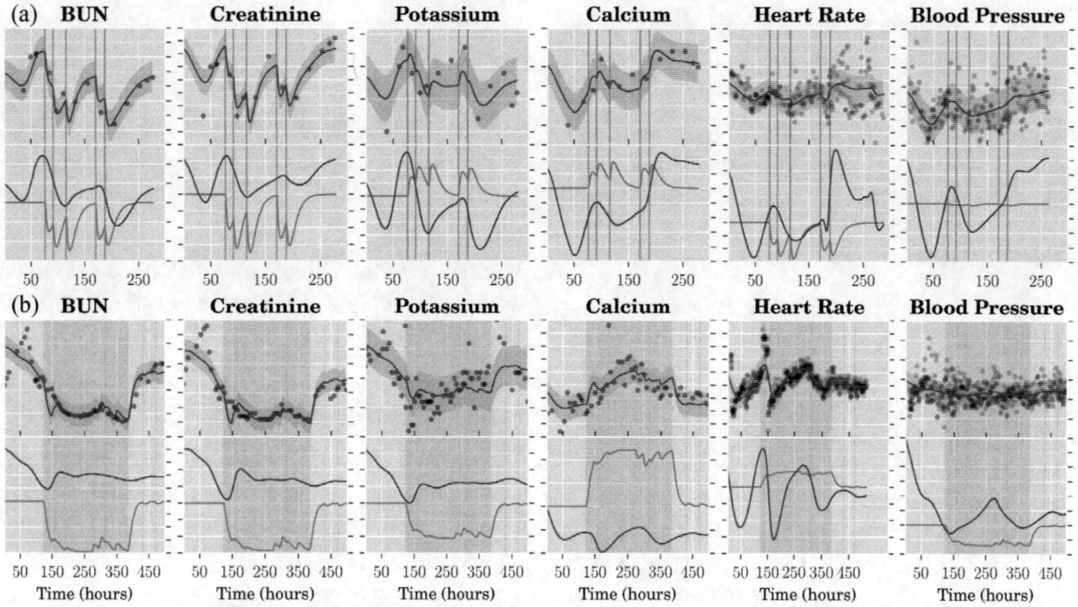

Figure 6: The observations (dots), the model's learned fits (blue line, top row) and mixed-effects (blue line, bottom row, shifted down for viewing) and treatment response (red line, bottom row) decompositions for 6 marker trajectories of two patients receiving (a) IHD (purple vertical lines) (b) CRRT (cyan shaded regions).

Quantitative Results: Fig. 5 shows NRMSE and standard error for prediction horizons of 1 to 7 days for each method. We see that the proposed method achieves better NRMSE than BART and LSTM. Further, the rate of increase of NRMSE as a function of prediction horizon is smaller for the proposed method than the baselines. Neither BART nor LSTM can naturally model treatment response. This is especially apparent on the subset of patients who received treatment in the test region: for a prediction horizon of 7 days on these patients, the model does 15% better than BART and 8% better than LSTM.

Qualitative Results: In order to demonstrate the potential of our model as an exploratory analysis tool, we examine in detail the latent treatment response structure it uncovers on the kidney function data.

Fig. 6a,b show the model's learned fits (top row) and mixed-effects and treatment response decompositions (bottom row) for six physiologic trajectories of two patients, a patient receiving IHD (Fig 6a) and a patient receiving CRRT (Fig. 6b). We can see that the proposed model can fit the overall trajectories in these signals well.

The learned decompositions qualitatively match clinical knowledge of dialysis. Both types of dialysis are used to lower BUN and creatinine levels in the blood. This is seen in both patients, for whom the proposed model learns a negative treatment response curve (red line in the bottom row). Further, we see that the observed values of BUN and creatinine return to elevated values once treatment is discontinued, as would be clinically relevant.

In order to quantitatively compare the relative impact of each treatment type j, we define a criterion to compute its maximum effect on every signal d, ($\mathcal{I}_{jd}$). Since the 2nd order LTI systems used in the treatment response components are normalized, the maximum amplitude of the estimated treatment response curves is bounded by the volume (dose) of the treatment input signal, $x(t)$, multiplied by the corresponding coefficient χ. Thus, we compute $\mathcal{I}_{ijd} = \chi_{ijd} \times [\max_t x_{ij}(t)]$ for each individual i.

Since dialysis is primarily used for managing waste products like BUN and creatinine, and electrolytes like calcium and potassium, the estimated effect of CRRT and IHD on these signals should be higher than the estimated effects on vital signals. This matches what our model learns: on average across the population, the maximum treatment effect of dialysis ($\mathcal{I}$) on BUN (-5.14), creatinine (-3.39), potassium (-0.57), and calcium (2.03) is greater than $\mathcal{I}$ on heart rate (1.48) and blood pressure (-0.08), which can be indirectly affected by dialysis.

As we qualitatively saw in Fig. 6, dialysis decreases BUN and creatinine. This is consistent with the average $\mathcal{I}$ of these two signals which are both negative. We find that the maximum effect of BUN is significantly less than 0 using a one-sided t-test with p-value 0.015, though it is not significant for the max effect of creatinine at the 0.05-level with p-value 0.065.

While CRRT and IHD are expected to have similar outcomes with respect to BUN and creatinine, IHD sessions are shorter with more aggressive dosing. The proposed model captures this difference: $\mathcal{I}_{\text{BUN}}$ and $\mathcal{I}_{\text{creatinine}}$ are significantly lower for CRRT than for IHD with p-values 0.0002 and 0.013, calculated using a one-sided t-test.

The ability of the model to extract these clinically-validated relationships from the sparse, unaligned, multivariate data shows its capability as an exploratory tool.

5 CONCLUSION

In this paper, we propose a flexible Bayesian semi-parametric approach for modeling multivariate outcomes over time. The proposed method provides a unified way to model continuous response over time to highly flexible dose functions (i.e. functions with continuous changes in dose level over time). For this, we model the treatment response curves using linear time-invariant dynamical systems. Further, our approach enables learning of structure in the response function that may be shared across multiple signals. Finally, using both simulated and real datasets, we show significant gains in performance for predicting outcomes.

It is worth noting that in the potential outcomes framework, estimation of the causal effect is precluded by the need to justify a set of generally untestable assumptions (Gill and Robins, 2001); e.g., see Lok (2008); Schulam and Saria (2017) for assumptions needed for continuous-time potential outcomes. When these conditions hold, the proposed method provides a highly flexible and accurate means for jointly modeling the multivariate potential outcomes. Further, while our approach relies on regularization to decompose the observed data into shared and signal-specific components, we need new methods for constraining the model in order to guarantee posterior consistency of the sub-components of this model.

Acknowledgements

The authors would like to thank Yanbo Xu for valuable discussions.

References

Abadi, M., Agarwal, A., Barham, P., et al. (2014). Tensorflow: Large-scale machine learning on heterogeneous distributed systems. Technical report.

Álvarez, M. A. and Lawrence, N. D. (2009). Computationally efficient convolved multiple output gaussian processes. *Journal of Machine Learning Research*, 12:1459–1500.

Bang, H. and Robins, J. M. (2005). Doubly robust estimation in missing data and causal inference models. *Biometrics*, 61(4):962–973.

Bottou, L., Peters, J., Quiñonero-Candela, J., et al. (2013). Counterfactual reasoning and learning systems: The example of computational advertising. *Journal of Machine Learning Research*, 14(1):3207–3260.

Byrd, R. H., Lu, P., Nocedal, J., and Zhu, C. (1995). A limited memory algorithm for bound constrained optimization. *SIAM Journal on Scientific Computing*, 16(5):1190–1208.

Card, D. (1999). The causal effect of education on earnings. *Handbook of Labor Economics*, 3:1801–1863.

Chipman, H. A., George, E. I., McCulloch, R. E., et al. (2010). BART: Bayesian additive regression trees. *The Annals of Applied Statistics*, 4(1):266–298.

Chou, K.-J., Lee, P.-T., Chen, C.-L., et al. (2006). Physiological changes during hemodialysis in patients with intradialysis hypertension. *Kidney International*, 69(10):1833–1838.

Cutler, D. J. (1978). Linear systems analysis in pharmacokinetics. *Journal of Pharmacokinetics and Pharmacodynamics*, 6(3):265–282.

Ghassemi, M., Pimentel, M. A., Naumann, T., et al. (2015). A multivariate timeseries modeling approach to severity of illness assessment and forecasting in icu with sparse, heterogeneous clinical data. In *AAAI*, pages 446–453.

Gill, R. D. and Robins, J. M. (2001). Causal inference for complex longitudinal data: the continuous case. *Annals of Statistics*, pages 1785–1811.

Golnaraghi, F. and Kuo, B. (2010). Automatic control systems. *Complex Variables*, 2:1–1.

Green, D. P. and Kern, H. L. (2012). Modeling heterogeneous treatment effects in survey experiments with Bayesian additive regression trees. *Public opinion quarterly*, pages 491–511.

Greenland, S. (1995). Dose-response and trend analysis in epidemiology: alternatives to categorical analysis. *Epidemiology*, pages 356–365.

Hensman, J., de G Matthews, A. G., et al. (2016). GPflow. https://github.com/GPflow/GPflow.

Hensman, J., Fusi, N., and Lawrence, N. D. (2013). Gaussian Processes for Big Data. In *UAI*.

Hensman, J. and Matthews, A. (2015). Scalable variational Gaussian process classification. In *AISTATS*, volume 38, pages 1–9.

Hill, J. L. (2011). Bayesian nonparametric modeling for causal inference. *Journal of Computational and Graphical Statistics*, 20(1):217–240.

Hochreiter, S. and Schmidhuber, J. (1997). Long short-term memory. *Neural Computation*, 9(8):1735–1780.

Hong, G. and Yu, B. (2008). Effects of kindergarten retention on children's social-emotional development: an application of propensity score method to multivariate, multilevel data. *Developmental Psychology*, 44(2):407.

Johnson, B. A. and Tsiatis, A. A. (2005). Semiparametric inference in observational duration-response studies, with duration possibly right-censored. *Biometrika*, 92(3):605–618.

Li, L., Chen, S., Kleban, J., and Gupta, A. (2015). Counterfactual estimation and optimization of click metrics in search engines: A case study. In *Int. Conf. on WWWW*, pages 929–934. ACM.

Lipton, Z. C., Kale, D. C., and Wetzel, R. (2016). Directly modeling missing data in sequences with RNNs: Improved classification of clinical time series. In *Machine Learning for Healthcare*, pages 1–17.

Liu, Z. and Hauskrecht, M. (2016). Learning adaptive forecasting models from irregularly sampled multivariate clinical data. In *AAAI*.

Lok, J. J. (2008). Statistical modeling of causal effects in continuous time. *The Annals of Statistics*, pages 1464–1507.

Moodie, E. E. and Stephens, D. A. (2012). Estimation of dose–response functions for longitudinal data using the generalised propensity score. *Statistical Methods in Medical Research*, 21(2):149–166.

Pannu, N. and Gibney, R. N. (2005). Renal replacement therapy in the intensive care unit. *Therapeutics and Clinical Risk Management*, 1(2):141.

Pearl, J. et al. (2009). Causal inference in statistics: An overview. *Statistics Surveys*, 3:96–146.

Rasmussen, C. E. and Williams, C. (2006). *Gaussian processes for machine learning*. MIT Press.

Rich, B., Moodie, E. E., and Stephens, D. A. (2016). Optimal individualized dosing strategies: A pharmacologic approach to developing dynamic treatment regimens for continuous-valued treatments. *Biometrical Journal*, 58(3):502–517.

Robins, J. (1987). A graphical approach to the identification and estimation of causal parameters in mortality studies with sustained exposure periods. *Journal of Chronic Diseases*, 40:139S–161S.

Robins, J. M., Hernan, M. A., and Brumback, B. (2000). Marginal structural models and causal inference in epidemiology.

Rosenbaum, P. R. and Rubin, D. B. (1984). Reducing bias in observational studies using subclassification on the propensity score. *Journal of the American statistical Association*, 79(387):516–524.

Rubin, D. B. (1974). Estimating causal effects of treatments in randomized and nonrandomized studies. *Journal of Educational Psychology*, 66(5):688.

Rubin, D. B. (1976). Inference and missing data. *Biometrika*, 63(3):581–592.

Saeed, M., Lieu, C., Raber, G., and Mark, R. G. (2002). Mimic II: a massive temporal ICU patient database to support research in intelligent patient monitoring. In *Computers in Cardiology, 2002*, pages 641–644.

Schnabel, T., Swaminathan, A., Singh, A., Chandak, N., and Joachims, T. (2016). Recommendations as treatments: Debiasing learning and evaluation. *CoRR, abs/1602.05352*.

Schulam, P. and Saria, S. (2016). Integrative analysis using coupled latent variable models for individualizing prognoses. *Journal of Machine Learning Research*, 17(234):1–35.

Schulam, P. and Saria, S. (2017). What-if reasoning with counterfactual Gaussian processes. *arXiv preprint arXiv:1703.10651*.

Seeger, M., Teh, Y.-W., and Jordan, M. (2005). Semiparametric latent factor models. Technical report.

Shargel, L., Andrew, B., and Wu-Pong, S. (2005). *Applied biopharmaceutics & pharmacokinetics*, volume 270. McGraw-Hill New York:.

Silva, R. (2016). Observational-interventional priors for dose-response learning. In *Advances in Neural Information Processing Systems*, pages 1561–1569.

Tao, Y. (2016). *Semiparametric regression and machine learning methods for estimating optimal dynamic treatment regimes*. PhD thesis, The University of Michigan.

Titsias, M. K. (2009). Variational model selection for sparse Gaussian process regression. In *AISTATS*.

Verbeke, G. and Molenberghs, G. (2009). *Linear mixed models for longitudinal data*. Springer Science & Business Media.

Westreich, D., Cole, S. R., Young, J. G., et al. (2012). The parametric g-formula to estimate the effect of highly active antiretroviral therapy on incident aids or death. *Statistics in Medicine*, 31(18):2000–2009.

Wilke, R., Xu, H., Denny, J., Roden, D., Krauss, R., and otherwise (2011). The emerging role of electronic medical records in pharmacogenomics. *Clinical Pharmacology & Therapeutics*, 89(3):379–386.

Xu, Y., Xu, Y., and Saria, S. (2016). A Bayesian nonparametric approach for estimating individualized treatment-response curves. In *Machine Learning for Healthcare*, pages 282–300.

A Appendix

We observe N_{id} samples from each signal d of every individual i; $\mathbf{y}_{id} = y_{id}(\mathbf{t}_{id}) = \{y_{id}(t_{idn}), \forall n = 1, 2, ..., N_{id}\}$. We denote the collection of observations of D longitudinal signals by $\mathbf{y}_i = \{\mathbf{y}_{i1}, ..., \mathbf{y}_{iD}\}, \forall i$. We also observe the treatments given to each individual i, $\mathbf{x}_{ijd}(t), \forall t, j, d$. We let $\mathbf{x}_i = \{\mathbf{x}_{i1}, ..., \mathbf{x}_{iJ}\}, \forall i$, be the collection of treatment inputs of all types.

For each latent function, we define a set of inducing input-output pairs $\mathbf{Z}, \mathbf{u}$, where $\mathbf{Z}$ are some pseudo-inputs, known as inducing points, and $\mathbf{u}$ are the values of the Gaussian process at $\mathbf{Z}$. We place the inducing points $\mathbf{Z}$ on a grid. We define a variational distribution for $\mathbf{u}$, $q(\mathbf{u}) = \mathcal{GP}(\mathbf{m}, \mathbf{S})$, where $\mathbf{m}$ and $\mathbf{S}$ are variational parameters. Using $q(\mathbf{u})$ we compute a variational GP distribution for each shared latent function: $q(\mathbf{g}) = \mathcal{GP}(\boldsymbol{\mu}_g, \boldsymbol{\Sigma}_g)$, where $\boldsymbol{\mu}_g = \mathbf{K_{NZ}}\mathbf{K_{ZZ}^{-1}}\mathbf{m}$ and $\boldsymbol{\Sigma}_g = \mathbf{K_{NN}} - \mathbf{K_{NZ}}\mathbf{K_{ZZ}^{-1}}(\mathbf{I} - \mathbf{S}\mathbf{K_{ZZ}^{-1}})\mathbf{K_{ZN}}$, with $\mathbf{K_{NZ}} = K(\mathbf{t}, \mathbf{Z})$. We similarly obtain $q(\mathbf{v}_d) = \mathcal{GP}(\boldsymbol{\mu}_{v_d}, \boldsymbol{\Sigma}_{v_d}), \forall d$, for signal-specific latent functions.

Here, to simplify the notation, we assume $\mathbf{t}_{id} = \mathbf{t}_i, \forall d$, and write $\mathbf{K_{NN}} = K_i(\mathbf{t}_i, \mathbf{t}_i')$. We emphasize that the observations from different signals need not be aligned for our learning and inference algorithm.

We obtain the variational distribution $q(\mathbf{f})$ by taking the linear combinations of the variational distributions for individual latent GPs: $q(\mathbf{f}_d) = \mathcal{GP}(\boldsymbol{\mu}_d, \boldsymbol{\Sigma}_d)$, where $\boldsymbol{\mu}_d = \rho_d\boldsymbol{\mu}_g + \kappa_d\boldsymbol{\mu}_{v_d}$ and $\boldsymbol{\Sigma}_d = \rho_d^2\boldsymbol{\Sigma}_g + \kappa_d^2\boldsymbol{\Sigma}_{v_d}$.

The log-likelihood of the observations and local model parameters for each individual is $\log p(\mathbf{y}_i, \Theta_i) = \log p(\mathbf{y}_i|\Theta_i) + \log p(\Theta_i)$, where we dropped the explicit conditioning on $\mathbf{x}_i$. Using sparse GP approximations and Jensen's inequality, we compute a variational lower bound for $\log p(\mathbf{y}_i|\Theta_i)$:

$$\begin{aligned}\log p(\mathbf{y}_i|\Theta_i) &= \log \int p(\mathbf{y}_i|\mathbf{f}_i)p(\mathbf{f}_i|\mathbf{u}_i)p(\mathbf{u}_i)\, \mathrm{d}\mathbf{f}_i\, \mathrm{d}\mathbf{u}_i \\ &\leq E_{q(\mathbf{f}_i)} \log p(\mathbf{y}_i|\mathbf{f}_i, \Theta_i) - \mathrm{KL}(q(\mathbf{u}_i)||p(\mathbf{u}_i)) \\ &= Q_i(\mathbf{y}_i; \Theta_i)\,, \end{aligned} \tag{6}$$

where, $q(\mathbf{f}_i) = E_{q(\mathbf{u}_i)}p(\mathbf{f}_i|\mathbf{u}_i)$. Also, $\mathrm{KL}(q(\mathbf{u}_i)||p(\mathbf{u}_i))$ is the Kullback-Leibler divergence between $q(\mathbf{u}_i)$ and $p(\mathbf{u}_i)$ which we compute analytically. We note that conditioned on $\mathbf{f}_i$, the distribution of $\mathbf{y}_i$ factorizes over all signals. Thus, we have $E_{q(\mathbf{f}_i)} \log p(\mathbf{y}_i|\mathbf{f}_i, \Theta_i) = \sum_d[\log m_{id}(\mathbf{t}_{id}) + E_{q(\mathbf{f}_{id})} \log p(\mathbf{y}_{id}|\mathbf{f}_{id})]$, where m_{id} is the sum of the treatment response component and the fixed-effect terms. The expectation $E_{q(\mathbf{f}_{id})} \log p(\mathbf{y}_{id}|\mathbf{f}_{id})$ is also available in closed-form (Titsias, 2009; Hensman et al., 2013). Given (6), we compute the evidence lower bound (ELBO) for each individual: $\mathrm{ELBO}_i = Q_i(\mathbf{y}_i; \Theta_i) + \log p(\Theta_i)$.

Interpreting and using CPDAGs with background knowledge

Emilija Perković
Seminar for Statistics
ETH Zurich, Switzerland
perkovic@stat.math.ethz.ch

Markus Kalisch
Seminar for Statistics
ETH Zurich, Switzerland
kalisch@stat.math.ethz.ch

Marloes H. Maathuis
Seminar for Statistics
ETH Zurich, Switzerland
maathuis@stat.math.ethz.ch

Abstract

We develop terminology and methods for working with maximally oriented partially directed acyclic graphs (maximal PDAGs). Maximal PDAGs arise from imposing restrictions on a Markov equivalence class of directed acyclic graphs, or equivalently on its graphical representation as a completed partially directed acyclic graph (CPDAG), for example when adding background knowledge about certain edge orientations. Although maximal PDAGs often arise in practice, causal methods have been mostly developed for CPDAGs. In this paper, we extend such methodology to maximal PDAGs. In particular, we develop methodology to read off possible ancestral relationships, we introduce a graphical criterion for covariate adjustment to estimate total causal effects, and we adapt the IDA and joint-IDA frameworks to estimate multi-sets of possible causal effects. We also present a simulation study that illustrates the gain in identifiability of total causal effects as the background knowledge increases. All methods are implemented in the R package `pcalg`.

1 INTRODUCTION

Directed acyclic graphs (DAGs) are used for causal reasoning (e.g., Pearl, 2009), where directed edges represent direct causal effects. In general, it is impossible to learn a DAG from (observational) data. Instead, one can learn a completed partially directed acyclic graph (CPDAG) (e.g., Spirtes et al., 2000; Chickering, 2002), which usually contains some undirected edges and represents a Markov equivalence class of DAGs (see Section 2 for definitions).

Maximally oriented partially directed acyclic graphs (maximal PDAGs) generally contain fewer undirected edges than their corresponding CPDAGs and thus represent fewer DAGs. They arise in various scenarios, for example when adding background knowledge about edge orientations to a CPDAG (Meek, 1995), when imposing a partial ordering (tiers) of variables before conducting causal structure learning (Scheines et al., 1998), in causal structure learning from both observational and interventional data (Hauser and Bühlmann, 2012; Wang et al., 2017), or in structure learning under certain model restrictions (Hoyer et al., 2008; Ernest et al., 2016; Eigenmann et al., 2017).

Maximal PDAGs appear in the literature under various names, such as interventional essential graphs (Hauser and Bühlmann, 2012; Wang et al., 2017), distribution equivalence patterns (Hoyer et al., 2008), aggregated PDAGs (Eigenmann et al., 2017) or simply CPDAGs with background knowledge (Meek, 1995). We refer to them as maximal PDAGs in this paper.

Maximal PDAGs can represent more information about causal relationships than CPDAGs. However, this additional information has not been fully exploited in practice, since causal methods that are applicable to CPDAGs are not directly applicable to general maximal PDAGs.

We now illustrate the difficulties and differences in working with maximal PDAGs, as opposed to CPDAGs. Consider the CPDAG $\mathcal{C}$ in Figure 1a. All DAGs represented by $\mathcal{C}$ (see Figure 1b) have the same adjacencies and unshielded colliders as $\mathcal{C}$. The undirected edge $A-B$ in $\mathcal{C}$ means that there exists a DAG represented by $\mathcal{C}$ that contains $A \rightarrow B$, as well as a DAG that contains $A \leftarrow B$. Conversely, if $A \rightarrow B$ was in $\mathcal{C}$, then $A \rightarrow B$ would be in all DAGs represented by $\mathcal{C}$.

The paths $B - D$, $B - C - D$ and $B - A - D$ are possibly directed paths in $\mathcal{C}$, and hence B is a possible ancestor of D in $\mathcal{C}$. In Figure 1b, we see that there indeed

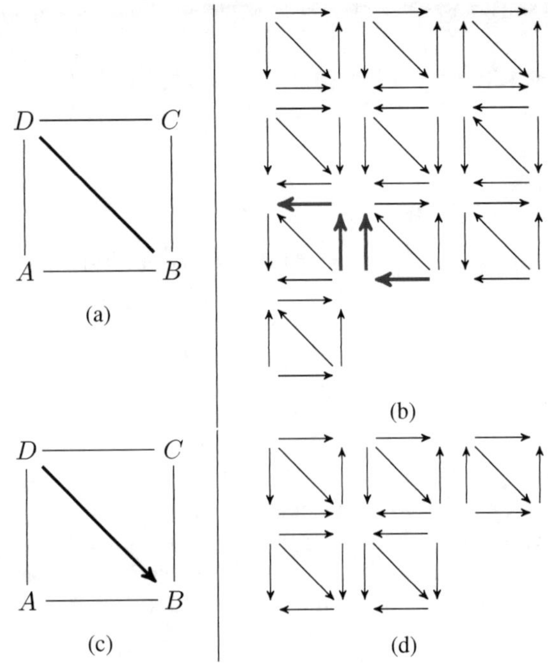

Figure 1: (a) CPDAG $\mathcal{C}$, (b) all DAGs represented by $\mathcal{C}$, (c) maximally oriented PDAG $\mathcal{G}$, (d) all DAGs represented by $\mathcal{G}$.

exist DAGs represented by $\mathcal{C}$ that contain directed paths $B \to D$, $B \to C \to D$, or $B \to A \to D$, and B is an ancestor of D in half of the DAGs represented by $\mathcal{C}$.

Now suppose that we know from background knowledge that $D \to B$. Adding $D \to B$ to $\mathcal{C}$ results in the maximal PDAG $\mathcal{G}$ in Figure 1c. The DAGs represented by $\mathcal{G}$, shown in Figure 1d, are exactly the first five DAGs of Figure 1b. Again, all DAGs represented by $\mathcal{G}$ have the same adjacencies and unshielded colliders as $\mathcal{G}$. Moreover, the interpretation of directed and undirected edges is the same as in the CPDAG.

In Figure 1c, paths $B - C - D$ and $B - A - D$ look like possibly directed paths from B to D, so that one could think that B is a possible ancestor of D. However, due to $D \to B$ and the acyclicity of DAGs, B is not an ancestor of D in any DAG represented by $\mathcal{G}$. Hence, we need a new way of reading off possible ancestral relationships.

An important difference between maximal PDAGs and CPDAGs, is that the former can contain partially directed cycles while the latter cannot. In Figure 1c, $D \to B - C - D$ and $D \to B - A - D$ are examples of such cycles. As a consequence, the important property of CPDAGs which states that if $D \to B - C$ is in a CPDAG $\mathcal{C}$, then $D \to C$ is also in $\mathcal{C}$ (Lemma 1 from Meek, 1995), does not hold in maximal PDAGs.

Furthermore, let $\mathcal{C}_{undir}$ denote the subgraph of a CPDAG $\mathcal{C}$ that contains only the undirected edges from $\mathcal{C}$. It is well known that $\mathcal{C}_{undir}$ is triangulated (chordal) and that the connected components of $\mathcal{C}_{undir}$ can be oriented into DAGs without unshielded colliders, independently of each other and the other edges in $\mathcal{C}$, to form all DAGs represented by $\mathcal{C}$ (see the proof of Theorem 4 in Meek, 1995). This result is not valid in maximal PDAGs. To see this, consider the undirected component $\mathcal{G}_{undir}$ of the maximal PDAG $\mathcal{G}$ in Figure 1c. Then $\mathcal{G}_{undir}$ is $A - B - C - D - A$ and is not triangulated. Orienting $A-B-C-D-A$ into a DAG always leads to at least one unshielded collider. This unshielded collider in $\mathcal{G}_{undir}$ must occur at A or C, so that it is shielded in $\mathcal{G}$ by the edge $D \to B$. Hence, one can no longer orient $\mathcal{G}_{undir}$ independently of the directed edges.

Previous work on maximal PDAGs deals with these issues in two ways, by considering special cases of maximal PDAGs that do not contain partially directed cycles and that retain the same path interpretations as CPDAGs (van der Zander and Liśkiewicz, 2016), or by exhaustively searching the space of DAGs represented by the maximal PDAG to find a solution consistent with all these DAGs (Hyttinen et al., 2015).

In this paper, we develop methodology to work with general maximal PDAGs directly. In **Section 2**, we introduce terminology and definitions. In **Section 3**, we define possible causal relationships in maximal PDAGs and construct a method to easily read these off from a given maximal PDAG.

In **Section 4**, we consider the problem of estimating (possible) total causal effects in maximal PDAGs. In **Section 4.1**, we give a necessary and sufficient graphical criterion for computing total causal effects in maximal PDAGs via covariate adjustment. Our criterion is called the b-adjustment criterion ('b' for background), and builds on Shpitser et al. (2010); Shpitser (2012) and Perković et al. (2015, 2017). We also construct fast algorithms for finding all adjustment sets in maximal PDAGs, using results from van der Zander et al. (2014). In **Section 4.2**, we no longer focus on total causal effects that are identifiable via covariate adjustment, but rather consider computing all possible total causal effects of a node set $\mathbf{X}$ on a node Y in a maximal PDAG $\mathcal{G}$, and collect all these values in a multi-set. Such an approach already exists for CPDAGs under the name (joint-)IDA (Maathuis et al., 2009, 2010; Nandy et al., 2017). We develop an efficient semi-local version of (joint-)IDA that is applicable to maximal PDAGs.

In **Section 5**, we discuss our implementation and present a simulation study where we apply our b-adjustment criterion and semi-local IDA algorithm to CPDAGs with various amounts of added background knowledge. We demonstrate that background knowledge can help considerably in identifying total causal effects via covariate adjustment and in reducing the number of unique values in estimated multi-sets of possible total causal effects. We close with a discussion in **Section 6**. All proofs can be found in the supplementary material.

2 PRELIMINARIES

Nodes, edges and subgraphs. A graph $\mathcal{G} = (\mathbf{V}, \mathbf{E})$ consists of a set of nodes (variables) $\mathbf{V} = \{X_1, \dots, X_p\}$ and a set of edges $\mathbf{E}$. There is at most one edge between any two nodes, and two nodes are *adjacent* if an edge connects them. We call $\rightarrow$ a directed and $-$ a undirected edge. An *induced subgraph* $\mathcal{G}' = (\mathbf{V}', \mathbf{E}')$ of $\mathcal{G} = (\mathbf{V}, \mathbf{E})$ consists of a subset of nodes $\mathbf{V}' \subseteq \mathbf{V}$ and edges $\mathbf{E}' \subseteq \mathbf{E}$ where $\mathbf{E}'$ are all edges in $\mathbf{E}$ between nodes in $\mathbf{V}'$.

Paths. A *path* p from X to Y in $\mathcal{G}$ is a sequence of distinct nodes $\langle X, \dots, Y \rangle$ in which every pair of successive nodes is adjacent. A node V *lies on a path* p if V occurs in the sequence of nodes. If $p = \langle X_1, X_2, \dots, X_k, \rangle, k \geq 2$, then X_1 and X_k are *endpoints* of p, and any other node $X_i, 1 < i < k$, is a *non-endpoint* node on p. A *directed path* or *causal path* from X to Y is a path from X to Y in which all edges are directed towards Y, that is $X \rightarrow \cdots \rightarrow Y$. A *possibly directed path* or *possibly causal path* from X to Y is a path from X to Y that does not contain an edge directed towards X. A *non-causal* path from X to Y contains at least one edge directed towards X. Throughout, we will refer to a path p from X to Y as non-causal (causal) if and only if it is non-causal (causal) from X to Y. For two disjoint subsets $\mathbf{X}$ and $\mathbf{Y}$ of $\mathbf{V}$, a path from $\mathbf{X}$ to $\mathbf{Y}$ is a path from some $X \in \mathbf{X}$ to some $Y \in \mathbf{Y}$. A path from $\mathbf{X}$ to $\mathbf{Y}$ is *proper* (w.r.t. $\mathbf{X}$) if only its first node is in $\mathbf{X}$. If $\mathcal{G}$ and $\mathcal{G}^*$ are two graphs with identical adjacencies and p is a path in $\mathcal{G}$, then the *corresponding path* p^* in $\mathcal{G}^*$ consists of the same node sequence as p.

Partially directed and directed cycles. A directed path from X to Y, together with $Y \rightarrow X$, forms a *directed cycle*. A *partially directed cycle* is formed by a possibly directed path from X to Y, together with $Y \rightarrow X$.

Subsequences and subpaths. A *subsequence* of a path p is obtained by deleting some nodes from p without changing the order of the remaining nodes. A subsequence of a path is not necessarily a path. For a path $p = \langle X_1, X_2, \dots, X_m \rangle$, the *subpath* from X_i to X_k $(1 \leq i \leq k \leq m)$ is the path $p(X_i, X_k) = \langle X_i, X_{i+1}, \dots, X_k \rangle$.

Ancestral relationships. If $X \rightarrow Y$, then X is a *parent* of Y. If $X - Y$, then X is a *sibling* of Y. If there is a causal path from X to Y, then X is an *ancestor* of Y, and Y is a *descendant* of X. We also use the convention that every node is a descendant and an ancestor of itself. The sets of parents, siblings, ancestors and descendants of X in $\mathcal{G}$ are denoted by $\mathrm{Pa}(X, \mathcal{G})$, $\mathrm{Sib}(X, \mathcal{G})$, $\mathrm{An}(X, \mathcal{G})$ and $\mathrm{De}(X, \mathcal{G})$ respectively. For a set of nodes $\mathbf{X} \subseteq \mathbf{V}$, we let $\mathrm{Pa}(\mathbf{X}, \mathcal{G}) = \cup_{X \in \mathbf{X}} \mathrm{Pa}(X, \mathcal{G})$, with analogous definitions for $\mathrm{Sib}(\mathbf{X}, \mathcal{G})$, $\mathrm{An}(\mathbf{X}, \mathcal{G})$ and $\mathrm{De}(\mathbf{X}, \mathcal{G})$.

Colliders, shields and definite status paths. If a path p contains $X_i \rightarrow X_j \leftarrow X_k$ as a subpath, then X_j is a *collider* on p. A path $\langle X_i, X_j, X_k \rangle$ is an *(un)shielded triple* if X_i and X_k are (not) adjacent. A path is *unshielded* if all successive triples on the path are unshielded. A node X_j is a *definite non-collider* on a path p if there is at least one edge out of X_j on p, or if $X_i - X_j - X_k$ is a subpath of p and $\langle X_i, X_j, X_k \rangle$ is an unshielded triple. A node is of *definite status* on a path if it is a collider, a definite non-collider or an endpoint on the path. A path p is of definite status if every node on p is of definite status.

D-connection and blocking. A definite status path p from X to Y is *d-connecting* given a node set $\mathbf{Z}$ ($X, Y \notin \mathbf{Z}$) if every definite non-collider on p is not in $\mathbf{Z}$, and every collider on p has a descendant in $\mathbf{Z}$. Otherwise, $\mathbf{Z}$ blocks p.

DAGs, PDAGs and CPDAGs. A *directed graph* contains only directed edges. A *partially directed graph* may contain both directed and undirected edges. A directed graph without directed cycles is a *directed acyclic graph* (DAG). A *partially directed acyclic graph* (PDAG) is a partially directed graph without directed cycles.

Two disjoint node sets $\mathbf{X}$ and $\mathbf{Y}$ in a DAG $\mathcal{D}$ are *d-separated* given a node set $\mathbf{Z}$ (pairwise disjoint with $\mathbf{X}$ and $\mathbf{Y}$) if and only if every path from $\mathbf{X}$ to $\mathbf{Y}$ is blocked by $\mathbf{Z}$. Several DAGs can encode the same d-separation relationships. Such DAGs form a *Markov equivalence class* which is uniquely represented by a *completed partially directed acyclic graph* (CPDAG) (Meek, 1995). A directed edge $X \rightarrow Y$ in a CPDAG $\mathcal{C}$ corresponds to $X \rightarrow Y$ in every DAG in the Markov equivalence class represented by $\mathcal{C}$. For any undirected edge $X - Y$ in a CPDAG $\mathcal{C}$, the Markov equivalence class represented by $\mathcal{C}$ contains a DAG with $X \rightarrow Y$ and a DAG with $X \leftarrow Y$.

A PDAG $\mathcal{G}'$ is *represented* by another PDAG $\mathcal{G}$ (equivalently $\mathcal{G}$ represents $\mathcal{G}'$) if $\mathcal{G}'$ and $\mathcal{G}$ have the same adjacencies and unshielded colliders and every directed edge $X \rightarrow Y$ in $\mathcal{G}$ is also in $\mathcal{G}'$.

Maximal PDAGs. A PDAG $\mathcal{G}$ is a *maximally oriented* PDAG if and only if the edge orientations in $\mathcal{G}$ are closed under the orientation rules in Figure 2. Throughout, we will refer to maximally oriented PDAGs as *maximal PDAGs*.

Algorithm 1: ConstructMaxPDAG

Data: maximal PDAG $\mathcal{G}$, background knowledge $\mathbf{R}$
Result: maximal PDAG $\mathcal{G}'$ or FAIL
Let $\mathcal{G}' = \mathcal{G}$;
while $\mathbf{R} \neq \emptyset$ **do**
  Choose an edge $\{X \to Y\}$ in $\mathbf{R}$;
  $\mathbf{R} = \mathbf{R} \setminus \{X \to Y\}$;
  if $\{X - Y\}$ *or* $\{X \to Y\}$ *is in* $\mathcal{G}'$ **then**
    Orient $\{X \to Y\}$ in $\mathcal{G}'$;
    Close the edge orientations under the rules in Figure 2 in $\mathcal{G}'$;
  else
    FAIL;
  end
end

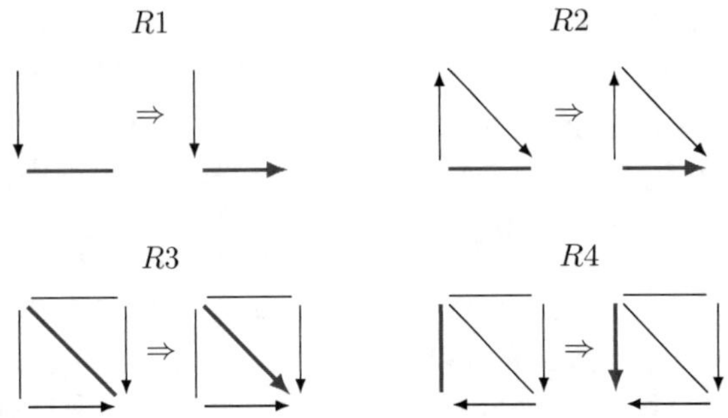

Figure 2: The orientation rules from Meek (1995). If the graph on the left-hand side of a rule is an induced subgraph of a PDAG $\mathcal{G}$, then *orient* the blue undirected edge ($-$) as shown on the right-hand side of the rule.

Let $\mathbf{R}$ be a set of required directed edges representing background knowledge. Algorithm 1 of Meek (1995) describes how to incorporate background knowledge $\mathbf{R}$ in a maximal PDAG $\mathcal{G}$. If Algorithm 1 does not return a FAIL, then it returns a new maximal PDAG $\mathcal{G}'$ that is represented by $\mathcal{G}$. Background knowledge $\mathbf{R}$ is *consistent* with maximal PDAG $\mathcal{G}$ if and only if Algorithm 1 does not return a FAIL (Meek, 1995).

$\mathcal{G}$ and $[\mathcal{G}]$. If $\mathcal{G}$ is a maximal PDAG, then $[\mathcal{G}]$ denotes every maximal PDAG represented by $\mathcal{G}$. Thus, $[\mathcal{G}]$ contains all DAGs represented by $\mathcal{G}$, but also all PDAGs (with the same adjacencies and unshielded colliders) that contain more orientations than $\mathcal{G}$.

Causal DAGs and PDAGs. A density f of $\mathbf{V} = \{X_1, \dots, X_p\}$ is *consistent* with a DAG $\mathcal{D} = (\mathbf{V}, \mathbf{E})$ if it factorizes as $f(\mathbf{V}) = \prod_{i=1}^{p} f(X_i | Pa(X_i, \mathcal{G}))$ (Pearl, 2009). A DAG is *causal* if every edge $X_i \to X_j$ in $\mathcal{D}$ represents a direct causal effect of X_i on X_j (wrt $\mathbf{V}$). A PDAG is *causal* if it represents a causal DAG.

We consider interventions $do(\mathbf{X} = \mathbf{x})$ (for $\mathbf{X} \subseteq \mathbf{V}$) or $do(\mathbf{x})$ for shorthand, which represent outside interventions that set $\mathbf{X}$ to $\mathbf{x}$ (Pearl, 2009). A density f of $\mathbf{V} = \{X_1, \dots, X_p\}$ is *consistent with a causal DAG* $\mathcal{D} = (\mathbf{V}, \mathbf{E})$ if all post-intervention densities $f(\mathbf{v}|do(\mathbf{x}))$ factorize as:

$$f(\mathbf{v}|do(\mathbf{x})) = \\ = \begin{cases} \prod_{X_i \in \mathbf{V} \setminus \mathbf{X}} f(x_i | \operatorname{Pa}(x_i, \mathcal{D})), & \text{if } \mathbf{X} = \mathbf{x}, \\ 0, & \text{otherwise.} \end{cases} \quad (1)$$

Equation (1) is known as the truncated factorization formula (Pearl, 2009), manipulated density formula (Spirtes et al., 2000) or the g-formula (Robins, 1986). A density f is *consistent with a causal PDAG* $\mathcal{G}$ if it is consistent with a causal DAG in $[\mathcal{G}]$.

3 POSSIBLY CAUSAL RELATIONSHIPS IN MAXIMAL PDAGs

A basic task for causal reasoning based on a maximal PDAG $\mathcal{G}$ is reading off possible causal relationships between nodes directly from $\mathcal{G}$. The alternative is of course to list all DAGs in $[\mathcal{G}]$ and to read off the causal relationship in each DAG. If $\mathcal{G}$ has many undirected edges, this task quickly becomes a computational burden. We show that possible causal relationships can be read off from the maximal PDAG directly if we modify the definitions of possibly causal and non-causal paths.

In Definition 3.1, we define a *b-possibly causal* path and its complement the *b-non-causal* path for maximal PDAGs. Throughout, we use the prefix *b-* (for background) to distinguish from the analogous terms for CPDAGs. Lemma 3.2 demonstrates the soundness of Definition 3.1.

Definition 3.1. ***(b-possibly causal path, b-non-causal path)*** *Let $p = \langle X = V_0, \dots, V_k = Y \rangle$, $k \geq 1$ be a path from node X to node Y in a maximal* PDAG *$\mathcal{G}$. We say that p is b-possibly causal in $\mathcal{G}$ if and only if no edge $V_i \leftarrow V_j, 0 \leq i < j \leq k$ is in $\mathcal{G}$. Otherwise, we say that p is b-non-causal path in $\mathcal{G}$.*

Remark. Note that Definition 3.1 involves edges that are not on p.

Lemma 3.2. *Let p^* be a path from X to Y in a maximal* PDAG *$\mathcal{G}$. If p^* is b-non-causal in $\mathcal{G}$, then for every* DAG *$\mathcal{D}$ in $[\mathcal{G}]$ the corresponding path in $\mathcal{D}$ is non-causal. By contraposition, if p is a causal path in at least one* DAG *$\mathcal{D}$ in $[\mathcal{G}]$, then the corresponding path in $\mathcal{G}$ is b-possibly causal.*

Note that since every CPDAG is also a maximal PDAG, all results in this paper subsume existing results for

CPDAGs. We now define *b-possible descendants* (*b-possible ancestors*) in a maximal PDAG.

Definition 3.3. (b-PossDe($\mathbf{X}, \mathcal{G}$) *and* b-PossAn($\mathbf{X}, \mathcal{G}$)) *Let* $\mathbf{X}$ *be a node set in a maximal* PDAG $\mathcal{G}$. *Then* W *is a b-possible descendant (b-possible ancestor) of* $\mathbf{X}$ *in* $\mathcal{G}$, *and we write* $W \in$ b-PossDe($\mathbf{X}, \mathcal{G}$) ($W \in$ b-PossAn($\mathbf{X}, \mathcal{G}$)) *if and only if* $W \in \mathbf{X}$ *or there is a node* $X \in \mathbf{X}$ *and a b-possibly causal path from* X *to* W *(*W *to* X*) in* $\mathcal{G}$.

Example 3.4. *We use this example to illustrate b-possibly causal paths and b-possible descendants. Consider* CPDAG $\mathcal{C}$ *in Figure 1a and maximal* PDAG $\mathcal{G}$ *in Figure 1c. We see that* $B - C - D$ *is a b-possibly causal path in* $\mathcal{C}$, *and a b-non-causal path in* $\mathcal{G}$ *due to* $D \to B$ *in* $\mathcal{G}$. *Conversely,* $D - C - B$ *is a b-possibly causal path in both* $\mathcal{C}$ *and* $\mathcal{G}$.

Furthermore, b-PossDe($B, \mathcal{C}$) $= \{A, B, C, D\}$ *and* b-PossDe($B, \mathcal{G}$) $= \{A, B, C\}$. *The b-possible descendants of* A, C *and* D *nodes are the same in* $\mathcal{G}$ *and* $\mathcal{C}$.

3.1 EFFICIENTLY FINDING ALL B-POSSIBLE DESCENDANTS/ANCESTORS

The b-possibly causal paths present an elegant extension of the notion of possibly causal paths from CPDAGs to maximal PDAGs. Nevertheless, finding all b-possible descendants by checking the b-possibly causal status of a path is non trivial, since it involves considering many edges not on the path. This is cumbersome if the graphs we are dealing with are large and/or dense.

To solve this issue, we use Lemma 3.6 (analogous to Lemma B.1 in Zhang, 2008) to only consider paths which are unshielded and hence, of definite status. We then only need consider the edges which are on the definite status paths (Lemma 3.5). Thus, the task of finding all b-possible descendants (ancestors) of $\mathbf{X}$ in a maximal PDAG $\mathcal{G} = (\mathbf{V}, \mathbf{E})$ can be done using a depth first search algorithm with computational complexity $O(|\mathbf{V}| + |\mathbf{E}|)$.

Lemma 3.5. *Let* $p^* = \langle V_1, \dots, V_k \rangle$ *be a definite status path in a maximal* PDAG $\mathcal{G}$. *Then* p^* *is b-possibly causal if and only if there is no* $V_i \leftarrow V_{i+1}$, *for* $i \in \{1, \dots, k-1\}$ *in* $\mathcal{G}$.

Lemma 3.6. *Let* X *and* Y *be distinct nodes in a maximal* PDAG $\mathcal{G}$. *If* p *is s a b-possibly causal path from* X *to* Y *in* $\mathcal{G}$, *then a subsequence* p^* *of* p *forms a b-possibly causal unshielded path from* X *to* Y *in* $\mathcal{G}$.

4 ESTIMATING TOTAL CAUSAL EFFECTS WITH MAXIMAL PDAGS

After inferring the existence of a possibly non-zero total causal effect of $\mathbf{X}$ on $\mathbf{Y}$ in a maximal PDAG $\mathcal{G}$ by finding a b-possible causal path from X to Y, the natural question to ask is, how big is this effect? How do we calculate this effect using observational data? Throughout, let $\mathcal{G} = (\mathbf{V}, \mathbf{E})$ represent a causal maximal PDAG, and let $\mathbf{X}$, $\mathbf{Y}$ and $\mathbf{Z}$ be pairwise disjoint subsets of $\mathbf{V}$. We are interested in the total causal effect of $\mathbf{X}$ on $\mathbf{Y}$.

4.1 ADJUSTMENT IN MAXIMAL PDAGs

The most commonly used tool for estimating total causal effects from observational data is covariate adjustment. We first define the concept of a adjustment sets for maximal PDAGs.

Definition 4.1. ***(Adjustment set)*** *Let* $\mathbf{X}, \mathbf{Y}$ *and* $\mathbf{Z}$ *be pairwise disjoint node sets in a causal maximal* PDAG $\mathcal{G}$. *Then* $\mathbf{Z}$ *is an adjustment set relative to* $(\mathbf{X}, \mathbf{Y})$ *in* $\mathcal{G}$ *if for any density* f *consistent with* $\mathcal{G}$ *we have*

$$f(\mathbf{y}|do(\mathbf{x})) = \begin{cases} f(\mathbf{y}|\mathbf{x}) & \textit{if } \mathbf{Z} = \emptyset, \\ \int_{\mathbf{z}} f(\mathbf{y}|\mathbf{x},\mathbf{z}) f(\mathbf{z}) d\mathbf{z} & \textit{otherwise.} \end{cases}$$

Thus, if $\mathbf{Z}$ is an adjustment set relative to $(\mathbf{X}, \mathbf{Y})$ in $\mathcal{G}$, we do not need to find the true underlying causal DAG in order to find the post-intervention density $f(\mathbf{y}|do(\mathbf{x}))$.

Under the assumption that the density consistent with the underlying causal DAG can be generated by a linear structural equation model (SEM) with additive noise (see Ch.5 in Pearl, 2009, for definition of SEMs), covariate adjustment allows the researcher to estimate the total causal effect by performing one multiple linear regression (see Nandy et al., 2017, for the non-Gaussian noise result). In this setting, if $\mathbf{Z}$ is an adjustment set relative to some nodes X, Y in $\mathcal{G}$, then the coefficient of X in the linear regression of Y on X and $\mathbf{Z}$ is the total causal effect of X on Y.

There has been recent work on finding graphical criteria for sets that satisfy Definition 4.1 relative to some $(\mathbf{X}, \mathbf{Y})$. The first such criterion was the back-door criterion (Pearl, 2009), which is sound but not complete for adjustment (wrt Definition 4.1). The sound and complete adjustment criterion for DAGs was introduced in Shpitser et al. (2010); Shpitser (2012) and extended to more general graph classes in Perković et al. (2015, 2017). Furthermore, van der Zander and Liśkiewicz (2016) presented an adjustment criterion that can be used in maximal PDAGs that do not contain partially directed cycles. None of these criteria is applicable to general maximal PDAGs.

We present our b-adjustment criterion in Definition 4.3, building on the results of Shpitser et al. (2010); Shpitser (2012) and Perković et al. (2015, 2017). Our criterion, as well as other results presented in this section, is phrased in the same way as the results in Perković et al. (2015, 2017). The only difference is the use of b-possibly causal paths as opposed to possibly causal paths. This similarity is intentional, as it makes our results easier to follow and further demonstrates that the results for DAGs and CPDAGs can be leveraged for maximal PDAGs. The proofs do not follow from previous results and require special consideration, especially due to the partially directed cycles that can occur in maximal PDAGs. In DAGs and CPDAGs our b-adjustment criterion reduces to the adjustment criteria from Shpitser et al. (2010); Shpitser (2012) and Perković et al. (2015, 2017). For consistency however, we will refer to the b-adjustment criterion for all graph types.

To define our b-adjustment criterion, we first introduce the concept of the b-forbidden set for maximal PDAGs. The b-forbidden set contains all nodes that cannot be used for adjustment.

Definition 4.2. (b-Forb$(\mathbf{X},\mathbf{Y},\mathcal{G})$) *Let $\mathbf{X}$ and $\mathbf{Y}$ be disjoint node sets in a maximal* PDAG $\mathcal{G}$. *We define the b-forbidden set relative to* $(\mathbf{X},\mathbf{Y})$ *as:*

$$\text{b-Forb}(\mathbf{X},\mathbf{Y},\mathcal{G}) = \{W' \in \mathbf{V} : W' \in \text{b-PossDe}(W,\mathcal{G}), \text{ for some } W \notin \mathbf{X} \text{ which lies on a proper b-possibly causal path from } \mathbf{X} \text{ to } \mathbf{Y} \text{ in } \mathcal{G}\}.$$

Definition 4.3. ***(b-adjustment criterion)*** *Let $\mathbf{X},\mathbf{Y}$ and $\mathbf{Z}$ be pairwise disjoint node sets in a maximal* PDAG $\mathcal{G}$. *Then $\mathbf{Z}$ satisfies the b-adjustment criterion relative to* $(\mathbf{X},\mathbf{Y})$ *in $\mathcal{G}$ if:*

- ***(b-amenability)*** *all proper b-possibly causal paths from $\mathbf{X}$ to $\mathbf{Y}$ start with a directed edge out of $\mathbf{X}$ in $\mathcal{G}$,*
- ***(b-forbidden set)*** $\mathbf{Z} \cap \text{b-Forb}(\mathbf{X},\mathbf{Y},\mathcal{G}) = \emptyset$,
- ***(b-blocking)*** *all proper b-non-causal definite status paths from $\mathbf{X}$ to $\mathbf{Y}$ are blocked by $\mathbf{Z}$ in $\mathcal{G}$.*

In Theorem 4.4 we show that the b-adjustment criterion is sound and complete for adjustment. Furthermore, in Theorem 4.6 we show that there exists an adjustment set if and only if the specific set b-Adjust$(\mathbf{X},\mathbf{Y},\mathcal{G})$ (Definition 4.5) is an adjustment set relative to $(\mathbf{X},\mathbf{Y})$ in $\mathcal{G}$.

Theorem 4.4. *Let $\mathbf{X},\mathbf{Y}$ and $\mathbf{Z}$ be pairwise disjoint node sets in a causal maximal* PDAG $\mathcal{G}$. *Then $\mathbf{Z}$ is an adjustment set (Definition 4.1) relative to $(\mathbf{X},\mathbf{Y})$ in $\mathcal{G}$ if and only if $\mathbf{Z}$ satisfies the b-adjustment criterion (Definition 4.3) relative to $(\mathbf{X},\mathbf{Y})$ in $\mathcal{G}$.*

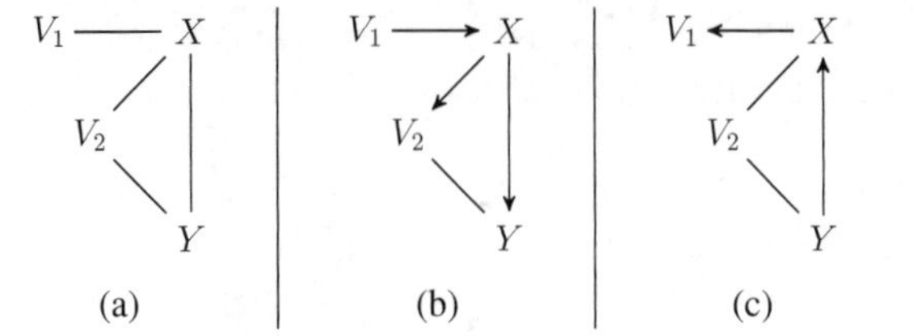

Figure 3: (a) CPDAG $\mathcal{C}$, (b) maximal PDAG $\mathcal{G}_1$, (c) maximal PDAG $\mathcal{G}_2$ used in Example 4.7.

Definition 4.5. (b-Adjust$(\mathbf{X},\mathbf{Y},\mathcal{G})$) *Let $\mathbf{X}$ and $\mathbf{Y}$ be disjoint node sets in a maximal* PDAG $\mathcal{G}$. *We define*

$$\text{b-Adjust}(\mathbf{X},\mathbf{Y},\mathcal{G}) = \text{b-PossAn}(\mathbf{X}\cup\mathbf{Y},\mathcal{G}) \setminus (\mathbf{X}\cup\mathbf{Y}\cup \text{b-Forb}(\mathbf{X},\mathbf{Y},\mathcal{G})).$$

Theorem 4.6. *Let $\mathbf{X}$ and $\mathbf{Y}$ be disjoint node sets in a maximal* PDAG $\mathcal{G}$. *There exists a set that satisfies the b-adjustment criterion relative to $(\mathbf{X},\mathbf{Y})$ in $\mathcal{G}$ if and only if* b-Adjust$(\mathbf{X},\mathbf{Y},\mathcal{G})$ *satisfies the b-adjustment criterion relative to $(\mathbf{X},\mathbf{Y})$ in $\mathcal{G}$.*

Example 4.7. *We use this example to illustrate the b-adjustment criterion. Consider Figure 3 with a* CPDAG $\mathcal{C}$ *in (a), and two maximal* PDAGs $\mathcal{G}_1$ *and* $\mathcal{G}_2$ *in* $[\mathcal{G}]$ *in (b) and (c). Maximal* PDAG $\mathcal{G}_1$ $(\mathcal{G}_2)$ *can be obtained from* $\mathcal{C}$ *by adding* $V_1 \to X$ $(Y \to X)$ *as background knowledge and completing the orientation rules from Figure 2.*

$\mathcal{C}$ is not b-amenable relative to (X,Y) due to $X - Y$ and $X - V_2 - Y$. Hence, there is no adjustment set (no set satisfies Definition 4.3) relative to (X,Y) in $\mathcal{G}$.

On the other hand, $\mathcal{G}_1$ is b-amenable relative to (X,Y) and b-Forb$(X,Y,\mathcal{G}_1) = \{V_2,Y\}$. *Since there are no b-non-causal paths from X to Y in $\mathcal{G}_1$ any set of nodes disjoint with* b-Forb$(X,Y,\mathcal{G}_1)\cup\{X,Y\}$ *satisfies the b-adjustment criterion relative to (X,Y). Hence, all valid adjustment sets relative to (X,Y) in $\mathcal{G}_1$ are $\emptyset$ and $\{V_1\}$.*

Maximal PDAG $\mathcal{G}_2$ *is also b-amenable relative to (X,Y) (since $X - V_2 - Y$ is a b-non-causal path). Since $X \leftarrow Y$ is in $\mathcal{G}_2$,* b-Forb$(X,Y,\mathcal{G}_2) = \emptyset$. *However, since $X \leftarrow Y$ is a proper b-non-causal definite status path from X to Y that cannot be blocked by any set of nodes, there is no adjustment set (no set satisfies Definition 4.3) relative to (X,Y) in $\mathcal{G}_2$. Nevertheless, since $Y \notin$* b-PossDe$(X,\mathcal{G}_2)$, *we can conclude that the total causal effect of X on Y in $\mathcal{G}_2$ is zero.*

4.1.1 Constructing adjustment sets

Checking whether $\mathbf{Z}$ is an adjustment set relative to $(\mathbf{X},\mathbf{Y})$ in $\mathcal{G}$ requires checking the three conditions in Definition 4.3: b-amenability, b-forbidden set and b-blocking. Checking the b-amenability condition or the b-forbidden set condition is computationally straightforward and depends only on constructing the set of all b-possible descendants of $\mathbf{X}$. Naively checking the b-blocking condition, however, requires keeping track of all paths between $\mathbf{X}$ and $\mathbf{Y}$. This scales very poorly with the size of the graph. To deal with this issue we rely on Lemma C.3 in the supplement, which is analogous to Lemma 10 in Perković et al., 2017.

If $\mathcal{G}$ is b-amenable and $\mathbf{Z}$ satisfies the b-forbidden set condition relative to $(\mathbf{X}, \mathbf{Y})$, then in order to verify that $\mathbf{Z}$ satisfies the b-blocking condition in $\mathcal{G}$ it is enough to verify that $\mathbf{Z}$ satisfies the b-blocking condition in one DAG in $[\mathcal{G}]$ ((iii) in Lemma C.3 in the supplement). In van der Zander et al. (2014), the authors propose fast algorithms to verify the b-blocking condition and construct adjustment sets in DAGs. Using the above mentioned result we can leverage these for use in maximal PDAGs.

The computational complexity of finding one DAG $\mathcal{D}$ in $[\mathcal{G}]$ is $O(|\mathbf{V}||\mathbf{E}|)$, as shown in Dor and Tarsi (1992). The computational complexity of verifying whether a set satisfies the b-adjustment criterion in $\mathcal{D}$ is $O(|\mathbf{V}| + |\mathbf{E}|)$, as shown in van der Zander et al. (2014). Furthermore, the computational complexity of listing all or all minimal adjustment sets in $\mathcal{D}$, is at most polynomial in $|\mathbf{V}|$ and $|\mathbf{E}|$ per output set, as shown in van der Zander et al. (2014). The complexity of verifying the b-blocking condition in $\mathcal{G}$ when exploiting the results of Lemma C.3, Dor and Tarsi (1992) and van der Zander et al. (2014) is polynomial in $|\mathbf{V}|$ and $|\mathbf{E}|$ and listing all or all minimal adjustment sets in $\mathcal{G}$ is polynomial in $|\mathbf{V}|$ and $|\mathbf{E}|$ per output set.

4.2 IDA AND JOINT-IDA IN MAXIMAL PDAGs

It is not always possible to find an adjustment set relative to $(\mathbf{X}, \mathbf{Y})$ in a maximal PDAG $\mathcal{G}$. For example, if the total causal effect of $\mathbf{X}$ on $\mathbf{Y}$ differs in some distinct DAGs in $[\mathcal{G}]$, then this effect is not identifiable in $\mathcal{G}$, and is certainly not identifiable via adjustment.

The IDA algorithm for CPDAGs from Maathuis et al. (2009) was developed with precisely this issue in mind. In order to estimate the possible total causal effects of a node X on a node Y based on a CPDAG $\mathcal{C}$ one can consider listing all DAGs in $[\mathcal{C}]$ and estimating the total causal effect of X on Y in each. Since this effect may differ between different DAGs in $\mathcal{G}$, the output of such an algorithm is a multi-set of possible total causal effects of X on Y. The joint-IDA algorithm for CPDAGs from Nandy et al. (2017) employs the same idea to estimate the possible total joint causal effect of a node set $\mathbf{X}$ on a node Y.

The IDA and joint-IDA algorithms use all possible (joint) parent sets of $\mathbf{X}$ in the DAGs in $[\mathcal{G}]$. If Y is not a parent of X in a causal DAG $\mathcal{D}$, it is well known that $\mathrm{Pa}(X, \mathcal{D})$ is an adjustment set relative to (X, Y) in $\mathcal{D}$ (Pearl, 2009).

Algorithm 2: Semi-locally find all joint parent sets of $\mathbf{X} = (X_1, \ldots, X_k), k \geq 1$, in a maximal PDAG $\mathcal{G}$.

Data: maximal PDAG $\mathcal{G}$, $\mathbf{X} = \{X_1, \ldots, X_k\}, k \geq 1$
Result: Multi-set $\mathbf{PossPa}$ of all joint parent sets of $\mathbf{X}$

```
PossPa = ∅;
Sib_1 = {A : A − X_1 in G};
if k > 1 then
 | Sib_i = {A : A − X_i in G} \ {X_1, ..., X_{i−1}};
end
forall S_i ⊆ Sib_i, i = 1, ..., k, do
    LocalBg = ∪_{i=1}^k {A → X_i : A ∈ S_i} ∪
              ∪_{i=1}^k {X_i → A : A ∈ Sib_i \ S_i};
    if ConstructMaxPDAG(G, LocalBg) ≠ FAIL
     then
        add (Pa(X_1, G) ∪ S_1, ..., Pa(X_k, G) ∪ S_k) to
        PossPa;
    end
end
```

The (joint-)IDA algorithm has different algorithmic variants for finding (joint) parent sets: global, local and semi-local. The global variant applies the above mentioned idea of listing all DAGs represented by a CPDAG $\mathcal{C}$ in order to find all possible (joint) parent sets of $\mathbf{X}$. This method can be applied directly to a maximal PDAG $\mathcal{G}$, but scales poorly with the number of undirected edges in $\mathcal{G}$. The local variant of IDA from Maathuis et al. (2009) and the semi-local variant of joint-IDA from Nandy et al. (2017) dramatically reduce the computational complexity of the algorithm. However, they are not applicable to maximal PDAGs, as we demonstrate in Examples 4.8 and 4.9.

In Algorithm 2, we present our semi-local variant for finding possible (joint) parent sets in maximal PDAGs. This algorithm exploits the soundness and completeness of orientations in the maximal PDAG (Meek, 1995). To find a possible parent set of X, Algorithm 2 simply considers all $\mathbf{S} \subseteq \mathrm{Sib}(X, \mathcal{G})$ and imposes $S \to X$ and $X \to \bar{S}$, for all $S \in \mathbf{S}$, and $\bar{S} \in \mathrm{Sib}(X, \mathcal{G}) \setminus \mathbf{S}$ as background knowledge called $\mathbf{LocalBg}$. If this background knowledge is consistent with $\mathcal{G}$, then $\mathbf{S} \cup \mathrm{Pa}(X, \mathcal{G})$ is a possible parent set of X. In case of joint interventions ($|\mathbf{X}| = k > 1$), Algorithm 2 does this for every $X_i \in \mathbf{X}, i \in \{1, \ldots, k\}$ and $(\mathrm{Pa}(X_1, \mathcal{G}) \cup \mathbf{S}_1, \ldots, \mathrm{Pa}(X_k, \mathcal{G}) \cup \mathbf{S}_k)$ is the possible joint parent set of $\mathbf{X}$.

Since the local IDA and semi-local joint-IDA are not applicable to maximal PDAGs, we can only compare the computational complexity of our Algorithm 2 with the local IDA and semi-local joint-IDA by applying them all to a CPDAG. In this case, Algorithm 2 will in general be slower than local IDA, as it requires closing the orientation rules of Meek (1995), but also in general somewhat faster than semi-local joint IDA, since it does not require orienting an entire undirected component of the CPDAG. We compare the runtimes of local IDA and our semi-local IDA in an empirical study in Section D of the supplement.

4.2.1 Examples

Example 4.8. *Consider the maximal* PDAG $\mathcal{G}$ *in Figure 1c. Suppose we want to estimate the total causal effect of* C *on* A *in* $\mathcal{G}$. *All possible parent sets of* C *according to Algorithm 2 are:* $\emptyset, \{D\}, \{B, D\}$. *These are also all possible parent sets of* C *according to Figure 1d.*

We now show that local IDA cannot be applied. For every $\mathbf{S} \subseteq \mathrm{Sib}(C, \mathcal{G})$, *local IDA from Maathuis et al. (2009) orients* $S - C$ *as* $S \rightarrow C$ *for every* $S \in \mathbf{S}$. *If this does not introduce a new unshielded collider* $\rightarrow C \leftarrow$ *it returns* $\mathrm{Pa}(C, \mathcal{G}) \cup \mathbf{S}$ *as a valid parent set. Local IDA returns the following sets as the possible parent sets of* C: $\emptyset, \{B\}, \{D\}, \{B, D\}$. *However, parent set* $\{B\}$ *means adding* $B \rightarrow C$ *and* $C \rightarrow D$ *and this introduces a cycle due to* $D \rightarrow B$. *Hence,* $\{B\}$ *will never be a parent set of* C *in* $[\mathcal{C}]$ *and local IDA is not valid for maximal* PDAGs.

Example 4.9. *Consider again the maximal* PDAG $\mathcal{G}$ *in Figure 1c. Suppose we want to estimate the total causal effect of* (C, D) *on* A *in* $\mathcal{G}$. *All possible joint parent sets of* (C, D) *according to Algorithm 2 are:* $(\emptyset, \{C\}), (\{D\}, \emptyset), (\{B, D\}, \emptyset), (\{B, D\}, \{A\})$. *These are also all possible joint parent sets of* (C, D) *according to Figure 1d.*

Semi-local joint-IDA from Nandy et al. (2017) would attempt to learn all possible joint parent sets of (C, D) *by orienting the undirected component* $A - B - C - D - A$ *on* $\mathcal{G}$ *into all possible* DAGs *without unshielded colliders. However, it is not possible to orient* $A - B - C - D - A$ *into a* DAG *without creating an unshielded collider. Hence, semi-local joint-IDA is not valid for maximal* PDAGs.

5 IMPLEMENTATION AND SIMULATION STUDY

We investigated the effect of including background knowledge into a CPDAG in a simulation study using `R (3.3.3)` and the R-package `pcalg (2.4-6)` (Kalisch et al., 2012) where the following functions were added or modified: `isValidGraph()`, `addBgKnowledge()`, `adjustment()`, `gac()`, `ida()`, `jointIda()`. Details about the simulation can be found in the package vignette.

We first sampled 1000 settings that were used to generate graphs later on. The following settings were drawn uniformly at random: the number of nodes $p \in \{20, 30, ..., 100\}$, and the expected neighborhood size $E[N] \in \{3, 4, ..., 10\}$.

For each of these 1000 settings, 20 DAGs were randomly generated and then transformed into the corresponding CPDAG. This resulted in 20 000 CPDAGs. For each graph, we randomly chose a node X and then randomly chose a node Y that was connected to X but was not a parent of X in the true underlying DAG. Furthermore, for each DAG we generated a data set with sample size $n = 200$.

For each of the 20 000 CPDAGs, we then generated additional maximal PDAGs by replacing a fraction of randomly chosen undirected edges by the true directed edges of the underlying DAG and applying the orientation rules in Figure 2 to further orient edges if possible. The fraction of background knowledge varied through all values in the set $\{0, 0.1, \ldots, 0.9, 1\}$, resulting in eleven maximal PDAGs. Note that a fraction of 0 corresponds to the CPDAG and a fraction of 1 corresponds to the true underlying DAG.

For each of the 220 000 maximal PDAGs $\mathcal{G}$ we analyzed two questions:

Q1: Is there a set that satisfies the b-adjustment criterion relative to (X, Y) in $\mathcal{G}$?

Q2: What is the multi-set of possible total causal effects of X on Y given $\mathcal{G}$ and the sampled data of the corresponding DAG? In particular, what is the number of unique estimates in the multi-set?

The results for question (**Q1**) are shown in Figure 4. We see that without any background knowledge around 90% of all total causal effects could be identified via adjustment, while around 70% of the non-zero total causal effects could be identified via adjustment. When the proportion of background knowledge increases, the fraction of total causal effects that we identify via adjustment increases, both for all total causal effects and for the non-zero total causal effects. With 100% background knowledge, the maximal PDAG is identical to the true underlying DAG and identification of the total causal effect of X on Y via covariate adjustment is always possible, since X is a single intervention and Y is not a parent of X in the DAG (Pearl, 2009).

The results for questions (**Q2**) are shown in Figure 5, restricting ourselves to the 4315 CPDAGs that had more

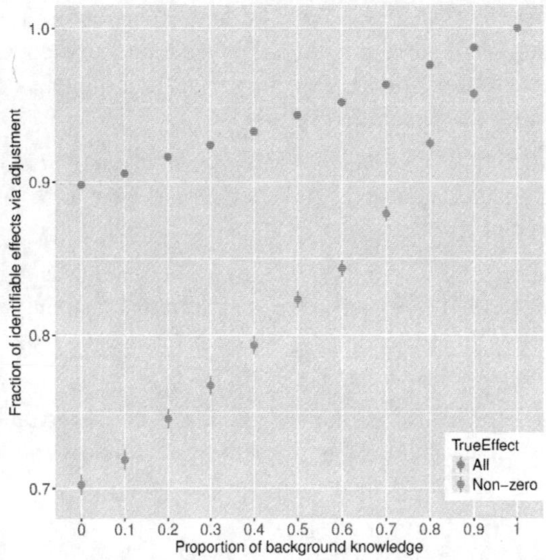

Figure 4: Fraction of total causal effects that are identifiable with our adjustment criterion, with respect to the proportion of background knowledge. Red: all simulations; blue: those simulations where the true total causal effect is non-zero. Error bars indicate standard errors and are partly too small to be seen.

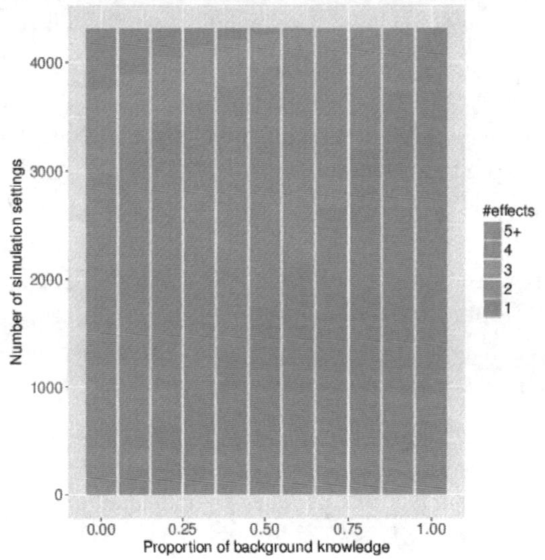

Figure 5: Stacked barplot of the number of unique possible total causal effects in the multi-sets of our semi-local IDA, with respect to the proportion of background knowledge. The results are restricted to the 4315 CPDAGs (out of 20 000) that have more than one unique estimated possible total causal effect in the multi-set.

than one unique estimate in the multi-set. When including background knowledge, the fraction of multi-sets with exactly one unique estimate gradually increases. Finally, with 100% background knowledge, the maximal PDAG is identical to the true underlying DAG and the multi-set always contains one unique element.

6 DISCUSSION

Although maximal PDAGs typically contain more orientation information than CPDAGs, this additional information has not been fully exploited in practice, due to a lack of understanding and methodology for maximal PDAGs. Our paper aims to make an important step in bridging this gap and in opening the way for the use of maximal PDAGs in practice.

This paper introduces various tools for working with maximal PDAGs. In particular, we are now able to read off possible ancestral relationships directly from a maximal PDAG and to estimate (possible) total causal effects when a maximal PDAG is given. Since CPDAGs and DAGs are special cases of maximal PDAGs, our b-adjustment criterion and semi-local (joint-)IDA methods for maximal PDAGs generalize existing results for CPDAGs and DAGs (Maathuis et al., 2009; Shpitser et al., 2010; Perković et al., 2015, 2017; Nandy et al., 2017). All methods are implemented in the `R` package `pcalg`.

The examples and the simulation study in our paper involve maximal PDAGs generated by adding background knowledge to a CPDAG. Nevertheless, we emphasize that maximal PDAGs can arise in many different ways, e.g., by adding background knowledge before structure learning (Scheines et al., 1998), by structure learning from a combination of observational and interventional data (Hauser and Bühlmann, 2012; Wang et al., 2017), or by structure learning for certain restricted model classes (Hoyer et al., 2008; Ernest et al., 2016; Eigenmann et al., 2017).

It would be interesting to extend our methods to settings with hidden variables, e.g., considering partial ancestral graphs (PAGs; Richardson and Spirtes, 2002; Ali et al., 2005) with background knowledge. An important missing link for such an extension is a clear understanding of PAGs with background knowledge. In particular, one would need to develop complete orientation rules for PAGs with background knowledge, analogous to the work of Meek (1995). Once this is in place, it seems feasible to generalize graphical criteria for covariate adjustment in PAGs (Perković et al., 2015, 2017) and an IDA type method for PAGs, called LV-IDA (Malinsky and Spirtes, 2017).

Acknowledgements

This work was supported in part by Swiss NSF Grant 200021_172603.

References

Ali, A. R., Richardson, T. S., Spirtes, P. L., and Zhang, J. (2005). Towards characterizing Markov equivalence classes for directed acyclic graphs with latent variables. In *Proceedings of UAI 2005*.

Chickering, D. M. (2002). Optimal structure identification with greedy search. *J. Mach. Learn. Res.*, 3:507–554.

Dor, D. and Tarsi, M. (1992). A simple algorithm to construct a consistent extension of a partially oriented graph. *Technicial Report R-185, Cognitive Systems Laboratory, UCLA*.

Eigenmann, M., Nandy, P., and Maathuis, M. H. (2017). Structure learning of linear Gaussian structural equation models with weak edges. In *Proceedings of UAI 2017*.

Ernest, J., Rothenhäusler, D., and Bühlmann, P. (2016). Causal inference in partially linear structural equation models: identifiability and estimation. arXiv:1607.05980.

Hauser, A. and Bühlmann, P. (2012). Characterization and greedy learning of interventional Markov equivalence classes of directed acyclic graphs. *J. Mach. Learn. Res.*, 13:2409–2464.

Hoyer, P. O., Hyvarinen, A., Scheines, R., Spirtes, P. L., Ramsey, J., Lacerda, G., and Shimizu, S. (2008). Causal discovery of linear acyclic models with arbitrary distributions. In *Proceedings of UAI 2008*, pages 282–289.

Hyttinen, A., Eberhardt, F., and Järvisalo, M. (2015). Do-calculus when the true graph is unknown. In *Proceedings of UAI 2015*, pages 395–404.

Kalisch, M., Mächler, M., Colombo, D., Maathuis, M. H., and Bühlmann, P. (2012). Causal inference using graphical models with the R package pcalg. *J. Stat. Softw.*, 47(11):1–26.

Maathuis, M. H., Colombo, D., Kalisch, M., and Bühlmann, P. (2010). Predicting causal effects in large-scale systems from observational data. *Nat. Methods*, 7:247–248.

Maathuis, M. H., Kalisch, M., and Bühlmann, P. (2009). Estimating high-dimensional intervention effects from observational data. *Ann. Stat.*, 37:3133–3164.

Malinsky, D. and Spirtes, P. (2017). Estimating bounds on causal effects in high-dimensional and possibly confounded systems. *Int. J. of Approx. Reason.*

Meek, C. (1995). Causal inference and causal explanation with background knowledge. In *Proceedings of UAI 1995*, pages 403–410.

Nandy, P., Maathuis, M. H., and Richardson, T. S. (2017). Estimating the effect of joint interventions from observational data in sparse high-dimensional settings. *Ann. Stat.*, 45(2):647–674.

Pearl, J. (2009). *Causality: Models, Reasoning, and Inference*. Cambridge University Press, New York, NY, second edition.

Perković, E., Textor, J., Kalisch, M., and Maathuis, M. H. (2015). A complete generalized adjustment criterion. In *Proceedings of UAI 2015*, pages 682–691.

Perković, E., Textor, J., Kalisch, M., and Maathuis, M. H. (2017). Complete graphical characterization and construction of adjustment sets in Markov equivalence classes of ancestral graphs. *J. Mach. Learn. Res.* to appear.

Richardson, T. S. and Spirtes, P. (2002). Ancestral graph Markov models. *Ann. Stat.*, 30:962–1030.

Robins, J. M. (1986). A new approach to causal inference in mortality studies with a sustained exposure period-application to control of the healthy worker survivor effect. *Math. Mod.*, 7:1393–1512.

Scheines, R., Spirtes, P., Glymour, C., Meek, C., and Richardson, T. (1998). The TETRAD project: constraint based aids to causal model specification. *Multivar. Behav. Res.*, 33(1):65–117.

Shpitser, I. (2012). Appendum to "On the validity of covariate adjustment for estimating causal effects". Personal communication.

Shpitser, I., VanderWeele, T., and Robins, J. M. (2010). On the validity of covariate adjustment for estimating causal effects. In *Proceedings of UAI 2010*, pages 527–536.

Spirtes, P., Glymour, C., and Scheines, R. (2000). *Causation, Prediction, and Search*. MIT Press, Cambridge, MA, second edition.

van der Zander, B. and Liśkiewicz, M. (2016). Separators and adjustment sets in Markov equivalent DAGs. In *Proceedings of AAAI 2016*, pages 3315–3321.

van der Zander, B., Liśkiewicz, M., and Textor, J. (2014). Constructing separators and adjustment sets in ancestral graphs. In *Proceedings of UAI 2014*, pages 907–916.

Wang, Y., Solus, L., Yang, K. D., and Uhler, C. (2017). Permutation-based causal inference algorithms with interventions. arXiv:1705.10220.

Zhang, J. (2008). On the completeness of orientation rules for causal discovery in the presence of latent confounders and selection bias. *Artif. Intell.*, 172:1873–1896.

Supplement to "Interpreting and using CPDAGs with background knowledge"

Emilija Perković
Seminar for Statistics
ETH Zurich, Switzerland
perkovic@stat.math.ethz.ch

Markus Kalisch
Seminar for Statistics
ETH Zurich, Switzerland
kalisch@stat.math.ethz.ch

Marloes H. Maathuis
Seminar for Statistics
ETH Zurich, Switzerland
maathuis@stat.math.ethz.ch

This is the supplement of the paper "Interpreting and using CPDAGs with background knowledge", which we refer to as the "main text".

A PRELIMINARIES

Paths. If $p = \langle X_1, X_2, \dots, X_k, \rangle, k \geq 2$ is a path, then with $-p$ we denote the path $\langle X_k, \dots, X_2, X_1 \rangle$. The *length* of a path equals the number of edges on the path. We denote the concatenation of paths by $\oplus$, so that for example $p = p(X_1, X_m) \oplus p(X_m, X_k)$ for $1 \leq m \leq k$.

Definition A.1. *(Distance-from-**Z**) Let* $\mathbf{X}, \mathbf{Y}$ *and* $\mathbf{Z}$ *be pairwise disjoint node sets in a maximal* PDAG $\mathcal{G}$. *Let* p *be a path from* $\mathbf{X}$ *to* $\mathbf{Y}$ *in* $\mathcal{G}$ *such that every collider* C *on* p *has a b-possibly causal path to* $\mathbf{Z}$. *Define the* distance-from-$\mathbf{Z}$ *of collider* C *to be the length of a shortest b-possibly causal path from* C *to* $\mathbf{Z}$, *and define the* distance-from-$\mathbf{Z}$ *of* p *to be the sum of the distances from* $\mathbf{Z}$ *of the colliders on* p.

Lemma A.2. *(Lemma A.7 in Ernest et al., 2016) Let* X *and* Y *be nodes in a maximal* PDAG $\mathcal{G}$ *such that* $X - Y$ *is in* $\mathcal{G}$. *Let* $\mathcal{G}' = \text{ConstructMaxPDAG}(\mathcal{G}, \{X \to Y\})$. *For any* $Z, W \in \mathbf{V}$ *if* $Z \to W$ *is in* $\mathcal{G}'$ *and* $Z - W$ *is in* $\mathcal{G}$, *then* $W \in \text{De}(Y, \mathcal{G}')$.

Lemma A.3. *(cf. Lemma A.8 in Ernest et al., 2016) Let* X *be a node in a maximal* PDAG $\mathcal{G}$. *Then there is a maximal* PDAG $\mathcal{G}'$ *in* $[\mathcal{G}]$ *such that* $X \to S$ *is in* $\mathcal{G}'$ *for all* $S \in \text{Sib}(X, \mathcal{G})$.

B PROOFS FOR SECTION 3

Proof of Lemma 3.2. Since $p^* = \langle X = V_0, \dots, V_k = Y \rangle$, $k \geq 1$ is b-non-causal in $\mathcal{G}$, we have $V_i \leftarrow V_j$ in $\mathcal{G}$ for some i, j such that $0 \leq i < j \leq k$. Let $\mathcal{D}$ be an arbitrary DAG in $[\mathcal{G}]$ and let p be the path corresponding to p^* in $\mathcal{D}$. Since $V_i \leftarrow V_j$ in $\mathcal{D}$, $p(V_i, V_j)$ is non-causal from V_i to V_j in $\mathcal{D}$. Hence, p is b-non-causal in $\mathcal{D}$. □

Proof of Lemma 3.5. One direction is trivial and we only prove that if there is no $V_i \leftarrow V_{i+1}$, for $i \in \{1, \dots, k-1\}$ in $\mathcal{G}$, then p^* is b-possibly causal in $\mathcal{G}$. Suppose for a contradiction that p^* is b-non-causal, that is, there is an edge $V_j \leftarrow V_r$, for $1 \leq j < r \leq k$, where $r \neq j+1$.

Since there is no $V_i \leftarrow V_{i+1}$ for any $i \in \{1, \dots, k-1\}$ in $\mathcal{G}$, $V_i - V_{i+1}$ or $V_i \to V_{i+1}$ is in $\mathcal{G}$ for every $i \in \{1, \dots, k-1\}$. Let $\mathcal{D}$ be a DAG in $[\mathcal{G}]$ that contains $V_1 \to V_2$ and let p be the path corresponding to p^* in $\mathcal{D}$. Since p^* is of definite status in $\mathcal{G}$ and since no $V_i \leftarrow V_{i+1}$, $i \in \{1, \dots, k-1\}$ is in $\mathcal{G}$, it follows that p^* contains only definite non-colliders. Then since $V_1 \to V_2$ is on p, p is a causal path in $\mathcal{D}$. But then $p(V_j, V_r)$ together with $V_j \leftarrow V_r$ create a directed cycle in $\mathcal{D}$. □

Lemma 3.6 is analogous to Lemma B.1 in Zhang (2008) and the proof follows the same reasoning as well.

Proof of Lemma 3.6. The proof is by induction on the length of p. Let $p = \langle X = V_1, \dots, V_k = Y \rangle$. Suppose that $k = 3$. Then either p is unshielded, or there is an edge $X - Y$ or $X \to Y$ in $\mathcal{G}$ ($X \leftarrow Y$ is not in $\mathcal{G}$ since p is b-possibly causal).

For the induction step suppose that the lemma holds for paths of length $n-1$ and let $k = n$. Then either p is unshielded, or there is a node V_i, $i > 1$ on p, such that $V_{i-1} - V_{i+1}$ or $V_{i-1} \to V_{i+1}$ is in $\mathcal{G}$ ($V_{i-1} \leftarrow V_{i+1}$ is not in $\mathcal{G}$ since p is b-possibly causal). Then $p' = p(X, V_{i-1}) \oplus \langle V_{i-1}, V_{i+1} \rangle \oplus p(V_{i+1}, Y)$ is a b-possibly causal path from X to Y of length $n-1$ and p' is a subsequence of p. □

The following lemma is analogous to Lemma 7.2 in Maathuis and Colombo (2015) and follows directly from our definitions of b-possibly causal paths and definite status paths.

Lemma B.1. *Let* $p = \langle V_1, \dots, V_k \rangle$ *be a b-possibly*

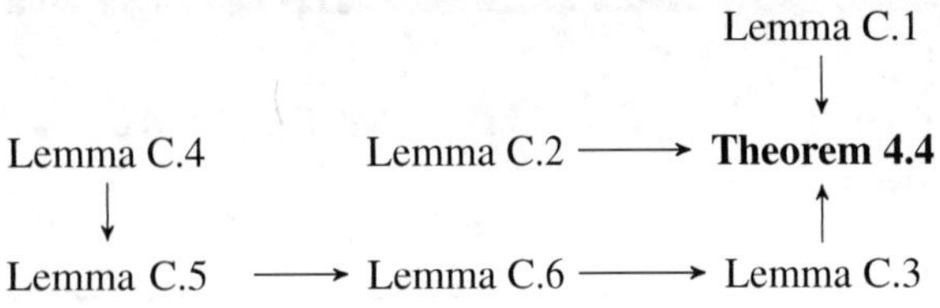

Figure 1: Proof structure of Theorem 4.4.

causal definite status path in a maximal PDAG $\mathcal{G}$. *If there is a node* $i \in \{1, \ldots, n-1\}$ *such that* $V_i \to V_{i+1}$, *then* $p(V_i, V_k)$ *is a causal path in* $\mathcal{G}$.

C PROOFS FOR SECTION 4.1 OF THE MAIN TEXT

C.1 PROOF OF THEOREM 4.4

Figure 1 shows how all lemmas fit together to prove Theorem 4.4. Theorem 4.4 is closely related to Theorem 3.6 for CPDAGs from Perković et al. (2017). Since every CPDAG is a maximal PDAG, all the results presented here subsume the existing results for CPDAGs. Throughout, we inform the reader when our results and proofs differ from the existing ones for CPDAGs.

Proof of Theorem 4.4. This proof is basically the same as the proof of Theorem 3.6 from Perković et al. (2017), except that instead of using Lemmas 3.12, 3.13 and 3.14 from Perković et al. (2017), we need to use Lemmas C.1, C.2 and C.3. We give the entire proof for completeness.

Suppose first that $\mathbf{Z}$ satisfies the b-adjustment criterion relative to $(\mathbf{X}, \mathbf{Y})$ in the maximal PDAG $\mathcal{G}$. We need to show that $\mathbf{Z}$ is an adjustment set (Definition 4.1) relative to $(\mathbf{X}, \mathbf{Y})$ in every DAG $\mathcal{D}$ in $[\mathcal{G}]$. By applying Lemmas C.1, C.2 and C.3 in turn, it directly follows that $\mathbf{Z}$ satisfies the b-adjustment criterion relative to $(\mathbf{X}, \mathbf{Y})$ in any DAG $\mathcal{D}$ in $[\mathcal{G}]$. Since the b-adjustment criterion reduces to the adjustment criterion (Shpitser et al., 2010; Shpitser, 2012) in DAGs and the adjustment criterion is sound for DAGs, $\mathbf{Z}$ is an adjustment set relative to $(\mathbf{X}, \mathbf{Y})$ in $\mathcal{D}$.

To prove the other direction, suppose that $\mathbf{Z}$ does not satisfy the b-adjustment criterion relative to $(\mathbf{X}, \mathbf{Y})$ in $\mathcal{G}$. First, suppose that $\mathcal{G}$ violates the b-amenability condition relative to $(\mathbf{X}, \mathbf{Y})$. Then by Lemma C.1, there is no adjustment set relative to $(\mathbf{X}, \mathbf{Y})$ in $\mathcal{G}$. Otherwise, suppose $\mathcal{G}$ is b-amenable relative to $(\mathbf{X}, \mathbf{Y})$. Then $\mathbf{Z}$ violates the b-forbidden set condition or the b-blocking condition. We need to show $\mathbf{Z}$ is not an adjustment set in at least one DAG $\mathcal{D}$ in $[\mathcal{G}]$. Suppose $\mathbf{Z}$ violates the forbidden set condition. Then by Lemma C.2, it follows that there exists a DAG $\mathcal{D}$ in $[\mathcal{G}]$ such that $\mathbf{Z}$ does not satisfy the b-adjustment criterion relative to $(\mathbf{X}, \mathbf{Y})$ in $\mathcal{D}$. Since the b-adjustment criterion reduces to the adjustment criterion (Shpitser et al., 2010; Shpitser, 2012) in DAGs and the adjustment criterion is complete for DAGs, it follows that $\mathbf{Z}$ is not an adjustment set relative to $(\mathbf{X}, \mathbf{Y})$ in $\mathcal{D}$. Otherwise, suppose $\mathbf{Z}$ satisfies the forbidden set condition, but violates the b-blocking condition. Then by Lemma C.3, it follows that there is a DAG $\mathcal{D}$ in $[\mathcal{G}]$ such that $\mathbf{Z}$ does not satisfy the b-adjustment criterion relative to $(\mathbf{X}, \mathbf{Y})$ in $\mathcal{D}$. Since the b-adjustment criterion reduces to the adjustment criterion (Shpitser et al., 2010; Shpitser, 2012) in DAGs and the adjustment criterion is complete for DAGs, it follows that $\mathbf{Z}$ is not an adjustment set relative to $(\mathbf{X}, \mathbf{Y})$ in $\mathcal{D}$. □

Lemma C.1. *Let* $\mathbf{X}$ *and* $\mathbf{Y}$ *be disjoint node sets in a maximal* PDAG $\mathcal{G}$. *If* $\mathcal{G}$ *violates the b-amenability condition relative to* $(\mathbf{X}, \mathbf{Y})$, *then there is no adjustment set relative to* $(\mathbf{X}, \mathbf{Y})$ *in* $\mathcal{G}$.

Proof. This lemma is related to Lemma 3.12 from Perković et al. (2017). The proofs are not the same due to the differences between CPDAGs and maximal PDAGs. We will point out where the two proofs diverge.

Suppose that $\mathcal{G}$ violates the b-amenability condition relative to $(\mathbf{X}, \mathbf{Y})$. We will show that in this case one can find DAGs $\mathcal{D}_1$ and $\mathcal{D}_2$ in $[\mathcal{G}]$, such that there is no set that satisfies the b-adjustment criterion relative to $(\mathbf{X}, \mathbf{Y})$ in both $\mathcal{D}_1$ and $\mathcal{D}_2$.

Since $\mathcal{G}$ is not b-amenable relative to $(\mathbf{X}, \mathbf{Y})$, there is a proper b-possibly causal path q^* from a node $X \in \mathbf{X}$ to a node $Y \in \mathbf{Y}$ that starts with a undirected edge. Let $q'^* = \langle X = V_0, V_1, \ldots, V_k = Y \rangle, k \geq 1$ (where $V_1 = Y$ is allowed) be a shortest subsequence of q^* such that q'^* is also a proper b-possibly causal path that starts with a undirected edge in $\mathcal{G}$.

Suppose first that q'^* is of definite status in $\mathcal{G}$. Let $\mathcal{D}_1$ be a DAG in $[\mathcal{G}]$ that contains $X \to V_1$ and let $\mathcal{D}_2$ be a DAG in $[\mathcal{G}]$ that has no additional edges into V_1 as compared to $\mathcal{G}$ (Lemma A.3). Then the path corresponding to q'^* in $\mathcal{D}_1$ is causal, whereas the path corresponding to q'^* in $\mathcal{D}_2$ is b-non-causal and contains no colliders. Hence, no set can satisfy both the b-forbidden set condition in $\mathcal{D}_1$ and the b-blocking condition in $\mathcal{D}_2$ relative to $(\mathbf{X}, \mathbf{Y})$.

Otherwise, q'^* is not of definite status in $\mathcal{G}$. In the proof of Lemma 3.12 from Perković et al. (2017), the authors show that if q'^* is not of definite status, this leads to a contradiction. However, q'^* can be of non-definite status in $\mathcal{G}$ and this is where the proofs diverge.

By Lemma 3.6, $q'^*(V_1, Y)$ must be unshielded and hence, of definite status in $\mathcal{G}$, since otherwise we can choose a shorter b-possibly causal path. Since q'^* is not of definite status and $q'^*(V_1, Y)$ is of definite status, it follows that V_1 is not of definite status on q'^*. Then $\langle X, V_1, V_2 \rangle$ is a shielded triple. By choice of q'^*, $X - V_1$ is in $\mathcal{G}$. Additionally, since V_1 is not of definite status on q'^*, $V_1 - V_2$ must be in $\mathcal{G}$. This implies that $X - V_1 - V_2$ is in $\mathcal{G}$ and $X \in \text{Adj}(V_2, \mathcal{G})$. Moreover, we must have $X \to V_2$, since $X - V_2$ contradicts the choice of q'^*, and $X \leftarrow V_2$ contradicts that q'^* is b-possibly causal in $\mathcal{G}$.

Let $\mathcal{D}_1$ be a DAG in $\mathcal{G}$ that has no additional edges into V_1 as compared to $\mathcal{G}$ (Lemma A.3). Let q_1 be the path corresponding to q'^* in $\mathcal{D}_1$. Then q_1 is of the form $X \leftarrow V_1 \to V_2 \to \cdots \to Y$ in $\mathcal{D}_1$. Since $X \to V_2 \to \cdots \to Y$ is a proper causal path in $\mathcal{D}_1$, $\{V_2, \dots, V_{k-1}\} \subseteq \text{b-Forb}(\mathbf{X}, \mathbf{Y}, \mathcal{D}_1)$. Hence, any set that satisfies the b-blocking condition and the b-forbidden set condition relative to $(\mathbf{X}, \mathbf{Y})$ in $\mathcal{D}_1$ must contain V_1 and not $\{V_2, \dots, V_{k-1}$.

Let $\mathcal{D}_2$ be a DAG in $\mathcal{G}$ that has no additional edges into V_2 as compared to $\mathcal{G}$ (Lemma A.3). Let q_2 be the path corresponding to q'^* in $\mathcal{D}_2$. Since $X \to V_2 \to V_1$ is in $\mathcal{D}_2$, $X \to V_1$ is in $\mathcal{D}_2$ (Rule $R2$). Then q_2 is of the form $X \to V_1 \leftarrow V_2 \to \cdots \to Y$ in $\mathcal{D}_2$. Hence, any set that satisfies the b-forbidden set condition and the b-blocking condition relative to $(\mathbf{X}, \mathbf{Y})$ in $\mathcal{D}_1$, violates the b-blocking condition relative to $(\mathbf{X}, \mathbf{Y})$ in $\mathcal{D}_2$. □

Lemma C.2. *Let* $\mathbf{X}$ *and* $\mathbf{Y}$ *be disjoint node sets in a maximal* PDAG $\mathcal{G}$. *If* $\mathcal{G}$ *is b-amenable relative to* $(\mathbf{X}, \mathbf{Y})$, *then the following statements are equivalent:*

(i) $\mathbf{Z}$ *satisfies the b-forbidden set condition (see Definition 4.3) relative to* $(\mathbf{X}, \mathbf{Y})$ *in* $\mathcal{G}$.

(ii) $\mathbf{Z}$ *satisfies the b-forbidden set condition relative to* $(\mathbf{X}, \mathbf{Y})$ *in every* DAG *in* $[\mathcal{G}]$.

Proof. This lemma is related to Lemma 3.14 from Perković et al. (2017), but instead of using Lemma A.9 and Lemma A.10 from Perković et al. (2017), we use Lemma 3.6 and Lemma B.1.

By Lemma 3.2 $\text{b-Forb}(\mathbf{X}, \mathbf{Y}, \mathcal{D}) \subseteq \text{b-Forb}(\mathbf{X}, \mathbf{Y}, \mathcal{G})$ hence, (i)⇒(ii) holds. We now prove ¬ (i)⇒ ¬ (ii).

Let $V \in \mathbf{Z} \cap \text{b-Forb}(\mathbf{X}, \mathbf{Y}, \mathcal{G})$. Then $V \in \text{b-PossDe}(W, \mathcal{G})$ for some $W = V_i$ on a proper b-possibly causal path $p = \langle X = V_0, V_1, \dots, V_k = Y \rangle, 1 \leq i \leq k$ from $X \in \mathbf{X}$ to $Y \in \mathbf{Y}$. Let $q = p(X, W)$, $r = p(W, Y)$ and let s be a b-possibly causal path from W to V, where r and s are allowed to be of zero length (if $W = Y$ and/or $W = V$).

Let q', r' and s' be subsequences of q, r and s that form unshielded b-possibly causal paths, with r' and s' possibly of zero length (Lemma 3.6). Then q' must start with a directed edge, otherwise $q' \oplus r'$ would violate the b-amenability condition. Hence, q' must be causal in $\mathcal{G}$ (Lemma B.1).

Let $\mathcal{D}$ be a DAG in $[\mathcal{G}]$ that has no additional edges into W as compared to $\mathcal{G}$ (Lemma A.3). Then since r' and s' are unshielded and b-possibly causal, the paths corresponding to r' and s' in $\mathcal{D}$ are causal (or of zero length). Hence, $V \in \text{b-Forb}(\mathbf{X}, \mathbf{Y}, \mathcal{D})$, so that $\mathbf{Z} \cap \text{b-Forb}(\mathbf{X}, \mathbf{Y}, \mathcal{D}) \neq \emptyset$. □

The final lemma needed to prove Theorem 4.4 is Lemma C.3. This lemma relies on Lemma C.6, which depends on Lemma C.4, C.5 and C.6. We first give Lemma C.3 with its proof. This is followed by Lemmas C.4, C.5 and C.6 with their proofs.

Lemma C.3. *Let* $\mathbf{X}$ *and* $\mathbf{Y}$ *be disjoint node sets in a maximal* PDAG $\mathcal{G}$. *If* $\mathcal{G}$ *is b-amenable relative to* $(\mathbf{X}, \mathbf{Y})$ *and* $\mathbf{Z}$ *satisfies the b-forbidden set condition relative to* $(\mathbf{X}, \mathbf{Y})$ *in* $\mathcal{G}$, *then the following statements are equivalent:*

(i) $\mathbf{Z}$ *satisfies the b-blocking condition (see Definition 4.3) relative to* $(\mathbf{X}, \mathbf{Y})$ *in* $\mathcal{G}$.

(ii) $\mathbf{Z}$ *satisfies the b-blocking condition relative to* $(\mathbf{X}, \mathbf{Y})$ *in every* DAG *in* $[\mathcal{G}]$.

(iii) $\mathbf{Z}$ *satisfies the b-blocking condition relative to* $(\mathbf{X}, \mathbf{Y})$ *in a* DAG $\mathcal{D}$ *in* $[\mathcal{G}]$.

Proof of Lemma C.3. This lemma is related to Lemma 3.15 from Perković et al. (2017),but instead of using Lemma B.6 from Perković et al. (2017), we use Lemma C.6.

To prove ¬ (i)⇒ ¬ (iii) let p be a proper b-non-causal definite status path from $\mathbf{X}$ to $\mathbf{Y}$ that is d-connecting given $\mathbf{Z}$ in $\mathcal{G}$. The path corresponding to p in any DAG $\mathcal{D}$ in $[\mathcal{G}]$ is proper, non-causal (Lemma 3.2) and d-connecting given $\mathbf{Z}$.

The implication ¬ (iii)⇒ ¬ (ii) trivially holds, so it is only left to prove that ¬ (ii)⇒ ¬ (i). Thus, assume there is a DAG $\mathcal{D}$ in $[\mathcal{G}]$ such that a proper b-non-causal path from $\mathbf{X}$ to $\mathbf{Y}$ in $\mathcal{D}$ is d-connecting given $\mathbf{Z}$. Among the shortest proper non-causal paths from $\mathbf{X}$ to $\mathbf{Y}$ that are d-connecting given $\mathbf{Z}$ in $\mathcal{D}$, choose a path p with a minimal distance-from-$\mathbf{Z}$ (Definition A.1). Let p^* in $\mathcal{G}$ be the path corresponding to p in $\mathcal{D}$. By Lemma C.6, p^* is a proper b-non-causal definite status path from $\mathbf{X}$ to $\mathbf{Y}$ that is d-connecting given $\mathbf{Z}$. □

Lemma C.4. *Let* $\mathbf{X}, \mathbf{Y}$ *and* $\mathbf{Z}$ *be pairwise disjoint node sets in a maximal* PDAG $\mathcal{G}$. *Let* $\mathbf{Z}$ *satisfy the b-amenability condition and the b-forbidden set condition* *relative to* $(\mathbf{X}, \mathbf{Y})$ *in* $\mathcal{G}$. *Let* $\mathcal{D}$ *be a* DAG *in* $[\mathcal{G}]$ *and let* $p = \langle X = V_0, V_1, \dots, V_k = Y\rangle, k \geq 1$, *be a proper non-causal path from* $X \in \mathbf{X}$ *to* $Y \in \mathbf{Y}$ *that is d-connecting given* $\mathbf{Z}$ *in* $\mathcal{D}$. *Let* p^* *in* $\mathcal{G}$ *denote the path corresponding to* p. *Then:*

(i) Let $i, j \in \mathbb{N}, 0 < i < j \leq k$, *such that there is an edge* $\langle V_i, V_j\rangle$ *in* $\mathcal{G}$. *The path* $p^*(X, V_i) \oplus \langle V_i, V_j\rangle \oplus p^*(V_j, Y)$ *(*$p^*(V_j, Y)$ *is possibly of zero length) is a proper b-non-causal path in* $\mathcal{G}$. *For* $j = i + 1$, *this implies that* p^* *is a proper b-non-causal path.*

(ii) If $X \leftarrow V_1$ *and* $V_1 \rightarrow V_2$ *are not in* $\mathcal{G}$ *and there is an edge* $\langle X, V_2\rangle$ *in* $\mathcal{G}$, *then* $q^* = \langle X, V_2\rangle \oplus p^*(V_2, Y)$, *(*$p^*(V_2, Y)$ *is possibly of zero length) is a proper b-non-causal path in* $\mathcal{G}$.

Proof. This lemma is related to Lemma B.3 from Perković et al. (2017). In particular, (i) in Lemma C.4 and (i) in Lemma B.3 from Perković et al. (2017) and their proofs match. The result in (ii) differs in both statement and proof from (ii)-(iii) in Lemma B.3 from Perković et al. (2017).

All paths considered are proper as they are subsequences of p^*, which corresponds to p.

(i) We use proof by contradiction. Thus, suppose that $q^* = p^*(X, V_i) \oplus \langle V_i, V_j\rangle \oplus p^*(V_j, Y)$ is b-possibly causal in $\mathcal{G}$. Then $\{V_1, \dots, V_i, V_j, \dots, V_k\} \subseteq$ b-Forb$(\mathbf{X}, \mathbf{Y}, \mathcal{G})$. Since $\mathcal{G}$ is b-amenable relative to $(\mathbf{X}, \mathbf{Y})$, q^* and $p^*(X, V_i)$ as well must start with $X \rightarrow V_1$. Then p also starts with $X \rightarrow V_1$ and since p is non-causal, there is at least one collider on p. Let $V_r, r \geq 1$, be the collider closest to X on p, then $V_r \in$ b-Forb$(\mathbf{X}, \mathbf{Y}, \mathcal{D})$. Since p is d-connecting given $\mathbf{Z}$, $\mathbf{Z} \cap \text{De}(V_r, \mathcal{D}) \neq \emptyset$. Since $\text{De}(V_r, \mathcal{D}) \subseteq$ b-Forb$(\mathbf{X}, \mathbf{Y}, \mathcal{D})$ and since b-Forb$(\mathbf{X}, \mathbf{Y}, \mathcal{D}) \subseteq$ b-Forb$(\mathbf{X}, \mathbf{Y}, \mathcal{G})$, this contradicts $\mathbf{Z} \cap$ b-Forb$(\mathbf{X}, \mathbf{Y}, \mathcal{G}) = \emptyset$.

(ii) We again use proof by contradiction. Suppose neither $X \leftarrow V_1$ nor $V_1 \rightarrow V_2$ are in $\mathcal{G}$ and q^* is a b-possibly causal path. Since $\mathcal{G}$ is b-amenable relative to $(\mathbf{X}, \mathbf{Y})$, $X \rightarrow V_2$ is in $\mathcal{G}$ and $\{V_2, \dots, V_k\} \subseteq$ b-Forb$(\mathbf{X}, \mathbf{Y}, \mathcal{G})$. Since $V_1 \rightarrow V_2$ is not in $\mathcal{G}$, either $V_1 - V_2$ or $V_1 \leftarrow V_2$ is in $\mathcal{G}$. Hence, $V_1 \in$ b-PossDe$(V_2, \mathcal{G})$. Since b-PossDe$(V_2, \mathcal{G}) \subseteq$ b-Forb$(\mathbf{X}, \mathbf{Y}, \mathcal{G})$, it follows that $V_1 \in$ b-Forb$(\mathbf{X}, \mathbf{Y}, \mathcal{G})$.

Suppose that $V_1 \leftarrow V_2$ is in $\mathcal{G}$. Then $X \rightarrow V_2 \rightarrow V_1$ and rule $R2$ implies that $X \rightarrow V_1$ is in $\mathcal{G}$. Then $X \rightarrow V_1 \leftarrow V_2$, so since p is d-connecting given $\mathbf{Z}$, $\mathbf{Z} \cap \text{De}(V_1, \mathcal{D}) \neq \emptyset$. But $\text{De}(V_1, \mathcal{D}) \subseteq$ b-PossDe$(V_1, \mathcal{G}) \subseteq$ b-Forb$(\mathbf{X}, \mathbf{Y}, \mathcal{G})$, which contradicts that $\mathbf{Z} \cap$ b-Forb$(\mathbf{X}, \mathbf{Y}, \mathcal{G}) = \emptyset$.

Otherwise, $V_1 - V_2$ is in $\mathcal{G}$. Additionally, $X \rightarrow V_2$ is in $\mathcal{G}$ and $p^*(V_2, Y)$ is b-possibly causal. So since p^* is b-non-causal (from (i)), $X \leftarrow V_1$ must be in $\mathcal{G}$. This contradicts our assumption in (ii). □

Lemma C.5. *Let* $\mathbf{X}, \mathbf{Y}$ *and* $\mathbf{Z}$ *be pairwise disjoint node sets in a maximal* PDAG $\mathcal{G}$. *Let* $\mathbf{Z}$ *satisfy the b-amenability condition and the b-forbidden set condition relative to* $(\mathbf{X}, \mathbf{Y})$ *in* $\mathcal{G}$. *Let* $\mathcal{D}$ *be a* DAG *in* $[\mathcal{G}]$ *and let* p *be a shortest proper non-causal path from* $\mathbf{X}$ *to* $\mathbf{Y}$ *that is d-connecting given* $\mathbf{Z}$ *in* $\mathcal{D}$. *Let* p^* *in* $\mathcal{G}$ *be corresponding path to* p *in* $\mathcal{D}$. *Then* p^* *is a proper b-non-causal definite status path in* $\mathcal{G}$ *such that for every subpath* $C_l \rightarrow C \leftarrow C_r$ *of* p^* *there is no edge* $\langle C_l, C_r\rangle$ *in* $\mathcal{G}$.

Proof. This lemma is related to Lemma B.4 from Perković et al. (2017). Our lemma additionally contains the result that if $\langle C_l, C, C_r\rangle$ is a subpath of p^*, then there is no edge $\langle C_l, C_r\rangle$ in $\mathcal{G}$. The proofs of this lemma and Lemma B.4 from Perković et al. (2017) overlap for cases (1)-(3) and then diverge after that.

Path p^* is proper and b-non-causal ((i) in Lemma C.4) in $\mathcal{G}$, so it is only left to prove that it is of definite status and that for any subpath $C_l \rightarrow C \leftarrow C_r$ of p^* there is no edge $\langle C_l, C_r\rangle$ in $\mathcal{G}$. Let $p^* = \langle X = V_0, V_1, \dots, V_k = Y\rangle, k > 1, X \in \mathbf{X}, Y \in \mathbf{Y}$. We first prove that p^* is of definite status, by contradiction.

Hence, suppose that a node on p^* is not of definite status. Let $V_i, i \geq 1$, be the node closest to X on p^* that is not of definite status. Then $\langle V_{i-1}, V_i, V_{i+1}\rangle$ is shielded in $\mathcal{G}$ and there is an edge between V_{i-1} and V_{i+1} in $\mathcal{G}$. Let $q = p(X, V_{i-1}) \oplus \langle V_{i-1}, V_{i+1}\rangle \oplus p(V_{i+1}, Y)$ in $\mathcal{D}$. Let q^* be the path corresponding to q in $\mathcal{G}$. Then q^* is proper and b-non-causal (Lemma C.4) in $\mathcal{G}$. Hence, q is also a proper non-causal path (Lemma 3.2). Since p is a shortest proper b-non-causal path from X to Y that is d-connecting given $\mathbf{Z}$, it follows that q must be blocked by $\mathbf{Z}$. The collider/non-collider status of all nodes, except possibly V_{i-1} and V_{i+1}, is the same on p and q. Hence, V_{i-1} or V_{i+1} block q, so $V_{i-1} \neq X$ or $V_{i+1} \neq Y$. We now discuss the different cases for the collider/non-collider status of V_{i-1} and V_{i+1} on p and q and derive a contradiction in each case.

(1) V_{i-1} is a non-collider on p, a collider on q and $\text{De}(V_{i-1}, \mathcal{D}) \cap \mathbf{Z} = \emptyset$. Then $V_{i+1} \rightarrow V_{i-1} \rightarrow V_i$ and rule $R2$ implies that $V_i \leftarrow V_{i+1}$ is in $\mathcal{D}$. Since p is d-connecting given $\mathbf{Z}$, $\text{De}(V_i, \mathcal{D}) \cap \mathbf{Z} \neq \emptyset$. As $\text{De}(V_i, \mathcal{D}) \subseteq \text{De}(V_{i-1}, \mathcal{D})$, this contradicts $\text{De}(V_{k-1}, \mathcal{D}) \cap \mathbf{Z} = \emptyset$.

(2) V_{i+1} is a non-collider on p, a collider on q and $\text{De}(V_{i+1}, \mathcal{D}) \cap \mathbf{Z} = \emptyset$. This case is symmetric to

case (1) and the same argument leads to a contradiction.

(3) V_{i-1} is a collider on p, a non-collider on q and $V_{i-1} \in \mathbf{Z}$. Since V_{i-1} is of definite status on p^* it follows that $V_{i-2} \rightarrow V_{i-1} \leftarrow V_i$ is in $\mathcal{G}$. This implies V_i is a definite non-collider on p^*, which is a contradiction.

(4) V_{i+1} is a collider on p, a non-collider on q and $V_{i+1} \in \mathbf{Z}$. Then $V_i \rightarrow V_{i+1} \leftarrow V_{i+2}$ and $V_{i-1} \leftarrow V_{i+1}$ is in $\mathcal{D}$. V_{i+1} is not of definite status on p^*, otherwise V_i would be of definite status on p^*. Thus, there is an edge $\langle V_i, V_{i+2} \rangle$ in $\mathcal{G}$. The path $r = p(X, V_i) \oplus \langle V_i, V_{i+2} \rangle \oplus p(V_{i+2}, Y)$ is proper, b-non-causal (Lemma C.4) and shorter than p. Hence, r must be blocked by $\mathbf{Z}$ in $\mathcal{D}$. The collider/non-collider status of all nodes except possibly V_i and V_{i+2} is the same on r and p, so either V_i or V_{i+2} must block r.

Since $V_i \rightarrow V_{i+1} \rightarrow V_{i-1}$ is in $\mathcal{G}$, rule $R2$ implies that $V_{i-1} \leftarrow V_i$ is in $\mathcal{G}$. Since $V_{i-1} \leftarrow V_i$ is on both r and p, V_i cannot block r. Additionally, $V_{i+1} \leftarrow V_{i+2}$ is in $\mathcal{D}$ so V_{i+2} is a non-collider on p. Thus, V_{i+2} must be a collider on r and $\text{De}(V_{i+2}, \mathcal{D}) \cap \mathbf{Z} = \emptyset$. However, by assumption in (4), $V_{i+1} \in \mathbf{Z}$ and $V_{i+1} \in \text{De}(V_{i+2}, \mathcal{D})$.

Lastly, let $C_l \rightarrow C \leftarrow C_r$ be a subpath of p^* and suppose for a contradiction that there is an edge $\langle C_l, C_r \rangle$ in $\mathcal{G}$. Let $q^* = p^*(X, C_l) \oplus \langle C_l, C_r \rangle \oplus p^*(C_r, Y)$. Then q^* is proper and b-non-causal (Lemma C.4) in $\mathcal{D}$. Let q in $\mathcal{D}$ be the path corresponding to q^* in $\mathcal{G}$. Then q is a proper non-causal path from X to Y that is shorter than p, so q must be blocked by $\mathbf{Z}$. Then as above, either C_l or C_r must block q.

Since C_l (C_r) is a non-collider on p, it must be a collider on q and $\text{De}(C_l, \mathcal{D}) \cap \mathbf{Z} \neq \emptyset$ ($\text{De}(C_r, \mathcal{D}) \cap \mathbf{Z} \neq \emptyset$). Since p is d-connecting given $\mathbf{Z}$, $\text{De}(C, \mathcal{D}) \cap \mathbf{Z} \neq \emptyset$. Additionally, $\text{De}(C_l, \mathcal{D}) \supseteq \text{De}(C, \mathcal{D})$ ($\text{De}(C_r, \mathcal{D}) \supseteq \text{De}(C, \mathcal{D})$), which contradicts $\text{De}(C_l, \mathcal{D}) \cap \mathbf{Z} \neq \emptyset$ ($\text{De}(C_r, \mathcal{D}) \cap \mathbf{Z} \neq \emptyset$). □

Lemma C.6. *Let* $\mathbf{X}, \mathbf{Y}$ *and* $\mathbf{Z}$ *be pairwise disjoint node sets in a maximal* PDAG $\mathcal{G}$. *Let* $\mathbf{Z}$ *satisfy the b-amenability condition and the b-forbidden set condition relative to* $(\mathbf{X}, \mathbf{Y})$ *in* $\mathcal{G}$. *Let* $\mathcal{D}$ *be a DAG in* $[\mathcal{G}]$ *and let* p *be a path with minimal* distance-from-$\mathbf{Z}$ *among the shortest proper non-causal paths from* $\mathbf{X}$ *to* $\mathbf{Y}$ *that are d-connecting given* $\mathbf{Z}$ *in* $\mathcal{D}$. *Let* p^* *in* $\mathcal{G}$ *be the path corresponding to* p *in* $\mathcal{D}$. *Then* p^* *is a proper b-non-causal definite status path from* $\mathbf{X}$ *to* $\mathbf{Y}$ *that is d-connecting given* $\mathbf{Z}$ *in* $\mathcal{G}$.

Proof. This lemma is related to Lemma B.6 from Perković et al. (2017). The line of reasoning used in this first part of this proof overlaps with the proof of Lemma B.6. We will point out where the two proofs diverge.

From Lemma C.5 we know that p^* is a proper b-non-causal definite status path from $\mathbf{X}$ to $\mathbf{Y}$ in $\mathcal{G}$. We only need to prove that it is also d-connecting given $\mathbf{Z}$ in $\mathcal{G}$.

Since p is d-connecting given $\mathbf{Z}$ in $\mathcal{D}$ and p^* is of definite status, it follows that no definite non-collider on p^* is in $\mathbf{Z}$ and that every collider on p^* has a possible descendant in $\mathbf{Z}$ (Lemma C.4). Since every collider on p^* has a b-possibly causal path to $\mathbf{Z}$, by Lemma 3.6 there is b-possibly causal definite status path from every collider on p^* to a node in $\mathbf{Z}$. Let C be an arbitrary collider on p^* and let d^* be a shortest b-possibly causal definite status path from C to a node in $\mathbf{Z}$. It is only left to show that d^* is causal in $\mathcal{G}$, since then $C \in \text{An}(\mathbf{Z}, \mathcal{G})$.

If d^* starts with a directed edge out of C, then d^* is causal in $\mathcal{G}$ (Lemma B.1). Otherwise, $d^* = C - S \dots Z, Z \in \mathbf{Z}$ (possibly $S = Z$). We will prove that this leads to a contradiction. Hence, let $C_l \rightarrow C \leftarrow C_r$ be a subpath of p^*.

From this point onwards, this proof deviates somewhat from the proof of Lemma B.6 from Perković et al. (2017), due to the additional result in Lemma C.5. Since $C_l \rightarrow C - S$ ($C_r \rightarrow C - S$) is in $\mathcal{G}$, rule $R1$ and $R2$ imply that either $C_l \rightarrow S$ or $C_l - S$ ($C_r \rightarrow S$ or $C_r - S$) is in $\mathcal{G}$. Suppose that $C_l - S$ is in $\mathcal{G}$. Since $C_l \notin \text{Adj}(C_r, \mathcal{G})$ (Lemma C.5), $C_r - S$ must be in $\mathcal{G}$, otherwise $C_l - S \leftarrow C_r$ violates $R1$ in $\mathcal{G}$. But then $C_l \rightarrow C \leftarrow C_r$, $C_l - S - C_r$ and $C - S$ violate $R3$ in $\mathcal{G}$.

Hence, $C_l \rightarrow S$ is in $\mathcal{G}$. Then $C_r \rightarrow S$ must be in $\mathcal{G}$, otherwise $C_l \notin \text{Adj}(C_r, \mathcal{G})$ and $C_l \rightarrow S - C_r$ violates $R1$. Now, depending on whether S is a node on p, we can derive the final contradiction.

Suppose S is not on p. Then if $S \notin \mathbf{X} \cup \mathbf{Y}$, $p(X, C_l) \oplus \langle C_l, S, C_r \rangle \oplus p(C_r, Y)$ is a proper non-causal path from $\mathbf{X}$ to $\mathbf{Y}$ in $\mathcal{D}$ that is of the same length as p, but with a shorter distance-from-$\mathbf{Z}$ than p and d-connecting given $\mathbf{Z}$. This contradicts our choice of p. Otherwise, suppose $S \in \mathbf{X}$. Then $\langle S, C_r \rangle \oplus p(C_r, Y)$ contradicts our choice of p. Otherwise, $S \in \mathbf{Y}$. Then $S \notin \text{b-Forb}(\mathbf{X}, \mathbf{Y}, \mathcal{G})$ otherwise, $Z \in \text{b-Forb}(\mathbf{X}, \mathbf{Y}, \mathcal{G})$ since $Z \in \text{b-PossDe}(S, \mathcal{G})$. Since $S \notin \text{b-Forb}(\mathbf{X}, \mathbf{Y}, \mathcal{G})$, it follows that $S \notin \text{b-Forb}(\mathbf{X}, \mathbf{Y}, \mathcal{D})$, so $p(X, C_r) \oplus \langle C_l, S \rangle$ is a non-causal path from $\mathbf{X}$ to $\mathbf{Y}$ in $\mathcal{D}$. Then $p(X, C_r) \oplus \langle C_l, S \rangle$ contradicts our choice of p.

Otherwise, S must be on p. Hence, $S \notin \mathbf{X}$. Suppose first that S is on $p(X, C_r)$. Let $q = p(X, S) \oplus \langle S, C_r \rangle \oplus p(C_r, Y)$. Since q is proper, non-causal and shorter than p, we only need to prove that q is d-connecting given $\mathbf{Z}$ to derive a contradiction. For this we only need to discuss the collider/non-collider status of S on q. If S is a collider on q, then q is d-connecting given $\mathbf{Z}$. Otherwise, S is a non-collider on q. Then since $S \leftarrow C_r$ is on q, S must also be a non-collider on p. Since p is d-connecting given $\mathbf{Z}$, $S \notin \mathbf{Z}$. Thus, q must be d-connecting given $\mathbf{Z}$ in $\mathcal{G}$.

Otherwise, S is on $p(C_r, Y)$. Then let $r = p(X, C_l) \oplus \langle C_l, S \rangle \oplus p(S, Y)$. Since $S \notin$ b-Forb$(\mathbf{X}, \mathbf{Y}, \mathcal{G})$ (otherwise $Z \in$ b-Forb$(\mathbf{X}, \mathbf{Y}, \mathcal{G})$ since $Z \in$ b-PossDe$(S, \mathcal{G})$) and since r is proper, it follows that r is a non-causal path. Hence, we only need to prove that r is d-connecting given $\mathbf{Z}$ to derive a contradiction. For this we again only discuss the collider/non-collider status of S on q. If S is a collider on r, r is d-connecting given $\mathbf{Z}$. Otherwise, S is a non-collider on r. Then since $C_l \rightarrow S$ is on q, S must also be a non-collider on p. Since p is d-connecting given $\mathbf{Z}$, $S \notin \mathbf{Z}$. Thus, r must be d-connecting given $\mathbf{Z}$ in $\mathcal{G}$. □

C.2 PROOF OF THEOREM 4.6

Proof of Theorem 4.6. This theorem is related to Theorem 4.3 from Perković et al. (2017). This proof relies on similar line of reasoning however since Theorem 4.3 from Perković et al. (2017) states a somewhat different result and relies on a few lemmas for the proof, we do not make a direct comparison between the two as we did with the result presented in Section C.

We only need to prove that if there is a set that satisfies the b-adjustment criterion relative to $(\mathbf{X}, \mathbf{Y})$ in $\mathcal{G}$, then b-Adjust$(\mathbf{X}, \mathbf{Y}, \mathcal{G})$ also satisfies the b-adjustment criterion relative to $(\mathbf{X}, \mathbf{Y})$ in $\mathcal{G}$. Hence, assume that $\mathbf{Z}$ satisfies the b-adjustment criterion relative to $(\mathbf{X}, \mathbf{Y})$ in $\mathcal{G}$ and that b-Adjust$(\mathbf{X}, \mathbf{Y}, \mathcal{G})$ does not satisfy the b-adjustment criterion relative to $(\mathbf{X}, \mathbf{Y})$ in $\mathcal{G}$. We will show that this leads to a contradiction.

Since $\mathbf{Z}$ is an adjustment set relative to $(\mathbf{X}, \mathbf{Y})$ in $\mathcal{G}$ (Theorem 4.4), $\mathcal{G}$ is b-amenable relative to $(\mathbf{X}, \mathbf{Y})$. By construction b-Adjust$(\mathbf{X}, \mathbf{Y}, \mathcal{G})$ satisfies the b-forbidden set condition, so it must violate the b-blocking condition. Let $p = \langle X = V_0, V_1, \dots, V_k = Y \rangle, k \geq 1, X \in \mathbf{X}, Y \in \mathbf{Y}$ be a shortest proper b-non-causal definite status paths from $\mathbf{X}$ to $\mathbf{Y}$ in $\mathcal{G}$ that is d-connecting given b-Adjust$(\mathbf{X}, \mathbf{Y}, \mathcal{G})$. Since $\mathbf{Z}$ blocks p, $k > 1$. So there is at least one non-endpoint node on p.

Since p is d-connecting given b-Adjust$(\mathbf{X}, \mathbf{Y}, \mathcal{G})$ and b-Adjust$(\mathbf{X}, \mathbf{Y}, \mathcal{G})$ = b-PossAn$(\mathbf{X} \cup \mathbf{Y}, \mathcal{G}) \setminus (\mathbf{X} \cup \mathbf{Y} \cup$ b-Forb$(\mathbf{X}, \mathbf{Y}, \mathcal{G}))$ any collider on p is in b-PossAn$(\mathbf{X} \cup \mathbf{Y}, \mathcal{G})$. Additionally, no collider C on p is in b-Forb$(\mathbf{X}, \mathbf{Y}, \mathcal{G})$ otherwise, De$(C, \mathcal{G}) \subseteq$ b-Forb$(\mathbf{X}, \mathbf{Y}, \mathcal{G})$ and b-Forb$(\mathbf{X}, \mathbf{Y}, \mathcal{G}) \cap$ b-Adjust$(\mathbf{X}, \mathbf{Y}, \mathcal{G})$ = $\emptyset$ contradicts that p is d-connecting given b-Adjust$(\mathbf{X}, \mathbf{Y}, \mathcal{G})$. Thus, every collider on p is in b-PossAn$(\mathbf{X} \cup \mathbf{Y}, \mathcal{G}) \setminus$ b-Forb$(\mathbf{X}, \mathbf{Y}, \mathcal{G})$.

Any definite non-collider on p is a b-possible ancestor of X, Y or a collider on p. Hence, any definite non-collider on p is in b-PossAn$(\mathbf{X} \cup \mathbf{Y}, \mathcal{G})$. Since p is d-connecting given b-Adjust$(\mathbf{X}, \mathbf{Y}, \mathcal{G})$, no definite non-collider on p is in b-Adjust$(\mathbf{X}, \mathbf{Y}, \mathcal{G})$. Then since b-Adjust$(\mathbf{X}, \mathbf{Y}, \mathcal{G})$ = b-PossAn$(\mathbf{X} \cup \mathbf{Y}, \mathcal{G}) \setminus (\mathbf{X} \cup \mathbf{Y} \cup$ b-Forb$(\mathbf{X}, \mathbf{Y}, \mathcal{G}))$, every definite non-collider on p is in $\mathbf{X} \cup \mathbf{Y} \cup$ b-Forb$(\mathbf{X}, \mathbf{Y}, \mathcal{G})$. Since p is proper, no definite non-collider on p is in $\mathbf{X}$. Additionally, if there was a definite non-collider V on p such that $V \in \mathbf{Y} \setminus$ b-Forb$(\mathbf{X}, \mathbf{Y}, \mathcal{G})$, then $p(X, V)$ would be a shorter proper b-non-causal definite status path in $\mathcal{G}$ that is d-connecting given b-Adjust$(\mathbf{X}, \mathbf{Y}, \mathcal{G})$. Hence, any definite non-collider on p must be in b-Forb$(\mathbf{X}, \mathbf{Y}, \mathcal{G})$.

Suppose that there is no collider on p. Then since $\mathbf{Z}$ blocks p, a non-collider on p must be in $\mathbf{Z}$. This contradicts that $\mathbf{Z}$ satisfies the b-forbidden set condition. Thus, there is a collider on p so let $V_{i-1} \rightarrow V_i \leftarrow V_{i+1}$ be a subpath of p. If there is a definite non-collider on p, then V_{i-1} or V_{i+1} is a non-collider on p. Suppose without loss of generality that V_{i-1} is a definite non-collider on p. Then $V_{i-1} \in$ b-Forb$(\mathbf{X}, \mathbf{Y}, \mathcal{G})$. Since $V_{i-1} \rightarrow V_i$ is in $\mathcal{G}$, $V_i \in$ b-Forb$(\mathbf{X}, \mathbf{Y}, \mathcal{G})$, which contradicts that V_i is a collider on p. Thus, there is no definite non-collider on p.

Since there is at least one collider on p and no definite non-collider is on p, it follows that p is of the form $X \rightarrow V_1 \leftarrow Y$ in $\mathcal{G}$. Since $V_1 \in$ b-PossAn$(\mathbf{X} \cup \mathbf{Y}, \mathcal{G}) \setminus$ b-Forb$(\mathbf{X}, \mathbf{Y}, \mathcal{G})$, let q be a shortest b-possibly causal definite status path from V_1 to a node in $\mathbf{X} \cup \mathbf{Y}$. Then $q = \langle V_1, \dots, V \rangle$, for some $V \in \mathbf{X} \cup \mathbf{Y}$. Then $V \in \mathbf{X}$ otherwise, $V_1 \in$ b-Forb$(\mathbf{X}, \mathbf{Y}, \mathcal{G})$.

Thus, $r = (-p)(Y, V_1) \oplus q$ is a b-possibly causal path, so let r' be an unshielded subsequence of r that forms a b-possibly causal path from Y to $\mathbf{X}$ in $\mathcal{G}$. Since $(-r)$ is a proper path with respect to $\mathbf{X}$, $(-r')$ is also a proper path with respect to $\mathbf{X}$. Then $(-r')$ must be a b-non-causal path otherwise, $Y \in$ b-Forb$(\mathbf{X}, \mathbf{Y}, \mathcal{G})$ which also implies $V_1 \in$ b-Forb$(\mathbf{X}, \mathbf{Y}, \mathcal{G})$. Since r' is also unshielded, $(-r')$ is a proper b-non-causal definite status path from $\mathbf{X}$ to $\mathbf{Y}$ in $\mathcal{G}$. Thus, $\mathbf{Z}$ must block $(-r')$. Since r' is b-possibly causal, $(-r')$ does not contain a collider, so a definite non-collider on $(-r')$ must be in $\mathbf{Z}$. However, all definite non-colliders on $(-r')$ are also on q, so $\mathbf{Z}$ cannot block both $(-r')$ and p in $\mathcal{G}$. □

D EMPIRICAL STUDY

The following empirical study compares the runtimes of local IDA and our semi-local IDA on CPDAGs. We consider the 20 000 simulation settings described in the paper. The times are recorded in seconds on an Intel(R) Core(TM) i7-4765T CPU 2.00GHz processor running under Fedora 24 and using R version 3.4.0 and pcalg version 2.4-6.) The summary is given in Table 1.

	Median	Mean	Max
Local IDA	0.003	0.003	0.009
Semi-local IDA	0.003	0.016	4.881

Table 1: Median, mean and max computation times of local IDA and semi-local IDA.

We see that the median computation times are identical for both methods. The mean and maximum computation times, however, are larger for semi-local IDA. This indicates some outliers in the computation time of semi-local IDA. This could be explained by the presence of a small number of CPDAGs where our semi-local method is forced to orient a large subgraph of the CPDAG.

We also investigated the difference in runtimes between semi-local IDA and local IDA as a function of the number of variables (p) and the expected neighborhood size ($E[N]$), these results are given in Table 2 and Table 3 respectively. We see that the mean difference in runtimes increases with p, while there is not a very clear relationship with neighborhood size.

p	mean difference
20	0.009
30	0.007
40	0.010
50	0.009
60	0.016
70	0.013
80	0.014
90	0.015
100	0.021

Table 2: The mean runtime difference aggregated according to the number of variables (p).

$E[N]$	mean difference
3	0.016
4	0.013
5	0.013
6	0.011
7	0.009
8	0.011
9	0.015
10	0.014

Table 3: The mean runtime difference aggregated according to the expected neighborhood size ($E[N]$).

References

Ernest, J., Rothenhäusler, D., and Bühlmann, P. (2016). Causal inference in partially linear structural equation models: identifiability and estimation. arXiv:1607.05980.

Maathuis, M. H. and Colombo, D. (2015). A generalized back-door criterion. *Ann. Stat.*, 43:1060–1088.

Perković, E., Textor, J., Kalisch, M., and Maathuis, M. H. (2017). Complete graphical characterization and construction of adjustment sets in Markov equivalence classes of ancestral graphs. *J. Mach. Learn. Res.* to appear.

Shpitser, I. (2012). Appendum to "On the validity of covariate adjustment for estimating causal effects". Personal communication.

Shpitser, I., VanderWeele, T., and Robins, J. M. (2010). On the validity of covariate adjustment for estimating causal effects. In *Proceedings of UAI 2010*, pages 527–536.

Zhang, J. (2008). On the completeness of orientation rules for causal discovery in the presence of latent confounders and selection bias. *Artif. Intell.*, 172:1873–1896.

Causal Consistency of Structural Equation Models

Paul K. Rubenstein[*12], **Sebastian Weichwald**[*13], **Stephan Bongers**[4], **Joris M. Mooij**[4]
Dominik Janzing[1], **Moritz Grosse-Wentrup**[1], **Bernhard Schölkopf**[1]
[*]Equal contribution
[1]Empirical Inference, MPI for Intelligent Systems, [2]Machine Learning Group, University of Cambridge,
[3]Max Planck ETH Center for Learning Systems, [4]Informatics Institute, University of Amsterdam

Abstract

Complex systems can be modelled at various levels of detail. Ideally, causal models of the same system should be consistent with one another in the sense that they agree in their predictions of the effects of interventions. We formalise this notion of consistency in the case of Structural Equation Models (SEMs) by introducing *exact transformations* between SEMs. This provides a general language to consider, for instance, the different levels of description in the following three scenarios: (a) models with large numbers of variables versus models in which the 'irrelevant' or unobservable variables have been marginalised out; (b) micro-level models versus macro-level models in which the macro-variables are aggregate features of the micro-variables; (c) dynamical time series models versus models of their stationary behaviour. Our analysis stresses the importance of well specified interventions in the causal modelling process and sheds light on the interpretation of cyclic SEMs.

1 INTRODUCTION

Physical systems or processes in the real world are complex and can be understood at various levels of detail. For instance, a gas in a volume consists of a large number of molecules. But instead of modelling the motions of each particle individually (micro-level), we may choose to consider macroscopic properties of their motions such as temperature and pressure. Our decision to use such macroscopic properties is first necessitated by practical considerations. Indeed, for all but extremely simple cases, making a measurement of all the individual molecules is practically impossible and our resources insufficient for modelling the $\sim 10^{22}$ particles present per litre of ideal gas. Furthermore, the decision for a macroscopic description level is also a pragmatic one: if we only wish to reason about temperature and pressure, a model of 10^{22} particles is ill-suited.

Statistical physics explains how higher-level concepts such as temperature and pressure arise as statistical properties of a system of a large number of particles, justifying the use of a macro-level model as a useful transformation of the micro-level model [1]. However, in many cases aggregate or indirect measurements of a complex system form the basis of a macroscopic description of the system, with little theory to explain whether this is justified or how the micro- and macro-descriptions stand in relation to each other.

Due to deliberate modelling choice or the limited ability to observe a system, differing levels of model descriptions are ubiquitous and occur, amongst possibly others, in the following three settings:

(a) Models with large numbers of variables versus models in which the 'irrelevant' or unobservable variables have been marginalised out [3]; e. g. modelling blood cholesterol levels and risk of heart disease while ignoring other blood chemicals or external factors such as stress.
(b) Micro-level models versus macro-level models in which the macro-variables are aggregate features of the micro-variables [4, 5, 9, 11, 17]; e. g. instead of modelling the brain as consisting of 100 billion neurons it can be modelled as averaged neuronal activity in distinct functional brain regions.
(c) Dynamical time series models versus models of their stationary behaviour [6, 8, 11–13, 15]; e. g. modelling only the final ratios of reactants and products of a time evolving chemical reaction.

In the context of causal modelling, such differing model levels should be consistent with one another in the sense that they agree in their predictions of the effects of interventions. The particular causal models we focus on in this

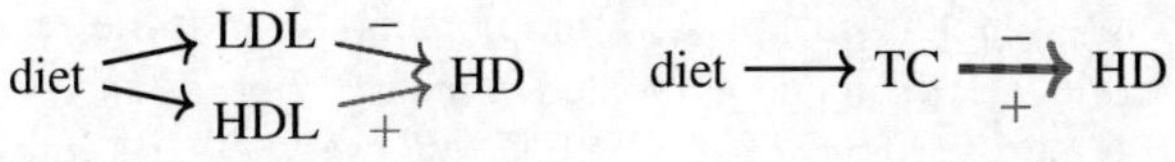

(a) (b)

Figure 1: As illustrated by (a), the current consensus is that LDL (resp. HDL) has a negative (resp. positive) effect on heart disease (HD). Considering TC = LDL + HDL to be a causal variable as in (b) leads to problems: two diets promoting raised LDL levels and raised HDL levels have the same effect on TC but opposite effects on heart disease. Hence different studies come to contradictory conclusions about the effect of TC on heart disease.

paper are Structural Equation Models (SEMs, Section 2, Section 3) [16, 19].

In Section 4, we introduce the notion of an exact transformation between two SEMs, providing us with a general framework to evaluate when two models can be thought of as causal descriptions of the same system. An important novel idea of this paper is to explicitly make use of a natural ordering on the set of interventions. On a high level, if an SEM can be viewed as an exact transformation of another SEM, we are provided with an explicit correspondence between the two models in such a way that causal reasoning on both levels is consistent. We discuss this notion of consistency in detail in Sections 4.4 and 4.5.

In Section 5 we apply this mathematical framework and prove the exactness of transformations belonging to each of the three categories listed above, with practical implications for the following questions in causal modelling: When can we model only a subsystem of a more complex system? When does a micro-level system admit a causal description in terms of macro-level features? How do cyclic SEMs arise? The fact that these distinct problems can all be considered using the language of transformations between SEMs demonstrates the generality of our approach. We close in Section 6 with a discussion.

1.1 A HISTORICAL MOTIVATION: CHOLESTEROL AND HEART DISEASE

In the following we give an example of the problems that can arise when there exists no consistent correspondence between two causal models, i. e. neither model can be viewed as an exact transformation of the other. This example falls into category (b) of the differing model levels listed above and was used by [18] to illustrate problems in the causal modelling process.

Historically, the level of total cholesterol in the blood (TC) was thought to be an important variable in determining risk of heart disease (HD). To investigate this, different experiments were carried out in which patients were assigned to different diets in order to raise or lower TC. Conflicting evidence was found by different experiments: some found that higher TC had the effect of lowering HD, while others found the opposite (cf. Figure 1b) [20, 21].

From our point of view, this problem (seemingly conflicting studies) arose from trying to perform an 'invalid' transformation of the 'true' underlying model (cf. Figure 1a). According to the American Heart Association, the current scientific consensus is that the two types of blood cholesterol, low-density lipoprotein (LDL) and high-density lipoprotein (HDL), have a negative and positive effect on HD respectively. Assigning diets that raise LDL or HDL both raise TC but have different effects on HD. It is therefore not possible to transform the model in Figure 1a into the model in Figure 1b without leading to conflict: in order to reason about the causes of HD we need to consider the variables LDL and HDL separately.

2 STRUCTURAL EQUATION MODELS

SEMs are a widely used framework in causal modelling, with applications in neuroscience, economics and the social sciences [2, 16]. In this section we introduce them as an abstract mathematical object; in Section 3 we describe their use as a causal modelling tool. Readers already familiar with SEMs should note that our definition is more general and deviates from the standard definition of SEMs in the following ways: we do not require that all possible perfect interventions be modelled; we do not assume independence of exogenous variables;[1] and we do not require acyclicity.

Definition 1 (Structural Equation Model (SEM)). *Let $\mathbb{I}_X$ be an index set. An SEM $\mathcal{M}_X$ over variables $X = (X_i : i \in \mathbb{I}_X)$ taking value in $\mathcal{X}$ is a triple $\left(\mathcal{S}_X, \mathcal{I}_X, \mathbb{P}_E\right)$ where*

- *$\mathcal{S}_X$ is a set of structural equations, i. e. it is a set of equations $X_i = f_i\left(X, E_i\right)$ for $i \in \mathbb{I}_X$;*
- *$(\mathcal{I}_X, \leq_X)$ is a subset of all perfect interventions equipped with a natural partial ordering (see below), i. e. it is an index set where each index corresponds to a particular perfect intervention on some of the X variables;*
- *$\mathbb{P}_E$ is a distribution over the exogenous variables $E = (E_i : i \in \mathbb{I}_X)$;*
- *with $\mathbb{P}_E$-probability one, under any intervention $i \in \mathcal{I}_X$ there is a unique solution $x \in \mathcal{X}$ to the intervened structural equations. This ensures that for any*

[1] Exogenous variables are also referred to as *noise variables* in the literature. Our relaxation of the assumption of independent exogenous variables means our models may be considered a type of semi-Markovian causal model.

intervention $i \in \mathcal{I}_X$, $\mathcal{M}_X$ induces a well-defined distribution over $\mathcal{X}$.[2]

In an SEM, each X_i is a function of the X-variables and the exogenous variable E_i. In this mathematical model, a perfect intervention on a single variable $\mathrm{do}(X_i = x_i)$ is realised by replacing the structural equation for variable X_i in $\mathcal{S}_X$ with $X_i = x_i$. Perfect interventions on multiple variables, e.g. $\mathrm{do}(X_i = x_i, X_j = x_j)$, are similarly realised by replacing the structural equations for each variable individually. Elements of $\mathcal{I}_X$ correspond to perfectly intervening on a subset of the X variables, setting them to some particular combination of values.

$\mathcal{I}_X$ has a natural partial ordering in which, for interventions $i, j \in \mathcal{I}_X$, $i \leq_X j$ if and only if i intervenes on a subset of the variables that j intervenes on and sets them equal to the same values as j. For example, $\mathrm{do}(X_i = x_i) \leq_X \mathrm{do}(X_i = x_i, X_j = x_j)$.[3] The observation that this structure is important is a contribution of this paper. We make crucial use of it in the next section.

The purpose of the following example is to illustrate how SEMs are written in our notation and to provide and example of a restricted set of interventions $\mathcal{I}_X$.

Example 2. *Consider the following SEM defined over the variables $\{B_1, B_2, L\}$*

$$\mathcal{S}_X = \{B_1 = E_1,\ B_2 = E_2,\ L = \mathrm{OR}(B_1, B_2, E_3)\}$$
$$\mathcal{I}_X = \{\varnothing,\ \mathrm{do}(B_1 = 0),\ \mathrm{do}(B_2 = 0),\ \mathrm{do}(B_1 = 0, B_2 = 0)\},$$
$$\{E_1, E_2, E_3\} \overset{iid}{\sim} \mathrm{Bernoulli}(0.5)$$

where by the element $\varnothing \in \mathcal{I}$ we denote the null-intervention corresponding to the unintervened SEM.

3 SEMS FOR CAUSAL MODELLING

In addition to being abstract mathematical objects, SEMs are used in causal modelling to describe distributions of variables and how they change under interventions [16]. The do-interventions as abstract manipulations of SEMs are understood as corresponding to actual (or potentially only hypothetical) physical implementations in the real world, i. e. the model is 'rooted in reality'. For instance, if a binary variable B_1 in an SEM reflects whether a light bulb is emitting light, then $\mathrm{do}(B_1 = 0)$ could be achieved by flipping the light switch or by removing the light bulb.

The SEM in Example 2 could be thought of as a simple causal model of two light bulbs B_1 and B_2 and the presence of light L in a room with a window. Suppose that we have no access to the light switch and there are no curtains in the room but that we can intervene by removing the light bulbs. We can model this restricted set of interventions by $\mathcal{I}_X$, i. e. the do-intervention on the SEM side $\mathrm{do}(B_1 = 0)$ corresponds to removing the light bulb B_1.

The partial ordering of $\mathcal{I}_X$ corresponds to the ability to compose physical implementations of interventions. The fact that we can first remove light bulb B_1 ($\mathrm{do}(B_1 = 0)$) and then afterwards remove light bulb B_2 (resulting in the combined intervention $\mathrm{do}(B_1 = 0, B_2 = 0)$) is reflected in the partial ordering via the relation $\mathrm{do}(B_1 = 0) \leq_X \mathrm{do}(B_1 = 0, B_2 = 0)$.

4 TRANSFORMATIONS BETWEEN SEMS

We now work towards our definition of an exact transformation between SEMs. Our core idea is to analyse the correspondence between different levels of modelling by considering one model to be a transformation of the other. We discuss in Section 4.4 how causal reasoning in two SEMs relate when one SEM can be viewed as an exact transformation of the other and in Section 4.5 we illustrate what can go wrong when this is not the case.

4.1 DISTRIBUTIONS IMPLIED BY AN SEM

Usually, a statistical model implies a single joint distribution over all variables once its parameters are fixed. SEMs are different in that, once the parameters are fixed, an SEM implies a family of joint distributions over the random variables, one for each intervention. That is, for each intervention $i \in \mathcal{I}_X$, the SEM $\mathcal{M}_X$ defines a distribution over $\mathcal{X}$ which we denote by $\mathbb{P}_X^{\mathrm{do}(i)}$. Throughout, we will denote the null-intervention corresponding to the unintervened setting by $\varnothing \in \mathcal{I}_X$. We can write the poset of all distributions implied by the SEM $\mathcal{M}_X$ as

$$\mathcal{P}_X := \left(\left\{\mathbb{P}_X^{\mathrm{do}(i)} \ :\ i \in \mathcal{I}_X\right\}, \leq_X\right)$$

where $\leq_X$ is the partial ordering inherited from $\mathcal{I}_X$, i. e. $\mathbb{P}_X^{\mathrm{do}(i)} \leq_X \mathbb{P}_X^{\mathrm{do}(j)} \iff i \leq_X j$.[4]

[2] That is, with probability one over the exogenous variables E, for each draw $E = e$ there exists a unique value $x \in \mathcal{X}$ such that e and x satisfy the intervened structural equations. The distribution of E in conjunction with $\mathcal{S}_X$ then implies a distribution over $\mathcal{X}$ for each intervention $i \in \mathcal{I}_X$ via these unique solutions. If the SEM is acyclic, this is always satisfied; we impose this condition because we also consider *cyclic* SEMs [3].

[3] Informally, this means that j can be performed after i without having to change or undo any of the changes to the structural equations made by i. Not all pairs of elements must be comparable: for instance, if $i = \mathrm{do}(X_1 = x_1)$ and $j = \mathrm{do}(X_2 = x_2)$, then neither $i \leq_X j$ nor $j \leq_X i$.

[4] More formally, one would need to define $\mathcal{P}_X$ to be the poset of *tuples* $\left(i, \mathbb{P}_X^{\mathrm{do}(i)}\right)$ to avoid problems in the case that $\mathbb{P}_X^{\mathrm{do}(i)} =$

Note that $\mathcal{P}_X$ contains all of the information in $\mathcal{M}_X$ about the different distributions implied by the SEM and, importantly, how they are related via the interventions.[5]

4.2 TRANSFORMATIONS OF RANDOM VARIABLES

Suppose we have a function $\tau : \mathcal{X} \to \mathcal{Y}$ which maps the variables of the SEM $\mathcal{M}_X$ to another space $\mathcal{Y}$. Observe that since X is a random variable, $\tau(X)$ is also a random variable. For any distribution $\mathbb{P}_X$ on $\mathcal{X}$ we thus obtain the distribution of the variable $\tau(X)$ on $\mathcal{Y}$ as $\mathbb{P}_{\tau(X)} = \tau\left(\mathbb{P}_X\right)$ via the push-forward measure.

In particular, for each intervention $i \in \mathcal{I}_X$ we can define the induced distribution $\mathbb{P}^i_{\tau(X)} = \tau\left(\mathbb{P}^{\mathrm{do}(i)}_X\right)$. We can write the poset of distributions on $\mathcal{Y}$ that are induced by the original SEM $\mathcal{M}_X$ and the transformation τ as

$$\mathcal{P}_{\tau(X)} := \left(\left\{\mathbb{P}^i_{\tau(X)} \ : \ i \in \mathcal{I}_X\right\}, \leq_X\right)$$

where $\leq_X$ is the partial ordering inherited from $\mathcal{P}_X$ (and in turn from $\mathcal{I}_X$).

$\mathcal{P}_{\tau(X)}$ is just a structured collection of distributions over $\mathcal{Y}$, indexed by interventions $\mathcal{I}_X$ on the $\mathcal{X}$-level; importantly, the indices are *not* interventions on the $\mathcal{Y}$-level.

4.3 EXACT TRANSFORMATIONS BETWEEN SEMS

Although $\mathcal{P}_{\tau(X)}$ is a poset of distributions over $\mathcal{Y}$, there does not necessarily exist an SEM $\mathcal{M}_Y$ over $\mathcal{Y}$ that implies it. For instance, if there is some intervention $i \in \mathcal{I}_X \setminus \{\varnothing\}$ such that none of the variables Y_i is constant under the distribution $\mathbb{P}^i_{\tau(X)}$, then $\mathbb{P}^i_{\tau(X)}$ could not possibly be expressed as arising from a do-intervention $j \in \mathcal{I}_Y \setminus \{\varnothing\}$ in any SEM over $\mathcal{Y}$.[6]

The case in which there *does* exist an SEM $\mathcal{M}_Y$ that implies $\mathcal{P}_{\tau(X)}$ is special, motivating our main definition.

Definition 3 (Exact Transformations between SEMs)**.** *Let $\mathcal{M}_X$ and $\mathcal{M}_Y$ be SEMs and $\tau : \mathcal{X} \to \mathcal{Y}$ be a function. We say $\mathcal{M}_Y$ is an* exact *τ-transformation of $\mathcal{M}_X$ if there exists a* surjective order-preserving *map $\omega : \mathcal{I}_X \to \mathcal{I}_Y$ such that*

$$\mathbb{P}^i_{\tau(X)} = \mathbb{P}^{\mathrm{do}(\omega(i))}_Y \quad \forall i \in \mathcal{I}_X$$

where $\mathbb{P}^i_{\tau(X)}$ is the distribution of the $\mathcal{Y}$-valued random variable $\tau(X)$ with $X \sim \mathbb{P}^{\mathrm{do}(i)}_X$.

Order-preserving means that $i \leq_X j \implies \omega(i) \leq_Y \omega(j)$. It is important that the converse need not in general hold as this would imply that ω is injective,[7] and hence also bijective. This would constrain the ways in which $\mathcal{M}_Y$ can be 'simpler' than $\mathcal{M}_X$.[8] That ω is surjective ensures that for any do-intervention $j \in \mathcal{I}_Y$ on $\mathcal{M}_Y$ there is at least one corresponding intervention on the $\mathcal{M}_X$ level, namely an element of $\omega^{-1}(\{j\}) \subseteq \mathcal{I}_X$. The following two results follow immediately from the definition (cf. proofs in Appendix A).

Lemma 4. *The identity mapping and permuting the labels of variables are both exact transformations.*

This is a good sanity check; it would be problematic if this were not the case and the labelling of our variables mattered. Similarly, compositions of exact transformations are also exact.

Lemma 5 (Transitivity of exact transformations)**.** *If $\mathcal{M}_Z$ is an exact τ_{ZY}-transformation of $\mathcal{M}_Y$ and $\mathcal{M}_Y$ is an exact τ_{YX}-transformation of $\mathcal{M}_X$, then $\mathcal{M}_Z$ is an exact $(\tau_{ZY} \circ \tau_{YX})$-transformation of $\mathcal{M}_X$.*

The following theorem is a consequence of the fact that ω is order-preserving. This is a mathematical formalisation of the sense in which an exact transformation preserves causal reasoning, which will be elaborated upon in the next subsection.

Theorem 6 (Causal consistency under exact transformations)**.** *Suppose that $\mathcal{M}_Y$ is an exact τ-transformation of $\mathcal{M}_X$ and ω is a corresponding surjective order-preserving mapping between interventions. Let $i, j \in \mathcal{I}_X$ be interventions such that $i \leq_X j$. Then the following diagram commutes:*

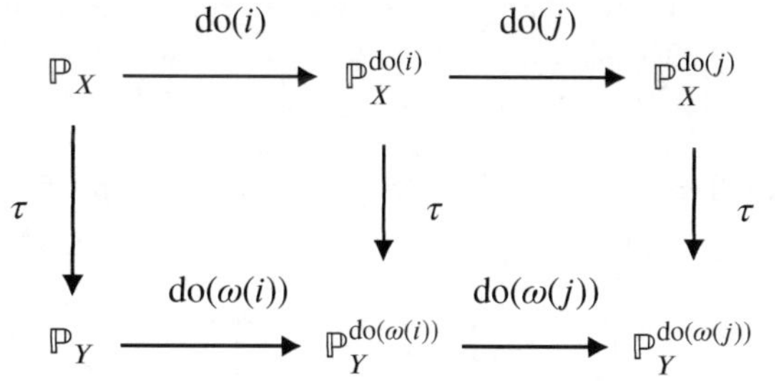

Proof. Let $i, j \in \mathcal{I}_X$ be interventions with $i \leq_X j$. The

$\mathbb{P}^{\mathrm{do}(j)}_X$ for some $i \neq_X j$. Doing so would not require a change to Definition 3 or affect the further results of this paper. To avoid notational burden in our exposition, we omit this treatment.

[5] For example, the distribution over the variables X in the observational setting, $\mathbb{P}^{\varnothing}_X$, changes to $\mathbb{P}^{\mathrm{do}(i)}_X$ if we implement the intervention do(i), and the partial ordering contains all information about which interventions can be composed.

[6] This problem is elaborated upon in [7].

[7] Since $\omega(i) = \omega(j) \iff \left(\omega(i) \leq_Y \omega(j)\right) \wedge \left(\omega(j) \leq_Y \omega(i)\right)$, which, if the converse held, would imply that $\left(i \leq_X j\right) \wedge \left(j \leq_X i\right)$, which is equivalent to $i = j$.

[8] For instance, if it were necessary that ω be bijective, Theorems 9 and 11 would not hold.

commutativity of the left square of the diagram follows immediately from the definition of an exact transformation. It remains to be shown that the right square of the diagram commutes. By definition we have that $\tau\left(\mathbb{P}_X^{\mathrm{do}(i)}\right) = \mathbb{P}_Y^{\mathrm{do}(\omega(i))}$ and $\tau\left(\mathbb{P}_X^{\mathrm{do}(j)}\right) = \mathbb{P}_Y^{\mathrm{do}(\omega(j))}$. Thus, we only have to show that $\mathbb{P}_Y^{\mathrm{do}(\omega(i))} \leq_Y \mathbb{P}_Y^{\mathrm{do}(\omega(j))}$ as elements of $\mathcal{P}_Y$, i. e. that the arrow $\mathbb{P}_Y^{\mathrm{do}(\omega(i))} \xrightarrow{\mathrm{do}(\omega(j))} \mathbb{P}_Y^{\mathrm{do}(\omega(j))}$ exists. This follows from the order-preservingness of ω. □

4.4 CAUSAL INTERPRETATION OF EXACT TRANSFORMATIONS

The notion of an exact transformation between SEMs was motivated by the desire to analyse the correspondence between two causal models describing the same system at different levels of detail. The purpose of this section is to show that if one SEM can be viewed as an exact transformation of the other, then both can sensibly be thought of as causal models of the same system. In the following, we assume that $\mathcal{M}_Y$ is an exact τ-transformation of $\mathcal{M}_X$ with ω the corresponding map between interventions.

Surjectivity of ω ensures that any intervention in $\mathcal{I}_Y$ can be viewed as an $\mathcal{M}_Y$-level representative of some intervention on the $\mathcal{M}_X$-level. Consequently, if do-interventions on the $\mathcal{M}_X$-level are in correspondence with physical implementations, then surjectivity of ω ensures that do-interventions on the $\mathcal{M}_Y$-level have at least one corresponding physical implementation, i. e. if $\mathcal{M}_X$ is 'rooted in reality', then so is $\mathcal{M}_Y$.

Commutativity of the left hand part of the diagram ensures that the effects of interventions are consistently modelled by $\mathcal{M}_X$ and $\mathcal{M}_Y$. Suppose we want to reason about the effects on the $\mathcal{M}_Y$-level caused by the intervention $j \in \mathcal{I}_Y$. For example, we may wish to reason about how the temperature and pressure of a volume of gaseous particles is affected by being heated. We could perform this reasoning by considering any corresponding $\mathcal{M}_X$-level intervention $i \in \omega^{-1}(\{j\})$ and considering the distribution this implies over $\mathcal{Y}$ via τ. In our example, this would correspond to considering how heating the volume of gas could be modelled by changing the motions of all the gaseous particles and then computing the temperature and pressure of the volume of particles. Commutativity of the left hand part of the diagram implies that $\mathcal{M}_X$ and $\mathcal{M}_Y$ are consistent in the sense that $\mathcal{M}_Y$ allows us to immediately reason about the effect of the intervention $j \in \mathcal{I}_Y$ while being equivalent to performing the steps above. That is, we can reason directly about temperature and pressure when heating a volume of gas without having to perform the intermediate steps that involve the microscopic description of the system.

Commutativity of the right hand side of the diagram ensures that once an intervention that fixes a subset of the variables has been performed, we can still consistently reason about the effects of further interventions on the remaining variables in $\mathcal{M}_X$ and $\mathcal{M}_Y$. Furthermore, it ensures that compositionality of do-interventions on the $\mathcal{M}_X$-level carries over to the $\mathcal{M}_Y$-level, i. e. if the intervention j on the $\mathcal{M}_X$-level can be performed additionally to the intervention i in $\mathcal{M}_X$—that is, $i \leq_X j$—, then the same is true of their representations in $\mathcal{M}_Y$.

If $\mathcal{M}_X$ and $\mathcal{M}_Y$ are models of the same system and it has been established that $\mathcal{M}_Y$ is an exact τ-transformation of $\mathcal{M}_X$ for some mapping τ, then the commutativity of the whole diagram in Theorem 6 ensures that they are causally consistent with one another in the sense described in the preceding paragraphs. If we wish to reason about the effects of interventions on the $\mathcal{Y}$-variables then it suffices to use the model $\mathcal{M}_Y$, rather than the (possibly more complex) model $\mathcal{M}_X$. In particular, this means that we can view the $\mathcal{Y}$-variables as causal entities, rather than only functions of underlying 'truly' causal entities. Only if this is the case, causal statements such as 'raising temperature increases pressure' or 'LDL causes heart disease' are meaningful.

4.5 WHAT CAN GO WRONG WHEN A TRANSFORMATION IS NOT EXACT?

In the previous section we argued that our definition of exact transformations between SEMs is a sensible formalisation of causal consistency. In this section we will try to give the reader an intuition for why weakening the conditions of our definition would be problematic. In particular we focus on the requirement that ω be order-preserving, which we view as one of the core ideas of our paper.

The requirement that ω be surjective is, as discussed above, required so that all interventions on the $\mathcal{M}_Y$-level have a corresponding intervention on the $\mathcal{M}_X$-level. If we were to only require that ω be surjective (but not order-preserving), the observational distribution of $\mathcal{M}_X$ may be mapped to an interventional distribution of $\mathcal{M}_Y$, as illustrated by the following example (cf. Figure 2 for an illustration).

Example 7. *Consider the SEM* $\mathcal{M}_X = \{\mathcal{S}_X, \mathcal{I}_X, \mathbb{P}_E\}$ *over* $\mathcal{X} = \mathbb{R}^3$ *where*

$$\mathcal{S}_X = \{X_1 = E_1,\ X_2 = E_2,\ X_3 = X_1 + X_2 + E_3\}$$
$$\mathcal{I}_X = \{\emptyset,\ \mathrm{do}(X_2 = 0),\ \mathrm{do}(X_1 = 0,\ X_2 = 0)\},$$
$$E_1 \sim \mathbb{P}_{E_1},\ E_2 = -E_1,\ E_3 \sim \mathbb{P}_{E_3}$$

where $\mathbb{P}_{E_1}$ *and* $\mathbb{P}_{E_3}$ *are arbitrary distributions. Let* $\tau : \mathcal{X} \to \mathcal{Y} = \mathbb{R}^2$ *be the mapping such that*

$$\tau(x_1, x_2, x_3) = (y_1, y_2) = (x_1 + x_2, x_3)$$

(a) SEM $\mathcal{M}_X$ (b) SEM $\mathcal{M}_Y$

Figure 2: Graphical illustration of parent-child relationships for the examples in Section 4.5. The micro-level model $\mathcal{M}_X$ depicted in (a) is to be transformed into the macro-level model $\mathcal{M}_Y$ depicted in (b) which is a coarser descriptions as in it only considers the sum of X_1 and X_2. In Section 4.5 we give examples of what can go wrong if the transformation is not exact.

Let $\mathcal{M}_Y = \{\mathcal{S}_Y, \mathcal{I}_Y, \mathbb{P}_F\}$ *be an SEM over* $\mathcal{Y}$ *with*

$$\mathcal{S}_Y = \{Y_1 = F_1,\ Y_2 = Y_1 + F_2\}$$
$$\mathcal{I}_Y = \{\varnothing,\ \mathrm{do}(Y_1 = 0)\},$$
$$F_1 \sim \mathbb{P}_{E_1},\ F_2 \sim \mathbb{P}_{E_3}$$

Let $\omega : \mathcal{I}_X \to \mathcal{I}_Y$ *be defined by*

$$\omega : \begin{cases} \varnothing & \mapsto \mathrm{do}(Y_1 = 0) \\ \mathrm{do}(X_2 = 0) & \mapsto \varnothing \\ \mathrm{do}(X_1 = 0,\ X_2 = 0) & \mapsto \mathrm{do}(Y_1 = 0) \end{cases}$$

Then it is true that $\mathbb{P}^i_{\tau(X)} = \mathbb{P}^{\mathrm{do}(\omega(i))}_Y$ *for all* $i \in \mathcal{I}_X$*, while* ω *is not order-preserving and* $\omega(\varnothing) \neq \varnothing$*.*

If the SEMs in the above example were used to model the same system, it would be problematic that the observational setting of $\mathcal{M}_X$—a description of the system when not having physically performed any intervention—would correspond to an interventional setting in $\mathcal{M}_Y$, conversely suggesting that the system *had* been intervened upon.

To avoid the above conflict, we could demand in addition to surjectivity that ω map the null intervention of $\mathcal{M}_X$ to the null intervention of $\mathcal{M}_Y$. This additional assumption would ensure commutativity of the left-hand part of the diagram in Theorem 6. However, as the following example shows, this would not ensure that the right-hand part of the diagram commutes for all pairs of interventions $i \leq_X j$, since in this case the arrow from $\mathbb{P}^{\mathrm{do}(\omega(i))}_Y$ to $\mathbb{P}^{\mathrm{do}(\omega(j))}_Y$ may not exist.[9]

Example 8. *Let* $\mathcal{X}, \mathcal{Y}$ *and* τ *be as in Example 7. Consider the SEM* $\mathcal{M}_X = \{\mathcal{S}_X, \mathcal{I}_X, \mathbb{P}_E\}$ *where*

$$\mathcal{S}_X = \{X_1 = E_1,\ X_2 = E_2,\ X_3 = X_1 + X_2 + E_3\}$$
$$\mathcal{I}_X = \{\varnothing,\ \mathrm{do}(X_2 = 0),\ \mathrm{do}(X_1 = 0,\ X_2 = 0)\},$$
$$E_1 = 1,\ E_2 \sim \mathbb{P}_{E_2},\ E_3 \sim \mathbb{P}_{E_3}$$

[9]By definition of the poset $\mathcal{P}_Y$, this arrow exists if and only if $\omega(i) \leq_Y \omega(j)$.

where $\mathbb{P}_{E_2}$ *and* $\mathbb{P}_{E_3}$ *are arbitrary distributions. Let* $\mathcal{M}_Y = \{\mathcal{S}_Y, \mathcal{I}_Y, \mathbb{P}_F\}$ *be the SEM over* $\mathcal{Y}$ *with*

$$\mathcal{S}_Y = \{Y_1 = 1 + F_1,\ Y_2 = Y_1 + F_2\}$$
$$\mathcal{I}_Y = \{\varnothing,\ \mathrm{do}(Y_1 = 0),\ \mathrm{do}(Y_1 = 1)\},$$
$$F_1 \sim \mathbb{P}_{E_2},\ F_2 \sim \mathbb{P}_{E_3}$$

Let $\omega : \mathcal{I}_X \to \mathcal{I}_Y$ *be defined by*

$$\omega : \begin{cases} \varnothing & \mapsto \varnothing \\ \mathrm{do}(X_2 = 0) & \mapsto \mathrm{do}(Y_1 = 1) \\ \mathrm{do}(X_1 = 0,\ X_2 = 0) & \mapsto \mathrm{do}(Y_1 = 0) \end{cases}$$

Then it is true that $\mathbb{P}^i_{\tau(X)} = \mathbb{P}^{\mathrm{do}(\omega(i))}_Y$ *for all* $i \in \mathcal{I}_X$ *and* $\omega(\varnothing) = \varnothing$*, although* ω *is not order-preserving.*

If the above SEMs were used as models of the same system, they would not suffer from the problem illustrated in Example 7. Suppose now, however, that we have performed the intervention $\mathrm{do}(X_2 = 0)$ in $\mathcal{M}_X$, corresponding to the intervention $\mathrm{do}(Y_1 = 1)$ in $\mathcal{M}_Y$. If we wish to reason about the effect of the intervention $\mathrm{do}(X_1 = 0,\ X_2 = 0)$ in $\mathcal{M}_X$, we run into a problem. $\mathcal{M}_X$ suggests that $\mathrm{do}(X_1 = 0,\ X_2 = 0)$ could be implemented by performing an additional action on top of $\mathrm{do}(X_2 = 0)$. In contrast, $\mathcal{M}_Y$ suggests that implementing the corresponding intervention $\mathrm{do}(Y_1 = 0)$ would conflict with the already performed intervention $\mathrm{do}(Y_1 = 1)$.

5 EXAMPLES OF EXACT TRANSFORMATIONS

In the introduction we motivated the problem considered in this paper by listing three settings in which differing model levels naturally occur. Having now introduced the notion of an exact transformation between SEMs, we provide in this section examples of exact transformations falling into each of these categories. The fact that a single framework can be used to draw an explicit correspondence between differing model levels in each of these settings demonstrates the generality of our framework.

Observe that in each of the following examples, the particular set of interventions considered is important. If we were to allow larger sets of interventions $\mathcal{I}_X$ in the SEM $\mathcal{M}_X$, the transformations given would not be exact. This highlights the importance to the causal modelling process of carefully considering the set of interventions. All proofs are found in the Appendix.

5.1 MARGINALISATION OF VARIABLES

In the following two Theorems we consider two operations that can be performed on SEMs, namely marginalisation of childless or non-intervened variables, and prove that these are exact transformations. That is, an SEM can be simplified into an SEM with fewer variables by either of these operations without losing any causal content concerning the remaining variables.

Thus if the SEM $\mathcal{M}_Y$ can be obtained from another SEM $\mathcal{M}_X$ by successively performing the operations in the following theorems, then $\mathcal{M}_Y$ is an exact transformation of $\mathcal{M}_X$ and hence the two models are causally consistent. This formally explains why we can sensibly consider causal models that focus on a subsystem $\mathcal{M}_Y$ of a more complex system $\mathcal{M}_X$ (cf. Figure 3). For a measure-theoretic treatment of marginalisation in SEMs, see [3].

Theorem 9 (Marginalisation of childless variables)**.** *Let $\mathcal{M}_X = (\mathcal{S}_X, \mathcal{I}_X, \mathbb{P}_E)$ be an SEM and suppose that $\mathbb{I}_Z \subset \mathbb{I}_X$ is a set of indices of variables with no children, i. e. if $i \in \mathbb{I}_Z$ then X_i does not appear in the right-hand side of any structural equation in $\mathcal{S}_X$. Let $\mathcal{Y}$ be the set in which $Y = \left(X_i : i \in \mathbb{I}_X \setminus \mathbb{I}_Z\right)$ takes value. Then the transformation $\tau : \mathcal{X} \to \mathcal{Y}$ mapping*

$$\tau : \left(x_i : i \in \mathbb{I}_X\right) = x \mapsto y = \left(x_i : i \in \mathbb{I}_X \setminus \mathbb{I}_Z\right)$$

naturally gives rise to an SEM $\mathcal{M}_Y$ that is an exact τ-transformation of $\mathcal{M}_X$, corresponding to marginalising out the childless variables X_i for $i \in \mathbb{I}_Z$.

Theorem 10 (Marginalisation of non-intervened variables)**.** *Let $\mathcal{M}_X = (\mathcal{S}_X, \mathcal{I}_X, \mathbb{P}_E)$ be an* acyclic *SEM and suppose that $\mathbb{I}_Z \subset \mathbb{I}_X$ is a set of indices of variables that are not intervened upon by any intervention $i \in \mathcal{I}_X$. Let $\mathcal{Y}$ be the set in which $Y = \left(X_i : i \in \mathbb{I}_X \setminus \mathbb{I}_Z\right)$ takes value. Then the transformation $\tau : \mathcal{X} \to \mathcal{Y}$ mapping*

$$\tau : \left(x_i : i \in \mathbb{I}_X\right) = x \mapsto y = \left(x_i : i \in \mathbb{I}_X \setminus \mathbb{I}_Z\right)$$

naturally gives rise to an SEM $\mathcal{M}_Y$ that is an exact τ-transformation of $\mathcal{M}_X$, corresponding to marginalising out the never-intervened-upon variables X_i for $i \in \mathbb{I}_Z$.

The assumption of acyclicity made in Theorem 10 can be relaxed to allow marginalisation of non-intervened variables in cyclic SEMs, at the expense of extra technical conditions (see Section 3 of [3]).

We remind the reader that our definition of an SEM does not require that the exogenous E-variables be independent. Theorem 10 would not hold if this restriction were made (which is usually the case in the literature); marginalising out a common parent node will in general result in its children having dependent exogenous variables.

5.2 MICRO- TO MACRO-LEVEL

Transformations from micro- to macro-levels may arise in situations in which the micro-level variables can be observed via a 'coarse' measurement device, represented by the function τ, e. g. we can use a thermometer to measure the temperature of a gas, but not the motions of the individual particles. They may also arise due to deliberate modelling choice when we wish to describe a system using higher level features, e. g. viewing the motor cortex as a single entity responsible for movements, rather than as a collection of individual neurons.

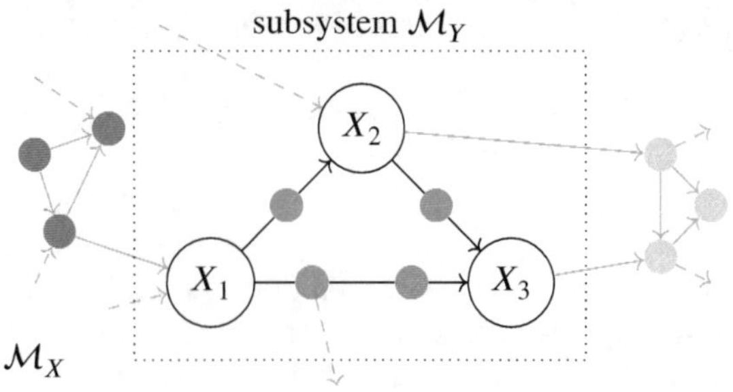

Figure 3: Suppose that there is a complex model $\mathcal{M}_X$ but that we only wish to model the distribution over X_1, X_2, X_3 and how it changes under some interventions on X_1, X_2, X_3. By Theorem 9, we can ignore downstream effects (●) after grouping them together as one multivariate variable and by Theorem 10 we can ignore intermediate steps of complex mechanisms (●) and treat upstream causes as noise fluctuations (●). That is, we can exactly transform the complex SEM $\mathcal{M}_X$ into a simpler model $\mathcal{M}_Y$ by marginalisation.

In such situations, our framework of exact transformations allows one to investigate whether such a macro-level model admits a causal interpretation. The following theorem provides an exact transformation between a micro-level model $\mathcal{M}_X$ and a macro-level model $\mathcal{M}_Y$ in which the variables are aggregate features of variables in $\mathcal{M}_X$ obtained by averaging (cf. Figure 4).

Theorem 11 (Micro- to macro-level)**.** *Let $\mathcal{M}_X = \left(\mathcal{S}_X, \mathcal{I}_X, \mathbb{P}_{E,F}\right)$ be a linear SEM over the variables $W = \left(W_i : 1 \leq i \leq n\right)$ and $Z = \left(Z_i : 1 \leq i \leq m\right)$ with*

$$\mathcal{S}_X = \left\{W_i = E_i : 1 \leq i \leq n\right\} \cup \left\{ Z_i = \sum_{j=1}^{n} A_{ij} W_j + F_i : 1 \leq i \leq m \right\}$$

$$\mathcal{I}_X = \Big\{ \varnothing,\ \mathrm{do}(W = w),\ \mathrm{do}(Z = z),\ \mathrm{do}(W = w, Z = z) : w \in \mathbb{R}^n,\ z \in \mathbb{R}^m \Big\}$$

and $(E, F) \sim \mathbb{P}$ where $\mathbb{P}$ is any distribution over $\mathbb{R}^{n+m}$ and A is a matrix.

Assume that there exists an $a \in \mathbb{R}$ such that each column of A sums to a. Consider the following transformation

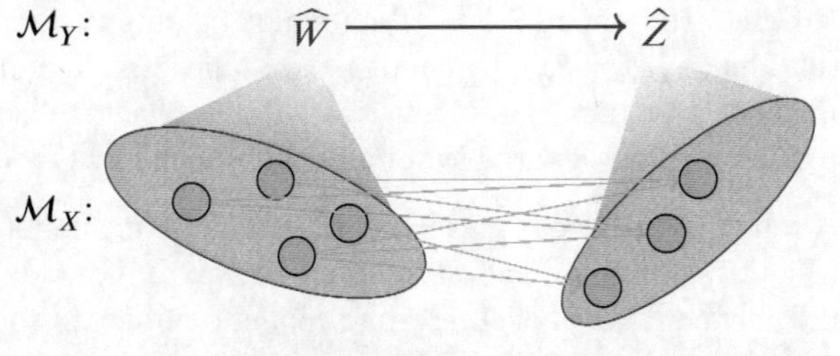

Figure 4: An illustration of the setting considered in Theorem 11. The micro-variables $W_1, \ldots, W_n$ and $Z_1, \ldots, Z_m$ in the SEM $\mathcal{M}_X$ can be averaged to derive macro-variables $\widehat{W}$ and $\widehat{Z}$ in such a way that the resulting macro-level SEM $\mathcal{M}_Y$ is an exact transformation of the micro-level SEM $\mathcal{M}_X$.

that averages the W and Z variables:

$$\tau : \mathcal{X} \to \mathcal{Y} = \mathbb{R}^2$$
$$\begin{pmatrix} W \\ Z \end{pmatrix} \mapsto \begin{pmatrix} \widehat{W} \\ \widehat{Z} \end{pmatrix} = \begin{pmatrix} \frac{1}{n}\sum_{i=1}^n W_i \\ \frac{1}{m}\sum_{j=1}^m Z_j \end{pmatrix}$$

Further, let $\mathcal{M}_Y = \left(\mathcal{S}_Y, \mathcal{I}_Y, \mathbb{P}_{\widehat{E},\widehat{F}}\right)$ *over the variables* $\left\{\widehat{W}, \widehat{Z}\right\}$ *be an SEM with*

$$\mathcal{S}_Y = \left\{\widehat{W} = \widehat{E},\ \widehat{Z} = \frac{a}{m}\widehat{W} + \widehat{F}\right\}$$
$$\mathcal{I}_Y = \Big\{\varnothing,\ \mathrm{do}(\widehat{W} = \widehat{w}),\ \mathrm{do}(\widehat{Z} = \widehat{z}),$$
$$\mathrm{do}(\widehat{W} = \widehat{w}, \widehat{Z} = \widehat{z}) : \widehat{w} \in \mathbb{R},\ \widehat{z} \in \mathbb{R}\Big\}$$
$$\widehat{E} \sim \frac{1}{n}\sum_{i=1}^n E_i, \quad \widehat{F} \sim \frac{1}{m}\sum_{i=1}^m F_i$$

Then $\mathcal{M}_Y$ *is an exact* τ*-transformation of* $\mathcal{M}_X$.

5.3 STATIONARY BEHAVIOUR OF DYNAMICAL PROCESSES

In this section we provide an example of an exact transformation between an SEM $\mathcal{M}_X$ describing a time-evolving system and another SEM $\mathcal{M}_Y$ describing the system after it has equilibrated. In this setting, τ could be thought of as representing our ability to only measure the time-evolving system at a single point in time, after the transient dynamics have taken place.

In particular, we consider a discrete-time linear dynamical system with identical noise and provide the explicit form of an SEM that models the distribution of the equilibria under each intervention (cf. Figure 5).[10]

Theorem 12 (Discrete-time linear dynamical process with identical noise)**.** *Let* $\mathcal{M}_X = \left(\mathcal{S}_X, \mathcal{I}_X, \mathbb{P}_E\right)$ *over the variables* $\left\{X_t^i : t \in \mathbb{Z},\ i \in \{1, \ldots, n\}\right\}$ *be a linear SEM with*

$$\mathcal{S}_X = \left\{ X_{t+1}^i = \sum_{j=1}^n A_{ij} X_t^j + E_t^i \ :\ i \in \{1, \ldots, n\}, t \in \mathbb{Z} \right\}$$
$$\text{i. e. } X_{t+1} = AX_t + E_t$$
$$\mathcal{I}_X = \left\{ \mathrm{do}(X_t^j = x_j\ \forall t \in \mathbb{Z}, \forall j \in J) : x \in \mathbb{R}^{|J|},\ J \subseteq \{1, \ldots, n\} \right\}$$
$$E_t = E\ \forall t \in \mathbb{Z} \text{ where } E \sim \mathbb{P}$$

where $\mathbb{P}$ *is any distribution over* $\mathbb{R}^n$ *and A is a matrix.*

Assume that the linear mapping $v \mapsto Av$ *is a contraction. Then the following transformation is well-defined under any intervention* $i \in \mathcal{I}_X$*:*[11]

$$\tau : \mathcal{X} \to \mathcal{Y}$$
$$(x_t)_{t\in\mathbb{Z}} \mapsto y = \lim_{t\to\infty} x_t$$

Let $\mathcal{M}_Y = \left(\mathcal{S}_Y, \mathcal{I}_Y, \mathbb{P}_F\right)$ *be the (potentially cyclic) SEM over the variables* $\left\{Y^i : i \in \{1, \ldots, n\}\right\}$ *with*

$$\mathcal{S}_Y = \left\{ Y^i = \frac{\sum_{j\neq i} A_{ij} Y^j}{1 - A_{ii}} + \frac{F^i}{1 - A_{ii}} \ :\ i \in \{1, \ldots, n\} \right\}$$
$$\mathcal{I}_Y = \left\{ \mathrm{do}(Y^j = y_j\ \forall j \in J) : y \in \mathbb{R}^{|J|},\ J \subseteq \{1, \ldots, n\} \right\}$$
$$F \sim \mathbb{P}$$

Then $\mathcal{M}_Y$ *is an exact* τ*-transformation of* $\mathcal{M}_X$.

The above theorem demonstrates how a linear additive SEM can arise as a result of making observations of a dynamical process. This supports one interpretation of SEMs as a description of a dynamical process that equilibrates quickly compared to its external environment.[12] The framework of exact transformations allows us to explain in a precise way the sense in which such equilibrium models can be used as causal descriptions of an underlying dynamical process.

[10]Note that the assumption that the transition dynamics be linear can be relaxed to more general non-linear mappings. In this case, however, the structural equations of $\mathcal{M}_Y$ can only be written in terms of implicit solutions to the structural equations of $\mathcal{M}_X$. For purposes of exposition, we stick here to the simpler case of linear dynamics.

[11]In Appendix D.1 we show that A being a contraction mapping ensures that the sequence $(X_t)_{t\in\mathbb{Z}}$ defined by $\mathcal{M}_X$ converges everywhere under any intervention $i \in \mathcal{I}_X$. That is, for any realisation $(x_t)_{t\in\mathbb{Z}}$ of this sequence, its limit $\lim_{t\to\infty} x_t$ as a sequence of elements of $\mathbb{R}^n$ exists.

[12]This interpretation corresponds to the assumption that the noise in the dynamical model is constant through time, and is used by e. g. [10, 12, 14, 15] and [13] to meaningfully interpret cyclic SEMs.

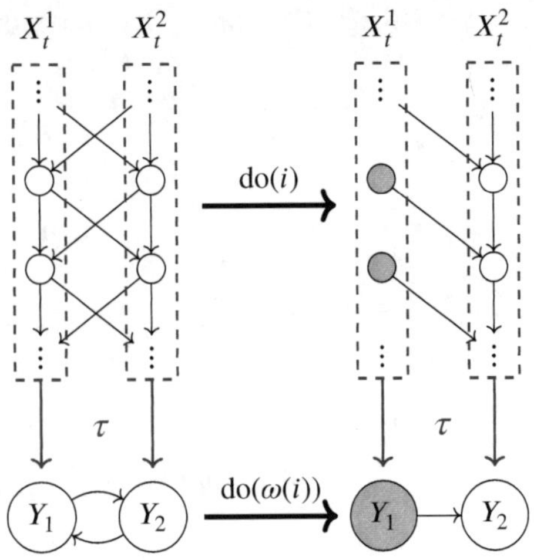

Figure 5: An illustration of the setting considered in Theorem 12. The discrete-time dynamical process is exactly transformed into a model describing its equilibria.

This result also sheds light on the interpretation of cyclic causal models. One interpretation of the structural equations of an acyclic SEM is that they represent a temporally ordered series of mechanisms by which data are generated. This is not possible in the case that the SEM exhibits cycles: there does not exist a partial ordering on the variables and hence one cannot think of each variable being generated temporally downstream of its parents. By showing that cyclic SEMs can arise as exact transformations of *acyclic* SEMs, we provide an interpretation of cyclic SEMs that does not suffer from the above problem.

6 DISCUSSION AND FUTURE WORK

It's turtles all the way down! There is no such thing as a 'correct' model, but in this paper we introduced the notions of exact transformations between SEMs to evaluate when two SEMs can be viewed as causally consistent models of the same system. Illustrating how these notions can be used in order to relate differing model levels, we proved in Section 5 the exactness of transformations occurring in three different settings. These have implications for the following questions in causal modelling: When can we model only a subsystem of a more complex system? When does a micro-level system admit a causal description in terms of macro-level features? How do cyclic causal models arise?

Our work has implications for other problems in causal modelling. It suggests that ambiguous manipulations [18] may be thought of as arising due to the application of an inexact transformation to an SEM $\mathcal{M}_X$. This was illustrated in Section 1.1 in which LDL and HDL cholesterol were only measured via their sum TC, resulting in a model that suffered from the problem of ambiguous manipulations (cf. Figure 1b) since it was not an exact transformation of the underlying model (cf. Figure 1a). This is related to the problem of causal variable definition as studied by [7].

A future line of enquiry would be to generalise the notion of an exact transformation in order to analyse the trade-off between model accuracy and model complexity for causal modelling using SEMs. For a transformation to be exact, we require that the posets $\mathcal{P}_{\tau(X)}$ and $\mathcal{P}_Y$ be equal. One could imagine a 'softening' of this requirement such that the distributions in the posets are required to be only approximately equal. A slightly inaccurate model with a small number of variables may be preferable to an accurate but complex model.

We discussed the importance of an order-preserving ω to ensure a notion of causal consistency between two SEMs. It would be interesting to better understand the conditions under which different properties of consistency between causal models hold – for instance, counterfactual reasoning, which we have not discussed in this paper.

While we have introduced the notion of an exact transformation, we have not provided any criterion to choose from amongst the set of all possible exact transformations of an SEM. Foundational work in a similar direction to ours has been done by [4, 5], who consider a particular discrete setting. They provide algorithms to learn a transformation of a micro-level model to a macro-level model with desirable information-theoretic properties. We conjecture that our framework may lead to extensions of their work, e. g. to the continuous setting.

Finally, suppose that we have made observations of an underlying system $\mathcal{M}_X$ via a measurement device τ, and that we want to fit an SEM $\mathcal{M}_Y$ from a restricted model class to our data. By using our framework, asking whether or not $\mathcal{M}_Y$ admits a causal interpretation consistent with $\mathcal{M}_X$ reduces to asking whether the transformation is exact. More generally, by fixing any two of $\mathcal{M}_X$, τ and $\mathcal{M}_Y$, we can ask what properties must be fulfilled by the third in order for the two models to be causally consistent. We hope that this may lead to the practical use of SEMs being theoretically grounded.

Acknowledgements

We thank Tobias Mistele for valuable early feedback. Stephan Bongers was supported by NWO, the Netherlands Organization for Scientific Research (VIDI grant 639.072.410). This project has received funding from the European Research Council (ERC) under the European Union's Horizon 2020 research and innovation programme (grant agreement n° 639466).

References

[1] R. Balian. *From microphysics to macrophysics*. Springer, 1992.

[2] K. A. Bollen. *Structural equations with latent variables*. John Wiley & Sons, 2014.

[3] S. Bongers, J. Peters, B. Schölkopf, and J. M. Mooij. Structural causal models: Cycles, marginalizations, exogenous reparametrizations and reductions. *arXiv preprint arXiv:1611.06221*, 2016.

[4] K. Chalupka, P. Perona, and F. Eberhardt. Visual causal feature learning. In *Proceedings of the Thirty-First Conference on Uncertainty in Artificial Intelligence*, pages 181–190. AUAI Press, 2015.

[5] K. Chalupka, P. Perona, and F. Eberhardt. Multi-level cause-effect systems. In *The 19th International Conference on Artificial Intelligence and Statistics.*, 2016.

[6] D. Dash and M. J. Druzdzel. Caveats for causal reasoning with equilibrium models. *Lecture notes in computer science*, pages 192–203, 2001.

[7] F. Eberhardt. Green and grue causal variables. *Synthese*, 193(4):1029–1046, 2016.

[8] F. M. Fisher. A correspondence principle for simultaneous equation models. *Econometrica: Journal of the Econometric Society*, pages 73–92, 1970.

[9] E. P. Hoel, L. Albantakis, and G. Tononi. Quantifying causal emergence shows that macro can beat micro. *Proceedings of the National Academy of Sciences*, 110(49):19790–19795, 2013.

[10] A. Hyttinen, F. Eberhardt, and P. O. Hoyer. Learning linear cyclic causal models with latent variables. *Journal of Machine Learning Research*, 13(Nov): 3387–3439, 2012.

[11] Y. Iwasaki and H. A. Simon. Causality and model abstraction. *Artificial Intelligence*, 67(1):143–194, 1994.

[12] G. Lacerda, P. L. Spirtes, J. Ramsey, and P. O. Hoyer. Discovering cyclic causal models by independent components analysis. In *Proceedings of the Twenty-Fourth Conference Annual Conference on Uncertainty in Artificial Intelligence*, 2008.

[13] J. M. Mooij and T. Heskes. Cyclic causal discovery from continuous equilibrium data. In *Proceedings of the Twenty-Ninth Conference Annual Conference on Uncertainty in Artificial Intelligence*, 2013.

[14] J. M. Mooij, D. Janzing, T. Heskes, and B. Schölkopf. On causal discovery with cyclic additive noise models. In J. Shawe-Taylor, R. Zemel, P. Bartlett, F. Pereira, and K. Weinberger, editors, *Advances in Neural Information Processing Systems 24 (NIPS*2011)*, pages 639–647, 2011.

[15] J. M. Mooij, D. Janzing, and B. Schölkopf. From Ordinary Differential Equations to Structural Causal Models: the deterministic case. In *Proceedings of the Twenty-Ninth Conference Annual Conference on Uncertainty in Artificial Intelligence*, pages 440–448, 2013.

[16] J. Pearl. *Causality*. Cambridge University Press, 2009.

[17] H. A. Simon and A. Ando. Aggregation of variables in dynamic systems. *Econometrica: journal of the Econometric Society*, pages 111–138, 1961.

[18] P. Spirtes and R. Scheines. Causal inference of ambiguous manipulations. *Philosophy of Science*, 71 (5):833–845, 2004.

[19] P. Spirtes, C. N. Glymour, and R. Scheines. *Causation, prediction, and search*. MIT press, 2000.

[20] D. Steinberg. *The Cholesterol Wars: The Skeptics vs the Preponderance of Evidence*. Academic Press, 2011.

[21] A. S. Truswell. *Cholesterol and beyond: the research on diet and coronary heart disease 1900-2000*. Springer Science & Business Media, 2010.

Appendix

A PROOFS FOR SECTION 4.3: ELEMENTARY EXACT TRANSFORMATIONS

Lemma 4. *The identity mapping and permuting the labels of variables are both exact transformations. That is, if $\mathcal{M}_X$ is an SEM and $\pi : \mathbb{I}_X \to \mathbb{I}_X$ is a bijection then the transformation*

$$\tau : \mathcal{X} \to \mathcal{Y}$$
$$(x_i : i \in \mathbb{I}_X) \mapsto (x_{\pi(i)} : i \in \mathbb{I}_X)$$

naturally gives rise to an SEM $\mathcal{M}_Y$ that is an exact τ-transformation of $\mathcal{M}_X$, corresponding to relabelling the variables.

Proof of Lemma 4. Consider the SEM $\mathcal{M}_Y$ obtained from $\mathcal{M}_X$ by replacing, for all $i \in \mathbb{I}_X$, any occurrence of X_i in the structural equations $\mathcal{S}_X$ and interventions $\mathcal{I}_X$ by $Y_{\pi(i)}$ and leaving the distribution over the exogenous variables unchanged. □

Proof of Lemma 5 (Transitivity of exact transformations). Let $\omega_{ZY} : \mathcal{I}_Y \to \mathcal{I}_Z$ and $\omega_{YX} : \mathcal{I}_X \to \mathcal{I}_Y$ be the mappings between interventions corresponding to the exact transformations τ_{ZY} and τ_{YX} respectively and define $\omega_{ZX} = \omega_{ZY} \circ \omega_{YX} : \mathcal{I}_X \to \mathcal{I}_Z$. Then ω_{ZX} is surjective and order-preserving since both ω_{ZY} and ω_{YX} are surjective and order-preserving. Since τ_{ZY} and τ_{YX} are exact it follows that for all $i \in \mathcal{I}_X$

$$\mathbb{P}^{i}_{\tau_{ZX}(X)} = \mathbb{P}^{\omega_{ZY}(\omega_{YX}(i))}_{\tau_{ZY}(\tau_{YX}(X))} = \mathbb{P}^{\mathrm{do}(\omega_{ZX}(i))}_{Z}$$

i. e. $\mathcal{M}_Z$ is an τ_{ZX}-exact transformation of $\mathcal{M}_X$. □

B PROOFS FOR SECTION 5.1: MARGINALISATION OF VARIABLES

Proof of Theorem 9 (Marginalisation of childless variables). By Lemma 5 it suffices to proof this for marginalisation of one childless variable. Without loss of generality, let X_1 be the childless variable to be marginalised out.

Let $\mathcal{M}_Y = (\mathcal{S}_Y, \mathcal{I}_Y, \mathbb{P}_F)$ be the SEM where

- the structural equations $\mathcal{S}_Y$ are obtained from $\mathcal{S}_X$ by removing the structural equation corresponding to the childless variable X_1;
- $\mathcal{I}_Y$ is the image of the map $\omega : \mathcal{I}_X \to \mathcal{I}_Y$ that drops any reference to the variable X_1 (e. g. $\mathrm{do}(X_1 = x_1, X_2 = x_2) \in \mathcal{I}_X$ would be mapped to $\mathrm{do}(X_2 = x_2) \in \mathcal{I}_Y$);
- $F = (E_i : i \in \mathbb{I}_X \setminus \{1\})$ are the remaining noise variables distributed according to their marginal distribution under $\mathbb{P}_E$.

By construction, ω is surjective and order-preserving. Let $i \in \mathcal{I}_X$ be any intervention. The variable X_1 being childless ensures that the law on the remaining variables $X_k, k \in \mathbb{I}_X \setminus \{1\}$ that we obtain by *marginalisation* of the childless variable, i. e. $\mathbb{P}^{i}_{\tau(X)}$, is equivalent to the law one obtains by simply *dropping* the childless variable, which is exactly what the law under $\mathcal{M}_Y$ amounts to, i. e. $\mathbb{P}^{\omega(\mathrm{do}(i))}_{Y}$. □

Proof of Theorem 10 (Marginalisation of non-intervened variables). By Lemma 5 it suffices to proof this for marginalisation of one never-intervened-upon variable. Without loss of generality, let X_1 be the never-intervened-upon variable to be marginalised out. By acyclicity of the SEM $\mathcal{M}_X$, the structural equation corresponding to variable X_1 is of the form $X_1 = f_1\left(\mathbf{X}_{\mathrm{pa}(1)}, E_1\right)$ and X_1 does not appear in the structural equation for any of its ancestors.

Now let $\mathcal{M}_Y = (\mathcal{S}_Y, \mathcal{I}_Y, \mathcal{P}_F)$ be the SEM where

- $\mathcal{I}_Y = \mathcal{I}_X$;

- $F_i = ((E_i, E_1) : i \in \mathbb{I}_X \setminus \{1\})$ are the noise variables distributed as implied by $\mathbb{P}_E$;
- the structural equations $\mathcal{S}_Y$ are obtained from $\mathcal{S}_X$ by removing the structural equation of X_1 and replacing any occurrence of X_1 in the right-hand side of the structural equations of children of X_1 by $f_1\left(\mathbf{X}_{\mathrm{pa}(1)}, E_1\right)$, yielding $X_i = f_i\left(f_1\left(\mathbf{X}_{\mathrm{pa}(1)}, E_1\right), \mathbf{X}_{\mathrm{pa}(i)}, E_i\right)$.

Note that the structural equations of the resulting SEM are still acyclic and are all of the form $X_i = h_i\left(\mathbf{X}_{\setminus i}, F_i\right)$. Then $\mathcal{M}_Y$ is, by construction, an τ-exact transformation of $\mathcal{M}_X$ for $\omega = \mathrm{id}$. □

C PROOF FOR SECTION 5.2: MICRO- TO MACRO-LEVEL

Proof of Theorem 11. We begin by defining a mapping between interventions

$$\begin{aligned} \omega : \mathcal{I}_X &\to \mathcal{I}_Y \\ \varnothing &\mapsto \varnothing \\ \mathrm{do}(W = w) &\mapsto \mathrm{do}\left(\widehat{W} = \frac{1}{n}\sum_{i=1}^{n} w_i\right) \\ \mathrm{do}(Z = z) &\mapsto \mathrm{do}\left(\widehat{Z} = \frac{1}{m}\sum_{i=1}^{m} z_i\right) \\ \mathrm{do}(W = w, Z = z) &\mapsto \mathrm{do}\left(\widehat{W} = \frac{1}{n}\sum_{i=1}^{n} w_i, \widehat{Z} = \frac{1}{m}\sum_{i=1}^{m} z_i\right) \end{aligned}$$

Note that ω is surjective and order-preserving (in fact, it is an order embedding). Therefore, it only remains to show that the distributions implied by $\tau(X)$ under any intervention $i \in \mathcal{I}_X$ agree with the corresponding distributions implied by $\mathcal{M}_Y$. That is, we have to show that

$$\mathbb{P}^{i}_{\tau(X)} = \mathbb{P}^{\mathrm{do}(\omega(i))}_{Y} \quad \forall i \in \mathcal{I}_X$$

In the observational setting, the distribution over $\mathcal{Y}$ is implied by the following equations:

$$\begin{aligned} \widehat{W} &= \frac{1}{n}\sum_{i=1}^{n} W_i = \frac{1}{n}\sum_{i=1}^{n} E_i \\ \widehat{Z} &= \frac{1}{m}\sum_{i=1}^{m} Z_i = \frac{1}{m}\sum_{i=1}^{m}\left(\sum_{j=1}^{n} A_{ij}W_j + F_i\right) = \frac{a}{m}\widehat{W} + \frac{1}{m}\sum_{i=1}^{m} F_i \end{aligned}$$

Since the distributions of the exogenous variables in $\mathcal{M}_Y$ are given by $\widehat{E} \sim \frac{1}{n}\sum_{i=1}^{n} E_i$, $\widehat{F} \sim \frac{1}{m}\sum_{i=1}^{m} F_i$, it follows that $\mathbb{P}^{\mathrm{do}(\varnothing)}_{\tau(X)}$ and $\mathbb{P}^{\mathrm{do}(\varnothing)}_{Y}$ agree. Similarly, the push-forward measure on $\mathcal{Y}$ induced by the intervention $\mathrm{do}(W = w) \in \mathcal{I}_X$ is given by

$$\begin{aligned} \widehat{W} &= \frac{1}{n}\sum_{i=1}^{n} W_i = \frac{1}{n}\sum_{i=1}^{n} w_i \\ \widehat{Z} &= \frac{1}{m}\sum_{i=1}^{m} Z_i = \frac{1}{m}\sum_{i=1}^{m}\left(\sum_{j=1}^{n} A_{ij}W_j + F_i\right) = \frac{a}{m}\widehat{W} + \frac{1}{m}\sum_{i=1}^{m} F_i \end{aligned}$$

which is the same as the distribution induced by the ω-corresponding intervention $\mathrm{do}\left(\widehat{W} = \frac{1}{n}\sum_{i=1}^{n} w_i\right)$ in $\mathcal{M}_Y$.

Similar reasoning shows that this also holds for the interventions $\mathrm{do}(Z = z)$ and $\mathrm{do}(W = w, Z = z)$.

□

D PROOF FOR SECTION 5.3: STATIONARY BEHAVIOUR OF DYNAMICAL PROCESSES

Proof of Theorem 12. We begin by defining a mapping between interventions

$$\omega : \mathcal{I}_X \to \mathcal{I}_Y$$
$$\mathrm{do}(X_t^j = x_j \;\; \forall t \in \mathbb{Z}, \, \forall j \in J) \mapsto \mathrm{do}(Y^j = x_j \; \forall j \in J)$$

Note that ω is surjective and order-preserving (in fact, it is an order embedding). Therefore, it only remains to show that the distributions implied by $\tau(X)$ under any intervention $i \in \mathcal{I}_X$ agree with the corresponding distributions implied by $\mathcal{M}_Y$. That is, we have to show that

$$\mathbb{P}^i_{\tau(X)} = \mathbb{P}_Y^{\mathrm{do}(\omega(i))} \quad \forall i \in \mathcal{I}_X$$

For this we consider, without loss of generality, the distribution arising from performing the $\mathcal{M}_X$-level intervention

$$i = \mathrm{do}(X_t^j = x_j \; \forall t \in \mathbb{Z}, \forall j \leq m \leq n) \in \mathcal{I}_X$$

for $m \in [n]$ (for $m = 0$ this amounts to the null-intervention).

Since A is a contraction mapping, it follows from Lemma 15 that for any intervention in $\mathcal{I}_X$, the sequence of random variables X_t defined by $\mathcal{M}_X$ converges everywhere. That is, there exists a random variable X_* such that $X_t \xrightarrow[t\to\infty]{\text{everywhere}} X_*$. In the case of the intervention i above, the random variable X_* satisfies:

$$\begin{cases} X_*^k = x_k & \text{if } k \leq m \\ X_*^k = \sum_j A_{kj} X_*^j + E^k & \text{if } m < k \leq n \end{cases} \tag{1}$$

Since $\tau(X) = \lim_{t\to\infty} X_t$, it follows from the definition of X_* that $\tau(X) = X_*$, and hence $\tau(X)$ also satisfies the equations above. It follows (rewriting the second line in Equation 1 above) that under the push-forward measure $\mathbb{P}^i_{\tau(X)} = \tau\left(\mathbb{P}_X^{\mathrm{do}(i)}\right)$ the distribution of the random variable $\tau(X) = X_*$ is given by:

$$\begin{cases} X_*^k = x_k & \text{if } k \leq m \\ X_*^k = \frac{\sum_{j\neq k} A_{kj} X_*^j}{1-A_{kk}} + \frac{E^k}{1-A_{kk}} & \text{if } m < k \leq n \end{cases}$$

We need to compare this to the law of Y as implied by $\mathcal{M}_Y$ under the intervention $\omega(i)$, i. e. $\mathbb{P}_Y^{\mathrm{do}(\omega(i))}$. The $\mathcal{M}_Y$-level intervention $\omega(i)$ corresponding to i is

$$\omega(i) = \mathrm{do}(Y^j = x_j \; \forall j \leq m \leq n) \in \mathcal{I}_Y$$

and so the structural equations of $\mathcal{M}_Y$ under the intervention $\omega(\mathrm{do}(i))$ are

$$\begin{cases} Y^k = x_k & \text{if } k \leq m \\ Y^k = \frac{\sum_{j\neq k} A_{kj} Y^j}{1-A_{kk}} + \frac{F^k}{1-A_{kk}} & \text{if } m < k \leq n \end{cases}$$

Since $F \sim E$ it indeed follows that $\tau(X) \sim Y$, i. e. $\mathbb{P}^i_{\tau(X)} = \mathbb{P}_Y^{\mathrm{do}(\omega(i))}$.

Thus $\mathcal{M}_Y$ is an exact τ-transformation of $\mathcal{M}_X$. □

D.1 CONTRACTION MAPPING AND CONVERGENCE

The following Lemmata show that A being a contraction mapping ensures that the sequence $(X_t)_{t\in\mathbb{Z}}$ defined by $\mathcal{M}_X$ in Theorem 12 converges everywhere under any intervention $i \in \mathcal{I}_X$. That is, for any realisation $(x_t)_{t\in\mathbb{Z}}$ of this sequence, its limit $\lim_{t\to\infty} x_t$ as a sequence of elements of $\mathbb{R}^n$ exists.

Lemma 13. *Suppose that the function*

$$\begin{aligned} f : \mathbb{R}^n &\to \mathbb{R}^m \\ x &\mapsto f(x) \end{aligned}$$

is a contraction mapping. Then, for any $e \in \mathbb{R}^m$, so is the function

$$\begin{aligned} f^* : \mathbb{R}^n &\to \mathbb{R}^m \\ x &\mapsto f(x) + e \end{aligned}$$

Proof. By definition, there exists $c < 1$ such that for any $x, y \in \mathbb{R}^n$,

$$\|f^*(x) - f^*(y)\| = \|(f(x) + e) - (f(y) + e)\| = \|f(x) - f(y)\| \leq c\|x - y\|$$

and hence f^* is a contraction mapping. □

Lemma 14. *Suppose that the function*

$$\begin{aligned} f : \mathbb{R}^n &\to \mathbb{R}^n \\ x = \begin{pmatrix} x_1 \\ \vdots \\ x_n \end{pmatrix} &\mapsto \begin{pmatrix} f_1(x) \\ \vdots \\ f_n(x) \end{pmatrix} \end{aligned}$$

is a contraction mapping. Then for any $m \leq n$, and $x_i^* \in \mathbb{R}$, $i \in [m]$, so is the function

$$\begin{aligned} f^* : \mathbb{R}^n &\to \mathbb{R}^n \\ x = \begin{pmatrix} x_1 \\ \vdots \\ x_n \end{pmatrix} &\mapsto \begin{pmatrix} x_1^* \\ \vdots \\ x_m^* \\ f_{m+1}(x) \\ \vdots \\ f_n(x) \end{pmatrix} \end{aligned}$$

Proof. By definition, there exists $c < 1$ such that for any $x, y \in \mathbb{R}^n$,

$$\begin{aligned} \|f^*(x) - f^*(y)\| = \left\| \begin{pmatrix} x_1^* \\ \vdots \\ x_m^* \\ f_{m+1}(x) \\ \vdots \\ f_n(x) \end{pmatrix} - \begin{pmatrix} x_1^* \\ \vdots \\ x_m^* \\ f_{m+1}(y) \\ \vdots \\ f_n(y) \end{pmatrix} \right\| = \left\| \begin{pmatrix} 0 \\ \vdots \\ 0 \\ f_{m+1}(x) - f_{m+1}(y) \\ \vdots \\ f_n(x) - f_n(y) \end{pmatrix} \right\| &\leq \left\| \begin{pmatrix} f_1(x) - f_1(y) \\ \vdots \\ f_n(x) - f_n(y) \end{pmatrix} \right\| \\ &= \|f(x) - f(y)\| \\ &\leq c\|x - y\| \end{aligned}$$

and hence f^* is a contraction mapping. □

Lemma 15. *Consider the SEM $\mathcal{M}_X$ in Theorem 12, and suppose that the linear map $A : \mathbb{R}^n \to \mathbb{R}^n$ is a contraction mapping. Then, for any intervention $i \in \mathcal{I}_X$, the sequence of X_t converges everywhere.*

Proof. Consider, without loss of generality, the intervention

$$\mathrm{do}(X_t^j = x_j \ \forall t \in \mathbb{Z}, \forall j \leq m \leq n) \in \mathcal{I}_X$$

for $m \in [n]$ (for $m = 0$ this amounts to the null-intervention). The structural equations under this intervention are

$$\begin{cases} X_{t+1}^k = x_k & \text{if } k \leq m \\ X_{t+1}^k = \sum_j A_{kj} X_t^j + E^k & \text{if } m < k \leq n \end{cases}$$

and thus the sequence X_t can be seen to transition according to the function $f = g \circ h$, where

$$\begin{aligned} h : \mathbb{R}^n &\to \mathbb{R}^n \\ v &\mapsto w = Av + E \end{aligned}$$

$$\begin{aligned} g : \mathbb{R}^n &\to \mathbb{R}^n \\ w = \begin{pmatrix} w_1 \\ \vdots \\ w_n \end{pmatrix} &\mapsto \begin{pmatrix} x_1 \\ \vdots \\ x_m \\ w_{m+1} \\ \vdots \\ w_n \end{pmatrix} \end{aligned}$$

By Lemma 13 and Lemma 14, f is a contraction mapping for any fixed E. Thus, by the contraction mapping theorem, the sequence of X_t converges everywhere to a unique fixed point. □

Stein Variational Adaptive Importance Sampling

Jun Han **Qiang Liu**
Computer Science, Dartmouth College, Hanover, NH 03755
{jun.han.gr, qiang.liu}@dartmouth.edu

Abstract

We propose a novel adaptive importance sampling algorithm which incorporates Stein variational gradient decent algorithm (SVGD) with importance sampling (IS). Our algorithm leverages the nonparametric transforms in SVGD to iteratively decrease the KL divergence between importance proposals and target distributions. The advantages of our algorithm are twofold: 1) it turns SVGD into a standard IS algorithm, allowing us to use standard diagnostic and analytic tools of IS to evaluate and interpret the results, and 2) it does not restrict the choice of the importance proposals to predefined distribution families like traditional (adaptive) IS methods. Empirical experiments demonstrate that our algorithm performs well on evaluating partition functions of restricted Boltzmann machines and testing likelihood of variational auto-encoders.

1 INTRODUCTION

Probabilistic modeling provides a fundamental framework for reasoning under uncertainty and modeling complex relations in machine learning. A critical challenge, however, is to develop efficient computational techniques for approximating complex distributions. Specifically, given a complex distribution $p(\boldsymbol{x})$, often known only up to a normalization constant, we are interested estimating integral quantities $\mathbb{E}_p[f]$ for test functions f. Popular approximation algorithms include particle-based methods, such as Monte Carlo, which construct a set of independent particles $\{\boldsymbol{x}_i\}_{i=1}^n$ whose empirical averaging $\frac{1}{n}\sum_{i=1}^n f(\boldsymbol{x}_i)$ forms unbiased estimates of $\mathbb{E}_p[f]$, and variational inference (VI), which approximates p with a simpler surrogate distribution q by minimizing a KL divergence objective function within a predefined parametric family of distributions. Modern variational inference methods have found successful applications in highly complex learning systems (e.g., Hoffman et al., 2013; Kingma & Welling, 2013). However, VI critically depends on the choice of parametric families and does not generally provide consistent estimators like particle-based methods.

Stein variational gradient descent (SVGD) is an alternative framework that integrates both the particle-based and variational ideas. It starts with a set of initial particles $\{\boldsymbol{x}_i^0\}_{i=1}^n$, and iteratively updates the particles using adaptively constructed deterministic variable transforms:

$$\boldsymbol{x}_i^\ell \leftarrow \boldsymbol{T}_\ell(\boldsymbol{x}_i^{\ell-1}), \quad \forall i = 1, \dots, n,$$

where $\boldsymbol{T}_\ell$ is a variable transformation at the ℓ-th iteration that maps old particles to new ones, constructed adaptively at each iteration based on the most recent particles $\{\boldsymbol{x}_i^{\ell-1}\}_{i=1}^n$ that guarantee to push the particles "closer" to the target distribution p, in the sense that the KL divergence between the distribution of the particles and the target distribution p can be iteratively decreased. More details on the construction of $\boldsymbol{T}_\ell$ can be found in Section 2.

In the view of measure transport, SVGD iteratively transports the initial probability mass of the particles to the target distribution. SVGD constructs a path of distributions that bridges the initial distribution q_0 to the target distribution p,

$$q_\ell = (\boldsymbol{T}_\ell \circ \cdots \circ \boldsymbol{T}_1)\sharp q_0, \quad \ell = 1, \dots, K. \tag{1}$$

where $\boldsymbol{T}\sharp q$ denotes the push-forward measure of q through the transform $\boldsymbol{T}$, that is the distribution of $\boldsymbol{z} = \boldsymbol{T}(\boldsymbol{x})$ when $\boldsymbol{x} \sim q$.

The story, however, is complicated by the fact that the transform $\boldsymbol{T}_\ell$ is practically constructed on the fly *depending* on the recent particles $\{\boldsymbol{x}_i^{\ell-1}\}_{i=1}^n$, which introduces complex dependency between the particles at the next iteration, whose theoretical understanding requires mathematical tools in interacting particle systems (e.g., Braun & Hepp, 1977; Spohn, 2012; Del Moral, 2013) and propagation of chaos (e.g., Sznitman, 1991). As a result, $\{\boldsymbol{x}_i^\ell\}_{i=1}^n$ can not be viewed as i.i.d. samples from q_ℓ. This makes it difficult to analyze the results of SVGD and quantify their bias and variance.

In this paper, we propose a simple modification of SVGD that "decouples" the particle interaction and returns particles i.i.d. drawn from q_ℓ; we also develop a method to iteratively keep track of the importance weights of these particles, which makes it possible to give consistent, or unbiased estimators within finite number of iterations of SVGD.

Our method integrates SVGD with importance sampling (IS) and combines their advantages: it leverages the SVGD dynamics to obtain high quality proposals q_ℓ for IS and also turns SVGD into a standard IS algorithm, inheriting the interpretability and theoretical properties of IS. Another advantage of our proposed method is that it provides an SVGD-based approach for estimating intractable normalization constants, an inference problem that the original SVGD does not offer to solve.

Related Work Our method effectively turns SVGD into a nonparametric, adaptive importance sampling (IS) algorithm, where the importance proposal q_ℓ is adaptively improved by the optimal transforms $\boldsymbol{T}_\ell$ which maximally decreases the KL divergence between the iterative distribution and the target distribution in a function space. This is in contrast to the traditional adaptive importance sampling methods (e.g., Cappé et al., 2008; Ryu & Boyd, 2014; Cotter et al., 2015), which optimize the proposal distribution from predefined distribution families $\{q_{\boldsymbol{\theta}}(\boldsymbol{x})\}$, often mixture families or exponential families. The parametric assumptions restrict the choice of the proposal distributions and may give poor results when the assumption is inconsistent with the target distribution p. The proposals q_ℓ in our method, however, are obtained by recursive variable transforms constructed in a nonparametric fashion and become more complex as more transforms $\boldsymbol{T}_\ell$ are applied. In fact, one can view q_ℓ as the result of pushing q_0 through a neural network with ℓ-layers, constructed in a non-parametric, layer-by-layer fashion, which provides a much more flexible distribution family than typical parametric families such as mixtures or exponential families.

There has been a collection of recent works (such as Rezende & Mohamed, 2015; Kingma et al., 2016; Marzouk et al., 2016; Spantini et al., 2017), that approximate the target distributions with complex proposals obtained by iterative variable transforms in a similar way to our proposals q_ℓ in (1). The key difference, however, is that these methods explicitly parameterize the transforms $\boldsymbol{T}_\ell$ and optimize the parameters by back-propagation, while our method, by leveraging the nonparametric nature of SVGD, constructs the transforms $\boldsymbol{T}_\ell$ sequentially in closed forms, requiring no back-propagation.

The idea of constructing a path of distributions $\{q_\ell\}$ to bridge the target distribution p with a simpler distribution q_0 invites connection to ideas such as annealed importance sampling (AIS) (Neal, 2001) and path sampling (PS) (Gelman & Meng, 1998). These methods typically construct an annealing path using geometric averaging of the initial and target densities instead of variable transforms, which does not build in a notion of variational optimization as the SVGD path. In addition, it is often intractable to directly sample distributions on the geometry averaging path, and hence AIS and PS need additional mechanisms in order to construct proper estimators.

Outlines The reminder of this paper is organized as follows. Section 2 discusses Stein discrepancy and SVGD. We propose our main algorithm in Section 3, and a related method in Section 4. Section 5 provides empirical experiments and Section 6 concludes the paper.

2 STEIN VARIATIONAL GRADIENT DESCENT

We introduce the basic idea of Stein variational gradient descent (SVGD) and Stein discrepancy. The readers are referred to Liu & Wang (2016) and Liu et al. (2016) for more detailed introduction.

Preliminary We always assume $\boldsymbol{x} = [x_1, \cdots, x_d]^\top \in \mathbb{R}^d$ in this paper. Given a positive definite kernel $k(\boldsymbol{x}, \boldsymbol{x}')$, there exists an unique reproducing kernel Hilbert space (RKHS) $\mathcal{H}_0$, formed by the closure of functions of form $f(\boldsymbol{x}) = \sum_i a_i k(\boldsymbol{x}, \boldsymbol{x}_i)$ where $a_i \in \mathbb{R}$, equipped with inner product $\langle f,\ g\rangle_{\mathcal{H}_0} = \sum_{ij} a_i k(\boldsymbol{x}_i, \boldsymbol{x}_j) b_j$ for $g(\boldsymbol{x}) = \sum_j b_j k(\boldsymbol{x}, \boldsymbol{x}_j)$. Denote by $\mathcal{H} = \mathcal{H}_0^d = \mathcal{H}_0 \times \cdots \times \mathcal{H}_0$ the vector-valued function space formed by $\boldsymbol{f} = [f_1, \ldots, f_d]^\top$, where $f_i \in \mathcal{H}_0$, $i = 1, \ldots, d$, equipped with inner product $\langle \boldsymbol{f},\ \boldsymbol{g}\rangle_{\mathcal{H}} = \sum_{l=1}^d \langle f_l,\ g_l\rangle_{\mathcal{H}_0}$, for $\boldsymbol{g} = [g_1, \ldots, g_d]^\top$. Equivalently, $\mathcal{H}$ is the closure of functions of form $\boldsymbol{f}(\boldsymbol{x}) = \sum_i \boldsymbol{a}_i k(\boldsymbol{x}, \boldsymbol{x}_i)$ where $\boldsymbol{a}_i \in \mathbb{R}^d$ with inner product $\langle \boldsymbol{f},\ \boldsymbol{g}\rangle_{\mathcal{H}} = \sum_{ij} \boldsymbol{a}_i^\top \boldsymbol{b}_j k(\boldsymbol{x}_i, \boldsymbol{x}_j)$ for $\boldsymbol{g}(\boldsymbol{x}) = \sum_i \boldsymbol{b}_i k(\boldsymbol{x}, \boldsymbol{x}_i)$. See e.g., Berlinet & Thomas-Agnan (2011) for more background on RKHS.

2.1 Stein Discrepancy as Gradient of KL Divergence

Let $p(\boldsymbol{x})$ be a density function on $\mathbb{R}^d$ which we want to approximate. We assume that we know $p(\boldsymbol{x})$ only up to a normalization constant, that is,

$$p(\boldsymbol{x}) = \frac{1}{Z}\bar{p}(\boldsymbol{x}), \qquad Z = \int \bar{p}(\boldsymbol{x}) d\boldsymbol{x}, \tag{2}$$

where we assume we can only calculate $\bar{p}(\boldsymbol{x})$ and Z is a normalization constant (known as the partition function) that is intractable to calculate exactly. We assume that $\log p(\boldsymbol{x})$ is differentiable w.r.t. $\boldsymbol{x}$, and we have access to $\nabla \log p(\boldsymbol{x}) = \nabla \log \bar{p}(\boldsymbol{x})$ which does not depend on Z.

The main idea of SVGD is to use a set of sequential deterministic transforms to iteratively push a set of particles

$\{\boldsymbol{x}_i\}_{i=1}^n$ towards the target distribution:

$$\begin{aligned}\boldsymbol{x}_i &\leftarrow \boldsymbol{T}(\boldsymbol{x}_i), \qquad \forall i = 1, 2, \cdots, n \\ \boldsymbol{T}(\boldsymbol{x}) &= \boldsymbol{x} + \epsilon\boldsymbol{\phi}(\boldsymbol{x}),\end{aligned} \tag{3}$$

where we choose the transform $\boldsymbol{T}$ to be an additive perturbation by a velocity field $\boldsymbol{\phi}$, with a magnitude controlled by a step size ϵ that is assumed to be small.

The key question is the choice of the velocity field $\boldsymbol{\phi}$; this is done by choosing $\boldsymbol{\phi}$ to maximally decrease the KL divergence between the distribution of particles and the target distribution. Assume the current particles are drawn from q, and $\boldsymbol{T}\sharp q$ is the distribution of the updated particles, that is, $\boldsymbol{T}\sharp q$ is the distribution of $\boldsymbol{x}' = \boldsymbol{T}(\boldsymbol{x}) = \boldsymbol{x} + \epsilon\boldsymbol{\phi}(\boldsymbol{x})$ when $\boldsymbol{x} \sim q$. The optimal $\boldsymbol{\phi}$ should solve the following functional optimization:

$$\mathbb{D}(q \,||\, p) \stackrel{def}{=} \max_{\boldsymbol{\phi}\in\mathcal{F}:\, ||\boldsymbol{\phi}||_{\mathcal{F}}\leq 1} \left\{ -\frac{d}{d\epsilon}\mathrm{KL}(\boldsymbol{T}\sharp q \,||\, p)\,\Big|_{\epsilon=0} \right\}, \tag{4}$$

where $\mathcal{F}$ is a vector-valued normed function space that contains the set of candidate velocity fields $\boldsymbol{\phi}$.

The maximum negative gradient value $\mathbb{D}(q \,||\, p)$ in (4) provides a discrepancy measure between two distributions q and p and is known as *Stein discrepancy* (Gorham & Mackey, 2015; Liu et al., 2016; Chwialkowski et al., 2016): if $\mathcal{F}$ is taken to be large enough, we have $\mathbb{D}(q \,||\, p) = 0$ iff there exists no transform to further improve the KL divergence between p and q, namely $p = q$.

It is necessary to use an infinite dimensional function space $\mathcal{F}$ to obtain good transforms, which then casts a challenging functional optimization problem. Fortunately, it turns out that a simple closed form solution can be obtained by taking $\mathcal{F}$ to be an RKHS $\mathcal{H} = \mathcal{H}_0 \times \cdots \mathcal{H}_0$, where $\mathcal{H}_0$ is a RKHS of scalar-valued functions, associated with a positive definite kernel $k(x, x')$. In this case, Liu et al. (2016) showed that the optimal solution of (4) is $\boldsymbol{\phi}^*/||\boldsymbol{\phi}^*||_{\mathcal{H}}$, where

$$\boldsymbol{\phi}^*(\cdot) = \mathbb{E}_{\boldsymbol{x}\sim q}[\nabla_{\boldsymbol{x}} \log p(\boldsymbol{x})k(\boldsymbol{x}, \cdot) + \nabla_{\boldsymbol{x}}k(\boldsymbol{x}, \cdot)]. \tag{5}$$

In addition, the corresponding Stein discrepancy, known as kernelized Stein discrepancy (KSD) (Liu et al., 2016; Chwialkowski et al., 2016; Gretton et al., 2009; Oates et al., 2016), can be shown to have the following closed form

$$\mathbb{D}(q \,||\, p) = ||\boldsymbol{\phi}^*||_{\mathcal{H}} = \left(\mathbb{E}_{x,x'\sim q}[\kappa_p(\boldsymbol{x}, \boldsymbol{x}')]\right)^{1/2}, \tag{6}$$

where $\kappa_p(x, x')$ is a positive definite kernel defined by

$$\begin{aligned}\kappa_p(\boldsymbol{x}, \boldsymbol{x}') &= \boldsymbol{s}_p(\boldsymbol{x})^\top k(\boldsymbol{x}, \boldsymbol{x}')\boldsymbol{s}_p(\boldsymbol{x}') + \boldsymbol{s}_p(\boldsymbol{x})^\top \nabla_{\boldsymbol{x}'}k(\boldsymbol{x}, \boldsymbol{x}') \\ &+ \boldsymbol{s}_p(\boldsymbol{x}')^\top \nabla_{\boldsymbol{x}}k(\boldsymbol{x}, \boldsymbol{x}') + \nabla_{\boldsymbol{x}} \cdot (\nabla_{\boldsymbol{x}'}k(\boldsymbol{x}, \boldsymbol{x}')).\end{aligned} \tag{7}$$

where $\boldsymbol{s}_p(\boldsymbol{x}) \stackrel{def}{=} \nabla \log p(\boldsymbol{x})$. We refer to Liu et al. (2016) for the derivation of (7), and further treatment of KSD in Chwialkowski et al. (2016); Oates et al. (2016); Gorham & Mackey (2017).

2.2 Stein Variational Gradient Descent

In order to apply the derived optimal transform in the practical SVGD algorithm, we approximate the expectation $\mathbb{E}_{\boldsymbol{x}\sim q}[\cdot]$ in (5) using the empirical averaging of the current particles, that is, given particles $\{\boldsymbol{x}_i^\ell\}_{i=1}^n$ at the ℓ-th iteration, we construct the following velocity field:

$$\boldsymbol{\phi}_{\ell+1}(\cdot) = \frac{1}{n}\sum_{j=1}^n [\nabla \log p(\boldsymbol{x}_j^\ell)k(\boldsymbol{x}_j^\ell, \cdot) + \nabla_{\boldsymbol{x}_j^\ell}k(\boldsymbol{x}_j^\ell, \cdot)]. \tag{8}$$

The SVGD update at the ℓ-th iteration is then given by

$$\begin{aligned}\boldsymbol{x}_i^{\ell+1} &\leftarrow \boldsymbol{T}_{\ell+1}(\boldsymbol{x}_i^\ell), \\ \boldsymbol{T}_{\ell+1}(\boldsymbol{x}) &= \boldsymbol{x} + \epsilon\boldsymbol{\phi}_{\ell+1}(\boldsymbol{x}).\end{aligned} \tag{9}$$

Here transform $\boldsymbol{T}_{\ell+1}$ is adaptively constructed based on the most recent particles $\{\boldsymbol{x}_i^\ell\}_{i=1}^n$. Assume the initial particles $\{\boldsymbol{x}_i^0\}_{i=1}^n$ are i.i.d. drawn from some distribution q_0, then the pushforward maps of $\boldsymbol{T}_\ell$ define a sequence of distributions that bridges between q_0 and p:

$$q_\ell = (\boldsymbol{T}_\ell \circ \cdots \circ \boldsymbol{T}_1)\sharp q_0, \quad \ell = 1, \ldots, K, \tag{10}$$

where q_ℓ forms increasingly better approximation of the target p as ℓ increases. Because $\{\boldsymbol{T}_\ell\}$ are nonlinear transforms, q_ℓ can represent highly complex distributions even when the original q_0 is simple. In fact, one can view q_ℓ as a deep residual network (He et al., 2016) constructed layer-by-layer in a fast, nonparametric fashion.

However, because the transform $\boldsymbol{T}_\ell$ depends on the previous particles $\{\boldsymbol{x}_i^{\ell-1}\}_{i=1}^n$ as shown in (8), the particles $\{\boldsymbol{x}_i^\ell\}_{i=1}^n$, after the zero-th iteration, depend on each other in a complex fashion, and do not, in fact, straightforwardly follow distribution q_ℓ in (10). Principled approaches for analyzing such interacting particle systems can be found in Braun & Hepp (e.g., 1977); Spohn (e.g., 2012); Del Moral (e.g., 2013); Sznitman (e.g., 1991). The goal of this work, however, is to provide a simple method to "decouple" the SVGD dynamics, transforming it into a standard importance sampling method that is amendable to easier analysis and interpretability, and also applicable to more general inference tasks such as estimating partition function of unnormalized distribution where SVGD cannot be applied.

3 DECOUPLING SVGD

In this section, we introduce our main Stein variational importance sampling (SteinIS) algorithm. Our idea is simple. We initialize the particles $\{\boldsymbol{x}_i^0\}_{i=1}^n$ by i.i.d. draws from an initial distribution q_0 and partition them into two sets, including a set of *leader particles* $\boldsymbol{x}_A^\ell = \{\boldsymbol{x}_i^\ell \colon i \in A\}$ and *follower particles* $\boldsymbol{x}_B^\ell = \{\boldsymbol{x}_i^\ell \colon i \in B\}$, with $B = \{1, \ldots, n\} \setminus A$, where the leader particles $\boldsymbol{x}_A^\ell$ are responsible for constructing the transforms, using the standard

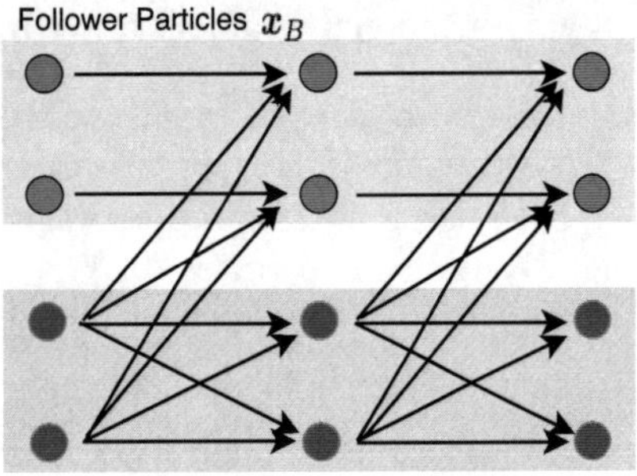

Figure 1: Our method uses a set of leader particles x_A^ℓ (green) to construct the transform map T_ℓ, which follower particles x_B^ℓ follows subsequently. The leader particles x_A^ℓ are interactive and dependent on each other. The follower particles x_B^ℓ can be viewed as i.i.d. draws from q_ℓ, given fixed leader particles x_A^ℓ.

SVGD update (9), while the follower particles x_B^ℓ simply follow the transform maps constructed by x_A^ℓ and do not contribute to the construction of the transforms. In this way, the follower particles x_B^ℓ are independent conditional on the leader particles x_A^ℓ.

Conceptually, we can think that we first construct all the maps T_ℓ by evolving the leader particles x_A^ℓ, and then push the follower particles through T_ℓ in order to draw exact, i.i.d. samples from q_ℓ in (10). Note that this is under the assumption the leader particles x_A^ℓ has been observed and fixed, which is necessary because the transform T_ℓ and distribution q_ℓ depend on x_A^ℓ.

In practice, however, we can simultaneously update both the leader and follower particles, by a simple modification of the original SVGD (9) shown in Algorithm 1 (step 1-2), where the only difference is that we restrict the empirical averaging in (8) to the set of the leader particles x_A^ℓ. The relationship between the particles in set A and B can be more easily understood in Figure 1.

Calculating the Importance Weights Because q_ℓ is still different from p when we only apply finite number of iterations ℓ, which introduces deterministic biases if we directly use x_B^ℓ to approximate p. We address this problem by further turning the algorithm into an importance sampling algorithm with importance proposal q_ℓ. Specifically, we calculate the importance weights of the particles $\{x_i^\ell\}$:

$$w_i^\ell = \frac{\bar{p}(x_i^\ell)}{q_\ell(x_i^\ell)}, \tag{11}$$

where $\bar{p}$ is the unnormalized density of p, that is, $p(x) = \bar{p}(x)/Z$ as in (2). In addition, the importance weights in (11) can be calculated based on the following formula:

$$q_\ell(x^\ell) = q_0(x^0) \prod_{j=1}^{\ell} |\det(\nabla_x T_j(x^{j-1}))|^{-1}, \tag{12}$$

Algorithm 1 Stein Variational Importance Sampling

Goal: Obtain i.i.d. importance sample $\{x_i^K,\ w_i^K\}$ for p.
Initialize x_A^0 and x_B^0 by i.i.d. draws from q_0.
Calculate $\{q_0(x_i^0)\}, \forall i \in B$.
for iteration $\ell = 0, \ldots, K-1$ **do**
1. Construct the map using the leader particles x_A^ℓ

$$\phi_{\ell+1}(\cdot) = \frac{1}{|A|} \sum_{j \in A} [\nabla \log p(x_j^\ell) k(x_j^\ell, \cdot) + \nabla_{x_j^\ell} k(x_j^\ell, \cdot)].$$

2. Update both the leader and follower particles

$$x_i^{\ell+1} \leftarrow x_i^\ell + \epsilon \phi_{\ell+1}(x_i^\ell), \quad \forall i \in A \cup B.$$

3. Update the density values (for $i \in B$) by

$$q_{\ell+1}(x_i^{\ell+1}) = q_\ell(x_i^\ell) \cdot |\det(I \ + \ \epsilon \nabla_x \phi_{\ell+1}(x_i^\ell))|^{-1}$$

end for
Calcuate $w_i^K = p(x_i^K)/q_K(x_i^K), \forall i \in B$.
Outputs: i.i.d. importance sample $\{x_i^K,\ w_i^K\}$ for $i \in B$.

---

where T_ℓ is defined in (9) and we assume that the step size ϵ is small enough so that each T_ℓ is an one-to-one map. As shown in Algorithm 1 (step 3), (12) can be calculated recursively as we update the particles.

With the importance weights calculated, we turn SVGD into a standard importance sampling algorithm. For example, we can now estimate expectations of form $\mathbb{E}_p f$ by

$$\hat{\mathbb{E}}_p[f] = \frac{\sum_{i \in B} w_i^\ell f(x_i^\ell)}{\sum_{i \in B} w_i^\ell},$$

which provides a consistent estimator of $\mathbb{E}_p f$ when we use finite number ℓ of transformations. Here we use the self normalized weights because $\bar{p}(x)$ is unnormalized. Further, the sum of the unnormalized weights provides an unbiased estimation for the normalization constant Z:

$$\hat{Z} = \frac{1}{|B|} \sum_{i \in B} w_i^\ell,$$

which satisfies the unbiasedness property $\mathbb{E}[\hat{Z}] = Z$. Note that the original SVGD does not provide a method for estimating normalization constants, although, as a side result of this work, Section 4 will discuss another method for estimating Z that is more directly motivated by SVGD.

We now analyze the time complexity of our algorithm. Let $\alpha(d)$ be the cost of computing $s_p(x)$ and $\beta(d)$ be the cost of evaluating kernel $k(x, x')$ and its gradient $\nabla k(x, x')$. Typically, both $\alpha(d)$ and $\beta(d)$ grow linearly with the dimension d. In most cases, $\alpha(d)$ is much larger than $\beta(d)$. The complexity of the original SVGD with $|A|$ particles is $O(|A|\alpha(d) + |A|^2\beta(d))$, and the complexity of Algorithm 1 is $O(|A|\alpha(d) + |A|^2\beta(d) + |B||A|\beta(d) + |B|d^3)$, where the $O(|B|d^3)$ complexity comes from calculating the determinant of the Jacobian matrix, which is expensive when dimension d is high, but is the cost to pay for having a consistent importance sampling estimator in finite iterations and for being able to estimate the normalization constant Z. Also, by calculating the effective sample size based on the importance weights, we can assess the accuracy of the estimator, and early stop the algorithm when a confidence threshold is reached.

One way to speed up our algorithm in empirical experiments is to parallelize the computation of Jacobian matrices for all follower particles in GPU. It is possible, however, to develop efficient approximation for the determinants by leveraging the special structure of the Jacobean matrix; note that

$$\nabla_{\boldsymbol{y}} \boldsymbol{T}(\boldsymbol{y}) = I + \epsilon A,$$
$$A = \frac{1}{n}\sum_{j=1}^{n} [\nabla_{\boldsymbol{x}} \log p(\boldsymbol{x}_j)^\top \nabla_{\boldsymbol{y}} k(\boldsymbol{x}_j, \boldsymbol{y}) + \nabla_{\boldsymbol{x}} \nabla_{\boldsymbol{y}} k(\boldsymbol{x}_j, \boldsymbol{y})].$$

Therefore, $\nabla_{\boldsymbol{y}} \boldsymbol{T}(\boldsymbol{y})$ is close to the identity matrix I when the step size is small. This allows us to use Taylor expansion for approximation:

Proposition 1. *Assume $\epsilon < 1/\rho(A)$, where $\rho(A)$ is the spectral radius of A, that is, $\rho(A) = \max_j |\lambda_j(A)|$ and $\{\lambda_j\}$ are the eigenvalues of A. We have*

$$\det(I + \epsilon A) = \prod_{k=1}^{d} (1 + \epsilon a_{kk}) + O(\epsilon^2), \tag{13}$$

where $\{a_{kk}\}$ are the diagonal elements of A.

Proof. Use the Taylor expansion of $\det(I + \epsilon A)$. □

Therefore, one can approximate the determinant with approximation error $O(\epsilon^2)$ using linear time $O(d)$ w.r.t. the dimension. Often the step size is decreasing with iterations, and a way to trade-off the accuracy with computational cost is to use the exact calculation in the beginning when the step size is large, and switch to the approximation when the step size is small.

3.1 Monotone Decreasing of KL divergence

One nice property of algorithm 1 is that the KL divergence between the iterative distribution q_ℓ and p is monotonically decreasing. This property can be more easily understood by considering our iterative system in continuous evolution time as shown in Liu (2017). Take the step size ϵ of the transformation defined in (3) to be infinitesimal, and define the continuos time $t = \epsilon\ell$. Then the evolution equation of random variable $\boldsymbol{x}^t$ is governed by the following nonlinear partial differential equation (PDE),

$$\frac{d\boldsymbol{x}^t}{dt} = \mathbb{E}_{\boldsymbol{x}\sim q_t}[\boldsymbol{s}_p(\boldsymbol{x})k(\boldsymbol{x}, \boldsymbol{x}^t) + \nabla_{\boldsymbol{x}} k(\boldsymbol{x}, \boldsymbol{x}^t)], \tag{14}$$

where t is the current evolution time and q_t is the density function of $\boldsymbol{x}^t$. The current evolution time $t = \epsilon\ell$ when ϵ is small and ℓ is the current iteration. We have the following proposition (see also Liu (2017)):

Proposition 2. *Suppose random variable $\boldsymbol{x}^t$ is governed by PDE (14), then its density q_t is characterized by*

$$\frac{\partial q_t}{\partial t} = -\mathrm{div}(q_t \mathbb{E}_{\boldsymbol{x}\sim q_t}[\boldsymbol{s}_p(\boldsymbol{x})k(\boldsymbol{x}, \boldsymbol{x}^t) + \nabla_{\boldsymbol{x}} k(\boldsymbol{x}, \boldsymbol{x}^t)]), \tag{15}$$

where $\mathrm{div}(\boldsymbol{f}) = \mathrm{trace}(\nabla \boldsymbol{f}) = \sum_{i=0}^{d} \partial f_i(\boldsymbol{x})/\partial x_i$, and $\boldsymbol{f} = [f_1, \ldots, f_d]^\top$.

The proof of proposition 2 is similar to the proofs of proposition 1.1 in Jourdain & Méléard (1998). Proposition 2 characterizes the evolution of the density function $q_t(\boldsymbol{x}^t)$ when the random variable $\boldsymbol{x}^t$ is evolved by (14). The continuous system captured by (14) and (15) is a type of Vlasov process which has wide applications in physics, biology and many other areas (e.g., Braun & Hepp, 1977). As a consequence of proposition 2, one can show the following nice property:

$$\frac{d\mathrm{KL}(q_t \,||\, p)}{dt} = -\mathbb{D}(q_t \,||\, p)^2 < 0, \tag{16}$$

which is proved by theorem 4.4 in Liu (2017). Equation (16) indicates that the KL divergence between the iterative distribution q_t and p is monotonically decreasing with a rate of $\mathbb{D}(q_t \,||\, p)^2$.

4 A PATH INTEGRATION METHOD

We mentioned that the original SVGD does not have the ability to estimate the partition function. Section 3 addressed this problem by turning SVGD into a standard importance sampling algorithm in Section 3. Here we introduce another method for estimating KL divergence and normalization constants that is more directly motivated by the original SVGD, by leveraging the fact that the Stein discrepancy is a type of gradient of KL divergence. This method does not need to estimate the importance weights but has to run SVGD to converge to diminish the Stein discrepancy between intermediate distribution q_ℓ and p. In addition, this method does not perform as well as Algorithm 1 as we find empirically. Nevertheless, we find this idea is conceptually interesting and useful to discuss it.

Recalling Equation (4) in Section 2.1, we know that if we perform transform $\boldsymbol{T}(\boldsymbol{x}) = \boldsymbol{x} + \epsilon\boldsymbol{\phi}^*(\boldsymbol{x})$ with $\boldsymbol{\phi}^*$ defined in (5), the corresponding decrease of KL divergence would

Algorithm 2 SVGD with Path Integration for estimating $\mathrm{KL}(q_0 \,||\, p)$ and $\log Z$

1: **Input:** Target distribution $p(x) = \bar{p}(x)/Z$; an initial distribution q_0.
2: **Goal:** Estimating $\mathrm{KL}(q_0 \,||\, p)$ and the normalization constant $\log Z$.
3: Initialize $\hat{K} = 0$. Initialize particles $\{\boldsymbol{x}_i^0\}_{i=1}^n \sim q_0(\boldsymbol{x})$.
4: Compute $\hat{\mathbb{E}}_{q_0}[\log(q_0(\boldsymbol{x})/\bar{p}(\boldsymbol{x}))]$ via sampling from q_0.
5: **while** iteration ℓ **do**
6:
$$\hat{K} \leftarrow \hat{K} + \epsilon \hat{\mathbb{D}}(q_\ell \,||\, p)^2,$$
$$\boldsymbol{x}_i^{\ell+1} \leftarrow \boldsymbol{x}_i^\ell + \boldsymbol{\phi}_{\ell+1}(\boldsymbol{x}_i^\ell),$$
where $\hat{\mathbb{D}}(q_\ell \,||\, p)$ is defined in (19).
7: **end while**
8: Estimate $\mathrm{KL}(q_0 \,||\, p)$ by $\hat{K}$ and $\log Z$ by $\hat{\mathbb{D}} - \hat{\mathbb{E}}_{q_0}[\log(q_0(\boldsymbol{x})/\bar{p}(\boldsymbol{x}))]$.

be

$$\begin{aligned}\mathrm{KL}(q \,||\, p) - \mathrm{KL}(\boldsymbol{T}\sharp q \,||\, p) &\approx \epsilon \cdot ||\boldsymbol{\phi}^*||_{\mathcal{H}} \cdot \mathbb{D}(q \,||\, p) \\ &\approx \epsilon \cdot \mathbb{D}(q \,||\, p)^2,\end{aligned} \tag{17}$$

where we used the fact that $\mathbb{D}(q \,||\, p) = ||\boldsymbol{\phi}^*||_{\mathcal{H}}$, shown in (6). Applying this recursively on q_ℓ in (17), we get

$$\mathrm{KL}(q_0 \,||\, p) - \mathrm{KL}(q_{\ell+1} \,||\, p) \approx \sum_{j=0}^{\ell} \epsilon \cdot \mathbb{D}(q_j \,||\, p)^2.$$

Assuming $\mathrm{KL}(q_\ell \,||\, p) \to 0$ when $\ell \to \infty$, we get

$$\mathrm{KL}(q_0 \,||\, p) \approx \sum_{\ell=0}^{\infty} \epsilon \cdot \mathbb{D}(q_\ell \,||\, p)^2. \tag{18}$$

By (6), the square of the KSD can be empirically estimated via V-statistics, which is given as

$$\hat{\mathbb{D}}(q_\ell \,||\, p)^2 = \frac{1}{n^2} \sum_{i,j=1}^{n} \kappa(\boldsymbol{x}_i^\ell, \boldsymbol{x}_j^\ell). \tag{19}$$

Overall, equation (18) and (19) give an estimator of the KL divergence between q_0 and $p = \bar{p}(\boldsymbol{x})/Z$. This can be transformed into an estimator of the log normalization constant $\log Z$ of p, by noting that

$$\log Z = \mathrm{KL}(q_0 \,||\, p) - \mathbb{E}_{q_0}[\log(q_0(\boldsymbol{x})/\bar{p}(\boldsymbol{x}))], \tag{20}$$

where the second term can be estimated by drawing a lot of samples to diminish its variance since the samples from q_0 is easy to draw. The whole procedure is summarized in Algorithm 2.

5 EMPIRICAL EXPERIMENTS

We study the empirical performance of our proposed algorithms on both simulated and real world datasets. We start with toy examples to numerically investigate some theoretical properties of our algorithms, and compare it with traditional adaptive IS on non-Gaussian, multi-modal distributions. We also employ our algorithm to estimate the partition function of Gaussian-Bernoulli Restricted Boltzmann Machine(RBM), a graphical model widely used in deep learning (Welling et al., 2004; Hinton & Salakhutdinov, 2006), and to evaluate the log likelihood of decoder models in variational autoencoder (Kingma & Welling, 2013).

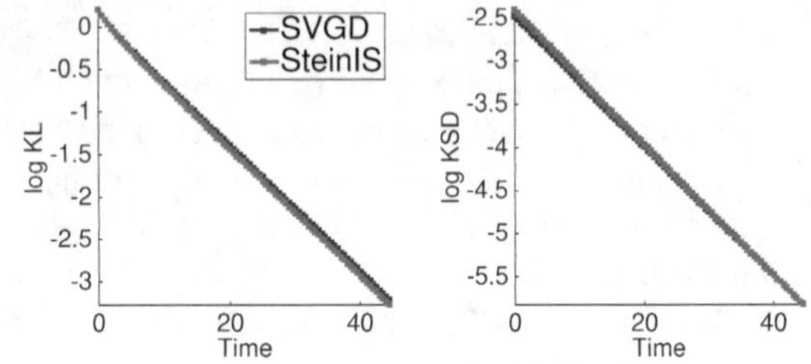

(a) KL (b) KSD

Figure 2: GMM with 10 mixture components. $d = 1$. In SVGD, 500 particles are evolved. In SteinIS, $|A| = 200$ and $|B| = 500$. For SVGD and SteinIS, all particles are drawn from the same Gaussian distribution $q_0(\boldsymbol{x})$.

We summarize some hyperparameters used in our experiments. We use RBF kernel $k(\boldsymbol{x}, \boldsymbol{x}') = \exp(-\|\boldsymbol{x} - \boldsymbol{x}'\|^2/h)$, where h is the bandwidth. In most experiments, we let $h = \mathrm{med}^2/(2\log(|A|+1))$, where med is the median of the pairwise distance of the current leader particles $\boldsymbol{x}_A^\ell$, and $|A|$ is the number of leader particles. The step sizes in our algorithms are chosen to be $\epsilon = \alpha/(1+\ell)^\beta$, where α and β are hyperparameters chosen from a validation set to achieve best performance. When $\epsilon \leq 0.1$, we use first-order approximation to calculate the determinants of Jacobian matrices as illustrated in proposition 1.

In what follows, we use "AIS" to refer to the annealing importance sampling with Langevin dynamics as its Markov transitions, and use "HAIS" to denote the annealing importance sampling whose Markov transition is Hamiltonian Monte Carlo (HMC). We use "transitions" to denote the number of intermediate distributions constructed in the paths of both SteinIS and AIS. A transition of HAIS may include L leapfrog steps, as implemented by Wu et al. (2016).

5.1 Gaussian Mixtures Models

We start with testing our methods on simple 2 dimensional Gaussian mixture models (GMM) with 10 randomly generated mixture components. First, we numerically investigate the convergence of KL divergence between the particle distribution q_t (in continuous time) and p. Sufficient particles are drawn and infinitesimal step ϵ is taken to closely simulate the continuous time system, as defined by (14),

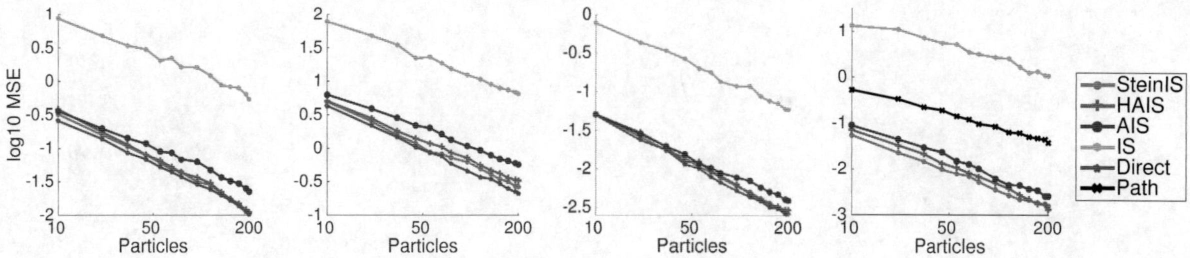

(a) $\mathbb{E}[x]$ (b) $\mathbb{E}[x^2]$ (c) $\mathbb{E}[\cos(wx+b)]$ (d) Partition Function

Figure 3: 2D GMM with 10 randomly generated mixture components. (a)-(c) shows mean square error(MSE) for estimating $\mathbb{E}_p[h(x)]$, where $h(\boldsymbol{x}) = x_j,\ x_j^2,\ \cos(wx_j + b)$ with $w \sim \mathcal{N}(0, 1)$ and $b \in \text{Uniform}([0, 1])$ for $j = 1, 2$, and the normalization constant (which is 1 in this case). We used 800 transitions in SteinIS, HAIS and AIS, and take $L = 1$ in HAIS. We fixed the size of the leader particles $|A|$ to be 100 and vary the size of follower particles $|B|$ in SteinIS. The initial proposal q_0 is the standard Gaussian. "Direct" means that samples are directly drawn from p and is not applicable in (d). "IS" means we directly draw samples from q_0 and apply standard importance sampling. "Path" denotes path integration method in Algorithm 2 and is only applicable to estimate the partition function in (d). The MSE is averaged on each coordinate over 500 independent experiments for SteinIS, HAIS, AIS and Direct, and over 2000 independent experiments for IS. SVGD has similar results (not shown for clarity) as our SteinIS on (a), (b), (c), but can not be applied to estimate the partition function in task (d). The logarithm base is 10.

(15) and (16). Figrue 2(a)-(b) show that the KL divergence $\text{KL}(q_t, p)$, as well as the squared Stein discrepancy $\mathbb{D}(q_t, p)^2$, seem to decay exponentially in both SteinIS and the original SVGD. This suggests that the quality of our importance proposal q_t improves quickly as we apply sufficient transformations. However, it is still an open question to establish the exponential decay theoretically; see Liu (2017) for a related discussion.

We also empirically verify the convergence property of our SteinIS as the follower particle size $|B|$ increases (as the leader particle size $|A|$ is fixed). We apply SteinIS to estimate $\mathbb{E}_p[h(x)]$, where $h(\boldsymbol{x}) = x_j,\ x_j^2$ *or* $\cos(wx_j+b)$ with $w \sim \mathcal{N}(0, 1)$ and $b \sim \text{Uniform}([0, 1])$ for $j = 1, 2$, and the partition function (which is trivially 1 in this case). From Figure 3, we can see that the mean square error(MSE) of our algorithms follow the typical convergence rate of IS, which is $O(1/\sqrt{|B|})$, where $|B|$ is the number of samples for performing IS. Figure 3 indicates that SteinIS can achieve almost the same performance as the exact Monte Carlo (which directly draws samples from the target p), indicating the proposal q_ℓ closely matches the target p.

5.2 Comparison between SteinIS and Adaptive IS

In the following, we compare SteinIS with traditional adaptive IS (Ryu & Boyd, 2014) on a probability model $p(\boldsymbol{x})$, obtained by applying nonlinear transform on a three-component Gaussian mixture model. Specifically, let $\widetilde{q}$ be a 2D Gaussian mixture model, and $\boldsymbol{T}$ is a nonlinear transform defined by $\boldsymbol{T}(\boldsymbol{z}) = [a_1 z_1 + b_1, a_2 z_1^2 + a_3 z_2 + b_2]^\top$, where $\boldsymbol{z} = [z_1, z_2]^\top$. We define the target p to be the distribution of $\boldsymbol{x} = \boldsymbol{T}(\boldsymbol{z})$ when $\boldsymbol{z} \sim \widetilde{q}$. The contour of the target density p we constructed is shown in Figure 4(h). We test our SteinIS with $|A| = 100$ particles and visualize in Figure 4(a)-(d) the density of the evolved distribution q_ℓ using kernel density estimation, by drawing a large number of follower particles. We compare our method with the adaptive IS by (Ryu & Boyd, 2014) using a proposal family formed by Gaussian mixture with 200 components. The densities of the proposals obtained by adaptive IS at different iterations are shown in Figure 4(e)-(g). We can see that the evolved proposals of SteinIS converge to the target density $p(\boldsymbol{x})$ and approximately match $p(\boldsymbol{x})$ at 2000 iterations, but the optimal proposal of adaptive IS with 200 mixture components (at the convergence) can not fit $p(\boldsymbol{x})$ well, as indicated by Figure 4(g). This is because the Gaussian mixture proposal family (even with upto 200 components) can not closely approximate the non-Gaussian target distribution we constructed. We should remark that SteinIS can be applied to refine the optimal proposal given by adaptive IS to get better importance proposal by implementing a set of successive transforms on the given IS proposal.

Qualitatively, we find that the KL divergence (calculated via kernel density estimation) between our evolved proposal q_ℓ and p decreases to ≤ 0.003 after 2000 iterations, while the KL divergence between the optimal adaptive IS proposal and the target p can be only decreased to 0.42 even after sufficient optimization.

5.3 Gauss-Bernoulli Restricted Boltzmann Machine

We apply our method to estimate the partition function of Gauss-Bernoulli Restricted Boltzmann Machine (RBM), which is a multi-modal, hidden variable graphical model. It consists of a continuous observable variable $\boldsymbol{x} \in \mathbb{R}^d$ and a binary hidden variable $\boldsymbol{h} \in \{\pm 1\}^{d'}$, with a joint probability

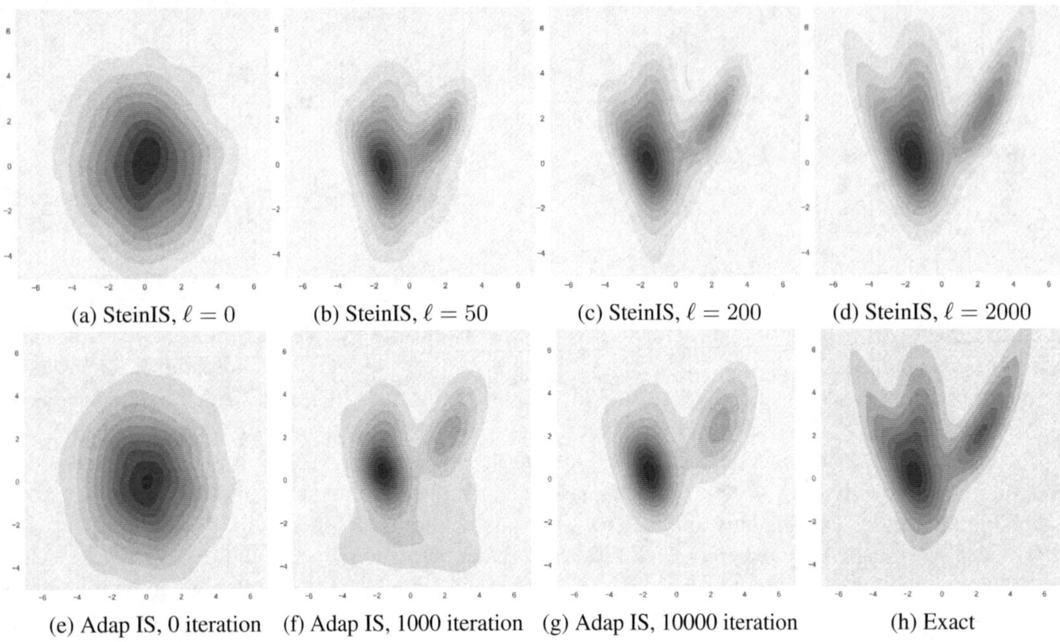

(a) SteinIS, $\ell = 0$ (b) SteinIS, $\ell = 50$ (c) SteinIS, $\ell = 200$ (d) SteinIS, $\ell = 2000$

(e) Adap IS, 0 iteration (f) Adap IS, 1000 iteration (g) Adap IS, 10000 iteration (h) Exact

Figure 4: Evolution of the contour of density functions for SteinIS and Adaptive IS. The top row (a)-(d) shows the contours of the evolved density functions in SteinIS, and bottom row (c)-(g) are the evolved contours of the traditional adaptive IS with Gaussian mixture proposals. (h) is the contour of the target density p. The number of the mixture components for adaptive IS is 200 and the number of leader particles for approximating the map in SteinIS is also 200.

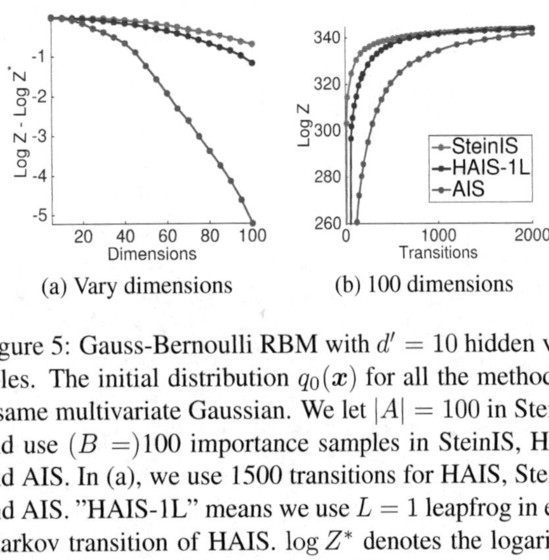

(a) Vary dimensions (b) 100 dimensions

Figure 5: Gauss-Bernoulli RBM with $d' = 10$ hidden variables. The initial distribution $q_0(\boldsymbol{x})$ for all the methods is a same multivariate Gaussian. We let $|A| = 100$ in SteinIS and use $(B =)100$ importance samples in SteinIS, HAIS and AIS. In (a), we use 1500 transitions for HAIS, SteinIS and AIS. "HAIS-1L" means we use $L = 1$ leapfrog in each Markov transition of HAIS. $\log Z^*$ denotes the logarithm of the exact normalizing constant. All experiments are averaged over 500 independent trails.

density function of form

$$p(\boldsymbol{x}, \boldsymbol{h}) = \frac{1}{Z}\exp(\boldsymbol{x}^{\mathrm{T}}B\boldsymbol{h} + b^{\mathrm{T}}\boldsymbol{x} + c^{\mathrm{T}}\boldsymbol{h} - \frac{1}{2}\|\boldsymbol{x}\|_2^2), \quad (21)$$

where $p(\boldsymbol{x}) = \frac{1}{Z}\sum_{\boldsymbol{h}} p(\boldsymbol{x}, \boldsymbol{h})$ and Z is the normalization constant. By marginalzing the hidden variable h, we can show that $p(\boldsymbol{x})$ is

$$p(\boldsymbol{x}) = \frac{1}{Z}\exp(b^{\mathrm{T}}\boldsymbol{x} - \frac{1}{2}\|\boldsymbol{x}\|_2^2)\prod_{i=1}^{d'}[\exp(\varphi_i) + \exp(-\varphi_i)],$$

where $\varphi = B^{\mathrm{T}}\boldsymbol{x} + c$, and its score function $\boldsymbol{s}_p$ is easily derived as

$$\boldsymbol{s}_p(\boldsymbol{x}) = \nabla_{\boldsymbol{x}} \log p(\boldsymbol{x}) = b - \boldsymbol{x} + B\frac{\exp(2\varphi) - 1}{\exp(2\varphi) + 1}.$$

In our experiments, we simulate a true model $p(\boldsymbol{x})$ by drawing b and c from standard Gaussian and select B uniformly random from $\{0.5, -0.5\}$ with probability 0.5. The dimension of the latent variable $\boldsymbol{h}$ is 10 so that the probability model $p(\boldsymbol{x})$ is the mixture of 2^{10} multivariate Gaussian distribution. The exact normalization constant Z can be feasibly calculated using the brute-force algorithm in this case. Figure 5(a) and Figure 5(b) shows the performance of SteinIS on Gauss-Bernoulli RBM when we vary the dimensions of the observed variables and the number of transitions in SteinIS, respectively. We can see that SteinIS converges slightly faster than HAIS which uses one leapfrog step in each of its Markov transition. Even with the same number of Markov transitions, AIS with Langevin dynamics converges much slower than both SteinIS and HAIS. The better performance of HAIS comparing to AIS was also observed by Sohl-Dickstein & Culpepper (2012) when they first proposed HAIS.

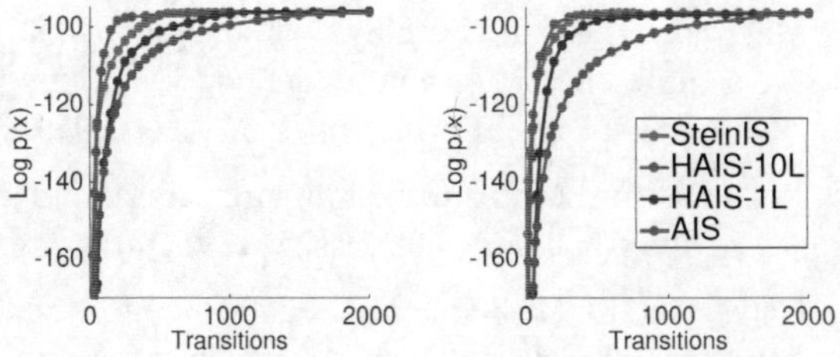

(a) 20 hidden variables (b) 50 hidden variables

Figure 6: Calculating the testing log-likelihood $\log p(x)$ for the deep generative model on MNIST. The initial distribution q_0 used in SteinIS, HAIS and AIS is a same multivariate Gaussian. We let $|A| = 60$ in SteinIS and use 60 samples for each image to implement IS in HAIS and AIS. "HAIS-10L" and "HAIS-1L" denote using $L = 10$ and $L = 1$ in each Markov transition of HAIS, respectively. The log-likelihood $\log p(x)$ is averaged over 1000 images randomly chosen from MNIST. Figure (a) and (b) show the results when using 20 and 50 hidden variables, respectively. Note that the dimension of the observable variable $\boldsymbol{x}$ is fixed, and is the size of the MNIS images.

5.4 Deep Generative Models

Finally, we implement our SteinIS to evaluate the log-likelihoods of the decoder models in variational autoencoder (VAE) (Kingma & Welling, 2013). VAE is a directed probabilistic graphical model. The decoder-based generative model is defined by a joint distribution over a set of latent random variables $\boldsymbol{z}$ and the observed variables $\boldsymbol{x} : p(\boldsymbol{x}, \boldsymbol{z}) = p(\boldsymbol{x} \mid \boldsymbol{z})p(\boldsymbol{z})$. We use the same network structure as that in Kingma & Welling (2013). The prior $p(\boldsymbol{z})$ is chosen to be a multivariate Gaussian distribution. The log-likelihood is defined as $p(\boldsymbol{x}) = \int p(\boldsymbol{x} \mid \boldsymbol{z})p(\boldsymbol{z})d\boldsymbol{z}$, where $p(\boldsymbol{x} \mid \boldsymbol{z})$ is the Bernoulli MLP as the decoder model given in Kingma & Welling (2013). In our experiment, we use a two-layer network for $p(\boldsymbol{x} \mid \boldsymbol{z})$, whose parameters are estimated using a standard VAE based on the MNIST training set. For a given observed test image $\boldsymbol{x}$, we use our method to sample the posterior distribution $p(\boldsymbol{z}|\boldsymbol{x}) = \frac{1}{p(\boldsymbol{x})}p(\boldsymbol{x}|\boldsymbol{z})p(\boldsymbol{z})$, and estimate the partition function $p(x)$, which is the testing likelihood of image $\boldsymbol{x}$.

Figure 6 also indicates that our SteinIS converges slightly faster than HAIS-1L which uses one leapfrog step in each of its Markov transitions, denoted by HAIS-1L. Meanwhile, the running time of SteinIS and HAIS-1L is also comparable as provided by Table 1. Although HAIS-10L, which use 10 leapfrog steps in each of its Markov transition, converges faster than our SteinIS, it takes much more time than our SteinIS in our implementation since the leapfrog steps in the Markov transitions of HAIS are sequential and can not be parallelized. See Table 5.4. Compared with HAIS and AIS, our SteinIS has another advantage: if we want to increase the transitions from 1000 to 2000 for better accuracy, SteinIS can build on the result from 1000 transitions and just need to run another 1000 iterations, while HAIS cannot take advantage of the result from 1000 transitions and have to independently run another 2000 transitions.

Table 1: Running Time (in seconds) on MNIST, using the same setting as in Figure 6. We use 1000 transitions in all methods to test the running time.

Dimensions of z	10	20	50
SteinIS	224.40	226.17	261.76
HAIS-10L	600.15	691.86	755.44
HAIS-1L	157.76	223.30	256.23
AIS	146.75	206.89	230.14

6 CONCLUSIONS

In this paper, we propose an nonparametric adaptive importance sampling algorithm which leverages the nonparametric transforms of SVGD to maximumly decrease the KL divergence between our importance proposals and the target distribution. Our algorithm turns SVGD into a typical adaptive IS for more general inference tasks. Numerical experiments demonstrate that our SteinIS works efficiently on the applications such as estimating the partition functions of graphical models and evaluating the log-likelihood of deep generative models. Future research includes improving the computational and statistical efficiency in high dimensional cases, more theoretical investigation on the convergence of $\mathrm{KL}(q_\ell \,||\, p)$, and incorporating Hamiltonian Monte Carlo into our SteinIS to derive more efficient algorithms.

Acknowledgments

This work is supported in part by NSF CRII 1565796. We thank Yuhuai Wu from Toronto for his valuable comments.

References

Berlinet, Alain and Thomas-Agnan, Christine. *Reproducing kernel Hilbert spaces in probability and statistics*. Springer Science & Business Media, 2011.

Braun, W and Hepp, K. The Vlasov dynamics and its fluctuations in the 1/n limit of interacting classical particles. *Communications in mathematical physics*, 56(2): 101–113, 1977.

Cappé, Olivier, Douc, Randal, Guillin, Arnaud, Marin, Jean-Michel, and Robert, Christian P. Adaptive importance sampling in general mixture classes. *Statistics and Computing*, 18(4):447–459, 2008.

Chwialkowski, Kacper, Strathmann, Heiko, and Gretton, Arthur. A kernel test of goodness of fit. In *Proceedings of the International Conference on Machine Learning (ICML)*, 2016.

Cotter, Colin, Cotter, Simon, and Russell, Paul. Parallel adaptive importance sampling. *arXiv preprint arXiv:1508.01132*, 2015.

Del Moral, Pierre. *Mean field simulation for Monte Carlo integration*. CRC Press, 2013.

Gelman, Andrew and Meng, Xiao-Li. Simulating normalizing constants: From importance sampling to bridge sampling to path sampling. *Statistical science*, pp. 163–185, 1998.

Gorham, Jackson and Mackey, Lester. Measuring sample quality with Stein's method. In *Advances in Neural Information Processing Systems*, pp. 226–234, 2015.

Gorham, Jackson and Mackey, Lester. Measuring sample quality with kernels. *arXiv preprint arXiv:1703.01717*, 2017.

Gretton, Arthur, Fukumizu, Kenji, Harchaoui, Zaid, and Sriperumbudur, Bharath K. A fast, consistent kernel two-sample test. In *Advances in neural information processing systems*, pp. 673–681, 2009.

He, Kaiming, Zhang, Xiangyu, Ren, Shaoqing, and Sun, Jian. Deep residual learning for image recognition. In *Proceedings of the IEEE Conference on Computer Vision and Pattern Recognition*, pp. 770–778, 2016.

Hinton, Geoffrey E and Salakhutdinov, Ruslan R. Reducing the dimensionality of data with neural networks. *science*, 313(5786):504–507, 2006.

Hoffman, Matthew D, Blei, David M, Wang, Chong, and Paisley, John William. Stochastic variational inference. *Journal of Machine Learning Research*, 14(1):1303–1347, 2013.

Jourdain, B and Méléard, S. Propagation of chaos and fluctuations for a moderate model with smooth initial data. In *Annales de l'Institut Henri Poincare (B) Probability and Statistics*, volume 34, pp. 727–766. Elsevier, 1998.

Kingma, Diederik P and Welling, Max. Auto-encoding variational Bayes. *arXiv preprint arXiv:1312.6114*, 2013.

Kingma, Diederik P, Salimans, Tim, Jozefowicz, Rafal, Chen, Xi, Sutskever, Ilya, and Welling, Max. Improved variational inference with inverse autoregressive flow. In *Advances in Neural Information Processing Systems*, pp. 4743–4751, 2016.

Liu, Qiang. Stein variational gradient descent as gradient flow. *arXiv preprint arXiv:1704.07520*, 2017.

Liu, Qiang and Wang, Dilin. Stein variational gradient descent: A general purpose Bayesian inference algorithm. In *Advances In Neural Information Processing Systems*, pp. 2370–2378, 2016.

Liu, Qiang, Lee, Jason D, and Jordan, Michael I. A kernelized Stein discrepancy for goodness-of-fit tests. In *Proceedings of the International Conference on Machine Learning (ICML)*, 2016.

Marzouk, Youssef, Moselhy, Tarek, Parno, Matthew, and Spantini, Alessio. An introduction to sampling via measure transport. *arXiv preprint arXiv:1602.05023*, 2016.

Neal, Radford M. Annealed importance sampling. *Statistics and Computing*, 11(2):125–139, 2001.

Oates, Chris J, Girolami, Mark, and Chopin, Nicolas. Control functionals for Monte Carlo integration. *Journal of the Royal Statistical Society: Series B (Statistical Methodology)*, 2016.

Rezende, Danilo and Mohamed, Shakir. Variational inference with normalizing flows. In *Proceedings of The 32nd International Conference on Machine Learning*, pp. 1530–1538, 2015.

Ryu, Ernest K and Boyd, Stephen P. Adaptive importance sampling via stochastic convex programming. *arXiv preprint arXiv:1412.4845*, 2014.

Sohl-Dickstein, Jascha and Culpepper, Benjamin J. Hamiltonian annealed importance sampling for partition function estimation. *arXiv preprint arXiv:1205.1925*, 2012.

Spantini, Alessio, Bigoni, Daniele, and Marzouk, Youssef. Inference via low-dimensional couplings. *arXiv preprint arXiv:1703.06131*, 2017.

Spohn, Herbert. *Large scale dynamics of interacting particles*. Springer Science & Business Media, 2012.

Sznitman, Alain-Sol. Topics in propagation of chaos. In *Ecole d'été de probabilités de Saint-Flour XIX1989*, pp. 165–251. Springer, 1991.

Welling, Max, Rosen-Zvi, Michal, and Hinton, Geoffrey E. Exponential family harmoniums with an application to information retrieval. In *Nips*, volume 4, pp. 1481–1488, 2004.

Wu, Yuhuai, Burda, Yuri, Salakhutdinov, Ruslan, and Grosse, Roger. On the quantitative analysis of decoder-based generative models. *arXiv preprint arXiv:1611.04273*, 2016.

Continuously tempered Hamiltonian Monte Carlo

Matthew M. Graham
School of Informatics
University of Edinburgh

Amos J. Storkey
School of Informatics
University of Edinburgh

Abstract

Hamiltonian Monte Carlo (HMC) is a powerful Markov chain Monte Carlo (MCMC) method for performing approximate inference in complex probabilistic models of continuous variables. In common with many MCMC methods, however, the standard HMC approach performs poorly in distributions with multiple isolated modes. We present a method for augmenting the Hamiltonian system with an extra continuous temperature control variable which allows the dynamic to bridge between sampling a complex target distribution and a simpler unimodal base distribution. This augmentation both helps improve mixing in multimodal targets and allows the normalisation constant of the target distribution to be estimated. The method is simple to implement within existing HMC code, requiring only a standard leapfrog integrator. We demonstrate experimentally that the method is competitive with annealed importance sampling and simulating tempering methods at sampling from challenging multimodal distributions and estimating their normalising constants.

1 INTRODUCTION

Applications of *Markov chain Monte Carlo* (MCMC) methods to perform inference in challenging statistical physics problems were among the earliest uses of the first modern electronic computers [38]. In the years since, MCMC methods have become a mainstay for performing approximate inference in complex probabilistic models in most fields of computational science. Statistical physics in particular has continued to contribute to key developments of MCMC methodology, such as tempering methods [17, 30, 41] and gradient-based dynamics [11].

The aim in MCMC methods is to construct an aperiodic and irreducible Markov chain which leaves a target distribution invariant, so that samples from the chain can be used to form Monte Carlo estimates of expectations with respect to the target distribution. Several general purpose constructions have been developed for specifying valid Markov transition operators for arbitrary target distributions, including Metropolis–Hastings methods [21, 31], slice sampling [9, 35] and Gibbs sampling [13, 16].

While these methods give a basis for constructing chains that will asymptotically give correct inferences, producing algorithms that will give reasonable results in a practical amount of time is still a major challenge. For the restricted case of target distributions defined by densities that are differentiable functions of a real-valued vector variable, *Hamiltonian Monte Carlo* (HMC)[1] [11, 36] provides a framework for defining efficient Markov chains that exploit the gradient of the target density.

Although HMC is able to efficiently explore contiguous regions of high probability density in a target distribution, as with most MCMC methods using local moves it struggles to move between isolated modes in multimodal target distributions [36]. Tempering methods [17, 30, 41] which augment the state space with an temperature variable are often used to improve exploration in multimodal distributions. As the temperature variable is typically discrete however it cannot be included in HMC updates.

In this paper we present an alternative *continuous tempering* approach which instead augments the state with a continuous temperature variable. This allows use of HMC to jointly update both the temperature and original state, making the method simple to use with existing HMC implementations. The proposed approach both improves exploration of multimodal densities and also provides estimates of the typically unknown normalising constant of the target density, which is often an important inferential quantity in its own right for model comparison [15].

[1] Originally termed *Hybrid Monte Carlo* in [11].

2 HAMILTONIAN MONTE CARLO

HMC can be used to perform inference whenever the target distribution of interest is defined on a random vector $\mathbf{x} \in \mathbb{R}^D = \mathcal{X}$, by a density function which is differentiable and has support almost everywhere in $\mathcal{X}$. Distributions with bounded support can often be mapped to an equivalent unbounded distribution by performing a change of variables via a smooth bijective map [8, 24]. We will follow the common convention of defining the target density in a Boltzmann-Gibbs form in terms of a real-valued *potential energy* function $\phi : \mathcal{X} \to \mathbb{R}$ and a (typically unknown) normalising constant Z,

$$\mathrm{p}_{\mathbf{x}}(\boldsymbol{x}) = \frac{1}{Z} \exp(-\phi(\boldsymbol{x})). \tag{1}$$

The key idea of HMC is to simulate a Hamiltonian dynamic in an extended state space to form long-range proposals for a Metropolis accept-reject step with a high probability of acceptance. The *target vector* $\mathbf{x}$ is augmented with a *momentum vector* $\mathbf{p} \in \mathbb{R}^D$. Typically the momentum is chosen to be independent of $\mathbf{x}$ with marginal $\mathrm{p}_{\mathbf{p}}(\boldsymbol{p}) \propto \exp(-\tau(\boldsymbol{p}))$, with a joint density

$$\mathrm{p}_{\mathbf{x},\mathbf{p}}(\boldsymbol{x}, \boldsymbol{p}) = \mathrm{p}_{\mathbf{x}}(\boldsymbol{x})\, \mathrm{p}_{\mathbf{p}}(\boldsymbol{p}) \propto \exp(-\phi(\boldsymbol{x}) - \tau(\boldsymbol{p})). \tag{2}$$

With analogy to classical dynamics, $\tau(\boldsymbol{x})$ is referred to as the *kinetic energy* and $h(\boldsymbol{x}, \boldsymbol{p}) = \phi(\boldsymbol{x}) + \tau(\boldsymbol{p})$ is termed the *Hamiltonian*. By construction, marginalising the joint density over the momenta recovers $\mathrm{p}_{\mathbf{x}}(\boldsymbol{x})$.

Each HMC update involves a discrete-time simulation of the canonical Hamiltonian dynamic

$$\frac{\mathrm{d}\boldsymbol{x}}{\mathrm{d}t} = \frac{\partial h}{\partial \boldsymbol{p}}^{\mathsf{T}} = \frac{\partial \tau}{\partial \boldsymbol{p}}^{\mathsf{T}} \qquad \frac{\mathrm{d}\boldsymbol{p}}{\mathrm{d}t} = -\frac{\partial h}{\partial \boldsymbol{x}}^{\mathsf{T}} = -\frac{\partial \phi}{\partial \boldsymbol{x}}^{\mathsf{T}} \tag{3}$$

which conserves the Hamiltonian and is time-reversible and volume-preserving. Through choice of an appropriate symplectic integrator such as the popular leapfrog (Störmer-Verlet) scheme, the simulated discrete time dynamic remains exactly time-reversible and volume-preserving and also approximately conserves the Hamiltonian even over long simulated trajectories [28].

The discrete-time dynamic is used to generate a new proposed state $(\boldsymbol{x}', \boldsymbol{p}')$ given the current state $(\boldsymbol{x}, \boldsymbol{p})$ and this proposal accepted or rejected in a Metropolis step with acceptance probability $\min\{1, \exp(h(\boldsymbol{x}, \boldsymbol{p}) - h(\boldsymbol{x}', \boldsymbol{p}'))\}$. Due to the approximate Hamiltonian conservation the acceptance probability is typically close to one, and so HMC is able to make long-range moves in high-dimensional state-spaces while still maintaining high acceptance rates, a significant improvement over the behaviour typical of simpler Metropolis–Hastings methods in high-dimensions.

The energy conservation property which gives this desirable behaviour also however suggests that standard HMC updates are unlikely to move between isolated modes in a target distribution. The Hamiltonian is approximately conserved over a trajectory therefore $\phi(\boldsymbol{x}') - \phi(\boldsymbol{x}) \approx \tau(\boldsymbol{p}) - \tau(\boldsymbol{p}')$. Typically a quadratic kinetic energy $\tau(\boldsymbol{p}) = \boldsymbol{p}^{\mathsf{T}} \boldsymbol{M}^{-1} \boldsymbol{p} \,/\, 2$ is used corresponding to a Gaussian marginal density on the momentum. As this kinetic energy is bounded below by zero, the maximum change in potential energy over a trajectory is approximately equal to the initial kinetic energy.

At equilibrium the momenta will have a Gaussian distribution and so the kinetic energy a χ^2 distribution with mean $D/2$ and variance D [2, 36]. If potential energy barriers significantly larger than $\sim D$ separate regions of the configuration state space the HMC updates are unlikely to move across the barriers meaning impractically long sampling runs will be needed for effective ergodicity.

3 THERMODYNAMIC METHODS

A common approach in MCMC methods for dealing with multimodal target distributions is to introduce a concept of temperature. In statistical mechanics, the Boltzmann distribution on a configuration $\mathbf{x}$ of a mechanical system with energy function ϕ and in thermal equilibrium with a heat bath at temperature T is defined by a probability density $\exp(-\beta\phi(\boldsymbol{x}))/z(\beta)$ where $\beta = (k_B T)^{-1}$ is the *inverse temperature*, k_B is Boltzmann's constant and $z(\beta)$ is the *partition function*. At high temperatures ($\beta \to 0$) the density function becomes increasingly flat across the target state space and, correspondingly, energy barriers between different regions of the state space become lower.

In the above statistical mechanics formulation, if $\mathbf{x} \in \mathbb{R}^D$ the distribution in the limit $\beta \to 0$ has an improper flat density across the target state space. More usefully from a statistical perspective we can use an inverse temperature variable $\beta \in [0, 1]$ to geometrically bridge between a simple *base distribution* with normalised density $\exp(-\psi(\boldsymbol{x}))$ at $\beta = 0$ and the target distribution at $\beta = 1$

$$\pi(\boldsymbol{x} \mid \beta) = \exp(-\beta\phi(\boldsymbol{x}) - (1-\beta)\psi(\boldsymbol{x})), \tag{4}$$

$$z(\beta) = \int_{\mathcal{X}} \exp(-\beta\phi(\boldsymbol{x}) - (1-\beta)\psi(\boldsymbol{x}))\,\mathrm{d}\boldsymbol{x}. \tag{5}$$

Several approaches to introducing a system temperature in to MCMC methods have been proposed. In *simulated tempering* (ST) [30] an ordered set of inverse temperatures are chosen

$$\{\beta_n\}_{n=0}^{N} : 0 = \beta_0 < \beta_1 < \cdots < \beta_N = 1, \tag{6}$$

and a joint distribution defined with density

$$\mathrm{p}_{\mathbf{x},\beta}(\boldsymbol{x}, \beta_n) \propto \pi(\boldsymbol{x} \mid \beta_n) \exp(w_n), \tag{7}$$

where $\{w_n\}_{n=0}^N$ are a set of prior weights associated with each inverse temperature. Alternating MCMC updates of $\beta \mid \mathbf{x}$ and $\mathbf{x} \mid \beta$ are performed, with $\mathbf{x}$ samples for which $\beta = 1$ converging in distribution to the target. Updates of the inverse temperature variable can propose moves to a limited set of neighbouring inverse temperatures or sample β independently from its conditional $\mathrm{p}_{\beta|\mathbf{x}}(\beta_n \mid \boldsymbol{x})$.

The ratio of the marginal densities of $\mathrm{p}_\beta(1)$ and $\mathrm{p}_\beta(0)$ can be related to the usually unknown normalising constant Z for the target density by

$$Z = \exp(w_0 - w_N)\, \mathrm{p}_\beta(1)/\mathrm{p}_\beta(0), \tag{8}$$

allowing estimation of Z from a ST chain by computing the ratio of counts of samples with $\beta = 1$ and $\beta = 0$. As an alternative [7] proposes to instead use a '*Rao-Blackwellised*' estimator for Z based on the identity

$$\mathrm{p}_\beta(\beta_n) = \int_{\mathcal{X}} \mathrm{p}_{\beta|\mathbf{x}}(\beta_n \mid \boldsymbol{x}) \mathrm{p}_{\mathbf{x}}(\boldsymbol{x})\, \mathrm{d}\boldsymbol{x} \tag{9}$$

which indicates $\mathrm{p}_\beta(\beta_n)$ can be estimated by averaging the conditional probabilities $\mathrm{p}_{\beta|\mathbf{x}}(\beta_n \mid \boldsymbol{x})$ across samples of $\mathbf{x}$ from the joint in (7). The authors empirically demonstrate this estimator can give significantly improved estimation accuracy over the simpler count-based estimator.

A problem for ST methods is that as $\mathrm{p}_\beta(\beta_n) \propto z(\beta_n)\exp(w_n)$ and the partition function can vary across several orders of magnitude, the chain can mix poorly between inverse temperatures. This is often tackled with an iterative approach in which initial pilot runs are used to estimate $\mathrm{p}_\beta(\beta_n)$ and the weights $\{w_n\}_{n=0}^N$ set so as to try to flatten out this marginal distribution [18].

An alternative is *parallel tempering* (PT) [12, 17, 41], where multiple Markov chains on the target state are run in parallel, with the nth chain having an associated inverse temperature β_n defined as in (6). MCMC updates are performed on each chain which leave a distribution with unnormalised density $\pi(\boldsymbol{x} \mid \beta_n)$ invariant. Interleaved with these updates, exchanges of the states of the chains at adjacent inverse temperatures (β_n, β_{n+1}) are proposed in a Metropolis–Hastings step. Parallel tempering sidesteps the issue with mixing between inverse temperatures in ST by keeping the inverse temperatures for the chains fixed, at a cost of a significantly increased state size.

Annealed Importance Sampling (AIS) [34] is another thermodynamic ensemble method, closely related to *Tempered Transitions* [33] and often the 'go-to' method for normalising constant estimation in the machine learning literature e.g [39, 43]. In AIS an ordered set of inverse temperatures are defined as in (6) and a corresponding series of transition operators $\{\mathsf{T}_n\}_{n=1}^{N-1}$. Each T_n leaves a distribution with unnormalised density $\pi(\boldsymbol{x} \mid \beta_n)$ invariant. Assuming the base distribution corresponding to $\beta_0 = 0$ can be sampled from independently, an independent state $\boldsymbol{x}^{(0)}$ from this distribution is generated and then the transition operators applied in a fixed sequence $\mathsf{T}_1 \dots \mathsf{T}_{N-1}$ to generate a chain of intermediate states $\{\boldsymbol{x}^{(n)}\}_{n=1}^{N-1}$. The product of ratios

$$r = \prod_{n=0}^{N-1} \left(\pi\left(\boldsymbol{x}^{(n)} \mid \beta_{n+1}\right)/\pi\left(\boldsymbol{x}^{(n)} \mid \beta_n\right)\right) \tag{10}$$

is an importance weight for the final state $\boldsymbol{x}^{(N-1)}$ with respect to the target distribution (1) and also an unbiased estimator for Z. By simulating multiple independent runs of this process, a set of importance weighted samples can be computed to estimate expectations with respect to the target (1) and the weights r used to unbiasedly estimate Z. Due to Jensen's inequality the unbiased estimate of Z corresponds to a stochastic lower bound on $\log Z$ [20].

In cases where an exact sample from the target distribution can be generated, running reversed AIS from the target to base distribution allow calculating an unbiased estimate of Z^{-1} and so a stochastic upper bound on $\log Z$ [20]. This combination of stochastically lower bounding $\log Z$ by forward AIS runs and stochastically upper bounding by reverse AIS runs is termed *bidirectional Monte Carlo*.

4 CONTINUOUS TEMPERING

In all three of AIS, PT and ST the choice of the discrete inverse temperature schedule (6) is key to getting the methods to perform well in complex high dimensional distributions [1, 3, 33]. To get reasonable performance it may be necessary to do preliminary pilot runs to guide the number of inverse temperatures and spacing between them to use, adding to the computational burden and difficulty of using these methods in a black-box fashion. A natural question is therefore whether it is possible to use a continuously varying inverse temperature variable.

Path sampling [15] proposes this approach, defining a general *path* as a function parametrised by β which continuously maps between the target density $\exp(-\phi(\boldsymbol{x}))/Z$ at $\beta = 1$ and a base density $\exp(-\psi(\boldsymbol{x}))$ at $\beta = 0$, with the geometric bridge in (4) a particular example. A joint target $\mathrm{p}_{\mathbf{x},\beta}(\boldsymbol{x}, \beta) \propto \pi(\boldsymbol{x} \mid \beta)\, \rho(\beta)$ is defined with $\rho(\beta)$ a chosen prior on the inverse temperature variable analogous to the weights $\{w_n\}_{n=0}^N$ in simulated tempering. In [15] it is proposed to construct a Markov chain leaving the joint density invariant by alternating updates of $\mathbf{x} \mid \beta$ and $\beta \mid \mathbf{x}$. Samples from the joint system can be used to estimate Z via the *thermodynamic integration* identity

$$\log Z = \int_0^1 \int_{\mathcal{X}} \frac{\mathrm{p}_{\mathbf{x},\beta}(\boldsymbol{x}, \beta)}{\mathrm{p}_\beta(\beta)} \frac{\partial \log \pi(\boldsymbol{x} \mid \beta)}{\partial \beta}\, \mathrm{d}\boldsymbol{x}\, \mathrm{d}\beta. \tag{11}$$

Adiabatic Monte Carlo [3] also proposes using a continuously varying inverse temperature variable, here specifically in the context of HMC. The original Hamiltonian system $(\mathbf{x}, \mathbf{p})$ is further augmented with a continuous inverse temperature coordinate $\beta \in [0, 1]$. A *contact Hamiltonian* is defined on the augmented system,

$$h_c(\boldsymbol{x}, \boldsymbol{p}, \beta) = \beta\phi(\boldsymbol{x}) + (1-\beta)\psi(\boldsymbol{x}) + \frac{1}{2}\boldsymbol{p}^{\mathsf{T}}\boldsymbol{M}^{-1}\boldsymbol{p} + \log z(\beta) + h_0 \tag{12}$$

this defining a corresponding *contact Hamiltonian flow*,

$$\frac{\mathrm{d}\boldsymbol{x}}{\mathrm{d}t} = \frac{\partial h_c}{\partial \boldsymbol{p}}^{\mathsf{T}}, \quad \frac{\mathrm{d}\boldsymbol{p}}{\mathrm{d}t} = \frac{\partial h_c}{\partial \beta}\boldsymbol{p} - \frac{\partial h_c}{\partial \boldsymbol{x}}^{\mathsf{T}}, \quad \frac{\mathrm{d}\beta}{\mathrm{d}t} = h_c - \frac{\partial h_c}{\partial \boldsymbol{p}}\boldsymbol{p}. \tag{13}$$

The contact Hamiltonian flow restricted to the zero level-set of the contact Hamiltonian (which the initial state can always be arranged to lie in by appropriately choosing the arbitrary constant h_0) generates trajectories which exactly conserve the contact Hamiltonian and extended state space volume element, and correspond to the thermodynamical concept of a reversible adiabatic process.

For a quadratic kinetic energy, $\frac{\mathrm{d}\beta}{\mathrm{d}t}$ is always non-positive and so forward simulation of the contact Hamiltonian flow generates non-increasing trajectories in β (and backwards simulation generates non-decreasing trajectories in β). In the ideal case this allows the inverse temperature range $[0, 1]$ to be coherently traversed without the random-walk exploration inherent to simulated tempering.

Simulating the contact Hamiltonian flow is non-trivial in practice however: the contact Hamiltonian (12) depends on the log partition function $\log z(\beta)$, the partial derivatives of which require computing expectations with respect to $\pi(\boldsymbol{x} \mid \beta)$ which for most problems is intractable to do exactly. Moreover the contact flow can encounter meta-stabilities whereby $\frac{\mathrm{d}\beta}{\mathrm{d}t}$ becomes zero and the flow halts at an intermediate β meaning the flow no longer defines a bijection between $\beta = 0$ and $\beta = 1$. This can be ameliorated by regular resampling of the momenta however this potentially increases random-walk behaviour.

An alternative *extended Hamiltonian approach* for simulating a system with a continuously varying inverse temperature was proposed recently in the statistical physics literature [19]. The inverse temperature of the system is indirectly set via an auxiliary variable, which we will term a *temperature control variable* $\mathrm{u} \in \mathbb{R}$. This control variable is mapped to an interval $[s, 1]$, $0 < s < 1$ via a smooth piecewise defined function $\beta : \mathbb{R} \to [s, 1]$, with the conditions that for a pair of thresholds (θ_1, θ_2) with $0 < \theta_1 < \theta_2$, $\beta(u) = 1 \ \forall\ |u| \leq \theta_1$, $\beta(u) = s \ \forall\ |u| \geq \theta_2$ and $s < \beta(u) < 1 \ \forall\ \theta_1 < |u| < \theta_2$.

Unlike Adiabatic Monte Carlo, an additional momentum variable v corresponding to u is also introduced. Although seemingly a minor difference this simplifies the implementation of the approach significantly as the system retains a symplectic structure and can continue to be viewed within the usual Hamiltonian dynamics framework. An *extended Hamiltonian* is defined on the augmented system

$$\tilde{h}(\boldsymbol{x}, u, \boldsymbol{p}, v) = \beta(u)\phi(\boldsymbol{x}) + \omega(u) + \frac{1}{2}\boldsymbol{p}^{\mathsf{T}}\boldsymbol{M}^{-1}\boldsymbol{p} + \frac{v^2}{2m} \tag{14}$$

where ω is a 'confining potential' on u and m is the mass (marginal variance) associated with v. This extended Hamiltonian is separable with respect to the extended configuration $(\mathbf{x}, \mathrm{u})$ and extended momentum $(\mathbf{p}, \mathrm{v})$ and so can be efficiently simulated using a standard leapfrog integrator. In [19] the extended Hamiltonian dynamics are integrated using a Langevin scheme without Metropolis adjustment and shown to improve mixing in several molecular dynamics problems.

Due to the condition $\beta(u) = 1 \ \forall\ |u| < \theta_1$, the set of sampled configuration states $\mathbf{x}$ which have associated $|\mathrm{u}| < \theta_1$ will (assuming the dynamic is ergodic and Metropolis adjustment were used) asymptotically converge in distribution to the target, and so can be used to estimate expectations without any importance re-weighting. The β function is required to be bounded below by a $s > 0$ in [19] due to the base density being bridged to being an improper uniform density on $\mathcal{X}$. The partition function $z(\beta) \to \infty$ as $\beta \to 0$ in this case, which would imply an infinite density for regions in the extended state space where $\beta(\mathrm{u}) = 0$. Even with a non-zero lower bound on β, the large variations in $z(\beta(\mathrm{u}))$ across different u values can lead to the dynamic poorly exploring the u dimension.

In [19] this issue is tackled by introducing an adaptive history-dependent biasing potential on u to try to achieve a flat density across a bounded interval $|\mathrm{u}| < \theta_2$, using for example metadynamics [25]. The resulting non-Markovian updates bias the invariant distribution of the target state however this can be accounted for either by a re-weighting scheme [5], or using a vanishing adaptation.

5 PROPOSED METHOD

As in [19] we define an extended Hamiltonian on an augmented state $(\mathbf{x}, \mathrm{u})$ with associated momenta $(\mathbf{p}, \mathrm{v})$,

$$\tilde{h}(\boldsymbol{x}, u, \boldsymbol{p}, v) = \beta(u)(\phi(\boldsymbol{x}) + \log\zeta) + (1-\beta(u))\psi(\boldsymbol{x}) - \log\left|\frac{\partial\beta}{\partial u}\right| + \frac{1}{2}\boldsymbol{p}^{\mathsf{T}}\boldsymbol{M}^{-1}\boldsymbol{p} + \frac{v^2}{2m}. \tag{15}$$

As with the approach of [19], this Hamiltonian is separable and the corresponding dynamic can be efficiently simulated with a leapfrog integrator. The reversible and volume-preserving simulated dynamic can then be used as a proposal generating mechanism on the joint space ($\mathbf{x}$, u, $\mathbf{p}$, v) for a Metropolis–Hastings step as in standard HMC. We will term this approach of running HMC in the extended joint space *joint continuous tempering*.

In contrast to [19] we propose to use a smooth monotonically increasing map $\beta : \mathbb{R} \to [0, 1]$ as the inverse temperature function, with our default choice in all experiments being the logistic sigmoid $\beta(u) = (1 + \exp(-u))^{-1}$.

As previously ψ is the negative logarithm of a simple *normalised* base density, which (as we will motivate in the next section) we will usually choose to be an approximation to the target density (1). Similarly the $\log \zeta$ term will be chosen to be an approximation to $\log Z$.

We can marginalise out the momenta from the joint distribution defined by this Hamiltonian, giving a joint density

$$\mathrm{p}_{\mathbf{x},\mathrm{u}}(\boldsymbol{x}, u) \propto \left|\frac{\partial \beta}{\partial u}\right| \exp\Big(-\beta(u)(\phi(\boldsymbol{x}) + \log \zeta) - (1 - \beta(u))\psi(\boldsymbol{x})\Big). \tag{16}$$

If we define a variable $\mathrm{\beta} = \beta(\mathrm{u})$ and use the change of variables formula for a density, we further have that

$$\mathrm{p}_{\mathbf{x},\mathrm{\beta}}(\boldsymbol{x}, \beta) \propto \frac{1}{\zeta\beta} \exp(-\beta\phi(\boldsymbol{x}) - (1 - \beta)\psi(\boldsymbol{x})) \tag{17}$$

The bijectivity between u and $\mathrm{\beta}$ is useful as although if simulating a Hamiltonian dynamic we will generally wish to work with u as it is unbounded, the conditional density on $\mathrm{\beta}$ given $\mathbf{x}$ has a tractable normalised form

$$\mathrm{p}_{\mathrm{\beta}|\mathbf{x}}(\beta \mid \boldsymbol{x}) = \frac{\exp(-\beta\Delta(\boldsymbol{x}))\Delta(\boldsymbol{x})}{1 - \exp(-\Delta(\boldsymbol{x}))}, \tag{18}$$

with $\Delta(\boldsymbol{x}) = \phi(\boldsymbol{x}) + \log \zeta - \psi(\boldsymbol{x})$. This corresponds to an exponential distribution with rate parameter $\Delta(\boldsymbol{x})$ truncated to $[0, 1]$. As an alternative to the joint updates, another option is therefore to form a Markov chain which leaves (17) invariant by alternating independently sampling $\mathrm{\beta}$ from its conditional given $\mathbf{x}$ and performing a transition which leaves the conditional on $\mathbf{x}$ given $\mathrm{\beta}$ invariant, similar to the suggested approach in [15]. We will term this Gibbs sampling type procedure as *Gibbs continuous tempering*.

Further we can use (18) to write the marginal density $\mathrm{p}_{\mathrm{\beta}}$

$$\mathrm{p}_{\mathrm{\beta}}(\beta) = \mathbb{E}\left[\frac{\exp(-\beta\Delta(\mathbf{x}))\Delta(\mathbf{x})}{1 - \exp(-\Delta(\mathbf{x}))}\right]. \tag{19}$$

By integrating the joint (17) over $\mathcal{X}$ we also have that

$$\mathrm{p}_{\mathrm{\beta}}(\beta) = \frac{1}{C\zeta^{\beta}} \int_{\mathcal{X}} \pi(\boldsymbol{x} \mid \beta)\,\mathrm{d}\boldsymbol{x} = \frac{z(\beta)}{C\zeta^{\beta}} \Rightarrow \mathrm{p}_{\mathrm{\beta}}(0) = \frac{1}{C},\ \mathrm{p}_{\mathrm{\beta}}(1) = \frac{Z}{C\zeta}, \tag{20}$$

for an unknown normalising constant C of the joint, and so for MCMC samples $\left\{\boldsymbol{x}^{(s)}, \beta^{(s)}\right\}_{s=1}^{S}$ from the joint (17)

$$Z = \frac{\mathrm{p}_{\mathrm{\beta}}(1)}{\mathrm{p}_{\mathrm{\beta}}(0)}\zeta = \lim_{S\to\infty} \frac{\sum_{s=1}^{S}\left(w_1\left(\boldsymbol{x}^{(s)}\right)\right)}{\sum_{s=1}^{S}\left(w_0\left(\boldsymbol{x}^{(s)}\right)\right)}\zeta, \tag{21}$$

with $w_0(\boldsymbol{x}) = \dfrac{\Delta(\boldsymbol{x})}{1 - \exp(-\Delta(\boldsymbol{x}))}$, $w_1(\boldsymbol{x}) = \dfrac{\Delta(\boldsymbol{x})}{\exp(\Delta(\boldsymbol{x})) - 1}$.

This can be seen to be a continuous analogue of the *Rao-Blackwellised* estimator (9) used in [7]. Similarly we can calculate consistent estimates of expectations with respect to the target density $\mathrm{p}_{\mathbf{x}|\mathrm{\beta}}(\boldsymbol{x} \mid 1) = \exp(-\phi(\boldsymbol{x}))/Z$ as importance weighted sums

$$\mathbb{E}\left[f(\mathbf{x}) \mid \mathrm{\beta} = 1\right] = \frac{\int_{\mathcal{X}} f(\boldsymbol{x})\,\mathrm{p}_{\mathrm{\beta}|\mathbf{x}}(1 \mid \boldsymbol{x})\,\mathrm{p}_{\mathbf{x}}(\boldsymbol{x})\,\mathrm{d}\boldsymbol{x}}{\int_{\mathcal{X}} \mathrm{p}_{\mathrm{\beta}|\mathbf{x}}(1 \mid \boldsymbol{x})\,\mathrm{p}_{\mathbf{x}}(\boldsymbol{x})\,\mathrm{d}\boldsymbol{x}} \approx \frac{\sum_{s=1}^{S}\left(w_1\left(\boldsymbol{x}^{(s)}\right) f\left(\boldsymbol{x}^{(s)}\right)\right)}{\sum_{s=1}^{S}\left(w_1\left(\boldsymbol{x}^{(s)}\right)\right)}. \tag{22}$$

We can also estimate expectations with respect to the base density $\mathrm{p}_{\mathbf{x}|\mathrm{\beta}}(\boldsymbol{x} \mid 0) = \exp(-\psi(\boldsymbol{x}))$ using

$$\mathbb{E}\left[f(\mathbf{x}) \mid \mathrm{\beta} = 0\right] \approx \frac{\sum_{s=1}^{S}\left(w_0\left(\boldsymbol{x}^{(s)}\right) f\left(\boldsymbol{x}^{(s)}\right)\right)}{\sum_{s=1}^{S}\left(w_0\left(\boldsymbol{x}^{(s)}\right)\right)}. \tag{23}$$

Often the base density will have known moments (e.g. mean and covariance of a Gaussian base density) which can be compared to the estimates calculated using (23) to check for convergence problems. Convergence of the estimates to the true moments is not a sufficient condition for convergence of the chain to the target joint density (17) but is necessary.

6 CHOOSING A BASE DENSITY

By applying Hölder's and Jensen's inequalities we can bound $\mathrm{p}_{\mathrm{\beta}}(\beta)$ (see Appendix A for details)

$$\frac{1}{C}\left(\frac{Z}{\zeta}\right)^{\beta} \exp\left(-\beta d^{b\to t}\right) \leq \mathrm{p}_{\mathrm{\beta}}(\beta) \leq \frac{1}{C}\left(\frac{Z}{\zeta}\right)^{\beta}, \tag{24}$$

where $d^{b\to t}$ indicates the *Kullback–Leibler* (KL) divergence from the base to target distribution

$$d^{b\to t} = \int_{\mathcal{X}} \exp(-\psi(\boldsymbol{x})) \log\left(\frac{\exp(-\psi(\boldsymbol{x}))}{\exp(-\phi(\boldsymbol{x}))/Z}\right) \mathrm{d}\boldsymbol{x}. \tag{25}$$

If $\zeta = Z$ the upper-bound is constant. If additionally we had $d^{b\to t} = 0$, the bound becomes tight and we would have a flat marginal density on $\mathrm{\beta}$, which we should improve mixing in the $\mathrm{\beta}$ dimension. In reality we do not know Z and cannot choose a base distribution such that

$d^{b \to t} = 0$ as we wish to use a simple distribution amenable to exploration. However under the constraint of the base distribution allowing exploration, a reasonable heuristic is to minimise the KL divergence to the target distribution. Further we want ζ as close to Z as possible.

Variational inference is an obvious route for tackling both problems, allowing us to fit a base density in a simple parametric family (e.g. Gaussian) by directly minimising the KL divergence (25) while also giving a lower bound on $\log Z$. In some cases we can use variational methods specifically aimed at the target distribution family. More generally methods such as *Automatic Differentiation Variational Inference* (ADVI) [24] provide a black-box framework for fitting variational approximations to differentiable target densities. In models such as Variational Autoencoders [23, 37] a parametric variational approximation to the target density of interest (e.g. posterior on latent space) is fitted during training of the original model, in which case it provides a natural choice for the base distribution as observed in [43].

A potential problem is that the classes of target distribution that we are particularly interested in applying our approach to — those with multiple isolated modes — are precisely the same distributions that simple variational approximations will tend to fit poorly, the divergence (25) being minimised favouring 'mode-seeking' solutions [4], which usually fit only one mode well. This both limits how small the divergence from the base to target can be made, but also crucially is undesirable as we wish to use the base distribution to move between modes in the target. One option would be to instead to minimise the reversed form of the KL divergence from the target to base distribution, this tending to produce 'mode-covering' solutions that match global moments (and can also be used to produce an analogous lower bound on the marginal density to that for $d^{b \to t}$ in (24) as shown in Appendix A). Methods such as *expectation propagation* (EP) [32] do allow moment-matching approximations to be found and may be a good option in some cases. Another possibility would be to use an alternative divergence in a variational framework that favours mode-covering solutions, with methods using the χ-divergence [10] and Rényi divergence [29] having been recently proposed in this context.

A further alternative is to fit multiple local variational approximations $\{q_i(\boldsymbol{x})\}_{i=1}^{L}$ by minimising the variational objective from multiple random parameter initialisations (discarding any duplicate solutions as measured by some distance tolerance between the variational parameters), each approximating a single mode well. We can then combine these local approximations into a global approximation $q(\boldsymbol{x})$, for example using a mixture model

$$q(\boldsymbol{x}) = \frac{1}{\zeta} \sum_{i=1}^{L} \left(\exp(\ell_i) q_i(\boldsymbol{x})\right), \quad \zeta = \sum_{i=1}^{L} \exp(\ell_i), \quad (26)$$

with ℓ_i the final variational objective value for q_i ($\log Z$ minus the KL divergence from q_i to target distribution). If the local approximations had non-overlapping support this would lead to a global approximation which is guaranteed to be at least as close in KL divergence as any of the local approximations and a $\log \zeta$ which is at least as tight a lower bound on $\log Z$ as any of the individual ℓ_i [45]. A mixture distribution is unlikely to itself be a good choice of base distribution however, as it will tend to be multimodal. We can therefore instead use a base distribution with moments matched to the fitted mixture, e.g. a Gaussian $\exp[-\psi(\boldsymbol{x})]$ with mean and covariance matched to the mean and covariance of the mixture $q(\boldsymbol{x})$.

For complex target distributions it will sometimes remain difficult to find a reasonable ψ and $\log \zeta$ which well approximate ϕ and $\log Z$. If the KL divergence from the base to target distribution is high, the bounds on the marginal in (24) become increasingly loose and this tends to lead to low densities on intermediate inverse temperatures. This reduces the ability of the MCMC dynamic to move between the inverse temperatures corresponding to the target and base distributions and so the mixing gain from the augmentation. Similarly from (20) the density ratio $\mathrm{p}_\beta(1) / \mathrm{p}_\beta(0)$ is $\exp(\log Z - \log \zeta)$, and so for large $|\log Z - \log \zeta|$ the dynamic will tend to spend most of the time close to $\beta = 1$ if $\log Z > \log \zeta$ or $\beta = 0$ if $\log Z < \log \zeta$. In the former case there will be limited gain from using the extended space while in the latter the variance of the estimator in (22) will be comparable to directly using an importance sampling estimator for the target using samples from the base distribution.

A natural approach to try to ameliorate these effects is to use an iterative 'bootstrap' method. An initial ψ and $\log \zeta$ are chosen for example using a Gaussian variational approximation to the target density as described above. A Markov chain which leaves the joint density (17) invariant is then simulated. The samples from this chain can then be used to both compute an estimate for $\log Z$ using (21) and updated estimates of the target density mean and covariance using (22). A new Gaussian base density can then be specified with the updated mean and covariance estimates and $\log \zeta$ chosen to be the updated $\log Z$ estimate. Samples of the new joint density can then be used to update $\log \zeta$ and ψ again and so on. This is analogous to the iterative approaches often used in ST to choose the prior weights on the inverse temperatures [7, 18].

7 EXPERIMENTS

We performed a series of experiments comparing our proposed approaches to existing methods. Code for running all experiments is available at `https://git.io/cthmc`. Appendix A shows an additional illustrative example.

7.1 BOLTZMANN MACHINE RELAXATIONS

As a first experiment we performed inference in Gaussian mixture relaxations of a set of ten synthetic Boltzmann machine distributions [44]. The parameters of the Boltzmann machine distributions were randomly generated so that the corresponding relaxations are highly multimodal and so challenging to explore well. A 2D projection of samples from one generated distribution illustrating this multimodality is shown in Figure 5 in Appendix C.

The moments of the relaxation distributions can be calculated from the moments of the original discrete Boltzmann machine distribution, which for models with a small number of binary units D_B (30 in our experiments) can be computed exactly by exhaustive iteration across the 2^{D_B} discrete states. This allows ground truth moments to be calculated against which convergence can be checked. The parametrisation used is described in in Appendix B. A Gaussian base density and approximate normalising constant ζ was fit to each the 10 relaxation target densities by matching moments to a mixture of variational Gaussian approximations (individually fitted using a mean-field approach based on the underlying Boltzmann machine distribution) as described in section 6.

Plots showing the *root mean squared error* (RMSE) in estimates of $\log Z$ and the mean and covariance of the relaxation distribution against computational run time for different sampling methods are shown in Figure 1. The RMSE values are normalised by the RMSEs of the corresponding estimated moments used in the base density (and $\log \zeta$) such that values below unity indicate an improvement in accuracy over the variational approximation. The curves shown are RMSEs averaged over 10 independent runs for each of the 10 generated parameter sets, with the filled regions indicating ± 3 standard errors of the mean. The free parameters of all methods were tuned on one parameter set and these values then fixed across all runs. All methods used a shared Theano [42] implementation running on a Intel Core i5-2400 quad-core CPU for the HMC updates and so run times are roughly comparable.

For ST, *Rao Blackwellised* estimators were used as described in [7], with HMC-based updates of the target state $\mathbf{x} \mid \beta$ interleaved with independent sampling of $\beta \mid \mathbf{x}$, and 1000 β_n values used. For AIS, HMC updates were used for the transition operators and separate runs with 1000, 5000 and 10000 β_n values used to obtain estimates at different run times. For the tempering approaches run times correspond to increasing numbers of MCMC samples.

The two *continuous tempering* (CT) approaches, Gibbs CT and joint CT, both dominate in terms of having lower average RMSEs in all three moment estimates across all run times, with joint CT showing marginally better performance on estimates of $\log Z$ and $\mathbb{E}[\mathbf{x}]$. The tempering approaches seem to outperform AIS here, possibly as the highly multimodal nature of the target densities favours the ability of tempered dynamics to move the inverse temperature both up and down and so in and out of modes in the target density, unlike AIS where the fixed temperature updates are more likely to end up with chains confined to a single mode after the initial transitions for low β_n.

7.2 HIERARCHICAL REGRESSION MODEL

As a second experiment, we apply our joint continuous tempering approach to perform Bayesian inference in a hierarchical regression model for predicting indoor radon measurements [14]. To illustrate the ease of integrating our approach in existing HMC-based inference software, this experiment was performed with the Python package PyMC3 [40], with its ADVI feature used to fit the base density and its implementation of the adaptive *No U-Turn Sampler* (NUTS) [22] HMC variant used to sample from the extended space.

The regression target in the dataset is measurements of the amount of radon gas $\mathrm{y}^{(i)}$ in $N = 919$ households. Two continuous regressors $\boldsymbol{x}^{(i)}$ and one categorical regressor $c^{(i)}$ are provided per household. A multilevel regression model defined by the factor graph in 2a was used. The model includes five scalar parameters $(\sigma_{\mathbf{a}}, \mu_{\mathbf{a}}, \sigma_{\mathbf{b}}, \mu_{\mathbf{b}}, \varepsilon)$, an 85-dimensional intercept vector $\mathbf{a}$ and a two-dimensional regressor coefficients vector $\mathbf{b}$, giving 92 parameters in total. As an example task, we consider inferring the marginal likelihood of the data under the model. Estimation of the marginal likelihood from MCMC samples of the target density alone is non-trivial, with approaches such as the harmonic mean estimator having high variance. Here we try to establish if our approach can be used in a black-box fashion to compute a reasonable estimate of the marginal likelihood.

As our 'ground truth' we use a large batch of long AIS runs (average across 100 runs of 10000 inverse temperatures) on a separate Theano implementation of the model. We use ADVI to fit a diagonal covariance Gaussian variational approximation to the target density and use this as the base density. NUTS chains, initialised at samples from the base density, were then run on the extended space for 2500 iterations. The samples from these chain were used to compute estimates of the normalising constant (marginal likelihood) using the estimator (21). The results are shown in Figure 2. It can be seen that estimates from the NUTS chains in the extended continuously tempered space quickly converge to a marginal likelihood estimate very close to the AIS estimate, and significantly improve over the final lower bound on the marginal likelihood that ADVI converges to.

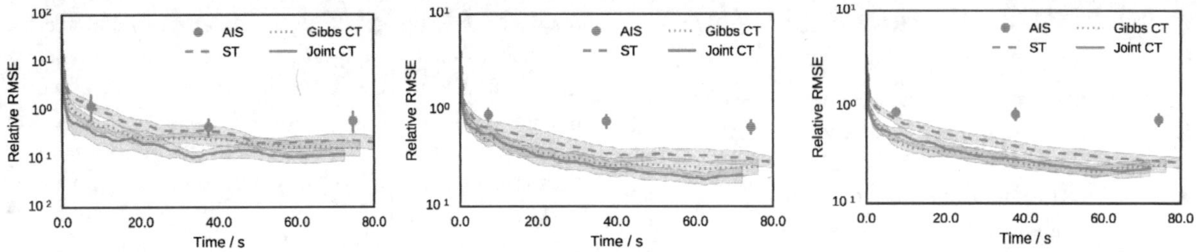

(a) log Z (b) $\mathbb{E}[\mathbf{x}]$ (c) $\mathbb{E}\left[\mathbf{x}\mathbf{x}^{\mathsf{T}}\right] - \mathbb{E}[\mathbf{x}]\,\mathbb{E}[\mathbf{x}]^{\mathsf{T}}$

Figure 1: RMSEs in empirical moments estimated from MCMC samples against run time for various thermodynamic ensemble MCMC methods run on Gaussian Boltzmann machine relaxation target distributions. All RMSEs are relative to the RMSE of the corresponding approximate moments calculated using the moment-matched variational mixtures, so values below 1 represent improvement on deterministic approximation. For AIS points across time axis represent increasing number of inverse temperatures: $(1, 5, 10) \times 10^3$. For ST, Gibbs CT and joint CT curves show RMSEs for expectations calculated with increasing number of samples from chains. All curves / points show mean across 10 runs for each of 10 generated parameter sets. Filled regions / error bars show ± 3 standard errors of mean.

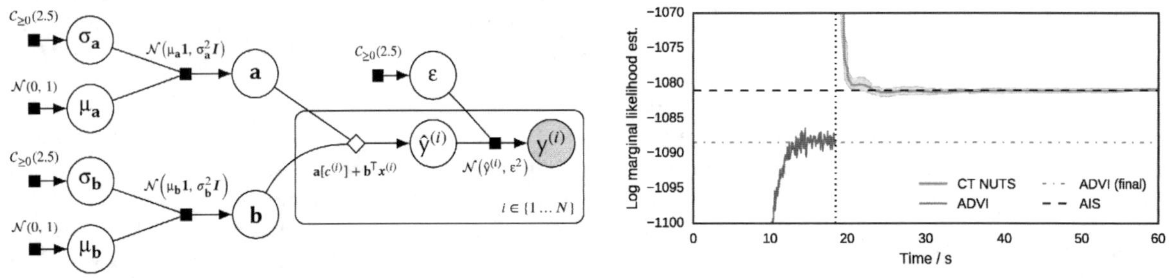

(a) Factor graph of hierarchical model. (b) Log marginal likelihood estimates.

Figure 2: (a) Factor graph for hierarchical regression model for *Radon* data. Factor notation - $\mathcal{N}(\mu, \sigma)$: normal distribution with mean μ, (co-)variance σ; $\mathcal{C}_{\geq 0}(\gamma)$ half-Cauchy distribution with scale γ; $\diamond$ deterministic factor. (b) Log marginal likelihood estimates against run time for hierarchical regression model. Black dashed line shows estimated log marginal likelihood from a long AIS run which is used as a proxy ground truth. The noisy blue curve shows the *evidence lower bound* ADVI objective over training and the red dot-dashed line the final converged value used for log ζ. The green curve shows log marginal likelihood estimates using samples from NUTS chains running on the extended joint density in the estimator (21), with the run time corresponding to increasing samples being included in the estimator (offset by initial ADVI run time). Curve shows mean over 10 runs and filled region ± 3 standard errors of mean.

7.3 GENERATIVE IMAGE MODELS

For our final experiments, we compared the efficiency of our CT approaches to ST and AIS for marginal likelihood estimation in decoder-based generative models for images. Use of AIS in this context was recently proposed in [43]. Specifically we estimate the joint marginal likelihood of 1000 generated binary images under the Bernoulli decoder distribution of two *importance weighted autoencoder* (IWAE) [6] models. Each IWAE has one stochastic hidden layer and a 50-dimensional latent space, with the two models trained on binarised versions of the MNIST [27] and Omniglot [26] datasets using the code at `https://github.com/yburda/iwae`. The generated images used are shown in Appendix D.

By performing inference on the per-image posterior densities on the latent representation given image, the joint marginal likelihood of the images can be estimated as the product of estimates of the normalising constants of the individual posterior densities. The use of generated images allows *bidirectional Monte Carlo* (BDMC) [20] to be used to 'sandwich' the marginal likelihood with stochastic upper and lower bounds formed with long forward and backward AIS runs (averages over 16 independent runs with 10000 inverse temperatures as used in [43]).

As the per-image latent representations are conditionally independent given the images, chains on all the posterior densities can be run in parallel, with the experiments in this section run on a NVIDIA Tesla K40 GPU to ex-

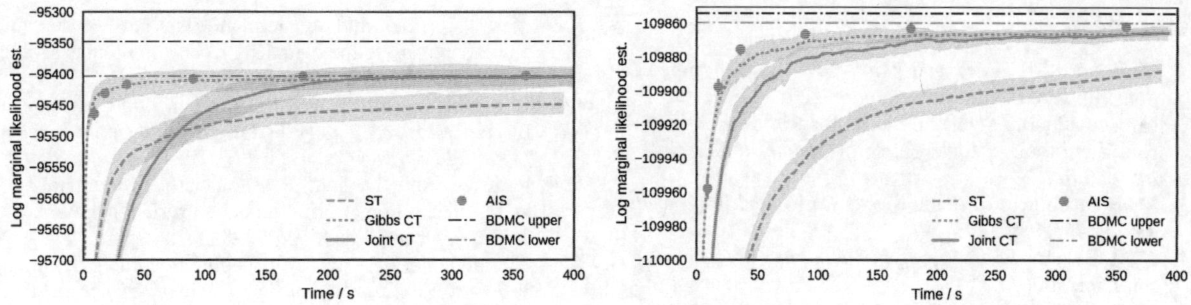

(a) MNIST log marginal likelihood estimates.

(b) Omniglot log marginal likelihood estimates.

Figure 3: Estimates of the log joint marginal likelihood of 1000 generated images under the Bernoulli decoder distributions of two IWAE models trained on the MNIST and Omniglot datasets against computation time. The black / red dashed lines show stochastic upper / lower bounds calculated using long BDMC runs. For AIS points across time axis represent increasing number of inverse temperatures: (50, 100, 200, 500, 1000, 2000). For ST, Gibbs CT and joint CT curves show estimates calculated with an increasing number of samples from chains. All curves / points show mean across 10 runs. Filled regions / error bars show ± 3 standard errors of mean.

ploit this inherent parallelism. The encoder of the trained IWAE models is an inference network which outputs the mean and diagonal covariance of a Gaussian variational approximation to the posterior density on the latent representation given an image and so was used to define per-image Gaussian base densities as suggested in [43]. Similarly the per-image $\log \zeta$ values were set using importance-weighted variational lower bound estimates for the per-image marginal likelihoods.

The results are shown in Figure 3, with the curves / points showing average results across 10 independent runs and filled regions / bars ± 3 standard error of means for the estimates. Here Gibbs CT and AIS perform similarly, with joint CT converging less quickly and simulated tempering significantly less efficient. The quick convergence of AIS and Gibbs CT here suggests the posterior densities are relatively easy for the dynamics to explore and well matched by the Gaussian base densities, limiting the gains from any more coherent exploration of the extended space by the joint CT updates. The higher per-leapfrog-step costs of the HMC updates in the extended space therefore mean the joint CT approach is less efficient overall here. The poorer performance of simulated tempering here is in part due to the generation of the discrete random indices becoming a bottleneck in the GPU implementation.

8 DISCUSSION

The approach we have presented is a simple but powerful extension to existing tempering methods which can both help exploration of distributions with multiple isolated modes and allow estimation of the normalisation constant of the target distribution. A key advantage of the joint CT method is its ease of implementation - it simply requires running HMC in an extended state space and so can easily be used for example within existing probabilistic programming software such as PyMC3 [40] and Stan [8]. By updating the temperature jointly with the original target state, it is also possible to leverage adaptive HMC variants such as NUTS [22] to perform tempered inference in a 'black-box' manner without the need to separately tune the updates of the inverse temperature variable.

The Gibbs CT method also provides a relatively black-box framework for tempering. Compared to ST it removes the need to choose the number and spacing of discrete inverse temperatures and also replaces generation of a discrete random variate from a categorical distribution when updating β given $\mathbf{x}$ (which as seen in Section 7.3 can become a computational bottleneck) with generation of a truncated exponential variate (which can be performed efficiently by inverse transform sampling). Compared to the joint CT approach, the Gibbs approach is less simple to integrate in to existing HMC code due to the separate β updates, but eliminates the need to tune the temperature control mass value m and achieved similar or better sampling efficiency in the experiments in Section 7.

Acknowledgements

We thank Ben Leimkuhler for introducing us to the extended Hamiltonian continuous tempering approach and to the anonymous reviewers of an earlier workshop paper for their useful feedback. This work was supported in part by grants EP/F500386/1 & BB/F529254/1 for the University of Edinburgh Doctoral Training Centre in Neuroinformatics & Computational Neuroscience from the UK Engineering & Physical Sciences Research Council (EPSRC), Biotechnology & Biological Sciences Research Council (BBSRC) & Medical Research Council (MRC).

References

[1] G. Behrens, N. Friel, and M. Hurn. Tuning tempered transitions. *Statistics and computing*, 2012.

[2] M. Betancourt. A general metric for Riemannian manifold Hamiltonian Monte Carlo. In *Geometric Science of Information*. 2013.

[3] M. Betancourt. Adiabatic Monte Carlo. *arXiv preprint arXiv:1405.3489*, 2014.

[4] C. M. Bishop. *Pattern recognition and machine learning*. Springer, 2006.

[5] M. Bonomi, A. Barducci, and M. Parrinello. Reconstructing the equilibrium Boltzmann distribution from well-tempered metadynamics. *Journal of computational chemistry*, 2009.

[6] Y. Burda, R. Grosse, and R. Salakhutdinov. Importance weighted autoencoders. In *Proceedings of the International Conference on Learning Representations (ICLR)*, 2016.

[7] D. Carlson, P. Stinson, A. Pakman, and L. Paninski. Partition functions from Rao-Blackwellized tempered sampling. In *Proceedings of The 33rd International Conference on Machine Learning*, 2016.

[8] B. Carpenter, A. Gelman, M. Hoffman, D. Lee, B. Goodrich, M. Betancourt, M. A. Brubaker, J. Guo, P. Li, and A. Riddell. Stan: A probabilistic programming language. *Journal of Statistical Software*, 2016.

[9] P. Damlen, J. Wakefield, and S. Walker. Gibbs sampling for Bayesian non-conjugate and hierarchical models by using auxiliary variables. *Journal of the Royal Statistical Society: Series B (Statistical Methodology)*, 1999.

[10] A. B. Dieng, D. Tran, R. Ranganath, J. Paisley, and D. M. Blei. The χ-divergence for approximate inference. *arXiv preprint arXiv:1611.00328*, 2016.

[11] S. Duane, A. D. Kennedy, B. J. Pendleton, and D. Roweth. Hybrid Monte Carlo. *Physics Letters B*, 1987.

[12] D. J. Earl and M. W. Deem. Parallel tempering: theory, applications, and new perspectives. *Physical Chemistry Chemical Physics*, 2005.

[13] A. E. Gelfand and A. F. Smith. Sampling-based approaches to calculating marginal densities. *Journal of the American Statistical Association*, 1990.

[14] A. Gelman and J. Hill. *Data analysis using regression and multilevel/hierarchical models*, chapter 12: Multilevel Linear Models. Cambridge University Press, 2006.

[15] A. Gelman and X.-L. Meng. Simulating normalizing constants: From importance sampling to bridge sampling to path sampling. *Statistical science*, 1998.

[16] S. Geman and D. Geman. Stochastic relaxation, Gibbs distributions, and the Bayesian restoration of images. *IEEE Transactions on pattern analysis and machine intelligence*, 1984.

[17] C. J. Geyer. Markov chain Monte Carlo maximum likelihood. *Computer Science and Statistics*, 1991.

[18] C. J. Geyer and E. A. Thompson. Annealing Markov chain Monte Carlo with applications to ancestral inference. *Journal of the American Statistical Association*, 1995.

[19] G. Gobbo and B. J. Leimkuhler. Extended Hamiltonian approach to continuous tempering. *Physical Review E*, 2015.

[20] R. Grosse, Z. Ghahramani, and R. P. Adams. Sandwiching the marginal likelihood using bidirectional Monte Carlo. *arXiv preprint arXiv:1511.02543*, 2015.

[21] W. K. Hastings. Monte Carlo sampling methods using Markov chains and their applications. *Biometrika*, 1970.

[22] M. D. Hoffman and A. Gelman. The No-U-turn sampler: adaptively setting path lengths in Hamiltonian Monte Carlo. *Journal of Machine Learning Research*, 2014.

[23] D. P. Kingma and M. Welling. Auto-encoding variational Bayes. In *Proceedings of the International Conference on Learning Representations (ICLR)*, 2014.

[24] A. Kucukelbir, D. Tran, R. Ranganath, A. Gelman, and D. M. Blei. Automatic differentiation variational inference. *arXiv preprint arXiv:1603.00788*, 2016.

[25] A. Laio and M. Parrinello. Escaping free-energy minima. *Proceedings of the National Academy of Sciences*, 2002.

[26] B. M. Lake, R. Salakhutdinov, and J. B. Tenenbaum. Human-level concept learning through probabilistic program induction. *Science*, 2015.

[27] Y. LeCun, L. Bottou, Y. Bengio, and P. Haffner. Gradient-based learning applied to document recognition. *Proceedings of the IEEE*, 1998.

[28] B. Leimkuhler and S. Reich. *Simulating Hamiltonian dynamics*. Cambridge University Press, 2004.

[29] Y. Li and R. E. Turner. Rényi divergence variational inference. In *Advances in Neural Information Processing Systems*, 2016.

[30] E. Marinari and G. Parisi. Simulated tempering: a new Monte Carlo scheme. *Europhysics Letters*, 1992.

[31] N. Metropolis, A. W. Rosenbluth, M. N. Rosenbluth, A. H. Teller, and E. Teller. Equation of state calculations by fast computing machines. *The Journal of Chemical Physics*, 1953.

[32] T. P. Minka. Expectation propagation for approximate Bayesian inference. *Proceedings of the Seventeenth conference on Uncertainty in Artificial Intelligence*, 2001.

[33] R. M. Neal. Sampling from multimodal distributions using tempered transitions. *Statistics and Computing*, 1996.

[34] R. M. Neal. Annealed importance sampling. *Statistics and Computing*, 2001.

[35] R. M. Neal. Slice sampling. *Annals of statistics*, 2003.

[36] R. M. Neal. MCMC using Hamiltonian dynamics. *Handbook of Markov Chain Monte Carlo*, 2011.

[37] D. J. Rezende, S. Mohamed, and D. Wierstra. Stochastic backpropagation and approximate inference in deep generative models. In *Proceedings of The 31st International Conference on Machine Learning*, 2014.

[38] C. Robert and G. Casella. A short history of Markov Chain Monte Carlo: subjective recollections from incomplete data. *Statistical Science*, 2011.

[39] R. Salakhutdinov and I. Murray. On the quantitative analysis of deep belief networks. In *Proceedings of the 25th International Conference on Machine learning*, 2008.

[40] J. Salvatier, T. V. Wiecki, and C. Fonnesbeck. Probabilistic programming in Python using PyMC3. *PeerJ Computer Science*, 2016.

[41] R. H. Swendsen and J.-S. Wang. Replica Monte Carlo simulation of spin-glasses. *Physical Review Letters*, 1986.

[42] Theano Development Team. Theano: A Python framework for fast computation of mathematical expressions. *arXiv e-prints*, abs/1605.02688, 2016.

[43] Y. Wu, Y. Burda, R. Salakhutdinov, and R. Grosse. On the quantitative analysis of decoder-based generative models. *arXiv preprint arXiv:1611.04273*, 2016.

[44] Y. Zhang, Z. Ghahramani, A. J. Storkey, and C. A. Sutton. Continuous relaxations for discrete Hamiltonian Monte Carlo. In *Advances in Neural Information Processing Systems*, 2012.

[45] O. Zobay. Mean field inference for the Dirichlet process mixture model. *Electronic Journal of Statistics*, 2009.

A One-dimensional bimodal target

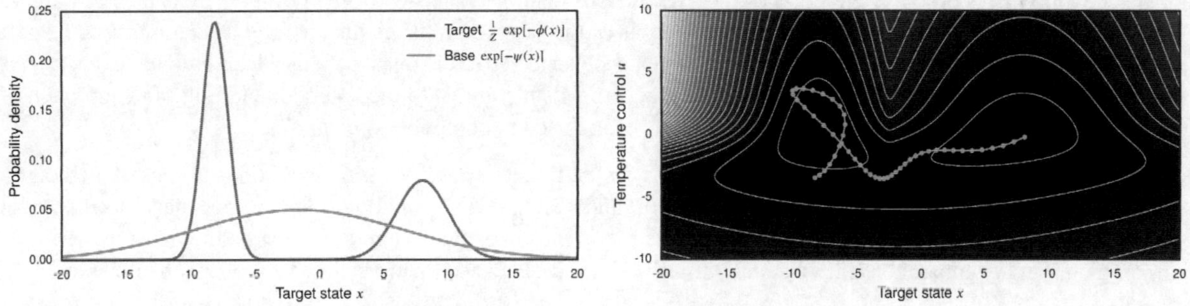

(a) Target (blue curve) & base (green curve) density functions. (b) Joint energy (contour plot) & example trajectory (green curve).

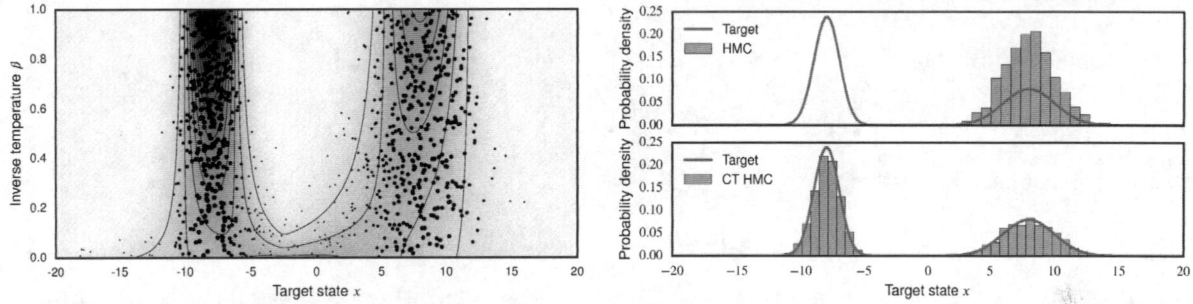

(c) Joint density (contour plot) and CT HMC samples (circles). (d) Histograms from HMC (top) and CT HMC (bottom) samples.

Figure 4: Visualisations of *continuous tempering* (CT) in a bimodal univariate target density. (a) A two-component Gaussian mixture target density (blue curve) and Gaussian base density (green curve) with mean and variance matched to the target. (b) The extended potential energy on the target state x and temperature control variable u (contour plot - dark colours indicate low energy) and an example simulated Hamiltonian trajectory in the joint space (green curve). The temperature control variable bridges the base and target densities lowering energy barriers in the target space. (c) Joint density on the target state x and inverse temperature β (17) (contour plot, dark colours indicate high density) and samples from a CT HMC chain run in the joint space (circles, size of each circle is proportional to $p_{\beta|x}(1 \mid x)$ and so larger symbols indicate a greater weighting in estimates of expectations with respect to the target (22)). (d) Example target state sample histograms from running standard HMC in the original target density (top) and running HMC in the extended joint space (bottom).

We give here an illustrative example of the gains of the proposed approach over standard HMC in target densities with isolated modes. We use a one-dimensional Gaussian mixture density with two separated Gaussian components as the target density, shown by the blue curve in Figure 4a. Although performance in this toy univariate model is not necessarily reflective of that in more realistic higher-dimensional models, it has the advantage of allowing the joint density on x and $\beta = \beta(u)$ to be directly visualised.

For the base density $\exp[-\psi(x)]$ we use a univariate Gaussian with mean and variance matched to those of the target density (corresponding to the Gaussian density minimising the KL divergence from the target to base distribution), shown by the green curve in Figure 4a. We also set $\log \zeta = \log Z$ and so the performance here represents a 'best-case' scenario for the continuous tempering approach.

The resulting potential energy $(-\log p_{x,u})$ on the extended (x, u) space is shown in Figure 4b. For positive temperature control values (and so inverse temperature values close to 1), the energy surface tends increasingly to the double-well potential corresponding to the target distribution, with a high energy barrier between the two modes. For negative temperature control values the energy surface tends towards the single quadratic well corresponding to the Gaussian base density. The resulting joint energy surface allows for paths between the values of the target state x corresponding to the two modes which have much lower potential energy barriers than the potential barrier between the two modes in the original target space, allowing simulated Hamiltonian trajectories such as that shown in green to more easily explore the target state space.

Samples from a HMC chain on the extended joint space are shown in Figure 4c, with the joint density on (x, β) (17) shown in the background as a contoured heat map. It can be seen that the Hamiltonian dynamic is able to explore the joint space well with good coverage of all of the high density regions. The size of the points in 4c is proportional to $w_1(x) = p_{\beta|x}(1 \mid x)$ and so reflects the importance weights of the samples in the estimator for expectations with respect to the target in (22). Importantly even points for which β is close to zero can contribute significantly to the expectations if the corresponding x value is probable under the target: this is in contrast to the extended Hamiltonian approach of [19] where only a subset of points corresponding to β = 1 are used to compute expectations.

The final panel, Figure 4d shows empirical histograms on the target variable x estimated from samples of a chain on the extended space (joint continuous tempering, bottom) and standard HMC on the original target space (top). As can be seen the standard HMC approach gets stuck in one mode thus does not assign any mass to the other mode in the histogram, unlike the tempered chain which identifies both modes and accurately estimates their relative masses.

B Bounding the inverse temperature marginal density

We have a joint density on (**x**, β)

$$p_{\mathbf{x},\beta}(\boldsymbol{x}, \beta) = \frac{1}{C} \exp(-\beta\phi(\boldsymbol{x}) - \beta \log \zeta - (1-\beta)\psi(\boldsymbol{x})). \tag{27}$$

The resulting marginal density on β is

$$p_{\beta}(\beta) = \int_{\mathcal{X}} p_{\mathbf{x},\beta}(\boldsymbol{x}, \beta)\, \mathrm{d}\boldsymbol{x} = \frac{1}{C\zeta^{\beta}} \int_{\mathcal{X}} \exp(-\beta\phi(\boldsymbol{x}) - (1-\beta)\psi(\boldsymbol{x}))\, \mathrm{d}\boldsymbol{x}. \tag{28}$$

To derive an upper-bound on $p_{\beta}(\beta)$ we use Hölder's inequality

$$\int_{\mathcal{X}} g(\boldsymbol{x})h(\boldsymbol{x})\, \mathrm{d}\boldsymbol{x} \leq \left(\int_{\mathcal{X}} |g(\boldsymbol{x})|^{\frac{1}{a}}\, \mathrm{d}\boldsymbol{x}\right)^{a} \left(\int_{\mathcal{X}} |h(\boldsymbol{x})|^{\frac{1}{1-a}}\, \mathrm{d}\boldsymbol{x}\right)^{1-a} \tag{29}$$

where $a \in [0, 1]$ and g and h are measurable functions. We also use the definitions

$$\int_{\mathcal{X}} \exp(-\phi(\boldsymbol{x}))\, \mathrm{d}\boldsymbol{x} = Z \quad \text{and} \quad \int_{\mathcal{X}} \exp(-\psi(\boldsymbol{x}))\, \mathrm{d}\boldsymbol{x} = 1. \tag{30}$$

From (28) we have that

$$p_{\beta}(\beta) = \frac{1}{C\zeta^{\beta}} \int_{\mathcal{X}} \left(\exp(-\phi(\boldsymbol{x}))^{\beta}\right)\left(\exp(-\psi(\boldsymbol{x}))^{1-\beta}\right) \mathrm{d}\boldsymbol{x}. \tag{31}$$

Applying Hölder's inequality (29) with $g(\boldsymbol{x}) = \exp(-\phi(\boldsymbol{x}))^{\beta}$, $h(\boldsymbol{x}) = \exp(-\psi(\boldsymbol{x}))^{1-\beta}$ and $a = \beta$

$$p_{\beta}(\beta) \leq \frac{1}{C\zeta^{\beta}} \left(\int_{\mathcal{X}} \left|\exp(-\phi(\boldsymbol{x}))^{\beta}\right|^{\frac{1}{\beta}} \mathrm{d}\boldsymbol{x}\right)^{\beta} \left(\int_{\mathcal{X}} \left|\exp(-\psi(\boldsymbol{x}))^{1-\beta}\right|^{\frac{1}{1-\beta}} \mathrm{d}\boldsymbol{x}\right)^{1-\beta} \tag{32}$$

$$= \frac{1}{C\zeta^{\beta}} \left(\int_{\mathcal{X}} \exp(-\phi(\boldsymbol{x}))\, \mathrm{d}\boldsymbol{x}\right)^{\beta} \left(\int_{\mathcal{X}} \exp(-\psi(\boldsymbol{x}))\, \mathrm{d}\boldsymbol{x}\right)^{1-\beta}. \tag{33}$$

Substituting the definitions in (30) gives

$$p_{\beta}(\beta) \leq \frac{1}{C}\left(\frac{Z}{\zeta}\right)^{\beta}. \tag{34}$$

To derive a lower-bound on $p_{\beta}(\beta)$, we use Jensen's inequality

$$\varphi\left(\int_{\mathcal{X}} g(\boldsymbol{x})q(\boldsymbol{x})\, \mathrm{d}\boldsymbol{x}\right) \geq \int_{\mathcal{X}} \varphi(g(\boldsymbol{x}))q(\boldsymbol{x})\, \mathrm{d}\boldsymbol{x}, \tag{35}$$

for a concave function φ, normalised density $q : \int_{\mathcal{X}} q(\boldsymbol{x})\, \mathrm{d}\boldsymbol{x} = 1$ and measurable g. The logarithm of (28) gives

$$\log p_{\beta}(\beta) + \beta \log \zeta + \log C = \log\left(\int_{\mathcal{X}} \exp(-\beta(\phi(\boldsymbol{x}) - \psi(\boldsymbol{x}))) \exp(-\psi(\boldsymbol{x}))\, \mathrm{d}\boldsymbol{x}\right). \tag{36}$$

Applying Jensen's inequality (35) with $\varphi = \log$, $q = \exp(-\psi)$ and $g = \exp(-\beta(\phi - \psi))$

$$\log \mathrm{p}_\beta(\beta) + \log C + \beta \log \zeta \geq \beta \int_{\mathcal{X}} (\psi(\boldsymbol{x}) - \phi(\boldsymbol{x})) \exp(-\psi(\boldsymbol{x}))\, \mathrm{d}\boldsymbol{x} \tag{37}$$

$$= \beta \int_{\mathcal{X}} (\log Z - \log Z - \log \exp(-\psi(\boldsymbol{x}) + \phi(\boldsymbol{x}))) \exp(-\psi(\boldsymbol{x}))\, \mathrm{d}\boldsymbol{x} \tag{38}$$

$$= \beta \log Z - \beta \int_{\mathcal{X}} \exp(-\psi(\boldsymbol{x})) \log\left(\frac{\exp(-\psi(\boldsymbol{x}))}{\exp(-\phi(\boldsymbol{x}))/Z} \right) \mathrm{d}\boldsymbol{x}. \tag{39}$$

Recognising the integral in the last line as the *Kullback–Leibler* (KL) divergence $d^{b \to t}$ from the base density $\exp(-\psi(\boldsymbol{x}))$ to the target density $\exp(-\phi(\boldsymbol{x}))/Z$

$$d^{b \to t} = \int_{\mathcal{X}} \exp(-\psi(\boldsymbol{x})) \log\left(\frac{\exp(-\psi(\boldsymbol{x}))}{\exp(-\phi(\boldsymbol{x}))/Z} \right) \mathrm{d}\boldsymbol{x}, \tag{40}$$

and taking the exponential of both sides and rearranging we have

$$\mathrm{p}_\beta(\beta) \geq \frac{1}{C} \left(\frac{Z}{\zeta} \right)^\beta \exp\left(-\beta d^{b \to t}\right). \tag{41}$$

By instead noting (28) can be rearranged into the form

$$\log \mathrm{p}_\beta(\beta) + \log C + \beta \log \zeta - \log Z = \log\left(\int_{\mathcal{X}} \exp(-(1-\beta)(\psi(\boldsymbol{x}) - \phi(\boldsymbol{x}))) \frac{1}{Z} \exp(-\phi(\boldsymbol{x}))\, \mathrm{d}\boldsymbol{x} \right), \tag{42}$$

by an equivalent series of steps we can also derive a bound using the reversed form of the KL divergence

$$d^{t \to b} = \int_{\mathcal{X}} \frac{1}{Z} \exp(-\phi(\boldsymbol{x})) \log\left(\frac{\exp(-\phi(\boldsymbol{x}))/Z}{\exp(-\psi(\boldsymbol{x}))} \right) \mathrm{d}\boldsymbol{x}. \tag{43}$$

from the target to the base distribution, giving that

$$\mathrm{p}_\beta(\beta) \geq \frac{1}{C} \left(\frac{Z}{\zeta} \right)^\beta \exp\left(-(1-\beta) d^{t \to b}\right). \tag{44}$$

C Gaussian mixture Boltzmann machine relaxations

We define a *Boltzmann machine distribution* on a signed binary state $\mathbf{s} \in \{-1, +1\}^{D_B} = \mathcal{S}$ as

$$\mathrm{p}_{\mathbf{s}}(\boldsymbol{s}) = \frac{1}{Z_B} \exp\left(\frac{1}{2} \boldsymbol{s}^\mathsf{T} \boldsymbol{W} \boldsymbol{s} + \boldsymbol{s}^\mathsf{T} \boldsymbol{b} \right) \qquad Z_B = \sum_{\boldsymbol{s} \in \mathcal{S}} \left(\exp\left(\frac{1}{2} \boldsymbol{s}^\mathsf{T} \boldsymbol{W} \boldsymbol{s} + \boldsymbol{s}^\mathsf{T} \boldsymbol{b} \right) \right). \tag{45}$$

We introduce an auxiliary real-valued vector random variable $\mathbf{x} \in \mathbb{R}^D$ with a Gaussian conditional distribution

$$\mathrm{p}_{\mathbf{x}|\mathbf{s}}(\boldsymbol{x} \mid \boldsymbol{s}) = \frac{1}{(2\pi)^{D/2}} \exp\left(-\frac{1}{2} \left(\boldsymbol{x} - \boldsymbol{Q}^\mathsf{T} \boldsymbol{s} \right)^\mathsf{T} \left(\boldsymbol{x} - \boldsymbol{Q}^\mathsf{T} \boldsymbol{s} \right) \right) \tag{46}$$

with $\boldsymbol{Q}$ a $D_B \times D$ matrix such that $\boldsymbol{Q}\boldsymbol{Q}^\mathsf{T} = \boldsymbol{W} + \boldsymbol{D}$ for some diagonal $\boldsymbol{D}$ which makes $\boldsymbol{W} + \boldsymbol{D}$ positive semi-definite. In our experiments, based on the observation in [44] that minimising the maximum eigenvalue of $\boldsymbol{W} + \boldsymbol{D}$ decreases the maximal separation between the Gaussian components in the relaxation, we set $\boldsymbol{D}$ as the solution to the semi-definite programme

$$\min_{\boldsymbol{D}} \left(\lambda_{\text{MAX}}(\boldsymbol{W} + \boldsymbol{D}) \right) \,:\, \boldsymbol{W} + \boldsymbol{D} \succeq 0 \tag{47}$$

where λ_{MAX} denotes the maximal eigenvalue. In general the optimised $\boldsymbol{W} + \boldsymbol{D}$ lies on the semi-definite cone and so has rank less than D_B hence a $\boldsymbol{Q}$ can be found such that $D < D_B$. The resulting joint distribution on $(\mathbf{x},\ \mathbf{s})$ is

$$\mathrm{p}_{\mathbf{x},\mathbf{s}}(\boldsymbol{x}, \boldsymbol{s}) = \frac{1}{(2\pi)^{D/2} Z_B} \exp\left(-\frac{1}{2}\boldsymbol{x}^\mathsf{T}\boldsymbol{x} + \boldsymbol{s}^\mathsf{T}\boldsymbol{Q}\boldsymbol{x} - \frac{1}{2}\boldsymbol{s}^\mathsf{T}\boldsymbol{Q}\boldsymbol{Q}^\mathsf{T}\boldsymbol{s} + \frac{1}{2}\boldsymbol{s}^\mathsf{T}\boldsymbol{W}\boldsymbol{s} + \boldsymbol{s}^\mathsf{T}\boldsymbol{b}\right) \tag{48}$$

$$= \frac{1}{(2\pi)^{D/2} Z_B} \exp\left(-\frac{1}{2}\boldsymbol{x}^\mathsf{T}\boldsymbol{x} + \boldsymbol{s}^\mathsf{T}(\boldsymbol{Q}\boldsymbol{x} + \boldsymbol{b}) - \frac{1}{2}\boldsymbol{s}^\mathsf{T}\boldsymbol{D}\boldsymbol{s}\right) \tag{49}$$

$$= \frac{1}{(2\pi)^{D/2} Z_B \exp\left(\frac{1}{2}\operatorname{Tr}(\boldsymbol{D})\right)} \exp\left(-\frac{1}{2}\boldsymbol{x}^\mathsf{T}\boldsymbol{x}\right) \prod_{i=1}^{D_B} \left(\exp\left(s_i\left(\boldsymbol{q}_i^\mathsf{T}\boldsymbol{x} + b_i\right)\right)\right), \tag{50}$$

where $\left\{\boldsymbol{q}_i^\mathsf{T}\right\}_{i=1}^{D_B}$ are the D_B rows of $\boldsymbol{Q}$. We can marginalise over the binary state $\mathbf{s}$ as each s_i is conditionally independent of all the others given $\mathbf{x}$ in the joint distribution. This gives the *Boltzmann machine relaxation* density on $\mathbf{x}$

$$\mathrm{p}_{\mathbf{x}}(\boldsymbol{x}) = \frac{2^{D_B}}{(2\pi)^{D/2} Z_B \exp\left(\frac{1}{2}\operatorname{Tr}(\boldsymbol{D})\right)} \exp\left(-\frac{1}{2}\boldsymbol{x}^\mathsf{T}\boldsymbol{x}\right) \prod_{i=1}^{D_B} \left(\cosh\left(\boldsymbol{q}_i^\mathsf{T}\boldsymbol{x} + b_i\right)\right), \tag{51}$$

which is a structured Gaussian mixture density with 2^{D_B} components. If we define $\mathrm{p}_{\mathbf{x}}(\boldsymbol{x}) = \frac{1}{Z}\exp(-\phi(\boldsymbol{x}))$ with

$$\phi(\boldsymbol{x}) = \frac{1}{2}\boldsymbol{x}^\mathsf{T}\boldsymbol{x} - \sum_{i=1}^{D_B} \left(\log\cosh\left(\boldsymbol{q}_i^\mathsf{T}\boldsymbol{x} + b_i\right)\right), \tag{52}$$

then the normalisation constant Z of the relaxation density can be related to the normalising constant of the corresponding Boltzmann machine distribution by

$$\log Z = \log Z_B + \frac{1}{2}\operatorname{Tr}(\boldsymbol{D}) + \frac{D}{2}\log(2\pi) - D_B \log 2. \tag{53}$$

It can also be shown that the first and second moments of the relaxation distribution are related to the first and second moments of the corresponding Boltzmann machine distribution by

$$\mathbb{E}[\mathbf{x}] = \int_{\mathcal{X}} \boldsymbol{x} \sum_{\boldsymbol{s}\in\mathcal{S}} \left(\mathrm{p}_{\mathbf{x}|\mathbf{s}}(\boldsymbol{x} \mid \boldsymbol{s})\,\mathrm{p}_{\mathbf{s}}(\boldsymbol{s})\right) \mathrm{d}\boldsymbol{x} = \sum_{\boldsymbol{s}\in\mathcal{S}} \left(\int_{\mathcal{X}} \boldsymbol{x}\,\mathcal{N}\left(\boldsymbol{x}; \boldsymbol{Q}^\mathsf{T}\boldsymbol{s}, \boldsymbol{I}\right) \mathrm{d}\boldsymbol{x}\,\mathrm{p}_{\mathbf{s}}(\boldsymbol{s})\right) = \mathbb{E}\left[\boldsymbol{Q}^\mathsf{T}\mathbf{s}\right] = \boldsymbol{Q}^\mathsf{T}\,\mathbb{E}[\mathbf{s}], \tag{54}$$

$$\text{and } \mathbb{E}\left[\mathbf{x}\mathbf{x}^\mathsf{T}\right] = \sum_{\boldsymbol{s}\in\mathcal{S}} \left(\int_{\mathcal{X}} \boldsymbol{x}\boldsymbol{x}^\mathsf{T}\,\mathcal{N}\left(\boldsymbol{x}; \boldsymbol{Q}^\mathsf{T}\boldsymbol{s}, \boldsymbol{I}\right) \mathrm{d}\boldsymbol{x}\,\mathrm{p}_{\mathbf{s}}(\boldsymbol{s})\right) = \mathbb{E}\left[\boldsymbol{Q}^\mathsf{T}\mathbf{s}\mathbf{s}\boldsymbol{Q} + \boldsymbol{I}\right] = \boldsymbol{Q}^\mathsf{T}\,\mathbb{E}\left[\mathbf{s}\mathbf{s}^\mathsf{T}\right]\boldsymbol{Q} + \boldsymbol{I}. \tag{55}$$

The weight parameters $\boldsymbol{W}$ of the Boltzmann machine distributions used in the experiments in Section 7.1 were generated using an eigendecomposition based method. A uniformly distributed (with respect to the Haar measure) random orthogonal matrix $\boldsymbol{R}$ was sampled. A vector of eigenvalues $\boldsymbol{e}$ was generated by sampling independent zero-mean unit-variance normal variates $n_i \sim \mathcal{N}(\cdot;\ 0,\ 1)\ \forall i \in \left\{1, \dots D_B\right\}$ and then setting $e_i = s_1 \tanh(s_2 n_i)\ \forall i \in \left\{1, \dots D_B\right\}$, with $s_1 = 6$ and $s_2 = 2$ in the experiments. This generates eigenvalues concentrated near $\pm s_1$ with this empirically observed to lead to systems which tended to be highly multimodal. A symmetric matrix $\boldsymbol{V} = \boldsymbol{R}\operatorname{diag}(\boldsymbol{e})\boldsymbol{R}^\mathsf{T}$ was then computed and the weights $\boldsymbol{W}$ set such that $W_{i,j} = V_{i,j}\ \forall i \neq j$ and $W_{i,i} = 0\ \forall i \in \left\{1, \dots D_B\right\}$. The biases $\boldsymbol{b}$ where generated using $b_i \sim \mathcal{N}\left(\cdot; 0, 0.1^2\right)\ \forall i \in \left\{1, \dots D_B\right\}$. An example of a two-dimensional projection of independent samples from a Boltzmann machine relaxation density with $D = 27$ ($D_B = 28$), and $\boldsymbol{W}$ and $\boldsymbol{b}$ generated as just described in shown in figure 5. As can be seen even when projected down to two-dimensions the resulting density shows multiple separated modes.

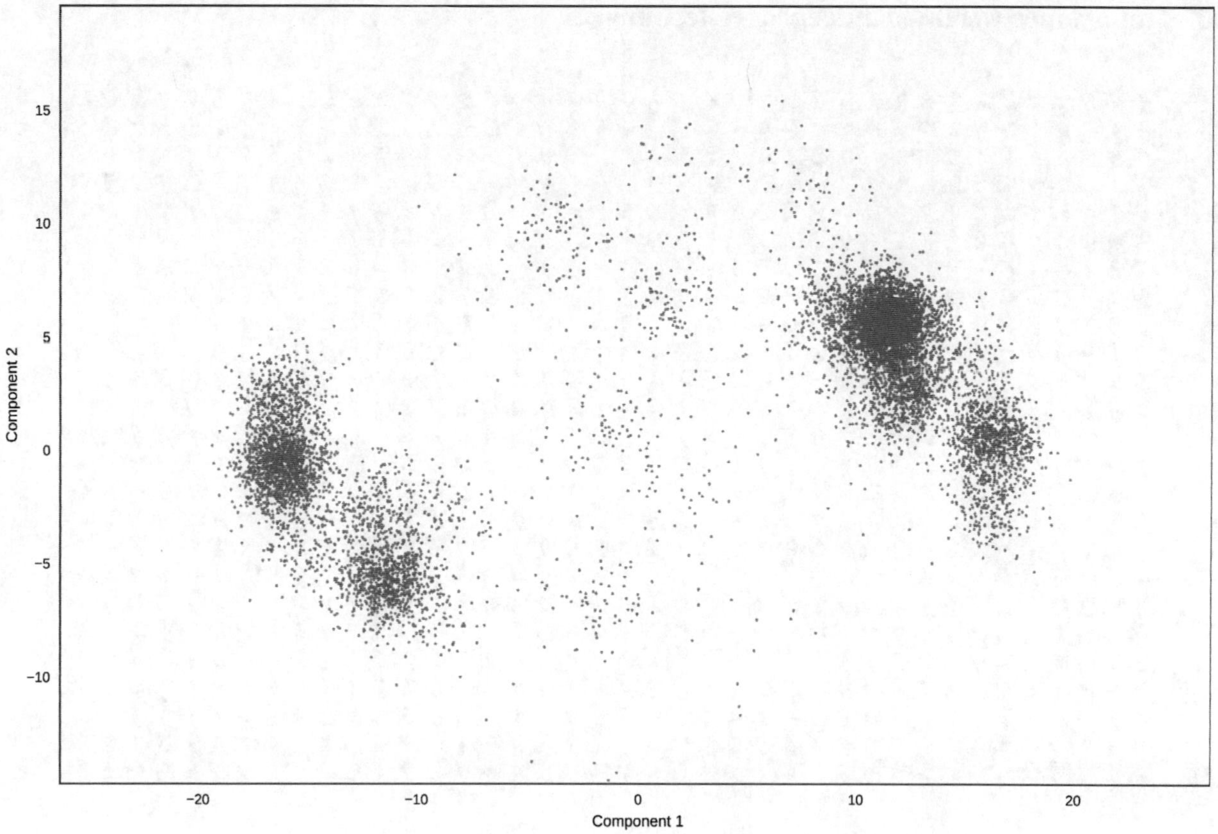

Figure 5: Two-dimensional projection of 10000 independent samples from a Gaussian mixture relaxation of a Boltzmann machine distribution. The parameters $\boldsymbol{W}$ and $\boldsymbol{b}$ of the Boltzmann machine distribution where generated as described in Section C, with here $D_B = 28$ (rather than $D_B = 30$ as in the experiments) as independent sampling from larger systems exceeded the memory available on the workstation used. The two components shown correspond to the two eigenvectors of the generated basis $\boldsymbol{R}$ with the largest corresponding eigenvalues.

D Importance weighted autoencoder test images

Figure 6: MNIST test images.

Figure 7: Omniglot test images.

Determinantal Point Processes for Mini-Batch Diversification

Cheng Zhang
Disney Research
Pittsburgh, PA, USA
cheng.zhang@disneyresearch.com

Hedvig Kjellström
KTH Royal Institute of Technology
Stockholm, Sweden
hedvig@kth.se

Stephan Mandt
Disney Research
Pittsburgh, PA, USA
stephan.mandt@disneyresearch.com

Abstract

We study a mini-batch diversification scheme for stochastic gradient descent (SGD). While classical SGD relies on uniformly sampling data points to form a mini-batch, we propose a non-uniform sampling scheme based on the Determinantal Point Process (DPP). The DPP relies on a similarity measure between data points and gives low probabilities to mini-batches which contain redundant data, and higher probabilities to mini-batches with more diverse data. This simultaneously balances the data and leads to stochastic gradients with lower variance. We term this approach Diversified Mini-Batch SGD (DM-SGD). We show that regular SGD and a biased version of stratified sampling emerge as special cases. Furthermore, DM-SGD generalizes stratified sampling to cases where no discrete features exist to bin the data into groups. We show experimentally that our method results more interpretable and diverse features in unsupervised setups, and in better classification accuracies in supervised setups.

1 INTRODUCTION

Stochastic gradient descent (SGD) is one of the most important algorithms for scalable machine learning [7, 36, 27]. SGD optimizes an objective function by successively following noisy estimates of its gradient based on mini-batches from a large underlying dataset. We usually assure that this gradient is unbiased, meaning that the expected stochastic gradient equals the true gradient. When combined with a suitably decreasing learning rate schedule, the algorithm converges to a local optimum of the objective [7].

Often we are not interested in learning an unbiased estimator of the gradient, but are rather willing to introduce some bias. There are many reasons for why this might be the case. First, biased SGD schemes such as momentum [34], iterate averaging [40], or preconditioning [9, 16, 43, 46] may reduce the stochastic gradient noise or ease the optimization problem, and therefore often lead to faster convergence. Another reason is that we may decide to actively select samples based on their relevance or difficulty levels such as boosting [10], or because we believe that our dataset is in some respect imbalanced [12]. In this paper, we propose and investigate a biased mini-batch subsampling scheme for imbalanced data.

Real-world data sets are naturally imbalanced. For instance, the sports topic appears more often in the news than biology; the internet contains more images of young people than of senior people, and Youtube has more videos of cats than of bees or ants. Aiming to maximize the probability of generating such training data, machine learning models will refine the dominant information with redundancy but ignore the important but scarce data. For example, a model trained on Youtube data might be very sensitive to different cats but unable to recognize ants. We may therefore decide to try to learn on a more balanced data set by actively selecting diversified mini-batches.

The currently most common tool for mini-batch diversification is stratified sampling [30, 48]. In this approach, one groups the data into a finite set of *strata* based on discrete or continuous features such as a label or cluster assignment. To re-balance the data set, the data can then be subsampled such that each stratum occurs with equal probability in the mini-batch (in the following, we refer to this method as *biased stratified sampling*). Unfortunately, the data are not always amenable to biased stratified sampling because discrete features may not exist, or the data may not be unambiguously clustered. Instead of subsampling based on discrete strata, it would be desirable to diversify the mini-batch based on a soft similarity measure between data points. As we show in this paper, this can be achieved using Determinantal Point Processes (DPPs) [19].

The DPP is a point process which mimics repulsive interactions between samples. Being based on a similarity matrix between the data points, a draw from a DPP yields diversified subsets of the data. The main contribution of this paper is using this mechanism to diversify the mini-batches in stochastic gradient-based learning and analyzing this setup theoretically. In more detail, our main achievements are:

- We present a mini-batch diversification scheme based on DPPs for stochastic gradient algorithms. This approach requires a similarity measure among data points, which can be constructed using low-level features of the data. Since the sampling strategy is independent of the learning objective, diversified mini-batches can be precomputed in parallel and reused for different learning tasks. Our approach applies to both supervised and unsupervised models.
- We prove that our method is a generalization of stratified sampling and i.i.d. mini-batch sampling. Both cases emerge for specific similarity kernels of the data.
- We theoretically analyze the conditions under which the variance of the DM-SGD gradient gets reduced. We also give an unbiased version of DM-SGD which optimizes the original objective without re-balancing the data.
- We carry out extensive experiments on several models and datasets. Our approach leads to faster learning and higher classification accuracies in deep supervised learning. For topic models we find that that the resulting document features are more interpretable and are better suited for subsequent supervised learning tasks.

Our paper is structured as follows. In Section 2 we list related work. Section 3 discusses our main concepts of a diversifed risk, and discuses the DM-SGD method. Section 4 discusses theoretical properties of our approach such as variance reduction. Finally, in Section 5, we give empirical evidence that our approach leads to higher classification accuracy and better feature extractions than i.i.d. sampling.

2 RELATED WORK

We revisit the most relevant prior work based on the following aspects. *Diversification and Stratification* comprises methods which aim at re-balancing the empirical distribution of the data. *Variance reduction* summarizes stochastic gradient methods that aim at faster convergence by reducing the stochastic gradient noise. Finally, we list related applications and extensions of *determinantal point processes*.

Diversification and stratification. Since our method suggests to diversify the mini-batches by of non-uniform subsampling from the data, it relates to stratification methods.

Stratification [30, 29] assumes that the data decomposes into disjoint sub-datasets, called strata. These are formed based on certain criteria such as a class-label. Instead of uniformly sampling from the whole dataset, each stratum is sub-sampled independently, which reduces the variance of the estimator of interest.

Stratified sampling has been suggested as a variance reduction method for stochastic gradient algorithms [11, 48]. If one subsamples the same number of data points from every stratum to form a mini-batch as in [48], one naturally balances the training procedure. This approach was also used in [1]. Our work relates closely to this type of biased stratified sampling. It is different in that it does not rely on discrete strata, but only requires a measure a measure of similarity between data points to achieve a similar effect. This applies more broadly.

Variance reduction. Besides re-balancing the dataset, our approach also reduces the variance of the stochastic gradients. Several ways of variance reduction of stochastic gradient algorithms have been proposed, an important class relying on control variates [26, 32, 35, 44, 38]. A second class of methods relies on non-uniform sampling of mini-batches [8, 11, 33, 39, 48, 49]. None of these methods rely on similarity measures between data points.

Our approach is most closely related to clustering-based sampling (CBS) [11] and stratified sampling (StS) [48]. StS applies stratified sampling to SGD and builds on pre-specified strata. For every stratum, the same number of data points are uniformly selected, and then re-weighted according to the size of the stratum to make the sampling scheme un-biased. CBS uses a similar strategy, but does not require a pre-speficied set of strata. Instead, the strata are formed by pre-clustering the raw data with k-means. (Thus, if the data are clustered based on a class label, CBS is identical to StS.) The problem is that the data are not always amenable to clustering. Second, both StS and CBS ignore the within-cluster variations between data points. In contrast, our approach relies on a continuous measure of similarity between samples. We furthermore show that it is a strict generalization of both setups for particular choices of similarity kernels.

Determinantal point processes. The DPP [19, 25] has been proposed [20, 22, 45] and advanced [4, 23, 24] in the machine learning community in the recent years. It has been applied in subset sampling [18, 24] and results filtering [22].

The DPP has also been used as a diversity-enhancing prior in Bayesian models [20, 45]. In big data setups, the data may overwhelm the prior such that the strength of the prior has to scale with the number of data points; introducing a bias. The approach is furthermore constrained to hierarchical Bayesian models, while our approach applies to all empirical risk minimization problems.

Recently, efficient algorithms have been proposed to make sampling using the DPP more scalable. In the traditional formulation, mini-batch sampling costs $\mathcal{O}(Nk^3)$, with an initial fixed cost of diagonalizing the similarity matrix [19], where N is the size of the data and k is the size of the mini-batch. Recent scalable versions of the DPP rely on core-sets and low-rank approximations and scale more favorably [4, 24]. These versions were used in our large-scale experiments.

3 METHOD

Our method, DM-SGD, uses a version of the DPP for mini-batch sampling in stochastic gradient descent. We show that this balances the underlying data distribution and simultaneously accelerates the convergence due to variance reduction. We briefly revisit DPP first, and then introduce our mini-batch diversification method. Theoretical aspects are then discussed in Section 4.

3.1 DETERMINANTAL POINT PROCESSES

A point process is a collection of points randomly located in some mathematical space. The most prominent example is the Poisson process on the real line [17], which models independently occurring events. In contrast, the DPP [19, 25] models repulsive correlations between these points.

In this paper, we restrict ourselves to a finite set of N points. Denote by $L \in \mathbb{R}^{N\times N}$ a similarity kernel matrix between these points, e.g. based on spatial distances or some other criterion. L is real, symmetric and positive definite, and its elements L_{ij} are some appropriately defined measure of similarity between the i_{th} and j_{th} data. The DPP assigns a probability to subsampling any subset Y of $\{1,\ldots,N\}$, which is proportional to the determinant of the sub-matrix L_Y of L which indexes the subset,

$$\mathscr{P}(Y) = \frac{det(L_Y)}{det(L+I)} \propto det(L_Y). \tag{1}$$

For instance, if $Y = \{i, j\}$ consists of only two elements, then $\mathscr{P}(Y) \propto L_{ii}L_{jj} - L_{ij}L_{ji}$. Because L_{ij} and L_{ji} measure the similarity between elements i and j, being more similar lowers the probability of co-occurrence. On the other hand, when the subset is very diverse, the determinant is bigger and correspondingly its co-occurrence is more likely. The DPP thus naturally diversifies the selection of subsets.

In this paper, we propose to use the DPP to diversify mini-batches. In practice, the mini-batch size is usually constrained by empirical bounds or hardware restrictions. In this case, we want to use DPP conditioned on a given size k. Therefore, a slightly modified version of the DPP is needed, which is called k-DPP [18]. It assigns probabilities to subsets of size k,

$$\mathscr{P}_L^k(Y) = \frac{det(L_Y)}{\sum_{|Y'|=k} det(L_{Y'})}. \tag{2}$$

Apart from conditioning on the size of the subset of points, the k-DPP has the same diversification effect as the DPP [18]. In order to have a fixed mini-batch size we use the k-DPP in this work.

3.2 MINI-BATCH DIVERSIFICATION

The diversifying property of the k-DPP makes it well-suited to diversify mini-batches. We first discuss our learning objective—the diversified risk. We then introduce our algorithm and qualitatively discuss its properties.

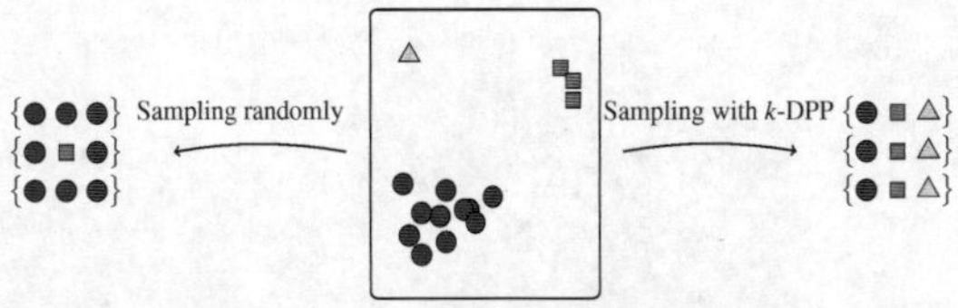

Figure 1: Sampling mini-batches using the k-DPP. For an imbalanced dataset, our method results in diversified mini-batches.

Expected, empirical, and diversified risk. Many problems in machine learning amount to minimizing some loss function $\ell(x,\theta)$ which both depends on a set of parameters θ and on data x. In probabilistic modeling, ℓ could be the negative logarithm of the likelihood of a probabilistic model, or a variational lower bound [6, 14]. We often thereby assume that the data were generated as draws from some underlying unknown data-generating distribution $p_{\text{data}}(x)$, also called the population distribution. To best generalize to unseen data, we would ideally like to minimize this function's expectation under p_{data},

$$J(\theta) = \mathop{\mathbb{E}}_{x\sim p_{\text{data}}} [\ell(x;\theta)] \tag{3}$$

This objective function is also called expected risk [7]. Since $p_{\text{data}}(x)$ is unknown and we believe that our observed data are in some sense a representative draw from the population distribution, we can replace the expectation by an expectation over the *empirical* distribution of the data p_{emp}, which leads to the empirical risk [7],

$$\hat{J}(\theta) = \mathop{\mathbb{E}}_{x\sim p_{\text{emp}}} [\ell(x;\theta)] = \frac{1}{N}\sum_{i=1}^{N} \ell(x_i,\theta). \tag{4}$$

A typical goal in machine learning is not to minimize the empirical risk with high accuracy, but to learn model parameters that generalize well to unseen data. For every data point in a test set, we wish our model to have high predictive accuracy. If this test set is more balanced than the training set (for instance, because it contains all classes to equal proportions in a classification setup), we would naturally like to train our model on a more balanced training set than the original one without throwing away data. In this work, we present a systematic way to achieve this goal based on biased subsampling of the training data. We term the collection of all samples generated from biased subsampling the *balanced dataset*.

To this end, we introduce the *diversified risk*, where we average the loss function over diversified mini-batches $\vec{x}$ of size k,

$$J^*(\theta) = \tfrac{1}{k} \mathop{\mathbb{E}}_{\vec{x}\sim \text{k-DPP}} [\ell(\vec{x};\theta)], \tag{5}$$

Due to the repulsive nature of k-DPP, similar data points are less likely to co-occur in the same draw. Thus, data points which are very different from the rest are more likely to be sampled and obtain a higher weight, as illustrated in Figure 2 (e).

The diversified risk depends both on the mini-batch size and on the similarity kernel L of the data. A more theoretical analysis of the diversified risk is carried out in Section 4.

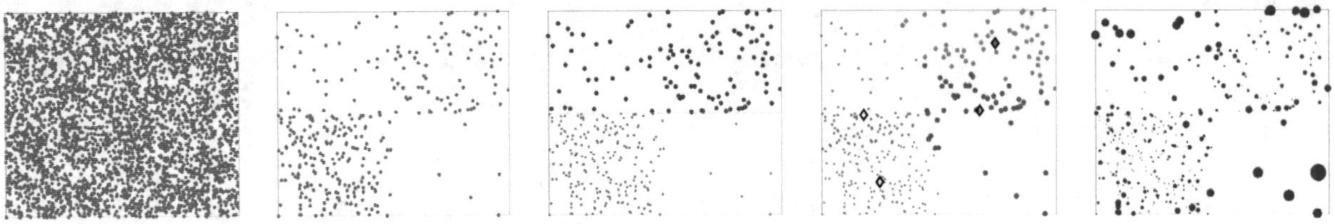

(a) True population (b) Dataset (c) Stratified Sampling (d) Pre-clustering (K-means) (e) k-DPP sampling

Figure 2: Visualization of different non-uniform data subsampling schemes on toy data. Panel (a) shows a homogeneous distribution of data. We assume that we only observe an imbalanced subset, shown in panel (b). Panels (c), (d), (e) demonstrate different biased sampling methods that aim at restoring balance in the data. Thicknesses of data points thereby indicate their sampling frequency. Biased stratified sampling (c) relies on dividing the feature space vertically along certain dimensions, whereas pre-clustering (d) defines the strata as clusters obtained from k-means [11] (we used $k = 4$). The black diamonds show the cluster centers and data are colored with respect to their cluster membership. Panel (e) shows the results using the k-DPP, using an RPF kernel of spatial distances as similarity measure between data points. In this example, the k-DPP best restores the balance of the original data set.

Algorithm. Our proposed algorithm directly optimizes the diversified risk in Eq. 5. To this end, we propose SGD updates on diversified mini-batches of fixed size k,

$$\theta_{t+1} = \theta_t - \rho_t \frac{1}{k} \sum_{i \in B} \nabla \ell(\theta, x_i), \quad B \sim \text{k}-\text{DPP}. \qquad (6)$$

Above, $B \subset \{1, \ldots, N\}$ is a collection of k indices, drawn from the k-DPP. In every stochastic gradient step, we thus sample mini-batches from the k-DPP and carry out an update with decreasing learning rate ρ_t.

Sampling from the k-DPP first requires an eigendecomposition of its kernel. This decomposition can also be approximated and has to be computed only once for one dataset. Drawing a sample then has the computational complexity $\mathcal{O}(Nk^3)$, where k is the mini-batch size, which is much more efficient since k is commonly small. This approach is briefly summarized in Algorithm 1; details on the sampling procedure are given in the supplementary material. For more details, we refer to [19] and to [4, 24] for more efficient sampling procedures.

Algorithm 1 DM-SGD

Input: Data X, mini-batch size k, eigendecomposition $\{(v_n, \lambda_n)\}_{n=1}^N$ of similarity matrix K.
for $t = 0$ *to MaxIter* **do**
  Sample a mini-batch using the k-DPP
  Sample k eigenvectors V using eigenvalues;
  Sample mini-batch $\vec{x}$ of size k using V. (See supplement.)
  Update parameters
  $\theta_{t+1} = \theta_t + \rho_t g^*(\theta_t; \vec{x})$ (g^* is the gradient estimate)
end

Stochastic Variational Inference (SVI) employs SGD for training probabilistic graphical models, such as Latent Dirichlet Allocation (LDA). Every SVI update involves an inner loop. Algorithm 2 shows an application of DM-SGD to SVI for LDA [6]. We thus term it *DM-SVI*.

Algorithm 2 DM-SVI

We adopt the notation from [13].
for $t = 0$ *to MaxIter* **do**
  Sample a mini-batch using the k-DPP;
  Update variational parameters;
  for $j = 0$ *to Mini-batch Size* **do**
    Update local variational parameters (e.g. ϕ and λ for LDA) for mini-batch.
  end
  Compute the intermediate global parameters as if the mini-batch is replicated $\frac{D}{S}$ times.
  (e.g. $\tilde{\lambda}_{kw} = \eta + \frac{D}{S} \sum_{s=1}^{S} n_{tw} \phi_{twk}$ for LDA)
  Update the current estimate of the global variational parameters with $\rho_t = (\tau_0 + t)^{-k}$.
  $\lambda = (1 - \rho_t)\lambda + \rho_t \tilde{\lambda}$
end

Variance reduction and connections to biased stratified sampling. Dividing the data into different strata and sampling data from each stratum with adjusted probabilities may reduce the variance of SGD. This insight forms the basis of stratified sampling [48], and the related pre-clustering based method [11]. As we will demonstrate rigorously in the next section, our approach also enjoys variance reduction but does not require an artificial partition of the data into clusters.

For many models, the gradient varies smoothly as a function of the data. Subsampling data from diversified regions in data space will therefore decorrelate the gradient contributions. This, in turn, may reduce the variance of the stochastic gradient. To some degree, methods such as biased stratified sampling or pre-clustering sample data from diversified regions, but ignore the fact that gradients *within* clusters may still be highly correlated. If the data are not amenable to clustering, this variance may be just as large as the inter-cluster variance. Our approach does not rely on the notion of clusters. Instead, we have a continuous measure of similarity between samples, given by the similarity kernel. This applies more broadly.

In Figure 2, we investigate how well our subsampling procedure using the k-DPP allows us to recover an original distribution of data from which we only observe an imbalanced subset. Panel (a) shows the original (uniform) distribution of data points, and (b) shows the observed data set which we use to re-estimate the original dataset. While biased stratified sampling (c) or pre-clustering based on k-means (d) need an artificial way of dividing the data into finitely many strata and re-balance their corresponding weights, our approach (e) relies on a continuous similarity measure between data and takes into account both intra-strata and inter-strata variations.

Computational overhead. Sampling from the k-DPP implies a computational overhead over classical SGD. Regarding the overall runtime, the benefits of the approach therefore come mainly into play in setups where each gradient update is expensive. One example is stochastic variational inference for models with local latent variables. For example, in LDA, the computational bottleneck is to update the per-document topic proportions. The time spent on sampling a mini-batch using the k-DPP is only about 10% of the time to infer these local variables and estimate the gradient (See Table 1 in Section 5). Spending this tiny overhead on actively selecting training examples is well invested as the resulting stochastic gradient has a lower variance.

Since the sampling procedure is independent of the learning algorithm, we can parallelize it or even draw the samples as a pre-processing step and reuse them for different hyperparameter settings. Moreover, there are approximate versions of k-DPP sampling which are scalable to big datasets [4, 23]. In this paper, we use the *fast k-DPP* [23] in our large-scale experiments (Section 5.3).

4 THEORETICAL CONSIDERATIONS

In this section, we give the theoretical foundation of the DM-SGD scheme. We first prove that biased stratified sampling and pre-clustering emerge as special cases of our algorithm for particular choices of the kernel matrix L. We then prove that the diversified risk of DM-SGD is a re-weighted variant of the empirical risk, where the weights are given by the marginal likelihoods of the k-DPP (we also present an unbiased DM-SGD scheme which approximates the true gradients, but which performs less favorably in practice). Last, we investigate under which circumstances DM-SGD reduces the variance of the stochastic gradient.

Notation. For what follows, let $m_i \in \{0,1\}$ denote a variable which indicates whether the i_{th} data point was sampled under the k-DPP. Furthermore, let $\mathbb{E}[\cdot] = \mathbb{E}_{m\sim \text{k-DPP}}[\cdot]$ always denote the expectation under the k-DPP. This lets us express the expectation $F(x) = \sum_i f(x_i)$ which depends additively on the data points x_i as

$$\mathbb{E}[\textstyle\sum_{i=1}^N m_i f(x_i)] \equiv \underset{x\sim \text{k-DPP}}{\mathbb{E}}[F(x)] \tag{7}$$

Next, we introduce short hand notations for first and second moments. Denote the marginal probability for a point x_i being sampled as

$$b_i \equiv \mathbb{E}[m_i], \tag{8}$$

which has an analytic form and can be computed efficiently. We also introduce the correlation matrix

$$C_{ij} = \frac{\mathbb{E}[(m_i - b_i)(m_j - b_j)]}{\mathbb{E}[m_i]\,\mathbb{E}[m_j]} = \frac{\mathbb{E}[m_i m_j]}{b_i b_j} - 1. \tag{9}$$

In contrast to minibatch SGD where $\mathbb{E}[m_i m_j] = \mathbb{E}[m_i]\,\mathbb{E}[m_j]$ and hence $C_{ij} = 0$, this is no longer true under the k-DPP. Instead, the correlation can be both negative (when data points are similar) and even positive (when data points are very dissimilar).

Lastly, let $g(\theta, x) = \sum_{i=1}^N g(\theta, x_i)$ denote the gradient of the empirical risk, which is the batch gradient, and $g(\theta, x_i)$ its individual contributions from the data x_i.

We first prove that our algorithm captures two important limiting cases, namely (biased) stratified sampling and pre-clustering.

Proposition 1. Biased stratified sampling (StS) [48], where data from different strata are subsampled with equal probability, is equivalent to DM-SGD with a similarity matrix L, defined as a block-diagonal matrix with

$$L_{ij} = \begin{cases} 1 & H_i = H_j \\ 0 & H_i \neq H_j, \end{cases} \tag{10}$$

where H_i denotes the label for the stratum of data point i.

Proof. It is enough to show that a draw A from the k-DPP which has multiple data points with the same strata assignment has probability zero.

Let $A = a \cup \bar{a}$, where a is a collection of indices which come from the same stratum, and $\bar{a}$ is its disjoint complement. Because of the block-structure of L, we have that

$$\det(L_A) = \det(L_a)\det(L_{\bar{a}}).$$

However, $\det(L_a) = 0$ because it is a matrix of all-ones. Therefore, $\det(L_A) = 0$, and hence A has zero probability under the k-DPP. Therefore, every draw from the k-DPP with L_{ij} defined as above contains at most one data point from each stratum. When k is the same as the number of classes, we recover StS. If k is smaller than the number of classes, we provide a direct generalization of StS. □

Proposition 2. Pre-clustering [11] results as a special case of DM-SGD, with $L_{ij} = 1$ if the data points i and j are assigned to the same cluster, and otherwise $L_{ij} = 0$.

It is furthermore simple to see that regular minibatch SGD results from DM-SGD when choosing the identity kernel.

Next, we analyze the objective function of DM-SGD. We prove that the diversified risk (Eq. 5) is given by a re-weighted version of the empirical risk (Eq. 4) of the data.

Proposition 3. The diversified risk (Eq. 5) can be expressed as a re-weighted empirical risk with the marginal k-DPP weights b_i,

$$J^*(\theta) = \frac{1}{k}\sum_{i=1}^{N} b_i \ell(x_i,\theta).$$

As $b_i \to k/N$ in case of a trivial similarity kernel $L = I$, this quantity just becomes the empirical risk.

Proof. We employ the indicators m_i defined above:

$$kJ^*(\theta) = \mathop{\mathbb{E}}_{x\sim\text{kDPP}}[\ell(x;\theta)] = \mathbb{E}[\sum_{i=1}^{N} m_i \ell(x_i;\theta)]$$
$$= \sum_{i=1}^{N} \mathbb{E}[m_i]\ell(x_i;\theta) = \sum_{i=1}^{N} b_i \ell(x_i;\theta).$$

□

The following corollary allows us to construct an unbiased stochastic gradient based on DM-SGD in case we are not interested in re-balancing the population.

Proposition 4. The following SGD scheme leads to an unbiased stochastic gradient:

$$\theta_{t+1} = \theta_t - \rho_t \frac{1}{k}\sum_{i\in B}\frac{1}{b_i}\nabla\ell(\theta,x_i), \quad B\sim \text{kDPP}. \tag{11}$$

This is a simple consequence of the identity $\mathbb{E}[\sum_{i=1}^{N}\frac{m_i}{b_i}g(\theta;x_i)] = \sum_{i=1}^{N}\mathbb{E}[\frac{m_i}{b_i}]g(\theta;x_i) = g(\theta,x)$.

Finally, we investigate under which circumstances the DM-SGD gradient has a lower variance compared to simple mini-batch SGD on the diversified risk. To this end, consider the gradient components $g(x_i,\theta)$, $g(x_i,\theta)$ of data points i and j, respectively, as well as their correlation C_{ij} under the k-DPP. A sufficient condition for BN-SGD to reduce the variance is given as follows.

Theorem 1. Assume that for all data points x_i and x_j and for all parameters θ in a region of interest, the scalar product $g(x_i,\theta)^\top g(x_j,\theta)$ is always positive (negative) whenever the correlation C_{ij} is negative (positive), respectively, i.e.

$$\forall_{i\neq j} : C_{ij}\, g(x_i,\theta)^\top g(x_j,\theta) < 0. \tag{12}$$

Then, DM-SGD has a lower variance than SGD.

Remark. The sufficient conditions outlined in Theorem 1 are very strong, but its proof provides us with valuable insights of why variance reduction occurs.

Proof. To begin with, define

$$g^F(\theta,x) = \tfrac{1}{k}\sum_{i=1}^{N} b_i\, g(\theta,x_i), \tag{13}$$
$$g^*(\theta,x) = \tfrac{1}{k}\sum_{i=1}^{N} m_i\, g(\theta,x_i), \tag{14}$$

where g^* is the DM-SGD gradient and $g^F = \mathbb{E}[g^*]$ is the full gradient of the diversified risk.

We denote the difference between the expected and stochastic gradient as

$$\Delta g = g^* - g^F = \tfrac{1}{k}\sum_{i=1}^{N}(b_i - m_i)\, g(\theta,x_i), \tag{15}$$

By construction, this quantity has expectation zero. We are interested in the trace of the stochastic gradient covariance,

$$Var(g^*) = \text{Tr}(Cov(g^*)) = \mathbb{E}[\Delta g^\top \Delta g]. \tag{16}$$

This quantity can be expressed as

$$Var(g^*) = \frac{1}{k^2}\sum_{i,j=1}^{N} \underbrace{\mathbb{E}[(m_i - b_i)(m_j - b_j)]}_{\mathbb{E}[m_i m_j] - b_i b_j} g(x_i,\theta)^\top g(x_j,\theta)$$

We can furthermore compute

$$\mathbb{E}[m_i m_j] = \mathbb{E}[m_i^2]\delta_{ij} + \mathbb{E}[m_i m_j](1-\delta_{ij})$$
$$= \mathbb{E}[m_i]\delta_{ij} + (C_{ij}+1) b_i b_j (1-\delta_{ij}),$$

where δ_{ij} is the Kronecker symbol (we used $m_i^2 = m_i$).

Collecting all terms, the variance can be written as

$$Var(g^*) = \frac{1}{k^2}\sum_{i=1}^{N}(b_i - b_i^2)\,||g(x_i,\theta)||_2^2$$
$$+ \frac{1}{k^2}\sum_{i\neq j} C_{ij} b_i b_j g(x_i,\theta)^\top g(x_j,\theta).$$

The first term is just the variance of regular mini-batch SGD, where we sample each data point with probability proportional to b_i, which also optimizes the diversified risk. This term is always positive because $b_i < 1$ and thus $b_i > b_i^2$.

The second term can be both positive and negative. By a clever choice of similarity kernel and resulting correlation function C_{ij} (as defined in Eq. 9), the second term may therefore reduce the variance. We immediately see that this condition exactly corresponds to Eq. 12. This proves our claim. □

Discussion of Theorem 1. If the similarity kernel L relies on spatial distances, nearby data points x_i and x_j have a negative correlation C_{ij} under the k-DPP. However, if the loss function is smooth, $g(x_i,\theta)$ and $g(x_j,\theta)$ tend to align (i.e. have a positive scalar product). Eq. 12 is therefore naturally satisfied for these points. C_{ij} can also be positive: since some combinations of data points are less likely to co-occur, others must be more likely to co-occur. Since these points tend to be far apart, it is reasonable to assume that their gradients show no tendency to align. It is therefore plausible to assume that for these points, Eq. 12 also applies[1].

To summarize, if the condition in Eq. 12 is met, we can guarantee variance reduction relative to mini-batch SGD, and we have given arguments why it is plausible that these are met to some degree when using DM-SGD with a distance-dependent similarity kernel. In our experimental section we show that DM-SGD has a faster learning curve, which we attribute to this phenomenon.

[1] We only need to assure that the negative contributions outweigh the positive ones to see variance reduction.

5 EXPERIMENTS

We evaluate the performance of our method in different settings. In Section 5.1 we demonstrate the usage of DM-SGD for Latent Dirichlet Allocation (LDA) [6], an unsupervised probabilistic topic model. We show that the learned diversified topic representations are better suited for subsequent text classification. In Section 5.2 we evaluate the supervised scenario based on multinomial (softmax) logistic regression with imbalanced data. We compare against stratified sampling, which emerges naturally in this example. In section 5.3 we show that our method also maintains performance on the balanced MNIST data set, where we tested convolutional neural networks. In all the experiments, we pre-sample the mini-batch indices using the k-DPP implementation from [19] for small datasets, and from [23] for big datasets. In this way, sampling is treated as a pre-scheduling step and can easily be parallelized. We found that our approach finds more diversified feature representations (in unsupervised setups) and higher predictive accuracies (in supervised setups). We also found that the k-DPP converges within fewer passes through the data compared to standard minibatch sampling due to variance reduction.

5.1 TOPIC LEARNING WITH LDA

We follow Algorithm 2 for LDA. Firstly, we demonstrate the performance of DM-SVI on synthetic data with LDA. We show that by balancing our mini-batches, we find a much better recovery of the topics that were used to generate the data. Second, we use a real-world news dataset. We demonstrate that we can learn more diverse topics that are also better features for text classification tasks.

In this setting, stratified sampling is not applicable since there is no discrete feature such as a class label available. With only word frequencies available, no simple criterion can be used to divide the data into meaningful strata.

5.1.1 SYNTHETIC DATA

We generate a synthetic dataset (shown in the supplementary material) following the generative process of LDA with a fixed global latent parameter (the graphical topics). We choose distinct patterns as shown in Figure 3 (a), where each row represents a topic and each column represents a word. To generate an imbalanced data set, we use different Dirichlet priors for the per document topic distribution θ. 300 documents are generated with prior (0.5 0.5 0.01 0.01 0.01); 50 with prior (0.01 0.5 0.5 0.5 0.01) and 10 with prior (0.01 0.01 0.01 0.5 0.5). Hence, the first two topics are used very often in the corpus. Topic 3 and 4 are shown a few times and topic 5 appears very rarely.

We fit LDA to recover the topics of the synthetic data using traditional SVI and our proposed DM-SVI respectively. Here, the raw data occurence x is used to construct the similarity matrix $L = xx^T$. We check how well the global parameters are recovered. Fully recovered latent variables

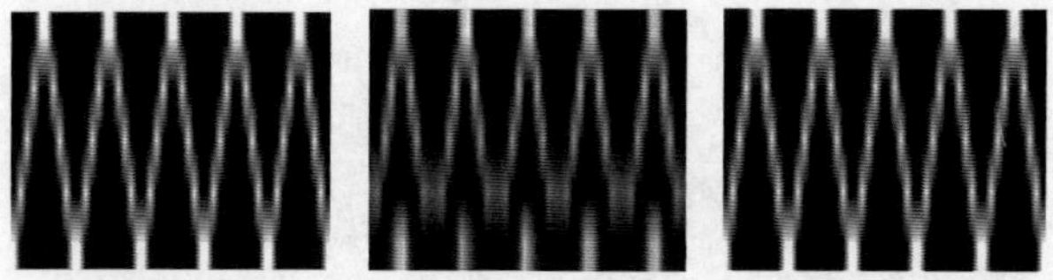

(a) Ground Truth (b) Est w. SVI LDA (c) Est w. **DM-SVI**

Figure 3: Per topic word distribution for the synthetic data. Each row presents a topic and each column presents a word. (a) shows the ground truth with which the synthetic data is generated using LDA. (b) shows the estimation of this latent variable with LDA using traditional stochastic variational inference (SVI). (c) shows the estimation of this latent variable with DM-SVI

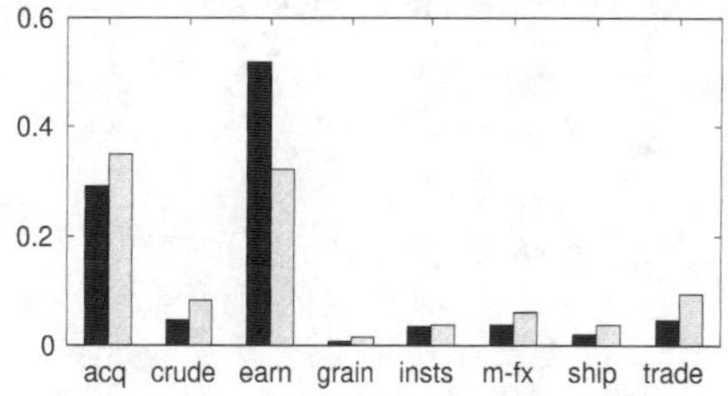

Figure 4: The frequency of class labels of the training dataset (in blue) and of the balanced dataset (in yellow). While explicit class label information is withheld, the algorithm partially balances class contributions.

indicate that the model is able to capture its underlying structure of the data. Figure 3 (b) shows the estimated per topic words distribution with SVI and Figure 3 (c) shows the result with our proposed DM-SVI.

In Figure 3 (b), we see that the first three topics are recovered using traditional SVI. Topic four is roughly recovered but with information from topic five mixed in. The last topic is not recovered at all, instead, it is a repetition of the first topic. This shows the drawback of the traditional method: when the data is not balanced, the model creates redundant topics to refine the likelihood of the dense data but ignores the scarce data even when they carry important information. In Figure 3 (c), we see that all the topics are correctly recovered thanks to the balanced dataset.

5.1.2 R8 NEWS DATA EXPERIMENT

We also evaluate the effect of DM-SVI on the Reuters news R8 dataset [3]. This dataset contains eight classes of news with an extremely imbalanced number of documents per class, as shown in Figure 4 (a). To measure similarities between documents, we represent each document with a vector x of the tf-idf [37] scores of each word in the document. Then define an annealed linear kernel $L(x_i, x_j) = x_i^\rho x_j^\rho$ with parameter $\rho = 0.1$, which is more sensitive to small feature overlap. We run LDA with SVI and DM-SVI with one effective pass through the data, where we set the mini-batch size to 80 and use 30 topics.

We first compare the frequencies at which documents with particular labels were sub-sampled. While Figure 4 shows

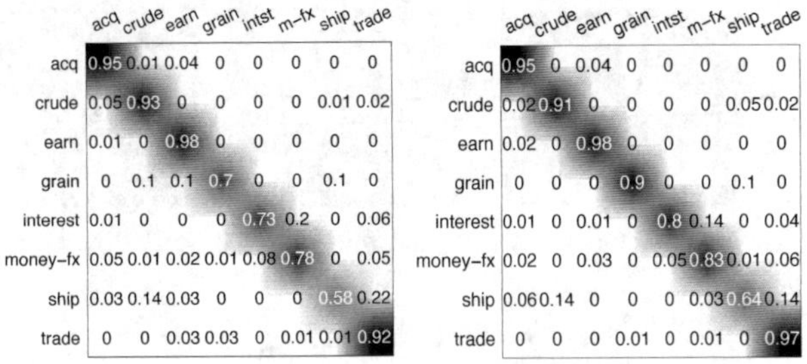

(a) CM w.SVI (b) CM w.**DM-SVI**.

Figure 5: Confusion matrix for text classification based on LDA features obtained from SVI (a) and the proposed DM-SVI (b). DM-SVI features lead to better accuracies.

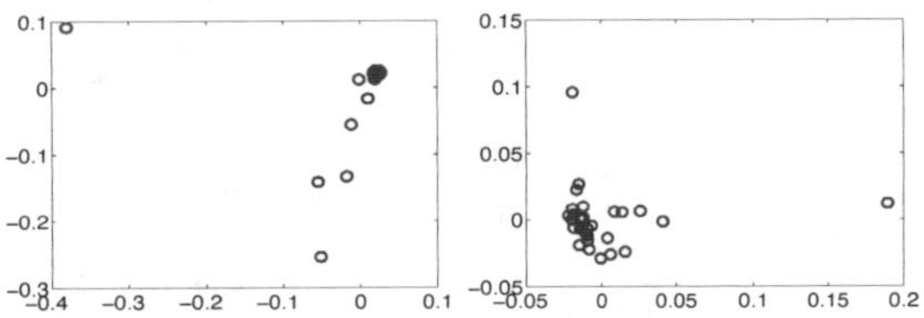

(a) First 2 PC w. SVI (b) First 2 PC w. **DM-SVI**

Figure 6: First 2 principle components of topic word distributions. DM-SVI topic vectors (b) are more diverse compared to SVI (a).

the actual frequency of these classes in the original data set compared with the frequency of these classes over the balanced dataset (a collection of sampled mini-batches using the k-DPP). We can see that the number of documents is more balanced among different classes.

To demonstrate that DM-SVI leads to a more useful topic representation, we classify each document in the test-set based on the learned topic proportions with a linear SVM. The global variable (per-topic word distribution) is only trained on the training set. The resulting confusion matrices are shown in Figure 5 using traditional SVI and DM-SVI respectively. With traditional SVI, the average performance over 8 classes is 82.11%; the total accuracy (number of correctly classified documents over number of test documents) is 94.11%. With DM-SVI, the average performance over 8 classes is 87.24% and the total accuracy is 94.7%.

Thus the overall classification performance is improved using DM-SVI features, and especially the performance on the classes with few documents (such as "grain" and "ship") is improved significantly.

We also visualize the first two principal components (PC) of the the global topics in Figure 6. In traditional SVI, many topics are redundant and share large parts of their vocabulary, resulting in a single dense cluster. In contrast, we see that the topics in DM-SVI are more spread out. In this regard, DM-SVI achieves a similar effect as when using diversity priors as in [20] without the need to grow the prior with the data. The top words from each topic are shown in the appendix, where we present more evidence that the

Size	k = 10	k =30	k=50	k=80
Relative cost	0.114%	1.097%	3.191%	8.971%

Table 1: LDA on the R8 dataset. Relative cost of mini-batch sampling as a fraction of the cost of a gradient update. Different values of mini-batch size k are shown.

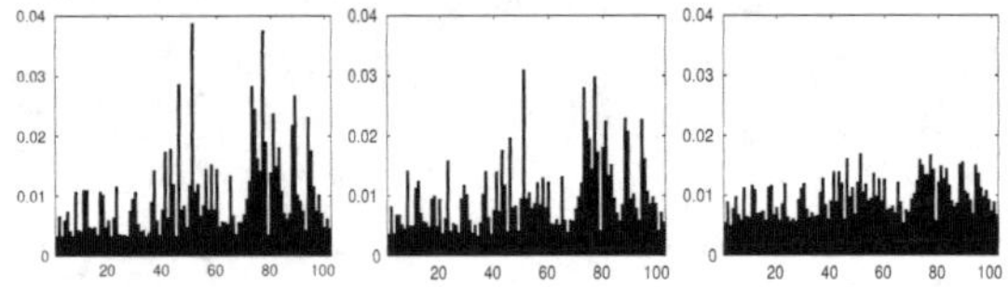

(a) Labels (b) $w = 0.3$ (c) $w = 0.9$

Figure 7: The frequency of data in each class of the training dataset and of the balanced dataset using different weights w (Eq. 17). There are 102 classes of flowers in total and each bar presents the percentage of data belongs to one class. Minibatch size 50 is used as an example here for (b) and (c).

topics learned by DM-SVI are more diverse.

The relative costs of sampling per iteration for LDA is shown in Table 1. Because every local update is expensive, the relative overhead of mini-batch sampling is small. More details are given in the appendix.

5.2 MULTICLASS LOGISTIC REGRESSION

In this section, we demonstrate DM-SGD on a fine-grained classification task. The Oxford 102 flower dataset [31, 41] is used here for evaluation.

Many datasets in computer vision are balanced even though the true collected dataset is extremely imbalanced. The true reason is that the performance of machine learning models usually suffer from imbalanced training data. One example is the Oxford 102 flower dataset which contains 1020 images in the training set with 10 images per class. However, in the test set, 6149 images are available with high imbalance. In this experiment, we make the learning task harder. We use the original testing set for training and use the original training set for testing. This setting demonstrates the real life scenario where we only can collect data with bias but wish the model to perform well in all different situations. Off-the-shelf CNN features [41] are used in this experiment. A pre-trained VGG16 network [42] is used for the feature extraction. We use the first fully connected layer as features, since [5] shows that this layer is most robust.

The similarity kernel L of the k-DPP was constructed as follows. We chose a linear kernel $L = FF^\top$, where F is a weighted concatenation of the fc1 features X_{fc1} and the labels a one-hot-vector representation of the class label H,

$$F = [(1-w)X_{fc1} \;\; wH], \quad 0 \leq w \leq 1. \qquad (17)$$

This kernel construction enables the population to be balanced both among classes and within classes. When w is large, the algorithm focuses more on the class labels. When w is small, balancing is performed mostly based on the fea-

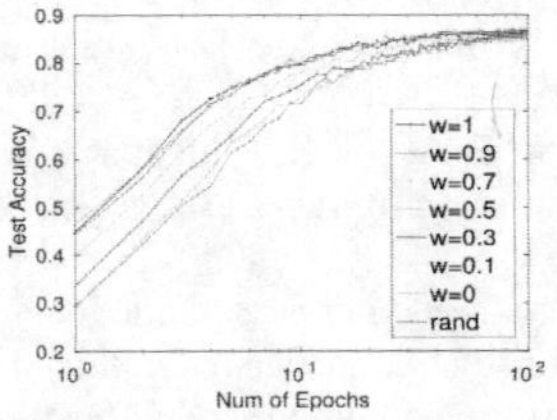

(a) k=50, Top3: 0.9, 0.7, 1; Best: 86.7% Baseline:84.7%

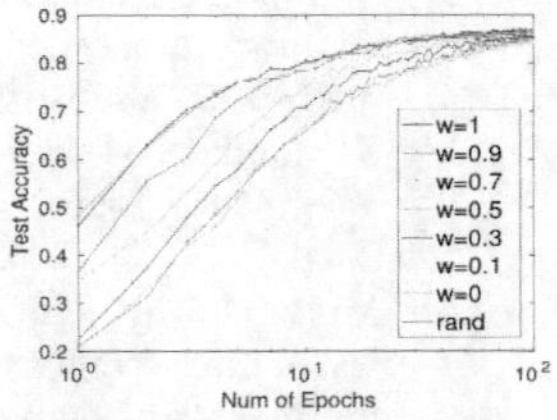

(b) k=80, Top3: 0.9, 0.7, 1; Best: 86.7% Baseline:81.8%

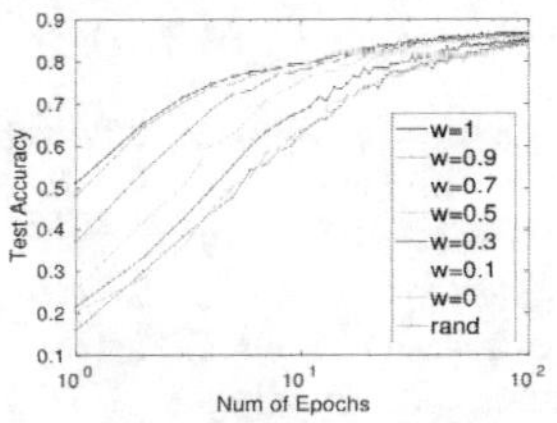

(c) k=102, Top3: 1, 0.9, 0.7; Best: 86.5% Baseline:84.5%

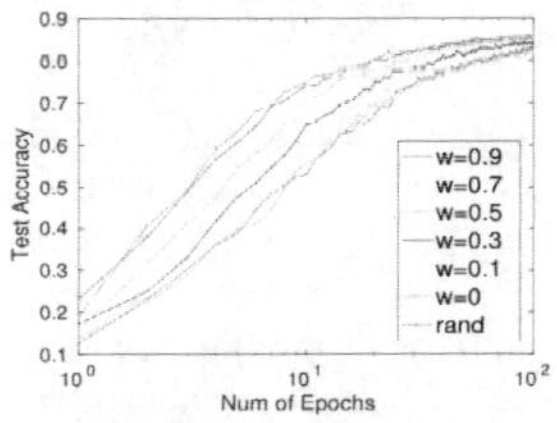

(d) k=150, Top3: 0.7, 0.5, 0.9; Best: 85.5% Baseline:83.1%

Figure 8: Test accuracy as a function of training epochs on the Oxford 102 multi-class classification task. We show DM-SGD for different values of w, with $w = 1$ being biased stratified sampling (see Eq. 17 and the discussion below). The plot caption indicates the batch size k and the three best performing values of w. 'Rand' indicates regular SGD sampling. We listed the final test accuracy after convergence, where "Best" indicates the best performance within our DM-SGD experiments, and "Baseline" indicates regular SGD as our baseline. The improvement is up to 5%.

tures. The weighting factor w is a free parameter. As $w = 1$ results in stratified sampling (see Theorem 1), this baseline is naturally captured in our approach.

In this setting, the class label is a natural criterion to divide the data into strata. One can then re-sample the same amount of data from each stratum in order to re-balance the data set. Such a mechanism constrains the mini-batch size to be $k = sM$ where M is the number of classes/strata and s is a positive integer. As proved in Section 4, when $k = M$ and $w = 1$, DM-SGD is equivalent to this type of (biased) stratified sampling.

Figure 7 shows the percentage of data in each class for the original dataset and with the balanced dataset. It shows that with larger w, the dataset is more balanced among classes. More examples are shown in the supplementary material.

We demonstrate this application with a standard linear Softmax classifier for multi-class classification. In our case, the inputs are the off-the-shelf CNN fc1 feature (X_{fc1}). We can also view this procedure as fine-tuning a neural network.

Figure 8 shows how the test accuracy changes with respect to each training epoch. We compare the DM-SGD with different weights against random sampling. The learning rate schedule is kept the same among different experiments. Different mini-batch sizes k are used, which is shown in the caption of each panel in the figure. We can see that with DM-SGD, we can reach a high model performance more rapidly. Additionally, for a classification task, balancing data with

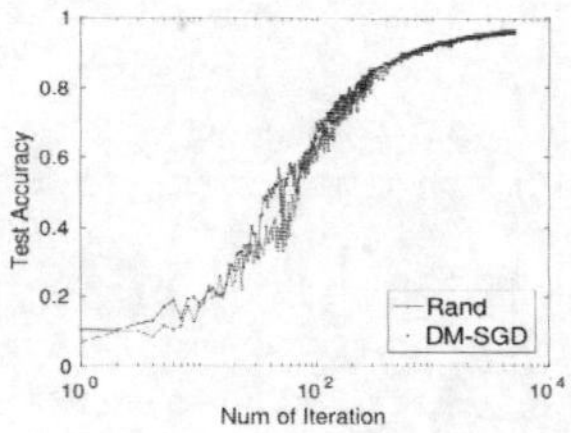

(a) k=10

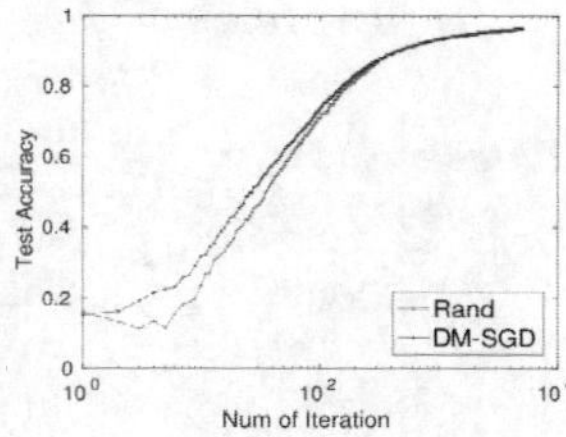

(b) k=200

Figure 9: Same quantities shown as in Fig. 8, but for the MNIST data set, which is more balanced.

respect to classes is important since the performance is better in general for bigger w. On the other hand, the feature information is essential as well since the best performance is mostly obtained with $w = 0.9$ and $w = 0.7$. Comparing these plots, we can see that the performance benefits more when the mini-batch size is comparably small. Small mini-batches in general are preferred due to low cost and our method can maximize the usage of small mini-batches.

5.3 CNN CLASSIFICATION ON MNIST

Finally, we show the performance of our method in a scenario where the dataset is balanced, which is less preferable scenario for DM-SGD. Here we consider the MNIST dataset [21], which contains approximately the same number of examples per hand-written digits. Since our method is independent of the model, we can use any low level data statistics. Here, we demonstrate DM-SGD with raw data features and apply it to training a CNN. Here, we construct the similarity kernel using a RBF kernel. For the low level feature, we use the normalized raw pixel value X directly. To encode both class information and label information, we use $F = [(1-w)X \quad wH]$ to compute the similarities matrix, where $w = 0.5$ for this experiment. We use half of the training data from MNIST to train a 5-layer CNN as in [2]. Figure 9 shows the test accuracy from each iteration with mini-batch size 10 and 200 respectively. We can see that even if the data are balanced, DM-SGD still performs better than random sampling due to its variance reduction property.

6 CONCLUSION

We proposed a diversified mini-batch sampling scheme based on determinantal point processes. Our method, DM-SGD, builds on a similarity matrix between the data points and suppresses the co-occurance of similar data points in the same mini-batch. This leads to a training outcome which generalizes better to unseen data. We also derived sufficient conditions under which the method reduces the variance of the stochastic gradient, leading to faster learning. We showed that our approach generalizes both stratified sampling and pre-clustering. In the future, we will explore the possibility to further improve the efficiency of the algorithm with data reweighing [28] and tackle imbalanced learning problems involving different modalities for supervised [47] and multi-modal [15] settings.

References

[1] Image classification with imagenet. https://github.com/soumith/imagenet-multiGPU.torch/blob/master/dataset.lua.

[2] Multilayer convolutional network. https://www.tensorflow.org/get_started/mnist/pros.

[3] R8 dataset. http://csmining.org/index.php/r52-and-r8-of-reuters-21578.html.

[4] R. H. Affandi, A. Kulesza, E. B. Fox, and B. Taskar. Nystrom approximation for large-scale determinantal processes. In *AISTATS*, pages 85–98, 2013.

[5] H. Azizpour, A. Sharif Razavian, J. Sullivan, A. Maki, and S. Carlsson. From generic to specific deep representations for visual recognition. In *CVPR WS*, pages 36–45, 2015.

[6] D. M. Blei, A. Y. Ng, and M. I. Jordan. Latent Dirichlet Allocation. *JMLR*, 3:993–1022, 2003.

[7] L. Bottou. Large-scale machine learning with stochastic gradient descent. In *COMPSTAT*, pages 177–186. 2010.

[8] D. Csiba and P. Richtarik. Importance sampling for minibatches. *arXiv:1602.02283*, 2016.

[9] J. Duchi, E. Hazan, and Y. Singer. Adaptive subgradient methods for online learning and stochastic optimization. *JMLR*, 12(Jul):2121–2159, 2011.

[10] Y. Freund and R. E. Schapire. A desicion-theoretic generalization of on-line learning and an application to boosting. In *EuroCOLT*, pages 23–37. Springer, 1995.

[11] T.F Fu and Z.H. Zhang. CPSG-MCMC: Clustering-based preprocessing method for stochastic gradient MCMC. In *AISTATS*, 2017.

[12] H. He and E. A. Garcia. Learning from imbalanced data. *TKDE*, 21(9):1263–1284, 2009.

[13] M. Hoffman, F. R. Bach, and D. M. Blei. Online learning for latent dirichlet allocation. In *NIPS*, pages 856–864, 2010.

[14] M. I. Jordan, Z. Ghahramani, T. S. Jaakkola, and L. K. Saul. An introduction to variational methods for graphical models. *Machine learning*, 37(2):183–233, 1999.

[15] A. Joulin, L. van der Maaten, A. Jabri, and N. Vasilache. Learning visual features from large weakly supervised data. In *ECCV*, 2016.

[16] D. Kingma and J. Ba. Adam: A method for stochastic optimization. *arXiv:1412.6980*, 2014.

[17] J. F. C. Kingman. *Poisson processes*. Wiley Online Library, 1993.

[18] A. Kulesza and B. Taskar. k-DPPs: Fixed-size determinantal point processes. In *ICML*, pages 1193–1200, 2011.

[19] A. Kulesza and B. Taskar. Determinantal point processes for machine learning. *arXiv:1207.6083*, 2012.

[20] J. T. Kwok and R. P. Adams. Priors for diversity in generative latent variable models. In *NIPS*, pages 2996–3004, 2012.

[21] Y. LeCun, L. Bottou, Y. Bengio, and P. Haffner. Gradient-based learning applied to document recognition. *Proceedings of the IEEE*, 86(11):2278–2324, 1998.

[22] D. Lee, G. Cha, M. H. Yang, and S. Oh. Individualness and determinantal point processes for pedestrian detection. In *ECCV*, pages 330–346, 2016.

[23] C. T. Li, S. Jegelka, and S. Sra. Fast DPP sampling for nyströom with application to kernel methods. *arXiv:1603.06052*, 2016.

[24] C.T. Li, S. Jegelka, and S. Sra. Efficient sampling for k-determinantal point processes. *arXiv:1509.01618*.

[25] O. Macchi. The coincidence approach to stochastic point processes. *Advances in Applied Probability*.

[26] S. Mandt and D. M. Blei. Smoothed gradients for stochastic variational inference. In *NIPS*, pages 2438–2446, 2014.

[27] S. Mandt, M. D. Hoffman, and D. M. Blei. Stochastic gradient descent as approximate Bayesian inference. *arXiv:1704.04289*, 2017.

[28] S. Mandt, J. McInerney, F. Abrol, R. Ranganath, and D. M. Blei. Variational Tempering. In *AISTATS*, pages 704–712, 2016.

[29] M. D. McKay, R. J. Beckman, and W. J. Conover. Comparison of three methods for selecting values of input variables in the analysis of output from a computer code. *Technometrics*, 21(2):239–245, 1979.

[30] J. Neyman. On the two different aspects of the representative method: the method of stratified sampling and the method of purposive selection. *Journal of the Royal Statistical Society*, 97(4):558–625, 1934.

[31] M. E. Nilsback and A. Zisserman. Automated flower classification over a large number of classes. In *ICVGIP*, 2008.

[32] J. Paisley, D. Blei, and M. Jordan. Variational bayesian inference with stochastic search. *arXiv:1206.6430*, 2012.

[33] D. Perekrestenko, V. Cevher, and M. Jaggi. Faster coordinate descent via adaptive importance sampling. In *AISTATS*, 2017.

[34] B. T. Polyak. Some methods of speeding up the convergence of iteration methods. *USSR Computational Mathematics and Mathematical Physics*, 4(5):1–17, 1964.

[35] R. Ranganath, S. Gerrish, and D. M. Blei. Black box variational inference. In *AISTATS*, pages 814–822, 2014.

[36] H. Robbins and D. Siegmund. A convergence theorem for non negative almost supermartingales and some applications. In *Herbert Robbins Selected Papers*, pages 111–135. Springer, 1985.

[37] S. Robertson. Understanding inverse document frequency: on theoretical arguments for IDF. *Journal of documentation*, 60(5):503–520, 2004.

[38] T. Salimans and D.A. Knowles. On using control variates with stochastic approximation for variational bayes and its connection to stochastic linear regression. *arXiv:1401.1022*.

[39] M. Schmidt, R. Babanezhad, M. O. Ahmed, A. Defazio, A. Clifton, and A. Sarkar. Non-uniform stochastic average gradient method for training conditional random fields. In *AISTATS*, 2015.

[40] M. Schmidt, N. Le Roux, and F. Bach. Minimizing finite sums with the stochastic average gradient. *Mathematical Programming*, pages 1–30, 2013.

[41] A. Sharif Razavian, H. Azizpour, J. Sullivan, and S. Carlsson. Cnn features off-the-shelf: an astounding baseline for recognition. In *CVPR WS*, pages 806–813, 2014.

[42] K. Simonyan and A. Zisserman. Very deep convolutional networks for large-scale image recognition. *arXiv:1409.1556*, 2014.

[43] T. Tieleman and G. Hinton. Lecture 6.5-RMSPROP: Divide the gradient by a running average of its recent magnitude. *COURSERA: Neural networks for machine learning*.

[44] C. Wang, X. Chen, A. J. Smola, and E. P. Xing. Variance reduction for stochastic gradient optimization. In *NIPS*, pages 181–189, 2013.

[45] P.T. Xie, Y.T. Deng, and E. Xing. Diversifying restricted boltzmann machine for document modeling. In *ACM SIGKDD*, pages 1315–1324. ACM, 2015.

[46] M. D. Zeiler. ADADELTA: an adaptive learning rate method. *arXiv:1212.5701*, 2012.

[47] C. Zhang and H. Kjellström. How to Supervise Topic Models. In *ECCV WS*, 2014.

[48] P.L. Zhao and T. Zhang. Accelerating minibatch stochastic gradient descent using stratified sampling. *arXiv:1405.3080*.

[49] P.L. Zhao and T. Zhang. Stochastic optimization with importance sampling for regularized loss minimization. In *ICML*, pages 1–9, 2015.

A SUPPLEMENT

Algorithm 3 shows the details of how to sample a mini-batch using k-DPP [19] which is used for the DM-SGD and DM-SVI algorithm in the paper.

Algorithm 3 Mini-batch Sampling

Input: Mini-batch size k, eigendecomposition $\{(v_n, \lambda_n)\}_{n=1}^{N}$ of similarity matrix L.

Compute the elementary symmetric polynomials

$e_0^n \leftarrow 1 \forall n \in \{0,1,2,...,N\}$

$e_0^l \leftarrow 1 \forall l \in \{1,2,...,k\}$

for $l = 1,2,...,k$ **do**

  for $n = 1,2,...,N$ **do**

    $e_l^n \leftarrow e_l^{n-1} + \lambda_n e_{l-1}^{n-1}$

  end

end

for t=*1 to Number of subset samples to generate* **do**

  Sampling k **eigenvectors** V **with indices** J

  $J \leftarrow \emptyset$

  $l \leftarrow k$

  for $n = N,...,2,1$ **do**

    if $l = 0$ **then**

      break;

    end

    if $u \sim U[0,1] \leq \lambda_n \frac{e_{l-1}^{n-1}}{e_l^n}$ **then**

      $J \leftarrow J \cup \{n\}$

      $l \leftarrow l - 1$

    end

  end

  Sample k **data points indexed by** Y **using** V.

  $V \leftarrow \{v_i\}_{i \in J}$

  $Y \leftarrow \emptyset$

  while $|V| > 0$ **do**

    Select i with $Pr(i) = \frac{1}{|V|} \sum_{v \in V} (v^T e_i)^2$

    $Y \leftarrow Y \cup i$ $V \leftarrow V_{\perp}$, an orthonormal basis for the subspace of V orthogonal to e_i

  end

  Output: Y

end

Table 2 and 3 show the top words using $K = 30$ for LDA using traditional SVI and our proposed DM-SVI respectively. We can see that the topics that are learned by DM-SVI are more diverse and rare topics such as grain (colored in blue) are captured.

Figure 10 shows the synthetic data that are used in the LDA experiment. Each row represents a document and each column represents a word.

The sampling time in seconds for the R8 dataset is listed in Table 4. There are 5485 training documents. The first row in the table shows the sampling time for different mini-batch sizes k and different versions of k-DPP sampling. In

Topic 1	pct shares stake and group investment securities stock commission firm
Topic 2	year pct and for last lower growth debt profits company
Topic 3	and merger for will approval companies corp acquire into letter
Topic 4	and for canadian company management pacific bid southern court units
Topic 5	baker official and that treasury western policy administration study budget
Topic 6	and president for executive chief shares plc company chairman cyclops
Topic 7	bank pct banks rate rates money interest and reuter today
Topic 8	and unit inc sale sell reuter company systems corp terms
Topic 9	mln stg and reuter months year for plc market pretax
Topic 10	and national loan federal savings reuter association insurance estate real
Topic 11	trade and for bill not united imports that surplus south
Topic 12	and february for china january gulf issue month that last
Topic 13	market dollar that had and will exchange system currency west
Topic 14	dlrs quarter share for company earnings year per and fiscal
Topic 15	billion mln tax year profit credit marks francs net pct
Topic 16	usair inc twa reuter trust air department chemical diluted piedmont
Topic 17	and will union spokesman not two that reuter security port
Topic 18	offer share tender shares that general and gencorp dlrs not
Topic 19	and company for that board proposal group made directors proposed
Topic 20	that japan japanese and world industry government for told officials
Topic 21	american analysts and that analyst chrysler shearson express stock not
Topic 22	loss profit mln reuter cts net shr dlrs qtr year
Topic 23	mln dlrs and assets for dlr operations year charge reuter
Topic 24	mln net cts shr revs dlrs qtr year oper reuter
Topic 25	cts april reuter div pay prior record qtly march sets
Topic 26	dividend stock split for two reuter march payable record april
Topic 27	oil and prices crude for energy opec petroleum production bpd
Topic 28	agreement for development and years program technology reuter conditions agreed
Topic 29	and foreign that talks for international industrial exchange not since
Topic 30	corp inc acquisition will company common shares reuter stock purchase

Table 2: Top 10 words for each topics learned from LDA with traditional SVI.

Topic 1	oil and that prices for petroleum dlrs energy crude field
Topic 2	pct and that rate market banks term rates this will
Topic 3	billion and pct mln group marks sales year capital rose
Topic 4	and saudi oil gulf that arabia december minister prices for
Topic 5	and dlrs debt for brazil southern mln will medical had
Topic 6	and grain that will futures for program farm certificates agriculture
Topic 7	bank banks rate and pct interest rates for foreign banking
Topic 8	and union for national seamen california port security that strike
Topic 9	and trade that for dollar deficit gatt not exports economic
Topic 10	and financial for sale inc services reuter systems agreement assets
Topic 11	dollar and for yen mark march that dealers sterling market
Topic 12	and for south unit equipment reuter two will state corp
Topic 13	and firm stock company will for pct not share that
Topic 14	and world that talks economic official for countries system monetary
Topic 15	and gencorp for offer general company partners that dlrs share
Topic 16	mln canada canadian stg and pct will air that royal
Topic 17	usair and twa that analysts not for pct analyst piedmont
Topic 18	and that for companies not years study this areas overseas
Topic 19	trade and bill for house that reagan foreign states committee
Topic 20	company dlrs offer stock and for corp share shares mln
Topic 21	dlrs year and quarter company for earnings will tax share
Topic 22	mln cts net loss dlrs profit reuter shr year qtr
Topic 23	exchange paris and rates that treasury baker allied for western
Topic 24	and shares inc for group dlrs pct offer reuter share
Topic 25	merger and that pacific texas hughes baker commerce for company
Topic 26	and american company subsidiary china french reuter pct for owned
Topic 27	japan japanese and that trade officials for government industry pact
Topic 28	oil opec mln bpd prices production ecuador and output crude
Topic 29	and that had shares block for mln government not san
Topic 30	mln pct and profits dlrs year for billion company will

Table 3: Top 10 words for each topics learned from LDA with DM-SVI.

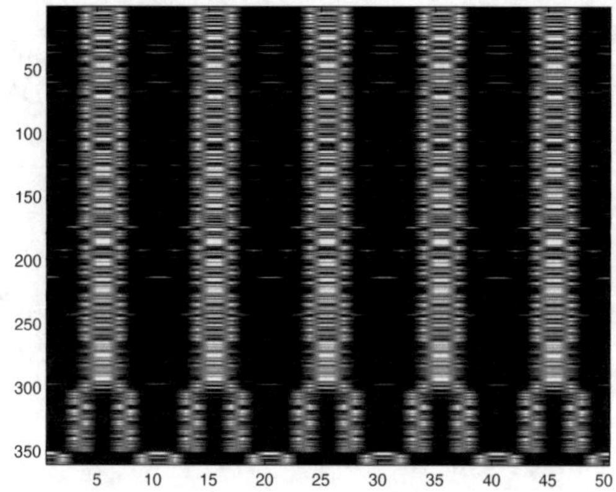

Figure 10: Synthetic data used to train the LDA model in the main paper. Each row presents a document and each column represents a word. Documents share topics with highly imbalanced proportions.

Size	k = 10	k =30	k=50	k=80
Fast k-DPP	0.001	0.0139	0.0541	0.2199
k-DPP	0.0098	0.1468	0.6438	2.6698
LDA	0.8777	1.2530	1.6414	2.2312

Table 4: Sampling time (in sec) for LDA on the R8 dataset with different mini-batch sizes.

practice, we use the original implementation from [23] with $M = 100$. To compare with the traditional k-DPP, we listed the elapsed time with [19]. The last row shows the running time per local LDA update, excluding sampling.

The computational time for training a neural network highly depends on the network structure and implementation details. For example, when using only one softmax layer as in the flower experiment, the cost per gradient step is in the milliseconds. In this setup, k-DPP is not effective from a runtime perspective, but still results in better final classification accuracies. However, the cost for each gradient step for a simple 5 layer NN as in the MNIST experiment with $K = 100$ is 1.294 seconds. In the latter case, this time is comparable to k-DPP sampling (0.7941 sec) see Table 5. We thus expect our methods to benefit expensive models and imbalanced training datasets more.

Figure 11 shows the bar plots of the frequency of images in each class for Oxford Flower dataset using the number of classes as the mini-batch size. With this setting, we can see that when $w = 1$, DM-SGD is equivalent to StS.

Size	k = 10	k =100	k=200
Fast k-DPP	0.0012	0.7941	5.4216
NN cost	0.166948	1.29452	2.64811

Table 5: Five Layer NN trained on MNIST with different mini-batch sizes. Top row: sampling time (in sec) using the fast k-DPP approach. Bottom row: run time for each update step (excluding mini-batch sampling).

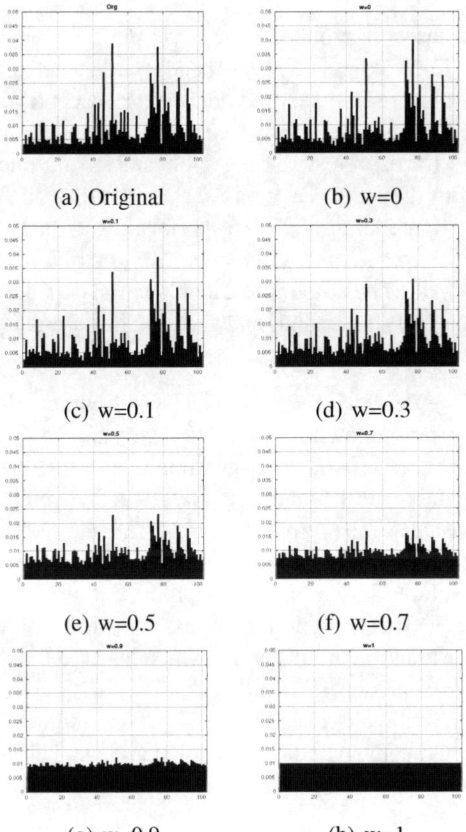

(a) Original (b) w=0

(c) w=0.1 (d) w=0.3

(e) w=0.5 (f) w=0.7

(g) w=0.9 (h) w=1

Figure 11: The frequency of images in each class for Oxford Flower dataset, with $k = 102$.

An Efficient Minibatch Acceptance Test for Metropolis-Hastings

Daniel Seita[1], **Xinlei Pan**[1], **Haoyu Chen**[1], **John Canny**[1,2]
[1] University of California, Berkeley, CA
[2] Google Research, Mountain View, CA
{seita,xinleipan,haoyuchen,canny}@berkeley.edu

Abstract

We present a novel Metropolis-Hastings method for large datasets that uses small expected-size minibatches of data. Previous work on reducing the cost of Metropolis-Hastings tests yield variable data consumed per sample, with only constant factor reductions versus using the full dataset for each sample. Here we present a method that can be tuned to provide arbitrarily small batch sizes, by adjusting either proposal step size or temperature. Our test uses the noise-tolerant Barker acceptance test with a novel additive correction variable. The resulting test has similar cost to a normal SGD update. Our experiments demonstrate several order-of-magnitude speedups over previous work.

1 INTRODUCTION

Markov chain Monte Carlo (MCMC) sampling is a powerful method for computation on intractable distributions. We are interested in large dataset applications, where the goal is to sample a posterior distribution $p(\theta|x_1, \ldots, x_N)$ of parameter θ for large N. The Metropolis-Hastings method (M-H) generates sample candidates from a proposal distribution q which is in general different from the target distribution p, and decides whether to accept or reject based on an acceptance test. The acceptance test is usually a Metropolis test [Metropolis et al., 1953, Hastings, 1970].

Many state-of-the-art machine learning methods, and deep learning in particular, are based on minibatch updates (such as SGD) to a model. Minibatch updates produce many improvements to the model for each pass over the dataset, and have high sample efficiency. In contrast, conventional M-H requires calculations over the full dataset to produce a new sample. Recent results from [Korattikara et al., 2014] and [Bardenet et al., 2014] perform approximate (bounded error) acceptance tests using subsets of the full dataset. The amount of data consumed for each test varies significantly from one minibatch to the next. By contrast, [Maclaurin and Adams, 2014, Bardenet et al., 2016] perform exact tests but require a lower bound on the parameter distribution across its domain. The amount of data reduction depends on the accuracy of this bound, and such bounds are only available for relatively simple distributions.

Here we derive a new test which incorporates the variability in minibatch statistics as *a natural part of the test* and requires less data per iteration than prior work. We use a Barker test function [Barker, 1965], which makes our test naturally error tolerant. The idea of using a noise-tolerant Barker's test function was suggested but not explored empirically in [Bardenet et al., 2016] section 6.3. But the asymptotic test statistic CDF and the Barker function are different, which leads to fixed errors for the approach in [Bardenet et al., 2016]. Here, we show that the difference between the distributions can be corrected with an additive random variable. This leads to a test which is fast, and whose error can be made arbitrarily small.

We note that this approach is fundamentally different from prior work. It makes no assumptions about the form of, and requires no global bounds on the posterior parameter distribution. It is exact in the limit as batch size increases by the Central Limit Theorem. This is not true of [Korattikara et al., 2014] and [Bardenet et al., 2014] which use tail bounds and provide only approximate tests even with arbitrarily large batches of data. Our test is also exact under the assumptions of Korattikara et al. [2014] that the log probability ratios of batches are normally distributed about their mean. Rather than tail bounds, our approach uses moment estimates from the data to determine how far the minibatch posteriors deviate from a normal distribution. These bounds carry through to the overall accuracy of the test.

Our test is applicable when the variance (over data samples) of the log probability ratio between the proposal and the current state is small enough (less than 1). It's not clear at first why this quantity should be bounded, but it is natural for well-specified models running Metropolis-Hastings sampling with optimal proposals [Roberts and Rosenthal, 2001] on a full dataset. If the posterior parameter distribution is a unit-variance normal distribution, then the posterior for N samples will have variance $1/N$. There is simply not enough information in $M \ll N$ samples to locate and efficiently sample from this posterior. This is not a property of any particular proposal or test, but of the information carried by the data. The variance condition succinctly captures the condition that the minibatch carries enough information to generate a sample. While we cannot expect to generate independent samples from the posterior using only a small subset of the data, there are three situations where we can exploit small minibatches:

1. Increase the temperature K of the target distribution. Log likelihoods scale as $1/K$, and so the variance of the likelihood ratio will vary as $1/K^2$. As we demonstrate in Section 6.2, higher temperature can be advantageous for parameter exploration.
2. For continuous distributions, reduce the proposal step size (i.e. generate correlated samples). The variance of the log acceptance probability scales as the square of proposal step size.
3. Utilize Hamiltonian Dynamics for proposals and tests. Here the dynamics itself provide shaping to the posterior distribution, and the M-H test is only needed to correct quantization error. In terms of the information carried by the samples, this approach is not limited by the data in a particular minibatch since momentum is carried over time and "remembered" across multiple minibatches.

We note that case two above is characteristic of Gibbs samplers applied to large datasets [Dupuy and Bach, 2016]. Such samplers represent a model posterior via counts over an entire dataset of N samples. When a minibatch of M samples is used to update the model, the counts for these samples only are updated. This creates "steps" of $O(M/N)$ in the model parameters, and correlated samples from the model posterior. Correlated samples are still very useful in high-dimensional ML problems with multi-modal posteriors since they correspond to a finer-scale random walk through the posterior landscape. The contributions of this paper are as follows:

- We develop a new, more efficient (in samples per test) minibatch acceptance test with quantifiable error bounds. The test uses a novel additive correction variable to implement a Barker test based on minibatch mean and variance.
- We compare our new test and prior approaches on several datasets. We demonstrate several order-of-magnitude improvements in sample efficiency, and that the batch size distribution is short-tailed.

2 PRELIMINARIES

In the Metropolis-Hastings method [Gilks and Spiegelhalter, 1996, Brooks et al., 2011], a difficult-to-compute probability distribution $p(\theta)$ is sampled using a Markov chain $\theta_1, \ldots, \theta_T$. The sample θ_{t+1} at time $t+1$ is generated using a candidate θ' from a (simpler) proposal distribution $q(\theta'|\theta_t)$, filtered by an acceptance test. The acceptance test is usually a Metropolis test. The Metropolis test has acceptance probability:

$$\alpha(\theta_t, \theta') = \frac{p(\theta')q(\theta_t|\theta')}{p(\theta_t)q(\theta'|\theta_t)} \wedge 1 \tag{1}$$

where $a \wedge b$ denotes $\min(a, b)$. With probability $\alpha(\theta_t, \theta')$, we accept θ' and set $\theta_{t+1} = \theta'$, otherwise set $\theta_{t+1} = \theta_t$. The test is often implemented with an auxiliary random variable $u \sim \mathcal{U}(0, 1)$ with a comparison $u < \alpha(\theta_t, \theta')$; here, $\mathcal{U}(a, b)$ denotes the uniform distribution on the interval $[a, b]$. For simplicity, we drop the subscript t for the current sample θ_t and denote it as θ.

The acceptance test guarantees detailed balance, which means $p(\theta)p(\theta'|\theta) = p(\theta')p(\theta|\theta')$, where $p(\theta'|\theta)$ is the probability of a transition from state θ to θ'. Here, $p(\theta'|\theta) = q(\theta'|\theta)\alpha(\theta, \theta')$. This condition, together with ergodicity, guarantees that the Markov chain has a unique stationary distribution $\pi(\theta) = p(\theta)$. For Bayesian inference, the target distribution is $p(\theta|x_1, \ldots, x_N)$. The acceptance probability is now:

$$\alpha(\theta, \theta') = \frac{p_0(\theta') \prod_{i=1}^{N} p(x_i|\theta')q(\theta|\theta')}{p_0(\theta) \prod_{i=1}^{N} p(x_i|\theta)q(\theta'|\theta)} \wedge 1 \tag{2}$$

where $p_0(\theta)$ is the prior. Computing samples this way requires all N data points, but this is very expensive for large datasets.

To address this challenge, [Korattikara et al., 2014, Bardenet et al., 2014] perform approximate Metropolis-Hasting tests using sequential hypothesis testing. At each iteration, a subset of data is sampled and used to test whether to accept θ' using an approximation to $\alpha(\theta, \theta')$. If the approximate test does not yield a decision, the minibatch size is increased and the test repeated. This process continues until a decision. These methods either invoke the asymptotic CLT and assume that finite batch errors are normally distributed [Korattikara et al., 2014] or use a concentration bound [Bardenet et al., 2014]. We refer to these algorithms, respectively, as AUSTEREMH and MHSUBLHD. While both show useful reductions in the number of samples required, they suffer from two drawbacks: (i) They are approximate, and always yield a decision with a finite error, (ii) They both require exact, dataset-wide bounds that depend on θ (see Section 5).[1] We discuss a worst-case scenario in Section 2.2.

2.1 NOTATION

Following [Bardenet et al., 2014], we write the test $u < \alpha(\theta, \theta')$ equivalently as $\Lambda(\theta, \theta') > \psi(u, \theta, \theta')$, where[2]

$$\begin{aligned}\Lambda(\theta, \theta') &= \sum_{i=1}^{N} \log \frac{p(x_i|\theta')}{p(x_i|\theta)},\\ \psi(u, \theta, \theta') &= \log\left(u \frac{q(\theta'|\theta)p_0(\theta)}{q(\theta|\theta')p_0(\theta')}\right).\end{aligned} \tag{3}$$

To simplify notation, we assume that temperature $K = 1$ (saving T to indicate the number of samples to draw). Temperature appears as an exponential on each likelihood, $p(x_i|\theta)^{1/K}$, so the effect would be to act as a $1/K$ factor on $\Lambda(\theta, \theta')$.

To reduce computational effort, an unbiased estimate of $\Lambda(\theta, \theta')$ based on a minibatch $\{x_1^*, \ldots, x_b^*\}$ can be used:

$$\Lambda^*(\theta, \theta') = \frac{N}{b} \sum_{i=1}^{b} \log \frac{p(x_i^*|\theta')}{p(x_i^*|\theta)}. \tag{4}$$

Finally, it will be convenient for our analysis to define $\Lambda_i(\theta, \theta') = N \log(\frac{p(x_i|\theta')}{p(x_i|\theta)})$. Thus, $\Lambda(\theta, \theta')$ is the mean of $\Lambda_i(\theta, \theta')$ over the entire dataset, and $\Lambda^*(\theta, \theta')$ is the mean of the $\Lambda_i(\theta, \theta')$ in its minibatch.

Since minibatches contains randomly selected samples, the values Λ_i are i.i.d. random variables.[3] By the Central Limit Theorem, we expect $\Lambda^*(\theta, \theta')$ to be approximately Gaussian. The acceptance test then becomes a statistical test of the hypothesis that $\Lambda(\theta, \theta') > \psi(u, \theta, \theta')$ by establishing that $\Lambda^*(\theta, \theta')$ is substantially larger than $\psi(u, \theta, \theta')$.

2.2 A WORST-CASE GAUSSIAN EXAMPLE

Let $x_1, \ldots, x_N$ be i.i.d. $\mathcal{N}(\theta, 1)$ with known variance $\sigma^2 = 1$ and (unknown) mean $\theta = 0.5$. We use a uniform prior on θ. The log likelihood ratio is

$$\Lambda^*(\theta, \theta') = N(\theta' - \theta)\left(\frac{1}{b}\sum_{i=1}^{b} x_i^* - \theta - \frac{\theta' - \theta}{2}\right) \tag{5}$$

which is normally distributed over selection of the Normal samples x_i^*. Since the x_i^* have unit variance, their mean has variance $1/b$, and the variance of $\Lambda^*(\theta, \theta')$ is $\sigma^2(\Lambda^*) = (\theta' - \theta)^2 N^2 / b$. In order to pass a hypothesis test that $\Lambda > \psi$, there needs to be a large enough gap (several $\sigma(\Lambda^*)$) between $\Lambda^*(\theta, \theta')$ and $\psi(u, \theta, \theta')$.

The posterior is a Gaussian centered on the sample mean μ, and with variance $1/N$ (i.e., $\mathcal{N}(\mu, 1/N)$). In one dimension, an efficient proposal distribution has the same variance as the target distribution [Roberts and Rosenthal, 2001], so we use a proposal based on $\mathcal{N}(\theta, 1/N)$. It is symmetric $q(\theta'|\theta) = q(\theta|\theta')$, and since we assumed a uniform prior, $\psi(u, \theta, \theta') = \log u$. Our worst-case scenario is specified in Lemma 1.

Lemma 1. *For the model in Section 2.2, there exists a fixed (independent of N) constant c such that with probability $\geq c$ over the joint distribution of (θ, θ', u),* AUSTEREMH *and* MHSUBLHD *consume all N samples.*

Proof. See Appendix, Section A.1. □

Similar results can be shown for other distributions and proposals by identifying regions in product space (θ, θ', u) such that the hypothesis test needs to separate nearly-equal values. It follows that the accelerated tests from prior work require at least a constant fraction $\geq c$ in the amount of data consumed per test compared to full-data tests, so their speed-up is $\leq 1/c$. The issue is the use of tail bounds to separate $\Lambda - \psi$ from zero; for certain input/random u combinations, this difference can be arbitrarily close to zero. We avoid this by using the *approximately normal* variation in Λ^* to *replace* the variation due to u.

2.3 MCMC POSTERIOR INFERENCE

There is a separate line of MCMC work drawing principles from statistical physics. One can apply Hamiltonian Monte Carlo (HMC) [Neal, 2010] methods which generate high acceptance *and* distant proposals when run on full batches of data. Recently Langevin Dynamics [Welling and Teh, 2011, Ahn et al., 2012] has been applied to Bayesian estimation on minibatches of data. This simplified dynamics uses local proposals and avoids M-H tests by using small proposal steps whose acceptance approaches 1 in the limit. However, the constraint on proposal step size is severe, and the state space exploration reduces to a random walk. Full minibatch HMC for minibatches was described in [Chen

[1] We obtained the authors code for both and found that they scanned the entire dataset at each step to obtain these estimates.

[2] Our definitions differ from those in [Bardenet et al., 2014] by a factor of N to simplify our analysis later.

[3] The analysis assumes sampling with replacement although implementations on typical large datasets will approximate this by sampling without replacement.

et al., 2014] which allows momentum-augmented proposals with larger step sizes. However, step sizes are still limited by the need to run accurately without M-H tests. By providing an M-H test with similar cost to standard gradient steps, our work opens the door to applying those methods with much more aggressive step sizes without loss of accuracy.

3 A NEW MH ACCEPTANCE TEST

3.1 LOG-LIKELIHOOD RATIOS

For our new M-H test, we denote the exact and approximate log likelihood ratios as Δ and Δ^*, respectively. First, Δ is defined as

$$\Delta(\theta, \theta') = \log \frac{p_0(\theta') \prod_{i=1}^N p(x_i|\theta') q(\theta|\theta')}{p_0(\theta) \prod_{i=1}^N p(x_i|\theta) q(\theta'|\theta)}, \quad (6)$$

where p_0, p, and q match the corresponding functions within Equation (2). We separate out terms dependent and independent of the data as:

$$\Delta(\theta, \theta') = \underbrace{\sum_{i=1}^N \log \frac{p(x_i|\theta')}{p(x_i|\theta)}}_{\Lambda(\theta,\theta')} - \psi(1, \theta, \theta'). \quad (7)$$

A minibatch estimator of Δ, denoted as Δ^*, is

$$\Delta^*(\theta, \theta') = \underbrace{\frac{N}{b} \sum_{i=1}^b \log \frac{p(x_i^*|\theta')}{p(x_i^*|\theta)}}_{\Lambda^*(\theta,\theta')} - \psi(1, \theta, \theta'). \quad (8)$$

Note that Δ and Δ^* are evaluated on the full dataset and a minibatch of size b respectively. The term N/b means $\Delta^*(\theta, \theta')$ is an unbiased estimator of $\Delta(\theta, \theta')$.

The key to our test is a smooth acceptance function. We consider functions other than the classical Metropolis test that satisfy the detailed balance condition needed for accurate posterior estimation. A class of suitable functions is specified as follows:

Lemma 2. *If $g(s)$ is any function such that $g(s) = \exp(s) g(-s)$, then the acceptance function $\alpha(\theta, \theta') \triangleq g(\Delta(\theta, \theta'))$ satisfies detailed balance.*

This result is used in [Barker, 1965] to define the Barker acceptance test.

3.2 BARKER (LOGISTIC) ACCEPTANCE FUNCTION

For our new MH test we use the Barker logistic [Barker, 1965] function: $g(s) = (1 + \exp(-s))^{-1}$. Straightforward arithmetic shows that it satisfies the condition in Lemma 2. It is slightly less efficient than the Metropolis test, since its acceptance rate for vanishing likelihood difference is 0.5. However we will see that its overall sample efficiency is much higher than the earlier methods. See Appendix B for additional discussion.

Assume we begin with the current sample θ and a candidate sample θ', and that $V \sim \mathcal{U}(0, 1)$ is a uniform random variable. We accept θ' if $g(\Delta(\theta, \theta')) > V$, and reject otherwise. Since $g(s)$ is monotonically increasing, its inverse $g^{-1}(s)$ is well-defined and unique. So an equivalent test is to accept θ' iff

$$\Delta(\theta, \theta') > X = g^{-1}(V) \quad (9)$$

where X is a random variable with the logistic distribution (its CDF is the logistic function). To see this notice that $\frac{dV}{dX} = g'$, that g' is the density corresponding to a logistic CDF, and finally that $\frac{dV}{dX}$ is the density of X. The density of X is symmetric, so we can equivalently test whether

$$\Delta(\theta, \theta') + X > 0 \quad (10)$$

for a logistic random variable X.

3.3 A MINIBATCH ACCEPTANCE TEST

We now describe acceptance testing using the minibatch estimator $\Delta^*(\theta, \theta')$. From Equation (8), $\Delta^*(\theta, \theta')$ can be represented as a constant term plus the mean of b IID terms $\Lambda_i(\theta, \theta')$ of the form $N \log \frac{p(x_i^*|\theta')}{p(x_i^*|\theta)}$. As b increases, $\Delta^*(\theta, \theta')$ therefore has a distribution which approaches a normal distribution by the Central Limit Theorem. We now describe this using an asymptotic argument and defer specific bounds between the CDFs of $\Delta^*(\theta, \theta')$ and a Gaussian to Section 5.

In the limit, since Δ^* is normally distributed about its mean Δ, we can write

$$\Delta^* = \Delta + X_{\text{norm}}, \quad X_{\text{norm}} \sim \bar{\mathcal{N}}(0, \sigma^2(\Delta^*)), \quad (11)$$

where $\bar{\mathcal{N}}(0, \sigma^2(\Delta^*))$ denotes a distribution which is approximately normal with variance $\sigma^2(\Delta^*)$. But to perform the test in Equation (10) we want $\Delta + X$ for a logistic random variable X (call it $X_{\log}$ from now on). In [Bardenet et al., 2016] it was proposed to use Δ^* in a Barker test, and tolerate the fixed error between the logistic and normal distributions.

Our approach is to instead decompose $X_{\log}$ as

$$X_{\log} = X_{\text{norm}} + X_{\text{corr}}, \quad (12)$$

where we assume $X_{\text{norm}} \sim \mathcal{N}(0, \sigma^2)$ and that X_{corr} is a zero-mean "correction" variable with density $C_\sigma(X)$.

The two variables are added (i.e., their distributions convolve) to form $X_{\log}$. This decomposition requires an appropriate C_σ, which we derive in Section 4. Using X_{corr} samples from $C_\sigma(X)$, the acceptance test is now

$$\Delta + X_{\log} = (\Delta + X_{\text{norm}}) + X_{\text{corr}} = \Delta^* + X_{\text{corr}} > 0. \tag{13}$$

Therefore, assuming the variance of Δ^* is small enough, if we have an estimate of Δ^* from the current data minibatch, we test acceptance by adding a random variable X_{corr} and then accept θ' if the result is positive (and reject otherwise).

If $\bar{\mathcal{N}}(0, \sigma^2(\Delta^*))$ is exactly $\mathcal{N}(0, \sigma^2(\Delta^*))$, the above test is exact, and as we show in Section 5, if there is a maximum error ϵ between the CDF of $\bar{\mathcal{N}}(0, \sigma^2(\Delta^*))$ and the CDF of $\mathcal{N}(0, \sigma^2(\Delta^*))$, then our test has an error of at most ϵ relative to the full batch version.

4 THE CORRECTION DISTRIBUTION

Our test in Equation (13) requires knowing the distribution of X_{corr}. In Section 5, we show that the test accuracy depends on the absolute error between the CDFs of $X_{\text{norm}} + X_{\text{corr}}$ and $X_{\log}$. Consequently, we need to minimize this in our construction of X_{corr}. More formally, let $\Phi_{s_X} = \Phi(X/s_X)$ where Φ is the standard normal CDF[4], $S(X)$ be the logistic function, and $C_\sigma(X)$ be the *density* of the correction X_{corr} distribution. Our goal is to solve:

$$C_\sigma^* = \arg\min_{C_\sigma} |\Phi_\sigma * C_\sigma - S| \tag{14}$$

where $*$ denotes convolution. To compute C_σ, we assume the input Y and another variable X lie in the intervals $[-V, V]$ and $[-2V, 2V]$, respectively. We discretize the convolution by discretizing X and Y into $4N+1$ and $2N+1$ values respectively. If $i \in \{-2N, \dots, 2N\} = \mathcal{I}$ and $j \in \{-N, \dots, N\} = \mathcal{J}$, then we can write $X_i = i(V/N)$ and $Y_j = j(V/N)$, and the objective can be written as:

$$C_\sigma^* = \arg\min_{C_\sigma} \max_{i \in \mathcal{I}} \left| \sum_{j \in \mathcal{J}} \Phi_\sigma(X_i - Y_j) C_\sigma(Y_j) - S(X_i) \right|.$$

Now define matrix M and vectors u and v such that $M_{ij} = \Phi_\sigma(X_i - Y_j)$, $u_j = C_\sigma(Y_j)$, and $v_i = S(X_i)$, where the indices i and j are appropriately translated to be non-negative for M, u, and v. The problem is now to minimize $\|Mu - v\|_\infty$ with the density non-negative constraint $u > 0$. We approximate this with least squares:

$$u^* = \arg\min_u \|Mu - v\|_2^2 + \lambda \|u\|_2^2, \tag{15}$$

[4]Hence, Φ_{s_X} is the CDF of a zero-mean Gaussian with standard deviation s_X.

Algorithm 1 MHMINIBATCH acceptance test.

Input: number of samples T, minibatch size m, error bound δ, pre-computed correction $C_1(X)$ distribution, initial sample θ_1.
Output: a chain of T samples $\{\theta_1, \dots, \theta_T\}$.
for $t = 1$ **to** T **do**
  -Propose a candidate θ' from proposal $q(\theta' | \theta_t)$.
  -Draw a minibatch of m points $\{x_1^*, \dots, x_m^*\}$.
  -Compute $\Delta^*(\theta_t, \theta')$ and sample variance $s_{\Delta^*}^2$.
  -Estimate moments $\mathbb{E}[|\Lambda_i - \Lambda|]$ and $\mathbb{E}[|\Lambda_i - \Lambda|^3]$ from the sample, and error ϵ from Corollary 1.
  while $s_{\Delta^*}^2 \geq 1$ **or** $\epsilon > \delta$ **do**
    -Draw m more samples to augment the minibatch, update Δ^*, $s_{\Delta^*}^2$ and ϵ estimates.
  end while
  -Draw $X_{\text{nc}} \sim \mathcal{N}(0, 1 - s_{\Delta^*}^2)$ and $X_{\text{corr}} \sim C_1(X)$.
  if $\Delta^* + X_{\text{nc}} + X_{\text{corr}} > 0$ **then**
    -Accept the candidate, $\theta_{t+1} = \theta'$.
  else
    -Reject and re-use the old sample, $\theta_{t+1} = \theta_t$.
  end if
end for

---

with regularization λ. The solution is well-known from the normal equations ($u^* = (M^T M + \lambda I)^{-1} M^T v$) and in practice yields an acceptable L_∞ norm.

With this approach, there is no guarantee that $u^* \geq 0$. However, we have some flexibility in the choice of σ in Equation (14). As we decrease the variance of X_{norm}, the variance of X_{corr} grows by the same amount and is in fact the result of convolution with a Gaussian whose variance is the difference. Thus as σ decreases, $C_\sigma(X)$ grows and approaches the derivative of a logistic function at $\sigma = 0$. It retains some weak negative values for $\sigma > 0$ but removal of those leads to small error. We use $N = 4000$ and $\lambda = 10$ for our experiments, which empirically provided excellent performance. See Table 3 in Appendix C.1 for detailed L_∞ errors for different settings. Algorithm 1 describes our procedure, MHMINIBATCH. A few points:

- It uses an adaptive step size so as to use the smallest possible average minibatch size. Unlike previous work, the size distribution is short-tailed.
- An additional normal variable X_{nc} is added to Δ^* to produce a variable with unit variance. This is not mathematically necessary, but allows us to use a single correction distribution C_1 with $\sigma = 1$ for X_{corr}, saving on memory footprint.
- The sample variance of Δ^* is denoted as $s_{\Delta^*}^2$ and is proportional to $\|\theta' - \theta\|_2^2$.

5 ANALYSIS

We now derive error bounds for our M-H test and the target distribution it generates. In Section 5.1, we present bounds on the absolute and relative error (in terms of the CDFs) of the distribution of Δ^* versus a Gaussian. We then show in Section 5.2 that these bounds are preserved after the addition of other random variables (e.g., X_{nc} and X_{corr}). It then follows that the acceptance test has the same error bound.

5.1 BOUNDING THE ERROR OF Δ^* FROM A GAUSSIAN

We use the following quantitative central-limit result:

Lemma 3. *Let $X_1, \ldots, X_n$ be a set of zero-mean, independent, identically-distributed random variables with sample mean $\bar{X}$ and sample variance s_X^2 where:*

$$\bar{X} = \frac{1}{n}\sum_{i=1}^{n} X_i, \quad s_X = \frac{1}{n}\left(\sum_{i=1}^{n}(X_i - \bar{X})^2\right)^{\frac{1}{2}}. \tag{16}$$

Then the t-statistic $t = \bar{X}/s_X$ has a distribution which is approximately normal, with error bounded by:

$$\sup_x |\Pr(t < x) - \Phi(x)| \leq \frac{6.4\mathbb{E}[|X|^3] + 2\mathbb{E}[|X|]}{\sqrt{n}}. \tag{17}$$

Proof. See Appendix, Section A.2. □

Lemma 3 demonstrates that if we know $\mathbb{E}[|X|]$ and $\mathbb{E}[|X|^3]$, we can bound the error of the normal approximation, which decays as $O(n^{-\frac{1}{2}})$. Making the change of variables $y = xs_X$, Equation (17) becomes

$$\sup_y \left|\Pr(\bar{X} < y) - \Phi\left(\frac{y}{s_X}\right)\right| \leq \frac{6.4\mathbb{E}[|X|^3] + 2\mathbb{E}[|X|]}{\sqrt{n}} \tag{18}$$

showing that the distribution of $\bar{X}$ approaches the normal distribution $\mathcal{N}(0, s_X)$ whose standard deviation is s_X, as measured from the sample.

To apply this to our test, let $X_i = \Lambda_i(\theta, \theta') - \Lambda(\theta, \theta')$, so that the X_i are zero-mean, i.i.d. variables. If instead of all n samples, we only extract a subset of b samples corresponding to our minibatch, we can connect $\bar{X}$ with our Δ^* term: $\bar{X} = \Delta^*(\theta, \theta') - \Delta(\theta, \theta')$, so that $s_X = s_{\Delta^*}$. We can now substitute into Equation (18) and displace by the mean, giving:

Corollary 1.

$$\sup_y \left|\Pr(\Delta^* < y) - \Phi\left(\frac{y - \Delta}{s_{\Delta^*}}\right)\right| \leq \frac{6.4\mathbb{E}[|X|^3] + 2\mathbb{E}[|X|]}{\sqrt{b}} \tag{19}$$

where the upper bound can be expressed as $\epsilon(\theta, \theta', b)$. Corollary 1 shows that the distribution of Δ^* approximates a Normal distribution with mean Δ and variance $s_{\Delta^*}^2$. Furthermore, it bounds the error with *estimable quantities*: both $\mathbb{E}[|X|]$ and $\mathbb{E}[|X|^3]$ can be estimated as means of $|\Lambda_i - \Lambda|$ and $|\Lambda_i - \Lambda|^3$, respectively, on each minibatch. We expect this will often be accurate enough on minibatches with hundreds of points, but otherwise bootstrap CIs can be computed.

5.2 ADDING RANDOM VARIABLES

We next relate the CDFs of distributions and show that bounds are preserved after adding random variables.

Lemma 4. *Let $P(x)$ and $Q(x)$ be two CDFs satisfying $\sup_x |P(x) - Q(x)| \leq \epsilon$ with x in some real range. Let $R(y)$ be the* density *of another random variable y. Let P' be the convolution $P * R$ and Q' be the convolution $Q * R$. Then $P'(z)$ (resp. $Q'(z)$) is the CDF of sum $z = x + y$ of independent random variables x with CDF $P(x)$ (resp. $Q(x)$) and y with density $R(y)$. Then*

$$\sup_x |P'(x) - Q'(x)| \leq \epsilon. \tag{20}$$

Proof. See Appendix, Section A.3. □

From Lemma 4, we have the following Corollary:

Corollary 2. *If $\sup_y |\Pr(\Delta^* < y) - \Phi(\frac{y-\Delta}{s_{\Delta^*}})| \leq \epsilon(\theta, \theta', b)$, then*

$$\sup_y |\Pr(\Delta^* + X_{\mathrm{nc}} + X_{\mathrm{corr}} < y) - S(y - \Delta)| \leq \epsilon(\theta, \theta', b)$$

where $S(x)$ is the standard logistic function, and X_{nc} and X_{corr} are generated as per Algorithm 1.

Proof. See Appendix, Section A.4. □

Corollary 2 shows that the bounds from Section 5.1 are preserved after adding random variables, so our test remains accurate. In fact we can do better ($O(n^{-1})$ instead of $O(n^{-1/2})$) by using a more precise limit distribution under an additional assumption. We review this in Appendix A.5.

5.3 BOUNDS ON THE STATIONARY DISTRIBUTION

Bounds on the error of an M-H test imply bounds on the stationary distribution of the Markov chain under appropriate conditions. Such bounds were derived in both [Korattikara et al., 2014] and [Bardenet et al., 2014]. We include the result from [Korattikara et al., 2014] (Theorem 1) here: Let $d_v(P, Q)$ denote the total variation distance between two distributions P and Q. Let $\mathcal{T}_0$ denote the transition kernel of the exact Markov chain, $\mathcal{S}_0$ denote the exact posterior distribution, and $\mathcal{S}_\epsilon$ denote the stationary distribution of the approximate transition kernel.

Lemma 5. *If $\mathcal{T}_0$ satisfies the contraction condition $d_v(P\mathcal{T}_0, \mathcal{S}_0) < \eta d_v(P, \mathcal{S}_0)$ for some constant $\eta \in [0, 1)$ and all probability distributions P, then*

$$d_v(S_0, S_\epsilon) \leq \frac{\epsilon}{1-\eta} \tag{21}$$

where ϵ is the bound on the error in the acceptance test.

6 EXPERIMENTS

Here we compare with the most similar prior works [Korattikara et al., 2014] and Bardenet et al. [2014]. In [Korattikara et al., 2014], an asymptotic CLT is used to argue that a modified standard M-H test can be used on subsets of the data. This assumes knowledge of dataset-wide mean μ_{std} each iteration (it depends on θ). Determining μ_{std} exactly requires a scan over the entire dataset, or some model-specific bounds. [Korattikara et al., 2014] also propose a conservative variant which assumes $\mu_{\text{std}} = 0$ and avoids the scan. We refer to the conservative version as AUSTEREMH(C) and the non-conservative variant as AUSTEREMH(NC). We analyze both in this section.

In [Bardenet et al., 2014] concentration bounds are used with a similar modification to the standard M-H test (MHSUBLHD method). For MHSUBLHD, the required global bound is denoted $C_{\theta,\theta'}$ which once again depends on θ and so must be recomputed at each step, or estimated in a model-specific way. We obtained sample code for both methods from the authors, and found that both AUSTEREMN(NC) and MHSUBLHD scanned the entire dataset at each iteration to derive these bounds. We do not include the cost of doing this in our experiments, since otherwise there would be no improvement over testing the full dataset. However, it should be kept in mind that such bounds must be provided to these methods. Our test by contrast uses a quantitative form of the CLT which rely on measurable statistics from a *single* minibatch. It therefore requires no dataset-wide scans, and can be used, e.g. on streams of data.

In Sections 6.1 and 6.2, we benchmark MHMINIBATCH against MHSUBLHD, AUSTEREMH(C) and AUSTEREMH(NC). Hyperparameters for the latter were optimized using a grid-search over minibatch sizes m and per-test thresholds ϵ described in Appendix C.2.1. Throughout our descriptions, we refer to a *trial* as the period when an algorithm collects all its desired samples $\{\theta_1, \ldots, \theta_T\}$, generally with $T = 3000$ or $T = 5000$.

6.1 MIXTURE OF GAUSSIANS

This model is adapted from [Welling and Teh, 2011] by increasing the number of samples to 1 million. The parameters are $\theta = \langle\theta_1, \theta_2\rangle$, and the generation process is

$$\begin{aligned} \theta &\sim \mathcal{N}(0, \text{diag}(\sigma_1^2, \sigma_2^2)) \\ x_i &\sim 0.5 \cdot \mathcal{N}(\theta_1, \sigma_x^2) + 0.5 \cdot \mathcal{N}(\theta_1 + \theta_2, \sigma_x^2). \end{aligned} \tag{22}$$

We set $\sigma_1^2 = 10, \sigma_2^2 = 1$ and $\sigma_x^2 = 2$. We fix $\theta = \langle 0, 1\rangle$. The original paper sampled 100 data points and estimated the posterior. We are interested in performance on larger problems and so sampled 1,000,000 points to form the posterior of $p(\theta)\prod_{i=1}^{1,000,000} p(x_i|\theta)^{1/K}$ with the same prior from Equation (22). This produces a much sharper posterior with two very narrow peaks. Our goal is to reproduce the original posterior, so we adjust the temperature to $K = 10,000$. Taking logs, we get the target as shown in the far right of Figure 1.

We benchmark with AUSTEREMH(C) and MHSUBLHD. We initialized MHMINIBATCH and MHSUBLHD with $m = 50$. For AUSTEREMH(C), we set the error bound ϵ to 0.005. For MHSUBLHD, we increase sizes geometrically with $\gamma = 1.5$ and use parameters $p = 2, \delta = 0.01$. All methods collect 3000 samples using a random walk proposer with covariance matrix $\text{diag}(0.15, 0.15)$, which means the M-H test is responsible for shaping the sample distribution.

Figure 1 shows scatter plots of the resulting θ samples for the three methods, with darker regions indicating a greater density of points. There are no obvious differences, showing that MHMINIBATCH reaches an acceptable posterior. We further measure the similarity between each set of samples and the actual posterior. Due to space constraints, results are in Appendix C.2.2.

Figure 2 shows that MHMINIBATCH dominates in terms of speed and efficiency. The histograms of the (final) minibatch sizes used each iteration show that our method consumes significantly less data; the distribution is short-tailed and the mean is 172, more than an order of magnitude better compared to the other two methods (averages are 12562 and 67508). We further ran 10 runs of mixture of Gaussians experiments and report minibatch sizes in Table 1. Sizes correspond to the running times of the methods, excluding the likelihood computation of all data points for AUSTEREMH(NC) and MHSUBLHD, which would drastically increase running time.

6.2 LOGISTIC REGRESSION

We next test logistic regression for the binary classification of 1s versus 7s on the MNIST [LeCun and Cortes,

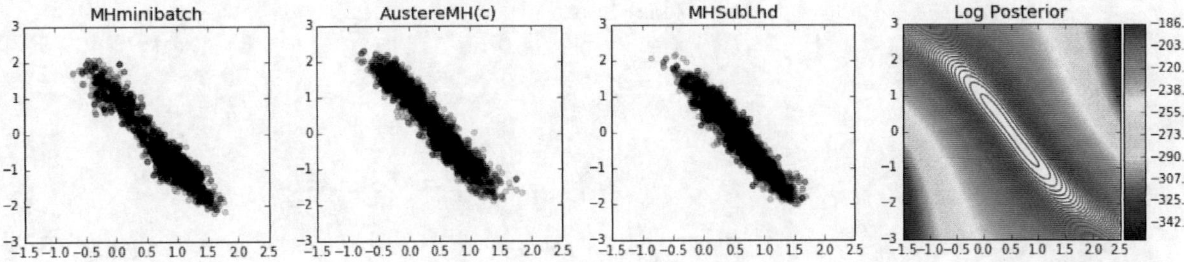

Figure 1: The log posterior contours and scatter plots of sampled θ values using different methods.

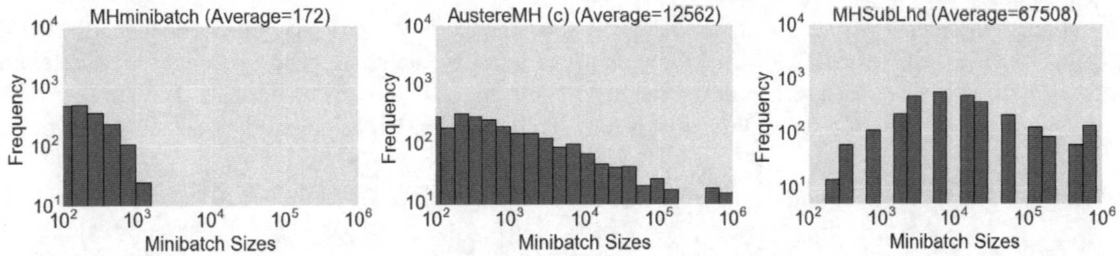

Figure 2: Minibatch sizes used in Section 6.1's experiment. The axes have the same (log-log scale) range.

Table 1: Average minibatch sizes ($\pm$ one standard deviation) on the Gaussian mixture model. The averages are taken over 10 independent trials (3000 samples each).

Method	Average of MB Sizes
MHMINIBATCH	182.3 ± 11.4
AUSTEREMH(C)	13540.5 ± 1521.4
MHSUBLHD	65758.9 ± 3222.6

1998] dataset and (a subset of) infinite MNIST [Loosli et al., 2007]. For the former, extracting all 1s and 7s resulted in 13,000 training samples, and for the latter, we used 87,000 additional (augmented) 1s and 7s to get 100,000 training samples. Both datasets use the same test set, with 2,163 samples. Henceforth, we call them MNIST-13k and MNIST-100k, respectively.

For all methods, we impose a uniform prior on θ and again use a random walk proposer, with covariance matrix $0.05I$ for MNIST-13k and $0.01I$ for MNIST-100k. The default temperature setting is a constant at $K = 100$ for MNIST-13k and MNIST-100k. Performance of all methods implicitly relies on the step size and temperature. Setting temperature too low or step size too high will result in slow convergence for all methods. For MNIST-13k, each method generated 5000 samples for ten independent trials; due to MNIST-100k's higher computational requirements, the methods generated 3000 samples for five independent trials. For additional parameter settings and an investigation on tuning step sizes, see Appendix C.3.

For MHSUBLHD, we tried to use the provided symbolic bound for $C_{\theta,\theta'}$ described in [Bardenet et al., 2014], but it was too high and provided no performance benefit. Instead we use the empirical $C_{\theta,\theta'}$ from the entire dataset.

The first two subplots of Figure 3 display the prediction accuracy on both datasets for all methods as a function of the cumulative training points processed.[5] To generate the curves, for each of the sampled vectors θ_t, $t \in \{1, \dots, T\}$, we use θ_t as the logistic regression parameter. The results indicate that our test is more efficient, obtaining convergence more than an order of magnitude faster than AUSTEREMH(NC) and several orders of magnitude compared to AUSTEREMH(C) and MHSUBLHD. We also observe the advantage of having higher temperature from the third plot in Figure 3, which plots average performance and one standard deviation for MHMINIBATCH over 10 trials. During the exploration period, the accuracy rapidly increases, and then after 400 samples, we switch the temperature to 1, but this requires the step size to decrease, hence the smaller changes in accuracy.

Figure 4 shows log-log histograms of minibatch sizes for the methods on MNIST-100k. (Figure 5 in Appendix C.3 contains results for MNIST-13k.) The histograms only represent one representative trial; Table 2 contains the

[5] The curves do not span the same length over the x-axis since the methods consume different amounts of data.

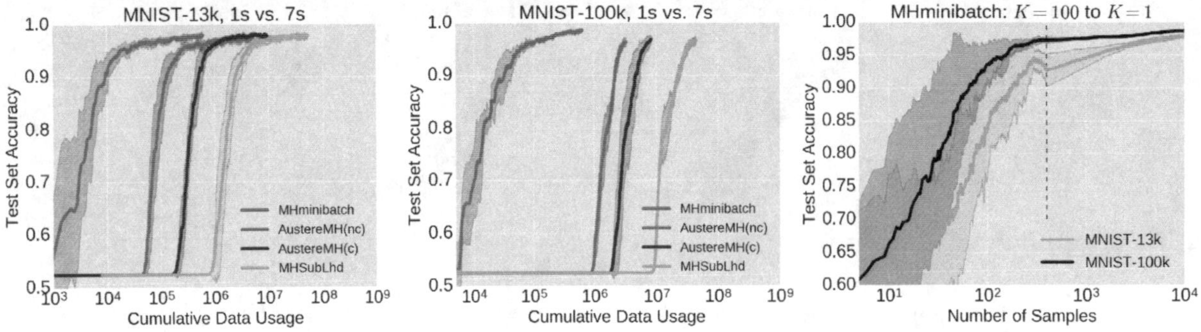

Figure 3: Binary classification accuracy of the MCMC methods on the 1s vs 7s logistic regression task for MNIST-13k (left plot) and MNIST-100k (middle plot) as a function of cumulative data usage. The right plot reports performance of MHMINIBATCH on both datasets when the temperature starts at 100 and drops to 1 after a "burn-in" period of 400 samples (vertical dashed line) of θ. For all three plots, one standard deviation is indicated by the shaded error regions.

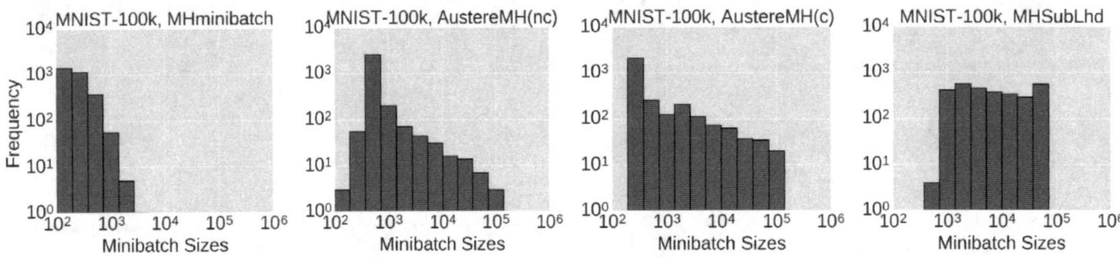

Figure 4: Minibatch sizes for a representative trial of logistic regression on MNIST-100k (analogous to Figure 2). Both axes are on a log scale and have the same ranges across the three histograms. See Section 6.2 for details.

Table 2: Average minibatch sizes ($\pm$ one standard deviation) on logistic regression on MNIST-13k and MNIST-100k. The averages are taken over 10 independent trials (5000 samples each) for MNIST-13k and 5 independent trials (3000 samples each) for MNIST-100k.

Method/Data	**MNIST-13k**	**MNIST-100k**
MHMINIBATCH	125.4 ± 9.2	216.5 ± 7.9
AUSTEREMH(NC)	973.8 ± 49.8	1098.3 ± 44.9
AUSTEREMH(C)	1924.3 ± 52.4	2795.6 ± 364.0
MHSUBLHD	10783.4 ± 78.9	14977.3 ± 582.0

average of the average minibatch sizes ($\pm$ one standard deviation) across all trials. MHMINIBATCH, with average minibatch sizes of 125.4 and 216.5 for MNIST-13k and MNIST-100k, respectively, consumes more than 7x and 4x fewer data points than the next-best method, AUSTEREMH(NC). We reiterate, however, that both AUSTEREMH(NC) and MHSUBLHD require computing $\log p(x_i|\theta)$ and $\log p(x_i|\theta')$ for all x_i each iteration. Our results here do not count that extra data consumption. Only our method and AUSTEREMH(C) rely solely on the minibatch of data each iteration.

7 CONCLUSIONS AND DISCUSSIONS

We have derived an M-H test for minibatch MCMC which approximates full data tests. We present theoretical results and experimentally show the benefits of our test on Gaussian mixtures and a logistic regression experiment.

A priority is to extend our work to methods such as Hamiltonian Monte Carlo and Langevin Dynamics which use efficient but asymmetric proposals. While there are various approaches to symmetrizing these proposals, they have high cost in the context of minibatch MCMC. Instead we plan to extend our method to log proposal ratios which have similar structure (whole-dataset mean plus additive noise) to the log probability ratio. These can be similarly absorbed in the Barker test.

Other possibilities for future work include integrating our algorithm with [Korattikara et al., 2014] by applying both tests each iteration, utilizing the variance reduction techniques suggested in [Chen and Ghahramani, 2016], and providing recipe for how to use our algorithm following the framework of [Ma et al., 2015].

References

Sungjin Ahn, Anoop Korattikara Balan, and Max Welling. Bayesian Posterior Sampling via Stochastic Gradient Fisher Scoring. In *Proceedings of the 29th International Conference on Machine Learning (ICML)*, 2012.

Rémi Bardenet, Arnaud Doucet, and Chris Holmes. Towards Scaling up Markov chain Monte Carlo: An Adaptive Subsampling Approach. In *Proceedings of the 31st International Conference on Machine Learning (ICML)*, 2014.

Rémi Bardenet, Arnaud Doucet, and Chris Holmes. On Markov Chain Monte Carlo Methods for Tall Data. *Journal of Machine Learning Research (JMLR)*, 2016.

A. A. Barker. Monte-Carlo Calculations of the Radial Distribution Functions for a Proton-Electron Plasma. *Australian Journal of Physics*, 18:119–133, 1965.

V. Bentkus, F. Gotze, and W.R.vanZwet. An Edgeworth Expansion for Symmetric Statistics. *Annals of Statistics*, 25(2), 1997.

Steve Brooks, Andrew Gelman, Galin Jones, and Xiao-Li Meng. *Handbook of Markov Chain Monte Carlo*. CRC press, 2011.

T. Chen, E.B. Fox, and C. Guestrin. Stochastic Gradient Hamiltonian Monte Carlo. In *Proceedings of the 31st International Conference on Machine Learning (ICML)*, 2014.

Yutian Chen and Zoubin Ghahramani. Scalable Discrete Sampling as a Multi-Armed Bandit Problem. In *Proceedings of the 33nd International Conference on Machine Learning, ICML*, 2016.

Christophe Dupuy and Francis Bach. Online but Accurate Inference for Latent Variable Models with Local Gibbs Sampling. *arXiv preprint arXiv:1603.02644*, 2016.

W.R. Gilks and DJ Spiegelhalter. *Markov chain Monte Carlo in practice*. Chapman & Hall/CRC, 1996.

W. K. Hastings. Monte Carlo Sampling Methods Using Markov Chains and Their Applications. *Biometrika*, 57:97–109, 1970.

Anoop Korattikara, Yutian Chen, and Max Welling. Austerity in MCMC Land: Cutting the Metropolis-Hastings Budget. In *Proceedings of the 31st International Conference on Machine Learning (ICML)*, 2014.

Yann LeCun and Corinna Cortes. MNIST Handwritten Digit Database. 1998. URL `http://yann.lecun.com/exdb/mnist/`.

Gaëlle Loosli, Stéphane Canu, and Léon Bottou. Training Invariant Support Vector Machines using Selective Sampling. In Léon Bottou, Olivier Chapelle, Dennis DeCoste, and Jason Weston, editors, *Large Scale Kernel Machines*, pages 301–320. MIT Press, Cambridge, MA., 2007.

Y. Ma, T. Chen, and E.B. Fox. A Complete Recipe for Stochastic Gradient MCMC. In *Advances in Neural Information Processing Systems 28*, 2015.

Dougal Maclaurin and Ryan P. Adams. Firefly Monte Carlo: Exact MCMC with Subsets of Data. In *Proceedings of the Thirtieth Conference on Uncertainty in Artificial Intelligence, (UAI)*, 2014.

Nicholas Metropolis, Arianna W. Rosenbluth, Marshall N. Rosenbluth, Augusta H. Teller, and Edward Teller. Equation of State Calculations by Fast Computing Machines. *The Journal of Chemical Physics*, 21, 1953.

Radford M. Neal. MCMC Using Hamiltonian Dynamics. *Handbook of Markov Chain Monte Carlo*, 54: 113–162, 2010.

Y. Novak. On Self-Normalized Sums and Student's Statistic. *Theory of Probability and its Applications*, 49(2):336–344, 2005.

Gareth O. Roberts and Jeffrey S. Rosenthal. Optimal Scaling for Various Metropolis-Hastings Algorithms. *Statistical Science*, 16(4):351367, 2001.

Max Welling and Yee Whye Teh. Bayesian Learning via Stochastic Gradient Langevin Dynamics. In *Proceedings of the 28th International Conference on Machine Learning (ICML)*, 2011.

Appendix

This appendix is divided into three major sections. Appendix A provides the proofs that we omitted from the main text due to space constraints. Appendix B elaborates on our choice of the Barker logistic function. Finally, Appendix C presents further details on the correction distribution numerical derivation and on our three main experiments to assist understanding and reproducibility.

A PROOFS OF LEMMAS AND COROLLARIES

A.1 PROOF OF LEMMA 1

Choose $(\theta' - \theta) \in \pm\frac{1}{\sqrt{N}}[0.5, 1]$ (event 1) and $(\theta - 0.5) \in \pm\frac{1}{\sqrt{N}}[0.5, 1]$ filtered for matching sign (event 2). As discussed in Lemma 1, both $q(\theta'|\theta)$ and $p(\theta|x_1, \ldots, x_N)$ have variance $1/N$. If we denote Φ as the CDF of the standard normal distribution, then the former event occurs with probability $p_0 = 2(\Phi(\sqrt{N}\frac{1}{\sqrt{N}}) - \Phi(\sqrt{N}\frac{0.5}{\sqrt{N}})) = 2(\Phi(1) - \Phi(0.5)) \approx 0.2997$. The latter event, because we restrict signs, occurs with probability $p_1 = \Phi(1) - \Phi(0.5) \approx 0.14988$.

These events together guarantee that $\Lambda^*(\theta, \theta')$ is negative by inspection of Equation (23) below. This implies that we can find a $u \in (0, 1)$ so that $\psi(u, \theta, \theta') = \log u < 0$ equals $\mathbb{E}[\Lambda^*(\theta, \theta')]$. Specifically, choose u_0 to satisfy $\log u_0 = \mathbb{E}[\Lambda^*(\theta, \theta')]$. Using $\mathbb{E}[x_i^*] = 0.5$ and Equation (5), we see that

$$\log u_0 = N(\theta' - \theta)\frac{1}{b} \cdot \mathbb{E}\left[\sum_{i=1}^{b} x_i^* - \theta - \frac{\theta' - \theta}{2}\right] = -N(\theta' - \theta)\left(\theta - 0.5 + \frac{\theta' - \theta}{2}\right). \tag{23}$$

Next, consider the minibatch acceptance test $\Lambda^*(\theta, \theta') \not\approx \psi(u, \theta, \theta')$ used in [Korattikara et al., 2014] and [Bardenet et al., 2014] , where $\not\approx$ means "significantly different from" under the distribution over samples. This is

$$\Lambda^*(\theta, \theta') \not\approx \psi(u_0, \theta, \theta') \iff N(\theta' - \theta) \cdot \frac{1}{b}\sum_{i=1}^{b} x_i^* - \theta - \frac{\theta' - \theta}{2} \not\approx \log u_0 \tag{24}$$

$$\iff \frac{1}{b}\sum_{i=1}^{b} x_i^* - \left(\theta + \frac{\theta' - \theta}{2} + \frac{\log u_0}{N(\theta' - \theta)}\right) \not\approx 0 \tag{25}$$

$$\iff \frac{1}{b}\sum_{i=1}^{b} x_i^* - 0.5 \not\approx 0. \tag{26}$$

Since the x_i^* have mean 0.5, the resulting test with our chosen u_0 will never correctly succeed and must use all N data points. Furthermore, if we sample values of u near enough to u_0, the terms in parenthesis will not be sufficiently different from 0.5 to allow the test to succeed.

The choices above for θ and θ' guarantee that

$$\log u_0 \in -[0.5, 1][0.75, 1.5] = [-1.5, -0.375]. \tag{27}$$

Next, consider the range of u values near u_0:

$$\log u \in \log u_0 + [-0.5, 0.375]. \tag{28}$$

The size of the range in u is at least $\exp([-2, -1.125]) \approx [0.13534, 0.32465]$ and occurs with probability at least $p_2 = 0.18932$. With u in this range, we rewrite the test as:

$$\frac{1}{b}\sum_{i=1}^{b} x_i^* - 0.5 \quad \not\approx \quad \frac{\log u/u_0}{N(\theta' - \theta)} \tag{29}$$

so that, as in Equation (26), the LHS has expected value zero. Given our choice of intervals for the variables, we can compute the range for the right hand side (RHS) assuming[6] that $\theta' - \theta > 0$:

$$\min\{\text{RHS}\} = \frac{-0.5}{\sqrt{N}\cdot 0.5} = -\frac{1}{\sqrt{N}} \quad \text{and} \quad \max\{\text{RHS}\} = \frac{0.375}{\sqrt{N}\cdot 0.5} = \frac{0.75}{\sqrt{N}} \tag{30}$$

Thus, the RHS is in $\frac{1}{\sqrt{N}}[-1, 0.75]$. The standard deviation of the LHS given the interval constraints is at least $0.5/\sqrt{b}$. Consequently, the gap between the LHS and RHS in Equation (29) is at most $2\sqrt{b/N}$ standard deviations, limiting the range in which the test will be able to "succeed" without requiring more samples.

The samples θ, θ' and u are drawn independently and so the probability of the conjunction of these events is $c = p_0 p_1 p_2 = 0.0085$.

A.2 PROOF OF LEMMA 3

The following bound is given immediately after Corollary 2 from [Novak, 2005]:

$$-6.4\mathbb{E}[|X|^3] - 2\mathbb{E}[|X|] \leq \sup_x |\Pr(t < x) - \Phi(x)|\sqrt{n} \leq 1.36\mathbb{E}[|X|^3]. \tag{31}$$

This bound applies to $x \geq 0$. Applying the bound to $-x$ when $x < 0$ and combining with $x > 0$, we obtain the weaker but unqualified bound in Equation (17).

A.3 PROOF OF LEMMA 4

We first observe that

$$P'(z) - Q'(z) = \int_{-\infty}^{+\infty} (P(z-x) - Q(z-x))R(x)dx,$$

and since $\sup_x |P(x) - Q(x)| \leq \epsilon$ it follows that $\forall z$:

$$-\epsilon = \int_{-\infty}^{+\infty} -\epsilon R(x)dx \leq \int_{-\infty}^{+\infty} (P(z-x) - Q(z-x))R(x)dx \leq \int_{-\infty}^{+\infty} \epsilon R(x)dx = \epsilon, \tag{32}$$

as desired.

A.4 PROOF OF COROLLARY 2

We apply Lemma 4 twice. First take:

$$P(y) = \Pr(\Delta^* < y) \quad \text{and} \quad Q(y) = \Phi\left(\frac{y - \Delta}{s_{\Delta^*}}\right) \tag{33}$$

and convolve with the distribution of X_n which has density $\phi(X/\sigma_n)$ where $\sigma_n^2 = 1 - s_{\Delta^*}^2$. This yields the next iteration of P and Q:

$$P'(y) = \Pr(\Delta^* + X_{\text{nc}} < y) \quad \text{and} \quad Q'(y) = \Phi(y - \Delta) \tag{34}$$

Now we convolve with the distribution of X_{corr}:

$$P''(y) = \Pr(\Delta^* + X_{\text{nc}} + X_{\text{corr}} < y) \quad \text{and} \quad Q''(y) = S(y - \Delta) \tag{35}$$

Both steps preserve the error bound $\epsilon(\theta, \theta', b)$. Finally $S(y - \Delta)$ is a logistic CDF centered at Δ, and so $S(y - \Delta) = \Pr(\Delta + X_{\text{log}} < y)$ for a logistic random X_{log}. We conclude that the probability of acceptance for the actual test $\Pr(\Delta^* + X_{\text{nc}} + X_{\text{corr}} > 0)$ differs from the exact test $\Pr(\Delta + X_{\text{log}} > 0)$ by at most ϵ.

[6] If $\theta' - \theta < 0$, then the range would be $\frac{1}{\sqrt{N}}[-0.75, 1]$ but this does not matter for the purposes of our analysis.

A.5 IMPROVED ERROR BOUNDS BASED ON SKEW ESTIMATION

We show that the CLT error bound can be improved to $O(n^{-1})$ using a more precise limit distribution under an additional assumption. Let μ_i denote the ith moment, and b_i denote the ith absolute moment of X. If Cramer's condition holds:

$$\lim_{t\to\infty} \sup |\mathbb{E}[\exp(itX)]| < 1, \tag{36}$$

then Equation 2.2 in Bentkus et al.'s work on Edgeworth expansions [Bentkus et al., 1997] provides:

Lemma 6. *Let $X_1, \ldots, X_n$ be a set of zero-mean, independent, identically-distributed random variables with sample mean $\hat{X}$ and with t defined as in Lemma 3. If X satisfies Cramer's condition, then*

$$\sup_x \left| \Pr(t < x) - G\left(x, \frac{\mu_3}{b_2^{3/2}}\right) \right| \leq \frac{c(\epsilon, b_2, b_3, b_4, b_{4+\epsilon})}{n}$$

where

$$G_n(x, y) = \Phi(x) + \frac{y(2x^2+1)}{6\sqrt{n}} \Phi'(x). \tag{37}$$

Lemma 6 shows that the average of the X_i has a more precise, skewed CDF limit $G_n(x, y)$ where the skew term has weight proportional to a certain measure of skew derived from the moments: $\mu_3 / b_2^{3/2}$. Note that if the X_i are symmetric, the weight of the correction term is zero, and the CDF of the average of the X_i converges to $\Phi(x)$ at a rate of $O(n^{-1})$.

Here the limit $G_n(x, y)$ is a normal CDF plus a correction term that decays as $n^{-1/2}$. Importantly, since $\phi''(x) = x^2\phi(x) - \phi(x)$ where $\phi(x) = \Phi'(x)$, the correction term can be rewritten giving:

$$G_n(x, y) = \Phi(x) + \frac{y}{6\sqrt{n}}(2\phi''(x) + 3\phi(x)) \tag{38}$$

From which we see that $G_n(x, y)$ is a linear combination of $\Phi(x)$, $\phi(x)$ and $\phi''(x)$. In Algorithm 1, we correct for the difference in σ between Δ^* and the variance needed by X_{corr} using X_{nc}. This same method works when we wish to estimate the error in Δ^* vs $G_n(x, y)$. Since all of the component functions of $G_n(x, y)$ are derivatives of a (unit variance) $\Phi(x)$, adding a normal variable with variance σ' increases the variance of all three functions to $1 + \sigma'$. Thus we add X_{nc} as per Algorithm 1 preserving the limit in Equation (38).

The deconvolution approach can be used to construct a correction variable X_{corr} between $G_n(x, y)$ and $S(x)$ the standard logistic function. An additional complexity is that $G_n(x, y)$ has additional parameters y and n. Since these act as a single multiplier $\frac{y}{6\sqrt{n}}$ in Equation (38), its enough to consider a function $g(x, y')$ parametrized by $y' = \frac{y}{6\sqrt{n}}$. This function can be computed and saved offline. As we have shown earlier, errors in the "limit" function propagate directly through as errors in the acceptance test. To achieve a test error of 10^{-6} (close to single floating point precision), we need a y' spacing of 10^{-6}. It should not be necessary to tabulate values all the way to $y' = 1$, since y' is scaled inversely by the square root of minibatch size. Assuming a max y' of 0.1 requires us to tabulate about 100,000. Since our x resolution is 10,000, this leads to a table with about 1 billion values, which can comfortably be stored in memory. However, if $g(x, y)$ is moderately smooth in y, it should be possible to achieve similar accuracy with a much smaller table. We leave further analysis and experiments with $g(x, y)$ as future work.

B WHY THE BARKER LOGISTIC FUNCTION?

Regarding our choice of the Logistic function, a test function $f(x)$ for Metropolis-Hastings must satisfy Lemma 2. In addition, it must be monotone, bounded by $[0, 1]$ and be such that $\lim_{x\to-\infty} f(x) = 0$ and $\lim_{x\to\infty} f(x) = 1$. While many functions satisfy this, including the classical test $f(x) = \min\{\exp(x), 1\}$, the Logistic function is the *unique* function in this class which is anti-symmetric about 0.5, so it represents the (unique) CDF of a symmetric random variable. Our method requires approximating this with the sum of a Gaussian random variable (which is symmetric) and a correction. The Logistic CDF L and Gaussian CDF Φ are extremely close even without correction; more precisely, the CDF error from the closest Gaussian CDF — which we numerically determined to have standard

Table 3: Errors (L_∞) in $X_{\text{norm}} + X_{\text{corr}}$ versus X_{log}, with $N = 4000$ (top row) and $N = 2000$ (bottom row).

$N = 2000$	$\sigma = 0.8$	$N = 2000$	$\sigma = 0.9$	$N = 2000$	$\sigma = 1.0$	$N = 2000$	$\sigma = 1.1$
λ	L_∞ error	λ	L_∞ error	λ	L_∞ error	λ	L_∞ error
100	2.6e-3	100	3.3e-3	100	4.4e-3	100	6.8e-3
10	4.0e-4	10	6.4e-4	10	1.3e-3	10	**4.6e-3**
1	6.7e-5	1	1.6e-4	1	**1.1e-3**	1	7.5e-3
0.1	1.4e-5	0.1	**1.3e-4**	0.1	2.0e-3	0.1	1.3e-2
0.01	**5.0e-6**	0.01	2.7e-4	0.01	3.6e-3	0.01	2.4e-2

$N = 4000$	$\sigma = 0.8$	$N = 4000$	$\sigma = 0.9$	$N = 4000$	$\sigma = 1.0$	$N = 4000$	$\sigma = 1.1$
λ	L_∞ error	λ	L_∞ error	λ	L_∞ error	λ	L_∞ error
100	8.3e-4	100	1.2e-3	100	1.9e-3	100	**4.3e-3**
10	1.3e-4	10	2.6e-4	10	**8.9e-4**	10	6.0e-3
1	2.5e-5	1	**1.0e-4**	1	1.6e-3	1	1.0e-2
0.1	**6.7e-6**	0.1	2.0e-4	0.1	2.8e-3	0.1	1.2e-2
0.01	7.4e-6	0.01	3.9e-4	0.01	5.2e-3	0.01	3.5e-2

Table 4: Gaussian Mixture Model statistics ($\pm$ one standard deviation over 10 trials).

Metric/Method	MHMINIBATCH	AUSTEREMH(C)	MHSUBLHD
Equation 39	-1307.0 ± 229.5	-1386.9 ± 322.4	-1295.1 ± 278.0
Chi-Squared	4502.3 ± 1821.8	5216.9 ± 3315.8	3462.3 ± 1519.5

deviation approximately 1.7 — satisfies $\sup_x |L(x) - \Phi(x/1.7)| < 0.01$. Said another way, the error between the Logistic and Gaussian CDFs is less than 1%. With our correction we can make this error orders of magnitude smaller.

While not a proof of optimality, it is unlikely that a non-symmetric test function $f(x)$ — representing a skewed variable — would do better. It would require a highly-skewed correction variable, and likely require a much narrower normal distribution (and hence more samples).

C ADDITIONAL EXPERIMENT DETAILS

C.1 OBTAINING THE CORRECTION DISTRIBUTION (SECTION 4)

In Section 4, we described our derivation of the correction distribution C_σ for random variable X_{corr}. Table 3 shows our L_∞ error results for the convolution (Equation (14)) based on various hyperparameter choices. We test using $N = 2000$ and $N = 4000$ points for discretization within a range of $X_{\text{corr}} \in [-20, 20]$, covering essentially all the probability mass. We also vary σ from 0.8 to 1.1.

We observe the expected tradeoff. With smaller σ, our C_σ is closer to the ideal distribution (as judged by L_∞ error), but this imposes a stricter upper bound on the sample variance of Δ^* before our test can be applied, which thus results in larger minibatch sizes. Conversely, a more liberal upper bound means we avail ourselves of smaller minibatch sizes, but at the cost of a less stable derivation for C_σ.

We chose $N = 4000, \sigma = 1$, and $\lambda = 10$ to use in our experiments, which empirically exhibits excellent performance. This is reflected in the description of MHMINIBATCH in Algorithm 1, which assumes that we used $\sigma = 1$ but we reiterate that the choice is arbitrary so long as $0 < \sigma < \sqrt{\pi^2/3} \approx 1.814$, the standard deviation of the standard logistic distribution, since there must be some variance left over for X_{corr}.

C.2 GAUSSIAN MIXTURE MODEL EXPERIMENT (SECTION 6.1)

C.2.1 Grid Search

For the Gaussian mixture experiment, we use the conservative method from [Korattikara et al., 2014], which avoids the need for recomputing log likelihoods of each data point each iteration by choosing baseline minibatch sizes m and per-test thresholds ϵ beforehand, and then using those values for the entirety of the trials. We experimented with the following values, which are similar to the values reported in [Korattikara et al., 2014]:

- $\epsilon \in \{0.001, 0.005, 0.01, 0.05, 0.1, 0.2\}$
- $m \in \{50, 100, 150, 200, 250, 300, 350, 400, 450, 500\}$

and chose the (m, ϵ) pairing which resulted in the lowest expected data usage given a selected upper bound on the error. Through personal communication with Korattikara et al. [2014], we were able to use their same code to compute expected data usage and errors.

The main difference between AUSTEREMH(C) and AUSTEREMH(NC)[7] is that the latter needs to run a grid search each iteration (i.e. after each time it makes an accept/reject decision for one sample θ_t). We use the same ϵ and m candidates above for AUSTEREMH(NC).

C.2.2 Gaussian Mixture Model Metrics

We discretize the posterior coordinates into bins with respect to the two components of θ. The probability P_i of a sample falling into bin i is the integral of the true posterior over the bin's area. A single sample should therefore be multinomial with distribution P, and a set of n (ideally independent) samples is $\text{Multinomial}(P, n)$. This distribution is simple and we can use it to measure the quality of the samples rather than use general purpose tests like KL-divergence or likelihood-ratio, which are problematic with zero counts.

For large n, the per-bin distributions are approximated by Poissons with parameter $\lambda_i = P_i n$. Given samples $\{\theta_1, \dots, \theta_T\}$, let c_j denote the number of individual samples θ_i that fall in bin j out of N_{bins} total. We have

$$\log p(c_1, \dots, c_{N_{\text{bins}}} | P_1, \dots, P_{N_{\text{bins}}}) = \sum_{j=1}^{N_{\text{bins}}} c_j \log(nP_j) - nP_j - \log(\Gamma(c_j + 1)). \tag{39}$$

Table 4 shows the likelihoods. To facilitate interpretation we perform significance tests using Chi-Squared distribution (also in Table 4). The table provides the mean likelihood value and mean Chi-Squared test statistics value as well as their standard deviations. Our likelihood values lies between [Korattikara et al., 2014] and [Bardenet et al., 2014], but we note that we are not aiming to optimize the likelihood values or the Chi-Squared statistics. We use these values to show the extent of correctness.

C.3 LOGISTIC REGRESSION EXPERIMENT (SECTION 6.2)

Figure 5 shows the histograms for the four methods on one representative trial of MNIST-13k, indicating similar relative performance of the four methods as in Figure 4 (which uses MNIST-100k). In particular, MHMINIBATCH exhibits a shorter-tailed distribution and consumes nearly an order of magnitude fewer data points compared to AUSTEREMH(NC), the next-best method; see Table 2 for details.

Next, we investigate the impact of the step size σ for the random walk proposers with covariance matrix σI. Note that I is 784×784 as we did not perform any downsampling or data preprocessing other than rescaling the pixel values to lie in $[0, 1]$.

For this, we use the larger dataset MNIST-100k, and test with $\sigma \in \{0.005, 0.01, 0.05\}$. We keep other parameters consistent with the experiments in Section 6.2, in particular, keeping the initial minibatch size $m = 100$, which is also the amount the minibatch increments by if we need more data. Figure 6 indicates minibatch histograms (again, using the log-log scale) for one trial of MHMINIBATCH using each of the step sizes. We observe that by tuning

[7] AUSTEREMH(NC) is used in Section 6.2.

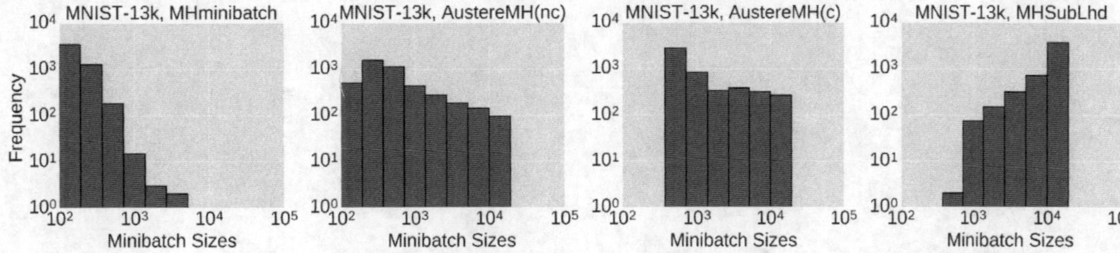

Figure 5: Minibatch sizes for a representative trial of logistic regression on MNIST-13k (analogous to Figure 2). Both axes are on a log scale and have the same ranges across the three histograms. See Section 6.2 for details.

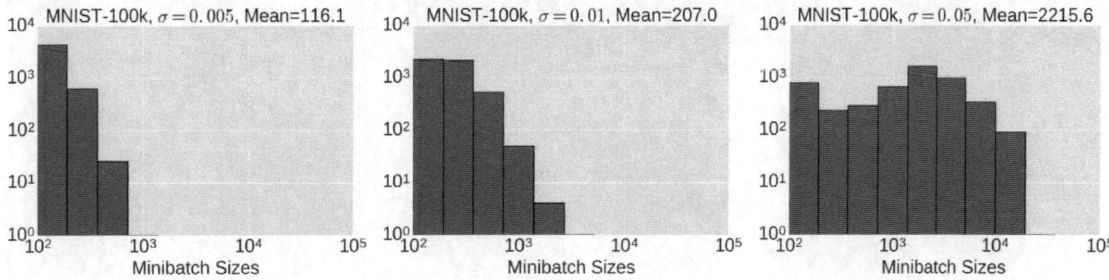

Figure 6: Effect of changing the proposal step size σ for MHMINIBATCH.

MHMINIBATCH, we are able to adjust the average number of data points in a minibatch across a wide range of values. Here, the smallest step size results in an average of just 116.1 data points per minibatch, while increasing to $\sigma = 0.05$ (the step size used for MNIST-13k) results in an average of 2215.6. This relative trend is also present for both AUSTEREMH variants and MHSUBLHD.

Table 5 indicates the relevant parameter settings for the logistic regression experiments. Unless otherwise stated, values apply to all methods tested. For values from [Korattikara et al., 2014] or [Bardenet et al., 2014], we use their notation ($\Delta^*, m, \epsilon, \gamma, p$, and δ) to be consistent.

Table 5: Parameters for the logistic regression experiments.

Value	**MNIST-13k**	**MNIST-100k**
Temperature K	100	100
Number of samples T	5000	3000
Number of trials	10	5
Step size σ for random walk proposer with covariance σI	0.05	0.01
MHMINIBATCH and MHSUBLHD minibatch size m	100	100
AUSTEREMH(C) chosen Δ^* bound	0.1	0.2
AUSTEREMH(C) minibatch size m from grid search	450	300
AUSTEREMH(C) per-test threshold ϵ from grid search	0.01	0.01
AUSTEREMH(NC) chosen Δ^* bound	0.05	0.1
MHSUBLHD γ	2.0	2.0
MHSUBLHD p	2	2
MHSUBLHD δ	0.01	0.01

Stochastic Bandit Models for Delayed Conversions

Claire Vernade
LTCI, Telecom ParisTech,
Université Paris-Saclay

Olivier Cappé
LIMSI, CNRS,
Université Paris-Saclay

Vianney Perchet
CMLA, ENS Paris-Saclay,
Université Paris-Saclay
& Criteo Research

Abstract

Online advertising and product recommendation are important domains of applications for multi-armed bandit methods. In these fields, the reward that is immediately available is most often only a proxy for the actual outcome of interest, which we refer to as a *conversion*. For instance, in web advertising, clicks can be observed within a few seconds after an ad display but the corresponding sale –if any– will take hours, if not days to happen. This paper proposes and investigates a new stochastic multi-armed bandit model in the framework proposed by Chapelle (2014) –based on empirical studies in the field of web advertising– in which each action may trigger a future reward that will then happen with a stochastic delay. We assume that the probability of conversion associated with each action is unknown while the distribution of the conversion delay is known, distinguishing between the (idealized) case where the conversion events may be observed whatever their delay and the more realistic setting in which late conversions are censored. We provide performance lower bounds as well as two simple but efficient algorithms based on the UCB and KLUCB frameworks. The latter algorithm, which is preferable when conversion rates are low, is based on a Poissonization argument, of independent interest in other settings where aggregation of Bernoulli observations with different success probabilities is required.

1 INTRODUCTION

Characterizing the relationship between marketing actions and users' decisions is of prime importance in advertising, product recommendation and customer relationship management. In online advertising a key aspect of the problem is that whereas marketing actions can be taken very fast –typically in less than a tenth of a second, if we think of an ad display–, user's buying decisions will happen at a much slower rate [7, 4, 18]. In the following, we refer to a user's decision of interest under the generic term of *conversion*. Chapelle, in [4], while analyzing data from the real-time bidding company Criteo, observed that, on average, only 35% of the conversions occurred within the first hour. Furthermore, about 13% of the conversions could be attributed to ad display that were more than two weeks old. Another interesting observation from this work is the fact that the delay distribution could be reasonably well fitted by an exponential distribution, particularly when conditioning on context variables that are available to the advertiser.

The present work addresses the problem of sequentially learning to select relevant items in the context where the feedback happens with long delays. By long we mean in particular that the feedback associated with a fraction of the actions taken by the learner will be practically unobserved because they will happen with an excessive delay. In the example cited above, if we were to run an online algorithm during two weeks, at least 13% of the actions would not receive an observable feedback because of delays. A related situation occurs if the online algorithm is run during, say, one month, but its memory is limited to a sliding window of two weeks. In Section 2 below we introduce models suitable for addressing these two related situations in the framework of multi-armed bandits.

Delayed feedback is a topic that has been considered before in the reinforcement learning literature and we defer the precise comparison between existing approaches and the proposed framework to Section 3. In a nutshell however, the distinctive features of our approach is to consider potentially infinite stochastic delays, resulting in some feedback being *censored* (ie. not observable). Existing works on delayed bandits focus on cases where the feedback is observed after some delay, typically assumed to be finite. In contrast, we assume that delays are random with a distribution that may have an unbounded support – although we require that it has finite expectation. As a result, some conversion events cannot be observed within any finite horizon and the proposed learning algorithm must take this uncertainty into account.

In Section 2, we propose discrete-time stochastic multi-armed bandit models to address the problem of long delays with possibly censored feedback. We distinguish two situations that correspond to the cases mentioned informally above: In the *uncensored* model, conversions can be assumed to be eventually observed after some possibly arbitrarily long delay; In the *censored* model, it is assumed that the environment imposes that the conversions related to actions cannot be observed anymore after a finite window of m time steps.

Assuming that the delay distribution is known, we prove problem-dependent lower bounds on the regret of any uniformly efficient bandit algorithm for the censored and uncensored models in Section 4.

In Section 5, we describe efficient anytime policies relying on optimistic indices, based on the UCB [1] or KLUCB [5] algorithms. The latter uses a Poissonization argument that can be of independent interest in other bandit models. In typical scenarios where the conversion rates are less than one percent, using the KLUCB variant will ensure a much faster learning and provides near-optimal perfomance on the long run (see Theorem 11).

These algorithms are analyzed in Section 6, showing that they reach close to optimal asymptotic performance. In Section 7 we discuss the implementation of these methods, showing that it is further simplified in the case of geometrically distributed delays, and we illustrate their performance on simulated data.

2 A STOCHASTIC MODEL FOR THE DELAYS

We now describe our bandit setting for delayed conversion events, inspired by [4]. We first consider the setting in which delays may be potentially unbounded and then consider the case where censoring occurs.

2.1 GENERAL BANDIT MODEL UNDER DELAYED FEEDBACK

At each round $t \in \mathbb{N}^*$, the learner chooses an arm $A_t \in \{1, \ldots, K\}$. This action simultaneously triggers two independent random variables:

- $C_t \in \{0, 1\}$, is the *conversion indicator* that is equal to 1 only if the action A_t will lead to a conversion;
- $D_t \in \mathbb{N}$, is *the delay* indicating the number of time steps needed before the conversion – if any – be disclosed to the learner.

At each round t, the agent then receives an integer-valued reward Y_t which corresponds to the number of observed conversions at time t:

$$Y_t = \sum_{s=1}^{t} C_s \mathbb{1}\{D_s = t - s\}.$$

In the following, we will use the short-hand notation $X_{s,t} = C_s \mathbb{1}\{D_s \leq t - s\}$, for $s \leq t$ to denote the possible contribution of the action taken at time s to the conversion(s) observed at a later time t. We emphasize that even if the actual reward of the learner is the sum of the conversions, we assume that the agent also observes all the individual contributions $(X_{s,t})_{1 \leq s \leq t}$ at time t triggered by actions taken before time t.

The above mechanism implies that if $C_t = 1$, the learner will observe D_t at time $t + D_t$, whereas if $C_t = 0$, the delay will not be directly observable. In particular, if at time t, $X_{s,u} = 0$, for all $s \leq u \leq t$, it is impossible to decide whether $C_s = 0$ or if $C_s = 1$ but $D_s > t - s$. Formally, the history of the algorithm is the σ-field generated by $\mathcal{H}_t := (X_{s,u})_{1 \leq u \leq t, 1 \leq s \leq u}$.

We consider the stochastic model under the following basic assumptions:

$$C_t | \mathcal{H}_{t-1} \sim \text{Bernoulli}(\theta_{A_t}),$$
$$D_t | \mathcal{H}_{t-1} \sim \text{distribution with CDF } \tau,$$

and C_t, D_t are conditionally independent given $\mathcal{H}_{t-1}$.

Lemma 1. *Denote by $a^* \in \{1, \ldots, K\}$ an index such that $\theta_a^* \geq \theta_k$, for $k \in \{1, \ldots, K\}$, and define by $r(T) = \sum_{t=1}^{T} Y_t$ the cumulated reward of the learner and by $r^*(T)$ the cumulated reward obtained by an oracle playing $A_t = a^*$ at each round. The expected regret of the learner is given by*

$$L(T) = \mathbb{E}\left[r^*(T) - r(T)\right] = \sum_{s=1}^{T} \mathbb{E}\left[\theta_{a^*} - \theta_{A_s}\right] \tau_{T-s} \tag{1}$$

where by definition $\tau_{T-s} = \mathbb{P}(D_s \leq T - s)$. Denoting $\mathbb{E}[N_k(T)] := \sum_{s=1}^{T-1} \mathbb{1}\{A_s = k\}$, it holds that

$$L(T) \leq \sum_{k=1}^{K} (\theta_{a^*} - \theta_k) N_k(t)$$

and if $\mu = \mathbb{E}[D_s] < \infty$,

$$\sum_{k=1}^{K} (\theta_{a^*} - \theta_k) N_k(t) - L(T) \leq \mu \sum_{k=1}^{K} (\theta_{a^*} - \theta_k). \tag{2}$$

Proof The cumulated reward at time T satisfies

$$r(T) = \sum_{t=1}^{T} Y_t = \sum_{t=1}^{T}\sum_{s=1}^{t} C_s \mathbf{1}\{D_s = t-s\}$$
$$= \sum_{s=1}^{T} C_s \mathbf{1}\{D_s \le T-s\} = \sum_{s=1}^{T} X_{s,T},$$

where the index T stands for the time at which all past conversions are observed while s is the index at which the action has been taken. Hence Eq. (1) is obtained by

$$\mathbb{E}\left[\sum_{t=1}^{T} r(T)\right] = \mathbb{E}\left[\sum_{t=1}^{T} Y_t\right]$$
$$= \sum_{s=1}^{T} \mathbb{E}\left[X_{s,T}\right] = \sum_{s=1}^{T} \theta_{A_s}\tau_{T-s}.$$

Obviously the fact that $\tau_{T-s} \le 1$ implies that $L(T)$ is upper bounded by $\sum_{k=1}^{K}(\theta_{a^\star} - \theta_k)N_k(t)$, which corresponds to the usual regret formula in the bandit model with explicit immediate feedback. To upper bound the difference, note that

$$\sum_{k=1}^{K}(\theta_{a^\star} - \theta_k)N_k(t) - L(T)$$
$$= \sum_{k=1}^{K}(\theta_{a^\star} - \theta_k)\sum_{s=1}^{T}\mathbf{1}\{A_s = k\}(1-\tau_{T-s})$$
$$\le \sum_{k=1}^{K}(\theta_{a^\star} - \theta_k)\sum_{n=0}^{\infty}(1-\tau_n) = \mu\sum_{k=1}^{K}(\theta_{a^\star} - \theta_k).$$

■

2.2 THRESHOLDED DELAYS: CENSORED OBSERVATIONS

The model with m-thresholded delays takes into account the fact that a conversion can only be observed within m steps after the action occurred. This basically changes the expression of the expected instantaneous reward Y_t which becomes,

$$Y_t = \sum_{s=t-m}^{t} C_s \mathbf{1}\{D_s = t-s\}$$

and the future contributions of each action are capped to the next m time steps: $(X_{s,t})_{t-m\le s\le t}$. The history of the algorithm only consists of $\mathcal{H}_t = \sigma((X_{s,u})_{1\le u\le t, u-m\le s\le u})$ and the regret expression of Lemma 1 can be split into two terms corresponding to old pulls and the m most recent pulls:

$$\sum_{s=1}^{T-m}(\theta_{a^\star} - \mathbb{E}[\theta_{A_s}])\tau_m + \sum_{s=T-m+1}^{T}(\theta_{a^\star} - \mathbb{E}[\theta_{A_s}])\tau_{T-s} \quad (3)$$

In the remaining, for $(p,q) \in [0,1]^2$, we will denote by $d(p,q) = p\log(p/q) + (1-p)\log((1-p)/(1-q))$ the binary entropy between p and q, that is the Kullback-Leibler divergence between Bernoulli distributions with parameters p and q. Moreover, without loss of generality, we will assume that $a^* = 1$ is the unique optimal arm of the considered bandit problems and denote by $\theta^* = \theta_1$ the optimal conversion rate.

3 RELATED WORK ON DELAYED BANDITS

Delayed feedback recently received increasing attention in the bandit and online learning literature due to its various applications ranging from online advertising [4] to distributed optimization [10, 3]. Indeed, delayed feedback have been extensively considered in the context of Markov Decision Processes (MDPs) [12, 19]. However, the present work focuses on unbounded delays and the models considered therein would result in an infinite space MDP for which even the planning problem would be challenging. In contrast, the lack of memory in bandits makes it possible to propose relatively simple algorithms even in the case where the delays may be very long. For a review of previous works in online learning in the stochastic and non-stochastic settings, see [8] and references therein. The latter work tackles the more general problem of partial monitoring under delayed feedback, with Sections 3.2 and 4 of the paper focusing on the stochastic delayed bandit problem. A key insight from this work is that, in minimax analysis, delay increases the regret in a multiplicative way in adversarial problems, and in an additive way in stochastic problems.

The algorithm of [9] relies on a queuing principle termed Q-PMD that uses an optimistic bandit referred to as "BASE" to perform exploration; in [9] UCB is chosen as BASE strategy while the follow-up work [8] also considers the use of KLUCB. The idea is to store all the observations that arrive at the same time t in a FIFO buffer and to feed BASE with the information related to an arm k only when this arm is about to be chosen. It means that the number of draws of an arm as well as the cumulated sum of the subsequent rewards are only updated whenever the observation arrives to the learner. Meanwhile, the algorithm acts as if nothing happened.

However, in the setting considered in the present work,

updating counts only after the observations are eventually received cannot lead to a practical algorithm: Whenever a click is received, the associated reward is 1 by definition, otherwise the ambiguity between non-received and negative feedback remains. Thus, the empirical average of the rewards for each arm computed by the updating mechanism of Q-PMD sticks to 1 and does not allow to compare the arms. As a consequence, the Q-PMD policy cannot be used for the models described in Section 2, except in the specific case of the uncensored delay model with bounded delays: Then there is no censoring anymore as one only needs to wait long enough (longer than the maximal possible delay) to reveal with certainty the exact value of the feedback.

Also, [16] notices that the empirical performances of this queuing-based heuristic are not fully satisfying because of the lack of variability in the decisions made by the policy while waiting for feedback. Their suggestion is to use random policies instead of deterministic ones in order to improve the overall exploration. Note that even though we stick to deterministic, history-based, policies, this problem is taken care of by our algorithm thanks to the use of the CDF of the delays that allow us to correct the confidence intervals continuously after a pull has been made.

Another possible way to handle bounded delays would be to plan ahead the sequence of pulls by batches, following the principles of Explore Then Commit, see [17]. With finite delays, a new un-necessary batch of exploration pulls might be started before the algorithm enters the exploitation (or commitment) phase. The extra cost would therefore be the maximal observable delay. Although these techniques are random and not deterministic, they have the same drawbacks as the other ones: The policy is not updated while waiting for feedback and, as a consequence, cannot handle arbitrarily large delays.

An obvious limitation of our work is that we assume that the delay distribution is known. We believe that it is a realistic assumption however as the delay distribution can be identified from historical data as reported in [4]. In addition, as we assume that the same delay distribution is shared by all actions, it is natural to expect that estimating the delay distribution on-line can be done at no additional cost in terms of performance. Perhaps more interestingly, it is possible to extend the model so as to include cases where the context of each action is available to the learner and determines the distribution of the corresponding delay, using for instance the generalized linear modeling of [4]. In particular, the same algorithms can be used in this case, by considering the proper CDFs corresponding to different instances. Of course the analysis to be described below would need to be extended to cover also this contextual case.

4 LOWER BOUND ON THE REGRET

The purpose of this section is to provide lower bounds on the regret of *uniformly efficient* algorithms in the two different settings of the Stochastic Delayed Bandit problem that we consider. This class of policies, introduced by [15], refers to algorithms such that for any bandit model ν, and any $\alpha \in (0,1)$, $\mathbb{E}[R(T)]/T^\alpha \to 0$ when $T \to \infty$.

Our results rely on changes of measure argument that are encapsulated in Lemma 1 of [13], or more recently, and more generally, in Inequality (F) of [6]. Those results can actually be reformulated as a lower bound on the expected log-likelihood ratio of the observations under the originally considered bandit model θ and the alternative one θ'

$$\mathbb{E}[\ell_T] = \mathbb{E}_\theta \left[\frac{p_\theta((X_{s,t})_{1\le t\le T, 1\le s\le t})}{p_{\theta'}((X_{s,t})_{1\le t\le T, 1\le s\le t})} \right].$$

The following inequality is obtained using proof techniques from Appendix B of [13] that are detailed in Appendix B.

$$\liminf_{T\to\infty} \frac{\mathbb{E}[\ell_T]}{\log(T)} \ge 1. \tag{4}$$

To obtain explicit regret lower bounds for the models introduced in Section 2, we compute below the expected log-likelihood ratio corresponding to these two models.

Lemma 2. *In the censored delayed feedback setting, the expected log-likelihood ratio is given by*

$$\mathbb{E}_\theta\left[\ell_T\right] = \sum_{s=1}^{T-m} d(\theta_{A_s}\tau_m, \theta'_{A_s}\tau_m) + \sum_{s=T-m}^{T} d(\theta_{A_s}\tau_{T-s}, \theta'_{A_s}\tau_{T-s}).$$

In the uncensored setting, the above sum is not split and we have

$$\mathbb{E}_\theta\left[\ell_T\right] = \sum_{s=1}^{T} d(\theta_{A_s}\tau_{T-s}, \theta'_{A_s}\tau_{T-s}).$$

Proof Given $\mathcal{H}_{s-1}$, $(X_{s,s},\ldots,X_{s,T})$ can be equal to

- $(0,\ldots,0)$, with proba. $(1-\theta_{A_s}) + \theta_{A_s}(1-\tau_{T-s})$,
- $(0,\ldots,0,1,1,\ldots,1)$ with proba. $\theta_{A_s}\delta_{u-s}$, for $u = s,\ldots,T$ (u denotes the position of 1 in the vector), where $\delta_k = \mathbb{P}(D_s \le k)$.

Hence,

$$\mathbb{E}_\theta\left[\log \frac{p_\theta(X_{s,s},\dots,X_{s,T})}{p_{\theta'}(X_{s,s},\dots,X_{s,T}}\middle|\mathcal{H}_{s-1}\right]$$
$$= \log\frac{1-\theta_{A_s}\tau_{T-s}}{1-\theta'_{A_s}\tau_{T-s}}(1-\theta_{A_s}\tau_{T-s})$$
$$+\sum_{u=s}^{T}\log\frac{\theta_{A_s}\delta_{u-s}}{\theta'_{A_s}\delta_{u-s}}\theta_{A_s}\delta_{u-s}$$
$$= \log\frac{1-\theta_{A_s}\tau_{T-s}}{1-\theta'_{A_s}\tau_{T-s}}(1-\theta_{A_s}\tau_{T-s}) + \log\frac{\theta_{A_s}}{\theta'_{A_s}}\theta_{A_s}\tau_{T-s}$$
$$= d(\theta_{A_s}\tau_{T-s}, \theta'_{A_s}\tau_{T-s}).$$

The equivalent expression for the censored case is easily deduced from the same calculations. ■

4.1 CENSORED SETTING

Using our notations, the following theorem provides a problem-dependent lower bound on the regret.

Theorem 3. *The regret of any uniformly efficient algorithm is bounded from below by*

$$\liminf_{T\to\infty}\frac{R(T)}{\log(T)} \geq \sum_{k\neq k^*}\frac{\tau_m(\theta^*-\theta_k)}{d(\tau_m\theta_k,\tau_m\theta^*)}.$$

Proof The details of the proof can be found in Appendix B but we provide here a sketch of the main argument. The log-likelihood ratio is given by Lemma 2:

$$\mathbb{E}_\theta[\ell_T] = \sum_{s=1}^{T-m} d(\theta_{A_s}\tau_m, \theta'_{A_s}\tau_m)$$
$$+\sum_{s=T-m}^{T} d(\theta_{A_s}\tau_{T-s}, \theta'_{A_s}\tau_{T-s}),$$

which is bounded from below by Eq.(4). However, obtaining a lower bound on the regret requires to decompose this quantity into $(K-1)$ terms depending on the suboptimal arms. For a fixed arm $k \neq 1$, we consider $\theta' = (\theta_1,\dots,\theta_{k-1},\theta_1+\epsilon,\dots,\theta_K)$ for which the expected log-likelihood ratio is

$$\mathbb{E}[N_k(T)]d(\tau_m\theta_k, \tau_m(\theta_1+\epsilon))$$
$$+\sum_{s=T-m}^{T} d(\theta_k\tau_{T-s}, (\theta_1+\epsilon)\tau_{T-s}) \geq \mathbb{E}_\theta[\ell_T].$$

Divide by $\log(T)$ and let T to infinity, to get the result for $\epsilon \to 0$, as the second term in the l.h.s. is bounded. ■

This lower bound implies that the delayed bandits problem with trespassing probability τ_m is as hard as solving the scaled bandit problem with expected rewards $(\tau_m\theta_1,\dots,\tau_m\theta_K)$. In the long run, one cannot learn faster than the heuristic approach discarding the last m observations and considerimg the fictitious bandit model with parameters $(\tau_m\theta_1,\dots,\tau_m\theta_K)$. However, on horizons of the order of m time-steps, we will show empirically in Section 7 that taking delay distributions into account allows for much faster learning. Note also that the convexity of the function $\tau \to d(\tau p, \tau q)$ proved in Lemma 15 implies that the regret lower bound is a monotonically increasing function of τ_m. Hence, either reduced values of m or longer values of the expected delay μ actually make the problem harder.

4.2 UNCENSORED SETTING

In the uncensored model, the same argument shows that the lower bound does not differ from the classical Lai & Robbins Lower Bound [15].

Theorem 4. *The regret of any uniformly efficient algorithm in the Uncensored Delays Setting is bounded from below by*

$$\liminf_{T\to\infty}\frac{R(T)}{\log(T)} \geq \sum_{k\neq k^*}\frac{(\theta^*-\theta_k)}{d(\theta_k,\theta^*)}.$$

The full proof of this result is similar to the proof of Theorem 3 and can be found in Appendix B.

5 DELAY-CORRECTED ESTIMATORS AND CONFIDENCE INTERVALS

In this section, for a fixed arm $k \in \{1,\dots,K\}$, we define a conditionally unbiased estimator for the conversion rate θ_k. Then, based on suitable concentration results we derive optimistic indices: a delay-corrected UCB as in [1] as well as a delay-corrected KLUCB as in [5].

5.1 PARAMETER ESTIMATOR

Define the sum of rewards up to time t as

$$S_k(t) = \sum_{s=1}^{t}\sum_{u=1}^{s} X_{u,s}\mathbb{1}\{A_u = k\}.$$

We recall that we defined the exact number of pulls of arm k up to time t as $N_k(t) := \sum_{s=1}^{t-1}\mathbb{1}\{A_s = k\}$. However, defining an estimator of θ_k that is unbiased – when conditioning on the selections of arms – requires to consider a delay-corrected count $\tilde{N}(t)$ taking into account the probability of having eventually observed the reward associated with each previous pull of k. We distinguish the expression of $\tilde{N}(t)$ according to whether feedback is censored or not.

Censored model. When rewards cannot be disclosed after m rounds following the action, the current available information on the pulls is split into two main groups: The 'oldest' pulls, censored if not observed yet, and the most recent ones. Namely, we now define $\tilde{N}_k(t)$ as

$$\tilde{N}_k(t) = \sum_{s=1}^{t-m} \mathbb{1}\{A_s = k\}\tau_m + \sum_{s=t-m+1}^{t-1} \mathbb{1}\{A_s = k\}\tau_{t-s}.$$

Overall, the conversion rate estimator is defined as

$$\hat{\theta}_k(t) = \frac{S_k(t)}{\tilde{N}_k(t)}. \tag{5}$$

Remark 5. *In the uncensored case, defining* $\tilde{N}_k(t) := \sum_{s=1}^{t} \mathbb{1}\{A_s = k\}\tau_{t-s}$. *leads to an equivalent definition of* $\hat{\theta}_k(t)$ *as a conditionally unbiased estimator.*

5.2 UCB INDEX

We first define a delay-corrected UCB-index for bounded rewards.

Concentration bound. Using the self-normalized concentration inequality of Proposition 8 of [14], yields the following result, that we recall here for completeness.

Proposition 6. *Let* k *be an arm in* $\{1, ..., K\}$, *then for any* $\beta > 0$ *and for all* $t > 0$,

$$\mathbb{P}\left(\theta_k > \hat{\theta}_k(t) + \sqrt{\frac{N_k(t)}{\tilde{N}_k(t)}}\sqrt{\frac{\beta}{2\tilde{N}_k(t)}}\right) < \beta e \log(t) e^{-\beta}.$$

Upper-confidence Bound. Thus, an UCB index for $\hat{\theta}_k(t)$ may be defined as

$$U_k^{\text{UCB}}(t) = \hat{\theta}_k(t) + \sqrt{\frac{N_k(t)}{\tilde{N}_k(t)}}\sqrt{\frac{\beta_\epsilon(t)}{2\tilde{N}_k(t)}},$$

where $\beta\epsilon(t)$ is a suitable slowly growing exploration function (see below). This upper confidence interval is scaled by $N_k(t)/\tilde{N}_k(t)$ when compared to the classical UCB index. This ratio gets bigger when the (τ_d)'s are small for large delays d, that is when the median delay is large: The longer we need to wait for observations to come, the largest our uncertainty about our current cumulated reward.

5.3 KLUCB INDEX

Concentration bound. We first state a concentration inequality that controls the underestimation probability based on an alternative Chernoff bound for a sum of independent binary random variables (Lemma 13 proved in Appendix A).

This lemma only holds for a sequence of pulls fixed before-hand, independently of realizations, i.e., the values of A_t do not depend on the sequence of X_s. Although with a restrictive scope, it provides intuition on the construction of the algorithm.

Lemma 7. *Assume that the sequence of pulls is fixed beforehand and let* k *be an arm in* $\{1, ..., K\}$. *Then for any* $\delta > 0$ *and for all* $t > 0$,

$$\mathbb{P}\left(\left\{\hat{\theta}_k(t) < \theta_k\right\} \cap \left\{\tilde{N}_k(t) d_{\text{Pois}}(\hat{\theta}_k(t), \theta_k) > \delta\right\}\right) < e^{-\delta}.$$

where $d_{\text{Pois}}(p, q) = p \log p/q + q - p$ *denotes the Poisson Kullback-Leibler divergence.*

To get upper confidence bounds for θ_k from Lemma 7, we follow [5] and define the KL-UCB index by

$$U_k^{\text{KL}}(t) = \max\Big\{q \in [\hat{\theta}_k(t), 1] : \tilde{N}_k(t) d_{\text{Pois}}(\hat{\theta}_k(t), q) \leq \beta_\epsilon(t)\Big\}.$$

Using $\beta_\epsilon(t) = \beta$, this KL-UCB index satisfies a result analogous to Proposition 6 (see Proposition 14 in Appendix A.1):

$$\mathbb{P}\left(\theta_k > U_k^{\text{KL}}(t)\right) \leq e\lceil \beta \log(t) \rceil e^{-\beta}.$$

Even though the Kullback-Leibler divergence does not have the same expression for Bernoulli and Poisson random variables, the following lemma (proved in Appendix A.1) shows that for a certain range or parameters they are actually very close.

Lemma 8. *For* $0 < p < q < 1$,

$$(1 - q) d(p, q) \leq d_{\text{Pois}}(p, q) \leq d(p, q).$$

6 ALGORITHMS

Algorithm 1 present the scheme common to both the censored and uncensored cases, which differ only by the definition of the parameter estimator. In both cases, one may also consider either of the two UCB or KL-UCB index defined in the previous section, resulting in the DelayedUCB and DelayedKLUCB algorithms. We provide a finite-time analysis of the regret of these algorithms, when using an exploration function of the form $\beta_\epsilon(t) = (1 + \epsilon)\log(t)$, for some positive ϵ.

Algorithm 1 – DelayedUCB and DelayedKLUCB.

Require: K, CDF parameters $(\tau_d)_{d\geq 0}$, threshold $m > 0$ if feedback is censored.
Initialization: First K rounds, play each arm once.
for $t > K$ **do**
  Compute $S_k(t)$ and $\tilde{N}_k(t)$ for all k according to the assumed feedback model (censored or not),
  Compute $\hat{\theta}_k(t)$ for al k,
  For a given choice of algorithm $\mathcal{A} \in \{\text{KLUCB}, \text{UCB}\}$,
  $A_t \leftarrow \arg\max_k U_k^{\mathcal{A}}(t)$.
  Observe reward Y_t and all individual feedback $(X_s, t)_{s\leq t}$
end for

Finite-time Analysis of DelayedUCB.

Theorem 9. *In the censored setting, the regret of DelayedUCB is bounded from above by*

$$L_{\text{UCB}}(T) \leq (1+\epsilon)\log(T)\sum_{k\neq *}\frac{1}{2\tau_m\Delta_k} + o_{\epsilon,m}(\log(T)).$$

Proof Outline of the proof (cf Appendix C.1):

1. First upper-bound the regret using Lemma 1 in the uncensored case:
$$R(T) \leq \sum_{k>1}\Delta_k\mathbb{E}[N_k(T)],$$
and bounding the first m losses by 1 in the censored case:
$$R(T) \leq m + \sum_{k>1}\tau_m\Delta_k\mathbb{E}\left[\sum_{t>m}^{T}\mathbb{1}\{A_t = k\}\right].$$

2. Then, decompose the event $\mathbb{1}\{A_t = k\}$ as in [1]
$$\sum_{t>m}^{T}\mathbb{1}\{A_t = k\} \leq \sum_{t>m}^{T}\mathbb{1}\left\{U_1^{\text{UCB}}(t) < \theta_1\right\}$$
$$+ \sum_{t>m}^{T}\mathbb{1}\left\{A_{t+1} = k, U_k^{\text{UCB}}(t) \geq \theta_1\right\}.$$

3. Remark that the first sum is handled by Proposition 6 so it suffices to control the second sum.
$$\mathbb{E}\left[\mathbb{1}\left\{A_{t+1} = k, U_k^{\text{UCB}}(t) \geq \theta_1\right\}\right]$$
$$\leq \frac{(1+\epsilon)\log(T)}{2\tau_m^2\Delta_i^2}$$
$$+ \sum_{s>\frac{(1+\epsilon)\log(T)}{2\Delta_i^2}} \mathbb{P}\left(U_k^{\text{UCB}}(t) \geq \theta_i + \Delta_i\right).$$

The last term is actually $O(\sqrt{\log(T)})$, giving the desired result. Details, as well as explicit constants and dependencies can be found in Appendix C.1. ■

Corollary 10. *In the uncensored setting, we also assume that there exists $c > 0$ such that $1 - \tau_m \leq \frac{c}{m}$ for all $m \geq 1$. Then, is bounded from above by*

$$L_{\text{UCB}}(T) \leq \frac{1+\epsilon}{1-\epsilon}\log(T)\sum_{k>1}\frac{1}{2\Delta_k} + o_{\epsilon,m}(\log(T)).$$

Proof The analysis of DelayedUCB given in Appendix C.1 (in the censored setting) shows that the performances of DelayedUCB in the uncensored setting can be upper-bounded by its performances in the censored setting, where the threshold m can be arbitrarily fixed to some value. Choosing m will only have an impact on the analysis of the algorithm. The specific choice of m satisfying $\tau_m \geq 1 - \epsilon$ gives the claimed result. As indicated in Appendix C.1, the dependency of $o_{\epsilon,m}(\log(T))$ is actually only linear in m. As a consequence, along with the assumption on the decay of $1 - \tau_m$, this yields that the overall dependency in the parameter m is reduced to $1/\epsilon$. ■

We emphasize that the assumption that $1 - \tau_m \leq 1/m$, is actually rather natural. Indeed, if $1 - \tau_m \leq c/m^\gamma$, for some constants $c, \gamma > 0$, then the finiteness requirement on the expected delay is satisfied if and only if $\gamma > 1$.

Finite-time Analysis of DelayedKLUCB.

Theorem 11. *For any $\eta > 0$, the regret of DelayedKLUCB is bounded in the censored setting as*

$$L_{\text{KLUCB}}(T) \leq (1+\eta)\frac{\beta_\epsilon(t)}{1-\theta_1}\sum_{k>1}\frac{\tau_m\Delta_k}{d(\tau_m\theta_k, \tau_m\theta_1)}$$
$$+ o_{\epsilon,m,\eta}(\log(T)).$$

Proof Outline of the proof (cf. AppendixC.2):

1. We start by decomposing the regret according to the different types of unfavorable events. Note that thanks to the upper bound on the regret provided by Lemma 1, we need to control on the number of suboptimal pulls $\mathbb{E}[N_k(T)]$ for arms $k > 1$.
$$\mathbb{E}[N_k(T)] \leq m + \mathbb{E}\left[\sum_{t=m+1}^{T}\mathbb{1}\{U_1(t) < \theta_1\}\right]$$
$$+ \mathbb{E}\left[\sum_{t=m+1}^{T}\mathbb{1}\{A(t) = k, U_k(t) \geq \theta_1\}\right].$$

2. The first sum is handled by Theorem 14 in Appendix A which shows that it is $o(\log(T))$. For the second term, we bound the indices using the fact

that $\tilde{N}_k(t) \geq \tau_m N_k(t-m)$ to obtain

$$U_k^{\mathrm{KL}}(t) \leq U_k^{\mathrm{KL}+}(t)$$
$$:= \arg\max_{q \in [\hat{\theta}_k, 1]} \{q | \tau_m d_{\mathrm{Pois}}(\hat{\theta}_k(t), q) \leq \frac{\beta_\epsilon(t)}{N_k(t-m)}\}.$$

Notice that the $U_k^{\mathrm{KL}+}(t)$ indices are well defined for $t > m$.

3. Then, we proceed as in the proof of Theorem 10 in Appendix B.2 of [9]. For any $\eta > 0$, we define the characteristic number of pulls

$$K_k(T) = \frac{(1+\eta)\beta_\epsilon(t)}{d_{\mathrm{Pois}}(\tau_m \theta_k, \tau_m \theta_1)},$$

and we prove

$$\sum_{s \geq K_k(T)} \mathbb{P}\left(\tau_m s d_{\mathrm{Pois}}(\hat{\theta}_{k,s}, \theta_1) \leq \beta_\epsilon(t)\right)$$
$$= o_{\epsilon,m,\eta}(\log T)$$

using Fact 2 of [2] for exponential families.

■

Corollary 12. *In the uncensored setting, under the same hypothesis than in Corollary 10, namely that there exists a constant c such that* $1 - \tau_m \leq \frac{c}{m}$ *for all* $m \leq 1$. *Then, the regret of* DelayedKLUCB *is bounded from above as*

$$L_{\mathrm{KLUCB}}(T) \leq \frac{\beta_\epsilon(t)}{1-\theta_1} \sum_{k>1} \frac{(1+\eta)(1-\epsilon)\Delta_k}{d((1-\epsilon)\theta_k, (1-\epsilon)\theta_1)}$$
$$+ o_{\eta,\epsilon}(\log(T)).$$

Proof As for the proof of Corollary 10, the performance of DelayedKLUCB in the uncensored case can be bounded as in the censored case by a specific choice of $m(\epsilon)$ such that $\tau_m \geq 1 - \epsilon$, namely $m(\epsilon) \geq c/\epsilon$. As shown in the proof of Theorem 11 in the censored case, the dependency in m of the term of rest is linear, reducing to $1/\epsilon$. ■

Naive benchmark: The DISCARDING policy. An obvious benchmark algorithm in the censored setting is to use the regular UCB and KLUCB policies only using the first $t - m$ pulls and observed rewards at each time t. In that case the empirical average considered is simply $\hat{\theta}_k^m(t) = S_k(t-m)/\tau_m N_k(t-m)$ and the corresponding optimistic indices are

$$U^m(t) = \hat{\theta}_k^m(t) + \sqrt{\beta_\epsilon(t)/2\tau_m N_k(t-m)},$$
$$U_k^{m|\mathrm{KL}}(t) = \max_{q \in [\hat{\theta}_k^m, 1]} \left\{q | \tau_m d_{\mathrm{Pois}}(\hat{\theta}_k^m, q) \leq \frac{\beta_\epsilon(t)}{N(t-m)}\right\}.$$

These indices can only be computed after at least m rounds. The proof technique used for the analysis of our algorithms in the censored case actually shows that the DISCARDINGUCB and DISCARDINGKLUCB policies are asymptotically optimal. Nonetheless, in practice it is very undesirable to have an arbitrarily long linear regret phase at the beginning of the learning until the threshold m is reached. This is especially true if the threshold m is large as compared to the horizon T. In that case, we empirically show in Section 7 that our algorithms achieve drastically improved short-horizon performance.

7 EXPERIMENTS

In this section we perform simulations in our two delayed feedback frameworks. The algorithms described in the previous section will be denoted D-UCB and D-KLUCB in the censored setting, and UD-UCB and UD-KLUCB in the uncensored setting.

As a matter of fact, the bottleneck of such policies is to compute $\tilde{N}(t)$ which is theoretically a weighted sum over all past actions and, without any assumption on the weights $(\tau_s)_{s \geq 0}$, it requires to store all previous rewards and recompute $\tilde{N}(t)$ at each iteration.

Following the conclusions of [4], we assume all along this section that the delays follow a geometric distribution with parameter $\lambda := 1/\mu$. This assumption allows us to implement our algorithms in a computationally, memory-efficient manner. Indeed, for each $s \geq 0$, we now have $(1 - \tau_{s+1}) = \lambda(1 - \tau_s)$ and this remark provides a sequential updating scheme of the quantity $\tilde{N}_k(t)$ for $k \in [K]$. In the uncensored setting, we have:

$$\tilde{N}_k(t) = \sum_{s=1}^{t} (1 - \lambda^{t-s+1}) \mathbb{1}\{A_s = k\} = N_k(t) - O_k(t),$$

where $O_k(t)$ is updated after each round as follows

$$O_k(t+1) \leftarrow \lambda O_k(t) + \mathbb{1}\{A_t = k\}. \qquad (6)$$

In the censored setting, however, one must still keep track of some of the previous pulls in order to compute

$$\tilde{N}_k(t) = N_k(t-m)\tau_m + \sum_{s=t-m+1}^{t-1} \mathbb{1}\{A_s = k\}\tau_{t-s}.$$

In practice this can be done by maintaining a buffer of size m containing the last m pulls that are multiplied by the probability of observing a reward with the delay corresponding to their current position in the buffer. In addition to this buffer, we add old pulls in a separate count $N_k(t-m)$ for which the weight will stay τ_m.

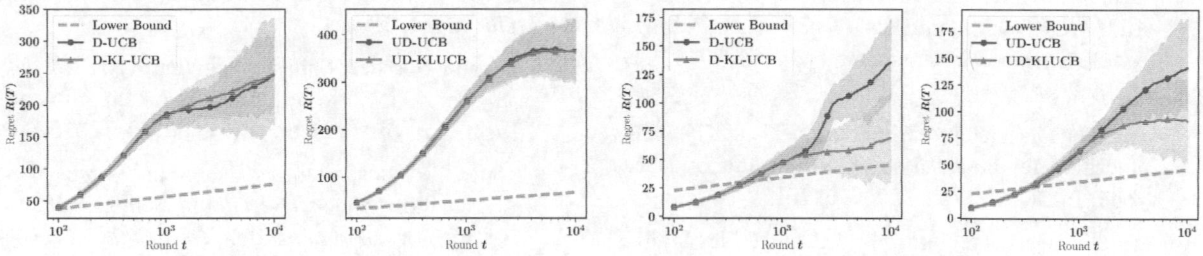

(a) $\theta_H = (0.5, 0.4, 0.3)$. (b) $\theta_L = (0.1, 0.05, 0.03)$.

Figure 1: Expected regret of D-UCB and D-KLUCB (censored setting), and UD-UCB and UD-KLUCB (uncensored setting) for two bandit problems: $\theta_H = (0.5, 0.4, 0.3)$, $\theta_L = (0.1, 0.05, 0.03)$. For all experiments, $T = 10000$, $\mu = 500$, $m = 1000$ (if censored) and the results are averaged over 100 runs.

Comparing DelayedUCB and DelayedKLUCB. We compare the regret of both delayed bandits policies in the censored and uncensored setting for $T = 10000$, $\mu = 500$ and $m = 1000$.

Simulations on Figure 1, for two problems, $\theta_H = (0.5, 0.4, 0.3)$ on the left, and $\theta_L = (0.1, 0.05, 0.03)$ on the right, display the classical pattern that while UCB-based algorithms perform satisfactorily for central values (close to 0.5) of the conversion rate, they are clearly sub-optimal with more realistic values for the conversion rate. The two right plots also confirm that, for the KLUCB-based algorithms, the loss with respect to the optimal regret growth rate due to the use of the Poisson divergence is – as expected from Theorem 11 – not significant for low values (here $\theta^* = 0.1$) of the conversion rates.

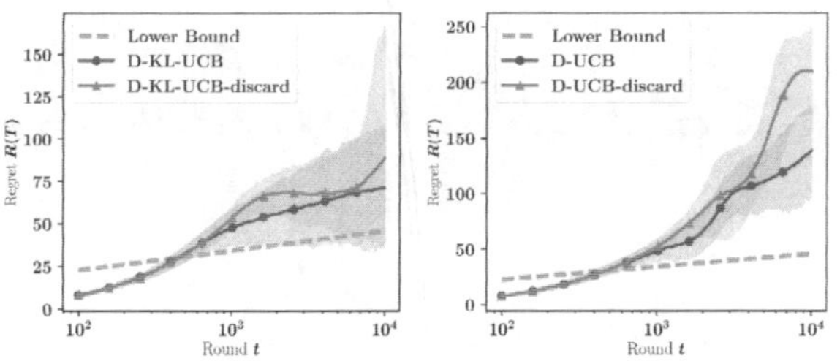

Figure 2: Expected regret of D-UCB and D-KLUCB in the censored setting vs the equivalent discarding policies when $\mu = 500$ and $m = 1000$. Results are averaged over 200 independent runs.

DelayedUCB and DelayedKLUCB vs. DISCARDING. In this section, we illustrate the good empirical initial performance of DelayedUCB and DelayedKLUCB, when compared to the heuristic DISCARDING approach presented in Section 6.

Figure 2 compares results for both DelayedUCB and DelayedKLUCB with $\theta = (0.1, 0.05, 0.03)$, $T = 10000$, $\mu = 500$ and $m = 1000$ in the censored setting. We observe that discarding policies incur a linear regret phase at the beginning of the learning and happen to catch up with the expected regret growth rate only after a large number of rounds. These figures reveal a non-negligible gap in performance between the naive DISCARDING approach and our delay-adapted quasi-optimal algorithms.

8 CONCLUSION

The stochastic delayed bandit setting introduced in this work addresses an important problem in many applications where the feedback associated to each action is delayed and censored, due to the ambiguity between conversions that will never happen and conversions that will occur at some later – perhaps unobservable– time. Under the hypothesis that the distribution of the delay is known, we provided a complete analysis of this model as well as simple and efficient algorithms. An interesting generalization of the present work would be to relax the model hypothesis and estimate the delay distribution on-the-go, possibly using context-dependent delay distributions.

References

[1] Peter Auer, Nicolo Cesa-Bianchi, and Paul Fischer. Finite-time analysis of the multiarmed bandit problem. *Machine learning*, 47(2-3):235–256, 2002.

[2] Olivier Cappé, Aurélien Garivier, Odalric-Ambrym Maillard, Rémi Munos, Gilles Stoltz, et al. Kullback–leibler upper confidence bounds for optimal sequential allocation. *The Annals of Statistics*, 41(3):1516–1541, 2013.

[3] Nicolo Cesa-Bianchi, Claudio Gentile, Yishay Mansour, and Alberto Minora. Delay and cooperation in nonstochastic bandits. In *29th Annual Conference on Learning Theory*, pages 605–622, 2016.

[4] Olivier Chapelle. Modeling delayed feedback in

display advertising. In *Proceedings of the 20th ACM SIGKDD international conference on Knowledge discovery and data mining*, pages 1097–1105. ACM, 2014.

[5] Aurélien Garivier and Olivier Cappé. The KL-UCB algorithm for bounded stochastic bandits and beyond. In *COLT*, pages 359–376, 2011.

[6] Aurélien Garivier, Pierre Menard, and Gilles Stoltz. Explore first, exploit next: The true shape of regret in bandit problems (*to appear*). *Mathematics of Operations Research*, 2017.

[7] Wendi Ji, Xiaoling Wang, and Dell Zhang. A probabilistic multi-touch attribution model for online advertising. In *Proceedings of the 25th ACM International on Conference on Information and Knowledge Management*, pages 1373–1382. ACM, 2016.

[8] Pooria Joulani, András György, and Csaba Szepesvári. Online learning under delayed feedback. *CoRR*, abs/1306.0686, 2013.

[9] Pooria Joulani, Andras Gyorgy, and Csaba Szepesvari. Online learning under delayed feedback. In *Proceedings of The 30th International Conference on Machine Learning*, pages 1453–1461, 2013.

[10] Kwang-Sung Jun, Kevin Jamieson, Robert Nowak, and Xiaojin Zhu. Top arm identification in multi-armed bandits with batch arm pulls. In *The 19th International Conference on Artificial Intelligence and Statistics (AISTATS)*, 2016.

[11] Sumeet Katariya, Branislav Kveton, Csaba Szepesvari, Claire Vernade, and Zheng Wen. Stochastic rank-1 bandits. *arXiv preprint arXiv:1608.03023*, 2016.

[12] Konstantinos V Katsikopoulos and Sascha E Engelbrecht. Markov decision processes with delays and asynchronous cost collection. *IEEE transactions on automatic control*, 48(4):568–574, 2003.

[13] Emilie Kaufmann, Olivier Cappé, and Aurélien Garivier. On the complexity of best arm identification in multi-armed bandit models. *The Journal of Machine Learning Research*, 2015.

[14] Paul Lagrée, Claire Vernade, and Olivier Cappé. Multiple-play bandits in the position-based model. In *Advances in Neural Information Processing Systems*, 2016.

[15] Tze Leung Lai and Herbert Robbins. Asymptotically efficient adaptive allocation rules. *Advances in applied mathematics*, 6(1):4–22, 1985.

[16] Travis Mandel, Yun-En Liu, Emma Brunskill, and Zoran Popović. The queue method: Handling delay, heuristics, prior data, and evaluation in bandits. In *Twenty-Ninth AAAI Conference on Artificial Intelligence*, 2015.

[17] Vianney Perchet, Philippe Rigollet, Sylvain Chassang, and Eric Snowberg. Batched bandit problems. *The Annals of Statistics*, 44(2):660–681, 2016.

[18] Rómer Rosales, Haibin Cheng, and Eren Manavoglu. Post-click conversion modeling and analysis for non-guaranteed delivery display advertising. In *Proceedings of the fifth ACM international conference on Web search and data mining*, pages 293–302. ACM, 2012.

[19] Thomas J Walsh, Ali Nouri, Lihong Li, and Michael L Littman. Learning and planning in environments with delayed feedback. *Autonomous Agents and Multi-Agent Systems*, 18(1):83–105, 2009.

A Concentration results

A.1 Poissonization of the KL indices

We require variants of Lemma 9 and Theorem 10 in [5] adapted to our setting.

Lemma 13. *For $\theta \in [0,1]$, $(\tau_i)_{1\leq i\leq L} \in [0,1]$, let $(X_{i,j})_{1\leq i\leq L, j\geq 1}$ be a collection of independent Bernoulli random variables such that $\mathbb{E}(X_{i,j}) = \tau_i\theta$ and $(\epsilon_{i,j}) \in \{0,1\}$ associated deterministic indicators. For $1 \leq i \leq L$, denote by $n_i = \sum_{j=1}^{\infty} \epsilon_{i,j}$ and whe shall assume that all n_i are finite an that at least one of them is non-zero. Let $X = \sum_{i=1}^{L}\sum_{j=1}^{\infty} \epsilon_{i,j}X_{i,j}$ and denote by $\phi(\lambda) = \log \mathbb{E}\left[\exp(\lambda X)\right]$ its log-Laplace transform and by $\phi^*(x) = \sup_\lambda x\lambda - \phi(\lambda)$ the associated convex conjugate (Fenchel–Legendre transform).*

Then, for all $\lambda \in \mathbb{R}$,

$$\phi(\lambda) \leq \left(\sum_{i=1}^{L} \tau_i n_i\right) \theta\left(e^\lambda - 1\right), \tag{7}$$

and, for all $x \geq 0$,

$$\phi^*(x) \geq \left(\sum_{i=1}^{L} \tau_i n_i\right) d_{\text{Pois}}\left(\frac{x}{\sum_{i=1}^{L} \tau_i n_i}, \theta\right), \tag{8}$$

where $d_{\text{Pois}}(p,q) = p\log p/q + q - p$ denotes the Poisson Kullback-Leibler divergence.

Proof By direct calculation,

$$\phi(\lambda) = \sum_{i=1}^{L} n_i \log\left(1 - \tau_i\theta + \tau_i\theta e^\lambda\right).$$

The function $\tau_i \to \log\left(1 - \tau_i\theta + \tau_i\theta e^\lambda\right)$ is a strictly concave function on $[0,1]$ and we upper bound it by its tangent in 0, that is,

$$\log\left(1 - \tau_i\theta + \tau_i\theta e^\lambda\right) \leq \tau_i\theta(e^\lambda - 1),$$

which yields (7) upon summing on i.

The r.h.s. of (7) is easily recognized as the log-Laplace transform of the Poisson distribution with expectation $\left(\sum_{i=1}^{L} \tau_i n_i\right)\theta$. To obtain (8), we use the observations that $x\lambda - a\left(e^\lambda - 1\right)$ is maximized for $\lambda = \log(x/a)$ where it is equal to $d_{\text{Pois}}(x,a)$ as well as the fact that $d_{\text{Pois}}(\tau x, \tau a) = \tau d_{\text{Pois}}(x,a)$. ■

Lemma 13 bounds the log-Laplace transform of the Bernoulli distribution with that of the Poisson distribution with the same mean and uses the stability of the Poisson distribution. Using $d_{\text{Pois}}(p,q)$ instead of $d(p,q)$ –where $d(p,q) = p\log p/q + (1-p)\log[1-p)/(1-q)$ denotes the Bernoulli Kullback-Leibler divergence– will of course induce a performance gap, which is however not significant for low values of the probabilities as shown by the Lemma 8, which we recall below.

Lemma 8. *For $0 < p < q < 1$,*

$$(1-q)d(p,q) \leq d_{\text{Pois}}(p,q) \leq d(p,q).$$

Proof For the upper bound,

$$d(p,q) - d_{\text{Pois}}(p,q) = (1-p)\log\frac{1-p}{1-q} - (q-p) = -(1-p)\log(1+\frac{p-q}{1-p}) + (p-q) \geq 0,$$

using $-\log(1+x) \geq -x$.

For the lower bound,

$$d_{\text{Pois}}(p,q) - (1-q)d(p,q) = qp\log\frac{p}{q} + q - p - (1-q)(1-p)\log\left(\frac{1-p}{1-q}\right). \tag{9}$$

One has $d_{\text{Pois}}(q,q) = d(q,q) = 0$ and the derivative of (9) wrt. p is equal to

$$q \log \frac{p}{q} + (1-q) \log \left(\frac{1-p}{1-q} \right) = -d(q,p) \leq 0.$$

Hence, $d_{\text{Pois}}(p,q) - (1-q)d(p,q)$ is positive when $p \leq q$. ■

We can now prove the concentration result stated in Lemma 7 that we recall below for readability purpose.

Lemma 7. *Assume that the sequence of pulls is fixed beforehand and let k be an arm in $\{1, ..., K\}$. Then for any $\delta > 0$ and for all $t > 0$,*

$$\mathbb{P}\left(\left\{ \hat{\theta}_k(t) < \theta_k \right\} \cap \left\{ \tilde{N}_k(t) d_{\text{Pois}}(\hat{\theta}_k(t), \theta_k) > \delta \right\} \right) < e^{-\delta}.$$

where $d_{\text{Pois}}(p,q) = p \log p/q + q - p$ denotes the Poisson Kullback-Leibler divergence.

Proof To bound $\mathbb{P}(\hat{\theta}_k(t) < x) = \mathbb{P}(S_k(t) < \tilde{N}_k(t)x)$, for $0 < x < \theta_k$, apply Chernoff's method using the result of Lemma 13 to obtain

$$\mathbb{P}(\hat{\theta}_k(t) < x) \leq e^{-\tilde{N}_k(t) d_{\text{Pois}}(x, \theta_k)}.$$

Using that $x \mapsto d_{\text{Pois}}(x, \theta_k)$ is decreasing on $[0, \theta_k]$, we can apply it on both side of the inequality on the left-hand side to obtain

$$\mathbb{P}\left(\left\{ \hat{\theta}_k(t) < \theta_k \right\} \cap \left\{ \tilde{N}_k(t) d_{\text{Pois}}(\hat{\theta}_k(t), \theta_k) > \tilde{N}_k(t) d_{\text{Pois}}(x, \theta_k) \right\} \right) \leq e^{-\tilde{N}_k(t) d_{\text{Pois}}(x, \theta_k)}.$$

Denoting $\delta = \tilde{N}_k(t) d_{\text{Pois}}(x, \theta_k)$ yields the desired result. ■

Theorem 14. *Consider $(\tau_i)_{1 \leq i \leq L} \in [0,1]$, $\theta \in (0,1)$, and independent sequences $(X_i(s))_{s \geq 1}$ of independent Bernoulli random variables such that $\mathbb{E} X_i(s) = \tau_i \theta$. Let $\mathcal{F}_t$ denote an increasing sequence of sigma-fields, such that for each t and all i, $\sigma(X_i(1), \ldots, X_i(t)) \subset \mathcal{F}_t$. Also consider a predictable sequence of indicator variables $\epsilon_i(s) \in \{0,1\}$, that is, such that $\sigma(\epsilon_1(t+1), \ldots, \epsilon_L(t+1)) \subset \mathcal{F}_t$.*

Define

$$S_i(t) = \sum_{s=1}^{t} \epsilon_i(s) X_i(s), \qquad N_i(t) = \sum_{s=1}^{t} \epsilon_i(s);$$

and the pooled quantities

$$S(t) = \sum_{i=1}^{L} S_i(t), \qquad N(t) = \sum_{i=1}^{L} N_i(t), \qquad \tilde{N}(t) = \sum_{i=1}^{L} \tau_i N_i(t), \qquad \hat{\theta}(t) = \frac{S(t)}{\tilde{N}(t)}.$$

The KLUCB index, defined as,

$$U^{\text{KL}}(n) = \max \left\{ q \in \left[\hat{\theta}(n), \theta_M \right] \,:\, \tilde{N}(n) d_{\text{Pois}}(\hat{\theta}(n), q) \leq \delta \right\}.$$

satisfies

$$\mathbb{P}\left(U(n) \leq \theta \right) \leq e \lceil \delta \log(n) \rceil e^{-\delta}.$$

Proof The proof is analogous to that of Theorem 10 of [5] and we only detail the step that differs, namely, the identification of the supermartingale W_t^{λ}.

Define, $W_0^{\lambda} = 1$ and, for $t \geq 1$,

$$W_t^{\lambda} = \exp\left(\lambda S(t) - \tilde{N}(t) \theta \left(e^{\lambda} - 1 \right) \right).$$

$$\mathbb{E}\left[\exp(\lambda(S(t+1)-S(t)))\,|\mathcal{F}_t\right] = \mathbb{E}\left[\exp\left(\lambda\sum_{i=1}^{L}\epsilon_i(t+1)X_i(t+1)\right)\Bigg|\,\mathcal{F}_t\right]$$
$$\leq \exp\left(\left(\sum_{i=1}^{L}\tau_i\epsilon_i(t+1)\right)\theta\left(e^{\lambda}-1\right)\right)$$
$$= \exp\left(\left(\tilde{N}(t+1)-\tilde{N}(t)\right)\theta\left(\theta e^{\lambda}-1\right)\right),$$

where we have used (7) and the definition of $\tilde{N}(t)$. Multiplying both sides of the inequality by $\exp\left(\lambda S(t)-\tilde{N}(t+1)\theta\left(e^{\lambda}-1\right)\right)$ show that $\mathbb{E}W_{t+1}^{\lambda} \leq \mathbb{E}W_t^{\lambda}$ and hence that W_t^{λ} is a supermartingale.

The rest of the proof is as in [5] replacing $N(t)$ by $\tilde{N}(t)$ and $\phi_\mu(\lambda)$ by $\theta\left(e^{\lambda}-1\right)$. ■

B Details on the Lower Bound Results

We provide here the details of the proof of Theorems 4 and 3. The key result that we use is a lower bound on the log-likelihood ratio under two alternative bandit models θ and θ' that do not have the same best arm. Namely, according to Lemma 1 of [13], we have

$$\liminf_{T\to\infty}\frac{\mathbb{E}[\ell_T]}{\log(T)} \geq 1.$$

Now, considering specific changes of measures θ' that only modify the distribution of one single suboptimal arm, we are going to obtain lower bounds on each expected number of pulls $\mathbb{E}[N_k(T)]$ for $k \neq 1$ as in Appendix B of [13].

Uncensored Setting: As argued in Section 4, in the uncensored setting the likelihood of the observations is

$$\mathbb{E}_\theta\left[\ell_T\right] = \sum_{s=1}^{T} d(\theta_{A_s}\tau_{T-s}, \theta'_{A_s}\tau_{T-s}).$$

Now, fix arm $k \neq 1$ and for $\epsilon > 0$, consider $\theta' = (\theta_1, \ldots, \theta_{k-1}, \theta_1+\epsilon, \ldots, \theta_K)$. For this change of measure, the expected log-likelihood only contains the terms involving arm k:

$$\mathbb{E}_\theta\left[\ell_T\right] = \sum_{s=1}^{T}\mathbb{1}\{A_s = k\}d(\theta_k\tau_{T-s}, (\theta_1+\epsilon)\tau_{T-s}).$$

Now, in order to obtain an expression that involves $\mathbb{E}[N_k(T)]$, we need to bound from above this sum using Lemma 5 of the Appendix B of [11], which we recall here for completeness.

Lemma 15. *Let p, q be any fixed real numbers in $(0,1)$. The function $f : \alpha \mapsto d(\alpha p, \alpha q)$ is convex and increasing on $(0,1)$. As a consequence, for any $\alpha < 1$, $d(\alpha p, \alpha q) < d(p,q)$.*

Thus, for each $s \geq 1$ we have $\tau_{T-s} \leq 1$ and according to the above result,

$$d(\theta_k, (\theta_1+\epsilon)) \geq d(\theta_k\tau_{T-s}, (\theta_1+\epsilon)\tau_{T-s})$$

and

$$\mathbb{E}[N_k(T)]d(\theta_k, \theta_1+\epsilon) \geq \sum_{s=1}^{T}\mathbb{1}\{A_s = k\}d(\theta_k\tau_{T-s}, (\theta_1+\epsilon)\tau_{T-s}).$$

We obtain

$$\liminf_{T\to\infty}\frac{\mathbb{E}[N_k(T)]d(\theta_k, \theta_1+\epsilon)}{\log(T)} \geq \liminf_{T\to\infty}\frac{\mathbb{E}[\ell_T]}{\log(T)} \geq 1.$$

Letting $\epsilon \to 0$ yields

$$\liminf_{T\to\infty}\frac{\mathbb{E}[N_k(T)]}{\log(T)} \geq \frac{1}{d(\theta_k, \theta_1)}.$$

In order to bound the expected regret L_T, we use the inequality (2) from Lemma 1:

$$L_T \geq \sum_{k=2}^{K} (\theta_1 - \theta_k) \left(\mathbb{E}[N_k(t)] - \mu \right),$$

where $\mu = \mathbb{E}[D_s]$. We now lower bound each $\mathbb{E}[N_k(t)]$ and under the assumption that $\mathbb{E}[D_s] < \infty$ and we use that $\liminf_{T\to\infty} \mu/\log(T) = 0$ to obtain

$$\liminf_{T\to\infty} \frac{L_T}{\log(T)} \geq \liminf_{T\to\infty} \frac{\sum_{k=2}^{K} (\theta_1 - \theta_k) \left(\mathbb{E}[N_k(t)] - \mu \right)}{\log(T)} \geq \sum_{k=2}^{K} \frac{(\theta_1 - \theta_k)}{d(\theta_k, \theta_1)}.$$

Censored Setting: The proof in the Censored Setting follows the same step as the proof above expect for the fact that we do not require Lemma 5 of [11] in order to bound the log-likelihood ratio. We directly have

$$\mathbb{E}_\theta \left[\ell_T \right] = \sum_{s=1}^{T-m} d(\theta_{A_s} \tau_m, \theta'_{A_s} \tau_m) + \sum_{s=T-m}^{T} d(\theta_{A_s} \tau_{T-s}, \theta'_{A_s} \tau_{T-s}).$$

Proceeding as above and considering the adequate change of measure involving only one suboptimal arm k and taking $\epsilon \to 0$, we obtain

$$\liminf_{T\to\infty} \frac{\mathbb{E}[N_k(T)] d(\tau_m \theta_k, \tau_m \theta_1) + \sum_{s=T-m}^{T} d(\theta_k \tau_{T-s}, \theta_1 \tau_{T-s})}{\log(T)} = \liminf_{T\to\infty} \frac{\mathbb{E}[N_k(T)] d(\tau_m \theta_k, \tau_m \theta_1)}{\log(T)} \geq 1,$$

where we used the fact that the second term of the sum in the left-hand side is finite. The end of the proof is similar to the uncensored setting case treated above where we can simply bound the regret according to Eq. (3) as

$$L_T \geq \sum_{k=2}^{k} \tau_m (\theta_1 - \theta_k) \mathbb{E}[N_k(T-m)] + \sum_{s=T-m+1}^{T} \tau_{T-s} (\theta_1 - \theta_{A_s})$$

in order to obtain the asymptotic lower bound.

C Analysis of DelayedUCB and DelayedKLUCB

In order to control the empirical averages of the rewards of each arm for different values of $N_k(t)$, we introduce the notation $\hat{\theta}_{k,s} := \sum_{u=1}^{s} X_{k,u}/s$ for the mean over the first s pulls of k.

C.1 DelayedUCB

In this section, we provide the complete proof of Theorem 9.

We decompose the regret after bounding by 1 the first m losses of the policy :

$$L_{\text{UCB}}(T) \leq m + \sum_{k>1} \tau_m \Delta_k \mathbb{E} \left[\sum_{t>m}^{T} \mathbb{1}\{A_t = k\} \right].$$

Hence we only need to bound the number of suboptimal pulls, as in the seminal proof by [1]. For any suboptimal $k > 1$, we have:

$$\begin{aligned} \mathbb{E}[N_k(T)] \leq 1 + &\sum_{t=K+1}^{T} \mathbb{P}\left(U_1^{\text{UCB}}(t) < \theta_1 \right) \\ &+ \sum_{t=K+1}^{T} \mathbb{P}\left(A_{t+1} = k, U_k^{\text{UCB}}(t) \geq \theta_1 \right). \end{aligned}$$

While the first term is simply handled by Proposition 6 and is $O(1/\epsilon^3) = o(\log(T)$, the second one must be controlled as in the original proof of UCB1 by [1] using the fact that for all $t > m$,

$$\frac{N_k(t)}{\tilde{N}_k(t)} \leq \frac{N_k(t-m)+m}{\tilde{N}_k(t)} \leq \frac{1}{\tau_m} + \frac{m}{\tau_m N_k(t-m)}$$

that allows us to upper-bound the optimistic indices as

$$\hat{\theta}_k(t) + \left(\frac{1}{\tau_m} + \frac{m}{\tau_m N_k(t-m)}\right)\sqrt{\frac{\beta_\epsilon(t)}{2N_k(t)}} \geq U_k^{\mathrm{UCB}}(t).$$

Then, we use this upper bound on the indices in order to bound the relevant sum of probabilities.

$$\begin{aligned}
&\sum_{t=m+1}^{T} \mathbb{P}\left(A_{t+1} = k, U_k^{\mathrm{UCB}}(t) \geq \theta_1\right) \\
&\leq \mathbb{E}\left[\sum_{s\geq 1} \mathbb{1}\left\{\hat{\theta}_{i,s} + \left(\frac{1}{\tau_m} + \frac{m}{\tau_m s}\right)\sqrt{\frac{\beta_\epsilon(t)}{2s}} \geq \theta_i + \Delta_i\right\}\right].
\end{aligned}$$

In order to upper-bound this expectation, we first introduce the quantity $\underline{s}_i > 0$ defined by

$$\left(\frac{1}{\tau_m} + \frac{m}{\tau_m \underline{s}_i}\right)\sqrt{\frac{\beta_\epsilon(t)}{2\underline{s}_i}} = \Delta_i,$$

that we rewrite, with the introduction of $\gamma_i > 0$, as

$$\underline{s}_i = \frac{\beta_\epsilon(t)}{2\tau_m^2 \Delta_i^2}(1+\gamma_i)^2 \quad \text{so that we get} \quad \left(1 + \frac{m}{\underline{s}_i}\right)\frac{1}{1+\gamma_i} = 1.$$

Simple computations finally leads to, if $\gamma_i \leq 1$,

$$\frac{2m\tau_m^2\Delta_i^2}{\beta_\epsilon(t)} = \gamma_i(1+\gamma_i)^2 \leq 4\gamma_i.$$

As a consequence, if T is big enough (so that the left hand side is smaller than 4), we get that

$$\underline{s}_i \leq \frac{(1+\varepsilon)\log(T)}{2\tau_m^2\Delta_i^2}(1+\gamma_i)^2 \leq \frac{(1+\varepsilon)\log(T)}{2\tau_m^2\Delta_i^2}(1+3\gamma_i) \leq \frac{(1+\varepsilon)\log(T)}{2\tau_m^2\Delta_i^2} + m.$$

We now focus on the sum to upper-bound:

$$\begin{aligned}
\mathbb{E}\left[\sum_{s\geq 1} \mathbb{1}\left\{\hat{\theta}_{i,s} + \left(\frac{1}{\tau_m} + \frac{m}{\tau_m s}\right)\sqrt{\frac{\beta_\epsilon(t)}{2s}} \geq \theta_i + \Delta_i\right\}\right] &\leq \lceil \underline{s}_i \rceil + 1 + \sum_{s > \lceil \underline{s}_i \rceil} e^{-2s\left(\Delta_i - \left(\frac{1}{\tau_m} + \frac{m}{\tau_m s}\right)\sqrt{\frac{\beta_\epsilon(t)}{2s}}\right)^2} \\
&\leq \underline{s}_i + 2 + \sum_{s > \lceil \underline{s}_i \rceil} e^{-2\left(\sqrt{s}\Delta_i - \left(1 + \frac{m}{\underline{s}_i}\right)\sqrt{\frac{\beta_\epsilon(t)}{2\tau_m^2}}\right)^2},
\end{aligned}$$

where we used the Chernoff's inequality for bounded random variables.

Standard computations (comparisons between sums and integrals) give the following

$$\begin{aligned}\sum_{s>\lceil \underline{s}_i \rceil} e^{-2\left(\sqrt{s}\Delta_i - \left(1+\frac{m}{\underline{s}_i}\right)\sqrt{\frac{\beta_\epsilon(t)}{2\tau_m^2}}\right)^2} &\leq \int_{\underline{s}_i}^{\infty} e^{-2\left(\sqrt{s}\Delta_i - \left(1+\frac{m}{\underline{s}_i}\right)\sqrt{\frac{\beta_\epsilon(t)}{2\tau_m^2}}\right)^2} ds \\ &\leq \frac{1}{2\Delta_i^2}\left(1+\frac{\sqrt{2\pi}}{4}\left(1+\frac{m}{\underline{s}_i}\right)\sqrt{\frac{\beta_\epsilon(t)}{2\tau_m^2}}\right) \\ &\leq \frac{1}{2\Delta_i^2}\left(1+\frac{\sqrt{2\pi}}{4}\sqrt{\underline{s}_i}\Delta_i\right) \\ &\leq \frac{1}{2\Delta_i^2}\left(1+\frac{\sqrt{\pi}}{4}\sqrt{\frac{(1+\epsilon)\log(T)}{\tau_m^2}}+\frac{\sqrt{\pi}}{4}\sqrt{m}\right).\end{aligned}$$

As a consequence, we have just proved that

$$\sum_{t=m+1}^{T} \mathbb{P}\left(A_{t+1}=k, U_k^{\mathrm{UCB}}(t) \geq \theta_1\right) \leq \frac{(1+\epsilon)\log(T)}{2\tau_m^2\Delta_i^2} + o(\log(T)).$$

More precisely, combining all our claims yields that

$$L_{\mathrm{UCB}}(T) \leq \frac{(1+\epsilon)\log(T)}{2\tau_m^2\Delta_i} + O\left(\frac{1}{\Delta_i}\sqrt{\frac{(1+\epsilon)\log(T)}{2\tau_m^2}}\right) + O\left(\frac{1}{\Delta_i}\frac{1}{\epsilon^3}\right) + O\left(\frac{\sqrt{m}}{\Delta_i}+m\right),$$

and the result follows.

C.2 DelayedKLUCB

We follow the steps of [5] and decompose the regret as

$$\begin{aligned}\mathbb{E}[N_k(T)] &\leq 1+m-K\sum_{t=m+1}^{T} \mathbb{P}\left(U_1^{\mathrm{KL}}(t)<\theta_1\right)+\sum_{t=m+1}^{T} \mathbb{P}\left(A_{t+1}=k, U_k^{\mathrm{KL}}(t)\geq\theta_1\right) \\ &\leq 1+m-K+\sum_{t=m+1}^{T} \mathbb{P}\left(U_1^{\mathrm{KL}}(t)<\theta_1\right)+\sum_{t=m+1}^{T} \mathbb{P}\left(A_{t+1}=k, U_k^{\mathrm{KL}}(t)\geq\theta_1\right).\end{aligned}$$

The first term of the above sum is handled by Theorem 14 that shows that it is $o(\log(T))$. We must now bound the second sum corresponding to the cases when suboptimal indices reach the optimal mean θ_1. To proceed, we simply notice that for all t, $\tilde{N}_k(t) \geq \tau_m N_k(t-m)$. We define an alternative optimistic index that upper bounds $U_k^{\mathrm{KL}}(t)$ for $t > m$:

$$U_k^{\mathrm{KL}}(t) \leq \underset{q\in[\hat{\theta}_k,1]}{\arg\max}\{q|\tau_m N_k(t-m) d_{\mathrm{Pois}}(\hat{\theta}_k(t),q) \leq \beta_\epsilon(t)\} := U_k^{\mathrm{KL}+}(t).$$

Now we can finish the proof following the steps of the proof of Theorem 2 in [5]. First, we denote

$$K_k(T) = \frac{(1+\eta)\beta_\epsilon(t)}{d(\tau_m\theta_k, \tau_m\theta_1)}$$

and we decompose the second sum after bounding the first $K_k(T)$ terms by 1 and bounding the remaining terms in a similar way as in Lemma 11 of [9]:

$$\begin{aligned}\sum_{t=m+1}^{T} \mathbb{P}\left(A_{t+1}=k, U_k^{\mathrm{KL}+}(t) \geq \theta_1\right) &\leq K_k(T) + \sum_{t \geq K_k(T)+m+1} \mathbb{P}\left(A_{t+1}=k, U_k^{\mathrm{KL}+}(t) \geq \theta_1\right) \\ &\leq K_k(T) + \mathbb{E}\left[\sum_{t \geq K_k(T)+m+1} \sum_{s=1}^{t} \mathbb{1}\left\{A_{t+1}=k, N_k(t-m)=s, \tau_m s d_{\mathrm{Pois}}(\hat{\theta}_{k,s}, \theta_1) \leq \beta_\epsilon(t)\right\}\right] \\ &\leq K_k(T) + \mathbb{E}\left[\sum_{s=K_k(T)}^{T} \mathbb{1}\left\{\tau_m s d_{\mathrm{Pois}}(\hat{\theta}_{k,s}, \theta_1) \leq \beta_\epsilon(t)\right\} \sum_{t=s}^{T} \mathbb{1}\left\{A_{t+1}=k, N_k(t-m)=s\right\}\right] \\ &\leq K_k(T) + m \sum_{s \geq K_k(T)} \mathbb{P}\left(\tau_m s d_{\mathrm{Pois}}(\hat{\theta}_{k,s}, \theta_1) \leq \beta_\epsilon(t)\right) \\ &\leq K_k(T) + \frac{m C_2(\eta)}{T^{f(\eta)}},\end{aligned}$$

where the last inequality comes from the fact that for all $s \in \{1, \ldots, T\}$, $\sum_{t=1}^{T} \mathbb{1}\{A_{t+1}=k, N_k(t-m)=s\} \leq m$ and from the proof of Fact 2 for exponential family bandits in [2] that proves the existence of the constants $C_2(\eta)$ and $f(\eta)$ that achieve the bound.

We can now upper bound the regret thanks to the decomposition provided by equation 3:

$$L_{\mathrm{KLUCB}}(T) \leq m + \sum_{k>1} \tau_m \Delta_k \mathbb{E}\left[N_k(T)\right] \leq (1+\eta)\beta_\epsilon(t) \sum_{k=2}^{K} \frac{\tau_m \Delta_k}{d_{\mathrm{Pois}}(\tau_m\theta_k, \tau_m\theta_1)} + o(\log(T)).$$

To obtain the final result, we use Lemma 8 that shows that for $\theta_k < \theta_1$, $d_{\mathrm{Pois}}(\tau_m\theta_k, \tau_m\theta_1) > (1 - \tau_m\theta_1) d(\tau_m\theta_k, \tau_m\theta_1)$. Thus,

$$L_{\mathrm{KLUCB}}(T) \leq m + (1+\eta)\frac{\beta_\epsilon(t)}{1-\tau_m\theta_1} \sum_{k=2}^{K} \frac{\tau_m \Delta_k}{d(\tau_m\theta_k, \tau_m\theta_1)} + o(\log(T)).$$

D Additionnal experiments on delay agnostic policies

As a last additional contribution to this work, we suggest a distribution-agnostic heuristic that estimates the CDF parameters $(\tau_d)_{d\geq 0}$ in an online fashion. Indeed, as the delay distribution is assumed to be shared between actions, each observed reward provides an information on the delays that can be exploited to estimate the CDF without having to deal with the exploration-exploitation dilemma.

Uncensored setting. In the Uncensored setting and under the geometric assumption on the distribution of the delays, the entire CDF can be retrieved using an estimate of the unique parameter $\lambda = 1/\mu$. To this aim, we build an estimate the expected delay at round t, $\hat{\mu}(t)$, using a stochastic approximation process with decreasing weights $\alpha_t = 1/t^\gamma$ for $1 \geq \gamma \geq 0.5$. When an observation D_t arrives we update

$$\hat{\mu}(t) \leftarrow (1-\alpha_t)\hat{\mu}(t) + \alpha_t D_t.$$

Then we use this estimator as a plug-in quantity to compute $O_k(t)$ defined in (6) for all k.

Censored setting. In the Censored setting however, no observation comes after the threshold m and this does not allow us to directly estimate the expected delay μ as the longest observations are censored. To circumvent this problem, we choose to estimate biased parameters for $\tau_1, \ldots, \tau_m$. Concretely, we initialize counts for the observed delay values $\delta_0 = (0, \ldots, 0) \in \mathbb{N}^{m+1}$ (delay can be null). Then, after each observation D_t, we increment all the counts δ_s for $s \geq D_t$. Then, the biased empirical CDF is obtained by normalizing those counts by the total number of observations received up to time t, $n_d(t)$. We emphasize that the obtained estimators are biased: For each

$s \in \{0, \ldots, m\}$, $\mathbb{E}[\delta_s(t)/n_d(t)] = \tau_s/\tau_m$ as all observed delays are smaller or equal to m. Thus, plugging those estimates in $\tilde{N}_k(t)$ actually allows to have an estimate of $\tilde{N}_k(t)/\tau_m$ instead of $\tilde{N}_k(t)$ and consequently an estimate of $\tau_m\theta_k$ instead of θ_k.

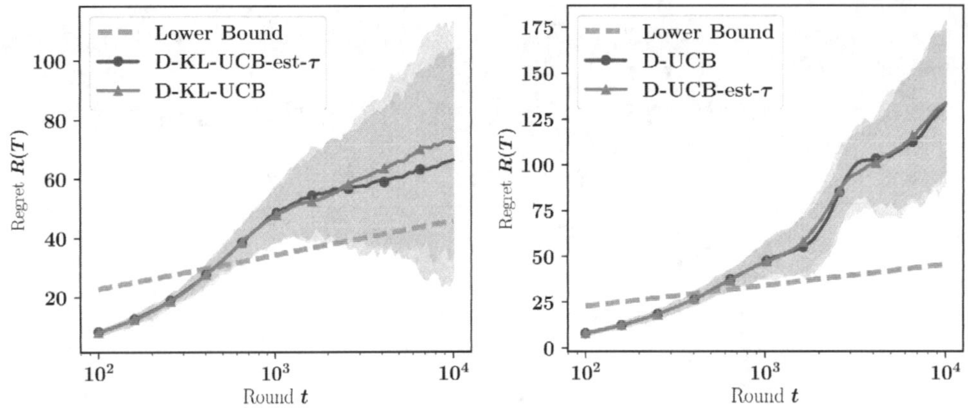

Figure 3: Expected regret of DelayedKLUCB with and without online estimation of the CDF in both the censored and uncensored setting. Results are averaged over 100 independent runs.

Figure 3 compares both our policies to its equivalent, delay-agnostic heuristic using the same confidence intervals with plug-in estimates of the $(\tau_d)_{d \geq 0}$. It is clear from these experiments that using delay parameters estimated on-the-go does not hurt the cumulated regret overall.

A Practical Method for Solving Contextual Bandit Problems Using Decision Trees

Ryan McNellis
IEOR Department
Columbia University

Adam N. Elmachtoub
IEOR Department
Columbia University

Sechan Oh
Moloco
Palo Alto, CA 94301

Marek Petrik
Dept. of Computer Science
University of New Hampshire

Abstract

Many efficient algorithms with strong theoretical guarantees have been proposed for the contextual multi-armed bandit problem. However, applying these algorithms in practice can be difficult because they require domain expertise to build appropriate features and to tune their parameters. We propose a new method for the contextual bandit problem that is simple, practical, and can be applied with little or no domain expertise. Our algorithm relies on decision trees to model the context-reward relationship. Decision trees are non-parametric, interpretable, and work well without hand-crafted features. To guide the exploration-exploitation trade-off, we use a bootstrapping approach which abstracts Thompson sampling to non-Bayesian settings. We also discuss several computational heuristics and demonstrate the performance of our method on several datasets.

1 INTRODUCTION

Personalized recommendation systems play a fundamental role in an ever-increasing array of settings. For example, many mobile and web services earn revenue primarily from targeted advertising (Yuan and Tsao, 2003; Dhar and Varshney, 2011). The effectiveness of this strategy is predicated upon intelligently assigning the right ads to users based on contextual information. Other examples include assigning treatments to medical patients (Kim et al., 2011) and recommending web-based content such as news articles to subscribers (Li et al., 2010).

In this paper, we tackle the problem where little or no prior data is available, and an algorithm is required to "learn" a good recommendation system in real time as users arrive and data is collected. This problem, known as the *contextual bandit problem* (or contextual multi-armed bandit problem), relies on an algorithm to navigate the *exploration-exploitation* trade-off when choosing recommendations. Specifically, it must simultaneously exploit knowledge from data accrued thus far to make high-impact recommendations, while also exploring recommendations which have a high degree of uncertainty in order to make better decisions in the future.

The contextual bandit problem we consider can be formalized as follows (Langford and Zhang, 2008). At each time point, a user arrives and we receive a vector of information, henceforth referred to as the *context*. We must then choose one of K distinct *actions* for this user. Finally, a random outcome or *reward* is observed, which is dependent on the user and action chosen by the algorithm. Note that the probability distribution governing rewards for each action is unknown and depends on the observed context. The objective is to maximize the total rewards accrued over time. In this paper, we focus on settings in which rewards are binary, observing a *success* or a *failure* in each time period. However, our algorithm does not rely on this assumption and may also be used in settings with continuous reward distributions.

A significant number of algorithms have been proposed for the contextual bandit problem, often with strong theoretical guarantees (Auer, 2002; Filippi et al., 2010; Chu et al., 2011; Agarwal et al., 2014). However, we believe that many of these algorithms cannot be straightforwardly and effectively applied in practice for personalized recommendation systems, as they tend to exhibit at least one of the following drawbacks.

1. *Parametric modeling assumptions*. The vast majority of bandit algorithms assume a parametric relationship between contexts and rewards (Li et al., 2010; Filippi et al., 2010; Abbasi-Yadkori et al., 2011; Agrawal and Goyal, 2013). To use such algorithms in practice, one must first do some fea-

ture engineering and transform the data to satisfy the parametric modeling framework. However, in settings where very little prior data is available, it is often unclear how to do so in the right way.

2. *Unspecified constants in the algorithm.* Many bandit algorithms contain unspecified parameters which are meant to be tuned to control the level of exploration (Auer, 2002; Li et al., 2010; Filippi et al., 2010; Allesiardo et al., 2014). Choosing the wrong parameter values can negatively impact performance (Russo and Van Roy, 2014), yet choosing the right values is difficult since little prior data is available.

3. *Ill-suited learners for classification problems.* It is commonly assumed in the bandit literature that the relationship between contexts and rewards is governed by a linear model (Li et al., 2010; Abbasi-Yadkori et al., 2011; Agrawal and Goyal, 2013). Although such models work well in regression problems, they often face a number of issues when estimating probabilities from binary response data (Long, 1997).

In the hopes of addressing all of these issues, we propose a new algorithm for the contextual bandit problem which we believe can be more effectively applied in practice. Our approach uses decision tree learners to model the context-reward distribution for each action. Decision trees have a number of nice properties which make them effective, requiring no data modification or user input before being fit (Friedman et al., 2001). To navigate the exploration-exploitation tradeoff, we use a parameter-free bootstrapping technique that emulates the core principle behind Thompson sampling. We also provide a computational heuristic to improve the speed of our algorithm. Our simple method works surprisingly well on a wide array of simulated and real-world datasets compared to well-established algorithms for the contextual bandit problem.

2 LITERATURE REVIEW

Most contextual bandit algorithms in the existing literature can be categorized along two dimensions: (i) the base learner and (ii) the exploration algorithm. Our method uses decision tree learners in conjunction with bootstrapping to handle the exploration-exploitation trade-off. To the best of our knowledge, the only bandit algorithm which applies such learners is BanditForest (Féraud et al., 2016), using random forests as the base learner with decision trees as a special case. One limitation of the algorithm is that it depends on four problem-specific parameters requiring domain expertise to set: two parameters directly influence the level of exploration, one controls the depth of the trees, and one determines the number of trees in the forest. By contrast, our algorithm requires no tunable parameters in its exploration and chooses the depth internally when building the tree. Further, BanditForest must sample actions uniformly-at-random until all trees are completely learned with respect to a particular context. As our numerical experiments show, this leads to excessive selection of low-reward actions, causing the algorithm's empirical performance to suffer. NeuralBandit (Allesiardo et al., 2014) is an algorithm which uses neural networks as the base learner. Using a probability specified by the user, it randomly decides whether to explore or exploit in each step. However, choosing the right probability is rather difficult in the absence of data.

Rather than using non-parametric learners such as decision trees and neural nets, the vast majority of bandit algorithms assume a parametric relationship between contexts and rewards. Commonly, such learners assume a monotonic relationship in the form of a linear model (Li et al., 2010; Abbasi-Yadkori et al., 2011; Agrawal and Goyal, 2013) or a Generalized Linear Model (Filippi et al., 2010; Li et al., 2011). However, as with all methods that assume a parametric structure in the context-reward distribution, manual transformation of the data is often required in order to satisfy the modeling framework. In settings where little prior data is available, it is often quite difficult to "guess" what the right transformation might be. Further, using linear models in particular can be problematic when faced with binary response data, as such methods can yield poor probability estimates in this setting (Long, 1997).

Our method uses bootstrapping in a way which "approximates" the behavior of Thompson sampling, an exploration algorithm which has recently been applied in the contextual bandit literature (Agrawal and Goyal, 2013; Russo and Van Roy, 2014). Detailed in Section 4.2, Thompson sampling is a Bayesian framework requiring a parametric response model, and thus cannot be straightforwardly applied when using decision tree learners. The connection between bootstrapping and Thompson sampling has been previously explored in Eckles and Kaptein (2014), Osband and Van Roy (2015), and Tang et al. (2015), although these papers either focus on the context-free case or only consider using parametric learners with their bootstrapping framework. Baransi et al. (2014) propose a sub-sampling procedure which is related to Thompson sampling, although the authors restrict their attention to the context-free case.

Another popular exploration algorithm in the contextual

bandit literature is Upper Confidence Bounding (UCB) (Auer, 2002; Li et al., 2010; Filippi et al., 2010). These methods compute confidence intervals around expected reward estimates and choose the action with the highest upper confidence bound. UCB-type algorithms often rely on a tunable parameter controlling the width of the confidence interval. Choosing the right parameter value can have a huge impact on performance, but with little problem-specific data available this can be quite challenging (Russo and Van Roy, 2014). Another general exploration algorithm which heavily relies on user input is Epoch-Greedy (Langford and Zhang, 2008), which depends on an unspecified (non-increasing) function to modulate between exploration and exploitation.

Finally, a separate class of contextual bandit algorithms are those which select the best policy from an exogenous finite set, such as Dudik et al. (2011) and Agarwal et al. (2014). The performance of such algorithms depends on the existence of a policy in the set which performs well empirically. In the absence of prior data, the size of the required set may be prohibitively large, resulting in poor empirical and computational performance. Furthermore, in a similar manner as UCB, these algorithms require a tunable parameter that influences the level of exploration.

3 PROBLEM FORMULATION

In every time step $t = 1, \dots, T$, a user arrives with an M-dimensional context vector $x_t \in \mathbb{R}^M$. Using x_t as input, the algorithm chooses one of K possible actions for the user at time t. We let $a_t \in \{1, ..., K\}$ denote the action chosen by the algorithm. We then observe a random, binary reward $r_{t,a_t} \in \{0, 1\}$ associated with the chosen action a_t and context x_t. Our objective is to maximize the cumulative reward over the time horizon.

Let $p(a, x)$ denote the (unknown) probability of observing a positive reward, given that we have seen context vector x and offered action a. We define the *regret* incurred at time t as

$$\max_a E[r_{t,a}] - E[r_{t,a_t}] = \max_a p(a, x_t) - p(a_t, x_t)\,.$$

Intuitively, the regret measures the expected difference in reward between a candidate algorithm and the best possible assignment of actions. An equivalent objective to maximizing cumulative rewards is to minimize the T-period *cumulative regret*, $R(T)$, which is defined as

$$R(T) = \sum_{t=1}^{T} \max_a p(a, x_t) - p(a_t, x_t)\,.$$

In our empirical studies, we use cumulative regret as the performance metric for assessing our algorithm.

4 PRELIMINARIES

4.1 DECISION TREES

Our method uses decision tree learners in modeling the relationship between contexts and success probabilities for each action. Decision trees have a number of desirable properties: they handle both continuous and binary response data efficiently, are robust to outliers, and do not rely on any parametric assumptions about the response distribution. Thus, little user configuration is required in preparing the data before fitting a decision tree model. They also have the benefit of being highly interpretable, yielding an elegant visual representation of the relationship between contexts and rewards (Friedman et al., 2001). Figure 1 provides a diagram of a decision tree model for a particular sports advertisement. Observe that the tree partitions the context space into different regions, referred to as *terminal nodes* or *leaves*, and we assume that each of the users belonging to a certain leaf has the same success probability.

There are many efficient algorithms proposed in the literature for estimating decision tree models from training data. In our numerical experiments, we used the CART algorithm with pruning as described by Breiman et al. (1984). Note that this method does not rely on any tunable parameters, as the depth of the tree is selected internally using cross-validation.

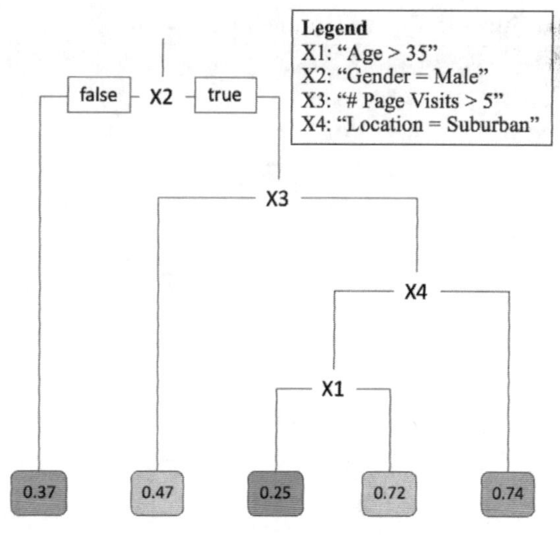

Figure 1: A decision tree modeling the distribution of rewards for a golf club advertisement. Terminal nodes display the success probability corresponding to each group of users.

4.2 THOMPSON SAMPLING FOR CONTEXTUAL BANDITS

Our algorithm was designed to mimic the behavior of Thompson sampling, a general algorithm for handling the exploration-exploitation trade-off in bandit problems. In addition to having strong performance guarantees relative to UCB (Russo and Van Roy, 2014), Thompson sampling does not contain unspecified constants which need to be tuned for proper exploration. Thus, there is sufficient motivation for using this method in our setting.

In order to provide intuition for our algorithm, we describe how Thompson sampling works in the contextual bandit case. To begin, assume that each action a has a set of unknown parameters θ_a governing its reward distribution, $P(r_a|\theta_a, x_t)$. For example, when using linear models with Thompson sampling, $E[r_a|\theta_a, x_t] = x_t'\theta_a$. We initially model our uncertainty about θ_a using a pre-specified prior distribution, $P(\theta_a)$. As new rewards are observed for action a, we update our model accordingly to its so-called posterior distribution, $P(\theta_a|D_{t,a})$. Here, $D_{t,a}$ represents the set of context/reward pairs corresponding to times up to t that action a was offered, i.e., $D_{t,a} = \{(x_s, r_{s,a}) : s \leq t-1, a_s = a\}$.

Thompson sampling behaves as follows. During each time step, every action's parameters θ_a are first randomly sampled according to posterior distribution $P(\theta_a|D_{t,a})$. Then, Thompson sampling chooses the action which maximizes expected reward with respect to the sampled parameters. In practice, this can be implemented according to the pseudocode given in Algorithm 1.

Algorithm 1: ThompsonSampling()

```
for t = 1, ..., T do
    Observe context vector x_t
    for a = 1, ..., K do
        Sample θ̃_{t,a} from P(θ_a | D_{t,a})
    end
    Choose action a_t = arg max_a E[r_a | θ̃_{t,a}, x_t]
    Update D_{t,a_t} and P(θ_{a_t} | D_{t,a_t}) with (x_t, r_{t,a_t})
end
```

5 THE BOOTSTRAPPING ALGORITHM

5.1 BOOTSTRAPPING TO CREATE A "THOMPSON SAMPLE"

As decision trees are inherently non-parametric, it is not straightforward to mathematically define priors and posteriors with respect to these learners, making Thompson sampling difficult to implement. However, one can use bootstrapping to simulate the behavior of sampling from a posterior distribution, the intuition for which is discussed below.

Recall that data $D_{t,a}$ is the set of observations for action a at time t. If we had access to many i.i.d. datasets of size $|D_{t,a}|$ for action a, we could fit a decision tree to each one and create a *distribution* of trees. A Thompson sample could then be generated by sampling a random tree from this collection. Although assuming access to these datasets is clearly impractical in our setting, we can use bootstrapping to approximate this behavior. We first create a large number of bootstrapped datasets, each one formed by sampling $|D_{t,a}|$ context-reward pairs from $D_{t,a}$ with replacement. Then, we fit a decision tree to each of these bootstrapped datasets. A "Thompson sample" is then a randomly selected tree from this collection. Of course, an equivalent and computationally more efficient procedure is to simply fit a decision tree to a *single* bootstrapped dataset. This intuition serves as the basis for our algorithm.

Following Tang et al. (2015), let $\tilde{D}_{t,a}$ denote the dataset obtained by bootstrapping $D_{t,a}$, i.e. sampling $|D_{t,a}|$ observations from $D_{t,a}$ with replacement. Denote the decision tree fit on $\tilde{D}_{t,a}$ by $\tilde{\theta}_{t,a}$. Finally, let $\hat{p}(\tilde{\theta}, x_t)$ denote the estimated probability of success from using decision tree $\tilde{\theta}$ on context x_t.

At each time point, the bootstrapping algorithm simply selects the action which maximizes $\hat{p}(\tilde{\theta}_{t,a}, x_t)$. See Algorithm 2 for the full pseudocode. Although our method is given with respect to decision tree models, note that this bootstrapping framework can be used with any base learner, such as logistic regression, random forests, and neural networks.

Algorithm 2: TreeBootstrap()

```
for t = 1, ..., T do
    Observe context vector x_t
    for a = 1, ..., K do
        Sample bootstrapped dataset D̃_{t,a} from D_{t,a}
        Fit decision tree θ̃_{t,a} to D̃_{t,a}
    end
    Choose action a_t = arg max_a p̂(θ̃_{t,a}, x_t)
    Update D_{t,a_t} with (x_t, r_{t,a_t})
end
```

Observe that TreeBootstrap may eliminate an action after a single observation if its first realized reward is a failure, as the tree constructed from the resampled dataset in subsequent iterations will always estimate a success probability of zero. There are multiple solutions to address this issue. First, one can force the algorithm to continue offering each action a until a success is observed (or an action a is eliminated after a certain threshold number of failures). This is the approach used in our numerical experiments. Second, one can add fabricated prior data of one success and one failure for each action, where the associated context for the prior is that of the first data point observed. The prior data prohibit the early termination of arms, and their impact on the prediction accuracy becomes negligible as the number of observations increases.

5.2 MEASURING THE SIMILARITY BETWEEN BOOTSTRAPPING AND THOMPSON SAMPLING

Here we provide a simple result that quantifies how close the Thompson sampling and bootstrapping algorithms are in terms of the actions chosen in each time step. Measuring the closeness of the two algorithms in the contextual bandit framework is quite challenging, and thus we focus on the standard (context-free) multi-armed bandit problem in this subsection. Suppose that the reward from choosing each action, i.e., $r_{t,a}$, follows a Bernoulli distribution with an unknown success probability. At a given time t, let n_a denote the total number of times that action a has been chosen, and let p_a denote the proportion of successes observed for action a.

In standard multi-armed bandits with Bernoulli rewards, Thompson sampling first draws a random sample of the true (unknown) success probability for each action a according to a Beta distribution with parameters $\alpha_a = n_a p_a$ and $\beta_a = n_a(1 - p_a)$. It then chooses the action with the highest sampled success probability. Conversely, the bootstrapping algorithm samples n_a observations with replacement from action a's observed rewards, and the generated success probability is then the proportion of successes observed in the bootstrapped dataset. Note that this procedure is equivalent to generating a binomial random variable with number of trials n_a and success rate p_a, divided by n_a.

In Theorem 1 below, we bound the difference in the probability of choosing action a when using bootstrapping versus Thompson sampling. For simplicity, we assume that we have observed at least one success and one failure for each action, i.e. $n_a \geq 2$ and $p_a \in (0, 1)$ for all a.

Theorem 1. *Let a_t^{TS} be the action chosen by the Thompson sampling algorithm, and let a_t^B be the action chosen by the bootstrapping algorithm given data (n_a, p_a) for each action $a \in \{1, 2, \dots, K\}$. Then,*

$$|P(a_t^{TS} = a) - P(a_t^B = a)| \leq C_a(p_1, ..., p_K) \sum_{a=1}^{K} \frac{1}{\sqrt{n_a}}$$

holds for every $a \in \{1, 2, \dots, K\}$, for some function $C_a(p_1, ..., p_K)$ of $p_1, ..., p_K$.

Note that both algorithms will sample each action infinitely often, i.e. $n_a \to \infty$ as $t \to \infty$ for all a. Hence, as the number of time steps increases, the two exploration algorithms choose actions according to increasingly similar probabilities. Theorem 1 thus sheds some light onto how quickly the two algorithms converge to the same action selection probabilities. A full proof is provided in the Supplementary Materials section.

5.3 EFFICIENT HEURISTICS

Note that TreeBootstrap requires fitting K decision trees from scratch at each time step. Depending on the method used to fit the decision trees as well as the size of M, K, and T, this can be quite computationally intensive. Various online algorithms have been proposed in the literature for training decision trees, referred to as Incremental Decision Trees (IDTs) (Crawford, 1989; Utgoff, 1989; Utgoff et al., 1997). Nevertheless, Algorithm 2 does not allow for efficient use of IDTs, as the bootstrapped dataset for an action significantly changes at each time step.

However, one could modify Algorithm 2 to instead use an *online* method of bootstrapping. Eckles and Kaptein (2014) propose a different bootstrapping framework for bandit problems which is more amenable to online learning algorithms. Under this framework, we begin by initializing B null datasets for every action, and new context-reward pairs are added in real time to each dataset with probability $1/2$. We then simply maintain $K \times B$ IDTs fit on each of the datasets, and a "Thompson sample" then corresponds to randomly selecting one of an action's B IDTs. Note that there is an inherent tradeoff with respect to the number of datasets per action, as larger values of B come with both higher approximation accuracy to the original bootstrapping framework and increased computational cost.

We now propose a heuristic which only requires maintaining one IDT per action, as opposed to $K \times B$ IDTs. Moreover, only one tree update is needed per time period. The key idea is to simply maintain an IDT $\hat{\theta}_{t,a}$ fit on each action's dataset $D_{t,a}$. Then, using the leaves of the trees to partition the context space into regions, we treat each region as a standard multi-arm bandit (MAB) problem. More specifically, let $N_1(\hat{\theta}_{t,a}, x_t)$ denote the number of successes in the leaf node of $\hat{\theta}_{t,a}$ corresponding to

x_t, and analogously define $N_0(\hat{\theta}_{t,a}, x_t)$ as the number of failures. Then, we simply feed this data into a standard MAB algorithm, where we assume action a has observed $N_1(\hat{\theta}_{t,a}, x_t)$ successes and $N_0(\hat{\theta}_{t,a}, x_t)$ failures thus far. Depending on the action we choose, we then update the corresponding IDT of that action and proceed to the next time step.

Algorithm 3 provides the pseudocode for this heuristic using the standard Thompson sampling algorithm for multi-arm bandits. Note that this requires a prior number of successes and failures for each context region, S_0 and F_0. In the absence of any problem-specific information, we recommend using the uniform prior $S_0 = F_0 = 1$.

Algorithm 3: TreeHeuristic()

```
for t = 1, ..., T do
    Observe context vector x_t
    for a = 1, ..., K do
        Sample TS_{t,a} ~
          Beta(N_1(θ̂_{t,a}, x_t) + S_0, N_0(θ̂_{t,a}, x_t) + F_0)
    end
    Choose action a_t = arg max_a TS_{t,a}
    Update tree θ̂_{t,a_t} with (x_t, r_{t,a_t})
end
```

Both TreeBootstrap and TreeHeuristic are algorithms which aim to emulate the behavior of Thompson Sampling. TreeHeuristic is at least $O(K)$ times faster computationally than TreeBootstrap, as it only requires refitting one decision tree per time step – the tree corresponding to the sampled action. However, TreeHeuristic sacrifices some robustness in attaining these computational gains. In each iteration of TreeBootstrap, a new decision tree is resampled for every action to account for two sources of uncertainty: (a) global uncertainty in the tree structure (i.e. are we splitting on the right variables?) and (b) local uncertainty in each leaf node (i.e., are we predicting the correct probability of success in each leaf?). Conversely, TreeHeuristic keeps the tree structures fixed and only resamples the data in leaf nodes corresponding to the current context – thus, TreeHeuristic only accounts for uncertainty (b), not (a). Note that if both the tree structures *and* the leaf node probability estimates were kept fixed, this would amount to a pure exploitation policy.

6 EXPERIMENTAL RESULTS

We assessed the empirical performance of our algorithm using the following sources of data as input:

1. A simulated "sports ads" dataset with decision trees for each offer governing reward probabilities.
2. Four classification datasets obtained from the UCI Machine Learning Repository (Lichman, 2013): *Adult*, *Statlog (Shuttle)*, *Covertype*, and *US Census Data (1990)*.

We measured the cumulative regret incurred by TreeBootstrap on these datasets, and we compare its performance with that of TreeHeuristic as well as several benchmark algorithms proposed in the bandit literature.

6.1 BENCHMARK ALGORITHMS

We tested the following benchmarks in our computational experiments:

1. *Context-free MAB*. To demonstrate the value of using contexts in recommendation systems, we include the performance of a context-free multi-arm bandit algorithm as a benchmark. Specifically, we use context-free Thompson sampling in our experiments.

2. *BanditForest*. To the best of our knowledge, BanditForest is the only bandit algorithm in the literature which uses decision tree learners. Following the approach used in their numerical studies, we first recoded each continuous variable into five binary variables before calling the algorithm. Note this is a necessary preprocessing step, as the algorithm requires all contexts to be binary. The method contains two tunable parameters which control the level of exploration, δ and ϵ, which we set to the values tested in their paper: $\delta = 0.05$, and $\epsilon \sim$ Uniform$(0.4, 0.8)$. Additionally, two other tunable parameters can be optimized: the depth of each tree, D, and the number of trees in the random forest, L. We report the values of these parameters which attained the best cumulative regret with respect to our time horizon: $L = 3$ and $D = 4, 2, 4, 5$, and 2 corresponding to the simulated sports-advertising dataset, *Adult*, *Shuttle*, *Covertype*, and *Census*, respectively. Note that the optimal parameter set varies depending on the dataset used. In practice, one cannot know the optimal parameter set in advance without any prior data, and so the performance we report may be optimistic.

3. *LinUCB*. Developed by Li et al. (2010), LinUCB is one of the most cited contextual bandit algorithms in the recent literature. The method calls for fitting a ridge regression model on the context-reward data for each action (with regularization parameter $\lambda = 1$). We then choose the action with the highest upper confidence bound with respect to a new context's estimated probability of success. All contexts

were scaled to have mean 0 and variance 1 before calling the algorithm, and all categorical variables were binarized. Due to the high-dimensionality of our datasets (particularly after binarization), the predictive linear model requires sufficient regularization to prevent overfitting. In the hopes of a fairer comparison with our algorithm, we instead select the regularization parameter from a grid of candidate values using cross-validation. We report the best cumulative regret achieved when varying the UCB constant α among a grid of values from 0.0001 to 10. Similar to the BanditForest case, the optimal parameter depends on the dataset.

4. *LogisticUCB*. As we are testing our algorithms using classification data, there is significant motivation to use a logistic model, as opposed to a linear model, in capturing the context-reward relationship. Filippi et al. (2010) describe a bandit algorithm using a generalized linear modeling framework, of which logistic regression is a special case. However, the authors tackle a problem formulation which is slightly different than our own. In their setting, each *action* has an associated, nonrandom context vector x_a, and the expected reward is a function of a single unknown parameter $\theta : E[r_t|x_a] = \mu(x_a^T\theta)$ (here, μ is the so-called inverse link function). Extending their algorithm to our setting, we give the full pseudocode of LogisticUCB in the Supplementary Materials section. We take all of the same preprocessing steps as in LinUCB, and we report the cumulative regret corresponding to the *best* UCB constant. For the same reasons as above, we use regularized logistic regression in practice with cross-validation to tune the regularization parameter.

5. *OfflineTree*. Recall that the simulated sports-advertising dataset was constructed using decision tree truths. Thus, it is meaningful to compare TreeBootstrap with a regret of zero, as it is possible in theory for estimated decision trees to capture the truth exactly. However, as the four UCI datasets are all composed of real observations, there will always be part of the "truth" which decision trees cannot capture. Our benchmark OfflineTree measures this error, serving as a meaningful *lower bound* against which we can compare our algorithm. Described in detail in Algorithm 4, it can essentially be thought of as the offline classification error of decision trees with respect to a held-out test set. In our experimental results, we report the difference in cumulative regret on the UCI datasets between the candidate algorithms and OfflineTree.

Algorithm 4: OfflineTree()

```
For each observation (x, y), define w_a(x, y) as follows:
  w_a(x, y) = 1 if y = a, and
  w_a(x, y) = 0 if y ≠ a
Hold out T random observations, {x_t}_{1≤t≤T}
for a = 1, ..., K do
    Fit tree θ̂_a on remaining data using w_a(x, y) as the
    response variable
end
for t = 1, ..., T do
    Observe context vector x_t
    Choose action a_t = arg max_a p̂(θ̂_a, x_t)
end
```

6.2 SPORTS ADVERTISING DATASET

First, TreeBootstrap was tested under an idealistic setting – a simulated dataset where the context-reward model is a decision tree for each action. We frame this dataset in the context of sports web-advertising. Whenever a user visits the website, we must offer ads for one of $K = 4$ different products: golf clubs, basketball nets, tennis rackets, and soccer balls. We receive a reward of 1 if the user clicks the ad; otherwise, we receive no reward.

Figure 1 provides an example of the decision tree used to simulate the golf advertisement rewards, as well as information about the $M = 4$ (binary) contextual variables available for each user. Figure 2 provides the cumulative regret data for the tested methods. As expected, our algorithm outperforms the other benchmark methods which do not use decision tree learners, and the performance of TreeBootstrap and TreeHeuristic are very similar. Moreover, the regret seems to converge to zero for our decision tree algorithms as the number of observed users becomes large. Finally, note how BanditForest eventually achieves a regret comparable to the other algorithms, but nonetheless incurs a much higher cumulative regret. This is due to the fact that the algorithm takes most of the time horizon to exit its "pure exploration" phase, an observation which also holds across all the UCI datasets.

6.3 UCI REPOSITORY DATASETS

We next evaluated our algorithm on four classification datasets from the UCI Machine Learning Repository (Lichman, 2013): *Adult*, *Statlog (Shuttle)*, *Covertype*, and *US Census Data (1990)*. The response variables used were *occupation*, *Cover_Type*, and *dOccup* for *Adult*, *Covertype*, and *Census*, respectively, while for *Shuttle* we used the variable corresponding to the last column of the dataset. We first ran a preprocessing step remov-

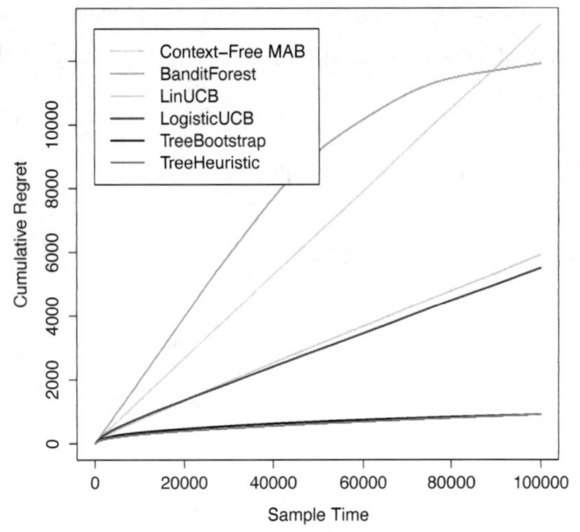

Figure 2: Cumulative regret incurred on the (simulated) sports advertising dataset.

ing classes which were significantly underrepresented in each dataset (i.e., less than 0.05% of the observations). After preprocessing, these datasets had $K = 12, 4, 7$, and 9 classes, respectively, as well as $M = 14, 9, 54$, and 67 contextual variables. We then constructed a bandit problem from the data in the following way: a regret of 0 (otherwise 1) is incurred if and only if the algorithm predicts the class of the data point correctly. This framework for adapting classification data for use in bandit problems is commonly used in the literature (Allesiardo et al., 2014; Agarwal et al., 2014; Féraud et al., 2016).

Figure 4 shows the cumulative regret of TreeBootstrap compared with the benchmarks on the UCI datasets. Recall that we plot regret relative to OfflineTree. In all cases, our heuristic achieves a performance equal to or better than that of TreeBootstrap. Note that LogisticUCB outperforms LinUCB on all datasets except *Covertype*, which demonstrates the value of using learners in our setting which handle binary response data effectively.

LinUCB and LogisticUCB outperform our algorithm on two of the four UCI datasets (*Adult* and *Census*). However, there are several caveats to this result. First, recall that we only report the cumulative regret of LinUCB and LogisticUCB with respect to the best exploration parameter, which is impossible to know a priori. Figure 3 shows LinUCB's cumulative regret curves corresponding to each value of the exploration parameter α implemented on the *Adult* dataset. We overlay this on a plot of the cumulative regret curves associated with TreeBootstrap and our heuristic. Note that TreeBootstrap and TreeHeuristic outperformed LinUCB in at least half of the parameter settings attempted. Second, the difference in cumulative regret between TreeBootstrap and Linear/Logistic UCB on *Adult* and *Census* appears to approach a constant as the time horizon increases. This is due to the fact that decision trees will capture the truth eventually given enough training data. Conversely, in settings such as the sports ad dataset, *Covertype*, and *Shuttle*, it appears that the linear/logistic regression models have already converged and fail to capture the context-reward distribution accurately. This is most likely due to the fact that feature engineering is needed for the data to satisfy the GLM framework. Thus, the difference in cumulative regret between Linear/Logistic UCB and TreeBootstrap will become arbitrarily large as the time horizon increases. Finally, note that we introduce regularization into the linear and logistic regressions, tuned using cross-validation, which improve upon the original framework for LinUCB and Logistic UCB.

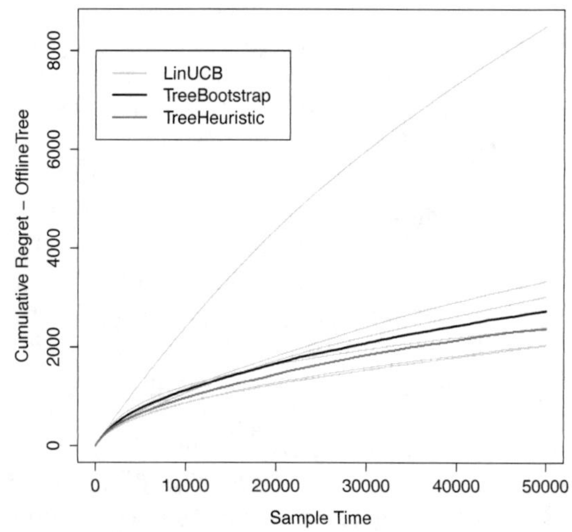

Figure 3: Cumulative regret incurred on the *Adult* dataset. The performance of LinUCB is given with respect to all values of the tuneable parameter attempted: $\alpha = 0.0001, 0.001, 0.01, 0.1, 1, 10$

7 CONCLUSION

We propose a contextual bandit algorithm, TreeBootstrap, which can be easily and effectively applied in practice. We use decision trees as our base learner, and we handle the exploration-exploitation trade-off using bootstrapping in a way which approximates the behavior of Thompson sampling. As our algorithm requires fitting multiple trees at each time step, we provide a computational heuristic which works well in practice. Empirically, our methods' performance is quite competitive and robust compared to several well-known algorithms.

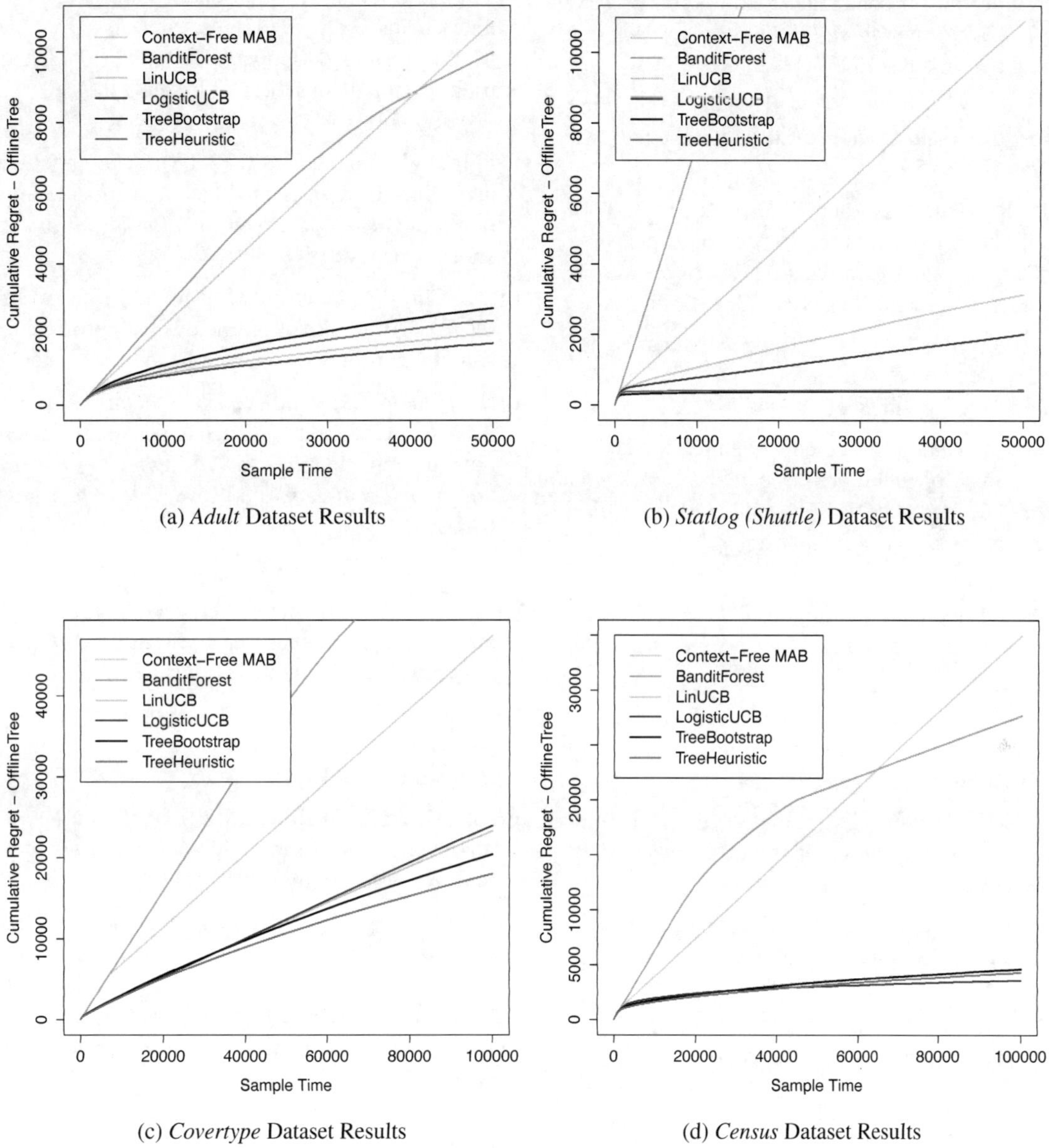

(a) *Adult* Dataset Results

(b) *Statlog (Shuttle)* Dataset Results

(c) *Covertype* Dataset Results

(d) *Census* Dataset Results

Figure 4: Cumulative regret incurred on various classification datasets from the UCI Machine Learning Repository. A regret of 0 (otherwise 1) is incurred iff a candidate algorithm predicts the class of the data point correctly.

References

Abbasi-Yadkori, Y., Pál, D., and Szepesvári, C. (2011). Improved algorithms for linear stochastic bandits. In *Advances in Neural Information Processing Systems*, pages 2312–2320.

Agarwal, A., Hsu, D., Kale, S., Langford, J., Li, L., and Schapire, R. (2014). Taming the monster: A fast and simple algorithm for contextual bandits. In *Proceedings of The 31st International Conference on Machine Learning*, pages 1638–1646.

Agrawal, S. and Goyal, N. (2013). Thompson sampling for contextual bandits with linear payoffs. In *ICML (3)*, pages 127–135.

Allesiardo, R., Féraud, R., and Bouneffouf, D. (2014). A neural networks committee for the contextual bandit problem. In *International Conference on Neural Information Processing*, pages 374–381. Springer.

Auer, P. (2002). Using confidence bounds for exploitation-exploration trade-offs. *Journal of Machine Learning Research*, 3(Nov):397–422.

Baransi, A., Maillard, O.-A., and Mannor, S. (2014). Sub-sampling for multi-armed bandits. In *Joint European Conference on Machine Learning and Knowledge Discovery in Databases*, pages 115–131. Springer.

Breiman, L., Friedman, J., Stone, C. J., and Olshen, R. A. (1984). *Classification and regression trees*. CRC press.

Chu, W., Li, L., Reyzin, L., and Schapire, R. E. (2011). Contextual bandits with linear payoff functions. In *AISTATS*, volume 15, pages 208–214.

Crawford, S. L. (1989). Extensions to the cart algorithm. *International Journal of Man-Machine Studies*, 31(2):197–217.

Dhar, S. and Varshney, U. (2011). Challenges and business models for mobile location-based services and advertising. *Communications of the ACM*, 54(5):121–128.

Dudik, M., Hsu, D., Kale, S., Karampatziakis, N., Langford, J., Reyzin, L., and Zhang, T. (2011). Efficient optimal learning for contextual bandits. *arXiv preprint arXiv:1106.2369*.

Eckles, D. and Kaptein, M. (2014). Thompson sampling with the online bootstrap. *arXiv preprint arXiv:1410.4009*.

Féraud, R., Allesiardo, R., Urvoy, T., and Clérot, F. (2016). Random forest for the contextual bandit problem. In *Proceedings of the 19th International Conference on Artificial Intelligence and Statistics*, pages 93–101.

Filippi, S., Cappe, O., Garivier, A., and Szepesvári, C. (2010). Parametric bandits: The generalized linear case. In *Advances in Neural Information Processing Systems*, pages 586–594.

Friedman, J., Hastie, T., and Tibshirani, R. (2001). *The elements of statistical learning*, volume 1. Springer series in statistics Springer, Berlin.

Kim, E. S., Herbst, R. S., Wistuba, I. I., Lee, J. J., Blumenschein, G. R., Tsao, A., Stewart, D. J., Hicks, M. E., Erasmus, J., Gupta, S., et al. (2011). The battle trial: personalizing therapy for lung cancer. *Cancer discovery*, 1(1):44–53.

Langford, J. and Zhang, T. (2008). The epoch-greedy algorithm for multi-armed bandits with side information. In *Advances in neural information processing systems*, pages 817–824.

Li, L., Chu, W., Langford, J., Moon, T., and Wang, X. (2011). An unbiased offline evaluation of contextual bandit algorithms with generalized linear models.

Li, L., Chu, W., Langford, J., and Schapire, R. E. (2010). A contextual-bandit approach to personalized news article recommendation. In *Proceedings of the 19th international conference on World wide web*, pages 661–670. ACM.

Lichman, M. (2013). UCI machine learning repository.

Long, J. S. (1997). Regression models for categorical and limited dependent variables. *Advanced quantitative techniques in the social sciences*, 7.

Osband, I. and Van Roy, B. (2015). Bootstrapped thompson sampling and deep exploration. *arXiv preprint arXiv:1507.00300*.

Russo, D. and Van Roy, B. (2014). Learning to optimize via posterior sampling. *Mathematics of Operations Research*, 39(4):1221–1243.

Tang, L., Jiang, Y., Li, L., Zeng, C., and Li, T. (2015). Personalized recommendation via parameter-free contextual bandits. In *Proceedings of the 38th International ACM SIGIR Conference on Research and Development in Information Retrieval*, pages 323–332. ACM.

Utgoff, P. E. (1989). Incremental induction of decision trees. *Machine learning*, 4(2):161–186.

Utgoff, P. E., Berkman, N. C., and Clouse, J. A. (1997). Decision tree induction based on efficient tree restructuring. *Machine Learning*, 29(1):5–44.

Yuan, S.-T. and Tsao, Y. W. (2003). A recommendation mechanism for contextualized mobile advertising. *Expert Systems with Applications*, 24(4):399–414.

Supplementary Materials For "A Practical Method for Solving Contextual Bandit Problems Using Decision Trees"

1 Proof of Theorem 1

For the standard multi-armed bandit problem, let n_k be the number of total observed responses for action k and p_k be the observed success rate for action k (proportion of success responses out of total observed responses). For simplicity, we assume that we have observed at least one success and one failure for each action, i.e. $n_k \geq 2$ and $p_k \in (0, 1)$ for all k. Then, the following theorem holds:

Theorem 1. *Let a_t^{TS} be the action chosen by the Thompson sampling algorithm, and let a_t^B be the action chosen by the bootstrapping algorithm given data (n_k, p_k) for each action $k \in \{1, 2, \ldots, K\}$. Then,*

$$|P(a_t^{TS} = k) - P(a_t^B = k)| \leq C_k(p_1, ..., p_K) \sum_{j=1}^{K} \frac{1}{\sqrt{n_j}}$$

holds for every $k \in \{1, 2, \ldots, K\}$, for some function $C_k(p_1, ..., p_K)$ of $p_1, ..., p_K$.

To prove the theorem, we first provide a few lemmas. The proofs for all lemmas are given in Section 2 of this supplementary materials document. For notational convenience, we define $\alpha_k = n_k p_k$ and $\beta_k = n_k(1 - p_k)$, which indicate the number of success and failure responses observed so far for action k. For each action $k \in \{1, 2, \ldots, K\}$, the Thompson sampling algorithm first draws a random sample of the true (unknown) success probability according to a beta distribution with parameters α_k and β_k, and it then chooses the action with the highest success probability. The bootstrapping algorithm samples n_k observations with replacement from action k's observed rewards, and the generated success probability is then the proportion of successes observed in the bootstrapped dataset. This procedure is equivalent to generating a binomial random variable with n_k trials and p_k success rate, divided by n_k. The following lemma shows how close the distributions of these two random probability estimates are in terms of the number of available data points for each action.

Lemma 1. *Let X be a beta random variable with integer parameters $\alpha > 0$ and $\beta > 0$, and let Y be a binomial random variable with n trials and success rate p, where $\alpha + \beta = n$ and $p = \frac{\alpha}{n}$. Then,*

$$\max_{z \in [0,1]} \left| P(X \leq z) - P\left(\frac{Y}{n} \leq z\right) \right| \leq \frac{c(p)}{\sqrt{n}},$$

for some function $c(p)$ that is independent of n.

We now provide a second lemma which will prove useful in deriving Theorem 1. Recall that for each $k \in \{1, 2, \ldots, K\}$, n_k is the total number of observations and p_k is the observed success rate. Let p_k^{TS}

be the randomly drawn success probability of action k by the Thompson sampling algorithm and let p_k^B be the randomly drawn success probability of action k by the bootstrapping algorithm. Under each algorithm $h \in \{TS, B\}$, an action is chosen arbitrarily from the set $M^h := \{k : p_k^h \geq p_j^h \text{ for every } j \neq k\}$. In the Thompson sampling algorithm, p_k^{TS} is sampled from a continuous (beta) distribution, and thus M^{TS} will have cardinality one almost surely. Hence,

$$P(a_t^{TS} = k) = P(p_k^{TS} \geq p_j^{TS} \text{ for every } j \neq k) \,. \tag{1}$$

However, these events are not necessarily equivalent with respect to the bootstrapping algorithm. Since p_k^B is sampled using a discrete (binomial) distribution, it is possible that two actions will have the same sampled probabilities. Thus, it is possible for an action $k \in M^B$ to not be chosen if there exists another action $l \in M^B$. We provide a lemma which examines the difference in these two events:

Lemma 2. *For some function $b(p_k)$ that is independent of n_k,*

$$|P(a_t^B = k) - P(p_k^B \geq p_j^B \text{ for every } j \neq k)| \leq \frac{b(p_k)}{\sqrt{n_k}}(1 + O(1/n_k)) \,.$$

We can now proceed with the derivation of the theorem. We define $err_k(z|X) := P(p_k^{TS} \leq z|X) - P(p_k^B \leq z|X)$ with respect to some random variable X. Assuming X is independent of p_k^{TS} and p_k^B (but not necessarily of z), then it follows from Lemma 1 that $|err_k(z|X)| \leq \frac{c(p_k)}{\sqrt{n_k}}$ for some function $c(p_k)$ that is independent of n_k. Note that this result also holds for the function $\widetilde{err}_k(z|X) := P(p_k^B \leq z|X) - P(p_k^{TS} \leq z|X)$.

Note that the events $\{p_k^h \geq p_j^h\}$ for $j \neq k$ are independent conditioned on p_k^h. Hence, using (1) we have

$$\begin{aligned} P(a_t^{TS} = k) &= E_{p_k^{TS}}\left[P(p_k^{TS} \geq p_j^{TS} \text{ for every } j \neq k | p_k^{TS})\right] \\ &= E_{p_k^{TS}}\left[\prod_{j \neq k} P(p_k^{TS} \geq p_j^{TS} | p_k^{TS})\right] \\ &= E_{p_k^{TS}}\left[\prod_{j \neq k} \left(P(p_k^{TS} \geq p_j^B | p_k^{TS}) + err_j(p_k^{TS} | p_k^{TS})\right)\right] \,. \end{aligned} \tag{2}$$

In the expansion of the product (2), only one term does not include $err_j(p_k^{TS}|p_k^{TS})$. This term is given as

$$
\begin{aligned}
& E_{p_k^{TS}}\left[\prod_{j\neq k} P(p_k^{TS} \geq p_j^B | p_k^{TS})\right] \\
= \; & E_{p_k^{TS}}\left[P(p_k^{TS} \geq p_j^B \text{ for every } j \neq k | p_k^{TS})\right] \\
= \; & E_{p_j^B, j\neq k}\left[P(p_k^{TS} \geq \max_{j\neq k} p_j^B | p_j^B, j \neq k)\right] \\
= \; & E_{p_j^B, j\neq k}\left[P(p_k^{B} \geq \max_{j\neq k} p_j^B | p_j^B, j \neq k) + \widetilde{err}_k(\max_{j\neq k} p_j^B | p_j^B, j \neq k)\right] \\
= \; & P(p_k^B \geq \max_{j\neq k} p_j^B) + E_{p_j^B, j\neq k}[\widetilde{err}_k(\max_{j\neq k} p_j^B | p_j^B, j \neq k)] \\
= \; & P(a_t^B = k) + (P(p_k^B \geq \max_{j\neq k} p_j^B) - P(a_t^B = k)) + E_{p_j^B, j\neq k}[\widetilde{err}_k(\max_{j\neq k} p_j^B | p_j^B, j \neq k)]\,. \qquad (3)
\end{aligned}
$$

The rest of (2) is the sum of multiplications of $K-1$ terms of $P(p_k^{TS} \geq p_j^B | p_k^{TS})$ and $err_j(p_k^{TS}|p_k^{TS})$. Because $P(p_k^{TS} \geq p_j^B | p_k^{TS}) \leq 1$ and $|err_j| \leq \frac{c(p_j)}{\sqrt{n_j}}$ from Lemma 1, the rest can be bounded by $\prod_{j\neq k}\left(1 + \frac{c(p_j)}{\sqrt{n_j}}\right) - 1$. Hence, applying Lemma 1 and Lemma 2 to (3), we have

$$
\begin{aligned}
& |P(a_t^{TS} = k) - P(a_t^B = k)| \\
\leq \; & |P(p_k^B \geq \max_{j\neq k} p_j^B) - P(a_t^B = k)| + |E_{p_j^B, j\neq k}[\widetilde{err}_k(\max_{j\neq k} p_j^B | p_j^B, j \neq k)]| + \prod_{j\neq k}\left(1 + \frac{c(p_j)}{\sqrt{n_j}}\right) - 1 \\
\leq \; & \frac{b(p_k)}{\sqrt{n_k}}(1 + O(1/n_k)) + \frac{c(p_k)}{\sqrt{n_k}} + \prod_{j\neq k}\left(1 + \frac{c(p_j)}{\sqrt{n_j}}\right) - 1\,. \qquad (4)
\end{aligned}
$$

Note that the error term from Sterling's approximation, $O(1/n_k)$, can be bounded from above by a constant. Furthermore, for any set S of actions,

$$
\prod_{s\in S} \frac{c(p_s)}{\sqrt{n_s}} \leq \frac{1}{\sqrt{n_t}} \prod_{s\in S} c(p_s) \qquad \forall t \in S\,.
$$

One can then use these facts to manipulate (4) to prove the desired result:

$$
|P(a_t^{TS} = k) - P(a_t^B = k)| \leq C_k(p_1, ..., p_K) \sum_{j=1}^{K} \frac{1}{\sqrt{n_j}}\,,
$$

where $C_k(p_1, ..., p_K)$ is a function of $p_1, ..., p_K$. □

2 Proof of Auxiliary Lemmas

Lemma 1. *Let X be a beta random variable with integer parameters $\alpha > 0$ and $\beta > 0$, and let Y be a binomial random variable with n trials and success rate p, where $\alpha + \beta = n$ and $p = \frac{\alpha}{n}$. Then,*

$$\max_{z\in[0,1]} \left| P(X \leq z) - P\left(\frac{Y}{n} \leq z\right) \right| \leq \frac{c(p)}{\sqrt{n}},$$

for some function $c(p)$ that is independent of n.

Proof. For notational convenience, we define $q = \frac{\beta}{n} = 1 - p$, and we denote the p.d.f., and the c.d.f. of a standard normal random variable by $\phi(\cdot)$ and $\Phi(\cdot)$, respectively. We will first show that, for each $z \in [0,1]$, $P(X \leq z)$ and $P\left(\frac{Y}{n} \leq z\right)$ can be approximated using normal c.d.f.'s $\Phi(\frac{\sqrt{n}(z-p)}{\sqrt{pq+(z-p)^2}})$ and $\Phi(\frac{\sqrt{n}(z-p)}{\sqrt{pq}})$, respectively. Finally, we will bound the difference in these approximations and apply the triangle inequality:

$$\begin{aligned}\left| P(X \leq z) - P\left(\frac{Y}{n} \leq z\right) \right| \leq& \left| P(X \leq z) - \Phi(\frac{\sqrt{n}(z-p)}{\sqrt{pq+(z-p)^2}}) \right| \\ &+ \left| \Phi(\frac{\sqrt{n}(z-p)}{\sqrt{pq}}) - \Phi(\frac{\sqrt{n}(z-p)}{\sqrt{pq+(z-p)^2}}) \right| \\ &+ \left| P(\frac{Y}{n} \leq z) - \Phi(\frac{\sqrt{n}(z-p)}{\sqrt{pq}}) \right| \end{aligned} \quad (5)$$

We first bound the normal approximation for $P\left(\frac{Y}{n} \leq z\right)$. From the Berry - Esseen theorem, we have

$$|P(\sqrt{n}\frac{(Y/n-p)}{\sqrt{pq}} \leq x) - \Phi(x)| \leq \frac{C(p^2+q^2)}{\sqrt{npq}}$$

for every x, which implies that

$$|P(\frac{Y}{n} \leq z) - \Phi(\frac{\sqrt{n}(z-p)}{\sqrt{pq}})| \leq \frac{C(p^2+q^2)}{\sqrt{npq}} \quad (6)$$

holds for every $z \in [0,1]$.

Next, we will show that $P(X \leq z)$ can be approximated by a similar (but not exactly the same) function, $\Phi(\frac{\sqrt{n}(z-p)}{\sqrt{pq+(z-p)^2}})$. Note that the beta random variable X has the same distribution as $\frac{A}{A+B}$, where A and B are independent Gamma random variables with shape parameters α and β, respectively. We first derive an approximation for the c.d.f. of Gamma random variables. Suppose that Γ is Gamma distributed with an integer shape parameter $m > 0$. Because Γ has the same distribution as the sum of m independent exponential random variables with parameter 1, from the Berry - Esseen theorem we have

$$|P(\sqrt{m}(\Gamma/m - 1) \leq x) - \Phi(x)| \leq \frac{C\rho}{\sqrt{m}}, \quad (7)$$

where ρ is the third-order absolute moment of the unit exponential distribution.

Let N_1 and N_2 be independent standard normal random variables, and define

$$g(z) := P((\sqrt{\alpha}N_1 + \alpha)(1-z) \le (\sqrt{\beta}N_2 + \beta)z)\,.$$

Then, from the triangle inequality we have that for all $z \in (0,1)$:

$$\begin{aligned} & |P(X \le z) - g(z)| = |P(A(1-z) \le Bz) - g(z)| \\ \le\ & |P(A(1-z) \le Bz) - P((\sqrt{\alpha}N_1+\alpha)(1-z) \le Bz)| + |P((\sqrt{\alpha}N_1+\alpha)(1-z) \le Bz) - g(z)|\,. \end{aligned}$$

From (7), we have

$$\begin{aligned} & |P(A(1-z) \le Bz) - P((\sqrt{\alpha}N_1+\alpha)(1-z) \le Bz)| \\ =\ & \left|E_B\left[P(A(1-z) \le Bz|B) - P((\sqrt{\alpha}N_1+\alpha)(1-z) \le Bz|B)\right]\right| \\ \le\ & E_B\left[\left|P(A(1-z) \le Bz|B) - P((\sqrt{\alpha}N_1+\alpha)(1-z) \le Bz|B)\right|\right] \\ \le\ & \frac{C\rho}{\sqrt{\alpha}}\,. \end{aligned}$$

Similarly, again from (7), we have

$$\begin{aligned} & |P((\sqrt{\alpha}N_1+\alpha)(1-z) \le Bz) - g(z)| \\ =\ & \left|E_{N_1}\left[P((\sqrt{\alpha}N_1+\alpha)(1-z) \le Bz|N_1) - P(\sqrt{\alpha}N_1(1-z) - \sqrt{\beta}N_2 z \le nz - \alpha|N_1)\right]\right| \\ \le\ & E_{N_1}\left[\left|P((\sqrt{\alpha}N_1+\alpha)(1-z) \le Bz|N_1) - P(\sqrt{\alpha}N_1(1-z) - \sqrt{\beta}N_2 z \le nz - \alpha|N_1)\right|\right] \\ \le\ & \frac{C\rho}{\sqrt{\beta}}\,. \end{aligned}$$

Finally, because $-N_2$ is a standard normal random variable and the sum of two independent normal random variables is a standard normal random variable, we have

$$\begin{aligned} g(z) &= P(\sqrt{\alpha}N_1(1-z) - \sqrt{\beta}N_2 z \le nz - \alpha) \\ &= \Phi\left(\frac{nz-\alpha}{\sqrt{\alpha(1-z)^2 + \beta z^2}}\right) = \Phi\left(\frac{\sqrt{n}(z-p)}{\sqrt{pq + (z-p)^2}}\right), \end{aligned}$$

which concludes that

$$|P(X \le z) - \Phi(\frac{\sqrt{n}(z-p)}{\sqrt{pq+(z-p)^2}})| \le \frac{C\rho}{\sqrt{np}} + \frac{C\rho}{\sqrt{nq}} \tag{8}$$

holds for every $z \in [0,1]$.

Finally, we provide a bound for $|\Phi(\frac{\sqrt{n}(z-p)}{\sqrt{pq}}) - \Phi(\frac{\sqrt{n}(z-p)}{\sqrt{pq+(z-p)^2}})|$. For notational convenience, we define $d := \frac{z-p}{\sqrt{pq}}$. Then, the difference is given as $|\Phi(\sqrt{n}d) - \Phi(\frac{\sqrt{n}d}{\sqrt{1+d^2}})|$. Because $\Phi(y)$ is concave in y for $y \ge 0$, for every $d \geq 0$ we have

$$
\begin{aligned}
|\Phi(\sqrt{n}d) - \Phi(\frac{\sqrt{n}d}{\sqrt{1+d^2}})| &= \Phi(\sqrt{n}d) - \Phi(\frac{\sqrt{n}d}{\sqrt{1+d^2}}) \\
&\leq \left(\sqrt{n}d - \frac{\sqrt{n}d}{\sqrt{1+d^2}}\right)\phi(\frac{\sqrt{n}d}{\sqrt{1+d^2}}) \\
&= (\sqrt{1+d^2}-1)\frac{\sqrt{n}d}{\sqrt{1+d^2}}\phi(\frac{\sqrt{n}d}{\sqrt{1+d^2}}) \\
&\leq (\sqrt{1+d^2}-1)\phi(1) \\
&= \left(\frac{d^2}{\sqrt{1+d^2}+1}\right)\phi(1) \\
&\leq \frac{d^2}{2}\phi(1)\,,
\end{aligned}
$$

where the first inequality is from the concavity of $\Phi(\cdot)$ and the second inequality is from the fact that $x\phi(x)$ is maximized at $x=1$ for $x \geq 0$. We define $f(d) := \Phi(\sqrt{n}d) - \Phi(\frac{\sqrt{n}d}{\sqrt{1+d^2}})$ and $d^*(n) := \arg\max_{d\geq 0} f(d)$. Then, for every $d \geq 0$, $\Phi(\sqrt{n}d) - \Phi(\frac{\sqrt{n}d}{\sqrt{1+d^2}}) \leq \Phi(\sqrt{n}d^*(n)) - \Phi(\frac{\sqrt{n}d^*(n)}{\sqrt{1+d^*(n)^2}}) \leq \frac{d^*(n)^2}{2}\phi(1)$.

We will later show that $d^*(n)^4 < \frac{30\ln(10)}{n}$. Hence,

$$
|\Phi(\frac{\sqrt{n}(z-p)}{\sqrt{pq}}) - \Phi(\frac{\sqrt{n}(z-p)}{\sqrt{pq+(z-p)^2}})| \leq \frac{\phi(1)\sqrt{30\ln(10)}}{2\sqrt{n}} \tag{9}
$$

holds for every $z \geq p$. The case of $z < p$ can be shown via symmetry.

Finally, from applying the bounds (6), (8), and (9) to equation (5), we have that

$$
\left|P(X \leq z) - P\left(\frac{Y}{n} \leq z\right)\right| \leq \frac{C(p^2+q^2)}{\sqrt{npq}} + \frac{C\rho}{\sqrt{np}} + \frac{C\rho}{\sqrt{nq}} + \frac{\phi(1)\sqrt{30\ln(10)}}{2\sqrt{n}}\,,
$$

which proves the lemma.

It remains to show that $d^*(n)^4 < \frac{30\ln(10)}{n}$. The first-order condition for $d^*(n)$ is given as

$$
f'(d) = \sqrt{n}\phi(\sqrt{n}d) - \sqrt{n}(1+d^2)^{-\frac{3}{2}}\phi(\frac{\sqrt{n}d}{\sqrt{1+d^2}}) = 0\,.
$$

Note that $f(d)$ is nonnegative and differentiable on $d \geq 0$. Since $f(0) = 0$, then if $\lim_{d\to\infty} f'(d) \leq 0$ we can conclude that there exists a global maximizer of $f(d)$ over $d \geq 0$ which satisfies the first-order condition. $f'(d) \leq 0$ can be simplified as

$$
\begin{aligned}
\exp\left(-\frac{nd^2}{2} + \frac{nd^2}{2(1+d^2)}\right) &\leq (1+d^2)^{-\frac{3}{2}} \\
-\frac{nd^4}{2(1+d^2)} &\leq -\frac{3}{2}\ln(1+d^2) \\
n &\geq \frac{3(1+d^2)\ln(1+d^2)}{d^4}\,.
\end{aligned}
$$

Note that the right hand side approaches zero as $d \to \infty$, proving that $\lim_{d\to\infty} f'(d) \leq 0$. Thus, $d^*(n)$ satisfies the first-order condition, given in a simplified form below:

$$n = \frac{3(1+d^2)\ln(1+d^2)}{d^4}.$$

Note that

$$\frac{d}{dx}\left(\frac{(1+x)\ln(1+x)}{x^2}\right) = \frac{\ln(1+x)}{x^2} + \frac{1}{x^2} - 2\frac{(1+x)\ln(1+x)}{x^3}$$
$$= \frac{1}{x^3}\left(x - (x+2)\ln(x+1)\right) \leq 0,$$

because $(x-(x+2)\ln(x+1))$ is decreasing in x and is zero when $x = 0$. Hence, $d^*(n)$ is decreasing in n.

From the first-order condition and the decreasing property of $d^*(n)$, we have

$$d^*(n)^4 = \frac{3(1+d^*(n)^2)\ln(1+d^*(n)^2)}{n} \leq \frac{3(1+d^*(1)^2)\ln(1+d^*(1)^2)}{n}.$$

From the decreasing property and the first-order condition, we can show that $d^*(1) < 3$, which implies that $\frac{3(1+d^*(1)^2)\ln(1+d^*(1)^2)}{n} < \frac{30\ln(10)}{n}$. □

Lemma 2. *For some function $b(p_k)$ that is independent of n_k,*

$$|P(a_t^B = k) - P(p_k^B \geq p_j^B \text{ for every } j \neq k)| \leq \frac{b(p_k)}{\sqrt{n_k}}(1 + O(1/n_k)).$$

Proof. Note that

$$\begin{aligned} P(p_k^B \geq p_j^B \text{ for every } j \neq k) &= P(p_k^B \geq \max_{j\neq k} p_j^B) \\ &= P(p_k^B \geq \max_{j\neq k} p_j^B, a_t^B = k) + P(p_k^B \geq \max_{j\neq k} p_j^B, a_t^B \neq k) \\ &= P(a_t^B = k) + P(p_k^B \geq \max_{j\neq k} p_j^B, a_t^B \neq k). \end{aligned}$$

Let Y_k denote the binomial variable associated with p_k^B for each action k, i.e. $Y_k := n_k p_k^B$. Then,

$$\begin{aligned} |P(a_t^B = k) - P(p_k^B \geq \max_{j\neq k} p_j^B)| &= P(p_k^B \geq \max_{j\neq k} p_j^B, a_t^B \neq k) \\ &\leq P(p_k^B = \max_{j\neq k} p_j^B) \\ &= P(Y_k = n_k \max_{j\neq k} p_j^B) \\ &\leq \max_i P(Y_k = i) \\ &= \max_i \binom{n_k}{i} p_k^i (1-p_k)^{n_k - i}. \end{aligned}$$

One can show that the binomial p.d.f. with parameters (n,p) is maximized when $i = \lfloor (n+1)p \rfloor$. Using the fact that $n_k p_k$ is an integer and that $p_k \in (0,1)$, $\lfloor (n_k+1)p_k \rfloor = \lfloor n_k p_k + p_k \rfloor = n_k p_k$. Further, through applying Stirling's formula, $n! = \sqrt{2\pi n}\left(\frac{n}{e}\right)^n (1 + O(1/n))$, one obtains

$$\begin{aligned}
\binom{n_k}{n_k p_k} &= \frac{n_k!}{(n_k p_k)!(n_k - n_k p_k)!} \\
&= \sqrt{\frac{n_k}{2\pi n_k p_k (n_k - n_k p_k)}} \left(\frac{n_k}{n_k p_k}\right)^{n_k p_k} \left(\frac{n_k}{n_k - n_k p_k}\right)^{n_k - n_k p_k} (1 + O(1/n_k)) \\
&= \frac{1}{\sqrt{2\pi n_k p_k (1-p_k)}} \left(\frac{1}{p_k}\right)^{n_k p_k} \left(\frac{1}{1-p_k}\right)^{n_k - n_k p_k} (1 + O(1/n_k)) .
\end{aligned}$$

Thus,

$$\begin{aligned}
&\max_i \binom{n_k}{i} p_k^i (1-p_k)^{n_k - i} \\
&= \binom{n_k}{n_k p_k} p_k^{n_k p_k} (1-p_k)^{n_k - n_k p_k} \\
&= \frac{1}{\sqrt{2\pi n_k p_k (1-p_k)}} \left(\frac{1}{p_k}\right)^{n_k p_k} \left(\frac{1}{1-p_k}\right)^{n_k - n_k p_k} p_k^{n_k p_k} (1-p_k)^{n_k - n_k p_k} (1 + O(1/n_k)) \\
&= \frac{1}{\sqrt{2\pi n_k p_k (1-p_k)}} (1 + O(1/n_k)) ,
\end{aligned}$$

which proves the lemma. □

3 Pseudocode for Logistic UCB

Algorithm 0: LogisticUCB()

Define $\mathcal{L}(y) = \frac{e^y}{1+e^y}$
Define $\rho(s) = \sqrt{M \log s \log(sT/\delta)}$

Initialize $t_a = 0, X_{t,a} = I_M \; \forall a = 1, ..., K$

for $t = 1, ..., T$ **do**
  Observe context vector x_t
  for $a = 1, ..., K$ **do**
    $UCB_{t,a} = \mathcal{L}(x_t^T \hat{\theta}_{t,a_t}) + \rho(t_a) ||x_t||_{X_{t,a}^{-1}}$
  end
  Choose action $a_t = \arg\max_a UCB_{t,a}$

  Update $t_{a_t} = t_{a_t} + 1, X_{t+1,a_t} = X_{t,a_t} + x_t x_t^T$
  Update $\hat{\theta}_{t,a_t}$ with (x_t, r_{t,a_t})
end

Analysis of Thompson Sampling for Stochastic Sleeping Bandits

Aritra Chaterjee, Ganesh Ghalme, Shweta Jain, Rohit Vaish and **Y. Narahari**
Department of Computer Science and Automation, Indian Institute of Science, Bangalore, India
{aritra.chatterjee, ganesh.ghalme, jainshweta, rohit.vaish, hari}@csa.iisc.ernet.in

Abstract

We study a variant of the stochastic multi-armed bandit problem where the set of available arms varies arbitrarily with time (also known as the *sleeping bandit* problem). We focus on the Thompson Sampling algorithm and consider a regret notion defined with respect to the best *available* arm. Our main result is an $\mathcal{O}(\log T)$ regret bound for Thompson Sampling, which generalizes a similar bound known for this algorithm from the classical bandit setting. Our bound also matches (up to constants) the best-known lower bound for the sleeping bandit problem. We show via simulations that Thompson Sampling outperforms the UCB-style AUER algorithm for the sleeping bandit problem.

1 INTRODUCTION

In the classical *multi-armed bandit* (MAB) problem, an algorithm is required to choose one of the K available actions in each of the T rounds. Each choice of action generates a stochastic reward drawn from an unknown but fixed distribution. The goal of the algorithm is to maximize its expected sum of rewards over the T rounds, relative to the best-fixed action in hindsight (in other words, minimize its *regret*).

The MAB framework can model a variety of situations that involve sequential decision-making, such as online advertising, network routing, and cloud computing (refer to the survey by Bubeck and Cesa-Bianchi, 2012 for other applications). In many of these settings, however, not all of the actions are available at all stages. Indeed, some advertisers might choose to stay away from the auction due to budget constraints, some links might be unavailable due to congestion, and some servers might be unavailable due to maintenance - forcing the algorithm to work only with the set of *available* actions. Such problems fall under the *sleeping multi-armed bandit* (SMAB) model, which generalizes the standard MAB framework.

In the SMAB model, at each round, the algorithm is required to select an action from a set of *available* arms. Just like in the classical setting, the algorithm receives a stochastic reward based on the chosen action. However, unlike the classical setting, the performance of the algorithm can no longer be evaluated relative to a single fixed action, since each action might become unavailable at some stage of the algorithm. For this reason, the regret of an algorithm for SMAB (for a given set of availabilities of arms) is measured relative to the best *available* action in hindsight (refer to Section 3.1 for a formal definition). The overall regret of the algorithm is given by the worst-case regret over all settings of availabilities (i.e., under adversarial selection of the available arms).

The SMAB problem was first studied by Kleinberg et al. (2010) for both stochastic and adversarial rewards, and under adversarial availabilities. Their analysis focuses on the AUER algorithm, which is a variant of the well-known UCB1 algorithm for the classical MAB problem (Auer et al., 2002). Kleinberg et al. (2010) provide an $\mathcal{O}(\log T)$ bound on the regret of AUER and show that this is information-theoretically optimal (up to constants). However, their regret bound lacks a fine-grained dependence on the structure of availability of the arms.

Our interest in this paper is in studying the SMAB problem for a different algorithm called *Thompson Sampling* (Thompson, 1933). This algorithm has generated significant interest recently due to its impressive theoretical and empirical properties in the classical MAB setting (Chapelle and Li, 2011; Kaufmann et al., 2012; Agrawal and Goyal, 2012, 2013a). In this paper, we evaluate the performance of Thompson Sampling for the SMAB problem both from a theoretical and an empirical standpoint.

Our contributions

- On the theoretical side, we provide an $\mathcal{O}(\log T)$ regret bound for Thompson Sampling for the SMAB problem (Corollary 1). This bound generalizes the bound known for this algorithm from the classical setting (Kaufmann et al., 2012), and also matches (up to constants) the information-theoretic lower bound for the SMAB problem (Kleinberg et al., 2010). An interesting feature of our bound is that it provides a fine-grained dependence of the regret on the availabilities of the arms (Theorem 1).
- On the empirical side, we show through simulations on synthetic datasets that Thompson Sampling outperforms AUER algorithm for various settings of availabilities (Section 5). We also find that the performance of Thompson Sampling (across availabilities) is consistent with the prediction of our regret bound in Theorem 1.

2 RELATED WORK

The SMAB problem was first considered by Kleinberg et al. (2010). They formulate the notion of regret as the difference between the expected cumulative reward of algorithm and the expected reward from an optimal policy which picks arms according to the *best ordering* in hindsight. For this notion of regret, Kleinberg et al. (2010) proved an $\Omega(\log T)$ lower bound on regret for any algorithm for SMAB (Proposition 2), and provided a UCB-style algorithm (AUER) with a matching upper bound up to constants (Proposition 3). The notion of regret used in our work (defined in Section 3.1) is equivalent to that of Kleinberg et al. (2010) as in both cases the optimal policy picks the best among the available arms according to a fixed and unknown ordering. Follow-up work by Kanade et al. (2009) and Kanade and Steinke (2014) has studied settings where the rewards are adversarial while the availability of arms is either stochastic or adversarial.

The work of Kaufmann et al. (2012) on Thompson Sampling for the classical MAB setting is closest to ours. They provided an asymptotically-optimal regret bound - generalizing the previously-known logarithmic bound of Agrawal and Goyal (2012). Our regret bound can be seen as a generalization of this result to the sleeping MAB problem. However, unlike Kaufmann et al. (2012), our regret guarantee is not asymptotically-optimal.

Thompson Sampling can be adapted to several other variations of the classical MAB problem such as the budgeted MAB problem (Xia et al., 2015), multi-pull MAB problem (Komiyama et al., 2015) and contextual MAB problem (Agrawal and Goyal, 2013b). Several papers (Gentile et al., 2014; Li et al., 2016) have studied UCB-based algorithms for the contextual MAB setting, but Li and Chapelle (2012) showed through detailed simulations that Thompson Sampling performs competitively even in such settings.

3 PRELIMINARIES

3.1 THE MODEL

An instance of the *sleeping multi-armed bandit* (SMAB) problem is a tuple $\langle [K], \{\mu_i\}_{i\in[K]}, \{A_t\}_{t\in[T]}\rangle$, where $[K]$ denotes the set of arms $\{1, 2, \ldots, K\}$, $\mu_i \in (0, 1)$ denotes the Bernoulli parameter for arm i, $A_t \subseteq [K]$ denotes the set of available arms at time instant t, and the parameter $T \in \mathbb{N}$ denotes the *time horizon*. For simplicity, we will assume that $\mu_1 > \mu_2 > \cdots > \mu_K$. When $A_t = [K]$ at each time t, we recover the classical MAB model.

Table 1: Notation

Notation	Definition
$[K]$	Set of arms.
T	Time horizon (or the number of rounds).
A_t	Set of arms available at time t.
$\mathcal{A}$	Availability sequence $\{A_1, \ldots, A_T\}$.
μ_i	Bernoulli parameter (or mean) for arm i.
i_t	Arm pulled at time t.
r_t	Reward obtained at time t.
i_t^*	Best available (or optimal) arm at time t.
$\theta_{i,t}$	Thompson sample of arm i at time t.
$s_{i,t}$	Number of successful pulls of arm i until time t.
$n_{i,t}$	Number of pulls of arm i until time t.
$\Delta_{i,j}$	$\lvert\mu_i - \mu_j\rvert$.
$\delta_{i,j}$	$\Delta_{i,j}/2$.
$a_{i,t}$	Number of times arm i is available until time t.
$N_{i,j}(t)$	Number of times arm j is pulled until time t when some arm in $[i]$ is available.
$L_{i,j}$	$32/\Delta_{i,j}^2$.
$w_{i,t}$	Number of times arm i is optimal until time t.
$e_{i,t}$	$\sqrt{4\ln(w_{i,t})/n_{i,t}}$.
$Q_{i,j}$	$4\ln(w_{i,t})/\delta_{i,j}^2$.

An *algorithm* for SMAB is specified as follows: At each time instant t, the algorithm receives as input the set of available arms A_t. The algorithm then outputs the index of an arm $i_t \in A_t$, and observes a reward r_t drawn i.i.d. from a Bernoulli distribution with parameter μ_{i_t}. The arm i_t is said to be *pulled* by the algorithm at time t.

The performance of an algorithm for SMAB problem is measured in terms of its *regret*. In order to formalize this, let $\mathcal{A} := \{A_1, \ldots, A_T\}$ denote the sequence of the availability sets (we call $\mathcal{A}$ the *availability sequence*). For any time instant t, let $i_t \in A_t$ denote the arm pulled by the algorithm, and let $i_t^* \in \arg\max_{i \in A_t} \mu_i$ denote the best available (or *optimal*) arm. Then, the expected regret of the algorithm for a given availability sequence $\mathcal{A}$ is,

$$R_{\mathcal{A}}(T) = \mathbb{E}\left[\sum_{t=1}^{T} \mu_{i_t^*} - \mu_{i_t}\right],$$

where the expectation is taken over the random choices $\{i_t\}_{t \in [T]}$ made by the algorithm. The overall expected regret $R(T)$ of the algorithm is defined as its expected regret for the worst-case availability sequence, i.e.,

$$R(T) = \max_{\mathcal{A}} R_{\mathcal{A}}(T).$$

From here onwards, we will call $R(T)$ the *regret* of the algorithm, and $R_{\mathcal{A}}(T)$ the *availability-specific regret*. We remark that the time horizon T is used only in the analysis of regret, and is not used by the algorithm in deciding which arm to pull. Table 1 provides a list of the key notation used in the paper.

3.2 THOMPSON SAMPLING ALGORITHM FOR SMAB

Algorithm 1: Thompson Sampling (TS-SMAB)

Input : Set of arms $[K]$.
Output: Set of pulls $\{i_t\}_{t=1}^{T}$.

Initialize $s_{i,1} = 0$ and $n_{i,1} = 0$ for all $i \in [K]$.
for $t \leftarrow 1$ **to** T **do**
    Observe the set of available arms $A_t \subseteq [K]$.
    Sample $\theta_{i,t} \sim \text{Beta}(s_{i,t} + 1, n_{i,t} - s_{i,t} + 1)$ for each arm $i \in A_t$.
    Pull the arm $i_t \in \arg\max_{i \in A_t} \theta_{i,t}$. (ties are broken lexicographically)
    Observe reward $r_t \sim \text{Bernoulli}(\mu_{i_t})$.
    Update posterior
$$s_{i_t,t+1} \leftarrow s_{i_t,t} + r_t$$
$$n_{i_t,t+1} \leftarrow n_{i_t,t} + 1$$
    for $j \neq i_t$ **do**
$$s_{j,t+1} \leftarrow s_{j,t}$$
$$n_{j,t+1} \leftarrow n_{j,t}$$
    end
end

In this work, we focus on the *Thompson Sampling* algorithm for the SMAB problem (denoted by TS-SMAB). Algorithm 1 presents a pseudo-code of TS-SMAB. At each time instant t, the algorithm observes the set of available arms A_t, and draws samples from Beta distributions for each available arm. The arm with the largest sample is pulled by the algorithm, and the Beta posteriors are updated based on the observed reward.

We remark that that the rewards are considered to be Bernoulli distributed throughout the paper. However, the algorithm and regret analysis can be adapted to more general reward distributions with support $[0, 1]$ by the simple extension provided by Agrawal and Goyal (2012) (Algorithm 2).

4 REGRET ANALYSIS

Our main result is a logarithmic bound on the availability-specific regret of TS-SMAB (Theorem 1). This bound is stated in terms of $a_{j,T}$, which is the number of times arm j is available until time T, i.e., $a_{j,T} = |\{t \in [T] : j \in A_t\}|$. This directly leads to an $\mathcal{O}(\log T)$ regret bound for TS-SMAB in Corollary 1.

Theorem 1. *The availability-specific regret of TS-SMAB is given by*

$$R_{\mathcal{A}}(T) \leq \sum_{i<j} \frac{32 \ln(a_{j,T})}{\Delta_{i,j}^2} \cdot \Delta_{i,i+1} + \mathcal{O}(1),$$

where $\Delta_{i,j} = |\mu_i - \mu_j|$ denotes the absolute difference of the mean rewards of the arms i and j.

In order to facilitate comparison with the existing results, we will make two simplifications to the bound in Theorem 1: First, we will upper bound the term $a_{j,T}$ by T (thereby removing the dependence on $\mathcal{A}$). Second, we will use Proposition 1 below to rewrite the dependence on the Δ parameters.

Proposition 1 (Kleinberg et al., 2010)**.**

$$\sum_{j=2}^{K} \sum_{i=1}^{j-1} \Delta_{i,j}^{-2} \Delta_{i,i+1} \leq 2 \sum_{i=1}^{K-1} \Delta_{i,i+1}^{-1}.$$

Corollary 1. *The regret of TS-SMAB is given by*

$$R(T) \leq 64 \ln(T) \cdot \sum_{i=1}^{K-1} \frac{1}{\Delta_{i,i+1}} + \mathcal{O}(1).$$

We can now compare our regret bound in Corollary 1 with the known results. First, we observe that our bound is *information-theoretically optimal*, i.e., it matches (up to problem-independent constants) the following lower bound for SMAB problem due to Kleinberg et al. (2010):

Proposition 2 (Kleinberg et al., 2010)**.** *Let $\mu_i \in (a, b)$ for all $i \in [K]$ and some $0 < a < b < 1$, s.t. $\mu_1 > \mu_2 > \ldots > \mu_K$. Then, the regret of any algorithm for SMAB is at least*

$$\Omega\left(\ln(T) \cdot \sum_{i=1}^{K-1} \frac{1}{\Delta_{i,i+1}}\right).$$

Next, we remark that our bound in Corollary 1 for TS-SMAB is identical to that of the AUER algorithm for SMAB.

Proposition 3 (Kleinberg et al., 2010)**.** *The regret of AUER algorithm for SMAB is given by*

$$R(T) \leq 64 \ln(T) \cdot \sum_{i=1}^{K-1} \frac{1}{\Delta_{i,i+1}} + \mathcal{O}(1).$$

Finally, our bound in Corollary 1 matches the bound for Thompson Sampling for *classical* MAB setting up to problem-dependent constants.

Proposition 4 (Kaufmann et al., 2012)**.** *Let $A_t = [K]$ for all $t \in [T]$. Then, the availability-specific regret of TS-SMAB is given by*

$$R_{\mathcal{A}}(T) \leq \sum_{i=2}^{K} \frac{\ln(T) + \ln\ln(T)}{\mathrm{KL}(\mu_i, \mu_1)} + \mathcal{O}(1).$$

4.1 PROOF OF MAIN RESULT (THEOREM 1)

Our proof for the regret bound in Theorem 1 relies on a key lemma (Lemma 1), which bounds the expected number of *suboptimal* pulls of any arm. A suboptimal pull is said to occur at time t if the algorithm pulls an arm $j \in A_t$ when a better arm i is available, i.e., $i_t = j$ and $\mu_i > \mu_j$. We use $N_{i,j}(t)$ to denote the number of times a fixed arm j is pulled until time t whenever some arm in the set $\{1, \ldots, i\}$ is available, i.e., $N_{i,j}(t) = |\{t' \in [T] : t' \leq t, i_{t'} = j, A_{t'} \cap [i] \neq \emptyset\}|$.

Lemma 1 (Bound on suboptimal pulls)**.** *For any pair of arms i and j such that $\mu_i > \mu_j$, we have*

$$\mathbb{E}[N_{i,j}(T)] \leq L_{i,j} \ln(a_{j,T}) + \mathcal{O}(1),$$

where $L_{i,j} = 32/\Delta_{i,j}^2$.

We will now present the proof of Theorem 1, followed by the proof of Lemma 1.

Proof of Theorem 1. We reduce the problem of upper-bounding the availability-specific regret to upper-bounding the expected number of suboptimal pulls.

$$R_{\mathcal{A}}(T) = \mathbb{E}\left[\sum_{i<j} (N_{i,j} - N_{i-1,j})\Delta_{i,j}\right]$$

$$= \mathbb{E}\left[\sum_{i<j} N_{i,j}(\Delta_{i,j} - \Delta_{i+1,j})\right]$$

(we follow the convention $N_{0,j} = 0$)

$$= \sum_{i<j} \Delta_{i,i+1} \cdot \mathbb{E}[N_{i,j}]$$

$$\leq \sum_{i<j} \Delta_{i,i+1} \cdot [L_{i,j} \ln(a_{j,T}) + \mathcal{O}(1)]$$

(Using Lemma 1)

$$= \sum_{i<j} \frac{32 \ln(a_{j,T})}{\Delta_{i,j}^2} \cdot \Delta_{i,i+1} + \mathcal{O}(1). \qquad \square$$

4.2 PROOF OF KEY LEMMA (LEMMA 1)

Our proof of Lemma 1 makes use of three intermediate results—Lemmas 2 to 4. Below, we state each of these results, followed by the proof of Lemma 1.

Our first two results (Lemmas 2 and 3) formalize the idea that pulling an arm j sufficiently many times results in the concentration of its Thompson samples around the mean. The proofs of these results follow from standard concentration arguments, and are deferred to the appendix (Sections B.1 and B.2).

Lemma 2. *Let $i, j \in [K]$ be a pair of arms such that $i < j$, and let $L_{i,j} = 32/\Delta_{i,j}^2$. Then, at any time $t \leq T$,*

$$\mathbb{P}(\theta_{j,t} \geq \mu_j + \Delta_{i,j}/2, n_{j,t} \geq L_{i,j} \ln(a_{j,T})) \leq 2a_{j,T}^{-3}.$$

Lemma 3. *Let $e_{i,t} = \sqrt{\frac{4\ln(w_{i,t})}{n_{i,t}}}$ for any arm i. Then, at any time t, we have,*

$$\mathbb{P}(\theta_{i,t} \leq \mu_i - e_{i,t}) \leq w_{i,t}^{-2},$$

where $w_{i,t}$ denotes the number of times arm i is the best available arm until time t.

Our next result (Lemma 4) is at the heart of our analysis, and is also technically the most involved. It associates the number of "optimal appearances" of an arm (i.e., the time instants at which a given arm is the best available arm) with the number of times it is pulled by the algorithm. More formally, for a given arm $i \in [K]$, let $w_{i,t}$ denote the number of time instants (until time t) where i is the best available arm. Then, Lemma 4 states that the number of times arm i is pulled by TS-SMAB (denoted by $n_{i,t}$) cannot be much smaller than $w_{i,t}$.

Lemma 4. *For each arm $i \in [K]$, there exist constants $b \in (0, 1)$ and $C_{i,b} < \infty$ such that*

$$\sum_{t \geq 1} \mathbb{P}\big(n_{i,t} \leq w_{i,t}^b\big) \leq C_{i,b}.$$

The proof of Lemma 4 extensively uses the techniques of Kaufmann et al. (2012), and is covered in Section 4.3. We now present the proof of Lemma 1 using Lemmas 2 to 4.

Proof of Lemma 1. Let $\zeta_{i,j}$ denote the set of all time instants until T for which the set of available arms includes the arm j and some arm in the set $\{1,\dots,i\}$, i.e., $\zeta_{i,j} = \{t \in [T] : A_t \cap [i] \neq \emptyset, j \in A_t\}$. Thus, $|\zeta_{i,j}| \geq N_{i,j}(T)$. We therefore have

$$\begin{aligned}
&\mathbb{E}[N_{ij}(T)] \\
&\leq \sum_{t\in\zeta_{i,j}} \mathbb{P}(i_t = j, A_t \cap [i] \neq \emptyset) \\
&\leq \sum_{t\in\zeta_{i,j}} \mathbb{P}(i_t = j, A_t \cap [i] \neq \emptyset, n_{j,t} \geq L_{i,j}\ln(a_{j,T})) \\
&\quad + L_{i,j}\ln(a_{j,T}). \qquad (1)
\end{aligned}$$

The first term on the right can be analyzed as follows:

$$\begin{aligned}
&\sum_{t\in\zeta_{i,j}} \mathbb{P}(i_t = j, A_t \cap [i] \neq \emptyset, n_{j,t} \geq L_{i,j}\ln(a_{j,T})) \\
&\leq \sum_{t\in\zeta_{i,j}} \mathbb{P}\Bigg(\underbrace{\theta_{j,t} \geq \theta_{h_t,t}}_{E_1}, \underbrace{n_{j,t} \geq L_{i,j}\ln(a_{j,T})}_{E_2}\Bigg),
\end{aligned}$$

where $h_t := \arg\max_{k\in[i]\cap A_t} \mu_k$ denotes the best available arm in the set $\{1,\dots,i\}$, and the event E_1 follows from the semantics of Thompson Sampling. We now use

$$\begin{aligned}
\mathbb{P}(E_1E_2) &= \mathbb{P}(E_1E_2E_3) + \mathbb{P}(E_1E_2E_3^c) \\
&\leq \mathbb{P}(E_1E_3) + \mathbb{P}(E_2E_3^c).
\end{aligned}$$

Thus,

$$\begin{aligned}
&\sum_{t\in\zeta_{i,j}} \mathbb{P}(i_t = j, A_t \cap [i] \neq \emptyset, n_{j,t} \geq L_{i,j}\ln(a_{j,T})) \\
&\leq \sum_{t\in\zeta_{i,j}} \mathbb{P}\Bigg(\underbrace{\theta_{j,t} \geq \theta_{h_t,t}}_{E_1}, \underbrace{\mu_j + \delta_{i,j} > \theta_{j,t}}_{E_3}\Bigg) \\
&\quad + \sum_{t\in\zeta_{i,j}} \mathbb{P}\Bigg(\underbrace{\theta_{j,t} \geq \mu_j + \delta_{i,j}}_{E_3^c}, \underbrace{n_{j,t} \geq L_{i,j}\ln(a_{j,T})}_{E_2}\Bigg), \\
&\qquad\qquad (\text{where } \delta_{i,j} = \Delta_{i,j}/2) \\
&\leq \sum_{t\in\zeta_{i,j}} \mathbb{P}(\mu_j + \delta_{i,j} \geq \theta_{h_t,t}) + \sum_{t\in\zeta_{i,j}} 2a_{j,T}^{-3} \\
&\qquad\qquad (\text{Using Lemma 2}) \\
&\leq \sum_{t\in\zeta_{i,j}} \mathbb{P}(\mu_j + \delta_{i,j} \geq \theta_{h_t,t}, \theta_{h_t,t} > \mu_{h_t} - e_{h_t,t}) \\
&\quad + \sum_{t\in\zeta_{i,j}} \mathbb{P}(\theta_{h_t,t} \leq \mu_{h_t} - e_{h_t,t}) + \sum_{i=1}^{a_{j,T}} 2a_{j,T}^{-3} \\
&\leq \sum_{t\in\zeta_{i,j}} \mathbb{P}(\mu_j + \delta_{i,j} \geq \mu_{h_t} - e_{h_t,t}) + \sum_{t\in\zeta_{i,j}} w_{h_t,t}^{-2} + 2a_{j,T}^{-2} \\
&\qquad\qquad (\text{Using Lemma 3}) \\
&\leq \sum_{t\in\zeta_{i,j}} \mathbb{P}(\mu_j + \delta_{h_t,j} \geq \mu_{h_t} - e_{h_t,t}) + \sum_{t\in\zeta_{i,j}} w_{h_t,t}^{-2} + \mathcal{O}(1) \\
&\leq \sum_{t\in\zeta_{i,j}} \mathbb{P}(-\delta_{h_t,j} \geq -e_{h_t,j}) + \sum_{t\in\zeta_{i,j}} w_{h_t,t}^{-2} + \mathcal{O}(1) \\
&\leq \sum_{t\in\zeta_{i,j}} \mathbb{P}(n_{h_t,t} \leq Q_{h_t,j}) + \sum_{k\leq i}\sum_{w_{k,t}\geq 1} w_{k,t}^{-2} + \mathcal{O}(1) \\
&\qquad\qquad \Big(Q_{h_t,j} := \tfrac{4\ln(w_{h_t,t})}{\delta_{h_t,j}^2}.\Big) \\
&\leq \sum_{t\in\zeta_{i,j}} \mathbb{P}\Big(n_{h_t,t} \leq Q_{h_t,j}, Q_{h_t,j} \leq w_{h_t,t}^b\Big) \\
&\quad + \sum_{t\in\zeta_{i,j}} \mathbb{P}\Big(n_{h_t,t} \leq Q_{h_t,j}, Q_{h_t,j} > w_{h_t,t}^b\Big) + \mathcal{O}(1) \\
&\leq \sum_{t\in\zeta_{i,j}} \mathbb{P}\Big(n_{h_t,t} \leq w_{h_t,t}^b\Big) + \sum_{t\in\zeta_{i,j}} \mathbb{P}\Big(Q_{h_t,j} > w_{h_t,t}^b\Big) \\
&\quad + \mathcal{O}(1) \\
&\leq \sum_{k\leq i}\sum_{w_{k,t}\geq 1} \mathbb{P}\Big(n_{k,t} \leq w_{k,t}^b\Big) + \sum_{k\leq i}\sum_{w_{k,t}\geq 1} \mathbb{P}\Big(Q_{k,j} > w_{k,t}^b\Big) \\
&\quad + \mathcal{O}(1) \\
&\leq \sum_{k\leq i} C_{k,b} + \mathcal{O}(1) + \mathcal{O}(1) \qquad (\text{Using Lemma 4}) \\
&= \mathcal{O}(1).
\end{aligned}$$

The $\mathcal{O}(1)$ bound on the term $\mathbb{P}\Big(Q_{k,j} > w_{k,t}^b\Big)$ follows from the observation that $Q_{k,j}$ is logarithmic in $w_{k,t}$, while $w_{k,t}^b$ is a polynomial. Along with Equation (1), the above bound gives the desired result. □

4.3 PROOF OF LEMMA 4

Outline of the proof: The description of the proof is made convenient by defining three different timescales. We use the term *original timeline* to refer to the time instants $t = 1, 2, \dots$ and so on. The top-row in Figure 1 shows the original timeline. For a fixed arm i, let *i-awake timeline* denote the set of time instants for which arm i is available, shown as the middle row in Figure 1. Let $\tau_j^{(i)}$ denote the time instant (according to the original timeline) at which arm i is pulled for the jth time (where $\tau_0^{(i)} := 0$). Consider the time interval (on the i-awake timeline) between the jth and $(j+1)^{\text{th}}$ pulls of arm i (i.e., between $\tau_j^{(i)}$ and $\tau_{j+1}^{(i)}$). For this interval, let $\xi_j^{(i)}$ denote the set of time instants when arm i is the best available arm, i.e., $\xi_j^{(i)} = \Big\{t \in [T] : \tau_j^{(i)} < t < \tau_{j+1}^{(i)}, i \in A_t, A_t \cap [i-1] = \emptyset\Big\}$.

We refer to the set $\xi_j^{(i)}$ as the *i-optimal timeline*. Hence, the three timelines defined above are zoomed in (or

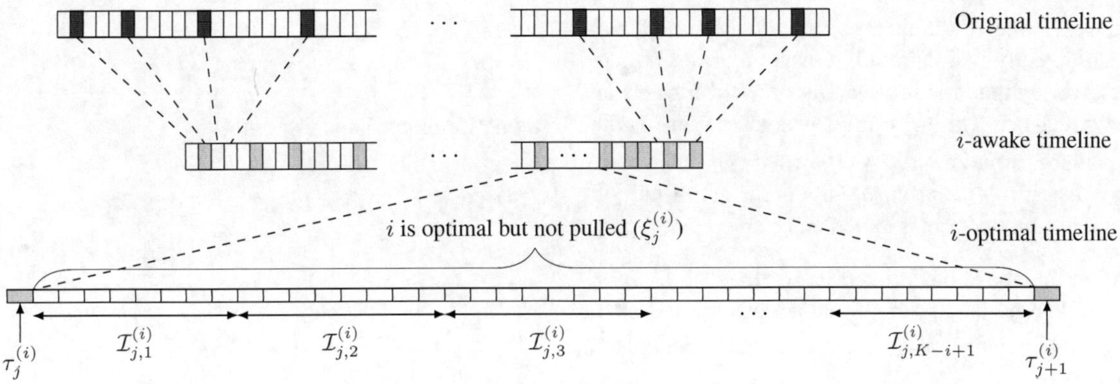

Figure 1: The top row shows the original timeline, and the highlighted squares denote the time instants when arm i is available. The middle row shows the i-awake timeline (i.e., time instants when arm i is always available), and the highlighted squares represent the pulls of arm i. The bottom row zooms into the time instants between consecutive pulls of arm i, and shows the set of time instants where arm i is the best available arm but not pulled.

zoomed out) versions of each other.

Our goal in the proof will be to show that the i-optimal timeline cannot be too long. In other words, we will show that there cannot be a long run of time instants where arm i is the best available arm but is not pulled by the algorithm. This, in turn, will help us argue that the number of pulls of arm i (namely, $n_{i,t}$) cannot "lag behind" the number of optimal appearances of arm i (namely, $w_{i,t}$), giving us the desired result.

More specifically, we define $E_j^{(i)}$ as the event that the length of the i-optimal timeline ($|\xi_j^{(i)}|$) is at least $w_{i,t}^{1-b} - 1$. Under this event, starting from the instant $\tau_j^{(i)}$, we divide the i-optimal timeline into $(K-i+1)$ intervals, denoted by $\mathcal{I}_{j,l}^{(i)}$ for $l \in [K-i+1]$, each of length $\left\lceil \frac{w_{i,t}^{1-b}-1}{K-i+1} \right\rceil$ for some constant $b \in (0,1)$. (Hence, it is possible that the tail-end of the i-optimal timeline is not covered by these intervals). This division is shown in the bottom row in Figure 1.

Our proof is structured as follows:

- Step 1 of the proof reduces the problem to analyzing the event $E_j^{(i)}$.
- Steps 2 and 3 analyze the two mutually disjoint and exhaustive events, namely $E_j^{(i)} \cap F_{j,l}^{(i)}$ and $E_j^{(i)} \cap \overline{F_{j,l}^{(i)}}$, obtained via decomposition of the event $E_j^{(i)}$. The former describes the event where all suboptimal actions have been played sufficiently many times by the end of the interval $\mathcal{I}_{j,K-i}^{(i)}$, so that their samples are well-concentrated. Therefore, the probability of pulling a suboptimal arm during the interval $\mathcal{I}_{j,K-i+1}^{(i)}$ is very small. The latter describes the event that some suboptimal arm has not been played sufficiently often. For this case, we show that at the end of each interval $\mathcal{I}_{j,l}^{(i)}$, the algorithm must sample some (underexplored) suboptimal arm sufficiently many times. Since there are at least as many intervals as there are suboptimal arms, this gives a probability bound on the second event as well.

It is worth pointing out that the above proof outline closely follows the arguments of Kaufmann et al. (2012), who consider the analysis of Thompson Sampling in the classical MAB setting. The important difference lies in the conceptualization of the i-awake and the i-optimal timelines: In the model of Kaufmann et al. (2012), arm 1 is always available, hence analysis with respect to the original timeline suffices. In the SMAB problem, however, this is no more the case, and therefore we need to make the above arguments over different timescales.

Proof of Lemma 4. Let us fix an arm i. For any arm $a > i$, let $n_{a,t}^{(i)}$ denote the number of pulls of arm a over all time instants until time t whenever i is the best available arm. Notice that $\sum_{a>i} n_{a,t}^{(i)} = \sum_{j=0}^{n_{i,t}} \left|\xi_j^{(i)}\right|$.

Step 1: Reducing the problem to the analysis of $E_j^{(i)}$.

$$\begin{aligned}
&\mathbb{P}\left(n_{i,t} \le w_{i,t}^{b}\right)\\
&\le \mathbb{P}\left(n_{i,t}^{(i)} \le w_{i,t}^{b}\right) = \mathbb{P}\left(\sum_{a>i} n_{a,t}^{(i)} \ge w_{i,t} - w_{i,t}^{b}\right)\\
&\le \mathbb{P}\left(\exists j \in \left\{0, \dots, \lfloor w_{i,t}^{b} \rfloor\right\} : \left|\xi_j^{(i)}\right| \ge w_{i,t}^{1-b} - 1\right)\\
&\le \sum_{j=0}^{\lfloor w_{i,t}^{b} \rfloor} \mathbb{P}\Big(\underbrace{\left|\xi_j^{(i)}\right| \ge w_{i,t}^{1-b} - 1}_{E_j^{(i)}}\Big).
\end{aligned} \tag{2}$$

Next, we formalize the idea of sampling a suboptimal arm "sufficiently many times". Given an arm a (where $a > i$), we say that a is *saturated* at time t if it has been pulled at least $L_{i,a} \ln(w_{i,t})$ times whenever arm i is the best available arm, i.e., $n_{a,t}^{(i)} \geq L_{i,a} \ln(w_{i,t})$. Otherwise, we say that arm a is *unsaturated*, and the act of pulling such an unsaturated arm is called an *interruption*.

Based on the above definitions, let us define $F_{j,l}^{(i)}$ to be the event that at least l suboptimal actions are saturated by the end of the interval $\mathcal{I}_{j,l}^{(i)}$. We also let $\gamma_{j,l}^{(i)}$ denote the number of interruptions during $\mathcal{I}_{j,l}^{(i)}$. A simple decomposition of $E_j^{(i)}$ gives us

$$\mathbb{P}\left(E_j^{(i)}\right) = \mathbb{P}\left(E_j^{(i)} \cap F_{j,K-i}^{(i)}\right) + \mathbb{P}\left(E_j^{(i)} \cap \overline{F_{j,K-i}^{(i)}}\right). \quad (3)$$

We analyze the two terms separately in Steps 2 and 3.

Step 2: In this step, we analyze the first term in Equation (3). Observe that the event $E_j^{(i)} \cap F_{j,K-i}^{(i)}$ implies that only the saturated arms are pulled during $\mathcal{I}_{j,K-i+1}^{(i)}$. Let $A := \{E_j^{(i)} \cap F_{j,K-i}^{(i)}\}$. Then,

$$\begin{aligned}
&\mathbb{P}\left(E_j^{(i)} \cap F_{j,K-i}^{(i)}\right) \\
&\leq \mathbb{P}\left(\left\{\exists t' \in \mathcal{I}_{j,K-i+1}^{(i)}, a > i : \theta_{a,t'} > \mu_a + \delta_{i,a}\right\} \cap A\right) \\
&\quad + \mathbb{P}\left(\left\{\forall t' \in \mathcal{I}_{j,K-i+1}^{(i)}, a > i : \theta_{a,t'} \leq \mu_a + \delta_{i,a}\right\} \cap A\right) \\
&\leq \mathbb{P}\Big(\exists t' \in \mathcal{I}_{j,K-i+1}^{(i)}, a > i : \theta_{a,t'} > \mu_a + \delta_{i,a}, \\
&\qquad\qquad n_{a,t}^{(i)} > L_{i,a} \ln(w_{i,t})\Big) \\
&\quad + \mathbb{P}\left(\left\{\forall t' \in \mathcal{I}_{j,K-i+1}^{(i)}, a > i : \theta_{a,t'} \leq y_i\right\} \cap A\right). \\
&\qquad\qquad (\text{where } y_i = \mu_{i+1} + \delta_{i,i+1})
\end{aligned}$$

We now use the following two results (Lemmas 5 and 6) whose proofs are deferred to the appendix (Sections B.3 and B.4).

Lemma 5. *For any fixed arm $a > i$,*

$$\mathbb{P}\left(\exists\, t' \in \mathcal{I}_{j,l}^{(i)} : \theta_{a,t'} \geq \mu_a + \delta_{i,a}, n_{a,t'}^{(i)} \geq L_{i,a} \ln(w_{i,t})\right) \leq 2 w_{i,t}^{-2+b}.$$

Lemma 6. *There exists a constant $\lambda_0 > 1$ such that for all $\lambda \in (1, \lambda_0)$, for any interval $\mathcal{J}^{(i)} \subseteq \cup_{l \in [K-i+1]} \mathcal{I}_{j,l}^{(i)}$ and for every positive function f, we have*

$$\begin{aligned}
&\mathbb{P}\left(\{\forall s \in \mathcal{J}^{(i)} : \theta_{i,s} \leq y_i\} \cap \{\left|\mathcal{J}^{(i)}\right| \geq f(t)\}\right) \\
&\leq (\alpha_i)^{f(t)} + C_{\lambda,i} \frac{1}{f(t)^{\lambda}} e^{-j d_{\lambda,i}},
\end{aligned}$$

where $C_{\lambda,i} > 0$, $d_{\lambda,i} > 0$, $\alpha_i = \left(\frac{1}{2}\right)^{1-\mu_{i+1}-\delta_i}$ and $y_i = \mu_{i+1} + \delta_{i,i+1}$ for every $i \in \{1, \ldots, K-1\}$.

Using Lemmas 5 and 6, we get

$$\begin{aligned}
&\mathbb{P}\left(E_j^{(i)} \cap F_{j,K-i}^{(i)}\right) \\
&\leq \frac{2}{w_{i,t}^{2+b}} + (\alpha_i)^{\frac{w_{i,t}^{1-b}-1}{K-i+1}} + C_{\lambda,i} \left(\frac{w_{i,t}^{1-b} - 1}{K-i+1}\right)^{-\lambda} e^{-j d_{\lambda,i}} \\
&= \frac{2}{w_{i,t}^{2+b}} + g(i, b, j, t).
\end{aligned}$$

Thus, $b < 1 - \frac{1}{\lambda} \Rightarrow \sum_{w_{i,t} \geq 1} \sum_{j \leq w_{i,t}^b} g(i, j, b, t) < +\infty.$

Step 3: This step provides the analysis for the second term in Equation (3). We claim that for any $2 \leq l \leq K$ and any time instant t greater than some constant $N_{i,b}$,

$$\mathbb{P}\left(E_j^{(i)} \cap \overline{F_{j,l-1}^{(i)}}\right) \leq (l-2)\left(\frac{2}{w_{i,t}^{2+b}} + f(i, b, j, t)\right).$$

We prove the above through induction over l. First, for the base case, observe that there exists a constant $N_{i,b}$ such that $w_{i,t} \geq N_{i,b} \Rightarrow \left\lceil \frac{w_{i,t}^{1-b}-1}{(K-i+1)^2} \right\rceil \geq L^{(i)} \ln(w_{i,t})$, (where $L^{(i)} = \max_{j>i} L_{i,j} = L_{i,i+1}$) which implies that at least one arm will be saturated by the end of interval $\mathcal{I}_{j,1}^{(i)}$. Hence for $w_{i,t} \geq N_{i,b}$, we have $\mathbb{P}\left(E_j^{(i)} \cap \overline{F_{j,1}^{(i)}}\right) = 0$. Next, we assume that the induction hypothesis holds for some $2 \leq l \leq K-i$.

Then,

$$\begin{aligned}
&\mathbb{P}\left(E_j^{(i)} \cap \overline{F_{j,l}^{(i)}}\right) \\
&\leq \mathbb{P}\left(E_j^{(i)} \cap \overline{F_{j,l-1}^{(i)}}\right) + \mathbb{P}\left(E_j^{(i)} \cap \overline{F_{j,l}^{(i)}} \cap F_{j,l-1}^{(i)}\right) \\
&\leq (l-2)\left(\frac{2}{w_{i,t}^{2+b}} + f(i, b, j, t)\right) \\
&\quad + \mathbb{P}\left(E_j^{(i)} \cap \overline{F_{j,l}^{(i)}} \cap F_{j,l-1}^{(i)}\right).
\end{aligned}$$

Hence, we need to show that

$$\mathbb{P}\left(E_j^{(i)} \cap \overline{F_{j,l}^{(i)}} \cap F_{j,l-1}^{(i)}\right) \leq \frac{2}{w_{i,t}^{2+b}} + f(i, b, j, t).$$

Observe that the event $E_j^{(i)} \cap \overline{F_{j,l}^{(i)}} \cap F_{j,l-1}^{(i)}$ implies that exactly $(l-1)$ arms are saturated at the beginning of interval $\mathcal{I}_{j,l}^{(i)}$, and no new arm is saturated during this interval. Hence, no unsaturated arm can be pulled more than $L^{(i)}\ln(w_{i,t})$ times, and thus, there cannot be more than $L^{(i)}(K-i)\ln(w_{i,t})$ interruptions during this interval. Let $\mathcal{S}_l^{(i)}$ denote the set of saturated arms at the end of $\mathcal{I}_{j,l}^{(i)}$. Then,

$$\begin{aligned}
&\mathbb{P}\Big(E_j^{(i)} \cap \overline{F_{j,l}^{(i)}} \cap F_{j,l-1}^{(i)}\Big)\\
&< \mathbb{P}\Big(E_j^{(i)} \cap F_{j,l-1}^{(i)} \cap \Big\{\gamma_{j,l}^{(i)} \le L^{(i)}(K-i)\ln(w_{i,t})\Big\}\Big)\\
&\le \mathbb{P}\Big(\Big\{\exists t' \in \mathcal{I}_{j,l}^{(i)}, a \in \mathcal{S}_{l-1}^{(i)} : \theta_{a,t'} > \mu_a + \delta_{i,a}\Big\}\\
&\qquad\qquad \cap E_j^{(i)} \cap F_{j,l-1}^{(i)}\Big)\\
&\quad + \underbrace{\mathbb{P}\Big(\Big\{\forall t' \in \mathcal{I}_{j,l}^{(i)}, a \in \mathcal{S}_{l-1}^{(i)} : \theta_{a,t'} \le \mu_a + \delta_{i,a}\Big\} \cap E_j^{(i)} \cap F_{j,l-1}^{(i)} \cap \Big\{\gamma_{j,l}^{(i)} \le L^{(i)}(K-i)\ln(w_{i,t})\Big\}\Big)}_{B}\\
&\le \mathbb{P}\Big(\exists t' \in \mathcal{I}_{j,l}^{(i)}, a > i : \theta_{a,t'} > \mu_a + \delta_{i,a},\\
&\qquad\qquad n_{a,t'}^{(i)} > L_{i,a}\ln(w_{i,t})\Big) + \mathbb{P}(B)\\
&\le \frac{2}{w_{i,t}^{2+b}} + \mathbb{P}(B). \qquad \text{(Using Lemma 5)}
\end{aligned}$$

In order to bound $\mathbb{P}(B)$, we define for $k \in \{0,\ldots,\gamma_{j,l}^{(i)}\}$, the random intervals $\mathcal{J}_k^{(i)}$ as the time range between k^{th} and $(k+1)^{\text{th}}$ interruption in $\mathcal{I}_{j,l}^{(i)}$. The event B implies there is an interval of $\mathcal{I}_{j,l}^{(i)}$ of length $\left\lceil \frac{w_{i,t}^{1-b}-1}{L^{(i)}(K-i)^2\ln(w_{i,t})}\right\rceil$ during which there are no interruptions, which, in turn, implies that the Thompson samples of the unsaturated arms are smaller than the highest Thompson sample of the saturated arms. Thus,

$$\begin{aligned}
&\mathbb{P}(B)\\
&\le \mathbb{P}\Bigg(\Bigg\{\exists k \in \{0,\ldots,\gamma_{j,l}^{(i)}\} : |\mathcal{J}_k^{(i)}| \ge \frac{w_{i,t}^{1-b}-1}{L^{(i)}(K-i)^2\ln(w_{i,t})}\Bigg\}\\
&\qquad \cap \{\forall t' \in \mathcal{I}_{j,l}^{(i)}, a \in \mathcal{S}_{l-1}^{(i)} : \theta_{a,t'} \le y_i\} \cap E_j^{(i)} \cap F_{j,l-1}^{(i)}\Bigg)\\
&\qquad\qquad \text{(where } y_i = \mu_{i+1} + \delta_{i,i+1})\\
&\le \sum_{k=1}^{(K-i)L^{(i)}\ln(w_{i,t})} \mathbb{P}\Bigg(\Bigg\{|\mathcal{J}_k^{(i)}| \ge \frac{w_{i,t}^{1-b}-1}{L^{(i)}(K-i)^2\ln(w_{i,t})}\Bigg\}\\
&\qquad \cap \{\forall s \in \mathcal{J}_k^{(i)}, a > i : \theta_{a,s} \le y_i\} \cap E_j^{(i)}\Bigg)\\
&\le \sum_{k=1}^{(K-i)L^{(i)}\ln(w_{i,t})} \mathbb{P}\Bigg(\Bigg\{|\mathcal{J}_k^{(i)}| \ge \frac{w_{i,t}^{1-b}-1}{L^{(i)}(K-i)^2\ln(w_{i,t})}\Bigg\}\\
&\qquad \cap \{\theta_{i,s} \le y_i\} \cap E_j^{(i)}\Bigg)
\end{aligned}$$

$$\begin{aligned}
&\le (K-i)L^{(i)}\ln(w_{i,t})(\alpha_i)^{\frac{w_{i,t}^{1-b}-1}{L^{(i)}(K-i)^2\ln(w_{i,t})}}\\
&\quad + C_{\lambda,i}\frac{L^{(i)}(K-i)\ln(w_{i,t})}{\left(\frac{w_{i,t}^{1-b}-1}{L^{(i)}(K-i)^2\ln(w_{i,t})}\right)^{\lambda}}e^{-jd_{\lambda,i}}\\
&:= f(i,b,j,t).
\end{aligned}$$

Once again we get $\sum_{w_{i,t}\ge 1}\sum_{j\le w_{i,t}^b} f(i,j,b,t) < +\infty$.

Putting it all together: From Equation (3) we get

$$\begin{aligned}
\mathbb{P}\Big(E_j^{(i)}\Big) &\le (K-i-1)\Bigg(\frac{2}{w_{i,t}^{2+b}} + f(i,b,j,t)\Bigg)\\
&\quad + \frac{2}{w_{i,t}^{2+b}} + g(i,b,j,t)\\
&\le \frac{2(K-i)}{w_{i,t}^{2+b}} + Kf(i,b,j,t) + g(i,b,j,t).
\end{aligned}$$

Thus, from Equation (2) we obtain

$$\begin{aligned}
&\sum_{t\ge 1}\mathbb{P}\Big(n_{i,t} \le w_{i,t}^b\Big)\\
&\le N_{i,b} + \sum_{w_{i,t}\ge 1}\sum_{j\le a_{i,t}^b}[Kf(i,b,j,t) + g(i,b,j,t)]\\
&\quad + 2(K-i)\sum_{w_{i,t}\ge 1}\sum_{j\le w_{i,t}^b}\frac{1}{w_{i,t}^{2+b}}\\
&\le N_{i,b} + \sum_{w_{i,t}\ge 1}\sum_{j\le w_{i,t}^b}[Kf(i,b,j,t) + g(i,b,j,t)]\\
&\quad + 2(K-i)\sum_{w_{i,t}\ge 1}\frac{1}{w_{i,t}^2}\\
&\le C_{i,b},
\end{aligned}$$

where, $C_{i,b}$ is some finite constant, as desired. □

5 EXPERIMENTAL RESULTS

In this section, we describe our experimental results comparing the performance of TS-SMAB and AUER algorithms for the SMAB problem. We work with SMAB instances where $K = 10$, $T = 10^5$, $\mu_1 = 0.5$, and $\Delta_{i,i+1} = 0.01$ for all $i \in [K-1]$. We consider the following three settings of the availability sequences of the arms: (1) The *classical MAB* setting, where each arm is available at every time instant, (2) the *changing suboptimal arm* setting, where arm 1 is always available, along with one other suboptimal arm (which changes constantly), i.e., $A_1 = \{1,2\}$, $A_2 = \{1,3\}$,..., $A_K = \{1,K\}$, $A_{K+1} = \{1,2\}$ and so on, and (3) the *random availability* setting, where each arm is (independently) available at every time instant with probability 0.5.

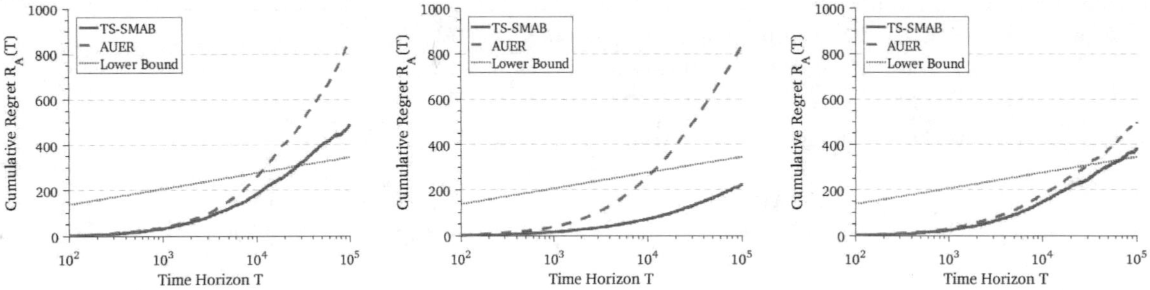

Figure 2: Comparing the regret of AUER and TS-SMAB algorithms for each of the three availability settings.

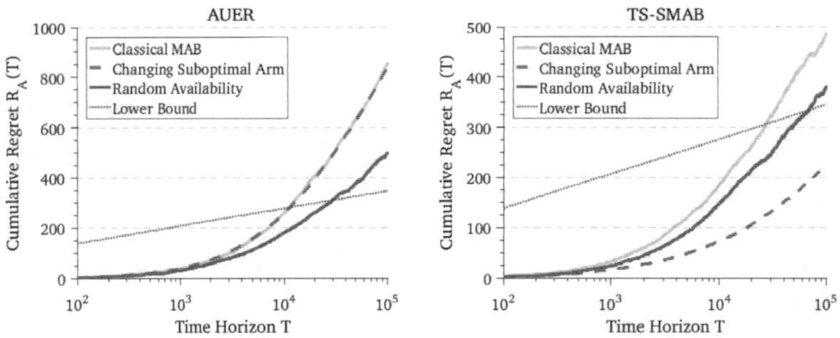

Figure 3: Evaluating each algorithm (AUER and TS-SMAB) across all three availability settings.

Figures 2 and 3 present our results. Each plot in Figure 2 compares the performance of TS-SMAB and AUER for one of the three availability settings described above. Each plot in Figure 3 pertains to a fixed algorithm, and evaluates its performance across the three availability settings. The regret values in each case are averaged over 1000 runs of the algorithm for each value of the time horizon T. We remark that the figures plot the actual expected regret accumulated in the simulations and not the theoretical upper bounds on the regret. We also plot the function $30\ln(T)$ as a proxy for the lower bound for SMAB (refer to Proposition 2).

Figure 2 shows that TS-SMAB outperforms AUER for each of the three availability settings described above, with the contrast being the most pronounced for the "changing suboptimal arm" setting.

Figure 3 shows how each of the two algorithms - AUER and TS-SMAB - performs across a range of availability settings.The performance of TS-SMAB is in agreement with our bound on the availability-specific regret from Theorem 1, which is maximized when $a_{j,T} = T$ for all $j \in [K]$ (as in the classical MAB setting), closely followed by the case when $a_{j,T} \approx T/2$ (as in the random availability setting), and is the smallest when $a_{j,T} = T/(K-1)$ for $j \in \{2, \ldots, K\}$ (as in the changing suboptimal arm setting). By contrast, the regret of AUER for the classical and the 'changing suboptimal arms' setting is nearly indistinguishable.

6 CONCLUDING REMARKS

We studied the sleeping multi-armed bandit problem with stochastic rewards and adversarial availabilities, and showed an $\mathcal{O}(\log T)$ regret bound for the Thompson Sampling algorithm (TS-SMAB). We also showed experimentally that TS-SMAB outperforms the AUER algorithm for various settings of availabilities, and discussed how our bounds capture the dependence of the regret of TS-SMAB on the structure of the availabilities.

As part of future work, it would be interesting to find out whether TS-SMAB is asymptotically optimal. It would also be of general interest to investigate problem independent bounds on the regret. Lastly, we intend to reproduce our experimental results on real world datasets.

Acknowledgments

The work reported here is partially supported by and is a part of the ongoing project *Disaster Recovery using Game Theory and Multiagent Systems* sponsored by the Defence Research and Development Organisation (DRDO), Government of India.

References

Agrawal, S. and Goyal, N. (2012). Analysis of Thompson Sampling for the multi-armed bandit problem. In *25th Annual Conference on Learning Theory, COLT 2012*, pages 39.1–39.26.

Agrawal, S. and Goyal, N. (2013a). Further optimal regret bounds for Thompson Sampling. In *Proceedings of the 16th International Conference on Artificial Intelligence and Statistics, AISTATS 2013*, pages 99–107.

Agrawal, S. and Goyal, N. (2013b). Thompson Sampling for contextual bandits with linear payoffs. In *Proceedings of the 30th International Conference on Machine Learning, ICML 2013*, pages 127–135.

Auer, P., Cesa-Bianchi, N., and Fischer, P. (2002). Finite-time analysis of the multiarmed bandit problem. *Machine Learning 2002*, 47(2-3):235–256.

Bubeck, S. and Cesa-Bianchi, N. (2012). Regret analysis of stochastic and nonstochastic multi-armed bandit problems. *Foundations and Trends in Machine Learning 2012*, 5(1):1–122.

Chapelle, O. and Li, L. (2011). An empirical evaluation of Thompson Sampling. In *25th Annual Conference on Neural Information Processing Systems (NIPS) 2011*, pages 2249–2257.

Gentile, C., Li, S., and Zappella, G. (2014). Online clustering of bandits. In *Proceedings of the 31st International Conference on Machine Learning (ICML-14)*, pages 757–765.

Hoeffding, W. (1963). Probability inequalities for sums of bounded random variables. *Journal of the American Statistical Association, 1963*, 58(301):13–30.

Kanade, V., McMahan, H. B., and Bryan, B. (2009). Sleeping experts and bandits with stochastic action availability and adversarial rewards. In *Proceedings of the 12th International Conference on Artificial Intelligence and Statistics, AISTATS 2009*, pages 272–279.

Kanade, V. and Steinke, T. (2014). Learning hurdles for sleeping experts. *ACM Transactions on Computation Theory, TOCT 2014*, 6(3):11:1–11:16.

Kaufmann, E., Korda, N., and Munos, R. (2012). Thompson Sampling: An asymptotically optimal finite-time analysis. In *23rd International Conference on Algorithmic Learning Theory, ALT 2012*, pages 199–213.

Kleinberg, R., Niculescu-Mizil, A., and Sharma, Y. (2010). Regret bounds for sleeping experts and bandits. *Machine Learning 2010*, 80(2-3):245–272.

Komiyama, J., Honda, J., and Nakagawa, H. (2015). Optimal regret analysis of Thompson Sampling in stochastic multi-armed bandit problem with multiple plays. In *Proceedings of the 32nd International Conference on Machine Learning, ICML 2015*, pages 1152–1161.

Li, L. and Chapelle, O. (2012). Open problem: Regret bounds for thompson sampling. In *25th Annual Conference on Learning Theory, COLT 2012*, pages 43.1–43.3.

Li, S., Karatzoglou, A., and Gentile, C. (2016). Collaborative filtering bandits. In *Proceedings of the 39th International ACM SIGIR conference on Research and Development in Information Retrieval*, pages 539–548. ACM.

Thompson, W. R. (1933). On the likelihood that one unknown probability exceeds another in view of the evidence of two samples. *Biometrika*, 25(3/4):285–294.

Xia, Y., Li, H., Qin, T., Yu, N., and Liu, T. (2015). Thompson Sampling for budgeted multi-armed bandits. In *Proceedings of the 24th International Joint Conference on Artificial Intelligence, IJCAI 2015*, pages 3960–3966.

Appendix A Preliminaries

We will extensively use the following two facts from probability theory. The first fact is a well known Hoeffding's inequality, and the second fact connects the cdfs of Beta and Binomial random variables.

Fact 1. ***Hoeffding's inequality (Hoeffding, 1963)*** *Let $X_1, \ldots, X_n$ be independent and bounded random variables with $X_i \in [a, b]$ for all i, where $-\infty < a \leq b < \infty$. Then,*

$$\mathbb{P}\left(\sum_{i=1}^{n} |X_i - \mathbb{E}[X_i]| \geq t\right) \leq 2\exp\left\{-\frac{2t^2}{n(b-a)^2}\right\}.$$

We have the following simple observation using Fact 1.

Observation 1. *For all $n, p \in [0, 1], \delta \geq 0$,*

$$F^B_{n+1,p}(np - n\delta) \leq e^{-2n\delta^2}.$$

Proof.

$$\begin{aligned} F^{\mathrm{B}}_{n+1,p}(r) &= (1-p)F^{\mathrm{B}}_{n,p}(r) + pF^{\mathrm{B}}_{n,p}(r-1) \\ &\leq (1-p)F^{\mathrm{B}}_{n,p}(r) + pF^{\mathrm{B}}_{n,p}(r) \\ &= F^{\mathrm{B}}_{n,p}(r). \end{aligned}$$

Using Fact 1 we have $F^{\mathrm{B}}_{n,p}(np - n\delta) \leq e^{-2n\delta^2}$. Combining that with the above identity gives us the proof. □

Fact 2. ***Beta-Binomial link (Agrawal and Goyal, 2012)*** *Let $F^{Beta}_{a,b}$ be the cdf of a Beta distribution with parameters a and b, and $F^B_{n,p}$ be the cdf of a Binomial distribution with parameters n and p. Then,*

$$F^{Beta}_{\alpha,\beta}(y) = 1 - F^{B}_{\alpha+\beta-1,y}(\alpha - 1).$$

Appendix B Omitted Proofs

B.1 Proof of Lemma 2

Lemma 2. *Let $i, j \in [K]$ be a pair of arms such that $i < j$, and let $L_{i,j} = 32/\Delta^2_{i,j}$. Then, at any time $t \leq T$,*

$$\mathbb{P}(\theta_{j,t} \geq \mu_j + \Delta_{i,j}/2, n_{j,t} \geq L_{i,j}\ln(a_{j,T})) \leq 2a^{-3}_{j,T}.$$

Proof. For simplicity of notation, let $\delta_{i,j} = \Delta_{i,j}/2$. We also introduce $\hat{\mu}_{i,t}$ as the empirical mean of arm i until time t. We use the fact that $\hat{\mu}_{i,t} = s_{i,t}/n_{i,t}$ in the following proof.

$$\begin{aligned} &\mathbb{P}(\theta_{j,t} \geq \mu_j + \delta_{i,j}, n_{j,t} \geq L_{i,j}\ln(a_{j,T})) \\ &\leq \underbrace{\mathbb{P}\left(\theta_{j,t} \geq \mu_j + \delta_{i,j}, \hat{\mu}_{j,t} \leq \mu_j + \frac{\delta_{i,j}}{2}, n_{j,t} \geq L_{i,j}\ln(a_{j,T})\right)}_{A} \\ &\quad + \underbrace{\mathbb{P}\left(\hat{\mu}_{j,t} > \mu_j + \frac{\delta_{i,j}}{2}, n_{j,t} \geq L_{i,j}\ln(a_{j,T})\right)}_{B} \end{aligned}$$

Bounding term A:

$$\begin{aligned} &\mathbb{P}\left(\theta_{j,t} \geq \mu_j + \delta_{i,j}, \hat{\mu}_{j,t} \leq \mu_i + \frac{\delta_{i,j}}{2}, n_{j,t} \geq L_{i,j}\ln(a_{j,T})\right) \\ &\leq \sum_{l=L_{i,j}\ln(a_{j,T})}^{a_{j,T}} \mathbb{P}\left(\theta_{j,t} \geq \hat{\mu}_{j,t} + \frac{\delta_{i,j}}{2}, n_{j,t} = l\right) \\ &= \sum_{l=L_{i,j}\ln(a_{j,T})}^{a_{j,T}} \left(1 - F^{\mathrm{Beta}}_{s_{i,t}+1, l-s_{i,t}+1}\left(\hat{\mu}_{j,t} + \frac{\delta_{i,j}}{2}\right)\right) \\ &= \sum_{l=L_{i,j}\ln(a_{j,T})}^{a_{j,T}} F^{\mathrm{B}}_{n_{j,t}+1, \hat{\mu}_{j,t}+\frac{\delta_{i,j}}{2}}(s_{i,t}) \qquad \text{(Using Fact 2)} \\ &\leq \sum_{l=L_{i,j}\ln(a_{j,T})}^{a_{j,T}} \exp\left\{-\frac{l\delta^2_{i,j}}{2}\right\} \qquad \text{(Using Observation 1)} \\ &\leq a_{j,T}\exp\left\{-\frac{L_{i,j}\ln(a_{j,T})\delta^2_{i,j}}{2}\right\} \\ &= a_{j,T}e^{-4\ln(a_{j,T})} = a^{-3}_{j,T} \end{aligned}$$

Bounding term B:

$$\begin{aligned} &\mathbb{P}\left(\hat{\mu}_{j,t} > \mu_i + \frac{\delta_{i,j}}{2}, n_{i,t} \geq L_{i,j}\ln(a_{j,T})\right) \\ &= \sum_{l=L_{i,j}\ln(a_{j,T})}^{a_{j,T}} \mathbb{P}\left(\hat{\mu}_{j,t} > \mu_i + \frac{\delta_{i,j}}{2}, n_{i,t} = l\right) \\ &\leq \sum_{l=L_{i,j}\ln(a_{j,T})}^{a_{j,T}} \exp\left\{-\frac{l\delta^2_{i,j}}{2}\right\} \qquad \text{(Using Fact 1)} \\ &\leq a_{j,T}\exp\left\{-\frac{L_{i,j}\ln(a_{j,T})\delta^2_{i,j}}{2}\right\} \\ &\leq a_{j,T}e^{-4\ln(a_{j,T})} \leq a^{-3}_{j,T} \end{aligned}$$

□

B.2 Proof of Lemma 3

Lemma 3. *Let $e_{i,t} = \sqrt{\frac{4\ln(w_{i,t})}{n_{i,t}}}$ for any arm i. Then, at any time t, we have,*

$$\mathbb{P}(\theta_{i,t} \leq \mu_i - e_{i,t}) \leq w^{-2}_{i,t},$$

where $w_{i,t}$ denotes the number of times arm i is the best available arm until time t.

Proof.

$$\mathbb{P}(\theta_{i,t} \le \mu_i - e_{i,t}) = F^{\text{Beta}}_{s_{i,t}+1, n_{i,t}-s_{i,t}+1}(\mu_i - e_{i,t})$$
$$= 1 - F^{\text{B}}_{n_{i,t}+1, \mu_i - e_{i,t}}(s_{i,t}) \quad \text{(Using Fact 2)}$$

Let $X_{1,l} \sim \text{Bernoulli}(\mu_i - e_{i,t})$ and $X_{2,l} \sim \text{Bernoulli}(\mu_i)$ be Bernoulli r.v.s. and let $Z_l = X_{2,l} - X_{1,l}$ be a discreet r.v. with values in $\{-1, 0, 1\}$ and mean $e_{i,t}$. Then,

$$\begin{aligned}
&= 1 - \mathbb{P}\left(\sum_{l=1}^{n_{i,t}+1} X_{1,l} \le \sum_{l=1}^{n_{i,t}} X_{2,l}\right) \\
&= \mathbb{P}\left(\sum_{l=1}^{n_{i,t}} X_{2,l} < \sum_{l=1}^{n_{i,t}+1} X_{1,l}\right) \\
&= \mathbb{P}\left(\sum_{l=1}^{n_{i,t}} Z_l < 1\right) \\
&= \mathbb{P}\left(\sum_{l=1}^{n_{i,t}} Z_l \le 0\right) \qquad \text{(As } X_{1,l} \le 1\text{)} \\
&= \mathbb{P}\left(\sum_{l=1}^{n_{i,t}} (Z_l - e_{i,t}) \le -n_{i,t} e_{i,t}\right) \\
&\le \exp\left\{-\frac{2 n_{i,t}^2 e_{i,t}^2}{4 n_{i,t}}\right\} \qquad \text{(Using Fact 1)} \\
&= e^{-2\ln(w_{i,t})} = w_{i,t}^{-2}
\end{aligned}$$

□

B.3 Proof of Lemma 5

Lemma 5. *For any fixed arm $a > i$,*

$$\mathbb{P}\left(\exists t' \in \mathcal{I}_{j,l}^{(i)} : \theta_{a,t'} \ge \mu_a + \delta_{i,a}, n_{a,t'}^{(i)} \ge L_{i,a} \ln(w_{i,t})\right) \le 2 w_{i,t}^{-2+b}.$$

Proof.

$$\begin{aligned}
&\mathbb{P}\left(\theta_{a,t'} \ge \mu_a + \delta_{i,a}, n_{a,t'}^{(i)} \ge L_{i,a} \ln(w_{i,t})\right) \le \\
&\underbrace{\mathbb{P}\left(\theta_{a,t'} \ge \mu_a + \delta_{i,a}, \hat{\mu}_{a,t'} \le \mu_a + \frac{\delta_{i,a}}{2}, n_{a,t'}^{(i)} \ge L_{i,a} \ln(w_{i,t})\right)}_{A} \\
&+ \underbrace{\mathbb{P}\left(\hat{\mu}_{a,t'} > \mu_a + \frac{\delta_{i,a}}{2}, n_{a,t'}^{(i)} \ge L_{i,a} \ln(w_{i,t})\right)}_{B}
\end{aligned}$$

Bounding term A:

$$\begin{aligned}
&\mathbb{P}\left(\theta_{a,t'} \ge \mu_a + \delta_{i,a}, \hat{\mu}_{a,t'} \le \mu_a + \frac{\delta_{i,a}}{2}, n_{a,t'}^{(i)} \ge L_{i,a} \ln(w_{i,t})\right) \\
&\le \sum_{l = L_{i,a} \ln(w_{i,t})}^{w_{i,t}} \mathbb{P}\left(\theta_{a,t'} \ge \hat{\mu}_{a,t'} + \frac{\delta_{i,a}}{2}, n_{a,t'}^{(i)} = l\right) \\
&= \sum_{l = L_{i,a} \ln(w_{i,t})}^{w_{i,t}} \left(1 - F^{\text{Beta}}_{s_{a,t'}+1, n_{a,t'}-s_{a,t'}+1}\left(\hat{\mu}_{a,t'} + \frac{\delta_{i,a}}{2}\right)\right) \\
&= \sum_{l = L_{i,a} \ln(w_{i,t})}^{w_{i,t}} F^{\text{B}}_{n_{a,t'}+1, \hat{\mu}_{a,t'} + \frac{\delta_{i,a}}{2}}(s_{a,t'}) \qquad \text{(Using Fact 2)} \\
&\le \sum_{l = L_{i,a} \ln(w_{i,t})}^{w_{i,t}} \exp\left\{-\frac{n_{a,t'} \delta_{i,a}^2}{2}\right\} \qquad \text{(Using Observation 1)} \\
&\le w_{i,t} \exp\left\{-\frac{L_{i,a} \ln(w_{i,t}) \delta_{i,a}^2}{2}\right\} \\
&= w_{i,t} e^{-4\ln(w_{i,t})} = w_{i,t}^{-3}
\end{aligned}$$

Bounding term B:

$$\begin{aligned}
&\mathbb{P}\left(\hat{\mu}_{a,t'} > \mu_a + \frac{\delta_{i,a}}{2}, n_{a,t'}^{(i)} \ge L_{i,a} \ln(w_{i,t})\right) \\
&= \sum_{l = L_{i,a} \ln(w_{i,t})}^{w_{i,t}} \mathbb{P}\left(\hat{\mu}_{a,t'} > \mu_a + \frac{\delta_{i,a}}{2}, n_{a,t'}^{(i)} = l\right) \\
&\le \sum_{l = L_{i,a} \ln(w_{i,t})}^{w_{i,t}} \exp\left\{-\frac{n_{a,t'} \delta_{i,a}^2}{2}\right\} \qquad \text{(Using Fact 1)} \\
&\le w_{i,t} \exp\left\{-\frac{L_{i,a} \ln(w_{i,t}) \delta_{i,a}^2}{2}\right\} \\
&\le w_{i,t} e^{-4\ln(w_{i,t})} \le w_{i,t}^{-3}
\end{aligned}$$

Thus we get,

$$\mathbb{P}\left(\theta_{a,t'} \ge \mu_a + \delta_{i,a}, n_{a,t'}^{(i)} \ge L_{i,a} \ln(w_{i,t})\right) \le 2 w_{i,t}^{-3}$$

Now,

$$\begin{aligned}
&\mathbb{P}\left(\exists t' \in \mathcal{I}_{j,l}^{(i)}, a > i : \theta_{a,t'} > \mu_a + \delta_{i,a}, n_{a,t'}^{(i)} > L_{i,a} \ln(w_{i,t})\right) \\
&\le \sum_{t' \in \mathcal{I}_{j,l}^{(i)}} \sum_{a > i} \mathbb{P}\left(\theta_{a,t'} \ge \mu_a + \delta_{i,a}, n_{a,t'}^{(i)} \ge L_{i,a} \ln(w_{i,t})\right) \\
&\le \sum_{t' \in \mathcal{I}_{j,l}^{(i)}} \sum_{a > i} 2 w_{i,t}^{-3} \\
&\le \frac{w_{i,t}^{1-b}}{K - i} \cdot (K - i) \cdot 2 w_{i,t}^{-3} = 2 w_{i,t}^{-(2+b)}
\end{aligned}$$

□

B.4 Proof of Lemma 6

Lemma 6. *There exists a constant $\lambda_0 > 1$ such that for all $\lambda \in (1, \lambda_0)$, for any interval $\mathcal{J}^{(i)} \subseteq \cup_{l \in [K-i+1]} \mathcal{I}_{j,l}^{(i)}$ and for every positive function f, we have*

$$\begin{aligned}
&\mathbb{P}\left(\{\forall s \in \mathcal{J}^{(i)} : \theta_{i,s} \le y_i\} \cap \{|\mathcal{J}^{(i)}| \ge f(t)\}\right) \\
&\le (\alpha_i)^{f(t)} + C_{\lambda,i} \frac{1}{f(t)^{\lambda}} e^{-j d_{\lambda,i}},
\end{aligned}$$

where $C_{\lambda,i} > 0$, $d_{\lambda,i} > 0$, $\alpha_i = \left(\frac{1}{2}\right)^{1-\mu_{i+1}-\delta_i}$ and $y_i = \mu_{i+1} + \delta_{i,i+1}$ for every $i \in \{1, \ldots, K-1\}$.

Proof. Recall that $\tau_j^{(i)}$ denotes the time of occurrence of the jth pull of arm i and $\xi_j^{(i)}$ denotes the i-optimal time-line between the jth and $(j+1)^{th}$ pull of arm i. Hence, on the interval $\mathcal{J}^{(i)}$ (included in $\xi_j^{(i)}$ by hypothesis) arm i has a fixed posterior Beta$(s_{i,\tau_j^{(i)}}+1, j-s_{i,\tau_j^{(i)}}+1)$ distribution when conditioned on $s_{i,\tau_j^{(i)}}$. Thus,

$$\mathbb{P}\Big(\theta_{i,s} \leq y_i \mid s \in \mathcal{J}^{(i)}\Big) \leq F^{\text{Beta}}_{s_i+1,j-s_i+1}(y_i) \quad \text{(Using } s_i = s_{i,\tau_j^{(i)}}\text{)}$$
$$= 1 - F^{\text{B}}_{j+1,y_i}(s_i) \quad \text{(Using Fact 2)}$$

This gives us,

$$\begin{aligned}
&\mathbb{P}\Big(\forall s \in \mathcal{J}^{(i)}, \theta_{i,s} \leq y_i\Big) \\
&= \mathbb{E}\Big[\mathbb{P}\Big(\forall s \in \mathcal{J}^{(i)}, \theta_{i,s} \leq y_i \mid s_{i,\tau_j^{(i)}}\Big)\Big] \\
&\leq \mathbb{E}\Big[\Big(1 - F^{\text{B}}_{j+1,y_i}\Big(s_{i,\tau_j^{(i)}}\Big)\Big)^{|\mathcal{J}^{(i)}|}\Big] \\
&\leq \mathbb{E}\Big[\Big(1 - F^{\text{B}}_{j+1,y_i}\Big(s_{i,\tau_j^{(i)}}\Big)\Big)^{f(t)}\Big] \\
&= \sum_{s=0}^{j}\Big(1 - F^{\text{B}}_{j+1,y_i}\Big(s_{i,\tau_j^{(i)}}\Big)\Big)^{f(t)} f^{\text{B}}_{j,\mu_i}(s) \\
&\leq \sum_{s=0}^{j} \exp\Big(-f(t)(1-y)F^{\text{B}}_{j+1,y}(s)\Big) f^{\text{B}}_{j,\mu_i}(s)
\end{aligned}$$

Using $F^{\text{B}}_{j+1,y_i}(s) = (1-y_i)F^{\text{B}}_{j,y_i}(s) + y_i F^{\text{B}}_{j,y_i}(s-1) \geq (1-y_i)F^{\text{B}}_{j+1,y_i}(s)$ we get:

$$\begin{aligned}
&\leq \sum_{s=0}^{j} \exp\Big(-f(t)(1-y_i)F^{\text{B}}_{j,y}(s)\Big) f^{\text{B}}_{j,\mu_i}(s) \\
&\leq \sum_{s=0}^{\lfloor y_i j \rfloor} \exp\Big(-f(t)(1-y_i)F^{\text{B}}_{j,y_i}(s)\Big) f^{\text{B}}_{j,\mu_i}(s) + \sum_{s=\lceil y_i j \rceil}^{j} \Big(\frac{1}{2}\Big)^{(1-y_i)f(t)} f^{\text{B}}_{j,\mu_i}(s) \\
&\leq \underbrace{\sum_{s=0}^{\lfloor y_i j \rfloor} \exp\Big(-f(t)(1-y_i)F^{\text{B}}_{j,y_i}(s)\Big) f^{\text{B}}_{j,\mu_i}(s)}_{E} + \sum_{s=\lceil y_i j \rceil}^{j} \Big(\frac{1}{2}\Big)^{(1-y_i)f(t)}
\end{aligned}$$

For every $\lambda > 1, \forall x > 0, x^\lambda \exp(-x) \leq \left(\frac{\lambda}{e}\right)^\lambda$. Taking $C_\lambda = \left(\frac{\lambda}{e}\right)^\lambda$, we get the following upper-bound:

$$\begin{aligned}
(E) &\leq \frac{C_\lambda}{(f(t)(1-y_i))^\lambda} \sum_{s=0}^{\lfloor y_i j \rfloor} \frac{f^{\text{B}}_{j,\mu_i}(s)}{\left(F^{\text{B}}_{j,y_i}(s)\right)^\lambda} \\
&\leq \frac{C_\lambda}{(f(t)(1-y_i))^\lambda} \sum_{s=0}^{\lfloor y_i j \rfloor} \frac{f^{\text{B}}_{j,\mu_i}(s)}{\left(f^{\text{B}}_{j,y_i}(s)\right)^\lambda}
\end{aligned}$$

Now,

$$\begin{aligned}
\frac{f^{\text{B}}_{j,\mu_i}(s)}{\left(f^{\text{B}}_{j,y_i}(s)\right)^\lambda} &= \frac{\binom{j}{s}\mu_i^s(1-\mu_i)^{j-s}}{\binom{j}{s}^\lambda (y^\lambda)^s((1-y)^\lambda)^{j-s}} \\
&\leq \frac{\mu_i^s(1-\mu_i)^{j-s}}{(y^\lambda)^s((1-y)^\lambda)^{j-s}} \\
&\leq \left(\frac{1-\mu_i}{(1-y)^\lambda}\right)^j \left(\frac{\mu_i(1-y)^\lambda}{y^\lambda(1-\mu_i)}\right)^s
\end{aligned}$$

Let $R_\lambda(\mu_i, y_i) = \frac{\mu_i(1-y_i)^\lambda}{y^\lambda(1-\mu_i)}$. There exists some $\lambda_1 > 1$ such that, if $\lambda < \lambda_1, R_\lambda > 1$. More precisely,

$$\lambda_1(\mu_i, y_i) = \begin{cases} \frac{\ln\left(\frac{\mu_i}{1-\mu_i}\right)}{\ln\left(\frac{y_i}{1-y_i}\right)} & \text{, if } y > \frac{1}{2} \\ +\infty & \text{, if } y < \frac{1}{2} \end{cases}$$

For $1 < \lambda < \lambda_1$:

$$\begin{aligned}
\sum_{s=0}^{\lfloor y_i j \rfloor} \frac{f^{\text{B}}_{j,\mu_i}(s)}{\left(f^{\text{B}}_{j,y_i}(s)\right)^\lambda} &\leq \left(\frac{1-\mu_i}{(1-y)^\lambda}\right)^j \sum_{s=0}^{\lfloor y_i j \rfloor} R_\lambda^s \\
&= \left(\frac{1-\mu_i}{(1-y)^\lambda}\right)^j \frac{R_\lambda^{\lfloor y_i j \rfloor + 1}}{R_\lambda - 1} \\
&\leq \left(\frac{1-\mu_i}{(1-y)^\lambda}\right)^j \frac{R_\lambda}{R_\lambda - 1} R_\lambda^{y_i j} \\
&= \frac{R_\lambda}{R_\lambda - 1}\left(\frac{1-\mu_i}{(1-y)^\lambda}\right)^{j-y_i j}\left(\frac{\mu_i}{y^\lambda}\right)^{y_i j} \\
&= \frac{R_\lambda}{R_\lambda - 1} e^{-j d_\lambda(y_i,\mu_i)}
\end{aligned}$$

where,

$$\begin{aligned}
d_\lambda(y_i, \mu_i) &= y_i \ln\left(\frac{y_i^\lambda}{\mu_i}\right) + (1-y_i)\ln\left(\frac{(1-y_i)^\lambda}{1-\mu_i}\right) \\
&= \lambda[y_i \ln(y_i) + (1-y_i)\ln(1-y_i)] \\
&\quad - [y_i \ln(\mu_i) + (1-y_i)\ln(1-\mu_i)]
\end{aligned}$$

which is an affine function of λ with negative slope $(y_i \ln(y_i) + (1-y_i)\ln(1-y_i) < 0)$ for all $y \in (0,1)$ and $d_1(y_i, \mu_i) = KL(y_i, \mu_i)$. Hence, for fixed $0 < y_i < \mu_i \leq 1$ this function is positive whenever

$$\lambda < \frac{y_i \ln(\mu_i) + (1-y_i)\ln(1-\mu_i)}{y_i \ln(y_i) + (1-y_i)\ln(1-y_i)} =: \lambda_2(\mu_i, y_i)$$

Clearly, $\lambda_2(\mu_i, y_i) > 1$ and we know from Kaufmann et al. (2012) that $\lambda_2 \leq \lambda_1$. So we choose $\lambda_0(\mu_i, y_i) = \lambda_2(\mu_i, y_i)$.

To conclude the proof we define $d_{\lambda,i} := d_\lambda(y_i, \mu_i)$ and $C_{\lambda,i} := C_\lambda(1-y_i)^{-\lambda}\frac{R_\lambda}{1-R_\lambda}$. □

The Total Belief Theorem

Chunlai Zhou[1,2], Fabio Cuzzolin[3]
[1]DEKE(MOE), Computer Science Dept., Renmin University, Beijing, CHINA
[2]State Key Lab of Computer Science, Institute of Software, Chinese Academy of Sciences, Beijing, CHINA
[3]Artificial Intelligence and Vision, Department of Computing and Communication Technologies,
Oxford Brookes University, Oxford, UK
czhou@ruc.edu.cn, fabio.cuzzolin@brookes.ac.uk

Abstract

In this paper, motivated by the treatment of conditional constraints in the data association problem, we state and prove the generalisation of the law of total probability to belief functions, as finite random sets. Our results apply to the case in which Dempster's conditioning is employed. We show that the solution to the resulting total belief problem is in general not unique, whereas it is unique when the a-priori belief function is Bayesian. Examples and case studies underpin the theoretical contributions. Finally, our results are compared to previous related work on the generalisation of Jeffrey's rule by Spies and Smets.

1 INTRODUCTION

A number of researchers have been working on the generalisation to belief functions (BFs) of a fundamental result of probability theory: the law of total probability. The latter is sometimes called 'Jeffrey's rule' [14, 15, 26, 13], for it is mathematically equivalent to a rule for updating a probability distribution based on a new distribution with values on a smaller set of events. Both laws concern the way non-conditional, joint models can be soundly built from conditional information and unconditional information.

A motivating example comes from *data association* [27, 22, 3]. There, a number of targets moving in the space are tracked by one or more cameras, appearing in an image sequence as unlabeled feature points [4]. When the targets belong to an object for which a topological model is known, an evidential solution can be proposed by expressing the prior, logical information carried by the body model in term of belief functions on a suitable frame of discernment (see [5], Chapter 7). In particular, a rigid motion constraint from each link in the topological model can be derived and expressed in a *conditional* way – in order to test the rigidity of the motion of two observed feature points at time k, we need to know the correct association between targets and features at time $k-1$. To construct an overall BF describing the association, such conditional pieces of information need to be combined. This requires us to equip the theory of belief functions with a law of total probability.
Another problem in which a total belief problem arises is example-based pose estimation [11], as soon as a regression framework based on belief functions is applied.

The generalisation of Jeffrey's rule to belief functions has been mainly studied by Spies [30] and Smets [28]. Ruspini [23] also reported results on deduction assuming approximate knowledge about the truth of conditional propositions. Spies [30] proved the existence of a solution to the generalisation of Jeffrey's rule to belief functions within his original conditioning framework. Smets also proposed generalisations of Jeffrey's rule based on both geometric and Dempster's conditioning [28].

1.1 CONTRIBUTIONS AND OUTLINE

In this paper we first provide a formal statement of the problem. Namely, we seek to combine conditional belief functions defined over disjoint subsets of a frame of discernment, while simultaneously constraining the resulting total belief function to be compatible with a second BF defined on the coarsening of the original frame.
We then adapt Smets' original proof of his well-known generalized Bayesian Theorem to construct a total belief function and show that it satisfies the prescribed marginalization and conditioning properties. The problem is shown to be equivalent to building a square linear system with positive solution, whose columns are associated with the focal elements (non-zero mass events) of the candidate total BF.

We first recall the necessary definitions from belief theory (Section 2). We then briefly review the belief-theoretical solution to the motivating data association problem (Section 3). In Section 4 we provide the formal statement of the total belief theorem and give a constructive proof for it. We show how to translate a total belief problem to a group of linear equations and analyze its possible solutions. Finally, Section 5 runs a critical comparison between our result and previous relevant work by Spies and Smets on the generalisation of Jeffrey's rule to belief functions. Section 6 concludes the paper.

2 BELIEF FUNCTIONS

2.1 BELIEF MEASURES

A *mass function* [2] over a *frame of discernment* Θ is a set function [8, 7] $m : 2^\Theta \rightarrow [0, 1]$ defined on the collection 2^Θ of all subsets of Θ such that: $m(\emptyset) = 0$, $\sum_{A\subset\Theta} m(A) = 1$. The quantity $m(A)$ is called the *basic probability number* or 'mass' [17, 16] assigned to A, and measures the belief committed exactly to $A \in 2^\Theta$. The elements of the power set 2^Θ associated with non-zero values of m are called the *focal elements* of m. The *belief function* associated with a mass function $m : 2^\Theta \rightarrow [0, 1]$ is the set function $b : 2^\Theta \rightarrow [0, 1]$ defined as: $b(A) = \sum_{B\subseteq A} m(B)$. The domain Θ on which a belief function is defined is usually interpreted as the set of possible answers to a given problem, exactly one of which is the correct one. For each subset ('event') $A \subseteq \Theta$ the quantity $b(A)$ takes on the meaning of 'degree of belief' that the truth lies in A, and represents the total belief committed to a set of possible outcomes A by the available evidence m. Given a belief function b, we can obtain its corresponding mass function m as follows: $m(A) = \sum_{B\subseteq A}(-1)^{|A\setminus B|} b(B)$ for all $A \subseteq \Theta$. The belief function b is called *Bayesian* if $m(A) = 0$ for all non-singletons A. It is called *categorical* if it has only one focal set. And it is called *vacuous* if Θ is the only focal element. A vacuous belief represents a state of total ignorance. The corresponding *plausibility function* $pl : 2^\Omega \rightarrow [0, 1]$ is defined by $pl(A) = \sum_{E\cap A\neq\emptyset} m(E)$ for all $A \subseteq \Theta$. For m, b and pl, if we know any one of them, then we can determine the other two.

2.2 CONDITIONING

In Bayesian reasoning, where all evidence comes in the form of a proposition A being true, conditioning (as we know) is performed via Bayes' rule. In belief theory, however, the onus is on combining the belief function representing our current knowledge state with a new one encoding the new evidence. After an initial proposal by Dempster, several other aggregation operators have been proposed, based on different assumptions on the nature and properties of the sources of evidence to combine.

Definition 1. *The* orthogonal sum *or* Dempster's combination $b_1 \oplus b_2 : 2^\Theta \rightarrow [0, 1]$ *of two belief functions* $b_1 : 2^\Theta \rightarrow [0, 1]$, $b_2 : 2^\Theta \rightarrow [0, 1]$ *defined on the same frame of discernment* Θ *is the unique BF on* Θ *whose focal elements are all the possible intersections of focal elements of* b_1 *and* b_2*, and whose mass is given by:*

$$(m_1 \oplus m_2)(A) = \frac{\sum_{i,j:A_i\cap B_j=A} m_1(A_i)m_2(B_j)}{1 - \sum_{i,j:A_i\cap B_j=\emptyset} m_1(A_i)m_2(B_j)},$$

where m_i *denotes the mass function related to* b_i.

Belief functions can also be conditioned, rather than combined, whenever they need to be updated based on similar hard evidence. However, just as in the case of combination rules, a variety of conditioning operators can be defined for belief functions [9, 12, 10, 6, 33], many of them generalisations of Bayes' rule itself. In particular, Dempster's rule of combination naturally induces a conditioning operator, as follows. Given a conditioning event $A \subseteq \Theta$, the 'logical' (or 'categorical', in Smets' terminology) belief function b_A such that $m(A) = 1$ is combined via Dempster's rule with the a-priori belief function b. The resulting belief function $b \oplus b_A$ is the conditional belief function given A *a la Dempster*, denoted by $b(A|B)$.

Suppose that $\Theta' \supseteq \Theta$ and m is a mass function over Θ. The mass function m can be identified with a mass function $\overrightarrow{m}_{\Theta'}$ over the larger frame Θ': for any $E' \subseteq \Theta'$, $\overrightarrow{m}_{\Theta'}(E') = m(E)$ if $E' = E\cup(\Theta'\setminus\Theta)$ and $\overrightarrow{m}_{\Theta'}(E') = 0$ otherwise. Such $\overrightarrow{m}_{\Theta'}$ is called the *conditional embedding* (or *ballooning extension*) of m into Θ'. When the context is clear, we can drop the subscript Θ'.

2.3 OUTER REDUCTIONS

Suppose that Θ is a *finer* frame than Ω. This means that the elements $\omega_1, \cdots, \omega_{|\Omega|}$ of Ω correspond to a partition $\Pi_1, \cdots, \Pi_{|\Omega|}$ of Θ: a subset $\{\omega_{i_1}, \cdots \omega_{i_k}\}$ of Ω has the same meaning as the subset $\Pi_{i_1} \cup \cdots \cup \Pi_{i_k}$ of Θ. This identification can represented by a mapping $\rho : 2^\Omega \rightarrow 2^\Theta$ such that $\rho(\{\omega_i\}) = \Pi_i (1 \leq i \leq |\Omega|)$ and $\rho(\{\omega_{i_1}, \cdots \omega_{i_k}\}) = \cup_{j=1}^k \rho(\omega_{i_j}) = \cup_{j=1}^k \Pi_{i_j}$. The partition $\Pi_1, \cdots, \Pi_{|\Omega|}$ of Θ as a basis defines a subalgebra $\mathbb{A}^\rho$ of 2^Θ as a Boolean algebra with set operations, which is isomorphic to the set algebra $\mathbb{A} = 2^\Omega$.

In the theory of evidence, two frames are called *compatible* if and only if they concern propositions which can be both expressed in terms of propositions of a common, finer frame [25]. In particular, two compatible frames must admit a common refinement, i.e., a frame which is a refinement of both. Each collection of compatible frames has many common refinements. In particular, if $\Theta_1, ..., \Theta_n$ are elements of a family of compatible frames $\mathcal{F}$, then there exists a unique frame $\Theta \in \mathcal{F}$ such that:

1. $\exists$ a refining $\rho_i : 2^{\Theta_i} \to 2^{\Omega}$ for all $i = 1, ..., n$;
2. $\forall \theta \in \Theta\ \exists \theta_i \in \Theta_i\ \forall i = 1, ..., n$ such that:

$$\{\theta\} = \rho_1(\{\theta_1\}) \cap ... \cap \rho_n(\{\theta_n\}).$$

This unique frame is called the *minimal refinement* $\Theta_1 \otimes \cdots \otimes \Theta_n$ of the collection $\Theta_1, ..., \Theta_n$, and is the simplest space in which we can compare propositions pertaining to different compatible frames.

If Θ_1 and Θ_2 are two compatible frames, then two belief functions $b_1 : 2^{\Theta_1} \to [0,1]$, $b_2 : 2^{\Theta_2} \to [0,1]$ can potentially be expression of the same body of evidence. Two belief functions b_1 and b_2 defined over two compatible frames Θ_1 and Θ_2 are said to be *consistent* if $b_1(A_1) = b_2(A_2)$ whenever $\rho_1(A_1) = \rho_2(A_2)$, $A_1 \subseteq \Theta_1$, $A_2 \subseteq \Theta_2$, where ρ_i is the refining between Θ_i and the minimal refinement $\Theta_1 \otimes \Theta_2$ of Θ_1 and Θ_2. When the two belief functions are defined on frames connected by a refining $\rho : 2^{\Theta_1} \to 2^{\Theta_2}$ (i.e., Θ_2 is a refinement of Θ_1), b_1 and b_2 are consistent iff: $b_1(A) = b_2(\rho(A)), \forall A \subseteq \Theta_1$.

Definition 2. *The* outer reduction *associated with a refining* $\rho : 2^{\Omega} \to 2^{\Theta}$ *is the mapping* $\overline{\rho} : 2^{\Theta} \to 2^{\Omega}$ *defined as, for any* $E \in 2^{\Theta}$,

$$\overline{\rho}(E) := \{\omega \in \Omega : \rho(\{\omega\}) \cap E \neq \emptyset\}.$$

Note that, for any $E \subseteq \Theta$, $\rho(\overline{\rho}(E))$ is the smallest element of $\mathbb{A}^{\rho}$ that contains E. So $\rho(\overline{\rho}(E))$ is called the *upper approximations* of E in $\mathbb{A}^{\rho}$, respectively. Given a belief function b over Θ with the refining mapping $\rho : 2^{\Omega} \to 2^{\Theta}$, its *marginal* $b \restriction_{\Omega}$ over Ω is defined as follows: $(b \restriction_{\Omega})(\{\omega_{i_1}, \cdots, \omega_{i_k}\}) = b(\Pi_{i_1} \cup \cdots \cup \Pi_{i_k})$. The corresponding mass function is:

$$(m \restriction_{\Omega})(\{\omega_{i_1}, \cdots, \omega_{i_k}\}) = \sum_{\substack{E \subseteq \Theta, \\ \overline{\rho}(E) = \{\omega_{i_1}, \cdots, \omega_{i_k}\}}} m(E). \tag{1}$$

A mass function m over Ω can be extended to a mass function $m^{\uparrow\Theta}$ over the finer frame Θ: $m^{\uparrow\Theta}(E) = m(\{\omega_{i_1}, \cdots, \omega_{i_k}\})$ if E is a union of some partition classes $\Pi_{i_1}, \cdots, \Pi_{i_k}$, $m^{\uparrow\Theta}(E) = 0$ otherwise. Such $m^{\uparrow\Theta}$ is called the *vacuous extension* of m. When the context is clear, we will omit the subscript Θ. Trivially, vacuous extension is the inverse of marginalization.

3 DATA ASSOCIATION WITH BFS

In data association we are given a sequence of images $\{I(k), k\}$, each containing a number of feature points $\{t_i(k)\}$ at time k which are projections of real world targets $\{T_1, ..., T_M\}$. We seek the correspondences $t_i(k) \longleftrightarrow t_j(k+1)$ between feature points in consecutive images which are projections of the same target.

3.1 CONDITIONAL CONSTRAINTS

If we assume that targets represent fixed positions on an articulated body connected by a rigid link, we can address the association task in critical situations in which several targets coalesce (*model-based* data association) via a set of logical constraints on the admissible positions of the targets. We can identify, among others [5]: (i) a 'prediction' constraint which encodes the likelihood of a measurement in the current image being associated with a measurement of the past image (e.g. produced by a Kalman filter [27] in joint probabilistic data association [4]); (ii) a *rigid motion* constraint, acting on pairs of targets T_{j_1}, T_{j_2} connected by a rigid link in the model:

$$\|t_i(k) - t_j(k)\| \cong \|t_{i'}(k-1) - t_{j'}(k-1)\|,$$

assuming that $t_i(k), t_{i'}(k-1)$ are both projections of T_{j_1}, and $t_j(k), t_{j'}(k-1)$ are images of T_{j_2}.
All such constraints can be expressed as belief functions over a suitable frame of discernment. However, whereas prediction information inherently concerns associations between feature points belonging to consecutive images, the rigid motion constraint depends on the target-to-measurement associations (e.g. $t_{i'}(k-1) \sim T_{j_1}, t_{j'}(k-1) \sim T_{j_2}$) estimated at the previous step.

3.2 A FAMILY OF ASSOCIATIONS FRAMES

We thus need to introduce a *past target-to-feature* associations frame: $\Theta_M^{k-1} \doteq \{t_i(k-1) \leftrightarrow T_j, i = 1, ..., n(k-1), j = 1, ..., M\}$, a *feature-to-feature* associations frame: $\Theta_k^{k-1} \doteq \{t_i(k-1) \leftrightarrow t_j(k), \forall i = 1, ..., n(k-1)\ \forall j = 1, ..., n(k)\}$, and a *current target-to-feature* associations frame: $\Theta_M^k \doteq \{t_i(k) \leftrightarrow T_j, \forall i = 1, ..., n(k)\ \forall j = 1, ..., M\}$. These form a family of compatible frames, as they are all connected by refining maps (see Figure 1). Prediction belief functions (i), for instance, will live on Θ_k^{k-1}. The belief estimate of the associations at time $k-1$ will live on Θ_M^{k-1}. The BFs encoding the various constraints can thus be combined on their minimal refinement $\Theta_M^{k-1} \otimes \Theta_k^{k-1}$. Marginalizing the resulting BF back onto the current target-to-feature association frame Θ_M^k yields the current best estimate.

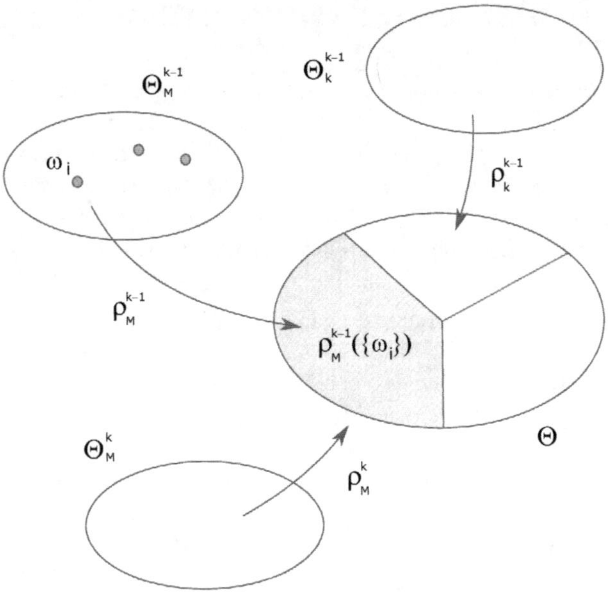

Figure 1: The family of past and present association frames. All the constraints of the model-based association problem are combined over the common refinement Θ and then marginalized onto the current association frame Θ_M^k to yield a belief estimate of the current feature-to-model association.

3.3 TOTAL BELIEF FOR DATA ASSOCIATION

The rigid motion constraint, however, generates an entire set of (conditional) belief functions $b_i : 2^{\rho_M^{k-1}(\{\omega_i\})} \to [0,1]$, each defined over an element $\rho_M^{k-1}(\{\omega_i\})$ of the disjoint partition of $\Theta = \Theta_M^{k-1} \otimes \Theta_k^{k-1}$ induced there by its coarsening Θ_M^{k-1} (the past target-to-feature frame, see Figure 1 again), where $\omega_i \in \Theta_M^{k-1}$ is the i-th possible association at time $k-1$. Merging all pieces of evidence on Θ thus requires combining these conditional belief functions into a single 'total' BF, which is eventually pooled with those generated by the remaining evidence.

4 THE TOTAL BELIEF THEOREM

4.1 TOTAL PROBABILITY

Suppose P is defined on a σ-algebra $\mathbb{A}$, and that a new probability measure P' on a sub-algebra $\mathbb{B}$ of $\mathbb{A}$. We seek an updated probability P'' which:

- meets the probability values specified by P' for events in the sub-algebra $\mathbb{B}$;
- is such that $\forall\, B \in \mathbb{B}$, $X, Y \subset B$, $X, Y \in \mathbb{A}$

$$\frac{P''(X)}{P''(Y)} = \begin{cases} \frac{P(X)}{P(Y)} & if\ P(Y) > 0 \\ 0 & if\ P(Y) = 0. \end{cases}$$

It can be proven that there is a unique solution to the above problem, given by *Jeffrey's rule*, also called the *law of total probability*:

$$P''(A) = \sum_{B \in \mathbb{B}} P(A|B)P'(B). \qquad (2)$$

The initial probability measure 'stands corrected' by the second one on a number of events (but not all). The law of total probability thus generalises standard conditioning, as the special case in which $P'(B) = 1$ for some B and the sub-algebra $\mathbb{B}$ reduced to a single event B.

4.2 CONSTRAINTS

The law of total probability involves, given a subalgebra of events $\mathbb{B}$: (i) a prior probability $P(B)$ on the events of $\mathbb{B}$, and (ii) a family of conditional probabilities $P(A|B)$ for every event in $\mathbb{B}$. In particular, $\mathbb{B}$ can be the subalgebra associated with the power set of a disjoint partition of the original sample space.

Abstracting from the data association problem, we can then state the conditions an overall, total belief function b must obey, given a set of conditional belief functions $b_i : 2^{\Pi_i} \to [0,1]$ over the elements Π_i of the partition $\Pi = \{\Pi_1, ..., \Pi_{|\Omega|}\}$ of a frame Θ induced by a coarsening Ω.

1. *A-priori constraint*: the marginal on the coarsening Ω of the frame Θ of the candidate total belief function b must coincide with a given *a-priori* b.f. $b_0 : 2^\Omega \to [0,1]$.

As we showed above, in the data association problem the *a-priori* constraint is represented by the BF encoding the estimate of the past feature-to-model association $M \leftrightarrow m(k-1)$, defined over Θ_k^{k-1} (Figure 1). It ensures that the belief total function is compatible with the last available estimate.

2. *Conditional constraint*: the belief function $b(\cdot|\Pi_i)$ obtained by (Dempster's) conditioning the total belief function b with respect to each element Π_i of the partition Π must coincide with the corresponding given conditional belief function b_i:

$$b(\cdot|\Pi_i) = b \oplus b_{\Pi_i} = b_i \quad \forall i = 1, ..., N,$$

where $m_{\Pi_i} : 2^\Theta \to [0,1]$ is such that:

$$m_{\Pi_i}(A) = \begin{cases} 1 & A = \Pi_i \\ 0 & A \subseteq \Theta, A \neq \Pi_i. \end{cases} \qquad (3)$$

4.3 FORMULATION AND PROOF

The generalization of the total probability theorem to the theory of belief functions – the *total belief theorem* – thus reads as follows (Figure 2).

Theorem 1. *Suppose Θ and Ω are two frames of discernment, and $\rho : 2^\Omega \to 2^\Theta$ a given refining between them. Let b_0 be a belief function defined over $\Omega = \{\omega_1, ..., \omega_{|\Omega|}\}$. Suppose there exists a collection of belief functions $b_i : 2^{\Pi_i} \to [0,1]$, where $\Pi = \{\Pi_1, ..., \Pi_{|\Omega|}\}$, $\Pi_i = \rho(\{\omega_i\})$, is the partition of Θ induced by its coarsening Ω. Then, there exists a total belief function $b : 2^\Theta \to [0,1]$ such that:*

- *(P1) $b \oplus b_{\Pi_i} = b_i \ \forall i = 1, ..., |\Omega|$, where b_{Π_i} is the categorical belief function with mass m_{Π_i} (3);*
- *(P2) b_0 is the marginal of b on Ω, $b_0 = b\lceil_\Omega$.*

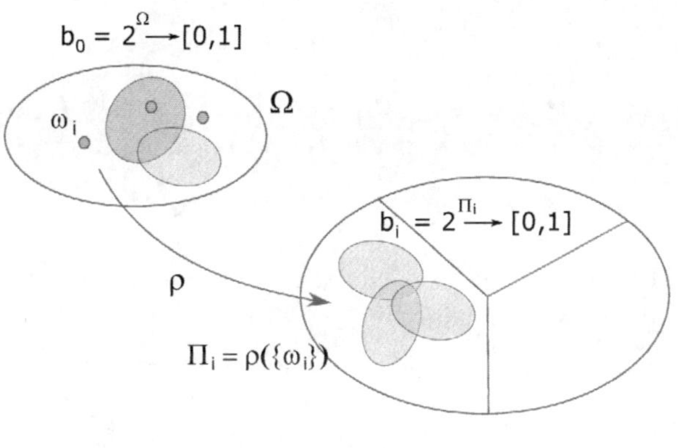

Figure 2: Pictorial representation of the total belief theorem hypotheses.

The theorem's proof makes use of the two lemmas that follow. We adapt Smets' original proof of the generalized Bayesian Theorem [29] to the refinement framework presented here, which is more general than his multivariate setting in which only Cartesian products of frames are considered. As usual, we denote by m_0 and m_i the mass functions of b_0 and b_i, respectively. Their sets of focal elements are denoted by $\mathcal{E}_\Omega$ and $\mathcal{E}_i$, respectively. For the collection of belief functions $b_i : 2^{\Pi_i} \to [0,1]$, let $\overrightarrow{b_i}$ be the conditional embedding of b_i into Θ and $\overrightarrow{b}$ denote the Dempster combination of all $\overrightarrow{b_i}$, i.e., $\overrightarrow{b} = \overrightarrow{b_1} \oplus \cdots \oplus \overrightarrow{b_{|\Omega|}}$, with mass function $\overrightarrow{m}$.

Lemma 1. *The belief function $\overrightarrow{b}$ over Θ satisfies the following two properties: (1) each focal element $\overrightarrow{e}$ of $\overrightarrow{b}$ is the union of exactly one focal element e_i of each of the conditional belief function b_i; (2) the marginal $\overrightarrow{b}\lceil_\Omega$ on Ω is the vacuous belief function over Ω.*

Proof. Each focal element $\overrightarrow{e_i}$ of $\overrightarrow{b_i}$ is of the form $(\bigcup_{j \neq i} \Pi_j) \cup e_i$ where e_i is some focal element of b_i. In other words, $\overrightarrow{e_i} = (\Theta \setminus \Pi_i) \cup e_i$. Since $\overrightarrow{b}$ is the Dempster combination of $\overrightarrow{b_i}$s, it is easy to see that each focal element $\overrightarrow{e}$ of $\overrightarrow{b}$ is the union of exactly one focal element e_i from each conditional belief function b_i. In other words, $\overrightarrow{e} = \bigcup_{i=1}^{|\Omega|} e_i$ where $e_i \in \mathcal{E}_i$, and condition (1) is proven.

Let $\overrightarrow{\mathcal{E}}$ denote the set of all focal elements of $\overrightarrow{b}$, namely:

$$\overrightarrow{\mathcal{E}} = \{\overrightarrow{e} \subseteq \Theta : \overrightarrow{e} = \textstyle\bigcup_{i=1}^{|\Omega|} e_i \text{ where } e_i \text{ is a focal element of } b_i\}.$$

Note that e_i's coming from different conditional belief functions b_i's are disjoint. For each $\overrightarrow{e} \in \overrightarrow{\mathcal{E}}$, $\bar{\rho}(\overrightarrow{e}) = \Omega$. It follows from Eq. (1) that $\overrightarrow{m}\lceil_\Omega(\Omega) = 1$ and hence the marginal of $\overrightarrow{b}$ on Ω is the vacuous belief function there.

□

Let $b_0^{\uparrow\Theta}$ be the vacuous extension of b_0 from Ω to Θ. We define the desired total belief function b to be the Dempster combination of $b_0^{\uparrow\Theta}$ and $\overrightarrow{b}$, namely:

$$b := b_0^{\uparrow\Theta} \oplus \overrightarrow{b}. \quad (4)$$

Lemma 2. *The belief function b defined in (4) over Θ satisfies the following two properties:*

1. *$b \oplus b_{\Pi_i} = b_i$ for all $i = 1, \cdots, |\Omega|$ where b_{Π_i} is the categorical belief function with the mass function: $m_{\Pi_i}(A) = 1$ if $A = \Pi_i$, and is 0, otherwise.;*
2. *b_0 is the marginal of b on Ω, i.e., $b_0 = b\lceil_\Omega$,*

i.e., is a valid total belief function.

Proof. Let $\overrightarrow{m}$ and m_i be the mass functions corresponding to $\overrightarrow{b}$ and b_i, respectively. For each $\overrightarrow{e} = \bigcup_{i=1}^{|\Omega|} e_i \in \overrightarrow{\mathcal{E}}$ where $e_i \in \mathcal{E}_i$, $\overrightarrow{m}(\overrightarrow{e}) = \Pi_{i=1}^{|\Omega|} m_i(e_i)$. Let $\mathcal{E}_\Omega^{\uparrow\Theta}$ denote the set of focal elements $b_0^{\uparrow\Theta}$. Since $b_0^{\uparrow\Theta}$ is the vacuous extension of b_0, $\mathcal{E}_\Omega^{\uparrow\Theta} = \{\rho(e_\Omega) : e_\Omega \in \mathcal{E}_\Omega\}$. Each element of $\mathcal{E}_\Omega^{\uparrow\Theta}$ is actually the union of some equivalence classes Π_i of the partition Π. Since each focal element of $b_0^{\uparrow\Theta}$ intersects with all focal elements $\overrightarrow{e} \in \overrightarrow{\mathcal{E}}$,

$$\sum_{e_\Omega \in \mathcal{E}_\Omega, \overrightarrow{e} \in \overrightarrow{\mathcal{E}}, \rho(e_\Omega) \cap \overrightarrow{e} \neq \emptyset} m_0^{\uparrow\Theta}(\rho(e_\Omega))\overrightarrow{m}(\overrightarrow{e}) = 1. \quad (5)$$

Thus, the normalization factor in the Dempster combination $b_0^{\uparrow\Theta} \oplus \overrightarrow{b}$ is equal to 1.

Now, let $\mathcal{E}$ denote the set of focal elements of the belief function $b = b_0^{\uparrow\Theta} \oplus \overrightarrow{b}$. By Dempster's sum (1) each element e of $\mathcal{E}$ is the union of focal elements of some conditional belief functions b_i, i.e., $e = e_{j_1} \cup e_{j_2} \cup \cdots \cup e_{j_K}$ for some K such that $\{j_1, \cdots, j_K\} \subseteq \{1, \cdots, |\Omega|\}$ and e_{j_l} is a focal element of $b_{j_l} (1 \leq l \leq K)$. Let m denote the mass function for b.

For each such $e \in \mathcal{E}$, $e = \rho(e_\Omega) \cap \vec{e}$ for some $e_\Omega \in \mathcal{E}_\Omega$ and $\vec{e} \in \vec{\mathcal{E}}$, so that $e_\Omega = \bar{\rho}(e)$. Thus we have

$$
\begin{aligned}
(m_0^{\uparrow\Theta} \oplus \vec{m})(e) &= \sum_{\substack{e_\Omega \in \mathcal{E}_\Omega, \vec{e} \in \vec{\mathcal{E}}, \\ \rho(e_\Omega) \cap \vec{e} = e}} m_0^{\uparrow\Theta}(\rho(e_\Omega)) \vec{m}(\vec{e}) \\
&= \sum_{e_\Omega \in \mathcal{E}_\Omega, \vec{e} \in \vec{\mathcal{E}}, \rho(e_\Omega) \cap \vec{e} = e} m_0(e_\Omega) \vec{m}(\vec{e}) \\
&= m_0(\bar{\rho}(e)) \sum_{\vec{e} \in \vec{\mathcal{E}}, \rho(\bar{\rho}(e)) \cap \vec{e} = e} \vec{m}(\vec{e}) \\
&= m_0(\bar{\rho}(e)) m_{j_1}(e_{j_1}) \cdots m_{j_K}(e_{j_K}) \prod_{j \notin \{j_1, \cdots, j_K\}} \sum_{e \in \mathcal{E}_j} m_j(e) \\
&= m_0(\bar{\rho}(e)) m_{j_1}(e_{j_1}) \cdots m_{j_K}(e_{j_K}), \qquad (6)
\end{aligned}
$$

as $\vec{m}(\vec{e}) = \prod_{i=1}^n m_i(e_i)$ whenever $\vec{e} = \cup_{i=1}^n e_i$.

Without loss of generality, we consider the conditional mass function $m(e_1|\Pi_1)$ where e_1 is a focal element of b_1 and Π_1 is the first partition class associated with the partition Π, and show that $m(e_1|\Pi_1) = m_1(e_1)$. In order to obtain $m(e_1|\Pi_1)$, which is equal to $\frac{\sum_{e \in \mathcal{E}, e \cap \Pi_1 = e_1} m(e)}{pl(\Pi_1)}$, in the following we separately compute $\sum_{e \in \mathcal{E}, e \cap \Pi_1 = e_1} m(e)$ and $pl(\Pi_1)$. For any $e \in \mathcal{E}$, if $e \cap \Pi_1 \neq \emptyset$, $\bar{\rho}(e)$ is a subset of Ω including ω_1.

$$
\begin{aligned}
pl(\Pi_1) &= \sum_{e \in \mathcal{E}, e \cap \Pi_1 \neq \emptyset} m(e) \\
&= \sum_{C \subseteq \{\Pi_2, \cdots, \Pi_{|\Omega|}\}} \left(\sum_{\rho(\bar{\rho}(e)) = \Pi_1 \cup (\bigcup_{E \in C} E)} m(e) \right) \\
&= \sum_{C \subseteq \{\Pi_2, \cdots, \Pi_{|\Omega|}\}} m_0^{\uparrow\Theta} \left(\Pi_1 \cup \bigcup_{E \in C} E \right) \\
&\quad \left(\sum_{e_1 \in \mathcal{E}_1} m_1(e_1) \prod_{\Pi_l \in C} \sum_{e_l \in \mathcal{E}_l} m_l(e_l) \right) \\
&= \sum_{C \subseteq \{\Pi_2, \cdots, \Pi_{|\Omega|}\}} m_0^{\uparrow\Theta} \left(\Pi_1 \cup \bigcup_{E \in C} E \right) \\
&= \sum_{e_\Omega \in \mathcal{E}_\Omega, \omega_1 \in e_\Omega} m_0(e_\Omega) = pl_0(\{\omega_1\}). \qquad (7)
\end{aligned}
$$

Similarly,

$$
\begin{aligned}
\sum_{e \in \mathcal{E}, e \cap \Pi_1 = e_1} m(e) &= \sum_{C \subseteq \{\Pi_2, \cdots, \Pi_{|\Omega|}\}} \sum_{\rho(\bar{\rho}(e)) = \bigcup_{E \in C} E} m(e_1 \cup e) \\
&= m_1(e_1) \sum_{C \subseteq \{\Pi_2, \cdots, \Pi_{|\Omega|}\}} m_0^{\uparrow\Theta} \left(\Pi_1 \cup \bigcup_{E \in C} E \right) \prod_{\Pi_l \in C} \sum_{e_l \in \mathcal{E}_l} m_l(e_l) \\
&= m_1(e_1) \sum_{C \subseteq \{\Pi_2, \cdots, \Pi_{|\Omega|}\}} m_0^{\uparrow\Theta} \left(\Pi_1 \cup \bigcup_{E \in C} E \right) \\
&= m_1(e_1) \sum_{e_\Omega \in \mathcal{E}_\Omega, \omega_1 \in e_\Omega} m_0(e_\Omega) = m_1(e_1) pl_0(\{\omega_1\}). \qquad (8)
\end{aligned}
$$

From Eqs. (7) and (8) it follows that $m(e_1|\Pi_1) = \frac{\sum_{e \in \mathcal{E}, e \cap \Pi_1 = e_1} m(e)}{pl(\Pi_1)} = m_1(e_1)$. This proves property 1. Proving 2. is much easier. For any $e_\Omega := \{\omega_{j_1}, \cdots, \omega_{j_K}\} \in \mathcal{E}_\Omega$,

$$
\begin{aligned}
m \upharpoonright_\Omega (e_\Omega) &= \sum_{\bar{\rho}(e) = e_\Omega} m(e) \\
&= m_0^{\uparrow\Theta}(\rho(e_\Omega)) \prod_{l=1}^{K} \sum_{e \in \mathcal{E}_{j_l}} m_{j_l}(e) = m_0^{\uparrow\Theta}(\rho(e_\Omega)) = \qquad (9)
\end{aligned}
$$

$= m_0(e_\Omega)$. It follows that $b \upharpoonright_\Omega = b_0$, hence the thesis.

□

The proof of the main Theorem 1 immediately follows from Lemmas 1 and 2.

Example 1. *Suppose that the considered coarsening* $\Omega := \{\omega_1, \omega_2, \omega_3\}$ *induces a partion* Π *of* Θ: $\{\Pi_1, \Pi_2, \Pi_3\}$. *Also suppose that the considered conditional belief function* b_1 *defined on* Π_1 *has two focal elements* e_1^1 *and* e_1^2; *the conditional belief function* b_2 *defined on* Π_2 *has a single focal element* e_2^1; b_3 *defined on* Π_3 *has two focal elements* e_3^1 *and* e_3^2 *(See Figure 3).*

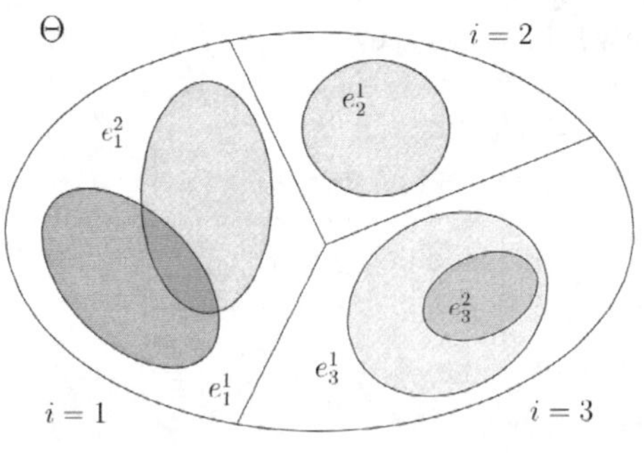

Figure 3: The conditional belief functions considered in our case study. The set-theoretical relations between their focal elements are immaterial to the solution.

According to Lemma 1, Dempster's combination $\vec{b}$ *of* *the conditional embeddings of the b_i's has 4 focal elements, which are listed as follows:*

$$e_1 = e_1^1 \cup e_2^1 \cup e_3^1, \quad e_2 = e_1^1 \cup e_2^1 \cup e_3^2$$
$$e_3 = e_1^2 \cup e_2^1 \cup e_3^1, \quad e_4 = e_1^2 \cup e_2^1 \cup e_3^2$$

The four focal total elements can be represented as "elastic bands" as in Figure 4.

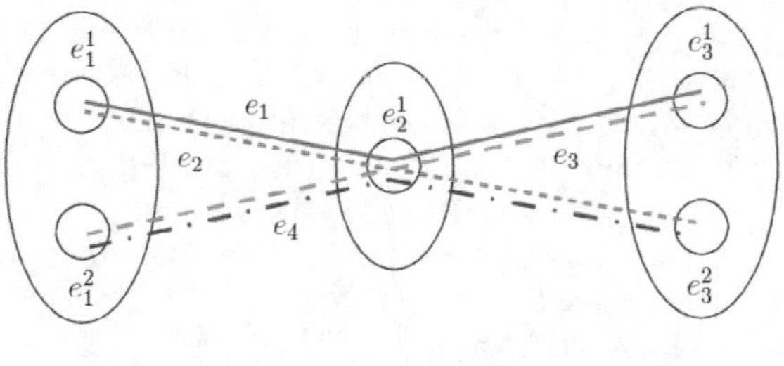

Figure 4: Graphical representation of the four possible focal elements of $\overrightarrow{b}$ in our case study.

Without loss of generality, we assume that a prior b_0 on Ω has each subset of Ω as a focal element, i.e., $\mathcal{E}_\Omega = 2^\Omega$. It follows that each focal element e of the total belief function $b := \overrightarrow{b} \oplus b_0^{\uparrow\Theta}$ is the union of some focal elements from different *conditional belief functions b_is. So the set $\mathcal{E}$ of the focal elements of b is $\{e = \bigcup_{1 \le i \le I} e_i : 1 \le I \le 3, e_i \in \mathcal{E}_i\}$ and is the union of the following three sets:*

$$\mathcal{E}_{I=1} := \mathcal{E}_1 \cup \mathcal{E}_2 \cup \mathcal{E}_3$$
$$\mathcal{E}_{I=2} := \{e \cup e' : (e, e') \in \mathcal{E}_i \times \mathcal{E}_j, 1 \le i, j \le 3, i \neq j\}$$
$$\mathcal{E}_{I=3} := \{e_1 \cup e_2 \cup e_3 : e_i \in \mathcal{E}_i, 1 \le i \le 3\}.$$

So the cardinality $|\mathcal{E}| = 5 + 8 + 4 = 17$. According to Eq. (6), it is very easy to compute the corresponding total mass function m. For example, for the two focal elements $e_1^1 \cup e_3^2$ and $e_1^1 \cup e_2^1 \cup e_3^2$ we have:

$$m(e_1^1 \cup e_3^2) = m_0(\{w_1, w_3\}) m_1(e_1^1) m_3(e_3^2)$$
$$m(e_1^1 \cup e_2^1 \cup e_3^2) = m_0(\Omega) m_1(e_1^1) m_2(e_2^1) m_3(e_3^2).$$

Since we assume that a topological model is known (Section 3), in this paper we take a closed-world approach and hence adopt normalized mass functions. Under an open-world assumption in which mass functions are not necessarily normalized, Theorem 1 does not hold any more. In the unnormalized case, however, a weaker form of (P1) exists. Let $m \circledcap m_{\Pi_i}$ denote Smets' conjunctive combination of m and the categorical mass function m_{Π_i} [29]. For any two focal elements e_1 and e_2 of m_i, $\frac{(m \circledcap m_{\Pi_i})(e_1)}{(m \circledcap m_{\Pi_i})(e_2)} = \frac{m_i(e_1)}{m_i(e_2)}$. Constraint (P2), instead, does not seem to be easily generalizable to unnormalized mass functions.

4.4 NUMBER OF SOLUTIONS

The total belief function b obtained in Theorem 1 is *not unique*. Assume that b^* is a total belief function satisfies the two properties in Theorem 1. Let m^* and $\mathcal{E}^*$ denote its mass function and the set of its focal elements, respectively. Without loss of generality, we still assume that the prior b_0 has every subset of Ω as its focal element, i.e., $\mathcal{E}_\Omega = 2^\Omega$. From the second property that $b^* \oplus b_{\Pi_i} = b_i (1 \le i \le |\Omega|)$, we derive that each focal element of b^* must be a union of focal elements of some conditional belief functions b_is. For, if e^* is a focal element of b^* and $e^* = e_l \cup e'$ where $\emptyset \neq e_l \subseteq \Pi_l$ and $e' \subseteq \Theta \setminus \Pi_l$ for some $1 \le l \le |\Omega|$, then $m_l(e_l) = (m^* \oplus m_{\Pi_l})(e_l) > 0$ and hence $e_l \in \mathcal{E}_l$. So we must have that $\mathcal{E}^* \subseteq \mathcal{E}$, where $\mathcal{E}$ is the set of focal elements of the total belief function b obtained in Theorem 1: $\mathcal{E} = \{\bigcup_{j \in J} e_j : J \subseteq \{1, \cdots, |\Omega|\}, e_j \in \mathcal{E}_j\}$.

In order to find b^* (or m^*), we need to solve a group of linear equations which correspond to the constraints dictated in the two properties. We specify the mass $m^*(e)$ of each focal element $e \in \mathcal{E}$ of the total solution (4) as an unknown variable. There are $|\mathcal{E}|$ variables in the group.

From Properties (P1) and (P2) we know that $pl_0(\omega_i) = pl^*(\Pi_i)(1 \le i \le |\Omega|)$ where pl_0 and pl^* are the corresponding plausibility functions of b_0 and b^*, respectively. In addition, Property (P1) implies the system of linear constraints:

$$\left\{ \sum_{e \cap \Pi_i = e_i, e \in \mathcal{E}} m^*(e) = m_i(e_i) pl_0(\omega_i), \quad \forall i \forall e_i \in \mathcal{E}_i. \right. \tag{10}$$

The total number of such equations is $\sum_{j=1}^{|\Omega|} |\mathcal{E}_j|$. Since, for each $1 \le i \le |\Omega|$, $\sum_{e \in \mathcal{E}_i} m_i(e) = 1$, system (10) include a group of $\sum_{j=1}^{|\Omega|} |\mathcal{E}_j| - |\Omega|$ *independent* linear equations, which we denote as G_1. From property (P2) (the marginal of b^* on Ω is b_0) follow the constaints:

$$\left\{ \sum_{e \in \mathcal{E}, \overline{p}(e) = C} m^*(e) = m_0(C), \quad \forall \emptyset \neq C \subseteq \Omega. \right. \tag{11}$$

The total number of linear equations in (11) is the number of all nonempty subsets of Ω. Since $\sum_{C \subseteq \Omega} m_0(C) = 1$, there is a subset of $|2^\Omega| - 2$ independent linear equations in (11), denoted by G_2.

The groups of constraints G_1 and G_2 are independent for, although for each $1 \le i \le |\Omega|$ $\sum_{w_i \in C, C \subseteq \Omega} m_0(C) = pl_0(w_i), m_i(e_i) \sum_{w_i \in C, C \subseteq \Omega} \sum_{e \in \mathcal{E}, \overline{p}(e) = C} m^*(e)$ is not generally identical to $\sum_{e \cap \Pi_i = e_i, e \in \mathcal{E}} m^*(e)$. Therefore, the union $G := G_1 \cup G_2$ completely specifies Properties (P1) and (P2) in Theorem 1. Since $|G_1| = \sum_{j=1}^{|\Omega|} |\mathcal{E}_j| -$

$|\Omega|$ and $|G_2| = |2^\Omega| - 2$, the cardinality of the union group G is $|G| = \sum_{j=1}^{|\Omega|} |\mathcal{E}_j| - |\Omega| + |2^\Omega| - 2$.

From Theorem 1, we know that the system of equations G is solvable and has at least a positive solution (in which each variable has a positive value). This implies that $|\mathcal{E}| \geq |G|$, i.e., the number of variables must be no less than that of the indepedent linear equations in G. If $|\mathcal{E}| > |G|$, in particular, we can apply the Fourier-Motzkin elimination method [24] to show that G has *another distinct positive* solution b^* (i.e., such that $m^*(e) \geq 0 (e \in \mathcal{E})$).

Example 2. *We employ Example 1 to illustrate the whole process to find the total belief function b^*. We further assume that m_0 and $m_i (1 \leq i \leq 3)$ take numerical values:*

- $m_1(e_1^1) = \frac{1}{2} = m_1(e_1^2); m_2(e_2^1) = 1; m_3(e_3^1) = \frac{1}{3}, m_3(e_3^2) = \frac{2}{3}$;
- $m_0(\{\omega_1\}) = m_0(\{\omega_2\}) = m_0(\{\omega_3\}) = \frac{1}{16}$; $m_0(\{\omega_1, \omega_2\}) = \frac{2}{16}, m_0(\{\omega_2, \omega_3\}) = \frac{4}{16}, m_0(\{\omega_1, \omega_3\}) = \frac{3}{16}; m_0(\Omega) = \frac{1}{4}$.

If we follow the above prescribed process to translate the two properties into a group G of linear equations, we obtain 17 unknown variables $m^*(e) (e \in \mathcal{E})$ ($|\mathcal{E}| = 17$) and 8 indepedent linear equations ($|G| = 8$). From Theorem 1, we can construct a positive solution m defined according to Eq. (6). For this example:

$$m(\{e_1^1, e_2^1, e_3^1\}) = m_0(\Omega) m_1(e_1^1) m_2(e_2^1) m_3(e_3^1) = \frac{1}{24},$$

$$m(\{e_1^2, e_2^1, e_3^2\}) = m_0(\Omega) m_1(e_1^2) m_2(e_2^1) m_3(e_3^2) = \frac{1}{12}.$$

When solving the equation group G via the Fourier-Motzkin elimination method, we choose $m^*(\{e_1^1, e_2^1, e_3^1\})$ and $m^*(\{e_1^2, e_2^1, e_3^2\})$ to be the last two variables to be eliminated. Moreover, there is a sufficiently small postive number ϵ such that $m^*(\{e_1^1, e_2^1, e_3^1\}) = \frac{1}{24} - \epsilon > 0$, $m^*(\{e_1^2, e_2^1, e_3^2\}) = \frac{1}{12} + \epsilon$, and all other varaibles also take positive values. It is easy to see that such obtained m^* is different from m obtained in Theorem 1.

However, when the prior b_0 is Bayesian, the total belief function obtained according to Eq. (6) is the unique one satisfying the two properties in Theorem 1.

Corollary 1. *For the belief function b_0 over Ω and conditional belief functions b_i over Π_i in Theorem 1, if b_0 is Bayesian (a probability function) such that $b_0(\omega_i) > 0$ for all $1 \leq i \leq |\Omega|$, then there is a unique total belief function $b : 2^\Theta \to [0, 1]$ such that:*

1. *$b \oplus b_{\Pi_i} = b_i$ for all $i = 1, \cdots, |\Omega|$ where b_{Π_i} is the categorical belief function with $m_{\Pi_i}(A) = 1$ if $A = \Pi_i$, and is 0, o.w.;*
2. *b_0 is the marginal of b on Ω, i.e., $b_0 = b \restriction_\Omega$.*

Moreover, the total mass function m of b is:

$$m(e) = \begin{cases} m_i(e) b_0(\omega_i) & \textit{if } e \in \mathcal{E}_i \textit{ for some } i, \\ 0 & \textit{otherwise.} \end{cases}$$

Proof. It is easy to check that the total mass function m defined above satisfies the two properties. Now we need to show that it is unique. Assume that b_0 is Bayesian such that $b_0(\omega_i) > 0$ for all i and m is the mass function of a total belief function b satisfying the two properties. Since $b_0 = b \restriction_\Omega$, each focal element e of b is a subset of some equivalence class Π_k for some $1 \leq k \leq |\Omega|$. Together with the first requirement that $b \oplus b_{\Pi_i} = b_i$, it implies that $pl(\Pi_i) = b(\Pi_i) = b_0(\omega_i)$ for all $1 \leq i \leq |\Omega|$ and $\mathcal{E} = \bigcup_{j=1}^{|\Omega|} \mathcal{E}_j$. For any $e \in \mathcal{E}$, $e \in \mathcal{E}_k$ for some $1 \leq k \leq |\Omega|$. It follows that $(m \oplus m_{\Pi_k})(e) = \frac{m(e)}{pl(\Pi_k)} = m_k(e)$ and hence $m(e) = m_k(e) pl(\Pi_k) = m_k(e) b_0(\omega_k)$. If $e \notin \bigcup_{i=1}^{|\Omega|} \mathcal{E}_i$, $e \notin \mathcal{E}$ and hence $m(e) = 0$. So we have shown that the total mass function m is the unique one satisfying the two properties. □

Corollary 1 recalls a more general characterization of uniqueness [1]: if $Bel(A, B) = Bel(A|B) \oplus Bel(B)$, then it will be unique when $Bel(A|B)$ is defined for all primitive elements of B and $Bel(B)$ is Bayesian, or $Bel(A|B)$ is defined for all subsets of B.

4.5 GENERALISATION

If the first requirement (P1) is modified to include conditional constraints with respect to unions of equivalence classes, the approach used to prove Theorem 1 does not work.

For each nonempty subset $\{i_1, \cdots, i_J\} \subseteq \{1, \cdots, |\Omega|\}$, let $b_{\bigcup_{j=1}^J \Pi_{i_j}}$ and $b_{i_1 \cdots i_J}$ denote the categorical belief function with as only focal element $\bigcup_{j=1}^J \Pi_{i_j}$ and a conditional belief function on $\bigcup_{j=1}^J \Pi_{i_j}$, respectively.

We can introduce a new requirement by generalising Property (P1):

- $(P1') : b \oplus b_{\bigcup_{j=1}^J \Pi_{i_j}} = b_{i_1 \cdots i_J}$ for every nonempty subset $\{i_1, \cdots, i_J\} \subseteq \{1, \cdots, |\Omega|\}$.

Let $\vec{b}_{i_1 \cdots i_J}$ denote the conditional embeddings of $b_{i_1 \cdots i_J}$ and $\vec{b}_{new}$ the Dempster combination of all these conditional embeddings. Let $b_{new} = \vec{b}_{new} \oplus b_0^{\uparrow \Theta}$. In the following example, we show that b_{new} satisfies neither $(P1')$ nor $(P2)$.

Example 3. *We continue Example 2 with an additional categorical conditional belief function b_{12} on $\Pi_1 \cup \Pi_2$ with the only focal element e_{new} where $e_{new} = e_1^3 \cup e_2^2$ for some $e_1^3 \subseteq \Pi_1$ and $e_2^2 \subseteq \Pi_2$ such that $e_1^3 \cap e_1^1 \neq \emptyset, e_1^3 \cap e_1^2 = \emptyset$ and $e_2^2 \cap e_2^1 = \emptyset$. It is easy to check that $b_{new} = (\overrightarrow{b} \oplus \overrightarrow{b}_{12}) \oplus b_0^{\uparrow\Theta}$ satisfies neither $P1'$ nor $P2$.*

5 RELATION TO GENERALISED JEFFREY'S RULES

In spirit, our approach in this paper is similar to Spies' Jeffrey's rule for belief functions in [30]. His total belief function is also the Dempster combination of the prior on the subalgebra generated by the partion Π of Θ with conditional belief functions on each equivalence class Π_i. Moreover, he showed that this total belief function satisfies the two properties in Theorem 1. However, his definition of conditional belief function is different from the one used in this paper, derived from Dempster's rule of combination. His definition falls within the framework of random sets, so that a conditional belief function there is a *second-order* belief function whose focal elements are conditional events which are sets of subsets of the underlying frame of discernment. The biggest difference between Spies' approach and ours is thus that his framework depends on probabilities while ours doesn't. It would be interesting to explore the connection of our total belief theorem to his Jeffrey's rule for BFs.

Smets [28] also generalized Jeffrey's rule within the framework of models based on belief functions, without relying on probabilities. Recall that ρ is a refining mapping from 2^Ω to 2^Θ and $\mathbb{A}^\rho$ is the Boolean algebra generated by the set of equivalence classes Π_i associated with the refining mapping ρ. Contrary to our total belief theorem which assumes conditional constraints only with respect to the equivalence classes Π_i (the atoms of $\mathbb{A}^\rho$), Smets' generalized Jeffrey's rule considers constraints with respect to unions of equivalence classes, i.e., arbitrary elements of $\mathbb{A}^\rho$. Given two belief functions b_1 and b_2 over Θ, his general idea is to find a BF b_3 there such that:

- (Q1) its marginal on Ω is the same as that of b_1, i.e., $b_3 \upharpoonright_\Omega = b_1 \upharpoonright_\Omega$;
- (Q2) its conditional constraints w.r.t. elements of $\mathbb{A}^\rho$ are the same as those of b_2.

Let m be a mass function over Θ. Smets defines two kinds of conditioning for conditional constraints: for any $E \in \mathbb{A}^\rho$ and $e \subseteq E$ such that $\rho(\bar{\rho}(e)) = E$,

- $m^{in}(e|E) := \frac{m(e)}{\sum_{\rho(\bar{\rho}(e'))=E} m(e')}$;
- $m^{out}(e|E) := \frac{m(e|E)}{\sum_{\rho(\bar{\rho}(e'))=E} m(e'|E)}$.

The first one is the well-known geometric conditioning, whereas the second one is called 'outer conditioning'. Both are distinct from Dempster's rule of conditioning used in this paper. From these two conditioning rules, he obtaines two different forms of generalized Jeffrey's rule: for any $e \subseteq \Theta$,

- $m_3^{in}(e) = m_1^{in}(e|E)m_2(E)$ where $E = \rho(\bar{\rho}(e))$;
- $m_3^{out}(e) = m_1^{out}(e|E)m_2(E)$.

Both m_3^{in} and m_3^{out} satisfy (Q1). As for (Q2), m_3^{in} applies whereas m_3^{out} only *partially* does, since $(m_3^{out})^{in}(e|E) = m_1^{out}(e|E)$ [34].

Finally, in [18] Ma *et al* define a new Jeffrey's rule where the conditional constraints are indeed defined according to Dempster's rule of combination, and w.r.t. the whole power set of the frame instead of a subalgebra as in Smets' framework. In their rule, however, the conditional constraints are not preserved by their total belief functions.

6 CONCLUSIONS

In this paper we stated and proved the generalisation of the law of total probability to belief measures, for the case in which Dempster's conditioning is employed. We showed that the solution is not unique, whereas it is unique when the a-priori belief function is Bayesian. A critical comparison with Spies' and Smets' results on generalised Jeffrey's rules was also conducted.

These results can be further extended in a number of ways. For instance, distinct versions of the law of total belief may arise by replacing Dempster's conditioning with other accepted forms of conditioning for belief functions, such as credal [9], geometric [31], conjunctive and disjunctive [28] conditioning. As belief functions are a special type of coherent lower probabilities, which in turn can be seen as a special class of lower previsions (consult [32], Section 5.13), marginal extension [19] can be applied to them to obtain a total lower prevision. The relationship between marginal extension and the law of total belief needs therefore to be understood.
Finally, fascinating relationships exist between the total belief problem and transversal matroids [20], on one hand, and the theory of positive linear systems [21], on the other, as hinted at in this paper, which will be investigated in the near future.

References

[1] B. Almond, *Graphical Belief Modeling*, Chapman and Hall/CRC, 1995.

[2] T. Augustin, *Modeling weak information with generalized basic probability assignments*, Data Analysis and Information Systems, pp. 101–113, 1996.

[3] A. Ayoun & Ph. Smets., *Data association in multi-target detection using the transferable belief model*, Int.. J. Intell. Systems **16**(10), 1167–82, 2001.

[4] Y. Bar-Shalom & T. E. Fortmann, *Tracking and data association*, Academic Press, Inc., 1988.

[5] F. Cuzzolin, *Visions of a generalized probability theory*, Lambert Academic Publishing, 2014.

[6] D. Denneberg, *Conditioning (updating) non-additive probabilities*, AOR **52**, 21–42, 1994.

[7] D. Denneberg & M. Grabisch, *Interaction transform of set functions over a finite set*, Information Sciences **121**, 149–170, 1999.

[8] D. Dubois & H. Prade, *A set theoretical view of belief functions*, International Journal of Intelligent Systems **12** (1986), 193–226.

[9] R. Fagin & J.Y. Halpern, *A new approach to updating beliefs*, Proc. of UAI, pp. 347–374, 1991.

[10] I. Gilboa & D. Schmeidler, *Updating ambiguous beliefs*, J. Economic Theory **59**, 33–49, 1993.

[11] W. Gong & F. Cuzzolin, *A belief-theoretical approach to example-based pose estimation*, IEEE Transactions on Fuzzy Systems, 2017.

[12] J. Y. Jaffray, *Bayesian updating and belief functions*, IEEE Tr. SMC **22**, 1144–1152, 1992.

[13] R. Jeffrey, *Conditioning, kinematics, and exchangeability*, Causation, chance, and credence **1**, 221–255, 1988.

[14] ______, *The logic of decision*, Mc Graw, 1965.

[15] ______, *Dracula meets wolfman: Acceptance vs. partial belief*, pp. 157–185, Springer, 1970.

[16] R. Kruse, D. Nauck & F. Klawonn, *Reasoning with mass*, Proc. of UAI, 182–187, 1991.

[17] R. Kruse, E. Schwecke & F. Klawonn, *On a tool for reasoning with mass distribution*, Proc. of IJCAI, vol. 2, pp. 1190–1195, 1991.

[18] J. Ma, W. Liu, D. Dubois & H. Prade, *Bridging Jeffrey's rule, AGM revision and Dempster conditioning in the theory of evidence*, International Journal on AI Tools **20 (4)**, 691–720, 2011.

[19] E. Miranda & G. de Cooman, *Marginal extension in the theory of coherent lower previsions*, Int. J. of Approximate Reasoning **46** (1), 188–225, 2007.

[20] J. G. Oxley, *Matroid theory*, Oxford University Press, 1992.

[21] S. Rinaldi & L. Farina, *I sistemi lineari positivi: teoria e applicazioni*, Cittá Studi Edizioni, 1998.

[22] B. Ristic & Ph. Smets, *The TBM global distance measure for the association of uncertain combat ID declarations*, Inform. Fusion **7**(3), 276–284, 2006.

[23] E. H. Ruspini, *Approximate deduction in single evidential bodies*, CoRR **abs/1304.3104**, 2011.

[24] A. Schrijver, *Theory of Linear and Integer Progamming*, John Wiley & Sons, 1986.

[25] G. Shafer, *A mathematical theory of evidence*, Princeton University Press, 1976.

[26] ______, *Jeffrey's rule of conditioning*, Philosophy of Sciences **48**, 337–362, 1981.

[27] P. Smets and B. Ristic, *Kalman filter and joint tracking and classification in the TBM framework*, Proc. of ICIF, vol. 1, pp. 46–53, 2004.

[28] P. Smets, *Jeffrey's rule of conditioning generalized to belief functions*, Proc. of UAI, 500–505, 1993.

[29] ______, *Belief functions : The disjunctive rule of combination and the generalized Bayesian theorem*, IJAR **9**, 1–35, 1993.

[30] M. Spies, *Conditional events, conditioning, and random sets*, IEEE Tr. SMC **24**, 1755–1763, 1994.

[31] P. Suppes & M. Zanotti, *On using random relations to generate upper and lower probabilities*, Synthese **36**, 427–440, 1977.

[32] P. Walley, *Statistical reasoning with imprecise probabilities*, Chapman and Hall, 1991.

[33] C. Yu & F. Arasta, *On conditional belief functions*, IJAR **10**, 155–172, 1994.

[34] C. Zhou, M. Wang, and B. Qin, *Belief-kinematics Jeffrey's rules in the theory of evidence*, Proc. of UAI, 917–926, 2014.

Complexity of Solving Decision Trees with Skew-Symmetric Bilinear Utility

Hugo Gilbert
Sorbonne Universités, UPMC Univ Paris 06
CNRS, LIP6 UMR 7606
4 place Jussieu
75005 Paris, France

Olivier Spanjaard
Sorbonne Universités, UPMC Univ Paris 06
CNRS, LIP6 UMR 7606
4 place Jussieu
75005 Paris, France

Abstract

We study the complexity of solving decision trees with a Skew-Symmetric Bilinear (SSB) utility function. The SSB model is an extension of Expected Utility (EU) with enhanced descriptive possibilities. Unlike EU, the optimality principle does not hold for SSB, which makes its optimization trickier. We show that determining an SSB optimal plan is NP-hard if one only considers deterministic plans while it is polynomial time if one allows randomized plans. With the Weighted EU model (a special case of SSB), the problem becomes polynomial in both settings. Our numerical tests show the operationality of the methods.

1 INTRODUCTION

This paper deals with planning under risk. In this setting, an agent repeatedly chooses actions to perform in order to maximize a given decision criterion. A solution to a planning problem is a plan, *i.e.* a sequence of actions conditioned by events. The difficulty of finding the optimal plan relies in the fact that actions' consequences are uncertain. Thus, a plan results in a probability distribution over possible outcomes (*i.e.* lotteries) and comparing plans amounts to comparing their respective lotteries. A popular decision criterion to compare lotteries is the Expected Utility (EU) model (von Neumann and Morgenstern, 1947). In this model, preferences over the set $\mathcal{X}$ of possible outcomes are modeled using a utility function which assigns a numerical value to each element $x \in \mathcal{X}$. Then, the preferences are lifted from outcomes to lotteries using expectation. More formally, a lottery p is preferred to a lottery q, denoted by $p \succ q$, iff $u(p) > u(q)$, with $u(p) = \sum_{x \in \mathcal{X}} p(x)u(x)$[1]. However, despite its appeal from a *normative* viewpoint, the EU model does not make it possible to describe all observed preferences (*descriptive* viewpoint). We present here two examples of observed preferences that EU cannot accommodate while they seem rational.

Example 1 (Gardner's dice)**.** *Consider three dice (Gardner, 1970): die A with faces $(1,4,4,4,4,4)$, die B with faces $(3,3,3,3,3,6)$ and die C with faces $(2,2,2,5,5,5)$. Consider a very simple two-player game where each player throws a die, and the player which throws the highest value wins. The probability to win with A (resp. B, C) against B (resp. C, A) is $25/36$ (resp. $21/36$, $21/36$). Thus, there is a "winning cycle": A wins against B, B wins against C and C wins against A. In this situation, it is therefore not possible to represent the preferences over dice by using an EU criterion (i.e., assigning a utility to each face in order to evaluate each die by the expected utility of the rolled face) because EU is not able to account for* intransitive *preferences.*

Example 2 (Allais' paradox)**.** *We present in Table 1 a very simple variant of this well-known paradox (variant by Kahneman and Tversky, 1979). Each row corresponds to a lottery p, q, p' or q' and each cell indicates the probability to win* 0\$, 3000\$ *or* 4000\$. *Allais' paradox stipulates that most people prefer lottery p to lottery q but prefer lottery q' to lottery p'. However, lottery p' (resp. q') is simply the mixture of lottery p (resp. q), with probability* 0.25, *and a sure amount of* 0\$, *with probability* 0.75. *Thus, those preferences violate the* independence *axiom which holds in EU theory. In short, the independence axiom states that $p \succ q \Rightarrow \alpha p + (1-\alpha)r \succ \alpha q + (1-\alpha)r$ where r is any lottery, $\alpha \in (0,1)$ and $\alpha p + (1-\alpha)r$ denotes the mixture where p (resp. r) is obtained with probability α (resp. $1-\alpha$). This makes it impossible to account for such preferences with the EU model.*

In this paper, we study two models able to cope with the preferences observed in the above examples: the Skew-Symmetric Bilinear (SSB) utility model (Fishburn, 1984b, 1982) is able to account for intransitive and non-

[1] with $p(x)$ the probability that p yields outcome x.

x	0$	3000$	4000$
$p(x)$	0	1	0
$q(x)$	0.2	0	0.8
$p'(x)$	0.75	0.25	0
$q'(x)$	0.8	0	0.2

Table 1: Allais' paradox.

independent preferences, while the Weighted Expected Utility (WEU) model (Chew, 1983; Fishburn, 1983) copes with non-independent preferences. Note that the WEU model is a subclass of the SSB model. Our aim is to identify the complexity of determining an optimal plan according to each of these two models in a sequential decision problem under risk.

A standard way of modeling a sequential decision problem under risk is to use a *decision tree* representing all decision steps and possible events. In a decision tree, the number of plans exponentially increases with the number of decision steps, thus the problem of choosing a plan is of combinatorial nature. The choice of a plan can be made in several manners according to the behavior of the Decision Maker (DM). We now briefly describe the most studied types of behaviors. A *consequentialist* DM selects a plan looking only at the possible futures (regardless of the past or counterfactual history); among consequentialist DMs, the *sophisticated* ones select a plan starting from the anticipated future decisions and rolling back to the present (in a recursive manner); on the contrary, a *resolute* DM considers all possible plans from the present time, chooses one and commits to it without deviating thereafter. The behavior of a resolute DM is therefore non-consequentialist because her choices in the future will depend on past and counterfactual events.

Note that an EU optimizer is both sophisticated and resolute. This is related to the fact that the Bellman optimality principle holds for the EU criterion (i.e., a subplan of an optimal plan is optimal). However, it is not the case for criteria able to account for intransitive and/or non-independent preferences because, contrary to the EU model, they violate the Bellman optimality principle. A DM whose behavior is consistent with the SSB/WEU model is thus either sophisticated or resolute. For a sophisticated DM, determining an optimal plan for the SSB/WEU model can be performed with a usual rolling back procedure. The drawback is the possibility to act as a *money pump* (Tversky, 1969). As in the Gardner's dice example, assume a DM prefers A to B, B to C, and C to A. It is reasonable to assume that she is willing to pay a small amount ε of money to replace A (resp. C, B) by C (resp. B, A). Consider now a sequential decision problem where the DM initially receives die A for free, then is proposed to switch for C, then to switch for B, then to switch for A, where each exchange has a cost of ε. A sophisticated DM will make all exchanges, ending up with die A as initially, but having spent an amount of 3ε (for a sufficiently small ε). Furthermore, even if the preferences are transitive, it is known that a sophisticated DM with non-independent preferences may end up with a stochastically dominated plan (Hammond, 1988).

	SSB	WEU
deterministic	NP-hard	P
randomized	P	P

Table 2: Synthesis of the contributions.

Interestingly, a resolute DM consistent with SSB is subject to none of these drawbacks. For a resolute DM, there are several manners to define an optimal strategy:

– *Dictatorship of the root*: the "root" refers to the situation at the start of the decision process; with this criterion, the DM chooses a plan that maximizes the SSB/WEU score at the root. The use of this criterion has been advocated by McClennen (1990).

– *Resolute choice with selves*: it consists in considering the present decision situation as well as each possible future decision situations as a self who represents the DM at the time and state when the decision is made (Jaffray, 1998); one then aims at determining a plan achieving a compromise between the different selves of the DM, i.e. a plan that remains suitable for all selves.

In this paper, we study the former approach (dictatorship of the root). We distinguish between two settings regarding the set of feasible plans. In the *deterministic* setting (most prominent one in the literature), one focuses on plans where a decision is deterministically selected in each possible decision situation. In the *randomized* setting, one considers the enlarged set of plans where a decision is randomly selected (according to a predefined probability distribution) in each possible situation.

After proving that, in the deterministic setting, "optimizing" (in a sense to be formalized later) an SSB utility function in a decision tree is NP-hard, we will see that, interestingly, optimizing a WEU function in a decision tree can be done in polynomial time. To the best of our knowledge, WEU is the first class of criteria able to cope with Allais' paradox and which does not lead to an NP-hard problem for determining an optimal plan. Table 2 summarizes our contributions.

2 RELATED WORKS

Several non-EU models have been investigated in sequential decision making under uncertainty.

Rank-Dependent Utility (RDU) model. The RDU model proposed by Quiggin (1993), where one specifies a probability distortion function, is compatible with Allais' paradox. Nielsen and Jaffray (2006) have studied the solution of sequential decision problems with RDU, under the resolute choice with selves paradigm. They proposed an operational approach eliminating any plan that appears to be largely suboptimal for RDU in some decision situation. Their approach returns an RDU-optimal plan (viewed from the root) among the remaining ones, such that no other plan stochastically dominates it. Jeantet et al. (2012) proposed another implementation of RDU theory in decision trees. The difference with the previous approach is that the cooperation between selves is formalized through the use of a weighted max regret criterion, where regrets measure RDU losses. Lastly, Jeantet and Spanjaard (2008) investigated the solution of sequential decision problems with the RDU model, under the dictatorship of the root paradigm. They showed that the problem is NP-hard and designed a branch and bound procedure to solve it.

Imprecise Probabilities. When probabilities are imprecise (i.e., a set of probability measures should be taken into account in the decisions instead of a single measure), several decision criteria can be used to evaluate a plan. In this setting, a pessimistic DM will make the decision that maximizes the worst possible expected utility. This is known as the Γ-maximin criterion. Conversely, an optimistic agent will make the decision that maximizes the best possible expected utility. This is known as the Γ-maximax criterion. Kikuti et al. (2011) proposed algorithms enabling a sophisticated DM to determine her preferred plan w.r.t. both criteria. Their algorithms rely on linear/multilinear programming. Subsequently, Fargier et al. (2011) studied the optimization of the Γ-maximin criterion under the dictatorship of the root paradigm. They showed that even the evaluation of a plan according to the Γ-maximin criterion is NP-hard, and proposed a procedure to determine an optimal plan derived from preliminary results by Huntley and Troffaes (2008). The Hurwicz criterion for imprecise probabilities is a convex combination of the Γ-maximin and the Γ-maximax criteria that can model intermediate attitudes w.r.t. ambiguity (Jaffray and Jeleva, 2007). The optimization of the Hurwicz criterion has been studied under the dictatorship of the root paradigm (Jeantet and Spanjaard, 2009). Once again, the determination of an optimal plan for the Hurwicz criterion is NP-hard.

Skew-Symmetric Bilinear utility. The use of SSB utilities in finite horizon Markov decision processes has been studied by Gilbert et al. (2015) under the dictatorship of the root paradigm. The authors showed that an optimal randomized policy always exists, and designed a game-theoretic solution procedure. This work was latter extended to the setting of reinforcement learning (Gilbert et al., 2016) and was used in a document treatment chain application (Nicart et al., 2016). The complexity of determining an SSB optimal plan remains an open question, which we address in this paper for sequential decision problems represented by decision trees.

Before describing the formalism of decision trees, we present the SSB and WEU models in the next section.

3 SSB AND WEU MODELS

3.1 The SSB model

In the SSB model (Fishburn, 1984b, 1982), the preferences of the agent under certainty are represented via a binary functional φ over pairs of outcomes $(x,y) \in \mathcal{X}^2$, with $x > y \Leftrightarrow \varphi(x,y) > 0$. The value $\varphi(x,y)$ measures the intensity with which the agent prefers outcome x to y. Function φ is assumed to be skew-symmetric and bilinear w.r.t. the mixture operation on lotteries. More formally, skew-symmetry means that $\varphi(x,y) = -\varphi(y,x)$, and bilinearity means that $\varphi(\sum_i \lambda_i p_i, q) = \sum_i \lambda_i \varphi(p_i,q)$ and $\varphi(p, \sum_i \lambda_i q_i) = \sum_i \lambda_i \varphi(p,q_i)$, where $\sum_i \lambda_i p_i$ is the lottery p defined by $p(x) = \sum \lambda_i p_i(x)$. The preferences are then lifted to probability distributions by expectation: $p \succ q \Leftrightarrow \varphi(p,q) = \sum_{x,y \in \mathcal{X}^2} p(x)q(y)\varphi(x,y) > 0$. SSB utility theory has strong descriptive abilities. Not only can it account for Allais' paradox but it can also allow intransitive preferences which have been observed in various experiments.

Example 3 (Gardner's dice cont'd)**.** *Gardner's dice correspond to the following lotteries on $\mathcal{X} = \{1,\dots,6\}$:*

	1	2	3	4	5	6
p_A	1/6	0	0	5/6	0	0
p_B	0	0	5/6	0	0	1/6
p_C	0	1/2	0	0	1/2	0

By setting $\varphi(x,y) = 1$ if $x > y$, and $\varphi(x,y) = -1$ if $x < y$, $\varphi(p,q)$ corresponds then to the probability that p beats q minus the probability that q beats p. The obtained SSB utilities in the example are:

$$\begin{aligned}\varphi(p_A,p_B) &= 25/36 - 11/36 &= 14/36,\\ \varphi(p_B,p_C) &= 21/36 - 15/36 &= 6/36,\\ \varphi(p_C,p_A) &= 21/36 - 15/36 &= 6/36.\end{aligned}$$

Thus, $\varphi(p_A,p_B)>0$, $\varphi(p_B,p_C)>0$ and $\varphi(p_C,p_A)>0$, which is consistent with the relation "more likely to win" between dice (i.e., $p_A \succ p_B \succ p_C \succ p_A$).

As SSB utility can lead to intransitive preferences, the existence of an *optimal* lottery is not obvious. Given a set $\mathcal{L} = \{p_1,\dots,p_n\}$ of lotteries, the SSB criterion induces a *weighted tournament* on $\mathcal{L}$, i.e., for each pair p,q of lotteries such that $\varphi(p,q) > 0$, $\varphi(p,q)$ represents the intensity with which p is preferred to q. Multiple rules exist for determining the winner(s) of a weighted tournament (Fischer et al., 2016). We adopt in this paper the minimax rule (Young, 1977), also known as Condorcet's rule or the Simpson-Kramer method, where each lottery p is evaluated by the highest intensity with which another lottery is preferred to p, and one selects a lottery with minimal evaluation. More formally, one seeks a lottery p in $\arg\min_{p\in\mathcal{L}} \max_{q\in\mathcal{L}} \varphi(q,p)$.

If one enlarges the set of possible lotteries to the convex hull $CH(\mathcal{L})$ of $\mathcal{L}$ where $CH(\mathcal{L}) = \{p : p=\sum_{i=1}^{n}\lambda_i p_i$ with $\sum_{i=1}^{n}\lambda_i=1$ and $\lambda_i\geq 0, \forall i\}$, Fishburn (1984a) showed that an optimal lottery $p\in CH(\mathcal{L})$ w.r.t. the minimax rule has the desirable property that $\varphi(p,q)\geq 0$ for all q. However, a DM may not accept to use a mixed lottery (i.e., a lottery in $CH(\mathcal{L})\setminus\mathcal{L}$). Thus, we study both optimization in $\mathcal{L}$ and in $CH(\mathcal{L})$.

The WEU criterion is a special case of SSB utilities, that enforces transitivity while still being able to cope with Allais' paradox. This is the topic of the next section.

3.2 The WEU model

The Weighted Expected Utility (WEU) theory, developed by Chew (1983), is obtained from the SSB utility theory by adding a transitivity axiom (Fishburn, 1983). The WEU criterion relies on two functions u and w (with $w > 0$) defined on $\mathcal{X}$ such that $\varphi(x,y) = u(x)w(y) - u(y)w(x)$. These two functions are lifted to lotteries by linearity in probabilities: $u(p) = \sum_{x\in\mathcal{X}} p(x)u(x)$ and $w(p) = \sum_{x\in\mathcal{X}} p(x)w(x)$. Consequently: $p \succ q \Leftrightarrow u(p)w(q) - u(q)w(p) > 0$ which can be rewritten as:

$$p \succ q \Leftrightarrow v(p) = u(p)/w(p) > v(q) = u(q)/w(q) \quad (1)$$

In the sequel, we will continue to use v to denote the ratio u/w. As WEU assigns a score $v(p)$ to each lottery p, it is unable to accommodate intransitive preferences. However, it can still accommodate Allais' paradox:

Example 4 (Allais' paradox cont'd). *We rescale the possible gains in Table 1 from interval* $[0, 4000]$ *to interval* $[0, 1]$ *(3000 becomes 3/4 and 4000 becomes 1). Consider the pair of functionals* (u, w) *defined by* $u(x) = x^2$ *and* $w(x) = 1 - \sqrt{x} + x^2$*, leading to the following values:*

	p	q	p'	q'
u	0.5625	0.8	0.1406	0.2
w	0.6965	1	0.9241	1

We can easily check that the WEU model using these two functions is compatible with Allais' paradox:

- $u(p)w(q) - u(q)w(p) \approx 0.005 > 0 \Rightarrow p \succ q$
- $u(q')w(p') - u(p')w(q') \approx 0.044 > 0 \Rightarrow q' \succ p'$

Before investigating the optimization of SSB and WEU utilities in sequential decision problems, we recall the formalism of decision trees in the next section.

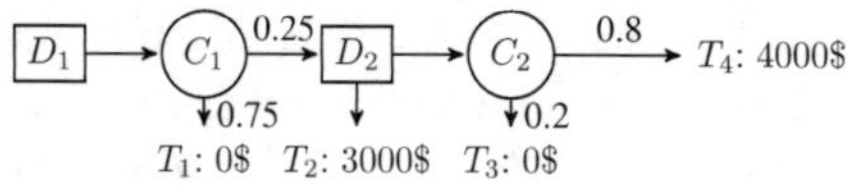

Figure 1: Allais' paradox as a decision tree problem.

4 DECISION TREE

A decision tree represents a sequential decision problem with three types of nodes: the *decision nodes* (represented by squares), the *chance nodes* (represented by circles), and the terminal nodes (the leaves of the tree). The branches starting from a decision node correspond to different possible decisions, while the ones starting from a chance node correspond to different possible events, the probabilities of which are known. The values indicated at the leaves correspond to the resulting outcomes. Such a decision tree is given in Figure 1. This decision tree is related to Allais' paradox. Indeed in node D_2, the agent needs to choose between lotteries p and q while in node D_1, the two possible plans yield lotteries p' and q', where p, q, p' and q' are as defined in Example 2.

More formally, a decision tree $\mathcal{T}$ is composed of a set of nodes $\mathcal{N}$ and a set of edges $\mathcal{E}$. The root node is denoted by N_r and the set of decision nodes, chance nodes and terminal nodes are respectively denoted by $\mathcal{N}_D$, $\mathcal{N}_C$ and $\mathcal{N}_T$. We define $\mathcal{E}_D := \{(D,N) \in \mathcal{E} : D \in \mathcal{N}_D\}$. Every edge $E = (C,N) \in \mathcal{E}$ such that $C \in \mathcal{N}_C$ is weighted by probability p_E of the corresponding event; every terminal node $T \in \mathcal{N}_T$ is labeled by the resulting outcome $o(T)$. Lastly, $\mathcal{S}(N)$ denotes the set of successors of N.

A plan in a decision tree is called a *strategy*. A strategy δ corresponds to a set $\mathcal{E}_\delta \subseteq \mathcal{E}_D$. The set of all feasible strategies is denoted by Δ. Let $\chi^\delta := (\chi_E)_{E\in\mathcal{E}_D}$ denote the incidence vector of a strategy δ (i.e., $\chi_E = 1$ if $E \in \mathcal{E}_\delta$ and $\chi_E = 0$ otherwise). The set of feasible strategies can be characterized as the incidence vectors satisfying the following constraints:

$$\sum_{N\in\mathcal{S}(N_r)} \chi_{(N_r,N)} = 1$$

$\forall D \in \mathcal{N}_D$:

if $\chi_{(D,C)} = 0$ then $\sum_{N\in\mathcal{S}(D')} \chi_{(D',N)} = 0 \quad \forall D' \in \mathcal{S}(C)\cap\mathcal{N}_D$

otherwise $\sum_{N\in\mathcal{S}(D')} \chi_{(D',N)} = 1 \quad \forall D' \in \mathcal{S}(C)\cap\mathcal{N}_D$

For instance, in Figure 1, $\mathcal{E}_D$ includes the three edges $E_1{=}(D_1,C_1)$, $E_2{=}(D_2,C_2)$ and $E_3{=}(D_2,T_2)$, and there are two possible deterministic strategies characterized by incidence vectors $(\chi_{E_1}{=}1, \chi_{E_2}{=}1, \chi_{E_3}{=}0)$ and $(\chi_{E_1}{=}1, \chi_{E_2}{=}0, \chi_{E_3}{=}1)$.

By abuse of notation, we will denote a strategy indifferently by δ or χ^δ. Following the same convention, we will denote by Δ both the set of feasible strategies and the set of corresponding incidence vectors.

Randomized strategies are obtained by relaxing the domain of variables χ_E from $\{0,1\}$ to $[0,1]$ while keeping the same constraints. In the decision tree represented in Figure 1, an example of a randomized strategy is given by vector $(\chi_{E_1} = 1, \chi_{E_2} = 0.5, \chi_{E_3} = 0.5)$. This corresponds to the situation where the DM in decision node D_2 will choose with equal probabilities to go either in T_2 or in C_2. We denote by $\widehat{\Delta}$ the set of feasible randomized strategies (or the corresponding incidence vectors).

As usual in sequential decision under risk, a strategy δ induces a lottery p_δ over outcomes. Let p_N^δ denote the probability to reach node N when following strategy δ. Values p_N^δ can be recursively computed as follows:

$p_{N_r}^\delta = 1$

$\forall D \in \mathcal{N}_D, \forall N \in \mathcal{S}(D), p_N^\delta = p_D^\delta * \chi_{(D,N)}^\delta$

$\forall C \in \mathcal{N}_C, \forall N \in \mathcal{S}(C), p_N^\delta = p_C^\delta * p_{(C,N)}$

The lottery over outcomes p_δ induced by δ is defined by $p_\delta(x) = \sum_{T \in \mathcal{N}_T : o(T)=x} p_T^\delta$ for $x \in \mathcal{X}$.

Let $P = \{p_\delta : \delta \in \Delta\}$ denote the image of deterministic strategies in the space of lotteries, and $\widehat{P} = \{p_\delta : \delta \in \widehat{\Delta}\}$ denote the image of randomized strategies in the space of lotteries. It is worth noting that $CH(P) = \widehat{P}$, where $CH(P) = \{p_\delta : \delta \in CH(\Delta)\}$. This is due to Carathéodory's theorem. As a consequence of this observation, optimizing over $\widehat{P}$ is equivalent to optimizing over $CH(P)$, and therefore there always exists a strategy $\delta \in \widehat{\Delta}$ such that $\varphi(p_\delta, p_{\delta'}) \geq 0$ for all feasible strategies $\delta' \in \widehat{\Delta}$ (by Fishburn's result recalled in Section 3.1).

Note that the number of deterministic strategies can possibly grow exponentially with the size of the decision tree, i.e. the number of decision nodes (this number has indeed the same order of magnitude as the number of nodes in $\mathcal{T}$). Indeed, one easily shows that there are $\Theta(2^{\sqrt{|\mathcal{N}_\mathcal{D}|}})$ strategies in a complete binary decision tree $\mathcal{T}$. For this reason, even in the deterministic setting, it is necessary to develop an optimization algorithm to determine the optimal strategy. It is well known that the rolling back method makes it possible to compute in linear time an optimal strategy w.r.t. EU. Indeed such a strategy satisfies the optimality principle: any substrategy of an optimal strategy is itself optimal, where a substrategy is the restriction of a strategy in $\mathcal{T}$ to a subtree. Starting from the leaves, one computes recursively for each node the EU of an optimal substrategy: the optimal EU for a chance node equals the expectation of the optimal utilities of its successors; the optimal EU for a decision node equals the maximum EU of it's successors.

Unfortunately, note that any criterion able to cope with Allais' paradox necessarily violates the optimality principle. Indeed in the decision tree represented in Figure 1 such a criterion would have $\{(D_2, T_2)\}$ as optimal substrategy from node D_2. However, the optimal strategy from node D_1 is $\{(D_1, C_1), (D_2, C_2)\}$. For this reason, the optimization of such criteria in a decision tree is tricky. This is the topic of the following sections. The optimization problems we consider are:

$$(\mathcal{R}): \ \min_{\delta \in \widehat{\Delta}} \max_{\delta' \in \widehat{\Delta}} \varphi(p_{\delta'}, p_\delta)$$
$$(\mathcal{D}): \ \min_{\delta \in \Delta} \max_{\delta' \in \Delta} \varphi(p_{\delta'}, p_\delta)$$

Problem $(\mathcal{R})$ (resp. $(\mathcal{D})$) aims at determining an optimal randomized (resp. deterministic) strategy for the SSB criterion. If $\varphi(p,q) = w(q)u(p) - w(p)u(q)$, then the problem amounts to determine an optimal WEU strategy.

5 OPTIMIZING THE SSB CRITERION

We start by presenting a Linear Program (LP) involving a polynomial number of variables and constraints (in the size of the decision tree) for solving optimization problem $(\mathcal{R})$. Thus, by polynomial complexity of linear programming (Khachiyan, 1980), determining an SSB optimal randomized strategy in a decision tree is a polynomial time problem. To this end, we start by noting that:

$$\max_{\delta' \in \widehat{\Delta}} \varphi(p_{\delta'}, p_\delta) = \max_{\delta' \in \Delta} \varphi(p_{\delta'}, p_\delta)$$

for any $\delta \in \widehat{\Delta}$. Indeed, if $\Delta = \{\delta_1, \ldots, \delta_n\}$, then there exist $\lambda_i \geq 0$ summing up to 1 such that $p_{\delta'} = \sum_{i=1}^n \lambda_i p_{\delta_i}$ and we have the following sequence of relations:

$$\varphi(\sum_i \lambda_i p_{\delta_i}, p_\delta) = \sum_{i=1}^n \lambda_i \varphi(p_{\delta_i}, p_\delta) \leq \max_i \varphi(p_{\delta_i}, p_\delta).$$

We now rewrite the objective function in a way highlighting the fact that determining a strategy δ' that is most preferred to strategy δ can be done by rolling back the decision tree $\mathcal{T}$ with a particular utility function V_δ.
By linearity of φ, we have:

$$\max_{\delta' \in \Delta} \varphi(p_{\delta'}, p_\delta) = \max_{\delta' \in \Delta} \sum_{x \in \mathcal{X}} p_{\delta'}(x) \varphi(x, p_\delta)$$

This latter expression can be rewritten as follows:

$$\max_{\delta' \in \Delta} \sum_{x \in \mathcal{X}} p_{\delta'}(x) \varphi(x, p_\delta) = \max_{\delta' \in \Delta} \sum_{x \in \mathcal{X}} p_{\delta'}(x) V_\delta(x)$$

where utilities $V_\delta(x)$ are defined by $V_\delta(x) = \varphi(x, p_\delta)$.

We now give the two classes of constraints involved in our LP to solve optimization problem $(\mathcal{R})$. The first class of constraints involves a set of variables p_N, describing all feasible randomized strategies $\delta \in \widehat{\Delta}$, where p_N is the probability that node N is reached with strategy δ:

$$p_{N_r} = 1$$
$$p_D = \sum_{N \in \mathcal{S}(D)} p_N, \forall D \in \mathcal{N}_D$$
$$p_{(C,N)} p_C = p_N, \ \forall C \in \mathcal{N}_C, \ \forall N \in \mathcal{S}(C)$$
$$p_N \geq 0, \forall N \in \mathcal{N}$$

The strategy δ (more precisely, its incidence vector χ^{δ}) can be recovered from variables p_N by using equation $\chi^{\delta}_{(D,N)} = p_N/p_D$ for each edge $(D,N) \in \mathcal{E}_D$. The second class of constraints aims at determining $\max_{\delta' \in \Delta} \sum_{x \in \mathcal{X}} p_{\delta'}(x)V_\delta(x)$ for a given strategy δ. As indicated above, this value can be computed by rolling back the decision tree, which amounts to satisfy the following Bellman's equations, where q_N denotes the EU value in node N according to utility function V_δ:

$$
\begin{aligned}
q_T &= V_\delta(o(T)), \forall T \in \mathcal{N}_T \\
q_C &= \sum_{N \in \mathcal{S}(C)} p_{(C,N)} q_N, \forall C \in \mathcal{N}_C \\
q_D &\geq q_N, \forall N \in \mathcal{S}(D),\ \forall D \in \mathcal{N}_D \\
q_N &\in \mathbb{R}, \forall N \in \mathcal{N}
\end{aligned}
$$

We have therefore $q_{N_r} = \max_{\delta' \in \Delta} \sum_{x \in \mathcal{X}} p_{\delta'}(x)V_\delta(x)$. Putting together the objective function $\min q_{N_r}$ and both classes of constraints, and replacing values $V_\delta(o(T))$ by $\sum_{T' \in \mathcal{N}_T} p_{T'}\varphi(o(T), o(T'))$, we obtain the final program $\mathcal{P}_{SSB}$ given below, that enables to determine an SSB optimal randomized strategy in polynomial time.

$$
\mathcal{P}_{SSB} \left\{
\begin{aligned}
&\min q_{N_r} \\
&p_{N_r} = 1 \\
&p_D = \sum_{N \in \mathcal{S}(D)} p_N, \forall D \in \mathcal{N}_D \\
&p_{(C,N)} p_C = p_N,\ \forall C \in \mathcal{N}_C,\ \forall N \in \mathcal{S}(C) \\
&q_T = \sum_{T' \in \mathcal{N}_T} p_{T'} \varphi(o(T), o(T')), \forall T \in \mathcal{N}_T \\
&q_C = \sum_{\forall N \in \mathcal{S}(C)} p_{(C,N)} q_N, \forall C \in \mathcal{N}_C \\
&q_D \geq q_N, \forall N \in \mathcal{S}(D),\ \forall D \in \mathcal{N}_D \\
&p_N \geq 0, \forall N \in \mathcal{N} \\
&q_N \in \mathbb{R}, \forall N \in \mathcal{N}
\end{aligned}
\right.
$$

We now prove that the determination of an SSB optimal *deterministic* strategy in a decision tree is an NP-hard problem, where the size of the instance is the number of involved decision nodes.

Theorem 1. *Finding an optimal deterministic SSB strategy in a decision tree (solving $\mathcal{D}$) is an* NP*-hard problem.*

Proof. To ease the presentation, the proof is divided into two parts. While the first part contains all the important ideas of the proof, it proves the result with an SSB utility function which expresses intransitive preferences over the (certain) outcomes of the trees. As this property can seem unnatural or restrictive, the second part of the proof extends the result to an SSB utility function with transitive preferences over the outcomes of the trees.

Part 1: The proof relies on a polynomial reduction from 3-SAT, which can be stated as follows:

INSTANCE: a set X of boolean variables, a collection $\mathcal{C}$ of clauses on X such that $|c| = 3$ for every clause $c \in \mathcal{C}$.
QUESTION: does there exist an assignment of truth values to the boolean variables of X that satisfies simultaneously all the clauses in $\mathcal{C}$?

Let $X = \{x_1, \ldots, x_n\}$ and $\mathcal{C} = \{c_1, \ldots, c_m\}$. The polynomial generation of a decision tree from an instance of 3-SAT is performed as follows. An example is provided in Figure 2. One defines a decision node X_i for every variable $x_i \in X$. Each node X_i has two children: the first one (chance node denoted by T_i) corresponds to the statement "x_i is true" while the second one (chance node denoted by F_i) corresponds to "x_i is false". The subset of clauses which includes the positive (resp. negative) literal x_i (resp. $\overline{x_i}$) is denoted by $\{c_{i_1}, \ldots, c_{i_j}\} \subset \mathcal{C}$ (resp. $\{c_{i'_1}, \ldots, c_{i'_k}\} \subset \mathcal{C}$). For every clause c_{i_h} (resp. $c_{i'_h}$) one generates a child of T_i (resp. F_i) denoted by c_{i_h} (resp. $c_{i'_h}$). These children are terminal nodes. Moreover, one generates an additional child of T_i (resp. F_i) denoted by c_0, corresponding to a fictive clause. Node T_i (resp. F_i) has therefore $j+1$ (resp. $k+1$) children. One adds a chance node C predecessor of all decision nodes x_i and a decision node D as root with C as child. Lastly, for every clause c_i in $\mathcal{C}$ one adds a child $\overline{c}_i$ to the root, a terminal node. The obtained decision tree involves $n+1$ decision nodes, $2n+1$ chance nodes and at most $2n(m+1)+m$ terminal nodes. There is a bijection between the assignments of truth values and the subset of deterministic strategies that choose chance node C at the root: one sets $x_i = 1$ in problem 3-SAT iff edge (x_i, T_i) is included in the strategy, and $x_i = 0$ otherwise. An assignment such that the entire expression is true in 3-SAT corresponds to a strategy such that every clause c_i, $i = 1 \ldots m$ is a possible outcome. To complete the reduction, we need to specify the SSB function φ and the probabilities in the tree such that property $(\mathcal{P})$ holds:

$(\mathcal{P})$ If the 3-SAT formula is (resp. is not) satisfiable, then any SSB optimal deterministic strategy reaches (resp. does not reach) every clause c_i, for $i \in \{1, \ldots, m\}$, with non null probability.

We set the probabilities in the following way. The edges starting from C have probabilities $1/n$. The edges leading to leaves $c_{i=1\ldots m}$ have probabilities $1/m$. Thus, if c_i ($i \in \{1, \ldots, m\}$) is a possible outcome of a strategy then the probability of obtaining c_i is greater than $1/nm$. The SSB function φ is defined to have the three following properties. Let p_δ be the lottery resulting from strategy δ. i) If c_i ($i \in \{1, \ldots, m\}$) is reached with a non null probability with strategy δ then $\varphi(p_\delta, \overline{c}_i) > 0$, ii) otherwise $\varphi(p_\delta, \overline{c}_i) < 0$. iii) Given two strategies δ and δ' both containing edge (D, C), $\varphi(p_\delta, p_{\delta'}) = 0$. Indeed, it is easy to see that i), ii) and iii) imply $(\mathcal{P})$. Those conditions are satisfied by the SSB function φ defined by: $\forall i, j \in \{0, \ldots, m\}, \varphi(c_i, c_j) = 0$;

$\forall i \in \{1, \ldots, m\}, \forall j \neq i \in \{0, \ldots, m\}, \varphi(\overline{c}_i, c_j) = 1;$
$\forall i \in \{1, \ldots, m\}, \varphi(c_i, \overline{c}_i) = nm.$

Indeed, in this case, properties ii) and iii) obviously hold. To see that i) is also satisfied, note that as the probability of obtaining c_i is greater than $1/nm$ if c_i is reached with a non null probability with strategy δ and $\varphi(c_j, \overline{c}_i) = -1, \forall j \neq i$ by skew symmetry, then:
$\varphi(p_\delta, \overline{c}_i) \geq \varphi(c_i, \overline{c}_i)/nm - (1 - 1/nm) = 1/nm > 0$
where $1 - 1/nm$ is an upper bound on the probability to reach another consequence than c_i with δ.

Part 2: Part 1 of the proof uses an SSB utility function with intransitive preferences on the outcomes of the tree (as $\overline{c}_i \succ c_j \succ \overline{c}_j \succ c_i \succ \overline{c}_i$) which can seem unnatural. Thus, we now consider another SSB utility function defined on $\mathbb{R}^2$ by $\varphi(x, y)$ equal to 1 (resp. $0, -1$) if $x > y$ (resp. $x = y, x < y$). The decision tree considered is the same as in the first part of the proof, but now, terminal nodes are replaced by the following lotteries:

$$\forall i \in \{0, \ldots, m\} : c_i = (i, 0.5; -i, 0.5)$$
$$\forall i \in \{1, \ldots, m\} :$$
$$\overline{c}_i = (i - 0.5, p; -i - 0.5, p; m + 1, 1 - 2p)$$

with $p \in (nm/(1 + 2nm), 0.5)$. The number of terminal nodes is now upper bounded by $6n(m + 1) + 3m$. One can check that with those changes, properties i), ii) and iii) (and therefore property $(\mathcal{P})$) of part 1 still hold. But now, the preferences on the clauses are transitive. □

Note that the associated decision problem "Given α, does there exist a deterministic strategy δ such that $\max_{\delta' \in \Delta} \varphi(p_{\delta'}, p_\delta) \leq \alpha$?" is actually NP-complete. It belongs to NP because, if an oracle provides a strategy δ, one can obtain in polynomial time the value $\max_{\delta' \in \Delta} \varphi(p_{\delta'}, p_\delta)$ by rolling back the decision tree with utility function V_δ as defined at the beginning of the section. It can be proved NP-hard by using similar arguments as in the proof of Theorem 1.

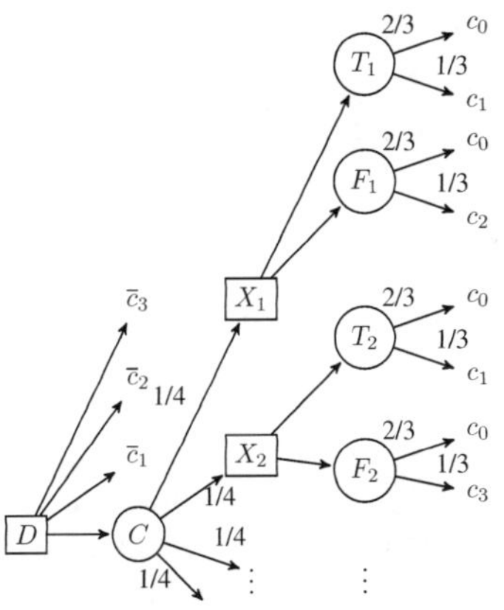

Figure 2: Portion of the decision tree obtained for 3-SAT formula: $(x_1 \vee x_2 \vee x_3) \wedge (\overline{x_1} \vee x_3 \vee x_4) \wedge (\overline{x_2} \vee \overline{x_3} \vee \overline{x_4})$.

6 OPTIMIZING THE WEU CRITERION

We first show that, with the WEU criterion, solving optimization problem $(\mathcal{R})$ is equivalent to solving optimization problem $(\mathcal{D})$. We recall that SSB $\equiv$ WEU for $\varphi(p, q) = u(p)w(q) - u(q)w(p)$ and that $\varphi(p_{\delta^*}, p_\delta) \geq 0$, $\forall \delta \in \Delta$ for strategy $\delta^* \in \Delta$ maximizing ratio $u(p_\delta)/w(p_\delta)$ (see Section 3.2).

Let $\Delta = \{\delta_1, \ldots, \delta_n\}$. For any strategy $\delta \in \widehat{\Delta}$, there exists positive λ_i's summing up to 1 such that $p_\delta = \sum_{i=1}^{n} \lambda_i p_{\delta_i}$. By bilinearity of φ, we have:

$$\varphi(p_{\delta_j}, \sum_i \lambda_i p_{\delta_i}) = \sum_{i=1}^{n} \lambda_i \varphi(p_{\delta_j}, p_{\delta_i}) \quad \forall j \in \{1, \ldots, n\} \quad (2)$$

For $\delta_j = \delta^*$, we have $\varphi(p_{\delta_j}, p_{\delta_i}) \geq 0$ for all i. Hence, by positivity of λ_i's, we can deduce that $\varphi(p_{\delta^*}, \sum_i \lambda_i p_{\delta_i}) \geq 0$ and therefore p_{δ^*} is preferred to any randomized strategy.

Conversely, consider an optimal strategy $\delta \in \widehat{\Delta}$ for problem $\mathcal{R}$. Let $p_\delta = \sum_i \lambda_i p_{\delta_i}$. In Equation 2, by optimality of δ, we should have $\sum_{i=1}^{n} \lambda_i \varphi(p_{\delta_j}, p_{\delta_i}) \leq 0$ for all $j \in \{1, \ldots, n\}$. For $\delta_j = \delta^*$, it holds that $\varphi(p_{\delta_j}, p_{\delta_i}) \geq 0$ for all i, and therefore $\lambda_i \varphi(p_{\delta_j}, p_{\delta_i}) = 0$ for all i. Consequently, $\lambda_i > 0 \Rightarrow \varphi(p_{\delta_j}, p_{\delta_i}) = 0$. Stated differently, it means that all deterministic strategies δ_i such that $\lambda_i > 0$ are optimal for problem $(\mathcal{D})$.

Therefore, for the WEU criterion, solving $(\mathcal{D})$ could be performed with the three following steps: 1) solve $(\mathcal{R})$ with program $\mathcal{P}_{SSB}$ to find an optimal randomized strategy δ_r^*; 2) derive from δ_r^* an equivalent mixed strategy δ_m^* (i.e., a probability distribution over deterministic strategies which yields the same probability distribution over the outcomes of the tree); 3) pick any deterministic strategy sampled by δ_m^* with non null probability. This approach could be performed in polynomial time by using a linear programming approach for step 2) (see e.g. Mastin et al., 2015). Instead of developing this approach, we show how to solve directly problem $(\mathcal{D})$ for a WEU criterion as it will reveal simpler and more efficient.

As shown by Equation 1, optimizing a WEU function entails the maximization of ratio $u(p)/w(p)$. Interestingly, fractional programming is a subfield of operational research dedicated to this type of objective functions (Schaible and Ibaraki, 1983; Stancu-Minasian, 2012). Several solution methods have been developed in this domain to optimize objective functions taking the form of a ratio of two linear functions (we recall that in WEU, functions u and w are linear w.r.t. mixtures). We adapt and present below two of these methods: Megiddo's method (1979) and Dinkelbach's method (1967). Megiddo's method yields a procedure that is polynomial in the number of decision nodes of the decision tree. This proves that solving a decision tree w.r.t.

to the WEU model is a polynomial time problem. Both algorithms are based on a simple idea: solving a decision tree w.r.t. the WEU model can be done by using multiple launches of a sub-routine which solves the decision tree according to the EU model using a utility function V_λ of the form $V_\lambda(x) = u(x) - \lambda w(x)$. The validity of the algorithms stems from the following observation:

Observation 1. *Given $\lambda \in \mathbb{R}$, let δ_λ denote an optimal EU strategy for utility function V_λ and $V_\lambda(p_{\delta_\lambda})$ denote its expected utility. Then, the sign of $V_\lambda(p_{\delta_\lambda})$ is determined by the position of λ w.r.t. λ^* (we recall that λ^* is the optimal value of a deterministic strategy w.r.t. WEU): 1) If $\lambda = \lambda^*$, then $V_\lambda(p_{\delta_\lambda}) = 0$ and δ_λ is an optimal deterministic strategy according to WEU. 2) If $\lambda > \lambda^*$, then $V_\lambda(p_{\delta_\lambda}) < 0$. Indeed, there is no strategy $\delta \in \Delta$ such that $u(p_\delta)/w(p_\delta) > \lambda$. 3) If $\lambda < \lambda^*$, then $V_\lambda(p_{\delta_\lambda}) > 0$.*

Determining a WEU optimal strategy thus amounts to the following optimization problem, where λ^* is unknown:

$$\max_{\delta \in \Delta} V_{\lambda^*}(p_\delta) \tag{3}$$

6.1 Megiddo's Method

The first algorithm is an adaptation of the method proposed by Megiddo (1979) to solve combinatorial optimization problems with rational objective functions. In our setting, this method can be explained as follows.

As the WEU optimal value λ^* is unknown, the idea is to solve the decision tree with a partially specified utility function V_{λ^*}. The method proceeds by interleaving a bi-objective rolling back procedure with an incremental refinement of the specification of λ^*. A (sub)strategy δ is evaluated by the two objective functions $u(p_\delta)$ and $w(p_\delta)$. If λ^* is known to belong to interval $[\lambda_l, \lambda_u]$, then $V_{\lambda^*}(p_\delta) \in [u(p_\delta) - \lambda_u w(p_\delta), u(p_\delta) - \lambda_l w(p_\delta)]$. When comparing two lotteries p_δ and $p_{\delta'}$ in the course of the rolling back procedure, several cases can occur:

i) If $u(p_\delta) - \lambda w(p_\delta) \leq$ (resp. $\geq$) $u(p_{\delta'}) - \lambda w(p_{\delta'})$ for $\lambda \in \{\lambda_l, \lambda_u\}$ then $V_\lambda(p_\delta) \leq$ (resp. $\geq$) $V_\lambda(p_{\delta'})$ for $\lambda \in [\lambda_l, \lambda_u]$, therefore $V_{\lambda^*}(p_\delta) \leq (\geq)\ V_{\lambda^*}(p_{\delta'})$ and strategy δ (resp. δ') can be discarded.

ii) Otherwise, there exists a single value $\lambda_{\delta,\delta'} \in [\lambda_l, \lambda_u]$ such that $u(p_\delta) - \lambda_{\delta,\delta'} w(p_\delta) = u(p_{\delta'}) - \lambda_{\delta,\delta'} w(p_{\delta'})$. Let δ'' denote an optimal strategy for utility function $V_{\lambda_{\delta,\delta'}}$ (obtained by rolling back). Two subcases can occur:

– If $V_{\lambda_{\delta,\delta'}}(p_{\delta''}) <$ (resp. $>$) 0, then $\lambda >$ (resp. $<$) λ^* by Observation 1 and interval $[\lambda_l, \lambda_u]$ is updated to $[\lambda_l, \lambda_{\delta,\delta'}]$ (resp. $[\lambda_{\delta,\delta'}, \lambda_u]$). After this update, either $u(p_\delta) - \lambda w(p_\delta) \leq u(p_{\delta'}) - \lambda w(p_{\delta'})$ for $\lambda \in \{\lambda_l, \lambda_u\}$ or $u(p_\delta) - \lambda w(p_\delta) \geq u(p_{\delta'}) - \lambda w(p_{\delta'})$ for $\lambda \in \{\lambda_l, \lambda_u\}$ which brings us back to case i).

– If $V_{\lambda_{\delta,\delta'}}(p_{\delta''}) = 0$, then $\lambda_{\delta,\delta'} = \lambda^*$ and δ'' is an optimal WEU strategy. Thus, the method can be stopped.

As the number of comparisons of lotteries in the rolling back method is upper bounded by $|\mathcal{N}_C| + |\mathcal{N}_T|$, the number of standard rolling back methods (in $O(|\mathcal{N}|)$) launched by Megiddo's method to find an optimal WEU strategy is also upper bounded by $|\mathcal{N}_C| + |\mathcal{N}_T|$. The complexity of the method is therefore $O(|\mathcal{N}^2|)$.

In practice, the initial values of variables λ_l and λ_u may impact the performance of the method. For instance, a "good" initialization can be obtained by computing the optimal deterministic strategy δ_u (resp. δ_w) maximizing (resp. minimizing) EU with utility function u (resp. w). Variable λ_l can then be set to $u(\delta_u)/w(\delta_u)$ and λ_u to $\max\{0, u(\delta_u)/w(\delta_w)\}$.

6.2 Dinkelbach's method

The second algorithm has not the polynomial time guarantee of the first one, but is more efficient in practice. Let $RB(V)$ denote an optimal EU strategy in Δ obtained by rolling back the decision tree with utility function V on the leaves (RB for "Rolling Back"). The optimization problem (3) can be solved by computing a sequence of strategies in Δ through recursive equation:

$$\delta_{t+1} = RB(V_{v(p_{\delta_t})})$$

where $v(p_{\delta_t}) = u(p_{\delta_t})/w(p_{\delta_t})$. A direct corollary from Observation 1 is that while $v(p_{\delta_t}){<}\lambda^*$, $v(p_{\delta_{t+1}}){>}v(p_{\delta_t})$. Note that, by definition of λ^*, we cannot have $v(p_{\delta_t}) > \lambda^*$. Therefore, the sequence $(v(p_{\delta_t}))_{t \in \mathbb{N}}$ is strictly increasing until reaching λ^*. Value λ^* is always reached after a finite number of iterations as there is a finite number of values in $\{v(p_\delta) : \delta \in \Delta\}$. After a finite number of iterations, we will thus have $v(p_{\delta_t}) = v(p_{\delta_{t+1}})$ which means that an optimal WEU strategy has been found. While the initial strategy δ_0 can be any feasible strategy in Δ, a "good" choice of δ_0 may increase the efficiency of the approach. For instance, δ_0 can be chosen as an optimal EU strategy according to utility function V_0.

7 NUMERICAL TESTS

We now present the results of our numerical test[2].

Random instances. Our tests were performed on complete binary decision trees. The depth of these decision trees varies from 5 to 20 (21 to 349525 decision nodes), with an alternation of decision nodes and chance nodes. At every terminal node T, outcome $o(T)$ is uniformly drawn in interval $[0, 500]$. The mapping u (resp. w) from $[0, 500]$ to $[0, 100]$ (resp. $[1, 100]$) is randomly gen-

[2]Methods coded in C++ using Gurobi 5.6.3 for LPs. Times are wall-clocked on a 2.4 GHz Intel Core i5 with 8GB RAM.

	depth	5	10	15	20
DIN	time (sec)	<0.001	<0.001	0.019	0.91
	nbsr	2.2	2.98	3.1	3.66
DIN^{WI}	time (sec)	<0.001	<0.001	0.019	0.789
	nbsr	3.04	3.72	4.06	4.24
MEG	time (sec)	<0.001	<0.001	0.039	3.572
	nbsr	2.02	2.74	5.52	14.38
MEG^{WI}	time (sec)	<0.001	0.001	0.074	4.77
	nbsr	0.52	6.02	11.02	19.16

Table 3: Computation times and number of sub-routine (nbsr in the table) launched for our solution procedures for WEU.

erated while enforcing nondecreasingness (resp. nonincreasingness). Imposing these monotonicity conditions on u and w ensures that $v = u/w$ is a nondecreasing function of outcomes. Table 3 presents the performances of Dinkelbach's method and Megiddo's method (denoted by DIN and MEG from now on) as the depth of the decision tree increases. For each depth level, we give the average computation time over 50 instances in seconds as well as the average number of times the sub-routine rolling back the decision tree for a given utility function V_λ was used. Initialization of both methods where performed as described in the previous section.

The results show that both methods are very efficient, solving trees of depth 20 in less than 1 sec (resp. 4 sec) for DIN (resp. MEG). Method DIN seems to perform best as it requires to launch less sub-routine algorithms.

To measure the impact of the quality of the initialization, we computed the same results for these two methods launched with weak initializations. They are denoted by DIN^{WI} and MEG^{WI} in the table (WI for weak initialization). While DIN^{WI} is initialized with a random initial strategy δ_0, MEG^{WI} starts with the loose lower and upper bounds $\lambda_l = 0$ and $\lambda_u = u(500)/w(0)$.

We observe that a weak initialization does not seem to highly impact the performance of the two methods (DIN^{WI} even achieves better performances than DIN on decision trees of depth 20).

We also tested solving $\mathcal{P}_{SSB}$ on the same trees with SSB utility function φ defined by $\varphi(x, y) = 1$ (resp. 0,-1) if $x > y$ (resp. $x = y$, $x < y$). Note that (as illustrated by Example 3), this function may model intransitive preferences. The computation times were averaged over 50 instances. They exponentially increase with the depth of the tree, raising from 2.796 sec for depth 10 to 73.722 sec for depth 12. This is not surprising as $|\mathcal{N}|$ (and thus the number of variables in $\mathcal{P}_{SSB}$) exponentially increases with the depth of the tree.

Application to Who wants to be a millionaire? *Who wants to be a millionaire?* is a popular game show, were a contestant must answer a sequence of 15 questions with 4 possible answers. The questions enable the contestant

		model 1	model 2
DIN	time (sec)	0.017	73.307
	nbsr	2.5	2.4
MEG	time (sec)	0.036	104.1
	nbsr	4.1	2.6

Table 4: Computation times and number of sub-routine (nbsr in the table) launched DIN and MEG .

to earn increasing sums of money but are also of increasing difficulties. If the answer given is wrong then the contestant leaves the game with no money except what was earned at the last guarantee point (questions 5 and 10). At each question, the contestant can also decide to stop. She then leaves with the money won so far. We used the Spanish version of the game modeled by Perea and Puerto (2007) where the monetary values of the questions range from 150€ (question 1) to 300000€ (question 15). Lastly, the contestant has three lifelines that can be used once during the game: Phone a friend, 50:50, and Ask the audience. We tested our solution methods for two models of this game. While model 1 (which contains around 70000 nodes) is the original one proposed by Perea and Puerto, model 2 (which contains around 80 million nodes) is a refinement proposed by Jeantet and Spanjaard (2008) to take into account the fact that the candidate may or may not (with a certain probability) know the answer to a given question. The results are averaged over 20 instances where functions of the form $u = x^\alpha$ and $w = 300001^\beta - x^\beta$ were used. For each instance, parameters α and β were uniformly sampled in (0,1). Our numerical results are given in Table 4. We observe that both methods DIN and MEG are efficient and that they require very few calls to their sub-routine.

8 CONCLUSION

We showed that determining an SSB optimal strategy in a decision tree is an NP-hard problem while it becomes polynomial when considering randomized strategies. Regarding the special case of WEU, both the deterministic and the randomized settings collapse as there always exists a WEU optimal strategy which is deterministic. Determining such an optimal strategy is polynomial time by instantiating fractional programming methods. As far as we know, it is the first polynomial time complexity result in sequential decision making under risk for a decision model encompassing Allais' paradox.

For future work, it would be interesting to investigate how these results extend to other frameworks (e.g., finite horizon MDPs). It seems that at least pseudo-polynomial solution methods could be obtained by simple adaptations of the methods proposed here to augmented MDPs (where the states are augmented with the accumulated rewards (Liu and Koenig, 2006)).

References

S. Chew (1983). A generalization of the quasilinear mean with applications to the measurement of income inequality and decision theory resolving the Allais paradox. *Econometrica* :1065–1092.

W. Dinkelbach (1967). On nonlinear fractional programming. *Management science* **13**(7):492–498.

H. Fargier, G. Jeantet, and O. Spanjaard (2011). Resolute choice in sequential decision problems with multiple priors. In *Proceedings of IJCAI 2011*. 2120–2125.

F. Fischer, O. Hudry, and R. Niedermeier (2016). Weighted tournament solutions. In *Handbook of Computational Social Choice*, Cambridge University Press. 85–102.

P. Fishburn (1984a). Dominance in SSB utility theory. *Journal of Economic Theory* **34**(1):130–148.

P. Fishburn (1984b). SSB utility theory: an economic perspective. *Math. Social Sciences* **8**(1):63 – 94.

P. C. Fishburn (1982). Nontransitive measurable utility. *Journal of Mathematical Psychology* **26**:31–67.

P. C. Fishburn (1983). Transitive measurable utility. *Journal of Economic Theory* **31**(2):293–317.

M. Gardner (1970). Mathematical games: The paradox of nontransitive dice and the elusive principle of indifference. *Sci. Amer.* **223**:110–114.

H. Gilbert, O. Spanjaard, P. Viappiani, and P. Weng (2015). Solving MDPs with skew symmetric bilinear utility functions. In *Proc. of IJCAI 2015*. 1989–1995.

H. Gilbert, B. Zanuttini, P. Viappiani, P. Weng, and E. Nicart (2016). Model-free reinforcement learning with skew-symmetric bilinear utilities. In *UAI 2016*.

P. Hammond (1988). Consequentialist foundations for expected utility. *Theory and decision* **25**(1):25–78.

N. Huntley and M. C. Troffaes (2008). An efficient normal form solution to decision trees with lower previsions. In *Soft Methods for Handling Variability and Imprecision*, Springer. 419–426.

J.-Y. Jaffray (1998). Implementing resolute choice under uncertainty. In *Proceedings of UAI 1998*. Morgan Kaufmann Publishers Inc., 282–288.

J.-Y. Jaffray and M. Jeleva (2007). Information processing under imprecise risk with the Hurwicz criterion. In *Proc. of ISIPTA 2007*. 233–242.

G. Jeantet, P. Perny, and O. Spanjaard (2012). Sequential decision making with rank dependent utility: a minimax regret approach. In *AAAI 2012*. 1931–1937.

G. Jeantet and O. Spanjaard (2008). Rank-dependent probability weighting in sequential decision problems under uncertainty. In *Proc. of ICAPS 2008*. 148–155.

G. Jeantet and O. Spanjaard (2009). Optimizing the Hurwicz criterion in decision trees with imprecise probabilities. In *Proc. of ADT 2009*. 340–352.

D. Kahneman and A. Tversky (1979). Prospect theory: An analysis of decisions under risk. *Econometrica* :263–291.

L. G. Khachiyan (1980). Polynomial algorithms in linear programming. *USSR Computational Mathematics and Mathematical Physics* **20**(1):53–72.

D. Kikuti, F. G. Cozman, and R. Shirota Filho (2011). Sequential decision making with partially ordered preferences. *Artif. Intelligence* **175**(7-8):1346–1365.

Y. Liu and S. Koenig (2006). Functional value iteration for decision-theoretic planning with general utility functions. In *Proc. of AAAI 2006*. vol. 21, 1186.

A. Mastin, P. Jaillet, and S. Chin (2015). Randomized minmax regret for combinatorial optimization under uncertainty. In *Proc. of ISAAC 2015*. 491–501.

E. F. McClennen (1990). *Rationality and dynamic choice: Foundational explorations*. Cambridge university press.

N. Megiddo (1979). Combinatorial optimization with rational objective functions. *Math. Oper. Res.* **4**(4):414–424.

J. von Neumann and O. Morgenstern (1947). *Theory of games and economic behaviour*. Princeton Univ Press.

E. Nicart, B. Zanuttini, H. Gilbert, B. Grilhères, and F. Praca (2016). Building document treatment chains using reinforcement learning and intuitive feedback. In *Proc. of ICTAI 2016*. 635–639.

T. D. Nielsen and J.-Y. Jaffray (2006). Dynamic decision making without expected utility: An operational approach. *European J. of Op. Research* **169**(1):226–246.

F. Perea and J. Puerto (2007). Dynamic programming analysis of the TV game "Who wants to be a millionaire?". *European J. of Op. Research* **183**(2):805–811.

J. Quiggin (1993). *Generalized expected utility theory: the rank-dependent model*. Kluwer.

S. Schaible and T. Ibaraki (1983). Fractional programming. *European J. of Op. Research* **12**(4):325–338.

I. Stancu-Minasian (2012). *Fractional programming: theory, methods and applications*, vol. 409. Springer Science & Business Media.

A. Tversky (1969). Intransitivity of preferences. *Preference, Belief, and Similarity* :433.

H. Young (1977). Extending Condorcet's rule. *Journal of Economic Theory* **16**(2):335–353.

Stochastic Segmentation Trees for Multiple Ground Truths

Jake Snell
University of Toronto
Vector Institute

Richard S. Zemel
University of Toronto
Vector Institute
Canadian Institute for Advanced Research

Abstract

A strong machine learning system should aim to produce the full range of valid interpretations rather than a single mode in tasks involving inherent ambiguity. This is particularly true for image segmentation, in which there are many sensible ways to partition an image into regions. We formulate a tree-structured probabilistic model, the *stochastic segmentation tree*, that represents a distribution over segmentations of a given image. We train this model by optimizing a novel objective that quantifies the degree of match between statistics of the model and ground truth segmentations. Our method allows learning of both the parameters in the tree and the structure itself. We demonstrate on two datasets, including the challenging Berkeley Segmentation Dataset, that our model is able to successfully capture the range of ground truths and to produce novel plausible segmentations beyond those found in the data.

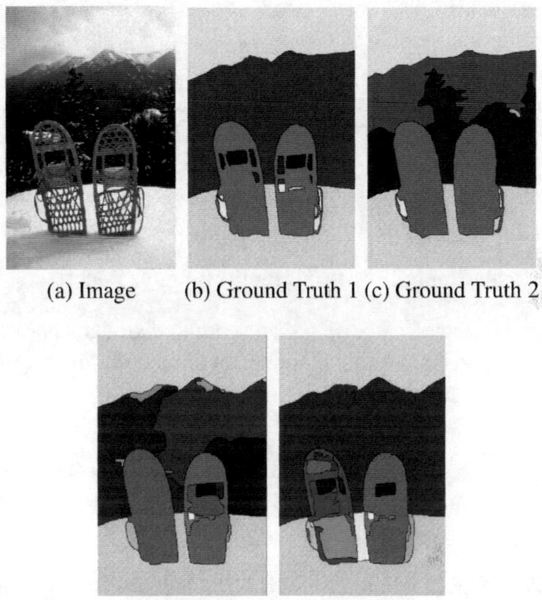

(a) Image (b) Ground Truth 1 (c) Ground Truth 2

(d) Sample 1 (e) Sample 2

Figure 1: Multiple ground truths from the Berkeley Segmentation Dataset and samples from our model. Stochastic segmentation trees produce segmentations that generalize through novel combinations of the level of detail in different areas of the image.

1 INTRODUCTION

Humans have a remarkable ability to resolve ambiguity in real-world situations. For example, a skilled interpreter knows that many valid translations of a sentence to a target language exist, and which is the most appropriate depends on context. Yet even in the absence of disambiguating information, humans are able to internally represent a wide range of plausible interpretations when presented with a stimulus. As the central aim of AI is to build machines that can reason about the world in a human-like way, strong AI systems should also be able to maintain a distribution over plausible outputs when confronted with an ambiguous task. Many current machine learning approaches are unable to do this despite the prevalence of ambiguity in domains such as natural language parsing, machine translation, image caption generation, and visual scene understanding.

Tasks involving ambiguity can often naturally be cast as structured output learning problems, in which outputs have internal dependencies. Examples of structured outputs are natural language sentences or paths in a graph. It is often infeasible to independently model each element of the exponentially large structured output spaces typically considered in such problems. Fortunately, graphical models provide a powerful and flexible framework for building rich distributions over structured output spaces. This is a boon for tasks involving ambiguity as they tend to naturally have multiple ground truths, each reflecting a different yet correct interpretation of the input. For example, the Berkeley Segmentation Dataset (BSD) (Martin et al., 2001; Arbelaez et al., 2011) contains segmentations of natural images collected from multiple human annotators. Due to variability in interpretation or attention, some annotators provided more detailed segmentations or emphasized different contour types than others (Hou et al., 2013). See Figure 1 for an example of such variation.

In this work we introduce the *stochastic segmentation tree* (SST) model, which treats multiple ground truths as samples from a target distribution and learns to predict a distribution specific to the given image. Motivated by the observation that biological visual systems parse scenes according to a hierarchy (Sharon et al., 2006), the model first builds a tree-structured latent region hierarchy of the image. It then predicts a distribution over binary variables corresponding to nodes in the tree that indicate which regions in the tree should be grouped in the same segment.

We make a number of contributions in this paper:

- We introduce an aim that to our knowledge is novel, of producing for a single test input multiple valid structured outputs that directly capture variations in ground truths (GTs).
- We formulate a probabilistic model, a *stochastic segmentation tree*, that represents a distribution over segmentations of a given image.
- We develop a method of forming a tree specific to a given image, and assigning probabilities to its nodes, from a base set of pixels or superpixels (groupings of pixels).
- We define a novel objective that quantifies the degree of match between the model and ground truth segmentations, and formulate an optimization method that allows learning of both the parameters in a tree and the tree structure itself.

2 RELATED WORK

The first line of research related to our SSTs concerns learning systems that produce multiple structured outputs. Many of these approaches can be viewed as structured output generalizations of common multi-label prediction, in which an input can be associated with any number of outputs. One way this can be done is to redefine the output space to be over sets rather than single outputs (Lampert, 2011). Another strategy is to train an ensemble of models to produce multiple hypotheses at test time, either independently (Guzman-Rivera et al., 2012) or in a cascade (Dey et al., 2015). Multiple outputs can also be produced by applying a specialized inference procedure, such as Diverse M-Best MAP (Batra et al., 2012; Yadollahpour et al., 2013; Kirillov et al., 2015) or Diverse Beam Search (Vijayakumar et al., 2016). These approaches have some overlap with our SSTs but differ in aims and formulation. None of these methods produce alternative valid interpretations given an input but instead predict a set of outputs such that one of them is good. Others have attempted to model diverse (and thereby multiple) outputs more directly via Structured DPPs (Kulesza et al., 2012; Gillenwater et al., 2012).

Our model is closely related to approaches that build a graphical model whose structure is conditioned on input data. For example, Wong & Mooney (2006) learn a set of context-free grammar rules which are used to produce a parse tree for a given natural language sentence. They also learn model parameters that define a distribution over meaning representations for the predicted parse tree. Their graphical model parameters are globally learned whereas ours are predicted by the model given the input. The machine translation model of Tromble et al. (2008) forms a distribution over sentences via paths through a translation lattice given a source sentence.

Our model also relates to structured output models, but differ in the training and evaluation criteria. Structured output models are conventionally trained with maximum likelihood given the ground truths for each input. Models are typically evaluated, however, via a task-specific loss comparing a single model output against the ground truths. Examples of task losses include mean average precision for rankings and BLEU (Papineni et al., 2002) for text generation. This disconnect between training and test has spurred many attempts to minimize task loss at training time (Hazan et al., 2010; Song et al., 2015; Shen et al., 2015; Ranzato et al., 2015). These training procedures often improve task loss performance at test but require additional loss-augmented inference or dynamic programming steps during training. In contrast, our method constructs a target distribution from the ground truths and learns to minimize the distance between the model and target distributions. When the model is amenable to such distance computation, this is a more efficient way to learn than task loss minimization since no inference is required. Moreover, the evaluation of model outputs against multiple ground truths via a task loss depends on specific characteristics of the (often few in number) ground truths. BLEU, for example, compares a model generated sentence against n-grams found in ground truth sentences. Yet replacing words in the ground truth sentences with direct synonyms would likely be equally plausible outputs. Using domain knowledge to construct a target distribution invariant to such low-level variations is a more direct way to train and evaluate models, and is the approach we take in this work.

We now review approaches specific to image segmentation. The goal of image segmentation is to partition an image into meaningful regions. Several task losses are used to measure segmentation performance; one of the most popular is the Probabilistic Rand Index (Unnikrishnan & Hebert, 2005), a generalization of Rand Index (Rand, 1971) to the single output multiple ground-truth setting. A common approach to image segmentation is to form a hierarchical region grouping, in which regions of finer-scale segmentations are subregions of those at coarser scales, and then cut the tree to obtain an output segmentation. The gPb-OWT-UCM (Arbelaez et al., 2011) algorithm (called UCM, hereafter) utilizes the oriented watershed transform on gPb (Maire et al., 2008) boundaries, followed by greedy merging of regions. It forms a weighted boundary map such that thresholding it at any level produces a valid segmentation, and the threshold value controls the scale. Jain et al. (2011) propose a method that learns to agglomerate superpixels into hierarchies, by learning a similarity function based on ground-truth clustered data. The agglomerative region clustering method (Ren & Shakhnarovich, 2013) uses a learned boundary probability model to merge regions until the estimated probability of merging is below a threshold. Arbelaez et al. (2014) propose a multiscale combinatorial grouping that uses a fast normalized cuts algorithm to produce a hierarchical segmentation that leverages information across different scales.

In general, these methods provide alternative approaches to construct the visual hierarchy from the image; our primary aim is to utilize this tree structure to generate alternative segmentations. The two approaches that most resemble our model are first the work by Ion et al. (2011), which composes multiple figure-ground hypotheses obtained by applying constraints at different locations and scales, into multiple larger interpretations of the entire image. More recently, Hu et al. (2015) propose a probabilistic generative model for segmentations, which can efficiently generate segmentations of varying granularity; unlike our SSTs this work does not propose a novel tree construction process, and more importantly, is trained via maximum likelihood as opposed to matching the set of human annotations.

3 SST MODEL

Our SST model produces multiple segmentation hypotheses from a single image in three steps: (1) a tree structure is constructed; (2) probabilities are associated with nodes in the tree; (3) sample segmentations are generated from the tree based on the node probabilities. Here we detail these steps, initially assuming that the tree structure is given. We first describe how nodes in a tree relate to regions of an image, and how a binary labeling of nodes in such a tree corresponds to a segmentation of the image. We then present the probabilistic model over segmentations based on these binary labelings, and a metric comparing the model samples to ground-truth segmentations of an image that can be used to evaluate a multiple segmentation system. This metric is then the objective utilized in learning the network that predicts the node probabilities from an image at test time. Finally at the end of this section we describe our own procedure for generating trees, which is also based on this metric.

3.1 PROBABILISTIC TREE MODEL

A segmentation can be represented as a vector of numbers, where each pixel is assigned a particular region index $r \in \mathcal{R}$. In such a representation, pixels assigned the same index r are considered to be grouped together. An alternative representation of the same information is as a symmetric binary matrix $\mathbf{S}$, where $S_{ij} = 1$ if pixel i and j are assigned to the same region, and $S_{ij} = 0$ otherwise. We adopt this representation here.

We also utilize a third representation of a segmentation, with respect to a *segmentation tree*. A segmentation tree has M leaves, one for each of M non-overlapping and complete image superpixels. A superpixel $m \in \{1, ..., M\}$ represents a grouping of contiguous pixels in the image; we denote the set of pixels assigned to superpixel m as $C(m)$. As a slight abuse of notation, we use m to denote both a superpixel and its corresponding leaf in the tree. Each internal node k represents a grouping of pixels that is the union of pixels assigned to its children: $C(k) = C(\ell(k)) \cup C(r(k))$, where $\ell(k)$ and $r(k)$ are the left and right child of k, respectively. This assignment of nodes to left and right children of parent nodes define the tree structure.

Given a particular tree structure, a segmentation is a set of binary values $\mathbf{t}$, where each leaf m has $t_m = 1$, and the binary value t_k associated with each internal tree node k represents whether or not the set of pixels in its left child and the pixels of the right child belong to the same image region:

$$t_k = 1 \Rightarrow S_{ij} = 1, \quad \forall i \in C(\ell(k)), j \in C(r(k)) \quad (1)$$

These binary values are constrained to ensure that the values in the pairwise pixel matrix $\mathbf{S}$ correspond to a valid segmentation. This is achieved by forcing $t_k = 0$ if either $t_{\ell(k)} = 0$ or $t_{r(k)} = 0$. This constraint results in tree labelings in which any path that starts at a leaf and

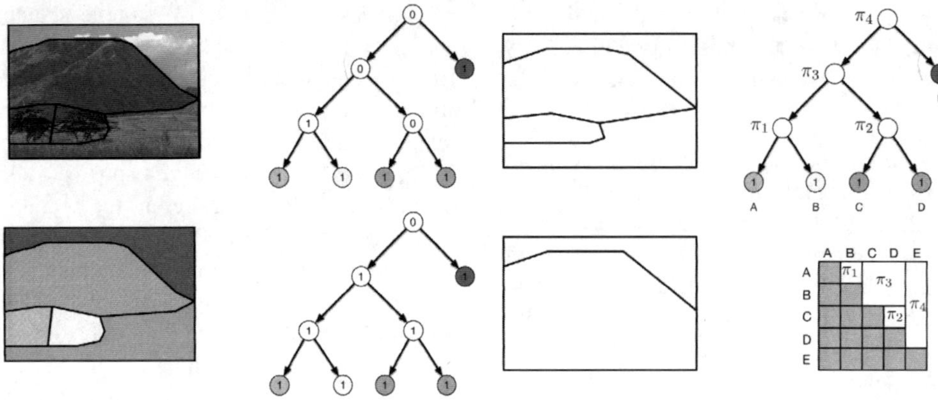

Figure 2: Left: image and color-coded superpixels. Middle: two sample segmentations, with corresponding binary values ($\mathbf{t}$) of the segmentation tree. Right: each node k in the tree has an associated marginal probability π_k, which governs a specific region of the pairwise segmentation matrix.

ends at the root has an initial value of 1, and if the value switches to 0 along the path then it stays at 0 through the root.

The last node along this path with a value of 1 defines a sub-tree of superpixels that all belong to the same image region, which corresponds to a block in the segmentation matrix. The relationship between the tree labeling $\mathbf{t}$ and the matrix $\mathbf{S}$ is illustrated in Figure 2.

In order to represent the variety of segmentations of a given image, with different levels of detail in different regions, we formulate a probabilistic model based on a leaf-to-root sampling scheme. The probabilities are assigned to nodes in the tree, which directly correspond to probabilities in the segmentation matrix. These equations define the SST probabilistic model:

$$P(t_k = 1|\mathbf{t}_{-k}) \;=\; \begin{cases} p_k & \text{if } t_{\ell(k)} = t_{r(k)} = 1 \\ 0 & \text{otherwise} \end{cases} \qquad (2)$$

where $\mathbf{t}_{-k}$ is the vector of binary values associated with the nodes below k in the tree. Given this definition, and a sampling scheme that samples binary values t_k starting at the leaves and moving up the tree, then it can be shown that the marginal probability π_k that node k takes on value 1 is a product of the local probability of that node and the marginals of its children:

$$\pi_k \equiv P(t_k = 1) = \prod_{d \in subTree(k)} p_d \;=\; p_k \pi_{\ell(k)} \pi_{r(k)} \qquad (3)$$

where $subTree(k)$ are all the nodes in the sub-tree rooted at node k.

The probabilistic model plays an important role in our system, specifying a distribution over segmentations of an image, which can be sampled to generate hypothesized segmentations. An example probability vector $P(\mathbf{t})$ for a given tree, and some corresponding samples are illustrated in Figure 2.

3.2 EVALUATING AN SST

The aim of the stochastic segmentation tree is to produce segmentations such that their statistics match the statistics of the reference segmentations for a given image. One metric that is well-suited to this goal is the *Hellinger distance*, which is a metric for comparing two distributions.

In our setting we utilize the marginal pairwise probabilities as the underlying probabilities to be compared via the Hellinger distance. For the model, the marginal probability that pixel i is in the same segment as pixel j is captured by π_k, where $i \in C(\ell(k))$ and $j \in C(r(k))$, or vice versa. Given a set of ground-truth segmentations $\{\mathbf{S}^1, ..., \mathbf{S}^U\}$, the target marginals q_{ij} can be computed easily: $q_{ij} = \frac{1}{U}\sum_u S^u_{ij}$. The squared-Hellinger distance $D(\pi, q)$ is defined to be:

$$1 - \frac{1}{\binom{N}{2}}\left(D_0 + \sum_{\substack{k,i \in C(\ell(k)) \\ j \in C(r(k))}} \left[\sqrt{\pi_k q_{ij}} + \sqrt{(1-\pi_k)(1-q_{ij})}\right]\right) \qquad (4)$$

where N is the number of pixels. Here D_0 is the summed Hellinger distance of each of the super-pixels, which sums over the SST leaves of any errors in the superpixellation; these errors are constant and cannot be repaired by the SST.

We propose that matching pairwise statistics is an appropriate goal for the multiple-segmentation scenario. Intuitively, the metric considers all pairs of pixels in the image, and compares how often that pair are grouped together by humans versus the model. An alternative is

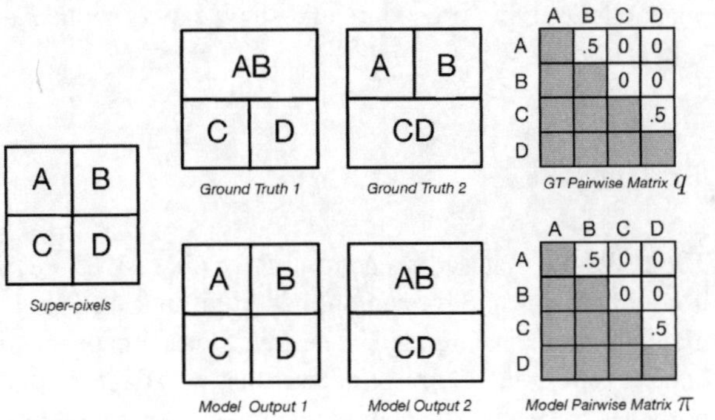

Figure 3: Illustration of the properties of the Hellinger distance as it relates to segmentations. In this scenario, there are four superpixels and two ground truth segmentations. When viewed in the pairwise matrix form, both the ground truth and model distributions are identical despite the fact that the model outputs segmentations not found in the ground truths. We hypothesize that these are sensible generalizations.

to attempt to match higher order statistics between the model and ground-truth segmentations, e.g., triplets of pixels, but given that typically only a small reference set of segmentations are available, these higher-order statistics are not as reliable. A visualization of the properties of the Hellinger distance is shown in Figure 3.

3.3 NETWORK TO ESTIMATE NODE MARGINALS

If the reference segmentations are available, the node probabilities and their corresponding marginals for a given tree structure can be optimized (e.g., via gradient descent) to minimize the Hellinger objective (Equation 4). At test time, however, with no reference segmentation these node marginals must be estimated from the image. We formulate a neural network that estimates node marginals, and optimize it to minimize the Hellinger objective on the training set. Then given a tree for a test image, we can estimate marginals, and sample segmentations.

Our network to estimate the marginals π_k for any node k is a three layer feed-forward neural net. The inputs to the network consist of visual features extracted from regions corresponding to $\ell(k)$ and $r(k)$, as well as a small number of geometric features of the regions, including centroid location and size. The first layer of the network applies the same weights to these features of the left and right regions. The second layer takes as input the concatenation of the hidden left and right representations with their element-wise squared difference. The third and final layer connects to the network output, a single sigmoid unit, which is the estimated marginal probability for the $\ell(k)$, $r(k)$ merge. The same network is used to predict merge marginal probabilities throughout the entire tree.

Learning is performed via SGD with backpropagation, to minimize the Hellinger distance with respect to the parameters of our model. This is made simpler by the fact that $D(\pi, q)$ decomposes over nodes of the tree. The learned network predicts marginal probabilities independently for each node and therefore it is possible that the network's predictions are not consistent with our tree assumptions from Section 3.1. For example, if the marginal probability predicted at a certain node is greater than that predicted at either of its children, there will be no setting of the conditional node probabilities $\mathbf{p}$ consistent with the network outputs that also satisfies Equation 3. Thus as a final step, we perform a separate constrained optimization using L-BFGS (Liu & Nocedal, 1989) to find the setting of $\mathbf{p}$ that has minimal Hellinger distance to the marginals outputted by the network while still obeying our tree assumptions. We then recompute the marginal probabilities corresponding to this setting of $\mathbf{p}$ using Equation 3 and treat these reconciled marginals as the final outputs of the model.

Sample segmentations can be generated from the model using a simple bottom-up procedure. The non-terminal nodes in the tree are traversed in bottom-up order. For each node k, draw $x_k \sim \text{Uniform}(0, 1)$. If $x_k < p_k$ and $t_{\ell(k)} = t_{r(k)} = 1$, then $t_k \leftarrow 1$. Otherwise, $t_k \leftarrow 0$. This setting of $\mathbf{t}$ defines a segmentation that is a sample from the model (see Figure 2 for a example $\mathbf{t}$ and the corresponding segmentation).

3.4 TREE CONSTRUCTION

The discussion above assumed the tree structure was given, as could be provided by some existing segmentation tree algorithm such as UCM (Arbelaez et al., 2011) or ISCRA (Ren & Shakhnarovich, 2013). Here we extend our formulation to also construct a tree for a given image. Our tree construction algorithm, called SST-SwapTree, begins with an arbitrary tree structure and seeks to iteratively improve it by making moves within the space of tree structures. We consider swaps, in which the subtree rooted at a node in the tree is exchanged with the subtree rooted at another node. Refer to Figure 4 for an illustration of a sample swap. Alternate strategies for constructing trees, such as agglomerative clustering, are possible but we opt to iteratively improve tree structures rather than building them from scratch for two main reasons. First, maintaining valid tree structures makes it easier to track performance throughout the tree building process. Second, it is simpler to estimate the effect of a move on the entire tree structure because the global con-

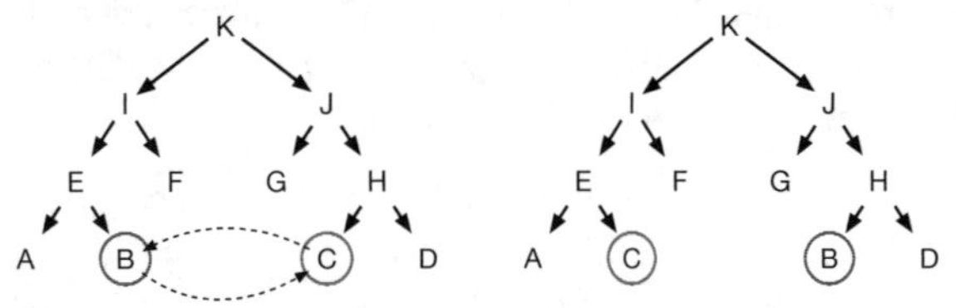

Figure 4: An example swap. **Left**: The tree structure before swapping B and C. **Right**: The structure after the swap. Note that when non-leaf nodes are swapped, their descendants also accompany them in the swap.

text is known, as opposed to agglomerative clustering in which part of the tree structure does not yet exist.

At each iteration of SST-SWAPTREE, the first step involves enumerating allowable swaps. A swap between nodes is allowable if neither is a descendant of the other, as otherwise the resulting structure is ill-defined. It also must preserve the property that children of any non-terminal node in the tree are neighboring. Both of these properties can be checked efficiently (see the supplementary material for details).

The next step involves scoring a swap. The key idea in this step is that any tree can be evaluated based on the minimum achievable Hellinger distance between the tree and the ground-truth segmentations. Hence a swap can be scored based on how it much it lowers this minimum distance. At training time we have access to the ground truth segmentations, and so the minimum achievable Hellinger distance for a given structure can be easily computed via numerical minimization of $D(\pi, q)$ with respect to π. At test time however this is not possible, so instead we utilize our learned network that estimates node marginals to approximate the change in achievable Hellinger distance effected by a swap, which determines its score. Every iteration of the algorithm greedily selects the highest scoring swap and produces a new tree structure. This procedure is repeated for a fixed number of iterations chosen based on validation performance. Space does not permit a detailed description here of our SST-SWAPTREE algorithm for enumerating and scoring swaps, and so further details can be found in the supplementary material.

4 EXPERIMENTS

In order to assess the effectiveness of SSTs in producing multiple plausible segmentations, we learned models on two segmentation datasets: the Berkeley Segmentation Dataset 500 (BSDS500) (Arbelaez et al., 2011) and the Penn-Fudan pedestrian parsing dataset (Bo & Fowlkes, 2011; Wang et al., 2007). In this section, we first describe the datasets we used. We then provide details of our model training procedure and show experimental results.

4.1 DATASETS

The BSDS500 dataset is a natural fit for our task because it contains multiple human-annotated ground truth segmentations for each image. The Penn-Fudan pedestrian dataset is a semantic image dataset that we adapt for our purposes by generating four synthetic GT segmentations per example, each of which represents a different prototypical parse of the image. We generate these GTs based on merging different body parts in different segmentations. Details of the merging algorithm, along with visualizations of several ground truths and corresponding images are shown in the supplementary material.

The BSDS500 dataset contains predefined training, validation, and test splits of 200, 100, and 200 examples, respectively. The Penn-Fudan dataset contains only 169 examples, so we randomly created five splits with 20% of the examples as test and the remainder divided into training and validation in an 80%-20% ratio. The reported evaluation results for this dataset are averaged over test predictions across the five splits.

4.2 SST TRAINING DETAILS

We took the regions output by the UCM algorithm, prior to thresholding, as the leaves of our trees. For BSDS500 this yielded a large number of leaves per image, so we thresholded the weighted contour map for each example independently such that 100 regions remained. All methods, including baselines, used the same base-level regions.

Our network for estimating marginal probabilities used two sets of features as input. The first are visual features computed by average-pooling activations from the fourth convolutional layer of the VGG-19 network (Simonyan & Zisserman, 2014). The second set were geometric features regarding the regions. Both sets of features have the benefit that the features of a parent region can efficiently be computed given features of the child regions.

The marginal probability estimation network was trained with SGD using the Adam optimizer (Kingma & Ba, 2014). Early stopping was done on the Hellinger distance of the model merge probability assigned trees on the validation set. Dropout was used on the first two layers of the network for regularization. Further training and architectural details are contained in the supplementary material.

4.3 RESULTS

We evaluate the learned SST models along with several baselines, which we describe here. We distinguish between methods that produce a single output and those that generate multiple outputs.

Of the single output baselines, the simplest is SUPERPIXELS, the segmentation consisting of the starting base-level regions themselves. BOYKOV-JOLLY is a baseline inspired by Boykov & Jolly (2001) in which strengths between regions are computed as a monotonically increasing function of the squared difference in mean intensity between them. This induces a tree structure, which can be thresholded at any strength in order to form a segmentation. UCM SINGLE is the standard single segmentation produced by UCM, based on thresholding the hierarchy at the threshold yielding the best performance on the validation set.

For multiple-output baselines, we consider an extension of UCM SINGLE, in which a Gaussian distribution over thresholds is constructed. Multiple segmentations can be generated by first sampling a threshold from this Gaussian, and then generating a segmentation by merging regions until this threshold is reached. The mean of this Gaussian is set to the corresponding UCM SINGLE threshold and the variance is tuned on the validation set. We call this extension UCM MULTIPLE.

We compare these baselines to two methods utilizing SSTs. SST-UTREE is our model trained using the UCM tree structures as described in Section 4.2. SST-SWAPTREE is a modified version of the procedure described in Section 3.4 to iteratively improve the trees generated by UCM. The only modification we made was to use the true node marginals when choosing swaps to make. As such these tree structures are oracle trees in that they can only be computed if the optimal π_k^* is known at test time. This tests whether our tree construction procedure produces better trees, provided the $\hat{\pi}$ estimator is sufficiently accurate. The final Hellinger distance computed on the tree structures does however use the network marginal outputs to assign probabilities to each node in the procedure described in Section 3.3.

We also evaluate the methods on a multiple output variant of the Rand Index that we call *matching Rand Index (MRI)*. For each method a set of candidate segmentations is first generated by sampling from the model. Then an optimal matching is found between these and the ground-truth segmentations; this can easily be computed via a max-weighted bipartite matching algorithm. Each ground truth matches the segmentation from the candidate set with the greatest Rand Index with respect to itself, subject to the constraint that no two ground truths match the same model output. The MRI is then the mean Rand Index of the matched segmentations. The MRI results are shown in Table 2. For methods that output a single segmentation we report its average Rand Index to the ground-truths; MRI simplifies to probabilistic Rand Index (PRI) (Unnikrishnan & Hebert, 2005) in this setting. For the multiple output methods we include results with both 50 and 100 samples drawn from the respective models. SST significantly outperforms the baselines here even though it was trained to optimize Hellinger distance, demonstrating that Hellinger is a sensible objective for training models in a multiple output setting. Also, the SST-SWAPTREE MRI shows the gains obtained by improving the tree structure.

Table 1: Test Hellinger distances (lower is better). The first methods all output a single segmentation, while the others output several.

Method	BSDS 500	Penn-Fudan
SUPERPIXELS	0.1451	0.3485
BOYKOV-JOLLY	0.1447	0.3172
UCM SINGLE	0.1315	0.2974
UCM MULTIPLE	0.1315	0.2971
SST-UTREE	0.0864	0.2070
SST-SWAPTREE	**0.0689**	**0.1901**

Table 2: Test matching Rand Index (higher is better).

Method	Samples	BSDS 500	Penn-Fudan
SUPERPIXELS	1	0.8107	0.6366
BOYKOV-JOLLY	1	0.8111	0.6612
UCM SINGLE	1	0.8247	0.6813
UCM MULTIPLE	50	0.8687	0.7037
SST-UTREE	50	0.8786	0.7160
SST-SWAPTREE	50	**0.9116**	**0.7726**
UCM MULTIPLE	100	0.8718	0.7072
SST-UTREE	100	0.8813	0.7180
SST-SWAPTREE	100	**0.9148**	**0.7792**

Segmentations sampled from the SST-UTREE model are visualized in Figure 5 for BSDS500. We observe that the samples vary across regions of the image, capturing the idea of generating segmentations at different levels of granularity.

4.4 APPLICATION OF SST: SEMANTIC SEGMENTATION

The stochastic segmentation tree provides an informative representation of the image structure. The tree, with each node assigned its own well-calibrated probability of the associated merge, describes a rich distribution over

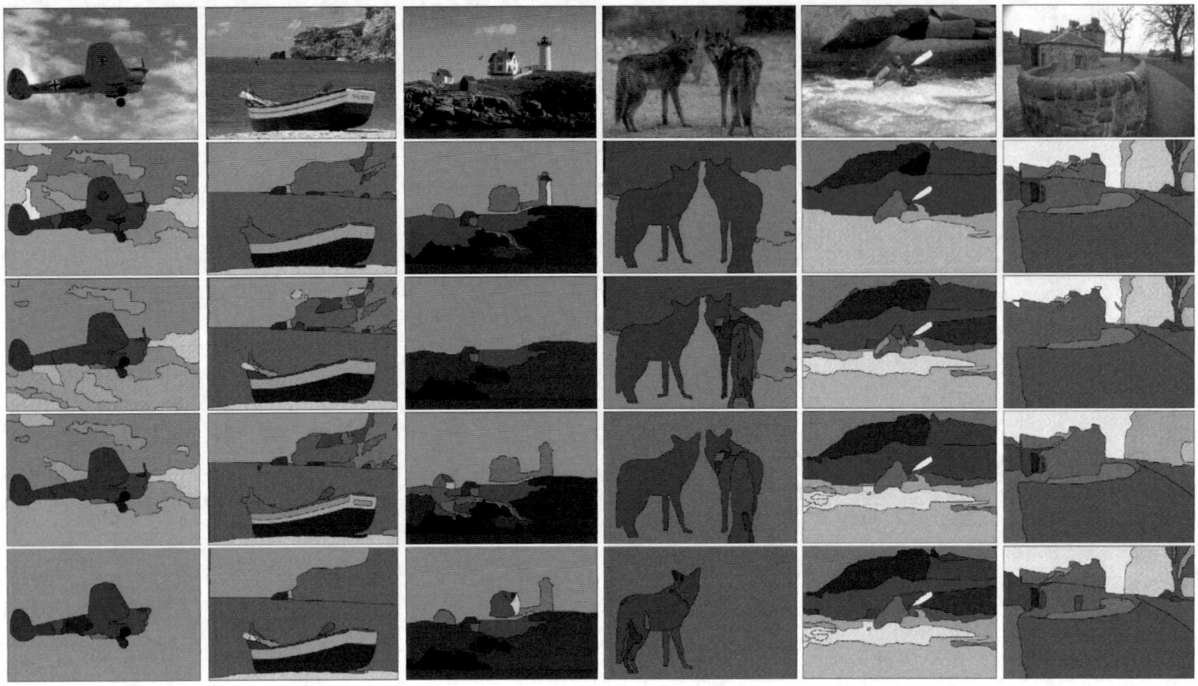

Figure 5: Samples from the SST-UTREE model on BSDS500. From top to bottom: image, samples 1-4 from the model. All images are from the test set.

segmentations. In addition, there are a number of potential applications of SSTs. Any algorithm $\mathcal{A}$ that uses superpixels as inputs could benefit from this rich representation. If $\mathcal{A}$ wants k superpixels, the SST can produce multiple instances with approximately the same number, but with varying granularity in different regions of the image. Other existing tree-based methods do not have the same ability. For example, UCM generates alternative segmentations, but these obey a fixed ordering, so they cannot produce higher granularity in one region and lower in another in one segmentation, and vice versa in a second segmentation. Running $\mathcal{A}$ on each of these superpixel inputs provides a natural measure of uncertainty in the algorithm's output.

Here we explore one such algorithm, semantic segmentation, that utilizes superpixels as inputs. In semantic segmentation, the goal is to assign each pixel in an image one of a fixed set of labels. We consider a scenario in which an SST is used to generate multiple segmentations, which are used as superpixel input to a semantic segmentation algorithm. In order to decouple the effects of the specific segmentation algorithm from the performance of the SST as a superpixel generator, we consider an oracle setting in which each region is assigned a single label that gives the highest segmentation accuracy as measured by Hamming distance or intersection-over-union (IOU) between the semantic segmentation and the ground truth.

Our experiments use the Penn-Fudan dataset, as they already contain semantic segmentation labels. We varied the sigmoid output bias of our SST-UTREE model in order to encourage it to generate superpixelations with various numbers of regions per image. We chose the biases to produce roughly 30, 50, 80, and 100 superpixels per image, and computed both the oracle segmentation accuracy and number of segments of 1,000 samples from our model on each test example. The results are shown in Figure 6 for Hamming distance and in Figure 7 for mean intersection-over-union (IOU). IOU was computed for each of the 12 non-background classes in the Penn-Fudan dataset and then averaged across classes to produce mean IOU. For comparison, we also display the oracle segmentation accuracy of the UCM SINGLE algorithm over a range of thresholds and the BOYKOV-JOLLY baseline. The oracle accuracy of SST-UTREE is higher for each of these scenarios than either UCM SINGLE or BOYKOV-JOLLY. In order to illustrate how the sampled segmentations vary, Figure 8 shows sampled oracle segmentations from the SST-UTREE model that produces roughly 50 superpixels per image.

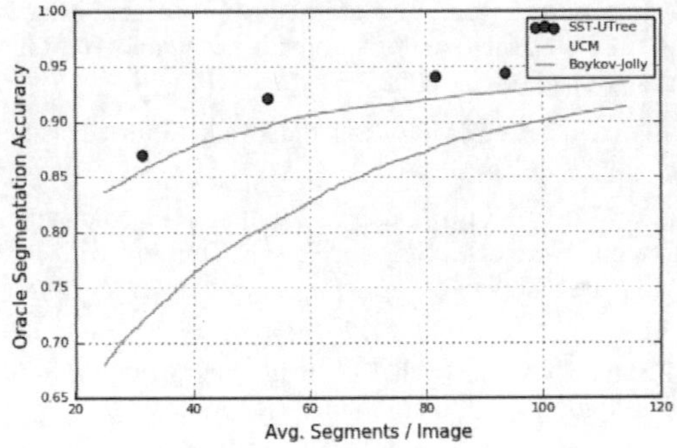

Figure 6: Oracle segmentation accuracy (Hamming) for SST-UTREE, UCM-SINGLE, and BOYKOV-JOLLY on the Penn-Fudan dataset.

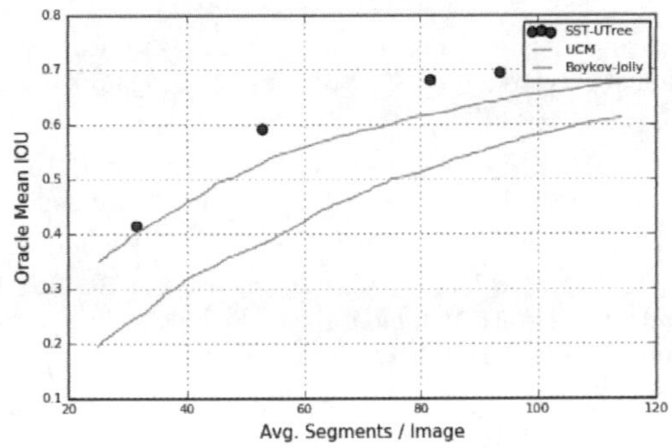

Figure 7: Oracle segmentation accuracy (mean IOU) for SST-UTREE, UCM-SINGLE, and BOYKOV-JOLLY on the Penn-Fudan dataset.

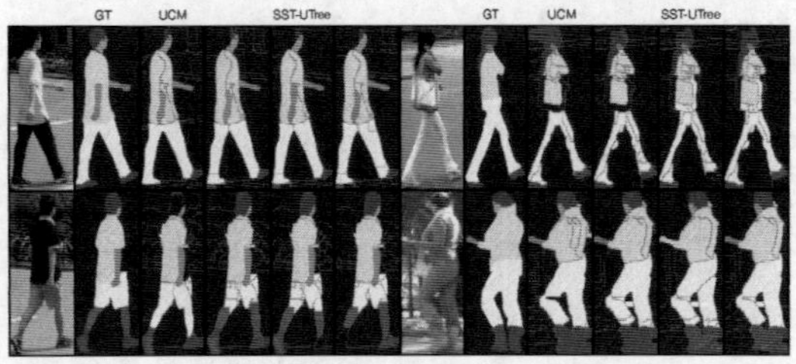

Figure 8: Oracle segmentation visualizations. From left to right: image, ground truth segmentation, UCM-SINGLE oracle segmentation, and oracle segmentations from three samples from SST-UTREE. Superpixels were generated from the $\sim$50 superpixels per image setting for both UCM-SINGLE and SST-UTREE. Superpixels are outlined in red.

5 CONCLUSION & FUTURE WORK

We have presented a model for producing multiple segmentations. The model extends current hierarchical segmentation approaches by formulating a probabilistic model using its structure. The probabilistic objective, based on the Hellinger distance, provides a fairly simple metric for evaluating and training this model. We formulate a learning approach to estimate merge probabilities for the internal nodes of a given tree. We then utilize this same estimator in order to optimize the tree structure, based on a sequence of sub-tree swaps, which effectively improves our loss function. We tested the model against two strong baselines, the standard Boykov-Jolly as well as a top current segmentation approach. The model provides a significant win on two datasets, including the challenging BSDS500. We also showed its utility in semantic segmentation, as a method of forming superpixels at different levels of granularity.

We are currently investigating a number of directions, including further improvements in the tree construction procedure. If the complexity of using multiple tree structures can be managed, this should provide a performance boost as well. Multiple trees would allow the model to handle diversity in the segmentations that go beyond that captured in a single tree, such as alternative groupings of ambiguous regions. In addition, allowing the merge probability estimator to take into account more information about regions, such as the level of the tree, and features at multiple levels, may also be beneficial.

The proper treatment of ambiguity is important to the future progress in AI. We believe that predicting the structure and parameters of a graphical model given an input, as we have done here for image segmentation, is applicable to other domains as well. Such models facilitate the minimization of distance to a target distribution constructed from multiple ground truths, which when appropriately built according to the task is a sensible objective. We hypothesize that this approach can be used to improve both training and evaluation of models in a wide range of important domains, particularly in tasks involving ambiguity in computer vision and natural language processing.

Acknowledgements

We thank Chris Williams and Raquel Urtasun for their helpful comments. This research was supported by Samsung and the Natural Sciences and Engineering Research Council of Canada.

References

Arbelaez, P., Maire, M., Fowlkes, C., and Malik, J. Contour Detection and Hierarchical Image Segmentation. *IEEE PAMI*, 2011.

Arbelaez, P., Pong-Tuset, J., Barron, J., Marques, F., and Malik, J. Multiscale Combinatorial Grouping. In *CVPR*, 2014.

Batra, Dhruv, Yadollahpour, Payman, Guzman-Rivera, Abner, and Shakhnarovich, Gregory. Diverse M-Best Solutions in Markov Random Fields. In *ECCV*, 2012.

Bo, Y. and Fowlkes, C. Shape-based Pedestrian Parsing. In *CVPR*, 2011.

Boykov, Y. and Jolly, M.-P. Interactive Graph Cuts for Optimal Boundary & Region Segmentation of Objects in N-D Images. In *ICCV*, 2001.

Dey, Debadeepta, Ramakrishna, Varun, Hebert, Martial, and Bagnell, J Andrew. Predicting Multiple Structured Visual Interpretations. In *ICCV*, 2015.

Gillenwater, Jennifer, Kulesza, Alex, and Taskar, Ben. Discovering Diverse and Salient Threads in Document Collections. In *EMNLP*, 2012.

Guzman-Rivera, A., Batra, D., and Kohli, P. Multiple Choice Learning: Learning to Produce Multiple Structured Outputs. In *NIPS*, 2012.

Hazan, Tamir, Keshet, Joseph, and McAllester, David A. Direct Loss Minimization for Structured Prediction. In *NIPS*, 2010.

Hou, X., Yuille, A., and Koch, C. Boundary Detection Benchmarking: Beyond F-Measures. In *CVPR*, 2013.

Hu, Shell X, Williams, Christopher KI, and Todorovic, Sinisa. Tree-Cut for Probabilistic Image Segmentation. *arXiv preprint arXiv:1506.03852*, 2015.

Ion, A, Carreira, J, and Sminchisescu, C. Image Segmentation by Figure-Ground Composition into Maximal Cliques. *ICCV*, 2011.

Jain, V., Turaga, S., Briggman, K., Helmstaedter, M., Denk, W., and Seung, H. S. Learning to Agglomerate Superpixel Hierarchies. In *NIPS*, 2011.

Kingma, Diederik and Ba, Jimmy. Adam: A method for stochastic optimization. *arXiv preprint arXiv:1412.6980*, 2014.

Kirillov, Alexander, Savchynskyy, Bogdan, Schlesinger, Dmitrij, Vetrov, Dmitry, and Rother, Carsten. Inferring M-Best Diverse Labelings in a Single One. In *ICCV*, 2015.

Kulesza, Alex, Taskar, Ben, et al. Determinantal point processes for machine learning. *Foundations and Trends in Machine Learning*, 5(2–3):123–286, 2012.

Lampert, C. Maximum Margin Multi-Label Structured Prediction. In *NIPS*, 2011.

Liu, Dong C and Nocedal, Jorge. On the Limited Memory BFGS Method for Large Scale Optimization. *Mathematical programming*, 45(1-3):503–528, 1989.

Maire, Michael, Arbeláez, Pablo, Fowlkes, Charless, and Malik, Jitendra. Using Contours to Detect and Localize Junctions in Natural Images. In *CVPR*, 2008.

Martin, D., Fowlkes, C., Tal, D., and Malik, J. A Database of Human Segmented Natural Images and its Application to Evaluating Segmentation Algorithms and Measuring Ecological Statistics. In *ICCV*, 2001.

Papineni, Kishore, Roukos, Salim, Ward, Todd, and Zhu, Wei-Jing. BLEU: a Method for Automatic Evaluation of Machine Translation. In *ACL*, 2002.

Rand, W. Objective Criteria for the Evaluation of Clustering Methods. *JASA*, 12 1971.

Ranzato, Marc'Aurelio, Chopra, Sumit, Auli, Michael, and Zaremba, Wojciech. Sequence Level Training with Recurrent Neural Networks. *arXiv preprint arXiv:1511.06732*, 2015.

Ren, Z. and Shakhnarovich, G. Image Segmentation by Cascaded Region Agglomeration. In *CVPR*, 2013.

Sharon, E., Galun, M., Sharon, D., Basri, R., and Brandt, A. Hierarchy and Adaptivity in Segmenting Visual Scenes. *Nature*, 442(7104):810–813, August 2006.

Shen, Shiqi, Cheng, Yong, He, Zhongjun, He, Wei, Wu, Hua, Sun, Maosong, and Liu, Yang. Minimum Risk Training for Neural Machine Translation. *arXiv preprint arXiv:1512.02433*, 2015.

Simonyan, Karen and Zisserman, Andrew. Very deep convolutional networks for large-scale image recognition. *arXiv preprint arXiv:1409.1556*, 2014.

Song, Yang, Schwing, Alexander G, Zemel, Richard S, and Urtasun, Raquel. Direct Loss Minimization for Training Deep Neural Nets. *arXiv preprint arXiv:1511.06411*, 2015.

Tromble, Roy W, Kumar, Shankar, Och, Franz, and Macherey, Wolfgang. Lattice Minimum Bayes-Risk Decoding for Statistical Machine Translation. In *EMNLP*, 2008.

Unnikrishnan, Ranjith and Hebert, Martial. Measures of Similarity. In *IEEE ACV*, 2005.

Vijayakumar, Ashwin K, Cogswell, Michael, Selvaraju, Ramprasath R, Sun, Qing, Lee, Stefan, Crandall, David, and Batra, Dhruv. Diverse beam search: Decoding diverse solutions from neural sequence models. *arXiv preprint arXiv:1610.02424*, 2016.

Wang, L., Shi, J., Song, G., and Shen, I. Object Detection Combining Recognition and Segmentation. In *ACCV 2007*, 2007.

Wong, Yuk Wah and Mooney, Raymond J. Learning for Semantic Parsing with Statistical Machine Translation. In *ACL*, 2006.

Yadollahpour, Payman, Batra, Dhruv, and Shakhnarovich, Gregory. Discriminative Re-ranking of Diverse Segmentations. In *CVPR*, 2013.

A DETAILS OF SST-SWAPTREE ALGORITHM

Our tree construction algorithm begins with an arbitrary tree structure and seeks to iteratively improve it by making moves within the space of tree structures. We consider swaps, in which the subtree rooted at a node in the tree is exchanged with the subtree rooted at another node. Refer to Figure 4 for an illustration of a sample swap.

We now present the details of how we efficiently compute and score allowable swaps in order to decide which move to make. This procedure continues for a fixed number of iterations chosen based on validation performance.

A.1 COMPUTATION OF ALLOWABLE SWAPS

We consider only swaps that satisfy two criteria. The first is that a swap must not be between a node and an ancestor of that node. We do not consider such swaps because the subtree rooted at each of two nodes overlap and therefore the position of any shared descendants after the swap is ill-defined. For example, a swap between node B and node I in Figure 4 would not be allowable.

The second criterion is that the swap must preserve the property that the children of any nonterminal node in the tree are neighboring. We call this property the *neighboring-region* property. Informally, the neighboring-region property ensures that for two children of a parent node k to be siblings, at least one of the superpixels corresponding to the left sibling must be adjacent to one of the superpixels corresponding to the right. If this condition is satisfied, we say that Neigh$(C(\ell(k)), C(r(k)))$. More precisely, the neighboring-region property is satisfied by a tree if for every non-terminal node k in the tree, $N(C(\ell(k))) \cap C(r(k)) \neq \varnothing$, where $N(S) = \left(\bigcup_{s \in S} \text{Adj}(s)\right) \setminus S$ denotes the set of superpixels directly adjacent to the superpixels contained in set S but not including the elements of S itself, and Adj(s) denotes the set of superpixels directly adjacent to superpixel s. Note that the neighboring-region property is symmetric in that it could equally well be expressed as $N(C(r(k))) \cap C(\ell(k)) \neq \varnothing$ for each non-terminal node k.

Finding swaps that satisfy the first criterion is simple. We begin by iterating over each node i in the tree. For each node i, we can search for potential swap partners j by traversing the path from i to the root. For each node k along this path (excluding i itself), we search the the subtree rooted at the child of k not belonging to that path for potential swap partners j. For example, if B were being considered for a swap in Figure 4, the path to the root (excluding B) would be E $\rightarrow$ I $\rightarrow$ K. We would therefore search the subtrees rooted at A, F, and J for nodes that could be swapped with B.

Satisfying the second criterion relies on two observations that hold for all swaps between nodes i and j: (a) any node not on the path from i to j will continue to satisfy the neighboring-region property after the swap, and (b) the lowest common ancestor $k = LCA(i, j)$ will maintain the neighboring-region property after the swap. Observation (a) is due to the fact that the regions corresponding to these nodes do not change as a result of the swap. For example, in Figure 4, the path from node B to C is B $\rightarrow$ E $\rightarrow$ I $\rightarrow$ K $\rightarrow$ J $\rightarrow$ H $\rightarrow$ C. A swap between B and C will not affect the subtrees rooted at A, F, G, or D, and therefore we do not need to check the neighboring-region property for these nodes. In addition, if there were any nodes above K in the example tree, they would not need to be checked either since the region corresponding to K in the tree does not change as a result of the swap. Furthermore, the subtrees rooted at i and j themselves do not change as a result of the swap and thus do not need to be checked.

To show observation (b) holds, assume without loss of generality that i is a descendant of $\ell(k)$ and j is a descendant of $r(k)$ (the right child of k). We know that prior to the swap, Neigh$(C(\ell(k)), C(r(k)))$ is true. Thus Neigh$((C(\ell(k)) \setminus C(i)) \cup C(i), (C(r(k)) \setminus C(j)) \cup C(j))$ is also true. For k to satisfy the neighboring-region property after the swap, it must be the case that Neigh$((C(\ell(k)) \setminus C(i)) \cup C(j), (C(r(k)) \setminus C(j)) \cup C(i))$. If $\ell(k) \neq i$, then we know that Neigh$(C(\ell(k)) \setminus C(i), C(i))$, otherwise the subtree rooted at $\ell(k)$ would not have satisfied the neighboring-region property prior to the swap. Similarly, if $r(k) \neq j$, then we know that Neigh$(C(r(k)) \setminus C(j), C(j))$. If both $\ell(k) = i$ and $r(k) = j$, then the neighboring-region property is satisfied trivially after the swap, because otherwise Neigh$(C(\ell(k)), C(r(k)))$ would not be true prior to the swap.

Therefore we must only check the nodes along the path from i to j that are not either the $LCA(i, j)$ or i or j themselves. Let m be such a node along the path from i to $LCA(i, j)$. Without loss of generality, assume that i is a descendant of $\ell(m)$. Define the set of *critical superpixels* in i relative to a node h to be Crit$(i, h) = C(i) \cap N(C(h))$. For m to have satisfied the neighboring-region property prior to the swap, it must be the case that Crit$(\ell(m), r(m)) \neq \varnothing$. If Crit$(\ell(m), r(m)) =$ Crit$(i, r(m))$, i.e. all critical superpixels of $\ell(m)$ relative to $r(m)$ are also contained in $C(i)$, then we say i is *critical* relative to $r(m)$.

If i is critical relative to $r(m)$, we know m will not satisfy the neighboring-region property after a swap involving i unless the region of the replacement node j is neighboring to the region of $r(m)$. We can thus add a *critical constraint* on j due to m that $C(j) \cap N(r(m)) \neq \varnothing$. Any such constraints can be accumulated as we traverse the path from i to $LCA(i, j)$, and we must check that the candidate node j satisfies all constraints. Similarly we must check that i satisfies all critical constraints collected along the path from j to $LCA(i, j)$. If all such constraints are satisfied then the swap between i and j is allowable.

A.2 SWAP SCORING

In this section we outline the algorithm used to assign scores to potential swaps. We first examine the minimum achievable Hellinger distance for a given tree structure. Then we show how to compute the change in minimum achievable Hellinger distance resulting from a swap. Finally, we derive an approximation to the change in Hellinger distance that can be computed given only information known at test time.

A.2.1 Minimum Achievable Hellinger Distance

When iteratively making swaps, we seek to decrease Hellinger distance achievable by the tree. In other words, we wish to decrease

$$\min_{\mathbf{p}} D(\pi, q) = 1 - \frac{1}{\binom{N}{2}} \sum_k \sum_{\substack{i \in C(\ell(k)) \\ j \in C(r(k))}} \left[\sqrt{\pi_k q_{ij}} + \sqrt{(1-\pi_k)(1-q_{ij})} \right] - \frac{1}{\binom{N}{2}} \sum_m \sum_{\substack{i,j \in C(m) \\ i<j}} \sqrt{q_{ij}}, \tag{5}$$

where the summation involving k is over nonterminal nodes in the tree, the summation involving m is over leafs of the tree, $\mathbf{p}$ is a vector of probabilities (one for each nonterminal node), and $\pi_k = p_k \pi_{\ell(k)} \pi_{r(k)}$ is the marginal probability of node k.

When scoring swaps it is more convenient to consider minimization directly over $\boldsymbol{\pi}$ because the summations decompose over nodes:

$$1 - \frac{1}{\binom{N}{2}} \sum_m \sum_{\substack{i,j \in C(m) \\ i<j}} \sqrt{q_{ij}} - \sum_k \max_{\pi_k} \left[\sqrt{\pi_k} \left(\frac{1}{\binom{N}{2}} \sum_{\substack{i \in C(\ell(k)) \\ j \in C(r(k))}} \sqrt{q_{ij}} \right) + \sqrt{1-\pi_k} \left(\frac{1}{\binom{N}{2}} \sum_{\substack{i \in C(\ell(k)) \\ j \in C(r(k))}} \sqrt{1-q_{ij}} \right) \right] \tag{6}$$

$$= 1 - \frac{1}{\binom{N}{2}} \sum_m \sum_{\substack{i,j \in C(m) \\ i<j}} \sqrt{q_{ij}} - \sum_k \max_{\pi_k} \left[Q(\ell(k), r(k)) \sqrt{\pi_k} + \tilde{Q}(\ell(k), r(k)) \sqrt{1-\pi_k} \right], \tag{7}$$

where we define

$$Q(s_1, s_2) \equiv \frac{1}{\binom{N}{2}} \sum_{\substack{i \in C(s_1) \\ j \in C(s_2)}} \sqrt{q_{ij}}, \text{ and } \tilde{Q}(s_1, s_2) \equiv \frac{1}{\binom{N}{2}} \sum_{\substack{i \in C(s_1) \\ j \in C(s_2)}} \sqrt{1-q_{ij}}. \tag{8}$$

The value π_k^* that minimizes Equation 7 is

$$\pi_k^* = \frac{Q(\ell(k), r(k))^2}{Q(\ell(k), r(k))^2 + \tilde{Q}(\ell(k), r(k))^2}, \tag{9}$$

and the term of the summation involving k resulting from substituting in π_k^* becomes

$$\max_{\pi_k} \left[Q(\ell(k), r(k))\sqrt{\pi_k} + \tilde{Q}(\ell(k), r(k))\sqrt{1-\pi_k} \right] = \sqrt{Q(\ell(k), r(k))^2 + \tilde{Q}(\ell(k), r(k))^2} \tag{10}$$

$$= \|z(\ell(k), r(k))\|_2, \tag{11}$$

where $z(s_1, s_2) \in \mathbb{R}^2$ and is defined to be

$$z(s_1, s_2) \equiv [Q(s_1, s_2), \tilde{Q}(s_1, s_2)]. \tag{12}$$

A.2.2 Effect of a Swap on Minimum Achievable Hellinger Distance

Most terms in the expression for $D(\pi, q)$ from Equation 5 will not change as a result of a swap of s_1 and s_2. The terms that do change are those corresponding to nodes along the path from s_1 to s_2, not including s_1 and s_2 themselves. Let k be a node along the path from s_1 to $LCA(s_1, s_2)$, not including the endpoints. Define $u(k)$ to be the child of k that is not an ancestor of s_1, and $g(k)$ to be the child of k that is an ancestor of s_1. Then the decrease in $D(\pi, q)$ due to k from making the swap is:

$$\Delta_k(s_1, s_2) = \|z(g(k) \setminus s_1, u(k)) + z(s_2, u(k))\| - \|z(g(k) \setminus s_1, u(k)) + z(s_1, u(k))\| \tag{13}$$

The change in $D(\pi, q)$ due to a node along the path from s_2 to $LCA(s_1, s_2)$ is similar to Equation 13 but with the roles of s_1 and s_2 reversed.

At the $LCA(s_1, s_2)$ the change is

$$\begin{aligned}\Delta_{LCA}(s_1, s_2) =& \|z(g(LCA) \setminus s_1, h(LCA) \setminus s_2) + z(s_1, s_2) + z(g(LCA) \setminus s_1, s_1) + z(s_2, h(LCA) \setminus s_2)\| - \\ & \|z(g(LCA) \setminus s_1, h(LCA) \setminus s_2) + z(s_1, s_2) + z(g(LCA) \setminus s_1, s_2) + z(s1, h(LCA) \setminus s_2)\|,\end{aligned} \tag{14}$$

where LCA is used as shorthand for $LCA(s_1, s_2)$. The total change in $D(\pi, q)$ is then

$$\sum_{k \in path(s_1, LCA(s_1, s_2))} \Delta_k(s_1, s_2) + \sum_{k \in path(s_2, LCA(s_1, s_2))} \Delta_k(s_2, s_1) + \Delta_{LCA}(s_1, s_2). \tag{15}$$

A.2.3 Approximating the Effect of a Swap

The quantity in Equation 15 depends on the values of q_{ij} for the relevant pixel pairs, which will be unknown at test time. We note that from Equations 9 and 12 that

$$z(s_1, s_2) = \|z(s_1, s_2)\|_2[\sqrt{\pi_k^*}, \sqrt{1 - \pi_k^*}]. \tag{16}$$

We choose to bound this based on the product of the size of the regions:

$$\|\boldsymbol{z}(s_1, s_2)\|_2 \leq \frac{|C(s_1)||C(s_2)|}{\binom{N}{2}}, \tag{17}$$

with equality iff either $q_{ij} = 1$ for all $i \in C(s_1), j \in C(s_2)$ or $q_{ij} = 0$ for all $i \in C(s_1), j \in C(s_2)$. If we have an estimate $\hat{\pi}(s_1, s_2)$ of any two regions s_1 and s_2, we can combine Equations 16 and 17 to obtain an estimate for $\boldsymbol{z}(s_1, s_2)$:

$$\hat{\boldsymbol{z}}(s_1, s_2) \approx \frac{|C(s_1)||C(s_2)|}{\binom{N}{2}}[\sqrt{\hat{\pi}(s_1, s_2)}, \sqrt{1 - \hat{\pi}(s_1, s_2)}]. \tag{18}$$

At test time, we can therefore use model predictions of $\boldsymbol{\pi}$ to estimate the change in Hellinger distance by plugging the approximate $\hat{\boldsymbol{z}}$ values from Equation 18 into the change in Hellinger distance from Equation 15.

B ADDITIONAL EXPERIMENTAL DETAILS

B.1 ADDITIONAL DATASET DETAILS

We generated four synthetic ground truth segmentations per example in the Penn-Fudan pedestrian dataset, each of which represents a different prototypical parse of the image. The original semantic segmentation labels contained thirteen classes: background, hair, face, upper and lower clothes, and left and right arms, hands, legs, and shoes. The first synthetic ground truth treats each of these semantic classes as a separate region. The second merges hair with face, hand with corresponding arm, and shoe with corresponding leg. The third further merges all lower body classes, upper body classes, and head classes together. The fourth and final ground truth segmentation distinguishes only between background and non-background semantic classes. When forming the ground truths, regions were split as necessary to ensure that each is spatially contiguous. Visualizations of several ground truths and corresponding images are shown in Figure 9.

B.2 ADDITIONAL SST TRAINING DETAILS

Our network for estimating marginal probabilities used two sets of features as input. The first are visual features extracted from VGG-19 (Simonyan & Zisserman, 2014). Each image was run through the net, and the activations just prior to the second max-pooling operation were recorded (fourth convolutional layer). These activations were then upsampled back to the original image size using nearest neighbor interpolation, thereby producing 128 features for each pixel. These features were average-pooled within the base-level regions to give 128 visual features for each. The second set were geometric features regarding the regions and their relations. These features included: centroids of the parent, left, and right regions; difference and absolute difference between the left and right centroids; coordinates of the top left and bottom right bounding box corners of each region; height and width of the regions; normalized number of pixels of each region (maximum of 1); the difference and absolute difference of the normalized number of pixels in the child regions; and the difference between the parent normalized number of pixels and minimum (respectively maximum) of child normalized number of pixels. All coordinates were expressed relative to the image size such that both x and y coordinates ranged from -1 to 1. This resulted in 35 additional geometric features, yield 163 features total.

Each set of features has the benefit that the features of a parent region can efficiently be computed given features of the child regions. All features were normalized to have zero mean and unit variance across the training examples.

For BSDS500, the first layer of the marginal estimation network had 128 hidden units and the second layer had 64. For Penn-Fudan the first layer had 32 hidden units and the second had 16. ReLU activations with dropout were used for the first and second layers. The final layer had a single sigmoid output and no dropout.

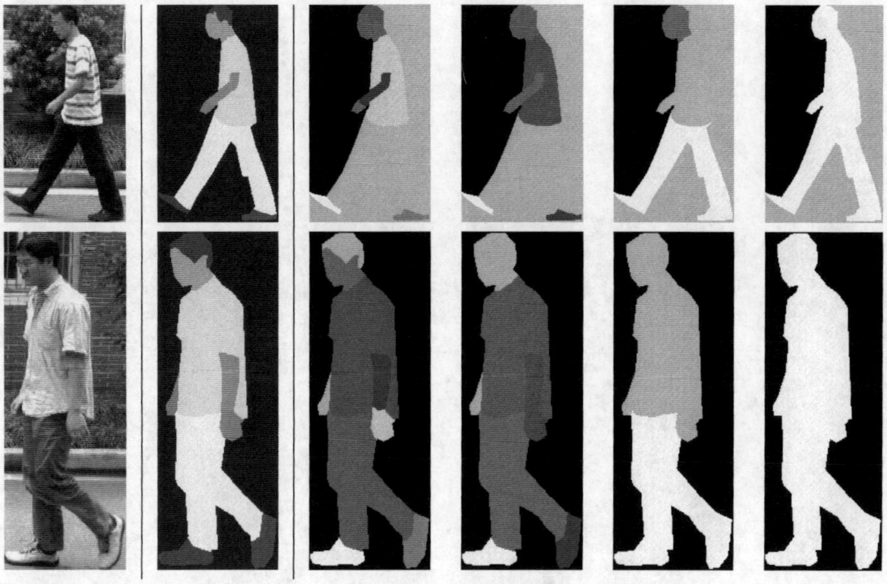

Figure 9: Example synthetic ground truths created for the Penn-Fudan dataset. From left to right: image, semantic segmentation labels, ground truths 1-4. The colors shown in the ground truths are not semantically meaningful: they are chosen to simply be maximally distinguishable for ease of visualization.

B.3 ADDITIONAL DETAILS REGARDING BOYKOV-JOLLY BASELINE

In BOYKOV-JOLLY, a strength is computed between any two adjacent base-level regions s_1 and s_2 as the mean of $1 - \frac{\exp(-(I_i - I_j)^2)}{2\sigma^2}$, where pixel $i \in s_1$ and pixel $j \in s_2$. Here $I_i \in [0, 1]$ denotes the mean intensity at pixel i across color channels. Merges are then sequentially made between regions in order of ascending strength. The strength between two arbitrary regions r_1 and r_2 is defined to be the minimum superpixel strength between two adjacent superpixels s_1 and s_2 such that $s_1 \in r_1$ and $s_2 \in r_2$. Merges continue in this way until a single region remains. This sequence of merges induces a segmentation tree, which can be thresholded by any strength from 0 to 1 in order to form a segmentation. In the results presented in Tables 1 and 2 of the main paper, a single threshold and σ with the best validation performance were chosen via grid search.

B.4 ADDITIONAL SAMPLES

We show additional samples from the SST-UTREE algorithm trained on BSDS 500 in Figure 10 and representative samples from SST-UTREE on Penn-Fudan in Figure 11.

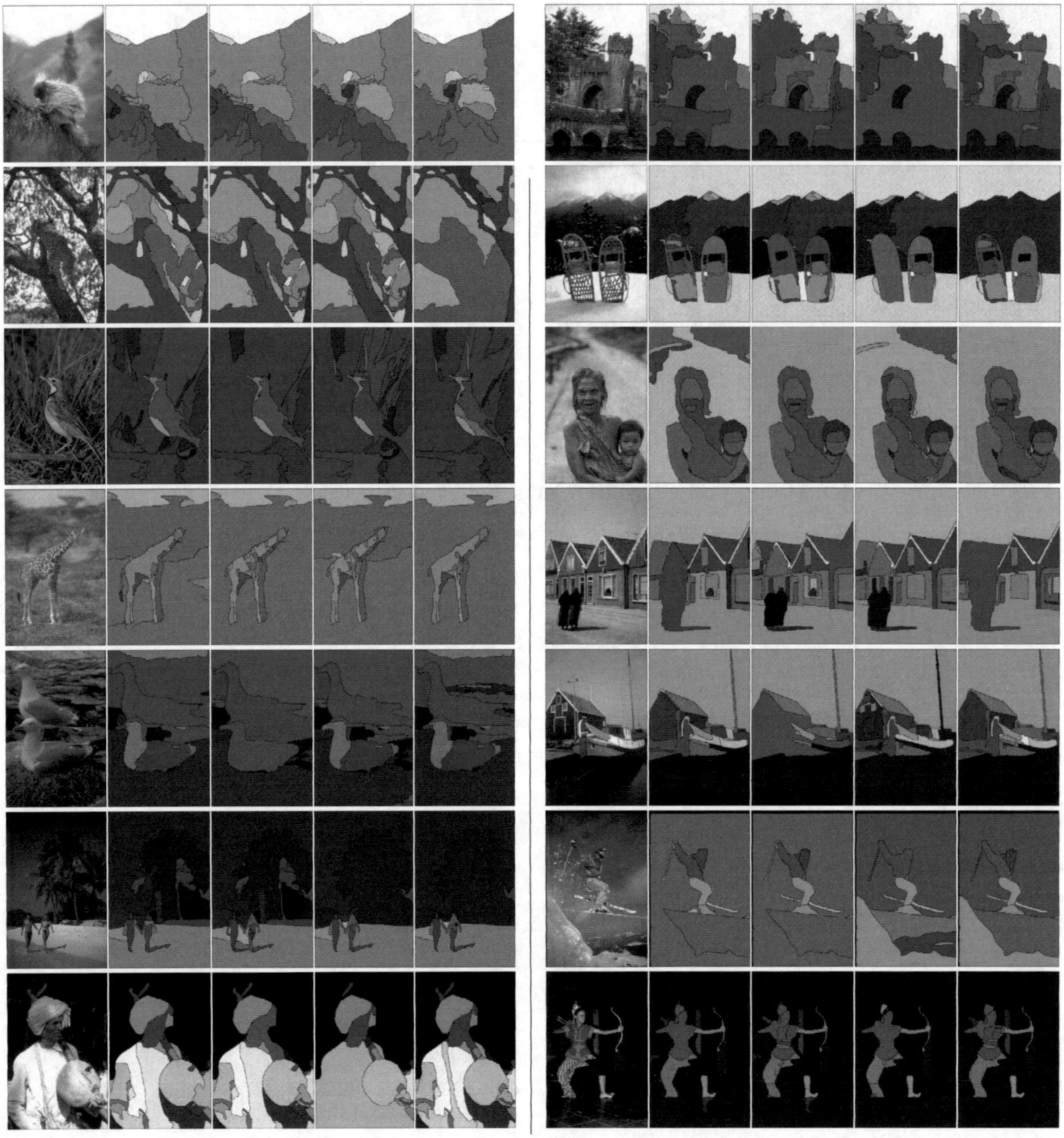

Figure 10: Samples from the SST-UTREE model on BSDS500. From left to right: image, samples 1-4 from the model. All images are from the test set.

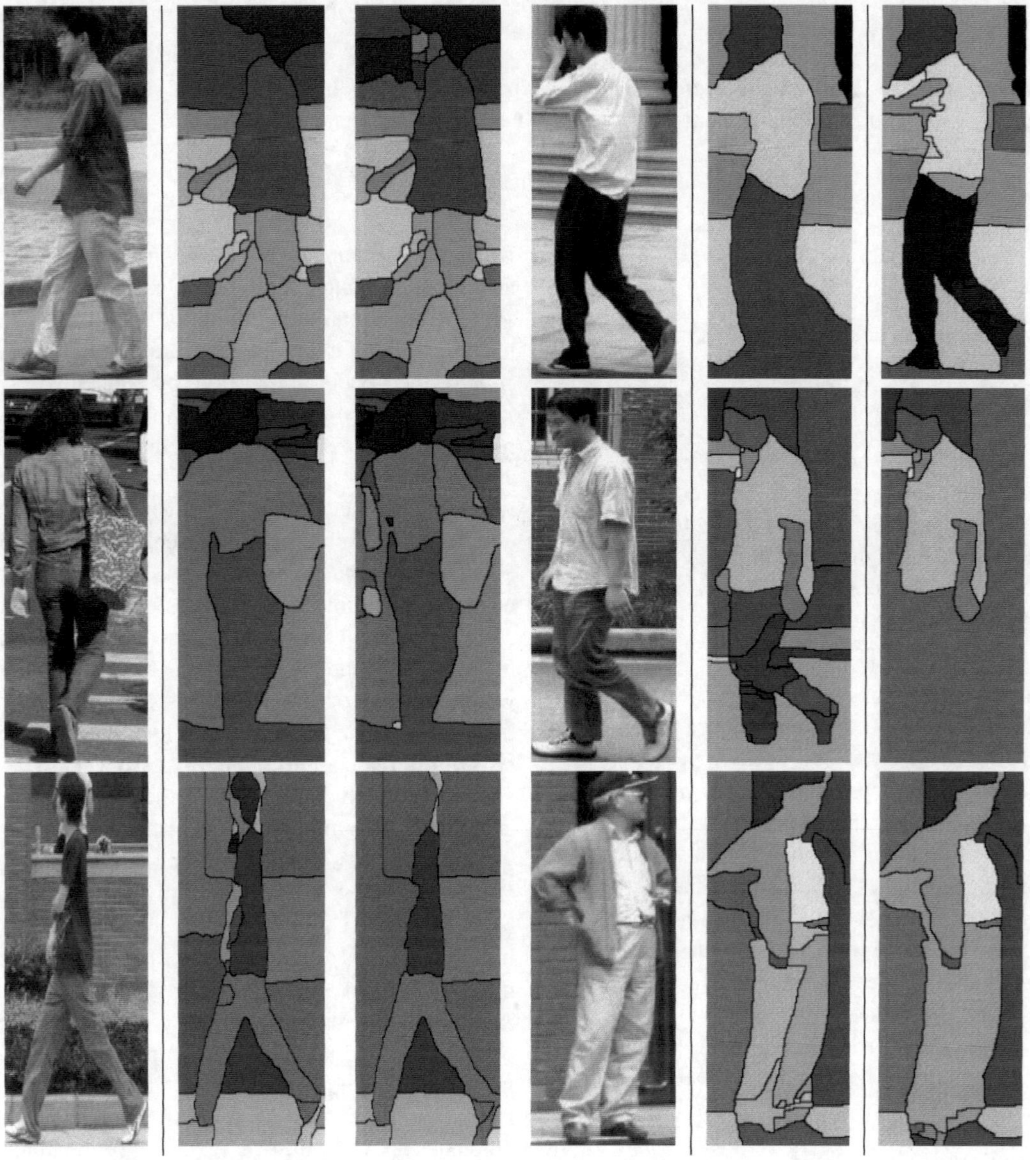

Figure 11: Representative samples from the SST-UTREE model on Penn-Fudan. Within each pane, from left to right: image, samples 1-2 from the corresponding test model. Note that for visualization purposes, the images and segmentations have been resized to the same dimensions; in the actual dataset the sizes vary.

Efficient Online Learning for Optimizing Value of Information: Theory and Application to Interactive Troubleshooting

Yuxin Chen
Caltech

Jean-Michel Renders
Xerox Research Center Europe

Morteza Haghir Chehreghani
Xerox Research Center Europe

Andreas Krause
ETH Zurich

Abstract

We consider the optimal value of information problem, where the goal is to sequentially select a set of tests with a minimal cost, so that one can efficiently make the best decision based on the observed outcomes. Existing algorithms are either heuristics with no guarantees, or scale poorly (with exponential run time in terms of the number of available tests). Moreover, these methods assume a known distribution over the test outcomes, which is often not the case in practice.

We propose a sampling-based online learning framework to address the above issues. First, assuming the distribution over hypotheses is known, we propose a *dynamic hypothesis enumeration* strategy, which allows efficient information gathering with strong theoretical guarantees. We show that with sufficient amount of samples, one can identify a near-optimal decision with high probability. Second, when the parameters of the hypotheses distribution are unknown, we propose an algorithm which learns the parameters progressively via posterior sampling in an *online* fashion. We further establish a rigorous bound on the expected regret. We demonstrate the effectiveness of our approach on a real-world interactive troubleshooting application, and show that one can efficiently make high-quality decisions with low cost.

1 INTRODUCTION

Optimal information gathering for decision making is a central challenge in artificial intelligence. A classical approach for decision making is the decision-theoretic *value of information* (VoI) [15], where one needs to find an optimal testing policy which achieves the maximal value of information. Informally, the goal of the optimal policy is to reduce the uncertainty about some *hidden state* of the system in question, by efficiently probing it via a sequence of *tests* and observations, so that one can make the best *decision* with the minimal cost. For example, consider the automated troubleshooting problem, where a customer reaches a contact center and wants to resolve some problem with her cell phone. To provide a solution, a virtual agent has to ask the customer a few questions regarding the symptoms of the cellphone to diagnose the root-cause. Here, "decision" corresponds to the solution, "hidden state" corresponds to the root-cause which we want to learn about, "tests" correspond to questions on the symptoms, and the "hypothesis space" consists of full realizations of all tests. We want to develop a virtual agent, which can identify the best solution for the customer with a minimal set of questions asked.

Optimization of VoI. The optimal VoI problem has been studied in various contexts, including active learning [10, 29], Bayesian experimental design [6], policy making [27] and probabilistic planning [17, 30], etc. We refer interested readers to §6 for a more detailed review of the related work. Deriving optimal policies is NP-hard in general [5]; however, under certain conditions some approximation results are known. In particular, if test outcomes are deterministic functions of the hidden state (i.e., noise-free setting), then a simple greedy algorithm, namely *generalized binary search* (GBS), is guaranteed to provide a near-optimal approximation of the optimal policy in terms of the cost [20]. These results have recently been generalized to decision making, where information gathering policies no longer aim to resolve all uncertainty of the hidden state – but just enough to make the optimal decision. Such problem, known as the *Decision Region Determination* (DRD) problem [16], relates the problem of learning the optimal policy with maximal utility, to the problem that aims at resolving the uncertainty amongst the decisions. Following this line of work, Javdani et al. [16] and Chen et al. [8] propose a principled framework for optimizing the VoI using surrogate objective functions. The theoretical guarantees of these algorithms rely on the fact that the objective functions exhibit *adaptive submodularity* [12], a natural diminishing returns property that generalizes the classical notion of submodularity to adaptive policies. It follows that a simple greedy policy can provide near-optimal approximation to the optimal (intractable) solution.

Limitations of existing methods. In many data-intensive decision making applications, however, evaluating these surrogate objectives is expensive. First, let us assume that the underlying distribution over hypotheses is given. At each iteration, one needs to perform a greedy search over the tests and find the one that myopically maximizes the expected gain in the corresponding objective, whose runtime depends linearly on the size of the support of the probability distribution over the hypotheses. However, with the size of the hypothesis space growing exponentially in the number of tests, it is often computationally prohibitive to work with the original distribution. Second, in practice, the underlying distribution over hypotheses is often unknown, and requires to be estimated (and learned) over time. Within an online framework for solving the troubleshooting problem, we assume that the virtual agent does not possess a perfect knowledge of which root-causes correspond to which symptoms. Thus, to provide better diagnosis in the long run, the virtual agent must engage customers to answer more explorative questions during each session, while not spamming the customer with excessive queries.

Our contribution. In this paper, we make contributions to both fronts. First, assuming that the prior over hypotheses is given, we propose an efficient hypothesis enumeration scheme, which makes the class of adaptive submodular surrogates practically feasible, while still preserving strong theoretical guarantees. In particular, through a "divide-and-conquer" strategy, we generate the most probable hypotheses conditioning on each hidden state with a novel and efficient *priority search* procedure, and then merge them over all states to compute their marginal likelihood. In comparison with prior art, our sampling scheme utilizes the specific structure of the underlying model, and thereby offers increased efficiency and better approximation guarantees.

As our second contribution, we integrate our hypothesis enumeration strategy for optimizing VoI into an *online* sequential information gathering framework, where the conditional probabilities of test outcomes given the hidden states are unknown, and can only be learned from data in an online fashion. For instance, in troubleshooting, the conditional probabilities of symptoms given a root-cause might be unknown. For this purpose, we employ a *posterior sampling* approach, where for each decision-making session (i.e., for each customer), we first sample parameters of the conditional probability distributions according to their probabilities of being "optimal" (in the sense that they reflect the true parameters), and then use our hypothesis enumeration algorithm to generate hypotheses for that session.

We further establish a rigorous bound on the *expected regret* (defined in terms of the value of information) of our algorithm. Our online learning strategy can be interpreted as Thompson sampling across multiple sessions of interaction. Several recent empirical simulations [7, 14, 28] and theoretical studies [1, 4, 19] have demonstrated the effectiveness of Thompson sampling in different settings. However, different from our framework, the classical usage of Thompson sampling [32] suggests to choose an action according to its probability of being optimal, i.e. the action which maximizes the reward in expectation; whereas in our model, the "action" can be interpreted as the set of tests performed in one decision-making session.

Finally, we demonstrate our online learning framework on a real-world troubleshooting platform. Our empirical results show that one can efficiently run the "submodular surrogate"-based approaches with our dynamic hypothesis enumeration strategy, while achieving much better performance comparing with existing commonly-used heuristics (we observe a 16% improvement on the average cost on our troubleshooting dataset). Our experiments under the online setting imply that our framework encourages efficient exploration, which, combined with the hypothesis enumeration algorithm, leads to efficient online learning of the optimal VoI.

2 VALUE OF INFORMATION

In this section we introduce basic notations, and formally state the VoI problem and existing methods for solving it.

Formulating VoI as a DRD problem. Let $Y \in \mathcal{Y} \triangleq \{y_1, \ldots, y_m\}$ be a random variable that represents some *hidden state*, upon which we want to make a *decision*. The reward of making decision $d \in \mathcal{D}$ for hidden state $y \in \mathcal{Y}$ is modeled by a utility function $u : \mathcal{D} \times \mathcal{Y} \to [0, 1]$. We are given a set of *tests* $\mathcal{T} \triangleq \{1, \ldots, n\}$ of *binary* outcomes; performing each test $t \in \mathcal{T}$ reveals some information about Y, and incurs some cost which is given by a cost function $c : \mathcal{T} \to \mathbb{R}_{\geq 0}$. Let $\mathcal{H}$ denote the ground set of *hypotheses*; each hypothesis $h \in \mathcal{H}$ corresponds to a possible realization of the outcomes of all tests in $\mathcal{T}$. In other words, the *outcome* of test t can be modeled as a deterministic function of h, i.e., $g_t : \mathcal{H} \to \{0, 1\}$. Let $X_t \in \{0, 1\}$ be the random variable corresponding to the outcome of test t, and $H = [X_1, \ldots, X_n]$ be the random variable over $\mathcal{H}$. We use x_t to denote the observed outcome of test t. Crucially, we assume that X_i's are *conditionally independent* given the hidden state Y, i.e., $\mathbb{P}[Y, X_1, \ldots, X_m] = \mathbb{P}[Y] \prod_{i=1}^{n} \mathbb{P}[X_i \mid Y]$. In such *offline* setting, we assume that the parameters of the above distributions are given.

Denote the set of performed tests by $\mathcal{A}$ and their outcome vector by $\mathbf{x}_{\mathcal{A}}$. We define $U(d \mid \mathbf{x}_{\mathcal{A}}) \triangleq \mathbb{E}_y[u(y, d) \mid \mathbf{x}_{\mathcal{A}}]$ to be the expected utility of making decision d after observing $\mathbf{x}_{\mathcal{A}}$. The *value* of a specific set of observations $\mathbf{x}_{\mathcal{A}}$ is then defined as: $\mathrm{VoI}(\mathbf{x}_{\mathcal{A}}) \triangleq \max_{d \in \mathcal{D}} U(d \mid \mathbf{x}_{\mathcal{A}})$, i.e., the maximum expected utility achievable when acting upon observations $\mathbf{x}_{\mathcal{A}}$. For each decision $d \in \mathcal{D}$, we define its associated *decision region* as $\mathcal{R}_d \triangleq \{h : U(d \mid h) = \mathrm{VoI}(h)\}$, i.e., the set of hypotheses for which d is the optimal decision.

Formally, a *policy* $\pi : 2^{\mathcal{T} \times \{0,1\}} \to \mathcal{T}$ is a partial mapping from the set of test-observation pairs to (the next) tests. The expected cost of a policy π is $\mathrm{cost}_{av}(\pi) \triangleq \mathbb{E}_h \left[\sum_{i:(i,x_i) \in \mathcal{S}(\pi,h)} c(i)\right]$, and worst-case cost is $\mathrm{cost}_{wc}(\pi) \triangleq \max_h \sum_{i:(i,x_i) \in \mathcal{S}(\pi,h)} c(i)$, where $\mathcal{S}(\pi, h)$ represents the set of tests (and their outcomes) seen by π given that hypothesis h happens. The goal of the DRD problem is to find an optimal policy π^* with a minimal cost (expected or worst-case), such that upon termination, there exists at least one decision region that contains all hypotheses consistent with the observations acquired by the policy. Formally, we seek

$$\pi^* \in \arg\min_{\pi} \mathrm{cost}(\pi), \quad \text{s.t. } \forall h \, \exists d : \mathcal{H}(\mathcal{S}(\pi, h)) \subseteq \mathcal{R}_d. \tag{1}$$

where $\mathcal{H}(\mathcal{S}(\pi, h)) = \{h' \in \mathcal{H} : (i, x) \in \mathcal{S}(\pi, h) \Rightarrow g_i(h') = x\}$ is the set of hypotheses consistent with $\mathcal{S}(\pi, h)$.

The *Equivalence Class Edge Cutting* algorithm. For simplicity, we consider the special case of the DRD problem where the decision regions are disjoint[1]. In such case, the DRD problem reduces to the *equivalence class determination* problem, which can be solved near-optimally by the *Equivalence Class Edge Cutting* (EC^2) algorithm [13].

As is illustrated in Fig. 1, EC^2 employs an edge-cutting strategy based on a weighted graph $G = (\mathcal{H}, E)$, where vertices represent hypotheses, and edges link hypotheses that we want to distinguish between. Formally, $E \triangleq \bigcup_{d \neq d'} \{\{h, h'\} : h \in \mathcal{R}_d, h' \in \mathcal{R}_{d'}\}$ consists of all (unordered) pairs of root-causes corresponding to different target decisions (see Fig. 1b). We define a weight function $w : E \to \mathbb{R}_{\geq 0}$ by $w(\{h, h'\}) \triangleq \mathbb{P}[h] \cdot \mathbb{P}[h']$, i.e., as the product of the probabilities of its incident root-causes. We extend the weight function on sets of edges $E' \subseteq E$, as the sum of weight of all edges $\{h, h'\} \in E'$, i.e., $w(E') \triangleq \sum_{\{h,h'\} \in E'} w(\{h, h'\})$.

Performing test $t \in \mathcal{T}$ with outcome x_t is said to "*cut*" an edge, if at least one of its incident root-causes is inconsistent with x_t (See Fig. 1c): Formally, the set of edges cut by observing x_t is $E(x_t) \triangleq \{\{h, h'\} \in E : \mathbb{P}[x_t \mid h] = 0 \vee \mathbb{P}[x_t \mid h'] = 0\}$. EC^2 then greedily selects the test that maximizes the total expected weight of edges cut per unit cost. The performance guarantee of EC^2 relies on the fact that the objective function (i.e., the total weight of edges cut) is *adaptive submodular*, and *strongly adaptive monotone* [12]. In particular, let $p_{\min} \triangleq \min_{h \in \mathcal{H}} \mathbb{P}[h]$ denote the minimal prior probability of any hypothesis; the expected cost of EC^2 is bounded by an $O(\log(1/p_{\min}) + 1)$ factor[2] of the minimal expected cost.

3 EFFICIENT OPTIMIZATION OF VOI VIA HYPOTHESIS ENUMERATION

Note that to compute the exact EC^2 objective, we have to enumerate all hypotheses in $\mathcal{H}$ of non-zero prior probability. The total number of hypotheses is exponential with respect to the number of tests; hence, direct application of EC^2 does not scale up to several hundreds of tests or more. To facilitate efficient optimization, we must consider effective sampling schemes to explore the hypothesis space. We aim to maintain a "confident set" of hypotheses to efficiently approximate the EC^2 objective. Concretely, we consider the following problem:

The optimal hypothesis enumeration problem. Assume the prior $\mathbb{P}[Y]$ on the hidden state is known, and the prior distribution over hypotheses are fully specified by the conditional probability distribution table (CPT): $\boldsymbol{\theta} = [\theta_{ij}]_{n \times m}$, where $\theta_{ij} \triangleq \mathbb{P}[X_i = 1 \mid Y = y_j]$ for test $i \in [n]$ and hidden state $j \in [m]$. Let $\tilde{\mathcal{H}}$ be the set of hypotheses sampled from the CPT. Clearly, an "ideal" set $\tilde{\mathcal{H}}$ for EC^2 should be (1) rich enough to enclose promising candidates of *true* underlying hypotheses, and (2) compact enough so that it excludes hypotheses that are extremely rare and ensures feasibility of the algorithm. To this end, we define the *coverage* of $\tilde{\mathcal{H}}$ as its total proba-

[1]Note that our algorithmic framework can also be directly applied to the general DRD setting with overlapping decision regions.

[2]Throughout this paper all the logs are in base 2.

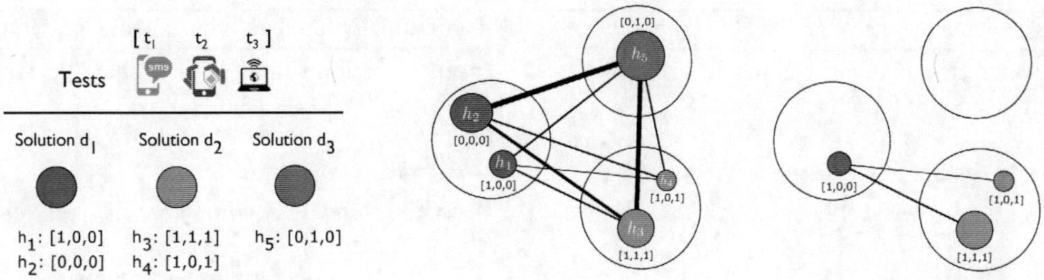

(a) A troubleshooting example (b) Initialization of EC^2 (c) Observing $X_1 = 1$

Figure 1: Illustration of the EC^2 algorithm of [13]. Fig. (a) shows an illustrative example of the troubleshooting problem. In this example, we assume that there are three possible troubleshooting decisions we can make (i.e., solutions); each of them corresponds to one or many hypotheses (e.g., realizations of test outcomes). The goal is to identify the best solution for a given problem as quickly as possible. In (b), we initialize EC^2, by drawing edges between all pairs of hypotheses (solid circles) that are mapped into different decisions (hollow circles). In (c), we perform test 1 and observe $X_1 = 1$. As a result, all the edges incident to hypotheses $h_2 : [0, 0, 0]$ and $h_5 : [0, 1, 0]$ are cut/ removed.

bility mass: $Z(\tilde{\mathcal{H}}) = \sum_{h \in \tilde{\mathcal{H}}} \mathbb{P}[h]$, and the coverage of $\tilde{\mathcal{H}}$ conditioning on y as $Z(\tilde{\mathcal{H}} \mid y) = \sum_{h \in \tilde{\mathcal{H}}} \mathbb{P}[h \mid Y = y]$. We aim to attain a high coverage over $\mathcal{H}$ using samples, while keeping the sample size as small as possible. Formally, to achieve $1 - \eta$ coverage, we seek

$$\tilde{\mathcal{H}}^* = \underset{\tilde{\mathcal{H}}: Z(\tilde{\mathcal{H}}) \geq 1-\eta}{\arg\min} |\tilde{\mathcal{H}}|.$$

Existing approaches for generating hypotheses, such as Monte-Carlo sampling, often require a large sample size to reach a certain coverage of the total probability mass. To illustrate this, let us consider a simple multinomial distribution that describes the probability distribution of four mutually exclusive hypotheses (h_1, h_2, h_3, h_4), with probabilities (0.94, 0.03, 0.02, 0.01). A Monte-Carlo hypothesis generator simply samples hypotheses according to their probabilities (as we were rolling a dice). If we require to observe a subset of hypotheses that cover at least 98% of the total probability mass (i.e. h_1, h_2 and at least one of h_3 or h_4) with a confidence level of at least 99%, then we need at least a sample of average size 174, to cover the "rare" observations.

Dynamic hypothesis enumeration. The problem of the Monte-Carlo approach is that it is ignorant of the structure of the VoI problem. Instead, our method aims at providing the most likely configurations – covering up to a pre-specified fraction of the total probability mass – in an efficient and adaptive way. In a nutshell, we adaptively maintain a pool of hypotheses that constitute a small sample with sufficient coverage. In particular, our hypothesis enumeration scheme consists of two modules: (1) Algorithm 1 *locally* enumerates the *most likely* hypotheses for each hidden state, which will cover – by taking the union over all hidden states – at least

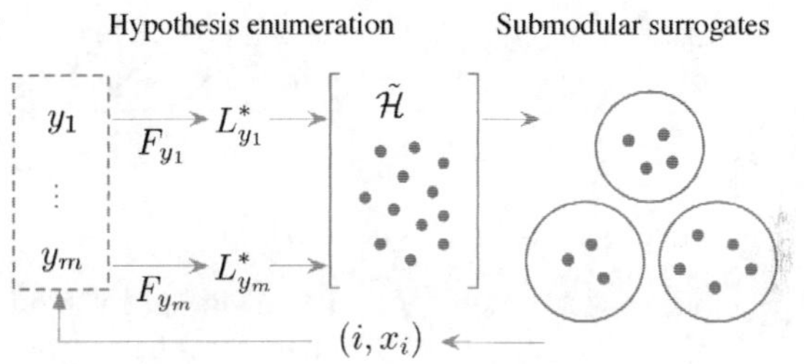

Figure 2: The dynamic hypothesis enumeration framework for optimizing VoI.

$(1 - \eta)$ fraction of the total probability mass of all hypotheses; and (2) Algorithm 2, as illustrated in Fig. 2, provides a *global* mechanism that, after observing a test outcome, adaptively filters out inconsistent hypotheses and *re-generates* new hypotheses by calling Algorithm 1.

3.1 ENUMERATING HYPOTHESES

The basic module of our hypothesis enumeration framework is a "local" hypothesis generator, which enumerates the most likely hypotheses for any given hidden state. It incrementally builds a Directed Acyclic Graph[3] (DAG) of hypotheses, starting from the most likely configuration. At each step, the leaf nodes of the DAG represent the current *candidate frontier*, i.e., the set of hypotheses that dominate all other candidate hypotheses in terms of likelihood. This set is used to generate the remaining hypotheses through a "children generation" mechanism: the next most likely hypothesis of *candidate frontier* is identified, and its (at most two) children

[3]Note that this DAG is used as a data structure for hypothesis enumeration, and is *different* from the (undirected) weighted graph used for running the EC^2 algorithm.

Algorithm 1: Generate the most likely hypotheses for y

1 **Input**: Hidden state y, Conditional probability table $\boldsymbol{\theta}$, coverage threshold η, (optional) frontier F_y;
begin
2   Sort tests in decreasing order of $\mathbb{P}[X_i = 1 \mid y]$;
  foreach $i \in \{1, \ldots, n\}$ **do**
3     $p_i \leftarrow \log(\mathbb{P}[X_i = 1 \mid y])$;
4     $q_i \leftarrow \log(\mathbb{P}[X_i = 0 \mid y])$;
  if F_y *is empty* **then**
5     $F_y \leftarrow \{h_1 = [1, 1, \ldots, 1]\}$, with log-weight $\lambda_y(h_1) = \sum_i \log p_i$;
6     $L^*_y \leftarrow \emptyset$;
  while $\sum_{h \in L^*_y} \exp(\lambda_y(h)) < 1 - \eta$ **do**
7     $h^* \leftarrow \arg\max_{h \in F_y} \lambda_y(h)$;
8     $F_y \leftarrow F_y \setminus \{h^*\}$, $L^*_y \leftarrow L^*_y \cup \{h^*\}$;
9   Generate (at most) 2 children h_{c_1}, h_{c_2} from h^*;
10     $F_y \leftarrow F_y \cup \{h_{c_1}, h_{c_2}\}$;
11   **Output**: Most likely hypotheses L^*_y for y, log-probabilities $\lambda_y(h) = \log(\mathbb{P}[h \mid y, \mathbf{x}_{\mathcal{A}}])$, and F_y.

Algorithm 2: Iterative Filtering and Re-sampling

1 **Input**: Conditional probability table $\boldsymbol{\theta}$, Prior $\mathbb{P}[Y]$, coverage threshold η;
begin
2   $\tilde{\mathcal{H}} \leftarrow \emptyset$;
  while *stopping condition for* EC^2 *not reached* **do**
    foreach $y \in \{y_1, \ldots, y_m\}$ **do**
3   Call Algorithm 1 to generate L^*_y;
4       $\tilde{\mathcal{H}} \leftarrow \tilde{\mathcal{H}} \cup L^*$;
    foreach $h \in \tilde{\mathcal{H}}$ **do**
5       $p(h \mid \mathbf{x}_{\mathcal{A}}) \leftarrow \sum_y \exp(\lambda_y(h)) \cdot \mathbb{P}[y \mid \mathbf{x}_{\mathcal{A}}]$;
6   Run EC^2 to determine the next test t;
    $\mathcal{A} \leftarrow \mathcal{A} \cup \{t\}$;
7   Observe x_t; $\mathbf{x}_{\mathcal{A}} \leftarrow \mathbf{x}_{\mathcal{A}} \cup \{x_t\}$;
8   Update $\mathbb{P}[y \mid \mathbf{x}_{\mathcal{A}}]$;
9     $\lambda_y(h) \leftarrow \lambda_y(h) - \log \mathbb{P}[x_t \mid y]$;
10   Filter out inconsistent hypotheses in L^*_y and F_y;
11   Remove test t from the list of available tests;
12   **Output**: (test - outcome) vectors $\mathbf{x}_{\mathcal{A}}$, decision d

are added as new leaf nodes to the DAG.

The input of Algorithm 1 consists of the given hidden state value y, the associated outcome probability vector over n tests, i.e., $\mathbb{P}[x_i \mid y]$ ($i = 1, \ldots, n$), and the threshold of coverage η. Optionally, it might be given a candidate frontier F_y, which is defined as a list of consistent hypotheses h with their log-probability weights $\lambda_y(h) = \mathbb{P}[h \mid y, \mathbf{x}_{\mathcal{A}}]$ conditioned on the hidden state value y and current observations $\mathbf{x}_{\mathcal{A}}$. F_y is obtained as a by-product when calling the same module for the same y at the previous iterations, and is used as a seed set of nodes to further expand the DAG.

W.l.o.g., we can assume that tests' outcomes are defined in such a way that $\mathbb{P}[X_i = 1 \mid y] \geq 0.5$.[4] Initially (line 2), the tests are rearranged in decreasing order of $\mathbb{P}[X_i = 1 \mid y]$. Thereby, the last test will be the one with the highest uncertainty; hence flipping the sign of this test will have the minimal effect on the overall likelihood. The generator then proceeds to enumerate the most likely hypotheses corresponding to the given hidden state y. At line 9, the two children hypotheses are generated as follows. For the first child, if the last (right-most) bit of h^* is 1, we then create h_{c_1} by switching the last bit to 0. For instance, the child hypothesis h_{c_1} of $h^* = [0, 1, 1, 0, \mathbf{1}]$ is $[0, 1, 1, 0, \mathbf{0}]$. Its log-probability is obtained by $\lambda_y(h_{c_1}) = \lambda_y(h^*) + q_n - p_n$. For the second child, we first need to locate the right-most "$[1, 0]$" pair in h^* (if there exists any; otherwise we do nothing), and the create h_{c_2} by switching "$[1, 0]$" into "$[0, 1]$". For instance, the child hypothesis h_{c_2} of $h^* = [0, 1, \mathbf{1}, \mathbf{0}, 1]$ is $[0, 1, \mathbf{0}, \mathbf{1}, 1]$. Its associated log-probability is computed by $\lambda_y(h_{c_2}) = \lambda_y(h^*) + q_i - p_i + p_{i+1} - q_{i+1}$, where i is the bit index of the "1" in the right-most "$[1, 0]$" pair.

As output, Algorithm 1 produces a ranked list L^*_y of the most likely hypotheses for a given y, and their log-probabilities $\lambda_y(h) = \log(\mathbb{P}[h \mid y, \mathbf{x}_{\mathcal{A}}])$, such that $\sum_{h \in L^*_y} \exp(\lambda_y(h)) \geq 1 - \eta$. In addition, it also produces a residual frontier F_y that will be used as a new "seed" list for the next iteration.

3.2 ITERATIVE FILTERING AND HYPOTHESIS RE-SAMPLING

After generating the most likely hypotheses for each hidden state, we merge them into a global set and compute their marginal likelihoods. We dynamically re-generate new hypotheses as more observations are made. This step is necessary in order to constantly guarantee that the sample set covers at least $1 - \eta$ of the total remaining mass, after new observations become available.

As shown in Algorithm 2, the global iterative filtering and re-sampling module consists of a global loop, where after initializing all ranked lists L^*_y to $\emptyset$ and $\mathbb{P}[y \mid \mathbf{x}_{\mathcal{A}} = \emptyset]$ to the prior distribution over the hidden states, it iteratively performs the following sequences of operations: First, for each hidden state y, it calls Algorithm 1 to generate enough hypotheses so that L^*_y covers at least $(1 - \eta)$ of its current mass, i.e., $Z(L^*_y \mid y, \mathbf{x}_{\mathcal{A}}) \geq 1 - \eta$ (line 3). L^*_y might not be initially empty due to a

[4] Otherwise, we can redefine a test with flipped labels.

previous call to Algorithm 1. In this case, the generator produces only new additional hypotheses starting from the frontier F_y until the desired coverage is achieved. This step is not necessary for the y's that are inconsistent with $\mathbf{x}_{\mathcal{A}}$, i.e., for those hidden states whose posterior distribution given $\mathbf{x}_{\mathcal{A}}$ is zero.

Once we merge the hypotheses associated with each hidden state (line 4), the sample set $\tilde{\mathcal{H}}$ covers at least $(1-\eta)$ fraction of the total mass that is consistent with all the observations up to $\mathbf{x}_{\mathcal{A}}$: $Z(\tilde{\mathcal{H}} \mid \mathbf{x}_{\mathcal{A}}) = \sum_{h \in \tilde{\mathcal{H}}} \mathbb{P}[h \mid \mathbf{x}_{\mathcal{A}}] \geq \sum_y \sum_{h \in L_y^*} \mathbb{P}[h \mid y, \mathbf{x}_{\mathcal{A}}] \mathbb{P}[y \mid \mathbf{x}_{\mathcal{A}}] \geq \sum_y (1-\eta) \mathbb{P}[y \mid \mathbf{x}_{\mathcal{A}}] = (1-\eta)$. The procedure is then followed by performing EC^2 on $\tilde{\mathcal{H}}$ to identify the next test to be performed (see Fig. 2).

3.3 UPPER BOUNDS ON THE COST

Assume that we only enumerate the hypotheses *once* at the beginning of each experiment, i.e., we do not regenerate the hypotheses after observing the outcome of a test. If the underlying true hypothesis is included in the sampled set $\tilde{\mathcal{H}}$, then by construction, Algorithm 2 is guaranteed to make the optimal decision. Otherwise, with small probability it fails to output the optimal decision. Theorem 1 states a trade-off between the size of $\tilde{\mathcal{H}}$ and the expected cost of Algorithm 2.

Theorem 1. *Suppose we have generated hypotheses $\tilde{\mathcal{H}}$ with coverage $1-\eta$. Define $\tilde{p}_{\min} = \min_{h \in \tilde{\mathcal{H}}} \frac{\mathbb{P}[h]}{1-\eta}$. Let $\pi^g_{\tilde{\mathcal{H}}}$ be the policy induced by Algorithm 2, OPT be the optimal policy on the original distribution of $\mathcal{H}$, and $c(\mathcal{T})$ be the cost of performing all tests. Then, it holds that* $\mathrm{cost}_{av}(\pi^g_{\tilde{\mathcal{H}}}) \leq (2 \ln(1/\tilde{p}_{\min}) + 1) \mathrm{cost}_{av}(\mathsf{OPT}) + \eta \cdot c(\mathcal{T})$. *Moreover, if we stop running $\pi^g_{\tilde{\mathcal{H}}}$ once it cuts all edges on $\tilde{\mathcal{H}}$, then with probability at least $1-\eta$, $\pi^g_{\tilde{\mathcal{H}}}$ outputs the optimal decision with* $\mathrm{cost}_{wc}(\pi^g_{\tilde{\mathcal{H}}}) \leq (2 \ln(1/\tilde{p}_{\min}) + 1) \mathrm{cost}_{wc}(\mathsf{OPT})$.

We defer the proof to the supplemental material. Note that the expected cost is computed w.r.t. the original hypothesis distribution $\mathbb{P}[H \mid H \in \mathcal{H}]$. Theorem 1 establishes a bound between the cost of the greedy algorithm on the samples $\tilde{\mathcal{H}}$, and the cost of the optimal algorithm on the total population $\mathcal{H}$. The quality of the bound depends on η, as well as the structure of the problem (which determines $\tilde{p}_{\min}$). Running the greedy policy on a larger set of samples leads to a lower failure rate, although $\tilde{p}_{\min}$ might be significantly smaller for small η. Further, with adaptive re-sampling we constantly maintain a $1-\eta$ coverage on posterior distribution over $\mathcal{H}$. With similar reasoning, we can show that the greedy policy with adaptively-resampled posteriors yields a lower failure rate than the greedy policy which only samples the hypotheses once at the start of the session.

4 ONLINE LEARNING FOR OPTIMIZING VOI

In the online setting, the exact decision making model (i.e., the conditional probability table of test outcomes given the hidden state) is unknown, and we need to learn the model as we get more feedback. We employ an efficient *posterior sampling* strategy, described as follows. Suppose that initially we have access to a prior over the model parameters, for example, in the troubleshooting application, we assume a Beta prior on the parameters $[\theta_{ij}]_{n \times m}$ of the CPT, In the beginning of session ℓ, we sample $\boldsymbol{\theta}^{(\ell)}$ from $B(\boldsymbol{\alpha}^{(\ell)}, \boldsymbol{\beta}^{(\ell)})$. In particular, for each (root-cause - symptom) pair (y_j, x_i), we simply generate the parameter $\theta_{ij}^{(\ell)} = \mathbb{P}[x_i = 1 \mid y_j]$ from $B(\alpha_{ij}^{(\ell)}, \beta_{ij}^{(\ell)})$, where α_{ij}, β_{ij} depend on historical data. Then we run Algorithm 2 with $\boldsymbol{\theta}^{(\ell)}$ to sequentially pick tests for session ℓ. When a decision making session is over, we observe y_ℓ, together with a set of test-outcome pairs. We then update the distribution on $\boldsymbol{\theta}$ before we enter the next conversation. See Algorithm 3 for details[5].

Algorithm 3: Online sequential decision making

Input: α_{ij}, β_{ij} parameters of Beta distributions, prior $\mathbb{P}_{\mathcal{Y}}[Y]$, sessions / test scenarios $\{S_1, \dots S_k\}$;
begin
  Set $\alpha_{ij}^{(1)} \leftarrow \alpha_{ij}; \beta_{ij}^{(1)} \leftarrow \beta_{ij}$ for all i, j;
  foreach $\ell = 1 \dots k$ **do**
    $A \leftarrow \emptyset, \mathbf{x}_{\mathcal{A}} \leftarrow \emptyset$;
    Draw $\boldsymbol{\theta}^{(\ell)} = \{\theta_{ij}^{(\ell)} \sim B(\alpha_{ij}^{(\ell)}, \beta_{ij}^{(\ell)})\}$;
    Call Algorithm 2 to engage session ℓ;
    Observe $\mathbf{x}_{\mathcal{A}}$ and hidden state y_ℓ with index ϑ;
    foreach $(i, x_i) \in \mathbf{x}_{\mathcal{A}}$ **do**
      if $x_i = 1$ **then**
        Set $\alpha_{i\vartheta}^{\ell+1} \leftarrow \alpha_{i\vartheta}^{\ell} + 1$;
      else
        Set $\beta_{i\vartheta}^{\ell+1} \leftarrow \beta_{i\vartheta}^{\ell} + 1$;

4.1 ONLINE REGRET BOUND

Suppose we have drawn $\boldsymbol{\theta}(\ell)$ for session ℓ. Denote the optimal policy w.r.t. this distribution by OPT_ℓ, and the policy induced by Algorithm 2 by $\pi^g_{\tilde{\mathcal{H}}_\ell}$. Further let $\tilde{p}_{\min,\ell} = \min_{h \in \tilde{\mathcal{H}}_\ell} \mathbb{P}[h]/1-\eta$. By definition, all *feasible* policies that satisfy the condition of the DRD problem (Problem (1)) achieve the same VoI (at different costs). Hence, Theorem 1 implies that with probability

[5]For simplicity, we assume that the prior $\mathbb{P}[Y]$ over root-causes is given. In principle, we can drop this assumption, and instead assume a prior over the parameters of $\mathbb{P}[Y]$ so that we can sample from it, similarly as how we sample $\boldsymbol{\theta} \sim B(\boldsymbol{\alpha}, \boldsymbol{\beta})$.

at least $1-\eta$, running Algorithm 2 at session ℓ achieves the same VoI with OPT_ℓ, with at most $(2\ln(1/\tilde{p}_{\min})+1)$ times of the optimal cost.

In principle, we want to design an adaptive policy for each session that is competitive with the *hindsight-optimal* policy that knows the true distribution. We define the expected *regret* of a policy $\pi^g_{\tilde{\mathcal{H}}_\ell}$ at session ℓ with respect to the *true* distribution as

$$\tilde{\Delta}_\ell = \mathrm{VoI}^*(\pi^g_{\tilde{\mathcal{H}}_\ell}) - \mathrm{VoI}^*(\pi^*),$$

where $\mathrm{VoI}^*(\pi) = \mathbb{E}_h[\max_{d\in\mathcal{D}} \mathbb{E}_y[u(y,d) \mid \mathcal{S}(\pi,h)]]$ denotes the expected utility of policy π w.r.t. the *true* distribution to be learned, and π^* denotes the optimal policy (w.r.t. the true distribution). Suppose we are given a fixed budget τ for performing tests in each session. Define the expected regret incurred by running policies $\{\pi_1,\dots,\pi_k\}$ over k sessions as $\mathrm{Regret}(k,\tau) = \sum_{i=1}^k \tilde{\Delta}_i$. We establish the following bound on the expected regret of running Algorithm 3:

Theorem 2. *Fix* $\eta \in (0,1)$. *Let* $\tau = (2\ln(1/\delta)+1)\, c^{wc}_{\mathsf{OPT}}$, *where* $\delta = \min_t \tilde{p}_{\min,\ell}$ *denotes the minimal probability of any hypothesis in the sampled distributions, and* c^{wc}_{OPT} *denotes the worst-case cost of the optimal algorithm over any of the* k *sessions. Then, Algorithm 3 achieves expected regret*

$$\mathbb{E}[\mathrm{Regret}(k,\tau)] = O\left(\tau S\sqrt{nk\tau\log(Snk\tau)} + k\eta\right),$$

where S *is the total number of possible realizations of* τ *tests, and* n *is the number of tests.*

To prove Theorem 2, we view the Optimal VoI problem as optimizing a (finite horizon) Partially Observable Markov Decision Process (POMDP) over repeated episodes of a fixed horizon τ. The parameter S in the regret bound corresponds to the number of (reachable) belief states of the POMDP. Once we have established this connection, we can interpret the online learning problem as a reinforcement learning problem via posterior sampling, in a similar way to Osband et al. [24]. Notice that a conservative bound on S in $2^{\binom{n}{\tau}}$, which is doubly-exponential in the horizon. However, in practice, the number of reachable belief states is limited by the structure of the problem (e.g., configuration of the CPTs), and hence could be far smaller. In any case, Theorem 2 implies that the expected regret of Algorithm 3 in the limit (as $k\to\infty$) is bounded by η/τ.

5 EXPERIMENTAL RESULTS

Data set and experimental setup. We carry out our experiments on a *real-world* troubleshooting platform.

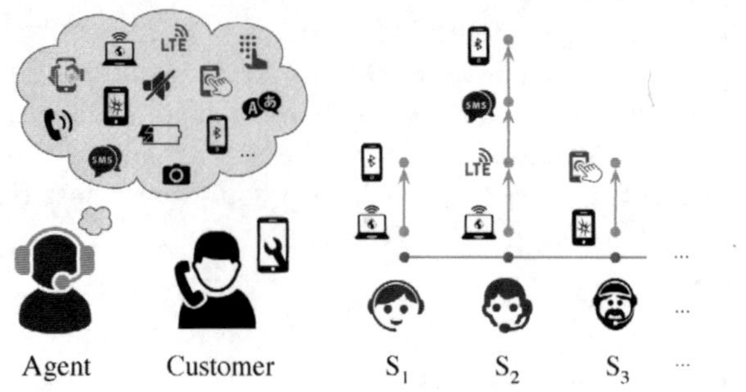

Figure 3: Online troubleshooting: customers reach a call center for diagnosis of their devices. The troubleshooting virtual agent resolves their issues by sequentially asking each customer a series of diagnosis questions.

Our data is collected from contact center agents and knowledge workers who solve complex troubleshooting problems for mobile devices (see Fig. 3). These training data involve around 1100 root-causes (the possible values of the hidden state Y) and 950 tests (questions on symptoms customers may encounter) with binary outcomes. From the training data, we derived a distribution over $[X_1,\dots,X_n]$ and Y as $\mathbb{P}[x_1,\dots,x_n,y] = \mathbb{P}_\mathcal{Y}[y]\prod_{i=1}^n \mathbb{P}[x_i \mid y]$, where $\mathbb{P}_\mathcal{Y}[y]$ is the prior distribution over the root-causes which we assume to be uniform.

We simulated over 10,000 test scenarios (10 scenarios for each y), where a customer enters the system with an initial symptom x_{t_0} (i.e. a test outcome) with probability $\mathbb{P}[x_{t_0} \mid y]$. Each scenario corresponds a to a root-cause y and an underlying hypothesis h. The number of decisions is the number of root-causes (which correspond to making a diagnosis), plus one extra decision of "give-up". Intuitively, if two root-causes result in the same symptoms, then the virtual agent cannot decide which one is the true root-cause, and therefore will forward such case to a human agent, corresponding to the "give-up" decision. In practice, introducing such "give-up" decision guarantees that there are no overlaps between decision regions. The utility function $u(d,y)$ corresponds to the cost of mis-prediction (either by mispredicting a root-cause, or simply "give-up"), which is specified by the business *domain expert* as: $u(d,y) =$ (1) 0 if d^* is "give-up"; (2) 1 if $d^* = y$; and (3) -19 if $d^* \in \mathcal{Y} \wedge d^* \neq y$. In this way, the "give-up" decision is optimal when the posterior distribution over Y given *all* test outcomes has no "peak" value higher than 95%.

Information gathering with full knowledge of θ. In our experiments we set the coverage parameter $\eta = 0.02$. In addition to EC^2, we also run Algorithm 2 with several other different subroutines (by replacing EC^2 at line 6 of Algorithm 2): myopic Value of Information (VoI), Information Gain (IG), and Uncertainty Sampling (US).

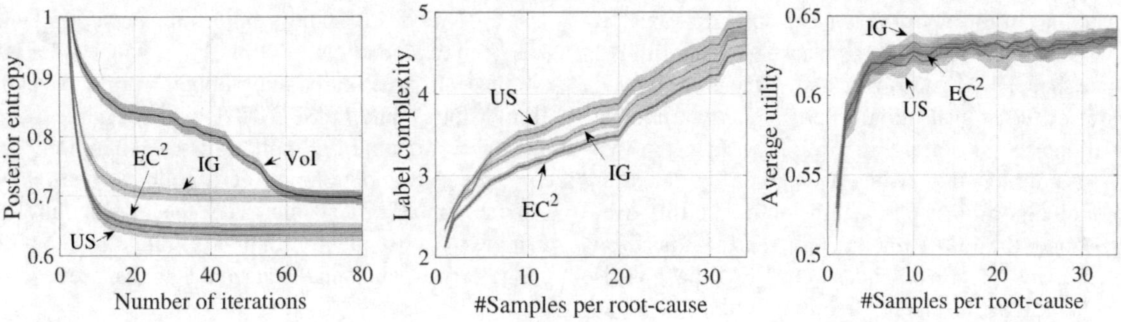

(a) Budget VS. Conditional Entropy (b) Cost VS. # Samples (c) Utility VS. # Samples

Figure 4: Experimental results by running Algorithm 2 with different subroutines under the *offline* setting.

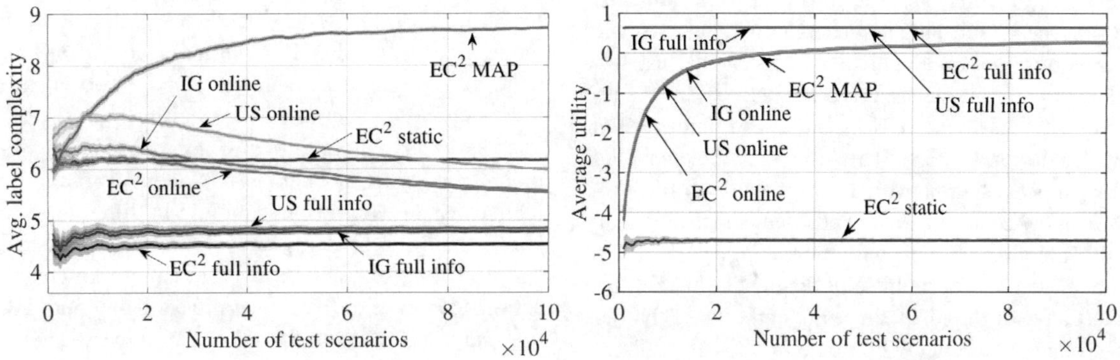

Figure 5: Experimental results by running Algorithm 3 with different subroutines under the *online* setting.

The myopic VoI criterion greedily picks the test leading to the highest expected utility[6]; the IG (resp., US) criterion picks tests that greedily maximizing the reduction of entropy over the decision regions (resp., hypotheses).

Fig. 4a shows the expected entropy on Y while increasing the test budget. Clearly, myopic VoI performs comparably worse than others. In Fig. 4b and Fig. 4c, we report the average label complexity (i.e., the expected number of tests required to solve a case), and the average utility of making decisions while varying the maximal number of samples allowed for each root-cause[7]. We see that as we generate hypotheses more extensively, all algorithms require more tests in order to make a decision; on the other hand, the quality of decisions also increases with more samples. This behavior is reasonable, since having too few samples excludes a large amount of good candidates which in turn leads to poor utility. Moreover, there is a $\sim$16% improvement in the average query complexity when using EC^2. This shows clear advantage of using submodular surrogates for this kind of sequential problem: EC^2 by construction is "less myopic".

[6]Myopic VoI does *not* require enumeration of hypotheses.

[7]The EC^2, IG and US scores of a test can be computed efficiently in *linear* time w.r.t. the number of hypotheses.

Online sequential information gathering We evaluate our online learning framework (Algorithm 3) over 100,000 simulated test scenarios. For the initial distribution over the CPT parameters, we set Beta priors $B(\boldsymbol{\alpha}, \boldsymbol{\beta})$ on the CPT, where α_{ij}/β_{ij} are set to be roughly proportional to the ratio between the number of positive and negative symptoms (i.e., $(x_i = 1, y_j)$ and $(x_i = 0, y_j)$ pairs) in the training set. Then we inject noise into these estimates, by flipping the values of α_{ij} and β_{ij} with some small probability. In our experiments, we assume a uniform prior distribution over root-causes.

Fig. 5 demonstrates the behavior of the three algorithms. In our experiments, we set a maximal budget for each session/test scenario, and keep running the policy till it identifies a decision region or exceeds the budget. At the end of session ℓ, we report the average label complexity (i.e., the accumulated mean of the number of questions asked over ℓ sessions) and the average utility (i.e., the accumulated means of the utility over ℓ sessions). In "EC^2 MAP", we update the CPT with their MAP estimators. We observe that its cost is much higher as it does not encourage exploration as much as the other online methods. In "EC^2 static", we run EC^2 only based on the initial sample of CPT without any updates. In the "full info" versions of the algorithms, the ground truth CPT is used, while in the "online" versions, we use Algorithm 3 to update the CPT's. The Y axis shows the accumulated means of different evaluation criteria. The two notable observations are in order: First, by integrating the two levels of sampling strategy, the average utility (a.k.a reward) of all algorithms approach the optimal utility over time. Second, the EC^2 variants consistently outperform the alternatives in terms of query complexity, which is consistent with the results in the offline setting.

6 RELATED WORK

Bayesian experimental design for troubleshooting. There has been substantial research in diagnosis and troubleshooting using graphical models in the last two decades, in particular using Bayesian networks. One research question is how to perform efficient inference. For example, Nielsen et al. [23] focuses on efficient belief updating in Bayesian networks, in particular in the context of troubleshooting; Ricks and Mengshoel [26] consider the inference problem with more complex Bayesian network structures for multi-fault diagnosis. In contrast, we focus on an orthogonal direction, in the sense that we assume one can efficiently compute the posterior distribution over Y (i.e., the inference itself is tractable), and aim to minimize the cost of the troubleshooting policy.

Optimal VoI. Many greedy heuristics have been proposed for optimizing VoI; for instance, Breese and Heckerman [3] proposes a myopic policy for the single fault troubleshooting problem, which chooses the action/test that minimizes the expected cost of fixing the device in question. Their objective function can be viewed as a particular form of the myopic VoI. Unfortunately, unlike the greedy algorithms based on submodular surrogates, these algorithms can perform arbitrarily badly [13, 21].

Sampling-based Bayesian inference. In [13], the authors suggest to use a rejection sampling approach to estimate the original distribution over hypotheses for the DRD problem. Another work, which is similar to our work in spirit, suggests to generate hypotheses in descending order of prior likelihood [22] for approximate inference in hybrid Bayesian networks. In comparison, our sampling scheme is based on the specific structure of the underlying model, which potentially offers increased efficiency and better approximation guarantees.

Sequential decision making as POMDP. Value of information is known as a reward function in Partially Observable Markov Decision Process [17, 30], where each belief state represents a set of tests and their outcomes. Unfortunately, this gives us an exponentially large state space. The idea of using samples to speed up planning has been explored, e.g., POMCP [25] which is based on Monte Carlo tree search that samples from states and action histories, and DESPOT [31] which samples scenarios for evaluation of all policies at each iteration. These approaches rely on a finite set of policy to be evaluated. As the number of tests increases, they will require more samples. Consequently, they are limited to short planning horizons and small state and action spaces.

Online learning. Many different schemes have been investigated in online learning [2] and online decision making [11, 18]. We look into a different setting, where we integrate sequential information gathering into an *online* learning framework wherein we learn the decision model over time. For this purpose, we lift our framework into a higher level sampling procedure, whose goal is to sample appropriately the decision model parameters. Several recent empirical simulations [7, 14, 28] and theoretical studies [1, 4, 19] have demonstrated the effectiveness of Thompson sampling in different settings. However, different from our framework, the classical usage of Thompson sampling [32] suggests to choose an action according to the probability of being optimal, i.e. the action which maximizes the reward in expectation.

7 CONCLUSION

We pursue practical and efficient approaches for the challenging problem of optimal VoI: (1) For a given prior over hypothesis space, we propose a novel hypothesis enumeration strategy for efficient optimization of VoI, and show that it compensates the inefficiency of the popular "submodular surrogate"-based greedy algorithms, while still enjoying provable theoretical guarantees; (2) when the prior is unknown, we propose an efficient, principled online learning framework with low expected regret in the long run. In addition, we demonstrate promising empirical performance of our framework on a real-world troubleshooting platform. We believe that our work is an important step towards practical and robust adaptive information acquisition systems.

Acknowledgments

We would like to thank the anonymous reviewers and Christopher Dance for their helpful comments. This work was done in part while Andreas Krause was visiting the Simons Institute for the Theory of Computing. This work was supported in part by ERC StG 307036, a Microsoft Research Faculty Fellowship, an SNSF Early Postdoc.Mobility Fellowship and a Google European Doctoral Fellowship.

References

[1] Shipra Agrawal and Navin Goyal. Analysis of thompson sampling for the multi-armed bandit problem. In *COLT*, 2012.

[2] Avrim Blum. On-line algorithms in machine learning. In *Developments from a June 1996 Seminar on Online Algorithms: The State of the Art*, 1998.

[3] John S. Breese and David Heckerman. Decision-theoretic troubleshooting: A framework for repair and experiment. In *UAI*, 1996.

[4] Sebastien Bubeck and Che-Yu Liu. Prior-free and prior-dependent regret bounds for thompson sampling. In *NIPS*, 2013.

[5] V. T. Chakaravarthy, V. Pandit, S. Roy, P. Awasthi, and M. Mohania. Decision trees for entity identification: Approximation algorithms and hardness results. In *SIGMOD/PODS*, 2007.

[6] K. Chaloner and I. Verdinelli. Bayesian experimental design: A review. *Statistical Science*, 1995.

[7] Olivier Chapelle and Lihong Li. An empirical evaluation of thompson sampling. In *NIPS*, 2011.

[8] Y. Chen, S. Javdani, A. Karbasi, J. Andrew Bagnell, S. Srinivasa, and A. Krause. Submodular surrogates for value of information. In *AAAI*, 2015.

[9] Y. Chen, S. H. Hassani, and A. Krause. Near-optimal bayesian active learning with correlated and noisy tests. In *AISTATS*, 2017.

[10] S. Dasgupta. Analysis of a greedy active learning strategy. In *NIPS*, 2004.

[11] Dean P. Foster and Rakesh Vohra. Regret in the on-line decision problem. *Games and Economic Behavior*, 29:735, 1999.

[12] D. Golovin and A. Krause. Adaptive submodularity: Theory and applications in active learning and stochastic optimization. *JAIR*, 2011.

[13] D. Golovin, A. Krause, and D. Ray. Near-optimal bayesian active learning with noisy observations. In *NIPS*, 2010.

[14] T. Graepel, J. Q. Candela, T. Borchert, and R. Herbrich. Web-scale bayesian click-through rate prediction for sponsored search advertising in microsoft's bing search engine. In *ICML*, 2010.

[15] R. A. Howard. Information value theory. In *IEEE T. Syst. Sci. Cyb.*, 1966.

[16] S. Javdani, Y. Chen, A. Karbasi, A. Krause, D. Bagnell, and S. Srinivasa. Near-optimal bayesian active learning for decision making. In *AISTATS*, 2014.

[17] L. P. Kaelbling, M. L. Littman, and A. R. Cassandra. Planning and acting in partially observable stochastic domains. *Artificial Intelligence*, 1998.

[18] Adam Kalai and Santosh Vempala. Efficient algorithms for online decision problems. In *J. Comput. Syst. Sci*, pages 26–40, 2003.

[19] Emilie Kaufmann, Nathaniel Korda, and Rémi Munos. Thompson sampling: An asymptotically optimal finite-time analysis. In *ALT*, 2012.

[20] S. Rao Kosaraju, Teresa M. Przytycka, and Ryan S. Borgstrom. On an optimal split tree problem. In *WADS*, 1999.

[21] A. Krause and C. Guestrin. Optimal value of information in graphical models. *JAIR*, 2009.

[22] Uri Lerner and Ronald Parr. Inference in hybrid networks: Theoretical limits and practical algorithms. In *UAI*, 2001.

[23] T. Nielsen, P.-H. Wuillemin, F. Jensen, and U. Kjaerulff. Using robdds for inference in bayesian networks with troubleshooting as an example. In *UAI*, 2000.

[24] Ian Osband, Dan Russo, and Benjamin Van Roy. (more) efficient reinforcement learning via posterior sampling. In *NIPS*, 2013.

[25] Joelle Pineau, Geoffrey Gordon, and Sebastian Thrun. Anytime point-based approximations for large pomdps. *JAIR*, 27(1):335–380, 2006.

[26] Brian Ricks and Ole J. Mengshoel. Diagnosis for uncertain, dynamic and hybrid domains using bayesian networks and arithmetic circuits. *International Journal of Approximate Reasoning*, 2014.

[27] M. C. Runge, S. J. Converse, and J. E. Lyons. Which uncertainty? using expert elicitation and expected value of information to design an adaptive program. *Biological Conservation*, 2011.

[28] Steven L. Scott. A modern bayesian look at the multi-armed bandit. *Appl. Stoch. Model. Bus. Ind.*, 26(6):639–658, 2010.

[29] B. Settles. *Active Learning*. Morgan & Claypool, 2012.

[30] Richard D. Smallwood and Edward J. Sondik. The optimal control of partially observable markov processes over a finite horizon. *Operations Research*, 21(5):1071–1088, 1973.

[31] Adhiraj Somani, Nan Ye, David Hsu, and Wee Sun Lee. Despot: Online pomdp planning with regularization. In *NIPS*, 2013.

[32] William R. Thompson. On the likelihood that one unknown probability exceeds another in view of the evidence of two samples. *Biometrika*, 1933.

A OPTIMIZING VOI VIA SUBMODULAR SURROGATES

We have discussed three orthogonal aspects for the optimal VoI problem, namely, (1) the *sampling scheme* for hypothesis enumeration, (2) the *online learning* framework, and (3) the *choice of algorithms* for optimizing VoI. In this paper we focus on the first two aspects, and propose a general framework integrating the three components. Inevitably, the discussion of our algorithmic framework is grounded on existing submodular surrogate-based approaches for the VoI problem. We give more details of this class of algorithms in this section.

A.1 SUBMODULARITY AND ITS IMPLICATIONS.

The EC^2 objective function introduced in §2 is *adaptive submodular*, and *strongly adaptive monotone*. Formally, let $\mathbf{x}_\mathcal{A}$ and $\mathbf{x}_\mathcal{B}$ be two observation vectors. We call $\mathbf{x}_\mathcal{A}$ a *subrealization* of $\mathbf{x}_\mathcal{B}$, denoted as $\mathbf{x}_\mathcal{A} \preceq \mathbf{x}_\mathcal{B}$, if the index set $\mathcal{A} \subseteq \mathcal{B}$ and $\mathbb{P}\left[\mathbf{x}_\mathcal{B} \mid \mathbf{x}_\mathcal{A}\right] > 0$. A function $f : 2^{\mathcal{T}\times\{0,1\}} \to \mathbb{R}$ is called *adaptive submodular* w.r.t. a distribution $\mathbb{P}$, if for any $\mathbf{x}_\mathcal{A} \preceq \mathbf{x}_\mathcal{B}$ and any test t it holds that $\Delta(t \mid \mathbf{x}_\mathcal{A}) \geq \Delta(t \mid \mathbf{x}_\mathcal{B})$, where $\Delta(t \mid \mathbf{x}_\mathcal{A}) := \mathbb{E}_{x_t}\left[f(\mathbf{x}_{\mathcal{A}\cup\{t\}}) - f(\mathbf{x}_\mathcal{A}) \mid \mathbf{x}_\mathcal{A}\right]$ (i.e., "adding information earlier helps more"). Further, function f is called *strongly adaptively monotone* w.r.t. $\mathbb{P}$, if for all $\mathcal{A}$, $t \notin \mathcal{A}$, and $x_t \in \{0,1\}$, it holds that $f(\mathbf{x}_\mathcal{A}) \leq f(\mathbf{x}_{\mathcal{A}\cup\{t\}})$ (i.e., "adding information never hurts"). For adaptive optimization problems satisfying adaptive submodularity and strongly adaptive monotonicity, the policy that greedily, upon having observed $\mathbf{x}_\mathcal{A}$, selects the test $t^* \in \arg\max_t \Delta(t \mid \mathbf{x}_\mathcal{A})/c(t)$, is guaranteed to attain near-minimal cost [13].

A.2 GENERAL APPROACHES BASED ON SUBMODULAR SURROGATES.

It is noteworthy to mention that our results are not restricted to EC^2, and can be readily generalized to settings where regions are *overlapped*. In such cases, we can use the DIRECT algorithm [8], and prove something similar with Theorem 1: in the upperbound, we get $(r \cdot \log(1/\tilde{p}_{\min}) + 1)\,\mathrm{cost}_{wc}(\mathsf{OPT})$ (for the worst-case cost) and $(r \cdot \log(1/\tilde{p}_{\min}) + 1)\,\mathrm{cost}_{av}(\mathsf{OPT}) + \eta c(\mathcal{T})$ (for the average-case / expected cost), where r measures the amount of "overlap". The analysis follows closely from the proof of Theorem 1 in §C. More generally, Theorem 1 (with modified multiplicative constant) also applies to greedy algorithms whose objective function (1) is adaptive submodular, and (2) rely on a finite set of hypotheses. Other examples satisfying these conditions include GBS [12] and HEC [16].

Furthermore, since our framework is orthogonal to the choice of the submodular surrogate-based algorithms, we can also easily extend our analysis to handle the (more) practical setting where test outcomes are *noisy*. In such settings, one can no longer "cut-away" edges as suggested by the EC^2 algorithm, since with noisy observations one cannot "eliminate" any of the hypotheses (i.e., setting their probability mass to 0). In practice, after observing the outcome of a test, we can perform Bayesian updates on the posterior over H instead of eliminating those hypotheses that are "inconsistent" with the observation. Analogous to the analysis of Theorem 1, we can establish a bound on the *worst-case* cost of such greedy policy, based on the recent results of [9]. Since the theoretical question of handling noisy tests is beyond the scope of this paper, we omit the proof details for this setting.

B IMPLEMENTATION DETAILS OF ALGORITHM 1

In the main paper, we have stated the pseudo code of our dynamic hypothesis enumeration algorithms. Due to space limit we only provide a concise description of the main idea behind the framework. In this section, we elaborate Algorithm 1 by providing more intuitions and implementation details, as well as additional clarifications for better understanding of the algorithm.

The DAG. We use a DAG represents the hypotheses enumeration process, and is *not* a data structure which we actually adopted in Algorithm 1. Rather, algorithmically we are maintaining a "candidate frontier" F_y for each hidden state y, which corresponds to the set of "leaf" hypotheses (i.e., nodes of the DAG which have no outgoing edges), as a seed set to generate more hypotheses. Algorithm 1 enumerates hypotheses in decreasing order of probabilities $\mathbb{P}\left[h \mid y\right]$. The directed edges in the DAG indicate the relations between the conditional probabilities: if there is a directed edge from node h_1 to h_2 in the DAG, it indicates that $\mathbb{P}\left[h_1 \mid y\right] \geq \mathbb{P}\left[h_2 \mid y\right]$. Other than this, we do not use the edge for any other purposes.

Implementation details. In practice, the underlying distributions are often highly concentrated, such that a few number of hypotheses cover a significant part of the total mass. On the other hand, there are many configurations with very small (but non-null) probabilities. Algorithm 1 exploits such structural assumption, and generates the most likely hypotheses in the following four steps:

- *Step* 1 (line 2):
  Test definitions are possibly switched, in a way that $\mathbb{P}[X_i = 1 \mid y] \geq 0.5 \quad \forall i$ (i.e., when $\mathbb{P}[X_i = 1 \mid y] < 0.5$, we consider the complementary event $\bar{X}_i$ as the new test outcome so that $\mathbb{P}\left[\bar{X}_i = 1 \mid y\right] = 1 - \mathbb{P}[X_i = 1 \mid y] \geq 0.5$); test indices are re-ranked in decreasing order of $\mathbb{P}[X_i = 1 \mid y]$;
- *Step* 2 (line 3, 4):
  For $i = 1, \ldots, n$, compute $p_i \triangleq \log(\mathbb{P}[X_i = 1 \mid y])$, and $q_i \triangleq \log(\mathbb{P}[X_i = 0 \mid y])$;
- *Step* 3 (line 5, 6):
  If F_y is empty, initialize F_y with the configuration $h_1 = [1 \ldots 1]$ with log-weight $\lambda_y(h_1) = \sum_i p_i$; set $L_y^* = \emptyset$.
- *Step* 4 (line 7-10): while $\sum_{h \in L_y^*} \exp(\lambda_y(h)) < (1 - \eta)$
  - *Step* 4a: Choose the element h^* from F_y such that $\lambda_y(h^*)$ is maximum;
  - *Step* 4b: Remove h^* from F_y and push it into L_y^*;
  - *Step* 4c (line 9): Generate (at most) 2 children from h^* and add them to F_y if they were not already present in F_y.

In the main paper, we have given detailed description of how to generate the two children configurations (h_{c_1} and h_{c_2}) in Step 4c. We provide some additional insight to facilitate better understanding of the procedure:

- *Child* 1: Once we have re-ranked the tests in decreasing order of $\mathbb{P}[X = 1 \mid y]$ in Step 1, the last test in the ordered list will have the smallest probability (conditioning on y) of being realized to its more likely outcome, and hence is the most uncertain one. If follows that if we flip the outcome of such test, we will generate a new hypothesis h with the highest $\mathbb{P}[h \mid y]$ among the unseen hypotheses. The first child is generated exactly in this way: if the last (right-most) bit of h^* is 1, we then create h_{c_1} by switching the last bit to 0. For instance, the child hypothesis h_{c_1} of $h^* = [0, 1, 1, 0, 1]$ is $[0, 1, 1, 0, 0]$. Its log-probability is obtained by $\lambda_y(h_{c_1}) = \lambda_y(h^*) + q_n - p_n$.
- *Child* 2: Besides flipping the last bit, the next most-likely hypothesis can also be the one with two bit edits of an existing hypothesis: Find the right-most "$[1, 0]$" pair in h^* (if there exists any; otherwise we do nothing), and the create h_{c_2} by switching "$[1, 0]$" into "$[0, 1]$". For instance, the child hypothesis h_{c_2} of $h^* = [0, 1, 1, 0, 1]$ is $[0, 1, 0, 1, 1]$. Its associated log-probability is computed by $\lambda_y(h_{c_2}) = \lambda_y(h^*) + q_i - p_i + p_{i+1} - q_{i+1}$, where i is the bit index of the "1" in the right-most "$[1, 0]$" pair.

C PROOFS OF THE MAIN THEOREMS

C.1 PROOF OF THEOREM 1

In this section, we provide proofs for the upper bounds on the cost of Algorithm 2. In the analysis, we assume that we only sample the hypotheses *once* in the beginning of each experiment (i.e., we don't resample after each iteration).

Proof. The main idea of the proof is illustrated in Fig. 6.

Bound on the expected cost We first prove the upper bound on the expected cost of the algorithm. We use p to denote the true distribution over the hypotheses $h \in \mathcal{H}$, and $\tilde{p}$ be the sampled distribution. That is, $p(h) = \mathbb{P}[h]$, and

$$\tilde{p}(h) = \begin{cases} \mathbb{P}[h] / (1 - \eta), & \text{for } h \in \tilde{\mathcal{H}}; \\ 0, & \text{otherwise.} \end{cases} \tag{2}$$

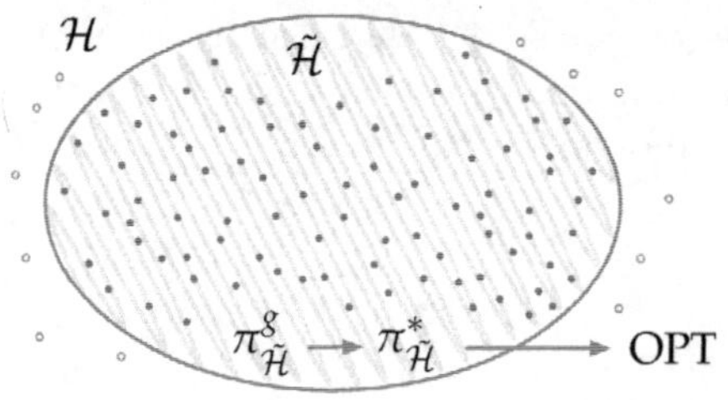

Figure 6: Depicting the main idea behind the proof. We introduce $\pi^*_{\tilde{\mathcal{H}}}$ (the optimal policy on the sampled distribution) as an auxiliary policy to connect $\pi^g_{\tilde{\mathcal{H}}}$ with OPT. If the realized hypothesis $h^* \in \tilde{\mathcal{H}}$, then $\pi^g_{\tilde{\mathcal{H}}}$ efficiently identifies the decision. Otherwise, (with probability at most η) $\pi^g_{\tilde{\mathcal{H}}}$ randomly chooses tests, and the cost can be at most $c(\mathcal{T})$.

For any policy π, let $\mathrm{cost}_{\tilde{p}}(\pi) \triangleq \mathbb{E}_{h\sim\tilde{p}(h)}[c(\mathcal{S}(\pi,h))]$ denote the expected cost of π w.r.t. $\tilde{p}$. Then, the expected cost of π w.r.t. the true distribution p satisfies

$$\begin{aligned}
\mathrm{cost}(\pi) &= \sum_{h\in\mathcal{H}} p(h)c(\mathcal{S}(\pi,h)) \\
&= \sum_{h\in\tilde{\mathcal{H}}} p(h)c(\mathcal{S}(\pi,h)) + \sum_{h\in\mathcal{H}\setminus\tilde{\mathcal{H}}} p(h)c(\mathcal{S}(\pi,h)) \\
&\overset{\text{Eq. (2)}}{=} (1-\eta)\sum_{h\in\tilde{\mathcal{H}}} \tilde{p}(h)c(\mathcal{S}(\pi,h)) + \sum_{h\in\mathcal{H}\setminus\tilde{\mathcal{H}}} p(h)c(\mathcal{S}(\pi,h)) \\
&= (1-\eta)\,\mathrm{cost}_{\tilde{p}}(\pi) + \sum_{h\in\mathcal{H}\setminus\tilde{\mathcal{H}}} p(h)\underbrace{c(\mathcal{S}(\pi,h))}_{\le c(\mathcal{T})} \qquad (3)\\
&\le (1-\eta)\,\mathrm{cost}_{\tilde{p}}(\pi) + \eta\cdot c(\mathcal{T}). \qquad (4)
\end{aligned}$$

The second term on the RHS of Eq. (3) is non-negative, which gives

$$\begin{aligned}
(1-\eta)\,\mathrm{cost}_{\tilde{p}}(\pi) &= \mathrm{cost}(\pi) - \sum_{h\in\mathcal{H}\setminus\tilde{\mathcal{H}}} p(h)c(\mathcal{S}(\pi,h)) \\
&\le \mathrm{cost}(\pi) \qquad (5)
\end{aligned}$$

Let $\pi^*_{\tilde{p}}$ be the optimal policy w.r.t. the sampled distribution $\tilde{p}$. By Theorem 3 of [13] we get

$$\mathrm{cost}_{\tilde{p}}\left(\pi^g_{\tilde{\mathcal{H}}}\right) \le (2\ln(1/\tilde{p}_{\min})+1)\,\mathrm{cost}_{\tilde{p}}\left(\pi^*_{\tilde{\mathcal{H}}}\right). \qquad (6)$$

Therefore,

$$\begin{aligned}
\mathrm{cost}(\pi^g_{\tilde{\mathcal{H}}}) &\overset{\text{Eq. (4)}}{\le} (1-\eta)\,\mathrm{cost}_{\tilde{p}}(\pi^g_{\tilde{\mathcal{H}}}) + \eta\cdot c(\mathcal{T}) \\
&\overset{\text{Eq. (6)}}{\le} (1-\eta)\,(2\ln(1/\tilde{p}_{\min})+1)\,\mathrm{cost}_{\tilde{p}}\left(\pi^*_{\tilde{\mathcal{H}}}\right) \\
&\quad + \eta\cdot c(\mathcal{T}).
\end{aligned}$$

By definition we know $\mathrm{cost}_{\tilde{p}}\left(\pi^*_{\tilde{\mathcal{H}}}\right) \le \mathrm{cost}_{\tilde{p}}(\mathsf{OPT})$. Hence

$$\begin{aligned}
\mathrm{cost}(\pi^g_{\tilde{\mathcal{H}}}) &\le (1-\eta)\,(2\ln(1/\tilde{p}_{\min})+1)\,\mathrm{cost}_{\tilde{p}}(\mathsf{OPT}) + \eta\cdot c(\mathcal{T}) \\
&\overset{\text{Eq. (5)}}{\le} (2\ln(1/\tilde{p}_{\min})+1)\,\mathrm{cost}(\mathsf{OPT}) + \eta\cdot c(\mathcal{T}),
\end{aligned}$$

which completes the first part of the proof.

Bound on the worst-case cost. Next, we provide the proof for bound on the worst-case cost. Analogous to the previous analysis, we consider two possible scenarios: (i) the realized hypotheses (i.e., the full realization vector) $h^* \in \tilde{\mathcal{H}}$; and (ii) $h^* \notin \tilde{\mathcal{H}}$.

For any policy π, the worst-case cost of π satisfies

$$\begin{aligned}\mathrm{cost}_{wc}(\pi) &= \max_{h \in \mathcal{H}} c(\mathcal{S}(\pi, h)) \\ &= \max\{\max_{h \in \tilde{\mathcal{H}}} c(\mathcal{S}(\pi, h)), \max_{h \in \mathcal{H} \setminus \tilde{\mathcal{H}}} c(\mathcal{S}(\pi, h))\}.\end{aligned}$$

Since policy $\pi^g_{\tilde{\mathcal{H}}}$ terminates if there is no edge left on $\tilde{\mathcal{H}}$, then $\max_{h \in \mathcal{H} \setminus \tilde{\mathcal{H}}} c(\mathcal{S}(\pi, h)) \leq \max_{h \in \tilde{\mathcal{H}}} c(\mathcal{S}(\pi, h)$. Therefore,

$$\begin{aligned}\mathrm{cost}_{wc}(\pi^g_{\tilde{\mathcal{H}}}) &= \max_{h \in \tilde{\mathcal{H}}} c\left(\mathcal{S}\left(\pi^g_{\tilde{\mathcal{H}}}, h\right)\right) \\ &\overset{\text{(a)}}{\leq} (2 \ln (1/\tilde{p}_{\min}) + 1) \max_{h \in \tilde{\mathcal{H}}} c\left(\mathcal{S}\left(\pi^*_{\tilde{\mathcal{H}}}, h\right)\right) \\ &\leq (2 \ln (1/\tilde{p}_{\min}) + 1) \max_{h \in H} c\left(\mathcal{S}\left(\mathsf{OPT}, h\right)\right).\end{aligned}$$

Step (a) in the above equation follows from Theorem A.12 of [12].

Therefore, when $\pi^g_{\tilde{\mathcal{H}}}$ terminates, with probability at least $1 - \eta$, it succeeds to output the correct decision with cost $(2 \ln (1/\tilde{p}_{\min}) + 1) \mathrm{cost}_{wc}(\mathsf{OPT})$. □

C.2 PROOF OF THEOREM 2

In this section, we prove the bound on the expected regret of our online learning algorithm.

Proof of Theorem 2. One way to model the non-myopic value of information problem is to view it as a (finite horizon) Partially Observable Markov Decision Process (POMDP), where each (belief-) state represents the selected tests and observed outcome of each test. Formally, the POMDP can be written as

$$M \triangleq \left(\mathcal{B}, \mathcal{T}, R^M, P^M, \tau, \rho\right). \tag{7}$$

Here, $\mathcal{B}$ is the set of belief states, $\mathcal{T}$ is the set of actions (i.e., tests), $R^M_t(b)$ is the (expected) reward associated with action t while in belief state b, $P^M_t(b' \mid b)$ denotes the probabiliy of transitioning to state b' if action t is selectedwhile in state b, τ is the time horizon for each session, and ρ is the initial belief state distribution.

In our problem, the *transition probabilities* P^M can be fully specified by the conditional probabilities of the test outcomes given the hidden state $\mathbb{P}[x_t \mid y]$; the *prior* distribution ρ on belief states can be specified by the prior distribution on the hypotheses $\mathbb{P}[y]$, and $\mathbb{P}[x_t \mid y]$. The *reward* R^M for running a policy π on M is the utility achieved upon termination of the policy. More specifically, we can interpret the reward function R^M as follows: we get reward 0 as the policy keeps selecting new tests, but get (expected) reward $\mathrm{VoI}(\mathcal{S}(\pi, h)) \triangleq \max_{d \in \mathcal{D}} \mathbb{E}_h[u(h, d) \mid \mathcal{S}(\pi, h)]$ if the policy terminates upon observing $\mathcal{S}(\pi, h)$ and suggests a decision. The reward function measures the expected (total) utility one can get by making a decision after running policy π.

We now consider running Algorithm 3 over k sessions of fixed duration τ. Following the previous discussion, the problem is equivalent to learning to optimize a random finite horizon POMDP of length τ in k repeated episodes of interaction. To establish the regret bound of Theorem 2, we need the following result:

Theorem 3 (Theorem 1 of [24])**.** *Consider the problem of learning to optimize a random finite horizon (PO)MDP* $M = \left(\mathcal{B}, \mathcal{T}, R^M, P^M, \tau, \rho\right)$ *in k repeated episodes, and consider running the following algorithm: at the start of each episode it updates the prior distribution over the MDP and takes one sample from the posterior, and then follows the policy that is optimal for this sampled MDP. For any prior distribution on the MDPs, it holds that*

$$\mathbb{E}[\mathit{Regret}(k, \tau)] = O\left(\tau |\mathcal{B}| \sqrt{k \tau |\mathcal{T}| \log(k \tau |\mathcal{B}| |\mathcal{T}|)}\right).$$

Theorem 3 implies that the posterior sampling strategy as employed in Algorithm 3 allows efficient learning of the MDP, given that one can find the *optimal* policy for the sampled MDP at each episode. However, since finding the optimal policy is NP-hard, in practice we can only *approximate* the optimal policy. In Algorithm 3, we consider running the greedy policy (i.e., Algorithm 2) in each episode to solve the sampled MDP:

Corollary 4. *Let M be a sampled MDP, and c^{wc}_{OPT} be the worst-case cost of the optimal algorithm on M. Consider running Algorithm 2 for $\tau = (2\ln(1/\delta) + 1)\, c^{wc}_{\mathsf{OPT}}$ steps. Then, with probability at least $1 - \eta$, it achieves the optimal VoI on M.*

Proof of Corollary 4. By Theorem 1, we know that the greedy policy finds the target decision region with probability at least $1 - \eta$. Furthermore, by definition we know that each decision region $\mathcal{R}_d = \{h : U(d \mid h) = \mathrm{VoI}(h)\}$ represents an optimal action for any of its enclosed hypotheses. In other words, a policy that successfully outputs a decision region achieves the optimal VoI. □

Denote the optimal policy on the sampled MDP in episode i as OPT_i. From Corollary 4, we know that Algorithm 2 achieves optimal utility with probability at least $1 - \eta$. Hence, the expected "regret" of Algorithm 2 over OPT_i is

$$\mathrm{Reg}(\text{Algorithm } 2) \overset{\text{(a)}}{\leq} (1 - \eta) \cdot 0 + \eta \cdot 1 = \eta. \tag{8}$$

Here, Step (a) is due to the fact that the utility is normalized so that $U \in [0, 1]$. Note that Reg(Algorithm 2) in Equation (8) refers to the difference between the value of Algorithm 2 and the value of the optimal policy on the sampled MDP (not the optimal policy for the true MDP). In other words, the price of not following the optimal policy is at most η.

By Theorem 3, we know that following OPT_i for episode i achieves expected regret $O\left(\tau|\mathcal{B}|\sqrt{k\tau|\mathcal{T}|\log(k\tau|\mathcal{B}||\mathcal{T}|)}\right)$. Further, we know that the price of approximating the optimal policy at episode i is at most η. Combining these two results we get

$$\begin{aligned}\mathbb{E}[\mathrm{Regret}(k, \tau)] &= O\left(\tau|\mathcal{B}|\sqrt{k\tau|\mathcal{T}|\log(k\tau|\mathcal{B}||\mathcal{T}|)}\right) + \sum_{i=1}^{k} \eta \\ &= O\left(\tau|\mathcal{B}|\sqrt{k\tau|\mathcal{T}|\log(k\tau|\mathcal{B}||\mathcal{T}|)} + \eta k\right),\end{aligned}$$

where $|\mathcal{B}| = S$ represents the number of the belief states, $|\mathcal{T}| = n$ represents the number of tests. Hence it completes the proof. □

D ADDITIONAL RESULTS

In §3.3 of the main paper (i.e., Upper Bounds on the Cost), we have provided upper bounds on the expected/worst-case cost of the greedy policy w.r.t. *non-adaptively* sampled prior. In this section, we provide preliminary results for the case with adaptive re-sampling, where we constantly maintain a $1 - \eta$ coverage on posterior distribution over $\mathcal{H}$.

D.1 LOWER BOUND ON THE EXPECTED EC^2 UTILITY

Theorem 5. *Let k, ℓ be positive integers[8], f be the EC^2 objective function, $\pi^g_{\tilde{\mathcal{H}},[\ell]}$ be the greedy policy with budget ℓ on $\tilde{\mathcal{H}}$, and $\pi^*_{\mathcal{H},[k]}$ be the optimal policy that achieves the maximal expected utility under budget k on $\mathcal{H}$, Then,*

$$f_{avg}\left(\pi^g_{\tilde{\mathcal{H}},[\ell]}\right) \geq \left(1 - e^{-\ell/k}\right) f_{avg}\left(\pi^*_{\mathcal{H},[k]}\right) - k\epsilon,$$

where $\epsilon = 2\eta\left(1 - \left(\frac{1}{k}\right)^{\ell}\right)$, and $f_{avg}(\pi) \triangleq \mathbb{E}_h[f(\mathcal{S}(\pi, h))]$ denotes the expected utility of running policy π w.r.t. the original distribution.

[8]If we assume unit cost for all tests, then k, ℓ are the number of tests selected. Otherwise, with non-uniform test costs, k, ℓ are the budget on the cost of selected items.

Note that the above result applies to the EC^2 algorithm with *adaptive-resampled* posteriors at each iteration. The additive term $k\epsilon$ on the RHS is due to the incompleteness of the samples provided by the sampling algorithm. The main intuition behind the proof is that, due to the effect of resampling, the expected one-step gain of the greedy policy $\pi^g_{\tilde{\mathcal{H}},[\ell]}$ on the sampled distribution suffers a small loss at each iteration, comparing to the greedy algorithm on the true distribution. The loss will be accumulated after ℓ rounds, leading to a cumulative loss of up to $k\epsilon$ in the lower bound.

We defer the proof of Theorem 5 to the next subsection (§D.2). In the following we show that an additive term is necessary in the lower bound. That is, we cannot remove the additive term (for example, we cannot push it into the multiplicative term involving $1 - e^{-\ell/k}$).

Suppose the hidden state take two values y_1, y_2 and there are two test t_1, t_2. Let $\eta = 0.1$. The conditional probabilities for the test outcomes are as follows: $p(t_1 = 1 \mid y_1) = p(t_1 = 1 \mid y_2) = 1, p(t_2 = 1 \mid y_1) = 0.001, p(t_2 = 1 \mid y_2) = 0$. There are only two hypotheses with non-zero probability, i.e., $h_1 = (1, 0)$ and $h_2 = (1, 1)$. Further assume there are two distinct decisions d_1, d_2 that are optimal for hypotheses h_1 is h_2 respectively.

However, the sampler will output only one hypothesis $h_1 = (1, 0)$, since $p(h_1 \mid y_1) > 1 - \eta$ and $p(h_2 \mid y_2) > 1 - \eta$. Assume that we further add infinitely many "dummy tests", i.e., for all t in this set, $p(t = 1 \mid y) = 0$ for all y. Then the greedy algorithm will choose those tests with high probability, since the gain for all tests over $\tilde{\mathcal{H}}$ is 0; whereas a smarter algorithm will pick test t_2, because we can identify the target region (and hence obtain a positive gain) upon observing its outcome.

D.2 PROOF OF THEOREM 5

Assume that the cumulative probability of the enumerate hypotheses is at least $1-\eta$, i.e., using our sampling algorithm we enumerate $1 - \eta$ fraction of the total mass.

Denote the set of sampled hypotheses by $\tilde{\mathcal{H}}$, and the expected gain of test t on $\tilde{\mathcal{H}}$ by $\Delta_{\tilde{\mathcal{H}}}(t \mid \cdot)$. Suppose we run the greedy algorithm based on $\tilde{\mathcal{H}}$. We want to show that the following lemma holds:

Lemma 6. *Suppose $\tilde{\mathcal{H}} \subseteq \mathcal{H}$ and $p(\tilde{\mathcal{H}}, \mathbf{x}_\mathcal{A}) \geq (1 - \eta)p(\mathcal{H}, \mathbf{x}_\mathcal{A})$. Let $\tilde{t} \triangleq \arg\max_t \Delta_{\tilde{\mathcal{H}}}(t \mid \mathbf{x}_\mathcal{A})$ be the test with the maximal gain on $\tilde{\mathcal{H}}$ in the* EC^2 *objective function. Then for any test t, it holds that*

$$\Delta_\mathcal{H}(\tilde{t} \mid \mathbf{x}_\mathcal{A}) \geq \Delta_\mathcal{H}(t \mid \mathbf{x}_\mathcal{A}) - 2\eta p(\mathbf{x}_\mathcal{A})^2.$$

That is, the test $\tilde{t}$ which achieves the maximal gain on $\tilde{\mathcal{H}}$ will achieve a gain on $\mathcal{H}$ which is no less than $\varepsilon \triangleq 2\eta p(\mathbf{x}_\mathcal{A})^2$ below the maximal gain of any test. In the following we provide the proof of Lemma 6.

Proof. Clearly, if we can show that for any test t, the gain of t over $\tilde{\mathcal{H}}$ and the gain of t over $\mathcal{H}$ are at most ε apart, i.e.,

$$\Delta_\mathcal{H}(t \mid \mathbf{x}_\mathcal{A}) \leq \Delta_{\tilde{\mathcal{H}}}(t \mid \mathbf{x}_\mathcal{A}) + \varepsilon, \tag{9}$$

then we know that $\Delta_\mathcal{H}(t^* \mid \mathbf{x}_\mathcal{A}) \leq \Delta_{\tilde{\mathcal{H}}}(t^* \mid \mathbf{x}_\mathcal{A}) + \varepsilon \leq \Delta_{\tilde{\mathcal{H}}}(\tilde{t} \mid \mathbf{x}_\mathcal{A}) + \varepsilon$.

In the following, we show that inequality (9) holds.

The conditional expected gain of test t over observed tests $\mathbf{x}_\mathcal{A}$ is

$$\begin{aligned}\Delta_{\tilde{\mathcal{H}}}(t \mid \mathbf{x}_\mathcal{A}) &= \mathbb{E}[\delta_{\tilde{\mathcal{H}}}(x_t \mid \mathbf{x}_\mathcal{A})] \\ &= p(x_t = 1 \mid \mathbf{x}_\mathcal{A})\delta_{\tilde{\mathcal{H}}}(x_t = 1 \mid \mathbf{x}_\mathcal{A}) + p(x_t = 0 \mid \mathbf{x}_\mathcal{A})\delta_{\tilde{\mathcal{H}}}(x_t = 0 \mid \mathbf{x}_\mathcal{A}).\end{aligned}$$

Here $\delta_{\tilde{\mathcal{H}}}(x_t \mid \mathbf{x}_\mathcal{A})$ denotes the conditional benefit of test t if its outcome is realized as x_t. Note that we can compute the probability terms $p(x_t = 1 \mid \mathbf{x}_\mathcal{A})$ and $p(x_t = 0 \mid \mathbf{x}_\mathcal{A})$ *exactly* from the CPT $\{\theta_{ij}\}_{n \times m}$ via Bayesian update, i.e., $p(x_t \mid \mathbf{x}_\mathcal{A}) = \sum_y p(x_t, y \mid \mathbf{x}_\mathcal{A}) = \frac{\sum_y p(y)p(\mathbf{x}_\mathcal{A}|y)p(x_t|y)}{\sum_y p(y)p(\mathbf{x}_\mathcal{A}|y)}$. What remains to be approximated is the gain for each specific realization. For EC^2 object function, the gain of observing x_t over hypothesis set $\mathcal{H}$ after having observed $\mathbf{x}_\mathcal{A}$ is

$$\delta_\mathcal{H}(x_t \mid \mathbf{x}_\mathcal{A}) = \sum_{i>j}(p(\mathcal{R}_i, \mathbf{x}_\mathcal{A})p(\mathcal{R}_j, \mathbf{x}_\mathcal{A}) - p(\mathcal{R}_i, \mathbf{x}_\mathcal{A}, x_t)p(\mathcal{R}_j, \mathbf{x}_\mathcal{A}, x_t)),$$

where $\mathcal{R}_i$ represent the set of hypotheses in *region / equivalence class* i.

We define short-hand notation $\gamma_i := p(\mathcal{R}_i \setminus \tilde{\mathcal{R}}_i, \mathbf{x}_\mathcal{A})$, where $\tilde{\mathcal{R}}_i$ denotes the sampled hypotheses of the ith decision region. The difference in the gain of t over $\mathcal{H}$ and $\tilde{\mathcal{H}}$ can be expressed as

$$\begin{aligned}
&\delta_{\mathcal{H}}(x_t \mid \mathbf{x}_\mathcal{A}) - \delta_{\tilde{\mathcal{H}}}(x_t \mid \mathbf{x}_\mathcal{A}) \\
&= \sum_{i>j} \Big(p(\mathcal{R}_i, \mathbf{x}_\mathcal{A}) p(\mathcal{R}_j, \mathbf{x}_\mathcal{A}) - p(\tilde{\mathcal{R}}_i, \mathbf{x}_\mathcal{A}) p(\tilde{\mathcal{R}}_j, \mathbf{x}_\mathcal{A}) \Big) - \\
&\qquad \sum_{i>j} (p(\mathcal{R}_i, \mathbf{x}_\mathcal{A}, x_t) p(\mathcal{R}_j, \mathbf{x}_\mathcal{A}, x_t) - p(\tilde{\mathcal{R}}_i, \mathbf{x}_\mathcal{A}, x_t) p(\tilde{\mathcal{R}}_j, \mathbf{x}_\mathcal{A}, x_t)\Big) \\
&\leq \sum_{i>j} (p(\mathcal{R}_i, \mathbf{x}_\mathcal{A}) p(\mathcal{R}_j, \mathbf{x}_\mathcal{A}) - p(\tilde{\mathcal{R}}_i, \mathbf{x}_\mathcal{A}) p(\tilde{\mathcal{R}}_j, \mathbf{x}_\mathcal{A})\Big) \\
&= \sum_{i>j} \Big(\Big(p(\tilde{\mathcal{R}}_i, \mathbf{x}_\mathcal{A}) + \gamma_i \Big) \Big(p(\tilde{\mathcal{R}}_j, \mathbf{x}_\mathcal{A}) + \gamma_j \Big) - p(\tilde{\mathcal{R}}_i, \mathbf{x}_\mathcal{A}) p(\tilde{\mathcal{R}}_j, \mathbf{x}_\mathcal{A}) \Big) \\
&= \sum_{i>j} \Big(\gamma_i \Big(\gamma_j + p(\tilde{\mathcal{R}}_j, \mathbf{x}_\mathcal{A}) \Big) + \gamma_j p(\tilde{\mathcal{R}}_i, \mathbf{x}_\mathcal{A}) \Big) \\
&= \sum_{i>j} \Big(\gamma_i p(\mathcal{R}_j, \mathbf{x}_\mathcal{A}) + \gamma_j p(\tilde{\mathcal{R}}_i, \mathbf{x}_\mathcal{A}) \Big) \\
&\leq \sum_i \gamma_i \sum_j p(\mathcal{R}_j, \mathbf{x}_\mathcal{A}) + \sum_j \gamma_j \sum_i p(\tilde{\mathcal{R}}_i, \mathbf{x}_\mathcal{A}).
\end{aligned}$$

By the definition of γ_i we know that

$$\sum_i \gamma_i = p\left(\bigcup_i \left(\mathcal{R}_i \setminus \tilde{\mathcal{R}}_i \right), \mathbf{x}_\mathcal{A} \right) \overset{(a)}{=} p\left(\left(\bigcup_i \mathcal{R}_i \setminus \bigcup_i \tilde{\mathcal{R}}_i \right), \mathbf{x}_\mathcal{A} \right) = p\left(\mathcal{H} \setminus \tilde{\mathcal{H}}, \mathbf{x}_\mathcal{A} \right) \leq \eta p(\mathbf{x}_\mathcal{A}).$$

Step (a) is because of the assumption that $\mathcal{R}_i$'s do not overlap. Hence,

$$\begin{aligned}
\Delta_{\mathcal{H}}(t \mid \mathbf{x}_\mathcal{A}) - \Delta_{\tilde{\mathcal{H}}}(t \mid \mathbf{x}_\mathcal{A}) &= \mathbb{E}[\delta_{\tilde{\mathcal{H}}}(x_t \mid \mathbf{x}_\mathcal{A})] \\
&\leq \eta p(\mathbf{x}_\mathcal{A}) \sum_j p(\mathcal{R}_j, \mathbf{x}_\mathcal{A}) + \eta p(\mathbf{x}_\mathcal{A}) \sum_i p(\tilde{\mathcal{R}}_i, \mathbf{x}_\mathcal{A}) \\
&\leq 2\eta p(\mathbf{x}_\mathcal{A})^2. \qquad (10)
\end{aligned}$$

Combining Equation (9) and (10) we finish the proof. □

Next, we provide the proof of Theorem 5 using the Lemma 6.

Proof of Theorem 5. The key of the proof is to bound the one-step gain of the policy $\pi^g_{\tilde{\mathcal{H}},[\ell]}$.

$$\begin{aligned}
&f_{avg}(\pi^g_{\tilde{\mathcal{H}},[i+1]}) - f_{avg}(\pi^g_{\tilde{\mathcal{H}},[i]}) \\
&\overset{\text{Lemma 6}}{\geq} \mathbb{E}\left[\max_t(\Delta(t \mid \mathbf{x}_\mathcal{A})) - 2\eta \right] \\
&\overset{(a)}{\geq} \mathbb{E}\left[\frac{\Delta(\pi^*_{\mathcal{H},[k]} \mid \mathbf{x}_\mathcal{A})}{k} - 2\eta \right] \\
&= \mathbb{E}\left[\frac{f_{avg}(\pi^*_{\mathcal{H},[k]} @ \pi^g_{\tilde{\mathcal{H}},[i]}) - f_{avg}(\pi^g_{\tilde{\mathcal{H}},[i]})}{k} - 2\eta \right] \\
&\overset{(b)}{\geq} \mathbb{E}\left[\frac{f_{avg}(\pi^*_{\mathcal{H},[k]}) - f_{avg}(\pi^g_{\tilde{\mathcal{H}},[i]})}{k} - 2\eta \right].
\end{aligned}$$

Here $\pi^*_{\mathcal{H},[k]}@\pi^g_{\tilde{\mathcal{H}},[i]}$ denotes the concatenated policy of $\pi^*_{\mathcal{H},[k]}$ and $\pi^g_{\tilde{\mathcal{H}},[i]}$ (i.e., we first run $\pi^g_{\tilde{\mathcal{H}},[i]}$, and then run $\pi^*_{\mathcal{H},[k]}$ from scratch, ignoring the observations made by $\pi^g_{\tilde{\mathcal{H}},[i]}$).

The proof structure follows closely from the proof of Theorem A.10 in [12]: Step (a) follows from from the adaptive submodularity of f, and step (b) is due to monotonicity of f_{avg}. Define $\Delta_i := f_{avg}(\pi^*_{\mathcal{H},[k]}) - f_{avg}(\pi^g_{\tilde{\mathcal{H}},[i]})$, from the above equation we get $\Delta_\ell \leq \left(1 - \frac{1}{k}\right)^l \Delta_0 + \sum_{i=0}^{l} \left(1 - \frac{1}{k}\right)^i$. Hence, $f_{avg}\left(\pi^g_{\tilde{\mathcal{H}},[\ell]}\right) \geq \left(1 - e^{-\ell/k}\right) f_{avg}\left(\pi^*_{\mathcal{H},[k]}\right) - 2k\eta\left(1 - \left(\frac{1}{k}\right)^\ell\right)$. □

Counting Markov Equivalence Classes by Number of Immoralities

Adityanarayanan Radhakrishnan
Laboratory for Information and
Decision Systems, and Institute for
Data, Systems and Society
Massachusetts Institute of Technology
Cambridge, MA, USA

Liam Solus
Department of Mathematics
KTH Royal Institute of Technology
Stockholm, Sweden

Caroline Uhler
Laboratory for Information and
Decision Systems, and Institute for
Data, Systems and Society
Massachusetts Institute of Technology
Cambridge, MA, USA

Abstract

Two directed acyclic graphs (DAGs) are called Markov equivalent if and only if they have the same underlying undirected graph (i.e. skeleton) and the same set of immoralities. When using observational data alone and typical identifiability assumptions, such as faithfulness, a DAG model can only be determined up to Markov equivalence. Therefore, it is desirable to understand the size and number of Markov equivalence classes (MECs) combinatorially. In this paper, we address this enumerative question using a pair of generating functions that encode the number and size of MECs on a skeleton G, and in doing so we connect this problem to classical problems in combinatorial optimization. The first generating function is a graph polynomial that counts the number of MECs on G by their number of immoralities. Using connections to the independent set problem, we show that computing a DAG on G with the maximum possible number of immoralities is NP-hard. The second generating function counts the MECs on G according to their size. Via computer enumeration, we show that this generating function is distinct for every connected graph on p nodes for all $p \leq 10$.

1 INTRODUCTION

Graphical models based on directed acyclic graphs (DAGs) are widely used to represent complex causal systems in applications ranging from computational biology to epidemiology, and sociology (Friedman et al., 2000; Pearl, 2000; Robins et al., 2000; Spirtes et al., 2001). A DAG entails a set of conditional independence (CI) relations through the Markov properties. Two DAGs are said to be *Markov equivalent* if they entail the same CI relations. Verma and Pearl (1992) show that a *Markov equivalence class* (MEC) is determined by the underlying undirected graph (or *skeleton*) and the placement of immoralities, i.e. induced subgraphs of the form $X \to Z \leftarrow Y$. From observational data alone, a DAG can only be identified up to Markov equivalence, and it is therefore important to describe the set of MECs and their sizes. For instance, if the MECs are large in size, then causal inference algorithms that operate in the space of MECs as compared to DAGs could significantly increase efficiency. In a similar fashion, the general problem of understanding the size and number of MECs on a given skeleton is statistically relevant. Causal discovery algorithms such as the PC algorithm (Spirtes et al., 2001) first learn a skeleton and then orient the edges. If the number of MECs on the learned skeleton is relatively small, it may not be necessary to complete the orientation step in order to determine the true MEC. This paper focuses on the complexity of deciding the number and size of MECs on a fixed skeleton.

The literature on the MEC enumeration problem is surprisingly sparse, and it can be summarized in terms of two important perspectives: (1) enumerate all MECs on p nodes (as in (Gillespie and Perlman, 2001)), and (2) enumerate all MECs of a given size (as in (Gillespie, 2006; Steinsky, 2003; Wagner, 2013; He and Yu, 2016)). The characterization of Markov equivalence of Verma and Pearl (1992) results in a representation of a MEC by a graph with directed and undirected edges known as the *essential graph* (Andersson et al., 1997) (or *cPDAG* (Chickering, 2002) or *maximally oriented graph* (Meek, 1995)). Gillespie and Perlman (Gillespie et al., 2001) use this characterization to identify all MECs on $p \leq 10$ nodes; namely, they fix a skeleton on p nodes, and then count the number of ways to compatibly place immoralities within the skeleton. The study of He and Yu (2016) counts the size of a *single* MEC in terms of the *core graph* of its essential graph. The works (Gillespie, 2006;

Steinsky, 2003; Wagner 2013) give inclusion-exclusion formulae for MECs of a fixed size by utilizing the structure of the essential graph. However, since essential graphs can be complicated, these formulae are only realizable for constrained classes of MECs. Namely, (Steinsky, 2003) and (Wagner, 2013) only consider MECs of size one, and (Gillespie, 2006) must fix the undirected edges of the essential graphs to be enumerated. These results show that the enumeration of MECs by number of nodes and size is a difficult problem in general.

A common approach to difficult graphical structure enumeration problems is to specify a type of graph for which to solve the problem. The purpose of this paper is to study the MEC enumeration problem from this perspective. This approach is used in classic combinatorial optimization problems such as the enumeration of independent sets, matchings, and colorings (Ellis-Monaghan and Merino, 2011; Levit and Mandrescu, 2005). In each case, it is typical to consider a generating function $P(G;x) := \sum_{k\geq 0} \alpha_k(G)x^k$, that when evaluated at $x = 1$ returns the desired statistic for the graph G. Such a generating function is called a *graph polynomial*. For example, the *independence polynomial* of G is the graph polynomial in which $\alpha_k(G)$ is the number of independent sets of size k in G. Researchers can gain useful information about the original enumeration problem by studying the properties and coefficients of a graph polynomial. For instance, the independence polynomial of G encodes the total number of independent sets (or the *Fibonacci number* of G) (Prodinger and Tichy, 1982), the maximum size of an independent set (or *independence number* of G) (van Lint and Wilson, 2001), and the number of independent sets of a fixed size (Levit and Mandrescu, 2005); all of which have been studied extensively. These refined statistics work together to give a complete understanding of the problem of enumerating independent sets for G. Here, we are interested in the combinatorial statistics of a graph G:

(1) $M(G)$, the total number of MECs on G,

(2) $m(G)$, the maximum number of immoralities on G,

(3) $m_k(G)$, the number of ways to place exactly k immoralities on G, and

(4) $M(G)_{\text{freq}} := (s_1(G), s_2(G), \ldots)$, where $s_k(G)$ denotes the number of MECs on G of size k.

The first three statistics fit together naturally in the graph polynomial presentation

$$M(G;x) := \sum_{k=0}^{m(G)} m_k(G)x^k,$$

since then $M(G;1) = M(G)$. Similarly, we can express the vector $M(G)_{\text{freq}}$ as a graph polynomial of the form $\sum_{k\geq 0} s_k(G)x^k$. However, it is perhaps more natural to encode the entries of $M(G)_{\text{freq}}$ in the arithmetic function

$$S(G;x) := \sum_{k\geq 0} \frac{s_k(G)}{k^x}.$$

We then have that $S(G;0) = M(G) = M(G;1)$, and both generating functions are multiplicative with respect to disjoint unions of graphs. That is,

$$M(G \sqcup H; X) = M(G;x)M(H;x), \text{ and}$$
$$S(G \sqcup H; X) = S(G;x)S(H;x),$$

where $G \sqcup H$ denotes the disjoint union of two graphs G and H.

We are interested in the complexity of computing the combinatorial statistics associated to the generating functions $M(G;x)$ and $S(G;x)$. The resulting theorems inform the complexity of computing the number and size of MECs on a fixed skeleton G. Our first main theorem, proven in Section 2.2, establishes the difficulty of computing a MEC on a skeleton G with many immoralities.

Theorem 1.1. *Given an undirected graph G, the problem of computing a DAG $\mathcal{G}$ with skeleton G and $m(G)$ immoralities is NP-hard.*

In analogy to the independence number of G, we call $m(G)$ the *immorality number of* G. This number is natural to consider when one attempts to enumerate the MECs on G by counting all compatible placements of immoralities. Here, we use the notion of NP-hardness as defined in (Chapter 5, Garey and Johnson, 1979). We will prove Theorem 1.1 in Section 2 via a reduction of the minimum vertex cover problem. To do so, we first prove a correspondence between minimum vertex covers of a given triangle-free graph G and minimum decompositions of G into non-overlapping stars, which we call *minimum star decompositions*. As with most NP-hard problems, restricting to special cases can make the problem tractable. In this case, the connection with minimum star decompositions allows us to compute $m(G)$ in some special cases. In particular, we can compute $m(G)$ for triangle-free graphs whose minimum star decompositions are isomorphic as forests, and we apply this result to recover $m(G)$ for the complete bipartite graph $K_{p,p}$ and some special types of circulant graphs.

Our second complexity result is computer-aided and observational. In order to study the generating functions $M(G;x)$ and $S(G;x)$, we developed a computer program for the enumeration of the combinatorial statistics (1), (2), (3), and (4) that expands on the original program of Gillespie and Perlman (2001). Using this program, we prove the following intriguing theorem.

Theorem 1.2. *The arithmetic generating function $S(G; x)$ is distinct for every connected graph G on p nodes for all $p \leq 10$.*

Theorem 1.2 can be viewed as a complexity result in the sense that it tells us that recovering the complete set of statistics $M(G)_{\text{freq}}$ for some unknown connected graph G from observational data alone is equally hard as recovering G itself. In Section 3, we describe our computer program for the computation of the statistics (1), (2) (3), and (4), and verify Theorem 1.2.

2 IMMORALITY NUMBERS AND STAR DECOMPOSITIONS

In this section, we show that computing the immorality number $m(G)$ of a graph G is an NP-hard problem by showing that it is a reduction of the problem of computing minimum vertex covers of G. Recall that a *vertex cover* of G is a subset S of vertices of G for which each edge of G is incident to some vertex in S. A classic problem in combinatorial optimization is to identify a vertex cover of minimum size for a given graph G. Formally stated, this is the search problem

Problem 2.1. MINIMUM VERTEX COVER

INPUT: An undirected graph $G = (V, E)$.

OUTPUT: A subset $C \subset V$ such that for all edges $\{u, v\} \in E$ either $u \in C$ or $v \in C$ and $|C|$ is minimized with respect to this property.

The decision version of this problem is called VERTEX COVER (Karp, 1972) and is stated as follows.

Problem 2.2. VERTEX COVER

INPUT: An undirected graph $G = (V, E)$ and a nonnegative integer k.

PROPERTY: G has a vertex cover of size less than or equal to k.

A search problem Π is said to be *NP-hard* if there is a polynomial time Turing reduction from an NP-complete Π' problem to Π (Chapter 5, Garey and Johnson, 1979). That is, if we are given a polynomial time algorithm A for solving Π, then there exists a polynomial time algorithm for solving Π' using A as a hypothetical subroutine. In (Poljak, 1974), it is shown that VERTEX COVER is NP-complete even when restricted to triangle-free graphs. Moreover, given a polynomial time algorithm for solving MINIMUM VERTEX COVER, we can certainly derive a polynomial time algorithm to solve VERTEX COVER (for triangle-free graphs or otherwise). Thus, MINIMUM VERTEX COVER is NP-hard for both triangle-free and arbitrary graphs. Analogously, we consider the following search and decision problems related to the computation of the immorality number $m(G)$.

Problem 2.3. MAXIMUM IMMORALITIES

INPUT: An undirected graph $G = (V, E)$.

OUTPUT: A DAG $\mathcal{G}$ with skeleton G and $m(G)$ immoralities.

Problem 2.4. IMMORALITES

INPUT: An undirected graph $G = (V, E)$ and a nonnegative integer k.

PROPERTY: There is a DAG $\mathcal{G}$ with skeleton G having at least k immoralities.

In the following, we will identify a polynomial time Turing reduction of MINIMUM VERTEX COVER to MAXIMUM IMMORALITIES when restricted to triangle-free graphs. A polynomial time solution to MAXIMUM IMMORALITIES would trivially yield a polynomial time solution to the same problem in the triangle-free case. Since this would in turn solve an NP-complete problem, we can conclude that the general instance of MAXIMUM IMMORALITIES is NP-hard. This will prove Theorem 1.1.

In order to reduce MINIMUM VERTEX COVER to MAXIMUM IMMORALITIES for triangle-free graphs, we will utilize a notion of *star decompositions* of G. We then use this connection to compute $m(G)$ in the special cases of the complete bipartite graph $K_{p,p}$ and a family of circulant graphs.

2.1 STAR DECOMPOSITIONS

Let $G = (V, E)$ be a connected, undirected graph, and let $K_{p,q}$ denote the complete bipartite graph with nodes partitioned into a collection of size p and a collection of size q. Recall that a *p-star* is the complete bipartite graph $K_{1,p}$ and its *center* is the unique degree p node. A collection of stars $\{S_1, \ldots, S_k\}$ is called a *star decomposition of G* if each S_i is a subgraph of G and each edge of G is an edge of exactly one star in the collection. Our definition of star decomposition is a bit more general than the standard notion studied in graph decompositions. The classic notion of a star decomposition adds the requirement that the stars $S_1, \ldots, S_k$ are all isomorphic to one another. While the literature on which graphs admit a star decomposition of this type is quite extensive (Cain, 1974; Cohen and Tarsi, 1991; Ushio et al., 1978), there is substantially less work relating to the more general notion we use here (Lin and Shyu, 1996).

In the following, the *trivial star* refers to $K_{1,0}$, and the *size* of a star S is the size of its edge set, which we denote by $|S|$. The *size* of a star decomposition $\mathcal{S}$ is the number of stars in the decomposition, and it is denoted $|\mathcal{S}|$. Given a star decomposition $\mathcal{S} = \{S_1, \ldots, S_k\}$ let $v(\mathcal{S}) \in \mathbb{R}^k$ denote the vector of the sizes of stars in $\mathcal{S}$ ordered greatest-to-least from left-to-right. So if $|S_1| \geq \cdots \geq |S_k|$ then $v(\mathcal{S}) = (|S_1|, |S_2|, \ldots, |S_k|)$. If $\mathcal{S}$ is a star decomposition of size k with cardinality vector $v(\mathcal{S}) \in \mathbb{R}^k$, for $m \geq k$ we embed $v(\mathcal{S}) \in \mathbb{R}^m$ by appending zeros to the right end of $v(\mathcal{S}) \in \mathbb{R}^k$. Notice that this corresponds to appending trivial stars to $\mathcal{S}$. We call a star decomposition of G *reduced* if it contains no trivial stars. Notice that the largest reduced star decomposition contains at most $|E|$ stars. A *minimum* star decomposition of G contains the minimum number of stars over all star decompositions of G. Notice that a minimum star decomposition will always be reduced. Since the maximum number of stars in a reduced star decomposition of G is $|E|$, then any minimum star decomposition contains at most $|E|$ stars. Also, given a star decomposition $\mathcal{S}$, we call the set of all centers of stars in $\mathcal{S}$ the *center set of* $\mathcal{S}$, and we denote it by $C(\mathcal{S})$. Note that if a star consists only of a single edge, then we simply choose one of its endpoints to be the center node.

For any DAG $\mathcal{G}$ on the undirected graph G we can construct a star decomposition of G as follows. For each node $v \in V$, consider the substar S_v in G whose center is v and whose edges are those directed into v in the DAG $\mathcal{G}$. The *star decomposition of G induced by $\mathcal{G}$* is then

$$\mathcal{S}(\mathcal{G}) := \{S_v : v \in V\}.$$

Notice that an induced star decomposition will not be reduced, and may contain intervals $K_{1,1}$.

Remark 2.1. Not all star decompositions of a graph G are induced by some DAG on G. For example, any graph has a star decomposition consisting of precisely its set of edges. In the case of the 4-cycle, for instance, this decomposition cannot arise from a DAG.

Since a star decomposition induced by a DAG always contains at least one trivial star, we make the following important definition. A minimum star decomposition of G is *induced* by a DAG $\mathcal{G}$ on G if it is a reduction of the star decomposition induced by $\mathcal{G}$.

Example 2.1. Consider C_4, the cycle on 4 nodes. Up to isomorphism, C_4 admits the three reduced star decompositions depicted in Figure 1. From this we can see that the minimum star decompositions of C_4 are all isomorphic to $\{K_{1,2}, K_{1,2}\}$. The two right-most star decompositions in Figure 1 are each induced by DAGs. For example, the middle decomposition is induced by the DAG $\mathcal{G}_1$ and the

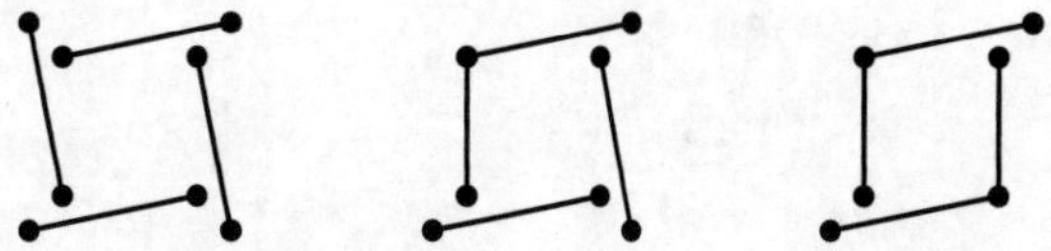

Figure 1: The three nonisomorphic reduced star decompositions of the 4-cycle

right-most decomposition is induced by the DAG $\mathcal{G}_2$ as depicted in Figure 2. The left-most star decomposition in Figure 1 is the maximum cardinality reduced star decomposition of the 4-cycle, which consists of exactly one copy of $K_{1,1}$ for each edge of C_4.

Example 2.1 demonstrates the properties of minimum star decompositions that we will use to study the immorality number of triangle-free graphs. Notice first that the center set of each star decomposition is a vertex cover of C_4 and that the minimum vertex covers of G are center sets of minimum star decompositions. Indeed, there exists a many-to-one correspondence between minimum star decompositions and minimum vertex covers of G.

Lemma 2.5. *Suppose $\mathcal{S}$ is a minimum star decomposition with center set $C(\mathcal{S})$. Then $C(\mathcal{S})$ is a minimum vertex cover of G.*

Proof. Recall that the center set $C(\mathcal{S})$ of any star decomposition $\mathcal{S}$ is a vertex cover of G. Therefore, any minimum star decomposition has to be at least as large as any minimum vertex cover of G. Suppose that for any minimum vertex cover C of G we can find a star decomposition of G with center set C. Then it follows that any minimum star decomposition has size exactly that of a minimum vertex cover of G. Moreover, the center set of any minimum star decomposition must be a minimum vertex cover. Thus, to complete the proof, we need only show that any minimum vertex cover of G is the center set of some star decomposition of G.

For a node v of a graph G we let $N[v]$ denote the neighbors of v in G including the node v itself. Suppose that $C = \{c_1, \ldots, c_k\}$ is a minimum vertex cover of G. Let $\mathcal{S}(C) = \{S_1, \ldots, S_k\}$ denote the star decomposition of

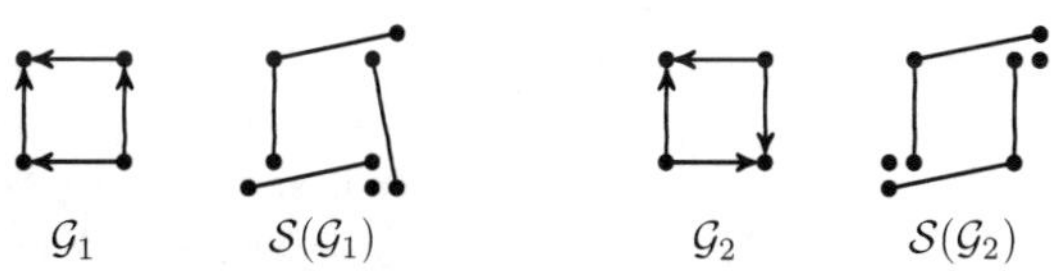

Figure 2: The DAGs $\mathcal{G}_1$ and $\mathcal{G}_2$ and their induced (nonreduced) star decompositions.

G given by setting

$$S_1 := \langle N[c_1] \rangle,$$
$$S_i := \langle N[c_i] \backslash (\cup_{j \leq i} N[c_j]) \rangle, \text{for } i > 1.$$

Since $\mathcal{S}$ is a star decomposition of G with center set C, this completes the proof. □

Lemma 2.6. *Suppose C is a minimum vertex cover of G and $\mathcal{S}$ is any star decomposition of G with center set C. Then $\mathcal{S}$ is a minimum star decomposition.*

Proof. Recall that the center set $C(\mathcal{S})$ of any star decomposition $\mathcal{S}$ of G is a vertex cover of G. Thus, just as stated in the proof of Lemma 2.5, we know that any star decomposition of G is at least as large as any minimum vertex cover of G. By the construction in the proof of Lemma 2.5, we know in fact that this lower bound is tight. Thus, any star decomposition with center set that is a minimum vertex cover must have minimum size. □

Lemma 2.7. *Suppose $\mathcal{S}$ is a minimum star decomposition of G with cardinality vector $v(\mathcal{S}) \in \mathbb{R}^{|E|}$ such that $v(\mathcal{S})^T v(\mathcal{S})$ is maximum over all star decompositions of G. Then $\mathcal{S}$ is induced by some DAG with skeleton G.*

Proof. Note first that any star decomposition $\mathcal{S} = \{S_1, \dots, S_k\}$ of G is induced by some directed, but not necessarily acyclic, graph $\mathcal{G}(\mathcal{S})$. Namely, $\mathcal{G}(\mathcal{S})$ is the directed graph whose arrows are given by directing all edges of S_i so that their heads are at the center node of S_i for all $i \in [k]$. Since each edge of G appears in exactly one star in $\mathcal{S}$, this definition yields a unique directed graph.

For the sake of contradiction, suppose $\mathcal{S}$ is a minimum star decomposition of G for which $v(\mathcal{S})^T v(\mathcal{S})$ is maximized, but $\mathcal{S}$ is not induced by a DAG. Then $\mathcal{S}$ is induced by the directed graph $\mathcal{G}(\mathcal{S})$ constructed in the previous paragraph. By assumption, $\mathcal{G}(\mathcal{S})$ contains some directed cycles. Notice that if v is any node contained in a directed cycle, then $v \in C(\mathcal{S})$ since v has nonzero indegree in $\mathcal{G}(\mathcal{S})$.

Let v_0 be a node of highest indegree that is contained in a directed cycle in $\mathcal{G}(\mathcal{S})$. Reverse all arrows pointing outwards from v_0 that are in a directed cycle and denote the resulting directed graph by $\mathcal{G}(\mathcal{S})_1$. The center set of the (reduced) induced star decomposition of $\mathcal{G}(\mathcal{S})_1$ is contained in the center set of $\mathcal{S}$ since all nodes on any directed cycle in $\mathcal{G}(\mathcal{S})$ are contained in $C(\mathcal{S})$. Therefore, since $\mathcal{S}$ is a minimum star decomposition of G, then so is $\mathcal{S}(\mathcal{G}(\mathcal{S})_1)$. Moreover, since we only reversed the direction of arrows in cycles with indegree at most that of v_0, it follows that

$$v(\mathcal{S})^T v(\mathcal{S}) < v(\mathcal{S}(\mathcal{G}(\mathcal{S})_1))^T v(\mathcal{S}(\mathcal{G}(\mathcal{S})_1)).$$

However, this is a contradiction to the assumption that $v(\mathcal{S})^T v(\mathcal{S})$ is maximum over all star decompositions of G.

□

In some special instances, when the minimum star decompositions of a graph G are well-understood, we can use this theory to compute $m(G)$. Recalling Example 2.1, notice that the minimum star decompositions of C_4 are all isomorphic to one another as forests, and each minimum star decomposition of C_4 is induced by a DAG. With this example in mind, we prove the following theorem.

Theorem 2.8. *Let G be a triangle-free, undirected graph whose minimum star decompositions are all isomorphic to one another as forests. Then given any minimum star decomposition $\mathcal{S}(G) = \{S_1, \dots, S_k\}$ of G the immorality number of G is*

$$m(G) = \sum_{i=1}^{k} \binom{|S_i|}{2}.$$

Proof. Since the maximum size of a minimum star decomposition is $|E|$, we can simply assume $k = |E|$ by filling out the set with trivial stars. That is, without loss of generality we assume that all star decompositions considered have the same cardinality $k = |E|$, but may contain trivial stars. A minimum star decomposition is then simply one with the maximum number of trivial stars.

Recall that for every DAG $\mathcal{G}$ on G we can construct the induced star decomposition $\mathcal{S}(\mathcal{G}) = \{S_1, \dots, S_k\}$. Since G is triangle-free, the number of immoralities in $\mathcal{G}$ is precisely $\sum_{i=1}^{k} \binom{|S_i|}{2}$. Each such induced star decomposition admits a vector in $\mathbb{R}^k$ for each permutation $\sigma \in S_k$ of cardinalities $(|S_{\sigma(1)}|, |S_{\sigma(2)}|, \dots, |S_{\sigma(k)}|) \in \mathbb{R}^k$, and we let $v(\mathcal{G})$ denote any one of these vectors. More generally, any star decomposition $\mathcal{S}$ of G admits such a vector of cardinalities for each permutation $\sigma \in S_k$, any one of which we denote by $v(\mathcal{S}) \in \mathbb{R}^k$. Let $\mathcal{V}(G)$ denote the set of all possible choices of vectors $v(\mathcal{S})$ for all possible star decompositions of G. Then our goal is to maximize the objective function $\sum_{i=1}^{k} \binom{x_i}{2}$ over the set $\mathcal{V}(G) \subset \mathbb{Z}_{\geq 0}^k$. Since the objective function satisfies

$$\sum_{i=1}^{k} \binom{x_i}{2} = \frac{1}{2} \left(\sum_{i=1}^{k} x_i^2 - \sum_{i=1}^{k} x_i \right),$$

and for all $(x_1, \dots, x_k) \in \mathcal{V}(G)$, we have that $\sum_{i=1}^{k} x_i = |E| = k$, then we are interested in solving the integer optimization problem

$$\begin{array}{ll} \text{maximize} & \mathbf{x}^T\mathbf{x} \\ \text{subject to} & \sum_{i=1}^k x_i = k, \\ & \mathbf{x} \in \mathbb{Z}_{\geq 0}^k, \\ & \mathbf{x} \in \mathcal{V}(G). \end{array}$$

The presentation of this optimization problem is redundant, but it is to emphasize the fact that any vector in $\mathcal{V}(G)$ lies in the kth dilate of the probability simplex Δ_k, which we denote by $k\Delta_k$. Therefore, we are simply maximizing the length over all vectors in the probability simplex that also lie in the set $\mathcal{V}(G)$. Since the value of $\mathbf{x}^T\mathbf{x}$ strictly increases as we approach the boundary of $k\Delta_k$ then the star decompositions with the maximum number of trivial stars will yield the maximum value of the objective function. These are the minimum star decompositions, all of which are isomorphic as trees, and therefore have the same vectors $v(\mathcal{S})$ up to a permutation of coordinates. Since we have assumed that at least one of these star decompositions is induced by a DAG, it follows that the maximum value of the original objective function $\sum_{i=1}^k \binom{x_i}{2}$ is the immorality number of G. □

Collectively, Lemmas 2.5, 2.7, and Theorem 2.8 allow us to prove Theorem 1.1.

2.2 PROOF OF THEOREM 1.1

Let G be a triangle-free graph, and suppose that we have a polynomial time algorithm that returns a DAG $\mathcal{G}^*$ with skeleton G for which $\mathcal{G}^*$ has the maximum number of immoralities. By Lemma 2.7 and Theorem 2.8, we know that the maximum value of $\sum_{i=1}^{|E|} \binom{|S_i|}{2}$ is achieved by a minimum star decomposition induced by a DAG. Since the value of $\sum_{i=1}^{|E|} \binom{|S_i|}{2}$ is exactly equal to the number of immoralities in a DAG with a triangle-free skeleton, it follows that our DAG $\mathcal{G}^*$ induces a minimum star decomposition $\mathcal{S}(\mathcal{G}^*)$ that maximizes $\sum_{i=1}^{|E|} \binom{|S_i|}{2}$. We know by Lemma 2.5 that the center set $C(\mathcal{S}(\mathcal{G}^*))$ is a minimum vertex cover of G. Therefore, we have a polynomial time algorithm for computing a minimum vertex cover of the triangle-free graph G. It is clear that a polynomial time algorithm for MAXIMUM IMMORALITIES for arbitrary graphs trivially yields a polynomial time algorithm for MAXIMUM IMMORALITIES for triangle-free graphs. Therefore, since MINIMUM VERTEX COVER is NP-complete for triangle-free graphs, we know that the general instance of MAXIMUM IMMORALITIES is NP-hard. This completes the proof of Theorem 1.1. □

Remark 2.2. Recall that there is trivially a polynomial time Turing reduction of MINIMUM VERTEX COVER to VERTEX COVER. Conversely, it is well-known that VERTEX COVER is *self-reducible*. That is, given a polynomial time algorithm for VERTEX COVER one can find a polynomial time algorithm solving MINIMUM VERTEX COVER. Collectively, this says that solving MINIMUM VERTEX COVER is no more or no less hard than solving VERTEX COVER. Since the former direction is trivial, the critical observation made here is the self-reducibility of VERTEX COVER.

The proof of self-reducibility for VERTEX COVER is standard across many NP-complete structural search problems for graphs, and it goes as follows. Given a graph $G = (V, E)$, the minimum size of a vertex cover must be between 0 and $|V|$. Thus, by a binary search, we can determine in polynomial time the size k^* of a minimum vertex cover of G. Then, to recover a vertex cover C with size k^* of G, we first pick a vertex v and delete it from G. If the resulting graph has a vertex cover of size $k^* - 1$, then v is in a minimum vertex cover of G, if not we return the vertex v, and repeat with another vertex. Iterating this procedure produces a minimum vertex cover of G in polynomial time.

While the self-reducibility of many other graph structure search problems are proved using a similar argument, this proof is unusable for IMMORALITIES. The analogous argument for IMMORALITIES would require considering all subsets of neighbors of the node v and deleting the corresponding star. Since the number of such queries for a given vertex v is only bounded by $\binom{\deg(v)}{2}$, this algorithm is not polynomial in time. However, this does not prove that IMMORALITIES is not self-reducible, nor does it prove that IMMORALITIES is not NP-complete.

2.3 EXAMPLES OF IMMORALITY NUMBERS

As with most NP-hard problems, the problem may become tractable when restricted to special cases. We now present a few cases in which star decompositions allow us to compute $m(G)$ via an application of Theorem 2.8. For some graphs, Theorem 2.8 makes the computation of $m(G)$ very simple. For instance, the unique minimum star decomposition of a star S_p is itself, and therefore $m(G) = \binom{p}{2}$. Similarly, the graph $K_{2,p}$ can be decomposed into two stars, both of which are isomorphic to $K_{1,p}$, in precisely one way, and therefore this is its unique minimum star decomposition. It follows from Theorem 2.8 that $m(K_{2,p}) = 2\binom{p}{2}$. On the other hand, Theorem 2.8 certainly has its limitations. For instance, let $S_2(p,q)$ denote the gluing of a p-star and a q-star; i.e. an edge $\{i,j\}$ with p leaves attached to i and q leaves attached to j). Then, Theorem 2.8 implies that $m(G_2(p,p)) = \binom{p+1}{2} + \binom{p}{2}$. However, if $p \neq q$, then the minimum star decompositions of $G_2(p,q)$ are all size two but need not be isomorphic. Therefore, Theorem 2.8

does not apply.

In general, it can be difficult to determine if the minimum star decompositions of a graph are all isomorphic. We end this section by computing $m(G)$ for some slightly more complicated graphs, thereby illustrating the rapidly increasing difficulty level of the problem. In subsection 2.3.1 we compute $m(G)$ for the complete bipartite graph $K_{p,p}$ and in subsection 2.3.2 for some special circulant graphs.

2.3.1 The complete bipartite graph $K_{p,p}$

Gillespie and Perlman (2001) note that the maximum number of induced 3-paths over all skeletons on p nodes, for each $p \leq 10$ is given by the complete bipartite graph $K_{\lfloor \frac{p}{2} \rfloor, \lceil \frac{p}{2} \rceil}$. The number of induced 3-paths in the graph $K_{\lfloor \frac{p}{2} \rfloor, \lceil \frac{p}{2} \rceil}$ is quickly seen to be $a_p = \lfloor \frac{p}{2} \rfloor \lceil \frac{p}{2} \rceil \frac{p-2}{2}$, which is sequence A111384 of the *Online Encyclopedia of Integer Sequences* (OEIS, 2003). Since induced 3-paths in an undirected graph G are exactly the possible locations of immoralities in a DAG with skeleton G, it is reasonable to ask for the immorality number of the complete bipartite graph $K_{p,p}$. As one would hope, the immorality number of $K_{p,p}$ turns out to be exactly one half the number of induced 3-paths. We now use Theorem 2.8 to compute the immorality number of $K_{p,p}$ via star decompositions. To do so, we make one additional observation.

Lemma 2.9. *The minimum star decompositions of $K_{p,p}$ are all isomorphic to*

$$\underbrace{\{K_{1,p}, K_{1,p}, \ldots, K_{1,p}\}}_{p \text{ times}}.$$

Proof. We prove a slightly stronger statement. Let $N[v]$ denote the subgraph of a graph G induced by the vertex v and its set of neighbors. Let the vertices of $K_{p,p}$ be the partitioned set $A \sqcup B$ where $A := \{a_1, \ldots, a_p\}$ and $B := \{b_1, \ldots, b_p\}$. We claim that the minimum star decompositions of $K_{p,p}$ are only $\{N[a_i] : i \in [p]\}$ and $\{N[b_i] : i \in [p]\}$. To see this assume otherwise. Suppose that $\{S_1, \ldots, S_k\}$ is a minimum star decomposition of $K_{p,p}$, and let c_i denote the center of star S_i for all $i \in [k]$. We also set $C := \{c_1, \ldots, c_k\}$.

Suppose first that $k = p$ and that $A \cap C \neq \emptyset$ and $B \cap C \neq \emptyset$. Without loss of generality, assume that $A \cap C = \{a_1, \ldots, a_\ell\}$ for some $\ell < k$. Then for all $i > \ell$ it must be that $b_i \in B \cap C$, since otherwise the edge $\{a_i, b_i\}$ would not appear in any star in $\{S_1, \ldots, S_k\}$. Since $k = p$, it follows that $B \cap C = \{b_{\ell+1}, \ldots, b_p\}$. However, this means that for all $i \leq \ell$ and $j \geq \ell + 1$, the edges $\{a_j, b_i\}$ are not in any star, which is a contradiction.

Now suppose that $k < p$. It is quick to see that if $C \subset A$ or $C \subset B$ then there exist edges of $K_{p,p}$ not contained in stars. So $A \cap C \neq \emptyset$. The proof then follows from applying the same argument as in the case when $k = p$ to derive a contradiction. □

Theorem 2.10. *The immorality number of $K_{p,p}$ is $p\binom{p}{2}$.*

Proof. Notice that $K_{p,p}$ is triangle-free. By Lemma 2.9, the minimum star decompositions of $K_{p,p}$ are all isomorphic as forests. Moreover, any such minimum star decomposition is induced by a DAG $\mathcal{G}$ on $K_{p,p}$ that has exactly p sinks located along either the node set A or B. The result then follows from Theorem 2.8. □

2.3.2 Some triangle-free circulants

Circulant graphs are natural generalizations of the cycle graphs, and both their independence polynomials and independence numbers have been studied extensively (Brown and Hoshino, 2011; Hoshino, 2008). However, there is no general formula for the Fibonacci number, the independence number, nor the independence polynomial of these graphs. Similarly, computing $M(G; x)$ or $S(G; x)$ is difficult for a general circulant. However, as a corollary to Theorem 2.8, we can compute the immorality number of some triangle-free circulants.

Recall that a circulant on p nodes is a graph whose nodes are identified with the elements of the cyclic group $\mathbb{Z}/p\mathbb{Z}$ of order p, and whose edges are given by a specified *connection set* $C \subset \mathbb{Z}/p\mathbb{Z}$. In the undirected setting, we assume C is closed under additive inverses. The circulant on p nodes with connection set C is denoted $X(p, C)$ and has edges $\{i, j\}$ for all pairs i and j satisfying $i - j \in C$. We often abbreviate the connection set C via a subset of $[\lfloor \frac{p}{2} \rfloor]$ by omitting the additive inverse of each element.

Corollary 2.11. *Let p be even, and suppose that $X(p, C)$ is a triangle-free circulant graph containing a p-cycle for which the maximum independent subset is of size $\frac{p}{2}$. Then*

$$m(X(p, C)) = \frac{p}{2}\binom{2|C|}{2}.$$

Proof. Recall that a set of nodes in a graph G is a minimum vertex cover if and only if its complement is an independent set in G. Since $X(p, C)$ contains a p-cycle, then without loss of generality we can assume that $1 \in C$. Since $1 \in C$ and the maximum independent subset of $X(p, C)$ is equal to the one of C_p of size $p/2$, then any minimum independent set is given by selecting precisely every other vertex of the graph as we walk along the p-cycle given by $1 \in C$. Moreover, such a vertex set is also a minimum vertex cover. Thus, if $\{c_1, \ldots, c_{\frac{p}{2}}\}$ is a maximum independent set in $X(p, C)$, then there is only one possible star decomposition with center set $\{c_1, \ldots, c_{\frac{p}{2}}\}$, namely

$$\{\langle N[c_1]\rangle, \ldots, \langle N[c_{\frac{p}{2}}]\rangle\} \simeq \{K_{1,2|C|}, \ldots, K_{1,2|C|}\}.$$

Since the only two maximum independent sets in $X(p, C)$ share this property, it follows from Lemma 2.6 that all minimum star decompositions of G are isomorphic. Thus, by Theorem 2.8 we conclude that $m(X(p, C)) = \frac{p}{2}\binom{2|C|}{2}$. □

Notice that Corollary 2.11 applies to any triangle free circulant with p even, $1 \in C$, which has all other elements of C being odd. On the other hand, we cannot apply the same techniques to compute the immorality numbers for p odd, since such circulants may contain nonisomorphic minimum star decompositions.

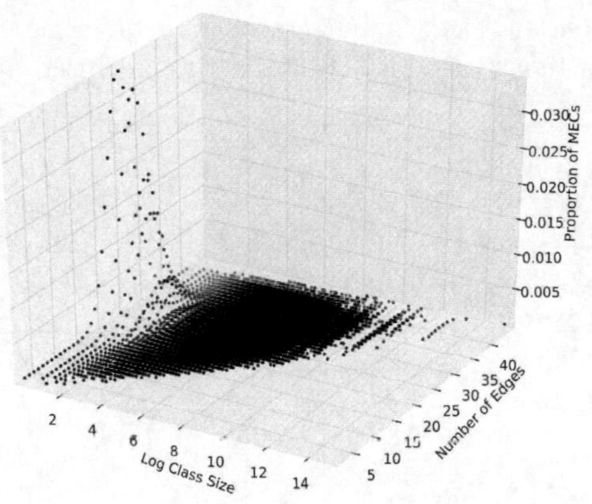

Figure 3: The proportion of MECs on connected graphs with 10 nodes by log class size and number of edges.

3 COMPUTATIONAL ANALYSIS

In this section, we describe the computer program we used to test our conjectures and collect relevant statistics. This program can be found at `https://github.com/aradha/mec_generation_tool`, and it expands on the first computer program written for the enumeration of MECs presented (Gillespie and Perlman, 2001). For each skeleton on $p \leq 10$ nodes, the Gillespie and Perlman algorithm logged the maximum number of induced 3-paths, the maximum number of MECs, the total number of MECs, and the size of each class. Our program expands on this original program in two ways: for skeletons on $p \leq 10$ nodes, our program collects more data about each skeleton, and it produces all such data for all triangle-free skeletons on $p \leq 12$ nodes. The new program now catalogues the same information as the original Gillespie and Perlman algorithm for each skeleton as well as the degree sequence of the skeleton, the number of triangles, and the number of immoralities per MEC. This additional data, especially in the triangle-free setting, allows us to more carefully analyze how the structure of the skeleton impacts the number and size of its associated MECs. In the following, we first provide a brief description of the algorithm and the hashing scheme used. We then validate Theorem 1.2 and discuss the analogous result in the case of unconnected graphs.

3.1 THE ALGORITHM

There are three main components in our program's data pipeline which we now describe. The first component is the main class that reads in skeleton data generated using tools from `nauty` and `Traces` (McKay and Piperno, 2014). The second component is a DAG generator that directly generates all DAGs on a given skeleton. Such a generator is realized using the algorithm published by Barbosa and Swarcfiter (1999). It is essential to directly generate all DAGs rather than generating all directed graphs and then pruning out the ones containing cycles, since the number of DAGs dominates the number of directed graphs for a large number of vertices.

The final main component is a DAG enumerator that generates the frequency vector $M(G)_{\text{freq}}$ when given the DAGs on a given skeleton G. In order to generate the number of MECs of each size on a given skeleton, this component creates a bit representation for each MEC by first creating a bit mask of the possible immoralities that could occur in the skeleton. Each DAG is then traversed. If three vertices are found to be in an immorality then the Cantor pairing function is used to hash the triple of their integer labels to the location of the bit in the immorality bit mask. Since the Cantor pairing function is invertible and since the number of vertices in each graph is small, we have a valid, non-overflowing hash function. After comparing the resulting hashes for all DAGs on the given skeleton, a pair of integers is returned for each MEC: the number of immoralities in the MEC and the size of the MEC. It is an important feature of the algorithm that this component of the pipeline has access to data on the given skeleton. This allows us to collect data on the skeleton in relation to each MEC. Using this, for each skeleton we record the number of induced 3-paths, the degree sequence, the number of edges, and the number of triangles. To handle the around 12 million undirected graphs on 10 nodes, we split these graphs into approximately 500 files across 10 directories, allocating 16 threads to process each directory. Running this process in parallel takes 5 days as compared to the 253 CPU hours (approximately 94 days) by Gillispie and Perlman.

Table 1: The 10-node graphs with the same $S(G;x)$ function. Here, nK_p denotes n disjoint copies of K_p.

Class Size(s)	Skeleton 1	Skeleton 2
24	$K_4 \sqcup 6K_1$	$K_3 \sqcup 2K_2 \sqcup 3K_1$
48	$K_4 \sqcup K_2 \sqcup 4K_1$	$K_3 \sqcup 3K_2 \sqcup K_1$
144	$K_4 \sqcup K_3 \sqcup 3K_1$	$2K_3 \sqcup 2K_2$
720	$K_6 \sqcup 4K_1$	$K_5 \sqcup K_3 \sqcup 2K_1$
1440	$K_6 \sqcup K_2 \sqcup 2K_1$	$K_5 \sqcup K_3 \sqcup K_2$
2880	$K_6 \sqcup 2K_2$	$K_5 \sqcup K_4 \sqcup K_1$
72, 24	$K_4 \sqcup I_3 \sqcup 3K_1$	$K_3 \sqcup I_3 \sqcup 2K_2$

3.2 CORRECTNESS OF THE ALGORITHM

To verify the correctness of our implementation, we matched our program's output with that of the algorithm in (Gillespie and Perlman, 2001). In Figure 3 for instance, we can use our program to reproduce the same distribution of the proportion of MECs with respect to class size and number of edges as in (Figure 4, Gillespie and Perlman, 2001).

We also compared performance in terms of speed and memory utilization. Our program runs in nearly the exact time measured by Gillespie and Perlman: we measured that our algorithm also takes around three minutes for eight vertices and only a few seconds or milliseconds for fewer vertices. We do, however, have better memory utilization than Gillespie and Perlman as the number of bits we store for hashes is dependent on the number of possible immoralities in the skeleton rather than on the number of possible triples of vertices. We also use Java to do our data processing. Thus, since we only need a print out of the data collected in subsection 3.1 (3) for each skeleton processed, the garbage collector clears out our hash map allocation after each skeleton. This allows us to not only log the class size and the number of MECs per skeleton, but also the number of immoralities per class as well as the number of induced 3-paths, the degree sequence, the number of edges, and the number of triangles. Thus, despite the fact that our algorithm only matches the Gillespie and Perlman algorithm in time, it is collecting significantly more data per skeleton.

3.3 VALIDITY OF THEOREM 1.2

After running the algorithm on all connected graphs with up to ten nodes, we verified that there was no pair of skeleta with $p \leq 10$ nodes that have the same frequency vector $M(G)_{\text{freq}}$. This indicates that the MEC frequency vectors $M(G)_{\text{freq}}$ (or equivalently the arithmetic generating functions $S(G;x)$) bijectively map to skeletons of connected graphs up to ten nodes. Similarly, when we ran our algorithm on all graphs with ten nodes including graphs that were not necessarily connected, we found that the only collisions occurred on graphs G and H with the following property: Let $G = G_1 \sqcup \cdots \sqcup G_m$ and $H = H_1 \sqcup \cdots \sqcup H_n$ be the decompositions of G and H into connected components. Let $G \cap H$ denote the set consisting of the connected components that are shared between G and H up to isomorphism. Now let $G \setminus G \cap H = G_{i_1} \sqcup \cdots \sqcup G_{i_m}$ and $H \setminus G \cap H = H_{j_1} \sqcup \cdots \sqcup H_{j_n}$, where $i_1, \ldots, i_m \in [m]$ and $j_1, \ldots, j_n \in [n]$, be the remaining subgraphs. Then $\prod_{k=1}^{m} |G_{i_k}| = \prod_{\ell=1}^{n} |H_{j_\ell}|$. Over all graphs with ten nodes, there are seven such examples that occurred. These are shown in Table 1.

4 Discussion

Understanding the number and size of MECs is important since it tells us about the complexity of DAG model recovery. Algorithms such as the PC algorithm first learn a skeleton and then orient its edges. If the number of MECs with the learned skeleton is small, the orientation step may be unnecessary. Therefore, it is desirable to know the size and number of MECs with a given skeleton. In this paper, we introduced a pair of generating functions, $M(G;x)$ and $S(G;x)$, that count the number of MECs on a skeleton G by their number of immoralities and size, respectively. This constitutes a novel approach to the MEC enumeration problem that yields connections to classically studied problems in combinatorial optimization. We observed that computing the degree of $M(G;x)$ for triangle-free graphs relates to the vertex-cover problem for G and its associated star decompositions. These connections allowed us to prove that computing the degree of $M(G;x)$ is NP-hard, thus demonstrating that counting the number of MECs on G must be hard as well. Alternatively, we observed the complexity of enumerating MECs by size by showing that $S(G;x)$ is distinct for every connected graph G on $p \leq 10$ nodes. The connections to classical problems revealed here suggest that the number of MECs for sparse graphs can be better understood by a closer examination of $M(G;x)$ and $S(G;x)$. In particular, it is natural to ask how $M(G;x)$ relates to the enumeration of vertex covers for fixed families of sparse graphs. Future work is required to address questions of this nature.

Acknowledgements

We thank Brendan McKay for helpful advice in the use of the programs `nauty` and `Traces`. Liam Solus was supported by an NSF Mathematical Sciences Postdoctoral Research Fellowship (DMS - 1606407). Caroline Uhler was partially supported by DARPA (W911NF-16-1-0551), NSF (1651995) and ONR (N00014-17-1-2147).

References

S. A. Andersson, D. Madigan, and M. D. Perlman. *A characterization of Markov equivalence classes for acyclic digraphs.* Annals of Stat. 25.2 (1997): 505–541.

V. C. Barbosa and J. L. Szwarcfiter. *Generating all the acyclic orientations of an undirected graph.* Information Processing Letters 72.1 (1999): 71–74.

J. Brown and R. Hoshino. *Well-covered circulant graphs.* Discrete Mathematics 311.4 (2011): 244–251.

P. Cain. *Decomposition of complete graphs into stars.* Bulletin of the Australian Mathematical Society 10.01 (1974): 23–30.

D. M. Chickering. *Learning equivalence classes of Bayesian-network structures.* Journal of Machine Learning Research 2 (2002): 445–498.

E. Cohen and M. Tarsi. *NP-completeness of graph decomposition problems.* Journal of Complexity 7.2 (1991): 200–212.

J. A. Ellis-Monaghan and C. Merino. *Graph polynomials and their applications I: The Tutte polynomial.* Structural Analysis of Complex Networks. Birkhäuser Boston, 2011. 219–255.

N. Friedman, M. Linial, I. Nachman and D. Peter. *Using Bayesian networks to analyze expression data.* Journal of Computational Biology 7 (2000): 601–620.

M. R. Garey and D. S. Johnson. *Computers and intractability: a guide to the theory of NP-completeness.* A Series of Books in the Mathematical Sciences. WH Freeman and Company, New York, NY 25.27 (1979): 141.

S. B. Gillispie. *Formulas for counting acyclic digraph Markov equivalence classes.* Journal of Statistical Planning and Inference 136.4 (2006): 1410-1432.

S. B. Gillispie and M. D. Perlman. *Enumerating Markov equivalence classes of acyclic digraph models.* Proc. of the Seventeenth Conference on Uncertainty in Artificial Intelligence. Morgan Kaufmann Publishers Inc., 2001.

Y. He and B. Yu. *Formulas for counting the sizes of Markov equivalence classes of directed acyclic graphs.* Preprint available on the arXiv: `https://arxiv.org/pdf/1610.07921.pdf` (2016).

R. Hoshino. *Independence polynomials of circulant graphs.* Library and Archives Canada, 2008.

R. M. Karp *Reducibility among combinatorial problems.* Complexity of Computer Computations. Springer US (1972): 85–103.

V. E. Levit and E. Mandrescu. *The independence polynomial of a graph – a survey.* Proceedings of the 1st International Conference on Algebraic Informatics. Vol. 233254. 2005.

C. Lin, and T-W. Shyu. *A necessary and sufficient condition for the star decomposition of complete graphs.* Journal of Graph Theory 23.4 (1996): 361–364.

J. H. van Lint and R. M. Wilson. *A Course in Combinatorics.* Cambridge University Press, 2001.

B. D. McKay and A. Piperno. *Practical graph isomorphism, II.* J. of Symbolic Comp. 60 (2014): 94–112.

C. Meek. *Causal inference and causal explanation with background knowledge.* Proc. of the Eleventh Conference on Uncertainty in Artificial Intelligence (1995): 403–410.

J. Pearl. *Causality: Models, Reasoning, and Inference.* Cambridge University Press, Cambridge, 2000.

S. Poljak. *A note on stable sets and colorings of graphs.* Commentationes Mathematicae Universitatis Carolinae 15.2 (1974): 307–309.

H. Prodinger and R. F. Tichy. *Fibonacci numbers of graphs.* Fibonacci Quarterly 20.1 (1982): 16–21.

J. M. Robins, M. A. Hernán and B. Brumback. *Marginal structural models and causal inference in epidemiology.* Epidemiology 11.5 (2000): 550–560.

N. J. Sloane. *The On-Line Encyclopedia of Integer Sequences.* (2003).

P. Spirtes, C. N. Glymour and R. Scheines. *Causation, Prediction, and Search.* MIT Press, Cambridge, 2001.

B. Steinsky. *Enumeration of labelled chain graphs and labelled essential directed acyclic graphs.* Discrete Mathematics 270.1 (2003): 267-278.

K. Ushio, S. Tazawa and S. Yamamoto. *On claw-decomposition of a complete multipartite graph.* Hiroshima Mathematical Journal 8.1 (1978): 207–210.

T. Verma and J. Pearl. *An algorithm for deciding if a set of observed independencies has a causal explanation.* Proc. of the Eighth International Conference on Uncertainty in Artificial Intelligence. Morgan Kaufmann Publishers Inc., 1992.

S. Wagner. *Asymptotic enumeration of extensional acyclic digraphs.* Algorithmica 66.4 (2013): 829–847.

Real-Time Resource Allocation for Tracking Systems

Yash Satsangi
University of Amsterdam

Shimon Whiteson
University of Oxford

Frans A. Oliehoek
University of Liverpool
University of Amsterdam

Henri Bouma
TNO, The Netherlands

Abstract

Automated tracking is key to many computer vision applications. However, many tracking systems struggle to perform in real-time due to the high computational cost of detecting people, especially in ultra high resolution images. We propose a new algorithm called *PartiMax* that greatly reduces this cost by applying the person detector only to the relevant parts of the image. PartiMax exploits information in the particle filter to select k of the n candidate *pixel boxes* in the image. We prove that PartiMax is guaranteed to make a near-optimal selection with error bounds that are independent of the problem size. Furthermore, empirical results on a real-life dataset show that our system runs in real-time by processing only 10% of the pixel boxes in the image while still retaining 80% of the original tracking performance achieved when processing all pixel boxes.

1 INTRODUCTION

Automated tracking is a key component of countless computer vision applications such as maintaining surveillance, studying traffic flows, and counting the number of people in a scene [Smeulders et al., 2014]. Consequently, in recent years many tracking systems have been proposed that make it possible to track people in a variety of challenging settings [La Cascia et al., 2000; Benfold and Reid, 2011; Smeulders et al., 2014]. However, these approaches still cannot perform real-time tracking on ultra high resolution videos (e.g., 5000×4000 pixels).

In particular, the *detection* stage, i.e., identifying an object in a scene, is the main computational bottleneck for systems that work on the *tracking-by-detection* principle [Benfold and Reid, 2011]. For example, Figure 1 shows a wide-view scene recorded by a camera mounted on top of a building [Schutte et al., 2016]. Successful tracking depends on detecting the person in the image by applying a trained detector to many *pixel boxes*. Since the scene records a wide landscape, the pixel boxes must be relatively small (e.g., 180×180), yielding approximately 7000 pixel boxes per image. Consequently, performing a *brute force detection* (BD) that applies the person detector to all 7000 pixel boxes is extremely computationally intensive and prohibitive to do in real time.

Figure 1: A wide-view scene recorded by a rooftop camera; the cyan rectangle shows an example pixel box.

In this paper, we propose a new tracking system that greatly reduces the cost of detection and thus enables real-time tracking on systems with ultra high resolution images or many cameras. The main idea is to perform *selective detection* (SD), i.e., apply the person detector not on all n pixel boxes, but only a carefully selected subset of k pixel boxes, while retaining performance guarantees, as shown in Figure 2. To do so, we build on existing techniques for *sensor selection*, which

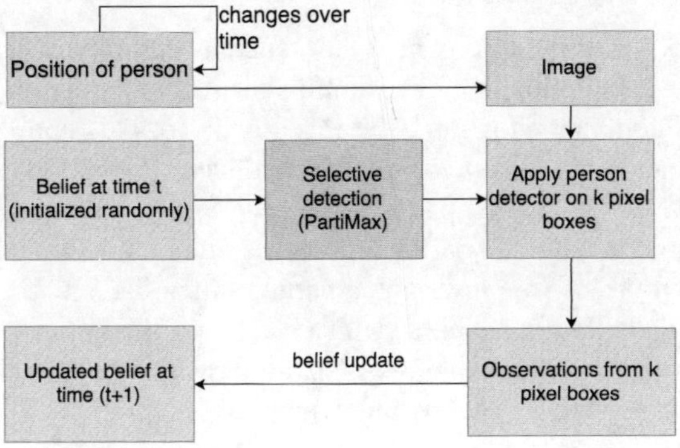

Figure 2: Proposed tracking system with PartiMax, our proposed selective detection method, highlighted in red.

select the k out of n sensors with the highest *utility* in a multi-sensor network. Sensor selection is challenging because there are $\binom{n}{k}$ ways to perform the selection, and computing the best one would use up the same scarce computational resources we aim to intelligently allocate. Fortunately, when the utility function possesses certain characteristics, including *submodularity*, a near-optimal selection can be found using *greedy maximization*, which evaluates the utility function only $\mathcal{O}(nk)$, instead of $\binom{n}{k}$, times. In addition, *stochastic greedy maximization* [Mirzasoleiman et al., 2015] further reduces the number of evaluations of the utility function by evaluating the utility function only for a random subset of pixel boxes of size r, where $r << n$.

However, for selective detection in real-time, even stochastic greedy maximization is too expensive because computing typical utility functions such as *information gain* or *expected coverage* requires marginalizing out the observation that each candidate sensor would generate. In fact, in real-life settings with high dimensional state and/or observation spaces, evaluating information gain or expected coverage even once can be prohibitively expensive.

We start by proposing a utility function for selective detection called *particle coverage* that approximates the probability of detecting a person in a given set of pixel boxes. We show that particle coverage approximates expected coverage under certain conditions, but is much faster to compute. Then, we propose *PartiMax*. Unlike (stochastic) greedy maximization, which treats utility evaluation as a black-box, PartiMax maintains and updates the particle coverage of each pixel box in every iteration of greedy maximization, leading to large computational savings, as the particle coverage of each pixel box is not evaluated from scratch in each iteration. Furthermore, instead of selecting a subset of pixel boxes *randomly* in every iteration like stochastic greedy maximization, PartiMax samples pixel boxes with high particle coverage leading to superior tracking performance.

Since sampling pixel boxes with high particle coverage without computing the particle coverage is not trivial, we propose a sampling algorithm that is guaranteed to sample a pixel box with probability directly proportional to its particle coverage. It does so by employing *tile coding*, a popular representation in reinforcement learning that discretizes continuous spaces.

We show that, given access to a sampling algorithm like the one we propose, PartiMax is guaranteed to return a solution with tight error bounds that are independent of the problem size, i.e., independent of both n and k. Although PartiMax is designed for the particle coverage function, our bound applies generally to maximization over a set function.

Finally, we use PartiMax for selective detection to build a real-time tracking system, which we apply to a real-life dataset. Our results show that our tracking system retains 80% of its performance despite processing only 10% of each image and running in real time.

2 RELATED WORK

Most detection systems, e.g., [Felzenszwalb et al., 2010; Dollár et al., 2014], including those based on convolutional neural networks [Tian et al., 2015; Redmon et al., 2016], process the whole image and are thus not computationally efficient enough for our setting, due to the high resolution and depth of scene of the images.

Some work does identify the relevant region of interest in an image [Kim et al., 2012], e.g., by generating *proposals* (see [Hosang et al., 2015] and references therein) or saliency points [Shtrom et al., 2013]. These methods, however, are based on the properties (or low-level features) of the entire image (since they do not consider the belief state) and often generate thousands of proposals/saliency points per image. In fact, selective detection can be coupled with these methods to selectively generate saliency points.

Recently developed models of visual attention [Mnih et al., 2014; Denil et al., 2012] come closest to our work in spirit. However, they use model-free deep reinforcement learning methods to identify relevant region to apply a trained detector on [Mnih et al., 2014], while we learn the model of the world from the data and use it to plan online to find the relevant regions to which to apply a trained detector.

Our work builds off the vast existing sensor selection literature. Most work uses utility functions involving information gain [Tham and Han, 2013; Wang et al., 2005;

Satsangi et al., 2016] and expected coverage [Spaan and Lima, 2009], which are too expensive for real-time systems. Other approaches do not consider partial observability [Natarajan et al., 2012] or do not scale to large state and observation spaces [Natarajan et al., 2012; Satsangi et al., 2015]. Methods based on dynamic programming [Williams et al., 2007] or linear programming [Williams et al., 2006] or focusing on occlusions [Gupta et al., 2007] are also limited to smaller state and observation spaces.

For submodular function maximization, the most related methods are those of [Mirzasoleiman et al., 2015] and [Badanidiyuru and Vondrák, 2014]. We significantly improve upon these methods for sensor selection by introducing a novel method with lower computational cost and thereby making them applicable to real-time tracking.

3 BACKGROUND

3.1 BASIC SETUP

Let $\mathcal{X} = \{1, 2 \ldots n\}$ denote the set of all pixel boxes and i denote a single pixel box in $\mathcal{X}$. $\mathcal{A}^+$ denotes the set of all possible subsets of $\mathcal{X}$ of size less than or equal to k, $\mathcal{A}^+ = \{\mathcal{A} \subseteq \mathcal{X} : |\mathcal{A}| \leq k\}$. For the image shown in Figure 1 the size of one pixel box was chosen to be 180 x 180 pixels. The true location of the person is a hidden variable denoted by s and S is the set of all possible values s can take.[1] The observation vector $\mathbf{z} = \langle z_1, z_2 \ldots z_n \rangle$ denotes the result of applying the detector to each pixel box, i.e., each z_i denotes an estimate of whether a person appears in the pixel box i. If a pixel box i is not selected for detection, then $z_i = \emptyset$. Ω is the set of all possible values $\mathbf{z}$ can take. The *belief* $b(s)$ is a probability distribution over s. Given $\mathcal{A}$ and $\mathbf{z}$, $b(s)$ can be updated using Bayes rule.

When there are many possible states, it is not possible to maintain $b(s)$ exactly. Thus, we use particle filters, described below, to maintain and update belief $b(s)$. Below we also describe greedy maximization, which is essential to our setup, as it selects k pixel boxes out of n in $\mathcal{O}(n \times k)$ time instead of $\mathcal{O}\binom{n}{k}$.

3.2 PARTICLE FILTERS

When there are many possible states, it is infeasible to update $b(s)$ exactly. Instead, we can use *particle filters* [Doucet et al., 2001], sequential Monte Carlo algorithms for approximate inference in partially observable scenarios that are commonly used to track people in complex situations. The true belief $b(s)$ is approximated with a *particle belief* $\mathcal{B}$, a collection of m samples from $b(s)$, called particles: $\mathcal{B} = \{s_1, s_2 \ldots s_m\}$. Although weighted particle filters are often used for tracking, we use an unweighted particle filter since it can be efficiently implemented with a black-box simulator without the need to explicitly model the accuracy of the person detector or the motion dynamics.

Given the particle belief $\mathcal{B}$, a subset of sensors $\mathcal{A}$ and observation $\mathbf{z}$, particle beliefs can be updated using a *Monte Carlo belief update* [Silver and Veness, 2010]. For each particle $s_l \in \mathcal{B}$, the next state s'_l is sampled from $\Pr(s'|s)$ (under the Markov assumption) to form $\mathcal{B}' : \{s'_l : s'_l \sim \Pr(s'_l|s_l) \wedge s_l \in \mathcal{B}\}$. With enough samples, $\mathcal{B}'$ approximates the probability distribution: $b'(s') = \sum_{s \in S} \Pr(s'|s) b(s)$.

For each $s'_l \in \mathcal{B}'$, the corresponding $\mathbf{z}_l$ is drawn from $\Pr(\mathbf{z}|s'_l, \mathcal{A})$. If $\mathbf{z}_l = \mathbf{z}$, then s'_l is added to the updated belief $\mathcal{B}^{\mathcal{A}}_{\mathbf{z}}$. Otherwise, the particle is discarded. To avoid particle degeneracy, a common problem with particle filters, we combine the belief update with new particles introduced by adding random particles sampled from S to the existing particle set. $\mathcal{B}^{\mathcal{A}}_{\mathbf{z}}$ approximates the probability distribution $b^{\mathcal{A}}_{\mathbf{z}}(s') = \frac{\Pr(\mathbf{z}|\mathcal{A},s')b'(s')}{\Pr(\mathbf{z}|b,\mathcal{A})}$.

3.3 GREEDY MAXIMIZATION

Given a set function $F(\mathcal{A})$, where $\mathcal{A} \in \mathcal{A}^+$, *greedy maximization* computes $\mathcal{A}^G$, which approximately maximizes F by building a subset of k pixel boxes iteratively. In particular, in each of its k iterations, greedy maximization adds to a partial solution the pixel box that maximizes the *marginal gain*:

$$\Delta_F(i|\mathcal{A}) = F(\mathcal{A} \cup i) - F(\mathcal{A}), \qquad (1)$$

of adding i to $\mathcal{A}$, i.e., it adds $\arg\max_{i \in \mathcal{X} \setminus \mathcal{A}^G} \Delta_F(i|\mathcal{A}^G)$ to $\mathcal{A}^G$ as shown in Algorithm 1.

Algorithm 1 `greedyMax`$(F, \mathcal{X}, k)$

1: $\mathcal{A}^G \leftarrow \emptyset$
2: **for** $l = 1$ *to* k **do**
3: $\quad \mathcal{A}^G \leftarrow \mathcal{A}^G \cup \arg\max_{i \in \mathcal{X} \setminus \mathcal{A}^G} \Delta_F(i|\mathcal{A}^G)$
4: **end for**
5: return $\mathcal{A}^G$

Nemhauser et al. [1978] showed that greedy maximization is guaranteed to have bounded error under certain conditions:

Theorem 1. *[Nemhauser et al., 1978] If F is non-negative, monotone and submodular, then* $F(\mathcal{A}^G) \geq$

[1] For simplicity, we sometimes assume there is only one person in the scene and the hidden variable is a vector in the Euclidean space. However, our methods and theoretical results extend easily to multiple people, as shown in Section 7.

$(1 - e^{-1})F(\mathcal{A}^*)$, *where* $\mathcal{A}^* = \arg\max_{A \in \mathcal{A}^+} F(A)$.

Submodularity is a property of set functions that formalizes the notion of diminishing returns: $F : 2^{\mathcal{X}} \rightarrow \mathbb{R}$ is submodular if for every $\mathcal{A}_M \subseteq \mathcal{A}_N \subseteq \mathcal{X}$ and $i \in \mathcal{X} \setminus \mathcal{A}_N$,

$$\Delta_F(i|\mathcal{A}_M) \geq \Delta_F(i|\mathcal{A}_N). \quad (2)$$

Thus, the marginal gain of adding an element to a smaller set $\mathcal{A}_M$ is always greater than or equal to the marginal gain of adding the same element to a bigger subset $\mathcal{A}_N$ such that $\mathcal{A}_M \subseteq \mathcal{A}_N \subseteq \mathcal{X}$. If this is true for all possible values of $\mathcal{A}_N, \mathcal{A}_M$, and i, then F is submodular.

3.4 STOCHASTIC GREEDY MAXIMIZATION

Stochastic greedy maximization, shown in Algorithm 2, further reduces costs by randomly sampling a subset $\mathcal{R}$ of size r from $\mathcal{X}$ in each iteration of greedy maximization and then selecting the element from $\mathcal{R}$ that maximizes the marginal gain. It computes a subset $\mathcal{A}^S$ by adding in each iteration $\arg\max_{i \in \mathcal{R}} \Delta_F(i|\mathcal{A}^S)$, where $\mathcal{R}$ is a subset of $\mathcal{X} \setminus \mathcal{A}^S$ of size r. Mirzasoleiman et al. [2015] showed that stochastic greedy maximization is also guaranteed to have bounded error.

Algorithm 2 `stochastic-greedy-max`$(F, \mathcal{X}, k, r)$

1: $\mathcal{A}^S \leftarrow \emptyset$
2: **for** $m = 1$ *to* k **do**
3: $\quad \mathcal{R} \leftarrow$ random sample of size r from $\mathcal{X} \setminus \mathcal{A}^S$.
4: $\quad \mathcal{A}^S \leftarrow \mathcal{A}^S \cup \arg\max_{i \in \mathcal{R}} \Delta_F(i|\mathcal{A}^S)$
5: **end for**
6: return $\mathcal{A}^S$

Theorem 2. *[Mirzasoleiman et al., 2015] If F is non-negative, monotone and submodular, then* $\mathbb{E}[F(\mathcal{A}^S)] \geq (1 - e^{-1} - \epsilon)F(\mathcal{A}^*)$, *where* $r = \frac{n}{k}\log(\frac{1}{\epsilon})$.

3.5 UTILITY FUNCTIONS

For tracking tasks, F is often defined as *information gain* [Cover and Thomas, 1991; Krause and Guestrin, 2005; Tham and Han, 2013]:

$$IG_b(\mathcal{A}) = H_b(s) - H_b^{\mathcal{A}}(s|\mathbf{z}), \quad (3)$$

where $H_b(s)$ is the *entropy* of s and $H_b^{\mathcal{A}}(s|\mathbf{z})$ is the *conditional entropy* of s given $\mathbf{z}$ [Cover and Thomas, 1991].

It can also be defined as *expected coverage* [Spaan and Lima, 2009]. Let $\mathcal{I}_{\mathcal{B}'}^j$ be the set of particles in $\mathcal{B}'$ that are *covered* by pixel box j, $\mathcal{I}_{\mathcal{B}'}^j = \{s' \in \mathcal{B}' : j \text{ covers } s'\}$. A pixel box j covers s' if a person in state s' is visible in

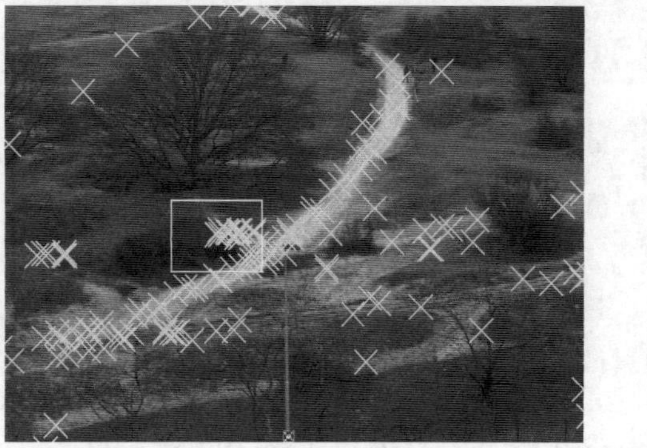

Figure 3: Particle belief: the yellow rectangle shows a pixel box and the particles it covers.

pixel box j. The expected coverage is defined as:

$$F_{\mathcal{B}'}(\mathcal{A}) = \sum_{\mathbf{z}} \Pr(\mathbf{z}|\mathcal{B}', \mathcal{A}) f_{\mathcal{B}_{\mathbf{z}}^{\mathcal{A}}}(\mathcal{A}), \quad (4)$$

where $f_{\mathcal{B}}(\mathcal{A}) = |\cup_{j \in \mathcal{A}} \mathcal{I}_{\mathcal{B}}^j|$. Expected coverage belongs to a general class of coverage functions that have been widely considered [Spaan and Lima, 2009]. In tracking, expected coverage is suitable because of the presence of partial observability, necessitating the expectation across $\mathbf{z}$. Expected coverage is appropriate for sensor selection or selective detection because it rewards selecting pixel boxes that have the highest probability of detecting a target. The underlying assumption is that the observations generated by the person detector are informative enough to detect a person correctly when present inside the pixel box, and are not informative enough if a person is absent from the pixel box. This is barely a restrictive assumption, as most useful person detectors satisfy it.

4 PARTICLE COVERAGE UTILITY FUNCTION

The utility functions described above are too expensive to compute in many practical settings, as they require marginalizing out observations, which is infeasible for real-time systems. In this section, we propose the *particle coverage function* (PCF) for selective detection, which does not require computing $\mathcal{B}_{\mathbf{z}}^{\mathcal{A}}$ and approximates expected coverage. PCF is defined as follows:

$$PCF_{\mathcal{B}'}(\mathcal{A}) = f_{\mathcal{B}'}(\mathcal{A}) = |\cup_{j \in \mathcal{A}} \mathcal{I}_{\mathcal{B}'}^j|. \quad (5)$$

$PCF_{\mathcal{B}'}(\mathcal{A})$ is simply the number of particles in $\mathcal{B}'$ that are covered by $\mathcal{A}$. In Figure 3, the particle coverage is the number of cyan particles that fall in the yellow pixel box. As opposed to expected coverage $F_{\mathcal{B}'}$, PCF does not involve an expectation over $\mathbf{z}$ nor does it require computing the resulting beliefs $\mathcal{B}_{\mathbf{z}}^{\mathcal{A}}$. PCF equals expected coverage under certain conditions, including the following.

Assumption 1. *For every $s' \in S$, $\mathcal{A} \subseteq \mathcal{X}$, there exist $\mathbf{z}_{s',\mathcal{A}}$ and $\bar{\mathbf{z}}_{s',\mathcal{A}}$ in Ω such that if s' is covered by $\mathcal{A}$, $\Pr(\mathbf{z}_{s',\mathcal{A}}|s',\mathcal{A}) = 1$ and if s' is not covered by $\mathcal{A}$, then $\Pr(\bar{\mathbf{z}}_{s',\mathcal{A}}|s',\mathcal{A}) = 1$.*

This assumption implies that any partial observability is due to perceptual aliasing, not noise in the sensors. Given Assumption 1, it is straightforward to show that expected coverage is equal to the particle coverage.

Theorem 3. *If Assumption 1 holds for a given $\mathcal{A}$, then $F_{\mathcal{B}'}(\mathcal{A}) = PCF_{\mathcal{B}'}(\mathcal{A})$.*

Proof. Expected coverage can be expressed as $F_{\mathcal{B}'}(\mathcal{A}) = \sum_{\mathbf{z}\in\Omega} \Pr(\mathbf{z}|\mathcal{B}',\mathcal{A}) f_{\mathcal{B}_{\mathbf{z}}^{\mathcal{A}}}(\mathcal{A})$. In case a negative detection is observed, that is the person is not in the space covered by $\mathcal{A}$ the resulting belief will not have any particle within the space covered by $\mathcal{A}$ due to Assumption 1 and thus resulting coverage is zero. If a positive detection is observed, that is the person is inside the space covered by $\mathcal{A}$ then all the particles in resulting belief will fall within the space that is covered by $\mathcal{A}$ resulting: $f_{\mathcal{B}_{\mathbf{z}}^{\mathcal{A}}}(\mathcal{A}) = m$. This implies, $F_{\mathcal{B}'}(\mathcal{A}) = \sum_{\mathbf{z}\in\Omega} \Pr(\mathbf{z}|\mathcal{B}',\mathcal{A})m$, where $\mathbf{z}$ is a positive observation that can be obtained only if a state is covered by $\mathcal{A}$. The probability of getting a positive detection according to $\mathcal{B}'$ is the sum of particles covered by $\mathcal{A}$ in $\mathcal{B}'$ divided by m. Thus, $F_{\mathcal{B}'}(\mathcal{A}) = \frac{PCF_{\mathcal{B}'}(\mathcal{A})}{m} \times m = PCF_{\mathcal{B}'}(\mathcal{A})$. □

In cases where Assumption 1 does not hold, particle coverage can be considered an approximation to expected coverage. Its key advantage is that computing $f_{\mathcal{B}'}$ does not require hypothetical belief updates, as one can iterate over the particle belief and simply count the number of particles that are covered by $\mathcal{A}$, making it practical for real-time applications. Moreover, it is a member of a class of coverage functions that are known to be submodular [Krause and Golovin, 2014; Takamura and Okumura, 2009] so we can employ greedy maximization to approximately maximize $f_{\mathcal{B}'}$. Our experiments show that $f_{\mathcal{B}'}$ is a good choice of utility function for selective detection in real time, leading to excellent tracking performance at a fraction of the computational cost.

Note that we formulate Assumption 1 merely for analysis purposes: to describe a set of cases in which particle coverage and expected coverage are identical. Assumption 1 is not a restrictive condition for applying PartiMax, described below. On the contrary, in the Experiments section we present excellent results for PartiMax on a real-life dataset for which Assumption 1 does not hold.

Furthermore, while we define particle coverage for the case of an unweighted particle filter, the concept is more general. In essence, the particle coverage of a pixel box is the cumulative probability mass concentrated on the states that are covered by the pixel box. Thus, any method that approximates a belief can be used to compute particle coverage by simply computing the probability mass concentrated on a set of states. For example, for a weighted particle filter, the particle coverage of a pixel box is just the sum of the weights of the particles covered by the pixel box.

5 PARTIMAX

In this section, we propose *PartiMax*, which combines the complementary benefits of PCF and stochastic greedy maximization for selective detection. Moreover, rather than merely naively applying them together, we exploit the unique structure of PCF to develop a better approach for sampling pixel boxes that is guaranteed to sample pixel boxes with high coverage, thus offering a further increase in performance. PartiMax is based on the key insight that sampling pixel boxes with a probability that is directly proportional to their particle coverage leads to strong theoretical guarantees on the expected utility. Thus, we prove error bounds for PartiMax that are independent of the number of available pixel boxes n, the number of particles in the particle filter m, or the number of pixel boxes to be selected k.

Greedy maximization and stochastic greedy maximization assume oracle access to the utility function and thus compute the marginal gain for every pixel box in every iteration. Generally, computing particle coverage function given a pixel box requires iterating over the particles to count how many fall in the space covered by the pixel box. Unlike greedy maximization, PartiMax does not explicitly compute particle coverage for each pixel box on the fly but instead maintains the particle coverage of each pixel box by updating it in every iteration. Using an approach inspired by *tile coding* [Sutton and Barto, 1998], a popular reinforcement learning technique for coding continuous state spaces, PartiMax is able to compute and maintain the particle coverage of every pixel box without having to visit n pixel boxes or m particles in every iteration.

A tile coding consists of many *tilings*. Each tiling is a set of *tiles*, which in our setting are pixel boxes. The pixel boxes in a tiling partition the state space S, i.e., they are disjoint and completely cover S. For example, Figure 4 shows two tilings in blue and yellow. Typically, different tilings have the same size pixel boxes but start at a fixed offset from each other, as in the figure. Since the pixel boxes in a given tiling form a partition, there is exactly

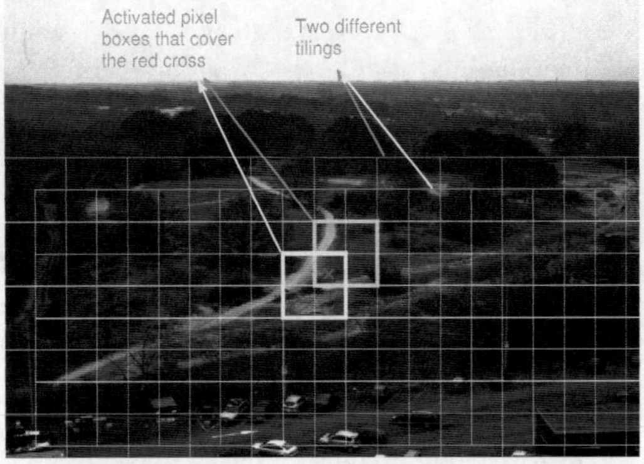

Figure 4: An example tile coding with two tilings. The highlighted tiles show the two pixel boxes that cover the red cross.

one pixel box in each tiling that covers a given state s'. If we represent each tiling as an array, locating the pixel box that covers a given state s' requires only simple arithmetic involving the size of the pixel boxes and the offset between the tilings. Figure 4 highlights the two pixel boxes, one in each tiling, that cover a given state (red cross). Thus, by representing the entire space of pixel boxes as multiple tilings, the set of pixel boxes $\mathcal{T}_{s'}$ that covers a given state s' can be identified in constant time.

In reinforcement learning, tile codings are used to discretize continuous state spaces in order to approximate a value function. Here, we use it differently, just as a scheme for dividing an image into overlapping pixel boxes. The benefit of this approach is that it enables PartiMax to maintain Δ_f efficiently, by providing constant-time access to the set $\mathcal{T}_{s'}$ of all pixel boxes that cover a given state s', i.e., $\mathcal{T}_{s'} = \{i \in \mathcal{X} : i \text{ covers } s'\}$.

Algorithm 3 PartiMax$(\mathcal{B}', \mathcal{X}, k)$

$\langle \Phi, \Delta_f \rangle \leftarrow$ `initialize`$(\mathcal{B}', \mathcal{X})$
$\mathcal{A}^S \leftarrow \emptyset$.
for $l = 1$ *to* k **do**
  $\mathcal{R} \leftarrow$ `sampleP`$(r, \mathcal{B}', \mathcal{X}, \mathcal{A}^S)$
  $i' \leftarrow \arg\max_{i \in \mathcal{R}} \Delta_f(i|\mathcal{A}^S)$.
  $\mathcal{A}^S \leftarrow \mathcal{A}^S \cup i'$
  $\langle \Delta_f, \Phi \rangle \leftarrow$ `update`$(\Delta_f, \Phi, i', \mathcal{A}^S, \mathcal{X})$
end for
return $\mathcal{A}^S$

Algorithm 3 shows pseudocode for PartiMax. It starts by calling `initialize` (Algorithm 4), which returns two data structures, Φ and Δ_f. $\Phi(i|\emptyset)$ stores for each i the set of particles in $\mathcal{B}'$ that i covers; and $\Delta_f(i|\emptyset)$ is the number of particles that are covered by i. For each particle $s' \in \mathcal{B}'$, `initialize` calls `covers`, which uses the tile coding to find the set of pixel boxes $\mathcal{T}_{s'}$ that cover

Algorithm 4 initialize$(\mathcal{B}', \mathcal{X})$

$\Phi(i|\emptyset) \leftarrow \emptyset \forall\, i \in \mathcal{X}$
$\Delta_f(i|\emptyset) \leftarrow 0 \,\forall\, i \in \mathcal{X}$
for $s' \in \mathcal{B}'$ **do**
  $\mathcal{T}_{s'} \leftarrow$ `covers`(s')
  $\Phi(i|\emptyset) \leftarrow \Phi(i|\emptyset) \cup \{s'\} \,\forall i \in \mathcal{T}_{s'}$
  $\Delta_f(i|\emptyset) = \Delta_f(i|\emptyset) + 1 \,\forall i \in \mathcal{T}_{s'}$
end for
return $\langle \Phi, \Delta_f \rangle$

that particle. For every activated pixel box, $i \in \mathcal{T}_{s'}$, $\Delta_f(i|\emptyset)$ is incremented and s' is added to the set of particles $\Phi(i|\emptyset)$.

Once Φ and Δ_f are returned by `initialize`, PartiMax proceeds like stochastic greedy maximization, adding in each iteration the pixel box i' that maximizes the marginal gain from $\mathcal{R}$. Since going over all pixel boxes is too expensive, PartiMax calls Algorithm 5 to obtain $\mathcal{R}$, a subset of $\mathcal{X}$ of size r ($r << n$). However, unlike stochastic greedy maximization, $\mathcal{R}$ is not sampled uniformly randomly but instead Algorithm 5 samples from a distribution such that the probability that i is included in $\mathcal{R}$ is directly proportional to the particle coverage of i.

Algorithm 5 sampleP$(r, \mathcal{B}', \mathcal{X}, \mathcal{A}^S)$

$\mathcal{R} \leftarrow \emptyset$
while $|\mathcal{R}| < r$ **do**
  $s' \sim \text{Unif}(\mathcal{B}')$
  if s' is not covered by $\mathcal{A}^S$ **then**
    $\mathcal{T}_{s'} \leftarrow$ `covers`(s')
    $i \sim \text{Unif}(\mathcal{T}_{s'})$ // uniformly random sample from $\mathcal{T}_{s'}$
    $\mathcal{R} \leftarrow \mathcal{R} \cup i$
  end if
end while
return $\mathcal{R}$

Algorithm 6 update$(\Delta_f, \Phi, i', \mathcal{A}^S, \mathcal{X})$

for $s' \in \Phi(i')$ **do**
  $\mathcal{T}_{s'} \leftarrow$ `covers`(s')
  $\Delta_f(i|\mathcal{A}^S) = \Delta_f(i|\mathcal{A}^S) - 1 \,\forall i \in \mathcal{T}_{s'}$
  $\Phi(i|\mathcal{A}^S) \leftarrow \Phi(i|\mathcal{A}^S) \setminus s' \,\forall i \in \mathcal{T}_{s'}$
end for
return $\langle \Delta_f, \Phi \rangle$

In general, sampling from such a distribution would be difficult, but with PCF we can do this efficiently. Algorithm 5 first uniformly randomly samples a particle from the belief. If the particle is not covered by $\mathcal{A}^S$, then it uses tile coding to find the set of pixel boxes $\mathcal{T}_{s'}$ that cover s' and adds a pixel box uniformly randomly from $\mathcal{T}_{s'}$. This is repeated until r pixel boxes are added to $\mathcal{R}$.

At the end of each iteration, PartiMax calls `update` (Algorithm 6), which updates $\Delta_f(i|\mathcal{A}^S)$ and $\Phi(i|\mathcal{A}^S)$ for every $i \in \cup_{s' \in \Phi(i'|\mathcal{A}^S)} \mathcal{T}_{s'}$. It starts by iterating over the particles s' in $\Phi(i'|\mathcal{A}^S)$ and for each particle uses the tile coding to find $\mathcal{T}_{s'}$. For every pixel box $i \in \mathcal{T}_{s'}$, $\Delta_f(i|\mathcal{A}^S)$ is decremented and s' is removed from $\Phi(i|\mathcal{A}^S)$, to account for the fact that i' now covers s' and thus the marginal gain of i is reduced. The marginal gain of every other i remains unchanged. Similarly, $\Phi(i|\mathcal{A}^S)$ is updated by subtracting s' from $\Phi(i|\mathcal{A}^S)$ for every i in $\mathcal{T}_{s'}$.

6 ANALYSIS

We now establish bounds on the cumulative error of PartiMax that are independent of the problem size. We start with a lemma that shows that the probability of adding i to $\mathcal{R}$ via Algorithm 5 is directly proportional to the marginal gain of i.

Lemma 1. *Let* $i = \texttt{sampleP}(1, \mathcal{B}', \mathcal{X}, \mathcal{A}^S)$ *then* $\Pr_{\mathcal{A}^S}(i = i_j) = c\Delta(i_j|\mathcal{A}^S)$, *where* $c = \frac{1}{tm}$ *is a constant.*

Proof. The probability that a given pixel box i_j is sampled in $\mathcal{T}_{s'}$ (in line 5) is the number of particles covered by i_j in $\mathcal{B}'$ that are not covered by $\mathcal{A}^S$, which is $\Delta_f(i_j|\mathcal{A}^S)$:

$$\Pr(i_j \in \mathcal{T}_{s'}) = \frac{1}{m}\Delta_f(i_j|\mathcal{A}^S). \tag{6}$$

Since there is exactly one pixel box that covers a given state in each of the t tilings, the total number of pixel boxes, that is the size of $\mathcal{T}_{s'}$ is t. Since Algorithm 5 samples uniformly randomly from $\mathcal{T}_{s'}$, then the probability of selecting i_j from $\mathcal{T}_{s'}$ is $\frac{1}{|\mathcal{T}_{s'}|} = \frac{1}{t}$. Thus,

$$\Pr(i = i_j) = \frac{1}{t}\frac{1}{m}\Delta_f(i_j|\mathcal{A}^S). \tag{7}$$

□

Next, we show that PartiMax is guaranteed to be near-optimal.

Theorem 4. *Let F be a set function over a collection of sets $\mathcal{A}^+ = \{\mathcal{A}_1, \mathcal{A}_2 \ldots \mathcal{A}_v\}$ and let $\mathcal{A}^* = \arg\max_{\mathcal{A} \in \mathcal{A}^+} F(\mathcal{A})$, let $\mathcal{A}' = \arg\max_{\mathcal{A} \in \mathcal{R}} F(\mathcal{A})$, such that $\mathcal{R}$ is formed by sampling r sets from a probability distribution such that probability of sampling $\mathcal{A}$ is $\Pr(\mathcal{A}) = cF(\mathcal{A})$, where c is constant. Then,*

$$F(\mathcal{A}^*) - \mathbb{E}F(\mathcal{A}') \leq (\frac{r}{1+r})^r F(\mathcal{A}^*). \tag{8}$$

Proof. Let $p_1, p_2 \ldots p_v$ denote $P(\mathcal{A}_1), P(\mathcal{A}_2) \ldots P(\mathcal{A}_v)$ respectively. Also without loss of generality, we assume $p_1 \geq p_2 \geq \ldots p_v$. Consequently, it follows, $F(\mathcal{A}_1) \geq F(\mathcal{A}_2) \geq \cdots \geq F(\mathcal{A}_v)$. Note $\mathcal{A}^* = \mathcal{A}_1$. The expected value of $F(\mathcal{A}')$ is at least as much as:

$$\mathbb{E}[F(\mathcal{A}')] \geq (1 - (1-p_1)^r)F(\mathcal{A}_1). \tag{9}$$

The term on the right corresponds to the case, when $\mathcal{A}_1$ is sampled at least once in $\mathcal{R}$, then we are guaranteed to get $\mathcal{A}' = \mathcal{A}_1$. The rest of the cases when $\mathcal{A}_1$ is not sampled in $\mathcal{R}$, we ignore, thus giving us the above bound on $\mathbb{E}[F(\mathcal{A}')]$. Thus,

$$F(\mathcal{A}_1) - \mathbb{E}[F(\mathcal{A}')] \leq F(\mathcal{A}_1) - (1-(1-p_1)^r)F(\mathcal{A}_1).$$

Since $cp_1 = F(\mathcal{A}_1)$, the above equation can be written as:

$$F(\mathcal{A}_1) - \mathbb{E}[F(\mathcal{A}')] \leq cp_1 - (1-(1-p_1)^r)cp_1. \tag{10}$$

On differentiating the right hand side with respect to p_1 and equating it to zero, we find that the maxima of right hand size occurs at $p_1 = (1/(r+1))$. Thus substituting this in the above equation we get,

$$F(\mathcal{A}_1) - \mathbb{E}[F(\mathcal{A}')] \leq (r/(r+1))^r F(\mathcal{A}_1).$$

□

The above theorem guarantees that, granted access to a probability distribution such that $\Pr(\mathcal{A}) = cF(\mathcal{A})$, there exists a tight theoretical guarantee for selecting $\mathcal{A}' = \arg\max_{\mathcal{A} \in \mathcal{R}} F(\mathcal{A})$, independent of the problem size.

Directly applying Theorem 4 and Lemma 1 yields the following lemma, which shows that the marginal gain of PartiMax $\Delta_f(i'|\mathcal{A}^S)$ in each iteration is at least $(1 - (\frac{r}{r+1})^r)\Delta_f(i^*|\mathcal{A}^S)$, where $i^* = \arg\max_{i \in \mathcal{X} \setminus \mathcal{A}^S} \Delta(i|\mathcal{A}^S)$.

Lemma 2. *Let* $i^* = \arg\max_{i \in \mathcal{X} \setminus \mathcal{A}^S} \Delta_f(i|\mathcal{A}^S)$ *and let* $i' = \arg\max_{i \in \mathcal{R}} \Delta_f(i|\mathcal{A}^S)$, *where* $\mathcal{R} = \texttt{sampleP}(\texttt{r}, \mathcal{B}', \mathcal{X}, \mathcal{A}^S)$.

$$\Delta_f(i^*|\mathcal{A}^S) - \mathbb{E}\Delta_f(i'|\mathcal{A}^S) \leq (\frac{r}{r+1})^r \Delta_f(i^*|\mathcal{A}^S).$$

Proof. Using $\mathcal{X} \setminus \mathcal{A}^S$ as $\mathcal{A}^+$, i^* as $\mathcal{A}^*$, i' as $\mathcal{A}'$ and applying Theorem 4 and Lemma 1 yields the desired result. □

Lemma 2 in turn yields the following theorem:

Theorem 5.

$$\mathbb{E}[f(\mathcal{A}^S)] \geq (1 - e^{-1} - (r/(r+1)^r))f(\mathcal{A}^*). \tag{11}$$

Proof. Let $\mathcal{A}^* = \{i_1^*, i_2^*, \ldots, i_k^*\}$ and $\mathcal{A}_m^S = \{i_1^S, i_2^S, \ldots, i_m^S\}$ be the solution returned by PartiMax after $m \leq k$ iterations. Let $\mathcal{A}^P = \mathcal{A}^* \setminus \mathcal{A}_m^S = \{i_1^P, \ldots, i_j^P\}$ and let $\mathcal{A}_l^P$ be the first l elements of $\mathcal{A}^P$, with $\mathcal{A}_0^P = \emptyset$. Note that $\mathbb{E}f(\mathcal{A}^* \cup \mathcal{A}_m^S)$ can be expressed as:

$$\mathbb{E}[f(\mathcal{A}^* \cup \mathcal{A}_m^S)] = \mathbb{E}[f(\mathcal{A}_m^S)] + \sum_{l=1}^{j} \mathbb{E}[\Delta_f(i_l^P | \mathcal{A}_m^S \cup \mathcal{A}_{l-1}^P\})].$$

f is monotonic, $\mathbb{E}[f(\mathcal{A}^* \cup \mathcal{A}_m^S)] \geq \mathbb{E}[f(\mathcal{A}^*)]$, and by submodularity, $\sum_{l=1}^{j} \mathbb{E}[\Delta_f(i_l^P | \mathcal{A}_m^S)] \geq \sum_{l=1}^{j} \mathbb{E}[\Delta_f(i_l^P | \mathcal{A}_m^S \cup \mathcal{A}_{l-1}^P\})]$. Thus,

$$\mathbb{E}[f(\mathcal{A}_m^S)] + \sum_{i \in \mathcal{A}^P} \mathbb{E}[\Delta_f(i | \mathcal{A}_m^S)] \geq f(\mathcal{A}^*). \tag{12}$$

From Lemma 2, $\mathbb{E}[f(\mathcal{A}_{m+1}^S) - f(\mathcal{A}_m^S)] \geq \Delta_f(i^* | \mathcal{A}_m^S) - (\frac{r}{r+1})^r \Delta_f(i^* | \mathcal{A}_m^S)$. Also, since $|\mathcal{A}^P| \leq k$,

$$\begin{aligned}\mathbb{E}[f(\mathcal{A}_{m+1}^S) - f(\mathcal{A}_m^S)] + (\frac{r}{r+1})^r \Delta_f(i^* | \mathcal{A}_m^S)) \\ \geq \frac{1}{k}[f(\mathcal{A}^*) - \mathbb{E}[f(\mathcal{A}_m^S)]].\end{aligned} \tag{13}$$

By induction on m the desired result can be obtained. ([Krause and Golovin, 2014; Mirzasoleiman et al., 2015; Satsangi et al., 2015]) □

The above theorem establishes a bound on the error of PartiMax that is independent of the size of the problem and thus remains tight even for large values of n. Furthermore, the above result shows that, as the size of $\mathcal{R}$ increases, PartiMax's performance is guaranteed to converge to that of greedy maximization.

While we have shown these results for PartiMax for selective detection, Theorem 4 is applicable to any problem that involves maximization over a set function where we can sample from a probability distribution such that the probability of sampling a subset $\mathcal{A}$ is directly proportional to the value of that subset specified by the set function F. Also note that Theorem 4 does not make any assumptions about F and is applicable to any set function, submodular or not.

7 EXPERIMENTS

We evaluated PartiMax on a dataset containing approximately 2100 trajectories of people recorded by a camera taking 5120×3840 resolution images running at 6 frames per second [Schutte et al., 2016]. The trajectories were generated using the *ACF* detector [Dollár et al., 2014] and in-camera tracking [Schutte et al., 2016]. These tracks were used to learn the *motion model* of the people walking in the scene, as described below.

We model the state s as the person's position and velocity, $s = \langle x, y, v_x, v_y \rangle$, where x and y describe position and v_x and v_y describe velocity. Both x and y are integers in $\{0, \ldots, 5000\}$. We use a motion model that predicts the next position as:

$$x_{next} = x_{curr} + v_x^{curr} + \mathcal{N}(0, \sigma_x), \tag{14}$$

for x and analogously for y. We use a maximum likelihood estimate of σ_x learned from the data.

Each pixel box was 180×180 and each tiling had a 60×30 offset from the previous one. This offset was chosen because it is the size of the average *bounding box* required to bound a detected person in the scene. This setup yields approximately 7000 pixel boxes per image.

We assume access to a detector that determines with 90% accuracy whether a person is located within a given pixel box and gives a noisy observation about the location of the person if detected. Using the motion model and this detector, we maintain a particle belief $\mathcal{B}$ about the person's location using an unweighted particle filter with 250 particles. Multi-person tracking uses a separate particle filter for each person.

In our experiments, each algorithm selects k pixel boxes to which to apply the detector. To evaluate its performance, we sample a test trajectory from the dataset and try to track the person's movement, starting with a random belief $\mathcal{B}$ and updating it at each timestep using the observations generated from the selected pixel boxes. At each timestep, the agent is asked to predict the position of the person in the scene and gets a reward of +1 for correct predictions and 0 otherwise. Performance is quantified as the total cumulative reward aggregated by the agent at the end of a trajectory over a series of 50 timesteps.

The experiments were run for over 140 trajectories for 8 independent runs for 1 person tracking and 6 independent runs for 3 and 5 person tracking.

As a baseline, we compare against an efficient version of greedy maximization (GM+PCF) (in red in plots) that employs tile coding to maintain the particle coverage of each pixel box. GM+PCF is the same as PartiMax but, instead of selecting the pixel box with the highest particle coverage, in each iteration from $\mathcal{R}$, GM+PCF selects it from $\mathcal{X}$. A naive implementation of greedy maximization that computes the particle coverage of each pixel box in every iteration by going over the entire belief was too slow for a complete run and required 160 seconds to select $k = 40$ from $n = 7200$ for one-person tracking. GM+PCF returns the same solution as greedy maximization but is faster. Simple baselines like downsampling are

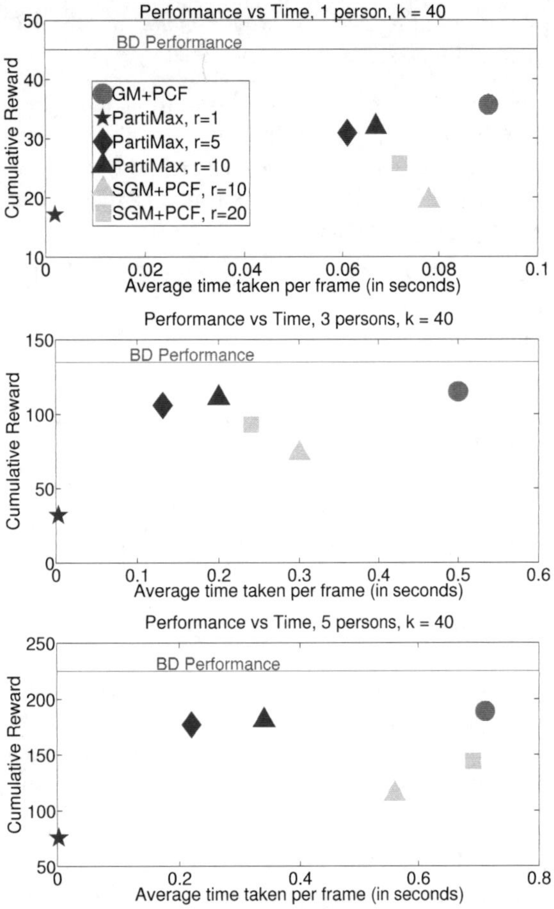

Figure 5: Total correct predictions vs. CPU time (seconds) for tracking one (top), three (middle) and five (bottom) people. The closer to the top-left corner, the better.

not useful as the tracking system must still process thousands of pixel boxes even if the image is downsampled by a factor of 4 or 8. Furthermore, downsampling precludes detection of high level features about the person like the color of his/her clothes, etc., thus defeating the purpose of deploying a high resolution camera.

We also compare to stochastic greedy maximization (in green in the plots) that randomly samples a subset $\mathcal{R}$ from $\mathcal{X}$ but employs tile coding to maintain the particle coverage of each pixel box. A naive implementation of stochastic greedy maximization that computes particle coverage of each pixel box from scratch takes around 0.83 seconds for $k = 40$ and $r = 10$ for one person tracking. The combination of SGM + PCF returns the same solution as stochastic greedy maximization, but faster.

Figure 5 shows a detailed comparison between PartiMax, greedy maximization, and stochastic greedy maximization when tracking 1, 3, or 5 people with $k = 40$. The y-axis shows the cumulative correct predictions averaged over multiple trajectories that the agent made using observations from each algorithm and the x-axis shows the time taken by each algorithm to select 40 out of 7200 pixel boxes. Thus, the top left corner indicates good tracking performance at a low computational cost. The brown line in the figure shows the tracking performance when the brute force detection is used, that is the person detector is applied to the entire image (except the part containing sky), which takes approximately 2.5 seconds.

The blue diamond and triangle at the top left corner of each plot show the superior performance and computational efficiency of PartiMax compared to the baselines. PartiMax not only matches the performance of greedy maximization, it does so extremely efficiently with a low value of r, thanks to the sampling scheme we propose. Stochastic greedy maximization's tracking performance suffers due to its random sampling, while the computational cost of GM+PCF increases with the number of people. PartiMax combines the best of both of these baselines and performs better both in terms of tracking performance and computational cost. In fact, as the number of people in the scene increases, PartiMax scales much better than any other algorithm. Overall, PartiMax is able to retain 80% percent of BD's tracking performance but is at least 10 times faster.

8 CONCLUSIONS & FUTURE WORK

This paper proposed a new tracking system that selectively processes only a fraction of an image to track people in real time. We proposed a new algorithm PartiMax that exploits submodularity to quickly identify the most relevant regions in an image. We applied our tracking system to a real-life dataset and showed that it retains 80% of tracking performance even while processing only a fraction of each image and running in real time. In future we plan to apply PartiMax to sensor selection tasks and other applications that involves maximizing coverage functions.

Acknowledgements

We thank TNO for providing us with the dataset used in our experiments. We also thank the STW User Committee for its advice regarding active perception for tracking systems. This research is supported by the Dutch Technology Foundation STW (project #12622), which is part of the Netherlands Organisation for Scientific Research (NWO), and which is partly funded by the Ministry of Economic Affairs. Frans Oliehoek is funded by NWO Innovational Research Incentives Scheme Veni #639.021.336.

References

A. Badanidiyuru and J. Vondrák. Fast algorithms for maximizing submodular functions. In *ICML*, 2014.

B. Benfold and I. Reid. Stable multi-target tracking in real-time surveillance video. In *CVPR*, 2011.

T.M. Cover and J.A. Thomas. *Entropy, relative entropy and mutual information*. Wiley-Interscience, 1991.

M. Denil, L. Bazzani, H. Larochelle, and N. de Freitas. Learning where to attend with deep architectures for image tracking. *Neural computation*, 2012.

P. Dollár, R. Appel, S. Belongie, and P. Perona. Fast feature pyramids for object detection. *TPAMI*, 36(8), 2014.

A. Doucet, N. De Freitas, and N. Gordon. *Sequential Monte Carlo methods in practice*. Springer Science & Business Media, 2001.

P. Felzenszwalb, Girshick, D McAllester, and D. Ramanan. Object detection with discriminatively trained part-based models. *TPAMI*, 32(9), 2010.

A. Gupta, A. Mittal, and L.S. Davis. Cost: An approach for camera selection and multi-object inference ordering in dynamic scenes. In *ICCV*, 2007.

J. Hosang, M. Omran, R. Beneson, and B. Schiele. Taking a deeper look at pedestrians. In *CVPR*, 2015.

K. Kim, D. Lee, and I. Essa. Detecting regions of interest in dynamic scenes with camera motions. In *CVPR*. IEEE, 2012.

A. Krause and D. Golovin. Submodular function maximization. Cambridge University Press, 2014.

A. Krause and C. Guestrin. Near-optimal nonmyopic value of information in graphical models. In *UAI*, 2005.

M. La Cascia, S. Sclaroff, and V. Athitsos. Fast, reliable head tracking under varying illumination: An approach based on registration of texture-mapped 3D models. *TPAMI*, 2000.

B. Mirzasoleiman, A. Badanidiyuru, A. Karbasi, J. Vondrák, and A. Krause. Lazier than lazy greedy. In *AAAI*, 2015.

V. Mnih, N. Heess, A. Graves, et al. Recurrent models of visual attention. In *NIPS*, 2014.

P. Natarajan, T.N. Hoang, K.H. Low, and M. Kankanhalli. Decision-theoretic approach to maximizing observation of multiple targets in multi-camera surveillance. In *AAMAS*, 2012.

G.L. Nemhauser, L.A. Wolsey, and M.L. Fisher. An analysis of approximations for maximizing submodular set functions. *Mathematical Programming*, 14, 1978.

J. Redmon, S. Divvala, R. Girshick, and A. Farhadi. You only look once: unified real-time object detection. 2016.

Y. Satsangi, S. Whiteson, and F. Oliehoek. Exploiting submodular value functions for faster dynamic sensor selection. In *AAAI*, 2015.

Y. Satsangi, S. Whiteson, and F. Oliehoek. PAC greedy maximization with efficient bounds on information gain for sensor selection. In *IJCAI 2016*, July 2016.

K. Schutte, G. Burghouts, N. Van der Stap, V. Westerwoudt, et al. Long-term behavior understanding based on the expert-based combination of short-term observations in high-resolution CCTV. In *SPIE*, volume 9995, 2016.

E. Shtrom, G. Leifman, and A. Tal. Saliency detection in large point sets. In *ICCV*, 2013.

D. Silver and J. Veness. Monte-Carlo planning in large POMDPs. In *NIPS*, 2010.

A. Smeulders, D. Chu, R. Cucchiara, S. Calderara, A. Dehghan, and M. Shah. Visual tracking: An experimental survey. *TPAMI*, 2014.

M.T.J. Spaan and P.U. Lima. A decision-theoretic approach to dynamic sensor selection in camera networks. In *ICAPS*, 2009.

R.S. Sutton and A.G. Barto. *Reinforcement learning: An introduction*, volume 1. MIT press Cambridge, 1998.

H. Takamura and M. Okumura. Text summarization model based on maximum coverage problem and its variant. In *Conf. Europ. Chapter Assoc. Comp. Ling.*, 2009.

C.-K. Tham and M. Han. Information-driven sensor selection for energy-efficient human motion tracking. In *IEEE Int. Conf. Distr. Comp. in Sensor Syst.*, 2013.

Y. Tian, P. Luo, X. Wang, and X. Tang. Pedestrian detection aided by deep learning semantic tasks. In *CVPR*, 2015.

H. Wang, K. Yao, and D. Estrin. Information-theoretic approaches for sensor selection and placement in sensor networks for target localization and tracking. *IEEE J. Comm. and Networks*, 2005.

J.L. Williams, J.W. Fisher III, and A.S. Willsky. Sensor management for multiple target tracking with heterogeneous sensor models. In *SPIE*, volume 6235, 2006.

J.L. Williams, J.W. Fisher, and A.S. Willsky. Approximate dynamic programming for communication-constrained sensor network management. *IEEE Trans. Signal Proc.*, 55(8), 2007.

Synthesis of strategies in influence diagrams

Manuel Luque and **Manuel Arias** and **Francisco J. Díez**
Dept. Artificial Intelligence, UNED
Juan del Rosal, 16
28040 Madrid, Spain
{mluque,marias,fjdiez}@dia.uned.es

Abstract

Influence diagrams (IDs) are a powerful tool for representing and solving decision problems under uncertainty. The objective of evaluating an ID is to compute the expected utility and an optimal strategy, which consists of a policy for each decision. Every policy is usually represented as a table containing a column for each decision scenario, i.e., for each configuration of the variables on which it depends. The no-forgetting assumption, which implies that the decision maker always remembers all past observations and decisions, makes the policies grow exponentially with the number of variables in the ID. For human experts it is very difficult to understand the strategy contained in huge policy tables, not only for their size, but also because the vast majority of columns correspond to suboptimal or impossible scenarios and are hence irrelevant. This makes it difficult to extract the rules of action, to debug the model, and to convince the experts that the recommendations of the ID are reasonable. In this paper, we propose a method that presents the strategy in the form of a compact tree. It has been implemented in OpenMarkov, an open-source software tool for probabilistic graphical models. This facility was essential when evaluating an influence diagram for the mediastinal staging of non-small cell lung cancer; the optimal strategy, whose biggest policy table contained more than 15,000 columns, was synthesized into a tree of only 5 leaves.

1 INTRODUCTION

Influence diagrams (IDs) are a graphical framework for representing and solving uncertain decision problems (Howard and Matheson, 1984; Bielza et al., 2010). The evaluation of an ID consists in obtaining the expected utility and an optimal strategy, formed by a policy for each decision in the model. Every policy is usually represented by a table containing a column for each decision scenario, i.e., for each configuration of the variables whose values are known when making the decision. For example, the ID in Figure 1 contains two decision nodes, drawn as squares: whether to do a test (T) and whether to apply a therapy (D). It has two chance nodes, drawn as circles that represent the presence of the disease (X) and the result of the test (Y). The domains of these variables are $\{+t, \neg t\}$, $\{+d, \neg d\}$, $\{+x, \neg x\}$, $\{+y, \neg y, np\}$ respectively, where $+y$ denotes a positive result of the test, $\neg y$ a negative result, and np means that the test has not been performed. It also contains two utility nodes, drawn as hexagons, which represent the cost and benefit of the therapy (U_1) and the cost of the test (U_2). Figure 2b shows the optimal policy for the decision D in the form of a table that contains a column for each configuration of T and Y, the variables known when making decision D, as shown in OpenMarkov, an open-source tool for probabilistic graphical models.[1] The two lower rows correspond to the two values for D: $+d$ (apply the therapy) or $\neg d$ (no therapy). They represent a probability distribution for D given each configuration of T and Y. When there is one optimal option, its probability is 1; in OpenMarkov that cell is colored in red. When there is a tie between two or more optimal options, all of them are assigned the same probability. The optimal policy for decision T is shown in Figure 2a. The optimal strategy consists of these two policy tables.

This way of representing the strategy faces several problems. First, the no-forgetting assumption, which implies that the decision maker always remembers all past observations and decisions, makes the policy tables grow exponentially with the number of variables known when making them. In our example, the policy for D in Figure 2b contains $3 \times 2 = 6$ columns. Second, many of the columns in the table may correspond to scenarios that are impossible due to structural constraints of the problem. Thus, when we decide not to do the test ($T = \neg t$), the test results

[1] See `www.openmarkov.org`.

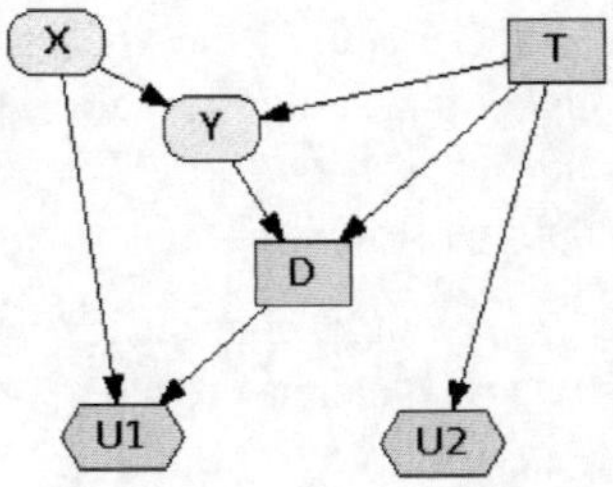

Figure 1: An ID for the decide-test problem.

+t	1
¬t	0

(a) Policy for T.

T	¬t	¬t	¬t	+t	+t	+t
Y	np	¬y	+y	np	¬y	+y
+d	0	0.5	0.5	0.5	0	1
¬d	1	0.5	0.5	0.5	1	0

(b) Policy for D.

Figure 2: Optimal policy tables for the ID in Figure 1. Different numerical parameters in the ID may lead to different optimal policies, but the structure of the tables would always be the same.

$Y = +y$ and $Y = \neg y$ are impossible; when we decide to do it, the value $Y = np$ (test not performed) is impossible. Therefore, three of the columns in Figure 2b are irrelevant, regardless of the numerical parameters of the problem (sensitivity, specificity, costs, etc.) and should be removed from the table. Third, depending on the values of the numerical parameters, some columns may correspond to suboptimal scenarios. This is the case for the column $\{T = \neg t, Y = np\}$ when the optimal decision is to do the test and for the columns $\{T = +t, Y = +y\}$ and $\{T = +t, Y = \neg t\}$ when the optimal decision is to do it. Therefore, in this example only one or two out of the 6 columns in Figure 2b are relevant for the optimal strategy.

In general, the proportion of irrelevant columns grows exponentially with the number of variables. For example, MEDIASTINET is an influence diagram for lung cancer (it is explained in further detail in Sec. 3.3.2); the policy table for the last decision in this ID contains 15,552 columns, but only 5 of them make part for the optimal strategy; even worse, the relevant columns cannot be detected by just analyzing this table, because they depend on the probabilities of its configurations and on the optimal policies for previous decisions. The problem is that standard algorithms for the evaluation of IDs only return the policy tables, without being able to extract the relevant columns nor to combine the optimal choices for different decisions into a single representation that can be easily understood by human experts.

For this reason, we have developed an algorithm that builds a strategy tree by using dynamic programming; more precisely, it extends the variable elimination algorithm described by Jensen and Nielsen (2007) and refined by Luque and Díez (2010). The version proposed in this paper builds the strategy tree at the same time it operates with the probability and utility potentials to compute the maximum expected utility.

The remainder of this paper is structured as follows. Section 2 presents the definitions of influence diagrams and their evaluation. Section 3 presents the algorithm for computing the tree representation of the strategy. Section 4 contains the conclusions and proposes some lines for future research.

2 FOUNDATIONS

2.1 INFLUENCE DIAGRAMS

In this paper a capital letter (X) denotes a variable and a lower-case letter (x) a generic value of the corresponding variable. A bold capital letter ($\mathbf{X}$) denotes a set of variables and a bold lower-case letter ($\mathbf{x}$) a configuration of them. When there is an arc $X \rightarrow Y$ in a graph, we say that X is a parent of Y and Y is a child of X. $Pa(X)$ is the set of parents of X and $pa(X)$ is a configuration of $Pa(X)$.

Influence diagrams (Howard and Matheson, 1984) are a framework for representing and solving probabilistic decision problems. Formally, an *influence diagram* (ID) consists of an acyclic directed graph having three disjoint sets of nodes: decisions ($\mathbf{V}_D$), chance nodes ($\mathbf{V}_C$) and utility nodes ($\mathbf{V}_U$). Decision nodes represent the actions that are under the direct control of the decision maker; they are represented graphically as squares or rectangles. Chance nodes represent uncertain events; they are drawn as ovals or rounded rectangles. Utility nodes quantify the decision maker's preferences and are depicted as diamonds or hexagons. In medical IDs, utility nodes represent health outcomes (quality of life, morbidity, mortality...), and sometimes economic costs. The parents of a node can only be of type chance or decision, i.e., utility nodes have no children.

An ID contains three types of arcs, depending on the type of node they go into. Arcs into chance nodes represent probabilistic dependencies. Arcs into decision nodes represent availability of information or temporal precedence between decisions; thus, an arc from a node X into a decision node D means that the value taken by X is known when making the decision. Arcs into utility nodes indicate the domain of the associated utility functions.

We assume that a directed path connects all the decision nodes, which induces a total ordering of the decisions, $\{D_1, D_2, \ldots, D_n\}$. This order partitions $\mathbf{V}_C$ into a collection of disjoint subsets, $\{\mathbf{C}_0, \mathbf{C}_1, \ldots, \mathbf{C}_n\}$, and induces a *partial order* $\prec$ in $\mathbf{V}_C \cup \mathbf{V}_D$:

$$\mathbf{C}_0 \prec \{D_1\} \prec \mathbf{C}_1 \prec \ldots \prec \{D_n\} \prec \mathbf{C}_n . \quad (1)$$

The variables known to the decision maker when deciding on D_j are called *informational predecessors* of D_j and denoted *iPred*(D_j). We assume the *no-forgetting* hypothesis, which states that the decision maker remembers all previous decisions and observations. In particular, *iPred*(D_j) is the set of variables that occurs before D_j under $\prec$: *iPred*$(D_j) = \mathbf{C}_0 \cup \{D_1\} \cup \mathbf{C}_1 \cup \ldots \cup \{D_{j-1}\} \cup \mathbf{C}_{j-1}$.

The quantitative information that defines an ID is given by: (1) a conditional probability $P(X|pa(X))$ assigned to each chance node X for each configuration of its parents, $pa(X)$, and (2) a potential $\psi_U(pa(U))$ assigned to each utility node U, which maps each configuration of its parents onto a real number. (A *potential* is a real-valued function over a set of variables.) When there are several utility nodes in the ID, we assume that there is an implicit sum among them.

2.2 EVALUATION OF IDs

2.2.1 Policies and strategies

A *policy* for a decision D is a probability distribution defined over D and conditioned on the set of its informational predecessors, $P_D(d|iPred(D))$. If P_D is degenerate, i.e., consisting of only ones and zeros, we say that the policy is *deterministic*; otherwise, we say it is *stochastic*.

A *strategy* Δ for an ID is a set of policies, one for each decision, $\{P_D \mid D \in \mathbf{V}_D\}$. If every policy in the strategy Δ is deterministic, then Δ is said to be *deterministic*; otherwise Δ is *stochastic*.

A strategy Δ *induces* a joint probability distribution over $\mathbf{V}_C \cup \mathbf{V}_D$ defined as follows:

$$P_\Delta(\mathbf{v}_C, \mathbf{v}_D) = P(\mathbf{v}_C \mid \mathbf{v}_D) \prod_{D \in \mathbf{V}_D} P_D(d|iPred(D)) \,. \tag{2}$$

where $P(\mathbf{v}_C \mid \mathbf{v}_D)$ is the product of the conditional probabilities:

$$P(\mathbf{v}_C \mid \mathbf{v}_D) = \prod_{X \in \mathbf{V}_C} P(x|pa(X)) \,.$$

We define the *expected utility under the strategy* Δ, denoted by EU(Δ), as:

$$\text{EU}(\Delta) = \sum_{\mathbf{v}_C} \sum_{\mathbf{v}_D} P_\Delta(\mathbf{v}_C, \mathbf{v}_D)\, \psi(\mathbf{v}_C, \mathbf{v}_D). \tag{3}$$

where $\psi(\mathbf{v}_C, \mathbf{v}_D)$ is the sum of the utilities:

$$\psi(\mathbf{v}_C, \mathbf{v}_D) = \sum_{U \in \mathbf{V}_U} \psi_U(pa(X)) \,.$$

An *optimal strategy* is a strategy Δ_{opt} that maximizes the expected utility:

$$\Delta_{opt} = \arg\max_{\Delta \in \boldsymbol{\Delta}} \text{EU}(\Delta), \tag{4}$$

where $\boldsymbol{\Delta}$ is the set of all the strategies for the ID. Each policy in an optimal strategy is said to be an *optimal policy*. The *maximum expected utility* (*MEU*) is the expected utility under an optimal strategy.

The evaluation of an ID consists in finding the *MEU* and an optimal strategy. It can be proved (Cowell et al., 1999) that

$$MEU = \sum_{\mathbf{c}_0} \max_{d_1} \ldots \max_{d_n} \sum_{\mathbf{c}_n} P(\mathbf{v}_C \mid \mathbf{v}_D)\, \psi(\mathbf{v}_C, \mathbf{v}_D) \,. \tag{5}$$

The optimal policy for decision D_i is (in the case of a tie, any of the values of D_i that maximize that expression can be arbitrarily chosen):

$$\delta_{D_i}(\text{iPred}(D_i)) = \arg\max_{d_i \in D_i} \sum_{\mathbf{c}_i} \max_{d_{i+1}} \ldots \sum_{\mathbf{c}_{n-1}} \max_{d_n} \sum_{\mathbf{c}_n} P(\mathbf{v}_C \mid \mathbf{v}_D)\, \psi(\mathbf{v}_C, \mathbf{v}_D) \,. \tag{6}$$

2.2.2 Variable elimination

One of the algorithms for evaluating IDs is variable elimination with division of potentials (Jensen and Nielsen, 2007). It operates on the set of probability potentials $\mathbf{\Phi}$ and the set utility potentials $\mathbf{\Psi}$ of the ID by eliminating the variables in the opposite order of $\prec$: first each of the variables in $\mathbf{C}_n$, then D_n, then those in $\mathbf{C}_{n-1}$, then D_{n-1}, etc., as indicated in line 5 of Algorithm 1. It returns the *MEU* and an optimal strategy, in the form of a set of policies, $\boldsymbol{\Delta}$—see also (Luque and Díez, 2010) for a more detailed explanation and justification of this algorithm.

3 SYNTHESIZING THE STRATEGY

3.1 DEFINITION OF STRATEGY TREE

In this section we show that, instead of representing the strategy as a set of policy tables, it is more efficient to use a *strategy tree*, which by definition has the following properties:

1. it has three types of nodes: chance, decision and *nil*;
2. every non-terminal node X represents a decision or a chance variable of the ID (but several chance nodes in the tree may correspond to the same node in the ID);
3. every terminal node is *nil* and its parent is a decision;
4. each decision node has exactly one child;
5. the ancestors of a decision node D in the tree are informational predecessors of D in the ID; and
6. each arc outgoing from a node X is labeled with a non-empty subset of states of X, and each state labels at most one arc.

1 **Function** `variableElimination(ID)`:
   Result: $\{MEU, \mathbf{\Delta}\}$
2 $\mathbf{\Phi} \leftarrow$ probability potentials in the ID;
3 $\mathbf{\Psi} \leftarrow$ utility potentials in the ID;
4 $\mathbf{\Delta} \leftarrow \varnothing$; // strategy (set of policies)
5 $\mathbf{V} \leftarrow$ ordered array of $\{\mathbf{V}_C \cup \mathbf{V}_D\}$;
6 **while** $\mathbf{V}$ *is not empty* **do**
7     $X \leftarrow$ first variable in $\mathbf{V}$;
8   // take out the potentials that depend on X
9     $\mathbf{\Phi}_X \leftarrow \{\phi \in \mathbf{\Phi} \mid X \in dom(\phi)\}$;
10     $\mathbf{\Phi} \leftarrow \mathbf{\Phi} \setminus \mathbf{\Phi}_\mathbf{X}$;
11     $\mathbf{\Psi}_X \leftarrow \{\psi \in \mathbf{\Psi} \mid X \in dom(\psi)\}$;
12     $\mathbf{\Psi} \leftarrow \mathbf{\Psi} \setminus \mathbf{\Psi}_\mathbf{X}$;
13   // compute the joint probability and the total
14   // utility for the potentials that depend on X
15     $\phi_{\text{joint}} \leftarrow \prod_{\phi \in \mathbf{\Phi}_X} \phi$;
16     $\psi_{\text{total}} \leftarrow \sum_{\psi \in \mathbf{\Psi}_X} \psi$;
17   **if** $X \in \mathbf{V_C}$ **then**
18         $\phi_{\text{marg}} \leftarrow \sum_x \phi_{\text{joint}}$;
19         $\phi_{\text{cond}} \leftarrow \phi_{\text{joint}} / \phi_{\text{marg}}$;
20         $\psi_{\text{new}} \leftarrow \sum_x \phi_{\text{cond}} \cdot \psi_{\text{total}}$;
21   **else** // X is a decision
22   // then ϕ_{joint} does not depend on X
23         $\phi_{\text{marg}} \leftarrow \text{project}_x\, \phi_{\text{joint}}$;
24         $\psi_{\text{new}} \leftarrow \max_x \psi_{\text{total}}$;
25   // find the optimal policy for this decision
26         $\delta_X \leftarrow \arg\max_x \psi_{\text{total}}$;
27         $\mathbf{\Delta} \leftarrow \mathbf{\Delta} \cup \{\delta_X\}$;
28   // store the new potentials
29     $\mathbf{\Phi} \leftarrow \mathbf{\Phi} \cup \{\phi_{\text{marg}}\}$
30     $\mathbf{\Psi} \leftarrow \mathbf{\Psi} \cup \{\psi_{\text{new}}\}$
31 $\psi_{\text{final}} \leftarrow \sum_{\psi \in \mathbf{\Psi}_X} \psi$
32 // ψ_{final} does not depend on any variable;
33 // it contains just one value
34 *MEU* $\leftarrow$ first value of ψ_{final}
35 **return** $\{\text{MEU}, \mathbf{\Delta}\}$

Algorithm 1: Variable elimination with division of potentials.

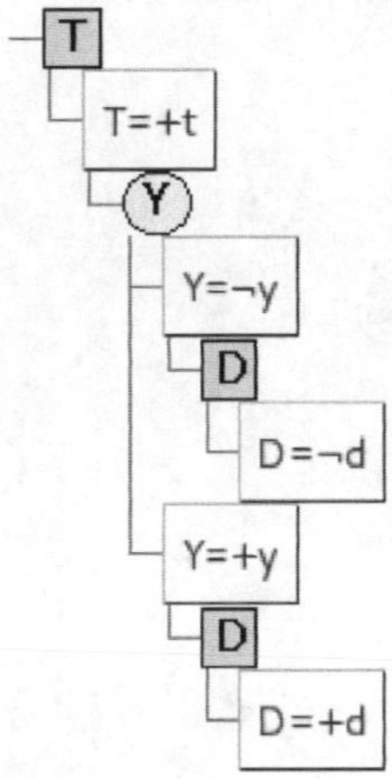

Figure 3: A strategy tree for the ID in Figure 1 as shown in OpenMarkov. Terminal nodes are not displayed because they convey no information. The size and structure of the optimal strategy depends on the numerical parameters of the ID.

Figure 3 shows a strategy tree for the ID in Figure 1.

3.2 ALGORITHM FOR BUILDING THE STRATEGY TREE

In the original variable elimination method (Algorithm 1) each probability potential assigns a real number to each configuration of its variables, $\phi(\mathbf{x}) \in \mathbb{R}$, and the same holds for utility potentials, $\psi(\mathbf{x}) \in \mathbb{R}$. However, the modified version that we present in this paper operates with *extended utility potentials*, such that $\psi^*(\mathbf{x}) = (u, s) \in \mathbb{R} \times \mathcal{S}$, where $\mathcal{S}$ is the space of strategies (in the form of trees). We denote by $u(\psi^*(\mathbf{x}))$ and $s(\psi^*(\mathbf{x}))$ the utility and the strategy of ψ^*, respectively, for configuration $\mathbf{x}$. We describe now the modifications that must be introduced in the algorithm. We do not discuss the computation of utilities because it is the same as in the original version.

3.2.1 Initialization

In line 3 of Algorithm 1 the utility potentials must be extended by assigning to each configuration $\mathbf{x}$ the strategy tree that only contains one node, *nil*. The utility does not change: $u(\psi^*(\mathbf{x})) = \psi(\mathbf{x})$.

3.2.2 Elimination of a decision

The elimination of decision D is determined by the potential $\psi^*_{\text{total}}(d, \mathbf{y})$—cf. line 24 in Algorithm 1—where $\mathbf{Y}$ is the set of variables that coexist with D in at least one potential. In the same way as the utility is computed by taking the highest utility and discarding the others, the strategy $s(\psi^*_{\text{new}}(\mathbf{y}))$ is built by making D the root of the tree and drawing one branch labeled with $x = \arg\max_{x'} u(\psi^*_{\text{total}}(x', \mathbf{y}))$. For example, when eliminating

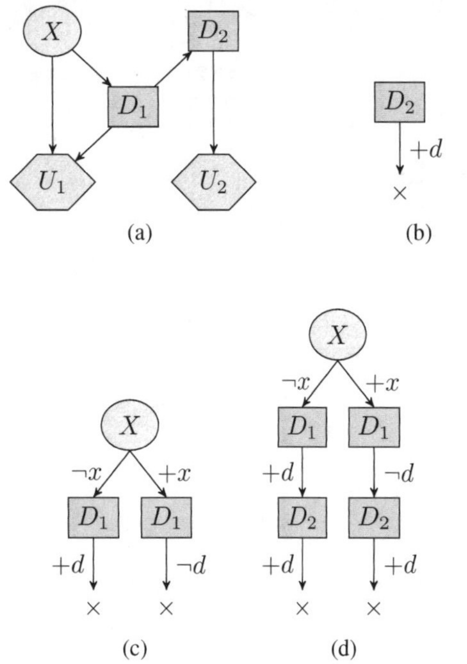

Figure 4: (a) An influence diagram with two decisions; the order is $X \prec D_1 \prec D_2$. (b) Strategy in the potential ψ_2^* obtained when eliminating D_2. (c) Strategy in the potential ψ_1^* obtained after eliminating D_1 and X. (d) Strategy in the potential $[\psi_1^* + \psi_2^*](x)$ computed at line 31 in Algorithm 1; it is built by replacing each *nil* node in (c) with the tree in (b).

D_2 for the ID in Figure 4b, $\mathbf{Y} = \varnothing$ and $s(\psi^*_{\text{new}}(\blacklozenge))$ is the tree shown in Figure 4b—"♦" is the only configuration of the empty set.

In the case of a tie between two or more states of X, it is possible to label the branch with all of them instead of randomly selecting one; users should be informed that when a branch outgoing from a decision is labeled with several states it means that they are all optimal and it is indifferent to choose any of them.

Please note that in the modified version of Algorithm 1 lines 26 and 27 should be removed because now it is not necessary to build a policy table for any decision.

3.2.3 Elimination of a chance variable

The elimination of a chance variable X is performed by multiplying a conditional probability $\phi_{\text{cond}}(x|\mathbf{y})$ and an extended utility potential $\psi^*_{\text{total}}(x, \mathbf{y})$ and then marginalizing for X in order to obtain $s(\psi_{\text{new}}(\mathbf{y}))$—cf. line 20 in Algorithm 1—where $\mathbf{Y}$ is the set of variables coexisting with X in at least one potential. In the most simple case, the strategy for each configuration $\mathbf{y}$ is built by making X the root of the tree and adding a branch for each state x and copying $s(\psi^*_{\text{total}}(x, \mathbf{y}))$ in that branch. For example, when eliminating X for the ID in Figure 4b, the two decisions have already been eliminated and $\mathbf{Y} = \varnothing$; $s(\psi^*_{\text{new}}(\blacklozenge))$ is the tree shown in Figure 4c.

However, it is often possible to build a simplified tree by applying these rules:

1. When no decision has been eliminated yet, $s(\psi^*_{\text{total}}(x, \mathbf{y})) = nil$ for all x. In this case, it is more efficient to make $s(\psi_{\text{new}}(\mathbf{y})) = nil$, because it does not make sense to include in the strategy tree a variable that is not an informational predecessor of any decision. This is the reason why the strategy in Figure 3 does not contain any node for variable X (*Disease*), whose value is never known.

2. When $\phi_{\text{cond}}(x|\mathbf{y}) = 0$, the value x must not generate a branch. For example, the node Y in Figure 3 has no outgoing branch for np because when the test is done the probability of "test not performed" is 0. This way the algorithm avoids adding branches corresponding to impossible scenarios.

3. When $\phi_{\text{cond}}(x|\mathbf{y}) = 1$ for a certain value x, X must not make part of the strategy—at least for configuration $\mathbf{y}$—and we should just make $s(\psi_{\text{new}}(\mathbf{y})) = s(\psi^*_{\text{total}}(x, \mathbf{y}))$. The reason is that a variable that can only take one value in a certain scenario does not contribute any information and would be unnecessary in the strategy tree. For example, if the optimal decision for T in the ID of Figure 1 were $\neg t$ (not to do the test) the probability of $Y = np$ (test not performed) would be 1 and it would not make sense to include Y and its only branch, np, in the strategy.

4. When there are two states x_1 and x_2 such that $s(\psi^*_{\text{total}}(x_1, \mathbf{y})) = s(\psi^*_{\text{total}}(x_2, \mathbf{y}))$, both of them must be put in the same branch (instead of having two branches with the same strategy).

3.2.4 Sum of extended utility potentials

In lines 16 and 31 the modified version of Algorithm 1 has to sum extended utility potentials. Let $\psi_1^*(\mathbf{x}_1)$ and $\psi_2^*(\mathbf{x}_2)$ be two such potentials, $\mathbf{x}$ a configuration of $\mathbf{X} = \mathbf{X}_1 \cup \mathbf{X}_2$, $s_1 = s(\psi_1^*(\mathbf{x}^{\downarrow \mathbf{X}_1}))$—where $\mathbf{x}^{\downarrow \mathbf{X}_1}$ is the projection of $\mathbf{x}$ onto $\mathbf{X}_1$, i.e., the configuration of $\mathbf{X}_1$ compatible with $\mathbf{x}$—and $s_2 = s(\psi_2^*(\mathbf{x}^{\downarrow X_2}))$. The strategy $s([\psi_1 + \psi_2](\mathbf{x}))$ is the result of connecting s_1 and s_2 by adding arcs from the leaves of the one to the root of the other, as shown in Figure 4d.

3.2.5 Termination

In the traditional version of variable elimination, ψ_{final} is obtained after eliminating all the variables (line 31). Hence, we have $MEU = \psi_{\text{final}}(\blacklozenge)$. Analogously, in the modified version we have $MEU = u(\psi^*_{\text{final}}(\blacklozenge))$ and the optimal strategy is $s(\psi^*_{\text{final}}(\blacklozenge))$.

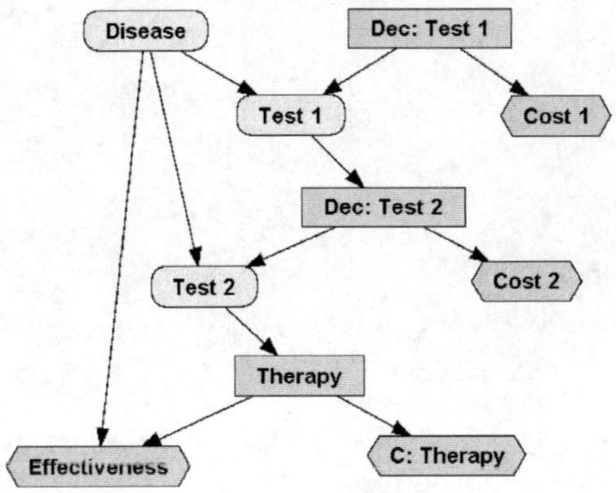

Figure 5: An ID for a hypothetical medical problem.

The interpretation of the tree returned by the algorithm is straightforward by reading each chance node as an "if" statement. For example, the strategy shown in Figure 3 can be read as follows: "do the test; if the result is positive, apply the therapy; if it is negative, do not apply it".

3.3 MORE COMPLEX EXAMPLES

3.3.1 AN ID WITH TWO TESTS

Let us extend the above example by adding a second test, such as the result of the first (when performed) is available before deciding whether to do the second, as shown in Figure 1. There are two therapies, incompatible with each other, which implies that there is only one decision about therapy, with three possible values: *therapy 1*, *therapy 2*, and *no therapy*.

Each decision about a test has two possible values (to do it or not) and the result of each test has three possible values (*positive*, *negative*, and *not performed*). Therefore, the policy table for *Therapy* has $2 \times 3 \times 2 \times 3 = 36$ columns, regardless of the numerical parameters of the model (sensitivities, specificities, costs, etc.). However, the optimal strategy does not depend on the parameters. For example, just by multiplying the three costs by a common factor—i.e., keeping the proportion among them—we may obtain 6 different strategies; four of them are shown in Figure 6. When the costs are very high, the optimal strategy is not to do any test nor to apply any therapy (Fig. 6a); in this case, the strategy tree contains just one node. In other cases the optimal strategy tree has up to 23 nodes, with 4 leaves. These trees show the optimal strategy much more clearly than the set of three policy tables, having 1, 6, and 36 columns respectively; we should note that even though this is a very small ID, the proportion of irrelevant columns in the last table ranges from 88% to 97%, depending on the numerical parameters.

3.3.2 MEDIASTINET

MEDIASTINET (Luque et al., 2016a) is an ID for the mediastinal staging of non-small cell lung cancer, which consists in determining whether there is metastasis in the mediastinum (this is represented by node *N2_N3* in Fig. 7), because it is the key factor for selecting a therapy for this type of cancer. Initially a CT scan is performed to all patients; the result is represented by the node *CT_scan*. Then the doctor can perform different diagnostic tests—*TBNA*, *PET*, *EBUS*, *EUS*, and mediastinoscopy (*MED*)— and then decides which *Treatment* to apply. Therefore, the ID contains 8 chance variables and 5 decisions; the number of columns in their respective policy tables is 2, 12, 72, 1,296, and 15,552. The number of relevant columns is 2 (100%), 3 (25%), 3 (4.2%), 5 (0.39%), and 5 (0.032%, i.e., 1 in every 3,110).

Given that the algorithm presented in this paper has been incorporated into the most recent version of OpenMarkov, we invite the reader to try it as follows: download the ID MEDIASTINET,[2] open it with OpenMarkov, compile it (with the thunder button), accepting the default values to convert it into a unicriterion problem, right-click on the last decision and have a look at the optimal policy table. Then click the S button and check that the strategy tree only contains 5 leaves, as shown in Figure 8.

4 CONCLUSIONS AND FUTURE WORK

A problem of representing the optimal strategy as a set of policy tables is that their size grows exponentially with the number of informational predecessors for each decision. The first attempt to alleviate it was to transform each policy table into a list-based representation (Fernández del Pozo et al., 2005), but this approach is unsatisfactory because those lists can still be very large and because the issue is not how to compact the whole table, but how to present the few relevant columns intuitively, which cannot not be found out by examining each single policy.

The approach presented in this paper is completely different: it represents each strategy as a tree (instead of a set of tables) and uses an extended version of the variable elimination algorithm (Jensen and Nielsen, 2007) that builds the tree at the same time as it computes the maximum expected utility. Other inference algorithms, such as arc reversal (Olmsted, 1983), can be adapted in the same way.

Our algorithm has been incorporated to OpenMarkov, an open-source tool for probabilistic graphical models. In this paper we have applied it to two toy examples and to MEDIASTINET, an influence diagram for a real medical problem (Luque et al., 2016a), whose policy table for the last decision contained more than 15,000 columns; in contrast,

[2] `www.probmodelxml.org/networks/id/ID-mediastinet-ce.pgmx`.

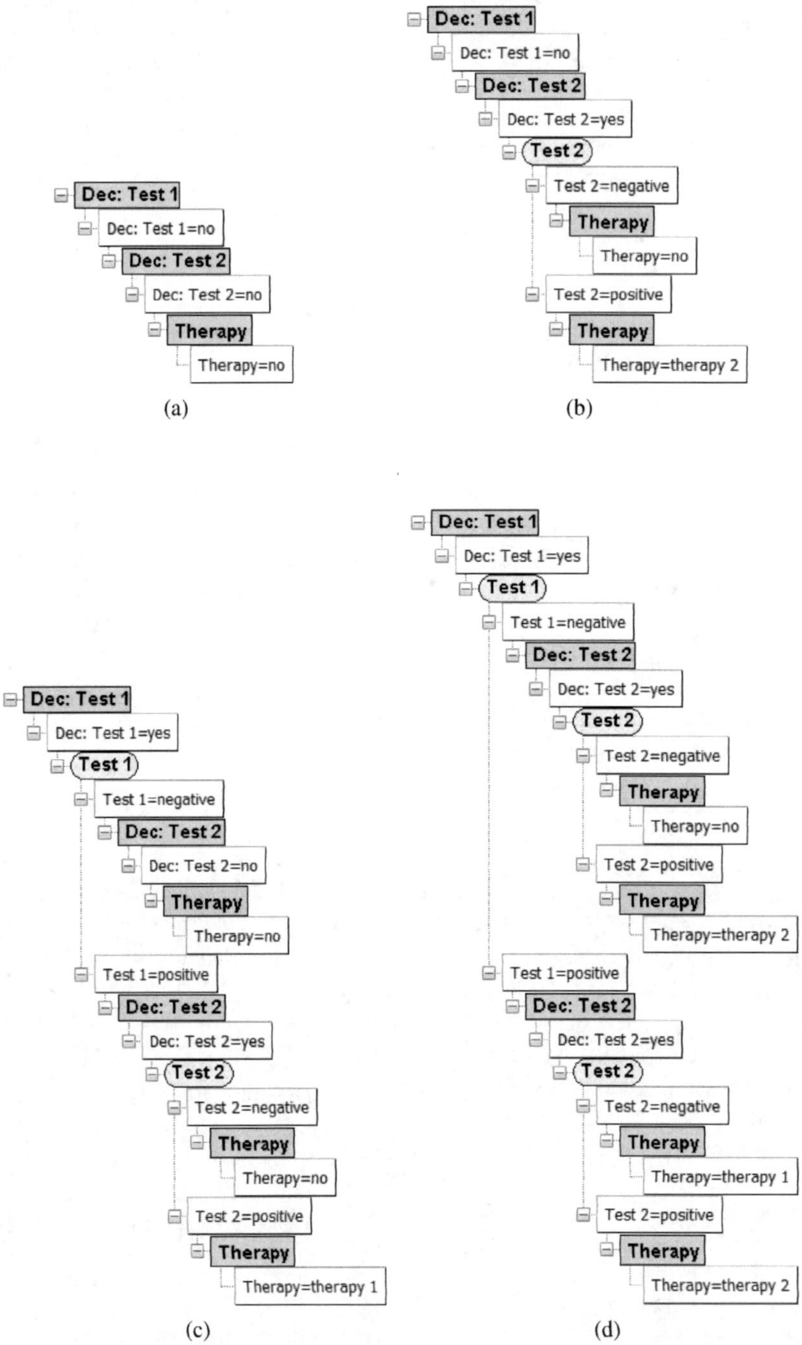

Figure 6: Optimal strategy trees for different assignments of costs for the ID in Figure 5.

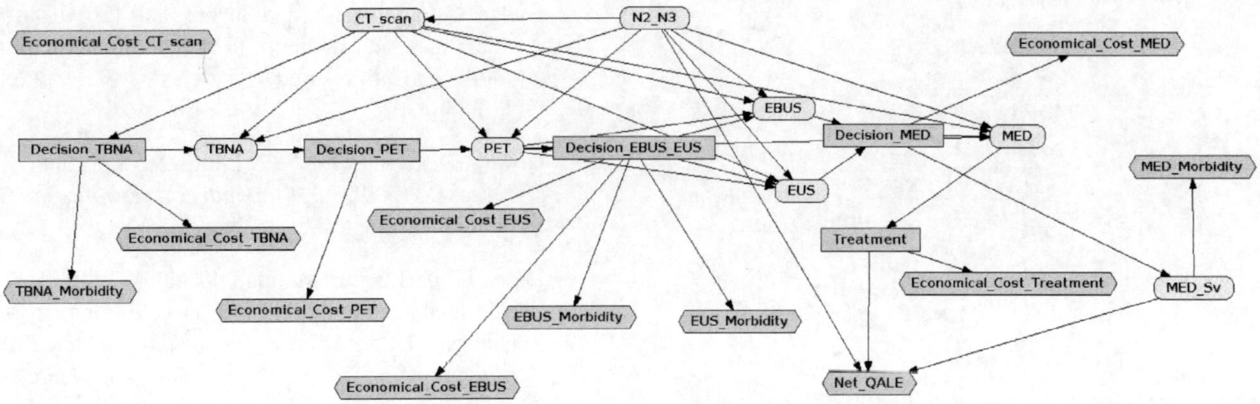

Figure 7: Influence diagram of MEDIASTINET.

the strategy tree for this ID contains only 5 leaves, which proves that only 0.03% of the columns in that table are relevant.

A limitation of the construction of the strategy tree is that in the worst case the number of leaves grows exponentially with the number of chance variables that are informational predecessors of the last decision—previous decisions do not increase the number of leaves because each decision node in the tree has just one outgoing branch—but, as we have seen in the examples, the tree is usually much smaller.

An open line for future research is how to reduce the size of the strategy tree, because there are some problems for which the resulting tree, even though much smaller than the policy tables, is still large—for instance, in the ID Arthronet.[3] In some cases reordering the chance variables between consecutive decisions might lead to significant reductions. Another approach would be to apply coalescence (Olmsted, 1983), i.e., to collapse the subtrees that appear several times in the tree. For example, in Figure 8 there are two identical subtrees having *Decision_PET* as the root; collapsing them would transform the tree into an acyclic directed graph with only 3 leaves.

Another research topic is to adapt this method to other representation frameworks for uncertain decision problems, such as decision analysis networks (DANs), an alternative to IDs for asymmetric decision problems (Díez et al., 2012), and Markov IDs (Díez et al., 2017), an extension of IDs especially designed for cost-effective analysis in health economics.

We are interested in evaluating the proposed algorithm on a large set of models. But, given that there are very few real-world non-small IDs, we will have to find a method for randomly generating IDs whose structure is similar to those we would expect to find in real-world problems. One possibility for addressing this issue would be to use parametrized templates, as in (Luque et al., 2016b).

Acknowledgments

This work has been supported by the Spanish Government under grants TIN2009-09158, PI13/02446, and TIN2016-77206-R, and co-financed by the European Regional Development Fund. We wish to thank the members of our research group for many fruitful discussions. We also thank all developers of OpenMarkov for providing a basis for our implementation.

[3] www.probmodelxml.org/networks/id/ID-arthronet-ce.pgmx.

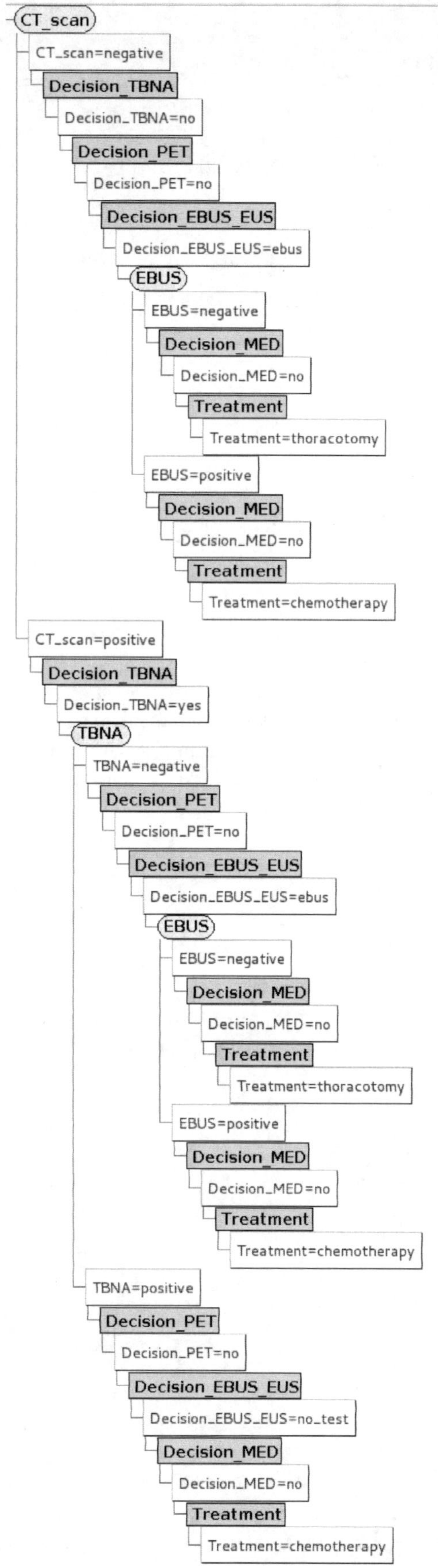

Figure 8: Optimal strategy tree for MEDIASTINET.

References

Bielza, C., Gómez, M., and Shenoy, P. P. (2010). Modeling challenges with influence diagrams: Constructing probability and utility models. *Decision Support Systems*, 49:354 – 364.

Cowell, R. G., Dawid, A. P., Lauritzen, S. L., and Spiegelhalter, D. J. (1999). *Probabilistic Networks and Expert Systems*. Springer-Verlag, New York.

Díez, F. J., Luque, M., and König, C. (2012). Decision analysis networks. In Cano, A., Gómez, M., and Nielsen, T. D., editors, *Proceedings of the Sixth European Workshop on Probabilistic Graphical Models (PGM'12)*, pages 83–90, Granada, Spain.

Díez, F. J., Yebra, M., Bermejo, I., Palacios-Alonso, M. A., Arias, M., Luque, M., and Pérez-Martín, J. (2017). Markov influence diagrams: A graphical tool for cost-effectiveness analysis. *Medical Decision Making*, 37:183–195.

Fernández del Pozo, J. A., Bielza, C., and Gómez, M. (2005). A list-based compact representation for large decision tables management. *European Journal of Operational Research*, 160:638–662.

Howard, R. A. and Matheson, J. E. (1984). Influence diagrams. In Howard, R. A. and Matheson, J. E., editors, *Readings on the Principles and Applications of Decision Analysis*, pages 719–762. Strategic Decisions Group, Menlo Park, CA.

Jensen, F. V. and Nielsen, T. D. (2007). *Bayesian Networks and Decision Graphs*. Springer-Verlag, New York, second edition.

Luque, M. and Díez, F. J. (2010). Variable elimination for influence diagrams with super-value nodes. *International Journal of Approximate Reasoning*, 51:615 – 631.

Luque, M., Díez, F. J., and Disdier, C. (2016a). Optimal sequence of tests for the mediastinal staging of non-small cell lung cancer. *BMC Medical Informatics and Decision Making*, 16:1–14.

Luque, M., Nielsen, T. D., and Jensen, F. V. (2016b). Anytime decision-making based on unconstrained influence diagrams. *International Journal of Intelligent Systems*, 31:379–398.

Olmsted, S. M. (1983). *On Representing and Solving Decision Problems*. PhD thesis, Dept. Engineering-Economic Systems, Stanford University, CA.

Embedding Senses via Dictionary Bootstrapping

Byungkon Kang
byungkon@ajou.ac.kr
Ajou University
Suwon, Korea

Kyung-Ah Sohn
kasohn@ajou.ac.kr
Ajou University
Suwon, Korea

Abstract

This paper addresses the problem of embedding senses of a plain word according to its context. Natural language is inherently ambiguous, due to the presence of many multi-sensed words. Such ambiguity might have undesirable influence over many text-mining tools, including word embedding. Traditional word embedding techniques have focused on identifying which words tend to co-occur with one another in order to derive close embeddings for such words. However, the effectiveness of this approach is largely susceptible to the validity and neutrality of the training corpus. To address this problem, we propose to use the dictionary as the authoritative corpus for computing the word embeddings. The basic idea is to simultaneously embed the definition sentence while disambiguating words. Since dictionaries list a set of disambiguated senses, the proposed procedure yields sense embeddings which exhibit semantic characteristics comparable to plain word embeddings.

1 INTRODUCTION

Recent advances in neural network technology have influenced the field of natural language processing (NLP) to progress towards using distributed representations for solving its problems. One notable example is the concept of *word embedding*, or word vectors, popularized by Mikolov et al. [2013]. This framework allows one to represent the semantics of each word in the vocabulary as a Euclidean vector. The basic concept is to have words with similar semantics be "embedded" as nearby points in the Euclidean space. The initial success of Mikolov et al. [2013] has led to the proposal of many variants (Hill et al. [2016], Iacobacci et al. [2015], Pennington et al. [2014]).

The advantage of operating with embedding vectors is that they allow for continuous operations, which are prevalent in most machine learning algorithms, to be applied to discrete objects. For example, one many take a dot product between any two word vectors to measure the similarity.

However, word embeddings are likely to suffer from corrupted samples. To be more concrete, most current algorithms used to embed words are heavily dependent on the corpora they use. The embedding algorithms work by taking co-occurrence statistics of words, and computes a set of vectors that best reflects such co-occurrences. Naturally, words that co-occur frequently will tend to have close-by vector representations. In other words, socio-linguistic norms are likely to influence the embeddings. While this approach may bear intuitive justification, it can sometimes have detrimental effects: Report by Bolukbasi et al. [2016] indicates that such word embeddings inadvertently exhibit sexist relationships.

Another shortcoming of word embedding is related to the processing of out-of-vocabulary (OOV) words. OOV words are words that have not been seen during the training phase of the embedding. Since OOV words lack sufficient amount of context on which embedding computation is based, there is not enough information to derive the embedding. Algorithms such as Skipthought (Kiros et al. [2015]) attempt to work around this issue by performing linear regression to extrapolate new vectors for the OOV word. Techniques motivated by morphological analysis exist as well (Zhang et al. [2015]), where convolution is performed on character level of the word to extract meaningful representation inherent in the morphemes. However, such methods are either approximate, or language dependent, and hence fail to capture the precise semantics of the embedding.

Finally, typical word embedding frameworks largely ignore the issue of word sense ambiguity. Most of the frequently-used words have multiple senses that are only discernible by their uses in context. Therefore, blindly using the corpora might yield embeddings that contain such unresolved ambiguities. There exists a work by Vilnis and McCallum [2015] that embeds each word as a multivariate Gaussian distribution, whose covariance matrix represents the degree of ambiguity. But it fails to mention how such ambiguities might be resolved.

In this work, we propose to use a dictionary to improve the above-mentioned problems of traditional word embedding frameworks. Since a dictionary is considered to contain precise, authoritative description of each word's semantics, using it will alleviate problems associated with corrupt samples. We also introduce a method to simultaneously learn a sentence embedding while disambiguating plain words.

Related Works This section serves as a brief survey of previous efforts that are best related to our proposal. We begin with the dictionary embedding by Hill et al. [2016]. In this work, the authors use dictionary definitions to enhance previous embeddings. However the focus is mainly on improving phrase representation. In fact, they use pre-existing word embeddings to learn phrase representation. Also, they do not distinguish various senses of the plain words, which is the greatest difference from our work.

Sense embedding has been pursued by Iacobacci et al. [2015] as well. In this SensEmbed framework, the embedding of individual senses is computed in the same manner as skip-gram or continuous bag-of-word embeddings (Mikolov et al. [2013]) are computed. One important preprocessing is to run an external word sense diambiguation (WSD) algorithm to label the senses of interest in the plain-word corpora. However, this requires that the WSD algorithm be accurate enough to be of good use. In contrast, our work combines the process of WSD with the embedding computation.

1.1 CONTRIBUTIONS

Although there have been previous works such as those by Hill et al. [2016] and Iacobacci et al. [2015] that resemble ours, we propose the following contributions that differ from theirs.

- Leveraging small-sized corpus to learn embeddings: Many word embedding algorithms such as Pennington et al. [2014] and Mikolov et al. [2013] require massive amount of text data in order to successfully gather co-occurrence statistics. However, this approach becomes infeasible when we wish to deal with a minor language that lacks electronic corpora. Our method uses a dictionary, which is considered to be the minimal text required to learn the basics of a language. A dictionary is much smaller than the corpora required by other embedding algorithms, hence it is more economical to use one.

- Automatic sense-disambiguation: When embedding a sentence, one often encounters multi-sensed words with ambiguity, such as "bank" or "paper". Such words can be disambiguated via use of context, or surrounding words in the sentence. Our model is able to learn which sense of the given ambiguous word carries most weight in assigning a proper semantic to the sentence embedding.

- Out-of-vocabulary (OOV) word processing: One of the difficulties involved with previous word-embedding techniques is dealing with words that do not appear in the known vocabulary. Skip-gram, for example, require a large amount of text that contain the OOV word in question in order to learn the embedding. However, since our approach to embedding a word uses a dictionary, all we need is the definition sentence of the OOV word. Intuitively, this is the minimally-required information one uses to learn the meaning of a new word.

2 PRELIMINARY

In our setting, we are given a vocabulary $V = \{v_1, \cdots, v_N\}$ with N words, and each word v_i is paired with a definition string $d(v_i) = \{d_i^1, d_i^2, \cdots, d_i^k | d_i^j \in O\}$. We assume that the words comprising the definition sentences belongs to a different set O. All words $v_i \in V$ are *disambiguated*, and are expressed using the WordNet (Miller [1995]) format to denote various senses of a word. That is, each sense of a word w is expressed as: w.POS.sense_num. POS is one of 'n', 'v', 'a', 'r' for noun, verb, adjective, and adverb, and 'sense_num' is a natural number indicating the count of the word. For example, the fifth noun sense of the word 'bank' is written as `bank.n.5`. On the other hand, the words $d_i^j \in O$ that make up the definition are *ambiguous*. In the following, the terms "word" and "sense" refer to disambiguated words (*e.g.*, `bank.n.5`), and "plain word" to ambiguous words (*e.g.*, "bank").

The triple $(V, O, d())$ forms a *dictionary* in a traditional sense. This dictionary is *closed*, meaning that all plain words that appear in the definition string must also have their corresponding senses present in V.

The types of definition strings $d(v_i)$ need not necessarily be confined to dictionary definition, as long as the contents contain sufficient information to describe the target word v_i. It could be as large as Wikipedia articles, but we settle for WordNet definitions for this work in order to quickly demonstrate the feasibility. Our goal is to compute, or refine a vector representation $e_i \in \mathbb{R}^D$ for each $v_i \in V$ using only the dictionary - hence the name *Dictionary bootstrapping*.

The most intuitive way to compute the embedding e_i of word v_i is to assign the embedding of its definition $d(v_i)$. The embedding of $d(v_i)$ is acquired from a recurrent neural network (RNN: Hochreiter and Schmidhuber [1997]). However, we will see in Section 3.2 that such a sequential RNN can be replaced by a simpler RNN.

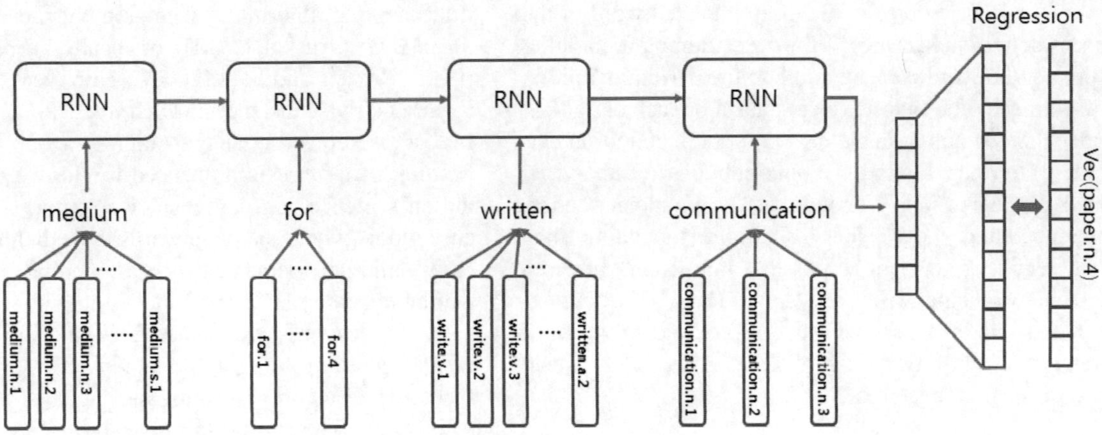

Figure 1: Proposed architecture for Dictionary Bootstrapping

3 ALGORITHM

One shortcoming of this sequeuntial RNN approach is that we only use the plain words of the definition sentence to derive an embedding. This might not pose much problem when we are dealing only with dictionaries, where the definitions of the words are given in a precise and unambiguous manner. But it would be better to devise a method that is capable of computing an embedding regardless of the ambiguity of the input sentence.

3.1 RESOLVING AMBIGUITIES

In order to reflect the ambiguity of the plain words, we let each plain word be modeled as a convex combination of its individual disambiguations, where the coefficients are determined by the context. For a plain word d_i, let $s(d_i) = \{v_i^1, \cdots, v_i^k\}$ denote the set of all disambiguated words of d_i. For example, $s(\text{`apple'}) = \{\texttt{apple.n.1}, \texttt{apple.n.2}\}$. With abuse of notation, we will also use $s(d_i)$ as the set of vectors corresponding to the disambiguated words. Then we represent a plain word d_i as

$$d_i = \sum_{v_j \in s(d_i)} \alpha_{ji} v_j, \text{ where } \sum_j \alpha_{ji} = 1, \alpha_{ji} \geq 0 \quad (1)$$

The coefficients α_{ji}'s denote the importance of each respective word v_j in relation to a plain word d_i in the context of v_j.

Let α_{ji} be the probability of the disambiguation for d_i being word $v_j \in s(d_i)$ given the context d_{-i} in the definition sentence[1]: $\alpha_{ji} \triangleq \Pr(v_j|d_{-i})$. We apply Bayes' rule to further expand this probability:

$$\alpha_{ji} = \frac{\Pr(v_j)\Pr(d_{-i}|v_j)}{\sum_{v_k \in s(d_i)} \Pr(v_k)\Pr(d_{-i}|v_k)} \quad (2)$$

[1]We have used the shorthand notation d_{-i} to mean the set $\{d_1, \cdots, d_{i-1}, d_{i+1}, \cdots, d_k\}$.

The prior $\Pr(v_j)$ allows the designer to incorporate preexisting knowledge about the language of interest. For example, one might wish to reflect the fact that only the first few senses of a certain plain word are active majority of the time. This is achievable by assigning $\Pr(v_j) \propto \exp(-j)$ so later senses receive exponentially smaller probabilities. In case such an assumption does not hold, a uniform prior $\Pr(v_j) = |s(d_i)|^{-1}$ will suffice.

To compute the probability $\Pr(d_{-i}|v_j)$, we make the assumption that the probability of "observing" the plain words in d_{-i}'s in the context is conditionally independent given the disambiguated word v_j in question. That is,

$$\Pr(d_{-i}|v_j) = \prod_{d_m \in d_{-i}} \Pr(d_m|v_j). \quad (3)$$

Next, we specify the form of $\Pr(d_m|v_j)$ to complete Equation 3.

$$\Pr(d_m|v_j) \propto \exp\left(\frac{\tau}{|s(d_m)|} \sum_{v_k \in s(d_m)} v_k^T L v_j\right).$$

That is, the probability is defined as the average of similarities between v_j and the senses of d_m, parameterized by $L \in \mathbb{R}^{D \times D}$. To ensure we are computing a valid inner-product, we restrict L to be positive-definite. τ is a hyper-parameter that controls the "temperature" of the softmax distribution.

This way of modeling sense-disambiguation is motivated by how humans look up new words in the dictionary: When we encounter an ambiguous plain word w in a sentence S, we must select among w's various senses. The method we use to choose the sense is a simple comparison between the definitions of w's senses and the plain words in S. Our approach can be thought of as a simplification of this process where we use the sense embedding instead of directly using the definitions.

To train the parameters, we need a supervised signal. To this end, it is tempting to add a a classification layer at the end of our RNN to predict the disambiguated word of the current definition sentence. However, training a classifier to predict the word corresponding to the current definition is ill-founded, due to insufficient data: For each class (*i.e.*, word), there is only a single data point (*i.e.*, definition embedding) to train. Instead, we opt to obtain the supervised signal via regression. For word $v_i \in V$ and its definition embedding e_i, let u_i be v_i's current embedding Then our objective is to learn a (possibly non-linear) function $f_\theta : \mathbb{R}^D \to \mathbb{R}^D$ that will take e_i to produce u_i. For our experiments, we take f_θ to be a two-layered neural network parameterized by layer weights $\Theta_0 = \{W_1, W_2\}$. Thus, our cost function becomes

$$J = \frac{1}{N} \sum_{i=1}^{N} \|f_{\Theta_0}(e_i) - u_i\|_2^2 + \lambda_0 \|\Theta_0\|_1, \quad (4)$$

where we add an L1-regularization term to prevent overfitting.

Although we have dropped the idea of using a classification layer, we suggest that the classification layer might become useful in the presence of additional data. For example, if we were to use Wordnet resources freely, then we could reformulate the class structure that better reflects the semantic hierarchy of the words. Then we will have sufficient training data for each class for our classification layer.

Of course, regular sentences we normally encounter will not be definitions of any words in general. But we expect this algorithm to learn the correct semantics associated with the sentence we process by training on word-definition pairs.

3.2 MESSAGE-PASSING-BASED RNN

In theory, directly assigning the definition embedding e_i to v_i appears to be a sound way to represent v_i. This intuition naturally yields an iterative fixed-point iteration procedure $v_i \leftarrow e_i$ until convergence.

However, this process converges to bad embeddings empirically. This is because of the premature usage of v_i's by the RNN training procedure. That is, the RNN takes a convex combination of each of the senses per plain word of the sentence, but the embeddings of such senses have not yet converged. Furthermore, the random initialization of the senses seems to exacerbate the matter.

Here, we propose to use a simple form of a definition embedding that not only addresses this problem, but also reduces the number of parameters. Furthermore, it can potentially leverage good pre-existing embeddings to quickly stabilize the learning of disambiguated word embeddings. We will explain towards the end of this section, how this approach is a simplification of the typical RNN-based definition encoding.

The main idea is to approach the embedding task as simultaneously finding the clustering of the words and their coordinates. A typical approach to this problem is to use manifold learning algorithms such as multi-dimensional scaling (MDS: Kruskal [1964]) or locally-linear embedding (LLE: Roweis and Saul [2000]). However, such methods require pairwise distances, which we lack.

Instead, we construct an embedding model where the embedding of a word is influenced by the words in its definition sentence. In particular, we assume a linear influence model where the plain words in the definition are linearly combined to update the corresponding disambiguated word embedding. Our model takes doubly-convex combination of the words, where the first level combines the plain words according to some pre-computed weights, and the second level combines each disambiguated word of each plain word. The second level is achieved by the α_{ji}'s we train via Equation 4. This process is illustrated in Figure 3.2 for the word `paper.n.4`.

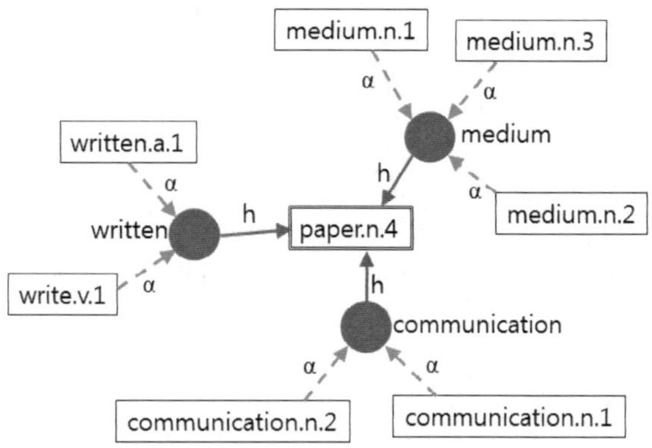

Figure 2: Illustration of passing influences.

Thus, the update formula takes the following recursive form for each word v_i:

$$v_i \leftarrow \sum_{d \in d(v_i)} h_d \sum_{v_j \in s(d)} \alpha_{ji} v_j. \quad (5)$$

The plain word weights h_d are normalized for each disambiguated word v_i, and can be pre-computed as constants. In our work, we initialize them as the inverse document frequency (IDF) of the corresponding plain words, but any weighting scheme is allowed. Intuitively, words that are defined using similar words (*i.e.*, words with similar meaning) will have higher chance of receiving and passing influences among themselves, and hence result in closer embedding.

In the context of graphical model, our procedure is reminiscent of the belief propagation algorithm on the graph formed by all the words in the dictionary. The plain and disambiguated words consist the vertex set, where a plain word receives directed edges from its disambiguated words, and a disambiguated word receives directed edges from the plain words in its definition. The edges are weighted with either h_d or α_{ji} accordingly as in Figure 3.2. Under this interpretation, the updates to v_i are similar to the log-messages from the variable nodes, that are summed up.

Unfortunately, the graph we work with is not a tree. Therefore the convergence of the update is not guaranteed. We work around this issue by the following measure.
We introduce another parameter $\beta_t \in (0,1)$ that changes over each iteration epoch t, to balance between stabilization and update:

$$v_i \leftarrow (1-\beta_t)v_i + \beta_t \left(\sum_{d \in d(v_i)} h_d \sum_{v_j \in s(d)} \alpha_{ji} v_j \right). \quad (6)$$

High value of β_t will aggressively reflect the update coming from the message-passing encoder, while lower β_t will be more conservative and retain previous value of v_i. When training, we start with a high value of β_t and gradually decrease β_t over t. By decreasing β_t, we can now ensure convergence of our update procedure.
This update rule can be loosely thought of as an unnormalized version of random walk, where each word receives influences from the plain words that constitute its definition. We call it unnormalized because the outgoing influences do not add up to 1. Under this intuition, the random walker sends unnormalized influence to its neighbors. Then, words sharing similar words will receive roughly similar influences, thus leading an approximate clustering of the semantics.

Simplified RNN Finally, we point out that the message-passing-based update can be thought of as a simplified RNN computation in its own right. This RNN has an identity activation function, and operates by simply accumulating the inputs ignoring the order. Such a view has also been adopted by (Hill et al. [2016]) under the name of *Bag-of-words (BOW) neural language model*. Although it may appear to be a crude way to encode sentences, this method becomes effective when encoding short phrases. Since most definition "sentences" we deal in this work are actually phrase-level expressions, the use of BOW is justified.

3.3 OVERALL TRAINING

Our approach to word embedding involves two phases: a regressor training phase and a message-passing-based update phase. These two phases are intertwined in that the variables updated in one phase is used as constants in the other. Therefore, we take an alternating training scheme where we fix one set of the variables while training for the others.
When training the regressor (and other related parameters), we freeze the disambiguated word vectors v_i's and update the parameters $\Theta = \{L, \Theta_0\}$. We would ideally have to train the RNN until convergence, but we only run K rounds of stochastic gradient descent on L_1 in practice.
On the other hand, we spend more time on the message-passing-based updates, since we found that such fixed-point iteration converge relatively quickly. The iteration is stopped when the maximum difference between the previous value and the update is smaller than some small threshold ϵ. Notice that the updates are *in-place*, meaning that the new values are updated immediately rather than postponed for a batch update. This allows the recently-updated values to be used as soon as possible for quicker convergence. Our full training procedure is outlined in Algorithm 1.

Algorithm 1 Overall algorithm

```
Input: K, β_0 ∈ (0,1), learning rate γ, ε
For training epoch t = 0, 1, ···
repeat
    // Repeat the regressor training for K iterations
    for i = 1, ···, K do
        Θ ← Θ − γ ∂J/∂Θ (See Eqn 4 for J)
        Update α_ji's using Θ (Eqn 2)
    end for
    // Run iteration for message-passing RNN
    repeat
        Δ ← −∞
        for Each word v_i ∈ V do
            v_new ← v_i + β_t(Σ h_d Σ α_ji v_j − v_i) (Eqn 6)
            Δ ← max{|v_new − v_i|, Δ}
            v_i ← v_new
        end for
    until Δ < ε
    β_{t+1} ← β_t β_0
until Converged
```

3.4 EXTENSION WITH BASE VECTORS

In the current presentation, we model the updates to vector v_i to be a function of purely its neighbors. In this section, we provide a generalized extension to our scheme, where each v_i can also take a pre-trained vector b_i into account when updating. This becomes possible by a simple modification to Equation 5:

$$v_i \leftarrow b_i + \sum_{d \in d(v_i)} h_d \sum_{v_j \in s(d)} \alpha_{ji} v_j. \quad (7)$$

The vectors b_i are called *base vectors*, since they provide base representations. The b_i's are supposed to be given as pre-trained vectors but we briefly discuss how to lift this assumption. We begin by treating each definition as a short document and perform topic modeling on them to compute topic distributions of each word. For example, latent Dirichlet allocation (LDA: (Blei et al. [2003])) with k topics yields a k-dimensional probability vector for each word. Using these topic vectors, we are able to compute the distance between any given two words using various distance metrics such as the Bhattacharyya distance, or the Jensen-Shannon distance. Such distances are gathered into an $N \times N$ matrix that are input to MDS. Performing MDS on this matrix results in the vector representations of each word that reflects the given distances. While these vectors may not be the best representations, we expect them to be good-enough initial values for our approach. This approach works better when the definitions we have are of moderate length. If not, one should consider using topic models that are specialized to short texts (*e.g.*, Yan et al. [2013]).

In Section 3.5, we give a scenario where this initialization scheme becomes more useful. For the experiments, we do not use the base vectors when computing the embeddings.

3.5 APPLICATIONS

Next we discuss about potential applications of our approach. There exist several well-known solutions for some of the fields we address, but we stress that our structure is particularly well-suited for such problems.

WORD SENSE DISAMBIGUATION

Word sense disambiguation (WSD) is a task where one has to identify the correct sense of a plain word. An instance of this problem is usually given in a sentence where the plain word can be interpreted in a variety of ways for each of its senses. For example, the word `paper` in the sentence "He submitted a *paper* to the professor" would refer to the sense `paper.n.5`, whose meaning is "a scholarly article".

As such, disambiguating plain words involves comparing each of the senses to the surrounding words in the context. This is exactly how our model operates to assign weights on the senses. To perform WSD, we simply input the given sentence that contains the plain word w to disambiguate into our RNN model, and read off the computed α_{wj}'s.

OUT-OF-VOCABULARY EMBEDDING

One important shortcoming of all word embedding is the processing of out-of-vocabulary (OOV) words. Most word embedding algorithms heavily relies on co-occurrence patterns in order to compute embeddings. However, rarely occurring words or newly created words will likely have few or no context data to use to compute the embeddings.

Our model, on the other hand, is able to compute the embeddings of any new word as long as its definition is provided as well. There is one other restriction that states the definition should consist of known words only, but this natural to expect. In fact, a closed set of related definitions is the minimally required information to learn the meaning of a new word.

The process of embedding an unknown word is simple: Run the definition through the RNN to compute the α_{ji}'s and use them to perform a single step update (Equation 5) on the unknown word.

ENCYCLOPEDIA EMBEDDING

So far, we have worked with a type of dictionary with limited information. We have implicitly assumed that each definition is a sentence. However, there are much richer resources nowadays that we can use in place of a simple dictionary.

One prominent example is Wikipedia, which contains multi-sentence and multi-modal definitions of concepts.

Furthermore, the entries are hyperlinked, so our random walk framework naturally yields a local iterative algorithm. That is, in hyperlinked environments, Equation 7 can be thought as the Bellman equation (Bellman [2003]). The b_i would represent the contents of page i, while the h_d's and the α_{ji}'s merge to become the random walk probability of jumping from i to its outgoing neighbor j.

One factor to consider is the embedding of the entry document, which is significantly different from embedding a single sentence. One should employ multi-modal embedding techniques to form a summary vector of the document. Note that representing a document generally requires an object more complex than a single vector. However, we conjecture that sufficiently high-dimensional vector should work well for documents that are highly focused on a single concept.

4 EXPERIMENTS

To show the effect of sense embeddings, we perform both qualitative and quantitative experiments. The qualitative results will mainly show the relationship among the embedded words, and the quantitative results will aim on solving the word-sense disambiguation (WSD) task.

For the setting of our experiments, the only training corpus we use is the list of words and their definitions extracted from WordNet (Miller [1995]). We first select a small group of "seed words" from the English Wikipedia corpora, by choosing the 10,000 most commonly occuring plain words. Based on this set of seed words, we prune out words that are not in the WordNet, and traverse the WordNet definition tree over the current pool of plain words used in the definitions. Words (senses) that form the plain words newly-encountered along the traversal are also added into the vocabulary list. As the final refinement, we removed words that occur less than three times in other definitions. This last step filters out words like minor proper nouns and scholar jargons. The final dictionary collected this way consists of $|V| = 82,831$ words whose definitions are formed by $|O| = 38,730$ plain words.

One disadvantage of using WordNet is that the definitions are limited to words having one of four parts-of-speeches (POSs): noun, verb, adjective, and adverb. This means all stop-words including prepositions, conjunctions, and articles are left out of the main vocabulary. While it is crucial to hold on to the stop-words to correctly learn the semantics of a sentence, we ignore them in this work. The reason for doing so is twofold: 1) we would like to assess how well our algorithm can learn the embeddings in the face of limited vocabulary, and 2) full integration of stop-words into the vocabulary might require sophisticated pre- and post-processing. We use no other linguistic/textual resources in this work.

As for the parameters of the model, we use the following setting.

- The trainable inner-product matrix L is factored into $L = UU$, where U is a diagonal matrix with non-zero elements. The optimization of Equation 4 is performed with respect to U instead of L.
- The decay schedule for β_t is computed as $\beta_t = 0.8^{t+1}$. Values of $\beta_0 = 0.7$ yielded similar results. $\Pr(d_m|v_j)$ being roughly uniform, due to exponentiating small values.
- The parameters Θ_0 and the word vectors $\{v_j\}$ are randomly initialized from the interval $(-0.1, 0.1)$. Word vectors are $D = 300$ dimensional.
- The per-plain-word coefficients $\{h_d\}$ for all $d \in O$ are computed as the IDF values over the dictionary. plain word d, and normalizing them over the plain words occurring in each word $v \in V$.
- The priors are initialized as uniform distributions: $\Pr(v_i) = |s(d_i)|^{-1}$
- We perform $K = 5$ steps of stochastic gradient descent on Equation 4 with learning rate $\gamma = 0.05$, followed by iterative update of the word vectors. The iteration is stopped when the update size becomes smaller than $\epsilon = 10^{-3}$. The size of the mini-batches is set to 64.

4.1 QUALITATIVE RESULTS

The first experiment we perform is examining the nearest neighbors of some often-confused words when in their plain form. Table 1 shows the seven words we examine for their nearest neighbors.

Table 1: Definitions of words used in Table 2.

Word	Definition
hood.n.1	A violent young criminal.
hood.n.2	A protective covering part of a plant.
paper.n.1	A material made of cellulose pulp.
paper.n.5	A scholarly article.
bank.n.1	Sloping land.
bank.n.5	A stock held in reserve for future use.
apple.n.1	Fruit with red or yellow or green skin.

The measure used to retrieve the nearest neighbor is the cosine similarity: $sim(\mathbf{x}, \mathbf{y}) = \mathbf{x} \cdot \mathbf{y} / \|\mathbf{x}\| \|\mathbf{y}\|$. Notice that the definitions are terse, and often seem to have insufficient information to learn the precise meaning. The list of nearest neighbors for seven selected words is given in Table 2.

Most of the retrieved words generally fall within the same category as the target word. There are two exceptions, however, that are underlined in the table.

The first one is `chiwere.n.1`, whose definition is "Language spoken by the Sioux people". We conjecture that this phenomenon is because of the flow of influence starting with `paper.n.1` → `card.n.1` → `michigan.n.3`[2] → `sioux.n.1` → `chiwere.n.1`. The reason of why the intermediate words did not appear in the nearest neighbors seems to be their definition lengths: longer definition tends to dampen the influence of the composing words in our BOW model. On the other hand, `chiwere.n.1` is relatively short and contains the plain word 'Sioux' which has an extremely high IDF. This, combined with the high IDF values of the intermediate words, boosted up the relatedness to `paper.n.1`.

The second exception is `hereafter.r.2`, whose definition is "in a future life or state". The influence from `bank.n.5` seems to have been passed via the term 'future'. Although its meaning is not entirely different from that of `bank.n.5`, it does seem a bit odd to be included in the neighbor list.

On a passing note, the nearest neighbors of `apple.n.1` are all valid, despite their deceiving forms. `cortland.n.1`, `delicious.n.1`, and `baldwin.n.3` are all types of apples.

The next set of experiments involves visualizing the embeddings in 2-dimension using t-SNE (van der Maaten and Hinton [2008]). First, we examine how analogical transformation of some words are reflected in their embeddings. The analogies we examine are liquid-solid and female-male relationships. For the former experiment, we take six words `drink.n.3`, `drink.v.1`, `magma.n.1`, `food.n.1`, `eat.v.1`, and `rock.n.1` and project their embeddings onto the 2-D plane. The first three words are related to liquid objects, and the last three are their solid counterparts. For example, `magma.n.1` is a liquid form of `rock.n.1`.

We can see from Figure 4.1 that the liquid versions are all generally located upward relative to the solid ones.

The second analogy is that of female-male relationship. The words used in this set are the gender-swapped version of the same concepts. Similarly to the previous embedding, we observe a somewhat consistent relative positioning in Figure 4.1.

Finally, we demonstrate that using an unprejudiced dictionary eliminates gender-biased embeddings such as those pointed out by Bolukbasi et al. [2016]. For this plotting, we compare the relative positions of four occupations `fireman.n.1`, `policeman.n.1`, `housewife.n.1`,

[2]A type of card game which has been mistaken as `michigan.n.1` when encoding `sioux.n.1`

Table 2: Nearest neighbors of select senses, with obvious "false neighbors" underlined.

Word	5 Nearest Neighbors
hood.n.1	bully.n.2, thugee.n.1, thuggery.n.1, muscleman.n.1, criminalism.n.1
hood.n.2	sheath.n.1, roof.n.1, skin.n.1, mask.n.4, roof.n.2
paper.n.1	cellulose.n.1, cellulosic.n.1, cellulose_xanthate.n.1, pulp.n.3, <u>chiwere.n.1</u>
paper.n.5	scholarly.a.1, unscholarly.a.1, tome.n.1, orientalism.n.1, memoir.n.2
bank.n.1	sloping.a.1, acclivitous.a.1, slop.v.3, hipped.a.1, highland.n.1
bank.n.5	store.n.2, forehanded.a.2, <u>hereafter.r.2</u>, stock.v.5, future.a.2
apple.n.1	cortland.n.1, winesap.n.1, delicious.n.1, corer.n.1, baldwin.n.3

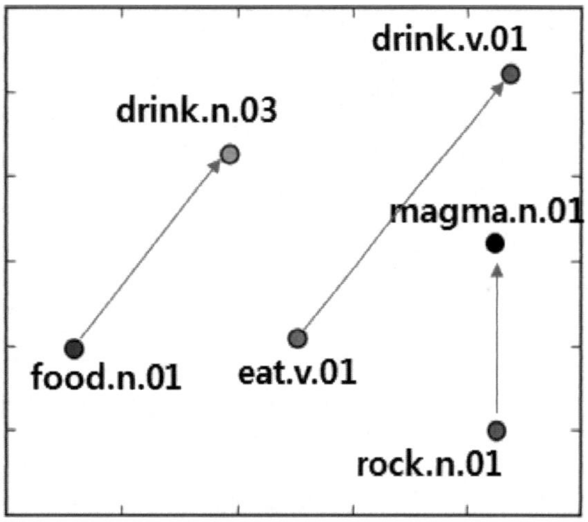

Figure 3: Liquid-solid relationship.

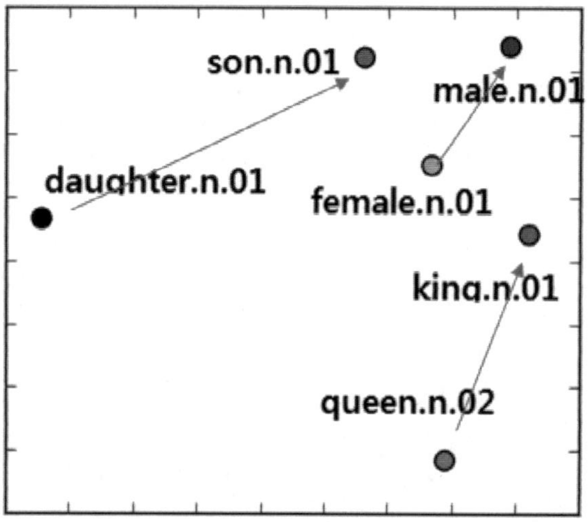

Figure 4: Gender relationship.

and seamstress.n.1, compared to two anchor words man.n.1 and woman.n.1. The first two occupations have been historically regarded as masculine jobs, while the last two were thought as feminine jobs (as shown etymologically). However, Figure 4.1 shows that our dictionary-based embeddings ignore such stereotypes; the positions of the occupations do not exihibit any patterns relative to the embeddings of man.n.1 and woman.n.1. This is not surprising, since the definitions for the four occupations used contain almost no gender-specific words, with the exception of housewife.n.1, whose definition is "A wife who manages a household while her husband earns the family income".

4.2 WORD SENSE DISAMBIGUATION RESULTS

Finally, we report result on the word sense disambiguation (WSD) task (Jurgens and Klapaftis [2013]). The evaluation set for this task had been provided by the SemEval2013 workshop, and we compare the performance of our approach to those of four other participants of the then-held competition. In addition to the participants, we also ran five baseline algorithms that rely on traditional WSD algorithms. These include: 1) the Lesk algorithm (Lesk [1986]), the adaptive Lesk (Banerjee and Pedersen [2002]), cosine Lesk (which uses cosines to compute overlaps), path similarity-based disambiguation (Leacock and Chodorow [1998]), and information-theoretic approach (Lin [1998]). Of these, we only report the result for the adaptive Lesk since it outperformed the other four[3].

The WSD task we address asks us to identify the correct sense of a particular word in context. The input is a sentence with a designated plain word in the sentence to disambiguate. The output should either be a single identified sense or multiple senses each labeled with applicability weights. SemEval provides five different evaluation metrics, but we only show three; two from the F1 measure family and one from the clustering measure family. The first is the well-known Jaccard index and the second is the weighted NDCG metric that computes a weighted F1 score. The third is the fuzzy NMI metric which views the weighted sense identification as a fuzzy clustering. We direct the readers to the cited paper for more information.

When identifying the sense, our algorithm simply computes the α_{ji} coefficients via Equation 2 and the trained

[3]The baseline algorithms are collectively implemented by the PyWSD package (https://github.com/alvations/pywsd)

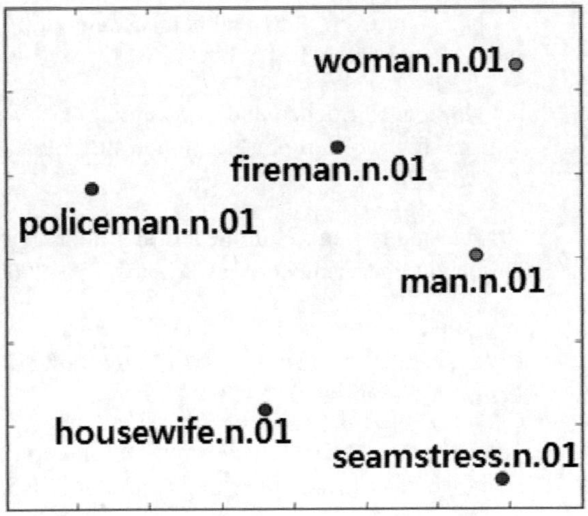

Figure 5: Gender-neutral embedding.

sense embeddings. Then we remove the senses receiving α_{ji} weights below a threshold of 0.02. For the Jaccard measure, we select the sense with the highest weight, since the Jaccard index does not account for the weights. Other than a straightforward thresholding, we perform no extra operations to fine-tune the final outcome. The result of our system is given in Table 3.

Despite the high Fuzzy NMI score, the Jaccard index and

Table 3: Results of the SemEval2013 WSD task. Duplicate entries indicate multiple submissions.

Algorithm	Jaccard	WNDCG	FuzzyNMI
AI-KU1	0.197	**0.387**	0.065
AI-KU2	0.197	0.215	0.035
AI-KU3	0.244	0.332	0.039
Unimelb1	0.218	0.365	0.056
Unimelb2	0.213	0.371	0.060
UoS1	0.192	0.315	0.047
UoS2	0.232	0.374	0.045
La Sapienza1	0.149	0.311	-
La Sapienza2	0.149	0.383	-
ALesk (baseline)	**0.254**	0.293	0.041
DiBoots (ours)	0.209	0.370	**0.074**

the WNDCG score do not stand out. But keep in mind that we only use a relatively small-sized corpus for an unsupervised training, and perform no post-processing on the WSD output. The competing algorithms, on the other hand, make heavy use of large corpora such as ukWaC (Ferraresi et al. [2008]) and Wikipedia, to train systems specifically targeted for the WSD task. Table 4 contrasts the amount of resources used by the competitors against ours. WN-sim is a WordNet-based similarity measure that reflects the entire ontological tree of WordNet. While there is room for improvement, we claim that our algorithm provides a good

Table 4: Comparison of resource requirements. WN-sim and WN-dict refer to the WordNet similarity functions and dictionary, respectively. The corpora ukWaC and Wikipedia each consist of 2 billion and 800 million English words.

System	Corpora	External Algorithms
AI-KU	ukWaC	Fastsub, S-CODE, K-means
Unimelb	Wikipedia	Hierarichical Dir. Proc.
UoS	ukWaC	Depend. parser, MaxMax
La Sapienza	ukWaC	PageRank, WN-sim.
DiBoots	WN-dict	-

starting-ground for NLP applications.

5 DISCUSSION

Our algorithm does provide promising aspects in the field of word embedding. While we do not achieve state-of-the art results in the problems we address, the performance is more than reasonable given the 6.9 MB dictionary size. Furthermore, we do not process the text in any way, other than simple case-lowering.

One interesting direction of improvement lies with language pre-processing: We have ignored the POS tag, tense, numbers, and compound nouns in this work. But such are the important factors for properly encoding the semantics. For example, the term “rocky mountain” should be treated as a single compound noun instead of two as we do. Also, as mentioned above, the restriction of WordNet definitions to four major POS categories has excluded the processing of many important conjunctions and prepositions such as “and” and “for”. In order to better-reflect the meaning of the definition sentence, we must devise a method to bring in these words.

Another interesting direction is with combining existing embeddings, motivated by Table 2. The nearest neighbors of the word `apple.n.1` are all valid apples, but are unfamiliar to the general public. Other embeddings such as GloVe will retrieve more user-friendly words, since they are trained to recognize naturally co-occurring word pairs such as apple-banana or apple-fruit. While the nearest neighbors DiBoots retrieves might be “more correct” than words such as `banana.n.1`, they might be inadequate for non-professionals. After all, acquiring precise semantics from the dictionary is often not what people expect. In that respect, using our algorithm to fine-tune existing co-occurrence-based embeddings seems like a desirable combination.

Acknowledgement B.Kang and K.-A. Sohn are supported by the National Research Foundation of Korea (NRF) grant funded by the Ministry of Education [NRF-2016R1A6A3A11932796 and NRF-2016R1D1A1B03933875, respectively.]

References

S. Banerjee and T. Pedersen. An adapted Lesk algorithm for word sense disambiguation using WordNet. In *Proceedings of CICLing*, 2002.

R. Bellman. *Dynamic Programming*. Dover Publications, Incorporated, 2003. ISBN 0486428095.

D. Blei, A. Ng, and M. Jordan. Latent Dirichlet allocation. *Journal of Machine Learning Research*, 3, 2003.

T. Bolukbasi, K. Chang, J. Zou, V. Saligrama, and A. Kalai. Man is to computer programmer as woman is to homemaker? Debiasing word embeddings. In *Proceedings of NIPS*, 2016.

A. Ferraresi, E. Zanchetta, M. Baroni, and S. Bernardini. Introducing and evaluating ukWaC, a very large web-derived corpus of english. In *Proceedings of the 4-th Web as Corpus (WAC) Workshop*, 2008.

F. Hill, K. Cho, A. Korhonen, and Y. Bengio. Learning to understand phrases by embedding the dictionary. *Transactions of the Association for Computational Linguistics*, 4, 2016.

S. Hochreiter and J. Schmidhuber. Long short-term memory. *Neural Computation*, 9, 1997.

I. Iacobacci, M. T. Pilehvar, and R. Navigli. SensEmbed: Learning sense embeddings for word and relational similarity. In *Proceedings of IJCNLP*, 2015.

D. Jurgens and I. Klapaftis. SemEval-2013 Task 13: Word sense induction for graded- and non-graded senses. In *Proceedings of International Workshop on Semantic Evaluation*, 2013.

R. Kiros, Y. Zhu, R. Salakhutdinov, R. S. Zemel, A. Torralba, R. Urtasun, and S. Fidler. Skip-thought vectors. In *Proceedings of NIPS*, 2015.

J. Kruskal. Nonmetric multidimensional scaling: a numerical method. *Psychometrika*, 29, 1964.

C. Leacock and M. Chodorow. Combining local context and wordnet similarity for word sense identification. *Computational Linguistics*, 24, 1998.

M. Lesk. Automatic sense disambiguation using machine readable dictionaries: how to tell a pine cone from an ice cream cone. In *Proceedings of SIGDOC*, 1986.

D. Lin. An information-theoretic definition of similarity. In *Proceedings of ICML*, 1998.

T. Mikolov, I. Sutskever, K. Chen, G. Corrado, and J. Dean. Distributed representations of words and phrases and their compositionality. In *Proceedings of NIPS*, 2013.

G. Miller. WordNet: A lexical database for english. *Communications of the ACM*, 38, 1995.

J. Pennington, R. Socher, and C. Manning. GloVe: Global vectors for word representation. In *Proceedings of EMNLP*, 2014.

S. Roweis and L. Saul. Nonlinear dimensionality reduction by locally linear embedding. *Science*, 290, 2000.

L. van der Maaten and G. Hinton. Visualizing high-dimensional data using t-SNE. *Journal of Machine Learning Research*, 9, 2008.

L. Vilnis and A. McCallum. Word representation via gaussian embedding. In *Proceedings of ICLR*, 2015.

X. Yan, J. Guo, Y. Lan, and X. Cheng. A biterm topic model for short texts. In *Proceedings of WWW*, 2013.

X. Zhang, J. Zhao, and Y. LeCun. Character-level convolutional networks for text classification. In *Proceedings of NIPS*, 2015.

Importance Sampled Stochastic Optimization for Variational Inference

Joseph Sakaya
Helsinki Institute for Information Technology HIIT
Department of Computer Science
University of Helsinki, Finland

Arto Klami
Helsinki Institute for Information Technology HIIT
Department of Computer Science
University of Helsinki, Finland

Abstract

Variational inference approximates the posterior distribution of a probabilistic model with a parameterized density by maximizing a lower bound for the model evidence. Modern solutions fit a flexible approximation with stochastic gradient descent, using Monte Carlo approximation for the gradients. This enables variational inference for arbitrary differentiable probabilistic models, and consequently makes variational inference feasible for probabilistic programming languages. In this work we develop more efficient inference algorithms for the task by considering importance sampling estimates for the gradients. We show how the gradient with respect to the approximation parameters can often be evaluated efficiently without needing to re-compute gradients of the model itself, and then proceed to derive practical algorithms that use importance sampled estimates to speed up computation. We present importance sampled stochastic gradient descent that outperforms standard stochastic gradient descent by a clear margin for a range of models, and provide a justifiable variant of stochastic average gradients for variational inference.

1 INTRODUCTION

Variational inference considers parametric approximations for posterior densities of probabilistic models. Following Jordan et al. (1999) the classical variational approximation algorithms are based on coordinate descent algorithms for which individual steps of the algorithm are often carried out analytically. This limits the use of variational approximation to models with conjugate priors (or simple extensions of those) and restricts the family of potential approximating distributions based on analytic tractability.

Recent advances in variational approximation have lead to a phase transition; instead of closed-form updates, the approximation is nowadays often fit using generic gradient descent techniques instead – for a good overview see, *e.g.*, Gal (2016). The key behind these advances is in using Monte Carlo approximation to estimate the gradient of the objective function that is an integral over the approximating distribution. This can be done in two alternative ways. The *reparameterization estimate* (Titsias and Lázaro-Gredilla, 2014; Kingma and Welling, 2014; Salimans and Knowles, 2013) allows expressing the gradient of the objective function using the gradients of the model itself, whereas the *score function estimate* (Ranganath et al., 2014) is based on gradients of the approximation. Given the new family of algorithms we can apply variational approximation for a considerably wider range of probabilistic models, enabling for example use of variational inference as the inference backend in probabilistic programming languages (Kucukelbir et al., 2017; Salvatier J, 2016; Tran et al., 2016).

The main research efforts in variational inference are nowadays geared towards making the approach applicable to a still wider family of models, by constructing even more flexible approximations (Rezende and Mohamed, 2015; Ranganath et al., 2016; Kingma et al., 2016) or by generalizing the gradient estimators (Ruiz et al., 2016; Naesseth et al., 2017). The question of how exactly the resulting optimization problem is solved has largely remained unattended to – practically all authors are satisfied with standard stochastic gradient descent (SGD) as the underlying optimizer, although some effort has been put into improving convergence by reducing the variance of the gradient estimate near the optimum (Roeder et al., 2017).

We turn our attention to the optimizer itself, looking into ways of speeding up the computation of gradient-based variational approximation. Practically all of the computational effort during learning goes into evaluating the gradient of the model (or the approximation if using the score-function estimate). Our contribution is in reducing the number of times we need to evaluate the gradient of the model during the optimization process, based on an importance sampling scheme specifically designed for optimization problems where the gradients are computed using Monte Carlo approximation.

The key observation is that the gradient of the objective function with respect to the parameters of the approximation consists of two parts. One part is the gradient of the model itself, evaluated at parameter values drawn from the approximation, whereas the other part is the gradient of the transformation used in the reparameterization estimate. We show that the gradient required for optimization can be computed for the newly updated approximation without recomputing the first part, which is computationally heavier. Instead, we can re-use existing computation by appropriately modifying and re-weighting the available terms.

We show how to formulate this idea in a justified manner, by constructing an importance sampling estimate for the gradient. Importance sampling is typically used for cases where one cannot sample from the distribution of interest but instead has to resort to sampling from a related proposal distribution. In our case we could sample from the distribution of interest – the current approximation – but choose not to, since by using an earlier approximation as a proposal we can avoid costly computation. The idea is conceptually similar to the way Gelman et al. (2017) reuses samples from previous iterations in expectation propagation.

Since the advances in our case are related to the computation of the gradient itself, the idea can readily be combined with several optimization algorithms. In this work, we derive practical algorithms extending standard SGD and stochastic average gradients (Schmidt et al., 2017). We demonstrate them in learning a variational approximation for several probabilistic models, showing how they improve the convergence speed in a model-independent manner.

In the following we first give a brief overview of the state-of-the-art in gradient-based variational approximation, covering both the gradient estimates and stochastic optimization algorithms in Section 2. We then proceed to describe the importance sampling estimate for the gradient in Section 3, followed by practical optimization algorithms outlined in Section 4. Empirical experiments and illustrations are provided in Section 5.

2 BACKGROUND

2.1 VARIATIONAL APPROXIMATION

Variational inference refers to approximating the posterior distribution $p(z|x)$ of a probabilistic model $p(x, z)$ using a distribution $q_\lambda(z)$ parameterized by λ. Usually this is achieved by maximizing a lower bound $\mathcal{L}(\lambda)$ for the evidence (also called the marginal likelihood) $p(x)$:

$$\mathcal{L}(\lambda) = \int q_\lambda(z) \log \frac{p(x,z)}{q_\lambda(z)} \, \delta z \leq p(x). \quad (1)$$

Traditionally, the problem has been made tractable by assuming a factorized mean-field approximation $q_\lambda(z) = \prod_i q_{\lambda_i}(z_i)$ and models with conjugate priors, resulting in closed-form coordinate ascent algorithms specific for individual models – for a full derivation and examples, see, *e.g.*, Blei et al. (2016).

In recent years several novel types of algorithms applicable for a wider range of models have been proposed (Titsias and Lázaro-Gredilla, 2014; Kingma and Welling, 2014; Salimans and Knowles, 2013; Ranganath et al., 2014), based on direct gradient-based optimization of the lower bound (1). The core idea behind these algorithms is in using Monte Carlo estimates for the loss and its gradient

$$\nabla_\lambda \mathcal{L}(\lambda) = \nabla_\lambda \mathbb{E}_{q_\lambda(z)}[\log p(x,z) - \log q_\lambda(z)]. \quad (2)$$

Given such estimates, the inference problem can be solved by standard gradient descent algorithms. This enables inference for non-conjugate likelihoods and for complex models for which closed-form updates would be hard to derive, making variational inference a feasible inference strategy for probabilistic programming languages (Kucukelbir et al., 2017; Tran et al., 2016; Salvatier J, 2016). In the following, we briefly describe two alternative strategies of estimating the gradient. In Section 3 we will then show how the proposed importance sampling technique is applied for both cases.

2.1.1 REPARAMETERIZATION ESTIMATE

The reparameterization estimate for (1) (and consequently (2)) is based on representing the approximation $q_\lambda(z)$ using a differentiable transformation $z = f(\epsilon, \lambda)$ of an underlying standard distribution $\phi(\epsilon)$ that does not have any free parameters. The core idea of how this enables computing the gradient was developed simultaneously by Kingma and Welling (2014); Salimans and Knowles (2013) and Titsias and Lázaro-Gredilla (2014) with many of the mathematical details visible already in the early work by Opper and Archambeau (2009). Plugging the transformation $f(\cdot)$ into (1) gives

$$\mathcal{L}(\lambda) = \int \phi(\epsilon) \log \frac{p(x, f(\epsilon,\lambda))|\det_{J_f}(\epsilon,\lambda)|}{\phi(\epsilon)} \, \delta\epsilon,$$

where the integral is over the standard distribution that does not depend on z, and $|\det_{J_f}(\epsilon,\lambda)|$ is the absolute value of the determinant of the Jacobian of $f(\epsilon,\lambda)$. Consequently, it can be replaced by a stochastic approximation

$$\mathcal{L}(\lambda) = \frac{1}{M}\sum_{m=1}^{M} \log \frac{p(x, f(\epsilon_m,\lambda))|\det_{J_f}(\epsilon_m,\lambda)|}{\phi(\epsilon_m)},$$

where ϵ_m is drawn from $\phi(\epsilon)$. We can now easily compute the gradients using the chain rule, by first differentiating $\log p(x, f(\epsilon,\lambda))$ w.r.t z and then $z = f(\epsilon,\lambda)$ w.r.t λ, resulting in

$$\nabla_\lambda \mathcal{L}(\lambda) \approx \frac{1}{M} \sum_{m=1}^{M} [\nabla_z \log p(x, z_m) \nabla_\lambda f(\epsilon_m, \lambda) \quad (3)$$
$$+ \nabla_\lambda |\det_{J_f}(\epsilon_m, \lambda)|] .$$

The combination of the standard distribution $\phi(\epsilon)$ and the transformation $f(\epsilon, \lambda)$ defines the approximation family. For example, $\phi(\epsilon) = \mathcal{N}(0, I)$ and $f(\epsilon, \lambda = \{\mu, L\}) = \mu + L\epsilon$ defines arbitrary Gaussian approximations (Opper and Archambeau, 2009; Titsias and Lázaro-Gredilla, 2014), where L is the Cholesky factor of the covariance. To create richer approximations we can concatenate multiple transformations; Kucukelbir et al. (2017) combines the transformation above with a rich family of univariate transformations designed for different kinds of parameter constraints. For example, by using $f(\epsilon, \lambda = \{\mu, L\}) = \text{Softplus}(\mu + L\epsilon)$ we can approximate parameters constrained for positive values. Alternatively, we can directly reparameterize other common distributions such as Gamma or Dirichlet – see Naesseth et al. (2017); Ruiz et al. (2016) for details.

2.1.2 SCORE FUNCTION ESTIMATE

An alternative estimate for (2) can be derived based on manipulation of the log-derivatives; the use of the estimate for simulation of models was originally presented by Kleijnen and Rubinstein (1995) and its use for variational approximation by Ranganath et al. (2014). The estimate for $\nabla_\lambda \mathcal{L}(\lambda)$ is provided by

$$\mathbb{E}_{q_\lambda(z)}[(\log p(x, z) - \log q_\lambda(z)) \nabla_\lambda \log q_\lambda(z)],$$

which again leads into a straightforward Monte Carlo approximation of $\nabla_\lambda \mathcal{L}(\lambda)$ as

$$\frac{1}{M} \sum_{m=1}^{M} (\log p(x, z_m) - \log q_\lambda(z_m)) \nabla_\lambda \log q_\lambda(z_m), \quad (4)$$

where $z_m \sim q_\lambda(z)$. The notable property of this technique is that it does not require derivatives of the model (that is, $\log p(x, z)$) itself, but instead relies solely on derivatives of the approximation. This is both a pro and a con; the model does not need to be differentiable, but at the same time the estimate is not using the valuable information the model gradient provides. This is shown to result in considerably higher variance compared to the reparameterization estimate, often by orders of magnitude. Variance reduction techniques (Ranganath et al., 2014) help, but for differentiable models the reparameterization technique is typically considerably more efficient (Naesseth et al., 2017; Ruiz et al., 2016).

2.2 STOCHASTIC GRADIENT OPTIMIZATION

Given estimates for the gradient (2) computed with either method, the optimization problem[1] is solved by standard gradient descent techniques. In practice all of the automatic variational inference papers have resorted to stochastic gradient descent (SGD) on mini-batches, adaptively tuning the step lengths with the state-of-the-art techniques.

In recent years several more advanced stochastic optimization algorithms have been proposed, such as stochastic average gradients (SAG) (Schmidt et al., 2017), stochastic variance reduced gradients (SVRG) (Johnson and Zhang, 2013), and SAGA that combines elements of both (Schatz et al., 2014). However, to our knowledge these techniques have not been successfully adapted for automatic variational inference. In Section 4.2 we will present a new variant of SAG that works also when the gradients are estimated as Monte Carlo approximations, and therefore briefly describe below the basic idea behind stochastic average gradients.

SAG performs gradient updates based on an estimate for the full batch gradient, obtained by summing up gradients stored for individual data points (or for mini-batches to save memory). Whenever a data point is seen again during the optimization the stored gradient for that point is replaced by the gradient evaluated at the current parameter values. The full gradient estimate hence consists of individual gradients estimated for different parameter values; the most recently computed gradients are accurate but the ones computed long time ago may correspond to vastly different parameter values. This introduces bias (Schatz et al., 2014), but especially towards the convergence the variance of the estimated full batch gradient is considerably smaller than that of the latest mini-batch, speeding up convergence.

3 METHOD

All gradient-based optimization algorithms follow the same basic pattern of computing a gradient for a mini-batch of samples and updating the parameters. The computational effort required goes almost solely into evaluating the gradient of the loss. To speed up the optimization, we next present a technique that allows computationally lighter evaluation of the gradient in scenarios where the gradient is computed using a Monte Carlo approximation. The presentation here is based on the reparameterization estimate (3) that benefits more off this treatment – as will become evident later – but for completeness we discuss also the score function estimate (4) in Section 3.2.

The Monte Carlo approximation for estimating the gradient depends on the data x and a set of M parameters

[1] Here cast as minimization of negative evidence, to maintain consistent terminology with gradient descent literature

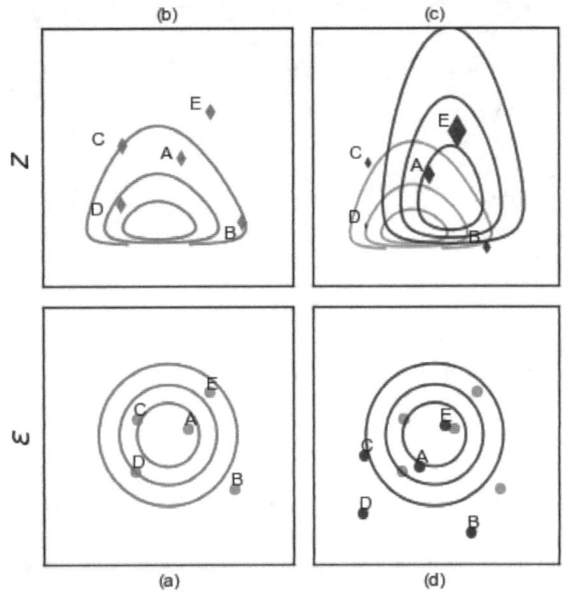

Figure 1: **Importance sampling illustration for reparametrization gradients**: A Monte Carlo estimate for the model evidence lower bound is obtained by drawing M (here 5) samples z_m from the approximation $q(\lambda)$ depicted by the contours in top left panel. The reparameterization estimate does this by actually drawing the samples ϵ_m from a standard distribution depicted in the bottom left panel, transforming them to the parameter space with $f(\epsilon, \lambda)$. The importance sampling estimate for the evidence lower bound of another approximation $q(\lambda')$ (top right) is obtained by keeping z_m fixed and computing the $\epsilon'_m = f^{-1}(z_m, \lambda')$ that would have been required as draws from the standard distribution (bottom right) to produce them. The estimate then re-weights the already computed log-likelihoods $\log p(x, z_m)$ with $w_m = \frac{\phi(\epsilon'_m)}{\phi(\epsilon_m)}$ to approximate the evidence lower bound; here sample E has higher probability under the new approximation, shown as larger diamond, and sample D has lower probability. The same basic procedure applies also for estimating the gradients instead of the evidence.

z_m drawn from the current approximation. As highlighted in (3), the actual computation factorizes into $\nabla_z p(x, z_m)$ that depends only on x and z_m and into $\nabla_\lambda f(\epsilon, \lambda)$ and $\nabla_\lambda |\det_{J_f}(\epsilon_m, \lambda)|$ that depend only on ϵ_m and λ. The former part is typically considerably more computationally expensive. The observation that the slower part does not directly depend on the parameters hints that it should be possible to avoid re-computing the term even if the approximation changes, and this indeed is the case as explained next.

Assume we have already estimated the gradient at some parameters λ, implying that we have also evaluated $\nabla_z p(x, z_m)$ for some set of z_m. The question now is how to estimate the gradient at parameters $\lambda' = \lambda + \delta$ that are (typically only slightly) different. It turns out this can be done using the well-known concept of *importance sampling* originally designed for approximating expectations when we cannot directly draw samples from the density of interest. In our case, however, we *could* draw samples directly from the new approximation, but *choose not to* since the gradient can be estimated also using the old approximation as a proposal distribution. That is, we are using importance sampling for an unusual reason but can still use all the standard tools.

Typically, we use importance sampling to find the expectation of a function $f(z)$ over the target distribution $p(z)$ if we are able to draw samples only from a proposal distribution $q(z)$. The expectation of $f(z)$ over $p(z)$ can then be approximated by

$$\mathbb{E}[f] = \int \frac{p(z)}{q(z)} f(z) q(z)\, \delta z = \frac{1}{M} \sum_{m=1}^{M} \frac{p(z_m)}{q(z_m)} f(z_m). \quad (5)$$

The quantities $w_m = p(z_m)/q(z_m)$ are the *importance weights* that correct the bias introduced by sampling from the wrong distribution $q(z)$ (Bishop, 2006). The weights w_m are non-negative and tend to zero when $p(z)$ is completely mismatched to $q(z)$, and $w_m > 1$ when the sample z_m is more likely under the $p(z)$. The estimate above is unbiased, but has high – potentially infinite – variance when $q(z)$ and $p(z)$ are dissimilar. Next we show how importance sampling can be used for evaluating the reparameterization gradient (3).

To save computation we want to re-use the model gradients $\nabla_z \log p(x, z_m)$ already available for certain values of z_m and hence need to consider estimates that keep these values fixed. This means we need to find the ϵ'_m under the new approximation $q_{\lambda'}(z)$ that correspond to these values, by computing $\epsilon'_m = f^{-1}(z_m, \lambda')$. Given these values we can evaluate the necessary quantities to compute both the importance weights and the other terms ($\nabla_\lambda f(\epsilon'_m, \lambda')$ and $\nabla_\lambda |\det_{J_f}(\epsilon_m, \lambda)|$) required for evaluating the gradient itself.

The resulting importance sampling estimate for (3) is

$$\nabla^i_\lambda \mathcal{L}(\lambda) \approx \frac{1}{M} \sum_{m=1}^{M} \big[\nabla_z \log p(x, z_m) \nabla_\lambda f(\epsilon'_m, \lambda') \quad (6)$$
$$+ \nabla_\lambda |\det_{J_f}(\epsilon'_m, \lambda')| \big] \times w_m,$$

where the i in $\nabla^i_\lambda \mathcal{L}(\lambda)$ refers to the importance-sampled estimate of the gradient. The computationally expensive part of the gradient $\nabla_z \log p(x, z_m)$ is already available and need not be computed. The rest of the terms are efficient to evaluate, and hence the whole gradient estimate is obtained in a fraction of a time compared to computing

Algorithm 1: Importance sampled gradients

input : Samples z_m and ϵ_m, gradient $\nabla_z p(x, z_m)$, transformation $f()$, current approximation λ'

output: Importance sampled gradients $\nabla^i_\lambda \mathcal{L}(\lambda)$

$\epsilon'_m \leftarrow f^{-1}(z_m, \lambda')$

$w_m \leftarrow \frac{\phi(\epsilon'_m)}{\phi(\epsilon_m)}$

Calculate $\nabla^i_\lambda \mathcal{L}(\lambda)$ using (6)

it from scratch. The importance weights are provided by

$$w_m = \frac{\phi(\epsilon'_m)}{\phi(\epsilon_m)} \tag{7}$$

and hence only require evaluating densities of the standard distribution underlying the approximation. The above description is summarized in Algorithm 1 and illustrated graphically in Figure 1.

It is also worth noting that if $f(\cdot)$ is constructed as a series of transformations, for example as element-wise transformations of reparameterized normal distribution as done by (Kucukelbir et al., 2017), then parts of the term $\nabla_\lambda |\det_{J_f}(\epsilon'_m, \lambda')|$ can (and naturally should) also be re-used. This is, however, of secondary importance compared to the computational saving of re-using $\nabla_z \log p(x, z_m)$.

A practical challenge with importance sampling is that for high-dimensional densities the weights w_m easily tend to zero. Variational approximation is, however, often conducted for approximations that factorize over the parameters of the approximation as $q(\lambda) = \prod_s q(\lambda_{S_s})$, where $\{S_s\}$ is a partitioning of the parameter vector. The importance sampling estimate can – and should – be done for each factor separately, since the gradient $\nabla_z \log p(x, z_m)$ can be computed for each approximation factor independently even if $\log p(x, z_m)$ itself does not factorize. We show in Section 5.1 that the technique helps at least until factors consisting of roughly ten parameters.

3.1 REPARAMETERIZATION GRADIENT EXAMPLE

To further clarify the derivation above, we next illustrate the procedure for the common scenario of Gaussian reparameterization combining $\phi(\epsilon) = \mathcal{N}(0, I)$ with $z = \mu + L\epsilon$, denoting $\lambda = \{\mu, L\}$. Given a set of z_m drawn from $q(\lambda)$ we want to estimate the gradient evaluated at λ' using (6).

First we compute $\epsilon'_m = f^{-1}(z_m, \lambda') = L^{-1}(z_m - \mu)$ and evaluate $\phi(\epsilon'_m)$ under the standard normal distribution. The weight w_m can then readily be evaluated using (7), computing $\phi(\epsilon_m)$ as well if it has not already been evaluated because of being used for another importance sampling estimate.

To compute the gradient (6) we need to re-compute $\nabla_\lambda f(\epsilon'_m, \lambda')$ and $\nabla_\lambda |\det_{J_f}(\epsilon'_m, \lambda')|$. For μ these terms are simply identity and zero, whereas for L we get z_m and $\nabla_L \log|L'| \equiv \Delta_{L'}$. The exact form of $\Delta_{L'}$ depends on the assumptions made for L; see Titsias and Lázaro-Gredilla (2014) for details. The final importance sampled estimate for the gradient is then

$$\nabla^i_\mu \mathcal{L}(\mu', L') \approx \frac{1}{M} \sum_{m=1}^{M} w_m \nabla_z \log p(x, z_m)$$

$$\nabla^i_L \mathcal{L}(\mu', L') \approx \frac{1}{M} \sum_{m=1}^{M} w_m \left[\nabla_z \log p(x, z_m) \epsilon'_m + \Delta_{L'}\right].$$

An important observation here is that the importance sampling procedure does not merely re-weight the terms $\nabla_z \log p(x, z_m)$, but in addition the transformation that converts them into the λ space changes because of the new values of ϵ'_m. These values depend on the approximation parameters in a non-linear fashion and hence the gradient itself is a non-linear transformation of the gradient evaluated at λ (for a graphical illustration, see Figure 2). This is crucially important for development of the practical optimization algorithms in Section 4; if the transformation was linear then the importance sampling estimate would not necessarily provide improvement over careful adaptation of element-wise learning rates.

3.2 SCORE FUNCTION ESTIMATE

Above we discussed the importance sampling estimate from the perspective of the reparameterization estimate. For completeness we also show how it can be applied for the score function estimate, and discuss why it is less useful there.

The Monte Carlo approximation for the score function (4) is obtained directly by drawing samples from the approximation $q(\lambda)$. To approximate the gradient for $q(\lambda')$ we merely use the standard importance sampling equation (5) to obtain the approximation

$$\frac{1}{M} \sum_{m=1}^{M} w_m \left[\log p(x, z_m) - \log q_\lambda(z_m)\right] \nabla_\lambda \log q_\lambda(z_m),$$

where $w_m = \frac{q(z|\lambda')}{q(z|\lambda)}$. This is still an unbiased estimate, but the computational saving is typically smaller than in the reparameterization case. We do not need to evaluate $\log p(x, z_m)$ since the samples z_m are kept constant, but all other terms need to be computed again and evaluating the gradient of the approximation is not cheap. This estimate is only useful when the evaluation of the log probability utterly dominates the total computation.

Algorithm 2: Importance sampled SGD

input : data X, model $p(x, z)$, the variational approximation $q_\lambda(z)$, threshold t
output: variational parameters λ^*

while *$\mathcal{L}(\lambda)$ has not converged* **do**
  if *random_uniform* $< t$ **then**
    Retrieve last stored z_m, ϵ_m and $\nabla_z \log p(x, z_m)$
    Update $\nabla_\lambda \mathcal{L}$ using Algorithm (1)
  else
    Draw mini-batch x from X
    $\epsilon_m \sim \phi(\epsilon)$
    $z_m \leftarrow f(\epsilon_m, \lambda)$
    Update $\nabla_\lambda \mathcal{L}$ using Equation (3)
    Store z_m, ϵ_m and $\nabla_z \log p(x, z_m)$
  end
  Update $\lambda \leftarrow \lambda + \rho \nabla_\lambda \mathcal{L}(\lambda)$
end

4 ALGORITHMS

In the following we describe example optimization algorithms based on the importance sampling idea. The details are provided for a straightforward variant of SGD and for a generalization of stochastic average gradients, but other related algorithms could be instantiated as well.

4.1 IMPORTANCE SAMPLED SGD

Stochastic gradient descent estimates the gradient based on a mini-batch and then takes a step along the gradient direction, typically using adaptive learning rates such as those by Kingma and Ba (2015); Duchi et al. (2010).

The importance sampled SGD (I-SGD; Algorithm 2) follows otherwise the same pattern, but for each mini-batch we conduct several gradient steps instead of just one. For the first one we evaluate the gradient directly using (2). After updating the approximation we apply Algorithm 1 to obtain an importance-sampled estimate for the gradient evaluated at the new parameter values, and proceed to take another gradient step using that estimate. For each step we use a proper estimate for the mini-batch gradient that can, after the first evaluation, be computed in a fraction of a time. After taking a few steps we then proceed to analyze a new mini-batch, again needing to compute the gradient from scratch since now x has changed.

After passing through the whole data we have evaluated $\log p(x, z)$ and its gradient once for every data point, just as in standard SGD. However, we have taken considerably more gradient steps, possibly by a factor of ten. Alternatively, we can think of it as performing more updates given a constant number of model gradient evaluations.

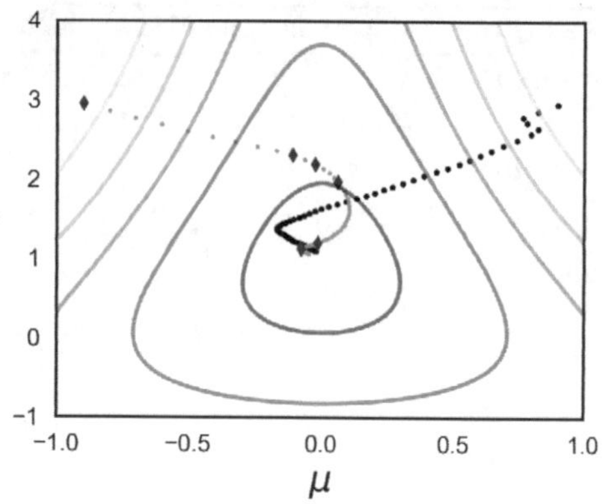

Figure 2: **Illustration of I-SGD.** I-SGD learns to approximate the posterior of a univariate normal distribution (parameterized by mean and precision) by computing the gradient of the evidence lower bound only a few times from scratch, indicated by red diamonds. Between these operations it performs multiple gradient steps (small red dots) using importance sampling estimates for the gradient that can be computed in a fraction of a time, while still following a non-linear trajectory between the red diamonds. For comparison, standard SGD, needs to estimate the full gradient for every step (blue dots).

A practical detail concerns the choice of how many steps to take for each mini-batch. This choice is governed by two aspects. On one hand we should not use the importance sampled estimate if the approximation has changed too much since computing the $\nabla_z \log p(x, z_m)$ terms, recognized typically as w_m tending to zero. On the other hand, we should not take too many steps even if the approximation does not change dramatically, since the gradient is still based on just a single mini-batch.

The empirical experiments in this paper are run with a simple heuristic that randomly determines whether to take another step with the current mini-batch or to proceed to the next one. This introduces a single tuning parameter t that controls the expected number of steps per mini-batch. The algorithm is robust for this choice; we obtain practical speedups with values ranging from $t = 0.5$ to $t = 0.9$. Finally, importance-sampling could in principle result in very large gradients if $w_m \gg 1$ for some m; we never encountered this in practice, but a safe choice is to proceed to the next batch if that happens.

For a practical illustration of the algorithm, see Figure 2 that approximates the posterior over the mean and precision of a normal model. Here $t = 0.9$ and hence we take on average 9 importance-sampled gradient steps for each mini-batch. The I-SGD algorithm reaches the optimum in roughly as many steps as conventional SGD but achieves it almost ten times faster.

Algorithm 3: Importance sampled SAG

input : data X, model $p(x, z)$, the variational approximation $q_\lambda(z)$, batches B
output: variational parameters λ^*

while *$\mathcal{L}(\lambda)$ has not converged* **do**
  foreach *mini-batch x_b in X* **do**
    $\epsilon_m^b \sim \phi(\epsilon)$
    $z_m^b \leftarrow f(\epsilon_m, \lambda)$
    Calculate $\nabla_\lambda^b \mathcal{L}$ using Equation (3)
    Store z_m^b, ϵ_m^b and $\nabla_z^b \log p(x_b, z_m)$
    foreach *mini-batch x_c in $X \backslash \{x_b\}$* **do**
      Retrieve z_m^c, ϵ_m^c and $\nabla_z^c \log p(x_c, z_m)$
      Update $\nabla_\lambda^c \mathcal{L}$ using Algorithm (1)
    end
    $\nabla_\lambda \mathcal{L} \leftarrow \sum_{n=1}^B \nabla_\lambda^n \mathcal{L}$
    Update $\lambda \leftarrow \lambda + \rho \nabla_\lambda \mathcal{L}(\lambda)$
  end
end

4.2 IMPORTANCE SAMPLED SAG

Stochastic average gradients (Schmidt et al., 2017) stores the batch gradient and iteratively updates it for the samples in a given mini-batch. In the following we derive a variant of SAG (Algorithm 3) that uses importance sampling to both re-weight and update the gradients for the historical mini-batches using (6), helping to detect and avoid using stale gradients whose parameter values have changed so much since computing them.

When visiting a new mini-batch we compute the gradient using (3). For all previously visited mini-batches we compute the importance weights and modify the gradient according to (6). The whole gradient is formed by summing up the terms for all mini-batches. It is important to note that the importance sampling changes the weight of the gradient, decreasing it towards zero for the mini-batches evaluated under clearly different parameter settings, and transforms the gradient to better match one that would have been calculated under the current approximation.

This algorithm provides a justified version of SAG for automatic variational inference. The computational cost is higher than for standard SAG since we need to evaluate the importance weights and compute the terms related to the gradient of the transformation for all past mini-batches. There is, however, no additional memory overhead and the amount of evaluations for the gradient of the model itself is the same. This overhead for importance sampling the gradients for other batches is not negligible, but usually still small enough that the resulting algorithm outperforms a naive implementation of SAG because of vastly more accurate gradient estimates, as shown in Section 5.3. In case updating the past gradients becomes too costly, a simple remedy is to use only the latest K mini-batches for some reasonable choice of K.

5 EXPERIMENTS

In this section we first demonstrate how the behavior of importance sampling depends on the dimensionality of the approximation. We then empirically compared both I-SGD and I-SAG for real variational inference tasks on a range of alternative models and settings.

5.1 DIMENSIONALITY OF THE APPROXIMATION

Figure 3 studies importance weights of approximations factorized at different granularities on a 100-dimensional diagonal multivariate Gaussian. An important observation is that even if importance sampling itself fails for factors of high dimensionality, the I-SGD algorithm degrades gracefully. For low-dimensional factors, up to at least 5-10 dimensions, we can safely take 5-10 steps with each mini-batch while still having accurate gradient estimates. When the dimensionality of individual factors reaches around 25 the weights tend to zero already after a single gradient step, but the algorithm does not break down. It merely needs to proceed immediately to the next step, reverting back to standard SGD.

5.2 IMPORTANCE SAMPLED SGD

We show in Figure 4 how I-SGD consistently bests SGD for a variety of different models, especially for the reparameterization estimate. For these experiments we use fully factorized mean-field approximation,

We first apply the reparameterization estimate for three probabilistic models: (a) a diagonal multivariate Gaussian with a standard normal prior on the mean and Gamma priors on the precisions, trained on $N = 50000$ data points of $D = 500$ dimensions; (b) a Bayesian linear regression model with standard normal priors on the weights and a Gamma prior on the precision with $N = 50000$ and $D = 500$; and (c) a Gaussian mixture model with the usual conjugate priors, $N = 10000$, $D = 2$ and $K = 25$ clusters. We used fully factorized variational approximations for all models, with $\mathrm{Softplus}$ transforms for the positively constrained precision parameters and the stick breaking transform for the mixture weights of the last model. For all three choices the I-SGD algorithm with $t = 0.9$ converges to the same optimal solution as SGD, but does so in roughly an order of magnitude faster. For fair comparison the size of the mini-batch, the initial learning rate were chosen for each method to work well for SGD, forcing I-SGD to use the same choices. For both algorithms, we used M = 1 sample to estimate the gradients and Adam (Kingma and Ba, 2015) to adaptively control the learning rate during optimization.

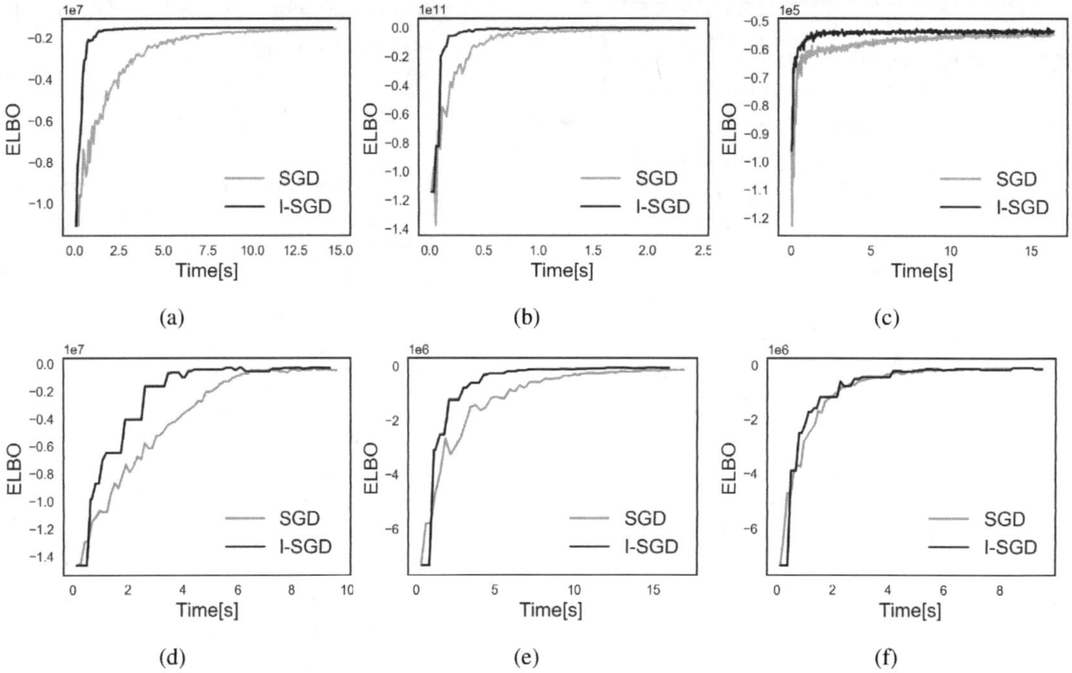

Figure 4: **Performance of I-SGD on different models and gradient estimates**: We evaluate the performance of I-SGD for reparameterization gradients in the top row and for score function gradients on the bottom row. For the reparameterization gradients our algorithm converges an order of magnitude faster than SGD for all three models. The computational savings in score function gradient is directly proportional to the complexity of the model's log-probability and the simplicity of the variational approximation; in (d) evaluating the model dominates the total cost whereas in (f) the advantage of I-SGD is lost because less computation is saved. For description of the models refer to Section 5.2.

We then compare I-SGD and SGD using the score function estimates on a Poisson likelihood with a single Gamma prior on the rate (d), and Bayesian linear regression models with large (e) and small (f) mini-batch. The variational approximations used were the same as the priors. For the sub-plots (d) and (e) evaluating the log-probability takes long compared to evaluating the gradient of the approximation because of a large mini-batch size, and hence I-SGD is faster. With a smaller mini-batch size (f) the advantage is lost because evaluating the gradient of the approximation starts to dominate. We used $M = 100$ samples and did not consider variance reduction techniques for simplicity.

5.3 IMPORTANCE SAMPLED SAG

Figure 5 compares the I-SAG algorithm (Algorithm 3) against naive implementation of SAG (Schmidt et al., 2017). Both algorithms are initialized by passing once through the data with I-SGD, to provide the initial estimate for the full batch gradient.

While SAG eventually converges to the right solution, the progress is slow and erratic due to stale mini-batch gradients being accumulated into the full gradient. I-SAG fixes the issue by not only down-weighting gradients corresponding to mini-batches visited several updates ago, but also by transforming the gradients to match the current approximation. The additional computation required for adapting the gradients for other mini-batches results in a computational overhead of, here, roughly 30% per iteration, but the improved accuracy of the batch gradient estimate is more than enough to overcome this.

Stochastic running average (SRA) provides another baseline that down-weights older mini-batches exponentially. Similar to I-SAG, it avoids using mini-batches with badly outdated gradient estimates, by using a simple weighting scheme without transforming the gradients. It outperforms SAG, but converges more slowly than I-SAG. Hence, I-SAG is stable implementation of SAG for variational inference, outperforming the alternative of running averages often considered as a remedy for the issues of SAG.

6 DISCUSSION

Automatic variational inference using automatically differentiated gradients has in recent years become a feasible technique for inference for a wide class of probabilistic models, extending the scope of variational approximations beyond simple conjugate models towards practical probabilistic inference engines. While standard computational platforms and advances in convex optimization are read-

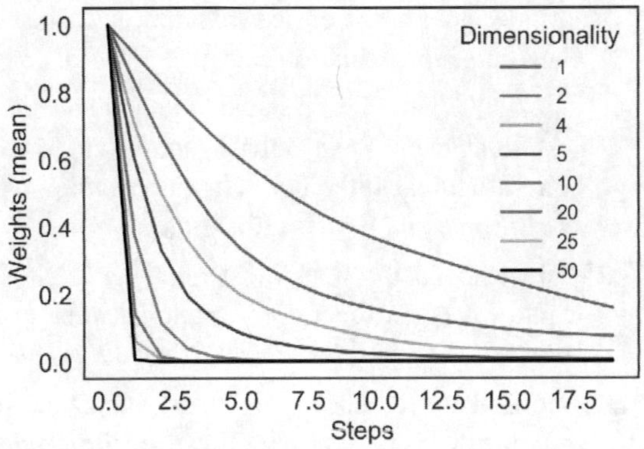

Figure 3: **Importance sampling and dimensionality**: Illustration of the behavior of the importance sampling weights during optimization for approximations of varying dimensionality. The approximation $q(\theta|\lambda)$ is over a 100-dimensional space and is factorized as $\prod_i q(\theta_{S_i}|\lambda_i)$ so that the color of the line indicates the size of each term; for example, the purple line corresponds to factorized approximation with 20 terms of 5 variables. For fully factorized approximation (blue line) and still for factors of 5-10 dimensions the weights decay slowly and it pays off to take a few gradient steps before re-calculating the gradient. For factors of 25 (yellow line) or more dimensions the weights drop to zero practically immediately. The I-SGD algorithm still works, but does not give any speed advantage.

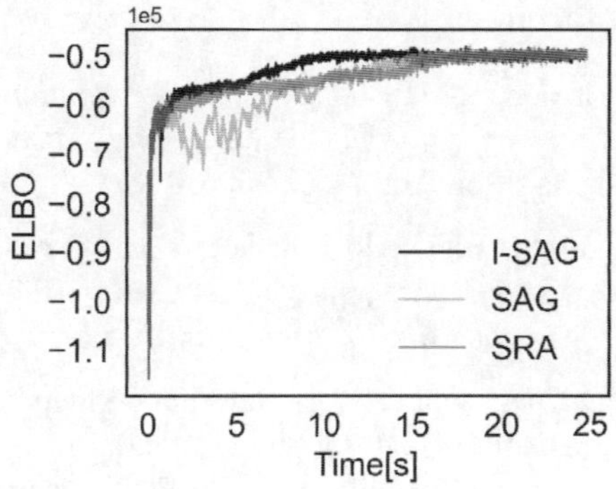

Figure 5: **Importance Sampled Stochastic Average Gradient**: Standard SAG algorithm (yellow line) performs poorly when using Monte Carlo approximation for the gradients. This can be in part overcome by considering a running average (SRA) of the mini-batch gradients instead (blue line, with $\alpha = 0.9$ as the decay factor), letting the algorithm ignore stale gradients. The I-SAG algorithm (red line) outperforms both because it down-weights mini-batch gradients evaluated earlier in a more justified manner and because it also transforms the historical gradients to match the current approximation instead of using them directly.

ily applicable for gradient-based variational inference, the need to use Monte Carlo approximation to estimate the gradients necessarily induces a computational overhead – with very few samples the gradients are noisy whereas the cost grows linearly as a function of the samples.

Our work addressed this central element, discussing ways to speed up the gradient-based inference of variational approximations. By highlighting how the gradient computation separates into two steps we derived an importance-sampling estimate for the gradient that often only needs to evaluate the computationally cheaper part to provide the estimate. Skipping the computationally costly evaluation of the gradient of the model itself as often as possible lead to a practical speedup that is independent of other improvements provided by more advanced optimization algorithms (Johnson and Zhang, 2013; Schatz et al., 2014). Our method relies on the inverse transformation being unique and efficient to compute. This might not be the case for complex structured approximations or approximations parameterized by neural networks; we leave more efficient extensions for such cases as future work.

We demonstrated the core idea in creating a more efficient stochastic gradient descent algorithm for both reparameterization (Titsias and Lázaro-Gredilla, 2014; Kucukelbir et al., 2017) and score function (Ranganath et al., 2014) estimates used for variational inference. In addition, we formulated a theoretically justified variant of stochastic average gradients (Schmidt et al., 2017) applicable for variational inference. The idea, however, extends well beyond these special cases. For example, the rejection sampling variational inference (Naesseth et al., 2017) can be readily combined with our importance sampling strategy and is expected to result in a similar speedup.

Our main focus was in practically applicable algorithms, with much of the theoretical analysis left for future work. Two particular directions are immediately apparent: (a) The decision of when to use importance sampling estimates and (b) the behavior for approximations that do not factorize into reasonably small factors. In this work we showed how simple randomized procedure for determining whether to re-compute the gradient for a new mini-batch results in practical and robust algorithm, but more theoretically justified decisions such as inspecting for example the variance of the importance sampling estimate could be considered. The proposed algorithms are efficient for approximating factors of dimensionality up to roughly ten; for factors of higher dimensionality the algorithms revert back to the standard variants since all gradients need to be computed from scratch for every iteration.

Acknowledgements

This work was financed by the Academy of Finland (decision number 266969) and by the *Scalable Probabilistic Analytics* project of Tekes, the Finnish funding agency for innovation.

References

Christopher M. Bishop. *Pattern Recognition and Machine Learning (Information Science and Statistics)*. Springer-Verlag New York, Inc., 2006.

David M. Blei, Alp Kucukelbir, and Jon D. McAuliffe. Variational inference: a review for statisticians. *arXiv:1601.00670*, 2016.

John Duchi, Elad Hazan, and Yoram Singer. Adaptive subgradient methods for online learning and stochastic optimization. Technical report, EECS Department, University of California, Berkeley, 2010.

Yarin Gal. *Uncertainty in deep learning*. PhD thesis, University of Cambridge, 2016.

Andrew Gelman, Aki Vehtari, Pasi Jylänki, Tuomas Sivula, Dustin Tran, Swupnil Sahai, Paul Blomstedt, John P. Cunningham, David Schiminovich, and Christian Robert. Expectation propagation as a way of life: A framework for bayesian inference on partitioned data. *arXiv:1412.4869*, 2017.

Rie Johnson and Tong Zhang. Accelerating stochastic gradient descent using predictive variance reduction. In *Advances in Neural Information Processing Systems*, 2013.

Michael I. Jordan, Zoubin Ghahramani, Tommi S. Jaakkola, and Lawrence K. Saul. An introduction to variational methods for graphical models. *Machine Learning*, 37(2), 1999.

Diederik P. Kingma and Jimmy Ba. Adam: a method for stochastic optimization. In *The International Conference on Learning Representations*, 2015.

Diederik P. Kingma and Max Welling. Auto-encoding variational Bayes. In *The International Conference on Learning Representations*, 2014.

Diederik P. Kingma, Tim Salimans, Rafal Józefowicz, Xi Chen, Ilya Sutskever, and Max Welling. Improving variational autoencoders with inverse autoregressive flow. In *Advances in Neural Information Processing Systems*, 2016.

Jack Kleijnen and R.Y. Rubinstein. Optimization and sensitivity analysis of computer simulation models by the score function method. Discussion paper, Tilburg University, Center for Economic Research, 1995.

Alp Kucukelbir, Dustin Tran, Rajesh Ranganath, Andrew Gelman, and David M. Blei. Automatic differentiation variational inference. *Journal of Machine Learning Research*, 18(14):1–45, 2017.

Christian A. Naesseth, Francisco J. R. Ruiz, Scott W. Linderman, and David M. Blei. Reparameterization gradients through acceptance-rejection sampling algorithms. In *Proceedings of the 20th International Conference on Artificial Intelligence and Statistics*, 2017.

Manfred Opper and Cedric Archambeau. The variational Gaussian approximation revisited. *Neural computation*, 21(3), 2009.

Rajesh Ranganath, Sean Gerrish, and David M Blei. Black box variational inference. In *Proceedings of Artificial Intelligence and Statistics*, 2014.

Rajesh Ranganath, Dustin Tran, Jaan Altosaar, and David M. Blei. Operator variational inference. In *Advances in Neural Information Processing Systems*, 2016.

Danilo Jimenez Rezende and Shakir Mohamed. Variational inference with normalizing flows. In *Proceedings of International Conference on Machine Learning*, 2015.

Geoffrey Roeder, Yuhuai Wu, and David Duvenaud. Sticking the landing: An asymptotically zero-variance gradient estimator for variational inference. *arXiv:1703.09194*, 2017.

Francisco J. R. Ruiz, Michalis K. Titsias, and David M. Blei. The generalized reparameterization gradient. In *Advances in Neural Information Processing Systems*, 2016.

Tim Salimans and David A. Knowles. Fixed-form variational posterior approximation through stochastic linear regression. *Bayesian Analysis*, 8(4), 2013.

Fonnesbeck C. Salvatier J, Wiecki TV. Probabilistic programming in Python using PyMC3. *PeerJ Computer Science 2:e55*, 2016.

Thomas Schatz, Vijayaditya Peddinti, Xuan-Nga Cao, Francis R. Bach, Hynek Hermansky, and Emmanuel Dupoux. Evaluating speech features with the minimal-pair ABX task (II): resistance to noise. In *Annual Conference of the International Speech Communication Association*, 2014.

Mark W. Schmidt, Nicolas Le Roux, and Francis R. Bach. Minimizing finite sums with the stochastic average gradient. *Mathematical Programming*, 162:83, 2017. doi: 10.1007/s10107-016-1030-6.

Michalis Titsias and Miguel Lázaro-Gredilla. Doubly stochastic variational Bayes for non-conjugate inference. In *Proceedings of International Conference on Machine Learning*, 2014.

Dustin Tran, Alp Kucukelbir, Adji B. Dieng, Maja Rudolph, Dawen Liang, and David M. Blei. Edward: A library for probabilistic modeling, inference, and criticism. *arXiv:1610.09787*, 2016.

Multi-dueling Bandits with Dependent Arms

Yanan Sui
Caltech
Pasadena, CA 91125
ysui@caltech.edu

Vincent Zhuang
Caltech
Pasadena, CA 91125
vzhuang@caltech.edu

Joel W. Burdick
Caltech
Pasadena, CA 91125
jwb@robotics.caltech.edu

Yisong Yue
Caltech
Pasadena, CA 91125
yyue@caltech.edu

Abstract

The dueling bandits problem is an online learning framework for learning from pairwise preference feedback, and is particularly well-suited for modeling settings that elicit subjective or implicit human feedback. In this paper, we study the problem of *multi-dueling bandits with dependent arms*, which extends the original dueling bandits setting by simultaneously dueling multiple arms as well as modeling dependencies between arms. These extensions capture key characteristics found in many real-world applications, and allow for the opportunity to develop significantly more efficient algorithms than were possible in the original setting. We propose the SELFSPARRING algorithm, which reduces the multi-dueling bandits problem to a conventional bandit setting that can be solved using a stochastic bandit algorithm such as Thompson Sampling, and can naturally model dependencies using a Gaussian process prior. We present a no-regret analysis for multi-dueling setting, and demonstrate the effectiveness of our algorithm empirically on a wide range of simulation settings.

1 INTRODUCTION

In many online learning settings, particularly those that involve human feedback, reliable feedback is often limited to pairwise preferences (e.g., "is A better than B?"). Examples include implicit or subjective feedback for information retrieval and various recommender systems (Chapelle et al., 2012; Sui & Burdick, 2014). This setup motivates the dueling bandits problem (Yue et al., 2012), which formalizes the problem of online regret minimization via preference feedback.

The original dueling bandits setting ignores many real world considerations. For instance, in personalized clinical recommendation settings (Sui & Burdick, 2014), it is often more practical for subjects to provide preference feedback on several actions (or treatments) simultaneously rather than just two. Furthermore, the action space can be very large, possibly infinite, but often has a low-dimensional dependency structure.

In this paper, we address both of these challenges in a unified framework, which we call *multi-dueling bandits with dependent arms*. We extend the original dueling bandits problem by simultaneously dueling multiple arms as well as modeling dependencies between arms using a kernel. Explicitly formalizing these real-world characteristics provides an opportunity to develop principled algorithms that are much more efficient than algorithms designed for the original setting. For instance, most dueling bandits algorithms suffer regret that scales linearly with the number of arms, which is not practical when the number of arms is very large or infinite.

For this setting, we propose the SELFSPARRING algorithm, inspired by the Sparring algorithm from Ailon et al. (2014), which algorithmically reduces the multi-dueling bandits problem into a conventional muilti-armed bandit problem that can be solved using a stochastic bandit algorithm such as Thompson Sampling (Chapelle & Li, 2011; Russo & Van Roy, 2014). Our approach can naturally incorporate dependencies using a Gaussian process prior with an appropriate kernel.

While there have been some prior work on multi-dueling (Brost et al., 2016) and learning from pairwise preferences over kernels (Gonzalez et al., 2016), to the best of our knowledge, our approach is the first to address to both in a unified framework. We are also the first to provide a regret analysis of the multi-dueling setting. We further demonstrate the effectiveness of our approach over conventional dueling bandits approaches in a wide range of simulation experiments.

2 BACKGROUND

2.1 Dueling Bandits

The original dueling bandits problem is a sequential optimization problem with relative feedback. Let $\mathcal{B} = \{b_1, \ldots, b_K\}$ be the set of K bandits (or arms). At each iteration, the algorithm duels or compares a single pair of arms b_i, b_j from the set of K arms (b_i and b_j can be identical). The outcome of each duel between b_i and b_j is an independent sample of a Bernoulli random variable. We define the probability that arm b_i beats b_j as:

$$P(b_i \succ b_j) = \phi(b_i, b_j) + 1/2,$$

where $\phi(b_i, b_j) \in [-1/2, 1/2]$ denotes the stochastic preference between b_i and b_j, thus $b_i \succ b_j \Leftrightarrow \phi(b_i, b_j) > 0$. We assume there is a total ordering, and WLOG that $b_i \succ b_j \Leftrightarrow i < j$.

The setting proceeds in a sequence of iterations or rounds. At each iteration t, the decision maker must choose a pair of bandits $b_t^{(1)}$ and $b_t^{(2)}$ to compare, and observes the outcome of that comparison. The quality of the decision making is then quantified using a notion of cumulative regret of T iterations:

$$R_T = \sum_{t=1}^{T} \left[\phi(b_1, b_t^{(1)}) + \phi(b_1, b_t^{(2)}) \right]. \tag{1}$$

When the algorithm has converged to the best arm b_1, then it can simply duel b_1 against itself, thus incurring no additional regret. In the recommender systems setting, one can interpret (1) as a measure of how much the user(s) would have preferred the best bandit over the the ones presented by the algorithm.

To date, there have been several algorithms proposed for the stochastic dueling bandits problem, including Interleaved Filter (Yue et al., 2012), Beat the Mean (Yue & Joachims, 2011), SAVAGE (Urvoy et al., 2013), RUCB (Zoghi et al., 2014, 2015b), Sparring (Ailon et al., 2014; Dudík et al., 2015), RMED (Komiyama et al., 2015), and DTS (Wu & Liu, 2016). Our proposed approach, SELFSPARRING, is inspired by Sparring, which along with RUCB-style algorithms are the best performing methods. In contrast to Sparring, which has no theoretical guarantees, we provide no-regret guarantees for SELFSPARRING, and demonstrate significantly better performance in the multi-dueling setting.

Previous work on extending the original dueling bandits setting have been largely restricted to settings that duel a single pair of arms at a time. These include continuous-armed convex dueling bandits (Yue & Joachims, 2009), contextual dueling bandits which also introduces the von Neumann winner solution concept (Dudík et al., 2015), sparse dueling bandits that focuses on the Borda winner solution concept (Jamieson et al., 2015), Copeland dueling bandits that focuses on the Copeland winner solution concept (Zoghi et al., 2015a), and adversarial dueling bandits (Gajane et al., 2015). In contrast, our work studies the complementary directions of how to formalize multiple duels simultaneously, as well as how to reduce the dimensionality of modeling the action space using a low-dimensional similarity kernel.

Recently, there have been increasing interest in studying personalization settings that simultaneously elicit multiple pairwise comparisons. Example settings include information retrieval (Hofmann et al., 2011; Schuth et al., 2014, 2016) and clinical treatment (Sui & Burdick, 2014). There have also been some previous work on multi-dueling bandits settings (Brost et al., 2016; Sui & Burdick, 2014; Schuth et al., 2016), however the previous approaches are limited in their scope and lack rigorous theoretical guarantees. In contrast, our approach can handle a wide range of multi-dueling mechanisms, has near-optimal regret guarantees, and can be easily composed with kernels to model dependent arms.

2.2 Multi-armed Bandits

Our proposed algorithm, SELFSPARRING, utilizes a multi-armed bandit (MAB) algorithm as a subroutine, and so we provide here a brief formal description of the conventional MAB problem for completeness. The stochastic MAB problem (Robbins, 1952) refers to an iterative decision making problem where the algorithm repeatedly chooses among K actions (or bandits or arms). In contrast to the dueling bandits setting, where the feedback is relative between two arms, here, we receive an absolute reward that depends on the arm selected. We assume WLOG that every reward is bounded between $[0, 1]$.[1] The goal then is to minimize the cumulative regret compared to the best arm:

$$R_T^{\text{MAB}} = \sum_{t=1}^{T} \left[\mu^1 - \mu(b_t) \right], \tag{2}$$

where b_t denotes the arm chosen at time t, $\mu(b)$ denotes the expected reward of arm b, and $\mu^1 = \operatorname{argmax}_b \mu(b)$. Popular algorithms for the stochastic setting include UCB (upper confidence bound) algorithms (Auer et al., 2002a), and Thompson Sampling (Chapelle & Li, 2011; Russo & Van Roy, 2014).

In the adversarial setting, the rewards are chosen in an adversarial fashion, rather than sampled independently

[1] So long as the rewards are bounded, one can shift and rescale them to fit within $[0, 1]$.

Algorithm 1 Thompson Sampling for Bernoulli Bandits

1: For each arm $i = 1, 2, \cdots, K$, set $S_i = 0$, $F_i = 0$.
2: **for** $t = 1, 2, \ldots$ **do**
3: For each arm $i = 1, 2, \cdots, K$, sample θ_i from $Beta(S_i + 1, F_i + 1)$
4: Play arm $i(t) := \text{argmax}_i\, \theta_i(t)$, observe reward r_t
5: $S_i \leftarrow S_i + r_t$, $F_i \leftarrow F_i + 1 - r_t$
6: **end for**

from some underlying distribution. In this case, regret (2) is rephrased as the difference in the sum of rewards. The predominant algorithm for the adversarial setting is EXP3 (Auer et al., 2002b).

2.3 Thompson Sampling

The specific MAB algorithm used by our SELFSPARRING approach is Thompson Sampling. Thompson Sampling is a stochastic algorithm that maintains a distribution over the arms, and chooses arms by sampling (Chapelle & Li, 2011). This distribution is updated using reward feedback. The entropy of the distribution thus corresponds to uncertainty regarding which is the best arm, and flatter distributions lead to more exploration.

Consider the Bernoulli bandits setting where observed rewards are either 1 (win) or 0 (loss). Let S_i and F_i denote the historical number of wins and losses of arm i, and let D_t denote the set of all parameters at round t:

$$D_t = \{S_1, \cdots, S_K; F_1, \cdots, F_K\}_t.$$

For brevity, we often represent D_t by D, since only the current iteration matters at run-time. The sampling process of Beta-Bernoulli Thompson Sampling given D is:

- For each arm i, sample $\theta_i \sim Beta(S_i + 1, F_i + 1)$.
- Choose the arm with maximal θ_i.

In other words, we model the average utility of each arm using a Beta prior, and rewards for arm i as Bernoulli distributed according to latent mean utility θ_i. As we observe more rewards, we can compute the posterior, which is also Beta distributed by conjugation between Beta and Bernoulli. The sampling process above can be shown to be sampling for the following distribution:

$$P(i|D) = P(i = \operatorname*{argmax}_b \theta_b|D). \quad (3)$$

Thus, any arm i is chosen with probability that it has maximal reward under the Beta posterior. Algorithm 1 describes the Beta-Bernoulli Thompson Sampling algorithm, which we use as a subroutine for our approach. Thompson Sampling enjoys near-optimal regret guarantees in the stochastic MAB setting, as given by the lemma below (which is a direct consequence of main theorems in Agrawal & Goyal (2012); Kaufmann et al. (2012)).

Lemma 1. *For the K-armed stochastic MAB problem, Thompson Sampling has expected regret:* $\mathbb{E}[R_T^{MAB}] = \mathcal{O}\left(\frac{K}{\Delta}\ln T\right)$, *where* Δ *is the difference between expected rewards of the best two arms.*

2.4 Gaussian Processes & Kernels

Normally, when one observes measurements about one arm (in both dueling bandits and conventional multi-armed bandits), one cannot use that measurement to infer anything about other arms – i.e., the arms are independent. This limitation necessarily implies that regret scales linearly w.r.t. the number of arms K, since each arm must be explored at least once to collect at least one measurement about it. We will use Gaussian processes and kernels to model dependencies between arms.

For simplicity, we present Gaussian processes in the context of multi-armed bandits. We will describe how to apply them to multi-dueling bandits in Section 3 A Gaussian process (GP) is a probability measure over functions such that any linear restriction is multivariate Gaussian. A GP is fully determined by its mean and a positive definite covariance operator, also known as a kernel. A $GP(\mu(b), k(b, b'))$ is a probability distribution across a class of "smooth" functions, which is parameterized by a kernel function $k(b, b')$ that characterizes the smoothness of f. One can think of f has corresponding to the reward function in the standard MAB setting.

We assume WLOG that $\mu(b) = 0$, and that our observations are perturbed by i.i.d. Gaussian noise, i.e., for samples at points $A_T = [b_1 \ldots b_T]$, we have $y_t = f(b_t) + n_t$ where $n_t \sim \mathcal{N}(0, \sigma^2)$ (we will relax this later). The posterior over f is then also Gaussian with mean $\mu_T(b)$, covariance $k_T(b, b')$ and variance $\sigma_T^2(b)$ that satisfy:

$$\mu_T(b) = k_T(b)^T(\mathcal{K}_T + \sigma^2 I)^{-1} y_T$$
$$k_T(b, b') = k(b, b') - k_T(x)^T(\mathcal{K}_T + \sigma^2 I)^{-1} k_T(b')$$
$$\sigma_T^2(b) = k_T(b, b),$$

where $k_T(b) = [k(b_1, b) \ldots k(b_T, b)]^T$ and $\mathcal{K}_T$ is the positive definite kernel matrix $[k(x, x')]_b x, b' \in A_T]$.

Posterior inference updates the mean reward estimates for all the arms that share dependencies (as specified by the kernel) with the arms selected for measurement. Thus one can show that MAB algorithms using Gaussian processes have regret that scale linearly w.r.t. the dimensionality of the kernel rather than the number of arms (which can now be infinite) (Srinivas et al., 2010).

3 MULTI-DUELING BANDITS

We now formalize the multi-dueling bandits problem. We inherit all notation from original dueling bandits setting (Section 2.1). The key difference is that the algorithm now selects a (multi-)set S_t of arms at each iteration t, and observes outcomes of duels between some pairs of arms in S_t. For example, in information retrieval this can be implemented via multi-leaving (Schuth et al., 2014) the ranked lists of the subset, S_t, of rankers and then inferring the relative quality of the lists (and the corresponding rankers) from user feedback.

In general, we assume the number of arms being dueled at each iteration is some fixed constant $m = |S_t|$. When $m = 2$, the problem reduces to the original dueling bandits setting. Extending the regret formulation from the original setting (1), we can write the regret as:

$$R_T = \sum_{t=1}^{T} \sum_{b \in S_t} \phi(b_1, b). \tag{4}$$

The goal then is to select subsets of arms S_t so that the cumulative regret (4) is minimized. Intuitively, all arms have to be selected a small number of times in order to be explored, but the goal of the algorithm is to minimize the number of times when suboptimal arms are selected. When the algorithm has converged to the best arm b_1, then it can simply choose S_t to only contain b_1, thus incurring no additional regret.

Our setting differs from Brost et al. (2016) in two ways. First, we play a fixed, rather than variable, number of arms at each iteration. Furthermore, we focus on total regret, rather than the instantaneous average regret in a single iteration; in many applications (e.g., Sui & Burdick (2014)), playing each arm incurs its own regret .

Feedback Mechanisms. Simultaneously dueling multiple arms opens up multiple options for collecting feedback. For example, in some applications it may be viable to collect all pairwise feedback for all chosen arms S_t. In other applications, it is more realistic to only observe the "winner" of S_t, in which we observe feedback that one $b \in S_t$ wins against all other arms in S_t, but nothing about pairwise preferences between the other arms.

Approximate Linearity. One assumption that we leverage in developing our approach is *approximate linearity*, which fully generalizes the linear utility-based dueling bandits setting studied in Ailon et al. (2014). For any triplet of bandits $b_i \succ b_j \succ b_k$ and some constant $\gamma > 0$:

$$\phi(b_i, b_k) - \phi(b_j, b_k) \geq \gamma \phi(b_i, b_j). \tag{5}$$

To understand Approximate Linearity, consider the special case when the preference function follows the form

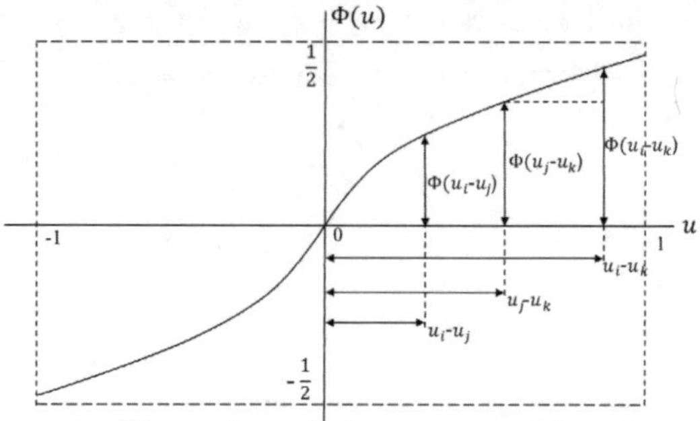

Figure 1: Illustration of Approximate Linearity. The curve represents $\Phi(\cdot)$ with support on $[-1, 1]$. Monotonicity guarantees Approximate Linearity for some γ.

$\phi(b_i, b_j) = \Phi(u_i - u_j)$, where u_i is a bounded utility measure of b_i. Approximate linearity of $\phi(\cdot, \cdot)$ is equivalent to having $\Phi(\cdot)$ be not far from some linear function on its bounded support (see Figure 1), and is satisfied by any continuous monotonic increasing function. When Φ is linear, then our setting reduces to the utility-based dueling bandits setting of Ailon et al. (2014).[2]

4 ALGORITHMS & RESULTS

We start with a high-level description of our general framework, called SELFSPARRING, which is inspired by the Sparring algorithm from Ailon et al. (2014). The high-level strategy is to reduce the multi-dueling bandits problem to a multi-armed bandit (MAB) problem that can be solved using a MAB algorithm, and ideally lift existing MAB guarantees to the multi-dueling setting.

Algorithm 2 describes the SELFSPARRING approach. SELFSPARRING uses a stochastic MAB algorithm such as Thompson sampling as a subroutine to independently sample the set of m arms, S_t to duel. The distribution of S_t is generally not degenerate (e.g., all the same arm) unless the algorithm has converged. In contrast, the Sparring algorithm uses m MAB algorithms to control the choice of the each arm, which essentially reduces the conventional dueling bandits problem to two multi-armed bandit problems "sparring" against each other.

SELFSPARRING takes as input S the total set of arms, m the number of arms to be dueled at each iteration, and η the learning rate for posterior updates. S can be a finite set of K arms for independent setting, or a continuous action space of arms for kernelized setting. A prior

[2]Compared to the assumptions of Yue et al. (2012), Approximate Linearity is a stricter requirement than strong stochastic transitivity, and is a complementary requirement to stochastic triangle inequality. In particular, stochastic triangle inequality requires that the curve in Figure 1 exhibits diminishing returns in the top-right quadrant (i.e., is sub-linear), whereas Approximate Linearity requires that the curve be not too far from linear.

Algorithm 2 SELFSPARRING

```
input arms 1, ..., K in space S, m the number of arms
      drawn at each iteration, η the learning rate
1: Set prior D_0 over S
2: for t = 1, 2, ... do
3:    for j = 1, ..., m do
4:       select arm i_j(t) using D_{t-1}
5:    end for
6:    Play m arms {i_j(t)}_j and observe m×m pairwise
      feedback matrix R = {r_ij ∈ {0, 1, ∅}}_{m×m}
7:    update D_{t-1} using R to obtain D_t
8: end for
```

Algorithm 3 INDSELFSPARRING

```
input m the number of arms drawn at each iteration, η
      the learning rate
1: For each arm i = 1, 2, ··· , K, set S_i = 0, F_i = 0.
2: for t = 1, 2, ... do
3:    for j = 1, ..., m do
4:       For each arm i = 1, 2, ··· , K, sample θ_i from
         Beta(S_i + 1, F_i + 1)
5:       Select i_j(t) := argmax_i θ_i(t)
6:    end for
7:    Play m arms {i_j(t)}_j, observe pairwise feedback
      matrix R = {r_jk ∈ {0, 1, ∅}}_{m×m}
8:    for j, k = 1, ..., m do
9:       if r_jk ≠ ∅ then
10:         S_j ← S_j + η · r_jk, F_j ← F_j + η(1 − r_jk)
11:      end if
12:   end for
13: end for
```

distribution D_0 is used to initialize the sampling process over S. In the t-th iteration, SELFSPARRING selects m arms by sampling over the distribution D_{t-1} as shown in line 2 of Algorithm 2. The preference feedback can be any type of comparisons ranging from full comparison over the m arms (a full matrix for R, aka 'all pairs") to single comparison of one pair (just two valid entries in R). The posterior distribution over arms D_t then gets updated by R and the prior D_{t-1}.

We specialize SELFSPARRING in two ways. The first, INDSELFSPARRING (Algorithm 3), is the independent-armed version of SELFSPARRING. The second, KERNELSELFSPARRING (Algorithm 4), uses Gaussian processes to make predictions about preference function f based on noisy evaluations over comparisons. We emphasize here that SELFSPARRING is very modular approach, and is thus easy to implement and extend.

4.1 Independent Arms Case

INDSELFSPARRING (Algorithm 3) instantiates SELFSPARRING using Beta-Bernoulli Thompson sampling. The posterior Beta distributions D_t over the arms are updated by the preference feedback within the iteration and the prior Beta distributions D_{t-1}.

We present a no-regret guarantee of INDSELFSPARRING in Theorem 2 below. We now provide a high-level outline of the main components leading to the result. Detail proofs are deferred to the supplementary material.

Our first step is to prove that INDSELFSPARRING is asymptotically consistent, i.e., it is guaranteed (with high probability) to converge to the best bandit. In order to guarantee consistency, we first show that all arms are sampled infinitely often in the limit.

Lemma 2. *Running INDSELFSPARRING with infinite time horizon will sample each arm infinitely often.*

In other words, Thompson sampling style algorithms do not eliminate any arms. Lemma 2 also guarantees concentration of any statistical estimates for each arm as $t \to \infty$. We next show that the sampling of INDSELFSPARRING will concentrate around the optimal arm.

Theorem 1. *Under Approximate Linearity, INDSELFSPARRING converges to the optimal arm b_1 as running time $t \to \infty$: $\lim_{t\to\infty} \mathbb{P}(b_t = b_1) = 1$.*

Theorem 1 implies that INDSELFSPARRING is asymptotically no-regret. As $t \to \infty$, the Beta distribution for each arm i is converging to $P(b_i \succ b_1)$, which implies converging to only choosing the optimal arm.

Most existing dueling bandits algorithm chooses one arm as a "reference" arm and the other arm as a competing arm for exploration/exploitation (in the $m = 2$ setting). If the distribution over reference arms never changes, then the competing arm is playing against a fixed "environment", i.e., it is a standard MAB problem. For general m, we can analogously consider choosing only one arm against a fixed distribution over all the other arms. Using Thompson sampling, the following lemma holds.

Lemma 3. *Under Approximate Linearity, selecting only one arm via Thompson sampling against a fixed distribution over the remaining arms leads to optimal regret w.r.t. choosing that arm.*

Lemma 3 and Theorem 1 motivate the idea of analyzing the regret of each individual arm against near-fixed (i.e., converging) environments.

Theorem 2. *Under Approximate Linearity, INDSELFSPARRING converges to the optimal arm with asymptotically optimal no-regret rate of $\mathcal{O}(K \ln(T)/\Delta)$.*

Theorem 2 shows an no-regret guarantee for INDSELF-

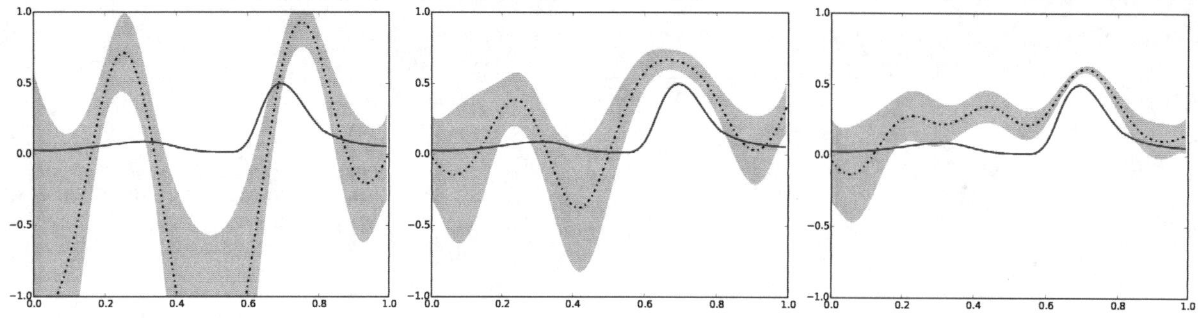

(a) 5 iterations (b) 20 iterations (c) 100 iterations

Figure 2: Evolution of a GP preference function in KERNELSELFSPARRING; dashed lines correspond to the mean and shaded areas to ± 2 standard deviations. The underlying utility function was sampled randomly from a GP with a squared exponential kernel with lengthscale parameter 0.2, and the resulting preference function is shown in blue. The GP finds the best arm with high confidence.

Algorithm 4 KERNELSELFSPARRING

input Input space S, GP prior (μ_0, σ_0), m the number of arms drawn at each iteration
for $t = 1, 2, \ldots$ **do**
  for $j = 1, \ldots, m$ **do**
    Sample f_j from $(\mu_{t-1}, \sigma_{t-1})$
    Select $i_j(t) := \text{argmax}_x f_j(x)$
  end for
  Play m arms $\{i_j(t)\}_j$, observe pairwise feedback matrix $R = \{r_{jk} \in \{0, 1, \emptyset\}\}_{m \times m}$
  for $j, k = 1, \ldots, m$ **do**
    if $r_{jk} \neq \emptyset$ **then**
      apply Bayesian update using $(i_j(t), r_{jk})$ to obtain (μ_t, σ_t)
    end if
  end for
end for

SPARRING that asymptotically matches the optimal rate of $\mathcal{O}(K \ln(T)/\Delta)$ up to constant factors. In other words, once $t > C$ for some problem-dependent constant C, the regret of INDSELFSPARRING matches information-theoretic bounds up to constant factors (see Yue et al. (2012) for lower bound analysis).[3] The proof technique follows two major steps: (1) prove the convergence of INDSELFSPARRING as shown in Theorem 1; and (2) bound the expected total regret for sufficiently large T.

4.2 Dependent Arms Case

We use Gaussian processes (see Section 2.4) to model dependencies among arms. Applying Gaussian processes is not straightforward, since the underlying utility function is not directly observable or does not exist. We instead use Gaussian processes to model the preference function $f(b)$ corresponding to the preference of choosing b over the perfect "environment" of competing arms. Like in the independent arms case (Section 4.1), the perfect environment corresponds to having all the remaining arms be deterministically selected as the best arm b_1: $f(b) = P(b \succ b_1)$. We model $f(b)$ as a sample from a Gaussian process $GP(\mu(b), k(b, b'))$. Note that this setup is analogous to the independent arms case, which uses a Beta prior to estimate the probability of each arm defeating the environment (and converges to competing against the best environment).

Algorithm 4 describes KERNELSELFSPARRING, which instantiates SELFSPARRING using a Gaussian process Thompson sampling algorithm. The input space S can be continuous. At each iteration t, m arms are sampled using the Gaussian process prior D_{t-1}. The posterior D_t is then updated by the responses R and the prior.

Figure 2 illustrates the optimization process in a one-dimensional example. The underlying preference function against the best environment is shown in blue. Dashed lines are the mean function of GP. Shaded areas are ± 2 standard deviations regions (high confidence regions). Figures 2(a)(b)(c) represent running KERNEL-SELFSPARRING algorithm at 5, 20, and 100 iterations. The GP model can be observed to be converging to the preference function against the best environment.

We conjecture that it is possible to prove no-regret guarantees that scale w.r.t. the dimensionality of the kernel. However, there does not yet exist suitable regret analyses for Gaussian Process Thompson Sampling in the kernelized MAB setting to leverage.

[3] A finite-time guarantee requires more a refined analysis of C, and is an interesting direction for future work.

Name	Distribution of Utilities of arms
1good	1 arm with utility 0.8, 15 arms with utility 0.2
arith	1 arm with utility 0.8, 15 arms forming an arithmetic sequence between 0.7 and 0.2

Table 1: 16-arm synthetic datasets used for experiments.

5 EXPERIMENTS

5.1 Simulation Settings & Datasets

Synthetic Functions. We evaluated on a range of 16-arm synthetic settings derived from the utility-based dueling bandits setting of Ailon et al. (2014). For the multi-dueling setting, we used the following preference functions:

$$\text{linear:} \quad \phi(x, y) - 1/2 = (1 + x - y)/2$$
$$\text{logit:} \quad \phi(x, y) - 1/2 = (1 + \exp(y - x))^{-1}$$

and the utility functions shown in Table 1 (generalized from those in Ailon et al. (2014)). Note that although these preference functions do not satisfy approximate linearity over their entire domains, they do for the utility samples (over the a finite subset of arms).

MSLR Dataset. Following the evaluation setup of Brost et al. (2016), we also used the Microsoft Learning to Rank (MSLR) WEB30k dataset, which consists of over 3 million query-document pairs labeled with relevance scores (Liu et al., 2007). Each pair is scored along 136 features, which can be treated as rankers (arms). For any subset of arms, we can estimate a preference matrix using the expected probability over the entire dataset of one arm beating another using top-10 interleaving and a perfect-click model. We simulate user feedback by using team-draft multileaving (Schuth et al., 2014).

5.2 Vanilla Dueling Bandits Experiments

We first compare against the vanilla dueling bandits setting of dueling a single pair of arms at a time. These experiments are included as a sanity check to confirm that SELFSPARRING (with $m = 2$) is a competitive algorithm in the original dueling bandits setting, and are not the main focus of our empirical analysis.

We empirically evaluate against a range of conventional dueling bandit algorithms, including:

- **Interleaved Filter (IF)** (Yue et al., 2012)
- **Beat the Mean (BTM)** (Yue & Joachims, 2011)
- **RUCB** (Zoghi et al., 2014)
- **MergeRUCB** (Zoghi et al., 2015b)
- **Sparring + UCB1** (Ailon et al., 2014)
- **Sparring + EXP3** (Dudík et al., 2015)
- **RMED1** (Komiyama et al., 2015)
- **Double Thompson Sampling** (Wu & Liu, 2016)

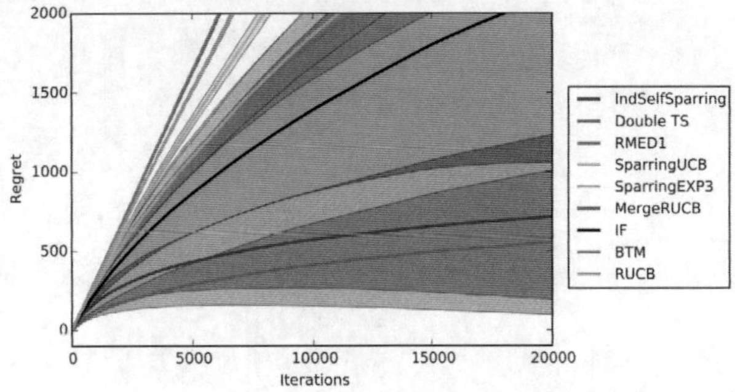

Figure 3: Vanilla dueling bandits setting. Average regret for top nine algorithms on logit/arith. Shaded regions correspond to one standard deviation.

For Double Thompson Sampling and INDSELFSPARRING, we set the learning rates to be 2.5 and 3.5 as optimized over a separate dataset of uniformly sampled utility functions. We use $\alpha = 0.51$ for RUCB/MergeRUCB, $\gamma = 1$ for BTM, and $f(K) = 0.3K^{1.01}$ for RMED1.

Results. For each scenario, we run each algorithm 100 times for 20000 iterations. For brevity, we show in Figure 3 the average regret of one synthetic simulation along with shaded one standard-deviation areas. We observe that SELFSPARRING is competitive with the best performing methods in the original dueling bandits setting. More complete experiments that replicate Ailon et al. (2014) are provided in the supplementary material, and demonstrate the consistency of this result.

Double Thompson Sampling (DTS) is the best performing approach in Figure 3, which is a fairly consistent result in the extended results in the supplementary material. However, given their high variances they are essentially comparable w.r.t. all other algorithms. Furthermore, INDSELFSPARRING has the advantage of being easily extensible to the more realistic multi-dueling and kernelized settings, which is not true of DTS.

5.3 Multi-Dueling Bandits Experiments

We next evaluate the multi-dueling setting with independent arms. We compare against the main existing approaches that are applicable to the multi-dueling setting, including the MDB algorithm (Brost et al., 2016), and the multi-dueling extension of Sparring, which we refer to as MultiSparring (Ailon et al., 2014). Following

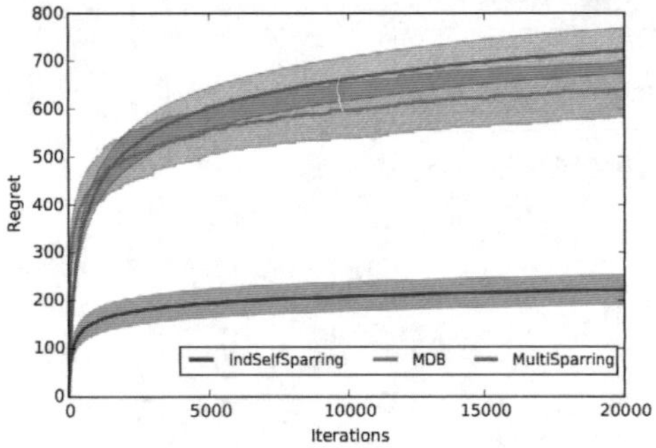

Figure 4: Multi-dueling regret for linear/1good setting

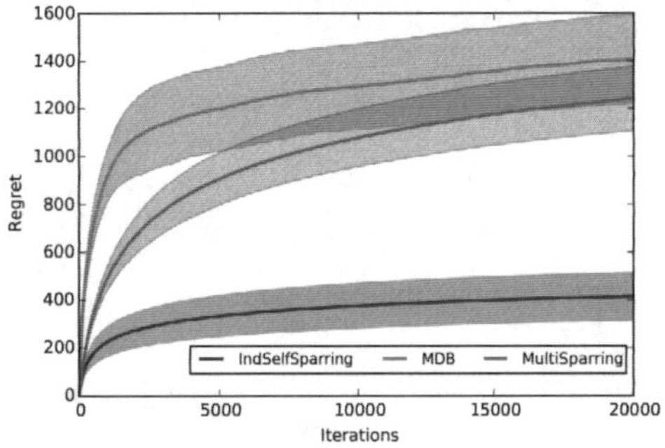

Figure 5: Multi-dueling regret for linear/arith setting

Brost et al. (2016), we use $\alpha = 0.5$ and $\beta = 1.5$ for the MDB algorithm. For INDSELFSPARRING, we set learning rate to be the default 1. Note that the vast majority dueling bandits algorithms are not easily applicable to the multi-dueling setting. For instance, RUCB-style algorithms treat the two arms asymmetrically, which is not easily generalized to multi-dueling.

Results on Synthetic Experiments. We test $m = 4$ on the linear 1good and arith datasets in Figure 4 and Figure 5, respectively. We observe that INDSELFSPARRING significantly outperforms competing approaches.

Results on MSLR Dataset. Following the simulation setting of Brost et al. (2016) on the MSLR dataset (see Section 5.1), we compared against the MDB algorithm over the same collection of 50 randomly sampled 16-arm subsets. We ensured that each 16-arm subset had a Condorcet winner; in general it is likely for any random subset of arms in the MSLR dataset to have a Condorcet winner (Zoghi et al., 2015a). Figure 6 shows the results, where we again see that INDSELFSPARRING enjoys significantly better performance.

5.4 Kernelized (Multi-)Dueling Experiments

We finally evaluate the kernelized setting for both the 2-dueling and the multi-dueling case. We evaluate KERNELSELFSPARRING against BOPPER (Gonzalez et al., 2016) and Sparring (Ailon et al., 2014) with GP-UCB

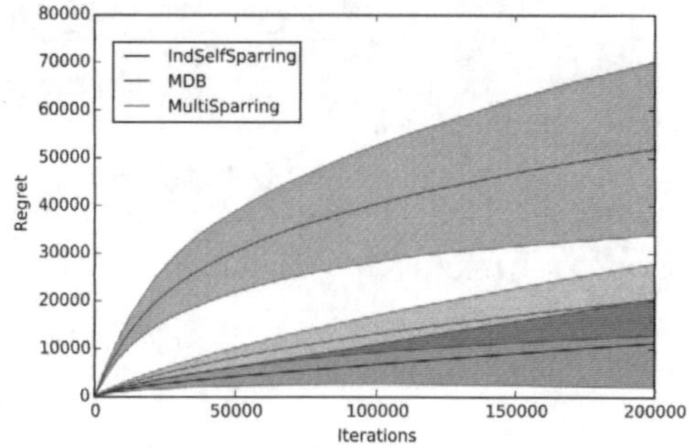

Figure 6: Multi-dueling regret for MSLR-30K experiments

(Srinivas et al., 2010). BOPPER is a Bayesian optimization method can be applied to kernelized 2-dueling setting (but not multi-dueling). Sparring with GP-UCB, which refer to as GP-Sparring, is essentially a variant of our KERNELSELFSPARRING approach but maintains a m GP-UCB bandit algorithms (one controlling each choice of arm to be dueled), rather than just a single one.

KERNELSELFSPARRING and GP-Sparring use GPs that model the preference function, i.e. are one-sided, whereas BOPPER uses a GP to model the entire preference matrix. Following Srinivas et al. (2010), we use a squared exponential kernel with lengthscale parameter 0.2 for both GP-Sparring and KERNELSELFSPARRING, and use a squared exponential kernel with parameter 1 for BOPPER. We initialize all GPs with a zero-mean prior, and use sampling noise variance $\sigma^2 = 0.025$. For GP-Sparring, we use the scaled-down version of β_t as suggested by Srinivas et al. (2010).

We use the Forrester and Six-Hump Camel functions as utility functions on $[0, 1]$ and $[0, 1]^2$, respectively, as in Gonzalez et al. (2016). Similarly, we use the same uniform discretizations of 30 and 64 points for the Forrester and Six-Hump Camel settings respectively, and use the logit link function to generate preferences.

Since the BOPPER algorithm is computationally expen-

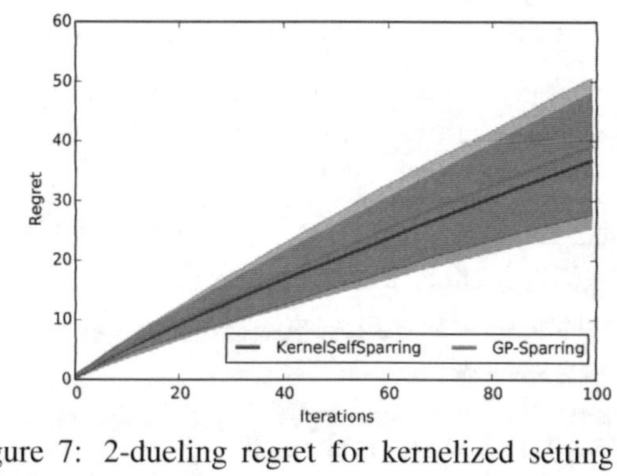

Figure 7: 2-dueling regret for kernelized setting with synthetic preferences

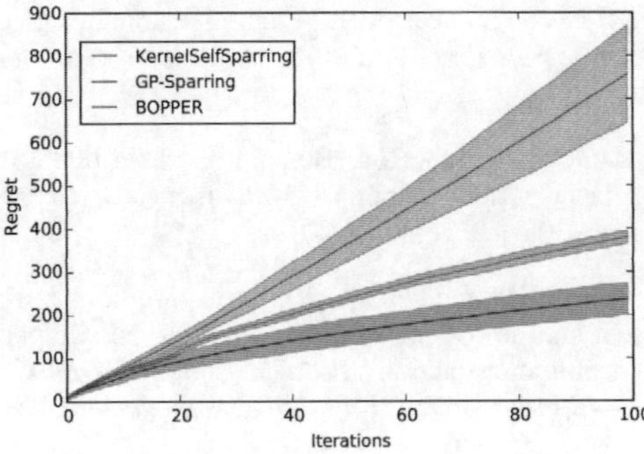

Figure 8: 2-dueling regret for kernelized setting with Forrester objective function

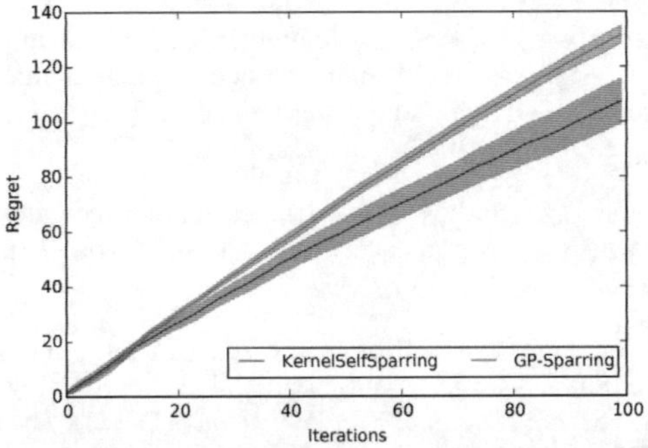

Figure 9: 2-dueling regret for kernelized setting with Six-Hump Camel objective function

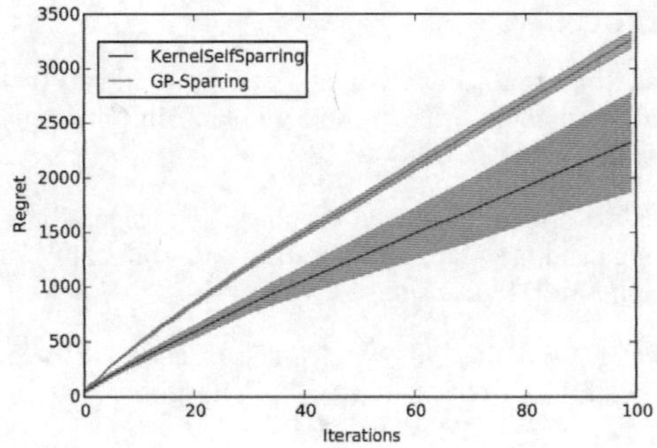

Figure 10: Multi-dueling regret for kernelized setting with Forrester objective function

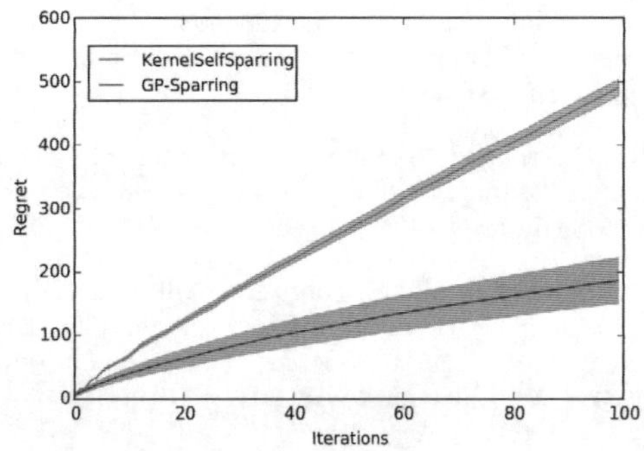

Figure 11: Multi-dueling regret for kernelized setting with Six-Hump Camel objective function

sive, we only include it in the Forrester setting, and run each algorithm 20 times for 100 iterations. In the Six-Hump Camel setting, we run KERNELSELFSPARRING and GP-Sparring for 500 iterations 100 times each. Results are presented in Figures 8 and 9, where we observe much better performance from KERNELSELFSPARRING against both BOPPER and GP-Sparring.

In the kernelized multi-dueling setting, we compare against GP-Sparring. We run each algorithm for 100 iterations 50 times on the Forrester and Six-Hump Camel functions, and plot their regrets in Figures 10 and 11 respectively. We use $m = 4$ for both algorithms, and the same discretization as in the standard dueling case. We again observe significant performance gains of our KERNELSELFSPARRING approach.

6 CONCLUSIONS

We studied multi-dueling bandits with dependent arms. This setting extends the original dueling bandits setting by dueling multiple arms per iteration rather than just two, and modeling low-dimensional dependencies between arms rather than treat each arm independently. Both extensions are motivated by practical real-world considerations such as in personalized clinical treatment (Sui & Burdick, 2014). We proposed SELFSPARRING, which is simple and easy to extend, e.g., by integrating with kernels to model dependencies across arms. Our experimental results demonstrated significant reduction in regret compared to state-of-the-art dueling bandit algorithms. Generally, relative benefits compared to dueling bandits increased with the number of arms being compared. For SELFSPARRING, the incurred regret did not increase substantially as the number of arms increased.

Our approach can be extended in several important directions. Most notably, the theoretical analysis could be improved. For instance, it would be more desirable to provide explicit finite-time regret guarantees rather than asymptotic ones. Furthermore, an analysis of the kernelized multi-dueling setting is also lacking. From a more practical perspective, we assumed that the choice of arms does not impact the feedback mechanism (e.g., all pairs), which is not true in practice (e.g., humans can have a hard time distinguishing very different arms).

Acknowledgments. This work was funded in part by NSF Awards #1564330 & #1637598, JPL PDF IAMS100224, a Bloomberg Data Science Research Grant, and a gift from Northrop Grumman.

References

Agrawal, Shipra and Goyal, Navin. Analysis of thompson sampling for the multi-armed bandit problem. In *Conference on Learning Theory (COLT)*, 2012.

Ailon, Nir, Karnin, Zohar, and Joachims, Thorsten. Reducing dueling bandits to cardinal bandits. In *International Conference on Machine Learning (ICML)*, 2014.

Auer, Peter, Cesa-Bianchi, Nicolo, and Fischer, Paul. Finite-time analysis of the multiarmed bandit problem. *Machine learning*, 47(2-3):235–256, 2002a.

Auer, Peter, Cesa-Bianchi, Nicolo, Freund, Yoav, and Schapire, Robert E. The nonstochastic multiarmed bandit problem. *SIAM Journal on Computing*, 32(1):48–77, 2002b.

Brost, Brian, Seldin, Yevgeny, Cox, Ingemar J, and Lioma, Christina. Multi-dueling bandits and their application to online ranker evaluation. In *ACM Conference on Information and Knowledge Management*, 2016.

Chapelle, Olivier and Li, Lihong. An empirical evaluation of thompson sampling. In *Advances in Neural Information Processing Systems (NIPS)*, 2011.

Chapelle, Olivier, Joachims, Thorsten, Radlinski, Filip, and Yue, Yisong. Large-scale validation and analysis of interleaved search evaluation. *ACM Transactions on Information Systems (TOIS)*, 30(1):6:1–6:41, 2012.

Dudík, Miroslav, Hofmann, Katja, Schapire, Robert E, Slivkins, Aleksandrs, and Zoghi, Masrour. Contextual dueling bandits. In *Conference on Learning Theory (COLT)*, 2015.

Gajane, Pratik, Urvoy, Tanguy, and Clérot, Fabrice. A relative exponential weighing algorithm for adversarial utility-based dueling bandits. In *International Conference on Machine Learning (ICML)*, 2015.

Gonzalez, Javier, Dai, Zhenwen, Damianou, Andreas, and Lawrence, Neil D. Bayesian optimisation with pairwise preferential returns. In *NIPS Workshop on Bayesian Optimization*, 2016.

Hofmann, Katja, Whiteson, Shimon, and De Rijke, Maarten. A probabilistic method for inferring preferences from clicks. In *ACM Conference on Information and Knowledge Management*, 2011.

Jamieson, Kevin, Katariya, Sumeet, Deshpande, Atul, and Nowak, Robert. Sparse dueling bandits. In *International Conference on Artificial Intelligence and Statistics (AISTATS)*, 2015.

Kaufmann, Emilie, Korda, Nathaniel, and Munos, Rémi. Thompson sampling: An asymptotically optimal finite-time analysis. In *Algorithmic Learning Theory (ALT)*, 2012.

Komiyama, Junpei, Honda, Junya, Kashima, Hisashi, and Nakagawa, Hiroshi. Regret lower bound and optimal algorithm in dueling bandit problem. In *COLT*, pp. 1141–1154, 2015.

Liu, Tie-Yan, Xu, Jun, Qin, Tao, Xiong, Wenying, and Li, Hang. Letor: Benchmark dataset for research on learning to rank for information retrieval. In *SIGIR 2007 workshop on learning to rank for information retrieval*, pp. 3–10, 2007.

Robbins, Herbert. Some aspects of the sequential design of experiments. *Bulletin of the American Mathematical Society*, 1952.

Russo, Daniel and Van Roy, Benjamin. Learning to optimize via posterior sampling. *Mathematics of Operations Research*, 39(4):1221–1243, 2014.

Schuth, Anne, Sietsma, Floor, Whiteson, Shimon, Lefortier, Damien, and de Rijke, Maarten. Multileaved comparisons for fast online evaluation. In *ACM Conference on Conference on Information and Knowledge Management*, 2014.

Schuth, Anne, Oosterhuis, Harrie, Whiteson, Shimon, and de Rijke, Maarten. Multileave gradient descent for fast online learning to rank. In *ACM Conference on Web Search and Data Mining*, 2016.

Srinivas, Niranjan, Krause, Andreas, Kakade, Sham, and Seeger, Matthias. Gaussian process optimization in the bandit setting: No regret and experimental design. In *International Conference on Machine Learning (ICML)*, 2010.

Sui, Yanan and Burdick, Joel. Clinical online recommendation with subgroup rank feedback. In *ACM Conference on Recommender Systems (RecSys)*, 2014.

Urvoy, Tanguy, Clerot, Fabrice, Féraud, Raphael, and Naamane, Sami. Generic exploration and k-armed voting bandits. In *International Conference on Machine Learning (ICML)*, 2013.

Wu, Huasen and Liu, Xin. Double thompson sampling for dueling bandits. In *Advances in Neural Information Processing Systems*, 2016.

Yue, Yisong and Joachims, Thorsten. Interactively optimizing information retrieval systems as a dueling bandits problem. In *International Conference on Machine Learning (ICML)*, 2009.

Yue, Yisong and Joachims, Thorsten. Beat the mean bandit. In *International Conference on Machine Learning (ICML)*, 2011.

Yue, Yisong, Broder, Josef, Kleinberg, Robert, and Joachims, Thorsten. The k-armed dueling bandits problem. *Journal of Computer and System Sciences*, 78(5):1538–1556, 2012.

Zoghi, Masrour, Whiteson, Shimon, Munos, Remi, and de Rijke, Maarten. Relative upper confidence bound for the k-armed dueling bandit problem. In *International Conference on Machine Learning (ICML)*, 2014.

Zoghi, Masrour, Karnin, Zohar S, Whiteson, Shimon, and de Rijke, Maarten. Copeland dueling bandits. In *Advances in Neural Information Processing Systems*, pp. 307–315, 2015a.

Zoghi, Masrour, Whiteson, Shimon, and de Rijke, Maarten. Mergerucb: A method for large-scale online ranker evaluation. In *ACM International Conference on Web Search and Data Mining (WSDM)*, 2015b.

A Proofs

This section provides the proof sketch of Lemmas and Theorems mentioned in the main paper.

Lemma 1. For the K-armed stochastic MAB problem, Thompson Sampling has expected regret: $\mathbb{E}[R_T^{\text{MAB}}] = \mathcal{O}\left(\frac{K}{\Delta}\ln T\right)$, where Δ is the difference between expected rewards of the best two arms.

Proof. This lemma is a direct result from Theorem 2 of Agrawal & Goyal (2012) and Theorem 1 of Kaufmann et al. (2012). □

Lemma 2. Running INDSELFSPARRING with infinite time horizon will sample each arm infinitely often.

Proof. Proof by contradiction.
Let $B(x;\alpha,\beta) = \int_0^x t^{\alpha-1}(1-t)^{\beta-1}dt$. Then the CDF of Beta distribution with parameters (α, β) is

$$F(x;\alpha,\beta) = \frac{B(x;\alpha,\beta)}{B(1;\alpha,\beta)}.$$

Suppose arm b can only be sampled in finite number of iterations. Then there exists finite upper bound T_b for $\alpha_b + \beta_b$. For any given $x \in (0,1)$, the probability of sampling values of arm b θ_b greater than x is

$$P(\theta_b > x) = 1 - F(x;\alpha_b,\beta_b)$$
$$\geq 1 - F(x;1,T_b-1) = (1-x)^{T_b-1} > 0$$

Then by running INDSELFSPARRING, the probability of choosing arm b after it has been chosen T_b times:

$$P(\theta_b \geq max_i\{\theta_{b_i}\}) \geq \prod_i P(\theta_b \geq \theta_{b_i})$$

is strictly non-zero. That violates any fixed upper bound T_b. □

Theorem 1. Under Approximate Linearity, INDSELFSPARRING converges to the optimal arm b_1 as running time $t \to \infty$: $\lim_{t\to\infty} \mathbb{P}(b_t = b_1) = 1$.

Proof. INDSELFSPARRING keeps one Beta distribution $Beta(\alpha_i(t), \beta_i(t))$ for each arm b_i at time step t. Let $\hat{\mu}_i(t) = \frac{\alpha_i(t)}{\alpha_i(t)+\beta_i(t)}$, $\hat{\sigma}_i^2(t) = \frac{\alpha_i(t)\beta_i(t)}{(\alpha_i(t)+\beta_i(t))^2(\alpha_i(t)+\beta_i(t)+1)}$ be the empirical mean and variance for arm b_i.
Obviously, $\hat{\sigma}_i^2(t) \to 0$ as $(\alpha_i(t) + \beta_i(t)) = (S_i(t) + F_i(t)) \to \infty$. By Lemma 2 we have $(S_i(t) + F_i(t)) \to \infty$ as $t \to \infty$. That shows every Beta distribution is concentrating to a Dirac function at $\hat{\mu}_i(t)$ when $t \to \infty$.

Define $\hat{\mu}(t) = [\hat{\mu}_1(t), \cdots, \hat{\mu}_K(t)]^T \in [0,1]^K$ to be the vector of means of all arms. Then $\mu = \{\mu_i = P(b_i \succ b_1)\}_{i=1,\cdots,K}$ is a stable point for INDSELFSPARRING in the K dimensional mean space.

Suppose there exists another stable point $\nu \in [0,1]^K (\nu \neq \mu)$ for INDSELFSPARRING, consider the following two possibilities: (1) $\nu_1 = max_i\{\nu_i\}$ and (2) $\nu_1 < max_i\{\nu_i\} = \nu_j$.

Since the Beta distributions for each arm b_i is concentrating to Dirac functions at ν_i, $P(\theta_i > \theta_j) \in [\mathbb{I}(\nu_i > \nu_j) - \delta, \mathbb{I}(\nu_i > \nu_j) + \delta]$ for any fixed $\delta > 0$ with high probability.

If (1) holds, then ν_1 will converge to $\frac{1}{2} = \mu_1$ and ν_i will converge to $P(b_i \succ b_1) = \mu_i$. Thus $\nu = \mu$. Contradict to $\nu \neq \mu$.

If (2) holds, then ν_j will converge to $\frac{1}{2} = \mu_1$ and $\nu_1 \in [P(b_1 \succ b_j) - \delta, P(b_1 \succ b_j) + \delta]$ for any fixed $\delta > 0$ with high probability. Since $P(b_1 \succ b_j) \geq \frac{1}{2} + \Delta$, $\nu_1 \in [P(b_1 \succ b_j) - \delta, P(b_1 \succ b_j) + \delta] \geq \frac{1}{2} + \Delta - \delta$. Since δ can be arbitrarily small, we have $\nu_1 \geq \frac{1}{2} + \Delta - \delta > \frac{1}{2} + \delta > \nu_j$. That contradict to $\nu_1 < \nu_j$.

In summary, $\mu = \{\mu_i = P(b_i \succ b_1)\}_{i=1,\cdots,K}$ is the only stable point in the mean space. As $\hat{\mu}(t) \to \mu$, $\mathbb{P}(b_t = b_1) \to 1$.

Define $\mathbb{P}_t = [P_1(t), P_2(t), ..., P_K(t)]$ as the probabilities of picking each arm at time t. Let $\mathbb{P} = \{\mathbb{P}_t\}_{t=1,2,...}$ be the sequence of probabilities w.r.t. time. Assume INDSELFSPARRING is non-convergent. It is equivalent to say that $\mathbb{P}$ is not converging to a fixed distribution. Then $\exists\delta > 0$ and arm i s.t. the sequence of probabilities $\{P_i(t)\}_t$ satisfies:

$$\limsup_{t\to\infty} P_i(t) - \liminf_{t\to\infty} P_i(t) > \delta$$

w.h.p. which is equivalent of having:

$$\limsup_{t\to\infty} \hat{\mu}_i(t) - \liminf_{t\to\infty} \hat{\mu}_i(t) > \epsilon$$

w.h.p. for some fixed $\epsilon > 0$. This violates the stability of INDSELFSPARRING in the K dimensional mean space as shown above. So as $t \to \infty$, $\hat{\mu}(t) \to \mu$, $\mathbb{P}(b_t = b_1) \to 1$.

□

Lemma 3. Under Approximate Linearity, selecting only one arm via Thompson sampling against a fixed distribution over the remaining arms leads to optimal regret w.r.t. choosing that arm.

Proof. We first prove the results for $m = 2$. Results for any $m > 2$ can be proved in a similar way.

Consider Player 1 drawing arms from a fixed distribution L. Player 2's drawing strategy is an MAB algorithm $\mathcal{A}$.

Let $R_A(T)$ be the regret of algorithm $\mathcal{A}$ within horizon T. $B(T) = \sup \mathbb{E}[R_A(T)]$ is the supremum of the expected regret of $\mathcal{A}$.

The reward of Player 2 at iteration t is $\phi(b_{2t}, b_{1t})$. Reward of keep playing the optimal arm is $\phi(b_1, b_{1t})$. So the total regret after T rounds is

$$R_A(T) = \sum_{t=1}^{T} [\phi(b_1, b_{1t}) - \phi(b_{2t}, b_{1t})]$$

Since Approximate Linearity yields

$$\phi(b_1, b_{1t}) - \phi(b_{2t}, b_{1t}) \geq \gamma \cdot \phi(b_1, b_{2t})$$

We have

$$\mathbb{E}[R_A(T)] = \mathbb{E}\mathbb{E}_{b_{1t}\sim L}\left[\sum_{t=1}^{T} [\phi(b_1, b_{1t}) - \phi(b_{2t}, b_{1t})\right]$$

$$\geq \mathbb{E}\mathbb{E}_{b_{1t}\sim L}\left[\sum_{t=1}^{T} \gamma \cdot \phi(b_1, b_{2t})\right]$$

$$= \gamma \cdot \mathbb{E}\left[\sum_{t=1}^{T} \phi(b_1, b_{2t})\right] = \gamma \cdot \mathbb{E}[R(T)]$$

So the total regret of Player 2 is bounded by

$$\mathbb{E}[R(T)] \leq \frac{1}{\gamma}\mathbb{E}[R_A(T)] \leq \frac{1}{\gamma} \sup \mathbb{E}[R_A(T)] = \frac{1}{\gamma} B(T)$$

□

Corollary 1. *If approximate linearity holds, competing with a drifting but converging distribution of arms guarantees the one-side convergence for Thompson Sampling.*

Proof. Let D_t be the drifting but converging distribution and $D_t \to D$ as $t \to \infty$. Let b_T be the drifting mean bandit of D_T after T iterations. Since D_t is convergent, $\exists T > K$ such that

$$\phi(\sup_{t>T} b_T, \inf_{t>T} b_T) < \phi(b_1, b_2)$$

where $\phi(b_1, b_2)$ is the preference between the best two arms. The mean value of feedback by playing arm i is $\phi(b_i, b_T)$. If b_T is fixed, by Lemma3, Thompson sampling converges to the arm: $i^* = \text{argmax}_i\, \phi(b_i, b_T)$. For drifting b_T, define $b^+ = \sup_{t>T} b_T$ and $b^- = \inf_{t>T} b_T$.

Thompson sampling convergence to the optimal arm implies that:

$$\phi(b_1, b^+) > \phi(b_i, b^-)$$

for all $i \neq 1$. Consider:

$$\begin{aligned} &\phi(b_1, b^+) - \phi(b_2, b^-) \\ &= \phi(b_1, b^+) - \phi(b_2, b^-) + \phi(b_1, b^-) - \phi(b_1, b^-) \\ &= \phi(b_1, b^-) - \phi(b_2, b^-) + \phi(b_2, b^+) - \phi(b_1, b^-) \\ &\geq \gamma \cdot [\phi(b_1, b_2) - \phi(b^+, b^-)] > 0 \end{aligned}$$

by approximate linearity.

So we have $\phi(b_1, b^+) > \phi(b_2, b^-)$. Since $\phi(b_2, b^-) > \phi(b_i, b^-)$ for $i > 2$. Then we have

$$\phi(b_1, b^+) > \phi(b_i, b^-)$$

holds for all $i \neq 1$. So Thompson sampling converge to the optimal arm. □

Theorem 2. Under Approximate Linearity, INDSELFSPARRING converges to the optimal arm with asymptotically optimal no-regret rate of $\mathcal{O}(K \ln(T)/\Delta)$. Where Δ is the difference between the rewards of the best two arms.

Proof. Theorem 1 provides the convergence guarantee of INDSELFSPARRING. Corollary 1 shows one-side convergence for playing against a converging distribution.

Since INDSELFSPARRING converges to the optimal arm b_1 as running time $t \to \infty$: $\lim_{t\to\infty} \mathbb{P}(b_t = b_1) = 1$. For $\forall\delta > 0$, there exists $C(\delta) > 0$ such that for any $t > C(\delta)$, the following condition holds w.h.p.: $P(b_t = b_1) \geq 1 - \delta$.

For the triple of bandits $b_1 \succ b_i \succ b_K$, Approximate Linearity guarantees:

$$\phi(b_i, b_K) < \phi(b_1, b_K) \leq \omega$$

holds for some fixed $\omega > 0$ and $\forall i \in \{2, \cdots, K-1\}$. With small δ, the competing environment of any Player p is bounded. If $\delta < \frac{\Delta}{\Delta+\omega}$, $(1-\delta)\cdot(-\Delta) + \delta \cdot \phi(b_2, b_K) < 0 = 1 \cdot \phi(b_1, b_1)$. The competing environment can be considered as unbiased and the theoretical guarantees for Thompson sampling for stochastic multi-armed bandit is valid (up to a constant factor).

Then INDSELFSPARRING has an no-regret guarantee that asymptotically matches the optimal rate of $\mathcal{O}(K \ln(T)/\Delta)$ up to constant factors, which proves Theorem 2.

□

B Further Experiments

We run further experiments on 16-arm synthetic datasets. The distributions of utilities of arms are shown in Table 2. We compared the performances of 8 algorithms and 15 scenarios as shown in Figure 12.

Name	Distribution of Utilities of arms
1good	1 arm with utility 0.8, 15 arms with utility 0.2
2good	1 arm with utility 0.8, 1 arms with utility 0.7, 14 arms with utility 0.2
6good	1 arm with utility 0.8, 5 arms with utility 0.7, 10 arms with utility 0.2
arith	1 arm with utility 0.8, 15 arms forming an arithmetic sequence between 0.7 and 0.2
geom	1 arm with utility 0.8, 15 arms forming a geometric sequence between 0.7 and 0.2

Table 2: 16-arm synthetic datasets used for experiments.

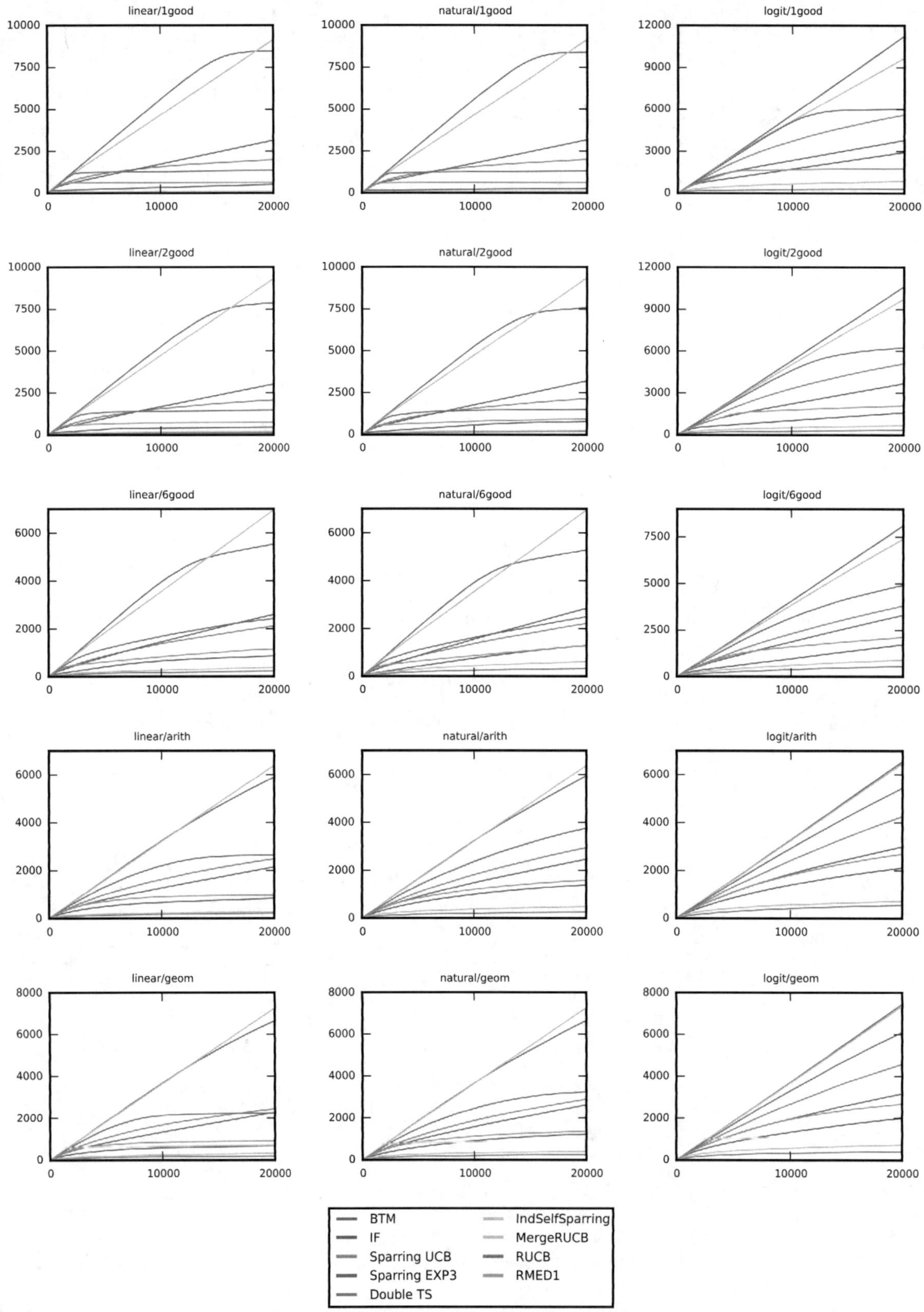

Figure 12: Average regret vs iterations for each of 8 algorithms and 15 scenarios.

Convex-constrained Sparse Additive Modeling and Its Extensions

Junming Yin
Eller College of Management
University of Arizona
Tucson, AZ 85721

Yaoliang Yu
School of Computer Science
University of Waterloo
Waterloo, ON, N2L3G1

Abstract

Sparse additive modeling is a class of effective methods for performing high-dimensional nonparametric regression. In this work we show how shape constraints such as convexity/concavity and their extensions, can be integrated into additive models. The proposed sparse difference of convex additive models (SDCAM) can estimate most continuous functions without any *a priori* smoothness assumption. Motivated by a characterization of difference of convex functions, our method incorporates a natural regularization functional to avoid overfitting and to reduce model complexity. Computationally, we develop an efficient backfitting algorithm with linear per-iteration complexity. Experiments on both synthetic and real data confirm that our method is competitive against state-of-the-art sparse additive models, with improved performance in most scenarios.

1 INTRODUCTION

Regression, which aims at predicting a real-valued response from a set of covariates, is an important form of supervised learning and has been widely studied in machine learning and statistics. More precisely, consider the following model:

$$Y = m(X) + \xi,$$

where the covariate $X \in \mathbb{R}^p$ and the noise $\xi \in \mathbb{R}$ are both random. It is common in practice to assume $\mathbb{E}(\xi|X) = 0$, hence $m(\mathbf{x}) = \mathbb{E}(Y|X = \mathbf{x})$ is the regression function that we aim to estimate based on a set of data samples $\{(\mathbf{x}_i, y_i) : i = 1, \ldots, n\}$. Asymptotic consistency for certain estimators (such as least-squares) is well-known, although the rate of convergence can be arbitrarily slow (Györfi et al., 2002). Meaningful and precise rates of convergence have been obtained if the regression function $m(\mathbf{x})$ is smooth, or, as we see more recently (Groeneboom & Jongbloed, 2014), if $m(\mathbf{x})$ satisfies certain shape restrictions (e.g., linear, monotonic, convex, or log-concave). However, even under such extra regularity conditions, the rate of convergence, quite disappointingly, still degrades quickly as the dimension p increases—a phenomenon widely known as the "curse of dimensionality."

Additive modeling (Hastie & Tibshirani, 1990) is a class of convenient tools to combat the curse of dimensionality, by making further assumption that the regression function $m(\mathbf{x})$ can be decomposed (approximately) into a sum of *univariate* component functions, each acting on a separate covariate. More precisely,

$$m(\mathbf{x}) \approx \mu + \sum_{j=1}^{p} f_j(x_j), \tag{1}$$

where $\mu \in \mathbb{R}$ is the intercept and each component f_j is a univariate function of x_j only. By restricting itself to the additive form (1), the class of additive models can bring in several advantages:

- dimensionality: a celebrated result of Stone (1985) reveals that when each component f_j is smooth, the additive models can achieve the same (optimal) rate of convergence for general p as they can for $p = 1$.
- interpretability: each component function can be easily visualized and inspected.
- computability: by decomposing the multivariate estimation problem into a set of univariate ones we can greatly simplify the underlying computations.

Previous works have also studied additive models where some interactions among covariates are allowed (Hastie & Tibshirani, 1990; Tyagi et al., 2016; Kandasamy & Yu, 2016).

Our main interest in this work is to incorporate certain shape constraints of component functions, such as convexity and its extension, into the procedure of estimating high dimensional additive models. In modern applications it is not uncommon that the number of covariates p is comparable with or even greatly exceeds the number of samples n that one can possibly (afford to) collect. However, the true regression function may only depend on a small number of important covariates, at least approximately. In the case of additive modeling, it amounts to identifying those few nonzero functional components in (1) based on a set of data samples (Ravikumar et al., 2008; Yin et al., 2012). It is also equally important that the regression function is usually subject to certain *a priori* regularity conditions. For instance, many functions that arise in econometrics (Varian, 1982, 1984), actuarial science (Grenander, 1956), statistics (Groeneboom & Jongbloed, 2014), and optimization (Hannah & Dunson, 2013; Hannah et al., 2014) *tend* to be convex/concave or monotonic (Barlow et al., 1972). However, such *a priori* knowledge can be imprecise and sometimes even wrong, e.g., convex functions are mistakenly believed to be concave. Therefore, we need our estimation procedure of additive models to be robust against the prior knowledge of component functions, such as their shape constraints.

More precisely, we make the following contributions in this work:

- We propose a sparse convex additive model to estimate convex (and monotonic) component functions in high dimensional additive modeling.
- To address potential robustness issue, we next propose the sparse difference of convex additive models (SDCAM) that can estimate most continuous functions, being smooth or not, that we use in practice. We discover three surprising properties of SDCAM: (1) If naively formulated, SDCAM is bound to overfit the training data; (2) By relating to a less-known characterization of difference of convex functions, we show how to add a very natural regularization functional to SDCAM to avoid overfitting and to reduce model complexity; (3) Despite the well-known fact that minimizing a difference of convex function is generally intractable, estimating a difference of convex function, as in SDCAM, can be achieved very efficiently.
- We propose an efficient backfitting algorithm for SDCAM with linear per-iteration complexity. It includes many prior algorithms as special cases.
- We test SDCAM on both synthetic and real data. Overall, SDCAM achieved competitive model selection and prediction accuracy against state-of-the-art sparse additive models. SDCAM also leads to some interesting new discovery on the Boston housing data.

This paper proceeds as follows. In the next section §2, we first introduce some background and related work. Then, we present the new sparse difference of convex additive models (SDCAM) in §3. Experimental results are reported in §4. Finally, we conclude in §5.

2 BACKGROUND AND RELATED WORK

In this section, we briefly review shape-constrained functions that are used in additive modeling before.

Recall that we are interested in estimating a multivariate function[1] $m : [0,1]^p \to \mathbb{R}$, based on i.i.d. samples $\{(\mathbf{x}_i, y_i) : i = 1, \dots, n\}$ from the following model

$$Y = m(X) + \xi,$$

where ξ is a random noise that is independent of X. To combat the curse of dimensionality, additive models try to find an additive approximation of the regression function

$$m(\mathbf{x}) = \mathbb{E}(Y|X = \mathbf{x}) \approx \mu + \sum_{j=1}^{p} f_j(x_j).$$

For the sake of model identifiability, we assume each univariate component function f_j is centered, i.e.,

$$\mathbb{E}(f_j(X_j)) = 0, j = 1, \dots, p.$$

As a consequence, an unbiased estimator of μ is simply the sample mean of the observed responses $\{y_i\}$. In what follows, we always first subtract this sample mean from the responses y_i hence the intercept μ can be omitted from the model.

2.1 ISOTONIC FUNCTIONS

Bacchetti (1989) first studied the isotonic additive modeling, in which each component function f_j is restricted to be isotonic, i.e., in the function class

$$\mathcal{M}_j := \{f : [0,1] \to \mathbb{R} \,|\, \mathbb{E}(f(X_j)) = 0, f \text{ is increasing}\}.$$

Given n samples $\{(\mathbf{x}_i, y_i) : i = 1, \dots, n\} \subseteq [0,1]^p \times \mathbb{R}$, the isotonic additive regression solves the following least squares estimation problem:

$$\min_{\forall j, f_j \in \mathcal{M}_j} \sum_{i=1}^{n} \Big(y_i - \sum_{j=1}^{p} f_j(x_{ij})\Big)^2. \tag{2}$$

Since the objective function depends on each f_j only at observed values, we can simplify (2) as follows: First,

[1]For simplicity, we assume the domain of the regression function is $[0,1]^p$ throughout the paper.

we sort each of the p covariates $\mathbf{x}_j \in \mathbb{R}^n$ separately in increasing order. Throughout this work we use the *tilde notation* $\tilde{\mathbf{x}}_j$ to represent this operation (w.r.t. $\mathbf{x}_j$), that is, $\tilde{\mathbf{x}}_j = P_j \mathbf{x}_j$ for a permutation matrix P_j such that

$$\tilde{x}_{1j} \leq \tilde{x}_{2j} \leq \cdots \leq \tilde{x}_{nj}.$$

Note that different covariates may require different permutations of the indexes in order to be sorted increasingly. Next, we introduce the component fits $\mathbf{z}_j \in \mathbb{R}^n$ on the observed values: $z_{ij} = f_j(x_{ij}), i = 1, \ldots, n$, and $\tilde{z}_{ij} = f_j(\tilde{x}_{ij})$ as a permuted version of $\mathbf{z}_j$, according to $\mathbf{x}_j$. Since all shape constraints in this work are with respect to the covariates $\mathbf{x}_j$, the monotonicity of the function f_j reduces to that of the vector $\tilde{\mathbf{z}}_j$. Lastly, we approximate the centering constraint $\mathbb{E}(f_j(X_j)) = 0$ by the empirical average over the samples. Thus, we arrive at the following *finite-dimensional* least squares problem:

$$\min_{\forall j, \tilde{\mathbf{z}}_j \in \mathcal{I} \cap \mathcal{H}} \sum_{i=1}^{n} \Big(y_i - \sum_{j=1}^{p} z_{ij}\Big)^2, \qquad (3)$$

where $\mathcal{H} := \{\mathbf{z} \in \mathbb{R}^n : \sum_{i=1}^n z_i = 0\}$ is the centering constraint and

$$\mathcal{I} := \{\mathbf{z} \in \mathbb{R}^n : z_1 \leq z_2 \leq \cdots \leq z_n\} \qquad (4)$$

is the isotonic (monotonic) cone. In what follows, one should keep in mind that $\tilde{\mathbf{z}}_j = P_j \mathbf{z}_j$ where the permutation matrix P_j satisfies $\tilde{\mathbf{x}}_j = P_j \mathbf{x}_j$.

Bacchetti (1989) developed a backfitting (i.e., block coordinate descent) algorithm for solving (3) while ignoring the centering constraint $\mathbf{z}_j \in \mathcal{H}$: in each step, all components except for one $\mathbf{z}_j$ are fixed, and the well-known pool-adjacent-violators (PAV) algorithm (Barlow et al., 1972) is applied to optimize $\mathbf{z}_j$ under the isotonic constraint $\mathcal{I}$. Oracle property of the backfitting estimator was later investigated by Mammen & Yu (2007).

Similar to standard additive models, isotonic additive modeling can fail in the high-dimensional setting ($p > n$). Fang & Meinshausen (2012) proposed the LASSO-Isotone (LISO) estimator, with the aim to incorporate the idea of sparsity into isotonic additive regression. Specifically, the total variation of component fits $\mathbf{z}_j$ were added to the objective function of problem (3) as a LASSO-style penalty:

$$\min_{\forall j, \tilde{\mathbf{z}}_j \in \mathcal{I} \cap \mathcal{H}} \sum_{i=1}^{n} \Big(y_i - \sum_{j=1}^{p} z_{ij}\Big)^2 + \sum_{j=1}^{p} \lambda_t \|\tilde{\mathbf{z}}_j\|_{\mathsf{tv}}, \qquad (5)$$

where the total variation

$$\|\tilde{\mathbf{z}}_j\|_{\mathsf{tv}} := \sum_{i=2}^{n} |\tilde{z}_{ij} - \tilde{z}_{i-1,j}|$$

simplifies to $\tilde{z}_{nj} - \tilde{z}_{1j}$ under the isotonic constraint $\tilde{\mathbf{z}}_j \in \mathcal{I}$. An iterative procedure called LISO-backfitting was applied to solve the LISO optimization problem (5).

2.2 FUNCTIONS OF BOUNDED VARIATION

The set of all isotonic functions $\mathcal{M}_j$ forms a convex cone in the vector space of all functions

$$\mathcal{F} := \{f \mid f : [0,1] \to \mathbb{R}\}.$$

It is thus natural to consider the subspace generated by isotonic functions, i.e., all functions that can be written as the difference of two increasing functions:

$$\mathcal{BV}_j := \{f \in \mathcal{F} \mid f = f_1 - f_2, f_1 \in \mathcal{M}_j, f_2 \in \mathcal{M}_j\}.$$

As is well-known in real analysis (Apostol, 1974, Theorem 6.13), the above class of functions coincides with the class of functions of bounded variation, i.e., functions f whose total variation is finite:

$$\|f\|_{\mathsf{tv}} := \sup_{\mathcal{P}} \sum_{i=2}^{n} |f(x_i) - f(x_{i-1})| < \infty,$$

where the supremum is taken over n and all partitions $\mathcal{P} = \{0 \leq x_1 \leq x_2 \leq \cdots \leq x_n \leq 1\}$ of $[0, 1]$.

The class of bounded variation functions motivates the development of the fused lasso additive model (FLAM), in which each component function f_j is estimated to be piecewise constant with a small number of adaptively chosen knots (Petersen et al., 2016). FLAM solves the following regularized least squares problem using block coordinate descent:

$$\min_{\forall j, \mathbf{z}_j \in \mathcal{H}} \sum_{i=1}^{n} \Big(y_i - \sum_{j=1}^{p} z_{ij}\Big)^2 + \sum_{j=1}^{p} \big(\lambda_t \|\tilde{\mathbf{z}}_j\|_{\mathsf{tv}} + \lambda_s \|\mathbf{z}_j\|_2\big),$$

where the total variation seminorm $\|\tilde{\mathbf{z}}_j\|_{\mathsf{tv}}$ encourages each component function to be piecewise constant and the ℓ_2 norm $\|\mathbf{z}_j\|_2$ imposes sparsity on the component functions to conduct variable selection. The centering constraint $\mathbf{z}_j \in \mathcal{H}$, however, is dropped in the implementation of FLAM, and the intercept μ has to be re-estimated in each iteration.

3 CONVEX-CONSTRAINED SPARSE ADDITIVE MODELS

Motivated by the previous work, in this section we study a related but different shape constraint, namely convexity, in sparse additive modeling. That is, each non-zero component function f_j is restricted to the following function class

$$\mathcal{C}_j := \{f : [0,1] \to \mathbb{R} \mid \mathbb{E}(f(X_j)) = 0, f \text{ is convex}\}.$$

Although there is a certain overlap between the two function classes $\mathcal{M}_j$ and $\mathcal{C}_j$, their "sizes" are quite different: the metric entropy of $\mathcal{M}_j$ (under the ℓ_∞ distance) is known to be of the order ϵ^{-1}(van der Vaart & Wellner, 2000, Theorem 2.7.5), while the metric entropy of the class of convex and uniformly bounded functions is of the significantly smaller order $\epsilon^{-1/2}$ (Guntuboyina & Sen, 2013).

Chen & Samworth (2016) studied a related problem where each component function in a generalized additive (index) model is required to obey a certain shape restriction, such as monotonicity, convexity, or the combination of the two (see their Table 1). In the case that it is a standard additive model and all the component functions are constrained to be convex, the resulting convex additive regression solves the following constrained least squares problem:

$$\min_{\forall j, f_j \in \mathcal{C}_j} \sum_{i=1}^{n} \Big(y_i - \sum_{j=1}^{p} f_j(x_{ij})\Big)^2. \tag{6}$$

Chen & Samworth (2016) applied an active set algorithm to solve (6) using basis expansion, which results in np parameters hence unfortunately can fail to work well in the high-dimensional setting. In fact, in their simulation study and real data examples, the dimensionality of covariates being considered is no larger than 10.

3.1 SPARSE CONVEX ADDITIVE MODEL (SCAM)

To deal with high dimensionality under the reasonable assumption that most covariates are irrelevant, we propose the following penalized optimization problem:

$$\min_{\forall j, f_j \in \mathcal{C}_j} \sum_{i=1}^{n} \Big(y_i - \sum_{j=1}^{p} f_j(x_{ij})\Big)^2 + \lambda_s \sum_{j=1}^{p} \|f_j\|_2, \tag{7}$$

where $\|f_j\|_2 := \sqrt{\mathbb{E}(f_j^2(X_j))}$ is the L_2 norm of component function f_j w.r.t. the marginal distribution of X_j. When p is large and λ_s is chosen appropriately, the L_2 norm in (7) will set many irrelevant component functions f_j to zero hence achieving model selection. Our model (7) here is inspired by SpAM (Ravikumar et al., 2008), which first considered the L_2 group norm in nonparametric additive modeling. The difference is that SpAM relies on linear smoothers to estimate *smooth* component functions while we are interested in getting *convex* component functions $\mathcal{C}_j$—a shape constraint that SpAM cannot explicitly take into account. We note in passing that a similar model to (7) (with group ℓ_∞ norm instead) appeared as the first stage of the screening procedure in the recent work of Xu et al. (2016),

Following the discussion from §2.1, we can simplify the infinite-dimensional problem (7) by first sorting each of the p covariates[2]. Again, we use the tilde notation to signal this sorting operation w.r.t. the corresponding covariate. Then, we introduce the fits $\mathbf{z}_j \in \mathbb{R}^n$ on the observed values, i.e., $z_{ij} = f_j(x_{ij}), i = 1\dots, n$, and make the substitution in the objective of (7). Lastly, we approximate the centering constraint $\mathbb{E}(f_j(X_j)) = 0$ and L_2 norm $\|f_j\|_2 := \sqrt{\mathbb{E}(f_j^2(X_j))}$ by the empirical average over the samples, leading to the *finite-dimensional* problem of the sparse convex additive model (SCAM):

$$\min_{\forall j, \tilde{\mathbf{z}}_j \in \mathcal{K}_j \cap \mathcal{H}} \sum_{i=1}^{n} \Big(y_i - \sum_{j=1}^{p} z_{ij}\Big)^2 + \lambda_s \sum_{j=1}^{p} \|\mathbf{z}_j\|_2, \tag{8}$$

where again $\mathcal{H} := \{\mathbf{z} \in \mathbb{R}^n : \sum_{i=1}^n z_i = 0\}$ is the empirical centering constraint and

$$\mathcal{K}_j := \left\{\mathbf{z} \in \mathbb{R}^n : \frac{z_2 - z_1}{\tilde{x}_{2j} - \tilde{x}_{1j}} \leq \cdots \leq \frac{z_n - z_{n-1}}{\tilde{x}_{nj} - \tilde{x}_{n-1,j}}\right\}. \tag{9}$$

Here, we use an important observation from the celebrated work of Hildreth (1954), namely, the convex cone constraint $\mathcal{K}_j$ is both sufficient and necessary to guarantee the underlying component function f_j to be convex. Note that had we not assumed the additive form $m(\mathbf{x}) \approx \sum_j f_j(x_j)$, we would have to deal with n^2 linear constraints (see for instance Boyd & Vandenberghe (2004, §6.5.5)) instead of only n simple ones. Therefore, the additive modeling assumption is not only useful in combating the curse of dimensionality; it also leads to computationally more convenient formulations.

Moreover, we can further combine monotonicity with convexity, as studied in Chen & Samworth (2016, Table 1). For instance, if some component function f_j is believed to be both convex and monotonically increasing, then we need only replace the cone $\mathcal{K}_j$ defined in (9) by

$$\mathcal{K}'_j := \left\{\mathbf{z} \in \mathbb{R}^n : 0 \leq \frac{z_2 - z_1}{\tilde{x}_{2j} - \tilde{x}_{1j}} \leq \cdots \leq \frac{z_n - z_{n-1}}{\tilde{x}_{nj} - \tilde{x}_{n-1,j}}\right\}. \tag{10}$$

As we shall see, this change will have very minimal effect on our backfitting algorithm hence below we do not discuss such straightforward extensions in details.

3.2 SPARSE DIFFERENCE OF CONVEX ADDITIVE MODEL (SDCAM)

The qualitative convex assumption in (7) is natural in many applications, but perhaps we can only expect it to hold *approximately*? Besides, what if we were wrong

[2]For simplicity, we assume that the observed values of each covariate are distinct. It is straightforward to extend to the case where ties can possibly arise.

and the component function f_j is in fact *concave*? In this section we propose a convenient extension to address such robustness issue.

The idea is to work with a larger class of functions. In particular, in parallel with §2.2, we consider class of difference of convex (DC) functions:

$$\mathcal{DC}_j := \{f \in \mathcal{F} \mid f = f_1 - f_2, f_1 \in \mathcal{C}_j, f_2 \in \mathcal{C}_j\}.$$

Clearly, $\mathcal{DC}_j$ is the vector space generated by $\mathcal{C}_j$. From the definition it is also clear that all convex functions, as well as all concave functions, are DC. In fact, most continuous functions (convex or not, smooth or not) we use in practice are DC. For comparison purpose we state the following fact:

Theorem 1. $\mathcal{M}_j \subset \mathcal{BV}_j \supset \mathcal{DC}_j \supset \mathcal{C}_j$.

As an example, we note that simple step functions are of bounded variation but they are not DC, since all DC functions are continuous (except perhaps at the boundaries of the domain). The difference is large in terms of metric entropy: $O(\epsilon^{-1})$ for $\mathcal{BV}_j$ versus $O(\epsilon^{-1/2})$ for $\mathcal{DC}_j$. As a result, searching in the space of DC functions is "easier" than in the space of bounded variation functions.

However, if we naively replace $\mathcal{C}_j$ with $\mathcal{DC}_j$ in the constraint of (7), the solution will severely overfit to the data, due to the following result:

Theorem 2. *For any sample* $\{(\mathbf{x}_i, y_i) : i = 1, \dots, n\} \subseteq [0,1]^p \times \mathbb{R}$ *such that* $\mathbf{x}_i \neq \mathbf{x}_j$ *for all* $1 \leq i \neq j \leq n$, *there always exists a multivariate*[3] *DC function* $f : [0,1]^p \to \mathbb{R}$ *such that for all* $i = 1, \dots, n$, $f(\mathbf{x}_i) = y_i$.

Proof. We only need to consider the special case of $p = 1$, which can be proved much more easily. However, we provide a proof for any p because this will provide another justification for the use of additive models.

Since $\mathbf{x}_i \neq \mathbf{x}_j$ for any $i \neq j$, we can put a bump function f_i around a small neighborhood N_i of each $\mathbf{x}_i$, such that $N_i \cap N_j = \emptyset$ for any $i \neq j$ and $f_i(\mathbf{z}) = 0$ iff $\mathbf{z} \notin N_i$. For instance, we can choose

$$f_i(\mathbf{z}) = \begin{cases} y_i e^{\frac{p}{\delta^2}} \prod_{j=1}^{p} e^{-\frac{1}{\delta^2 - (z_j - x_{ij})^2}}, & \text{if } \|\mathbf{z} - \mathbf{x}_i\|_\infty < \delta \\ 0, & \text{otherwise} \end{cases}$$

for some sufficiently small positive δ. Note that $f_i(\mathbf{x}_i) = y_i$ and f_i is twice (in fact infinitely many times) continuously differentiable. Now consider $f(\mathbf{z}) = \sum_{i=1}^{n} f_i(\mathbf{z})$. Since the functions f_i have non-overlapping support, $f(\mathbf{x}_i) = f_i(\mathbf{x}_i) = y_i$ for all $i = 1, \dots, n$. Moreover, the Hessian $\nabla^2 f$ is bounded from below. Therefore, for γ sufficiently large, the function $f(\mathbf{z}) + \gamma \|\mathbf{z}\|_2^2$ is convex, which implies that f is DC.

The centering constraint $\mathbb{E}(f(X_j)) = 0$ can also be satisfied, by choosing a centered bump function, or we can add an extra point $\mathbf{x}_0 \notin \{\mathbf{x}_1, \dots, \mathbf{x}_n\}$ and an additional component f_0 with suitable y_0 to cancel the integrals of $f_1, \dots, f_n$. □

[3]The definition of multivariate DC functions is a straightforward extension of the univariate case.

Therefore, naively estimating DC functions as in (7) would always lead to zero training error, effectively memorizing the training samples. The fundamental reason is that the class of DC functions is too rich. Thus, we need a complexity measure to penalize those estimators that use very "complex" DC functions. Fortunately, this can be achieved through the following characterization of DC functions of one variable:

Theorem 3 ((Roberts & Varberg, 1973, §14))**.** *Let* $f : [0,1] \to \mathbb{R}$ *be a function with finite one-sided derivatives at* 0 *and* 1. *Then* f *is DC iff*

$$\|f\|_{\mathcal{DC}} := \sup_{\mathcal{P}} \sum_{i=2}^{n-1} \left| \frac{f(x_{i+1}) - f(x_i)}{x_{i+1} - x_i} - \frac{f(x_i) - f(x_{i-1})}{x_i - x_{i-1}} \right| < \infty,$$

where the supremum is taken over n *and the partitions* $\mathcal{P} = \{0 \leq x_1 < x_2 < \cdots < x_n \leq 1\}$ *of* $[0,1]$.

In particular, if f is convex, then $\|f\|_{\mathcal{DC}} = f'_-(1) - f'_+(0)$, which explains the assumption of finite one-sided derivatives. Moreover, $\|f\|_{\mathcal{DC}} = 0$ iff f is affine, i.e., $f(x) = ax + b$ for some constant a and b. Essentially, the seminorm $\|f\|_{\mathcal{DC}}$ measures how fast the slope of f changes. If f is twice continuously differentiable, then

$$\|f\|_{\mathcal{DC}} = \int_0^1 |f''(x)| \, \mathrm{d}x.$$

Note that it is crucial here that f is a *univariate* function. For multivariate DC functions, we still do not have a convenient characterization as in Theorem 3.

Leveraging on the above result, we propose to estimate DC functions by solving the following penalized least squares formulation:

$$\min_{\forall j, f_j \in \mathcal{DC}_j} \sum_{i=1}^{n} \Big(y_i - \sum_{j=1}^{p} f_j(x_{ij})\Big)^2 + \sum_{j=1}^{p} (\lambda_d \|f_j\|_{\mathcal{DC}} + \lambda_s \|f_j\|_2), \tag{11}$$

where the constant λ_d controls the "degree of DC" of each f_j while the constant λ_s controls the number of effective components f_j (i.e., sparsity). We see again here that the additive assumption is not only useful in interpretability but also in computability: it allows us to use the convenient complexity measure $\|\cdot\|_{\mathcal{DC}}$.

As before, we can simplify (11), which we call sparse difference of convex additive model (SDCAM), as:

$$\min_{\forall j, \tilde{\mathbf{z}}_j \in \mathcal{H}} \sum_{i=1}^{n} (y_i - \sum_{j=1}^{p} z_{ij})^2 + \sum_{j=1}^{p} (\lambda_d \|\tilde{\mathbf{z}}_j\|_{\mathcal{DC}_j} + \lambda_s \|\mathbf{z}_j\|_2), \quad (12)$$

where for $\mathbf{z} \in \mathbb{R}^n$ we define

$$\|\mathbf{z}\|_{\mathcal{DC}_j} := \sum_{i=2}^{n-1} \left| \frac{z_{i+1} - z_i}{\tilde{x}_{i+1,j} - \tilde{x}_{ij}} - \frac{z_i - z_{i-1}}{\tilde{x}_{ij} - \tilde{x}_{i-1,j}} \right|. \quad (13)$$

Note that we have suppressed the dependence of $\|\cdot\|_{\mathcal{DC}_j}$ on $\tilde{\mathbf{x}}_j$ (the sorted version of $\mathbf{x}_j$). It is clear that we can easily incorporate further monotonic or convex constraints (or both) in (12), by adding $\tilde{\mathbf{z}}_j \in \mathcal{I}$ (c.f. (4)) or $\tilde{\mathbf{z}}_j \in \mathcal{K}_j$ (c.f. (9)) or $\tilde{\mathbf{z}}_j \in \mathcal{K}'_j$ (c.f. (10)). On the other hand, the following variation may be useful in estimating *approximately* convex functions:

$$\|\mathbf{z}\|_{\mathcal{AC}_j} := \sum_{i=2}^{n-1} \max \left\{ \frac{z_i - z_{i-1}}{\tilde{x}_{ij} - \tilde{x}_{i-1,j}} - \frac{z_{i+1} - z_i}{\tilde{x}_{i+1,j} - \tilde{x}_{ij}}, 0 \right\}.$$

Indeed, $\|\mathbf{z}\|_{\mathcal{AC}_j} = 0$ iff the underlying function is convex. We note in passing that Tibshirani (2014) used a simplified form of (13) for trend filtering. However, the connection to DC functions and the implication for additive models are not investigated.

It is well-known in optimization that minimizing a DC function in general is intractable. However, our proposed procedure SDCAM for *estimating* a DC function is a tractable convex problem hence amenable to global and efficient algorithms, as we show next.

3.3 BACKFITTING ALGORITHM

We propose to solve SDCAM in (12) using a *modified* backfitting algorithm (i.e., block coordinate gradient). In each iteration, we fix all component fits except for one $\mathbf{z}_j$, and we solve the resulting subproblem:

$$\min_{\tilde{\mathbf{z}}_j \in \mathcal{H}} \tfrac{1}{2}\|\tilde{\mathbf{r}}_j - \tilde{\mathbf{z}}_j\|_2^2 + \lambda_d \|\tilde{\mathbf{z}}_j\|_{\mathcal{DC}_j} + \lambda_s \|\tilde{\mathbf{z}}_j\|_2, \quad (14)$$

where $\tilde{\mathbf{r}}_j \in \mathbb{R}^n$ is the partial residual that removes the contribution of $\tilde{\mathbf{z}}_j$. To show how we can solve (14), it is helpful to recall the following concept:

Definition 1 (Proximal Map (Moreau, 1965)). For any closed convex function $f : \mathbb{R}^n \to \mathbb{R} \cup \{\infty\}$, we define its proximal map as:

$$\forall \mathbf{r} \in \mathbb{R}^n, \ \ \mathsf{P}_f^\eta(\mathbf{r}) = \operatorname*{argmin}_{\mathbf{z} \in \mathbb{R}^n} \tfrac{1}{2\eta}\|\mathbf{z} - \mathbf{r}\|_2^2 + f(\mathbf{z}),$$

and we write $\mathsf{P}_f = \mathsf{P}_f^1$.

Note that the proximal map is a nonlinear map from $\mathbb{R}^n$ to $\mathbb{R}^n$. With this definition we can write the solution to (14) succinctly as $\mathsf{P}_{\lambda_d\|\cdot\|_{\mathcal{DC}_j} + \lambda_s\|\cdot\|_2 + \mathcal{H}}(\tilde{\mathbf{r}}_j)$, where we abuse the notation $\mathcal{H}$ as its indicator function

$$\iota_{\mathcal{H}}(\mathbf{z}) = \begin{cases} 0, & \text{if } \mathbf{z} \in \mathcal{H} \\ \infty, & \text{if } \mathbf{z} \notin \mathcal{H} \end{cases}.$$

Then, we can solve the subproblem (14) based on the following decomposition result:

Theorem 4. *The solution to subproblem* (14) *can be computed as*

$$\mathsf{P}_{\lambda_d\|\cdot\|_{\mathcal{DC}_j} + \lambda_s\|\cdot\|_2 + \mathcal{H}}(\tilde{\mathbf{r}}_j) = \mathsf{P}^{\lambda_s}_{\|\cdot\|_2}\left[\mathsf{P}_{\mathcal{H}}(\mathsf{P}^{\lambda_d}_{\|\cdot\|_{\mathcal{DC}_j}}(\tilde{\mathbf{r}}_j))\right].$$

Proof. We first note that both $\lambda_d\|\cdot\|_{\mathcal{DC}_j}$ and $\mathcal{H}$ are positive homogeneous, hence we have

$$\mathsf{P}_{\lambda_d\|\cdot\|_{\mathcal{DC}_j} + \lambda_s\|\cdot\|_2 + \mathcal{H}}(\tilde{\mathbf{r}}_j) = \mathsf{P}^{\lambda_s}_{\|\cdot\|_2}\left[\mathsf{P}_{\lambda_d\|\cdot\|_{\mathcal{DC}_j} + \mathcal{H}}(\tilde{\mathbf{r}}_j)\right],$$

according to Yu (2013, Theorem 4). Next, by verifying the sufficient condition in Yu (2013, Theorem 1), we have

$$\mathsf{P}_{\lambda_d\|\cdot\|_{\mathcal{DC}_j} + \mathcal{H}}(\tilde{\mathbf{r}}_j) = \mathsf{P}_{\mathcal{H}}(\mathsf{P}^{\lambda_d}_{\|\cdot\|_{\mathcal{DC}_j}}(\tilde{\mathbf{r}}_j)).$$

Combining the previous two claims we complete the proof. □

It is well-known that $\mathsf{P}_{\mathcal{H}}$ amounts to subtracting the average and $\mathsf{P}^{\lambda_s}_{\|\cdot\|_2}(\mathbf{r}) = \left(1 - \frac{\lambda_s}{\|\mathbf{r}\|_2}\right)_+ \mathbf{r}$, where $(t)_+ := \max\{t, 0\}$, is the block soft thresholding operator. Thus, we need only find a way to compute $\mathsf{P}^{\lambda_d}_{\|\cdot\|_{\mathcal{DC}_j}}(\tilde{\mathbf{r}}_j)$, i.e.,

$$\mathsf{P}^{\lambda_d}_{\|\cdot\|_{\mathcal{DC}_j}}(\tilde{\mathbf{r}}_j) = \operatorname*{argmin}_{\tilde{\mathbf{z}} \in \mathbb{R}^n} \tfrac{1}{2}\|\tilde{\mathbf{z}} - \tilde{\mathbf{r}}_j\|_2^2 + \lambda_d \|\tilde{\mathbf{z}}\|_{\mathcal{DC}_j}.$$

With a suitable change of variables[4], the problem is equivalent to solving

$$\min_{s \in \mathbb{R}, \mathbf{w} \in \mathbb{R}^{n-1}} \frac{1}{2}\left\| A_j \binom{s}{\mathbf{w}} - \tilde{\mathbf{r}}_j \right\|_2^2 + \lambda_d \|\mathbf{w}\|_{\text{tv}}, \quad (15)$$

where

$$A_j = \begin{bmatrix} 1 & 0 & 0 & \cdots & 0 \\ 1 & \tilde{x}_{2j} - \tilde{x}_{1j} & 0 & \cdots & 0 \\ 1 & \tilde{x}_{2j} - \tilde{x}_{1j} & \tilde{x}_{3j} - \tilde{x}_{2j} & \cdots & 0 \\ \vdots & \vdots & \vdots & \ddots & \vdots \\ 1 & \tilde{x}_{2j} - \tilde{x}_{1j} & \tilde{x}_{3j} - \tilde{x}_{2j} & \cdots & \tilde{x}_{nj} - \tilde{x}_{n-1,j} \end{bmatrix}.$$

[4]Define $s = \tilde{z}_1$ and $w_i = \frac{\tilde{z}_{i+1} - \tilde{z}_i}{\tilde{x}_{i+1,j} - \tilde{x}_{ij}}, i = 1, \ldots n-1$. Hence, $\tilde{\mathbf{z}} = A_j \binom{s}{\mathbf{w}}$ and $\|\tilde{\mathbf{z}}\|_{\mathcal{DC}_j} = \|\mathbf{w}\|_{\text{tv}}$.

Algorithm 1 Modified backfitting algorithm for Sparse Difference of Convex Additive Model (SDCAM)

input: $X \in \mathbb{R}^{n \times p}$, $\mathbf{y} \in \mathbb{R}^n$, $\lambda_d, \lambda_s \geq 0$, step size $\eta > 0$

1 $Z \leftarrow \mathbf{0}_{n \times p}$ // initialization
2 $\mathbf{r} \leftarrow \mathbf{y} - \mathsf{mean}(\mathbf{y})$ // remove mean μ
3 **while** *not converged* **do**
4   select some component $j \in \{1, 2, \ldots, p\}$
5     $\mathbf{r} \leftarrow \mathbf{r} + Z_{.j}$ // remove current component
6     $\tilde{\mathbf{r}} \leftarrow \pi(\mathbf{r})$ // permute according to $\mathbf{x}_j$
7     $\tilde{\mathbf{z}} \leftarrow \pi(Z_{.j})$ // permute according to $\mathbf{x}_j$
8   **for** $k = 1, \ldots, \max$ **do**
9         $\binom{s}{\mathbf{w}} \leftarrow \binom{s}{\mathbf{w}} - \eta \cdot A_j^\top(\tilde{\mathbf{z}} - \tilde{\mathbf{r}})$ // grad step
10         $\mathbf{w} \leftarrow \mathsf{P}^{\eta}_{\lambda_d \|\cdot\|_{\mathrm{tv}}}(\mathbf{w})$ // $\mathsf{P}_{\mathcal{I}}$ for SCAM (8)
11         $\tilde{\mathbf{z}} \leftarrow A_j \binom{s}{\mathbf{w}}$ // substitution
12     $\tilde{\mathbf{z}} \leftarrow \tilde{\mathbf{z}} - \mathsf{mean}(\tilde{\mathbf{z}})$ // computing $\mathsf{P}_{\mathcal{H}}$
13     $\tilde{\mathbf{z}} \leftarrow \left(1 - \frac{\lambda_s}{\|\tilde{\mathbf{z}}\|_2}\right)_+ \tilde{\mathbf{z}}$ // computing $\mathsf{P}^{\lambda_s}_{\|\cdot\|_2}$
14     $Z_{.j} \leftarrow \pi^{-1}(\tilde{\mathbf{z}})$ // inverse permute
15     $\mathbf{r} \leftarrow \mathbf{r} - Z_{.j}$ // add component back

Since the proximal map $\mathsf{P}^{\eta}_{\lambda_d \|\cdot\|_{\mathrm{tv}}}$ can be computed in linear time using the algorithm in Davies & Kovac (2001), we can solve (15) hence $\mathsf{P}^{\lambda_d}_{\|\cdot\|_{\mathcal{DC}_j}}(\mathbf{r}_j)$ iteratively using the accelerated proximal gradient algorithm (Beck & Teboulle, 2009; Nesterov, 2013).

We summarize the entire computational procedure for SDCAM in Algorithm 1. The necessary modifications for the SCAM problem (8) should be clear: we only need to replace the proximal map $\mathsf{P}^{\eta}_{\lambda_d \|\cdot\|_{\mathrm{tv}}}$ by $\mathsf{P}_{\mathcal{I}}$ in line 10, i.e., projecting onto the isotonic cone $\mathcal{I}$ in (4). Importantly, note that the matrix A_j appears only in two matrix-vector products $A_j^\top(\tilde{\mathbf{z}} - \tilde{\mathbf{r}})$ and $A_j\binom{s}{\mathbf{w}}$. By exploiting the special structure in A_j, we observe that we do *not* need to maintain A_j explicitly (since there are only n unique entries), and both matrix-vector products can be computed in $O(n)$ time using cumulative sums. Thus, the per-iteration complexity of Algorithm 1 is linear in the sample size n. Moreover, we can prove that Algorithm 1 converges to the global minimum at a sublinear rate by casting it under the block coordinate descent framework of Tseng (2001).

3.4 INTERPOLATION

SDCAM, as well as any other nonparametric additive models, only yield the function value estimates $z_{ij} = f(x_{ij})$ on the observed training data X. As more and more data are observed, it is possible to estimate the entire function f asymptotically. However, for a given finite sample size, there are infinitely many candidate function estimates that all yield the same fits z_{ij} on the training data. To fix a particular choice, we can construct a function estimate by some form of smoothing or interpolation. For instance, the recent work of Canini et al. (2016) performed interpolation through a *fixed* lattice in the domain. In our experiments, we simply use linear interpolation to get a piece-wise linear function estimate, although in principle higher order interpolations can also be used. Note that we do not extrapolate the function values outside the range of the training data, because Balázs et al. (2015) showed that a naive extrapolation can lead to large or even infinite generalization errors.

4 EXPERIMENTS

In this section, we compare the performance of SDCAM to SpAM (Ravikumar et al., 2008) and FLAM (Petersen et al., 2016) on both simulated and real data. SpAM is implemented using Gaussian kernel smoothers with the plug-in bandwidth. We do not compare to LISO (Fang & Meinshausen, 2012) or SCAM because they achieve similar performance as SDCAM when the shape parameters are set correctly and perform much worse when the shape constraints do not apply hence are misspecified.

4.1 SIMULATION STUDY

We generate samples $X \in \mathbb{R}^{n \times p}$ and $\mathbf{y} \in \mathbb{R}^n$ with $n = 100, p = 1000$ according to $y_i = \sum_{j=1}^4 f_j(x_{ij}) + \epsilon_i$, where $x_{ij} \sim \mathrm{Uniform}(-2.5, 2.5)$ and $\epsilon_i \sim \mathcal{N}(0, \sigma^2)$. Two different values of σ are chosen so that the signal-to-noise ratio $\mathrm{SNR} = 3$ or 5, respectively. In other words, only the first 4 component functions are nonzero and the other 996 variables are irrelevant. We consider the following three scenarios for the choice of $f_1, \ldots, f_4$:

- Scenario 1: all of them are piecewise constant (Figure 1 (a)).
- Scenario 2: all of them are smooth (Figure 1 (b)).
- Scenario 3: f_2 is smooth and the rest of them are piecewise linear (Figure 1 (c)).

For each combination of scenario and SNR level, we simulate training, validation, and test sets of the same size ($n = 100, p = 1000$). Validation sets are used to choose the optimal tuning parameter (or parameter pair) for all algorithms, and test sets are used to calculate the mean squared error (MSE) to evaluate the prediction accuracy of the estimated models. Table 1 summarizes the performance of each method in terms of precision/recall for sparsity pattern recovery, estimated model size, and test set MSE over 100 random data replicates.

As expected, FLAM achieves the lowest test set MSE in Scenario 1 because it employs a total variation regularizer to encourage the estimated functions to be piecewise constant (see also Figure 1 (a)). SDCAM performs com-

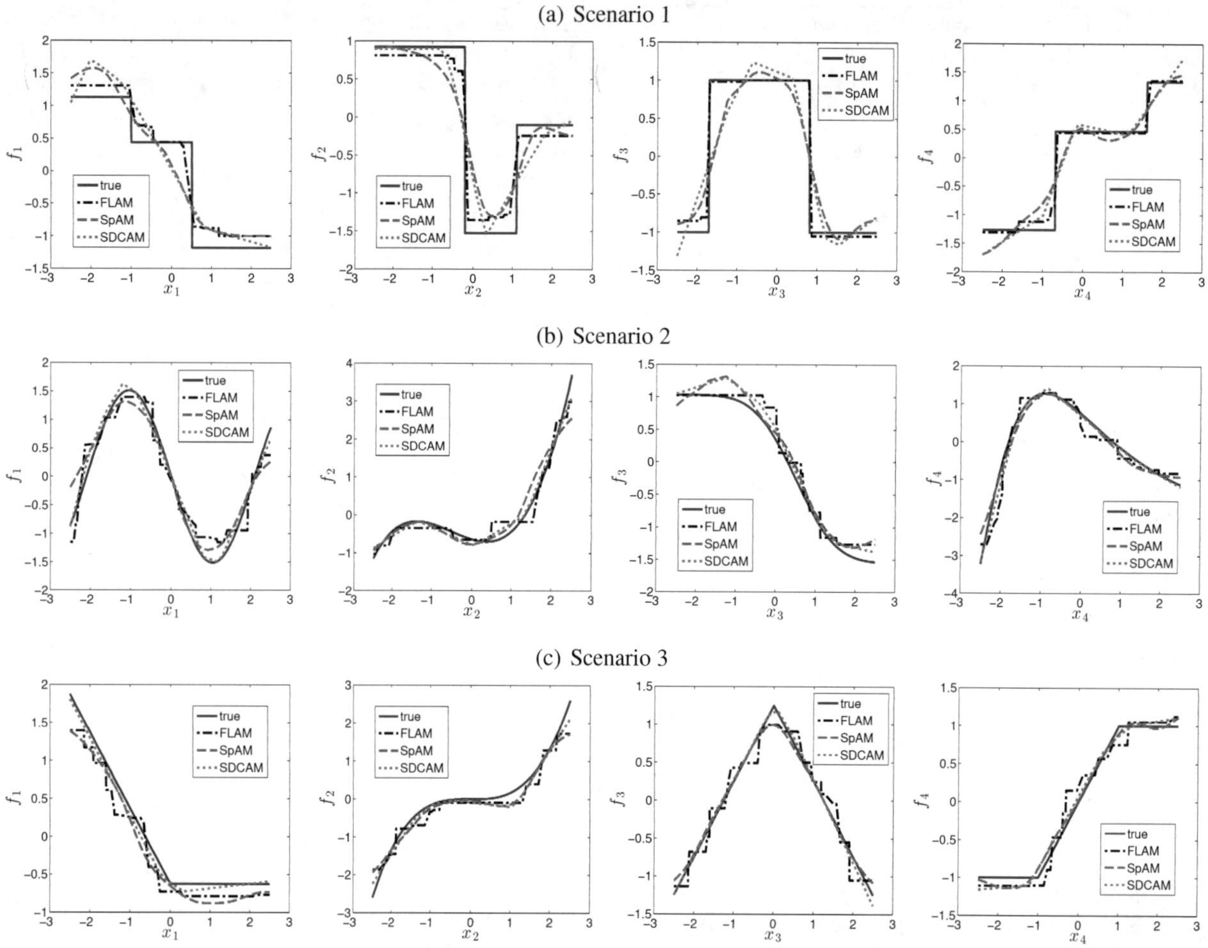

Figure 1: Typical examples of component fits $\hat{f}_1, \hat{f}_2, \hat{f}_3, \hat{f}_4$ in three simulation scenarios, with $n = 100$, $p = 1000$, and SNR $= 5$. The true component functions are plotted in solid blue lines. All models are estimated using the optimal tuning parameter (or parameter pair) that achieves the minimum validation set MSE.

parably to SpAM in this scenario, in which neither is able to capture the sharp transition of values in the discontinuous functions.

In Scenario 2 where all relevant component functions are smooth, SDCAM outperforms SpAM, with FLAM being the worst option. Although SDCAM estimates seem to be quite similar to SpAM fits for the 4 true components (see Figure 1 (b)), SDCAM has the best precision score. That means, it is more effective in eliminating irrelevant variables and their spurious fits in the estimated models, which in turn can greatly improve the test set MSE.

Scenario 3 is particularly interesting: all the true component functions are DC but only f_2 is smooth. SDCAM achieves the best performance in such a mixed scenario, because SpAM cannot well handle the estimation of nonsmooth functions (in this case, piecewise linear functions) and smooth functions are unfavorable to FLAM. It is also worth noting that the SDCAM estimates tend to be less biased on the boundaries of the domain compared to SpAM fits, which are based on the smoothing technique (Figure 1 (c)).

4.2 REAL DATA

We consider the Boston housing data that contains $n = 506$ observations of housing values (`medv`) in suburbs of Boston. Following Härdle et al. (2004) and Ravikumar et al. (2008), 10 original covariates are chosen to be included in the study: `crim`, `indus`, `nox`, `rm`, `age`, `dis`, `tax`, `ptratio`, `b`, `lstat`. We first rescale each variable to the interval $[0, 1]$, and then add spurious variables randomly drawn from $\mathrm{Uniform}(0, 1)$ to produce three datasets of $p = 30, 40$, and 50, respectively. For each such dataset, 10-fold cross-validation is used to select the optimal tuning parameter, and the final models are estimated on all the samples with the chosen value. Table 2 shows the proportion of 100 random cross-validation partitions that can correctly eliminate spurious variables in the final models. The performance of SDCAM is very consistent across

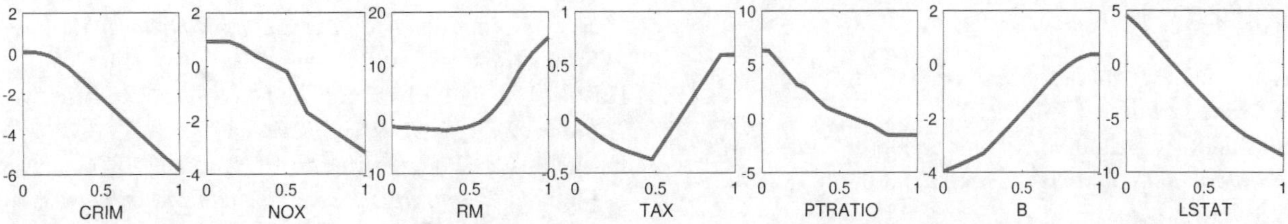

Figure 2: SDCAM estimates on the Boston housing data, with $p = 50$. Plotted are the fitted functions on the 7 selected variables. The remaining 43 components are all constant zero.

method	precision	recall	model size	MSE
Scenario 1, SNR = 3				
SpAM	0.87 (0.19)	0.99 (0.04)	4.93 (1.86)	1.15 (0.39)
FLAM	0.82 (0.21)	1.00 (0.00)	5.48 (2.60)	0.85 (0.24)
SDCAM	0.86 (0.17)	0.99 (0.05)	4.78 (1.14)	1.32 (0.41)
Scenario 1, SNR = 5				
SpAM	0.92 (0.14)	1.00 (0.00)	4.54 (1.14)	0.72 (0.20)
FLAM	0.78 (0.22)	1.00 (0.00)	5.73 (2.27)	0.43 (0.13)
SDCAM	0.93 (0.13)	1.00 (0.00)	4.41 (0.96)	0.75 (0.18)
Scenario 2, SNR = 3				
SpAM	0.87 (0.19)	0.99 (0.03)	4.91 (1.52)	0.89 (0.36)
FLAM	0.80 (0.20)	1.00 (0.00)	5.48 (2.14)	0.95 (0.29)
SDCAM	0.93 (0.12)	1.00 (0.00)	4.38 (0.78)	0.64 (0.14)
Scenario 2, SNR = 5				
SpAM	0.92 (0.14)	1.00 (0.00)	4.51 (1.17)	0.47 (0.17)
FLAM	0.76 (0.19)	1.00 (0.00)	5.70 (1.74)	0.49 (0.16)
SDCAM	0.98 (0.06)	1.00 (0.00)	4.10 (0.30)	0.25 (0.04)
Scenario 3, SNR = 3				
SpAM	0.92 (0.16)	1.00 (0.00)	4.57 (1.39)	0.47 (0.10)
FLAM	0.86 (0.16)	1.00 (0.00)	4.84 (1.17)	0.55 (0.11)
SDCAM	0.97 (0.08)	1.00 (0.00)	4.15 (0.41)	0.41 (0.06)
Scenario 3, SNR = 5				
SpAM	0.98 (0.07)	1.00 (0.00)	4.11 (0.34)	0.21 (0.04)
FLAM	0.77 (0.19)	1.00 (0.00)	5.62 (1.85)	0.26 (0.06)
SDCAM	0.99 (0.05)	1.00 (0.00)	4.06 (0.24)	0.15 (0.02)

Table 1: Performance of different methods in the simulation study, with $n = 100$ and $p = 1000$. Shown are the mean (standard error) of precision/recall for sparsity pattern recovery, estimated model size, and test set MSE over 100 random data replicates.

different cross-validation partitions (and across different values of p) and is significantly better than the other two methods, demonstrating its superior ability in identifying irrelevant factors.

Because the SpAM and FLAM estimates are very sensitive to the choice of cross-validation partition, we only report the SDCAM fits for $p = 50$ in Figure 2. The results are largely compatible with two previous

	SpAM	FLAM	SDCAM
$p = 30$	0.76	0.83	0.99
$p = 40$	0.87	0.85	0.99
$p = 50$	0.87	0.87	0.99

Table 2: The proportion of 100 random cross-validation partitions for the Boston housing data that can correctly eliminate irrelevant variables in the final models.

studies (Ravikumar et al., 2008; Fang & Meinshausen, 2012): (1) the fitted patterns on selected `crim`, `rm`, `ptratio`, and `lstat` are quite similar; (2) `indus`, `age`, and `dis` are regarded to be irrelevant or have small effects; (3) there is a certain effect from `nox`, which was claimed to be large in Fang & Meinshausen (2012) and borderline in Ravikumar et al. (2008). Perhaps the most striking finding is a fairly large effect of `tax`, which were estimated to be insignificant in these two studies. Nevertheless, our function estimate of $f_7(\texttt{tax})$ is largely compatible with the fitted pattern reported in Härdle et al. (2004, Figure 8.3).

5 CONCLUSIONS

We have shown how to integrate shape constraints such as convexity into sparse additive models. The proposed sparse difference of convex additive model (SDCAM) can successfully estimate most additive continuous functions even in the presence of many irrelevant features. We propose a natural regularization functional in SDCAM to avoid overfitting and to reduce model complexity, and we develop an efficient backfitting algorithm with linear per-iteration complexity. Experiments on both synthetic and real data confirm that our method is competitive against state-of-the-art alternatives. Encouraged by our experiments, in the future we plan to study the model selection consistency of SDCAM and to investigate the bias-variance tradeoff when estimating a non-additive regression function.

Acknowledgements

We thank the reviewers for their comments. This work is partly supported by Eller College Dean's Research Grant (JY) and NSERC (YY).

References

Apostol, T. M. *Mathematical Analysis*. Addison-Wesley, Second edition, 1974.

Bacchetti, P. Additive isotonic models. *Journal of the American Statistical Association*, 84(405):289–294, 1989.

Balázs, G., György, A., and Szepesvári, C. Near-optimal max-affine estimators for convex regression. In *AISTATS*, 2015.

Barlow, R. E., Bartholomew, D. J., Bremner, J. M., and Brunk, H. D. *Statistical inference under order restrictions: The theory and application of isotonic regression*. John Wiley & Sons, 1972.

Beck, A. and Teboulle, M. A fast iterative shrinkage-thresholding algorithm for linear inverse problems. *SIAM Journal on Imaging Sciences*, 2(1):183–202, 2009.

Boyd, S. and Vandenberghe, L. *Convex Optimization*. Cambridge University Press, 2004.

Canini, K., Cotter, A., Gupta, M. R., Fard, M. Milani, and Pfeifer, J. Fast and flexible monotonic functions with ensembles of lattices. In *NIPS*, 2016.

Chen, Y. and Samworth, R. J. Generalized additive and index models with shape constraints. *Journal of Royal Statistical Society, Series B*, 78(4):729–754, 2016.

Davies, P. L. and Kovac, A. Local extremes, runs, strings and multiresolution. *The Annals of Statistics*, 29(1):1–65, 2001.

Fang, Z. and Meinshausen, N. Lasso isotone for high-dimensional additive isotonic regression. *Journal of Computational and Graphical Statistics*, 21(1):72–91, 2012.

Grenander, U. On the theory of mortality measurement. *Scandinavian Actuarial Journal*, 39(2):125–153, 1956.

Groeneboom, P. and Jongbloed, G. *Nonparametric Estimation under Shape Constraints: Estimators, Algorithms and Asymptotics*. Cambridge University Press, 2014.

Guntuboyina, A. and Sen, B. Covering numbers for convex functions. *IEEE Transactions on Information Theory*, 59(4):1957–1965, 2013.

Györfi, L., Kohler, M., Krzyzak, A., and Walk, H. *A Distribution-Free Theory of Nonparametric Regression*. Springer, 2002.

Hannah, L. A. and Dunson, D. B. Multivariate convex regression with adaptive partitioning. *Journal of Machine Learning Research*, 14:3261–3294, 2013.

Hannah, L. A., Powell, W. B., and Dunson, D. B. Semi-convex regression for metamodeling-based optimization. *SIAM Journal on Optimization*, 24(2):573–597, 2014.

Härdle, W., Sperlich, S., Müller, M., and Werwatz, A. *Nonparametric and Semiparametric Models*. Springer, 2004.

Hastie, T. J. and Tibshirani, R. J. *Generalized Additive Models*. Chapman & Hall/CRC, 1990.

Hildreth, C. Point estimates of ordinates of concave functions. *Journal of the American Statistical Association*, 49(267):598–619, 1954.

Kandasamy, K. and Yu, Y. Additive approximations in high dimensional nonparametric regression via the SALSA. In *ICML*, 2016.

Mammen, E. and Yu, K. Additive isotonic regression. In *Asymptotics: Particles, Processes and Inverse Problems*, volume 55, pp. 179–195, 2007.

Moreau, J. J. Proximité et dualtité dans un espace Hilbertien. *Bulletin de la Société Mathématique de France*, 93:273–299, 1965.

Nesterov, Y. Gradient methods for minimizing composite functions. *Mathematical Programming, Series B*, 140:125–161, 2013.

Petersen, A., Witten, D., and Simon, N. Fused lasso additive model. *Journal of Computational and Graphical Statistics*, 25(4):1005–1025, 2016.

Ravikumar, P., Lafferty, J., Liu, H., and Wasserman, L. SpAM: Sparse additive models. In *NIPS*. 2008.

Roberts, A. W. and Varberg, D. E. *Convex Functions*. Academic Press, 1973.

Stone, C. J. Additive regression and other nonparametric models. *The Annals of Statistics*, 13(2):689–705, 1985.

Tibshirani, R. J. Adaptive piecewise polynomial estimation via trend filtering. *The Annals of Statistics*, 42(1): 285–323, 2014.

Tseng, P. Convergence of a block coordinate descent method for nondifferentiable minimization. *Journal of Optimization Theory and Applications*, 109(3):475–494, 2001.

Tyagi, H., Kyrillidis, A., Gärtner, B., and Krause, A. Learning sparse additive models with interactions in high dimensions. In *AISTATS*, 2016.

van der Vaart, A. W. and Wellner, J. A. *Weak Convergence and Empirical Processes: With Applications to Statistics*. Springer, 2000.

Varian, H. R. The nonparametric approach to demand analysis. *Econometrica*, 50(4):945–973, 1982.

Varian, H. R. The nonparametric approach to production analysis. *Econometrica*, 52(3):579–597, 1984.

Xu, M., Chen, M., and Lafferty, J. Faithful variable screening for high-dimensional convex regression. *The Annals of Statistics*, 44(6):2624–2660, 2016.

Yin, J., Chen, X., and Xing, E. P. Group sparse additive models. In *ICML*, 2012.

Yu, Y. On decomposing the proximal map. In *NIPS*, 2013.

Stein Variational Policy Gradient

Yang Liu
UIUC
liu301@illinois.edu

Prajit Ramachandran
UIUC
prajitram@gmail.com

Qiang Liu
Dartmouth
qiang.liu@dartmouth.edu

Jian Peng
UIUC
jianpeng@illinois.edu

Abstract

Policy gradient methods have been successfully applied to many complex reinforcement learning problems. However, policy gradient methods suffer from high variance, slow convergence, and inefficient exploration. In this work, we introduce a maximum entropy policy optimization framework which explicitly encourages parameter exploration, and show that this framework can be reduced to a Bayesian inference problem. We then propose a novel Stein variational policy gradient method (SVPG) which combines existing policy gradient methods and a repulsive functional to generate a set of diverse but well-behaved policies. SVPG is robust to random initializations and can easily be implemented in a parallel manner. On several continuous control problems, we find that SVPG versions of REINFORCE and advantage actor-critic algorithms are greatly improved in terms of both average return and data efficiency.

1 INTRODUCTION

Recent advances in policy gradient methods and deep learning have demonstrated their applicability for complex reinforcement learning problems. Instead of deriving a policy from a value function, policy gradient methods directly optimize a parametrized policy with gradients approximated from rollout trajectories. Deep neural networks trained with policy gradient methods have demonstrated impressive performance on continuous control, vision-based navigation and Atari games (Schulman et al., 2015b, Kakade, 2002, Schulman et al., 2015a, Mnih et al., 2016). However, these algorithms are not yet applicable for hard real-world tasks, partially due to high variance, slow convergence, and insufficient exploration. Because of the non-convexity of neural-network policies, the performance of trained agents is often very sensitive to their initializations.

In this work, we introduce the Stein variational policy gradient (SVPG) method, a new policy optimization method that leverages a recent Stein variational gradient descent method (Liu and Wang, 2016) to allow simultaneous exploitation and exploration of multiple policies. Unlike traditional policy optimization which attempts to learn a single policy, we model a distribution of policy parameters, where samples from this distribution will represent strong policies. We first introduce a framework that optimizes this distribution of policy parameters with (relative) entropy regularization. The (relative) entropy term explicitly encourages exploration in the parameter space while also optimizing the expected utility of polices drawn from this distribution. We show that this framework can be reduced to a Bayesian inference problem in which we generate samples of policy parameters from a posterior. We then use Stein variational gradient descent (SVGD) to optimize this distribution. SVGD leverages efficient deterministic dynamics to transport a set of particles to approximate given target posterior distributions. It combines the advantages of MCMC, which does not confine the approximation within a parametric family, and variational inference, which converges fast due to deterministic updates that utilize the gradient. Specifically, in SVPG a policy gradient estimator is applied to improve policy parameter particles while a repulsive functional is used to diversify these particles to enable parameter exploration.

In our experiments, we implementing SVPG on top of existing policy gradient methods, including REINFORCE (Williams, 1992) and advantageous actor critic, improves average return on continuous control problems. The SVPG versions enjoy better data efficiency through explicit parameter exploration. SVPG is also more robust to different initializations. Because of its simplicity and generality, we believe that SVPG provides a generic tool that can be broadly applied to boost the performance of existing policy optimization methods.

2 PRELIMINARIES

We introduce the background of reinforcement learning and discuss different policy gradient estimation methods.

2.1 REINFORCEMENT LEARNING

Reinforcement learning considers agents which are able to take a sequence of actions in an environment and experience at most one scalar reward per action. The task of the agents is to learn a policy that maximizes cumulative rewards.

Formally, consider an agent operating over time $t \in \{1, \ldots, T\}$. At time t the agent is in an environment state s_t and produces an action $a_t \in A$. The agent will then observe a new state s_{t+1} and receive a scalar reward $r_t \in R$. The set of possible actions A can be discrete or continuous. The goal of reinforcement learning is to find a policy $\pi(a_t|s_t)$ for choosing an action in state s_t to maximize a utility function (or expected return)

$$J(\pi) = \mathbf{E}_{s_0,a_0,\ldots}[\sum_{t=0}^{\infty} \gamma^t r(s_t, a_t)],$$

where $0 \leq \gamma \leq 1$ is a discount factor; $a_t \sim \pi(a_t|s_t)$ is drawn from the policy; $s_{t+1} \sim P(s_{t+1}|s_t, a_t)$ is generated by the environmental dynamics. In this work, we consider policy $\pi(a_t|s_t)$ to be a stochastic policy which defines the distribution over actions given the current state s_t. In the model free setting, we assume that the environmental dynamics $P(s_{t+1}|s_t, a_t)$ is unknown. The state value function

$$V^{\pi}(s_t) = \mathbf{E}_{a_t,s_{t+1},\ldots}[\sum_{i=0}^{\infty} \gamma^i r(s_{t+i}, a_{t+i})]$$

is the expected return by policy π from state s_t. The state-action function

$$Q^{\pi}(s_t, a_t) = \mathbf{E}_{s_{t+1},a_{t+1},\ldots}[\sum_{i=0}^{\infty} \gamma^i r(s_{t+i}, a_{t+i})]$$

is the expected return by policy π after taking action a_t at state s_t.

2.2 POLICY GRADIENT ESTIMATION

In policy-based reinforcement learning approaches, policy $\pi(a|s;\theta)$ is parameterized by θ and is iteratively improved by updating θ to optimize the utility function $J(\theta)$; here by an abuse of notation, we denote $J(\theta) = J(\pi(a|s;\theta))$. There are two main approaches to estimate policy gradient from rollout samples.

Finite difference methods. It is possible to estimate the gradient $\nabla_\theta J(\theta)$ using finite difference methods. Instead of computing the finite difference for each individual parameter, rollout efficient methods such as SPSA (Spall, 1998), PEPG (Sehnke et al., 2010) and evolutionary strategy approximations (Hansen, 2006, Mannor et al., 2003) have been proposed. The key idea of such methods is to use a small number of random perturbations to approximate the gradient values of all parameters simultaneously. In particular, the following stochastic finite difference approximation has recently been shown to be highly effective over several complex domains (Salimans et al., 2017):

$$\nabla_\theta J(\theta) \approx \frac{1}{m} \sum_{i=1}^{m} \frac{J(\theta + h\xi_i)\xi_i}{h}, \tag{1}$$

where ξ_i are drawn from standard Gaussian $\mathcal{N}(0, I)$. When h is very small, this estimate provides an accurate approximation of $\nabla_\theta J(\theta)$.

Likelihood ratio methods. Policy gradient algorithms, such as the well-known REINFORCE (Williams, 1992), estimate the gradient $\nabla_\theta J(\theta)$ from rollout samples generated by $\pi(a|s;\theta)$ using the likelihood ratio trick. Specifically, REINFORCE uses the following approximator of the policy gradient

$$\nabla_\theta J(\theta) \approx \sum_{t=0}^{\infty} \nabla_\theta \log \pi(a_t|s_t;\theta) R_t \tag{2}$$

based on a single rollout trajectory, where $R_t = \sum_{i=0}^{\infty} \gamma^i r(s_{t+i}, a_{t+i})$ is the accumulated return from time step t. It was shown that this gradient is an unbiased estimation of $\nabla_\theta J(\theta)$. With a careful choice of baseline function $b(s_t)$, another estimate of policy gradient

$$\nabla_\theta J(\theta) \approx \sum_{t=0}^{\infty} \nabla_\theta \log \pi(a_t|s_t;\theta)(R_t - b(s_t)) \tag{3}$$

was shown to be unbiased but with smaller variance. It is common to use the value function $V^{\pi}(s_t)$ as the baseline. $R_t - V^{\pi}(s_t)$ is an estimate of advantage function $A^{\pi}(s_t, a_t) = Q^{\pi}(s_t, a_t) - V^{\pi}(s_t)$.

$$\nabla_\theta J(\theta) \approx \sum_{t=0}^{\infty} \nabla_\theta \log \pi(a_t|s_t;\theta)(R_t - V^{\pi}(s_t)) \tag{4}$$

This method is also known as advantage actor critic (A2C) (Schulman et al., 2015b, Mnih et al., 2016). In practice, multiple rollouts are sometimes used to estimate these policy gradient in a batch.

3 STEIN VARIATIONAL POLICY GRADIENT

This section introduces our main framework. We start with introducing a maximum entropy policy optimization framework for learning upper level policies in Section 3.1, and then develop our Stein variational policy gradient in Section 3.2.

3.1 MAXIMUM ENTROPY POLICY OPTIMIZATION

Instead of finding a single policy θ, here we consider the policy parameter θ as a random variable and seek a distribution $q(\theta)$ to optimize the expected return. We also introduce a *default* parameter distribution q_0 to incorporate prior domain knowledge of parameters or provide the regularization of θ. We formulate the optimization of q as the following regularized expected utility problem:

$$\max_q \left\{ \mathbf{E}_{q(\theta)}[J(\theta)] - \alpha \mathbf{D}(q \| q_0) \right\}, \tag{5}$$

where q maximizes the expected utility, regularized by a relative entropy or Kullback-Leibler (KL) divergence $\mathbf{D}(q\|q_0)$ with a "prior distribution" q_0,

$$\mathbf{D}(q\|q_0) = \mathbf{E}_{q(\theta)}[\log q(\theta) - \log q_0(\theta)].$$

If we use an uninformative (and improper) prior $q_0(\theta) = const$, the second KL term is simplified to the entropy $\mathbf{H}(q) = \mathbf{E}_{q(\theta)}[-\log q(\theta)]$ of q. The optimization

$$\max_q \left\{ \mathbf{E}_{q(\theta)}[J(\theta)] + \alpha \mathbf{H}(q) \right\}, \tag{6}$$

then explicitly encourages exploration in the θ parameter space according to the principle of maximum entropy.

By taking the derivative of the objective function in (Eq. (5)) and setting it to zero, we can show that the optimal distribution of policy parameter θ of the above optimization is

$$q(\theta) \propto \exp\left(\frac{1}{\alpha} J(\theta)\right) q_0(\theta). \tag{7}$$

This formulation is equivalent to a Bayesian formulation of parameter θ, where $q(\theta)$ can be seen as the "posterior" distribution; $\exp(J(\theta)/\alpha)$ is the "likelihood" function; $q_0(\theta)$ is the prior distribution. The coefficient α can be viewed as a temperature parameter that controls the strength of exploration in the parameter space. When $\alpha \to 0$, samples drawn from $q(\theta)$ will be around global optima (or optimum) of the expected return $J(\theta)$.

A similar idea of entropy regularization has been investigated in the context of bounded relational decision-makers to trade off utility and information costs (Wolpert, 2006, Ortega and Braun, 2011). Learning upper level policies are also discussed in (Salimans et al., 2017), in which the $q(\theta)$ distribution is often assumed to follow certain parametric form, such as a Gaussian distribution, whose parameters are optimized to maximize the expected reward (their method does not use entropy regularization and hence is non-Bayesian). Our method does not require a parametric assumption on $q(\theta)$. In many other works, entropy regularization has been proposed directly on policy π. For example, TRPO (Schulman et al., 2015a) enforces a relative entropy constraint to make sure the current policy stays close to a previous policy. Recently (Haarnoja et al., 2017) proposed to leverage the maximum entropy principle on policies and derived a deep energy-based policy optimization method.

3.2 STEIN VARIATIONAL GRADIENT DESCENT

Traditional Bayesian inference approaches that are used to draw samples from the posterior distribution $q(\theta)$, such as MCMC, may suffer from slow convergence or oscillations due to the high-variance and stochastic nature of estimating $J(\theta)$. Accurate estimation of $J(\theta)$ for a single policy often requires a large number of rollout samples. Instead of utilizing $J(\theta)$, we hope to use the gradient information $\nabla_\theta J(\theta)$ which provides a noisy direction in which to update the policy. For this purpose, here we use the Stein variational gradient descent (SVGD) for Bayesian inference (Liu and Wang, 2016). SVGD is a nonparametric variational inference algorithm that leverages efficient deterministic dynamics to transport a set of particles $\{\theta_i\}_{i=1}^n$ to approximate given target posterior distributions $q(\theta)$. SVGD combines the benefits of typical MCMC and variational inference in that it does not confine the approximation within parametric families, unlike traditional variational inference methods, and converges faster than MCMC due to the deterministic updates that efficiently leverage gradient information. Thus SVGD has a number of advantages that are critical for policy exploration and optimization.

Briefly, SVGD iteratively updates the "particles" $\{\theta_i\}$ via

$$\theta_i \leftarrow \theta_i + \epsilon \phi^*(\theta_i),$$

where ϵ is a step size and $\phi(\cdot)$ is a function in the unit ball of a reproducing kernel Hilbert space (RKHS) $\mathcal{H} = \mathcal{H}_0 \times \cdots \mathcal{H}_0$ of $d \times 1$ vector-valued functions, chosen to maximumly decrease the KL divergence between the particles and the target distribution in that sense that

$$\phi^* \leftarrow \max_{\phi \in \mathcal{H}} \{ -\frac{d}{d\epsilon} \mathbf{D}(\rho_{[\epsilon\phi]} \| q), \quad s.t. \quad ||\phi||_{\mathcal{H}} \leq 1\},$$

where $\rho_{[\epsilon\phi]}$ denotes the distribution of $\theta' = \theta + \epsilon\phi(\theta)$, and the distribution of θ is ρ. Liu and Wang (2016) showed that this functional optimization yields a closed form solution,

$$\phi^*(\theta) = \mathbb{E}_{\vartheta \sim \rho}[\nabla \log q(\vartheta) k(\vartheta, \theta) + \nabla_\vartheta k(\vartheta, \theta)],$$

where $k(x, x')$ is the positive definite kernel associated with the RKHS $\mathcal{H}_0$. By replacing the expectation $\mathbb{E}_{\vartheta \sim \rho}$ with an empirical averaging on the current particles $\{\theta_i\}$, we can derive the following Stein variational gradient

$$\hat{\phi}(\theta_i) = \frac{1}{n} \sum_{j=1}^{n} \left[\nabla_{\theta_j} \log q(\theta_j) k(\theta_j, \theta_i) + \nabla_{\theta_j} k(\theta_j, \theta_i) \right] \tag{8}$$

In this update, $\hat{\phi}$ includes two important terms that play different roles.

Algorithm 1 Stein Variational Policy Gradient

Input: Learning rate ϵ, kernel $k(x, x')$, temperature, initial policy particles $\{\theta_i\}$.
for iteration $t = 0, 1, .., T$ **do**
  for particle $i = 0, 1, .., n$ **do**
    Compute $\nabla_{\theta_i} J(\theta_i)$ e.g., by Eq. (1)-Eq. (4).
  end for
  for particle $i = 0, 1, .., n$ **do**

$$\Delta\theta_i \leftarrow \frac{1}{n}\sum_{j=1}^{n}[\nabla_{\theta_j}\left(\frac{1}{\alpha}J(\theta_j) + \log q_0(\theta_j)\right)k(\theta_j, \theta_i) + \nabla_{\theta_j}k(\theta_j, \theta_i)]$$

$$\theta_i \leftarrow \theta_i + \epsilon\Delta\theta_i$$

  end for
end for

The first term involves the gradient $\nabla_\theta \log q(\theta)$ which drives the policy particles θ_i towards the high probability regions of q with information sharing across similar particles. The second term $\nabla_{\theta_j} k(\theta_j, \theta_i)$ pushes the particles away from each other, diversifying the policies. Note that without the second term, all the particles would collapse to the local modes of $\log q$ and the algorithm would reduce to the typical gradient ascent for maximum a posteriori (MAP). In particular, if we just use one particle ($n = 1$) and choose the kernel with $\nabla_\theta k(\theta, \theta) = 0$, then SVGD is reduced to a single chain of gradient ascent for MAP.

Applying SVGD to the posterior in Eq. (7), we introduce the Stein Variational Policy Gradient method (SVPG) that estimates the policy gradient $\nabla_\theta J(\theta)$ using existing methods, such as those we introduced in Eq. (1) -Eq. (4).

$$\hat{\phi}(\theta_i) = \frac{1}{n}\sum_{j=1}^{n}[\nabla_{\theta_j}\left(\frac{1}{\alpha}J(\theta_j) + \log q_0(\theta_j)\right)k(\theta_j, \theta_i) + \nabla_{\theta_j}k(\theta_j, \theta_i)] \tag{9}$$

Note that here the magnitude of α adjusts the relative importance between the policy gradient and the prior term $\nabla_{\theta_j}\left(\frac{1}{\alpha}J(\theta_j) + \log q_0(\theta_j)\right)k(\theta_j, \theta_i)$ and the repulsive term $\nabla_{\theta_j} k(\theta_j, \theta_i)$. A suitable α provides a good trade-off between exploitation and exploration. If α is too large, the Stein gradient would only drive the particles to be consistent with the prior q_0. As $\alpha \to 0$, this algorithm is reduced to running n copies of independent policy gradient algorithms, if $\{\theta_i\}$ are initialized very differently. In practice, we found that with a reasonable α, SVPG consistently outperforms the original versions of several policy gradient methods on continuous control tasks. A careful annealing scheme of α allows efficient exploration in the beginning of training and later focuses on exploitation towards the end of training.

4 RELATED WORK

Policy gradient techniques have recently shown strong results for deep reinforcement learning. Trust region policy optimization (Schulman et al., 2015a) optimizes its policy by establishing a trust region centered at its current policy. Asynchronous advantage actor-critic (A3C) (Mnih et al., 2016) runs multiple agents asynchronously in parallel to train an actor-critic architecture. Numerous works have built on top of A3C (Jaderberg et al., 2016, Mirowski et al., 2016) to solve difficult environments like navigating a 3D maze (Beattie et al., 2016). Recent work has also explored sample efficient policy gradients (Gu et al., 2016, Wang et al., 2016). Notably, all such methods and improvements can be applied to SVPG without any modification.

There has been a wealth of prior work to encourage exploration in reinforcement learning. For example, entropy penalties (Williams and Peng, 1991, Mnih et al., 2016) are used to learn a smoother policy by penalizing the model when the distribution over actions is too sharp. Recent work (Nachum et al., 2016) has explicitly attempted to explore under-appreciated rewards through importance sampling of trajectories over the current policy.

Intrinsic motivation techniques have recently gained popularity in the deep reinforcement learning setting. These techniques (Singh et al., 2004, Storck et al., 1995) attempt to train the agent with rewards beyond those given from the environment. For example, the notion of curiosity can be used to encourage exploration by giving the agent additional rewards for visiting novel states. Novelty can be measured though Bayesian methods (Mohamed and Rezende, 2015, Houthooft et al., 2016), where information gain is used as a proxy for curiosity. Count-based methods (Bellemare et al., 2016, Ostrovski et al., 2017) produce a reward inversely proportional to the number of times a state has been visited, using a density model to approximate visits in large state spaces. SVPG is compatible with these reward shaping (Ng et al., 1999) procedures since it does not impose any constraints on the parameters and gradients.

Prior work has also explored the use of different agents to collect experience in parallel. Nair et al. (2015) developed a system called GORILA that deployed multiple actors in parallel to collect experience. Agents differed slightly in parameters due to the asynchronous nature of their training procedure. Mnih et al. (2016) extended this idea by sampling different exploration ϵ hyperparameters for the ϵ-greedy policy of different agents. Agents with different sets of parameters was also explored by Osband et al. (2016) to encourage deep exploration. In practice, all their agents were trained with the same gradient update. In contrast, SVPG uses different updates for each agent and explicitly encourages diversity through the kernel gradient term.

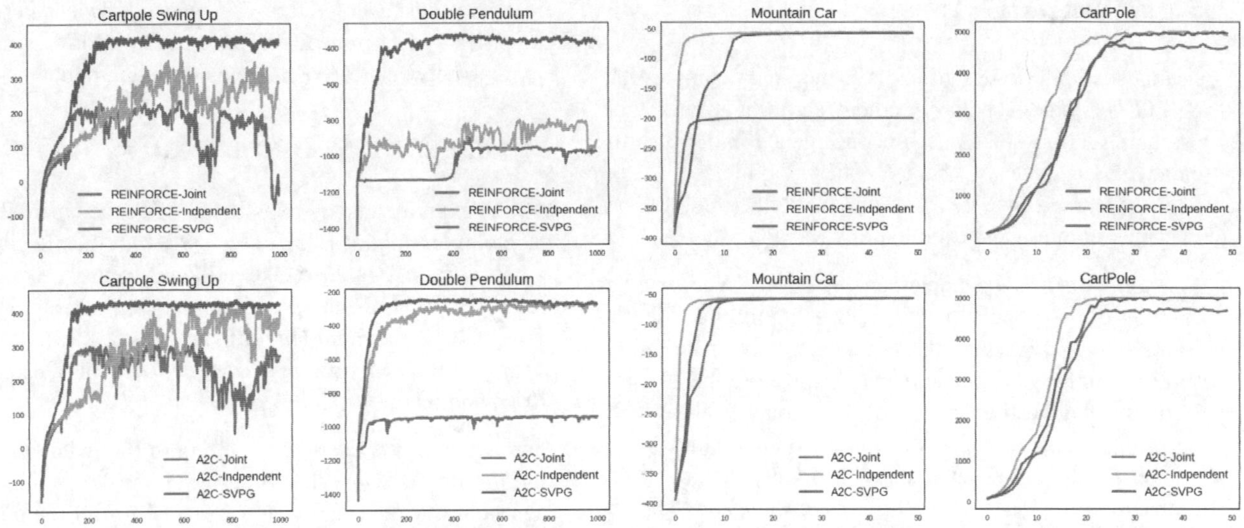

Figure 1: **Learning curves by SVPG and two baseline versions.** The x-axis denotes the training iteration while the y-axis denotes the average return achieved by the policy. Since all three algorithms use the same number of samples per iteration, the x-axis is also proportional to the total number of samples used in training.

Table 1: Best test return and the number of episodes required to reach within 5/% of the maximum return.

A2C	Joint	episodes	Independent	episodes	SVPG	episodes
Cartpole Swing Up	308.71	189	419.62	474	**436.84**	**171**
Double Pendulum	-938.73	46	-256.64	638	**-244.85**	**199**
REINFORCE	Joint	episodes	Independent	episodes	SVPG	episodes
Cartpole Swing Up	232.96	253	391.46	594	**426.69**	**238**
Double Pendulum	-892.31	446	-797.45	443	**-319.66**	**327**

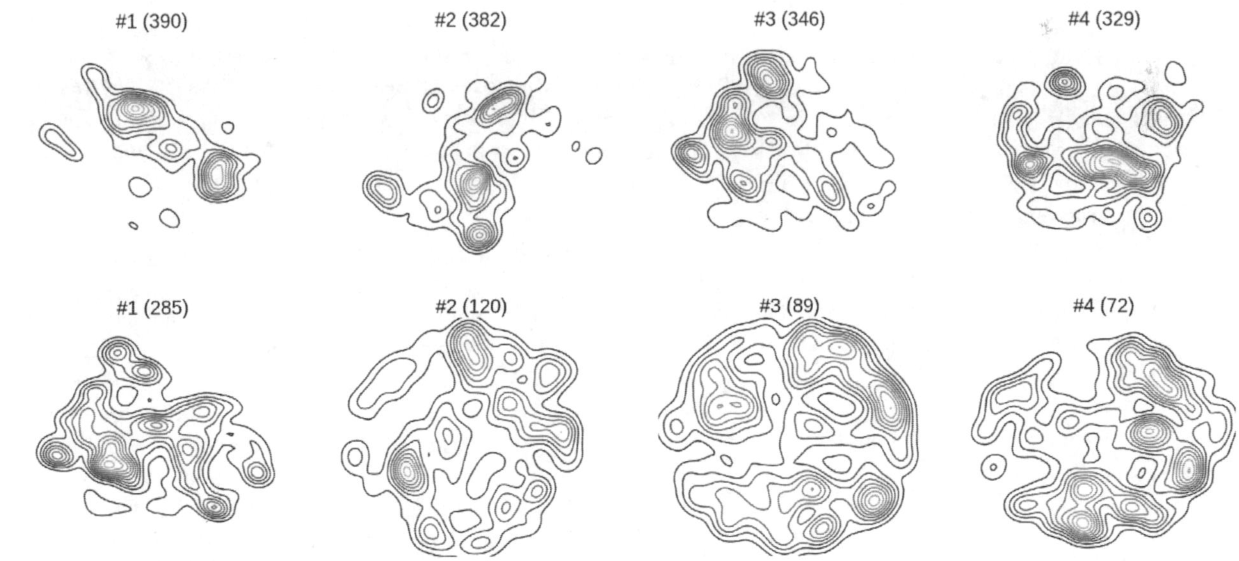

Figure 2: **State visitation density by REINFORCE-SVPG/Independent algorithms.** The state visitation landscapes of the best four policies learned by SVPG (first row) and Independent agents (second row). The value in the parenthesis is the average return of a policy. All states are projected from a 4D space into a 2D space by t-SNE (Maaten and Hinton, 2008).

5 EXPERIMENTS

In this section, we design experiments to 1) compare the SVPG versions of policy gradient algorithms with their original versions in terms of convergence and data efficiency, 2) analyze the characteristics of policies simultaneously learned by SVPG, 3) investigate the trade-off between exploration and exploitation in SVPG.

For comparisons, we implement SVPG and the original versions of two popular policy gradient algorithms: the REINFORCE (Eq (2)) and the advantage actor critic (A2C) (Eq (4)). In the A2C implementations, we use the generalized advantage estimator (GAE) (Schulman et al., 2015b) for critic, which is implemented in the rllab toolkit (Schulman et al., 2015b, Duan et al., 2016). Only the policy parameters are updated by SVPG, while the critics are updated with the their normal TD-error gradient. After training, the agent that gives the best average return is selected.

We use the flat improper prior $\log q_0(\theta) = 1$ in all our experiments. For SVGD, we follow Liu and Wang (2016) to use the Gaussian RBF kernel $k(\vartheta, \theta) = \exp(-||\theta - \vartheta||_2^2/h)$ with the bandwidth h chosen to be $med^2/\log(n+1)$ where med denotes the median of pairwise distances between the particles $\{\theta_i\}$. This simple heuristic allows the bandwidth to adaptively change as the particles move, ensuring that there is always a significant number of particles that interact with each other.

Since SVPG is a multi-agent method that simultaneously trains a number of policies, we design two implementations of original REINFORCE and A2C as baselines:[1]

- **REINFORCE/A2C-Joint**: We train a single agent with the same amount of data as used by multiple agents in SVPG. Assume that we use m transition samples for each of the n agents by SVPG during each iteration, we use in total nm samples per iteration to train a single agent here. In this way, we can also view this joint version as a parallel policy gradient implementation with n threads, each accumulating the gradient information in parallel. This joint variation enjoys better gradient estimation, but SVPG's multiple agents will provide more exploration. This experiment tries to determine whether the repulsive functional in SVPG will encourage exploration that lead to better policies.

- **REINFORCE/A2C-Independent**: We train multiple agents independently with no communication among them. So for each of the n agents, we use m samples to calculate the gradient. After training, the agent that gives best average return is selected. This experiment tries to determine the importance of information sharing between different agents through gradients.

[1] In addition, we compared SVPG with the Stochastic Gradient Langevin Dynamics (Welling and Teh, 2011). Results can be found at `https://github.com/largelymfs/svpg_REINFORCE/blob/master/uai.pdf`

5.1 EXPERIMENTAL SETTING

All the experiments are constructed with the OpenAI rllab development toolkit (Duan et al., 2016). Specifically, we benchmark on four classical continuous control tasks: Cartpole Swing-Up, Double Pendulumn, Cartpole, and MountainCar. The maximal length of trajectories is set to 500. Details of these environments can be found in (Duan et al., 2016) and on the GitHub website[2].

Here we describe the default setting of the policy gradient algorithms we test on these control tasks. We used a Gaussian policy with a diagonal covariance for all these tasks. The mean is parameterized by a neural networks with three hidden layers (100-50-25 hidden units) and $\tanh$ as the activation function. The log standard deviation is parameterized by a linear function, as suggested in (Duan et al., 2016, Schulman et al., 2015a). The SVPG and Independent algorithms used $m = 10000$ samples for policy gradient estimation for each of the $n = 16$ agents. We found that the choice of m is quite robust as long as it is not too small. For the Joint version, the number of samples used in each iteration is $nm = 160,000$. For A2C, we set $\lambda = 1$ for the generalized advantage estimation as suggested in (Duan et al., 2016). In the SVPG algorithms, we set $\alpha = 10$, which seems to find a good trade-off between exploration and exploitation in these tasks. We also investigate this hyperparameter in a later experiment. We used ADAM (Kingma and Ba, 2014) to adjust the step-size of gradient descent in all algorithms. For the two easy tasks, Mountain Car and Cartpole, all agents are trained for 50 iterations with 5 re-runs. For the two complex tasks, Cartpole Swing-Up and Double Pendulum, we train all agents up to 1000 iterations with 5 re-runs with different random seeds.

5.2 CONVERGENCE AND DATA EFFICIENCY

The learning curves of algorithms are shown in Figure 1. On the two easy tasks, Mountain Car and Cartpole, almost all algorithms can successfully solve them in around 20 iterations (except of REINFORCE-Joint on Mountain Car). On the two more challenging tasks, the differences between algorithms are substantial. On Cartpole Swing-Up, REINFORCE-SVPG and A2C-SVPG converges substantially faster than the corresponding baselines. A2C-Independent is able to achieve the desirable performance after more than 800 iterations, while all other baselines cannot converge after 1,000 iterations. On Double Pendulum, We also performed the same training with a different batch size $m = 5000$ and observed similar results. The variances

[2] https://github.com/openai/rllab

of the SVPG algorithms are close to those of the Independent versions, but much smaller than the Joint versions, probably due to the robustness of multiple agents. These results demonstrate that SVPG is able to improve the training convergence of policy gradient algorithms.

5.3 SVPG LEARNS GOOD AND DIVERSE POLICIES

We further investigate the quality and diversity of the policies learned by SVPG.

First, we compute the best test returns of the policies learned by all algorithms and counted how many episodes each policy needed to achieve the 95% of its best return. Results are shown in Table 1. SVPG versions clearly outperforms policies learned by Joint and Independent versions, in terms of both best test returns and the episodes required to achieve 95% of the return.

Second, we compare the quality of all policies learned by SVPG and Independent versions. It is worth noting that in Independent versions, parameter exploration is only done through random initialization, while in SVPG, parameter exploration is explicitly done through repulsion. Thus it is possible that SVPG can better explore the parameter landscape and find multiple good local optima or solutions. We compute average returns of all policies with 50,000 test transitions on Cartpole Swing-Up. The results are then averaged across 5 re-runs with different training random seeds. The sorted policies are shown in Figure 3. SVPG has found many good policies, while only the very top policies learned by Independent algorithms can achieve satisfactory performance.

Third, we visualize the diversity of the policies learned by SVPG algorithms. Since SVPG learns policies simultaneously, it is possible that all the top policies are very similar. It is worth noting that good policies cannot be starkly different from each other. To illustrate the diversity of the learned policies in SVPG approach, we generated the state-visitation landscape of individual policies. We chose the best four policies learned by REINFORCE-SVPG and the best four by REINFORCE-Independent on Carptole Swing-up, and randomly generate 100 test trajectories for each policy. Then all states are projected into 2D space with the t-SNE algorithm (Maaten and Hinton, 2008, Van Der Maaten, 2014, Ulyanov, 2016) for visualization. Then we plotted the density contours of state-visitation frequencies for each policy in Figure 2. Note that the 2D projection may introduce artifacts in the visualization.

Notwithstanding artifacts, it seems that the state visitation landscapes of the policies learned by SVPG are different from each other. Each policy covers certain regions in the projected state space with high visitation frequencies. Three policies learned by the Independent algorithm (#2-#4) are quite similar to each other, but it average return of these policies are far from the best average return. It is worth noting that the best policy by the Independent algorithm looks similar to SVPG policy #3, and it is possible that they are close to a same local optimum.

These observations indicate that SVPG can learn robust and diverse policies thanks to the balance between information sharing and repulsive forces.

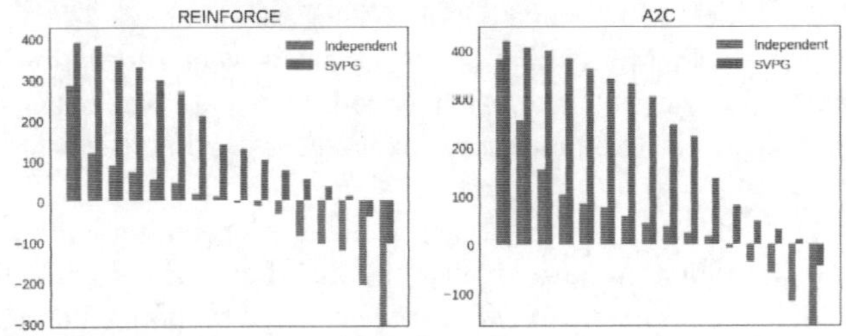

Figure 3: Average return comparison for all agents learned by the SVPG and Independent algorithms.

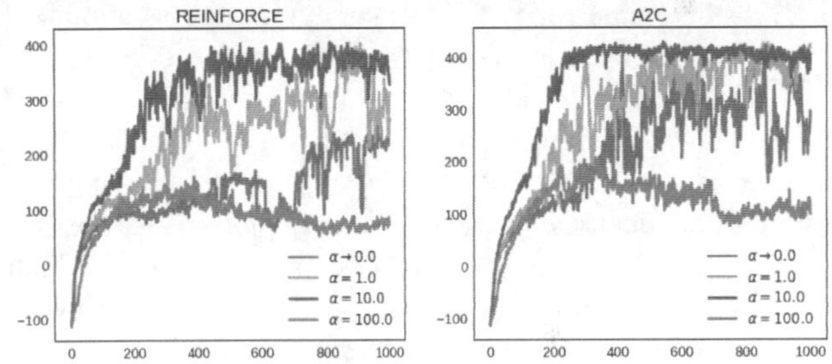

Figure 4: The influence of the temperature hyperparameter in REINFORCE/A2C-SVPG.

5.4 EXPLORATION AND EXPLOITATION

The above results demonstrate that SVPG can better explore in the parameter space than the original policy gradient methods. In SVPG, the temperature hyperparameter α controls the trade-off between exploration, which is driven by the repulsion between parameters of different policies and exploitation, which is driven by policy gradient. Lower temperatures make the algorithm focus on exploitation, as the first term with the policy gradient becomes much more important than the second repulsive term. Higher temperature will drive the policies to be more diverse. That is,

$$\sum_{j=1}^{n}[\underbrace{\nabla_{\theta_j} J(\theta_j) k(\theta_j, \theta_i)}_{exploitation} + \alpha \times \underbrace{\nabla_{\theta_j} k(\theta_j, \theta_i)}_{exploration}].$$

Figure 4 shows training curves with different values of the temperature hyperparameter α (batch size $m = 5,000$).

When the temperature is very high (e.g. $\alpha = 100$), exploration dominates exploitation. Policies are repelled too much from each other, which prevents them from converging to a good set of policies. When the temperature is too low ($\alpha \rightarrow 0$), exploitation dominates exploration. The algorithm is then similar to training a set of independent policies. As training proceeding, the Euclidean distances between parameters of policies become large. As a result, both information sharing and inter-agent exploration are no longer effective. An intermediate $\alpha = 10$ well balances between exploration and exploitation, and outperforms other temperatures for both A2C and REINFORCE. We believe that a good annealing scheme of α enables efficient exploration in the beginning of policy training and while focusing on exploitation in the later stage for policy tuning.

6 CONCLUSION

In this work, we first introduced a maximum entropy policy optimization framework. By modeling a distribution of policy parameters with the (relative) entropy regularization, this framework explicitly encourages exploration in the parameter space while also optimizing the expected utility of polices generated from this distribution. We showed that this framework can be reduced to a Bayesian inference problem and then propose the Stein variational policy gradient to allow simultaneous exploitation and exploration of multiple policies. In our experiments, we evaluated the SVPG versions of REINFORCE and A2C on several continuous control tasks and found that they greatly improved the performance of the original policy gradient methods. We also performed extensive analysis of SVPG to demonstrate its robustness and the ability to generate diverse policies. Due to its simplicity, we expect that SVPG provides a generic approach to improve existing policy gradient methods. The parallel nature of SVPG also makes it attractive to be implemented in distributed systems.

There are many potential future directions we hope to explore. First we plan to evaluate the empirical performance of SVPG in other RL domains. Furthermore, the choices of kernel in SVPG may be critical for high dimensional RL problems, and future work can explore the impact of the choice of different kernel functions. For example, it is possible to design a layer-wise kernel for deep neural network policies. Another direction is to study the trade-off between exploration and exploitation in SVPG. Currently, we simply choose a fixed α to control the ratio between the policy gradient and the repulsive terms. Smart annealing schemes of α may lead to an improved and adaptive trade-off. Finally, it would be very interesting to develop SVPG versions of other policy optimization methods, such as natural policy gradient and trust region policy optimization.

Acknowledgements

The authors appreciate the insightful feedback from anonymous reviewers. This work is supported in part by NSF CRII 1565796.

References

Beattie, C., Leibo, J. Z., Teplyashin, D., Ward, T., Wainwright, M., Küttler, H., Lefrancq, A., Green, S., Valdés, V., Sadik, A., et al. (2016). Deepmind lab. *arXiv preprint arXiv:1612.03801*.

Bellemare, M., Srinivasan, S., Ostrovski, G., Schaul, T., Saxton, D., and Munos, R. (2016). Unifying count-based exploration and intrinsic motivation. In *Advances in Neural Information Processing Systems*, pages 1471–1479.

Duan, Y., Chen, X., Houthooft, R., Schulman, J., and Abbeel, P. (2016). Benchmarking deep reinforcement learning for continuous control. In *Proceedings of the 33rd International Conference on Machine Learning (ICML)*.

Gu, S., Lillicrap, T., Ghahramani, Z., Turner, R. E., and Levine, S. (2016). Q-prop: Sample-efficient policy gradient with an off-policy critic. *arXiv preprint arXiv:1611.02247*.

Haarnoja, T., Tang, H., Abbeel, P., and Levine, S. (2017). Reinforcement learning with deep energy-based policies. *arXiv preprint arXiv:1702.08165*.

Hansen, N. (2006). The cma evolution strategy: a comparing review. In *Towards a new evolutionary computation*, pages 75–102. Springer.

Houthooft, R., Chen, X., Duan, Y., Schulman, J., De Turck, F., and Abbeel, P. (2016). Vime: Variational information maximizing exploration. In *Advances in Neural Information Processing Systems*, pages 1109–1117.

Jaderberg, M., Mnih, V., Czarnecki, W. M., Schaul, T., Leibo, J. Z., Silver, D., and Kavukcuoglu, K. (2016). Reinforcement learning with unsupervised auxiliary tasks. *arXiv preprint arXiv:1611.05397*.

Kakade, S. (2002). A natural policy gradient. *Advances in neural information processing systems*, 2:1531–1538.

Kingma, D. and Ba, J. (2014). Adam: A method for stochastic optimization. *arXiv preprint arXiv:1412.6980*.

Liu, Q. and Wang, D. (2016). Stein variational gradient descent: A general purpose bayesian inference algorithm. In *Advances In Neural Information Processing Systems*, pages 2370–2378.

Maaten, L. v. d. and Hinton, G. (2008). Visualizing data using t-sne. *Journal of Machine Learning Research*, 9(Nov):2579–2605.

Mannor, S., Rubinstein, R. Y., and Gat, Y. (2003). The cross entropy method for fast policy search. In *ICML*, pages 512–519.

Mirowski, P., Pascanu, R., Viola, F., Soyer, H., Ballard, A., Banino, A., Denil, M., Goroshin, R., Sifre, L., Kavukcuoglu, K., et al. (2016). Learning to navigate in complex environments. *arXiv preprint arXiv:1611.03673*.

Mnih, V., Badia, A. P., Mirza, M., Graves, A., Lillicrap, T. P., Harley, T., Silver, D., and Kavukcuoglu, K. (2016). Asynchronous methods for deep reinforcement learning. In *International Conference on Machine Learning*.

Mohamed, S. and Rezende, D. J. (2015). Variational information maximisation for intrinsically motivated reinforcement learning. In *Advances in neural information processing systems*, pages 2125–2133.

Nachum, O., Norouzi, M., and Schuurmans, D. (2016). Improving policy gradient by exploring under-appreciated rewards. *arXiv preprint arXiv:1611.09321*.

Nair, A., Srinivasan, P., Blackwell, S., Alcicek, C., Fearon, R., De Maria, A., Panneershelvam, V., Suleyman, M., Beattie, C., Petersen, S., et al. (2015). Massively parallel methods for deep reinforcement learning. *arXiv preprint arXiv:1507.04296*.

Ng, A. Y., Harada, D., and Russell, S. (1999). Policy invariance under reward transformations: Theory and application to reward shaping. In *ICML*, volume 99, pages 278–287.

Ortega, D. A. and Braun, P. A. (2011). Information, utility and bounded rationality. In *International Conference on Artificial General Intelligence*, pages 269–274. Springer.

Osband, I., Blundell, C., Pritzel, A., and Van Roy, B. (2016). Deep exploration via bootstrapped dqn. In *Advances In Neural Information Processing Systems*, pages 4026–4034.

Ostrovski, G., Bellemare, M. G., Oord, A. v. d., and Munos, R. (2017). Count-based exploration with neural density models. *arXiv preprint arXiv:1703.01310*.

Salimans, T., Ho, J., Chen, X., and Sutskever, I. (2017). Evolution strategies as a scalable alternative to reinforcement learning. *arXiv preprint arXiv:1703.03864*.

Schulman, J., Levine, S., Abbeel, P., Jordan, M. I., and Moritz, P. (2015a). Trust region policy optimization. In *ICML*, pages 1889–1897.

Schulman, J., Moritz, P., Levine, S., Jordan, M., and Abbeel, P. (2015b). High-dimensional continuous control using generalized advantage estimation. *arXiv preprint arXiv:1506.02438*.

Sehnke, F., Osendorfer, C., Rückstieß, T., Graves, A., Peters, J., and Schmidhuber, J. (2010). Parameter-exploring policy gradients. *Neural Networks*, 23(4):551–559.

Singh, S. P., Barto, A. G., and Chentanez, N. (2004). Intrinsically motivated reinforcement learning. In *NIPS*, volume 17, pages 1281–1288.

Spall, J. C. (1998). An overview of the simultaneous perturbation method for efficient optimization. *Johns Hopkins apl technical digest*, 19(4):482–492.

Storck, J., Hochreiter, S., and Schmidhuber, J. (1995). Reinforcement driven information acquisition in non-deterministic environments. In *Proceedings of the international conference on artificial neural networks, Paris*, volume 2, pages 159–164. Citeseer.

Ulyanov, D. (2016). Muticore-tsne. `https://github.com/DmitryUlyanov/Muticore-TSNE`.

Van Der Maaten, L. (2014). Accelerating t-sne using tree-based algorithms. *Journal of machine learning research*, 15(1):3221–3245.

Wang, Z., Bapst, V., Heess, N., Mnih, V., Munos, R., Kavukcuoglu, K., and de Freitas, N. (2016). Sample efficient actor-critic with experience replay. *arXiv preprint arXiv:1611.01224*.

Welling, M. and Teh, Y. W. (2011). Bayesian learning via stochastic gradient langevin dynamics. In *Proceedings of the 28th International Conference on Machine Learning (ICML-11)*, pages 681–688.

Williams, R. J. (1992). Simple statistical gradient-following algorithms for connectionist reinforcement learning. *Machine learning*, 8(3-4):229–256.

Williams, R. J. and Peng, J. (1991). Function optimization using connectionist reinforcement learning algorithms. *Connection Science*, 3(3):241–268.

Wolpert, D. H. (2006). Information theorythe bridge connecting bounded rational game theory and statistical physics. In *Complex Engineered Systems*, pages 262–290. Springer.

Causal Discovery from Temporally Aggregated Time Series

Mingming Gong*†, Kun Zhang†, Bernhard Schölkopf‡, Clark Glymour†, Dacheng Tao♯
*Centre for Artificial Intelligence, FEIT, University of Technology Sydney, NSW, Australia
†Department of Philosophy, Carnegie Mellon University, Pittsburgh, USA
‡Max Plank Institute for Intelligent Systems, Tübingen, Germany
♯School of Information Technologies, FEIT, University of Sydney, NSW, Australia

Abstract

Discovering causal structure of a dynamical system from observed time series is a traditional and important problem. In many practical applications, observed data are obtained by applying subsampling or temporally aggregation to the original causal processes, making it difficult to discover the underlying causal relations. Subsampling refers to the procedure that for every k consecutive observations, one is kept, the rest being skipped, and recently some advances have been made in causal discovery from such data. With temporal aggregation, the local averages or sums of k consecutive, non-overlapping observations in the causal process are computed as new observations, and causal discovery from such data is even harder. In this paper, we investigate how to recover causal relations at the original causal frequency from temporally aggregated data when k is known. Assuming the time series at the causal frequency follows a vector autoregressive (VAR) model, we show that the causal structure at the causal frequency is identifiable from aggregated time series if the noise terms are independent and non-Gaussian and some other technical conditions hold. We then present an estimation method based on non-Gaussian state-space modeling and evaluate its performance on both synthetic and real data.

1 INTRODUCTION

Causal modeling (Spirtes et al., 2001; Pearl, 2000) of time series data has been widely applied in many fields such as econometrics (Ghysels et al., 2016), neuroscience (Zhou et al., 2014), and climate science (Van Nes et al., 2015). Classical causal discovery approaches, e.g., Granger causality test (Granger, 1969), usually assume that the data measurement frequency matches the true causal frequency of the underlying physical process. However, since the true causal frequency is usually unknown, the time series data are often measured at the frequency lower than the causal frequency. For example, some econometric indicators such as GDP and non-farm payroll are usually recorded at quarterly and monthly scales. Causal interactions between the processes, however, may take place at the weekly or fortnightly scales (Ghysels et al., 2016). In neuroscience, imaging technologies have relatively low temporal resolutions, while many high frequency neuronal interactions are important for understanding neuronal dynamics (Zhou et al., 2014). In these situations, the available observations have a lower resolution than the underlying causal process.

There are two typical schemes to generate low-resolution or low-frequency data from high-frequency ones (Silvestrini & Veredas, 2008; Marcellino, 1999). One is by subsampling: for every k consecutive observations, one is kept, the rest being skipped. The other is temporally aggregation, i.e., taking the local averages or sums of k consecutive, non-overlapping observations from the underlying causal process as new observations. For instance, the time series of interest, money supply, and temperature are usually obtained by subsampling; in contrast, the U.S. nominal GDP was obtained by aggregation – it refers to a total number of dollars spent over a time period.

Numerous contributions have been made on analyzing the effects of the above two schemes to generate low-resolution data on the properties of the time series such as estimated causal relations and exogeneity (Tiao, 1972; Weiss, 1984; Granger, 1987; Marcellino, 1999; Rajaguru & Abeysinghe, 2008). These studies found that temporal aggregation can lead to errors in the estimated causal relations if not properly addressed. For example, Breitung & Swanson (2002) examined the impact of temporal aggregation on Granger causality in vector autoregressive (VAR) models and found that the results of Granger causal analysis heavily depend on temporal aggregation.

Recovering the high frequency causal relations from temporally aggregated data is a very hard problem due to information loss in the aggregation process. A classical way to discover high frequency causal relations from temporally aggregated data is to first disaggregate the low frequency time series to high frequency ones and then apply standard causal discovery methods on the disaggregated data. Temporal disaggregation of low resolution time series has been extensively studied in the econometric and statistical literature (Boot et al., 1967; Stram & Wei, 1986; Harvey & Chung, 2000; Moauro & Savio, 2005; Proietti, 2006), which is clearly an even harder problem than discovering causal relations.

Recently, a set of methods have been proposed to estimate the causal structure at the causal frequency from *subsampled* data without resorting to disaggregation techniques (Hyttinen et al., 2016; Gong et al., 2015; Plis et al., 2015a; Danks & Plis, 2013). Plis et al. (2015a,b) first inferred the causal structure from the subsampled data, and then searched for the causal structure at the causal frequency from the causal structure inferred in the first step. Based on this framework, Hyttinen et al. (2016) proposed a much faster inference method using a general purpose Boolean constraint solver. Gong et al. (2015) proposed a model-based approach and examined the identifiability of the underlying vector autoregressive model (VAR) at the causal frequency from subsampled time series. They showed that the causal transition matrix is identifiable if the noise process is non-Gaussian. This work was recently extended to mixed frequency data by structural VAR modeling (Tank et al., 2017) . However, how to estimate causal relations from aggregated data still remains unknown.

Compared to subsampling, *temporal aggregation* is perhaps more widely used to produce low-resolution time series, especially in economics and finance. However, the effect of temporal aggregation is more complex, and accordingly it is technically more difficult to recover the underlying causal relations from such data. Specifically, because the noise terms are generated by a larger number of independent components and thus the mixing matrix contains a more complicated structure, the estimation is both statistically and computationally harder.

The objective of this paper is to seek a possible solution to this problem, by studying the theoretical identifiability of the underlying causal relations and developing a practical causal discovery algorithm. Following (Gong et al., 2015), we assume that the high-frequency data follow a VAR model, the error terms are non-Gaussian, and there are no confounders (Geiger et al., 2015). We show that the original causal relation can be estimated from the aggregated data with known k, under a set of technical conditions.

Moreover, we propose an estimation method based on non-Gaussian state-space modeling of the aggregated data. Since the exact inference in the non-Gaussian state-space model is intractable, we estimate the model parameters using the particle stochastic approximation EM (PSAEM) algorithm (Lindsten, 2013; Svensson et al., 2014), which combines the efficient conditional particle filter with ancestor sampling (CPF-AS) (Lindsten et al., 2014) with the stochastic approximation EM (SAEM) algorithm (Delyon et al., 1999). Interestingly, in the extreme case where the aggregation factor k becomes larger and larger, we show that the observed time series will become independent and identically distributed (*i.i.d.*), and we study to what extent the underlying time-delayed causal relations can be recovered from the instantaneous dependence in the observed data.

2 EFFECT OF TEMPORAL AGGREGATION

In the linear case, Granger causal analysis Granger (1969) can be done by fitting the following first-order VAR model (Sims, 1980):

$$\mathbf{x}_t = \mathbf{A}\mathbf{x}_{t-1} + \mathbf{e}_t, \tag{1}$$

where $\mathbf{x}_t = (x_{t,1}, x_{t,2}, ..., x_{t,n})^\intercal$ is the vector of the observed data, $\mathbf{e}_t = (e_{t,1}, ..., e_{t,n})^\intercal$ is the temporally and contemporaneously independent noise process, and $\mathbf{A}$ is the causal transition matrix containing temporal causal relations.

2.1 WITH A FINITE k

Gong et al. (2015) studied causal discovery from subsampled data. With subsampling, the observations $\tilde{\mathbf{x}}^s_{1:T} \triangleq (\tilde{\mathbf{x}}^s_1, \tilde{\mathbf{x}}^s_2, ..., \tilde{\mathbf{x}}^s_T) = (\mathbf{x}_1, \mathbf{x}_{1+k}, ..., \mathbf{x}_{1+(T-1)k})$ follow

$$\begin{aligned}\tilde{\mathbf{x}}^s_t &= \mathbf{A}\mathbf{x}_{1+(t-1)k-1} + \mathbf{e}_{1+(t-1)k} \\ &= \mathbf{A}(\mathbf{A}\mathbf{x}_{1+(t-1)k-2} + \mathbf{e}_{1+(t-1)k-1}) + \mathbf{e}_{1+(t-1)k} \\ &= ... \\ &= \mathbf{A}^k\tilde{\mathbf{x}}^s_{t-1} + \sum_{l=0}^{k-1} \mathbf{A}^l \mathbf{e}_{1+(t-1)k-l},\end{aligned} \tag{2}$$

which turns out to be a VAR model with temporally independent and contemporaneously dependent noise process. They demonstrated that it is possible to identify the high-resolution causal relation $\mathbf{A}$ from the low-resolution observations $\tilde{\mathbf{x}}^s_{1:T}$ if the noise terms are non-Gaussian.

In this paper, we are concerned with the temporally aggregated data $\tilde{\mathbf{x}}_{1:T} \triangleq (\tilde{\mathbf{x}}_1, \tilde{\mathbf{x}}_2, ..., \tilde{\mathbf{x}}_T)$, which are obtained by taking the average (or sum) of every non-overlapping k points, i.e., $\tilde{\mathbf{x}}_t = \frac{1}{k}\sum_{i=1}^k \mathbf{x}_{i+(t-1)k}$, where

$$\mathbf{x}_{i+(t-1)k} = \mathbf{A}^k\mathbf{x}_{i+(t-2)k} + \sum_{l=0}^{k-1} \mathbf{A}^l \mathbf{e}_{i+(t-1)k-l}.$$

Taking the average of the above equation over $i = 1, 2, \ldots, k$, we have

$$\tilde{\mathbf{x}}_t = \frac{\mathbf{A}^k}{k}\sum_{i=1}^k \mathbf{x}_{i+(t-2)k} + \frac{1}{k}\sum_{i=1}^k \Big(\sum_{l=0}^{k-1} \mathbf{A}^l \mathbf{e}_{i+(t-1)k-l}\Big)$$

$$= \mathbf{A}^k\tilde{\mathbf{x}}_{t-1} + \frac{1}{k}\Big(\sum_{m=0}^{k-1}(\sum_{n=0}^{m}\mathbf{A}^n)\mathbf{e}_{tk-m}$$
$$+ \sum_{m=1}^{k-1}(\sum_{n=m}^{k-1}\mathbf{A}^n)\mathbf{e}_{(t-1)k-m+1}\Big), \quad (3)$$

which is a vector autoregressive-moving-average (VARMA) model with one autoregressive term and two moving-average terms:

$$\tilde{\mathbf{x}}_t = \mathbf{A}^k\tilde{\mathbf{x}}_{t-1} + \vec{\mathbf{e}}_t$$
$$= \mathbf{A}^k\tilde{\mathbf{x}}_{t-1} + \mathbf{M}_0\boldsymbol{\epsilon}_t + \mathbf{M}_1\boldsymbol{\epsilon}_{t-1}, \quad (4)$$

where $\boldsymbol{\epsilon}_t = \frac{1}{k}[\mathbf{e}_{tk}, \mathbf{e}_{tk-1}, \ldots, \mathbf{e}_{(t-1)k+1}]^\intercal$, $\mathbf{M}_0 = [\mathbf{I}, \mathbf{I} + \mathbf{A}, \ldots, \sum_{n=0}^{k-1}\mathbf{A}^n]$, and $\mathbf{M}_1 = [\sum_{n=1}^{k-1}\mathbf{A}^n, \ldots, \mathbf{A}^{k-1}, \mathbf{0}]$. Here, $\mathbf{I}$ represents the $n\times n$ identity matrix, and $\mathbf{0}$ represents the $n \times n$ zero matrix. We call $(\mathbf{A}, \mathbf{e}, k)$ the representation of the k-th order aggregated time series $\tilde{\mathbf{x}}$. Clearly $\mathbf{A}$ cannot be recovered by simply fitting a VAR model on $\tilde{\mathbf{x}}_t$, as done by Granger causal analysis. Even if we using VARMA modeling, we are only guaranteed to identify $\mathbf{A}^k$ instead of the original $\mathbf{A}$. In Section 3, we will show under what conditions can we identify the causal relation $\mathbf{A}$ at the causal frequency from the aggregated time series $\tilde{\mathbf{x}}_{1:T}$.

2.2 WHEN $k \to \infty$

Interestingly, causal discovery from aggregated data with a large aggregation factor k seems to have a wide range of applications. For instance, in the stock market, the causal influences between stocks take place very quickly (as indicated by the efficient market hypothesis), but we usually work with low-frequency data such as daily returns. The daily return is the sum of high-frequency returns within the same day. Discovering the causal interactions between stocks from their daily returns then become a problem of causal discovery from aggregated data with a large k.

When the aggregation factor k is very large, $\vec{\mathbf{e}}_t$ becomes a mixture of numerous independent components. Fortunately, we can use a simple model to approximate the generating process of the aggregated data. From (1), we have

$$\sum_{i=1}^{k}\mathbf{x}_{i+(t-1)k+1} = \mathbf{A}\sum_{i=1}^{k}\mathbf{x}_{i+(t-1)k} + \sum_{i=1}^{k}\mathbf{e}_{i+(t-1)k+1},$$

that is,

$$\tilde{\mathbf{x}}_t = \frac{1}{k}\sum_{i=1}^{k}\mathbf{x}_{i+(t-1)k+1}$$
$$= \mathbf{A}\Big[\frac{1}{k}\sum_{i=1}^{k}\mathbf{x}_{i+(t-1)k+1} - \frac{1}{k}(\mathbf{x}_{1+tk} - \mathbf{x}_{1+(t-1)k})\Big] +$$
$$\frac{1}{k}\sum_{i=1}^{k}\mathbf{e}_{i+(t-1)k+1}.$$

Denote by $\bar{\mathbf{e}}_t$ the error term above, i.e., $\bar{\mathbf{e}}_t = \frac{1}{k}\sum_{i=1}^{k}\mathbf{e}_{i+(t-1)k+1}$. Note that $\bar{\mathbf{e}}_t$ has contemporaneous independent components. Since

$$\frac{1}{k}(\mathbf{x}_{1+tk} - \mathbf{x}_{1+(t-1)k}) \to 0, \text{ as } k \to \infty,$$

we have

$$\tilde{\mathbf{x}}_t = \mathbf{A}\tilde{\mathbf{x}}_t + \bar{\mathbf{e}}_t, \quad (5)$$

as $k \to \infty$. This is a linear instantaneous causal model for the components of $\tilde{\mathbf{x}}_t$ because the components of the total error term, $\bar{\mathbf{e}}_t$, are still contemporaneously independent. When the error terms are non-Gaussian, it has the same form as the Linear, Non-Gaussian Model (LiNG) (Lacerda et al., 2008); when the causal relations are further assumed to be acyclic, it follows the form of the Linear, Non-Gaussian Acyclic Model (LiNGAM) (Shimizu et al., 2006). The difference is that in LiNG or LiNGAM, the self-loop influences, A_{ii}, are assumed to be zero. We will also investigate the identifiably of $\mathbf{A}$ in this case in Section 3.

3 IDENTIFIABILITY OF CAUSAL RELATIONS IN A

We investigate the identifiability of the high-resolution causal transition matrix $\mathbf{A}$ from the aggregated time time series $\tilde{\mathbf{x}}_{1:T}$. In other words, suppose $\tilde{\mathbf{x}}$ also admits another representation $(\mathbf{A}', \mathbf{e}', k)$, we aim to see whether it is always the case that $\mathbf{A} = \mathbf{A}'$ as the sample size $T \to \infty$. If the noise terms follow the Gaussian distribution, $\mathbf{A}$ is usually not identifiable (Palm & Nijman, 1984). Recently, it has been shown that $\mathbf{A}$ is identifiable from subsampled time series if the noise terms are non-Gaussian (Gong et al., 2015). However, this does not give rise to the identifiability of $\mathbf{A}$ from aggregated time series – the latter is much more difficult to see as the aggregated model described in (3) has a more complicated structure. Here, we show that, in the exact model (3), $\mathbf{A}$ is identifiable from the aggregated data under appropriate conditions; furthermore, as $k \to \infty$, the approximate model (5) holds, and $\mathbf{A}$ is partially identifiable from the aggregated data, but the identification procedure is computationally much more efficient.

First, we will show that $\mathbf{A}^k$ can be identified by fitting the VARMA model (4). We make the following assumption.

*A*1. At least one of the τ-step ($\tau \geq 2$) delayed cross covariance matrices of $\tilde{\mathbf{x}}_t$, $\mathbb{E}[\tilde{\mathbf{x}}_{t-1}\tilde{\mathbf{x}}_{t-\tau}^\intercal]$, is invertible.

Since $\boldsymbol{\epsilon}_t$ is both temporally and contemporaneously independent, $\boldsymbol{\epsilon}_t$ and $\boldsymbol{\epsilon}_{t-1}$ are independent of $\tilde{\mathbf{x}}_{t-\tau}$, which implies that

$$\mathbb{E}[\boldsymbol{\epsilon}_t\tilde{\mathbf{x}}_{t-\tau}^\intercal] = 0, \ \mathbb{E}[\boldsymbol{\epsilon}_{t-1}\tilde{\mathbf{x}}_{t-\tau}^\intercal] = 0.$$

Multiplying both sides of (4) from the right side by $\tilde{\mathbf{x}}_{t-\tau}^{\intercal}$ and taking the expectation, we have

$$\begin{aligned}&\mathbb{E}[\tilde{\mathbf{x}}_t\tilde{\mathbf{x}}_{t-\tau}^{\intercal}]\\&= \mathbf{A}^k\mathbb{E}[\tilde{\mathbf{x}}_{t-1}\tilde{\mathbf{x}}_{t-\tau}^{\intercal}] + \mathbf{M}_0\mathbb{E}[\epsilon_t\tilde{\mathbf{x}}_{t-\tau}^{\intercal}] + \mathbf{M}_1\mathbb{E}[\epsilon_{t-1}\tilde{\mathbf{x}}_{t-\tau}^{\intercal}]\\&= \mathbf{A}^k\mathbb{E}[\tilde{\mathbf{x}}_{t-1}\tilde{\mathbf{x}}_{t-\tau}^{\intercal}]. \qquad (6)\end{aligned}$$

Under the assumption A_1, we can first see that $\mathbf{A}^k$ is identifiable:

$$\mathbf{A}^k = \mathbb{E}[\tilde{\mathbf{x}}_t\tilde{\mathbf{x}}_{t-\tau}^{\intercal}] \cdot \mathbb{E}[\tilde{\mathbf{x}}_{t-1}\tilde{\mathbf{x}}_{t-\tau}^{\intercal}]^{-1}. \qquad (7)$$

3.1 IDENTIFIABILITY WITH FINITE k

Substituting the above equation into (3), one can then find $\vec{\mathbf{e}}_t$, which is defined to be linear mixtures of $(2k-1)$ noise terms, i.e., $\mathbf{e}_{tk}, \mathbf{e}_{tk-1}, \ldots,$ and $\mathbf{e}_{(t-2)k+2}$. In the following, we will concentrate on the identifiablity of $\mathbf{A}$ from $\vec{\mathbf{e}}$.

Let

$$\mathbf{H} \triangleq [\mathbf{I}, \mathbf{I}+\mathbf{A}, \ldots, \sum_{l=0}^{k-1}\mathbf{A}^l, \sum_{l=1}^{k-1}\mathbf{A}^l, \ldots, \sum_{l=k-2}^{k-1}\mathbf{A}^l, \mathbf{A}^{k-1}]. \qquad (8)$$

The error terms in (3) correspond to the following mixing procedure of random vectors:

$$\vec{\mathbf{e}} = \mathbf{H}\tilde{\mathbf{e}}, \text{ where} \qquad (9)$$
$$\tilde{\mathbf{e}} = (e_1^{(0)}, ..., e_n^{(0)}, e_1^{(1)}, ..., e_n^{(1)}, ..., e_1^{(2k-2)}, ..., e_n^{(2k-2)})^{\intercal}.$$

Here, $\mathbf{e}^l = (e_1^{(l)}, ..., e_n^{(l)})^{\intercal}$ together with the time index t represent $\mathbf{e}_{tk-l}$. The components of $\tilde{\mathbf{e}}$ are independent, and for each i, $e_i^{(l)}$, $l = 0, ..., 2k-2$, have the same distribution p_{e_i}. Under the condition that p_{e_i} is non-Gaussian for each i, $\mathbf{H}$ can be estimated up to the permutation and scaling indeterminacies (including the sign indeterminacy) of the columns, as given in the following proposition.

Proposition 1. *Suppose that all p_{e_i} are non-Gaussian. Given k and $\tilde{\mathbf{x}}_{1:T}$ generated according to (3), $\mathbf{H}$ can be determined up to permutation and scaling of columns.*

For the proof of Proposition 1, please refer to (Gong et al., 2015).

We make the following assumptions on the underlying dynamic process (1) and the distributions p_{e_i}, and then we have the identifiability result for the causal transition matrix $\mathbf{A}$.

A2. The system is stable, in that all eigenvalues of $\mathbf{A}$ have modulus smaller than one.

A3. The distributions p_{e_i} are different for different i after re-scaling by any non-zero scale factor, their characteristic functions are all analytic (or they are all non-vanishing), and none of them has an exponent factor with a polynomial of degree at least 2.

The following identifiability result on $\mathbf{A}$ states that in various situations, $\mathbf{A}$ for the original high frequency data is fully identifiable.

Theorem 1. *Suppose all of e_{it} are non-Gaussian, and that the data $\tilde{\mathbf{x}}_t$ are generated by (3) and that it also admits another kth order aggregation representation $(\mathbf{A}', \mathbf{e}', k)$. Let assumptions A1 and A2 hold. When the number of observed data points $T \to \infty$, the following statements are true.*

(i) $\mathbf{A}'$ can be represented as $\mathbf{A}' - \mathbf{I} = (\mathbf{A} - \mathbf{I})\mathbf{D}$, where $\mathbf{D}$ is a diagonal matrix with 1 or -1 on its diagonal. If we constrain all the self influences, represented by diagonal entries of $\mathbf{A}$ and $\mathbf{A}'$, to be no greater than 1, then $\mathbf{A}' = \mathbf{A}$.

(ii) If each p_{e_i} is asymmetric, we have $\mathbf{A}' = \mathbf{A}$.

A complete proof of Theorem 1 can be found in Section 6.

3.2 IDENTIFIABILITY AS $k \to \infty$

We have shown that $\mathbf{A}$ is identifiable from aggregated data (3) when k is finite. However, when k becomes larger, estimating $\mathbf{A}$ will encounter more difficulty because more independent components in (9) are involved. When $k = \infty$, it is not necessary for Proposition 1, as well as Theorem 1, to hold, because $\vec{\mathbf{e}}$ in (9) is the mixture of an infinite number of independent components.

Interestingly, as $k \to \infty$, $\tilde{\mathbf{x}}_t$ follows an instantaneous causal model in the i.i.d. case, as shown in (5). We will then answer the following two questions. In this case, can we still estimate $\mathbf{A}$ from aggregated data? If we can, is there an efficient procedure to do so?

Equation (5) implies $(\mathbf{I}-\mathbf{A})\tilde{\mathbf{x}}_t = \bar{\mathbf{e}}_t$. That is, applying the linear transformation $(\mathbf{I}-\mathbf{A})$ on $\tilde{\mathbf{x}}_t$ produces independent components, as components of $\bar{\mathbf{e}}_t$. This can be achieved by the independent component analysis (ICA) procedure (Hyvärinen et al., 2001), and $(\mathbf{I}-\mathbf{A})$ can be estimated up to row scaling and permutation indeterminacies. We then have the following observations.

First, the diagonal entries of $\mathbf{A}$, A_{ii}, which represent the self influences or "self-loops" of the time-delayed causal relations, cannot be determined (Lacerda et al., 2008). (Here we have assumed $A_{ii} \neq 1$.) This is because the scale of each row of $(\mathbf{I}-\mathbf{A})$ is unknown, and so is $(1 - A_{ii})$.

Let $\mathbf{D}_\mathbf{A}$ be the diagonal matrix with $A_{11}, A_{22}, ..., A_{nn}$ on its diagonal. Equation (5) is equivalent to

$$\begin{aligned}&(\mathbf{I}-\mathbf{D}_\mathbf{A})\tilde{\mathbf{x}}_t = (\mathbf{A}-\mathbf{D}_\mathbf{A})\tilde{\mathbf{x}}_t + \bar{\mathbf{e}}_t\\ \Rightarrow &\tilde{\mathbf{x}}_t = \underbrace{(\mathbf{I}-\mathbf{D}_\mathbf{A})^{-1}(\mathbf{A}-\mathbf{D}_\mathbf{A})}_{\triangleq \mathbf{A}_{NoSelfLoop}}\tilde{\mathbf{x}}_t + (\mathbf{I}-\mathbf{D}_\mathbf{A})^{-1}\bar{\mathbf{e}}_t.\end{aligned} \qquad (10)$$

Secondly, suppose there is no feedback loop between the processes after removing the self-loops, meaning that $(\mathbf{A} - \mathbf{D}_\mathbf{A})$ can be permuted to a strictly lower-triangular matrix by equal row and column permutations. According to the LiNGAM model, which assumes these is no self-loop, $(\mathbf{I} - \mathbf{D}_\mathbf{A})^{-1}(\mathbf{A} - \mathbf{D}_\mathbf{A})$ in (10) can be uniquely estimated (Shimizu et al., 2006). In other words, if one applies LiNGAM analysis on $\tilde{\mathbf{x}}_t$, the estimated causal coefficients from th ith variable to the jth variable is actually $(1 - A_{jj})^{-1}A_{ji}$. From this we can see whether A_{ji} is zero or not; furthermore, if the self-loops A_{jj} are given by prior knowledge, then $\mathbf{A}$ is fully identifiable.

Thirdly, suppose there exist feedback loops between the processes after removing the self-loops. In this case, $(\mathbf{A} - \mathbf{D}_\mathbf{A})$ cannot be permuted to a strictly lower-triangular matrix by equal row and column permutations. The identifiability of $\mathbf{A}$ in (5) has been studied by Lacerda et al. (2008): suppose the feedback loops are disjoint, although in theory there are multiple solutions to $\mathbf{A}^{NoSelfLoop}$, the most stable solution (the product of the coefficients in $\mathbf{A}^{NoSelfLoop}$ along each loop is minimized) is unique.

4 ESTIMATING THE CAUSAL RELATIONS FROM AGGREGATED DATA

In this section, we present the algorithm to estimate $\mathbf{A}$ from aggregated data with finite k. Clearly, the larger k, the more difficult it is to estimate $\mathbf{A}$ from aggregated data. Therefore, when k is relatively large (say, larger than 6), we advocate the methods given in Section 3.2 to partially estimate $\mathbf{A}$.

Since the identifiability of $\mathbf{A}$ from aggregated data relies on the non-Gaussianity of the error terms, we use Gaussian mixtures to represent their distributions. It is natural to do parameter estimation with the Expectation-Maximization algorithm, which, unfortunately, involves a large number of Gaussian components. To avoid this issue, we propose to use the Stochastic Approximation EM (SAEM) algorithm, as a variant of EM, and further resort to conditional particle filtering with ancestor sampling (CPF-AS) to achieve computational efficiency.

4.1 STATE-SPACE MODELING

We can consider (3) as a special *state-space* model:

$$\begin{aligned}\tilde{\mathbf{x}}_t &= \mathbf{A}^k \tilde{\mathbf{x}}_{t-1} + \mathbf{H}\tilde{\mathbf{e}}_t \\ &= \mathbf{A}^k \tilde{\mathbf{x}}_{t-1} + \begin{bmatrix}\mathbf{I} & \sum_{l=0}^{1}\mathbf{A}^l & \dots & \sum_{l=0}^{k-1}\mathbf{A}^l & \sum_{l=1}^{k-1}\mathbf{A}^l & \dots & \sum_{l=k-2}^{k-1}\mathbf{A}^l & \mathbf{A}^{k-1}\end{bmatrix} \begin{bmatrix}\tilde{\mathbf{e}}_t^{(0)} \\ \tilde{\mathbf{e}}_t^{(1)} \\ \vdots \\ \tilde{\mathbf{e}}_t^{(2k-2)}\end{bmatrix},\end{aligned} \quad (11)$$

where

$$\begin{bmatrix}\tilde{\mathbf{e}}_t^{(0)} \\ \tilde{\mathbf{e}}_t^{(1)} \\ \vdots \\ \tilde{\mathbf{e}}_t^{(2k-2)}\end{bmatrix} = \mathbf{F}\begin{bmatrix}\tilde{\mathbf{e}}_{t-1}^{(0)} \\ \tilde{\mathbf{e}}_{t-1}^{(1)} \\ \vdots \\ \tilde{\mathbf{e}}_{t-1}^{(2k-2)}\end{bmatrix} + \begin{bmatrix}\mathbf{e}_{tk} \\ \mathbf{e}_{tk-1} \\ \vdots \\ \mathbf{e}_{(t-1)k+1} \\ \mathbf{0}_{(nk-n)\times 1}\end{bmatrix},$$

$$\mathbf{F} = \begin{bmatrix}\mathbf{0}_{nk\times(nk-n)} & \mathbf{0}_{nk\times(nk)} \\ \mathbf{I}_{(nk-n)\times(nk-n)} & \mathbf{0}_{(nk-n)\times(nk)}\end{bmatrix},$$

$\tilde{\mathbf{e}}_t^{(l)} = \mathbf{e}_{tk-l}$, and the noise terms $\mathbf{e}_{tk}, \mathbf{e}_{tk-1}, ..., \mathbf{e}_{(t-1)k+1}$ share the same distribution for the same channel and are mutually independent. Since the non-Gaussianity is essential to the identifiability of $\mathbf{A}$, we use a Gaussian mixture model to represent each channel of noise term $\mathbf{e}$, i.e., $p_{e_i} = \sum_{c=1}^{m} w_{i,c}\mathcal{N}(e_i|\mu_{i,c}, \sigma_{i,c}^2)$, where $w_{i,c} \geq 0$, and $\sum_{c=1}^{m}\pi_{i,c} = 1$, for $i = 1, ..., n$. Correspondingly, each channel of $\tilde{\mathbf{e}}$ is also represented by a Gaussian mixture model.

We aim to estimate the parameters $\mathbf{A}$ and the noise terms (if necessary) in the above state-space model. We introduce the additional latent variable $\tilde{\mathbf{z}}_t = (\tilde{z}_{t,1}, ..., \tilde{z}_{t,nk})^\intercal$, in which $\tilde{z}_{t,j} \in \{1, \dots, m\}$, to model the distribution of noise terms $\tilde{\mathbf{e}}_t$ by Gaussian mixture models. The joint distribution of the state-space model (11) over both observed and unobserved variables is given by

$$\begin{aligned}&p(\tilde{\mathbf{x}}_{1:T}, \tilde{\mathbf{e}}_{1:T}, \tilde{\mathbf{z}}_{1:T}) = p(\tilde{\mathbf{z}}_1)p(\tilde{\mathbf{e}}_1|\tilde{\mathbf{z}}_1)p(\tilde{\mathbf{x}}_1|\tilde{\mathbf{e}}_1) \\ &\prod_{t=2}^{T} p(\tilde{\mathbf{z}}_t)p(\tilde{\mathbf{e}}_t|\tilde{\mathbf{e}}_{t-1}, \tilde{\mathbf{z}}_t)p(\tilde{\mathbf{x}}_t|\tilde{\mathbf{x}}_{t-1}, \tilde{\mathbf{e}}_t).\end{aligned} \quad (12)$$

The distributions in (12) are specified as follows:

$$p(\tilde{\mathbf{z}}_t) = \prod_{j=1}^{nk} p(\tilde{z}_{t,j}) = \prod_{j=1}^{nk} \tilde{\pi}_{j,\tilde{z}_{t,j}}, \quad (13a)$$

$$p(\tilde{\mathbf{e}}_t|\tilde{\mathbf{e}}_{t-1}, \tilde{\mathbf{z}}_t) = \mathcal{N}(\tilde{\mathbf{e}}_t|\mathbf{F}\tilde{\mathbf{e}}_{t-1} + \tilde{\boldsymbol{\mu}}_t, \tilde{\boldsymbol{\Sigma}}_t), \quad (13b)$$

$$p(\tilde{\mathbf{x}}_t|\tilde{\mathbf{e}}_t, \tilde{\mathbf{x}}_{t-1}) = \mathcal{N}(\tilde{\mathbf{x}}_t|\mathbf{A}^k\tilde{\mathbf{x}}_{t-1} + \mathbf{H}\tilde{\mathbf{e}}_t, \boldsymbol{\Lambda}). \quad (13c)$$

Since there are no additional additive noise terms in the model, we fix $\boldsymbol{\Lambda}$ to a small value in our estimation algorithm for regularization. $\tilde{\boldsymbol{\mu}}_t$ is the conditional mean of $\tilde{\mathbf{e}}_t$, i.e., $\tilde{\boldsymbol{\mu}}_t = [\tilde{\mu}_{1,\tilde{z}_{t,1}}, \dots, \tilde{\mu}_{nk,\tilde{z}_{t,nk}}, \mathbf{0}_{1\times n(k-1)}]^\intercal$. $\tilde{\boldsymbol{\Sigma}}_t$ is a diagonal matrix containing the conditional variance parameters of $\tilde{\mathbf{e}}_t$, i.e., $\tilde{\boldsymbol{\Sigma}}_t = \text{diag}([\tilde{\sigma}^2_{1,\tilde{z}_{t,1}}, \dots, \tilde{\sigma}^2_{nk,\tilde{z}_{t,nk}}, \mathbf{0}_{1\times n(k-1)}])$. According to the structure of $\tilde{\mathbf{e}}$, the parameters $\tilde{\pi}_{j,\tilde{z}_{t,j}}$, $\tilde{\mu}_{j,\tilde{z}_{t,j}}$, and $\tilde{\sigma}_{j,\tilde{z}_{t,j}}$ are controlled by the parameters of $\mathbf{e}$, i.e., $\tilde{\pi}_{i+nl,c} = \pi_{i,c}$, $\tilde{\mu}_{i+nl,c} = \mu_{i,c}$, and $\tilde{\sigma}_{i+nl,c} = \sigma_{i,c}$, for $i = 1, ..., n$, $l = 0, ..., k-1$, and $c = 1, ..., m$.

4.2 STOCHASTIC APPROXIMATION EM

The expectation-maximization (EM) algorithm is usually adopted to find the maximum likelihood estimation of the parameters in a probabilistic model with unobserved variables. We can estimate the parameters $\theta = (\mathbf{A}, w_{i,c}, \mu_{i,c}, \sigma_{i,c})$ in (12) using the EM algorithm that iteratively maximizes the lower bound of the marginal log-likelihood $p_\theta(\tilde{\mathbf{x}}_{1:T}) = \log \sum_{\tilde{\mathbf{z}}_{1:T}} \int p_\theta(\tilde{\mathbf{x}}_{1:T}, \tilde{\mathbf{e}}_{1:T}, \tilde{\mathbf{z}}_{1:T}) d_{\tilde{\mathbf{e}}_{1:T}}$. In the E-step, at the k-th iteration, given the parameters θ_{k-1} estimated from the $(k-1)$-th iteration, the EM algorithm firstly computes the posterior distribution $p_{\theta_{k-1}}(\tilde{\mathbf{z}}_{1:T}, \tilde{\mathbf{e}}_{1:T}|\tilde{\mathbf{x}}_{1:T})$ and then computes the lower bound $\mathcal{Q}(\theta, \theta_{k-1}) = \sum_{\tilde{\mathbf{z}}_{1:T}} \int p_{\theta_{k-1}}(\tilde{\mathbf{z}}_{1:T}, \tilde{\mathbf{e}}_{1:T}|\tilde{\mathbf{x}}_{1:T}) \log p_\theta(\tilde{\mathbf{x}}_{1:T}, \tilde{\mathbf{e}}_{1:T}, \tilde{\mathbf{z}}_{1:T}) d_{\tilde{\mathbf{e}}_{1:T}}$. In the M-step, the parameters are updated as $\theta_k = \arg\max_\theta \mathcal{Q}(\theta, \theta_{k-1})$.

However, we note that the number of Gaussian mixtures in the posterior distribution grows exponentially with the dimension of the time series, n, the number of aggregation factor, k, and the duration of time series T. Therefore, computing the exact posterior $p_{\theta_{k-1}}(\tilde{\mathbf{z}}_{1:T}, \tilde{\mathbf{e}}_{1:T}|\tilde{\mathbf{x}}_{1:T})$ and $\mathcal{Q}(\theta, \theta_{k-1})$ is intractable in this situation. A possible solution is to adopt the monte carlo EM (MCEM) algorithm (Wei & Tanner, 1990), which approximately calculates $\mathcal{Q}(\theta, \theta_{k-1})$ using samples drawn from the posterior distribution $p_{\theta_{k-1}}(\tilde{\mathbf{z}}_{1:T}, \tilde{\mathbf{e}}_{1:T}|\tilde{\mathbf{x}}_{1:T})$. However, MCEM makes inefficient use of generated samples, as it discards samples generated in the previous EM iterations. Therefore, a large number of sample points are required for each iteration, which is computationally expensive when the sampling method is complex.

To reduce the number of simulated sample points, we propose to use the stochastic approximation EM (SAEM) algorithm (Delyon et al., 1999), which only requires of a single realization of the unobserved variables at each iteration. At the k-th iteration, the E-step and M-step are replaced by the following:

E-step: Generate a single sample point $\tilde{\mathbf{z}}_{1:T}[k]$ from the posterior $p_{\theta_{k-1}}(\tilde{\mathbf{z}}_{1:T}|\tilde{\mathbf{x}}_{1:T})$, and compute

$$\begin{aligned}\hat{\mathcal{Q}}_k(\theta) &= (1-\gamma_k)\hat{\mathcal{Q}}_{k-1}(\theta) \\ &+ \gamma_k \int p_{\theta_{k-1}}(\tilde{\mathbf{e}}_{1:T}|\tilde{\mathbf{z}}_{1:T}[k], \tilde{\mathbf{x}}_{1:T}) \\ &\log p_\theta(\tilde{\mathbf{x}}_{1:T}, \tilde{\mathbf{e}}_{1:T}, \tilde{\mathbf{z}}_{1:T}[k]) d_{\tilde{\mathbf{e}}_{1:T}}. \end{aligned} \quad (14)$$

M-step: Update parameters by $\theta_k = \arg\max_\theta \hat{\mathcal{Q}}_k(\theta)$.

In (14), $\{\gamma_k\}_{k=1}^{\infty}$ is a sequence of decreasing step sizes satisfying $\sum_{k=1}^{\infty} \gamma_k = \infty$ and $\sum_{k=1}^{\infty} \gamma_k^2 < \infty$. Here we use Rao-Blackwellization (Svensson et al., 2014) to avoid sampling $\tilde{\mathbf{e}}_{1:T}$ because it is analytically integrable. It has been shown in (Delyon et al., 1999) that the resulting sequence $\{\theta_k\}_{k\geq 1}$ will converge to a stationary point of $p_\theta(\tilde{\mathbf{x}}_{1:T})$ under weak assumptions.

4.3 CONDITIONAL PARTICLE FILTER WITH ANCESTOR SAMPLING

In our model, sampling from the posterior $p_{\theta_{k-1}}(\tilde{\mathbf{z}}_{1:T}|\tilde{\mathbf{x}}_{1:T})$ is usually performed using forward filter/backward simulator particle smoother, which typically requires a large number of particles to generate a smooth backward trajectory $\tilde{\mathbf{z}}_{1:T}[k]$. To reduce the number of required particles, we use the Markovian version of SAEM (Kuhn & Lavielle, 2004), which samples from a Markov kernel $\mathcal{M}_{\theta_{t-1}}$, leaving the posterior distribution invariant. Specifically, let $\tilde{\mathbf{z}}_{1:T}[k-1]$ be the previous draw from the Markov kernel, the current state is sampled by $\tilde{\mathbf{z}}_{1:T}[k] \sim \mathcal{M}_{\theta_{k-1}}(\cdot|\tilde{\mathbf{z}}_{1:T}[k-1])$. Following (Lindsten, 2013; Svensson et al., 2014), we construct the Markov kernel using Rao-Blackwellized conditional particle filter with ancestor sampling (RB-CPF-AS) (Lindsten et al., 2014), which was originally proposed for Gibbs sampling.

The machinery inside RB-CPF-AS resembles a standard particle filter, with two main differences: one particle trajectory is deterministically set to a reference trajectory $\tilde{\mathbf{z}}'_{1:T}$, and the ancestors of the reference trajectory are randomly chosen and stored during the algorithm execution. Algorithm 1 gives a brief description of the RB-CPF-AS algorithm. Let $\{\tilde{\mathbf{z}}^i_{1:t-1}, w^i_{t-1}\}_{i=1}^N$ be the approximation of $p_\theta(\tilde{\mathbf{z}}_{1:t-1}|\tilde{\mathbf{x}}_{1:t-1})$, RB-CPF-AS propagates this sample to time t by introducing the auxiliary variables $\{a^i_t\}_{i=1}^N$, referred to as *ancestor indices*. To generate $\tilde{\mathbf{z}}^i_t$ for the first $N-1$ particle trajectories, we first sample the ancestor index according to $P(a^i_t = j) \propto w^j_{t-1}$, and then sample $\tilde{\mathbf{z}}^i_{t,j}$ according to $p_\theta(\tilde{\mathbf{z}}_t|\tilde{\mathbf{z}}^{a^i_t}_{t-1}) = \prod_{j=1}^{nk} p_\theta(\tilde{z}_{t,j})$. The first $N-1$ trajectories are then augmented as $\tilde{\mathbf{z}}^i_{1:t} = \{\tilde{\mathbf{z}}^{a^i_t}_{1:t-1}, \tilde{\mathbf{z}}^i_t\}$. The N-th particle is set to the reference particle, $\tilde{\mathbf{z}}^N_t = \tilde{\mathbf{z}}'_t$, and the ancestor index a^N_t is sampled according to

$$\begin{aligned} &P(a^N_t = i) \\ &\propto p_\theta(\tilde{\mathbf{z}}^i_{1:t-1}|\tilde{\mathbf{z}}'_{t:T}, \tilde{\mathbf{x}}_{1:T}) \\ &\propto p_\theta(\tilde{\mathbf{x}}_{t:T}, \tilde{\mathbf{z}}'_{t:T}|\tilde{\mathbf{x}}_{1:t-1}, \tilde{\mathbf{z}}^i_{1:t-1}) p_\theta(\tilde{\mathbf{z}}^i_{1:t-1}|\tilde{\mathbf{x}}_{1:t-1}), \end{aligned} \quad (15)$$

where $p_\theta(\tilde{\mathbf{z}}^i_{1:t-1}|\tilde{\mathbf{x}}_{1:t-1}) = w^i_{t-1}$ and

$$\begin{aligned} &p_\theta(\tilde{\mathbf{x}}_{t:T}, \tilde{\mathbf{z}}'_{t:T}|\tilde{\mathbf{x}}_{1:t-1}, \tilde{\mathbf{z}}^i_{1:t-1}) \\ &\propto |\mathbf{M}^i_{t-1}|^{-1/2} \exp(-\frac{1}{2}\eta^i_{t-1}). \end{aligned} \quad (16)$$

Conditioned on $\tilde{\mathbf{z}}^i_{1:T}$, we can calculate $p(\tilde{\mathbf{e}}_{1:T}|\tilde{\mathbf{z}}^i_{1:T}, \tilde{\mathbf{x}}_{1:T})$ using Kalman filter and Rauch-Tung-Striebel (RTS) smoother. The filtering, prediction, and smoothing PDFs are

$$p_\theta(\tilde{\mathbf{e}}_t|\tilde{\mathbf{z}}^i_{1:t}, \tilde{\mathbf{x}}_{1:t}) = \mathcal{N}(\tilde{\mathbf{e}}_t|\hat{\boldsymbol{\mu}}^i_{f,t}, \hat{\boldsymbol{\Sigma}}^i_{f,t}), \quad (17a)$$

$$p_\theta(\tilde{\mathbf{e}}_{t+1}|\tilde{\mathbf{z}}^i_{1:t}, \tilde{\mathbf{x}}_{1:t}) = \mathcal{N}(\tilde{\mathbf{e}}_{t+1}|\hat{\boldsymbol{\mu}}^i_{p,t}, \hat{\boldsymbol{\Sigma}}^i_{p,t}), \quad (17b)$$

$$p_\theta(\tilde{\mathbf{e}}_t|\tilde{\mathbf{z}}^i_{1:T}, \tilde{\mathbf{x}}_{1:T}) = \mathcal{N}(\tilde{\mathbf{e}}_t|\hat{\boldsymbol{\mu}}^i_{s,t}, \hat{\boldsymbol{\Sigma}}^i_{s,t}), \quad (17c)$$

respectively. Let $\|\mathbf{e}\|^2_{\mathbf{\Omega}} = \mathbf{e}^\intercal \mathbf{\Omega} \mathbf{e}$ and $\hat{\mathbf{\Sigma}}^i_{f,t} = \mathbf{\Gamma}^i_{f,t}\mathbf{\Gamma}^{i,\intercal}_{f,t}$. In (16),

$$\mathbf{M}^i_t = \mathbf{\Gamma}^{i,\intercal}_{f,t}\mathbf{\Omega}_t\mathbf{\Gamma}^i_{f,t} + \mathbf{I}, \tag{18a}$$

$$\eta^i_t = \|\hat{\boldsymbol{\mu}}^i_{f,t}\|^2_{\mathbf{\Omega}_t} - 2\boldsymbol{\lambda}^\intercal_t\hat{\boldsymbol{\mu}}^i_{f,t} - \|\mathbf{\Gamma}^{i,\intercal}_{f,t}(\boldsymbol{\lambda}_t - \mathbf{\Omega}_t\hat{\boldsymbol{\mu}}^i_{f,t})\|^2_{\mathbf{M}^{-1}_t}, \tag{18b}$$

where

$$\mathbf{\Omega}_t = \mathbf{F}^\intercal(\mathbf{I} - \hat{\mathbf{\Omega}}_{t+1}\tilde{\mathbf{\Sigma}}^{'1/2}_{t+1}\mathbf{\Upsilon}^{-1}_{t+1}\tilde{\mathbf{\Sigma}}^{'1/2}_{t+1})\hat{\mathbf{\Omega}}_{t+1}\mathbf{F}, \tag{19a}$$

$$\boldsymbol{\lambda}_t = \mathbf{F}^\intercal(\mathbf{I} - \hat{\mathbf{\Omega}}_{t+1}\tilde{\mathbf{\Sigma}}^{'1/2}_{t+1}\mathbf{\Upsilon}^{-1}_{t+1}\tilde{\mathbf{\Sigma}}^{'1/2}_{t+1})(\hat{\boldsymbol{\lambda}}_{t+1} - \hat{\mathbf{\Omega}}_{t+1}\tilde{\boldsymbol{\mu}}^{'}_{t+1}), \tag{19b}$$

$$\hat{\mathbf{\Omega}}_t = \mathbf{\Omega}_t + \mathbf{H}^\intercal\mathbf{\Lambda}^{-1}\mathbf{H}, \tag{19c}$$

$$\hat{\boldsymbol{\lambda}}_t = \boldsymbol{\lambda}_t + \mathbf{H}^\intercal\mathbf{\Lambda}^{-1}(\tilde{\mathbf{x}}_t - \mathbf{A}^k\tilde{\mathbf{x}}_{t-1}), \tag{19d}$$

$$\mathbf{\Upsilon}_t = \tilde{\mathbf{\Sigma}}^{'1/2}_t\hat{\mathbf{\Omega}}_t\tilde{\mathbf{\Sigma}}^{'1/2}_t + \mathbf{I}, \tag{19e}$$

$$\tilde{\boldsymbol{\mu}}^{'}_t = [\tilde{\mu}_{1,\tilde{z}^{'}_{t,1}}, \ldots, \tilde{\mu}_{nk,\tilde{z}^{'}_{t,nk}}, \mathbf{0}_{1\times n(k-1)}]^\intercal, \tag{19f}$$

$$\tilde{\mathbf{\Sigma}}^{'}_t = \mathrm{diag}([\tilde{\sigma}^2_{1,\tilde{z}^{'}_{t,1}}, \ldots, \tilde{\sigma}^2_{nk,\tilde{z}^{'}_{t,nk}}, \mathbf{0}_{1\times n(k-1)}]). \tag{19g}$$

With $\mathbf{\Omega}_T = 0$ and $\boldsymbol{\lambda}_T = 0$, $\{\mathbf{\Omega}_t, \boldsymbol{\lambda}_t\}^T_{t=1}$ can be computed recursively for $\tilde{\mathbf{z}}^{'}_{1:T}$ using (19a)-(19g). Once all the ancestors $\{a^i_t\}^N_{i=1}$ have been sampled, we can calculate the new particle weights as follows

$$\begin{aligned} w^i_t &\propto p_\theta(\tilde{\mathbf{x}}_t|\tilde{\mathbf{z}}^i_{1:t}, \tilde{\mathbf{x}}_{1:t-1}) \\ &= \mathcal{N}(\tilde{\mathbf{x}}_t|\mathbf{F}\hat{\boldsymbol{\mu}}^i_{p,t+1} + \mathbf{A}^k\tilde{\mathbf{x}}_{t-1}, \mathbf{F}\hat{\mathbf{\Sigma}}^i_{p,t+1}\mathbf{F}^\intercal + \mathbf{\Lambda}). \end{aligned} \tag{20}$$

After all the particle trajectories have been generated, we obtain $\tilde{\mathbf{z}}_{1:T}[k]$ by sampling from these trajectories according to the weights $\{W^i_T\}^N_{i=1}$ at time T.

4.4 PARAMETER UPDATE

At the k-th M step, given the sample $\tilde{\mathbf{z}}_{1:T}[k]$ drawn by RB-CPF-AS, we can obtain $p_{\theta_{k-1}}(\tilde{\mathbf{e}}_t|\tilde{\mathbf{z}}_{1:T}[k], \tilde{\mathbf{x}}_{1:T}) = \mathcal{N}(\tilde{\mathbf{e}}_t|\hat{\boldsymbol{\mu}}_{s,t}, \hat{\mathbf{\Sigma}}_{s,t})$ using the RTS smoother. Then we have

$$\begin{aligned} &\int p_{\theta_{k-1}}(\tilde{\mathbf{e}}_{1:T}|\tilde{\mathbf{z}}_{1:T}, \tilde{\mathbf{x}}_{1:T})\log p_\theta(\tilde{\mathbf{x}}_{1:T}, \tilde{\mathbf{e}}_{1:T}, \tilde{\mathbf{z}}_{1:T})d_{\tilde{\mathbf{e}}_{1:T}} \\ &= \sum_{t=1}^T \log p(\tilde{\mathbf{z}}_t) \\ &\quad - \frac{1}{2}\sum_{t=1}^T \int q(\tilde{\mathbf{e}}^{'}_t)(\tilde{\mathbf{e}}^{'}_t - \tilde{\boldsymbol{\mu}}^{'}_t)^\intercal\tilde{\mathbf{\Sigma}}^{'-1}_t(\tilde{\mathbf{e}}^{'}_t - \tilde{\boldsymbol{\mu}}^{'}_t)d\tilde{\mathbf{e}}^{'}_t + \log|\tilde{\mathbf{\Sigma}}_t| \\ &\quad - \frac{1}{2}\sum_{t=1}^T \int q(\tilde{\mathbf{e}}_t)(\tilde{\mathbf{y}}_t - \mathbf{H}\tilde{\mathbf{e}}_t)^\intercal\mathbf{\Lambda}^{-1}(\tilde{\mathbf{y}}_t - \mathbf{H}\tilde{\mathbf{e}}_t)d\tilde{\mathbf{e}}_t \\ &\quad + \text{const}, \end{aligned} \tag{21}$$

where $\tilde{\mathbf{z}}_t = \tilde{\mathbf{z}}_t[k]$, $\tilde{\mathbf{e}}^{'}_t = [\mathbf{e}^\intercal_{tk}, \mathbf{e}^\intercal_{tk-1}, \ldots, \tilde{\mathbf{e}}^\intercal_{(t-1)k+1}]^\intercal$, $\tilde{\boldsymbol{\mu}}^{'}_t = [\tilde{\mu}_{1,\tilde{z}_{t,1}}, \ldots, \tilde{\mu}_{nk,\tilde{z}_{t,nk}}]^\intercal$, $\tilde{\mathbf{\Sigma}}^{'}_t = \mathrm{diag}([\tilde{\sigma}^2_{1,\tilde{z}_{t,1}}, \ldots, \tilde{\sigma}^2_{nk,\tilde{z}_{t,nk}}])$, $\tilde{\mathbf{y}}_t = \tilde{\mathbf{x}}_t - \mathbf{A}^k\tilde{\mathbf{x}}_{t-1}$, and $q(\tilde{\mathbf{e}}_t) = p_{\theta_{k-1}}(\tilde{\mathbf{e}}_t|\tilde{\mathbf{z}}_{1:T}, \tilde{\mathbf{x}}_{1:T})$.

Algorithm 1: RB-CPF-AS

Input: $\tilde{\mathbf{z}}^{'}_{1:T} = \tilde{\mathbf{z}}_{1:T}[k-1]$, $\theta = \theta_{k-1}$
Output: $\tilde{\mathbf{z}}_{1:T}[k] \sim \mathcal{M}_{\theta_{k-1}}(\cdot|\tilde{\mathbf{z}}_{1:T}[k-1])$
Compute $\{\mathbf{\Omega}_t, \boldsymbol{\lambda}_t\}^T_{t=1}$ according to (19a)-(19g)
Draw $\tilde{\mathbf{z}}^i_1$ with $\tilde{\mathbf{z}}^i_1 \sim p_\theta(\tilde{\mathbf{z}}_1)$ for $i = 1, \ldots, N$
Compute $\boldsymbol{\mu}^i_1$, $\mathbf{\Sigma}^i_1$, and w^i_1 for $i = 1, \ldots, N$
for *t=2 to T* **do**
  Draw a^i_t with $P(a^i_t = j) \propto w^j_{t-1}$for $i = 1, \ldots, N$
  // Resampling and ancestor sampling
  Draw $\tilde{\mathbf{z}}^i_t$ with $\tilde{\mathbf{z}}^i_t \sim p_\theta(\tilde{\mathbf{z}}_t)$ for $i = 1, \ldots, N$
  Compute $\{\mathbf{M}^i_{t-1}, \eta^i_{t-1}\}$ according to (18a) and (18b)
  Draw a^i_N according to (15) for $i = 1, \ldots, N$
  // Particle propagation
  Set $\tilde{\mathbf{z}}^i_{1:t} = \{\tilde{\mathbf{z}}^{a^i_t}_{1:t-1}, \tilde{\mathbf{z}}^i_t\}$ for $i = 1, \ldots, N$
  Set $\hat{\boldsymbol{\mu}}^i_{f,1:t-1} = \hat{\boldsymbol{\mu}}^{a^i_t}_{f,1:t-1}$, $\hat{\boldsymbol{\mu}}^i_{p,1:t-1} = \hat{\boldsymbol{\mu}}^{a^i_t}_{p,1:t-1}$,
  $\hat{\mathbf{\Sigma}}^i_{f,1:t-1} = \hat{\mathbf{\Sigma}}^{a^i_t}_{f,t-1}$, $\hat{\mathbf{\Sigma}}^i_{p,1:t-1} = \hat{\mathbf{\Sigma}}^{a^i_t}_{p,1:t-1}$
  // Weighting
  Compute $\hat{\boldsymbol{\mu}}^i_{f,t}$, $\hat{\boldsymbol{\mu}}^i_{p,t}$, $\hat{\mathbf{\Sigma}}^i_{f,t}$, and $\hat{\mathbf{\Sigma}}^i_{p,t}$
  Compute weights w^i_t according to (20)
Draw J with $P(J = j) \propto W^j_T$ and set $\tilde{\mathbf{z}}_{1:T}[k] = \tilde{\mathbf{z}}^J_{1:T}$.

It can be seen that we only need sufficient statistics $\int \tilde{\mathbf{e}}_t q(\tilde{\mathbf{e}}_t)d\tilde{\mathbf{e}}_t$ and $\int \tilde{\mathbf{e}}_t\tilde{\mathbf{e}}^\intercal_t q(\tilde{\mathbf{e}}_t)d\tilde{\mathbf{e}}_t$ to maximize (21). Denoting a sufficient statistics at the k-th iteration as S^k, we use $\mathbb{S}^k = (1 - \gamma_k)\mathbb{S}^k + \gamma_k S^k$ to maximize $\hat{Q}_k(\theta)$. To maximize $\hat{Q}_k(\theta)$ with respect to $\mathbf{A}$, we compute the gradient of $\mathbf{A}$ in terms involving $\mathbf{A}^k$ and $\mathbf{H}$ and apply a conjugate gradient descent method as done in Gong et al. (2015).

5 EXPERIMENTS

In this section, we conduct empirical studies of the two estimation methods presented in Section 3.2 and Section 4 on both synthetic and real data to show their effectiveness.

5.1 SIMULATED DATA

We conduct a series of simulations to investigate the effectiveness of the proposed estimation methods. Following (Gong et al., 2015), we generated the data at the casual frequency using the VAR model (1) with randomly generated matrix $\mathbf{A}$ and independent Gaussian mixture noises $\mathbf{e}_t$. The elements in $\mathbf{A}$ were drawn from a uniform distribution $\mathcal{U}(-0.5, 0.5)$. The Gaussian mixture model contains two components for each channel. The parameters were $w_{1,1} = 0.2$, $w_{1,2} = 0.8$, $w_{2,1} = 0.3$, $w_{2,2} = 0.7$,$\mu_{i,1} = 0$, $\mu_{i,2} = 0$, $\sigma^2_{i,1} = 1e-4$, $\sigma^2_{1,2} = .1$, and $\sigma^2_{2,2} = 0.2$. Low-resolution observations were obtained by aggregating the high-resolution data using aggregation factor k. Similarly, we also generated data with Gaussian noise (by setting $\sigma_{1,c}^2 = 0.01$, $\sigma_{2,c}^2 = 0.02$) for comparison of different methods. We tested data with dimension $n = 2$, aggregation factor $k = 2$ and 3, and sample size $T = 150$ and 300, respectively. For comparison,we replaced the Gaussian mixture models in our method with Gaussian noise models, leading to a method based on Gaussian noises. We denote the method proposed in Section 4 that performs causal discovery from temporally aggregated data as $\text{CDTA}_{\text{finite}}$ and the corresponding Gaussian counterpart as $\text{CDTA}_{\text{Gauss}}$. We also compare with the NG-EM method (Gong et al., 2015) on the aggregated data with non-Gaussian noises. The experiments are repeated for 10 replications .

Table 1 shows the mean squared error (MSE) of the estimated causal transition matrix $\mathbf{A}$. It can be seen that as the sample size T increases, both the proposed $\text{CDTA}_{\text{finite}}$ and the baseline method $\text{CDTA}_{\text{Gauss}}$ obtain smaller estimation errors. On the non-Gaussian data, $\text{CDTA}_{\text{Gauss}}$ produces much higher errors than $\text{CDTA}_{\text{finite}}$. On the Gaussian data, neither $\text{CDTA}_{\text{finite}}$ nor $\text{CDTA}_{\text{Gauss}}$ can obtain accurate estimations. This is because the estimation algorithms can converge to many possible solutions that have the same marginal likelihood, if the data noises are Gaussian or the estimation algorithms assume a Gaussian noise model. The results are consistent with the theoretical results that the causal relations might not be uniquely determined using Gaussian noise models. It can also be seen that the NG-EM method fails on the aggregated data, because NG-EM is proposed for subsampled rather than aggregated data.

Further, we examined the performance of the method described in Section 3.2, denoted as $\text{CDTA}_{\text{infty}}$, with finite k values. To achieve so, we generated aggregated data with $\mathbf{A} = \begin{bmatrix} 0.8 & 0.1 \\ 0.6 & 0.7 \end{bmatrix}$, aggregation factor $k = 2, 3, 4, 10$, and the same Gaussian mixture noise parameters described above. The true $\mathbf{A}^{\text{NoSelfLoop}}$ in this case can be calculated as $\mathbf{A}^{\text{NoSelfLoop}} = \begin{bmatrix} 0 & 0.5 \\ 2 & 0 \end{bmatrix}$. Using the linear instantaneous non-Gaussian model, we can obtain the estimations of $\mathbf{A}^{\text{NoSelfLoop}}$ on the aggregated data. The results for $k = 2, 3, 4, 10$ are given as follows:

$$\hat{\mathbf{A}}_2^{\text{NoSelfLoop}} = \begin{bmatrix} 0 & 0.52 \\ -13.5 & 0 \end{bmatrix}, \hat{\mathbf{A}}_3^{\text{NoSelfLoop}} = \begin{bmatrix} 0 & 0.47 \\ 1.43 & 0 \end{bmatrix},$$
$$\hat{\mathbf{A}}_4^{\text{NoSelfLoop}} = \begin{bmatrix} 0 & 0.44 \\ 1.61 & 0 \end{bmatrix}, \hat{\mathbf{A}}_{10}^{\text{NoSelfLoop}} = \begin{bmatrix} 0 & 0.51 \\ 2.03 & 0 \end{bmatrix}. \quad (22)$$

It seems that when $k \geq 4$, the linear instantaneous non-Gaussian causal model (10), which assumes that there is no self-loop, can estimate the corresponding $\mathbf{A}^{\text{NoSelfLoop}}$ accurately and very efficiently, at the cost of losing the self-loops in the original process. However, the self-loops can be estimated with $\text{CDTA}_{\text{finite}}$ when k is reasonably large. As a cautionary notice, researchers should carefully interpret the estimated parameters produced by linear instantaneous causal models, which assume there is no self-loop; as a consequence, the linear instantaneous non-Gaussian causal model produces $(1 - A_{jj})^{-1} A_{ji}$, whose magnitude can be very different from the true causal parameter A_{ji}.

5.2 REAL DATA

We conducted experiments on the Temperature Ozone data (Mooij et al., 2016) and the macroeconomic data used in (Moneta, 2008). These two time series are collected by averaging the records during specified time intervals. For example, the Temperature Ozone data contain daily mean values of ozone and temperature of year 2009 in Chaumont and Switzerland. The macroeconomic data contain quarterly US macro variables for the period 1947:2 to 1994:1.

Temperature Ozone. The Temperature Ozone data is the 50th causal-effect pair from the website `https://webdav.tuebingen.mpg.de/cause-effect/`. The data have records of ozone density X and daily mean temperature$Y$. The ground truth is causal relation is $Y \to X$. We first applied $\text{CDTA}_{\text{infty}}$ on the data, resulting in $\mathbf{A}^{\text{NoSelfLoop}} = \begin{bmatrix} 0 & 0.65 \\ 0.65 & 0 \end{bmatrix}$. From this result, we can find that instantaneous effects exist in both directions. This could possibly caused by aggregation with a small k as the estimated $\mathbf{A}^{\text{NoSelfLoop}}$ is likely to be inaccurate. We then estimated the causal matrix by $\text{CDTA}_{\text{finite}}$. The estimated transition matrix $\mathbf{A}$ for $k = 1, 2, 3$ is $\begin{bmatrix} 0.8418 & 0.0945 \\ 0.0165 & 0.9785 \end{bmatrix}$, $\begin{bmatrix} 0.8426 & 0.1151 \\ 0.0220 & 0.9702 \end{bmatrix}$, $\begin{bmatrix} 0.8360 & 0.1150 \\ 0.0172 & 0.9729 \end{bmatrix}$, respectively. It seems that the estimated matrices sensibly captured the self-influences and cross-influences between the ozone and temperature processes.

Macroeconomic Data The data are quarterly U.S. observational on real aggregated macroeconomic variables. Here we consider the causal relations between two variables, including real balances X and price inflation Y. X denotes the logarithm of per captita M2 minus the logarithm of the implicit price deflator. Y is the log of the implicit price deflator at the time t minus log of the implicit price deflator at the time $t - 1$. Again, we first applied the $\text{CDTA}_{\text{infty}}$ to find the rough estimation of causal relations excluding self-loops. The estimated $\mathbf{A}^{\text{NoSelfLoop}}$ is $\begin{bmatrix} 0 & 0 \\ 0.3074 & 0 \end{bmatrix}$. This indicates that no influence from effect to cause can be estimated from the instantaneous dependencies, which is consistent with the ground truth. We also employed $\text{CDTA}_{\text{finite}}$ to obtain the estimation of a complete causal transition matrix $\mathbf{A}$. The estimated transition matrix $\mathbf{A}$ for $k = 1, 2, 3, 4$ is $\begin{bmatrix} 1.009 & -0.0013 \\ 0.1718 & 0.5796 \end{bmatrix}$, $\begin{bmatrix} 0.9007 & -0.0011 \\ 0.2024 & 0.6420 \end{bmatrix}$, $\begin{bmatrix} 0.8503 & -0.0005 \\ 0.1378 & 0.7091 \end{bmatrix}$, respectively. We can see that $\mathbf{A}$ gives weaker responses from effect Y to cause X as k increases. If we consider $k = 4$ as the aggregation factor, then we can calculate from the estimated $\mathbf{A}$ that $\mathbf{A}^{\text{NoSelfLoop}} = \begin{bmatrix} 0 & 0.033 \\ 0.4737 & 0 \end{bmatrix}$, which is close to the results estimated by $\text{CDTA}_{\text{infty}}$.

6 CONCLUSION

In this paper, we have investigate the problem of discovering high frequency causal relations from temporally aggregated time series. When the aggregation factor is finite, we proved

Methods \ Data	non-Gaussian noise				Gaussian noise			
	k=2		k=3		k=2		k=3	
	T=150	T=300	T=150	T=300	T=150	T=300	T=150	T=300
$\text{CDTA}_{\text{finite}}$	**2.10e-4**	**1.19e-4**	**8.17e-4**	**7.36e-4**	1.42e-2	3.67e-3	7.63e-3	9.69e-3
$\text{CDTA}_{\text{Gauss}}$	1.28e-2	4.49e-3	1.20e-2	7.22e-3	1.13e-2	3.08e-3	6.26e-2	9.07e-3
NG-EM	8.75e-2	8.51e-2	5.27e-1	1.88e-1	-	-	-	-

Table 1: MSE of different methods on simulated non-Gaussian and Gaussian data. The results are shown for subsampling factors ($k = 2, 3$) and lengths of data ($T = 150, 300$).

that the causal relations are fully identifiable if the underlying causal relations are linear and the noise process is non-Gaussian. We also show that the causal matrix that removes self-loops is identifiable from instantaneous dependencies, when the aggregation factor goes to infinity. Based on these results, we propose an algorithm to recover the complete causal matrix when the aggregation factor is relatively small an an very efficient algorithm to partially recover the matrix when the aggregation factor is relatively large. Future work will focus on automatically estimating the aggregation factor k from data.

APPENDIX: PROOF OF THEOREM 1

Proof. Here we consider the limit when $T \to \infty$. According to the identifiability results of $\mathbf{A}^k$ (7), we have

$$\mathbf{A}^k = \mathbf{A}'^k. \tag{23}$$

We then consider the remaining error term $\vec{\mathbf{e}}_t$. The corresponding random vector $\vec{\mathbf{e}}$ follows both the representation (9) and

$$\mathbf{H}' \triangleq [\mathbf{I}, \ldots, \sum_{l=0}^{k-1} \mathbf{A}'^l, \sum_{l=1}^{k-1} \mathbf{A}'^l, \ldots, \sum_{l=k-2}^{k-1} \mathbf{A}'^l, \mathbf{A}'^{k-1}]. \tag{24}$$

$$\tilde{\mathbf{e}}' = (e'^{(0)}_1, ..., e'^{(0)}_n, e'^{(1)}_1, ..., e'^{(1)}_n, ..., e'^{(2k-2)}_1, ..., e'^{(2k-2)}_n)^\intercal \tag{25}$$

with $e'^{(l)}_i$, $l = 0, ..., 2k-2$, having the same distribution $p_{e'_i}$.

According to Proposition 1, each column of $\mathbf{H}'$ is a scaled version of a column of $\mathbf{H}$. Denote by $H_{ln+i}, l = 0, ..., 2k-2; i = 1, ..., n$, the $(ln+i)$th column of $\mathbf{H}$, and similarly for H'_{ln+i}. According to the Uniqueness Theorem in Eriksson & Koivunen (2004), we know that under condition A2, for each i, there exists one and only one j such that the distribution of $e^{(l)}_i$, $l = 0, ..., 2k-2$ (which have the same distribution), is the same as the distribution of $e'^{(l)}_j$, $l = 0, ..., 2k-2$, up to changes of location and scale. As a consequence, the columns $\{H'_{ln+j} \mid l = 0, ..., 2k-2\}$ correspond to $\{H_{ln+i} \mid l = 0, ..., 2k-2\}$ up to the permutation and scaling arbitrariness.

According to the structure of $\mathbf{H}$, $\forall\, m \le k-1$, $H_{kn+i} = H_{m+i} + H_{m+k+i}$, and similarly we have $\forall\, m \le k-1$, $H'_{kn+j} = H'_{m+j} + H'_{m+k+j}$. Hence, H_{kn+i} is proportional to H'_{kn+j}, i.e., $H'_{kn+j} = \lambda_{ki} H_{kn+i}$. Assume that $\sum_{l=0}^{1} \mathbf{A}'^l, \ldots, \sum_{l=0}^{k-1} \mathbf{A}'^l, \sum_{l=1}^{k-1} \mathbf{A}'^l, \ldots, \sum_{l=k-2}^{k-1} \mathbf{A}'^l$, $\mathbf{A}'^{k-1}$ are non-diagonal matrices, we have $H'_j = \lambda_{0i} H_i$. Since H_i and H'_j must be columns of $\mathbf{I}$, as implied by the structure of $\mathbf{H}$ and $\mathbf{H}'$, we can see that $\lambda_{0i} = 1$ and that $i = j$. Consequently, λ_{ki} must be 1 or -1. Let $\mathbf{B} = \mathbf{I} + \mathbf{A} + \ldots + \mathbf{A}^{k-1}$ and $\mathbf{B}' = \mathbf{I} + \mathbf{A}' + \ldots + \mathbf{A}'^{k-1}$, we thus have $\mathbf{B} = \mathbf{B}'\mathbf{D}$, where $\mathbf{D}$ is a diagonal matrix with 1 or -1 as its diagonal entries. Moreover, because $\mathbf{AB} - \mathbf{B} = \mathbf{A}^k - \mathbf{I}$ and $\mathbf{A}'\mathbf{B}' - \mathbf{B}' = \mathbf{A}'^k - \mathbf{I}$, and $\mathbf{A}^k = \mathbf{A}'^k$, we have

$$\mathbf{A}' - \mathbf{I} = (\mathbf{A} - \mathbf{I})\mathbf{D}. \tag{26}$$

If both $\mathbf{A}'$ and $\mathbf{A}$ have diagonal entries which are smaller than 1, $\mathbf{D}$ must be the identity matrix, i.e., $\mathbf{A}' = \mathbf{A}$. Therefore statement (i) is true.

If each p_{e_i} is asymmetric, e_i and $-e_i$ have different distributions. Consequently, the representation (24) does not hold any more if one changes the signs of a subset of, but not all, non-zero elements of $\{H'_{ln+j} \mid l = 0, ..., 2k-2\}$. This implies that for non-zero H_{ln+i}, λ_{li}, including λ_{0i}, have the same sign, and they are therefore 1 since $\lambda_{0i} = 1$. $\lambda_{ki} = 1$ leads to $\mathbf{D} = \mathbf{I}$ and thus gives $\mathbf{A}' = \mathbf{A}$. That is, (ii) is true. □

Acknowledgements

The authors would like to thank Dr. Tongliang Liu for helpful discussions. DT and MG would like to acknowledge the support from DP-140102164, FT-130101457, and LP-150100671. CG and KZ would like to acknowledge the support from NIH-1R01EB022858-01 FAIN-R01EB022858, NIH-1R01LM012087, and NIH-5U54HG008540-02 FAIN-U54HG008540.

References

Boot, J.CG., Feibes, W., and Lisman, J. Hubertus C. Further methods of derivation of quarterly figures from annual data. *Applied Statistics*, pp. 65–75, 1967.

Breitung, J. and Swanson, N. R. Temporal aggregation and spurious instantaneous causality in multiple time series models. *Journal of Time Series Analysis*, 23:651–665, 2002.

Danks, D. and Plis, S. Learning causal structure from undersampled time series. In *JMLR: Workshop and Conference Proceedings*, 2013.

Delyon, B., Lavielle, M., and Moulines, E. Convergence of a stochastic approximation version of the em algorithm. *Annals of statistics*, pp. 94–128, 1999.

Eriksson, J. and Koivunen, V. Identifiability, separability, and uniqueness of linear ICA models. *IEEE Signal Processing Letters*, 11(7):601–604, 2004.

Geiger, P., Zhang, K., Gong, M., Schölkopf, B., and Janzing, D. Causal inference by identification of vector autoregressive processes with hidden components. In *32nd International Conference on Machine Learning*, pp. 1917–1925. Microtome Publishing, 2015.

Ghysels, E., Hill, J.B., and Motegi, K. Testing for granger causality with mixed frequency data. *Journal of Econometrics*, 192(1): 207–230, 2016.

Gong, M., Zhang, K., Schölkopf, B., Tao, D., and Geiger, P. Discovering temporal causal relations from subsampled data. In *ICML*, pp. 1898–1906, 2015.

Granger, Clive WJ. Investigating causal relations by econometric models and cross-spectral methods. *Econometrica: Journal of the Econometric Society*, pp. 424–438, 1969.

Granger, Clive WJ. Implications of aggregation with common factors. *Econometric Theory*, 3(02):208–222, 1987.

Harvey, A. C. and Chung, C. H. Estimating the underlying change in unemployment in the uk. *Journal of the Royal Statistics Society, Series A*, 163:303–309, 2000.

Hyttinen, A., Plis, S., Järvisalo, M., Eberhardt, F., and Danks, D. Causal discovery from subsampled time series data by constraint optimization. In *International Conference on Probabilistic Graphical Models*, pp. 216–227, 2016.

Hyvärinen, A., Karhunen, J., and Oja, E. *Independent Component Analysis*. John Wiley & Sons, Inc, 2001.

Kuhn, E. and Lavielle, M. Coupling a stochastic approximation version of em with an mcmc procedure. *ESAIM: Probability and Statistics*, 8:115–131, 2004.

Lacerda, G., Spirtes, P., Ramsey, J., and Hoyer, P. O. Discovering cyclic causal models by independent components analysis. In *Proceedings of the 24th Conference on Uncertainty in Artificial Intelligence (UAI2008)*, Helsinki, Finland, 2008.

Lindsten, F. An efficient stochastic approximation em algorithm using conditional particle filters. In *Acoustics, Speech and Signal Processing (ICASSP), 2013 IEEE International Conference on*, pp. 6274–6278. IEEE, 2013.

Lindsten, F., Jordan, M. I, and Schön, T.B. Particle gibbs with ancestor sampling. *Journal of Machine Learning Research*, 15 (1):2145–2184, 2014.

Marcellino, M. Some consequences of temporal aggregation in empirical analysis. *Journal of Business and Economic Statistics*, 17:129–136, 1999.

Moauro, F. and Savio, G. Temporal disaggregation using multivariate structural time series models. *Journal of Econometrics*, 8:210–234, 2005.

Moneta, A. Graphical causal models and vars: an empirical assessment of the real business cycles hypothesis. *Empirical Economics*, 35(2):275–300, 2008.

Mooij, J. M, Peters, J., Janzing, D., Zscheischler, J., and Schölkopf, B. Distinguishing cause from effect using observational data: methods and benchmarks. *Journal of Machine Learning Research*, 17(32):1–102, 2016.

Palm, F. C. and Nijman, T. E. Missing observations in the dynamic regression model. *Econometrica*, 52:1415–1435, 1984.

Pearl, J. *Causality: Models, Reasoning, and Inference*. Cambridge University Press, Cambridge, 2000.

Plis, S., Danks, D., Freeman, C., and Calhoun, V. Rate-agnostic (causal) structure learning. In *Advances in neural information processing systems*, pp. 3303–3311, 2015a.

Plis, S., Danks, D., and Yang, J. Mesochronal structure learning. In *Proceedings of the 31st Conference on Uncertainty in Artificial Intelligence*, volume 31. NIH Public Access, 2015b.

Proietti, T. Temporal disaggregation by state space methods: Dynamic regression methods revisited. *The Econometrics Journal*, 9:357–372, 2006.

Rajaguru, G. and Abeysinghe, T. Temporal aggregation, cointegration and causality inference. *Economics Letters*, 101:223–226, 2008.

Shimizu, S., Hoyer, P.O., Hyvärinen, A., and Kerminen, A.J. A linear non-Gaussian acyclic model for causal discovery. *Journal of Machine Learning Research*, 7:2003–2030, 2006.

Silvestrini, A. and Veredas, D. Temporal aggregation of univariate and multivariate time series models: A survey. *Journal of Economic Surveys*, 22:458–497, 2008.

Sims, C. A. Macroeconomics and reality. *Econometrica*, 48:1–48, 1980.

Spirtes, P., Glymour, C., and Scheines, R. *Causation, Prediction, and Search*. MIT Press, Cambridge, MA, 2nd edition, 2001.

Stram, Daniel O and Wei, William WS. A methodological note on the disaggregation of time series totals. *Journal of Time Series Analysis*, 7(4):293–302, 1986.

Svensson, A., Schön, T.B., and Lindsten, F. Identification of jump markov linear models using particle filters. In *Decision and Control (CDC), 2014 IEEE 53rd Annual Conference on*, pp. 6504–6509. IEEE, 2014.

Tank, A., Fox, E.B., and Shojaie, A. Identifiability and estimation of structural vector autoregressive models for subsampled and mixed frequency time series. *arXiv preprint arXiv:1704.02519*, 2017.

Tiao, George C. Asymptotic behaviour of temporal aggregates of time series. *Biometrika*, pp. 525–531, 1972.

Van Nes, E.H., Scheffer, M., Brovkin, V., Lenton, T.M., Ye, H., Deyle, E., and Sugihara, G. Causal feedbacks in climate change. *Nature Climate Change*, 5(5):445–448, 2015.

Wei, G.CG. and Tanner, M.A. A monte carlo implementation of the em algorithm and the poor man's data augmentation algorithms. *Journal of the American statistical Association*, 85 (411):699–704, 1990.

Weiss, A. Systematic sampling and temporal aggregation in time series models. *Journal of Econometrics*, 26:271–281, 1984.

Zhou, D., Zhang, Y., Xiao, Y., and Cai, D. Analysis of sampling artifacts on the granger causality analysis for topology extraction of neuronal dynamics. *Frontiers in computational neuroscience*, 8, 2014.

Efficient Solutions for Stochastic Shortest Path Problems with Dead Ends

Felipe Trevizan
Data61, CSIRO
Australian National University
felipe.trevizan@anu.edu.au

Florent Teichteil-Königsbuch
Airbus
Central Research & Technology
florent.teichteil-koenigsbuch@airbus.com

Sylvie Thiébaux
Data61, CSIRO
Australian National University
sylvie.thiebaux@anu.edu.au

Abstract

Many planning problems require maximizing the probability of goal satisfaction as well as minimizing the expected cost to reach the goal. To model and solve such problems, there have been several attempts at extending Stochastic Shortest Path problems (SSPs) to deal with dead ends and optimize a dual optimization criterion. Unfortunately these extensions lack either theoretical robustness or practical efficiency. We study a new, perhaps more natural optimization criterion capturing these problems, the Min-Cost given Max-Prob (MCMP) criterion. This criterion leads to the minimum expected cost policy among those with maximum success probability, and accurately accounts for the cost and risk of reaching dead ends. Moreover, it lends itself to efficient solution methods that build on recent heuristic search algorithms for the dual representation of stochastic shortest paths problems. Our experiments show up to one order of magnitude speed-up over the state of the art.

INTRODUCTION

Stochastic Shortest Path Problems (SSPs) [Bertsekas and Tsitsiklis, 1991] are the *de facto* model for planning in stochastic environments in which an agent need to reach a goal state while minimizing the cost of doing so. Most theoretical results regarding SSPs assume that there are no dead ends in the environment, yet this is hardly the case in practice. Unfortunately, if dead ends are unavoidable, i.e., the probability of reaching the goal is always less than 1, SSPs implicitly become a multi-objective optimization problem with two potentially conflicting objectives: the maximization of the probability to reach the goal and the minimization of the expected cost to reach the goal.

To illustrate the conflict between these two objectives, consider a factory that can use either a human employee or a robot to manufacture a fragile good. Let the cost of the actions represent the cost in dollars of the actions for both the human (e.g., fraction of their salary) and the robot (e.g., cost of energy to perform the action) and the dead ends represent states in which the good cannot be manufactured anymore and the source materials are wasted. For this example, the robot is not capable of perfectly grasping the fragile source materials but if it succeeds ($p_r = 0.9$), the good can be perfectly manufactured due to the robots precision at an expected cost of \$100 for the electric energy used. Alternatively, human employees perfectly handle the fragile source materials; however, they lack the precision of the robot and can only complete the manufacture of the good with probability $p_h = 0.95$ with an expected labour cost of \$500. The conflict appears when these two options are compared: is it worth paying the extra \$400 to increase the probability of producing the good from 0.9 to 0.95?

One approach, known as Finite-Penalty [Mausam and Kolobov, 2012], is to assign a finite and fixed penalty D for not reaching the goal. For instance, the expected cost of assigning a human employee and a robot in the factory example is $475 + 0.05D$ and $90 + 0.1D$, respectively. Although intuitive, Finite-Penalty has the drawback of labelling any state with expected cost greater than D as a dead end. In our example, if the source materials cost \$10 and we use this value as dead-end penalty D, then using either the human or the robot are considered solutions that never reach the goal since their expected costs is greater than $D = 10$. Although it might be easy to derive a good value for D in our factory example, this is not the case for domain-independent planning (i.e., for algorithms that do not use knowledge of the problem being solved) which is the scope of this paper. For instance, there is no domain-independent method to derive D automatically given a problem description. There is also no known method to learn a function that returns, for all planning problems, a value of D that is always large enough but never so large that it leads to numerical instability or increased CPU time.

In order to avoid the need for the fixed penalty D (and its drawbacks), one can ignore the expected cost and maximize only the probability to reach the goal. This approach, known as Max-Prob [Kolobov et al., 2011], would always choose the human employee in the factory example; however it would be unable to distinguish between different employees with the same probability of success but with different pay rates. To be able to distinguish such cases in addition to getting rid of finite penalties for dead ends, two similar approaches have been proposed: S^3P [Teichteil-Königsbuch, 2012] and iSSPUDE [Kolobov et al., 2012]. Both approaches minimize the expected cost to reach the goal in a transformed SSP in which dead ends are removed and whose feasible solutions are exactly the same as the solutions that maximizes the probability of reaching the goal in the original problem. Unfortunately, computing this dead-end-free SSP potentially requires enumerating all the possible Max-Prob solutions which, as we later show, can be extremely inefficient.

In this paper, we introduce a new optimization criterion for SSPs with dead ends, the Min-Cost given Max-Prob (MCMP) criterion, which leads to the minimum expected cost policy among those with maximum success probability. MCMP differs from S^3P and iSSPUDE on how paths leading to dead ends are accounted for. This difference results in no transformation from the original SSP to a dead-end-free SSP being required, whether a priori or on-the-fly. As we show in our experiments, the optimal MCMP solution for SSPs can be computed up to 1 order of magnitude faster than its respective S^3P and iSSPUDE solution.

This performance improvement is due to how search is performed in the space of Max-Prob solutions: S^3P and iSSPUDE potentially compute the probability of reaching the goal for all the states reachable under any Max-Prob policy from the initial state. In contrast, MCMP need only find the maximum probability of reaching the goal from the initial state, and then search in the original SSP search space for a solution that minimizes the expected cost and reaches the goal with that probability. This allows MCMP to explore the original SSP search space using heuristics for both the probability of reaching the goal and the expected cost of reaching the goal. Moreover, the MCMP criterion is naturally expressed using dual formulation of SSPs and can trivially accommodate cost constraints; therefore, it also trivially applies to Constrained SSPs [Altman, 1999], which is not possible using S^3P or iSSPUDE.

NOTATION AND BACKGROUND

A Stochastic Shortest Path problem (SSP) [Bertsekas and Tsitsiklis, 1991] is a tuple $\mathbb{S} = \langle \mathsf{S}, s_0, \mathsf{G}, \mathsf{A}, P, C \rangle$ in which: S is the finite set of states; $s_0 \in \mathsf{S}$ is the initial state; $\mathsf{G} \subseteq \mathsf{S}$ is the non-empty set of goal states; A is the finite set of actions; $P(s'|s,a)$ is the probability that s' is reached after applying action a in state s; and $C(s,a) \in \mathbb{R}^*_+$ is the cost of applying action a in state s. We represent by $\mathsf{A}(s)$ the actions applicable in state s.

A solution to an SSP is a policy π mapping from states to actions. We denote by Π the set of all (deterministic) policies for $\mathbb{S}$. A trace $T_{\pi,s}$ is a sequence of states $s\, s_1 s_2 \ldots$ visited when following $\pi \in \Pi$ from s. We denote the i-th state of $T_{\pi,s}$ by $T^i_{\pi,s}$ and require that $P(T^{i+1}_{\pi,s}|T^i_{\pi,s}, \pi(T^i_{\pi,s})) > 0$ for all pairs $T^i_{\pi,s}T^{i+1}_{\pi,s} \in T_{\pi,s}$. If s is omitted, then s_0 is implied. Also, π is omitted when clear from context.

A trace T can be finite or infinite. If finite, the last state s of T is either a goal state (i.e., $s \in \mathsf{G}$) or there is no applicable action in s (i.e., $\mathsf{A}(s) = \emptyset$). Moreover, for a finite trace T, its probability is $P(T) = \prod_{i=1}^{|T|} P(T^{i+1}|T^i, \pi(T^i))$ and its cost is $C(T) = \sum_{i=1}^{|T|} C(T^i, \pi(T^i))$. Infinite traces happen when the execution of π enters a cycle that never reaches the goal, getting trapped there forever. Since action costs are strictly positive, the cost of any infinite trace is infinity.

We denote by $\mathsf{T}_{\pi,s}$ the set of all traces of π from s. Notice that $\mathsf{T}_{\pi,s}$ may be an infinite set (e.g., if an action prescribed by π has a positive probability of looping). We also partition $\mathsf{T}_{\pi,s}$ into the set of traces that reach the goal ($\mathsf{T}^{\mathsf{G}}_{\pi,s}$) and its complement $\mathsf{T}^{\mathsf{DE}}_{\pi,s}$, i.e, the set of traces that do not reach the goal. While every trace in $\mathsf{T}^{\mathsf{G}}_{\pi,s}$ is finite (because its last state must be a goal state), $\mathsf{T}^{\mathsf{DE}}_{\pi,s}$ can have infinite traces, that is, traces that loop indefinitely without reaching a goal state. We use the same notation simplifications for $\mathsf{T}_{\pi,s}$ and its partitions as for traces.

Most results and algorithms for SSPs assume that there are no unavoidable dead ends, i.e., there exists a policy for which the goal can be reached from the initial state with probability 1. Using our trace notation, this is equivalent to assuming that there exists a policy π such that $\mathsf{T}^{\mathsf{DE}}_{\pi,s_0} = \emptyset$. When this assumption holds, the optimal solution of an SSP is characterized by a unique fixed-point solution for the following set of equations, known as Bellman equations:

$$V^*(s) = \min_{a \in A(s)} C(s,a) + \sum_{s' \in \mathsf{S}} P(s'|s,a) V^*(s')$$

for all $s \in \mathsf{S} \setminus \mathsf{G}$ and $V^*(s_g) = 0$ for all $s_g \in \mathsf{G}$. Any greedy policy w.r.t. to the optimal value function V^* (i.e., by applying argmin instead of $\min$) is an optimal policy.

In the presence of dead ends, the Bellman equations might diverge resulting in the optimal solution to be ill-defined. This is always the case when the problem has unavoidable dead ends. Several criteria have been proposed to characterize the optimal solution of SSPs with dead ends, such as the Finite-Penalty criterion:

Definition 1 (Finite-Penalty). *Given a dead-end penalty $D \in \mathbb{R}^*_+$, find a greedy policy for the unique fixed-point solution of:*

$$V^*_{FP}(s) = \min\{D, \min_{a \in \mathsf{A}(s)} C(s,a) + \sum_{s' \in \mathsf{S}} P(s'|s,a) V^*_{FP}(s')\}$$

for all $s \in \mathsf{S} \setminus \mathsf{G}$ and $V^*_{FP}(s_g) = 0$ for all $s_g \in \mathsf{G}$.

The Finite-Penalty criterion is equivalent to solving the SSP $\mathbb{S}' = \langle \mathsf{S}, s_0, \mathsf{G}, \mathsf{A}', P', C' \rangle$ where, for all $s \in \mathsf{S}$, $\mathsf{A}'(s) = \mathsf{A}(s) \cup \{\text{give-up}\}$, $C'(s, \text{give-up}) = D$, $C'(s,a) = C(s,a)$ for $a \in \mathsf{A}(s)$, and $P(s_g|s, \text{give-up}) = 1$ for any $s_g \in \mathsf{G}$. Notice that $\mathbb{S}'$ has no dead ends and can be solved using any algorithm for SSPs.

A drawback of the Finite-Penalty criterion is that every state with expected cost of reaching the goal greater than the dead-end penalty D is considered a dead end, regardless of its maximum probability of reaching the goal. E.g.,

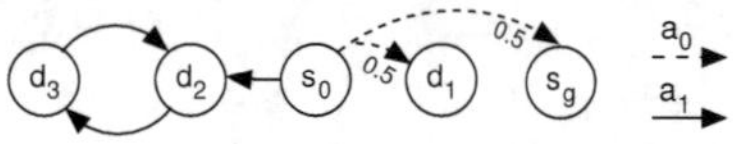

Figure 1: Example of SSP with multiple fixed-point solutions for P^*. The goal set is $\mathsf{G} = \{s_g\}$ and $P^*(s_0) = 0.5$.

consider a simple SSP with two states s_0 and s_g ($G=\{s_g\}$) and one action a s.t. $P(s_g|s_0,a)=p>0$ and $P(s_0|s_0,a)=1-p$. If $C(s,a)/p$ is greater than D then s_0 is considered a dead end under the Finite-Penalty criterion and its optimal policy prescribes the "give-up" action for s_0 even though the probability of reaching s_g from s_0 is 1. To overcome this, an alternative is to directly maximize the probability of reaching the goal, a criterion known as Max-Prob:

Definition 2 (Max-Prob)**.** *Find a policy π that maximizes the probability of reaching any goal state $s_g \in \mathsf{G}$ when following π from s_0, i.e.,* $\text{argmax}_{\pi \in \sqcap} P(\mathsf{T}^{\mathsf{G}}_{\pi,s_0})$. *We denote by p^{max} this maximum probability and by $\sqcap^{MP}$ the set of all Max-Prob policies, i.e.,* $\{\pi \in \sqcap | P(\mathsf{T}^{\mathsf{G}}_{\pi,s_0}) = p^{max}\}$.

The optimal solution under the Max-Prob criterion can be computed by solving a problem $\mathcal{M}$ in which everything stays the same as in the original SSP $\mathbb{S}$ except that we want to *maximize* the expected sum, over all traces $T \in \mathsf{T}_{\pi,s_0}$, of the function $R(s,a) = \sum_{s_g \in \mathsf{G}} P(s_g|s,a)$. We denote the solution of the Bellman equations for $\mathcal{M}$ as P^* and $P^*(s)$ represents the maximum probability of reaching the goal from $s \in \mathsf{S}$ (thus $p^{\max}$ equals $P^*(s_0)$). Also, $P^*(s) \in [0,1]$ for all s even if $\mathcal{M}$ has unavoidable dead ends; however, the Bellman equations for $\mathcal{M}$ can have several non-optimal fixed-point solutions. For instance, the SSP in Fig. 1 has the following *non-optimal* fixed-point solution for $\mathcal{M}$: $P(d_1) = 0$ and $P(s_g) = P(s_0) = P(d_2) = P(d_3) = 1$.

One approach to compute P^* (and avoid being trapped in a non-optimal solution) is to apply value iteration on $\mathcal{M}$ after initializing the algorithm with 1 for all $s_g \in \mathsf{G}$ and 0 otherwise. Another approach is to solve $\mathcal{M}$ using heuristic search algorithms such as FRET [Kolobov et al., 2011] and FRET-π [Steinmetz et al., 2016]. Both these algorithms iterate between: (i) finding a fixed-point solution for P^* using any optimal heuristic search algorithm for SSPs; and (ii) post processing the candidate solution to remove cycles that have not converged to P^*. In our example from Fig. 1, step (ii) would identify the loop between d_2 and d_3 and update $P(d_2)$ and $P(d_3)$ to 0.

In addition to the non-optimal fixed-point solutions, the Max-Prob criterion has another drawback: all policies in $\sqcap^{MP}$ are equally good for Max-Prob, independently of their expected cost. The S^{3}P criterion addresses this isssue:

Definition 3 (S^{3}P [Teichteil-Königsbuch, 2012])**.** *Find a policy*

$$\pi = \underset{\pi \in \sqcap^{MP}}{\text{argmin}} \ \mathbf{E}[C(T) \,|\, T \in \mathsf{T}^{\mathsf{G}}_{\pi,s_0}].$$

The S^{3}P criterion is inspired by the evaluation metric used at the International Probabilistic Planning Competition (IPPC) up to 2008 [Younes et al., 2005, Bryce and Buffet, 2008] that accounted both for the proportion of simulations of a policy that reached the goal and for the average cost accumulated by these policies only when they reached the goal. Thus, S^{3}P only considers policies in $\sqcap^{MP}$ and the traces of these policies that reach the goal. Moreover, given our assumption of $C(s,a) > 0$ for all $s \in \mathsf{S}$ and $a \in \mathsf{A}(s)$, the S^{3}P criterion is equivalent to the iSSPUDE criterion [Kolobov et al., 2012]. Given P^*, the S^{3}P optimal solution of an SSP is equivalent to the optimal solution of the following transformed SSP [Kolobov et al., 2012]:

Definition 4 (P^*-SSP)**.** *Given an SSP $\langle \mathsf{S}, s_0, \mathsf{G}, \mathsf{A}, P, C\rangle$ and its P^*, the P^*-SSP is the tuple $\langle \mathsf{S}, s_0, \mathsf{G}, \mathsf{A}', P', C\rangle$ where: $\mathsf{A}'(s) = \mathsf{A}(s)$ if $P^*(s) > 0$ and empty otherwise; and $P'(s'|s,a) = P(s'|s,a)P^*(s')/P^*(s)$ if $P^*(s) > 0$ and 0 otherwise.*

Since P^*-SSP has no dead ends, any SSP algorithm can be used for solving it. In practice, P^* can be computed on-the-fly while solving the P^*-SSP, as we do in our experiments.

MCMP CRITERION

As shown in the previous section, the S^{3}P criterion extends the Max-Prob criterion by ranking Max-Prob policies according to their expected cost when the traces reaching dead ends are ignored. One drawback of this approach is that, when executing an S^{3}P optimal policy $\pi^*_{\text{S}^3\text{P}}$, unavoidable dead ends will still be reached and the cost of doing so will also be incurred; therefore the optimal value computed by the S^{3}P algorithms might be different from the expected cost obtained by an execution $\pi^*_{\text{S}^3\text{P}}$. In this section we adress this issue, but first let us define the function ψ that truncates a trace at the first encountered dead end state:

Definition 5 (ψ)**.** *Let $\psi\colon \mathsf{T} \mapsto \mathsf{T}$ be the function:*

$$\psi(s_i s_{i+1} \cdots) = \begin{cases} s_i & \text{if } |T|=1 \text{ or } P(\mathsf{T}^{\mathsf{G}}_{s_i})=0 \\ s_i\,\psi(s_{i+1}\cdots) & \text{otherwise} \end{cases}$$

Notice that the $\psi(T)$ is always a finite trace since either a goal is reached or a state s_i with probability 0 of reaching the goal ($P(\mathsf{T}^{\mathsf{G}}_{s_i}) = 0$) is reached and $s_{i+1}s_{i+2}\cdots$ are ignored. Moreover, $\psi(T) = T$ for all $T \in \mathsf{T}^{\mathsf{G}}$.

Our optimal criterion for SSPs with dead ends, the Min-Cost given Max-Prob (MCMP) is defined in Definition 6 and, although it does not distinguish the different traces reaching the same dead end, it differs from S^{3}P because MCMP considers the complete set of traces T_{π,s_0}. Example 1 illustrates the differences between S^{3}P and MCMP and show that their optimal policies can be different.

Definition 6 (MCMP)**.** *The Min-Cost Max-Prob (MCMP) problem is to find a policy*

$$\pi = \underset{\pi \in \sqcap^{MP}}{\text{argmin}} \ \mathbf{E}[C(\psi(T))].$$

Example 1. *Consider the SSP in Fig. 2. There are two possible policies in this SSP: π_0 that always applies a_0 and π_1 that always applies a_1. The probability of reaching s_g for*

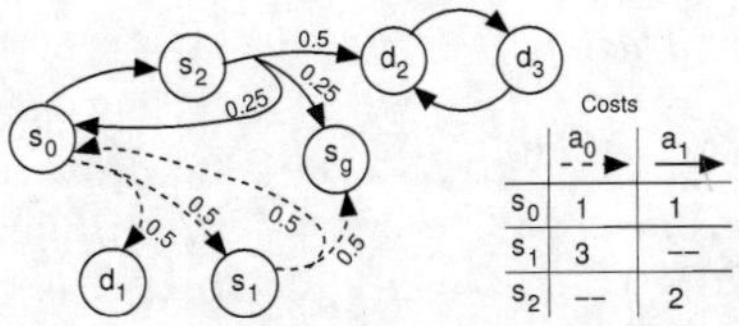

Figure 2: Example of SSP. The goal is $\mathsf{G} = \{s_g\}$. The initial state is s_0 and states d_1, d_2 and d_3 are dead ends. See Example 1 for more details.

each one of them is: $P(\mathsf{T}^{\mathsf{G}}_{s_0,\pi_0}) = .5(.5 + .5P(\mathsf{T}^{\mathsf{G}}_{s_0,\pi_0})) = 1/3$ *and* $P(\mathsf{T}^{\mathsf{G}}_{s_0,\pi_1}) = .25 + .25P(\mathsf{T}^{\mathsf{G}}_{s_0,\pi_1}) = 1/3$, *thus* $\Pi^{MP} = \{\pi_0, \pi_1\}$ *and* $p^{max} = 1/3$. *For the* S^3P *criterion, we have:*

π_0: *Only traces of the form* $(s_0 s_1)^+ s_g$ *are considered, where* $(s_0 s_1)^+$ *represent 1 or more repetitions of the sequence* $s_0 s_1$. *The expected cost of* π_0 *is* $V^{\pi_0}_{S^3P}(s_0) = (\sum_{i=1}^{\infty}(0.5 \times 0.5)^i (1+3)i)/p^{max} = 16/3$.

π_1: *Only* $(s_0 s_2)^+ s_g$ *traces are considered. The expected cost of* π_1 *is* $V^{\pi_1}_{S^3P}(s_0) = (\sum_{i=1}^{\infty}(1 \times 0.25)^i (1+2)i)/p^{max} = 4$.

For MCMP, we have:

π_0: *All traces in* T_{π_0,s_0} *are finite since* $A(d_1) = \emptyset$. *Thus* $\psi(T) = T$ *for all* $T \in \mathsf{T}_{\pi_0,s_0}$. *Since* s_g *is reached with probability* $p^{max} = 1/3$, *then* s_1 *is visited in expectation* $p^{max}/0.5 = 2/3$ *and* s_0 *visited* $(2/3)/0.5 = 4/3$. *Thus,* $V^{\pi_0}_{MCMP}(s_0) = 4/3 + 3 \times 2/3 = 10/3$.

π_1: *Since* d_2 *is the first state in the infinite loop* $d_2 d_3 d_2 \cdots$, $\psi(s_0 \cdots s_2 d_2 d_3 d_2 \cdots) = s_0 \cdots s_2 d_2$. *Thus, we only need to consider the expected number of times the costs* $C(s_0, a_1) = 1$ *and* $C(s_2, a_1) = 2$ *are incurred. Since* s_g *is reached with probability* $p^{max} = 1/3$, *then* s_0 *and* s_1 *are visited in expectation* $p^{max}/0.25 = 4/3$. *Therefore* $V^{\pi_1}_{MCMP}(s_0) = 4/3(1+2) = 4$.

Therefore, $V^{\pi_0}_{MCMP}(s_0) < V^{\pi_1}_{MCMP}(s_0) = V^{\pi_1}_{S^3P}(s_0) < V^{\pi_0}_{S^3P}(s_0)$, *and the optimal policy according to the MCMP and* S^3P *criteria is* π_0 *and* π_1, *respectively.*

As illustrated above, ignoring the traces that reaches dead ends can lead to unexpected optimal policies. In the case of our factory scenario from the introduction, the S^{3}P criterion would consider that we do not have to pay for electricity or the employee wages if a failure happened when producing the good. In contrast, the MCMP criterion accounts for all the cost until a dead end is reached, therefore, the electricity and employee wages are considered.

ALGORITHM FOR MCMP

Although it might seem costly to detect the infinite traces and prune them, this can be efficiently done by solving LP 1 using the heuristic search algorithm i-dual [Trevizan et al., 2016] (more below). This LP is a modified version of the dual LP for SSPs with no dead ends [Altman, 1999]. Its variables are the policy's occupation measures $x_{s,a}$ representing the expected number of times action $a \in A(s)$ will be executed in state s.

$$\min_x \sum_{s \in \mathsf{S}, a \in \mathsf{A}} x_{s,a} C(s,a) \quad \text{s.t. (C1) – (C6)} \qquad \text{(LP 1)}$$

$$x_{s,a} \geq 0 \qquad \forall s \in \mathsf{S}, a \in \mathsf{A}(s) \quad \text{(C1)}$$

$$in(s) = \sum_{s' \in \mathsf{S}, a \in \mathsf{A}(s')} x_{s',a} P(s|s', a) \qquad \forall s \in \mathsf{S} \quad \text{(C2)}$$

$$out(s) = \sum_{a \in \mathsf{A}(s)} x_{s,a} \qquad \forall s \in \mathsf{S} \setminus \mathsf{G} \quad \text{(C3)}$$

$$out(s) - in(s) \leq 0 \qquad s \in \mathsf{S} \setminus (\mathsf{G} \cup \{s_0\}) \quad \text{(C4)}$$

$$out(s_0) - in(s_0) \leq 1 \qquad \text{(C5)}$$

$$\sum_{s_g \in \mathsf{G}} in(s_g) = p^{\max} \qquad \text{(C6)}$$

The modifications in LP 1 from the regular dual LP are on constraint C4 – C6. These modifications implicitly allow states to choose a give-up action as in the Finite-Penalty criterion; however, this implicit give-up action *has cost zero*. The implicit give-up actions are encoded in C4 and C5 by upper bounding the conservation of flow instead of using an equality constraint. Formally, C4 is equivalent to $out(s) - in(s) + x_{s,\text{give-up}} = 0$ for $x_{s,\text{give-up}} \geq 0$ and $C(s, \text{give-up}) = 0$, thus not affecting the objective value. Moreover, C6 constrains the solution found by LP 1 to be in Π^{MP} because it enforces that, from the one unit of flow injected in the system (C5), $p^{\max}$ units of flow reach the goal ($p^{\max}$ is a constant for LP 1). Therefore, the implicit give-up actions are only used when strictly necessary, as otherwise not enough flow would reach the goal. They are used in a state s that either: has no applicable action, in which case $out(s)$ can only be zero while $in(s)$ might be greater than 0; or is an infinite loop that never reaches the goal, in which case the give-up action avoids an infinite cost.

Computing the MCMP solution using LP 1 has the advantage that it only requires $p^{\max}$, which can be computed by finding any Max-Prob policy $\pi \in \Pi^{\text{MP}}$. In contrast, the S^{3}P criterion requires the P^*-SSP, thus all Max-Prob policies will be considered in the worst case. Another advantage is that we can solve LP 2 to compute $p^{\max}$ and, since the optimal solution x^* for LP 2 (below) is a feasible solution for LP 1, we can use x^* to *warm start* the search in LP 1.

$$\max_x \sum_{s_g \in \mathsf{G}} in(s_g) \quad \text{s.t. (C1) – (C3), (C7) – (C8)} \qquad \text{(LP 2)}$$

$$out(s) - in(s) = 0 \qquad \forall s \in \mathsf{S} \setminus (\mathsf{G} \cup \{s_0\}) \quad \text{(C7)}$$

$$out(s_0) - in(s_0) = 1 \qquad \text{(C8)}$$

LP 2 uses the original dual SSP flow constraints (C7 and C8) and it represents the dual formulation for the Max-Prob problem: we inject one unit of flow in s_0 and maximize the flow reaching the sink, i.e., the goal. Its optimal value is $p^{\max}$ and its optimal solution x^* can be converted into an optimal Max-Prob policy $\pi^*_{\text{MP}}(s) = a$ where $a \in A(s)$ is the only action such that $x_{s,a} > 0$ [Altman,

1999]. Differently from the space explored by Value Iteration, FRET, and FRET-π, the dual space explored by LP 2 does not contain non-optimal fixed-point solutions. For instance, in the SSP shown in Fig. 1, the dual formulation prevents any flow from reaching d_2 because, by C7, we have: $out(d_2) - in(d_2) = x_{d_2,a_1} - (x_{s_0,a_1} + x_{d_3,a_1}) = x_{s_0,a_1} = 0$.

Lastly, i-dual [Trevizan et al., 2016] can be used to efficiently solve LP 1 and LP 2 using heuristic search. Given an SSP, i-dual generates and solves increasingly large LPs (in the dual representation) to solve the current SSP. A parameter of i-dual is a cost heuristic for SSPs and this heuristic is used for choosing what states should be expanded to generate the next LP. I-dual can be trivially adapted for the MCMP criterion as follows. For solving LP 1 (MCMP second phase), LP 1 is used as template in line 12 of the original i-dual pseudo-code. Notice that, the heuristic for this stage is any cost heuristic for SSPs, e.g., $h^{\max}$ [Teichteil-Königsbuch et al., 2011], h^{roc} and h^{pom} [Trevizan et al., 2017]. Similarly, the first stage of MCMP (Max-Prob) can be solved by using LP 2 as template for the generation of LPs in line 12 of i-dual. It is important to notice that, for the first stage of MCMP, the cost of actions is ignored (LP 2 does not uses the cost function of the SSP) and the heuristic passed as a parameter to i-dual is a (admissible) Max-Prob heuristic, i.e., a (upper) bound on P^*. For both stages, the dead-end penalties required by i-dual are ignored since both LP 1 and LP 2 do not use them. The parameter $p^{\max}$ of LP 2 is obtained as the objective function of the last LP generated by i-dual when solving the first stage of MCMP.

RELATIONS BETWEEN CRITERIA

A property of the MCMP criterion, independently of the approach used to solve it, is that a dead-end penalty can be easily incorporated to the MCMP solution without the need to re-solve the problem. Formally, given $p^{\max}$ and $V^*_{\text{MCMP}}(s_0)$, the optimal solution cost for s_0 with dead-end penalty D is $V^*_{\text{MCMP}}(s_0) + (1 - p^{\max})D$. This is equivalent to use $C(\psi(T)) + D$ as the cost for all traces $T \in \mathsf{T}^{\text{DE}}$ since $\mathbf{E}[C(\psi(T)) + D | T \in \mathsf{T}^{\text{DE}}] = \mathbf{E}[C(\psi(T)) | T \in \mathsf{T}^{\text{DE}}] + D$.

The advantage of this approach over Finite-Penalty is that states s s.t. $P(\mathsf{T}^{\mathsf{G}}_s) > 0$ can have expected value greater than D, that is, the planner cannot avoid a large expected cost solution from s by using the give-up action. For instance, consider Example 1 and let the dead-end penalty be $D = 0.5$. For Finite-Penalty, we have $V^{\pi_0}_{\text{FP}}(s_0) = V^{\pi_1}_{\text{FP}}(s_0) = 0.5$ since $C(s_0, a_0) = C(s_0, a_1) = 1 > D$; moreover, $\pi^*_{\text{FP}}(s_0) =$ give-up. Alternatively, for MCMP, the optimal policy is π_0 and its expected cost with the dead-end penalty is $10/3 + 0.5 \times 2/3 = 11/3$.

This intuition that the MCMP criterion captures the expected cost from s_0 more accurately than Finite-Penalty is formalized in the following theorem:

Theorem 1. *Let V^*_{FP} and V^*_{MCMP} be the optimal solution of Finite-Penalty and MCMP, respectively, for the same SSP and $D \in \mathbb{R}^*_+$ be the dead-end penalty used by Finite-Penalty. Then*

$$V^*_{FP}(s_0) \leq V^*_{MCMP}(s_0) + (1 - p^{max})D$$

Proof Sketch. Notice that $V^*_{\text{FP}}(d) = D$ for all $d \in \mathsf{S}$ such that $P(\mathsf{T}^{\mathsf{G}}_d) = 0$ since d either (i) has no applicable action and thus it is assigned a cost of D; or (ii) is in a loop that never reaches the goal, thus it has infinite expected cost and the min operator of Finite-Penalty limits its expected cost to D. Therefore, $(1 - p^{\max})D$ is equivalent to the expected cost incurred in the Finite-Penalty for all such states d. Moreover, by the definition of Finite-Penalty, $V^*_{\text{FP}}(s) \leq D$ for all $s \in \mathsf{S}$ even if $P(\mathsf{T}^{\mathsf{G}}_s) = 1$. Thus Finite-Penalty considers states with expected cost greater than D as dead ends. However, this is not the case for MCMP and $V^*_{\text{MCMP}}(s)$ can be arbitrarily large since it accounts for the real costs of transitions independently of D. Thus, $V^*_{\text{FP}}(s_0) - (1 - p^{\max})D \leq V^*_{\text{MCMP}}(s_0)$. □

Similarly to MCMP, we can add a dead-end penalty in S^{3}P criterion, i.e., define $C(T) = D$ for $T \in \mathsf{T}^{\text{DE}}$. Formally,

$$\begin{aligned}
&\mathbf{E}[C(T)] \\
&= p^{\max}\,\mathbf{E}[C(T)|T \in \mathsf{T}^{\mathsf{G}}] + (1 - p^{\max})\,\mathbf{E}[C(T)|T \in \mathsf{T}^{\text{DE}}] \\
&= p^{\max} V^*_{\text{S}^3\text{P}}(s_0) + (1 - p^{\max})\,\mathbf{E}[C(T)|T \in \mathsf{T}^{\text{DE}}] \\
&\geq p^{\max} V^*_{\text{S}^3\text{P}}(s_0) + (1 - p^{\max})D
\end{aligned}$$

Thus, we are effectively approximating the cost of all traces reaching a dead end by D. Unfortunately, it is not always the case that this extension of the S^{3}P criterion captures the expected cost from s_0 more accurately than Finite-Penalty as shown in the following theorem:

Theorem 2. *Let V^*_{FP} and $V^*_{S^3P}$ be the optimal solution of Finite-Penalty and S^{3}P, respectively, for the same SSP and $D \in \mathbb{R}^*_+$ be the dead-end penalty used by Finite-Penalty. Then $p^{max} V^*_{S^3P}(s_0) + (1 - p^{max})D$ is neither a lower nor an upper bound for V^*_{FP} as a function of D.*

Proof. Consider the SSP in Fig. 2 with the following modifications: (i) there is only action a_0; and (ii) $C(s_0, a_0) = C(s_1, a_0) = c \in \mathbb{R}^*_+$. As shown in Example 1, $p^{\max} = 1/3$ and $V^*_{\text{S}^3\text{P}}(s_0) = 8c/3$. For Finite-Penalty, we have: $V^*_{\text{FP}}(s_0) = \min\{D, c + .5D + .5V^*_{\text{FP}}(s_1)\} = \min\{D, c + .5D + .5(\min\{D, c + .5V^*_{\text{FP}}(s_0)\})\} = \min\{D, 2c + 2D/3\}$. Thus, if $0 < c < 3D/8$ then $V^*_{\text{S}^3\text{P}}(s_0)/p^{\max} + (1 - p^{\max})D = 8c/3 + 2D/3 < V^*_{\text{FP}}(s_0) \leq D$ and if $c > 3D/8$, then $V^*_{\text{FP}}(s_0) = D < 8c/3 + 2D/3$. □

Lastly, the following theorem shows that, by considering the traces leading to dead ends, the MCMP criterion captures the expected cost from s_0 more accurately than S^{3}P:

Theorem 3. *Let $V^*_{S^3P}$ and V^*_{MCMP} be the optimal solution of S^{3}P and MCMP, respectively, for the same SSP. Then $p^{max} V^*_{S^3P}(s_0) \leq V^*_{MCMP}(s_0)$.*

Proof. This follows from their respective definitions: $V^*_{\text{MCMP}}(s_0) = \mathbf{E}[C(\psi(T)] = p^{\max}\,\mathbf{E}[C(\psi(T))|T \in \mathsf{T}^{\mathsf{G}}] + (1 - p^{\max})\,\mathbf{E}[C(\psi(T))|T \in \mathsf{T}^{\text{DE}}] \geq p^{\max}\,\mathbf{E}[C(\psi(T))|T \in \mathsf{T}^{\mathsf{G}}] = p^{\max} V^*_{\text{S}^3\text{P}}(s_0)$. □

MCMP FOR CONSTRAINED SSPs

Another advantage of implementing the MCMP criterion via LP 1 and LP 2 is that we can add cost constraints to both LPs, and thus easily apply the MCMP criterion to Constrained SSPs (C-SSPs) [Altman, 1999]. In a C-SSP, multiple cost functions capture potentially competing objectives (e.g., time, money). One of these objectives is optimized whilst constraining the others.

Formally, a C-SSP $\langle \mathsf{S}, s_0, \mathsf{G}, \mathsf{A}, P, \vec{C}, \vec{u} \rangle$ is an SSP whose cost function is replaced by a vector of $n+1$ cost functions $\vec{C} = [C_0, \ldots, C_n]$ and a vector of n bounds $\vec{u} = [u_1, \ldots, u_n]$ ($u_j > 0$ for all j). We call C_0 the *primary cost* and the other cost functions the *secondary costs*. An optimal solution for a C-SSP is a *stochastic* policy $\pi : \mathsf{S} \mapsto \mathsf{A} \times [0,1]$, which minimizes the expected primary cost C_0 to reach the goal G from the s_0, subject to the expected values of the secondary cost C_j being upper bounded by u_j for $j \in \{1, \ldots, n\}$. These stochastic policies are needed to optimally account for trade-offs between the various cost functions, but do not alter the complexity of optimally solving C-SSPs which remains polynomial in the size of the C-SSP [Dolgov and Durfee, 2005].

Currently, the only approach to solve C-SSP with dead ends is Finite-Penalty [Trevizan et al., 2016] and, as shown in Section 3, the MCMP criterion has several advantages over Finite-Penalty. We can apply MCMP to C-SSPs by replacing $C(s,a)$ with $C_0(s,a)$ in LP 1 and augmenting both LP 2 and LP 1 with constraints of the form:

$$\sum_{s \in \mathsf{S}, a \in \mathsf{A}(s)} x_{s,a} C_j(s,a) \leq u_j \qquad \forall j \in \{1, \ldots, n\} \qquad \text{(C9)}$$

As before, i-dual can be used to optimally solve these LPs using heuristic search, provided admissible heuristics $H_j(s) \leq V_j^*(s)$ are available for each of the cost functions C_j. The only difference with the SSP case is that the policies in Π^{MP} are now potentially stochastic.

EMPIRICAL EVALUATION

In this section, we empirically evaluate different algorithms for solving SSPs using the $\mathrm{S}^3\mathrm{P}$ and MCMP criteria and C-SSPs using the Finite-Penalty and MCMP criteria. All our experiments were conducted on a cluster of Intel E5-2660 run at 2.60GHz and, unless noted otherwise, we enforced a cputime and memory cutoff of 30 minutes and 10Gb, respectively. We used Gurobi 6.5 as LP solver and our results are averaged over 30 runs using different random seeds. The coverage for each planner is the number of runs in which a given planner successfully finds the optimal solution for the same problem under different random seeds.

Experiments on SSPs

We implemented two planners for $\mathrm{S}^3\mathrm{P}$. The first planner computes P^* using FRET [Kolobov et al., 2012] (LRTDP [Bonet and Geffner, 2003] is used as Find-and-Revise algorithm) and then solves P^*-SSP using LRTDP. The second planner is the same as the first one but FRET-π is used instead of FRET. We implemented the P^*-SSP using a lazy evaluation of P^*, i.e., FRET and FRET-π are called on-demand to give values for P^*. Every time we computed $P^*(s)$, we also cached the values of any other state s' in which $P^*(s')$ has also converged. This lazy approach is particularly beneficial for FRET-π since its focused search can find $P^*(s)$ for a single optimal policy as opposed to FRET that converges over the union of the greedy policies; therefore, the heuristic search performed by LRTDP in the second stage can avoid the query of P^* for states that are too expensive to visit. We refer to these planners for $\mathrm{S}^3\mathrm{P}$ as FRET and FRET-π.

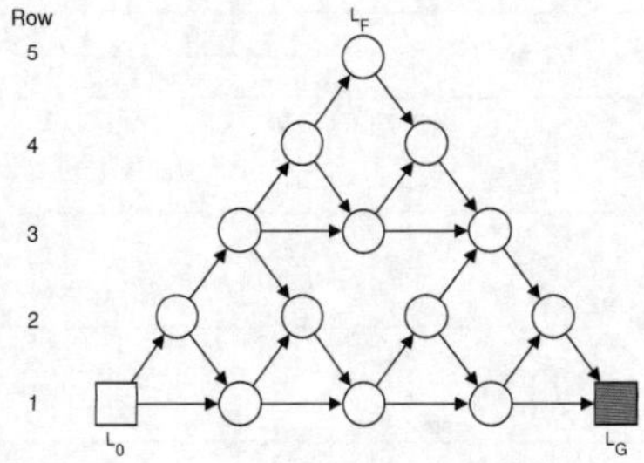

Figure 3: Map for the triangle tireworld problem #2. The goal is to reach location L_G from location L_0. Location L_F represents the opposite corner from L_0 and L_G.

To solve SSPs using the MCMP criterion, we implemented i-dual to solve both LP 2 and LP 1 and use the solution of the former to warm start the latter. For all planners considered in this section, we used $h^{\max}$ over the all-outcomes determinization as heuristic for both stages [Teichteil-Königsbuch et al., 2011]. The Max-Prob version of $h^{\max}$ returns 0 if no solution is found, i.e., a queried state is a dead end, and 1 otherwise. We consider problems in the following domains:

Exploding Blocks World. From the IPPC'08 [Bryce and Buffet, 2008], this domain is a probabilistic extension of the deterministic blocks world in which blocks can explode and destroy other blocks or the table. All actions have the same effects as in their deterministic blocks world counterpart and put-down and put-on-block have the probabilistic side effect of detonating the block being held and destroying the table or the block below with probability 0.4 and 0.1, respectively. Once a block or the table is destroyed, nothing can be placed on them, and destroyed blocks cannot be moved; therefore, problems in this domain can have unavoidable dead ends. Also, each block detonates only once and, after its detonation, the block can be safely moved. We use the corrected version of this domain that forbids a block to be placed on top of itself.

Triangle Tireworld. From [Little et al., 2007] and used in the IPPCs, this domain represents a car that has to travel between locations in triangular map (Fig. 3) to reach a goal

#	planner	cov.	Avg. Time (s) Total	MaxPr	Avg # States Expl. 1st stage	2nd stage
1	MCMP	30	0.1	0.1	746	197
	FRET	30	0.5	0.4	3676	92
	FRET-π	30	0.2	0.1	676	95
2	MCMP	30	0.7	0.4	1639	1205
	FRET	30	2.7	2.7	5631	188
	FRET-π	30	9.6	1.6	2112	202
3	MCMP	30	0.2	0.1	730	447
	FRET	30	8.6	8.4	63160	452
	FRET-π	30	54.9	0.6	4871	493
4	MCMP	30	0.7	0.4	1987	1868
	FRET	30	20.5	20.4	32358	1227
	FRET-π	30	48.4	7.2	11826	1337
5	MCMP	30	0.3	0.3	1107	210
	FRET	30	89.0	88.9	60040	249
	FRET-π	30	19.7	14.3	6525	272
7	MCMP	30	114.3	1.3	2675	50519
	FRET-π	7	1568.2	764.8	2316519	77928
9	MCMP	30	108.2	31.2	19209	40553

Table 1: Results for the Exploding Blocks World problems. # is the problem number in IPPC'08.

#	planner	cov.	Avg. Time (s) Total	MaxPr	Avg # States Expl. 1st stage	2nd stage
3	MCMP	30	1.4	0.2	2454	6459
	FRET	30	4.3	3.5	41944	17706
	FRET-π	30	3.9	3.1	32151	17750
4	MCMP	30	125.4	1.0	6973	108097
	FRET	30	115.9	98.8	777722	299921
	FRET-π	30	95.8	79.0	555260	299734

Table 2: Results for the Triangle Tireworld problems. # is the problem number in IPPC'08.

location from its initial location. When the car moves, a flat tire happens with probability 0.5 and the car becomes unable to move if neither the car nor the location have a spare tire. Problems in this domain are such that only the longest path (i.e., to move from L_0 to L_F then to L_G) has enough spare tires to reach the goal with probability 1; therefore, these problems have avoidable dead ends.

Reversed Triangle Tireworld. This is a variation of the triangle tireworld that we designed to illustrate the tradeoffs between the S^3P and MCMP algorithms. The difference between the original and the reverse triangle tireworld is only the location of the spare tires: for the reversed tireworld, the spare tires are available in every locations in rows 1 to r (Fig. 3) where r is a parameter of the problem. Therefore, for all r, the policy representing the shortest path from L_0 to L_G has probability 1 of reaching the goal in the reversed tire world; moreover, this policy is always the optimal policy. As with the original triangle tireworld, the problems in this domain have avoidable dead ends. The reversed tireworld problems highlight the tradeoffs between the different algorithms because the parameter r controls the size of Π^{MP} while maintaining the same optimal policy under all SSP criteria. Moreover, the cost heuristic $h^{\max}$ used for solving these problems guides the cost optimization of the different criteria directly to the optimal policy; therefore, narrowing down the differences in performance to the differences in the search approaches over Π^{MP}.

Results. For the exploding blocks world (Tab. 1), i-dual is the only planner to obtain 100% coverage in all the problems and to scale up to problem #9. Moreover, i-dual is always the fastest planner and its speed-up ranges from 2x to 40x compared to the second best planner. The performance gains from i-dual come mainly from its first stage (columns 5 and 6 in Tab. 1) that efficiently computes $p^{\max}$ without exploring too many states. This efficiency is due to the search in the dual space which does not contain local maxima, as opposed to the search in the primal space performed by FRET and FRET-π that need to escape local maxima (i.e., fixed-point solutions for P^* that are not optimal). For instance, both FRET and FRET-π need to escape loopy policies in which a detonated block is picked up and then placed in its previous location similarly to loop between d_2 and d_3 in Fig. 1. Notice that these loopy policies can happen in any problem with reversible actions, i.e., loops between doing and undoing an action.

For the triangle tireworld (Tab. 2), all planners scaled up to instance #4 and both FRET and FRET-π are faster than i-dual in the largest instance. Although this domain is acyclic and represents the best case scenario for FRET and FRET-π (there is only one fixed-point solution for P^*), i-dual still spends less time computing $p^{\max}$. Moreover, i-dual explores considerably fewer states in both stages: up to 80x less for the first stage and 3x less for the second stage. The underperformance of i-dual is because the triangle tireworld was designed to mislead planners and heuristics based on the all-outcomes determinization: the second stage of i-dual is constantly misdirected towards dead ends by $h^{\max}$ and has to infer that those states do not reach the goal with probability 1 (this can be verified by the average time spent in the second stage, i.e., column 5 minus column 6 in Tab. 2). In other words, the main advantage of i-dual, namely the usage of the cost heuristics to prune the search in the Max-Prob space, is lost and becomes an overhead since we still need to compute the heuristic cost. Notice that both FRET and FRET-π do not suffer for the misdirection of $h^{\max}$ in the second stage because the P^*-SSP is a trivial SSP since it has only one policy. As we demonstrate in the reversed triangle tireworld experiments, this behavior is an exception caused by the fact that $|\Pi^{MP}| = 1$.

For the reversed triangle tireworld (Tab. 3), i-dual scales up to all problems while: FRET solves only the instances with small r since $|\Pi^{MP}|$ is small for them; and FRET-π scales up to all values of r for tire04 but fails to obtain 100% coverage for the larger values of r for tire05. The total time speed up obtained by i-dual is up to 293x and 17x w.r.t. FRET and FRET-π. This large difference in performance is due to how i-dual combines the search for the policy with minimal cost and a policy with maximum probability to reach the goal in its second phase, enabling it to prune large areas of the state space when these are proven too costly, irrespective of their P^* value. Notice that our implementation of the P^*-SSP performs a lazy evaluation of P^*, which also allows both FRET and FRET-π to avoid

#	r	planner	cov.	Avg. Time (s) Total	MaxPr	Avg # States Expl. 1st stage	2nd stage
4	1	MCMP	30	0.8	0.2	1014	3766
		FRET	30	1.3	1.0	6186	3011
		FRET-π	30	1.2	1.0	5877	3006
	2	MCMP	30	3.1	0.7	4949	7500
		FRET	30	92.1	89.8	808958	27396
		FRET-π	30	30.6	29.6	227976	27520
	3	MCMP	30	3.7	0.6	3937	8573
		FRET	30	481.7	470.9	4394767	40018
		FRET-π	30	53.7	52.2	418872	39978
	4	MCMP	30	4.0	0.8	4790	8699
		FRET	30	1174.6	1148.3	10695787	43191
		FRET-π	30	84.3	82.5	654374	43214
	5	MCMP	30	4.2	1.0	5716	8692
		FRET-π	30	83.6	81.7	662169	43260
	6	MCMP	30	4.2	1.0	5491	8695
		FRET-π	30	86.3	84.5	682331	43549
	7	MCMP	30	4.1	0.9	5218	8698
		FRET-π	30	86.2	84.4	681039	43280
	8	MCMP	30	4.2	1.0	5553	8695
		FRET-π	30	87.1	85.3	682876	43280
	9	MCMP	30	4.1	0.9	5211	8688
		FRET-π	30	85.9	84.1	682290	43280
5	1	MCMP	30	6.4	0.4	1948	15780
		FRET	30	8.1	6.9	25192	12223
		FRET-π	30	7.3	6.1	23911	12225
	2	MCMP	30	43.7	2.2	10067	41243
		FRET-π	30	386.0	375.4	1999963	190251
	3	MCMP	30	75.5	2.2	9018	52572
		FRET-π	29	789.9	771.5	4180058	313663
	4	MCMP	30	80.9	2.4	9392	54931
		FRET-π	28	1217.6	1193.7	6599042	359568
	5	MCMP	30	83.3	2.5	10568	55315
		FRET-π	26	1268.4	1244.3	6987555	366708
	6	MCMP	30	83.3	3.6	13869	55300
		FRET-π	25	1384.1	1358.9	7517924	368086
	7	MCMP	30	82.6	3.2	12211	55189
		FRET-π	26	1395.6	1369.6	7635691	366690
	8	MCMP	30	82.4	3.2	12684	55282
		FRET-π	24	1381.5	1356.5	7481011	366047
	9	MCMP	30	79.8	3.6	13588	55261
		FRET-π	25	1374.6	1349.3	7612778	364596
	10	MCMP	30	81.4	3.2	12174	55303
		FRET-π	24	1380.3	1354.9	7489997	366921
	11	MCMP	30	81.0	2.9	11705	55246
		FRET-π	26	1406.8	1381.5	7707530	367452

Table 3: Results for the Reversed Triangle Tireworld problems. # is of the problem number of the original Triangle Tireworld and r is number of rows with spare tires.

querying P^* for regions of the state space that have a high expected cost. Nonetheless, both FRET and FRET-π still compute P^* for a large number of states due to their primal space search procedure: they explore millions of states to answer the P^* queries while i-dual explores less than 15000 states, resulting in up to 1435x and 476x speed-up w.r.t. FRET and FRET-π in the first stage.

The reversed tireworld experiment also shows that the worst-case scenario for FRET and FRET-π is more than simply problems without dead ends, as claimed in [Kolobov et al., 2012, Sec. 8]: rather, their worst-case scenarios are problems with a large number of Max-Prob solutions (i.e., large $|\Pi^{MP}|$) with small intersection between the reachable states of the policies $\pi \in \Pi^{MP}$. This is because S^3P minimizes the expected cost in the P^*-SSP thus, in the worst case, the complete space of the P^*-SSP is explored and this space is exactly the union of all states reachable from s_0 using any Max-Prob policy.

r	b	criteria	Avg Time (s) Total	MaxPr	Avg # States Expl. 1st stage	2nd stage	Pr. Goal
4	10	$D=25$	19.19	–	–	31769	0.45
		$D=50$	32.50	–	–	42085	0.64
		MCMP	74.23	25.20	38020	48742	0.66
	12	$D=25$	18.72	–	–	32501	0.54
		$D=50$	95.08	–	–	55039	0.76
		MCMP	255.00	96.28	60338	60217	0.76
	14	$D=25$	21.78	–	–	33455	0.62
		$D=50$	66.99	–	–	56489	0.84
		MCMP	145.59	61.71	63504	60256	0.84
	16	$D=25$	21.31	–	–	34954	0.70
		$D=50$	61.47	–	–	59496	0.91
		MCMP	136.12	52.65	68378	60607	0.91
	18	$D=25$	17.95	–	–	30920	0.77
		$D=50$	83.94	–	–	63682	0.99
		MCMP	183.88	77.96	85720	62185	0.99
	20	$D=25$	19.09	–	–	31092	0.83
		$D=50$	68.10	–	–	53574	1.00
		MCMP	174.48	90.05	88807	53581	1.00
5	10	$D=25$	44.84	–	–	55658	0.45
		$D=50$	219.54	–	–	87220	1.00
		MCMP	298.50	11.95	30801	87177	1.00
	12	$D=25$	47.12	–	–	57209	0.54
		$D=50$	146.11	–	–	88210	1.00
		MCMP	213.32	19.30	41866	88276	1.00
	14	$D=25$	51.43	–	–	58558	0.62
		$D=50$	158.94	–	–	90003	1.00
		MCMP	230.69	24.74	47667	89812	1.00
	16	$D=25$	57.42	–	–	58811	0.70
		$D=50$	160.72	–	–	90074	1.00
		MCMP	262.99	58.33	69568	90127	1.00
	18	$D=25$	31.54	–	–	47196	0.77
		$D=50$	163.79	–	–	90329	1.00
		MCMP	257.68	46.60	64807	90352	1.00
	20	$D=25$	31.80	–	–	47295	0.83
		$D=50$	161.53	–	–	90484	1.00
		MCMP	321.12	109.91	92912	90465	1.00

Table 4: Results for the constrained reversed tireworld problems. All problems considered are based on the problem #4 of the original tireworld domain. r and b represent the number of rows with available spare tires and the budget to buy spare tires, respectively. For Finite-Penalty, the dead-end penalty D is displayed on the criteria column. All planners obtained 100% coverage for these problems.

Experiments on Constrained SSPs

To illustrate the feasibility of solving C-SSPs using the MCMP criterion, we compare i-dual using the Finite-Penalty and MCMP criteria in an extension of the reversed tireworld domain. In this extension, the main cost function is the same as before and represents travel time, and we added a secondary cost function to represent the money spent buying spare tires. For these problems, if a location l has an available spare tire, the planner has to pay \$1, \$5, or \$10 to buy that spare if l is, respectively, a cheap, regular, or expensive location. We set all the outside locations (i.e., in the direct path from L_0 to L_F and L_F to L_G) as cheap locations. All internal locations from rows 1 to $\lceil n/3 \rceil$, $\lceil n/3 \rceil+1$ to $2\lceil n/3 \rceil$, and $2\lceil n/3 \rceil+1$ to n (where n is the total number of rows) are, respectively, expensive, regular and cheap. Thus, the more direct a path from L_0 to L_G is, more money is necessary in expectation to buy spare tires.

For the constrained reversed tireworld, we use a cost constraint over the secondary cost function, that is, we enforce a maximum expected amount of money that can be used for buying spare tires. Therefore, if spare tire budget b is too small, no policy will be able to reach the goal with probability 1 even if the unconstrained problem has no dead end. For this experiment, we used the tire04 problem and let the parameters r and b vary, and we also used a different values of dead-end penalty D. Tab. 4 shows the results for selected combinations of r, b, and d. As the last column shows, $D = 25$ is too small as a dead-end penalty and solutions that can reach the goal with higher probability are unduely pruned, while $D = 50$ is large enough for all parametrizations, except $r = 4$ and $b = 10$ in which the MCMP reaches the goal with a larger probability. Regarding runtime, i-dual using the MCMP criterion takes close to the double of the time of the finite-penalty $D = 50$, showing that it is feasible to use MCMP as a criterion for C-SSPs. Moreover, the solution for the Max-Prob stage (i.e., solution of LP 2) is computed quite fast (which can be as small as 1/10 of the total time of the finite-penalty approaches) and already satisfies the cost constraints by design; therefore, the Min-Cost stage can be seen as an iterative refinement procedure that can be stopped at anytime.

CONCLUSION AND FUTURE WORK

In this paper, we presented MCMP, a natural optimization criterion for stochastic shortest paths problems with dead ends, which results in the minimum expected cost policy among those with maximum success probability. We also proposed an efficient solution method for MCMP, which leverages recent work on heuristic search in the dual space. Unlike the Finite-Penalty method [Kolobov et al., 2012], our approach does not suffer from having to guess an appropriate dead-end penalty. In comparison to other robust criteria such as S^3P and iSSPUDE [Teichteil-Königsbuch, 2012, Kolobov et al., 2012], MCMP more accurately reflects the expected cost of reaching dead ends, and as shown by our experiments, often provides a substantial computational advantage.

This computational advantage comes from applying heuristic search on the dual representation of SSPs: the Max-Prob problem is directly optimized by the flow objective function of the dual space which prevents heuristic search algorithms to be trapped in non-optimal fixed-point solutions. Alternatively, heuristic search algorithms in the primal representation optimize a reward function that indirectly represents the Max-Prob problem and are susceptible to converge to non-optimal fixed-point solutions. Thus, they need to detect if the current fixed-point solution is optimal or not and post-process the solution in the latter case. Moreover, our approach to solve MCMP is able to prune the search space using simultaneously heuristics for both the probability of reaching the goal and the expected cost of reaching the goal. Observe that this computational advantage of our approach does not transfer to S^3P or iSSPUDE, as they require (a priori or on-the-fly) the Max-Prob solution.

Another optimization criterion that can avoid the infinite cost associated with being trapped in a dead end is the Average Reward criterion [Puterman, 1994]. For SSPs, this criterion minimizes the average cost of the traces $T_{\pi,s}$ generated by π of size 1 to N for $N \to \infty$. This limiting sum allows policies to always have a finite value regardless of their probability of reaching dead ends. The drawback of the Average Reward criterion is that neither heuristic search algorithms nor heuristics for them have been proposed; therefore the full state space reachable from the initial state must be considered to solve any given problem. As a result, any algorithm for solving SSPs using the Average Reward criterion will not scale up to the large problems considered in this paper.

The related work for explicitly handling the conflict of optimizing goal probability reachability and expected cost includes three classes of approaches. The first, to which MCMP belongs, is ordered objective optimization where goal probability reachability is the primary objective. This includes S^3P and iSSPUDE, as well as earlier work studying the merits of Max-Prob, SSP, and discounted MDP models to handle robotics environments with dead ends [Koenig and Liu, 2002].

The second class of approaches are constrained MDPs, where one of the objective is viewed as a constraint while the other is optimized. Work in this area ranges from the seminal work of Altman [1999] to the recent work by Trevizan et al [2016] on i-dual which our approach builds on. Steinmetz et al. [2016] also consider the *At-Least-Prob* criterion for which an extra parameter $\underline{p} \in (0, 1]$ is given and the solution is to find a policy that reaches the goal with probability greater or equal to $\underline{p}$. LP 1 can be trivially adapted by replacing C6 with $\sum_{s_g \in \mathsf{G}} in(s_g) \geq \underline{p}$ to efficiently generate policies that minimize the expected cost whilst satisfying *At-Least-Prob* criterion.

A third class of relevant approaches are multi-objective MDPs viewing goal probability reachability and cost as competing objectives. However, multi-objective approaches are often more appropriate in a setting where a set of alternative policies (e.g. pareto sets of non-dominated policies) needs to be computed because the way of prioritising these objectives is unknown or too difficult to elicit a priori [Roijers et al., 2013]. Also, multi-objective MDPs are rather expensive to solve [Chatterjee et al., 2006], and existing work has focused on discounted MDPs.

As future work, we plan to improve our algorithm for MCMP even further. We suspect that i-dual is somewhat overkill as it can also solve problems requiring stochastic policies whereas MCMP only requires deterministic policies for SSPs. It is known that in the general case, it is harder to compute deterministic than stochastic policies for C-SSPs (NP-hard vs polynomial) [Dolgov and Durfee, 2005]. However, it should be possible to avoid this complexity increase in the case of MCMP and take advantage of the deterministic nature of optimal policies for SSPs.

Acknowledgements
This research was funded by AFOSR grant FA2386-15-1-4015.

References

[Altman, 1999] Altman, E. (1999). *Constrained Markov Decision Processes*, volume 7. CRC Press.

[Bertsekas and Tsitsiklis, 1991] Bertsekas, D. and Tsitsiklis, J. (1991). An Analysis of Stochastic Shortest Path Problems. *Mathematics of Operations Research*, 16(3):580–595.

[Bonet and Geffner, 2003] Bonet, B. and Geffner, H. (2003). Labeled RTDP: improving the convergence of real-time dynamic programming. In *Proc. Int. Conf. on Automated Planning and Scheduling*.

[Bryce and Buffet, 2008] Bryce, D. and Buffet, O. (2008). 6th Int. Planning Competition: Uncertainty Track. In *3rd Int. Probabilistic Planning Competition (IPPC-ICAPS'08)*.

[Chatterjee et al., 2006] Chatterjee, K., Majumdar, R., and Henzinger, T. A. (2006). Markov decision processes with multiple objectives. In *STACS 2006, 23rd Annual Symposium on Theoretical Aspects of Computer Science, Marseille, France, February 23-25, 2006, Proceedings*, pages 325–336.

[Dolgov and Durfee, 2005] Dolgov, D. A. and Durfee, E. H. (2005). Stationary deterministic policies for constrained mdps with multiple rewards, costs, and discount factors. In *Proc. Int. Joint Conf. on Artificial Intelligence*.

[Koenig and Liu, 2002] Koenig, S. and Liu, Y. (2002). The interaction of representations and planning objectives for decision-theoretic planning tasks. *J. Exp. Theor. Artif. Intell.*, 14(4):303–326.

[Kolobov et al., 2012] Kolobov, A., Mausam, and Weld, D. S. (2012). A theory of goal-oriented mdps with dead ends. In *Proc. Conf. on Uncertainty in Artificial Intelligence (UAI)*.

[Kolobov et al., 2011] Kolobov, A., Mausam, Weld, D. S., and Geffner, H. (2011). Heuristic search for generalized stochastic shortest path mdps. In *Proc. International Conference on Automated Planning and Scheduling (ICAPS)*.

[Little et al., 2007] Little, I., Thiebaux, S., et al. (2007). Probabilistic planning vs. replanning. In *ICAPS Workshop on IPC: Past, Present and Future*.

[Mausam and Kolobov, 2012] Mausam and Kolobov, A. (2012). *Planning with Markov Decision Processes*. Morgan & Claypool.

[Puterman, 1994] Puterman, M. (1994). *Markov Decision Processes: Discrete Stochastic Dynamic Programming*. John Wiley & Sons, Inc.

[Roijers et al., 2013] Roijers, D. M., Vamplew, P., Whiteson, S., and Dazeley, R. (2013). A survey of multi-objective sequential decision-making. *J. Artif. Intell. Res. (JAIR)*, 48:67–113.

[Steinmetz et al., 2016] Steinmetz, M., Hoffmann, J., and Buffet, O. (2016). Revisiting foal probability analysis in probabilistic planning. In *Proc. Int. Conf. on Automated Planning and Scheduling*.

[Teichteil-Königsbuch, 2012] Teichteil-Königsbuch, F. (2012). Stochastic safest and shortest path problems. In *Proc. AAAI Conf. on Artificial Intelligence*.

[Teichteil-Königsbuch et al., 2011] Teichteil-Königsbuch, F., Vidal, V., and Infantes, G. (2011). Extending Classical Planning Heuristics to Probabilistic Planning with Dead-Ends. In *Proc. AAAI Conf. on Artificial Intelligence*.

[Trevizan et al., 2017] Trevizan, F., Thiébaux, S., , and Haslum, P. (2017). Occupation Measure Heuristics for Probabilistic Planning. In *Proc. of 27th Int. Conf. on Automated Planning and Scheduling (ICAPS)*.

[Trevizan et al., 2016] Trevizan, F., Thiébaux, S., Santana, P., and Williams, B. (2016). Heuristic Search in Dual Space for Constrained Stochastic Shortest Path Problems. In *Proc. Int. Conf. on Automated Planning and Scheduling (ICAPS)*.

[Younes et al., 2005] Younes, H. L. S., Littman, M. L., Weissman, D., and Asmuth, J. (2005). The first probabilistic track of the international planning competition. *J. Artif. Int. Res.*, 24(1):851–887.

Probabilistic Program Abstractions

Steven Holtzen and **Todd Millstein** and **Guy Van den Broeck**
Computer Science Department
University of California, Los Angeles
{sholtzen,todd,guyvdb}@cs.ucla.edu

Abstract

Abstraction is a fundamental tool for reasoning about complex systems. Program abstraction has been utilized to great effect for analyzing deterministic programs. At the heart of program abstraction is the relationship between a concrete program, which is difficult to analyze, and an abstract program, which is more tractable. Program abstractions, however, are typically not probabilistic. We generalize non-deterministic program abstractions to probabilistic program abstractions by explicitly quantifying the non-deterministic choices. Our framework upgrades key definitions and properties of abstractions to the probabilistic context. We also discuss preliminary ideas for performing inference on probabilistic abstractions and general probabilistic programs.

1 INTRODUCTION & MOTIVATION

Program abstractions are a richly studied method from the programming languages community for reasoning about intractably complex programs (Cousot and Cousot, 1977). An abstraction is typically an over-approximation to a program: any execution that is possible in the original program is contained within the abstraction. Over-approximation allows abstractions to be used to prove *program invariants*: any property of all executions in the abstraction is also true of all executions in the original program. To achieve this goal while being more tractable than the concrete program, abstractions work on a simplified domain. The abstraction selectively models particular aspects of the original program while utilizing non-determinism to conservatively model the rest.

Non-deterministic abstractions are useful for verifying properties such as reachability in a concrete program. However, abstractions are decidedly not probabilistic: they are concerned with the possible, not the probable. Therefore, they fail to support more nuanced queries such as probabilistic reachability, or probabilistic program inference. We seek to enhance the program abstraction framework by explicitly quantifying the non-deterministic choices made in the abstraction, turning the program abstraction into a probabilistic model. That is, our probabilistic abstractions are themselves probabilistic programs, which have been the subject of intense study recently (e.g., Goodman et al. (2008); Fierens et al. (2013); Wood et al. (2014); Carpenter et al. (2016)).

The key contribution of this paper is the development of a foundational theory for probabilistic program abstractions. We define probabilistic abstractions as a natural generalization of traditional abstractions, using random variables as the abstraction mechanism instead of non-determinism. We also formalize the relationship between a probabilistic abstraction and a concrete program, again generalizing from the non-deterministic setting. This includes semantics in both the concrete and abstract domain, the connection between these semantics, and the notion of a sound probabilistic over-approximation.

A well-known construction of non-deterministic program abstractions is that of a *predicate abstraction* (Graf and Saïdi, 1997; Ball et al., 2001). It induces an abstraction relative to a given set of Boolean predicates about the program state. We define *probabilistic predicate abstractions*, which are represented by a simple Bernoulli probabilistic program, as an instance of our framework, and a generalization of classical predicate abstraction.

We conclude with a discussion of ideas for performing inference in probabilistic predicate abstractions, building on *model checking* techniques from the programming languages community and *weighted model counting* from the artificial intelligence community. We then discuss how probabilistic abstractions could be used to simplify inference in probabilistic concrete programs.

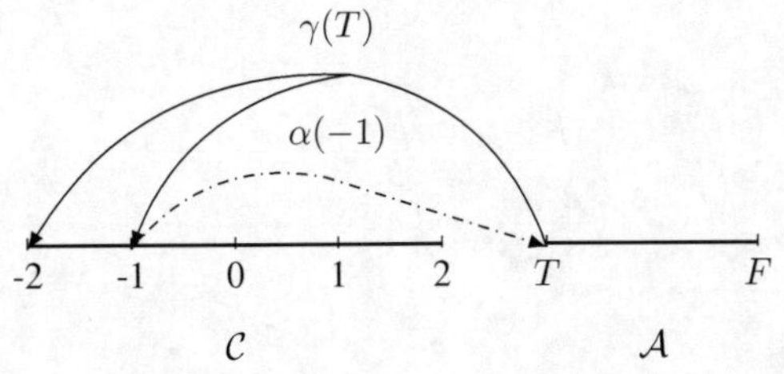

Figure 1: Visualization of a simple predicate domain. The five concrete states over an integer variable x in the range $[-2, 2]$ are abstracted to two states based on the valuation of the predicate $(x < 0)$. We see, for example, that $\alpha(-1) = T$, and $\gamma(T) = \{-2, -1\}$).

2 NON-DETERMINISTIC PROGRAM ABSTRACTION

In this section we provide the semantics and properties of an *over-approximate non-deterministic* abstraction and provide an example of a particular class of over-approximations known as predicate abstractions.

2.1 SEMANTICS AND PROPERTIES

A concrete program is a syntactic object written $\mathcal{C}$. The semantics of a concrete program, which for simplicity we also denote $\mathcal{C}$, is a function from input states to output states over some concrete domain $\mathcal{D}_\mathcal{C}$. Concrete states are total assignments to all variables in the concrete domain, which we denote $z \in \mathcal{D}_\mathcal{C}$.

In general, the problem of proving that a given program satisfies a desired invariant is undecidable. Advances in theorem proving techniques such as Satisfiability Modulo Theory (SMT) solvers (e.g., De Moura and Bjørner (2008)) render reasoning in many useful theories tractable, yet there exist common program structures that lie outside of supported theories.

The framework of abstract interpretation (Cousot and Cousot, 1977) provides a general technique for relating a concrete program $\mathcal{C}$ to another program $\mathcal{A}$ which we refer to as an *abstraction*. We describe a specialization of the abstract interpretation framework.

Definition 2.1. Abstract semantics of an abstraction. The abstract semantics of an abstraction $\mathcal{A}$, which for simplicity we also denote $\mathcal{A}$, is a function from input states to sets of output states over an abstract domain $\mathcal{D}_\mathcal{A}$, written $\mathcal{A} : \mathcal{D}_\mathcal{A} \to 2^{\mathcal{D}_\mathcal{A}}$.

Intuitively, the nondeterminism in the abstract semantics of an abstraction represents uncertainty due to the loss of information in abstracting $\mathcal{C}$ to $\mathcal{A}$. We represent this non-determinism as a set of possible abstract states, denoted $a \in \mathcal{D}_\mathcal{A}$. To relate concrete programs with abstractions we introduce two mappings between concrete and abstract states.

Definition 2.2. Abstraction and concretization functions. An *abstraction function* for $\mathcal{D}_\mathcal{C}$ and $\mathcal{D}_\mathcal{A}$ is a function $\alpha : \mathcal{D}_\mathcal{C} \to \mathcal{D}_\mathcal{A}$ that maps each concrete state to its abstract representative. A *concretization function* for $\mathcal{D}_\mathcal{C}$ and $\mathcal{D}_\mathcal{A}$ is a function $\gamma : \mathcal{D}_\mathcal{A} \to 2^{\mathcal{D}_\mathcal{C}}$ that maps each abstract state to a set of concrete states. When applied to sets, γ and α respectively concretize or abstract each element of the set.

Abstraction and concretization functions are related.

Definition 2.3. Compatibility. An abstraction function α and concretization function γ are *compatible* if $z \in \gamma(\alpha(z))$ for all $z \in \mathcal{D}_\mathcal{C}$. As an extension, the two functions are *strongly compatible* if they are compatible and for any a and $z \in \gamma(a)$, we have that $z \notin \gamma(a')$ for any $a' \neq a$.

A *predicate domain* is a well-studied abstract domain induced by a given sequence of predicates $(p_1, \ldots, p_n)$ about the concrete state. The abstract domain $\mathcal{D}_\mathcal{A}$ consists of n Boolean variables $(b_1, \ldots, b_n)$ and so has 2^n possible elements, one for each valuation to the n variables. For instance, suppose $\mathcal{D}_\mathcal{C}$ consists of a single integer variable x whose value is in the range $[-2, 2]$. The single predicate $(x < 0)$ induces an abstract domain with two possible states, representing the concrete states where $(x < 0)$ is true and false. See Figure 1 for a visualization. The abstraction function α maps each concrete state z to the abstract state $(p_1(z), \ldots, p_n(z))$, and the concretization function γ maps each abstract state a to the set of concrete states consistent with it: $\{z \in \mathcal{D}_\mathcal{C} \mid (p_1(z), \ldots, p_n(z)) = a\}$. The functions α and γ are strongly compatible for predicate domains.

Intuitively, an abstraction represents a set of possible concrete programs, which is formalized as follows:

Definition 2.4. Concrete semantics of an abstraction. The concrete semantics of an abstraction $\mathcal{A}$, given compatible abstraction and concretization functions α and γ, is a function $[\![\mathcal{A}]\!] : \mathcal{D}_\mathcal{C} \to 2^{\mathcal{D}_\mathcal{C}}$ defined as follows:

$$[\![\mathcal{A}]\!](z) = \gamma(\mathcal{A}(\alpha(z))),$$

where γ is applied to each element of $\mathcal{A}(\alpha(z))$.

Ultimately we wish to prove properties about a particular concrete program $\mathcal{C}$ by reasoning about some simpler abstract program $\mathcal{A}$. From the above definition of an abstraction's concrete semantics we immediately obtain the following criterion for relating a specific concrete program $\mathcal{C}$ to $\mathcal{A}$:

Definition 2.5. Sound over-approximation. Let $\mathcal{A}$ be some abstract program with compatible abstraction and

```
if(x<0) {
  x = 0
} else {
  x = x + 1
}
```

Figure 2: A simple concrete program over an integer variable x.

concretization functions α and γ. The tuple $(\mathcal{A}, \alpha, \gamma)$ is a sound over-approximation of $\mathcal{C}$ if for all $z \in \mathcal{D}_\mathcal{C}$, $\mathcal{C}(z) \in [\![\mathcal{A}]\!](z)$.

In other words, $\mathcal{A}$ is sound for $\mathcal{C}$ if the result of any concrete execution of $\mathcal{C}$ is contained within the possible concretizations of the result of $\mathcal{A}$ executed on the abstracted input. Sound over-approximations can be used to verify *safety* properties of programs, which intuitively express the fact that certain "bad" things never happen (e.g., no null dereferences will occur). Every safety property can be formalized as a requirement that some set $\mathcal{B}$ of "bad" states in the concrete program never be reached. To prove that $\mathcal{C}(z) \notin \mathcal{B}$ for each concrete state z, it suffices to prove that $\gamma([\![\mathcal{A}]\!](a)) \cap \mathcal{B} = \emptyset$ for each abstract state $a \in \mathcal{D}_\mathcal{A}$, where $\mathcal{A}$ is a sound over-approximation of $\mathcal{C}$.

In general, the construction of an abstraction is a careful balance between *precision*, the fidelity of the abstraction to the original concrete program, and *tractability*, how difficult the abstraction is to construct and reason about. For abstract predicate domains, adding more predicates to the domain increases precision but also makes the abstraction more costly to produce and analyze.

The semantics above treats programs $\mathcal{C}$ and $\mathcal{A}$ as black-box input-output functions. Nevertheless, the semantics straightforwardly generalizes to assign meaning to every single line of code in the programs, allowing us to establish a sound over-approximation throughout.

2.2 PREDICATE ABSTRACTION

A *predicate abstraction* is a well-studied program abstraction whose abstract domain is a predicate domain (Graf and Saïdi, 1997; Ball et al., 2001) (see the previous section for the definition of a predicate domain). Predicate abstractions are known as *Boolean programs*: the domain $\mathcal{D}_\mathcal{A} = \{T, F\}^n$. Safety checking in Boolean programs is decidable: a Boolean program has a finite set of states over a fixed number of Boolean variables, making it decidable to obtain the set of reachable states. Given a concrete program $\mathcal{C}$ and a set of n predicates $(p_1, \ldots, p_n)$ over the concrete domain $\mathcal{D}_\mathcal{C}$, the goal of the predicate abstraction process is to construct an abstract Boolean program $\mathcal{A}$ that forms a sound over-approximation of $\mathcal{C}$ and is as precise as possible relative to the given predicates.

We use the simple program in Figure 2 as an example to illustrate the predicate abstraction process. The Boolean program induced by the predicates x<-4 and x<3 is shown in Figure 3. Following the notation of Ball et al. (2001), the $\star$ operator represents nondeterministic choice, and the Boolean variable associated with predicate p is denoted $\{p\}$. We describe the predicate abstraction process for branches and assignments in turn.

```
if(*) {
  assume({x<3})
  {x<-4}, {x<3} = F, T
} else {
  assume(!{x<-4})
  {x<-4}, {x<3} =
     choose(F, !{x<3} ∨ !{x<-4}),
     choose({x<-4}, !{x<3})
}
```

Figure 3: A predicate abstraction of the program in Figure 2 induced by the predicates x<-4 and x<3. Note that predicate updates that are abstractions of the same concrete assignment statement are updated simultaneously.

2.2.1 Abstracting Branches

Consider a conditional statement of the form

```
if (p) {···} else {···}
```

in the concrete program. Let $\mathtt{p}^T$ denote the strongest propositional formula over the predicates $p_1, \ldots, p_n$ that is implied by p and $\mathtt{p}^F$ denote the strongest propositional formula over the predicates $p_1, \ldots, p_n$ that is implied by !p. These formulas represent the most precise information we can know inside the *then* and *else* branches respectively, given the predicates in the abstraction. They can be obtained through queries to an SMT solver, assuming that p and the n predicates are all in decidable logical theories; see Ball et al. (2001) for details. The predicate abstraction process translates the above conditional as follows in the Boolean program:

```
if (*) {
  assume({p^T}) ...
} else {
  assume({p^F}) ...
}
```

Here $\{\mathtt{p}^T\}$ is $\mathtt{p}^T$ but with each predicate p_i replaced by its Boolean counterpart $\{p_i\}$, and similarly for $\{\mathtt{p}^F\}$. The statement assume(φ), which is standard in the programming languages community, silently ignores executions which do not satisfy φ. Note that $\{\mathtt{p}^T\}$ and $\{\mathtt{p}^F\}$ can simultaneously be true, which allows the execution to nondeterministically take either branch of the conditional.

In the program of Figure 2, we know that x<0 is true

in the *then* clause. In Figure 3, the strongest information our abstraction can know at that point is that (the Boolean variable corresponding to) `x<3` is true. Similarly, `x<0` is false in the *else* branch in Figure 2, while the abstraction in Figure 3 only knows that `x<-4` is false.

2.2.2 Abstracting Assignment Statements

Consider an assignment statement of the form `x = e` in the concrete program. In the corresponding point of the abstract program we must *simultaneously* update the values of all Boolean variables to reflect the update to the value of `x`. Suppose we want to update the variable $\{p_i\}$. Let p_i^T denote the weakest propositional formula over the predicates $p_1, \ldots, p_n$ such that p_i^T holding before the assignment `x = e` suffices to ensure that p_i will be true after the assignment. Similarly let p_i^F denote the weakest propositional formula over the predicates $p_1, \ldots, p_n$ such that p_i^F holding before the assignment `x = e` suffices to ensure that p_i will be false after the assignment. Again an SMT solver can be used to obtain these formulas, leveraging the standard notion of the *weakest precondition* of an assignment statement with respect to a predicate (Dijkstra, 1976). The predicate abstraction process updates the Boolean variable $\{p_i\}$ as follows in the Boolean program:

$\{p_i\}$ = choose($\{p_i^T\}$, $\{p_i^F\}$)

Here choose(φ_1, φ_2) returns T if φ_1 is satisfied, otherwise returns F if φ_2 is satisfied, and otherwise chooses nondeterministically between T and F.

Consider the assignment statement `x = 0` in Figure 2. The abstraction process described above will assign `{x<3}` in the Boolean program to choose(T, F), which simplifies to just T as shown in Figure 3. More interestingly, consider the assignment statement `x = x + 1` in Figure 2. If `x<-4` is true before the assignment, then we can be sure that `x<3` is true afterward. If `x<3` is false before the assignment, then we can be sure that `x<3` is false afterward. If neither of these is the case, then the abstraction does not have enough information to know the value of `x<3` after the assignment. Hence in the Boolean program `{x<3}` is assigned to `choose({x<-4}, !{x<3})`.

Invariants Multiple predicates that involve the same variable are typically constrained in some way. For example, the predicates `{{x<3}, {x<-4}}` are constrained due to the relationship `{x<-4}`$\Rightarrow$`{x<3}`. This constraint is an invariant which increases the precision of the abstraction with minimal decrease in tractability. We call this constraint $\mathcal{I}$, and we can enforce it simply by inserting an assume($\mathcal{I}$) statement after each set of assignments.

2.2.3 Proving Program Invariants

A predicate abstraction is a sound over-approximation of the original concrete program. Further, because a Boolean program has a finite set of possible states at each point in the program, it can be exhaustively explored via a form of *model checking*, which conceptually executes the program in all possible ways (Ball and Rajamani, 2000). Model checking produces the set of reachable states at each point in the program, and this information can be used to verify invariants of the original program.

Consider the Boolean program in Figure 3. All executions of this program end in a state where the Boolean variable `{x<-4}` has the value F. This implies that `x` always ends in a value greater than or equal to `-4` in the original program in Figure 2. On the other hand, our predicate abstraction is not precise enough to verify that `x` always ends in a nonnegative value, though that is true of the original program. A different choice of predicates would enable such reasoning in the abstraction.

Selecting predicates The selection of predicates is clearly a critical component of an effective predicate abstraction. In this work we focus on the definition and construction of probabilistic predicate abstractions given a fixed set of predicates, leaving automated selection of predicates for future work. The programming languages community has developed several approaches to the problem of predicate selection. A common approach is to use a form of *counterexample-driven refinement*, which iteratively adds predicates until the abstraction is precise enough to prove or disprove the desired property of the concrete program (e.g., Ball and Rajamani (2002)). Extending these techniques to the probabilistic context is a challenging and exciting research problem.

3 PROBABILISTIC PROGRAM ABSTRACTION

The primary contribution of this paper is the extension of the non-deterministic program abstractions of the previous section to the probabilistic context. We begin by defining a simple probabilistic programming language. Syntactically, our probabilistic predicate abstractions will simply be probabilistic programs in this language. Next, we generalize the abstraction semantics of Section 2.1 to the probabilistic context, and define soundness criteria for probabilistic program abstractions. Finally, we generalize the predicate abstraction process from Section 2.2 to the probabilistic context by placing distributions on the non-deterministic choices.

3.1 PROBABILISTIC PROGRAMMING

We define a simple probabilistic programming language, BERN, which contains only (1) Boolean variables; (2) Boolean operators; (3) Boolean assignments; (4) `if` statements; (5) a `flip`(θ) operator, which is a Bernoulli random variable with parameter θ; and (6) an `observe`(φ) statement, which ignores executions that do not satisfy some condition φ. Note that `observe` statements can also be captured by a conditional probability query on the distribution.

An extension to BERN is to introduce a `goto` construct, which would allow it to reason about underlying concrete programs with arbitrary control flow. The predicate abstraction framework makes reasoning about loopy concrete programs tractable (Ball et al., 2001); however, we defer generalizing the semantics of loopy probabilistic predicate abstractions to future work. As an example of a BERN program, one can construct a program that encodes a Bayesian network ⓐ $\rightarrow$ ⓑ:

```
a = flip(θ1)
if(a)  { b = flip(θ2)}
else   { b = flip(θ3)}
observe(b)
```

This probabilistic program defines the conditional probability of each event by utilizing the control-flow features of BERN. For example, $\Pr(b \mid \neg a) = \theta_3$. The `observe` statement conditions the Bayesian network on some evidence: thus, queries about a in this program correspond to $\Pr(a \mid b)$.

Probabilistic programming has proven a natural tool for the construction of generative statistical models. As such, infrastructure for computing queries on probabilistic programs has begun to develop in the AI and programming languages communities (Carpenter et al., 2016; Goodman et al., 2008; Wood et al., 2014; Fierens et al., 2013).

3.2 PROBABILISTIC SEMANTICS

Section 2.1 identifies both the abstract and concrete semantics of a program abstraction. We generalize these non-deterministic semantics to probabilistic semantics by producing families of compatible probability distributions described by constraints on their support.

Since syntactically abstractions will be probabilistic programs, the abstract semantics of a probabilistic abstraction are simply the semantics of that program, broadly defined.

Definition 3.1. Abstract semantics. Let $a_i, a_o \in \mathcal{D}_\mathcal{A}$. The abstract semantics of a probabilistic abstraction $\mathcal{A}$, denoted $\Pr_\mathcal{A}(a_o \mid a_i)$, is a *conditional probability distribution* over abstract domain $\mathcal{D}_\mathcal{A}$, which describes the probability of transitioning from an initial set of states a_i to an output state a_o under the abstraction $\mathcal{A}$.

To define the concrete semantics of a probabilistic abstraction, we first need to generalize the concretization function γ to the probabilistic context.

Definition 3.2. Concretization distribution. Let $z \in \mathcal{D}_\mathcal{C}$ and $a \in \mathcal{D}_\mathcal{A}$. A concretization distribution is a *conditional probability distribution* $\Pr_\gamma(z \mid a)$ that describes the probability of concretizing an abstract state a to some concrete state z.

In the non-deterministic setting, we were concerned only with membership in the set γ. Here, we generalized γ to the probabilistic context by placing a distribution over possible concretizations.[1] Concretization distributions and abstraction functions are related as follows:

Definition 3.3. Compatibility. An abstraction function α and concretization distribution $\Pr_\gamma$ are *compatible* when, for all $z \in \mathcal{D}_\mathcal{C}$, $\Pr_\gamma(z \mid \alpha(z)) > 0$. Furthermore, these functions are *strongly compatible* if they are compatible and for any a and z such that $\Pr_\gamma(z \mid a) > 0$, we have that $\Pr_\gamma(z \mid a') = 0$ for all $a' \neq a$.

We are now in a position to define the concrete semantics of a probabilistic abstraction.

Definition 3.4. Concrete semantics. Let $z_i, z_o \in \mathcal{D}_\mathcal{C}$ be some input and output concrete states. The concrete semantics of an abstraction $\mathcal{A}$ given a compatible abstraction function α and concretization distribution $\Pr_\gamma$ is a *conditional probability distribution* describing the probability of transitioning from z_i to z_o:

$$\Pr_{[\![\mathcal{A}]\!]}(z_o \mid z_i) = \sum_{a_o \in \mathcal{D}_\mathcal{A}} \Pr_\gamma(z_o \mid a_o) \Pr_\mathcal{A}(a_o \mid \alpha(z_i)).$$

In the case when α and $\Pr_\gamma$ are strongly compatible, we can refine the above definition:

Proposition 3.1. Let $z_o, z_i \in \mathcal{D}_\mathcal{C}$. For strongly compatible α and $\Pr_\gamma$, there exists a single a_o for which $\Pr_\gamma(z_o \mid a_o) > 0$. Thus the sum may be collapsed:

$$\Pr_{[\![\mathcal{A}]\!]}(z_o \mid z_i) = \Pr_\gamma(z_o \mid a_o) \Pr_\mathcal{A}(a_o \mid \alpha(z_i)).$$

As an example, we saw previously that predicate domains allow for strongly compatible concretization and abstraction functions. We see in Figure 4 a probabilistic extension to non-deterministic predicate abstraction.

Under the probabilistic semantics, we can define a probabilistic analog of the over-approximation property of $\mathcal{A}$ as a constraint on the support of $\Pr_{[\![\mathcal{A}]\!]}$.

[1] For continuous concrete domains, concretization distributions directly generalize to concretization densities.

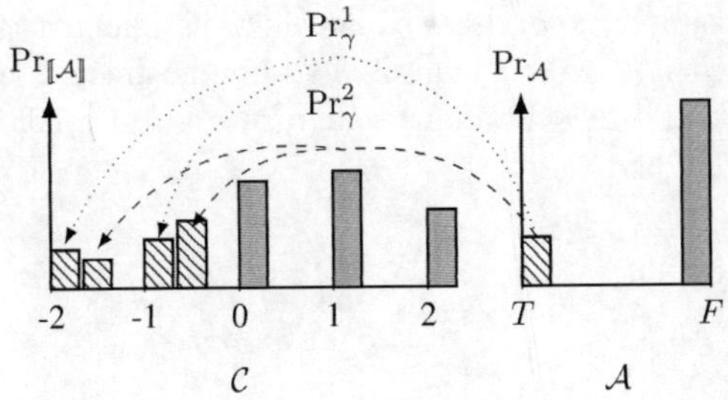

Figure 4: Probabilistic predicate abstraction over domain $\mathcal{D}_{\mathcal{A}}$ ={{x<0}}. Distribution $\Pr_{[\![\mathcal{A}]\!]}$ over $\mathcal{D}_{\mathcal{C}}$ is generated by (1) a distribution over abstract states $\Pr_{\mathcal{A}}$ and (2) one of two concretization distributions: $\Pr_\gamma^1$ or $\Pr_\gamma^2$.

Definition 3.5. Sound probabilistic over-approximation. Let $\mathcal{A}$ be a probabilistic program abstraction with compatible abstraction function α and concretization distribution $\Pr_\gamma$. Then the tuple ($\mathcal{A}$, α, $\Pr_\gamma$) is a sound probabilistic over-approximation of concrete program $\mathcal{C}$ if for all $z \in \mathcal{D}_{\mathcal{C}}$, $\Pr_{[\![\mathcal{A}]\!]}(\mathcal{C}(z) \mid z) > 0$.

3.2.1 Non-Deterministic Semantics

A sound probabilistic over-approximation is a generalization of a sound non-deterministic over-approximation in the sense that it provides a distribution over feasible states. Thus a sound probabilistic over-approximation has a corresponding sound non-deterministic over-approximation, which we make precise in the following definitions:

Definition 3.6. Non-deterministic semantics. Let $\mathcal{A}$ be a probabilistic program abstraction with compatible concretization distribution $\Pr_\gamma$ and abstraction function α. Then there is a corresonding non-deterministic concretization function $\gamma(a)_\downarrow = \{z \mid \Pr_\gamma(z \mid a) > 0)\}$ and abstract non-deterministic program $\mathcal{A}(a)_\downarrow = \{a' \mid \Pr_{\mathcal{A}}(a' \mid a) > 0)\}$.

We observe that $\gamma(a)_\downarrow$ is compatible with α if $\Pr_\gamma$ is compatible with α. Further, soundness of a probabilistic abstraction implies soundness of its corresponding non-deterministic abstraction, and vice versa:

Theorem 3.1. Non-deterministic sound over-approximation. For any probabilistic program abstraction $\mathcal{A}$ with compatible concretization distribution $\Pr_\gamma$ and abstraction function α, the tuple $(\mathcal{A}, \alpha, \Pr_\gamma)$ is a sound probabilistic over-approximation to concrete program $\mathcal{C}$ if and only if the tuple $(\mathcal{A}(\cdot)_\downarrow, \alpha, \gamma(\cdot)_\downarrow)$ is a sound non-deterministic over-approximation to $\mathcal{C}$.

3.2.2 Concretization Invariance

The concrete semantics $\Pr_{[\![\mathcal{A}]\!]}$ are necessary for reasoning about the concrete domain. However, directly analyzing $\Pr_{[\![\mathcal{A}]\!]}$ is made difficult by the necessity of selecting some compatible concretization distribution $\Pr_\gamma$. Significantly, in the case when a concrete query can be precisely represented using a set of abstract states, $\mathcal{A}$ alone provides sufficient structure to compute a probability in $\Pr_{[\![\mathcal{A}]\!]}$ independent of the choice of $\Pr_\gamma$:

Theorem 3.2. Concretization distribution invariance. Let $\mathcal{A}$ be a probabilistic program abstraction with strongly compatible concretization distribution $\Pr_\gamma$ and abstraction function α. For any $z_i \in \mathcal{D}_{\mathcal{C}}$ and $a_o \in \mathcal{D}_{\mathcal{A}}$,

$$\Pr_{[\![\mathcal{A}]\!]}(a_o|z_i) \overset{\text{def}}{=} \sum_{z_o \in \gamma(a_o)_\downarrow} \Pr_{[\![\mathcal{A}]\!]}(z_o|z_i) = \Pr_{\mathcal{A}}(a_o|\alpha(z_i)).$$

In other words, the probability of an abstracted event occurring in the concrete semantics is equivalent to the probability of that event in the abstract semantics, regardless of the concretization distribution.

We see a visualization of this theorem in Figure 4. Regardless of whether $\Pr_\gamma^1$ or $\Pr_\gamma^2$ are chosen,

$$\begin{aligned}\Pr_{[\![\mathcal{A}]\!]}\left(\gamma(\alpha(x=-1))_\downarrow)\right) &= \Pr_{[\![\mathcal{A}]\!]}(\{-1,-2\}) \\ &= \Pr_{\mathcal{A}}(\{x<0\}).\end{aligned}$$

As a consequence, queries performed on the abstraction $\mathcal{A}$ represent queries performed on the set of all possible strongly-compatible concretization distributions. Thus, even though in the probabilistic setting we must reason about a distribution over concrete states, we can still lift our analyses to the abstract domain, similar to the benefits of non-deterministic abstraction in Section 2.2.3.

3.3 PROBABILISTIC PREDICATE ABSTRACTIONS

Thus far we have seen a semantics for a probabilistic program abstraction, but we do not yet have a way to generate one for a particular program. In this section, we seek to generalize predicate abstraction to the probabilistic domain, and show that in general a probabilistic predicate abstraction is a family of Boolean probabilistic programs with Bernoulli `flip` parameters.

3.3.1 Branch Statements

We saw in Section 2.2.1 that a predicate abstraction of an `if` statement is of the form

```
if(*) {assume(α) ... } else {assume(β) ...}
```

where α and β represent the most precise information we can know about the state of predicates at the *then* and *else* branches of the program. The behavior of the abstraction is non-deterministic in the case when both α and β hold. A probabilistic predicate abstraction of this statement should explicitly quantify the probability of choosing a particular path when either path is possible in the abstraction.

To do so, we first rewrite the predicate abstraction's `if` statement equivalently as follows:

```
if(¬β ∨ (α ∧ ∗)) { ... } else { ... }
```

As in the original formulation, this version ensures that the *then* clause will not be taken if α is false and the *else* clause will not be taken if β is false.[2] The non-deterministic choice $\star$ then determines which path to take when both predicates are true.

A probabilistic predicate abstraction must represent a distribution over paths when α and β both hold. Under the semantics of BERN, we may do so simply by replacing the non-deterministic choice with a `flip`:

```
if(¬β ∨ (α ∧ flip(θ))) { ... } else { ... }
```

Thus a probabilistic version of the predicate abstraction in Figure 3 would have an `if` statement with guard `{x<-4}∨({x<3}∧flip(θ))`, where θ represents the conditional probability that the branch is taken given $-4 \leq x < 3$. As long as $0 < \theta < 1$, all concrete executions are contained within the support of this probabilistic program abstraction, implying that it is a sound probabilistic over-approximation.

3.3.2 Assignment Statements

Section 2.2.2 showed that a concrete assignment is abstracted to a set of predicate assignments of the form γ = `choose(α, β)`, where γ is a predicate and α and β encode the most precise update we can make to γ. The abstraction behaves non-deterministically: it may assign γ to either `true` or `false` when neither α nor β holds. Thus, the probabilistic generalization of an assignment statement needs to represent the conditional probability of γ given $\neg\alpha \wedge \neg\beta$.

First, we re-write the `choose` statement, introducing a non-deterministic $\star$ operator similar to the previous section. We may write an equivalent update to γ:

```
γ = α ∨ (¬β ∧ ⋆)
```

As above, in BERN we then replace $\star$ with a Bernoulli random variable:

```
γ = α ∨ (¬β ∧ flip(θ))
```

[2]Note that by construction α and β cannot both be false.

For example, under this strategy the assignment statement `x=x+1` from Figure 3 would be abstracted to the following BERN program statements, given predicates `{x<-3}` and `{x<4}`:

```
{x<-4}, {x<3} =
    ({x<-4} ∧ {x<3} ∧ flip(θ1)),
    ({x<-4} ∨ ({x<3} ∧ flip(θ2)))
```

3.4 INVARIANTS

In the non-deterministic case, enforcing invariants among predicates is a lightweight procedure of inserting `assume` statements in order to increase the precision of the abstraction. Analogously, in the probabilistic case, we wish to represent distributions over predicates while disallowing inconsistent predicate states. In this section we explore the consequences of enforcing invariants on the abstraction.

An initial approach to enforcing invariants is to straightforwardly generalize the non-deterministic procedure by inserting `observe(`$\mathcal{I}$`)` statements between each assignment, where $\mathcal{I}$ is the invariant which must hold over the predicates. For example, for the concrete program `x=x+10` with the predicates `{x<-4}` and `{x<3}`, we generate the following abstraction:

```
{x<-4}, {x<3} =
    ({x<-4} ∧ {x<3} ∧ flip(θ1)),
    ({x<-4} ∧ {x<3} ∧ flip(θ2))
observe({x<-4}⇒{x<3})
```

A key downside is that the parameters no longer have a *local semantics*: conditioning correlates the otherwise independent flips. This complicates the probability computation, which now involves a partition function.

Therefore we present an alternative abstraction construction procedure which preserves the local semantics of the parameters of the abstraction while enforcing invariants over predicates. Consider again the concrete program `x=x+10`. We generate an abstraction using the same predicates as before. However, instead of simply inserting `observe` statements, we utilize control flow in order to effectively condition on the previously assigned value:

```
{x<3} = {x<3} ∧ {x<-4} ∧ flip(θ1)
if({x<3}) {
  {x<-4} = {x<-4} ∧ flip(θ2)
} else {
  {x<-4} = F
}
```

This abstraction, which we call *structurally dependent*, updates each predicate sequentially, considering all previous decisions. Each concrete statement is abstracted to several abstract statements which utilize control flow to disallow invalid states. The state `{x<-4}∧!{x<3}` is guaranteed to have 0 probability without the use of `observe` statements. Further, the parameters have a local interpretation as a conditional probability: it is not necessary to compute a partition function to compute the probability of a particular predicate configuration.

Fundamentally, these two methods of constructing the abstraction represent different factorizations of the distribution. In the non-deterministic context with invariant enforcement, these two abstractions are equivalent.

4 DISCUSSION

This paper focuses on the definition and key properties of probabilistic program abstractions. In this section we discuss natural next steps for the work. Traditional nondeterministic program abstractions are typically used to produce the set of reachable program states, in order to verify invariants. The analogous operation on a probabilistic program abstraction is inference. First we discuss possible approaches to inference for probabilistic predicate abstractions, by leveraging both model checking and weighted model counting. Second, we discuss how the ability to perform inference on a probabilistic abstraction could be a key enabler for a new approach to performing inference on more general probabilistic programs. The main idea is to reduce inference on a probabilistic program to the task of choosing particular `flip` probabilities for a corresponding probabilistic abstraction.

4.1 INFERENCE FOR PROBABILISTIC PREDICATE ABSTRACTIONS

We believe that existing techniques from the programming languages literature which are designed for working with non-deterministic Boolean programs can be extended to perform inference on BERN programs. We can then use weighted model counting to evaluate queries. We note that abstractions allow one to query the marginal probability of an event at any point in the program, not merely upon program termination.

Probabilistic Model Checking The problem of computing the set of reachable states in a Boolean program is known as the *model checking problem* and has been extensively studied by the programming languages community. Commonly one represents the set of reachable states at any point in the program as some Boolean knowledge base Δ. In many existing tools, Δ is represented using a binary decision diagram (Ball and Rajamani, 2000). Inference in BERN is thus an extension to the traditional model checking paradigm in which we introduce weighted variables for the state of each `flip`. During model checking, we treat each `flip` as an unconstrained Boolean variable.

```
a = unif [0, 10)
if (a < 5) { b = unif [0, 10) }
  else { b = unif [0, 20) }
if (b < 5) { c = unif [0, 10) }
  else { c = unif [0, 20) }
```

(a) Probabilistic program for Bayesian network ⓐ → ⓑ → ⓒ.

```
{a<5} = flip(1/2)
if({a<5}) { {b<5} = flip(1/2) }
  else { {b<5} = flip(1/4) }
if({b<5}) { {c<5} = flip(1/2) }
  else { {c<5} = flip(1/4) }
```

(b) Probabilistic abstraction with `{a<5}`, `{b<5}`, and `{c<5}`.

Figure 5: A concrete probabilistic program and a probabilistic abstraction for computing $\Pr_{[\![\mathcal{A}]\!]}(c < 5)$.

For example, consider the probabilistic predicate abstraction statement `{x<4} = {x<4} ∧ flip(`θ`)`. We assume Δ = `{x<4}` prior to execution of statement. Following this statement, Δ' = `({x<4}∧flip(`θ`)) ∨ (!{x<4} ∧ !flip(`θ`))`. See Ball and Rajamani (2000) for more details.

Weighted Model Counting Whereas model checking is usually concerned with determining whether $\mathcal{A}$ can reach a particular state, in probabilistic program inference we are concerned with the weighted sum of reachable states, where the weights are induced by the parameters of the `flip`s in each model. The programming languages community has two primary methodologies for computing the set of reachable states in a Boolean program: (1) knowledge compilation to binary decision diagrams (Ball and Rajamani, 2000), and (2) satisfiability methods (Donaldson et al., 2011). Both of these approaches can be generalized to perform weighted model counting for inference in BERN.

The knowledge compilation approach to model checking is already capable of performing weighted model counting due to the nature of the queries efficiently supported by a binary decision diagram (Darwiche and Marquis, 2001), and is used for inference in discrete probabilistic programs (Fierens et al., 2013) and Bayesian networks (Chavira and Darwiche, 2008). The satisfiability approach to model checking can be extended to perform weighted model counting. This problem is #P-hard (Valiant, 1979), but a number of recent approximation methods have been explored (Chakraborty et al., 2013; Belle et al., 2015b; Zhao et al., 2016); see Gomes et al. (2009) for a survey of the subject.

4.2 INFERENCE FOR GENERAL PROBABILISTIC PROGRAMS

Consider the probabilistic program in Figure 5a and suppose we want to evaluate $\Pr_{[\![\mathcal{C}]\!]}(c < 5)$. We will sketch an approach to doing so using probabilistic predicate abstractions.

Figure 5b shows a probabilistic predicate abstraction for our original probabilistic program, induced by the predicates `{a<5}`, `{b<5}`, and `{c<5}`. Initially each `flip` has its own parameter to represent its probability. In the figure, we show particular values for each parameter, which were computed by performing queries on fragments of the original concrete program. For example, the concrete assignment `a = unif[0, 10)` is abstracted to `{a<5} = flip(1/2)` by computing $\Pr(a < 5)$ on this single statement of the concrete program. The other parameters can be learned similarly. The key point is that each of these queries is much easier to evaluate in the original program than the actual query of interest, as they are over smaller fragments of the program.

Now we show that the abstraction captures enough detail to answer our query precisely. Computing the weighted model count using the approach described in the previous subsection, we see that:

$$\Pr_{\mathcal{A}}(\texttt{\{c<5\}}) = \overbrace{0.5 \cdot 0.5 \cdot 0.5}^{\texttt{\{a<5\},\{b<5\},\{c<5\}}} + \overbrace{0.5 \cdot 0.5 \cdot 0.25}^{\texttt{\{a<5\},!\{b<5\},\{c<5\}}}$$
$$+ \underbrace{0.5 \cdot 0.25 \cdot 0.5}_{\texttt{!\{a<5\},\{b<5\},\{c<5\}}} + \underbrace{0.5 \cdot 0.75 \cdot 0.25}_{\texttt{!\{a<5\},!\{b<5\},\{c<5\}}} = \frac{11}{32}.$$

The result is in fact the answer to the original query.

In this way, the inference problem on $\mathcal{C}$ is decomposed into two, potentially much simpler, problems: (i) fixing the parameters of an abstraction, and (ii) weighted model counting on the abstraction. There remains considerable theoretical work to formally connect the semantics of the probabilistic abstraction with a probabilistic concrete program, as well as practical work to realize the benefits of the approach on desired applications.

5 RELATED WORK

Probabilistic reasoning and static analysis. Several recent works leverage a probabilistic model to guide refinements of a program abstraction (Grigore and Yang, 2016; Zhang et al., 2017). However, the abstractions themselves are not probabilistic. Gehr et al. (2016) use static analysis of a probabilistic program to decompose the problem of inference along paths, which are then dispatched to specialized integration tools depending on the constraints of each path; this work analyzes the original concrete program and does not rely on abstractions.

Probabilistic abstract interpretation. Probabilistic abstract interpretation is used to reason about programs with probabilistic semantics, for example to place upper bounds on the probability of a particular path (Monniaux, 2000) or construct Monte-Carlo methods (Monniaux, 2001); this line of work does not explore the connections between abstractions and probabilistic programs, nor does it model concrete program marginals. However, our work does not reason about unbounded loops. The framework of Cousot and Monerau (2012) is a highly general framework for reasoning about programs using probabilistic abstract interpretation; however, they do not consider the abstraction itself to be a statistical model.

Probabilistic programming systems. Many systems have been developed within the AI and programming languages communities that tackle the problem of probabilistic program inference, but few utilize abstractions. Systems such as Church (Goodman et al., 2008), Anglican (Wood et al., 2014), Stan (Carpenter et al., 2016), BLOG (Milch et al., 2005), and others directly analyze the concrete program. Weighted model counting and knowledge compilation have been used to perform probabilistic program inference (Fierens et al., 2013); they also do not leverage program abstractions. Several probabilistic inference approaches capture distributions in continuous domains by using Boolean predicates, either as an approximation (Michels et al., 2016) or as an exact representation (Belle et al., 2015a). Finally, program abstraction with the purpose of inference is an instance of approximate lifted inference (Kersting, 2012): the abstract domain groups together sets of concrete states, with the aim of reasoning at the higher level.

6 CONCLUSION

Probabilistic program abstractions are currently unexplored territory for aiding in the analysis of programs, despite the popularity of probabilistic programming. We provided a formal framework, derived useful properties, and described probabilistic predicate abstractions techniques. Much theoretical and practical work remains to be done in exploring alternative characterizations, showing relationships between concrete programs and their abstractions, and building practical probabilistic abstraction tools. We hope our framework provides the foundational theory to enable these advances in the future.

Acknowledgements

This work is partially supported by NSF grants #CCF-1527923, #IIS-1657613, and #IIS-1633857, and by DARPA grant #N66001-17-2-4032. S.H. is supported by a National Physical Sciences Consortium Fellowship.

References

T. Ball and S. K. Rajamani. Bebop: A symbolic model checker for boolean programs. In *SPIN Model Checking and Software Verification*, pages 113–130, 2000.

T. Ball and S. K. Rajamani. The SLAM project: Debugging system software via static analysis. In *Proc. of POPL*, pages 1–3, 2002.

T. Ball, R. Majumdar, T. Millstein, and S. K. Rajamani. Automatic predicate abstraction of c programs. In *Proc. of PLDI*, pages 203–213, 2001.

V. Belle, A. Passerini, and G. Van den Broeck. Probabilistic inference in hybrid domains by weighted model integration. In *Proc. of IJCAI*, pages 2770–2776, 2015a.

V. Belle, G. Van den Broeck, and A. Passerini. Hashing-based approximate probabilistic inference in hybrid domains. In *Proc. of UAI*, pages 141–150, 2015b.

B. Carpenter, A. Gelman, M. Hoffman, D. Lee, B. Goodrich, M. Betancourt, M. A. Brubaker, P. Li, and A. Riddell. Stan: A probabilistic programming language. *J. Statistical Software*, VV(Ii), 2016.

S. Chakraborty, K. S. Meel, and M. Y. Vardi. A scalable approximate model counter. In *Proc. of CP*, pages 200–216, 2013.

M. Chavira and A. Darwiche. On probabilistic inference by weighted model counting. *J. Artificial Intelligence*, 172(6-7):772–799, Apr. 2008.

P. Cousot and R. Cousot. Abstract interpretation: A unified lattice model for static analysis of programs by construction or approximation of fixpoints. In *Proc. of POPL*, pages 238–252, 1977.

P. Cousot and M. Monerau. Probabilistic abstract interpretation. In *Proc. of ESOP*, pages 169–193, 2012.

A. Darwiche and P. Marquis. A Knowledge Compilation Map. *Proc. of IJCAI*, 17:175–182, 2001.

L. De Moura and N. Bjørner. Z3: An efficient smt solver. In *Proc. of TACAS/ETAPS*, pages 337–340, Berlin, Heidelberg, 2008.

E. W. Dijkstra. *A Discipline of Programming*. Prentice-Hall, Englewood Cliffs, New Jersey, 1976.

A. Donaldson, A. Kaiser, D. Kroening, and T. Wahl. Symmetry-aware predicate abstraction for shared-variable concurrent programs. In *Proc. of CAV*, volume 6806 of *LNCS*, pages 356–371. Springer, 2011.

D. Fierens, G. Van den Broeck, J. Renkens, D. Shterionov, B. Gutmann, I. Thon, G. Janssens, and L. De Raedt. Inference and learning in probabilistic logic programs using weighted boolean formulas. *J. Theory and Practice of Logic Programming*, 15(3): 358 – 401, 2013.

T. Gehr, S. Misailovic, and M. Vechev. Psi: Exact symbolic inference for probabilistic programs. *Proc. of ESOP/ETAPS*, 9779:62–83, 2016.

C. P. Gomes, A. Sabharwal, and B. Selman. Model counting. In A. Biere, M. Heule, H. van Maaren, and T. Walsh, editors, *Handbook of Satisfiability*, volume 185 of *Frontiers in Artificial Intelligence and Applications*, pages 633–654. IOS Press, 2009.

N. D. Goodman, V. K. Mansinghka, D. M. Roy, K. Bonawitz, and J. B. Tenenbaum. Church: A language for generative models. In *Proc. of UAI*, pages 220–229, 2008.

S. Graf and H. Saïdi. Construction of abstract state graphs with PVS. In *Proc. of CAV*, volume 1254, pages 72–83. Springer-Verlag, June 1997.

R. Grigore and H. Yang. Abstraction Refinement Guided by a Learnt Probabilistic Model. *Proc. of POPL*, pages 485–498, 2016.

K. Kersting. Lifted probabilistic inference. In *Proc. of ECAI*, pages 33–38, 2012.

S. Michels, A. Hommersom, and P. J. F. Lucas. Approximate probabilistic inference with bounded error for hybrid probabilistic logic programming. In *Proc. of IJCAI*, pages 3616–3622, 2016.

B. Milch, B. Marthi, S. Russell, D. Sontag, D. L. Ong, and A. Kolobov. Blog: Probabilistic models with unknown objects. In *Proc. of IJCAI*, pages 1352–1359, 2005.

D. Monniaux. Abstract interpretation of probabilistic semantics. In *International Symposium on Static Analysis*, pages 322–339, 2000.

D. Monniaux. An abstract monte-carlo method for the analysis of probabilistic programs. *SIGPLAN Not.*, 36 (3):93–101, Jan. 2001.

L. G. Valiant. The complexity of computing the permanent. *J. Theoretical Computer Science*, 8:189–201, 1979.

F. Wood, J. W. van de Meent, and V. Mansinghka. A new approach to probabilistic programming inference. In *Proc. of AISTATS*, pages 1024–1032, 2014.

X. Zhang, X. Si, and M. Naik. Combining the logical and the probabilistic in program analysis. In *Proc. ACM SIGPLAN International Workshop on Machine Learning and Programming Languages*, pages 27–34, 2017.

S. Zhao, S. Chaturapruek, A. Sabharwal, and S. Ermon. Closing the gap between short and long xors for model counting. In *Proc. of AAAI*, pages 3322–3329, 2016.

Communication-Efficient Distributed Primal-Dual Algorithm for Saddle Point Problems

Yaodong Yu*
Nanyang Technological University
ydyu@ntu.edu.sg

Sulin Liu*
Nanyang Technological University
liusl@ntu.edu.sg

Sinno Jialin Pan
Nanyang Technological University
sinnopan@ntu.edu.sg

Abstract

Primal-dual algorithms, which are proposed to solve reformulated convex-concave saddle point problems, have been proven to be effective for solving a generic class of convex optimization problems, especially when the problems are ill-conditioned. However, the saddle point problem still lacks a distributed optimization framework where primal-dual algorithms can be employed. In this paper, we propose a novel communication-efficient distributed optimization framework to solve the convex-concave saddle point problem based on primal-dual methods. We carefully design local subproblems and a central problem such that our proposed distributed optimization framework is communication-efficient. We provide a convergence analysis of our proposed algorithm, and extend it to address non-smooth and non-strongly convex loss functions. We conduct extensive experiments on several real-world datasets to demonstrate competitive performance of the proposed method, especially on ill-conditioned problems.

1 INTRODUCTION

In the era of big data, developing distributed machine learning algorithms has become increasingly important yet challenging. In this work, we focus on developing a new distributed optimization algorithm for regularized *empirical risk minimization* (ERM), which is a generic class of convex optimization problems that arises often from machine learning. Specifically, our goal is to minimize the empirical loss defined over n data samples:

$$\min_{\mathbf{x}\in\mathbb{R}^d} \mathcal{P}(\mathbf{x}) = \frac{1}{n}\sum_{i=1}^{n}\phi_i(a_i^\top \mathbf{x}) + g(\mathbf{x}), \quad (1)$$

where $a_1, ..., a_n \in \mathbb{R}^d$ are feature vectors of n data points, $\phi_i : \mathbb{R} \to \mathbb{R}$ is a convex loss function with the linear predictor $a_i^\top \mathbf{x}$, for $i = 1, ..., n$, and $g : \mathbb{R}^d \to \mathbb{R}$ is a convex regularization function for the predictor $\mathbf{x} \in \mathbb{R}^d$. Suppose that a distributed system consists of K machines, and each machine has access only a subset $\mathcal{P}_k$ of the data $[n] := \{1, ..., n\}$, where $\{\mathcal{P}_k\}_{k=1}^K$ is a given partition of the dataset $[n]$, and we denote by $n_k = |\mathcal{P}_k|$.

1.1 COMMUNICATION-EFFICIENT DISTRIBUTED OPTIMIZATION

One of the most important issues in distributed optimization is the communication efficiency because communication between machines is much more expensive than reading data from the memory on local machines. Therefore, more and more efforts have been made in proposing communication-efficient methods in distributed optimization (Jaggi et al., 2014, Ma et al., 2015, Reddi et al., 2016, Shamir et al., 2014, Smith et al., 2015, Yang, 2013). The basic idea behind these methods is to carefully design local computation and communication in a distributed system. To achieve this goal, existing methods usually decompose the optimization problem into K local subproblems, denoted by $\mathcal{L}_k$, with respect to local data of each machine. After each local machine performs an arbitrary optimization method on $\mathcal{L}_k$ and solves it approximately, updated information from local machines is sent to a central node to carry out a central update. This allows one to control the trade-off between communication and local computation, which is more flexible in distributed setting.

In general, existing communication-efficient methods can be classified into two categories. A first category

*Indicates equal contributions.

is referred to as *gradient*-type, which aims to decompose the problem (1) into K local subproblems and solve each subproblem using gradient descent methods, such as stochastic variance reduced gradient (SVRG) (Johnson and Zhang, 2013), on each local machine independently, and then update the optimization variables by doing an average of local variables of each machine (Reddi et al., 2016, Shamir et al., 2014).

The second one is referred to as *coordinate*-type, which usually focuses on solving the dual problem of (1),

$$\max_{\boldsymbol{\alpha}\in\mathbb{R}^n} \mathcal{D}(\boldsymbol{\alpha}) = \frac{1}{n}\sum_{i=1}^{n} -\phi_i^*(\alpha_i) - g^*(-\frac{1}{n}\sum_{i=1}^{n}\alpha_i a_i), \quad (2)$$

where ϕ_i^* is the conjugate function of ϕ_i, $\boldsymbol{\alpha}$ is the dual variable vector with the i-th element being α_i. This category of methods decomposes the dual problem (2) into K local subproblems with regard to each machine, and employs a coordinate-type method, such as stochastic dual coordinate ascent method (SDCA) (Shalev-Shwartz and Zhang, 2013), to solve each local subproblem. After each local subproblem is approximately solved, the central node takes an average/add step according to the local update from each machine (Jaggi et al., 2014, Ma et al., 2015, Yang, 2013). Our proposed method falls into this category.

There are two limitations of the *coordinate*-type approach. One limitation is that most existing coordinate-type methods fail to match the communication complexity lower bounds proved in (Arjevani and Shamir, 2015). For example, when ϕ_i is $(1/\gamma)$-smooth, g is λ-strongly convex, and $R = \max_i \|a_i\|_2$ in problem (1), then the *condition number* is defined as

$$\kappa = R^2/(\lambda\gamma), \quad (3)$$

and the lower bound of communication complexity obtained in (Arjevani and Shamir, 2015) is $\tilde{\mathcal{O}}\left(\sqrt{\kappa}\log(1/\epsilon)\right)$ in order to achieve an ϵ-suboptimal solution (Nesterov, 2013). Since these *coordinate*-type methods (Jaggi et al., 2014, Ma et al., 2015, Yang, 2013) could be seen as a distributed version of SDCA, and the iteration complexity of SDCA is $\tilde{\mathcal{O}}\left(\kappa\log(1/\epsilon)\right)$, the communication complexity of these methods (Jaggi et al., 2014, Ma et al., 2015, Yang, 2013) is $\tilde{\mathcal{O}}\left(\kappa\log(1/\epsilon)\right)$, which does not match the optimal communication complexity. The problem could get worse when problem (1) is ill-conditioned, i.e., $\kappa \gg 1$. The other limitation is that it is not straight-forward to extend existing coordinate-type approaches (Jaggi et al., 2014, Ma et al., 2015, Yang, 2013) to deal with different regularization forms of the regularization term $g(\cdot)$ other than ℓ_2 regularization.

1.2 OUR APPROACH

To overcome the limitations mentioned above, we propose a novel communication-efficient distributed framework with a primal-dual algorithm for saddle point problems (Chambolle and Pock, 2011, Zhang and Xiao, 2015b). The reasons that we focus on developing distributed framework for saddle point problems are three folds:

1. It has been shown that saddle point algorithms are able to obtain comparable and even more stable performance than other state-of-the-art techniques for convex optimization (Chambolle and Pock, 2011, Yu et al., 2015, Zhang and Xiao, 2015b).

2. Primal-dual coordinate algorithms for saddle point problems are able to reach the optimal iteration complexity as proved by Zhang and Xiao (2015b).

3. Since primal-dual algorithms keep both primal and dual variables in optimization, they are able to deal with different kinds of regularization terms $g(\cdot)$, such as ℓ_1-regularization, naturally.

Therefore, we aim to develop a distributed primal-dual algorithm which can inherit the above three properties in a distributed environment. To be specific, we first reformulate problem (1) as a convex-concave saddle point problem through convex conjugation, which keeps both primal and dual variables in optimization. We then decompose the saddle point problem into carefully designed local subproblems, which can be solved independently by each machine with respect to its local data. After the local subproblems are solved approximately, the updated local dual variables of each machine are sent to a central node. Based on all the updates of local dual variables, we construct a central problem and get the central update of the primal variables on the central node. Finally, the central node sends the updated primal variables and aggregated dual variables to each local machine for next local optimization iteration. Details will be described in Section 3.

As will be discussed in Section 4 and Section 5, by carefully designing the local subproblems and the central problem, our algorithm is able to reach the communication complexity lower bounds, and deal with different kinds of regularization terms. As the parameter λ of the regularization function $g(\cdot)$ is usually on the order of $1/\sqrt{n}$ or $1/n$ for many machine learning problems, we are especially interested in solving problem (1) under the distributed setting when it is ill-conditioned. With an extremely large-scale dataset, the *condition number* in (3) could be relatively large ($\kappa \gg 1$). We will show through experiments in Section 6 that our proposed algorithm can obtain better and more stable performance on ill-conditioned problems compared to other communication-efficient distributed optimization methods. Moreover, we provide a solution to extend our algorithm to deal with non-smooth and non-strongly convex optimization problems in Section 5.

1.3 OTHER RELATED WORK

Besides the communication-efficient distributed optimization methods reviewed above, there exist other parallel and distributed optimization techniques. For example, a well-known approach for solving problem (1) is to perform a gradient descent method implemented in a distributed system. Each local machine computes its local gradient and sends it to the central node. The central node aggregates the local gradient to take a gradient step and updates $\mathbf{x}$, and then broadcasts it back to each local machine for the next iteration updates. If the accelerated gradient descent method (Nesterov, 2013) is used, one can obtain the iteration complexity $\tilde{\mathcal{O}}\left(\sqrt{\kappa}\log(1/\epsilon)\right)$. Another popular technique is distributed alternating direction method of multipliers (ADMM) (Boyd et al., 2011, Shi et al., 2014), whose complexity is $\tilde{\mathcal{O}}\left(\sqrt{\kappa}\log(1/\epsilon)\right)$ under certain conditions. Recently, Zhang and Xiao (2015a) proposed a distributed algorithm based on the inexact damped Newton method, which matches the communication complexity lower bound $\tilde{\mathcal{O}}\left(\sqrt{\kappa}\log(1/\epsilon)\right)$. For more related distributed and parallel optimization methods, we refer the readers to (Arjevani and Shamir, 2015, Chang et al., 2014, Duchi et al., 2013, Zhang et al., 2012) for a more comprehensive literature of the related work.

2 PRELIMINARIES

In this section, we introduce first-order primal-dual algorithms for convex-concave saddle point problems in a single machine. To begin with, we reformulate the primal problem (1) as a convex-concave saddle point problem through convex conjugation, and the saddle point reformulation is widely applied in machine learning (Dai et al., 2016, Zhang and Xiao, 2015b). Based on the definition of convex conjugate, we replace each component function $\phi_i(a_i^\top \mathbf{x})$ by

$$\phi_i(a_i^\top \mathbf{x}) = \sup_{y_i \in \mathbb{R}} \left\{ y_i \langle a_i, \mathbf{x}\rangle - \phi_i^*(y_i) \right\},$$

where $\phi_i^*(y_i) = \sup_{\alpha\in\mathbb{R}} \{\alpha y_i - \phi_i(\alpha)\}$ is the convex conjugate of ϕ_i, then we arrive at a convex-concave saddle point problem

$$\min_{\mathbf{x}\in\mathbb{R}^d} \max_{\mathbf{y}\in\mathbb{R}^n} f(\mathbf{x}, \mathbf{y}), \tag{4}$$

where

$$f(\mathbf{x}, \mathbf{y}) \stackrel{\text{def}}{=} \frac{1}{n}\sum_{i=1}^{n} \left(y_i\langle a_i, \mathbf{x}\rangle - \phi_i^*(y_i)\right) + g(\mathbf{x}),$$

where $\mathbf{y} \in \mathbb{R}^n$ is referred to as a vector of dual variables with its i-th element denoted by y_i, and each y_i is associated with a data point a_i. Under the assumption that ϕ_i is $(1/\gamma)$-smooth, g is λ-strongly convex, and each ϕ_i^* is γ-strongly convex, the saddle point problem (4) has a unique solution, which is denoted by $(\mathbf{x}^\star, \mathbf{y}^\star)$.

Based on the reformulated problem (4), we could rewrite the optimization problem as

$$\min_{\mathbf{x}\in\mathbb{R}^d} \max_{\mathbf{y}\in\mathbb{R}^n} f(\mathbf{x}, \mathbf{y}) = \frac{1}{n}\langle A\mathbf{y}, \mathbf{x}\rangle - \Phi^*(\mathbf{y}) + g(\mathbf{x}),$$

where $A = [a_1, ..., a_n]$ and $\Phi^*(\mathbf{y}) = \frac{1}{n}\sum_{i=1}^n \phi_i^*(y_i)$. This is the generic saddle point problem (Chambolle and Pock, 2011). To solve this optimization problem, the basic idea is to alternatingly maximize f with repect to $\mathbf{y}$, and minimize f with respect to $\mathbf{x}$, which is

$$\begin{aligned}
\mathbf{y}^{(t+1)} &= \arg\max_{\mathbf{y}\in\mathbb{R}^n} \frac{1}{n}\langle A\mathbf{y}, \bar{\mathbf{x}}^{(t)}\rangle - \Phi^*(\mathbf{y}) - \frac{\|\mathbf{y}-\mathbf{y}^{(t)}\|_2^2}{2\sigma n}, \\
\mathbf{x}^{(t+1)} &= \arg\min_{\mathbf{x}\in\mathbb{R}^d} \frac{1}{n}\langle A\mathbf{y}^{(t+1)}, \mathbf{x}\rangle + g(\mathbf{x}) + \frac{\|\mathbf{x}-\mathbf{x}^{(t)}\|_2^2}{2\tau}, \\
\bar{\mathbf{x}}^{(t+1)} &= \mathbf{x}^{(t+1)} + \theta\left(\mathbf{x}^{(t+1)} - \mathbf{x}^{(t)}\right),
\end{aligned}$$

where the parameters τ and σ control the quadratic regularization terms with respect to $\mathbf{x}$ and $\mathbf{y}$, respectively, which is similar to the use of step size in primal methods. And $\bar{\mathbf{x}}^{(t+1)}$ is the extrapolation from $\mathbf{x}^{(t)}$ and $\mathbf{x}^{(t+1)}$ with parameter $\theta \in [0, 1]$. Here, $\theta\left(\mathbf{x}^{(t+1)} - \mathbf{x}^{(t)}\right)$ is similar to the momentum term in Nesterov acceleration (Nesterov, 2013). There have been various primal-dual coordinate algorithms designed based on the above scheme, such as (Chambolle and Pock, 2011, Yu et al., 2015, Zhang and Xiao, 2015b). Among them, Yu et al. (2015), Zhang and Xiao (2015b) developed stochastic versions of the primal-dual algorithm for the saddle point problem. Suppose ϕ_i is $(1/\gamma)$-smooth and g is λ-strongly convex, most existing algorithms (Chambolle and Pock, 2011, Yu et al., 2015, Zhang and Xiao, 2015b) can achieve linear convergence rate to obtain an ϵ-accurate solution. The (expected) iteration complexity of these methods is $\tilde{\mathcal{O}}\left(\sqrt{\kappa}\log(1/\epsilon)\right)$, which is desired on ill-conditioned problems.

3 DISTRIBUTED SADDLE-POINT FRAMEWORK

In this section, we present our proposed communication-efficient **Di**stributed **S**addle **P**oint **A**lgorithm (DiSPA) in detail. Assume that the dataset $\{a_i\}_{i=1}^n$ is distributed over K local machines, each machine k has access to a subset $\mathcal{P}_k$ of the data with size of n_k. Here we define K local vectors of $\mathbf{y}$ by using the notation $\mathbf{y}_{[k]} \in \mathbb{R}^n$ for $k = 1, ..., K$:

$$\left(\mathbf{y}_{[k]}\right)_i = \begin{cases} y_i, & \text{if } i \in \mathcal{P}_k, \\ 0, & \text{otherwise,} \end{cases}$$

and K local data matrix of A by using the notation $A_{[k]} \in \mathbb{R}^{d \times n}$ for $k = 1, ..., K$:

$$\left(A_{[k]}\right)_i = \begin{cases} a_i, & \text{if } i \in \mathcal{P}_k, \\ \mathbf{0}, & \text{otherwise,} \end{cases}$$

where $\left(A_{[k]}\right)_i$ denotes the i-th column of $A_{[k]}$, and $\mathbf{0}$ is a d-dimensional vector of all zeros. According to the data partition, we decompose the problem (4) into K local subproblems, and define the associated central problem. The core idea is to solve the defined **local subproblems** on each local machine independently, and then centralize the updated information of each machine to solve a easy **central problem**.

3.1 LOCAL SUBPROBLEMS

We define a local subproblem of the original saddle point problem (4) for machine k, which only requires accessing data that is available locally, i.e., $\mathcal{P}_k$. Specifically, each local subproblem of machine k at t-iteration is defined as

$$\min_{\mathbf{x} \in \mathbb{R}^d} \max_{\mathbf{y}_{[k]} \in \mathbb{R}^n} \mathcal{L}_k^{(t)}(\mathbf{x}, \mathbf{y}_{[k]}), \tag{5}$$

where

$$\begin{aligned} \mathcal{L}_k^{(t)}(\mathbf{x}, \mathbf{y}_{[k]}) :=& \frac{1}{n} \sum_{j \in \mathcal{P}_k} \left(y_j \langle a_j, \mathbf{x} \rangle - \phi_j^*(y_j)\right) + g(\mathbf{x}) \\ &+ \frac{1}{n} \sum_{i \notin \mathcal{P}_k} y_i^{(t-1)} \langle a_i, \mathbf{x} \rangle + r_k^{(t)}(\mathbf{x}, \mathbf{y}_{[k]}), \end{aligned}$$

and

$$r_k^{(t)}(\mathbf{x}, \mathbf{y}_{[k]}) = \frac{\|\mathbf{x} - \mathbf{x}^{(t-1)}\|_2^2}{2\tau} - \frac{K \|\mathbf{y}_{[k]} - \mathbf{y}_{[k]}^{(t-1)}\|_2^2}{2\sigma n}.$$

Each local subproblem is related to the solution obtained in the previous iteration $\left(\mathbf{x}^{(t-1)}, \mathbf{y}^{(t-1)}\right)$, and we will define the parameters τ, σ later. The first two terms can be regarded as a local version of the original saddle point problem (4). The third term $\frac{1}{n} \sum_{i \notin \mathcal{P}_k} y_i^{(t-1)} \langle a_i, \mathbf{x} \rangle = \frac{1}{n} \langle \sum_{l \neq k} A_{[l]} \mathbf{y}_{[l]}^{(t-1)}, \mathbf{x} \rangle$ in (5) can be interpreted as the interaction with other local subproblems. And the quadratic regularization term $r_k^{(t)}(\mathbf{x}, \mathbf{y}_{[k]})$ is used to enforce $\mathbf{x}$ and $\mathbf{y}_{[k]}$ not to move too far away from solution obtained at the previous iteration.

To solve the local subproblem $\mathcal{L}_k^{(t)}(\mathbf{x}, \mathbf{y}_{[k]})$, we could apply primal-dual coordinate type of methods (Yu et al., 2015, Zhang and Xiao, 2015b). The input needed for solving the local subproblem would be $\mathbf{x}^{(t-1)}$ and $A\mathbf{y}^{(t-1)}$, as the term $\sum_{l \neq k} A_{[l]} \mathbf{y}_{[l]}^{(t-1)}$ can be expressed as $\left(A\mathbf{y}^{(t-1)} - A_{[k]} \mathbf{y}_{[k]}^{(t-1)}\right)$ and machine k has access to $\left(A_{[k]}, \mathbf{y}_{[k]}^{(t-1)}\right)$. By denoting our local optimization algorithm used as 'Local-DiSPA', we could denote the procedure of solving the local subproblem as $\left(\mathbf{x}_k^{(t)}, \mathbf{y}_{[k]}^{(t)}\right) \leftarrow$ Local-DiSPA$(\mathbf{x}^{(t-1)}, A\mathbf{y}^{(t-1)})$. Note that in our framework, each local subproblem is only required to be solved approximately.

3.2 CENTRAL PROBLEM

Let $\left(\mathbf{x}_k^{(t)}, \mathbf{y}_{[k]}^{(t)}\right)$ denote the approximate solution obtained by solving $\mathcal{L}_k^{(t)}(\mathbf{x}, \mathbf{y}_{[k]})$ on machine k. Let $\mathbf{y}^{(t)} = \sum_{k=1}^K \mathbf{y}_{[k]}^{(t)}$, we define a central problem at t-iteration as

$$\mathbf{x}^{(t)} = \arg\min_{\mathbf{x} \in \mathbb{R}^d} \mathcal{C}^{(t)}(\mathbf{x}), \tag{6}$$

where

$$\mathcal{C}^{(t)}(\mathbf{x}) := \frac{1}{n} \sum_{i=1}^n y_i^{(t)} \langle a_i, \mathbf{x} \rangle + g(\mathbf{x}) + \frac{\|\mathbf{x} - \mathbf{x}^{(t-1)}\|_2^2}{2\tau}.$$

The central update involves two steps. Firstly, updated local $A_{[k]} \mathbf{y}_{[k]}^{(t)} \in \mathbb{R}^d$ are sent to the central node. After that, we solve (6) on the central node, and then send the updated $\mathbf{x}^{(t)} \in \mathbb{R}^d$ and $A\mathbf{y}^{(t)} \in \mathbb{R}^d$ of the t-iteration back to each local machine. The central update could be viewed as minimizing the original saddle point problem (4) over $\mathbf{x}$ with updated $\mathbf{y}^{(t)}$. Also, we should observe that the parameter τ defined in (5) and (6) is the same parameter, which is one of the key points of our framework.

3.3 OVERALL ALGORITHM DESCRIPTION

The overall algorithm of DiSPA is presented in Algorithm 1. Firstly, we distribute the initial dual variable $\mathbf{y}^{(0)}$ to K local machines, and aggregate $A_{[k]} \mathbf{y}_{[k]}^{(0)}$ from all machines to compute $A\mathbf{y}^{(0)} \leftarrow \sum_{k=1}^K A_{[k]} \mathbf{y}_{[k]}^{(0)}$. After that, the initial primal variables $\mathbf{x}^{(0)}$ and the transformed dual variables $A\mathbf{y}^{(0)}$ are sent to each machine (Steps 2-4). Secondly, each machine performs optimization on its own local subproblem $\mathcal{L}_k^{(t)}(\mathbf{x}, \mathbf{y}_{[k]})$, using a primal-dual algorithm, such as SPDC (Zhang and Xiao, 2015b), and sends its local update $A_{[k]} \mathbf{y}_{[k]}^{(t)} \in \mathbb{R}^d$ to the central

Algorithm 1 DiSPA($f, \mathbf{x}^{(0)}, \mathbf{y}^{(0)}, \tau, \sigma, T$)

1: **Input:** Data points $\{a_i\}_{i=1}^n$ distributed across K machines $\{\mathcal{P}_k\}_{k=1}^K$, parameters $\tau, \sigma \in \mathbb{R}$, initial primal variables $\mathbf{x}^{(0)} \in \mathbb{R}^d$ and initial dual variables $\mathbf{y}^{(0)} \in \mathbb{R}^n$.
2: Distribute $\mathbf{y}^{(0)}$ to K machines as $\mathbf{y}_{[k]}^{(0)}$ for each.
3: Each machine compute $A_{[k]}\mathbf{y}_{[k]}^{(0)}$, and send it back to the central node.
4: Perform $A\mathbf{y}^{(0)} \leftarrow \sum_{k=1}^K A_{[k]}\mathbf{y}_{[k]}^{(0)}$ on the central node, and send $\mathbf{x}^{(0)}$ and $A\mathbf{y}^{(0)}$ to each machine
5: **for** $t = 1, 2, ..., T$ **do**
6:     **for** $k \in [K]$ in parallel over all machines **do**
7:         $\left(\mathbf{x}_k^{(t)}, \mathbf{y}_{[k]}^{(t)}\right) \leftarrow$Local-DiSPA$(\mathbf{x}^{(t-1)}, A\mathbf{y}^{(t-1)})$
8:         Send $A_{[k]}\mathbf{y}_{[k]}^{(t)}$ to the central node
9:     **end for**
10:     $A\mathbf{y}^{(t)} \leftarrow \sum_{k=1}^K A_{[k]}\mathbf{y}_{[k]}^{(t)}$ (on the central node)
11:     $\mathbf{x}^{(t)} \leftarrow \arg\min_{\mathbf{x}\in\mathbb{R}^d} \mathcal{C}^{(t)}(\mathbf{x})$ (on the central node)
12:     Send $\mathbf{x}^{(t)}$ and $A\mathbf{y}^{(t)}$ back to each machine
13: **end for**
14: **Output:** $(\mathbf{x}^{(T)}, \mathbf{y}^{(T)})$

node. The goal of this internal procedure is to approximately solve each local subproblem. We refer this procedure as the inner loop, which is stated in Steps 6-9 of Algorithm 1. Thirdly, with the local updates $A_{[k]}\mathbf{y}_{[k]}^{(t)}$'s, the central node aggregates them to compute $A\mathbf{y}^{(t)}$, and solves the defined central problem $\mathcal{C}^{(t)}(\mathbf{x})$ to get the update of $\mathbf{x}^{(t)}$ (Steps 10-11 of Algorithm 1). Finally, the central node sends ($\mathbf{x}^{(t)}$ and $A\mathbf{y}^{(t)}$) back to each machine in order to start the next round of local optimization (Step 12), we refer Steps 5-13 as the outer loop of our algorithm.

Note that, on one hand, the essential information that the central problem requires can be represented by the vectors $\left\{A_{[k]}\mathbf{y}_{[k]}^{(t)}\right\}$'s of each local machine, which are of dimension of d. On the other hand, each local machine only requires $\left(\mathbf{x}^{(t)}, A\mathbf{y}^{(t)}\right)$, which is of $2d$ dimensions, from the central node.

4 CONVERGENCE ANALYSIS

Before we present our main convergence results, we make some assumptions on the objective functions and the local suboptimality on each local subproblem.

Assumption 1. *Each $\phi_i(\cdot)$ is convex and differentiable, and $\phi_i(\cdot)$ is $(1/\gamma)$-smooth, i.e.,*

$$|\phi_i'(a) - \phi_i'(b)| \le (1/\gamma)|a - b|, \quad \forall a, b \in \mathbb{R}.$$

Assumption 2. *$g(\cdot)$ is λ-strongly convex i.e. for $\forall x, y \in \mathbb{R}^d$ and $g'(y) \in \partial g(y)$,*

$$g(x) \ge g(y) + g'(y)(x - y) + \frac{\lambda}{2}\|x - y\|_2^2.$$

Assumption 3. *There exists constants $\Omega_{\mathbf{x}}, \Omega_{\mathbf{y}} > 0$ such that*

$$\max_t \|\mathbf{x}^{(t)} - \mathbf{x}^\star\|_2 \le \Omega_{\mathbf{x}},$$
$$\max_t \|\mathbf{y}^{(t)} - \mathbf{y}^\star\|_2 \le \Omega_{\mathbf{y}},$$

where $(\mathbf{x}^{(t)}, \mathbf{y}^{(t)})$ is t-iteration update of Algorithm 1, and $(\mathbf{x}^\star, \mathbf{y}^\star)$ is the optimal solution of (4).

Assumption 4. *Each local machine k produces an approximate solution $\left(\mathbf{x}_k^{(t)}, \mathbf{y}_{[k]}^{(t)}\right)$ that satisfies*

$$\mathbb{E}\left[\left\|\mathbf{y}_{[k]}^{(t)} - \hat{\mathbf{y}}_{[k]}^{(t)}\right\|_2\right] \le \hat{\Theta}\left\|\mathbf{y}_{[k]}^{(t-1)} - \hat{\mathbf{y}}_{[k]}^{(t)}\right\|_2,$$

and

$$\mathbb{E}[(f(\hat{\mathbf{x}}_k^{(t)}, \hat{\mathbf{y}}_{[k]}^{(t)}) - f(\hat{\mathbf{x}}_k^{(t)}, \mathbf{y}_{[k]}^{(t)}))]$$
$$\le \tilde{\Theta}\left(f(\hat{\mathbf{x}}_k^{(t)}, \hat{\mathbf{y}}_{[k]}^{(t)}) - f(\hat{\mathbf{x}}_k^{(t)}, \mathbf{y}_{[k]}^{(t-1)})\right),$$

where $\hat{\Theta}, \tilde{\Theta} < 1$, and $\left(\hat{\mathbf{x}}_k^{(t)}, \hat{\mathbf{y}}_{[k]}^{(t)}\right)$ is the optimal solution of local subproblem $\mathcal{L}_k^{(t)}\left(\mathbf{x}, \mathbf{y}_{[k]}\right)$.

Assumption 5. *There exist constants c', $c'' > 0$, and the approximate solution $\mathbf{y}^{(t)} = \sum_{k=1}^K \mathbf{y}_{[k]}^{(t)}$ satisfies*

$$\mathbb{E}[\blacktriangle] \le \Theta(f(\mathbf{x}^{(t-1)}, \mathbf{y}^\star) - f(\mathbf{x}^\star, \mathbf{y}^{(t-1)})),$$

and $\blacktriangle$ is defined as

$$\blacktriangle = \sum_{k=1}^K (f(\hat{\mathbf{x}}_k^{(t)}, \hat{\mathbf{y}}_{[k]}^{(t)}) - f(\hat{\mathbf{x}}_k^{(t)}, \mathbf{y}_{[k]}^{(t)})) + \frac{M}{n}\|\mathbf{y}^{(t)} - \hat{\mathbf{y}}^{(t)}\|_2,$$

where $M = c'\Omega_{\mathbf{x}} + c''\Omega_{\mathbf{y}}$, and $\Theta \in (0, 1)$ is a pre-defined constant.

Note that Assumptions 4 and 5 imply that the local subproblems need to be solved approximately to some extent. As the local subproblems are saddle point problems, we can apply different kinds of algorithms for saddle point problems to solve them, such as (Chambolle and Pock, 2011, Yu et al., 2015, Zhang and Xiao, 2015b), which include both stochastic and non-stochastic optimization methods.

To analyse the convergence behavior of our distributed algorithm, we need to characterize the connection between local subproblems and central update on the central node. Based on the relationship between the central update $\mathbf{x}^{(t)}$ and the local optimal solution $\left(\hat{\mathbf{x}}_k^{(t)}, \hat{\mathbf{y}}_{[k]}^{(t)}\right)$, we can get the convergence guarantee of Algorithm 1. All proofs can be found in Appendix.

Lemma 1. *Suppose that Assumptions 1-5 hold. Let $(\mathbf{x}^\star, \mathbf{y}^\star)$ be the unique saddle point of $f(\mathbf{x}, \mathbf{y})$ defined in (4), and define*

$$\Delta^{(t)} = f(\mathbf{x}^{(t)}, \mathbf{y}^\star) - f(\mathbf{x}^\star, \mathbf{y}^{(t)}) + \frac{1+\tau\lambda}{2\tau}\|\mathbf{x}^{(t)} - \mathbf{x}^\star\|_2^2 + \frac{2K^2 + 2K\sigma\gamma - 1}{4\sigma n K}\|\mathbf{y}^{(t)} - \mathbf{y}^\star\|_2^2.$$

If the parameters τ and σ are chosen such that $\tau\sigma = \frac{1}{4R^2}$ and $\sigma > \frac{1}{2K\gamma}$, then for $t \geq 1$, the proposed DiSPA (Algorithm 1) achieves

$$\mathbb{E}[\Delta^{(t)}] \leq \Theta \mathbb{E}[\Delta^{(t-1)}], \tag{7}$$

where $\Theta = \max\{\frac{1}{1+(\frac{\sigma\gamma}{K} - \frac{1}{2K^2})}, \frac{1}{1+\tau\lambda}\}$.

Theorem 1. *Suppose that Assumptions 1-5 hold, and the parameters $\tau = \gamma/(4R^2)$, $\sigma = 1/\gamma$ and $K \leq \kappa$. In order for Algorithm 1 to obtain*

$$\mathbb{E}[\|\mathbf{x}^{(T)} - \mathbf{x}^\star\|_2^2] \leq \epsilon,$$

it suffices to have the number of communication iterations T satisfy

$$T \geq \left(1 + \frac{4R^2}{\lambda\gamma}\right) \log\left(\frac{C}{\epsilon}\right),$$

where $C = \frac{\Delta^{(0)}}{\frac{\lambda}{2}\left(1+\frac{4R^2}{\lambda\gamma}\right)}$.

Based on Lemma 1 and Theorem 1, we can get the communication complexity of Algorithm 1. By taking $\tau = \frac{\gamma}{4R^2}$ and $\sigma = \frac{1}{\gamma}$, the communication complexity of Algorithm 1 is $\tilde{\mathcal{O}}(\kappa \log(1/\epsilon))$. This does not match the optimal communication complexity. In the next section, we derive an accelerated version of DiSPA that attains the optimal communication complexity.

5 EXTENSION OF DISPA

In this section, we derive two extensions of DiSPA. The first extension applies a generic acceleration scheme proposed by Lin et al. (2015) to obtain an accelerated version of DiSPA. The second one extends our algorithm to handle non-smooth and non-strongly convex loss functions with convergence guarantee.

5.1 ACCELERATION

The communication complexity of our algorithm derived in Theorem 1 is $\tilde{\mathcal{O}}(\kappa \log(1/\epsilon))$ in order to achieve an ϵ-suboptimal solution, which does not match the lower bound proved in (Arjevani and Shamir, 2015). Based on the 'Catalyst' acceleration scheme proposed by Lin et al. (2015), we develop the accelerated DiSPA to achieve the optimal communication complexity. 'Catalyst' is a generic scheme for accelerating first-order optimization methods, similar to classical gradient descent schemes of Nesterov acceleration. It is a natural choice for distributed optimization algorithms that solve local subproblem approximately in each communication iteration. Based on Catalyst acceleration, we modify the original objective function by adding a quadratic term

$$f^{(t)}(\mathbf{x}, \mathbf{y}) = f(\mathbf{x}, \mathbf{y}) + \frac{\vartheta}{2}\|\mathbf{x} - \mathbf{z}^{(t-1)}\|_2^2,$$

where $\vartheta > 0$ is a parameter defined in Catalyst, $\mathbf{z}^{(t)}$ is obtained by an extrapolation step similar to the acceleration scheme in (Nesterov, 2013). With a carefully selected parameter ϑ, we can develop an accelerated version of DiSPA described in Algorithm 2, which achieves the optimal communication complexity. We refer to the accelerated distributed saddle point algorithm as A-DiSPA.

Theorem 2. *Suppose Assumption 1-5 hold and assume $\vartheta = \frac{4R^2}{\gamma} - \lambda > 0$, if the parameters in Catalyst are chosen as $T_s = \tilde{O}(1)$, $q = \lambda/(\lambda + \vartheta)$, $\alpha_0 = \sqrt{q}$. The total communication iterations of Algorithm 2 for achieving $\mathcal{P}(\mathbf{x}^{(T)}) - \mathcal{P}(\mathbf{x}^\star) < \epsilon$ is $\tilde{O}\left(\sqrt{\kappa}\log\left(\frac{1}{\epsilon}\right)\right)$.*

The 'Catalyst' acceleration scheme is applied widely to accelerate different kinds of optimization methods (Reddi et al., 2016). As the 'acceleration' quadratic term is related to the primal variable $\mathbf{x}$ and the saddle point problem keeps the primal variable, it is convenient to apply this acceleration scheme to DiSPA and achieve the optimal communication complexity.

5.2 NON-SMOOTH OR/AND NON-STRONGLY CONVEX FUNCTIONS

The communication complexity bounds in Theorem 1 and Theorem 2 are developed under the Assumptions 1 and 2, which means that the derivative of $\phi_i(\cdot)$ needs to be $(1/\gamma)$-Lipschitz continuous and $g(\cdot)$ needs to be λ-strongly convex. For general loss functions in machine learning, both assumptions may fail, for example, when $\phi_i(\cdot)$ is hinge loss and $g(\cdot)$ is ℓ_1-regularization term. Therefore, we aim to develop an extension of Algorithm 2 to deal with non-smooth and non-strongly convex loss functions.

To be concise, we only consider the case when $\phi_i(\cdot)$ is non-smooth and $g(\cdot)$ is non-strongly convex. The key idea here is to apply a perturbation term to analyze the non-smooth and non-strongly convex setting, which is commonly used in many optimization methods (Reddi et al., 2016, Zhang and Xiao, 2015b). Here we assume that neither $\phi_i(\cdot)$ is smooth nor $g(\cdot)$ is strongly convex.

Algorithm 2 A-DiSPA

1: **Input:** Data points $\{a_i\}_{i=1}^n$ distributed across K machines $\{\mathcal{P}_k\}_{k=1}^K$, parameters $\tau, \sigma, \vartheta, \alpha_0 \in \mathbb{R}$, initial primal variable $\mathbf{x}^{(0)}$ generated on the central node, initial local dual variables $\mathbf{y}^{(0)}$ generated on local machines, optimization algorithm DiSPA, number of inner iterations T_s of DiSPA.
2: **Initialization:** $q = \lambda/(\lambda + \vartheta), \mathbf{z}^{(0)} = \mathbf{x}^{(0)}, t = 1$
3: **while** stopping criterion is not satisfied **do**
4: $\quad (\mathbf{x}^{(t)}, \mathbf{y}^{(t)}) = \text{DiSPA}(f^{(t)}, \mathbf{x}^{(t-1)}, \mathbf{y}^{(t-1)}, \tau, \sigma, T_s)$
5: $\quad$ Compute $\alpha_t \in (0, 1)$ from equation

$$\alpha_t^2 = (1 - \alpha_t)\alpha_{t-1}^2 + q\alpha_t$$

6: $\quad$ Compute $\mathbf{z}^{(t)} = \mathbf{x}^{(t)} + \beta_t(\mathbf{x}^{(t)} - \mathbf{x}^{(t-1)})$, where $\beta_t = \frac{\alpha_{t-1}(1-\alpha_{t-1})}{\alpha_{k-1}^2 + \alpha_t}$
7: $\quad t = t + 1$
8: **end while**
9: **Output** $\mathbf{x}^{(t)}$

In particular, we consider the following modified saddle point function

$$f_\epsilon(\mathbf{x}, \mathbf{y}) \overset{\text{def}}{=} \frac{1}{n} \sum_{i=1}^n \left(y_i \langle a_i, \mathbf{x} \rangle - \left(\phi_i^*(y_i) + \frac{\epsilon}{2} y_i^2 \right) \right) + \left(g(\mathbf{x}) + \frac{\epsilon}{2} \|\mathbf{x}\|_2^2 \right), \tag{8}$$

where $\epsilon > 0$ is a pre-defined scalar. $f_\epsilon(\mathbf{x}, \mathbf{y})$ can be regarded as an approximation of the original saddle point problem $f(\mathbf{x}, \mathbf{y})$. We then obtain that both $\phi_i^*(y_i) + \frac{\epsilon}{2} y_i^2$ and $g(\mathbf{x}) + \frac{\epsilon}{2}\|\mathbf{x}\|_2^2$ are ϵ-strongly convex. In the following corollary, we show that the perturbed function $f_\epsilon(\mathbf{x}, \mathbf{y})$ is a good approximation of the origin function $f(\mathbf{x}, \mathbf{y})$.

Corollary 1. *Assume that ϕ_i is convex and L_ϕ-Lipschitz continuous, and g is convex. Let $(\mathbf{x}^\star, \mathbf{y}^\star)$ be the unique saddle point of $f(\mathbf{x}, \mathbf{y})$, and $(\mathbf{x}_\epsilon^\star, \mathbf{y}_\epsilon^\star)$ be the unique saddle point of $f_\epsilon(\mathbf{x}, \mathbf{y})$. Then we have*

$$\mathcal{P}(\mathbf{x}_\epsilon^\star) - \mathcal{P}(\mathbf{x}^\star) \le \frac{\epsilon}{2} \left(\|\mathbf{x}^\star\|_2^2 + L_\phi^2 \right).$$

As a result, we could apply Algorithm 2 to the perturbed function $f_\epsilon(\mathbf{x}, \mathbf{y})$. By applying Theorem 2 and the relationship between $f_\epsilon(\mathbf{x}, \mathbf{y})$ and $f(\mathbf{x}, \mathbf{y})$, we obtain that the communication complexity of Algorithm 2 for non-smooth and non-strongly convex functions is $\tilde{O}\left((1/\epsilon) \log\left(\frac{1}{\epsilon^2}\right)\right)$, and the proof is similar to the one in (Zhang and Xiao, 2015b).

6 NUMERICAL EXPERIMENTS

In this section, we conduct numerical experiments of DiSPA and A-DiSPA on several real-world distributed datasets. We compare the performance of our algorithms with the state-of-the-art distributed optimization algorithm CoCoA+ (Ma et al., 2015).

For our experiments, we solve the standard binary classification task with datasets obtained from LIBSVM datasets (Chang and Lin, 2011). The statistics of the datasets are summarized in Table 1. Our goal is to minimize the regularized empirical risk with smoothed hinge loss:

$$\min_{\mathbf{x} \in \mathbb{R}^d} \mathcal{P}(\mathbf{x}) = \frac{1}{n} \sum_{i=1}^n \phi_i(a_i^\top \mathbf{x}) + \frac{\lambda}{2} \|\mathbf{x}\|_2^2.$$

For each task, the data point takes the form of (a_i, b_i), where a_i is a feature vector, $b_i \in \{1, -1\}$ is the corresponding class label and associated with loss function ϕ_i. The smoothed hinge loss function (Shalev-Shwartz and Zhang, 2013) ϕ_i is defined as

$$\phi_i(z) = \begin{cases} 0 & \text{if } b_i z \ge 1, \\ 1 - b_i z - \frac{\gamma}{2} & \text{if } b_i z \le 1 - \gamma, \\ \frac{1}{2\gamma}(1 - b_i z)^2 & \text{otherwise,} \end{cases}$$

where ϕ_i is $(1/\gamma)$-smooth. We set $\gamma = 1$ in our experiments. The conjugate function of ϕ_i is $\phi_i^*(\beta) = b_i\beta + \frac{\gamma}{2}\beta^2$ for $b_i\beta \in [-1, 0]$ and $+\infty$ otherwise.

Table 1: Three Datasets for Numerical Experiments

DATASET	# SAMPLES n	# FEATURES d
RCV1	677,399	47,236
Realsim	72,309	20,958
Covtype	581,012	54

6.1 IMPLEMENTATION DETAILS

We implement DiSPA, A-DiSPA and CoCoA+ in Petuum (Xing et al., 2015). For DiSPA and A-DiSPA, we use SPDC (Zhang and Xiao, 2015b) as the local solver, and use SDCA (Shalev-Shwartz and Zhang, 2013) as the local solver for CoCoA+. When doing comparison among different algorithms, we run the same number of local iterations on local machines (i.e., iterations of SDCA or SPDC) before communication with the central node. We compare different algorithms based on communication iterations. From our results, we find that DiSPA converges faster when parameters τ and σ are large, which is similar to the findings reported in (Johnson and Zhang, 2013, Zhang and Xiao, 2015a). We adopt

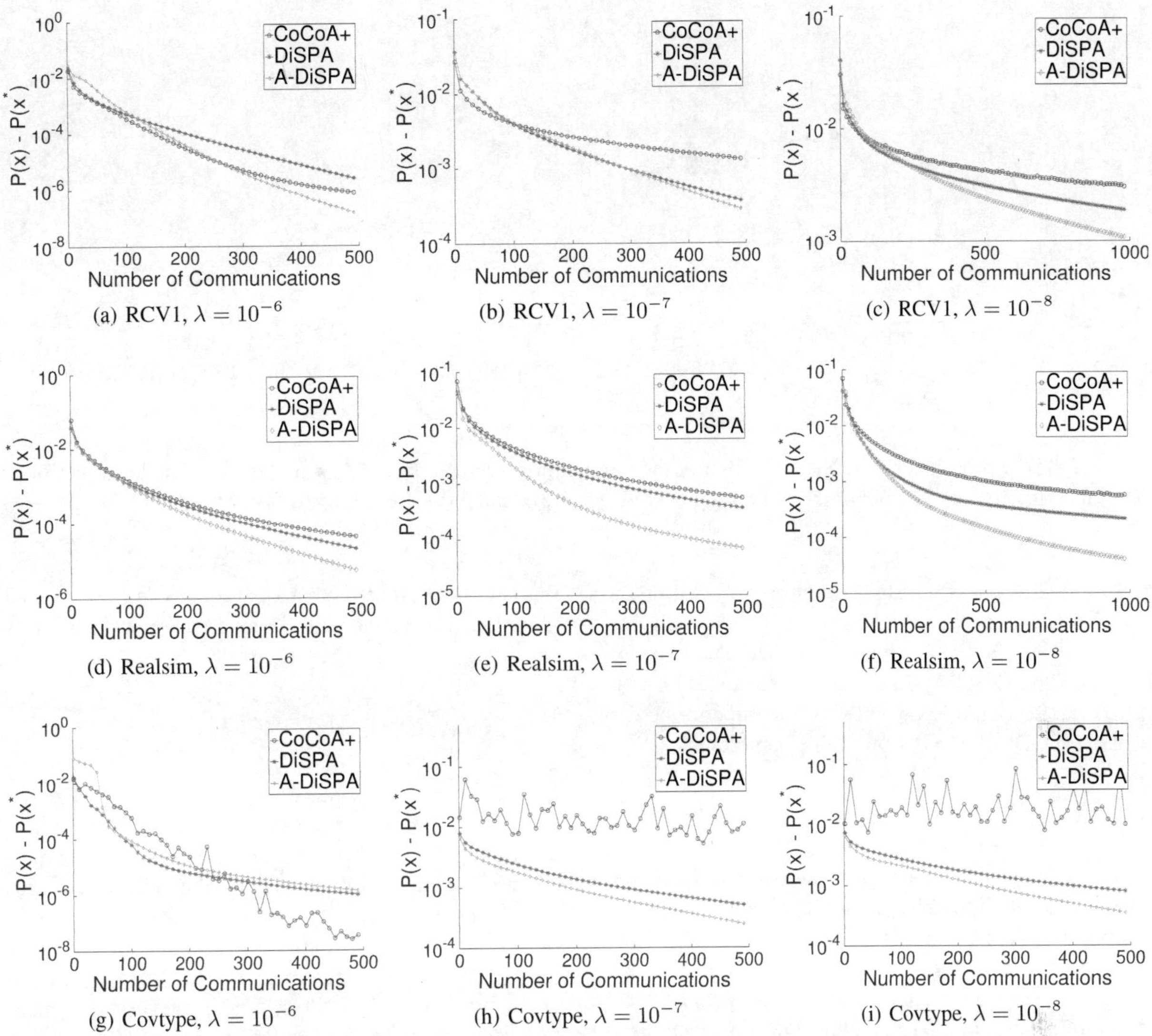

(a) RCV1, $\lambda = 10^{-6}$ (b) RCV1, $\lambda = 10^{-7}$ (c) RCV1, $\lambda = 10^{-8}$

(d) Realsim, $\lambda = 10^{-6}$ (e) Realsim, $\lambda = 10^{-7}$ (f) Realsim, $\lambda = 10^{-8}$

(g) Covtype, $\lambda = 10^{-6}$ (h) Covtype, $\lambda = 10^{-7}$ (i) Covtype, $\lambda = 10^{-8}$

Figure 1: Comparison of DiSPA, A-DiSPA and CoCoA+ on three datasets: RCV1, Realsim, Covtype. The horizontal axis is the number of communications, and the vertical axis is the optimality gap $(P(\mathbf{x}^{(T)}) - P(\mathbf{x}^\star))$. Each plot contains a comparison of CoCoA+ (blue, circle), DiSPA (red, asterisk) and A-DiSPA (yellow, diamond). All the plots are shown on log-y scale . The number of local iterations performed in each communication iteration is 5,000 for Realsim, and 10,000 iterations for RCV1 and Covtype.

tuned parameters τ and σ from a predefined range. For CoCoA+, we present the results of the selected optimal parameter σ'.

6.2 COMPARISON BETWEEN DISPA AND COCOA+

We compare DiSPA and CoCoA+ on three datasets: RCV1, Realsim, Covtype, across different values of the regularization parameter λ. To be specific, the regularization parameter λ is set to be $\lambda \in \{10^{-6}, 10^{-7}, 10^{-8}\}$ on the three datasets. Both DiSPA and CoCoA+ are implemented on 16 machines ($K = 16$). For both DiSPA and CoCoA+, the numbers of local iterations performed in each communication iteration are the same.

In Figure 1, the results show that the performance of DiSPA is comparable with CoCoA+. We can see that when $\lambda = 10^{-6}$, DiSPA has comparable convergence performance with regard to CoCoA+. On all the three datasets, when $\lambda \in \{10^{-7}, 10^{-8}\}$, DiSPA converges to the optimal solution faster and more stable than CoCoA+. We also notice that the performance of Co-

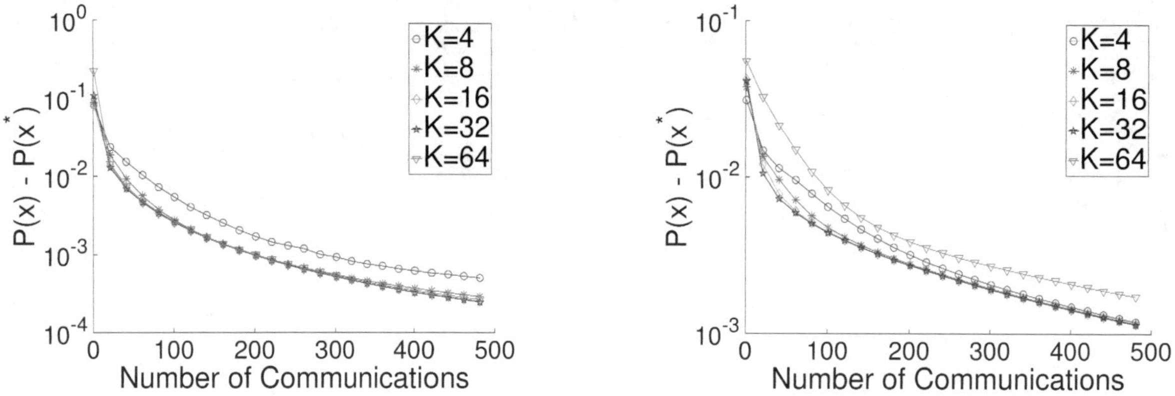

(a) Realsim, $\lambda = 10^{-7}$ (b) RCV1, $\lambda = 10^{-7}$

Figure 2: The performance of DiSPA with increasing number of machines, $K \in \{4, 8, 16, 32, 64\}$. The local iterations performed in each communication iteration is 1,000 for Realsim, and 5,000 iterations for RCV1.

CoA+ on Covtype is not stable compared to that on the other two datasets, especially when λ is very small, i.e., $\lambda = 10^{-7}$ or $\lambda = 10^{-8}$, which is consistent with the experimental results of CoCoA+ on Covtype in Reddi et al. (2016). In Section 6.3, we will show the superior performance of A-DiSPA on ill-conditioned problems.

6.3 COMPARISON OF DISPA AND A-DISPA

In Figure 1, we also compare A-DiSPA and DiSPA to show the acceleration obtained by applying Catalyst acceleration. We compare DiSPA and A-DiSPA on three datasets (RCV1, Realsim, Covtype) across different regularization parameter under the same settings as mentioned in Section 6.2. The results show that when problem is ill-conditioned, i.e. $\kappa = R^2/(\lambda\gamma) \gg 1$, A-DiSPA converges substantially faster than DiSPA. This confirms our theoretical analysis, as the communication complexity of A-DiSPA is $\tilde{O}\left(\sqrt{\kappa}\log\left(\frac{1}{\epsilon}\right)\right)$ and DiSPA is $\tilde{O}\left(\kappa\log\left(\frac{1}{\epsilon}\right)\right)$.

6.4 SCALABILITY

Since scalability is an important metric of distributed optimization algorithms, in Figure 2, we study the scalability of DiSPA by observing the numerical performance with increasing number of machines. We conduct experiments on two datasets (RCV1, Realsim), and the machine number is set to be $K \in \{4, 8, 16, 32, 64\}$. For comparison, we keep the iterations and parameters τ, σ the same for each dataset. The experiments show that DiSPA can scale effectively with number of machines, which confirms our theory in Section 4. We observe that performance slightly drops on RCV1 with 64 machines, this is possibly because that local subproblems are solved with higher accuracy which may affect the effectiveness of aggregation in the central update.

7 CONCLUSION

In this work, we present a novel distributed optimization framework for solving the saddle point problem, which can be applied to solving a generic class of convex optimization problems. We provide the theoretical guarantee of our algorithms, and show that the accelerated algorithm can achieve the optimal communication complexity. We also extend our algorithm for solving non-smooth and non-strongly convex loss functions. The experimental results demonstrate that our algorithms obtain better performance compared to the state-of-the-art distributed optimization method.

Acknowledgements

This work is supported by NTU Singapore Nanyang Assistant Professorship (NAP) grant M4081532.020, Singapore MOE AcRF Tier-2 grant MOE2016-T2-2-060, and MOE AcRF Tier-1 grant 2016-T1-001-159.

References

Y. Arjevani and O. Shamir. Communication complexity of distributed convex learning and optimization. In *Advances in Neural Information Processing Systems*, pages 1756–1764, 2015.

S. Boyd, N. Parikh, E. Chu, B. Peleato, and J. Eckstein. Distributed optimization and statistical learning via the alternating direction method of multipliers.

Foundations and Trends® in Machine Learning, 3(1): 1–122, 2011.

A. Chambolle and T. Pock. A first-order primal-dual algorithm for convex problems with applications to imaging. *Journal of Mathematical Imaging and Vision*, 40(1):120–145, 2011.

C.-C. Chang and C.-J. Lin. LIBSVM: A library for support vector machines. *ACM Transactions on Intelligent Systems and Technology*, 2:27:1–27:27, 2011. Software available at `http://www.csie.ntu.edu.tw/~cjlin/libsvm`.

T.-H. Chang, A. Nedic, and A. Scaglione. Distributed constrained optimization by consensus-based primal-dual perturbation method. *IEEE Transactions on Automatic Control*, 59(6):1524–1538, 2014.

B. Dai, N. He, Y. Pan, B. Boots, and L. Song. Learning from conditional distributions via dual kernel embeddings. *arXiv preprint arXiv:1607.04579*, 2016.

J. Duchi, M. I. Jordan, and B. McMahan. Estimation, optimization, and parallelism when data is sparse. In *Advances in Neural Information Processing Systems*, pages 2832–2840, 2013.

M. Jaggi, V. Smith, M. Takác, J. Terhorst, S. Krishnan, T. Hofmann, and M. I. Jordan. Communication-efficient distributed dual coordinate ascent. In *Advances in Neural Information Processing Systems*, pages 3068–3076, 2014.

R. Johnson and T. Zhang. Accelerating stochastic gradient descent using predictive variance reduction. In *Advances in Neural Information Processing Systems*, pages 315–323, 2013.

H. Lin, J. Mairal, and Z. Harchaoui. A universal catalyst for first-order optimization. In *Advances in Neural Information Processing Systems*, pages 3384–3392, 2015.

C. Ma, V. Smith, M. Jaggi, M. Jordan, P. Richtarik, and M. Takac. Adding vs. averaging in distributed primal-dual optimization. In *Proceedings of The 32nd International Conference on Machine Learning*, pages 1973–1982, 2015.

Y. Nesterov. *Introductory lectures on convex optimization: A basic course*, volume 87. Springer Science & Business Media, 2013.

S. J. Reddi, J. Konečný, P. Richtárik, B. Póczós, and A. Smola. Aide: Fast and communication efficient distributed optimization. *arXiv preprint arXiv:1608.06879*, 2016.

S. Shalev-Shwartz and T. Zhang. Stochastic dual coordinate ascent methods for regularized loss minimization. *Journal of Machine Learning Research*, 14(Feb):567–599, 2013.

O. Shamir, N. Srebro, and T. Zhang. Communication-efficient distributed optimization using an approximate newton-type method. In *Proceedings of The 31st International Conference on Machine Learning*, pages 1000–1008, 2014.

W. Shi, Q. Ling, K. Yuan, G. Wu, and W. Yin. On the linear convergence of the admm in decentralized consensus optimization. *IEEE Transactions on Signal Processing*, 62(7):1750–1761, 2014.

V. Smith, S. Forte, M. I. Jordan, and M. Jaggi. L1-regularized distributed optimization: A communication-efficient primal-dual framework. *arXiv preprint arXiv:1512.04011*, 2015.

E. P. Xing, Q. Ho, W. Dai, J. K. Kim, J. Wei, S. Lee, X. Zheng, P. Xie, A. Kumar, and Y. Yu. Petuum: A new platform for distributed machine learning on big data. *IEEE Transactions on Big Data*, 1(2):49–67, 2015.

T. Yang. Trading computation for communication: Distributed stochastic dual coordinate ascent. In *Advances in Neural Information Processing Systems*, pages 629–637, 2013.

A. W. Yu, Q. Lin, and T. Yang. Doubly stochastic primal-dual coordinate method for regularized empirical risk minimization with factorized data. *CoRR, abs/1508.03390*, 2015.

Y. Zhang and L. Xiao. Disco: Distributed optimization for self-concordant empirical loss. In *Proceedings of the 32nd International Conference on Machine Learning*, pages 362–370, 2015a.

Y. Zhang and L. Xiao. Stochastic primal-dual coordinate method for regularized empirical risk minimization. In *Proceedings of The 32nd International Conference on Machine Learning*, pages 353–361, 2015b.

Y. Zhang, M. J. Wainwright, and J. C. Duchi. Communication-efficient algorithms for statistical optimization. In *Advances in Neural Information Processing Systems*, pages 1502–1510, 2012.

Appendix

A Lemmas for Convergence Analysis of DiSPA

We first introduce the lemma that characterizes the optimality condition of local subproblem $\mathcal{L}_k^{(t)}(\mathbf{x}, \mathbf{y}_{[k]})$.

Lemma 2. *Assume that each $\phi_i(\cdot)$ is $(1/\gamma)$-smooth and $g(\cdot)$ is λ-strongly convex, $R = \max\{\|a_1\|_2, ...\|a_n\|_2\}$. Let $(\hat{\mathbf{x}}_k^{(t)}, \hat{\mathbf{y}}_{[k]}^{(t)})$ be the optimal solution of $\mathcal{L}_k^{(t)}(\mathbf{x}, \mathbf{y}_{[k]})$, $k = 1, 2, ..., K$. Based on the strongly convexity, we have*

$$\mathcal{L}_k^{(t)}(\mathbf{x}, \hat{\mathbf{y}}_{[k]}^{(t)}) \geq \mathcal{L}_k^{(t)}(\hat{\mathbf{x}}_k^{(t)}, \hat{\mathbf{y}}_{[k]}^{(t)}) + \left(\frac{1}{2\tau} + \frac{\lambda}{2}\right) \|\mathbf{x} - \hat{\mathbf{x}}_k^{(t)}\|^2, \quad \forall \mathbf{x} \in \mathbb{R}^d$$

$$\mathcal{L}_k^{(t)}(\hat{\mathbf{x}}_k^{(t)}, \mathbf{y}_{[k]}) \leq \mathcal{L}_k^{(t)}(\hat{\mathbf{x}}_k^{(t)}, \hat{\mathbf{y}}_{[k]}^{(t)}) - \left(\frac{K}{2\sigma n} + \frac{\gamma}{2n}\right) \|\mathbf{y}_{[k]} - \hat{\mathbf{y}}_{[k]}^{(t)}\|^2, \quad \forall \mathbf{y}_{[k]} \in \mathbb{R}^n$$

Proof. Based on the definition of the saddle point, we can notice that $-\mathcal{L}_k^{(t)}(\hat{\mathbf{x}}^{(t)}, \mathbf{y}_{[k]})$ is a $(\frac{K}{\sigma n} + \frac{\gamma}{n})$-strongly convex function and minimized by $\hat{\mathbf{y}}_{[k]}^{(t)}$, which implies

$$-\mathcal{L}_k^{(t)}(\hat{\mathbf{x}}^{(t)}, \mathbf{y}_{[k]}) \geq -\mathcal{L}_k^{(t)}(\hat{\mathbf{x}}^{(t)}, \hat{\mathbf{y}}_{[k]}^{(t)}) + \left(\frac{K}{2\sigma n} + \frac{\gamma}{2n}\right) \|\mathbf{y}_{[k]} - \hat{\mathbf{y}}_{[k]}^{(t)}\|^2, \quad \forall \mathbf{y}_{[k]} \in \mathbb{R}^n$$

Also notice that $\mathcal{L}_k^{(t)}(\mathbf{x}, \hat{\mathbf{y}}_{[k]}^{(t)})$ is a $(\frac{1}{\tau} + \lambda)$-strongly convex function minimized by $\hat{\mathbf{x}}_k^{(t)}$, which implies

$$\mathcal{L}_k^{(t)}(\mathbf{x}, \hat{\mathbf{y}}_{[k]}^{(t)}) \geq \mathcal{L}_k^{(t)}(\hat{\mathbf{x}}_k^{(t)}, \hat{\mathbf{y}}_{[k]}^{(t)}) + \left(\frac{1}{2\tau} + \frac{\lambda}{2}\right) \|\mathbf{x} - \hat{\mathbf{x}}_k^{(t)}\|^2, \quad \forall \mathbf{x} \in \mathbb{R}^d$$

□

Based on the optimality condition of $\mathcal{L}_k^{(t)}(\mathbf{x}, \mathbf{y}_{[k]})$ and the central update $\mathbf{x}^{(t)}$ on central worker, we can get the connection between local subproblems and central update on central worker.

Lemma 3 (Relationship between local optimal solution and central update)**.** *Assume that each $\phi_i(\cdot)$ is $(1/\gamma)$-smooth and $g(\cdot)$ is λ-strongly convex, $R = \max\{\|a_1\|_2, ...\|a_n\|_2\}$. Let $(\hat{\mathbf{x}}_k^{(t)}, \hat{\mathbf{y}}_{[k]}^{(t)})$ be the optimal solution of $\mathcal{L}_k^{(t)}(\mathbf{x}, \mathbf{y}_{[k]})$, $k = 1, 2, ..., K$. Let $\mathbf{x}^{(t)} = \arg\min_{\mathbf{x} \in \mathbb{R}^d} \mathcal{C}^{(t)}(\mathbf{x})$, it holds that*

$$\frac{(K-1)^2}{4\sigma n K} \|\mathbf{y}^{(t-1)} - \mathbf{y}^{(t)}\|_2^2 + \mathbf{\Lambda}' \geq \left(\frac{3}{4\tau} + \lambda\right) \sum_{k=1}^{K} \|\mathbf{x}^{(t)} - \hat{\mathbf{x}}_k^{(t)}\|_2^2 \tag{9}$$

where $\mathbf{\Lambda}' = \frac{1}{n} \sum_{k=1}^{K} (\hat{\mathbf{y}}_{[k]}^{(t)} - \mathbf{y}_{[k]}^{(t)})^\top A^\top (\mathbf{x}^{(t)} - \hat{\mathbf{x}}_k^{(t)})$ and $1/\tau = 4\sigma R^2$.

Proof. Based on lemma 2, we could get that for $k = 1, 2, ..., K$,

$$\frac{1}{n} \sum_{j \in \mathcal{P}_k} \hat{y}_j^{(t)} \langle a_j, \mathbf{x}^{(t)} - \hat{\mathbf{x}}_k^{(t)} \rangle + \frac{1}{n} \sum_{i \notin \mathcal{P}_k} y_i^{(t-1)} \langle a_i, \mathbf{x}^{(t)} - \hat{\mathbf{x}}_k^{(t)} \rangle + g(\mathbf{x}^{(t)}) - g(\hat{\mathbf{x}}_k^{(t)}) + \frac{\|\mathbf{x}^{(t)} - \mathbf{x}^{(t-1)}\|_2^2}{2\tau} \geq$$
$$\frac{\|\hat{\mathbf{x}}_k^{(t)} - \mathbf{x}^{(t-1)}\|_2^2}{2\tau} + \left(\frac{1}{2\tau} + \frac{\lambda}{2}\right) \|\mathbf{x}^{(t)} - \hat{\mathbf{x}}_k^{(t)}\|_2^2$$

Since $\mathbf{x}^{(t)}$ minimizes the function $\mathcal{C}^{(t)}(\mathbf{x})$, which means that for $k = 1, 2, ..., K$, we have

$$\frac{1}{n} \sum_{i=1}^{n} y_i^{(t)} \langle a_i, \hat{\mathbf{x}}_k^{(t)} - \mathbf{x}^{(t)} \rangle + g(\hat{\mathbf{x}}_k^{(t)}) - g(\mathbf{x}^{(t)}) + \frac{\|\hat{\mathbf{x}}_k^{(t)} - \mathbf{x}^{(t-1)}\|_2^2}{2\tau} \geq \frac{\|\mathbf{x}^{(t)} - \mathbf{x}^{(t-1)}\|_2^2}{2\tau} + \left(\frac{1}{2\tau} + \frac{\lambda}{2}\right) \|\mathbf{x}^{(t)} - \hat{\mathbf{x}}_k^{(t)}\|_2^2$$

Sum up the above two inequalities, we can get

$$\frac{1}{n}\sum_{j\in\mathcal{P}_k}\hat{y}_j^{(t)}\langle a_j,\mathbf{x}^{(t)}-\hat{\mathbf{x}}_k^{(t)}\rangle+\frac{1}{n}\sum_{i\notin\mathcal{P}_k}y_i^{(t-1)}\langle a_i,\mathbf{x}^{(t)}-\hat{\mathbf{x}}_k^{(t)}\rangle+\frac{1}{n}\sum_{i=1}^{n}y_i^{(t)}\langle a_i,\hat{\mathbf{x}}_k^{(t)}-\mathbf{x}^{(t)}\rangle\geq\left(\frac{1}{\tau}+\lambda\right)\|\mathbf{x}^{(t)}-\hat{\mathbf{x}}_k^{(t)}\|_2^2$$

$$\frac{1}{n}\sum_{j\in\mathcal{P}_k}\left(\hat{y}_j^{(t)}-y_j^{(t)}\right)\langle a_j,\mathbf{x}^{(t)}-\hat{\mathbf{x}}_k^{(t)}\rangle+\frac{1}{n}\sum_{i\notin\mathcal{P}_k}\left(y_i^{(t-1)}-y_i^{(t)}\right)\langle a_i,\mathbf{x}^{(t)}-\hat{\mathbf{x}}_k^{(t)}\rangle\geq\left(\frac{1}{\tau}+\lambda\right)\|\mathbf{x}^{(t)}-\hat{\mathbf{x}}_k^{(t)}\|_2^2$$

$$\frac{1}{n}(\hat{\mathbf{y}}_{[k]}^{(t)}-\mathbf{y}_{[k]}^{(t)})^\top A^\top(\mathbf{x}^{(t)}-\hat{\mathbf{x}}_k^{(t)})+\frac{1}{n}\sum_{l\neq k}(\mathbf{y}_{[l]}^{(t-1)}-\mathbf{y}_{[l]}^{(t)})^\top A^\top(\mathbf{x}^{(t)}-\hat{\mathbf{x}}_k^{(t)})\geq\left(\frac{1}{\tau}+\lambda\right)\|\mathbf{x}^{(t)}-\hat{\mathbf{x}}_k^{(t)}\|_2^2$$

We need to upper bound the second term on the left-hand-side of the above inequality. Since $\|a_i\|_2\leq R$, and we assume that $1/\tau=4\sigma R^2$, then

$$\begin{aligned}\left|\frac{1}{n}\sum_{l\neq k}(\mathbf{y}_{[l]}^{(t-1)}-\mathbf{y}_{[l]}^{(t)})^\top A^\top(\mathbf{x}^{(t)}-\hat{\mathbf{x}}_k^{(t)})\right|&\leq\frac{\|\mathbf{x}^{(t)}-\hat{\mathbf{x}}_k^{(t)}\|_2^2}{4\tau}+\frac{\|\sum_{l\neq k}A(\mathbf{y}_{[l]}^{(t-1)}-\mathbf{y}_{[l]}^{(t)})\|_2^2}{n^2/\tau}\\&\leq\frac{\|\mathbf{x}^{(t)}-\hat{\mathbf{x}}_k^{(t)}\|_2^2}{4\tau}+\frac{(\sum_{i\notin\mathcal{P}_k}|y_i^{(t-1)}-y_i^{(t)}|\cdot\|a_i\|)^2}{4\sigma R^2n^2}\\&\leq\frac{\|\mathbf{x}^{(t)}-\hat{\mathbf{x}}_k^{(t)}\|_2^2}{4\tau}+\frac{(K-1)}{4\sigma nK}\sum_{l\neq k}\|\mathbf{y}_{[l]}^{(t-1)}-\mathbf{y}_{[l]}^{(t)}\|_2^2\end{aligned}$$

Combine the above two inequalities,

$$\frac{(K-1)}{4\sigma nK}\sum_{l\neq k}\|\mathbf{y}_{[l]}^{(t-1)}-\mathbf{y}_{[l]}^{(t)}\|_2^2+\frac{1}{n}(\hat{\mathbf{y}}_{[k]}^{(t)}-\mathbf{y}_{[k]}^{(t)})^\top A^\top(\mathbf{x}^{(t)}-\hat{\mathbf{x}}_k^{(t)})\geq\left(\frac{3}{4\tau}+\lambda\right)\|\mathbf{x}^{(t)}-\hat{\mathbf{x}}_k^{(t)}\|_2^2$$

Sum up the above inequality over $k=1,2,...,K$, and denote $\mathbf{\Lambda}'=\frac{1}{n}\sum_{k=1}^K(\hat{\mathbf{y}}_{[k]}^{(t)}-\mathbf{y}_{[k]}^{(t)})^\top A^\top(\mathbf{x}^{(t)}-\hat{\mathbf{x}}_k^{(t)})$, we have

$$\frac{(K-1)^2}{4\sigma nK}\|\mathbf{y}^{(t-1)}-\mathbf{y}^{(t)}\|_2^2+\mathbf{\Lambda}'\geq\left(\frac{3}{4\tau}+\lambda\right)\sum_{k=1}^K\|\mathbf{x}^{(t)}-\hat{\mathbf{x}}_k^{(t)}\|_2^2$$

□

Lemma 3 shows that the distance between $\mathbf{x}^{(t)}$ and $\hat{\mathbf{x}}_k^{(t)}$ can be control by the update of $\mathbf{y}^{(t)}$ in each iteration.

B Proofs of Convergence for DiSPA and A-DiSPA

B.1 Proof of Lemma 1

Proof. We start from characterizing the relationship between $\mathbf{x}^{(t)}$ and $\mathbf{x}^\star$ after the t-update in Algorithm 1. According to the definition of $\mathbf{x}^{(t)}$, we have $\mathcal{C}^{(t)}(\mathbf{x}^\star)\geq\mathcal{C}^{(t)}(\mathbf{x}^{(t)})+\left(\frac{1}{2\tau}+\frac{\lambda}{2}\right)\|\mathbf{x}^{(t)}-\mathbf{x}^\star\|_2^2$, i.e.,

$$\frac{1}{n}\sum_{i=1}^{n}y_i^{(t)}\langle a_i,\mathbf{x}^\star-\mathbf{x}^{(t)}\rangle+g(\mathbf{x}^\star)-g(\mathbf{x}^{(t)})+\frac{\|\mathbf{x}^\star-\mathbf{x}^{(t-1)}\|_2^2}{2\tau}\geq\frac{\|\mathbf{x}^{(t)}-\mathbf{x}^{(t-1)}\|_2^2}{2\tau}+\left(\frac{1}{2\tau}+\frac{\lambda}{2}\right)\|\mathbf{x}^{(t)}-\hat{\mathbf{x}}^\star\|_2^2 \quad (10)$$

We also could derive the inequality characterizing the relation between $\hat{\mathbf{y}}^{(t)}=\sum_{k=1}^K\hat{\mathbf{y}}_{[k]}^{(t)}$ and $\mathbf{y}^\star$. For $k=1,2,...,K$, we have

$$\hat{\mathbf{y}}_{[k]}^{(t)}=\arg\max_{\mathbf{y}_{[k]}\in\mathbb{R}^n}\mathcal{L}_k^{(t)}(\hat{\mathbf{x}}_k^{(t)},\mathbf{y}_{[k]})$$

Since $\phi_i(\cdot) is (1/\gamma)$-smooth, we have $\phi_i^*(\cdot)$ is γ-strongly convex, therefore, for $k=1,2,...,K$, $\forall j\in\mathcal{P}_k$

$$(\hat{y}_j^{(t)}-y_j^\star)\langle a_j,\hat{\mathbf{x}}_k^{(t)}\rangle+\left(\phi_j^*(y_j^\star)-\phi_j^*(\hat{y}_j^{(t)})\right)+\frac{K(y_j^\star-y_j^{(t-1)})^2}{2\sigma}\geq\frac{K(\hat{y}_j^{(t)}-y_j^{(t-1)})^2}{2\sigma}+\left(\frac{K}{2\sigma}+\frac{\gamma}{2}\right)(\hat{y}_j^{(t)}-y_j^\star)^2$$

Sum up the above inequality over j, we have

$$\sum_{j\in\mathcal{P}_k}(\hat{y}_j^{(t)}-y_j^\star)\langle a_j,\hat{\mathbf{x}}_k^{(t)}\rangle+\sum_{j\in\mathcal{P}_k}\left(\phi_j^*(y_j^\star)-\phi_j^*(\hat{y}_j^{(t)})\right)+\frac{K\|\mathbf{y}_{[k]}^\star-\mathbf{y}_{[k]}^{(t-1)}\|_2^2}{2\sigma}\geq\frac{K\|\hat{\mathbf{y}}_{[k]}^{(t)}-\mathbf{y}_{[k]}^{(t-1)}\|_2^2}{2\sigma}+\left(\frac{K}{2\sigma}+\frac{\gamma}{2}\right)\|\mathbf{y}_{[k]}^\star-\hat{\mathbf{y}}_{[k]}^{(t)}\|_2^2$$

Sum up the above inequality over $k=1,2,...,K$ and multiplying both sides by $1/n$,

$$\begin{aligned}&\frac{1}{n}\sum_{k=1}^{K}\sum_{j\in\mathcal{P}_k}(\hat{y}_j^{(t)}-y_j^\star)\langle a_j,\hat{\mathbf{x}}_k^{(t)}\rangle+\frac{1}{n}\sum_{i=1}^{n}\left(\phi_i^*(y_j^\star)-\phi_i^*(\hat{y}_j^{(t)})\right)+\frac{K\|\mathbf{y}^\star-\mathbf{y}^{(t-1)}\|_2^2}{2\sigma n}\\&\geq\frac{K\|\hat{\mathbf{y}}^{(t)}-\mathbf{y}^{(t-1)}\|_2^2}{2\sigma n}+\left(\frac{K}{2\sigma n}+\frac{\gamma}{2n}\right)\|\mathbf{y}^\star-\hat{\mathbf{y}}^{(t)}\|_2^2\end{aligned}\tag{11}$$

In addition, we consider a combination of the saddle-point function values at different points, we have

$$\begin{aligned}&\left(f(\mathbf{x}^{(t)},\mathbf{y}^\star)-f(\mathbf{x}^\star,\mathbf{y}^\star)\right)+\left(f(\mathbf{x}^\star,\mathbf{y}^\star)-f(\mathbf{x}^\star,\mathbf{y}^{(t)})\right)\\&=\left(\frac{1}{n}\sum_{i=1}^{n}y_i^\star\langle a_i,\mathbf{x}^{(t)}\rangle-\frac{1}{n}\sum_{i=1}^{n}\phi_i^*(y_i^\star)+g(\mathbf{x}^{(t)})\right)-\left(\frac{1}{n}\sum_{i=1}^{n}y_i^{(t)}\langle a_i,\mathbf{x}^\star\rangle-\frac{1}{n}\sum_{i=1}^{n}\phi_i^*(y_i^{(t)})+g(\mathbf{x}^\star)\right)\\&=\left(g(\mathbf{x}^{(t)})-g(\mathbf{x}^\star)\right)+\frac{1}{n}\sum_{i=1}^{n}\left(\phi_i^*(y_i^{(t)})-\phi_i^*(y_i^\star)\right)+\left(\frac{1}{n}\sum_{i=1}^{n}y_i^\star\langle a_i,\mathbf{x}^{(t)}\rangle-\frac{1}{n}\sum_{i=1}^{n}y_i^{(t)}\langle a_i,\mathbf{x}^\star\rangle\right)\end{aligned}$$

Then we add (10) and (11) to the above equality, which implies

$$\begin{aligned}&\frac{1}{n}\sum_{k=1}^{K}\sum_{j\in\mathcal{P}_k}(\hat{y}_j^{(t)}-y_j^\star)\langle a_j,\hat{\mathbf{x}}_k\rangle+\frac{1}{n}\sum_{i=1}^{n}y_i^{(t)}\langle a_i,\mathbf{x}^\star-\mathbf{x}^{(t)}\rangle+\frac{1}{n}\sum_{i=1}^{n}y_i^\star\langle a_i,\mathbf{x}^{(t)}\rangle-\frac{1}{n}\sum_{i=1}^{n}y_i^{(t)}\langle a_i,\mathbf{x}^\star\rangle\\&+\frac{1}{n}\sum_{i=1}^{n}\left(\phi_i^*(y_i^{(t)})-\phi_i^*(\hat{y}_i^{(t)})\right)+\frac{\|\mathbf{x}^\star-\mathbf{x}^{(t-1)}\|_2^2}{2\tau}+\frac{K\|\mathbf{y}^\star-\mathbf{y}^{(t-1)}\|_2^2}{2\sigma n}\\&\geq\left(f(\mathbf{x}^{(t)},\mathbf{y}^\star)-f(\mathbf{x}^\star,\mathbf{y}^\star)\right)+\left(f(\mathbf{x}^\star,\mathbf{y}^\star)-f(\mathbf{x}^\star,\mathbf{y}^{(t)})\right)\\&+\frac{\|\mathbf{x}^{(t)}-\mathbf{x}^{(t-1)}\|_2^2}{2\tau}+\frac{K\|\hat{\mathbf{y}}^{(t)}-\mathbf{y}^{(t-1)}\|_2^2}{2\sigma n}+\left(\frac{1}{2\tau}+\frac{\lambda}{2}\right)\|\mathbf{x}^{(t)}-\mathbf{x}^\star\|_2^2+\left(\frac{K}{2\sigma n}+\frac{\gamma}{2n}\right)\|\mathbf{y}^\star-\hat{\mathbf{y}}^{(t)}\|_2^2\end{aligned}$$

which implies that

$$\begin{aligned}&\frac{1}{n}\sum_{k=1}^{K}\sum_{j\in\mathcal{P}_k}(\hat{y}_j^{(t)}-y_j^\star)\langle a_j,\hat{\mathbf{x}}_k-\mathbf{x}^{(t)}\rangle+\frac{1}{n}\sum_{i=1}^{n}(\hat{y}_i^{(t)}-y_i^{(t)})\langle a_i,\mathbf{x}^{(t)}\rangle+\frac{1}{n}\sum_{i=1}^{n}\left(\phi_i^*(y_i^{(t)})-\phi_i^*(\hat{y}_i)\right)\\&+\frac{\|\mathbf{x}^\star-\mathbf{x}^{(t-1)}\|_2^2}{2\tau}\|^2+\frac{K\|\mathbf{y}^\star-\mathbf{y}^{(t-1)}\|_2^2}{2\sigma n}\\&\geq\left(f(\mathbf{x}^{(t)},\mathbf{y}^\star)-f(\mathbf{x}^\star,\mathbf{y}^\star)\right)+\left(f(\mathbf{x}^\star,\mathbf{y}^\star)-f(\mathbf{x}^\star,\mathbf{y}^{(t)})\right)+\frac{\|\mathbf{x}^{(t)}-\mathbf{x}^{(t-1)}\|_2^2}{2\tau}+\frac{K\|\hat{\mathbf{y}}^{(t)}-\mathbf{y}^{(t-1)}\|_2^2}{2\sigma n}\\&+\left(\frac{1}{2\tau}+\frac{\lambda}{2}\right)\|\mathbf{x}^{(t)}-\mathbf{x}^\star\|_2^2+\left(\frac{K}{2\sigma n}+\frac{\gamma}{2n}\right)\|\mathbf{y}^\star-\hat{\mathbf{y}}^{(t)}\|_2^2\end{aligned}$$

We need to upper bound the first term on the left-hand-side of the above inequality, assume that $1/\tau = 4\sigma R^2$, we have

$$
\begin{aligned}
|\frac{1}{n}\sum_{j\in\mathcal{P}_k}(\hat{y}_j^{(t)} - y_j^\star)\langle a_j, \hat{\mathbf{x}}_k^{(t)} - \mathbf{x}^{(t)}\rangle| &= |\frac{1}{n}(\hat{\mathbf{y}}_{[k]}^{(t)} - \mathbf{y}_{[k]}^\star)^\top A^\top(\hat{\mathbf{x}}_k^{(t)} - \mathbf{x}^{(t)})| \\
&\le \frac{\|\hat{\mathbf{x}}_k^{(t)} - \mathbf{x}^{(t)}\|_2^2}{4\tau} + \frac{\|A(\hat{\mathbf{y}}_{[k]}^{(t)} - \mathbf{y}_{[k]}^\star)\|_2^2}{n^2/\tau} \\
&\le \frac{\|\hat{\mathbf{x}}_k^{(t)} - \mathbf{x}^{(t)}\|_2^2}{4\tau} + \frac{(\sum_{j\in\mathcal{P}_k}|\hat{y}_j^{(t)} - y_j^\star|\cdot\|a_j\|)^2}{4\sigma R^2 n^2} \\
&\le \frac{\|\hat{\mathbf{x}}_k^{(t)} - \mathbf{x}^{(t)}\|_2^2}{4\tau} + \frac{\|\hat{\mathbf{y}}_{[k]}^{(t)} - \mathbf{y}_{[k]}^\star\|_2^2}{4\sigma n K}
\end{aligned}
$$

then we can get the upper bound

$$
\frac{1}{n}\sum_{k=1}^{K}\sum_{j\in\mathcal{P}_k}(\hat{y}_j^{(t)} - y_j^\star)\langle a_j, \hat{\mathbf{x}}_k - \mathbf{x}^{(t)}\rangle \le \sum_{k=1}^{K}\frac{\|\hat{\mathbf{x}}_k^{(t)} - \mathbf{x}^{(t)}\|_2^2}{4\tau} + \frac{\|\hat{\mathbf{y}}^{(t)} - \mathbf{y}^\star\|_2^2}{4\sigma n K}
$$

next we denote that

$$
\mathbf{\Lambda}'' = \frac{1}{n}\sum_{i=1}^{n}(\hat{y}_i^{(t)} - y_i^{(t)})\langle a_i, \mathbf{x}^{(t)}\rangle + \frac{1}{n}\sum_{i=1}^{n}\left(\phi_i^*(y_i^{(t)}) - \phi_i^*(\hat{y}_i)\right)
$$

Combining the above inequality and equation, we derive that

$$
\begin{aligned}
&\sum_{k=1}^{K}\frac{\|\hat{\mathbf{x}}_k^{(t)} - \mathbf{x}^{(t)}\|_2^2}{4\tau} + \frac{\|\mathbf{x}^\star - \mathbf{x}^{(t-1)}\|_2^2}{2\tau} + \frac{K\|\mathbf{y}^\star - \mathbf{y}^{(t-1)}\|_2^2}{2\sigma n} + \mathbf{\Lambda}'' \\
&\ge \left(f(\mathbf{x}^{(t)}, \mathbf{y}^\star) - f(\mathbf{x}^\star, \mathbf{y}^\star)\right) + \left(f(\mathbf{x}^\star, \mathbf{y}^\star) - f(\mathbf{x}^\star, \mathbf{y}^{(t)})\right) + \frac{\|\mathbf{x}^{(t)} - \mathbf{x}^{(t-1)}\|_2^2}{2\tau} + \frac{K\|\hat{\mathbf{y}}^{(t)} - \mathbf{y}^{(t-1)}\|_2^2}{2\sigma n} \\
&\quad + \left(\frac{1}{2\tau} + \frac{\lambda}{2}\right)\|\mathbf{x}^{(t)} - \mathbf{x}^\star\|_2^2 + \left(\frac{K}{2\sigma n} + \frac{\gamma}{2n} - \frac{1}{4\sigma n K}\right)\|\mathbf{y}^\star - \hat{\mathbf{y}}^{(t)}\|_2^2
\end{aligned}
$$

Based on the inequality (9) in lemma 3, we could get that

$$
\begin{aligned}
&\sum_{k=1}^{K}\frac{\|\hat{\mathbf{x}}_k^{(t)} - \mathbf{x}^{(t)}\|_2^2}{4\tau} + \frac{(K-1)^2}{4\sigma n K}\|\mathbf{y}^{(t-1)} - \mathbf{y}^{(t)}\|_2^2 + \frac{\|\mathbf{x}^\star - \mathbf{x}^{(t-1)}\|_2^2}{2\tau} + \frac{K\|\mathbf{y}^\star - \mathbf{y}^{(t-1)}\|_2^2}{2\sigma n} + \mathbf{\Lambda}' + \mathbf{\Lambda}'' \\
&\ge \left(f(\mathbf{x}^{(t)}, \mathbf{y}^\star) - f(\mathbf{x}^\star, \mathbf{y}^\star)\right) + \left(f(\mathbf{x}^\star, \mathbf{y}^\star) - f(\mathbf{x}^\star, \mathbf{y}^{(t)})\right) + \frac{\|\mathbf{x}^{(t)} - \mathbf{x}^{(t-1)}\|_2^2}{2\tau} + \frac{K\|\hat{\mathbf{y}}^{(t)} - \mathbf{y}^{(t-1)}\|_2^2}{2\sigma n} \\
&\quad + \left(\frac{3}{4\tau} + \lambda\right)\sum_{k=1}^{K}\|\mathbf{x}^{(t)} - \hat{\mathbf{x}}_k^{(t)}\|_2^2 + \left(\frac{1}{2\tau} + \frac{\lambda}{2}\right)\|\mathbf{x}^{(t)} - \mathbf{x}^\star\|_2^2 + \left(\frac{K}{2\sigma n} + \frac{\gamma}{2n} - \frac{1}{4\sigma n K}\right)\|\mathbf{y}^\star - \hat{\mathbf{y}}^{(t)}\|_2^2
\end{aligned}
$$

Since we can rewrite $\|\mathbf{y} - \hat{\mathbf{y}}^{(t)}\|_2^2 = \|\mathbf{y} - \mathbf{y}^{(t)}\|_2^2 + \|\mathbf{y}^{(t)} - \hat{\mathbf{y}}^{(t)}\|_2^2 + 2(\mathbf{y} - \mathbf{y}^{(t)})^\top(\mathbf{y}^{(t)} - \hat{\mathbf{y}}^{(t)})$, then we denote that

$$
\begin{aligned}
\mathbf{\Lambda}''' = &-\left(\frac{K}{2\sigma n} + \frac{\gamma}{2n} - \frac{1}{4\sigma n K}\right)\left(\|\mathbf{y}^{(t)} - \hat{\mathbf{y}}^{(t)}\|_2^2 + 2(\mathbf{y}^\star - \mathbf{y}^{(t)})^\top(\mathbf{y}^{(t)} - \hat{\mathbf{y}}^{(t)})\right) \\
&- \frac{K}{2\sigma n}\left(\|\mathbf{y}^{(t)} - \hat{\mathbf{y}}^{(t)}\|_2^2 + 2(\mathbf{y}^{(t-1)} - \mathbf{y}^{(t)})^\top(\mathbf{y}^{(t)} - \hat{\mathbf{y}}^{(t)})\right)
\end{aligned}
$$

Based on the definition of $\mathbf{\Lambda}'''$, we derive that

$$
\begin{aligned}
&\frac{\|\mathbf{x}^\star - \mathbf{x}^{(t-1)}\|_2^2}{2\tau} + \frac{K\|\mathbf{y}^\star - \mathbf{y}^{(t-1)}\|_2^2}{2\sigma n} + \mathbf{\Lambda}' + \mathbf{\Lambda}'' + \mathbf{\Lambda}''' \\
&\ge \left(f(\mathbf{x}^{(t)}, \mathbf{y}^\star) - f(\mathbf{x}^\star, \mathbf{y}^\star)\right) + \left(f(\mathbf{x}^\star, \mathbf{y}^\star) - f(\mathbf{x}^\star, \mathbf{y}^{(t)})\right) \\
&\quad + \left(\frac{1}{2\tau} + \frac{\lambda}{2}\right)\|\mathbf{x}^{(t)} - \mathbf{x}^\star\|_2^2 + \left(\frac{K}{2\sigma n} + \frac{\gamma}{2n} - \frac{1}{4\sigma n K}\right)\|\mathbf{y}^\star - \mathbf{y}^{(t)}\|_2^2 + \mathbf{\Lambda}^\sharp
\end{aligned}
$$

where we define

$$\boldsymbol{\Lambda}^\sharp = \frac{\|\mathbf{x}^{(t)} - \mathbf{x}^{(t-1)}\|_2^2}{2\tau} + \left(\frac{1}{2\tau} + \lambda\right)\sum_{k=1}^K \|\mathbf{x}^{(t)} - \hat{\mathbf{x}}_k^{(t)}\|_2^2 + \left(\frac{K}{2\sigma n} - \frac{(K-1)^2}{4\sigma n K}\right)\|\mathbf{y}^{(t)} - \mathbf{y}^{(t-1)}\|_2^2$$

Assume that $\Theta \geq 0$, then we can obtain

$$\begin{aligned}
&\Theta\left(f(\mathbf{x}^{(t-1)}, \mathbf{y}^\star) - f(\mathbf{x}^\star, \mathbf{y}^\star)\right) + \Theta\left(f(\mathbf{x}^\star, \mathbf{y}^\star) - f(\mathbf{x}^\star, \mathbf{y}^{(t-1)})\right) \\
&\frac{\|\mathbf{x}^\star - \mathbf{x}^{(t-1)}\|_2^2}{2\tau} + \frac{K\|\mathbf{y}^\star - \mathbf{y}^{(t-1)}\|_2^2}{2\sigma n} + \boldsymbol{\Lambda} \\
\geq &\left(f(\mathbf{x}^{(t)}, \mathbf{y}^\star) - f(\mathbf{x}^\star, \mathbf{y}^\star)\right) + \left(f(\mathbf{x}^\star, \mathbf{y}^\star) - f(\mathbf{x}^\star, \mathbf{y}^{(t)})\right) + \Theta\left(f(\mathbf{x}^{(t-1)}, \mathbf{y}^\star) - f(\mathbf{x}^\star, \mathbf{y}^{(t-1)})\right) \\
&+ \left(\frac{1}{2\tau} + \frac{\lambda}{2}\right)\|\mathbf{x}^{(t)} - \mathbf{x}^\star\|_2^2 + \left(\frac{K}{2\sigma n} + \frac{\gamma}{2n} - \frac{1}{4\sigma n K}\right)\|\mathbf{y}^\star - \mathbf{y}^{(t)}\|_2^2 + \boldsymbol{\Lambda}^\sharp
\end{aligned}$$

where $\boldsymbol{\Lambda} = \boldsymbol{\Lambda}' + \boldsymbol{\Lambda}'' + \boldsymbol{\Lambda}'''$ and $\boldsymbol{\Lambda}^\sharp > 0$.

In order to get the convergence guarantee of our algorithm, we need to get the upper bound of $\boldsymbol{\Lambda}$, based on the definition of $\boldsymbol{\Lambda}$, we could get

$$\begin{aligned}
\boldsymbol{\Lambda} \leq &\frac{1}{n}\sum_{k=1}^K (\hat{\mathbf{y}}_{[k]}^{(t)} - \mathbf{y}_{[k]}^{(t)})^\top A^\top(\mathbf{x}^{(t)} - \hat{\mathbf{x}}_k^{(t)}) + \frac{1}{n}(\hat{\mathbf{y}}^{(t)} - \mathbf{y}^{(t)})^\top A^\top \mathbf{x}^{(t)} + \frac{1}{n}\sum_{i=1}^n \left(\phi_i^*(y_i^{(t)}) - \phi_i^*(\hat{y}_i)\right) \\
&+ \left(\frac{K}{\sigma n} + \frac{\gamma}{n} - \frac{1}{2\sigma n K}\right)(\mathbf{y}^\star - \mathbf{y}^{(t)})^\top(\hat{\mathbf{y}}^{(t)} - \mathbf{y}^{(t)}) + \frac{K}{\sigma n}(\mathbf{y}^{(t-1)} - \mathbf{y}^{(t)})^\top(\hat{\mathbf{y}}^{(t)} - \mathbf{y}^{(t)})
\end{aligned}$$

based on the assumption, then we could get that

$$\boldsymbol{\Lambda} \leq \frac{M}{n}\|\hat{\mathbf{y}}^{(t)} - \mathbf{y}^{(t)}\|_2 + \sum_{k=1}^K \left(f(\hat{\mathbf{x}}_k^{(t)}, \hat{\mathbf{y}}_{[k]}^{(t)}) - f(\hat{\mathbf{x}}_k^{(t)}, \mathbf{y}_{[k]}^{(t)})\right)$$

where $M = 4\sqrt{n}R\,\Omega_{\mathbf{x}} + \left(\frac{3K}{\sigma} + \gamma\right)\Omega_{\mathbf{y}} = c'\Omega_{\mathbf{x}} + c''\Omega_{\mathbf{y}}$ as defined in Assumption 5. Based on the assumption

$$\mathbb{E}[\boldsymbol{\Lambda}] \leq \hat{\Theta}\frac{M}{n}\|\mathbf{y}^{(t-1)} - \hat{\mathbf{y}}^{(t)}\|_2 + \tilde{\Theta}\sum_{k=1}^K \left(f(\hat{\mathbf{x}}_k^{(t)}, \hat{\mathbf{y}}_{[k]}^{(t)}) - f(\hat{\mathbf{x}}_k^{(t)}, \mathbf{y}_{[k]}^{(t-1)})\right)$$

where $\hat{\Theta} < 1$, $\tilde{\Theta} < 1$ are defined in Assumption 4, and define the parameter Θ as

$$\Theta = \max\left\{\frac{1}{1 + \left(\frac{\sigma\gamma}{K} - \frac{1}{2K^2}\right)}, \frac{1}{1 + \tau\lambda}\right\} \tag{12}$$

based on Assumption 5, and we could get that

$$\mathbb{E}[\blacktriangle] = \mathbb{E}[\frac{M}{n}\|\hat{\mathbf{y}}^{(t)} - \mathbf{y}^{(t)}\|_2 + \sum_{k=1}^K \left(f(\hat{\mathbf{x}}_k^{(t)}, \hat{\mathbf{y}}_{[k]}^{(t)}) - f(\hat{\mathbf{x}}_k^{(t)}, \mathbf{y}_{[k]}^{(t)})\right)] \leq \Theta\left(f(\mathbf{x}^{(t-1)}, \mathbf{y}^\star) - f(\mathbf{x}^\star, \mathbf{y}^{(t-1)})\right)$$

Then we could get our finial conclusion

$$\mathbb{E}[\Delta^{(t)}] \leq \Theta\mathbb{E}[\Delta^{(t-1)}]$$

where we require that

$$\sigma > \frac{1}{2K\gamma}, \quad \tau\sigma = \frac{1}{4R^2} \tag{13}$$

□

B.2 Proof of Theorem 1

Proof. By Lemma 1, for each $t > 0$, we have $\mathbb{E}[\Delta^{(t)}] \leq \Theta^t \mathbb{E}[\Delta^{(0)}]$, according to the definition of C, we have

$$\mathbb{E}[\|\mathbf{x}^{(t)} - \mathbf{x}^\star\|_2^2] \leq \Theta^t C \tag{14}$$

In order to obtain $\Theta^T C \leq \epsilon$, which needs

$$T \geq -\frac{\log(C/\epsilon)}{\log(\Theta)}$$

Suppose the parameters τ, σ are set as

$$\sigma = \frac{1}{\gamma}, \quad \tau = \frac{\gamma}{4R^2}$$

Then according to the definition of Θ

$$\Theta = \max\left\{\frac{1}{1+(\frac{\sigma\gamma}{K} - \frac{1}{2K^2})}, \frac{1}{1+\tau\lambda}\right\} = \max\left\{\frac{1}{1+(\frac{1}{K} - \frac{1}{2K^2})}, \frac{1}{1+(\lambda\gamma)/(4R^2)}\right\}$$

As long as $\frac{1}{K} - \frac{1}{2K^2} \geq \frac{1}{K} - \frac{1}{2K} = \frac{1}{2K} \geq \frac{\lambda\gamma}{4R^2}$, since we assume $K \leq \kappa$. Then we have

$$\Theta = \frac{1}{1+(\lambda\gamma)/(4R^2)} = 1 - \frac{1}{1+(4R^2)/(\lambda\gamma)}$$

Thus we can get

$$T \geq -\frac{\log(C/\epsilon)}{\log(\Theta)} = \frac{\log(C/\epsilon)}{-\log\left(1 - \frac{1}{1+(4R^2)/(\lambda\gamma)}\right)}$$

where we apply the inequality $\log(1-x) \leq -x$ in the last inequality and we could get the conclusion. □

B.3 Convergence guarantee of primal-dual gap

Next we derive the convergence rate of primal-dual gap based on Theorem 1.

Lemma 4 (Yu et al. (2015)). *Suppose Assumption 1,2 holds, Let $(\mathbf{x}^\star, \mathbf{y}^\star)$ is the unique saddle-point of $f(\mathbf{x}, \mathbf{y})$, and $R = \max_{1\leq i\leq n} \|a_i\|_2$. Then for any point $(\mathbf{x}, \mathbf{y}) \in dom(g) \times dom(\phi^*)$, we have*

$$\mathcal{P}(\mathbf{x}) \leq f(\mathbf{x}, \mathbf{y}^\star) + \frac{R^2}{2\gamma}\|\mathbf{x} - \mathbf{x}^\star\|_2^2, \; \mathcal{D}(\mathbf{y}) \geq f(\mathbf{x}^\star, \mathbf{y}) - \frac{R^2}{2\lambda n}\|\mathbf{y} - \mathbf{y}^\star\|_2^2 \tag{15}$$

Corollary 2. *Suppose Assumption A holds and the parameters τ, σ, Θ are set as in (12), (13). Then the iterates of Algorithm 1 satisfy*

$$\mathbb{E}[\mathcal{P}(\mathbf{x}^{(T)}) - \mathcal{D}(\mathbf{y}^{(T)})] \leq \epsilon$$

it suffices to have the number of communication iterations T satisfy,

$$T \geq \left(1 + \frac{4R^2}{\lambda\gamma}\right) \log\left(\left(1 + \frac{R^2}{\lambda\gamma}\right)\frac{C}{\epsilon}\right)$$

.

Proof. Based on Lemma 4, we have

$$\begin{aligned}
\mathcal{P}(\mathbf{x}^{(t)}) - \mathcal{D}(\mathbf{y}^{(t)}) &= \mathcal{P}(\mathbf{x}^{(t)}) - \mathcal{P}(\mathbf{x}^\star) + \mathcal{D}(\mathbf{y}^\star) - \mathcal{D}(\mathbf{y}^{(t)}) \\
&\leq f(\mathbf{x}^{(t)}, \mathbf{y}^\star) + \frac{R^2}{2\gamma}\|\mathbf{x}^{(t)} - \mathbf{x}^\star\|_2^2 - f(\mathbf{x}^\star, \mathbf{y}^{(t)}) + \frac{R^2}{2\lambda n}\|\mathbf{y}^{(t)} - \mathbf{y}^\star\|_2^2 \\
&\leq \left(1 + \frac{R^2}{\lambda\gamma}\right)\Delta^{(t)}
\end{aligned}$$

Similar to Theorem 1, we could get the conclusion.

□

B.4 Proof of Theorem 2

Proof. If the parameters τ, σ in Algorithm 2 are set as

$$\tau = \frac{\gamma}{4R^2}, \quad \sigma = \frac{1}{\gamma}$$

then based on Lemma 1, we have

$$\Theta = \max\left\{\frac{1}{1+(\frac{\sigma\gamma}{K} - \frac{1}{2K^2})}, \frac{1}{1+\tau\lambda}\right\} = \max\left\{\frac{1}{1+(\frac{1}{K} - \frac{1}{2K^2})}, \frac{1}{1+\frac{\lambda\gamma}{4R^2}}\right\}$$

assume that $K \geq 2$, and $(\frac{1}{K} - \frac{1}{2K^2}) \geq \frac{\lambda\gamma}{4R^2}$, which means we focus on the situation that $\kappa = \frac{R^2}{\lambda\gamma} \gg 1$. Then we could get that

$$\Theta = \frac{1}{1+\frac{\lambda\gamma}{4R^2}} = 1 - \frac{1}{1+\frac{4R^2}{\lambda\gamma}}$$

Based on Corollary 2, we could get that

$$\mathcal{P}(\mathbf{x}^{(t)}) - \mathcal{P}(\mathbf{x}^\star) \leq \mathcal{P}(\mathbf{x}^{(t)}) - \mathcal{D}(\mathbf{y}^{(t)}) \leq \left(1 + \frac{R^2}{\lambda\gamma}\right)\Delta^{(t)} \leq C'\Theta^t\left(\mathcal{P}(\mathbf{x}^{(0)}) - \mathcal{P}(\mathbf{x}^\star)\right)$$

where C' is a constant and $C' > 0$ and $\mathcal{P}(\cdot)$ is defined in (1). If we apply DiSPA on $f^{(t)}$ defined in Section 5.1, then based on Proposition 3.2 of Lin et al. (2015), the $\tau_{\mathcal{M}}$ defined in Proposition 3.2 equals

$$\tau_{\mathcal{M}} = \frac{1}{1+\frac{4R^2}{(\lambda+\vartheta)\gamma}}$$

where ϑ is the parameter defined in Section 5.1. We could get that $\tau_{\mathcal{M}} \approx \frac{(\lambda+\vartheta)\gamma}{4R^2}$ since $\kappa \gg 1$. Now apply Proposition 3.2 in Lin et al. (2015), we could get the global linear rate of convergence withe parameter $\tau_{\mathcal{A},F}$,

$$\tau_{\mathcal{A},F} = \tilde{O}\left(\tau_{\mathcal{M}}\sqrt{\lambda}/\sqrt{\lambda+\vartheta}\right) = \tilde{O}\left(\frac{(\lambda+\vartheta)\gamma\sqrt{\lambda}}{4R^2\sqrt{\lambda+\vartheta}}\right)$$

if we take ϑ as $\vartheta = \frac{4R^2}{\gamma} - \lambda$, then we can get that the communication complexity of the A-DiSPA for achieving $\mathcal{P}(\mathbf{x}^{(T)}) - \mathcal{P}(\mathbf{x}^\star) < \epsilon$ is $\tilde{O}\left(\sqrt{\kappa}\log\left(\frac{1}{\epsilon}\right)\right)$. □

Robust Model Equivalence using Stochastic Bisimulation for N-Agent Interactive DIDs

Muthukumaran Chandrasekaran
University of Georgia
Athens, GA, USA 30602
mkran@uga.edu

Junhuan Zhang
Beihang University
Beijing, China 100191
junhuan.zhang@gmail.com

Prashant Doshi
University of Georgia
Athens, GA, USA 30602
pdoshi@cs.uga.edu

Yifeng Zeng
Teesside University
Middlesbrough, UK TS1 3BX
y.zeng@tees.ac.uk

Abstract

I-DIDs suffer disproportionately from the curse of dimensionality dominated by the exponential growth in the number of models over time. Previous methods for scaling I-DIDs identify notions of equivalence between models, such as behavioral equivalence (BE). But, this requires that the models be solved first. Also, model space compression across agents has not been previously investigated. We present a way to compress the space of models across agents, possibly with different frames, and do so without having to solve them first, using stochastic bisimulation. We test our approach on two non-cooperative partially observable domains with up to 20 agents.

1 INTRODUCTION

Autonomous agents must be capable of perceiving the environment, interact with other agents, and make rational decisions to achieve their goals under uncertainty. Interactive partially observable markov decision process (I-POMDP) [19] is a recognized framework that models the decision-making process of a self-interested agent in a partially observable multiagent setting. I-POMDPs cover an important portion of the multiagent planning problem space [10, 15]. Applications in diverse areas such as security [23, 21], robotics [26, 25], ad hoc teams [6, 7] and human behavior modeling [12, 27] testify to its wide appeal while motivating better scalability.

Interactive dynamic influence diagrams [14] provide a graphical and naturally factored representation for I-POMDPs. They compactly represent the problem of how an agent should act in an uncertain environment shared with others with unknown behaviors. I-DIDs typically handle the uncertainty over the other agents' behaviors by maintaining a belief over a large but finite set of models, and updating it over time [22]. However, I-DIDs suffer disproportionately from the curse of dimensionality [14]. The curse of dimensionality is dominated by the exponential growth in the number of models over time. Toward this, previous methods for scaling I-DIDs identify notions of equivalence between models, such as behavioral equivalence (BE) [28]. But, this requires that the models be solved first [28, 8]. All existing approaches group models that differ only in their beliefs while sharing a common frame (i.e., transition, observation, and reward functions). Hence, they have been evaluated on domains involving one other agent only.

Is there a way to compress the space of models across agents, possibly with different frames, and do so without having to solve them first? To answer this question, we draw upon the well-known concept of *stochastic bisimulation* [18, 4], which allows us to establish equivalence relationships (bisimilarity) between models under conditions of uncertainty. An exact bisimilar relation between two models (say, DIDs) implies that, for all the actions, the expected immediate rewards are equal and transitions occur to models that are themselves bisimilar. The base case requires we transition to beliefs that are the same.

However, this notion of exact bisimilarity is too stringent to use in practice because it requires that the frames of agents agree exactly. Obviously, this is not robust because even a small change in the rewards or the transition probabilities cause these models to appear dissimilar although their solutions may not be different. Therefore, we are motivated to measure the *degree* to which two models with differing frames may be bisimilar. Ferns *et.* al [16, 17] define a distance metric, called the *bisimulation metric*, that varies relative to the quantitative difference between two MDPs. We leverage the theoretical guarantees of this metric and generalize it to partially observable settings. Hence, for the first time in the context of I-DIDs, we can operate on models across one or more frames whose "similarity" can be measured by using our generalized metric. We are excited about the prospects of this metric: computational savings achievable by pruning *similar* models across agents, and the ability to do so without having to solve the models first.

Specifically, the contributions of this paper are three-fold: (i) We leverage the existing equivalence notion of stochastic bisimulation and extend Ferns et. al's bisimulation metrics for MDPs [16, 17] to partially observable settings represented by models such DIDs. We formally define and use this metric to quantitatively measure the *similarity* between any two models in the space of models that the subject agent ascribes to the other agents in its I-DID. (ii) Using a tolerance parameter ϵ, we present a way to partition the model space into ϵ-bisimiar regions using *barycentric subdivision* [20]. We also present a way to mitigate the combinatorial explosion due to barycentric subdividing by merging all those adjacent regions which, when merged, continue to satisfy the ϵ-bisimiarity constraints. (iii) Finally, we generalize I-DIDs to N-agents and compare the performance of our model space compression technique against a baseline I-DID solver that uses the current state-of-the-art BE-based technique – discriminative model updates (DMU) [28] – on two non-cooperative multiagent domains exhibiting partial observability with up to 20 agents.

2 RELATED WORK

Previous notions of equivalence like stochastic bisimulation and trajectory equivalence between states have been used in the context of model abstraction to provide a principled way to reduce a model into something more compact [18, 4]. The reduced model can then be solved using traditional solvers utilizing much lesser computational power than what would have been needed otherwise. However, exact equivalence is too stringent to use in practice. In their first piece of related work, Ferns *et.* al devised metrics which quantitatively measured the degree of similarity between states in an MDP [16]. More recently, they went on to extend their metrics to MDPs with continuous states [17]. In the context of I-DIDs, previous efforts focus predominantly on addressing their *curse of dimensionality* which is *in part* due to exponential growth in the number of models over time[1] [14, 13, 11, 5, 28, 8], and the *curse of history* due to exponential increase in the size of the model solutions – policy trees and actions – with the planning horizon [30, 29]. All these approaches identify some notion of *equivalence* between models – including behavioral equivalence (BE), action equivalence (AE), and value equivalence (VE) – and require solving of *all* the models and comparing their solutions. A few approaches exploit the spatial closeness of beliefs in order to identify equivalence between models [14] while others operate directly on candidate model solutions instead of the model specifications [28]. A general limitation of the former – utilizing the spatial proximity of beliefs – is that it is less likely that two such models will result in the same behavior if their frames (say, the transition or reward functions) were different. The latter, however, continue to apply, albeit with increased computational complexity, even if there was some uncertainty in the frames.

[1]The curse of dimensionality in I-DIDs can also be due to the exponential growth in the model space with the number of agents.

3 BACKGROUND

We briefly review I-DIDs next followed by the concept of stochastic bisimulation for MDPs.

3.1 INTERACTIVE DIDs (I-DIDs)

Representation We illustrate a generic two time-slice level $l > 0$ I-DID with $N = 2$ agents in Fig. 1. I-DIDs have a

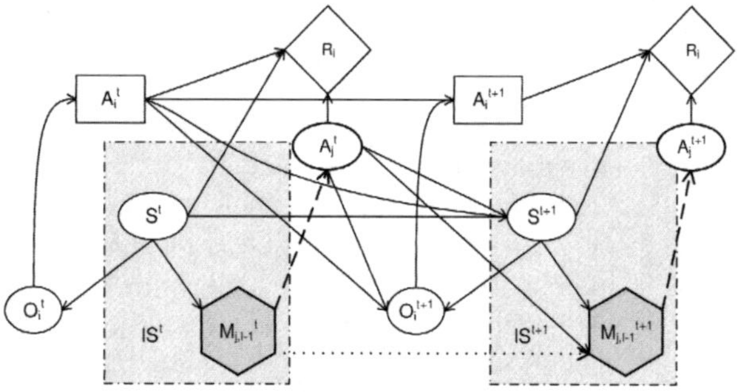

Figure 1: A generic two time-slice level l I-DID for agent i situated with one other agent j.

model node (denoted by the hexagonal node) in addition to the nodes already present in traditional DIDs. DIDs utilize chance nodes to model the uncertainty in the subject agent i's decision making problem through random variables such as those for modeling the physical state, S, and the agent's observations, O_i. They additionally use decision nodes and utility nodes to model the agent's actions, A_i, and reward function, R_i, respectively. In addition to the model node, I-DIDs also have a chance node, A_j, to represent the distribution over actions of the other agent j. The model node $M_{j,l-1}$ in the I-DID houses a candidate set of computable *intentional models* (and possibly *subintentional models*) ascribed by i to agent j. Subscript $l-1$ denotes the *strategy level* indicating the cognitive capability of the other agent j. A model in the model node may be a level $l-1$ I-DID or a DID. The recursion ends at level 0, when the models are DIDs. We note that the other agents' level is one less than that of i which follows from established previous hierarchical formulations in game theory [1, 3] and decision theory [19]. In order to operationalize this formulation of I-DIDs, the state space is augmented with the models of the other agents, referred to as the *interactive state space*, IS_i (shown in Fig. 1). A link from the chance node, S, to the model node, $M_{j,l-1}$, represents agent i's beliefs over j's models. Specifically, it is a probability distribution in the conditional probability table (CPT) of the chance node, $Mod[M_j]$ (in Fig. 2). An individual model of an agent j, denoted $m_{j,l-1}$, is a 2-tuple

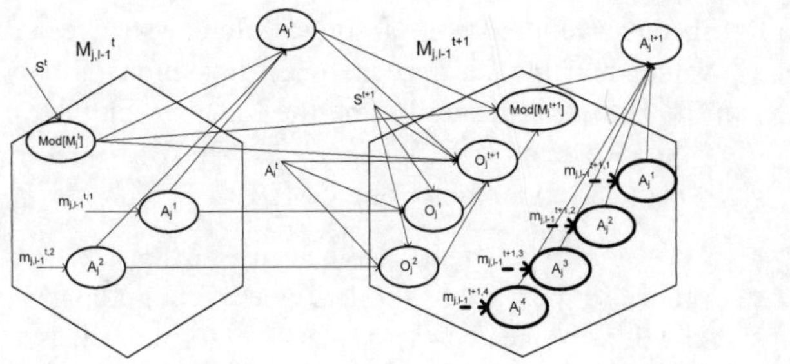

Figure 2: Implementation of the model update link using standard dependency links and chance nodes.

$< b_{j,l-1}, \hat{\theta}_j >$ where $b_{j,l-1}$ is the level $l-1$ belief, which is the probability distribution over j's interactive state space, and $\hat{\theta}_j$ is agent j's *frame* that encompasses the decision, observation, transition, and utility nodes. Solutions to the model are the predicted behavior of j and are encoded into the chance node, A_j, through a dashed link, called a *policy link*. Connecting A_j with other nodes in the I-DID structures how agent j's actions influence i's decision-making process. As agent j acts and receives observations over time, its models should be updated. A dotted link, called the *model update link*, from $M^t_{j,l-1}$ to $M^{t+1}_{j,l-1}$ in Fig. 1 denotes the update of the model node over time. For example, two models, $m^{t,1}_{j,l-1}$ and $m^{t,2}_{j,l-1}$, are updated into four models at time $t+1$ (shown in Fig. 2). Models at $t+1$ reflect the updated belief of j, and their solutions provide the probability distributions for the corresponding action node. We may implement the model node, the policy link, and the model update link using chance nodes and standard dependency links, as shown in Fig. 2, and transform an I-DID into a traditional DID.

Solution We outline a generic procedure for solving I-DIDs below and refer the readers to [13, 28] for more information. The solution for a level l I-DID expanded over T time steps proceeds in a bottom-up manner. In order to solve the subject agent i's I-DID at level l, all models of the other agent j at level $l-1$ must first be solved. The solution to a level $l-1$ model $m_{j,l-1}$ is j's policy that prescribes an optimal decision in A_j initially given its belief $b_{j,l-1}$, and the actions thereafter conditional on its observations in O_j up to time T. We perform this process for each level $l-1$ model of j and obtain the fully expanded level l model.

3.2 EQUIVALENCE USING STOCHASTIC BISIMULATION

Stochastic bisimulation can be used to define equivalence relations between states in stochastic processes. Givan *et.* al extended the notion of stochastic bisimulation to probabilistic transition systems with rewards in the context of MDPs [18] providing a principled way for model abstraction in MDPs with pleasing theoretically guarantees.

The 4-tuple $\langle S, A, T, R \rangle$ defines an MDP with a finite set of physical states S and actions A, transition function $T : S \times A \rightarrow \Delta(S)$, and reward function $R : S \times A \rightarrow \mathbb{R}$. A bisimulation relation between states in an MDP is defined as follows:

Definition 1 (Stochastic bisimulation relation). *An equivalence relation $E \subseteq S \times S$ between two states $s, s' \in S$ is a* ***stochastic bisimulation relation*** *if whenever sEs', then the following holds $\forall a \in A$: (i) $R(s,a) = R(s',a)$, and (ii) $\forall C \in S/E$, $T(s,a)(C) = T(s',a)(C)$.*

where, S/E is the state partition induced by E and $T(s,a)(C) = \sum_{s'' \in C} T(s,a,s'')$. Stochastic bisimulation, $\approx$, is the largest stochastic bisimulation relation.

Givan et. al show an iterative procedure to compute the stochastic bisimulation (henceforth simply bisimulation) partition. Castro *et.* al extend bisimulation to partially observable settings [4] in the context of a *belief MDP*. A *belief MDP* equivalently converts a POMDP into a MDP with a continuous state space comprising of the entire belief simplex. We note that DIDs are just graphical representations of belief MDPs.

A belief MDP is a 4-tuple $M = \langle B, A, \mathcal{T}, \rho \rangle$, where B denotes the belief simplex; A is the set of actions; $\mathcal{T} : B \times A \rightarrow \Delta(B)$ is the belief-transition function; $\rho : B \times A \rightarrow \mathbb{R}$ is the reward function. $\rho(b,a)$ and $\mathcal{T}(b,a)(b')$ are defined below:

$$\rho(b,a) = \sum_{s \in S} R(s,a) b(s) \tag{1}$$

$$\mathcal{T}(b,a)(b') = \sum_{\omega \in \Omega} Pr(b'|b,a,\omega) Pr(\omega|a,b) \tag{2}$$

$$Pr(b'|a,b,\omega) = \begin{cases} 1 & \text{if } b' = \tau(b,a,\omega). \\ 0 & \text{otherwise.} \end{cases}$$

$$\tau(b,a,\omega) \triangleq b'(s') = \frac{O(s',a,\omega) \sum_{s \in S} T(s,a,s') b(s)}{Pr(\omega|a,b)}$$

$$Pr(\omega|a,b) = \sum_{s' \in S} O(s',a,\omega) \sum_{s \in S} T(s,a,s') b(s)$$

where, $O(s',a,\omega)$ denotes the probability of observing ω given the state s' and action a. Castro et. al defines *stochastic bisimulation* between 2 beliefs as follows:

Definition 2 (Belief bisimulation relation). *A relation $E \subseteq B \times B$ is a* ***belief bisimulation relation*** *if whenever bEc, then the following holds: (i) $\forall a \in A$ $\rho(b,a) = \rho(c,a)$, (ii) $\forall a \in A$, $\forall \omega \in \Omega$ $O(b,a,\omega) = O(c,a,\omega)$, (iii) $\forall a \in A$, $\forall \omega \in \Omega$ $\tau(b,a,\omega)$ and $\tau(c,a,\omega)$ are belief bisimilar. (Def. 3).*

Definition 3 (Belief bisimilarity). *Two belief states b, c are **bisimilar**, denoted $b \approx c$, if there exists a belief bisimulation relation E such that bEc.*

We note that *belief bisimulation* has a recursive definition. In other words, in order for two belief states to be *bisimilar*, their updated beliefs need to also be *bisimilar*. This in turn implies that their corresponding belief transition functions must also be equal. Therefore, if $\tau(b, a, \omega) E \tau(c, a, \omega)$ (*Condition (iii) in Def. 2*), it follows that for any arbitrary belief $g \in B/E$ and action $a \in A, Pr(g|b, a) = Pr(g|c, a)$, and vice versa; where $Pr(g|b, a) = \sum_{b' \in g} \mathcal{T}(b, a)(b')$ and B/E denotes the partition of B into E-equivalence classes. Stochastic bisimulation is the largest belief bisimulation relation.

Unfortunately, the equivalence notion of stochastic bisimulation is too stringent because it requires that the rewards and transition probabilities agree exactly. This is not robust because even small perturbations in rewards or transition probabilities will cause states to appear dissimilar. This motivates the use of a distance metric to evaluate the degree to which two models may be bisimilar. Previously, Ferns *et* al. introduced metrics for computing the *degree* of bisimilarity between two states in an MDPs – and hence the MDPs themselves – with theoretical bounds on the solution quality due to the induced approximations [16, 17]. In general, they used a semimetric as a distance function that quantifies how far apart two states are in the MDP.

Definition 4 (Semimetric). *A semimetric on S is a map $d : S \times S \to [0, \infty)$ s.t. for every triple s, s', and $s'' \in S$, (i) $s = s' \Rightarrow d(s, s') = 0$, (ii) $d(s, s') = d(s', s)$, and (iii) $d(s, s'') \leq d(s, s') + d(s', s'')$*

If the converse of Condition (i) was true, then d would be a proper *metric*. This allows the possibility of the distance between s and s' to be 0 even if s and s' are distinct. Let D be the set of all semimetrics on S that assigns a distance of at most 1. Note that every semimetric d induces an equivalence relation, E, on S, obtained by equating the states assigned a distance of zero by d. For convenience, we will refer to semimetrics as just metrics hereafter.

Definition 5 (Bisimulation metric). *We say that $d \in D$ is a bisimulation relation metric if it measures the bisimulation relation, E, as defined in Def. 1. The bisimulation relation metric d is a bisimulation metric if E is a stochastic bisimulation, $\approx$.*

Ferns et. al construct the bisimulation metrics as a linear combination of a metric on the rewards and a metric on the transition probability distributions.

$$d(s, s') = \max_{a \in A} c_R\,(R(s, a) - R(s', a)) + c_T\, d_p(\mathcal{T}(s, a), \mathcal{T}'(s', a)) \tag{3}$$

where d_p is some probability metric, and c_R and c_T are constants between 0 and 1. The constants represent the respective weights on the absolute difference between reward values and the distance between transition probabilities. The latter is measured using the Kantorovich metric [24], which we detail next. We set $c_T = \gamma$ and $c_R = 1 - \gamma$ where γ is the discount factor of the MDPs.

The Kantorovich metric has been used extensively in recent years as a measure of similarity between 2 probability distributions because it can be elegantly formulated as a linear program computable in polynomial time with several appealing theoretical properties applicable within our context probabilistic concurrency (like in stochastic processes)[2]. In general, behavioral equivalences for probabilistic processes such as MDPs involve a *lifting* operation that converts a relation on states into a relation on distributions of states. This nicely corresponds to the way the Kantorovich metric works – in 2 levels: it considers both (i) the distances between the underlying states, and (ii) the distances between the probability distributions over those states. We detail the linear program used to compute the Kantorovich metric, $T_K(d)$, below:

Definition 6 (Kantorovich metric). *Let C be a block in the partition of states S induced by the equivalence relation, E. Given $d \in \mathcal{D}$, the Kantorovich metric, denoted $T_K(d)$, applied to finite probability distributions P and Q each over S is defined by the following linear program:*

$$T_K(d)(P, Q) = \max_{v_C} \sum\nolimits_{C \in S/E} (P(C) - Q(C))\, v_C$$
$$\textit{subject to}: \; v_C - v_D \leq \min_{i \in C, j \in D} d(s_i, s_j) \;\; \forall C, D$$
$$0 \leq v_C \leq 1 \;\; \forall C$$

and $T_K(d)(P, Q) = 0 \Leftrightarrow P(C) = Q(C), \forall C \in S/E$.

where d is the underlying cost function between two states and $P(C) = \sum_{s \in C} P(s)$. As $d \in D$ is a metric, the solution to the above LP (i.e. the Kantorovich metric distance) is also a metric. Therefore, the bisimulation metric can be expressed in terms of the Kantorovich metric.

The following lemmas are a direct consequence of Def. 5 and Def. 6:

Lemma 1. *Let $M = \langle S, A, T, R \rangle$ and $M' = \langle S, A, T', R' \rangle$ be two MDPs sharing the same set of actions and a common state space S. If $d \in \mathcal{D}$ is a bisimulation metric, then $\forall s, s' \in S$ $d(s, s') = 0$ iff $\forall a \in A$:*

$$R(s, a) - R(s', a) = 0, \quad T_K(d)(\mathcal{T}(s, a), \mathcal{T}'(s', a)) = 0$$

Lemma 2. *If $d \in \mathcal{D}$ satisfies Lemma 1, then*

$$d(s, s') = 0 \Rightarrow s \approx s' \; (i.e.\ s, s'\ are\ bismilar)$$

[2]Commonly used KL divergence is not a proper metric, unlike the Kantorovich metric. The latter is also known by several other names including Monge-Kantorovich, Kantorovich-Rubinstein, Wasserstein, and Earth Movers Distance.

Given Lemmas 1 and 2, the next theorem follows in a straightforward manner.

Theorem 1. *If $d \in \mathcal{D}$ is a bisimulation metric defined on S (i.e. satisfies Lemma 1), then for all s, s' ($\in S$) coming from M, M' respectively,*

$$d(s, s') = 0 \Rightarrow M \approx M' \text{ (i.e. } M, M' \text{ are bismilar)}$$

The Kantorovich metric leverages a few theoretical results from *fixed-point* theory [16, 17]. It preserves the point-wise partial ordering that the set of probability metrics $\mathcal{D}$ (on S) is equipped with: $\forall d, d' \in \mathcal{D}$ $d \leq d'$ iff $d(s, s') \leq d'(s, s')$. As a result, $T_K : \mathcal{D} \to \mathcal{D}$ is shown to be continuous given that the partial ordering is $\omega - complete$. We can then define the *bisimulation metric* based on the Kantorovich probability metric as follows:

Definition 7 (Bisimulation metric using Kantorovich metric). *Let $c_R, c_T \geq 0$ with $c_R + c_T \leq 1$. Define a continuous function $F : \mathcal{D} \to \mathcal{D}$ as,*

$$F(d)(s, s') = \max_{a \in A} c_R \, (R(s, a) - R(s', a)) + c_T \, T_K(d)(\mathcal{T}(s, a), \mathcal{T}'(s', a))$$

Then F has a least fixed-point, d^*, and d^* is a bisimulation metric.

The existence of the fixed-point is proven in [16]. Ferns *et* al. also show that $s \approx s' \iff d^*(s, s') = 0$. Note that d^* can be computed to some degree of accuracy by iterative applications of F for a proportional number of steps. This essentially reduces to computing a Kantorovich metric at each iteration for every action and pair of states.

4 MODEL SPACE COMPRESSION FOR N-AGENT I-DIDS

Stochastic bisimulation presents a principled way to establish equivalence relationships between models with different frames without having to solve them first. We seek to incorporate this idea within the context of I-DIDs allowing for model space compression across agents – whom may have different frames – for the first time. Toward this, we generalize the existing 2-agent I-DIDs to N agents.

4.1 GENERALIZATION TO N-AGENTS

We illustrate an example generic two time-slice level $l > 0$ I-DID for agent i situated with 2 other agents j and k in Fig. 3. Notice that we added a model node and a chance node representing the distribution over an agent's actions linked together using a *policy link*, for each other agent.

The subject agent i's reward, transition, and observation functions are impacted by the other agents' actions. Therefore, we note an exponential explosion in the size of the

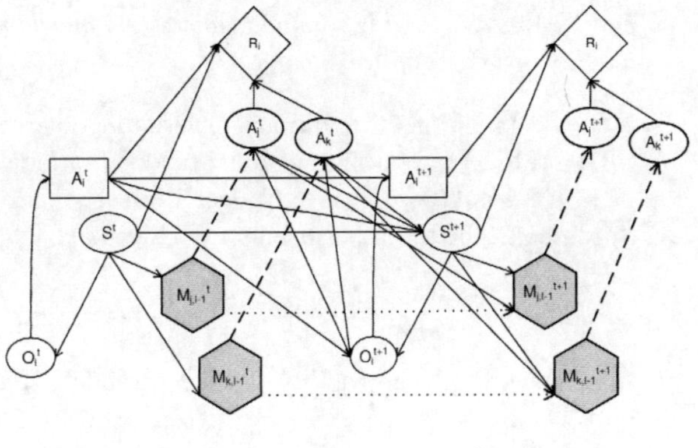

Figure 3: A generic two time-slice level l I-DID for agent i situated with two other agents j and k.

CPTs of the chance nodes S^{t+1} and O_i^{t+1}, and the reward function R_i with increasing numbers of other agents in the setting. As mentioned earlier, in the expansion step of agent i's I-DID, we must update the belief over interactive states of i, which includes the physical states and other agents' models, over time. For simplicity, we assume that given the belief over the physical states and the corresponding distribution over the actions of the other agent, agent i's belief over the other agents' models is conditionally independent and can be factored. Consequently, we can update the models of each other agent independently of other agents' models. The exponential growth in the number of models in the model node over time is further impacted by the number of other agents in the setting. The *model update links* for agents j and k from their corresponding model nodes at time t to time $t + 1$ – denoted by dotted links – are shown in Fig. 1. Models at $t+1$ reflect the updated beliefs of j and k, and their solutions provide the probability distributions for their corresponding action nodes.

4.2 BISIMULATION METRICS

Incorporating *exact* stochastic bisimulation for model compression in I-DIDs may be impractical because it is sensitive to variations in the numerical values of the parameters of the models as mentioned previously. Therefore, leveraging the notion of stochastic bisimulation for POMDPs from Castro *et* al [4] and the bisimulation metrics for MDPs from Ferns *et* al [16], we generalize the bisimulation metrics to POMDPs. We will operationalize its use as a quantitative measure of similarity between level-0 models (DIDs) ascribed by the subject agent (at level-1) to the others in the model nodes of the I-DID. We will limit the scope of this work to level-1 I-DIDs as we believe this is a good and necessary first step in the generalization to I-DIDs at higher levels. We redefine the bisimulation metrics in the context of belief states in DIDs next:

Definition 8 (Belief bisimulation metric). *We say that $d \in D$ measures the belief bisimulation relation metric if it measures the belief bisimulation relation E as defined in*

Def. 2. We say that d is a belief bisimulation metric if E is a belief bisimulation ≈.

First, we transform the traditional reward function of belief MDPs (Eq. 1) into a binary-valued random variable, $\mathcal{R} : B \times A \to \Delta(\{0,1\})$ using Cooper's transformation [9]. Specifically, the reward distribution $\mathcal{R}(b,a)$ is:

$$Pr(\mathcal{R}(b,a) = 1|\rho(b,a)) = \frac{\rho(b,a) - \rho_{min}}{\rho_{max} - \rho_{min}} \tag{4}$$

In other words, the probability of selecting and de-selecting the reward $\rho(b,a)$ is given by $Pr(\mathcal{R}(b,a) = 1|\rho(b,a))$ and $1 - Pr(\mathcal{R}(b,a) = 1|\rho(b,a))$ respectively.

We may redefine the bisimulation relation of Def. 2 by replacing the traditional reward function in the first constraint of the definition with the corresponding stochastic reward.

Next, we construct the bisimulation metric for level-0 models – represented as DIDs – as a linear combination of two metrics; one on the stochastic reward and one on the belief transition probabilities. Both metrics can now be defined using the Kantorovich metric and can be computed using a linear program similar to the one in Definition 6.

$$\begin{aligned} d(b,b') = \max_{a \in A} \; & c_R \, T_K(d)(\mathcal{R}(b,a), \mathcal{R}'(b',a)) \\ & + c_T \, T_K(d)(\mathcal{T}(b,a), \mathcal{T}'(b',a)) \end{aligned} \tag{5}$$

where c_R and c_T are as defined previously.

We can also rewrite the lemmas 1 and 2 and theorem 1 in our context next. Let M and M' be two level-0 models sharing the same set of actions and a common belief space B. Let $b, b' \in B$ be the corresponding initial beliefs of the two models respectively.

Lemma 3. *If $d \in \mathcal{D}$ is a belief bisimulation metric, then $\forall b, b' \in B$, $d(b,b') = 0$ iff $\forall a \in A$:*

$$\begin{aligned} & T_K(d)(\mathcal{R}(b,a), \mathcal{R}'(b',a)) = 0, \text{ and} \\ & T_K(d)(\mathcal{T}(b,a), \mathcal{T}'(b',a)) = 0 \end{aligned}$$

Lemma 4. *If $d \in \mathcal{D}$ satisfies Lemma 3, then*

$$d(b,b') = 0 \Rightarrow b \approx b' \text{ (i.e. } b, b' \text{ are bismilar)}$$

Theorem 2. *If $d \in \mathcal{D}$ is a belief bisimulation metric defined on B (i.e. satisfies Lemma 3), then for all b, b' ($\in B$) coming from M, M' respectively,*

$$d(b,b') = 0 \Rightarrow M \approx M' \text{ (i.e. } M, M' \text{ are bismilar)}$$

Next, we may redefine the belief bisimulation metric based on the Kantorovich metric analogous to Definition 7.

Definition 9 (Belief bisimulation metric). *Let $c_R, c_T \geq 0$ with $c_R + c_T \leq 1$. Define a continuous fn. $F : \mathcal{D} \to \mathcal{D}$ as,*

$$\begin{aligned} F(d)(b,b') = \; & \max_{a \in A} \; c_R \, T_K(d)(\mathcal{R}(b,a), \mathcal{R}'(b',a)) \\ & + c_T \, T_K(d)(\mathcal{T}(b,a), \mathcal{T}'(b',a)) \end{aligned} \tag{6}$$

Then F has a least fixed-point, d^*, and d^* is a belief bisimulation metric.

The proofs for the above lemmas and theorem can be trivially generalized from [16]. The theoretical results concerning fixed-point metrics from [16] also apply here.

4.3 COMPUTING STOCHASTIC BISIMULATION

In the previous section, we developed a metric which when equal to zero, establishes an exact bisimulation relation between beliefs. This metric also varies smoothly relative to the differences in the reward and transition probabilities. Therefore, we may choose a tolerance parameter $\epsilon \in [0,1]$ and cluster models that are in the ϵ-neighborhoods: all models within a cluster are *ϵ-bisimilar* (denoted by $\approx_\epsilon$). More formally,

Definition 10 (Approximately bisimilar). *If $d \in \mathcal{D}$ is a bisimulation metric, then $b, b' \in B$, $d(b,b') \leq \epsilon$ iff $\forall a \in A$*

$$\begin{aligned} & T_K(d)(\mathcal{R}(b,a), \mathcal{R}'(b',a)) \leq \epsilon, \text{ and} \\ & T_K(d)(\mathcal{T}(b,a), \mathcal{T}'(b',a)) \leq \epsilon \end{aligned} \tag{7}$$

Let $d(b,b') \leq \epsilon \Rightarrow b \approx_\epsilon b'$ and subsequently $M \approx_\epsilon M'$ (i.e. M, M' are ϵ-bisimilar) from Theorem 2.

Consider an $(|S|-1)$-dimensional belief simplex B, and a partition P of B. We seek to find a *partition* P^*, called the *bisimulation partition*, that divides B into a disjoint set of convex regions (i.e. *blocks*) such that any two arbitrary models within a block in P^* are *ϵ-bisimilar* (as defined in Def. 10). As each block is convex, we may sufficiently represent a block using its finite set of vertex beliefs that make up its *convex hull*. For example, we illustrate a $2D$ belief simplex B in Fig. 4(a).

Algorithm 1 Bisimulation Partitioning

```
Input: ε
Let P = {B} /* trivial one block partition */
while P ∋ B1, B2 s.t. P ≠ split_ε(B1, B2, P) do
    P = split_ε(B1, B2, P)
P* = the equivalence relation given by P
Output: P*
```

The algorithm for computing the *bisimulation partition* is outlined in Alg. 1. We start with a trivial 1-block partition $P = \{B\}$ (line 1). We split the block if the boundary beliefs are not pairwise ϵ-bisimilar using *barycentric subdivision* (line 3). As we note in Def. 2, the check for ϵ-bisimilarity between two beliefs is recursive. We require that their updated beliefs also be pairwise ϵ-bisimilar, and so on. To that end, we define *stability* of a block $B1$ with respect to block $B2$ as when all pairs of boundary beliefs of $B1$ satisfy Lemma 10 of being carried into block $B2$ for every action $a \in A$ (line 2). We terminate when all blocks in the partition are *stable* with respect to each other. This final partition is a *bisimulation partition* (line 4).

Barycentric Subdivision Barycentric subdivision presents a principled way to *exactly* divide a convex n-dimensional

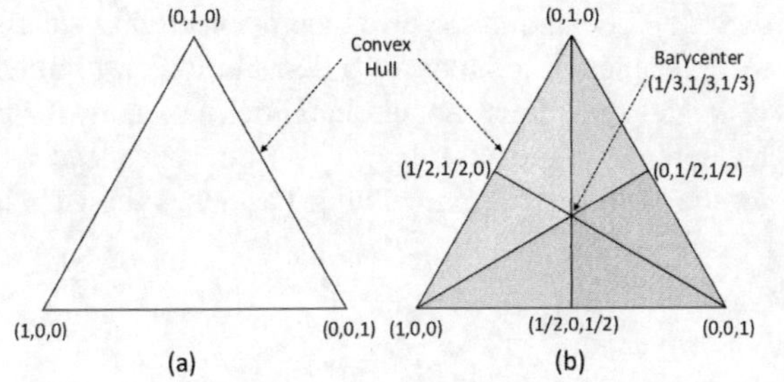

Figure 4: (a) A $2D$ belief simplex whose convex hull is represented using 3 boundary belief points. (b) Six $2D$ sub-simplices resulting from 1 *split*.

simplex into disjoint and convex sub-simplices with the same dimension by connecting the *barycenters* (or centroids) of their faces, *and* guarantee convergence to a *fixed point* [3]. Fig. 4(b) shows how a 2D simplex will look like after one *split* operation. One split operation on an n-dimensional simplex will result in $(n+1)!$ sub-simplices. This is evidently one of the bottlenecks of this approach; it is combinatorial with respect to the dimensionality of the state space. Since our split methodology may not result in a *minimal* partition, we additionally implement a ***merge***$_\epsilon$ method that combines all adjacent blocks – sharing a common $n-1$ dimensional face – which, when merged, continue to preserve the stability constraints.

4.4 SOLVING I-DID USING BISIMULATION

As a first step in our algorithm Solving I-DID (Alg. 2), we compute the final bisimulation partition, P^*, of the belief simplex after ***merge***$_\epsilon$ (line 3). We then solve one representative model m_c per block $C \in P^*$, by randomly picking a candidate model that lies within the block and solving it (lines 4-7). Note that the model can be of *any* other agent. We denote π_C as the solution to the block and assign it to be the solutions for all candidate models of all other agents that lie within that block. Of course, we also transfer the probability mass of all the candidates to their corresponding representatives. The rest of the solution for the I-DID proceeds in the usual manner as in [13].

5 EXPERIMENTS

We implemented our algorithm (shown in Alg. 2) and evaluated its performance against Doshi *et.* al's discriminative model update algorithm (DMU) [13, 28], a state-of-the-art BE technique.

[3]In the worst case, after ∞ splits, each sub-simplex constitutes 1 belief point which is *bismilar w.r.t.* itself.

Algorithm 2 Solving I-DID

Inputs: level $l \geq 1$ I-DID or level 0 DID, horizon T, tolerance parameter ϵ

Preprocessing:Partitioning

1: $P^* \leftarrow$ Bisimulation Partitioning (ϵ) (from Alg. 1)
2: $P^* \leftarrow \text{merge}_\epsilon(P^*)$
3: **for** each $C \in P^*$ **do**
4:    Pick $m_c \in \mathcal{M}_{-i,l-1}$ s.t. $m_c \in C$
5:    Let $\pi_{m_c} \leftarrow$ solution of m_c.
6:    $\pi_C \leftarrow \pi_{m_c}$
7: **for** each $j = 1 \ldots N$ **do**
8:    **for** each $m_j \in \mathcal{M}_{j,l-1}$ **do**
9:       $\pi_{m_j} \leftarrow \pi_C \; s.t \; C \ni m_j$

Expansion Phase

10: **for** t from 0 to $T-1$ **do**
11:    **if** $l \geq 1$ **then**
12:       **for** j from 0 to N **do**
         Populate $M^{t+1}_{j,l-1}$
13:          **for** each $m^t_j \in \mathcal{M}^t_{j,l-1}$ **do**
14:             Let $OPT(m^t_j) \leftarrow \pi^t_{m_j}$
15:             Map the decision node of the solved model, $OPT(m^t_j)$, to the corresponding A_j
16:          **for** each $m^t_j \in \mathcal{M}^t_{j,l-1}$ **do**
17:             **for** each $a_j \in OPT(m^t_j)$ **do**
18:                **for** each $o_j \in O_j$ (part of m^t_j) **do**
19:                   Update j's belief, $b^{t+1}_j \leftarrow \tau(b^t_j, a_j, o_j)$
20:                   $m^{t+1}_j \leftarrow$ New I-DID (or DID) with b^{t+1}_j
21:                   $\mathcal{M}^{t+1}_{j,l-1} \overset{\cup}{\leftarrow} \{m^{t+1}_j\}$
22:          Add node $M^{t+1}_{j,l-1}$, and the model update link
23:    Add the nodes and links for $t+1$ time slice
24:    Establish the CPTs for chance and utility nodes

Solution Phase

25: **if** $l \geq 1$ **then**
26:    Represent the model nodes, policy links and the model update links as in Fig. 3 to obtain the DID
27: Apply the standard look-ahead and backup method to solve the expanded DID

Output: π_i

5.1 PROBLEM DOMAINS

We experimented on two multiagent problem domains with up to 20 agents: the multiagent tiger problem [19], and a slightly larger, more contemporary, solar energy storage problem inspired by Tesla's *solar city* initiative, modified from [31].

5.1.1 Multiagent Tiger, $Tiger$

In the multiagent tiger problem, N agents are tasked with finding a pot of gold hiding behind one of 2 closed doors.

Behind the other door is a ferocious tiger. The agents receive a positive reward for opening the door that leads to the gold but get penalized for opening the door that hides the tiger. The agents may open the left door or the right door, or listen. Upon performing the listen action, the agents receive one of 2 observations – growl from the left or growl from the right – indicating the probable location of the tiger. Additionally, the agents hear creaks originating from the direction of the door that was possibly opened by the other agent - creak from the left or creak from right - or silence if no door was opened. Upon performing *open* actions, the tiger's location randomly resets.

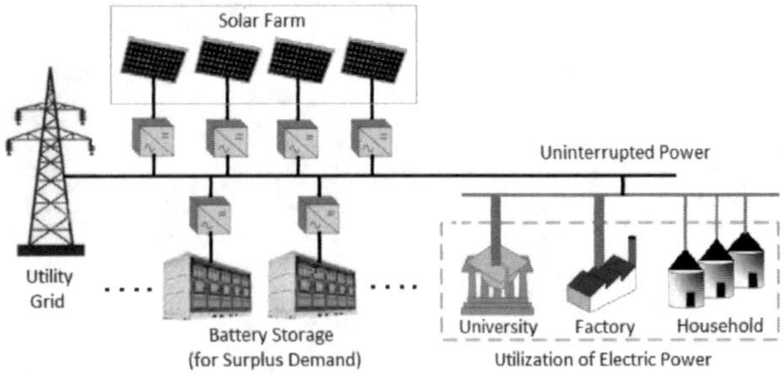

Figure 5: $Solar$ domain with the utility company (subject agent) and 5 consumers (other agents): a university, a factory, and 3 households.

5.1.2 Solar Energy Storage, $Solar$

The solar energy storage problem, on the other hand, is slightly more contemporary and trending right now. It is the consequence of the fact that much of the renewable energy generation is intermittent: wind or solar power generation peaks are often around times of low demand. Therefore, companies like Tesla offer massive batteries that store electricity during the day when the supply is abundant and discharge it, on demand, even after the sun goes down. Utility companies that own solar farms use these batteries for when there is surplus demand. We consider the problem faced by our subject agent (i.e. utility companies) in deciding how much battery storage it needs to buy to fully sustain the demand from $N-1$ different consumers as illustrated in Fig. 5. Let C_{max} be the maximum total electricity storage capacity in the batteries procured by the utility company. There is a fixed per-unit cost for energy procurement and a fixed positive return for per-unit sale to each consumer. The state space constitutes the difference between supply and expected demand in terms of percentage of C_{max}. Each consumer agent may have a different rate of electricity consumption depending on their own usage and the amount of electricity produced in-house (using solar panels or Tesla Energy's home batteries). The utility company may choose to draw 0, 1, or 2 units of electricity generated from its batteries. Similarly, each consumer may draw up to 2 units of electricity from the grid at a time. The state space is not fully observable to the agent because the expected demand in the next step is uncertain. We assume the existence of a data-driven demand forecast model that generates the observation probabilities indicating the possible demand in the next step. A two-time slice level l I-DID for the $Solar$ problem involving 3 agents is shown in Fig.6.

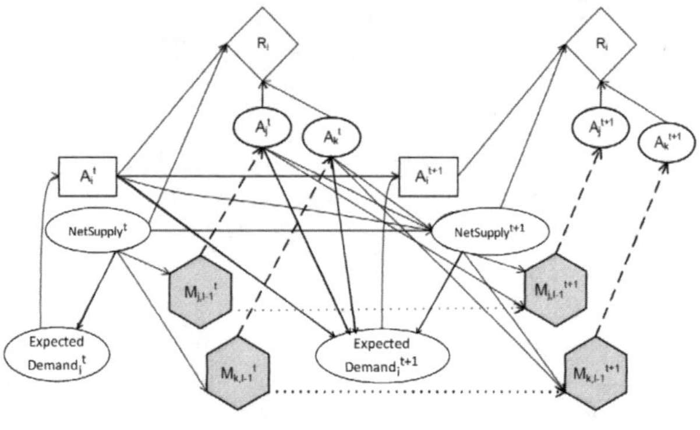

Figure 6: A generic two time-slice level l I-DID for the $Solar$ problem for the utility company agent i situated with two other consumer agents j and k.

Table 1: Domain dimensions and input parameters.

Domain	$\lvert\mathcal{M}^0_{-i}\rvert$	Dimension
Tiger	1000	$\lvert S\rvert = 2, \lvert A\rvert = 3, \lvert\Omega_i\rvert = 6, \lvert\Omega_{j\neq i}\rvert = 2$
Solar	2000	$\lvert S\rvert = 6, \lvert A\rvert = 3, \lvert\Omega_i\rvert = 3, \lvert\Omega_{j\neq i}\rvert = 3$

We summarize the domain parameters in Table 1. We compare run time performances and average reward over 10 trials of our approach I-DID BIS against DMU. Next, for the $Tiger$ problem, we scale in the number of agents and demonstrate significant savings in terms of the number of models solved for varying tolerance values. Our computing configuration included an Intel 2.7GHz processor, 32GB RAM and Linux.

5.2 VALIDATION

First we focus on generating solutions for an N-agent I-DID using our bisimulation approach I-DID BIS for both the multiagent tiger (denoted $Tiger$) and multiagent solar energy storage (denoted $Solar$) problem domains, and comparing their average expected utility over 10 trials against the solutions generated by DMU. We expect that the solution quality approaches that of DMU validating the correctness of our solutions. We vary the number of agents $N \in \{3, 5, 8\}$ and the horizons $T \in \{3, 5, 10, 15\}$ while fixing the candidate model space for each other agent $\lvert\mathcal{M}_{j\neq i}\rvert = 1000$ and 2000, and the tolerance parameter $\epsilon = 0.1$ and 0.14 for $Tiger$ and $Solar$ problems respectively. Expectedly, we note in Table 2 that the solution quality in terms of average reward over 10 trials for I-DID BIS was equal to that of DMU in 8 out of the 13 runs with different input parameter settings. In the remaining runs, the average expected utility of I-DID BIS solutions was slightly smaller compared to that of DMU, but not statistically significantly. This empirically verifies the correctness of our approach.

Table 2: Performance Comparison: I-DID BIS vs DMU

Domain	N	T	I-DID BIS Time (in sec)	I-DID BIS Avg Reward	DMU Time (in sec)	DMU Avg Reward	Speedup
Tiger	3	5	0.0071	14	2.611	14	368
		10	0.486	77.5	187.992	77.5	387
		15	27.301	135.5	11351.7	135.5	416
	5	5	0.806	77.5	5.953	88.5	7
		10	13.291	108.5	390.878	113	29
		15	76.474	135.5	22993.62	143.5	301
	8	5	9.166	86	17.115	86	2
		10	24.174	108	609.261	108	25
Solar	3	5	2.09	8.5	13.561	9	6
		10	18.983	23.5	437.22	23.5	23
	5	5	4.41	9	21.877	9	5
		10	53.847	106	693.22	108.5	13
	8	3	7.23	8.5	24.55	8.5	3

5.3 RUN TIME FOR SOLVING I-DIDS

Table 2 also shows how our algorithm stacks up against DMU in terms of computation time. We expect better run times in I-DID BIS because it only solves one model per block in the bisimulation partition whereas DMU requires that all initial models of the other agents be solved first before we start noticing its benefits. However, in I-DID BIS, there is a one-time overhead for computing the bisimulation partition. We test for varying ϵ, increasing number of agents N and planning horizons T for the 2 problem domains described earlier. Despite the overhead, we observe that our algorithm, I-DID BIS, takes orders of magnitude lesser time for solving the I-DID compared to DMU indicating that the benefits of solving lesser number of models outweigh the cost of computing the partition. We show the speedup of I-DID BIS with respect to DMU in Table 2. As expected, increasing N and T imply increasing run times.

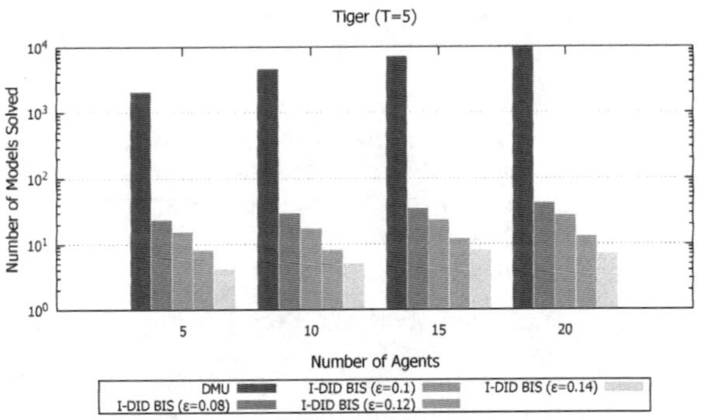

Figure 7: Savings in terms of the total number of models of the other agents solved for different ϵ values in the $Tiger$ domain with up to 20 agents. We also compare with DMU.

5.4 SCALABILITY

Next, we scale in the number of agents and illustrate in Fig. 7, the number of models solved for varying tolerance parameter values $\epsilon = \{0.08, 0.1, 0.12, 0.14\}$ for the $Tiger$ domain. We fix the planning horizon to $T = 5$ and the number of initial models of the other agents in our subject agent's I-DID to be $|\mathcal{M}_{j \neq i}| = 500$. As expected, we observe that the number of equivalence classes – and therefore the number of models solved – reduces with increasing ϵ. Again, because DMU ends up having to solve all initial models of the others, we note a significant increase in the number of models solved compared to I-DID BIS. Consequently, the time taken to solve the I-DID is expected to be orders of magnitude higher.

We note that we reached the memory cap on how much we can scale I-DIDs within HUGIN EXPERT [2], a well-known API for solving multistage influence diagrams. A general hurdle is that further scalability of ID-based graphical models is also limited by the absence of state-of-the-art techniques for solving DIDs within commercial implementations such as HUGIN EXPERT that predominantly rely on solving the entire DID in main memory. Although newer versions of HUGIN use limited memory IDs, a more scalable approach for solving multistage IDs would help drive further scalability of I-DID solutions.

6 CONCLUSION

In conclusion, we directly address the curse of dimensionality in I-DIDs due to exponential growth in the number of models over time. We successfully defined, implemented, and tested a metric to quantitatively measure the *similarity* between any two models in the space of models that the subject agent ascribes to the other agents in a partially observable setting within the context of an I-DID. Using such a metric, we were able to partition the belief space into equivalence classes using barycentric subdivision without having to solve the models first. This is the first time this has ever been done. Toward this, we generalized I-DIDs to N-agents and compared the performance of our model space compression technique against a baseline I-DID solver that uses the current state-of-the-art BE-based technique on two multiagent domains exhibiting partial observability with up to 20 agents. Our approach could benefit from a better partitioning technique because barycentric subdivision leads to a combinatorial explosion in the number of partitions generated after every split with the size of the state space. In any case, we think that this is a good first step in the right direction toward scaling I-DID solutions.

Acknowledgements

This research is supported in part by a grant from ONR N-00-0-141310870 and a grant from NSF IIA-1444182.

References

[1] Brandenburger Adam and Eddie Dekel. Hierarchies of beliefs and common knowledge. *International Journal of Game Theory*, 1993.

[2] Stig K. Andersen, Kristian G. Olesen, Finn V. Jensen, and Frank Jensen. Hugin: A shell for building bayesian belief universes for expert systems. In *IJCAI*, 1989.

[3] Robert J. Aumann. Interactive epistemology i: Knowledge. *International Journal of Game Theory*, 28(3):263–300, 1999.

[4] Pablo Samuel Castro, Prakash Panangaden, and Doina Precup. Equivalence relations in fully and partially observable markov decision processes. In *IJCAI*, volume 9, pages 1653–1658, 2009.

[5] Muthukumaran Chandrasekaran, Prashant Doshi, and Yifeng Zeng. Approximate solutions of interactive dynamic influence diagrams using epsilon-behavioral equivalence. In *11th International Symposium on Artificial Intelligence and Mathematics*, 2010.

[6] Muthukumaran Chandrasekaran, Prashant Doshi, Yifeng Zeng, and Yingke Chen. Team behavior in interactive dynamic influence diagrams with applications to ad hoc teams (extended abstract). In *Autonomous Agents and Multi-Agent Systems Conference (AAMAS)*, pages 1559–1560, 2014.

[7] Muthukumaran Chandrasekaran, Prashant Doshi, Yifeng Zeng, and Yingke Chen. Can bounded and self-interested agents be teammates? application to planning in ad hoc teams. *Autonomous Agents and Multi-Agent Systems*, 31(4):821–860, July 2017.

[8] Ross Conroy, Yifeng Zeng, and Jing Tang. Approximating value equivalence in interactive dynamic influence diagrams using behavioral coverage. In *IJCAI*, 2016.

[9] Gregory F Cooper. A method for using belief networks as influence diagrams. In *Proceedings of the Fourth Workshop on Uncertainty in Artificial Intelligence (UAI)*, pages 55–63, 1988.

[10] Prashant Doshi. Decision making in complex multiagent settings: A tale of two frameworks. *AI Magazine*, 33(4):82–95, 2012.

[11] Prashant Doshi, Muthukumaran Chandrasekaran, and Yifeng Zeng. Epsilon-subjective equivalence of models for interactive dynamic influence diagrams. In *WIC/ACM/IEEE WI-IAT*, 2010.

[12] Prashant Doshi, Xia Qu, Adam Goodie, and Diana Young. Modeling recursive reasoning in humans using empirically informed interactive POMDPs. In *International Autonomous Agents and Multiagent Systems Conference (AAMAS)*, pages 1223–1230, 2010.

[13] Prashant Doshi and Yifeng Zeng. Improved approximation of interactive dynamic influence diagrams using discriminative model updates. In *AAMAS*, pages 907–914, 2009.

[14] Prashant Doshi, Yifeng Zeng, and Qiongyu Chen. Graphical models for interactive pomdps: Representations and solutions. *JAAMAS*, 18(3):376–416, 2009.

[15] Edmund Durfee and Shlomo Zilberstein. *Multiagent Systems*, chapter Multiagent Planning, Control and Execution, pages 485–546. MIT Press, second edition, 2013.

[16] Norm Ferns, Prakash Panangaden, and Doina Precup. Metrics for finite markov decision processes. In *Proceedings of Uncertainty in Artificial Intelligence (UAI-04)*, July 2004.

[17] Norm Ferns, Prakash Panangaden, and Doina Precup. Bisimulation metrics for continuous markov decision processes. *SIAM Journal on Computing*, 40(6):1662–1714, 2011.

[18] R. Givan, T. Dean, and M. Greig. Equivalence notions and model minimization in markov decision processes. *Artificial Intelligence*, 147:163–223, 2003.

[19] Piotr Gmytrasiewicz and Prashant Doshi. A framework for sequential planning in multiagent settings. *JAIR*, 24:49–79, 2005.

[20] J.R. Munkres. *Elements of Algebraic Topology*. Advanced book classics. Avalon Publishing, 1984.

[21] Brenda Ng, Carol Meyers, Kofi Boakye, and John Nitao. Towards applying interactive POMDPs to real-world adversary modeling. In *Innovative Applications in Artificial Intelligence (IAAI)*, pages 1814–1820, 2010.

[22] David Pynadath and Stacy Marsella. Minimal mental models. In *AAAI*, pages 1038–1044, 2007.

[23] Richard Seymour and Gilbert L. Peterson. A trust-based multiagent system. In *IEEE International Conference on Computational Science and Engineering*, pages 109–116, 2009.

[24] L. Nisonovich Vaserstein. Markov processes over denumerable products of spaces, describing large systems of automata. *Problemy Peredachi Informatsii*, 5(3):64–72, 1969.

[25] Fangju Wang. An I-POMDP based multi-agent architecture for dialogue tutoring. In *International Conference on Advanced ICT and Education (ICAICTE-13)*, pages 486–489, 2013.

[26] Mark P. Woodward and Robert J. Wood. Learning from humans as an i-pomdp. *CoRR*, abs/1204.0274, 2012.

[27] Michael Wunder, Michael Kaisers, John Yaros, and Michael Littman. Using iterated reasoning to predict opponent strategies. In *International Conference on Autonomous Agents and Multi-Agent Systems (AAMAS)*, pages 593–600, 2011.

[28] Yifeng Zeng and Prashant Doshi. Exploiting model equivalences for solving interactive dynamic influence diagrams. *JAIR*, 43:211–255, 2012.

[29] Yifeng Zeng, Prashant Doshi, Yingke Chen, Yinghui Pan, Hua Mao, and Muthukumaran Chandrasekaran. Approximating behavioral equivalence for scaling solutions of i-dids. *Knowledge and Information Systems*, 49(2):511–552, 2016.

[30] Yifeng Zeng, Prashant Doshi, Yinghui Pan, Hua Mao, Muthukumaran Chandrasekaran, and Jian Luo. Utilizing partial policies for identifying equivalence of behavioral models. In *AAAI*, pages 1083–1088, 2011.

[31] Ronghuo Zheng, Ying Xu, Nilanjan Chakraborty, and Katia P Sycara. A crowdfunding model for green energy investment. In *IJCAI*, pages 2669–2676, 2015.

Adversarial Sets for Regularising Neural Link Predictors

Pasquale Minervini[1] **Thomas Demeester**[2] **Tim Rocktäschel**[3] **Sebastian Riedel**[1]
University College London, London, United Kingdom[1]
Ghent University - iMinds, Ghent, Belgium[2]
University of Oxford, Oxford, United Kingdom[3]

Abstract

In adversarial training, a set of models learn together by pursuing competing goals, usually defined on *single* data instances. However, in relational learning and other non-*i.i.d* domains, goals can also be defined over *sets* of instances. For example, a link predictor for the IS-A relation needs to be consistent with the *transitivity* property: if IS-A(x_1, x_2) and IS-A(x_2, x_3) hold, IS-A(x_1, x_3) needs to hold as well. Here we use such assumptions for deriving an *inconsistency loss*, measuring the degree to which the model violates the assumptions on an adversarially-generated set of examples. The training objective is defined as a minimax problem, where an *adversary* finds the most offending adversarial examples by maximising the inconsistency loss, and the model is trained by jointly minimising a supervised loss and the inconsistency loss on the adversarial examples. This yields the first method that can use function-free Horn clauses (as in Datalog) to regularise any neural link predictor, with complexity independent of the domain size. We show that for several link prediction models, the optimisation problem faced by the adversary has efficient closed-form solutions. Experiments on link prediction benchmarks indicate that given suitable prior knowledge, our method can significantly improve neural link predictors on all relevant metrics.

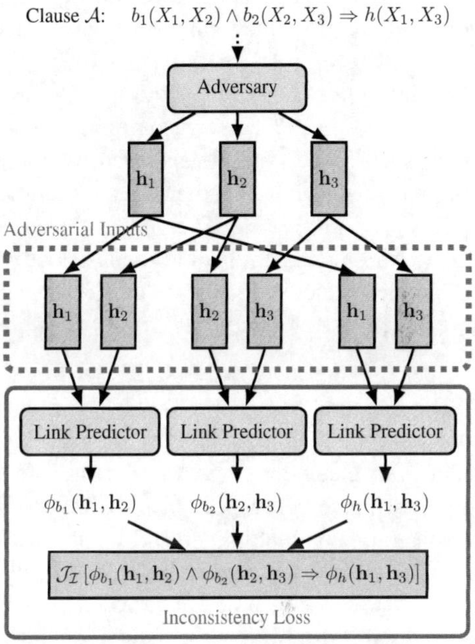

Figure 1: Overview of regularisation via adversarial sets for neural link prediction. Given a clause $\mathcal{A}$ with variables $\{X_1, X_2, X_3\}$, an adversary maps each variable to an adversarial entity embedding that maximises an inconsistency loss, while the discriminator is trained by minimising the link prediction and inconsistency loss.

1 INTRODUCTION

Adversarial training [Dalvi et al., 2004, Goodfellow et al., 2014, Szegedy et al., 2014] is a learning setting where two or more models learn together by pursuing competing goals. Adversarial learning has received increasing attention in recent years, mainly motivated by the observation that neural networks can be vulnerable to carefully-crafted adversarial examples [Goodfellow et al., 2014]. Adding additional loss terms to training objectives for enforcing models to be robust to adversarial examples can be very beneficial, for instance in the context of image synthesis [Dosovitskiy et al., 2015].

Such competing goals are generally defined on *single* data instances. For example, in Generative Adversarial Networks (GANs) [Goodfellow et al., 2014], a generator is trained to synthesise single *fake* data instances (*e.g.* images) that are classified as *real* by a discriminator, while the discriminator is trained to discriminate between single *real* and *fake* data instances. However, for relational tasks such as *link prediction* or *knowledge base population* [Nickel et al., 2012, Riedel et al., 2013b, Socher et al., 2013, Chang et al., 2014, Toutanova et al., 2015, Neelakantan et al., 2015], where objects can interact with each other, such goals can also be defined in terms of several instances.

For instance, consider the hypernymy relation IS-A. Since state-of-the-art link predictors rank or score pairs in isolation [Bordes et al., 2013, Toutanova et al., 2015, Trouillon et al., 2016], they cannot explicitly account for the transitivity property of IS-A. This means that a predictor might infer IS-A(x_1, x_2) and IS-A(x_2, x_3), but not IS-A(x_1, x_3). In this case, encouraging transitivity to hold for such models can be achieved by defining a goal on three related inputs rather than a single input: $\{(x_1, x_2), (x_2, x_3), (x_1, x_3)\}$. The goal of the adversary would be to find inputs that lead to inconsistent predictions, while the predictor's goal would be restoring consistency on such sets of inputs.

In this paper, we introduce Adversarial Set Regularisation (ASR), a general and scalable method for regularising neural link prediction models by using background knowledge. Our method is summarised by the *adversarial training* architecture in Fig. 1. In ASR, we first define a set of constraints on multiple problem instances in the form of function-free First-order Logic (FOL) clauses. From these clauses we then derive an *inconsistency loss* that measures the extent to which constraints are violated.

The learning architecture is composed of two models, an *adversary* and a *discriminator*, having two competing goals. The *adversary* tries to find a set of adversarial input representations for which, according to the discriminator (a link prediction model), the constraints do not hold. Such a set is found by maximising the inconsistency loss. The *discriminator*, on the other hand, uses the inconsistency loss on the adversarial input representations for regularising its training process.

Our proposed training algorithm, described in Sect. 3, can be seen as a zero-sum game involving two players, where: i) one player, the link predictor, has to predict a target graph over a set of *real* inputs, while ensuring global consistency over a set of *generated adversarial* inputs; and ii) the other player, the adversary, has to generate adversarial input representations such that the link predictor fails at constructing consistent graphs.

The link prediction model is trained by jointly minimising both the data loss and the inconsistency loss on the adversarial input sets by updating the model, while the adversary maximises the inconsistency loss by changing the input sets. Another interpretation is that the adversary acts as an *adaptive regulariser* for training neural link predictors.

Our method is related to Rocktäschel et al. [2015] and its variant KALE [Guo et al., 2016], which also minimise an inconsistency loss over sets of instances. A core difference with the proposed approach is that, instead of generating adversarial examples in representation space, they select random entities from the training and test sets. This generally leads to less effective updates, since the random entities can already satisfy the imposed constraints. Furthermore, they also enforce consistency not just by changing the relation-specific parameters, but also by changing the distributed representations of the entity inputs. This can lead to poor generalisation on entities less frequently sampled during training. Demeester et al. [2016] overcome this problem, but their approach only works for a single type of model and simple clauses. Our approach has no such restrictions, and we formally show that it is a generalisation of their work.

We show empirically that, by training on adversarial input sets, the link prediction model becomes indeed more robust. In experiments, we use our approach to inject prior assumptions into several state-of-the-art models, indicating the general nature of our approach. The regularised models outperform the original models on real-world data sets, namely WN18 and FB122. Moreover, using the same constraints and experimental setup, we outperform KALE both in terms of absolute performance, and in terms of relative improvements when compared to their underlying base models.

Our contributions are threefold: i) we introduce a novel approach to regularise neural link prediction models based on prior relational assumptions, such as transitivity – this is the first work that uses adversarial input sets for doing so; ii) we present an optimisation algorithm for solving the underlying minimax problem; and iii) we derive closed form solutions for the inner maximisation problem that enable faster training, provide intuitive insights into the goal of the adversary, and show that the method of Demeester et al. [2016] can be derived from our framework.

In the next sections we first briefly introduce the link prediction problem and state-of-the-art link prediction models. Then we present our adversarial approach to injecting prior knowledge. We conclude with experimental results and a discussion.

2 LINK PREDICTION

In this work, we focus on the problem of *predicting missing links* in large, multi-relational networks such as FREEBASE. In the literature, this problem is referred to as *link prediction*. We specifically focus on *knowledge graphs*, *i.e.*, graph-structured knowledge bases where factual information is stored in the form of relationships between entities. Link prediction in knowledge graphs is also known as *knowledge base population*. We refer to Nickel et al. [2016] for a recent survey on approaches for this problem.

A knowledge graph $\mathcal{G} \triangleq \{(r, a_1, a_2)\} \subseteq \mathcal{R} \times \mathcal{E} \times \mathcal{E}$ can be formalised as a set of triples (facts) consisting of a relation type $r \in \mathcal{R}$ and two entities $a_1, a_2 \in \mathcal{E}$, respectively referred to as the *subject* and the *object* of the triple. Each triple (r, a_1, a_2) encodes a relationship of type r between a_1 and a_2, represented by the fact $r(a_1, a_2)$.

Link prediction in knowledge graphs is often simplified to a *learning to rank* problem, where the objective is to find a score or ranking function $\phi_r^{\boldsymbol{\theta}} : \mathcal{E} \times \mathcal{E} \mapsto \mathbb{R}$ for a relation r that can be used for ranking triples according to the likelihood that the corresponding facts hold true.

2.1 Neural Link Prediction

Recently, a specific class of link predictors received a growing interest [Nickel et al., 2016]. These predictors can be understood as multi-layer neural networks. Given a triple $\mathbf{x} = (r, a_1, a_2)$, the associated score $\phi_r^{\boldsymbol{\theta}}(a_1, a_2)$ is given by a neural network architecture encompassing an *encoding layer* and a *scoring layer*.

In the encoding layer, the subject and object entities a_1 and a_2 are mapped to low-dimensional vector representations (embeddings) $\mathbf{h}_1 \triangleq \mathbf{h}(a_1) \in \mathbb{R}^k$ and $\mathbf{h}_2 \triangleq \mathbf{h}(a_2) \in \mathbb{R}^k$, produced by an encoder $\mathbf{h}^{\gamma} : \mathcal{E} \rightarrow \mathbb{R}^k$ with parameters $\boldsymbol{\gamma}$. This layer can be pre-trained [Vylomova et al., 2016] or, more commonly, learnt from data by back-propagating the link prediction error to the encoding layer [Bordes et al., 2013, Nickel et al., 2016, Trouillon et al., 2016].

In the scoring layer, the entity representations $\mathbf{h}_1$ and $\mathbf{h}_2$ are scored by a function $\phi_r^{\boldsymbol{\theta}}(\mathbf{h}_1, \mathbf{h}_2)$, parametrised by $\boldsymbol{\theta}$.

Summarising, the high-level architecture is defined as:

$$\begin{aligned} \mathbf{h}_1, \mathbf{h}_2 &\triangleq \mathbf{h}^{\gamma}(a_1), \mathbf{h}^{\gamma}(a_2) \\ \phi_r(a_1, a_2) &\triangleq \phi_r^{\boldsymbol{\theta}}(\mathbf{h}_1, \mathbf{h}_2) \end{aligned}$$

Ideally, more likely triples should be associated with higher scores, while less likely triples should be associated with lower scores.

While the literature has produced a multitude of encoding and scoring strategies, for brevity we overview only a small subset of these. However, we point out that our method makes no further assumptions about the network architecture other than the existence of an argument encoding layer.

2.2 Encoding Layer

Given an entity $a \in \mathcal{E}$, the entity encoder $\mathbf{h}^{\gamma}$ is usually implemented as a simple embedding layer $\mathbf{h}^{\gamma}(a) \triangleq [\gamma]_a$, where $\boldsymbol{\gamma}$ is an embedding matrix [Nickel et al., 2016]. For pre-trained embeddings, the embedding matrix is fixed. Note that other encoding mechanisms are conceivable, such as recurrent or convolutional neural networks.

2.3 Scoring Layer

DistMult DISTMULT [Yang et al., 2015] represents each relation r using a parameter vector $\boldsymbol{\theta}_r \in \mathbb{R}^k$, and scores a link of type r between $(\mathbf{h}_1, \mathbf{h}_2)$ using the following scoring function:

$$\phi_r^{\boldsymbol{\theta}}(\mathbf{h}_1, \mathbf{h}_2) \triangleq \langle \boldsymbol{\theta}_r, \mathbf{h}_1, \mathbf{h}_2 \rangle \triangleq \sum_{i=1}^{k} \boldsymbol{\theta}_{r,i} \mathbf{h}_{1,i} \mathbf{h}_{2,i},$$

where $\langle \cdot, \cdot, \cdot \rangle$ denotes the tri-linear dot product.

ComplEx COMPLEX [Trouillon et al., 2016] is an extension of DISTMULT using complex-valued embeddings while retaining the mathematical definition of the dot product. In this model, the scoring function is defined as follows:

$$\phi_r^{\boldsymbol{\theta}}(\mathbf{h}_1, \mathbf{h}_2) \triangleq \operatorname{Re}\left(\langle \boldsymbol{\theta}_r, \mathbf{h}_1, \overline{\mathbf{h}_2} \rangle\right),$$

where $\boldsymbol{\theta}_r, \mathbf{h}_1, \mathbf{h}_2 \in \mathbb{C}^k$ are complex vectors, $\overline{\mathbf{x}}$ denotes the complex conjugate of $\mathbf{x}$, and $\operatorname{Re}(\mathbf{x}) \in \mathbb{R}^k$ denotes the real part of $\mathbf{x}$.

2.4 Training

Training neural link predictors amounts to minimising a loss function defined over a target graph $\mathcal{G}$ of triples $\{(r, a_1, a_2)\}$. Since such graphs usually only contain positive examples (true facts), a common strategy is to generate negative examples by *corrupting* the triples in the graph [Rendle et al., 2009, Bordes et al., 2013, Yang et al., 2015, Nickel et al., 2016].

Formally, given a triple (r, a_1, a_2), negative examples are generated by a corruption process δ defined by:

$$\begin{aligned} &\delta(r, a_1, a_2) \triangleq \\ &\qquad \{(r, \tilde{a_1}, a_2) \mid \tilde{a_1} \in \mathcal{E}\} \cup \{(r, a_1, \tilde{a_2}) \mid \tilde{a_2} \in \mathcal{E}\}. \end{aligned}$$

The main motivation for this negative sampling strategy is the Local Closed World Assumption (LCWA) [Dong et al., 2014]. According to the LCWA, if a triple exists in the graph, other triples obtained by corrupting either the subject or the object of the triples not appearing in the graph can be considered as negative examples.

Similarly to Bordes et al. [2013], we learn the model parameters $\boldsymbol{\theta}$ and γ by minimising a *hinge loss* $\mathcal{J}_{\mathcal{F}}$, referred to as *fact loss*, defined over positive and negative examples:

$$\mathcal{J}_{\mathcal{F}}(\mathcal{G};\boldsymbol{\theta},\gamma) \triangleq \sum_{(r,a_1,a_2)\in\Omega} \left[1 - y_r(a_1,a_2)\cdot\phi_r^{\boldsymbol{\theta}}(\mathbf{h}^{\gamma}(a_1),\mathbf{h}^{\gamma}(a_2))\right]_+, \quad (1)$$

where $\mathcal{N} \triangleq \{\tilde{\mathbf{x}} \mid \mathbf{x} \in \mathcal{G} \wedge \tilde{\mathbf{x}} \in \delta(\mathbf{x})\}$ is the set of negative examples (triples) generated by corrupting the triples in $\mathcal{G}$, $\Omega \triangleq \mathcal{G} \cup \mathcal{N}$ is a set containing both positive and negative examples, and $y_r(a_1,a_2) = \pm 1$ is an indicator function with value 1 if $(r,a_1,a_2) \in \mathcal{G}$, and -1 otherwise.

For several neural link prediction models, the fact scores can be trivially increased by increasing the magnitude of entity embeddings. A common solution is to either regularise the entity representations [Yang et al., 2015, Trouillon et al., 2016], or require them to live in subspaces such as the unit cube [Demeester et al., 2016] $\{\mathbf{h} \mid \mathbf{h} \in [0,1]^k\}$, or in the unit sphere [Bordes et al., 2013] $\{\mathbf{h} \mid \|\mathbf{h}\|_2^2 = 1\}$.

3 ADVERSARIAL SETS

Even though the training data may be consistent with various assumptions we can make about the graph, on sets of unseen triples the local nature of the classifiers may still lead to inconsistencies. Taking the IS-A example, we may see a high score for (IS-A, CAT, FELINE) and (IS-A, FELINE, ANIMAL), but a low score for (IS-A, CAT, ANIMAL), violating the transitivity property of the IS-A hypernymy relation.

To address this problem, we generate *adversarial input sets*, and encourage the model to fix its inconsistencies with respect to these inputs. More specifically, we find a set of adversarial entity embeddings as inputs to the scoring layer of the model, instead of a set of actual entity pairs. This has two core benefits. First, it allows us to solve a continuous optimisation problem (over embeddings) as opposed to a combinatorial one (over actual entities). The former can even have closed form solutions, as shown in Sect. 3.3. Second, it forces the model to learn general correlations between relations, as opposed to knowledge about specific facts and entities through the encoder.

For clarity, we now consider a single assumption $\mathcal{A}$, such as the transitivity of relation r. Generalising to multiple assumptions only requires instantiating one adversary and one inconsistency loss for each of the assumptions. In this work, we use Horn Clauses, a subset of FOL formulae, to express our assumptions. For example, transitivity of the hypernym relation can be expressed by:

$$\text{IS-A}(X_1,X_2) \wedge \text{IS-A}(X_2,X_3) \Rightarrow \text{IS-A}(X_1,X_3), \quad (2)$$

where the atom on the right-hand side of the implication is referred to as the *head* of the clause, the conjunction of atoms on the left-hand side is referred to as the *body* of the clause, and all variables are universally quantified.

Let an *adversarial input set* $\mathcal{S}$ define a mapping from the free variables in $\mathcal{V}$ in $\mathcal{A}$ to k-dimensional embeddings – *i.e.* $\mathcal{S} : \mathcal{V} \mapsto \mathbb{R}^k$. We call $\mathcal{S}$ a *set* because it implicitly specifies a set of adversarial inputs to the scoring layers of the neural link predictors associated with the atoms in $\mathcal{A}$. For example, in the case of the transitivity clause in Eq. (2), a mapping $\mathcal{S}$ with $\mathcal{S}(X_1) = \mathbf{h}_1$, $\mathcal{S}(X_2) = \mathbf{h}_2$ and $\mathcal{S}(X_3) = \mathbf{h}_3$ will define the set of inputs $(\mathbf{h}_1,\mathbf{h}_2)$, $(\mathbf{h}_2,\mathbf{h}_3)$ and $(\mathbf{h}_1,\mathbf{h}_3)$ to the scoring layer $\phi_{\text{IS-A}}$.

Given the adversarial input set $\mathcal{S}$, the *inconsistency loss* $\mathcal{J}_{\mathcal{I}}(\mathcal{A};\boldsymbol{\theta},\mathcal{S})$ measures the degree to which assumption $\mathcal{A}$ is violated on $\mathcal{S}$ with model parameters $\boldsymbol{\theta}$. It is computed as a function of the neural link prediction scores on the adversarial inputs in $\mathcal{S}$. For the transitivity clause in Eq. (2), the inconsistency loss is computed as a function of $\phi_{\text{IS-A}}(\mathbf{h}_1,\mathbf{h}_2)$, $\phi_{\text{IS-A}}(\mathbf{h}_2,\mathbf{h}_3)$ and $\phi_{\text{IS-A}}(\mathbf{h}_1,\mathbf{h}_3)$.

Our loss function is then a linear combination of the fact loss function in Eq. (1) and the inconsistency loss $\mathcal{J}_{\mathcal{I}}$:

$$\mathcal{J}(\mathcal{G},\mathcal{A};\boldsymbol{\theta},\gamma,\mathcal{S}) \triangleq \mathcal{J}_{\mathcal{F}}(\mathcal{G};\boldsymbol{\theta},\gamma) + \alpha\mathcal{J}_{\mathcal{I}}(\mathcal{A};\boldsymbol{\theta},\mathcal{S}),$$

where $\alpha \in \mathbb{R}$ controls the extent to which the assumption $\mathcal{A}$ should be enforced.

Our adversarial training algorithm attempts to find input sets $\mathcal{S}$ with maximal inconsistency, and model parameters $\boldsymbol{\theta},\gamma$ that minimise such an inconsistency. This can be formalised by the following minimax problem:

$$\min_{\boldsymbol{\theta},\gamma}\max_{\mathcal{S}} \mathcal{J}(\mathcal{G},\mathcal{A};\boldsymbol{\theta},\gamma,\mathcal{S}). \quad (3)$$

Note that the search over possible $\mathcal{S}$ needs to take into account the unit sphere or cube constraints mentioned earlier: for any variable $X_i \in \mathcal{V}$, the corresponding k-dimensional embedding $\mathcal{S}(X_i)$ should live on the same subspace (*e.g.* unit sphere or unit cube) as the entity embeddings.

To instantiate this framework we need to be able to map an assumption $\mathcal{A}$ to an inconsistency loss $\mathcal{J}_{\mathcal{I}}(\mathcal{A}; \boldsymbol{\theta}, \mathcal{S})$, and to solve the optimisation problem in Eq. (3).

3.1 Inconsistency Losses

Given an assumption $\mathcal{A}$ expressed as a FOL clause BODY $\Rightarrow$ HEAD, as in Eq. (2), our goal is defining a loss term $\mathcal{J}_{\mathcal{I}}(\mathcal{S})$ that assesses the degree to which $\mathcal{A}$ is violated on a set of adversarial inputs $\mathcal{S}$.

Recall that we represent $\mathcal{S} : \mathcal{V} \mapsto \mathbb{R}^k$ as a binding of the free variables $\mathcal{V}$ in $\mathcal{A}$ to adversarially-trained embeddings in $\mathbb{R}^k$. This means that in practice we have to search over variable-to-embedding bindings.

We construct the inconsistency loss $\mathcal{J}_{\mathcal{I}}$ compositionally, by first calculating $\phi(\text{HEAD})$ and $\phi(\text{BODY})$, respectively representing the scores for the head and body of the clause, based on the binding of variables to embeddings defined by $\mathcal{S}$. Subsequently, we test whether the head score is lower than the body score, *i.e.*, $\phi(\text{HEAD}) < \phi(\text{BODY})$ [Demeester et al., 2016]. If so, we assign a penalty proportional to the margin between body score and the head score. This yields the following inconsistency loss:

$$\mathcal{J}_{\mathcal{I}}(\text{BODY} \Rightarrow \text{HEAD}) \triangleq [\phi(\text{BODY}) - \phi(\text{HEAD})]_+ .$$

The motivation for this loss is that implications can be understood as "whenever the body is true, the head has to be true as well". In terms of neural link prediction models, this translates into "the score of the head should at least be as large as the score of the body".

For calculating the inconsistency loss, we need to specify how to calculate the scores of the head and body. To score a single atom, we simply map the free variables with the corresponding embeddings contained in the adversarial set $\mathcal{S}$ and apply the neural link predictor scoring function:

$$\phi\left(r\left(X_i, X_j\right)\right) = \phi_r\left(\mathcal{S}(X_i), \mathcal{S}(X_j)\right).$$

This gives us the score of the head atom, and the scores of the atoms within the body. Similarly to the product t-norm used in Rocktäschel et al. [2015], we use the Gödel t-norm, a continuous generalisation of the conjunction operator in logic [Gupta and Qi, 1991] to score the body of a clause, *i.e.*, a conjunction of several atoms:

$$\phi(A \wedge B) \triangleq \min\{\phi(A), \phi(B)\},$$

where A and B are clause atoms. This allows us to back-propagate through a conjunction of atoms. For disjunction one can use $\phi(A \vee B) \triangleq \max\{\phi(A), \phi(B)\}$, and for negation $\phi(\neg A) \triangleq -\phi(A)$, which allows the use of arbitrary function-free FOL clauses as in Rocktäschel et al. [2015]. However, in our experiments we only use Horn clauses, and leave the investigation of more complex clauses for future work.

Algorithm 1 Solving the minimax problem in Eq. (3) via Projected Stochastic Gradient Descent

Require: No. of epochs $\{\tau_a, \tau_d, \tau\}$, learning rates $\{\boldsymbol{\eta}^a, \boldsymbol{\eta}\}$
1: **main** AdversarialSetTraining($\mathcal{A}$)
2: Randomly initialise $\{\boldsymbol{\theta}_0, \gamma_0\}$
3: **for** $i \in \{1, \ldots, \tau\}$ **do**
4: $\mathcal{S}_i \leftarrow$ FindAdversarialSet($\mathcal{A}, \boldsymbol{\theta}_{i-1}$)
5: $(\boldsymbol{\theta}_i, \gamma_i) \leftarrow$ TrainDiscriminator($\mathcal{G}, \boldsymbol{\theta}_{i-1}, \gamma_{i-1}, \mathcal{S}_i$)
6: **end for**
7: **return** $\boldsymbol{\theta}_\tau, \gamma_\tau$
8: **end main**
9: **function** FindAdversarialSet($\mathcal{A}, \boldsymbol{\theta}$)
10: Randomly initialise $\mathcal{S}_0$
11: **for** $i = 1, \ldots, \tau_a$ **do**
12: $\mathbf{h}_j \leftarrow \text{proj}(\mathbf{h}_j),\ \forall \mathbf{h}_j \in \mathcal{S}$
13: $g_i \leftarrow \nabla_{\mathcal{S}} \mathcal{J}_{\mathcal{I}}(\mathcal{A}; \boldsymbol{\theta}, \mathcal{S}_{i-1})$
14: $\mathcal{S}_i \leftarrow \mathcal{S}_{i-1} + \eta_i^a g_i$
15: **end for**
16: **return** $\mathcal{S}_{\tau_a}$
17: **end function**
18: **function** TrainDiscriminator($\mathcal{G}, \boldsymbol{\theta}, \gamma, \mathcal{S}$)
19: $\boldsymbol{\theta}_0 \leftarrow \boldsymbol{\theta}, \gamma_0 \leftarrow \gamma$
20: **for** $i = 1, \ldots, \tau_d$ **do**
21: $\mathbf{h}_j \leftarrow \text{proj}(\mathbf{h}_j),\ \forall j \in \{1, \ldots, |\mathcal{E}|\}$
22: $g_i \leftarrow \nabla_{\langle \boldsymbol{\theta}, \gamma \rangle} \mathcal{J}(\mathcal{G}, \mathcal{A}; \boldsymbol{\theta}_{i-1}, \gamma_{i-1}, \mathcal{S})$
23: $(\boldsymbol{\theta}_i, \gamma_i) \leftarrow (\boldsymbol{\theta}_{i-1}, \gamma_{i-1}) - \eta_i g_i$
24: **end for**
25: **return** $\boldsymbol{\theta}_{\tau_d}, \gamma_{\tau_d}$
26: **end function**

3.2 Optimisation

To optimise the minimax objective in Eq. (3), we alternate between two optimisation processes, as shown in Alg. 1. On line 4, the algorithm finds an adversarial set $\mathcal{S}$ by maximising the inconsistency loss using τ_a-many Gradient Ascent iterations. On line 5, the link prediction model is trained by jointly minimising the fact loss and the inconsistency loss on the adversarial input set $\mathcal{S}$ via τ_d-many Stochastic Gradient Descent iterations.

In our implementation of Alg. 1, we enforce all entity and adversarial embeddings to live either on the unit cube, *i.e.*, $\text{proj}(\mathbf{h}) \triangleq \min(\max(\mathbf{h}, \mathbf{0}), \mathbf{1})$, or on the unit sphere, *i.e.*, $\text{proj}(\mathbf{h}) \triangleq \mathbf{h} / \|\mathbf{h}\|_2$. At the beginning of the training process, we initialise the neural link predictor parameters $\{\boldsymbol{\theta}, \gamma\}$ using uniform Xavier initialisation [Glorot and Bengio, 2010]. When searching for the adversarial set $\mathcal{S}$ that maximises the inconsistency loss, we initialise $\mathcal{S}$ using randomly sampled entity embeddings. Note that this algorithm is independent of the specific neural link prediction model used, and applicable to any function-free FOL clause.

Table 1: Closed form expressions $\mathcal{J}_{\mathcal{I}}^{\max}$ for DISTMULT and COMPLEX on three types of clauses. For DISTMULT $\boldsymbol{\delta} = \boldsymbol{\theta}_b - \boldsymbol{\theta}_r \in \mathbb{R}^k$, and for COMPLEX, $\boldsymbol{\delta} = \boldsymbol{\theta}_b - \boldsymbol{\theta}_r = \overline{\boldsymbol{\zeta}} \in \mathbb{C}^k$, for entity embeddings restricted to the unit sphere (left) and unit cube (right) subspaces.

Clause	Model	Unit Sphere	Unit Cube
$r(X_1, X_2) \Rightarrow r(X_2, X_1)$	DISTMULT	0	0
	COMPLEX	$\max_i \{2\lvert\boldsymbol{\theta}^{\mathrm{I}}_{r,i}\rvert\}$	$2\sum_i \lvert\boldsymbol{\theta}^{\mathrm{I}}_{r,i}\rvert$
$b(X_1, X_2) \Rightarrow r(X_1, X_2)$	DISTMULT	$\max_i \{\lvert\delta_i\rvert\}$	$\sum_i \max\{0, \delta_i\}$
	COMPLEX	$\max_i \left\{\sqrt{(\delta^{\mathrm{R}}_i)^2 + (\delta^{\mathrm{I}}_i)^2}\right\}$	$\sum_i \max(0, \delta^{\mathrm{R}}_i) + \max(\delta^{\mathrm{R}}_i, \lvert\delta^{\mathrm{I}}_i\rvert)$
$b(X_1, X_2) \Rightarrow r(X_2, X_1)$	DISTMULT	$\max_i \{\lvert\delta_i\rvert\}$	$\sum_i \max\{0, \delta_i\}$
	COMPLEX	$\max_j \left\{\sqrt{(\zeta^{\mathrm{R}}_i)^2 + (\zeta^{\mathrm{I}}_i)^2}\right\}$	$\sum_i \max(0, \zeta^{\mathrm{R}}_i) + \max(\zeta^{\mathrm{R}}_i, \lvert\zeta^{\mathrm{I}}_i\rvert)$

3.3 Closed Form Solutions

While the algorithm above is much more efficient than grounding out the clauses over the entity space (as in Rocktäschel et al. [2015]), it still requires the inner loop of maximising the inconsistency loss. Compared to closed-form analytical solutions, the inner optimisation loop can be computationally less efficient, require more hyperparameters (learning rate, number of iterations etc.) and offer fewer guarantees on whether the global optimum is found.

In some cases, it is possible to analytically calculate the solution $\mathcal{J}_{\mathcal{I}}^{\max}(\mathcal{A};\boldsymbol{\theta})$ to the inner optimisation problem of maximising the inconsistency loss $\mathcal{J}_{\mathcal{I}}(\mathcal{A};\boldsymbol{\theta},\mathcal{S})$ with respect to the adversarial set $\mathcal{S}$:

$$\mathcal{J}_{\mathcal{I}}^{\max}(\mathcal{A};\boldsymbol{\theta}) \triangleq \max_{\mathcal{S}} \mathcal{J}_{\mathcal{I}}(\mathcal{A};\boldsymbol{\theta},\mathcal{S}).$$

When $\mathcal{J}_{\mathcal{I}}^{\max}$ is known up front, the inner training loop disappears. We will call this approach the *Closed-Form* Adversarial Set Regularisation (*cASR*) method, as opposed to the more general iterative method in Alg. 1. We derive $\mathcal{J}_{\mathcal{I}}^{\max}$ for several types of clauses, both for DISTMULT and COMPLEX, as shown in Tab. 1. Full derivations are provided in the supplementary material.

Let's consider the closed-form inconsistency loss $\mathcal{J}_{\mathcal{I}}^{\max}$ for simple clauses of the form $b(X_1, X_2) \Rightarrow r(X_1, X_2)$, and let $\boldsymbol{\theta}_b, \boldsymbol{\theta}_r$ denote the predicate embeddings of predicates b and r, respectively. From Tab. 1 we can see that the expressions in the unit sphere case are independent of the sign of $\boldsymbol{\theta}_{b,i} - \boldsymbol{\theta}_{r,i}$, indicating that the non-symmetric implications cannot be explicitly modelled with unit sphere constraints. Both our theoretical and experimental results indicate that unit cube constraints used by Demeester et al. [2016] are indeed better suited for rule injection. Also note that the lifted clause injection method by Demeester et al. [2016] can be seen as a special case of this formulation, which is however limited to a single neural link prediction model and a small subset of clauses.

Figure 2: $\mathcal{J}_{\mathcal{I}}^{\max}$ contours for simple implications with COMPLEX, for varying $\boldsymbol{\theta}_{b,i} - \boldsymbol{\theta}_{r,i}$, for unit sphere (left) and unit cube (right) constraints.

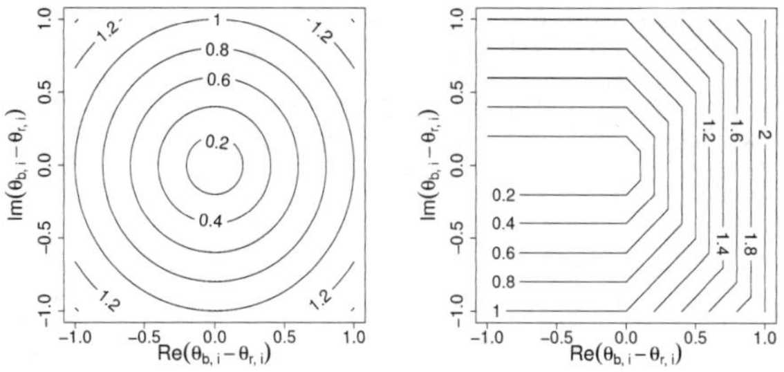

(a) Unit Sphere (b) Unit Cube

Fig. 2 shows contours of the contribution to $\mathcal{J}_{\mathcal{I}}^{\max}$ from component $\boldsymbol{\theta}_{b,i} - \boldsymbol{\theta}_{r,i}$, for simple implications with COMPLEX. We observe the rotation-symmetric behaviour for the unit sphere constraints (Fig. 2a). In contrast, for unit cube constraints (Fig. 2b) we see the quite different impact of the real part (on its own a scaled version of the expression for DISTMULT) and that the imaginary part contributes as soon as its absolute value exceeds the real part.

Minimising $\mathcal{J}_{\mathcal{I}}^{\max}$ for unit sphere constraints in COMPLEX boils down to encouraging $\boldsymbol{\theta}_{r,i} \approx \boldsymbol{\theta}_{b,i}$, for both real and imaginary parts, whereas for unit cube constraints it encourages an ordering relation of the real parts $\mathrm{Re}(\boldsymbol{\theta}_{r,i}) \geq \mathrm{Re}(\boldsymbol{\theta}_{b,i})$, and the equality of the imaginary parts $\mathrm{Im}(\boldsymbol{\theta}_{r,i}) \approx \mathrm{Im}(\boldsymbol{\theta}_{b,i})$.

4 RELATED WORK

Rocktäschel et al. [2014, 2015] provide a framework for jointly maximising the probability of observed facts and propositionalised First-Order Logic clauses. Wang et al. [2015] show how different types of clauses can be included after training the model by using Integer Linear Programming. Recently, Wang and Cohen [2016] propose a method for embedding facts and clauses using matrix factorisation. However, all these approaches ground the clauses in the training data. This limits their scalability to comparably small knowledge bases that contain only few entities. As mentioned in Demeester et al. [2016], such problems provide an important motivation for *lifted* clause injection methods that do not rely on grounding of clauses, but rather regularise relation representations directly and ensure that the assumptions hold on the whole entity embedding space, improving generalisation. Dong et al. [2014], Nickel et al. [2014] and Wang et al. [2015] propose combining observable patterns in the form of clauses and latent features for link prediction tasks. However, in these models, clauses are not used for learning better distributed representations of entities and relation types.

Our model is related to MODEL FSL proposed by Demeester et al. [2016], where they use very simple clauses for defining a partial ordering among relation embeddings. Moreover, their approach is limited to the simple matrix factorisation MODEL F by Riedel et al. [2013a], while ASR extends and improves over MODEL FSL. First, it can be used for injecting arbitrarily complex first-order logic clauses, such as the transitivity clause in Eq. (2). Second, it can be used jointly with any knowledge graph embedding model. Furthermore, it also improves over the general clause-injection methods by Rocktäschel et al. [2015] and Guo et al. [2016] since it avoids generating possible groundings of a clause. Gaifman models [Niepert, 2016] and related works train latent representations using features derived from subregions of a knowledge base: in such models, one can define relationships between subregions.

5 EXPERIMENTS

We now present our experimental results, starting by describing the experimental setup and hyper-parameters, both on synthetic and real-world data-sets. All models were implemented in TensorFlow, and source code is available on-line.[1]

Experimental Setup for Synthetic Data In order to investigate the effect of ASR on particular types of clauses, we created the following small synthetic knowledge base. We randomly sampled subject-object pairs from a low-dimensional entity space (with probability 0.1, and for $|\mathcal{E}| = 30$). With each of these pairs, we created facts by combining them with 15 relations in $\mathcal{R}$ with probability 0.1, resulting in 135 training facts. Besides those, we created clauses by randomly combining relations into the appropriate clause template, *i.e.* symmetry constraints, implications, and transitivity. For each experiment on a particular type of clause, 10 different clauses of that type were applied together. The training facts contain no evidence of these clauses. Each new fact that could be inferred based on the clauses was added as a positive item to the test data, together with a negative example obtained by corrupting its subject-object pair.

Experimental Setup for Real Data We also evaluate the proposed method on WORDNET (WN18) and FREEBASE (FB122) jointly with the set of rules released by Guo et al. [2016]. WORDNET [Miller, 1995] is a lexical knowledge base for the English language, where entities correspond to word senses, and relationships define lexical relations between them. The WN18 dataset consists of a subset of WORDNET, containing 40,943 entities, 18 relation types, and 151,442 triples. FREEBASE [Bollacker et al., 2007] is a large knowledge graph that stores general facts about the world. The FB122 dataset is a subset of FREEBASE regarding the topics of *people*, *location* and *sports*, and contains 9,738 entities, 122 relation types, and 112,476 triples. For both data sets, we used the fixed training, validation, test sets and rules provided by Guo et al. [2016]; a subset of the rules is shown in Tab. 2. Note that a subset of the test triples can be inferred by deductive logic inference. For such a reason, following Guo et al. [2016], we also partition the test set in two subsets, namely Test-I and Test-II: Test-I contains triples that *cannot* be inferred by deductive logic inference, while Test-II contains all remaining test triples. Statistics for the data sets are shown in Tab. 3.

Hyper-parameters We ran a grid search for the embedding dimension $k \in \{20, 50, 100, 150, 200\}$, the margin $\gamma \in \{1, 2, 5, 10\}$, the weight of the adversarial loss $\alpha \in \{1, 10, 10^2, 10^3, 10^4\}$, the number of iterations for the discriminator and the adversary $\tau_d, \tau_a \in \{1, 10\}$, fixed the number of epochs to $\tau = 100$, and decided the optimal subspace $\mathcal{U}$ among either unit cube or unit sphere. We use AdaGrad [Duchi et al., 2011] for automatically selecting the optimal learning rate, with an initial value of 0.1. For the synthetic dataset experiments, we use the same settings, fixing the hyper-parameters to $k = 20, \gamma = 1, \alpha = 1, \tau_d = 10$ and $\tau_a = 1$.

Evaluation Metrics For evaluating each model, we measure the quality of the ranking of test triples in terms of *Mean Reciprocal Rank* (MRR) and *HITS@k* [Bordes et al., 2013, Nickel et al., 2016]. MRR and Hits@K are two standard evaluation measures on these data sets and are used in two settings: *raw* and *filtered* [Bordes et al., 2013]. Our results are reported in the *filtered* setting, where metrics are computed after removing all the other known triples appearing in the training, validation or test sets from the ranking. This is motivated by observing that ranking a test triple lower than another true triple should not be penalised. For the experiments on synthetic data, we calculate the Area Under the Precision-Recall Curve (AUC-PR), based on the test data consisting of true facts and a single corruption of each true fact. Each experiment is repeated 10 times with different randomly generated train facts, test facts, and clauses. The reported AUC-PR values are averaged over these runs.

[1] `https://github.com/uclmr/inferbeddings`

Table 2: Examples of the clauses used for FREEBASE (FB122) and WORDNET (WN18).

/PEOPLE/PERSON/NATIONALITY(X_1, X_2) $\wedge$ /LOCATION/COUNTRY/OFFICIAL_LANGUAGE(X_2, X_3) $\Rightarrow$ /PEOPLE/PERSON/LANGUAGES(X_1, X_3)	
/COUNTRY/ADMINISTRATIVE_DIVISIONS(X_1, X_2) $\wedge$ /ADMINISTRATIVE_DIVISION/CAPITAL(X_2, X_3) $\Rightarrow$ /LOCATION/CONTAINS(X_1, X_3)	
/LOCATION/COUNTRY/CAPITAL(X_1, X_2) $\Rightarrow$ /LOCATION/LOCATION/CONTAINS(X_1, X_2)	
_HYPERNYM(X_1, X_2) $\Rightarrow$ _HYPONYM(X_2, X_1)	_HYPONYM(X_1, X_2) $\Rightarrow$ _HYPERNYM(X_2, X_1)
_HAS_PART(X_1, X_2) $\Rightarrow$ _PART_OF(X_2, X_1)	_PART_OF(X_1, X_2) $\Rightarrow$ _HAS_PART(X_2, X_1)

Table 3: Statistics for the data sets.

Dataset	$\lvert\mathcal{E}\rvert$	$\lvert\mathcal{R}\rvert$	#Train	#Valid	#Test-I	#Test-II
FB122	9,738	122	91,638	9,595	5,057	6,186
WN18	40,943	18	141,442	5,000	1,394	3,606

6 RESULTS AND DISCUSSION

In this section, we describe our findings on the synthetic, WORDNET (WN18) and FREEBASE (FB122) datasets.

6.1 Synthetic Data

ASR We tested the effectiveness of adversarial training for five different types of clauses in the synthetic data setup described in Section 5. Table 6 shows the resulting AUC-PR, where entity embeddings lie on the unit cube or on the unit sphere, and with vs. without iterative adversarial training ($\alpha = 0$ and $\alpha = 1$, respectively). DISTMULT and COMPLEX are able to encode the various types of clauses into the relation and argument representations. In line with arguments given above, the results for unit cube entities are generally better than their counterparts on the unit sphere, both on the standard models and with ASR. The most complex type of clauses (*i.e.* the transitivity over three different relations) yields lower absolute AUC-PR values than simpler clauses. Nonetheless, we observe a significant increase in scores due to the clauses. A noticeable case where the standard models cannot be improved is for DISTMULT on the clause that expresses symmetry (the first clause in Table 1). This is unsurprising since symmetry is satisfied by construction in DISTMULT. This experiment confirms that ASR is able to encode different types of clauses (unlike Demeester et al. [2016]), and for different models (unlike Rocktäschel et al. [2015]).

Closed-Form Solutions Using the closed-form expressions for $\mathcal{J}_{\mathcal{I}}^{\max}$ given in Table 1, we performed the synthetic data set experiments again. The results, shown in Table 7, indicate that the optimal adversarial training is also able to encode clauses into the trained embeddings. As with the iterative method, unit cube constraints perform better than on the unit sphere. For the synthetic data experiments, no hyper-parameter optimisation was performed, and we used the same number of discriminator training cycles as for the results presented in Table 6. Compared to the iterative method, closed form results on the unit sphere are consistently weaker. This is in line with our earlier observations that their symmetric character is not suited for modelling asymmetry in clauses. In any case, we observed a strong reduction in training time: the runs based on closed-form expressions took around a fifth the time of the corresponding iterative runs.

6.2 Link Prediction in Freebase and Wordnet

We compare the proposed Adversarial Set Regularisation (ASR) method with KALE, a recently proposed neural link prediction model that also leverages rules during the training process, the Translating Embeddings model (TRANSE) [Bordes et al., 2013], DISTMULT and COMPLEX. In particular, we compare ASR with two strong KALE variants: KALE-PRE, which augments training triples by means of logic inference, and KALE-JOINT, which jointly considers training triples and rules during training [Guo et al., 2016]. Results for TRANSE and KALE are reported from Guo et al. [2016].

In experiments, we use ASR for regularising the learning process in DISTMULT and COMPLEX – we denote the resulting models by *ASR*-DISTMULT and *ASR*-COMPLEX: we retain the original formulations of the scoring functions ϕ_r, but train the models by solving the minimax optimisation problem in Eq. (3) using Alg. 1.

Results for FREEBASE are reported in Tab. 4. We can see that *ASR*-COMPLEX yields better results both in comparison with KALE and with the un-regularised model COMPLEX. When comparing DISTMULT with its ASR-regularised extension, we note an improvement from 0.628 to 0.675 for MRR, and from 72.9% to 75.2% for Hits@10. Similarly, when comparing COMPLEX with its extension *ASR*-COMPLEX, we note an improvement from 0.641 to 0.698 for MRR, and from 71.9% to 75.7% for Hits@10. Also note that ASR, when used jointly with COMPLEX and DISTMULT, yields larger relative improvements in comparison with KALE (a model inspired by TRANSE) and TRANSE.

Improvements are even more evident if we consider the FB122 results in Test-II, where test facts are directly related to the logic clauses. We can see that, in terms of MRR, the proposed regularisation method improves

Table 4: Link prediction results on the Test-I, Test-II and and Test-ALL on FB122, filtered setting.

		Test-I				Test-II				Test-ALL			
		Hits@N (%)			MRR	Hits@N (%)			MRR	Hits@N (%)			MRR
		3	5	10		3	5	10		3	5	10	
FB122	TRANSE [Bordes et al., 2013]	36.0	41.5	48.1	0.296	77.5	82.8	88.4	0.630	58.9	64.2	70.2	0.480
	KALE-PRE [Guo et al., 2016]	35.8	41.9	49.8	0.291	82.9	86.1	89.9	0.713	61.7	66.2	71.8	0.523
	KALE-JOINT [Guo et al., 2016]	**38.4**	**44.7**	**52.2**	0.325	79.7	84.1	89.6	0.684	61.2	66.4	72.8	0.523
	DISTMULT [Yang et al., 2015]	36.0	40.3	45.3	0.313	92.3	93.8	94.7	0.874	67.4	70.2	72.9	0.628
	ASR-DISTMULT	36.3	40.3	44.9	0.330	98.0	99.0	99.2	0.948	70.7	73.1	75.2	0.675
	cASR-DISTMULT	37.0	40.4	45.1	0.337	96.7	98.6	99.3	0.933	70.1	72.7	75.1	0.669
	COMPLEX [Trouillon et al., 2016]	37.0	41.3	46.2	0.329	91.4	91.9	92.4	0.887	67.3	69.5	71.9	0.641
	ASR-COMPLEX	37.3	41.0	45.9	0.338	**99.2**	**99.3**	**99.4**	**0.984**	**71.7**	**73.6**	**75.7**	**0.698**
	cASR-COMPLEX	37.9	41.7	46.2	**0.339**	97.7	**99.3**	**99.4**	0.954	71.1	**73.6**	75.6	0.680

Table 5: Results on WN18 with limited training data – *i.e.* 20%, 30%, 40% and 50% of the training set.

	Training data		20%	30%	40%	50%
WN18	Hits@10	COMPLEX	38.9	46.6	54.1	60.5
		ASR-COMPLEX	**39.9**	**47.1**	**54.8**	**61.1**
	MRR	COMPLEX	0.356	0.418	0.480	0.538
		ASR-COMPLEX	**0.366**	**0.423**	**0.484**	**0.540**

Table 6: AUC-PR results for *ASR*-DISTMULT and *ASR*-COMPLEX on synthetic datasets with various types of clauses (with $r \neq s \neq t$). Comparison of standard models without clauses ($\alpha = 0$) and iterative adversarial training with clauses ($\alpha = 1$), with unit cube or unit sphere constraints on the entity embeddings.

Clauses	Model	$\alpha = 0$ Unit Cube	$\alpha = 0$ Unit Sphere	$\alpha = 1$ Unit Cube	$\alpha = 1$ Unit Sphere
$r(X_1, X_2)$	DISTMULT	**96.0**	95.7	95.9	95.6
$\Rightarrow r(X_2, X_1)$	COMPLEX	45.0	42.4	90.6	**91.2**
$r(X_1, X_2)$	DISTMULT	59.2	61.3	**86.3**	79.2
$\Rightarrow s(X_1, X_2)$	COMPLEX	60.8	61.2	**85.8**	79.7
$r(X_1, X_2)$	DISTMULT	59.6	59.1	**76.6**	73.1
$\Rightarrow s(X_2, X_1)$	COMPLEX	54.7	51.4	**87.5**	81.0
$r(X_1, X_2) \wedge r(X_2, X_3)$	DISTMULT	45.0	37.5	**65.9**	45.8
$\Rightarrow r(X_1, X_3)$	COMPLEX	40.9	36.3	**54.8**	42.5
$r(X_1, X_2) \wedge s(X_2, X_3)$	DISTMULT	41.9	39.5	44.9	**49.8**
$\Rightarrow t(X_1, X_3)$	COMPLEX	39.1	37.8	40.3	**45.4**

Table 7: AUC-PR results on synthetic datasets for adversarial training with closed form expressions.

Clause	Model	$\alpha = 1$ Unit Cube	$\alpha = 1$ Unit Sphere
$r(X_1, X_2)$	DISTMULT	**97.3**	95.2
$\Rightarrow r(X_2, X_1)$	COMPLEX	**91.7**	90.1
$r(X_1, X_2)$	DISTMULT	**85.0**	69.5
$\Rightarrow s(X_1, X_2)$	COMPLEX	**83.6**	75.5
$r(X_1, X_2)$	DISTMULT	**76.9**	67.8
$\Rightarrow s(X_2, X_1)$	COMPLEX	**80.2**	73.9

the MRR from 0.874 to 0.948 for DISTMULT, and from 0.887 to 0.984 for COMPLEX.

We ran the same experiments on WN18 (see the supplemental material for more exhaustive results) but did not notice any significant improvements. One reason can be that the neural link prediction model has enough training data to *learn* the WN18 rules by itself. For this reason, we also evaluate ASR in settings where the availability of training data is limited. More specifically, at training time, we use a limited sample of the training triples (*i.e.* 20%, 30%, ...) whose predicate appears in the head of a clause. Results are available in Tab. 5: we note that, in a limited data regime, ASR yields some marginal improvements on WN18. In Tab. 4 we also report results for the closed-form solutions described in Sect. 3.3 and derived in the Appendix, denoted by *cASR*-COMPLEX and *cASR*-DISTMULT. In both cases, the closed form solutions for the inner adversarial training loop yield similar results to their iterative counterparts, improving on all baselines.

7 CONCLUSIONS

In this paper, we introduced Adversarial Set Regularisation (ASR), a general and scalable method for regularising neural link prediction models. In the proposed method, an assumption is used for deriving an *inconsistency loss* measuring the degree to which the model violates the assumption on an adversarially-trained set of input representations. The training objective is defined as a zero-sum game, where an adversary finds the most offending set of input representations by maximising the inconsistency loss, and the model uses the inconsistency loss on such a set for regularising its training process. Our results demonstrate that incorporating prior assumptions in the form of FOL clauses gives a steady improvement over neural link prediction models, especially when the availability of training data is limited. Furthermore, the proposed method yields consistent improvements over the recently-proposed KALE method.

Acknowledgements

We are immensely grateful to Jeff Mitchell, Johannes Welbl, and Jason Naradowsky for useful discussions. This work has been supported by the Research Foundation - Flanders (FWO), Ghent University - iMinds, a Google PhD Fellowship in Natural Language Processing, an Allen Distinguished Investigator Award, and a Marie Curie Career Integration Award.

References

K. D. Bollacker, R. P. Cook, and P. Tufts. Freebase: A Shared Database of Structured General Human Knowledge. In *AAAI*, pages 1962–1963, 2007.

A. Bordes, N. Usunier, A. García-Durán, J. Weston, and O. Yakhnenko. Translating Embeddings for Modeling Multi-relational Data. In *NIPS*, pages 2787–2795, 2013.

K.-W. Chang, W.-t. Yih, B. Yang, and C. Meek. Typed Tensor Decomposition of Knowledge Bases for Relation Extraction. In *EMNLP*, 2014.

N. N. Dalvi, P. M. Domingos, Mausam, S. K. Sanghai, and D. Verma. Adversarial Classification. In *KDD*, pages 99–108. ACM, 2004.

T. Demeester, T. Rocktäschel, and S. Riedel. Lifted rule injection for relation embeddings. In *EMNLP*, pages 1389–1399, 2016.

X. Dong, E. Gabrilovich, G. Heitz, W. Horn, N. Lao, K. Murphy, T. Strohmann, S. Sun, and W. Zhang. Knowledge Vault: A Web-Scale Approach to Probabilistic Knowledge Fusion. In *KDD*, pages 601–610, 2014.

A. Dosovitskiy, J. Tobias Springenberg, and T. Brox. Learning to generate chairs with convolutional neural networks. In *ICVPR*, pages 1538–1546, 2015.

J. C. Duchi, E. Hazan, and Y. Singer. Adaptive Subgradient Methods for Online Learning and Stochastic Optimization. *JMLR*, 12:2121–2159, 2011.

X. Glorot and Y. Bengio. Understanding the difficulty of training deep feedforward neural networks. In *AISTATS*, volume 9 of *JMLR Proceedings*, pages 249–256. JMLR.org, 2010.

I. J. Goodfellow, J. Pouget-Abadie, M. Mirza, B. Xu, D. Warde-Farley, S. Ozair, A. C. Courville, and Y. Bengio. Generative Adversarial Nets. In *NIPS*, pages 2672–2680, 2014.

S. Guo, Q. Wang, L. Wang, B. Wang, and L. Guo. Jointly Embedding Knowledge Graphs and Logical Rules. In *EMNLP*, pages 192–202, 2016.

M. M. Gupta and J. Qi. Theory of t-norms and fuzzy inference methods. *Fuzzy Sets Syst.*, 40(3):431–450, Apr. 1991.

G. A. Miller. Wordnet: A lexical database for english. *Commun. ACM*, 38(11):39–41, 1995.

A. Neelakantan, B. Roth, and A. McCallum. Compositional Vector Space Models for Knowledge Base Completion. *arXiv preprint arXiv:1504.06662*, 2015.

M. Nickel, V. Tresp, and H.-P. Kriegel. Factorizing YAGO: Scalable Machine Learning for Linked Data. In *WWW*, pages 271–280, 2012.

M. Nickel, X. Jiang, and V. Tresp. Reducing the Rank in Relational Factorization Models by Including Observable Patterns. In *NIPS*, pages 1179–1187, 2014.

M. Nickel, K. Murphy, V. Tresp, and E. Gabrilovich. A review of relational machine learning for knowledge graphs. *Proceedings of the IEEE*, 104(1):11–33, 2016.

M. Niepert. Discriminative gaifman models. In *NIPS*, pages 3405–3413, 2016.

S. Rendle, C. Freudenthaler, Z. Gantner, and L. Schmidt-Thieme. BPR: Bayesian Personalized Ranking from Implicit Feedback. In *UAI*, pages 452–461. AUAI Press, 2009.

S. Riedel, L. Yao, A. McCallum, and B. M. Marlin. Relation Extraction with Matrix Factorization and Universal Schemas. In *NAACL-HLT*, pages 74–84, 2013a.

S. Riedel, L. Yao, A. McCallum, and B. M. Marlin. Relation Extraction with Matrix Factorization and Universal Schemas. In *NAACL-HLT*, pages 74–84, 2013b.

T. Rocktäschel, M. Bosnjak, S. Singh, and S. Riedel. Low-Dimensional Embeddings of Logic. In *ACL Workshop on Semantic Parsing (SP'14)*, 2014.

T. Rocktäschel, S. Singh, and S. Riedel. Injecting Logical Background Knowledge into Embeddings for Relation Extraction. In *NAACL-HLT*, pages 1119–1129, 2015.

R. Socher, D. Chen, C. D. Manning, and A. Y. Ng. Reasoning With Neural Tensor Networks for Knowledge Base Completion. In *NIPS*, pages 926–934, 2013.

C. Szegedy, W. Zaremba, I. Sutskever, J. Bruna, D. Erhan, I. J. Goodfellow, and R. Fergus. Intriguing properties of neural networks. In *ICLR*, 2014.

K. Toutanova, D. Chen, P. Pantel, P. Choudhury, and M. Gamon. Representing Text for Joint Embedding of Text and Knowledge Bases. *ACL*, 2015.

T. Trouillon, J. Welbl, S. Riedel, É. Gaussier, and G. Bouchard. Complex Embeddings for Simple Link Prediction. In *ICML*, pages 2071–2080, 2016.

E. Vylomova, L. Rimell, T. Cohn, and T. Baldwin. Take and Took, Gaggle and Goose, Book and Read: Evaluating the Utility of Vector Differences for Lexical Relation Learning. In *ACL*, 2016.

Q. Wang, B. Wang, and L. Guo. Knowledge Base Completion Using Embeddings and Rules. In *IJCAI*, pages 1859–1866, 2015.

W. Y. Wang and W. W. Cohen. Learning First-Order Logic Embeddings via Matrix Factorization. In *IJCAI*, pages 2132–2138, 2016.

B. Yang, W. Yih, X. He, J. Gao, and L. Deng. Embedding Entities and Relations for Learning and Inference in Knowledge Bases. In *ICLR*, 2015.

Supplementary Material

A Closed Form Solutions for Maximum Violation Loss for Simple Implications

Let $\phi_r(\mathbf{h}_1, \mathbf{h}_2)$ be a scoring function for a relation r defined over pairs of entity vectors $\mathbf{h}_1$ and $\mathbf{h}_2$, such as the scoring function in DISTMULT or COMPLEX. In the following, we assume that all entity embeddings live on a subspace $\mathcal{U} \subseteq \mathbb{R}^k$. The subspace $\mathcal{U}$ can either correspond to the unit sphere – *i.e.* $\mathcal{U} \triangleq \{\mathbf{h} \mid \|\mathbf{h}\|_2 = 1\}$ – or to the unit cube – *i.e.* $\mathcal{U} \triangleq \{\mathbf{h} \mid \mathbf{h} \in [0, 1]^k\}$.

Let us consider a mapping $\mathcal{S} : \mathcal{V} \mapsto \mathbb{R}^k$ from variables to k-dimensional embeddings, where $\mathbf{h}_i = \mathcal{S}(X_i), \forall i$.

Given a clause expressing a simple implication in the form $b(X_1, X_2) \Rightarrow r(X_1, X_2)$, we would like to maximise the inconsistency loss $\mathcal{J}_\mathcal{I}$ associated to the clause:

$$\mathcal{J}_\mathcal{I}^{\max} = \max\left(0, \mathcal{J}^{\max}\right)$$
$$\text{with} \quad \mathcal{J}^{\max} = \max_{\mathbf{h}_1, \mathbf{h}_2 \in \mathcal{U}} \left(\phi_b(\mathbf{h}_1, \mathbf{h}_2) - \phi_r(\mathbf{h}_1, \mathbf{h}_2)\right).$$

The following sections show how to directly derive $\mathcal{J}_\mathcal{I}^{\max}$ for various models and entity embedding space restrictions. One way to solve the maximisation problem is via the Karush–Kuhn–Tucker (KKT) conditions – we refer to Boyd and Vandenberghe [2004] for more details.

A.1 DISTMULT

In the following, we focus on the Bilinear-Diagonal model (DISTMULT), proposed by Yang et al. [2015], and provide the corresponding derivations for different choices of the entity embedding subspace $\mathcal{U}$.

We want to solve the following optimisation problem:

$$\begin{aligned}\mathcal{J}^{\max} &= \max_{\mathbf{h}_1, \mathbf{h}_2 \in \mathcal{U}} \left(\phi_b(\mathbf{h}_1, \mathbf{h}_2) - \phi_r(\mathbf{h}_1, \mathbf{h}_2)\right) \\ &= \max_{\mathbf{h}_1, \mathbf{h}_2 \in \mathcal{U}} \langle \boldsymbol{\theta}_b, \mathbf{h}_1, \mathbf{h}_2 \rangle - \langle \boldsymbol{\theta}_r, \mathbf{h}_1, \mathbf{h}_2 \rangle \\ &= \max_{\mathbf{h}_1, \mathbf{h}_2 \in \mathcal{U}} \langle \boldsymbol{\delta}, \mathbf{h}_1, \mathbf{h}_2 \rangle,\end{aligned}$$

where $\boldsymbol{\delta} \triangleq \boldsymbol{\theta}_b - \boldsymbol{\theta}_r$.

A.1.1 Unit Sphere

Assume that the subspace $\mathcal{U}$ corresponds to a the unit sphere, *i.e.* $\forall x \in \mathcal{E} : \|\mathbf{h}_x\|_2^2 = 1$. The Lagrangian is:

$$\mathcal{L} = -\langle \boldsymbol{\delta}, \mathbf{h}_1, \mathbf{h}_2 \rangle + \lambda_1(\|\mathbf{h}_1\|_2^2 - 1) + \lambda_2(\|\mathbf{h}_2\|_2^2 - 1).$$

Imposing stationarity: $\nabla_{\mathbf{h}_1} \mathcal{L} = 0$ and $\nabla_{\mathbf{h}_2} \mathcal{L} = 0$ gives:

$$\begin{aligned}-\boldsymbol{\delta} \odot \mathbf{h}_2 + 2\lambda_1 \mathbf{h}_1 = 0 \\ -\boldsymbol{\delta} \odot \mathbf{h}_1 + 2\lambda_2 \mathbf{h}_2 = 0\end{aligned}$$

in which $\odot$ denotes the component-wise multiplication. For $\lambda_1 \neq 0$, a simple substitution leads to:

$$-\boldsymbol{\delta}^2 \odot \mathbf{h}_2 + 4\lambda_1\lambda_2 \mathbf{h}_2 = 0,$$

with the notation $\boldsymbol{\delta} \odot \boldsymbol{\delta} = \boldsymbol{\delta}^2$. As a result, $4\lambda_1\lambda_2 = \delta_i^2$ for components i with $h_{1,i} \neq 0$. Given the symmetry of the equations, the same requirements $4\lambda_1\lambda_2 = \delta_i^2$ hold for components $h_{2,i} \neq 0$.

We search for $\mathbf{h}_1$ and $\mathbf{h}_2$, such that δ_i^2 is constant for their non-zero components. Construct $\mathbf{h}_1$ and $\mathbf{h}_2$ such that only their component j is non-zero: $\forall i \neq j : h_{1,i} = h_{2,i} = 0$, whereas $h_{1,j} = \pm 1$, $h_{2,j} = \pm 1$ (given the unit sphere constraint). The contribution of component j to $\langle \boldsymbol{\delta}, \mathbf{h}_1, \mathbf{h}_2 \rangle$ depends on $h_{1,i} h_{2,i}$ which can take values ± 1. As a result:

$$\mathcal{J}^{\max} = \max_j |\delta_j|.$$

In the case where several components δ_j have the same value, then all $h_{1,i}$ and $h_{2,i}$ need to be zero for $i \neq j$, but due to the normalisation constraint, the highest value of $\sum_j h_{1_j} h_{2_j}$ is found for a single index j if both components take the value ± 1.

Finally, since $\mathcal{J}^{\max}$ is always non-negative, we find:

$$\boxed{\mathcal{J}_{\mathcal{I}}^{\max} = \max_j |\boldsymbol{\theta}_{b,j} - \boldsymbol{\theta}_{r,j}|}$$

A.1.2 Unit cube

For the entity embeddings to be constrained in the unit cube, their subspace is set to $\mathcal{U} = [0,1]^k \subset \mathbb{R}^k$. This corresponds to reducing the entity embeddings to approximately Boolean embeddings(see Demeester et al. [2016]).

The Lagrangian becomes:

$$\mathcal{L} = -\langle \boldsymbol{\delta}, \mathbf{h}_1, \mathbf{h}_2 \rangle + \sum_i \left[\boldsymbol{\mu}_1 \odot (\mathbf{h}_1 - \mathbf{1}) + \boldsymbol{\mu}_2 \odot (\mathbf{h}_2 - \mathbf{1}) \right]_i$$

with $\forall i : h_{1,i} - 1 \leq 0, h_{2,i} - 1 \leq 0$ (primal feasibility), $\forall i : \mu_{1,i} \geq 0, \mu_{2,i} \geq 0$ (dual feasibility), $\forall i : \mu_{1,i}(h_{1,i} - 1) = 0,\ \mu_{2,i}(h_{2,i} - 1) = 0$ (complementary slackness). In fact, we should add KKT multipliers for the conditions $-h_{1,i} \leq 0, -h_{2,i} \leq 0$ as well. These don't change the results, if we ensure the unit cube restrictions are satisfied.

Imposing stationarity, or $\nabla_{\mathbf{h}_1} \mathcal{L} = 0$ and $\nabla_{\mathbf{h}_2} \mathcal{L} = 0$, we get:

$$-\boldsymbol{\delta} \odot \mathbf{h}_2 + \boldsymbol{\mu}_1 = 0$$
$$-\boldsymbol{\delta} \odot \mathbf{h}_1 + \boldsymbol{\mu}_2 = 0$$

This can be solved component-wise, or for any component i:

$$\mu_{1i} = \delta_i h_{2,i}$$
$$\mu_{2i} = \delta_i h_{1,i}$$

Dual feasibility dictates that $\mu_{1i} \geq 0$ and $\mu_{2i} \geq 0$, such that $h_{2,i} = 0$ and $h_{1,i} = 0$ for any components where $\delta_i < 0$.

For the other components, we have $\delta_i \geq 0$, such that while satisfying the unit cube constraints the highest value of the objective becomes $\mathcal{J}_i^{\max} = \delta_i$ for $h_{1,i} = h_{2,i} = 1$.

Finally, we find:

$$\boxed{\mathcal{J}_{\mathcal{I}}^{\max} = \sum_j \max(0, \boldsymbol{\theta}_{b,j} - \boldsymbol{\theta}_{r,j}),}$$

which is exactly the same expression as the lifted loss for simple implications with unit cube entity embeddings introduced by Demeester et al. [2016] for MODEL F (which can be seen as a special case of DISTMULT where the subject embeddings are replaced by entity pair embeddings, and all object embedding components are set to 1).

A.2 COMPLEX

In COMPLEX, proposed by Trouillon et al. [2016], the scoring function ϕ is defined as follows:

$$\phi_r^{\boldsymbol{\theta}}(\mathbf{h}_1, \mathbf{h}_2) \triangleq \langle \boldsymbol{\theta}_r, \mathbf{h}_1, \overline{\mathbf{h}_2} \rangle^{\mathrm{R}}$$

where $\mathbf{x}^{\mathrm{R}} \triangleq \mathrm{Re}(\mathbf{x})$ and $\mathbf{x}^{\mathrm{I}} \triangleq \mathrm{Im}(\mathbf{x})$ denote the real and imaginary part of $\mathbf{x}$, respectively. In the following, we analyse the cases where entity embeddings live on the unit sphere (*i.e.* $\forall x \in \mathcal{E} : \|\mathbf{h}_x\|_2^2 = 1$) and in the unit cube (*i.e.*$\forall x \in \mathcal{E} : \mathbf{h}_x^{\mathrm{R}} \in [0,1]^k,\ \mathbf{h}_x^{\mathrm{I}} \in [0,1]^k$).

We want to solve the following maximisation problem:

$$\mathcal{J} = \max_{\mathbf{h}_1, \mathbf{h}_2 \in \mathcal{U}} \left(\phi_b(\mathbf{h}_1, \mathbf{h}_2) - \phi_r(\mathbf{h}_1, \mathbf{h}_2) \right)$$
$$= \max_{\mathbf{h}_1, \mathbf{h}_2 \in \mathcal{U}} \langle \boldsymbol{\delta}, \mathbf{h}_1, \overline{\mathbf{h}_2} \rangle^{\mathrm{R}},$$

with the complex vector $\boldsymbol{\delta} = \boldsymbol{\theta}_b - \boldsymbol{\theta}_r$.

To keep notations simple, we will continue to work with complex vectors as much as possible. For the Lagrangian $\mathcal{L}$, the pair of stationarity equations with respect to the real and imaginary part of a variable (say $\mathbf{h}_1$), can be taken together as follows:

$$\nabla_{\mathbf{h}_1^{\mathrm{R}}} \mathcal{L} + j \nabla_{\mathbf{h}_1^{\mathrm{I}}} \mathcal{L} = 0$$

and we introduce the notation $\nabla_{\mathbf{h}_1} \mathcal{L} \triangleq \nabla_{\mathbf{h}_1^{\mathrm{R}}} \mathcal{L} + j \nabla_{\mathbf{h}_1^{\mathrm{I}}} \mathcal{L}$, with j the imaginary unit. For the remainder, we need the following:

$$\begin{aligned}
\nabla_{\mathbf{h}_1} \langle \boldsymbol{\delta}, \mathbf{h}_1, \overline{\mathbf{h}_2} \rangle^{\mathrm{R}} &= \frac{1}{2} \nabla_{\mathbf{h}_1} \left(\langle \boldsymbol{\delta}, \mathbf{h}_1, \overline{\mathbf{h}_2} \rangle + \langle \overline{\boldsymbol{\delta}}, \overline{\mathbf{h}_1}, \mathbf{h}_2 \rangle \right) \\
&= \frac{1}{2} \left(\boldsymbol{\delta} \odot \overline{\mathbf{h}_2} + j \left(j \boldsymbol{\delta} \odot \overline{\mathbf{h}_2} \right) + \overline{\boldsymbol{\delta}} \odot \mathbf{h}_2 + j \left(-j \overline{\boldsymbol{\delta}} \odot \mathbf{h}_2 \right) \right) \\
&= \overline{\boldsymbol{\delta}} \odot \mathbf{h}_2 \\
\nabla_{\mathbf{h}_2} \langle \boldsymbol{\delta}, \mathbf{h}_1, \overline{\mathbf{h}_2} \rangle^{\mathrm{R}} &= \boldsymbol{\delta} \odot \mathbf{h}_1
\end{aligned}$$

A.2.1 Unit sphere

We now restrict the subject and object embeddings to live on the unit sphere, *i.e.* $\forall x \in \mathcal{E} : \|\mathbf{h}_x\|_2^2 = 1$. Given that the adversarial entity embeddings need to live on the unit sphere, the Lagrangian can be defined as follows:

$$\begin{aligned}
\mathcal{L}(\mathbf{h}_1, \mathbf{h}_2, \lambda_1, \lambda_2) = &- \langle \boldsymbol{\delta}, \mathbf{h}_1, \overline{\mathbf{h}_2} \rangle^{\mathrm{R}} \\
&+ \lambda_1 \left(\|\mathbf{h}_1\|_2^2 - 1 \right) \\
&+ \lambda_2 \left(\|\mathbf{h}_2\|_2^2 - 1 \right)
\end{aligned}$$

with real-valued Lagrange multipliers λ_1 and λ_2, and in which $\|\mathbf{h}_1\|_2^2 \triangleq \left\|\mathbf{h}_1^{\mathrm{R}}\right\|_2^2 + \left\|\mathbf{h}_1^{\mathrm{I}}\right\|_2^2$ is the L2 norm of the complex vector $\mathbf{h}_1$. With the expressions for $\nabla_{\mathbf{h}_1} \langle \boldsymbol{\delta}, \mathbf{h}_1, \overline{\mathbf{h}_2} \rangle^{\mathrm{R}}$ and $\nabla_{\mathbf{h}_2} \langle \boldsymbol{\delta}, \mathbf{h}_1, \overline{\mathbf{h}_2} \rangle^{\mathrm{R}}$ above, the stationarity conditions can be written out as follows:

$$\begin{aligned}
-\overline{\boldsymbol{\delta}} \odot \mathbf{h}_2 + 2\lambda_1 \mathbf{h}_1 &= 0 \\
-\boldsymbol{\delta} \odot \mathbf{h}_1 + 2\lambda_2 \mathbf{h}_2 &= 0
\end{aligned}$$

Substituting into each other, we find:

$$\begin{aligned}
4\lambda_1\lambda_2 \mathbf{h}_1 &= \overline{\boldsymbol{\delta}} \odot \boldsymbol{\delta} \odot \mathbf{h}_1, \qquad (\lambda_2 \neq 0) \\
4\lambda_1\lambda_2 \mathbf{h}_2 &= \boldsymbol{\delta} \odot \overline{\boldsymbol{\delta}} \odot \mathbf{h}_2, \qquad (\lambda_1 \neq 0)
\end{aligned}$$

As a result, we require $4\lambda_1\lambda_2 = |\delta_i|^2$ for components i with $h_{1,i} \neq 0$ or $h_{2,i} \neq 0$. As in the case with DistMult, take $h_{1,i} = h_{2,i} = 0$ for each component $i \neq j$, such that for component j, we need $|h_{1,j}| = |h_{2,j}| = 1$, such that $|h_{1,j} \overline{h_{2,j}}| = 1$. In order to maximise the contribution of that component to the loss, we choose the argument of the complex number $h_{1,j}\overline{h_{2,j}}$ such that $\delta_j h_{1,j} \overline{h_{2,j}}$ falls on the positive real axis. As a result:

$$\boxed{\mathcal{J}_{\mathcal{I}}^{\max} = \max_j |b_j - r_j| = \max_j \sqrt{(\boldsymbol{\theta}_{b,j}^{\mathrm{R}} - \boldsymbol{\theta}_{r,j}^{\mathrm{R}})^2 + (\boldsymbol{\theta}_{b,j}^{\mathrm{I}} - \boldsymbol{\theta}_{r,j}^{\mathrm{I}})^2}}$$

A.2.2 Unit cube

This case can be solved with the KKT conditions again, but instead we provide a shorter, less formal, derivation. It is clear that we can maximise the objective by maximising each component independently. For component i we need to optimise the following:

$$\delta_i^{\mathrm{R}} {h_{1,i}}^{\mathrm{R}} {h_{2,i}}^{\mathrm{R}} + \delta_i^{\mathrm{R}} {h_{1,i}}^{\mathrm{I}} {h_{2,i}}^{\mathrm{I}} + \delta_i^{\mathrm{I}} {h_{1,i}}^{\mathrm{R}} {h_{2,i}}^{\mathrm{I}} - \delta_i^{\mathrm{I}} {h_{1,i}}^{\mathrm{I}} {h_{2,i}}^{\mathrm{R}}$$

Regrouping gives:

$$\alpha \delta_i^{\mathrm{R}} + \beta \delta_i^{\mathrm{I}},$$

with $\alpha = {h_{1,i}}^{\mathrm{R}}{h_{2,i}}^{\mathrm{R}} + {h_{1,i}}^{\mathrm{I}}{h_{2,i}}^{\mathrm{I}}$ and $\beta = {h_{1,i}}^{\mathrm{R}}{h_{2,i}}^{\mathrm{I}} - {h_{1,i}}^{\mathrm{I}}{h_{2,i}}^{\mathrm{R}}$. We know $0 \leq \alpha \leq 2$, $-1 \leq \beta \leq 1$ and $\alpha + |\beta| \leq 2$. This allows maximising the objective as follows:

$$\boxed{\mathcal{J}_{\mathcal{I}}^{\max} = \sum_i \max(\delta_i^{\mathrm{R}}, 0) + \max(\delta_i^{\mathrm{R}}, |\delta_i^{\mathrm{I}}|)}$$

B Simple Implications with Swapped Arguments

Given a clause expressing a simple implication with swapped arguments, in the form $b(X_1, X_2) \Rightarrow r(X_2, X_1)$, we would like to maximise the inconsistency loss $\mathcal{J}_{\mathcal{I}}$ associated to the clause, *i.e.*:

$$\begin{aligned} &\mathcal{J}_{\mathcal{I}}^{\max} = \max\left(0, \mathcal{J}^{\max}\right) \\ &\text{with} \quad \mathcal{J}^{\max} = \max_{\mathbf{h}_1, \mathbf{h}_2 \in \mathcal{U}} \left(\phi_b(\mathbf{h}_1, \mathbf{h}_2) - \phi_r(\mathbf{h}_2, \mathbf{h}_1)\right). \end{aligned}$$

B.1 DISTMULT

Due to symmetry, the same close form expressions as for the simple implications hold.

B.2 COMPLEX

We want to solve the following maximisation problem:

$$\begin{aligned} \mathcal{J}^{\max} &= \max_{\mathbf{h}_1, \mathbf{h}_2 \in \mathcal{U}} \left(\phi_b(\mathbf{h}_1, \mathbf{h}_2) - \phi_r(\mathbf{h}_2, \mathbf{h}_1)\right) \\ &= \max_{\mathbf{h}_1, \mathbf{h}_2 \in \mathcal{U}} \langle \boldsymbol{\theta}_b, \mathbf{h}_1, \overline{\mathbf{h}_2} \rangle^{\mathrm{R}} - \langle \boldsymbol{\theta}_r, \mathbf{h}_2, \overline{\mathbf{h}_1} \rangle^{\mathrm{R}} \\ &= \max_{\mathbf{h}_1, \mathbf{h}_2 \in \mathcal{U}} \langle \boldsymbol{\theta}_b, \mathbf{h}_1, \overline{\mathbf{h}_2} \rangle^{\mathrm{R}} - \langle \overline{\boldsymbol{\theta}_r}, \overline{\mathbf{h}_2}, \mathbf{h}_1 \rangle^{\mathrm{R}} \\ &= \max_{\mathbf{h}_1, \mathbf{h}_2 \in \mathcal{U}} \langle \boldsymbol{\theta}_b - \overline{\boldsymbol{\theta}_r}, \mathbf{h}_1, \overline{\mathbf{h}_2} \rangle^{\mathrm{R}} \\ &= \max_{\mathbf{h}_1, \mathbf{h}_2 \in \mathcal{U}} \langle \boldsymbol{\zeta}, \mathbf{h}_1, \overline{\mathbf{h}_2} \rangle^{\mathrm{R}} \end{aligned}$$

This has the same form as the simple implications case, but with $\boldsymbol{\theta}_r$ replaced by $\overline{\boldsymbol{\theta}_r}$, or, more specifically, $\boldsymbol{\theta}_r^{\mathrm{I}}$ by $-\boldsymbol{\theta}_r^{\mathrm{I}}$.

B.2.1 Unit sphere

Under unit sphere constraints, $\mathcal{J}_{\mathcal{I}}^{\max}$ has the following value:

$$\boxed{\mathcal{J}_{\mathcal{I}}^{\max} = \max_i \sqrt{(\boldsymbol{\theta}_{b,i}^{\mathrm{R}} - \boldsymbol{\theta}_{r,i}^{\mathrm{R}})^2 + (\boldsymbol{\theta}_{b,i}^{\mathrm{I}} + \boldsymbol{\theta}_{r,i}^{\mathrm{I}})^2}} \tag{4}$$

B.2.2 Unit cube

With $\zeta_i^{\mathrm{R}} = \boldsymbol{\theta}_{b,i}^{\mathrm{R}} - \boldsymbol{\theta}_{r,i}^{\mathrm{R}}$ and $\zeta_i^{\mathrm{I}} = \boldsymbol{\theta}_{b,i}^{\mathrm{I}} + \boldsymbol{\theta}_{r,i}^{\mathrm{I}}$:

$$\boxed{\mathcal{J}_{\mathcal{I}}^{\max} = \sum_i \max(\zeta_i^{\mathrm{R}}, 0) + \max(\zeta_i^{\mathrm{R}}, |\zeta_i^{\mathrm{I}}|)}$$

C Symmetry

Given a clause expressing a simple implication with swapped arguments, in the form $r(X_1, X_2) \Rightarrow r(X_2, X_1)$, we would like to maximise the inconsistency loss $\mathcal{J}_{\mathcal{I}}$ associated to the clause, *i.e.*:

$$\begin{aligned} &\mathcal{J}_{\mathcal{I}}^{\max} = \max\left(0, \mathcal{J}^{\max}\right) \\ &\text{with} \quad \mathcal{J}^{\max} = \max_{\mathbf{h}_1, \mathbf{h}_2 \in \mathcal{U}} \left(\phi_r(\mathbf{h}_1, \mathbf{h}_2) - \phi_r(\mathbf{h}_2, \mathbf{h}_1)\right). \end{aligned}$$

Note that this is a special case of Appendix B where $r = b$.

C.1 DISTMULT

Since DISTMULT is symmetric, the gradient for symmetry clauses is zero, *i.e.*, all relations already satisfy symmetry.

C.2 COMPLEX

We want to solve the following maximisation problem:

$$\begin{aligned}\mathcal{J}^{\max} &= \max_{\mathbf{h}_1,\mathbf{h}_2\in\mathcal{U}} \left(\phi_r(\mathbf{h}_1,\mathbf{h}_2) - \phi_r(\mathbf{h}_2,\mathbf{h}_1)\right) \\ &= \max_{\mathbf{h}_1,\mathbf{h}_2\in\mathcal{U}} \langle \boldsymbol{\theta}_r - \overline{\boldsymbol{\theta}_r}, \mathbf{h}_1, \overline{\mathbf{h}_2}\rangle^{\mathrm{R}}\end{aligned}$$

C.2.1 Unit sphere

From Eq. (4) with $\boldsymbol{\theta}^{\mathrm{R}}_{r,i} = \boldsymbol{\theta}^{\mathrm{R}}_{b,i}$ and $\boldsymbol{\theta}^{\mathrm{I}}_{r,i} = \boldsymbol{\theta}^{\mathrm{I}}_{b,i}$ we get:

$$\boxed{\mathcal{J}^{\max} = \max_i 2|\boldsymbol{\theta}^{\mathrm{I}}_{r,i}|}$$

C.2.2 Unit cube

Similarly, with $\boldsymbol{\theta}^{\mathrm{R}}_{r,i} = \boldsymbol{\theta}^{\mathrm{R}}_{b,i}$ and $\boldsymbol{\theta}^{\mathrm{I}}_{r,i} = \boldsymbol{\theta}^{\mathrm{I}}_{b,i}$ we get:

$$\boxed{\mathcal{J}^{\max} = 2\sum_i |\boldsymbol{\theta}^{\mathrm{I}}_{r,i}|}$$

D Link Prediction Results

Table 8: Link prediction results on the Test-I, Test-II and and Test-ALL on FB122, filtered setting.

		Test-I				Test-II				Test-ALL			
		Hits@N (%)			MRR	Hits@N (%)			MRR	Hits@N (%)			MRR
		3	5	10		3	5	10		3	5	10	
FB122	TRANSE [Bordes et al., 2013]	36.0	41.5	48.1	0.296	77.5	82.8	88.4	0.630	58.9	64.2	70.2	0.480
	KALE-PRE [Guo et al., 2016]	35.8	41.9	49.8	0.291	82.9	86.1	89.9	0.713	61.7	66.2	71.8	0.523
	KALE-JOINT [Guo et al., 2016]	**38.4**	**44.7**	**52.2**	0.325	79.7	84.1	89.6	0.684	61.2	66.4	72.8	0.523
	DISTMULT [Yang et al., 2015]	36.0	40.3	45.3	0.313	92.3	93.8	94.7	0.874	67.4	70.2	72.9	0.628
	ASR-DISTMULT	36.3	40.3	44.9	0.330	98.0	99.0	99.2	0.948	70.7	73.1	75.2	0.675
	cASR-DISTMULT	37.0	40.4	45.1	0.337	96.7	98.6	99.3	0.933	70.1	72.7	75.1	0.669
	COMPLEX [Trouillon et al., 2016]	37.0	41.3	46.2	0.329	91.4	91.9	92.4	0.887	67.3	69.5	71.9	0.641
	ASR-COMPLEX	37.3	41.0	45.9	0.338	**99.2**	**99.3**	**99.4**	**0.984**	**71.7**	**73.6**	**75.7**	**0.698**
	cASR-COMPLEX	37.9	41.7	46.2	**0.339**	97.7	**99.3**	**99.4**	0.954	71.1	**73.6**	75.6	0.680
WN18	TRANSE [Bordes et al., 2013]	57.4	72.3	80.1	0.306	87.5	95.6	98.7	0.511	79.1	89.1	93.6	0.453
	KALE-PRE [Guo et al., 2016]	60.6	74.5	81.1	0.322	96.4	98.6	99.6	0.612	86.4	91.9	94.4	0.532
	KALE-JOINT [Guo et al., 2016]	65.5	76.3	82.1	0.338	93.3	95.4	97.2	0.787	85.5	90.1	93.0	0.662
	DISTMULT [Yang et al., 2015]	80.6	81.6	82.6	0.796	96.7	98.4	99.5	0.872	92.3	93.7	94.9	0.850
	ASR-DISTMULT	**81.4**	**82.0**	**82.9**	0.801	96.7	98.4	99.5	0.869	92.4	93.8	94.9	0.851
	COMPLEX [Trouillon et al., 2016]	81.0	81.8	82.5	**0.803**	**99.9**	**100**	**100**	**0.996**	**94.7**	**95.0**	**95.1**	**0.942**
	ASR-COMPLEX	81.0	81.8	82.5	**0.803**	**99.9**	**100**	**100**	**0.996**	**94.7**	**95.0**	**95.1**	**0.942**

Supplementary References

[sup1] S. Boyd and L. Vandenberghe. *Convex Optimization*. Cambridge University Press, New York, NY, USA, 2004. ISBN 0521833787.

AUTHOR INDEX

AUTHOR INDEX

AUTHOR INDEX